The Broadview Anthology of BRITISH LITERATURE

Volume 3
The Restoration and the Eighteenth Century

Second Edition

The Broadview Anthology of British Literature

The Medieval Period
The Renaissance and the Early Seventeenth Century
The Restoration and the Eighteenth Century
The Age of Romanticism
The Victorian Era
The Twentieth Century and Beyond

The Broadview Anthology of

BRITISH LITERATURE

Volume 3
The Restoration and the Eighteenth Century

Second Edition

GENERAL EDITORS

Joseph Black, University of Massachusetts
Leonard Conolly, Trent University
Kate Flint, University of Southern California
Isobel Grundy, University of Alberta
Don LePan, Broadview Press
Roy Liuzza, University of Tennessee
Jerome J. McGann, University of Virginia
Anne Lake Prescott, Barnard College
Barry V. Qualls, Rutgers University
Claire Waters, University of California, Davis

broadview press

BROADVIEW PRESS — www.broadviewpress.com
Peterborough, Ontario, Canada

Founded in 1985, Broadview Press remains a wholly independent publishing house. Broadview's focus is on academic publishing; our titles are accessible to university and college students as well as scholars and general readers. With over 600 titles in print, Broadview has become a leading international publisher in the humanities, with world-wide distribution. Broadview is committed to environmentally responsible publishing and fair business practices.

LIBRARY AND ARCHIVES CANADA CATALOGUING IN PUBLICATION

The Broadview anthology of British literature / general editors, Joseph Black ... [et al].—2nd ed.

Includes bibliographical references and indexes.
Contents: v.1. The Medieval period — v.2. The Renaissance and the early seventeenth century — v.3. The Restoration and the eighteenth century — v.4. The age of romanticism — v. 5. The Victorian era — v.6. The twentieth century and beyond.
ISBN 978-1-55481-047-5 (v.3).

1. English literature. I. Black, Joseph Laurence, 1962–

PR1109.B77 2009 820.8 C2009-901366-5

Broadview Press handles its own distribution in North America
PO Box 1243, Peterborough, Ontario K9J 7H5, Canada
555 Riverwalk Parkway, Tonawanda, NY 14150, USA
Tel: (705) 743-8990; Fax: (705) 743-8353
email: customerservice@broadviewpress.com

Distribution is handled by Eurospan Group in the UK, Europe, Central Asia, Middle East, Africa, India, Southeast Asia, Central America, South America, and the Caribbean. Distribution is handled by Footprint Books in Australia and New Zealand.

Broadview Press acknowledges the financial support of the Government of Canada for our publishing activities.

Canada

Typeset by Kathryn Brownsey
Cover design by Lisa Brawn

PRINTED IN CANADA

Contributing Editors and Writers

Managing Editor — Don LePan
Assistant Managing Editor — Laura Buzzard
Developmental Editors — Laura Buzzard, Jennifer McCue
Editorial Coordinator — Jennifer McCue
General Academic and Textual Editors — Laura Cardiff, Colleen Franklin, Morgan Rooney
Design Coordinator — Kathryn Brownsey

Contributing Editors

Katherine O. Acheson
Suzy Anger
Phanuel Antwi
Melissa Bachynski
Robert Barrett
Gisele Baxter
Donald Beecher
Sandra Bell
Emily Bernhard Jackson
Joseph Black
Carol Blessing
Robert Boenig
Sarika Bose
Matthieu Boyd
Benjamin Bruch
Laura Buzzard
Michael Calabrese
Laura Cardiff
Lisa Celovsky
Noel Chevalier
Mita Choudhury
Youngjin Chung
Massimo Ciavolella
Anna Clark
Elisha Cohn
Thomas J. Collins
Leonard Conolly
Darryl Domingo
Annmarie Drury
Dianne Dugaw
Siân Echard
Rose Eckert-Jantzie
Warren Edminster
Rachel Eisendrath
Garrett Epp
Michael Faletra
Emily Farrell
Christina Fawcett
Christina Fitzgerald
Adrienne Fitzpatrick
Andrew Fleck
Melissa Free
Maura Giles Watson
Stephen Glosecki
Amanda Goldrick-Jones
Katie Gramich
Erik Gray
John Greenwood
Isobel Grundy
Stephen Guy-Bray
Douglas Hayes
Peter C. Herman
Heather Hill-Vasquez
John Holmes
Diane Jakacki
Eleanor Johnson
Ian Johnston
Susan Kattwinkel
Michael Keefer
Amy King
David Klausner
Scott Kleinman
Chris Koenig-Woodyard
Gary Kuchar
Roger P. Kuin
Lydia K. Lake
Wendy Lee
Don LePan
Ruth Lexton
Roy Liuzza
Kirsten Lodge
Marie Loughlin
D.L. Macdonald
Hugh Magennis
Anne McWhir
Tobias Menely
Britt Mize
Alexander Mueller
Ian Munro
Sarah Neville
Meghan Nieman
David Oakleaf
Maureen Okun
Philip S. Palmer
Virginia Philipson
Jude Polsky
Anne Lake Prescott
Joyce Rappaport
Joseph Rezek
Shelby Richardson
Terry Robinson
Herbert Rosengarten
Jason Rudy
Janice Schroeder
Chester Scoville
John T. Sebastian
Kelly Stage
Emily Steiner
Ashley Streeter
Martha Stoddard-Holmes
Julie Sutherland
David Swain
Carol Symes
Andrew Taylor
Peggy Thompson
Jane Tolmie
Rebecca Totaro
David Townsend
Yevgeniya Traps
Melissa Valiska Gregory
Martine van Elk
Fred Waage
Andrea Walkden
Craig Walker
Claire Waters
David Watt
William Weaver

Vivienne Westbrook
David Williams
Adrienne Williams Boyarin
James Winny

CONTRIBUTING WRITERS

Laura Cardiff
Jude Polsky
Victoria Abboud
Jane Beal
Jennifer Beauvais
Rachel Bennett
Emily Bernhard Jackson
Rebecca Blasco
Jess Boland
Matthieu Boyd
Julie Brennan
Andrew Bretz
Laura Buzzard
Paul Johnson Byrne
Emily Cargan
Darryl Domingo
Victoria Duncan
Adrienne Eastwood
Wendy Eberle-Sinatra
Zachary Edwards
Peter Enman
Emily Farrell
Christina Fawcett
Joanne Findon
Jane Grove
Camille Isaacs
Erik Isford
John Geddert
Shoshannah Jones Square
Stephanie King
Chris Koenig-Woodyard
Gabrielle L'Archeveque
Philip Laven
Jessica Legacy
Don LePan
Anna Lepine
Kelly Loewen
John McIntyre
Brett McLenithan
Carrie Nartkler
Byron Nelson
Robin Norris
Kenna Olsen
Kendra O'Neal Smith
Laura Pellerine
Tiffany Percival
Virginia Philipson
Allison Pitcher
Andrew Reszitnyk
Dave Ross
Nora Ruddock
Jason Rudy
Anne Salo
Janice Schroeder
Carrie Shanafelt
Nicole Shukin
Helena Snopek
James Soderholm
Anne Sorbie
Martha Stoddard-Holmes
Jenna Stook
Ashley Streeter
Alexandria Stuart
Candace Taylor
Kaitlyn Till
Yevgeniya Traps
David Van Belle
Deirdra Wadden
Shari Watling
Matthew Williams
Bj Wray
Nicole Zylstra

LAYOUT AND TYPESETTING

Kathryn Brownsey
Susan Chamberlain

ILLUSTRATION FORMATTING AND ASSISTANCE

Cheryl Baldwin
Lisa Brawn
Eileen Eckert

PRODUCTION COORDINATORS

Tara Lowes
Tara Trueman

PERMISSIONS COORDINATORS

Merilee Atos
Chris Griffin
Emily Cargan
Amy Nimegeer
Jennifer Elsayed

PROOFREADERS

Jennifer Bingham
Judith Earnshaw
Anne Hodgetts
Joe Davies
Martin Boyne
Rose Eckert-Jantzie
Amy Neufeld
Lucy Conolly
Lynn Fraser
Lynn Neufeld

Editorial Advisors

Contents

Preface xxiii

Acknowledgments xxxi

The Restoration and the Eighteenth Century xxxv
  Religion, Government, and Party Politics xxxvi
  Empiricism, Skepticism, and Religious Dissent xxxix
  Industry, Commerce, and the Middle Class xlii
  Ethical Dilemmas in a Changing Nation xlvi
  Print Culture li
  Poetry lv
  Theater lix
  The Novel lxii
  The Development of the English Language lxix

History of the Language and of Print Culture lxxii

Margaret Cavendish 1
  The Poetess's Hasty Resolution 3
  An Excuse for so Much Writ Upon My Verses 3
  Of the Theme of Love 3
  A Woman Drest by Age 3
  A Dialogue Betwixt the Body and the Mind 3
  The Hunting of the Hare 4
  from *The Description of a New World, Called the Blazing World* 6
    from To the Reader 6
    The Description of a New World, Called the Blazing World 6
    [The Lady Becomes Empress] 7
    [The Empress Brings the Duchess of Newcastle to Be Her Scribe] 9
    [The Duchess and the Empress Create Their Own Worlds] 9
    The Epilogue to the Reader 11
  from *Sociable Letters* 11
    55 11
    143 12
    163 13
  The Convent of Pleasure 13
  from *A True Relation of My Birth, Breeding, and Life*
    (sites.broadviewpress.com/bablonline)

John Aubrey (sites.broadviewpress.com/bablonline)
  from *Brief Lives*
    Francis Bacon, Viscount St. Albans
    John Milton
    Andrew Marvell

John Bunyan 32
from *The Pilgrim's Progress* 34
The Author's Apology for His Book 34
from The Second Part 55

John Dryden 69
Absalom and Achitophel: A Poem 72
Mac Flecknoe 87
from Religio Laici or A Layman's Faith 90
To the Memory of Mr. Oldham 91
A Song for St. Cecilia's Day 92
Cymon and Iphigenia, from Boccace 93
from *An Essay of Dramatic Poesy* 101

Samuel Pepys 112
from *The Diary* 114
In Context: Other Accounts of the Great Fire 138
The Great Fire of London, 1666 138
from *The London Gazette* (3–10 September 1666) 138

Contexts: Mind and God, Faith and Science 143
from Thomas Sprat, *The History of the Royal Society of London, for the Improving of Natural Knowledge* (1667) 146
from Section 5. A Model of Their Whole Design 146
from Section 20. Their Manner of Discourse 146
from Section 22. A Defence of the Royal Society, in Respect of the Ancients 147
Philosophical Transactions 149
Introduction to the First Issue (1665) 149
"An Account of a Very Odd Monstrous Calf" (1665) 149
from Robert Boyle, "Trials Proposed by Mr. Boyle to Dr. Lower to Be Made by Him for the Improvement of Transfusing Blood out of One Live Animal into Another" (1666) 149
Thomas Coxe, "An Account of Another Experiment of Transfusion, *viz.* of Bleeding a Mangy into a Sound Dog" 150
from Will Chesselden, "An Account of Some Observations Made by a Young Gentleman Who Was Born Blind, or Lost His Sight So Early, That He Had No Remembrance of Ever Having Seen, and Was Couched Between 13 and 14 Years of Age" 151
from Sir Isaac Newton, "A Letter of Mr. Isaac Newton, Professor of the Mathematics in the University of Cambridge, Containing His New Theory about Light and Colours" (1671) 151
from Benjamin Franklin, *The Autobiography of Benjamin Franklin* 153
from Joseph Priestley, *Experiments and Observations on Different Kinds of Air* 155
from The Preface 155
from The Introduction 157

from John Locke, *An Essay Concerning Human Understanding* 159
from Book 2, "Of Ideas," Chapter 1 159
from Book 2, Chapter 23 160
from Robert Hooke, *Micrographia: Or Some Physiological Descriptions of Minute Bodies Made by Magnifying Glasses, with Observations and Inquiries Thereupon* 161
The Epistle Dedicatory. To the King 161
To the Royal Society 161
from The Preface 161
from Observation 1. Of the Point of a Small Sharp Needle 163
from Observation 39. Of the Eyes and Head of a Great Drone-Fly, and of Several Other Creatures 165
from Margaret Cavendish, *Observations upon Experimental Philosophy, To Which Is Added, The Description of a New Blazing World* 167
from Preface to the Ensuing Treatise 167
from *The Description of a New World, Called the Blazing World* 168
from Voltaire, *Micromegas* 171
Chapter 4: What happened to them upon this our globe 171
Chapter 5: The experiments and reasonings of the two travellers 172
from Chapter 6: What happened to them in their intercourse with men 173
Chapter 7: A conversation with men 174
from Sir Isaac Newton, Letter to Richard Bentley (10 December 1692) 177
from James Thomson, "A Poem Sacred to the Memory of Sir Isaac Newton" 179
Mark Akenside, "Hymn to Science" 180
from Margaret Bryan, *A Compendious System of Astronomy* 181
from Lecture 1 181
from Benjamin Franklin, Letter to Joseph Priestley (8 September 1780) 182
Isaac Watts, "Against Idleness and Mischief" 182
Isaac Watts, "Man Frail, and God Eternal" 183
from David Hume, *An Enquiry Concerning Human Understanding* 183
from Section 10: "Of Miracles" 183
from James Boswell, *The Life of Samuel Johnson* 185
from *The Spectator* No. 7 (8 March 1711) 186
William Hogarth, *Credulity, Superstition, and Fanaticism: A Medley* 187
from Erasmus Darwin, *Loves of the Plants* 189
from the Advertisement 189
from the Proem 189
from Loves of the Plants 189
from Mary Astell, *A Serious Proposal to the Ladies* 190
from Judith Drake, *An Essay in Defense of the Female Sex* 192
from Eliza Haywood, *The Female Spectator* No. 10 (February 1745) 194

Aphra Behn 196
The Disappointment 197
On a Juniper Tree, Cut Down to Make Busks 199

To the Fair Clarinda 200
The Feigned Courtesans (sites.broadviewpress.com/bablonline)
Oroonoko: or, The Royal Slave. A True History 201

William Wycherley 238
The Country Wife 239

John Wilmot, Earl of Rochester 290
A Satire on Charles II 291
A Satire against Reason and Mankind 292
Love and Life: A Song 294
The Disabled Debauchee 295
A Letter from Artemisia in the Town to Chloe in the Country 296
The Imperfect Enjoyment 299
Impromptu on Charles II 300
In Context: The Lessons of Rochester's Life 301

Daniel Defoe 302
A True Relation of the Apparition of One Mrs. Veal 304
from *Robinson Crusoe* 308
from Chapter 3 309
Chapter 4 313
Chapter 5 323
Chapter 6 329
In Context: Illustrating *Robinson Crusoe* 336
from *A Journal of the Plague Year* 338

Anne Finch, Countess of Winchilsea 348
from The Spleen: A Pindaric Poem 349
The Introduction 350
A Letter to Daphnis, 2 April 1685 351
To Mr. F., Now Earl of W. 351
The Unequal Fetters 353
By neer resemblance that Bird betray'd 353
A Nocturnal Reverie 354

Mary Astell 355
from *A Serious Proposal to the Ladies* 356
from *Reflections upon Marriage* 362
from The Preface 362

Jonathan Swift 373
The Progress of Beauty 375
A Description of a City Shower 376
Stella's Birthday, written in the year 1718 377

Stella's Birthday (1727) 378
The Lady's Dressing Room 379
Verses on the Death of Dr Swift, D.S.P.D. 381
Gulliver's Travels 389
Part One: A Voyage To Lilliput 391
Part Two: A Voyage to Brobdingnag 420
Part Three: A Voyage to Laputa 452
Part Four: A Voyage to the Country of The Houyhnhnms 484
In Context: *Gulliver's Travels* in Its Time 519
from Letter from Swift to Alexander Pope, 29 September 1725 519
from Letter from Swift to Alexander Pope, 26 November 1725 520
Letter from "Richard Sympson" to Benjamin Motte, 8 August 1726 521
from Letter from John Gay and Alexander Pope to Swift, 17 November 1726 522
from Letter from Alexander Pope to Swift, 26 November 1726 523
A Modest Proposal 523
In Context: Sermons and Tracts: Backgrounds to *A Modest Proposal* 528
from Jonathan Swift, "Causes of the Wretched Condition of Ireland" 528
from Jonathan Swift, *A Short View of the State of Ireland* 530

Joseph Addison 533
from *The Spectator* 534
No. 285 [On the Language of *Paradise Lost*] 534
No. 414 [Nature, Art, Gardens] 538

John Gay (sites.broadviewpress.com/bablonline)
The Beggar's Opera

Alexander Pope 540
from *An Essay on Criticism* (complete text @ sites.broadviewpress.com/bablonline) 542
Windsor-Forest 548
The Rape of the Lock: An Heroi-Comical Poem in Five Cantos 555
Elegy to the Memory of an Unfortunate Lady 568
Eloisa to Abelard 570
from *An Essay on Man* 575
The Design 575
Epistle 1 575
Epistle 2 579
An Epistle from Mr. Pope to Dr. Arbuthnot 584
Epistle 2. To a Lady 591
Epistle 4. To Richard Boyle, Earl of Burlington 597

Lady Mary Wortley Montagu 602
Saturday; The Small Pox 603
The Reasons that Induced Dr. S. to Write a Poem Called The Lady's Dressing Room 605

The Lover: A Ballad 606
Epistle from Mrs. Y[onge] to Her Husband 607
The Spectator No. 573 [From the President of the Widow's Club] (28 July 1714) .. 608
A Plain Account of the Inoculating of the Smallpox by a Turkey Merchant 611
Selected Letters 612
To Wortley, 28 March 1710 612
To Philippa Mundy, 25 September 1711 613
To Philippa Mundy, c. 2 November 1711 614
To Wortley, c. 26 July 1712 614
From Wortley, 13 August 1712 615
To Wortley, 15 August 1712 616
To Wortley, 15 August 1712 616
To Lady Mar, 17 November 1716 617
To Lady——, 1 April 1717 617
To Lady Mar, 1 April 1717 619
To [Sarah Chiswell], 1 April 1717 621
To Alexander Pope, September 1718 622
To Lady Mar, September 1727 623
To Lady Bute, 5 January 1748 624
To Lady Bute, 19 February 1750 624
To Wortley, 10 October 1753 626
To Lady Bute, 30 November[?] 1753 626
To Sir James Steuart, 14 November 1758 628

ELIZA HAYWOOD 630
Fantomina: or, Love in a Maze 631
IN CONTEXT: The Eighteenth-Century Sexual Imagination 647
from *A Present for a Servant-Maid* 647
from *Venus in the Cloister; or, The Nun in Her Smock* 649

CONTEXTS: PRINT CULTURE, STAGE CULTURE 651
from Nahum Tate, *The History of King Lear* 653
from Act 5 653
from Colley Cibber, *An Apology for the Life of Mr. Colley Cibber* 654
from Jeremy Collier, *A Short View of the Immorality and Profaneness of the English Stage* 655
Introduction 655
from Chapter 1: The Immodesty of the Stage 655
from Chapter 4: The Stage-Poets Make Their Principal Persons Vicious and Reward Them at the End of the Play 656
from Joseph Addison, *The Spectator* No. 18 (21 March 1711) 657
from The Licensing Act of 1737 658
from The Statute of Anne 659
from James Boswell, *The Life of Samuel Johnson* 661
Joseph Addison, *The Tatler* No. 224 (14 September 1710) 661
from Samuel Johnson, *The Idler* No. 30 (11 November 1758) 663

from Clara Reeve, *The Progress of Romance* 664
from James Lackington, *Memoirs of the Forty-Five First Years of the Life of James Lackington, Bookseller* 665
from Thomas Erskine, *Speech as Prosecution in the Seditious-Libel Trial of Thomas Williams for Publishing* Age of Reason, *by Thomas Paine* 667

CONTEXTS: EIGHTEENTH-CENTURY PERIODICALS AND PRINTS 668
Daniel Defoe, Introduction, *A Weekly Review of the Affairs of France* No. 1 (sites.broadviewpress.com/bablonline)
from Richard Steele, *The Tatler* No. 21 [The Gentleman; The Pretty Fellow] (sites.broadviewpress.com/bablonline)
from Joseph Addison, *The Tatler* No. 155 [The Political Upholsterer] (6 April 1710) 670
from *The Female Tatler* No. 1 [Introduction, Advertisment] (8 July 1709) 672
Richard Steele, *The Spectator* No. 11 [Inkle and Yarico] (13 March 1711) 673
Joseph Addison, *The Spectator* No. 112 [Sir Roger at Church] (19 July 1711) 676
from Joseph Addison, *The Spectator* No. 127 [On the Hoop Petticoat] (26 July 1711) 676
John Hughes, *The Spectator* No. 302 [Emilia] (sites.broadviewpress.com/bablonline)
The Walpole Print War (sites.broadviewpress.com/bablonline)
Bolingbroke, "*Remarks on the History of England*: Letter 5," *The Craftsman* No. 215
James Pitt, "A Continuation of the Observations on Mr. Oldcastle's Remarks upon the English History," *The London Journal* No. 577
Lady Mary Wortley Montagu, *The Nonsense of Common-Sense* No. 5 [On Publishing] (17 January 1738) 681
from Eliza Haywood, *The Female Spectator* Book 1 [The Author's Intent] (sites.broadviewpress.com/bablonline)
from Eliza Haywood, *The Female Spectator* Book 1 [Erminia] (April 1744) 684
Samuel Johnson, *The Rambler* No. 148 [On Parental Tyranny] (17 August 1751) . 686
from Samuel Richardson, *The Rambler* No. 97 [Change in the Manners of Women] (19 February 1751) 690
Samuel Johnson, *The Rambler* No. 114 [On Capital Punishment] (20 April 1751) 693
Samuel Johnson, *The Rambler* No. 170 [Misella, A Prostitute] and No. 171 [Misella's Story Continued] (sites.broadviewpress.com/bablonline)
Henry Fielding, *The Covent-Garden Journal* No. 4 [A Modern Glossary] (sites.broadviewpress.com/bablonline)
from Henry Fielding, *The Covent-Garden Journal* No. 6 [Mortality of Print] (21 January 1752) 695
Henry Fielding, *The Covent-Garden Journal* No. 31 [Criticism of Shakespeare] (sites.broadviewpress.com/bablonline)
from Frances Brooke, *The Old Maid* No. 13 [The Foundling Hospital] (7 February 1756) 698
from Frances Brooke, *The Old Maid* No. 18 [On *King Lear*] (sites.broadviewpress.com/bablonline)

from Sir Joshua Reynolds, *The Idler* [On Beauty] (sites.broadviewpress.com/bablonline)
Oliver Goldsmith, Letter 3, *The Public Ledger* No. 15 [The Citizen of the World Observes British Fashion] (29 January 1760) 700
Pierre Joseph Boudier de Villemert, "Of the Studies Proper for Women," *The Lady's Museum* No. 1 (sites.broadviewpress.com/bablonline)
François Fénelon, "Of the Importance of the Education of Daughters," *The Lady's Museum* No. 4 (sites.broadviewpress.com/bablonline)
from John Wilkes, *The North Briton* No. 45 [The King's Speech] (sites.broadviewpress.com/bablonline)
Prints 703

James Thomson 708
Winter 709
Spring (sites.broadviewpress.com/bablonline)
Summer
Autumn
Rule, Britannia 715

Henry Fielding 716
The Tragedy of Tragedies: or, the Life and Death of Tom Thumb the Great 718
In Context (materials online at sites.broadviewpress.com/bablonline)

Samuel Johnson 759
The Vanity of Human Wishes: The Tenth Satire of Juvenal Imitated 761
On the Death of Dr. Robert Levett 766
from *The Rambler*
No. 4 [On Fiction] (31 March 1750) 766
No. 12 [Cruelty of Employers] (28 April 1750) 769
No. 60 [On Biography] (13 October 1750) 771
No. 155 [On Becoming Acquainted with Our Real Characters] (10 September 1751) 774
from *The Idler*
No. 26 [Betty Broom] (14 October 1758) 776
No. 29 [Betty Broom, cont.] (4 November 1758) 778
No. 31 [On Idleness] (18 November 1758) 779
No. 49 [Will Marvel] (24 March 1759) 780
No. 81 [On Native Americans] (3 November 1759) 782
from *A Dictionary of the English Language* 783
from The Preface 783
Selected Entries 785
from The Preface to *The Works of William Shakespeare* 786
from *Lives of the English Poets* 793
from John Milton 793
from Alexander Pope 797
Letters 800
To the Right Honourable Earl of Chesterfield, 7 February 1755 800

To Mrs. Thrale, 10 July 1780 801
To Mrs. Thrale, 19 June 1783 801
To Mrs. Thrale, 2 July 1784 803
To Mrs. Thrale, 8 July 1784 803

THOMAS GRAY 804
Ode on a Distant Prospect of Eton College 805
Ode on the Death of a Favourite Cat, Drowned in a Tub of Gold Fishes 806
Sonnet on the Death of Mr. Richard West 807
Elegy Written in a Country Churchyard 807
The Bard (sites.broadviewpress.com/bablonline)

POPULAR BALLADS 810
Robin Hood and Alan a Dale 810
Edward, Edward 812
Tam Lin 813
The Death of Robin Hood 817
A Lyke-Wake Dirge 819
Mary Hamilton 820

HORACE WALPOLE (sites.broadviewpress.com/bablonline)
The Castle of Otranto
Chapter 1
Chapter 2
Chapter 3
Chapter 4
Chapter 5
IN CONTEXT: The Origins of *The Castle of Otranto*
from a Letter by Walpole to the Reverend William Cole, 9 March 1765
IN CONTEXT: Reactions to *The Castle of Otranto*
from *The Monthly Review*; or, *Literary Journal* Volume 32 (1764)
from *The Monthly Review*; or, *Literary Journal* Volume 32 (1765)
from William Warburton, a footnote to line 146 of Alexander Pope's poem *First Epistle to the Second Book of Horace Imitated*, in Warburton's edition of Pope's verse
from William Hazlitt, "On the English Novelists" (1819)
from Sir Walter Scott, "Introduction" to the 1811 edition of *The Castle of Otranto*

WILLIAM COLLINS (sites.broadviewpress.com/bablonline)
Ode to Fear

CHRISTOPHER SMART 822
from *Jubilate Agno*
[MY CAT JEOFFRY] 823

Contexts: Transatlantic Currents 825
Slavery 827
from Richard Ligon, *A True & Exact History of the Island of Barbados* 827
from John Woolman, "Considerations on the Keeping of Negroes" 828
from John Bicknell and Thomas Day, "The Dying Negro, A Poem" (sites.broadviewpress.com/bablonline)
from William Cowper, *The Task* (sites.broadviewpress.com/bablonline)
from Book 2
from Book 4
Hannah More, "Slavery: A Poem" 830
Ann Yearsley, "A Poem on the Inhumanity of the Slave-Trade" 834
Immigration to America 840
from Ebenezer Cooke, *The Sotweed Factor* (sites.broadviewpress.com/bablonline)
from William Moraley, *The Infortunate: The Voyage and Adventures of William Moraley, an Indentured Servant* 840
from Gottlieb Mittelberger, *Journey to Pennsylvania* (sites.broadviewpress.com/bablonline)
from Lady Lucan, "On the Present State of Ireland" 842
from Commissioners of the Customs in Scotland, *Report on the Examination of the Emigrants from the Counties of Caithness and Sutherland on Board the Ship Bachelor of Leith Bound to Wilmington in North Carolina* 844
from Benjamin Franklin, *Information to Those Who Would Remove to America* . 846
from J. Hector St. John Crèvecoeur, *Letters from an American Farmer* 848
from Anonymous, *Look Before You Leap* 851
from The Preface 851
from Israel Potter, *Life and Remarkable Adventures of Israel R. Potter* (sites.broadviewpress.com/bablonline)
General Wolfe and the Fall of Quebec 852
from "Anecdotes Relating to the Battle of Quebec" 852
from Thomas Cary, "Abram's Plains" (sites.broadviewpress.com/bablonline)
from Horace Walpole, *Memoirs of the Last Ten Years of the Reign of King George II* 853
Colonists and Native People 855
from Mary Rowlandson, *A Narrative of the Captivity and Restoration of Mrs. Mary Rowlandson* (sites.broadviewpress.com/bablonline)
from William Penn, "A Letter from William Penn, Proprietary and Governor of Pennsylvania in America, to the Committee of the Free Society of Traders of that Province Residing in London" (sites.broadviewpress.com/bablonline)
from Samson Occom, *A Short Narrative of My Life* (sites.broadviewpress.com/bablonline)
Benjamin Franklin, "Remarks Concerning the Savages of North America" (sites.broadviewpress.com/bablonline)
William Wordsworth, "Complaint of a Forsaken Indian Woman" 855
from Susannah Johnson, *The Captive American or A Narrative of the Suffering of Mrs. Johnson During Four Years Captivity with the Indians and French* . . . 857

from the Introduction 857
from Chapter 1 857
from Chapter 3 859
from Chapter 4 859
from Chapter 5 859
American Independence 861
from Edmund Burke, "Speech on Conciliation with the Colonies" 861
from Samuel Johnson, *Taxation No Tyranny; an Answer to the Resolutions and Addresses of the American Congress* (sites.broadviewpress.com/bablonline)
from Benjamin Franklin, *The Autobiography of Benjamin Franklin* 863
from Richard Price, *Observations on the Nature of Civil Liberty, the Principles of Government, and the Justice and Policy of the War with America* 864
from Part 2 864
from Section 1, Of the Justice of the War with America 864
from Section 3, Of the Policy of the War with America 865
Thomas Jefferson, "A Declaration by the Representatives of the United States of America, in General Congress Assembled" 865
from Thomas Paine, *The American Crisis* 869
Number 1 869
from Richard Price, *Observations on the Importance of the American Revolution* ... 871
from Judith Sargent Murray, "The Gleaner Contemplates the Future Prospects of Women in this 'Enlightened Age'" (sites.broadviewpress.com/bablonline)

Contexts: The Abolition of Slavery (sites.broadviewpress.com/bablonline)
(Please note that this Contexts section also appears in volume 4 of the bound-book component of the anthology. It is included here as well for the benefit of those focusing on slavery in the context of Restoration and eighteenth-century literature.)
from John Newton, *A Slave Trader's Journal*
from Quobna Ottobah Cugoano, *Thoughts and Sentiments on the Evil and Wicked Traffic of the Slavery and Commerce of the Human Species*
from Alexander Falconbridge, *Account of the Slave Trade on the Coast of Africa*
William Cowper, "Sweet Meat Has Sour Sauce" or, The Slave-Trader in the Dumps
from William Wilberforce, "Speech to the House of Commons," 13 May 1789
Proponents of Slavery
from Rev. Robert Boncher Nicholls, *Observations, Occasioned by the Attempts Made in England to Effect the Abolition of the Slave Trade*
from Anonymous, *Thoughts on the Slavery of Negroes, as It Affects the British Colonies in the West Indies: Humbly Submitted to the Consideration of Both Houses of Parliament*
from Gordon Turnbull, *An Apology of Negro Slavery; or, the West India Planters Vindicated from the Charge of Inhumanity*
from Mary Wollstonecraft, *A Vindication of the Rights of Men*
Anna Laetitia Barbauld, "Epistle to William Wilberforce, Esq., on the Rejection of the Bill for Abolishing the Slave Trade"

William Blake, Images of Slavery
from Samuel Taylor Coleridge, *On the Slave Trade*
from William Earle, *Obi; or, the History of Three-Fingered Jack*
Mary Robinson, Poems on Slavery
"The African"
"The Negro Girl"
from Dorothy Wordsworth, *The Grasmere Journal*
from Thomas Clarkson, *The History of the Rise, Progress and Accomplishment of the Abolition of the African Slave Trade*
from Matthew Gregory Lewis, *Journal of a West India Proprietor*

OLIVER GOLDSMITH 872
The Deserted Village 873

WILLIAM COWPER 879
Light Shining Out of Darkness 880
from *The Task* 880
Advertisement 880
from Book 1: The Sofa 881
from Book 6: The Winter Walk at Noon 883
The Castaway 886
The Retired Cat 887
On the Loss of the Royal George 888
My Mary 889

JAMES BOSWELL (sites.broadviewpress.com/bablonline)
from *London Journal*
Introduction
from *The Life of Samuel Johnson*

LABORING-CLASS POETS 890
Stephen Duck 891
The Thresher's Labour (1730) 891
The Thresher's Labour (1736 edition) (sites.broadviewpress.com/bablonline)
Mary Collier 894
The Woman's Labour: To Mr. Stephen Duck 894
Mary Leapor 898
An Epistle to a Lady 898
To a Gentleman with a Manuscript Play 899
Crumble Hall 900
Elizabeth Hands 902
On the Supposition of an Advertisement Appearing in a Morning Paper, of the Publication of a Volume of Poems, by a Servant Maid 902

Contexts: Town and Country 904
from John Gay, *Trivia* 906
Joseph Addison, *The Spectator* No. 69 (19 May 1711) 914
from Daniel Defoe, "On Trade" (from *The Complete English Tradesman*), Letter 22, "Of the Dignity of Trade in England More Than in Other Countries" 916
from *The Female Tatler* No. 9 (25–27 July 1709) 917
from *The Female Tatler* No. 67 (7–9 December 1709) 918
from Anonymous, *The Character of a Coffee-House, with the Symptoms of a Town-Wit* .. 919
from Anonymous, *Coffee-Houses Vindicated* 920
from Richard Steele, *The Spectator* No. 155 (28 August 1711) 921
William Hogarth, *Marriage A-la-Mode* 922
Joseph Addison, *The Spectator* No. 119 (17 July 1711) 928
from John Gay, *The Shepherd's Week* 933
from Lady Mary Wortley Montagu, *Six Town Eclogues* 935
from Joseph Addison, *The Spectator* No. 414 (25 June 1712) 938
from Alexander Pope, Letter to Edward Blount, 2 June 1725 941
from John Dyer, *The Fleece* 942
from Edmund Burke, *A Philosophical Enquiry into the Origin of Our Ideas of the Sublime and the Beautiful* 943
Of the Sublime 943
Of the Passion Caused by the Sublime 944
The Sublime and Beautiful Compared 944

Hester Thrale Piozzi 945
from *Hester Thrale's Journal* 946
Selected Letters (sites.broadviewpress.com/bablonline)
To Samuel Johnson, 4 July 1784
To Samuel Johnson, 15 July 1784
To the Ladies of Liangollen, 2 May 1800
To the Reverend Leonard Chappelow, 13 May 1800
To the Reverend Robert Gray, 13 May 1801
To the Reverend Chappelow, 18 June 1804
To Penelope Sophia Pennington, 19 August 1804

Olaudah Equiano or Gustavus Vassa 952
from *The Interesting Narrative of the Life of Olaudah Equiano* 953
Chapter 1 953
Chapter 2 960
Chapter 5 (sites.broadviewpress.com/bablonline)
Chapter 7
In Context: Reactions to Olaudah Equiano's Work 968
from *The Analytic Review* (May 1789) 968
from *The Gentleman's Magazine* (June 1789) 968
from *The Monthly Review* (June 1789) 969
from *The General Magazine and Impartial Review* (July 1789) 969

RICHARD BRINSLEY SHERIDAN 970
The School for Scandal 972

FRANCES BURNEY (sites.broadviewpress.com/bablonline)
The Witlings
IN CONTEXT: Journals and Letters
from Letter from Frances Burney to Susanna Burney, 3 September 1778
from Letter from Frances Burney to Dr. Charles Burney, c. 13 August 1779
from Oliver Goldsmith's "An Essay on the Theatre"

PHILLIS WHEATLEY 1016
To Maecenas 1017
To the King's Most Excellent Majesty 1018
On Being Brought from Africa to America 1018
To the Right Honorable William, Earl of Dartmouth 1019
To S.M. a Young African Painter, on Seeing His Works 1019
A Farewell to America: To Mrs. S.W. 1020
A Funeral Poem on the Death of C.E., An Infant of Twelve Months 1021
On the Death of the Reverend Mr. George Whitefield 1022
IN CONTEXT: Letters Concerning Black or Slave Writers 1025
Copy of a Letter sent by the Author's Master to the Publisher, Boston (14 November 1772) 1025
from *The Massachusetts Gazette and Boston Post Boy and Advertisers* (21 March 1774) 1025
from Thomas Jefferson, Notes on the State of Virginia 1026

APPENDICES

READING POETRY 1027

MAPS 1047

MONARCHS AND PRIME MINISTERS 1051

GLOSSARY OF TERMS 1056

TEXTS AND CONTEXTS: CHRONOLOGICAL CHART (sites.broadviewpress.com/bablonline)

BIBLIOGRAPHY (sites.broadviewpress.com/bablonline)

PERMISSIONS ACKNOWLEDGMENTS 1079

INDEX OF FIRST LINES 1081

INDEX OF AUTHORS AND TITLES 1083

Preface

A Fresh Approach

The publication of the first edition of this anthology in 2006 was widely hailed as an exciting achievement, with many academics concluding that its comprehensiveness, its consistency, its visual appeal, and its fresh approach made the Broadview the "new standard" in anthologies of British literature. We are also taking a fresh approach in issuing new editions of the anthology's volumes. Rather than publishing a second edition of each of the six volumes simultaneously, we are publishing new editions of the individual volumes at the rate of approximately one per year. If all goes according to plan, each volume will thus appear in a new edition every six years. We recognize that some competitors have in recent years made it a practice to issue new editions more frequently than that, but our feeling is that it is better to allow several years to elapse between editions—not least of all, as a new edition may represent a considerable inconvenience to academics teaching from the anthology. (The approach also has real practical advantages for a smaller publisher such as Broadview; rather than gearing up for a massive process of revision every few years and then gearing down again in the wake of publication, we can proceed at a steady pace with the work of updating and revising.)

For the second edition of this volume a considerable number of changes have been made. In several cases the selections from canonical authors have been expanded; there is more Pepys, more Defoe, more Swift, more Pope, and more Johnson. Fielding's *Tragedy of Tragedies* is a major addition to the anthology's representation of the drama of the period. Additional chapters from Equiano's *Interesting Narrative* have been added, and the selection of work by Mary Astell is larger too. The importance of periodical literature to the period is now recognized through the inclusion of a substantial new section of material.

Some of the most important additions to the volume are to the contextual materials; the sections on "Town and Country" and on "Mind and God, Faith and Science" are expanded, and a wide-ranging section entitled "Transatlantic Currents" has been added. The volume also includes additional visual material—including four more pages of color illustrations.

Inevitably, some selections have been dropped from the bound book; these will all remain available, however, as part of the anthology's website component. Perhaps the most significant works in this category are *The Castle of Otranto* and *The Witlings*; as well as remaining available on the website, these works—like *The Rover, Joseph Andrews, Evelina*, and approximately 100 other titles from the period—are available as stand-alone volumes in the Broadview Editions series, and may be ordered with this volume (at little or no additional cost to the student) in a shrink-wrapped combination package.

Of the General Editors, Isobel Grundy of the University of Alberta has played the largest part (so far as the "Restoration and the Eighteenth Century" volume is concerned) in choosing and preparing material for publication. As with the previous edition of the volume, many people outside the General Editors group have also made important contributions to the preparation of this material. Particular thanks should go to Darryl Domingo of the University of Memphis (who played an instrumental role in the very difficult editorial task of preparing the text of Fielding's *Tragedy of Tragedies*); and to Developmental Editor Laura Buzzard, who took the lead in expanding the range of textual materials for this edition. Laura Cardiff and Yevgeniya Traps also made significant contributions—as did Jennifer McCue, Developmental Editor for the anthology as a whole, and Kathryn Brownsey, who coordinates design and typesetting.

Enlisting the help of a substantial number of people is entirely consistent with the approach we have followed from the start with *The Broadview Anthology*. Rather than dividing up the vast amount of work entailed in preparing such a large anthology among a relatively small number of academics, and asking each of them to handle on their own the work of choosing, annotating, and preparing introductions to texts in their particular areas of specialization, we chose to involve a large number of contributors in the process (as the pages following the title page to this volume attest), and to encourage a high degree of collaboration at every level. First and foremost are the distinguished academics who serve as our General Editors for the project, but in all there have literally been hundreds of people involved at various stages in researching, drafting headnotes or annotations, reviewing material, editing material, and carrying out the work of designing and typesetting the texts and other materials. That approach allowed us to draw on a diverse range of talent, and to prepare the first edition of a large anthology with extraordinary efficiency. It has also facilitated the maintenance of a high degree of consistency. Material has been reviewed and revised in-house at Broadview, by outside editors, by a variety of academics with a diverse range of backgrounds and academic specialities, and by our team of General Editors for the project as a whole. The aim has been not only to ensure accuracy but also to make sure that the same standards be applied throughout the anthology to matters such as coverage provided in introductions, level of annotation, tone of writing, and student accessibility.

As with the first edition, our General Editors have throughout taken the lead in the process of making selections for the anthology. Several core principles have guided those selections. We have endeavored to provide a selection that is broadly representative, while also being mindful of the importance of choosing texts that have the capacity to engage readers' interest today. We have for the most part made it a policy to include long works in their entirety or not at all; works from the Restoration and the Eighteenth Century included in their entirety in the anthology include *Oroonoko*, *Gulliver's Travels*, and *Fantomina*. And over the full six volumes of *The Broadview Anthology* readers will find a range of works (among them Barbauld's *Eighteen Hundred and Eleven*, Smith's *Beachy Head*, Tennyson's *In Memoriam*, and Meredith's *Modern Love*) that are often excerpted in (or omitted from) other anthologies. Where editions of works are available separately in our acclaimed Broadview Editions series, we have often decided to omit them from the anthology, on the grounds that those wishing to teach one or more such works may easily do so in a combination package with the anthology. On such grounds we have decided against including, for example, *Utopia*, *Twelfth Night*, *Frankenstein*, *Pride and Prejudice*, or *Heart of Darkness*.

Any discussion of what is distinctive about *The Broadview Anthology of British Literature* must focus above all on the contents. In every volume of the anthology there is material that is distinctive and fresh—including not only selections by lesser-known writers but also less familiar selections from canonical writers. The anthology takes a fresh approach too to a great many canonical texts. The first volume of the anthology includes not only Roy Liuzza's translation of *Beowulf* (widely acclaimed as the most engaging and reliable translation available), but also new translations by Liuzza of many other works of Old English poetry and prose. Unique to the first volume of this anthology are a verse translation of *Judith* by Stephen Glosecki, and translations by Claire Waters of several of the *Lais* of Marie De France. The present volume includes a ground-breaking selection of work by laboring-class poets and a unique group of materials on the development of print culture over the period. "The Victorian Era" includes "The Story of Little Dombey" and "Sikes and Nancy"—two short works developed by Dickens out of his novels and shaped into concise new works for presentation in performance. Volume 6 includes not only Woolf and Joyce but also Dorothy Richardson—an author who arguably did more than either of her more famous contemporaries to introduce "stream of consciousness" fiction into English literature.

In a number of cases the distinctive physical form of the anthology facilitates the presentation of content in an engaging and practical fashion. Notably, the adoption of a two-column format allows for some translations (the Marie de France *Lais*, the James Winny translation of *Sir Gawain and the Green Knight*) to be presented in parallel column format alongside the original texts, allowing readers to experience something of the flavor of the original, while providing convenient access to an accessible translation. Similarly, scenes from the Quarto version of *King Lear* are presented alongside the comparable sections of the Folio text, and passages from four translations of the Bible are laid out parallel to each other for ready comparison.

The large trim-size, two-column format also allows for greater flexibility in the presentation of visual materials. Throughout our intent is to make this an anthology that is fully alive to the connections between literary and visual culture, from the discussion of the CHI-RHO page of the Lindisfarne Gospels in the first volume of the anthology (and the accompanying color illustration) to the inclusion in Volume 6 of a number of selections (including Graham Greene's "The Basement Room," Hanif Kureishi's "My Son the Fanatic," Tom Stoppard's "Professional Foul," and several skits from "Monty Python's Flying Circus") that may be discussed in connection with film or television versions. Along the way appear several full-page illustrations from the Ellesmere manuscript of Chaucer's *Canterbury Tales* and illustrations to a wide variety of other works, from *Robinson Crusoe* and *Gulliver's Travels* to *A Christmas Carol* and *The Road to Wigan Pier*.

CONTEXTUAL MATERIALS

Illustrations are also an important component of the background materials that form an important part of the anthology. These materials are presented in two ways. Several "Contexts" sections on particular topics or themes appear in each volume of the anthology, presented independent of any particular text or author. These include broadly based groupings of material on such topics as "Religion and Spiritual Life," "Print Culture," "India and the Orient," "The Abolition of Slavery," "The New Art of Photography," and "The End of Empire." The groups of "In Context" materials each relate to a particular text or author. They range from the genealogical tables provided as a supplement to *Beowulf*; to materials on "The Eighteenth-Century Sexual Imagination" (presented in conjunction with Haywood's *Fantomina*); to a selection of materials relating to the Peterloo massacre (presented in conjunction with Percy Shelley's "The Mask of Anarchy"); to materials on "'The Vilest Scramble for Loot' in Central Africa" (presented in conjunction with Conrad's "An Outpost of Progress"). For the most part these contextual materials are, as the word suggests, included with a view to setting texts in their broader literary, historical, and cultural contexts; in some cases, however, the materials included in "Contexts" sections are themselves literary works of a high order. The autobiographical account by Eliza M. of nineteenth-century life in Cape Town, for example (included in the section in Volume 5 on "Race and Empire"), is as remarkable for its literary qualities as it is for the light it sheds on the realities of colonial life. In the inclusion of texts such as these, as well as in other ways, the anthology aims to encourage readers to explore the boundaries of the literary and the non-literary, and the issue of what constitutes a "literary text."

WOMEN'S PLACE

A central element of the broadening of the canon of British literature in recent generations has of course been a great increase in the attention paid to texts by women writers. As one might expect from a publisher that has played an important role in making neglected works by women writers widely available, this anthology reflects the broadening of the canon quantitatively, by including a substantially larger number of women writers than have earlier anthologies of British literature. But it also reflects this broadening in other ways. In many anthologies of literature (anthologies of British literature, to be sure, but also anthologies of literature of a variety of other sorts) women writers are set somewhat apart, referenced in introductions and headnotes only in relation to issues of gender, and treated as important only for the fact of their being women writers. *The Broadview Anthology* strenuously resists such segregation; while women writers are of course discussed in relation to gender issues, their texts are also presented and discussed alongside those by men in a wide variety of other contexts, including seventeenth-century religious and political controversies, the abolitionist movement, and World War I pacifism. Texts by women writers are front and center in the discussion of the development of realism in nineteenth-century fiction. And when it comes to the twentieth century, both Virginia Woolf and Dorothy Richardson are included alongside James Joyce as practitioners of groundbreaking modernist narrative techniques.

"BRITISH," "ENGLISH," "IRISH," "SCOTTISH," "WELSH," "OTHER"

The broadening of English Studies, in conjunction with the expansion and subsequent contraction of British power and influence around the world, has considerably complicated the issue of exactly how inclusive anthologies should be. In several respects this anthology (like its two main competitors) is significantly more inclusive than its title suggests, including a number of non-British writers whose works connect in important ways with the traditions of British literature. We endeavor to portray the fluid and multilingual reality of the medieval period through the inclusion not only of works in Old and Middle English but also, where other cultures interacted with the nascent "English" language and "British" culture, works in Latin, in French, and in Welsh.

In later periods the word "British" becomes deeply problematic in different respects, but on balance we have preferred it to the only obvious alternative, "English." There are several objections to the latter in this context. Perhaps most obviously, "English" excludes authors or texts not only from Ireland but also from Scotland and from Wales, both of which retain to this day cultures quite distinct from that of the English. "English literature," of course, may also be taken to mean "literature written in English," but since the anthology does not cover *all* literature written in English (most obviously in excluding American literature), the ambiguity would not in this case be helpful.

The inclusion of Irish writers presents a related but even more tangled set of issues. At the beginning of the period covered by the six volumes of this anthology we find works, such as the *Book of Kells*, that may have been created in what is now England, in what is now Scotland, in what is now Ireland—or in some combination of these. Through most of the seventeenth, eighteenth, and nineteenth centuries almost the whole of Ireland was under British control—but for the most part unwillingly. In the period covered in the last of the six volumes Ireland was partitioned, with Northern Ireland becoming a part of the United Kingdom and the Republic of Ireland declared independent of Britain on 6 December 1921. Less than two months earlier, James Joyce had completed *Ulysses*, which was first published as a complete work the following year (in Paris, not in Britain). It would be obviously absurd to regard Joyce as a British writer up to just before the publication of *Ulysses*, and an Irish writer thereafter. And arguably he and other Irish writers should never be regarded as British, whatever the politics of the day. If on no other grounds than their overwhelming influence on and connection to the body of literature written in the British Isles, however, we have included Irish writers—among them Swift, Sheridan, Wilde, Shaw, Beckett, Bowen, Muldoon, and Heaney as well as Joyce—throughout this anthology. We have also endeavored to give a real sense in the introductions to the six volumes of the anthology, in the headnotes to individual authors, and in the annotations to the texts themselves, of the ways in which the histories and the cultures of England, Ireland, Scotland, and Wales, much as they interact with one another, are also distinct.

Also included in this anthology are texts by writers from areas that are far removed geographically from the British Isles but that are or have been British possessions. Writers such as Mary Rowlandson, Olaudah Equiano, and Phillis Wheatley are included, as they spent all or most of their lives living in what were then British colonial possessions. Writers who came of age in an independent United States, on the other hand, are not included, unless (like T.S. Eliot) they subsequently put down roots in Britain and became important British literary figures. Substantial grey areas, of course, surround such issues. One might well argue, for example, that Henry James merits inclusion in an anthology of British literature, or that W.H. Auden and Thom Gunn are more American poets than British ones. But the chosen subject matter of James's work has traditionally been considered to mark him as having remained an American writer, despite having spent almost two-thirds of his life in England. And both Auden and Gunn so clearly made a mark in Britain before crossing the Atlantic that it would seem odd to exclude them from these pages on the grounds of their having lived the greater part of their adult lives in America. One of our competitors includes Sylvia Plath in their anthology of British literature; Plath lived in England for only five of her thirty years, though, and her poetry is generally agreed to have more in common with the traditions of

Lowell, Merwin, and Sexton than with the currents of British poetry in the 1950s and '60s.

As a broad principle, we have been open to the inclusion of twentieth and twenty-first century work in English not only by writers from the British Isles but also by writers from British possessions overseas, and by writers from countries that were once British possessions and have remained a part of the British Commonwealth. In such cases we have often chosen selections that relate in one way or another to the tradition of British literature and the British colonial legacy. Of the Judith Wright poems included, several relate to her coming to terms with the British colonial legacy in Australia; similarly, both the Margaret Atwood and the Alice Munro selections include work in which these Canadian authors attempt to recreate imaginatively the experience of British emigrants to Canada in the nineteenth century; the Chinua Achebe story in the anthology concerns the divide between British colonial culture and traditional Nigerian culture; and so on. (For convenience the anthology's last volume groups most of the post-World War II non-British authors together, following the "Contexts: The End of Empire" section; for the most part, the contents for all volumes are arranged chronologically according to the birthdate of each author.)

THE HISTORY OF LANGUAGE, AND OF PRINT CULTURE

Among the liveliest discussions we had at meetings of our General Editors were those concerning the issue of whether or not to bring spelling and punctuation into accord with present-day practice. We finally decided that, in the interests of making the anthology accessible to the introductory student, we should *in most cases* bring spelling and punctuation in line with present-day practice. An important exception has been made for works in which modernizing spelling and punctuation would alter the meaning or the aural and metrical qualities. In practice this means that works before the late sixteenth century tend to be presented either in their original form or in translation, whereas later texts tend to have spelling and punctuation modernized. But where spelling and punctuation choices in later texts are known (or believed on reliable authority) to represent conscious choice on the part of the author rather than simply the common practice of the time, we have in those cases, too, made an exception and retained the original spelling and punctuation. (Among these are texts by Edmund Spenser, by William Cowper, by William Blake, John Clare, and several other poets of the Romantic era, by Bernard Shaw, and by contemporary figures such as Linton Kwesi Johnson.)

Beyond this, we all agreed that we should provide for readers a real sense of the development of the language and of print culture. To that end we have included in each volume examples of texts in their original form—in some cases through the use of pages shown in facsimile, in others by providing short passages in which spelling and punctuation have not been modernized. A list of these appears near the beginning of each volume of the anthology.

We have also included a section of the history of the language as part of the introduction to each volume. And throughout the anthology we include materials—visual as well as textual—relating to the history of print culture.

A DYNAMIC AND FLEXIBLE ANTHOLOGY

Almost all major book publishing projects nowadays are accompanied by an adjunct website, and most large-scale anthologies are accompanied by websites that provide additional background materials in electronic form. The website component of this anthology, on the other hand, is precisely that—a *component* of the anthology itself. The notion of a website of this sort grew organically out of the process of trying to winnow down the contents of the first edition of the anthology to a manageable level—the point at which all the material to be included would fit within the covers of bound books that would not be overwhelmingly heavy. And we simply could not do it. After we had made a very substantial round of cuts we were still faced with a table of contents in which each volume was at least 200 or 300 pages longer than our agreed-upon maximum. Our solution was not to try to cut anything more, but rather to select a range of material to be made available in a website component of the anthology. This material is in every way produced according to the same high standards of the material in the bound books; the editorial standards, the procedures for annotation, the author introductions, and the page design and layout—all are the same. The texts on the web, in short, are not "extra" materials; they are an integral part of the full anthology. In accordance with that principle, we have been careful to include a wide range of texts by lesser-known writers within the bound books, and a number of texts by canonical writers within the web component of the anthology.

The latter may be used in a variety of ways. Most obviously, readings from the web component are available to any purchaser of the book. Instructors who adopt *The Broadview Anthology of British Literature* as a course text are also granted permission to reproduce any web material for which Broadview holds copyright in a supplementary coursepack. An alternative for instructors who want to "create their own" anthology is to provide the publisher with a desired table of contents; Broadview will then make available to students through their university bookstore a custom-made coursepack with precisely those materials included. Other options are available too. Volumes of the anthology itself may of course be shrink-wrapped together at special prices in any desired combination. They may also (for a modest additional charge) be combined in a shrink-wrapped package with one or more of the over 400 volumes in the Broadview Editions series.

We anticipate that over the years the web-based component of the anthology will continue to grow—every year there is a greater choice of web-based texts in the anthology. And we now offer (in partnership with Symtext) an all-electronic option for using the anthology. But we never foresee the day when the web will be the only option; we expect physical books always to remain central to Broadview's approach to publishing.

THE BROADVIEW LIST

One of the reasons we were able to bring a project of this sort to fruition in a relatively short time was that we were able to draw on the resources of the full Broadview list: the many titles in the Broadview Editions series, and also the considerable range of other Broadview anthologies. As the contributors' pages and the permissions acknowledgments pages indicate, a number of Broadview authors have acted as contributing editors to this volume, providing material from other volumes that has been adapted to suit the needs of the present anthology; we gratefully acknowledge their contribution.

As it has turned out, the number of cases where we have been able to draw on the resources of the Broadview list in the full sense, using in these pages texts and annotations in very much the same form in which they appear elsewhere, has been relatively small; whether because of an issue such as the level of textual modernization or one of style of annotation, we have more often than not ended up deciding that the requirements of this anthology were such that we could not use material from another Broadview source as-is. But even in these cases we often owe a debt of gratitude to the many academics who have edited outstanding editions and anthologies for Broadview. For even where we have not drawn directly from them, we have often been inspired by them—inspired to think of a wider range of texts as possibilities than we might otherwise have done, inspired to think of contextual materials in places where we might otherwise not have looked, inspired by the freshness of approach that so many of these titles exemplify.

EDITORIAL PROCEDURES AND CONVENTIONS, APPARATUS

The in-house set of editorial guidelines for *The Broadview Anthology of British Literature* runs to over 40 pages, covering everything from conventions for the spacing of marginal notes, to the use of small caps for the abbreviations CE and BCE, to the approach we have adopted to references in author headnotes to name changes. Perhaps the most important core principle in the introductions to the various volumes, in the headnotes for each author, in the introductions in "Contexts" sections, and in annotations throughout the anthology, is to endeavor to provide a sufficient amount of information to enable students to read and interpret these texts, but without making evaluative judgments or imposing particular interpretations. In practice that is all a good deal more challenging than it sounds; it is often extremely difficult to describe why a particular author is considered to be important without using language that verges on the interpretive or the evaluative. But it is a fine line that we have all agreed is worth trying to walk; we hope that readers will find that the anthology achieves an appropriate balance.

ANNOTATION: It is also often difficult to make judgments as to where it is appropriate to provide an explanatory annotation for a word or phrase. Our policy has been to annotate where we feel it likely that most first- or second-year students are likely to have difficulty understanding the denotative meaning. (We have made it a practice not to provide notes discussing connotative meanings.) But in practice the vocabularies and levels of verbal facility of first- and second-year students may vary enormously, both from institution to institution and within any given college or university class. On the whole, we provide somewhat more annotation than our competitors, and somewhat less interpretation. Again, we hope that readers will find that the anthology has struck an appropriate balance.

THE ETHICS AND POLITICS OF ANNOTATION: On one issue regarding annotation we have felt that principles are involved that go beyond the pedagogical. Most anthologies of British literature allow many words or phrases of a racist, sexist, anti-Semitic, or homophobic nature either to pass entirely without comment, or to be glossed with apologist comments that leave the impression that such comments were excusable in the past, and may even be unobjectionable in the present. Where derogatory comments about Jewish people and money-lending are concerned, for example, anthologies often leave the impression that money-lending was a pretty unsavory practice that Jewish people entered by choice; it has been all too rare to provide readers with any sense of the degree to which English society consistently discriminated against Jews, expelling them entirely for several centuries, requiring them to wear physical marks identifying their Jewish status, prohibiting them from entering most professions, and so on. *The Broadview Anthology* endeavors in such cases, first of all, not to allow such words and phrases to pass without comment; and second, to gloss without glossing over.

DATES: We make it a practice to include the date when a work was first made public, whether publication in print or, in the case of dramatic works, made public through the first performance of the play. Where that date is known to differ substantially from the date of composition, a note to this effect is included in parentheses. With medieval works, where there is no equivalent to the "publication" of later eras, where texts often vary greatly from one manuscript copy to another, and where knowledge as to date of original composition is usually imprecise, the date that appears at the end of each work is an estimate of the date of the work's origin in the written form included in the anthology. Earlier oral or written versions are of course in some cases real possibilities.

TEXTS: Where translations appear in this anthology, a note at the bottom of the first page indicates what translation is being used. Similar notes also address overall textual issues where choice of copy text is particularly significant. Reliable editions of all works are listed in the bibliography for the anthology, which is included as part of the website component rather than in the bound books, to facilitate ready revision. (In addition to information as to reliable editions, the bibliography provides for each author and for each of the six periods select lists of important or useful historical and critical works.) Copyright information for texts not in the public domain, however, is provided within the bound books in a section listing Permissions Acknowledgments.

INTRODUCTIONS: In addition to the introductory headnotes for each author included in the anthology, each "Contexts" section includes a substantial introduction, and each volume includes an introduction to the period as a whole. These introductions to the six volumes of the anthology endeavor to provide a sense not only of the broad picture of literary developments in the period, but also of the historical, social, and political background, and of the cultural climate. Readers should be cautioned that, while there is inevitably some overlap between information presented here and information presented in the author headnotes, an effort has been made to avoid such repetition as much as possible; the general introduction to each period should thus be read in conjunction with the author headnotes. The general introductions aim not only to provide an overview of ways in which texts and authors included in these pages may connect with one another, but also to give readers a sense of connection with a range of other writers and texts of the period.

READING POETRY: For much of the glossary and for the "Reading Poetry" section that appears as part of the appendices to each volume we have drawn on the superb material prepared by Herbert Rosengarten and Amanda Goldrick-Jones for *The Broadview Anthology of Poetry*; this section provides a concise but comprehensive introduction to the study of poetry. It includes discussions of diction, imagery, poetic figures, and various poetic forms, as well as offering an introduction to prosody.

MAPS: Also appearing within each of the bound books are maps especially prepared for this anthology, including, for each volume, a map of Britain showing towns and features of relevance during the pertinent period; a map showing the counties of Britain and of Ireland; maps both of the London area and of the inner city; and world maps indicating the locations of some of the significant places referenced in the anthology, and for later volumes showing the extent of Britain's overseas territories.

GLOSSARY: Some other anthologies of British literature include both glossaries of terms and essays introducing students to various political and religious categories in British history. Similar information is included in *The Broadview Anthology of British Literature*, but we have adopted a more integrated approach, including political and religious terms along with literary ones in a convenient general glossary. While we recognize that "googling" for information of this sort is often the student's first resort (and we acknowledge too the value of searching the web for the wealth of background reference information available there), we also recognize that information culled from the Internet is often far from reliable; it is our intent, through this glossary, through our introductions and headnotes, and through the wealth of accessible annotation in the anthology, to provide as part of the anthology a reliable core of information in the most convenient and accessible form possible.

OTHER MATERIALS: A chart of Monarchs and Prime Ministers is also provided within these pages. A range of other adjunct materials may be accessed through *The Broadview Anthology of British Literature* website. "Texts and Contexts" charts for each volume provide a convenient parallel reference guide to the dates of literary texts and historical developments. "Money in Britain" provides a thumbnail sketch of the world of pounds, shillings, and pence, together with a handy guide to estimating the current equivalents of monetary values from earlier eras. And the website offers, too, a variety of aids for the student and the instructor. An up-to-date list of these appears on the site.

Acknowledgments

The names of those on the Editorial Board that shaped this anthology appear on the title page, and those of the many who contributed directly to the writing, editing, and production of the project on the following two pages. Special acknowledgment for this new edition should go to Developmental Editor Jennifer McCue, who has been instrumental in tying together all the vast threads of this project and in making it a reality; to Senior Editor Laura Buzzard, who has led the way in drafting introductory materials and annotations for the new material, and done so with great skill and unfailing grace; to Kathryn Brownsey, who has been responsible for design and typesetting, and has continued to do a superb job and to maintain her good spirits even when faced with near-impossible demands; to Joe Davies, for the range of his general knowledge as well as for his keen eye as our primary proofreader for the entire project; to Merilee Atos, who has done superb work on the vast job of clearing permissions for the anthology; and to Leslie Dema, Nora Ruddock, and Christine Handley, who have ably and enthusiastically taken the lead with marketing matters.

The academic general editors and all of us in-house at Broadview owe an enormous debt of gratitude to the hundreds of academics who have offered assistance at various stages of this project. In particular we would like to express our appreciation and our thanks to the following:

Rachel Ablow, University of Rochester
Katherine Acheson, University of Waterloo
Kenet Adamson, Southwestern Community College
Bryan Alexander, Middlebury College
Sharon Alker, Whitman College
James Allard, Brock University
Ella Allen, St. Thomas University
Rosemary Allen, Georgetown College
Laurel Amtower, San Diego State University
Robert Anderson, Oakland University
Christopher Armitage, University of North Carolina, Chapel Hill
Clinton Atchley, Henderson State University
Gerry Baillargeon, University of Victoria
John Baird, University of Toronto
William Baker, Northern Illinois University
Karen Bamford, Mount Allison University
John Batchelor, University of Newcastle
Lynn Batten, University of California, Los Angeles
Stephen Behrendt, University of Nebraska
Alexandra Bennett, Northern Illinois University
John Beynon, California State University, Fresno
Daniel Bivona, Arizona State University
Robert E. Bjork, Arizona State University
John Black, Moravian College
Scott Black, Villanova University
Rita Bode, Trent University
Robert Boenig, Texas A & M University
Matthew Borushko, Stonehill College
Rick Bowers, University of Alberta
Patricia Brace, Columbus State University
David Brewer, Ohio State University
William Brewer, Appalachian State University
Susan Brown, University of Guelph
Sylvia Brown, University of Alberta
Sheila Burgar, University of Victoria
Catherine Burroughs, Wells College
Rebecca Bushnell, University of Pennsylvania
Michael Calabrese, California State University
Elizabeth Campbell, Oregon State University
Gregory Castle, Arizona State University
Cynthia Caywood, University of San Diego

Jane Chance, Rice University
Ranita Chatterjee, California State University, Northridge
William Christmas, San Francisco State University
Nancy Cirillo, University of Illinois, Chicago
Eric Clarke, University of Pittsburgh
Jeanne Clegg, University of Aquila, Italy
Thomas J. Collins, University of Western Ontario
Thomas L. Cooksey, Armstrong Atlantic State University
Kevin Cope, Louisiana State University
David Cowart, University of South Carolina
Catherine Craft-Fairchild, University of St. Thomas
Roger Davis, Red Deer College
Carol Davison, University of Windsor
Alexander Dick, University of British Columbia
Len Diepeveen, Dalhousie University
Mary Dockray-Miller, Lesley College
James Doelman, Brescia University College, University of Western Ontario
Frank Donoghue, Ohio State University
Chris Downs, Saint James School
Alfred Drake, Chapman University
Ian Duncan, University of California, Berkeley
Julie Early, University of Alabama, Huntsville
Roxanne Eberle, University of Georgia
Siân Echard, University of British Columbia
Garrett Epp, University of Alberta
Joshua Eyler, Columbus State University
Ruth Feingold, St. Mary's College, Maryland
Dino Franco Felluga, Perdue University
Joanne Findon, Trent University
Larry Fink, Hardin Simmons University
Daniel Fischlin, University of Guelph
Christina Fitzgerald, University of Toledo
Verlyn Flieger, University of Maryland
Robert Forman, St. John's University
Allyson Foster, Hunter College
Lorcan Fox, University of British Columbia
Roberta Frank, Yale University
Jeff Franklin, University of Colorado, Denver
Maria Frawley, George Washington University
Mark Fulk, Buffalo State College
Constance Fulmer, Pepperdine University
Christine Gallant, Georgia State University
Andrew Galloway, Cornell University
Michael Gamer, University of Pennsylvania
Barbara Gates, University of Delaware
Jonathan C. Glance, Mercer University
Susan Patterson Glover, Laurentian University
Daniel Gonzalez, University of New Orleans
Jan Gorak, University of Denver
Chris Gordon-Craig, University of Alberta
Ann-Barbara Graff, Georgia Tech University
Bruce Graver, Providence College
Mary Griffin, Kwantlen University College
Michael Griffin, formerly of Southern Illinois University
George C. Grinnell, University of British Columbia, Okanagan
Elisabeth Gruner, University of Richmond
Bonnie Gunzenhauser, Roosevelt University
Kevin Gustafson, University of Texas at Arlington
Stephen Guy-Bray, University of British Columbia
Ruth Haber, Worcester State College
Dorothy Hadfield, University of Guelph
Margaret Hadley, University of Calgary
Robert Hampson, Royal Holloway University of London
Carol Hanes, Howard College
Michael Hanly, Washington State University
Lila Harper, Central Washington State University
Joseph Harris, Harvard University
Katherine Harris, San Jose State University
Anthony Harrison, North Carolina State University
John Hart, Motlow State Community College
Douglas Hayes, Lakehead University
Jennifer Hellwarth, Allegheny University
David Herman, Ohio State University
Peter Herman, San Diego State University
Kathy Hickock, Iowa State University
John Hill, US Naval Academy
Thomas Hill, Cornell University
Elizabeth Hodgson, University of British Columbia
Jim Hood, Guilford College
Joseph Hornsby, University of Alabama
Scott Howard, University of Denver
Jennifer Hughes, Averett University
Sylvia Hunt, Georgian College
Tara Hyland-Russell, St. Mary's College
Catherine Innes-Parker, University of Prince Edward Island

Jacqueline Jenkins, University of Calgary
John Johansen, University of Alberta
Gordon Johnston, Trent University
Richard Juang, Susquehanna University
Michael Keefer, University of Guelph
Sarah Keefer, Trent University
Lloyd Kermode, California State University, Long Beach
Brandon Kershner, University of Florida
Jon Kertzer, University of Calgary
Waqas Khwaja, Agnes State C ollege
Helen Killoran, Ohio University
Gordon Kipling, University of California, Los Angeles
Anne Klinck, University of New Brunswick
Elizabeth Kraft, University of Georgia
Mary Kramer, University of Massachusetts, Lowell
Wai-Leung Kwok, San Francisco State University
Marilyn Lantz, East Mississippi Community College
Kate Lawson, University of Waterloo
Linda Leeds, Bellevue Community College
Mary Elizabeth Leighton, University of Victoria
Eric Lindstrom, University of Vermont
William Liston, Ball State University
Sharon Locy, Loyola Marymount University
Ross MacKay, Malaspina University-College
Peter Mallios, University of Maryland
Arnold Markley, Penn State University
Louis Markos, Houston Baptist University
Nick Mason, Brigham Young University
Pamela McCallum, University of Calgary
Patricia McCormack, Itawamba Community College
Kristen McDermott, Central Michigan University
John McGowan, University of North Carolina
Brian McHale, Ohio State University
Jim McKeown, McLennan Community College
Thomas McLean, University of Otago, New Zealand
Susan McNeill-Bindon, University of Alberta
Jodie Medd, Carleton University
Rod Michell, Thompson Rivers University
David Miller, Mississippi College
Kitty Millett, San Francisco State University
Britt Mize, Texas A&M University
Richard Moll, University of Western Ontario
Amy L. Montz, Texas A&M University
Monique Morgan, McGill University
John Morillo, North Carolina State University
Lucy Morrison, Salisbury University
Lorri Nandrea, University of Wisconsin-Steven's Point
Mara Narain, Texas Christian University
Byron Nelson, West Virginia University
Carolyn Nelson, West Virginia University
Claudia Nelson, Southwest Texas State University
Holly Faith Nelson, Trinity Western University
John Niles, University of Wisconsin, Madison
Michael North, University of California, Los Angeles
Mary Anne Nunn, Central Connecticut State University
David Oakleaf, University of Calgary
Tamara O'Callaghan, Northern Kentucky University
Karen Odden, Assistant Editor for *Victorian Literature and Culture* (formerly of University of Wisconsin, Milwaukee)
Erika Olbricht, Pepperdine University
Patrick O'Malley, Georgetown University
Patricia O'Neill, Hamilton College
Delilah Orr, Fort Lewis College
John Pagano, Barnard College
Kirsten Parkinson, Hiram College
Diana Patterson, Mount Royal College
Cynthia Patton, Emporia State University
Russell Perkin, St. Mary's University
Marjorie G. Perloff, Stanford University
Jim Persoon, Grand Valley State University
John Peters, University of North Texas
Todd Pettigrew, Cape Breton University
Alexander Pettit, University of North Texas
Jennifer Phegley, The University of Missouri, Kansas City
John Pollock, San Jose State University
Mary Poovey, New York University
Gautam Premnath, University of Massachusetts, Boston
Regina Psaki, University of Oregon
Laura Quinney, Brandeis University
Katherine Quinsey, University of Windsor
Tilottama Rajan, University of Western Ontario
Geoff Rector, University of Ottawa
Margaret Reeves, Atkinson College, York University
Cedric Reverand, University of Wyoming
Gerry Richman, Suffolk University
John Rickard, Bucknell University
Michelle Risdon, Lake Tahoe Community College

David Robinson, University of Arizona
Solveig C. Robinson, Pacific Lutheran University
Laura Rotunno, Pennsylvania State University, Altoona
Brian Rourke, New Mexico State University
Christopher Rovee, Louisiana State University
Nicholas Ruddick, University of Regina
Jason Rudy, University of Maryland
Donelle Ruwe, Northern Arizona University
Michelle Sauer, Minot State University
SueAnn Schatz, Lock Haven University of Pennsylvania
Dan Schierenbeck, Central Missouri State University
Norbert Schürer, California State University, Long Beach
Debora B. Schwartz, California Polytechnic University
Janelle A. Schwartz, Loyola University
John T. Sebastian, Loyola University
David Seed, University of Liverpool
Karen Selesky, University College of the Fraser Valley
Carol Senf, Georgia Tech University
Sharon Setzer, North Carolina State University
Lynn Shakinovsky, Wilfred Laurier University
John Sider, Westmont College
Judith Slagle, East Tennessee State University
Johanna Smith, University of Texas at Arlington
Sharon Smulders, Mount Royal College
Jason Snart, College of DuPage
Malinda Snow, Georgia State University
Goran Stanivukovic, St. Mary's University
Thomas Steffler, Carleton University
Richard Stein, University of Oregon
Eric Sterling, Auburn University Montgomery
James Stokes, University of Wisconsin, Stevens Point
Mary-Ann Stouck, Simon Fraser University
Nathaniel Strout, Hamilton College
Brad Sullivan, Western New England College
Lisa Surridge, University of Victoria
Joyce A. Sutphen, Gustavus Adolphus College
Beth Sutton-Ramspeck, Ohio State University
Nanora Sweet, University of Missouri, St. Louis
Dana Symons, Simon Fraser University
Andrew Taylor, University of Ottawa
Elizabeth Teare, University of Dayton
Doug Thorpe, University of Saskatchewan
Jane Toswell, University of Western Ontario
Kim Trainor, University of British Columbia
Herbert Tucker, University of Virginia
John Tucker, University of Victoria
Mark Turner, King's College, University of London
Eleanor Ty, Wilfrid Laurier University
Deborah Tyler-Bennett, Loughborough University
Kirsten Uszkalo, University of Alberta
Lisa Vargo, University of Saskatchewan
Gina Luria Walker, The New School, New York City
Kim Walker, Victoria University of Wellington
Miriam Wallace, New College of Florida
Orrin Wang, University of Maryland
Hayden Ward, West Virginia State University
David Watt, University of Manitoba
Ruth Wehlau, Queen's University
Lynn Wells, University of Regina
Dan White, University of Toronto at Mississauga
Patricia Whiting, Carleton University
Thomas Willard, University of Arizona
Tara Williams, Oregon State University
Chris Willis, Birkbeck University of London
Lisa Wilson, SUNY College at Potsdam
Ed Wiltse, Nazareth College
Anne Windholz, Augustana College
Susan Wolfson, Princeton University
Kenneth Womack, Pennsylvania State University
Gillen Wood, University of Illinois, Urbana-Champaign
Carolyn Woodward, University of New Mexico
Julia Wright, Wilfrid Laurier University
Julian Yates, University of Delaware
Arlene Young, University of Manitoba
Lisa Zeitz, University of Western Ontario

The Restoration and the Eighteenth Century

Between 1660, when the Stuart monarchy was restored, and the close of the eighteenth century, the people of England (then more commonly referred to as "English" than "British," despite the official creation of Great Britain with the 1707 Act of Union) underwent numerous changes—in how they earned their living, by whom they were ruled, and how they responded to that government, in where they tended to live, and in the ways they envisioned themselves and their relationship with the world around them.

Over the course of the eighteenth century the population of the nation doubled to roughly ten million, with the most significant growth occurring in London, where the population grew from half a million in 1700 to over a million in 1800. Approximately one-tenth of the nation's population resided in its capital city, which in the seventeenth century had already become the largest city in Europe. Regional migration (from Scotland and Ireland as well as from other parts of the nation) accounted for much of this growth, but international immigrants—from Germany, Poland, Africa, and the Caribbean, for example—made up a significant portion of the city's new residents, and often formed discrete communities. More than half the city's inhabitants were women, many of whom, seeking employment as domestic help, joined the large numbers of those who left their rural homes to earn a living in the city. While developments in medicine and sanitation improved the quality of life and lowered the death rate, the English population remained quite young (with the percentage of the population over 60 never reaching higher than 8 percent), particularly in London. In the rural areas large tracts of land were enclosed for the cultivation of crops or for grazing livestock as agriculture increasingly shifted from subsistence farming into a business and demands for food from the growing urban population increased.

On average, the English people were significantly wealthier at the end of this period than they had been at its beginning. The national income increased more than fivefold—from 43 million to 222 million pounds. Industrial and financial revolutions spurred the further growth of a hitherto small though highly significant class of people, the merchant middle class, and led to a demand for a plethora of new goods that these people imported, manufactured, and sold. From a nation of farmers England was increasingly becoming, in Adam Smith's famous phrase, "a nation of shopkeepers."

Samuel Scott, "Entrance to the Fleet River" (c. 1750). Scott's style was influenced by that of Canaletto, the Italian master of city painting who lived in London intermittently from 1746 to 1755. The entrance to the Fleet River from the Thames in London is now hidden from view by the Thames Embankment.

Of London's million people, a growing percentage (though still a small one by modern standards) was literate, able to afford books, and in possession of the leisure time necessary for reading. In 1782, bookseller James Lackington claimed that the reading public had quadrupled since the early 1770s. While a substantial proportion of publications continued to be collections of sermons or devotion manuals, the new reading public also demanded news in the form of newspapers and periodicals, and fiction in a new, capacious form, the novel. The first provincial paper was launched in 1701, and by 1760 over 150 had been started. The first public libraries were founded in 1725 in Bath and Edinburgh, and by 1800 there were 122 libraries in London and 268 more in the rest of the country.

In the eighteenth century the term "British" became more and more far-reaching. For centuries the Scots had periodically fought the English to preserve their independence, but with the 1707 Act of Union that struggle ended. The kingdom of Scotland joined with that of England and Wales, and the Scottish people became subjects of the new Great Britain. Because several colonies along the eastern seaboard of North America declared independence during this period, students of American history often have the sense that Britain was a shrinking colonial power during this era; in fact the opposite is true. After the Treaty of Utrecht that ended the War of Spanish Succession, the people of the Hudson Bay Territory, as well as those of Acadia and Newfoundland (in what are now eastern provinces of Canada), became colonial British subjects. The same thing happened to the remaining inhabitants of Canada and many of those of India after the 1763 Treaty of Paris, which ended the Seven Years' War (now sometimes referred to as the first of the world wars). That treaty formalized England's supremacy in Canada and paved the way for an extensive British Empire in India. Under it, England also received control of Grenada, France's American territory east of the Mississippi, and the Spanish colony of Florida.

With the restoration of the monarchy in the late seventeenth century, the English people attempted to move beyond centuries of religious strife that had culminated in a bitter civil war. The animosity between the established Anglican Church, the Nonconformists and descendants of the former "Puritans," and the "papists," which had dominated political life, did not disappear (laws discriminating against religious minorities, such as Catholics, remained in place), but increasingly these religious debates were subsumed into broader political debates between parties with established party ideologies. Whereas previously any formal opposition to the government was apt to be regarded as treason (as it was in the case of Algernon Sidney and William Russell in 1683), during the eighteenth century the concept of a legitimate ongoing opposition to government began to take root. Political parties were born, and Parliament and the press became arenas for sanctioned political debate. By 1800 England could boast a political system that was the envy of its neighbors for its stability, effectiveness, and perceived fairness.

RELIGION, GOVERNMENT, AND PARTY POLITICS

The period began, however, with an attempt to reverse, rather than embrace, change. When Charles II landed at Dover, returning from exile in France and restoring the Stuart monarchy, many English people hoped they could return to the old order that had been shattered by civil war. Charles was crowned King in 1661, but the new monarch governed as if this were the eleventh, rather than the first, year of his rule—symbolically erasing the intervening years of civil war, Commonwealth, and Interregnum. The Act of Oblivion formally forgave many (though not all) convicted rebels, furthering the illusion that the turmoil of the preceding years could be erased. With the restoration of the monarchy came that of the established church, but Charles II promised some changes from the disastrous rule of Charles I before the civil war, including increased tolerance of Protestant dissenters and a monarchy that would rule in conjunction with Parliament, rather than in opposition to it. Underlying religious and constitutional issues continued to threaten the stability of the nation, however. Charles was ostensibly a member of the Anglican Church, but his brother, James, Duke of York, remained staunchly and publicly Catholic, with the avowed aim of establishing his faith as the national one. Though Charles had many children, he produced none with his wife; as a result, James remained next in line for the throne. These issues came to a head with the "Popish Plot" of 1678, in which Titus Oates presented perjured testimony suggesting that a Jesuit plot existed to assassinate the King and reestablish Catholic rule in England. A sharp divide arose between Successionists, who supported Charles II and his brother James, and Exclusionists, who sought to exclude James from the line of succession and to appoint James, Duke of Monmouth (one of the King's Protestant illegitimate children), in his place. To restore order Charles asserted his absolute monarchical authority, dissolving Parliament and preventing the passage of the Exclusion Bill. (It is this assertion of royal authority that Poet Laureate John Dryden celebrates in his 1681 poem *Absalom and Achitophel.*)

J.M. Wright, "Charles II" (1661).

The division between Successionists and Exclusionists led to a more lasting one between England's emerging political parties—the Whigs and the Tories. The Tories, made up primarily of landed gentry and rural clergymen, developed out of the Successionist faction; Tories (whose party name was a former term for Irish-Catholic or Royalist bandits) were characterized by their support for the monarchy and for continuing all the privileges of the Anglican Church— that is to say, by a desire to maintain the status quo. From the Exclusionist faction emerged the opposing Whig party, which represented the new moneyed interests (of big landowners and merchants), as well as Dissenters. The Whigs (a previous name for Scottish Covenanters) supported stronger Parliamentary authority, the interests and development of commerce, and somewhat more religious tolerance. These parties established themselves more and more securely in the British political arena as the eighteenth century progressed.

As many Protestants had feared, the Catholic James II did indeed come to the throne when Charles died in 1685. James promised to honor the supremacy of the Anglican Church, but soon began to back away from that promise—suspending the Test Act (which had required all holders of office to take Communion in an Anglican church) and installing Catholics in senior positions in the army, the universities, and the government. The birth of James's son raised in many minds the specter of a Catholic dynasty of rulers, and plans to remove the monarch began to take shape. Secret negotiations resulted in William of Orange, husband of James's elder, Protestant daughter Mary, marching on London with a small army in what became known as the Glorious (or Bloodless) Revolution of 1688. At William's approach James fled to exile in France—though he retained some loyal supporters in England (who were referred to as "Jacobites," from *Jacobus*, the Latin form of "James"). Parliament sanctioned the joint crowning of King William III and Queen Mary II, announcing that, rather than having conquered anything or overthrown anyone, William had simply arrived, found the throne vacant, and installed himself as its rightful occupant. (In fact Mary, as a direct descendant, was first offered the Crown, but she was too dutiful a wife to reign without her husband.) Despite the best efforts of Parliament to paper over the dynastic change, Jacobites continued through the first half of the eighteenth century to affirm that James's son and grandson (known to others as the

"Old Pretender" and the "Young Pretender," respectively) were the legitimate rulers of the nation, and major Jacobite uprisings threatened the peace in 1715 and 1745.

AN
ARGUMENT,
Shewing, that a
Standing Army
Is inconſiſtent with
A Free Government, and abſolutely deſtructive to the Conſtitution of the Engliſh Monarchy.

Cervus Equum pugna melior communibus herbis
Pellebat, donec minor in certamine longo
Imploravit opes hominis frænumq; recepit.
Sed poſtquam victor violens diſceſſit ab hoſte,
Non Equitem dorſo, non frænum depulit ore.
Horat. Epiſt. 10.

LONDON;
Printed in the Year 1697.

Title page of an anonymous 1697 pamphlet. The issue of whether or not the government should be allowed to retain a standing army was a highly contentious one in the last years of the seventeenth century—and one that revived many of the strong feelings of the Civil War and Interregnum; until William III's 1697 decision to maintain a permanent army in the wake of the Peace of Ryswick, the only English ruler to have maintained a standing army in peacetime was Oliver Cromwell.

The reign of William and Mary restored a Protestant monarchy, and it was one that promised increased tolerance. The Toleration Act of 1689 granted religious freedoms to some Dissenters (though not to Catholics) if they swore their allegiance to the Crown. Jews during this period were allowed to worship (London's first synagogue was built in 1701) but were deprived of most civil rights. A Bill of Rights reaffirmed the powers of Parliament and limited the control of the Crown. The reign of the successor to William and Mary, Mary's sister Anne (who reigned from 1702 to 1714), marked a period of commercial growth and expansion abroad. During the war with France known variously as Queen Anne's War and the War of the Spanish Succession (1702–13), England won a number of victories under John Churchill, Duke of Marlborough, which brought the nation new territory in North America, as well as control over the slave trade from Africa to the Caribbean and Spanish America. Anne's reign was the first in which a Tory government ruled (from 1710 to 1714), much to the joy of Tory writers Jonathan Swift, Alexander Pope, John Gay, and others. However, a rivalry between two important Tory ministers—Robert Harley, Earl of Oxford, and Henry St. John, Viscount Bolingbroke—weakened the party, and when George I (James II's Protestant grandson and the first British king from the house of Hanover) ascended the throne in 1714, the Whigs resumed control of Parliament.

The reigns of the first three Hanoverian kings, George I, II, and III, took the nation through the second decade of the nineteenth century and marked a period of continued economic growth, industrialization, expansion of foreign trade—and an important development in the growth of Parliamentary power. Both George I and II were born in Germany and were unfamiliar with the language, culture, or government of their new country. As a result, they intervened little in the day-to-day affairs of the nation. In the absence of a strong monarchy, the political scene was dominated from 1721 to 1742 by Robert Walpole, a Whig minister who had risen to power after the economic bubble and subsequent stock market crash of 1720 known as the "South Sea Bubble." Many government ministers were among the thousands ruined through overheated speculation in the South Sea Company's shares, but

Walpole remained untainted by the ensuing scandal, and consolidated his hold on the reins of government. The unprecedented degree of power with which he aggrandized himself earned him the derogatory nickname among his opponents of "prime minister"—an insult that had become an official title by the time Walpole left office. The centralization of power proved to have considerable benefits; under his corrupt but firm and efficient rule the government enjoyed a long period of stability. Walpole cultivated commerce and avoided conflict as much as possible.

If Walpole was anxious to maintain the peace, others saw a willingness to wage war as a necessity if Britain wished to continue to increase its wealth and power. Subsequent prime ministers—William Pitt most prominent among them—entered the nation into a series of wars fought to protect their foreign trade against encroachments by France, Spain, and Austria. It was under Pitt (and under George III, who took the throne in 1760 and reigned until 1820) that Britain emerged as the world's most significant colonial power. But George's reign was hardly one of untroubled success. The loss of the American colonies in 1783 was a blow to both British commerce and British pride, and religious intolerance continued to cause problems at home; a partial repeal of the penal laws, which had restricted the freedoms of Catholics, led to the Gordon Riots of 1780, in which a reactionary Protestant mob ruled the streets for ten days, defacing Catholic public buildings, and even threatening known Catholics. George himself suffered from mental instability (likely caused by a metabolic disorder called porphyria), and descriptions of his bouts of madness—such as that given by Frances Burney in her journal—were a source of concern for many of his subjects.

EMPIRICISM, SKEPTICISM, AND RELIGIOUS DISSENT

The eighteenth century was an age of great scientific advancement, during which the English people increasingly seemed to possess the capacity to uncover laws governing the universe. Sir Isaac Newton (1642–1727) was the hero of the age, and vast numbers of scientific advances were either directly or indirectly attributed to him. As Alexander Pope says in a famous couplet, "Nature and Nature's laws lay hid in Night; / God said Let Newton be! and all was Light." In *Principia Mathematica* (1687), *Optics* (1704), and other works, Newton laid out the laws of gravity, celestial mechanics, and optics. Perhaps as important as the discoveries themselves was the scientific approach to causes and effects that Newton exemplified. In the first of the four rules in the *Principia* for arriving at knowledge he puts the matter succinctly: "We are to admit no more causes of natural things than such as are both true and sufficient to explain the appearances.… Nature is pleased with simplicity, and affects not the pomp of superfluous causes."

Other scientific advances included improvements in navigation, the successful determination of the shape of the earth and the measurement of its distance from the sun, and improved knowledge of physical and chemical properties—for example, Robert Boyle determined that the pressure and volume of a gas are inversely proportionate (Boyle's Law). In 1752 Benjamin Franklin demonstrated that lightning is an electrical discharge; Franklin, a colonial British subject who lived for much of his adult life in England, was admitted to the Royal Society the following year in recognition of his scientific achievements. Later in the century Linnaeus's system of taxonomy was accepted among naturalists, and increased study of fossils led to the discovery, through the examination of lava-based soil from volcanic eruptions, that the earth was much older than the 6000 years allowed by biblical tradition. Largely as a follow-up to these geological discoveries, comprehensive theories of evolution began to be put forward in the last decades of the century.

More than ever before, citizens felt they could understand the world through logic, reasoning, and close attention to detail, rather than through faith. A plethora of new instruments for observing, measuring, and quantifying (most notably, the microscope and the telescope) opened up whole new realms of the universe, from microscopic organisms to other planets, for examination. The influential Royal Society of London for the Improving of Natural Knowledge, founded in 1662, helped to organize scientific enquiry and championed empiricism—the belief that through observation, experimentation, and experience humans could ascertain the truth. The Royal Society also helped to spread knowledge of scientific discoveries and advances; the British Museum, for example, was founded in 1759 with the donation of the private collection of a former president of the Royal Society, physician and botanist Sir Hans Sloane. In all walks of life Britons began to experience a desire to keep records of the observed minutiae of their everyday lives. Notable among them was Samuel Pepys, a naval administrator in London who rose to be secretary of the Admiralty, systematically restructured the navy, and became president of the Royal Society—yet is nevertheless remembered primarily as a diarist. His diary provides a unique record of the daily goings-on of his native city, including details of business, religion, science, literature, theater, and music; Pepys brought to the diary form the same sort of passion for detail that James Boswell would later bring to his biography of Samuel Johnson. For the nearly ten years (1660–69) that Pepys kept his diary, he related all that he saw around him, compressing remarkable detail into each page through use of his own private shorthand. When it was finally decoded and certain selections published in 1825, the diary gave readers an extraordinary glimpse of life during the Restoration, including such momentous events as the landing of Charles II at Dover in 1660 and the Great Fire of London in 1666.

Another member of the Royal Society whose career was founded on a fascination for detail was antiquarian and biographer John Aubrey. Aubrey's desire to preserve as complete a record of the past as possible led him to write a natural history of Wiltshire (his home county), a survey of ancient sites across Britain (including Avebury, some twenty miles from Stonehenge, which he is credited with "discovering"), and a scrappy collection of notes which, collected and published after his death as *Brief Lives*, brought together biographical sketches of some of the dominant figures of his time (including John Milton and Francis Bacon). His studies in archaeological history were unique at their time; similarly, his studies in folklore led him to write the first English work entirely devoted to that topic. And Aubrey's inquiry into the ways in which practices and conventions such as prices, weights, measures, dress, handwriting, navigation, and astronomy have changed over time anticipated the strategies followed in modern historical research.

Rather as a turn toward personal observation increasingly marked secular life in the late seventeenth and eighteenth centuries, so too did many people advocate a turn inward in spiritual life, to one's own conscience and personal faith in God. One such thinker was John Bunyan, a preacher who staunchly defended the primacy of one's own conscience over the dictates of organized religion. In 1660 the Anglican Church began to move against dissenting sects, jailing nonconformist preachers such as Bunyan. Though he was offered release if he promised to stop preaching, Bunyan chose to remain in jail, continuing to preach and write religious manuals and a spiritual autobiography, *Grace Abounding to the Chief of Sinners* (1666), while in prison. He defended his calling and, by remaining loyal to his beliefs, inspired many of his converts to do the same. Released after 12 years, Bunyan was yet again imprisoned in 1675; it was during this second sentence that he wrote *The Pilgrim's Progress*, a religious allegory in which Christian is a traveler putting this world resolutely behind him in order to achieve the perilous journey to salvation and the next world. It became the most popular work of prose fiction of the seventeenth century.

The ways of thinking of Bunyan, on one hand, and of Aubrey and Pepys, on the other, epitomize two approaches to interpreting the world—approaches that continued to clash throughout the seventeenth century. The ever-growing belief that through close observation the order of the universe could be uncovered was often at odds with religious beliefs, particularly as a result of the influential theories of philosopher John Locke. Locke, sometimes referred to as the "Newton of the mind," took Newton's theories and scientific reasoning and applied them to epistemological questions, asking how we come to know and understand. In his *Essay Concerning Human Understanding* (1690), Locke (drawing on Aristotle) advances the theory that the mind is a *tabula rasa* (blank slate) at birth and acquires ideas through experience. The theory had enormous implications for the study of the human mind and for educational practice, but its impact on theology was also profound. If we have no innate ideas concerning our own existence or the world around us, no more do we

John Michael Wright, *Astraea Returns to Earth*, 1660. The prophecy of the Roman poet Virgil of a golden age ruled over by Astraea, virgin goddess of Justice, is alluded to in the painting. A cherub holds the image of the new monarch, Charles II, as Astraea returns to earth.

Jan Siberechts, *Landscape with Rainbow, Henley-on-Thames*, c. 1690. Siberechts came to London from Flanders around 1675, and played an influential part in the development of an English tradition of landscape art.

Edward Haytley, *View of the Temple Pond at Beachborough Manor*, 1744–46.

John Singleton Copley, *Brook Watson and the Shark*, 1778. Copley (1738–1814) and Benjamin West were the leading British historical artists of the second half of the eighteenth century. This painting depicts a 1749 incident in the West Indies. Watson, a 14-year-old British orphan, was attacked while swimming in Havana harbor; his shipmates came to the rescue and Watson lost a leg but survived. Copley, born and raised in the British colony of Massachusetts, moved to London in 1774 at the age of 28, and never returned to America.

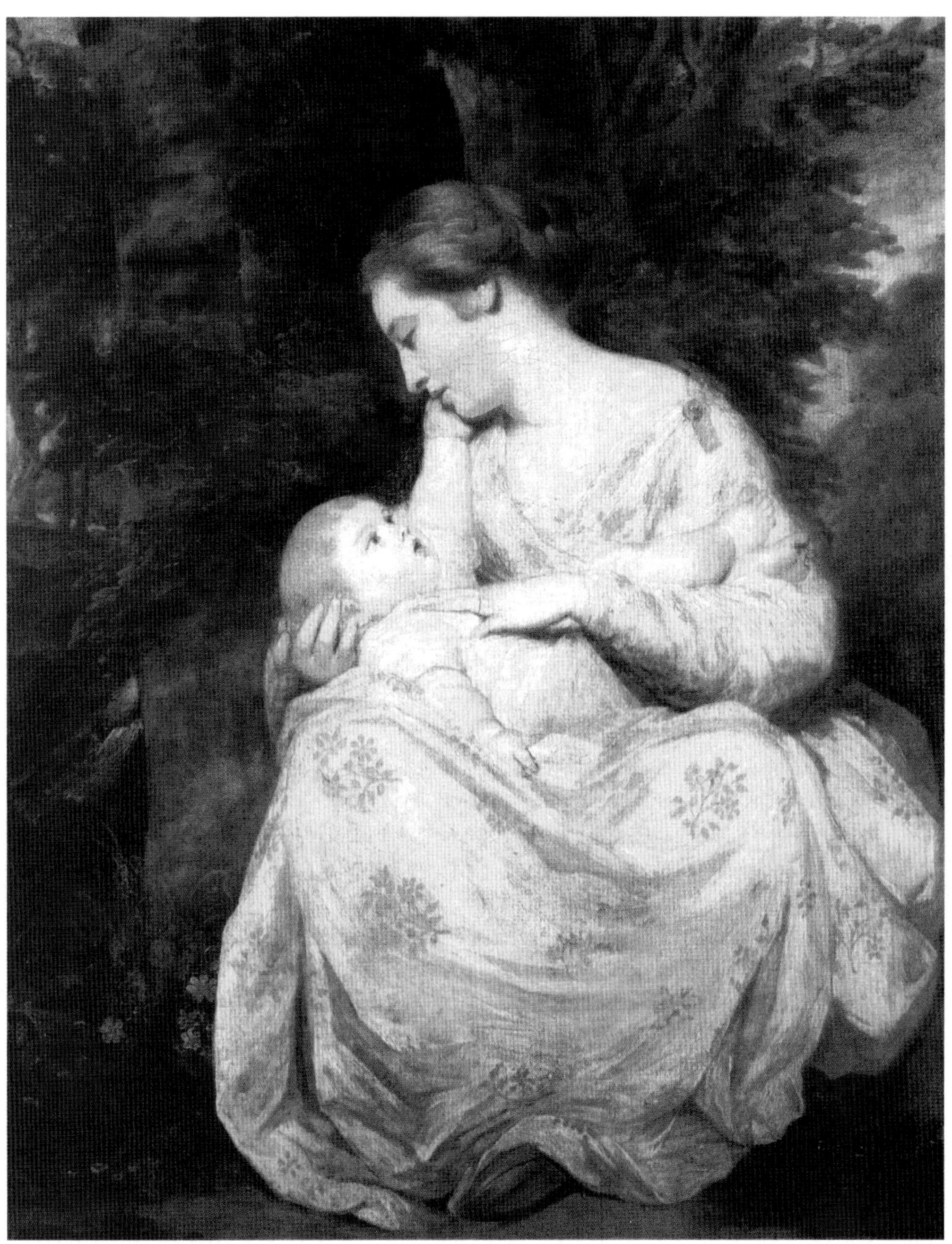

Sir Joshua Reynolds, *Mrs. Susanna Hoare and Child*, 1763–64. The goldsmith Richard Hoare began banking out of his shop in Cheapside in 1672, and the Hoare family became established landed gentry in the eighteenth century. Hoare & Company still operates today as a private bank.

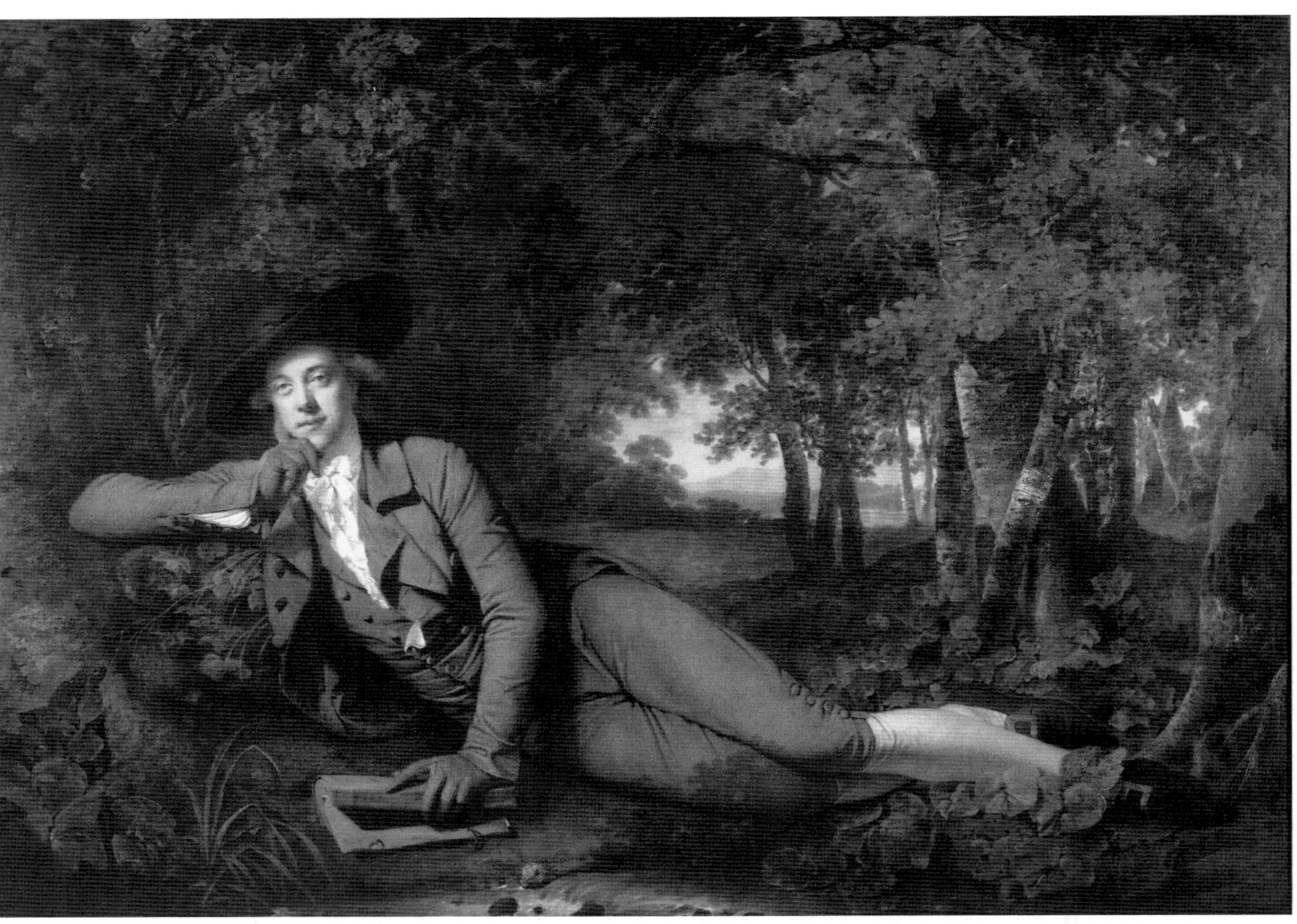

Joseph Wright of Derby, *Sir Brooke Boothby*, 1781. Boothby, sometimes described as epitomizing the "Man of Feeling," was a friend of Jean-Jacques Rousseau and was instrumental in making Rousseau's *Confessions* available in England. The word "Rousseau" appears on the spine of the book that Boothby holds in this portrait.

George Stubbs, *The Reapers*, 1785. This is one of two paired images; a detail of the other, *The Haymakers*, appears on the cover of this volume.

Angelica Kauffmann, *The Artist in the Character of Design Listening to the Inspiration of Poetry*, 1782. The Swiss-born Kauffmann moved to London in 1766, and established herself as a highly successful artist; she was a founding member of the Royal Academy of Arts.

William Hogarth, *Heads of Six of Hogarth's Servants*, c. 1750–55. For an artist to make his servants the subject of his art was highly unusual in the mid eighteenth century. The picture, which Hogarth hung in his studio, is a composite—the figures are painted from unrelated studies rather than posed together.

Joseph Wright of Derby, *An Experiment on a Bird in the Air Pump*, 1768. In the early 1660s, Royal Society member Robert Boyle used a pump like this one for several experiments involving air and air pressure; the most striking was his experiment examining the effects of air deprivation on animals. Boyle describes the experiment on a hen-sparrow:

> *When we put her into the receiver … she seemed to be dead within seven minutes … but upon the speedy turning of the key, the fresh air flowing in began slowly to revive her, so that after some pantings she opened her eyes and regained her feet, and in about ½ of an hour after, threatened to make an escape at the top of the glass, which had been unstoppered to let the fresh air upon her. But the receiver being closed the second time, she was killed with violent convulsions within five minutes.…*

By the 1760s, the air deprivation experiment was a mainstay of traveling lecturers, who performed demonstrations in natural philosophy for the entertainment and education of the general public. Wright's painting depicts such an experiment and the varied reactions of its viewers.

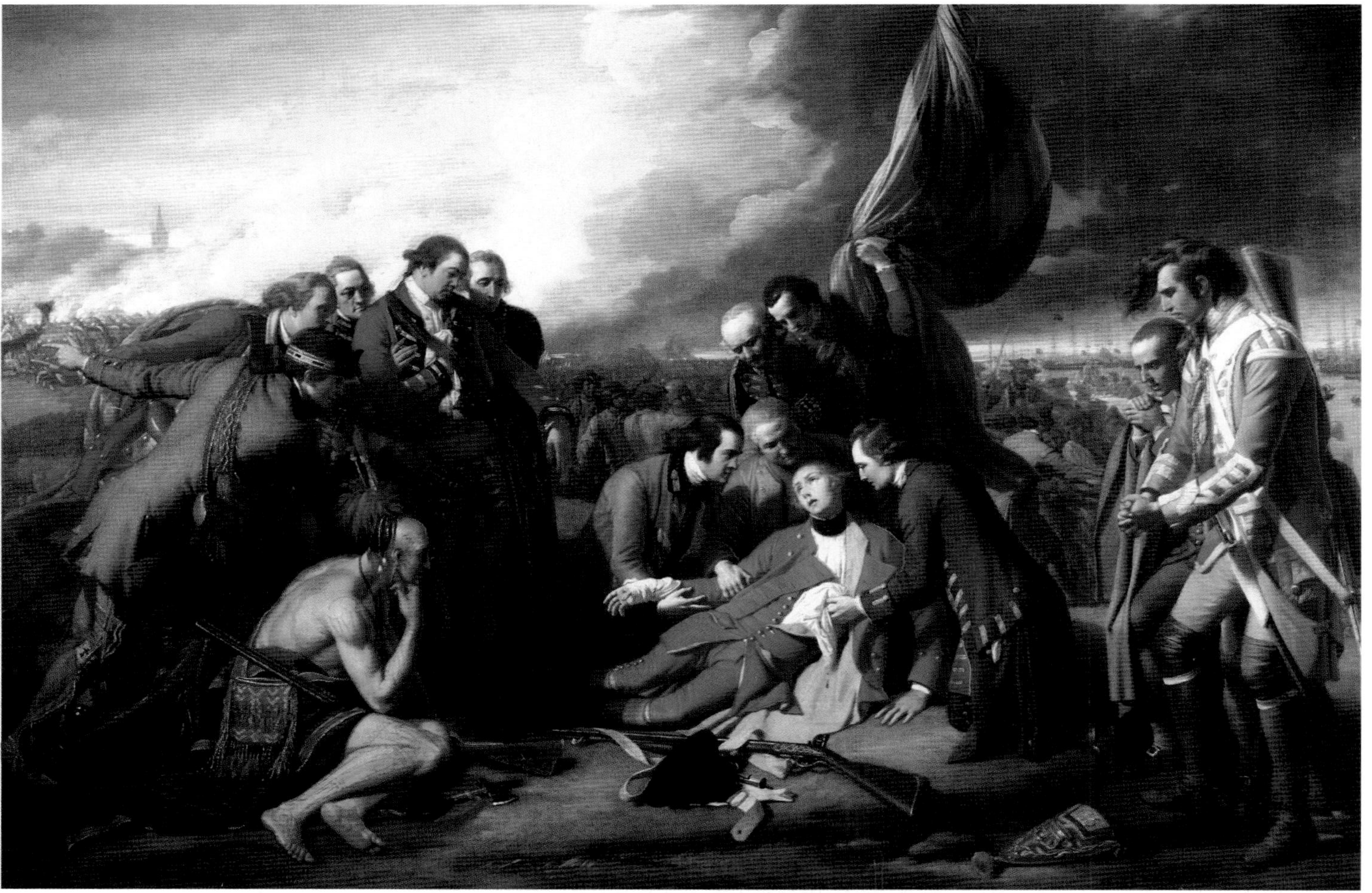

Benjamin West, *The Death of General Wolfe*, 1770. In 1759, General James Wolfe led British troops to a decisive victory over the French forces at Quebec City, dying from battle wounds in the hour of his success. Reproduced again and again in prose, poetry, and painting, his story became a beloved popular legend. Of the many imaginings of the dramatic scene, West's was by far the most famous—it was, in fact, the most reproduced of any image in eighteenth-century England. The work depicts the moment at which the dying Wolfe, concerned only with the outcome of the battle, was informed that the English were winning; upon hearing this, he reportedly expressed his satisfaction, and died.

Anonymous, *Portrait of Dido Elizabeth Belle and Lady Elizabeth Murray*, c. 1777. From the collection of the Earl of Mansfield, Scone Palace, Perth, Scotland. In its portrayal of a black woman and a white woman as equals—or at least near equals—this double portrait is highly unusual for its time. On the left is Dido Elizabeth Belle, the mixed-race daughter of British admiral John Lindsay and Maria Belle, an African slave. Almost immediately after her birth, Dido was sent to England to be raised by her great-uncle, Lord Chief Justice Mansfield. Growing up with her cousin, Lady Elizabeth Murray (on the right), Dido occupied an unconventional position in the Mansfield household, treated much better than a servant but not as well as Elizabeth (although, because Elizabeth was a legitimate heir and Dido was illegitimate, this unequal treatment might have occurred even if both had been white). Dido and Elizabeth were close companions and moved in the same social circles.

Lord Mansfield is well known for his influential decision on Somersett's Case (1772), a dispute in which the recaptured slave James Somersett, with the help of abolitionist activists, challenged the legality of slavery in England. Mansfield ruled in Somersett's favor; the language he uses limits the decision to the particular case, but many interpreted his verdict to mean that slavery was outlawed on English soil (although not in the colonies); the ruling thus had a considerable impact on behavior. Mansfield had great affection and admiration for his great-niece Dido, and it has been speculated that his relationship to her may have influenced his progressive ruling.

possess any innate notions as to the existence of God. Instead, in Locke's view, we must arrive at the idea of God through a chain of reasoning. Through intuiting knowledge of our own existence as humans and of the world around us, we proceed to a knowledge of the existence of God through the logical necessity of a "First Cause" to account for our existence. By emphasizing the role that external evidence can play in finding a path to theological truth, Locke brought about an explosion in Deism, or natural theology. Locke's theories, like those of Newton, offered rational grounds for belief in God. For many, the perfectly ordered universe gave in its very being evidence of the God who had created it, for this order could not have arisen out of chaos without a creator (the cosmological argument), nor could it have been designed with such incomparable artistry (the argument from design). (Joseph Addison poetically summed up this belief in the periodical *The Spectator*, saying the planets are in reason's ear "Forever singing as they shine / The hand that made us is divine.") Popular throughout the later eighteenth century was the concept of God as a mechanic or mathematician who does not necessarily need to intervene in the working of his creation, which he has ordered so that it runs smoothly on its own.

Empiricism brought about new forms of religious belief, but for many the logical end of empiricist thinking was a profound religious skepticism. As geological discoveries challenged the truth of the Scriptures, and as the mysteries of the universe seemed ready to be solved one by one, some began to feel that there might no longer be room for God in this rational, enlightened universe. The leading skeptic of his day was David Hume. As Boswell famously recorded it, Hume was asked on his deathbed if "it was not possible that there might be a future state" after death, to which Hume replied that "it was possible that a piece of coal put upon the fire would not burn." Despite his evident lack of faith in the existence of any afterlife, Hume was not a full-fledged atheist; he stated repeatedly that he accepted the argument from design. "I infer an infinitely perfect architect from the infinite art and contrivance which is displayed in the whole fabric of the universe," he declared. Yet Hume was rightly regarded as the foe of many common manifestations of Christian belief, including belief in divine Providence as well as faith in an afterlife. In his *Natural History of Religion* (1757), Hume took an almost anthropological approach to religious belief, examining the histories of various religions through the ages and concluding that religions tend to arise from passion, fear, imagination, or desire, and that they are products of various cultures and thus evolve slowly over time. He claimed that any member of humanity who seeks the protection of faith tends to do so "from a consciousness of his imbecility and misery, rather than from any reasoning." And, both in his major work *An Enquiry Concerning Human Understanding* and in his most controversial essay, "Of Miracles," Hume voices a thoroughgoing skepticism concerning supernatural claims:

> It is a general maxim worthy of our attention, "That no testimony is sufficient to establish a miracle, unless the testimony be of such a kind that its falsehood would be more miraculous than the fact which it endeavors to establish...." When anyone tells me, that he saw a dead man restored to life, I immediately consider with myself whether it be more probable that this person should either deceive or be deceived, or that the fact which he relates should really have happened. I weigh the one miracle against the other; and according to the superiority which I discover, I pronounce my decision, and always reject the greater miracle.

Hume's skepticism was shared by many freethinkers, but Samuel Johnson doubtless represented the majority view in his disdain for Hume, and in his unwavering belief in miracles. In his *Life of Johnson* Boswell records Johnson's view that "although God has made Nature to operate by certain fixed laws, yet it is not unreasonable to think that he may suspend those laws in order to establish a system highly advantageous to mankind."

In the face of increasing skepticism, many Christian apologists sought to defend their beliefs by using the same rational tools employed by the freethinkers. Various mathematical and logistical arguments were also published, endeavoring to provide scientific support for the truth of the scriptures. Joseph Butler, for example, argued for the truth of revelation using historical evidence in *The Analogy of Religion Natural and Revealed to the Constitution and Course of Nature* (1736). Others responded by disregarding the rational arguments of skeptics altogether, turning instead to powerful appeals to the emotions in their efforts to reaffirm faith. Methodism, an evangelical movement that originated within the Church of England, is perhaps the most important example here. Led by John Wesley, Methodism spread rapidly in new industrial villages and poorer areas. Methodist preachers spoke their gospel to common people—often out in the fields or in barns because they were barred from preaching in churches. With its emphasis on faith as the only path to salvation, its strong reliance on hymns, and its fervent and energetic sermons, Methodism won many converts.

Throughout the century the debate over free-thinking was a heated one in England—citizens heard freethinkers denounced from pulpits, read attacks on them in the press, and even saw them pilloried or imprisoned for blasphemy. Despite public alarm, however, these blasphemous thinkers made up a very small minority of the population, and posed little real threat to the established Church. As Johnson famously said to Boswell, "Sir, there is a great cry about infidelity; but there are, in reality, very few infidels." The Church continued as an arm of the state, serving as both political body and spiritual leader. "Papists" were a minority, despite the fears their presence evoked among Protestants.

More and more homes contained copies of at least a few books—most commonly the Bible, a prayer book, and John Bunyan's *The Pilgrim's Progress*. After those three, James Thomson's *Seasons* may well have been the most popular book of the age. Many homes would also have held copies of devotional manuals such as William Law's *A Serious Call* and a few of the most popular fictional works of the time, many of which—such as Daniel Defoe's *Robinson Crusoe*, for example—contained a strong moral message.

INDUSTRY, COMMERCE, AND THE MIDDLE CLASS

While religious and secular debates continued, the scientific advances that had helped to incite them changed the physical face of the nation. The first crude steam engine was invented in 1698 by Thomas Savery, a military engineer, as a means of removing water from mines. In *The Miner's Friend; or, an Engine to Raise Water by Fire, Described* (1702), however, Savery includes a chapter on "The Uses that this Engine may be applied Unto" that shows a dawning awareness of the far-reaching possibilities for such a device:

> (1) It may be of great use for palaces, for the nobilities or gentlemen's houses: for by a cistern on the top of a house, you may with a great deal of ease and little charge, throw what quantity of water you have occasion for to the top of any house; which water in its fall makes you what sorts of fountains you please and supply any room in the house. And it is of excellent use in case of fire, of which more hereafter. (2) Nothing can be more fit for serving cities and towns with water, except a crank-work by the force of a river.... (3) As for draining fens and marshes ... it is much cheaper, and every way easier, especially where coals are water borne, to continue the discharge of any quantities of water by our engine than it can be done by any horse engines what so ever. (4) I believe it may be made very useful to ships, but I dare not meddle with that matter; and leave it to the judgment of those who are the best judges of maritime affairs.

The steam engine—particularly following Thomas Newcomen's pioneering use of pistons in 1712 and James Watt's invention of a condenser (patented in 1769) to make its functioning more efficient—was the driving force behind an Industrial Revolution in Britain that both literally and figuratively gathered steam throughout the eighteenth century. And the fuel that fed it, coal, took a central place in British life. Coal had begun to be used extensively as a heating fuel in the later Middle Ages, as the forests were depleted, and its domestic use accelerated during the "Little Ice Age" that brought colder-than-average winters to Britain through most of the seventeenth and eighteenth centuries. The industrial use of coal grew rapidly throughout the era as well; by 1700 Britain was mining and burning far more coal than the rest of the world. In the early years of the eighteenth century, Daniel Defoe marveled at the "prodigious fleets of ships which come constantly in with coals for this increasing city [London]," and at the vast numbers of coal pits and the "prodigious heaps, I may say mountains of coal which are dug up at every pit" in Newcastle. But if coal made possible warmer dwellings and industrial growth, it was most certainly a mixed blessing. The life of a miner was nasty, brutish, and short. The mines themselves were extraordinarily dangerous, and the mine operators in Newcastle created what may have been the first industrial slums. London by 1700 was already a blackened city; according to the essayist Thomas Nourse, "when men think to take the sweet air, they suck into their lungs this sulphurous stinking powder." Nourse concluded that "of all the cities perhaps of Europe, there is not a more nasty and a more unpleasant place."

London firefighters, c. 1720. The machine is filled by hand at the front as the pumping mechanism is operated at the sides.

If coal mining and the steam engine both accelerated the Industrial Revolution, so too did modifications in factory design and in the production process, which enabled goods to be produced more quickly and in larger quantities. And with the industrial revolution came a financial revolution. Today investment banking has become the epitome of a respectable profession, but before the late seventeenth century moneylending was for the most part both informal and disreputable. With the founding of the Bank of England in 1694 the country took a decisive step toward the provision for loans at stable interest rates and toward the creation of a permanent national debt (the bank's primary purpose was to lend to the government, not to individuals or private companies). Also vital to financing the growth of business and industry was the rise of equity financing, the division of a company's ownership into equal shares made available for sale to the general public. Though the London Stock Exchange did not exist on any formally regulated basis until 1801, the exchange dates its existence to 1698, when one John Casting began to issue a list of the current prices of company shares and of commodities on a regular basis from "this Office in Jonathan's Coffee-house." The invention of paper money and of checks also helped to facilitate economic fluidity, and virtual free trade resulted from the breaking of a number of government monopolies in the late seventeenth century. Put together, these developments placed Britain firmly on the road toward the system that would come to be known as "capitalism" (the word "capitalism" was not coined until the mid-nineteenth century, but the *Oxford English Dictionary* records the first use of "capital" as occurring in 1708 with the issuance of "An Act for Enlarging the Capital Stock of the Bank of England"). By the early eighteenth century it had become relatively respectable to make money with money, and for the first time moneyed interests dominated landed ones. By the end of the century Britain was the richest nation in the world.

With the extension of trade and the development of more—and more sophisticated—manufactured goods, the nation found itself with a new driving force—one of relentless growth, expansion, and mercantilism. Goods and people could more easily move throughout the nation thanks to developments in transportation. The first Turnpike Trust was passed in 1663, and by 1770 there were 519 trusts, covering nearly 15,000 miles of road. In such trusts, a group of people (usually including a treasurer, a surveyor, and many of the landowners through whose property the road passed) would be granted (by an Act of Parliament) responsibility for managing the road, and would earn money for its upkeep through the establishment and maintenance of toll gates. A canal system was also begun, first to extend natural waterways and then to connect different river systems, bringing more inland coalfields and manufacturing districts within reach. Boats and coaches began for the first time to keep regular schedules, and time-keeping became an exact science as British clock-makers worked to meet the needs of their nation. A new group of consumers was established, as the merchant class began producing goods not only designed for the aristocracy, but for fellow members of the middle class, who struggled to keep up with the ever-changing dictates of fashion. And for the first time periodicals and newspapers were filled with advertisements for consumer goods.

A booming leisure industry was created to feed the demands of the growing middle class, particularly in London, where urban entertainment flourished. For the first time women from middle-class families entered the public sphere, and the result was something of a cultural revolution. Before 1700 these women (for example merchants' or doctors' wives and daughters) could attend few public social activities, even in larger provincial towns—the only places at which it was proper to be seen included the church, county fairs, and races. By the last decades of the century, however, such a woman's social calendar could include concerts, plays, lectures, debates, balls, exhibitions, and assemblies. Significant architectural changes occurred to feed this leisure industry: shopping streets were laid out, old public buildings were rebuilt, therapeutic spas and bath houses were constructed, and massive pleasure gardens, such as those at Vauxhall and Ranelagh, were laid out. With the advent of town planning, it became fashionable to design town centers in an octagonal pattern, which facilitated movement into the business center at the town core.

The growing power of the middle class and the influence of its values and ideals were evident in the changes that occurred in the theater between the Restoration and the mid-eighteenth century. The theaters, which had been closed in 1642 by Puritan decree, were reopened with the restoration of the monarchy in 1660. Charles II, returning from exile in France (the theater center of Europe) and anxious to signal a new era, indulged the public's keen appetite for the theater by licensing two public London theaters. In the atmosphere and layout of the playhouses and in the plays performed, Restoration theater showed a marked difference from its Elizabethan predecessor. While in Elizabethan theater almost every stratum of society could be found, except royalty, this was no longer true of the Restoration playhouses, which, for the first time in history, the King attended. Restoration playhouses were much smaller and more exclusive; while the Globe Theatre sat between two and three thousand people, Restoration playhouses held between two and three hundred. Prices were therefore significantly higher, and beyond the means of most citizens. The audience consisted almost entirely of young and well-to-do fashionable people from the western end of London (the "Town"), who were closely affiliated with the court. As a group they were united in their Royalist leanings and love of wit, and mostly shared an attitude of skepticism and cynicism coupled with anti-Puritanism. Authors wrote with this audience in mind; they fed their audience's desire for singing, dancing, elaborate costumes, glittering sets, and brilliant spectacles. They also wrote an extraordinary number of scathingly witty and entertaining comedies; the Restoration and early eighteenth century was something of a golden age for the English stage. Among the many comedies from this period that have continued to be revived into our own age are William Wycherley's *The Country Wife* (1675), Aphra Behn's *The Rover* (1677), John Vanbrugh's *The Relapse* (1677), William Congreve's *The Way of the World* (1700), and Susanna Centlivre's *A Bold Stroke for a Wife* (1718), as well as John Gay's ballad opera *The Beggar's Opera*.

While the fashionable set flocked to the theater in these years, members of the respectable middle classes, who leaned more toward Puritan religious notions and who typically resided in the original city of London (now the East End)—while people of rank lived in what was then the separate city of Westminster (now the West End)—tended to avoid the theaters, which were situated in the liminal area between London and Westminster. By the end of the seventeenth century Puritan opposition to the stage was again becoming more vocal. Jeremy Collier's famous attack on contemporary theater, *A Short View of the Immorality and Profaneness of the English Stage* (1698), was effectively answered in principle by Congreve's "Amendments Upon Mr. Collier's False and Imperfect Citations, etc." and John Dennis's "The Usefulness of the Stage," but the sorts of views that Collier had expressed continued to gain ground among the populace at large, and Congreve, like other playwrights, hastened to pay lip service to the new climate of opinion by, for instance, replacing "Oh God" with "Oh Heaven" in his characters' lines. Collier's anger was chiefly drawn by bad (that is, irreligious) language and by the representation of either clergymen or ladies as less than exemplary. In 1737 Parliament passed a new Licensing Act, restricting London theater to two tightly controlled venues. Some modern readers may find the raucous, grossly physical and demeaning satire of such pieces as *A Vision of the Golden Rump* (the play which made Walpole's case for the need for censorship) offensive in itself, but to the eighteenth-century censor the point was the attack on Robert Walpole.

"The North Prospect of the Square in Birmingham," engraving (1732). The Square, an exclusive residential complex, began to be constructed around 1700.

As a result of the Licensing Act restrictions, writers who a generation earlier might have been drawn to the stage began increasingly to try their hand at the novel. The drama that remained gave prominent place to moralizing and sentimentality, and placed considerable emphasis on decorum. The theater continued to sparkle intermittently (the mid-eighteenth century was the era of renowned actor, theater manager, and playwright David Garrick), but it was not until the last quarter of the century that satirical social comedy made a brilliant comeback on the stage with plays such as Oliver Goldsmith's *She Stoops to Conquer* (1773), Richard Sheridan's *The School for Scandal* (1777), and Hannah Cowley's *The Belle's Stratagem* (1780).

Ethical Dilemmas in a Changing Nation

In the Middle Ages and through much of the sixteenth century most Britons saw themselves as living in an age of decline or of stasis, and even in the seventeenth century a sense of the world as a place in which continual improvements were to be expected was limited to the well-educated. But in the eighteenth century a sense of the inevitability of progress—a sense that would crest in the nineteenth and early twentieth centuries—became more and more general. Prosperity unquestionably played its part in fostering this change; so too did various technological and medical advancements. Increased sanitation and improvements in hygiene had reduced the death rate, particularly in the army. The use of citrus to prevent scurvy was discovered in 1754, and James Cook had sailed around the globe without a single sailor dying of it. (Tragically, though, Cook's expeditions spread suffering and death through venereal disease to various populations in the South Pacific, most notably in Tahiti.) Improvements in preventative medicine had also reduced the death rate, and the first preventative injections began in England with inoculation against smallpox, a process popularized largely by the unflagging efforts of woman-of-letters Lady Mary Wortley Montagu, who had observed the practice in Turkey. Many new hospitals were founded, while increased understanding of the workings of the nervous system and of psychological or physiological disorders brought about more humane treatment for those suffering from mental diseases—who were formerly believed to be possessed by demonic spirits, and were therefore locked up in terrible conditions and even put on display for visitors, as at St. Mary's of Bethlehem ("Bedlam"). St. Luke's Hospital in London, where poet Christopher Smart was an early inmate, was founded in 1751. Increased investigations into the relationship between the body and mind led to detailed studies of hypochondria, depression, and hysteria. George Chine's *The English Malady* (1733) investigated the complaint (believed to be especially common in England) known as "the vapors" or "spleen," a vague melancholia and malaise from which James Boswell, amongst others, suffered.

While most English people believed that new advances benefited society, an understanding of them was growing to be beyond the grasp of the average educated individual. The numerous scientific and technological developments led inevitably toward greater specialization, and the new disciplines of physics, astronomy, and chemistry grew increasingly complex. Until the eighteenth century most educated gentlemen could keep up to date with discoveries and theories in all areas of knowledge, but this was now no longer the case. While many writers, such as Margaret Cavendish in her 1666 work *Description of a New Blazing World* (a precursor of the genre we now call "science fiction"), enjoyed speculating about where the path of the new knowledge might lead, for others the effect was far more disorienting. Swift's satire of poorly formulated and ill-conceived experimental science in Book Three of *Gulliver's Travels*, for example, gives voice to the widely shared sense that some of the new lines of inquiry were not only incomprehensible, but also ridiculous. As the world broadened, it became increasingly difficult for individuals to understand the complex societal machine of which they formed a small part—and this broadening was often perceived as a threat to social coherence. When Alexander Pope, in his *Essay on Man*, attacks scientists who are too absorbed in minutiae to see the bigger picture, he reflects a common belief that individuals must keep the interests of society as a whole in mind.

Any references to "the average educated individual" in this period are of course still very far from denoting the whole population. One of the new notions of the Reformation was the idea that education should be universal—for all classes of society, and for females as well as for males. John Knox, the Scottish Protestant leader, was the first to give practical shape to such radical notions, formulating in the 1560s a plan for incorporating schools into every church. Implementation of such a plan occurred only slowly and fitfully; the Scottish Highlands lagged behind the rest of Britain in levels of education as a result of the lack of books in Gaelic. But by the late eighteenth century the system had put down deep roots, and Scotland was the only area in Europe in which over half of the citizenry was formally educated.

In England it was coming to be considered proper that female members of the gentry should be tutored, and boarding schools, although decried by the intelligentsia, were increasingly popular for middle-class girls. But the idea of universal education for all women and men was given serious consideration only by a few, and higher education for women remained a subject for jokes. Some women did strongly protest the philosophical and theological assumptions that denied that women have the capacity to improve their minds. Mary Astell's 1694 *A Serious Proposal to the Ladies* (probably the most famous of such early proto-feminist texts) was not only an important call for the education of women but also one of the first works to inquire into the degree to which humans' search for truth may be influenced by prejudice. In this she challenges Locke's theory that we are born as blank slates; Astell argues instead that people are born into families, towns, cities, and countries that provide pre-existing conditions and help to shape human prejudices. In a similar vein Bathsua Makin, in her *Essay to Revive the Ancient Education of Gentlewomen* (1673) had already declared,

> "Custom, when it is inveterate, has a mighty influence: it has the force of nature itself. The barbarous custom to breed women low is grown general amongst us, and has prevailed so far, that it is verily believed (especially amongst a sort of debauched sots) that women are not endued with such reason as men; nor capable of improvement by education, as they are. It is looked upon as a monstrous thing to pretend the contrary.... To offer to the world the liberal education of women is to deface the image of God in man." At least a few men shared such views—Daniel Defoe, for example, refers to the denial of learning to women as "one of the most barbarous customs in the world"—but it would be two hundred years before such views became those of the majority.

Susana Highmore Duncombe, *Vignette with Two Ladies Conversing in a Park, with Athena Chasing Away Cupid* (c. 1785). Duncombe's parents held advanced views regarding the education of young women; she learned French, Latin, and Italian, was taught to draw by her father (the painter Joseph Highmore, also remembered as illustrator of Richardson's *Pamela*), and published both translations of Italian poets and her own verse.

The new celebration of mercantilism—and the acceptance of selfishness that this mercantilism implied—posed moral dilemmas that Enlightenment habits of thought encouraged many individuals to explore. If people allowed themselves to be driven by their own self-interest, would they ignore the greater good of society as a whole? How should other peoples (as well as other individual people) be treated? These questions became more complex and vexing as England expanded geographically and its citizens found themselves part of an ever-larger community. With the Seven Years' War Britain became a major colonial power, and its position in relation to the rest of the world changed dramatically. This too was generally assumed to be "progress," both for England and for the areas it came to control. The appropriation of wealth from India and the Indies, for example, was justified by citing England's supposed cultural and technological superiority, from which it was supposed that the indigenous populations would themselves benefit, and by arguing that the British were saving the Hindus from the oppressive Muslim Mughal emperors. But some English people voiced different beliefs concerning the morality of colonial expansion and trade. While many saw the future of the nation as dependent on aggressive expansion of trade and the colonial empire, others supported international trade but were morally opposed to expansion. Many writers—including Jonathan Swift and Samuel Johnson—have left memorable denunciations of colonial land-grabbing and many more of involvement in the slave trade.

English participation in the slave trade had begun to grow significantly in the seventeenth century, and by the mid-eighteenth century close to 50,000 slaves were being transported across the Atlantic annually by British ships. But by that time stirrings of conscience about the morality of the practice of slavery were also evident. Here is how Samuel Johnson (as reported by Boswell) thought the matter through:

> It must be agreed that in most ages many countries have had part of their inhabitants in a state of slavery; yet it may be doubted whether slavery can ever be supposed the natural condition of man. It is impossible not to conceive that men in their original state were equal; and very difficult to imagine how one would be subjected to another but by violent compulsion. An individual may, indeed, forfeit his liberty by a crime; but he cannot by that crime forfeit the liberty of his children. What is true of a criminal seems true likewise of a captive. A man may accept life from a conquering enemy on condition of perpetual servitude; but it is very doubtful whether he can entail that servitude on his descendants; for no man can stipulate without commission for another. The condition which he himself accepts, his son or grandson would have rejected.

As Johnson's thoughts suggest, the questioning of the moral grounds for slavery arose to a significant extent from the consideration of broader inquiries concerning human nature. Many theorists of the time, such as Anthony Ashley Cooper, the third Earl of Shaftesbury, claimed people naturally attained the greatest possible level of happiness by being good to others. Because humanity is inherently sociable, that argument went, those acts and characteristics that are most virtuous are also those that are best for society as a whole. In Pope's *Essay on Man* (1733–34), for example, self-interest is seen as beneficial (through God's foresight) to others as well as to the self. Each individual's "ruling passion" causes him or her to seek "a sev'ral goal"; thus, by gratifying one's own desires, one also works together as part of a larger framework. David Hume also argued, though from a rather different standpoint, that the cultivation of virtue would advance the general good; Hume emphasized the importance of the feelings or "sentiments"—what we would today call the emotions—in leading us to a sense of what is right—and emphasized, too, the role that habit can play in cultivating patterns of good behavior.

There were some, however, who took a more pessimistic view of human nature and society. Bernard Mandeville, the most controversial of early eighteenth-century moral theorists, saw self-interest purely as selfishness, a quality that, in the natural state of human beings, would not allow for the interests of others. Ethical behavior, in Mandeville's view, is in essence a by-product of our vanity. It arises purely from the human desire to be recognized and praised. There is no place in Mandeville's world for appeals to conscience; morality is only driven by pride and shame. According to Mandeville, a wealthy society depends on people having and indulging their vices, such as greed and vanity, because these lead to full employment and a buoyant economy—whereas a pious, self-denying society will lead to unemployment and general poverty. In other words, general Puritan reform would bring economic collapse. Mandeville's defense of the financial benefits of the consumer society is in many ways strikingly modern.

The ideas of Adam Smith concerning human nature are in some respects closely connected with those of Mandeville, but Smith's understanding of both morality and economics is more complex and nuanced. Even as Smith puts forward the notion that self-interest can work to the benefit of all through the mechanism of the "invisible hand," Smith does not see selfishness itself as a virtue. He accepts that altruism exists, recognizing that, however selfish "man may be supposed, there are evidently some principles in his nature that interest him in the fortune of others and render their happiness necessary to him, though he derives nothing from it except the pleasure of seeing it." And Smith devotes considerable effort to discussing the ways in which selfishness acts *against* the public interest, and must be curbed. Though "civil government" was said to have been instituted "for the security of property," he concluded that it had been "in reality instituted for the defense of the rich against the poor, or of those who have some property against those who have none at all." Far from giving free rein to commercial interests, Smith concluded that the interests of business people "is never exactly the same with that of the public," and that they "have generally an interest to deceive and even to oppress the public."

Most people accepted the more optimistic view of human nature, and the theories such as those of Shaftesbury and Hume led to a growing cult of sentiment, in which people celebrated what they saw as their natural sympathetic responses to human suffering (and, to a lesser extent, to human joy). Social reform movements grew as the English people sought the pleasure that charitable acts would bring them. As the growing trend of social improvement became not only

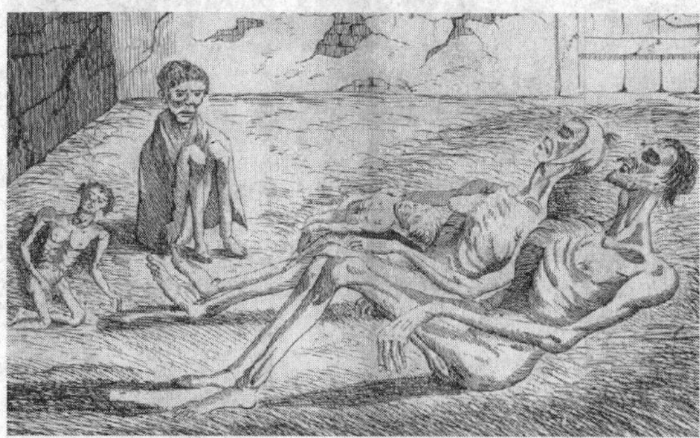

A View of the Poor House of Datchworth, detail from an engraving in Philip Thicknesse's *Four Persons Found Starved to Death, at Datchworth* (1769).

THE

DESERTED VILLAGE,

A

POEM.

By Dr. GOLDSMITH

LONDON:

Printed for W. Griffin, at Garrick's Head, in Catharine-street, Strand.

MDCCLXX.

Title page, Oliver Goldsmith's *The Deserted Village* (1770). Outrage against extremes of hardship and inequality caused by such "rural improvement" practices as enclosure (of formerly common land) and engrossment (the practice of replacing a larger number of rural tenants with a much smaller number) was stirred in the 1760s by a variety of works, among them Thicknesse's shocking account of an incident in Hertfordshire, and Oliver Goldsmith's long poem lamenting the disappearance of rural and village society in the face of the greed of wealthy landowners: "the man of wealth and pride / Takes up a space that many poor supplied."

popular, but also fashionable, there was much sentimental posturing, and many supposedly benevolent actions were, in reality, motivated by selfish desires for social acceptance or prestige. Works such as Oliver Goldsmith's "The Deserted Village" (1770), however, show the deepening sense of obligation that many truly felt toward their fellow citizens. (Goldsmith also shows this sense of responsibility taken to extremes in his comedy *The Good-Natured Man* [1768], which features a hero who is almost pathologically incapable of considering his own needs in relation to anybody else's.)

Questions concerning the goodness of human nature were also linked with debates concerning the best form of government—debates that attained particular urgency with the American and French Revolutions. Thomas Paine's *Common Sense* (1776) brought the issues of the goodness of government to the forefront for many eighteenth-century citizens of both England and the colonies. For Paine, an Englishman with limited formal education who moved to the colony of Pennsylvania in 1774, when he was 37, government was at best a necessary evil to be endured, and its dictatorial tendencies must be curbed. The constitution of England was, according to Paine, an amalgam of republican elements with the remains of monarchical and despotic ones. The very idea of a monarch, in his view, went against the principle of human equality: and "'tis a form of government which the word of God bears testimony against, and blood will attend it." Blood was shed over such issues only on the American side of the Atlantic, but *Common Sense* went through five editions in London, with editions also appearing in Newcastle and Edinburgh.

A Coffee House, engraving, 1668. The first London coffee house opened in 1652.

Print Culture

Whatever British people's opinions on issues of morality, philosophy, government, or technology, they soon found themselves with a multitude of new forums in which to express those opinions, thanks to the booming print trade. The religious controversies of the seventeenth-century English civil wars had done much to fuel a desire for printed information, whether in the form of prophecies, sermons, news, or political controversy. Censorship under the Licensing Act, which had loosened under Charles I at the approach of the civil war, was briefly revived following the Restoration, but in 1695 the old Licensing Act was allowed to lapse. Newfound freedom of the press sparked a rise in writing of all kinds, whether political or religious treatises, satires, or debates. The production of newspapers, journals, miscellanies (what we would call anthologies, with mostly contemporary content), and pamphlets increased greatly, and printed materials began to sell in unprecedented numbers. Short or serial publications were cheaper than novels or volumes of poetry and made information accessible to a much larger portion of the population. Defoe's *Robinson Crusoe* (1719), for example, was far more widely read after it was reprinted in the *Original London Post* in installments three times a week.

Gradually, a new reading public emerged. Though reading had always been a social activity, with literate members of a family reading the Bible or news to others, for example, in the eighteenth century reading and writing became activities that occurred in public spaces that were often designed solely for that purpose. With the rise of coffee houses—of which it was estimated London had roughly 3,000 by the end of the eighteenth century—British subjects could come together to read and debate. Libraries and literary clubs provided alternative spaces for such activities, and ones in which women were welcome (as they were not in coffee houses). Literary clubs such as the Scriblerus Club of Alexander Pope, John Gay, Jonathan Swift, Thomas Parnell, and John Arbuthnot or Dr. Johnson's Literary Club (both all male) originated in the eighteenth century. Many of these groups, such as that gathered informally around Samuel Richardson, were of mixed company or made up predominantly of women, such as the bluestocking society organized by Elizabeth Montagu. (Though this society included men, the term "bluestocking" soon came to be a derisive term for a bookish woman.) During the period, people frequently read aloud, and many guides were published to instruct people in the best practices of reading to others. The anxiety that Frances Burney describes in her journal at being asked to read to Queen Charlotte demonstrates the importance placed on this new art.

With new print technology and the development of the newspaper, as well as the new popularity of the essay as a literary form and the new social space of the city (where the majority of the reading public was located) came the rise of the periodical—of which by far the most influential was Richard Steele's *The Tatler* and his and Joseph Addison's *The Spectator*. These periodicals organized themselves around the coffee-house culture and embraced the conversation and public debate that they fostered. *The Spectator* (1711–14) advertised itself as being organized around the meetings of a fictitious club, the Spectator Club, which claimed to comprise a country gentleman, a London merchant, a retired soldier, a clergyman, a lawyer, and a gentleman born to a hereditary estate. Addison claimed that each copy of *The Spectator* was read by as many as twenty people as a result of coffee-shop circulation. With this large an audience, Addison greatly influenced the beliefs of his society and the ways in which that society saw itself. He popularized the theories of Newton and Locke, bringing them to the average gentleman (and also explicitly aiming to include strong female representation among his readership), and substantially influenced the aesthetic tastes of his day. Anthologies, miscellanies, and periodicals also provided a forum for women writers. Future bluestocking Elizabeth Carter worked for the *Gentleman's Magazine*, and there were numerous women who occasionally contributed to such magazines. Several specifically female periodicals were also published, such as *The Female Tatler*, Eliza Haywood's *The Female Spectator*, and Charlotte Lennox's *The Lady's Museum*. These offered a public space for women writers, editors, and critics.

As a result of these changes in print culture, the individual reader had a sense of him or herself as part of a larger reading community in which debate was freely engaged, and conversation between various readers and writers was a central part of most publications. Writers frequently responded to, continued, or revised one another's work. Collaborative work became popular, and frequently arose out of literary groups. Meanwhile, booksellers produced anthologies of both poems and prose, such as Dodsley's *Collection of Poems* (1748–58).

During this period criticism came into its own as a separate genre. Though writers had always commented on and responded to one another's work, they often did so more privately. In manuscript culture, for example, texts would be annotated with marginal comments arguing with, supporting, or even summarizing an author's points. Thomas More's *Utopia* contains printed marginal notes of this sort, probably written by his friend and supporter Erasmus. With the decline of manuscript circulation, this sort of private literary conversation became public, separate works of criticism became more common, and Dryden included critical introductions in his own work. With this genre of writing about literature and about authors themselves, some literary personalities approached the status of celebrities. Samuel Johnson, for example, observed to Boswell a few years before his death, "I believe there is hardly a day in which there is not something about me in the newspapers."

All these developments in print culture marked a dramatic change from the previous century, when publishing one's own work had been seen as "vulgar"; it had been thought that the lofty aims of art or high-culture conversation transcended material concerns such as money or a desire for fame. Some seventeenth-century authors had circulated their works in manuscript for years (even if after that they took steps to publish them), and many works were not published at all during an author's lifetime. In the eighteenth century some authors still continued the practice of publishing anonymously, particularly in the first half of the century, even if their identity was commonly known. Samuel Johnson, a bookseller's son who famously declared, "No man but a blockhead ever wrote, except for money," did not sign his name on any of his early work.

Because writers often played with the new print culture, using various means to disguise their authorship, the question of attribution can be a difficult one for scholars of the eighteenth century. Readers at the time generally assumed they could solve the mysteries of authorship, but they were frequently incorrect. Authors carefully avoided publishing any autobiographical or blatantly self-promotional material. Letters were occasionally saved and prepared for posthumous publication by their authors, but in 1739 Pope startled his peers by becoming one of the first literary figures to oversee the publication of his own letters. Pope avoided much of the scandal that this would ordinarily have caused through employing intricate subterfuge. Throughout his career he had an antagonistic relationship with the notoriously immoral publisher Edmund Curll, who frequently attacked Pope in print and published pirated copies of his works and those of his friends, such as Jonathan Swift, John Gay, and Lady Mary Wortley Montagu. Pope arranged for some of his correspondence to fall into Curll's hands, and when the publisher printed this supposedly pirated edition, Pope was justified in releasing the official edition of his letters—an edition that he had significantly doctored (while pretending candor and sincerity) to present himself in a more favorable light.

While it became increasingly socially acceptable for people of high rank to publish their writing, advances in print technology and changes in the publishing industry also made it possible for men and women from various backgrounds to earn a living through writing. Before the eighteenth century, those who wished to support themselves by writing would have had to find themselves a rich aristocratic patron who would support them, and to whom they would dedicate their works. During the Restoration, Aphra Behn and John Dryden also supported themselves by writing for the stage, and in the eighteenth century Alexander Pope was the first to earn a living by subscription writing. His success marked a change in the writing and publishing industries. With subscription printing, all subscribers would make financial contributions in exchange for having their names appear on a page inside the work, just as the patron's name would have previously; in this way, a system of what Terry Eagleton refers to as "collective patronage" came into effect. By contributing money up front, subscribers helped defray the initial cost of printing. An author's friends often formed the bulk of subscribers, though many others might become subscribers either out of something akin to charity or for the prestige that came with illustrious publications. Dryden's *The Works of Virgil* (1697), which set the standard for the Latin translations that were highly esteemed and successful during this century, was one of the first works by an English poet to be financed in this manner, though in the seventeenth century much legal, scientific, and theological publishing was done in this way. Publishers (who usually doubled as and were known as new booksellers) also formed "congers," or partnerships, to share the costs of elaborate or expensive new works and of existing copyrights (because the copyright of works by dead authors could be sold on from one publisher to another).

The concept of copyright as we know it today first took shape in the early eighteenth century. In England from the sixteenth century onwards, the rights acquired by stationers or printers upon securing from the Stationers' Company a license to print books had been generally assumed to be property rights, with the understanding being that, as with other sorts of property, ownership was ongoing; English practice severely restricted the reproduction of literary works other than by their "owner." No formal copyright protection existed in English law, however, and from time to time editions would find their way into the English market from Scotland or Ireland (where intellectual property was less restricted). English publishers began to agitate to have perpetual "copy right" formalized in law, and the British Parliament eventually decided (in the 1709 Statute of Anne) to recognize and protect copyright. But rather than declaring copyright to be a property right held in perpetuity, Parliament restricted it to 14 years from publication (renewable in certain circumstances for a further 14 years)—after which anyone could publish competing editions of a work. Remarkably, publishers who had "owned" popular works refused to concede, and managed to persuade a succession of judges that the Statute of Anne had improperly authorized the uncompensated confiscation of private property. In defiance of what was seemingly set out in law, they succeeded for another 65 years in maintaining control over what we would now term "works in the public domain." Ironically, then, the Statute of Anne ushered in what William St. Clair has termed an "age of high monopoly" in the book trade. Together with the ending of official state censorship in 1695 and the gradual withdrawal of some other controls on the content of printed matter in the first half of the eighteenth century, the secure conditions under which British publishers operated fostered the production of large, beautifully produced volumes—and something of a golden era for the spread of Enlightenment culture. But the same conditions that favored the publication of expensive works of history and philosophy with a limited market slowed the spread of popular literature in book form—and the growth of a reading public. It was not until a 1774 legal case finally brought an end to the near-monopoly conditions that books started to become smaller and cheaper. That in turn led to a huge surge in reading across all social classes. In 1791, bookseller James Lackington described the degree to which things had changed: "According to the best estimation I have been able to make, I suppose that more than four times the number of books are sold now than were sold twenty years since.... In short, all ranks and degrees now READ."

An explosive growth in periodicals and newspapers, however, began much earlier. And with it came changes in the community of writers. A new term, "Grub Street," was used to describe the multitude of freelance writers who contributed for pay to the popular press. Many of these writers had little education, worked for meager wages, and lived in rundown apartments on London's Grub Street. With this profusion of "hack" writers (one of whom was Samuel Johnson in his early career), many feared that literature was becoming mired in trivial, everyday concerns. Alexander Pope was without a doubt the writer who most viciously satirized hack writers; his satirical masterpiece *The Dunciad* (1742) depicted a kingdom of dunces that included nearly every minor writer or publisher with whose work Pope had found fault.

Eighteenth-century theories of aesthetics sought to define what should be the lofty aims of true art (in order to separate the "true" art from the masses of popular writing), and often advocated avoiding the "low" details of the surrounding everyday world. Early in the eighteenth century John Gay wrote poetry of the tradespeople and messengers in the streets of London, with the often dirty or pungent details of their business. Later, in his essay on the theater, Oliver Goldsmith argued that the single word "low" as a term of contempt had made comedy virtually impossible. When he introduced bailiffs into a tea-party of his hero and heroine in *The Good-Natured Man* the audience was outraged, rather as if he had personally introduced them to actual bailiffs. Not only were certain aspects of satire out of bounds, but poets also felt that general principles, abstract propositions, or sensitive feelings were more worthy of their art than the material world. The empiricism of Locke and Hume shaped aesthetic theories according to which the artist's role was to embody sensory messages (through which individuals receive information about the outside world) in the imagery of his or her work. According to Locke, the mind passively receives impressions through our senses from external objects, and then combines these received simple ideas into complex ideas. Edmund Burke, in his *Enquiry into the Origin of Our Ideas of the Sublime and the Beautiful* (1757), follows Locke in asserting that the senses are the origin of all our ideas and pleasures. The reader experiences the work as a series of sensations, and its value lies in the emotional effect it produces and the way in which the artist produces this effect. In his treatise, Burke forms a distinction between the sublime and the beautiful—either of which, he maintains, may be the aim of a literary work. Our emotional response to something beautiful is a positive pleasure, or a social pleasure. Ideas that excite terror, on the other hand, and give us impressions of pain and danger, are sources of the sublime. We are impressed and astonished without being troubled by receiving ideas of pain and danger when we are in no actual danger ourselves, and thus we derive delight as a result of our desire for self-preservation.

Theories such as Burke's endeavored to link principles of aesthetics to those of morality and psychology. Such was also the case with the influential aesthetic theories of Henry Home, Lord Kames. For

Thomas Hickey, *Edmund Burke and Charles James Fox* (c. 1775). A friend in early life of Burke (who is best remembered for his later, conservative views), Fox went on to become a leader in Whig politics in the late eighteenth and early nineteenth centuries.

Kames, what we find beautiful in works of art is what improves us morally; for example, tragedy appeals to us in large part because it develops our sympathy for others. It is the nature of fine arts, Kames says in his *Elements of Criticism* (1762), to raise pleasurable emotions. Kames also expanded the definition of the fine arts to include practices not formerly considered, such as gardening (that is, landscape gardening or large-scale garden design, an artistic pursuit that flourished in the eighteenth century). According to Kames, the characteristics of gardens, such as their (loosely) regulated patterns, their color, and their utility, can raise pleasurable emotions such as gaiety, melancholy, surprise, wonder, or a sense of grandeur.

Increasingly as the eighteenth century progressed, those who valued the sublime in art sought the work of a wide variety of ancient societies as models. Alongside the well-established admiration for the complex social organization of ancient Greece and Rome, critics and

Paul Sandby, *Dolbadarn Castle and Llanberris Lake*, c. 1770. In the second half of the eighteenth century interest in travel to the more remote and wild regions of Britain (notably the Lake District, North Wales, and the Highlands of Scotland) greatly increased; Thomas Pennant's *Tour in Scotland* (1772), for example, went through five editions before 1790. Sandby's painting shows the ruins of a thirteenth-century castle set among craggy peaks in North Wales, viewed by a touring party.

artists began to celebrate the natural genius of what they saw as primitive and uneducated writers from uncivilized ages. These writers were seen as having created through spontaneous impulse, unimpeded by the conventions of civilization. Influential critics such as Sir William Temple also admired "exotic" cultures such as those of China and Peru. The Goths became another important model, as did the Celts and the Druids, and interest in medieval English literature increased greatly; the works of Chaucer found renewed popularity, and Alfred the Great became an object of admiration. It was during the eighteenth century that a field of genuine medieval scholarship arose, though romantic medievalism was also popular among poets; Thomas Gray was among the prominent poets who looked to medieval literature for inspiration. William Collins, for his part, purported to draw from ancient Persian writing in his *Persian Eclogues* (1742). All things Oriental exploded into fashion in the eighteenth century; the Orient became, in the minds of many English people, a place that embodied all the characteristics found lacking in British society. This led to admiration for the Orient as an ideal, uncorrupted place of wealth and leisure, but it did not provide the average reader with any understanding of the complex realities of these foreign cultures. Sir William Temple garnered much critical interest when he published an old Icelandic fragment, and Scottish poet James Macpherson captured public attention when he claimed to have discovered and translated primitive epics from the Scottish Highlands written about the legendary hero Ossian. Though *Ossian* was later discovered to have been almost entirely composed by Macpherson himself on the slenderest dependence on traditional ballads, the impact the work had upon the reading public testified to the high demand for works colored with the romantic appeal of antiquity.

POETRY

While many writers turned to the exotic or primitive as a source of inspiration or a means of indicating special knowledge (which would distinguish them from the masses of hack writers), there was in general a continued emphasis on Greek and Roman cultures as representing the origins of true art and literature. In the early part of the eighteenth century in particular, a knowledge of Greek and Latin languages and literature was seen as prerequisite for anyone who attempted to write in English. Allusions to Homer and Roman poets Horace, Virgil, Juvenal, and Ovid occur throughout the works of poets such as Dryden, Pope, and Swift, who saw themselves as the eighteenth-century disciples of these venerated ancient poets. In fact, because of the similarities between the creative and political climates of the early eighteenth century and those of ancient Rome during the reign of Augustus Caesar, the first few decades of the century are often referred to as the "Augustan Age." In the political climate that these poets saw as relatively stable, in comparison to the turmoil of the mid-seventeenth century following the Restoration, poetry was able to flourish—just as during the reign of Augustus Caesar, the first Roman emperor, patrons in this period of peace following Rome's civil war had increasingly used their wealth and leisure to enjoy and support the arts. In the Restoration and early eighteenth century, many leading literary figures tried their hands

Thomas Gainsborough, *Robert Andrews and his Wife, Frances* (c. 1748–49). Gainsborough is now regarded as one of the great artists of rural life in the eighteenth century. During his lifetime (1727–88) his portraits were far more in demand than were his landscapes of rural life; the latter came to be far more appreciated after his death. This canvas, which combines the two genres, is unfinished; a small area remains blank on Mrs. Andrews's lap.

at translations of the ancient poets. Dryden was the first writer of the period to tackle this sort of work on a large scale, producing English versions of the works of Virgil, Juvenal, and parts of Horace and Homer. Pope, as an aspiring poet, translated Homer's *Iliad* and *Odyssey*, and later produced imitations or freely updated adaptations of many poems by Horace. Poets combined these influences with important ones from the English tradition, including Chaucer, Shakespeare, Spenser, and Milton. (Because they attempted to fuse new elements with the classical, Pope, Dryden, and others were often referred to as "neoclassical" writers.)

Like the ancients, these neoclassical poets sought to convey truths about the world around them by investigating general aspects of human character or striking aspects of the natural realm. In contrast to earlier poets such as Donne and Milton, eighteenth-century poets sought a simplicity of language with which to convey pleasurable images of nature and the sublime to their readers. Nevertheless, the classical influence often resulted in Latinate syntax and diction, and highly allusive content. Eighteenth-century poetry is also highly visual, frequently relying on detailed descriptions and often personifying abstract aspects of human nature or elements of the physical world.

As in classical Rome, so in Restoration and eighteenth-century Britain, satire was a prominent poetic form and the most common path used by poets to comment on the particulars of their daily lives. Eighteenth-century poets looked back to Juvenal and Horace, the great classical satirists, and imitations of their models provided a forum for sharp yet elegantly styled attacks on the government. Despite this reliance on the ancients, poetry was intimately connected to current political and social events, and wielded a good deal of power. The more witty and technically masterful the poem, the more damaging the satire, and those who perfected the mode could ruin entire careers and ministries. Political satire in both poetry and prose could also cause trouble for writers in the politically charged climate in the late seventeenth and early eighteenth centuries. If well-written, however, such work often had the effect of silencing enemies. When Daniel Defoe was placed in the pillory after pleading guilty to charges of libel for his 1703 *The Shortest Way with the Dissenters* (a pamphlet parodying extremist High Churchman and facetiously advocating the mass torture of Dissenters), he turned the event to his advantage with his "Hymn to the Pillory," denouncing those who sentenced him. The government so admired his skill in doing this that the ministry hired him to publish a newspaper (the *Review*) that would report the news from a point of view that was sympathetic to the government. Another satirical art form that developed in the eighteenth century in conjunction with poetic satire was the political cartoon or caricature. Until the eighteenth and early nineteenth centuries cartoons were usually published anonymously to protect their authors from charges of libel. Nevertheless, the cartoon became a popular and often savage form of propaganda and of satire.

Poetic satire began as a means of political commentary, but it soon branched out to include almost all aspects of public life, and on occasion the minutiae of private life as well. Samuel Garth's *The Dispensary* (1699), for example, used the mock epic form to satirize the war between doctors and apothecaries over who would dispense medicine. Mock epic was a popular form for such ventures; its contrast between elevated style and mundane content accentuates the frivolity of whatever petty disputes or political intrigues are described. Pope's *The Rape of the Lock* (1712) is probably the most celebrated example of such a genre. Epic conventions such as the description of the battle scene become ridiculous when used to treat trivialities such as the theft of a piece of hair. By using the heroic couplet, writers could pair elevated and common subject matter in one rhyme. In these types of satire, poets had a very clear sense of their audience, which was often very small (in the case of *The Rape of the Lock*, the original audience was only two families, though in print the poem sold extremely well), and spoke directly to it. (This close relationship between writer and audience can cause difficulty for the contemporary reader who cannot be familiar with the highly specific references to people, events, and places of eighteenth-century London.)

After Pope, who stretched the heroic couplet in new directions, using it with unprecedented virtuosity, the form became less common. Blank verse, the form of James Thomson's *The Seasons* (1727) and William Cowper's *The Task* (1785), was an increasingly popular form that gave writers greater flexibility while still providing a set structure. More "common" poetic forms such as the ballad, hymn, and various stanzaic forms also gained in popularity as the century progressed.

While the neoclassical poets of the early part of the eighteenth century felt that "low" details of common life had little place in poetry (except in the realm of satire), in the later part of the century realism and attention to detail manifested themselves as well in various works, usually set outside the London scene. Wordsworth, in his 1800 preface to *Lyrical Ballads*, expressed concern that the novel had taken and sensationalized subjects and language that poetry needed to reclaim. He disliked the classical and what he felt to be the artificial tone of the important body of eighteenth-century poetry dealing with rural life and the world of work. These poems that dealt with the details of common life often took the form of the georgic, a genre named after Virgil's *Georgics*, which Addison defined as "some part of the science of husbandry [i.e., farming] put into a pleasing dress, and set off with all the beauties and embellishments of poetry." Unlike the pastoral, the most common type of poem in the sixteenth and seventeenth centuries dealing with nature, the georgic did not idealize nature or rural life, and was not highly stylized. Instead, georgics were digressive, often didactic, and unusually detailed, typically taking one very specific aspect of rustic life as a topic. William Somerville's *The Chase* (1735) described hunting, fishing, and sports, while Christopher Smart's *The Hop Garden* (1752) and James Grainger's *The Sugar Cane* (1764)—set in the West Indies—dealt with specificities of agriculture. John Dyer's *The Fleece* (1757) was the first such poem to include scenes in an industrial setting, linking traditional husbandry with the new commercialism. Often georgics used burlesque or subtle mockery in their treatment of their subjects, as in John Gay's *Wine* (1708), *Rural Sports* (1713), and *The Shepherd's Week* (1714). James Thomson's *The Seasons* (1730, following the individual appearances of the four poems, "Spring," "Summer," "Autumn," and "Winter," which, combined, make up the larger work), the most famous work to come out of this tradition, remained popular throughout this period and indeed through the nineteenth century.

The authors of many of these poems lacked first-hand experience of rural labor, but rural poets also began to find their own voice in this period. Appearing in the same year as *The Seasons* was *The Thresher's Labour*, a poem by Stephen Duck, a farm laborer taken up by patrons, which was commissioned as a poem "on his own labors." In contrast to Thomson's poem, *The Thresher's Labour* presents a harsher view of the agricultural cycle as a relentless master. Another poet writing of her own experience was Mary Collier; Collier's *The Woman's Labour* (1739)—written, without patrons, in response to Duck's poem—objected to his depiction of women workers as less important to rural labor than men.

George Stubbs, *Haymakers*, 1785. Stubbs (1724–1806), is known primarily for his equestrian pictures—scenes of hunting and horseracing. He was also active in other genres of painting, however; in the 1780s he began to concentrate largely on portrayals of daily life in rural England.

Some poets writing about the countryside directly challenged the vision of rural happiness so common in pastoral poetry. George Crabbe's *The Village* (1783) is one such poem. With its damning portraits of the failure both of individuals and of institutions to alleviate the suffering of the poor, and its diagnosis of social evils, it brought heightened realism to the genre. Charles Churchill found a similar parody of the pastoral helpful for political satire; his satirical portrait of Scotland, *The Prophecy of Famine: A Scots Pastoral* (1763), parodies the conventions of the pastoral, conveying Churchill's political concerns against a backdrop of waste and disease.

Close observation of nature could sometimes play a part in the introspective poetry of meditation, as in some work by Anne Finch, Countess of Winchilsea. Clergyman Thomas Parnell favored religious subject matter in his "Meditating on the Wounds of Christ" (1722), "On Divine Love" (1722), and "Hymn to Contentment" (1714). These poems, examining one aspect of human nature, often take the form of the hymn or ode. (William Collins's *Odes on Several Descriptive and Allegorical Subjects* [1746], which includes "Ode to Pity" and "Ode to Fear," is an important example.) A school of so-called graveyard poets might claim particular poems by several of these poets, though its leading representatives are Robert Blair's *The Grave* (1743) and Edward Young's *Night Thoughts* (1742–46). The meditative verse of these poets is suffused with melancholy and often features solitary, brooding figures who wander at night, a type largely inspired by Milton's *Il Penseroso* (1645). Gray's *Elegy Written in a Country Churchyard* (1751), which also employs aspects of this genre, features an isolated poet meditating on the generalities of life and death and lamenting the loss of poetic power and authority. Poetry's loss of force in contemporary society was a common complaint among these poets, and their works evince a lyrical nostalgia for the days when the poet's rich language and imagination held sway. Many were concerned that the true art of poetry would be lost without the flights of imagination and fantastical language they saw as the markers of poetry.

Theater

Following the restoration of the monarchy, English theater showed the influence of the French productions that the court had enjoyed while in exile. William Wycherley and Sir George Etherege composed comedies of wit like those of Molière, but with a narrow focus on the follies of a small class of people, the fashionable wits and beaux who were the theater's primary audience. They treated the particulars of the social life of the time, and satirized the more ridiculous and self-serving aspects of upper-class behavior; as in Molière's work, the humor of these plays relies on exaggeration and a highly stylized view of life, in which comic repartee and artful contrivance dominate. Referred to as "comedies of manners" or "social comedies," these plays often feature a witty, unprincipled, yet charismatic and charming libertine. The libertine-hero is ambivalently presented, generally an object of unmixed admiration to his own male circle and the available young women in the play, though more or less open to criticism from the audience. In Etherege's *The Man of Mode* (1676) the rake-hero gets off scot-free, rewarded for his heartless infidelities to other women with the hand of the witty and virginal heroine; Behn's rake-hero in *The Rover* (1677) is similarly rewarded, though he is not a cruel character and may be seen as having been (twice) genuinely in love in the course of the action. (After this play Behn arranged the offstage death of her witty heroine, in order to free the hero for fresh adventures in a sequel.) In Wycherley's *The Country Wife* (1675) a tradesman who marries for love may appear colorless beside the out-and-out rake whose continuing, obsessive pursuit of women leaves him isolated from his peers. Etherege, Behn, and Wycherley belonged to the earlier generation of Restoration playwrights. In the next generation, Vanbrugh (e.g., in *The Relapse* [1696]) and Congreve (e.g., in *The Way of the World* [1700]) opened the possibility of a charismatic rake not only marrying for love but attempting fidelity afterwards. These comedies are highly physical, with duels, disguises, and highly erotic scenes; their language is full of wordplay and sexual innuendo.

In Restoration theater women were hired for the first time to play the female parts. Their presence on stage (and the wide popularity that many of them achieved through the audience's knowledge or supposed knowledge about their private lives—as with Nell Gwynn, who eventually left the stage to become Charles II's mistress) incited playwrights to create provocative roles for them. The degree to which coarse or sexually suggestive language and behavior was being depicted on the stage in the late seventeenth century became a particular focus of complaint, and the portrayal of women was the most common source of outrage. Jeremy Collier's view was that

> Obscenity in any company is a rustic, uncreditable talent, but among women 'tis particularly rude. Such talk would be very affrontive in conversation and not endured by any lady of reputation. Whence then comes it to pass that those liberties which disoblige so much in conversation should entertain upon the stage? Do women leave all the regards to decency and conscience behind them when they come to the playhouse? In this respect the stage is faulty to a scandalous degree of nauseousness and aggravation.

Women were not only present on the stage; they were also writing plays for the stage for the first time in history. (Some women had written closet dramas before this, but none had been performed in a public theater.) Aphra Behn was one of the most successful dramatists of the age; her career began with *The Forced Marriage* (1670), a tragi-comedy about sexual relations and power struggles between the sexes. Behn had been preceded by a year by Frances Boothby's *Marcela* (1669). Delarivier Manley, Mary Pix, and Catharine Trotter soon followed in her footsteps, though all four women were considered morally suspect for embracing such an inherently public career. Susanna Centlivre, a leading professional playwright of the next generation, did not attract the censure her predecessors had. Her many published plays include the highly successful *The Busy Body* (1709).

Most of these women wrote more frequently in the genre of sophisticated farcical comedy than in the highly stylized tragedies that were popular at the time (Centlivre's one tragedy, *The Cruel Gift*, was written in collaboration with Nicholas Rowe). Set in remote times and places with spectacular scenes and effects, such tragedies tended to center on warrior/lovers torn between conflicting obligations in agonizing dilemmas. In this sort of heroic tragedy, the heroic couplet (written in iambic pentameter), championed by Dryden, was the meter of choice. While the heroic-couplet tragedy swiftly grew to enormous popularity, its downfall was just as sudden. George Villiers's famous burlesque *The Rehearsal* (1671), written in parody of Dryden and of the genre of heroic tragedy in general, was said to have helped hasten its end. From this point on, blank-verse tragedies, such as Thomas Otway's *Venice Preserved* (1682), gradually became more popular. In the theater, as in poetry, the eighteenth-century interest in (and admiration for) classical culture was prominent; the most popular tragedy of the time was Joseph Addison's *Cato* (1713). Adaptations and imitations of Shakespearean dramas were also common; Dryden's *All for Love* (1678), a revision of Shakespeare's *Antony and Cleopatra*, was the most successful of such adaptations in the period. The "she-tragedy," which detailed the dramatic fall of a heroine, was a popular new form of tragedy that appealed to the audience's sense of pity, especially for helpless women. These she-tragedies were removed from the current political and social scene, but featured historical settings that were often more precise or more recent than those of the heroic drama.

In the eighteenth century a new form of theatrical entertainment, the opera, came to England from Italy and became both a popular form of entertainment and a source of much derision. Critics could not comprehend the audience's desire to forego "legitimate" theater for entertainment featuring songs in languages they did not understand. In a *Spectator* article on the subject, Addison derisively declares that these operas seem to be written according to a rule "that nothing is capable of being well set to music that is not nonsense." With John Gay's *The Beggar's Opera* (1728), however, a new genre of opera was born—the ballad opera, to which the modern musical can trace its roots. Written in mockery of the rise of Italian opera in England, Gay's work derives its music from ballads and folk-songs. *The Beggar's Opera* became an instant success, inspiring numerous imitations and parodies, as well as a line of merchandise that included playing cards, fans, plates, and paintings.

One effect of Gay's play was to lessen the popularity of the Italian opera; another was to incur the displeasure of minister Robert Walpole: *The Beggar's Opera* was taken as a satire on the Prime Minister (though Gay never admitted to any such intention). Nevertheless, it was one of many real or supposed theatrical attacks on Walpole during his time in office. Henry Fielding's *Pasqual* (1736) was one of a series of works with which he targeted Walpole. Perceiving these satires as a threat to the authority of his ministry, Walpole sought to bring them to an end. He pushed through the Theatrical Licensing Act of 1737, the result of which was that the Lord Chamberlain had to approve plays before they could be produced. The political threat posed by the theater was curbed, and Walpole's control over his reputation was asserted.

William Hogarth, *The Laughing Audience* (1733). This etching depicts the audience at a theatrical performance. The three figures in the front are seated in the orchestra. Behind them (and separated by a spiked partition), commoners in the pit laugh uproariously—with the exception of one being jostled by an orange seller. One gentleman in the balcony has eyes only for a competing orange seller, while the interests of another are also engaged elsewhere.

Revivals of earlier plays, which had always been staples of the stage, helped to take the place of new plays. Those new plays that were produced tended to replace political with domestic concerns and biting wit with sentimentality and melodrama; theatrical productions were required to be much more respectful of conventional views, and playwrights had to be acutely aware of the public temper at any given time. The taste for decorum, overt moralizing, and warm human sentiments evident in the new sentimental comedies offered opportunities for female playwrights, who were seen as having authority in these emotional, domestic realms. Elizabeth Griffith and Frances Sheridan—and Elizabeth Inchbald and Joanna Baillie a few decades later—could argue for their inherent expertise in the matters depicted in their plays. Following a lengthy vogue for sentimental comedy in the mid-eighteenth century, new "laughing" comedies such as Oliver Goldsmith's *She Stoops to Conquer* (1773), Richard Brinsley Sheridan's *The School for Scandal* (1778), and Hannah Cowley's *The Belle's Stratagem* (1780) sought to reclaim comedy for satire and fun, though at least the threat of tears was still likely to accompany the laughter, and protagonists were lauded for their private, emotional virtue as well as teased about faults or follies.

THE NOVEL

With the rise of the reading public, the decline of literary patronage, and the increasing power and range of the influence of "booksellers," literature for the first time became a market commodity. As Daniel Defoe put it, writing "is become a very considerable branch of the English Commerce. The booksellers are the master manufacturers or employers. The several writers, authors, copiers, sub-writers, and all other operators with pen and ink are the workmen employed by the said master manufacturers." Literature was not only more popular and more widely disseminated, it was also to an unprecedented degree subject to economic laws, in which supply was determined by popular demand.

The growth and diversification of the reading public are two frequently cited reasons for the sudden rise of the popular form of the novel. As the century progressed, the influence of an educated elite who maintained an interest in (and knowledge of) classical letters declined; more and more, reading became a leisure activity undertaken for pleasure. Many of the new readers were females from well-off families. These readers sought increasingly realistic (rather than romantic-fantastical), detailed works that spoke to their own lives and the world around them. The periodical essay, in which the minute details of ordinary lives were described and analyzed, was instrumental in creating tastes to which the novel then catered. Articles gave practical information about domestic and public life and sought to improve the minds and morals of their readers while simultaneously providing entertainment. Novels also represented the new values and lifestyles of eighteenth-century Britain, in which older, rural, land-centered lifestyles were being replaced. The vast majority of novels were either entirely set in London or involved travel to that city. Defoe's *The Fortunes and Misfortunes of Moll Flanders* (1722) features a woman in London underground society without a family, education, or social position. It describes the specifics of the London criminal world as well as the potential for rehabilitation. When Moll is transported to the New World as a convicted felon (where, under the "Transportation Act" of 1718, regular shiploads of criminals were sent), she becomes both rich and penitent. Frances Burney's novel *Evelina, or the History of a Young Lady's Entrance into the World* (1778), like some of the articles in Eliza Haywood's *The Female Tatler*, opened up the intimate details of a female world to the public eye, giving male readers a glimpse of what it meant to be female and vulnerable.

The modern conception of "realism," often considered the novel's most defining characteristic, was not explicitly formulated as an aesthetic principle until the nineteenth and twentieth centuries, but owes its origin to the ideas of Descartes and Locke, who worked to advance the theory that truth can be discovered through the individual's senses. This new emphasis on individual experience and perception of reality lies at the heart of the eighteenth-century novel. Previous forms (such as the epic or pastoral elegy) demanded fidelity to certain set rules of the genre, and the author's skill was judged by his or her ability to adhere to accepted traditional models. In contrast, the primary aim of novels was the depiction of individual experience. In order to give primacy to an individual perception of reality, authors did not rely on allusions to or inspiration from classical sources, but sought their material in the actual, familiar world of daily experience. Daniel Defoe and Samuel Richardson were notable in that they did not take their plots from mythology, history, or pre-existing legend or literature.

The rise of the epistolary form is another important thread in the development of the novel. Aphra Behn pioneered epistolary fiction in the Restoration; her *Love Letters Between a Nobleman and His Sister* (meaning, in this case, sister-in-law) (1684–87), is an epistolary novel that also provides a subjective account of contemporary political events. (The form was also used by Mary Davys in a work published in 1725, but the epistolary novel did not gain wide popularity as a genre until well into the eighteenth century.) The century's countless newspapers generally had correspondents who wrote in from their various locations, summarizing local events, and publishers of periodicals often found letters—fictitious or otherwise—to be a popular method of creating a sense of sociability and of literary conversation. Late seventeenth-century writers had begun to explore various themes and concerns through collections of fictitious letters; Margaret Cavendish's *Sociable Letters* (1664), for example, imagines the written communication of two women living a short distance from one another, mixing discursive, serious letters (frequently critiquing marriage) with more comic, anecdotal letters. Travel narratives too began frequently to be cast as a series of letters from the traveler to those at home, describing his or her experiences. Richardson's first novel, *Pamela* (1740), developed out of a small book of sample letters Richardson wrote in order to educate his readers in the art of letter-writing; eventually he reworked the "sample" and incorporated it into a much larger prose narrative.

Behn's *Oroonoko* (1688) shows the influence of various forms of non-fiction on the development of the novel. Part novel or romance, part history, and part travel narrative, of novella length, it includes an extended description of natives and slaves in Africa and Guiana, economic details of colonial trade, and various of Behn's observations from the time she spent in Surinam in 1663 and 1664. As such works suggest, the development of the novel as a popular genre was a many-faceted process. The term "novel" can be misleading for the contemporary reader; by thinking of the various long prose narratives of the eighteenth century as novels, we unify them into one genre in a way that contemporary readers did not. The use of the term "novel," which identifies the genre only by its newness, was not in common use until the end of the seventeenth century, and when it was used, it typically denoted a short, romantic tale. (Its first use was to describe the various short tales within Boccaccio's fifteenth-century *Decameron.*) In the eighteenth century a variety of other names as well were given to what we now call novels, including "romance," "history," "adventure," "memoir," and "tale." The current conception of the novel—as a long prose fiction presenting more or less realistic characters—did not solidify until the time of Jane Austen and Sir Walter Scott. Aphra Behn, Daniel Defoe, and Samuel Richardson—each of whom has been named as the "founder" of the modern novel—each conceived of their fiction in very different terms, came to the novel from different writing backgrounds, and had different goals for their work. Samuel Richardson and Henry Fielding each significantly influenced the development of the novel, but these two men wrote in diametrically opposed styles and created works with what they saw as opposing aims. Richardson boasted that his epistolary mode allowed him to provide "familiar letters written as it were to the moment."

In response to Richardson's *Pamela; or, Virtue Rewarded* (1741), Fielding, one of the leading comic playwrights in England in the early part of the century, but at that point a writer who had not previously attempted prose fiction, wrote the anonymous *An Apology for the Life of Mrs. Shamela Andrews* (1741) to mock Richardson's style. Both *Shamela* and Eliza Haywood's *Anti-Pamela; or, Feigned Innocence Detected* (1741) question Richardson's representation of sexuality and class while mocking his style and the generic conventions he establishes for his novel. In contrast to Richardson's prurience and lack of humor, both works adopt a playful ironic tone that mockingly exposes

PAMELA:

OR,

VIRTUE Rewarded.

In a SERIES of

FAMILIAR LETTERS

FROM A

Beautiful Young DAMSEL,

To her PARENTS.

Now first Published

In order to cultivate the Principles of VIRTUE and RELIGION in the Minds of the YOUTH of BOTH SEXES.

A Narrative which has its Foundation in TRUTH and NATURE; and at the same time that it agreeably entertains, by a Variety of *curious* and *affecting* INCIDENTS, is intirely divested of all those Images, which, in too many Pieces calculated for Amusement only, tend to *inflame* the Minds they should *instruct*.

In TWO VOLUMES.

VOL. I.

LONDON:

Printed for C. RIVINGTON, in *St. Paul's Church-Yard*; and J. OSBORN, in *Pater-noster Row*.

MDCCXLI.

Title page, *Pamela; or Virtue Rewarded* (1741).

AN

APOLOGY

FOR THE

LIFE

OF

Mrs. SHAMELA ANDREWS.

In which, the many notorious FALSHOODS and MISREPRSENTATIONS of a Book called

PAMELA,

Are exposed and refuted; and all the matchless ARTS of that young Politician, set in a true and just Light.

Together with

A full Account of all that passed between her and Parson *Arthur Williams*; whose Character is represented in a manner something different from what he bears in *PAMELA*. The whole being exact Copies of authentick Papers delivered to the Editor.

Necessary to be had in all FAMILIES.

By Mr. *CONNY KEYBER*.

LONDON:

Printed for A. DODD, at the *Peacock*, without *Temple-bar*.
M. DCC. XLI.

Title page, *An Apology for the Life of Mrs. Shamela Andrews* (1741).

Pamela's virtue as feigned. Fielding's *Joseph Andrews* (1742), written about a hero who turns out to be Pamela's brother, works in a similar fashion, using the picaresque, ironic, and anti-romantic style of Cervantes's *Don Quixote* as a model.

These works demonstrate the ways in which novels and the cultural discourse surrounding them were in dialogue with one another as the generic shape of the novel gradually began to solidify. From its outset the novel was often a remarkably self-conscious form, however, and even as the genre was taking shape some writers were keen to play with its nascent conventions. Laurence Sterne's *Tristram Shandy*, in particular, does this with typographical oddities, direct addresses by author to reader about his difficulties in writing, and chapters printed out of order. Its chronology moves backward as well as forward. The narrator plays with the language through puns and *double entendres*, and frequently interrupts himself for digressions so lengthy that he professes to have difficulty keeping track of his own story. In this novel the narrator's private reality takes control of both the content and the form of the novel. Charlotte Lennox's *The Female Quixote* (1752), another work influenced by Cervantes, comments on the interrelationships between romance, female desire and social position, and the novel. Her heroine is, like Don Quixote, a dreamer who treats her life as if it were a plot from one of the numerous chivalric romances she reads. Lennox's novel demonstrates the mistakes that can be made if one thinks of life as resembling a popular romance; it also highlights the differences between the emerging novel and a genre from which most novel writers sought to distance themselves—the popular romance.

Many works that were, at the time, written in reaction to the genre of the novel are now regarded as being novels themselves. Jonathan Swift distrusted the individualist psychology, adjustable morals, and the faith in class mobility and commercialism that the novel represented; his *Gulliver's Travels* (1726)—which is not a novel, but follows an earlier form of non-naturalistic prose fiction—in some respects, as in the middle-class ordinariness of its protagonist, forecasts the direction of the emergent novel, and in some respects reads like a burlesque of the form. Gulliver can be seen as a parody of the typical, middle-class fictional subject; while the authority of narratives by early novelists, particularly Defoe, relied on the assumed fitness of a merchant class or low-life narrator (such as Robinson Crusoe, Moll Flanders, or Colonel Jack) to record modern life, Swift employs a naive narrator to obliquely advance social criticisms. Later in the eighteenth century, Samuel Johnson, who observed that novels were written "chiefly to the young, the ignorant, and the idle," felt these readers in particular required moral instruction and not the false optimism of a happy-ever-after ending. His *Rasselas* (1759) reacts against the moral ambiguities of the novel by offering a strictly moral and elaborately inconclusive tale meant to educate his readers by forcing them to think.

Women made up an increasing percentage of the novel's new writers, and as they struggled for literary authority they influenced the development of various modes of fiction. Of these female writers, Eliza Haywood (whom Fielding used as the basis of a stage figure named "Mrs. Novel") was the most prolific producer of novel titles before the late eighteenth century. Her first novel, *Love in Excess* (1719), published in the same year as *Robinson Crusoe*, was one of only two works to rival it in popularity. Although her later novels are less erotically charged, Haywood's reputation remained colored by her early work; along with Delarivier Manley and Aphra Behn, she was known for bawdy, sensational novels whose plots foregrounded sexual intrigue. Manley was famous for publishing "secret histories," such as *The New Atlantis* (1709)—for which she was arrested—which detailed scandals about contemporary political figures, passed off as fiction. John Cleland's *Fanny Hill; or, Memoirs of a Woman of Pleasure* (1749) may be one of the most famous of numerous scandalous texts—many disseminated by notorious bookseller Edmund Curll—that celebrated libertine attitudes of sexual behavior. Haywood's *Fantomina* (1725) and *The History of Miss Betsy Thoughtless* (1751), though they featured far less in the line of seduction or rape, were to some people even more shocking, since it was female sexuality they foregrounded, rather than male.

The new taste for sentiment made itself felt in fiction as in poetry and the theater. The "sentimental" in fiction may mean stories designed to fill the reader with anguished pity, or stories glorifying the sentimental as morally worthy. Sarah Fielding's *The Adventures of David Simple* (1744) was, like Richardson's *Pamela*, designed to display the elevated, refined, humanitarian feelings of its central characters, while the still fairly heavy incidence of seduction, rape, and false accusation is performed by palpably evil characters, and the moral design of the fiction is obvious. When Fielding added her *Volume the Last* to *David Simple* in 1753, she produced a disturbing tear-jerker in which the good characters are routed and largely destroyed by the bad ones. Sarah Scott's *The History of Sir George Ellison* (1770) claimed to depict "the life of a man more ordinarily good"; while Sir George succeeds in materially reforming at least the small section of the world around him, the sentimental character is often seen in vain opposition to a cruel world to which he or she could not be reconciled. Henry Mackenzie's *The Man of Feeling* (1771), for example, shows a character of sentiment too sensitive for the world. This sentiment was considered edifying and instructive as well as touching; as Johnson told Boswell of Samuel Richardson, "You must read him for the sentiment." The ideal characteristics of both sentimental heroes and heroines were traditionally feminine ones, such as sensitivity, compassion, and private virtue. Some women writers led and some opposed the movement to establish the sentimental, sensitive, often victimized heroine as the ideal model of femininity, often using heroines of this type to engage with political issues. Novels such as Frances Sheridan's *Memoirs of Miss Sidney Bidulph* (1761), or Elizabeth Griffith's three novels about women in unhappy marriages, explore women's virtue and vice, their status in the home, and their use of domestic power within the larger social structure. Often these works also express concern about the double standard of sexual morality.

Courtship novels were also a convenient mode for examining sentiment, sensibility, gender roles, and behavior. Frances Burney's *Cecilia* (1782), Elizabeth Inchbald's *A Simple Story* (1791), and Charlotte Smith's *Emmeline, the Orphan of the Castle* (1788) and *Celestina* (1791) all use the tale of a young girl's emergence into social life and the rituals of courtship to convey opinions on manners, fashions, morals, and changing sexual and national politics. An element of subversion is often built into the courtship genre, as the heroine looks critically upon the process she is undergoing. Jane Austen, who was an avid reader of Charlotte Smith's work, was strongly influenced by Smith's *Emmeline* when she wrote her *Sense and Sensibility* (1811); that novel marks a turn away from the cult of sensibility (upon which *Emmeline* relies) and toward a reassertion of rationalism.

Just as some poets began to feel that realism had robbed their art of its power and creativity, some novelists came to feel the novel's strict fidelity to realistic narrative to be stifling. Horace Walpole, frustrated with the confines of realism and rationalism, attempted in his *Castle of Otranto* (1764) to combine the realism of the novel's psychological representation with the imaginative resources of old romance, in which the supernatural and marvelous were allowed full play. Written as a trifle and in a spirit of pure fun, *Otranto* is now taken seriously as the first Gothic novel; it created a form that became predominant at the turn of the century. Popular Gothic works included Clara Reeve's *The Old English Baron* (1777), William Beckford's *Vathek* (1786), Matthew Lewis's *The Monk* (1796), William Godwin's *Caleb Williams* (1794) and *St. Leon* (1799), and the numerous novels of renowned Gothic novelist Ann Radcliffe, including *The Mysteries of Udolpho* (1794) and *The Italian* (1797). These novels investigated human responses to seemingly supernatural occurrences, things known (thanks to the advances of science and natural history) to be impossible. In an Enlightenment era, the Gothic examined dark mysteries, and their darkness was even more menacing in contrast to the light that had been thrown on the world around them. The "horror" Gothic associated with Matthew or "Monk" Lewis was strong on graveyard elements and corpses risen from the dead, while the "terror" Gothic associated primarily with Ann Radcliffe turned on the emotions awakened in a rational and balanced person by the threat of the supernatural or the unexplained. The generally formulaic plots of Gothic novels often involve the usurpation of a title or estate, a hidden crime, or a secret pact with the devil. They tend to feature stereotypical characters and take place in worlds temporally or geographically distanced from England. Many of the elements of Gothic fiction had been present decades earlier in other genres, such as Alexander Pope's heroic epistle *Eloisa to Abelard* (1717). Like a typical terror Gothic, the poem featured a heroine physically confined, isolated, and subjected to harrowing emotions. The surrounding landscape is highly symbolic, reflecting the psychological world of the character, which dominates the work, and the heroine's plight is rendered in highly expressive rhetoric full of rhapsodic feeling. The Gothic often expresses darker elements of marriage and family life: where the courtship novel offers an attractive young man, the Gothic novel offers a cruel patriarch. Gothic novels provided an ominous view of homes, which tend to be confining, isolating, and ill-omened structures whose occupants are threatened by insanity and hysteria. Forbidden themes (such as incest, necrophilia, and murder) are allowed to surface. The structures themselves often embodied the political and social tensions resulting from the integration of ancient or historical time, preserved in castles or abbeys, into a world which is in other respects modern. The Gothic setting of Charlotte Smith's *Emmeline, the Orphan of the Castle*, for example, allows Smith to explore social concerns such as English laws of primogeniture and women's social status and identity within the frame of a courtship novel. Her novel illustrates the ways in which the frightening, distorted world of the Gothic could also serve as a forum for social commentary—as it also does in William Godwin's *Caleb Williams* and in Eliza Fenwick's *Secresy* (1795).

As the British Empire expanded and Britons increasingly looked out beyond the borders of Europe, the scope of the British novel responded to this broader perspective. Restoration tragedy had favored exotic settings including the empires of the Mughals and the Aztecs. In the early eighteenth century, fiction writers like Daniel Defoe and Penelope Aubin made use of both the "East Indies" (roughly today's East Asia) and the West. *Robinson Crusoe* famously takes place on an uninhabited island in the Atlantic; Behn's *Oroonoko* takes its readers to the racially mixed society of Surinam; in Johnson's *Rasselas* the central characters come from Africa and journey through Egypt. An English appetite for non-fiction about the colonies was fed by Mary Rowlandson's narrative of her captivity and ransom by the Algonquin Native Americans, *A True History of the Captivity and Restoration of Mrs. Mary Rowlandson* (1682) and by *The Female American; or, The Adventures of Unca Eliza Winkfield* (1767), which is a novel in the guise of autobiography. Its narrator, the daughter of a Native-American princess and an English settler, is, like Robinson Crusoe, shipwrecked on an island in the Atlantic. This trans-Atlantic examination of issues of race, gender, and empire depicts a feminist utopian society in the cross-racial community its narrator discovers on her island. Fiction in which characters and settings spanned the Atlantic became common. Frances Brooke published *The History of Emily Montague* (1768), set in what is now Quebec, after living there for several years. Among those who more than once set a novel at least partly in the colonies were Charlotte Lennox, who had an American childhood, and Susanna Rowson, who became on balance more American than English, while Phebe Gibbes and Charlotte Smith took an interest in the colonies without ever having gone there. Smith's interest was political, and was shared with other radical or Jacobin writers: the protagonist of Robert Bage's *Hermsprong, or, Man as He Is Not* (1796) is by no means the only English radical hero to have been shaped by an upbringing among Native Americans. Rowson's *Reuben and Rachel* (1798) amounts at least in its earlier parts to an American melting-pot or birth-of-the-nation novel, while Elizabeth Hamilton's *Translations of the Letters of a Hindoo Rajah* (1796) continues the examination of Indian culture that Gibbes had launched in *Hartly House, Calcutta*, in 1789 (another novel which was widely taken for non-fiction).

Not only did the imaginary realms of fiction extend out into the world; the books themselves increasingly traveled outside Britain. Popular works such as novels by Fielding and Richardson would be shipped to the colonies or pirated by American printers. Across the continent, British literature was becoming more widely translated, read, and admired. *The Tatler* and *The Spectator* were read as far north as the Scottish Highlands, in addition to being sent across the Atlantic to the North American colonies. *Robinson Crusoe* was one of the first works of British literature to be widely acclaimed on the continent; in Germany and France the novel was more widely read than Chaucer, Shakespeare, or Milton at the time of its publication. The value of these older English writers also began to be more widely recognized internationally, however, as eighteenth-century poets, dramatists, and critics acknowledged their debt to these predecessors, extolling their merits and making international readers aware of the influence their contributions had made to contemporary writing. Johnson's *Dictionary* also contributed to the international recognition of British authors. In his account of the English language, Johnson's quotations from leading English authors from previous centuries not only illustrated the wealth and variety of usage, but were instrumental in the creation of a canon of works of established value. As the *Dictionary* gained international renown, so, too, did the authors Johnson quoted.

THE DEVELOPMENT OF THE ENGLISH LANGUAGE

One effect of the growth of print culture was to slow down the rate at which change in the language occurred; another was to make people more aware of the variations that did exist. Many came to the view that change in the language was in itself something to be resisted on principle, on the grounds that change allowed "corruptions" to be introduced to the language, and would make literary works of their present generation less accessible to future generations. In the late seventeenth century Dryden had expressed his desire that the English "might all write with the same certainty of words, and purity of phrase, to which the Italians first arrived, and after them the French"—in other words, a "purity" of linguistic standards set and enforced by the state, as the Accademia della Crusca had done in Italy since 1592 and the Académie française had done in France since 1635. Swift echoed Dryden in 1712 with "A Proposal for Correcting, Improving, and Ascertaining the English Tongue," which exerted considerable influence on educated opinion. Like Dryden, Swift called for the production of dictionaries and books of grammar that would codify practice and identify corrupt linguistic practices to be weeded out, and that would act as a retarding force against change. Swift wanted to "fix" the English language in two senses: "fix" in the sense of "repair damage" (he believed that numerous corruptions had been introduced to the language since the civil wars), and also "fix" in the sense of "set in a fixed position." In his view, it was "better that a language should not be wholly perfect, than that it should be perpetually changing."

Before the Restoration, books of grammar in England were generally books on the grammar of Latin. In the late sixteenth century, two short grammars of English had been published, and several more had followed in the first half of the seventeenth. In the late seventeenth century, though, and even more so in the eighteenth century, this trickle became a flood. Perhaps the most influential was Robert Lowth's *Short Introduction to English Grammar* (1762), which did much to establish a tradition of focusing such works largely on errors in grammar and usage. In the view of grammarians such as Thomas Sheridan (father of the playwright Richard), such errors carried moral weight: the "revival of the art of speaking, and the study of language," in Sheridan's view, might be expected to contribute "in great measure" to remedying the "evils of immorality, ignorance, and false taste." At the other end of the spectrum was Joseph Priestley, the theologian and scientist (discoverer of sulphur dioxide, ammonia, and the gas that was later given the name oxygen); Priestley's *Rudiments of English Grammar* (1761) staunchly resisted the prescriptive, maintaining in startlingly modern terms that "the custom of speaking is the original and only just standard of a language."

In the late eighteenth century the prescriptivists won the day over issues of grammar, and began to entrench a good many distinctions, rules, and standards of correctness that remain with us today. Among these were the creation of distinctions in meaning between the verbs "lie" and "lay," between "between" and "among," and between "shall" and "will"; the prohibition on degrees of such "absolute" qualities as roundness and perfection; and the prohibition of double negatives.

English dictionaries (the first of which had appeared in 1604) included only "hard words" through the seventeenth century. The first dictionary to aim at comprehensiveness was Nathaniel Bailey's *Universal Etymological English Dictionary* (1721). Bailey's work went through 27 editions before the end of the century, but it was Samuel Johnson's *Dictionary* (1755) that had the more lasting impact. The decisions Johnson made in writing his *Dictionary*—to include illustrative quotations and to break down definitions of each head word into distinct senses—became conventional for all later dictionaries. Perhaps Johnson's most controversial decision was to make the dictionary primarily descriptive rather than prescriptive in nature; though Johnson noted certain "improprieties and absurdities, which it is the duty of the lexicographer to correct or proscribe," he saw the main purpose of his dictionary as being to record how the language was being and had been used, not to dictate how it should be used.

Johnson agreed with Swift that the pre-Restoration language represented "the wheels of English undefiled," but he disagreed as to the appropriate response. Not only was he willing to record usages of which he disapproved in his dictionary; he also strenuously resisted calls for the establishment of a formal authority to regulate the language, approving of the way in which "Englishmen have always been moved by a spirit of personal liberty in the use of their language." In similar fashion Priestley declared that an academy regulating the language would be "unsuitable to the genius of a free nation." It was this nationalistic argument more than anything that swayed the English in the late eighteenth century against the French and Italian models.

Language, of course, continued to change throughout the period, albeit at a rather slower pace than in the sixteenth and early seventeenth centuries. It often changed in ways of which the prescriptivists disapproved—and often resisted change in directions they wished it to follow. Swift and many other prescriptivists had conceived a violent disapproval of the supposedly excessive number of monosyllabic words in English. Swift disapproved especially of the creation of shortened forms of longer words, such as *pozz* for *positive* and *mob* for *mobile*. (This last was long a particular pet peeve of Swift's, but late in life he finally admitted defeat in the face of the linguistic mob that adopted the shortened form.) But English has remained a language possessing a substantially larger percentage of monosyllabic words than do other European languages.

Swift disapproved too of the shortened pronunciation of words ending in the suffix *-ed*, which during his lifetime was typically pronounced as a separate syllable. This change in pronunciation was achieved initially through the use of an apostrophe, such that "changed" (which would have been pronounced "change-ed") became "chang'd," and "deserved" (which would have been pronounced with three syllables) became "deserv'd." "By leaving out a vowel to save a syllable," Swift asserted, "we form so jarring a sound, and so difficult to utter, that I have often wondered how it could ever obtain." His fulminations notwithstanding, the practice became more and more common. And, given the large number of such words in the English language, the development inevitably had a considerable effect on accentual syllabic verse in English—and on the way such poetry appeared on the page. Through most of the eighteenth century, printed English poetry is heavily populated by words ending in *-'d* rather than *-ed*. By century's end, however, these apostrophes start to disappear as the once-universal habit of pronouncing the *-ed* as a separate syllable became a thing of the past. In nineteenth, twentieth, and twenty-first century poetry the presumption runs the other way; to indicate, for example, that "despised" is to be pronounced as three syllables rather than two, a grave accent is used ("despisèd").[1]

Perhaps the most important structural change in the late seventeenth and eighteenth centuries was the spread of progressive verb forms, and in particular the development of the passive progressive. Where in the seventeenth century one would say "The church is building," in the eighteenth people began to say "The church is being built." This development occurred organically, and (despite what seems to us to be its obvious usefulness) was widely resisted by grammarians.

There were also a number of more superficial changes in the written forms of English. There remained no agreed-upon standards regarding capitalization and italics, but it was common practice to employ both liberally. Many writers made it a practice to capitalize all

[1] In this anthology spelling and punctuation are, as a rule, modernized; where an eighteenth century poem prints "chang'd" to indicate that the word should be pronounced as one syllable (where we would pronounce it as one syllable regardless), our practice is to modernize the spelling as "changed." (Where an eighteenth-century poem has "heav'n" rather than "heaven," on the other hand, we retain the apostrophe, as it indicates that the word should be pronounced differently from the manner in which we habitually do.)

abstract nouns, and some capitalized virtually all nouns. No conventions existed for the treatment of quotations in print (quotation marks were not commonly used in the modern style before the nineteenth century); some writers used dashes and paragraph breaks to aid the reader, while others left the reader to infer who was saying what, purely on the basis of interpolated phrases such as *he said*, *she replied*, and so on.

The spread of dictionaries—and of publishing itself—helped to "fix" English spelling, but it largely became fixed in a form that represented the English that had been spoken before the great shift in English pronunciation that had occurred in the fifteenth to seventeenth centuries. Thus were preserved the *t* in *castle*, the *k* in *knight*, the *gh* in *through*, and so on.

The American Revolution was accompanied by dissatisfaction in the new nation at using the language of the defeated imperial power. Noah Webster was among those who preferred to call the language used in the United States "American," and in 1789 Webster introduced a range of spelling changes designed both to rationalize spelling and to make the American variety distinctive from the English; the American spellings of *color*, *favor*, *honor*, *traveling*, and *theater* all took root as a result of Webster's initiative. (Over the following decades Webster came to acknowledge that he had lost the battle to call "American" a separate language, however; his 1828 dictionary was entitled *An American Dictionary of the English Language*.)

Above all, perhaps, the late seventeenth and eighteenth centuries were a period of growth for the English language. Words continued to be imported from other languages, perhaps most notably from French; it was a sign of the times that many now found these imports objectionable. In 1711, for example, Addison expressed his hope that "superintendents of our language" might be appointed "to hinder any words of a foreign coin from passing among us; and in particular to prohibit any French phrases from becoming current in our kingdom, when those of our own stamp are altogether as valuable." Even in the face of resistance such as this, *ballet* and *champagne* made their way across the Channel and entered English during this period, as did *connoisseur*, *dentist*, *negligee*, and *publicity*, along with a host of others. But the greatest growth came not in imports from France but in the coining of new scientific terms (often from Latin or Greek roots), from *abdomen* and *atom*, to *corolla* and *cortex*, to *genus* and *gravity*, on to *zoology*, and including thousands of more specialized terms that have never come into general circulation but have nonetheless contributed to the expansion in the communicative capacity of the English language.

History of the Language and of Print Culture

In an effort to provide for readers a direct sense of the development of the language and of print culture, examples of texts in their original form (and of illustrations) have been provided in each volume. A list of these within the present volume appears below in chronological order. An overview of developments in the history of language during this period appears on pages LXX to LXXII, and a "Contexts" section on various aspects of "Print Culture, Stage Culture" appears on pages 651–67.

The London Gazette, Sept 3–10, 1666, pp. 139–42.

"An Argument Shewing, that a Standing Army is inconsistent with a Free Government," title page of 1697 pamphlet, p. XXXIX.

John Wilmot, Earl of Rochester, "A Letter from Artemesia in the Town to Chloe in the Country," passage in original spelling and punctuation, p. 296; facsimile page from a late eighteenth-century edition of *Rochester's Life*, p. 301.

Anne Finch, Countess of Winchelsea, "By neer resemblance that Bird betray'd," poem in original spelling and punctuation, pp. 353–54.

Joseph Addison, *The Spectator* No. 112, facsimile, pp. 677–78.

Alexander Pope, *The Rape of the Lock*, illustrations from the 1714 edition, pp. 556, 558, 561, 563, 566.

Daniel Defoe, *Robinson Crusoe*, illustrations to various editions, pp. 336–38.

Eliza Haywood, *Fantomina*, passage in original spelling and punctuation, pp. 638–39.

Jonathan Swift, *Gulliver's Travels*, illustration from frontispiece to 1726 edition, p. 391; maps from the 1726 edition, pp. 421, 484; passages in original spelling and punctuation, pp. 442–44.

Samuel Richardson, *Pamela: or, Virtue Rewarded*, facsimile of 1741 title page, p. LXV.

Henry Fielding, *An Apology for the Life of Mrs. Shamela Andrews*, facsimile of 1741 title page, p. LXVI.

"God Save Our Lord, the King," facsimile from *The Gentleman's Magazine*, 1745, p. 687.

William Hogarth, *Marriage A-la-Mode* (series of engravings), pp. 922–27.

Hester Thrale Piozzi, *Hester Thrale's Journal*, passage in original spelling and punctuation, p. 950.

Margaret Cavendish
1623 – 1673

Margaret Cavendish was one of the most unusual, most prolific writers of the English Interregnum and Restoration periods. As a woman who published under her own name she was widely ridiculed by her social peers. Cavendish's reputation suffered for centuries; it was not until the late twentieth century that critics began to admire her eclectic range of interests and her passionate, personal style of writing.

Cavendish was born Margaret Lucas near Colchester, Essex, in 1623. She came from a rich family, the youngest of eight children of Thomas Lucas, Earl of Colchester, and Elizabeth Leighton Lucas. Her father died when she was two years old. Her mother raised her, and in doing so proved to be a strong, independent role model. Because she was a girl, Margaret was not formally educated, and received no training beyond rudimentary reading and writing skills.

In 1642 the Lucases's comfortable life was interrupted by the beginning of the English Civil War. Firmly in the Royalist camp, the family moved to Oxford, which was then the center of power for the Royalist faction. Margaret was impressed by the strength of character demonstrated by Queen Henrietta Maria (wife of Charles I) during the conflict, and she joined her court as a maid of honor, against the advice of her family. In 1644 she went with the Queen into exile in Paris. These were difficult years for Margaret Lucas. Separated from her family, she was very lonely. Painfully shy, she said very little in court, for fear of being thought foolish—and in a social culture that valued wit above all, she was mocked for her silence.

In 1645 she met and was wooed by William Cavendish, the recently widowed Marquess of Newcastle, who was also in exile for being a Royalist military commander. The age gap between the two was considerable: Margaret was 22, and William was 52, a difference so great that the Queen advised her against the match. But William proved to be persuasive—the two were married in December 1645.

Although William was a supportive husband, the marriage did not bring much financial stability. In 1649 the Royalists were defeated and King Charles I was beheaded. William was officially banished from England, and all of his estates were confiscated. The couple lived impoverished in exile, first in Paris, then in Antwerp. While living in Paris, however, Cavendish had the opportunity to meet some of the most influential thinkers of the time; Thomas Hobbes and René Descartes were dinner guests at the Cavendish household.

Cavendish went to England in 1651 to request compensation for the loss of William's property from the new government. Her petition failed, but during the two years that she spent in the endeavor, she began writing. She was to continue to write for the rest of her life.

In 1653 she published two volumes under her own name, *Poems, and Fancies* and *Philosophical Fancies*. This was not in itself an unusual event, but her sex made it an outrageous act. In Cavendish's time, women were expected to limit their activities to the private sphere; although women occasionally published, it was usually done under pseudonyms or under the writer's initials, not under her own, full name. (There was also a class issue; though members of the upper classes often wrote, they frequently felt it more dignified not to publish.) Public reaction was immediate. Cavendish was portrayed as a vulgar, attention-seeking pretender within her social circle. (No doubt it did not help that Cavendish's writing was often unconventional; Cavendish valued the passion of her writing more than the technical proficiency of its execution.) She also chose to forego the topic of love in her verse, arguing that it was too predictable a topic for a woman, and instead wrote poems about science, politics, and morality.

The negative reactions did not deter Cavendish from writing and publishing a torrent of works throughout the rest of her life. Her letters indicate that she was driven by a desire to be remembered by the world, and not just as the wife of a nobleman. As she wrote in one of her *Sociable Letters*,

> I should weep myself into water if I could have no other fame than rich coaches, lackeys, and what state and ceremony could produce, for my ambition flies higher, to worth and merit, not state and vanity; I would be known to the world by my wit, not by my folly, and I would have my actions be wise and just, as I might neither be ashamed nor afraid to hear of myself.

In 1655 Cavendish published two more books, *The World's Olio*, a broad-ranging book on politics, aesthetics, and science, and *Philosophical and Physical Opinions* (revised and reissued in 1668 as *Grounds of Natural Philosophy*), a discourse concerning the methods of the new philosophers. The next year she followed up with a collection of short prose and verse entitled *Nature's Pictures*, an eclectic collection of fables and romances, together with a short autobiography. She had planned to publish a book of closet drama, plays intended to be read rather than performed, but the manuscript was lost en route from Antwerp to England when the ship it was on sank. The publication, *Orations of Divers Sorts and Plays*, was delayed until 1662.

The Cavendishes returned to England in 1660 when the monarchy was restored and the new king, Charles II, named them Duke and Duchess of Newcastle. They regained their estate, albeit in a poorer condition than when they left it, and settled into a quieter life. Despite all of the ridicule, Cavendish had by this time become something of a literary celebrity. She was also considered a public curiosity; she disdained convention by dressing in men's waistcoats and cavalier hats, and choosing to bow, rather than curtsey.

She continued to publish, writing at least seven more books, including the remarkable *Description of a New World Called The Blazing World* (1666), a companion piece to a long scientific study called *Observations Upon Experimental Philosophy. Blazing World* is in some respects a precursor of the genre we now call science fiction. It begins as a record of the observations of a female protagonist who enters another world through a connection at the Earth's North Pole, but the book soon strays into the fields of natural science, philosophy, and even autobiography.

In 1668 Cavendish published a new volume of plays, *Plays Never Before Printed.* One of these, *The Convent of Pleasure*, has proved particularly compelling for recent commentators. In this play the heroine, Lady Happy, creates a man-free haven in her newly inherited estate, only to find the haven infiltrated by a man disguising himself as a woman.

Toward the end of her life, Cavendish spent her time revising and reissuing her body of work. She died, suddenly, on 15 December 1673 at the age of 50, and was buried in Westminster Abbey on 7 January 1674. Her husband died three years later; in the year of his death he published *Letters and Poems in Honour of the Incomparable Princess Margaret, Duchess of Newcastle.*

⌘⌘⌘

The Poetess's Hasty Resolution

Reading my verses, I like't them so well,
Self-love did make my judgment to rebel.
Thinking them so good, I thought more to write;
Considering not how others would them like.
I writ so fast, I thought, if I lived long,
A pyramid of fame to build thereon.
Reason, observing which way I was bent,
Did stay my hand, and ask't me what I meant;
"Will you," said she, "thus waste your time in vain,
On that which in the world small praise shall gain?
For shame, leave off," said she, "the printer spare,
He'll lose by your ill poetry, I fear
Besides, the world hath already such a weight
Of useless books, as it is over-fraught.
Then pity take, do the world a good turn,
And all you write cast in the fire, and burn."
Angry I was, and Reason struck away,
When I did hear what she to me did say.
Then all in haste I to the press it sent,
Fearing persuasion might my book prevent:
But now 'tis done, with grief repent do I,
Hang down my head with shame, blush, sigh, and cry.
Take pity, and my drooping spirits raise,
Wipe off my tears with handkerchiefs of praise.
—1653

An Excuse for so Much Writ Upon My Verses

Condemn me not for making such a coil° *fuss*
About my book, alas it is my child.
Just like a bird, when her young are in nest,
Goes in, and out, and hops and takes no rest;
But when their young are fledged, their heads out peep,
Lord what a chirping does the old one keep.
So I, for fear my strengthless child should fall
Against a door, or stool, aloud I call,
Bid have a care of such a dangerous place:
Thus write I much, to hinder all disgrace.
—1653

Of the Theme of Love

O love, how thou art tired out with rhyme!
Thou art a tree whereon all poets climb;
And from thy branches every one takes some
Of thy sweet fruit, which fancy feeds upon.
But now thy tree is left so bare, and poor,
That they can hardly gather one plum more.
—1653

A Woman Drest by Age

A milk-white hair-lace° wound up all her hairs, *head-band*
And a deaf coif[1] did cover both her ears,
A sober countenance about her face she ties,
And a dim sight doth cover half her eyes,
About her neck a kercher° of coarse skin, *kerchief*
Which Time had crumpled, and worn creases in,
Her gown was turned to melancholy black,
Which loose did hang upon her sides and back,
Her stockings cramps had knit, red worsted[2] gout,
And pains as garters tied her legs about.
A pair of palsy gloves her hands drew on,
With weakness stitched, and numbness trimmed upon.
Her shoes were corns, and hard skin sewed together,
Hard skin were soles, and corns the upper leather.
A mantle of diseases laps her round,
And thus she's dressed, till Death lays her in ground.
—1653

A Dialogue Betwixt the Body and the Mind

BODY. What bodies else but Man's did Nature make,
To join with such a mind, no rest can take;
That ebbs, and flows, with full and falling tide,
As minds dejected fall, or swell with pride:
In waves of passion roll to billows high,
Always in motion, never quiet lie.
Where thoughts like fishes swim the mind about,

[1] *coif* Close-fitting cap which covers the top, back, and sides of the head.

[2] *worsted* Type of woolen fabric.

Where the great thoughts the smaller thoughts eat out.
My body the barque° rows in mind's ocean wide, *row-boat*
Whose waves of passions beat on every side.
When that dark cloud of ignorance hangs low,
And winds of vain opinions strong do blow;
Then showers of doubts into the mind rain down,
In deep vast studies my barque of flesh is drowned.
MIND. Why doth the body thus complain, when I
Do help it forth of every misery?
For in the world your barque is bound to swim,
Nature hath rigged it out to traffic in.
Against hard rocks you break in pieces small,
If my invention help you not in all.
The lodestone° of attraction I find out, *magnet*
The card of observation guides about.
The needle of discretion points the way,
Which makes your barque get safe into each bay.
BODY. If I 'scape drowning in the wat'ry main,° *sea*
Yet in great mighty battles I am slain.
By your ambition I am forced to fight,
When many winds upon my body light.
For you care not, so you a fame may have,
To live, if I be buried in a grave.
MIND. If bodies fight, and kingdoms win, then you
Take all the pleasure that belongs thereto.
You have a crown, your head for to adorn,
Upon your body jewels are hung on.
All things are sought to please your senses five,
No drug unpractised to keep you alive.
And I, to set you up in high degree,
Invent all engines used in war to be.
'Tis I that make you in great triumph sit,
Above all other creatures high to get:
By the industrious arts, which I do find,
You other creatures in subjection bind:
You eat their flesh, and after that their skin,
When winter comes, you lap° your bodies in. *fold*
And so of every thing that Nature makes,
By my direction you great pleasure takes.
BODY. What though my senses all do take delight,
Yet you my entrails always bite.
My flesh eat up, that all my bones are bare,
With the sharp teeth of sorrow, grief and care.
Draws out my blood from veins, with envious spite,
Decays my strength with shame, or extreme fright.
With love extremely sick I lie,
With cruel hate you make me die.
MIND. Care keeps you from all hurt, or falling low,
Sorrow and grief are debts to friends we owe.
Fear makes men just, to give each one his own,
Shame makes civility, without there's none.
Hate makes good laws, that all may live in peace,
Love brings society, and gets increase.
Besides, with joy I make the eyes look gay,
With pleasing smiles they dart forth every way.
With mirth the cheeks are fat, smooth, rosy-red,
Your speech flares wit, when fancies fill the head.
If I were gone, you'd miss the company,
Wish we were joined again, or you might die.
—1653

The Hunting of the Hare

Betwixt two ridges of plowed land lay Wat,[1]
Pressing his body close to earth lay squat.
His nose upon his two forefeet close lies,
Glaring obliquely with his great gray eyes.
His head he always sets against the wind;
If turn his tail, his hairs blow up behind:
Which he too cold will grow, but he is wise,
And keeps his coat still down, so warm he lies.
Thus resting all the day, till sun doth set,
Then riseth up, his relief for to get.
Walking about until the sun doth rise,
Then back returns, down in his form he lies.
At last, poor Wat was found, as he there lay,
By huntsmen with their dogs, which came that way.
Seeing, gets up, and fast begins to run,
Hoping some ways the cruel dogs to shun.
But they by nature have so quick a scent,
That by their nose they trace what way he went.
And with their deep, wide mouths set forth a cry,
Which answered was by echoes in the sky.
Then Wat was struck with terror, and with fear,
Thinks every shadow still the dogs they were.
And running out some distance from the noise,
To hide himself, his thoughts he new employs.

[1] *Wat* Name for a hare.

Under a clod of earth in sand pit wide,
Poor Wat sat close, hoping himself to hide.
There long he had not sat, but straight his ears
The winding° horns and crying dogs he hears: *sounding*
Starting with fear, up leaps, then doth he run,
And with such speed, the ground scarce treads upon.
Into a great thick wood he straightway gets,
Where underneath a broken bough he sits.
At every leaf that with the wind did shake,
Did bring such terror, made his heart to ache.
That place he left, to champaign° plains he went, *open*
Winding about, for to deceive their scent.
And while they snuffling were, to find his track,
Poor Wat, being weary, his swift pace did slack.
On his two hinder legs for ease did sit,
His forefeet rubbed his face from dust and sweat.
Licking his feet, he wiped his ears so clean,
That none could tell that Wat had hunted been.
But casting round about his fair great eyes,
The hounds in full career° he near him spies: *speed*
To Wat it was so terrible a sight,
Fear gave him wings, and made his body light.
Though weary was before, by running long,
Yet now his breath he never felt more strong.
Like those that dying are, think health returns,
When 'tis but a faint blast, which life out burns.
For spirits seek to guard the heart about,
Striving with death, but death doth quench them out.
Thus they so fast came on, with such loud cries,
That he no hopes hath left, nor help espies.
With that the winds did pity poor Wat's case,
And with their breath the scent blew from the place.
Then every nose is busily employed,
And every nostril is set open, wide,
And every head doth seek a several way,
To find what grass, or track, the scent on lay.
Thus quick industry, that is not slack,
Is like to witchery, brings lost things back.
For though the wind had tied the scent up close,
A busy dog thrust in his snuffling nose:
And drew it out, with it did foremost run,
Then horns blew loud, for th'rest to follow on.
The great slow hounds their throats did set a bass,
The fleet swift hounds, as tenors next in place;
The little beagles, they a treble sing,
And through the air their voice a round did ring.
Which made a concert, as they ran along;
If they but words could speak, might sing a song,
The horns kept time, the hunters shout for joy,
And valiant seem, poor Wat for to destroy:
Spurring their horses to a full career,
Swim rivers deep, leap ditches without fear;
Endanger life and limbs, so fast will ride,
Only to see how patiently Wat died.
For why, the dogs so near his heels did get,
That they their sharp teeth in his breech did set;
Then tumbling down, did fall with weeping eyes,
Gives up his ghost, and thus poor Wat he dies.
Men whooping loud, such acclamations make,
As if the Devil they did prisoner take,
When they do but a shiftless creature kill;
To hunt, there needs no valiant soldier's skill.
But man doth think that exercise and toil,
To keep their health, is best, which makes most spoil,
Thinking that food and nourishment so good,
And appetite, that feeds on flesh and blood.
When they do lions, wolves, bears, tigers see,
To kill poor sheep, straight say, they cruel be;
But for themselves all creatures think too few,
For luxury, wish God would make them new.
As if that God made creatures for man's meat,
To give them life, and sense, for man to eat;
Or else for sport, or recreation's sake,
Destroy those lives that God saw good to make:
Making their stomachs graves, which full they fill
With murdered bodies that in sport they kill.
Yet man doth think himself so gentle, mild,
When he of creatures is most cruel wild.
And is so proud, thinks only he shall live,
That God a God-like nature did him give.
And that all creatures for his sake alone,
Was made for him, to tyrannize upon.

—1653

from *The Description of a New World, Called the Blazing World*

from To the Reader

… This is the reason why I added this piece of fancy to my philosophical observations,[1] and joined them as two worlds at the ends of their poles; both for my own sake, to divert my studious thoughts, which I employed in the contemplation thereof, and to delight the reader with variety, which is always pleasing. But lest my fancy should stray too much, I chose such a fiction as would be agreeable to the subject I treated of in the former parts; it is a description of a new world, not such as Lucian's, or the Frenchman's world in the moon,[2] but a world of my own creating, which I call the Blazing World: the first part whereof is romancical, the second philosophical, and the third is merely fancy, or (as I may call it) fantastical; which, if it add any satisfaction to you, I shall account myself a happy creatoress. If not, I must be content to live a melancholy life in my own world; I cannot call it a poor world, if poverty be only want of gold, silver, and jewels; for there is more gold in it than all the chemists[3] ever did, and (as I verily believe) will ever be able to, make. As for the rocks of diamonds, I wish with all my soul they might be shared amongst my noble female friends, and upon that condition, I would willingly quit my part; and of the gold I should only desire so much as might suffice to repair my noble lord and husband's losses:[4] for I am not covetous, but as ambitious as ever any of my sex was, is, or can be; which makes, that though I cannot be Henry the Fifth, or Charles the Second, yet I endeavour to be Margaret the First; and although I have neither power, time, nor occasion to conquer the world as Alexander and Caesar did; yet rather than not to be mistress of one, since Fortune and the Fates would give me none, I have made a world of my own; for which nobody, I hope, will blame me, since it is in everyone's power to do the like.

The Description of a New World, Called the Blazing World

A merchant travelling into a foreign country fell extremely in love with a young lady; but, being a stranger in that nation, and beneath her both in birth and wealth, he could have but little hopes of obtaining his desire. However, his love growing more and more vehement upon him, even to the slighting of all difficulties, he resolved at last to steal her away, which he had the better opportunity to do because her father's house was not far from the sea, and, she often using to gather shells upon the shore, accompanied not with above two or three of her servants, it encouraged him the more to execute his design. Thus, coming one time with a little light vessel, not unlike a packet-boat,[5] manned with some few seamen and well victualled,[6] for fear of some accidents which might perhaps retard their journey, to the place where she used to repair, he forced her away. But when he fancied himself the happiest man of the world, he proved to be the most unfortunate; for Heaven, frowning at his theft, raised such a tempest as they knew not what to do, or whither to steer their course; so that the vessel, both by its own lightness and the violent motion of the wind, was carried, as swift as an arrow out of a bow, towards the north pole, and in a short time reached the icy sea, where the wind forced it amongst huge pieces of ice. But, being little and light, it did, by assistance and favour of the gods to this virtuous lady, so turn and wind through those precipices as if it had been guided by some experienced pilot and skilful mariner. But alas! those few men which were in it, not

[1] *This … observations* *The Blazing World* was published in conjunction with *Observations upon Experimental Philosophy*, a critique of the method then championed by the Royal Society. Cavendish challenges the Society's belief that human perception—with the aid of machines such as microscopes and telescopes—could uncover the workings of the natural world.

[2] *not such … moon* References to Greek satirist Lucian (124–c. 200 CE), whose *True History* consists of a dialogue concerning an imaginary voyage, and to French author Cyrano de Bergerac, who wrote a story in this tradition about a voyage to the moon (*Histoire comique contenant les états et empires de la lune, 1657*).

[3] *chemists* I.e., alchemists.

[4] *my noble … losses* During the Civil Wars, William Cavendish was banished from England and his property confiscated.

[5] *packet-boat* Mail-boat; a small boat that regularly ferries mail and goods between two ports.

[6] *victualled* Supplied with provisions.

knowing whither they went, nor what was to be done in so strange an adventure, and not being provided for so cold a voyage, were all frozen to death; the young lady only, by the light of her beauty, the heat of her youth, and protection of the gods, remaining alive. Neither was it a wonder that the men did freeze to death; for they were not only driven to the very end or point of the pole of that world, but even to another pole of another world, which joined close to it; so that the cold, having a double strength at the conjunction of those two poles, was insupportable. At last the boat, still passing on, was forced into another world; for it is impossible to round this world's globe from pole to pole, so as we do from east to west; because the poles of the other world, joining to the poles of this, do not allow any further passage to surround the world that way; but if anyone arrives to either of these poles, he is either forced to return or to enter into another world....

But to return to the wandering boat and the distressed lady, she, seeing all the men dead, found small comfort in life. Their bodies, which were preserved all that while from putrefaction and stench by the extremity of cold, began now to thaw and corrupt; whereupon she, having not strength enough to fling them overboard, was forced to remove, out of her small cabin, upon the deck to avoid that nauseous smell; and, finding the boat swim between two plains of ice, as a stream that runs betwixt two shores, at last perceived land, but covered all with snow: from which came walking upon the ice strange creatures, in shape like bears, only they went upright as men. Those creatures, coming near the boat, catched hold of it with their paws, that served them instead of hands; some two or three of them entered first; and when they came out, the rest went in one after another. At last, having viewed and observed all that was in the boat, they spake to each other in a language which the lady did not understand, and, having carried her out of the boat, sunk it, together with the dead men.

The lady, now finding herself in so strange a place, and amongst such a wonderful kind of creatures, was extremely stricken with fear, and could entertain no other thoughts but that every moment her life was to be a sacrifice to their cruelty. But those bear-like creatures, how terrible soever they appeared to her sight, yet were they so far from exercising any cruelty upon her, that rather they showed her all civility and kindness imaginable; for she being not able to go upon the ice, by reason of its slipperiness, they took her up in their rough arms and carried her into their city, where, instead of houses, they had caves underground. And as soon as they entered the city, both males and females, young and old, flocked together to see this lady, holding up their paws in admiration. At last, having brought her into a certain large and spacious cave, which they intended for her reception, they left her to the custody of the females, who entertained her with all kindness and respect, and gave her such victuals as they were used to eat; but, seeing her constitution neither agreed with the temper of that climate, nor their diet, they were resolved to carry her into another island of a warmer temper; in which were men like foxes, only walking in an upright shape, who received their neighbours the bear-men with great civility and courtship, very much admiring this beauteous lady, and, having discoursed some while together, agreed at last to make her a present to the emperor of their world....

[The Lady Becomes Empress]

No sooner was the lady brought before the Emperor but he conceived her to be some goddess, and offered to worship her; which she refused, telling him (for by that time she had pretty well learned their language) that although she came out of another world, yet was she but a mortal; at which the Emperor, rejoicing, made her his wife and gave her an absolute power to rule and govern all that world as she pleased. But her subjects, who could hardly be persuaded to believe her mortal, tendered her all the veneration and worship due to a deity....

Their priests and governors were princes of the imperial blood, and made eunuchs[1] for that purpose; and as for the ordinary sort of men in that part of the world where the Emperor resided, they were of several complexions; not white, black, tawny, olive- or ash-coloured; but some appeared of an azure, some of a deep purple, some of a grass-green, some of a scarlet,

[1] *eunuchs* Castrated males. In Oriental and Roman courts, these men often dealt with important matters of state.

some of an orange-colour, &c. Which colours and complexions, whether they were made by the bare reflection of light, without the assistance of small particles, or by the help of well-ranged and ordered atoms, or by a continual agitation of little globules, or by some pressing and reacting motion, I am not able to determine. The rest of the inhabitants of that world were men of several different sorts, shapes, figures, dispositions, and humours, as I have already made mention heretofore; some were bear-men, some worm-men, some fish- or mer-men, otherwise called sirens; some bird-men, some fly-men, some ant-men, some geese-men, some spider-men, some lice-men, some fox-men, some ape-men, some jackdaw-men, some magpie-men, some parrot-men, some satyrs,[1] some giants, and many more which I cannot all remember. And of these several sorts of men, each followed such a profession as was most proper for the nature of their species, which the Empress encouraged them in, especially those that had applied themselves to the study of several arts and sciences; for they were as ingenious and witty in the invention of profitable and useful arts as we are in our world, nay, more; and to that end she erected schools and founded several societies. The bear-men were to be her experimental philosophers, the bird-men her astronomers, the fly-, worm-, and fish-men her natural philosophers, the ape-men her chemists, the satyrs her Galenic[2] physicians, the fox-men her politicians, the spider- and lice-men her mathematicians, the jackdaw-, magpie-, and parrot-men her orators and logicians, the giants her architects, &c. But before all things, she, having got a sovereign power from the Emperor over all the world, desired to be informed both of the manner of their religion and government, and to that end she called the priests and statesmen to give her an account of either. Of the statesmen she enquired, first, why they had so few laws. To which they answered that many laws made many divisions, which most commonly did breed factions, and at last break out into open wars. Next she asked why they preferred the monarchical form of government before any other. They answered that as it was natural for one body to have but one head, so it was also natural for a politic body to have but one governor; and that a commonwealth which had many governors was like a monster of many heads: besides, said they, a monarchy is a divine form of government, and agrees most with our religion; for as there is but one God, whom we all unanimously worship and adore with one faith, so we are resolved to have but one Emperor, to whom we all submit with one obedience.

Then the Empress, seeing that the several sorts of her subjects had each their churches apart, asked the priests whether they were of several religions. They answered her Majesty that there was no more but one religion in all that world, nor no diversity of opinions in that same religion; for though there were several sorts of men, yet had they all but one opinion concerning the worship and adoration of God. The Empress asked them whether they were Jews, Turks, or Christians. We do not know, said they, what religions those are; but we do all unanimously acknowledge, worship, and adore the Only, Omnipotent, and Eternal God, with all reverence, submission, and duty. Again the Empress enquired whether they had several forms of worship. They answered, no: for our devotion and worship consists only in prayers, which we frame according to our several necessities, in petitions, humiliations, thanksgiving, &c. Truly, replied the Empress, I thought you had been either Jews or Turks, because I never perceived any women in your congregations; but what is the reason you bar them from your religious assemblies? It is not fit, said they, that men and women should be promiscuously together in time of religious worship; for their company hinders devotion, and makes many, instead of praying to God, direct their devotion to their mistresses. But, asked the Empress, have they no congregation of their own, to perform the duties of divine worship as well as men? No, answered they: but they stay at home and say their prayers by themselves in their closets.[3] Then the Empress desired to know the reason why the priests and governors of their world were made eunuchs. They answered, to keep them from marriage: for women and children most commonly make disturbance both in church and state. But, said she, women and children have no employment in

[1] *satyrs* Creatures with partially human and partially bestial forms.

[2] *Galenic* Following the theories of Galen, Greek physician (131–201 CE), whose medical views revised those of Aristotle and were foundational to medical practice until the sixteenth century.

[3] *closets* Private inner chambers.

church or state. 'Tis true, answered they; but although they are not admitted to public employments, yet are they so prevalent with their husbands and parents that many times, by their importunate persuasions, they cause as much, nay, more, mischief secretly than if they had the management of public affairs....

[The Empress Brings the Duchess of Newcastle to Be Her Scribe]

After some time, when the spirits[1] had refreshed themselves in their own vehicles, they sent one of their nimblest spirits to ask the Empress whether she would have a scribe.... The Empress received the proffer which they made her, with all civility; and told him that she desired a spiritual scribe. The spirit answered that they could dictate, but not write, except they put on a hand or arm, or else the whole body, of man. The Empress replied, how can spirits arm themselves with gauntlets of flesh? As well, answered he, as man can arm himself with a gauntlet of steel. If it be so, said the Empress, then I will have a scribe. Then the spirit asked her whether she would have the soul of a living or a dead man. Why, said the Empress, can the soul quit a living body and wander or travel abroad? Yes, answered he, for according to Plato's doctrine there is a conversation of souls, and the souls of lovers live in the bodies of their beloved. Then I will have, answered she, the soul of some ancient famous writer, either of Aristotle, Pythagoras, Plato, Epicurus,[2] or the like. The spirit said that those famous men were very learned, subtle, and ingenious writers, but they were so wedded to their own opinions that they would never have the patience to be scribes. Then, said she, I'll have the soul of one of the most famous modern writers, as either of Galileo, Gassendus, Descartes, Helmont, Hobbes, H. More,[3] &c. The Spirit answered that they were fine ingenious writers, but yet so self-conceited that they would scorn to be scribes to a woman. But, said he, there's a lady, the Duchess of Newcastle, which, although she is not one of the most learned, eloquent, witty, and ingenious, yet is she a plain and rational writer, for the principle of her writings is sense and reason, and she will, without question, be ready to do you all the service she can. That lady, then, said the Empress, will I choose for my scribe, neither will the Emperor have reason to be jealous, she being one of my own sex. In truth, said the Spirit, husbands have reason to be jealous of platonic lovers, for they are very dangerous, as being not only very intimate and close, but subtle and insinuating. You say well, replied the Empress; wherefore I pray send me the Duchess of Newcastle's soul; which the spirit did; and after she came to wait on the Empress, at her first arrival the Empress embraced and saluted her with a spiritual kiss....

[The Duchess and the Empress Create Their Own Worlds]

One time, when the Duchess her soul was with the Empress, she seemed to be very sad and melancholy; at which the Empress was very much troubled, and asked her the reason of her melancholic humour. Truly, said the Duchess to the Empress (for between dear friends there's no concealment, they being like several parts of one united body), my melancholy proceeds from an extreme ambition.... My ambition is that I would fain be as you are, that is, an empress of a world, and I shall never be at quiet until I be one. I love you so well, replied the Empress, that I wish with all my soul, you had the fruition of your ambitious desire, and I shall not fail to give you my best advice how to accomplish it. The best informers are the immaterial spirits, and they'll soon tell you whether it be possible to obtain your wish. ... No sooner had the Empress said this, but some immaterial spirits came to visit her, of whom she

[1] *spirits* In addition to all the other inhabitants of the Blazing World, the Empress makes the acquaintance of the spirit-people, who inhabit the air and can travel between her old world and the Blazing World.

[2] *Aristotle ... Epicurus* Four classical philosophers, each of whom founded his own school of philosophy.

[3] *Galileo* Italian astronomer Galileo Galilei (1564–1642); *Gassendus* Pierre Gassendi (1592–1655), French mechanistic philosopher; *Descartes* René Descartes (1596–1650), French philosopher and mathematician; *Helmont* Jan Baptista van Helmont (1577–1644), French chemist and philosopher; *Hobbes* Thomas Hobbes (1588–1679), English philosopher, political scientist, and author; *H. More* Henry More (1614–87) English neo-Platonic philosopher.

inquired whether there were but three worlds in all, to wit, the Blazing World where she was in, the world which she came from, and the world where the Duchess lived? The spirits answered that there were more numerous worlds than the stars which appeared in these three mentioned worlds. Then the Empress asked whether it was not possible that her dearest friend the Duchess of Newcastle might be empress of one of them? Although there be numerous, nay, infinite worlds, answered the spirits, yet none is without government. … But we wonder, proceeded the spirits, that you desire to be empress of a terrestrial world, whenas you can create yourself a celestial world if you please. What, said the Empress, can any mortal be a creator? Yes, answered the spirits; for every human creature can create an immaterial world fully inhabited by immaterial creatures, and populous of immaterial subjects, such as we are, and all this within the compass of the head or skull; nay, not only so, but he may create a world of what fashion and government he will, and give the creatures thereof such motions, figures, forms, colours, perceptions, &c. as he pleases. … And since it is in your power to create such a world, what need you to venture life, reputation and tranquillity to conquer a gross material world? For you can enjoy no more of a material world then a particular creature is able to enjoy, which is but a small part, considering the compass of such a world; and you may plainly observe it by your friend the Empress here, which, although she possesses a whole world, yet enjoys she but a part thereof. … Why should you desire to be empress of a material world and be troubled with the cares that attend government whenas, by creating a world within your self, you may enjoy all, both in whole and in parts, without control or opposition, and may make what world you please, and alter it when you please, and enjoy as much pleasure and delight as a world can afford you? You have converted me, said the Duchess to the spirits, from my ambitious desire; wherefore I'll take your advice, reject and despise all the worlds without me, and create a world of my own. The Empress said, if I do make such a world, then I shall be mistress of two worlds, one within, and the other without me. That your Majesty may, said the spirits; and so left these two ladies to create two worlds within themselves: who did also part from each other until such time as they had brought their worlds to perfection. …

At last, when the Duchess saw that no patterns would do her any good in the framing of her world;[1] she was resolved to make a world of her own invention, … which world, after it was made, appeared so curious and full of variety, so well ordered and wisely governed that it cannot possibly be expressed by words, nor the delight and pleasure which the Duchess took in making this world of her own.

In the meantime the Empress was also making and dissolving several worlds in her own mind, and was so puzzled that she could not settle in any of them; wherefore she sent for the Duchess, who, being ready to wait on the Empress, carried her beloved world along with her, and invited the Empress's soul to observe the frame, order, and government of it. Her Majesty was so ravished with the perception of it that her soul desired to live in the Duchess's world; but the Duchess advised her to make such another world in her own mind; for, said she, your Majesty's mind is full of rational corporeal motions, and the rational motions of my mind shall assist you by the help of sensitive expressions, with the best instructions they are able to give you.

The Empress, being thus persuaded by the Duchess to make an imaginary world of her own, followed her advice; and after she had quite finished it, and framed all kinds of creatures proper and useful for it, strengthened it with good laws, and beautified it with arts and sciences; having nothing else to do, unless she did dissolve her imaginary world, or made some alterations in the Blazing World she lived in, which yet she could hardly do, by reason it was so well ordered that it could not be mended; for it was governed without secret and deceiving policy; neither was there any ambition, factions, malicious detractions, civil dissensions, or home-bred quarrels, divisions in religion, foreign wars, &c., but all the people live in a peaceful society, united tranquillity, and religious conformity; she was desirous

[1] *At last … world* Before resolving to create her own world, the Duchess attempts to follow the models of philosophers Thales, Pythagoras, Plato, Epicurus, Aristotle, Descartes, Hobbes, but with each world she encounters irreconcilable difficulties.

to see the world the Duchess came from, and observe therein the several sovereign Governments, Laws and Customs of several Nations....

The Epilogue to the Reader

By this poetical description you may perceive that my ambition is not only to be empress but authoress of a whole world; and that the worlds I have made, both the Blazing and the other Philosophical World, mentioned in the first part of this description, are framed and composed of the most pure, that is, the rational parts of matter, which are the parts of my mind; which creation was more easily and suddenly effected than the conquests of the two famous monarchs of the world, Alexander and Caesar. Neither have I made such disturbances and caused so many dissolutions of particulars, otherwise named deaths, as they did; for I have destroyed but some few men in a little boat, which died through the extremity of cold, and that by the hand of Justice, which was necessitated to punish their crime of stealing away a young and beauteous lady. And in the formation of those worlds I take more delight and glory than ever Alexander or Caesar did in conquering this terrestrial world; and though I have made my Blazing World a peaceable world, allowing it but one religion, one language, and one government; yet could I make another world, as full of factions, divisions, and wars as this is of peace and tranquillity; and the rational figures of my mind might express as much courage to fight as Hector and Achilles had; and be as wise as Nestor, as eloquent as Ulysses, and as beautiful as Helen.[1] But I esteeming peace before war, wit before policy, honesty before beauty; instead of the figures of Alexander, Caesar, Hector, Achilles, Nestor, Ulysses, Helen, &c., chose rather the figure of honest Margaret Newcastle, which now I would not change for all this terrestrial world; and if any should like the world I have made, and be willing to be my subjects, they may imagine themselves such, and they are such; I mean, in their minds, fancies, or imaginations; but if they cannot endure to be subjects, they may create worlds of their own, and govern themselves as they please: but yet let them have a care not to prove unjust usurpers and to rob me of mine; for, concerning the Philosophical World, I am Empress of it myself; and as for the Blazing World, it having an empress already, who rules it with great wisdom and conduct, which Empress is my dear Platonic friend; I shall never prove so unjust, treacherous, and unworthy to her as to disturb her government, much less to depose her from her imperial throne for the sake of any other; but rather choose to create another world for another friend.

—1666

from *Sociable Letters*[2]

Letter 55

Madam,

You were pleased in your last letter to tell me that you had been in the country and that you did almost envy the peasants for living so merrily. It is a sign, Madam, they live happily, for mirth seldom dwells with troubles and discontents; neither doth riches nor grandeur live so easily as that unconcerned freedom that is in low and mean fortunes and persons. For the ceremony of grandeur is constrained and bound with forms and rules, and a great estate and high fortune is not so easily managed as a less. A little is easily ordered, where much doth require time, care, wisdom, and study as considerations. But poor, mean peasants that live by their labour are for the most part happier and pleasanter than great rich persons that live in luxury and idleness; for idle time is tedious, and luxury is unwholesome, whereas labour is healthful and recreative, and surely

[1] *Hector and Achilles* The two heroes of Homer's epic poem *The Iliad*, about the Trojan War. The following characters also figure prominently in this work; *Nestor* Wise, elderly advisor to the Greeks during the Trojan War; *Ulysses* Hero of the Trojan War and Homer's *Odyssey*; *Helen* Wife of the Greek King Menelaus. Her extraordinary beauty prompted the Trojan Paris to steal her away, thus causing the Trojan War.

[2] *Sociable Letters* Book of fictitious letters in which Cavendish, as she says in her Preface, "endeavoured under the cover of letters to express the humours of mankind, and the actions of a man's life, by the correspondence of two ladies living at some short distance from each other."

country housewives take more pleasure in milking their cows, making their butter and cheese, and feeding their poultry than great ladies do in painting, curling, and adorning themselves. Also, they have more quiet & peaceable minds and thoughts, for they never, or seldom, look in a glass to view their faces. They regard not their complexions, nor observe their decays; they defy time's ruins of their beauties. They are not peevish and froward[1] if they look not as well one day as another; a pimple or spot in their skin tortures not their minds. They fear not the sun's heat, but out-face the sun's power. They break not their sleeps to think of fashions, but work hard to sleep soundly. They lie not in sweats to clear their complexions, but rise to sweat to get them food. Their appetites are not queasy with surfeits, but sharpened with fasting. They relish with more savour their ordinary coarse fare than those who are pampered do their delicious rarities, and for their mirth and pastimes they take more delight and true pleasure, and are more inwardly pleased and outwardly merry at their wakes, than the great ladies at their balls. And though they dance not with such art and measure, yet they dance with more pleasure and delight; they cast not envious, spiteful eyes at each other, but meet friendly and lovingly. But great ladies at public meetings take not such true pleasures, for their envy at each other's beauty and bravery disturbs their pastimes and obstructs their mirth. They rather grow peevish and froward through envy than loving and kind through society; so that whereas the country peasants meet with such kind hearts and unconcerned freedom as they unite in friendly jollity and depart with neighbourly love, the greater sort of persons meet with constrained ceremony, converse with formality, and for the most part depart with enmity. And this is not only amongst women, but amongst men, for there is amongst the better sort a greater strife for bravery than for courtesy, for place than friendship; and in their societies there is more vainglory than pleasure, more pride than mirth, and more vanity than true content. Yet in one thing the better sort of men, as the nobles and gentry, are to be commended, which is that, though they are oftener drunken and more debauched than peasants, having more means to maintain their debaucheries, yet at such times as at great assemblies they keep themselves more sober and temperate than peasants do, which are for the most part drunk at their departing. But to judge between the peasantry and nobles for happiness, I believe where there's one noble that is truly happy, there are a hundred peasants; not that there be more peasants than nobles, but that they are more happy, number for number, as having not the envy, ambition, pride, vainglory, to cross, trouble, and vex them, as nobles have. When I say nobles, I mean those that have been ennobled by time, as well as title, as the gentry. But, Madam, I am not a fit judge for the several sorts or degrees, or courses of lives, or actions of mankind, as to judge which is happiest; for happiness lives not in outward show or concourse, but inwardly in the mind, and the minds of men are too obscure to be known, and too various and inconstant to fix a belief in them. And since we cannot know ourselves, how should we know others? Besides, pleasure and true delight lives in everyone's own delectation. But let me tell you, my delectation is to prove myself,

Madam,

Your faithful friend and servant.

Letter 143

Madam,

I heard the ship was drowned wherein the man was that had the charge and care of my plays, to carry them into E. to be printed, I being then in A. Which when I heard, I was extremely troubled, and if I had not had the original of them by me, truly I should have been much afflicted, and accounted the loss of my twenty plays as the loss of twenty lives; for in my mind I should have died twenty deaths, which would have been a great torment, or I should have been near the fate of those plays and almost drowned in salt tears, as they in the salt sea. But they are destinated[2] to live, and, I hope, I in them when my body is dead and turned to dust. But I am so prudent and careful of my poor labours, which are my writing works, as I always keep the copies of them safely with me until they are printed, and then I commit the originals to the fire like parents which are

[1] *froward* Difficult to deal with or please.

[2] *destinated* Destined.

willing to die whenas they are sure of their children's lives, knowing when they are old and past breeding they are but useless in this world. But howsoever their paper bodies are consumed, like as the Roman Emperors, in funeral flames, I cannot say an eagle flies out of them, or that they turn into a blazing star, although they make a great blazing light when they burn. And so, leaving them to your approbation or condemnation, I rest,

Madam,

Your faithful friend and servant.

LETTER 163

Madam,

You were pleased to desire me to let my steward receive five hundred pounds for you here in this town, but you must have a little patience, for they will pay no money, although it be due, until these Christmas holy-days be past. I know not whether they are so strict as to receive none; methinks they should be apt to take, for they are all busy in entertainments, eating, drinking, and feasting. But I observe some things which I wonder at, viz. that money should pass, or move so slowly in matters or affairs of right and due, as debts, rewards, and gratitudes, or concerning honour, as generosity, or, for Heaven's sake, as charity, whenas in causes of injustice and wrong, as in bribes, or wars, or for vice and vanity, as for unlawful love, gaming, drinking, gluttonous feasting, vain shows, and superfluous bravery, it runs about with that swift speed that there is no catching hold of as to stay it. But it seems to be the minds of men that hold it from going forth to good and noble uses, and the appetites of men that make it run to base, wicked, vain, and foolish employments, so that we may perceive that the appetites have more power to do evil than the mind hath will to do good. But, Madam, my will hath a mind to serve you, although I have not means nor power to do it; yet in what I can, your Ladyship shall always find me,

Your most faithful friend and servant.

—1664

The Convent of Pleasure

A Comedy

CHARACTERS:

Three Gentlemen
Lady Happy
Madam Mediator
Monsieur Take-pleasure and Dick, his Man
Monsieur Facil
Monsieur Adviser
Monsieur Courtly
Lady Amorous
Lady Virtue
The Princess
Two Mean[1] Women
A Lady and her Maid
Two Ladies
A Distracted[2] Lady and her Maid
A Citizen's Wife
Two Ancient Ladies
A Gentleman and a Young Lady
A Shepherd
Sea-Nymphs
An Ambassador

ACT 1, SCENE 1

(*Enter Three Gentlemen.*)

FIRST GENTLEMAN. Tom, where have you been, you look so sadly of it?

SECOND GENTLEMAN. I have been at the funeral of the Lord Fortunate, who has left his daughter, the Lady Happy, very rich, having no other daughter but her.

FIRST GENTLEMAN. If she be so rich, it will make us all young men spend all our wealth in fine clothes, coaches, and lackeys, to set out our wooing hopes.

THIRD GENTLEMAN. If all her wooers be younger brothers, as most of us gallants are, we shall undo

[1] *Mean* Of low social status.

[2] *Distracted* Agitated.

ourselves upon bare hopes, without probability. But is she handsome, Tom?

SECOND GENTLEMAN. Yes, she is extreme handsome, young, rich, and virtuous.

FIRST GENTLEMAN. Faith, that is too much for one woman to possess.

SECOND GENTLEMAN. Not if you were to have her.

FIRST GENTLEMAN. No, not for me; but in my opinion too much for any other man.

(*Exeunt.*)

ACT 1, SCENE 2

(*Enter the Lady Happy and one of her attendants.*)

SERVANT. Madam, you being young, handsome, rich, and virtuous, I hope you will not cast away those gifts of nature, fortune, and heaven upon a person which cannot merit you.

LADY HAPPY. Let me tell you that riches ought to be bestowed on such as are poor and want means to maintain themselves; and youth, on those that are old; beauty, on those that are ill-favoured; and virtue, on those that are vicious: so that if I should place my gifts rightly, I must marry one that's poor, old, ill-favoured, and debauched.

SERVANT. Heaven forbid.

LADY HAPPY. Nay, Heaven doth not only allow of it, but commands it; for we are commanded to give to those that want.

(*Enter Madam Mediator to the Lady Happy.*)

MADAME MEDIATOR. Surely, Madam, you do but talk, and intend not to go where you say.

LADY HAPPY. Yes, truly, my words and intentions go even together.

MADAME MEDIATOR. But surely you will not encloister[1] yourself, as you say.

LADY HAPPY. Why, what is there in the public world that should invite me to live in it?

MADAME MEDIATOR. More than if you should banish yourself from it.

LADY HAPPY. Put the case I should marry the best of men, if any best there be; yet would a married life have more crosses and sorrows than pleasure, freedom, or happiness. Nay, marriage to those that are virtuous is a greater restraint than a monastery. Or should I take delight in admirers? They might gaze on my beauty and praise my wit, and I receive nothing from their eyes nor lips; for words vanish as soon as spoken, and sights are not substantial. Besides, I should lose more of my reputation by their visits than gain by their praises. Or, should I quit reputation and turn courtesan, there would be more lost in my health than gained by my lovers. I should find more pain than pleasure; besides, the troubles and frights I should be put to, with the quarrels and brouilleries[2] that jealous rivals make, would be a torment to me; and 'tis only for the sake of men when women retire not. And since there is so much folly, vanity and falsehood in men, why should women trouble and vex themselves for their sake; for retiredness bars the life from nothing else but men.

MADAME MEDIATOR. O yes, for those that encloister themselves bar themselves from all other worldly pleasures.

LADY HAPPY. The more fools they.

MADAME MEDIATOR. Will you call those fools that do it for the gods' sake?

LADY HAPPY. No, Madam, it is not for the gods' sake, but for opinion's sake; for can any rational creature think or believe the gods take delight in the creature's uneasy life? Or did they command or give leave to Nature to make senses for no use; or to cross, vex, and pain them? For what profit or pleasure can it be to the gods to have men or women wear coarse linen or rough woollen, or to flay their skin with hair-cloth,[3] or to eat or saw through their flesh with cords? Or what profit or pleasure can it be to the gods to have men eat more fish than flesh, or to fast? unless the gods did feed on such meat themselves; for then, for fear the gods should want it, it were fit for men to abstain from it. The like for

[1] *encloister* Enter into a cloister.

[2] *brouilleries* Contentions, quarrels.

[3] *flay* Inflict pain upon; *hair-cloth* I.e., hair shirt, a coarse, irritating garment (made of hair) worn next to the skin as a penance.

garments: for fear the gods should want fine clothes to adorn themselves, it were fit men should not wear them. Or what profit or pleasure can it be to the gods to have men to lie uneasily on the hard ground, unless the gods and Nature were at variance, strife, and wars; as if what is displeasing unto Nature were pleasing to the gods, and to be enemies to her were to be friends to them.

MADAME MEDIATOR. But being done for the gods' sake, it makes that which in Nature seems to be bad in divinity to be good.

LADY HAPPY. It cannot be good if it be neither pleasure nor profit to the gods; neither do men any thing for the gods', but their own, sake.

MADAME MEDIATOR. But when the mind is not employed with vanities, nor the senses with luxury, the mind is more free to offer its adorations, prayers, and praises to the gods.

LADY HAPPY. I believe the gods are better pleased with praises than fasting, but when the senses are dulled with abstinency, the body weakened with fasting, the spirits tired with watching, the life made uneasy with pain, the soul can have but little will to worship: only the imagination doth frighten it into active zeal, which devotion is rather forced than voluntary, so that their prayers rather flow out of their mouth than spring from their heart, like rainwater that runs through gutters, or like water that's forced up a hill by artificial pipes and cisterns. But those that pray not unto the gods, or praise them more in prosperity than adversity, more in pleasures than pains, more in liberty than restraint, deserve neither the happiness of ease, peace, freedom, plenty, and tranquillity in this world, nor the glory and blessedness of the next. And if the gods should take pleasure in nothing but in the torments of their creatures, and would not prefer those prayers that are offered with ease and delight, I should believe the gods were cruel. And what creature that had reason or rational understanding would serve cruel masters when they might serve a kind mistress, or would forsake the service of their kind mistress to serve cruel masters? Wherefore, if the gods be cruel, I will serve Nature; but the gods are bountiful and give all that's good, and bid us freely please ourselves in that which is best for us: and that is best what is most temperately used, and longest may be enjoyed, for excess doth waste itself and all it feeds upon.

MADAME MEDIATOR. In my opinion your doctrine and your intention do not agree together.

LADY HAPPY. Why?

MADAME MEDIATOR. You intend to live encloistered and retired from the world.

LADY HAPPY. 'Tis true, but not from pleasures; for I intend to encloister myself from the world to enjoy pleasure, and not to bury myself from it; but to encloister myself from the encumbered cares and vexations, troubles and perturbance of the world.

MADAME MEDIATOR. But if you encloister yourself, how will you enjoy the company of men, whose conversation is thought the greatest pleasure?

LADY HAPPY. Men are the only troublers of women; for they only cross and oppose their sweet delights and peaceable life. They cause their pains, but not their pleasures. Wherefore those women that are poor, and have not means to buy delights and maintain pleasures, are only fit for men; for, having not means to please themselves, they must serve only to please others. But those women where Fortune, Nature, and the gods are joined to make them happy were mad to live with men, who make the female sex their slaves. But I will not be so enslaved, but will live retired from their company. Wherefore, in order thereto, I will take so many noble persons of my own sex as my estate will plentifully maintain, such whose births are greater than their fortunes and are resolved to live a single life, and vow virginity. With these I mean to live encloistered with all the delights and pleasures that are allowable and lawful. My cloister shall not be a cloister of restraint, but a place for freedom, not to vex the senses but to please them.

For every sense shall pleasure take,
And all our lives shall merry make.
Our minds in full delight shall joy,
Not vexed with every idle toy.
Each season shall our caterers be,
To search the land, and fish the sea;
To gather fruit and reap the corn,
That's brought to us in plenty's horn;
With which we'll feast and please our taste,
But not luxurious make a waste.

We'll clothe ourselves with softest silk,
And linen fine as white as milk.
We'll please our sight with pictures rare;
Our nostrils with perfumèd air.
Our ears with sweet melodious sound,
Whose substance can be nowhere found;
Our taste with sweet delicious meat,
And savoury sauces we will eat:
Variety each sense shall feed,
And change in them new appetites breed.
Thus will in Pleasure's convent I
Live with delight, and with it die.

(*Exeunt.*)

ACT 2, SCENE 1

(*Enter Monsieur Take-pleasure and his man, Dick.*)

MONSIEUR TAKE-PLEASURE. Dick, am I fine today?

DICK. Yes, Sir, as fine as feathers, ribbons, gold, and silver can make you.

MONSIEUR TAKE-PLEASURE. Dost thou think I shall get the Lady Happy?

DICK. Not if it be her fortune to continue in that name.

MONSIEUR TAKE-PLEASURE. Why?

DICK. Because if she marry your Worship she must change her name; for the wife takes the name of her husband, and quits her own.

MONSIEUR TAKE-PLEASURE. Faith, Dick, if I had her wealth I should be happy.

DICK. It would be according as your Worship would use it; but, on my conscience, you would be more happy with the lady's wealth than the lady would be with your Worship.

MONSIEUR TAKE-PLEASURE. Why should you think so?

DICK. Because women never think themselves happy in marriage.

MONSIEUR TAKE-PLEASURE. You are mistaken; for women never think themselves happy until they be married.

DICK. The truth is, Sir, that women are always unhappy in their thoughts, both before and after marriage; for, before marriage they think themselves unhappy for want of a husband, and after they are married they think themselves unhappy for having a husband.

MONSIEUR TAKE-PLEASURE. Indeed, women's thoughts are restless.

(*Enter Monsieur Facil and Monsieur Adviser, to Monsieur Take-pleasure; all in their wooing accoutrements.*)

MONSIEUR TAKE-PLEASURE. Gentlemen, I perceive you are all prepared to woo.

MONSIEUR FACIL. Yes, faith, we are all prepared to be wooers. But whom shall we get to present us to the Lady Happy?

MONSIEUR ADVISER. We must set on bold faces and present ourselves.

MONSIEUR TAKE-PLEASURE. Faith, I would not give my hopes for an indifferent portion.

MONSIEUR FACIL. Nor I.

MONSIEUR ADVISER. The truth is, we are all stuffed with hopes, as cushions are with feathers.

(*Enter Monsieur Courtly.*)

MONSIEUR COURTLY. O gentlemen, gentlemen, we are all utterly undone.

MONSIEUR ADVISER. Why, what's the matter?

MONSIEUR COURTLY. Why, the Lady Happy hath encloistered herself, with twenty ladies more.

MONSIEUR ADVISER. The devil she hath!

MONSIEUR FACIL. The gods forbid.

MONSIEUR COURTLY. Whether it was the devil or the gods that have persuaded her to it, I cannot tell; but gone in she is.

MONSIEUR TAKE-PLEASURE. I hope it is but a blast of devotion, which will soon flame out.

(*Enter Madam Mediator.*)

MONSIEUR TAKE-PLEASURE. O Madam Mediator, we are all undone; the Lady Happy is encloistered.

MADAME MEDIATOR. Yes, Gentlemen, the more is the pity.

MONSIEUR ADVISER. Is there no hopes?

MADAME MEDIATOR. Faith, little.

MONSIEUR FACIL. Let us see the clergy to persuade her out, for the good of the Commonwealth.

MADAME MEDIATOR. Alas, gentlemen! they can do no good, for she is not a votress[1] to the gods, but to Nature.

MONSIEUR COURTLY. If she be a votress to Nature, you are the only person fit to be Lady Prioress; and so by your power and authority you may give us leave to visit your nuns sometimes.

MADAME MEDIATOR. Not but at a grate,[2] unless in time of building, or when they are sick; but howsoever, the Lady Happy is Lady Prioress herself, and will admit none of the masculine sex, not so much as to a grate, for she will suffer no grates about the cloister. She has also women physicians, surgeons, and apothecaries, and she is the chief confessor herself, and gives what indulgences or absolutions she pleaseth. Also, her house, where she hath made her convent, is so big and convenient and so strong as it needs no addition or repair. Besides, she has so much compass of ground within her walls as there is not only room and place enough for gardens, orchards, walks, groves, bowers, arbours, ponds, fountains, springs, and the like; but also conveniency for much provision, and hath women for every office and employment. For though she hath not above twenty ladies with her, yet she hath a numerous company of female servants, so as there is no occasion for men.

MONSIEUR TAKE-PLEASURE. If there be so many women, there will be the more use for men. But pray, Madam Mediator, give me leave rightly to understand you by being more clearly informed: you say the Lady Happy is become a votress to Nature. And if she be a votress to Nature, she must be a mistress to men.

MADAME MEDIATOR. By your favour, Sir, she declares that she hath avoided the company of men by retirement merely because she would enjoy the variety of pleasures which are in Nature; of which, she says, men are obstructers; for instead of increasing pleasure, they produce pain; and instead of giving content, they increase trouble. Instead of making the female sex happy, they make them miserable; for which she hath banished the masculine company for ever.

MONSIEUR ADVISER. Her heretical opinions ought not to be suffered, nor her doctrine allowed; and she ought to be examined by a masculine synod[3] and punished with a severe husband, or tortured with a deboist[4] husband.

MADAME MEDIATOR. The best way, gentlemen, is to make your complaints and put up a petition to the state, with your desires for a redress.

MONSIEUR COURTLY. Your counsel is good.

MONSIEUR FACIL. We will follow it, and go presently about it.

(*Exeunt.*)

ACT 2, SCENE 2

(*Enter the Lady Happy with her ladies; as also Madam Mediator.*)

LADY HAPPY. Ladies, give me leave to desire your confession whether or no you repent your retirement.

LADIES. Most excellent Lady, it were as probable a repentance could be in Heaven amongst angels as amongst us.

LADY HAPPY. Now, Madam Mediator, let me ask you, do you condemn my act of retirement?

MADAME MEDIATOR. I approve of it with admiration and wonder, that one that is so young should be so wise.

LADY HAPPY. Now give me leave to inform you how I have ordered this, our Convent of Pleasure. First, I have such things as are for our ease and conveniency; next, for pleasure and delight, as I have change of furniture for my house according to the four seasons of the year, especially our chambers: as in the spring, our chambers are hung with silk damask[5] and all other things suitable to it; and a great looking glass in each chamber, that we may view ourselves and take pleasure in our own beauties whilst they are fresh and young. Also, I have in each chamber a cupboard of such plate[6] as is useful, and whatsoever is to be used is there ready to be employed; also, I have all the floor strewed with sweet flowers. In

[1] *votress* Female votary; one who has made a special vow of devotion.

[2] *grate* Iron bars with which cloistered nuns are separated from the world and through which they speak to their visitors.

[3] *synod* Assembly of clergy.

[4] *deboist* Debauched.

[5] *damask* Rich fabric originally produced in the city of Damascus.

[6] *plate* Serving vessels of silver.

the summer I have all our chambers hung with taffety,[1] and all other things suitable to it, and a cupboard of porcelain and of plate, and all the floor strewed every day with green rushes or leaves, and cisterns placed near our beds' heads, wherein water may run out of small pipes made for that purpose. To invite repose in the autumn, all our chambers are hung with gilt leather, or frangipane;[2] also, beds and all other things suitable, and the rooms matted with very fine mats. In the winter our chambers must be hung with tapestry, and our beds of velvet, lined with satin, and all things suitable to it, and all the floor spread over with Turkey[3] carpets, and a cupboard of gilt plate; and all the wood for firing to be cypress and juniper; and all the lights to be perfumed wax. Also, the bedding and pillows are ordered according to each season; *viz.* to be stuffed with feathers in the spring and autumn, and with down in the winter, but in the summer to be only quilts, either of silk or fine Holland;[4] and our sheets, pillows, tablecloths and towels to be of pure fine Holland, and every day clean. Also, the rooms we eat in, and the vessels we feed withal, I have according to each season; and the linen we use to our meat to be pure fine diaper[5] and damask, and to change it fresh every course of meat. As for our galleries, staircases, and passages, they shall be hung with various pictures; and all along the wall of our gallery, as long as the summer lasts, do stand, upon pedestals, flower pots with various flowers; and in the winter, orange trees. And my gardens to be kept curiously,[6] and flourish in every season of all sorts of flowers, sweet herbs, and fruits, and kept so as not to have a weed in it; and all the groves, wildernesses, bowers, and arbours pruned, and kept free from dead boughs, branches, or leaves; and all the ponds, rivulets, fountains, and springs kept clear, pure, and fresh. Also, we will have the choicest meats every season doth afford, and that every day our meat be drest several ways, and our drink cooler or hotter according to the several seasons; and all our drinks fresh and pleasing. Change of garments are also provided, of the newest fashions for every season, and rich trimming, so as we may be accoutred properly, and according to our several pastimes; and our shifts[7] shall be of the finest and purest linen that can be bought or spun.

LADIES. None in this world can be happier.

LADY HAPPY. Now, ladies, let us go to our several pastimes, if you please.

(*Exeunt.*)

ACT 2, SCENE 3

(*Enter two ladies.*)

LADY AMOROUS. Madam, how do you, since you were married?

LADY VIRTUE. Very well, I thank you.

LADY AMOROUS. I am not so well as I wish I were.

(*Enter Madam Mediator to them.*)

MADAME MEDIATOR. Ladies, do you hear the news?

LADY VIRTUE. What news?

MADAME MEDIATOR. Why, there is a great foreign princess arrived, hearing of the famous Convent of Pleasure, to be one of Nature's devotees.

LADY AMOROUS. What manner of lady is she?

MADAME MEDIATOR. She is a princely brave woman, truly, of a masculine presence.

LADY VIRTUE. But, Madam Mediator, do they live in such pleasure as you say? For they'll admit you, a widow, although not us, by reason we are wives.

MADAME MEDIATOR. In so much pleasure as Nature never knew before this convent was. And for my part, I had rather be one in the Convent of Pleasure than Empress of the whole world; for every lady there enjoyeth as much pleasure as any absolute monarch can do, without the troubles and cares that wait on royalty. Besides, none can enjoy those pleasures they have unless they live such a retired or retreated life, free from the world's vexations.

[1] *taffety* Taffeta.

[2] *frangipane* Perfume made from the red jasmine flower.

[3] *Turkey* Turkish.

[4] *Holland* Type of linen fabric originally from Holland.

[5] *diaper* Type of simply patterned linen fabric.

[6] *curiously* Skillfully; fastidiously.

[7] *shifts* Undergarments.

LADY VIRTUE. Well, I wish I might see, and know what pleasures they enjoy.

MADAME MEDIATOR. If you were there, you could not know all their pleasure in a short time, for their varieties will require a long time to know their several changes. Besides, their pleasures and delights vary with the seasons; so that, what with the several seasons and the varieties of every season, it will take up a whole life's time.

LADY VIRTUE. But I could judge of their changes by their single principles.

MADAME MEDIATOR. But they have variety of one and the same kind.

LADY VIRTUE. But I should see the way or manner of them.

MADAME MEDIATOR. That you might.

(*Exeunt.*)

ACT 2, SCENE 4

(*Enter Monsieur Adviser, Courtly, Take-pleasure, and Facil.*)

MONSIEUR COURTLY. Is there no hopes to get those ladies out of their convent?

MONSIEUR ADVISER. No, faith, unless we could set the convent on fire.

MONSIEUR TAKE-PLEASURE. For Jupiter's sake, let us do it; let's everyone carry a fire-brand to fire it.

MONSIEUR COURTLY. Yes, and smoke them out, as they do a swarm of bees.

MONSIEUR FACIL. Let's go presently about it.

MONSIEUR ADVISER. Stay, there is a great princess there.

MONSIEUR TAKE-PLEASURE. 'Tis true, but when that princess is gone, we will surely do it.

MONSIEUR ADVISER. Yes, and be punished for our villainy.

MONSIEUR TAKE-PLEASURE. It will not prove villainy, for we shall do Nature good service.

MONSIEUR ADVISER. Why, so we do Nature good service when we get a wench with child, but yet the civil laws do punish us for it.

MONSIEUR COURTLY. They are not civil laws that punish lovers.

MONSIEUR ADVISER. But those are civil laws that punish adulterers.

MONSIEUR COURTLY. Those are barbarous laws that make love adultery.

MONSIEUR ADVISER. No, those are barbarous that make adultery love.

MONSIEUR FACIL. Well, leaving love and adultery, they are foolish women that vex us with their retirement.

MONSIEUR ADVISER. Well, gentlemen, although we rail at the Lady Happy for retiring, yet if I had such an estate as she, and would follow her example, I make no doubt but you would all be content to encloister yourselves with me upon the same conditions as those ladies encloister themselves with her.

MONSIEUR TAKE-PLEASURE. Not unless you had women in your convent.

MONSIEUR ADVISER. Nay, faith, since women can quit the pleasure of men, we men may well quit the trouble of women.

MONSIEUR COURTLY. But is there no place where we may peek into the convent?

MONSIEUR ADVISER. No, there are no grates, but brick and stone walls.

MONSIEUR FACIL. Let us get out some of the bricks or stones.

MONSIEUR ADVISER. Alas! the walls are a yard thick.

MONSIEUR FACIL. But nothing is difficult to willing minds.

MONSIEUR ADVISER. My mind is willing; but my reason tells me it is impossible; wherefore, I'll never go about it.

MONSIEUR TAKE-PLEASURE. Faith, let us resolve to put ourselves in women's apparel, and so by that means get into the convent.

MONSIEUR ADVISER. We shall be discovered.

MONSIEUR TAKE-PLEASURE. Who will discover us?

MONSIEUR ADVISER. We shall discover ourselves.

MONSIEUR TAKE-PLEASURE. We are not such fools as to betray ourselves.

MONSIEUR ADVISER. We cannot avoid it, for our very garb and behaviour, besides our voices, will discover us: for we are as untoward to make curtseys in petticoats as women are to make legs[1] in breeches, and it will be as great a difficulty to raise our voices to a treble sound as for women to press down their voices to a bass. Besides, we shall never frame our eyes and mouths to such coy dissembling looks and pretty simpering mopes and smiles as they do.

MONSIEUR COURTLY. But we will go as strong, lusty country wenches that desire to serve them in inferior places and offices, as cook-maids, laundry-maids, dairy-maids, and the like.

MONSIEUR FACIL. I do verily believe I could make an indifferent cook-maid, but not a laundry-, nor a dairy-maid; for I cannot milk cows, nor starch gorgets,[2] but I think I could make a pretty shift[3] to wash some of the ladies' night linen.

MONSIEUR TAKE-PLEASURE. But they employ women in all places in their gardens, and for brewing, baking, and making all sorts of things; besides, some keep their swine, and twenty such like offices and employments there are which we should be very proper for.

MONSIEUR FACIL. O yes, for keeping of swine belongs to men; remember the prodigal son.[4]

MONSIEUR ADVISER. Faith, for our prodigality we might be all swine-herds.

MONSIEUR COURTLY. Also, we shall be proper for gardens, for we can dig and set and sow.

MONSIEUR TAKE-PLEASURE. And we are proper for brewing.

MONSIEUR ADVISER. We are more proper for drinking, for I can drink good beer or ale when 'tis brewed; but I could not brew such beer or ale as any man could drink.

MONSIEUR FACIL. Come, come, we shall make a shift one way or other. Besides, we shall be very willing to learn and be very diligent in our services, which will give good and great content; wherefore, let us go and put these designs into execution.

MONSIEUR COURTLY. Content, content.

MONSIEUR ADVISER. Nay, faith, let us not trouble ourselves for it, 'tis in vain.

[1] *make legs* Bow.

[2] *gorgets* Ornamental collars.

[3] *shift* Attempt.

[4] *the prodigal son* In Luke 15.11–32, after the prodigal son wastes all the goods given to him by his father, he goes into the fields and feeds swine.

(*Exeunt.*)

ACT 3, SCENE 1

(*Enter the Princess and the Lady Happy with the rest of the ladies belonging to the convent.*)

LADY HAPPY. Madam, your Highness has done me much honour to come from a splendid court to a retired convent.

PRINCESS. Sweet Lady Happy, there are many that have quit their crowns and power for a cloister of restraint; then well may I quit a court of troubles for a convent of pleasure. But the greatest pleasure I could receive were to have your friendship.

LADY HAPPY. I should be ungrateful should I not be not only your friend, but humble servant.

PRINCESS. I desire you would be my mistress, and I your servant; and upon this agreement of friendship I desire you will grant me one request.

LADY HAPPY. Anything that is in my power to grant.

PRINCESS. Why then, I observing, in your several recreations, some of your ladies do accoutre themselves in masculine habits and act lovers' parts, I desire you will give me leave to be sometimes so accoutred and act the part of your loving servant.

LADY HAPPY. I shall never desire to have any other loving servant than yourself.

PRINCESS. Nor I any other loving mistress than yourself.

LADY HAPPY. More innocent lovers never can there be,
Than my most princely lover, that's a she.

PRINCESS. Nor never convent did such pleasures give,
Where lovers with their mistresses may live.

(*Enter a lady, asking whether they will see the play.*)

LADY. May it please your Highness, the play is ready to be acted.

(*The scene is opened, the Princess and L. Happy sit down, and the play is acted within the scene, the Princess and the L. Happy being spectators.*)

(*Enter one drest like a man, that speaks the Prologue.*)

Noble spectators, you shall see tonight
A play, which, though't be dull, yet's short to sight;
For, since we cannot please your ears with wit,
We will not tire your limbs, long here to sit

Act 3, Scene 2

(*Enter two mean women.*)

First Woman. O neighbour, well met. Where have you been?

Second Woman. I have been with my neighbour the cobbler's wife, to comfort her for the loss of her husband, who is run away with Goody[1] Mettle, the tinker's wife.

First Woman. I would to Heaven my husband would run away with Goody Shred, the butcher's wife; for he lies all day drinking in an ale-house, like a drunken rogue as he is, and when he comes home he beats me all black and blue, when I and my children are almost starved for want.

Second Woman. Truly neighbour, so doth my husband; and spends not only what he gets, but what I earn with the sweat of my brows, the whilst my children cry for bread, and he drinks that away that should feed my small children, which are too young to work for themselves.

First Woman. But I will go and pull my husband out of the ale-house, or I'll break their lattice-windows down.

Second Woman. Come, I'll go and help; for my husband is there too. But we shall be both beaten by them.

First Woman. I care not, for I will not suffer him to be drunk, and I and my children starve. I had better be dead.

(*Exeunt.*)

[1] *Goody* I.e., goodwife. Title given to married women of humble status.

Act 3, Scene 3

(*Enter a lady and her maid.*)

Lady. Oh, I am sick!

Maid. You are breeding a child, Madam.

Lady. I have not one minute's time of health.

(*Exeunt.*)

Act 3, Scene 4

(*Enter two ladies.*)

First Lady. Why weep you, Madam?

Second Lady. Have I not cause to weep when my husband hath played all his estate away at dice and cards, even to the clothes on his back?

First Lady. I have as much cause to weep then as you; for, though my husband hath not lost his estate at play, yet he hath spent it amongst his whores, and is not content to keep whores abroad, but in my house, under my roof; and they must rule as chief mistresses.

Second Lady. But my husband hath not only lost his own estate, but also my portion, and hath forced me with threats to yield up my jointure,[2] so that I must beg for my living, for anything I know as yet.

First Lady. If all married women were as unhappy as I, marriage were a curse.

Second Lady. No doubt of it.

(*Exeunt.*)

Act 3, Scene 5

(*Enter a lady as almost distracted, running about the stage, and her maid follows her.*)

Lady. Oh! my child is dead, my child is dead! What shall I do, what shall I do?

Maid. You must have patience, Madam.

[2] *jointure* Portion of an estate reserved for the wife's sole ownership after her husband's death. A husband could not legally spend his wife's jointure without first obtaining her permission.

LADY. Who can have patience to lose their only child? who can! Oh, I shall run mad, for I have no patience.

(*Runs off the stage. Exit Maid after her.*)

ACT 3, SCENE 6

(*Enter a citizen's wife as into a tavern, where a bush*[1] *is hung out, and meets some gentlemen there.*)

CITIZEN'S WIFE. Pray, gentlemen, is my husband, Mr. Negligent, here?

FIRST GENTLEMAN. He was, but he is gone some quarter of an hour since.

CITIZEN'S WIFE. Could he go, gentlemen?

SECOND GENTLEMAN. Yes, with a supporter.

CITIZEN'S WIFE. Out upon him! Must he be supported? Upon my credit, gentlemen, he will undo himself, and me too, with his drinking and carelessness, leaving his shop and all his commodities at sixes and sevens;[2] and his 'prentices and journeymen are as careless and idle as he. Besides, they cozen[3] him of his wares. But, was it a he—or she—supporter my husband was supported by?

FIRST GENTLEMAN. A she-supporter; for it was one of the maid-servants which belong to this tavern.

CITIZEN'S WIFE. Out upon him, knave! Must he have a she-supporter, in the Devil's name? But I'll go and seek them both out with a vengeance.

SECOND GENTLEMAN. Pray, let us entreat your stay to drink a cup of wine with us.

CITIZEN'S WIFE. I will take your kind offer, for wine may chance to abate choleric vapours, and pacify the spleen.[4]

FIRST GENTLEMAN. That it will, for wine and good company are the only abaters of vapours.

SECOND GENTLEMAN. It doth not abate vapours so much as cure melancholy.

CITIZEN'S WIFE. In truth, I find a cup of wine doth comfort me sometimes.

FIRST GENTLEMAN. It will cheer the heart.

SECOND GENTLEMAN. Yes, and enlighten the understanding.

CITIZEN'S WIFE. Indeed, and my understanding requires enlightening.

(*Exeunt.*)

ACT 3, SCENE 7

(*Enter a lady big with child, groaning as in labour, and a company of women with her.*)

LADY. Oh my back, my back will break! Oh! Oh! Oh!

FIRST WOMAN. Is the midwife sent for?

SECOND WOMAN. Yes, but she is with another lady.

LADY. Oh my back! Oh! Oh! Oh! Juno,[5] give me some ease.

(*Exeunt.*)

ACT 3, SCENE 8

(*Enter two ancient ladies.*)

FIRST LADY. I have brought my son into the world with great pains, bred him with tender care, much pains, and great cost; and must he now be hanged for killing a man in a quarrel? When he should be a comfort and staff of my age, is he to be my age's affliction?

SECOND LADY. I confess it is a great affliction; but I have had as great, having had but two daughters, and them fair ones, though I say it, and might have matched them well. But one of them was got with child to my great disgrace; th'other run away with my butler, not worth the droppings of his taps.[6]

[1] *bush* Sign-board of a tavern.

[2] *at sixes and sevens* I.e., in confusion and disarray.

[3] *cozen* Cheat.

[4] *choleric ... spleen* Vapors, or humors, were thought to be injurious exhalations from the organs. Of the four dominant humors, choler was thought to originate in the renal glands, while melancholy was produced by the spleen. The term "the vapors" was also used to refer to the morbid or hysterical condition these vapors could produce.

[5] *Juno* In Roman mythology, the goddess of childbirth and the wife of Jupiter, king of the gods.

[6] *the droppings ... taps* I.e., the spillage from his casks. Among the butler's duties was the distribution of the household's liquor.

FIRST LADY. Who would desire children, since they come to such misfortunes?

(*Exeunt.*)

ACT 3, SCENE 9

(*Enter one woman meeting another.*)

FIRST WOMAN. Is the midwife come? for my lady is in a strong labour.

SECOND WOMAN. No, she cannot come, for she hath been with a lady that hath been in strong labour these three days of a dead child, and 'tis thought she cannot be delivered.

(*Enter another woman.*)

THIRD WOMAN. Come away, the midwife is come.

FIRST WOMAN. Is the lady delivered, she was withall?

THIRD WOMAN. Yes, of life; for she could not be delivered, and so she died.

SECOND WOMAN. Pray tell not our lady so, for the very fright of not being able to bring forth a child will kill her.

(*Exeunt.*)

ACT 3, SCENE 10

(*Enter a gentleman, who meets a fair young lady.*)

GENTLEMAN. Madam, my Lord desires you to command whatsoever you please, and it shall be obeyed.

LADY. I dare not command, but I humbly entreat I may live quiet and free from his amours.

GENTLEMAN. He says he cannot live and not love you.

LADY. But he may live and not lie with me.

GENTLEMAN. He cannot be happy unless he enjoy you.

LADY. And I must be unhappy if he should.

GENTLEMAN. He commanded me to tell you that he will part from his lady for your sake.

LADY. Heaven forbid I should part man and wife.

GENTLEMAN. Lady, he will be divorced for your sake.

LADY. Heaven forbid I should be the cause of a divorce between a noble pair.

GENTLEMAN. You had best consent, for otherwise he will have you against your will.

LADY. I will send his Lordship an answer tomorrow; pray him to give me so much time.

GENTLEMAN. I shall, Lady.

(*Exit Gentleman.*)

(*Lady sola.*[1])

LADY. I must prevent my own ruin, and the sweet virtuous lady's, by going into a nunnery; wherefore, I'll put myself into one tonight:

There will I live, and serve the gods on high,
And leave this wicked world and vanity.

(*Exeunt.*)

(*One enters and speaks the Epilogue.*)

Marriage is a curse we find,
Especially to womankind:
From the cobbler's wife we see,
To ladies, they unhappy be.

LADY HAPPY. (*To the Princess.*) Pray, Servant, how do you like this play?

PRINCESS. My sweet Mistress, I cannot in conscience approve of it; for though some few be unhappy in marriage, yet there are many more that are so happy as they would not change their condition.

LADY HAPPY. O Servant, I fear you will become an apostate.[2]

PRINCESS. Not to you, sweet Mistress.

(*Exeunt.*)

(*Enter the Gentlemen.*)

FIRST GENTLEMAN. There is no hopes of dissolving this Convent of Pleasure.

[1] *sola* Latin: alone (feminine).

[2] *apostate* One who abandons his or her faith or abandons his or her party.

SECOND GENTLEMAN. Faith, not as I can perceive.

THIRD GENTLEMAN. We may be sure, this Convent will never be dissolved, by reason it is ennobled with the company of great Princesses, and glorified with a great fame; but the fear is that all the rich heirs will make convents, and all the young beauties associate themselves in such convents.

FIRST GENTLEMAN. You speak reason; wherefore, let us endeavour to get wives before they are encloistered.

(*Exeunt.*)

ACT 4, SCENE 1

(*Enter Lady Happy drest as a shepherdess. She walks very melancholy, then speaks, as to herself:*)

LADY HAPPY. My name is Happy, and so was my condition, before I saw this Princess; but now I am like to be the most unhappy maid alive. But why may not I love a woman with the same affection I could a man?

No, no, Nature is Nature, and still will be
The same she was from all eternity.

(*Enter the Princess in masculine shepherd's clothes.*)

PRINCESS. My dearest Mistress, do you shun my company? Is your servant become an offence to your sight?

LADY HAPPY. No, servant! your presence is more acceptable to me than the presence of our goddess Nature, for which she, I fear, will punish me for loving you more than I ought to love you.

PRINCESS. Can lovers love too much?

LADY HAPPY. Yes, if they love not well.

PRINCESS. Can any love be more virtuous, innocent, and harmless than ours?

LADY HAPPY. I hope not.

PRINCESS. Then let us please ourselves, as harmless lovers use to do.

LADY HAPPY. How can harmless lovers please themselves?

PRINCESS. Why very well, as to discourse, embrace, and kiss; so mingle souls together.

LADY HAPPY. But innocent lovers do not use to kiss.

PRINCESS. Not any act more frequent amongst us women-kind; nay, it were a sin in friendship should not we kiss: then let us not prove ourselves reprobates.

(*They embrace and kiss, and hold each other in their arms.*)

PRINCESS. These my embraces, though of female kind,
May be as fervent as a masculine mind.

(*The scene is opened; the Princess and L. Happy go in. A pastoral within the scene. The scene is changed into a green, or plain, where sheep are feeding, and a maypole*[1] *in the middle. L. Happy as a shepherdess and the Princess as a shepherd are sitting there.*)

(*Enter another shepherd, and woos the Lady Happy.*)

SHEPHERD. Fair Shepherdess, do not my suit deny,
O grant my suit, let me not for love die:
Pity my flocks, Oh, save their shepherd's life;
Grant you my suit, be you their shepherd's wife.

LADY HAPPY. How can I grant to everyone's request?
Each shepherd's suit lets me not be at rest;
For which I wish the winds might blow them far,
That no love-suit might enter to my ear.

(*Enter Madam Mediator in a shepherdess dress, and another shepherd.*)

SHEPHERD. Good Dame, unto your daughter speak for me.
Persuade her I your son-in-law may be:
I'll serve your swine, your cows bring home to milk;
Attend your sheep, whose wool's as soft as silk;
I'll plough your grounds, corn I'll in winter sow,
Then reap your harvest, and your grass I'll mow;
Gather your fruits in autumn from the tree.
All this and more I'll do, if y'speak for me.

SHEPHERDESS. My daughter vows a single life,
And swears, she ne'er will be a wife,
But live a maid, and flocks will keep,
And her chief company shall be sheep.

[1] *maypole* Pole decorated with flowers and greenery, painted with stripes, and set up in the middle of an open space for people to dance around during May-time celebrations.

(*The Princess, as a shepherd, speaks to the Lady Happy.*)

PRINCESS. My Shepherdess, your wit flies high,
Up to the sky,
And views the gates of Heaven,
Which are the planets seven;
Sees how fixed stars are placed,
And how the meteors waste;
What makes the snow so white,
And how the sun makes light;
What makes the biting cold
On every thing take hold;
And hail a mixed degree,
'Twixt snow and ice you see
From whence the winds do blow;
What thunder is, you know,
And what makes lightning flow
Like liquid streams, you show.
From sky you come to th'earth,
And view each creature's birth;
Sink to the centre deep,
Where all dead bodies sleep;
And there observe to know,
What makes the minerals grow;
How vegetables sprout,
And how the plants come out;
Take notice of all seed,
And what the earth doth breed;
Then view the springs below,
And mark how waters flow;
What makes the tides to rise
Up proudly to the skies,
And shrinking back descend,
As fearing to offend.
Also your wit doth view
The vapour and the dew,
In summer's heat, that wet
Doth seem like the earth's sweat;
In wintertime, that dew
Like paint's white to the view,
Cold makes that thick white dry;
As ceruse[1] it doth lie
On th'earth's black face, so fair
As painted ladies are;
But, when a heat is felt,
That frosty paint doth melt.
Thus Heav'n and earth you view,
And see what's old, what's new;
How bodies transmigrate,
Lives are predestinate.
Thus doth your wit reveal
What Nature would conceal.

LADY HAPPY. My Shepherd,
All those that live do know it,
That you are born a poet;
Your wit doth search mankind,
In body and in mind;
The appetites you measure,
And weigh each several pleasure;
Do figure every passion,
And every humour's fashion;
See how the fancy's wrought,
And what makes every thought;
Fathom conceptions low,
From whence opinions flow;
Observe the memory's length,
And understanding's strength,
Your wit doth reason find,
The centre of the mind,
Wherein the rational soul
Doth govern and control,
There doth she sit in state,
Predestinate by fate,
And by the gods' decree,
That sovereign she should be.
And thus your wit can tell
How souls in bodies dwell;
As that the mind dwells in the brain,
And in the mind the soul doth reign,
And in the soul the life doth last,
For with the body it doth not waste;
Nor shall wit like the body die,
But live in the world's memory.

PRINCESS. May I live in your favour, and be possessed with your love and person, is the height of my ambitions.

LADY HAPPY. I can neither deny you my love nor person.

[1] *ceruse* White lead, used as paint or as a cosmetic for the skin.

PRINCESS. In amorous pastoral verse we did not woo.
As other pastoral lovers use to do.
LADY HAPPY. Which doth express, we shall more constant be,
And in a married life better agree.
PRINCESS. We shall agree, for we true love inherit,
Join as one body and soul, or heav'nly spirit.

(*Here come rural sports, as country dances about the maypole. That pair which dances best is crowned King and Queen of the shepherds that year; which happens to the Princess and the Lady Happy.*)

LADY HAPPY (*To the Princess.*) Let me tell you, servant, that our custom is to dance about this maypole, and that pair which dances best is crowned King and Queen of all the shepherds and shepherdesses this year: which sport, if it please you, we will begin.

PRINCESS. Nothing, sweetest Mistress, that pleases you can displease me.

(*They dance. After the dancing the Princess and Lady Happy are crowned with a garland of flowers. A shepherd speaks.*)

[Written by my Lord Duke.[1]]

SHEPHERD. You've won the prize, and justly; so we all
Acknowledge it with joy, and offer here
Our hatchments[2] up, our sheep-hooks[3] as your due,
And scrips of corduant, and oaten pipe;[4]
So all our pastoral ornaments we lay
Here at your feet, with homage to obey
All your commands, and all these things we bring
In honour of our dancing Queen and King;
For dancing heretofore has got more riches
Then we can find in all our shepherds' breeches;
Witness rich Holmby.[5] Long then may you live,
And for your dancing, what we have we give.

(*A wassail is carried about and syllabubs.*[6]
Another shepherd speaks, or sings this that follows.)

[Written by my Lord Duke.]

SHEPHERD. The jolly wassail now do bring,
With apples drowned in stronger ale,
And fresher syllabubs, and sing;
Then each to tell their love-sick tale:
So home by couples, and thus draw
Ourselves by holy Hymen's[7] law.

(*The scene vanishes.*)

(*Enter the Princess, sola, and walks a turn or two in a musing posture, then views herself, and speaks.*)

PRINCESS. What have I on a petticoat, O Mars![8] thou god of war, pardon my sloth; but yet remember thou art a lover, and so am I. But you will say my kingdom wants me, not only to rule and govern it, but to defend it: but what is a kingdom in comparison of a beautiful mistress? Base thoughts fly off, for I will not go, did not only a kingdom, but the world, want me.

(*Exeunt.*)

(*Enter the Lady Happy, sola and melancholy; and after a short musing speaks.*)

LADY HAPPY. O Nature, O you gods above,
Suffer me not to fall in love;
O strike me dead here in this place
Rather than fall into disgrace.

---

[1] *Written ... Duke* This is one of three sections of the play written by Margaret Cavendish's husband, William Cavendish, Duke of Newcastle.

[2] *hatchments* Tablets displaying coats of arms.

[3] *sheep-hooks* I.e., shepherd's crooks.

[4] *scrips of corduant* I.e., small pieces of cordon, an ornamental cord or ribbon forming part of an insignia; *oaten pipe* The shepherd's pipe, the symbol of pastoral poetry.

[5] *Holmby* The name of the house that Queen Elizabeth I supposedly bestowed upon her Lord Chancellor, Sir Christopher Hatton, for his skill in dancing.

[6] *wassail* Spiced ale with which toasts were drunk at celebrations; *syllabubs* Drinks or dishes made of curdled cream and wine.

[7] *Hymen* In Greek mythology, the god of marriage.

[8] *Mars* Roman god of war and lover of Venus, the goddess of beauty and wife of Vulcan.

(*Enter Madam Mediator.*)

MADAME MEDIATOR. What, Lady Happy, solitary, alone! and musing like a disconsolate lover!

LADY HAPPY. No, I was meditating of holy things.

MADAME MEDIATOR. Holy things! what holy things?

LADY HAPPY. Why, such holy things as the gods are.

MADAME MEDIATOR. By my truth, whether your contemplation be of gods or of men, you are become lean and pale since I was in the convent last.

(*Enter the Princess.*)

PRINCESS. Come, my sweet mistress, shall we go to our sports and recreations?

MADAME MEDIATOR. Beshrew me,[1] your Highness hath sported too much, I fear.

PRINCESS. Why, Madam Mediator, say you so?

MADAME MEDIATOR. Because the Lady Happy looks not well; she is become pale and lean.

PRINCESS. Madam Mediator, your eyes are become dim with time; for my sweet mistress appears with greater splendor than the god of light.

MADAME MEDIATOR. For all you are a great Princess, give me leave to tell you,
I am not so old, nor yet so blind
But that I see you are too kind.

PRINCESS. Well, Madam Mediator, when we return from our recreations, I will ask your pardon for saying your eyes are dim; conditionally, you will ask pardon for saying my Mistress looks not well.

(*Exeunt.*)

(*The scene is opened, and there is presented a rock, as in the sea, whereupon sit the Princess and the Lady Happy; the Princess as the sea god Neptune, the Lady Happy as a sea goddess. The rest of the ladies sit somewhat lower, dressed like water-nymphs. The Princess begins to speak a speech in verse, and after her the Lady Happy makes her speech.*)

PRINCESS. I am the king of all the seas,
All wat'ry creatures do me please,
Obey my power and command,
And bring me presents from the land;
The waters open their flood-gates,
Where ships do pass, sent by the fates;
Which fates do yearly, as May-dew,[2]
Send me a tribute from Peru,
From other nations besides,
Brought by their servants, winds, and tides,
Ships fraught and men to me they bring;
My watery kingdom lays them in.
Thus from the earth a tribute I
Receive, which shows my power thereby.
Besides, my kingdom's richer far
Than all the earth and every star.

LADY HAPPY. I feed the sun, which gives them light,
And makes them shine in darkest night;
Moist vapour from my breast I give,
Which he sucks forth, and makes him live,
Or else his fire would soon go out,
Grow dark, or burn the world throughout.

PRINCESS. What earthly creature's like to me,
That hath such power and majesty?
My palaces are rocks of stone,
And built by Nature's hand alone;
No base, dissembling, coz'ning art
Do I employ in any part,
In all my kingdom large and wide,
Nature directs and doth provide
Me all provisions which I need,
And cooks my meat on which I feed.

LADY HAPPY. My cabinets are oyster shells,
In which I keep my Orient-pearls,
To open them I use the tide,
As keys to locks, which opens wide,
The oyster shells then out I take;
Those, Orient pearls and crowns do make;
And modest coral I do wear,
Which blushes when it touches air.
On silver waves I sit and sing,
And then the fish lie listening:
Then sitting on a rocky stone,
I comb my hair with fish's bone;

[1] *Beshrew me* Curse or imprecatory expression meaning, "The devil take me," or "Evil befall me."

[2] *May-dew* Dew gathered on May Day, or in the month of May, was said to have medicinal properties.

The whilst Apollo,[1] with his beams,
Doth dry my hair from wat'ry streams.
His light doth glaze the water's face,
Make the large sea my looking glass;
So when I swim on waters high,
I see myself as I glide by:
But when the sun begins to burn,
I back into my waters turn,
And dive unto the bottom low:
Then on my head the waters flow,
In curled waves and circles round;
And thus with waters am I crowned.

PRINCESS. Besides, within the waters deep,
In hollow rocks my court I keep;
Of ambergris[2] my bed is made,
Whereon my softer limbs are laid,
There take I rest; and whilst I sleep,
The sea doth guard, and safe me keep
From danger; and, when I awake,
A present of a ship doth make.
No prince on earth hath more resort,
Nor keeps more servants in his court;
Of mermaids you're waited on,
And mermen do attend upon
My person; some are councillors,
Which order all my great affairs;
Within my wat'ry kingdom wide,
They help to rule, and so to guide
The common-wealth; and are by me
Prefered unto an high degree.
Some judges are, and magistrates,
Decide each cause, and end debates;
Others, commanders in the war;
And some to governments prefer;
Others are Neptune's priests, which pray
And preach when is a holy day.
And thus with method order I,
And govern all with majesty;
I am sole monarch of the sea,
And all therein belongs to me.

(*A sea-nymph sings this following song.*)

1. We watery nymphs rejoice and sing
About god Neptune, our sea's king;
In sea-green habits, for to move
His god-head, for to fall in love.

2. That with his trident[3] he doth stay
Rough foaming billows, which obey:
And when in triumph he doth stride
His managed dolphin for to ride.

3. All his sea-people to his wish,
From whale to herring, subject fish
With acclamations do attend him,
And prays more riches still to send him.

(*Exeunt.*
The scene vanishes.)

ACT 5, SCENE 1

(*Enter the Princess and the Lady Happy; the Princess is in a man's apparel, as going to dance. They whisper some time, then the Lady Happy takes a ribbon from her arm and gives it to the Princess, who gives her another instead of that, and kisses her hand. They go in and come presently out again with all the company to dance. The music plays, and after they have danced a little while in comes Madam Mediator, wringing her hands and spreading her arms; and full of passion cries out.*)

MADAME MEDIATOR. O Ladies, Ladies! you're all betrayed, undone, undone; for there is a man disguised in the convent. Search and you'll find it.

(*They all skip from each other, as afraid of each other; only the Princess and the Lady Happy stand still together.*)

PRINCESS. You may make the search, Madam Mediator; but you will quit me, I am sure.

MADAME MEDIATOR. By my faith but I will not, for you are most to be suspected.

[1] *Apollo* Greek god of the sun.

[2] *ambergris* Wax-like substance found in tropical seas and in the intestines of the sperm whale, used to make perfumes.

[3] *trident* Three-pronged scepter or spear.

PRINCESS. But you say the man is disguised like a woman, and I am accoutred like a man.

MADAME MEDIATOR. Fiddle faddle, that is nothing to the purpose.

(*Enter an ambassador to the Prince; the ambassador kneels, the Prince bids him rise.*)

PRINCE. What came you here for?

AMBASSADOR. May it please your Highness, the lords of your council sent me to inform your Highness that your subjects are so discontented at your absence that if your Highness do not return into your kingdom soon, they'll enter this kingdom by reason they hear you are here. And some report as if your Highness were restrained as prisoner.

PRINCE. So I am, but not by the state, but by this fair lady, who must be your Sovereigness.

(*The Ambassador kneels and kisses her hand.*)

PRINCE. But since I am discovered, go from me to the councillors of this state and inform them of my being here, as also the reason, and that I ask their leave I may marry this lady; otherwise, tell them I will have her by force of arms.

(*Exit Ambassador.*)

MADAME MEDIATOR. O the Lord! I hope you will not bring an army to take away all the women; will you?

PRINCE. No, Madam Mediator, we will leave you behind us.

(*Exeunt.*)

ACT 5, SCENE 2

(*Enter Madam Mediator lamenting and crying with a handkerchief in her hand.*)

[Written by my Lord Duke.]

MADAME MEDIATOR. O gentlemen, that I never had been born; we're all undone and lost!

MONSIEUR ADVISER. Why, what's the matter?

MADAME MEDIATOR. Matter? nay, I doubt there's too much matter.

MONSIEUR ADVISER. How?

MADAME MEDIATOR. How never such a mistake; why, we have taken a man for a woman.

MONSIEUR ADVISER. Why, a man is for a woman.

MADAME MEDIATOR. Fiddle faddle, I know that as well as you can tell me; but there was a young man drest in woman's apparel, and entered our convent, and the gods know what he hath done. He is mighty handsome, and that's a great temptation to virtue; but I hope all is well. But this wicked world will lay aspersion upon anything or nothing; and therefore I doubt[1] all my sweet young birds are undone; the gods comfort them.

MONSIEUR COURTLY. But could you never discover it? nor have no hint he was a man?

MADAME MEDIATOR. No, truly. Only once I saw him kiss the Lady Happy; and you know women's kisses are unnatural, and me-thought they kissed with more alacrity than women use—a kind of titillation, and more vigorous.

MONSIEUR ADVISER. Why, did you not then examine it?

MADAME MEDIATOR. Why, they would have said I was but an old jealous fool, and laughed at me; but experience is a great matter. If the gods had not been merciful to me, he might have fallen upon me.

MONSIEUR COURTLY. Why, what if he had?

MADAME MEDIATOR. Nay, if he had I care not: for I defy the flesh as much as I renounce the devil, and the pomp of this wicked world. But if I could but have saved my young sweet virgins I would willingly have sacrificed my body for them; for we are not born for ourselves, but for others.

MONSIEUR ADVISER. 'Tis piously said; truly, lovingly, and kindly.

MADAME MEDIATOR. Nay, I have read *The Practice of Piety*;[2] but, further, they say he is a foreign prince, and they say they're very hot.

MONSIEUR COURTLY. Why, you are Madam Mediator, you must mediate and make a friendship.

[1] *doubt* Fear.

[2] *The Practice of Piety* Popular devotional manual written by Lewis Bayly, Bishop of Bangor, and published in 1612.

MADAME MEDIATOR. Od's body,[1] what do you talk of mediation, I doubt they are too good friends. Well, this will be news for court, town, and country, in private letters, in the Gazette, and in abominable ballads, before it be long, and jeered to death by the pretending wits. But, good Gentlemen, keep this as a secret, and let not me be the author, for you will hear abundantly of it before it be long.

MONSIEUR ADVISER. But, Madam Mediator, this is no secret; it is known all the town over, and the state is preparing to entertain the Prince.

MADAME MEDIATOR. Lord, to see how ill news will fly so soon abroad!

MONSIEUR COURTLY. Ill news indeed for us wooers.

MONSIEUR ADVISER. We only wooed in imagination, but not in reality.

MADAME MEDIATOR. But you all had hopes.

MONSIEUR ADVISER. We had so, but she only has the fruition; for it is said the Prince and she are agreed to marry; and the State is so willing, as they account it an honour, and hope shall reap much advantage by the match.

MADAME MEDIATOR. Yes, yes; but there is an old and true saying, "There's much between the cup and the lip."

(*Exeunt.*)

ACT 5, SCENE 3

(*Enter the Prince as bridegroom and the Lady Happy as bride, hand in hand under a canopy borne over their heads by men; the Magistrates march before, then the hautboys;*[2] *and then the bridal-guests, as coming from the church, where they were married.*

All the Company bids them joy. They thank them.)

MADAM MEDIATOR. Although your Highness will not stay to feast with your guests, pray dance before you go.

PRINCE. We will both dance and feast before we go; come, Madam, let us dance, to please Madam Mediator.

(*The Prince and Princess dance.*)

PRINCE. Now, noble friends, dance you; and the Princess and I will rest ourselves.

(*After they have danced, the Lady Happy, as now Princess, speaks to the Lady Virtue.*)

LADY HAPPY. (*Speaks to Lady Virtue.*) Lady Virtue, I perceive you keep mimic[3] still.

LADY HAPPY. (*To the Prince.*) Sir, this is the mimic I told you of.

LADY HAPPY. (*To Mimic.*) Mimic, will you leave your Lady and go with me?

MIMIC. I am a married man, and have married my Lady's maid, Nan, and she will keep me at home, do what I can; but you've now a mimic of your own, for the Prince has imitated a woman.

LADY HAPPY. What, you rogue, do you call me a fool?

MIMIC. Not I, please your Highness, unless all women be fools.

PRINCE. Is your wife a fool?

MIMIC. Man and wife, 'tis said, makes but one fool.

(*He kneels to the Prince.*)

MIMIC. I have an humble petition to your Highness.

PRINCE. Rise; what petition is that?

MIMIC. That your Highness would be pleased to divide the convent in two equal parts; one for fools, and th'other for married men, as mad men.

PRINCE. I'll divide it for virgins and widows.

MIMIC. That will prove a convent of pleasure indeed; but they will never agree, especially if there be some disguised Prince amongst them. But you had better bestow it on old decrepit and bed-rid matrons, and then it may be called the Convent of Charity, if it cannot possibly be named the Convent of Chastity.

PRINCE. Well, to show my charity, and to keep your wife's chastity, I'll bestow my bounty in a present, on the condition you speak the Epilogue. Come, noble friends, let us feast before we part.

---

[1] *Od's body* I.e., "God's body."

[2] *hautboys* Those who play the hautboy, a wooden wind instrument similar to the oboe.

[3] *mimic* Mime or jester.

(*Exeunt.*)

(*Mimic solus.*[1])

MIMIC. An Epilogue, says he; the devil an Epilogue have I: let me study.

(*He questions and answers himself.*)

MIMIC. I have it, I have it; no, faith, I have it not; I lie, I have it, I say, I have it not. Fie, mimic, will you lie? Yes, mimic, I will lie, if it be my pleasure. But I say, it is gone. What is gone? The Epilogue. When had you it? I never had it. Then you did not lose it. That is all one, but I must speak it, although I never had it. How can you speak it, and never had it? I marry,[2] that's the question; but words are nothing, and then an Epilogue is nothing, and so I may speak nothing. Then nothing be my speech.

(*He speaks the Epilogue.*)

Noble spectators, by this candlelight,
I know not what to say, but bid Good Night:
I dare not beg applause, our poetess then
Will be enraged, and kill me with her pen;
For she is careless, and is void of fear;
If you dislike her play she doth not care.
But I shall weep, my inward grief shall show
Through floods of tears that through my eyes will flow.
And so poor mimic he for sorrow die.
And then through pity you may chance to cry:
But if you please, you may a cordial give,
Made up with praise, and so he long may live.

FINIS.

—1668

[1] *solus* Latin: alone (masculine).

[2] *I marry* Expression used to demonstrate indignation or add emphasis.

John Bunyan

1628 – 1688

"In general, when the educated minority and the common people differ about the merit of a book, the opinion of the educated minority finally prevails. *The Pilgrim's Progress* is perhaps the only book about which, after the lapse of a hundred years, the educated minority has come over to the opinion of the common people." So wrote the renowned Victorian historian Thomas Macaulay in 1852, as John Bunyan's magnum opus was reaching the zenith of its popularity, acknowledged on all sides as one of the foundational texts of English literature and of the Christian faith and second perhaps only to the Bible in readership. Though it no longer occupies a central place in the literary or religious consciousness of the English-speaking world, John Bunyan's *The Pilgrim's Progress* remains one of the most significant allegorical works in English literature.

Bunyan was born in the small village of Elstow, near Bedford, in 1628. His father had descended from several centuries of yeoman farmers in Bedfordshire, but was forced to become a traveling tinker (a mender of pots and kettles) when the family fell on hard times. Despite his parents' struggle with poverty, Bunyan was sent to grammar school at an early age, where he learned to read and write. In 1644, shortly after the death of his mother, Bunyan enlisted into active military service during the English Civil War in accordance with a Parliamentary edict demanding 225 recruits from the town of Bedford. Although he had fulfilled his requirement for service in 1645, he joined another regiment and continued serving in the Parliamentary Army until 1647.

Shortly upon leaving the army, Bunyan took up his father's trade as a tinker and returned to Elstow. Although no record of his marriage has been found, it is presumed that he married within a year of his return. Little is known about Bunyan's first wife Mary (who died in 1655) except that she persuaded Bunyan to begin attending church regularly. It was also through Mary that Bunyan became familiar with Arthur Dent's *The Plaine Mans Path-Way to Heaven* and Lewis Bayly's *The Practice of Piety*. These written works and his wife's piety inspired him to give up all worldly amusements, and to begin a lifelong habit of introspection in an effort to gain spiritual nourishment. In 1653 Bunyan joined the Baptist Church of Bedford. The zeal with which Bunyan approached his religious conversion, together with his power of expression, soon made him prominent among his fellow Baptist Nonconformists (anyone who did not follow the doctrines of the Church of England); he began to be called upon to preach in Bedford and surrounding towns.

Bunyan's long history of imprisonment began in 1660 with the Restoration of Charles II. After many years of civil unrest, it was believed by the monarchy that national unity would be furthered through religious conformity. As a result, the Anglican Church began to persecute Nonconformist preachers. Initially sentenced to three months in prison, Bunyan refused to submit to the Church of England or to give up preaching, and as a result was kept in jail for twelve years. Bunyan was by no means idle while incarcerated. He studied, preached to his fellow prisoners, made boot laces to support his family, and wrote many works on religious themes—including his spiritual autobiography *Grace Abounding to the Chief of Sinners* (1666).

In 1672 Charles II issued the Declaration of Religious Indulgence; Bunyan was released from prison and given permission to preach once again. His reputation soon spread to such an extent that great crowds of Puritans reportedly flocked to hear him speak. So broad became his influence that his friends, and even his enemies, began to refer to him in jest as "Bishop Bunyan."

This period of religious freedom did not last for long. In 1673 Charles II repealed the Declaration of Religious Indulgence, and religious persecution of Nonconformists began once again. In March of 1675 a warrant for Bunyan's arrest was issued, and Bunyan was imprisoned in the county jail for another six months. In all probability it was in prison that Bunyan began to compose his most famous work *The Pilgrim's Progress from This World to That Which Is to Come*; the book was entered into the Stationers' Register on 22 December 1677, and licensed in February 1678. Bunyan himself reveals in the verse "apology" that serves as a preface to *The Pilgrim's Progress* that his inspiration for the work came to him suddenly "like sparks that from the coals of fire do fly." It is difficult for the present-day reader to apprehend imaginatively the force carried by the images that crowded into Bunyan's mind—mountains and quagmires, rivers and fiery furnaces, all freshly saturated with allegorical meaning. The story that Bunyan told recounted the many stages of Christian's journey from the City of Destruction to the Celestial City. Told in plain prose, *The Pilgrim's Progress* is very different in tone from that other most famous of English allegories, *The Faerie Queene*—but it may have had an even greater impact on English culture. Certainly few books have been more widely read than *The Pilgrim's Progress*. Several editions were published in Bunyan's lifetime, during a period when books and people who could read were relatively scarce. In over three centuries since its publication, *The Pilgrim's Progress* has been translated into almost every spoken language and literally hundreds of editions are still in existence, with new editions published every year. Many common phrases in use today, including "the house beautiful," "Vanity Fair," and "the slough of despond" find their origins in Bunyan's popular allegory. The popularity of the first edition of *The Pilgrim's Progress* led Bunyan to undertake further religious allegories including *The Life and Death of Mr. Badman* (1680), and *The Holy War* (1682). He then published *The Pilgrim's Progress, Part II* (1684).

During the last years of his life he enjoyed immense success and influence as a writer, administrator, and pastor-in-chief, and his services were in demand throughout England. In August 1688 he was called to London in order to counsel a father and son. After forty miles of riding through hard rain, he fell ill and took to bed in a friend's house. Fever took hold rapidly and he died on 31 August 1688.

⌘⌘⌘

from *The Pilgrim's Progress*

The Author's Apology for His Book

When at the first I took my pen in hand
Thus for to write, I did not understand
That I at all should make a little book
In such a mode; nay, I had undertook
To make another, which when almost done,
Before I was aware, I this begun.
And thus it was: I, writing of the way
And race of saints in this our gospel day,
Fell suddenly into an allegory
About their journey and the way to glory,
In more than twenty things, which I set down;
This done, I twenty more had in my crown,° *head*
And they again began to multiply,
Like sparks that from the coals of fire do fly.
Nay then, thought I, if that you breed so fast,
I'll put you by yourselves, lest you at last
Should prove *ad infinitum*,[1] and eat out
The book that I already am about.
Well, so I did; but yet I did not think
To show to all the world my pen and ink
In such a mode; I only thought to make
I knew not what; nor did I undertake
Thereby to please my neighbour; no, not I,
I did it my own self to gratify.
Neither did I but vacant seasons spend
In this my scribble; nor did I intend
But to divert myself in doing this,
From worser thoughts, which make me do amiss.
Thus I set pen to paper with delight,
And quickly had my thoughts in black and white.
For having now my method by the end,
Still as I pulled, it came; and so I penned
It down until it came at last to be,
For length and breadth, the bigness which you see.
Well, when I had thus put my ends together,
I showed them others, that I might see whether
They would condemn them or them justify.
And some said, "Let them live"; some, "Let them die."
Some said, "John, print it"; others said, "Not so."
Some said, "It might do good"; others said, "No."
Now was I in a strait,° and did not see *dilemma*
Which was the best thing to be done by me.
At last I thought, "Since you are thus divided,
I print it will," and so the case decided.

...

And now, before I do put up my pen,
I'll show the profit of my book, and then
Commit both thee and it unto that hand
That pulls the strong down and makes weak ones stand.
This book it chalketh out before thine eyes
The man that seeks the everlasting prize;
It shows you whence he comes, whither he goes,
What he leaves undone, also what he does;
It also shows you how he runs and runs
Till he unto the gate of glory comes.
It shows, too, who sets out for life amain,° *vehemently*
As if the lasting crown they would attain.
Here also you may see the reason why
They lose their labour and like fools do die.
This book will make a traveller of thee,
If by its counsel thou wilt ruled be;
It will direct thee to the Holy Land,
If thou wilt its directions understand.
Yea, it will make the slothful active be,
The blind, also, delightful things to see.
Art thou for something rare and profitable?
Wouldest thou see a truth within a fable?
Art thou forgetful? Wouldest thou remember
From New Year's Day to the last of December?
Then read my fancies; they will stick like burrs,
And may be to the helpless comforters.
This book is writ in such a dialect,
As may the minds of listless men affect.
It seems a novelty, and yet contains
Nothing but sound and honest gospel strains.
Wouldst thou divert thyself from melancholy?
Wouldst thou be pleasant, yet be far from folly?
Wouldst thou read riddles, and their explanation,
Or else be drowned in thy contemplation?
Dost thou love picking meat? Or wouldst thou see
A man i' th' clouds and hear him speak to thee?
Wouldst thou be in a dream and yet not sleep?
Or wouldst thou in a moment laugh and weep?

[1] *ad infinitum* Latin: without limit.

Wouldst thou lose thyself and catch no harm?
And find thyself again without a charm?
Wouldst read thyself and read thou knowest not what
And yet know whether thou art blest or not,
By reading the same lines? O then come hither,
And lay my book, thy head and heart together.

John Bunyan

As I walked through the wilderness of this world, I lighted on a certain place where was a den,[1] and I laid me down in that place to sleep, and as I slept I dreamed a dream. I dreamed, and behold I saw a man clothed with rags,[2] standing in a certain place, with his face from his own house, a book in his hand, and a great burden upon his back.[3] I looked, and saw him open the book, and read therein; and as he read he wept and trembled, and not being able longer to contain, he brake out with a lamentable cry, saying, "What shall I do?"[4]

In this plight therefore he went home and refrained himself as long as he could that his wife and children should not perceive his distress; but he could not be silent long, because that[5] his trouble increased. Wherefore at length he brake his mind[6] to his wife and children; and thus he began to talk to them, "O my dear wife," said he, "and you, the children of my bowels, I your dear friend am in myself undone, by reason of a burden that lieth hard upon me; moreover, I am for certain informed that this our city will be burned with fire from heaven, in which fearful overthrow both myself, with thee, my wife, and you, my sweet babes, shall miserably come to ruin; except (the which, yet I see not) some way of escape can be found, whereby we may be delivered." At this his relations were sore amazed; not for that they believed that what he said to them was true, but because they thought that some frenzy distemper[7] had got into his head; therefore, it drawing towards night, and they hoping that sleep might settle his brains, with all haste they got him to bed. But the night was as troublesome to him as the day; wherefore[8] instead of sleeping, he spent it in sighs and tears. So when the morning was come, they would[9] know how he did, and he told them worse and worse. He also set to talking to them again, but they began to be hardened.[10] They also thought to drive away his distemper by harsh and surly carriages[11] to him: sometimes they would deride; sometimes they would chide; and sometimes they would quite neglect him. Wherefore he began to retire himself to his chamber to pray for and pity them, and also to condole[12] his own misery; he would also walk solitarily in the fields, sometimes reading, and sometimes praying, and thus for some days he spent his time.

Now, I saw upon a time when he was walking in the fields that he was (as he was wont) reading in his book and greatly distressed in his mind; and as he read, he burst out, as he had done before, crying, "What shall I do to be saved?"

I saw also that he looked this way and that way, as if he would run; yet he stood still, because, as I perceived, he could not tell which way to go. I looked then and saw a man named Evangelist coming to him and asked, "Wherefore dost thou cry?" He answered, "Sir, I perceive, by the book in my hand, that I am condemned to die and after that to come to judgement; and I find that I am not willing to do the first, nor able to do the second."

Then said Evangelist, "Why not willing to die since this life is attended with so many evils?" The man answered, "Because I fear that this burden that is upon my back will sink me lower than the grave, and I shall fall into Tophet.[13] And, sir, if I be not fit to go to prison, I am not fit (I am sure) to go to judgement and from thence to execution; and the thoughts of these things make me cry."

[1] [Bunyan's note] The jail.

[2] *I saw … rags* Cf. Isaiah 64.6.

[3] *great burden upon his back* Cf. Psalms 38.4.

[4] *What shall I do?* Cf. Acts 16.30–31.

[5] *because that* Because.

[6] *brake his mind* Revealed his thoughts.

[7] *frenzy distemper* Mental derangement.

[8] *wherefore* Therefore.

[9] *would* Wished to.

[10] [Bunyan's note] Carnal physic for a sick soul.

[11] *carriages* Treatment; behavior.

[12] *condole* Lament.

[13] *Tophet* Hell; a place near Jerusalem where children were sacrificed to Moloch (2 Kings 23.10) and which became later a depository for refuse where fires continually burned, suggesting the torments of hell.

Then said Evangelist, "If this be thy condition, why standest thou still?" He answered, "Because I know not whither to go." Then he gave him a parchment roll, and there was written within, "Fly from the wrath to come."[1]

The man therefore read it, and looking up on Evangelist very carefully, said, "Whither must I fly?" Then said Evangelist, pointing with his finger over a very wide field, "Do you see yonder wicket-gate?"[2] The man said, "No." Then said the other, "Do you see yonder shining light?"[3] He said, "I think I do." Then said Evangelist, "Keep that light in your eye, and go up directly thereto; so shalt thou see the gate, at which when thou knockest, it shall be told thee what thou shalt do."[4]

So I saw in my dream that the man began to run. Now he had not run far from his own door, but his wife and children perceiving it, began to cry after him to return. But the man put his fingers in his ears and ran on crying, "Life, life, eternal life." So he looked not behind him, but fled towards the middle of the plain.[5]

The neighbours also came out to see him run,[6] and as he ran, some mocked, others threatened, and some cried after him to return. Now among those that did so, there were two that were resolved to fetch him back by force. The name of the one was Obstinate and the name of the other Pliable. Now by this time the man was got a good distance from them; but, however, they were resolved to pursue him, which they did and in little time they overtook him. Then said the man, "Neighbours, wherefore are you come?" They said, "To persuade you to go back with us." But he said, "That can by no means be. You dwell," said he, "in the City of Destruction[7] (the place also where I was born). I see it to be so, and dying there, sooner or later, you will sink lower than the grave, into a place that burns with fire and brimstone. Be content, good neighbours, and go along with me."

"What!" said Obstinate, "and leave our friends and our comforts behind us!"

"Yes," said Christian (for that was his name), "because, that all which you shall forsake is not worthy to be compared with a little of that that I am seeking to enjoy, and if you will go along with me, and hold it, you shall fare as I myself; for there where I go is enough and to spare. Come away and prove[8] my words."

OBSTINATE. "What are the things you seek, since you leave all the world to find them?"

CHRISTIAN. "I seek an 'inheritance, incorruptible, undefiled, and that fadeth not away,'[9] and it is laid up in Heaven, and fast[10] there, to be bestowed at the time appointed on them that diligently seek it. Read it so, if you will, in my book."

OBSTINATE. "Tush," said Obstinate, "away with your book; will you go back with us or no?"

CHRISTIAN. "No, not I," said the other, "because I have laid my hand to the plow."[11]

OBSTINATE. "Come, then, neighbour Pliable, let us turn again, and go home without him; there is a company of these crazed-headed coxcombs,[12] that when they take a fancy by the end are wiser in their own eyes than seven men that can render a reason."[13]

PLIABLE. Then said Pliable, "Don't revile; if what the good Christian says is true, the things he looks after are better than ours; my heart inclines to go with my neighbour."

OBSTINATE. "What! more fools still? Be ruled by me and go back; who knows whither such a brain-sick fellow will lead you? Go back, go back, and be wise."

CHRISTIAN. "Come with me, neighbour Pliable; there are such things to be had which I spoke of and many more glories besides; if you believe not me, read here in this book, and for the truth of what is expressed therein,

---

[1] *Fly from the wrath to come* Cf. Matthew 3.7.

[2] *Do you see yonder wicket-gate?* Cf. Matthew 7.13–14.

[3] *Do ... light?* Cf. Psalms 119.105; 2 Peter 1.19.

[4] [Bunyan's note] Christ and the way to Him cannot be found without the Word.

[5] *So ... plain* Cf. Genesis 19.17.

[6] [Bunyan's note] They that fly from the wrath to come are a gazing-stock to the world.

[7] *City of Destruction* Cf. Isaiah 19.18.

[8] *prove* Learn by experience.

[9] *inheritance ... away* From 1 Peter 1.4.

[10] *fast* Secure.

[11] *because ... plow* Cf. Luke 9.62.

[12] *coxcombs* Conceited, showy persons; the meaning derives from the hats in the shape of cocks' combs worn by jesters.

[13] *seven ... reason* From Proverbs 26.16.

behold all is confirmed by the blood of Him that made it."

Pliable. "Well, neighbour Obstinate," said Pliable, "I begin to come to a point; I intend to go along with this good man and to cast in my lot with him. But, my good companion, do you know the way to this desired place?"

Christian. "I am directed by a man whose name is Evangelist to speed me to a little gate that is before us, where we shall receive instruction about the way."

Pliable. "Come then, good neighbour, let us be going." Then they went both together.

Obstinate. "And I will go back to my place," said Obstinate. "I will be no companion of such misled fantastical fellows."

Now I saw in my dream that when Obstinate was gone back, Christian and Pliable went talking over the plain, and thus they began their discourse.

Christian. "Come, neighbour Pliable, how do you do? I am glad you are persuaded to go along with me, and had even Obstinate himself but felt what I have felt of the powers and terrors of what is yet unseen, he would not thus lightly have given us the back."[1]

Pliable. "Come, neighbour Christian, since there is none but us two here, tell me now further, what the things are and how to be enjoyed, whither we are going."

Christian. "I can better conceive of them with my mind than speak of them with my tongue. But yet since you are desirous to know, I will read of them in my book."

Pliable. "And do you think that the words of your book are certainly true?"

Christian. "Yes, verily, for it was made by Him that cannot lie."[2]

Pliable. "Well said; what things are they?"

Christian. "There is an endless kingdom to be inhabited and everlasting life to be given us, that we may inhabit that kingdom forever."

Pliable. "Well said, and what else?"

Christian. "There are crowns of glory to be given us, and garments that will make us shine like the sun in the firmament of heaven."

Pliable. "This is excellent, and what else?"

Christian. "There shall be no more crying, nor sorrow; for He that is owner of the place will wipe all tears from our eyes."[3]

Pliable. "And what company shall we have there?"

Christian. "There we shall be with seraphims and cherubims, creatures that will dazzle your eyes to look on them. There also you shall meet with thousands and ten thousands that have gone before us to that place; none of them are hurtful, but loving and holy, every one walking in the sight of God, and standing in his presence with acceptance forever. In a word, there we shall see the elders with their golden crowns. There we shall see the holy virgins with their golden harps.[4] There we shall see men that by the world were cut in pieces, burned in flames, eaten of beasts, drowned in the seas, for the love that they bare to the Lord of the place, all well and clothed with immortality, as with a garment."

Pliable. "The hearing of this is enough to ravish one's heart; but are these things to be enjoyed? How shall we get to be sharers hereof?"

Christian. "The Lord, the governor of that country, hath recorded in this book, the substance of which is: if we be truly willing to have it, he will bestow it upon us freely."

Pliable. "Well, my good companion, glad am I to hear of these things. Come on, let us mend our pace."

Christian. "I cannot go so fast as I would, by reason of this burden that is upon my back."

Now I saw in my dream, that just as they had ended this talk, they drew near to a very miry slough that was in the midst of the plain, and they, being heedless, did both fall suddenly into the bog. The name of the slough was Despond. Here therefore they wallowed for a time, being grievously bedaubed with the dirt; and Christian, because of the burden that was on his back, began to sink in the mire.

Pliable. Then said Pliable, "Ah, neighbour Christian, where are you now?"

Christian. "Truly," said Christian, "I do not know."

Pliable. At that Pliable began to be offended; and angrily said to his fellow, "Is this the happiness you have

[1] *given us the back* Turned away from us; disregarded us.

[2] *him ... lie* Cf. Titus 1.2: "In hope of eternal life, which God, that cannot lie, promised before the world began."

[3] *There ... eyes* Cf. Revelation 21.4.

[4] *In a word ... harps* Cf. Revelation 4.4, 5.11, 14.1–5.

told me all this while of? If we have such ill speed at our first setting out, what may we expect, 'twixt this and our journey's end? May I get out again with my life, you shall possess the brave[1] country alone for me." And with that he gave a desperate struggle or two and got out of the mire, on that side of the slough which was next to his own house. So away he went, and Christian saw him no more.

Wherefore Christian was left to tumble in the slough of Despond alone; but still he endeavoured to struggle to that side of the slough that was still further from his own house and next to the wicket-gate; the which he did, but could not get out, because of the burden that was upon his back. But I beheld in my dream that a man came to him, whose name was Help, and asked him what he did there?

CHRISTIAN. "Sir," said Christian, "I was bid go this way by a man called Evangelist, who directed me also to yonder gate, that I might escape the wrath to come. And as I was going thither, I fell in here."

HELP. "But why did you not look for the steps?"[2]

CHRISTIAN. "Fear followed me so hard, that I fled the next way and fell in."

HELP. "Then," said he, "give me thy hand." So he gave him his hand, and he drew him out, and set him upon sound ground, and bid him go on his way.[3]

Then I stepped to him that plucked him out and said, "Sir, wherefore, since over this place is the way from the City of Destruction to yonder gate, is it that this plat[4] is not mended that poor travellers might go thither with more security?" And he said unto me, "This miry slough is such a place as cannot be mended. It is the descent whither the scum and filth that attends conviction for sin doth continually run, and therefore is it called the Slough of Despond; for still as[5] the sinner is awakened about his lost condition, there ariseth in his soul many fears, and doubts, and discouraging apprehensions, which all of them get together, and settle in this place. And this is the reason of the badness of this ground.

"It is not the pleasure of the King that this place should remain so bad; his labourers also have, by the direction of His Majesty's surveyors, been for above this sixteen hundred years employed about this patch of ground, if perhaps it might have been mended. Yea, and to my knowledge," saith he, "here hath been swallowed up at least twenty thousand cart-loads, yea millions of wholesome instructions that have at all seasons been brought from all places of the King's dominions, and they that can tell say they are the best materials to make good ground of the place. If so be it might have been mended, but it is the Slough of Despond still and so will be when they have done what they can.

"True, there are, by the direction of the law-giver, certain good and substantial steps,[6] placed even through the very midst of this Slough; but at such time as this place doth much spew out its filth, as it doth against[7] change of weather, these steps are hardly seen; or if they be, men, through the dizziness of their heads, step besides, and then they are bemired to purpose, notwithstanding the steps be there; but the ground is good when they are once got in at the gate."

Now I saw in my dream that by this time Pliable was got home to his house again. So his neighbours came to visit him, and some of them called him wise man for coming back, and some called him fool for hazarding himself with Christian; others again did mock at his cowardliness, saying, "Surely since you began to venture, I would not have been so base to have given out for a few difficulties." So Pliable sat sneaking among them. But at last he got more confidence, and then they all turned their tales and began to deride poor Christian behind his back. And thus much concerning Pliable.

Now as Christian was walking solitary by himself, he espied one afar off come crossing over the field to meet him; and their hap[8] was to meet just as they were crossing the way of each other. The gentleman's name was Mr. Worldly Wiseman; he dwelt in the town of

[1] [Bunyan's note] It is not enough to be pliable. [*brave* Splendid.]

[2] [Bunyan's note] The promises.

[3] *So ... way* Cf. Psalms 40.2.

[4] *plat* Surface; piece of ground.

[5] *still as* Whenever.

[6] [Bunyan's note] The promises of forgiveness and acceptance to life by faith in Christ.

[7] *against* During.

[8] *hap* Chance, fortune.

Carnal Policy, a very great town, and also hard by[1] from whence Christian came. This man then meeting with Christian, and having some inkling of him, for Christian's setting forth from the City of Destruction was much noised[2] abroad, not only in the town where he dwelt, but also it began to be the town-talk in some other places, Master Worldly Wiseman therefore, having some guess of him, by beholding his laborious going, by observing his sighs and groans, and the like, began thus to enter into some talk with Christian.

Worldly Wiseman. "How now, good fellow, whither away after this burdened manner?"

Christian. "A burdened manner, indeed, as ever I think poor creature had. And whereas you ask me, 'Whither away,' I tell you, sir, I am going to yonder wicket-gate before me; for there, as I am informed, I shall be put into a way to be rid of my heavy burden."

Worldly Wiseman. "Hast thou a wife and children?"

Christian. "Yes, but I am so laden with this burden that I cannot take that pleasure in them as formerly; methinks, I am as if I had none."[3]

Worldly Wiseman. "Wilt thou hearken to me, if I give thee counsel?"

Christian. "If it be good, I will, for I stand in need of good counsel."

Worldly Wiseman. "I would advise thee then that thou with all speed get thyself rid of thy burden; for thou wilt never be settled in thy mind till then, nor canst thou enjoy the benefits of the blessing which God hath bestowed upon thee till then."

Christian. "That is that which I seek for, even to be rid of this heavy burden; but get it off myself I cannot, nor is there a man in our country that can take it off my shoulders; therefore am I going this way, as I told you, that I may be rid of my burden."

Worldly Wiseman. "Who bid thee go this way to be rid of thy burden?"

Christian. "A man that appeared to me to be a very great and honourable person; his name, as I remember, is Evangelist."

Worldly Wiseman. "I beshrew[4] him for his counsel; there is not a more dangerous and troublesome way in the world than is that unto which he hath directed thee; and that thou shalt find, if thou wilt be ruled by his counsel. Thou hast met with something (as I perceive) already; for I see the dirt of the Slough of Despond is upon thee; but that slough is the beginning of the sorrows that do attend those that go on in that way. Hear me, I am older than thou! Thou art like to meet with in the way which thou goest wearisomeness, painfulness, hunger, perils, nakedness, sword, lions, dragons, darkness, and in a word, death, and what not? These things are certainly true, having been confirmed by many testimonies. And why should a man so carelessly cast away himself by giving heed to a stranger?"

Christian. "Why, sir, this burden upon my back is more terrible to me than are all these things which you have mentioned. Nay, methinks I care not what I meet with in the way, so be I can also meet with deliverance from my burden."

Worldly Wiseman. "How camest thou by thy burden at first?"

Christian. "By reading this book in my hand."

Worldly Wiseman. "I thought so;[5] and it happened unto thee as to other weak men, who, meddling with things too high for them, do suddenly fall into thy distractions; which distractions do not only unman[6] men, as thine, I perceive, has done thee, but they run them upon desperate ventures, to obtain they know not what."

Christian. "I know what I would obtain; it is ease for my heavy burden."

Worldly Wiseman. "But why wilt thou seek for ease this way, seeing so many dangers attend it, especially since, hadst thou but patience to hear me, I could direct thee to the obtaining of what thou desirest, without the dangers that thou in this way wilt run thyself into; yea, and the remedy is at hand. Besides, I will add, that instead of those dangers thou shalt meet with much safety, friendship, and content."

Christian. "Pray, sir, open this secret to me."

[1] *hard by* Near.

[2] *noised* Talked about; broadcast.

[3] *Yes ... none* Cf. 1 Corinthians 7.29.

[4] *beshrew* Curse.

[5] [Bunyan's note] Worldly Wiseman does not like that men should be serious in reading the Bible.

[6] *unman* Deprive of manly qualities, especially courage or strength.

WORLDLY WISEMAN. "Why in yonder village (the village is named Morality) there dwells a gentleman whose name is Legality, a very judicious man (and a man of a very good name) that has skill to help men off with such burdens as thine are from their shoulders; yea, to my knowledge he hath done a great deal of good this way. Ay, and besides, he hath skill to cure those that are somewhat crazed in their wits with their burdens. To him, as I said, thou mayest go, and be helped presently. His house is not quite a mile from this place; and if he should not be at home himself, he hath a pretty[1] young man to[2] his son, whose name is Civility, that can do it (to speak on) as well as the old gentleman himself. There, I say, thou mayest be eased of thy burden, and if thou art not minded to go back to thy former habitations, as indeed I would not wish thee, thou mayest send for thy wife and children to thee to this village, where there are houses now stand empty, one of which thou mayest have at reasonable rates. Provision is there also cheap and good; and that which will make thy life the more happy is, to be sure; there thou shalt live by honest neighbours, in credit and good fashion."

Now was Christian somewhat at a stand, but presently he concluded, if this be true which this gentleman hath said, my wisest course is to take his advice; and with that he thus farther spoke.

CHRISTIAN. "Sir, which is my way to this honest man's house?"

WORLDLY WISEMAN. "Do you see yonder high hill?"[3]

CHRISTIAN. "Yes, very well."

WORLDLY WISEMAN. "By that hill you must go, and the first house you come at is his."

So Christian turned out of his way to go to Mr. Legality's house for help; but behold, when he was got now hard by the hill, it seemed so high, and also that side of it that was next the wayside did hang so much over that Christian was afraid to venture further, lest the hill should fall on his head. Wherefore there he stood still, and wotted[4] not what to do. Also his burden, now, seemed heavier to him than while he was in his way. There came also flashes of fire out of the hill that made Christian afraid that he should be burned;[5] here therefore he sweat, and did quake for fear.[6] And now he began to be sorry that he had taken Mr. Worldly Wiseman's counsel; and with that he saw Evangelist coming to meet him, at the sight also of whom he began to blush for shame. So Evangelist drew nearer, and nearer, and coming up to him, he looked upon him with a severe and dreadful countenance, and thus began to reason with Christian.

EVANGELIST. "What doest thou here?" said he, at which word Christian knew not what to answer; wherefore, at present, he stood speechless before him. Then said Evangelist farther, "Art not thou the man that I found crying, without the walls of the City of Destruction?"

CHRISTIAN. "Yes, dear sir, I am the man."

EVANGELIST. "Did not I direct thee the way to the little wicket-gate?"

CHRISTIAN. "Yes, dear sir," said Christian.

EVANGELIST. "How is it then that thou art so quickly turned aside, for thou art now out of the way?"

CHRISTIAN. "I met with a gentleman so soon as I had got over the Slough of Despond, who persuaded me that I might in the village before me find a man that could take off my burden."

EVANGELIST. "What was he?"

CHRISTIAN. "He looked like a gentleman, and talked much to me, and got me at last to yield; so I came hither. But when I beheld this hill, and how it hangs over the way, I suddenly made a stand, lest it should fall on my head."

EVANGELIST. "What said that gentleman to you?"

CHRISTIAN. "Why, he asked me whither I was going, and I told him."

EVANGELIST. "And what said he then?"

CHRISTIAN. "He asked me if I had a family, and I told him; but, said I, I am so laden with the burden that is on my back, that I cannot take pleasure in them as formerly."

EVANGELIST. "And what said he then?"

CHRISTIAN. "He bid me with speed get rid of my burden, and I told him 'twas ease that I sought. And

[1] *pretty* Fine; commendable.

[2] *to* As.

[3] [Bunyan's note] Mount Sinai.

[4] *wotted* Knew.

[5] *There … burned* Cf. Exodus 19.16, 18.

[6] *did quake for fear* Cf. Hebrews 12.21.

said I, I am therefore going to yonder gate to receive further direction how I may get to the place of deliverance. So he said that he would show me a better way, and short, not so attended with difficulties, as the way, sir, that you set me; which way, said he, will direct you to a gentleman's house that hath skill to take off these burdens. So I believed him, and turned out of that way into this, if haply[1] I might be soon eased of my burden; but when I came to this place, and beheld things as they are, I stopped for fear (as I said) of danger, but I now know not what to do."

EVANGELIST. "Then," said Evangelist, "stand still a little that I may show thee the words of God." So he stood trembling. Then said Evangelist, "See that ye refuse not him that speaketh; for if they escaped not who refused him that spake on earth, much more shall not we escape, if we turn away from him that speaketh from Heaven."[2] He said moreover, "Now the just shall live by faith; but if any man draws back, my soul shall have no pleasure in him."[3] He also did thus apply[4] them, "Thou art the man that art running into this misery, thou has began to reject the counsel of the Most High, and to draw back thy foot from the way of peace, even almost to the hazarding of thy perdition."

Then Christian fell down at his foot as dead, crying, "Woe is me, for I am undone."[5] At the sight of which Evangelist caught him by the right hand, saying, "All manner of sin and blasphemies shall be forgiven unto men;[6] be not faithless, but believing."[7] Then did Christian again a little revive, and stood up trembling, as at first, before Evangelist.

Then Evangelist proceeded, saying, "Give more earnest heed to the things that I shall tell thee of. I will now show thee who it was that deluded thee, and who 'twas also to whom he sent thee. The man that met thee is one Worldly Wiseman, and rightly is he so called; partly, because he favoureth only the doctrine of this world (therefore he always goes to the town of Morality to church) and partly because he loveth that doctrine best, for it saveth him from the cross; and because he is of this carnal temper, therefore he seeketh to prevent my ways, though right. Now there are three things in this man's counsel that thou must utterly abhor.

1. His turning thee out of the way.
2. His labouring to render the cross odious to thee.
3. And his setting thy feet in that way that leadeth unto the administration of death.

"First, thou must abhor his turning thee out of the way, yea, and thine own consenting thereto; because this is to reject the counsel of God, for the sake of the counsel of a Worldly Wiseman. The Lord says, 'Strive to enter in at the strait gate,'[8] the gate to which I sent thee; for 'strait is the gate that leadeth unto life, and few there be that find it.'[9] From this little wicket-gate, and from the way thereto hath this wicked man turned thee, to the bringing of thee almost to destruction; hate therefore his turning thee out of the way, and abhor thyself for hearkening to him.

"Secondly, thou must abhor his labouring to render the cross odious unto thee; for thou art to prefer it before the treasures in Egypt;[10] besides, the King of Glory hath told thee that he that 'will save his life shall lose it,'[11] and he that comes after him, 'and hates not his father and mother, and wife, and children, and brethren, and sisters, yea, and his own life also, he cannot be my disciple.'[12] I say, therefore, for a man to labour to persuade thee that that shall be thy death, without which, the truth hath said, thou canst not have eternal life, this doctrine thou must abhor.

"Thirdly, thou must hate his setting of thy feet in the way that leadeth to the ministration of death. And for this thou must consider to whom he sent thee and also how unable that person was to deliver thee from thy burden.

---

[1] *haply* By chance.

[2] *See ... Heaven* From Hebrews 12.25.

[3] *Now ... him* From Hebrews 10.38.

[4] *apply* Address.

[5] *Woe ... undone* From Isaiah 6.5.

[6] *All ... men* Cf. Matthew 12.31; Mark 3.28.

[7] *be ... believing* From John 20.27.

[8] *Strive ... gate* From Luke 13.24.

[9] *strait ... it* Cf. Matthew 7.13,14.

[10] *Secondly ... Egypt* Cf. Hebrews 11.26.

[11] *save ... it* From Mark 8.35.

[12] *and hates ... disciple* From Luke 14.26.

"He to whom thou wast sent for ease, being by name Legality, is the son of the bondwoman[1] which now is, and is in bondage with her children, and is in a mystery, this Mount Sinai, which thou hast feared will fall on thy head. Now if she with her children are in bondage, how canst thou expect by them to be made free? This Legality therefore is not able to set thee free from thy burden. No man was as yet ever rid of his burden by him, no, nor ever is like to be; ye cannot be justified by the works of the law, for by the deeds of the law no man living can be rid of his burden. Therefore Mr. Worldly Wiseman is an alien, and Mr. Legality a cheat; and for his son Civility, notwithstanding his simpering looks, he is but an hypocrite, and cannot help thee. Believe me, there is nothing in all this noise that thou hast heard of this sottish man, but a design to beguile thee of thy salvation, by turning thee from the way in which I had set thee." After this Evangelist called aloud to the heavens for confirmation of what he had said; and with that there came words and fire out of the mountain under which poor Christian stood, that made the hair of his flesh stand. The words were thus pronounced, "As many as are of the works of the law are under the curse: for it is written, Cursed is everyone that continueth not in all things which are written in the book of the law to do them."[2]

Now Christian looked for nothing but death, and began to cry out lamentably, even cursing the time in which he met with Mr. Worldly Wiseman, still calling himself a thousand fools for hearkening to his counsel; he also was greatly ashamed to think that this gentleman's arguments, flowing only from the flesh, should have that prevalency with him as to cause him to forsake the right way. This done, he applied himself again to Evangelist in words and sense as follows.

CHRISTIAN. "Sir, what think you? Is there hopes? May I now go back and go up to the wicket-gate? Shall I not be abandoned for this, and sent back from thence ashamed? I am sorry I have hearkened to this man's counsel, but may my sin be forgiven."

EVANGELIST. Then said Evangelist to him, "Thy sin is very great, for by it thou hast committed two evils; thou hast forsaken the way that is good, to tread in forbidden paths. Yet will the man at the gate receive thee, for he has good will for men. Only," said he, "take heed that thou turn not aside again, lest thou perish from the way when his wrath is kindled but a little."[3] Then did Christian address himself to go back, and Evangelist, after he had kissed him, gave him one smile, and bid him Godspeed; so he went on with haste; neither spake he to any man by the way; nor, if any man asked him, would he vouchsafe them an answer. He went like one that was all the while treading on forbidden ground, and could by no means think himself safe till again he was got into the way which he left to follow Mr. Worldly Wiseman's counsel; so in process of time Christian got up to the gate. Now over the gate there was written, "Knock and it shall be opened unto you."[4] He knocked therefore, more than once or twice, saying,

> May I now enter here? Will he within
> Open to sorry me, though I have been
> An undeserving rebel? Then shall I,
> Not fail to sing his lasting praise on high.

At last there came a grave person to the gate, named Good Will, who asked who was there, and whence he came, and what he would have?

CHRISTIAN. "Here is a poor burdened sinner. I come from the City of Destruction, but am going to Mount Zion, that I may be delivered from the wrath to come; I would therefore, sir, since I am informed that by this gate is the way thither, know if you are willing to let me in."

GOOD WILL. "I am willing with all my heart," said he; and with that he opened the gate.[5] ...

Then he began to go forward, but Discretion, Piety, Charity, and Prudence would accompany him down to the foot of the hill. So they went on together, reiterating their former discourses till they came to go down the hill. Then said Christian, "As it was difficult coming up, so (so far as I can see) it is dangerous going down."

[1] *He ... bondwoman* Cf. Galatians 4.21–31.

[2] *as many ... them* Cf. Galatians 3.10.

[3] *perish ... little* From Psalms 2.12.

[4] *Knock ... you* Cf. Matthew 7.8.

[5] [Bunyan's note] The gate will be opened to broken-hearted sinners.

"Yes," said Prudence, "so it is; for it is a hard matter for a man to go down into the Valley of Humiliation, as thou art now, and to catch no slip[1] by the way. Therefore," said they, "are we come out to accompany thee down the hill." So he began to go down, but very warily, yet he caught a slip or two.

Then I saw in my dream that these good companions (when Christian was gone down to the bottom of the hill) gave him a loaf of bread, a bottle of wine, and a cluster of raisins; and then he went on his way.

But now in this Valley of Humiliation poor Christian was hard put to it, for he had gone but a little way before he espied a foul fiend coming over the field to meet him; his name is Apollyon.[2] Then did Christian begin to be afraid and to cast in his mind whether to go back or to stand his ground. But he considered again that he had no armour for his back, and therefore thought that to turn the back to him might give him greater advantage with ease to pierce him with his darts; therefore he resolved to venture and stand his ground. For thought he, had I no more in mine eye, than the saving of my life, 'twould be the best way to stand.

So he went on, and Apollyon met him. Now the monster was hideous to behold; he was clothed with scales like a fish (and they are his pride); he had wings like a dragon, feet like a bear, and out of his belly came fire and smoke, and his mouth was as the mouth of a lion. When he was come up to Christian, he beheld him with a disdainful countenance, and thus began to question with him.

APOLLYON. "Whence come you, and whither you are bound?"

CHRISTIAN. "I come from the City of Destruction, which is the place of all evil, and am going to the City of Zion."

APOLLYON. "By this I perceive thou art one of my subjects, for all that country is mine; and I am the prince and god of it. How is it then that thou hast run away from thy king? Were it not that I hope thou mayest do me more service, I would strike thee now at one blow to the ground."

CHRISTIAN. "I was born indeed in your dominions, but your service was hard, and your wages such as a man could not live on, for the wages of sin is death;[3] therefore when I was come to years, I did as other considerate persons do, look out, if perhaps I might mend myself."

APOLLYON. "There is no prince that will thus lightly lose his subjects; neither will I as yet lose thee. But since thou complainest of thy service and wages, be content to go back; what our country will afford, I do here promise to give thee."

CHRISTIAN. "But I have let myself to another, even to the King of Princes, and how can I with fairness go back with thee?"

APOLLYON. "Thou hast done in this, according to the proverb, changed a bad for a worse. But it is ordinary for those that have professed themselves his servants after a while to give him the slip, and return again to me. Do thou so too, and all shall be well."

CHRISTIAN. "I have given him my faith, and sworn my allegiance to him; how then can I go back from this, and not be hanged as a traitor?"

APOLLYON. "Thou didst the same to me, and yet I am willing to pass by all, if now thou wilt yet turn again, and go back."

CHRISTIAN. "What I promised thee was in my nonage;[4] and besides, I count that the Prince under whose banner now I stand is able to absolve me, yea, and to pardon also what I did as to my compliance with thee. And besides (O thou destroying Apollyon), to speak truth, I like his service, his wages, his servants, his government, his company, and country better than thine; and therefore leave off to persuade me further. I am his servant, and I will follow him."

APOLLYON. "Consider again when thou art in cool blood, what thou art like to meet with in the way that thou goest. Thou knowest that for the most part his servants come to an ill end, because they are transgressors against me and my ways. How many of them have been put to shameful deaths! And besides, thou countest his service better than mine, whereas he never came yet from the place where he is to deliver any that served him out of our hands. But as for me, how many times, as all the world very well knows, have I delivered, either by

[1] *catch no slip* Avoid stumbling or falling.

[2] *his ... Apollyon* Cf. Revelation 9.11.

[3] *wages of sin is death* From Romans 6.23.

[4] *nonage* Youth; immaturity.

power or fraud, those that have faithfully served me from him and his though taken by them; and so I will deliver thee."

CHRISTIAN. "His forbearing at present to deliver them is on purpose to try their love, whether they will cleave to him to the end; and as for the ill end thou sayest they come to, that is most glorious in their account. For, for present deliverance, they do not much expect it; for they stay for their glory, and then they shall have it, when their Prince comes in his and the glory of the angels."

APOLLYON. "Thou hast already been unfaithful in thy service to him, and how dost thou think to receive wages of him?"

CHRISTIAN. "Wherein, O Apollyon, have I been unfaithful to him?"

APOLLYON. "Thou didst faint at first setting out, when thou wast almost choked in the Gulf of Despond. Thou didst attempt wrong ways to be rid of thy burden, whereas thou shouldest have stayed till thy Prince had taken it off. Thou didst sinfully sleep, and lose thy choice thing; thou wast also almost persuaded to go back at the sight of the lions; and when thou talkest of thy journey, and of what thou hast heard, and seen, thou art inwardly desirous of vainglory in all that thou sayest or doest."

CHRISTIAN. "All this is true, and much more, which thou hast left out; but the Prince whom I serve and honour is merciful, and ready to forgive. But besides, these infirmities possessed me in thy country, for there I sucked them in, and I have groaned under them, been sorry for them, and have obtained pardon of my Prince."

APOLLYON. Then Apollyon broke out into a grievous rage, saying, "I am an enemy of this Prince. I hate his person, his laws, and people. I am come out on purpose to withstand thee."

CHRISTIAN. "Apollyon, beware what you do, for I am in the King's highway, the way of holiness; therefore take heed to yourself."

APOLLYON. Then Apollyon straddled quite over the whole breadth of the way, and said, "I am void of fear in this matter; prepare thyself to die, for I swear by my infernal den that thou shalt go no further. Here will I spill thy soul." And with that he threw a flaming dart at his breast; but Christian had a shield in his hand, with which he caught it, and so prevented the danger of that. Then did Christian draw, for he saw 'twas time to bestir him; and Apollyon as fast made at him, throwing darts as thick as hail, by the which, notwithstanding all that Christian could do to avoid it, Apollyon wounded him in his head, his hand and foot;[1] this made Christian give a little back. Apollyon therefore followed his work amain,[2] and Christian again took courage and resisted as manfully as he could. This sore combat lasted for above half a day, even till Christian was almost quite spent. For you must know that Christian, by reason of his wounds, must needs grow weaker and weaker.

Then Apollyon, espying his opportunity, began to gather up close to Christian, and wrestling with him, gave him a dreadful fall; and with that Christian's sword flew out of his hand. Then said Apollyon, "I am sure of thee now," and with that, he had almost pressed him to death, so that Christian began to despair of life. But as God would have it, while Apollyon was fetching of[3] his last blow, thereby to make a full end of this good man, Christian nimbly reached out his hand for his sword and caught it, saying, "Rejoice not against me, O mine enemy! When I fall, I shall arise";[4] and with that, gave him a deadly thrust, which made him give back, as one that had received his mortal wound. Christian, perceiving that, made at him again, saying, "Nay, in all these things we are more than conquerors through him that loved us."[5] And with that, Apollyon spread forth his dragon's wings and sped him away, that Christian saw him no more.

In this combat no man can imagine, unless he had seen and heard as I did, what yelling and hideous roaring Apollyon made all the time of the fight; he spake like a dragon, and on the other side, what sighs and groans brast[6] from Christian's heart. I never saw him all the while give so much as one pleasant look, till he perceived he had wounded Apollyon with his two-edged

[1] [Bunyan's note] Christian wounded in his understanding, faith, and conversation.

[2] *amain* Vigorously.

[3] *fetching of* Dealing.

[4] *Rejoice ... arise* From Micah 7.8.

[5] *Nay ... us* From Romans 8.37.

[6] *brast* Burst.

sword; then indeed he did smile, and look upward; but 'twas the dreadfulest sight that ever I saw.…

Then I saw in my dream that when they[1] were got out of the wilderness, they presently saw a town before them, and the name of that Town is Vanity; and at the town there is a fair kept called Vanity Fair. It is kept all the year long; it beareth the name of Vanity Fair, because the town where 'tis kept is lighter than vanity, and also because all that is there sold or that cometh thither is Vanity. As is the saying of the wise, "All that cometh is vanity."[2]

This fair is no new erected business, but a thing of ancient standing; I will show you the original of it.

Almost five thousand years agone,[3] there were pilgrims walking to the Celestial City, as these two honest persons are; and Beelzebub, Apollyon, and Legion, with their companions, perceiving by the path that the pilgrims made that their way to the city lay through this town of Vanity, they contrived here to set up a fair, a fair wherein should be sold of all sorts of vanity and that it should last all the year long. Therefore at this fair are all such merchandise sold, as houses, lands, trades, places, honours, preferments, titles, countries, kingdoms, lusts, pleasures, and delights of all sorts, as whores, bawds, wives, husbands, children, masters, servants, lives, blood, bodies, souls, silver, gold, pearls, precious stones, and what not.

And, moreover, at this fair there is at all times to be seen jugglings, cheats, games, plays, fools, apes, knaves, and rogues, and that of all sorts.

Here are to be seen, too, and that for nothing, thefts, murders, adulteries, false swearers, and that of a blood-red colour.

And as in other fairs of less moment, there are the several rows and streets under their proper names, where such and such wares are vended. So here likewise, you have the proper places, rows, streets *(viz.*[4] countries and kingdoms), where the wares of this fair are soonest to be found. Here is the Britain Row, the French Row, the Italian Row, the Spanish Row, the German Row, where several sorts of vanities are to be sold. But as in other fairs, some one commodity is as the chief of all the fair, so the ware of Rome and her merchandise is greatly promoted in this fair. Only our English nation, with some others, have taken a dislike thereat.

Now, as I said, the way to the Celestial City lies just through this town, where this lusty fair is kept, and he that will go to the city, and yet not go through this town, must needs "go out of the world."[5] The Prince of Princes himself, when here, went through this town to his own country and that upon a fair day, too. Yea, and as I think it was Beelzebub, the chief lord of this fair, that invited him to buy of his vanities; yea, would have made him lord of the fair would he but have done him reverence as he went through the town. Yea, because he was such a person of honour, Beelzebub had him from street to street and showed him all the kingdoms of the world in a little time that he might, if possible, allure that Blessed One to cheapen[6] and buy some of his vanities.[7] But he had no mind to the merchandise and therefore left the town, without laying out so much as one farthing upon these vanities. This fair therefore is an ancient thing, of long standing, and a very great fair.

Now these pilgrims, as I said, must needs go through this fair. Well, so they did, but behold, even as they entered into the fair, all the people in the fair were moved and the town itself as it were in a hubbub about them, and that for several reasons; for,

First, the pilgrims were clothed with such kind of raiment as was diverse from the raiment of any that traded in that fair. The people therefore of the fair made a great gazing upon them. Some said they were fools, some they were bedlams,[8] and some they are outlandish[9] men.

Secondly, and as they wondered at their apparel, so they did likewise at their speech, for few could understand what they said. They naturally spoke the language of Canaan, but they that kept the fair were the men of

[1] *they* Christian and his fellow pilgrim, Faithful.

[2] *"All … vanity."* Cf. Ecclesiastes 11.8.

[3] *agone* Ago.

[4] *viz.* I.e., *videlicet* (Latin): that is to say.

[5] *go out of the world* From 1 Corinthians 5.10.

[6] *cheapen* Bargain for.

[7] *Yea … vanities* Cf. Matthew 4.8–9; Luke 4.5–7.

[8] *bedlams* The mentally ill, especially those discharged and licensed to beg; the word is a corruption of Bethlehem, after the Hospital of St. Mary of Bethlehem in London, an asylum for the mentally ill.

[9] *outlandish* Foreign, and hence exotic or bizarre in appearance.

this world. So that from one end of the fair to the other, they seemed barbarians[1] each to the other.

Thirdly, but that which did not a little amuse[2] the merchandisers was that these pilgrims set very light by[3] all their wares; they cared not so much as to look upon them, and if they called upon them to buy, they would put their fingers in their ears and cry, "Turn away mine eyes from beholding vanity,"[4] and look upwards, signifying that their trade and traffic was in heaven.

One chanced mockingly, beholding the carriages of the men, to say unto them, "What will ye buy?" But they, looking gravely upon him, said, "We buy the truth."[5] At that, there was an occasion taken to despise the men the more; some mocking, some taunting, some speaking reproachfully, and some calling upon others to smite them. At last things came to an hubbub, and great stir in the fair, insomuch that all order was confounded. Now was word presently brought to the great one of the fair, who quickly came down and deputed some of his most trusty friends to take these men into examination,[6] about whom the fair was almost overturned. So the men were brought to examination; and they that sat upon them, asked them whence they came, whither they went and what they did there in such an unusual garb? The men told them that they were pilgrims and strangers in the world and that they were going to their own country, which was the heavenly Jerusalem, and that they had given none[7] occasion to the men of the town, nor yet to the merchandisers, thus to abuse them and to let[8] them in their journey. Except it was, for that, when one asked them what they would buy, they said they would buy the truth. But they that were appointed to examine them did not believe them to be any other than bedlams and mad, or else such as came to put all things into a confusion in the fair. Therefore they took them and beat them and besmeared them with dirt, and then put them into the cage, that they might be made a spectacle to all the men of the fair. There therefore they lay, for some time, and were made the objects of any man's sport, or malice, or revenge. The great one of the fair laughing still at all that befell them. But the men being patient and not rendering railing[9] for railing, but contrariwise blessing and giving good words for bad and kindness for injuries done, some men in the fair that were more observing and less prejudiced than the rest began to check and blame the baser sort for their continual abuses done by them to the men. They therefore in angry manner let fly at them again, counting them as bad as the men in the cage, and telling them that they seemed confederates, and should be made partakers of their misfortunes. The other replied that for aught[10] they could see, the men were quiet and sober and intended nobody any harm, and that there were many that traded in their fair that were more worthy to be put into the cage, yea, and pillory, too, than were the men that they had abused. Thus, after divers[11] words had passed on both sides (the men behaving themselves all the while very wisely, and soberly before them) they fell to some blows among themselves and did harm one to another. Then were these two poor men brought before their examiners again, and there charged as being guilty of the late hubbub that had been in the fair. So they beat them pitifully, and hanged irons upon them, and led them in chains up and down the fair, for an example and a terror to others, lest any should further speak in their behalf or join themselves unto them. But Christian and Faithful behaved themselves yet more wisely and received the ignominy and shame that was cast upon them with so much meekness and patience that it won to their side (though but few in comparison of the rest) several of the men in the fair. This put the other party yet into a greater rage, insomuch that they concluded[12] the death of these two men. Wherefore they threatened that the cage nor irons should serve their turn, but that they should die, for the abuse they had done and for deluding the men of the fair.

[1] *barbarians* Foreigners.

[2] *amuse* Astonish.

[3] *set very light by* Gave scant regard to.

[4] *Turn ... vanity* From Psalms 119.37.

[5] *buy the truth* From Proverbs 23.23.

[6] *examination* Trial; inquisition.

[7] *none* No.

[8] *let* Hinder.

[9] *railing* Abuse.

[10] *aught* Anything.

[11] *divers* Various; sundry.

[12] *concluded* Decided in favor of.

Then were they remanded to the cage again, until further order should be taken with them. So they put them in and made their feet fast in the stocks.

Here also they called again to mind what they had heard from their faithful friend Evangelist, and was the more confirmed in their way and sufferings by what he told them would happen to them. They also now comforted each other that whose lot it was to suffer, even he should have the best on't;[1] therefore each man secretly wished that he might have that preferment, but committing themselves to the all-wise dispose[2] of him that ruleth all things, with much content they abode[3] in the condition in which they were, until they should be otherwise disposed of.

Then a convenient time being appointed, they brought them forth to their trial in order to their condemnation. When the time was come, they were brought before their enemies and arraigned; the judge's name was Lord Hategood. Their indictment was one and the same in substance, though somewhat varying in form; the contents whereof was this:

"That they were enemies to and disturbers of their trade; that they had made commotions and divisions in the town, and had won a party to their own most dangerous opinions, in contempt of the law of their prince."

Then Faithful began to answer that he had only set himself against that which had set itself against him that is higher than the highest. And, said he, "As for disturbance, I make none, being myself a man of peace; the party that were won to us were won by beholding our truth and innocence, and they are only turned from the worse to the better. And as to the king you talk of, since he is Beelzebub, the enemy of our Lord, I defy him and all his angels."

Then proclamation was made that they that had ought to say for their lord the king against the prisoner at the bar should forthwith appear and give in their evidence. So there came in three witnesses, to wit, Envy, Superstition, and Pickthank. They were then asked if they knew the prisoner at the bar and what they had to say for their lord the king against him.

Then stood forth Envy, and said to this effect, "My Lord, I have known this man a long time and will attest upon my oath before this honourable bench that he is—"

JUDGE. "Hold, give him his oath." So they swore him. Then he said, "My Lord, this man, notwithstanding his plausible name, is one of the vilest men in our country. He neither regardeth prince nor people, law nor custom, but doth all that he can to possess all men with certain of his disloyal notions, which he in the general calls principles of faith and holiness. And in particular, I heard him once myself affirm that Christianity and the customs of our town of Vanity were diametrically opposite and could not be reconciled. By which saying, my Lord, he doth at once not only condemn all our laudable doings, but us in the doing of them."

JUDGE. Then did the judge say to him, "Hast thou any more to say?"

ENVY. "My Lord, I could say much more, only I would not be tedious to the court. Yet if need be, when the other gentlemen have given in their evidence, rather than anything shall be wanting that will dispatch him, I will enlarge my testimony against him." So he was bid stand by. Then they called Superstition and bid him look upon the prisoner; they also asked what he could say for their lord the king against him. Then they swore him; so he began.

SUPERSTITION. "My Lord, I have no great acquaintance with this man, nor do I desire to have further knowledge of him. However this I know, that he is a very pestilent fellow, from some discourse that the other day I had with him in this town; for then talking with him, I heard him say that our religion was naught and such by which a man could by no means please God. Which sayings of his, my Lord, your Lordship very well knows what necessarily thence will follow, to wit, that we still do worship in vain, are yet in our sins, and finally shall be damned; and this is that which I have to say."

Then was Pickthank sworn and bid say what he knew, in behalf of their lord the king against the prisoner at the bar.

PICKTHANK. "My Lord, and you gentlemen all, this fellow I have known of a long time and have heard him speak things that ought not to be spoke. For he hath railed on our noble Prince Beelzebub and hath spoke

[1] *have the best on't* Be favored; have the advantage.

[2] *dispose* Disposition; control.

[3] *abode* Abided.

contemptibly of his honourable friends, whose names are the Lord Old Man, the Lord Carnal Delight, the Lord Luxurious, the Lord Desire of Vainglory, my old Lord Lechery, Sir Having Greedy, with all the rest of our nobility;[1] and he hath said, moreover, that if all men were of his mind, if possible, there is not one of these noblemen should have any longer a being in this town. Besides, he hath not been afraid to rail on you, my Lord, who are now appointed to be his judge, calling you an ungodly villain, with many other such like vilifying terms, with which he hath bespattered most of the gentry of our town." When this Pickthank had told his tale, the judge directed his speech to the prisoner at the bar, saying, "Thou renegade; heretic, and traitor, hast thou heard what these honest gentlemen have witnessed against thee."

FAITHFUL. "May I speak a few words in my own defence?"

JUDGE. "Sirrah, sirrah, thou deservest to live no longer, but to be slain immediately upon the place; yet that all men may see our gentleness towards thee, let us hear what thou hast to say."

FAITHFUL. "1. I say then in answer to what Mr. Envy hath spoken, I never said aught but this: that what rule or laws or custom or people were flat against the Word of God are diametrically opposite to Christianity. If I have said amiss in this, convince me of my error, and I am ready here before you to make my recantation.

"2. As to the second, to wit, Mr. Superstition, and his charge against me, I said only this: that in the worship of God there is required a divine faith; but there can be no divine faith without a divine revelation of the will of God. Therefore whatever is thrust into the worship of God that is not agreeable to divine revelation cannot be done but by a human faith, which faith will not profit to eternal life.

"3. As to what Mr. Pickthank hath said, I say (avoiding terms, as that I am said to rail, and the like) that the prince of this town, with all the rabblement his attendants, by this gentleman named, are more fit for a being in hell than in this town and country. And so the Lord have mercy upon me."

Then the judge called to the jury (who all this while stood by, to hear and observe), "Gentlemen of the jury, you see this man about whom so great an uproar hath been made in this town. You have also heard what these worthy gentlemen have witnessed against him; also you have heard his reply and confession. It lieth now in your breasts to hang him or save his life. But yet I think meet[2] to instruct you into our law.

"There was an act made in the days of Pharaoh the Great, servant to our prince, that lest those of a contrary religion should multiply and grow too strong for him, their males should be thrown into the river.[3] There was also an act made in the days of Nebuchadnezzar the Great,[4] another of his servants, that whoever would not fall down and worship his golden image should be thrown into a fiery furnace. There was also an act made in the days of Darius[5] that who so, for some time, called upon any god but his should be cast into the lion's den. Now the substance of these laws this rebel has broken, not only in thought (which is not to be borne[6]), but also in word and deed, which must therefore needs be intolerable.

"For that of Pharaoh, his law was made upon a supposition to prevent mischief, no crime being yet apparent; but here is a crime apparent. For the second and third, you see he disputeth against our religion, and for the treason he hath confessed, he deserveth to die the death."

Then went the jury out, whose names were Mr. Blind-man, Mr. No-good, Mr. Malice, Mr. Love-lust, Mr. Live-loose, Mr. Heady, Mr. High-mind, Mr. Enmity, Mr. Liar, Mr. Cruelty, Mr. Hate-light, and Mr. Implacable, who everyone gave in his private verdict against him among themselves, and afterwards unanimously concluded to bring him in guilty before the judge. And first Mr. Blind-man, the foreman, said, "I see clearly that this man is an heretic." Then said Mr. No-good, "Away with such a fellow from the earth." "Ay," said Mr. Malice, "for I hate the very looks of him." Then said Mr. Love-lust, "I could never endure

[1] [Bunyan's note] Sins are all Lords, and great ones.

[2] *meet* Appropriate.

[3] *act ... river* Cf. Exodus 1.22.

[4] *Nebuchadnezzar the Great* King of Babylon (605–562 BCE) during the Jewish exile there; as to the law referred to here, cf. Daniel 3.11.

[5] *Darius* Darius the Great, King of Persia 521–485 BCE; as to the law referred to here, cf. Daniel 6.7.

[6] *borne* Tolerated.

him." "Nor I," said Mr. Live-loose, "for he would always be condemning my way." "Hang him, hang him," said Mr. Heady. "A sorry scrub,"[1] said Mr. High-mind. "My heart riseth against him," said Mr. Enmity. "He is a rogue," said Mr. Liar. "Hanging is too good for him," said Mr. Cruelty. "Let's dispatch him out of the way," said Mr. Hate-light. Then said Mr. Implacable, "Might I have all the world given me, I could not be reconciled to him; therefore let us forthwith bring him in guilty of death." And so they did; therefore he was presently condemned, to be had from the place where he was to the place from whence he came, and there to be put to the most cruel death that could be invented.

They therefore brought him out to do with him according to their law; and first they scourged him, then they buffeted him, then they lanced his flesh with knives; after that they stoned him with stones, then pricked him with their swords, and last of all they burned him to ashes at the stake. Thus came Faithful to his end. Now, I saw that there stood behind the multitude a chariot and a couple of horses, waiting for Faithful, who (so soon as his adversaries had dispatched him) was taken up into it, and straightway[2] was carried up through the clouds, with sound of trumpet, the nearest way to the Celestial Gate. But as for Christian, he had some respite, and was remanded back to prison; so he there remained for a space. But he that overrules all things, having the power of their rage in his own hand, so wrought it about[3] that Christian for that time escaped them, and went his way.

And as he went he sang:

Well, Faithful, thou hast faithfully professed
Unto thy Lord. With him thou shalt be blest,
When faithless ones, with all their vain delights,
Are crying out under their hellish plights,
Sing, Faithful, sing; and let thy name survive;
For though they killed thee, thou art yet alive.

Now I saw in my dream that Christian went not forth alone, for there was one whose name was Hopeful (being made so by the beholding of Christian and Faithful in their words and behaviour, in their sufferings at the fair) who joined himself unto him, and entering into a brotherly covenant, told him that he would be his companion. Thus one died to make testimony to the truth, and another rises out of his ashes to be a companion with Christian. This Hopeful also told Christian that there were many more of the men in the fair that would take their time and follow after....

I saw then that they went on their way to a pleasant river, which David the King called the "river of God"[4] but John, "The river of the water of life."[5] Now their way lay just upon the bank of the river. Here therefore Christian and his companion walked with great delight; they drank also of the water of the river, which was pleasant and enlivening to their weary spirits. Besides, on the banks of this river, on either side, were green trees that bore all manner of fruit, and the leaves of the trees were good for medicine; with the fruit of these trees they were also much delighted, and the leaves they eat to prevent surfeits[6] and other diseases that are incident to those that heat their blood by travels. On either side of the river was also a meadow, curiously beautified with lilies. And it was green all the year long. In this meadow they lay down and slept, for here they might lie down safely. When they awoke, they gathered again of the fruit of the trees, and drank again of the water of the river, and then lay down again to sleep. Thus they did several days and nights. Then they sang,

Behold ye how these crystal streams do glide
(To comfort pilgrims) by the highway side;
The meadows green, besides their fragrant smell,
Yield dainties for them, and he that can tell
What pleasant fruit, yea, leaves, these trees do yield,
Will soon sell all that he may buy this field.

So when they were disposed to go on (for they were not, as yet, at their journey's end) they ate and drank and departed.

[1] *scrub* Mean, insignificant fellow.

[2] *straightway* Immediately.

[3] *wrought it about* Arranged it.

[4] *river of God* From Psalms 65.9.

[5] *The ... life* Cf. Revelations 22.1.

[6] *surfeits* Illnesses, especially those caused by intemperance or overeating.

Now I beheld in my dream that they had not journeyed far, but the river and the way, for a time, parted. At which they were not a little sorry, yet they durst not go out of the way. Now the way from the river was rough, and their feet tender by reason of their travels. So the soul of the pilgrims was much discouraged, because of the way.[1] Wherefore still as they went on, they wished for better way. Now a little before them there was on the left hand of the road a meadow and a stile[2] to go over into it, and that meadow is called By-path Meadow. Then said Christian to his fellow, "If this meadow lieth along by our wayside, let's go over into it."[3] Then he went to the stile to see, and behold a path lay along by the way on the other side of the fence. "'Tis according to my wish," said Christian. "Here is the easiest going; come, good Hopeful, and let us go over."

HOPEFUL. "But how if this path should lead us out of the way?"

CHRISTIAN. "That's not like,"[4] said the other. "Look, doth it not go along by the wayside?" So Hopeful, being persuaded by his fellow, went after him over the stile.[5] When they were gone over and were got into the path, they found it very easy for their feet; and withal,[6] they, looking before them, espied a man walking as they did (and his name was Vain Confidence). So they called after him, and asked him whither that way led. He said, "To the Celestial Gate." "Look," said Christian, "did not I tell you so? By this you may see we are right." So they followed, and he went before them. But behold the night came on, and it grew very dark; so that they that were behind lost the sight of him that went before.[7]

He therefore that went before (Vain Confidence by name), not seeing the way before him, fell into a deep pit, which was on purpose there made by the prince of those grounds to catch vainglorious fools withal, and was dashed in pieces with his fall.

Now Christian and his fellow heard him fall. So they called to know the matter, but there was none to answer, only they heard a groaning. Then said Hopeful, "Where are we now?" Then was his fellow silent, as mistrusting that he had led him out of the way. And now it began to rain, and thunder, and lighten in a very dreadful manner, and the water rose amain.

Then Hopeful groaned in himself, saying, "Oh that I had kept on my way!"

CHRISTIAN. "Who could have thought that this path should have led us out of the way?"

HOPEFUL. "I was afraid on't at very first, and therefore gave you that gentle caution. I would have spoke plainer, but that you are older than I."

CHRISTIAN. "Good brother, be not offended. I am sorry I have brought thee out of the way, and that I have put thee into such eminent[8] danger; pray, my brother, forgive me; I did not do it of an evil intent."

HOPEFUL. "Be comforted, my brother, for I forgive thee, and believe, too, that this shall be for our good."

CHRISTIAN. "I am glad I have with me a merciful brother. But we must not stand thus; let's try to go back again."

HOPEFUL. "But, good brother, let me go before."

CHRISTIAN. "No, if you please let me go first, that if there be any danger, I may be first therein, because by my means we are both gone out of the way."

HOPEFUL. "No," said Hopeful, "you shall not go first, for your mind, being troubled, may lead you out of the way again." Then for their encouragement, they heard the voice of one, saying, "Let thine heart be towards the highway, even the way that thou wentest: turn again."[9] But by this time the waters were greatly risen, by reason of which the way of going back was very dangerous. (Then I thought that it is easier going out of the way when we are in than going in when we are out.) Yet they adventured to go back; but it was so dark, and the flood was so high, that in their going back they had like to have been drowned nine or ten times.

[1] *So ... way* Cf. Numbers 21.4.

[2] *stile* Set of steps or rungs designed to allow passage over a fence or through a hedge to people while barring access to livestock.

[3] [Bunyan's note] One temptation does make way for another.

[4] *like* Likely.

[5] [Bunyan's note] Strong Christians may lead weak ones out of the way.

[6] *withal* Also; at the same time.

[7] [Bunyan's note] See what it is too suddenly to fall in with strangers.

[8] *eminent* Remarkable.

[9] *thine ... again* From Jeremiah 31.21.

Neither could they, with all the skill they had, get again to the stile that night. Wherefore, at last, lighting under a little shelter, they sat down there till the day brake; but being weary, they fell asleep. Now there was not far from the place where they lay a castle, called Doubting Castle, the owner whereof was Giant Despair, and it was in his grounds they now were sleeping; wherefore he getting up in the morning early, and walking up and down in his fields, caught Christian and Hopeful asleep in his grounds. Then with a grim and surly voice he bid them awake, and asked them whence they were and what they did in his grounds? They told him they were pilgrims and that they had lost their way. Then said the giant, "You have this night trespassed on me, by trampling in and lying on my grounds, and therefore you must go along with me." So they were forced to go, because he was stronger than they. They also had but little to say, for they knew themselves in a fault. The giant therefore drove them before him and put them into his castle, into a very dark dungeon, nasty and stinking to the spirit of these two men. Here then they lay from Wednesday morning till Saturday night, without one bit of bread or drop of drink, or any light, or any to ask how they did. They were therefore here in evil case and were far from friends and acquaintance. Now in this place, Christian had double sorrow, because 'twas through his unadvised haste that they were brought into this distress.

Now Giant Despair had a wife, and her name was Diffidence.[1] So when he was gone to bed, he told his wife what he had done, to wit, that he had taken a couple of prisoners and cast them into his dungeon for trespassing on his grounds. Then he asked her also what he had best to do further to them. So she asked him what they were, whence they came, and whither they were bound. And he told her. Then she counselled him that when he arose in the morning, he should beat them without mercy. So when he arose, he getteth him a grievous crabtree cudgel and goes down into the dungeon to them; and there, first falls to rating[2] of them as if they were dogs, although they gave him never a word of distaste; then he falls upon them, and beats them fearfully, in such sort, that they were not able to help themselves, or to turn them upon the floor. This done, he withdraws and leaves them, there to condole their misery and to mourn under their distress. So all that day they spent the time in nothing but sighs and bitter lamentations. The next night she talking with her husband about them further, and understanding that they were yet alive, did advise him to counsel them to make away themselves.[3] So when morning was come, he goes to them in a surly manner, as before, and perceiving them to be very sore with the stripes[4] that he had given them the day before, he told them that since they were never like to come out of that place, their only way would be forthwith to make an end of themselves, either with knife, halter[5] or poison. "For why," said he, "should you choose life, seeing it is attended with so much bitterness." But they desired him to let them go; with that he looked ugly upon them, and rushing to them, had doubtless made an end of them himself, but that he fell into one of his fits (for he sometimes in sunshine weather fell into fits) and lost (for a time) the use of his hand. Wherefore he withdrew and left them (as before) to consider what to do. Then did the prisoners consult between themselves, whether 'twas best to take his counsel or no, and thus they began to discourse.

CHRISTIAN. "Brother," said Christian, "what shall we do? The life that we now live is miserable. For my part, I know not whether is best to live thus or to die out of hand? My soul chooseth strangling rather than life,[6] and the grave is more easy for me than this dungeon. Shall we be ruled by the giant?"

HOPEFUL. "Indeed our present condition is dreadful, and death would be far more welcome to me than thus forever to abide. But yet let us consider; the Lord of the country to which we are going hath said thou shalt do no murder, no not to another man's person; much more then are we forbidden to take his counsel to kill ourselves. Besides, he that kills another can but commit murder upon his body; but for one to kill himself is to kill body and soul at once. And moreover, my brother, thou talkest of ease in the grave, but hast thou forgotten

[1] *Diffidence* Lack of faith.

[2] *rating* Angry condemnation or reprimand.

[3] *make away themselves* Commit suicide.

[4] *stripes* I.e., cuts made by the giant's beating.

[5] *halter* Rope with noose for hanging a person.

[6] *My … life* From Job 7.15.

the hell whither, for certain, the murderers go? For no murderer hath eternal life, &c. And, let us consider again, that all the law is not in the hand of Giant Despair. Others, so far as I can understand, have been taken by him, as well as we, and yet have escaped out of his hand. Who knows, but that God that made the world may cause that Giant Despair may die, or that, at some time or other, he may forget to lock us in; or, but he may in short time have another of his fits before us and may lose the use of his limbs, and if ever that should come to pass again, for my part, I am resolved to pluck up the heart of a man and to try my utmost to get from under his hand. I was a fool that I did not try to do it before. But, however, my brother, let's be patient, and endure awhile. The time may come that may give us a happy release, but let us not be our own murderers." With these words, Hopeful at present did moderate the mind of his brother; so they continued together (in the dark) that day, in their sad and doleful condition.

Well, towards evening the giant goes down into the dungeon again to see if his prisoners had taken his counsel; but when he came there, he found them alive, and, truly, alive was all. For now, what for want of bread and water, and by reason of the wounds they received when he beat them, they could do little but breathe. But, I say, he found them alive, at which he fell into a grievous rage and told them that seeing they had disobeyed his counsel, it should be worse with them than if they had never been born.

At this they trembled greatly, and I think that Christian fell into a swoon; but coming a little to himself again, they renewed their discourse about the giant's counsel, and whether yet they had best to take it or no. Now Christian again seemed to be for doing it, but Hopeful made his second reply as followeth.

HOPEFUL. "My brother," said he, "rememberest thou not how valiant thou hast been heretofore; Apollyon could not crush thee, nor could all that thou didst hear or see or feel in the Valley of the Shadow of Death; what hardship, terror, and amazement hast thou already gone through, and art thou now nothing but fear? Thou seest that I am in the dungeon with thee, a far weaker man by nature than thou art. Also this giant has wounded me as well as thee, and hath also cut off the bread and water from my mouth, and with thee I mourn without the light. But let's exercise a little more patience. Remember how thou playedst the man at Vanity Fair, and wast neither afraid of the chain nor cage, nor yet of bloody death. Wherefore let us (at least to avoid the shame that becomes not a Christian to be found in) bear up with patience as well as we can."

Now night being come again, and the giant and his wife being in bed, she asked him concerning the prisoners and if they had taken his counsel. To which he replied, "They are sturdy rogues. They choose rather to bear all hardship than to make away themselves." Then said she, "Take them into the castle-yard tomorrow, and show them the bones and skulls of those that thou hast already dispatched; and make them believe, e're a week comes to an end, thou also wilt tear them in pieces as thou hast done their fellows before them."

So when the morning was come, the giant goes to them again, and takes them into the castle-yard, and shows them, as his wife had bidden him. "These," said he, "were pilgrims as you are, once, and they trespassed in my grounds, as you have done; and when I thought fit, I tore them in pieces; and so within ten days I will do you. Go get you down to your den again." And with that he beat them all the way thither. They lay therefore all day on Saturday in a lamentable case, as before. Now when night was come, and when Mrs. Diffidence and her husband, the giant, were got to bed, they began to renew their discourse of their prisoners, and withal, the old giant wondered that he could neither by his blows, nor counsel, bring them to an end. And with that his wife replied, "I fear," said she, "that they live in hope that some will come to relieve them or that they have pick-locks about them, by the means of which they hope to escape." "And sayest thou so, my dear," said the giant, "I will therefore search them in the morning."

Well, on Saturday about midnight they began to pray and continued in prayer till almost break of day.

Now a little before it was day, good Christian, as one half amazed, broke out in this passionate speech, "What a fool," quoth he, "am I, thus to lie in a stinking dungeon, when I may as well walk at liberty? I have a key in my bosom,[1] called Promise, that will (I am persuaded) open any lock in Doubting Castle." Then said Hopeful, "That's good news; good brother, pluck it out of thy

[1] *bosom* Shirt-front, or front pocket.

bosom and try." Then Christian pulled it out of his bosom, and began to try at the dungeon door, whose bolt (as he turned the key) gave back, and the door flew open with ease, and Christian and Hopeful both came out. Then he went to the outward door that leads into the castle-yard, and with his key opened the door also. After he went to the iron gate, for that must be opened, too, but that lock went damnable hard; yet the key did open it. Then they thrust open the gate to make their escape with speed, but that gate, as it opened, made such a creaking that it waked Giant Despair, who, hastily rising to pursue his prisoners, felt his limbs to fail, for his fits took him again, so that he could by no means go after them. Then they went on and came to the King's highway again, and so were safe, because they were out of his jurisdiction....

Now I saw in my dream that by this time the pilgrims were got over the Enchanted Ground, and entering into the country of Beulah,[1] whose air was very sweet and pleasant. The way lying directly through it, they solaced themselves there for a season. Yet, here they heard continually the singing of birds, and saw every day the flowers appear in the earth, and heard the voice of the turtle[2] in the land.[3] In this country the sun shineth night and day; wherefore this was beyond the Valley of the Shadow of Death, and also out of the reach of Giant Despair; neither could they from this place so much as see Doubting Castle. Here they were within sight of the city they were going to. Also here met them some of the inhabitants[4] thereof. For in this land the Shining Ones commonly walked, because it was upon the borders of heaven. In this land also the contract between the bride and the bridegroom[5] was renewed. Yea, here, "as the bridegroom rejoiceth over the bride, so did their god rejoice over them."[6] Here they had no want of corn[7] and wine; for in this place they met with abundance of what they had sought for in all their pilgrimage. Here they heard voices from out of the city, loud voices, saying, "Say ye to the daughter of Zion, behold thy salvation cometh; behold his reward is with him."[8] Here all the inhabitants of the country called them, "The holy people, the redeemed of the Lord, sought out, &c."[9]

Now as they walked in this land they had more rejoicing than in parts more remote from the kingdom to which they were bound; and drawing near to the city, they had yet a more perfect view thereof. It was builded of pearls and precious stones. Also the street thereof was paved with gold, so that by reason of the natural glory of the city and the reflection of the sunbeams upon it, Christian with desire fell sick. Hopeful also had a fit or two of the same disease. Wherefore here they lay by it awhile, crying out because of their pangs, "If you see my beloved, tell him that I am sick of love."[10]

But being a little strengthened and better able to bear their sickness, they walked on their way, and came yet nearer and nearer where were orchards, vineyards, and gardens, and their gates opened into the highway. Now as they came up to these places, behold the gardener stood in the way, to whom the pilgrims said, "Whose goodly vineyards and gardens are these?" He answered, "They are the King's, and are planted here for his own delights and also for the solace of pilgrims." So the gardener had them into the vineyards, and bid them refresh themselves with the dainties. He also showed them there the King's walks and the arbours where he delighted to be. And here they tarried and slept.

Now I beheld in my dream that they talked more in their sleep at this time than ever they did in all their journey; and being in a muse[11] thereabout, the gardener said even to me, "Wherefore musest thou at the matter? It is the nature of the fruit of the grapes of these vineyards to go down so sweetly, as to 'cause the lips of them that are asleep to speak.'"[12]

So I saw that when they awoke, they addressed themselves to go up to the city. But, as I said, the

[1] *Beulah* Cf. Isaiah 62.4.

[2] *turtle* Turtledove.

[3] *singing ... land* Cf. Song of Solomon 2.12.

[4] [Bunyan's note] Angels.

[5] *the bride ... bridegroom* Christ and his Church.

[6] *as ... them* From Isaiah 62.5.

[7] *corn* Grain.

[8] *Say ... him* From Isaiah 62.11.

[9] *The ... &c.* From Isaiah 62.12.

[10] *I am sick of love* From Song of Solomon 5.8.

[11] *muse* Fit of abstraction.

[12] *Wherefore ... speak* Cf. Song of Solomon 1.

reflections of the sun upon the city (for "the city was pure gold")[1] was so extremely glorious, that they could not, as yet, with open face behold it but through an instrument made for that purpose.[2] So I saw that as they went on, there met them two men in raiment that shone like gold, also their faces shone as the light.

These men asked the pilgrims whence they came, and they told them. They also asked them where they had lodged, what difficulties and dangers, what comforts and pleasures they had met in the way, and they told them. Then said the men that met them, "You have but two difficulties more to meet with, and then you are in the city."

Christian then and his companion asked the men to go along with them. So they told them they would. "But," said they, "you must obtain it by your own faith." So I saw in my dream that they went on together till they came within sight of the gate.

Now I further saw that betwixt them and the gate was a river,[3] but there was no bridge to go over. The river was very deep; at the sight therefore of this river, the pilgrims were much astounded, but the men that went with them said, "You must go through, or you cannot come at the gate."

The pilgrims then began to inquire if there was no other way to the gate.[4] To which they answered, "Yes, but there hath not any, save two, to wit, Enoch and Elijah,[5] been permitted to tread that path since the foundation of the world, nor shall until the last trumpet shall sound." The pilgrims then, especially Christian, began to despond in his mind, and looked this way and that, but no way could be found by them by which they might escape the river. Then they asked the men if the waters were all of a depth. They said no, yet they could not help them in that case; for, said they, "You shall find it deeper or shallower, as you believe in the King of the place."[6]

They then addressed themselves to the water; and entering, Christian began to sink, and crying out to his good friend Hopeful, he said, "I sink in deep waters, the billows go over my head, all his waves go over me, Selah."[7]

Then said the other, "Be of good cheer, my brother. I feel the bottom, and it is good." Then said Christian, "Ah, my friend, the sorrows of death have compassed me about.[8] I shall not see the land that flows with milk and honey."[9] And with that, a great darkness and horror fell upon Christian, so that he could not see before him; also here he in great measure lost his senses, so that he could neither remember nor orderly talk of any of those sweet refreshments that he had met with in the way of his pilgrimage. But all the words that he spake still tended to discover that he had horror of mind and hearty fears that he should die in that river, and never obtain entrance in at the gate. Here also, as they that stood by perceived, he was much in the troublesome thoughts of the sins that he had committed, both since and before he began to be a pilgrim. 'Twas also observed that he was troubled with apparitions of hobgoblins and evil spirits. For ever and anon he would intimate so much by words. Hopeful therefore here had much ado to keep his brother's head above water. Yea, sometimes he would be quite gone down, and then ere a while he would rise up again half dead. Hopeful also would endeavour to comfort him, saying, "Brother, I see the gate, and men standing by it to receive us." But Christian would answer. "'Tis you, 'tis you they wait for. You have been Hopeful ever since I knew you." "And so have you," said he to Christian. "Ah, brother," said he, "surely if I was right, he would now arise to help me; but for my sins he hath brought me into the snare, and hath left me." Then said Hopeful, "My brother, you have quite forgot the text, where it's said of the wicked, 'There is no band in their death, but their strength is firm, they are not troubled as other men, neither are

[1] *So ... gold* Cf. Revelation 21.18.

[2] *they ... purpose* Cf. 2 Corinthians 3.18.

[3] [Bunyan's note] Death.

[4] [Bunyan's note] Death is not welcome to nature, though by it we pass out of this world into glory.

[5] *Enoch and Elijah* Cf. Genesis 5.24, Hebrews 11.5, 2 Kings 2.11-12. Both were "translated" alive into heaven, and did not "see death."

[6] [Bunyan's note] Angels help us not comfortably through death.

[7] *the billows ... over me* Cf. Jonah 2.3 and Psalms 42.7; *Selah* Expression of unknown meaning occurring frequently in the Psalms, thought to be a liturgical or musical direction; cf. Psalms 88.7.

[8] *compassed me about* Surrounded me.

[9] *land ... honey* Expression used frequently in the Old Testament to describe the promised land into which the Lord led the Israelites from Egypt; cf., for example, Exodus 3.8.

they plagued like other men.'[1] These troubles and distresses that you go through in these waters are no sign that God hath forsaken you, but are sent to try you, whether you will call to mind that which heretofore you have received of His goodness, and live upon Him in your distresses."

Then I saw in my dream that Christian was as in a muse a while; to whom also Hopeful added this word, "Be of good cheer. Jesus Christ maketh thee whole." And with that, Christian broke out with a loud voice, "Oh, I see him again! And he tells me, 'When thou passest through the waters, I will be with thee, and through the rivers, they shall not overflow thee.'"[2] Then they both took courage, and the enemy was after that as still as a stone, until they were gone over. Christian therefore presently found ground to stand upon; and so it followed that the rest of the river was but shallow. Thus they got over. Now upon the bank of the river, on the other side, they saw the two Shining Men again, who there waited for them. Wherefore being come up out of the river, they saluted them, saying, "We are ministering spirits, sent forth to minister for those that shall be heirs of salvation."[3] Thus they went along towards the gate. Now you must note that the city stood upon a mighty hill, but the pilgrims went up that hill with ease, because they had these two men to lead them up by the arms. Also they had left their mortal garments behind them in the river, for though they went in with them, they came out without them. They therefore went up here with much agility and speed, though the foundation upon which the city was framed was higher than the clouds. They therefore went up through the regions of the air, sweetly talking as they went, being comforted because they safely got over the river and had such glorious companions to attend them....

from THE SECOND PART

Courteous companions, some time since, to tell you my dream that I had of Christian, the pilgrim, and of his dangerous journey toward the Celestial Country, was pleasant to me and profitable to you. I told you then also what I saw concerning his wife and children, and how unwilling they were to go with him on pilgrimage; insomuch that he was forced to go on his progress without them, for he durst not run the danger of that destruction which he feared would come by staying with them in the City of Destruction. Wherefore, as I then showed you, he left them and departed.

Now it hath so happened, through the multiplicity of business, that I have been much hindered and kept back from my wonted[4] travels into those parts whence he went, and so could not till now obtain an opportunity to make further inquiry after whom he left behind, that I might give you an account of them. But having had some concerns that way of late, I went down again thitherward. Now, having taken up my lodgings in a wood about a mile off the place, as I slept I dreamed again.

And as I was in my dream, behold, an aged gentleman came by where I lay; and because he was to go some part of the way that I was travelling, methought I got up and went with him. So as we walked, and as travellers usually do, it was as if we fell into discourse. And our talk happened to be about Christian and his travels. For thus I began with the old man:

"Sir," said I, "what town is that there below that lieth on the left hand of our way?"

Then said Mr. Sagacity, for that was his name, "It is the City of Destruction, a populous place, but possessed with a very ill-conditioned and idle[5] sort of people."

"I thought that was that city," quoth I. "I went once myself through that town, and therefore know that this report you give of it is true."

SAGACITY. "Too true. I wish I could speak truth in speaking better of them that dwell therein."

"Well, sir," quoth I, "then I perceive you to be a well-meaning man, and so one that takes pleasure to hear and tell of that which is good. Pray, did you never hear what happened to a man sometime ago in this town, whose name was Christian, that went on pilgrimage up towards the higher regions?"

[1] *There ... men* Cf. Psalms 73.4–5.

[2] *When ... thee* From Isaiah 43.2.

[3] [Bunyan's note] The angels do wait for them so soon as they are passed out of this world. [Cf. Hebrews 1.14.]

[4] *wonted* Accustomed.

[5] *ill-conditioned* Evil; *idle* Vain, frivolous.

SAGACITY. "Hear of him! Ay, and I also heard of the molestations, troubles, wars, captivities, cries, groans, frights and fears that he met with and had in his journey. Besides, I must tell you, all our country rings of him. There are few houses that have heard of him and his doings, but have[1] sought after and got the records of his pilgrimage. Yea, I think I may say that his hazardous journey has got a many well-wishers to his ways. For though when he was here, he was fool in every man's mouth, yet now he is gone, he is highly commended of all. For 'tis said he lives bravely where he is. Yea, many of them that are resolved never to run his hazards,[2] yet have their mouths water at his gains."

"They may," quoth I, "well think, if they think anything that is true, that he liveth well, where he is. For he now lives at and in the Fountain of Life, and has what he has without labour and sorrow, for there is no grief mixed therewith."

SAGACITY. "Talk! The people talk strangely about him. Some say that he now walks in white,[3] that he has a chain of gold about his neck, that he has a crown of gold, beset with pearls, upon his head. Others say that the Shining Ones, that sometimes showed themselves to him in his journey, are become his companions, and that he is as familiar with them in the place where he is as here one neighbour is with another. Besides, 'tis confidently affirmed concerning him that the King of the place where he is has bestowed upon him already a very rich and pleasant dwelling at court; and that he every day eateth and drinketh, and walketh and talketh with him, and receiveth of the smiles and favours of him that is judge of all there. Moreover, it is expected of some that his Prince, the Lord of that country, will shortly come into these parts, and will know the reason, if they can give any, why his neighbours set so little by him and had him so much in derision when they perceived that he would be a pilgrim. For they say that now he is so in the affections of his Prince, and that his sovereign is so much concerned with the indignities that was cast upon Christian when he became a pilgrim, that he will look upon all as if done unto himself; and no marvel, for 'twas for the love that he had to his Prince that he ventured as he did."

"I dare say," quoth I, "I am glad on't. I am glad for the poor man's sake, for now that he has rest from his labour,[4] and for that he now reapeth the benefit of his tears with joy, and for that he is got beyond the gunshot of his enemies and is out of the reach of them that hate him. I also am glad for that a rumour of these things is noised abroad in this country. Who can tell but that it may work some good effect on some that are left behind? But, pray, sir, while it is fresh in my mind, do you hear anything of his wife and children? Poor hearts, I wonder in my mind what they do?"

SAGACITY. "Who? Christiana and her sons? They are like to do as well as did Christian himself; for though they all played the fool at the first, and would by no means be persuaded by either the tears or entreaties of Christian, yet second thoughts have wrought wonderfully with them. So they have packed up and are also gone after him."

"Better and better," quoth I. "But, what! wife and children and all?"

SAGACITY. "'Tis true, I can give you an account of the matter, for I was upon the spot at the instant and was thoroughly acquainted with the whole affair."

"Then," said I, "a man, it seems, may report it for a truth?"

SAGACITY. "You need not fear to affirm it. I mean that they are all gone on pilgrimage, both the good woman and her four boys. And being we are, as I perceive, going some considerable way together, I will give you an account of the whole of the matter.

"This Christiana (for that was her name from the day that she with her children betook themselves to a pilgrim's life), after her husband was gone over the river, and she could hear of him no more, her thoughts began to work in her mind. First, for that[5] she had lost her husband, and for that the loving bond of that relation was utterly broken betwixt them. For you know," said he to me, "nature can do no less but entertain the living with many a heavy cogitation in the remembrance of the loss of loving relations. This therefore of her husband

[1] *but have* That have not.

[2] *hazards* Risks.

[3] *Some … white* Cf. Revelation 3.4.

[4] *I … labour* Revelation 14.13.

[5] *for that* That.

did cost her many a tear. But this was not all, for Christiana did also begin to consider with herself, whether her unbecoming behaviour towards her husband was not one cause that she saw him no more, and that in such sort he was taken away from her. And upon this, came into her mind by swarms all her unkind, unnatural, and ungodly carriages to her dear friend, which also clogged her conscience and did load her with guilt. She was, moreover, much broken with recalling to remembrance the restless groans, brinish[1] tears, and self-bemoanings of her husband, and how she did harden her heart against all his entreaties, and loving persuasions (of her and her sons) to go with him. Yea, there was not anything that Christian either said to her or did before her, all the while that his burden did hang on his back, but it returned upon her like a flash of lightning and rent the caul of her heart in sunder;[2] specially that bitter outcry of his, 'What shall I do to be saved?' did ring in her ears most dolefully.

"Then said she to her children, 'Sons, we are all undone. I have sinned away your father, and he is gone. He would have had us with him, but I would not go myself. I also have hindered you of life.' With that, the boys fell all into tears and cried out to go after their father. 'Oh,' said Christiana, 'that it had been but our lot to go with him, then had it fared well with us beyond what 'tis like to do now. For though I formerly foolishly imagined, concerning the troubles of your father, that they proceeded of a foolish fancy that he had, or for that he was overrun with melancholy humours;[3] yet now 'twill not out of my mind but that they sprang from another cause, to wit, for that the light of light was given him, by, the help of which, as I perceive, he has escaped the snares of death.' Then they all wept again, and cried out, 'Oh, woe worth[4] the day.'

"The next night Christiana had a dream, and behold, she saw as if a broad parchment was opened before her, in which were recorded the sum of her ways, and the times, as she thought, looked very black upon her. Then she cried out aloud in her sleep, 'Lord have mercy upon me, a sinner,' and the little children heard her.

"After this she thought she saw two very ill-favoured[5] ones standing by her bedside, and saying, 'What shall we do with this woman? For she cries out for mercy waking and sleeping. If she be suffered to go on as she begins, we shall lose her as we have lost her husband. Wherefore we must, by one way or other, seek to take her off from the thoughts of what shall be hereafter; else all the world cannot help it but she will become a pilgrim.'[6]

"Now she awoke in a great sweat; also a trembling was upon her, but after a while she fell to sleeping again. And then she thought she saw Christian, her husband, in a place of bliss among many immortals, with an harp in his hand, standing and playing upon it before one that sat on a throne with a rainbow about his head. She saw also as if he bowed his head with his face to the paved work[7] that was under the Prince's feet, saying, 'I heartily thank my Lord and King for bringing of me into this place.' Then shouted a company of them that stood round about and harped with their harps;[8] but no man living could tell what they said but Christian and his companions.

"Next morning when she was up, had prayed to God and talked with her children awhile, one knocked hard at the door, to whom she spake out saying, 'If thou comest in God's name, come in.' So he said 'Amen,' and opened the door, and saluted her with 'Peace be to this house.' The which when he had done, he said, 'Christiana, knowest thou wherefore I am come?' Then she blushed and trembled; also her heart began to wax[9] warm with desires to know whence he came and what was his errand to her. So he said unto her, 'My name is Secret; I dwell with those that are high. It is talked of where I dwell as if thou hadst a desire to go thither. Also there is a report that thou art aware of the evil thou hast formerly done to thy husband in hardening of thy heart

[1] *brinish* Salty.

[2] *returned … lightning* Cf. Ezekiel 1.14; *rent … heart* Cf. Hosea 13.8; *caul* Covering; membrane; *in sunder* Apart.

[3] *humours* States of mind.

[4] *woe worth* A curse upon.

[5] *ill-favoured* Ugly.

[6] [Bunyan's note] Mark this, this is the quintessence of hell.

[7] *paved work* Pavement, or pavement-like surface; cf. Exodus 24.10.

[8] *Then … harps* Cf. Revelation 14.2.

[9] *wax* Grow.

against his way and in keeping of these thy babes in their ignorance. Christiana, the merciful one has sent me to tell thee that he is a God ready to forgive, and that he taketh delight to multiply pardon to offences. He also would have thee know that he inviteth thee to come into his presence, to his table, and that he will feed thee with the fat of his house and with the heritage of Jacob, thy father.[1]

"'There is Christian, thy husband that was, with legions more his companions, ever beholding that face that doth minister life to beholders. And they will all be glad when they shall hear the sound of thy feet step over thy Father's threshold.'

"Christiana at this was greatly abashed in herself and bowing her head to the ground. This visitor proceeded and said, 'Christiana, here is also a letter for thee which I have brought from thy husband's King.' So she took it and opened it, but it smelt after the manner of the best perfume; also it was written in letters of gold. The contents of the letter was, 'that the King would have her do as did Christian, her husband; for that was the way to come to his city, and to dwell in his presence with joy forever.' At this, the good woman was quite overcome; so she cried out to her visitor, 'Sir, will you carry me and my children with you that we also may go and worship this King?'

"'Then said the visitor, 'Christiana, the bitter is before the sweet. Thou must through[2] troubles, as did he that went before thee enter this Celestial City. Wherefore I advise thee to do as did Christian, thy husband. Go to the wicket-gate yonder, over the plain, for that stands in the head of the way up which thou must go, and I wish thee all good speed. Also I advise that thou put this letter in thy bosom, that thou read therein to thyself and to thy children until you have got it by root-of-heart.[3] For it is one of the songs that thou must sing while thou art in this house of thy pilgrimage.[4] Also this thou must deliver in at the further gate.'"

Now I saw in my dream that this old gentleman, as he told me this story, did himself seem to be greatly affected therewith. He moreover proceeded and said, "So Christiana called her sons together and began thus to address herself unto them, 'My sons, I have, as you may perceive, been of late under much exercise in my soul about the death of your father; not for that I doubt at all of his happiness, for I am satisfied now that he is well. I have also been much affected with the thoughts of mine own state and yours, which I verily believe is by nature miserable. My carriages also to your father in his distress is a great load to my conscience. For I hardened both mine own heart and yours against him and refused to go with him on pilgrimage.

"'The thoughts of these things would now kill me outright, but that for a dream which I had last night, and but that for the encouragement that this stranger has given me this morning. Come, my children, let us pack up and be gone to the gate that leads to the Celestial Country, that we may see your father and be with him and his companions in peace according to the laws of that land.'

"Then did her children burst out into tears for joy that the heart of their mother was so inclined. So their visitor bid them farewell, and they began to prepare to set out for their journey.

"But while they were thus about to be gone, two of the women that were Christiana's neighbours came up to her house and knocked at her door.[5] To whom she said as before, 'If you come in God's name, come in.' At this, the women were stunned, for this kind of language they used not to hear, or to perceive to drop from the lips of Christiana. Yet they came in. But, behold, they found the good woman a-preparing to be gone from her house.

"So they began and said, 'Neighbour, pray, what is your meaning by this?'

"Christiana answered and said to the eldest of them, whose name was Mrs. Timorous, 'I am preparing for a journey.' (This Timorous was daughter to him that met Christian upon the hill Difficulty; and would a[6] had him gone back for fear of the lions.)

[1] *heritage ... father* Cf. Isaiah 58.14.

[2] *through* Get through; overcome.

[3] *by root-of-heart* By heart, and also, perhaps, deeply felt.

[4] *For ... pilgrimage* Cf. Psalms 119.54.

[5] [Bunyan's note] Timorous comes to visit Christiana, with Mercy, one of her neighbours.

[6] *would a* Would have.

TIMOROUS. 'For what journey, I pray you?'

CHRISTIANA. 'Even to go after my good husband,' and with that she fell aweeping.

TIMOROUS. 'I hope not so, good neighbour. Pray, for your poor children's sake, do not so unwomanly cast away yourself.'

CHRISTIANA. 'Nay, my children shall go with me; not one of them is willing to stay behind.'

TIMOROUS. 'I wonder in my very heart, what, or who, has brought you into this mind.'

CHRISTIANA. 'Oh, neighbour, knew you but as much as I do, I doubt not but that you would go with me.'

TIMOROUS. 'Prithee, what new knowledge hast thou got that so worketh off[1] thy mind from thy friends and that tempteth thee to go nobody knows where?'

CHRISTIANA. Then Christiana replied, 'I have been sorely afflicted since my husband's departure from me, but specially since he went over the river. But that which troubleth me most is my churlish carriages to him when he was under his distress. Besides, I am now as he was then; nothing will serve me but going on pilgrimage. I was a-dreamed last night that I saw him. O, that my soul was with him! He dwelleth in the presence of the King of the country; he sits and eats with him at his table; he is become a companion of immortals, and has a house now given him to dwell in, to which, the best palaces on earth, if compared, seems to me to be but as a dunghill. The Prince of the place has also sent for me with promise of entertainment[2] if I shall come to him; his messenger was here even now and has brought me a letter which invites me to come.' And with that she plucked out her letter and read it and said to them, 'What now will you say to this?'

TIMOROUS. 'Oh, the madness that has possessed thee and thy husband, to run yourselves upon such difficulties! You have heard, I am sure, what your husband did meet with, even in a manner at the first step that he took on his way as our neighbour Obstinate yet can testify; for he went along with him, yea, and Pliable too, until they, like wise men, were afraid to go any further. We also heard over and above, how he met the lions, Apollyon, the Shadow of Death, and many other things. Nor is the danger he met with at Vanity Fair to be forgotten by thee. For if he, though a man, was so hard put to it,[3] what canst thou, being but a poor woman, do? Consider also that these four sweet babes are thy children, thy flesh and thy bones. Wherefore, though thou shouldst be so rash as to cast away thyself, yet for the sake of the fruit of thy body, keep thou at home.'[4]

"But Christiana said unto her, 'Tempt me not, my neighbour. I have now a price put into mine hand to get gain,[5] and I should be a fool of the greatest size if I should have no heart to strike in with the opportunity. And for that you tell me of all these troubles that I am like to meet with in the way, they are so far off from being to me a discouragement that they show I am in the right. The bitter must come before the sweet, and that also will make the sweet the sweeter. Wherefore, since you came not to my house in God's name, as I said, I pray you to be gone and not to disquiet me further.'

"Then Timorous all to[6] reviled her, and said to her fellow, 'Come neighbour Mercy, let's leave her in her own hands, since she scorns our counsel and company.' But Mercy was at a stand and could not so readily comply with her neighbour, and that for a twofold reason. First, her bowels[7] yearned over Christiana. So she said within herself, 'If my neighbour will needs be gone, I will go a little way with her and help her.' Secondly, her bowels yearned over her own soul, for what Christiana had said had taken some hold upon her mind. Wherefore she said within herself again, 'I will yet have more talk with this Christiana, and if I find truth and life in what she shall say, myself with my heart shall also go with her.' Wherefore Mercy began thus to reply to her neighbour Timorous.

MERCY. 'Neighbour, I did indeed come with you to see Christiana this morning, and since she is, as you see, a-taking of her last farewell of her country, I think to walk, this sunshine morning, a little way with her to

[1] *worketh off* Draws away.

[2] *entertainment* Hospitality.

[3] *hard put to it* Beset with difficulties.

[4] [Bunyan's note] The reasoning of the flesh.

[5] *price ... gain* Thing of value by which I might prosper.

[6] *all to* Quite.

[7] *bowels* Innermost tender feelings.

help her on the way.' But she told her not of her second reason, but kept that to herself.

TIMOROUS. 'Well, I see you have a mind to go a-fooling too; but take heed in time, and be wise. While we are out of danger we are out; but when we are in, we are in.' So Mrs. Timorous returned to her house, and Christiana betook herself to her journey. But when Timorous was got home to her house, she sends for some of her neighbours, to wit, Mrs. Bat's-eyes, Mrs. Inconsiderate, Mrs. Light-mind, and Mrs. Know-nothing. So when they were come to her house, she falls to telling of the story of Christiana and of her intended journey. And thus she began her tale,

TIMOROUS. 'Neighbours, having had little to do this morning, I went to give Christiana a visit, and when I came at the door I knocked, as you know 'tis our custom. And she answered, "If you come in God's name, come in." So in I went, thinking all was well. But when I came in, I found her preparing herself to depart the town, she and also her children. So I asked her what was her meaning by that. And she told me, in short, that she was now of a mind to go on pilgrimage as did her husband. She told me also of a dream that she had, and how the King of the country where her husband was had sent her an inviting letter to come thither.'

"Then said Mrs. Know-nothing, 'And what, Do you think she will go?'

TIMOROUS. 'Ay, go she will, whatever come on't. And methinks I know it by this: for that which was my great argument to persuade her to stay at home (to wit, the troubles she was like to meet with in the way), is one great argument with her to put her forward on her journey. For she told me in so many words, "The bitter goes before the sweet. Yea, and for as much as it so doth, it makes the sweet the sweeter."'

MRS. BAT'S-EYES. 'Oh, this blind and foolish woman,' said she. 'Will she not take warning by her husband's afflictions? For my part, I say if he was here again he would rest him content in a whole skin and never run so many hazards for nothing.'

"Mrs. Inconsiderate also replied, saying, 'Away with such fantastical fools from the town; a good riddance, for my part, I say of her. Should she stay where she dwells and retain this her mind, who could live quietly by her? For she will either be dumpish[1] or unneighbourly, or talk of such matters as no wise body can abide. Wherefore, for my part, I shall never be sorry for her departure. Let her go, and let better come in her room.[2] 'twas never a good world since these whimsical fools dwelt in it.'

"Then Mrs. Light-mind added as followeth. 'Come put this kind of talk away. I was yesterday at Madam Wanton's, where we were as merry as the maids. For who do you think should be there but I, and Mrs. Love-the-flesh, and three or four more, with Mr. Lechery, Mrs. Filth, and some others. So there we had music, and dancing, and what else was meet to fill up the pleasure. And I dare say my lady herself is an admirably well-bred gentlewoman, and Mr. Lechery is as pretty a fellow.'

"By this time Christiana was got on her way, and Mercy went along with her. So as they went, her children being there also, Christiana began to discourse. 'And Mercy,' said Christiana, 'I take this as an unexpected favour that thou shouldest set foot out-of-doors with me to accompany me a little in my way.'

MERCY. Then said young Mercy (for she was but young), 'If I thought it would be to purpose[3] to go with you, I would never go near the town any more.'

CHRISTIANA. 'Well, Mercy,' said Christiana, 'cast in thy lot with me. I well know what will be the end of our pilgrimage. My husband is where he would not but be for all the gold in the Spanish mines.[4] Nor shalt thou be rejected, though thou goest but upon my invitation. The King, who hath sent for me and my children, is one that delighteth in Mercy. Besides, if thou wilt, I will hire thee, and thou shalt go along with me as my servant. Yet we will have all things in common betwixt thee and me; only go along with me.'

MERCY. 'But how shall I be ascertained that I also shall be entertained? Had I but this hope from one that can tell, I would make no stick[5] at all, but would go, being helped by him that can help, though the way was never so tedious.'

[1] *dumpish* Melancholy.

[2] *room* Place; stead.

[3] *to purpose* Useful.

[4] *Spanish mines* I.e., in South America.

[5] *stick* Delay.

CHRISTIANA. 'Well, loving Mercy, I will tell thee what thou shalt do. Go with me to the wicket-gate, and there I will further inquire for thee,[1] and if there thou shalt not meet with encouragement, I will be content that thou shalt return to thy place. I also will pay thee for thy kindness which thou showest to me and my children in thy accompanying of us in our way as thou doest.'

MERCY. 'Then will I go thither and will take what shall follow, and the Lord grant that my lot may there fall even as the King of heaven shall have his heart upon me.'

"Christiana then was glad at her heart, not only that she had a companion, but also for that she had prevailed with this poor maid to fall in love with her own salvation. So they went on together, and Mercy began to weep. Then said Christiana, 'Wherefore weepeth my sister so?'

MERCY. 'Alas,' said she, 'who can but lament that shall but rightly consider what a state and condition my poor relations are in that yet remain in our sinful town? And that which makes my grief the more heavy is because they have no instructor, nor any to tell them what is to come.'

CHRISTIANA. 'Bowels becometh pilgrims. And thou dost for thy friends as my good Christian did for me when he left me. He mourned for that I would not heed nor regard him, but his Lord and ours did gather up his tears and put them into his bottle.[2] And now both I and thou, and these my sweet babes, are reaping the fruit and benefit of them. I hope, Mercy, these tears of thine will not be lost, for the truth hath said "That they that sow in tears shall reap in joy, in singing. And he that goeth forth and weepeth, bearing precious seed, shall doubtless come again with rejoicing, bringing his sheaves with him."'[3]

"Then said Mercy,

'Let the most blessed be my guide,
If't be his blessed will,
Unto his gate, into his fold,
Up to his holy hill.

And let him never suffer me
To swerve or turn aside
From his free grace and holy ways
What ere shall me betide.

And let him gather them of mine
That I have left behind.
Lord, make them pray they may be thine,
With all their heart and mind.'"

Now my old friend proceeded and said, "But when Christiana came up to the Slough of Despond, she began to be at a stand.[4] 'For,' said she, 'this is the place in which my dear husband had like to a been smothered with mud.' She perceived also that, notwithstanding the command of the King to make this place for pilgrims good, yet it was rather worse than formerly." So I asked if that was true. "Yes," said the old gentleman, "too true. For that many there be that pretend to be the King's labourers, and that say they are for mending the King's highway, that bring dirt and dung instead of stones, and so mar instead of mending.[5] Here Christiana therefore, with her boys, did make a stand. But said Mercy, 'Come, let us venture; only let us be wary.' Then they looked well to the steps and made a shift[6] to get staggeringly over. Yet Christiana had like to a been in, and that not once nor twice. Now they had no sooner got over, but they thought they heard words that said unto them, 'Blessed is she that believeth, for there shall be a performance of the things that have been told her from the Lord.'[7]

"Then they went on again, and said Mercy to Christiana, 'Had I as good ground to hope for a loving reception at the wicket-gate as you, I think no Slough of Despond would discourage me.'

"'Well,' said the other, 'you know your sore,[8] and I know mine; and, good friend, we shall all have enough evil before we come at our journey's end.

"'For can it be imagined that the people that design to attain such excellent glories as we do, and that are so

[1] [Bunyan's note] Christiana allures her to the gate which is Christ, and promiseth there to inquire for her.

[2] *Lord ... bottle* Cf. Psalms 56.8.

[3] *That ... him* From Psalms 126.5–6.

[4] *at a stand* Perplexed; unable to proceed.

[5] [Bunyan's note] Their own carnal conclusions, instead of the word of life.

[6] *made a shift* Managed somehow.

[7] *Blessed ... Lord* From Luke 1.45.

[8] *sore* Trouble.

envied that happiness as we are, but that we shall meet with what fears and scares, with what troubles and afflictions they can possibly assault us with, that hate us?'"

And now Mr. Sagacity left me to dream out my dream by myself. Wherefore methought I saw Christiana and Mercy, and the boys, go all of them up to the gate. To which, when they were come, they betook themselves to a short debate about how they must manage their calling at the gate and what should be said to him that did open to them. So it was concluded, since Christiana was the eldest, that she should knock for entrance, and that she should speak to him that did open, for the rest. So Christiana began to knock, and, as her poor husband did, she knocked and knocked again. But instead of any that answered, they all thought that they heard as if a dog came barking upon them, a dog, and a great one too; and this made the women and children afraid.[1] Nor durst they for a while dare to knock any more, for fear the mastiff should fly upon them. Now, therefore, they were greatly tumbled up and down in their minds and knew not what to do. Knock they durst not, for fear of the dog; go back they durst not, for fear that the keeper of that gate should espy them as they so went, and should be offended with them. At last they thought of knocking again, and knocked more vehemently than they did at the first. Then said the keeper of the gate, "Who is there?" So the dog left off[2] to bark, and he opened unto them.

Then Christiana made low obeisance and said, "Let not our Lord be offended with his handmaidens for that we have knocked at his princely gate." Then said the keeper, "Whence come ye, and what is that you would have?"

Christiana answered, "We are come from whence Christian did come and upon the same errand as he, to wit, to be, if it shall please you, graciously admitted by this gate into the way that leads to the Celestial City. And I answer, my Lord, in the next place, that I am Christiana, once the wife of Christian, that now is gotten above."

With that the keeper of the gate did marvel, saying, "What, is she become now a pilgrim, that but awhile ago abhorred that life?" Then she bowed her head and said, "Yes, and so are these my sweet babes also."

Then he took her by the hand and led her in, and said also, "Suffer the little children to come unto me,"[3] and with that he shut up the gate. This done, he called to a trumpeter that was above, over the gate, to entertain Christiana with shouting and sound of trumpet for joy. So he obeyed and sounded and filled the air with his melodious notes.

Now, all this while, poor Mercy did stand without, trembling and crying for fear that she was rejected. But when Christiana had gotten admittance for herself and her boys, then she began to make intercession for Mercy.

CHRISTIANA. And she said, "My Lord, I have a companion of mine that stands yet without, that is come hither upon the same account as myself, one that is much dejected in her mind, for that she comes, as she thinks, without sending for, whereas I was sent to by my husband's King to come."

Now Mercy began to be very impatient, for each minute was as long to her as an hour; wherefore she prevented Christiana from a fuller interceding for her by knocking at the gate herself.[4] And she knocked then so loud that she made Christiana to start. Then said the keeper of the gate, "Who is there?" And said Christiana, "It is my friend."

So he opened the gate and looked out, but Mercy was fallen down without[5] in a swoon, for she fainted and was afraid that no gate should be opened to her.

Then he took her by the hand and said, "Damsel, I bid thee arise."

"O, sir," said she, "I am faint. There is scarce life left in me." But he answered, "That one once said, 'When my soul fainted within me I remembered the Lord, and my prayer came in unto thee, into thy Holy Temple.'[6] Fear not, but stand upon thy feet and tell me wherefore thou art come."

MERCY. "I am come for that unto which I was never invited as my friend Christiana was. Hers was from the

[1] [Bunyan's note] The dog, the Devil, an enemy to prayer.

[2] *left off* Ceased.

[3] *Suffer ... me* From Mark 10.14.

[4] [Bunyan's note] The delays make the hungering soul theferventer.

[5] *without* Outside.

[6] *When ... Temple* Jonah 2.7.

King and mine was but from her. Wherefore I fear I presume."

"Did she desire thee to come with her to this place?"

Mercy. "Yes, and as my Lord sees, I am come. And if there is any grace and forgiveness of sins to spare, I beseech that I, thy poor handmaid, may be partaker thereof."

Then he took her again by the hand and led her gently in and said, "I pray for all them that believe on me, by what means soever they come unto me." Then said he to those that stood by, "Fetch something, and give it Mercy to smell on, thereby to stay her fainting." So they fetched her a bundle of myrrh,[1] and awhile after she was revived.

And now was Christiana, and her boys, and Mercy received of the Lord at the head of the way and spoke kindly unto by him.

Then said they yet further unto him, "We are sorry for our sins, and beg of our Lord his pardon and further information what we must do."

"I grant pardon," said he, "by word, and deed; by word in the promise of forgiveness; by deed in the way I obtained it. Take the first from my lips with a kiss, and the others as it shall be revealed."

Now I saw in my dream that he spoke many good words unto them whereby they were greatly gladdened. He also had them up to the top of the gate and showed them by what deed they were saved, and told them withal[2] that that sight[3] they would have again as they went along in the way, to their comfort.

So he left them awhile in a summer-parlour below, where they entered into talk by themselves. And thus Christiana began, "O Lord! How glad am I that we are got in hither!"

Mercy. "So you well may. But I, of all, have cause to leap for joy."

Christiana. "I thought, one time, as I stood at the gate (because I had knocked and none did answer), that all our labour had been lost, specially when that ugly cur made such a heavy barking against us."

Mercy. "But my worst fears was after I saw that you was taken into his favour and that I was left behind. Now, thought I, 'tis fulfilled which is written, 'Two women shall be grinding together; the one shall be taken, and the other left.'[4] I had much ado to forbear crying out, 'Undone, undone.'

"And afraid I was to knock any more; but when I looked up to what was written over the gate, I took courage. I also thought that I must either knock again or die. So I knocked; but I cannot tell how, for my spirit now struggled betwixt life and death."

Christiana. "Can you not tell how you knocked? I am sure your knocks were so earnest that the very sound of them made me start. I thought I never heard such knocking in all my life. I thought you would a come in by violent hand or a took the kingdom by storm."[5]

Mercy. "Alas, to be in my case.[6] Who that so was could but a done so? You saw that the door was shut upon me and that there was a most cruel dog thereabout. Who, I say, that was so faint hearted as I, that would not a knocked with all their might? But, pray, what said my Lord to my rudeness? Was he not angry with me?"

Christiana. "When he heard your lumbering noise, he gave a wonderful innocent smile. I believe what you did pleased him well enough, for he showed no sign to the contrary. But I marvel in my heart why he keeps such a dog. Had I known that afore, I fear I should not have had heart enough to a ventured myself in this manner. But now we are in, we are in, and I am glad with all my heart."

Mercy. "I will ask, if you please, next time he comes down, why he keeps such a filthy cur in his yard. I hope he will not take it amiss."

"Ay, do," said the children, "and persuade him to hang him, for we are afraid that he will bite us when we go hence."

---

[1] *Fetch … myrrh* Cf. Song of Solomon 1.13.

[2] *withal* As well.

[3] [Bunyan's note] Christ crucified seen afar off.

[4] *Two … left* From Matthew 24.41.

[5] *violent … storm* Cf. Matthew 11.12.

[6] *case* Circumstances.

So at last he came down to them again, and Mercy fell to the ground on her face before him and worshipped and said, "Let my Lord accept of the sacrifice of praise which I now offer unto him, with the calves of my lips."[1]

So he said to her, "Peace be to thee, stand up."

But she continued upon her face and said, "Righteous art thou, O Lord, when I plead with thee. Yet let me talk with thee of thy judgements. Wherefore dost thou keep so cruel a dog in thy yard, at the sight of which such women and children as we are ready to fly from thy gate for fear?"[2]

He answered and said, "That dog has another owner. He also is kept close in another man's ground; only my pilgrims hear his barking. He belongs to the castle which you see there at a distance but can come up to the walls of this place. He has frighted many an honest pilgrim, from worse to better, by the great voice of his roaring. Indeed, he that owneth him doth not keep him of any good will to me or mine, but with intent to keep the pilgrims from coming to me, and that they may be afraid to knock at this gate for entrance. Sometimes also he has broken out and has worried[3] some that I love; but I take all at present patiently. I also give my pilgrims timely help, so they are not delivered up to his power to do to them what his doggish nature would prompt him to. But what! my purchased one, I trow,[4] hadst thou known never so much before hand, thou wouldst not a been afraid of a dog.

"The beggars that go from door to door will, rather than they will lose a supposed alms, run the hazard of the bawling, barking, and biting, too, of a dog. And shall a dog, a dog in another man's yard, a dog whose barking I turn to the profit of pilgrims, keep any from coming to me? I deliver them from the lions, their darling from the power of the dog."[5] ...

After this, I beheld until they were come into the Land of Beulah,[6] where the sun shineth night and day. Here, because they was weary, they betook themselves awhile to rest. And because this country was common for pilgrims, and because the orchards and vineyards that were here belonged to the King of the Celestial Country, therefore they were licensed to make bold with[7] any of his things.

But a little while soon refreshed them here, for the bells did so ring, and the trumpets continually sound so melodiously, that they could not sleep, and yet they received as much refreshing as if they had slept their sleep never so soundly. Here also all the noise of them that walked the streets was, "More pilgrims are come to town." And another would answer saying, "And so many went over the water and were let in at the golden gates today." They would cry again, "There is now a legion of Shining Ones just come to town, by which we know that there are more pilgrims upon the road; for here they come to wait for them and to comfort them after all their sorrow." Then the pilgrims got up and walked to and fro. But how were their ears now filled with heavenly noises and their eyes delighted with celestial visions? In this land they heard nothing, saw nothing, felt nothing, smelt nothing, tasted nothing that was offensive to their stomach or mind. Only when they tasted of the water of the river over which they were to go, they thought that tasted a little bitterish to the palate, but it proved sweeter when 'twas down.[8]

In this place, there was a record kept of the names of them that had been pilgrims of old, and a history of all the famous acts that they had done. It was here also much discoursed how the river to some had had its flowings, and what ebbings it has had while others have gone over. It has been in a manner dry for some, while it has overflowed its banks for others.

In this place, the children of the town would go into the King's gardens and gather nosegays for the pilgrims and bring them to them with much affection. Here also grew camphor, with spikenard, and saffron, calamus, and cinnamon, with all its trees of frankincense, myrrh,

[1] *calves of my lips* A doubtful translation from Hebrew in the King James Bible, with the general meaning of an offering of praise; cf. Hosea 14.2.

[2] *Wherefore ... fear* Cf. Jeremiah 12.1–2.

[3] *worried* Attacked.

[4] *purchased* Freed for a price, as a slave might be ransomed; *trow* Believe.

[5] *I ... dog* Cf. Psalms 22.20–21.

[6] *Beulah* Cf. Isaiah 62.4.

[7] *licensed ... with* Permitted to use.

[8] [Bunyan's note] Death bitter to the flesh, but sweet to the soul.

and aloes, with all chief spices.[1] With these the pilgrims' chambers were perfumed while they stayed here; and with these were their bodies anointed to prepare them to go over the river when the time appointed was come.

Now while they lay here and waited for the good hour, there was a noise in the town that there was a post[2] come from the Celestial City with matter of great importance to one Christiana, the wife of Christian, the pilgrim. So inquiry was made for her, and the house was found out where she was; so the post presented her with a letter the contents whereof was, "Hail, good woman, I bring thee tidings that the Master calleth for thee and expecteth that thou shouldest stand in his presence, in clothes of immortality, within this ten days."

When he had read this letter to her, he gave her therewith a sure token that he was a true messenger and was come to bid her make haste to be gone. The token was an arrow with a point sharpened with love, let easily into her heart, which by degrees wrought so effectually with her that at the time appointed she must be gone.

When Christiana saw that her time was come, and that she was the first of this company that was to go over, she called for Mr. Great-heart, her guide, and told him how matters were. So he told her he was heartily glad of the news and could a been glad had the post came for him. Then she bid that he should give advice how all things should be prepared for her journey.

So he told her saying, "Thus and thus it must be, and we that survive will accompany you to the river-side."

Then she called for her children and gave them her blessing, and told them that she yet read with comfort the mark that was set in their foreheads, and was glad to see them with her there, and that they had kept their garments so white. Lastly, she bequeathed to the poor that little she had, and commanded her sons and her daughters to be ready against[3] the messenger should come for them.

When she had spoken these words to her guide and to her children, she called for Mr. Valiant-for-truth and said unto him, "Sir, you have in all places showed yourself true-hearted; be faithful unto death and my King will give you a crown of life.[4] I would also entreat you to have an eye to my children, and if at any time you see them faint, speak comfortably to them. For my daughters, my sons' wives, they have been faithful, and a fulfilling of the promise upon them will be their end." But she gave Mr. Stand-fast a ring.

Then she called for old Mr. Honest and said of him, "Behold, an Israelite indeed, in whom is no guile."[5] Then said he, "I wish you a fair day when you set out for Mount Zion, and shall be glad to see that you go over the river dry-shod." But she answered, "Come wet, come dry, I long to be gone. For however the weather is in my journey, I shall have time enough when I come there to sit down and rest me, and dry me."

Then came in that good man, Mr. Ready-to-halt,[6] to see her. So she said to him, "Thy travel hither has been with difficulty, but that will make thy rest the sweeter. But watch and be ready, for at an hour when you think not the messenger may come."

After him came in Mr. Despondency, and his daughter, Much-afraid, to whom she said, "You ought, with thankfulness forever, to remember your deliverance from the hands of Giant Despair, and out of Doubting Castle. The effect of that mercy is that you are brought with safety hither. Be ye watchful, and cast away fear. Be sober, and hope to the end."

Then she said to Mr. Feeble-mind, "Thou was delivered from the mouth of Giant Slaygood that thou mightest live in the light of the living forever and see thy King with comfort. Only I advise thee to repent thee of thy aptness to fear and doubt of his goodness before he sends for thee lest thou shouldest, when he comes, be forced to stand before him for that fault with blushing."

Now the day drew on that Christiana must be gone. So the road was full of people to see her take her journey. But, behold, all the banks beyond the river were full of horses and chariots which were come down from above to accompany her to the city gate. So she came forth and entered the river with a beckon of farewell to those that followed her to the river-side. The last word

[1] *trees ... spices* From Song of Solomon 4.14.

[2] [Bunyan's note] Messenger; here, a messenger of death sent to Christiana.

[3] *against* By the time that.

[4] *be faithful ... life* Cf. Revelations 2.10.

[5] *Behold ... guile* Cf. John 1.47.

[6] *halt* Limp.

she was heard to say here was, "I come, Lord, to be with thee and bless thee."[1]

So her children and friends returned to their place for that those that waited for Christiana had carried her out of their sight. So she went and called, and entered in at the gate with all the ceremonies of joy that her husband, Christian, had done before her.

At her departure her children wept, but Mr. Great-heart and Mr. Valiant played upon the well-tuned cymbal and harp, for joy. So all departed to their respective places.

In process of time there came a post to the town again, and his business was with Mr. Ready-to-halt. So he inquired him out and said to him, "I am come to thee in the name of him whom thou hast loved and followed though upon crutches. And my message is to tell thee that he expects thee at his table to sup with him in his kingdom the next day after Easter, wherefore prepare thy self for this journey."

Then he also gave him a token that he was a true messenger saying, "I have broken thy golden bowl and loosed thy silver cord."[2]

After this, Mr. Ready-to-halt called for his fellow pilgrims and told them saying, "I am sent for, and God shall surely visit you also." So he desired Mr. Valiant to make his will. And because he had nothing to bequeath to them that should survive him but his crutches and his good wishes, therefore thus he said, "These crutches I bequeath to my son that shall tread in my steps, with an hundred warm wishes that he may prove better than I have done."

Then he thanked Mr. Great-heart for his conduct and kindness and so addressed himself to this journey. When he came at the brink of the river he said, "Now I shall have no more need of these crutches since yonder are chariots and horses for me to ride on." The last words he was heard to say was, "Welcome, life." So he went his way.

After this, Mr. Feeble-mind had tidings brought him that the post sounded his horn at his chamber-door. Then he came in and told him saying, "I am come to tell thee that the Master has need of thee, and that in very little time thou must behold his face in brightness. And take this as a token of the truth of my message, 'Those that look out at the windows shall be darkened.'"[3]

Then Mr. Feeble-mind called for his friends and told them what errand had been brought unto him, and what token he had received of the truth of the message. Then he said, "Since I have nothing to bequeath to any, to what purpose should I make a will? As for my feeble mind, that I will leave behind me, for that I shall have no need of that in the place whither I go, nor is it worth bestowing upon the poorest pilgrim. Wherefore, when I am gone, I desire that you, Mr. Valiant, would bury it in a dunghill." This done, and the day being come in which he was to depart, he entered the river as the rest. His last words were, "Hold out, faith and patience." So he went over to the other side.

When days had many of them passed away Mr. Despondency was sent for. For a post was come, and brought this message to him, "Trembling man, these are to summon thee to be ready with thy King, by the next Lord's day, to shout for joy for thy deliverance from all thy doubtings."

And said the messenger, "That my message is true take this for a proof." So he gave him, "The grasshopper to be a burden unto him."[4] Now Mr. Despondency's daughter, whose name was Much-afraid, said, when she heard what was done, that she would go with her father. Then Mr. Despondency said to his friends, "Myself and my daughter, you know what we have been and how troublesomely we have behaved ourselves in every company. My will and my daughter's is that our desponds and slavish fears be by no man ever received, from the day of our departure, forever; for I know that after my death they will offer themselves to others. For, to be plain with you, they are ghosts, the which we entertained when we first began to be pilgrims and could never shake them off after. And they will walk about and seek entertainment of the pilgrims, but for our sakes shut ye the doors upon them."

When the time was come for them to depart they went to the brink of the river. The last words of Mr.

[1] *be with thee and bless thee* Cf. Genesis 26.3 and 26.24.

[2] *broken ... cord* Cf. Ecclesiastes 12.6.

[3] *Those ... darkened* Cf. Ecclesiastes 12.3.

[4] *The grasshopper ... him* Cf. Ecclesiastes 12.5.

Despondency were, "Farewell, night; welcome, day." His daughter went through the river singing, but none could understand what she said.

Then it came to pass, a while after, that there was a post in the town that inquired for Mr. Honest. So he came to the house where he was and delivered to his hand these lines, "Thou art commanded to be ready, against this day seven night, to present thyself before thy Lord, at His Father's house. And for a token that my message is true, 'All thy daughters of music shall be brought low.'"[1] Then Mr. Honest called for his friends and said unto them, "I die but shall make no will. As for my honesty, it shall go with me; let him that comes after be told of this." When the day that he was to be gone was come, he addressed himself to go over the river. Now the river at that time overflowed the banks in some places. But Mr. Honest in his lifetime had spoken to one Good-conscience to meet him there, the which he also did, and lent him his hand, and so helped him over. The last words of Mr. Honest were, "Grace reigns." So he left the world.

After this it was noised abroad that Mr. Valiant-for-truth was taken with a summons by the same post as the other, and had this for a token that the summons was true, "That his pitcher was broken at the fountain."[2] When he understood it, he called for his friends and told them of it. Then said he, "I am going to my Father's, and though with great difficulty I am got hither, yet now I do not repent me of all the trouble I have been at to arrive where I am. My sword I give to him that shall succeed me in my pilgrimage, and my courage and skill to him that can get it. My marks and scars I carry with me to be a witness for me that I have fought his battles who now will be my rewarder." When the day that he must go hence was come, many accompanied him to the river-side, into which, as he went, he said, "Death, where is thy sting?" And as he went down deeper he said, "Grave, where is thy victory?"[3] So he passed over, and the trumpets sounded for him on the other side.

Then there came forth a summons for Mr. Stand-fast (this Mr. Stand-fast was he that the rest of the pilgrims found upon his knees in the Enchanted Ground), for the post brought it him open in his hands. The contents whereof were that he must prepare for a change of life, for his Master was not willing that he should be so far from him any longer. At this, Mr. Stand-fast was put into a muse. "Nay," said the messenger, "you need not doubt of the truth of my message. For here is a token of the truth thereof, 'Thy wheel is broken at the cistern.'"[4] Then he called to him Mr. Great-heart, who was their guide, and said unto him, "Sir, although it was not my hap to be much in your good company in the days of my pilgrimage, yet since the time I knew you, you have been profitable to me. When I came from home, I left behind me a wife and five small children. Let me entreat you, at your return (for I know that you will go and return to your master's house, in hopes that you may yet be a conductor to more of the holy pilgrims), that you send to my family and let them be acquainted with all that hath, and shall happen, unto me. Tell them, moreover, of my happy arrival to this place, and of the present late blessed condition that I am in. Tell them also of Christian, and of Christiana, his wife, and how she and her children came after her husband. Tell them also of what a happy end she made and whither she is gone. I have little or nothing to send to my family, except it be prayers and tears for them; of which it will suffice, if thou acquaint them, if peradventure they may prevail." When Mr. Stand-fast had thus set things in order, and the time being come for him to hast him[5] away, he also went down to the river. Now there was a great calm at that time in the river; wherefore Mr. Standfast, when he was about half-way in, he stood awhile and talked to his companions that had waited upon him thither. And he said,

"This river has been a terror to many; yea, the thoughts of it also have often frighted me. But now, methinks, I stand easy. My foot is fixed upon that upon which the feet of the priests that bare the ark of the covenant stood while Israel went over this Jordan.[6] The

[1] *All ... low* Cf. Ecclesiastes 12.4.

[2] *pitcher ... fountain* Cf. Ecclesiastes 12.6.

[3] *Death ... victory* From 1 Corinthians 15.55.

[4] *wheel ... cistern* Cf. Ecclesiastes 12.6.

[5] *hast him* Hasten himself.

[6] *My foot ... Jordan* Cf. Joshua 3.17.

waters indeed are to the palate bitter and to the stomach cold. Yet the thoughts of what I am going to, and of the conduct that waits for me on the other side, doth lie as a glowing coal at my heart.

"I see myself now at the end of my journey; my toilsome days are ended. I am going now to see that head that was crowned with thorns and that face that was spit upon for me.

"I have formerly lived by hearsay and faith, but now I go where I shall live by sight and shall be with him in whose company I delight myself.

"I have loved to hear my Lord spoken of, and wherever I have seen the print of his shoe in the earth, there I have coveted[1] to set my foot too.

"His name has been to me as a civet-box,[2] yea, sweeter than all perfumes. His voice to me has been most sweet, and his countenance I have more desired than they that have most desired the light of the sun. His Word I did use to gather for my food and for antidotes against my faintings. He has held me, and I have kept me from mine iniquities. Yea, my steps hath he strengthened in his way."

Now while he was thus in discourse his countenance changed, his strong men bowed under him, and after he had said, "Take me, for I come unto thee," he ceased to be seen of them.

But glorious it was to see how the open region was filled with horses and chariots, with trumpeters and pipers, with singers and players on stringed instruments, to welcome the pilgrims as they went up and followed one another in at the beautiful gate of the city.

As for Christian's children, the four boys that Christiana brought with her, with their wives and children, I did not stay where I was till they were gone over. Also since I came away I heard one say that they were yet alive, and so would be for the increase of the Church in that place where they were for a time.

Shall it be my lot to go that way again, I may give those that desire it an account of what I here am silent about; meantime I bid my reader adieu.

—1684

[1] *coveted* Desired.

[2] *civet-box* Box for storing perfumes.

John Dryden
1631 – 1700

Few authors of the Restoration were as prolific as was John Dryden, and few rival his vigor, intellect and craftsmanship. Throughout his literary career, Dryden maintained a conscious awareness of his public role as an author, and his works give a fine sense of the changing moral, political, and intellectual enthusiasms of his day. He is perhaps best known for his poetic and dramatic works, yet he was with some justice referred to by Samuel Johnson as "the father of English criticism." He was, according to his contemporary William Congreve, "an improving writer to the last."

Born 9 August 1631, in Aldwinkle All Saints, Northamptonshire, Dryden grew up in the uneasy period of Civil War and Parliamentary Revolution. He was the son of Erasmus Dryden and Mary Pickering; both sides of Dryden's family were Puritans who were allied with the Parliamentary party against the King. He attended Westminster School where he received a humanist education, firmly grounded in the ideals of ancient Greece and Rome. His first poem, *Upon the Death of Lord Hastings* (a school-mate of Dryden's), was published in 1649 while he was still at Westminster. The following year, he was admitted to Trinity College, Cambridge. He graduated in 1654, the same year his father died, and left Dryden a small estate upon which to build his adult livelihood. Little is known about the years immediately following his departure from Cambridge, but there is evidence to suggest that (likely through the influence of his cousin, Sir Gilbert Pickering, Cromwell's Lord Chamberlain) Dryden found employment as an administrator in Oliver Cromwell's Protectorate.

The publication in 1659 of Dryden's *Heroic Stanzas to the Glorious Memory of Cromwell* effectively began his literary career. Always supportive of authority and troubled by civic unrest, Dryden celebrated the return of Charles II the following year with his poem *Astraea Redux*, a poem that confirmed his mastery of the heroic couplet. In it he expounded for the first time in his works the notion of a parallel between England and ancient Rome. Dryden's reputation as a prominent man of letters quickly gained ground; he was elected a Fellow of the Royal Society in 1662.

Dryden's first play, the comedy *The Wild Gallant* (1662), did little to herald the author's future success as a playwright. According to Samuel Pepys the play was "so poor a thing as I never saw in my life almost … the King did not seem pleased at all." Dryden soon found success with *The Indian Queen* (1664), co-authored with Sir Robert Howard, a principal investor in the King's Company and also a brother-in-law; Dryden had married Lady Elizabeth Howard the previous year. *The Indian Queen* featured the music of Dryden's contemporary Henry Purcell, and marked the beginning of Dryden's interest in developing the genre of heroic tragedy for the Restoration audience. Later heroic tragedies such as *The Indian Emperor* (1665), *Tyrannick Love* (1669), *The Conquest of Granada* (1670), and *Aureng-Zebe* (1675) featured sensational plots, extravagant pageantry, and noble heroes torn between love and honor. Consciously artificial and bombastic, these plays repeatedly demonstrated Dryden's mastery of the heroic rhyming couplet; he finally confessed, in the prologue for *Aureng-Zebe*, that he had "grown weary of his long-lov'd mistress, Rhyme." His next play, *All For Love* (1677), presented the story of Antony and Cleopatra using more flexible and natural blank verse.

Although Dryden had argued in his *Essay of Dramatic Poesy* (1668) that English plays could succeed even when they did not follow the classical unities of time, place, and action, he valued the unities highly, and *All for Love* observes them, in his own words "more exactly than, perhaps the English theatre requires." Its precise construction was far more in accord with the neoclassical spirit of the age than was Shakespeare's sprawling rendition of the same story, and *All for Love* enjoyed enormous success through to the late eighteenth century. Although seldom produced today, *All for Love* remains a milestone in the corpus of English tragedy, and is considered a masterpiece of the Restoration stage.

Dryden attained notoriety as well as fame amongst play-goers for his heroic tragedies; the King's Company produced a dramatic parody of Drydenesque heroic drama in *The Rehearsal* (1671), by George Villiers, Duke of Buckingham (and collaborators). Dryden's comedies also received a mixed reception: this genre did not seem to offer him the same degree of inspiration he found in serious drama. *Marriage à la Mode* (1671), however, felt by Dryden to be the best of his comic works, was a considerable success. It embodies much of the gaiety and exuberance of Restoration comedy, yet extends Dryden's exploration of the heroic form through its serious sub-plot.

Outside of the theater, Dryden continued to chronicle important public occasions in verse. In 1668 he succeeded William Davenant as Poet Laureate, and in 1670 was also appointed Historiographer Royal. These appointments not only afforded him a degree of financial security; they also established him as the leading public author of the English realm.

For the next decade Dryden devoted most of his artistry to works for the stage, but political and personal debate also drew him to satire. An ongoing rivalry with fellow author Thomas Shadwell prompted the satirical invective *Mac Flecknoe* (1678). Drawing on an obvious animosity towards his subject and a long-established mastery of classical history and literature, Dryden rendered Shadwell's ascension to the "throne of dullness" with great deftness and wit. With its playful use of heroic style, and its ironic grandiosity, the poem exemplifies the mock-epic form; it would influence Alexander Pope's *The Rape of the Lock* (1712) and *The Dunciad* (1728).

In 1681, Dryden responded to the atmosphere of political turbulence occasioned by the Popish Plot and the controversy over the line of succession with the majestic satire *Absalom and Achitophel*. By drawing a biblical parallel to contemporary events and personalities Dryden succeeded in offering the public a reasoned (if far from impartial) examination of the exclusion debate, while endowing the poem with such satiric invention that the fever of the moment was exposed as ridiculous. Especially popular in its day for its clever portraiture of contemporary figures and controlled allegorical representation of events, *Absalom and Achitophel* established Dryden as the leading satirical poet of the day.

Known as a public man of letters and as a commentator on the political and social events of his day, Dryden seldom offered personal revelation in his poetry. The majority of his poems are "occasional" writings, inspired by particular events or current debates. His two poems on the subject of religion, *Religio Laici* (1682) and *The Hind and the Panther* (1687) are his most personal. The ideal balance between religious faith and political authority had long been of interest to Dryden. In *Religio Laici*, a discursive statement of his beliefs, he defends the Church of England as a necessary intercessor against the excesses of private guidance in religious matters. In 1685, with the ascension of James II to the throne, Dryden himself converted to Catholicism. Although regarded by many as an opportunist and hypocrite for his conversion, Dryden refused to change his religious views when the Glorious Revolution of 1688 placed the Protestant William III and Mary II on the throne. As a result, Dryden was stripped of his laureateship and pension and entered a period of great personal and financial difficulty.

Without the security of public office and income, Dryden turned once again to the stage; producing works such as *Don Sebastian* (1690), *Amphitryton* (1690), and the opera *King Arthur* (1691), a successful collaboration with Henry Purcell. Far from slowing his literary efforts in later years, Dryden rejuvenated his career as a translator, publishing the satires of Juvenal and Persius (1693), and Virgil (1697). His final major work demonstrated strength of mind and continued vigor in his last years, combining his talents as poet, critic, and translator in *Fables Ancient and Modern* (1700). *Fables* contains a number of adaptations of tales from Homer, Ovid, Chaucer, and Boccaccio, as well as several original fables. Its preface also provided occasion for one of Dryden's most important critical essays.

Throughout his life Dryden wrote prefaces, dedications, and critical essays that interpreted and refined tradition in English literature. He sought to give precision to what he perceived as an unruly and languid English poetic form and championed the application of critical and historical principles to the creation and appreciation of artistic work. Of his critical works, the most noteworthy are *An Essay of Dramatic Poesy* (1668), an extended discussion on the nature of dramatic writing and of the degree to which classical principles should be applied; and The Preface to *Fables Ancient and Modern*, wherein Dryden defends his editorial influence as a translator, and offers a spirited defense of Chaucer's poetry. Although the critical preface did not originate with Dryden, no previous English author had developed the form as fully or as skillfully as he did.

In the first year of the new century Dryden succumbed to the gout that had long afflicted him; he refused amputation of an inflamed toe until the infection had spread beyond remedy. On 1 May 1700, it was reported in a London newspaper that "John Dryden Esq., departed his life, who for his poetry &c. excelled all others this age produced." He was buried in Westminster Abbey on 13 May 1700.

Absalom and Achitophel

Published in 1681, *Absalom and Achitophel* was composed in celebration of what Dryden saw as King Charles II's recent assertion of monarchical authority and recovery of political control. The previous years had been characterized by widespread political turmoil and the looming threat of civil war, which had begun with the "Popish Plot" of 1678. That year, Catholic convert Titus Oates testified to the existence of a Jesuit plot to assassinate the king, destroy London, and kill the Protestants in order to reestablish Catholic rule in England. Though this plot was later discovered to be a fabrication, at the time it created mass panic, particularly when the murdered body of prominent London Justice of the Peace Sir Edmund Berry Godfrey was discovered. Fears of Catholic invasion reinforced existing divisions between King Charles and his opponents and fueled the already bitter controversy concerning the successor to the English throne.

Though Charles had many illegitimate children, he had produced none with his wife; as a result, his Catholic brother, James, the Duke of York, would succeed him to the throne—a fact that dismayed many Protestants and divided the country into Successionists, who supported Charles and his brother James, and Exclusionists, who sought to pass a bill excluding James from the line of succession and appointing in his place James, Duke of Monmouth (a Protestant and one of the king's illegitimate children). Order was only restored when Charles dissolved Parliament, prevented the passage of the Exclusion Bill, and arrested opposition leader Lord Shaftesbury, who had tried twice to pass the bill.

Written while Shaftesbury was in jail awaiting trial, *Absalom and Achitophel* is often described as a "miniature epic" of the Popish plot, and the resulting exclusion debate, presented within the framework of the biblical story of King David's betrayal by his wayward son, Absalom, in 2 Samuel. Readers at the time would have been familiar with this story, and indeed various writers and politicians had already drawn parallels between Charles II and David, between Absalom and Monmouth, and between England and Israel. Dryden, however, used these established metaphors to exploit the biblical tale for a broad range of satiric possibilities that had been overlooked by other writers.

Dryden casts Shaftesbury in the role of Achitophel, Absalom's evil counselor who incites him to rebel against his father. Achitophel is made more evil by his association, in the poem, with Satan; conversely, David is seen as closer to the divine for having been anointed by God. Monmouth (as Absalom), led by Shaftesbury (Achitophel), tempts the English to abandon their King—an event which, described in epic language and within the framework of a biblical narrative, is portrayed as catastrophic, not merely for the English Parliament, but for all humanity. The happy resolution of events which Dryden foresees, however, will, according to the poem's closing lines, usher in an age of peace and justice.

In using his wit to demonstrate his loyalty to the king (without glossing over all the King's faults, particularly his promiscuity), to garner support for the Successionists, and to ridicule his enemies (without dealing too harshly with Monmouth, whom Charles still loved) Dryden was fulfilling some of the most difficult tasks of his office as Poet Laureate, while simultaneously succeeding in entertaining his audience.

⌘⌘⌘

Absalom and Achitophel: A Poem

In pious times, ere priestcraft did begin,
Before polygamy was made a sin;
When man on many multiplied his kind,
Ere one to one was cursedly confined;
When nature prompted and no law denied
Promiscuous use of concubine and bride;
Then Israel's monarch[1] after Heaven's own heart,
His vigorous warmth did variously impart
To wives and slaves; and, wide as his command,
Scattered his Maker's image through the land.
Michal,[2] of royal blood, the crown did wear,
A soil ungrateful to the tiller's care:
Not so the rest; for several mothers bore
To godlike David several sons before.
But since like slaves his bed they did ascend,
No true succession could their seed attend.
Of all this numerous progeny was none
So beautiful, so brave, as Absalom:[3]
Whether, inspired by some diviner lust,
His father got him with a greater gust,° *pleasure*
Or that his conscious destiny made way,
By manly beauty, to imperial sway.
Early in foreign fields he won renown,
With kings and states allied to Israel's crown:[4]
In peace the thoughts of war he could remove,
And seemed as he were only born for love.
Whate'er he did, was done with so much ease,
In him alone 'twas natural to please;
His motions all accompanied with grace;
And paradise was opened in his face.
With secret joy indulgent David viewed
His youthful image in his son renewed:
To all his wishes nothing he denied;
And made the charming Annabel[5] his bride.
What faults he had (for who from faults is free?)
His father could not, or he would not see.
Some warm excesses which the law forbore,
Were construed youth that purged by boiling o'er:
And Amnon's murder,[6] by a specious name,

[1] *Israel's monarch* David, King of Israel (here representing Charles II).

[2] *Michal* One of David's wives, here representing Catherine of Braganza, Charles's Queen. See 2 Samuel 6.12–23.

[3] *Absalom* David's son; here, James, Duke of Monmouth, Charles II's illegitimate son.

[4] *Early in foreign … Israel's crown* Monmouth fought as a soldier for France against Holland in 1672–73, and for Holland against France in 1678.

[5] *Annabel* Anne, Countess of Buccleuch (1651–1732).

[6] *Amnon's murder* In 2 Samuel 13.28–29, Absalom murders his half-brother Amnon for the rape of his sister Tamar.

Was called a just revenge for injured fame.
Thus praised and loved the noble youth remained,
While David, undisturbed, in Sion[1] reigned.
But life can never be sincerely° blest; *completely*
Heav'n punishes the bad, and proves° the best. *tests*
The Jews,[2] a headstrong, moody, murm'ring race,
As ever tried th' extent and stretch of grace;
God's pampered people, whom, debauched with ease,
No king could govern, nor no God could please
(Gods they had tried of every shape and size
That god-smiths could produce, or priests devise);
These Adam-wits,[3] too fortunately free,
Began to dream they wanted liberty;
And when no rule, no precedent was found,
Of men by laws less circumscribed and bound,
They led their wild desires to woods and caves,
And thought that all but savages were slaves.
They who, when Saul[4] was dead, without a blow,
Made foolish Ishbosheth[5] the crown forgo;
Who banished David did from Hebron[6] bring,
And with a general shout proclaimed him king:
Those very Jews, who, at their very best,
Their humor more than loyalty expressed,
Now wondered why so long they had obeyed
An idol monarch, which their hands had made;
Thought they might ruin him they could create,
Or melt him to that golden calf,[7] a state.° *republic*
But these were random bolts; no formed design
Nor interest made the factious crowd to join:
The sober part of Israel, free from stain,
Well knew the value of a peaceful reign;
And, looking backward with a wise affright,
Saw seams of wounds, dishonest° to the sight: *shameful*
In contemplation of whose ugly scars
They cursed the memory of civil wars.
The moderate sort of men, thus qualified,
Inclined the balance to the better side;
And David's mildness managed it so well,
The bad found no occasion to rebel.
But when to sin our biased nature leans,
The careful Devil is still at hand with means;
And providently pimps for ill desires:
The Good Old Cause[8] revived, a plot requires.
Plots, true or false, are necessary things,
To raise up commonwealths and ruin kings.
 Th' inhabitants of old Jerusalem
Were Jebusites;[9] the town so called from them;
And theirs the native right.
But when the chosen people[10] grew more strong,
The rightful cause at length became the wrong;
And every loss the men of Jebus bore,
They still were thought God's enemies the more.
Thus worn and weakened, well or ill content,
Submit they must to David's government:
Impoverished and deprived of all command,
Their taxes doubled as they lost their land;
And, what was harder yet to flesh and blood,
Their gods disgraced, and burnt like common wood.
This set the heathen priesthood[11] in a flame;
For priests of all religions are the same:
Of whatsoe'er descent their godhead be,
Stock, stone, or other homely pedigree,
In his defense his servants are as bold,
As if he had been born of beaten gold.
The Jewish rabbins,[12] though their enemies,
In this conclude them honest men and wise:
For 'twas their duty, all the learned think,
T' espouse his cause, by whom they eat and drink.
From hence began that Plot,[13] the nation's curse,

[1] *Sion* Jerusalem; here, London.

[2] *Jews* I.e., the English.

[3] *Adam-wits* False reasoners.

[4] *Saul* Former king of Israel; here, Oliver Cromwell, Lord Protector of England, Scotland, and Ireland from 1653 to 1658.

[5] *Ishbosheth* Here, Cromwell's son Richard, who succeeded his father as Lord Protector (from 1658 to 1659). See 2 Samuel 3–4.

[6] *Hebron* Here, Scotland, where Charles II had been crowned in 1651, prior to his ascension to the English throne in 1660. See 2 Samuel 5.1–5.

[7] *golden calf* The image worshiped by the Jews as Moses was on Mount Sinai (Exodus 32).

[8] *The Good Old Cause* Slogan of the Puritan rebellion; here it refers to the Commonwealth of 1649–53.

[9] *Jebusites* Jebus was the original name of Jerusalem. Jebusites inhabited Jerusalem before Benjamin's tribe. Here Dryden refers to Roman Catholics.

[10] *chosen people* Originally, the Jews; in this context, the Protestants.

[11] *heathen priesthood* Roman Catholic clergy.

[12] *rabbins* Here, Anglican priests.

[13] *that Plot* The Popish Plot of 1678.

Bad in itself, but represented worse;
Raised in extremes, and in extremes decried;
With oaths affirmed, with dying vows denied;
Not weighed or winnowed[1] by the multitude;
But swallowed in the mass, unchewed and crude.
Some truth there was, but dashed and brewed with lies,
To please the fools, and puzzle all the wise.
Succeeding times did equal folly call,
Believing nothing, or believing all.
Th' Egyptian rites the Jebusites embraced,
Where gods were recommended by their taste.[2]
Such sav'ry deities must needs be good,
As served at once for worship and for food.
By force they could not introduce these gods,
For ten to one in former days was odds;
So fraud was used (the sacrificer's trade):
Fools are more hard to conquer than persuade.
Their busy teachers mingled with the Jews,
And raked for converts even the court and stews:° *brothels*
Which Hebrew priests the more unkindly took,
Because the fleece[3] accompanies the flock.
Some thought they God's anointed[4] meant to slay
By guns, invented since full many a day:
Our author swears it not; but who can know
How far the Devil and Jebusites may go?
This Plot, which failed for want of common sense,
Had yet a deep and dangerous consequence:
For, as when raging fevers boil the blood,
The standing lake soon floats into a flood,
And ev'ry hostile humor, which before
Slept quiet in its channels, bubbles o'er;
So several factions from this first ferment
Work up to foam, and threat the government.
Some by their friends, more by themselves thought wise,
Opposed the pow'r to which they could not rise.
Some had in courts been great, and thrown from thence,
Like fiends were hardened in impenitence;
Some, by their monarch's fatal mercy, grown
From pardoned rebels kinsmen to the throne,
Were raised in pow'r and public office high;
Strong bands, if bands ungrateful men could tie.
Of these the false Achitophel[5] was first;
A name to all succeeding ages cursed:
For close designs, and crooked counsels fit;
Sagacious, bold, and turbulent of wit;
Restless, unfixed in principles and place;
In pow'r unpleased, impatient of disgrace:
A fiery soul, which, working out its way,
Fretted the pygmy body to decay,[6]
And o'er-informed the tenement of clay.
A daring pilot in extremity;
Pleased with the danger, when the waves went high,
He sought the storms; but, for a calm unfit,
Would steer too nigh the sands, to boast his wit.
Great wits are sure to madness near allied,
And thin partitions do their bounds divide;
Else why should he, with wealth and honor blest,
Refuse his age the needful hours of rest?
Punish a body which he could not please;
Bankrupt of life, yet prodigal of ease?
And all to leave what with his toil he won,
To that unfeathered two-legged thing,[7] a son;
Got, while his soul did huddled° notions try; *disordered*
And born a shapeless lump, like anarchy.[8]
In friendship false, implacable in hate,
Resolved to ruin or to rule the state.
To compass this the triple bond[9] he broke.
The pillars of the public safety shook,
And fitted Israel for a foreign yoke;[10]
Then seized with fear, yet still affecting fame,
Usurped a patriot's all-atoning name.
So easy still it proves in factious times,
With public zeal to cancel private crimes.
How safe is treason, and how sacred ill,

[1] *winnowed* Separated from inferior elements.

[2] *Egyptian rites ... taste* Refers to the Roman Catholic doctrine of transubstantiation, and the consumption of bread and wine during Mass.

[3] *fleece* Tithes.

[4] *God's annointed* The king.

[5] *Achitophel* Evil counselor of Absalom; see 2 Samuel. Here, Anthony Ashley Cooper (1621–83), First Earl of Shaftesbury.

[6] *A fiery ... decay* Shaftesbury's body was twisted and stunted as a result of illness.

[7] *unfeathered two-legged thing* Dryden refers to Plato's definition of a human as "a featherless biped."

[8] *a son ... anarchy* Dryden's allusion is uncertain.

[9] *triple bond* The 1668 alliance of England, Sweden, and Holland against France.

[10] *foreign yoke* That of France.

Where none can sin against the people's will!
Where crowds can wink, and no offense be known,
Since in another's guilt they find their own!
Yet fame deserved, no enemy can grudge;
The statesman we abhor, but praise the judge.
In Israel's courts ne'er sat an Abbethdin[1]
With more discerning eyes, or hands more clean;
Unbribed, unsought, the wretched to redress;
Swift of dispatch, and easy of access.
Oh, had he been content to serve the crown,
With virtues only proper to the gown;
Or had the rankness of the soil been freed
From cockle,° that oppressed the noble seed; *weeds*
David for him his tuneful harp had strung,
And Heav'n had wanted one immortal song.[2]
But wild Ambition loves to slide, not stand,
And Fortune's ice prefers to Virtue's land.
Achitophel, grown weary to possess
A lawful fame, and lazy happiness,
Disdained the golden fruit[3] to gather free,
And lent the crowd his arm to shake the tree.
Now, manifest of crimes contrived long since,
He stood at bold defiance with his prince;
Held up the buckler[4] of the people's cause
Against the crown, and skulked behind the laws.
The wished occasion of the Plot he takes;
Some circumstances finds, but more he makes.
By buzzing emissaries fills the ears
Of list'ning crowds with jealousies° and fears *suspicions*
Of arbitrary counsels brought to light,
And proves the king himself a Jebusite.
Weak arguments! which yet he knew full well
Were strong with people easy to rebel.
For, governed by the moon, the giddy Jews
Tread the same track when she the prime renews;[5]
And once in twenty years, their scribes record,

[1] *Abbethdin* Senior justice of the Jewish civil court. Shaftesbury was Lord Chancellor from 1672–73.

[2] *And Heav'n ... immortal song* Refers to Psalms 3 and 4, and also to 2 Samuel 18.33.

[3] *golden fruit* Forbidden fruit in the Garden of Eden.

[4] *buckler* Small round shield.

[5] *For ... renews* Dryden refers to the constitutional crises of 1640, 1660, and 1680 as following the lunar cycle, which lasts approximately 20 years.

By natural instinct they change their lord.
Achitophel still wants a chief, and none
Was found so fit as warlike Absalom:
Not that he wished his greatness to create
(For politicians neither love nor hate),
But, for he knew his title not allowed,
Would keep him still depending on the crowd,
That kingly pow'r, thus ebbing out, might be
Drawn to the dregs of a democracy.[6]
Him he attempts with studied arts to please,
And sheds his venom in such words as these:
"Auspicious prince, at whose nativity
Some royal planet ruled the southern sky;
Thy longing country's darling and desire;
Their cloudy pillar and their guardian fire:[7]
Their second Moses, whose extended wand
Divides the seas, and shows the promised land;
Whose dawning day in every distant age
Has exercised the sacred prophet's rage:° *inspiration*
The people's prayer, the glad diviners' theme,
The young men's vision, and the old men's dream![8]
Thee, savior, thee, the nation's vows confess,
And, never satisfied with seeing, bless:
Swift unbespoken pomps[9] thy steps proclaim,
And stammering babes are taught to lisp thy name.
How long wilt thou the general joy detain,
Starve and defraud the people of thy reign?
Content ingloriously to pass thy days
Like one of Virtue's fools that feeds on praise;
Till thy fresh glories, which now shine so bright,
Grow stale and tarnish with our daily sight.
Believe me, royal youth, thy fruit must be
Or gathered ripe, or rot upon the tree.
Heav'n has to all allotted, soon or late,
Some lucky revolution of their fate;
Whose motions if we watch and guide with skill
(For human good depends on human will),
Our Fortune rolls as from a smooth descent,
And from the first impression takes the bent;

[6] *democracy* Popular government (here used pejoratively).

[7] *Their cloudy pillar and their guardian fire* During the Exodus, Moses led the Israelites across the Red Sea, following a pillar of cloud by day and a pillar of fire by night.

[8] *young men's ... dream* Cf. Joel 2.28.

[9] *unbespoken pomps* Spontaneous honors or processions.

But, if unseized, she glides away like wind,
And leaves repenting Folly far behind.
Now, now she meets you with a glorious prize,
And spreads her locks before her as she flies.[1]
Had thus old David, from whose loins you spring,
Not dared, when Fortune called him, to be king,
At Gath[2] an exile he might still remain,
And heaven's anointing oil had been in vain.
Let his successful youth your hopes engage;
But shun th' example of declining age;
Behold him setting in his western skies,
The shadows lengthening as the vapors rise.
He is not now, as when on Jordan's sand[3]
The joyful people thronged to see him land,
Cov'ring the beach, and black'ning all the strand;
But, like the Prince of Angels, from his height
Comes tumbling downward with diminished light;[4]
Betrayed by one poor plot to public scorn
(Our only blessing since his cursed return),
Those heaps of people which one sheaf did bind,
Blown off and scattered by a puff of wind.
What strength can he to your designs oppose,
Naked of friends, and round beset with foes?
If Pharaoh's[5] doubtful succor he should use,
A foreign aid would more incense the Jews:
Proud Egypt would dissembled friendship bring;
Foment the war, but not support the king:
Nor would the royal party e'er unite
With Pharaoh's arms t' assist the Jebusite;
Or if they should, their interest soon would break,
And with such odious aid make David weak.
All sorts of men by my successful arts,
Abhorring kings, estrange their altered hearts
From David's rule: and 'tis the general cry,
'Religion, commonwealth, and liberty.'
If you, as champion of the public good,
Add to their arms a chief of royal blood,
What may not Israel hope, and what applause
Might such a general gain by such a cause?
Not barren praise alone, that gaudy flow'r
Fair only to the sight, but solid pow'r;
And nobler is a limited command,
Giv'n by the love of all your native land,
Than a successive title, long and dark,
Drawn from the moldy rolls of Noah's ark."
What cannot praise effect in mighty minds,
When flattery soothes, and when ambition blinds!
Desire of pow'r, on earth a vicious weed,
Yet, sprung from high, is of celestial seed:
In God 'tis glory; and when men aspire,
'Tis but a spark too much of heavenly fire.
Th' ambitious youth, too covetous of fame,
Too full of angels' metal[6] in his frame,
Unwarily was led from virtue's ways,
Made drunk with honor, and debauched with praise.
Half loath, and half consenting to the ill
(For loyal blood within him struggled still),
He thus replied: "And what pretense have I
To take up arms for public liberty?
My father governs with unquestioned right;
The faith's defender, and mankind's delight,
Good, gracious, just, observant of the laws:
And heav'n by wonders has espoused his cause.
Whom has he wronged in all his peaceful reign?
Who sues for justice to his throne in vain?
What millions has he pardoned of his foes,
Whom just revenge did to his wrath expose?
Mild, easy, humble, studious of our good,
Inclined to mercy, and averse from blood;
If mildness ill with stubborn Israel suit,
His crime is God's beloved attribute.
What could he gain, his people to betray,
Or change his right for arbitrary sway?
Let haughty Pharaoh curse with such a reign
His fruitful Nile, and yoke a servile train.
If David's rule Jerusalem displease,
The Dog Star[7] heats their brains to this disease.

[1] *But, if unseized … flies* Traditionally, Fortune (or Opportunity) is represented as a woman with flowing hair that can be seized as she approaches. She is bald behind, however, and once past cannot be grasped.

[2] *Gath* Here, Brussels, where Charles II spent the last years of his exile.

[3] *Jordan's sand* Here, Dover Beach, where Charles II landed in 1660.

[4] *Comes … light* Lucifer, once the light-bearer, was cast out of heaven for rebelling against God.

[5] *Pharaoh* Ruler of Egypt; here, Louis XIV of France.

[6] *angels' metal* Pun on both *metal* (mettle) and *angel* (a gold coin).

[7] *Dog Star* Sirius, which rises and sets with the mid-summer sun and is therefore associated with "midsummer madness" or the "dog days."

Why then should I, encouraging the bad,
Turn rebel and run popularly mad?
Were he a tyrant, who, by lawless might
Oppressed the Jews, and raised the Jebusite,
Well might I mourn; but nature's holy bands
Would curb my spirits and restrain my hands:
The people might assert their liberty,
But what was right in them were crime in me.
His favor leaves me nothing to require,
Prevents my wishes, and outruns desire.
What more can I expect while David lives?
All but his kingly diadem he gives:
And that"—But there he paused; then sighing, said—
"Is justly destined for a worthier head.
For when my father from his toils shall rest
And late augment the number of the blest,
His lawful issue shall the throne ascend,
Or the collat'ral line,[1] where that shall end.
His brother, though oppressed with vulgar spite,
Yet dauntless, and secure of native right,
Of every royal virtue stands possessed;
Still dear to all the bravest and the best.
His courage foes, his friends his truth proclaim;
His loyalty the king, the world his fame.
His mercy ev'n th' offending crowd will find,
For sure he comes of a forgiving kind.° *family*
Why should I then repine at heaven's decree,
Which gives me no pretense to royalty?
Yet O that fate, propitiously inclined,
Had raised my birth, or had debased my mind;
To my large soul not all her treasure lent,
And then betrayed it to a mean descent!
I find, I find my mounting spirits bold,
And David's part disdains my mother's mold.
Why am I scanted by a niggard° birth? *stingy*
My soul disclaims the kindred of her earth;
And, made for empire, whispers me within,
'Desire of greatness is a godlike sin.'"
Him staggering° so when hell's dire agent found, *wavering*
While fainting Virtue scarce maintained her ground,
He pours fresh forces in, and thus replies:
"Th' eternal god, supremely good and wise,
Imparts not these prodigious gifts in vain:
What wonders are reserved to bless your reign!
Against your will, your arguments have shown,
Such virtue's only giv'n to guide a throne.
Not that your father's mildness I contemn,
But manly force becomes the diadem.
'Tis true he grants the people all they crave;
And more, perhaps, than subjects ought to have:
For lavish grants suppose a monarch tame,
And more his goodness than his wit proclaim.
But when should people strive their bonds to break,
If not when kings are negligent or weak?
Let him give on till he can give no more,
The thrifty Sanhedrin[2] shall keep him poor;
And every shekel which he can receive,
Shall cost a limb of his prerogative.[3]
To ply him with new plots shall be my care;
Or plunge him deep in some expensive war;
Which when his treasure can no more supply,
He must, with the remains of kingship, buy.
His faithful friends our jealousies and fears
Call Jebusites, and Pharaoh's pensioners;
Whom when our fury from his aid has torn,
He shall be naked left to public scorn.
The next successor, whom I fear and hate,
My arts have made obnoxious to the state;
Turned all his virtues to his overthrow,
And gained our elders[4] to pronounce a foe.
His right, for sums of necessary gold,
Shall first be pawned, and afterward be sold;
Till time shall ever-wanting David draw,
To pass your doubtful title into law:
If not, the people have a right supreme
To make their kings; for kings are made for them.
All empire is no more than pow'r in trust,
Which, when resumed, can be no longer just.
Succession, for the general good designed,
In its own wrong a nation cannot bind;
If altering that the people can relieve,

[1] *collat'ral line* Line of succession through Charles's brother James, or his descendants.

[2] *Sanhedrin* Highest Jewish judicial council; here, Parliament.

[3] *prerogative* Royal prerogative, or special privileges, which Parliament sought to limit by controlling the Crown's money supply.

[4] *elders* Shaftesbury's supporters were members of the gentry and aristocracy.

Better one suffer than a nation grieve.[1]
The Jews well know their pow'r: ere Saul they chose,
God was their king, and God they durst depose.[2]
Urge now your piety, your filial name,
A father's right and fear of future fame;
The public good, that universal call,
To which even heav'n submitted, answers all.
Nor let his love enchant your generous mind;
'Tis Nature's trick to propagate her kind.
Our fond begetters, who would never die,
Love but themselves in their posterity.
Or let his kindness by th' effects be tried,
Or let him lay his vain pretense aside.
God said he loved your father; could he bring
A better proof than to anoint him king?
It surely showed he loved the shepherd well,
Who gave so fair a flock as Israel.
Would David have you thought his darling son?
What means he then, to alienate[3] the crown?
The name of godly he may blush to bear:
'Tis after God's own heart to cheat his heir.
He to his brother gives supreme command;
To you a legacy of barren land,[4]
Perhaps th' old harp, on which he thrums his lays,° *ballads*
Or some dull Hebrew ballad in your praise.
Then the next heir, a prince severe and wise,
Already looks on you with jealous eyes;
Sees through the thin disguises of your arts,
And marks your progress in the people's hearts.
Though now his mighty soul its grief contains,
He meditates revenge who least complains;
And, like a lion, slumb'ring in the way,
Or sleep dissembling, while he waits his prey,
His fearless foes within his distance draws,
Constrains his roaring, and contracts his paws;
Till at the last, his time for fury found,
He shoots with sudden vengeance from the ground;
The prostrate vulgar[5] passes o'er and spares,
But with a lordly rage his hunters tears.
Your case no tame expedients will afford:
Resolve on death, or conquest by the sword,
Which for no less a stake than life you draw;
And self-defense is nature's eldest law.
Leave the warm people no considering time;
For then rebellion may be thought a crime.
Prevail° yourself of what occasion gives, *avail*
But try your title while your father lives;
And that your arms may have a fair pretense,
Proclaim you take them in the king's defense;
Whose sacred life each minute would expose
To plots, from seeming friends, and secret foes.
And who can sound the depth of David's soul?
Perhaps his fear his kindness may control.
He fears his brother, though he loves his son,
For plighted vows too late to be undone.
If so, by force he wishes to be gained,
Like women's lechery, to seem constrained.° *forced*
Doubt not; but when he most affects the frown,
Commit a pleasing rape upon the crown.
Secure his person to secure your cause:
They who possess the prince, possess the laws."

He said, and this advice above the rest
With Absalom's mild nature suited best:
Unblamed of life (ambition set aside),
Not stained with cruelty, nor puffed with pride,
How happy had he been, if destiny
Had higher placed his birth, or not so high!
His kingly virtues might have claimed a throne,
And blest all other countries but his own.
But charming greatness since so few refuse,
'Tis juster to lament him than accuse.
Strong were his hopes a rival to remove,
With blandishments to gain the public love;
To head the faction while their zeal was hot,
And popularly prosecute the Plot.
To further this, Achitophel unites
The malcontents of all the Israelites;
Whose differing parties he could wisely join,
For several ends, to serve the same design:

[1] *Better one … grieve* Cf. John 11.50, in which the high priest Caiaphas says to the Pharisees about Jesus, "it is expedient for us that one man should die for the people, and that the whole nation perish not."

[2] *The Jews … durst depose* Before Saul, Israel was ruled by judges. Cromwell, the first Lord Protector, replaced the Rump Parliament in 1653.

[3] *alienate* Transfer into ownership of another person.

[4] *To you … land* Charles II promoted James to general in 1678 and banished Monmouth to Holland in the following year.

[5] *vulgar* Commoners.

The best (and of the princes some were such),
Who thought the pow'r of monarchy too much;
Mistaken men, and patriots in their hearts;
Not wicked, but seduced by impious arts.
By these the springs of property were bent,
And wound so high, they cracked the government.
The next for interest sought t' embroil the state,
To sell their duty at a dearer rate;
And make their Jewish markets of the throne,
Pretending public good, to serve their own.
Others thought kings an useless heavy load,
Who cost too much, and did too little good.
These were for laying honest David by,
On principles of pure good husbandry.° *management*
With them joined all th' haranguers of the throng,
That thought to get preferment by the tongue.
Who follow next, a double danger bring,
Not only hating David, but the king:
The Solymaean rout,[1] well-versed of old
In godly faction, and in treason bold;
Cow'ring and quaking at a conqu'ror's sword,
But lofty to a lawful prince restored;
Saw with disdain an ethnic[2] plot begun,
And scorned by Jebusites to be outdone.
Hot Levites[3] headed these; who, pulled before
From th' ark, which in the Judges' days they bore,
Resumed their cant, and with a zealous cry
Pursued their old belov'd theocracy:[4]
Where Sanhedrin and priest enslaved the nation,
And justified their spoils by inspiration:[5]
For who so fit for reign as Aaron's race,[6]
If once dominion they could found in grace?
These led the pack; though not of surest scent,
Yet deepest-mouthed° against the government. *loudest*
A numerous host of dreaming saints succeed,
Of the true old enthusiastic breed:[7]
'Gainst form and order they their pow'r employ,
Nothing to build, and all things to destroy.
But far more numerous was the herd of such,
Who think too little, and who talk too much.
These out of mere instinct, they knew not why,
Adored their fathers' God and property;
And, by the same blind benefit of fate,
The Devil and the Jebusite did hate:
Born to be saved, even in their own despite,
Because they could not help believing right.
Such were the tools; but a whole Hydra[8] more
Remains, of sprouting heads too long to score.
Some of their chiefs were princes of the land:
In the first rank of these did Zimri[9] stand;
A man so various, that he seemed to be
Not one, but all mankind's epitome:
Stiff in opinions, always in the wrong;
Was everything by starts, and nothing long;
But, in the course of one revolving moon,
Was chemist, fiddler, statesman, and buffoon:
Then all for women, painting, rhyming, drinking,
Besides ten thousand freaks° that died in thinking. *whims*
Blest madman, who could every hour employ,
With something new to wish, or to enjoy!
Railing° and praising were his usual themes; *criticizing*
And both (to show his judgment) in extremes:
So over-violent, or over-civil,
That every man, with him, was God or Devil.
In squandering wealth was his peculiar art:
Nothing went unrewarded but desert.
Beggared by fools, whom still he found too late,
He had his jest, and they had his estate.
He laughed himself from court; then sought relief

[1] *Solymaean rout* London rabble.

[2] *ethnic* Gentile; here, Roman Catholic.

[3] *Levites* Ancient Hebrew tribe, especially those who were Assistants to the Priestly class. During the exile of the Jews, the Levites carried the Ark of the Covenant. Here Dryden refers to Presbyterian clergymen who lost their church benefices with the Act of Conformity in 1662.

[4] *theocracy* System of government by God, or by priestly order; here, the Commonwealth.

[5] *inspiration* Members of non-conforming sects sometimes claimed divine inspiration, or direct contact with God.

[6] *Aaron's race* Priests of Israel, who were descendants of Aaron.

[7] *enthusiastic breed* Here, religious enthusiasts, used pejoratively.

[8] *Hydra* In Greek mythology the Hydra was a many-headed serpent that would sprout new heads whenever one was severed.

[9] *Zimri* George Villiers, Second Duke of Buckingham, a prominent Whig and supporter of Shaftesbury. He was the author of *The Rehearsal*, which satirized the heroic play and ridiculed Dryden. For biblical Zimris, see Numbers 25.6–15, 1 Kings 8–20, and 2 Kings 9.31.

By forming parties, but could ne'er be chief;
For, spite of him, the weight of business fell
On Absalom and wise Achitophel:
Thus, wicked but in will, of means bereft,
He left not faction, but of that was left.
    Titles and names 'twere tedious to rehearse
Of lords, below the dignity of verse.
Wits, warriors, Commonwealth's men, were the best;
Kind husbands, and mere nobles, all the rest.
And therefore, in the name of dullness, be
The well-hung Balaam[1] and cold Caleb,[2] free;
And canting Nadab[3] let oblivion damn,
Who made new porridge for the paschal lamb.[4]
Let friendship's holy band some names assure;
Some their own worth, and some let scorn secure.
Nor shall the rascal rabble here have place,
Whom kings no titles gave, and God no grace:
Not bull-faced Jonas,[5] who could statutes draw
To mean rebellion, and make treason law.
But he, though bad, is followed by a worse,
The wretch who heav'n's anointed dared to curse:
Shimei,[6] whose youth did early promise bring
Of zeal to God and hatred to his king,
Did wisely from expensive sins refrain,
And never broke the Sabbath, but for gain;
Nor ever was he known an oath to vent,
Or curse, unless against the government.
Thus heaping wealth, by the most ready way
Among the Jews, which was to cheat and pray,
The city, to reward his pious hate
Against his master, chose him magistrate.
His hand a vare° of justice did uphold; *staff*
His neck was loaded with a chain of gold.
During his office, treason was no crime;
The sons of Belial[7] had a glorious time;
For Shimei, though not prodigal of pelf,[8]
Yet loved his wicked neighbor as himself.
When two or three were gathered to declaim
Against the monarch of Jerusalem,
Shimei was always in the midst of them;
And if they cursed the king when he was by,
Would rather curse than break good company.
If any durst his factious friends accuse,
He packed a jury of dissenting Jews;
Whose fellow-feeling in the godly cause
Would free the suff'ring saint from human laws.
For laws are only made to punish those
Who serve the king, and to protect his foes.
If any leisure time he had from pow'r
(Because 'tis sin to misemploy an hour),
His business was, by writing, to persuade
That kings were useless, and a clog to trade;
And, that his noble style he might refine,
No Rechabite[9] more shunned the fumes of wine.
Chaste were his cellars, and his shrieval board° *sheriff's table*
The grossness of a city feast abhorred:
His cooks, with long disuse, their trade forgot;
Cool was his kitchen, though his brains were hot,
Such frugal virtue malice may accuse,
But sure 'twas necessary to the Jews:
For towns once burnt[10] such magistrates require
As dare not tempt God's providence by fire.
With spiritual food he fed his servants well,
But free from flesh that made the Jews rebel;
And Moses' laws he held in more account,
For forty days of fasting in the mount.[11]
To speak the rest, who better are forgot,

[1] *Balaam* Probably Theophilus Hastings, Earl of Huntingdon, who initially supported Shaftesbury, but returned his support to the King in 1681.See Numbers 13–14.

[2] *Caleb* Arthur Capel, Earl of Essex. See Number 13–14.

[3] *Nadab* William, Lord Howard of Escrick, a dissenting preacher. See Leviticus 10.1–2.

[4] *Who … lamb* Howard was said to have taken the sacrament with hot ale, known as "porridge," instead of wine.

[5] *Jonas* Sir William Jones, prosecutor of those accused in the Popish Plot, and then supporter of the Exclusion Bill against the succession of James, Duke of York.

[6] *Shimei* In 2 Samuel 16.5–14, Shimei curses David as he flees from Absalom's rebellion. Here, Slingsby Bethel, a London sheriff responsible for packing juries in order to thwart the prosecution of Shaftesbury and his supporters.

[7] *Belial* Fallen angel, a minister of Satan. Here, wicked or dissolute persons in general. Possibly also a pun on Balliol College, which was friendly to the Whigs during the Oxford Parliament of 1681.

[8] *prodigal of pelf* Free with money.

[9] *Rechabite* Jewish sect that abstained from wine drinking.

[10] *towns once burnt* Reference to the Great Fire of London in 1666.

[11] *And Moses' laws … fasting in the mount* Moses received God's commandments during a forty-day fast on Mount Sinai (Exodus 34.28).

Would tire a well-breathed witness of the Plot.
Yet, Corah,[1] thou shalt from oblivion pass:
Erect thyself, thou monumental brass,
High as the serpent of thy metal made,[2]
While nations stand secure beneath thy shade.
What though his birth were base, yet comets rise
From earthy vapors, ere they shine in skies.
Prodigious actions may as well be done
By weaver's issue,[3] as by prince's son.
This arch-attestor for the public good
By that one deed ennobles all his blood.
Who ever asked the witnesses' high race
Whose oath with martyrdom did Stephen[4] grace?
Ours was a Levite, and as times went then,
His tribe were God Almighty's gentlemen.
Sunk were his eyes, his voice was harsh and loud,
Sure signs he neither choleric° was nor proud: *hot-tempered*
His long chin proved his wit; his saintlike grace
A church vermilion, and a Moses' face.[5]
His memory, miraculously great,
Could plots, exceeding man's belief, repeat;
Which therefore cannot be accounted lies,
For human wit could never such devise.
Some future truths are mingled in his book;
But where the witness failed, the prophet spoke:
Some things like visionary flights appear;
The spirit caught him up, the Lord knows where,
And gave him his rabbinical degree,
Unknown to foreign university.[6]
His judgment yet his mem'ry did excel;
Which pieced his wondrous evidence so well,
And suited to the temper of the times,
Then groaning under Jebusitic crimes.
Let Israel's foes suspect his heav'nly call,
And rashly judge his writ apocryphal;[7]
Our laws for such affronts have forfeits made:
He takes his life, who takes away his trade.
Were I myself in witness Corah's place,
The wretch who did me such a dire disgrace
Should whet my memory, though once forgot,
To make him an appendix of my plot.
His zeal to heav'n made him his prince despise,
And load his person with indignities;
But zeal peculiar privilege affords,
Indulging latitude to deeds and words;
And Corah might for Agag's[8] murder call,
In terms as coarse as Samuel used to Saul.
What others in his evidence did join
(The best that could be had for love or coin),
In Corah's own predicament will fall;
For *witness* is a common name to all.

Surrounded thus with friends of every sort,
Deluded Absalom forsakes the court:
Impatient of high hopes, urged with renown,
And fired with near possession of a crown.
Th' admiring crowd are dazzled with surprise,
And on his goodly person feed their eyes:
His joy concealed, he sets himself to show,
On each side bowing popularly low;
His looks, his gestures, and his words he frames,
And with familiar ease repeats their names.
Thus formed by nature, furnished out with arts,
He glides unfelt into their secret hearts.
Then, with a kind compassionating look,
And sighs, bespeaking pity ere he spoke,
Few words he said; but easy those and fit,
More slow than Hybla-drops,[9] and far more sweet.

"I mourn, my countrymen, your lost estate;
Though far unable to prevent your fate:
Behold a banished man, for your dear cause
Exposed a prey to arbitrary laws!
Yet oh! that I alone could be undone,

[1] *Corah* Rebellious Levite; here, Titus Oates, the chief manufacturer of the Popish Plot.

[2] *the serpent of thy metal made* Moses erected a brass serpent to cure Jews suffering from snake bites (Numbers 21.4–9); metal also refers to Oates's "mettle," his spirit, or ambition.

[3] *By weaver's issue* By the child of a weaver. (Oates's father was a weaver.)

[4] *Stephen* First Christian martyr; he was stoned by false witnesses (Acts 6–7).

[5] *Moses' face* Moses's face shone with divine illumination after receiving God's commandments (Exodus 34.29–30).

[6] *And gave him … foreign university* Oates falsely claimed to have a Doctor of Divinity degree from the University of Salamanca.

[7] *apocryphal* Excluded from the Holy Canon.

[8] *Agag* Likely refers to Lord Stafford, accused by Oates and executed in 1680. For Samuel's denouncement of Saul see 1 Samuel 15.

[9] *Hybla-drops* Celebrated Sicilian honey noted for its sweetness.

Cut off from empire, and no more a son!
Now all your liberties a spoil are made;
Egypt and Tyrus[1] intercept your trade,
And Jebusites your sacred rites invade.
My father, whom with reverence yet I name,
Charmed into ease, is careless of his fame;
And, bribed with petty sums of foreign gold,
Is grown in Bathsheba's[2] embraces old;
Exalts his enemies, his friends destroys;
And all his pow'r against himself employs.
He gives, and let him give, my right away;
But why should he his own, and yours betray?
He only, he can make the nation bleed,
And he alone from my revenge is freed.
Take then my tears (with that he wiped his eyes),
'Tis all the aid my present pow'r supplies:
No court-informer can these arms accuse;
These arms may sons against their fathers use:
And 'tis my wish, the next successor's reign
May make no other Israelite complain."
    Youth, beauty, graceful action seldom fail;
But common interest always will prevail;
And pity never ceases to be shown
To him who makes the people's wrongs his own.
The crowd (that still° believe their kings oppress) *always*
With lifted hands their young Messiah bless:
Who now begins his progress to ordain
With chariots, horsemen, and a num'rous train;
From east to west his glories he displays,[3]
And, like the sun, the promised land surveys.
Fame runs before him as the morning star,
And shouts of joy salute him from afar:
Each house receives him as a guardian god,
And consecrates the place of his abode:
But hospitable treats did most commend
Wise Issachar,[4] his wealthy western friend.
This moving court, that caught the people's eyes,
And seemed but pomp, did other ends disguise:
Achitophel had formed it, with intent
To sound the depths, and fathom, where it went,
The people's hearts; distinguish friends from foes,
And try their strength, before they came to blows.
Yet all was colored with a smooth pretense
Of specious love, and duty to their prince.
Religion, and redress of grievances,
Two names that always cheat and always please,
Are often urged; and good King David's life
Endangered by a brother and a wife.[5]
Thus, in a pageant show, a plot is made,
And peace itself is war in masquerade.
O foolish Israel! never warned by ill,
Still the same bait, and circumvented still!
Did ever men forsake their present ease,
In midst of health imagine a disease;
Take pains contingent mischiefs to foresee,
Make heirs for monarchs, and for God decree?
What shall we think! Can people give away
Both for themselves and sons, their native sway?
Then they are left defenseless to the sword
Of each unbounded, arbitrary lord:
And laws are vain, by which we right enjoy,
If kings unquestioned can those laws destroy.
Yet if the crowd be judge of fit and just,
And kings are only officers in trust,
Then this resuming cov'nant was declared
When kings were made, or is forever barred.
If those who gave the scepter could not tie
By their own deed their own posterity,
How then could Adam bind his future race?
How could his forfeit on mankind take place?
Or how could heavenly justice damn us all,
Who ne'er consented to our father's fall?
Then kings are slaves to those whom they command,
And tenants to their people's pleasure stand.
Add, that the pow'r for property allowed
Is mischievously seated in the crowd;
For who can be secure of private right,
If sovereign sway may be dissolved by might?
Nor is the people's judgment always true:

[1] *Egypt and Tyrus* Here, France and Holland.

[2] *Bathsheba* Duchess of Portsmouth, Louise-Renée de Kéroualle, a mistress of Charles II who was popularly considered a French spy.

[3] *From … displays* Monmouth journeyed through western England in order to rally support.

[4] *Issachar* Thomas Thynne of Longleat, a wealthy Whig supporter who entertained Monmouth on his western journey. See Genesis 49.14–15.

[5] *Endangered … wife* Titus Oates accused Charles's Queen Catherine and his brother James of conspiring to murder him.

The most may err as grossly as the few;
And faultless kings run down, by common cry,
For vice, oppression, and for tyranny.
What standard is there in a fickle rout,
Which, flowing to the mark, runs faster out?
Nor only crowds, but Sanhedrins may be
Infected with this public lunacy,
And share the madness of rebellious times,
To murder monarchs for imagined crimes.[1]
If they may give and take whene'er they please,
Not kings alone (the Godhead's images),
But government itself at length must fall
To nature's state, where all have right to all.
Yet, grant our lords the people kings can make,
What prudent men a settled throne would shake?
For whatsoe'er their sufferings were before,
That change they covet makes them suffer more.
All other errors but disturb a state,
But innovation is the blow of fate.
If ancient fabrics nod, and threat to fall,
To patch the flaws, and buttress up the wall,
Thus far 'tis duty; but here fix the mark;
For all beyond it is to touch our ark.[2]
To change foundations, cast the frame anew,
Is work for rebels, who base ends pursue,
At once divine and human laws control,
And mend the parts by ruin of the whole.
The tamp'ring world is subject to this curse,
To physic their disease into a worse.
  Now what relief can righteous David bring?
How fatal 'tis to be too good a king!
Friends he has few, so high the madness grows:
Who dare be such, must be the people's foes:
Yet some there were, ev'n in the worst of days;
Some let me name, and naming is to praise.
  In this short file Barzillai[3] first appears;
Barzillai, crowned with honor and with years:
Long since, the rising rebels he withstood
In regions waste, beyond the Jordan's flood:

[1] *To ... crimes* Allusion to the execution of Charles I in 1649.

[2] *to touch our ark* To touch the Ark of the Covenant is to commit sacrilege.

[3] *Barzillai* Loyal supporter of David during Absalom's rebellion (2 Samuel 19.31–39). Here, James Butler, Duke of Ormond, a loyal supporter of both Charles I and Charles II.

Unfortunately brave to buoy the State;
But sinking underneath his master's fate:
In exile with his godlike prince he mourned;
For him he suffered, and with him returned.
The court he practiced, not the courtier's art:
Large was his wealth, but larger was his heart:
Which well the noblest objects knew to choose,
The fighting warrior, and recording Muse.
His bed could once a fruitful issue boast;
Now more than half a father's name is lost.
His eldest hope,[4] with every grace adorned,
By me (so Heav'n will have it) always mourned,
And always honored, snatched in manhood's prime
B' unequal fates, and Providence's crime:
Yet not before the goal of honor won,
All parts fulfilled of subject and of son;
Swift was the race, but short the time to run.
O narrow circle, but of pow'r divine,
Scanted in space, but perfect in thy line!
By sea, by land, thy matchless worth was known,
Arms thy delight, and war was all thy own:
Thy force, infused, the fainting Tyrians'[5] propped;
And haughty Pharaoh found his fortune stopped.
Oh ancient honor! Oh unconquered hand,
Whom foes unpunished never could withstand!
But Israel was unworthy of thy name:
Short is the date of all immoderate fame.
It looks as Heav'n our ruin had designed,
And durst not trust thy fortune and thy mind.
Now, free from earth, thy disencumbered soul
Mounts up, and leaves behind the clouds and starry pole:
From thence thy kindred legions mayst thou bring,
To aid the guardian angel of thy king. Here stop my
Muse, here cease thy painful flight;
No pinions° can pursue immortal height: *wings*
Tell good Barzillai thou canst sing no more,
And tell thy soul she should have fled before:
Or fled she with his life, and left this verse
To hang on her departed patron's hearse?
Now take thy steepy flight from Heav'n, and see
If thou canst find on earth another *he*:
Another *he* would be too hard to find;
See then whom thou canst see not far behind.

[4] *eldest hope* Ormond's son, Thomas, Earl of Ossory, died in 1680.

[5] *Tyrians* Here, the Dutch.

Zadoc[1] the priest, whom, shunning pow'r and place,
His lowly mind advanced to David's grace:
With him the Sagan[2] of Jerusalem,
Of hospitable soul, and noble stem;
Him of the western dome,[3] whose weighty sense
Flows in fit words and heavenly eloquence.
The prophets' sons,[4] by such example led,
To learning and to loyalty were bred:
For colleges on bounteous kinds depend,
And never rebel was to arts a friend.
To these succeed the pillars of the laws,
Who best could plead, and best can judge a cause.
Next them a train of loyal peers ascend;
Sharp-judging Adriel,[5] the Muses' friend,
Himself a Muse—in Sanhedrin's debate
True to his prince, but not a slave of state:
Whom David's love with honors did adorn,
That from his disobedient son were torn.[6]
Jotham[7] of piercing wit, and pregnant thought,
Indued by nature, and by learning taught
To move assemblies, who but only tried
The worse a while, then chose the better side;
Nor chose alone, but turned the balance too;
So much the weight of one brave man can do.
Hushai,[8] the friend of David in distress,
In public storms, of manly steadfastness:
By foreign treaties he informed his youth,
And joined experience to his native truth.
His frugal care supplied the wanting throne,
Frugal for that, but bounteous of his own:
'Tis easy conduct when exchequers flow,
But hard the task to manage well the low;
For sovereign power is too depressed or high,
When kings are forced to sell, or crowds to buy.
Indulge one labor more, my weary Muse,
For Amiel:[9] who can Amiel's praise refuse?
Of ancient race by birth, but nobler yet
In his own worth, and without title great:
The Sanhedrin long time as chief he ruled,
Their reason guided, and their passion cooled:
So dext'rous was he in the crown's defense,
So formed to speak a loyal nation's sense,
That, as their band was Israel's tribes in small,
So fit was he to represent them all.
Now rasher charioteers the seat ascend,
Whose loose careers his steady skill commend:
They like th' unequal ruler of the day,
Misguide the seasons, and mistake the way;[10]
While he withdrawn at their mad labor smiles,
And safe enjoys the sabbath of his toils.
    These were the chief, a small but faithful band
Of worthies, in the breach who dared to stand,
And tempt th' united fury of the land.
With grief they viewed such powerful engines bent,
To batter down the lawful government:
A numerous faction, with pretended frights,
In Sanhedrins to plume° the regal rights; *pluck*
The true successor from the court removed:[11]
The Plot, by hireling witnesses, improved.
These ills they saw, and, as their duty bound,
They showed the king the danger of the wound:
That no concessions from the throne would please,
But lenitives[12] fomented the disease;
That Absalom, ambitious of the crown,

[1] *Zadoc* David demanded that Zadoc and the Levites remain behind when he left the city during Absalom's rebellion (2 Samuel 8.17). Here Zadoc represents William Sancroft, Archbishop of Canterbury.

[2] *Sagan* Second-highest temple official. Here, Henry Compton, Bishop of London.

[3] *Him of the western dome* John Dolben, Dean of Westminster.

[4] *The prophet's sons* Students of Westminster School, where Dryden had been a King's Scholar.

[5] *Adriel* John Sheffield, Earl of Mulgrave. He was a patron and friend of Dryden's.

[6] *That from … were torn* In 1679, two high offices, Governor of Hull and Lord Lieutenant of Yorkshire, were transferred from Monmouth to Mulgrave.

[7] *Jotham* George Saville, Marquis of Halifax. Formerly associated with Shaftesbury, he helped defeat the Exclusion Bill in the House of Lords. See Judges 9.1–21.

[8] *Hushai* Laurence Hyde, Earl of Rochester and First Lord of the Treasury from 1679–85. He was another of Dryden's patrons. See 2 Samuel 16.

[9] *Amiel* Edward Seymour, Speaker of the House of Commons from 1673–78.

[10] *Misguide … way* Allusion to Phaethon, son of Apollo, who almost set the world afire when he could not control his father's chariot, which pulled the sun across the sky.

[11] *The true … removed* The Duke of York was banished from England for six months in 1679.

[12] *lenitives* Soothing medicines.

Was made the lure to draw the people down;
That false Achitophel's pernicious hate
Had turned° the Plot to ruin Church and State: *manipulated*
The council violent, the rabble worse;
That Shimei taught Jerusalem to curse.
With all these loads of injuries oppressed,
And long revolving, in his careful breast,
Th' event of things, at last, his patience tired,
Thus from his royal throne, by Heav'n inspired,
The godlike David spoke: with awful fear
His train their Maker in their master hear.
"Thus long have I, by native mercy swayed,
My wrongs dissembled, my revenge delayed:
So willing to forgive th' offending age,
So much the father did the king assuage.
But now so far my clemency they slight,
Th' offenders question my forgiving right.
That one was made for many, they contend;
But 'tis to rule; for that's a monarch's end.
They call my tenderness of blood, my fear;
Though manly tempers can the longest bear.
Yet, since they will divert my native course,
'Tis time to show I am not good by force.
Those heaped affronts that haughty subjects bring,
Are burdens for a camel, not a king:
Kings are the public pillars of the State,
Born to sustain and prop the nation's weight:
If my young Samson[1] will pretend a call
To shake the column, let him share the fall:
But, oh, that yet he would repent and live!
How easy 'tis for parents to forgive!
With how few tears a pardon might be won
From nature, pleading for a darling son!
Poor pitied youth, by my paternal care
Raised up to all the height his frame could bear:
Had God ordained his fate for empire born,
He would have giv'n his soul another turn:
Gulled° with a patriot's name, whose modern sense *tricked*
Is one that would by law supplant his prince:
The people's brave, the politician's tool;
Never was patriot yet, but was a fool.
Whence comes it that religion and the laws
Should more be Absalom's than David's cause?
His old instructor, ere he lost his place,
Was never thought indued with so much grace.
Good Heav'ns, how faction can a patriot paint!
My rebel ever proves my people's saint:
Would *they* impose an heir upon the throne?
Let Sanhedrins be taught to give their own.
A king's at least a part of government,
And mine as requisite as their consent;
Without my leave a future king to choose,
Infers a right the present to depose:
True, they petition me to approve their choice;
But Esau's hands suit ill with Jacob's voice.[2]
My pious subjects for my safety pray,
Which to secure, they take my pow'r away.
From plots and treasons Heav'n preserve my years,
But save me most from my petitioners.
Unsatiate as the barren womb or grave;
God cannot grant so much as they can crave.
What then is left but with a jealous eye
To guard the small remains of royalty?
The law shall still direct my peaceful sway,
And the same law teach rebels to obey:
Votes shall no more established power control—
Such votes as make a part exceed the whole:
No groundless clamors shall my friends remove,
Nor crowds have pow'r to punish ere they prove:
For gods and godlike kings, their care express,
Still to defend their servants in distress.
O that my pow'r to saving were confined:
Why am I forced, like Heav'n, against my mind,
To make examples of another kind?
Must I at length the sword of justice draw?
O curst effects of necessary law!
How ill my fear they by my mercy scan!° *judge*
Beware the fury of a patient man.
Law they require, let Law then show her face;
They could not be content to look on Grace,
Her hinder parts, but with a daring eye
To tempt the terror of her front and die.[3]

[1] *Samson* Biblical hero of enormous strength who killed himself by pulling down the Temple pillars while he stood under them. See Judges 13–16.

[2] *But Esau's … voice* In Genesis 27 Jacob disguised himself as his brother Esau by covering his hands with rough goat skin in order to receive his father's blessings.

[3] *To tempt … die* Moses was not allowed to see the face of God (Exodus 33.20–23).

By their own arts, 'tis righteously decreed,
Those dire artificers of death shall bleed.
Against themselves their witnesses will swear,
Till viper-like their mother Plot they tear:
And suck for nutriment that bloody gore,
Which was their principle of life before.
Their Belial with their Belzebub[1] will fight;
Thus on my foes, my foes shall do me right:
Nor doubt th' event; for factious crowds engage,
In their first onset, all their brutal rage.
Then let 'em take an unresisted course,
Retire and traverse, and delude their force:
But when they stand all breathless, urge the fight,
And rise upon 'em with redoubled might:
For lawful pow'r is still superior found,
When long driv'n back, at length it stands the ground."
He said. Th' Almighty, nodding, gave consent;
And peals of thunder shook the firmament.
Henceforth a series of new time began,
The mighty years in long procession ran:
Once more the godlike David was restored,
And willing nations knew their lawful lord.
—1681

Mac Flecknoe

The first of Dryden's satires, *Mac Flecknoe*, with its bawdy raillery against dull writers and ignorant, unimaginative readers, is often considered his liveliest and most humorous poem. Its primary target is Thomas Shadwell, a rival dramatist of Dryden who wrote "humor-comedy," a genre, perfected by Ben Jonson and popular during the Renaissance, in which characters are seen to be ruled by one dominant mood, or humor. Dryden's comedies of wit employed a style almost directly opposed to Shadwell's. More pertinently, Shadwell was politically a Whig, one of the party Dryden attacked in *Absalom and Achitophel*. For several years the two men had engaged in an ongoing quarrel—primarily conducted in prefaces of their respective plays—over the relative merits of their respective works. With *Mac Flecknoe*, Dryden moved the quarrel from the realm of polite literary debate to a more pointed attack and used his disagreement with Shadwell to voice his dissatisfaction with the literary society of his day.

In the poem, Shadwell has been chosen by the English poet Richard Flecknoe (a minor poet of the previous generation whose name was, at least for Dryden, synonymous with bad poetry) as heir to his kingdom of dullness—thus becoming "Mac," or the "son of" Flecknoe. In elevated language and an epic form, the poem proclaims a new ruler of the kingdom of dullness and provides a description of the coronation ceremony that takes as its model that of Charles II. Shadwell's royal procession though the city also satirically echoes the entry of Christ into Jerusalem. In this ironic vision of a world in which dullness is a virtue, and wit and sense are scourges of the earth, Shadwell comes to embody the void of cultural values that Dryden saw around him.

Though the poem may have been completed as early as 1678, Dryden made no move to publish it, most likely out of respect for Shadwell, and though the manuscript was circulated for several years it did not appear publicly until a pirated edition was published in 1682. Ironically, Shadwell was chosen to replace Dryden as Poet Laureate in 1688.

[1] *Belzebub* Devil, one of Satan's ministers.

Mac Flecknoe
Or, a Satire upon the True-Blue-Protestant Poet, T.S.

All human things are subject to decay,
And when fate summons, monarchs must obey.
This Flecknoe found, who, like Augustus,[1] young
Was called to empire, and had governed long;
In prose and verse, was owned, without dispute,
Through all the realms of Nonsense, absolute.
This aged prince, now flourishing in peace,
And blest with issue of a large increase,
Worn out with business, did at length debate
To settle the succession of the state;
And, pond'ring which of all his sons was fit
To reign, and wage immortal war with wit,
Cried: "'Tis resolved; for nature pleads that he
Should only rule, who most resembles me.
Sh—— alone my perfect image bears,
Mature in dullness from his tender years:
Sh—— alone, of all my sons, is he
Who stands confirmed in full stupidity.
The rest to some faint meaning make pretense,
But Sh—— never deviates into sense.
Some beams of wit on other souls may fall,
Strike through, and make a lucid interval;
But Sh——'s genuine night admits no ray,
His rising fogs prevail upon the day.
Besides, his goodly fabric[2] fills the eye,
And seems designed for thoughtless majesty:
Thoughtless as monarch oaks that shade the plain,
And, spread in solemn state, supinely reign.
Heywood and Shirley[3] were but types[4] of thee,
Thou last great prophet of tautology.[5]
Even I, a dunce of more renown than they,
Was sent before but to prepare thy way;[6]
And, coarsely clad in Norwich drugget,[7] came
To teach the nations in thy greater name.
My warbling lute, the lute I whilom° strung, *formerly*
When to King John of Portugal[8] I sung,
Was but the prelude to that glorious day,
When thou on silver Thames didst cut thy way,
With well-timed oars before the royal barge,
Swelled with the pride of thy celestial charge;
And big with hymn, commander of a host,
The like was ne'er in Epsom blankets[9] tossed.
Methinks I see the new Arion[10] sail,
The lute still trembling underneath thy nail.
At thy well-sharpened thumb from shore to shore
The treble squeaks for fear, the basses roar;
Echoes from Pissing Alley[11] Sh—— call,
And Sh—— they resound from Aston Hall.
About thy boat the little fishes throng,
As at the morning toast° that floats along. *sewage*
Sometimes, as prince of thy harmonious band,
Thou wield'st thy papers in thy threshing hand,
St. Andre's feet[12] ne'er kept more equal time,
Not ev'n the feet of thy own *Psyche's* rhyme;
Though they in number as in sense excel:
So just, so like tautology, they fell,
That, pale with envy, Singleton[13] forswore
The lute and sword, which he in triumph bore,
And vowed he ne'er would act Villerius[14] more."

[1] *Augustus* Octavius (later Augustus) Caesar became the first Roman emperor at the age of 32.

[2] *goodly fabric* Allusion to Shadwell's corpulence.

[3] *Heywood and Shirley* Thomas Heywood (1570?–1641), and James Shirley (1596–1666), popular dramatists prior to the closing of the theaters in 1642. They were not well known in Dryden's age.

[4] *types* Prefigurings, or imperfect symbols.

[5] *tautology* Unintentional repetition of the same meaning.

[6] *prepare thy way* John the Baptist is said to have been sent to prepare the way for Christ (Matthew 3.3).

[7] *Norwich drugget* Drugget is a coarse woolen cloth. Shadwell was from Norfolk.

[8] *King John of Portugal* Flecknoe boasted of this king's patronage.

[9] *Epsom blankets* Reference to two different plays by Shadwell, *Epsom Wells* and *The Virtuoso*. In the latter, the character of Sir Samuel Hearty is tossed in a blanket.

[10] *Arion* In Greek mythology, Arion was a celebrated musician who was saved from drowning by music-loving dolphins.

[11] *Pissing Alley* Route from London's Strand to the Thames.

[12] *St. Andre's feet* French dancer who choreographed Shadwell's opera *Psyche*. Dryden's suggestion here is that the metrical feet of Shadwell's poetry would be just as regular as a dancer's steps to the music—a comparison not intended as a compliment. The "threshing hand" of Shadwell is suggested to be beating out a mechanical rhythm.

[13] *Singleton* John Singleton, a musician at the Theatre Royal.

[14] *Villerius* Character in William Davenant's opera *The Siege of Rhodes*.

Here stopped the good old sire, and wept for joy
In silent raptures of the hopeful boy.
All arguments, but most his plays, persuade.
That for anointed dullness he was made.
  Close to the walls which fair Augusta[1] bind
(The fair Augusta much to fears inclined),[2]
An ancient fabric,° raised t' inform the sight, *building*
There stood of yore, and Barbican[3] it hight:° *was called*
A watchtower once; but now, so fate ordains,
Of all the pile an empty name remains.
From its old ruins brothel houses rise,
Scenes of lewd loves, and of polluted joys,
Where their vast courts the mother-strumpets keep,
And, undisturbed by watch, in silence sleep.
Near these a Nursery[4] erects its head,
Where queens are formed, and future heroes bred;
Where unfledged actors learn to laugh and cry,
Where infant punks° their tender voices try, *prostitutes*
And little Maximins[5] the gods defy.
Great Fletcher never treads in buskins here,
Nor greater Jonson dares in socks appear;[6]
But gentle Simkin[7] just reception finds
Amidst this monument of vanished minds:
Pure clinches° the suburbian Muse affords, *puns*
And Panton[8] waging harmless war with words.
Here Flecknoe, as a place to fame well known,
Ambitiously design'd his Sh——'s throne;
For ancient Dekker[9] prophesied long since,
That in this pile would reign a mighty prince,
Born for a scourge of wit, and flail of sense;
To whom true dullness should some *Psyches* owe,
But worlds of *Misers* from his pen should flow;
Humorists and *Hypocrites*[10] it should produce,
Whole Raymond families, and tribes of Bruce.[11]
  Now Empress Fame had published the renown
Of Sh——'s coronation through the town.
Roused by report of Fame, the nations meet,
From near Bunhill, and distant Watling Street.[12]
No Persian carpets spread th' imperial way,
But scattered limbs of mangled poets lay;
From dusty shops neglected authors come,
Martyrs of pies, and relics of the bum.[13]
Much Heywood, Shirley, Ogilby[14] there lay,
But loads of Sh—— almost choked the way.
Bilked stationers for yeomen stood prepared,
And Herringman was captain of the guard.[15]
The hoary prince in majesty appeared,
High on a throne of his own labors reared.
At his right hand our young Ascanius[16] sate,
Rome's other hope, and pillar of the state.
His brows thick fogs, instead of glories, grace,
And lambent dullness played around his face.
As Hannibal did to the altars come,

[1] *Augusta* London.

[2] *The fair Augusta ... inclined* The line alludes to fears and suspicions aroused by the Popish Plot.

[3] *Barbican* Fortification, or gatehouse in the ancient wall surrounding the city. The area was a disreputable district in Dryden's day.

[4] *Nursery* School for young actors founded by Lady Davenant in 1671.

[5] *Maximins* Raging emperor in Dryden's *Tyrannic Love*.

[6] *Great Fletcher ... socks appear* John Fletcher (1579–1625), playwright noted for his tragedies, and Ben Jonson (1573–1637), noted for his comedies. Buskins were high boots worn by tragic actors and socks were the slippers, or soft shoes, of Athenian comic actors.

[7] *Simkin* Common simple character in a farce.

[8] *Panton* Common farce character known for being a punster.

[9] *Dekker* Thomas Dekker (1572?–1632), prolific dramatist known for his plays about life in London. Jonson satirized him in *The Poetaster*.

[10] *Misers ... Humorists and Hypocrites* Titles of early plays by Shadwell.

[11] *Raymond ... Bruce* Characters in Shadwell's plays.

[12] *Bunhill ... Watling Street* Both Bunhill and Watling Street are within half a mile of the Nursery and are located within the inner City.

[13] *Martyrs of pies ... bum* Unsold books were sold for scrap paper, here used as wrapping paper for pieshops, or bakeries, and as toilet paper.

[14] *Ogilby* John Ogilby (1600–76), a poet and translator of Homer and Virgil.

[15] *Bilked stationers ... the guard* Publishers who lost money. Henry Herringman published both Dryden and Shadwell.

[16] *Ascanius* Son of Aeneas who was marked by the gods by a flickering flame around his head in Virgil's *Aeneid*.

Sworn by his sire a mortal foe to Rome,[1]
So Sh—— swore, nor should his vow be vain,
That he till death true dullness would maintain;
And, in his father's right, and realm's defense,
Ne'er to have peace with wit, nor truce with sense.
The king himself the sacred unction[2] made,
As king by office, and as priest by trade.
In his sinister° hand, instead of ball, *left*
He placed a mighty mug of potent ale;
Love's Kingdom[3] to his right he did convey,
At once his scepter, and his rule of sway;
Whose righteous lore the prince had practiced young,
And from whose loins recorded *Psyche*[4] sprung.
His temples, last, with poppies[5] were o'erspread,
That nodding seemed to consecrate his head.
Just at that point of time, if Fame not lie,
On his left hand twelve reverend owls[6] did fly.
So Romulus, 'tis sung, by Tiber's brook,[7]
Presage of sway from twice six vultures took.[8]
Th' admiring throng loud acclamations make,
And omens of his future empire take.
The sire then shook the honors of his head,
And from his brows damps of oblivion shed
Full on the filial dullness: long he stood,
Repelling from his breast the raging God;
At length burst out in this prophetic mood:
"Heavens bless my son, from Ireland let him reign
To far Barbadoes on the western main;
Of his dominion may no end be known,

[1] *As Hannibal … Rome* According to Livy, the Carthaginian general Hannibal was forced by his father to swear an oath against Rome as a young boy.

[2] *sacred unction* Sacramental oil used to anoint the monarch in coronation ceremonies.

[3] *Love's Kingdom* Play by Flecknoe (1664).

[4] *Psyche* Opera by Shadwell.

[5] *poppies* Alludes to Shadwell's use of opium as well as to the mental dullness that is associated with its use (and, in Dryden's view, with Shadwell's writing).

[6] *twelve reverend owls* Symbols of darkness or dullness.

[7] *Romulus … Tiber's brook* Romulus and Remus were the co-founders of Rome, through which the Tiber River runs.

[8] *from twice six vultures took* According to Plutarch, Romulus chose the site of Rome upon seeing twelve vultures to his brother Remus's six.

And greater than his father's be his throne;
Beyond *Love's Kingdom* let him stretch his pen!"
He paused, and all the people cried, "Amen."
Then thus continued he: "My son, advance
Still in new impudence, new ignorance.
Success let others teach, learn thou from me
Pangs without birth, and fruitless industry.
Let *Virtuosos* in five years be writ;
Yet not one thought accuse thy toil of wit.
Let gentle George[9] in triumph tread the stage,
Make Dorimant betray, and Loveit rage;
Let Cully, Cockwood, Fopling, charm the pit,
And in their folly show the writer's wit.
Yet still thy fools shall stand in thy defense,
And justify their author's want of sense.
Let 'em be all by thy own model made
Of dullness, and desire no foreign aid;
That they to future ages may be known,
Not copies drawn, but issue of thy own.
Nay, let thy men of wit too be the same,
All full of thee, and differing but in name.
But let no alien S—dl—y[10] interpose,
To lard with wit thy hungry *Epsom* prose.
And when false flowers of rhetoric thou wouldst cull,
Trust nature, do not labor to be dull;
But write thy best, and top; and, in each line,
Sir Formal's[11] oratory will be thine:
Sir Formal, though unsought, attends thy quill,
And does thy northern dedications fill.[12]
Nor let false friends seduce thy mind to fame,
By arrogating Jonson's hostile name.
Let father Flecknoe fire thy mind with praise,
And uncle Ogilby thy envy raise.
Thou art my blood, where Jonson has no part:
What share have we in nature, or in art?
Where did his wit on learning fix a brand,

[9] *George* Sir George Etherege (1636–92), a comedic dramatist. The names in the next couplet refer to characters from his plays.

[10] *S—dl—y* Sir Charles Sedley (1638–1701), poet and playwright. Dryden alludes to the rumor that Sedley contributed more than the prologue to Shadwell's *Epsom Wells*.

[11] *Sir Formal's* Sir Formal Trifle, "The Orator" from Shadwell's *The Virtuoso*.

[12] *northern dedications fill* Both Shadwell and Flecknoe dedicated several works to the Duke and Duchess of Newcastle.

And rail at arts he did not understand?
Where made he love in Prince Nicander's[1] vein,
Or swept the dust in *Psyche's* humble strain?
Where sold he bargains,[2] 'whip-stitch,[3] kiss my arse,'
Promised a play and dwindled to a farce?
When did his Muse from Fletcher scenes purloin,
As thou whole Eth'rege dost transfuse to thine?
But so transfused, as oil on water's flow,
His always floats above, thine sinks below.
This is thy province, this thy wondrous way,
New humors to invent for each new play:
This is that boasted bias of thy mind,
By which one way, to dullness, 'tis inclined;
Which makes thy writings lean on one side still,
And, in all changes, that way bends thy will.
Nor let thy mountain-belly make pretense
Of likeness; thine's a tympany[4] of sense.
A tun° of man in thy large bulk is writ, *large cask*
But sure thou'rt but a kilderkin° of wit. *small cask*
Like mine, thy gentle numbers feebly creep;
Thy tragic Muse gives smiles, thy comic sleep.
With whate'er gall thou sett'st thyself to write,
Thy inoffensive satires never bite.
In thy felonious heart though venom lies,
It does but touch thy Irish pen,[5] and dies.
Thy genius calls thee not to purchase fame
In keen iambics,[6] but mild anagram.
Leave writing plays, and choose for thy command
Some peaceful province in acrostic[7] land.
There thou may'st wings display and altars raise,[8]
And torture one poor word ten thousand ways.
Or, if thou wouldst thy diff'rent talent suit,
Set thy own songs, and sing them to thy lute."
He said: but his last words were scarcely heard
For Bruce and Longville had a trap prepared,[9]
And down they sent the yet declaiming bard.
Sinking he left his drugget robe behind,
Borne upwards by a subterranean wind.
The mantle fell to the young prophet's part,[10]
With double portion of his father's art.
—1682 (WRITTEN C. 1679)

from *Religio Laici*[11]
or A Layman's Faith

Dim, as the borrowed beams of moon and stars
To lonely, weary, wand'ring travellers,
Is Reason to the soul: and as on high,
Those rolling fires discover but the sky
Not light us here; so Reason's glimmering ray
Was lent, not to assure our doubtful way,
But guide us upward to a better day.
And as those nightly tapers° disappear *candles*
When day's bright Lord ascends our hemisphere;
So pale grows Reason at religion's sight;
So dies, and so dissolves in supernatural light.
Some few, whose lamp shone brighter, have been led
From cause to cause, to Nature's secret head;
And found that one first principle must be:
But what, or who, that UNIVERSAL HE;
Whether some soul encompassing this ball

[1] *Prince Nicander's* Character in *Psyche*.

[2] *sold he bargains* To "sell bargains" is to respond to an innocent question with a coarse response.

[3] *whip-stitch* Nonsense phrase frequently used by Sir Samuel Hearty in *The Virtuoso*.

[4] *tympany* Swelling of the abdomen due to excess gas.

[5] *Irish pen* Although neither Flecknoe, nor Shadwell were Irish, Dryden uses the term as a common seventeenth-century reference to barbarity and poverty.

[6] *iambics* Sharp satire was often written in iambic meter.

[7] *acrostic* Poem in which the first letter of every line spells out the name of the person, or thing that is the subject of the verse.

[8] *wings display and altars raise* Dryden refers to the style of emblematic verse used by George Herbert in *Easter Wings* and *The Altar*. In this form of poetry, the lines of the poem create the visual shape of the subject.

[9] *Bruce and Longville … prepared* In *The Virtuoso*, Bruce and Longville open a trap-door underneath Sir Formal Trifle as he makes a speech.

[10] *The mantle … prophet's part* In 2 Kings 2.8–14, the prophet Elijah is carried to heaven in a chariot of fire as his mantle falls to his successor Elisha.

[11] *Religio Laici* Dryden composed this poem in response to Father Richard Simon's *Critical History of the Old Testament*, which examines the many manuscript variants of the Old Testament and concludes that, as a result of these variants, Catholicism is justified in interpreting the Bible in light of its own traditions. Dryden attacked this argument as potentially leading to the denial of the authority of the Scriptures and presented instead the Biblically-based faith of the Church of England.

Unmade, unmoded; yet making, moving all;
Or various atoms interfering dance
Leapt into form (the noble work of chance),
Or this great all was from eternity;
Not even the stagirite[1] himself could see;
And Epicurus[2] guessed as well as he:
As blindly groped they for a future state;
As rashly judged of providence and fate:
But least of all could their endeavours find
What most concerned the good of human kind:[3]
For happiness was never to be found;
But vanished from them, like enchanted ground.
One thought content the good to be enjoyed:
This, every little accident destroyed:
The wiser madmen did for virtue toil:
A thorny, or at best a barren soil:
In pleasure some their glutton souls would steep;
But found their line too short, the well too deep;
And leaky vessels which no bliss could keep.
Thus, anxious thoughts in endless circles roll,
Without a centre where to fix the soul:
In this wild maze their vain endeavours end.
How can the less the greater comprehend?
Or finite reason reach infinity?
For what could fathom GOD were more than he.
—1682

To the Memory of Mr. Oldham[4]

Farewell, too little and too lately known,
Whom I began to think and call my own;
For sure our souls were near allied, and thine
Cast in the same poetic mould with mine.[5]
One common note on either lyre did strike,
And knaves and fools we both abhorred alike:
To the same goal did both our studies drive,
The last set out the soonest did arrive.
Thus Nisus fell upon the slippery place,
While his young friend performed and won the race.[6]
O early ripe! to thy abundant store
What could advancing age have added more?
It might (what Nature never gives the young)
Have taught the numbers[7] of thy native tongue;
But satire needs not those, and wit will shine
Through the harsh cadence of a rugged line:
A noble error, and but seldom made,
When poets are by too much force betrayed.
Thy generous fruits, though gathered ere their prime
Still showed a quickness;[8] and maturing time
But mellows what we write to the dull sweets of rhyme.
Once more, hail and farewell;[9] farewell though young,
But ah too short, Marcellus[10] of our tongue;
Thy brows with ivy, and with laurels bound;[11]
But fate and gloomy night encompass thee around.
—1684

[1] *stagirite* Aristotle.

[2] *Epicurus* Greek philosopher (c. 340-270 BCE) who founded a school in Athens.

[3] [Dryden's note] Opinions of the several sects of philosophers concerning the *summum bonum*. [*Summum bonum* Latin: greatest good.]

[4] *Mr. Oldham* John Oldham, (1653–83) English poet known for his 1681 *Satires upon the Jesuits* (which was, like Dryden's *Absalom and Achitophel*, inspired by the Popish plot) and for his translations of classical poems. Dryden, who greatly admired his work, published this poem as a memorial, prefixed to the *Remains of Mr. John Oldham in Verse and Prose* (1684).

[5] *For sure ... mine* An echo of lines 204–05 of Oldham's "David's Lamentation": "Oh, dearer than my soul! if I can call it mine, / For sure we had the same, 'twas very thine."

[6] *Thus ... race* In his *Aeneid*, Virgil tells the story of Nisus, who slips in a pool of blood during a foot race, impeding a rival and thus enabling his friend Euryalus to win.

[7] *numbers* Metrical patterns.

[8] *quickness* Liveliness; also, an acidity or sharpness (either of taste or of speech).

[9] *hail and farewell* Translation of the Latin "ave atque vale," from Roman poet Catullus's elegy for his brother.

[10] *Marcellus* Nephew and adopted son (and heir) of Augustus, Marcellus had a great military career but died at the age of twenty. Book 6 of Virgil's *Aeneid* ends with Aeneas being shown a vision of Marcellus: "... hov'ring mists around his brows are spread, / And night, with sable shades, involves his head."

[11] *Thy ... bound* Ivy denotes immortality, while laurels are awarded to victors.

A Song for St. Cecilia's Day[1]

I

From harmony, from heav'nly harmony
This universal frame° began: *structure*
When Nature underneath a heap
Of jarring atoms lay,
And could not heave her head,
The tuneful voice was heard from high:
"Arise, ye more than dead."
Then cold, and hot, and moist, and dry,[2]
In order to their stations leap,
And Music's pow'r obey.
From harmony, from heav'nly harmony
This universal frame began:
From harmony to harmony
Through all the compass of the notes it ran,
The diapason[3] closing full in man.

2

What passion cannot Music raise and quell!
When Jubal[4] struck the corded shell,
His list'ning brethren stood around,
And, wond'ring, on their faces fell
To worship that celestial sound.
Less than a god they thought there could not dwell
Within the hollow of that shell
That spoke so sweetly and so well.
What passion cannot Music raise and quell!

3

The trumpet's loud clangor
Excites us to arms,
With shrill notes of anger,
And mortal alarms.
The double double double beat
Of the thund'ring drum
Cries: "Hark! the foes come;
Charge, charge, 'tis too late to retreat."

4

The soft complaining flute
In dying notes discovers
The woes of hopeless lovers,
Whose dirge is whispered by the warbling lute.

5

Sharp violins proclaim
Their jealous pangs, and desperation,
Fury, frantic indignation,
Depth of pains, and height of passion,
For the fair, disdainful dame.

6

But O! what art can teach,
What human voice can reach,
The sacred organ's praise?
Notes inspiring holy love,
Notes that wing their heav'nly ways
To mend the choirs above.

7

Orpheus[5] could lead the savage race;
And trees unrooted left their place,
Sequacious of[6] the lyre;
But bright Cecilia raised the wonder high'r:
When to her organ vocal breath was giv'n,
An angel heard, and straight appeared,
Mistaking earth for heav'n.

GRAND CHORUS

As from the pow'r of sacred lays
The spheres began to move,

[1] *A Song ... Day* St. Cecilia, the patron saint of music, was celebrated in England on November 22 of each year. In London the Musical Society would commission an original composition as an ode for the occasion. This is the first of two odes composed by Dryden in honor of St. Cecilia; the second, *Alexander's Feast,* was written ten years later. Both were later set to music by Handel. (G.B. Draghi composed the original music to which the ode was set in 1687.)

[2] *cold ... dry* Refers to the Epicurean conception of the activity of atoms of the four elements: earth, fire, water, and air.

[3] *diapason* Combination of all the notes or parts of the harmony.

[4] *Jubal* "The father of all such as handle the harp and organ" (Genesis 4.21).

[5] *Orpheus* According to Ovid's *Metamorphoses*, Orpheus was able to charm trees, stones and wild beasts into following him by the beautiful playing of his lyre.

[6] *Sequacious of* Following.

And sung the great Creator's praise
To all the blest above;
So, when the last and dreadful hour
This crumbling pageant shall devour,
The trumpet shall be heard on high,[1]
The dead shall live, the living die,
And Music shall untune the sky.
—1687

Cymon and Iphigenia, from Boccace[2]

Poeta loquitur,[3]

Old as I am, for ladies' love unfit,
The pow'r of beauty I remember yet,
Which once inflamed my soul, and still inspires my wit.
If love be folly, the fever divine
Has felt that folly, though he censures mine;
Pollutes the pleasures of a chaste embrace,
Acts what I write, and propagates in grace,
With riotous excess, a priestly race:
Suppose him free, and that I forge th'offence,
He showed the way, perverting first my sense:
In malice witty, and with venom fraught,
He makes me speak the things I never thought.
Compute the gains of his ungoverned zeal;
Ill suits his cloth the praise of railing well!
The world will think that what we loosely write,
Though now arraigned, he read with some delight;
Because he seems to chew the cud again,
When his broad comment makes the text too plain:
And teaches more in one explaining page,
Than all the double meanings of the stage.

What needs he paraphrase on what we mean?
We were at worst but wanton; he's obscene.
I, nor my fellows, nor my self excuse;
But love's the subject of the comic muse:
Nor can we write without it, nor would you
A tale of only dry instruction view;
Nor love is always of a vicious kind,
But oft to virtuous acts inflames the mind,
Awakes the sleepy vigour of the soul,
And, brushing o'er, adds motion to the pool.
Love, studious how to please, improves our parts,
With polished manners, and adorns with arts.
Love first invented verse, and formed the rhyme,
The motion measured, harmonized the chime;
To lib'ral acts enlarged the narrow-souled:
Softened the fierce, and made the coward bold:
The world when waste, he peopled with increase,
And warring nations reconciled in peace.
Ormond, the first, and all the fair may find
In this one legend to their fame designed,
When beauty fires the blood, how love exalts the mind.

In that sweet isle, where Venus[4] keeps her court,
And every grace, and all the loves resort;
Where either sex is formed of softer earth,
And takes the bent of pleasure from their birth;
There lived a Cyprian lord, above the rest,
Wise, wealthy, with a num'rous issue blest.

But as no gift of fortune is sincere,
Was only wanting in a worthy heir:
His eldest born, a goodly youth to view,
Excelled the rest in shape, and outward show;
Fair, tall, his limbs with due proportion joined,
But of a heavy, dull, degenerate mind.
His soul belied the features of his face;
Beauty was there, but beauty in disgrace.
A clownish mien,° a voice with rustic found, *look*
And stupid eyes, that ever loved the ground.
He looked like nature's error; as the mind
And body were not of a piece designed,
But made for two, and by mistake in one were joined.

The ruling rod, the father's forming care,
Were exercised in vain, on wit's despair;
The more informed the less he understood,
And deeper sunk by flound'ring in the mud.

[1] *The … high* 1 Corinthians 15.52 describes the "last trump" as heralding the Resurrection and Last Judgment.

[2] *Cymon … Boccace* "Cymon and Iphigenia" is a translation of Italian poet Giovanni Boccaccio's poem "Filostrato" (c. 1341).

[3] *Poeta loquitur* Latin: The poet says.

[4] *Venus* Roman goddess of love.

Now scorned of all, and grown the public shame,
The people from Galesus changed his name,
And Cymon called, which signifies a brute;
So well his name did with his nature suit.

His father, when he found his labour lost,
And care employed that answered not the cost,
Chose an ungrateful object to remove,
And loathed to see what nature made him love;
So to his country farm the fool confined:
Rude work well suited with a rustic mind.
Thus to the wilds the sturdy Cymon went,
A squire among the swains,° and pleased with banishment. *country laborers*
His corn, and cattle, were his only care,
And his supreme delight a country fair.

It happened on a summer's holiday,
That to the greenwood-shade he took his way;
For Cymon shunned the church, and used not much to pray.
His quarterstaff,[1] which he could ne'er forsake,
Hung half before, and half behind his back.
He trudged along unknowing what he sought,
And whistled as he went, for want of thought.

By chance conducted, or by thirst constrained,
The deep recesses of the grove he gained;
Where in a plain, defended by the wood,
Crept through the matted grass a crystal flood,
By which an alabaster fountain stood:
And on the margin of the fount was laid
(Attended by her slaves) a sleeping maid.
Like Dian[2] and her nymphs, when tired with sport,
To rest by cool Eurotas[3] they resort:
The dame herself the goddess well expressed,
Not more distinguished by her purple vest
Than by the charming features of her face,
And ev'n in slumber a superior grace:
Her comely limbs composed with decent care,

[1] *quarterstaff* Six- or eight-foot long pole tipped with iron, a common weapon among the English peasantry.

[2] *Dian* Diana, virgin goddess of the moon and of the hunt.

[3] *Eurotas* Greek river that runs through the city of Sparta and empties into the Laconic Gulf.

Her body shaded with a slight cymar;[4]
Her bosom to the view was only bare:
Where two beginning paps° were scarcely spied, *nipples*
For yet their places were but signified:
The fanning wind upon her bosom blows,
To meet the fanning wind the bosom rose;
The fanning wind and purling streams continue her repose.

The fool of nature stood with stupid eyes
And gaping mouth, that testified surprise,
Fixed on her face, nor could remove his sight,
New as he was to love, and novice in delight:
Long mute he stood, and leaning on his staff,
His wonder witnessed with an idiot laugh;
Then would have spoke, but by his glimmering sense
First found his want of words, and feared offence:
Doubted for what he was he should be known,
By his clown accent, and his country tone.

Through the rude chaos thus the running light
Shot the first ray that pierced the native night:
Then day and darkness in the mass were mixed,
Till gathered in a globe, the beams were fixed:
Last shone the sun, who, radiant in his sphere,
Illumined heav'n and earth, and rolled around the year.

So reason in this brutal soul began:
Love made him first suspect he was a man;
Love made him doubt his broad barbarian sound;
By love his want of words, and wit, he found:
That sense of want prepared the future way
To knowledge, and disclosed the promise of a day.

What not his father's care, nor tutor's art
Could plant with pains in his unpolished heart,
The best instructor, love, at once inspired,
As barren grounds to fruitfulness are fired:
Love taught him shame, and shame with love at strife
Soon taught the sweet civilities of life;
His gross material soul at once could find
Somewhat in her excelling all her kind:
Exciting a desire till then unknown,
Somewhat unfound, or found in her alone.

[4] *cymar* Type of long robe.

This made the first impression in his mind,
Above, but just above, the brutal kind.
For beasts can like, but not distinguish too,
Nor their own liking by reflection know;
Nor why they like or this, or t'other face,
Or judge of this or that peculiar grace,
But love in gross, and stupidly admire;
As flies, allured by light, approach the fire.
Thus our man-beast, advancing by degrees,
First likes the whole, then sep'rates what he sees;
On sev'ral parts a sev'ral praise bestows,
The ruby lips, the well-proportioned nose,
The snowy skin, the raven-glossy hair,
The dimpled cheek, the forehead rising fair,
And ev'n in sleep itself a smiling air.
From thence his eyes descending viewed the rest,
Her plump round arms, white hands, and heaving breast.
Long on the last he dwelt, though every part
A pointed arrow sped to pierce his heart.

Thus in a trice° a judge of beauty grown, *instant*
(A judge erected from a country clown)
He longed to see her eyes in slumber hid;
And wished his own could pierce within the lid:
He would have waked her, but restrained his thought,
And love new-born the first good manners taught.
An awful fear his ardent wish withstood,
Nor durst disturb the goddess of the wood;
For such she seemed by her celestial face,
Excelling all the rest of human race:
And things divine by common sense he knew,
Must be devoutly seen at distant view:
So checking his desire, with trembling heart
Gazing he stood, nor would, nor could depart;
Fixed as a pilgrim wildered in his way,
Who dares not stir by night for fear to stray,
But stands with awful eyes to watch the dawn of day.

At length awaking, Iphigene the Fair
(So was the beauty called who caused his care)
Unclosed her eyes, and double day revealed,
While those of all her slaves in sleep were sealed.

The slavering cudden° propped upon his staff, *fool*
Stood ready gaping with a grinning laugh,
To welcome her awake, nor durst begin
To speak, but wisely kept the fool within.
Then she, "What make you, Cymon, here alone?"
(For Cymon's name was round the country known
Because descended of a noble race,
And for a soul ill sorted with his face.)

But still the sot stood silent with surprise,
With fixed regard on her new opened eyes,
And in his breast received th'envenomed dart,
A tickling pain that pleased amid the smart.
But conscious of her form, with quick distrust
She saw his sparkling eyes, and feared his brutal lust:
This to prevent she waked her sleepy crew,
And rising hasty took a short adieu.

Then Cymon first his rustic voice essayed,
With proffered service to the parting maid
To see her safe; his hand she long denied,
But took at length, ashamed of such a guide.
So Cymon led her home, and leaving there
No more would to his country clowns repair,
But sought his father's house with better mind,
Refusing in the farm to be confined.

The father wondered at the son's return,
And knew not whether to rejoice or mourn;
But doubtfully received, expecting still
To learn the secret causes of his altered will.
Nor was he long delayed; the first request
He made was like his brothers to be dressed,
And, as his birth required, above the rest.

With ease his suit was granted by his sire,
Distinguishing his heir by rich attire:
His body thus adorned, he next designed
With lib'ral arts to cultivate his mind:
He sought a tutor of his own accord,
And studied lessons he before abhorred.

Thus the man-child advanced, and learned so fast,
That in short time his equals he surpassed:
His brutal manners from his breast exiled,
His mien he fashioned, and his tongue he filed;
In every exercise of all admired,

He seemed, nor only seemed, but was, inspired:
Inspired by love, whose business is to please;
He rode, he fenced, he moved with graceful ease,
More famed for sense, for courtly carriage more,
Than for his brutal folly known before.

What then of altered Cymon shall we say,
But that the fire which choked in ashes lay,
A load too heavy for his soul to move,
Was upward blown below, and brushed away by love?
Love made an active progress through his mind,
The dusky parts he cleared, the gross refined;
The drowsy waked; and as he went impressed
The Maker's image on the human breast.
Thus was the man amended by desire,
And though he loved perhaps with too much fire,
His father all his faults with reason scanned,
And liked an error of the better hand;
Excused th'excess of passion in his mind,
By flames too fierce, perhaps too much refined:
So Cymon, since his sire indulged his will,
Impetuous loved, and would be Cymon still;
Galesus he disowned, and chose to bear
The name of fool confirmed, and bishoped[1] by the
fair.

To Cipseus by his friends his suit he moved,
Cipseus, the father of the fair he loved:
But he was pre-engaged by former ties,
While Cymon was endeav'ring to be wise:
And Iphigene, obliged by former vows,
Had giv'n her faith to wed a foreign spouse:
Her sire and she to Rhodian Pasimond,
Though both repenting, were by promise bound,
Nor could retract; and thus, as fate decreed,
Though better loved, he spoke too late to speed.

The doom was past; the ship, already sent,
Did all his tardy diligence prevent:
Sighed to herself the fair unhappy maid,
While stormy Cymon thus in secret said:
"The time is come for Iphigene to find
The miracle she wrought upon my mind:
Her charms have made me man, her ravished love
In rank shall place me with the blessed above.
For mine by love, by force she shall be mine,
Or death, if force should fail, shall finish my design."

Resolved he said: "And rigged with speedy care
A vessel strong, and well equipped for war."
The secret ship with chosen friends he stored;
And bent to die, or conquer, went aboard.
Ambushed he lay behind the Cyprian shore,
Waiting the sail that all his wishes bore;
Nor long expected, for the following tide
Sent out the hostile ship and beauteous bride.

To Rhodes the rival bark directly steered,
When Cymon sudden at her back appeared,
And stopped her flight: then standing on his prow
In haughty terms he thus defied the foe:
"Or strike your sails at summons, or prepare
To prove the last extremities of war."
Thus warned, the Rhodians for the fight provide;
Already were the vessels side by side,
These obstinate to save, and those to seize the bride.
But Cymon soon his crooked grapples cast,
Which with tenacious hold his foes embraced,
And, armed with sword and shield, amid the press he
passed.
Fierce was the fight, but hast'ning to his prey,
By force the furious lover freed his way:
Himself alone dispersed the Rhodian crew,
The weak disdained, the valiant overthrew;
Cheap conquest for his following friends remained,
He reaped the field, and they but only gleaned.[2]

His victory confessed[3] the foe's retreat,
And cast their weapons at the victor's feet.
Whom thus he cheered: "O Rhodian youth, I fought
For love alone, nor other booty sought;
Your lives are safe; your vessel I resign,
Yours be your own, restoring what is mine:
In Iphigene I claim my rightful due,
Robbed by my rival, and detained by you:

[1] *bishoped* Established; confirmed (i.e., through the religious rite of confirmation).

[2] *gleaned* Gathered or picked up after the reapers.

[3] *confessed* Was evidence of; attested to.

Your Pasimond a lawless bargain drove,
The parent could not sell the daughter's love;
Or if he could, my love disdains the laws,
And like a king by conquest gains his cause:
Where arms take place, all other pleas are vain;
Love taught me force, and force shall love maintain.
You, what by strength you could not keep, release,
And at an easy ransom buy your peace."

Fear on the conquered side soon signed th'accord,
And Iphigene to Cymon was restored:
While to his arms the blushing bride he took,
To seeming sadness she composed her look;
As if by force subjected to his will,
Though pleased, dissembling, and a woman still.
And, for she wept, he wiped her falling tears,
And prayed her to dismiss her empty fears;
"For yours I am," he said, "and have deserved
Your love much better, whom so long I served,
Than he to whom your formal father tied
Your vows and sold a slave, not sent a bride."
Thus while he spoke he seized the willing prey,
As Paris bore the Spartan spouse[1] away:
Faintly she screamed, and ev'n her eyes confessed
She rather would be thought, than was, distressed.

Who now exults but Cymon in his mind,
Vain hopes, and empty joys of human kind,
Proud of the present, to the future blind!
Secure of fate while Cymon plows the sea,
And steers to Candy with his conquered prey.
Scarce the third glass of measured hours was run,
When like a fiery meteor sunk the sun;
The promise of a storm; the shifting gales
Forsake by fits, and fill the flagging sails:
Hoarse murmurs of the main[2] from far were heard,
And night came on, not by degrees prepared,
But all at once; at once the winds arise,
The thunders roll, the forky lightning flies:
In vain the master issues out commands,
In vain the trembling sailors ply their hands:
The tempest unforeseen prevents their care,
And from the first they labour in despair.
The giddy ship betwixt the winds and tides
Forced back, and forwards in a circle rides,
Stunned with the diff'rent blows; then shoots amain,[3]
Till counterbuffed she stops, and sleeps again.
Not more aghast the proud archangel fell,
Plunged from the height of heav'n to deepest hell,[4]
Than stood the lover of his love possessed,
Now cursed the more, the more he had been blessed;
More anxious for her danger than his own,
Death he defies, but would be lost alone.

Sad Iphigene to womanish complaints
Adds pious prayers, and wearies all the saints;
Ev'n if she could, her love she would repent,
But since she cannot, dreads the punishment:
Her forfeit faith, and Pasimond betrayed,
Are ever present, and her crime upbraid.
She blames herself, nor blames her lover less,
Augments her anger as her fears increase;
From her own back the burden would remove,
And lays the load on his ungoverned love,
Which interposing durst in heav'n's despite
Invade, and violate another's right:
The pow'rs incensed awhile deferred his pain,
And made him master of his vows in vain:
But soon they punished his presumptuous pride;
That for his daring enterprise she died,
Who rather not resisted, than complied.

Then impotent of mind, with altered sense,
She hugged th'offender, and forgave th'offence,
Sex to the last: Meantime with sails declined
The wand'ring vessel drove before the wind:
Tossed, and retossed, aloft, and then alow;
Nor port they seek, nor certain course they know,
But ev'ry moment wait the coming blow.
Thus blindly driv'n, by breaking day they viewed
The land before 'em, and their fears renewed;

[1] *Spartan spouse* Helen, whom Paris stole from Menelaus, King of Sparta, thus starting the Trojan War.

[2] *main* Open sea.

[3] *amain* At full speed.

[4] *proud archangel … hell* Lucifer. See Isaiah 14.12: "How art thou fallen from heaven, O Lucifer, son of the morning! How art thou cut down to the ground, which didst weaken the nations!"

The land was welcome, but the tempest bore
The threatened ship against a rocky shore.

A winding bay was near; to this they bent,
And just escaped; their force already spent:
Secure from storms and panting from the sea,
The land unknown at leisure they survey;
And saw (but soon their sickly sight withdrew)
The rising tow'rs of Rhodes at distant view;
And cursed the hostile shore of Pasimond,
Saved from the seas, and shipwrecked on the ground.

The frighted sailors tried their strength in vain
To turn the stern, and tempt the stormy main;
But the stiff wind withstood the lab'ring oar,
And forced them forward on the fatal shore!
The crooked keel now bites the Rhodian strand,° *coast*
And the ship, moored, constrains the crew to land:
Yet still they might be safe because unknown,
But as ill fortune seldom comes alone.
The vessel they dismissed was driv'n before,
Already sheltered on their native shore;
Known each, they know: but each with change of cheer
The vanquished side exults; the victors fear;
Not them but theirs, made pris'ners e'er they fight,
Despairing conquest, and deprived of flight.

The country rings around with loud alarms,
And raw in fields the rude militia[1] swarms;
Mouths without hands, maintained at vast expense,
In peace a charge, in war a weak defense:
Stout once a month they march a blust'ring band,
And ever, but in times of need, at hand:
This was the morn when issuing on the guard,
Drawn up in rank and file they stood prepared
Of seeming arms to make a short essay,
Then hasten to be drunk, the business of the day.

The cowards would have fled, but that they knew
Themselves so many, and their foes so few;
But crowding on, the last the first impel;
Till overborn with weight the Cyprians fell.
Cymon enslaved, who first the war begun,
And Iphigene once more is lost and won.

Deep in a dungeon was the captive cast,
Deprived of day, and held in fetters fast:
His life was only spared at their request,
Whom taken he so nobly had released:
But Iphigenia was the ladies' care,
Each in their turn addressed to treat the fair;
While Pasimond and his the nuptial feast prepare.

Her secret soul to Cymon was inclined,
But she must suffer what her fates assigned;
So passive is the church of womankind.
What worse to Cymon could his fortune deal,
Rolled to the lowest spoke of all her wheel?
It rested to dismiss the downward weight,
Or raise him upward to his former height;
The latter pleased; and love (concerned the most)
Prepared th'amends, for what by love he lost.

The sire of Pasimond had left a son,
Though younger, yet for courage early known,
Ormisda called, to whom by promise tied,
A Rhodian beauty was the destined bride:
Cassandra was her name, above the rest
Renowned for birth, with fortune amply blessed.
Lysymachus, who ruled the Rhodian state,
Was then by choice their annual magistrate:
He loved Cassandra too, with equal fire,
But fortune had not favoured his desire;
Crossed by her friends, by her not disapproved,
Nor yet preferred, or like Ormisda loved:
So stood th'affair: some little hope remained,
That should his rival chance to lose, he gained.

Meantime young Pasimond his marriage pressed,
Ordained the nuptial day, prepared the feast;
And frugally resolved (the charge° to shun,° *expense / avoid*
Which would be double should he wed alone)
To join his brother's bridal with his own.

Lysymachus, oppressed with mortal grief,
Received the news, and studied quick relief.
The fatal day approached: if force were used,

[1] *militia* Locally-raised citizen army, a potential source of anti-monarchist action.

The magistrate his public trust abused,
To justice, liable as law required;
For when his office ceased, his pow'r expired:
While power remained, the means were in his hand
By force to seize, and then forsake the land:
Betwixt extremes he knew not how to move,
A slave to fame,[1] but more a slave to love:
Restraining others, yet himself not free,
Made impotent by pow'r, debased by dignity!
Both sides he weighed: but after much debate,
The man prevailed above the magistrate.

Love never fails to master what he finds,
But works a diff'rent way in diff'rent minds,
The fool enlightens, and the wise he blinds.
This youth proposing to possess, and 'scape,
Began in murder, to conclude in rape:
Unpraised by me, though heaven sometime may bless
An impious act with undeserved success:
The Great, it seems, are privileged alone
To punish all injustice but their own.
But here I stop, not daring to proceed,
Yet blush to flatter an unrighteous deed:
For crimes are but permitted, not decreed.

Resolved on force, his wit the praetor bent,
To find the means that might secure th'event;
Not long he laboured, for his lucky thought
In captive Cymon found the friend he sought;
Th'example pleased: the cause and crime the same;
An injured lover, and a ravished dame.
How much he durst he knew by what he dared,
The less he had to lose, the less he cared
To menage loathsome life when love was the reward.

This pondered well, and fixed on his intent,
In depth of night he for the pris'ner sent;
In secret sent, the public view to shun,
Then with a sober smile he thus begun:
"The pow'rs above who bounteously bestow
Their gifts and graces on mankind below,
Yet prove our merit first, nor blindly give
To such as are not worthy to receive:
For valour and for virtue they provide
Their due reward, but first they must be tried:
These fruitful seeds within your mind they sowed;
'Twas yours t'improve the talent they bestowed:
They gave you to be born of noble kind;
They gave you love to lighten up your mind
And purge the grosser parts; they gave you care
To please, and courage to deserve the fair.

"Thus far they tried you, and by proof they found
The grain entrusted in a grateful ground:
But still the great experiment remained,
They suffered you to lose the prize you gained;
That you might learn the gift was theirs alone,
And when restored, to them the blessing own.
Restored it soon will be; the means prepared,
The difficulty smoothed, the danger shared:
Be but yourself, the care to me resign,
Then Iphigene is yours, Cassandra mine.
Your rival Pasimond pursues your life,
Impatient to revenge his ravished wife,
But yet not his; tomorrow is behind,
And love our fortunes in one band has joined:
Two brothers are our foes; Ormisda mine,
As much declared as Pasimond is thine:
Tomorrow must their common vows be tied;
With love to friend and fortune for our guide,
Let both resolve to die, or each redeem a bride.

"Right I have none, nor hast thou much to plead;
'Tis force when done must justify the deed:
Our task performed we next prepare for flight;
And let the losers talk in vain of right:
We with the fair will sail before the wind,
If they are grieved, I leave the laws behind.
Speak thy resolves; if now thy courage droop,
Despair in prison, and abandon hope;
But if thou dar'st in arms thy love regain
(For liberty without thy love were vain),
Then second my design to seize the prey,
Or lead to second rape, for well thou know'st the way."

Said Cymon, overjoyed, "Do thou propose
The means to fight, and only show the foes;

[1] *fame* Good character or reputation.

For from the first, when love had fired my mind,
Resolved, I left the care of life behind."

To this the bold Lysymachus replied,
"Let heav'n be neuter, and the sword decide:
The spousals are prepared, already play
The minstrels, and provoke the tardy day:
By this the brides are waked, their grooms are dressed;
All Rhodes is summoned to the nuptial feast,
All but myself, the sole unbidden guest.
Unbidden though I am, I will be there,
And, joined by thee, intend to joy the fair.

"Now hear the rest; when day resigns the light,
And cheerful torches gild the jolly night,
Be ready at my call, my chosen few
With arms administered shall aid thy crew.
Then ent'ring unexpected will we seize
Our destined prey, from men dissolved in ease;
By wine disabled, unprepared for fight;
And, hast'ning to the seas, suborn[1] our flight:
The seas are ours, for I command the fort,
A ship well manned expects us in the port:
If they, or if their friends the prize contest,
Death shall attend the man who dares resist."

It pleased! The pris'ner to his hold retired,
His troop with equal emulation fired,
All fixed to fight, and all their wonted work required.

The sun arose; the streets were thronged around,
The palace opened, and the posts were crowned:
The double bridegroom at the door attends
Th'expected spouse, and entertains the friends:
They meet, they lead to church; the priests invoke
The pow'rs, and feed the flames with fragrant smoke:
This done they feast, and at the close of night
By kindled torches vary their delight,
These lead the lively dance, and those the brimming
bowls invite.

Now at th'appointed place and hour assigned,
With souls resolved the ravishers were joined.
Three bands are formed: the first is sent before
To favour the retreat, and guard the shore:
The second at the palace gate is placed,
And up the lofty stairs ascend the last:
A peaceful troop they seem with shining vests,
But coats of mail beneath secure their breasts.

Dauntless they enter, Cymon at their head,
And find the feast renewed, the table spread:
Sweet voices mixed with instrumental sounds
Ascend the vaulted roof, the vaulted roof rebounds.
When like the harpies[2] rushing through the hall
The sudden troop appears, the tables fall,
Their smoking load is on the pavement thrown;
Each ravisher prepares to seize his own:
The brides, invaded with a rude embrace,
Shriek out for aid, confusion fills the place.
Quick to redeem the prey their plighted lords
Advance; the palace gleams with shining swords.

But late is all defense, and succour[3] vain;
The rape is made, the ravishers remain:
Two sturdy slaves were only sent before
To bear the purchased prize in safety to the shore.
The troop retires, the lovers close the rear,
With forward faces not confessing fear:
Backward they move, but scorn their pace to mend,
Then seek the stairs, and with slow haste descend.

Fierce Pasimond, their passage to prevent,
Thrust full on Cymon's back in his descent;
The blade returned unbathed, and to the handle bent:
Stout Cymon soon remounts, and cleft in two
His rival's head with one descending blow:
And as the next in rank Ormisda stood,
He turned the point: the sword, inured to blood,
Bored his unguarded breast, which poured a purple
flood.

With vowed revenge the gath'ring crowd pursues,
The ravishers turn head, the fight renews;

[1] *suborn* Procure in a stealthy manner.

[2] *harpies* Mythological monsters that are half woman, half bird and are said to bring divine vengeance.

[3] *succour* Aid, reinforcements.

The hall is heaped with corps;[1] the sprinkled gore
Besmears the walls, and floats the marble floor,
Dispersed at length the drunken squadron flies,
The victors to their vessel bear the prize;
And hear behind loud groans, and lamentable cries.

The crew with merry shouts their anchors weigh,
Then ply their oars, and brush the buxom sea,
While troops of gathered Rhodians crowd the quay.
What should the people do, when left alone?
The governor and government are gone.
The public wealth to foreign parts conveyed;
Some troops disbanded, and the rest unpaid.
Rhodes is the sovereign of the sea no more;
Their ships unrigged, and spent their naval store;
They neither could defend, nor can pursue,
But grind their teeth, and cast a helpless view:
In vain with darts a distant war they try,
Short, and more short, the missive weapons fly.
Meanwhile the ravishers their crimes enjoy,
And flying sails, and sweeping oars employ;
The cliffs of Rhodes in little space are lost,
Jove's isle they seek; nor Jove denies his coast.

In safety landed on the Candian shore,
With generous wines their spirits they restore;
There Cymon with his Rhodian friend resides,
Both court and wed at once the willing brides.
A war ensues, the Cretans own their cause,
Stiff to defend their hospitable laws:
Both parties lose by turns; and neither wins,
'Till peace propounded by a truce begins.
The kindred of the slain forgive the deed,
But a short exile must for show precede;
The term expired, from Candia they remove;
And happy each at home enjoys his love.
—1700

[1] *corps* I.e., bodies.

from *An Essay of Dramatic Poesy*

It was that memorable day[2] in the first summer of the late war, when our navy engaged the Dutch; a day wherein the two most mighty and best appointed fleets which any age had ever seen, disputed the command of the greater half of the globe, the commerce of nations, and the riches of the universe. While these vast floating bodies, on either side, moved against each other in parallel lines, and our countrymen, under the happy conduct of his Royal Highness, went breaking, by little and little, into the line of the enemies; the noise of the cannon from both navies reached our ears about the City,[3] so that all men being alarmed with it, and in a dreadful suspense of the event which we knew was then deciding, every one went following the sound as his fancy led him; and leaving the town almost empty, some took towards the park, some cross the river, others down it; all seeking the noise in the depth of silence.

Among the rest, it was the fortune of Eugenius, Crites, Lisideius, and Neander,[4] to be in company together; three of them persons whom their wit and quality have made known to all the town; and whom I have chose to hide under these borrowed names, that they may not suffer by so ill a relation as I am going to make of their discourse.

Taking then a barge which a servant of Lisideius had provided for them, they made haste to shoot the bridge, and left behind them that great fall of waters which hindered them from hearing what they desired: after which, having disengaged themselves from many vessels which rode at anchor in the Thames, and almost blocked up the passage towards Greenwich, they ordered the watermen to let fall their oars more gently; and then, every one favouring his own curiosity with a strict silence, it was not long ere they perceived the air break about them like the noise of distant thunder, or of swallows in a chimney: those little undulations of sound, though almost vanishing before they reached them, yet

[2] *memorable day* 3 June 1665, when the English defeated the Dutch.

[3] *the City* London.

[4] *Eugenius* Charles Sackville (1638–1706), son of Richard, fifth Earl of Dorset; *Crites* Sir Robert Howard (1626–98); *Lisideius* Sir Charles Sedley (c. 1639–1701); *Neander* Dryden himself.

still seeming to retain somewhat of their first horror, which they had betwixt the fleets. After they had attentively listened till such time as the sound by little and little went from them, Eugenius, lifting up his head, and taking notice of it, was the first who congratulated to the rest that happy omen of our Nation's victory: adding, we had but this to desire in confirmation of it, that we might hear no more of that noise, which was now leaving the English coast. When the rest had concurred in the same opinion, Crites, a person of a sharp judgment, and somewhat too delicate a taste in wit, which the world have mistaken in him for ill-nature, said, smiling to us, that if the concernment of this battle had not been so exceeding great, he could scarce have wished the victory at the price he knew he must pay for it, in being subject to the reading of so many ill verses as he was sure would be made upon it. Adding that no argument could 'scape some of those eternal rhymers, who watch a battle with more diligence than the ravens and birds of prey; and the worst of them surest to be first in upon the quarry: while the better able either out of modesty writ not at all, or set that due value upon their poems, as to let them be often called for and long expected!

"There are some of those impertinent people you speak of," answered Lisideius, "who to my knowledge are already so provided, either way, that they can produce not only a panegyric upon the victory, but, if need be, a funeral elegy on the Duke; and after they have crowned his valour with many laurels, at last deplore the odds under which he fell, concluding that his courage deserved a better destiny." All the company smiled at the conceit of Lisideius; but Crites, more eager than before, began to make particular exceptions against some writers, and said, the public magistrate ought to send betimes to forbid them; and that it concerned the peace and quiet of all honest people, that ill poets should be as well silenced as seditious preachers.

"In my opinion," replied Eugenius, "you pursue your point too far; for as to my own particular, I am so great a lover of poesy, that I could wish them all rewarded, who attempt but to do well; at least, I would not have them worse used than Sylla the Dictator[1] did one of their brethren heretofore: *Quem in concione vidimus* (says Tully) *cum ei libellum malus poeta de populo subjecisset, quod epigramma in eum fecisset tantummodo alternis versibus longiusculis, statim ex its rebus quas tunc vendebat jubere ei praemium tribui, sub ea conditione ne quid postea scriberet.*"[2]

"I could wish with all my heart," replied Crites, "that many whom we know were as bountifully thanked upon the same condition—that they would never trouble us again. For amongst others, I have a mortal apprehension of two poets,[3] whom this victory, with the help of both her wings, will never be able to escape."

"'Tis easy to guess whom you intend," said Lisideius; "and without naming them, I ask you, if one of them does not perpetually pay us with clenches[4] upon words, and a certain clownish kind of raillery? if now and then he does not offer at a catachresis[5] or Clevelandism,[6] wresting and torturing a word into another meaning: in fine, if he be not one of those whom the French would call *un mauvais buffon*; one that is so much a well-willer to the satire, that he spares no man; and though he cannot strike a blow to hurt any, yet ought to be punished for the malice of the action, as our witches are justly hanged, because they think themselves so; and suffer deservedly for believing they did mischief, because they meant it."

[1] *Sylla the Dictator* Lucius Cornelius Sulla (c. 138–78 BCE), a Roman general and self-proclaimed dictator of the Roman Empire in 82 BCE. Sulla's dictatorship was notorious for its cruelty and illegal activity.

[2] *Quem in concione … scriberet* Latin: "Whom we saw in a gathering, when an amateurish poet of the people handed up a book to him with every other line a bit longer; immediately from those wares which he was then selling, he ordered a reward to be given to him but on the condition that he would not write afterwards" (Cicero, *Pro Archia* 10.25); *Tully* Marcus Tullius Cicero (c. 106–43 BCE), Roman orator, politician, and philosopher.

[3] *two poets* Likely Robert Wild and Richard Flecknoe (satirized by Dryden in *Mac Flecknoe*).

[4] *clenches* Puns.

[5] *catachresis* Misapplication of a word or phrase, or a strained figure of speech.

[6] *Clevelandism* Named for metaphysical poet John Cleveland (1613–58).

"You have described him," said Crites, "so exactly, that I am afraid to come after you with my other extremity of poetry. He is one of those who, having had some advantage of education and converse, knows better than the other what a poet should be, but puts it into practice more unluckily than any man; his style and matter are everywhere alike: he is the most calm, peaceable writer you ever read: he never disquiets your passions with the least concernment, but still leaves you in as even a temper as he found you; he is a very Leveller[1] in poetry: he creeps along with ten little words in every line, and helps out his numbers with *For to*, and *Unto*, and all the pretty expletives he can find, till he drags them to the end of another line; while the sense is left tired half way behind it: he doubly starves all his verses, first for want of thought, and then of expression; his poetry neither has wit in it, nor seems to have it; like him in Martial:

> *Pauper videri* Cinna *vult, est pauper*.[2]

"He affects plainness, to cover his want of imagination: when he writes the serious way, the highest flight of his fancy is some miserable antithesis, or seeming contradiction; and in the comic he is still reaching at some thin conceit, the ghost of a jest, and that too flies before him, never to be caught; these swallows which we see before us on the Thames are the just resemblance of his wit: you may observe how near the water they stoop, how many proffers they make to dip, and yet how seldom they touch it; and when they do, 'tis but the surface: they skim over it but to catch a gnat, and then mount into the air and leave it."

"Well, gentlemen," said Eugenius, "you may speak your pleasure of these authors; but though I and some few more about the town may give you a peaceable hearing, yet assure yourselves, there are multitudes who would think you malicious and them injured: especially him who you first described; he is the very Withers[3] of the city: they have bought more editions of his works than would serve to lay under all their pies at the Lord Mayor's Christmas. When his famous poem first came out in the year 1660, I have seen them reading it in the midst of 'Change time; nay so vehement they were at it, that they lost their bargain by the candles' ends; but what will you say, if he has been received amongst the great ones? I can assure you he is, this day, the envy of a great Person who is lord in the art of quibbling; and who does not take it well, that any man should intrude so far into his province."

"All I would wish," replied Crites, "is that they who love his writings, may still admire him, and his fellow poet: *Qui Bavium non odit, &c.*,[4] is curse sufficient."

"And farther," added Lisideius, "I believe there is no man who writes well, but would think himself[5] very hardly dealt with, if their admirers should praise anything of his: *Nam quos contemnimus, eorum quoque laudes contemnimus*."[6]

"There are so few who write well in this age," says Crites, "that methinks any praises should be welcome; they neither rise to the dignity of the last age, nor to any of the Ancients: and we may cry out of the writers of this time, with more reason than Petronius[7] of his, *Pace vestra liceat dixisse, primi omnium eloquentiam perdidists*:[8] you have debauched the true old poetry so far, that Nature, which is the soul of it, is not in any of your writings."

"If your quarrel," said Eugenius, "to those who now write, be grounded only on your reverence to antiquity, there is no man more ready to adore those great Greeks and Romans than I am: but on the other side, I cannot think so contemptibly of the age I live in, or so dishonourably of my own country, as not to judge we equal the Ancients in most kinds of poesy, and in some surpass

---

[1] *Leveller* Derogatory term for political radicals in favor of the abolition of social or economic inequalities. (Before the Restoration the term was used by members of that party to describe themselves.)

[2] *Pauper … pauper* Latin: "Cinna wishes to appear a pauper, and he is" (*Epigrams* 8.19).

[3] *Withers* Reference to poet George Wither (1588-1667).

[4] *Qui Bavium … &c* Latin: "Who does not hate Boevius, etc." (Virgil, *Eclogues* 3.90).

[5] *but would think himself* I.e., who would not think himself.

[6] *Nam quos … contemnimus* Latin: "For we detest those people who admire what we despise" (source unknown).

[7] *Petronius* Notable Roman author and satirist (c. 27–66 CE); his sole surviving work is the *Satyricon*.

[8] *Pace vestra … perdidists* Latin: "If I may say it, you [rhetoricians] are the first to have lost the eloquence of all who went before" (*Satyricon* 2).

them; neither know I any reason why I may not be as zealous for the reputation of our age, as we find the Ancients themselves in reference to those who lived before them. For you hear your Horace saying,

Indignor quidquam reprehendi, non quia crasse
Compositum, illepideve putetur, sed quia nuper.[1]

And after:

Si meliora dies, ut vina, poemata reddit,
Scire velim, pretium chartis quotus arroget annus?[2]

"But I see I am engaging in a wide dispute, where the arguments are not like to reach close on either side; for Poesy is of so large an extent, and so many both of the Ancients and Moderns have done well in all kinds of it, that in citing one against the other, we shall take up more time this evening than each man's occasions will allow him: therefore I would ask Crites to what part of poesy he would confine his arguments, and whether he would defend the general cause of the Ancients against the Moderns, or oppose any age of the Moderns against this of ours?"

Crites, a little while considering upon this demand, told Eugenius he approved his propositions, and if he pleased, he would limit their dispute to dramatic poesy; in which he thought it not difficult to prove, either that the Ancients were superior to the Moderns, or the last age to this of ours. …

Crites, being desired by the company to begin, spoke on behalf of the Ancients, in this manner:

"If confidence presage a victory, Eugenius, in his own opinion, has already triumphed over the Ancients: nothing seems more easy to him, than to overcome those whom it is our greatest praise to have imitated well; for we do not only build upon their foundation, but by their models. Dramatic poesy had time enough, reckoning from Thespis[3] (who first invented it) to Aristophanes,[4] to be born, to grow up, and to flourish in maturity. It has been observed of arts and sciences, that in one and the same century they have arrived to a great perfection; and no wonder, since every age has a kind of universal genius, which inclines those that live in it to some particular studies: the work then being pushed on by many hands, must of necessity go forward.

"Is it not evident, in these last hundred years (when the study of philosophy[5] has been the business of all the Virtuosi in Christendom), that almost a new nature has been revealed to us?—that more errors of the school have been detected, more useful experiments in philosophy have been made, more noble secrets in optics, medicine, anatomy, astronomy, discovered, than in all those credulous and doting ages from Aristotle to us?—so true is it, that nothing spreads more fast than science,[6] when rightly and generally cultivated.

"Add to this, the more than common emulation that was in those times of writing well; which though it be found in all ages and all persons that pretend to the same reputation, yet Poesy, being then in more esteem than now it is, had greater honours decreed to the professors of it, and consequently the rivalship was more high between them; they had judges ordained to decide their merit, and prizes to reward it; and historians have been diligent to record of Aeschylus, Euripides, Sophocles, Lycophron,[7] and the rest of them, both who they were that vanquished in these wars of the theatre, and how often they were crowned: while the Asian kings and Grecian commonwealths scarce afforded them a nobler subject than the unmanly luxuries of a debauched court, or giddy intrigues of a factious city. *Alit aemulatio ingenia* (says Paterculus[8]) *et nunc invidia, nunc admiratio*

[1] *Indignor … nuper* Latin: "It angers me when something is blamed, not for being poorly written or inelegant, but for being new" (Horace, *Epistles* 2.1.76–77).

[2] *Si … annus* Latin: "If poems improve with every passing day, as wine does, I should like to know which year is best for literature" (Horace, *Epistles* 2.1.34–35).

[3] *Thespis* First reported actor upon the stage in ancient Greece (in the sixth century BCE).

[4] *Aristophanes* Greek comic poet (c. 446–385 BCE); his plays are the only surviving examples of ancient Greek "Old Comedy," characterized by high-spirited satire of popular persons and events, as well as buffoonery and "low" humor.

[5] *philosophy* I.e., science.

[6] *science* I.e., knowledge.

[7] *Aeschylus, Euripides, Sophocles, Lycophron* Ancient Greek tragedians.

[8] *Paterculus* Marcus Velleius Paterculus (c. 19 BCE–c. 31 CE), Roman historian known for his *Historiae Romanae.*

incitationem accendit: Emulation is the spur of wit; and sometimes envy, sometimes admiration, quickens our endeavours.

"But now, since the rewards of honour are taken away, that virtuous emulation is turned into direct malice; yet so slothful, that it contents itself to condemn and cry down others, without attempting to do better: 'tis a reputation too unprofitable, to take the necessary pains for it; yet, wishing they had it is incitement enough to hinder others from it. And this, in short, Eugenius, is the reason why you have now so few good poets, and so many severe judges. Certainly, to imitate the Ancients well, much labour and long study is required; which pains, I have already shown, our poets would want encouragement to take, if yet they had ability to go through with it. Those Ancients have been faithful imitators and wise observers of that Nature which is so torn and ill represented in our plays; they have handed down to us a perfect resemblance of her; which we, like ill copiers, neglecting to look on, have rendered monstrous, and disfigured. But, that you may know how much you are indebted to those your masters, and be ashamed to have so ill requited them, I must remember you, that all the rules by which we practise the drama at this day (either such as relate to the justness and symmetry of the plot, or the episodical ornaments, such as descriptions, narrations, and other beauties, which are not essential to the play) were delivered to us from the observations which Aristotle made, of those poets, which either lived before him, or were his contemporaries: we have added nothing of our own, except we have the confidence to say our wit is better; of which none boast in this our age, but such as understand not theirs. Of that book which Aristotle has left us, περὶ τῆς Ποιητικῆς,[1] Horace his *Art of Poetry* is an excellent comment, and I believe, restores to us that Second Book of his concerning *Comedy*, which is wanting in him.

"Out of these two have been extracted the famous rules, which the French call *des trois unitez*, or, the three unities, which ought to be observed in every regular play; namely, of time, place, and action.

"The unity of time they comprehend in twenty-four hours, the compass of a natural day, or as near as it can be contrived; and the reason of it is obvious to every one—that the time of the feigned action, or fable of the play, should be proportioned as near as can be to the duration of that time in which it is represented: since therefore, all plays are acted on the theatre in a space of time much within the compass of twenty-four hours, that play is to be thought the nearest imitation of nature, whose plot or action is confined within that time; and, by the same rule which concludes this general proportion of time, it follows, that all the parts of it are to be equally subdivided; as namely, that one act take not up the supposed time of half a day, which is out of proportion to the rest; since the other four are then to be straitened within the compass of the remaining half: for it is unnatural that one act, which being spoke or written is not longer than the rest, should be supposed longer by the audience; 'tis therefore the poet's duty, to take care that no act should be imagined to exceed the time in which it is represented on the stage; and that the intervals and inequalities of time be supposed to fall out between the acts.

"This rule of time, how well it has been observed by the Ancients, most of their plays will witness; you see them in their tragedies (wherein to follow this rule, is certainly most difficult) from the very beginning of their plays, falling close into that part of the story which they intend for the action or principal object of it, leaving the former part to be delivered by narration: so that they set the audience, as it were, at the post where the race is to be concluded; and, saving them the tedious expectation of seeing the poet set out and ride the beginning of the course, you behold him not till he is in sight of the goal, and just upon you.

"For the second unity, which is that of place, the Ancients meant by it, that the scene ought to be continued through the play, in the same place where it was laid in the beginning: for the stage on which it is represented being but one and the same place, it is unnatural to conceive it many; and those far distant from one another. I will not deny but, by the variation of painted scenes, the fancy, which in these cases will contribute to its own deceit, may sometimes imagine it several places, with some appearance of probability; yet it still carries the greater likelihood of truth, if those places be sup-

[1] περὶ τῆς Ποιητικῆς *Poetics* of Aristotle.

posed so near each other, as in the same town or city; which may all be comprehended under the larger denomination of one place; for a greater distance will bear no proportion to the shortness of time which is allotted in the acting, to pass from one of them to another; for the observation of this, next to the Ancients, the French are to be most commended. They tie themselves so strictly to the unity of place, that you never see in any of their plays, a scene changed in the middle of an act: if the act begins in a garden, a street, or a chamber, 'tis ended in the same place; and that you may know it to be the same, the stage is so supplied with persons, that it is never empty all the time: he that enters the second, has business with him who was on before; and before the second quits the stage, a third appears who has business with him. This Corneille calls *la liaison des scenes*, the continuity or joining of the scenes; and 'tis a good mark of a well-contrived play, when all the persons are known to each other, and every one of them has some affairs with all the rest.

"As for the third unity, which is that of action, the Ancients meant no other by it than what the logicians do by their *finis*, the end or scope of any action; that which is the first in intention, and last in execution: now the poet is to aim at one great and complete action, to the carrying on of which all things in his play, even the very obstacles, are to be subservient; and the reason of this is as evident as any of the former.

"For two actions, equally laboured and driven on by the writer, would destroy the unity of the poem; it would be no longer one play, but two: not but that there may be many actions in a play, as Ben Jonson has observed in his *Discoveries*; but they must be all subservient to the great one, which our language happily expresses in the name of *underplots*: such as in Terence's *Eunuch*[1] is the difference and reconcilement of Thais and Phaedria, which is not the chief business of the play, but promotes the marriage of Chaerea and Chremes's sister, principally intended by the poet. There ought to be but one action, says Corneille,[2] that is, one complete action which leaves the mind of the audience in a full repose; but this cannot be brought to pass but by many other imperfect actions, which conduce to it, and hold the audience in a delightful suspense of what will be.

"If by these rules (to omit many other drawn from the precepts and practice of the Ancients) we should judge our modern plays, 'tis probable that few of them would endure the trial: that which should be business of a day, takes up in some of them an age; instead of one action, they are the epitomes of a man's life; and for one spot of ground (which the stage should represent) we are sometimes in more countries than the map can show us." ...

[Neander:] "But to return from whence I have digressed: I dare boldly affirm these two things of the English drama; first, that we have many plays of ours as regular as any of theirs,[3] and which, besides, have more variety of plot and characters; and secondly, that in most of the irregular plays of Shakespeare or Fletcher[4] (for Ben Jonson's are for the most part regular) there is a more masculine fancy and greater spirit in the writing, than there is in any of the French. I could produce, even in Shakespeare's and Fletcher's works, some plays which are almost exactly formed; as *The Merry Wives of Windsor*, and *The Scornful Lady*: but because (generally speaking) Shakespeare, who writ first, did not perfectly observe the laws of comedy, and Fletcher, who came nearer to perfection, yet through carelessness made many faults; I will take the pattern of a perfect play from Ben Jonson, who was a careful and learned observer of the dramatic laws, and from all his comedies I shall select *The Silent Woman*; of which I will make a short examen, according to those rules which the French observe."

As Neander was beginning to examine *The Silent Woman*, Eugenius, looking earnestly upon him; "I beseech you, Neander," said he, "gratify the company, and me in particular, so far, as before you speak of the play, to give us a character of the author; and tell us frankly your opinion, whether you do not think all writers, both French and English, ought to give place to him."

[1] *Terence's Eunuch* P. Terentius Afer, or Terence (185–159 BCE), a Roman comic playwright and author of *Eunuchus* (161 BCE).

[2] *Corneille* Pierre Corneille (1606–84), a French playwright.

[3] *of theirs* I.e., those of the French.

[4] *Fletcher* John Fletcher (1579–1625), a Jacobean poet and playwright, known for his tragicomedies and comedies of manners, who often collaborated with Francis Beaumont (1584–1616).

"I fear," replied Neander, "that in obeying your commands I shall draw a little envy on myself. Besides, in performing them, it will be first necessary to speak somewhat of Shakespeare and Fletcher, his rivals in poesy; and one of them, in my opinion, at least his equal, perhaps his superior.

"To begin, then, with Shakespeare. He was the man who of all modern, and perhaps ancient poets, had the largest and most comprehensive soul. All the images of Nature were still present to him, and he drew them, not laboriously, but luckily; when he describes any thing, you more than see it, you feel it too. Those who accuse him to have wanted learning, give him the greater commendation: he was naturally learned; he needed not the spectacles of books to read Nature; he looked inwards, and found her there. I cannot say he is every where alike; were he so, I should do him injury to compare him with the greatest of mankind. He is many times flat, insipid; his comic wit degenerating into clenches, his serious swelling into bombast. But he is always great, when some great occasion is presented to him; no man can say he ever had a fit subject for his wit, and did not then raise himself as high above the rest of poets,

Quantum lenta solent inter viburna cupressi.[1]

The consideration of this made Mr. Hales[2] of Eton say, that there was no subject of which any poet ever writ, but he would produce it much better treated of in Shakespeare; and however others are now generally preferred before him, yet the age wherein he lived, which had contemporaries with him Fletcher and Jonson, never equalled them to him in their esteem: and in the last King's court, when Ben's reputation was at highest, Sir John Suckling, and with him the greater part of the courtiers, set our Shakespeare far above him.

"Beaumont and Fletcher, of whom I am next to speak, had, with the advantage of Shakespeare's wit, which was their precedent, great natural gifts, improved by study: Beaumont especially being so accurate a judge of plays, that Ben Jonson, while he lived, submitted all his writings to his censure, and, 'tis thought, used his judgment in correcting, if not contriving, all his plots. What value he had for him, appears by the verses he writ to him; and therefore I need speak no farther of it. The first play that brought Fletcher and him in esteem was their *Philaster*: for before that, they had written two or three very unsuccessfully, as the like is reported of Ben Jonson, before he writ *Every Man in his Humour*. Their plots were generally more regular than Shakespeare's, especially those which were made before Beaumont's death; and they understood and imitated the conversation of gentlemen much better; whose wild debaucheries, and quickness of wit in repartees, no poet can ever paint as they have done. Humour, which Ben Jonson derived from particular persons, they made it not their business to describe: they represented all the passions very lively, but above all, love. I am apt to believe the English language in them arrived to its highest perfection: what words have since been taken in, are rather superfluous than ornamental. Their plays are now the most pleasant and frequent entertainments of the stage; two of theirs being acted through the year for one of Shakespeare's or Jonson's: the reason is, because there is a certain gaiety in their comedies, and pathos in their more serious plays, which suits generally with all men's humours. Shakespeare's language is likewise a little obsolete, and Ben Jonson's wit comes short of theirs.

"As for Jonson, to whose character I am now arrived, if we look upon him while he was himself (for his last plays were but his dotages), I think him the most learned and judicious writer which any theatre ever had. He was a most severe judge of himself, as well as others. One cannot say he wanted wit, but rather that he was frugal of it. In his works you find little to retrench or alter. Wit, and language, and honour also in some measure, we had before him; but something of art was wanting to the drama, till he came. He managed his strength to more advantage than any who preceded him. You seldom find him making love in any of his scenes, or endeavouring to move the passions; his genius was too sullen and saturnine to do it gracefully, especially when he knew he came after those who had performed both to such an height. Humour was his proper sphere; and in that he delighted most to represent mechanic

[1] *Quantum ... cupressi* Latin: "As do cypresses among pliant shrubs" (Virgil, *Eclogues* 1.25).

[2] *Mr. Hales* John Hales (1584–1656), who claimed he had heard Ben Jonson speak of Shakespeare's lack of learning.

people.[1] He was deeply conversant in the Ancients, both Greek and Latin, and he borrowed boldly from them: there is scarce a poet or historian among the Roman authors of those times whom he has not translated in *Sejanus* and *Catiline.* But he has done his robberies so openly, that one may see he fears not to be taxed by any law. He invades authors like a monarch; and what would be theft in other poets, is only victory in him. With the spoils of these writers he so represents old Rome to us, in its rites, ceremonies, and customs, that if one of their poets had written either of his tragedies, we had seen less of it than in him. If there was any fault in his language, 'twas that he weaved it too closely and laboriously, in his serious plays: perhaps too, he did a little too much Romanize our tongue, leaving the words which he translated almost as much Latin as he found them: wherein, though he learnedly followed the idiom of their language, he did not enough comply with the idiom of ours. If I would compare him with Shakespeare, I must acknowledge him the more correct poet, but Shakespeare the greater wit. Shakespeare was the Homer, or father of our dramatic poets; Jonson was the Virgil, the pattern of elaborate writing; I admire him, but I love Shakespeare. To conclude of him; as he has given us the most correct plays, so in the precepts which he has laid down in his *Discoveries*, we have as many and profitable rules for perfecting the stage, as any wherewith the French can furnish us.

"Having thus spoken of the author, I proceed to the examination of his comedy, *The* Silent Woman.

Examen of The Silent Woman

"To begin first with the length of the action; it is so far from exceeding the compass of a natural day, that it takes not up an artificial one. 'Tis all included in the limits of three hours and an half, which is no more than is required for the presentment on the stage. A beauty perhaps not much observed; if it had, we should not have looked on the Spanish translation of *Five Hours* with so much wonder. The scene of it is laid in London; the latitude of place is almost as little as you can imagine; for it lies all within the compass of two houses, and after the first act, in one. The continuity of scenes is observed more than in any of our plays, except his own *Fox* and *Alchymist.* They are not broken above twice or thrice at most in the whole comedy; and in the two best of Corneille's plays, the *Cid* and *Cinna,* they are interrupted once apiece. The action of the play is entirely one; the end or aim of which is the settling Morose's estate on Dauphine. The intrigue of it is the greatest and most noble of any pure unmixed comedy in any language; you see it in many persons of various characters and humours, and all delightful: as first, Morose, or an old man, to whom all noise but his own talking is offensive. Some who would be thought critics, say this humour of his is forced: but to remove that objection, we may consider him first to be naturally of a delicate hearing, as many are, to whom all sharp sounds are unpleasant; and secondly, we may attribute much of it to the peevishness of his age, or the wayward authority of an old man in his own house, where he may make himself obeyed; and this the poet seems to allude to in his name Morose. Besides this, I am assured from diverse persons, that Ben Jonson was actually acquainted with such a man, one altogether as ridiculous as he is here represented. Others say, it is not enough to find one man of such an humour; it must be common to more, and the more common the more natural. To prove this, they instance in the best of comical characters, Falstaff: there are many men resembling him; old, fat, merry, cowardly, drunken, amorous, vain, and lying. But to convince these people, I need but tell them, that humour is the ridiculous extravagance of conversation, wherein one man differs from all others. If then it be common, or communicated to many, how differs it from other men's? or what indeed causes it to be ridiculous so much as the singularity of it? As for Falstaff, he is not properly one humour, but a miscellany of humours or images, drawn from so many several men: that wherein he is singular is his wit, or those things he says *praeter expectatum,* unexpected by the audience; his quick evasions, when you imagine him surprised, which, as they are extremely diverting of themselves, so receive a great addition from his person; for the very sight of such an unwieldy old debauched fellow is a comedy alone. And here, having a place so proper for it, I cannot but enlarge somewhat upon this subject of humour into

[1] *mechanic people* Members of the working class; tradespeople.

which I am fallen. The ancients had little of it in their comedies; for the ἰὸ γελοῖον[1] of the Old Comedy, of which Aristophanes was chief, was not so much to imitate a man, as to make the people laugh at some odd conceit, which had commonly somewhat of unnatural or obscene in it. Thus, when you see Socrates brought upon the stage, you are not to imagine him made ridiculous by the imitation of his actions, but rather by making him perform something very unlike himself; something so childish and absurd, as by comparing it with the gravity of true Socrates, makes a ridiculous object for the spectators. In their New Comedy[2] which succeeded, the poets sought indeed to express the ἦθος[3] as in their tragedies the πάθος[4] of mankind. But this ἦθος contained only the general characters of men and manners; as old men, lovers, serving-men, courtezans, parasites, and such other persons as we see in their comedies; all which they made alike: that is, one old man or father, one lover, one courtezan, so like another, as if the first of them had begot the rest of every sort: *Ex homine hunc natum dicas.*[5] The same custom they observed likewise in their tragedies. As for the French, though they have the word *humeur* among them, yet they have small use of it in their comedies or farces; they being but ill imitations of the *ridiculum*, or that which stirred up laughter in the Old Comedy. But among the English 'tis otherwise: where by humour is meant some extravagant habit, passion, or affection, particular (as I said before) to some one person, by the oddness of which, he is immediately distinguished from the rest of men; which being lively and naturally represented, most frequently begets that malicious pleasure in the audience which is testified by laughter; as all things which are deviations from common customs are ever the aptest to produce it: though by the way this laughter is only accidental, as the person represented is fantastic or bizarre; but pleasure is essential to it, as the limitation of what is natural. The description of these humours, drawn from the knowledge and observation of particular persons, was the peculiar genius and talent of Ben Jonson; to whose play I now return.

"Besides Morose, there are at least nine or ten different characters and humours in *The Silent Woman*; all which persons have several concernments of their own, yet are all used by the poet, to the conducting of the main design to perfection. I shall not waste time in commending the writing of this play; but I will give you my opinion, that there is more wit and acuteness of fancy in it than in any of Ben Jonson's. Besides, that he has here described the conversation of gentlemen in the persons of True-Wit, and his friends, with more gaiety, air, and freedom, than in the rest of his comedies. For the contrivance of the plot, 'tis extreme elaborate, and yet withal easy; for the λῦόις, or untying of it, 'tis so admirable, that when it is done, no one of the audience would think the poet could have missed it; and yet it was concealed so much before the last scene, that any other way would sooner have entered into your thoughts. But I dare not take upon me to commend the fabric of it, because it is altogether so full of art, that I must unravel every scene in it to commend it as I ought. And this excellent contrivance is still the more to be admired, because 'tis comedy, where the persons are only of common rank, and their business private, not elevated by passions or high concernments, as in serious plays. Here every one is a proper judge of all he sees, nothing is represented but that with which he daily converses: so that by consequence all faults lie open to discovery, and few are pardonable. 'Tis this which Horace has judiciously observed:

> *Creditur, ex medio quia res arcessit, habere*
> *Sudoris minimum; sed habet Comedia tanto*
> *Plus oneris, quanto veniae minus.*[6]

"But our poet who was not ignorant of these difficulties, had prevailed himself of all advantages; as he

[1] ἰὸ γελοῖον Greek: the laughable.

[2] *New Comedy* Originating in ancient Greece and Rome in the fourth and third centuries BCE, New Comedy began to replace the farcical satires of Old Comedy with a wittier and more romantic form. Menander, Plautus, and Terence were writers associated with this style.

[3] ἦθος Greek: character.

[4] πάθος Greek: passion.

[5] *Ex homine ... dicas* Latin: "You would say he was born of the other man" (Terence, *Eunuch*, 460).

[6] *Creditur ... minus* Latin: "It is believed that comedy demands the least effort because it draws its subjects from the ordinary; but the less indulgence it has, the greater the work it needs" (Horace, *Epistles* 2. 1.168–70).

who designs a large leap takes his rise from the highest ground. One of these advantages is that which Corneille has laid down as the greatest which can arrive to any poem, and which he himself could never compass above thrice in all his plays; viz. the making choice of some signal and long-expected day, whereon the action of the play is to depend. This day was that designed by Dauphine for the settling of his uncle's estate upon him; which to compass, he contrives to marry him. That the marriage had been plotted by him long beforehand, is made evident by what he tells True-Wit in the second act, that in one moment he had destroyed what he had been raising many months.

"There is another artifice of the poet, which I cannot here omit, because by the frequent practice of it in his comedies he has left it to us almost as a rule; that is, when he has any character of humour wherein he would show a *coup de Maistre*, or his highest skill, he recommends it to your observation by a pleasant description of it before the person first appears. Thus, in *Bartholomew Fair* he gives you the pictures of Numps and Cokes, and in this those of Daw, Lafoole, Morose, and the Collegiate Ladies; all which you hear described before you see them. So that before they come upon the stage, you have a longing expectation of them, which prepares you to receive them favourably; and when they are there, even from their first appearance you are so far acquainted with them, that nothing of their humour is lost to you.

"I will observe yet one thing further of this admirable plot; the business of it rises in every act. The second is greater than the first; the third than the second; and so forward to the fifth. There too you see, till the very last scene, new difficulties arising to obstruct the action of the play; and when the audience is brought into despair that the business can naturally be effected, then, and not before, the discovery is made. But that the poet might entertain you with more variety all this while, he reserves some new characters to show you, which he opens not till the second and third act. In the second Morose, Daw, the Barber, and Otter; in the third the Collegiate Ladies: all which he moves afterwards in bywalks, or under-plots, as diversions to the main design, lest it should grow tedious, though they are still naturally joined with it, and somewhere or other subservient to it. Thus, like a skillful chess-player, by little and little he draws out his men, and makes his pawns of use to his greater persons.

"If this comedy and some others of his were translated into French prose (which would now be no wonder to them, since Moliere has lately given them plays out of verse, which have not displeased them), I believe the controversy would soon be decided betwixt the two nations, even making them the judges. But we need not call our heroes to our aid; be it spoken to the honour of the English, our nation can never want in any age such who are able to dispute the empire of wit with any people in the universe. And though the fury of a civil war, and power for twenty years together abandoned to a barbarous race of men, enemies of all good learning, had buried the Muses under the ruins of monarchy; yet, with the restoration of our happiness, we see revived Poesy lifting up its head, and already shaking off the rubbish which lay so heavy on it. We have seen since his Majesty's return, many dramatic poems which yield not to those of any foreign nation, and which deserve all laurels but the English. I will set aside flattery and envy: it cannot be denied but we have had some little blemish either in the plot or writing of all those plays which have been made within these seven years (and perhaps there is no nation in the world so quick to discern them, or so difficult to pardon them, as ours): yet if we can persuade ourselves to use the candour[1] of that poet, who, though the most severe of critics, has left us this caution by which to moderate our censures—

> *... ubi plura nitent in carmine, non ego paucis*
> *Offendar maculis*;[2]

if, in consideration of their many and great beauties, we can wink at some slight and little imperfections, if we, I say, can be thus equal to ourselves, I ask no favour from the French. And if I do not venture upon any particular judgment of our late plays, 'tis out of the consideration which an ancient writer gives me: *vivor-*

---

[1] *candour* Generosity in judgment.

[2] *ubi ... maculis* Latin: "where many beauties shine in a poem, I will not be bothered by little faults" (Horace, *The Art of Poetry* 2.351–52).

um, ut magna admiratio, ita censura difficilis:[1] betwixt the extremes of admiration and malice, 'tis hard to judge uprightly of the living. Only I think it may be permitted me to say, that as it is no lessening to us to yield to some plays, and those not many, of our own nation in the last age, so can it be no addition to pronounce of our present poets, that they have far surpassed all the Ancients, and the modern writers of other countries."

—1668

[1] *vivorum ... difficilis* Latin: "admiration for the living is great, censure is difficult" (Velleius Paterculus, *Historia Romana* 2.36.3).

Samuel Pepys

1633 – 1703

On 1 January 1660, a young civil servant named Samuel Pepys (pronounced "peeps") took pen in hand and began recording what has become one of the most important sources of information on the Restoration in London. Covering almost 10 years, from 1660 to 1669, Pepys's *Diary* offers an invaluable record of such momentous events as the Restoration of the Stuart monarchy in 1660, the Plague of 1665, and the Great Fire of London in 1666. Far from being a document of public record, however, Pepys's *Diary* records with tantalizing detail hundreds of scenes from his own personal and private life. As such, the *Diary* offers an uncensored and unaffected view of one man's tastes, preoccupations, desires, and pleasures in an age of social and political turbulence. Writing in shorthand, and often employing foreign words and phrases, particularly when describing his amorous affairs, Pepys evidently never intended his *Diary* to be read by any eyes but his own (it was not deciphered and published until more than a century after his death).

Samuel Pepys was born in London in 1633, above his father's prosperous tailor shop. The fifth of eleven children (only three of whom survived childhood), Pepys grew up amidst the Puritan home atmosphere of his parents John and Margaret Pepys. Distressed from an early age by a stone in his urinary system, Pepys wrote decades later: "I remember not my life without the pain of the stone in the kidneys ... till I was about twenty years of age." He was educated at St. Paul's School in London, and then attended Magdalene College, Cambridge as a scholarship student, taking his B.A. in 1654. A year later he married Elizabeth St. Michel, a penniless, fifteen-year-old French Protestant. As later entries in his *Diary* would reveal, Pepys found the marriage satisfactory, despite his criticisms of Elizabeth's unintellectual nature and alleged failures in domestic management—and despite the fact that it was a childless union (still a frequent source of marital discord at the time). As the *Diary* also reveals, Pepys engaged in a number of adulterous affairs. Nevertheless, the marriage was affectionate, and Pepys never remarried after his wife's death in 1669.

Shortly after his marriage, Pepys entered the personal service of his influential cousin Edward Montagu (later Earl of Sandwich). Commander of the Commonwealth fleet, Montagu engaged Pepys to manage his personal affairs while he was away at sea. In 1658, likely through Montagu's influence, Pepys became a clerk of the Exchequer and began his future in public administration. At the same time, the symptoms of his urinary ailment were recurring with agonizing frequency. Pepys agreed to a life-threatening surgical procedure to remove the offending kidney stone, and to his absolute delight the surgery was a success. In later years he celebrated the anniversary of this event with an annual dinner of thanksgiving with his friends and family. His continued good health is celebrated in the opening line of his *Diary* over a year later: "Blessed be God, at the end of the last year I was in very good health, without any sense of my old pain, but upon taking of cold."

As Pepys began his *Diary*, England was in tumult. Oliver Cromwell's death in 1658 had opened a period of Parliamentary upheaval and civil unrest. Pepys secured his future in public office through this difficult time by further attaching himself to the affairs of his cousin Montagu. Although Pepys and his cousin had long been supporters of Cromwell, the events following the Protector's death converted both to the Royalist cause. In 1660, Pepys went to sea as secretary to his cousin, returning on the flagship that carried King Charles II home to England. Having made valuable contacts with influential persons during the voyage, Pepys secured a high position as Clerk of the Acts with the royal navy, and distinguished himself significantly by reducing the cost of naval maintenance. His success in this post earned him accolades as "the right hand of the navy."

Having solidified his position in public office, Pepys enjoyed the security of home and income it afforded, and was able to indulge in many of his interests to a new degree. The pages of his *Diary* abound with tales of his frequent trips to the theater, not to mention his infatuations and illicit affairs with the actresses (who appeared on the English stage for the first time when Charles II reopened the London theaters). Pepys reveals his taste in fashion and his obvious love of social gatherings involving food and drink. He indulged his deep love of music, often singing with friends in his home, at taverns and coffeehouses, or playing his lute in the solitude of his room. Keenly observant by nature, and insatiably curious, Pepys began attending weekly meetings of the Royal Society to see experiments and hear lectures by leading minds of the day. He took a keen, though amateur, interest in scientific matters, and eventually he was appointed the Society's President, serving from 1684 to 1685.

Of all the events described by Pepys in his *Diary*, none illustrates more dramatically the value of first-hand commentary than his account of the Great Fire of 1666. Starting in a baker's shop in Pudding Lane on 2 September, the fire spread through the close-packed streets of London with terrifying speed. Citizens watched helplessly as their homes were consumed; the inferno raged for four days, during which 80 per cent of the city was reduced to rubble. By the end over 13,000 houses, 89 churches, 52 guild halls and the Cathedral of St. Paul's had burned in a disaster of unprecedented proportions. Pepys's contemporary (and fellow member of the Royal Society), architect Christopher Wren, was instrumental in the reconstruction of the city, including the provision of the designs for the new St. Paul's. (One interesting aspect of the reconstruction is that the fire prompted the introduction of the world's first set of building standards.)

By 1669 Pepys's eyesight had begun to trouble him a great deal. He became convinced that he was going blind, and reluctantly gave up maintaining his *Diary*. On 31 May 1669 he concluded his final entry: "And so I betake myself to that course, which is almost as much as to see myself go into my grave: for which, and all the discomforts that will accompany my being blind, the good God prepare me!" His fears proved unjustified, as he lived another thirty-four years without going blind, yet he never felt able to resume his confidential daily record. Soon after he finished with his *Diary*, Pepys and his wife embarked on a visit to France and Holland. Elizabeth fell ill during the journey, and after struggling home to London she died later that year at the age of twenty-nine.

Following the death of his wife, Pepys found distraction in his work at the Navy Office. In 1673, when the Test Act forced the Duke of York (Charles's Catholic brother James) to resign as Lord High Admiral, Pepys was installed in the newly created post of Secretary of the Admiralty by the King. He immediately enacted widespread reforms in naval operations, making the entire fleet more efficient than before. His efforts were interrupted in 1679 when he was falsely charged with, and imprisoned for, involvement in the Popish Plot (a plan that Titus Oates, an anti-Catholic protester, largely invented: he claimed that Jesuits were plotting to assassinate the King and hasten the succession of the openly Catholic James II). Although acquitted of any wrongdoing, Pepys was not re-installed in office until 1684. He continued in this official capacity when James II, an admirer of his talents, acceded to the throne in 1685. However, James's flight to France in 1688 heralded the end of Pepys's naval career. He officially discharged his last duty in 1689, and died in Clapham on 26 May 1703, after a lengthy illness.

⌘⌘⌘

from *The Diary*

MAY 1660[1]

21. So into my naked bed and slept till 9 o'clock, and then John Goods waked me, [by] and by the captain's boy brought me four barrels of Mallows oysters, which Captain Tatnell had sent me from Murlace.[2] The weather foul all this day also. After dinner, about writing one thing or other all day, and setting my papers in order, having been so long absent. At night Mr. Pierce, Purser (the other Pierce and I having not spoken to one another since we fell out about Mr. Edward), and Mr. Cook[3] sat with me in my cabin and supped with me, and then I went to bed. By letters that came hither in my absence, I understand that the Parliament had ordered all persons to be secured, in order to a trial, that did sit as judges in the late King's death[4] and all the officers too attending the Court. Sir John Lenthall moving in the House that all that had borne arms against the King should be exempted from pardon, he was called to the bar of the House, and after a severe reproof he was degraded his knighthood.[5] At Court I find that all things grow high. The old clergy talk as being sure of their lands again, and laugh at the Presbytery; and it is believed that the sales of the King's and Bishops' lands will never be confirmed by Parliament,[6] there being nothing now in any man's power to hinder them and the King[7] from doing what they have a mind, but everybody willing to submit to anything. We expect every day to have the King and Duke[8] on board as soon as it is fair. My Lord do nothing now, but offers all things to the pleasure of the Duke as Lord High Admiral. So that I am at a loss what to do.

22. Up very early, and now beginning to be settled in my wits again, I went about setting down my last four days' observations this morning. After that, was trimmed by a barber that has not trimmed me yet, my Spaniard being on shore. News brought that the two Dukes are coming on board, which, by and by, they did, in a Dutch boat, the Duke of York in yellow trimmings, the Duke of Gloucester[9] in grey and red. My Lord[10] went in a boat to meet them, the Captain, myself, and others, standing at the entering port. So soon as they were entered we shot the guns off round the fleet. After that they went to view the ship all over, and were most exceedingly pleased with it. They seem to be both very fine gentlemen. After that done, upon the quarter-deck table under the awning, the Duke of York and my Lord,

[1] *May 1660* In March 1660, Pepys accompanied his patron Edward Montagu, soon to become the 1st Earl of Sandwich, then recently reappointed General at Sea, on a mission to retrieve Charles II from the Netherlands, where he had been exiled during Oliver Cromwell's protectorate (1651–58). On 8 May 1660, the English Parliament formally named Charles II king, and Montagu was officially charged with bringing Charles home. This entry is thus written onboard ship.

[2] *naked bed* Reference to the then-common habit of sleeping naked; a bed in which one sleeps without undergarments; *John Goods* One of the Earl of Sandwich's servants; *Mallows* St. Malo, a port city in the Brittany region in the northwest of France; *Murlace* Morlaix, a village in Brittany.

[3] *Mr. Pierce ... the other Pierce* The ship's purser was Andrew Pearse; the "other" Pearse is James, the ship's surgeon; *Purser* Naval officer charged with supplies and accounts onboard a ship; *Mr. Edward* Edward Montagu, the Earl of Sandwich's son, then twelve years old. A few days earlier when they were spending time as tourists on shore, Pepys had left the boy with Pearse to look after him, and the two spent the night in another town without leaving Pepys any indication of where they had gone; *Mr. Cook* Another of Sandwich's servants.

[4] *late King's death* King Charles I, father of Charles II, was executed on 30 January 1649 during the English Civil War.

[5] *Sir John Lenthall ... degraded his knighthood* Lenthall was elected Member of Parliament in 1645 and knighted by Cromwell in 1658. The House's rebuke, apparently provoked by Lenthall's blanket condemnation of Cromwell's supporters, may have been politically motivated; the House did not, however, revoke his title, which ceased to exist at the end of Cromwell's protectorate.

[6] *The old ... by Parliament* Church and crown lands had been sold during Cromwell's rule, but most property was recovered by its original owners; *Presbytery* Clerical court.

[7] *King* Charles II.

[8] *Duke* James Stuart, Duke of York and Lord High Admiral. In 1685, he would become King of England and Ireland (as James II) and King of Scotland (as James VII).

[9] *Duke of Gloucester* Henry Stuart, youngest son of Charles I.

[10] *My Lord* Earl of Sandwich.

Mr. Coventry[1] and I spent an hour at allotting to every ship their service in their return to England; which having done, they went to dinner, where the table was very full: the two Dukes at the upper end, my Lord Opdam[2] next on one side, and my Lord on the other. Two guns given to every man while he was drinking the King's health, and so likewise to the Duke's health. I took down Monsieur d'Esquier[3] to the great cabin below, and dined with him in state alone with only one or two friends of his. All dinner the harper[4] belonging to Captain Sparling played to the Dukes. After dinner, the Dukes and my Lord to see the Vice and Rear-Admirals, and I in a boat after them. After that done, they made to the shore in the Dutch boat that brought them, and I got into the boat with them; but the shore was so full of people to expect their coming, as that it was as black (which otherwise is white sand), as every one could stand by another. When we came near the shore my Lord left them and came into his own boat, and General Pen[5] and I with him; my Lord being very well pleased with this day's work. By the time we came on board again, news is sent us that the King is on shore; so my Lord fired all his guns round twice, and all the fleet after him, which in the end fell into disorder, which seemed very handsome. The gun over against my cabin I fired myself to the King, which was the first time that he had been saluted by his own ships since this change; but holding my head too much over the gun, I had almost spoiled my right eye. Nothing in the world but going of guns almost all this day. In the evening we began to remove[6] cabins; I to the carpenter's cabin, and Dr. Clerke with me, who came on board this afternoon, having been twice ducked in the sea today coming from shore, and Mr. North and John Pickering[7] the like. Many of the King's servants came on board tonight; and so many Dutch of all sorts came to see the ship till it was quite dark, that we could not pass by one another, which was a great trouble to us all. This afternoon Mr. Downing[8] (who was knighted yesterday by the King) was here on board, and had a ship for his passage into England, with his lady and servants. By the same token he called me to him when I was going to write the order, to tell me that I must write him Sir G. Downing. My Lord lay in the roundhouse[9] tonight. This evening I was late writing a French letter myself by my Lord's order to Monsieur Kragh, Embassador de Denmarke à la Haye,[10] which my Lord signed in bed. After that I to bed, and the Doctor, and sleep well.

23. The Doctor and I waked very merry, only my eye was very red and ill in the morning from yesterday's hurt. In the morning came infinity of people on board from the King to go along with him. My Lord, Mr. Crew,[11] and others, go on shore to meet the King as he comes off from shore, where Sir R. Stayner[12] bringing His Majesty into the boat, I hear that His Majesty did with a great deal of affection kiss my Lord upon his first meeting. The King, with the two Dukes and Queen of Bohemia, Princess Royal, and Prince of Orange,[13] came

[1] *Mr. Coventry* Sir William Coventry served as secretary to the Duke of York following negotiations to restore Charles II to the throne. He and Pepys became well-acquainted and attached.

[2] *Lord Opdam* Jacob Obdam served as the supreme commander of the Dutch navy.

[3] *Monsieur d'Esquier* Sandwich's assistant.

[4] *harper* Harp player.

[5] *General Pen* Sir William Penn, an English admiral and, as of 1660, Commissioner of the Navy Board.

[6] *remove* I.e., remove to.

[7] *Dr. Clerke* Timothy Clarke, physician; *Mr. North and John Pickering* Sir Charles North and John Pickering, both sons of barons related to the Montagu family by marriage.

[8] *Mr. Downing* Sir George Downing, a diplomat sent by Cromwell to the Netherlands in 1657 to unite the Protestant countries in Europe and follow the activities of exiled supporters of the King. However, in 1660, he renounced his former allegiances and reconciled with Charles II, who, as Pepys notes, knighted him.

[9] *roundhouse* Set of cabins in the ship's rear part.

[10] *Monsieur Kragh … la Haye* Otto Krag, one of two Danish ambassadors to Charles II.

[11] *Mr. Crew* John Crew, a Member of Parliament who worked to restore Charles II to the throne.

[12] *Sir R. Stayner* Richard Stayner, a naval commander and friend of Montagu, who had the distinction of being knighted by both Cromwell and, after the Restoration, Charles II.

[13] *Queen of Bohemia* Sister of Charles I—and therefore aunt to the King and to the Duke of York; *Princess Royal* Sister to the King and to the Duke of York; *Prince of Orange* Son of the Princess Royal, William (who much later would become king) was nine years old in 1660.

on board, where I in their coming in kissed the King's, Queen's, and Princess's hands, having done the other before. Infinite shooting off of the guns and that in a disorder on purpose, which was better than if it had been otherwise. All day nothing but Lords and persons of honour on board, that we were exceeding full. Dined in a great deal of state, the royal company by themselves in the coach,[1] which was a blessed sight to see. I dined with Dr. Clerke, Dr. Quarterman, and Mr. Darcy[2] in my cabin. This morning Mr. Lucy came on board, to whom and his company of the King's guard in another ship my Lord did give three dozen of bottles of wine. He made friends between Mr. Pierce and me. After dinner the king and Duke altered the name of some of the ships, *viz.*[3] the *Nazeby* into *Charles*; the *Richard*, *James*; the *Speakers*, *Mary*; the *Dunbar* (which was not in company with us), the *Henry*; *Winsly*, *Happy Return*; *Wakefield*, *Richmond*; *Lambert*, the *Henrietta*; *Cheriton*, the *Speedwell*; *Bradford*, the *Success*. That done, the Queen, Princess Royal, and Prince of Orange took leave of the King, and the Duke of York went on board the *London*, and the Duke of Gloucester, the *Swiftsure*. Which done, we weighed anchor, and with a fresh gale and most happy weather we set sail for England. All the afternoon the King walked here and there, up and down (quite contrary to what I thought him to have been), very active and stirring. Upon the quarter-deck he fell into discourse of his escape from Worcester,[4] where it made me ready to weep to hear the stories that he told of his difficulties that he had passed through, as his travelling four days and three nights on foot, every step up to his knees in dirt, with nothing but a green coat and a pair of country breeches on, and a pair of country shoes that made him so sore all over his feet that he could scarce stir. Yet he was forced to run away from a miller and other company that took them for rogues. His sitting at table at one place, where the master of the house, that had not seen him in eight years, did know him, but kept it private; when at the same table there was one that had been of his own regiment at Worcester, could not know him, but made him drink the King's health, and said that the King was at least four fingers higher than he.[5] At another place he was by some servants of the house made to drink, that they might know him not to be a Roundhead,[6] which they swore he was. In another place at his inn, the master of the house, as the King was standing with his hands upon the back of a chair by the fire-side, kneeled down and kissed his hand, privately, saying that he would not ask him who he was, but bid God bless him whither he was going. Then the difficulty of getting a boat to get into France, where he was fain[7] to plot with the master thereof to keep his design from the four men and a boy (which was all his ship's company), and so got to Fécamp in France. At Rouen he looked so poorly that the people went into the rooms before he went away to see whether he had not stole something or other. In the evening I went up to my Lord to write letters for England, which he sent away with word of our coming, by Mr. Edw. Pickering.[8] The King supped alone in the coach; after that I got a dish, and we four supped in my cabin, as at noon. About bed-time my Lord Bartelett (who I had offered my service to before) sent for me to get him a bed, who with much ado I did get to bed to my Lord Middlesex[9]

[1] *the coach* I.e., the ship.

[2] *Dr. Quarterman* William Quartermaine, personal physician to Charles II; *Mr. Darcy* Marmaduke Darcy, companion to Charles II during his exile.

[3] *viz.* Abbreviation of the Latin *videlicet*, meaning "namely" or "that is to say." Ship names reflecting glory on the Commonwealth (e.g. the battle of Nazeby, a roundhead victory, and Richard, Oliver Cromwell's son) are giving way to royalist names, e.g. Charles and James.

[4] *Worcester* Site of an attempt by Charles II to regain the crown in 1651; Charles's forces were decisively defeated, and a £1000 reward was offered for Charles's arrest. The king's escape to France (the story of which was preserved for posterity by Pepys) was thus a thoroughly dangerous one, shadowed by the possibility of capture and execution.

[5] *the King … higher than he* Charles II was 1.88 meters (or 6′2″) in height, a size that distinguished him from other seventeenth-century men, who were generally significantly shorter. The king's conspicuous height made his escape after the Battle of Worcester all the more difficult.

[6] *Roundhead* Supporter of Parliament during the Civil War, named for their tendency to cut their hair close to their heads.

[7] *fain* Forced by circumstance.

[8] *Mr. Edw. Pickering* Edward Pickering, a relative of Sandwich's, whose tendency to gossip made him widely reviled.

[9] *Lord Bartelett* Apparently a mistake for Lord Berkeley, one of the six lords assigned to present a congratulatory speech to the restored king; *Lord Middlesex* Charles Sackville, also a member of the delegation sent to congratulate and welcome the King.

in the great cabin below, but I was cruelly troubled before I could dispose of him, and quit myself of him. So to my cabin again, where the company still was, and were talking more of the King's difficulties; as how he was fain to eat a piece of bread and cheese out of a poor boy's pocket; how, at a Catholic house, he was fain to lie in the priest's hole[1] a good while in the house for his privacy. After that our company broke up, and the Doctor and I to bed. We have all the Lords Commissioners on board us, and many others. Under sail all night, and most glorious weather.

OCTOBER 1660[2]

20. This morning one came to me to advise with me where to make me a window into my cellar in lieu of one which Sir W. Batten[3] had stopped up, and going down into my cellar to look I stepped into a great heap of ———, by which I found that Mr. Turner's house of office[4] is full and comes into my cellar, which do trouble me, but I shall have it helped. To my Lord's by land, calling at several places about business, where I dined with my Lord and Lady;[5] when he was very merry, and did talk very high how he would have a French cook, and a master of his horse, and his lady and child to wear black patches;[6] which methought was strange, but he is become a perfect courtier; and, among other things, my Lady saying that she could get a good merchant for her daughter Jem.,[7] he answered, that he would rather see her with a pedlar's[8] pack at her back, so she married a gentleman, than she should marry a citizen. This afternoon, going through London, and called at Crowe's the upholster's, in Saint Bartholomew's, I saw the limbs of some of our new traitors set upon Aldersgate, which was a sad sight to see; and a bloody week this and the last have been, there being ten hanged, drawn, and quartered.[9] Home, and after writing a letter to my uncle by the post, I went to bed.

NOVEMBER 1660

10. Up early. Sir Wm. Batten and I to make up an account of the wages of the officers and mariners at sea, ready to present to the Committee of Parliament this afternoon. Afterwards came the Treasurer and Comptroller,[10] and sat all the morning with us till the business was done. So we broke up, leaving the thing to be wrote over fair and carried to Trinity House for Sir Wm. Batten's hand.[11] When staying very long I found (as appointed) the Treasurer and Comptroller at Whitehall,[12] and so we went with a foul copy[13] to the Parliament house, where we met with Sir Thos. Clarges and Mr. Spry, and after we had given them good satisfaction we parted. The Comptroller and I to the coffee-

[1] *Catholic house* Charles II was repeatedly aided by Catholics. The King converted to Catholicism on his deathbed; *priest's hole* Hiding place for Catholic priests, particularly necessary in Elizabethan and Jacobean England during intense periods of persecution.

[2] *OCTOBER 1660* Pepys spent much of October 1660 making household repairs, bringing his house into accordance with his newly attained status and wealth.

[3] *Sir W. Batten* Sir William Batten, admiral and Surveyor of the Navy.

[4] ——— Samuel politely notes stepping into the toilet waste that has apparently collected in his neighbor's home; *Mr. Turner* Thomas Turner, General Clerk at the Navy Office; *house of office* Toilet.

[5] *Lady* Jemima Montagu, Countess of Sandwich, wife of Edward Montagu.

[6] *black patches* Artificial beauty spots, placed on the face. These became fashionable in the court of Charles I, though they were just as often ridiculed.

[7] *Jem.* Jemima Montagu, later Carteret, daughter of the Earl and Countess of Sandwich.

[8] *pedlar* Itinerant street seller. Sandwich would rather his daughter married an upper-class man, even if poor, than someone bourgeois ("citizen") even if rich.

[9] *traitors set … and quartered* On 13 October 1660, ten men involved in the execution of Charles I were hanged, drawn, and quartered. The limbs "upon Aldersgate" are the butchered quarters of these men, nailed up on one of the gateways to the City of London as an awful warning. Pepys, a witness to the event, writes in his entry for the day: "Thus it was my chance to see the King beheaded at Whitehall, and to see the first blood shed in revenge for the blood of the King at Charing Cross."

[10] *Comptroller* Head accountant.

[11] *Trinity House … Batten's hand* Batten was Master of Trinity House, the authority responsible for lighthouses and other markers for marine navigation.

[12] *Whitehall* Main residence of English monarchs from 1530 to 1698, when most of the palace was destroyed by fire.

[13] *foul copy* Draft.

house, where he showed me the state of his case; how the King did owe him about 6000*l*. But I do not see great likelihood for them to be paid, since they begin already in Parliament to dispute the paying of the just sea-debts, which were already promised to be paid, and will be the undoing of thousands if they be not paid. So to Whitehall to look but could not find Mr. Fox, and then to Mr. Moore[1] at Mr. Crew's, but missed of him also. So to Paul's Churchyard, and there bought Montelion,[2] which this year do not prove so good as the last was; so after reading it I burnt it. After reading of that and the comedy of the Rump,[3] which is also very silly, I went to bed. This night going home, Will[4] and I bought a goose.

20. About two o'clock my wife[5] wakes me, and comes to bed, and so both to sleep and the wench to wash.[6] I rose and with Will to my Lord's by land, it being a very hard frost, the first we have had this year. There I stayed with my Lord and Mr. Shepley,[7] looking over my Lord's accounts and to set matters straight between him and Shepley, and he did commit the viewing of these accounts to me, which was a great joy to me to see that my Lord do look upon me as one to put trust in. Hence to the organ, where Mr. Child[8] and one Mr. Mackworth (who plays finely upon the violin) were playing, and so we played till dinner and then dined, where my Lord in a very good humour and kind to me. After dinner to the Temple,[9] where I met Mr. Moore and discoursed with him about the business of putting out[10] my Lord's 3,000*l*., and that done, Mr. Shepley and I to the new Play-house near Lincoln's-Inn Fields (which was formerly Gibbon's tennis-court), where the play of *Beggar's Bush*[11] was newly begun; and so we went in and saw it, it was well acted: and here I saw the first time one Moone,[12] who is said to be the best actor in the world, lately come over with the King, and indeed it is the finest play-house, I believe, that ever was in England. From thence, after a pot of ale with Mr. Shepley at a house hard by, I went by link home, calling a little by the way at my father's and my uncle Fenner's,[13] where all pretty well, and so home, where I found the house in a washing pickle, and my wife in a very joyful condition when I told her that she is to see the Queen next Thursday, which puts me in mind to say that this morning I found my Lord in bed late, he having been with the King, Queen, and Princess, at the Cockpit all night, where General Monk[14] treated them; and after supper a play, where the King did put a great affront upon Singleton's[15] music, he bidding them stop and bade the French music play, which, my Lord says, do much outdo all ours. But while my Lord was rising, I

[1] *Mr. Fox* Sir Stephen Fox, Paymaster of the Forces and friend of Charles II; *Mr. Moore* Henry Moore, Sandwich's lawyer.

[2] *Paul's Churchyard* Center of London's book trade; *Montelion* John Phillips, under the pen name Montelion, published an annual series of parody astrological almanacs full of royalist political satire.

[3] *the Rump* Rump Parliament is the name given to the Parliament after it was purged, in December 1648, of members against the resolution to try Charles I for high treason. The term "Rump Parliament" has since come to mean a parliament remaining after the legitimate parliament has disbanded.

[4] *Will* Will Hewer, Pepys's chief clerk.

[5] *my wife* Elizabeth Pepys.

[6] *wench* Jane Birch, the Pepys's maid; *wash* I.e., begin the laundry.

[7] *Mr. Shepley* Sandwich's servant.

[8] *Mr. Child* William Child, organist and Master of the king's Wind Music.

[9] *Temple* Area in central London where many legal offices and associations are located.

[10] *putting out* Investing.

[11] *new Play-house … tennis-court* King's House, which first opened on 8 November 1660; *Beggar's Bush* Beaumont and Fletcher's 1647 comedy, revived in November 1660. The old form of tennis ("royal tennis") was played in a large indoor arena, suitable for conversion into a theater.

[12] *Moone* Michael Mohun, a celebrated London actor, who had previously held a commission in the king's army.

[13] *link* Lighted torch, here carried by a hired boy to guide people through the dark streets; *my father* John Pepys, a tailor; *uncle Fenner* Thomas Fenner, a master blacksmith, husband of Katherine Kite, sister of Samuel's mother.

[14] *Queen* Henrietta-Maria Stuart, wife of Charles I and mother of Charles II and James II, thus known as the Queen-Mother during Charles's reign; *Princess* Henrietta Stuart, youngest daughter of Charles I; *the Cockpit* Theater at Whitehall named from its former use in the cruel sport of cock-fighting; *General Monk* George Monk, 1st Duke of Albemarle, who played an integral part in the restoration of Charles II.

[15] *Singleton* John Singleton, musician to the king.

went to Mr. Fox's, and there did leave the gilt tankard for Mrs. Fox, and then to the counting-house to him, who hath invited me and my wife to dine with him on Thursday next, and so to see the Queen and Princesses.

JANUARY 1660/61

3. Early in the morning to the Exchequer,[1] where I told over what money I had of my Lord's and my own there, which I found to be 970*l.* Thence to Will's, where Spicer[2] and I eat our dinner of a roast leg of pork which Will did give us, and after that to the Theatre, where was acted *Beggars' Bush*, it being very well done; and here the first time that ever I saw women come upon the stage.[3] From thence to my father's, where I found my mother gone by Bird, the carrier, to Brampton, upon my uncle's great desire, my aunt[4] being now in despair of life. So home.

JULY 1662[5]

12. Up by five o'clock, and put things in my house in order to be laid up, against my workmen come on Monday to take down the top of my house, which trouble I must go through now, but it troubles me much to think of it. So to my office,[6] where till noon we sat, and then I to dinner and to the office all the afternoon with much business. At night with Cooper[7] at arithmetic, and then came Mr. Creed[8] about my Lord's accounts to even them, and he gone I to supper and to bed.

[1] *Exchequer* Government treasury.

[2] *Spicer* Jack Spicer, a clerk in the Exchequer.

[3] *the first time … the stage* Women were first allowed on the stage following the Restoration.

[4] *my mother* Margaret Pepys; *my uncle* Robert Pepys, oldest brother of Samuel's father, who resided in Brampton in Cambridgeshire; *my aunt* Anne Pepys, Robert's wife.

[5] *JULY 1662* In July of 1662, Pepys undertook a household renovation, with workmen removing the roof of the house in order to build additional stories.

[6] *my office* Navy Office, site of the Navy Board.

[7] *Cooper* Richard Cooper, sailing master, then unemployed, who Pepys hired to teach him mathematics.

[8] *Mr. Creed* John Creed, deputy treasurer to the Earl of Sandwich in the spring of 1660 and Pepys's rival for Sandwich's patronage.

18. Up very early, and got atop of my house, seeing the design of my work, and like it very well, and it comes into my head to have my dining-room wainscoted,[9] which will be very pretty. By-and-by by water to Deptford,[10] to put several things in order, being myself now only left in town, and so back again to the office, and there doing business all the morning and the afternoon also till night, and then comes Cooper for my mathematics, but, in good earnest, my head is so full of business that I cannot understand it as otherwise I should do. At night to bed, being much troubled at the rain coming into my house, the top being open.

19. Up early and to some business, and my wife coming to me I stayed long with her discoursing about her going into the country, and as she is not very forward so am I at a great loss whether to have her go or no because of the charge, and yet in some considerations I would be glad she was there, because of the dirtiness of my house and the trouble of having of a family there. So to my office, and there all the morning, and then to dinner and my brother Tom[11] dined with me only to see me. In the afternoon I went upon the river to look after some tar[12] I am sending down and some coals, and so home again; it raining hard upon the water, I put ashore and sheltered myself, while the King came by in his barge, going down towards the Downs[13] to meet the Queen: the Duke being gone yesterday. But methought it lessened my esteem of a king, that he should not be able to command the rain. Home, and Cooper coming (after I had dispatched several letters) to my mathematics, and so at night to bed in a chamber at Sir W. Pen's, my own house being so foul that I cannot lie there any longer, and there the chamber lies so as that I come into it over my leads[14] without going about, but yet I am not fully content with it, for there will be much trouble to have servants running over the leads to and fro.

[9] *wainscoted* Lined with wood panel-work.

[10] *Deptford* Location of royal dockyards, downriver from the City of London.

[11] *my brother Tom* Thomas Pepys, a tailor.

[12] *tar* Used as a timber preservative for ships.

[13] *the Downs* Part of the sea near the English Channel used as a base for ships patrolling the North Sea.

[14] *leads* Roof.

MAY 1663

9. … At noon dined at home with a heavy heart … and after dinner went out to my brother's, and thence to Westminster, where at Mr. Jervas's, my old barber, I did try two or three periwigs,[1] meaning to wear one; and yet I have no stomach [for it] but that the pains of keeping my hair clean is so great. He trimmed me, and at last I parted, but my mind was almost altered from my first purpose, from the trouble that I foresee will be in wearing them also. Thence by water home and to the office, where busy late, and so home to supper and bed. …

10. *Lord's Day.*[2] Up betimes, and put on a black cloth suit, with white lynings[3] under all, as the fashion is to wear, to appear under the breeches. So being ready walked to St. James's,[4] where I sat talking with Mr. Coventry, while he made himself ready, about several businesses of the Navy, and afterwards, the Duke being gone out, he and I walked to Whitehall together over the Park. …

OCTOBER 1663

29. Up, it being my Lord Mayor's day,[5] Sir Anthony Bateman. This morning was brought home my new velvet cloak, that is, lined with velvet, a good cloth the outside, the first that ever I had in my life, and I pray God it may not be too soon now that I begin to wear it. I had it this day brought, thinking to have worn it to dinner, but I thought it would be better to go without it because of the crowd, and so I did not wear it. We met a little at the office, and then home again and got me ready to go forth, my wife being gone forth by my consent before to see her father and mother, and taken her cook maid[6] and little girl to Westminster with her for them to see their friends. This morning in dressing myself and wanting a band,[7] I found all my bands that were newly made clean so ill smoothed that I crumpled them, and flung them all on the ground, and was angry with Jane, which made the poor girl mighty sad, so that I were troubled for it afterwards. At noon I went forth, and by coach to Guildhall[8] (by the way calling at Mr. Rawlinson's),[9] and there was admitted, and meeting with Mr. Proby[10] (Sir R. Ford's son), and Lieutenant-Colonel Baron, a city commander, we went up and down to see the tables; where under every salt[11] there was a bill of fare,[12] and at the end of the table the persons proper for the table. Many were the tables, but none in the Hall but the Mayor's and the Lords of the Privy Council[13] that had napkins or knives, which was very strange. We went into the Buttry,[14] and there stayed and talked, and then into the Hall again: and there wine was offered and they drunk, I only drinking some hypocras, which do not break my vow,[15] it being, to the best of my present judgment, only a mixed compound drink, and not any wine.[16] If I am mistaken, God forgive me! but I hope and do think I am not. By and by met with Creed; and we, with the others, went within the several Courts, and there saw the tables prepared for the Ladies and Judges and Bishops: all great sign of a great dinner to come. By and by about one

[1] *periwigs* Wigs, especially formal ones, commonly worn by men and women in the seventeenth century.

[2] *Lord's Day* Sunday.

[3] *lynings* Underclothes.

[4] *St. James's* St. James's Palace, the primary residence of James Stuart, near St. James's Park.

[5] *Lord Mayor's day* Day on which London's Lord Mayor holds a dinner and a lavish pageant.

[6] *cook maid* Kitchen maid.

[7] *band* Neckband for a shirt, a necessary component of seventeenth-century gentlemanly attire.

[8] *Guildhall* City of London's Town Hall.

[9] *Mr. Rawlinson's* Dan Rawlinson was the host of the Mitre, a London tavern.

[10] *Mr. Proby* Peter Proby, merchant. His father-in-law, Sir Richard Ford, was among those sent to request Charles II's return to England.

[11] *salt* Large salt-cellar.

[12] *bill of fare* Menu.

[13] *Privy Council* Body of royal advisors, made up of senior members of Parliament, both present and past.

[14] *Buttry* Room for storing liquor.

[15] *my vow* In July 1663, Samuel made a vow to abstain from "all strong drink," including wine.

[16] *hypocras … not any wine* Pepys was wrong. Hippocras is spiced wine.

o'clock, before the Lord Mayor came, come into the Hall, from the room where they were first led into, the Lord Chancellor (Archbishop before him), with the Lords of the Council, and other Bishops, and they to dinner. Anon comes the Lord Mayor, who went up to the lords, and then to the other tables to bid welcome; and so all to dinner. I sat near Proby, Baron, and Creed at the Merchant Strangers' table; where ten good dishes to a messe,[1] with plenty of wine of all sorts, of which I drunk none; but it was very unpleasing that we had no napkins nor change of trenchers,[2] and drunk out of earthen pitchers and wooden dishes. It happened that after the lords had half dined, came the French Ambassador, up to the lords' table, where he was to have sat; but finding the table set, he would not sit down nor dine with the Lord Mayor, who was not yet come, nor have a table to himself, which was offered; but in a discontent went away again. After I had dined, I and Creed rose and went up and down the house, and up to the ladys' room, and there stayed gazing upon them. But though there were many and fine, both young and old, yet I could not discern one handsome face there; which was very strange, nor did I find the lady that young Dawes married so pretty as I took her for,[3] I having here an opportunity of looking much upon her very near. I expected music, but there was none but only trumpets and drums, which displeased me. The dinner, it seems, is made by the Mayor and two Sheriffs[4] for the time being, the Lord Mayor paying one half, and they the other. And the whole, Proby says, is reckoned to come to about 7 or 800*l.* at most. Being wearied with looking upon a company of ugly women, Creed and I went away, and took coach and through Cheapside,[5] and there saw the pageants, which were very silly, and thence to the Temple, where meeting Greatorex, he and we to Hercules Pillars, there to show me the manner of his going about of draining of fenns,[6] which I desired much to know, but it did not appear very satisfactory to me, as he discoursed it, and I doubt[7] he will fail in it. Thence I by coach home, and there found my wife come home, and by and by came my brother Tom, with whom I was very angry for not sending me a bill with my things, so as that I think never to have more work done by him if ever he serves me so again, and so I told him. The consideration of laying out 32*l.* 12*s.* this very month in his very work troubles me also, and one thing more, that is to say, that Will having been at home all the day,[8] I doubt is the occasion that Jane has spoken to her mistress tonight that she sees she cannot please us and will look out to provide herself elsewhere, which do trouble both of us, and we wonder also at her, but yet when the rogue is gone I do not fear but the wench will do well. To the office a little, to set down my journal, and so home late to supper and to bed. The Queen[9] mends apace, they say; but yet talks idle still.

31. Up and to the office, where we sat all the morning, and at noon home to dinner, where Creed came and dined with me, and after dinner he and I upstairs, and I showed him my velvet cloak and other things of clothes, that I have lately bought, which he likes very well, and I took his opinion as to some things of clothes, which I purpose to wear, being resolved to go a little handsomer than I have hitherto. Thence to the office; where busy till night, and then to prepare my monthly account, about which I stayed till 10 or 11 o'clock at night, and to my great sorrow find myself 43*l.* worse than I was the last month, which was then 760*l.*, and now it is but 717*l.* But it hath chiefly arisen from my layings-out in clothes for myself and wife; viz., for her

[1] *messe* Meal course.

[2] *trenchers* Plates.

[3] *the lady ... her for* Earlier in the year, Samuel expressed envy toward Sir John Dawes, who, despite being "a simple man," had managed to marry a wealthy, "well-bred and handsome lady."

[4] *Sheriffs* Judicial officers immediately subordinate to the Lord Mayor.

[5] *Cheapside* London market street, often the site of important parades.

[6] *Greatorex* Robert Greatorex, inventor and maker of mathematical instruments, a long-time friend of Pepys; *Hercules Pillars* Tavern near the Temple district; *fenns* Marshes.

[7] *doubt* Suspect.

[8] *Will having ... the day* Will Hewer had been living with the Pepys family, causing some conflict in the household; the day before this entry, Samuel resolved to find him lodging elsewhere.

[9] *The Queen* Catherine of Braganza, daughter of John IV of Portugal and queen consort to Charles II. In October 1663, the Queen suffered a prolonged illness, perhaps the result of a miscarriage, her poor health made worse by her unhappiness with Charles's affairs, known publicly and therefore profoundly shameful to her.

about 12*l.*, and for myself 55*l.*, or thereabouts; having made myself a velvet cloak, two new cloth suits, black, plain both; a new shag[1] gown, trimmed with gold buttons and twist, with a new hat, and silk tops for my legs, and many other things, being resolved henceforward to go like myself. And also two periwigs, one whereof cost me 3*l.*, and the other 40*s.*—I have worn neither yet, but will begin next week, God willing. So that I hope I shall not need now to lay out more money a great while, I having laid out in clothes for myself and wife, and for her closet and other things without, these two months, this and the last, besides household expenses of victuals, &c., above 110*l.* But I hope I shall with more comfort labour to get more, and with better success than when, for want of clothes, I was forced to sneak like a beggar. Having done this I went home, and after supper to bed, my mind being eased in knowing my condition, though troubled to think that I have been forced to spend so much....

NOVEMBER 1663

3. Up and to the office, where busy all the morning, and at noon to the Coffee-house, and there heard a long and most passionate discourse between two doctors of physic, of which one was Dr. Allen, whom I knew at Cambridge, and a couple of apothecaries;[2] these maintaining chemistry against them Galenical physic;[3] and the truth is, one of the apothecaries whom they charged most, did speak very prettily, that is, his language and sense good, though perhaps he might not be so knowing a physician as to offer to contest with them. At last they came to some cooler terms, and broke up. I home, and there Mr. Moore coming by my appointment dined with me, and after dinner came Mr. Goldsborough, and we discoursed about the business of his mother,[4] but could come to no agreement in it but parted dissatisfied. By and by comes Chapman, the periwig-maker, and upon my liking it, without more ado I went up, and there he cut off my hair, which went a little to my heart at present to part with it; but, it being over, and my periwig on, I paid him 3*l.* for it; and away went he with my own hair to make up another of, and I by and by, after I had caused all my maids to look upon it; and they conclude it do become me; though Jane was mightily troubled for my parting of my own hair, and so was Besse, I went abroad to the Coffeehouse, and coming back went to Sir W. Pen and there sat with him and Captain Cocke[5] till late at night, Cocke talking of some of the Roman history very well, he having a good memory. Sir W. Pen observed mightily, and discoursed much upon my cutting off my hair, as he do of every thing that concerns me, but it is over, and so I perceive after a day or two it will be no great matter.

8. *Lord's Day.* Up, and it being late, to church[6] without my wife, and there I saw Pembleton come into the church and bring his wife with him, a good comely plain woman, and by and by my wife came after me all alone, which I was a little vexed at. I found that my coming in a periwig did not prove so strange to the world as I was afraid it would, for I thought that all the church would presently have cast their eyes all upon me, but I found no such thing. Here an ordinary lazy sermon of Mr. Mill's, and then home to dinner, and there Tom came and dined with us; and after dinner to talk about a new black cloth suit that I have a making, and so at church time to church again, where the Scot[7] preached, and I slept most of the time. Thence home, and I spent most of the evening upon Fuller's *Church*

[1] *shag* Velvet-like luxury fabric.

[2] *apothecaries* Makers and sellers of medicine.

[3] *Galenical physic* Galenical medicine (the approach still favored by most doctors at the time) treated disease with foods thought to balance the bodily humors, which were believed to control the health of the human body; the chemistry-based approach of the apothecaries would have somewhat more closely resembled that of modern scientific medicine.

[4] *Mr. Goldsborough ... his mother* Goldsborough's mother owed £10 to Samuel's uncle's estate.

[5] *Captain Cocke* George Cocke, a merchant who supplied goods to the navy.

[6] *church* St. Olave, an Anglican church.

[7] *the Scot* Young Scottish preacher who occasionally delivered the sermon at St. Olave.

History and Barckly's *Argeny*,[1] and so after supper to prayers and to bed, a little fearing my pain coming back again, myself continuing as costive as ever, and my physic[2] ended, but I had sent a porter today for more and it was brought me before I went to bed, and so with pretty good content to bed.

OCTOBER 1664

30. *Lord's Day*. Up, and this morning put on my new, fine, coloured cloth suit, with my cloak lined with plush, which is a dear and noble suit, costing me about 17*l.*[3] To church, and then home to dinner, and after dinner to a little music with my boy,[4] and so to church with my wife, and so home, and with her all the evening reading and at music with my boy with great pleasure, and so to supper, prayers, and to bed.

JUNE 1665

2. Lay troubled in mind abed a good while, thinking of my Tangier and victualling business,[5] which I doubt will fall. Up and to the Duke of Albemarle,[6] but missed him. Thence to the Harp and Ball and to Westminster Hall, where I visited "the flowers"[7] in each place, and so met with Mr. Creed, and he and I to Mrs. Croft's to drink and did, but saw not her daughter Borroughes. I away home, and there dined and did business. In the afternoon went with my tallies, made a fair end with Colvill and Viner,[8] delivering them 5000*l.* tallies to each and very quietly had credit given me upon other tallies of Mr. Colvill for 2000*l.* and good words for more, and of Mr. Viner too. Thence to visit the Duke of Albemarle, and thence my Lady Sandwich and Lord Crew. Thence home, and there met an express from Sir W. Batten at Harwich, that the fleet is all sailed from Solebay,[9] having spied the Dutch fleet at sea, and that, if the calms hinder not, they must needs now be engaged with them.[10] Another letter also come to me from Mr. Hater, committed by the Council this afternoon to the Gatehouse, upon the misfortune of having his name used by one, without his knowledge or privity, for the receiving of some powder that he had bought.[11] Up to Court about these two, and for the former was led up to my Lady Castlemayne's[12] lodgings, where the King and she and others were at supper, and there I read the letter and returned; and then to Sir G. Carteret[13] about Hater, and shall have him released tomorrow, upon my giving bail for his appearance, which I have promised to do. Sir G. Carteret did go on purpose to the King to ask this, and it was granted. So home at past 12, almost one o'clock in the morning. To my office till past two, and then home to supper and to bed.

6. Waked in the morning before 4 o'clock with great pain to piss, and great pain in pissing by having, I think, drank too great a draught of cold drink before going to bed. But by and by to sleep again, and then rose and to the office, where very busy all the morning, and at noon to dinner with Sir G. Carteret to his house with all our

[1] *Fuller's Church History* Thomas Fuller's *The Church-History of Britain* (1655); *Barckly's Argeny* John Barclay's *Argenis* (1621), a royalist historical allegory.

[2] *costive* Constipated; *physic* Purging medicine.

[3] *17l.* Some historians have noted the expense, remarking that a typical salary for a household servant would have been £2 or £3 per year.

[4] *my boy* Thomas Edwards, a servant in the Pepys household.

[5] *Tangier* Port city in northern Morocco, site of a British naval base; *victualling business* Food provision, here presumably for the navy. Later that year, Pepys was named Surveyor-General of Victualling for the navy, a highly lucrative position.

[6] *Duke of Albemarle* While James Stuart was at sea commanding the British in the Second Anglo-Dutch War, the Duke of Albemarle was performing the administrative duties of the Lord High Admiral.

[7] *"the flowers"* I.e., the pretty women.

[8] *tallies* Wooden sticks marked with notches representing debts or payments; *Colvil and Viner* John Colvill and Robert Viner, bankers, coin-makers, and financiers.

[9] *Solebay* English port town on the North Sea.

[10] *the fleet … with them* Second Anglo-Dutch War (1665–67), between England and the Dutch Republic, was beginning.

[11] *Mr. Hater* Thomas Hayter, one of Pepys's favorite clerks; *the Gatehouse* London prison; *privity* I.e., legal consent; *some powder … had bought* Hayter was accused of embezzling gunpowder from the King.

[12] *Lady Castlemayne* Barbara Palmer, Countess of Castlemaine, was a mistress of Charles II; her beauty and ability to manipulate the king resulted in a series of scandals in the court.

[13] *Sir G. Carteret* George Carteret, Treasurer of the Navy and a politician of considerable influence.

Board, where a good pasty[1] and brave discourse. But our great fear was some fresh news of the fleet, but not from the fleet, all being said to be well and beaten the Dutch, but I do not give much belief to it, and indeed the news come from Sir W. Batten at Harwich, and writ so simply that we all made good mirth of it. Thence to the office, where upon Sir G. Carteret's accounts, to my great vexation there being nothing done by the Controller[2] to right the King herein. I thence to my office and wrote letters all the afternoon, and in the evening by coach to Sir Ph. Warwicke's[3] about my Tangier business to get money, and so to my Lady Sandwich's, who, poor lady, expects every hour to hear of my Lord;[4] but in the best temper, neither confident nor troubled with fear, that I ever did see in my life. She tells me my Lord Rochester is now declaredly out of hopes of Mrs. Mallett,[5] and now she is to receive notice in a day or two how the King stands inclined to the giving leave for my Lord Hinchingbroke[6] to look after her, and that being done to bring it to an end shortly. Thence by coach home, and to my office a little, and so before 12 o'clock home and to bed.

7. This morning my wife and mother rose about two o'clock; and with Mercer,[7] Mary, the boy, and W. Hewer, as they had designed, took boat and down to refresh themselves on the water to Gravesend.[8] Lay till 7 o'clock, then up and to the office upon Sir G. Carteret's accounts again, where very busy; thence abroad and to the 'Change,[9] no news of certainty being yet come from the fleet. Thence to the Dolphin Tavern, where Sir J. Minnes, Lord Brunkard, Sir Thomas Harvy,[10] and myself dined, upon Sir G. Carteret's charge, and very merry we were, Sir Thomas Harvy being a very droll.[11] Thence to the office, and meeting Creed away with him to my Lord Treasurer's, there thinking to have met the goldsmiths, at Whitehall, but did not, and so appointed another time for my Lord to speak to them to advance us some money. Thence, it being the hottest day that ever I felt in my life, and it is confessed so by all other people the hottest they ever knew in England in the beginning of June, we to the New Exchange, and there drunk whey,[12] with much entreaty getting it for our money, and [they] would not be entreated to let us have one glass more. So took water and to Fox-Hall, to the Spring garden,[13] and there walked an hour or two with great pleasure, saving our minds ill at ease concerning the fleet and my Lord Sandwich, that we have no news of them, and ill reports run up and down of his being killed, but without ground. Here stayed pleasantly walking and spending but *6d.* till nine at night, and then by water to Whitehall, and there I stopped to hear news of the fleet, but none come, which is strange, and so by water home, where, weary with walking and with the mighty heat of the weather, and for my wife's not coming home, I staying walking in the garden till twelve at night, when it begun to lighten[14] exceedingly, through the greatness of the heat. Then despairing of her coming home, I to bed. This day, much against my will, I did in Drury Lane[15] see two or three houses marked with a red cross

[1] *Board* Navy Board, which administered the royal navy; *pasty* Meat pie, in the shape of a turnover.

[2] *Controller* Comptroller; manager of the royal accounts.

[3] *Sir Ph. Warwicke* Philip Warwick, secretary to the Lord Treasurer.

[4] *expects every … my Lord* Sandwich served as Lieutenant Admiral in the Second Anglo-Dutch War.

[5] *Lord Rochester* John Wilmot, 2nd Earl of Rochester, renowned libertine and important satirical poet; *Mrs. Mallet* Elizabeth Malet, a great beauty, according to Pepys, attracted Rochester's attention but refused his offer of marriage; he responded to her refusal by kidnapping the young woman in May 1665 and causing a scandal. Eventually, Elizabeth forgave him, and she married Rochester in 1667, becoming Countess of Rochester.

[6] *Lord Hinchingbroke* Edward Montagu, Sandwich's son.

[7] *Mercer* Mary Mercer, a companion to Mrs. Pepys.

[8] *Gravesend* Town on the Thames.

[9] *the 'Change* Royal Exchange, a commerce center built in 1565. It was sometimes known as the "Old Exchange."

[10] *Sir J. Minnes … Sir Thomas Harvy* Members of the Navy Board.

[11] *droll* Joker.

[12] *New Exchange* Built in 1608–09, the Exchange served as a commercial center, clustering many sellers of luxury goods; *whey* Liquid remainder of curdled milk, usually a by-product of cheese making.

[13] *Fox-Hall … Spring garden* New Spring Gardens, later known as Vauxhall Gardens.

[14] *it begun to lighten* I.e., there was thunder and lightning.

[15] *Drury Lane* London street of brothels, taverns, and theaters.

upon the doors, and "Lord have mercy upon us" writ there; which was a sad sight to me, being the first of the kind that, to my remembrance, I ever saw. It put me into an ill conception of myself and my smell, so that I was forced to buy some roll-tobacco to smell to and chaw, which took away the apprehension.[1]

8. About five o'clock my wife come home, it having lightened all night hard, and one great shower of rain. She come and lay upon the bed; I up and to the office, where all the morning. Alone at home to dinner, my wife, mother, and Mercer dining at W. Joyce's;[2] I giving her a caution to go round by the Half Moone to his house, because of the plague.[3] I to my Lord Treasurer's by appointment of Sir Thomas Ingram's, to meet the goldsmiths;[4] where I met with the great news at last newly come, brought by Bab May[5] from the Duke of York, that we have totally routed the Dutch; that the Duke himself, the Prince,[6] my Lord Sandwich, and Mr. Coventry are all well: which did put me into such joy that I forgot almost all other thoughts. The particulars I shall set down by and by. By and by comes Alderman Maynell and Mr. Viner, and there my Lord Treasurer did entreat them to furnish me with money upon my tallies, Sir Philip Warwicke before my Lord declaring the King's changing of the hand from Mr. Povy[7] to me, whom he called a very sober person, and one whom the Lord Treasurer would own in all things that I should concern myself with them in the business of money. They did at present declare they could not part with money at present. My Lord did press them very hard, and I hope upon their considering we shall get some of them. Thence with great joy to the Cocke-pitt;[8] where the Duke of Albermarle, like a man out of himself with content, new-told me all; and by and by comes a letter from Mr. Coventry's own hand to him, which he never opened (which was a strange thing), but did give it me to open and read, and consider what was fit for our office to do in it, and leave the letter with Sir W. Clerke; which upon such a time and occasion was a strange piece of indifference, hardly pardonable. I copied out the letter, and did also take minutes out of Sir W. Clerke's other letters; and the sum of the news is:

VICTORY OVER THE DUTCH,[9] JUNE 3RD, 1665.

This day they engaged; the Dutch neglecting greatly the opportunity of the wind they had of us, by which they lost the benefit of their fire-ships. The Earl of Falmouth, Muskerry, and Mr. Richard Boyle killed on board the Duke's ship, the *Royall Charles*, with one shot: their blood and brains flying in the Duke's face; and the head of Mr. Boyle striking down the Duke, as some say. Earl of Marlborough, Portland, Rear-Admiral Sansum (to Prince Rupert) killed, and Capt. Kirby and Ableson. Sir John Lawson wounded on the knee; hath had some bones taken out, and is likely to be well again. Upon receiving the hurt, he sent to the Duke for another to command the *Royall Oake*. The Duke sent Jordan out of the *St. George*, who did brave things in her. Capt. Jer. Smith of the *Mary* was second to the Duke, and stepped between him and Captain Seaton of the *Urania* (76 guns and 400 men), who had sworn to board the Duke; killed him, 200 men, and took the ship; himself losing 99 men, and never an officer saved but himself and lieutenant. His master indeed is saved, with his leg cut off: Admiral Opdam blown up, Trump killed, and said by Holmes; all the rest of their admirals, as they say,

[1] *ill conception … the apprehension* Body odor was considered an early sign of the plague, and tobacco was thought to protect from the disease.

[2] *W. Joyce* William Joyce, a relative of the Pepys family.

[3] *plague* The Great Plague (1665–66) killed an estimated 20 per cent of the English population.

[4] *Sir Thomas Ingram* Politician who served with Pepys on the committee governing Tangier; *goldsmiths* Francis Meynell and Thomas Viner, makers of English coins.

[5] *Bab May* Baptist May, a royal courtier.

[6] *the Prince* Prince Rupert of the Rhine, who served as a squadron commander during the Second Anglo-Dutch War.

[7] *Mr. Povy* Thomas Povey, appointed First Treasurer for Tangier in 1663. The position was reassigned to Pepys in May 1665, following Povy's failure to keep accounts in order.

[8] *Cocke-pitt* Cockpit, part of the Royal Palace at Whitehall so named from its former use in the cruel sport of cock-fighting.

[9] *VICTORY OVER THE DUTCH* The Battle of Lowestoft on 13 June (New Style) 1665 was a decisive success for the English in the Second Anglo-Dutch War, though the English failed to take full advantage of the Dutch defeat. The war ended in a Dutch victory.

> but Everson (whom they dare not trust for his affection to the Prince of Orange[1]), are killed: we having taken and sunk, as is believed, about 24 of their best ships; killed and taken near 8 or 10,000 men, and lost, we think, not above 700. A great[er] victory never known in the world. They are all fled, some 43 got into the Texell,[2] and others elsewhere, and we in pursuit of the rest.

Thence, with my heart full of joy; home, and to my office a little; then to my Lady Pen's, where they are all joyed and not a little puffed up at the good success of their father; and good service indeed is said to have been done by him.[3] Had a great bonfire at the gate; and I with my Lady Pen's people and others to Mrs. Turner's[4] great room, and then down into the street. I did give the boys 4*s.* among them, and mighty merry. So home to bed, with my heart at great rest and quiet, saving that the consideration of the victory is too great for me presently to comprehend.

15. Up, and put on my new stuff suit with close knees, which becomes me most nobly, as my wife says. At the office all day. At noon, put on my first laced band, all lace; and to Kate Joyce's[5] to dinner, where my mother, wife, and abundance of their friends, and good usage. Thence, wife and Mercer and I to the Old Exchange, and there bought two lace bands more, one of my seamstress, whom my wife concurs with me to be a pretty woman. So down to Deptford and Woolwich,[6] my boy and I. At Woolwich, discoursed with Mr. Sheldon[7] about my bringing my wife down for a month or two to his house, which he approves of, and, I think, will be very convenient. So late back, and to the office, wrote letters, and so home to supper and to bed. This day the newsbook (upon Mr. Moore's showing L'Estrange Captain Ferrers's letter[8]) did do my Lord Sandwich great right as to the late victory. The Duke of York not yet come to town. The towne grows very sickly, and people to be afeard of it; there dying this last week of the plague 112, from 43 the week before, whereof but [one] in Fanchurch-street, and one in Broad-street, by the Treasurer's office.

29. Up and by water to Whitehall, where the Court full of wagons and people ready to go out of town. To the Harp and Ball, and there drank and talked with Mary, she telling me in discourse that she lived lately at my neighbour's, Mr. Knightly, which made me forbear further discourse. This end of the town every day grows very bad of the plague. The Mortality Bill is come to 267;[9] which is about ninety more than the last: and of these but four in the City,[10] which is a great blessing to us. Thence to Creed, and with him up and down about Tangier business, to no purpose. Took leave again of Mr. Coventry; though I hope the Duke has not gone to stay, and so do others too. So home, calling at Somersett House,[11] where all are packing up too: the Queen-Mother setting out for France this day to drink Bourbon waters this year, she being in a consumption; and intends not to come till winter come twelvemonths.[12] So

[1] *whom they … of Orange* William III was born in the Dutch Republic and would become head of state there before he became King of England; his family thus had Dutch supporters.

[2] *Texell* Island belonging to the Netherlands. The final naval battle of the First Anglo-Dutch War took place there.

[3] *good service … by him* When Charles II granted William Penn a charter for governing the American province to be called Pennsylvania, his service during the Battle of Lowestoft was specifically cited in the document.

[4] *Mrs. Turner* Jane Turner, Samuel's cousin.

[5] *Kate Joyce* Samuel's cousin.

[6] *Deptford and Woolwich* Sites of royal dockyards outside the City.

[7] *Mr. Sheldon* Financial manager of the Woolwich Dockyard, living in Woolwich.

[8] *L'Estrange* Roger L'Estrange published *The Public Intelligencer*, the precursor of the *London Gazette*; *Captain Ferrers's letter* Ferrer, a captain in Sandwich's regiment, wrote a letter praising the Earl's actions in the Battle of Lowestoft.

[9] *Mortality Bill … to 267* The London Bills of Mortality were an official source of mortality statistics, issued to inform the population about plague outbreaks. In the week ending 27 June, the total number of deaths in London was 684, of which 267 were caused by the plague.

[10] *City* I.e., City of London, the part of the city falling within London's ancient boundaries. The financial and commercial centers were located in the City.

[11] *Somersett House* Palace used by Charles II.

[12] *consumption* Extreme wasting of the body, typically due to tuberculosis; *intends … twelvemonths* In fact, the Queen Mother never again returned to England; she died in August 1669, at her French chateau.

by coach home, where at the office all the morning, and at noon Mrs. Hunt[1] dined with us. Very merry, and she a very good woman. To the office, where busy a while putting some things in my office in order, and then to letters till night. About 10 o'clock home, the days being sensibly shorter before I have once kept a summer's day by shutting up office by daylight; but my life hath been still as it was in winter almost. But I will for a month try what I can do by daylight. So home to supper and to bed.

JULY 1665

30. *Lord's Day*. Up, and in my night gown, cap and neckcloth, undressed all day long, lost not a minute, but in my chamber, setting my Tangier accounts to rights. Which I did by night to my very heart's content, not only that it is done, but I find everything right, and even beyond what, after so long neglecting them, I did hope for. The Lord of Heaven be praised for it! Will was with me today, and is very well again. It was a sad noise to hear our bell to toll and ring so often today, either for deaths or burials; I think five or six times. At night weary with my day's work, but full of joy at my having done it, I to bed, being to rise betimes tomorrow to go to the wedding at Dagenhams.[2] So to bed, fearing I have got some cold sitting in my loose garments all this day.

31. Up, and very betimes by six o'clock at Deptford, and there find Sir G. Carteret, and my Lady ready to go: I being in my new coloured silk suit, and coat trimmed with gold buttons and gold broad lace round my hands, very rich and fine. By water to the Ferry, where, when we come, no coach there; and tide of ebb so far spent as the horse-boat could not get off on the other side the river to bring away the coach. So we were fain to stay there in the unlucky Isle of Doggs,[3] in a chill place, the morning cool, and wind fresh, above two if not three hours to our great discontent. Yet being upon a pleasant errand, and seeing that it could not be helped, we did bear it very patiently; and it was worth my observing, I thought, as ever anything, to see how upon these two scores, Sir G. Carteret, the most passionate man in the world, and that was in greatest haste to be gone, did bear with it, and very pleasant all the while, at least not troubled much so as to fret and storm at it. Anon the coach comes: in the meantime there coming a News thither with his horse to go over, that told us he did come from Islington this morning; and that Proctor the vintner[4] of the Miter in Wood-street, and his son, are dead this morning there, of the plague; he having laid out abundance of money there, and was the greatest vintner for some time in London for great entertainments. We, fearing the canonical hour[5] would be past before we got thither, did with a great deal of unwillingness send away the license and wedding ring. So that when we come, though we drove hard with six horses, yet we found them gone from home; and going towards the church, met them coming from church, which troubled us. But, however, that trouble was soon over; hearing it was well done: they being both in their old clothes; my Lord Crew giving her,[6] there being three coach fulls of them. The young lady mighty sad,[7] which troubled me; but yet I think it was only her gravity in a little greater degree than usual. All saluted[8] her, but I did not till my Lady Sandwich did ask me whether I had saluted her or no. So to dinner, and very merry we were; but yet in such a sober way as never almost any wedding was in so great families: but it was much better. After dinner company divided, some to cards, others to talk. My Lady Sandwich and I up to settle accounts, and pay her some money. And mighty kind she is to me, and would fain have had me gone down for company with her to Hinchingbroke;[9] but for my life I cannot. At night to supper, and so to talk; and which, methought, was the most extraordinary thing, all of us to prayers as

[1] *Mrs. Hunt* Neighbor of the Pepys family.

[2] *wedding at Dagenhams* Between Jemima Montagu, Sandwich's daughter, and Sir George Carteret's son Philip; *Dagenhams* Village on the Thames.

[3] *Isle of Doggs* I.e., Isle of dogs, an area of East London.

[4] *vintner* Wine-seller.

[5] *canonical hour* Interval between 8:00 a.m. and 12:00 p.m., the only hours during which the Church of England would perform weddings.

[6] *Lord Crew giving her* I.e., giving her away in marriage (because her father was at sea with the navy).

[7] *sad* I.e., serious.

[8] *saluted* Kissed.

[9] *Hinchingbroke* In Hertfordshire, country seat of the Earls of Sandwich.

usual, and the young bride and bridegroom too and so after prayers, soberly to bed; only I got into the bridegroom's chamber while he undressed himself, and there was very merry, till he was called to the bride's chamber, and into bed they went. I kissed the bride in bed, and so the curtains drawn with the greatest gravity that could be, and so good night. But the modesty and gravity of this business[1] was so decent, that it was to me indeed ten times more delightful than if it had been twenty times more merry and jovial. Whereas I feared I must have sat up all night, we did here all get good beds, and I lay in the same I did before with Mr. Brisband, who is a good scholar and sober man; and we lay in bed, getting him to give me an account of home, which is the most delightful talk a man can have of any traveller: and so to sleep. My eyes much troubled already with the change of my drink. Thus I ended this month with the greatest joy that ever I did any in my life, because I have spent the greatest part of it with abundance of joy, and honour, and pleasant journeys, and brave entertainments, and without cost of money; and at last live to see the business ended with great content on all sides. This evening with Mr. Brisband, speaking of enchantments and spells; I telling him some of my charms; he told me this of his own knowledge, at Bourdeaux, in France. The words these:

Voici un corps mort,
Raide comme un bâton,
Froid comme marbre,
Léger comme un esprit,
Levons te au nom de Jesus Christ.[2]

He saw four little girls, very young ones, all kneeling, each of them, upon one knee; and one begun the first line, whispering in the ear of the next, and the second to the third, and the third to the fourth, and she to the first. Then the first begun the second line, and so round quite through, and, putting each one finger only to a boy that lay flat upon his back on the ground, as if he was dead; at the end of the words, they did with their four fingers raise this boy as high as they could reach, and he[3] being there, and wondering at it, as also being afeard to see it, for they would have had him to have bore a part in saying the words, in the room of one of the little girls that was so young that they could hardly make her learn to repeat the words, did, for fear there might be some sleight used in it by the boy, or that the boy might be light, call the cook of the house, a very lusty fellow, as Sir G. Carteret's cook, who is very big, and they did raise him in just the same manner. This is one of the strangest things I ever heard, but he tells it me of his own knowledge, and I do heartily believe it to be true. I enquired of him whether they were Protestant or Catholic girls; and he told me they were Protestant, which made it the more strange to me. Thus we end this month, as I said, after the greatest glut of content that ever I had; only under some difficulty because of the plague, which grows mightily upon us, the last week being about 1700 or 1800 of the plague. My Lord Sandwich at sea with a fleet of about 100 sail, to the Northward, expecting De Ruyter, or the Dutch East India fleet.[4] My Lord Hinchingbroke coming over from France, and will meet his sister at Scott's-hall.[5] Myself having obliged both these families in this business very much; as both my Lady, and Sir G. Carteret and his Lady do confess exceedingly, and the latter do also now call me cousin, which I am glad of. So God preserve us all friends long, and continue health among us.

[1] *this business* Lord Hinchingbroke is Lord Sandwich's son and heir, and so brother of the recent bride, and "this business" is the wedding. Pepys has done a service to both families by helping to bring about the marriage between them, and Carteret calls him cousin because he is a distant cousin of the Montagu family (that of Lord and Lady Sandwich).

[2] *Voici un ... Jesus Christ* French: "Here lies a dead body, / Stiff as a stick, / Cold as marble, / Light as a spirit, / Rise in the name of Jesus Christ." This chant—similar to the present-day "light as a feather, stiff as a board"—is part of a game in which one person lies on the floor while others gather round the body, each placing one finger under it. When the chant is recited, the body is supposed to levitate. The game was especially popular during times of plague outbreak.

[3] *he* Mr. Brisband.

[4] *De Ruyter* Michiel Adriaenszoon de Ruyter, perhaps the most famous Dutch admiral and an integral force in both Anglo-Dutch Wars; *Dutch East India fleet* The Dutch East India Company, established in 1602, was a trading concern so powerful as to establish colonies and wage war. The company had a fleet of nearly five thousand ships. (In contrast, the English East India Company, chartered in 1600, had a fleet of some 2,690 ships.)

[5] *Scott's-hall* Country manor in southeast England.

AUGUST 1665

15. Up by 4 o'clock and walked to Greenwich,[1] where called at Captain Cocke's and to his chamber, he being in bed, where something put my last night's dream into my head, which I think is the best that ever was dreamt, which was that I had my Lady Castlemayne in my arms and was admitted to use all the dalliance I desired with her, and then dreamt that this could not be awake, but that it was only a dream; but that since it was a dream, and that I took so much real pleasure in it, what a happy thing it would be if when we are in our graves (as Shakespeare resembles it[2]) we could dream, and dream but such dreams as this, that then we should not need to be so fearful of death, as we are this plague time. Here I hear that news is brought Sir G. Carteret that my Lord Hinchingbroke is not well, and so cannot meet us at Cranborne tonight. So I to Sir G. Carteret's; and there was sorry with him for our disappointment. So we have put off our meeting there till Saturday next. Here I stayed talking with Sir G. Carteret, he being mighty free with me in his business, and among other things hath ordered Rider and Cutler[3] to put into my hands copper to the value of 5,000*l.* (which Sir G. Carteret's share it seems come to in it), which is to raise part of the money he is to lay out for a purchase for my Lady Jemimah. Thence he and I to Sir J. Minnes's[4] by invitation, where Sir W. Batten and my Lady, and my Lord Bruncker,[5] and all of us dined upon a venison pasty and other good meat, but nothing well dressed. But my pleasure lay in getting some bills signed by Sir G. Carteret, and promise of present payment from Mr. Fenn,[6] which do rejoice my heart, it being one of the heaviest things I had upon me, that so much of the little I have should lie (*viz.* near 1000*l.*) in the King's hands. Here very merry and (Sir G. Carteret being gone presently after dinner) to Captain Cocke's, and there merry, and so broke up and I by water to the Duke of Albemarle, with whom I spoke a great deal in private, they being designed to send a fleet of ships privately to the Streights.[7] No news yet from our fleet, which is much wondered at, but the Duke says for certain guns have been heard to the northward very much. It was dark before I could get home, and so land at Church-yard stairs, where, to my great trouble, I met a dead corpse of the plague, in the narrow ally just bringing down[8] a little pair of stairs. But I thank God I was not much disturbed at it. However, I shall beware of being late abroad again.

SEPTEMBER 1665

7. Up by 5 of the clock, mighty full of fear of an ague,[9] but was obliged to go, and so by water, wrapping myself up warm, to the Tower, and there sent for the Weekly Bill,[10] and find 8,252 dead in all, and of them 6,878 of the plague; which is a most dreadful number, and shows reason to fear that the plague hath got that hold that it will yet continue among us. Thence to Brainford, reading *The Villaine*,[11] a pretty good play, all the way. There a coach of Mr. Povy's stood ready for me, and he at his house ready to come in, and so we together merrily to Swakely,[12] Sir R. Viner's. A very pleasant place, bought by him of Sir James Harrington's lady. He took us up and down with great respect, and showed us all his house and grounds; and it is a place not very modern in the garden nor house, but the most uniform in all that ever I saw; and some things to excess. Pretty to see over the screen of the hall (put up by Sir J. Harrington, a Long Parliamentman) the King's head,

[1] *Greenwich* For safety during the plague, London's navy office relocated from the City to Greenwich, near Deptford.

[2] *Shakespeare resembles it* See *Hamlet* 3.1.65–66.

[3] *Rider and Cutler* Merchants who sold supplies to the navy.

[4] *Sir J. Minnes* John Mennes, Comptroller of the Navy.

[5] *Lord Bruncker* William Brouncker, a mathematician and natural philosopher.

[6] *Mr. Fenn* John Fenn, paymaster to the Navy Treasurer.

[7] *the Streights* Strait of Gibraltar, which connects the Atlantic Ocean and the Mediterranean Sea.

[8] *just bringing down* I.e., just being brought down.

[9] *ague* Illness.

[10] *the Tower* Tower of London, used as a prison for high-status inmates; *Weekly Bill* I.e., Bill of Mortality.

[11] *Brainford* Brentford, a few miles outside the City; *The Villaine* Play by Thomas Porter, first performed in 1662 and published the following year, which borrows heavily from Shakespeare's *Othello*.

[12] *Swakely* Viner's country house.

and my Lord of Essex on one side, and Fairfax[1] on the other; and upon the other side of the screen, the parson of the parish, and the lord of the manor and his sisters. The window-cases, door-cases, and chimneys of all the house are marble. He showed me a black boy that he had, that died of a consumption, and being dead, he caused him to be dried in an oven, and lies there entire in a box. By and by to dinner, where his lady I find yet handsome, but hath been a very handsome woman; now is old, hath brought him near 100,000*l.* and now he lives, no man in England in greater plenty, and commands both King and Council with his credit he gives them. Here was a fine lady a merchant's wife at dinner with us, and who should be here in the quality of a woman but Mrs. Worship's daughter, Dr. Clerke's niece, and after dinner Sir Robert led us up to his long gallery, very fine, above stairs (and better, or such, furniture I never did see), and there Mrs. Worship did give us three or four very good songs, and sings very neatly, to my great delight. After all this, and ending the chief business to my content about getting a promise of some money of him, we took leave, being exceedingly well treated here, and a most pleasant journey we had back, Povy and I, and his company most excellent in anything but business, he here giving me an account of as many persons at Court as I had a mind or thought of enquiring after. He tells me by a letter he showed me, that the King is not, nor hath been of late, very well, but quite out of humour; and, as some think, in a consumption, and weary of everything. He showed me my Lord Arlington's house that he was born in, in a town called Harlington: and so carried me through a most pleasant country to Brainford, and there put me into my boat, and good night. So I wrapt myself warm, and by water got to Woolwich[2] about one in the morning, my wife and all in bed.

[1] *Long Parliamentman* Lasting from 1640 until 1648, the so-called Long Parliament was called by Charles I. Its name derives from an Act of Parliament decreeing that it could only be dissolved through the agreement of its members, rather than by the King's will; *Fairfax* Thomas Fairfax, 3rd Lord Fairfax of Cameron, was the Parliamentarians' commander-in-chief during the English Civil War.

[2] *Woolwich* I.e., Mr. Sheldon's house in Woolwich, where Elizabeth was staying to avoid the plague.

10. *Lord's Day.* Walked home; being forced thereto by one of my watermen falling sick yesterday, and it was God's great mercy I did not go by water with them yesterday, for he fell sick on Saturday night, and it is to be feared of the plague. So I sent him away to London with his fellow; but another boat come to me this morning, whom I sent to Blackewall for Mr. Andrews.[3] I walked to Woolwich, and there find Mr. Hill,[4] and he and I all the morning at music and a song he hath set of three parts, methinks, very good. Anon comes Mr. Andrews, though it be a very ill day, and so after dinner we to music and sang till about 4 or 5 o'clock, it blowing very hard, and now and then raining, and wind and tide being against us, Andrews and I took leave and walked to Greenwich. My wife before I come out telling me the ill news that she hears that her father is very ill, and then I told her I feared of the plague, for that the house is shut up. And so she much troubled she did desire me to send them something; and I said I would, and will do so.

But before I come out there happened news to come to the by an express from Mr. Coventry, telling me the most happy news of my Lord Sandwich's meeting with[5] part of the Dutch; his taking two of their East India ships, and six or seven others, and very good prizes and that he is in search of the rest of the fleet, which he hopes to find upon the Wellbancke,[6] with the loss only of the *Hector*, poor Captain Cuttle. This news do so overjoy me that I know not what to say enough to express it, but the better to do it I did walk to Greenwich, and there sending away Mr. Andrews, I to Captain Cocke's, where I find my Lord Bruncker and his mistress, and Sir J. Minnes. Where we supped (there was also Sir W. Doyly and Mr. Evelyn[7]); but the receipt of this news did put us all into such an ecstasy of joy, that it inspired into Sir J. Minnes and Mr. Evelyn such

[3] *Mr. Andrews* Thomas Andrews, a merchant who sold supplies to the naval base in Tangier.

[4] *Mr. Hill* Thomas Hill, merchant and amateur musician, a close friend of Pepys.

[5] *meeting with* I.e., engaging in combat with.

[6] *Wellbancke* Area of the North Sea between northern England and the Netherlands.

[7] *Sir W. Doyly and Mr. Evelyn* Two of the four commissioners responsible for the navy's medical services during the Second Anglo-Dutch War. Like Pepys, John Evelyn was a diarist.

a spirit of mirth, that in all my life I never met with so merry a two hours as our company this night was. Among other humours, Mr. Evelyn's repeating of some verses made up of nothing but the various acceptations of may and can, and doing it so aptly upon occasion of something of that nature, and so fast, did make us all die almost with laughing, and did so stop the mouth of Sir J. Minnes in the middle of all his mirth (and in a thing agreeing with his own manner of genius), that I never saw any man so out-done in all my life; and Sir J. Minnes's mirth too to see himself out-done, was the crown of all our mirth. In this humour we sat till about ten at night, and so my Lord and his mistress home, and we to bed, it being one of the times of my life wherein I was the fullest of true sense of joy.

14. Up, and walked to Greenwich, and there fitted myself in several businesses to go to London, where I have not been now a pretty while. But before I went from the office news is brought by word of mouth that letters are just now brought from the fleet of our taking a great many more of the Dutch fleet, in which I did never more plainly see my command of my temper in my not admitting myself to receive any kind of joy from it till I had heard the certainty of it, and therefore went by water directly to the Duke of Albemarle, where I find a letter of the 12th from Solebay, from my Lord Sandwich, of the fleet's meeting with about eighteen more of the Dutch fleet, and his taking of most of them; and the messenger says they had taken three after the letter was wrote and sealed; which being twenty-one, and the fourteen took the other day, is forty-five sail; some of which are good, and others rich ships, which is so great a cause of joy in us all that my Lord and everybody is highly joyed thereat. And having taken a copy of my Lord's letter, I away back again to the Bear at the Bridge foot,[1] being full of wind and out of order, and there called for a biscuit and a piece of cheese and gill of sack,[2] being forced to walk over the Bridge, toward the 'Change, and the plague being all thereabouts. Here my news was highly welcome, and I did wonder to see the 'Change so full, I believe 200 people; but not a man or merchant of any fashion, but plain men all. And Lord! to see how I did endeavour all I could to talk with as few as I could, there being now no observation of shutting up of houses infected, that to be sure we do converse and meet with people that have the plague upon them. I to Sir Robert Viner's, where my main business was about settling the business of Debusty's[3] 5000*l.* tallies, which I did for the present to enable me to have some money, and so home, buying some things for my wife in the way. So home, and put up several things to carry to Woolwich, and upon serious thoughts I am advised by W. Griffin to let my money and plate[4] rest there, as being as safe as any place, nobody imagining that people would leave money in their houses now, when all their families are gone. So for the present that being my opinion, I did leave them there still. But, Lord! to see the trouble that it puts a man to, to keep safe what with pain a man hath been getting together, and there is good reason for it. Down to the office, and there wrote letters to and again about this good news of our victory, and so by water home late. Where, when I come home I spent some thoughts upon the occurrences of this day, giving matter for as much content on one hand and melancholy on another, as any day in all my life. For the first; the finding of my money and plate, and all safe at London, and speeding in my business of money this day. The hearing of this good news to such excess, after so great a despair of my Lord's doing anything this year; adding to that, the decrease of 500 and more, which is the first decrease we have yet had in the sickness since it begun: and great hopes that the next week it will be greater. Then, on the other side, my finding that though the Bill in general is abated, yet the City within the walls is increased, and likely to continue so, and is close to our house there. My meeting dead corpses of the plague, carried to be buried close to me at noon-day through the City in Fanchurch-street. To see a person sick of the sores,[5] carried close by me by Gracechurch in a hackney-

[1] *the Bear at the Bridge foot* Tavern at the foot of London Bridge.

[2] *gill of sack* Fourth of a pint of fortified white wine.

[3] *Debusty* Lawrence Debussy, merchant.

[4] *W. Griffin* Employee of the navy office; *plate* Gold or silver tableware.

[5] *sick of the sores* Sores were a common mark of the plague, and contact with open sores was a source of the disease's spread. Beginning in 1604, anyone in public found to have a plague sore could be whipped or even hanged.

coach.[1] My finding the Angell tavern, at the lower end of Tower-hill, shut up, and more than that, the alehouse at the Tower-stairs, and more than that, the person was then dying of the plague when I was last there, a little while ago, at night, to write a short letter there, and I overheard the mistress of the house sadly saying to her husband somebody was very ill, but did not think it was of the plague. To hear that poor Payne, my waiter, hath buried a child, and is dying himself. To hear that a labourer I sent but the other day to Dagenhams, to know how they did there, is dead of the plague; and that one of my own watermen, that carried me daily, fell sick as soon as he had landed me on Friday morning last, when I had been all night upon the water (and I believe he did get his infection that day at Brainford), and is now dead of the plague. To hear that Captain Lambert and Cuttle are killed in the taking these ships; and that Mr. Sidney Montague[2] is sick of a desperate fever at my Lady Carteret's, at Scott's-hall. To hear that Mr. Lewes[3] hath another daughter sick. And, lastly, that both my servants, W. Hewer and Tom Edwards, have lost their fathers, both in St. Sepulchre's parish, of the plague this week, do put me into great apprehensions of melancholy, and with good reason. But I put off the thoughts of sadness as much as I can, and the rather to keep my wife in good heart and family also. After supper (having eat nothing all this day) upon a fine tench[4] of Mr. Shelden's taking, we to bed.

SEPTEMBER 1666

1. Up and at the office all the morning, and then dined at home. Got my new closet[5] made mighty clean against tomorrow. Sir W. Penn and my wife and Mercer and I to *Polichenelly*,[6] but were there horribly frighted to see young Killigrew[7] come in with a great many more young sparks; but we hid ourselves, so as we think they did not see us. By and by they went away, and then we were at rest again; and so the play being done, we to Islington and there eat and drank and mighty merry—and so home, singing; and after a letter or two at the office, to bed.

2. *Lord's day.* Some of our maids sitting up late last night to get things ready against our feast today, Jane called us up, about 3 in the morning, to tell us of a great fire they saw in the City.[8] So I rose, and slipped on my nightgown and went to her window, and thought it to be on the back side of Mark Lane at the furthest; but being unused to such fires as followed, I thought it far enough off, and so went to bed again and to sleep. About 7 rose again to dress myself, and there looked out at the window and saw the fire not so much as it was, and further off. So to my closet to set things to rights after yesterday's cleaning. By and by Jane comes and tells me that she hears that above 300 houses have been burned down tonight by the fire we saw, and that it was now burning down all Fish Street by London Bridge. So I made myself ready presently, and walked to the Tower and there got up upon one of the high places, Sir J. Robinson's[9] little son going up with me; and there I did see the houses at that end of the bridge all on fire, and an infinite great fire on this and the other side the end of the bridge—which, among other people, did trouble me for poor little Michell[10] and our Sarah on the Bridge. So down, with my heart full of trouble, to the Lieutenant of the Tower, who tells me that it begun this morning in the King's baker's house in Pudding Lane, and that it hath burned down St. Magnes Church and most part of Fish Street already. So I down to the water-side and there got a boat and through bridge, and there saw

[1] *hackney-coach* Hired coach.

[2] *Mr. Sidney Montague* The Earl of Sandwich's father.

[3] *Mr. Lewes* Civil servant in navy administration.

[4] *tench* Carp-like fish.

[5] *closet* Small private room.

[6] *Polichenelly* Puppet play based on the Italian *commedia dell'arte* character of Polichinello.

[7] *young Killigrew* Possibly Henry Killigrew, younger brother to dramatist Thomas Killigrew.

[8] *the City* I.e., the City of London, the part of the city falling within London's ancient boundaries. The financial and commercial centers were located in the City.

[9] *Sir J. Robinson* Sir John Robinson was lieutenant of the Tower of London.

[10] *Michell* William Michell and his wife Betty kept a brandy shop near London Bridge. Betty had been one of Pepys's old flames, and is referred to earlier in the *Diary* as his "second wife," Sarah.

a lamentable fire. Poor Michell's house, as far as the Old Swan,[1] already burned that way and the fire running further, that in a very little time it got as far as the Steel-yard while I was there. Everybody endeavouring to remove their goods, and flinging into the River or bringing them into lighters[2] that lay off. Poor people staying in their houses as long as till the very fire touched them, and then running into boats or clambering from one pair of stair by the water-side to another. And among other things, the poor pigeons I perceive were loath to leave their houses, but hovered about the windows and balconies till they were some of them burned, their wings, and fell down.

Having stayed, and in an hour's time seen the fire rage every way, and nobody to my sight endeavouring to quench it, but to remove their goods and leave all to the fire; and having seen it get as far as the Steel-yard, and the wind mighty high and driving it into the city, and everything, after so long a drought, proving combustible, even the very stones of churches, and among other things, the poor steeple by which pretty Mrs. ——[3] lives, and whereof my old school-fellow Elborough is parson, taken fire in the very top and there burned till it fall down—I to Whitehall with a gentleman with me who desired to go off from the Tower to see the fire in my boat—to Whitehall, and there up to the King's closet in the chapel, where people came about me and I did give them an account dismayed them all; and word was carried in to the King, so I was called for and did tell the King and Duke of York what I saw, and that unless his Majesty did command houses to be pulled down, nothing could stop the fire. They seemed much troubled, and the King commanded me to go to my Lord Mayor from him and command him to spare no houses but to pull down before the fire every way. The Duke of York bid me tell him that if he would have any more soldiers, he shall; and so did my Lord Arlington afterward, as a great secret. Here meeting with Captain Cocke, I in his coach, which he lent me, and Creed with me, to Paul's;[4] and there walked along Watling Street as well as I could, every creature coming away loaden with goods to save—and here and there sick people carried away in beds. Extraordinary good goods carried in carts and on backs. At last met my Lord Mayor in Canning Street, like a man spent, with a handkerchief about his neck. To the King's message, he cried like a fainting woman, "Lord, what can I do? I am spent. People will not obey me. I have been pulling down houses. But the fire overtakes us faster than we can do it." That he needed no more soldiers; and that for himself, he must go and refresh himself, having been up all night. So he left me, and I him, and walked home—seeing people all almost distracted and no manner of means used to quench the fire. The houses too, so very thick thereabouts, and full of matter for burning, as pitch and tar, in Thames Street—and warehouses of oil and wines and brandy and other things. Here I saw Mr. Isaac Houblon, that handsome man—prettily dressed and dirty at his door at Dowgate, receiving some of his brother's things whose houses were on fire; and as he says, have been removed twice already, and he doubts (as it soon proved) that they must be in a little time removed from his house also—which was a sad consideration. And to see the churches all filling with goods, by people who themselves should have been quietly there at this time.

By this time it was about 12 o'clock, and so home and there find my guests, which was Mr. Wood and his wife, Barbary Shelden, and also Mr. Moone—she mighty fine, and her husband, for aught I see, a likely[5] man. But Mr. Moone's design and mine, which was to look over my closet and please him with the sight thereof, which he hath long desired, was wholly disappointed, for we were in great trouble and disturbance at this fire, not knowing what to think of it. However, we had an extraordinary good dinner, and as merry as at this time we could be.

While at dinner, Mrs. Batelier came to enquire after Mr. Woolfe and Stanes (who it seems are related to them), whose houses in Fish Street are all burned, and they in a sad condition. She would not stay in the fright.

[1] *Old Swan* Tavern in Thames Street.

[2] *lighters* Barges.

[3] *Mrs. ——* Mrs. Horsely, a pretty woman whom Pepys admired and pursued unsuccessfully.

[4] *Paul's* St. Paul's Cathedral.

[5] *likely* Capable.

As soon as dined, I and Moone away and walked through the City, the streets full of nothing but people and horses and carts loaded with goods, ready to run over one another, and removing goods from one burned house to another—they now removing out of Canning Street (which received goods in the morning) into Lumbard Street and further; and among others, I now saw my little goldsmith Stokes receiving some friend's goods, whose house itself was burned the day after. We parted at Paul's, he home and I to Paul's Wharf, where I had appointed a boat to attend me; and took in Mr. Carcasse and his brother, whom I met in the street, and carried them below and above bridge, to and again, to see the fire, which was now got further, both below and above, and no likelihood of stopping it. Met with the King and Duke of York in their barge, and with them to Queenhithe[1] and there called Sir Rd. Browne[2] to them. Their order was only to pull down houses apace, and so below bridge at the waterside; but little was or could be done, the fire coming upon them so fast. Good hopes there was of stopping it at the Three Cranes above, and at Buttolph's Wharf below bridge, if care be used; but the wind carries it into the City, so as we know not by the water-side what it doth there. River full of lighters and boats taking in goods, and good goods swimming in the water; and only, I observed that hardly one lighter or boat in three that had the goods of a house in, but there was a pair of virginals[3] in it. Having seen as much as I could now, I away to Whitehall by appointment, and there walked to St. James's Park, and there met my wife and Creed and Wood and his wife and walked to my boat, and there upon the water again, and to the fire up and down, it still increasing and the wind great. So near the fire as we could for smoke; and all over the Thames, with one's face in the wind you were almost burned with a shower of firedrops—this is very true—so as houses were burned by these drops and flakes of fire, three or four, nay five or six houses, one from another. When we could endure no more upon the water, we to a little alehouse on the Bankside over against the Three Cranes, and there stayed till it was dark almost and saw the fire grow; and as it grew darker, appeared more and more, and in corners and upon steeples and between churches and houses, as far as we could see up the hill of the City, in a most horrid malicious bloody flame, not like the fine flame of an ordinary fire. Barbary[4] and her husband away before us. We stayed till, it being darkish, we saw the fire as only one entire arch of fire from this to the other side the bridge, and in a bow up the hill, for an arch of above a mile long. It made me weep to see it. The churches, houses, and all on fire and flaming at once, and a horrid noise the flames made, and the cracking of houses at their ruin. So home with a sad heart, and there find everybody discoursing and lamenting the fire; and poor Tom Hater came with some few of his goods saved out of his house, which is burned upon Fish Street hill. I invited him to lie at my house, and did receive his goods: but was deceived in his lying there,[5] the noise coming every moment of the growth of the fire, so as we were forced to begin to pack up our own goods and prepare for their removal. And did by moonshine (it being brave,[6] dry, and moonshine and warm weather) carry much of my goods into the garden, and Mr. Hater and I did remove my money and iron chests into my cellar—as thinking that the safest place. And got my bags of gold into my office ready to carry away, and my chief papers of accounts also there, and my tallies into a box by themselves. So great was our fear, as Sir W. Batten had carts come out of the country to fetch away his goods this night. We did put Mr. Hater, poor man, to bed a little; but he got but very little rest, so much noise being in my house, taking down of goods.

3. About 4 o'clock in the morning, my Lady Batten sent me a cart to carry away all my money and plate and best things to Sir W. Rider's at Bednall Green; which I did, riding myself in my nightgown in the cart; and Lord, to see how the streets and the highways are crowded with people, running and riding and getting of carts at any rate to fetch away things. I find Sir W. Rider tired with being called up all night and receiving things from

[1] *Queenhithe* Harbor in Thames Street.

[2] *Sir Rd. Browne* I.e., Sir Richard Browne, a former Lord Mayor.

[3] *pair of virginals* Popular table-sized harpsichord.

[4] *Barbary* Actress Elizabeth Knepp, whom Pepys called "Barbary" because of her singing of *Barbary Allen*.

[5] *deceived in his lying there* Pepys felt mistaken to have extended the offer as the fire advanced.

[6] *brave* Fine.

several friends. His house full of goods—and much of Sir W. Batten and Sir W. Penn's. I am eased at my heart to have my treasure so well secured. Then home with much ado to find a way. Nor any sleep all this night to me nor my poor wife. But then, and all this day, she and I and all my people labouring to get away the rest of our things, and did get Mr. Tooker to get me a lighter to take them in, and we did carry them (myself some) over Tower Hill, which was by this time full of people's goods, bringing their goods thither. And down to the lighter, which lay at the next quay above the Tower dock. And here was my neighbour's wife, Mrs. ——,[1] with her pretty child and some few of her things, which I did willingly give way to be saved with mine. But there was no passing with anything through the postern, the crowd was so great.

The Duke of York came this day by the office and spoke to us, and did ride with his guard up and down the City to keep all quiet (he being now General, and having the care of all).

This day, Mercer being not at home, but against her mistress's order gone to her mother's, and my wife going thither to speak with W. Hewer, met her there and was angry; and her mother saying that she was not an apprentice girl, to ask leave every time she goes abroad, my wife with good reason was angry, and when she came home, bid her be gone again. And so she went away, which troubled me; but yet less than it would, because of the condition we are in fear of coming into in a little time, of being less able to keep one in her quality. At night, lay down a little upon a quilt of W. Hewer in the office (all my own things being packed up or gone); and after me, my poor wife did the like—we having fed upon the remains of yesterday's dinner, having no fire nor dishes, nor any opportunity of dressing anything.

4. Up by break of day to get away the remainder of my things, which I did by a lighter at the Iron-gate; and my hands so few, that it was the afternoon before we could get them all away.

Sir W. Penn and I to Tower Street, and there met the fire burning three or four doors beyond Mr. Howell's; whose goods, poor man (his trays and dishes, shovels &c., were flung all along Tower Street in the kennels,[2] and people working therewith from one end to the other), the fire coming on in that narrow street, on both sides, with infinite fury. Sir W. Batten, not knowing how to remove his wine, did dig a pit in the garden and laid it in there; and I took the opportunity of laying all the papers of my office that I could not otherwise dispose of. And in the evening Sir W. Penn and I did dig another and put our wine in it, and I my parmesan cheese as well as my wine and some other things.

The Duke of York was at the office this day at Sir W. Penn's, but I happened not to be within. This afternoon, sitting melancholy with Sir W. Penn in our garden and thinking of the certain burning of this office without extraordinary means, I did propose for the sending up of all our workmen from Woolwich and Deptford yards (none whereof yet appeared), and to write to Sir W. Coventry to have the Duke of York's permission to pull down houses rather than lose this office, which would much hinder the King's business. So Sir W. Penn he went down this night, in order to the sending them up tomorrow morning; and I wrote to Sir W. Coventry about the business, but received no answer.

This night Mrs. Turner (who, poor woman, was removing her goods all this day—good goods, into the garden, and knew not how to dispose of them)—and her husband supped with my wife and I at night in the office, upon a shoulder of mutton from the cook's, without any napkin or anything, in a sad manner but were merry. Only, now and then walking into the garden and saw how horridly the sky looks, all on fire in the night, was enough to put us out of our wits; and indeed it was extremely dreadful—for it looks just as if it was at us, and the whole heaven on fire. I after supper walked in the dark down to Tower Street, and there saw it all on fire at the Trinity house on that side and the Dolphin tavern on this side, which was very near us—and the fire with extraordinary vehemence. Now begins the practice of blowing up of houses in Tower Street, those next the Tower, which at first did frighten people more than anything; but it stopped the fire where it was done—it bringing down the houses to the

[1] *Mrs. ——* Mrs. Buckworth.

[2] *kennels* Gutters.

ground in the same places they stood, and then it was easy to quench what little fire was in it, though it kindled nothing almost. W. Hewer this day went to see how his mother did, and comes late home, but telling us how he hath been forced to remove her to Islington, her house in Pye Corner being burned. So that it is got so far that way and all the Old Bailey,[1] and was running down to Fleet Street. And Paul's is burned, and all Cheapside. I wrote to my father this night; but the post-house being burned, the letter could not go.

5. I lay down in the office again upon W. Hewer's quilt, being mighty weary and sore in my feet with going[2] till I was hardly able to stand. About 2 in the morning my wife calls me up and tells of new cries of "Fire!"—it being come to Barking Church, which is the bottom of our lane. I up; and finding it so, resolved presently to take her away; and did, and took my gold (which was about 2350*l.*), W. Hewer, and Jane down by Poundy's boat to Woolwich. But Lord, what a sad sight it was by moonlight to see the whole City almost on fire—that you might see it plain at Woolwich, as if you were by it. There when I came, I find the gates shut, but no guard kept at all; which troubled me, because of discourses now begun that there is plot in it and that the French had done it.[3] I got the gates open, and to Mr. Shelden's, where I locked up my gold and charged my wife and W. Hewer never to leave the room without one of them in it night nor day. So back again, by the way seeing my goods well in the lighters at Deptford and watched well by people. Home, and whereas I expected to have seen our house on fire, it being now about 7 o'clock, it was not. But to the fire, and there find greater hopes than I expected; for my confidence of finding our office on fire was such, that I durst not ask anybody how it was with us, till I came and saw it not burned. But going to the fire, I find, by the blowing up of houses and the great help given by the workmen out of the King's yards, sent up by Sir W. Penn, there is a good stop given to it, as well at Mark Lane end as ours—it having only burned the dial[4] of Barking Church, and part of the porch, and was there quenched. I up to the top of Barking steeple, and there saw the saddest sight of desolation that I ever saw. Everywhere great fires. Oil cellars and brimstone and other things burning. I became afeared to stay there long; and therefore down again as fast as I could, the fire being spread as far as I could see it, and to Sir W. Penn's and there eat a piece of cold meat, having eaten nothing since Sunday but the remains of Sunday's dinner.

Here I met with Mr. Young and Whistler; and having removed all my things, and received good hopes that the fire at our end is stopped, they and I walked into the town and find Fanchurch Street, Gracious Street, and Lumbard Street all in dust. The Exchange a sad sight, nothing standing there of all the statues or pillars but Sir Tho. Gresham's[5] picture in the corner. Walked into Moorfields (our feet ready to burn, walking through the town among the hot coals) and find that full of people, and poor wretches carrying their goods there, and everybody keeping his goods together by themselves (and a great blessing it is to them that it is fair weather for them to keep abroad[6] night and day); drank there, and paid twopence for a plain penny loaf.

Thence homeward, having passed through Cheapside and Newgate Market, all burned—and seen Anthony Joyce's house in fire. And took up (which I keep by me) a piece of glass of Mercer's chapel in the street, where much more was, so melted and buckled with the heat of the fire, like parchment. I also did see a poor cat taken out of a hole in the chimney joining to the wall of the Exchange, with the hair all burned off the body and yet alive. So home at night, and find there good hopes of saving our office—but great endeavours of watching all night and having men ready; and so we lodged them in the office, and had drink and bread and cheese for them. And I lay down and slept a good night about midnight—though when I rose, I hear that there had been a great alarm of French and Dutch being risen—which proved nothing. But it is a strange thing to see how long this time did look since Sunday, having been

[1] *Old Bailey* The area in which the Old Bailey, London's central criminal court, was located.

[2] *going* Walking.

[3] *French had done it* Pepys refers to rumors that the French had set the fire and were invading.

[4] *dial* Clock-face.

[5] *Sir Tho. Gresham's* I.e., Sir Thomas Gresham, who founded the Royal Exchange in 1568.

[6] *abroad* Outdoors.

always full of variety of actions, and little sleep, that it looked like a week or more. And I had forgot almost the day of the week.

MAY 1668

17. *Lord's Day.* Up, and put on my new stuff-suit with a shoulder-belt, according to the new fashion, and the bands of my vest and tunic laced with silk lace of the colour of my suit. And so, very handsome, to church, where a dull sermon and of a stranger, and so home; and there I find W. Howe,[1] and a younger brother of his, come to dine with me; and there comes Mercer, and brings with her Mrs. Gayet, which pleased me mightily; and here was also W. Hewer, and mighty merry; and after dinner to sing psalms. But Lord! to hear what an excellent bass this younger brother of W. Howe's sings, even to my astonishment, and mighty pleasant. By and by Gayet goes away, being a Catholic, to her devotions, and Mercer to church; but we continuing an hour or two singing, and so parted; and I to Sir W. Pen's, and there sent for a hackney-coach and he and she[2] and I out to take the gyre.[3] We went to Stepney,[4] and there stopped at the Trinity House, he to talk with the servants there against tomorrow, which is a great day for the choice of a new Master. And thence to Mile End,[5] and there eat and drank, and so home; and I supped with them—that is, eat some butter and radishes, which is my excuse for not eating of any other of their victuals, which I hate because of their sluttery:[6] and so home, and made my boy read to me part of Dr. Wilkins's new book of the *Real Character*;[7] and so to bed.

MAY 1669[8]

31. Up very betimes, and so continued all the morning, with W. Hewer, upon examining and stating my accounts, in order to the fitting myself to go abroad beyond sea, which the ill condition of my eyes, and my neglect for a year or two, hath kept me behindhand in, and so as to render it very difficult now and troublesome to my mind to do it; but I this day made a satisfactory entrance therein. Dined at home, and in the afternoon by water to Whitehall, calling by the way at Michell's, where I have not been many a day till just the other day; and now I met her mother there and knew her husband to be out of town. And here *je* did *baiser elle*, but had not opportunity *para hacer*[9] some with her as I would have offered if *je* had had it. And thence had another meeting with the Duke of York, at Whitehall, on yesterday's work and made a good advance: and so being called by my wife, we to the park, Mary Batelier,[10] and a Dutch gentleman, a friend of hers, being with us. Thence to "The World's End," a drinking-house by the park; and there merry, and so home late.

And thus ends all that I doubt I shall ever be able to do with my own eyes in the keeping of my journal, I being not able to do it any longer, having done now so long as to undo my eyes almost every time that I take a pen in my hand; and, therefore, whatever comes of it, I must forbear: and, therefore, resolve, from this time forward, to have it kept by my people in long-hand, and must therefore be contented to set down no more than is fit for them and all the world to know; or if there be anything, which cannot be much, now my amours to Deb.[11] are past, and my eyes hindering me in almost all

[1] *W. Howe* Sandwich's clerk.

[2] *she* Lady Penn.

[3] *take the gyre* I.e., walk around.

[4] *Stepney* Village outside the City of London.

[5] *Mile End* Between Stepney and the City of London.

[6] *sluttery* Filthiness.

[7] *Dr. Wilkins… Real Character* John Wilkins, a clergyman, writer, and scientific thinker, wrote *An Essay towards a Real Character and a Philosophical Language* (1688), in which he proposed a universal language to be used for international communication by diplomats, merchants, and travelers.

[8] *MAY 1669* At this point, Pepys began to notice the deterioration of his eyesight, which he attributed to the long hours he spent working and writing.

[9] *je did baiser elle* French: I did kiss her; *para hacer* Spanish: To do.

[10] *Mary Batelier* Neighbor of the Pepys family.

[11] *Deb.* Deborah Willet was hired to accompany and attend to Pepys's wife Elizabeth in 1668. Samuel became infatuated with her, and the two had an affair. When Elizabeth learned of the relationship, she threatened to attack Deb, and Pepys was forced to renounce her.

other pleasures, I must endeavour to keep a margin in my book open, to add, here and there, a note in short-hand with my own hand.

And so I betake myself to that course, which is almost as much as to see myself go into my grave: for which, and all the discomforts that will accompany my being blind, the good God prepare me!

S.P.

MAY 31, 1669

IN CONTEXT

The Great Fire of London, 1666

Other Accounts of the Great Fire

The painting above is of the Dutch school, after Jan Griffien the Elder; it dates from c. 1675. The old St. Paul's Cathedral is in the center of the picture.

from *The London Gazette* (3–10 September 1666)

Reproduced on the following four pages is the issue of *The London Gazette* that reported on the fire. As with most newspapers of the time, four pages constituted the entire publication.

THE LONDON GAZETTE.

Published by Authority.

From Monday, Septemb 3, to Monday, Septemp 10, 1666.

Whitehall, Sept. 8.

THE ordinary course of this paper having been interuppted by a sad and lamentable accident of Fire lately hapned in the City of *London*: it hath been thought fit for satisfying the minds of so many of His Majesties good Subjects who must needs be concerned for the Issue of so great an accident, to give this short, but true Accompt of it.

On the second instant, at one of the clock in the Morning, there hapned to break out, a sad in deplorable Fire in *Pudding-lane*, neer *New Fish-street*, which falling out at that hour of the night, and in a quarter of the Town so close built with wooden pitched houses spread itself so far before day, and with such distraction to the inhabitants and Neighbours, that care was not taken for the timely preventing the further diffusion of it, by pulling down houses, as ought to have been; so that this lamentable Fire in a short time became too big to be mastred by any Engines or working neer it. It fell out most unhappily too, That a violent Easterly wind fomented it, and kept it burning all that day, and the night following spreading itself up to *Grace-church-street* and downwards from *Cannon-street* to the Water-side, as far as the *Three Cranes in the Vintrey*.

The people in all parts about it, distracted by the vastness of it, and their particular care to carry away their Goods, many attempts were made to prevent the spreading of it by pulling down Houses, and making great Intervals, but all in vain, the Fire seizing upon the Timber and Rubbish, and so continuing it set even through those spaces, and raging in a bright flame all Monday and Teusday, not withstanding His Majesties own, and His Royal Highness's indefatigable and personal pains to apply all possible remedies to prevent it, calling upon and helping the people with their Guards; and a great number of Nobility and Gentry unwearidly assisting therein, for which they were requited with a thousand blessings from the poor distressed people. By the favour of God the Wind slackened a little on Teusday night & the Flames meeting with brick buildings at the *Temple*, by little and little it was observed to lose its force on that side, so that on Wednesday morning we began to hope well, and his Royal Highness never despairing or slackening his personal care wrought so well that day, assisted in some parts by the Lords of the Council before and behind it that a stop was put to it at the *Temple Church*, neer *Holborn-bridge*, *Pie-corner*, *Aldersgate*, *Cripple-gate*, neer the lower end of *Coleman-street*, at the end of *Basin-hall-street* by the *Postern* at the upper end of *Bishopsgate-street* and *Leadenhall-street*, at the *Standard* in *Cornhill* at the church in *Fenchurch street*, neer *Cloth-workers Hall* in *Mineing-lane*, at the middle of *Mark-lane*, and at the *Tower-dock*.

On Thursday by the blessing of God it was wholly beat down and extinguished. But so as that Evening it unhappily burst out again a fresh at the *Temple*, by the falling of some sparks (as is supposed) upon a Pile of Wooden buildings; but his Royal Highness who watched there that vvhole night in Person, by the great labours and diligence used, and especially by applying Powder to blow up the Houses about it, before day most happily mastered it.

Divers Strangers, Dutch and French were, during the fire, apprehended, upon suspicion that they contributed mischievously to it, who are all imprisoned, and Informations prepared to make a severe inquisition here upon by my Lord Chief Justice *Keeling*, assisted by some of the Lords of the Privy Council; and some principal Members of the City, notwithstanding which suspicion, the manner of the burning all along in a Train, and so blowen forwards in all its way by strong Winds, make us conclude the whole was an effect of an unhappy chance, or to speak better, the heavy hand of God upon us for our sins, shewing us the terrour of his Judgement in thus raising the Fire, and immediately after his miraculous and never to be acknowledged Mercy, in putting a stop to it when we were in the last despair, and that all attempts for quenching it however industriously pursued seemed insufficient. His Majesty then sat hourly in Councel, and ever since hath continued making rounds about the City in all parts of it where the danger and mischief was greatest, till this morning that he hath sent his Grace the Duke of *Albemarle*, whom he hath called for to assist him in this great occasion, to put his happy and successful hand to the finishing this memorable deliverance.

About the *Tower* the seasonable orders given for plucking down the Houses to secure the Magazines of Powder was more especially successful, that part being up the Wind, notwithstanding which it came almost to the very Gates of it. So as by this early provision the general Stores of War lodged in the *Tower* were entirely saved: And we have further this intimate cause to give God thanks, that the Fire did not happen where his Majesties Naval Stores are kept. So as though it has pleased God to visit us with his own hand, he hath not, by disfurnishing us with the means of carrying on the War, subjected us to our enemies.

It must be observed, that this fire happened in a part of the Town, vvhere tho the commodities vvere not very rich, yet they vvere so bulky that they could not vvell be removed, so that the Inhabitants of that part where it first began have sustained very great loss, but by the best enquiry vve can make, the other parts of the Town where the Commodities vvere of greater value, took the Alarum so early, that they saved most of their goods of value; which possibly may have diminished the loss, tho some think, that if the whole industry of the Inhabitants had been applyed to the stopping of the fire, and not to the saving of their particular *Goods*, the success might have been much better, not only to the publick, but to many of them in their own particulars.

Through this sad Accident it is easie to be imagined how many persons were necessitated to remove themselves and Goods into the open fields, where they were forced to continue some time, which could not but work compassion in the beholders, but his Majesties care was most signal in this occasion, who besides his personal pains was frequent in consulting all wayes for relieving those distressed persons, which produced so good effect, as well as by his Majesties Proclamations and the Orders issued to the Neighbour Justices of the Peace to encourage the sending in provisions to the Markets, which are publickly known, as by other directions, that when his Majesty, fearing lest other Orders might not yet have been sufficient, had commanded the Victualler of his Navy to send bread into *Moore-fields* for relief of the poor, which for the more speedy supply he sent in Bisket out of the Sea Stores; it was found that the Markets had been already so well supplyd that the people, being un-accustomed to that kind of Bread declined it, and so it was returned in greater part to his Majestys Stores again vvithout any use made of it.

And we cannot but observe to the confutation of all his Majesties enemies, who endeavour to perswade the vvorld abroard of great parties, and disaffection at home against his Majesties Government; that a greater instance of the affections of this City could never been given then hath now been given in this sad and deplorable Accident vvhen if at any time disorder might have been expected from the losses, distraction, and almost desperation of some people in their private fortune, thousands of people not having had habitations to cover them. And yet in all this time it hath been so far from any appearance of designs or attempts against his Majesties Government, that his Majesty and his Royal Brother, out of their care to stop and prevent the fire, frequently exposing their persons with very small attendants in all parts of the Town—sometimes even to be intermixed with those who laboured in the business, yet never the less there hath not been observed so much as a murmuring word to fall from any, but on the contrary, even those persons, whose losses rendered their conditions most desperate, and to be fit objects of others prayers, beholding those frequent instances of his Majesties care of his people, forgot their own misery, and filled the streets with their prayers for his Majesty, vvhose trouble they seemed to compassionate before their own.

A FARTHUR ACCOUNT OF THIS LAMENTABLE FIRE.

This dismal fire broke out at a baker's shop in *Pudding-lane*, by *Fish-street*, in the lower part of the city, neer Thames-street (among wooden houses ready to take fire & full of combustible goods) in *Billingsgate-ward;* which ward in a few hours was laid in ashes. As it began in the dead of the night when everybody was asleep, the darkness greatly increased the horror of the calamity; it rapidly rushed down the hill to the bridge; crossed *Thames-street* to *St. Mangus* church at the foot of the bridge; but having scaled and captured its fort, shot large volumes of flames into every place about it. The fire drifted back to the city again & roared with great violence through *Thames-street* aided by the combustible matter deposited there with such a fierce wind at its back as to strike with horror its beholders.

Fire! Fire! Fire! doth resound in every street, some starting out of their sleep & peeping through the windows half-dressed. Some in night dresses rushing wildly about the streets crying piteously & praying to God for assistance, women carrying children in their arms & the men looking quite bewildered. Many cripples were also seen hobbling about not knowing which way to go to get free from the flames which were raging all round them. No man that had the sence of human miseries could unconcertedly behold the frightful destruction made in one of the noblest Cities in the world.

What a confusion! the Lord Mayor of the city came with his officers, & *London* so famous for its wisdom can find neither hands nor brains to prevent its utter ruin. London must fall to the ground in ashes & who can prevent it? The fire raged mastery, & burnt dreadfully; by the fierce Easterly wind it spread quickly in all directions, overturning all so furiously that the whole city is brought into a desolation. That night most of the citizens had taken their last sleep; & when they went to sleep they little thought that when their ears were unlocked that such an enemy had invaded their City, & that they should see him with such fury break through their doors, & enter their rooms with such threatening countenance.

☞ It commenced on the Lord's day morning, never was there the like Sabbath in *London:* many churches were in flames that day; God seemed to come down and preach himself in them, as he did in *Sinai* when the mount burnt with fire: such warm preaching those churches never had before

& in other churches ministers had preached their farewell sermons.

Goods were moved hastily from the lower part of the City to the upper part, & some hopes were retained on Sunday that the fire would not reach them; they could scarcely imagine that a fire half a mile off could reach their houses. All means to stop it proved ineffectual; the wind blew so hard that flakes of flames & burning matters were carried across the streets & spread the fire in all directions, & when the evening came on the fire was more visible & dreadful & instead of the dark curtains of night which used to spread over the City the curtains had changed to yellow & at a distance the whole City appeared to be on fire, little sleep was taken that night, men busy in all directions pulling down & blowing up houses to stop its progress, but all to no purpose, for it made the most furious onset & drove back all opposers. Many were upon their knees in the night, pouring out tears before the Lord; interceding for poor London in the day of its calamity; but all in vain.

Sunday night the fire had got into *Cannon-street* & levelled it with the ground.

On Monday, *Grace-church-street* was all in flames & *Lombard-street* & *Fen-church-street*. The burning was in the shape of a bow, & a fearful bow it was!

Then the flames broke in on *Cornhill* that large & spacious street, & rapidly crossed the way by the train of wood that laid in the streets untaken away, which had been pulled from the houses to prevent its spreading & burned to the tops of the highest houses & to the bottom of the lowest cellars.

The *Royal Exchanges* was next invaded & burned quickly through all its galleries; by and bye down fell all the Kings upon their faces & the building on the top of them with such a noise as was dreadful; then the citizens trembled & fled away lest they should be devoured also.

Monday night was a dreadful night! The fire burst into *Cheapside* in four directions with such a dazzling glare and roaring noise by the falling of so many houses at one time, as to amaze any one who witnessed it.

On Tuesday the fire burned up the very bowels of *London* from *Bow-lane*, *Bread-street*, *Friday-street*, and *Old Change* the flames came up almost together.

Then the fire got on to *Paternoster Row*, *Newgate-street*, the *Old Bailey* and *Ludgate hill* & rushed down into *Fleet-street*. *St. Paul's church* though all of stone outward, and naked of houses about it strangely caught fire at the top; the lead melted & ran down as snow before the burning sun and the massy stones, with a hideous noise fell on the pavement.

Tuesday night was more dreadful than Monday night, for the flames having consumed the greatest part of the city; threatened the suburbs, and the poor were preparing to fly as well as they could with their luggage into the countries and villages.

On Wednesday the Lord had pity on them; the wind hushed & the fire burnt gently; then the citizens began to gather a little heart.

The following list of buildings destroyed in this terrible disaster hath been taken:—

13,200 Houses
87 Churches
6 Chapels
The Royal Exchange
The Custom House
Jail at Newgate
Three City gates
The Guildhall and
Four bridges.

Edenburg Aug 29 Scarce a day passes vvherein some Prizes are not bough in by our Privateers, amongst the rest one of them of six guns has lately siesed on a very rich Prize laden vvith Spices bound for *Denmark*, and in her (as 'tis said) a Natural Son of the King of *Denmark*.

Southwold Spt 2 A French vessel called the *Hope* of *Quellebeuf*, laden vvith 1750 firkins of Butter and 400 Pigs of Lead, vvas put ashore about a league to the south-ward of this Town, and split in pieces; but the Goods are most of them saved and preserved for the owners, it being one of those vessels that bought over the Lord Douglas' Regiment and vvas permitted to lade home.

Plymouth Sept. 2. Yesterday arrived here *Ostenders* laden vvith salt &c. from *Rochelle*, from vvhence they came the 16 of *August* last, and report the D. *de Beaufort* vvas then in there with his Fleet of about 40 sayl, great and small, Men of War and Fireships, vvhereof 3 Dutch; and vvere making all the preparations they could for the Sea, but their going out was uncertain.

Pendennis Sept 3. On Friday morning arrived here *La Signoria de la Gratia*, a Venetian Vessell, hired by Mr *Abraham Walwynn*, who laded Currans and Oyle at *Zanti* and *Gallipoli*, and vvere bound for *London*; by the vvay the *Venetians*, *Maltesians*, and other Italians vvith vvhom she was mann'd designed the destruction of the Merchant and those belonging to them; intending afterwards to carry off the ship vvith its fraight; and in execution of their purpose had fallen upon the Merchant vvhom they vvounded in several places, and had undoubtly kill'd him, but that Captain *Lucy* in the *Victory*, a Privateer, came by providence to its rescue, and seizing their principals secured them from further attempts.

Weymouth Sept 3. On the first instant a small French vessel vvith Ballast, taken by one of our Frigots, vvas sent in hither and by the vvay ran on ground in the storm, but by the assistance of several persons she got off, being robb'd vvhilst the lay there of all her Rigging Sayles, and Tackle.

Dublin Aug 28. On the 25 instant his Grace the Lord Lieutenant came safe to *Kilkenny*, intending from thence to visit all the most considerable places in *Munster*. The Lord Chancellour is vvell recovered, and vvas yesterday abroad and intends speedily to follow. All countries are in very good order, the Toryes no more heard of, and the Militia is generally settled in a very good posture.

Norwich September 5. The account of our Bill of Mortality for this last week runs thus, buried of all Diseases 162. Whereof of the Plague 147. Besides at the Pest house 12.

Portsmouth Septemb 7. Yesterday, his Grace the Lord General passed hence for *London*, leaving the Fleet refitted after the late Storm ready to put to Sea again vvith the first fair vvind.

N*Otice is hereby given, That Sir* Robert Viner *is now settld in the* Affrican *house near the middle of* Broard-street London, *where he intends to manage his affairs (as formerly in* Lumbard-*street) having by the good providence of God been entirely preserved by a timely and safe removal of all his concerns, almost twenty-four hours before the furious fire entered* Lumbard-*street.*

Also Alderman Meynell, *and Alderman* Backwell, *with divers others of* Lumbard Street, *being likewise preserved in their estates, do intend to settle in a few daies in or near* Broard Street.

THE *General Post-office is for the present held at the two Black Pillars in* Bridges Street, *over against the* Fleece Tavern, *Covent Garden, till a more convenient place can be found in London.*

Royal Charles in St. *Helen's* Road, Sept 2. On the 30th past, by six in the morning, our Fleet weighed Anchor at *Sole* Bay, but it proving a calm, and the tide against us, we were forced to come again to an Anchor before we had made a league of vvay, and so rid that day without farther intelligence of the Enemy.

The 31 by 7 in the morning we were under sayl, and stood a course towards the *Long-sand-head*, till about 11 at noon, when off *Balsey Cliffe*, we discovered the Enemy bearing S. and by E, whereupon we steered S.E., being assured by our Pilots to be clear of the *Galopes*, but yet we past not so well, but that this Ship struck upon the sand, but was so fortunate to get off again without prejudice: Which stop brought us into better order to steer after the Enemy with the White Squadron in the Van and the Blew in the Rear, till 12 at night, keeping the Wind, at which time we guess the Dutch were tacked, seeing them neer us, and some of our sternmost ships and the Enemy firing, which made us tack also and stand to the northward.

Sept I. We saw the Vice-Admiral of the Blew to the Leeward with some few ships, and finding the Dutch were gone away from us towards *Calais*, we stood a Course after them, and found some of them merely Anchored, and others standing in, but at our approach they all got Under sayle, and stood for *Bullogne* Road, haling in close to the shore, being sure to weather us if we pass the Point, the Wind then E. by N. and E.N.E. as much as we could carry our Topsails half-mast high: Whereupon we lay by short of the place till all our Fleet came up; but then the storm growing greater, and having no hopes, by reason of the ill-weather, of attempting further upon the enemy; who durst not adventure out of the shelter of the shoar. It was found best to lay bye and bring the Fleet together, and the next day to betake ourselves to St. *Helen's* Bay—the place appointed for our Rendezvous, as the most proper station to hinder the Enemies conjunction with the French, we being ready with the first fair wind to seek out the enemy.

In the storm two of our ships struck upon the *Riprap* Sands *viz.* the *Andrew* and the *Happy Return*, but we got well off again; The rest of our Fleet in good condition. What loss the enemy sustained by the storm we know not, only we are assured, they were forced to blow up one of their greatest ships; another a Flagship wholly disabled was seen driving before the vvind, and that several others of them were much damnified and disabled; and of the rest four vve could see run upon the Sands, and with great difficulty got off again.

Dover Sept 8 This afternoon the *Dutch* Fleet weighed from *Bullen Road*, and are now standing towards their own coast.

London Printed by Tho. Newcomb. 1666.

Mind and God, Faith and Science

CONTEXTS

In the seventeenth century, empiricism—the position that all legitimate knowledge is based on sensory experience—became an undeniable presence in British intellectual life. The reverberations of empiricism were felt in all the arts, from politics and religion to ethics and epistemology, but the impact registered most strongly in the development of experimentation as a way to investigate the material world. "Natural philosophy," as the study of the physical universe was then called, was beginning to resemble modern science.

Among the strongest champions of the new "experimental philosophy" were the members of the "Royal Society for the Improving of Natural Knowledge," initially an informal club that received an official charter from Charles II in 1662. As Thomas Sprat explains in his *History of the Royal Society*, members rejected the scientific tradition of Aristotle and other ancient and medieval thinkers, striving to accept as truth only what could be reasoned from observations. Their approach was based in large part on the changes to natural philosophy Francis Bacon had proposed earlier in the century;[1] where Aristotle had placed the highest value on conclusions deduced from premises already known, Bacon argued that natural philosophers should base their reasoning on facts gathered through experiments. This refusal of established doctrine sparked resistance in many quarters; Sprat's *History* was published shortly after the Society was founded as an explanation and defense of its practices.

The Society applied its new approach very widely; the first issue of *Philosophical Transactions*, the periodical issued by the Society, included articles that we would now place in such categories as astronomy, biology, geology, and practical technological innovation, as well as several descriptions of deformed animals. This broad field of study was called "experimental philosophy"—at this point, "science" was a much broader term, applied to philosophy and mathematics as well as to the study of nature. Within experimental philosophy, boundaries of specialization were not yet established, and Society members often developed multiple areas of expertise. Benjamin Franklin, for instance, is best known as a scientist for the work on electricity he describes in his *Autobiography*, but he also made discoveries in oceanography, meteorology, and the physics of light and temperature; such diversity of interest is typical of the best scientific minds of the period. Typical too was an informal and open approach. In his *Experiments and Observations on Different Kinds of Air*, for example, Joseph Priestley details his methods and equipment so that any reader could acquire the necessary skills and replicate his experiments. With enough leisure time, the right equipment, and the appropriate open-minded curiosity, the new science could be practiced by anyone (or at least any man—the Royal Society excluded female experimenters until the twentieth century).

The experimental philosophers of the Royal Society used scientific enquiry and empiricism to investigate the material universe. John Locke (also a member of the Society) embraced a similar approach in examining the nature of the human mind. In his *Essay Concerning Human Understanding*, Locke suggests that the mind is like a blank sheet of paper at birth. Deriving all knowledge through experience, it gathers information about the world, and then combines the simple ideas gleaned from experience into more complex ones.

---

[1] See Bacon's utopian work *The New Atlantis* (selection in the online component of this anthology, volume 2) for his ideas on how natural philosophy ought to be conducted.

While many embraced with enthusiasm the findings of the new science, some others viewed them with distrust. When Robert Hooke of the Royal Society published his *Micrographia*, primarily a collection of drawings and descriptions based on his discoveries with a microscope, its celebration of the powers of observation created a stir. Many who read it were amazed and entertained—Samuel Pepys called it "the most ingenious book that ever I read in my life"—but others were less confident of the value of information obtained in this way. Margaret Cavendish was among those who questioned the assumption that the microscope and its sister invention, the telescope, could provide valuable knowledge rather than mere fanciful distortion. Voltaire, although a supporter of the Royal Society, in *Micromegas* similarly invokes microscopic and telescopic distortions of scale in the course of investigating the relationship between reality and its human observers—and suggests that they may make "reality" a somewhat problematic concept.

If the emphasis that Locke and the experimental philosophers placed on what could be reasoned from the observable destabilized certain notions of reality, it also unsettled attitudes toward morality and religious faith. Excitement about the possibilities for progress that science held out competed with fears that the new ideas about the nature of truth would bring about the presumptuous rejection of traditional values and beliefs.

For Locke and many others, empiricism offered a means of explaining God through a chain of reasoning, and of providing rational grounds for religious belief. Isaac Newton, in a letter to the clergyman Richard Bentley, advanced the notion of "natural religion," arguing that a reasoned understanding of the spectacular order of the universe not only proves the necessity of a creator but also enhances one's appreciation of his grandeur. The poets Mark Akenside and James Thomson echoed this sentiment, praising scientific discovery for promising not only human dominion over the material world but also advances in morality and religion. Margaret Bryan, a schoolteacher and popular science writer, framed the pursuit of scientific knowledge for her students in terms of developing an appropriate relationship to God. Benjamin Franklin thought that scientific and ethical development were wholly unrelated, but he had endless ambitions for the material improvements science could offer. For others, religious faith remained untouched by scientific discovery; the hymns of Isaac Watts, a philosopher and an admirer of Newton and Locke, demonstrate a firm faith that eternal truth is founded not on scientific discovery but on the greatness of God. (As his "Against Idleness and Mischief" indicates, Watts's focus was on "works" as much as it was on faith; his call for children to emulate the "busy bee" remained an educational touchstone well into the twentieth century.)

Those who saw empirical reasoning as a threat to the primacy of faith, however, had real grounds for concern. David Hume, a particularly controversial thinker of the mid and late eighteenth century, recognized the possibility of an impasse between empirical reason and Christianity. Although Hume likely believed in God, he argued that "mere reason is insufficient to convince us" of the veracity of the Christian religion. As the excerpt in these pages from his "Of Miracles" demonstrates, he was profoundly skeptical of supernatural or miraculous occurrences—on which the Christian religion is quite largely based. A discussion of Hume's arguments by James Boswell and Samuel Johnson is also reprinted below.

In the midst of this intellectual turmoil, many people ill-equipped to choose between competing truth claims grasped for meaning wherever they could find it. The *Spectator* article on omens included below provides commentary on the sort of "superstitious folly" that was widespread in the period.

During the middle of the eighteenth century, the growing Methodist movement provided a different approach, endeavoring through emotional appeal to convey religious truth to those unmoved by rational considerations, or alienated, as many poorer people were, from the established church. Methodism, an evangelical movement that originated within the Church of England, spread rapidly in new industrial villages and poorer areas, where common people were drawn by its emphasis on faith as the only path to salvation, its strong reliance on hymns, and its fervent and energetic sermons—which are satirized in William Hogarth's engraving *Credulity, Superstition, and Fanaticism*, included here. Like the *Spectator* article, Hogarth's engraving speaks to the confusion of religious beliefs during the period, and to the hypocrisy that sometimes attended the most vociferous declarations of faith.

Raising theological objections to the new forms of scientific inquiry, some criticized them for failing to respect ethical values. Erasmus Darwin's *Loves of the Plants*, for example, a highly popular poem on botanical classification, provoked scandal in response to what was seen as its sexually licentious content. In other cases, scientific pursuits raised serious ethical problems almost inadvertently. Joseph Wright's painting *An Experiment on a Bird in the Air Pump* (reproduced in the color section of this volume) highlights the cruelty that was frequently involved in experimentation on animals—something that neither Joseph Priestley nor Robert Boyle appear to acknowledge in their discussions of mice and dogs as subjects for research.[1]

Empiricism also provided new ammunition to those advocating a turn away from tradition in some areas of ethics and politics. Both Mary Astell and Judith Drake, in the essays below, use Locke's ideas as a launching point for their own examinations of the evident inequalities in the education and social status of men and women. The portion of Mary Astell's *A Serious Proposal to the Ladies* reprinted here complicates Locke's ideas about how we acquire knowledge. Astell argues that prejudices, arising from social circumstances, plague us from birth and mar our ability to perceive truth. Her essay was one of the earliest and most famous of many texts advocating educational improvements for women; she goes on to propose the establishment of religious communities for "ladies of quality," funded by dowries and money earned from the establishment of a school. Judith Drake, in her *Essay in Defence of the Female Sex*, uses Locke's theories to argue that if both women and men are born equal, and females do not exhibit any difference in physiology that might make them mentally inferior, then they should be as capable of education and improvement as men. Her essay, framed as a letter to Princess Anne of Denmark, argues that the education of women will only improve society in all respects. The fictitious letter from Eliza Haywood's *Female Spectator* included here gives some sense of the ways in which such ideas concerning female education gained attention and support as the century progressed, though in simplified and more accessible forms.

⌘⌘⌘

[1] See also Anna Laetitia Barbauld's poem "The Mouse's Petition" in volume 4 of this anthology.

from Thomas Sprat, *The History of the Royal Society of London, for the Improving of Natural Knowledge* (1667)

from Section 5. A Model of Their Whole Design

I will here, in the first place, contract into few words the whole sum of [the Royal Society's] resolutions.... Their purpose is, in short, to make faithful records of all the works of nature or art which can come within their reach—that so the present age and posterity may be able to put a mark on the errors which have been strengthened by long prescription; to restore the truths that have lain neglected; to push on those which are already known to more various uses; and to make the way more passable to what remains unrevealed. This is the compass of their design. And to accomplish this they have endeavoured to separate the knowledge of nature from the colours of rhetoric, the devices of fancy, or the delightful deceit of fables. They have laboured to enlarge it from being confined to the custody of a few, or from servitude to private interests. They have striven to preserve it from being over-pressed by a confused heap of vain and useless particulars, or from being straitened and bounded up too much by general doctrines. They have tried to put it into a condition of perpetual increasing by settling an inviolable correspondence between the hand and the brain. They have studied to make it not only an enterprise of one season, or of some lucky opportunity, but a business of time—a steady, a lasting, a popular, an uninterrupted work. They have attempted to free it from the artifice,[1] and humours, and passions of sects;[2] to render it an instrument whereby mankind may obtain a dominion over *things*, and not only over one another's *judgments*. And lastly, they have begun to establish these reformations in philosophy, not so much by any solemnity of laws or ostentation of ceremonies, as by solid practice and examples; not by a glorious pomp of words, but by the silent, effectual, and unanswerable arguments of real productions.

from Section 20. Their Manner of Discourse

Thus they have directed, judged, conjectured upon, and improved experiments. But lastly, in these and all other businesses that have come under their care, there is one thing more about which the Society has been most solicitous;[3] and that is the manner of their discourse, which, unless they had been very watchful to keep in due temper, the whole spirit and vigour of their design had been soon eaten out by the luxury and redundance of speech. The ill effects of this superfluity of talking have already overwhelmed most other arts and professions, insomuch that when I consider the means of happy living and the causes of their corruption, I can hardly forbear ... concluding that eloquence ought to be banished out of all civil societies as a thing fatal to peace and good manners. To this opinion I should wholly incline, if I did not find that it is a weapon which may be as easily procured by bad men as good, and that if these should only cast it away and those retain it, the naked innocence of virtue would be upon all occasions exposed to the armed malice of the wicked. This is the chief reason that should now keep up the ornaments of speaking in any request, since they are so much degenerated from their original usefulness. They were at first, no doubt, an admirable instrument in the hands of wise men, when they were only employed to describe goodness, honesty, obedience, in larger, fairer, and more moving images; to represent truth clothed with bodies; and to bring knowledge back again to our very senses, from whence it was at first derived to our understandings. But now they are generally changed to worse uses: they make the fancy disgust[4] the best things, if they come sound[5] and unadorned; they are in open defiance against reason, professing not to hold much correspondence with that, but with its slaves, the passions; they give the mind a motion too changeable and bewitching to consist with right practice. Who can behold without indignation how many mists and

[1] *artifice* Clever deception.

[2] *sects* Groups of people united by dogmatic belief.

[3] *solicitous* Eagerly attentive.

[4] *fancy disgust* Imagination find distasteful.

[5] *sound* Solidly reasoned.

uncertainties these specious tropes and figures[1] have brought on our knowledge? How many rewards, which are due to more profitable and difficult arts, have been still snatched away by the easy vanity of fine speaking? For now I am warmed with this just anger, I cannot withhold myself from betraying the shallowness of all these seeming mysteries, upon which we writers and speakers look so big. And, in few words, I dare say that of all the studies of men, nothing may be sooner obtained than this vicious abundance of phrase, this trick of metaphors, this volubility of tongue, which makes so great a noise in the world.... It will suffice my present purpose to point out what has been done by the Royal Society towards the correcting of [eloquence's] excesses in natural philosophy, to which it is, of all others, a most professed enemy.

They have therefore been most rigorous in putting in execution the only remedy that can be found for this extravagance. And that has been a constant resolution to reject all the amplifications, digressions, and swellings of style, to return back to the primitive purity and shortness, when men delivered so many *things*, almost in an equal number of *words*. They have exacted from all their members a close, naked, natural way of speaking; positive expressions; clear senses; a native easiness; bringing all things as near the mathematical plainness as they can, and preferring the language of artisans, countrymen, and merchants before that of wits or scholars.

And here there is one thing not to be passed by, which will render this established custom of the Society well-nigh everlasting: and that is the general constitution of the minds of the English.... If there can be a true character given of the universal temper of any nation under heaven, then certainly this must be ascribed to our countrymen: that they have commonly an unaffected sincerity; that they love to deliver[2] their minds with a profound simplicity; that they have the middle qualities between the reserved, subtle southern and the rough, unhewn northern people; that they are not extremely prone to speak; that they are more concerned what others will think of the strength than of the fineness of what they say; and that an universal modesty possesses them. These qualities are so conspicuous and proper to our soil that we often hear them objected to us,[3] by some of our neighbour satirists, in more disgraceful expressions. For they are wont[4] to revile the English with a want of familiarity; with a melancholy dumpishness[5]; with slowness, silence, and with the unrefined sullenness of their behaviour. But these are only the reproaches of partiality or ignorance, for they ought rather to be commended for an honourable integrity; for a neglect of circumstances[6] and flourishes; for regarding things of greater moment[7] more than less; for a scorn to deceive as well as to be deceived; which are all the best endowments that can enter into a philosophical mind. So that even the position of our climate, the air, the influence of the heaven, the composition of the English blood, as well as the embraces of the ocean, seem to join with the labours of the Royal Society to render our country a land of experimental knowledge....

from SECTION 22. A DEFENCE OF THE ROYAL SOCIETY, IN RESPECT OF THE ANCIENTS

... I doubt not ... but it will come into the thoughts of many critics (of whom the world is now full) to urge against us that I have spoken a little too sparingly of the merits of former ages, and that this design seems to be promoted with a malicious intention of disgracing the merits of the ancients.

... [W]hat is this of which they accuse us? They charge us with immodesty in neglecting the guidance of wiser and more discerning men than ourselves. But is not this rather the greatest sign of modesty, to confess that we ourselves may err, and all mankind besides? To acknowledge the difficulties of science? And to submit our minds to all the least works of nature? What kind of behaviour do they exact[8] from us in this case? That we should reverence the footsteps of antiquity? We do it most unanimously. That we should subscribe to their

[1] *specious tropes and figures* Misleading turns of phrase and figures of speech.

[2] *deliver* I.e., speak.

[3] *objected to us* Raised as objections against us.

[4] *wont* Accustomed.

[5] *dumpishness* Dejection.

[6] *circumstances* Grand affectations.

[7] *moment* Importance.

[8] *exact* Demand.

sense before our own? We are willing in probabilities, but we cannot in matters of fact; for in them we follow the most ancient author of all others, even nature itself. Would they have us make our eyes behold things at no farther distance than they saw? That is impossible, seeing we have the advantage of standing upon their shoulders. They say it is insolence to prefer our own inventions before those of our ancestors. But do not even they the very same thing themselves, in all the petty matters of life? In the arts of war and government; in the making and abolishing of laws; nay, even in the fashion of their clothes they differ from them, as their humour or fancy leads them. We approach the ancients, as we behold their tombs, with veneration—but we would not therefore be confined to live in them altogether, nor would (I believe) any of those who profess to be most addicted[1] to their memories. They tell us that in this corruption of manners, and sloth of men's minds, we cannot go beyond those who searched so diligently and concluded so warily before us. But in this they are confuted by every day's experience. They object to us tradition, and the consent of all ages. But do we not yet know the deceitfulness of such words? Is any man that is acquainted with the craft of founding sects, or of managing votes in popular assemblies, ignorant how easy it is to carry things in a violent stream? And when an opinion has once mastered its first opposers and settled itself in men's passions or interests, how few there be that coldly consider what they admit, for a long time after? So that when they say that all antiquity is against us, 'tis true, in show,[2] they object to us the wisdom of many ages; but in reality they only confront us with the authority of a few leading men. Nay, what if I should say that this honour for the dead, which such men pretend to, is rather a worshipping of themselves than of the ancients? It may well be proved that they are more in love with their own commentaries than with the texts of those whom they seem to make their oracles—and that they chiefly dote on those theories which they themselves have drawn from, which it is likely are almost as far distant from the original meaning of their authors as the positions of the new philosophers themselves.

But to conclude this argument (for I am weary of walking in a road so trodden) I think I am able to confute such men by the practice of those very ancients to whom they stoop[3] so low. Did not they trust themselves and their own reasons? Did not they busy themselves in inquiry, make new arts, establish new tenets, overthrow the old, and order all things as they pleased, without any servile regard to their predecessors?...

In few words therefore, let such men believe that we have no thought of detracting from what was good in former times. But, on the contrary, we have a mind to bestow on them a solid praise, instead of a great and an empty. While we are raising new observations on nature, we mean not to abolish the old, which were well and judiciously established by them, no more than a king, when he makes a new coin of his own, does presently call in that which bears the image of his father. He only intends thereby to increase the current money of his kingdom and still permits the one to pass, as well as the other. It is probable enough that upon a fresh survey we may find many things true which they have before asserted; and then will not they receive a greater confirmation from this, our new and severe approbation,[4] than from those men who resign up[5] their opinions to their words only? It is the best way of honouring them, to separate the certain things in them from the doubtful, for that shows we are not so much carried towards them by rash affection as by an unbiased judgment. If we would do them the most right, it is not necessary we should be perfectly like them in all things. There are two principal ways of preserving the names of those that are passed: the one, by pictures; the other, by children. The pictures may be so made that they may far nearer resemble the original than children do their parents, and yet all mankind choose rather to keep themselves alive by children than by the other. It is best for the philosophers of this age to imitate the ancients as their children: to have their blood derived down to them, but to add a new complexion and life of their own—while those that

[1] *addicted* Devoted.

[2] *show* Appearance.

[3] *stoop* I.e., bow.

[4] *severe approbation* Austere approval.

[5] *resign up* Submit.

endeavour to come near them in every line and feature may rather be called their dead pictures, or statues, than their genuine offspring.

Philosophical Transactions

A periodical first issued by the Royal Society in 1665, and produced continuously ever since, *Philosophical Transactions* was the first journal in the world to devote itself exclusively to matters of science. Inclusive of anything that would contribute to the advancement of natural philosophy, its content ranged widely from significant discoveries, notably Isaac Newton's "New Theory about Light and Colours," to descriptions of curiosities such as "An Account of a Very Odd Monstrous Calf." Henry Oldenburg, the founder of the journal, was also the secretary of the Royal Society; his patron was Robert Boyle, a very productive participant in the Society as well as a frequent contributor to its *Transactions*.

Introduction to the First Issue (1665)

Whereas there is nothing more necessary for promoting the improvement of philosophical matters than the communicating, to such as apply their studies and endeavours that way, such things as are discovered or put in practice by others; it is therefore thought fit to employ the press as the most proper way to gratify those whose engagement in such studies, and delight in the advancement of learning and profitable discoveries, doth entitle them to the knowledge of what this kingdom, or other parts of the world, do from time to time afford, as well of the progress of the studies, labours, and attempts of the curious and learned in things of this kind, as of their complete discoveries and performances. To the end that, such productions being clearly and truly communicated, desires after solid and useful knowledge may be further entertained, ingenious endeavours and undertakings cherished, and those addicted to and conversant in such matters may be invited and encouraged to search, try, and find out new things, impart their knowledge to one another, and contribute what they can to the grand design of improving natural knowledge and perfecting all philosophical arts and sciences. All for the glory of God, the honour and advantage of these kingdoms, and the universal good of mankind.

"An Account of a Very Odd Monstrous Calf" (1665)

By the same noble person[1] was lately communicated to the Royal Society an account of a very odd monstrous birth, produced at Limmington in Hampshire, where a butcher, having caused a cow (which cast her calf[2] the year before) to be covered[3] that she might the sooner be fatted, killed her when fat, and opening the womb, which he found heavy to admiration, saw in it a calf, which had begun to have hair, whose hinder legs had no joints, and whose tongue was, Cerberus-like,[4] triple, to each side of his mouth one, and one in the midst. Between the forelegs and the hinder-legs was a great stone on which the calf rid. The *sternum*, or that part of the breast where the ribs lie, was also perfect stone; and the stone, on which it rid, weighed twenty pounds and a half. The outside of the stone was of greenish colour, but some small parts being broken off, it appeared a perfect freestone.[5] The stone, according to the letter of Mr. David Thomas, who sent his account to Mr. Boyle, is with Doctor Haughteyn of Salisbury, to whom he also referreth for further information.

from Robert Boyle, "Trials Proposed by Mr. Boyle to Dr. Lower to Be Made by Him for the Improvement of Transfusing Blood out of One Live Animal into Another" (1666)

... At the reading of [these questions], the author declared that of diverse of them he thought he could foresee the events, but yet judged it fit not to omit

[1] *the same noble person* Robert Boyle; the preceding article discusses his recent book, *An Experimental History of Cold.*

[2] *cast her calf* Gave birth to her calf prematurely.

[3] *covered* Kept in an enclosed yard.

[4] *Cerberus* Mythological giant dog with three heads.

[5] *freestone* Uniform rock suitable for delicate masonry.

them, because the importance of the theories they may give light to may make the trials recompense the pains, whether the success favour the affirmative or the negative of the question, by enabling us to determine the one or the other upon surer grounds than we could otherwise do....

The queries themselves follow.

1. Whether by this way of transfusing blood the disposition of individual animals of the same kind may not be much altered? (As whether a fierce dog, by being often quite new stocked with the blood of a cowardly dog, may not become more tame; & vice versa, &c?)...

4. Whether acquired habits will be destroyed or impaired by this experiment? (As whether a dog, taught to fetch and carry, or to dive after ducks, or to sett,[1] will after frequent and full recruits of the blood of dogs unfit for those exercises, be as good at them as before?)...

8. Whether a dog that is sick of some disease chiefly imputable to the mass of blood may be cured by exchanging it for that of a sound dog? And whether a sound dog may receive such diseases from the blood of a sick one, as are not otherwise of an infectious nature?

9. What will be the operation of frequently stocking (which is feasible enough) an old and feeble dog with the blood of young ones, as to liveliness, dullness, drowsiness, squeamishness, &c., et vice versa?

10. Whether a small young dog, by being often fresh stocked with the blood of a young dog of a larger kind, will grow bigger than the ordinary size of its own kind? ...

12. Whether, a purging medicine being given to the emittent dog a while before the operation, the recipient dog will be thereby purged, and how? (Which experiment may be hugely varied.)

13. Whether the operation may be successfully practised in case[2] the injected blood be that of an animal of another species, as of a calf into a dog, &c., and of a cold animal, as of a fish, or frog, or tortoise, into the vessels of a hot animal, and vice versa?...

[1] *sett* Indicate that it smells a wild animal.

[2] *in case* In a case where.

Thomas Coxe, "An Account of Another Experiment of Transfusion, *viz.*[3] of Bleeding a Mangy into a Sound Dog" (1666)

This was made by Mr. Thomas Coxe, and imparted likewise to the Royal Society in manner following.

I procured an old mongrel cur all overrun with the mange,[4] of a middle size, and having some hours before fed him plentifully with cheese-parings and milk, I prepared the jugular vein as we use to do the carotidal artery of the emittent animal, not designing anything further than to determine by experiment the infection of the recipient's blood. Then I made as strong a ligature upon the dog's neck as I durst for fear of choking him, to the end that the venal blood, which is much more sluggish in its motion and evacuation than the arterial, might be emitted with the greater advantage of impetus. Then I took a young land-spaniel of about the same bigness and prepared his jugular vein as is usually done in the recipient animal; the heartward part of the vein to receive the mangy dog's blood, and the headward part of it to discharge his own into a dish.

Having thus prepared them both and placed them in a convenient posture one to the other, I let slip the running knots, and by frequent compression of the neck (besides the ligature I had made) by reason of the tardy running of the venal blood out of the emittent, transfused about 14 or 16 ounces of the blood of the infected into the veins of the sound dog, as near as I could guess by the quantity of blood which ran into a dish from the recipient, supposing the recipient animal to lose near about the same proportion to what the emittent supplies.

The effect of which experiment was no alteration at all, any way, to be observed in the sound dog. But for the mangy dog, he was in about 10 days' or a fortnight's[5] space perfectly cured—which might with probability enough, I think, have been expected from

[3] *viz.* Abbreviation for the Latin *videlicet*, meaning "namely" or "that is to say."

[4] *the mange* Skin disease caused by mites.

[5] *fortnight* Two weeks.

the considerable evacuation[1] he made (perhaps the quickest and surest remedy for the cure of that sort of disease he was infected with, both in man and beast).

from Will Chesselden, "An Account of Some Observations Made by a Young Gentleman Who Was Born Blind, or Lost His Sight So Early, That He Had No Remembrance of Ever Having Seen, and Was Couched[2] Between 13 and 14 Years of Age" (1727)

Though we say of the gentleman that he was blind, as we do for all people who have ripe cataracts, yet they are never so blind from that cause but that they can discern day from night, and for the most part in a strong light distinguish black, white, and scarlet; but they cannot perceive the shape of anything.…

When he first saw, he was so far from making any judgment about distances that he thought all objects whatever touched his eyes (as he expressed it) as what he felt, did his skin, and thought no objects so agreeable as those which were smooth and regular, though he could form no judgment of their shape, or guess what it was in any object that was pleasing to him. He knew not the shape of anything, nor any one thing from another, no matter how different in shape or magnitude. But upon being told what things were, whose form he knew before from feeling, he would carefully observe, that he might know them again; but having too many objects to learn at once, he forgot many of them, and (as he said) forgot a thousand things in a day. One particular only (though it may appear trifling) I will relate: having often forgot which was the cat, and which the dog, he was ashamed to ask; but catching the cat (which he knew by feeling) he was observed to look at her steadfastly, and setting her down, said, So Puss! I shall know you another time. He was very much surprised that those things which he had liked best did not appear most agreeable to his eyes, expecting those persons would appear most beautiful that he loved most, and such things to be most agreeable to his sight that were to his taste. We thought he soon knew what pictures represented which were showed to him, but we found afterwards we were mistaken. For about two months after he was couched, he discovered at once they represented solid bodies, when to that time he considered them only as partly-coloured planes, or surfaces diversified with variety of paint. But even then he was no less surprised, expecting the pictures would feel like the things they represented, and was amazed when he found those parts which by their light and shadow appeared now round and uneven felt only flat like the rest, and asked which was the lying sense, feeling or seeing?…

At first he could bear but little sight, and the things he saw he thought extremely large. But upon seeing things larger, those first seen he conceived less, never being able to imagine any lines beyond the bounds he saw; the room he was in, he said, he knew to be part of the house, yet he could not conceive that the whole house could look bigger. Before he was couched, he expected little advantage from seeing worth undergoing an operation for, except reading and writing.… He said every new object was a new delight, and the pleasure was so great that he wanted[3] ways to express it.

from Sir Isaac Newton, "A Letter of Mr. Isaac Newton, Professor of the Mathematics in the University of Cambridge, Containing His New Theory about Light and Colours" (1671)

… I shall now proceed to acquaint you with [a] notable deformity in [light's] rays, wherein the origin of colours is unfolded, concerning which I shall lay down the doctrine first and then, for its examination, give you an instance or two of the experiments, as a specimen of the rest.

The doctrine you will find comprehended and illustrated in the following propositions:

1. As the rays of light differ in degrees of refrangibility,[4] so they also differ in their disposition to exhibit this or that particular colour. Colours are not qualifications[5] of light, derived from refractions or reflections of

[1] *evacuation* Discharge of blood.

[2] *Couched* Operated on.

[3] *wanted* Lacked.

[4] *refrangibility* Refractability.

[5] *qualifications* Conditions.

natural bodies (as 'tis generally believed), but original and connate[1] properties which in diverse rays are diverse. Some rays are disposed to exhibit a red colour and no other, some a yellow and no other, some a green and no other, and so of the rest. Nor are there only rays proper and particular to the more eminent colours, but even to all their intermediate gradations. …

3. The species of colour and degree of refrangibility proper to any particular sort of rays is not mutable by refraction, nor by reflection from natural bodies, nor by any other cause that I could yet observe. When any one sort of rays hath been well parted from those of other kinds, it hath afterwards obstinately retained its colour, notwithstanding my utmost endeavours to change it. I have refracted it with prisms and reflected it with bodies which in daylight were of other colours; I have intercepted it with the coloured film of air interceding two compressed plates of glass; transmitted it through coloured mediums and through mediums irradiated with other sorts of rays, and diversely terminated it; and yet could never produce any new colour out of it. It would by contracting or dilating become more brisk or faint and by the loss of many rays in some cases very obscure and dark; but I could never see it changed *in specie*.[2]

4. Yet seeming transmutations of colours may be made, where there is any mixture of diverse sorts of rays. For in such mixtures, the component colours appear not, but by their mutual allaying each other constitute a middling colour. And therefore if, by refraction or any other of the aforesaid causes, the difform[3] rays latent in such a mixture be separated, there shall emerge colours different from the colour of the composition. Which colours are not new generated, but only made apparent by being parted; for if they be again entirely mixed and blended together, they will again compose that colour which they did before separation. And for the same reason, transmutations made by the convening of diverse colours are not real; for when the difform rays are again severed, they will exhibit the very same colours which they did before they entered the composition—as you see blue and yellow powders, when finely mixed, appear to the naked eye green, and yet the colours of the component corpuscles[4] are not thereby transmuted, but only blended. For, when viewed with a good microscope, they still appear blue and yellow interspersedly.

5. There are therefore two sorts of colours: the one original and simple, the other compounded of these. The original or primary colours are red, yellow, green, blue, and a violet-purple, together with orange, indigo, and an indefinite variety of intermediate graduations.

6. The same colours *in specie* with these primary ones may be also produced by composition. For a mixture of yellow and blue makes green; of red and yellow makes orange; of orange and yellowish green makes yellow. And in general if any two colours be mixed which, in the series of those generated by the prism, are not too far distant one from another, they by their mutual alloy compound that colour which in the said series appeareth in the mid-way between them. But those which are situated at too great a distance do not so. Orange and indigo produce not the intermediate green, nor scarlet and green the intermediate yellow.

7. But the most surprising and wonderful composition was that of whiteness. There is no one sort of rays which alone can exhibit this. 'Tis ever compounded, and to its composition are requisite all the aforesaid primary colours, mixed in a due proportion. I have often with admiration beheld that all the colours of the prism, being made to converge and thereby to be again mixed as they were in the light before it was incident upon the prism, reproduced light entirely and perfectly white, and not at all sensibly differing from a direct light of the sun, unless when the glasses I used were not sufficiently clear; for then they would a little incline it to their colour.

…

13. … [T]he colours of all natural bodies have no other origin than this: that they are variously qualified to reflect one sort of light in greater plenty than another. And this I have experimented in a dark room by illuminating those bodies with uncompounded light of diverse colours. For by that means any body may be made to appear of any colour. They have there no appropriate colour, but ever appear of the colour of the light cast

[1] *connate* Innate.

[2] *in specie* Latin: in form.

[3] *difform* Of different forms.

[4] *corpuscles* Small particles.

upon them, but yet with this difference, that they are most brisk and vivid in the light of their own daylight colour....

These things being so, it can no longer be disputed whether there be colours in the dark, nor whether they be the qualities of the objects we see, no, nor perhaps whether light be a body. For since colours are the qualities of light, having its rays for their entire and immediate subject, how can we think those rays qualities also, unless one quality may be the subject of and sustain another; which in effect is to call it substance. We should not know bodies for substances were it not for their sensible qualities, and the principal of those[1] being now found due to something else, we have as good reason to believe that to be a substance also.

Besides, who ever thought any quality to be a heterogeneous aggregate, such as light is discovered to be. But to determine more absolutely what light is, after what manner refracted, and by what modes or actions it produceth in our minds the phantasms of colours, is not so easy. And I shall not mingle conjectures with certainties.

from Benjamin Franklin, *The Autobiography of Benjamin Franklin* (1793)

... [I]t may not be amiss here to give some account of the rise & progress of my philosophical reputation.

In 1746, being at Boston, I met there with a Dr. Spence, who was lately arrived from Scotland, and showed me some electric experiments. They were imperfectly performed, as he was not very expert; but, being on a subject quite new to me, they equally surprised and pleased me. Soon after my return to Philadelphia, our library company received from Mr. Peter Collinson, F.R.S.[2] of London a present of a glass tube, with some account of the use of it in making such experiments. I eagerly seized the opportunity of repeating what I had seen at Boston, and by much practice acquired great readiness in performing those, also, which we had an account of from England, adding a number of new ones. I say much practice, for my house was continually full, for some time, with people who came to see these new wonders. To divide a little this encumbrance among my friends, I caused a number of similar tubes to be blown at our glass-house, with which they furnished themselves, so that we had at length several performers. Among these, the principal was Mr. Kinnersley, an ingenious neighbour, who, being out of business, I encouraged to undertake showing the experiments for money, and drew up for him two lectures in which the experiments were ranged in such order, and accompanied with such explanations in such method, as that the foregoing should assist in comprehending the following. He procured an elegant apparatus for the purpose, in which all the little machines that I had roughly made for myself were nicely formed by instrument-makers. His lectures were well attended, and gave great satisfaction; and after some time he went through the Colonies, exhibiting them in every capital town, and picked up some money. In the West India islands, indeed, it was with difficulty the experiments could be made, from the general moisture of the air.

Obliged as we were to Mr. Collinson for his present of the tube, &c., I thought it right he should be informed of our success in using it, and wrote him several letters containing accounts of our experiments. He got them read in the Royal Society, where they were not at first thought worth so much notice as to be printed in their *Transactions*.[3] One paper, which I wrote for Mr. Kinnersley on the sameness of lightning with electricity, I sent to Dr. Mitchel, an acquaintance of mine, and one of the members also of that society, who wrote me word that it had been read but was laughed at by the connoisseurs. The papers, however, being shown to Dr. Fothergill, he thought them of too much value to be stifled, and advised the printing of them. Mr. Collinson then gave them to Cave[4] for publication in his *Gentleman's Magazine*; but he chose to print them separately in a pamphlet, and Dr. Fothergill wrote the preface. Cave, it

[1] *the principal of those* I.e., color.

[2] *Mr. Peter Collinson* Peter Collinson (1694–1768), a plant collector, maintained friendships with noteworthy scientists throughout the Western world; *F.R.S.* Fellow of the Royal Society.

[3] *Transactions* The early scientific periodical *Philosophical Transactions*, a journal of the Royal Society.

[4] *Cave* Edward Cave (1691–1754), creator and editor of *The Gentleman's Magazine*, a general interest digest.

seems, judged rightly for his profit, for by the additions that arrived afterward they swelled to a quarto volume, which has had five editions, and cost him nothing for copy-money.

It was, however, some time before those papers were much taken notice of in England. A copy of them happening to fall into the hands of the Count de Buffon, a philosopher deservedly of great reputation in France, and, indeed, all over Europe, he prevailed with M. Dalibard to translate them into French, and they were printed at Paris. The publication offended the Abbé Nollet, preceptor[1] in natural philosophy to the royal family and an able experimenter, who had formed and published a theory of electricity which then had the general vogue. He could not at first believe that such a work came from America, & said it must have been fabricated by his enemies at Paris, to decry his system. Afterwards, having been assured that there really existed such a person as Franklin at Philadelphia, which he had doubted, he wrote and published a volume of letters,[2] chiefly addressed to me, defending his theory & denying the verity of my experiments, and of the positions deduced from them. I once purposed answering the Abbé, and actually began the answer. But on consideration that my writings contained a description of experiments which anyone might repeat & verify, and if not to be verified, could not be defended; or of observations offered as conjectures, & not delivered dogmatically, therefore not laying me under any obligation to defend them; and reflecting that a dispute between two persons, writing in different languages, might be lengthened greatly by mistranslations, and thence misconceptions of one another's meaning, much of one of the Abbé's letters being founded on an error in the translation, I concluded to let my papers shift for themselves, believing it was better to spend what time I could spare from public business in making new experiments than in disputing about those already made. I therefore never answered M. Nollet, and the event gave me no cause to repent my silence; for my friend M. le Roy, of the Royal Academy of Sciences,[3] took up my cause and refuted him; my book was translated into the Italian, German, and Latin languages, and the doctrine it contained was by degrees universally adopted by the philosophers of Europe, in preference to that of the Abbé; so that he lived to see himself the last of his sect, except Monsieur B——, his *élève*[4] and immediate disciple.

What gave my book the more sudden and general celebrity was the success of one of its proposed experiments, made by Messrs. Dalibard & Delor at Marly,[5] for drawing lightning from the clouds. This engaged the public attention everywhere. M. Delor, who had an apparatus for experimental philosophy and lectured in that branch of science, undertook to repeat what he called the Philadelphia Experiments; and, after they were performed before the king & court, all the curious of Paris flocked to see them. I will not swell this narrative with an account of that capital experiment, nor of the infinite pleasure I received in the success of a similar one I made soon after with a kite at Philadelphia,[6] as both are to be found in the histories of electricity. Dr. Wright, an English physician, when at Paris, wrote to a friend who was of the Royal Society an account of the high esteem my experiments were in among the learned abroad, and of their wonder that my writings had been so little noticed in England. The society, on this, resumed the consideration of the letters that had been read to them, and the celebrated Dr. Watson drew up a summary account of them & of all I had afterwards sent

[1] *preceptor* Teacher.

[2] *letters* Jean Antoine Nollet's book *Letters on Electricity* (1753) defended his view that electricity is a fluid.

[3] *Royal Academy of Sciences* French counterpart to the Royal Society.

[4] *élève* French: student.

[5] *Dalibard & Delor at Marly* French naturalist Thomas-François Dalibard attracted lightning with an insulated metal pole at Marly-la-ville, near Paris; after his success, Delor and other French experimenters repeated his results.

[6] *a similar ... Philadelphia* In a letter to the *Royal Society*, Franklin describes his famous experiment involving a kite on a line of twine:

> To the end of the twine, next the hand, is to be tied a silk ribbon, and where the twine and silk join, a key may be fastened.
>
> The kite is to be raised when a thunder gust appears to be coming on ... & the person who holds the string must stand ... under some cover so that the silk ribbon may not be wet....
>
> When the rain has wet the kite & twine, so that it can conduct the electric fire freely, you will find it stream out plentifully from the key on the approach of your knuckle.

to England on the subject, which he accompanied with some praise of the writer. This summary was then printed in their *Transactions*; and some members of the society in London, particularly the very ingenious Mr. Canton, having verified the experiment of procuring lightning from the clouds by a pointed rod, and acquainting them with the success, they soon made me more than amends for the slight with which they had before treated me. Without my having made any application for that honour, they chose me a member and voted that I should be excused the customary payments, which would have amounted to twenty-five guineas; and ever since have given me their *Transactions gratis*.[1] They also presented me with the Gold Medal of Sir Godfrey Copley[2] for the Year 1753, the delivery of which was accompanied by a very handsome speech of the president, Lord Macclesfield, wherein I was highly honoured.

from Joseph Priestley, *Experiments and Observations on Different Kinds of Air* (1774–86)

from THE PREFACE

... I find it absolutely impossible to produce a work on this subject that shall be anything like complete. My first publication I acknowledged to be very imperfect, and the present, I am as ready to acknowledge, is still more so. But, paradoxical as it may seem, this will ever be the case in the progress of natural science, so long as the works of God are, like himself, infinite and inexhaustible. In completing one discovery we never fail to get an imperfect knowledge of others of which we could have no idea before, so that we cannot solve one doubt without creating several new ones.

Travelling on this ground resembles Pope's description of travelling among the Alps, with this difference: that here there is not only succession, but an increase of new objects and new difficulties.

So pleased at first the tow'ring Alps we try,
Mount o'er the vales, and seem to tread the sky.
Th'eternal snows appear already past,
And the first clouds and mountains seem the last,
But those attained, we tremble to survey
The growing labours of the lengthened way.
Th'increasing prospect tires our wand'ring eyes,
Hills peep o'er hills, and Alps on Alps arise.

Essay on Criticism[3]

Newton, as he had very little knowledge of air, so he had few doubts concerning it. Had Dr. Hales,[4] after his various and valuable investigations, given a list of all his desiderata,[5] I am confident that he would not have thought of one in ten that had occurred to me at the time of my last publication—and my doubts, queries, and hints for new experiments are very considerably increased after a series of investigations, which have thrown great light upon many things of which I was not able to give any explanation before.

I would observe farther that a person who means to serve the cause of science effectually must hazard his own reputation so far as to risk even mistakes in things of less moment. Among a multiplicity of new objects and new relations, some will necessarily pass without sufficient attention; but if a man be not mistaken in the principal objects of his pursuits, he has no occasion to distress himself about lesser things.

In the progress of his inquiries he will generally be able to rectify his own mistakes. Or, if little and envious souls should take a malignant pleasure in detecting them for him, and endeavouring to expose him, he is not worthy of the name of a philosopher if he has not strength of mind sufficient to enable him not to be disturbed at it. He who does not foolishly affect to be above the failings of humanity will not be mortified when it is proved that he is but a man.

In this work, as well as in all my other philosophical writings, I have made it a rule not to conceal the real

[1] *gratis* Latin: free.

[2] *Gold Medal ... Copley* The Copley Medal remains the Royal Society's most prestigious award.

[3] *Essay on Criticism* Alexander Pope's *An Essay on Criticism* (1709), lines 225–32.

[4] *Dr. Hales* Stephen Hales (1677–1761), a Fellow of the Royal Society, conducted experiments on plant interactions with air about forty years before Priestley.

[5] *desiderata* Latin: things desired.

views with which I have made experiments, because, though by following a contrary maxim I might have acquired a character[1] of greater sagacity, I think that two very good ends are answered by the method that I have adopted. For it both tends to make a narrative of a course of experiments more interesting, and likewise encourages other adventurers in experimental philosophy, showing them that by pursuing even false lights, real and important truths may be discovered, and that in seeking one thing we often find another.

In some respects, indeed, this method makes the narrative longer, but it is by making it less tedious; and in other respects I have written much more concisely than is usual with those who publish accounts of their experiments. In this treatise the reader will often find the result of long processes expressed in a few lines, and of many such in a single paragraph—each of which, if I had, with the usual parade, described it at large (explaining first the preparation, then reciting the experiment itself, with the result of it, and lastly making suitable reflections) would have made as many sections or chapters, and have swelled my book to a pompous and respectable size. But I have the pleasure to think that those philosophers who have but little time to spare for reading, which is always the case with those who *do* much themselves, will thank me for not keeping them too long from their own pursuits, and that they will find rather more in the volume than the appearance of it promises.

I do not think it at all degrading to the business of experimental philosophy to compare it, as I often do, to the diversion of hunting, where it sometimes happens that those who have beat the ground the most, and are consequently the best acquainted with it, weary themselves without starting any game,[2] when it may fall in the way of a mere passenger,[3] so that there is but little room for boasting in the most successful termination of the chase.

The best founded praise is that which is due to the man who, from a supreme veneration for the God of nature, takes pleasure in contemplating his works, and from a love of his fellow-creatures as the offspring of the same all-wise and benevolent parent, with a grateful sense and perfect enjoyment of the means of happiness of which he is already possessed, seeks, with earnestness, but without murmuring or impatience, that greater command of the powers of nature which can only be obtained by a more extensive and more accurate knowledge of them; and which alone can enable us to avail ourselves of the numerous advantages with which we are surrounded, and contribute to make our common situation more secure and happy.

Besides, the man who believes that there is a governor as well as a maker of the world (and there is certainly equal reason to believe both) will acknowledge his providence and favour at least as much in a successful pursuit of knowledge as of wealth. Which is a sentiment that entirely cuts off all boasting with respect to ourselves and all envy and jealousy with respect to others, and disposes us mutually to rejoice in every new light that we receive, through whose hands soever it be conveyed to us.

I shall pass for an enthusiast with some, but I am perfectly easy under the imputation because I am happy in those views which subject me to it. But considering the amazing improvements in natural knowledge which have been made within the last century, and the many ages abounding with men who had no other object but study in which, however, nothing of this kind was done, there appears to me to be a very particular providence in the concurrence of those circumstances which have produced so great a change. And I cannot help flattering myself that this will be instrumental in bringing about other changes in the state of the world, of much more consequence to the improvement and happiness of it.

This rapid progress of knowledge—which, like the progress of a wave of the sea, of sound, or of light from the sun, extends itself not this way or that way only, but in all directions—will, I doubt not, be the means under God of extirpating all error and prejudice, and of putting an end to all undue and usurped authority in the business of religion, as well as of science. And all the efforts of the interested friends of corrupt establishments of all kinds will be ineffectual for their support in this enlightened age, though, by retarding their downfall, they may make the final ruin of them more complete

[1] *character* Reputation.

[2] *starting any game* Forcing any game animals out of their lairs.

[3] *passenger* Person passing by on foot.

and glorious. It was ill policy in Leo the Xth to patronize polite literature.[1] He was cherishing an enemy in disguise. And the English hierarchy (if there be any thing unsound in its constitution) has equal reason to tremble even at an air-pump, or an electrical machine.

There certainly never was any period in which natural knowledge made such a progress as it has done of late years, and especially in this country. And they who affect to speak with supercilious contempt of the publications of the present age in general, or of the Royal Society in particular, are only those who are themselves engaged in the most trifling of all literary pursuits, who are unacquainted with all real science, and are ignorant of the progress and present state of it....

from THE INTRODUCTION

SECTION 2: *An account of the apparatus with which the following experiments were made.*

It will be seen that my apparatus for experiments on air is, in fact, nothing more than the apparatus of Dr. Hales, Dr. Brownrigg, and Mr. Cavendish,[2] diversified and made a little more simple. Yet notwithstanding the simplicity of this apparatus and the ease with which all the operations are conducted, I would not have any person who is altogether without experience to imagine that he shall be able to select any of the following experiments, and immediately perform it without difficulty or blundering. It is known to all persons who are conversant in experimental philosophy that there are many little attentions and precautions necessary to be observed in the conducting of experiments which cannot well be described in words, but which it is needless to describe, since practice will necessarily suggest them; though, like all other arts in which the hands and fingers are made use of, it is only much practice that can enable a person to go through complex experiments, of this or any other kind, with ease and readiness.

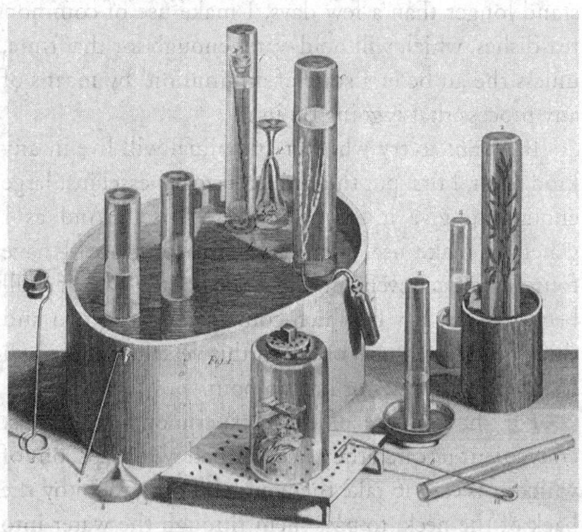

Joseph Priestley's illustration of his apparatus.

For experiments in which air will bear to be confined by water, I first used an oblong trough made of earthen ware (as *a*, fig. 1) about eight inches deep, at one end of which I put thin flat stones (*b, b*) about an inch or half an inch under the water, using more or fewer of them according to the quantity of water in the trough. But I have since found it more convenient to use a larger wooden trough of the same general shape, eleven inches deep, two feet long, and 1½ wide, with a shelf about an inch lower than the top instead of the flat stones abovementioned. This trough being larger than the former, I have no occasion to make provision for the water being higher or lower, the bulk of a jar or two not making so great a difference as did before.

The several kinds of air I usually keep in cylindrical jars (as *c, c*, fig. 1), about ten inches long and 2½ wide, being such as I have generally used for electrical batteries, but I have likewise vessels of very different forms and sizes adapted to particular experiments.

When I want to remove vessels of air from the large trough, I place them in pots or dishes of various sizes, to hold more or less water according to the time that I have occasion to keep the air (as fig. 2). These I plunge in water, and slide the jars into them, after which they may be taken out together and be set wherever it shall be most convenient. For the purpose of merely removing a jar of air from one place to another, where it is not to

---

[1] *Leo the Xth ... literature* Pope Leo X (1475–1521), a generous patron of humanist pursuits. He is best known for his financial corruption, which was a contributing factor in provoking the Protestant Reformation.

[2] *Dr. Hales ... Mr. Cavendish* Fellows of the Royal Society who conducted experiments on gases.

stand longer than a few days, I make use of common tea-dishes, which will hold water enough for that time, unless the air be in a state of diminution[1] by means of any process that is going on in it.

If I want to try whether an animal will live in any kind of air, I first put the air into a small vessel just large enough to give it room to stretch itself. And as I generally make use of mice for this purpose, I have found it very convenient to use the hollow part of a tall beer-glass (*d,* fig. 1) which contains between two and three ounce measures of air. In this vessel a mouse will live twenty minutes or half an hour.

For the purpose of these experiments it is most convenient to catch the mice in small wire traps, out of which it is easy to take them and, holding them by the back of the neck, to pass them through the water into the vessel which contains the air. If I expect that the mouse will live a considerable time, I take care to put into the vessel something on which it may conveniently sit, out of the reach of the water. If the air be good, the mouse will soon be perfectly at its ease, having suffered nothing by its passing through the water. If the air be supposed to be noxious, it will be proper (if the operator be desirous of preserving the mice for farther use) to keep hold of their tails, that they may be withdrawn as soon as they begin to show signs of uneasiness. But if the air be thoroughly noxious, and the mouse happens to get a full inspiration, it will be impossible to do this before it be absolutely irrecoverable.

In order to keep the mice, I put them into receivers open at the top and bottom, standing upon plates of tin perforated with many holes, and covered with other plates of the same kind, held down by sufficient weights (as fig. 3). These receivers stand upon a frame of wood, that the fresh air may have an opportunity of getting to the bottoms of them and circulating through them. In the inside I put a quantity of paper or tow,[2] which must be changed, and the vessel washed and dried, every two or three days. This is most conveniently done by having another receiver, ready cleaned and prepared, into which the mice may be transferred till the other shall be cleaned.

... [T]he most accurate method of procuring air from several substances by means of heat is to put them, if they will bear it, into phials full of quicksilver[3] with the mouths immersed in the same, and then throw the focus of a burning mirror upon them. For this purpose the phials should be made with their bottoms round and very thin, that they may not be liable to break with a pretty sudden application of heat.

If I want to expel air from any liquid, I nearly fill a phial with it and, having a cork perforated, I put through it, and secure with cement, a glass tube bended in the manner represented at *e,* fig. 1. I then put the phial into a kettle of water, which I set upon the fire and make to boil. The air expelled by the heat from the liquor contained in the phial issues through the tube, and is received in the basin of quicksilver (fig. 7). Instead of this suspended basin, I sometimes content myself with tying a flaccid bladder to the end of the tube in both these processes, that it may receive the newly generated air....

When I want to try whether any kind of air will admit a candle to burn in it, I make use of a cylindrical glass vessel (fig. 11) and a bit of wax candle (*a,* fig. 12) fastened to the end of a wire (*b*) and turned up in such a manner as to be let down into the vessel with the flame upwards. The vessel should be kept carefully covered till the moment that the candle is admitted. In this manner I have frequently extinguished a candle more than twenty times successively in a vessel of this kind, though it is impossible to dip the candle into it without giving the external air an opportunity of mixing with the air in the inside more or less.

[1] *For the purpose ... of diminution* More water would be necessary, for instance, if the experiment were left long enough for significant evaporation to occur, or if an aspect of the experiment (such as the application of heat) caused the volume of air in the jar to decrease, drawing more water into the jar.

[2] *tow* Flax or hemp fibers.

[3] *quicksilver* Mercury.

from John Locke, *An Essay Concerning Human Understanding* (1689)

from Book 2, "Of Ideas," Chapter 1

Let us then suppose the mind to be, as we say, white paper,[1] void of all characters, without any ideas. How comes it to be furnished? Whence comes it by that vast store, which the busy and boundless fancy of man has painted on it, with an almost endless variety? Whence has it all the materials of reason and knowledge? To this I answer, in one word, from *experience.* In that, all our knowledge is founded, and from that it ultimately derives itself. Our observation employed either about *external, sensible objects, or about the internal operations of our minds, perceived and reflected on by ourselves, is that which supplies our understandings with all the materials of thinking.* These two are the fountains of knowledge, from whence all the ideas we have, or can naturally have, do spring.

First, our senses, conversant about particular sensible objects, do convey into the mind several distinct perceptions of things, according to those various ways, wherein those objects do affect them; and thus we come by those ideas we have of yellow, white, heat, cold, soft, hard, bitter, sweet, and all those which we call sensible qualities, which when I say the senses convey into the mind, I mean, they from external objects convey into the mind what produces there those perceptions. This great source of most of the ideas we have, depending wholly upon our senses and derived by them to the understanding, I call *sensation.*

Secondly, the other fountain from which experience furnisheth the understanding with ideas is the *perception of the operations of our own minds* within us, as it is employed about the ideas it has got; which operations, when the soul comes to reflect on and consider, do furnish the understanding with another set of ideas, which could not be had from things without; and such are *perception, thinking, doubting, believing, reasoning, knowing, willing,* and all the different actings of our own minds; which we being conscious of, and observing in ourselves, do from these receive into our understandings, as distinct ideas, as we do from bodies affecting our senses. This source of ideas every man has wholly in himself. And though it be not sense, as having nothing to do with external objects, yet it is very like it, and might properly enough be called internal sense. But as I call the other *sensation,* so I call this *reflection,* the ideas it affords being such only as the mind gets by reflecting on its own operations within itself. By *reflection* then, in the following part of this discourse, I would be understood to mean that notice which the mind takes of its own operations, and the manner of them, by reason whereof there come to be ideas of these operations in the understanding. These two, I say, viz. external, material things, as the objects of sensation, and the operations of our own minds within, as the objects of reflection, are, to me, the only originals, from whence all our ideas take their beginnings. The term *operations* here I use in a large sense, as comprehending not barely the actions of the mind about its ideas, but some sort of passions arising sometimes from them, such as is the satisfaction or uneasiness arising from any thought.

The understanding seems to me not to have the least glimmering of any ideas which it doth not receive from one of these two. *External objects furnish the mind with the ideas of sensible qualities,* which are all those different perceptions they produce in us; and the *mind furnishes the understanding with ideas of its own operations.*

These, when we have taken a full survey of them, and their several modes, combinations, and relations, we shall find to contain all our whole stock of ideas; and that we have nothing in our minds which did not come in one of these two ways. Let anyone examine his own thoughts, and thoroughly search into his understanding, and then let him tell me, whether all the original ideas he has there are any other than of the objects of his senses, or of the operations of his mind, considered as objects of his reflection; and how great a mass of knowledge soever he imagines to be lodged there, he will, upon taking a strict view, see that he has *not any idea in his mind, but what one of these two have imprinted;*

[1] *white paper* The Latin phrase *tabula rasa,* meaning "blank (or erased) slate," is generally used to reference the concept Locke discusses here using the phrase "white paper." The term was first used in the sixteenth century in connection with the ideas of Aristotle, who, like Locke, believed our minds were born void and ready to receive impressions. It is now most often associated with Locke, who provided the most comprehensive articulation of the "blank slate" theory.

though, perhaps, with infinite variety compounded and enlarged by the understanding, as we shall see hereafter.

He that attentively considers the state of a child at his first coming into the world, will have little reason to think him stored with plenty of ideas that are to be the matter of his future knowledge. 'Tis by degrees he comes to be furnished with them. And though the ideas of obvious and familiar qualities imprint themselves before the memory begins to keep a register of time and order, yet 'tis often so late before some unusual qualities come in the way that there are few men that cannot recollect the beginning of their acquaintance with them; and if it were worthwhile, no doubt a child might be so ordered as to have but a very few, even of the ordinary ideas, 'till he were grown up to a man. But all that are born into the world being surrounded with bodies that perpetually and diversely affect them, variety of ideas, whether care be taken about it or no, are imprinted on the minds of children: light and colors are busy at hand everywhere, when the eye is but open; sounds and some tangible qualities fail not to solicit their proper senses and force an entrance to the mind. But yet, I think, it will be granted easily that if a child were kept in a place where he never saw any other but black and white till he were a man, he would have no more ideas of scarlet or green than he that from his childhood never tasted an oyster, or a pineapple, has of those particular relishes. ...

from BOOK 2, CHAPTER 23

But to return to the matter in hand, the ideas we have of substances, and the ways we come by them; I say our specific ideas of substances are nothing else but a collection of a certain number of simple ideas, considered as united in one thing. These ideas of substances, though they are commonly called simple apprehensions, and the names of them simple terms, yet in effect, are complex and compounded. Thus the idea which an Englishman signifies by the name *swan* is white color, long neck, red beak, black legs, and whole feet, and all these of a certain size, with a power of swimming in the water, and making a certain kind of noise, and, perhaps, to a man who has long observed those kind of birds, some other properties, which all terminate in sensible simple ideas, all united in one common subject.

Besides the complex ideas we have of material sensible substances, of which I have last spoken, by the simple ideas we have taken from those operations of our own minds, which we experiment daily in ourselves, as thinking, understanding, willing, knowing, and power of beginning motion, etc. co-existing in some substance, we are able to frame the complex idea *of an immaterial spirit*. And thus by putting together the ideas of thinking, perceiving, liberty, and power of moving themselves and other things, we have as clear a perception and notion of immaterial substances as we have of material. For putting together the ideas of thinking and willing, or the power of moving or quieting corporeal motion, joined to substance, of which we have no distinct idea, we have the idea of an immaterial spirit; and by putting together the ideas of coherent solid parts, and a power of being moved, joined with substance, of which likewise we have no positive idea, we have the idea of matter. The one is as clear and distinct an idea as the other: the idea of thinking, and moving a body, being as clear and distinct ideas as the ideas of extension, solidity, and being moved. ...

If we examine the idea we have of the incomprehensible Supreme Being, we shall find that we come by it the same way; and that the complex ideas we have both of God and separate spirits are made up of the simple ideas we receive from reflection; v.g.,[1] having, from what we experiment in ourselves, got the ideas of existence and duration; of knowledge and power; of pleasure and happiness; and of several other qualities and powers, which it is better to have than to be without. When we would frame an idea the most suitable we can to the Supreme Being, we enlarge every one of these with our idea of infinity; and so putting them together, make our complex idea of God. For that the mind has such a power of enlarging some of its ideas, received from sensation and reflection, has been already showed. ...

[1] *v.g.* For *verbi gratia* (Latin), meaning "for example."

from Robert Hooke, *Micrographia: Or Some Physiological Descriptions of Minute Bodies Made by Magnifying Glasses, with Observations and Inquiries Thereupon* (1665)

THE EPISTLE DEDICATORY. TO THE KING.[1]

I do here most humbly lay this small present at your Majesty's royal feet. And though it comes accompanied with two disadvantages, the meanness of the author, and of the subject; yet in both I am encouraged by the greatness of your mercy and your knowledge. By the one I am taught that you can forgive the most presumptuous offenders; and by the other, that you will not esteem the least work of nature or art unworthy your observation. Amidst the many felicities that have accompanied your Majesty's happy restoration[2] and government, it is none of the least considerable that philosophy and experimental learning have prospered under your royal patronage. And as the calm prosperity of your reign has given us the leisure to follow these studies of quiet and retirement, so it is just that the fruits of them should, by way of acknowledgement, be returned to your Majesty. There are, Sir, several other of your subjects, of your Royal Society, now busy about nobler matters: the improvement of manufactures and agriculture, the increase of commerce, the advantage of navigation, in all which they are assisted by your Majesty's encouragement and example. Amidst all those greater designs, I here presume to bring in that which is more proportionable to the smallness of my abilities, and to offer some of the least of all visible things to that mighty king, that has established an empire over the best of all invisible things of this world: the minds of men.

Your Majesty's most humble and most obedient subject and servant,

ROBERT HOOKE.

[1] *the King* Charles II, a generous patron of the sciences who granted the Society its charter and remained supportive of its activities.

[2] *your Majesty's happy restoration* Charles II's restoration to the throne six years earlier.

TO THE ROYAL SOCIETY.

After my address to our great founder and patron, I could not but think myself obliged, in consideration of those many engagements you have laid upon me, to offer these my poor labours to this most illustrious assembly. You have been pleased formerly to accept of these rude drafts.[3] I have since added to them some descriptions and some conjectures of my own. And therefore, together with your acceptance, I must also beg your pardon. The rules you have prescribed yourselves in your philosophical progress do seem the best that have ever yet been practised. And particularly that of avoiding dogmatizing and the espousal of any hypothesis not sufficiently grounded and confirmed by experiments. This way seems the most excellent, and may preserve both philosophy and natural history from its former corruptions. In saying which, I may seem to condemn my own course in this treatise, in which there may perhaps be some expressions which may seem more positive than your prescriptions will permit: and though I desire to have them understood only as conjectures and queries (which your method does not altogether disallow) yet if even in those I have exceeded, 'tis fit that I should declare that it was not done by your directions. For it is most unreasonable that you should undergo the imputation of the faults of my conjectures, seeing you can receive so small advantage of reputation by the slight observations of your most humble and most faithful servant,

ROBERT HOOKE.

from THE PREFACE.

It is the great prerogative of mankind above other creatures that we are not only able to behold the works of nature, or barely to sustain our lives by them, but we have also the power of considering, comparing, altering, assisting, and improving them to various uses. And as this is the peculiar privilege of human nature in general, so is it capable of being so far advanced by the helps of art and experience as to make some men excel others in their observations and deductions almost as much as

[3] *You have … rude drafts* Some of the material in *Micrographia* was originally used in demonstrations given for the Royal Society.

they do beasts. By the addition of such artificial instruments and methods, there may be, in some manner, a reparation made for the mischiefs and imperfection mankind has drawn upon itself by negligence, and intemperance, and a wilful and superstitious deserting the prescripts and rules of nature, whereby every man, both from a derived corruption, innate and born with him, and from his breeding and converse with men, is very subject to slip into all sorts of errors.

The only way which now remains for us to recover some degree of those former perfections seems to be by rectifying the operations of the senses, the memory, and reason, since upon the evidence, the strength, the integrity, and the right correspondence of all these, all the light by which our actions are to be guided is to be renewed, and all our command over things is to be established.

It is therefore most worthy of our consideration to recollect their several defects, that so we may the better understand how to supply[1] them, and by what assistances we may enlarge their power and secure them in performing their particular duties.

As for the actions of our senses, we cannot but observe them to be in many particulars much outdone by those of other creatures and, when at best, to be far short of the perfection they seem capable of. And these infirmities of the senses arise from a double cause, either from the disproportion of the object to the organ, whereby an infinite number of things can never enter into them, or else from error in the perception, that many things which come within their reach are not received in a right manner.

The like frailties are to be found in the memory; we often let many things slip away from us which deserve to be retained, and of those which we treasure up, a great part is either frivolous or false; and if good and substantial, either in tract of time obliterated, or at best so overwhelmed and buried under more frothy[2] notions that when there is need of them they are in vain sought for.

The two main foundations being so deceivable, it is no wonder that all the succeeding works which we build upon them, of arguing, concluding, defining, judging, and all the other degrees of reason, are liable to the same imperfection, being, at best, either vain or uncertain. So that the errors of the understanding are answerable to the two other, being defective both in the quantity and goodness of its knowledge; for the limits to which our thoughts are confined are small in respect of the vast extent of nature itself. Some parts of it are too large to be comprehended, and some too little to be perceived. And from thence it must follow that, not having a full sensation of the object, we must be very lame and imperfect in our conceptions about it, and in all the proportions which we build upon it; hence, we often take the shadow of things for the substance, small appearances for good similitudes, similitudes for definitions. And even many of those which we think to be the most solid definitions are rather expressions of our own misguided apprehensions than of the true nature of the things themselves.

The effects of these imperfections are manifested in different ways according to the temper and disposition of the several[3] minds of men. Some they incline to gross ignorance and stupidity, and others to a presumptuous imposing on other men's opinions, and a confident dogmatizing on matters whereof there is no assurance to be given.

Thus all the uncertainty and mistakes of humane actions proceed either from the narrowness and wandering of our senses, from the slipperiness or delusion of our memory, from the confinement or rashness of our understanding, so that 'tis no wonder that our power over natural causes and effects is so slowly improved, seeing we are not only to contend with the obscurity and difficulty of the things whereon we work and think, but even the forces of our own minds conspire to betray us.

These being the dangers in the process of human reason, the remedies of them all can only proceed from the real, the mechanical, the experimental philosophy, which has this advantage over the philosophy of discourse and disputation: that whereas that chiefly aims at the subtlety of its deductions and conclusions without much regard to the first groundwork, which ought to be well laid on the sense and memory; so this intends the

[1] *supply* I.e., compensate for.

[2] *frothy* Trifling; empty.

[3] *several* Individual.

right ordering of them all, and the making them serviceable to each other.

The first thing to be undertaken in this weighty work is a watchfulness over the failings and an enlargement of the dominion of the senses.

To which end it is requisite, first, that there should be a scrupulous choice, and a strict examination, of the reality, constancy, and certainty of the particulars that we admit. This is the first rise whereon truth is to begin, and here the most severe and most impartial diligence must be employed; the storing up of all without any regard to evidence or use will only tend to darkness and confusion. We must not therefore esteem the riches of our philosophical treasure by the number only, but chiefly by the weight; the most vulgar instances are not to be neglected, but above all, the most instructive are to be entertained. The footsteps of nature are to be traced, not only in her ordinary course, but when she seems to be put to her shifts,[1] to make many doublings and turnings, and to use some kind of art in endeavouring to avoid our discovery.

The next care to be taken in respect of the senses is a supplying of their infirmities with instruments and, as it were, the adding of artificial organs to the natural. This in one of them has been of late years accomplished, with prodigious benefit to all sorts of useful knowledge, by the invention of optical glasses. By the means of telescopes, there is nothing so far distant but may be represented to our view; and by the help of microscopes, there is nothing so small as to escape our inquiry; hence there is a new visible world discovered to the understanding. By this means the heavens are opened, and a vast number of new stars, and new motions, and new productions appear in them, to which all the ancient astronomers were utterly strangers. By this the Earth itself, which lies so near us under our feet, shows quite a new thing to us; and in every little particle of its matter, we now behold almost as great a variety of creatures as we were able before to reckon up in the whole universe itself.

It seems not improbable but that by these helps the subtlety of the composition of bodies, the structure of their parts, the various texture of their matter, the instruments and manner of their inward motions, and all the other possible appearances of things, may come to be more fully discovered; all which the ancient Peripatetics[2] were content to comprehend in two general and (unless further explained) useless words of *matter* and *form*. From whence there may arise many admirable advantages towards the increase of the operative and the mechanic knowledge to which this age seems so much inclined, because we may perhaps be enabled to discern all the secret workings of nature, almost in the same manner as we do those that are the productions of art, and are managed by wheels, and engines, and springs that were devised by human wit.

In this kind I here present to the world my imperfect endeavours, which though they shall prove no other way considerable, yet I hope they may be in some measure useful to the main design of a reformation in philosophy, if it be only by showing that there is not so much required towards it—any strength of imagination, or exactness of method, or depth of contemplation (though the addition of these, where they can be had, must needs produce a much more perfect composure)—as a sincere hand and a faithful eye, to examine and to record the things themselves as they appear....

The truth is, the science of nature has been already too long made only a work of the brain and the fancy; it is now high time that it should return to the plainness and soundness of observations on material and obvious things. It is said of great empires that the best way to preserve them from decay is to bring them back to the first principles and arts on which they did begin. The same is undoubtedly true in philosophy, that by wandering far away into invisible notions has almost quite destroyed itself, and it can never be recovered or continued but by returning into the same sensible paths in which it did at first proceed.

from OBSERVATION I. OF THE POINT OF A SMALL SHARP NEEDLE.

... We will begin these our inquiries ... with the observations of bodies of the most simple nature first, and so gradually proceed to those of a more compounded one.

[1] *put to her shifts* Forced to rely on her cunning.

[2] *Peripatetics* Followers of Aristotle.

In prosecution of which method, we shall begin with a physical point, of which kind the point of a needle is commonly reckoned for one—and is indeed, for the most part, made so sharp that the naked eye cannot distinguish any parts of it. It very easily pierces, and makes its way through all kind of bodies softer than itself. But if viewed with a very good microscope, we may find that the top of a needle (though as to the sense very sharp) appears a broad, blunt, and very irregular end, not resembling a cone, as is imagined, but only a piece of a tapering body with a great part of the top removed or deficient. The points of pins are yet more blunt, and the points of the most curious mathematical instruments do very seldom arrive at so great a sharpness; how much therefore can be built upon demonstrations made only by the productions of the ruler and compasses, he will be better able to consider that shall but view those points and lines with a microscope.

Now, though this point be commonly accounted the sharpest (whence when we would express the sharpness of a point the most superlatively, we say, "as sharp as a needle") yet the microscope can afford us hundreds of instances of points many thousand times sharper, such as those of the hairs, and bristles, and claws of multitudes of insects; the thorns, or crooks, or hairs of leaves, and other small vegetables.... Yet I doubt not but, were we able practically to make microscopes according to the theory of them, we might find hills, and dales, and pores, and a sufficient breadth or expansion to give all those parts elbow-room even in the blunt top of the very point of any of these so very sharp bodies. For certainly the quantity or extension of any body may be divisible *in infinitum*, though perhaps not the matter.

But to proceed. The image we have here exhibited in the first figure was the top of a small and very sharp needle, whose point (*a, a*) nevertheless appeared through the microscope above a quarter of an inch broad, not round nor flat, but irregular and uneven, so that it seemed to have been big enough to have afforded a hundred armed mites room enough to be ranged by each other without endangering the breaking one another's necks by being thrust off on either side. The

From *Schema* 2: The point of a needle and a period.

surface of which, though appearing to the naked eye very smooth, could not nevertheless hide a multitude of holes and scratches and ruggednesses from being discovered by the microscope to invest it, several of which inequalities (as A, B, C, seemed holes made by some small specks of rust; and D some adventitious[1] body that stuck very close to it) were casual.[2] All the rest that roughen the surface were only so many marks of the rudeness and bungling of art. So inaccurate is it in all its productions, even in those which seem most neat, that if examined with an organ more acute than that by which they were made, the more we see of their shape, the less appearance will there be of their beauty; whereas in the works of nature the deepest discoveries show us the greatest excellencies. An evident argument that he that was the author of all these things was no other than omnipotent, being able to include as great a variety of parts and contrivances in the yet smallest discernable point as in those vaster bodies (which comparatively are called also points) such as the Earth, sun, or planets. Nor need it seem strange that the Earth itself may be by analogy called a physical point: for as its body, though now so near us as to fill our eyes and fancies with a sense of the vastness of it, may, by a little distance and some convenient diminishing glasses, be made vanish into a scarce visible speck or point (as I have often tried on the moon and, when not too bright, on the sun itself). So could a mechanical contrivance successfully answer our

[1] *adventitious* I.e., not part of the needle.

[2] *were casual* Occurred by chance.

theory, we might see the least spot as big as the Earth itself; and discover, as Descartes also conjectures,[1] as great a variety of bodies in the moon, or planets, as in the Earth.

from OBSERVATION 39. OF THE EYES AND HEAD OF A GREAT DRONE-FLY, AND OF SEVERAL OTHER CREATURES.

I took a large grey drone-fly that had a large head, but a small and slender body in proportion to it, and cutting off its head, I fixed it with the forepart or face upwards upon my object plate. (This I made choice of rather than the head of a great blue fly because, my enquiry being now about the eyes, I found this fly to have, first, the biggest clusters of eyes in proportion to his head of any small kind of fly that I have yet seen, it being somewhat inclining towards the make of the large dragonflies. Next, because there is a greater variety in the knobs or balls of each cluster, then is of any small fly.) Then examining it according to my usual manner, by varying the degrees of light and altering its position to each kind of light, I drew that representation of it which is delineated in the 24 *Scheme*,[2] and found these things to be as plain and evident as notable and pleasant.

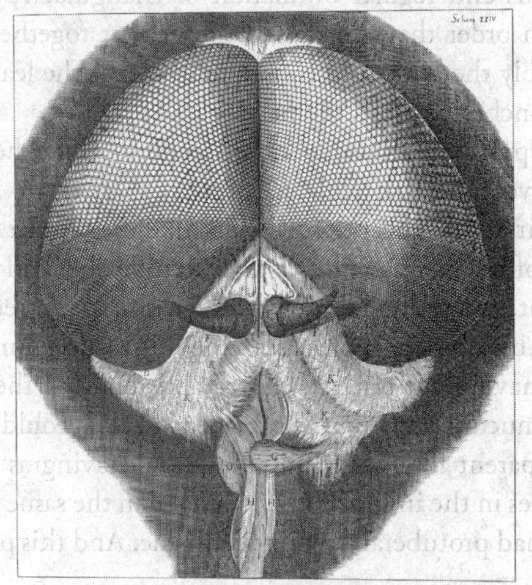

Schema 24: The eyes of a drone-fly.

First, that the greatest part of the face, nay, of the head, was nothing else but two large and protuberant bunches, or prominent parts, A B C D E A, the surface of each of which was all covered over, or shaped into a multitude of small hemispheres placed in a triagonal order, that being the closest and most compacted, and in that order, ranged over the whole surface of the eye in very lovely rows, between each of which, as is necessary, were left long and regular trenches, the bottoms of every of which were perfectly entire and not at all perforated or drilled through, which I most certainly was assured of by the regularly reflected image of certain objects which I moved to and fro between the head and the light. And by examining the cornea or outward skin after I had stripped it off from the several substances that lay within it, and by looking both upon the inside and against the light.

Next, that of those multitudes of hemispheres there were observable two degrees of bigness. The half of them that were lowermost and looked toward the ground or their own legs (namely, C D E), C D E being a pretty deal smaller than the other (namely, A B C E), A B C E, that looked upward and sideways or foreright and backward, which variety I have not found in any other small fly.

Thirdly, that every one of these hemispheres, as they seemed to be pretty near the true shape of a hemisphere, so was the surface exceeding smooth and regular, reflecting as exact, regular, and perfect an image of any object from the surface of them as a small ball of quicksilver[3] of that bigness would do, but nothing near so vivid, the reflection from these being very languid, much like the reflection from the outside of water, glass, crystal, &c. In so much that in each of these hemispheres, I have been able to discover a landscape of those things which lay before my window, one thing of which was a large tree, whose trunk and top I could plainly discover, as I could also the parts of my window, and my hand and fingers if I held it between the window and the object; a small draft of nineteen of which, as they appeared in the bigger magnifying glass to reflect the image of the two windows of my chamber, are delineated in the third figure of the 23 *Schema*.

[1] *Descartes also conjectures* See the tenth discourse in Descartes's *Optics* (1637).

[2] *Scheme* Diagrams (plural of *schema*).

[3] *quicksilver* Mercury.

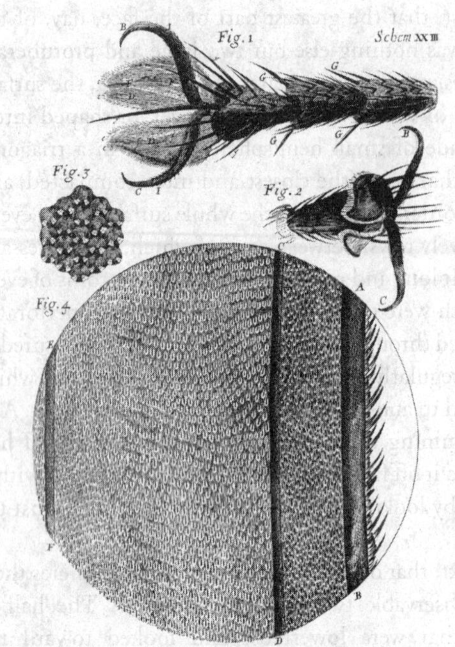

Schema 23: The feet of flies (figures 1 and 2), the wing of a fly (figure 4), and Hooke's windows reflected in the eyes of a drone-fly (figure 3).

Fourthly, that these rows were so disposed that there was no quarter visible from his head that there was not some of these hemispheres directed against, so that a fly may be truly said to have an eye every way, and to be really circumspect.[1] And it was further observable that that way where the trunk of his body did hinder his prospect backward, these protuberances were elevated, as it were, above the plane of his shoulders and back, so that he was able to see backwards also over his back.

Fifthly, in living flies I have observed, that when any small mote or dust which flies up and down the air chances to light upon any part of these knobs, as it is sure to stick firmly to it and not fall, ... so the fly presently makes use of his two fore-feet instead of eyelids, with which, as with two brooms or brushes, they being all bestuck with bristles, he often sweeps or brushes off whatever hinders the prospect of any of his hemispheres, and then, to free his legs from that dirt, he rubs them one against another, the pointed bristles or tenters[2] of which looking both one way, the rubbing of them to and fro one against another, does cleanse them in the same manner as I have observed those that card wool[3] to cleanse their cards by placing their cards so as the teeth of both look the same way, and then rubbing them one against another. In the very same manner do they brush and cleanse their bodies and wings, as I shall by and by show; other creatures have other contrivances for the cleansing and clearing their eyes.

Sixthly, that the number of the pearls or hemispheres in the clusters of this fly was near 14,000. Which I judged by numbering certain rows of them several ways, and casting up the whole content, accounting each cluster to contain about seven thousand pearls, three thousand of which were of a size, and consequently the rows not so thick, and the four thousand I accounted to be the number of the smaller pearls next the feet and proboscis. Other animals I observed to have yet a greater number, as the dragon-fly or adderbolt, and others to have a much less company, as an ant, &c. and several other small flies and insects.

Seventhly, that the order of these eyes or hemispheres was altogether curious and admirable, they being placed in all kind of flies and aerial animals in a most curious and regular ordination of triangular rows, in which order they are ranged the nearest together that possibly they can, and consequently leave the least pits or trenches between them....

Upon the anatomy or dissection of the head, I observed these particulars:

First, that this outward skin, like the cornea of the eyes of the greater animals, was both flexible and transparent, and seemed through the microscope perfectly to resemble the very substance of the cornea of a man's eye. For, having cut out the cluster and removed the dark and mucous stuff that is subjacent to it, I could see it transparent like a thin piece of skin, having as many cavities in the inside of it, and ranged in the same order, as it had protuberances on the outside. And this propri-

[1] *circumspect* I.e., able to see everywhere.

[2] *tenters* Hooks.

[3] *card wool* Separate wool fibers using brushes with hooked bristles, called cards.

ety[1] I found the same in all the animals that had it, whether flies or shellfish.

Secondly, I found that all animals that I have observed with those kind of eyes have within this cornea a certain clear liquor or juice, though in a very little quantity....

from Margaret Cavendish, *Observations upon Experimental Philosophy, To Which Is Added, The Description of a New Blazing World* (1666)

Cavendish was one of few eighteenth-century women who wrote on the subject of natural philosophy. Although she disagreed with the experimental methods of the Royal Society, she was not entirely on the side of tradition—she proposed her own system of nature in contradiction to Aristotle's. Her *Observations upon Experimental Philosophy* includes a concerted attack on the experimental philosophers' reliance on sensory perception, especially perception aided by scientific instruments, as exemplified in the role of the microscope in Hooke's *Micrographia*.

Along with her treatise, Cavendish published a work of fiction exploring similar ideas. In this tale, a woman travels via the North Pole to the Blazing World, an undiscovered realm populated by "bird-men," "bear-men," and other strange people, who make her their empress. In the selection below, she encounters the Blazing World's incarnation of the Royal Society. (For other selections from this work see the Cavendish section earlier in this volume.)

from PREFACE TO THE ENSUING TREATISE

I confess, there are many useless and superfluous books, and perchance mine will add to the number of them; especially it is to be observed that there have been, in this latter age, as many writers of natural philosophy as in former ages there have been of moral philosophy; which multitude, I fear, will produce such a confusion of truth and falsehood as the number of moral writers formerly did with their over-nice[2] divisions of virtues and vices, whereby they did puzzle their readers so that they knew not how to distinguish between them. The like, I doubt,[3] will prove amongst our natural philosophers, who by their extracted, or rather distracted arguments, confound both divinity and natural philosophy, sense and reason, nature and art, so much as in time we shall have rather a chaos than a well-ordered universe, by their doctrine. Besides, many of their writings are but parcels taken from the ancient; but such writers are like unconscionable men in civil wars, which endeavour to pull down the hereditary mansions of noblemen and gentlemen to build a cottage of their own; for so do they pull down the learning of ancient authors to render themselves famous in composing books of their own.... Truly, the art of augury[4] was far more beneficial than the lately invented micrography; for I cannot perceive any great advantage this art doth bring us. Also, the eclipse of the sun and moon was not found out by telescopes, nor the motions of the lodestone,[5] ... nor the art of guns and gunpowder, nor the art of printing and the like, by microscopes; nay, if it be true that telescopes make appear the spots in the sun and moon, or discover some new stars, what benefit is that to us? Or if microscopes do truly represent the exterior parts and superficies of some minute creatures, what advantageth it our knowledge? For unless they could discover their interior, corporeal, figurative motions, and the obscure actions of nature, or the causes which make such or such creatures, I see no great benefit or advantage they yield to man. Or if they discover how reflected light makes loose and superficial colours, such as no sooner perceived but are again dissolved, what benefit is that to man? For neither painters nor dyers can enclose and mix that atomical dust and those reflections of light to serve them for any use. Wherefore, in my opinion, it is both time and labour lost; for the inspection of the exterior parts of vegetables doth not give us any knowledge how to sow, set, plant, and graft, so that a gardener or husbandman will gain no advantage at all by this art. The inspection

[1] *propriety* Characteristic.

[2] *over-nice* Overly particular.

[3] *doubt* Fear.

[4] *augury* Ancient Roman method of predicting the future by studying omens in the natural world.

[5] *lodestone* I.e., compass.

of a bee through a microscope will bring him no more honey; nor the inspection of a grain, more corn; neither will the inspection of dusty atoms and reflections of light teach painters how to make and mix colours—although it may perhaps be an advantage to a decayed lady's face, by placing herself in such or such a reflection of light where the dusty atoms may hide her wrinkles. The truth is, most of these arts are fallacies rather than discoveries of truth; for sense deludes more than it gives a true information, and an exterior inspection through an optic glass is so deceiving that it cannot be relied upon....

from *The Description of a New World, Called the Blazing World*[1]

... [T]he Empress asked the bird-men of the nature of thunder and lightning, and whether it was not caused by roves[2] of ice falling upon each other. To which they answered that it was not made that way, but by an encounter of cold and heat, so that an exhalation, being kindled in the clouds, did dash forth lightning, and that there were so many rentings[3] of clouds as there were sounds and cracking noises. But this opinion was contradicted by others, who affirmed that thunder was a sudden and monstrous *blas* stirred up in the air, and did not always require a cloud; but the Empress, not knowing what they meant by *blas* (for even they themselves were not able to explain the sense of this word), liked the former better. And to avoid hereafter tedious disputes, and have the truth of the phenomena of celestial bodies more exactly known, commanded the bear-men, which were her experimental philosophers, to observe them through such instruments as are called telescopes. Which they did according to her Majesty's command; but these telescopes caused more differences and divisions amongst them than ever they had before. For some said they perceived that the sun stood still and the Earth did move about it; others were of opinion that they both did move; and others said again that the Earth stood still, and sun did move. Some counted more stars than others; some discovered new stars never seen before; some fell into a great dispute with others concerning the bigness of the stars; some said the moon was another world like their terrestrial globe, and the spots therein were hills and valleys; but others would have the spots to be the terrestrial parts and the smooth and glossy parts, the sea. At last, the Empress commanded them to go with their telescopes to the very end of the pole that was joined to the world she came from, and try whether they could perceive any stars in it, which they did, and, being returned to her Majesty, reported that they had seen three blazing-stars appear there, one after another in a short time, whereof two were bright, and one dim. But they could not agree neither in this observation: for some said it was but one star which appeared at three several times, in several places; and others would have them to be three several stars, for they thought it impossible that those three several appearances should have been but one star, because every star did rise at a certain time and appeared in a certain place, and did disappear in the same place. Next, it is altogether improbable, said they, that one star should fly from place to place, especially at such a vast distance, without a visible motion, in so short a time, and appear in such different places, whereof two were quite opposite and the third sideways. Lastly, if it had been but one star, said they, it would always have kept the same splendour, which it did not, for, as above mentioned, two were bright and one was dim. After they had thus argued, the Empress began to grow angry at their telescopes, that they could give no better intelligence; for, said she, now I do plainly perceive that your glasses are false informers and, instead of discovering the truth, delude your senses. Wherefore I command you to break them, and let the bird-men trust only to their natural eyes and examine celestial objects by the motions of their own sense and reason. The bear-men replied that it was not the fault of their glasses which caused such differences in their opinions, but the sensitive motions in their optic organs did not move alike, nor were their rational judgments always regular. To which the Empress answered that if their glasses were true informers, they would rectify their irregular sense and reason. But, said she, nature has made your sense and reason more

---

[1] *The Description ... Blazing World* Further selections from *The Blazing World* can be found in the Margaret Cavendish section of this volume.

[2] *roves* Shreds.

[3] *rentings* Tearings.

regular than art has your glasses, for they are mere deluders and will never lead you to the knowledge of truth. Wherefore I command you again to break them, for you may observe the progressive motions of celestial bodies with your natural eyes better than through artificial glasses. The bear-men, being exceedingly troubled at her Majesty's displeasure concerning their telescopes, kneeled down and in the humblest manner petitioned that they might not be broken; for, said they, we take more delight in artificial delusions than in natural truths. Besides, we shall want employments for our senses and subjects for arguments; for, were there nothing but truth, and no falsehood, there would be no occasion to dispute, and by this means we should want[1] the aim and pleasure of our endeavours in confuting and contradicting each other. Neither would one man be thought wiser than another, but all would either be alike knowing and wise, or all would be fools; wherefore we most humbly beseech your Imperial Majesty to spare our glasses, which are our only delight, and as dear to us as our lives. The Empress at last consented to their request, but upon condition that their disputes and quarrels should remain within their schools, and cause no factions or disturbances in state or government. The bear-men, full of joy, returned their most humble thanks to the Empress; and to make her amends for the displeasure which their telescopes had occasioned, told her Majesty that they had several other artificial optic-glasses, which they were sure would give her Majesty a great deal more satisfaction. Amongst the rest, they brought forth several microscopes, by the means of which they could enlarge the shapes of little bodies, and make a louse appear as big as an elephant, and a mite as big as a whale. First of all they showed the Empress a gray drone-fly,[2] wherein they observed that the greatest part of her face, nay, of her head, consisted of two large bunches all covered over with a multitude of small pearls or hemispheres in a trigonal order, which pearls were of two degrees, smaller and bigger. The smaller degree was lowermost, and looked towards the ground; the other was upward, and looked sideward, forward and backward. They were all so smooth and polished that they were able to represent the image of any object. The number of them was in all 14,000. After the view of this strange and miraculous creature, and their several observations upon it, the Empress asked them what they judged those little hemispheres might be. They answered that each of them was a perfect eye, by reason[3] they perceived that each was covered with a transparent cornea[4] containing a liquor within them which resembled the watery or glassy humour[5] of the eye. To which the Empress replied that they might be glassy pearls, and yet not eyes, and that perhaps their microscopes did not truly inform them. But they smilingly answered her Majesty that she did not know the virtue of those microscopes: for they did never delude, but rectify and inform the senses; nay, the world, said they, would be but blind without them, as it has been in former ages before those microscopes were invented.

After this, they took a charcoal[6] and, viewing it with one of their best microscopes, discovered in it an infinite multitude of pores—some bigger, some less—so close and thick that they left but very little space betwixt them to be filled with a solid body. And to give her imperial Majesty a better assurance thereof, they counted in a line of them an inch long no less than 2,700 pores, from which observation they drew this following conclusion, to wit, that this multitude of pores was the cause of the blackness of the coal. For, said they, a body that has so many pores, from each of which no light is reflected, must necessarily look black, since black is nothing else but a privation of light, or a want of reflection. But the Empress replied that if all colours were made by reflection of light, and that black was as much a colour as any other colour, then certainly they contradicted themselves in saying that black was made by want of reflection. However, not to interrupt your

[1] *want* Lack.

[2] *drone-fly* See Observation 39 from Robert Hooke's *Micrographia* (1665), elsewhere in this section.

[3] *by reason* I.e., which they knew because.

[4] *cornea* Clear outer layer at the front of the eye.

[5] *humour* Liquid (as in the *aqueous humour* and *vitreous humour* of the human eye).

[6] *charcoal* In observation 39 of *Micrographia*, Hooke writes that upon examination of charcoal "there will appear an infinite company of exceedingly small and very regular pores, so thick and so orderly set, and so close to one another that they leave very little room or space between them to be filled with a solid body." He counts 2,700 pores per inch.

microscopical inspections, said she, let us see how vegetables appear through your glasses; whereupon they took a nettle[1] and, by the virtue of the microscope, discovered that underneath the points of the nettle there were certain little bags or bladders containing a poisonous liquor, and when the points had made way into the interior parts of the skin, they like syringe-pipes served to convey that same liquor into them. To which observation the Empress replied that if there were such poison in nettles, then certainly in eating of them they would hurt us inwardly as much as they do outwardly. But they answered that it belonged to physicians more than to experimental philosophers to give reasons hereof; for they only made microscopical inspections and related the figures of the natural parts of creatures according to the presentation of their glasses.

Lastly, they showed the Empress a flea and a louse,[2] which creatures through the microscope appeared so terrible to her sight that they had almost put her into a swoon. The description of all their parts would be very tedious to relate, and therefore I'll forbear it at this present. The Empress, after the view of those strangely-shaped creatures, pitied much those that are molested with them, especially poor beggars, which although they have nothing to live on themselves, are yet necessitated to maintain and feed of their own flesh and blood a company of such terrible creatures called lice; who, instead of thanks, do reward them with pains and torment them for giving them nourishment and food. But after the Empress had seen the shapes of these monstrous creatures, she desired to know whether their microscopes could hinder their biting, or at least show some means how to avoid them? To which they answered that such arts were mechanical and below that noble study of microscopical observations. Then the Empress asked them whether they had not such sorts of glasses that could enlarge and magnify the shapes of great bodies as well as they had done of little ones. Whereupon they took one of their best and largest microscopes, and endeavoured to view a whale through it; but alas! the shape of the whale was so big that its circumference went beyond the magnifying quality of the glass. Whether the error proceeded from the glass or from a wrong position of the whale against the reflection of light, I cannot certainly tell. The Empress seeing the insufficiency of those magnifying-glasses, that they were not able to enlarge all sorts of objects, asked the bear-men whether they could not make glasses of a contrary nature to those they had showed her, to wit, such as instead of enlarging or magnifying the shape or figure of an object, could contract it beneath its natural proportion. Which, in obedience to her Majesty's commands, they did; and viewing through one of the best of them, a huge and mighty whale appeared no bigger than a sprat;[3] nay, through some no bigger than a vinegar-eel.[4] And through their ordinary ones, an elephant seemed no bigger than a flea; a camel no bigger than a louse; and an ostrich no bigger than a mite. To relate all their optic observations through the several sorts of their glasses would be a tedious work, and tire even the most patient reader, wherefore I'll pass them by. Only this was very remarkable and worthy to be taken notice of, that notwithstanding their great skill, industry and ingenuity in experimental philosophy, they could yet by no means contrive such glasses by the help of which they could spy out a vacuum, with all its dimensions; nor immaterial substances, non-beings, and mixed-beings; or such as are between something and nothing; which they were very much troubled at, hoping that yet, in time, by long study and practice, they might perhaps attain to it.

[1] *nettle* In observation 25 of *Micrographia*, Hooke writes that nettle contains "bladders or receptacles full of water or, as I guess, the liquor of the plant, which was poisonous, and those small bodkins [needles] were but the syringe-pipes ... which first made way into the skin ... served to convey that poisonous juice ... into the interior and sensible parts of the skin."

[2] *a flea and a louse* Hooke describes both insects in detail in *Micrographia*.

[3] *sprat* Little fish.

[4] *vinegar-eel* Worm-like creature about 2 millimeters long.

from Voltaire, *Micromegas*[1] (1752)

Popular in England and strongly influenced by English ideas, the French writer and philosopher Voltaire was an admirer of the Royal Society. His interest in the distortions of scale the telescope and microscope could produce is evident in the story of Micromegas. An inhabitant of a very large planet orbiting the star Sirius, Micromegas is almost 130,000 feet tall. He sets out to explore the universe and arrives at the planet Saturn—where he is amused to learn that the inhabitants are a mere 6,000 feet tall—and befriends a Saturnian who shares his interest in philosophical matters. Micromegas and the Saturnian "dwarf" decide to continue Micromegas's exploration together, and eventually make their way to Earth, landing "at the northern coast of the Baltic sea, on the 5th of July … in the year 1737."

CHAPTER 4

What happened to them upon this our globe.

After some repose, they breakfasted upon two mountains, which their attendants had very palatably dressed for them. Having done this, they very naturally wished to reconnoitre[2] the little spot where they were, and accordingly they traversed it at once from north to south. The ordinary paces of the Sirian and his attendants measured about thirty thousand royal feet each; the dwarfish Saturnian usually came panting behind, for he was compelled to take nearly a dozen strides for every single step of his fellow-traveller. Figure to yourself (if I may be allowed to compare my philosophers to so humble a resemblance of them) a little tiny spaniel dodging after a captain of Prussian grenadiers.[3]

As these strangers walked at a good round pace, they made the tour of the whole globe in six and thirty hours. The sun, it must be allowed, or rather the earth itself, makes a similar tour in one day; but it must be remembered that you travel much more at your ease when you turn on your own axis than when you walk a-foot. Behold them then returned to the place from whence they set out, after having had a glimpse of that almost imperceptible sea which is called the Mediterranean, and that other narrow puddle which surrounds this mole hill under the denomination of the Great Ocean—in stepping through which, the dwarf found no occasion to wet himself higher than his middle, while his companion scarcely moistened his heel. They did what they could, both in going and in returning through each hemisphere, to discover whether this globe was inhabited or not. They stooped, they lay down, they groped about; but neither their eyes nor their hands were proportioned to the diminutive beings who run up and down the earth. They did not receive the smallest hint which could lead them to suspect that we and our little brethren, the other inhabitants of this globe, had the honour to exist.

The dwarf, who sometimes judged too hastily, decided at once that there was no living creature upon the face of the whole earth; and his chief reason for this decision was that he had seen nobody. But Micromegas, in a polite manner, made him sensible of the fallacy of this mode of reasoning: "For," said he, "with the trifling powers of your eyesight, you are not able to perceive many stars of the fiftieth magnitude, which I can see distinctly; and yet would you conclude from thence that such stars do not exist?"

"But I have groped in every place with the greatest care," said the dwarf.

"Perhaps," replied the other, "your sense of feeling is bad."

"But then," said the dwarf, "this globe is so ill constructed; it is so irregular, and of so ridiculous a form; everything here seems in a chaos. Do but observe those little rivers, not one of which is in a straight line; those ponds which are neither round, square, oval, nor anything else; and all these little pointed pebbles with which the earth is bristled (meaning the mountains), and which have torn all the skin off my feet. Observe, too, the form of the whole globe, how flat it is at the poles; it turns round the sun in so clumsy a manner that the polar circles cannot possibly be cultivated. Upon my word, what principally makes me think the place unpeopled is that no man of sense would consent to live in it."

[1] *Micromegas* Translation by Leigh Hunt, 1807.

[2] *reconnoitre* Scout out.

[3] *Prussian grenadiers* Elite soldiers chosen for their strength and height and known for formidable discipline.

"Well," said Micromegas, "it is very probable that these are not the kind of men that do live here; but still there is some chance that the globe was not made for nothing. Everything seems irregular here, say you, because you see everything drawn by lines in Saturn and Jupiter; and probably it is for this very reason that there is so much confusion here. Have I not told you again and again, that in all my travels I have everywhere met with variety in nature?"

The Saturnian replied to every tittle[1] of this reasoning; and in all likelihood the dispute would never have been brought to a conclusion had it not luckily happened that Micromegas, in his eagerness to retort, broke the string of his diamond necklace; and thus his argument and his jewels fell to the ground together. The necklace was composed of very pretty karats of unequal sizes, the largest of them weighing not more than four hundred pounds, and the smallest only fifty. The dwarf, as he picked them up, perceived on lifting them to his eye that these diamonds, from the manner in which they were cut, formed excellent microscopes. He therefore took up one of these little microscopes of about six hundred feet in diameter, and applied it to his eye, while Micromegas chose out one of two thousand five hundred feet. They were excellent, but at first our travellers could discern nothing with all their assistance. They must be adjusted a little. Now the Saturnian thought he could descry an almost imperceptible atom which was gliding between two waves in the Baltic sea; it was a whale. He caught it with a curve of his little finger very dextrously, and, placing it carefully on his thumbnail, directed the Sirian's eye to it. The Sirian, when he had caught it, laughed most heartily at the excessive diminutiveness peculiar to the inhabitants of our globe. The Saturnian was now convinced that our world was inhabited, but with his usual hastiness insisted that it was by whales only; and, as he was a mighty reasoner, he began to conjecture how so insignificant an atom could move, and whether it could possess ideas, will, liberty. Micromegas was infinitely perplexed at all this; he pored over the animal very patiently, and the result of his minute examination was that he had no reason to believe that such a thing as a soul was lodged in the whole insect. The two travellers were hence inclined to think that there could be no such thing in the whole globe, when, by the assistance of their microscopes, they perceived something larger than a whale floating on the Baltic. All the world knows that at this time a whole volley of philosophers were returning from a voyage to the polar circle,[2] under which they had made diverse discoveries of which till then nobody had ever thought. The gazettes say that their ship ran ashore on the coast of Bohemia,[3] and that they were with great difficulty saved, but in this world one can never dive to the bottom of things. For my part, I shall ingenuously tell the story as it happened, without putting in anything of my own, which is no small effort in a modern historian.

CHAPTER 5
The experiments and reasonings of the two travellers.

Micromegas stretched out his hand very gently towards the place where the object appeared, and advancing two fingers, then drawing them back for fear of a disappointment, and afterwards slowly opening and closing them, he very dextrously caught the ship that contained these gentlemen and placed it on his thumbnail, taking care however not to squeeze it too much for fear of crushing it to atoms.

"Here," said the Saturnian dwarf, "is an animal very different from the former."

The Sirian placed the supposed animal in the hollow of his hand. The passengers and crew, who thought they had been blown up by a hurricane and seated upon a species of rock, began to bestir themselves. The sailors, having hoisted up some hogsheads[4] of wine, whirled them into the hand of Micromegas, and afterwards jumped there themselves. The mathematicians, having secured their quadrants, their sectors, and their Lapland

[1] *tittle* Smallest part.

[2] *All the world … polar circle* Pierre-Louis Moreau de Maupertuis led a 1735 expedition to northern Finland to measure the shape of the earth and confirmed Newton's assertion that the earth was flatter toward its poles. After Maupertuis returned to France, he published a sensational account of the dangers of his journey, including a shipwreck in the Baltic.

[3] *their ships … coast of Bohemia* This is unlikely, as Bohemia was a landlocked nation.

[4] *hogsheads* Large barrels.

mistresses,[1] climbed down upon the fingers of the Sirian, where they made such a disturbance that he at last felt something moving which gave him a tickling sensation. This was an iron crow[2] which they had thrust about a foot deep into his forefinger. From this prick, he judged that something had issued from the little animal he held in his hand, but did not at first suspect anything more; for the microscope, which could but just compass a whale and a ship, had no hold at all on so imperceptible a being as man. I do not intend here to shock the vanity of any man, but I am obliged to request the self-conceited to stop and make a little remark here with me. It is that, supposing the height of us men to be about five feet, we make no greater figure on the earth than an animal not the six hundred thousandth part of our thumb in stature would on a ball ten feet in circumference. Figure to yourself then a being capable of holding the whole globe in his hand, endued with organs proportionate to ours (and it may very well be supposed that there are many such), then conceive, if you please, what must they think of those battles that have gained us two villages, which we have been forced only to cede again?

I have no doubt that if some captain of grenadiers should read this work, he would pull up the caps of his whole company at least two feet higher; but I must forewarn him that, do what he will, he and his men will still be infinitely diminutive.

What marvellous address[3] then must our Sirian philosopher have had, to perceive the atoms of which I am about to speak! When Leeuwenhoek and Hartsoeker first saw, or thought they saw, the seed of which we are formed,[4] they did not make anything like so astonishing a discovery. What delight did Micromegas feel at seeing these little machines move about, in examining all their pranks, in following them through all their operations! With what transport did he exclaim! With what eager joy did he thrust one of his microscopes into the hands of his companion!

[1] *Lapland mistresses* This is a jibe at Maupertuis, who brought two Finnish women back to France at the end of his expedition.

[2] *iron crow* Crowbar.

[3] *address* Skill.

[4] *Leeuwenhoek and ... are formed* Innovators in microscopy, Antony van Leeuwenhoek and Nicolaas Hartsoeker in 1674 became the first to observe human sperm cells.

"I see them distinctly," cried they both at the same instant. "Don't you perceive them carrying burdens? Now they stoop down, and now they rise up again!" So saying, their very hands trembled with pleasure at seeing such uncommon objects, and with fear lest they should for a moment lose sight of them.

from CHAPTER 6

What happened to them in their intercourse with men.

Micromegas, who was a much narrower[5] observer than his dwarf, plainly discovered that the atoms conversed. This he remarked to his companion, who would not believe that such a puny species could possibly communicate their ideas: he had the gift of tongues[6] as well as the Sirian; he did not hear these puppets speak, and therefore he took it for granted that they did not speak; besides, how, in the name of the miraculous, could such imperceptible atoms possess the organs of articulation, and what could they possibly have to say to one another? In order to speak they must think, or something like it, and if these little creatures think, they must have something equivalent to a soul: now to attribute anything like a soul to such a race as this must be absolutely absurd.

"But we must endeavour to examine these insects in the first place; it will be time enough to speculate upon them by and bye."

"Very well," replied Micromegas, drawing forth a pair of scissors which he kept for the purpose of paring his nails, and instantly forming, of a slice which he cut from his thumb nail, a large speaking trumpet, like a vast tunnel, the muzzle of which he placed in his ear. The circumference of this tunnel enveloped the ship and its whole equipage;[7] and the most feeble voice could not fail to glide along the circular fibres of this bit of nail; so that thanks to his industry, the philosopher on high could hear distinctly every buzz of the insects below. In a few hours he began even to distinguish words in what they said, and at last he actually heard French. The dwarf did the same, though with more

[5] *narrower* More accurate.

[6] *gift of tongues* Ability to speak any language.

[7] *equipage* Crew and equipment.

difficulty. The astonishment of our travellers redoubled every instant; they now heard mites talking tolerably good sense; this freak of nature appeared to them most inexplicable. You may very well suppose that the Sirian and his dwarf turned with impatience to hold some conversation with these atoms, but the dwarf was afraid that the thunder of his voice, and even more so that of Micromegas's, would only deafen the mites without making them comprehend what was said. They must try to diminish its force then. Accordingly each placed in his mouth a sort of little toothpick, the thin end of which touched the vessel. The Sirian held the dwarf upon his knees, and the ship and its equipage upon his nail; he stooped his head and practised a low tone of voice. At length, after these and ten thousand other precautions, he ventured to begin his discourse thus:

"O ye invisible insects, to whom the hand of the Creator is pleased to give birth in the abyss of infinite littleness, I give him thanks that he hath deigned to disclose unto me secrets which seemed impenetrable. Perhaps, O atoms, the court of Sirius will not condescend to regard you, but for my part, I despise no creature, and offer you my protection."

If ever man was astounded, the people who heard this address were so. They were at a loss to conceive from whence it proceeded. The chaplain of the vessel repeated the prayers of exorcism, the sailors swore, and the philosophers of the ship formed a system; but whatever system it was, they could not guess who spoke to them by it. The dwarf of Saturn, whose voice was more gentle than that of Micromegas, then told them in a few words with what beings they had to deal. He related their voyage from Saturn, gave them to understand who this Mr. Micromegas was, and after having pitied their smallness, asked them if they had always been in this miserable state so near akin to annihilation, what they did in a globe which appeared to belong to whales, whether they were happy, if they multiplied, if they had souls, and a hundred other questions of this nature.

A certain mathematician of the crew, who was more courageous than the rest, shocked to hear his soul's existence doubted, took an observation of this spokesman with pinnules pointed on a quadrant, planted himself in two different stations, and at the third spoke thus.[1] "You flatter yourself, then, Sir, that because you are a thousand fathoms from top to toe, you must be a ——"

"A thousand fathoms," cried the dwarf. "In the name of God, how came he to know my height so exactly? A thousand fathoms! My dimensions to a hair! What! and has this atom measured me? He is a geometrician, forsooth, acquainted with my stature; and yet I, who can but just descry him with the assistance of a microscope, am left totally unacquainted with his!"...

Micromegas then pronounced these words. "I am convinced, more than ever convinced, how wrong it is to judge of anything by its apparent size. O God, who hast given intelligence to particles in all appearance so contemptible, the infinitely small costeth thee as little in its production as the infinitely great; and if it be possible that there are beings even less than these, yet still they may possess a mind superior to that of the stupendous animals I have seen in heaven, a single foot of whom would cover the whole globe on which I have perched." One of our little philosophers told him that he might rest assured that there were thinking beings who were much smaller than man.... After this, he gave him to understand that there were insects who are to bees what bees are to men, what the Sirian himself was to these vast animals he spoke of, and what these gigantic creatures must be to other substances before whom they appeared but as atoms. By degrees, the conversation became interesting, and Micromegas delivered himself thus.

CHAPTER 7

A conversation with men.

"O ye intelligent little atoms, in whom the Supreme Being hath been pleased to manifest his skill and omnipotence, you must certainly taste the purest joys in a globe like yours; for, seeing the small quantity of matter you are composed of, and appearing as you do all mind, you must pass your lives in nothing but the pleasures of love and of meditation; this is the true spiritual life. I

[1] *pinnules pointed on a quadrant* Sights on an observational instrument used for measuring angles; *planted himself ... spoke thus* Based on his measurements, the mathematician uses triangulation to calculate the Saturnian's height.

have hitherto been unsuccessful in finding real happiness, but here it must undoubtedly exist!"

At these words, all the little philosophers shook their heads in silence, till at length one of them more frank than the rest confessed in good earnest that, excepting a very small number of his fellow-inhabitants who were held in no estimation at all, they were an assembly of fools, knaves and miserable wretches. "We have more than enough matter about us," continued he, "to do a great deal of mischief, if mischief proceeds from matter, and more than enough spirit, if mischief proceeds from spirit. You must know, for instance, that at the very moment I am speaking, there are no less than a hundred thousand fools of our species covered with hats, who are slaying a hundred thousand other fools, who are covered with turbans, or else they are slain by the turbans;[1] and what is more, this has been the custom in almost every part of our earth from time immemorial."

The Sirian shuddered, and asked what could be the subject of these horrible quarrels among such pitiful little animals.

"It all turns," said the philosopher, "upon two or three heaps of dirt about as big as your heel: not that a single one of these millions who are cutting one another's throats cares a straw for the heaps of dirt; the question is whether they belong to a certain man called Sultan, or to another whom, I know not why, they dignify with the appellation of Caesar.[2] Neither the one nor the other of these men has ever seen, or ever will see, the contemptible nook in question; and scarcely one of these animals, the mutual cutthroats, has ever seen the animal in whose cause they cut."

"Wretches!" cried the Sirian indignantly. "Can anyone conceive so furious an excess of rage? I have a great mind to take two or three steps and crush the whole anthill of these ludicrous little assassins."

"You need not give yourself that trouble," replied one of the philosophers; "they will ruin themselves quite fast enough. Do you know that at the end of ten years, the hundredth part of these wretches will not be in existence, for even if they should not draw a single sword, hunger, fatigue and intemperance would carry almost all of them off. Besides, it is not they whom you ought to punish, it is those sedentary barbarians who from their closets give orders for the massacre of millions of their fellow-creatures, and who afterwards solemnly thank God for it."

The traveller felt himself touched with pity for this little human race, in whom he discovered such astonishing contrasts. "Since you are of the small number of the wise," said he to these gentlemen, "and since you perhaps never murder for money, tell me, I beseech you, what can your employment be."

"We dissect flies," said the philosopher, "we measure right lines, we calculate figures; we are agreed upon two or three points which we do understand, and we dispute upon two or three thousand which we do not."

The Sirian and the Saturnian immediately took it into their heads to interrogate these thinking atoms upon what they did understand. "How far do you measure," said one of them, "from the dog-star to the great star of the constellation Gemini?"

The philosophers bawled out at once, "Thirty-two degrees and a half."

"And how far do you reckon from hence to the moon?"

"Why, in round numbers, say sixty semi-diameters of the Earth."

"Of what specific gravity[3] is your atmosphere?" said the interrogator, thinking to pose them; but they answered him to a man that common air weighed about nine hundred times less than its similar quantity of the lightest water, and nineteen thousand times less than ducat gold.

The little Saturnian dwarf, astonished at their replies, was now tempted to take for wizards the very people to whom he had but a quarter of an hour before denied the possession of souls.

At length Micromegas said to them: "Since, gentlemen, you are so well acquainted with what is without you, you are no doubt better acquainted with what is

[1] *there are … the turbans* If this is a reference to a specific war as opposed to wars in particular, it is likely the Russo-Turkish War (1735–39), a conflict between the Russian Empire and the Ottoman Empire over territory north and east of the Black Sea.

[2] *Caesar* I.e., Tsar, a derivative of Caesar.

[3] *specific gravity* Relative density of a substance (in this case, the atmosphere) to that of another (such as water), which serves as a reference point.

within you. Tell me what is your soul, and how are its ideas formed?"

Here the philosophers bust out all together as they had done before. The oldest of them quoted Aristotle, another mentioned the name of Descartes, this talked of Malebranche, that of Leibniz, and a third talked of Locke.[1] An old peripatetic[2] confidently said aloud, "the soul is a perfection and a reason, by which it has the power to be what it is. This is what Aristotle expressly declares, page 633 of the Louvre edition:

> Ε'ντελεχεια ἐστι, &c.[3]

"I don't understand too much Greek," said the giant.

"Nor I neither," said the mite of a philosopher.

"Why then," replied the Sirian, "do you quote that same Aristotle in Greek?"

"Because," replied the philosopher, "it is right to quote what you don't understand at all in the language you understand the least."

Here the Cartesian[4] took up the discourse. "The soul," said he, "is a pure spirit, which has received in its formation every one of its metaphysical ideas,[5] and which, when formed, is obliged to go to school and learn anew what it once was so well acquainted with, and which it will never know again."

"It surely was not worthwhile," replied the animal of eight leagues, "for your soul to be thus wise in its embryo state, only to be thus ignorant when you have got a beard on your chin. But what do you understand by spirit?"

"Why do you ask me that question?" said the reasoner. "I have not a single idea on the subject...."

A little partisan of Locke hopped up presently.... "I know not," said he, "by what means I think, but this I know, that I have never had a single thought of which my senses were not the cause. That there are such things as immaterial and yet intelligent substances, I don't at all doubt: but that it is possible for God to communicate thought to matter, I cannot so readily believe. I revere eternal power, and it does not become me to set bounds to it. I affirm nothing, but content myself with believing that many more things are possible than are actually thought so."

The Sirian animal smiled; he did not think the last sage the least wise. And as for the dwarf of Saturn, he would actually have embraced this little disciple of Locke if it had not been for the unaccommodating disproportion there was between their sizes. But unluckily there was another animalcule[6] in a square cap, who cut short every one of these philosophical animalcules by saying that he knew that whole secret, and that it was to be found in the abridgment of St. Thomas.[7] He then eyed our two celestial inhabitants from top to toe, and maintained to their faces that their persons, their worlds, their suns, their stars, all were made solely for the convenience of man.

---

[1] *Aristotle* Widely influential ancient Greek philosopher who defined the soul as the essence of life, and assigned different types of soul to plants, animals, and people; *Descartes* Philosopher René Descartes (1596–1650) asserted a dualistic model in which the material body, governed by the laws of physics, is understood separately from the non-material mind or soul; *Malebranche* Catholic philosopher Nicolas Malebranche (1638–1715) argued that all human thought and movement depends on the active intervention of God, and that a clear understanding of the nature of the mind is impossible; *Leibniz* Prolific mathematician and philosopher Gottfried Leibniz (1646–1716) argued that the soul and the body are of the same material but do not interact directly; *Locke* Empiricist philosopher John Locke (1632–1704) took the mind to be a blank slate which acquired knowledge through the senses (see his *Essay Concerning Human Understanding,* above).

[2] *peripatetic* Follower of Aristotle.

[3] *Ε'ντελεχεια ἐστι, &c.* From *On the Soul*: "Soul is a certain actuality, a notion or form, of that which has the capacity to be endowed with soul" (2.414a.15).

[4] *Cartesian* Follower of Descartes.

[5] *received in ... metaphysical ideas* Descartes argues that some ideas are innate in the mind and can therefore be discovered through reasoning alone; these include the idea of God, as well as principles of mathematics, logic, and geometry. In making this argument, Descartes references but does not explicitly endorse the ancient Greek philosopher Plato's doctrine of recollection, the argument that human beings are born possessing all knowledge, and that learning means remembering what the soul knew in its original state. See Descartes's *Meditations on First Philosophy*, Meditation 5.

[6] *animalcule* Single-celled organism.

[7] *abridgment of St. Thomas* Thomas Aquinas writes in his *Summa Theologica* (1265–74) that "those creatures that are less noble than man exist for the sake of man" (1.65.2).

At this monstrous assertion, our two travellers could not help rolling upon one another in endeavouring to stifle that inextinguishable laughter which, according to Homer, is the portion of the Gods only; their shoulders and bodies went and came, and in the midst of all these convulsions, the ship, which the Sirian held on his nail, fell into the Saturnian's breeches-pocket. Our good folks searched for it a long time, and at last found the whole equipage up in one corner of it; they then adjusted everything exactly as it was before. The Sirian took up the ludicrous little mites again, and spoke to them with renewed affability, although at the bottom he was very mortified to find that if these creatures were infinitely small, their pride was infinitely great. However, he promised to write them a very nice book of philosophy, purposely for their use, and added that in this book they would be able to come at the truth of everything. In fact, before his departure he actually gave them this same book; it was carried to the Academy of Sciences[1] at Paris, but when the secretary opened it, he saw nothing but blank paper.

"Ah!" said he. "This is just what I suspected."

from Sir Isaac Newton, Letter to Richard Bentley (10 December 1692)

Sir,

When I wrote my treatise about our system, I had an eye upon such principles as might work with considering men for the belief of a deity, & nothing can rejoice me more than to find it useful for that purpose. But if I have done the public any service this way, 'tis due to nothing but industry & a patient thought.

As to your first query, it seems to me that if the matter of our sun & planets & all the matter in the universe was evenly scattered throughout all the heavens, & every particle had an innate gravity towards all the rest,[2] & the whole space throughout which this matter was scattered was but finite, the matter on the outside of this space would by its gravity tend towards all the matter on the inside & by consequence fall down to the middle of the whole space & there compose one great spherical mass. But if the matter was evenly diffused through an infinite space, it would never convene into one mass, but some of it convene into one mass & some into another so as to make an infinite number of great masses scattered at great distances from one another throughout all that infinite space. And thus might the sun and fixed stars be formed, supposing the matter were of a lucid[3] nature. But how the matter should divide itself into two sorts, & that part of it which is fit to compose a shining body should fall down into one mass & make a sun, & the rest which is fit to compose an opaque body should coalesce not into one great body like the shining matter but into many little ones. Or if the sun was at first an opaque body like the planets or the planets lucid bodies like the sun, how he alone should be changed into a shining body whilst all they continue opaque, or all they be changed into opaque ones whilst he remains unchanged, I do not think explicable by mere natural causes but am forced to ascribe it to the counsel & contrivance of a voluntary agent. The same power, whether natural or supernatural, which placed the sun in the center of the orbs of the six primary planets,[4] placed Saturn in the center of the orbs[5] of his satellites, five secondary planets[6] & Jupiter in the center of the orbs of his four secondary ones, & the Earth in the center of the moon's orb; & therefore, had this cause been a blind one without contrivance & design, the sun would have been a body of the same kind with Saturn, Jupiter, & the Earth, that is without light & heat. Why there is one body in our system qualified to give light & heat to all the rest I know no reason but because the author of the system thought it convenient, & why there is but one body of this kind I know no reason but because one was sufficient to warm & enlighten all the rest. For the Cartesian hypothesis[7] of

[1] *Academy of Sciences* French counterpart to the Royal Society.

[2] *an innate ... rest* Newton did not assume this to be true; he offered no hypothesis as to the cause of gravity, innate to matter or otherwise.

[3] *lucid* Radiant.

[4] *the six primary planets* Mercury, Venus, Earth, Mars, Jupiter, and Saturn were the only planets known to Newton.

[5] *orbs* Orbits.

[6] *secondary planets* Satellites that orbit planets.

[7] *Cartesian hypothesis* In his *Principles of Philosophy* (1644), Descartes hypothesizes that the universe is full of particles, and that the swirling of these particles in vortices creates the movement of

suns losing their light & then turning into comets, & comets into planets, can have no place in my system, & is plainly erroneous because it's certain that comets as often as they appear to us descend into the system of our planets lower than the orb of Jupiter & sometimes lower than the orbs of Venus & Mercury, & yet never stay here but always return from the sun with the same degrees of motion by which they approached him.

To your second query, I answer that the motions which the planets now have could not spring from any natural cause alone, but were impressed by an intelligent agent. For since comets descend into the region of our planets & here move all manner of ways—going sometimes the same way with the planets, sometimes the contrary way, & sometimes in cross ways in planes inclined to the plane of the ecliptic[1] at all kinds of angles—it's plain that there is no natural cause which could determine all the planets, both primary & secondary, to move the same way & in the same plane without any considerable variation.[2] This must have been the effect of counsel. Nor is there any natural cause which could give the planets those just degrees of velocity in proportion to their distances from the sun & other central bodies about which they move & to the quantity of matter contained in those bodies, which were requisite to make them move in concentric orbs about those bodies. Had the planets been as swift as comets in proportion to their distances from the sun (as they would have been, had their motions been caused by their gravity, whereby the matter at the first formation of the planets might fall from the remotest regions towards the sun) they would not move in concentric orbs but in such eccentric ones as the comets move in. Were all the planets as swift as Mercury or as slow as Saturn or his satellites, or were their several velocities otherwise much greater or less than they are (as they might have been had they arose from any other cause than their gravity), or had their distances from the centers about which they move been greater or less than they are with the same velocities; or had the quantity of matter in the sun or in Saturn, Jupiter, & the Earth, & by consequence their gravitating power, been greater or less than it is, the primary planets could not have revolved about the sun, nor the secondary ones about Saturn, Jupiter, & the Earth in concentric circles as they do, but would have moved in hyperbolas or parabolas or in ellipses very eccentric. To make this system, therefore, with all its motions, required a cause which understood & compared together the quantities of matter in the several bodies of the sun & planets & the gravitating powers resulting from thence, the several distances of the primary planets from the sun & secondary ones from Saturn, Jupiter, & the Earth, & the velocities with which these planets could revolve at those distances about those quantities of matter in the central bodies. And to compare & adjust all these things together in so great a variety of bodies argues that cause to be not blind & fortuitous, but very well skilled in mechanics & geometry.

To your third query, I answer that it may be represented that the sun may, by heating those planets most which are nearest to him, cause them to be better concocted[3] & more condensed by concoction. But when I consider that our Earth is much more heated in its bowels below the upper crust by subterraneous fermentations of mineral bodies then by the sun, I see not why the interior parts of Jupiter & Saturn might not be as much heated, concocted, & coagulated by those fermentations as our Earth is, & therefore this various density should have some other cause than the various distances of the planets from the sun, & I am confirmed in this opinion by considering that the planets of Jupiter & Saturn, as they are rarer[4] than the rest, so they are vastly greater & contain a far greater quantity of matter & have many satellites about them, which qualifications surely arose not from their being placed at so great a distance from the sun but were rather the cause why the creator placed them at that great distance. For by their

planets and other bodies in space. He thought that the matter in vortices eventually condensed into stars, which provided the material for comets and planets.

[1] *ecliptic* The path of the sun relative to the stars, as observed from Earth.

[2] *all the planets … variation* There are actually small differences in the orbits of the planets which would have been known to Newton; the planes of the orbits are close to the ecliptic, but do not line up precisely.

[3] *concocted* Refined by high temperature.

[4] *rarer* Not as dense.

gravitating powers they disturb one another's motions very sensibly, as I find by some late observations of Mr. Flamsteed,[1] & had they been placed much nearer to the sun & to one another they would by the same powers have caused a considerable disturbance in the whole system....

Lastly, I see nothing extraordinary in the inclination of the Earth's axis for proving a deity, unless you will urge it as a contrivance for winter & summer & for making the Earth habitable towards the poles, & that the diurnal rotations of the sun & planets, as they could hardly arise from any cause purely mechanical, so by being determined all the same way with the annual & menstrual[2] motions they seem to make up that harmony in the system which (as I explained above) was the effect of choice rather than of chance.

from James Thomson, "A Poem Sacred to the Memory of Sir Isaac Newton" (1727)

Shall the great soul of Newton quit this Earth,
To mingle with his stars; and every Muse,
Astonished into silence, shun the weight
Of honours due to his illustrious name?
But what can man? Even now the sons of light,
In strains high-warbled to seraphic lyre,[3]
Hail his arrival on the coast of bliss.
Yet am not I deterred, though high the theme,
And sung to harps of angels; for with you,
Ethereal flames! ambitious, I aspire
In Nature's general symphony to join.

And what new wonders can ye show your guest!
Who, while on this dim spot, where mortals toil
Clouded in dust, from motion's simple laws,
Could trace the secret hand of Providence,
Wide-working through his universal frame.[4]

Have ye not listened while he bound the suns
And planets to their spheres! th'unequal task
Of humankind[5] till then. Oft had they rolled
O'er erring man the year, and oft disgraced
The pride of schools, before their course was known
Full in its causes and effects to him,
All-piercing sage! who sat not down and dreamed
Romantic schemes, defended by the din
Of specious words,[6] and tyranny of names;[7]
But, bidding his amazing mind attend,
And with heroic patience years on years
Deep-searching, saw at last the system dawn,
And shine, of all his race, on him alone.

What were his raptures then! how pure! how strong!
And what the triumphs of old Greece and Rome,
By his diminished, but the pride of boys
In some small fray victorious! when instead
Of shattered parcels of this Earth usurped
By violence unmanly, and sore deeds
Of cruelty and blood, Nature herself
Stood all-subdued by him, and open laid
Her every latent° glory to his view. *concealed*
...

What wonder thence that his devotion swelled
Responsive to his knowledge? For could he,
Whose piercing mental eye diffusive saw
The finished university[8] of things,
In all its order, magnitude, and parts,

[1] *late observations of Mr. Flamsteed* John Flamsteed (1646–1719), Fellow of the Royal Society and founder of the Greenwich Observatory, made astronomical observations more accurate than any cataloged previously.

[2] *menstrual* In a monthly cycle.

[3] *seraphic lyre* Angelic harp.

[4] *from motion's ... universal frame* Newton showed that his laws of motion and law of universal gravitation applied to objects in space as well as on earth.

[5] *unequal task / Of humankind* I.e., task to which humankind was inferior.

[6] *specious words* Apparently true claims that would prove incorrect if examined.

[7] *tyranny of names* I.e., the dominance of the ideas of distinguished ancient thinkers such as Aristotle.

[8] *finished university* Complete wholeness; i.e., conformity to universal laws.

Forbear incessant to adore that Power
Who fills, sustains, and actuates the whole.
…
O Britain's boast!… Oh, look with pity down
On humankind, a frail erroneous race!
Assuage the madness of a frantic world!
But chiefly o'er thy country's cause preside,
And be her genius called! Her councils steer,
Correct her manners, and inspire her youth!
For, guilty as she is, she brought thee forth,
And glories in thy name; she points thee out
To all her sons, and bids them eye thy star:
While in expectance of th'arousing blast,
When time shall be no more, thy sacred dust
Sleeps with her kings, and dignifies the scene.

Mark Akenside, "Hymn to Science" (1739)

SCIENCE! thou fair effusive ray
From the great source of mental day,
Free, generous, and refined!
Descend with all thy treasures fraught,° *loaded*
Illumine° each bewildered thought, *illuminate*
And bless my labouring mind.

But first with thy resistless light,
Disperse those phantoms from my sight,
Those mimic shades of thee;
The scholiast's[1] learning, sophist's cant,[2]
The visionary bigot's[3] rant,
The monk's philosophy.[4]

O! let thy powerful charms impart
The patient head, the candid heart,
Devoted to thy sway;
Which no weak passions e'er mislead,
Which still with dauntless steps proceed
Where Reason points the way.

Give me to learn each secret cause;
Let number's, figure's, motion's laws
Revealed before me stand;
These to great Nature's scenes apply,
And round the globe, and through the sky,
Disclose her working hand.

Next, to thy nobler search resigned,
The busy, restless, human mind
Through ev'ry maze pursue;
Detect Perception where it lies,
Catch the ideas as they rise,
And all their changes view.

Say from what simple springs began
The vast, ambitious thoughts of man,
Which range beyond control;
Which seek eternity to trace,
Dive through th'infinity of space,
And strain to grasp THE WHOLE.

Her secret stores let Memory tell,
Bid Fancy quit her fairy cell,
In all her colours dressed;
While, prompt her sallies to control,[5]
Reason, the judge, recalls the soul
To Truth's severest test.

Then launch through Being's wide extent;
Let the fair scale, with just ascent,
And cautious steps, be trod;
And from the dead, corporeal mass,[6]
Through each progressive order pass
To Instinct, Reason, God.

There, Science! veil thy daring eye;
Nor dive too deep, nor soar too high,
In that divine abyss;
To Faith content thy beams to lend,
Her hopes t'assure, her steps befriend,
And light her way to bliss.

[1] *scholiast* Interpreter of ancient texts.

[2] *sophist's cant* Deceptive abuse of logic.

[3] *bigot* Blindly prejudiced person.

[4] *monk's philosophy* I.e., philosophy governed by religion as opposed to reason.

[5] *prompt her … to control* Quick to restrict the leaps of fancy.

[6] *dead, corporeal mass* I.e., matter.

Then downwards take thy flight again,
Mix with the policies of men,
And social nature's ties:
The plan, the genius of each state,
Its interest and its powers relate,
Its fortunes and its rise.

Through private life pursue thy course,
Trace every action to its source,
And means and motives weigh:
Put tempers, passions in the scale,
Mark what degrees in each prevail,
And fix the doubtful sway.[1]

That last, best effort of thy skill,
To form the life, and rule the will,
Propitious° pow'r! impart: *benevolent*
Teach me to cool my passion's fires,
Make me the judge of my desires,
The master of my heart.

Raise me above the vulgar's breath,
Pursuit of fortune, fear of death,
And all in life that's mean.° *lowly*
Still true to reason be my plan,
Still let my action speak the man,[2]
Through every various scene.

Hail! queen of manners, light of truth;
Hail! charm of age, and guide of youth;
Sweet refuge of distress:
In business, thou! exact, polite;
Thou giv'st retirement its delight,
Prosperity its grace.

Of wealth, power, freedom, thou! the cause;
Foundress of order, cities, laws,
Of arts inventress, thou!
Without thee what were human kind?
How vast their wants, their thoughts how blind!
Their joys how mean! how few!

Sun of the soul! thy beams unveil!
Let others spread the daring sail,
On Fortune's faithless sea;
While undeluded, happier I
From the vain tumult timely fly,
And sit in peace with thee.

[1] *fix the doubtful sway* Secure the uncertain rule.

[2] *speak the man* I.e., communicate my character.

from Margaret Bryan, *A Compendious System of Astronomy* (1797)

Margaret Bryan operated a school for girls in London, where she taught astronomy and physics; the following excerpt is from a compilation of her lectures. Her *Compendious System* marks the beginning of a period in which popular science writing, often by women, made the recent advances in natural philosophy accessible to general readers of both sexes.

from LECTURE I

Natural objects, when properly contemplated, continually admonish[3] us in the important science of divine wisdom, leading us to consider our situation in this sublunary[4] state, our connections and dependencies, from which we learn the duties required of us and the exertions we are capable of making.

From the consideration of our mental faculties, we infer the exalted idea of a future state of existence, so naturally rising in the intelligent mind, which reflects on the never-ceasing energy of the mental power, and its independency of all mortal circumstances.

Thus, perceiving what is the purer essence of our nature and what the grosser, we are conscious that our present existence was not the primary or principal intention of our Creator. Yet, as it is allotted us preparatory to that for which we were created, it claims our particular attention, becoming either advantageous to us or otherwise accordingly as we deal with the objects which surround us.

Our superiority in the scale of beings gives us the power of applying to our own use the gifts of provi-

[3] *admonish* Instruct.

[4] *sublunary* Of this world (as opposed to a superior spiritual one).

dence, by which we are surrounded, with the greatest advantage, not only so as to supply the necessities of our mortal nature, but also to derive considerable mental gratification from them.

Shall we then neglect rightly to use the gift of reason, and thereby become unworthy of such a boon, as well as lose all the benefits to be derived from it? Certainly not. Let us rather, on the contrary, so exercise and improve our understanding as to form a right judgement of the value of things, by which alone we can be enabled to conduct ourselves according to the proper circumstances of the state in which we are placed—a business which requires more caution in the investigation than young minds are apt to imagine, implying a thorough knowledge of the human mind, which can be obtained only by a careful examination of its capacities and infirmities.

Before entering upon this important investigation, my duty prompts me to offer some reflections on that hand which formed us; that divine mind which directs all our involuntary operations; and that benevolence which renders these operations instrumental to the comfort and happiness of all its creatures.

Yet, how can I presume to recount the works of the Almighty, or show the wisdom of his counsels! Far above the narrow scale of human inquiry, far out of the reach of the feeble efforts of human comprehension, are such investigations: yet are his attributes discoverable in his wise administration, made evident to us through the medium of our senses. Let us, then, receive these emanations of the divine mind shed down upon us, with joy and thankfulness; and, like the effects of the rays of the sun falling upon our crops of corn, which makes them yield forth their abundance, so let the influence of divine benevolence act on our minds, perfecting all that is good in us, and expanding our hearts with universal philanthropy.

This world is by no means barren of comforts to those who cultivate a relish for the delights it offers, avoiding satiety;[1] for, by a proper application of the objects of sense, we shall learn how to render the things of this life not only serviceable but delightful to us. …

How delightful is the task of inquiry! How important the advantages resulting from investigation! Amply is the searcher into nature rewarded by the extension of ideas and the strength of judgment acquired, by which the human understanding, soaring above vulgar prejudices, views the works of God with satisfaction, deriving consolation from every object in nature!

[1] *satiety* Complete satisfaction; i.e., the absence of curiosity.

from Benjamin Franklin, Letter to Joseph Priestley (8 September 1780)

Dear Sir,

… I always rejoice to hear of your being still employed in experimental researches into nature, and of the success you meet with. The rapid progress true science now makes occasions my regretting sometimes that I was born so soon. It is impossible to imagine the height to which may be carried in a 1000 years the power of man over matter. We may perhaps learn to deprive large masses of their gravity & give them absolute levity,[2] for the sake of easy transport. Agriculture may diminish its labour & double its produce. All diseases may by sure means be prevented or cured, not excepting even that of old age, and our lives lengthened at pleasure even beyond the antediluvian[3] standard. O that moral science were in as fair a way of improvement, that men would cease to be wolves to one another, and the human beings would at length learn what they now improperly call humanity.

Isaac Watts, "Against Idleness and Mischief" (1715)

How doth the little busy bee
Improve each shining hour,
And gather honey all the day
From every opening flower!

How skillfully she builds her cell!
How neat she spreads the wax!

[2] *absolute levity* Weightlessness.

[3] *antediluvian* From before the Flood; according to Genesis, the early patriarchs lived many hundreds of years, with lifespans gradually decreasing after the Flood.

And labours hard to store it well
With the sweet food she makes.

In works of labour, or of skill,
I would be busy too;
For Satan finds some mischief still° *always*
For idle hands to do.

In books, or work, or healthful play,
Let my first years be passed,
That I may give for every day
Some good account at last.

Isaac Watts, "Man Frail, and God Eternal"[1] (1719)

Our God, our help in ages past,
Our hope for years to come,
Our shelter from the stormy blast,
And our eternal home.

Under the shadow of Thy throne
Thy saints have dwelt secure.
Sufficient is Thine arm alone,
And our defense is sure.

Before the hills in order stood,
Or earth received her frame,
From everlasting Thou art God,
To endless years the same.

Thy word commands our flesh to dust,
Return, ye sons of men.
All nations rose from earth at first,
And turn to earth again.

A thousand ages in Thy sight
Are like an evening gone;
Short as the watch that ends the night,
Before the rising sun.

The busy tribes of flesh and blood
With all their lives and cares
Are carried downwards by thy flood,
And lost in following years.

Time, like an ever-rolling stream,
Bears all its sons away.
They fly forgotten, as a dream
Dies at the op'ning day.

Like flow'ry fields the nations stand
Pleased with the morning light.
The flow'rs beneath the mower's hand
Lie with'ring ere 'tis night.

Our God, our help in ages past,
Our hope for years to come,
Be Thou our guard while troubles last,
And our eternal home.

[1] *Man … Eternal* An imitation of lines 1–6 of Psalm 90.

from David Hume, *An Enquiry Concerning Human Understanding* (1748)

from SECTION 10: "OF MIRACLES"

A miracle is a violation of the laws of nature; and, as a firm and unalterable experience has established these laws, the proof against a miracle, from the very nature of the fact, is as entire as any argument from experience can possibly be imagined. Why is it more than probable that all men must die; that lead cannot, of itself, remain suspended in the air; that fire consumes wood, and is extinguished by water; unless it be, that these events are found agreeable to the laws of nature, and there is required a violation of these laws, or in other words, a miracle to prevent them? Nothing is esteemed a miracle if it ever happen in the common course of nature. It is no miracle that a man, seemingly in good health, should die on a sudden; because such a kind of death, though more unusual than any other, has yet been frequently observed to happen. But it is a miracle that a dead man should come to life, because that has never been observed in any age or country. There must, therefore, be a uniform experience against every miraculous event, otherwise the event would not merit that appellation. And as a uniform experience amounts to a proof, there is here a direct and full proof, from the nature of the fact, against the existence of any miracle; nor can such a proof be destroyed, or the miracle rendered credible, but by an opposite proof, which is superior.

The plain consequence is (and it is a general maxim worthy of our attention), "That no testimony is sufficient to establish a miracle, unless the testimony be of such a kind that its falsehood would be more miraculous than the fact which it endeavors to establish; and even in that case there is a mutual destruction of arguments, and the superior only gives us an assurance suitable to that degree of force which remains after deducting the inferior." When anyone tells me that he saw a dead man restored to life, I immediately consider with myself whether it be more probable that this person should either deceive or be deceived, or that the fact which he relates should really have happened. I weigh the one miracle against the other; and according to the superiority which I discover, I pronounce my decision, and always reject the greater miracle. If the falsehood of his testimony would be more miraculous than the event which he relates, then, and not till then, can he pretend to command my belief or opinion.

In the foregoing reasoning we have supposed that the testimony upon which a miracle is founded may possibly amount to an entire proof, and that the falsehood of that testimony would be a real prodigy. But it is easy to show that we have been a great deal too liberal in our concession, and that there never was a miraculous event established on so full an evidence.

For *first*, there is not to be found, in all history, any miracle attested by a sufficient number of men of such unquestioned good sense, education, and learning, as to secure us against all delusion in themselves; of such undoubted integrity, as to place them beyond all suspicion of any design to deceive others; of such credit and reputation in the eyes of mankind, as to have a great deal to lose in case of their being detected in any falsehood; and at the same time, attesting facts performed in such a public manner and in so celebrated a part of the world, as to render the detection unavoidable. All which circumstances are requisite to give us a full assurance in the testimony of men.

Secondly. We may observe in human nature a principle which, if strictly examined, will be found to diminish extremely the assurance which we might, from human testimony, have in any kind of prodigy. The maxim by which we commonly conduct ourselves in our reasonings is that the objects of which we have no experience resemble those of which we have; that what we have found to be most usual is always most probable; and that where there is an opposition of arguments, we ought to give the preference to such as are founded on the greatest number of past observations. But though, in proceeding by this rule, we readily reject any fact which is unusual and incredible in an ordinary degree, yet in advancing farther, the mind observes not always the same rule; but when anything is affirmed utterly absurd and miraculous, it rather the more readily admits of such a fact, upon account of that very circumstance which ought to destroy all its authority. The passion of surprise and wonder, arising from miracles, being an agreeable emotion, gives a sensible tendency towards the belief of those events from which it is derived. And this goes so far that even those who cannot enjoy this pleasure immediately, nor can believe those miraculous events of which they are informed, yet love to partake of the satisfaction at second-hand or by rebound, and place a pride and delight in exciting the admiration of others. ...

Thirdly. It forms a strong presumption against all supernatural and miraculous relations, that they are observed chiefly to abound among ignorant and barbarous nations; or if a civilized people has ever given admission to any of them, that people will be found to have received them from ignorant and barbarous ancestors, who transmitted them with that inviolable sanction and authority which always attend received opinions. When we peruse the first histories of all nations, we are apt to imagine ourselves transported into some new world, where the whole frame of nature is disjointed, and every element performs its operations in a different manner from what it does at present. Battles, revolutions, pestilence, famine, and death are never the effect of those natural causes which we experience. Prodigies, omens, oracles, judgments, quite obscure the few natural events that are intermingled with them. But as the former grow thinner every page, in proportion as we advance nearer the enlightened ages, we soon learn that there is nothing mysterious or supernatural in the case, but that all proceeds from the usual propensity of mankind towards the marvelous, and that, though this inclination may at intervals receive a check from sense and learning, it can never be thoroughly extirpated from human nature....

Upon the whole, then, it appears that no testimony for any kind of miracle has ever amounted to a probability, much less to a proof; and that, even supposing it amounted to a proof, it would be opposed by another proof derived from the very nature of the fact which it would endeavor to establish. It is experience only which gives authority to human testimony; and it is the same experience which assures us of the laws of nature. When, therefore, these two kinds of experience are contrary, we have nothing to do but subtract the one from the other and embrace an opinion, either on one side or the other, with that assurance which arises from the remainder. But, according to the principle here explained, this subtraction, with regard to all popular religions, amounts to an entire annihilation; and therefore we may establish it as a maxim, that no human testimony can have such force as to prove a miracle and make it a just foundation for any such system of religion....

What we have said of miracles may be applied, without any variation, to prophecies; and indeed, all prophecies are real miracles, and as such only can be admitted as proofs of any revelation. If it did not exceed the capacity of human nature to foretell future events, it would be absurd to employ any prophecy as an argument for a divine mission or authority from heaven. So that, upon the whole, we may conclude that the Christian religion not only was at first attended with miracles, but even at this day cannot be believed by any reasonable person without one. Mere reason is insufficient to convince us of its veracity. And whoever is moved by faith to assent to it, is conscious of a continued miracle in his own person, which subverts all the principles of his understanding, and gives him a determination to believe what is most contrary to custom and experience.

from James Boswell, *The Life of Samuel Johnson* (1791)

Next morning I found [Johnson] alone, and have preserved the following fragments of his conversation. Of a gentleman who was mentioned, he said, "I have not met with any man for a long time who has given me such general displeasure. He is totally unfixed in his principles, and wants to puzzle other people." I said his principles had been poisoned by a noted infidel writer,[1] but that he was, nevertheless, a benevolent good man. JOHNSON. "We can have no dependence upon that instinctive, that constitutional goodness which is not founded upon principle. I grant you that such a man may be a very amiable member of society. I can conceive him placed in such a situation that he is not much tempted to deviate from what is right; and as every man prefers virtue, when there is not some strong incitement to transgress its precepts, I can conceive him doing nothing wrong. But if such a man stood in need of money, I should not like to trust him; and I should certainly not trust him with young ladies, for *there* there is always temptation. Hume, and other skeptical innovators, are vain men, and will gratify themselves at any expense. Truth will not afford sufficient food to their vanity; so they have betaken themselves to error. Truth, sir, is a cow which will yield such people no more milk, and so they are gone to milk the bull. If I could have allowed myself to gratify my vanity at the expense of truth, what fame might I have acquired. Everything which Hume has advanced against Christianity had passed through my mind long before he wrote. Always remember this, that after a system is well settled upon positive evidence, a few partial objections ought not to shake it. The human mind is so limited that it cannot take in all the parts of a subject, so that there may be objections raised against anything. There are objections against a *plenum*, and objections against a *vacuum*; yet one of them must certainly be true."[2]

I mentioned Hume's argument against the belief of miracles, that it is more probable that the witnesses to the

[1] *noted infidel writer* I.e., Hume.

[2] *There are ... true* That is, either all space is full of matter (*plenum*), or there are parts of space that are empty of matter (*vacuum*).

truth of them are mistaken, or speak falsely, than that the miracles should be true.[1] JOHNSON. "Why, sir, the great difficulty of proving miracles should make us very cautious in believing them. But let us consider; although God has made nature to operate by certain fixed laws, yet it is not unreasonable to think that he may suspend those laws, in order to establish a system highly advantageous to mankind. Now the Christian religion is a most beneficial system, as it gives us light and certainty where we were before in darkness and doubt. The miracles which prove it are attested by men who had no interest in deceiving us; but who, on the contrary, were told that they should suffer persecution, and did actually lay down their lives in confirmation of the truth of the facts which they asserted. Indeed, for some centuries the heathens did not pretend to deny the miracles; but said they were performed by the aid of evil spirits. This is a circumstance of great weight. Then, sir, when we take the proofs derived from prophecies which have been so exactly fulfilled, we have most satisfactory evidence. Supposing a miracle possible, as to which, in my opinion, there can be no doubt, we have as strong evidence for the miracles in support of Christianity, as the nature of the thing admits."

from *The Spectator* No. 7 (8 March 1711)

Going yesterday to dine with an old acquaintance, I had the misfortune to find his whole family very much dejected. Upon asking him the occasion of it, he told me that his wife had dreamt a strange dream the night before, which they were afraid portended some misfortune to themselves, or to their children. At her coming into the room, I observed a settled melancholy in her countenance, which I should have been troubled for, had I not heard from whence it proceeded. We were no sooner sat down, but after having looked upon me a little while, "My dear," says she, turning to her husband, "you may now see the stranger that was in the candle last night." Soon after this, as they began to talk of family affairs, a little boy at the lower end of the table told her that he was to go into join-hand[2] on Thursday. "*Thursday!*" says she. "No, child, if it please God, you shall not begin upon Childermas-day,[3] tell your writing-master that Friday will be soon enough." I was reflecting with myself on the oddness of her fancy, and wondering that anybody would establish it as a rule to lose a day in every week. In the midst of these my musings, she desired me to reach her a little salt upon the point of my knife, which I did in such a trepidation and hurry of obedience that I let it drop by the way; at which she immediately startled, and said it fell towards her. Upon this I looked very blank and, observing the concern of the whole table, began to consider myself, with some confusion, as a person that had brought a disaster upon the family. The lady, however, recovering herself after a little space, said to her husband, with a sigh, "My dear, misfortunes never come single." …

I took my leave immediately after dinner, and withdrew to my own lodgings. Upon my return home, I fell into a profound contemplation on the evils that attend these superstitious follies of mankind; how they subject us to imaginary afflictions, and additional sorrows, that do not properly come within our lot. As if the natural calamities of life were not sufficient for it, we turn the most indifferent circumstances into misfortunes, and suffer as much from trifling accidents as from real evils. I have known the shooting of a star spoil a night's rest, and have seen a man in love grow pale and lose his appetite upon the plucking of a merry-thought.[4] A screech-owl at midnight has alarmed a family more than a band of robbers; nay, the voice of a cricket hath struck more terror than the roaring of a lion. There is nothing so inconsiderable, which may not appear dreadful to an imagination that is filled with omens and prognostics. A rusty nail, or a crooked pin, shoot up into prodigies. …

[1] *Hume's … true* See Hume's "Of Miracles," *An Enquiry Concerning Human Understanding* (1748).

[2] *join-hand* Cursive writing.

[3] *Childermas-day* Day of the Festival of the Innocents, commemorating the slaughter of the children by Herod (see Matthew 2.16). Also, the day of the week, throughout the year, that corresponds to the day of this festival.

[4] *merry-thought* Wishbone.

For my part, I should be very much troubled were I endowed with this divining quality, though it should inform me truly of everything that can befall me. I would not anticipate the relish of any happiness, nor feel the weight of any misery, before it actually arrives.

I know but one way of fortifying my soul against these gloomy presages and terrors of mind, and that is, by securing to myself the friendship and protection of that Being who disposes of events, and governs futurity. He sees, at one view, the whole thread of my existence, not only that part of it which I have already passed through, but that which runs forward into all the depths of eternity. When I lay me down to sleep, I recommend myself to His care. When I awake, I give myself up to His direction. Amidst all the evils that threaten me, I will look up to Him for help, and question not but He will either avert them, or turn them to my advantage. Though I know neither the time nor the manner of the death I am to die, I am not at all solicitous about it, because I am sure that He knows them both, and that He will not fail to comfort and support me under them.

William Hogarth, *Credulity, Superstition, and Fanaticism: A Medley* (1762)

This picture (reproduced on the following page) depicts a Methodist service observed through the barred window by an amazed "infidel." The ape-like faces of the congregation are contorted with emotion as they listen to their preacher, who speaks with such vehemence that his wig has flown off (revealing the characteristically shaved head, or tonsure, of a Catholic priest underneath) and the board above his head has cracked from the force of his voice. A sign above him reads "To St. Money-trap," and one below him reads, "I Speak as a Fool." On the pulpit are dolls representing Julius Caesar, Mrs. Veal (a gentlewoman who was famously said to have appeared to her friend on the day following her death, written up in a short story by Daniel Defoe), and Sir George Villiers.

Below, a minister shoves an icon down a woman's dress in a fit of what is portrayed as both sexual and religious ecstasy. A little devil whispers in the ears of two sleepers, and the unused "Poor's Box" grows cobwebs beside them (because to Hogarth emphasis on faith implies neglect of good works). At the lectern stands a clerk, possibly meant to represent Calvinist leader George Whitefield, with two disembodied cherubs with birds' wings, who are meant to satirize bad religious art. On the lectern is inscribed "Continually do Cry," and on its side is the text "Only Love to us be giv'n / Lord we ask no other Heav'n / Hymn by G. Whitfield Page 130." The man to the left of the picture, whose knife reads "Bloody," has often been thought to represent a converted Jew. He is killing lice. Below him a woman gives birth to rabbits (Mary Toft, who had falsely claimed to have done this in 1726, became a symbol of the power of credulity) and a shoe-shine boy watches while spitting nails. His gin bottle is corked with an icon and his basket contains "Whitfield's Journal" and rests upon "Demonology by K. James 1st."

In the bottom right corner is an enlarged human brain resting on "Wesley's Sermons" and "Glanvill on Witches." (Charles Wesley was one of the founders of Methodism, and Joseph Glanvill was a seventeenth-century Church of England clergyman who had gathered stories of witchcraft in the hope of proving its existence.) This brain forms the bulb of a thermometer measuring the level of "raving," which is only registering lukewarm. Another thermometer measures "vociferation" and is topped with a mouth yelling "Blood Blood Blood Blood." Above the entire congregation hangs a chandelier that depicts "A New and Correct Globe of Hell by Romaine."

Hogarth cites 1 John 4.1 below the engraving: "Believe not every spirit, but try the spirits whether they are of God: because many false prophets are gone out into the world."

William Hogarth, *Credulity, Superstition, and Fanaticism: A Medley* (1762).

from Erasmus Darwin, *Loves of the Plants* (1789)

Loves of the Plants elaborates and clarifies the system of plant classification first advanced by Swedish botanist Carl Linnaeus (1707–78), the originator of our modern method of taxonomy. To inspire the interest of general readers, Darwin composed his work as a long poem, lovingly anthropomorphizing more than eighty species. Because Darwin did not shy away from Linnaeus's sexualized language—and because Darwin's politics in general were unusually liberal—conservatives detested the work, which was nonetheless highly popular. *Loves of the Plants* contains the seeds of a surprisingly modern understanding of evolution, a concept that would be much more clearly articulated and demonstrated by Erasmus's more famous grandson, Charles, seventy years later.

from the ADVERTISEMENT

The general design of the following sheets is to enlist imagination under the banner of science; and to lead her votaries[1] from looser analogies, which dress out the imagery of poetry, to the stricter ones, which form the ratiocination[2] of philosophy. While their particular design is to induce the ingenious to cultivate the knowledge of botany by introducing them to the vestibule of that delightful science, and recommending to their attention the immortal works of the celebrated Swedish naturalist, Linnaeus.

from the PROEM

Lo, here a CAMERA OBSCURA[3] is presented to thy view, in which are lights and shades dancing on a whited canvass, and magnified into apparent life! If thou art perfectly at leisure for such trivial amusement, walk in and view the wonders of my ENCHANTED GARDEN.…

… [T]hou mayst contemplate [the plants] as diverse little pictures suspended over the chimney of a lady's dressing room, connected only by the slight festoon of ribbons. And which, though thou mayst not be acquainted with the originals, may amuse thee by the beauty of their persons, their graceful attitudes, or the brilliance of their dress.

FAREWELL.

from LOVES OF THE PLANTS

…

First the tall CANNA[4] lifts his curled brow
Erect to heaven, and plights his nuptial vow;
The virtuous pair, in milder regions born,
Dread the rude blast of Autumn's icy morn;
Round the chill fair° he folds his crimson vest, *beauty*
And clasps the timorous° beauty to his breast. *shy*
Thy love, CALLITRICHE,[5] two virgins share,
Smit° with thy starry eye and radiant hair;— *smitten*
On the green margin sits the youth, and laves° *washes*
His floating train of tresses in the waves;
Sees his fair features paint the streams that pass,
And bends for ever o'er the watery glass.
Two brother swains,° of COLLIN'S[6] gentle name, *suitors*
The same their features, and their forms the same,
With rival love for fair COLLINIA sigh,
Knit the dark brow, and roll the unsteady eye.
With sweet concern the pitying beauty mourns,
And sooths with smiles the jealous pair by turns.

…

[1] *votaries* Devotees.

[2] *ratiocination* Reasoning process.

[3] *CAMERA OBSCURA* Precursor to the camera, used to project images onto a screen in a dark room.

[4] [Darwin's note] Cane, or Indian Reed. One male and one female inhabit each flower. It is brought from between the tropics to our hot-houses, and bears a beautiful crimson flower.…

[5] [Darwin's note] Fine-Hair, Stargrass. One male and two females inhabit each flower. The upper leaves grow in form of a star; … its stems and leaves float far on the water, and are often so matted together as to bear a person walking on them. The male sometimes lives in a separate flower.

[6] [Darwin's note] Two males, one female. I have lately observed a very singular circumstance in this flower; the two males stand widely diverging from each other, and the female bends herself into contact first with one of them, and after some time leaves this, and applies herself to the other. It is probable one of the anthers [pollen vessels] may be mature before the other.…

Wooed with long care, CURCUMA[1] cold and shy
Meets her fond husband with averted eye:
Four beardless youths the obdurate° beauty move *unyielding*
With soft attentions of Platonic[2] love.
…
The fell° SILENE[3] and her sisters fair, *deadly*
Skilled in destruction, spread the viscous snare.
The harlot-band ten lofty bravoes° screen, *mercenaries*
And, frowning, guard the magic nets unseen.
Haste glittering nations, tenants of the air,
Oh, steer from hence your viewless course afar!
If with soft words, sweet blushes, nods, and smiles,
The three dread Sirens[4] lure you to their toils,
Limed[5] by their art in vain you point your stings,
In vain the efforts of your whirring wings!
Go, seek your gilded mates and infant hives,
Nor taste the honey purchased with your lives!
….

[1] [Darwin's note] Turmeric. One male and one female inhabit this flower; but there are besides four imperfect males, or filaments without anthers upon them, called by Linnaeus eunuchs…. In like manner some tribes of insects have males, females, and neuters among them: as bees, wasps, ants….

Other animals have marks of having in a long process of time undergone changes in some parts of their bodies, which may have been effected to accommodate them to new ways of procuring their food. The existence of teats on the breasts of male animals, and which are generally replete with a thin kind of milk at their nativity, is a wonderful instance of this kind. Perhaps all the productions of nature are in their progress to greater perfection? An idea countenanced by the modern discoveries and deductions concerning the progressive formation of the solid parts of the terraqueous [consisting of land and water] globe, and consonant to [consistent with] the dignity of the Creator of all things. [Darwin says in *The Temple of Nature* (1803) that "the solid parts of the globe are gradually enlarging, and consequently [the Earth must be] young, as the fluid parts are not yet all converted into solid ones" (1.4).]

[2] *Platonic* I.e., non-sexual.

[3] [Darwin's note] Catchfly. Three females and ten males inhabit each flower; the viscous material which surrounds the stalks under the flowers of this plant … is a curious contrivance to prevent various insects from plundering the honey or devouring the seed….

[4] *Sirens* In Greek mythology, a trio of supernatural women who lured passing sailors to shipwreck with their seductive song.

[5] *Limed* Captured in an adhesive.

Weak with nice° sense, the chaste MIMOSA[6] stands, *delicate*
From each rude touch withdraws her timid hands;
Oft as light clouds o'er-pass the Summer-glade,
Alarmed she trembles at the moving shade;
And feels, alive through all her tender form,
The whispered murmurs of the gathering storm;
Shuts her sweet eye-lids to approaching night;
And hails with freshened charms the rising light.
Veiled, with gay decency and modest pride,
Slow to the mosque she moves, an eastern bride;
There her soft vows unceasing love record,
Queen of the bright seraglio° of her Lord. *palace harem*
So sinks or rises with the changeful hour
The liquid silver[7] in its glassy tower.
So turns the needle to the pole it loves,[8]
With fine librations° quivering as it moves. *vibrations*

from Mary Astell, *A Serious Proposal to the Ladies* (1694)

[I advise that we] disengage ourselves from all our former prejudices, from our opinion of names, authorities, customs and the like, not give credit to anything any longer because we have once believed it, but because it carries clear and uncontested evidence along with it. I should think there needed no more to persuade us to this, than a consideration of the mischiefs these prejudices do us. These are the grand hindrance in our search after truth; these dispose us for the reception of error, and when we have imbibed confirm us in it; contract our souls and shorten our views; hinder the free range of our thoughts and confine them only to that

[6] [Darwin's note] The sensitive plant. Of the class Polygamy, one house [meaning individual plants have some flowers with each sex and some flowers with both]. Naturalists have not explained the immediate cause of the collapsing of the sensitive plant; the leaves meet and close in the night during the sleep of the plant, or when exposed to much cold in the day-time, in the same manner as when they are affected by external violence, folding their upper surfaces together, and in part over each other like scales or tiles, so as to expose as little of the upper surface as may be to the air….

[7] *liquid silver* Mercury (in a thermometer).

[8] *needle to … it loves* I.e., compass needle toward the north.

particular track which these have taken; and in a word, erect a tyranny over our free-born souls, whilst they suffer nothing to pass for true that has not been stamped at their own mint. But this is not all their mischief. They are really the root of skepticism; for when we have taken up an opinion of weak grounds and stiffly adhered to it, coming afterwards by some chance or other to be convinced of its falseness, the same disposition which induced us to receive the premises without reason now inclines us to draw as false a conclusion from them. And because we seemed once well assured of what now appears to have no thing in't to make us so, therefore we fancy there's nothing certain that all our notions are but probabilities, which stand or fall according to the ingenuity of their managers. And so from an unreasonable obstinacy we pass on to as unreasonable a levity; so smooth is the transition from believing too easily and too much, to the belief of just nothing at all.

But pray, where's the force of this argument, "This is true because such a person or such a number of men have said it." Or, which commonly weighs more, "because I myself, the dear idol of my own heart, have sometimes embraced and perhaps very zealously maintained it"? Were we to poll for truth, or were our own particular opinions th'infallible standard of it, there were reason to subscribe to the sentiments of the many, or to be tenacious of our own. But since Truth, though she is bright and ready to reveal herself to all sincere inquirers, is not often found by the generality of those who pretend to seek after her—Interest, Applause, or some other little sordid Passion being really the mistress they court—whilst she (like Religion in another case) is made use of for a stale[1] to carry on the design the better; since we're commonly too much under the power of inordinate affections to have our understandings always clear and our judgments certain, are too rash, too precipitate not to need the assistance of a calmer thought, a more serious review; Reason wills that we should think again, and not form our conclusions or fix our foot till we can honestly say that we have with our prejudice or prepossession viewed the matter in debate on all sides, seen it in every light, have no bias to incline us either way, but are only determined by Truth itself, shining brightly in our eyes, and not permitting us to resist the force and evidence it carries. This I'm sure is what rational creatures ought to do. What's then the reason that they do't not? …

Again self-love, an excellent principle when true, but the worst and most mischievous when mistaken, disposes us to be retentive of our prejudices and errors, especially when it is joined, as most commonly it is, with pride and conceitedness. The condition of our present state (as was said before), in which we feel the force of our passions e're we discern the strength of our reason, necessitates us to take up with such principles and reasonings to direct and determine these passions as we happen to meet with, though probably they are far from being just ones, and are such as education or accident, not right reason disposes us to. And being inured[2] and habituated to these, we at last take them for our own, for parts of our dear beloved selves, and are as unwilling to be divorced from them as we would be to part with a hand or an eye or any the most useful member. Whoever talks contrary to these received notions seems to banter us, to persuade us out of our very senses, and does that which our pride cannot bear: he supposes we've been all along deceived and must begin anew. We therefore, instead of depositing[3] our old errors, fish about for arguments to defend 'em, and do not raise hypotheses on the discoveries we have made of truth, but search for probabilities to maintain our hypotheses. And what's the result of all this? Having set out in a wrong way we're resolved to persist in it; we stumble in the dark and quarrel with those who would lead us out of it.

But is there no remedy for this disorder, since we hope that all are not irrecoverably lost, though too many are so enveloped in prejudice that there's little probability of disengaging them? Why, really, the best that I can think of at present is to resolve to be industrious, and to think no pains too much to purchase truth; to consider that our forefathers were men of like passions with us, and are therefore not to be credited on the score of authority, but of reason.…

'Tis a great mistake to fancy it a reproach to change our sentiments; the infamy lies on their side who

[1] *stale* Bait.

[2] *inured* Accustomed.

[3] *depositing* I.e., putting away.

willfully and unreasonably adhere to 'em.... But as there is an extreme on one hand in being too resolutely bent on our old opinions, so is there on the other in inordinately thirsting after novelty. An opinion is neither better nor worse for being old or new; the truth of it is the only thing considerable.

from Judith Drake, *An Essay in Defense of the Female Sex* (1696)

[*Some advantages to be allowed to the disparity of education.*[1]]

... Our company is generally by our adversaries represented as unprofitable and irksome to men of sense, and, by some of the more vehement sticklers against us, as criminal. These imputations, as they are unjust, especially the latter, so they savour[2] strongly of the malice, arrogance, and sottishness[3] of those that most frequently urge 'em, who are commonly either conceited fops,[4] whose success in their pretences to the favour of our sex has been no greater than their merit, and fallen very far short of their vanity and presumption, or a sort of morose, ill-bred, unthinking fellows, who appear to be men only by their habit[5] and beards, and are scarce distinguishable from brutes but by their figure and risibility.[6] But I shall wave these reflections at present, however just, and come closer to our argument. If women are not qualified for the conversation of ingenious men, or, to go yet further, their friendship, it must be because they want some one condition, or more, necessarily requisite to either. The necessary conditions of these are sense and good nature, to which must be added, for friendship, fidelity and integrity. Now, if any of these be wanting to our sex, it must be either because nature has not been so liberal as to bestow 'em upon us, or because due care has not been taken to cultivate those gifts to a competent measure in us.

The first of these causes is that which is most generally urged against us, whether it be in raillery or spite. I might easily cut this part of the controversy short by an irrefragable[7] argument, which is, that the express intent and reason for which woman was created, was to be a companion and help meet[8] to man; and that consequently those that deny 'em to be so must argue a mistake in Providence, and think themselves wiser than their Creator. But these gentlemen are generally such passionate admirers of themselves, and have such a profound value and reverence for their own parts,[9] that they are ready at any time to sacrifice their religion to the reputation of their wit, and, rather than lose their point, deny the truth of the history. There are others, that though they allow the story, yet affirm that the propagation and continuance of mankind was the only reason for which we were made; as if the wisdom that first made man could not without trouble have continued the species by the same or any other method, had not this been most conducive to His happiness, which was the gracious and only end of His Creation. But these superficial gentlemen wear their understandings like their clothes, always set and formal, and would no more talk than dress out of fashion; beaux that, rather than any part of their outward figure should be damaged, would wipe the dirt of their shoes with their handkerchief, and that value themselves infinitely more upon modish nonsense than upon the best sense against the fashion. But since I do not intend to make this a religious argument, I shall leave all further considerations of this nature to the divines,[10] whose more immediate business and study it is to assert the wisdom of Providence in the order and distribution of this world, against all that oppose it.

[*No distinction of sexes in souls.*] To proceed, therefore, if we be naturally defective, the defect must be either in soul or body. In the soul it can't be, if what I have heard some learned men maintain be true, that all

[1] *Some ... education* This heading is by Drake, as are all other pieces of italicized text in square brackets in this piece.

[2] *savour* I.e., smell.

[3] *sottishness* Folly.

[4] *fops* Fools.

[5] *habit* Clothing.

[6] *risibility* Faculty for laughter.

[7] *irrefragable* Incontrovertible.

[8] *meet* Mate.

[9] *parts* Abilities.

[10] *divines* Clergymen; theologians.

souls are equal and alike, and that consequently there is no such distinction as male and female souls; that there are not innate *ideas*, but that all the notions we have are derived from our external senses, either immediately, or by reflection. These metaphysical speculations, I must own, madam, require much more learning and a stronger head than I can pretend to be mistress of, to be considered as they ought. Yet so bold I may be as to undertake the defense of these opinions when any of our jingling opponents think fit to refute 'em.

[*No advantage in the organization of their bodies.*] Neither can it be in the body (if I may credit the report of learned physicians), for there is no difference in the organization of those parts which have any relation to, or influence over, the minds; but the brain, and all other parts (which I am not anatomist enough to name), are contrived as well for the plentiful conveyance of spirits,[1] which are held to be the immediate instruments of sensation, in women, as men. I see therefore no natural impediment in the structure of our bodies; nor does experience or observation argue any. We use all our natural faculties as well as men—nay, and our rational too, deducting only for the advantages before mentioned.[2]

[*Confirmed from experience of brutes.*] Let us appeal yet further to experience, and observe those creatures that deviate least from simple nature, and see if we can find any difference in sense or understanding between males and females. In these we may see nature plainest, who lie under no constraint of custom or laws but those of passion or appetite, which are nature's, and know no difference of education, nor receive any bias by prejudice. We see great distance in degrees of understanding, wit, cunning, and docility (call them what you please) between the several species of brutes. An ape, a dog, a fox, are by daily observation found to be more docile and more subtle than an ox, a swine, or a sheep. But a she ape is as full of, and as ready at, imitation as a he; a bitch will learn as many tricks in as short a time as a dog;[3] a female fox has as many wiles as a male. A thousand instances of this kind might be produced; but I think these are so plain that to instance more were a superfluous labour; I shall only once more take notice, that in brutes and other animals there is no difference betwixt male and female in point of sagacity, notwithstanding there is the same distinction of sexes that is between man and women. I have read that some philosophers have held brutes to be no more than mere machines, a sort of divine clockwork, that act only by the force of nice unseen springs without sensation, and cry out without feeling pain, eat without hunger, drink without thirst, fawn upon their keepers without seeing 'em, hunt hares without smelling, etc. Here, madam, is cover for our antagonists against the last argument so thick that there is no beating 'em out. For my part, I shall not envy 'em their refuge, let 'em lie like the wild Irish, secure within their bogs; the field is at least ours, so long as they keep to their fastnesses.[4] But to quit this topic, I shall only add, that if the learnedest He of 'em all can convince me of the truth of this opinion, He will very much stagger my faith; for hitherto I have been able to observe no difference between our knowledge and theirs, but a gradual one; and depend upon Revelation alone that our souls are immortal, and theirs not.

[*Experience of mankind.*] But if an argument from brutes and other animals shall not be allowed as conclusive (though I can't see why such an inference should not be valid, since the parity[5] of reason is the same on both sides in this case), I shall desire those that hold against us to observe the country people—I mean the inferior sort of them, such as, not having stocks[6] to follow husbandry[7] upon their own score, subsist upon their daily labour. For amongst these, though not so equal as that of brutes, yet the condition of the two sexes is more level than amongst gentlemen, city traders, or rich yeomen.[8] Examine them in their several businesses, and their capacities will appear equal; but talk to them of things indifferent, and out of the road of their constant employment, and the balance will fall on our

[1] *spirits* I.e., vital powers.

[2] *advantages before mentioned* Earlier Drake acknowledges that there are some disparities in learning and ingenuity between men and women, but she attributes these to men's "education, freedom of converse, and variety of business and company."

[3] *dog* I.e., a male dog.

[4] *fastnesses* Strongholds.

[5] *parity* Equality.

[6] *stocks* Capital.

[7] *husbandry* Farming.

[8] *yeomen* Owners of their own land.

side; the women will be found the more ready and polite. Let us look a little further, and view our sex in a state of more improvement amongst our neighbours the Dutch. There we shall find them managing not only the domestic affairs of the family, but making, and receiving all payments as well great as small, keeping the books, balancing the accounts, and doing all the business, even the nicest of merchants, with as much dexterity and exactness as their—or our—men can do. And I have often heard some of our considerable merchants blame the conduct of our countrymen in this point; that they breed our women so ignorant of business, whereas were they taught arithmetic, and other arts which require not much bodily strength, they might supply the places of abundance of lusty[1] men now employed in sedentary business; which would be a mighty profit to the nation, by sending those men to employments where hands and strength are more required, especially at this time when we are in such a want of people. Beside that it might prevent the ruin of many families, which is often occasioned by the death of merchants in full business, and leaving their accounts perplexed, and embroiled to a widow and orphans, who understanding nothing of the husband or father's business, occasions the rending, and oftentimes the utter confounding a fair estate; which might be prevented, did the wife but understand merchants' accounts, and were made acquainted with the books.

from Eliza Haywood, *The Female Spectator* No. 10 (February 1745)

We were beginning to lament the misfortunes our sex frequently fall into through the want[2] of those improvements we are doubtless capable of, when a letter, left for us at our publisher's, was brought in which happened to be on that subject, and cannot anywhere be more properly inserted than in this place.

To the Female Spectator

Ladies,

Permit me to thank you for the kind and generous task you have undertaken in endeavoring to improve the minds and manners of our unthinking sex. It is the noblest act of charity you could exercise in an age like ours, where the sense of good and evil is almost extinguished, and people desire to appear more vicious than they really are, that so they may be less unfashionable. This humor, which is too prevalent in the female sex, is the true occasion of the many evils and dangers to which they are daily exposed. No wonder the men of sense disregard us! and the dissolute triumph over that virtue they ought to protect!

Yet I think it would be cruel to charge the ladies with all the errors they commit; it is most commonly the fault of a wrong education, which makes them frequently do amiss, while they think they act not only innocently but uprightly. It is therefore only the men—and the men of understanding, too—who, in effect, merit the blame of this, and are answerable for all the misconduct we are guilty of. Why do they call us silly women, and not endeavor to make us otherwise? God and Nature has endued them with means, and custom has established them in the power of rendering our minds such as they ought to be. How highly ungenerous is it then to give us a wrong turn and then despise us for it!

The Mahometans indeed enslave their women, but then they teach them to believe their inferiority will extend to eternity. But our case is even worse than this; for while we live in a free country, and are assured from our excellent Christian principles that we are capable of those refined pleasures which last to immortality, our minds, our better parts, are wholly left uncultivated, and, like a rich soil neglected, bring forth nothing but noxious weeds.

There are, undoubtedly, no sexes in souls, and we are as able to receive and practice the impressions—not only of virtue and religion, but also of those sciences which the men engross to themselves—as they can be. Surely our bodies were not formed by the great Creator out of the finest mold, that our souls might be neglected like the coarsest of the clay?

O! would too imperious and too tenacious man be so just to the world as to be more careful of the educa-

[1] *lusty* Vigorous.

[2] *want* Lack.

tion of those females to whom they are parents or guardians! Would they convince them in their infancy that dress and show are not the essentials of a fine lady, and that true beauty is seated in the mind, how soon should we see our sex retrieve the many virtues which false taste has buried in oblivion! Strange infatuation, to refuse us what would so much contribute to their own felicity! Would not themselves reap the benefit of our amendment? Should we not be more obedient daughters, more faithful wives, more tender mothers, more sincere friends, and more valuable in every other station of life?

But I find I have let my pen run a much greater length than I at first intended. If I have said anything worthy your notice, or what you think the truth of the case, I hope you will mention this subject in some of your future essays; or if you find I have any way erred in my judgment, to set me right will be the greatest favor you can confer on,

Ladies,

Your constant reader,

And humble servant,

Cleora

Aphra Behn
1640 – 1689

Long recognized as the first professional woman writer in England, Aphra Behn is also known for a life of adventure and espionage, for libertine sexual views, and for helping to lay the foundation for the cause of women's rights. Behn was one of the most prolific dramatists of the Restoration period and has been credited with introducing into her plays to an unprecedented degree aspects of the life of the time not previously considered fit material for the stage. Her most successful work, *Oroonoko*, has come to be recognized as an important narrative of slavery. Much as Behn was successful and influential in her own day, by the late nineteenth century she was almost forgotten; the open treatment of sexuality in her work was condemned as too "coarse" to be deserving of a broad audience. In the twentieth century, however, her literary reputation soared, and she has been championed by feminists for creating a place for women in the writing world. Virginia Woolf wrote in *A Room of One's Own*: "All women together ought to let flowers fall upon the tomb of Aphra Behn, [...] for it was she who earned them the right to speak their minds."

Behn's parentage is not known with any certainty. Some believe she was born to a barber and his wife, the Amies, in Wye, Kent, but scholars now generally accept that she was born to a family called Johnson just outside Canterbury. In the late 1650s the family moved to Surinam in South America, where her father had been given an administrative post. He died on the voyage, but the family remained in Surinam until about 1663. Her stay in the then-British colony exposed Behn to what would become the setting of *Oroonoko* more than twenty years later; it is believed that she also began writing plays during this period. She married shortly after her return to England. Virtually nothing is known of Mr. Behn, who was a merchant of Dutch/German heritage. He may have died in 1664, possibly of the bubonic plague; at any rate, no record of him after this point has come down to us. Some time during this period, Behn was introduced to the court of Charles II. She was considered a witty conversationalist, and her travels to the colonies made her much sought after. Her knowledge of several languages, including Dutch, proved useful and in 1666 she became a spy for the King in Antwerp. She was Agent 160, also known as Astrea, a name she used later as a *non de plume.* She incurred a great deal of debt while working in the King's service, and when she returned to London in 1667 she may have been put briefly in debtors' prison.

Single and forced to earn a living, Behn became a writer out of necessity. She wrote in one of her prefaces that she was "forced to write for bread and not ashamed to own it." With the Restoration the theaters had been re-opened and women were for the first time appearing on the commercial stage in England, as they did in France. Behn was able to find a niche in a newly burgeoning theater world that was looking for new works to produce. Her first play was *The Forc'd Marriage* (1670). Its central theme—the human damage caused when parents forced their offspring, particularly daughters, to marry against their free choice—was present in many of her later plays as well. Behn would often use her plays to attack what she considered the wrongs of society. In the prefaces of the printed versions of her plays she would answer her critics and put forward her ideas on the position of women.

The world of Restoration drama was one tolerant of iconoclasm, and in that context it is less surprising than it might otherwise be that Behn became one of the most established dramatists of the time, writing approximately 20 plays in as many years. The years 1676–83 were her most successful period of writing, and from this period *The Rover* (1677) remains the play she is most known for. Like many of her plays, *The Rover* was a social comedy, involving a good deal of sexual adventure (and misadventure). It was said to be one of the King's favorite plays and it was frequently produced through to the end of the century.

Two years after the success of *The Rover*, Behn followed with a similar play, *The Feigned Courtesans*, which also proved to be extremely popular. In this play Behn again raises the issue of women with limited marital options; Marcella and Cornelia pose as prostitutes in order to avoid an arranged marriage for Marcella and the convent for Cornelia. The women use their wits to marry the husbands of their own choosing. In using the "oldest profession in the world" in this dramatic fashion, Behn makes a pointed commentary on the treatment of women as commodities in society at large.

Between 1683 and 1688 Behn did not produce as many plays, and instead turned her attention to other genres (poetry, letters, and novels). The most widely read and discussed of Behn's non-dramatic works is *Oroonoko: or, The Royal Slave*, published in 1688. Now widely regarded as one of the most important prose fiction narratives of the period in English literature, *Oroonoko* caused little stir initially; its great fame came later (and was inextricably involved) with that of Thomas Southerne's dramatic adaptation (1695). From not long thereafter until well into the nineteenth century *Oroonoko* remained a literary touchstone of the anti-slavery movement. The work details the journey of Oroonoko from royal prince to slave in Surinam, where he leads a failed slave uprising. It is not certain how much of the narrative is based on actual events; while Behn was in Surinam, it is possible that she encountered a figure like Oroonoko.

Behn's last few years were filled with poverty and illness. She was aging, and no longer sought after for her witty repartee. Although it is known that she died on 16 April 1689, few of the details are known. The epitaph on her tombstone in Westminster Abbey reads as follows: "Here lies a proof that wit can never be / Defence enough against mortality."

⌘⌘⌘

The Disappointment [1]

One day the amorous Lysander,[2]
By an impatient passion swayed,
Surprised fair Cloris,[3] that loved maid,
Who could defend herself no longer.
All things did with his love conspire;
The gilded planet° of the day, *sun*
In his gay chariot drawn by fire,
Was now descending to the sea,
And left no light to guide the world,
But what from Cloris' brighter eyes was hurled.

In a lone thicket made for love,
Silent as yielding maid's consent,
She with a charming languishment,
Permits his force, yet gently strove;
Her hands his bosom softly meet,
But not to put him back designed,
Rather to draw him on inclined;
Whilst he lay trembling at her feet,

[1] *The Disappointment* Cf. "The Imperfect Enjoyment," by Behn's contemporary, John Wilmot, Earl of Rochester. "The Disappointment" was first published alongside Rochester's poem in his 1680 volume *Poems on Several Occasions*.

[2] *Lysander* Common name for a shepherd in pastoral poetry.

[3] *Cloris* Common name for a shepherdess in pastoral poetry.

Resistance 'tis in vain to show;
She wants the power to say—"Ah! What d'ye do?"

Her bright eyes sweet, and yet severe,
Where love and shame confus'dly strive,
Fresh vigour to Lysander give;
And breathing faintly in his ear,
She cried—"Cease, cease—your vain desire,
Or I'll call out—what would you do?
My dearer honour ev'n to you
I cannot, must not give—retire,
Or take this life, whose chiefest part
I gave you with the conquest of my heart."

But he as much unused to fear,
As he was capable of love,
The blessed minutes to improve,
Kisses her mouth, her neck, her hair;
Each touch her new desire alarms,
His burning trembling hand he pressed
Upon her swelling snowy breast,
While she lay panting in his arms.
All her unguarded beauties lie
The spoils and trophies of the enemy.

And now without respect or fear,
He seeks the object of his vows,
(His love no modesty allows)
By swift degrees advancing—where
His daring hand that altar seized,
Where gods of love do sacrifice:
That awful throne, that paradise
Where rage is calmed, and anger pleased,
That fountain where delight still flows,
And gives the universal world repose.

Her balmy lips encount'ring his,
Their bodies, as their souls, are joined;
Where both in transports unconfined
Extend themselves upon the moss.
Cloris half dead and breathless lay;
Her soft eyes cast a humid light,
Such as divides the day and night;
Or falling stars, whose fires decay:
And now no signs of life she shows,
But what in short-breathed sighs returns and goes.

He saw how at her length she lay;
He saw her rising bosom bare;
Her loose thin robes, through which appear
A shape designed for love and play;
Abandoned by her pride and shame
She does her softest joys dispense,
Offering her virgin innocence
A victim to love's sacred flame;
While the o'er-ravished shepherd lies
Unable to perform the sacrifice.

Ready to taste a thousand joys,
The too transported hapless swain
Found the vast pleasure turned to pain;
Pleasure which too much love destroys.
The willing garments by he laid,
And heaven all opened to his view,
Mad to possess, himself he threw
On the defenceless lovely maid.
But oh what envious gods conspire
To snatch his power, yet leave him the desire!

Nature's support (without whose aid
She can no human being give)
Itself now wants the art to live;
Faintness its slackened nerves invade;
In vain th'enraged youth essayed
To call its fleeting vigour back,
No motion 'twill from motion take;
Excess of love his love betrayed.
In vain he toils, in vain commands;
The insensible fell weeping in his hand.

In this so amorous cruel strife,
Where love and fate were too severe,
The poor Lysander in despair
Renounced his reason with his life.
Now all the brisk and active fire
That should the nobler part inflame,
Served to increase his rage and shame,
And left no spark for new desire:

Not all her naked charms could move
Or calm that rage that had debauched his love.

Cloris returning from the trance
Which love and soft desire had bred,
Her timorous hand she gently laid
(Or guided by design or chance)
Upon that fabulous Priapus,[1]
That potent god, as poets feign;
But never did young shepherdess,
Gath'ring of fern upon the plain,
More nimbly draw her fingers back,
Finding beneath the verdant leaves, a snake,

Then Cloris her fair hand withdrew,
Finding that god of her desires
Disarmed of all his awful fires,
And cold as flow'rs bathed in the morning dew.
Who can the nymph's confusion guess?
The blood forsook the hinder place,
And strewed with blushes all her face,
Which both disdain and shame expressed:
And from Lysander's arms she fled,
Leaving him fainting on the gloomy bed.

Like lightning through the grove she hies,
Or Daphne from the Delphic god,[2]
No print upon the grassy road
She leaves, t'instruct pursuing eyes.
The wind that wantoned in her hair,
And with her ruffled garments played,
Discovered in the flying maid
All that the gods e'er made, of fair.
So Venus, when her love was slain,
With fear and haste flew o'er the fatal plain.[3]

The nymph's resentments none but I
Can well imagine or condole:
But none can guess Lysander's soul,
But those who swayed his destiny.
His silent griefs swell up to storms,
And not one god his fury spares;
He cursed his birth, his fate, his stars
But more the shepherdess's charms,
Whose soft bewitching influence
Had damned him to the hell of impotence.
—1680

On a Juniper Tree, Cut Down to Make Busks[4]

Whilst happy I triumphant stood,
The pride and glory of the wood;
My aromatic boughs and fruit,
Did with all other trees dispute.
Had right by nature to excel,
In pleasing both the taste and smell:
But to the touch I must confess,
Bore an ungrateful sullenness.
My wealth, like bashful virgins, I
Yielded with some reluctancy;
For which my value should be more,
Not giving easily my store.
My verdant branches all the year
Did an eternal beauty wear;
Did ever young and gay appear.
Nor needed any tribute pay,
For bounties from the God of Day:
Nor do I hold supremacy,
In all the wood o'er every tree.
But ev'n those too of my own race,
That grow not in this happy place.
But that in which I glory most,
And do my self with reason boast,
Beneath my shade the other day,
Young Philocles and Cloris[5] lay,
Upon my root she leaned her head,
And where I grew, he made their bed:
Whilst I the canopy more largely spread.

[1] *Priapus* Greek god of fertility, who is usually depicted with an enormous, erect phallus.

[2] *Daphne ... god* The nymph Daphne fled from the god Apollos' advances and was transformed into a laurel tree in her escape.

[3] *Venus ... plain* When Adonis was slain by a wild boar, Venus, the goddess of love, rushed to his side to help him.

[4] *Busks* Strips of wood used to stiffen corsets.

[5] *Philocles ... Cloris* Common names for a shepherd and shepherdess in pastoral poetry.

Their trembling limbs did gently press,
The kind supporting yielding grass:
Ne'er half so blest as now to bear
A swain so young, a nymph so fair:
My grateful shade I kindly lent,
And ev'ry aiding bough I bent
So low, as sometimes had the bliss
To rob the shepherd of a kiss,
Whilst he in pleasures far above
The sense of that degree of love:
Permitted ev'ry stealth I made,
Unjealous of his rival shade.
I saw 'em kindle to desire,
Whilst with soft sighs they blew the fire:
Saw the approaches of their joy,
He growing more fierce, and she less coy,
Saw how they mingled melting rays,
Exchanging love a thousand ways.
Kind was the force on ev'ry side,
Her new desire she could not hide:
Nor would the shepherd be denied.
Impatient he waits no consent
But what she gave by languishment,
The blessed minute he pursued;
Whilst Love, her fear, and shame subdued;
And now transported in his arms,
Yields to the conqueror all her charms,
His panting breast, to hers now joined,
They feast on raptures unconfined;
Vast and luxuriant, such as prove
The immortality of Love.
For who but a divinity,
Could mingle souls to that degree;
And melt 'em into ecstasy.
Now like the phoenix, both expire,
While from the ashes of their fire,
Sprung up a new, and soft desire.[1]
Like charmers, thrice they did invoke,
The god, and thrice new vigour took.
Nor had thy mystery ended there,
But Cloris reassumed her fear,
And chid° the swain, for having prest, *scolded*
What she alas would not resist:
Whilst he in whom Love's sacred flame,
Before and after was the same,
Fondly implored she would forget
A fault, which he would yet repeat.
From active joys with some they hast,° *hasten*
To a reflection on the past;
A thousand times my covert bless,
That did secure their happiness:
Their gratitude to ev'ry tree
They pay, but most to happy me;
The shepherdess my bark caressed,
Whilst he my root, Love's pillow, kissed;
And did with sighs, their fate deplore,
Since I must shelter 'em no more;
And if before my joys were such,
In having heard, and seen too much,
My grief must be as great and high,
When all abandoned I shall be,
Doomed to a silent destiny.
No more the charming strife to hear,
The shepherd's vows, the virgin's fear:
No more a joyful looker on,
Whilst Love's soft battle's lost and won.

With grief I bowed my murm'ring head,
And all my crystal dew I shed.
Which did in Cloris pity move,
Cloris whose soul is made of love;
She cut me down, and did translate
My being to a happier state.
No martyr for religion died
With half that unconsidering pride;
My top was on that altar laid,
Where Love his softest off'rings paid:
And was as fragrant incense burned,
My body into busks was turned:
Where I still guard the sacred store,
And of Love's temple keep the door.

—1684

[1] *phoenix ... desire* In Greek mythology, the phoenix was a bird that lived for hundreds of years. It was eventually set ablaze by the sun, but a young phoenix rose up again from the ashes.

To the Fair Clarinda, Who Made Love to[1] *Me, Imagined More than Woman*

Fair lovely maid, or if that title be
Too weak, too feminine for nobler thee,
Permit a name that more approaches truth:
And let me call thee, lovely charming youth.
This last will justify my soft complaint,[2]
While that may serve to lessen my constraint;
And without blushes I the youth pursue,
When so much beauteous woman is in view.
Against thy charms we struggle but in vain
With thy deluding form thou giv'st us pain,
While the bright nymph betrays us to the swain.[3]
In pity to our sex sure thou wert sent,
That we might love, and yet be innocent:
For sure no crime with thee we can commit;
Or if we should—thy form excuses it.
For who, that gathers fairest flowers believes
A snake lies hid beneath the fragrant leaves.

Thou beauteous wonder of a different kind,
Soft Cloris with the dear Alexis[3] joined;
When e'er the manly part of thee, would plead
Thou tempts us with the image of the maid,
While we the noblest passions do extend
The love to Hermes, Aphrodite[4] the friend.

—1688

Oroonoko: or, The Royal Slave. A True History

In the opening lines of *Oroonoko*, the narrator promises to give us a true history: "I was myself an eyewitness, to a great part, of what you will find here set down." This promise is not to be taken at face value, as it is highly contested how closely we ought to associate Aphra Behn's own experiences with those of her narrator, and equally uncertain whether the account of Oroonoko's life is purely fiction or possibly inspired by a real person or event. Oroonoko's name itself is almost certainly an invention; it could be derived from the name Oorondates used in Ancient Greek literature, inspired by the Orinoco river where an English population settled in South America, or taken from the oronoko variety of tobacco, which was grown on the plantations of Surinam.

Even if Oroonoko's story is likely imagined, Behn's depiction of its setting in Surinam, although certainly romanticized, is historically genuine, and is far more realistic and detailed than was typical of fiction at the time. Surinam was the site of a British colony between 1650 and 1667, after which it became a possession of the Dutch. Most of the Europeans mentioned by name in *Oroonoko* were actual members of the colony's upper classes during this time. Their primary goal as colonists was the cultivation of coffee, sugar cane, and other trade goods for export, and most of this work was done by African slaves under appalling conditions of violence and deprivation. The Englishman George Warren lamented in his 1667 *Impartial Description of Surinam* that slaves

[1] *Made Love to* I.e., expressed love toward.

[2] *complaint* Melancholy, wistful poem, often lamenting lost love.

[3] *nymph … swain* A nymph is a sexually desirable young woman; a swain is a young male suitor. The terms are commonly used to refer to a lover and his beloved in pastoral poetry.

[4] *Cloris with … dear Alexis* Cloris and Alexis are names typical of the pastoral tradition.

[5] *Hermes, Aphrodite* In Greek mythology, the god Hermes seduced Aphrodite, the goddess of love and beauty, and their union resulted in the birth of a beautiful boy, Hermaphroditus. The water spirit Salmacis fell in love with him and prayed for union with him; the gods merged their bodies to form one person of both sexes.

> are sold like dogs, and no better esteem'd but for their work-sake, which they perform all the week, with the severest usages for the slightest fault ... [T]heir lodging is a hard board, and their black skins their covering. These wretched miseries not seldom drive them to desperate attempts for the recovery of their liberty, endeavouring to escape.

Although there is no record of a large scale rebellion similar to the one the title character Oroonoko incites, some slaves did manage to escape the plantations, and the raids conducted by these refugees were a significant threat to colonists' safety. Behn's portrait of Surinam as plagued by unstable violent tension between races and classes is true to the political realities of the colony.

Despite a few dissenting voices that existed at the time of *Oroonoko*'s publication, on the whole popular opinion in Britain was not yet against slavery. While *Oroonoko* would later acquire a reputation as an abolitionist text, it was not initially perceived as one, and it is highly unlikely that Behn herself opposed slavery—in fact, evidence suggests that she might have been married to a slave trader. Her engagement with the issue is nonetheless progressive for its time, especially in its sympathetic portrayal of a black African hero and heroine; Oroonoko and Imoinda are much more virtuous than the general population of slaves—and, notably, than the majority of the white characters. On the subject of race, *Oroonoko* is also unusual in that, through its retelling of Oroonoko and Imoinda's initial love affair in their homeland, it provides one of the first accounts of West African native life attempted by a European writer. Although her depiction is far more fanciful than factual, a few aspects are true; for example, as she reports, warring tribes did sell their captives to the British as slaves. For the most part, however, Behn combines personal invention with whatever inaccurate information she might have been able to gather, manufacturing an intricate West African civilization that never actually existed. Her representation of native life in Surinam as an uncomplicated golden age is equally distorted.

While *Oroonoko*'s treatment of race is certainly of interest, it was probably not the political issue foremost in Behn's mind at the time of her writing. She composed *Oroonoko* in 1688, which was a period of upheaval for the British government due to James II's precarious position as king. As a Catholic advocating religious freedom, and as an absolutist monarch attempting to ignore the will of Parliament, James was faced with rapidly growing opposition from most of his subjects. The Glorious Revolution was approaching, and later in 1688, after *Oroonoko* was published, it would result in James's forced abdication of the throne. Behn was a vehement royalist who remained supportive of James II, and it is worth considering in the context of these events what Oroonoko might represent as a virtuous, legitimate prince deprived of his rightful class position. *Oroonoko*'s most hypocritical characters claim to be Christian but act otherwise, and this, too, can be read as an indictment of the revolutionaries, since James's Parliamentarian enemies supported the power of the Anglican Church.

Whatever immediate political intentions Behn might originally have had, the story's popular success did not arrive until after the Glorious Revolution had passed. In 1695, Thomas Southerne adapted Behn's story to the stage, and his play *Oroonoko: A Tragedy* was performed frequently for the next hundred years. Although Behn's work shared in the play's success—her book was reprinted shortly after Southerne's play was first performed—Southerne's reinterpretation came to color subsequent readings of the original. *Oroonoko: A Tragedy* differed from its predecessor in its increased emphasis on the romance between Oroonoko and the beautiful Imoinda, who was transformed from a black African into a white woman in Southerne's text and in nearly all of the other stage adaptations that followed. Southerne's first audiences were, it seemed, much more interested in the story's emotional qualities than in any political aspects; it was only as the abolitionist movement gained momentum in Britain that *Oroonoko* began to be interpreted as an ideological engagement with slavery. When abolitionism became popular in the late 1700's and early 1800's, stage versions of *Oroonoko* proliferated and were performed as contributions to the slavery debate. John Ferriar's 1778 adaptation *The Prince of Angola*, for instance, was presented as a reworking of the plot to accurately portray the injustices of slavery in South America. *The Prince of Angola*, described on its title page as "a tragedy, altered from the play of *Oroonoko* [a]nd adapted to the circumstances of the present times," corrected what Ferriar saw as pro-slavery tendencies in both Southerne's text and Behn's original. In most eyes, however, all versions of *Oroonoko* including Behn's became synonymous with anti-slavery sentiment—so much so that, while it was very successful elsewhere, all its stage incarnations were banned in the slave-trading port of Liverpool.

Valued alternately as superbly descriptive travel narrative, sensational tragedy, political allegory, and early abolitionist argument, *Oroonoko* has presented very different faces according to the contexts in which it has been read and reinterpreted. This is no less true for modern readers, who will find much that is problematically colonialist in its treatment of race, romance, and leadership, but will also find much that remains affecting and challenging.

Oroonoko: or, The Royal Slave. A True History

I do not pretend, in giving you the history of this royal slave, to entertain my reader with the adventures of a feigned hero, whose life and fortunes fancy may manage at the poet's pleasure; nor in relating the truth, design to adorn it with any accidents, but such as arrived in earnest to him. And it shall come simply into the world, recommended by its own proper merits, and natural intrigues; there being enough of reality to support it, and to render it diverting, without the addition of invention.

I was myself an eyewitness, to a great part, of what you will find here set down; and what I could not be witness of, I received from the mouth of the chief actor in this history, the hero himself, who gave us the whole transactions of his youth; and though I shall omit, for brevity's sake, a thousand little accidents of his life, which, however pleasant to us, where history was scarce, and adventures very rare, yet might prove tedious and heavy to my reader, in a world where he finds diversions for every minute, new and strange. But we who were perfectly charmed with the character of this great man, were curious to gather every circumstance of his life.

The scene of the last part of his adventures lies in a colony in America, called Surinam,[1] in the West Indies.

But before I give you the story of this gallant slave, 'tis fit I tell you the manner of bringing them to these new colonies; for those they make use of there, are not natives of the place; for those we live with in perfect amity, without daring to command them; but on the contrary, caress them with all the brotherly and friendly affection in the world; trading with them for their fish, venison, buffaloes, skins, and little rarities; as marmosets, a sort of monkey as big as a rat or weasel, but of a marvellous and delicate shape, and has face and hands like an human creature; and cousheries, a little beast in the form and fashion of a lion, as big as a kitten; but so exactly made in all parts like that noble beast, that it is it in miniature. Then for little parakeets, great parrots, macaws, and a thousand other birds and beasts of wonderful and surprising forms, shapes, and colours. For skins of prodigious snakes, of which there are some threescore[2] yards in length; as is the skin of one that may be seen at His Majesty's Antiquaries, where are also some rare flies,[3] of amazing forms and colours, presented to them by myself, some as big as my fist, some less; and all of various excellencies, such as art cannot imitate. Then we trade for feathers, which they order into all

[1] *Surinam* The first Dutch settlers arrived in Surinam (previously allocated as part of the territory of Guiana in South America and now called the Republic of Suriname) in the late 1500s. The Dutch West India Company took control of the territory in 1621, and it became officially a Dutch colony (Dutch Guiana) in 1667. Unable to find enough laborers among the native Indian tribes to support their rich sugar plantations, the Dutch brought in vast numbers of slaves from West Africa. There were frequent and violent slave uprisings, with many slaves being killed and others fleeing to the country's interior. In Voltaire's *Candide*, a native of Surinam says: "When we work in the sugar mills and catch our finger in the millstone, they cut off our hand; when we try to run away, they cut off our leg: both things have happened to me. It is at this price that you eat sugar in Europe."

[2] *threescore* Sixty.

[3] *flies* Butterflies.

shapes, make themselves little short habits of them, and glorious wreaths for their heads, necks, arms and legs, whose tinctures are inconceivable. I had a set of these presented to me, and I gave them to the King's Theatre, and it was the dress of the *Indian Queen*,[1] infinitely admired by persons of quality, and were inimitable. Besides these, a thousand little knacks, and rarities in nature, and some of art, as their baskets, weapons, aprons, etc. We dealt with them with beads of all colours, knives, axes, pins and needles, which they used only as tools to drill holes with in their ears, noses and lips, where they hang a great many little things, as long beads, bits of tin, brass, or silver, beat thin, and any shining trinket. The beads they weave into aprons about a quarter of an ell[2] long, and of the same breadth; working them very prettily in flowers of several colours of beads; which apron they wear just before them, as Adam and Eve did the fig leaves, the men wearing a long strip of linen, which they deal with us for. They thread these beads also on long cotton threads, and make girdles to tie their aprons to, which come twenty times, or more, about the waist, and then cross, like a shoulder-belt, both ways, and round their necks, arms and legs. This adornment, with their long black hair, and the face painted in little specks or flowers here and there, makes them a wonderful figure to behold. Some of the beauties which indeed are finely shaped, as almost all are, and who have pretty features, are very charming and novel; for they have all that is called beauty, except the colour, which is a reddish yellow; or after a new oiling, which they often use to themselves, they are of the colour of a new brick, but smooth, soft and sleek. They are extreme modest and bashful, very shy, and nice[3] of being touched. And though they are all thus naked, if one lives forever among them, there is not to be seen an indecent action, or glance; and being continually used to see one another so unadorned, so like our first parents before the fall, it seems as if they had no wishes; there being nothing to heighten curiosity, but all you can see, you see at once, and every moment see; and where there is no novelty, there can be no curiosity. Not but I have seen a handsome young Indian, dying for love of a very beautiful young Indian maid; but all his courtship was, to fold his arms, pursue her with his eyes, and sighs were all his language; while she, as if no such lover were present, or rather, as if she desired none such, carefully guarded her eyes from beholding him, and never approached him, but she looked down with all the blushing modesty I have seen in the most severe and cautious of our world. And these people represented to me an absolute idea of the first state of innocence, before man knew how to sin; and 'tis most evident and plain, that simple nature is the most harmless, inoffensive and virtuous mistress. 'Tis she alone, if she were permitted, that better instructs the world than all the inventions of man; religion would here but destroy that tranquillity they possess by ignorance, and laws would but teach them to know offence, of which now they have no notion. They once made mourning and fasting for the death of the English governor, who had given his hand to come on such a day to them, and neither came, nor sent, believing, when once a man's word was past, nothing but death could or should prevent his keeping it. And when they saw he was not dead, they asked him, what name they had for a man who promised a thing he did not do? The governor told them, such a man was a liar, which was a word of infamy to a gentleman. Then one of them replied, "Governor, you are a liar, and guilty of that infamy." They have a native justice, which knows no fraud; and they understand no vice, or cunning, but when they are taught by the white men. They have plurality of wives, which, when they grow old, they serve those that succeed them, who are young, but with a servitude easy and respected; and unless they take slaves in war, they have no other attendants.

Those on that continent where I was, had no king; but the oldest war captain was obeyed with great resignation.

A war captain is a man who has led them on to battle with conduct, and success, of whom I shall have occasion to speak more hereafter, and of some other of their customs and manners, as they fall in my way.

With these people, as I said, we live in perfect tranquility, and good understanding, as it behooves us

[1] *Indian Queen* This semi-opera (play that combined music and the spoken word), written by John Dryden and Sir Robert Howard, featured ornate costumes, in particular a dress made from exotic feathers.

[2] *ell* Unit of measurement equal to 45 inches.

[3] *nice* Reluctant.

to do; they knowing all the places where to seek the best food of the country, and the means of getting it; and for very small and invaluable trifles, supply us with what 'tis impossible for us to get; for they do not only in the wood, and over the savannahs, in hunting, supply the parts of hounds, by swiftly scouring through those almost impassable places, and by the mere activity of their feet, run down the nimblest deer, and other eatable beasts, but in the water, one would think they were gods of the rivers, or fellow citizens of the deep, so rare an art they have in swimming, diving, and almost living in water, by which they command the less swift inhabitants of the floods. And then for shooting, what they cannot take, or reach with their hands, they do with arrows, and have so admirable an aim, that they will split almost a hair; and at any distance that an arrow can reach, they will shoot down oranges, and other fruit, and only touch the stalk with the darts' points, that they may not hurt the fruit. So that they being, on all occasions, very useful to us, we find it absolutely necessary to caress[1] them as friends, and not to treat them as slaves; nor dare we do other, their numbers so far surpassing ours in that continent.

Those then whom we make use of to work in our plantations of sugar are negroes, black slaves altogether, which are transported thither in this manner.

Those who want slaves, make a bargain with a master, or captain of a ship, and contract to pay him so much apiece, a matter of twenty pound a head for as many as he agrees for, and to pay for them when they shall be delivered on such a plantation. So that when there arrives a ship laden with slaves, they who have so contracted, go aboard, and receive their number by lot; and perhaps in one lot that may be for ten, there may happen to be three or four men, the rest, women and children; or be there more or less of either sex, you are obliged to be contented with your lot.

Coramantien,[2] a country of blacks so called, was one of those places in which they found the most advantageous trading for these slaves; and thither most of our great traders in that merchandise trafficked; for that nation is very warlike and brave, and having a continual campaign, being always in hostility with one neighbouring prince or other, they had the fortune to take a great many captives; for all they took in battle, were sold as slaves, at least, those common men who could not ransom themselves. Of these slaves so taken, the general only has all the profit; and of these generals, our captains and masters of ships buy all their freights.

The King of Coramantien was himself a man of a hundred and odd years old, and had no son, though he had many beautiful black wives; for most certainly, there are beauties that can charm of that colour. In his younger years he had had many gallant men to his sons, thirteen of which died in battle, conquering when they fell; and he had only left him for his successor, one grandchild, son to one of these dead victors; who, as soon as he could bear a bow in his hand, and a quiver at his back, was sent into the field, to be trained up by one of the oldest generals, to war; where, from his natural inclination to arms, and the occasions given him, with the good conduct of the old general, he became, at the age of seventeen, one of the most expert captains, and bravest soldiers, that ever saw the field of Mars;[3] so that he was adored as the wonder of all that world, and the darling of the soldiers. Besides, he was adorned with a native beauty so transcending all those of his gloomy race, that he struck an awe and reverence, even in those that knew not his quality; as he did in me, who beheld him with surprise and wonder, when afterwards he arrived in our world.

He had scarce arrived at his seventeenth year, when fighting by his side, the general was killed with an arrow in his eye, which the Prince Oroonoko (for so was this gallant Moor[4] called) very narrowly avoided; nor had he, if the general, who saw the arrow shot, and perceiving it aimed at the Prince, had not bowed his head between, on purpose to receive it in his own body rather than it should touch that of the Prince, and so saved him.

'Twas then, afflicted as Oroonoko was, that he was proclaimed general in the old man's place; and then it was, at the finishing of that war, which had continued for two years, that the Prince came to court, where he

[1] *caress* Treat with kindness.

[2] *Coramantien* Region on the west coast of Africa (now Ghana), where the British held a fort and slave market.

[3] *Mars* Roman god of war.

[4] *Moor* Originally a native of North Africa of mixed Berber and Arab ancestry. Because Moors were regarded as being dark skinned, the term was often used to refer to black people in general.

had hardly been a month together, from the time of his fifth year to that of seventeen; and 'twas amazing to imagine where it was he learned so much humanity, or, to give his accomplishments a juster name, where 'twas he got that real greatness of soul, those refined notions of true honour, that absolute generosity, and that softness that was capable of the highest passions of love and gallantry, whose objects were almost continually fighting men, or those mangled, or dead, who heard no sounds, but those of war and groans. Some part of it we may attribute to the care of a Frenchman of wit and learning, who finding it turn to very good account to be a sort of royal tutor to this young Black, and perceiving him very ready, apt, and quick of apprehension, took a great pleasure to teach him morals, language and science, and was for it extremely beloved and valued by him. Another reason was, he loved, when he came from war, to see all the English gentlemen that traded thither; and did not only learn their language, but that of the Spaniards also, with whom he traded afterwards for slaves.

I have often seen and conversed with this great man, and been a witness to many of his mighty actions, and do assure my reader, the most illustrious courts could not have produced a braver man, both for greatness of courage and mind, a judgment more solid, a wit more quick, and a conversation more sweet and diverting. He knew almost as much as if he had read much: he had heard of, and admired the Romans; he had heard of the late civil wars in England, and the deplorable death of our great monarch,[1] and would discourse of it with all the sense, and abhorrence of the injustice imaginable. He had an extreme good and graceful mien, and all the civility of a well-bred great man. He had nothing of barbarity in his nature, but in all points addressed himself as if his education had been in some European court.

This great and just character of Oroonoko gave me an extreme curiosity to see him, especially when I knew he spoke French and English, and that I could talk with him. But though I had heard so much of him, I was as greatly surprised when I saw him as if I had heard nothing of him, so beyond all report I found him. He came into the room, and addressed himself to me, and some other women, with the best grace in the world. He was pretty tall, but of a shape the most exact that can be fancied; the most famous statuary[2] could not form the figure of a man more admirably turned from head to foot. His face was not of that brown, rusty black which most of that nation are, but a perfect ebony, or polished jet. His eyes were the most awful[3] that could be seen, and very piercing; the white of them being like snow, as were his teeth. His nose was rising and Roman, instead of African and flat. His mouth, the finest shaped that could be seen, far from those great turned lips, which are so natural to the rest of the Negroes. The whole proportion and air of his face was so noble, and exactly formed, that, bating[4] his colour, there could be nothing in nature more beautiful, agreeable and handsome. There was no one grace wanting, that bears the standard of true beauty. His hair came down to his shoulders, by the aids of art, which was, by pulling it out with a quill, and keeping it combed, of which he took particular care. Nor did the perfections of his mind come short of those of his person; for his discourse was admirable upon almost any subject; and whoever had heard him speak, would have been convinced of their errors, that all fine wit is confined to the white men, especially to those of Christendom; and would have confessed that Oroonoko was as capable even of reigning well, and of governing as wisely, had as great a soul, as politic maxims,[5] and was as sensible of power as any Prince civilized in the most refined schools of humanity and learning, or the most illustrious courts.

This Prince, such as I have described him, whose soul and body were so admirably adorned, was (while yet he was in the court of his grandfather) as I said, as capable of love, as 'twas possible for a brave and gallant man to be; and in saying that, I have named the highest degree of love; for sure, great souls are most capable of that passion.

[1] *civil wars ... monarch* In the 1640s King Charles I and the Royalists, his supporters, fought the Parliamentarians, led by Oliver Cromwell. The King was eventually captured and was executed in 1649.

[2] *statuary* Sculptor.

[3] *awful* Awe-inspiring.

[4] *bating* Excepting.

[5] *politic maxims* Judicious opinion in matters of policy.

I have already said the old general was killed by the shot of an arrow, by the side of this Prince, in battle, and that Oroonoko was made general. This old dead hero had one only daughter left of his race, a beauty that, to describe her truly, one need say only, she was female to the noble male; the beautiful black Venus,[1] to our young Mars; as charming in her person as he, and of delicate virtues. I have seen an hundred white men sighing after her, and making a thousand vows at her feet, all vain, and unsuccessful; and she was, indeed, too great for any but a prince of her own nation to adore.

Oroonoko coming from the wars (which were now ended) after he had made his court to his grandfather, he thought in honour he ought to make a visit to Imoinda, the daughter of his foster father, the dead general; and to make some excuses to her, because his preservation was the occasion of her father's death; and to present her with those slaves that had been taken in this last battle, as the trophies of her father's victories. When he came, attended by all the young soldiers of any merit, he was infinitely surprised at the beauty of this fair Queen of Night, whose face and person was so exceeding all he had ever beheld; that lovely modesty with which she received him, that softness in her look, and sighs, upon the melancholy occasion of this honour that was done by so great a man as Oroonoko, and a prince of whom she had heard such admirable things; the awfulness wherewith she received him, and the sweetness of her words and behaviour while he stayed, gained a perfect conquest over his fierce heart, and made him feel the victor could be subdued. So that having made his first compliments, and presented her a hundred and fifty slaves in fetters, he told her with his eyes that he was not insensible of her charms; while Imoinda, who wished for nothing more than so glorious a conquest, was pleased to believe she understood that silent language of newborn love, and from that moment, put on all her additions to beauty.

The Prince returned to court with quite another humour[2] than before; and though he did not speak much of the fair Imoinda, he had the pleasure to hear all his followers speak of nothing but the charms of that maid, insomuch that, even in the presence of the old King, they were extolling her, and heightening, if possible, the beauties they had found in her, so that nothing else was talked of, no other sound was heard in every corner where there were whisperers, but "Imoinda! Imoinda!"

'Twill be imagined Oroonoko stayed not long before he made his second visit, nor, considering his quality, not much longer before he told her, he adored her. I have often heard him say, that he admired by what strange inspiration he came to talk things so soft, and so passionate, who never knew love, nor was used to the conversation of women; but (to use his own words) he said, most happily, some new and till then unknown power instructed his heart and tongue in the language of love, and at the same time, in favour of him, inspired Imoinda with a sense of his passion. She was touched with what he said, and returned it all in such answers as went to his very heart, with a pleasure unknown before. Nor did he use those obligations ill that love had done him, but turned all his happy moments to the best advantage; and as he knew no vice, his flame aimed at nothing but honour, if such a distinction may be made in love, and especially in that country, where men take to themselves as many as they can maintain, and where the only crime and sin with woman is to turn her off, to abandon her to want, shame and misery. Such ill morals are only practised in Christian countries, where they prefer the bare name of religion, and, without virtue or morality, think that's sufficient. But Oroonoko was none of those professors; but as he had right notions of honour, so he made her such propositions as were not only and barely such, but, contrary to the custom of his country, he made her vows she should be the only woman he would possess while he lived; that no age or wrinkles should incline him to change, for her soul would be always fine, and always young; and he should have an eternal idea in his mind of the charms she now bore, and should look into his heart for that idea, when he could find it no longer in her face.

After a thousand assurances of his lasting flame, and her eternal empire over him, she condescended to receive him for her husband, or rather, received him, as the greatest honour the gods could do her.

There is a certain ceremony in these cases to be observed, which I forgot to ask him how performed; but

[1] *Venus* Roman goddess of love.

[2] *humour* Disposition.

'twas concluded on both sides that, in obedience to him, the grandfather was to be first made acquainted with the design; for they pay a most absolute resignation to the monarch, especially when he is a parent also.

On the other side, the old King, who had many wives, and many concubines, wanted not court flatterers to insinuate in his heart a thousand tender thoughts for this young beauty, and who represented her to his fancy as the most charming he had ever possessed in all the long race of his numerous years. At this character his old heart, like an extinguished brand, most apt to take fire, felt new sparks of love, and began to kindle, and now grown to his second childhood, longed with impatience to behold this gay thing, with whom, alas, he could but innocently play. But how he should be confirmed she was this wonder, before he used his power to call her to court (where maidens never came, unless for the king's private use) he was next to consider; and while he was so doing, he had intelligence brought him, that Imoinda was most certainly mistress to the Prince Oroonoko. This gave him some chagrin; however, it gave him also an opportunity, one day, when the Prince was a-hunting, to wait on a man of quality, as his slave and attendant, who should go and make a present to Imoinda, as from the Prince; he should then, unknown, see this fair maid, and have an opportunity to hear what message she would return the Prince for his present, and from thence gather the state of her heart, and degree of her inclination. This was put in execution, and the old monarch saw, and burnt; he found her all he had heard, and would not delay his happiness, but found he should have some obstacle to overcome her heart; for she expressed her sense of the present the Prince had sent her, in terms so sweet, so soft and pretty, with an air of love and joy that could not be dissembled, insomuch that 'twas past doubt whether she loved Oroonoko entirely. This gave the old King some affliction, but he salved it with this, that the obedience the people pay their king, was not at all inferior to what they paid their gods, and what love would not oblige Imoinda to do, duty would compel her to.

He was therefore no sooner got to his apartment, but he sent the royal veil to Imoinda, that is, the ceremony of invitation; he sends the lady, he has a mind to honour with his bed, a veil, with which she is covered and secured for the King's use; and 'tis death to disobey, besides, held a most impious disobedience.

'Tis not to be imagined the surprise and grief that seized this lovely maid at this news and sight. However, as delays in these cases are dangerous, and pleading worse than treason, trembling, and almost fainting, she was obliged to suffer herself to be covered and led away.

They brought her thus to court; and the King, who had caused a very rich bath to be prepared, was led into it, where he sat under a canopy in state, to receive this longed for virgin, whom he having commanded should be brought to him, they (after disrobing her) led her to the bath, and making fast the doors, left her to descend. The King, without more courtship, bade her throw off her mantle and come to his arms. But Imoinda, all in tears, threw herself on the marble on the brink of the bath, and besought him to hear her. She told him, as she was a maid, how proud of the divine glory she should have been of having it in her power to oblige her king; but as by the laws he could not, and from his royal goodness would not take from any man his wedded wife, so she believed she should be the occasion of making him commit a great sin, if she did not reveal her state and condition, and tell him she was another's, and could not be so happy to be his.

The King, enraged at this delay, hastily demanded the name of the bold man that had married a woman of her degree without his consent. Imoinda, seeing his eyes fierce, and his hands tremble, whether with age or anger, I know not, but she fancied the last, almost repented she had said so much, for now she feared the storm would fall on the Prince; she therefore said a thousand things to appease the raging of his flame, and to prepare him to hear who it was with calmness; but before she spoke, he imagined who she meant, but would not seem to do so, but commanded her to lay aside her mantle and suffer herself to receive his caresses; or, by his gods, he swore, that happy man whom she was going to name should die, though it were even Oroonoko himself. "Therefore," said he, "deny this marriage, and swear thyself a maid."

"That," replied Imoinda, "by all our powers I do, for I am not yet known to my husband."[1]

[1] *not yet … my husband* I.e., the marriage has not been consummated.

"'Tis enough," said the King, "'tis enough to satisfy both my conscience, and my heart." And rising from his seat, he went and led her into the bath, it being in vain for her to resist.

In this time the Prince, who was returned from hunting, went to visit his Imoinda, but found her gone, and not only so, but heard she had received the royal veil. This raised him to a storm, and in his madness they had much ado to save him from laying violent hands on himself. Force first prevailed, and then reason. They urged all to him that might oppose his rage; but nothing weighed so greatly with him as the King's old age, incapable of injuring him with Imoinda.[1] He would give way to that hope, because it pleased him most, and flattered best his heart. Yet this served not altogether to make him cease his different passions, which sometimes raged within him, and sometimes softened into showers. 'Twas not enough to appease him, to tell him, his grandfather was old, and could not that way injure him, while he retained that awful duty which the young men are used there to pay to their grave relations. He could not be convinced he had no cause to sigh and mourn for the loss of a mistress he could not with all his strength and courage retrieve. And he would often cry, "Oh my friends! Were she in walled cities, or confined from me in fortifications of the greatest strength; did enchantments or monsters detain her from me, I would venture through any hazard to free her. But here, in the arms of a feeble old man, my youth, my violent love, my trade in arms, and all my vast desire of glory avail me nothing. Imoinda is as irrecoverably lost to me, as if she were snatched by the cold arms of death. Oh! she is never to be retrieved. If I would wait tedious years, till fate should bow the old King to his grave, even that would not leave me Imoinda free; but still that custom that makes it so vile a crime for a son to marry his father's wives or mistress would hinder my happiness, unless I would either ignobly set an ill precedent to my successors, or abandon my country, and fly with her to some unknown world, who never heard our story."

But it was objected to him, that his case was not the same; for Imoinda being his lawful wife, by solemn contract, 'twas he was the injured man, and might, if he so pleased, take Imoinda back, the breach of the law being on his grandfather's side; and that if he could circumvent him, and redeem her from the otan, which is the palace of the King's women, a sort of seraglio,[2] it was both just and lawful for him so to do.

This reasoning had some force upon him, and he should have been entirely comforted, but for the thought that she was possessed by his grandfather. However, he loved so well that he was resolved to believe what most favoured his hope, and to endeavour to learn from Imoinda's own mouth, what only she could satisfy him in, whether she was robbed of that blessing,[3] which was only due to his faith and love. But as it was very hard to get a sight of the women, for no men ever entered into the otan, but when the King went to entertain himself with some one of his wives or mistresses, and 'twas death at any other time for any other to go in, so he knew not how to contrive to get a sight of her.

While Oroonoko felt all the agonies of love, and suffered under a torment the most painful in the world, the old King was not exempted from his share of affliction. He was troubled for having been forced by an irresistible passion to rob his son of a treasure he knew could not but be extremely dear to him, since she was the most beautiful that ever had been seen; and had besides, all the sweetness and innocence of youth and modesty, with a charm of wit surpassing all. He found that, however she was forced to expose her lovely person to his withered arms, she could only sigh and weep there, and think of Oroonoko, and oftentimes could not forbear speaking of him, though her life were, by custom, forfeited by owning her passion. But she spoke not of a lover only, but of a prince dear to him to whom she spoke; and of the praises of a man, who, till now, filled the old man's soul with joy at every recital of his bravery, or even his name. And 'twas this dotage on our young hero that gave Imoinda a thousand privileges to speak of him without offending, and this condescension in the old King that made her take the satisfaction of speaking of him so very often.

Besides, he many times enquired how the Prince bore himself; and those of whom he asked, being

[1] *incapable ... with Imoinda* I.e., the King will not be able to consummate his liaison with Imoinda due to his age.

[2] *seraglio* Harem.

[3] *that blessing* I.e., Imoinda's virginity.

entirely slaves to the merits and virtues of the Prince, still answered what they thought conduced best to his service, which was, to make the old King fancy that the Prince had no more interest in Imoinda, and had resigned her willingly to the pleasure of the King, that he diverted himself with his mathematicians, his fortifications, his officers, and his hunting.

This pleased the old lover, who failed not to report these things again to Imoinda, that she might, by the example of her young lover, withdraw her heart and rest better contented in his arms. But however she was forced to receive this unwelcome news, in all appearance, with unconcern, and content, her heart was bursting within, and she was only happy when she could get alone, to vent her griefs and moans with sighs and tears.

What reports of the Prince's conduct were made to the King, he thought good to justify as far as possibly he could by his actions; and when he appeared in the presence of the King, he showed a face not at all betraying his heart; so that in a little time the old man, being entirely convinced that he was no longer a lover of Imoinda, he carried him with him, in his train to the otan, often to banquet with his mistress. But as soon as he entered, one day, into the apartment of Imoinda, with the King, at the first glance from her eyes, notwithstanding all his determined resolution, he was ready to sink in the place where he stood, and had certainly done so, but for the support of Aboan, a young man, who was next to him, which, with his change of countenance, had betrayed him, had the King chanced to look that way. And I have observed, 'tis a very great error in those who laugh when one says, a Negro can change colour; for I have seen them as frequently blush, and look pale, and that as visibly as ever I saw in the most beautiful white. And 'tis certain that both these changes were evident, this day, in both these lovers. And Imoinda, who saw with some joy the change in the Prince's face, and found it in her own, strove to divert the King from beholding either, by a forced caress, with which she met him, which was a new wound in the heart of the poor dying Prince. But as soon as the King was busied in looking on some fine thing of Imoinda's making, she had time to tell the Prince with her angry, but love-darting eyes, that she resented his coldness, and bemoaned her own miserable captivity. Nor were his eyes silent, but answered hers again, as much as eyes could do, instructed by the most tender, and most passionate heart that ever loved. And they spoke so well, and so effectually, as Imoinda no longer doubted, but she was the only delight, and the darling of that soul she found pleading in them its right of love, which none was more willing to resign than she. And 'twas this powerful language alone that in an instant conveyed all the thoughts of their souls to each other, that they both found there wanted but opportunity to make them both entirely happy. But when he saw another door opened by Onahal, a former old wife of the King's who now had charge of Imoinda, and saw the prospect of a bed of state made ready with sweets and flowers for the dalliance of the King, who immediately led the trembling victim from his sight, into that prepared repose. What rage! What wild frenzies seized his heart! Which forcing to keep within bounds, and to suffer without noise, it became the more insupportable and rent his soul with ten thousand pains. He was forced to retire to vent his groans, where he fell down on a carpet, and lay struggling a long time, and only breathing now and then, "O Imoinda!" When Onahal had finished her necessary affair within, shutting the door, she came forth to wait, till the King called; and hearing someone sighing in the other room, she passed on, and found the Prince in that deplorable condition which she thought needed her aid. She gave him cordials, but all in vain, till finding the nature of his disease, by his sighs, and naming Imoinda. She told him he had not so much cause as he imagined to afflict himself; for if he knew the King so well as she did, he would not lose a moment in jealousy, and that she was confident that Imoinda bore, at this minute, part in his affliction. Aboan was of the same opinion, and both together, persuaded him to reassume his courage; and all sitting down on the carpet, the Prince said so many obliging things to Onahal, that he half persuaded her to be of his party. And she promised him she would thus far comply with his just desires, that she would let Imoinda know how faithful he was, what he suffered, and what he said.

This discourse lasted till the King called, which gave Oroonoko a certain satisfaction; and with the hope Onahal had made him conceive, he assumed a look as gay as 'twas possible a man in his circumstances could do; and presently after, he was called in with the rest who waited without. The King commanded music to be brought, and several of his young wives and mistresses came all together by his command, to dance before him, where Imoinda performed her part with an air and grace so passing all the rest, as her beauty was above them, and received the present, ordained as a prize. The Prince was every moment more charmed with the new beauties and graces he beheld in this fair one; and while he gazed and she danced, Onahal was retired to a window with Aboan.

This Onahal, as I said, was one of the cast[1] mistresses of the old King; and 'twas these (now past their beauty) that were made guardians, or governants[2] to the new, and the young ones, and whose business it was, to teach them all those wanton arts of love with which they prevailed and charmed heretofore in their turn and who now treated the triumphing happy ones with all the severity, as to liberty and freedom, that was possible, in revenge of those honours they rob them of envying them those satisfactions, those gallantries and presents, that were once made to themselves, while youth and beauty lasted, and which they now saw pass regardless by, and paid only to the bloomings. And certainly, nothing is more afflicting to a decayed beauty than to behold in itself declining charms, that were once adored, and to find those caresses paid to new beauties to which once she laid a claim to hear them whisper as she passes by, "That once was a delicate woman." These abandoned ladies therefore endeavour to revenge all the despites[3] and decays of time on these flourishing happy ones. And 'twas this severity that gave Oroonoko a thousand fears he should never prevail with Onahal to see Imoinda. But, as I said, she was now retired to a window with Aboan.

This young man was not only one of the best quality, but a man extremely well made, and beautiful; and coming often to attend the King to the otan, he had subdued the heart of the antiquated Onahal, which had not forgot how pleasant it was to be in love. And though she had some decays in her face, she had none in her sense and wit; she was there agreeable still, even to Aboan's youth, so that he took pleasure in entertaining her with discourses of love. He knew also, that to make his court to these she-favourites was the way to be great, these being the persons that do all affairs and business at court. He had also observed that she had given him glances more tender and inviting than she had done to others of his quality. And now, when he saw that her favour could so absolutely oblige the Prince, he failed not to sigh in her ear, and to look with eyes all soft upon her, and give her hope that she had made some impressions on his heart. He found her pleased at this, and making a thousand advances to him, but the ceremony ending, and the King departing, broke up the company for that day, and his conversation.

Aboan failed not that night to tell the Prince of his success, and how advantageous the service of Onahal might be to his amour with Imoinda. The Prince was overjoyed with this good news, and besought him, if it were possible, to caress her, so as to engage her entirely, which he could not fail to do, if he complied with her desires. "For then," said the Prince, "her life lying at your mercy, she must grant you the request you make in my behalf." Aboan understood him, and assured him he would make love so effectually, that he would defy the most expert mistress of the art, to find out whether he dissembled it or had it really. And 'twas with impatience they waited the next opportunity of going to the otan.

The wars came on, the time of taking the field approached, and 'twas impossible for the Prince to delay his going at the head of his army to encounter the enemy; so that every day seemed a tedious year, till he saw his Imoinda, for he believed he could not live, if he were forced away without being so happy. 'Twas with impatience therefore, that he expected the next visit the King would make; and, according to his wish, it was not long.

The parley of the eyes of these two lovers had not passed so secretly, but an old jealous lover could spy it; or rather, he wanted not flatterers who told him they observed it. So that the Prince was hastened to the camp, and this was the last visit he found he should make to the otan; he therefore urged Aboan to make the best of this last effort, and to explain himself so to Onahal, that she, deferring her enjoyment of her young

[1] *cast* Cast-off.

[2] *governants* Governesses.

[3] *despites* Injuries.

lover no longer, might make way for the Prince to speak to Imoinda.

The whole affair being agreed on between the Prince and Aboan, they attended the King, as the custom was, to the otan, where, while the whole company was taken up in beholding the dancing and antic[1] postures the women royal made, to divert the King, Onahal singled out Aboan, whom she found most pliable to her wish. When she had him where she believed she could not be heard, she sighed to him, and softly cried, "Ah, Aboan! When will you be sensible of my passion? I confess it with my mouth, because I would not give my eyes the lie; and you have but too much already perceived they have confessed my flame. Nor would I have you believe that because I am the abandoned mistress of a king I esteem myself altogether divested of charms. No, Aboan; I have still a rest[2] of beauty enough engaging, and have learned to please too well, not to be desirable. I can have lovers still, but will have none but Aboan."

"Madam," replied the half-feigning youth, "you have already, by my eyes, found you can still conquer; and I believe 'tis in pity of me, you condescend to this kind confession. But, Madam, words are used to be so small a part of our country courtship, that 'tis rare one can get so happy an opportunity as to tell one's heart; and those few minutes we have are forced to be snatched for more certain proofs of love than speaking and sighing; and such I languish for."

He spoke this with such a tone, that she hoped it true, and could not forbear believing it; and being wholly transported with joy, for having subdued the finest of all the King's subjects to her desires, she took from her ears two large pearls and commanded him to wear them in his. He would have refused them, crying, "Madam, these are not the proofs of your love that I expect; 'tis opportunity, 'tis a lone hour only, that can make me happy."

But forcing the pearls into his hand, she whispered softly to him, "Oh! Do not fear a woman's invention, when love sets her a-thinking." And pressing his hand, she cried, "This night you shall be happy. Come to the gate of the orange groves, behind the otan, and I will be ready, about midnight, to receive you." 'Twas thus agreed, and she left him, that no notice might be taken of their speaking together.

The ladies were still dancing, and the King, laid on a carpet, with a great deal of pleasure, was beholding them, especially Imoinda, who that day appeared more lovely than ever, being enlivened with the good tidings Onahal had brought her of the constant passion the Prince had for her. The Prince was laid on another carpet, at the other end of the room, with his eyes fixed on the object of his soul; and as she turned, or moved, so did they; and she alone gave his eyes and soul their motions. Nor did Imoinda employ her eyes to any other use, than in beholding with infinite pleasure the joy she produced in those of the Prince. But while she was more regarding him than the steps she took, she chanced to fall, and so near him as that leaping with extreme force from the carpet, he caught her in his arms as she fell; and 'twas visible to the whole presence, the joy wherewith he received her. He clasped her close to his bosom, and quite forgot that reverence that was due to the mistress of a king, and that punishment that is the reward of a boldness of this nature; and had not the presence of mind of Imoinda (fonder of his safety, than her own) befriended him in making her spring from his arms and fall into her dance again, he had, at that instant, met his death; for the old King, jealous to the last degree, rose up in rage, broke all the diversion, and led Imoinda to her apartment, and sent out word to the Prince to go immediately to the camp, and that if he were found another night in court, he should suffer the death ordained for disobedient offenders.

You may imagine how welcome this news was to Oroonoko, whose unseasonable transport and caress of Imoinda was blamed by all men that loved him; and now he perceived his fault, yet cried, that for such another moment, he would be content to die.

All the otan was in disorder about this accident; and Onahal was particularly concerned, because on the Prince's stay depended her happiness, for she could no longer expect that of Aboan. So that, e'er they departed, they contrived it so that the Prince and he should come both that night to the grove of the otan, which was all of oranges and citrons, and that there they should wait her orders.

[1] *antic* Bizarre.

[2] *rest* Remnant.

They parted thus, with grief enough, till night, leaving the King in possession of the lovely maid. But nothing could appease the jealousy of the old lover. He would not be imposed on, but would have it that Imoinda made a false step on purpose to fall into Oroonoko's bosom, and that all things looked like a design on both sides, and 'twas in vain she protested her innocence. He was old and obstinate, and left her more than half assured that his fear was true.

The King going to his apartment, sent to know where the Prince was, and if he intended to obey his command. The messenger returned, and told him he found the Prince pensive, and altogether unpreparing for the campaign, that he lay negligently on the ground, and answered very little. This confirmed the jealousy of the King, and he commanded that they should very narrowly and privately watch his motions, and that he should not stir from his apartment, but one spy or other should be employed to watch him. So that the hour approaching, wherein he was to go to the citron grove, and taking only Aboan along with him, he leaves his apartment, and was watched to the very gate of the otan, where he was seen to enter, and where they left him, to carry back the tidings to the King.

Oroonoko and Aboan were no sooner entered but Onahal led the Prince to the apartment of Imoinda, who, not knowing anything of her happiness, was laid in bed. But Onahal only left him in her chamber to make the best of his opportunity, and took her dear Aboan to her own, where he showed the height of complaisance for his Prince, when, to give him an opportunity, he suffered himself to be caressed in bed by Onahal.

The Prince softly wakened Imoinda, who was not a little surprised with joy to find him there, and yet she trembled with a thousand fears. I believe he omitted saying nothing to this young maid, that might persuade her to suffer him to seize his own, and take the rights of love; and I believe she was not long resisting those arms where she so longed to be; and having opportunity, night and silence, youth, love and desire, he soon prevailed, and ravished in a moment what his old grandfather had been endeavouring for so many months.

'Tis not to be imagined the satisfaction of these two young lovers, nor the vows she made him, that she remained a spotless maid till that night, and that what she did with his grandfather had robbed him of no part of her virgin honour, the gods in mercy and justice having reserved that for her plighted lord, to whom of right it belonged. And 'tis impossible to express the transports he suffered, while he listened to a discourse so charming from her loved lips, and clasped that body in his arms, for whom he had so long languished; and nothing now afflicted him, but his sudden departure from her; for he told her the necessity and his commands, but should depart satisfied in this, that since the old King had hitherto not been able to deprive him of those enjoyments which only belonged to him, he believed for the future he would be less able to injure him. So that, abating the scandal of the veil, which was no otherwise so, than that she was wife to another, he believed her safe, even in the arms of the King, and innocent; yet would he have ventured at the conquest of the world, and have given it all, to have had her avoided that honour of receiving the royal veil. 'Twas thus, between a thousand caresses, that both bemoaned the hard fate of youth and beauty, so liable to that cruel promotion; 'twas a glory that could well have been spared here, though desired, and aimed at by all the young females of that kingdom.

But while they were thus fondly employed, forgetting how time ran on, and that the dawn must conduct him far away from his only happiness, they heard a great noise in the otan, and unusual voices of men, at which the Prince, starting from the arms of the frighted Imoinda, ran to a little battle-axe he used to wear by his side; and having not so much leisure as to put on his habit,[1] he opposed himself against some who were already opening the door, which they did with so much violence, that Oroonoko was not able to defend it, but was forced to cry out with a commanding voice, "Whoever ye are that have the boldness to attempt to approach this apartment thus rudely, know that I, the Prince Oroonoko, will revenge it with the certain death of him that first enters. Therefore stand back, and know this place is sacred to love, and me this night; tomorrow 'tis the King's."

This he spoke with a voice so resolved and assured, that they soon retired from the door, but cried, "'Tis by the King's command we are come; and being satisfied

[1] *habit* Clothing.

by thy voice, O Prince, as much as if we had entered, we can report to the King the truth of all his fears, and leave thee to provide for thy own safety, as thou art advised by thy friends."

At these words they departed, and left the Prince to take a short and sad leave of his Imoinda, who trusting in the strength of her charms, believed she should appease the fury of a jealous king by saying she was surprised, and that it was by force of arms he got into her apartment. All her concern now was for his life, and therefore she hastened him to the camp, and with much ado, prevailed on him to go. Nor was it she alone that prevailed; Aboan and Onahal both pleaded, and both assured him of a lie that should be well enough contrived to secure Imoinda. So that, at last, with a heart sad as death, dying eyes, and sighing soul, Oroonoko departed, and took his way to the camp.

It was not long after the King in person came to the otan, where beholding Imoinda with rage in his eyes, he upbraided her wickedness and perfidy, and threatening her royal lover, she fell on her face at his feet, bedewing the floor with her tears and imploring his pardon for a fault which she had not with her will committed, as Onahal, who was also prostrate with her, could testify that, unknown to her, he had broke into her apartment, and ravished her. She spoke this much against her conscience; but to save her own life, 'twas absolutely necessary she should feign this falsity. She knew it could not injure the Prince, he being fled to an army that would stand by him against any injuries that should assault him. However, this last thought of Imoinda's being ravished changed the measures of his revenge, and whereas before he designed to be himself her executioner, he now resolved she should not die. But as it is the greatest crime in nature amongst them to touch a woman, after having been possessed by a son, a father, or a brother, so now he looked on Imoinda as a polluted thing, wholly unfit for his embrace; nor would he resign her to his grandson, because she had received the royal veil. He therefore removed her from the otan, with Onahal, whom he put into safe hands, with order they should be both sold off, as slaves, to another country, either Christian, or heathen; 'twas no matter where.

This cruel sentence, worse than death, they implored might be reversed; but their prayers were vain, and it was put in execution accordingly, and that with so much secrecy, that none, either without or within the otan, knew anything of their absence, or their destiny.

The old King, nevertheless, executed this with a great deal of reluctance; but he believed he had made a very great conquest over himself when he had once resolved, and had performed what he resolved. He believed now, that his love had been unjust, and that he could not expect the gods, or Captain of the Clouds (as they call the unknown power) should suffer a better consequence from so ill a cause. He now begins to hold Oroonoko excused, and to say, he had reason for what he did; and now everybody could assure the King, how passionately Imoinda was beloved by the Prince; even those confessed it now who said the contrary before his flame was abated. So that the King being old and not able to defend himself in war, and having no sons of all his race remaining alive, but only this, to maintain him on the throne, and looking on this as a man disobliged, first by the rape of his mistress, or rather, wife; and now by depriving him wholly of her, he feared, might make him desperate, and do some cruel thing, either to himself, or his old grandfather, the offender, he began to repent him extremely of the contempt he had, in his rage, put on Imoinda. Besides, he considered he ought in honour to have killed her for this offence, if it had been one. He ought to have had so much value and consideration for a maid of her quality, as to have nobly put her to death, and not to have sold her like a common slave, the greatest revenge, and the most disgraceful of any, and to which they a thousand times prefer death, and implore it as Imoinda did, but could not obtain that honour. Seeing therefore it was certain that Oroonoko would highly resent this affront, he thought good to make some excuse for his rashness to him, and to that end he sent a messenger to the camp with orders to treat with him about the matter, to gain his pardon, and to endeavour to mitigate his grief, but that by no means he should tell him she was sold, but secretly put to death; for he knew he should never obtain his pardon for the other.

When the messenger came, he found the Prince upon the point of engaging with the enemy, but as soon as he heard of the arrival of the messenger he commanded him to his tent, where he embraced him, and received him with joy, which was soon abated, by the downcast looks of the messenger, who was instantly demanded the cause by Oroonoko, who, impatient of delay, asked a thousand questions in a breath, and all concerning Imoinda. But there needed little return, for he could almost answer himself of all he demanded from his sighs and eyes. At last, the messenger casting himself at the Prince's feet and kissing them with all the submission of a man that had something to implore which he dreaded to utter, he besought him to hear with calmness what he had to deliver to him, and to call up all his noble and heroic courage to encounter with his words, and defend himself against the ungrateful things he must relate. Oroonoko replied, with a deep sigh, and a languishing voice, "I am armed against their worst efforts—for I know they will tell me, Imoinda is no more—and after that, you may spare the rest." Then, commanding him to rise, he laid himself on a carpet under a rich pavilion, and remained a good while silent, and was hardly heard to sigh. When he was come a little to himself, the messenger asked him leave to deliver that part of his embassy which the Prince had not yet divined, and the Prince cried, "I permit thee." Then he told him the affliction the old King was in for the rashness he had committed in his cruelty to Imoinda, and how he deigned to ask pardon for his offence, and to implore the Prince would not suffer that loss to touch his heart too sensibly which now all the gods could not restore him, but might recompense him in glory which he begged he would pursue; and that death, that common revenger of all injuries, would soon even the account between him and a feeble old man.

Oroonoko bade him return his duty to his lord and master, and to assure him there was no account of revenge to be adjusted between them; if there were, 'twas he was the aggressor, and that death would be just, and, maugre[1] his age, would see him righted; and he was contented to leave his share of glory to youths more fortunate, and worthy of that favour from the gods. That henceforth he would never lift a weapon, or draw a bow, but abandon the small remains of his life to sighs and tears, and the continual thoughts of what his lord and grandfather had thought good to send out of the world, with all that youth, that innocence, and beauty.

After having spoken this, whatever his greatest officers, and men of the best rank could do, they could not raise him from the carpet, or persuade him to action and resolutions of life, but commanding all to retire, he shut himself into his pavilion all that day, while the enemy was ready to engage; and wondering at the delay, the whole body of the chief of the army then addressed themselves to him, and to whom they had much ado to get admittance. They fell on their faces at the foot of his carpet, where they lay, and besought him with earnest prayers and tears, to lead them forth to battle, and not let the enemy take advantages of them, and implored him to have regard to his glory, and to the world that depended on his courage and conduct. But he made no other reply to all their supplications but this, that he had now no more business for glory; and for the world, it was a trifle not worth his care. "Go," continued he, sighing, "and divide it amongst you; and reap with joy what you so vainly prize, and leave me to my more welcome destiny."

They then demanded what they should do, and whom he would constitute in his room,[2] that the confusion of ambitious youth and power might not ruin their order, and make them a prey to the enemy. He replied, he would not give himself the trouble, but wished them to choose the bravest man amongst them, let his quality or birth be what it would, "For, O my friends!" said he, "it is not titles make men brave, or good, or birth that bestows courage and generosity, or makes the owner happy. Believe this, when you behold Oroonoko, the most wretched, and abandoned by fortune of all the creation of the gods." So turning himself about, he would make no more reply to all they could urge or implore.

The army beholding their officers return unsuccessful, with sad faces, and ominous looks, that presaged no good luck, suffered a thousand fears to take possession of their hearts, and the enemy to come even upon them, before they would provide for their safety by any defence; and though they were assured by some, who had a mind to animate them, that they should be immediately headed by the Prince, and that in the meantime Aboan had orders to command as general, yet they were so dismayed for want of that great example of bravery

[1] *maugre* Despite.

[2] *constitute … room* I.e., appoint as his successor.

that they could make but a very feeble resistance; and at last, downright, fled before the enemy, who pursued them to the very tents, killing them. Nor could all Aboan's courage, which that day gained him immortal glory, shame them into a manly defence of themselves. The guards that were left behind, about the Prince's tent, seeing the soldiers flee before the enemy, and scatter themselves all over the plain, in great disorder, made such outcries as roused the Prince from his amorous slumber, in which he had remained buried for two days, without permitting any sustenance to approach him. But, in spite of all his resolutions, he had not the constancy of grief to that degree as to make him insensible of the danger of his army; and in that instant he leapt from his couch, and cried, "Come, if we must die, let us meet death the noblest way; and 'twill be more like Oroonoko to encounter him at an army's head, opposing the torrent of a conquering foe, than lazily, on a couch, to wait his lingering pleasure, and die every moment by a thousand wrecking thoughts; or be tamely taken by an enemy and led a whining, lovesick slave, to adorn the triumphs of Jamoan, that young victor, who already is entered beyond the limits I had prescribed him."

While he was speaking, he suffered his people to dress him for the field; and sallying out of his pavilion, with more life and vigour in his countenance than ever he showed, he appeared like some divine power descended to save his country from destruction; and his people had purposely put him on all things that might make him shine with most splendour, to strike a reverend awe into the beholders. He flew into the thickest of those that were pursuing his men, and being animated with despair, he fought as if he came on purpose to die, and did such things as will not be believed that human strength could perform, and such as soon inspired all the rest with new courage and new order. And now it was that they began to fight indeed, and so, as if they would not be outdone even by their adored hero, who turning the tide of the victory, changing absolutely the fate of the day, gained an entire conquest; and Oroonoko having the good fortune to single out Jamoan, he took him prisoner with his own hand, having wounded him almost to death.

This Jamoan afterwards became very dear to him, being a man very gallant and of excellent graces, and fine parts, so that he never put him amongst the rank of captives, as they used to do, without distinction, for the common sale or market, but kept him in his own court, where he retained nothing of the prisoner but the name, and returned no more into his own country, so great an affection he took for Oroonoko; and by a thousand tales and adventures of love and gallantry, flattered[1] his disease of melancholy and languishment, which I have often heard him say had certainly killed him, but for the conversation of this Prince and Aboan, and the French governor he had from his childhood, of whom I have spoken before, and who was a man of admirable wit, great ingenuity and learning, all which he had infused into his young pupil. This Frenchman was banished out of his own country for some heretical notions he held; and though he was a man of very little religion, he had admirable morals, and a brave soul.

After the total defeat of Jamoan's army, which all fled, or were left dead upon the place, they spent some time in the camp, Oroonoko choosing rather to remain a while there in his tents, than enter into a palace, or live in a court where he had so lately suffered so great a loss. The officers therefore, who saw and knew his cause of discontent, invented all sorts of diversions and sports to entertain their Prince: so that what with those amusements abroad, and others at home, that is, within their tents, with the persuasions, arguments and care of his friends and servants that he more peculiarly prized, he wore off in time a great part of that chagrin and torture of despair which the first effects of Imoinda's death had given him; insomuch as having received a thousand kind embassies from the King, and invitations to return to court, he obeyed, though with no little reluctance; and when he did so, there was a visible change in him, and for a long time he was much more melancholy than before. But time lessens all extremes, and reduces them to mediums and unconcern; but no motives or beauties, though all endeavoured it, could engage him in any sort of amour, though he had all the invitations to it, both from his own youth and others' ambitions and designs.

Oroonoko was no sooner returned from this last conquest, and received at court with all the joy and magnificence that could be expressed to a young victor, who was not only returned triumphant, but beloved like

[1] *flattered* Cheered away.

a deity, when there arrived in the port an English ship.

This person had often before been in these countries, and was very well known to Oroonoko, with whom he had trafficked for slaves, and had used to do the same with his predecessors.

This commander was a man of a finer sort of address and conversation, better bred, and more engaging than most of that sort of men are; so that he seemed rather never to have been bred out of a court, than almost all his life at sea. This captain therefore was always better received at court, than most of the traders to those countries were, and especially by Oroonoko, who was more civilized, according to the European mode, than any other had been, and took more delight in the white nations, and, above all, men of parts and wit. To this captain he sold abundance of his slaves, and for the favour and esteem he had for him, made him many presents, and obliged him to stay at court as long as possibly he could. Which the captain seemed to take as a very great honour done him, entertaining the Prince every day with globes and maps, and mathematical discourses and instruments, eating, drinking, hunting and living with him with so much familiarity, that it was not to be doubted, but he had gained very greatly upon the heart of this gallant young man. And the captain, in return of all these mighty favours, besought the Prince to honour his vessel with his presence, some day or other, to dinner, before he should set sail, which he condescended to accept, and appointed his day. The captain, on his part, failed not to have all things in a readiness, in the most magnificent order he could possibly. And the day being come, the captain, in his boat, richly adorned with carpets and velvet cushions, rowed to the shore to receive the Prince, with another longboat, where was placed all his music and trumpets, with which Oroonoko was extremely delighted; who met him on the shore, attended by his French governor, Jamoan, Aboan, and about an hundred of the noblest of the youths of the court. And after they had first carried the Prince on board, the boats fetched the rest off, where they found a very splendid treat, with all sorts of fine wines, and were as well entertained, as 'twas possible in such a place to be.

The Prince having drunk hard of punch, and several sorts of wine, as did all the rest (for great care was taken, they should want nothing of that part of the entertainment) was very merry, and in great admiration of the ship, for he had never been in one before, so that he was curious of beholding every place, where he decently might descend. The rest, no less curious, who were not quite overcome with drinking, rambled at their pleasure fore and aft, as their fancies guided them: so that the captain, who had well laid his design before, gave the word and seized on all his guests; they clapping great irons suddenly on the Prince when he was leaped down in the hold to view that part of the vessel, and locking him fast down, secured him. The same treachery was used to all the rest; and all in one instant, in several places of the ship, were lashed fast in irons and betrayed to slavery. That great design over, they set all hands to work to hoist sail; and with as treacherous and fair a wind they made from the shore with this innocent and glorious prize, who thought of nothing less than such an entertainment.

Some have commended this act, as brave in the captain; but I will spare my sense of it, and leave it to my reader to judge as he pleases.

It may be easily guessed in what manner the Prince resented this indignity, who may be best resembled to a lion taken in a toil; so he raged, so he struggled for liberty, but all in vain; and they had so wisely managed his fetters, that he could not use a hand in his defence, to quit himself of a life that would by no means endure slavery; nor could he move from the place where he was tied to any solid part of the ship against which he might have beat his head, and have finished his disgrace that way, so that being deprived of all other means, he resolved to perish for want of food. And pleased at last with that thought, and toiled and tired by rage and indignation, he laid himself down, and sullenly resolved upon dying, and refused all things that were brought him.

This did not a little vex the captain, and the more so because he found almost all of them of the same humour, so that the loss of so many brave slaves, so tall and goodly to behold, would have been very considerable. He therefore ordered one to go from him (for he would not be seen himself) to Oroonoko, and to assure him he was afflicted for having rashly done so inhospitable a deed, and which could not be now remedied, since they were far from shore; but since he resented it in so high a nature, he assured him he would revoke his resolution, and set both him and his friends ashore on the next land they should touch at; and of this the messenger gave him his oath, provided he would resolve to live. And Oroonoko, whose honour was such as he never had violated a word in his life himself, much less a solemn asseveration,[1] believed in an instant what this man said, but replied he expected for a confirmation of this to have his shameful fetters dismissed. This demand was carried to the captain, who returned him answer that the offence had been so great which he had put upon the Prince, that he durst not trust him with liberty while he remained in the ship, for fear lest by a valour natural to him, and a revenge that would animate that valour, he might commit some outrage fatal to himself and the King his master, to whom his vessel did belong. To this Oroonoko replied, he would engage his honour to behave himself in all friendly order and manner, and obey the command of the captain, as he was lord of the King's vessel, and general of those men under his command.

This was delivered to the still doubting captain, who could not resolve to trust a heathen he said, upon his parole, a man that had no sense or notion of the God that he worshipped. Oroonoko then replied he was very sorry to hear that the captain pretended to the knowledge and worship of any gods who had taught him no better principles, than not to credit as he would be credited; but they told him the difference of their faith occasioned that distrust: for the captain had protested to him upon the word of a Christian, and sworn in the name of a great God, which if he should violate, he would expect eternal torment in the world to come. "Is that all the obligation he has to be just to his oath?" replied Oroonoko. "Let him know I swear by my honour, which to violate, would not only render me contemptible and despised by all brave and honest men, and so give myself perpetual pain, but it would be eternally offending and diseasing all mankind, harming, betraying, circumventing and outraging all men; but punishments hereafter are suffered by oneself; and the world takes no cognizances whether this god have revenged them, or not, 'tis done so secretly, and deferred so long; while the man of no honour suffers every moment the scorn and contempt of the honester world, and dies every day ignominiously in his fame, which is more valuable than life. I speak not this to move belief, but to show you how you mistake, when you imagine that he who will violate his honour, will keep his word with his gods." So turning from him with a disdainful smile, he refused to answer him when he urged him to know what answer he should carry back to his captain, so that he departed without saying any more.

The captain pondering and consulting what to do, it was concluded that nothing but Oroonoko's liberty would encourage any of the rest to eat, except the Frenchman, whom the captain could not pretend to keep prisoner, but only told him he was secured because he might act something in favour of the Prince, but that he should be freed as soon as they came to land. So that they concluded it wholly necessary to free the Prince from his irons that he might show himself to the rest, that they might have an eye upon him, and that they could not fear a single man.

This being resolved, to make the obligation the greater, the captain himself went to Oroonoko, where, after many compliments, and assurances of what he had already promised, he receiving from the Prince his parole, and his hand, for his good behaviour, dismissed his irons, and brought him to his own cabin, where, after having treated and reposed him a while, for he had neither eaten nor slept in four days before, he besought him to visit those obstinate people in chains, who refused all manner of sustenance, and entreated him to oblige them to eat, and assure them of their liberty the first opportunity.

Oroonoko, who was too generous not to give credit to his words, showed himself to his people, who were transported with excess of joy at the sight of their darling Prince, falling at his feet, and kissing and embracing them, believing, as some divine oracle, all he assured them. But he besought them to bear their chains with that bravery that became those whom he had seen act so nobly in arms, and that they could not give him greater proofs of their love and friendship, since 'twas all the security the captain (his friend) could have against the revenge, he said, they might possibly justly take, for the injuries sustained by him. And they all, with one

[1] *asseveration* Promise; oath.

accord, assured him they could not suffer enough when it was for his repose and safety.

After this they no longer refused to eat, but took what was brought them and were pleased with their captivity, since by it they hoped to redeem the Prince, who, all the rest of the voyage, was treated with all the respect due to his birth, though nothing could divert his melancholy; and he would often sigh for Imoinda, and think this a punishment due to his misfortune, in having left that noble maid behind him that fatal night in the otan, when he fled to the camp.

Possessed with a thousand thoughts of past joys with this fair young person, and a thousand griefs for her eternal loss, he endured a tedious voyage, and at last arrived at the mouth of the river of Surinam, a colony belonging to the King of England, and where they were to deliver some part of their slaves. There the merchants and gentlemen of the country going on board to demand those lots of slaves they had already agreed on, and amongst those the overseers of those plantations where I then chanced to be, the captain, who had given the word, ordered his men to bring up those noble slaves in fetters, whom I have spoken of; and having put them, some in one, and some in other lots, with women and children (which they call pickaninnies), they sold them off as slaves to several merchants and gentlemen, not putting any two in one lot, because they would separate them far from each other; not daring to trust them together, lest rage and courage should put them upon contriving some great action, to the ruin of the colony.

Oroonoko was first seized on and sold to our overseer, who had the first lot, with seventeen more of all sorts and sizes, but not one of quality with him. When he saw this, he found what they meant; for, as I said, he understood English pretty well; and being wholly unarmed and defenceless, so as it was in vain to make any resistance, he only beheld the captain with a look all fierce and disdainful, upbraiding him with eyes, that forced blushes on his guilty cheeks, he only cried in passing over the side of the ship, "Farewell, Sir! 'Tis worth my suffering to gain so true a knowledge both of you and of your gods by whom you swear." And desiring those that held him to forbear their pains, and telling them he would make no resistance, he cried, "Come, my fellow slaves, let us descend, and see if we can meet with more honour and honesty in the next world we shall touch upon." So he nimbly leapt into the boat, and showing no more concern, suffered himself to be rowed up the river with his seventeen companions.

The gentleman that bought him was a young Cornish gentleman, whose name was Trefry; a man of great wit, and fine learning, and was carried into those parts by the Lord ——, Governor, to manage all his affairs.[1] He reflecting on the last words of Oroonoko to the captain, and beholding the richness of his vest, no sooner came into the boat, but he fixed his eyes on him; and finding something so extraordinary in his face, his shape and mien, a greatness of look, and haughtiness in his air, and finding he spoke English, had a great mind to be enquiring into his quality and fortune; which, though Oroonoko endeavoured to hide by only confessing he was above the rank of common slaves, Trefry soon found he was yet something greater than he confessed, and from that moment began to conceive so vast an esteem for him, that he ever after loved him as his dearest brother, and showed him all the civilities due to so great a man.

Trefry was a very good mathematician, and a linguist, could speak French and Spanish; and in the three days they remained in the boat (for so long were they going from the ship to the plantation) he entertained Oroonoko so agreeably with his art and discourse, that he was no less pleased with Trefry, than he was with the Prince; and he thought himself, at least, fortunate in this, that since he was a slave, as long as he would suffer himself to remain so, he had a man of so excellent wit and parts for a master. So that before they had finished their voyage up the river, he made no scruple of declaring to Trefry all his fortunes and most part of what I have here related, and put himself wholly into the hands of his new friend, whom he found resenting all the injuries were done him, and was charmed with all the greatnesses of his actions, which were recited with that modesty and delicate sense, as wholly vanquished him, and subdued him to his interest. And he promised him on his word and honour, he would find the means to reconduct him to his own country again; assuring him,

[1] *Trefry … affairs* John Trefry was hired by the then-governor of Surinam, Lord Willoughby, to be his agent at his plantation at Parham.

he had a perfect abhorrence of so dishonourable an action, and that he would sooner have died, than have been the author of such a perfidy. He found the Prince was very much concerned to know what became of his friends, and how they took their slavery; and Trefry promised to take care about the enquiring after their condition, and that he should have an account of them.

Though, as Oroonoko afterwards said, he had little reason to credit the words of a backearary,[1] yet he knew not why, but he saw a kind of sincerity and awful truth in the face of Trefry; he saw an honesty in his eyes, and he found him wise and witty enough to understand honour, for it was one of his maxims, "A man of wit could not be a knave or villain."

In their passage up the river they put in at several houses for refreshment, and ever when they landed numbers of people would flock to behold this man; not but their eyes were daily entertained with the sight of slaves, but the fame of Oroonoko was gone before him, and all people were in admiration of his beauty. Besides, he had a rich habit on, in which he was taken, so different from the rest, and which the captain could not strip him of because he was forced to surprise his person in the minute he sold him. When he found his habit made him liable, as he thought, to be gazed at the more, he begged Trefry to give him something more befitting a slave, which he did, and took off his robes. Nevertheless, he shone through all and his osenbrigs (a sort of brown holland suit he had on) could not conceal the graces of his looks and mien; and he had no less admirers than when he had his dazzling habit on. The royal youth appeared in spite of the slave, and people could not help treating him after a different manner without designing it; as soon as they approached him they venerated and esteemed him; his eyes insensibly commanded respect, and his behaviour insinuated it into every soul. So that there was nothing talked of but this young and gallant slave, even by those who yet knew not that he was a prince.

I ought to tell you, that the Christians never buy any slaves but they give them some name of their own, their native ones being likely very barbarous, and hard to pronounce; so that Mr. Trefry gave Oroonoko that of Caesar, which name will live in that country as long as that (scarce more) glorious one of the great Roman, for 'tis most evident, he wanted no part of the personal courage of that Caesar, and acted things as memorable, had they been done in some part of the world replenished with people and historians that might have given him his due. But his misfortune was to fall in an obscure world, that afforded only a female pen to celebrate his fame, though I doubt not but it had lived from others' endeavours, if the Dutch, who, immediately after his time, took that country, had not killed, banished, and dispersed all those that were capable of giving the world this great man's life,[2] much better than I have done. And Mr. Trefry, who designed it, died before he began it, and bemoaned himself for not having undertook it in time.

For the future therefore, I must call Oroonoko Caesar, since by that name only he was known in our western world, and by that name he was received on shore at Parham House, where he was destined a slave. But if the King himself (God bless him) had come ashore, there could not have been greater expectations by all the whole plantation, and those neighbouring ones, than was on ours at that time; and he was received more like a governor than a slave. Notwithstanding, as the custom was, they assigned him his portion of land, his house, and his business, up in the plantation.

But as it was more for form than any design to put him to his task, he endured no more of the slave but the name, and remained some days in the house, receiving all visits that were made him, without stirring towards that part of the plantation where the Negroes were.

At last, he would needs go view his land, his house, and the business assigned him. But he no sooner came to the houses of the slaves, which are like a little town by itself, the Negroes all having left work, but they all came forth to behold him, and found he was that prince who had, at several times, sold most of them to these parts; and, from a veneration they pay to great men, especially if they know them, and from the surprise and awe they had at the sight of him, they all cast themselves at his feet, crying out, in their language, "Live, O King! Long live, O King!" And kissing his feet, paid him even divine homage.

[1] *backearary* From the word "buckra," meaning white man.

[2] *the Dutch ... life* The Dutch took control of Surinam from the British in 1667.

Several English gentlemen were with him, and what Mr. Trefry had told them, was here confirmed of which he himself before had no other witness than Caesar himself. But he was infinitely glad to find his grandeur confirmed by the adoration of all the slaves.

Caesar, troubled with their over-joy, and over-ceremony, besought them to rise, and to receive him as their fellow slave, assuring them, he was no better. At which they set up with one accord a most terrible and hideous mourning and condoling, which he and the English had much ado to appease. But at last they prevailed with them, and they prepared all their barbarous music, and everyone killed and dressed something of his own stock (for every family has their land apart, on which, at their leisure times, they breed all eatable things) and clubbing it together, made a most magnificent supper, inviting their grandee captain, their Prince, to honour it with his presence, which he did, and several English with him, where they all waited on him, some playing, others dancing before him all the time, according to the manners of their several nations, and with unwearied industry, endeavouring to please and delight him.

While they sat at meat Mr. Trefry told Caesar, that most of these young slaves were undone in love, with a fine she slave, whom they had had about six months on their land. The Prince, who never heard the name of love without a sigh, nor any mention of it without the curiosity of examining further into that tale, which of all discourses was most agreeable to him, asked, how they came to be so unhappy, as to be all undone for one fair slave? Trefry, who was naturally amorous, and loved to talk of love as well as anybody, proceeded to tell him, they had the most charming black that ever was beheld on their plantation, about fifteen or sixteen years old, as he guessed; that, for his part, he had done nothing but sigh for her ever since she came; and that all the white beauties he had seen, never charmed him so absolutely as this fine creature had done; and that no man, of any nation, ever beheld her, that did not fall in love with her; and that she had all the slaves perpetually at her feet; and the whole country resounded with the fame of Clemene, for so, said he, we have christened her. But she denies us all with such a noble disdain, that 'tis a miracle to see that she, who can give such eternal desires, should herself be all ice, and all unconcern. She is adorned with the most graceful modesty that ever beautified youth, the softest sigher—that, if she were capable of love, one would swear she languished for some absent happy man, and so retired, as if she feared a rape even from the God of Day,[1] or that the breezes would steal kisses from her delicate mouth. Her task of work some sighing lover every day makes it his petition to perform for her, which she accepts blushing, and with reluctance, for fear he will ask her a look for a recompense, which he dares not presume to hope, so great an awe she strikes into the hearts of her admirers. "I do not wonder," replied the Prince, "that Clemene should refuse slaves, being as you say so beautiful, but wonder how she escapes those who can entertain her as you can do. Or why, being your slave, you do not oblige her to yield."

"I confess," said Trefry, "when I have, against her will, entertained her with love so long, as to be transported with my passion, even above decency, I have been ready to make use of those advantages of strength and force nature has given me. But oh! she disarms me, with that modesty and weeping so tender and so moving, that I retire, and thank my stars she overcame me." The company laughed at his civility to a slave, and Caesar only applauded the nobleness of his passion and nature, since that slave might be noble, or, what was better, have true notions of honour and virtue in her. Thus passed they this night, after having received, from the slaves, all imaginable respect and obedience.

The next day Trefry asked Caesar to walk, when the heat was allayed, and designedly carried him by the cottage of the fair slave, and told him, she whom he spoke of last night lived there retired. "But," says he, "I would not wish you to approach, for, I am sure, you will be in love as soon as you behold her." Caesar assured him, he was proof against all the charms of that sex, and that if he imagined his heart could be so perfidious to love again, after Imoinda, he believed he should tear it from his bosom. They had no sooner spoke, but a little shock dog,[2] that Clemene had presented her, which she took great delight in, ran out, and she, not knowing anybody was there, ran to get it in again, and bolted out

---

[1] *the God of Day* Apollo, god of light, here represented by the sun.

[2] *shock dog* Small, long-haired dog.

on those who were just speaking of her. When seeing them, she would have run in again, but Trefry caught her by the hand, and cried, "Clemene, however you fly a lover, you ought to pay some respect to this stranger" (pointing to Caesar). But she, as if she had resolved never to raise her eyes to the face of a man again, bent them the more to the earth, when he spoke, and gave the Prince the leisure to look the more at her. There needed no long gazing, or consideration, to examine who this fair creature was. He soon saw Imoinda all over her; in a minute he saw her face, her shape, her air, her modesty, and all that called forth his soul with joy at his eyes, and left his body destitute of almost life. It stood without motion, and, for a minute, knew not that it had a being. And, I believe, he had never come to himself, so oppressed he was with over-joy, if he had not met with this allay,[1] that he perceived Imoinda fall dead in the hands of Trefry. This awakened him, and he ran to her aid, and caught her in his arms, where, by degrees, she came to herself; and 'tis needless to tell with what transports, what ecstasies of joy, they both a while beheld each other, without speaking, then snatched each other to their arms, then gaze again, as if they still doubted whether they possessed the blessing they grasped. But when they recovered their speech, 'tis not to be imagined what tender things they expressed to each other, wondering what strange fate had brought them again together. They soon informed each other of their fortunes, and equally bewailed their fate; but, at the same time, they mutually protested, that even fetters and slavery were soft and easy, and would be supported with joy and pleasure, while they could be so happy to possess each other, and to be able to make good their vows. Caesar swore he disdained the empire of the world, while he could behold his Imoinda, and she despised grandeur and pomp, those vanities of her sex, when she could gaze on Oroonoko. He adored the very cottage where she resided, and said, that little inch of the world would give him more happiness than all the universe could do, and she vowed, it was a palace, while adorned with the presence of Oroonoko.

Trefry was infinitely pleased with this novel,[2] and found this Clemene was the fair mistress of whom Caesar had before spoke, and was not a little satisfied, that heaven was so kind to the Prince, as to sweeten his misfortunes by so lucky an accident, and leaving the lovers to themselves, was impatient to come down to Parham House (which was on the same plantation) to give me an account of what had happened. I was as impatient to make these lovers a visit, having already made a friendship with Caesar, and from his own mouth learned what I have related, which was confirmed by his Frenchman, who was set on shore to seek his fortunes, and of whom they could not make a slave, because a Christian, and he came daily to Parham Hill to see and pay his respects to his pupil Prince. So that concerning and interesting myself in all that related to Caesar, whom I had assured of liberty as soon as the governor arrived, I hasted presently to the place where the lovers were, and was infinitely glad to find this beautiful young slave (who had already gained all our esteems, for her modesty and her extraordinary prettiness) to be the same I had heard Caesar speak so much of. One may imagine then, we paid her a treble respect; and though from her being carved in fine flowers and birds all over her body, we took her to be of quality before, yet, when we knew Clemene was Imoinda, we could not enough admire her.

I had forgot to tell you, that those who are nobly born of that country are so delicately cut and raced[3] all over the fore part of the trunk of their bodies, that it looks as if it were japanned,[4] the works being raised like high point round the edges of the flowers. Some are only carved with a little flower, or bird, at the sides of the temples, as was Caesar; and those who are so carved over the body, resemble our ancient Picts,[5] that are figured in the chronicles, but these carvings are more delicate.

From that happy day Caesar took Clemene for his wife, to the general joy of all people, and there was as much magnificence as the country would afford at the celebration of this wedding. And in a very short time after she conceived with child, which made Caesar even adore her, knowing he was the last of his great race. This

[1] *allay* Hindrance, cause of diminishment.

[2] *novel* Story.

[3] *raced* Engraved; i.e., ritual scarification.

[4] *japanned* Lacquered in the Japanese style.

[5] *Picts* From the Latin *pictii,* meaning painted, an ancient people of northern Britain who were said to have been ornately tattooed.

new accident made him more impatient of liberty, and he was every day treating with Trefry for his and Clemene's liberty, and offered either gold, or a vast quantity of slaves, which should be paid before they let him go, provided he could have any security that he should go when his ransom was paid. They fed him from day to day with promises, and delayed him, till the Lord Governor should come, so that he began to suspect them of falsehood, and that they would delay him till the time of his wife's delivery, and make a slave of that too, for all the breed is theirs to whom the parents belong. This thought made him very uneasy, and his sullenness gave them some jealousies[1] of him, so that I was obliged, by some persons who feared a mutiny (which is very fatal sometimes in those colonies that abound so with slaves that they exceed the whites in vast numbers), to discourse with Caesar, and to give him all the satisfaction I possibly could. They knew he and Clemene were scarce an hour in a day from my lodgings, that they ate with me, and that I obliged them in all things I was capable of: I entertained him with the lives of the Romans, and great men, which charmed him to my company, and her, with teaching her all the pretty works[2] that I was mistress of, and telling her stories of nuns, and endeavouring to bring her to the knowledge of the true God. But of all discourses Caesar liked that the worst, and would never be reconciled to our notions of the Trinity, of which he ever made a jest; it was a riddle, he said, would turn his brain to conceive, and one could not make him understand what faith was. However, these conversations failed not altogether so well to divert him, that he liked the company of us women much above the men, for he could not drink, and he is but an ill companion in that country that cannot. So that obliging him to love us very well, we had all the liberty of speech with him, especially myself, whom he called his Great Mistress; and indeed my word would go a great way with him. For these reasons, I had opportunity to take notice to him, that he was not well pleased of late, as he used to be, was more retired and thoughtful, and told him, I took it ill he should suspect we would break our words with him, and not permit both him and Clemene to return to his own kingdom, which was not so long away, but when he was once on his voyage he would quickly arrive there. He made me some answers that showed a doubt in him, which made me ask him, what advantage it would be to doubt? It would but give us a fear of him, and possibly compel us to treat him so as I should be very loath to behold: that is, it might occasion his confinement. Perhaps this was not so luckily spoke of me, for I perceived he resented that word, which I strove to soften again in vain. However, he assured me, that whatsoever resolutions he should take, he would act nothing upon the white people. And as for myself, and those upon that plantation where he was, he would sooner forfeit his eternal liberty, and life itself, than lift his hand against his greatest enemy on that place. He besought me to suffer no fears upon his account, for he could do nothing that honour should not dictate, but he accused himself for having suffered slavery so long; yet he charged that weakness on love alone, who was capable of making him neglect even glory itself, and, for which, now he reproaches himself every moment of the day. Much more to this effect he spoke, with an air impatient enough to make me know he would not be long in bondage, and though he suffered only the name of a slave, and had nothing of the toil and labour of one, yet that was sufficient to render him uneasy, and he had been too long idle, who used to be always in action, and in arms. He had a spirit all rough and fierce, and that could not be tamed to lazy rest, and though all endeavours were used to exercise himself in such actions and sports as this world afforded, as running, wrestling, pitching the bar,[3] hunting and fishing, chasing and killing tigers of a monstrous size, which this continent affords in abundance, and wonderful snakes, such as Alexander is reported to have encountered at the river of Amazons, and which Caesar took great delight to overcome; yet these were not actions great enough for his large soul, which was still panting after more renowned action.

Before I parted that day with him, I got, with much ado, a promise from him to rest yet a little longer with patience, and wait the coming of the Lord Governor, who was every day expected on our shore. He assured me he would, and this promise he desired me to know

[1] *jealousies* Apprehensions; suspicions.

[2] *works* Kinds of needlework.

[3] *pitching the bar* Throwing a heavy rod was considered both a game and a form of exercise.

was given perfectly in complaisance to me, in whom he had an entire confidence.

After this, I neither thought it convenient to trust him much out of our view, nor did the country who feared him; but with one accord it was advised to treat him fairly, and oblige him to remain within such a compass, and that he should be permitted, as seldom as could be, to go up to the plantations of the Negroes, or, if he did, to be accompanied by some that should be rather in appearance attendants than spies. This care was for some time taken, and Caesar looked upon it as a mark of extraordinary respect, and was glad his discontent had obliged them to be more observant to him. He received new assurance from the overseer, which was confirmed to him by the opinion of all the gentlemen of the country, who made their court to him. During this time that we had his company more frequently than hitherto we had had, it may not be unpleasant to relate to you the diversions we entertained him with, or rather he us.

My stay was to be short in that country, because my father died at sea, and never arrived to possess the honour was designed him (which was lieutenant-general of six and thirty islands, besides the continent of Surinam), nor the advantages he hoped to reap by them, so that though we were obliged to continue on our voyage, we did not intend to stay upon the place. Though, in a word, I must say thus much of it, that certainly had his late Majesty, of sacred memory, but seen and known what a vast and charming world he had been master of in that continent, he would never have parted so easily with it to the Dutch. 'Tis a continent whose vast extent was never yet known, and may contain more noble earth than all the universe besides; for, they say, it reaches from east to west, one way as far as China, and another to Peru. It affords all things both for beauty and use; 'tis there eternal spring, always the very months of April, May and June. The shades are perpetual, the trees, bearing at once all degrees of leaves and fruit, from blooming buds to ripe autumn, groves of oranges, lemons, citrons, figs, nutmegs, and noble aromatics, continually bearing their fragrancies. The trees appearing all like nosegays adorned with flowers of different kind; some are all white, some purple, some scarlet, some blue, some yellow; bearing, at the same time, ripe fruit and blooming young, or producing every day new. The very wood of all these trees have an intrinsic value above common timber, for they are, when cut, of different colours, glorious to behold, and bear a price considerable, to inlay withal. Besides this, they yield rich balm, and gums, so that we make our candles of such an aromatic substance, as does not only give a sufficient light, but, as they burn, they cast their perfumes all about. Cedar is the common firing, and all the houses are built with it. The very meat we eat, when set on the table, if it be native, I mean of the country, perfumes the whole room, especially a little beast called an armadillo, a thing which I can liken to nothing so well as a rhinoceros. 'Tis all in white armour so jointed, that it moves as well in it, as if it had nothing on. This beast is about the bigness of a pig of six weeks old. But it were endless to give an account of all the diverse wonderful and strange things that country affords, and which we took a very great delight to go in search of, though those adventures are oftentimes fatal and at least dangerous. But while we had Caesar in our company on these designs we feared no harm, nor suffered any.

As soon as I came into the country, the best house in it was presented me, called St. John's Hill. It stood on a vast rock of white marble, at the foot of which the river ran a vast depth down, and not to be descended on that side. The little waves still dashing and washing the foot of this rock, made the softest murmurs and purlings in the world, and the opposite bank was adorned with such vast quantities of different flowers eternally blowing,[1] and every day and hour new, fenced behind them with lofty trees of a thousand rare forms and colours, that the prospect was the most ravishing that sands can create. On the edge of this white rock, towards the river, was a walk or grove of orange and lemon trees, about half the length of the Mall[2] here, whose flowery and fruity branches meet at the top, and hindered the sun, whose rays are very fierce there, from entering a beam into the grove, and the cool air that came from the river made it not only fit to entertain people in, at all the hottest hours of the day, but refreshed the sweet blossoms, and made it always sweet and charming, and sure the whole globe of the world cannot show so delightful a place as

[1] *blowing* Blooming.

[2] *Mall* Tree-lined promenade in St. James's Park, London.

this grove was. Not all the gardens of boasted Italy can produce a shade to out-vie this, which nature had joined with art to render so exceeding fine. And 'tis a marvel to see how such vast trees, as big as English oaks, could take footing on so solid a rock, and in so little earth, as covered that rock, but all things by nature there are rare, delightful and wonderful. But to our sports.

Sometimes we would go surprising,[1] and in search of young tigers[2] in their dens, watching when the old ones went forth to forage for prey, and oftentimes we have been in great danger, and have fled apace for our lives, when surprised by the dams. But once, above all other times, we went on this design, and Caesar was with us, who had no sooner stolen a young tiger from her nest, but going off, we encountered the dam,[3] bearing a buttock of a cow, which he had torn off with his mighty paw, and going with it towards his den. We had only four women, Caesar, and an English gentleman, brother to Harry Martin, the great Oliverian.[4] We found there was no escaping this enraged and ravenous beast. However, we women fled as fast as we could from it, but our heels had not saved our lives, if Caesar had not laid down his cub, when he found the tiger quit her prey to make the more speed towards him, and taking Mr. Martin's sword desired him to stand aside, or follow the ladies. He obeyed him, and Caesar met this monstrous beast of might, size, and vast limbs, who came with open jaws upon him, and fixing his awful stern eyes full upon those of the beast, and putting himself into a very steady and good aiming posture of defence, ran his sword quite through his breast down to his very heart, home to the hilt of the sword. The dying beast stretched forth her paw, and going to grasp his thigh, surprised with death in that very moment, did him no other harm than fixing her long nails in his flesh very deep, feebly wounded him, but could not grasp the flesh to tear off any. When he had done this, he hollowed to us to return, which, after some assurance of his victory, we did, and found him lugging out the sword from the bosom of the tiger, who was laid in her blood on the ground. He took up the cub, and with an unconcern, that had nothing of the joy or gladness of a victory, he came and laid the whelp at my feet. We all extremely wondered at his daring, and at the bigness of the beast, which was about the height of an heifer, but of mighty, great, and strong limbs.

Another time, being in the woods, he killed a tiger, which had long infested that part, and borne away abundance of sheep and oxen, and other things, that were for the support of those to whom they belonged. Abundance of people assailed this beast, some affirming they had shot her with several bullets quite through the body, at several times, and some swearing they shot her through the very heart, and they believed she was a devil rather than a mortal thing. Caesar had often said, he had a mind to encounter this monster, and spoke with several gentlemen who had attempted her, one crying, I shot her with so many poisoned arrows, another with his gun in this part of her, and another in that. So that he remarking all these places where she was shot, fancied still he should overcome her, by giving her another sort of a wound than any had yet done, and one day said (at the table) "What trophies and garlands ladies will you make me, if I bring you home the heart of this ravenous beast, that eats up all your lambs and pigs?" We all promised he should be rewarded at all our hands. So taking a bow, which he chose out of a great many, he went up in the wood, with two gentlemen, where he imagined this devourer to be. They had not passed very far in it, but they heard her voice, growling and grumbling, as if she were pleased with something she was doing. When they came in view, they found her muzzling in the belly of a new ravished sheep, which she had torn open, and seeing herself approached, she took fast hold of her prey, with her forepaws, and set a very fierce raging look on Caesar, without offering to approach him, for fear, at the same time, of losing what she had in possession. So that Caesar remained a good while, only taking aim, and getting an opportunity to shoot her where he designed. 'Twas some time before he could accomplish it, and to wound her, and not kill her, would but have enraged her more, and endangered him. He had a quiver of arrows at his side, so that if one failed he could be supplied. At last, retiring a little, he gave her opportunity to eat, for he found she was

[1] *surprising* Raiding.

[2] *tigers* Pumas (cougars).

[3] *dam* Behn confuses the tiger's gender in the following message.

[4] *Oliverian* Martin owned Surinam plantations and had been a supporter of Oliver Cromwell.

ravenous, and fell to as soon as she saw him retire, being more eager of her prey than of doing new mischiefs. When he going softly to one side of her, and hiding his person behind certain herbage that grew high and thick, he took so good aim, that, as he intended, he shot her just into the eye, and the arrow was sent with so good a will, and so sure a hand, that it stuck in her brain, and made her caper, and become mad for a moment or two, but being seconded by another arrow, he fell dead upon the prey. Caesar cut him open with a knife, to see where those wounds were that had been reported to him, and why he did not die of them. But I shall now relate a thing that possibly will find no credit among men, because 'tis a notion commonly received with us, that nothing can receive a wound in the heart and live; but when the heart of this courageous animal was taken out, there were seven bullets of lead in it, and the wounds seamed up with great scars, and she lived with the bullets a great while, for it was long since they were shot. This heart the conqueror brought up to us, and 'twas a very great curiosity, which all the country came to see, and which gave Caesar occasion of many fine discourses, of accidents in war, and strange escapes.

At other times he would go a-fishing, and discoursing on that diversion, he found we had in that country a very strange fish, called, a numb eel[1] (an eel of which I have eaten) that while it is alive, it has a quality so cold, that those who are angling, though with a line of never so great a length, with a rod at the end of it, it shall, in the same minute the bait is touched by this eel, seize him or her that holds the rod with benumbedness, that shall deprive them of sense, for a while. And some have fallen into the water, and others dropped as dead on the banks of the rivers where they stood, as soon as this fish touches the bait. Caesar used to laugh at this, and believed it impossible a man could lose his force at the touch of a fish, and could not understand that philosophy,[2] that a cold quality should be of that nature. However, he had a great curiosity to try whether it would have the same effect on him it had on others, and often tried, but in vain. At last, the sought for fish came to the bait, as he stood angling on the bank; and instead of throwing away the rod, or giving it a sudden twitch out of the water, whereby he might have caught both the eel, and have dismissed the rod, before it could have too much power over him for experiment sake, he grasped it but the harder, and fainting fell into the river. And being still possessed of the rod, the tide carried him senseless as he was a great way, till an Indian boat took him up, and perceived, when they touched him, a numbness seize them, and by that knew the rod was in his hand, which, with a paddle (that is, a short oar) they struck away, and snatched it into the boat, eel and all. If Caesar were almost dead, with the effect of this fish, he was more so with that of the water, where he had remained the space of going a league,[3] and they found they had much ado to bring him back to life. But, at last, they did, and brought him home, where he was in a few hours well recovered and refreshed; and not a little ashamed to find he should be overcome by an eel, and that all the people, who heard his defiance, would laugh at him. But we cheered him up, and he, being convinced, we had the eel at supper; which was a quarter of an ell about, and most delicate meat, and was of the more value, since it cost so dear as almost the life of so gallant a man.

About this time we were in many mortal fears about some disputes the English had with the Indians, so that we could scarce trust ourselves, without great numbers, to go to any Indian towns, or place, where they abode, for fear they should fall upon us, as they did immediately after my coming away, and that it was in the possession of the Dutch, who used them not so civilly as the English, so that they cut in pieces all they could take, getting into houses, and hanging up the mother, and all her children about her, and cut a footman I left behind me, all in joints, and nailed him to trees.

This feud began while I was there, so that I lost half the satisfaction I proposed, in not seeing and visiting the Indian towns. But one day, bemoaning of our misfortunes upon this account, Caesar told us, we need not fear, for if we had a mind to go, he would undertake to be our guard. Some would, but most would not venture. About eighteen of us resolved, and took barge, and, after eight days, arrived near an Indian town. But approaching it, the hearts of some of our company failed, and they would not venture on shore, so we polled who

[1] *numb eel* Electric eel.

[2] *philosophy* Scientific phenomenon.

[3] *league* Approximately three miles.

would, and who would not. For my part, I said, if Caesar would, I would go. He resolved, so did my brother, and my woman, a maid of good courage. Now none of us speaking the language of the people, and imagining we should have a half diversion in gazing only and not knowing what they said, we took a fisherman that lived at the mouth of the river, who had been a long inhabitant there, and obliged him to go with us. But because he was known to the Indians, as trading among them, and being, by long living there, become a perfect Indian in colour, we, who resolved to surprise them, by making them see something they never had seen (that is, white people) resolved only myself, my brother, and woman should go. So Caesar, the fisherman, and the rest, hiding behind some thick reeds and flowers, that grew on the banks, let us pass on towards the town, which was on the bank of the river all along. A little distant from the houses, or huts, we saw some dancing, others busied in fetching and carrying of water from the river. They had no sooner spied us, but they set up a loud cry, that frighted us at first. We thought it had been for those that should kill us, but it seems it was of wonder and amazement. They were all naked, and we were dressed, so as is most commode[1] for the hot countries, very glittering and rich, so that we appeared extremely fine. My own hair was cut short, and I had a taffeta cap, with black feathers, on my head. My brother was in a stuff[2] suit, with silver loops and buttons, and abundance of green ribbon. This was all infinitely surprising to them, and because we saw them stand still, till we approached them, we took heart and advanced, came up to them, and offered them our hands, which they took, and looked on us round about, calling still for more company, who came swarming out, all wondering, and crying out "*tepeeme*," taking their hair up in their hands, and spreading it wide to those they called out to, as if they would say (as indeed it signified) "numberless wonders," or not to be recounted, no more than to number the hair of their heads. By degrees they grew more bold, and from gazing upon us round, they touched us, laying their hands upon all the features of our faces, feeling our breasts and arms, taking up one petticoat, then wondering to see another, admiring our shoes and stockings, but more our garters, which we gave them, and they tied about their legs, being laced with silver lace at the ends, for they much esteem any shining things. In fine,[3] we suffered them to survey us as they pleased, and we thought they would never have done admiring us. When Caesar, and the rest, saw we were received with such wonder, they came up to us, and finding the Indian trader whom they knew (for 'tis by these fishermen, called Indian traders, we hold a commerce with them; for they love not to go far from home, and we never go to them), when they saw him therefore they set up a new joy, and cried, in their language, "Oh! here's our *tiguamy*, and we shall now know whether those things can speak." So advancing to him, some of them gave him their hands, and cried, "*Amora tiguamy*," which is as much as, "How do you," or "Welcome friend," and all, with one din, began to gabble to him, and asked if we had sense, and wit? If we could talk of affairs of life, and war, as they could do? If we could hunt, swim, and do a thousand things they use? He answered them, we could. Then they invited us into their houses, and dressed venison and buffalo for us, and, going out, gathered a leaf of a tree, called a sarumbo leaf, of six yards long, and spread it on the ground for a tablecloth, and cutting another in pieces instead of plates, setting us on little bow Indian stools, which they cut out of one entire piece of wood, and paint, in a sort of japan work. They serve everyone their mess on these pieces of leaves, and it was very good, but too high seasoned with pepper. When we had eaten, my brother and I took out our flutes, and played to them, which gave them new wonder, and I soon perceived, by an admiration that is natural to these people, and by the extreme ignorance and simplicity of them, it were not difficult to establish any unknown or extravagant religion among them, and to impose any notions or fictions upon them. For seeing a kinsman of mine set some paper afire, with a burning-glass, a trick they had never before seen, they were like to have adored him for a god, and begged he would give them the characters or figures of his name, that they might oppose it against winds and storms, which he did, and they held it up in those seasons, and fancied it had a charm to conquer them, and kept it like a holy relic. They are very super-

[1] *commode* Suitable.

[2] *stuff* Wool.

[3] *In fine* In the end.

stitious, and called him the great *peeie*, that is, prophet. They showed us their Indian *peeie*, a youth of about sixteen years old, as handsome as nature could make a man. They consecrate a beautiful youth from his infancy, and all arts are used to complete him in the finest manner, both in beauty and shape. He is bred to all the little arts and cunning they are capable of, to all the legerdemain[1] tricks, and sleight of hand, whereby he imposes upon the rabble, and is both a doctor in physic and divinity. And by these tricks makes the sick believe he sometimes eases their pains, by drawing from the afflicted part little serpents, or odd flies, or worms, or any strange thing; and though they have besides undoubted good remedies, for almost all their diseases, they cure the patient more by fancy than by medicines, and make themselves feared, loved, and reverenced. This young *peeie* had a very young wife, who seeing my brother kiss her, came running and kissed me; after this, they kissed one another, and made it a very great jest, it being so novel, and new admiration and laughing went round the multitude, that they never will forget that ceremony, never before used or known. Caesar had a mind to see and talk with their war captains, and we were conducted to one of their houses, where we beheld several of the great captains, who had been at council. But so frightful a vision it was to see them no fancy can create; no such dreams can represent so dreadful a spectacle. For my part I took them for hobgoblins, or fiends, rather than men. But however their shapes appeared, their souls were very humane and noble, but some wanted their noses, some their lips, some both noses and lips, some their ears, and others cut through each cheek, with long slashes, through which their teeth appeared; they had several other formidable wounds and scars, or rather dismemberings. They had *comitias*, or little aprons before them, and girdles of cotton, with their knives naked, stuck in it, a bow at their backs, and a quiver of arrows on their thighs, and most had feathers on their heads of diverse colours. They cried "*Amora tigame*" to us at our entrance, and were pleased we said as much to them. They feted us, and gave us drink of the best sort, and wondered, as much as the others had done before, to see us. Caesar was marvelling as much at their faces, wondering how they should all be so wounded in war; he was impatient to know how they all came by those frightful marks of rage or malice, rather than wounds got in noble battle. They told us, by our interpreter, that when any war was waging, two men chosen out by some old captain, whose fighting was past, and who could only teach the theory of war, these two men were to stand in competition for the generalship, or Great War Captain, and being brought before the old judges, now past labour, they are asked, what they dare do to show they are worthy to lead an army? When he, who is first asked, making no reply, cuts off his nose, and throws it contemptibly on the ground, and the other does something to himself that he thinks surpasses him, and perhaps deprives himself of lips and an eye. So they slash on till one gives out, and many have died in this debate. And 'tis by a passive valour they show and prove their activity, a sort of courage too brutal to be applauded by our black hero; nevertheless he expressed his esteem of them.

In this voyage Caesar begot so good an understanding between the Indians and the English, that there were no more fears, or heartburnings during our stay, but we had a perfect, open, and free trade with them. Many things remarkable, and worthy reciting, we met with in this short voyage, because Caesar made it his business to search out and provide for our entertainment, especially to please his dearly adored Imoinda, who was a sharer in all our adventures; we being resolved to make her chains as easy as we could, and to compliment the Prince in that manner that most obliged him.

As we were coming up again, we met with some Indians of strange aspects, that is, of a larger size, and other sort of features, than those of our country. Our Indian slaves, that rowed us, asked them some questions, but they could not understand us, but showed us a long cotton string, with several knots on it, and told us, they had been coming from the mountains so many moons as there were knots. They were habited in skins of a strange beast, and brought along with them bags of gold dust, which, as well as they could give us to understand, came streaming in little small channels down the high mountains, when the rains fell, and offered to be the convoy to anybody, or persons, that would go to the mountains. We carried these men up to Parham, where they were kept till the Lord Governor came. And

[1] *legerdemain* Magic.

because all the country was mad to be going on this golden adventure, the governor, by his letters, commanded (for they sent some of the gold to him) that a guard should be set at the mouth of the river of Amazons (a river so called, almost as broad as the river of Thames), and prohibited all people from going up that river, it conducting to those mountains of gold. But we going off for England before the project was further prosecuted, and the governor being drowned in a hurricane,[1] either the design died, or the Dutch have the advantage of it. And 'tis to be bemoaned what His Majesty lost by losing that part of America.

Though this digression is a little from my story, however since it contains some proofs of the curiosity and daring of this great man, I was content to omit nothing of his character.

It was thus, for some time we diverted him. But now Imoinda began to show she was with child, and did nothing but sigh and weep for the captivity of her lord, herself, and the infant yet unborn, and believed, if it were so hard to gain the liberty of two, 'twould be more difficult to get that for three. Her griefs were so many darts in the great heart of Caesar, and taking his opportunity one Sunday, when all the whites were overtaken in drink, as there were abundance of several trades, and slaves for four years,[2] that inhabited among the Negro houses, and Sunday was their day of debauch (otherwise they were a sort of spies upon Caesar), he went pretending out of goodness to them, to feast amongst them, and sent all his music, and ordered a great treat for the whole gang, about three hundred Negroes. And about a hundred and fifty were able to bear arms, such as they had, which were sufficient to do execution with spirits accordingly. For the English had none but rusty swords, that no strength could draw from a scabbard, except the people of particular quality, who took care to oil them and keep them in good order. The guns also, unless here and there one, or those newly carried from England, would do no good or harm, for 'tis the nature of that county to rust and eat up iron, or any metals, but gold and silver. And they are very inexpert at the bow, which the Negroes and Indians are perfect masters of.

Caesar, having singled out these men from the women and children, made a harangue to them of the miseries, and ignominies of slavery; counting up all their toils and sufferings, under such loads, burdens, and drudgeries, as were fitter for beasts than men; senseless brutes, than human souls. He told them it was not for days, months, or years, but for eternity; there was no end to be of their misfortunes. They suffered not like men who might find a glory, and fortitude in oppression, but like dogs that loved the whip and bell, and fawned the more they were beaten. That they had lost the divine quality of men, and were become insensible asses, fit only to bear. Nay worse, an ass, or dog, or horse having done his duty, could lie down in retreat, and rise to work again, and while he did his duty endured no stripes, but men, villainous, senseless men, such as they, toiled on all the tedious week till Black Friday, and then, whether they worked or not, whether they were faulty or meriting, they promiscuously, the innocent with the guilty, suffered the infamous whip, the sordid stripes, from their fellow slaves till their blood trickled from all parts of their body, blood whose every drop ought to be revenged with a life of some of those tyrants that impose it. "And why," said he, "my dear friends and fellow sufferers, should we be slaves to an unknown people? Have they vanquished us nobly in fight? Have they won us in honourable battle? And are we, by the chance of war, become their slaves? This would not anger a noble heart, this would not animate a soldier's soul. No, but we are bought and sold like apes, or monkeys, to be the sport of women, fools and cowards, and the support of rogues, renegades, that have abandoned their own countries, for raping, murders, thefts and villainies. Do you not hear every day how they upbraid each other with infamy of life, below the wildest savages, and shall we render obedience to such a degenerate race, who have no one human virtue left, to distinguish them from the vilest creatures? Will you, I say, suffer the lash from such hands?"

They all replied, with one accord, "No, no, no; Caesar has spoke like a great captain, like a great king."

After this he would have proceeded, but was interrupted by a tall Negro of some more quality than the rest. His name was Tuscan, who bowing at the feet of

[1] *drowned in a hurricane* Lord Willoughby died at sea in 1666.

[2] *slaves for four years* Europeans could bind themselves to service in the colonies by contract, or indenture. Criminals were also shipped to the colonies to serve out sentences as laborers.

Caesar, cried, "My lord, we have listened with joy and attention to what you have said, and, were we only men, would follow so great a leader through the world. But oh! consider, we are husbands and parents too, and have things more dear to us than life: our wives and children unfit for travel, in these impassable woods, mountains and bogs. We have not only difficult lands to overcome, but rivers to wade, and monsters to encounter, ravenous beasts of prey—." To this, Caesar replied, that honour was the first principle in nature that was to be obeyed; but as no man would pretend[1] to that, without all the acts of virtue, compassion, charity, love, justice and reason, he found it not inconsistent with that, to take an equal care of their wives and children, as they would of themselves, and that he did not design, when he led them to freedom, and glorious liberty, that they should leave that better part of themselves to perish by the hand of the tyrant's whip. But if there were a woman among them so degenerate from love and virtue to choose slavery before the pursuit of her husband, and with the hazard of her life, to share with him in his fortunes, that such an one ought to be abandoned, and left as a prey to the common enemy.

To which they all agreed—and bowed. After this, he spoke of the impassable woods and rivers, and convinced them, the more danger, the more glory. He told them that he had heard of one Hannibal a great captain, had cut his way through mountains of solid rocks,[2] and should a few shrubs oppose them, which they could fire before them? No, 'twas a trifling excuse to men resolved to die, or overcome. As for bogs, they are with a little labour filled and hardened, and the rivers could be no obstacle, since they swam by nature, at least by custom, from their first hour of their birth. That when the children were weary they must carry them by turns, and the woods and their own industry would afford them food. To this they all assented with joy.

Tuscan then demanded, what he would do? He said, they would travel towards the sea; plant a new colony, and defend it by their valour; and when they could find a ship, either driven by stress of weather, or guided by providence that way, they would seize it, and make it a prize, till it had transported them to their own countries. At least, they should be made free in his kingdom, and be esteemed as his fellow sufferers, and men that had the courage, and the bravery to attempt, at least, for liberty. And if they died in the attempt it would be more brave, than to live in perpetual slavery.

They bowed and kissed his feet at this resolution, and with one accord vowed to follow him to death. And that night was appointed to begin their march; they made it known to their wives, and directed them to tie their hamaca[3] about their shoulder and under their arm like a scarf, and to lead their children that could go,[4] and carry those that could not. The wives who pay an entire obedience to their husbands obeyed, and stayed for them, where they were appointed. The men stayed but to furnish themselves with what defensive arms they could get, and all met at the rendezvous, where Caesar made a new encouraging speech to them, and led them out.

But, as they could not march far that night, on Monday early, when the overseers went to call them all together, to go to work, they were extremely surprised to find not one upon the place, but all fled with what baggage they had. You may imagine this news was not only suddenly spread all over the plantation, but soon reached the neighbouring ones, and we had by noon about six hundred men, they call the militia of the county, that came to assist us in the pursuit of the fugitives. But never did one see so comical an army march forth to war. The men, of any fashion,[5] would not concern themselves, though it were almost the common cause, for such revoltings are very ill examples, and have very fatal consequences oftentimes in many colonies. But they had a respect for Caesar, and all hands were against the Parhamites, as they called those of Parham plantation, because they did not, in the first place, love the Lord Governor, and secondly, they would have it, that Caesar was ill used, and baffled with.[6] And 'tis not impossible but some of the best in the country was of his counsel in this flight, and depriving us of all the slaves, so that they of the better sort

[1] *pretend* Claim to have or deserve.

[2] *Hannibal … rocks* Hannibal, the commander of the Carthaginians, crossed the Alps in 218 BCE on a mission to invade Rome.

[3] *hamaca* Hammock.

[4] *go* Walk.

[5] *fashion* Rank.

[6] *baffled with* Cheated.

would not meddle in the matter. The deputy governor, of whom I have had no great occasion to speak, and who was the most fawning fair-tongued fellow in the world, and one that pretended the most friendship to Caesar, was now the only violent man against him; and though he had nothing, and so need fear nothing, yet talked and looked bigger than any man. He was a fellow whose character is not fit to be mentioned with the worst of the slaves. This fellow would lead his army forth to meet Caesar, or rather to pursue him. Most of their arms were of those sort of cruel whips they call cat with nine tails; some had rusty useless guns for show, others old basket-hilts,[1] whose blades had never seen the light in this age, and others had long staffs, and clubs. Mr. Trefry went along, rather to be a mediator than a conqueror, in such a battle; for he foresaw, and knew, if by fighting they put the Negroes into despair, they were a sort of sullen fellows, that would drown, or kill themselves, before they would yield, and he advised that fair means was best. But Byam[2] was one that abounded in his own wit, and would take his own measures.

It was not hard to find these fugitives, for as they fled they were forced to fire and cut the woods before them, so that night or day they pursued them by the light they made, and by the path they had cleared. But as soon as Caesar found he was pursued, he put himself in a posture of defence, placing all the women and children in the rear, and himself, with Tuscan by his side, or next to him, all promising to die or conquer. Encouraged thus, they never stood to parley, but fell on pell-mell upon the English, and killed some, and wounded a good many, they having recourse to their whips, as the best of their weapons. And as they observed no order, they perplexed the enemy so sorely, with lashing them in the eyes. And the women and children, seeing their husbands so treated, being of fearful cowardly dispositions, and hearing the English cry out, "Yield and live, yield and be pardoned," they all ran in amongst their husbands and fathers, and hung about them, crying out, "Yield, yield, and leave Caesar to their revenge," that by degrees the slaves abandoned Caesar, and left him only Tuscan and his heroic Imoinda, who, grown big as she was, did nevertheless press near her lord, having a bow, and a quiver full of poisoned arrows, which she managed with such dexterity, that she wounded several, and shot the governor into the shoulder, of which wound he had like to have died, but that an Indian woman, his mistress, sucked the wound, and cleansed it from the venom. But however, he stirred not from the place till he had parleyed with Caesar, who he found was resolved to die fighting, and would not be taken; no more would Tuscan, or Imoinda. But he, more thirsting after revenge of another sort, than that of depriving him of life, now made use of all his art of talking, and dissembling, and besought Caesar to yield himself upon terms, which he himself should propose, and should be sacredly assented to and kept by him. He told him, it was not that he any longer feared him, or could believe the force of two men, and a young heroine, could overcome all them, with all the slaves now on their side also, but it was the vast esteem he had for his person, the desire he had to serve so gallant a man, and to hinder himself from the reproach hereafter, of having been the occasion of the death of a prince, whose valour and magnanimity deserved the empire of the world. He protested to him, he looked upon this action, as gallant and brave, however tending to the prejudice of his lord and master, who would by it have lost so considerable a number of slaves, that this flight of his should be looked on as a heat of youth, and rashness of a too forward courage, and an unconsidered impatience of liberty, and no more; and that he laboured in vain to accomplish that which they would effectually perform, as soon as any ship arrived that would touch on his coast. "So that if you will be pleased," continued he, "to surrender yourself, all imaginable respect shall be paid you; and yourself, your wife, and child, if it be here born, shall depart free out of our land." But Caesar would hear of no composition,[3] though Byam urged, if he pursued, and went on in his design, he would inevitably perish, either by great snakes, wild beasts, or hunger, and he ought to have regard to his wife, whose condition required ease, and not the fatigues of tedious travel, where she could not be secured from being devoured. But Caesar told him,

[1] *basket-hilts* Old-fashioned swords with basket-shaped guards on their hilts.

[2] *Byam* William Byam, deputy governor of Surinam under Lord Willoughby.

[3] *composition* Compromise.

there was no faith in the white men, or the gods they adored, who instructed them in principles so false, that honest men could not live amongst them; though no people professed so much, none performed so little; that he knew what he had to do, when he dealt with men of honour, but with them a man ought to be eternally on his guard, and never to eat and drink with Christians without his weapon of defence in his hand, and, for his own security, never to credit one word they spoke. As for the rashness and inconsiderateness of his action he would confess the governor is in the right, and that he was ashamed of what he had done, in endeavouring to make those free, who were by nature slaves, poor wretched rogues, fit to be used as Christians' tools; dogs, treacherous and cowardly, fit for such masters, and they wanted only but to be whipped into the knowledge of the Christian gods to be the vilest of all creeping things, to learn to worship such deities as had not power to make them just, brave, or honest. In fine, after a thousand things of this nature, not fit here to be recited, he told Byam, he had rather die than live upon the same earth with such dogs. But Trefry and Byam pleaded and protested together so much, that Trefry believing the governor to mean what he said, and speaking very cordially himself, generously put himself into Caesar's hands, and took him aside, and persuaded him, even with tears, to live, by surrendering himself, and to name his conditions. Caesar was overcome by his wit and reasons, and in consideration of Imoinda, and demanding what he desired, and that it should be ratified by their hands in writing, because he had perceived that was the common way of contract between man and man, amongst the whites. All this was performed, and Tuscan's pardon was put in, and they surrender to the governor, who walked peaceably down into the plantation with them, after giving order to bury their dead. Caesar was very much toiled with the bustle of the day, for he had fought like a Fury,[1] and what mischief was done he and Tuscan performed alone, and gave their enemies a fatal proof that they durst do anything, and feared no mortal force.

But they were no sooner arrived at the place, where all the slaves receive their punishments of whipping, but they laid hands on Caesar and Tuscan, faint with heat and toil; and, surprising them, bound them to two several stakes, and whipped them in a most deplorable and inhumane manner, rending the very flesh from their bones, especially Caesar, who was not perceived to make any moan, or to alter his face, only to roll his eyes on the faithless governor, and those he believed guilty, with fierceness and indignation. And, to complete his rage, he saw every one of those slaves, who, but a few days before, adored him as something more than mortal, now had a whip to give him some lashes, while he strove not to break his fetters, though, if he had, it were impossible. But he pronounced a woe and revenge from his eyes, that darted fire, that 'twas at once both awful and terrible to behold.

When they thought they were sufficiently revenged on him, they untied him, almost fainting with loss of blood, from a thousand wounds all over his body, from which they had rent his clothes, and led him bleeding and naked as he was, and loaded him all over with irons, and then rubbed his wounds, to complete their cruelty, with Indian pepper, which had like to have made him raving mad, and, in this condition, made him so fast to the ground that he could not stir, if his pains and wounds would have given him leave. They spared Imoinda, and did not let her see this barbarity committed towards her lord, but carried her down to Parham, and shut her up, which was not in kindness to her, but for fear she should die with the sight, or miscarry, and then they should lose a young slave, and perhaps the mother.

You must know, that when the news was brought on Monday morning, that Caesar had betaken himself to the woods, and carried with him all the Negroes, we were possessed with extreme fear, which no persuasions could dissipate, that he would secure himself till night, and then, that he would come down and cut all our throats. This apprehension made all the females of us fly down the river, to be secured, and while we were away, they acted this cruelty. For I suppose I had authority and interest enough there, had I suspected any such thing, to have prevented it, but we had not gone many leagues, but the news overtook us that Caesar was taken, and whipped like a common slave. We met on the river with Colonel Martin, a man of great gallantry, wit, and

[1] *Fury* One of the three Greek, and later Roman, avenging deities, who were terrifying in their aspects and behavior.

goodness, and, whom I have celebrated in a character of my new comedy,[1] by his own name, in memory of so brave a man. He was wise and eloquent, and, from the fineness of his parts, bore a great sway over the hearts of all the colony. He was a friend to Caesar, and resented this false dealing with him very much. We carried him back to Parham, thinking to have made an accommodation; when we came, the first news we heard was, that the governor was dead of a wound Imoinda had given him, but it was not so well. But it seems he would have the pleasure of beholding the revenge he took on Caesar, and before the cruel ceremony was finished, he dropped down, and then they perceived the wound he had on his shoulder was by a venomed arrow, which, as I said, his Indian mistress healed, by sucking the wound.

We were no sooner arrived, but we went up to the plantation to see Caesar, whom we found in a very miserable and inexpressible condition, and I have a thousand times admired how he lived, in so much tormenting pain. We said all things to him, that trouble, pity, and good nature could suggest, protesting our innocence of the fact, and our abhorrence of such cruelties, making a thousand professions of services to him, and begging as many pardons for the offenders, till we said so much, that he believed we had no hand in his ill treatment, but told us, he could never pardon Byam. As for Trefry, he confessed he saw his grief and sorrow, for his suffering, which he could not hinder, but was like to have been beaten down by the very slaves, for speaking in his defence. But for Byam, who was their leader, their head—and should, by his justice, and honour, have been an example to them—for him, he wished to live, to take a dire revenge of him, and said, "It had been well for him, if he had sacrificed me, instead of giving me the contemptible whip." He refused to talk much, but begging us to give him our hands, he took them, and protested never to lift up his, to do us any harm. He had a great respect for Colonel Martin, and always took his counsel, like that of a parent, and assured him, he would obey him in anything, but his revenge on Byam. "Therefore," said he, "for his own safety, let him speedily dispatch me, for if I could dispatch myself, I would not, till that justice were done to my injured person, and the contempt of a soldier. No, I would not kill myself, even after a whipping, but will be content to live with that infamy, and be pointed at by every grinning slave, till I have completed my revenge; and then you shall see that Oroonoko scorns to live with the indignity that was put on Caesar." All we could do could get no more words from him, and we took care to have him put immediately into a healing bath, to rid him of his pepper, and ordered a chirurgeon[2] to anoint him with healing balm, which he suffered, and in some time he began to be able to walk and eat. We failed not to visit him every day, and, to that end, had him brought to an apartment at Parham.

The governor was no sooner recovered, and had heard of the menaces of Caesar, but he called his council, who (not to disgrace them, or burlesque the government there) consisted of such notorious villains as Newgate never transported,[3] and possibly originally were such, who understood neither the laws of God or man, and had no sort of principles to make them worthy the name of men. But, at the very council table, would contradict and fight with one another, and swear so bloodily that 'twas terrible to hear, and see them. (Some of them were afterwards hanged, when the Dutch took possession of the place; others sent off in chains.) But calling these special rulers of the nation together, and requiring their counsel in this weighty affair, they all concluded, that (damn them) it might be their own cases, and that Caesar ought to be made an example to all the Negroes, to fright them from daring to threaten their betters, their lords and masters, and, at this rate, no man was safe from his own slaves, and concluded, *nemine contradicente*,[4] that Caesar should be hanged.

Trefry then thought it time to use his authority, and told Byam his command did not extend to his lord's plantation, and that Parham was as much exempt from the law as Whitehall;[5] and that they ought no more to touch the servants of the lord—(who there represented the King's person) than they could those about the King

[1] *character of my new comedy* George Marteen, in *The Younger Brother, or the Amorous Jilt* (1696).

[2] *chirurgeon* Surgeon.

[3] *Newgate … transported* London prison from which criminals were sometimes shipped out to the colonies.

[4] *nemine contradicente* Latin: unanimously.

[5] *Whitehall* Whitehall Palace, then the king's residence in London.

himself; and that Parham was a sanctuary, and though his lord were absent in person, his power was still in being there, which he had entrusted with him, as far as the dominions of his particular plantations reached, and all that belonged to it; the rest of the country, as Byam was lieutenant to his lord, he might exercise his tyranny upon. Trefry had others as powerful, or more, that interested themselves in Caesar's life, and absolutely said, he should be defended. So turning the governor, and his wise council, out of doors (for they sat at Parham House) we set a guard upon our landing place, and would admit none but those we called friends to us and Caesar.

The governor having remained wounded at Parham, till his recovery was completed, Caesar did not know but he was still there, and indeed, for the most part, his time was spent there, for he was one that loved to live at other people's expense, and if he were a day absent, he was then present there, and used to play, and walk, and hunt, and fish, with Caesar. So that Caesar did not at all doubt, if he once recovered strength, but he should find an opportunity of being revenged on him. Though, after such a revenge, he could not hope to live, for if he escaped the fury of the English mobile,[1] who perhaps would have been glad of the occasion to have killed him, he was resolved not to survive his whipping, yet he had, some tender hours, a repenting softness, which he called his fits of coward, wherein he struggled with love for the victory of his heart, which took part with his charming Imoinda there, but, for the most part, his time was passed in melancholy thought, and black designs. He considered, if he should do this deed, and die either in the attempt, or after it, he left his lovely Imoinda a prey, or at best a slave, to the enraged multitude; his great heart could not endure that thought. "Perhaps," said he, "she may be first ravished by every brute, exposed first to their nasty lusts, and then a shameful death." No, he could not live a moment under that apprehension, too insupportable to be borne. These were his thoughts, and his silent arguments with his heart, as he told us afterwards, so that now resolving not only to kill Byam, but all those he thought had enraged him, pleasing his great heart with the fancied slaughter he should make over the whole face of the plantation. He first resolved on a deed, that (however horrid it at first appeared to us all) when we had heard his reasons, we thought it brave and just. Being able to walk, and, as he believed, fit for the execution of his great design, he begged Trefry to trust him into the air, believing a walk would do him good, which was granted him, and taking Imoinda with him, as he used to do in his more happy and calmer days, he led her up into a wood, where, after (with a thousand sighs, and long gazing silently on her face, while tears gushed, in spite of him, from his eyes), he told her his design first of killing her, and then his enemies, and next himself, and the impossibility of escaping, and therefore he told her the necessity of dying. He found the heroic wife faster pleading for death than he was to propose it, when she found his fixed resolution, and, on her knees, besought him, not to leave her a prey to his enemies. He (grieved to death) yet pleased at her noble resolution, took her up, and embracing her, with all the passion and languishment of a dying lover, drew his knife to kill this treasure of his soul, this pleasure of his eyes. While tears trickled down his cheeks, hers were smiling with joy she should die by so noble a hand, and be sent in her own country (for that's their notion of the next world) by him she so tenderly loved, and so truly adored in this, for wives have a respect for their husbands equal to what any other people pay a deity, and when a man finds any occasion to quit his wife, if he love her, she dies by his hand, if not, he sells her, or suffers some other to kill her. It being thus, you may believe the deed was soon resolved on, and 'tis not to be doubted, but the parting, the eternal leave-taking of two such lovers, so greatly born, so sensible,[2] so beautiful, so young, and so fond, must be very moving, as the relation of it was to me afterwards.

All that love could say in such cases, being ended, and all the intermitting irresolutions being adjusted, the lovely, young, and adored victim lays herself down, before the sacrificer, while he, with a hand resolved, and a heart breaking within, gave the fatal stroke, first, cutting her throat, and then severing her, yet smiling, face from that delicate body, pregnant as it was with fruits of tenderest love. As soon as he had done, he laid the body decently on leaves and flowers, of which he made a bed, and concealed it under the same coverlid of nature, only her face he left yet bare to look on. But

[1] *mobile* Populace.

[2] *sensible* Sensitive.

when he found she was dead, and past all retrieve, never more to bless him with her eyes, and soft language, his grief swelled up to rage; he tore, he raved, he roared, like some monster of the wood, calling on the loved name of Imoinda. A thousand times he turned the fatal knife that did the deed, toward his own heart, with a resolution to go immediately after her, but dire revenge, which now was a thousand times more fierce in his soul than before, prevents him, and he would cry out, "No, since I have sacrificed Imoinda to my revenge, shall I lose that glory which I have purchased so dear, as at the price of the fairest, dearest, softest creature that ever nature made? No, no!" Then, at her name, grief would get the ascendant of rage, and he would lie down by her side, and water her face with showers of tears, which never were wont to fall from those eyes. And however bent he was on his intended slaughter, he had not power to stir from the sight of this dear object, now more beloved, and more adored than ever.

He remained in this deploring condition for two days, and never rose from the ground where he had made his sad sacrifice. At last, rousing from her side, and accusing himself with living too long, now Imoinda was dead, and that the deaths of those barbarous enemies were deferred too long, he resolved now to finish the great work; but offering to rise, he found his strength so decayed, that he reeled to and fro, like boughs assailed by contrary winds, so that he was forced to lie down again, and try to summon all his courage to his aid. He found his brains turn round, and his eyes were dizzy, and objects appeared not the same to him as they were wont to do; his breath was short, and all his limbs surprised with a faintness he had never felt before. He had not eaten in two days, which was one occasion of this feebleness, but excess of grief was the greatest; yet still he hoped he should recover vigour to act his design, and lay expecting it yet six days longer, still mourning over the dead idol of his heart, and striving every day to rise, but could not.

In all this time you may believe we were in no little affliction for Caesar, and his wife. Some were of opinion he was escaped never to return; others thought some accident had happened to him. But however, we failed not to send out a hundred people several ways to search for him. A party, of about forty, went that way he took, among whom was Tuscan, who was perfectly reconciled to Byam. They had not gone very far into the wood, but they smelt an unusual smell, as of a dead body, for stinks must be very noisome that can be distinguished among such a quantity of natural sweets, as every inch of that land produces. So that they concluded they should find him dead, or somebody that was so. They passed on towards it, as loathsome as it was, and made such a rustling among the leaves that lie thick on the ground, by continual falling, that Caesar heard he was approached, and though he had, during the space of these eight days, endeavoured to rise, but found he wanted strength, yet looking up, and seeing his pursuers, he rose, and reeled to a neighbouring tree, against which he fixed his back. And being within a dozen yards of those that advanced, and saw him, he called out to them, and bid them approach no nearer, if they would be safe, so that they stood still, and hardly believing their eyes, that would persuade them that it was Caesar that spoke to them, so much was he altered. They asked him, what he had done with his wife, for they smelt a stink that almost struck them dead. He, pointing to the dead body, sighing, cried, "Behold her there."

They put off the flowers that covered her with their sticks, and found she was killed, and cried out, "Oh monster! that hast murdered thy wife." Then asking him, why he did so cruel a deed.

He replied, he had no leisure to answer impertinent questions. "You may go back," continued he, "and tell the faithless governor, he may thank fortune that I am breathing my last, and that my arm is too feeble to obey my heart, in what it had designed him." But his tongue faltering, and trembling, he could scarce end what he was saying.

The English taking advantage by his weakness, cried, "Let us take him alive by all means."

He heard them; and, as if he had revived from a fainting, or a dream, he cried out, "No, gentlemen, you are deceived, you will find no more Caesars to be whipped, no more find a faith in me. Feeble as you think me, I have strength yet left to secure me from a second indignity." They swore all anew, and he only shook his head, and beheld them with scorn.

Then they cried out, "Who will venture on this single man? Will nobody?"

They stood all silent while Caesar replied, "Fatal will be the attempt to the first adventurer, let him assure himself," and, at that word, held up his knife in a menacing posture. "Look ye, ye faithless crew," said he, "'tis not life I seek, nor am I afraid of dying," and, at that word, cut a piece of flesh from his own throat, and threw it at them, "yet still I would live if I could, till I had perfected my revenge. But oh! it cannot be. I feel life gliding from my eyes and heart, and, if I make not haste, I shall yet fall a victim to the shameful whip." At that, he ripped up his own belly, and took his bowels and pulled them out, with what strength he could, while some, on their knees imploring, besought him to hold his hand.

But when they saw him tottering, they cried out, "Will none venture on him?"

A bold English cried, "Yes, if he were the devil" (taking courage when he saw him almost dead) and swearing a horrid oath for his farewell to the world he rushed on. Caesar with his armed hand met him so fairly, as stuck him to the heart, and he fell dead at his feet.

Tuscan seeing that, cried out, "I love thee, oh Caesar, and therefore will not let thee die, if possible." And, running to him, took him in his arms, but, at the same time, warding a blow that Caesar made at his bosom, he received it quite through his arm, and Caesar having not the strength to pluck the knife forth, though he attempted it, Tuscan neither pulled it out himself, nor suffered it to be pulled out, but came down with it sticking in his arm, and the reason he gave for it was, because the air should not get into the wound. They put their hands across, and carried Caesar between six of them, fainted as he was, and they thought dead, or just dying, and they brought him to Parham, and laid him on a couch, and had the chirurgeon immediately to him, who dressed his wounds, and sewed up his belly, and used means to bring him to life, which they effected. We ran all to see him; and, if before we thought him so beautiful a sight, he was now so altered, that his face was like a death's head blacked over, nothing but teeth, and eyeholes. For some days we suffered nobody to speak to him, but caused cordials to be poured down his throat, which sustained his life, and in six or seven days he recovered his senses. For, you must know, that wounds are almost to a miracle cured in the Indies, unless wounds in the legs, which rarely ever cure.

When he was well enough to speak, we talked to him, and asked him some questions about his wife, and the reasons why he killed her. And he then told us what I have related of that resolution, and of his parting, and he besought us, we would let him die, and was extremely afflicted to think it was possible he might live. He assured us, if we did not despatch him, he would prove very fatal to a great many. We said all we could to make him live, and gave him new assurances, but he begged we would not think so poorly of him, or of his love to Imoinda, to imagine we could flatter him to life again; but the chirurgeon assured him, he could not live, and therefore he need not fear. We were all (but Caesar) afflicted at this news; and the sight was gashly.[1] His discourse was sad; and the earthly smell about him so strong, that I was persuaded to leave the place for some time (being myself but sickly, and very apt to fall into fits of dangerous illness upon any extraordinary melancholy). The servants, and Trefry, and the chirurgeons, promised all to take what possible care they could of the life of Caesar, and I, taking boat, went with other company to Colonel Martin's, about three days' journey down the river, but I was no sooner gone, but the governor taking Trefry, about some pretended earnest business, a day's journey up the river, having communicated his design to one Banister,[2] a wild Irishman, and one of the council, a fellow of absolute barbarity, and fit to execute any villainy, but was rich. He came up to Parham, and forcibly took Caesar, and had him carried to the same post where he was whipped, and causing him to be tied to it, and a great fire made before him, he told him, he should die like a dog, as he was. Caesar replied, this was the first piece of bravery that ever Banister did, and he never spoke sense till he pronounced that word, and, if he would keep it, he would declare, in the other world, that he was the only man, of all the whites, that ever he heard speak truth. And turning to the men that bound him, he said, "My friends, am I to die, or to be whipped?"

And they cried, "Whipped! no; you shall not escape so well."

[1] *gashly* Ghastly.

[2] *Banister* Major James Banister, who succeeded Byam as deputy governor of Surinam.

And then he replied, smiling, "A blessing on thee," and assured them, they need not tie him, for he would stand fixed, like a rock, and endure death so as should encourage them to die. "But if you whip me," said he, "be sure you tie me fast."

He had learned to take tobacco, and when he was assured he should die, he desired they would give him a pipe in his mouth, ready lighted, which they did, and the executioner came, and first cut off his members, and threw them into the fire. After that, with an ill-favoured knife, they cut his ears, and his nose, and burned them; he still smoked on, as if nothing had touched him. Then they hacked off one of his arms, and still he bore up, and held his pipe. But at the cutting off the other arm, his head sunk, and his pipe dropped, and he gave up the ghost, without a groan, or a reproach. My mother and sister were by him all the while, but not suffered to save him, so rude and wild were the rabble, and so inhuman were the justices, who stood by to see the execution, who after paid dearly enough for their insolence. They cut Caesar in quarters, and sent them to several of the chief plantations. One quarter was sent to Colonel Martin, who refused it, and swore, he had rather see the quarters of Banister, and the governor himself, than those of Caesar, on his plantations, and that he could govern his Negroes without terrifying and grieving them with frightful spectacles of a mangled king.

Thus died this great man, worthy of a better fate, and a more sublime wit than mine to write his praise. Yet, I hope, the reputation of my pen is considerable enough to make his glorious name to survive to all ages, with that of the brave, the beautiful, and the constant Imoinda.

—1688

William Wycherley

1641 – 1716

Though he produced only four plays, William Wycherley is recognized as one of the leading playwrights of the Restoration period. Wycherley was born in Clive, near Shrewsbury, England, into a privileged family; his father was Daniel Wycherley, High Steward in the household of John Paulet, marquess of Winchester, at Basing House in Hampshire. Wycherley's father was a Royalist, and he sent Wycherley to France to be educated. While in France, Wycherley converted from Protestantism to Catholicism under the influence of his mentors, Madame and Marquis de Montausier. It was a theological shift of a sort that he was to make a number of times throughout his life, often changing his religion in order to suit his environment.

Wycherley's father brought him back to England in 1659, not long before the Restoration of Charles II, and enrolled him in Queen's College at Oxford University. For this he had to become a Protestant again. He left Oxford very quickly, without graduating, and began to study law. However, his attentions were focused less on work than on the court of Charles II, the new monarch, where his status as an eligible bachelor quickly made him a court favorite. Wycherley soon gave up on the law; he joined the navy, and went off to fight the Dutch. Through his favor with the court, he quickly became a Captain, but he resigned his commission within a week, turning to playwriting instead. Between 1671 and 1677, he published four plays: *Love in a Wood, or St. James's Park* (1671), a farce that takes place largely in the dark; *The Gentleman Dancing-Master* (1672), a comedy depicting a resourceful fourteen-year-old who deceives her father in order to marry the man she loves; *The Country Wife* (1675); and *The Plain Dealer* (1676), an adaptation of the French playwright Molière's *Le Misanthrope* that centers on a man who prides himself on his inability to tell a lie.

The Country Wife, Wycherley's best-known work, is a witty, ribald portrait of the London society in which he lived. It was first produced by the King's Company and performed at Drury Lane's Theatre Royal, likely on 12 January 1675. The play features broadly drawn characters and a plot full of misunderstandings, secrets, and *double entendres*, all elements that were typical of Restoration comedies. It was considered so bawdy that from the mid-eighteenth century it ceased to be performed in its original form. The famous actor David Garrick gutted the play of its sexual content and produced a tamer version called *The Country Girl* in 1766. The original text was not produced again on the English stage until 1924.

In the late 1670s Wycherley turned away from the stage and was engaged by Charles II as royal tutor. He was to be paid very well to teach the King's illegitimate son, James Scott (later Earl of Monmouth), and then offered a life-long pension once his services were no longer needed. However, his favor with the court ended abruptly in 1680 with his disastrous marriage to Laetitia-Isabella, the recent widow of the Earl of Drogheda. He had entered into this marriage as a means of paying off his sizeable debts; Laetitia-Isabella was a wealthy heiress. But his plan backfired badly. He had intended to keep his marriage to Laetitia-Isabella a secret; as a tutor he was an entirely unsuitable match for a woman of the nobility, and for such a gentleman to marry such an heiress against her family's wishes was seen as tantamount to robbery. Unfortunately for her, word of Wycherley's transgression quickly got out, and he was banished from the court of Charles II and from his position as royal tutor. The marriage itself was also a failure, but after one very unhappy year Isabella suddenly died in 1681. Her estate became tied up in litigation; Wycherley received nothing but her debts, and in 1682 was imprisoned as a debtor.

Wycherley's fortunes turned again when James II ascended the throne in 1685. The new monarch took a liking to the former playwright, believing that he had modeled the character of Manly in *The Plain Dealer* on him. Flattered, he had Wycherley released from debtors' prison, paid him a pension of £200 per year, and offered to settle all his debts. In gratitude to the King, who was deeply Catholic, Wycherley re-converted. Unfortunately, he felt too embarrassed to reveal the total amount of his debt to the King, and thus continued to owe money after his release from prison. During these years, Wycherley wrote no plays; he did write a number of poems, none of which are considered to be of the same caliber as his dramatic works. He also struck up an association with the young Alexander Pope, who revised and edited his poems.

Toward the end of his life, Wycherley married a young girl, Elizabeth Jackson, in order to keep his estate out of the hands of his nephew and sole heir, whom he felt had treated him badly. He was married to her for eleven days before his death at age 76 on 31 December 1716. He was buried in St. Paul's Church, Covent Garden, London.

⌘⌘⌘

The Country Wife

PROLOGUE

Spoken by Mr. Hart[1]

Poets, like cudgeled bullies, never do
At first or second blow submit to you
But will provoke you still, and ne'er have done,
Till you are weary first with laying on.
The late so baffled scribbler of this day,
Though he stands trembling, bids me boldly say
What we before most plays are used to do;
For poets out of fear first draw on you,
In a fierce prologue the still pit[2] defy,
And, ere you speak, like Kastrill[3] give the lie.[4]
But though our Bayes's[5] battles oft I've fought,
And with bruised knuckles their dear conquest bought;
Nay, never yet feared odds upon the stage,
In prologue dare not hector with the age,
But would take quarter from your saving hands,
Though Bayes within all yielding countermands,
Says you confed'rate wits no quarter give,
Therefore his play shan't ask your leave to live.
Well, let the vain, rash fop, by huffing so,
Think to obtain the better terms of you;
But we, the actors, humbly will submit,
Now, and at any time, to a full pit;
Nay, often we anticipate your rage,
And murder poets for you on our stage;
We set no guards upon our tiring room,[6]
But when with flying colors[7] there you come,
We patiently, you see, give up to you
Our poets, virgins, nay, our matrons too.

[1] *Mr. Hart* Charles Hart (d. 1683), actor, the first to play Mr. Horner.

[2] *pit* Fashionable men—"gallants" and "beaux"—sat in the pit and set themselves up as hard-to-please critics.

[3] *Kastrill* Character in Ben Jonson's *The Alchemist*.

[4] *give the lie* Accuse a person of lying, to his or her face.

[5] *Bayes's* Playwright's (i.e., Wycherley's). This is the name of the playwright-character mocked in the Duke of Buckingham's *The Rehearsal*.

[6] *tiring room* Dressing room.

[7] *with flying colors* I.e., like a besieging army, with flags or ensigns held aloft.

DRAMATIS PERSONAE

[MEN]

Mr. Horner
Mr. Harcourt
Mr. Dorilant
Mr. Pinchwife
Mr. Sparkish
Sir Jaspar Fidget
A boy
[Dr.] Quack
[Clasp, a bookseller]
[A person]
Waiters, servants, and attendants

[WOMEN]

Mrs. Margery Pinchwife
Mrs.[1] Alithea
My Lady Fidget
Mrs. Dainty Fidget
Mrs. Squeamish
Old Lady Squeamish
Lucy, Alithea's maid

THE SCENE: LONDON.

Indignor quicquam reprehendi, non quia crasse
Compositum illepideve putetur, sed quia nuper,
Nec veniam antiquis, sed honorem et praemia posci.[2]
Horat.

ACT 1, SCENE 1. [Horner's lodging.]

(*Enter Horner and Quack following him at a distance.*)

HORNER. (Aside.) A quack is as fit for a pimp as a midwife for a bawd; they are still but in their way both helpers of nature.—Well my dear doctor, hast thou done what I desired?

QUACK. I have undone you forever with the women and reported you throughout the whole Town[3] as bad as an eunuch with as much trouble as if I had made you one in earnest.

HORNER. But have you told all the midwives you know, the orange wenches[4] at the playhouses, the City husbands, and old fumbling keepers[5] of this end of the Town? For they'll be the readiest to report it.

QUACK. I have told all the chambermaids, waiting women, tirewomen,[6] and old women of my acquaintance, nay, and whispered it as a secret to 'em and to the whisperers of Whitehall,[7] so that you need not doubt 'twill spread, and you will be as odious to the handsome young women as—

HORNER. As the small pox. Well—

QUACK. And to the married women of this end of the Town as—

HORNER. As the great ones,[8] nay, as their own husbands.

QUACK. And to the City dames as Aniseed Robin[9] of filthy and contemptible memory, and they will frighten their children with your name, especially their females.

HORNER. And cry, "Horner's coming to carry you away!" I am only afraid 'twill not be believed. You told 'em 'twas by an English-French disaster and an English-French chirurgeon,[10] who has given me at once, not only a cure, but an antidote for the future against that damned malady and that worse distemper, love, and all other women's evils.

QUACK. Your late journey into France has made it the more credible, and your being here a fortnight before you appeared in public looks as if you apprehended the shame, which I wonder you do not. Well, I have been

[1] *Mrs.* "Mistress," used for both married and unmarried women.

[2] *Indignor ... posci* Latin: I am impatient that any work is censured, not because it is thought to be coarse or inelegant in style, but because it is modern, and that what is claimed for the ancients should be, not indulgence, but honor and rewards (Horace, *Epistles* 2.1.76-78).

[3] *Town* The fashionable world; London.

[4] *orange wenches* Women who sold oranges at the playhouses, and who were often prostitutes as well.

[5] *keepers* Men who kept mistresses.

[6] *tirewomen* Ladies' maids in charge of attire.

[7] *Whitehall* English royal palace and the area around it in Westminster.

[8] *the great ones* Great (or French) pox; i.e., syphilis.

[9] *Aniseed Robin* Notorious hermaphrodite.

[10] *English-French disaster ... English-French chirurgeon* French pox caught by an Englishman, treated by an English doctor practicing in France.

hired by young gallants to belie 'em t'other way, but you are the first would be thought a man unfit for women.

HORNER. Dear Mr. Doctor, let vain rogues be contented only to be thought abler men than they are; generally 'tis all the pleasure they have, but mine lies another way.

QUACK. You take, methinks, a very preposterous way to it and as ridiculous as if we operators in physic should put forth bills to disparage our medicaments with hopes to gain customers.

HORNER. Doctor, there are quacks in love as well as physic who get but the fewer and worse patients for their boasting; a good name is seldom got by giving it one's self, and women no more than honor are compassed by bragging. Come, come, doctor, the wisest lawyer never discovers[1] the merits of his cause till the trial; the wealthiest man conceals his riches, and the cunning gamester his play; shy husbands and keepers, like old rooks,[2] are not to be cheated but by a new unpracticed trick: false friendship will pass now no more than false dice upon 'em, no, not in the City.

(*Enter boy.*)

BOY. There are two ladies and a gentleman coming up.

HORNER. A pox! some unbelieving sisters of my former acquaintance, who, I am afraid, expect their sense should be satisfied of the falsity of the report.

(*Enter Sir Jaspar Fidget, Lady Fidget, and Dainty.*)

No—this formal fool and women!

QUACK. His wife and sister.

SIR JASPAR. My coach breaking just now before your door, sir, I look upon as an occasional[3] reprimand to me, sir, for not kissing your hands, sir, since your coming out of France, sir, and so my disaster, sir, has been my good fortune, sir, and this is my wife and sister, sir.

HORNER. What then, sir?

SIR JASPAR. My lady and sister, sir.—Wife, this is Master Horner.

LADY FIDGET. Master Horner, husband!

SIR JASPAR. My lady, my Lady Fidget, sir.

HORNER. So, sir.

SIR JASPAR. Won't you be acquainted with her, sir? (*Aside.*) So the report is true, I find by his coldness or aversion to the sex, but I'll play the wag with him.—Pray salute[4] my wife, my lady, sir.

HORNER. I will kiss no man's wife, sir, for him, sir; I have taken my eternal leave, sir, of the sex already, sir.

SIR JASPAR. (*Aside.*) Ha, ha, ha, I'll plague him yet.—Not know my wife, sir?

HORNER. I do know your wife, sir: she's a woman, sir, and consequently a monster, sir, a greater monster than a husband, sir.

SIR JASPAR. A husband! How, sir?

HORNER. (*Makes horns.*[5]) So, sir. But I make no more cuckolds, sir.

SIR JASPAR. Ha, ha, ha, Mercury, Mercury.[6]

LADY FIDGET. Pray Sir Jaspar, let us be gone from this rude fellow.

DAINTY. Who, by his breeding, would think he had ever been in France?

LADY FIDGET. Faugh, he's but too much a French fellow, such as hate women of quality and virtue for their love to their husbands, Sir Jaspar; a woman is hated by 'em as much for loving her husband as for loving their money. But pray, let's be gone.

HORNER. You do well, madam, for I have nothing that you came for. I have brought over not so much as a bawdy picture, new postures,[7] nor the second part of the *École des filles*,[8] nor—

QUACK. (*Apart to Horner.*) Hold for shame, sir. What d'ye mean? You'll ruin yourself forever with the sex.

[1] *discovers* Reveals.

[2] *rooks* Cheaters.

[3] *occasional* Timely; arising from the occasion.

[4] *salute* To greet with a kiss.

[5] *horns* Sign of a cuckold, a man whose wife is having an affair.

[6] *Mercury* God associated with wit (who wears a hat with wings resembling cuckold's horns); also, substance used to treat venereal disease.

[7] *new postures* Cf. *The Sixteen Postures*, by Giuliano Romano (1492–1546), drawings of sixteen sexual positions accompanied by sonnets by Pietro Aretino (1492–1556).

[8] *École des filles* Notoriously bawdy dialogues by Michel Millot (1655); the "second part," like the "new postures," was nonexistent.

SIR JASPAR. Ha, ha, ha, he hates women perfectly, I find.

DAINTY. What pity 'tis he should.

LADY FIDGET. Aye, he's a base rude fellow for it, but affectation makes not a woman more odious to them than virtue.

HORNER. Because your virtue is your greatest affectation, madam.

LADY FIDGET. How, you saucy fellow, would you wrong my honor?

HORNER. If I could.

LADY FIDGET. How d'ye mean, sir?

SIR JASPAR. Ha, ha, ha, no, he can't wrong your ladyship's honor, upon my honor; he, poor man—hark you in your ear—a mere eunuch.

LADY FIDGET. Oh filthy French beast! Faugh, faugh! Why do we stay? Let's be gone; I can't endure the sight of him.

SIR JASPAR. Stay but till the chairs[1] come; they'll be here presently.

LADY FIDGET. No, no.

SIR JASPAR. Nor can I stay longer: 'tis—let me see, a quarter and a half quarter of a minute past eleven; the Council[2] will be sat; I must away. Business must be preferred always before love and ceremony with the wise, Mr. Horner.

HORNER. And the impotent, Sir Jaspar.

SIR JASPAR. Aye, aye, the impotent Master Horner, ha, ha, ha!

LADY FIDGET. What, leave us with a filthy man alone in his lodgings?

SIR JASPAR. He's an innocent man now, you know. Pray stay, I'll hasten the chairs to you.—Mr. Horner, your servant. I should be glad to see you at my house. Pray, come and dine with me and play at cards with my wife after dinner; you are fit for women at that game yet, ha, ha! (*Aside.*) 'Tis as much a husband's prudence to provide innocent diversion for a wife as to hinder her unlawful pleasures, and he had better employ her than let her employ herself.—Farewell. (*Exit.*)

HORNER. Your servant, Sir Jaspar.

LADY FIDGET. I will not stay with him, faugh!

HORNER. Nay madam, I beseech you stay, if it be but to see I can be as civil to ladies yet as they would desire.

LADY FIDGET. No, no, faugh, you cannot be civil to ladies.

DAINTY. You as civil as ladies would desire!

LADY FIDGET. No, no, no, faugh, faugh, faugh!

(*Exeunt Lady Fidget and Dainty.*)

QUACK. Now I think, I, or you yourself rather, have done your business with the women.

HORNER. Thou art an ass. Don't you see already upon the report and my carriage, this grave man of business leaves his wife in my lodgings, invites me to his house and wife, who before would not be acquainted with me out of jealousy?

QUACK. Nay, by this means you may be the more acquainted with the husbands, but the less with the wives.

HORNER. Let me alone; if I can but abuse the husbands, I'll soon disabuse the wives. Stay—I'll reckon you up the advantages I am like to have by my stratagem: first, I shall be rid of all my old acquaintances, the most insatiable sorts of duns that invade our lodgings in a morning. And next to the pleasure of making a new mistress is that of being rid of an old one and of all old debts: love, when it comes to be so, is paid the most unwillingly.

QUACK. Well, you may be so rid of your old acquaintances, but how will you get any new ones?

HORNER. Doctor, thou wilt never make a good chemist,[3] thou art so incredulous and impatient. Ask but all the young fellows of the Town if they do not lose more time, like huntsmen, in starting the game than in running it down; one knows not where to find 'em, who will or will not. Women of quality are so civil, you can hardly distinguish love from good breeding, and a man is often mistaken. But now I can be sure, she that shows an aversion to me loves the sport, as those women that are gone, whom I warrant to be right. And then the next thing is, your women of honor, as you call 'em, are only chary of their reputations, not their persons, and 'tis scandal they would avoid, not men. Now may I have by the reputation of an eunuch the privileges of one and be

[1] *chairs* Sedans, portable chairs borne by chairmen.

[2] *Council* Possibly the Common Council, the administrative body of the City of London.

[3] *chemist* Alchemist, who needs both credulity and patience to see his experiments through.

seen in a lady's chamber in a morning as early as her husband, kiss virgins before their parents or lovers, and may be, in short, the *passe-partout* of the Town. Now, doctor.

QUACK. Nay, now you shall be the doctor, and your process is so new that we do not know but it may succeed.

HORNER. Not so new neither: *probatum est*,[1] doctor.

QUACK. Well, I wish you luck and many patients whilst I go to mine. (*Exit.*)

(*Enter Harcourt and Dorilant to Horner.*)

HARCOURT. Come, your appearance at the play yesterday has, I hope, hardened you for the future against the women's contempt and the men's raillery, and now you'll abroad as you were wont.

HORNER. Did I not bear it bravely?[2]

DORILANT. With a most theatrical impudence, nay, more than the orange wenches show there or a drunken vizard mask[3] or a great bellied[4] actress, nay, or the most impudent of creatures, an ill poet, or what is yet more impudent, a second-hand critic.

HORNER. But what say the ladies? Have they no pity?

HARCOURT. What ladies? The vizard masks, you know, never pity a man when all's gone though in their service.

DORILANT. And for the women in the boxes, you'd never pity them when 'twas in your power.

HARCOURT. They say 'tis pity, but all that deal with common women should be served so.

DORILANT. Nay I dare swear, they won't admit you to play at cards with them, go to plays with 'em, or do the little duties which other shadows of men are wont to do for 'em.

HORNER. Who do you call shadows of men?

DORILANT. Half men.

HORNER. What, boys?

DORILANT. Aye, your old boys, old *beaux garçons*,[5] who like superannuated stallions are suffered to run, feed, and whinny with the mares as long as they live, though they can do nothing else.

HORNER. Well, a pox on love and wenching; women serve but to keep a man from better company. Though I can't enjoy them, I shall you the more. Good fellowship and friendship are lasting, rational, and manly pleasures.

HARCOURT. For all that, give me some of those pleasures you call effeminate, too; they help to relish one another.

HORNER. They disturb one another.

HARCOURT. No, mistresses are like books: if you pore upon them too much, they doze you and make you unfit for company, but if used discreetly, you are the fitter for conversation[6] by 'em.

DORILANT. A mistress should be like a little country retreat near the Town, not to dwell in constantly but only for a night and away, to taste the Town the better when a man returns.

HORNER. I tell you, 'tis as hard to be a good fellow, a good friend, and a lover of women as 'tis to be a good fellow, a good friend, and a lover of money. You cannot follow both; then choose your side. Wine gives you liberty; love takes it away.

DORILANT. Gad, he's in the right on't.

HORNER. Wine gives you joy; love, grief and tortures, besides the chirurgeon's. Wine makes us witty; love, only sots.[7] Wine makes us sleep; love breaks it.

DORILANT. By the world, he has reason, Harcourt.

HORNER. Wine makes—

DORILANT. Aye, wine makes us—makes us princes; love makes us beggars, poor rogues, egad—and wine—

HORNER. So, there's one converted.—No, no, love and wine, oil and vinegar.

HARCOURT. I grant it: love will still be uppermost.

HORNER. Come, for my part I will have only those glorious manly pleasures of being very drunk and very slovenly.

[1] *probatum est* Tried and tested (literally, it is approved [Lat.]).

[2] *bravely* Excellently.

[3] *vizard mask* Masked prostitute.

[4] *great bellied* Pregnant.

[5] *beaux garçons* Fops (literally, pretty boys [Fr.]).

[6] *conversation* Social (or sexual) intercourse.

[7] *sots* Fools.

(*Enter boy.*)

BOY. Mr. Sparkish is below, sir.

HARCOURT. What, my dear friend! a rogue that is fond of me only, I think, for abusing him.

DORILANT. No, he can no more think the men laugh at him than that women jilt him, his opinion of himself is so good.

HORNER. Well, there's another pleasure by drinking, I thought not of: I shall lose his acquaintance because he cannot drink, and you know 'tis a very hard thing to be rid of him, for he's one of those nauseous offerers at wit who, like the worst fiddlers, run themselves into all companies.

HARCOURT. One that by being in the company of men of sense would pass for one.

HORNER. And may so to the short-sighted world, as a false jewel amongst true ones is not discerned at a distance; his company is as troublesome to us as a cuckold's when you have a mind to his wife's.

HARCOURT. No, the rogue will not let us enjoy one another, but ravishes our conversation, though he signifies no more to't than Sir Martin Mar-all's[1] gaping and awkward thrumming upon the lute does to his man's voice and music.

DORILANT. And to pass for a wit in Town shows himself a fool every night to us that are guilty of the plot.

HORNER. Such wits as he are, to a company of reasonable men, like rooks to the gamesters, who only fill a room at the table but are so far from contributing to the play that they only serve to spoil the fancy of those that do.

DORILANT. Nay, they are used like rooks, too—snubbed, checked, and abused—yet the rogues will hang on.

HORNER. A pox on 'em and all that force Nature and would be still what she forbids 'em; affectation is her greatest monster.

HARCOURT. Most men are the contraries to that they would seem: your bully, you see, is a coward with a long sword; the little humbly fawning physician with his ebony cane is he that destroys men.

DORILANT. The usurer, a poor rogue possessed of moldy bonds and mortgages, and we they call spendthrifts are only wealthy who lay out his money upon daily new purchases of pleasure.

HORNER. Aye, your arrantest cheat is your trustee or executor; your jealous man, the greatest cuckold; your churchman, the greatest atheist; and your noisy pert rogue of a wit, the greatest fop, dullest ass, and worst company, as you shall see. For here he comes.

(*Enter Sparkish to them.*)

SPARKISH. How is't, sparks, how is't? Well faith, Harry, I must rally thee a little, ha, ha, ha, upon the report in Town of thee, ha, ha, ha. I can't hold i'faith. Shall I speak?

HORNER. Yes, but you'll be so bitter then.

SPARKISH. Honest Dick and Frank here shall answer for me; I will not be extreme bitter, by the universe.

HARCOURT. We will be bound in ten thousand pound bond, he shall not be bitter at all.

DORILANT. Nor sharp, nor sweet.

HORNER. What, not downright insipid?

SPARKISH. Nay then, since you are so brisk and provoke me, take what follows: you must know, I was discoursing and rallying with some ladies yesterday, and they happened to talk of the fine new signs in Town.

HORNER. Very fine ladies, I believe.

SPARKISH. Said I, "I know where the best new sign is." "Where?" says one of the ladies. "In Covent Garden,"[2] I replied. Said another, "In what street?" "In Russell Street," answered I. "Lord," says another, "I'm sure there was ne'er a fine new sign there yesterday." "Yes, but there was," said I again, "and it came out of France and has been there a fortnight."

DORILANT. A pox, I can hear no more, prithee.

HORNER. No, hear him out; let him tune his crowd[3] a while.

HARCOURT. The worst music, the greatest preparation.

SPARKISH. Nay faith, I'll make you laugh. "It cannot

[1] *Sir Martin Mar-all* Foolish hero of John Dryden's play of that name (1667), who mimes a serenade to his mistress even after his hidden servant has stopped singing and playing his lute.

[2] *Covent Garden* Fashionable residential district that also housed the first theaters of the period.

[3] *crowd* Fiddle.

be," says a third lady. "Yes, yes," quoth I again. Says a fourth lady—

HORNER. Look to't, we'll have no more ladies.

SPARKISH. No? Then mark, mark, now. Said I to the fourth, "Did you never see Mr. Horner? He lodges in Russell Street, and he's a sign of a man, you know, since he came out of France." He, ha, he!

HORNER. But the devil take me if thine be the sign of a jest.

SPARKISH. With that they all fell a-laughing till they bepissed themselves. What, but it does not move you, me-thinks? Well, I see one had as good go to law without a witness as break a jest without a laugher on one's side.—Come, come, sparks, but where do we dine? I have left at Whitehall an earl to dine with you.

DORILANT. Why, I thought thou hadst loved a man with a title better than a suit with a French trimming to't.

HARCOURT. Go, to him again.

SPARKISH. No sir, a wit to me is the greatest title in the world.

HORNER. But go dine with your earl, sir; he may be exceptious.[1] We are your friends and will not take it ill to be left, I do assure you.

HARCOURT. Nay, faith he shall go to him.

SPARKISH. Nay, pray gentlemen.

DORILANT. We'll thrust you out if you wonnot. What, disappoint anybody for us?

SPARKISH. Nay, dear gentlemen, hear me.

HORNER. No, no, sir, by no means; pray go, sir.

SPARKISH. Why, dear rogues—

DORILANT. No, no.

(*They all thrust him out of the room.*)

ALL. Ha, ha, ha.

(*Sparkish returns.*)

SPARKISH. But sparks, pray hear me. What, d'ye think I'll eat then with gay shallow fops and silent coxcombs? I think wit as necessary at dinner as a glass of good wine, and that's the reason I never have any stomach when I eat alone. Come, but where do we dine?

HORNER. Ev'n where you will.

SPARKISH. At Chateline's.[2]

DORILANT. Yes, if you will.

SPARKISH. Or at the Cock.[3]

DORILANT. Yes, if you please.

SPARKISH. Or at the Dog and Partridge.[4]

HORNER. Aye, if you have a mind to't, for we shall dine at neither.

SPARKISH. Pshaw, with your fooling we shall lose the new play, and I would no more miss seeing a new play the first day than I would miss sitting in the wits' row;[5] therefore, I'll go fetch my mistress and away. (*Exit.*)

(*Enter Pinchwife.*)

HORNER. Who have we here, Pinchwife?

PINCHWIFE. Gentlemen, your humble servant.

HORNER. Well Jack, by thy long absence from the Town, the grumness[6] of thy countenance, and the slovenliness of thy habit, I should give thee joy, should I not, of marriage?

PINCHWIFE. (*Aside.*) Death, does he know I'm married, too? I thought to have concealed it from him at least.—My long stay in the country will excuse my dress, and I have a suit of law that brings me up to Town that puts me out of humor; besides, I must give Sparkish tomorrow five thousand pound to lie with my sister.[7]

HORNER. Nay, you country gentlemen, rather than not purchase, will buy anything, and he is a cracked title,[8] if we may quibble. Well, but am I to give thee joy? I heard thou wert married.

PINCHWIFE. What then?

[1] *exceptious* Likely to take offense.

[2] *Chateline's* Fashionable French restaurant in Covent Garden.

[3] *the Cock* Out of many taverns by that name, this probably refers to a less fashionable one in Bow Street, Covent Garden, frequented by Wycherley.

[4] *the Dog and Partridge* An unfashionable tavern in Fleet Street.

[5] *wits' row* Near the front of the theater pit.

[6] *grumness* Moroseness; gloominess.

[7] *Sparkish ... sister* Pinchwife is providing his sister with a dowry to enable her to marry Sparkish.

[8] *cracked title* Either Sparkish's patrimony or his genealogy is of questionable value.

HORNER. Why, the next thing that is to be heard is thou'rt a cuckold.

PINCHWIFE. (*Aside.*) Insupportable name.

HORNER. But I did not expect marriage from such a whoremaster as you: one that knew the Town so much and women so well.

PINCHWIFE. Why, I have married no London wife.

HORNER. Pshaw, that's all one: that grave circumspection in marrying a country wife is like refusing a deceitful pampered Smithfield[1] jade to go and be cheated by a friend in the country.

PINCHWIFE. (*Aside.*) A pox on him and his simile.—At least we are a little surer of the breed there, know what her keeping has been, whether foiled[2] or unsound.[3]

HORNER. Come, come, I have known a clap[4] gotten in Wales, and there are cozens,[5] justices, clerks, and chaplains in the country; I won't say coachmen. But she's handsome and young?

PINCHWIFE. (*Aside.*) I'll answer as I should do.—No, no, she has no beauty but her youth, no attraction but her modesty: wholesome, homely, and housewifely, that's all.

DORILANT. He talks as like a grazier[6] as he looks.

PINCHWIFE. She's too awkward, ill-favored, and silly[7] to bring to Town.

HARCOURT. Then methinks you should bring her to be taught breeding.

PINCHWIFE. To be taught! No sir, I thank you, good wives and private soldiers should be ignorant. [*Aside.*] I'll keep her from your instructions, I warrant you.

HARCOURT. (*Aside.*) The rogue is as jealous as if his wife were not ignorant.

HORNER. Why, if she be ill-favored, there will be less danger here for you than by leaving her in the country: we have such variety of dainties that we are seldom hungry.

DORILANT. But they have always coarse, constant, swingeing[8] stomachs in the country.

HARCOURT. Foul feeders indeed.

DORILANT. And your hospitality is great there.

HARCOURT. Open house, every man's welcome.

PINCHWIFE. So, so, gentlemen.

HORNER. But prithee, why wouldst thou marry her? If she be ugly, ill-bred, and silly, she must be rich then.

PINCHWIFE. As rich as if she brought me twenty thousand pound out of this Town, for she'll be as sure not to spend her moderate portion as a London baggage would be to spend hers, let it be what it would; so 'tis all one. Then because she's ugly, she's the likelier to be my own, and being ill-bred, she'll hate conversation and, since silly and innocent, will not know the difference betwixt a man of one-and-twenty and one of forty.

HORNER. Nine—to my knowledge. But if she be silly, she'll expect as much from a man of forty-nine as from him of one-and-twenty. But methinks wit is more necessary than beauty, and I think no young woman ugly that has it and no handsome woman agreeable without it.

PINCHWIFE. 'Tis my maxim: he's a fool that marries, but he's a greater that does not marry a fool. What is wit in a wife good for but to make a man a cuckold?

HORNER. Yes, to keep it from his knowledge.

PINCHWIFE. A fool cannot contrive to make her husband a cuckold.

HORNER. No, but she'll club with a man that can, and what is worse, if she cannot make her husband a cuckold, she'll make him jealous and pass for one, and then 'tis all one.

PINCHWIFE. Well, well, I'll take care for one: my wife shall make me no cuckold though she had your help, Mr. Horner. I understand the Town, sir.

DORILANT. (*Aside.*) His help!

HARCOURT. (*Aside.*) He's come newly to Town, it seems, and has not heard how things are with him.

HORNER. But tell me, has marriage cured thee of whoring, which it seldom does?

HARCOURT. 'Tis more than age can do.

HORNER. No, the word is, "I'll marry and live honest."[9] But a marriage vow is like a penitent gamester's oath

[1] *Smithfield* City market, known for its sharp practices.

[2] *foiled* Injured (of a horse); deflowered (of a woman).

[3] *unsound* Unhealthy, particularly suffering from venereal disease.

[4] *a clap* Gonorrhea.

[5] *cozens* Possibly "cozeners," meaning "cheats"; or "cousins," meaning "family friends or extended family members."

[6] *grazier* One who grazes cattle.

[7] *silly* Innocent, unsophisticated, usually rustic.

[8] *swingeing* Huge.

[9] *honest* Faithful.

and entering into bonds and penalties to stint himself to such a particular small sum at play for the future, which makes him but the more eager, and not being able to hold out, loses his money again and his forfeit to boot.

DORILANT. Aye, aye, a gamester will be a gamester whilst his money lasts, and a whoremaster, whilst his vigor.

HARCOURT. Nay, I have known 'em, when they are broke and can lose no more, keep a-fumbling with the box[1] in their hands to fool with only and hinder other gamesters.

DORILANT. That had wherewithal to make lusty stakes.

PINCHWIFE. Well gentlemen, you may laugh at me, but you shall never lie with my wife. I know the Town.

HORNER. But prithee, was not the way you were in better? Is not keeping better than marriage?

PINCHWIFE. A pox on't, the jades would jilt me; I could never keep a whore to myself.

HORNER. So then you only married to keep a whore to yourself. Well but let me tell you, women, as you say, are, like soldiers, made constant and loyal by good pay rather than by oaths and covenants. Therefore, I'd advise my friends to keep rather than marry since, too, I find by your example it does not serve one's turn, for I saw you yesterday in the eighteen-penny place[2] with a pretty country wench.

PINCHWIFE. (*Aside.*) How the devil! Did he see my wife then? I sat there that she might not be seen, but she shall never go to a play again.

HORNER. What, dost thou blush at nine-and-forty for having been seen with a wench?

DORILANT. No faith, I warrant 'twas his wife, which he seated there out of sight, for he's a cunning rogue and understands the Town.

HARCOURT. He blushes; then 'twas his wife, for men are now more ashamed to be seen with them in public than with a wench.

PINCHWIFE. (*Aside.*) Hell and damnation! I'm undone since Horner has seen her and they know 'twas she.

HORNER. But prithee, was it thy wife? She was exceedingly pretty. I was in love with her at that distance.

PINCHWIFE. You are like never to be nearer to her. Your servant, gentlemen. (*Offers to go.*)

HORNER. Nay, prithee stay.

PINCHWIFE. I cannot; I will not.

HORNER. Come, you shall dine with us.

PINCHWIFE. I have dined already.

HORNER. Come, I know thou hast not. I'll treat thee, dear rogue; thou shalt spend none of thy Hampshire money today.

PINCHWIFE. (*Aside.*) Treat me! So he uses me already like his cuckold.

HORNER. Nay, you shall not go.

PINCHWIFE. I must, I have business at home. (*Exit.*)

HARCOURT. To beat his wife: he's as jealous of her as a Cheapside[3] husband of a Covent Garden[4] wife.

HORNER. Why, 'tis as hard to find an old whoremaster without jealousy and the gout as a young one without fear or the pox.

As gout in age from pox in youth proceeds,
So wenching past, then jealousy succeeds:
The worst disease that love and wenching breeds.

(*Exeunt.*)

ACT 2, SCENE 1. [Pinchwife's lodging.]

(*Margery Pinchwife and Alithea, Pinchwife peeping behind at the door.*)

MARGERY. Pray sister,[5] where are the best fields and woods to walk in in London?

ALITHEA. A pretty question. Why sister, Mulberry Garden[6] and St. James's Park[7] and, for close[8] walks, the New Exchange.[9]

---

[1] *box* Dice cup (*double entendre*).

[2] *eighteen-penny place* Middle gallery in the theater, away from the gallants in the pit and boxes.

[3] *Cheapside* Business district.

[4] *Covent Garden* Area associated with prostitutes.

[5] *sister* I.e., sister-in-law. Alithea is Pinchwife's sister.

[6] *Mulberry Garden* Fashionable promenade within St. James's Park, at the site of the current Buckingham Palace.

[7] *St. James's Park* Very fashionable London district at the western end of Pall Mall.

[8] *close* Indoor.

[9] *New Exchange* Meeting place for bankers and merchants, as well as the location of a gallery of fashionable shops, located on the Strand in London. The original Exchange burned down in the fire of 1666.

MARGERY. Pray sister, tell me why my husband looks so grum here in Town and keeps me up so close and will not let me go a-walking nor let me wear my best gown yesterday?

ALITHEA. Oh, he's jealous, sister.

MARGERY. Jealous, what's that?

ALITHEA. He's afraid you should love another man.

MARGERY. How should he be afraid of my loving another man when he will not let me see any but himself?

ALITHEA. Did he not carry you yesterday to a play?

MARGERY. Aye, but we sat amongst ugly people; he would not let me come near the gentry, who sat under us, so that I could not see 'em. He told me none but naughty women sat there, whom they toused and moused, but I would have ventured for all that.

ALITHEA. But how did you like the play?

MARGERY. Indeed I was aweary of the play, but I liked hugeously the actors; they are the goodliest, properest men, sister.

ALITHEA. Oh, but you must not like the actors, sister.

MARGERY. Ay, how should I help it, sister? Pray sister, when my husband comes in, will you ask leave for me to go a-walking?

ALITHEA. (*Aside.*) A-walking, ha, ha! Lord, a country gentlewoman's leisure is the drudgery of a foot post,[1] and she requires as much airing as her husband's horses.

(*Enter Pinchwife.*)

But here comes your husband; I'll ask, though I'm sure he'll not grant it.

MARGERY. He says he won't let me go abroad for fear of catching the pox.[2]

ALITHEA. Fie, the small pox you should say.

MARGERY. Oh my dear, dear bud, welcome home. Why dost thou look so froppish? Who has nangered[3] thee?

PINCHWIFE. You're a fool.

(*Margery goes aside and cries.*)

ALITHEA. Faith so she is, for crying for no fault, poor, tender creature!

PINCHWIFE. What, you would have her as impudent as yourself, as arrant a jill-flirt,[4] a gadder, a magpie, and, to say all, a mere[5] notorious Town woman?

ALITHEA. Brother, you are my only censurer, and the honor of your family shall sooner suffer in your wife there than in me, though I take the innocent liberty of the Town.

PINCHWIFE. Hark you, mistress, do not talk so before my wife. The innocent liberty of the Town!

ALITHEA. Why pray, who boasts of any intrigue with me? What lampoon has made my name notorious? What ill women frequent my lodgings? I keep no company with any women of scandalous reputations.

PINCHWIFE. No, you keep the men of scandalous reputations company.

ALITHEA. Where? Would you not have me civil? answer 'em in a box at the plays? in the Drawing Room[6] at Whitehall? in St. James's Park? Mulberry Garden? or—

PINCHWIFE. Hold, hold, do not teach my wife where the men are to be found; I believe she's the worse for your Town documents[7] already. I bid you keep her in ignorance as I do.

MARGERY. Indeed, be not angry with her, bud; she will tell me nothing of the Town, though I ask her a thousand times a day.

PINCHWIFE. Then you are very inquisitive to know, I find?

MARGERY. Not I, indeed, dear. I hate London. Our place-house[8] in the country is worth a thousand of't. Would I were there again!

PINCHWIFE. So you shall, I warrant, but were you not talking of plays and players when I came in?—You are her encourager in such discourses.

MARGERY. No indeed, dear, she chid me just now for liking the playermen.

PINCHWIFE. (*Aside.*) Nay, if she be so innocent as to own to me her liking them, there is no hurt in't.—

[1] *foot post* One who delivers the mail (post) on foot.

[2] *pox* Smallpox. In Town usage, "pox" referred to venereal disease.

[3] *froppish* Fretful; peevish; *nangered* Angered (baby talk).

[4] *jill-flirt* Female flirt; wanton.

[5] *mere* No less than.

[6] *Drawing Room* Reception room at the royal palace.

[7] *documents* Lessons.

[8] *place-house* Chief residence of an estate.

Come my poor rogue, but thou lik'st none better than me?

MARGERY. Yes indeed, but I do: the playermen are finer folks.

PINCHWIFE. But you love none better than me?

MARGERY. You are mine own dear bud, and I know you; I hate a stranger.

PINCHWIFE. Aye my dear, you must love me only and not be like the naughty Town women, who only hate their husbands and love every man else, love plays, visits, fine coaches, fine clothes, fiddles, balls, treats, and so lead a wicked Town life.

MARGERY. Nay, if to enjoy all these things be a Town life, London is not so bad a place, dear.

PINCHWIFE. How! If you love me, you must hate London.

ALITHEA. (*Aside.*) The fool has forbid me discovering to her the pleasures of the Town, and he is now setting her agog upon them himself.

MARGERY. But husband, do the Town women love the playermen, too?

PINCHWIFE. Yes, I warrant you.

MARGERY. Ay, I warrant you.

PINCHWIFE. Why, you do not, I hope?

MARGERY. No, no, bud, but why have we no playermen in the country?

PINCHWIFE. Hah! Mrs. Minx, ask me no more to go to a play.

MARGERY. Nay, why, love? I did not care for going, but when you forbid me, you make me, as't were, desire it.

ALITHEA. (*Aside.*) So 'twill be in other things, I warrant.

MARGERY. Pray, let me go to a play, dear.

PINCHWIFE. Hold your peace; I wonnot.

MARGERY. Why, love?

PINCHWIFE. Why, I'll tell you.

ALITHEA. (*Aside.*) Nay, if he tell her, she'll give him more cause to forbid her that place.

MARGERY. Pray, why, dear?

PINCHWIFE. First, you like the actors, and the gallants may like you.

MARGERY. What, a homely country girl? No, bud, nobody will like me.

PINCHWIFE. I tell you, yes, they may.

MARGERY. No, no, you jest. I won't believe you; I will go.

PINCHWIFE. I tell you then that one of the lewdest fellows in Town, who saw you there, told me he was in love with you.

MARGERY. Indeed! Who, who, pray, who was't?

PINCHWIFE. (*Aside.*) I've gone too far and slipped before I was aware. How overjoyed she is!

MARGERY. Was it any Hampshire gallant, any of our neighbors? I promise you, I am beholding to him.

PINCHWIFE. I promise you, you lie, for he would but ruin you as he has done hundreds. He has no other love for women but that. Such as he look upon women like basilisks, but to destroy 'em.

MARGERY. Ay, but if he loves me, why should he ruin me? Answer me to that. Methinks he should not; I would do him no harm.

ALITHEA. Ha, ha, ha.

PINCHWIFE. 'Tis very well, but I'll keep him from doing you any harm, or me either.

(*Enter Sparkish and Harcourt.*)

But here comes company. Get you in, get you in.

MARGERY. But pray, husband, is he a pretty gentleman that loves me?

PINCHWIFE. In baggage, in. (*Thrusts her in; shuts the door.*) What, all the lewd libertines of the Town brought to my lodging by this easy coxcomb! S'death,[1] I'll not suffer it.

SPARKISH. Here Harcourt, do you approve my choice?—Dear little rogue, I told you I'd bring you acquainted with all my friends, the wits, and—

(*Harcourt salutes her.*)

PINCHWIFE. Aye, they shall know her as well as you yourself will, I warrant you.

SPARKISH. This is one of those, my pretty rogue, that are to dance at your wedding tomorrow, and him you must bid welcome ever to what you and I have.

PINCHWIFE. (*Aside.*) Monstrous!

SPARKISH. Harcourt, how dost thou like her, faith?—Nay dear, do not look down; I should hate to have a wife of mine out of countenance at any thing.

PINCHWIFE. Wonderful!

[1] *S'death* God's death (an oath).

SPARKISH. Tell me, I say, Harcourt, how dost thou like her? Thou hast stared upon her enough to resolve me.

HARCOURT. So infinitely well that I could wish I had a mistress, too, that might differ from her in nothing but her love and engagement to you.

ALITHEA. Sir, Master Sparkish has often told me that his acquaintance were all wits and railleurs,[1] and now I find it.

SPARKISH. No, by the universe, madam, he does not rally now; you may believe him. I do assure you, he is the honestest, worthiest, true-hearted gentleman—a man of such perfect honor, he would say nothing to a lady he does not mean.

PINCHWIFE. (*Aside.*) Praising another man to his mistress!

HARCOURT. Sir, you are so beyond expectation obliging, that—

SPARKISH. Nay, egad, I am sure you do admire her extremely; I see't in your eyes.—He does admire you, madam.—By the world, don't you?

HARCOURT. Yes, above the world or the most glorious part of it, her whole sex, and till now I never thought I should have envied you, or any man about to marry, but you have the best excuse for marriage I ever knew.

ALITHEA. Nay, now, sir, I'm satisfied you are of the society of the wits and railleurs since you cannot spare your friend, even when he is but too civil to you, but the surest sign is since you are an enemy to marriage, for that I hear you hate as much as business or bad wine.

HARCOURT. Truly madam, I never was an enemy to marriage till now because marriage was never an enemy to me before.

ALITHEA. But why, sir, is marriage an enemy to you now? because it robs you of your friend here? For you look upon a friend married as one gone into a monastery, that is, dead to the world.

HARCOURT. 'Tis indeed because you marry him. I see, madam, you can guess my meaning. I do confess heartily and openly I wish it were in my power to break the match. By heavens, I would!

SPARKISH. Poor Frank!

ALITHEA. Would you be so unkind to me?

HARCOURT. No, no, 'tis not because I would be unkind to you.

SPARKISH. Poor Frank! No, gad, 'tis only his kindness to me.

PINCHWIFE. (*Aside.*) Great kindness to you, indeed. Insensible fop, let a man make love[2] to his wife to his face!

SPARKISH. Come, dear Frank, for all my wife there that shall be, thou shalt enjoy me sometimes, dear rogue. By my honor, we men of wit condole for our deceased brother in marriage as much as for one dead in earnest. I think that was prettily said of me, hah, Harcourt? But come, Frank, be not melancholy for me.

HARCOURT. No, I assure you I am not melancholy for you.

SPARKISH. Prithee Frank, dost think my wife that shall be there a fine person?

HARCOURT. I could gaze upon her till I became as blind as you are.

SPARKISH. How, as I am! How?

HARCOURT. Because you are a lover, and true lovers are blind, stock-blind.

SPARKISH. True, true, but by the world, she has wit, too, as well as beauty. Go, go with her into a corner and try if she has wit; talk to her anything; she's bashful before me.

HARCOURT. Indeed, if a woman wants[3] wit in a corner, she has it nowhere.

ALITHEA. (*Aside to Sparkish.*) Sir, you dispose of me a little before your time.

SPARKISH. Nay, nay, madam, let me have an earnest of your obedience, or—Go, go, madam.

(*Harcourt courts Alithea aside.*)

PINCHWIFE. How, sir! if you are not concerned for the honor of a wife, I am for that of a sister. He shall not debauch her. Be a pander to your own wife, bring men to her, let 'em make love before your face, thrust 'em into a corner together, then leave 'em in private! Is this your Town wit and conduct?

SPARKISH. Ha, ha, ha, a silly wise rogue would make one laugh more than a stark fool, ha, ha! I shall burst. Nay, you shall not disturb 'em. I'll vex thee, by the world. (*Struggles with Pinchwife to keep him from Harcourt and Alithea.*)

[1] *railleurs* Those who banter or mock, a fashionable French word.

[2] *make love* Pay court.

[3] *wants* Lacks or needs.

ALITHEA. The writings are drawn, sir, settlements made; 'tis too late, sir, and past all revocation.

HARCOURT. Then so is my death.

ALITHEA. I would not be unjust to him.

HARCOURT. Then why to me so?

ALITHEA. I have no obligation to you.

HARCOURT. My love.

ALITHEA. I had his before.

HARCOURT. You never had it: he wants, you see, jealousy, the only infallible sign of it.

ALITHEA. Love proceeds from esteem; he cannot distrust my virtue. Besides, he loves me, or he would not marry me.

HARCOURT. Marrying you is no more sign of his love than bribing your woman, that he may marry you, is a sign of his generosity. Marriage is rather a sign of interest than love, and he that marries a fortune, covets a mistress, not loves her. But if you take marriage for a sign of love, take it from me immediately.

ALITHEA. No, now you have put a scruple in my head. But in short, sir, to end our dispute, I must marry him: my reputation would suffer in the world else.

HARCOURT. No, if you do marry him, with your pardon, madam, your reputation suffers in the world, and you would be thought in necessity for a cloak.

ALITHEA. Nay, now you are rude, sir.—Mr. Sparkish, pray come hither; your friend here is very troublesome and very loving.

HARCOURT. (*Aside to Alithea.*) Hold, hold—

PINCHWIFE. D'ye hear that?

SPARKISH. Why, d'ye think I'll seem to be jealous, like a country bumpkin?

PINCHWIFE. No, rather be a cuckold, like a credulous cit.[1]

HARCOURT. Madam, you would not have been so little generous[2] as to have told him.

ALITHEA. Yes, since you could be so little generous as to wrong him.

HARCOURT. Wrong him! No man can do't; he's beneath an injury: a bubble,[3] a coward, a senseless idiot, a wretch so contemptible to all the world but you that—

ALITHEA. Hold, do not rail at him, for since he is like to be my husband, I am resolved to like him. Nay, I think I am obliged to tell him you are not his friend.—Master Sparkish, Master Sparkish.

SPARKISH. What, what? Now, dear rogue, has not she wit?

HARCOURT. (*Speaks surlily.*) Not so much as I thought and hoped she had.

ALITHEA. Mr. Sparkish, do you bring people to rail at you?

HARCOURT. Madam—

SPARKISH. How! No, but if he does rail at me, 'tis but in jest, I warrant, what we wits do for one another and never take any notice of it.

ALITHEA. He spoke so scurrilously of you I had no patience to hear him; besides, he has been making love to me.

HARCOURT. (*Aside.*) True, damned, tell-tale woman.

SPARKISH. Pshaw, to show his parts.[4] We wits rail and make love often but to show our parts; as we have no affections, so we have no malice, we—

ALITHEA. He said you were a wretch, below an injury.

SPARKISH. Pshaw.

HARCOURT. (*Aside.*) Damned, senseless, impudent, virtuous jade! Well, since she won't let me have her, she'll do as good: she'll make me hate her.

ALITHEA. A common bubble.

SPARKISH. Pshaw.

ALITHEA. A coward.

SPARKISH. Pshaw, pshaw.

ALITHEA. A senseless, driveling idiot.

SPARKISH. How! Did he disparage my parts? Nay, then my honor's concerned. I can't put up that, sir.—By the world, brother, help me to kill him. (*Aside.*) I may draw[5] now, since we have the odds of him; 'tis a good occasion, too, before my mistress. (*Offers to draw.*)

ALITHEA. Hold, hold!

SPARKISH. What, what?

ALITHEA. (*Aside.*) I must not let 'em kill the gentleman neither, for his kindness[6] to me. I am so far from hating

[1] *cit* A businessman, as opposed to a gentleman. The City was the section of London in which trade was conducted; hence, a "cit" is a denizen of the City.

[2] *generous* Noble.

[3] *bubble* Dupe.

[4] *parts* Personal qualities.

[5] *draw* Withdraw a sword.

[6] *kindness* Affection.

him that I wish my gallant had his person and understanding. Nay, if my honor—

SPARKISH. I'll be thy death.

ALITHEA. Hold, hold! Indeed, to tell the truth, the gentleman said after all that what he spoke was but out of friendship to you.

SPARKISH. How! Say I am, I am a fool, that is, no wit, out of friendship to me?

ALITHEA. Yes, to try whether I was concerned enough for you, and made love to me only to be satisfied of my virtue, for your sake.

HARCOURT. (*Aside.*) Kind however—

SPARKISH. Nay, if it were so, my dear rogue, I ask thee pardon, but why would not you tell me so, faith?

HARCOURT. Because I did not think on't, faith.

SPARKISH. Come, Horner does not come, Harcourt, let's be gone to the new play.—Come, madam.

ALITHEA. I will not go if you intend to leave me alone in the box and run into the pit, as you use to do.

SPARKISH. Pshaw, I'll leave Harcourt with you in the box to entertain you, and that's as good. If I sat in the box, I should be thought no judge but of trimmings.—Come away, Harcourt, lead her down.

(*Exeunt Sparkish, Harcourt, and Alithea.*)

PINCHWIFE. Well, go thy ways, for the flower of the true Town fops, such as spend their estates before they come to 'em and are cuckolds before they're married. But let me go look to my own freehold.—How—

(*Enter My Lady Fidget, Dainty, and Mistress Squeamish.*)

LADY FIDGET. Your servant, sir. Where is your lady? We are come to wait upon her to the new play.

PINCHWIFE. New play!

LADY FIDGET. And my husband will wait upon you presently.

PINCHWIFE. (*Aside.*) Damn your civility.—Madam, by no means, I will not see Sir Jaspar here till I have waited upon him at home, nor shall my wife see you till she has waited upon your ladyship at your lodgings.

LADY FIDGET. Now we are here, sir—

PINCHWIFE. No, madam.

DAINTY. Pray, let us see her.

MRS. SQUEAMISH. We will not stir till we see her.

PINCHWIFE. (*Aside.*) A pox on you all. (*Goes to the door and returns.*) She has locked the door and is gone abroad.

LADY FIDGET. No, you have locked the door, and she's within.

DAINTY. They told us below she was here.

PINCHWIFE. [*Aside.*] Will nothing do?—Well it must out then: to tell you the truth, ladies, which I was afraid to let you know before lest it might endanger your lives, my wife has just now the small pox come out upon her. Do not be frightened, but pray, be gone ladies. You shall not stay here in danger of your lives. Pray get you gone, ladies.

LADY FIDGET. No, no, we have all had 'em.

MRS. SQUEAMISH. Alack, alack.

DAINTY. Come, come, we must see how it goes with her. I understand the disease.

LADY FIDGET. Come.

PINCHWIFE. (*Aside.*) Well, there is no being too hard for women at their own weapon, lying; therefore, I'll quit the field. (*Exit.*)

MRS. SQUEAMISH. Here's an example of jealousy.

LADY FIDGET. Indeed, as the world goes, I wonder there are no more jealous, since wives are so neglected.

DAINTY. Pshaw, as the world goes, to what end should they be jealous?

LADY FIDGET. Faugh, 'tis a nasty world.

MRS. SQUEAMISH. That men of parts, great acquaintance, and quality should take up with and spend themselves and fortunes in keeping little playhouse creatures, faugh!

LADY FIDGET. Nay, that women of understanding, great acquaintance, and good quality should fall a-keeping, too, of little creatures, faugh!

MRS. SQUEAMISH. Why, 'tis the men of quality's fault: they never visit women of honor and reputation as they used to do and have not so much as common civility for ladies of our rank but use us with the same indifferency and ill breeding as if we were all married to 'em.

LADY FIDGET. She says true. 'Tis an arrant shame women of quality should be so slighted; methinks birth, birth, should go for something. I have known men admired, courted, and followed for their titles only.

MRS. SQUEAMISH. Aye, one would think men of honor

should not love, no more than marry, out of their own rank.

DAINTY. Fie, fie upon 'em, they are come to think crossbreeding for themselves best, as well as for their dogs and horses.

LADY FIDGET. They are dogs and horses for't.

MRS. SQUEAMISH. One would think if not for love, for vanity a little.

DAINTY. Nay, they do satisfy their vanity upon us sometimes and are kind to us in their report, tell all the world they lie with us.

LADY FIDGET. Damned rascals, that we should be only wronged by 'em! To report a man has had a person, when he has not had a person, is the greatest wrong in the whole world that can be done to a person.

MRS. SQUEAMISH. Well, 'tis an arrant shame noble persons should be so wronged and neglected.

LADY FIDGET. But still 'tis an arranter shame for a noble person to neglect her own honor and defame her own noble person with little inconsiderable fellows, faugh!

DAINTY. I suppose the crime against our honor is the same with a man of quality as with another.

LADY FIDGET. How! No, sure the man of quality is likest one's husband, and therefore, the fault should be the less.

DAINTY. But then the pleasure should be the less.

LADY FIDGET. Fie, fie, fie, for shame sister! Whither shall we ramble? Be continent in your discourse, or I shall hate you.

DAINTY. Besides, an intrigue is so much the more notorious for the man's quality.

MRS. SQUEAMISH. 'Tis true, nobody takes notice of a private man, and therefore, with him 'tis more secret, and the crime's the less when 'tis not known.

LADY FIDGET. You say true. I'faith, I think you are in the right on't. 'Tis not an injury to a husband till it be an injury to our honors, so that a woman of honor loses no honor with a private person, and to say truth—

DAINTY. (*Apart to Mrs. Squeamish.*) So the little fellow is grown a private person—with her—

LADY FIDGET. But still my dear, dear honor.

(*Enter Sir Jaspar, Horner, Dorilant.*)

SIR JASPAR. Aye, my dear, dear of honor, thou hast still so much honor in thy mouth—

HORNER. (*Aside.*) That she has none elsewhere—

LADY FIDGET. Oh, what d'ye mean to bring in these upon us?

DAINTY. Faugh, these are as bad as wits!

MRS. SQUEAMISH. Faugh!

LADY FIDGET. Let us leave the room.

SIR JASPAR. Stay, stay, faith, to tell you the naked truth.

LADY FIDGET. Fie, Sir Jaspar, do not use that word "naked."

SIR JASPAR. Well, well, in short, I have business at Whitehall and cannot go to the play with you; therefore, would have you go—

LADY FIDGET. With those two to a play?

SIR JASPAR. No, not with t'other, but with Mr. Horner; there can be no more scandal to go with him than with Mr. Tattle or Master Limberham.[1]

LADY FIDGET. With that nasty fellow! No—no.

SIR JASPAR. Nay prithee dear, hear me. (*Whispers to Lady Fidget.*)

(*Horner, Dorilant drawing near Squeamish and Dainty.*)

HORNER. Ladies.

DAINTY. Stand off.

MRS. SQUEAMISH. Do not approach us.

DAINTY. You herd with the wits; you are obscenity all over.

MRS. SQUEAMISH. And I would as soon look upon a picture of Adam and Eve without fig leaves as any of you, if I could help it; therefore, keep off and do not make us sick.

DORILANT. What a devil are these?

HORNER. Why, these are pretenders to honor, as critics to wit, only by censuring others, and as every raw, peevish, out-of-humored, affected, dull, tea-drinking, arithmetical[2] fop sets up for a wit by railing at men of sense, so these for honor, by railing at the Court and ladies of as great honor as quality.

SIR JASPAR. Come Mr. Horner, I must desire you to go with these ladies to the play, sir.

HORNER. I, sir!

SIR JASPAR. Aye, aye, come, sir.

---

[1] *Limberham* Limber-jointed or weak-kneed person.

[2] *arithmetical* Precise.

HORNER. I must beg your pardon, sir, and theirs. I will not be seen in women's company in public again for the world.

SIR JASPAR. Ha, ha, strange aversion!

MRS. SQUEAMISH. No, he's for women's company in private.

SIR JASPAR. He—poor man—he! Ha, ha, ha.

DAINTY. 'Tis a greater shame amongst lewd fellows to be seen in virtuous women's company than for the women to be seen with them.

HORNER. Indeed madam, the time was I only hated virtuous women, but now I hate the other, too. I beg your pardon, ladies.

LADY FIDGET. You are very obliging, sir, because we would not be troubled with you.

SIR JASPAR. In sober sadness he shall go.

DORILANT. Nay, if he wonnot, I am ready to wait upon the ladies, and I think I am the fitter man.

SIR JASPAR. You, sir! no, I thank you for that. Master Horner is a privileged man amongst the virtuous ladies; 'twill be a great while before you are so. He, he, he, he's my wife's gallant, he, he, he. No, pray withdraw, sir, for as I take it, the virtuous ladies have no business with you.

DORILANT. And I am sure, he can have none with them. 'Tis strange a man can't come amongst virtuous women now but upon the same terms as men are admitted into the Great Turk's seraglio,[1] but heavens keep me from being an ombre[2] player with 'em. But where is Pinchwife? (*Exit.*)

SIR JASPAR. Come, come, man. What, avoid the sweet society of womankind? that sweet, soft, gentle, tame, noble creature woman, made for man's companion—

HORNER. So is that soft, gentle, tame, and more noble creature a spaniel, and has all their tricks: can fawn, lie down, suffer beating, and fawn the more, barks at your friends when they come to see you, makes your bed hard, gives you fleas and the mange sometimes, and all the difference is, the spaniel's the more faithful animal and fawns but upon one master.

SIR JASPAR. He, he, he.

MRS. SQUEAMISH. Oh, the rude beast!

DAINTY. Insolent brute!

LADY FIDGET. Brute! Stinking, mortified, rotten French wether,[3] to dare—

SIR JASPAR. Hold, an't[4] please your ladyship.—For shame, Master Horner, your mother was a woman. (*Aside.*) Now shall I never reconcile 'em.—Hark you, madam, take my advice in your anger: you know you often want one to make up your drolling pack of ombre players, and you may cheat him easily, for he's an ill gamester and consequently loves play. Besides, you know, you have but two old civil gentlemen (with stinking breaths, too) to wait upon you abroad. Take in the third into your service. The other are but crazy, and a lady should have a supernumerary gentleman-usher, as a supernumerary coach-horse, lest sometimes you should be forced to stay at home.

LADY FIDGET. But are you sure he loves play and has money?

SIR JASPAR. He loves play as much as you and has money as much as I.

LADY FIDGET. Then I am contented to make him pay for his scurrility; money makes up in a measure all other wants in men. (*Aside.*) Those whom we cannot make hold for gallants, we make fine.[5]

SIR JASPAR. (*Aside.*) So, so, now to mollify, to wheedle him.—Master Horner, will you never keep civil company? Methinks 'tis time now, since you are only fit for them. Come, come, man, you must e'en fall to visiting our wives, eating at our tables, drinking tea with our virtuous relations after dinner, dealing cards to 'em, reading plays and gazettes to 'em, picking fleas out of their shocks[6] for 'em, collecting receipts,[7] new songs, women, pages, and footmen for 'em.

HORNER. I hope they'll afford me better employment, sir.

SIR JASPAR. He, he, he! 'Tis fit you know your work before you come into your place, and since you are unprovided of a lady to flatter and a good house to eat at, pray frequent mine and call my wife "mistress," and she shall call you "gallant," according to the custom.

HORNER. Who, I?

[1] *Great Turk's seraglio* Harem of the Ottoman sultan.

[2] *ombre* Card game.

[3] *wether* Eunuch.

[4] *an't* And it; i.e., if it.

[5] *fine* To forfeit money.

[6] *shocks* Lapdogs.

[7] *receipts* Recipes or prescriptions.

SIR JASPAR. Faith, thou shalt for my sake; come, for my sake only.

HORNER. For your sake—

SIR JASPAR. Come, come, here's a gamester for you; let him be a little familiar sometimes. Nay, what if a little rude? Gamesters may be rude with ladies, you know.

LADY FIDGET. Yes, losing gamesters have a privilege with women.

HORNER. I always thought the contrary, that the winning gamester had most privilege with women, for when you have lost your money to a man, you'll lose anything you have, all you have, they say, and he may use you as he pleases.

SIR JASPAR. He, he, he! Well, win or lose, you shall have your liberty with her.

LADY FIDGET. As he behaves himself and for your sake, I'll give him admittance and freedom.

HORNER. All sorts of freedom, madam?

SIR JASPAR. Aye, aye, aye, all sorts of freedom thou canst take, and so go to her; begin thy new employment. Wheedle her, jest with her, and be better acquainted one with another.

HORNER. (*Aside.*) I think I know her already, therefore, may venture with her, my secret for hers.

(*Horner and Lady Fidget whisper.*)

SIR JASPAR. Sister, Cuz,[1] I have provided an innocent playfellow for you there.

DAINTY. Who, he!

MRS. SQUEAMISH. There's a playfellow indeed.

SIR JASPAR. Yes, sure. What, he is good enough to play at cards, blindman's buff, or the fool with sometimes.

MRS. SQUEAMISH. Faugh, we'll have no such playfellows.

DAINTY. No sir, you shan't choose playfellows for us, we thank you.

SIR JASPAR. Nay, pray hear me. (*Whispering to them.*)

LADY FIDGET. [*Aside to Horner.*] But poor gentleman, could you be so generous? so truly a man of honor, as for the sakes of us women of honor, to cause your self to be reported no man? no man! and to suffer your self the greatest shame that could fall upon a man, that none might fall upon us women by your conversation. But indeed, sir, as perfectly, perfectly the same man as before your going into France, sir, as perfectly, perfectly, sir?

HORNER. As perfectly, perfectly, madam. Nay, I scorn you should take my word; I desire to be tried only, madam.

LADY FIDGET. Well, that's spoken again like a man of honor; all men of honor desire to come to the test. But indeed, generally you men report such things of yourselves one does not know how or whom to believe, and it is come to that pass, we dare not take your words, no more than your tailors, without some staid servant of yours be bound with you. But I have so strong a faith in your honor, dear, dear, noble sir, that I'd forfeit mine for yours at any time, dear sir.

HORNER. No madam, you should not need to forfeit it for me: I have given you security already to save you harmless, my late reputation being so well known in the world, madam.

LADY FIDGET. But if upon any future falling out or upon a suspicion of my taking the trust out of your hands to employ some other, you yourself should betray your trust, dear sir? I mean, if you'll give me leave to speak obscenely, you might tell, dear sir.

HORNER. If I did, nobody would believe me: the reputation of impotency is as hardly recovered again in the world as that of cowardice, dear madam.

LADY FIDGET. Nay then, as one may say, you may do your worst, dear, dear, sir.

SIR JASPAR. Come, is your ladyship reconciled to him yet? Have you agreed on matters? For I must be gone to Whitehall.

LADY FIDGET. Why indeed, Sir Jaspar, Master Horner is a thousand, thousand times a better man than I thought him.—Cousin Squeamish, Sister Dainty, I can name him now. Truly not long ago, you know, I thought his very name obscenity, and I would as soon have lain with him as have named him.

SIR JASPAR. Very likely, poor madam.

DAINTY. I believe it.

MRS. SQUEAMISH. No doubt on't.

SIR JASPAR. Well, well, that your ladyship is as virtuous as any she, I know, and him all the Town knows, he, he, he. Therefore, now you like him, get you gone to your business together. Go, go, to your business, I say, pleasure, whilst I go to my pleasure, business.

LADY FIDGET. Come then, dear gallant.

[1] *Cuz* Cousin.

HORNER. Come away, my dearest mistress.

SIR JASPAR. So, so, why 'tis as I'd have it. (*Exit.*)

HORNER. And as I'd have it.

LADY FIDGET. Who for his business from his wife will run
Takes the best care to have her business done.

(*Exeunt.*)

ACT 3, SCENE 1. [Pinchwife's lodging.]

(*Alithea and Margery.*)

ALITHEA. Sister, what ails you, you are grown melancholy?

MARGERY. Would it not make anyone melancholy to see you go every day fluttering about abroad, whilst I must stay at home like a poor lonely, sullen bird in a cage?

ALITHEA. Aye sister, but you came young and just from the nest to your cage, so that I thought you liked it and could be as cheerful in't as others that took their flight themselves early and are hopping abroad in the open air.

MARGERY. Nay, I confess I was quiet enough till my husband told me what pure[1] lives the London ladies live abroad, with their dancing, meetings, and junketings, and dressed every day in their best gowns, and I warrant you, play at ninepins every day of the week, so they do.

(*Enter Pinchwife.*)

PINCHWIFE. Come, what's here to do? You are putting the Town pleasures in her head and setting her a-longing.

ALITHEA. Yes, after ninepins! You suffer none to give her those longings, you mean, but yourself.

PINCHWIFE. I tell her of the vanities of the Town like a confessor.

ALITHEA. A confessor! just such a confessor as he that by forbidding a silly ostler to grease the horses' teeth,[2] taught him to do't.

PINCHWIFE. Come Mistress Flippant, good precepts are lost when bad examples are still before us: the liberty you take abroad makes her hanker after it and out of humor at home, poor wretch! She desired not to come to London; I would bring her.

ALITHEA. Very well.

PINCHWIFE. She has been this week in Town and never desired, till this afternoon, to go abroad.

ALITHEA. Was she not at a play yesterday?

PINCHWIFE. Yes, but she ne'er asked me; I was myself the cause of her going.

ALITHEA. Then if she ask you again, you are the cause of her asking, and not my example.

PINCHWIFE. Well, tomorrow night I shall be rid of you, and the next day before 'tis light, she and I'll be rid of the Town and my dreadful apprehensions.—Come, be not melancholy, for thou shalt go into the country after tomorrow, dearest.

ALITHEA. Great comfort.

MARGERY. Pish, what d'ye tell me of the country for?

PINCHWIFE. How's this! What, pish at the country?

MARGERY. Let me alone; I am not well.

PINCHWIFE. Oh, if that be all—what ails my dearest?

MARGERY. Truly I don't know, but I have not been well since you told me there was a gallant at the play in love with me.

PINCHWIFE. Hah—

ALITHEA. That's by my example too.

PINCHWIFE. Nay, if you are not well but are so concerned because a lewd fellow chanced to lie and say he liked you, you'll make me sick, too.

MARGERY. Of what sickness?

PINCHWIFE. Oh, of that which is worse than the plague, jealousy.

MARGERY. Pish, you jeer. I'm sure there's no such disease in our receipt-book at home.

PINCHWIFE. No, thou never met'st with it, poor innocent. (*Aside.*) Well, if thou cuckold me, 'twill be my own fault, for cuckolds and bastards are generally makers of their own fortune.

MARGERY. Well but pray, bud, let's go to a play tonight.

PINCHWIFE. 'Tis just done; she comes from it.—But why are you so eager to see a play?

MARGERY. Faith dear, not that I care one pin for their talk there, but I like to look upon the playermen and would see, if I could, the gallant you say loves me; that's all, dear bud.

PINCHWIFE. Is that all, dear bud?

ALITHEA. This proceeds from my example.

[1] *pure* Fine; wonderful (a ruralism).

[2] *grease the horses' teeth* Ruse by which horses cannot eat what their owners have paid for.

MARGERY. But if the play be done, let's go abroad, however, dear bud.

PINCHWIFE. Come, have a little patience, and thou shalt go into the country on Friday.

MARGERY. Therefore, I would see first some sights to tell my neighbors of. Nay, I will go abroad, that's once.[1]

ALITHEA. I'm the cause of this desire, too.

PINCHWIFE. But now I think on't, who was the cause of Horner's coming to my lodging today? That was you.

ALITHEA. No, you, because you would not let him see your handsome wife out of your lodging.

MARGERY. Why, oh Lord! Did the gentleman come hither to see me indeed?

PINCHWIFE. No, no.—You are not cause of that damned question, too, Mistress Alithea? (*Aside.*) Well, she's in the right of it: he is in love with my wife—and comes after her. 'Tis so. But I'll nip his love in the bud, lest he should follow us into the country and break his chariot[2] wheel near our house on purpose for an excuse to come to't. But I think I know the Town.

MARGERY. Come, pray bud, let's go abroad before 'tis late, for I will go, that's flat and plain.

PINCHWIFE. (*Aside.*) So! The obstinacy already of a Town wife, and I must, whilst she's here, humor her like one.—Sister, how shall we do, that she may not be seen or known?

ALITHEA. Let her put on her mask.

PINCHWIFE. Pshaw, a mask makes people but the more inquisitive and is as ridiculous a disguise as a stage beard; her shape, stature, habit will be known, and if we should meet with Horner, he would be sure to take acquaintance with us, must wish her joy, kiss her, talk to her, leer upon her, and the devil and all. No, I'll not use her to a mask; 'tis dangerous, for masks have made more cuckolds than the best faces that ever were known.

ALITHEA. How will you do then?

MARGERY. Nay, shall we go? The Exchange will be shut, and I have a mind to see that.

PINCHWIFE. So—I have it. I'll dress her up in the suit we are to carry down to her brother, little Sir James; nay, I understand the Town tricks. Come, let's go dress her. A mask! No—a woman masked, like a covered dish, gives a man curiosity and appetite, when, it may be, uncovered, 'twould turn his stomach. No, no.

ALITHEA. Indeed, your comparison is something a greasy one. But I had a gentle gallant used to say, a beauty masked, like the sun in eclipse, gathers together more gazers than if it shined out.

(*Exeunt.*)

ACT 3, SCENE 2. The New Exchange.

(*Enter Horner, Harcourt, Dorilant. [Clasp at his booth.]*)

DORILANT. Engaged to women, and not sup with us?

HORNER. Aye, a pox on 'em all.

HARCOURT. You were much a more reasonable man in the morning and had as noble resolutions against 'em as a widower of a week's liberty.

DORILANT. Did I ever think to see you keep company with women in vain?

HORNER. In vain! No, 'tis since I can't love 'em, to be revenged on 'em.

HARCOURT. Now your sting is gone, you looked in the box amongst all those women like a drone in the hive: all upon you, shoved and ill-used by 'em all, and thrust from one side to t'other.

DORILANT. Yet he must be buzzing amongst 'em still, like other old beetle-headed, lickerish drones. Avoid 'em and hate 'em as they hate you.

HORNER. Because I do hate 'em and would hate 'em yet more, I'll frequent 'em. You may see by marriage, nothing makes a man hate a woman more than her constant conversation. In short, I converse with 'em, as you do with rich fools, to laugh at 'em and use 'em ill.

DORILANT. But I would no more sup with women unless I could lie with 'em, than sup with a rich coxcomb unless I could cheat him.

HORNER. Yes, I have known thee sup with a fool for his drinking; if he could set out your hand[3] that way only, you were satisfied, and if he were a wine-swallowing mouth, 'twas enough.

HARCOURT. Yes, a man drinks often with a fool, as he tosses with a marker, only to keep his hand in ure.[4] But do the ladies drink?

---

[1] *that's once* That's final, or positive; once and for all.

[2] *chariot* Light four-wheeled vehicle.

[3] *set out your hand* Furnish you.

[4] *tosses ... ure* Throws dice with a scorekeeper (i.e., one who doesn't play for money) to keep in practice.

HORNER. Yes sir, and I shall have the pleasure at least of laying 'em flat with a bottle and bring as much scandal that way upon 'em as formerly t'other.

HARCOURT. Perhaps you may prove as weak a brother amongst 'em that way as t'other.

DORILANT. Faugh, drinking with women is as unnatural as scolding with 'em, but 'tis a pleasure of decayed fornicators and the basest way of quenching love.

HARCOURT. Nay, 'tis drowning love instead of quenching it. But leave us for civil women, too!

DORILANT. Aye, when he can't be the better for 'em. We hardly pardon a man that leaves his friend for a wench, and that's a pretty lawful call.

HORNER. Faith, I would not leave you for 'em if they would not drink.

DORILANT. Who would disappoint his company at Lewis's[1] for a gossiping?

HARCOURT. Faugh, wine and women good apart, together as nauseous as sack[2] and sugar. But hark you, sir, before you go, a little of your advice; an old maimed general, when unfit for action, is fittest for counsel. I have other designs upon women than eating and drinking with them. I am in love with Sparkish's mistress, whom he is to marry tomorrow. Now how shall I get her?

(*Enter Sparkish, looking about.*)

HORNER. Why, here comes one will help you to her.

HARCOURT. He! He, I tell you, is my rival and will hinder my love.

HORNER. No, a foolish rival and a jealous husband assist their rivals' designs, for they are sure to make their women hate them, which is the first step to their love for another man.

HARCOURT. But I cannot come near his mistress but in his company.

HORNER. Still the better for you, for fools are most easily cheated when they themselves are accessories, and he is to be bubbled of his mistress, as of his money, the common mistress, by keeping him company.

SPARKISH. Who is that, that is to be bubbled? Faith, let me snack;[3] I han't met with a bubble since Christmas. Gad, I think bubbles are like their brother woodcocks, go out with the cold weather.

HARCOURT. (*Apart to Horner.*) A pox! He did not hear all, I hope.

SPARKISH. Come, you bubbling rogues, you. Where do we sup?—Oh Harcourt, my mistress tells me you have been making fierce love to her all the play long, ha, ha—but I—

HARCOURT. I make love to her?

SPARKISH. Nay, I forgive thee, for I think I know thee, and I know her, but I am sure I know myself.

HARCOURT. Did she tell you so? I see all women are like these of the Exchange, who, to enhance the price of their commodities, report to their fond[4] customers offers which were never made 'em.

HORNER. Aye, women are as apt to tell before the intrigue as men after it and so show themselves the vainer sex. But hast thou a mistress, Sparkish? 'Tis as hard for me to believe it as that thou ever hadst a bubble, as you bragged just now.

SPARKISH. Oh your servant, sir. Are you at your raillery, sir? But we were some of us beforehand with you today at the play. The wits were something bold with you, sir. Did you not hear us laugh?

HARCOURT. Yes, but I thought you had gone to plays to laugh at the poet's wit, not at your own.

SPARKISH. Your servant, sir. No, I thank you. Gad, I go to a play as to a country treat: I carry my own wine to one and my own wit to t'other, or else I'm sure I should not be merry at either, and the reason why we are so often louder than the players is because we think we speak more wit and so become the poet's rivals in his audience. For to tell you the truth, we hate the silly rogues, nay, so much that we find fault even with their bawdy upon the stage whilst we talk nothing else in the pit as loud.

HORNER. But why shouldst thou hate the silly poets? Thou hast too much wit to be one, and they, like whores, are only hated by each other, and thou dost scorn writing, I'm sure.

[1] *Lewis's* Presumably a tavern or eating house.

[2] *sack* Wine.

[3] *snack* Share; take part.

[4] *fond* Foolish.

SPARKISH. Yes, I'd have you to know, I scorn writing, but women, women, that make men do all foolish things, make 'em write songs, too; everybody does it. 'Tis e'en as common with lovers as playing with fans, and you can no more help rhyming to your Phyllis than drinking to your Phyllis.

HARCOURT. Nay, poetry in love is no more to be avoided than jealousy.

DORILANT. But the poets damned your songs, did they?

SPARKISH. Damn the poets! They turned 'em into burlesque, as they call it; that burlesque is a hocus-pocus trick they have got, which by the virtue of "*hictius doctius*,[1] topsey turvey," they make a wise and witty man in the world a fool upon the stage, you know not how, and 'tis, therefore, I hate 'em too, for I know not but it may be my own case, for they'll put a man into a play for looking asquint. Their predecessors were contented to make serving men only their stage fools, but these rogues must have gentlemen, with a pox to 'em, nay, knights. And indeed, you shall hardly see a fool upon the stage but he's a knight, and to tell you the truth, they have kept me these six years from being a knight in earnest, for fear of being knighted in a play and dubbed a fool.

DORILANT. Blame 'em not; they must follow their copy, the age.

HARCOURT. But why shouldst thou be afraid of being in a play, who expose yourself everyday in the playhouses and as public places?

HORNER. 'Tis but being on the stage instead of standing on a bench in the pit.

DORILANT. Don't you give money to painters to draw you like? And are you afraid of your pictures at length in a playhouse where all your mistresses may see you?

SPARKISH. A pox! Painters don't draw the small pox or pimples in one's face. Come, damn all your silly authors whatever, all books and booksellers, by the world, and all readers, courteous or uncourteous.

HARCOURT. But who comes here, Sparkish?

(*Enter Pinchwife and his wife in man's clothes; Alithea; Lucy, her maid.*)

SPARKISH. Oh hide me! There's my mistress, too. (*Hides himself behind Harcourt.*)

HARCOURT. She sees you.

SPARKISH. But I will not see her; 'tis time to go to Whitehall, and I must not fail the Drawing Room.

HARCOURT. Pray, first carry me and reconcile me to her.

SPARKISH. Another time, faith, the King will have supped.

HARCOURT. Not with the worse stomach for thy absence. Thou art one of those fools that think their attendance at the King's meals as necessary as his physicians', when you are more troublesome to him than his doctors or his dogs.

SPARKISH. Pshaw, I know my interest, sir. Prithee hide me.

HORNER. Your servant, Pinchwife.—What, he knows us not!

PINCHWIFE. (*To his wife aside.*) Come along.

MARGERY. Pray, have you any ballads? Give me sixpenny worth.

CLASP. We have no ballads.

MARGERY. Then give me *Covent Garden Drollery*,[2] and a play or two.—Oh here's *Tarugo's Wiles* and *The Slighted Maiden*.[3] I'll have them.

PINCHWIFE. (*Apart to her.*) No, plays are not for your reading. Come along. Will you discover yourself?

HORNER. Who is that pretty youth with him, Sparkish?

SPARKISH. I believe his wife's brother, because he's something like her, but I never saw her but once.

HORNER. Extremely handsome. I have seen a face like it, too. Let us follow 'em.

(*Exeunt Pinchwife, Margery; Alithea, Lucy, Horner, Dorilant following them.*)

HARCOURT. Come Sparkish, your mistress saw you and will be angry you go not to her; besides, I would fain be reconciled to her, which none but you can do, dear friend.

---

[1] *hictius doctius* Standard part of the magician's (juggler's) repertoire; perhaps from *hicce est doctus* (Latin: this is the doctor).

[2] *Covent Garden Drollery* Miscellany of songs, poems, prologues, and epilogues by various writers, including Wycherley, published in 1672.

[3] *Tarugo's Wiles* Comedy by Sir Thomas St. Serfe (1668); *The Slighted Maiden* Tragicomedy by Sir Robert Staplyton (1663).

SPARKISH. Well that's a better reason, dear friend. I would not go near her now for hers or my own sake, but I can deny you nothing, for though I have known thee a great while, never go,[1] if I do not love thee as well as a new acquaintance.

HARCOURT. I am obliged to you indeed, dear friend. I would be well with her only to be well with thee still, for these ties to wives usually dissolve all ties to friends. I would be contented she should enjoy you a-nights, but I would have you to my self a-days, as I have had, dear friend.

SPARKISH. And thou shalt enjoy me a-days, dear, dear friend, never stir,[2] and I'll be divorced from her sooner than from thee. Come along.

HARCOURT. (*Aside.*) So we are hard put to't when we make our rival our procurer, but neither she nor her brother would let me come near her now. When all's done, a rival is the best cloak to steal to a mistress under without suspicion, and when we have once got to her as we desire, we throw him off like other cloaks.

(*Exit Sparkish, Harcourt following him. Re-enter Pinchwife, Margery in man's clothes.*)

PINCHWIFE. (*To Alithea [offstage].*) Sister, if you will not go, we must leave you. (*Aside.*) The fool, her gallant, and she will muster up all the young saunterers of this place, and they will leave their dear seamstresses to follow us. What a swarm of cuckolds and cuckold-makers are here?—Come let's be gone, Mistress Margery.

MARGERY. Don't you believe that, I han't half my belly full of sights yet.

PINCHWIFE. Then walk this way.

MARGERY. Lord, what a power of brave signs are here! Stay—the Bull's Head, the Ram's Head, and the Stag's Head, dear—

PINCHWIFE. Nay, if every husband's proper sign here were visible, they would be all alike.

MARGERY. What d'ye mean by that, bud?

PINCHWIFE. 'Tis no matter—no matter, bud.

MARGERY. Pray tell me, nay, I will know.

PINCHWIFE. They would be all bulls', stags', and rams' heads.

(*Exeunt Pinchwife, Margery. Re-enter Sparkish, Harcourt, Alithea, Lucy at the other door.*)

SPARKISH. Come dear madam, for my sake, you shall be reconciled to him.

ALITHEA. For your sake, I hate him.

HARCOURT. That's something too cruel, madam, to hate me for his sake.

SPARKISH. Aye indeed, madam, too, too cruel to me to hate my friend for my sake.

ALITHEA. I hate him because he is your enemy, and you ought to hate him, too, for making love to me, if you love me.

SPARKISH. That's a good one! I hate a man for loving you! If he did love you, 'tis but what he can't help, and 'tis your fault not his, if he admires you. I hate a man for being of my opinion! I'll ne'er do't, by the world.

ALITHEA. Is it for your honor or mine to suffer a man to make love to me, who am to marry you tomorrow?

SPARKISH. Is it for your honor or mine to have me jealous? That he makes love to you is a sign you are handsome, and that I am not jealous is a sign you are virtuous. That, I think, is for your honor.

ALITHEA. But 'tis your honor, too, I am concerned for.

HARCOURT. But why, dearest madam, will you be more concerned for his honor than he is himself? Let his honor alone for my sake and his. He, he, has no honor—

SPARKISH. How's that?

HARCOURT. But what my dear friend can guard himself.

SPARKISH. Oh ho—that's right again.

HARCOURT. Your care of his honor argues his neglect of it, which is no honor to my dear friend here; therefore, once more, let his honor go which way it will, dear madam.

SPARKISH. Aye, aye, were it for my honor to marry a woman whose virtue I suspected and could not trust her in a friend's hands?

ALITHEA. Are you not afraid to lose me?

HARCOURT. He afraid to lose you, madam! No, no—you may see how the most estimable and most glorious creature in the world is valued by him. Will you not see it?

[1] *never go* Don't worry.

[2] *never stir* As above, don't worry.

SPARKISH. Right, honest Frank, I have that noble value for her that I cannot be jealous of her.

ALITHEA. You mistake him: he means you care not for me nor who has me.

SPARKISH. Lord madam, I see you are jealous. Will you wrest a poor man's meaning from his words?

ALITHEA. You astonish me, sir, with your want of jealousy.

SPARKISH. And you make me giddy, madam, with your jealousy and fears and virtue and honor; gad, I see virtue makes a woman as troublesome as a little reading or learning.

ALITHEA. Monstrous!

LUCY. (*Behind.*) Well, to see what easy husbands these women of quality can meet with! A poor chambermaid can never have such ladylike luck. Besides, he's thrown away upon her; she'll make no use of her fortune, her blessing. None to a gentleman for a pure cuckold, for it requires good breeding to be a cuckold.

ALITHEA. I tell you then plainly: he pursues me to marry me.

SPARKISH. Pshaw—

HARCOURT. Come madam, you see you strive in vain to make him jealous of me; my dear friend is the kindest creature in the world to me.

SPARKISH. Poor fellow.

HARCOURT. But his kindness only is not enough for me, without your favor; your good opinion, dear madam, 'tis that must perfect my happiness. Good gentleman, he believes all I say; would you would do so. Jealous of me! I would not wrong him nor you for the world.

(*Alithea walks carelessly to and fro.*)

SPARKISH. Look you there, hear him, hear him, and do not walk away so.

HARCOURT. I love you, madam, so—

SPARKISH. How's that! Nay—now you begin to go too far indeed.

HARCOURT. So much, I confess, I say I love you, that I would not have you miserable and cast yourself away upon so unworthy and inconsiderable a thing as what you see here. (*Clapping his hand on his breast, points at Sparkish.*)

SPARKISH. No, faith, I believe thou wouldst not, now his meaning is plain. But I knew before thou wouldst not wrong me nor her.

HARCOURT. No, no, heavens forbid the glory of her sex should fall so low as into the embraces of such a contemptible wretch, the last of mankind—my dear friend here—I injure him. (*Embracing Sparkish.*)

ALITHEA. Very well.

SPARKISH. No, no, dear friend, I knew it.—Madam, you see he will rather wrong himself than me in giving himself such names.

ALITHEA. Do not you understand him yet?

SPARKISH. Yes, how modestly he speaks of himself, poor fellow.

ALITHEA. Methinks he speaks impudently of yourself, since—before yourself, too, insomuch that I can no longer suffer his scurrilous abusiveness to you, no more than his love to me. (*Offers to go.*)

SPARKISH. Nay, nay, madam, pray stay. His love to you! Lord madam, has he not spoke yet plain enough?

ALITHEA. Yes indeed, I should think so.

SPARKISH. Well then, by the world, a man can't speak civilly to a woman now but presently[1] she says he makes love to her. Nay madam, you shall stay, with your pardon, since you have not yet understood him, till he has made an éclaircissement[2] of his love to you, that is, what kind of love it is.—Answer to thy catechism. Friend, do you love my mistress here?

HARCOURT. Yes, I wish she would not doubt it.

SPARKISH. But how do you love her?

HARCOURT. With all my soul.

ALITHEA. I thank him, methinks he speaks plain enough now.

SPARKISH. (*To Alithea.*) You are out[3] still.—But with what kind of love, Harcourt?

HARCOURT. With the best and truest love in the world.

SPARKISH. Look you there then: that is with no matrimonial love, I'm sure.

ALITHEA. How's that, do you say matrimonial love is not best?

[1] *presently* Instantly or immediately.

[2] *éclaircissement* Clarification.

[3] *out* Mistaken.

SPARKISH. [*Aside.*] Gad, I went too far ere I was aware.—But speak for thyself, Harcourt: you said you would not wrong me nor her.

HARCOURT. No, no, madam, e'en take him for Heaven's sake—

SPARKISH. Look you there, madam.

HARCOURT. Who should in all justice be yours, he that loves you most. (*Claps his hand on his breast.*)

ALITHEA. Look you there, Mr. Sparkish. Who's that?

SPARKISH. Who should it be? Go on, Harcourt.

HARCOURT. Who loves you more than women, titles, or fortune fools. (*Points at Sparkish.*)

SPARKISH. Look you there: he means me still, for he points at me.

ALITHEA. Ridiculous!

HARCOURT. Who can only match your faith and constancy in love.

SPARKISH. Aye.

HARCOURT. Who knows, if it be possible, how to value so much beauty and virtue.

SPARKISH. Aye.

HARCOURT. Whose love can no more be equaled in the world than that heavenly form of yours.

SPARKISH. No—

HARCOURT. Who could no more suffer a rival than your absence and yet could no more suspect your virtue than his own constancy in his love to you.

SPARKISH. No—

HARCOURT. Who, in fine, loves you better than his eyes that first made him love you.

SPARKISH. Aye.—Nay madam, faith you shan't go till—

ALITHEA. Have a care lest you make me stay too long—

SPARKISH. But till he has saluted[1] you, that I may be assured you are friends after his honest advice and declaration. Come pray, madam, be friends with him.

(*Enter Pinchwife, Margery.*)

ALITHEA. You must pardon me, sir, that I am not yet so obedient to you.

PINCHWIFE. What, invite your wife to kiss men? Monstrous! Are you not ashamed? I will never forgive you.

SPARKISH. Are you not ashamed that I should have more confidence in the chastity of your family than you have? You must not teach me: I am a man of honor, sir, though I am frank and free. I am frank, sir—

PINCHWIFE. Very frank, sir, to share your wife with your friends.

SPARKISH. He is an humble, menial friend, such as reconciles the differences of the marriage bed. You know man and wife do not always agree. I design him for that use, therefore, would have him well with my wife.

PINCHWIFE. A menial friend—you will get a great many menial friends by showing your wife as you do.

SPARKISH. What then, it may be I have a pleasure in't, as I have to show fine clothes at a playhouse the first day[2] and count money before poor rogues.

PINCHWIFE. He that shows his wife or money will be in danger of having them borrowed sometimes.

SPARKISH. I love to be envied and would not marry a wife that I alone could love; loving alone is as dull as eating alone. Is it not a frank age, and I am a frank person? And to tell you the truth, it may be I love to have rivals in a wife: they make her seem to a man still but as a kept mistress, and so good night, for I must to Whitehall.—Madam, I hope you are now reconciled to my friend, and so I wish you a good night, madam, and sleep if you can, for tomorrow you know I must visit you early with a canonical gentleman.[3]—Good night, dear Harcourt. (*Exit.*)

HARCOURT. Madam, I hope you will not refuse my visit tomorrow, if it should be earlier, with a canonical gentleman, than Mr. Sparkish's.

PINCHWIFE. (*Coming between Alithea and Harcourt.*) This gentlewoman is yet under my care; therefore, you must yet forbear your freedom with her, sir.

HARCOURT. Must, sir—

PINCHWIFE. Yes, sir, she is my sister.

HARCOURT. 'Tis well she is, sir—for I must be her servant, sir.—Madam—

PINCHWIFE. Come away, sister. We had been gone if it had not been for you and so avoided these lewd rake-hells who seem to haunt us.

(*Enter Horner, Dorilant to them.*)

HORNER. How now, Pinchwife?

PINCHWIFE. Your servant.

[1] *saluted* Kissed.

[2] *the first day* I.e., the first performance of a play.

[3] *canonical gentleman* Clergyman.

HORNER. What, I see a little time in the country makes a man turn wild and unsociable and only fit to converse with his horses, dogs, and his herds.

PINCHWIFE. I have business, sir, and must mind it. Your business is pleasure; therefore, you and I must go different ways.

HORNER. Well, you may go on, but this pretty young gentleman— (*Takes hold of Margery.*)

HARCOURT. The lady—

DORILANT. And the maid—

HORNER. Shall stay with us, for I suppose their business is the same with ours, pleasure.

PINCHWIFE. (*Aside.*) 'Sdeath, he knows her, she carries it so sillily, yet if he does not, I should be more silly to discover it first.

ALITHEA. Pray let us go, sir.

PINCHWIFE. Come, come—

HORNER. (*To Margery.*) Had you not rather stay with us?—Prithee Pinchwife, who is this pretty young gentleman?

PINCHWIFE. One to whom I'm a guardian. (*Aside.*) I wish I could keep her out of your hands—

HORNER. Who is he? I never saw any thing so pretty in all my life.

PINCHWIFE. Pshaw, do not look upon him so much. He's a poor bashful youth; you'll put him out of countenance. Come away, brother. (*Offers to take her away.*)

HORNER. Oh your brother!

PINCHWIFE. Yes, my wife's brother.—Come, come, she'll stay supper for us.

HORNER. I thought so, for he is very like her I saw you at the play with, whom I told you I was in love with.

MARGERY. (*Aside.*) Oh jiminy! Is this he that was in love with me? I am glad on't, I vow, for he's a curious fine gentleman, and I love him already, too. (*To Mr. Pinchwife.*) Is this he, bud?

PINCHWIFE. (*To his wife.*) Come away, come away.

HORNER. Why, what haste are you in? Why won't you let me talk with him?

PINCHWIFE. Because you'll debauch him. He's yet young and innocent, and I would not have him debauched for anything in the world. (*Aside.*) How she gazes on him! The devil—

HORNER. Harcourt, Dorilant, look you here: this is the likeness of that dowdy he told us of, his wife. Did you ever see a lovelier creature? The rogue has reason to be jealous of his wife, since she is like him, for she would make all that see her in love with her.

HARCOURT. And as I remember now, she is as like him here as can be.

DORILANT. She is indeed very pretty, if she be like him.

HORNER. Very pretty? a very pretty commendation! She is a glorious creature, beautiful beyond all things I ever beheld.

PINCHWIFE. So, so.

HARCOURT. More beautiful than a poet's first mistress of imagination.

HORNER. Or another man's last mistress of flesh and blood.

MARGERY. Nay, now you jeer, sir. Pray don't jeer me—

PINCHWIFE. Come, come. (*Aside.*) By heavens, she'll discover herself!

HORNER. I speak of your sister, sir.

PINCHWIFE. Aye, but saying she was handsome, if like him, made him blush. (*Aside.*) I am upon a rack—

HORNER. Methinks he is so handsome, he should not be a man.

PINCHWIFE. [*Aside.*] Oh there 'tis out! He has discovered her! I am not able to suffer any longer. (*To his wife.*) Come, come away, I say—

HORNER. Nay by your leave, sir, he shall not go yet.—Harcourt, Dorilant, let us torment this jealous rogue a little.

HARCOURT AND DORILANT. How?

HORNER. I'll show you.

PINCHWIFE. Come, pray let him go. I cannot stay fooling any longer. I tell you his sister stays supper for us.

HORNER. Does she? Come then we'll all go sup with her and thee.

PINCHWIFE. No, now I think on't, having stayed so long for us, I warrant she's gone to bed. (*Aside.*) I wish she and I were well out of their hands.—Come, I must rise early tomorrow, come.

HORNER. Well then, if she be gone to bed, I wish her and you a good night.—But pray, young gentleman, present my humble service to her.

MARGERY. Thank you heartily, sir.

PINCHWIFE. (*Aside.*) S'death, she will discover herself yet in spite of me.—He is something more civil to you, for your kindness to his sister, than I am, it seems.

HORNER. Tell her, dear sweet little gentleman, for all

your brother there, that you have revived the love I had for her at first sight in the playhouse.

MARGERY. But did you love her indeed and indeed?

PINCHWIFE. (*Aside.*) So, so.—Away, I say.

HORNER. Nay, stay. Yes, indeed and indeed, pray do you tell her so and give her this kiss from me. (*Kisses her.*)

PINCHWIFE. (*Aside.*) Oh heavens! What do I suffer! Now 'tis too plain he knows her and yet—

HORNER. And this and this— (*Kisses her again.*)

MARGERY. What do you kiss me for? I am no woman.

PINCHWIFE. (*Aside.*) So—there 'tis out.—Come, I cannot, nor will stay any longer.

HORNER. Nay, they shall send your lady a kiss, too. Here Harcourt, Dorilant, will you not?

(*They kiss her.*)

PINCHWIFE. (Aside.) How! Do I suffer this? Was I not accusing another just now for this rascally patience in permitting his wife to be kissed before his face? Ten thousand ulcers gnaw away their lips.—Come, come.

HORNER. Good night, dear little gentleman.—Madam, good night.—Farewell, Pinchwife. (*Apart to Harcourt and Dorilant.*) Did not I tell you I would raise his jealous gall?

(*Exeunt Horner, Harcourt, and Dorilant.*)

PINCHWIFE. So they are gone at last.—Stay, let me see first if the coach be at this door. (*Exit.*)

(*Horner, Harcourt, Dorilant return.*)

HORNER. What, not gone yet? Will you be sure to do as I desired you, sweet sir?

MARGERY. Sweet sir, but what will you give me then?

HORNER. Anything. Come away into the next walk.

(*Exit Horner, haling away Margery.*)

ALITHEA. Hold, hold, what d'ye do?

LUCY. Stay, stay, hold—

(*Alithea, Lucy struggling with Harcourt and Dorilant.*)

HARCOURT. Hold, madam, hold. Let him present him; he'll come presently. Nay, I will never let you go till you answer my question.

LUCY. For God's sake, sir, I must follow 'em.

DORILANT. No, I have something to present you with, too. You shan't follow them.

Pinchwife returns.

PINCHWIFE. Where? how? what's become of—? Gone! Whither?

LUCY. He's only gone with the gentleman, who will give him something, an't please your worship.

PINCHWIFE. Something—give him something, with a pox! Where are they?

ALITHEA. In the next walk only, brother.

PINCHWIFE. Only! Only! Where? Where? (*Exit and returns presently, then goes out again.*)

HARCOURT. What's the matter with him? Why so much concerned?—But dearest madam—

ALITHEA. Pray let me go, sir. I have said and suffered enough already.

HARCOURT. Then you will not look upon nor pity my sufferings?

ALITHEA. To look upon 'em, when I cannot help 'em, were cruelty, not pity; therefore, I will never see you more.

HARCOURT. Let me then, madam, have my privilege of a banished lover: complaining or railing and giving you but a farewell reason why, if you cannot condescend to marry me, you should not take that wretch my rival.

ALITHEA. He only, not you, since my honor is engaged so far to him, can give me a reason why I should not marry him, but if he be true and what I think him to me, I must be so to him. Your servant, sir.

HARCOURT. Have women only constancy when 'tis a vice and, like Fortune, only true to fools?

DORILANT. (*To Lucy, who struggles to get from him.*) Thou shalt not stir, thou robust creature. You see I can deal with you; therefore, you should stay the rather and be kind.

(*Enter Pinchwife.*)

PINCHWIFE. Gone, gone, not to be found! quite gone! Ten thousand plagues go with 'em! Which way went they?

ALITHEA. But into t'other walk, brother.

LUCY. Their business will be done presently sure, an't please your worship; it can't be long in doing, I'm sure on't.

ALITHEA. Are they not there?

PINCHWIFE. No, you know where they are, you infamous wretch, eternal shame of your family, which you do not dishonor enough yourself, you think, but you must help her to do it, too, thou legion of bawds!

ALITHEA. Good brother!

PINCHWIFE. Damned, damned sister!

ALITHEA. Look you here, she's coming.

(*Enter Margery in man's clothes, running with her hat under her arm, full of oranges and dried fruit, Horner following.*)

MARGERY. Oh dear bud, look you here what I have got! See.

PINCHWIFE. (*Aside, rubbing his forehead.*) And what I have got here, too, which you can't see.[1]

MARGERY. The fine gentleman has given me better things yet.

PINCHWIFE. Has he so? (*Aside.*) Out of breath and colored—I must hold yet.

HORNER. I have only given your little brother an orange, sir.

PINCHWIFE. (*To Horner.*) Thank you, sir. (*Aside.*) You have only squeezed my orange, I suppose, and given it me again, yet I must have a City patience. (*To his wife.*) Come, come away.

MARGERY. Stay, till I have put up my fine things, bud.

(*Enter Sir Jaspar Fidget.*)

SIR JASPAR. Oh, Master Horner, come, come, the ladies stay for you. Your mistress, my wife, wonders you make not more haste to her.

HORNER. I have stayed this half hour for you here, and 'tis your fault I am not now with your wife.

SIR JASPAR. But pray, don't let her know so much; the truth on't is I was advancing a certain project to his Majesty about—I'll tell you.

HORNER. No, let's go and hear it at your house.—Good night, sweet little gentleman. One kiss more. (*Kisses her.*) You'll remember me now, I hope.

DORILANT. What, Sir Jaspar, will you separate friends? He promised to sup with us, and if you take him to your house, you'll be in danger of our company, too.

SIR JASPAR. Alas gentlemen, my house is not fit for you: there are none but civil women there, which are not for your turn. He, you know, can bear with the society of civil women, now, ha, ha, ha. Besides he's one of my family;[2] he's—he, he, he.

DORILANT. What is he?

SIR JASPAR. Faith, my eunuch, since you'll have it, he, he, he.

(*Exit Sir Jaspar Fidget and Horner.*)

DORILANT. I rather wish thou wert his, or my cuckold.—Harcourt, what a good cuckold is lost there for want of a man to make him one; thee and I cannot have Horner's privilege, who can make use of it.

HARCOURT. Aye, to poor Horner 'tis like coming to an estate at threescore,[3] when a man can't be the better for't.

PINCHWIFE. Come.

MARGERY. Presently, bud.

DORILANT. Come, let us go, too. (*To Alithea.*) Madam, your servant. (*To Lucy.*) Good night, strapper.

HARCOURT. Madam, though you will not let me have a good day or night, I wish you one, but dare not name the other half of my wish.

ALITHEA. Good night, sir, forever.

MARGERY. I don't know where to put this. Here, dear bud, you shall eat it. Nay, you shall have part of the fine gentleman's good things, or treat as you call it, when we come home.

PINCHWIFE. Indeed I deserve it, since I furnished the best part of it. (*Strikes away the orange.*)
The gallant treats, presents, and gives the ball,
But 'tis the absent cuckold pays for all.

[1] *Aside … can't see* Reference to cuckold's horns.

[2] *family* Household.

[3] *threescore* Sixty (years of age).

ACT 4, SCENE 1. Pinchwife's house in the morning.

(*Lucy, Alithea dressed in new clothes.*)

LUCY. Well madam, now have I dressed you and set you out with so many ornaments and spent upon you ounces of essence and pulvillio,[1] and all this for no other purpose but as people adorn and perfume a corpse for a stinking second-hand grave, such or as bad I think Master Sparkish's bed.

ALITHEA. Hold your peace.

LUCY. Nay madam, I will ask you the reason why you would banish poor Master Harcourt forever from your sight? How could you be so hard-hearted?

ALITHEA. 'Twas because I was not hard-hearted.

LUCY. No, no, 'twas stark love and kindness, I warrant.

ALITHEA. It was so: I would see him no more because I love him.

LUCY. Hey day, a very pretty reason.

ALITHEA. You do not understand me.

LUCY. I wish you may yourself.

ALITHEA. I was engaged to marry, you see, another man, whom my justice will not suffer me to deceive or injure.

LUCY. Can there be a greater cheat or wrong done to a man than to give him your person without your heart? I should make a conscience of it.

ALITHEA. I'll retrieve it for him after I am married awhile.

LUCY. The woman that marries to love better will be as much mistaken as the wencher that marries to live better. No madam, marrying to increase love is like gaming to become rich: alas, you only lose what little stock you had before.

ALITHEA. I find by your rhetoric you have been bribed to betray me.

LUCY. Only by his merit that has bribed your heart, you see, against your word and rigid honor. But what a devil is this honor? 'Tis sure a disease in the head, like the megrim[2] or falling sickness,[3] that always hurries people away to do themselves mischief. Men lose their lives by it; women, what's dearer to 'em, their love, the life of life.

ALITHEA. Come, pray talk you no more of honor nor Master Harcourt. I wish the other would come to secure my fidelity to him and his right in me.

LUCY. You will marry him then?

ALITHEA. Certainly, I have given him already my word and will my hand, too, to make it good when he comes.

LUCY. Well, I wish I may never stick pin more, if he be not an arrant natural[4] to t'other fine gentleman.

ALITHEA. I own he wants the wit of Harcourt, which I will dispense withal for another want he has, which is want of jealousy, which men of wit seldom want.

LUCY. Lord madam, what should you do with a fool to your husband? You intend to be honest, don't you? Then that husbandly virtue, credulity, is thrown away upon you.

ALITHEA. He only that could suspect my virtue should have cause to do it; 'tis Sparkish's confidence in my truth that obliges me to be so faithful to him.

LUCY. You are not sure his opinion may last.

ALITHEA. I am satisfied 'tis impossible for him to be jealous after the proofs I have had of him. Jealousy in a husband, Heaven defend me from it! It begets a thousand plagues to a poor woman: the loss of her honor, her quiet, and her—

LUCY. And her pleasure.

ALITHEA. What d'ye mean, impertinent?

LUCY. Liberty is a great pleasure, madam.

ALITHEA. I say loss of her honor, her quiet, nay, her life sometimes, and what's as bad almost, the loss of this Town; that is, she is sent into the country, which is the last ill usage of a husband to a wife, I think.

LUCY. (*Aside.*) Oh does the wind lie there?—Then of necessity, madam, you think a man must carry his wife into the country if he be wise. The country is as terrible I find to our young English ladies as a monastery to those abroad. And on my virginity, I think they would rather marry a London gaoler than a high sheriff of a county, since neither can stir from his employment. Formerly women of wit married fools for a great estate, a fine seat, or the like, but now 'tis for a pretty seat only in Lincoln's Inn Fields, St. James's Fields, or the Pall Mall.[5]

1 *pulvillio* Powdered perfume.

2 *megrim* Headache or depression.

3 *falling sickness* Epilepsy.

4 *natural* Mentally challenged.

5 *Lincoln's Inns Fields, St. James's Fields, … the Pall Mall* Fashionable places in which to live in London.

(*Enter to them Sparkish and Harcourt dressed like a parson.*)

SPARKISH. Madam, your humble servant, a happy day to you and to us all.

HARCOURT. Amen.

ALITHEA. Who have we here?

SPARKISH. My chaplain, faith. Oh madam, poor Harcourt remembers his humble service to you and, in obedience to your last commands, refrains coming into your sight.

ALITHEA. Is not that he?

SPARKISH. No, fie, no, but to show that he ne'er intended to hinder our match, has sent his brother here to join our hands. When I get me a wife, I must get her a chaplain, according to the custom; this is his brother and my chaplain.

ALITHEA. His brother?

LUCY. (*Aside.*) And your chaplain, to preach in your pulpit then.

ALITHEA. His brother!

SPARKISH. Nay, I knew you would not believe it.—I told you, sir, she would take you for your brother Frank.

ALITHEA. Believe it!

LUCY. (*Aside.*) His brother! Ha, ha, he, he has a trick left still it seems.

SPARKISH. Come my dearest, pray let us go to church before the canonical hour[1] is past.

ALITHEA. For shame! You are abused still.

SPARKISH. By the world, 'tis strange now you are so incredulous.

ALITHEA. 'Tis strange you are so credulous.

SPARKISH. Dearest of my life, hear me: I tell you this is Ned Harcourt of Cambridge;[2] by the world, you see he has a sneaking college look. 'Tis true he's something like his brother Frank, and they differ from each other no more than in their age, for they were twins.

LUCY. Ha, ha, he.

ALITHEA. Your servant, sir. I cannot be so deceived, though you are. But come let's hear, how do you know what you affirm so confidently?

SPARKISH. Why, I'll tell you all. Frank Harcourt coming to me this morning to wish me joy and present his service to you, I asked him if he could help me to a parson, whereupon he told me he had a brother in Town who was in orders,[3] and he went straight away and sent him you see there to me.

ALITHEA. Yes, Frank goes, and puts on a black coat, then tells you he is Ned; that's all you have for't.

SPARKISH. Pshaw, pshaw, I tell you by the same token, the midwife put her garter about Frank's neck to know 'em asunder, they were so like.

ALITHEA. Frank tells you this, too.

SPARKISH. Aye, and Ned there too; nay, they are both in a story.

ALITHEA. So, so, very foolish.

SPARKISH. Lord, if you won't believe one, you had best try him by your chambermaid there, for chambermaids must needs know chaplains from other men, they are so used to 'em.[4]

LUCY. Let's see: nay, I'll be sworn he has the canonical smirk and the filthy, clammy palm of a chaplain.

ALITHEA. Well, most reverend doctor, pray let us make an end of this fooling.

HARCOURT. With all my soul, divine, heavenly creature, when you please.

ALITHEA. He speaks like a chaplain indeed.

SPARKISH. Why, was there not, "soul," "divine," "heavenly," in what he said?

ALITHEA. Once more, most impertinent blackcoat, cease your persecution and let us have a conclusion of this ridiculous love.

HARCOURT. (*Aside.*) I had forgot, I must suit my style to my coat, or I wear it in vain.

ALITHEA. I have no more patience left; let us make once an end of this troublesome love, I say.

HARCOURT. So be it, seraphic lady, when your honor shall think it meet and convenient so to do.

SPARKISH. Gad, I'm sure none but a chaplain could speak so, I think.

ALITHEA. Let me tell you, sir, this dull trick will not serve your turn. Though you delay our marriage, you shall not hinder it.

HARCOURT. Far be it from me, munificent patroness, to delay your marriage. I desire nothing more than to marry you presently, which I might do, if you yourself

[1] *canonical hour* Twelve o'clock noon, the hour after which marriages could not legally be performed.

[2] *of Cambridge* I.e., of Cambridge University.

[3] *in orders* I.e., Holy Orders—reference to a clergyman.

[4] *chambermaids … used to 'em* Alleged promiscuity between chambermaids and the clergy was a standard joke of the time.

would, for my noble, good-natured, and thrice generous patron here would not hinder it.

SPARKISH. No, poor man, not I, faith.

HARCOURT. And now, madam, let me tell you plainly, nobody else shall marry you, by heavens. I'll die first, for I'm sure I should die[1] after it.

LUCY. [*Aside.*] How his love has made him forget his function, as I have seen it in real parsons.

ALITHEA. That was spoken like a chaplain, too! Now you understand him, I hope.

SPARKISH. Poor man, he takes it heinously to be refused. I can't blame him; 'tis putting an indignity upon him not to be suffered. But you'll pardon me, madam, it shan't be; he shall marry us. Come away, pray madam.

LUCY. Ha, ha, he, more ado! 'Tis late.

ALITHEA. Invincible stupidity, I tell you he would marry me as your rival, not as your chaplain.

SPARKISH. (*Pulling her away.*) Come, come, madam.

LUCY. I pray, madam, do not refuse this reverend divine the honor and satisfaction of marrying you, for I dare say, he has set his heart upon't, good doctor.

ALITHEA. What can you hope or design by this?

HARCOURT. [*Aside.*] I could answer her, a reprieve for a day only often revokes a hasty doom; at worst, if she will not take mercy on me and let me marry her, I have at least the lover's second pleasure, hindering my rival's enjoyment, though but for a time.

SPARKISH. Come, madam, 'tis e'en twelve o'clock, and my mother charged me never to be married out of the canonical hours. Come, come. Lord, here's such a deal of modesty, I warrant, the first day.

LUCY. Yes, an't please your worship, married women show all their modesty the first day, because married men show all their love the first day.

(*Exeunt.*)

ACT 4, SCENE 2. A bedchamber.

(*Pinchwife, Margery.*)

PINCHWIFE. Come tell me, I say.

MARGERY. Lord, han't I told it an hundred times over?

PINCHWIFE. (*Aside.*) I would try, if in the repetition of the ungrateful tale, I could find her altering it in the least circumstance, for if her story be false, she is so too.—Come, how was't, baggage?

MARGERY. Lord, what pleasure you take to hear it, sure!

PINCHWIFE. No, you take more in telling it, I find, but speak. How was't?

MARGERY. He carried me up into the house next to the Exchange.

PINCHWIFE. So, and you two were only in the room.

MARGERY. Yes, for he sent away a youth that was there, for some dried fruit and China oranges.[2]

PINCHWIFE. Did he so? Damn him for it—and for—

MARGERY. But presently came up the gentlewoman of the house.

PINCHWIFE. Oh 'twas well she did. But what did he do whilst the fruit came?

MARGERY. He kissed me an hundred times and told me he fancied he kissed my fine sister, meaning me, you know, whom he said he loved with all his soul and bid me be sure to tell her so and to desire her to be at her window by eleven of the clock this morning, and he would walk under it at that time.

PINCHWIFE. (*Aside.*) And he was as good as his word, very punctual. A pox reward him for't.

MARGERY. Well, and he said if you were not within, he would come up to her, meaning me, you know, bud, still.

PINCHWIFE. (*Aside.*) So—he knew her certainly, but for this confession I am obliged to her simplicity.—But what, you stood very still when he kissed you?

MARGERY. Yes, I warrant you. Would you have had me discovered myself?

PINCHWIFE. But you told me he did some beastliness to you, as you called it. What was't?

MARGERY. Why, he put—

PINCHWIFE. What?

MARGERY. Why he put the tip of his tongue between my lips and so muzzled[3] me—and I said I'd bite it.

PINCHWIFE. An eternal canker seize it, for a dog!

MARGERY. Nay, you need not be so angry with him neither, for to say truth, he has the sweetest breath I ever knew.

PINCHWIFE. The devil—you were satisfied with it then and would do it again.

---

[1] *die* To suffer *la petite mort* ("the little death") of sexual orgasm.

[2] *China oranges* Sweet, thin-skinned oranges, a delicacy originally from China.

[3] *muzzled* French kissed.

MARGERY. Not unless he should force me.

PINCHWIFE. Force you, changeling! I tell you no woman can be forced.

MARGERY. Yes, but she may sure, by such a one as he, for he's a proper, goodly strong man; 'tis hard, let me tell you, to resist him.

PINCHWIFE. [*Aside.*] So, 'tis plain she loves him, yet she has not love enough to make her conceal it from me, but the sight of him will increase her aversion for me and love for him, and that love instruct her how to deceive me and satisfy him, all idiot as she is. Love, 'twas he gave women first their craft, their art of deluding; out of Nature's hands they came plain, open, silly, and fit for slaves, as she and Heaven intended 'em, but damned Love—well—I must strangle that little monster whilst I can deal with him.—Go fetch pen, ink, and paper out of the next room.

MARGERY. Yes bud. (*Exit.*)

PINCHWIFE. Why should women have more invention in love than men? It can only be because they have more desires, more soliciting passions, more lust, and more of the Devil.

(*Margery returns.*)

Come minx, sit down and write.

MARGERY. Aye, dear bud, but I can't do't very well.

PINCHWIFE. I wish you could not at all.

MARGERY. But what should I write for?

PINCHWIFE. I'll have you write a letter to your lover.

MARGERY. Oh Lord, to the fine gentleman a letter!

PINCHWIFE. Yes, to the fine gentleman.

MARGERY. Lord, you do but jeer; sure you jest.

PINCHWIFE. I am not so merry. Come write as I bid you.

MARGERY. What, do you think I am a fool?

PINCHWIFE. [*Aside.*] She's afraid I would not dictate any love to him; therefore, she's unwilling.—But you had best begin.

MARGERY. Indeed and indeed, but I won't, so I won't.

PINCHWIFE. Why?

MARGERY. Because he's in Town; you may send for him if you will.

PINCHWIFE. Very well, you would have him brought to you. Is it come to this? I say take the pen and write, or you'll provoke me.

MARGERY. Lord, what d'ye make a fool of me for? Don't I know that letters are never writ but from the country to London and from London into the country? Now he's in Town, and I am in Town, too; therefore, I can't write to him, you know.

PINCHWIFE. (*Aside.*) So, I am glad it is no worse; she is innocent enough yet.—Yes, you may when your husband bids you write letters to people that are in Town.

MARGERY. Oh may I so! Then I'm satisfied.

PINCHWIFE. Come begin. (*Dictates.*) "Sir"—

MARGERY. Shan't I say, "Dear Sir"? You know one says always something more than bare "Sir."

PINCHWIFE. Write as I bid you, or I will write whore with this penknife in your face.

MARGERY. Nay, good bud. (*She writes.*) "Sir"—

PINCHWIFE. "Though I suffered last night your nauseous, loathed kisses and embraces"—Write.

MARGERY. Nay, why should I say so? You know I told you he had a sweet breath.

PINCHWIFE. Write!

MARGERY. Let me but put out "loathed."

PINCHWIFE. Write I say!

MARGERY. Well then. (*Writes.*)

PINCHWIFE. Let's see what have you writ. (*Takes the paper and reads.*) "Though I suffered last night your kisses and embraces"—Thou impudent creature! Where is "nauseous" and "loathed"?

MARGERY. I can't abide to write such filthy words.

PINCHWIFE. (*Holds up penknife.*) Once more, write as I'd have you and question it not, or I will spoil thy writing with this. I will stab out those eyes that cause my mischief.

MARGERY. Oh Lord, I will! [*Writes.*]

PINCHWIFE. So—so—let's see now! (*Reads.*) "Though I suffered last night your nauseous, loathed kisses, and embraces." Go on: "Yet I would not have you presume that you shall ever repeat them." So—

(*She writes.*)

MARGERY. I have writ it.

PINCHWIFE. On then: "I then concealed myself from your knowledge to avoid your insolencies."

(*She writes.*)

MARGERY. So—

PINCHWIFE. "The same reason now I am out of your hands"—

(*She writes.*)

MARGERY. So—

PINCHWIFE. "Makes me own to you my unfortunate though innocent frolic of being in man's clothes"—

(*She writes.*)

MARGERY. So—

PINCHWIFE. "That you may forever more cease to pursue her who hates and detests you"—

(*She writes on.*)

MARGERY. So—h— (*Sighs.*)

PINCHWIFE. What, do you sigh?—"detests you—as much as she loves her husband and her honor."

MARGERY. I vow, husband, he'll ne'er believe I should write such a letter.

PINCHWIFE. What, he'd expect a kinder from you? Come now, your name only.

MARGERY. What, shan't I say "Your most faithful, humble servant till death"?

PINCHWIFE. No, tormenting fiend. (*Aside.*) Her style, I find, would be very soft.—Come wrap it up now whilst I go fetch wax and a candle[1] and write on the back side "For Mr. Horner." (*Exit.*)

MARGERY. "For Mr. Horner." So, I am glad he has told me his name. Dear Mr. Horner, but why should I send thee such a letter that will vex thee and make thee angry with me?—Well, I will not send it.—Aye, but then my husband will kill me, for I see plainly he won't let me love Mr. Horner.—But what care I for my husband?—I won't so, I won't send poor Mr. Horner such a letter.—But then my husband—But oh, what if I writ at bottom, "My husband made me write it"?—Aye, but then my husband would see't.—Can one have no shift?[2] Ah, a London woman would have had a hundred presently. Stay—what if I should write a letter and wrap it up like this and write upon't, too?—Aye, but then my husband would see't.—I don't know what to do.—But yet y'vads[3] I'll try, so I will, for I will not send this letter to poor Mr. Horner, come what will on't. (*She writes and repeats what she hath writ.*) "Dear, sweet Mr. Horner"—so—"My husband would have me send you a base, rude, unmannerly letter, but I won't,"—so—"and would have me forbid you loving me, but I won't,"—so—"and would have me say to you, I hate you, poor Mr. Horner, but I won't tell a lie for him,"—there—"for I'm sure if you and I were in the country at cards together,"—so—"I could not help treading on your toe under the table"—so—"or rubbing knees with you and staring in your face till you saw me"—very well—"and then looking down and blushing for an hour together."—so—"But I must make haste before my husband come, and now he has taught me to write letters, you shall have longer ones from me who am, dear, dear, poor dear Mr. Horner, your most humble friend and servant to command till death, Margery Pinchwife." Stay, I must give him a hint at bottom—so—now wrap it up just like t'other—so—now write "For Mr. Horner."—But oh now what shall I do with it? For here comes my husband.

(*Enter Pinchwife.*)

PINCHWIFE. (*Aside.*) I have been detained by a sparkish coxcomb who pretended a visit to me, but I fear 'twas to my wife.—What, have you done?

MARGERY. Aye, aye, bud, just now.

PINCHWIFE. Let's see't. What d'ye tremble for? What, you would not have it go?

MARGERY. Here. (*Aside.*) No, I must not give him that; so I had been served if I had given him this.

(*He opens and reads the first letter.*)

PINCHWIFE. Come, where's the wax and seal?

MARGERY. (*Aside.*) Lord, what shall I do now? Nay, then I have it.—Pray let me see't. Lord, you think me so arrant a fool, I cannot seal a letter? I will do't, so I will. (*Snatches the letter from him, changes it for the other, seals it, and delivers it to him.*)

---

[1] *wax and a candle* Pinchwife will melt the wax on the folded letter and press the end of the candle into the wax. When the wax has cooled, the letter will be sealed.

[2] *shift* Resource.

[3] *y'vads* In faith (rustic expression).

PINCHWIFE. Nay, I believe you will learn that and other things, too, which I would not have you.

MARGERY. So, han't I done it curiously?[1] (*Aside.*) I think I have: there's my letter going to Mr. Horner, since he'll needs have me send letters to folks.

PINCHWIFE. 'Tis very well, but I warrant, you would not have it go now?

MARGERY. Yes indeed, but I would, bud, now.

PINCHWIFE. Well, you are a good girl then. Come let me lock you up in your chamber till I come back, and be sure you come not within three strides of the window when I am gone, for I have a spy in the street.

(*Exit Margery. Pinchwife locks the door.*)

At least 'tis fit she think so. If we do not cheat women, they'll cheat us, and fraud may be justly used with secret enemies, of which a wife is the most dangerous. And he that has a handsome one to keep, and a frontier town, must provide against treachery rather than open force. Now I have secured all within, I'll deal with the foe without with false intelligence.

(*Holds up the letter and exits.*)

ACT 4, SCENE 3. Horner's lodging.

(*Quack and Horner.*)

QUACK. Well sir, how fadges[2] the new design? Have you not the luck of all your brother projectors,[3] to deceive only yourself at last?

HORNER. No, good domine[4] doctor, I deceive you, it seems, and others too, for the grave matrons and old rigid husbands think me as unfit for love as they are. But their wives, sisters, and daughters know, some of 'em, better things already.

QUACK. Already!

HORNER. Already, I say. Last night I was drunk with half a dozen of your civil persons, as you call 'em, and people of honor and so was made free of their society and dressing rooms forever hereafter and am already come to the privileges of sleeping upon their pallets, warming smocks, tying shoes and garters, and the like, doctor, already, already, doctor.

QUACK. You have made use of your time, sir.

HORNER. I tell thee, I am now no more interruption to 'em when they sing or talk bawdy than a little, squab, French page who speaks no English.

QUACK. But do civil persons and women of honor drink and sing bawdy songs?

HORNER. Oh amongst friends, amongst friends. For your bigots in honor are just like those in religion: they fear the eye of the world more than the eye of Heaven and think there is no virtue but railing at vice and no sin but giving scandal. They rail at a poor, little, kept player[5] and keep themselves some young, modest pulpit comedian to be privy to their sins in their closets,[6] not to tell 'em of them in their chapels.

QUACK. Nay, the truth on't is, priests amongst the women now have quite got the better of us lay confessors, physicians.

HORNER. And they are rather their patients, but—

(*Enter Lady Fidget, looking about her.*)

Now we talk of women of honor, here comes one. Step behind the screen there and but observe if I have not particular privileges with the women of reputation already, doctor, already.

LADY FIDGET. Well Horner, am not I a woman of honor? You see I'm as good as my word.

HORNER. And you shall see, madam, I'll not be behindhand with you in honor, and I'll be as good as my word, too, if you please but to withdraw into the next room.

LADY FIDGET. But first, my dear sir, you must promise to have a care of my dear honor.

HORNER. If you talk a word more of your honor, you'll make me incapable to wrong it. To talk of honor in the mysteries of love is like talking of Heaven or the Deity in an operation of witchcraft: just when you are employing the Devil, it makes the charm impotent.

LADY FIDGET. Nay, fie, let us not be smutty! But you talk of mysteries and bewitching to me; I don't understand you.

[1] *curiously* Skillfully.

[2] *fadges* Prospers.

[3] *projectors* Schemers.

[4] *domine* Master (of a profession).

[5] *player* Actress.

[6] *closets* Small private rooms, generally within bedchambers.

HORNER. I tell you, madam, the word "money" in a mistress's mouth at such a nick of time is not a more disheartening sound to a younger brother than that of "honor" to an eager lover like myself.

LADY FIDGET. But you can't blame a lady of my reputation to be chary.

HORNER. Chary! I have been chary of it already by the report I have caused of myself.

LADY FIDGET. Aye, but if you should ever let other women know that dear secret, it would come out. Nay, you must have a great care of your conduct, for my acquaintance are so censorious (oh 'tis a wicked censorious world, Mr. Horner), I say, are so censorious and detracting that perhaps they'll talk to the prejudice of my honor, though you should not let them know the dear secret.

HORNER. Nay madam, rather than they shall prejudice your honor, I'll prejudice theirs, and to serve you, I'll lie with 'em all, make the secret their own, and then they'll keep it. I am a Machiavel[1] in love, madam.

LADY FIDGET. Oh no, sir, not that way.

HORNER. Nay, the devil take me if censorious women are to be silenced any other way.

LADY FIDGET. A secret is better kept, I hope, by a single person than a multitude; therefore, pray do not trust anybody else with it, dear, dear Mr. Horner. (*Embracing him.*)

(*Enter Sir Jaspar Fidget.*)

SIR JASPAR. How now!

LADY FIDGET. (*Aside.*) Oh my husband—prevented—and what's almost as bad, found with my arms about another man. That will appear too much. What shall I say?—Sir Jaspar, come hither. I am trying if Mr. Horner were ticklish, and he's as ticklish as can be. I love to torment the confounded toad. Let you and I tickle him.

SIR JASPAR. No, your ladyship will tickle him better without me, I suppose. But is this your buying china? I thought you had been at the china house?

HORNER. (*Aside.*) China house, that's my cue; I must take it.—A pox, can't you keep your impertinent wives at home? Some men are troubled with the husbands, but I with the wives. But I'd have you to know, since I cannot be your journeyman by night, I will not be your drudge by day, to squire your wife about and be your man of straw, or scarecrow, only to pies and jays[2] that would be nibbling at your forbidden fruit. I shall be shortly the hackney gentleman-usher of the Town.

SIR JASPAR. (*Aside.*) He, he, he, poor fellow, he's in the right on't, faith: to squire women about for other folks is as ungrateful an employment as to tell money for other folks.—He, he, he, ben't angry, Horner—

LADY FIDGET. No, 'tis I have more reason to be angry, who am left by you to go abroad indecently alone or, what is more indecent, to pin myself upon such ill-bred people of your acquaintance, as this is.

SIR JASPAR. Nay prithee, what has he done?

LADY FIDGET. Nay, he has done nothing.

SIR JASPAR. But what d'ye take ill if he has done nothing?

LADY FIDGET. Ha, ha, ha! Faith, I can't but laugh, however. Why, d'ye think, the unmannerly toad would not come down to me to the coach. I was fain to come up to fetch him or go without him, which I was resolved not to do, for he knows china very well and has himself very good, but will not let me see it, lest I should beg some. But I will find it out and have what I came for yet.

(*Exit Lady Fidget, and locks the door, followed by Horner to the door.*)

HORNER. (*Apart to Lady Fidget.*) Lock the door, madam.—So, she has got into my chamber and locked me out. Oh the impertinency of womankind! Well Sir Jaspar, plain dealing is a jewel: if ever you suffer your wife to trouble me again here, she shall carry you home a pair of horns, by my Lord Mayor she shall; though I cannot furnish you myself, you are sure yet I'll find a way.

SIR JASPAR. (*Aside.*) Ha, ha, he, at my first coming in and finding her arms about him, tickling him it seems, I was half jealous, but now I see my folly.—He, he, he, poor Horner.

HORNER. Nay, though you laugh now, 'twill be my turn ere long. Oh women, more impertinent, more cunning, and more mischievous than their monkeys and to me almost as ugly.—Now is she throwing my things

[1] *Machiavel* Unscrupulous villain, from Niccolò Machiavelli, author of a treatise on political power, *The Prince.*

[2] *pies and jays* Birds; magpies and jackdaws.

about and rifling all I have, but I'll get into her the back way and so rifle her for it.

SIR JASPAR. Ha, ha, ha, poor angry Horner.

HORNER. Stay here a little. I'll ferret her out to you presently, I warrant. (*Exit at the other door.*)

SIR JASPAR. Wife, my Lady Fidget, wife, he is coming into you the back way.

(*Sir Jaspar calls through the door to his wife; she answers from within.*)

LADY FIDGET. Let him come, and welcome, which way he will.

SIR JASPAR. He'll catch you and use you roughly and be too strong for you.

LADY FIDGET. Don't you trouble yourself; let him if he can.

QUACK. (*Behind.*) This indeed I could not have believed from him nor any but my own eyes.

(*Enter Mistress Squeamish.*)

MRS. SQUEAMISH. Where's this woman-hater, this toad, this ugly, greasy, dirty sloven?

SIR JASPAR. [*Aside.*] So the women all will have him ugly. Methinks he is a comely person, but his wants make his form contemptible to 'em, and 'tis e'en as my wife said yesterday, talking of him, that a proper handsome eunuch was as ridiculous a thing as a gigantic coward.

MRS. SQUEAMISH. Sir Jaspar, your servant. Where is the odious beast?

SIR JASPAR. He's within in his chamber with my wife; she's playing the wag with him.

MRS. SQUEAMISH. Is she so? And he's a clownish[1] beast: he'll give her no quarter; he'll play the wag with her again, let me tell you. Come, let's go help her. What, the door's locked?

SIR JASPAR. Aye, my wife locked it.

MRS. SQUEAMISH. Did she so? Let us break it open then.

SIR JASPAR. No, no, he'll do her no hurt.

MRS. SQUEAMISH. No. (*Aside.*) But is there no other way to get into 'em? Whither goes this? I will disturb 'em.

(*Exit Squeamish at another door. Enter Old Lady Squeamish.*)

OLD LADY SQUEAMISH. Where is this harlotry, this impudent baggage, this rambling tomrig?[2]—Oh Sir Jaspar, I'm glad to see you here. Did you not see my vild[3] grandchild come in hither just now?

SIR JASPAR. Yes.

OLD LADY SQUEAMISH. Aye, but where is she then? Where is she? Lord, Sir Jaspar, I have e'en rattled myself to pieces in pursuit of her. But can you tell what she makes here? They say below, no woman lodges here.

SIR JASPAR. No.

OLD LADY SQUEAMISH. No—what does she here then? Say if it be not a woman's lodging, what makes she here? But are you sure no woman lodges here?

SIR JASPAR. No, nor no man neither: this is Mr. Horner's lodging.

OLD LADY SQUEAMISH. Is it so? Are you sure?

SIR JASPAR. Yes, yes.

OLD LADY SQUEAMISH. So then there's no hurt in't, I hope. But where is he?

SIR JASPAR. He's in the next room with my wife.

OLD LADY SQUEAMISH. Nay, if you trust him with your wife, I may with my Biddy. They say he's a merry, harmless man now, e'en as harmless a man as ever came out of Italy with a good voice[4] and as pretty harmless company for a lady as a snake without his teeth.

SIR JASPAR. Aye, aye, poor man.

(*Enter Mrs. Squeamish.*)

MRS. SQUEAMISH. I can't find 'em.—Oh are you here, Grandmother? I followed, you must know, my Lady Fidget hither; 'tis the prettiest lodging, and I have been staring on the prettiest pictures.

(*Enter Lady Fidget with a piece of china in her hand and Horner following.*)

LADY FIDGET. And I have been toiling and moiling for the prettiest piece of china, my dear.

[1] *clownish* Unsophisticated.

[2] *tomrig* Strumpet, tomboy.

[3] *vild* Wild.

[4] *man … good voice* Castrato, a male singer castrated as a youth to preserve a soprano or alto voice.

HORNER. Nay, she has been too hard for me, do what I could.

MRS. SQUEAMISH. Oh Lord, I'll have some china, too. Good Mr. Horner, don't think to give other people china and me none. Come in with me, too.

HORNER. Upon my honor I have none left now.

MRS. SQUEAMISH. Nay, nay, I have known you deny your china before now, but you shan't put me off so. Come—

HORNER. This lady had the last there.

LADY FIDGET. Yes indeed, madam, to my certain knowledge he has no more left.

MRS. SQUEAMISH. Oh but it may be he may have some you could not find.

LADY FIDGET. What, d'ye think if he had had any left, I would not have had it too? For we women of quality never think we have china enough.

HORNER. Do not take it ill. I cannot make china for you all, but I will have a roll-waggon[1] for you, too, another time.

MRS. SQUEAMISH. Thank you, dear toad.

LADY FIDGET. (*To Horner, aside.*) What do you mean by that promise?

HORNER. (*Apart to Lady Fidget.*) Alas, she has an innocent, literal understanding.

OLD LADY SQUEAMISH. Poor Mr. Horner. He has enough to do to please you all, I see.

HORNER. Aye madam, you see how they use me.

OLD LADY SQUEAMISH. Poor gentleman, I pity you.

HORNER. I thank you, madam. I could never find pity but from such reverend ladies as you are; the young ones will never spare a man.

MRS. SQUEAMISH. Come, come, beast, and go dine with us, for we shall want a man at ombre after dinner.

HORNER. That's all their use of me, madam, you see.

MRS. SQUEAMISH. Come sloven, I'll lead you to be sure of you. (*Pulls him by the cravat.*[2])

OLD LADY SQUEAMISH. Alas, poor man, how she tugs him. Kiss, kiss her! That's the way to make such nice[3] women quiet.

HORNER. No madam, that remedy is worse than the torment; they know I dare suffer anything rather than do it.

OLD LADY SQUEAMISH. Prithee, kiss her, and I'll give you her picture in little[4] that you admired so last night, prithee do.

HORNER. Well, nothing but that could bribe me. I love a woman only in effigy and good painting as much as I hate them. I'll do't, for I could adore the Devil well painted. (*Kisses Mrs. Squeamish.*)

MRS. SQUEAMISH. Faugh, you filthy toad! Nay, now I've done jesting.

OLD LADY SQUEAMISH. Ha, ha, ha, I told you so.

MRS. SQUEAMISH. Faugh, a kiss of his—

SIR JASPAR. Has no more hurt in't than one of my spaniel's.

MRS. SQUEAMISH. Nor no more good neither.

QUACK. (*Behind.*) I will now believe anything he tells me.

(*Enter Pinchwife.*)

LADY FIDGET. Oh Lord, here's a man, Sir Jaspar! My mask, my mask. I would not be seen here for the world.

SIR JASPAR. What, not when I am with you?

LADY FIDGET. No, no, my honor—let's be gone.

MRS. SQUEAMISH. Oh Grandmother, let us be gone. Make haste, make haste. I know not how he may censure us.

LADY FIDGET. Be found in the lodging of anything like a man? Away.

(*Exeunt Sir Jaspar, Lady Fidget, Old Lady Squeamish, Mrs. Squeamish.*)

QUACK. (*Behind.*) What's here, another cuckold? He looks like one, and none else sure have any business with him.

HORNER. Well, what brings my dear friend hither?

PINCHWIFE. Your impertinency.

HORNER. My impertinency! Why, you gentlemen that have got handsome wives think you have a privilege of saying anything to your friends and are as brutish as if you were our creditors.

PINCHWIFE. No sir, I'll ne'er trust you anyway.

HORNER. But why not, dear Jack? Why diffide[5] in me

[1] *roll-waggon* Cylindrical-shaped Chinese vase.

[2] *cravat* Neckerchief.

[3] *nice* Fastidious; delicate.

[4] *picture in little* Miniature.

[5] *diffide* Lack confidence.

thou knowst so well?

PINCHWIFE. Because I do know you so well.

HORNER. Han't I been always thy friend, honest Jack, always ready to serve thee, in love or battle, before thou wert married and am so still?

PINCHWIFE. I believe so; you would be my second[1] now indeed.

HORNER. Well then, dear Jack, why so unkind, so grum, so strange to me? Come, prithee kiss me, dear rogue. Gad, I was always, I say, and am still as much thy servant as—

PINCHWIFE. As I am yours, sir. What, you would send a kiss to my wife, is that it?

HORNER. So there 'tis. A man can't show his friendship to a married man but presently he talks of his wife to you. Prithee, let thy wife alone and let thee and I be all one, as we were wont. What, thou art as shy of my kindness as a Lombard Street[2] alderman of a courtier's civility at Locket's.[3]

PINCHWIFE. But you are over-kind to me, as kind as if I were your cuckold already, yet I must confess you ought to be kind and civil to me since I am so kind, so civil to you as to bring you this. Look you there, sir. (*Delivers him a letter.*)

HORNER. What is't?

PINCHWIFE. Only a love letter, sir.

HORNER. From whom? (*Reads.*)

How, this is from your wife!—hum—and hum—

PINCHWIFE. Even from my wife, sir. Am I not wondrous kind and civil to you now, too? (*Aside.*) But you'll not think her so.

HORNER. (*Aside.*) Hah, is this a trick of his or hers?

PINCHWIFE. The gentleman's surprised, I find. What, you expected a kinder letter?

HORNER. No faith, not I. How could I?

PINCHWIFE. Yes, yes, I'm sure you did. A man so well made as you are must needs be disappointed if the women declare not their passion at first sight or opportunity.

HORNER. [*Aside.*] But what should this mean? Stay, the postscript: "Be sure you love me whatsoever my husband says to the contrary, and let him not see this, lest he should come home and pinch me or kill my squirrel." It seems he knows not what the letter contains.

PINCHWIFE. Come, ne'er wonder at it so much.

HORNER. Faith, I can't help it.

PINCHWIFE. Now I think I have deserved your infinite friendship and kindness and have showed myself sufficiently an obliging kind friend and husband. Am I not so, to bring a letter from my wife to her gallant?

HORNER. Aye, the devil take me, art thou the most obliging, kind friend and husband in the world, ha, ha.

PINCHWIFE. Well, you may be merry, sir, but in short I must tell you, sir, my honor will suffer no jesting.

HORNER. What dost thou mean?

PINCHWIFE. Does the letter want a comment? Then know, sir, though I have been so civil a husband as to bring you a letter from my wife, to let you kiss and court her to my face, I will not be a cuckold, sir, I will not.

HORNER. Thou art mad with jealousy. I never saw thy wife in my life but at the play yesterday, and I know not if it were she or no. I court her, kiss her!

PINCHWIFE. I will not be a cuckold, I say; there will be danger in making me a cuckold.

HORNER. Why, wert thou not well cured of thy last clap?

PINCHWIFE. I wear a sword.

HORNER. It should be taken from thee lest thou shouldst do thyself a mischief with it. Thou art mad, man.

PINCHWIFE. As mad as I am and as merry as you are, I must have more reason from you ere we part, I say again, though you kissed and courted last night my wife in man's clothes, as she confesses in her letter.

HORNER. (*Aside.*) Hah!

PINCHWIFE. Both she and I say you must not design it again, for you have mistaken your woman, as you have done your man.

HORNER. (*Aside.*) Oh I understand something now.—Was that thy wife? Why wouldst thou not tell me 'twas she? Faith, my freedom with her was your fault, not mine.

PINCHWIFE. (*Aside.*) Faith, so 'twas.

HORNER. Fie, I'd never do't to a woman before her husband's face, sure.

PINCHWIFE. But I had rather you should do't to my wife before my face than behind my back, and that you shall never do.

[1] *second* In a duel, the friend who stands by a principal.

[2] *Lombard Street* In the City.

[3] *Locket's* Fashionable eating-house.

HORNER. No, you will hinder me.

PINCHWIFE. If I would not hinder you, you see by her letter, she would.

HORNER. Well, I must e'en acquiesce then and be contented with what she writes.

PINCHWIFE. I'll assure you 'twas voluntarily writ; I had no hand in't, you may believe me.

HORNER. I do believe thee, faith.

PINCHWIFE. And believe her too, for she's an innocent creature, has no dissembling in her, and so fare you well, sir.

HORNER. Pray however, present my humble service to her and tell her I will obey her letter to a tittle and fulfill her desires be what they will or with what difficulty soever I do't, and you shall be no more jealous of me, I warrant her, and you—

PINCHWIFE. Well then, fare you well, and play with any man's honor but mine, kiss any man's wife but mine, and welcome. (*Exit.*)

HORNER. Ha, ha, ha, doctor.

QUACK. It seems he has not heard the report of you or does not believe it.

HORNER. Ha, ha, now doctor, what think you?

QUACK. Pray let's see the letter. (*Reads.*) Hum—"for"—"dear"—"love you"—

HORNER. I wonder how she could contrive it! What say'st thou to't? 'Tis an original.

QUACK. So are your cuckolds, too, originals, for they are like no other common cuckolds, and I will henceforth believe it not impossible for you to cuckold the Grand Signior[1] amidst his guards of eunuchs, that I say.

HORNER. And I say for the letter, 'tis the first love letter that ever was without flames, darts, fates, destinies, lying, and dissembling in't.

(*Enter Sparkish pulling in Pinchwife.*)

SPARKISH. Come back! You are a pretty brother-in-law, neither go to church nor to dinner with your sister bride.

PINCHWIFE. My sister denies her marriage and you see is gone away from you dissatisfied.

SPARKISH. Pshaw, upon a foolish scruple that our parson was not in lawful orders and did not say all the Common Prayer,[2] but 'tis her modesty only, I believe. But let women be never so modest the first day, they'll be sure to come to themselves by night, and I shall have enough of her then. In the meantime, Harry Horner, you must dine with me; I keep my wedding at my aunt's in the Piazza.[3]

HORNER. Thy wedding! What stale maid has lived to despair of a husband, or what young one of a gallant?

SPARKISH. Oh your servant, sir. This gentleman's sister then—no stale maid.

HORNER. I'm sorry for't.

PINCHWIFE. (*Aside.*) How comes he so concerned for her?

SPARKISH. You sorry for't! Why, do you know any ill by her?

HORNER. No, I know none but by thee; 'tis for her sake, not yours, and another man's sake that might have hoped, I thought—

SPARKISH. Another man, another man, what is his name?

HORNER. Nay, since 'tis past, he shall be nameless. (*Aside.*) Poor Harcourt, I am sorry thou hast missed her.

PINCHWIFE. (*Aside.*) He seems to be much troubled at the match.

SPARKISH. Prithee, tell me.—Nay, you shan't go, brother.

PINCHWIFE. I must of necessity, but I'll come to you to dinner. (*Exit.*)

SPARKISH. But Harry, what, have I a rival in my wife already? But with all my heart, for he may be of use to me hereafter, for though my hunger is now my sauce and I can fall on heartily without. But the time will come, when a rival will be as good sauce for a married man to a wife as an orange to veal.

HORNER. Oh thou damned rogue, thou hast set my teeth on edge with thy orange.

SPARKISH. Then let's to dinner. There I was with you again. Come.

HORNER. But who dines with thee?

SPARKISH. My friends and relations, my brother Pinchwife, you see, of your acquaintance.

HORNER. And his wife?

---

[1] *Grand Signior* Sultan of Turkey.

[2] *Common Prayer* Marriage service within the Anglican *Book of Common Prayer.*

[3] *Piazza* Arcade around two sides of Covent Garden.

SPARKISH. No, gad, he'll ne'er let her come amongst us good fellows. Your stingy country coxcomb keeps his wife from his friends as he does his little firkin of ale for his own drinking, and a gentleman can't get a smack on't. But his servants, when his back is turned, broach it at their pleasure and dust it away, ha, ha, ha. Gad, I am witty, I think, considering I was married today, by the world, but come—

HORNER. No, I will not dine with you unless you can fetch her, too.

SPARKISH. Pshaw, what pleasure canst thou have with women now, Harry?

HORNER. My eyes are not gone. I love a good prospect[1] yet and will not dine with you unless she does too. Go fetch her, therefore, but do not tell her husband 'tis for my sake.

SPARKISH. Well, I'll go try what I can do. In the meantime, come away to my aunt's lodging; 'tis in the way to Pinchwife's.

HORNER. [*Apart to Quack.*] The poor woman has called for aid and stretched forth her hand, doctor; I cannot but help her over the pale[2] out of the briars.

(*Exeunt.*)

ACT 4, SCENE 4. Pinchwife's house.

(*Margery alone leaning on her elbow. A table, pen, ink, and paper.*)

MARGERY. Well 'tis e'en so: I have got the London disease they call love; I am sick of my husband and for my gallant. I have heard this distemper called a fever, but methinks 'tis liker an ague,[3] for when I think of my husband, I tremble and am in a cold sweat and have inclinations to vomit, but when I think of my gallant, dear Mr. Horner, my hot fit comes, and I am all in a fever indeed, and as in other fevers, my own chamber is tedious to me, and I would fain be removed to his, and then methinks I should be well. Ah poor Mr. Horner! Well, I cannot, will not stay here; therefore, I'll make an end of my letter to him, which shall be a finer letter than my last, because I have studied it like anything. Oh sick! sick! (*Takes the pen and writes.*)

(*Enter Mr. Pinchwife, who, seeing her writing, steals softly behind her and looking over her shoulder, snatches the paper from her.*)

PINCHWIFE. What, writing more letters?

MARGERY. Oh Lord, bud, why d'ye fright me so?

(*She offers to run out; he stops her and reads.*)

PINCHWIFE. How's this! Nay, you shall not stir, madam. "Dear, dear, dear, Mr. Horner"—very well—I have taught you to write letters to good purpose, but let's see't. "First I am to beg your pardon for my boldness in writing to you, which I'd have you to know I would not have done, had not you said first you loved me so extremely, which if you do, you will never suffer me to lie in the arms of another man, whom I loathe, nauseate, and detest." Now you can write these filthy words! But what follows? "Therefore, I hope you will speedily find some way to free me from this unfortunate match, which was never, I assure you, of my choice, but I'm afraid 'tis already too far gone; however, if you love me, as I do you, you will try what you can do, but you must help me away before tomorrow, or else, alas, I shall be forever out of your reach for I can defer no longer our—" (*The letter concludes.*) "Our"? What is to follow "our"? Speak! What? Our journey into the country, I suppose. Oh woman, damned woman! And Love, damned Love, their old tempter! For this is one of his miracles: in a moment he can make those blind that could see and those see that were blind, those dumb that could speak and those prattle who were dumb before, nay, what is more than all, make these dough-baked,[4] senseless, indocile animals, women, too hard for us, their politic lords and rulers, in a moment. But make an end of your letter, and then I'll make an end of you thus and all my plagues together. (*Draws his sword.*)

MARGERY. Oh Lord, oh Lord, you are such a passionate man, bud!

(*Enter Sparkish.*)

[1] *prospect* Scene; landscape.

[2] *pale* Fence.

[3] *ague* Fever.

[4] *dough-baked* Half-baked; foolish.

SPARKISH. How now, what's here to do?

PINCHWIFE. This fool here now!

SPARKISH. What, drawn upon your wife? You should never do that but at night in the dark when you can't hurt her. This is my sister-in-law, is it not? (*Pulls aside her handkerchief.*) Aye faith, e'en our country Margery, one may know her. Come, she and you must go dine with me; dinner's ready, come. But where's my wife? Is she not come home yet? Where is she?

PINCHWIFE. Making you a cuckold. 'Tis that they all do as soon as they can.

SPARKISH. What, the wedding day? No, a wife that designs to make a cully of her husband will be sure to let him win the first stake of love, by the world. But come, they stay dinner for us; come, I'll lead down, our Margery.

MARGERY. No sir, go, we'll follow you.

SPARKISH. I will not wag without you.

PINCHWIFE. This coxcomb is a sensible torment to me amidst the greatest in the world.

SPARKISH. Come, come, Madam Margery.

PINCHWIFE. No, I'll lead her my way. What, would you treat your friends with mine, for want of your own wife? (*Leads her to the other door and locks her in and returns. Aside.*) I am contented my rage should take breath.

SPARKISH. I told Horner this.

PINCHWIFE. Come now.

SPARKISH. Lord, how shy you are of your wife, but let me tell you, brother, we men of wit have amongst us a saying that cuckolding, like the small pox, comes with a fear, and you may keep your wife as much as you will out of danger of infection, but if her constitution incline her to't, she'll have it sooner or later, by the world, say they.

PINCHWIFE. (*Aside.*) What a thing is a cuckold, that every fool can make him ridiculous.—Well sir, but let me advise you, now you are come to be concerned because you suspect the danger, not to neglect the means to prevent it, especially when the greatest share of the malady will light upon your own head, for

Hows'e'er the kind wife's belly comes to swell,
The husband breeds[1] for her and first is ill.

ACT 5, SCENE 1. Pinchwife's house.

(*Enter Pinchwife and Margery. A table and candle.*)

PINCHWIFE. Come, take the pen and make an end of the letter, just as you intended. If you are false in a tittle, I shall soon perceive it and punish you with this as you deserve. (*Lays his hand on his sword.*) Write what was to follow. Let's see. "You must make haste and help me away before tomorrow, or else I shall be forever out of your reach, for I can defer no longer our—" What follows "our"?

MARGERY. Must all out then, bud? (*Margery takes the pen and writes.*) Look you there then.

PINCHWIFE. Let's see. "For I can defer no longer our—wedding. Your slighted Alithea." What's the meaning of this, my sister's name to't? Speak, unriddle!

MARGERY. Yes indeed, bud.

PINCHWIFE. But why her name to't? Speak—speak, I say!

MARGERY. Aye, but you'll tell her then again. If you would not tell her again—

PINCHWIFE. I will not. I am stunned; my head turns round. Speak.

MARGERY. Won't you tell her indeed and indeed?

PINCHWIFE. No. Speak, I say.

MARGERY. She'll be angry with me, but I had rather she should be angry with me than you, bud, and to tell you the truth, 'twas she made me write the letter and taught me what I should write.

PINCHWIFE. [*Aside.*] Hah! I thought the style was somewhat better than her own.—But how could she come to you to teach you, since I had locked you up alone?

MARGERY. Oh, through the keyhole, bud.

PINCHWIFE. But why should she make you write a letter for her to him, since she can write herself?

MARGERY. Why, she said because—for I was unwilling to do it.

PINCHWIFE. Because what? Because?

MARGERY. Because lest Mr. Horner should be cruel and refuse her, or vain afterwards and show the letter, she might disown it, the hand not being hers.

PINCHWIFE. (*Aside.*) How's this? Hah! Then I think I shall come to myself again. This changeling could not invent this lie. But if she could, why should she? She

[1] *breeds* Grows the cuckold's horns.

might think I should soon discover it. Stay—now I think on't, too, Horner said he was sorry she had married Sparkish, and her disowning her marriage to me makes me think she has evaded it for Horner's sake. Yet why should she take this course? But men in love are fools; women may well be so.—But hark you, madam, your sister went out in the morning and I have not seen her within since.

MARGERY. Alackaday, she has been crying all day above, it seems, in a corner.

PINCHWIFE. Where is she? Let me speak with her.

MARGERY. (*Aside.*) Oh Lord, then he'll discover all.—Pray hold, bud. What, d'ye mean to discover me? She'll know I have told you then. Pray bud, let me talk with her first.

PINCHWIFE. I must speak with her to know whether Horner ever made her any promise and whether she be married to Sparkish or no.

MARGERY. Pray dear bud, don't till I have spoken with her and told her that I have told you all, for she'll kill me else.

PINCHWIFE. Go then, and bid her come out to me.

MARGERY. Yes, yes, bud.

PINCHWIFE. Let me see—

MARGERY. [*Aside.*] I'll go, but she is not within to come to him. I have just got time to know of Lucy, her maid, who first set me on work, what lie I shall tell next, for I am e'en at my wit's end. (*Exit.*)

PINCHWIFE. Well, I resolve it: Horner shall have her. I'd rather give him my sister than lend him my wife, and such an alliance will prevent his pretensions to my wife, sure. I'll make him of kin to her, and then he won't care for her.

(*Margery returns.*)

MARGERY. Oh Lord, bud, I told you what anger you would make me with my sister.

PINCHWIFE. Won't she come hither?

MARGERY. No no, alackaday, she's ashamed to look you in the face, and she says if you go in to her, she'll run away downstairs and shamefully go herself to Mr. Horner, who has promised her marriage, she says, and she will have no other, so she won't—

PINCHWIFE. Did he so—promise her marriage? Then she shall have no other. Go tell her so, and if she will come and discourse with me a little concerning the means, I will about it immediately. Go.

(*Exit Margery.*)

His estate is equal to Sparkish's, and his extraction as much better than his as his parts are, but my chief reason is I'd rather be of kin to him by the name of brother-in-law than that of cuckold.

(*Enter Margery.*)

Well, what says she now?

MARGERY. Why, she says she would only have you lead her to Horner's lodging—with whom she first will discourse the matter before she talk with you, which yet she cannot do, for, alack poor creature, she says she can't so much as look you in the face; therefore, she'll come to you in a mask, and you must excuse her if she make you no answer to any question of yours till you have brought her to Mr. Horner, and if you will not chide her nor question her, she'll come out to you immediately.

PINCHWIFE. Let her come. I will not speak a word to her nor require a word from her.

MARGERY. Oh, I forgot: besides, she says, she cannot look you in the face though through a mask; therefore, would desire you to put out the candle.

PINCHWIFE. I agree to all; let her make haste.

(*Exit Margery; [Pinchwife] puts out the candle.*)

There, 'tis out. My case is something better: I'd rather fight with Horner for not lying with my sister than for lying with my wife, and of the two, I had rather find my sister too forward than my wife. I expected no other from her free education, as she calls it, and her passion for the Town. Well, wife and sister are names which make us expect love and duty, pleasure and comfort, but we find 'em plagues and torments and are equally, though differently, troublesome to their keeper, for we have as much ado to get people to lie with our sisters as to keep 'em from lying with our wives.

(*Enter Margery masked and in hoods and scarves and a nightgown*[1] *and petticoat of Alithea's, in the dark.*)

What, are you come, sister? Let us go then, but first let me lock up my wife. Mistress Margery, where are you?

MARGERY. Here, bud.

PINCHWIFE. Come hither, that I may lock you up.

(*Margery gives him her hand, but when he lets her go, she steals softly on the other side of him.*)

Get you in. (*Locks the door.*) Come, sister, where are you now?

(*[She] is led away by him for his sister Alithea.*)

ACT 5, SCENE 2. Horner's lodging.

(*Quack, Horner.*)

QUACK. That, all alone, not so much as one of your cuckolds here nor one of their wives? They use to take their turns with you as if they were to watch you.

HORNER. Yes, it often happens that a cuckold is but his wife's spy and is more upon family duty when he is with her gallant abroad hindering his pleasure than when he is at home with her playing the gallant. But the hardest duty a married woman imposes upon a lover is keeping her husband company always.

QUACK. And his fondness wearies you almost as soon as hers.

HORNER. A pox, keeping a cuckold company after you have had his wife is as tiresome as the company of a country squire to a witty fellow of the Town when he has got all his money.

QUACK. And as at first a man makes a friend of the husband to get the wife, so at last you are fain to fall out with the wife to be rid of the husband.

HORNER. Aye, most cuckold-makers are true courtiers: when once a poor man has cracked his credit for 'em, they can't abide to come near him.

QUACK. But at first to draw him in, are so sweet, so kind, so dear, just as you are to Pinchwife. But what becomes of that intrigue with his wife?

HORNER. A pox, he's as surly as an alderman that has been bit,[2] and since he's so coy, his wife's kindness is in vain, for she's a silly innocent.

QUACK. Did she not send you a letter by him?

HORNER. Yes, but that's a riddle I have not yet solved. Allow the poor creature to be willing, she is silly, too, and he keeps her up so close—

QUACK. Yes, so close that he makes her but the more willing and adds but revenge to her love, which two, when met, seldom fail of satisfying each other one way or other.

HORNER. What, here's the man we are talking of, I think.

(*Enter Pinchwife leading in his wife masked, muffled, and in her sister's gown.*)

HORNER. Pshaw.

QUACK. Bringing his wife to you is the next thing to bringing a love letter from her.

HORNER. What means this?

PINCHWIFE. The last time, you know, sir, I brought you a love letter; now you see a mistress. I think you'll say I am a civil man to you.

HORNER. Aye, the devil take me, will I say thou art the civilest man I ever met with, and I have known some. I fancy I understand thee now better than I did the letter, but hark thee in thy ear—

PINCHWIFE. What?

HORNER. Nothing but the usual question, man. Is she sound,[3] on thy word?

PINCHWIFE. What, you take her for a wench and me for a pimp?

HORNER. Pshaw, wench and pimp, paw[4] words. I know thou art an honest fellow and hast a great acquaintance among the ladies and perhaps hast made love for me rather than let me make love to thy wife—

PINCHWIFE. Come sir, in short, I am for no fooling.

HORNER. Nor I neither. Therefore, prithee, let's see her face presently; make her show, man. Art thou sure I don't know her?

PINCHWIFE. I am sure you do know her.

HORNER. A pox, why dost thou bring her to me then?

[1] *nightgown* Evening dress.

[2] *bit* Cheated.

[3] *sound* Healthy; here, free of venereal disease.

[4] *paw* Obscene.

PINCHWIFE. Because she's a relation of mine.

HORNER. Is she, faith, man? Then thou art still more civil and obliging, dear rogue.

PINCHWIFE. Who desired me to bring her to you.

HORNER. Then she is obliging, dear rogue.

PINCHWIFE. You'll make her welcome, for my sake, I hope.

HORNER. I hope she is handsome enough to make herself welcome. Prithee, let her unmask.

PINCHWIFE. Do you speak to her; she would never be ruled by me.

HORNER. Madam—

(*Margery whispers to Horner.*)

She says she must speak with me in private. Withdraw, prithee.

PINCHWIFE. (*Aside.*) She's unwilling, it seems, I should know all her undecent conduct in this business.—Well then, I'll leave you together and hope when I am gone you'll agree; if not, you and I shan't agree, sir.

HORNER. [*Aside.*] What means the fool?—If she and I agree, 'tis no matter what you and I do.

(*Whispers to Margery, who makes signs with her hand for [Pinchwife] to be gone.*)

PINCHWIFE. In the meantime, I'll fetch a parson and find out Sparkish and disabuse him. You would have me fetch a parson, would you not? [*Aside.*] Well then, now I think I am rid of her and shall have no more trouble with her. Our sisters and daughters, like usurers' money, are safest when put out, but our wives, like their writings, never safe but in our closets under lock and key. (*Exit.*)

(*Enter Boy.*)

BOY. Sir Jaspar Fidget, sir, is coming up.

HORNER. [*Aside to Quack.*] Here's the trouble of a cuckold now we are talking of. A pox on him! Has he not enough to do to hinder his wife's sport, but he must other women's, too?—Step in here, madam.

(*Exit Margery. Enter Sir Jaspar.*)

SIR JASPAR. My best and dearest friend.

HORNER. [*Aside to Quack.*] The old style, doctor.—Well, be short, for I am busy. What would your impertinent wife have now?

SIR JASPAR. Well guessed i'faith, for I do come from her.

HORNER. To invite me to supper. Tell her I can't come. Go.

SIR JASPAR. Nay, now you are out, faith, for my lady and the whole knot of the virtuous gang, as they call themselves, are resolved upon a frolic of coming to you tonight in a masquerade and are all dressed already.

HORNER. I shan't be at home.

SIR JASPAR. Lord, how churlish he is to women! Nay, prithee don't disappoint 'em; they'll think 'tis my fault. Prithee, don't. I'll send in the banquet and the fiddles, but make no noise on't, for the poor virtuous rogues would not have it known for the world that they go a-masquerading, and they would come to no man's ball but yours.

HORNER. Well, well—get you gone and tell 'em if they come, 'twill be at the peril of their honor and yours.

SIR JASPAR. He, he, he—we'll trust you for that. Farewell. (*Exit.*)

HORNER. Doctor, anon you too shall be my guest,
But now I'm going to a private feast.

[*Exeunt.*]

ACT 5, SCENE 3. The Piazza of Covent Garden.

(*Sparkish, Pinchwife.*)

SPARKISH. (The letter in his hand.) But who would have thought a woman could have been false to me? By the world, I could not have thought it.

PINCHWIFE. You were for giving and taking liberty; she has taken it only, sir, now you find in that letter. You are a frank person, and so is she, you see there.

SPARKISH. Nay, if this be her hand, for I never saw it.

PINCHWIFE. 'Tis no matter whether that be her hand or no. I am sure this hand, at her desire, led her to Mr. Horner, with whom I left her just now to go fetch a parson to 'em at their desire, too, to deprive you of her forever, for it seems yours was but a mock marriage.

SPARKISH. Indeed, she would needs have it that 'twas Harcourt himself in a parson's habit that married us, but

I'm sure he told me 'twas his brother Ned.

PINCHWIFE. Oh there 'tis out, and you were deceived, not she, for you are such a frank person. But I must be gone. You'll find her at Mr. Horner's; go and believe your eyes. (*Exit.*)

SPARKISH. Nay, I'll to her and call her as many crocodiles, sirens, harpies,[1] and other heathenish names as a poet would do a mistress who had refused to hear his suit, nay more, his verses on her. But stay, is not that she following a torch at t'other end of the Piazza, and from Horner's certainly? 'Tis so.

(*Enter Alithea following a torch and Lucy behind.*)

You are well met, madam, though you don't think so. What, you have made a short visit to Mr. Horner, but I suppose you'll return to him presently; by that time the parson can be with him.

ALITHEA. Mr. Horner and the parson, sir!

SPARKISH. Come madam, no more dissembling, no more jilting, for I am no more a frank person.

ALITHEA. How's this?

LUCY. (*Aside.*) So 'twill work, I see.

SPARKISH. Could you find out no easy country fool to abuse? None but me, a gentleman of wit and pleasure about the Town? But it was your pride to be too hard for a man of parts, unworthy, false woman, false as a friend that lends a man money to lose, false as dice, who undo those that trust all they have to 'em.

LUCY. (*Aside.*) He has been a great bubble by his similes, as they say.

ALITHEA. You have been too merry, sir, at your wedding dinner, sure.

SPARKISH. What, d'ye mock me too?

ALITHEA. Or you have been deluded.

SPARKISH. By you.

ALITHEA. Let me understand you.

SPARKISH. Have you the confidence—I should call it something else, since you know your guilt—to stand my just reproaches? You did not write an impudent letter to Mr. Horner, who I find now has clubbed with you in deluding me with his aversion for women, that I might not, forsooth, suspect him for my rival?

LUCY. (*Aside.*) D'ye think the gentleman can be jealous now, madam?

ALITHEA. I write a letter to Mr. Horner!

SPARKISH. Nay madam, do not deny it; your brother showed it me just now and told me likewise he left you at Horner's lodging to fetch a parson to marry you to him, and I wish you joy, madam, joy, joy, and to him, too, much joy and to myself, more joy for not marrying you.

ALITHEA. (*Aside.*) So I find my brother would break off the match, and I can consent to't, since I see this gentleman can be made jealous.—Oh Lucy, by his rude usage and jealousy, he makes me almost afraid I am married to him. Art thou sure 'twas Harcourt himself and no parson that married us?

SPARKISH. No madam, I thank you. I suppose that was a contrivance too of Mr. Horner's and yours to make Harcourt play the parson, but I would as little as you have him one now, no, not for the world, for shall I tell you another truth? I never had any passion for you till now, for now I hate you. 'Tis true I might have married your portion, as other men of parts of the Town do sometimes, and so, your servant, and to show my unconcernedness, I'll come to your wedding and resign you with as much joy as I would a stale wench to a new cully, nay, with as much joy as I would after the first night, if I had been married to you. There's for you, and so, your servant. (*Exit.*)

ALITHEA. How was I deceived in a man!

LUCY. You'll believe, then, a fool may be made jealous now? For that easiness in him that suffers him to be led by a wife will likewise permit him to be persuaded against her by others.

ALITHEA. But marry Mr. Horner? My brother does not intend it, sure. If I thought he did, I would take thy advice and Mr. Harcourt for my husband, and now I wish that if there be any over-wise woman of the Town, who, like me, would marry a fool for fortune, liberty, or title: first, that her husband may love play and be a cully[2] to all the Town but her and suffer none but Fortune to be mistress of his purse; then, if for liberty, that he may send her into the country under the conduct of some housewifely mother-in-law; and if for title, may the world give 'em none but that of cuckold.

LUCY. And for her greater curse, madam, may he not

[1] *sirens, harpies* According to Greek mythology, sirens lured sailors to destruction and harpies were monstrous creatures with claws and wings appended to a woman's body.

[2] *cully* Person who is easily deceived.

deserve it.

ALITHEA. Away, impertinent!—Is not this my old Lady Lanterlu's?[1]

LUCY. Yes, madam. (*Aside.*) And here I hope we shall find Mr. Harcourt.

(*Exeunt.*)

ACT 5, SCENE 4. Horner's lodging.

(*Horner, Lady Fidget, Dainty, Mrs. Squeamish. A table, banquet, and bottles.*)

HORNER. (*Aside.*) A pox, they are come too soon—before I have sent back my new mistress! All I have now to do is to lock her in that they may not see her.

LADY FIDGET. That we may be sure of our welcome, we have brought our entertainment with us and are resolved to treat thee, dear toad—

DAINTY. And that we may be merry to purpose, have left Sir Jaspar and my old Lady Squeamish quarreling at home at backgammon.

MRS. SQUEAMISH. Therefore, let us make use of our time, lest they should chance to interrupt us.

LADY FIDGET. Let us sit then.

HORNER. First that you may be private, let me lock this door and that, and I'll wait upon you presently.

LADY FIDGET. No sir, shut 'em only and your lips forever, for we must trust you as much as our women.[2]

HORNER. You know all vanity's killed in me; I have no occasion for talking.

LADY FIDGET. Now ladies, supposing we had drank each of us our two bottles, let us speak the truth of our hearts.

DAINTY AND MRS. SQUEAMISH. Agreed.

LADY FIDGET. By this brimmer,[3] for truth is nowhere else to be found. (*Aside to Horner.*) Not in thy heart, false man.

HORNER. (*Aside to Lady Fidget.*) You have found me a true man, I'm sure.

LADY FIDGET. (*Aside to Horner.*) Not every way.—But let us sit and be merry. (*Sings.*)

1.
Why should our damned tyrants oblige us to live
On the pittance of pleasure which they only give?
    We must not rejoice
    With wine and with noise.
In vain we must wake in a dull bed alone,
Whilst to our warm rival the bottle they're gone.
    Then lay aside charms
    And take up these arms.[4]

2.
'Tis wine only gives 'em their courage and wit;
Because we live sober to men, we submit.
    If for beauties you'd pass,
    Take a lick of the glass;
'Twill mend your complexions, and when they are gone,
The best red we have is the red of the grape.
    Then sisters lay't on
    And damn a good shape.

DAINTY. Dear brimmer! Well, in token of our openness and plain dealing, let us throw our masks over our heads.

HORNER. So 'twill come to the glasses anon.

MRS. SQUEAMISH. Lovely brimmer! Let me enjoy him first.

LADY FIDGET. No, I never part with a gallant till I've tried him. Dear brimmer that mak'st our husbands short-sighted—

DAINTY. And our bashful gallants bold—

MRS. SQUEAMISH. And for want of a gallant, the butler lovely in our eyes. Drink, eunuch.

LADY FIDGET. Drink, thou representative of a husband. Damn a husband—

DAINTY. And as it were a husband, an old keeper—

MRS. SQUEAMISH. And an old grandmother—

HORNER. And an English bawd and a French chirurgeon.

LADY FIDGET. Aye, we have all reason to curse 'em.

HORNER. For my sake, ladies.

LADY FIDGET. No, for our own, for the first spoils all young gallant's industry—

DAINTY. And the other's art makes 'em bold only with common women—

MRS. SQUEAMISH. And rather run the hazard of the vile distemper amongst them than of a denial amongst us.

[1] *Lady Lanterlu's* Lanterloo, or loo, a popular card game; from *lanturelu*, French for twaddle.

[2] *women* Waiting-women.

[3] *brimmer* Full glass.

[4] *arms* The glasses.

DAINTY. The filthy toads choose mistresses now as they do stuffs,[1] for having been fancied and worn by others—

MRS. SQUEAMISH. For being common and cheap—

LADY FIDGET. Whilst women of quality, like the richest stuffs, lie untumbled and unasked for.

HORNER. Aye, neat and cheap and new often they think best.

DAINTY. No sir, the beasts will be known by a mistress longer than by a suit—

MRS. SQUEAMISH. And 'tis not for cheapness neither—

LADY FIDGET. No, for the vain fops will take up druggets[2] and embroider 'em. But I wonder at the depraved appetites of witty men; they used to be out of the common road and hate imitation. Pray tell me, beast, when you were a man, why you rather chose to club with a multitude in a common house for an entertainment than to be the only guest at a good table.

HORNER. Why faith, ceremony and expectation are unsufferable to those that are sharp bent;[3] people always eat with the best stomach at an ordinary,[4] where every man is snatching for the best bit—

LADY FIDGET. Though he get a cut over the fingers. But I have heard people eat most heartily of another man's meat, that is, what they do not pay for.

HORNER. When they are sure of their welcome and freedom, for ceremony in love and eating is as ridiculous as in fighting: falling on[5] briskly is all should be done in those occasions.

LADY FIDGET. Well then, let me tell you, sir, there is nowhere more freedom than in our houses, and we take freedom from a young person as a sign of good breeding, and a person may be as free as he pleases with us, as frolic, as gamesome, as wild as he will.

HORNER. Han't I heard you all declaim against wild men?

LADY FIDGET. Yes, but for all that, we think wildness in a man as desirable a quality as in a duck or rabbit. A tame man, faugh!

HORNER. I know not, but your reputations frightened me as much as your faces invited me.

LADY FIDGET. Our reputation! Lord, why should you not think that we women make use of our reputation as you men of yours, only to deceive the world with less suspicion? Our virtue is like the stateman's religion, the Quaker's word, the gamester's oath, and the great man's honor: but to cheat those that trust us.

MRS. SQUEAMISH. And that demureness, coyness, and modesty that you see in our faces in the boxes at plays is as much a sign of a kind woman as a vizard-mask in the pit.

DAINTY. For I assure you, women are least masked when they have the velvet vizard on.

LADY FIDGET. You would have found us modest women in our denials only—

MRS. SQUEAMISH. Our bashfulness is only the reflection of the men's—

DAINTY. We blush when they are shame-faced.

HORNER. I beg your pardon, ladies, I was deceived in you devilishly. But why that mighty pretense to honor?

LADY FIDGET. We have told you, but sometimes 'twas for the same reason you men pretend business often: to avoid ill company, to enjoy the better and more privately those you love.

HORNER. But why would you ne'er give a friend a wink then?

LADY FIDGET. Faith, your reputation frightened us as much as ours did you, you were so notoriously lewd—

HORNER. And you so seemingly honest.

LADY FIDGET. Was that all that deterred you?

HORNER. And so expensive— (You allow freedom, you say?)

LADY FIDGET. Aye, aye.

HORNER. That I was afraid of losing my little money, as well as my little time, both which my other pleasures required.

LADY FIDGET. Money, faugh! You talk like a little fellow now. Do such as we expect money?

HORNER. I beg your pardon, madam, I must confess I have heard that great ladies, like great merchants, set but the higher prices upon what they have because they are not in necessity of taking the first offer.

DAINTY. Such as we make sale of our hearts?

MRS. SQUEAMISH. We bribed for our love? Faugh!

HORNER. With your pardon, ladies, I know, like great men in offices, you seem to exact flattery and attendance

[1] *stuffs* Material for clothing; cloth.

[2] *druggets* Coarse woven material.

[3] *sharp bent* Hungry.

[4] *ordinary* Dining room in a public house or tavern.

[5] *falling on* Commencing.

only from your followers, but you have receivers[1] about you and such fees to pay, a man is afraid to pass your grants;[2] besides, we must let you win at cards, or we lose your hearts, and if you make an assignation, 'tis at a goldsmith's, jeweler's, or china house, where for your honor you deposit to him, he must pawn his to the punctual cit, and so paying for what you take up, pays for what he takes up.

DAINTY. Would you not have us assured of our gallant's love?

MRS. SQUEAMISH. For love is better known by liberality than by jealousy—

LADY FIDGET. For one may be dissembled, the other not. (*Aside.*) But my jealousy can be no longer dissembled, and they are telling-ripe.—Come, here's to our gallants in waiting, whom we must name, and I'll begin: this is my false rogue. (*Claps him on the back.*)

MRS. SQUEAMISH. How!

HORNER. So all will out now—

MRS. SQUEAMISH. (*Aside to Horner.*) Did you not tell me 'twas for my sake only you reported yourself no man?

DAINTY. (*Aside.*) Oh wretch! Did you not swear to me 'twas for my love and honor you passed for that thing you do?

HORNER. So, so.

LADY FIDGET. Come, speak ladies. This is my false villain.

MRS. SQUEAMISH. And mine too.

DAINTY. And mine.

HORNER. Well then, you are all three my false rogues too, and there's an end on't.

LADY FIDGET. Well then, there's no remedy, sister sharers. Let us not fall out but have a care of our honor. Though we get no presents, no jewels of him, we are savers of our honor, the jewel of most value and use, which shines yet to the world unsuspected, though it be counterfeit.

HORNER. Nay and is e'en as good as if it were true, provided the world think so, for honor, like beauty now, only depends on the opinion of others.

LADY FIDGET. Well Harry Common, I hope you can be true to three. Swear. But 'tis no purpose to require your oath, for you are as often forsworn as you swear to new women.

HORNER. Come, faith madam, let us e'en pardon one another, for all the difference I find betwixt we men and you women, we forswear ourselves at the beginning of an amour, you, as long as it lasts.

(*Enter Sir Jaspar Fidget and Old Lady Squeamish.*)

SIR JASPAR. Oh my Lady Fidget, was this your cunning, to come to Mr. Horner without me? But you have been no where else, I hope?

LADY FIDGET. No, Sir Jaspar.

OLD LADY SQUEAMISH. And you came straight hither, Biddy?

MRS. SQUEAMISH. Yes indeed, Lady Grandmother.

SIR JASPAR. 'Tis well, 'tis well. I knew when once they were thoroughly acquainted with poor Horner, they'd ne'er be from him. You may let her masquerade it with my wife and Horner, and I warrant her reputation safe.

(*Enter boy.*)

BOY. Oh sir, here's the gentleman come whom you bid me not suffer to come up without giving you notice, with a lady, too, and other gentlemen.

HORNER. Do you all go in there, whilst I send 'em away.—And boy, do you desire 'em to stay below till I come, which shall be immediately.

(*Exeunt Sir Jaspar, [Old] Lady Squeamish, Lady Fidget, Dainty, Mrs. Squeamish.*)

BOY. Yes sir. (*Exit.*)

(*Exit Horner at the other door, and returns with Margery.*)

HORNER. You would not take my advice to be gone home before your husband came back. He'll now discover all, yet pray, my dearest, be persuaded to go home and leave the rest to my management; I'll let you down the back way.

MARGERY. I don't know the way home, so I don't.

HORNER. My man shall wait upon you.

MARGERY. No, don't you believe that I'll go at all. What, are you weary of me already?

[1] *receivers* Servants who must be paid for cooperation and silence.

[2] *pass your grants* Accept your favors.

HORNER. No my life, 'tis that I may love you long, 'tis to secure my love and your reputation with your husband; he'll never receive you again else.

MARGERY. What care I? D'ye think to frighten me with that? I don't intend to go to him again; you shall be my husband now.

HORNER. I cannot be your husband, dearest, since you are married to him.

MARGERY. Oh, would you make me believe that? Don't I see every day at London here, women leave their first husbands and go and live with other men as their wives? Pish, pshaw, you'd make me angry, but that I love you so mainly.

HORNER. So, they are coming up. In again, in, I hear 'em.

(*Exit Margery.*)

Well, a silly mistress is like a weak place, soon got, soon lost; a man has scarce time for plunder. She betrays her husband first to her gallant and then her gallant to her husband.

(*Enter Pinchwife, Alithea, Harcourt, Sparkish, Lucy, and a parson.*)

PINCHWIFE. Come madam, 'tis not the sudden change of your dress, the confidence of your asseverations, and your false witness there shall persuade me I did not bring you hither just now; here's my witness, who cannot deny it, since you must be confronted.—Mr. Horner, did not I bring this lady to you just now?

HORNER. (*Aside.*) Now must I wrong one woman for another's sake, but that's no new thing with me, for in these cases I am still on the criminal's side against the innocent.

ALITHEA. Pray speak, sir.

HORNER. (*Aside.*) It must be so. I must be impudent and try my luck; impudence uses to be too hard for truth.

PINCHWIFE. What, you are studying an evasion or excuse for her. Speak, sir.

HORNER. No, faith, I am something backward only to speak in women's affairs or disputes.

PINCHWIFE. She bids you speak.

ALITHEA. Aye, pray sir, do, pray satisfy him.

HORNER. Then truly, you did bring that lady to me just now.

PINCHWIFE. Oh ho!

ALITHEA. How, sir!

HARCOURT. How, Horner!

ALITHEA. What mean you, sir? I always took you for a man of honor.

HORNER. (*Aside.*) Aye, so much a man of honor that I must save my mistress, I thank you, come what will on't.

SPARKISH. So if I had had her, she'd have made me believe, the moon had been made of a Christmas pie.

LUCY. (*Aside.*) Now could I speak, if I durst, and solve the riddle, who am the author of it.

ALITHEA. Oh unfortunate woman! [*To Harcourt.*] A combination against my honor, which most concerns me now, because you share in my disgrace, sir, and it is your censure, which I must now suffer, that troubles me, not theirs.

HARCOURT. Madam, then have no trouble; you shall now see 'tis possible for me to love, too, without being jealous. I will not only believe your innocence myself, but make all the world believe it. (*Apart to Horner.*) Horner, I must now be concerned for this lady's honor.

HORNER. And I must be concerned for a lady's honor, too.

HARCOURT. This lady has her honor, and I will protect it.

HORNER. My lady has not her honor, but has given it me to keep, and I will preserve it.

HARCOURT. I understand you not.

HORNER. I would not have you.

MARGERY. (*Peeping in behind.*) What's the matter with 'em all?

PINCHWIFE. Come, come, Mr. Horner, no more disputing. Here's the parson; I brought him not in vain.

HARCOURT. No sir, I'll employ him, if this lady please.

PINCHWIFE. How, what d'ye mean?

SPARKISH. Aye, what does he mean?

HORNER. Why, I have resigned your sister to him; he has my consent.

PINCHWIFE. But he has not mine, sir. A woman's injured honor, no more than a man's, can be repaired or satisfied by any but him that first wronged it, and you shall marry her presently, or— (*Lays his hand on his sword.*)

(*Enter Margery.*)

MARGERY. Oh Lord, they'll kill poor Mr. Horner! Besides, he shan't marry her whilst I stand by and look on; I'll not lose my second husband so.

PINCHWIFE. What do I see?

ALITHEA. My sister in my clothes!

SPARKISH. Hah!

MARGERY. (*To Pinchwife.*) Nay, pray now don't quarrel about finding work for the parson; he shall marry me to Mr. Horner, for now I believe you have enough of me.

HORNER. Damned, damned, loving changeling.

MARGERY. Pray sister, pardon me for telling so many lies of you.

HARCOURT. I suppose the riddle is plain now.

LUCY. No, that must be my work, good sir, hear me. (*Kneels to Pinchwife, who stands doggedly, with his hat over his eyes.*)

PINCHWIFE. I will never hear woman again, but make 'em all silent thus— (*Offers to draw upon his wife.*)

HORNER. No, that must not be.

PINCHWIFE. You then shall go first; 'tis all one to me. (*Offers to draw on Horner, stopped by Harcourt.*)

HARCOURT. Hold—

(*Enter Sir Jaspar Fidget, Lady Fidget, Old Lady Squeamish, Dainty, Mrs. Squeamish.*)

SIR JASPAR. What's the matter, what's the matter, pray what's the matter, sir? I beseech you communicate, sir.

PINCHWIFE. Why, my wife has communicated, sir, as your wife may have done, too, sir, if she knows him, sir.

SIR JASPAR. Pshaw, with him, ha, ha, he!

PINCHWIFE. D'ye mock me, sir? A cuckold is a kind of wild beast, have a care, sir.

SIR JASPAR. No, sure you mock me, sir. He cuckold you! It can't be, ha, ha, he. Why, I'll tell you, sir. (*Offers to whisper.*)

PINCHWIFE. I tell you again, he has whored my wife and yours, too, if he knows her, and all the women he comes near. 'Tis not his dissembling, his hypocrisy can wheedle me.

SIR JASPAR. How! Does he dissemble? Is he a hypocrite? Nay, then—how—wife—sister, is he a hypocrite?

OLD LADY SQUEAMISH. A hypocrite! A dissembler! Speak, young harlotry, speak. How!

SIR JASPAR. Nay, then—oh my head too—oh thou libidinous lady!

OLD LADY SQUEAMISH. Oh thou harloting harlotry, hast thou done't then?

SIR JASPAR. Speak, good Horner. Art thou a dissembler, a rogue? Hast thou—

HORNER. Soh—

LUCY. (*Apart to Horner.*) I'll fetch you off and her too, if she will but hold her tongue.

HORNER. (*Apart to Lucy.*) Canst thou? I'll give thee—

LUCY. (*To Mr. Pinchwife.*) Pray have but patience to hear me, sir, who am the unfortunate cause of all this confusion. Your wife is innocent, I only culpable, for I put her upon telling you all these lies concerning my mistress in order to the breaking off the match between Mr. Sparkish and her to make way for Mr. Harcourt.

SPARKISH. Did you so, eternal rotten tooth? Then it seems my mistress was not false to me; I was only deceived by you.—Brother that should have been, now, man of conduct, who is a frank person now? To bring your wife to her lover—hah!

LUCY. I assure you, sir, she came not to Mr. Horner out of love, for she loves him no more—

MARGERY. Hold! I told lies for you, but you shall tell none for me, for I do love Mr. Horner with all my soul, and nobody shall say me nay. Pray don't you go to make poor Mr. Horner believe to the contrary. 'Tis spitefully done of you, I'm sure.

HORNER. (*Aside to Margery.*) Peace, dear idiot.

MARGERY. Nay, I will not peace.

PINCHWIFE. Not till I make you.

(*Enter Dorilant, Quack.*)

DORILANT. Horner, your servant. I am the doctor's guest; he must excuse our intrusion.

QUACK. But what's the matter, gentlemen? For Heaven's sake, what's the matter?

HORNER. Oh 'tis well you are come. 'Tis a censorious world we live in. You may have brought me a reprieve, or else I had died for a crime I never committed, and these innocent ladies had suffered with me; therefore, pray satisfy these worthy, honorable, jealous gentlemen that—(*Whispers.*)

QUACK. Oh I understand you. Is that all?—Sir Jasper, by heavens and upon the word of a physician, sir,—

(*Whispers to Sir Jaspar.*)

SIR JASPAR. Nay, I do believe you truly.—Pardon me, my virtuous lady and dear of honor.

OLD LADY SQUEAMISH. What, then all's right again.

SIR JASPAR. Aye, aye, and now let us satisfy him, too.

(*They whisper with Pinchwife.*)

PINCHWIFE. An eunuch! Pray no fooling with me.

QUACK. I'll bring half the chirurgeons in Town to swear it.

PINCHWIFE. They! They'll swear a man that bled to death through his wounds died of an apoplexy.[1]

QUACK. Pray hear me, sir. Why, all the Town has heard the report of him.

PINCHWIFE. But does all the Town believe it?

QUACK. Pray inquire a little and first of all these.

PINCHWIFE. I'm sure when I left the Town he was the lewdest fellow in't.

QUACK. I tell you, sir, he has been in France since. Pray ask but these ladies and gentlemen, your friend Mr. Dorilant.—Gentlemen and ladies, han't you all heard the late sad report of poor Mr. Horner?

ALL LADIES. Aye, aye, aye.

DORILANT. Why, thou jealous fool, dost thou doubt it? He's an arrant French capon.[2]

MARGERY. 'Tis false, sir, you shall not disparage poor Mr. Horner, for to my certain knowledge—

LUCY. Oh hold!

MRS. SQUEAMISH. (*Aside to Lucy.*) Stop her mouth!

LADY FIDGET. (*To Pinchwife.*) Upon my honor, sir, 'tis as true—

DAINTY. D'ye think we would have been seen in his company—

MRS. SQUEAMISH. Trust our unspotted reputations with him?

LADY FIDGET. (*Aside to Horner.*) This you get and we, too, by trusting your secret to a fool.

HORNER. Peace, madam. (*Aside to Quack.*) Well Doctor, is not this a good design that carries a man on unsuspected and brings him off safe?

PINCHWIFE. (*Aside.*) Well, if this were true, but my wife—

(*Dorilant whispers with Margery.*)

ALITHEA. Come brother, your wife is yet innocent, you see, but have a care of too strong an imagination, lest like an over-concerned, timorous gamester, by fancying an unlucky cast, it should come. Women and Fortune are truest still to those that trust 'em.

LUCY. And any wild thing grows but the more fierce and hungry for being kept up and more dangerous to the keeper.

ALITHEA. There's doctrine for all husbands, Mr. Harcourt.

HARCOURT. And I edify, madam, so much that I am impatient till I am one.

DORILANT. And I edify so much by example I will never be one.

SPARKISH. And because I will not disparage my parts, I'll ne'er be one.

HORNER. And I, alas, can't be one.

PINCHWIFE. But I must be one against my will, to a country wife, with a country murrain[3] to me.

MARGERY. (*Aside.*) And I must be a country wife still, too, I find, for I can't, like a City one, be rid of my musty husband and do what I list.

HORNER. Now sir, I must pronounce your wife innocent, though I blush whilst I do it, and I am the only man by her now exposed to shame, which I will straight drown in wine, as you shall your suspicion, and the ladies' troubles we'll divert with a ballet.—Doctor, where are your maskers?

LUCY. Indeed, she's innocent, sir. I am her witness, and her end of coming out was but to see her sister's wedding, and what she has said to your face of her love to Mr. Horner was but the usual innocent revenge on a husband's jealousy, was it not? Madam, speak.

MARGERY. (*Aside to Lucy and Horner.*) Since you'll have me tell more lies.—Yes indeed, bud.

PINCHWIFE. For my own sake, fain I would all believe:
Cuckolds, like lovers, should themselves deceive.
But— (*Sighs.*)
His honor is least safe (too late I find)
Who trusts it with a foolish wife or friend.

(*A dance of cuckolds.*)

[1] *apoplexy* Stroke.

[2] *capon* Domestic male fowl which has been castrated so that it will fatten for eating.

[3] *murrain* Infection, of livestock.

HORNER. Vain fops but court and dress and keep a pother
To pass for women's men with one another,
But he who aims by women to be prized,
First by the men, you see, must be despised.

[*Exeunt.*]

EPILOGUE

Spoken by Mrs. Knepp[1]

Now you, the vigorous, who daily here
O'er vizard mask in public domineer,
And what you'd do to her, if in place where;
Nay, have the confidence to cry, "Come out!"
Yet when she says, "Lead on!" you are not stout;
But to your well-dressed brother straight turn round
And cry, "Pox on her, Ned, she can't be sound!"
Then slink away, a fresh one to engage,
With so much seeming heat and loving rage,
You'd frighten listening actress on the stage;
Till she at last has seen you huffing come,
And talk of keeping in the tiring room,
Yet cannot be provoked to lead her home.
Next, you Falstaffs[2] of fifty, who beset
Your buckram maidenheads,[3] which your friends get;
And whilst to them you of achievements boast,
They share the booty and laugh at your cost.
In fine, you essenced boys, both old and young,
Who would be thought so eager, brisk, and strong,
Yet do the ladies, not their husbands, wrong;
Whose purses for your manhood make excuse,
And keep your Flanders mares for show, not use;
Encouraged by our woman's man today,
A Horner's part may vainly think to play;
And may intrigues so bashfully disown,
That they may doubted be by few or none;
May kiss the cards at picquet, ombre, loo,[4]
And so be thought to kiss the lady too;
But, gallants, have a care, faith, what you do.
The world, which to no man his due will give,
You by experience know you can deceive;
And men may still believe you vigorous,
But then we women—there's no cozening[5] us.

FINIS

—1675

[1] *Mrs. Knepp* Mary Knep or Knipp (died c. 1680), actress, first to play Lady Fidget.

[2] *Falstaffs* Reference to a character in Shakespeare's *Merry Wives of Windsor, 1 Henry IV*, and *2 Henry IV.*

[3] *buckram maidenheads* Cf. Shakespeare's *1 Henry IV*, 2.4.

[4] *picquet, ombre, loo* Card games.

[5] *cozening* Cheating.

John Wilmot, Earl of Rochester

1647 – 1680

John Wilmot, Earl of Rochester, so embodied the role of a Restoration rake that his writing risks being eclipsed by his notoriety. Although historically considered a minor writer, Rochester was a dynamic participant in the literary milieu of his day: a contributor to plays by John Fletcher and John Howard; an influential stage patron who was blamed by many for instigating a 1679 attack on Dryden, his arch rival, in Covent Garden; and a poet known and feared for his relentless satire and lampooning of contemporary court figures and mores.

Born in April 1647 at Ditchley, Oxfordshire, Wilmot became the second Earl of Rochester in 1658 after his Royalist father died in exile. (His mother favored the other side in the great political split of the time.) Rochester entered Wadham College, Oxford, in January 1660, but left within two years to embark on a three-year tour of Europe. He returned to the court of Charles II at the age of 17 and soon provided plenty of grist for the London gossip mills by abducting his future wife, Elizabeth Malet, in 1665—an impetuous plan that earned the young Earl several weeks in the Tower while plague ravaged the city. After his release in June 1665, Rochester volunteered for service against the Dutch by joining the English fleet under the command of the Earl of Sandwich. His courage earned him a reward of £750 from the King, who later made Rochester a Gentleman of the Bedchamber. Rochester eventually married Malet (who also wrote poetry) in January 1667, and the couple had four children; their relationship is believed to have been happy despite his frequent absences and affairs. A well-known philanderer and drinker, Rochester fathered an illegitimate daughter with one of his mistresses, the actress Elizabeth Barry, and he claimed to have been continually drunk for five years during his early twenties.

Rochester's relationship with Charles II was mercurial; the Earl was often in disgrace, but the King was seemingly unable to remain angry with him, in spite of his irreverent behavior and verse. In one serious breach of court etiquette, Rochester struck Thomas Killigrew in the King's presence in 1669, but the King was seen walking amicably with Rochester the day after the incident. In 1674, Rochester mistakenly gave the King a copy of verses concerning Charles II's sexual exploits, a manuscript that included such lines as, "Poor prince! thy prick, like thy buffoons at Court, / Will govern thee because it makes thee sport. / 'Tis sure the sauciest prick that e'er did swive, / The proudest, peremptoriest prick alive." For that offence Rochester was briefly banished from the Court, but the King granted him the lucrative Rangership of Woodstock Park only a few months later. In one of his more infamous adventures, a drunken Rochester, accompanied by equally inebriated friends, smashed the King's phallic glass sundials in Whitehall's Privy Garden, shouting as he did so, "What! Dost thou stand here to —— Time?"

Like many Court poets, Rochester circulated his work in manuscript and did not pursue publication. A collection of his poems that contained many false attributions appeared only months after his death in July 1680. (A second collection appeared in 1691, with several poems missing stanzas to avoid, according to the publisher, offending the reader.) It was not until the late twentieth century that reliable and unexpurgated texts of all Rochester's known work were published; in all, there are approximately 75 authentic Rochester poems in existence. Many of them are remarkably explicit sexually, even by today's standards; more generally, his verse is characterized by his unsparing honesty about the most personal of subjects (including love, religious belief or unbelief, and sexual failure and embarrassment). He also writes of his disinclination to trust anything beyond personal, usually physical, experience. In its style Rochester's verse is often (though by no means always) as polished and elegant as it is rude in its content.

At the end of his short life, his health ruined by alcoholism and venereal disease, the former skeptic retired to the country in April 1680 and underwent a surprising conversion to Christianity after listening to his mother's chaplain read Isaiah 53. He had already summoned clergyman Gilbert Burnet, his first biographer, to his London home in October 1679 after reading Burnet's *History of the Reformation*. Burnet recorded the details of their theological debates in his book, published after Rochester's death, entitled *Some Passages of the Life and Death of the Right Honourable John, Earl of Rochester*, but many doubted the validity of Rochester's deathbed conversion, claiming either that he was unbalanced due to illness or that Burnet's account was biased. His mother honored his request to burn his papers—an act which has no doubt contributed to the difficulty of determining an accurate Rochester canon. Authentic or not, his celebrated conversion has only added to the Rochester legend; his story was gladly seized upon by those wishing to transform him into a lesson in morality, the paradigm of the reformed rake.

⌘⌘⌘

A Satire on Charles II[1]

I' th' isle of Britain, long since famous grown
For breeding the best cunts in Christendom
There reigns, and oh! long may he reign and thrive,
The easiest King and best-bred man alive.
Him no ambition moves to get renown
Like the French fool,[2] that wanders up and down
Starving his people, hazarding[3] his crown.
Peace is his aim, his gentleness is such,
And love he loves, for he loves fucking much.

Nor are his high desires above his strength:
His scepter and his prick are of a length;[4]
And she may sway the one who plays with th'other,
And make him little wiser than his brother.[5]
Poor prince! thy prick, like thy buffoons at Court,
Will govern thee because it makes thee sport.
'Tis sure the sauciest prick that e'er did swive,[6]
The proudest, peremptoriest prick alive.
Though safety, law, religion, life lay on't,
'Twould break through all to make its way to cunt.
Restless he rolls about from whore to whore,
A merry monarch, scandalous and poor.

To Carwell,[7] the most dear of all his dears,
The best relief of his declining years,
Oft he bewails his fortune, and her fate:
To love so well, and be beloved so late.
For though in her he settles well his tarse,[8]
Yet his dull, graceless bollocks hang an arse.[9]
This you'd believe, had I but time to tell ye
The pains it costs to poor, laborious Nelly,[10]
Whilst she employs hands, fingers, mouth, and thighs,

---

[1] *A Satire on Charles II* Rochester was banished from court as a result of the King having read this poem. The circumstances are described in a letter dated 20 January 1674: "My lord Rochester fled from Court some time since for delivering (by mistake) into the King's hands a terrible lampoon of his own making against the King, instead of another the King asked him for."

[2] *the French fool* King Louis XIV (1638–1715).

[3] *hazarding* Putting at risk.

[4] *of a length* I.e., of the same length.

[5] *his brother* James (later King James II).

[6] *swive* Engage in sexual intercourse.

[7] *Carwell* Louise de Keroualle, Duchess of Portsmouth.

[8] *tarse* Penis.

[9] *hang an arse* Are slow or sluggish.

[10] *Nelly* Nell Gwyn, an actress and Charles II's best-known mistress. There were extensive rivalries among Charles's various mistresses, including Lady Castlemaine, Frances Stuart, Lucy Walters, and Moll Davis, as well as Gwyn and de Keroualle.

Ere she can raise the member she enjoys.
All monarchs I hate, and the thrones they sit on,
From the hector[1] of France to the cully[2] of Britain.
—1673/74

A Satire against Reason and Mankind

Were I (who to my cost already am
One of those strange prodigious creatures, man)
A spirit free to choose for my own share,
What case of flesh and blood I pleased to wear;
I'd be a dog, a monkey, or a bear.
Or any thing but that vain animal
Who is so proud of being rational.
The senses are too gross, and he'll contrive
A sixth to contradict the other five:
And before certain instinct will prefer
Reason, which fifty times for one does err.
Reason, an *ignis fatuus*[3] of the mind,
Which leaving light of nature, sense, behind;
Pathless and dangerous wand'ring ways it takes,
Through error's fenny° bogs and thorny brakes:° *swampy* / *briars*
Whilst the misguided follower climbs with pain
Mountains of whimsies heaped in his own brain;
Stumbling from thought to thought, falls headlong down
Into doubt's boundless sea, where like to drown,
Books bear him up a while, and make him try
To swim with bladders[4] of philosophy:
In hopes still to o'ertake th'escaping light,
The vapour dances in his dazzled sight,
Till spent, it leaves him to eternal night.
Then old age and experience hand in hand,
Lead him to death, and make him understand,
After a search so painful and so long
That all his life he has been in the wrong.
Huddled in dirt the reasoning engine lies,
Who was so proud, so witty and so wise.
Pride drew him in (as cheats their bubbles° catch) *victims*
And made him venture to be made a wretch.
His wisdom did his happiness destroy,
Aiming to know that world he should enjoy;
And wit was his vain frivolous pretence,
Of pleasing others at his own expense:
For wits are treated just like common whores,
First they're enjoyed and then kicked out of doors.
The pleasure past, a threat'ning doubt remains,
That frights th'enjoyer with succeeding pains:
Women and men of wit are dangerous tools,
And ever fatal to admiring fools.
Pleasure allures, and when the fops escape,
'Tis not that they're belov'd, but fortunate;
And therefore what they fear, at heart they hate.
But now methinks some formal band and beard
Takes me to task. Come on, sir, I'm prepared:
Then by your favour anything that's writ
Against this gibing, jingling knack called wit,
Likes me abundantly, but you take care
Upon this point not to be too severe.
Perhaps my muse were fitter for this part,
For, I profess, I can be very smart
On wit, which I abhor with all my heart.
I long to lash it in some sharp essay,
But your grand indiscretion bids me stay,
And turns my tide of ink another way.
What rage ferments in your degenerate mind,
To make you rail at reason and mankind?
Blest glorious man! to whom alone kind Heaven
An everlasting soul has freely given:
Whom his Creator took such care to make,
That from Himself He did the image take:
And this fair frame in shining reason dressed,
To dignify his nature above beast.
Reason, by whose aspiring influence
We take a flight beyond material sense;
Dive into mysteries, then soaring pierce
The flaming limits of the universe:
Search Heaven and Hell, find out what's acted there,
And give the world true grounds of hope and fear.
Hold mighty man, I cry; all this we know,
From the pathetic pen of Ingelo,[5]

[1] *hector* Noisy, blustery fellow, bully.

[2] *cully* One who is deceived.

[3] *ignis fatuus* Latin: foolish fire; also called will-o'-the-wisp. A phosphorescent light that hovers above marshy ground and is believed to be caused by the spontaneous combustion of inflammable gases emitted from decaying matter. Travelers attempting to follow this light would frequently become lost.

[4] *bladders* Inflated and used as a float.

[5] *Ingelo* Reverend Nathaniel Ingelo, author of the allegorical romance *Bentivolio and Urania* (1660).

From Patrick's Pilgrim, Sibbes' Soliloquies;[1]
And 'tis this very reason I despise.
This supernatural gift, that makes a mite
Think he's the image of the infinite;
Comparing his short life, void of all rest,
To the eternal, and the ever blest.
This busy puzzling stirrer up of doubt,
That frames deep mysteries, then finds them out;
Filling with frantic crowds of thinking fools
Those reverend bedlams,[2] colleges and schools;
Born on whose wings each heavy sot can pierce
The limits of the boundless universe.
So charming ointments make an old witch fly,
And bear a crippled carcass through the sky.
'Tis this exalted power whose business lies
In nonsense and impossibilities.
This made a whimsical philosopher
Before the spacious world his tub prefer.[3]
And we have modern cloistered coxcombs, who
Retire to think, 'cause they have nought to do:
But thoughts are given for action's government,
Where action ceases, thought's impertinent.
Our sphere of action is life's happiness,
And he who thinks beyond, thinks like an ass.
Thus whilst against false reasoning I inveigh,
I own right reason, which I would obey;
That reason which distinguishes by sense,
And gives us rules of good and ill from thence:
That bounds desires with a reforming will,
To keep them more in vigour, not to kill.
Your reason hinders, mine helps to enjoy,
Renewing appetites yours would destroy.
My reason is my friend, yours is a cheat,
Hunger calls out, my reason bids me eat;
Perversely yours your appetites does mock,
They ask for food, that answers what's a clock.
This plain distinction, Sir, your doubt secures,
'Tis not true reason I despise, but yours.

Thus I think reason righted, but for man,
I'll ne'er recant, defend him if you can.
For all his pride and his philosophy,
'Tis evident beasts are in their degree,
As wise at least, and better far than he.
Those creatures are the wisest who attain
By surest means, the ends at which they aim:
If therefore Jowler[4] finds and kills his hares,
Better than Meeres[5] supplies committee chairs;
Though one's a statesman, th'other but a hound,
Jowler in justice would be wiser found.
You see how far man's wisdom here extends;
Look next if human nature makes amends:
Whose principles most generous are and just,
And to whose morals you would sooner trust.
Be judge yourself, I'll bring it to the test,
Which is the basest creature, man or beast.
Birds feed on birds, beasts on each other prey,
But savage man alone does man betray:
Pressed by necessity they kill for food,
Man undoes man to do himself no good.
With teeth and claws by nature armed, they hunt
Nature's allowance to supply their want.
But man with smiles, embraces, friendship, praise,
Inhumanly his fellow's life betrays;
With voluntary pains works his distress,
Not through necessity, but wantonness.
For hunger or for love they fight and tear,
Whilst wretched man is still in arms for fear:
For fear he arms, and is of arms afraid,
By fear to fear successively betrayed.
Base fear! The source whence his best passion came,
His boasted honour, and his dear bought fame:
That lust of power, to which he's such a slave,
And for the which alone he dares be brave,
To which his various projects are designed,
Which makes him generous, affable and kind;
For which he takes such pains to be thought wise
And screws his actions in a forced disguise;
Leading a tedious life in misery
Under laborious mean hypocrisy:
Look to the bottom of his vast design,

[1] *Patrick's Pilgrim* Reference to *The Parable of the Pilgrim* (1665) by Simon Patrick, Bishop of Chichester and Ely; *Sibbes' Soliloquies* Sermons of Richard Sibbes (1577–1635), a Puritan apologist.

[2] *reverend bedlams* I.e., monasteries. "Bedlam," so called after London's Bedlam (originally, the Hospital of St. Mary of Bethlehem), a hospital for the mentally and emotionally ill.

[3] *whimsical ... prefer* Reference to the Greek Cynic philosopher Diogenes (c. 412-323 BCE), who is said to have temporarily resided in a large tub.

[4] *Jowler* Common name for a hunting dog.

[5] *Meeres* Sir Thomas Meeres (1635–1715), an industrious Lincoln MP who was a leading figure in the campaign against the Test Act, which imposed legal sanctions on Catholics and Dissenters.

Wherein man's wisdom, power and glory join;
The good he acts, the ill he does endure,
'Tis all from fear to make himself secure.
Merely for safety after fame we thirst;
For all men would be cowards if they durst.
And honesty's against all common sense;
Men must be knaves, 'tis in their own defence.
Mankind's dishonest, if you think it fair
Among known cheats to play upon the square,
You'll be undone—
Nor can weak truth your reputation save;
The knaves will all agree to call you knave.
Wronged shall he live, insulted o'er, oppressed,
Who dares be less a villain than the rest.
Thus, sir, you see what human nature craves,
Most men are cowards, all men should[1] be knaves.
The difference lies, as far as I can see,
Not in the thing itself, but the degree:
And all the subject matter of debate,
Is only who's a knave of the first rate.

ADDITION[2]
All this with indignation have I hurled
At the pretending part of the proud world,
Who swoll'n with selfish vanity, devise
False freedoms, holy cheats and formal lies,
Over their fellow slaves to tyrannize.
But if in court so just a man there be,
(In court a just man yet unknown to me)
Who does his needful flattery direct,
Not to oppress and ruin, but protect.
(Since flattery, which way so ever laid,
Is still a tax on that unhappy trade)
If so upright a statesman you can find,
Whose passions bend to his unbiased mind;
Who does his arts and policies apply,
To raise his country, not his family.
Nor while his pride owned avarice withstands,
Receives close bribes through friends' corrupted hands.
Is there a churchman who on God relies,
Whose life his faith and doctrine justifies;
Not one blown up with vain prelatic[3] pride,
Who for reproof of sins does man deride;
Whose envious heart makes preaching a pretence,
With his obstreperous saucy eloquence,
To chide at kings, and rail at men of sense.
Who from his pulpit vents more peevish lies,
More bitter railings, scandals, calumnies,
Than at a gossiping are thrown about
When the good wives get drunk and then fall out.
None of that sensual tribe, whose talents lie
In avarice, pride, sloth and gluttony,
Who hunt good livings,° but abhor good lives, *jobs*
Whose lust exalted to that height arrives,
They act° adultery with their own wives; *perform*
And ere a score of years completed be,
Can from the lofty pulpit proudly see
Half a large parish their own progeny.
Nor doting bishop, who would be adored
For domineering at the council board,
A greater fop in business at fourscore,[4]
Fonder of serious toys, affected more
Than the gay glittering fool at twenty proves,
With all his noise, his tawdry clothes and loves.
But a meek humble man of honest sense,
Who preaching peace does practice continence;° *chastity*
Whose pious life's a proof he does believe
Mysterious truths, which no man can conceive.
If upon earth there dwell such God-like men,
I'll here recant my paradox to them;
Adore those shrines of virtue, homage pay,
And, with the rabble world, their laws obey.
If such there be, yet grant me this at least,
Man differs more from man, than man from beast.
—1679

Love and Life: A Song

All my past life is mine no more;
The flying hours are gone,
Like transitory dreams giv'n o'er° *finished*
Whose images are kept in store
By memory alone.

Whatever is to come is not;
How can it then be mine?

[1] *should* I.e., wish to.

[2] *ADDITION* This second part was originally circulated separately.

[3] *prelatic* Characteristic of bishops.

[4] *fourscore* Eighty (four times a "score," or twenty).

The present moment's all my lot,[1]
And that as fast as it is got
Phyllis[2] is wholly thine.

Then talk not of inconstancy,
False hearts, and broken vows,
If I, by miracle can be
This livelong minute true to thee,
'Tis all that heav'n allows.
—1680

The Disabled Debauchee

As some brave admiral, in former war,
Deprived of force, but pressed with courage still,
Two rival fleets, appearing from afar,
Crawls to the top of an adjacent hill;

From whence (with thoughts full of concern) he views
The wise, and daring conduct of the fight,
And each bold action, to his mind renews,
His present glory, and his past delight;

From his fierce eyes, flashes of rage he throws,
As from black clouds, when lightning breaks away,
Transported, thinks himself amidst his foes,
And absent, yet enjoys the bloody day;

So when my days of impotence approach,
And I'm by pox° and wine's unlucky chance, *syphilis*
Forced from the pleasing billows of debauch,
On the dull shore of lazy temperance,

My pains at least some respite shall afford,
Whilst I behold the battles you maintain,
When fleets of glasses sail above the board,° *table*
From whose broadsides[3] volleys of wit shall rain.

Nor let the sight of honourable scars,
Which my too forward valour did procure,
Frighten new-listed° soldiers from the wars, *newly enlisted*
Past joys have more than paid what I endure.

Should any youth (worth being drunk) prove nice,[4]
And from his fair inviter meanly shrink,
'Twill please the ghost of my departed vice,[5]
If at my counsel, he repent and drink.

Or should some cold-complexioned[6] sot forbid,
With his dull morals, our night's brisk alarms,[7]
I'll fire his blood by telling what I did,
When I was strong, and able to bear arms.

I'll tell of whores attacked, their lords at home,
Bawds' quarters[8] beaten up, and fortress won,
Windows demolished, watches[9] overcome,
And handsome ills, by my contrivance done.

Nor shall our love-fits, Chloris,[10] be forgot,
When each the well-looked linkboy,[11] strove t' enjoy,
And the best kiss, was the deciding lot,
Whether the boy fucked you, or I the boy.

With tales like these, I will such thoughts inspire,
As to important mischief shall incline.
I'll make him long some ancient church to fire,
And fear no lewdness he's called to by wine.

Thus, statesmanlike, I'll saucily impose,
And safe from action valiantly advise,

[1] *Whatever ... my lot* Several critics read these lines as a paraphrase of a passage in Hobbes's *Leviathan*: "The present only has a being in nature; things past have a being in the memory only, but things to come have no being at all, the future being but a fiction of the mind."

[2] *Phyllis* Woman's name, common in pastoral poetry.

[3] *broadsides* Sides of a ship from which guns were fired; also sheets printed with news, ballads, proclamations, etc.

[4] *nice* Fastidious; fussy.

[5] *vice* Character in morality plays.

[6] *cold-complexioned* Reference to the medieval and Renaissance belief in the four humors, four liquids that constitute a person's temperament and physicality. Someone with a high proportion of the cold and moist phlegm would be considered phlegmatic, or calm and unemotional.

[7] *alarms* Signals calling men to arms or warning of danger.

[8] *Bawds' quarters* Houses kept by men or women for the purposes of prostitution.

[9] *watches* Watchmen or sentinels hired to keep order during the night.

[10] *Chloris* Woman's name, common in pastoral poetry.

[11] *linkboy* Boy hired to accompany people through the streets carrying a lighted link, or torch.

Sheltered in impotence, urge you to blows,
And being good for nothing else, be wise.
—1680

A Letter from Artemisia[1] in the Town to Chloe in the Country

Chloe, in verse by your command I write;
Shortly you'll bid me ride astride, and fight.
These talents better with our sex agree,
Than lofty flights of dang'rous poetry.
Amongst the men, I mean the men of wit
(At least they passed for such before they writ),
How many bold adventurers for the bays,[2]
(Proudly designing large returns of praise)
Who durst that stormy, pathless world explore,
Were soon dashed back, and wrecked on the dull shore,
Broke of that little stock, they had before?
How would a woman's tott'ring bark° be tossed, *ship*
Where stoutest ships (the men of wit) are lost?
When I reflect on this, I straight grow wise,
And my own self thus gravely I advise.
Dear Artemisia, poetry's a snare;
Bedlam[3] has many mansions: have a care.
Your muse diverts you, makes the reader sad;
You fancy, you're inspired, he thinks you mad.
Consider too, 'twill be discreetly done,
To make your self the fiddle° of the town, *jester*
To find th' ill-humoured pleasure at their need,
Cursed if you fail, and scorned, though you succeed.
Thus, like an arrant° woman, as I am, *notorious*
No sooner well convinced writing's a shame,
That whore is scarce a more reproachful name
Than poetess:
Like men that marry, or like maids that woo,
'Cause 'tis the very worst thing they can do,
Pleased with the contradiction and the sin,
Methinks I stand on thorns till I begin.
Y' expect at least to hear what loves have passed
In this lewd town since you and I met last.
What change has happened of intrigues, and whether
The old ones last, and who and who's together.
But how, my dearest Chloe, shall I set
My pen to write, what I would fain° forget, *willingly*
Or name that lost thing (love) without a tear
Since so debauched by ill-bred customs here?
Love, the most gen'rous passion of the mynde,
The softest refuge Innocence can fynde,
The safe directour of unguided youth,
Fraught with kind wishes, and secur'd by Trueth,
That Cordiall[4] dropp Heav'n in our Cup has throwne,
To make the nauseous draught of life goe downe,
On which one onely blessing God might rayse
In lands of Atheists Subsidyes of prayse
(For none did e're soe dull, and stupid prove,
But felt a God, and blest his pow'r in Love)
This onely Joy, for which poore Wee were made,
Is growne like play,° to be an Arrant Trade; *gaming*
The Rookes° creepe in, and it has gott of late *swindlers*
As many little Cheates, and Trickes, as that.
But what yet more a Womans heart would vexe,
'Tis cheifely carry'd on by our own Sexe,
Our silly Sexe, who borne, like Monarchs, free,
Turne Gipsyes for a meaner Liberty,[5]
And hate restraint, though but from Infamy.[6]
They call whatever is not Common, nice,° *fastidious*
And deafe to Natures rule, or Loves advice,
Forsake the pleasure, to pursue the Vice.
To an exact perfection they have wrought
The action, love, the passion is forgot.
'Tis below wit, they tell you, to admire,
And ev'n without approving they desire.
Their private wish obeys the public voice,
'Twist good and bad, whimsy decides, not choice.

[1] *Artemisia* Pen name, chosen perhaps as an allusion to a queen of Helicarnassus in Asia Minor. Artemisia joined Xerxes's forces during the Persian invasion of mainland Greece by commanding a small squadron of ships.

[2] *bays* Wreaths of laurel or bay leaves given in recognition of distinction in poetry.

[3] *Bedlam* Colloquial term for a hospital for the mentally ill, from the Hospital of Saint Mary of Bethlehem in London.

[4] *Cordiall* Invigorating medicine.

[5] *Turne ... Liberty* Turn into licentious and dishonorable people in order to be free in demeaning ways. The itinerant Romany people have been subject to systematic discrimination throughout Europe; as this line illustrates, the label that they have usually been given, "gypsies," has tended to have pejorative connotations.

[6] *Infamy* Disgraceful act.

Fashions grow up for taste, at forms they strike;
They know what they would have, not what they like.

Bovey's[1] a beauty, if some few agree
To call him so, the rest to that degree
Affected are, that with their ears they see.
Where I was visiting the other night,
Comes a fine lady with her humble knight,
Who had prevailed on her, through her own skill,
At his request, though much against his will,
To come to London.
As the coach stopped, we heard her voice, more loud
Than a great-bellied woman's in a crowd,
Telling the knight that her affairs require
He for some hours obsequiously retire.
I think she was ashamed to have him seen;
(Hard fate of husbands) the gallant had been,
Though a diseased, ill-favoured fool, brought in.
"Dispatch," says she, "that business you pretend,
Your beastly visit to your drunken friend;
A bottle ever makes you look so fine!
Methinks I long to smell you stink of wine.
Your country drinking breath's enough, to kill
Sour ale corrected with a lemon pill.
Prithee farewell—we'll meet again anon."
The necessary thing bows, and is gone.
She flies upstairs, and all the haste does show
That fifty antic° postures will allow, *ludicrous*
And then bursts out—"Dear madam, am not I
The altered'st creature breathing? Let me die,
I find my self ridiculously grown
Embarassé with being out of town,
Rude and untaught like any Indian queen;
My country nakedness is strangely seen."
How is love governed? Love, that rules the state,
And pray, who are the men most worn° of late? *fashionable*
When I was married fools were *à la mode*,° *in fashion*
The men of wit were then held *incommode*,° *unsuitable*
Slow of belief, and fickle in desire,
Who ere they'll be persuaded, must inquire
As if they came to spy, not to admire.
With searching wisdom fatal to their ease,
They still find out why what may, should not please;
Nay, take themselves for injured when we dare
Make 'em think better of us than we are;
And if we hide our frailties from their sights,
Call us deceitful jilts[2] and hypocrites.
They little guess who at our arts are grieved,
The perfect joy of being well deceived.
Inquisitive as jealous cuckolds[3] grow,
Rather than not be knowing, they will know
What, being known, creates their certain woe.
Women should these of all mankind avoid,
For wonder by clear knowledge is destroyed.
Woman, who is an arrant bird of night,
Bold in the dusk, before a fool's dull sight,
Should fly when reason brings the glaring light.
But the kind easy fool, apt to admire
Himself, trusts us; his follies all conspire
To flatter his and favour our desire.
Vain of his proper merit, he with ease
Believes we love him best who best can please.
On him our gross, dull, common flatt'ries pass,
Ever most joyful when most made an ass.
Heavy to apprehend, though all mankind
Perceive us false, the fop concerned is blind,
Who, doting on himself,
Thinks everyone that sees him of his mind.

These are true women's men.—Here forced to cease
Through want of breath, not will, to hold her peace,
She to the window runs, where she had spied
Her much esteemed dear friend, the monkey, tied.
With forty smiles, as many antic bows,
As if 't had been the lady of the house,
The dirty, chatt'ring monster she embraced,
And made it this fine tender speech at last:
"Kiss me, thou curious miniature of man.
How odd thou art. How pretty. How Japan.[4]
Oh I could live and die with thee." Then on
For half an hour in compliment she run.
I took this time to think what nature meant,
When this mixed thing into the world she sent,
So very wise, yet so impertinent.
One who knew everything, who, God thought fit,
Should be an ass through choice, not want of wit;
Whose foppery, without the help of sense,

[1] *Bovey's* Possibly a reference to Sir Ralph Bovey, a contemporary of Rochester.

[2] *jilts* Here, harlots or strumpets.

[3] *cuckolds* Husbands of unfaithful wives.

[4] *Japan* Fashionable, relating to the interest in Japanese goods.

Could ne'er have rose to such an excellence.
Nature's as lame in making a true fop
As a philosopher; the very top
And dignity of folly we attain
By studious search and labour of the brain,
By observation, counsel, and deep thought;
God never made a coxcomb° worth a groat.[1] *conceited fop*
We owe that name to industry and arts:
An eminent fool must be a fool of parts;
And such a one was she, who had turned o'er
As many books as men, loved much, read more,
Had a discerning wit; to her was known
Everyone's fault and merit but her own.
All the good qualities that ever blessed
A woman, so distinguished from the rest,
Except discretion only, she possessed.
"But now, *mon cher*, dear Pug,"[2] she cries, "*adieu*,"
And the discourse broke off does thus renew.

You smile to see me, whom the world perchance
Mistakes to have some wit, so far advance
The interest of fools, that I approve
Their merit more than men's of wit, in love.
But in our sex too many proofs there are
Of such whom wits undo and fools repair.
This in my time was so observed a rule,
Hardly a wench in town but had her fool.
The meanest common slut, who long was grown
The jest and scorn of every pit buffoon[3]
Had yet left charms enough to have subdued
Some fop or other fond° to be thought lewd. *eager*
Foster could make an Irish lord a Nokes,[4]
And Betty Morris[5] had her city cokes.° *dupes*
A woman's ne'er so ruined but she can
Be still revenged on her undoer, man.
How lost so e'er she'll find some lover more

[1] *groat* Silver coin equal to four pence.

[2] *Pug* Name at this date for a monkey rather than a dog.

[3] *pit buffoon* The pit, or the floor of the theater, was the preferred seating area for the fashionable men of London. This part of the audience was noted for its noisy and disruptive behavior; a "pit buffoon" would be such an audience member.

[4] *Foster* Foster may be a lower-class woman mentioned by John Muddyman in a 1671 letter to Rochester; *Nokes* James Nokes, actor in the Duke's Company who regularly played the role of a fool.

[5] *Betty Morris* Probably a prostitute. Betty Morris is also mentioned in Wilmot's "An Allusion to Horace" (111).

A lewd abandoned fool than she a whore.
That wretched thing Corinna, who had run
Through all the several ways of being undone,
Cozened° at first by love and living then *deceived*
By turning the too-dear-bought trick on men.[6]
Gay were the hours, and winged with joys they flew,
When first the town her early beauties knew,
Courted, admired, and loved, with presents fed,
Youth in her looks and pleasure in her bed,
Till fate, or her ill angel, thought it fit
To make her dote upon a man of wit,
Who found 'twas dull to love above a day,
Made his ill-natured jest, and went away.
Now scorned by all, forsaken and oppressed,
She's a *memento mori* ° to the rest. *reminder of death*
Diseased, decayed, to take up half a crown,
Must mortgage her long scarf and mantua gown.
Poor creature! who, unheard of as a fly,
In some dark hole must all the winter lie,
And want and dirt endure a whole half year,
That for one month she tawdry may appear.
In Easter term she gets her a new gown,
When my young master's worship comes to town,
From pedagogue[7] and mother just set free,
The heir and hopes of a great family,
Which, with strong ale and beef, the country rules,
And ever since the Conquest[8] have been fools.
And now with careful prospect to maintain
This character, lest crossing of the strain
Should mend the booby° breed, his friends provide *useless, stupid*
A cousin of his own to be his bride;
And thus set out—
With an estate, no wit, and a young wife
(The solid comforts of a coxcomb's life),
Dung-hill and pease forsook, he comes to town,
Turns spark,[9] learns to be lewd, and is undone.
Nothing suits worse with vice than want of sense;
Fools are still wicked at their own expense.
This o'ergrown schoolboy lost-Corinna wins,
And at first dash to make an ass begins:

[6] *turning ... men* Becoming a prostitute.

[7] *young master's ... pedagogue* University student in London during term break.

[8] *the Conquest* Norman Conquest of England, 1066 CE.

[9] *spark* Young man of smart dress and manners.

Pretends to like a man who has not known
The vanities nor vices of the town;
Fresh in his youth and faithful in his love,
Eager of joys, which he does seldom prove,
Healthful and strong, he does no pains endure,
But what the fair one he adores can cure.
Grateful for favours does the sex esteem,
And libels none for being kind to him.
Then of the lewdness of the times complains,
Rails at the wits and atheists and maintains
'Tis better than good sense, than pow'r or wealth,
To have a love untainted, youth, and health.
The unbred puppy, who had never seen
A creature look so gay or talk so fine,
Believes, then falls in love, and then in debt,
Mortgages all, ev'n to th' ancient seat,° *estate*
To buy this mistress a new house for life;
To give her plate° and jewels, robs his wife; *silver*
And when to the height of fondness he is grown,
'Tis time to poison him, and all's her own.
Thus meeting in her common[1] arms his fate,
He leaves her bastard heir to his estate;
And as the race of such an owl deserves,
His own dull lawful progeny he starves.
Nature, who never made a thing in vain,
But does each insect to some end ordain,
Wisely contrived kind-keeping fools, no doubt,
To patch up vices men of wit wear out.
Thus she ran on two hours, some grains of sense
Still mixed with volleys of impertinence.
But now 'tis time, I should some pity show
To Chloe, since I cannot choose but know
Readers must reap the dullness writers sow.
By the next post such stories I will tell
As joined with these shall to a volume swell,
As true as heaven, more infamous than hell;
But you are tired, and so am I. Farewell.
—1680

[1] *common* Also used by other men.

The Imperfect Enjoyment[2]

Naked she lay, clasped in my longing arms,
I filled with love, and she all over charms,
Both equally inspired with eager fire,
Melting through kindness,[3] flaming in desire;
With arms, legs, lips, close clinging to embrace,
She clips me to her breast, and sucks me to her face.
The nimble tongue (Love's lesser lightning) played
Within my mouth, and to my thoughts conveyed
Swift orders that I should prepare to throw,
The all-dissolving thunderbolt below.
My flutt'ring soul, sprung with the pointed kiss,
Hangs hov'ring o'er her balmy brinks of bliss.
But whilst her busy hand would guide that part,
Which should convey my soul up to her heart,
In liquid raptures I dissolve all o'er,
Melt into sperm, and spend° at every pore: *ejaculate*
A touch from any part of her had done 't,
Her hand, her foot, her very look's a cunt.
Smiling, she chides in a kind murm'ring noise,
And from her body wipes the clammy joys;
When with a thousand kisses, wand'ring o'er
My panting bosom, "Is there then no more?"
She cries. "All this to love and rapture's due,
Must we not pay a debt to pleasure too?"
But I, the most forlorn, lost man alive,
To show my wished obedience vainly strive,
I sigh alas! and kiss, but cannot swive.° *copulate*
Eager desires confound my first intent,
Succeeding shame does more success prevent,
And rage at last confirms me impotent.
Ev'n her fair hand, which might bid heat return
To frozen age, and make cold hermits burn,
Applied to my dead cinder, warms no more
Than fire to ashes, could past flames restore.
Trembling, confused, despairing, limber, dry,
A wishing, weak, unmoving lump I lie.
This dart of love, whose piercing point oft tried,
With virgin blood, ten thousand maids have dyed;
Which nature still directed with such art,

[2] *The Imperfect Enjoyment* Stemming from Ovid's *Amores*, the tradition of seventeenth-century "imperfect enjoyment" poems includes works by Aphra Behn and George Etherege, as well as by several French poets.

[3] *kindness* Instinct.

That it through every cunt reached every heart.
Stiffly resolved, 'twould carelessly invade
Woman or man, nor ought its fury stayed,
Where'er it pierced, a cunt it found or made.
Now languid lies in this unhappy hour,
Shrunk up and sapless, like a withered flow'r.
Thou treacherous, base, deserter of my flame,
False to my passion, fatal to my fame;
Through what mistaken magic dost thou prove
So true to lewdness, so untrue to love?
What oyster, cinder,[1] beggar, common whore,
Didst thou e'er fail in all thy life before?
When vice, disease, and scandal lead the way,
With what officious haste dost thou obey?
Like a rude, roaring hector[2] in the streets,
That scuffles, cuffs, and ruffles all he meets,
But if his king or country claim his aid,
The rakehell° villain shrinks and hides his head; *debauched*
Ev'n so thy brutal valour is displayed,
Breaks every stew,° does each small whore invade, *brothel*
But when great Love the onset does command,
Base recreant[3] to thy prince, thou dar'st not stand.
Worst part of me, and henceforth hated most,
Through all the town, a common fucking post,
On whom each whore relieves her tingling cunt,
As hogs on gates do rub themselves and grunt.
May'st thou to rav'nous chancres° be a prey, *syphilitic ulcers*
Or in consuming weepings waste away.
May strangury and stone[4] thy days attend,
May'st thou ne'er piss, who didst refuse to spend,
When all my joys did on false thee depend.
And may ten thousand abler pricks agree,
To do the wronged Corinna[5] right for thee.
—1680

Impromptu on Charles II

God bless our good and gracious King,
Whose promise none relies on;
Who never said a foolish thing,
Nor ever did a wise one.
—1707

[1] *oyster, cinder* Some of the poorest women on the streets, oyster women and cinder women were considered potential prostitutes.

[2] *hector* Rowdy young man.

[3] *recreant* One who is unfaithful to his or her duty.

[4] *strangury and stone* Diseases characterized by painful and slow urination.

[5] *Corinna* Woman's name, common in pastoral poetry.

In Context

The Lessons of Rochester's Life

ADVERTISEMENT.

ALL the lewd and profane poems and libels of the late Lord Rocheſter having been (contrary to his dying requeſt, and in defiance of religion, government, and common decency) publiſhed to the world; and (for the eaſier and ſurer propagation of vice) printed in penny-books, and cried about the ſtreets of this honourable city, without any offence or diſlike taken at them: it is humbly hoped that this ſhort diſcourſe, which gives a true account of the death and repentance of that noble lord, may likewiſe (for the ſake of his name) find a favourable reception among ſuch perſons; though the influence of it cannot be ſuppoſed to reach as far as the poiſon of the other books is ſpread; which, by the ſtrength of their own virulent corruption, are capable of doing more miſchief than all the plays, and fairs, and ſtews, in and about this town can do together.

Advertisement and opening page, Robert Parson's "Sermon Preached at Rochester's Funeral," facsimile page from a volume c. 1780 entitled *Rochester's Life,* which brought together Samuel Johnson's "Preface" to Rochester's works, Gilbert Burnet's account of *The Life and Death of John Rochester,* and Parson's sermon. Material of this sort concerning Rochester continued to be republished through the eighteenth century.

Daniel Defoe

1660 – 1731

In 1660 Daniel Foe was born to Alice and James Foe; his father was an eminent London and area tradesman and tallow chandler. His parents were Puritan Dissenters or Nonconformists (individuals who separated themselves from the national church) and at the age of ten, shortly after his mother's death, Daniel was sent to a private Nonconformist school in Dorking, and then to a notable academy for Dissenters run by Dr. Charles Morton. While in attendance at school, he was tutored according to a more unconventional curriculum than was commonplace; the study of Greek and Latin was underplayed in favor of a strong education in science, philosophy, civil law, and modern history.

By 1679, while many of his classmates prepared for careers in the ministry, Foe entered his father's world of trade. In his early twenties, he became a partner in a haberdashery, and quickly expanded his interests as a wholesaler of wine, tobacco, textiles, and other commodities. Foe was married in 1684 to Mary Tuffley, the daughter of a London merchant family. Mary Foe would live to bear her husband eight children, and the marriage survived over fifty years of political turbulence, personal danger, and financial ruin. It was shortly after his marriage that Foe began involving himself, often to his own personal and professional peril, in the capricious world of English politics.

An ardent Whig and a Dissenter, Foe strongly opposed the Catholic James II, and chose to fight in the failed Monmouth Rebellion of 1685. In consequence he was forced to spend much of the next two years in hiding; during this time he continued to speak in anonymous pamphlets against the King's religious policies. When the Glorious Revolution brought the Protestant William III to the throne in 1688, Foe offered his services to the new king—as an author and also as a secret agent. Ironically, Foe's business ventures met with disaster partly due to William's policies; when the new king went to war with France he lost many lucrative trading connections. These problems, compounded by the failure of some risky ventures into ship insurance, forced him to declare bankruptcy in 1692.

Never allowing his energy and pride to fail him, Foe began to focus on writing for his livelihood. It was at this period that he began to add the French *de* to his surname, as he launched into a long and prolific career as an essayist, poet, and novelist. In 1697 Defoe completed his first substantial book, *An Essay upon Projects*, followed four years later by his more popular *The True-Born Englishman*, in which he attacked "loyal" and "native" Britons who condemned their king for being a foreigner. The unexpected death of William III in 1702 once again brought Defoe's fortunes into doubt, as Queen Anne launched a new assault on Nonconformists. Undeterred, Defoe anonymously published *The Shortest Way with Dissenters*, a deliberately crafted hoax in which he mimicked the rhetoric of High Tory officials in an exaggerated argument for the extermination of all Dissenters. It did not take long for his enemies to discover the identity of the pamphlet's author, and a warrant was issued for Defoe's arrest. After four months of hiding, Defoe was arrested and sentenced to stand three times in the pillory, and to serve an indefinite period of time in Newgate Prison "at the Queen's pleasure." While in prison Defoe managed to arrange for publication of a mock ode, *Hymn to the Pillory* (1703), which was popularly sold in the streets; to the author's surprise, as he stood in the pillory he was pelted with flowers rather than with putrid vegetables.

In spite of his rise in popularity with the common reader, Defoe was in a bad state. His indefinite prison sentence had ruined his new business (as a partner in a brick and tile factory) and his ability to provide for his large family had grown extraordinarily limited. It was an ambitious Tory politician, Robert Harley, who brought about a change in Defoe's fortunes. Harley approached Defoe with an offer to work as a literary secret agent for the Tory cause; in return Harley arranged to pay some of Defoe's fines and debts, and secured his release from jail. Disillusioned with his Whig allies, Defoe accepted, and as a result of Harley's influence was released from prison in November, 1703.

From 1703 to 1714 Defoe served his Tory benefactors as a pamphleteer and political spy, traveling throughout England and Scotland and sending reports back to Harley on how the counties felt about the government. From 1704 to 1713 he wrote and edited the thrice-weekly periodical *A Review of the Affairs of France: and of All Europe, as Influenc'd by That Nation*, which offered commentary on foreign and domestic affairs, and published numerous other works, including his ambitious political poem in twelve books, *The History of the Union of Great Britain* (1709).

With the death of Queen Anne in 1714, the political tide turned once again, and the newly installed Whig leaders quickly realized the value of Defoe's position, engaging him to deliver "Tory" political messages infiltrated with the voice of the opposing Whig point of view. Although it has been said that Defoe's changing allegiances demonstrated a lack of principled politics, it has also plausibly been argued that his ability to take on the voice of another with conviction allowed him to play against both Whig and Tory extremes throughout the course of his party employment, and that his aim had generally been to advocate a reasonable and moderate course between partisan extremes.

It was not until the last decade of his life that Defoe turned to writing fiction. In 1719 he published what purported to be the true account of the strange and surprising adventures of one Robinson Crusoe, a mariner of York. Based on the actual accounts of William Selkirk, a castaway for four years on the remote island of Juan Fernandez, *Robinson Crusoe* was the first of Defoe's "true histories" in which the author imaginatively relayed the events and memoirs of a fictitious character's life, all the while creating a convincing air of truth behind every detail. *Robinson Crusoe* proved so popular that Defoe issued two sequels to the story, *The Farther Adventures of Robinson Crusoe* (1719), and *Reflections During the Life and Surprising Adventures of Robinson Crusoe* (1720). In the next five years he followed the success of these fictional "memoirs" with such works as *The Life, Adventures, and Pyracies of the Famous Captain Singleton* (1720), *The Fortunes and Misfortunes of the Famous Moll Flanders* (1721), *Colonel Jack* (1722), *A Journal of the Plague Year* (1722), and *Roxana* (1724). With these works Defoe secured his position as a leading popular author. His reputation among his contemporaries never rivaled that of Pope, Dryden, or other leading poets, but in the centuries since his work has arguably been at least as influential; Defoe is universally acknowledged as a founding figure in the history of the English novel.

In the final years of his life Defoe continued to publish considerable works of non-fiction according to his interests, including *A Tour Through the Whole Island of Great Britain* (1724–27), *The Great Law of Subordination Considered* (1724), and *The Complete English Tradesman* (1726). Becoming increasingly interested in the supernatural, he also published *The Political History of the Devil* (1726) and *An Essay on the History and Reality of Apparitions* (1727). Despite the success of his fictional narratives and his furious rate of publication, Defoe continued to struggle financially. In the last months before his death, he was forced into hiding in order to avoid debtor's prison. In an effort to hide his whereabouts, Defoe returned to the parish of his birth, where he died on 24 April 1731. He is buried in Bunhill Fields, where his grave lies amongst other notable Dissenters of his century, including John Bunyan, Isaac Watts, and William Blake.

⌘⌘⌘

A True Relation of the Apparition of One Mrs. Veal the Next Day after her Death to One Mrs. Bargrave at Canterbury the 8th of September, 1705[1]

The Preface

This relation is matter of fact, and attended with such circumstances as may induce any reasonable man to believe it. It was sent by a gentleman, a justice of peace at Maidstone, in Kent, and a very intelligent person, to his friend in London, as it is here worded; which discourse is attested by a very sober and understanding gentlewoman, a kinswoman of the said gentleman's, who lives in Canterbury, within a few doors of the house in which the within-named Mrs. Bargrave lives; who believes his kinswoman to be of so discerning a spirit as not to be put upon by any fallacy; and who positively assured him that the whole matter, as it is related and laid down, is really true; and what she herself had in the same words, as near as may be, from Mrs. Bargrave's own mouth, who, she knows, had no reason to invent and publish such a story, or any design to forge and tell a lie, being a woman of much honesty and virtue, and her whole life a course, as it were, of piety. The use which we ought to make of it is to consider that there is a life to come after this, and a just God, who will retribute to every one according to the deeds done in the body; and therefore to reflect upon our past course of life we have led in the world; that our time is short and uncertain; and that if we would escape the punishment of the ungodly, and receive the reward of the righteous, which is the laying hold of eternal life, we ought, for the time to come, to return to God by a speedy repentance, ceasing to do evil and learning to do well: to seek after God early, if happily he may be found of us, and lead such lives for the future, as may be well pleasing in his sight.

A Relation of the Apparition of Mrs. Veal

This thing is so rare in all its circumstances, and on so good authority, that my reading and conversation has not given me anything like it; it is fit to gratify the most ingenious and serious inquirer. Mrs. Bargrave is the person to whom Mrs. Veal appeared after her death; she is my intimate friend, and I can avouch for her reputation for these last fifteen or sixteen years on my own knowledge, and I can confirm the good character she had from her youth to the time of my acquaintance. Though, since this relation, she is calumniated by some people that are friends to the brother of this Mrs. Veal, who appeared; who think the relation of this appearance to be a reflection, and endeavour what they can to blast Mrs. Bargrave's reputation, and to laugh the story out of countenance. But by the circumstances thereof, and the cheerful disposition of Mrs. Bargrave, notwithstanding the ill-usage of a very wicked husband, there is not yet the least sign of dejection in her face; nor did I ever hear her let fall a desponding or murmuring expression; nay, not when actually under her husband's barbarity, which I have been witness to, and several other persons of undoubted reputation.

Now you must know that Mrs. Veal was a maiden[2] gentlewoman of about thirty years of age, and for some years last past had been troubled with fits, which were perceived coming on her by her going off from her discourse very abruptly to some impertinence. She was maintained by an only brother, and kept his house in Dover. She was a very pious woman, and her brother a very sober man to all appearance; but now he does all he can to null or quash the story. Mrs. Veal was intimately acquainted with Mrs. Bargrave from her childhood. Mrs. Veal's circumstances were then mean;[3] her father did not take care of his children as he ought, so that they were exposed to hardships; and Mrs. Bargrave, in those days, had as unkind a father, though she wanted neither for food nor clothing, whilst Mrs. Veal wanted for both. So that it was in the power of Mrs. Bargrave to

[1] *A True ... 1705* First published as an anonymous pamphlet, this work was originally thought to be an entirely fictional account, possibly written to support Charles Drelincourt's *Defense Against the Fears of Death*, which is repeatedly praised by Mrs. Veal. In the late nineteenth century, however, evidence came to light that the story was based, at least in part, on alleged fact. Defoe scholar George Aitkin published a Latin note recording an interview with a real Mrs. Bargrave, and other contemporary records of Mrs. Bargrave's story were discovered, including an account printed in the *Loyal Post*. Here Defoe gives his own account of the strange appearance of Mrs. Veal, using the perspective of a fictional friend.

[2] *Mrs. Veal ... maiden* During this time, the title Mrs. or mistress did not imply marriage.

[3] *mean* Poor.

be very much her friend in several instances, which mightily endeared Mrs. Veal; insomuch that she would often say, "Mrs. Bargrave, you are not only the best, but the only friend I have in the world, and no circumstance of life shall ever dissolve my friendship." They would often condole each other's adverse fortunes, and read together *Drelincourt upon Death*,[1] and other good books. And so, like two Christian friends, they comforted each other under their sorrow.

Sometime after, Mr. Veal's friends got him a place in the custom-house at Dover, which occasioned Mrs. Veal, by little and little, to fall off from her intimacy with Mrs. Bargrave, though there was never any such thing as a quarrel. But an indifference came on by degrees, till at last Mrs. Bargrave had not seen her in two years and a half; though above a twelvemonth of the time Mrs. Bargrave hath been absent from Dover, and this last half year has been in Canterbury about two months of the time, dwelling in a house of her own.

In this house, on the 8th of September, 1705, she was sitting alone in the forenoon, thinking over her unfortunate life, and arguing herself into a due resignation to Providence, though her condition seemed hard. And said she, "I have been provided for hitherto, and doubt not but I shall be still; and am well satisfied that my afflictions shall end when it is most fit for me." And then took up her sewing-work, which she had no sooner done but she hears a knocking at the door. She went to see who was there, and this proved to be Mrs. Veal, her old friend, who was in a riding-habit. At that moment of time the clock struck twelve at noon.

"Madam," says Mrs. Bargrave, "I am surprised to see you; you have been so long a stranger," but told her she was glad to see her, and offered to salute[2] her; which Mrs. Veal complied with till their lips almost touched; and then Mrs. Veal drew her hand across her own eyes and said, "I am not very well," and so waived it. She told Mrs. Bargrave she was going a journey, and had a great mind to see her first. "But," says Mrs. Bargrave, "how came you to take a journey alone? I am amazed at it, because I know you have a fond brother." "Oh!" says Mrs. Veal, "I gave my brother the slip and came away, because I had so great a desire to see you before I took my journey." So Mrs. Bargrave went in with her, into another room within the first, and Mrs. Veal sat her down in an elbow-chair,[3] in which Mrs. Bargrave was sitting when she heard Mrs. Veal knock. Then says Mrs. Veal, "My dear friend, I am come to renew our old friendship again, and beg your pardon for my breach of it; and if you can forgive me, you are the best of women." "O," says Mrs. Bargrave, "do not mention such a thing. I have not had an uneasy thought about it; I can easily forgive it." "What did you think of me?" said Mrs. Veal. Says Mrs. Bargrave, "I thought you were like the rest of the world, and that prosperity had made you forget yourself and me." Then Mrs. Veal reminded Mrs. Bargrave of the many friendly offices she did her in former days, and much of the conversation they had with each other in the times of their adversity; what books they read, and what comfort, in particular, they received from *Drelincourt's Book of Death*, which was the best, she said, on that subject ever wrote. She also mentioned Dr. Sherlock,[4] and two Dutch books which were translated, wrote upon death, and several others. But Drelincourt, she said, had the clearest notions of death, and of the future state, of any who had handled that subject. Then she asked Mrs. Bargrave whether she had Drelincourt. She said, "Yes." Says Mrs. Veal, "Fetch it." And so Mrs. Bargrave goes up stairs and brings it down. Says Mrs. Veal, "Dear Mrs. Bargrave, if the eyes of our faith were as open as the eyes of our body, we should see numbers of angels about us for our guard. The notions we have of heaven now are nothing like what it is, as Drelincourt says; therefore be comforted under your afflictions, and believe that the Almighty has a particular regard to you, and that your afflictions are marks of God's favour; and when they have done the business they are sent for, they shall be removed from you. And, believe me, my dear friend, believe what I say to you, one minute of future happiness will infinitely reward you for all your sufferings. For I can never believe" (and claps her hand upon her knee with great earnestness, which indeed ran through most of her discourse) "that ever God will suffer you to spend all your days in this afflicted state. But be assured that your

[1] *Drelincourt upon Death* French Protestant pastor and devotional writer Charles Drelincourt's *The Christian Defense against the Fears of Death* (1651).

[2] *salute* Kiss.

[3] *elbow-chair* Armchair.

[4] *Dr. Sherlock* William Sherlock (1640–1707), Church of England clergyman and author of *Practical Discourse upon Death* (1689).

afflictions shall leave you, or you them, in a short time." She spake in that pathetical and heavenly manner, that Mrs. Bargrave wept several times, she was so deeply affected with it. Then Mrs. Veal mentioned Dr. Horneck's *Ascetic*,[1] at the end of which he gives an account of the lives of the primitive Christians. Their pattern she recommended to our imitation, and said their conversation was not like this of our age. "For now," says she, "there is nothing but frothy, vain discourse, which is far different from theirs. Theirs was to edification, and to build one another up in faith; so that they were not as we are, nor are we as they were. But," says she, "we ought to do as they did. There was an hearty friendship among them; but where is it now to be found?" Says Mrs. Bargrave, "It is hard indeed to find a true friend in these days." Says Mrs. Veal, "Mr. Norris[2] has a fine copy of verses called *Friendship in Perfection*, which I wonderfully admire. Have you seen the book?" says Mrs. Veal. "No," says Mrs. Bargrave, "but I have the verses of my own writing out." "Have you?" says Mrs. Veal, "Then fetch them." Which she did from above stairs, and offered them to Mrs. Veal to read, who refused, and waived the thing, saying holding down her head would make it ache, and then desired Mrs. Bargrave to read them to her, which she did. As they were admiring friendship, Mrs. Veal said, "Dear Mrs. Bargrave, I shall love you for ever. In these verses there is twice used the word Elysium. Ah!" says Mrs. Veal, "these poets have such names for heaven." She would often draw her hand across her own eyes, and say, "Mrs. Bargrave, do not you think I am mightily impaired by my fits?" "No," says Mrs. Bargrave, "I think you look as well as ever I knew you."

After all this discourse, which the apparition put in much finer words than Mrs. Bargrave said she could pretend to, and as much more than she can remember (for it cannot be thought that an hour and three quarters' conversation could all be retained, though the main of it she thinks she does). She said to Mrs. Bargrave she would have her write a letter to her brother, and tell him she would have him give rings to such and such, and that there was a purse of gold in her cabinet, and that she would have two broad pieces given to her cousin Watson. Talking at this rate, Mrs. Bargrave thought that a fit was coming upon her, and so placed herself in a chair just before her knees, to keep her from falling to the ground if her fits should occasion it: for the elbow-chair, she thought, would keep her from falling on either side. And to divert Mrs. Veal, as she thought, she took hold of her gown sleeve several times, and commended it. Mrs. Veal told her it was a scoured[3] silk, and newly made up. But for all this, Mrs. Veal persisted in her request, and told Mrs. Bargrave she must not deny her, and she would have her tell her brother all their conversation, when she had opportunity. "Dear Mrs. Veal," says Mrs. Bargrave, "this seems so impertinent that I cannot tell how to comply with it; and what a mortifying story will our conversation be to a young gentleman?" "Well," says Mrs. Veal, "I must not be denied." "Why," says Mrs. Bargrave, "it is much better, methinks, to do it yourself." "No," says Mrs. Veal, "though it seems impertinent to you now, you will see more reason for it hereafter." Mrs. Bargrave then, to satisfy her importunity, was going to fetch a pen and ink; but Mrs. Veal said, "Let it alone now, and do it when I am gone; but you must be sure to do it." Which was one of the last things she enjoined her at parting; and so she promised her.

Then Mrs. Veal asked for Mrs. Bargrave's daughter. She said she was not at home. "But if you have a mind to see her," says Mrs. Bargrave, "I'll send for her." "Do," says Mrs. Veal. On which she left her and went to a neighbour's to see for her; and by the time Mrs. Bargrave was returning, Mrs. Veal was got without the door in the street, in the face of the beast-market on a Saturday, which is market-day, and stood ready to part as soon as Mrs. Bargrave came to her. She asked her why she was in such haste. She said she must be going, though perhaps she might not go her journey till Monday; and told Mrs. Bargrave she hoped she should see her again at her cousin Watson's before she went whither she was a-going. Then she said she would take her leave of her, and walked from Mrs. Bargrave in her view, till a turning interrupted the sight of her, which was three quarters after one in the afternoon.

Mrs. Veal died the 7th of September at twelve o'clock at noon, of her fits, and had not above four hours' senses before her death, in which time she

[1] *Dr. Horneck's Ascetic* Church of England clergyman Anthony Horneck's *The Happy Ascetic* (1681).

[2] *Mr. Norris* Clergyman and philosopher John Norris (1657–1712).

[3] *scoured* Treated with detergent.

received the sacrament. The next day after Mrs. Veal's appearing, being Sunday, Mrs. Bargrave was mightily indisposed with a cold and a sore throat, that she could not go out that day; but on Monday morning she sent a person to Captain Watson's to know if Mrs. Veal was there. They wondered at Mrs. Bargrave's inquiry, and sent her word that she was not there, nor was expected. At this answer Mrs. Bargrave told the maid she had certainly mistook the name, or made some blunder. And though she was ill, she put on her hood and went herself to Captain Watson's, though she knew none of the family, to see if Mrs. Veal was there or not. They said they wondered at her asking, for that she had not been in town; they were sure, if she had, she would have been there. Says Mrs. Bargrave, "I am sure she was with me on Saturday almost two hours." They said it was impossible, for they must have seen her if she had. In comes Captain Watson, while they were in dispute, and said that Mrs. Veal was certainly dead, and her escutcheons were making.[1] This strangely surprised Mrs. Bargrave, who went to the person immediately who had the care of them, and found it true. Then she related the whole story to Captain Watson's family, and what gown she had on, and how striped; and that Mrs. Veal told her it was scoured. Then Mrs. Watson cried out, "You have seen her indeed, for none knew but Mrs. Veal and myself that gown was scoured!" And Mrs. Watson owned that she described the gown exactly. "For," said she, "I helped her to make it up." This, Mrs. Watson blazed all about the town, and avouched the demonstration of the truth of Mrs. Bargrave's seeing Mrs. Veal's apparition. And Captain Watson carried two gentlemen immediately to Mrs. Bargrave's house to hear the relation of her own mouth. And then it spread so fast that gentlemen and persons of quality, the judicious and sceptical part of the world, flocked in upon her, which at last became such a task that she was forced to go out of the way. For they were, in general, extremely satisfied of the truth of the thing, and plainly saw that Mrs. Bargrave was no hypochondriac; for she always appears with such a cheerful air and pleasing mien that she has gained the favour and esteem of all the gentry, and it is thought a great favour if they can but get the relation from her own mouth. I should have told you before that Mrs. Veal told Mrs. Bargrave that her sister and brother-in-law were just come down from London to see her. Says Mrs. Bargrave, "How came you to order matters so strangely?" "It could not be helped," says Mrs. Veal. And her brother and sister did come to see her, and entered the town of Dover just as Mrs. Veal was expiring. Mrs. Bargrave asked her whether she would drink some tea. Says Mrs. Veal, "I do not care if I do; but I'll warrant you, this mad fellow" (meaning Mrs. Bargrave's husband) "has broke all your trinkets." "But," says Mrs. Bargrave, "I'll get something to drink in for all that." But Mrs. Veal waived it, and said, "It is no matter, let it alone." And so it passed.

All the time I sat with Mrs. Bargrave, which was some hours, she recollected fresh sayings of Mrs. Veal. And one material thing more she told Mrs. Bargrave, that old Mr. Breton allowed Mrs. Veal ten pounds a year, which was a secret, and unknown to Mrs. Bargrave till Mrs. Veal told it her. Mrs. Bargrave never varies in her story, which puzzles those who doubt of the truth, or are unwilling to believe it. A servant in the neighbour's yard adjoining to Mrs. Bargrave's house heard her talking to somebody an hour of the time Mrs. Veal was with her. Mrs. Bargrave went out to her next neighbour's the very moment she parted with Mrs. Veal, and told her what ravishing conversation she had with an old friend, and told the whole of it. *Drelincourt's Book of Death* is, since this happened, bought up strangely. And it is to be observed that notwithstanding all the trouble and fatigue Mrs. Bargrave has undergone upon this account, she never took the value of a farthing, nor suffered her daughter to take anything of anybody, and therefore can have no interest in telling the story.

But Mr. Veal does what he can to stifle the matter, and said he would see Mrs. Bargrave; but yet it is certain matter of fact that he has been at Captain Watson's since the death of his sister, and yet never went near Mrs. Bargrave. And some of his friends report her to be a liar, and that she knew of Mr. Breton's ten pounds a year. But the person who pretends to say so has the reputation of a notorious liar among persons whom I know to be of undoubted credit. Now Mr. Veal is more of a gentleman than to say she lies, but says a bad husband has crazed her. But she needs only present herself, and it will effectually confute that pretense. Mr. Veal says he asked his sister on her deathbed whether she

[1] *her escutcheons were making* Her funeral ornaments were being made.

had a mind to dispose of anything, and she said, "No." Now, the things which Mrs. Veal's apparition would have disposed of were so trifling, and nothing of justice aimed at in their disposal, that the design of it appears to me to be only in order to make Mrs. Bargrave so to demonstrate the truth of her appearance as to satisfy the world of the reality thereof, as to what she had seen and heard, and to secure her reputation among the reasonable and understanding part of mankind. And then again, Mr. Veal owns that there was a purse of gold, but it was not found in her cabinet, but in a comb-box. This looks improbable, for that Mrs. Watson owned that Mrs. Veal was so very careful of the key of the cabinet that she would trust nobody with it. And if so, no doubt she would not trust her gold out of it. And Mrs. Veal's often drawing her hand over her eyes, and asking Mrs. Bargrave whether her fits had not impaired her, looks to me as if she did it on purpose to remind Mrs. Bargrave of her fits, to prepare her not to think it strange that she should put her upon writing to her brother to dispose of rings and gold, which looked so much like a dying person's bequest; and it took accordingly with Mrs. Bargrave as the effects of her fits coming upon her, and was one of the many instances of her wonderful love to her, and care of her, that she should not be affrighted; which indeed appears in her whole management, particularly in her coming to her in the daytime, waiving the salutation, and when she was alone; and then the manner of her parting, to prevent a second attempt to salute her.

Now, why Mr. Veal should think this relation a reflection, as 'tis plain he does, by his endeavouring to stifle it, I cannot imagine, because the generality believe her to be a good spirit, her discourse was so heavenly. Her two great errands were to comfort Mrs. Bargrave in her affliction, and to ask her forgiveness for the breach of friendship, and with a pious discourse to encourage her. So that, after all, to suppose that Mrs. Bargrave could hatch such an invention as this from Friday noon till Saturday noon, supposing that she knew of Mrs. Veal's death the very first moment, without jumbling circumstances, and without any interest too, she must be more witty, fortunate, and wicked too, than any indifferent person, I dare say, will allow. I asked Mrs. Bargrave several times if she was sure she felt the gown. She answered modestly, "If my senses be to be relied on, I am sure of it." I asked her if she heard a sound when she clapped her hand upon her knee? She said she did not remember she did; but said she appeared to be as much a substance as I did, who talked with her. "And I may," said she, "be as soon persuaded that your apparition is talking to me now, as that I did not really see her." For I was under no manner of fear, and received her as a friend, and parted with her as such. "I would not," says she, "give one farthing to make anyone believe it. I have no interest in it; nothing but trouble is entailed upon me for a long time, for aught I know; and had it not come to light by accident, it would never have been made public." But now she says she will make her own private use of it, and keep herself out of the way as much as she can; and so she has done since. She says she had a gentleman who came thirty miles to her to hear the relation, and that she had told it to a room full of people at a time. Several particular gentlemen have had the story from Mrs. Bargrave's own mouth.

This thing has very much affected me, and I am as well satisfied as I am of the best-grounded matter of fact. And why we should dispute matter of fact because we cannot solve things of which we can have no certain or demonstrative notions, seems strange to me. Mrs. Bargrave's authority and sincerity alone would have been undoubted in any other case.

—1706

Robinson Crusoe

Defoe's work, often considered one of the earliest English novels, is based in part on the experiences of Alexander Selkirk, a sailor who, after a disagreement with his captain concerning some repairs to the ship, refused to sail any farther and was set down on the Island of Juan Fernandez, off the coast of Chile, in 1704. He survived the four and a half years on the island before his rescue in much the same manner as Crusoe does for his twenty-eight years.

In Defoe's novel, Crusoe chooses to devote his life to the sea (despite the disapproval of his father, who has encouraged him to study law). A ship he has enlisted on is later seized by Moorish pirates, who take Crusoe and the other sailors to North Africa to work as slaves. On a fishing expedition Crusoe and a young slave boy break free and sail down the African coast, where a Portuguese captain picks them up. Crusoe sells the slave boy to the captain before settling in Brazil, where he establishes himself as a plantation owner. The excerpt below recounts what happens next.

from *Robinson Crusoe*

from CHAPTER 3[1]

… To come, then, by the just degrees to the particulars of this part of my story. You may suppose that, having now lived almost four years in the Brasils, and beginning to thrive and prosper very well upon my plantation, I had not only learned the language, but had contracted acquaintance and friendship among my fellow-planters, as well as among the merchants at St. Salvadore,[2] which was our port; and that, in my discourses among them, I had frequently given them an account of my two voyages to the coast of Guinea,[3] the manner of trading with the negroes there, and how easy it was to purchase upon the coast for trifles—such as beads, toys, knives, scissors, hatchets, bits of glass, and the like—not only gold-dust, Guinea grains,[4] elephants' teeth, &c., but negroes for the service of the Brasils, in great numbers.

They listened always very attentively to my discourses on these heads, but especially to that part which related to the buying negroes, which was a trade at that time not only not far entered into, but as far as it was, had been carried on by the assientos,[5] or permission of the kings of Spain and Portugal, and engrossed[6] in the public, so that few negroes were brought, and those excessive dear.

It happened, being in company with some merchants and planters of my acquaintance and talking of those things very earnestly, three of them came to me next morning, and told me they had been musing very much upon what I had discoursed with them of the last night, and they came to make a secret proposal to me; and, after enjoining me secrecy,[7] they told me that they had a mind to fit out a ship to go to Guinea, that they had all plantations as well as I, and were straitened for nothing so much as servants; that as it was a trade that could not be carried on, because they could not publicly sell the negroes when they came home, so they desired to make but one voyage, to bring the negroes on shore privately and divide them among their own plantations; and, in a word, the question was whether I would go their super-cargo[8] in the ship to manage the trading part upon the coast of Guinea. And they offered me that I should have my equal share of the negroes, without providing any part of the stock.

This was a fair proposal, it must be confessed, had it been made to any one that had not had a settlement and plantation of his own to look after, which was in a fair way of coming to be very considerable, and with a good stock upon it. But for me that was thus entered and established, and had nothing to do but to go on as I had begun for three or four years more, and to have sent for the other hundred pound from England, and who in that time, and with that little addition, could scarce have failed of being worth three or four thousand pounds sterling, and that increasing too; for me to think of such a voyage was the most preposterous thing that ever man in such circumstances could be guilty of.

But I that was born to be my own destroyer could no more resist the offer than I could restrain my first rambling designs, when my father's good counsel was

[1] *CHAPTER 3* Defoe's original text did not contain chapter divisions, but these divisions, inserted after the original publication, are now commonly used and are here provided for reference.

[2] *St. Salvadore* Salvador da Bahia, then capital of Brazil.

[3] *Guinea* Region of West Africa.

[4] *Guinea grains* Seeds of a West African plant, used as a substitute for black pepper.

[5] *assientos* Spanish: contracts. Refers to agreements granting exclusive rights to the slave trade in the Spanish colonies.

[6] *engrossed* Held by exclusive possession.

[7] *enjoining me secrecy* I.e., requesting that I keep the conversation secret.

[8] *go their super-cargo* Travel as the officer who oversees the cargo and its exchange.

lost upon me. In a word, I told them I would go with all my heart, if they would undertake to look after my plantation in my absence and would dispose of it to such as I should direct if I miscarried. This they all engaged to do, and entered into writings or covenants to do so; and I made a formal will, disposing of my plantation and effects in case of my death, making the captain of the ship that had saved my life, as before, my universal heir, but obliging him to dispose of my effects as I had directed in my will, one half of the produce being to himself, and the other to be shipped to England.

In short, I took all possible caution to preserve my effects and keep up my plantation; had I used half as much prudence to have looked into my own interest, and have made a judgment of what I ought to have done, and not to have done, I had certainly never gone away from so prosperous an undertaking, leaving all the probable views of a thriving circumstance, and gone upon a voyage to sea, attended with all its common hazards; to say nothing of the reasons I had to expect particular misfortunes to myself.[1]

But I was hurried on, and obeyed blindly the dictates of my fancy rather than my reason; and accordingly, the ship being fitted out, and the cargo furnished, and all things done as by agreement by my partners in the voyage, I went on board in an evil hour: the first of September, 1659, being the same day eight year that I went from my father and mother at Hull, in order to act the rebel to their authority, and the fool to my own interests.

Our ship was about 120 tun burden,[2] carried 6 guns and 14 men besides the master, his boy, and myself. We had on board no large cargo of goods, except of such toys as were fit for our trade with the negroes, such as beads, bits of glass, shells, and odd trifles, especially little looking-glasses, knives, scissors, hatchets, and the like.

The same day I went on board we set sail, standing away to the northward upon our own coast, with design to stretch over for the African coast, when they came about 10 or 12 degrees of northern latitude, which it seems was the manner of their course in those days. We had very good weather, only excessive hot, all the way upon our own coast, till we came to the height of Cape St. Augustino;[3] from whence keeping farther off at sea we lost sight of land, and steered as if we were bound for the isle Fernand de Noronha,[4] holding our course N.E. by N. and leaving those isles on the east; in this course we passed the line[5] in about 12 days' time, and were by our last observation in 7 degrees 22 min. northern latitude, when a violent tornado or hurricane took us quite out of our knowledge. It began from the south-east, came about to the north-west, and then settled into the north-east, from whence it blew in such a terrible manner that for twelve days together we could do nothing but drive and, scudding away before it, let it carry us whither ever fate and the fury of the winds directed; and during these twelve days, I need not say that I expected every day to be swallowed up, nor indeed did any in the ship expect to save their lives.

In this distress, we had, besides the terror of the storm, one of our men die of the calenture,[6] and one man and the boy washed overboard. About the 12th day, the weather abating a little, the master made an observation as well as he could, and found that he was in about 11 degrees north latitude, but that he was 22 degrees of longitude difference west from Cape St. Augustino; so that he found he was upon the coast of Guiana, or the north part of Brasil, beyond the river Amazones, toward that of the river Orinoque,[7] commonly called the Great River; and began to consult with me what course he should take, for the ship was leaky and very much disabled, and he was going directly back to the coast of Brasil.

I was positively against that, and, looking over the charts of the sea-coast of America with him, we concluded there was no inhabited country for us to have recourse to till we came within the circle of the Caribbee

[1] *the reasons … to myself* Crusoe's earlier experiences have led him to believe that he is subject to an "evil influence" causing him to embark on adventures against his better judgment, and that these are fated to end in disaster.

[2] *tun burden* Measurement of a ship's capacity based on the weight of tuns (large wine casks). Crusoe's ship would have been able to carry 115 modern tons.

[3] *Cape St. Augustino* Town on the easternmost portion of Brazil's coastline.

[4] *Fernand de Noronha* About 370 miles north of Cape St. Augustino.

[5] *the line* The equator.

[6] *calenture* Heatstroke, often accompanied by hallucinations.

[7] *Orinoque* Orinoco River, the mouth of which is located near the northern coast of South America, north of the Amazon.

Islands, and therefore resolved to stand away for Barbadoes,[1] which, by keeping off at sea to avoid the indraft of the Bay or Gulf of Mexico, we might easily perform, as we hoped, in about fifteen days' sail; whereas we could not possibly make our voyage to the coast of Africa without some assistance both to our ship and to ourselves.

With this design we changed our course, and steered away N.W. by W. in order to reach some of our English islands, where I hoped for relief; but our voyage was otherwise determined, for being in the latitude of 12 deg. 18 min. a second storm came upon us, which carried us away with the same impetuosity westward and drove us so out of the very way of all human commerce that, had all our lives been saved as to the sea, we were rather in danger of being devoured by savages than ever returning to our own country.

In this distress, the wind still blowing very hard, one of our men early in the morning cried out, *Land*; and we had no sooner run out of the cabin to look out in hopes of seeing whereabouts in the world we were, but the ship struck upon a sand, and in a moment, her motion being so stopped, the sea broke over her in such a manner that we expected we should all have perished immediately, and we were immediately driven into our close quarters to shelter us from the very foam and spray of the sea.

It is not easy for anyone who has not been in the like condition to describe or conceive the consternation of men in such circumstances; we knew nothing where we were, or upon what land it was we were driven, whether an island or the main, whether inhabited or not inhabited; and as the rage of the wind was still great, though rather less than at first, we could not so much as hope to have the ship hold many minutes without breaking in pieces, unless the winds by a kind of miracle should turn immediately about. In a word, we sat looking upon one another and expecting death every moment, and every man acting accordingly, as preparing for another world, for there was little or nothing more for us to do in this; that which was our present comfort, and all the comfort we had, was that, contrary to our expectation, the ship did not break yet, and that the master said the wind began to abate.

Now, though we thought that the wind did a little abate, yet the ship having thus struck upon the sand, and sticking too fast for us to expect her getting off, we were in a dreadful condition indeed, and had nothing to do but to think of saving our lives as well as we could; we had a boat at our stern just before the storm, but she was first staved by dashing against the ship's rudder, and in the next place she broke away, and either sunk or was driven off to sea, so there was no hope from her; we had another boat on board, but how to get her off into the sea was a doubtful thing; however, there was no room to debate, for we fancied the ship would break in pieces every minute, and some told us she was actually broken already.

In this distress, the mate of our vessel laid hold of the boat, and with the help of the rest of the men, they got her flung over the ship's side and, getting all into her, let go and committed ourselves, being eleven in number, to God's mercy and the wild sea; for though the storm was abated considerably, yet the sea went dreadful high upon the shore, and might be well called *den wild zee*,[2] as the Dutch call the sea in a storm.

And now our case was very dismal indeed; for we all saw plainly that the sea went so high that the boat could not live, and that we should be inevitably drowned. As to making sail, we had none, nor, if we had, could we have done anything with it; so we worked at the oar towards the land, though with heavy hearts, like men going to execution; for we all knew that when the boat came nearer the shore, she would be dashed in a thousand pieces by the breach of the sea. However, we committed our souls to God in the most earnest manner; and, the wind driving us towards the shore, we hastened our destruction with our own hands, pulling as well as we could towards land.

What the shore was, whether rock or sand, whether steep or shoal, we knew not; the only hope that could rationally give us the least shadow of expectation was if we might happen into some bay or gulf, or the mouth of some river, where by great chance we might have run our boat in, or got under the lee of the land, and perhaps made smooth water. But there was nothing of this appeared; but as we made nearer and nearer the shore, the land looked more frightful than the sea.

[1] *Caribbee Islands* Chain of islands between South America and Puerto Rico; *Barbadoes* One of several English island colonies in this chain.

[2] *den wild zee* Dutch: the wild sea.

After we had rowed—or rather driven—about a league and a half,[1] as we reckoned it, a raging wave, mountain-like, came rolling astern of us and plainly bade us expect the *coup de grace*.[2] In a word, it took us with such a fury that it overset the boat at once; and, separating us as well from the boat, as from one another, gave us no time to say, O God! for we were all swallowed up in a moment.

Nothing can describe the confusion of thought which I felt when I sunk into the water; for though I swam very well, yet I could not deliver myself from the waves so as to draw breath till that wave, having driven me, or rather carried me, a vast way on towards the shore, and, having spent itself, went back and left me upon the land almost dry, but half-dead with the water I took in. I had so much presence of mind as well as breath left that, seeing myself nearer the main land than I expected, I got upon my feet and endeavoured to make on towards the land as fast as I could, before another wave should return and take me up again. But I soon found it was impossible to avoid it; for I saw the sea come after me as high as a great hill and as furious as an enemy which I had no means or strength to contend with; my business was to hold my breath, and raise myself upon the water if I could; and so, by swimming, to preserve my breathing and pilot myself towards the shore, if possible; my greatest concern now being that the sea, as it would carry me a great way towards the shore when it came on, might not carry me back again with it when it gave back towards the sea.

The wave that came upon me again buried me at once 20 or 30 foot deep in its own body; and I could feel myself carried with a mighty force and swiftness towards the shore a very great way; but I held my breath and assisted myself to swim still forward with all my might. I was ready to burst with holding my breath when, as I felt myself rising up, so to my immediate relief I found my head and hands shoot out above the surface of the water; and though it was not two seconds of time that I could keep myself so, yet it relieved me greatly, gave me breath and new courage. I was covered again with water a good while, but not so long but I held it out; and, finding the water had spent itself and began to return, I struck forward against the return of the waves, and felt ground again with my feet. I stood still a few moments to recover breath, and till the water went from me, and then took to my heels and ran with what strength I had farther towards the shore. But neither would this deliver me from the fury of the sea, which came pouring in after me again, and twice more I was lifted up by the waves and carried forwards as before, the shore being very flat.

The last time of these two had well near been fatal to me; for the sea, having hurried me along as before, landed me—or rather dashed me—against a piece of rock, and that with such force as it left me senseless, and indeed helpless, as to my own deliverance; for the blow, taking my side and breast, beat the breath, as it were, quite out of my body; and, had it returned again immediately, I must have been strangled in the water; but I recovered a little before the return of the waves, and, seeing I should be covered again with the water, I resolved to hold fast by a piece of the rock, and so to hold my breath, if possible, till the wave went back; now, as the waves were not so high as at first, being nearer land, I held my hold till the wave abated, and then fetched another run, which brought me so near the shore that the next wave, though it went over me, yet did not so swallow me up as to carry me away, and the next run I took, I got to the main land, where, to my great comfort, I clambered up the cliffs of the shore and sat me down upon the grass, free from danger, and quite out of the reach of the water.

I was now landed, and safe on shore, and began to look up and thank God that my life was saved in a case wherein there was, some minutes before, scarce any room to hope. I believe it is impossible to express to the life what the ecstasies and transports of the soul are, when it is so saved, as I may say, out of the very grave; and I do not wonder now at that custom, *viz.*[3] that when a malefactor[4] who has the halter about his neck is tied up and just going to be turned off,[5] and has a reprieve brought to him; I say, I do not wonder that they bring a surgeon with it to let his blood that very moment they tell him of it, that the surprise may not drive the animal spirits from the heart and overwhelm him:

[1] *about a ... half* Approximately 4.5 miles.

[2] *coup de grace* French: merciful killing blow.

[3] *viz.* Abbreviation of the Latin *videlicet*, meaning "namely; that is to say."

[4] *malefactor* Criminal.

[5] *turned off* Hanged.

For sudden joys, like griefs, confound at first.[1]

I walked about on the shore, lifting up my hands, and my whole being, as I may say, wrapped up in the contemplation of my deliverance, making a thousand gestures and motions which I cannot describe, reflecting upon all my comrades that were drowned, and that there should not be one soul saved but myself; for, as for them, I never saw them afterwards, or any sign of them, except three of their hats, one cap, and two shoes that were not fellows.

I cast my eyes to the stranded vessel, when, the breach and froth of the sea being so big, I could hardly see it, it lay so far off, and considered, Lord! how was it possible I could get on shore?

After I had solaced my mind with the comfortable part of my condition, I began to look round me to see what kind of place I was in and what was next to be done; and I soon found my comforts abate, and that, in a word, I had a dreadful deliverance: for I was wet, had no clothes to shift me,[2] nor anything either to eat or drink to comfort me; neither did I see any prospect before me but that of perishing with hunger or being devoured by wild beasts; and that which was particularly afflicting to me was that I had no weapon, either to hunt and kill any creature for my sustenance, or to defend myself against any other creature that might desire to kill me for theirs. In a word, I had nothing about me but a knife, a tobacco-pipe, and a little tobacco in a box; this was all my provision, and this threw me into such terrible agonies of mind that for a while I ran about like a madman; night coming upon me, I began with a heavy heart to consider what would be my lot if there were any ravenous beasts in that country, seeing at night they always come abroad for their prey.

All the remedy that offered to my thoughts at that time was to get up into a thick bushy tree, like a fir, but thorny, which grew near me, and where I resolved to sit all night, and consider the next day what death I should die, for as yet I saw no prospect of life; I walked about a furlong[3] from the shore to see if I could find any fresh water to drink, which I did, to my great joy; and having drank and put a little tobacco into my mouth to prevent hunger, I went to the tree and, getting up into it, endeavoured to place myself so that if I should sleep I might not fall; and, having cut me a short stick, like a truncheon, for my defence, I took up my lodging, and having been excessively fatigued, I fell fast asleep and slept as comfortably as, I believe, few could have done in my condition, and found myself more refreshed with it than I think I ever was on such an occasion.

Chapter 4

When I waked it was broad day, the weather clear, and the storm abated, so that the sea did not rage and swell as before. But that which surprised me most was that the ship was lifted off in the night from the sand where she lay, by the swelling of the tide, and was driven up almost as far as the rock which I at first mentioned, where I had been so bruised by the wave dashing me against it. This being within about a mile from the shore where I was, and the ship seeming to stand upright still, I wished myself on board, that at least I might save some necessary things for my use.

When I came down from my apartment in the tree, I looked about me again, and the first thing I found was the boat, which lay as the wind and the sea had tossed her up upon the land, about two miles on my right hand. I walked as far as I could upon the shore to have got to her, but found a neck or inlet of water between me and the boat which was about half a mile broad, so I came back for the present, being more intent upon getting at the ship, where I hoped to find something for my present subsistence.

A little after noon I found the sea very calm, and the tide ebbed so far out that I could come within a quarter of a mile of the ship. And here I found a fresh renewing of my grief; for I saw evidently that if we had kept on board we had been all safe—that is to say, we had all got safe on shore, and I had not been so miserable as to be left entirely destitute of all comfort and company, as I now was. This forced tears to my eyes again; but as there was little relief in that, I resolved, if possible, to get to the ship; so I pulled off my clothes—for the weather was hot to extremity—and took the water. But when I came to the ship my difficulty was still greater to know how to get on board; for, as she lay aground, and high out of

[1] *For sudden … at first* From Robert Wild's poem "Poetica Licentia" (1672).

[2] *shift me* Change my clothes.

[3] *furlong* 220 yards.

the water, there was nothing within my reach to lay hold of. I swam round her twice, and the second time I spied a small piece of rope, which I wondered I did not see at first, hung down by the fore-chains, so low as that with great difficulty I got hold of it, and by the help of that rope I got up into the forecastle of the ship. Here I found that the ship was bulged,[1] and had a great deal of water in her hold, but that she lay so on the side of a bank of hard sand, or rather earth, that her stern lay lifted up upon the bank, and her head low almost to the water. By this means all her quarter was free, and all that was in that part was dry; for you may be sure my first work was to search and to see what was spoiled and what was free. And first I found that all the ship's provisions were dry and untouched by the water; and, being very well disposed to eat, I went to the bread room and filled my pockets with biscuit, and ate it as I went about other things, for I had no time to lose. I also found some rum in the great cabin, of which I took a large dram, and which I had indeed need enough of to spirit me for what was before me. Now I wanted nothing but a boat to furnish myself with many things which I foresaw would be very necessary to me.

It was in vain to sit still and wish for what was not to be had; and this extremity roused my application. We had several spare yards,[2] and two or three large spars of wood, and a spare topmast or two in the ship; I resolved to fall to work with these, and I flung as many of them overboard as I could manage for their weight, tying every one with a rope, that they might not drive away. When this was done I went down the ship's side and, pulling them to me, I tied four of them together at both ends as well as I could, in the form of a raft, and, laying two or three short pieces of plank upon them crossways, I found I could walk upon it very well, but that it was not able to bear any great weight, the pieces being too light. So I went to work, and with a carpenter's saw I cut a spare topmast into three lengths, and added them to my raft with a great deal of labour and pains. But the hope of furnishing myself with necessaries encouraged me to go beyond what I should have been able to have done upon another occasion.

My raft was now strong enough to bear any reasonable weight. My next care was what to load it with, and how to preserve what I laid upon it from the surf of the sea; but I was not long considering this. I first laid all the planks or boards upon it that I could get, and, having considered well what I most wanted, I got three of the seamen's chests, which I had broken open and emptied, and lowered them down upon my raft; the first of these I filled with provisions—*viz.* bread, rice, three Dutch cheeses, five pieces of dried goat's flesh (which we lived much upon), and a little remainder of European corn, which had been laid by for some fowls which we brought to sea with us, but the fowls were killed. There had been some barley and wheat together; but, to my great disappointment, I found afterwards that the rats had eaten or spoiled it all. As for liquors, I found several cases of bottles belonging to our skipper, in which were some cordial waters, and, in all, about five or six gallons of rack.[3] These I stowed by themselves, there being no need to put them into the chest, nor any room for them. While I was doing this, I found the tide began to flow, though very calm, and I had the mortification to see my coat, shirt, and waistcoat, which I had left on shore upon the sand, swim away; as for my breeches, which were only linen, and open-kneed, I swam on board in them and my stockings. However, this set me upon rummaging for clothes, of which I found enough, but took no more than I wanted for present use, for I had other things which my eye was more upon—as, first, tools to work with on shore. And it was after long searching that I found out the carpenter's chest, which was, indeed, a very useful prize to me, and much more valuable than a shipload of gold would have been at that time. I got it down to my raft, whole as it was, without losing time to look into it, for I knew in general what it contained.

My next care was for some ammunition and arms. There were two very good fowling-pieces[4] in the great cabin, and two pistols. These I secured first, with some powder-horns[5] and a small bag of shot, and two old rusty swords. I knew there were three barrels of powder in the ship, but knew not where our gunner had stowed

[1] *bulged* Warping or bulging would cause gaps to open between the planks and make the ship take on water.

[2] *yards* Wooden spars that support and extend sails already hung on masts.

[3] *rack* Arrack, a name given by Europeans to liquor made by natives, especially that made from fermented rice, sugar, or coco-palm.

[4] *fowling-piece* Light gun (used for shooting birds).

[5] *powder-horns* Flasks for holding gunpowder.

them; but with much search I found them, two of them dry and good, the third had taken water. Those two I got to my raft with the arms. And now I thought myself pretty well freighted, and began to think how I should get to shore with them, having neither sail, oar, nor rudder; and the least capful of wind would have overset all my navigation.

I had three encouragements: 1. a smooth, calm sea; 2. the tide rising, and setting in to the shore; 3. what little wind there was blew me towards the land: and thus, having found two or three broken oars belonging to the boat, and, besides the tools which were in the chest, I found two saws, an axe, and a hammer, and with this cargo I put to sea. For a mile or thereabouts my raft went very well, only that I found it drive a little distant from the place where I had landed before; by which I perceived that there was some indraft of the water, and consequently I hoped to find some creek or river there, which I might make use of as a port to get to land with my cargo.

As I imagined, so it was. There appeared before me a little opening of the land, and I found a strong current of the tide set into it, so I guided my raft as well as I could to keep in the middle of the stream; but here I had like to have suffered a second shipwreck—which, if I had, I think verily would have broken my heart; for, knowing nothing of the coast, my raft ran aground at one end of it upon a shoal, and, not being aground at the other end, it wanted but a little that all my cargo had slipped off towards that end that was afloat, and so fallen into the water. I did my utmost, by setting my back against the chests, to keep them in their places, but could not thrust off the raft with all my strength; neither durst I stir from the posture I was in; but, holding up the chests with all my might, I stood in that manner near half-an-hour, in which time the rising of the water brought me a little more upon a level; and a little after, the water still rising, my raft floated again, and I thrust her off with the oar I had into the channel, and then, driving up higher, I at length found myself in the mouth of a little river, with land on both sides and a strong current of tide running up. I looked on both sides for a proper place to get to shore; for I was not willing to be driven too high up the river, hoping in time to see some ships at sea, and therefore resolved to place myself as near the coast as I could.

At length I spied a little cove on the right shore of the creek, to which with great pain and difficulty I guided my raft, and at last got so near that, reaching ground with my oar, I could thrust her directly in. But here I had like to have dipped all my cargo into the sea again; for that shore lying pretty steep—that is to say sloping—there was no place to land, but where one end of my float, if it ran on shore, would lie so high, and the other sink lower, as before, that it would endanger my cargo again. All that I could do was to wait till the tide was at the highest, keeping the raft with my oar like an anchor, to hold the side of it fast to the shore, near a flat piece of ground, which I expected the water would flow over; and so it did. As soon as I found water enough—for my raft drew about a foot of water—I thrust her upon that flat piece of ground, and there fastened, or moored, her by sticking my two broken oars into the ground, one on one side near one end, and one on the other side near the other end; and thus I lay till the water ebbed away and left my raft and all my cargo safe on shore.

My next work was to view the country and seek a proper place for my habitation, and where to stow my goods to secure them from whatever might happen. Where I was, I yet knew not; whether on the continent or on an island; whether inhabited or not inhabited; whether in danger of wild beasts or not. There was a hill not above a mile from me, which rose up very steep and high, and which seemed to overtop some other hills, which lay as in a ridge from it northward. I took out one of the fowling-pieces, and one of the pistols, and a horn of powder; and, thus armed, I travelled for discovery up to the top of that hill, where, after I had with great labour and difficulty got to the top, I saw my fate to my great affliction—*viz.* that I was in an island environed every way with the sea: no land to be seen except some rocks, which lay a great way off, and two small islands, less than this, which lay about three leagues to the west.

I found also that the island I was in was barren, and, as I saw good reason to believe, uninhabited except by wild beasts, of whom, however, I saw none. Yet I saw abundance of fowls, but knew not their kinds; neither when I killed them could I tell what was fit for food and what not. At my coming back, I shot at a great bird which I saw sitting upon a tree on the side of a great wood. I believe it was the first gun that had been fired there since the creation of the world. I had no sooner fired than from all parts of the wood there arose an innumerable number of fowls of many sorts, making a confused screaming and crying, and every one according to his usual note, but not one of them of any kind that I knew. As for the creature I killed, I took it to be a kind of hawk, its colour and beak resembling it, but it had no talons, or claws, more than common. Its flesh was carrion,[1] and fit for nothing.

Contented with this discovery, I came back to my raft and fell to work to bring my cargo on shore, which took me up the rest of that day. What to do with myself at night I knew not, nor indeed where to rest, for I was afraid to lie down on the ground, not knowing but some wild beast might devour me, though, as I afterwards found, there was really no need for those fears.

However, as well as I could I barricaded myself round with the chest and boards that I had brought on shore, and made a kind of hut for that night's lodging. As for food, I yet saw not which way to supply myself, except that I had seen two or three creatures like hares run out of the wood where I shot the fowl.

I now began to consider that I might yet get a great many things out of the ship which would be useful to me, and particularly some of the rigging and sails, and such other things as might come to land; and I resolved to make another voyage on board the vessel, if possible. And as I knew that the first storm that blew must necessarily break her all in pieces, I resolved to set all other things apart till I had got everything out of the ship that I could get. Then I called a council—that is to say in my thoughts—whether I should take back the raft; but this appeared impracticable: so I resolved to go as before, when the tide was down; and I did so, only that I stripped before I went from my hut, having nothing on but my chequered shirt, a pair of linen drawers, and a pair of pumps on my feet.

I got on board the ship as before, and prepared a second raft; and, having had experience of the first, I neither made this so unwieldy, nor loaded it so hard, but yet I brought away several things very useful to me. As first, in the carpenter's stores I found two or three bags full of nails and spikes, a great screw-jack,[2] a dozen or two of hatchets, and, above all, that most useful thing called a grindstone. All these I secured, together with several things belonging to the gunner, particularly two or three iron crows,[3] and two barrels of musket bullets, seven muskets, another fowling-piece with some small quantity of powder more, a large bagful of small shot, and a great roll of sheet-lead; but this last was so heavy I could not hoist it up to get it over the ship's side.

Besides these things, I took all the men's clothes that I could find, and a spare fore-topsail, a hammock, and some bedding; and with this I loaded my second raft and brought them all safe on shore, to my very great comfort.

I was under some apprehension during my absence from the land that at least my provisions might be devoured on shore. But when I came back I found no sign of any visitor; only there sat a creature like a wild cat upon one of the chests, which, when I came towards it, ran away a little distance and then stood still. She sat very composed and unconcerned, and looked full in my face, as if she had a mind to be acquainted with me. I presented my gun at her, but, as she did not understand it, she was perfectly unconcerned at it, nor did she offer to stir away; upon which I tossed her a bit of biscuit—though, by the way, I was not very free of it, for my store was not great. However, I spared her a bit, I say, and she went to it, smelled at it, and ate it, and looked (as if pleased) for more; but I thanked her and could spare no more, so she marched off.

Having got my second cargo on shore—though I was fain to open the barrels of powder and bring them by parcels, for they were too heavy, being large casks—I went to work to make me a little tent with the sail and some poles which I cut for that purpose. And into this tent I brought everything that I knew would spoil either with rain or sun; and I piled all the empty chests and casks up in a circle round the tent, to fortify it from any sudden attempt, either from man or beast.

When I had done this, I blocked up the door of the tent with some boards within, and an empty chest set up on end without; and, spreading one of the beds upon

[1] *carrion* I.e., flesh unfit for food.

[2] *screw-jack* Portable device used for lifting heavy objects. By turning a handle connected to a screw and a rack, the object is lifted from below.

[3] *crows* I.e., crowbars.

the ground, laying my two pistols just at my head and my gun at length by me, I went to bed for the first time, and slept very quietly all night, for I was very weary and heavy; for the night before I had slept little, and had laboured very hard all day to fetch all those things from the ship and to get them on shore.

I had the biggest magazine of all kinds now that ever was laid up, I believe, for one man. But I was not satisfied still; for while the ship sat upright in that posture I thought I ought to get everything out of her that I could; so every day at low water I went on board and brought away something or other; but particularly the third time I went I brought away as much of the rigging as I could, as also all the small ropes and rope-twine I could get, with a piece of spare canvas, which was to mend the sails upon occasion, and the barrel of wet gunpowder. In a word, I brought away all the sails, first and last; only that I was fain to cut them in pieces and bring as much at a time as I could, for they were no more useful to be sails, but as mere canvas only.

But that which comforted me more still was that, last of all, after I had made five or six such voyages as these and thought I had nothing more to expect from the ship that was worth my meddling with—I say, after all this, I found a great hogshead[1] of bread, three large runlets[2] of rum, or spirits, a box of sugar, and a barrel of fine flour. This was surprising to me because I had given over expecting any more provisions, except what was spoiled by the water. I soon emptied the hogshead of the bread and wrapped it up, parcel by parcel, in pieces of the sails, which I cut out; and, in a word, I got all this safe on shore also.

The next day I made another voyage, and now, having plundered the ship of what was portable and fit to hand out, I began with the cables. Cutting the great cable into pieces such as I could move, I got two cables and a hawser[3] on shore, with all the ironwork I could get; and, having cut down the spritsail-yard and the mizzen-yard,[4] and everything I could to make a large raft, I loaded it with all these heavy goods and came away. But my good luck began now to leave me; for this raft was so unwieldy and so overladen that, after I had entered the little cove where I had landed the rest of my goods, not being able to guide it so handily as I did the other, it overset and threw me and all my cargo into the water. As for myself, it was no great harm, for I was near the shore; but as to my cargo, it was a great part of it lost, especially the iron, which I expected would have been of great use to me; however, when the tide was out I got most of the pieces of the cable ashore, and some of the iron, though with infinite labour; for I was fain to dip for it into the water, a work which fatigued me very much. After this, I went every day on board and brought away what I could get.

I had been now thirteen days on shore and had been eleven times on board the ship, in which time I had brought away all that one pair of hands could well be supposed capable to bring; though I believe verily, had the calm weather held, I should have brought away the whole ship, piece by piece. But preparing the twelfth time to go on board, I found the wind began to rise. However, at low water I went on board, and though I thought I had rummaged the cabin so effectually that nothing more could be found, yet I discovered a locker with drawers in it, in one of which I found two or three razors and one pair of large scissors, with some ten or a dozen of good knives and forks. In another I found about thirty-six pounds value in money—some European coin, some Brasil, some pieces of eight, some gold, and some silver.

I smiled to myself at the sight of this money: "O drug!" said I, aloud, "what art thou good for? Thou art not worth to me—no, not the taking off the ground; one of those knives is worth all this heap; I have no manner of use for thee—e'en remain where thou art, and go to the bottom as a creature whose life is not worth saving." However, upon second thoughts I took it away; and, wrapping all this in a piece of canvas, I began to think of making another raft. But while I was preparing this, I found the sky overcast, and the wind began to rise, and in a quarter of an hour it blew a fresh gale from the shore. It presently occurred to me that it was in vain to pretend[5] to make a raft with the wind offshore, and that it was my business to be gone before the tide of flood began, otherwise I might not be able to reach the shore at all. Accordingly, I let myself down

[1] *hogshead* Large cask.

[2] *runlet* Vessel for storing liquid; cask.

[3] *hawser* Large rope used for mooring and warping.

[4] *spritsail-yard ... mizzen-yard* Wooden spars that support and extend the spritsail and mizzen sail.

[5] *pretend* Attempt.

into the water and swam across the channel, which lay between the ship and the sands—and even that with difficulty enough, partly with the weight of the things I had about me, and partly the roughness of the water; for the wind rose very hastily, and before it was quite high water it blew a storm.

But I had got home to my little tent, where I lay with all my wealth about me, very secure. It blew very hard all night, and in the morning when I looked out, behold, no more ship was to be seen! I was a little surprised, but recovered myself with the satisfactory reflection that I had lost no time, nor abated any diligence, to get everything out of her that could be useful to me; and that, indeed, there was little left in her that I was able to bring away if I had had more time.

I now gave over any more thoughts of the ship, or of anything out of her, except what might drive on shore from her wreck; as, indeed, diverse pieces of her afterwards did. But those things were of small use to me.

My thoughts were now wholly employed about securing myself against either savages, if any should appear, or wild beasts, if any were in the island; and I had many thoughts of the method how to do this, and what kind of dwelling to make—whether I should make me a cave in the earth, or a tent upon the earth; and, in short, I resolved upon both; the manner and description of which, it may not be improper to give an account of.

I soon found the place I was in was not fit for my settlement, because it was upon a low, moorish ground, near the sea, and I believed it would not be wholesome, and more particularly because there was no fresh water near it; so I resolved to find a more healthy and more convenient spot of ground.

I consulted several things in my situation, which I found would be proper for me: 1st, health and fresh water, I just now mentioned; 2ndly, shelter from the heat of the sun; 3rdly, security from ravenous creatures, whether man or beast; 4thly, a view to the sea, that if God sent any ship in sight, I might not lose any advantage for my deliverance, of which I was not willing to banish all my expectation yet.

In search of a place proper for this, I found a little plain on the side of a rising hill whose front towards this little plain was steep as a house-side, so that nothing could come down upon me from the top. On the one side of the rock there was a hollow place, worn a little way in, like the entrance or door of a cave, but there was not really any cave or way into the rock at all.

On the flat of the green just before this hollow place I resolved to pitch my tent. This plain was not above a hundred yards broad, and about twice as long, and lay like a green before my door; and, at the end of it, descended irregularly every way down into the low ground by the seaside. It was on the north-northwest side of the hill, so that it was sheltered from the heat every day till it came to a west-and-by-south sun, or thereabouts, which, in those countries, is near the setting.

Before I set up my tent I drew a half-circle before the hollow place which took in about ten yards in its semi-diameter from the rock, and twenty yards in its diameter from its beginning and ending.

In this half-circle I pitched two rows of strong stakes, driving them into the ground till they stood very firm like piles, the biggest end being out of the ground above five feet and a half, and sharpened on the top. The two rows did not stand above six inches from one another.

Then I took the pieces of cable which I had cut in the ship and laid them in rows, one upon another, within the circle, between these two rows of stakes, up to the top, placing other stakes in the inside, leaning against them, about two feet and a half high, like a spur to a post; and this fence was so strong that neither man nor beast could get into it or over it. This cost me a great deal of time and labour, especially to cut the piles in the woods, bring them to the place, and drive them into the earth.

The entrance into this place I made to be not by a door, but by a short ladder to go over the top; which ladder, when I was in, I lifted over after me; and so I was completely fenced in and fortified, as I thought, from all the world, and consequently slept secure in the night, which otherwise I could not have done; though, as it appeared afterwards, there was no need of all this caution from the enemies that I apprehended danger from.

Into this fence or fortress, with infinite labour, I carried all my riches, all my provisions, ammunition, and stores, of which you have the account above; and I made a large tent, which, to preserve me from the rains that in one part of the year are very violent there, I made double—one smaller tent within, and one larger tent above it—and covered the uppermost with a large tarpaulin, which I had saved among the sails.

And now I lay no more for a while in the bed which I had brought on shore, but in a hammock, which was indeed a very good one, and belonged to the mate of the ship.

Into this tent I brought all my provisions and everything that would spoil by the wet; and, having thus enclosed all my goods, I made up the entrance, which till now I had left open, and so passed and repassed, as I said, by a short ladder.

When I had done this, I began to work my way into the rock, and, bringing all the earth and stones that I dug down out through my tent, I laid them up within my fence, in the nature of a terrace, so that it raised the ground within about a foot and a half; and thus I made me a cave, just behind my tent, which served me like a cellar to my house.

It cost me much labour and many days before all these things were brought to perfection; and therefore I must go back to some other things which took up some of my thoughts. At the same time it happened, after I had laid my scheme for the setting up my tent and making the cave, that, a storm of rain falling from a thick, dark cloud, a sudden flash of lightning happened, and after that a great clap of thunder, as is naturally the effect of it. I was not so much surprised with the lightning as I was with the thought which darted into my mind as swift as the lightning itself—Oh, my powder! My very heart sank within me when I thought that at one blast all my powder might be destroyed; on which, not my defence only, but the providing my food, as I thought, entirely depended. I was nothing near so anxious about my own danger—though had the powder took fire I should never have known who had hurt me.

Such impression did this make upon me that after the storm was over I laid aside all my works, my building and fortifying, and applied myself to make bags and boxes, to separate the powder and to keep it a little and a little in a parcel, in the hope that, whatever might come, it might not all take fire at once; and to keep it so apart that it should not be possible to make one part fire another. I finished this work in about a fortnight; and I think my powder, which in all was about two hundred and forty pounds weight, was divided in not less than a hundred parcels. As to the barrel that had been wet, I did not apprehend any danger from that, so I placed it in my new cave, which in my fancy I called my kitchen; and the rest I hid up and down in holes among the rocks, so that no wet might come to it, marking very carefully where I laid it.

In the interval of time while this was doing, I went out once at least every day with my gun, as well to divert myself as to see if I could kill anything fit for food; and, as near as I could, to acquaint myself with what the island produced. The first time I went out I presently discovered that there were goats in the island, which was a great satisfaction to me; but then it was attended with this misfortune to me—*viz.* that they were so shy, so subtle, and so swift of foot, that it was the most difficult thing in the world to come at them; but I was not discouraged at this, not doubting but I might now and then shoot one, as it soon happened; for after I had found their haunts a little, I laid wait in this manner for them: I observed if they saw me in the valleys, though they were upon the rocks, they would run away, as in a terrible fright; but if they were feeding in the valleys and I was upon the rocks, they took no notice of me; from whence I concluded that, by the position of their optics, their sight was so directed downward that they did not readily see objects that were above them; so afterwards I took this method—I always climbed the rocks first, to get above them, and then had frequently a fair mark.

The first shot I made among these creatures, I killed a she-goat, which had a little kid by her which she gave suck to, which grieved me heartily; for when the old one fell, the kid stood stock still by her, till I came and took her up; and not only so, but when I carried the old one with me, upon my shoulders, the kid followed me quite to my enclosure; upon which I laid down the dam, and took the kid in my arms, and carried it over my pale,[1] in hopes to have bred it up tame; but it would not eat; so I was forced to kill it and eat it myself. These two supplied me with flesh a great while, for I ate sparingly and saved my provisions—my bread especially—as much as possibly I could.

Having now fixed my habitation, I found it absolutely necessary to provide a place to make a fire in, and fuel to burn: and what I did for that, and also how I enlarged my cave, and what conveniences I made, I shall give a full account of in its place. But I must now give

[1] *pale* Fence.

some little account of myself and of my thoughts about living, which, it may well be supposed, were not a few.

I had a dismal prospect of my condition; for as I was not cast away upon that island without being driven, as is said, by a violent storm, quite out of the course of our intended voyage, and a great way—*viz.* some hundreds of leagues—out of the ordinary course of the trade of mankind, I had great reason to consider it as a determination of Heaven that in this desolate place, and in this desolate manner, I should end my life. The tears would run plentifully down my face when I made these reflections; and sometimes I would expostulate with myself why Providence should thus completely ruin His creatures and render them so absolutely miserable; so without help, abandoned, so entirely depressed, that it could hardly be rational to be thankful for such a life.

But something always returned swift upon me to check these thoughts and to reprove me; and particularly one day, walking with my gun in my hand by the seaside, I was very pensive upon the subject of my present condition, when reason, as it were, expostulated with me the other way, thus: "Well, you are in a desolate condition, it is true; but pray remember, where are the rest of you? Did not you come, eleven of you in the boat? Where are the ten? Why were they not saved, and you lost? Why were you singled out? Is it better to be here or there?" And then I pointed to the sea. All evils are to be considered with the good that is in them, and with what worse attends them.

Then it occurred to me again how well I was furnished for my subsistence, and what would have been my case if it had not happened (which was a hundred thousand to one) that the ship floated from the place where she first struck and was driven so near to the shore that I had time to get all these things out of her. What would have been my case if I had been forced to have lived in the condition in which I at first came on shore, without necessaries of life, or necessaries to supply and procure them? "Particularly," said I, aloud (though to myself), "what should I have done without a gun, without ammunition, without any tools to make anything, or to work with; without clothes, bedding, a tent, or any manner of covering?" and that now I had all these to sufficient quantity and was in a fair way to provide myself in such a manner as to live without my gun when my ammunition was spent: so that I had a tolerable view of subsisting, without any want, as long as I lived; for I considered from the beginning how I would provide for the accidents that might happen, and for the time that was to come, even not only after my ammunition should be spent, but even after my health and strength should decay.

I confess I had not entertained any notion of my ammunition being destroyed at one blast—I mean my powder being blown up by lightning—and this made the thoughts of it so surprising to me when it lightened and thundered, as I observed just now.

And now being about to enter into a melancholy relation of a scene of silent life, such, perhaps, as was never heard of in the world before, I shall take it from its beginning and continue it in its order. It was by my account the 30th of September when, in the manner as above said, I first set foot upon this horrid island; when the sun, being to us in its autumnal equinox, was almost over my head; for I reckoned myself, by observation, to be in the latitude of nine degrees, twenty-two minutes north of the line.

After I had been there about ten or twelve days, it came into my thoughts that I should lose my reckoning of time for want of books and pen and ink, and should even forget the Sabbath days; but to prevent this, I cut with my knife upon a large post, in capital letters—and making it into a great cross, I set it up on the shore where I first landed—"I came on shore here on the 30th September 1659."

Upon the sides of this square post I cut every day a notch with my knife, and every seventh notch was as long again as the rest, and every first day of the month as long again as that long one; and thus I kept my calendar, or weekly, monthly, and yearly reckoning of time.

In the next place, we are to observe that among the many things which I brought out of the ship in the several voyages which, as above mentioned, I made to it, I got several things of less value, but not at all less useful to me, which I omitted setting down before; as, in particular, pens, ink, and paper; several parcels in the captain's, mate's, gunner's and carpenter's keeping; three or four compasses; some mathematical instruments, dials, perspectives, charts, and books of navigation; all which I huddled together, whether I might want them or no; also, I found three very good Bibles, which came to me in my cargo from England, and which I had packed up among my things; some Portuguese books also; and among them two or three Popish prayer-books, and several other books, all which I carefully secured. And I must not forget that we had in the ship a dog and two cats, of whose eminent history I may have occasion to say something in its place; for I carried both the cats with me; and, as for the dog, he jumped out of the ship of himself, and swam on shore to me the day after I went on shore with my first cargo, and was a trusty servant to me many years; I wanted nothing that he could fetch me, nor any company that he could make up to me; I only wanted to have him talk to me, but that would not do. As I observed before, I found pens, ink, and paper, and I husbanded them to the utmost; and I shall show that while my ink lasted, I kept things very exact, but after that was gone I could not, for I could not make any ink by any means that I could devise.

And this put me in mind that I wanted many things notwithstanding all that I had amassed together; and of these, ink was one; as also a spade, pickaxe, and shovel, to dig or remove the earth; needles, pins, and thread; as for linen, I soon learned to want that without much difficulty.

This want of tools made every work I did go on heavily, and it was near a whole year before I had entirely finished my little pale, or surrounded my habitation. The piles, or stakes, which were as heavy as I could well lift, were a long time in cutting and preparing in the woods, and more, by far, in bringing home; so that I spent sometimes two days in cutting and bringing home one of those posts, and a third day in driving it into the ground; for which purpose I got a heavy piece of wood at first, but at last bethought myself of one of the iron crows; which, however, though I found it, made driving those posts or piles very laborious and tedious work. But what need I have been concerned at the tediousness of anything I had to do, seeing I had time enough to do it in? Nor had I any other employment if that had been over, at least that I could foresee, except the ranging the island to seek for food, which I did, more or less, every day.

I now began to consider seriously my condition and the circumstances I was reduced to, and I drew up the state of my affairs in writing, not so much to leave them to any that were to come after me—for I was likely to have but few heirs—as to deliver my thoughts from daily poring over them and afflicting my mind; and as my reason began now to master my despondency, I began to comfort myself as well as I could, and to set the good against the evil, that I might have something to distinguish my case from worse; and I stated very impartially, like debtor and creditor, the comforts I enjoyed against the miseries I suffered, thus:

EVIL.	GOOD.
I am cast upon a horrible desolate island, void of all hope of recovery.	But I am alive, and not drowned, as all my ship's company was.
I am singled out and separated, as it were, from all the world to be miserable.	But I am singled out, too, from all the ship's crew to be spared from death; and He that miraculously saved me from death, can deliver me from this condition.
I am divided from mankind, a solitaire, one banished from human society.	But I am not starved and perishing on a barren place, affording no substance.
I have no clothes to cover me.	But I am in a hot climate, where, if I had clothes, I could hardly wear them.
I am without any defence, or means to resist any violence of man or beast.	But I am cast on an island, where I see no wild beasts to hurt me, as I saw on the coast of Africa; and what if I had been shipwrecked there?
I have no soul to speak to, or relieve me.	But God wonderfully sent the ship in near enough to the shore, that I have gotten out so many necessary things as will either supply my wants, or enable me to supply myself, even as long as I live.

Upon the whole, here was an undoubted testimony that there was scarce any condition in the world so miserable, but there was something *negative* or something *positive* to be thankful for in it; and let this stand as a direction from the experience of the most miserable of all conditions in this world: that we may always find in it something to comfort ourselves from, and to set, in the description of good and evil, on the credit side of the account.

Having now brought my mind a little to relish my condition, and given over looking out to sea to see if I could spy a ship—I say, giving over these things, I begun to apply myself to arrange my way of living, and to make things as easy to me as I could.

I have already described my habitation, which was a tent under the side of a rock, surrounded with a strong pale of posts and cables. But I might now rather call it a wall, for I raised a kind of wall up against it of turfs, about two feet thick on the outside; and after some time (I think it was a year and a half) I raised rafters from it, leaning to the rock, and thatched or covered it with boughs of trees and such things as I could get to keep out the rain, which I found at some times of the year very violent.

I have already observed how I brought all my goods into this pale, and into the cave which I had made behind me. But I must observe, too, that at first this was a confused heap of goods, which, as they lay in no order, so they took up all my place. I had no room to turn myself, so I set myself to enlarge my cave and work farther into the earth; for it was a loose sandy rock, which yielded easily to the labour I bestowed on it: and so when I found I was pretty safe as to beasts of prey, I worked sideways, to the right hand, into the rock; and then, turning to the right again, worked quite out, and made me a door to come out on the outside of my pale or fortification.

This gave me not only egress and regress, as it was a back way to my tent and to my storehouse, but gave me room to store my goods.

And now I began to apply myself to make such necessary things as I found I most wanted, particularly a chair and a table; for without these I was not able to enjoy the few comforts I had in the world. I could not write or eat, or do several things, with so much pleasure without a table.

So I went to work; and here I must needs observe that, as reason is the substance and origin of the mathematics, so by stating and squaring everything by reason, and by making the most rational judgment of things, every man may be, in time, master of every mechanic art. I had never handled a tool in my life; and yet, in time, by labour, application, and contrivance, I found at last that I wanted nothing but I could have made it, especially if I had had tools. However, I made abundance of things, even without tools; and some with no more tools than an adze and a hatchet, which perhaps were never made that way before, and that with infinite labour. For example, if I wanted a board, I had no other way but to cut down a tree, set it on an edge before me, and hew it flat on either side with my axe, till I brought it to be thin as a plank, and then dub it smooth with my adze. It is true, by this method I could make but one board out of a whole tree; but this I had no remedy for but patience, any more than I had for the prodigious deal of time and labour which it took me up to make a plank or board: but my time or labour was little worth, and so it was as well employed one way as another.

However, I made me a table and a chair, as I observed above, in the first place; and this I did out of the short pieces of boards that I brought on my raft from the ship. But when I had wrought out some boards as above, I made large shelves, of the breadth of a foot and a half, one over another all along one side of my cave, to lay all my tools, nails, and ironwork on; and, in a word, to separate everything at large into their places, that I might come easily at them. I knocked pieces into the wall of the rock to hang my guns and all things that would hang up; so that, had my cave been to be seen, it looked like a general magazine of all necessary things; and had everything so ready at my hand that it was a great pleasure to me to see all my goods in such order, and especially to find my stock of all necessaries so great.

And now it was that I began to keep a journal of every day's employment; for, indeed, at first I was in too much hurry—and not only hurry as to labour, but in too much discomposure of mind—and my journal would have been full of many dull things; for example, I must have said thus: "Sept. the 30th. After I had got to shore, and escaped drowning, instead of being thankful to God for my deliverance, having first vomited, with the great quantity of salt water which had got into my stomach, and recovering myself a little, I ran about the shore wringing my hands and beating my head and face, exclaiming at my misery, and crying out, 'I was undone, undone!' till, tired and faint, I was forced to lie down on the ground to repose, but durst not sleep for fear of being devoured."

Some days after this, and after I had been on board the ship, and got all that I could out of her, yet I could not forbear getting up to the top of a little mountain and looking out to sea, in hopes of seeing a ship; then fancy at a vast distance I spied a sail—please myself with the hopes of it—and then after looking steadily, till I was almost blind, lose it quite, and sit down and weep like a child, and thus increase my misery by my folly.

But having gotten over these things in some measure, and having settled my household staff and habitation, made me a table and a chair, and all as handsome about me as I could, I began to keep my journal; of which I shall here give you the copy (though in it will be told all these particulars over again) as long as it lasted; for having no more ink, I was forced to leave it off.

CHAPTER 5

The Journal

September 30, 1659. I, poor miserable Robinson Crusoe, being shipwrecked during a dreadful storm in the offing, came on shore on this dismal, unfortunate island, which I called "The Island of Despair"; all the rest of the ship's company being drowned, and myself almost dead.

All the rest of the day I spent in afflicting myself at the dismal circumstances I was brought to—*viz.* I had neither food, house, clothes, weapon, nor place to fly to—and, in despair of any relief, saw nothing but death before me, either that I should be devoured by wild beasts, murdered by savages, or starved to death for want of food. At the approach of night I slept in a tree for fear of wild creatures; but slept soundly, though it rained all night.

October 1. In the morning I saw, to my great surprise, the ship had floated with the high tide, and was driven on shore again much nearer the island; which, as it was some comfort, on one hand—for, seeing her set upright, and not broken to pieces, I hoped, if the wind abated, I might get on board, and get some food and necessaries out of her for my relief—so, on the other hand, it renewed my grief at the loss of my comrades, who I imagined, if we had all stayed on board, might have saved the ship, or, at least, that they would not have been all drowned as they were; and that, had the men been saved, we might perhaps have built us a boat out of the ruins of the ship to have carried us to some other part of the world. I spent great part of this day in perplexing myself on these things; but at length, seeing the ship almost dry, I went upon the sand as near as I could, and then swam on board. This day also it continued raining, though with no wind at all.

From the 1st of October to the 24th. All these days entirely spent in many several voyages to get all I could out of the ship, which I brought on shore every tide of flood upon rafts. Much rain also in the days, though with some intervals of fair weather; but it seems this was the rainy season.

Oct. 20. I overset my raft, and all the goods I had got upon it; but, being in shoal water, and the things being chiefly heavy, I recovered many of them when the tide was out.

Oct. 25. It rained all night and all day, with some gusts of wind, during which time the ship broke in pieces, the wind blowing a little harder than before, and was no more to be seen, except the wreck of her, and that only at low water. I spent this day in covering and securing the goods which I had saved, that the rain might not spoil them.

Oct. 26. I walked about the shore almost all day to find out a place to fix my habitation, greatly concerned to secure myself from any attack in the night, either from wild beasts or men. Towards night, I fixed upon a proper place, under a rock, and marked out a semicircle for my encampment, which I resolved to strengthen with a work, wall, or fortification, made of double piles, lined within with cables, and without with turf.

From the 26th to the 30th I worked very hard in carrying all my goods to my new habitation, though some part of the time it rained exceedingly hard.

The 31st, in the morning, I went out into the island with my gun to seek for some food and discover the country, when I killed a she-goat, and her kid followed me home, which I afterwards killed also, because it would not feed.

November 1. I set up my tent under a rock and lay there for the first night; making it as large as I could, with stakes driven in to swing my hammock upon.

Nov. 2. I set up all my chests and boards, and the pieces of timber which made my rafts, and with them formed a fence round me, a little within the place I had marked out for my fortification.

Nov. 3. I went out with my gun and killed two fowls like ducks, which were very good food. In the afternoon went to work to make me a table.

Nov. 4. This morning I began to order my times of work, of going out with my gun, time of sleep, and time of diversion—*viz.* every morning I walked out with my gun for two or three hours, if it did not rain; then employed myself to work till about eleven o'clock; then ate what I had to live on; and from twelve to two I lay down to sleep, the weather being excessively hot; and then, in the evening, to work again. The working part of this day and of the next were wholly employed in making my table, for I was yet but a very sorry workman, though time and necessity made me a complete natural mechanic soon after, as I believe they would do anyone else.

Nov. 5. This day went abroad with my gun and my dog and killed a wild cat; her skin pretty soft, but her flesh good for nothing. Every creature that I killed I took off the skins, and preserved them. Coming back by the seashore I saw many sorts of sea-fowls, which I did not understand; but was surprised, and almost frightened, with two or three seals, which, while I was gazing at, not well knowing what they were, got into the sea and escaped me for that time.

Nov. 6. After my morning walk I went to work with my table again, and finished it, though not to my liking; nor was it long before I learned to mend[1] it.

Nov. 7. Now it began to be settled fair weather. The 7th, 8th, 9th, 10th, and part of the 12th (for the 11th was Sunday) I took wholly up to make me a chair, and with much ado brought it to a tolerable shape, but never to please me; and even in the making I pulled it in pieces several times. *Note.* I soon neglected my keeping Sundays; for, omitting my mark for them on my post, I forgot which was which.

Nov. 13. This day it rained, which refreshed me exceedingly, and cooled the earth; but it was accompanied with terrible thunder and lightning, which frightened me dreadfully, for fear of my powder. As soon as it was over, I resolved to separate my stock of powder into as many little parcels as possible, that it might not be in danger.

Nov. 14, 15, 16. These three days I spent in making little square chests, or boxes, which might hold about a pound, or two pounds at most, of powder; and so, putting the powder in, I stowed it in places as secure and remote from one another as possible. On one of these three days I killed a large bird that was good to eat, but I knew not what to call it.

Nov. 17. This day I began to dig behind my tent into the rock, to make room for my further conveniency. *Note.* Three things I wanted exceedingly for this work—*viz.* a pickaxe, a shovel, and a wheelbarrow or basket—so I desisted from my work and began to consider how to supply that want, and make me some tools. As for the pickaxe, I made use of the iron crows, which were proper enough, though heavy; but the next thing was a shovel or spade; this was so absolutely necessary, that, indeed, I could do nothing effectually without it; but what kind of one to make I knew not.

Nov. 18. The next day in searching the woods I found a tree of that wood, or like it, which in the Brasils they call the iron-tree, for its exceeding hardness. Of this, with great labour, and almost spoiling my axe, I cut a piece, and brought it home, too, with difficulty enough, for it was exceeding heavy. The excessive hardness of the wood, and my having no other way, made me a long while upon this machine, for I worked it effectually by little and little into the form of a shovel or spade; the handle exactly shaped like ours in England, only that the board part having no iron shod upon it at bottom, it would not last me so long; however, it served well enough for the uses which I had occasion to put it to; but never was a shovel, I believe, made after that fashion, or so long in making.

I was still deficient, for I wanted a basket or a wheelbarrow. A basket I could not make by any means, having no such things as twigs that would bend to make wicker-ware—at least, none yet found out; and as to a

[1] *mend* Improve.

wheelbarrow, I fancied I could make all but the wheel; but that I had no notion of; neither did I know how to go about it; besides, I had no possible way to make the iron gudgeons[1] for the spindle or axis of the wheel to run in. So I gave it over, and so, for carrying away the earth which I dug out of the cave, I made me a thing like a hod,[2] which the labourers carry mortar in when they serve the bricklayers. This was not so difficult to me as the making the shovel: and yet this and the shovel, and the attempt which I made in vain to make a wheelbarrow, took me up no less than four days—I mean always excepting my morning walk with my gun, which I seldom failed, and very seldom failed also bringing home something fit to eat.

Nov. 23. My other work having now stood still because of my making these tools, when they were finished I went on; and, working every day as my strength and time allowed, I spent eighteen days entirely in widening and deepening my cave, that it might hold my goods commodiously. *Note.* During all this time I worked to make this room or cave spacious enough to accommodate me as a warehouse or magazine, a kitchen, a dining-room, and a cellar. As for my lodging, I kept to the tent; except that sometimes, in the wet season of the year, it rained so hard that I could not keep myself dry, which caused me afterwards to cover all my place within my pale with long poles, in the form of rafters, leaning against the rock, and load them with flags[3] and large leaves of trees, like a thatch.

December 10. I began now to think my cave or vault finished, when on a sudden (it seems I had made it too large) a great quantity of earth fell down from the top on one side; so much that, in short, it frighted me, and not without reason, too, for if I had been under it, I had never wanted a gravedigger. I had now a great deal of work to do over again, for I had the loose earth to carry out; and, which was of more importance, I had the ceiling to prop up, so that I might be sure no more would come down.

Dec. 11. This day I went to work with it accordingly, and got two shores, or posts, pitched upright to the top, with two pieces of boards across over each post. This I finished the next day; and, setting more posts up with boards, in about a week more I had the roof secured, and the posts, standing in rows, served me for partitions to part off the house.

Dec. 17. From this day to the 20th I placed shelves and knocked up nails on the posts to hang everything up that could be hung up; and now I began to be in some order within doors.

Dec. 20. Now I carried everything into the cave and began to furnish my house and set up some pieces of boards like a dresser, to order my victuals upon; but boards began to be very scarce with me; also, I made me another table.

Dec. 24. Much rain all night and all day. No stirring out.

Dec. 25. Rain all day.

Dec. 26. No rain, and the earth much cooler than before, and pleasanter.

Dec. 27. Killed a young goat and lamed another, so that I caught it and led it home in a string; when I had it at home, I bound and splintered up its leg, which was broke. *N.B.*[4] I took such care of it that it lived, and the leg grew well and as strong as ever; but by my nursing it so long it grew tame, and fed upon the little green at my door, and would not go away. This was the first time that I entertained a thought of breeding up some tame creatures, that I might have food when my powder and shot was all spent.

Dec. 28, 29, 30, 31. Great heats and no breeze, so that there was no stirring abroad, except in the evening, for food; this time I spent in putting all my things in order within doors.

January 1. Very hot still, but I went abroad early and late with my gun, and lay still in the middle of the day. This evening, going farther into the valleys which lay towards the centre of the island, I found there were plenty of goats, though exceedingly shy, and hard to come at; however, I resolved to try if I could not bring my dog to hunt them down.

Jan. 2. Accordingly, the next day I went out with my dog and set him upon the goats, but I was mistaken, for they all faced about upon the dog, and he knew his danger too well, for he would not come near them.

Jan. 3. I began my fence or wall; which, being still jealous of my being attacked by somebody, I resolved to

[1] *gudgeons* Pivots on which the wheels turn.

[2] *hod* Receptacle for carrying mortar, bricks, coal, etc., on the shoulder.

[3] *flags* Rushes.

[4] *N.B.* For *nota bene* (Latin: note well).

make very thick and strong. *N.B.* This wall being described before, I purposely omit what was said in the journal; it is sufficient to observe that I was no less time than from the 2nd of January to the 14th of April working, finishing, and perfecting this wall, though it was no more than about twenty-four yards in length, being a half-circle from one place in the rock to another place about eight yards from it, the door of the cave being in the centre behind it.

All this time I worked very hard, the rains hindering me many days—nay, sometimes weeks together—but I thought I should never be perfectly secure till this wall was finished; and it is scarce credible what inexpressible labour everything was done with, especially the bringing piles out of the woods and driving them into the ground; for I made them much bigger than I needed to have done.

When this wall was finished and the outside double fenced, with a turf wall raised up close to it, I perceived myself that if any people were to come on shore there, they would not perceive anything like a habitation; and it was very well I did so—as may be observed hereafter, upon a very remarkable occasion.

During this time I made my rounds in the woods for game every day when the rain permitted me, and made frequent discoveries in these walks of something or other to my advantage; particularly, I found a kind of wild pigeons, which build not as wood-pigeons, in a tree, but rather as house-pigeons, in the holes of the rocks; and taking some young ones, I endeavoured to breed them up tame, and did so; but when they grew older they flew away, which perhaps was at first for want of feeding them, for I had nothing to give them. However, I frequently found their nests and got their young ones, which were very good meat.

And now, in the managing my household affairs, I found myself wanting in many things which I thought at first it was impossible for me to make; as, indeed, with some of them it was. For instance, I could never make a cask to be hooped. I had a small runlet or two, as I observed before, but I could never arrive at the capacity of making one by them, though I spent many weeks about it. I could neither put in the heads, or join the staves so true to one another as to make them hold water; so I gave that also over.

In the next place, I was at a great loss for candles; so that as soon as ever it was dark, which was generally by seven o'clock, I was obliged to go to bed. I remembered the lump of beeswax with which I made candles in my African adventure, but I had none of that now. The only remedy I had was that when I had killed a goat I saved the tallow, and with a little dish made of clay, which I baked in the sun (to which I added a wick of some oakum) I made me a lamp; and this gave me light, though not a clear, steady light, like a candle. In the middle of all my labours it happened that, rummaging my things, I found a little bag which, as I hinted before, had been filled with corn for the feeding of poultry—not for this voyage, but before, as I suppose, when the ship came from Lisbon. The little remainder of corn that had been in the bag was all devoured by the rats, and I saw nothing in the bag but husks and dust; and being willing to have the bag for some other use (I think it was to put powder in, when I divided it for fear of the lightning, or some such use), I shook the husks of corn out of it on one side of my fortification, under the rock.

It was a little before the great rains just now mentioned that I threw this stuff away, taking no notice, and not so much as remembering that I had thrown anything there, when, about a month after, or thereabouts, I saw some few stalks of something green shooting out of the ground, which I fancied might be some plant I had not seen; but I was surprised and perfectly astonished when, after a little longer time, I saw about ten or twelve ears come out, which were perfect green barley, of the same kind as our European—nay, as our English barley.

It is impossible to express the astonishment and confusion of my thoughts on this occasion. I had hitherto acted upon no religious foundation at all; indeed, I had very few notions of religion in my head, nor had entertained any sense of anything that had befallen me otherwise than as chance, or, as we lightly say, what pleases God, without so much as inquiring into the end of Providence in these things, or His order in governing events for the world. But after I saw barley grow there, in a climate which I knew was not proper for corn,[1] and especially that I knew not how it came

[1] *corn* I.e., grain.

there, it startled me strangely, and I began to suggest that God had miraculously caused His grain to grow without any help of seed sown, and that it was so directed purely for my sustenance on that wild, miserable place.

This touched my heart a little, and brought tears out of my eyes, and I began to bless myself, that such a prodigy of nature should happen upon my account; and this was the more strange to me because I saw near it still, all along by the side of the rock, some other straggling stalks, which proved to be stalks of rice, and which I knew because I had seen it grow in Africa when I was ashore there.

I not only thought these the pure productions of Providence for my support, but, not doubting that there was more in the place, I went all over that part of the island where I had been before, peering in every corner, and under every rock, to see for more of it, but I could not find any. At last it occurred to my thoughts that I shook a bag of chickens' meat[1] out in that place; and then the wonder began to cease; and I must confess my religious thankfulness to God's providence began to abate too, upon the discovering that all this was nothing but what was common—though I ought to have been as thankful for so strange and unforeseen a providence as if it had been miraculous; for it was really the work of Providence to me, that should order or appoint that ten or twelve grains of corn should remain unspoiled, when the rats had destroyed all the rest, as if it had been dropped from heaven; as also, that I should throw it out in that particular place, where, it being in the shade of a high rock, it sprang up immediately; whereas, if I had thrown it anywhere else at that time, it had been burnt up and destroyed.

I carefully saved the ears of this corn, you may be sure, in their season, which was about the end of June; and, laying up every corn, I resolved to sow them all again, hoping in time to have some quantity sufficient to supply me with bread. But it was not till the fourth year that I could allow myself the least grain of this corn to eat, and even then but sparingly, as I shall say afterwards, in its order; for I lost all that I sowed the first season by not observing the proper time; for I sowed it just before the dry season, so that it never came up at all, at least not as it would have done; of which in its place.

[1] *meat* Food.

Besides this barley, there were, as above, twenty or thirty stalks of rice, which I preserved with the same care and for the same use, or to the same purpose—to make me bread, or rather food; for I found ways to cook it without baking, though I did that also after some time. But to return to my journal.

I worked excessive hard these three or four months to get my wall done; and the 14th of April I closed it up, contriving to go into it not by a door but over the wall, by a ladder, that there might be no sign on the outside of my habitation.

April 16. I finished the ladder; so I went up the ladder to the top, and then pulled it up after me and let it down in the inside. This was a complete enclosure to me; for within I had room enough, and nothing could come at me from without, unless it could first mount my wall.

The very next day after this wall was finished I had almost had all my labour overthrown at once, and myself killed. The case was thus: as I was busy in the inside, behind my tent, just at the entrance into my cave, I was terribly frighted with a most dreadful, surprising thing indeed; for all on a sudden I found the earth come crumbling down from the roof of my cave, and from the edge of the hill over my head, and two of the posts I had set up in the cave cracked in a frightful manner. I was heartily scared, but thought nothing of what was really the cause, only thinking that the top of my cave was fallen in, as some of it had done before. And for fear I should be buried in it I ran forward to my ladder, and not thinking myself safe there neither, I got over my wall for fear of the pieces of the hill which I expected might roll down upon me. I was no sooner stepped down upon the firm ground than I plainly saw it was a terrible earthquake, for the ground I stood on shook three times at about eight minutes' distance, with three such shocks as would have overturned the strongest building that could be supposed to have stood on the earth; and a great piece of the top of a rock which stood about half a mile from me next the sea fell down with such a terrible noise as I never heard in all my life. I perceived also the very sea was put into violent motion by it; and I believe the shocks were stronger under the water than on the island.

I was so much amazed with the thing itself, having never felt the like, nor discoursed with anyone that had, that I was like one dead or stupefied; and the motion of the earth made my stomach sick, like one that was tossed at sea. But the noise of the falling of the rock awakened me, as it were, and, rousing me from the stupefied condition I was in, filled me with horror; and I thought of nothing then but the hill falling upon my tent and all my household goods, and burying all at once; and this sunk my very soul within me a second time.

After the third shock was over and I felt no more for some time, I began to take courage; and yet I had not heart enough to go over my wall again, for fear of being buried alive, but sat still upon the ground, greatly cast down and disconsolate, not knowing what to do. All this while I had not the least serious religious thought; nothing but the common "Lord have mercy upon me!" And when it was over that went away too.

While I sat thus, I found the air overcast and grow cloudy, as if it would rain. Soon after that the wind arose by little and little, so that in less than half-an-hour it blew a most dreadful hurricane. The sea was all on a sudden covered over with foam and froth; the shore was covered with the breach of the water; the trees were torn up by the roots; and a terrible storm it was. This held about three hours, and then began to abate; and in two hours more it was quite calm, and began to rain very hard.

All this while I sat upon the ground, very much terrified and dejected, when on a sudden it came into my thoughts that these winds and rain being the consequences of the earthquake, the earthquake itself was spent and over, and I might venture into my cave again. With this thought my spirits began to revive; and the rain also helping to persuade me, I went in and sat down in my tent. But the rain was so violent that my tent was ready to be beaten down with it, and I was forced to go into my cave, though very much afraid and uneasy, for fear it should fall on my head.

This violent rain forced me to a new work—*viz.* to cut a hole through my new fortification, like a sink, to let the water go out, which would else have flooded my cave. After I had been in my cave for some time, and found still no more shocks of the earthquake follow, I began to be more composed. And now, to support my spirits, which indeed wanted it very much, I went to my little store and took a small sup of rum; which, however, I did then and always very sparingly, knowing I could have no more when that was gone.

It continued raining all that night and great part of the next day, so that I could not stir abroad; but, my mind being more composed, I began to think of what I had best do; concluding that if the island was subject to these earthquakes there would be no living for me in a cave, but I must consider of building a little hut in an open place which I might surround with a wall, as I had done here, and so make myself secure from wild beasts or men; for I concluded, if I stayed where I was, I should certainly one time or other be buried alive.

With these thoughts I resolved to remove my tent from the place where it stood, which was just under the hanging precipice of the hill; and which, if it should be shaken again, would certainly fall upon my tent; and I spent the two next days, being the 19th and 20th of April, in contriving where and how to remove my habitation.

The fear of being swallowed up alive made me that I never slept in quiet; and yet the apprehension of lying abroad without any fence was almost equal to it; but still, when I looked about, and saw how everything was put in order, how pleasantly concealed I was, and how safe from danger, it made me very loath to remove.

In the meantime, it occurred to me that it would require a vast deal of time for me to do this, and that I must be contented to venture where I was till I had formed a camp for myself, and had secured it so as to remove to it. So with this resolution I composed myself for a time, and resolved that I would go to work with all speed to build me a wall with piles and cables, &c., in a circle, as before, and set my tent up in it when it was finished; but that I would venture to stay where I was till it was finished, and fit to remove. This was the 21st.

April 22. The next morning I begin to consider of means to put this resolve into execution; but I was at a great loss about my tools. I had three large axes, and abundance of hatchets (for we carried the hatchets for traffic with the Indians); but, with much chopping and cutting knotty hard wood, they were all full of notches, and dull; and though I had a grindstone, I could not turn it and grind my tools too. This cost me as much thought as a statesman would have bestowed upon a grand point of politics, or a judge upon the life and death of a man. At length I contrived a wheel with a string, to turn it with my foot, that I might have both my hands at liberty. *Note.* I had never seen any such thing in England, or at least, not to take notice how it was done, though since I have observed, it is very common there; besides that, my grindstone was very large and heavy. This machine cost me a full week's work to bring it to perfection.

April 28, 29. These two whole days I took up in grinding my tools, my machine for turning my grindstone performing very well.

April 30. Having perceived my bread had been low a great while, now I took a survey of it, and reduced myself to one biscuit cake a day, which made my heart very heavy.

May 1. In the morning, looking towards the sea side, the tide being low, I saw something lie on the shore bigger than ordinary, and it looked like a cask; when I came to it, I found a small barrel and two or three pieces of the wreck of the ship, which were driven on shore by the late hurricane; and, looking towards the wreck itself, I thought it seemed to lie higher out of the water than it used to do. I examined the barrel which was driven on shore, and soon found it was a barrel of gunpowder; but it had taken water, and the powder was caked as hard as a stone; however, I rolled it farther on shore for the present, and went on upon the sands, as near as I could to the wreck of the ship, to look for more.

When I came down to the ship I found it strangely removed. The forecastle, which lay before buried in sand, was heaved up at least six feet, and the stern (which was broke in pieces and parted from the rest by the force of the sea, soon after I had left rummaging her) was tossed, as it were, up, and cast on one side; and the sand was thrown so high on that side next her stern, that whereas there was a great place of water before, so that I could not come within a quarter of a mile of the wreck without swimming I could now walk quite up to her when the tide was out. I was surprised with this at first, but soon concluded it must be done by the earthquake; and as by this violence the ship was more broke open than formerly, so many things came daily on shore which the sea had loosened, and which the winds and water rolled by degrees to the land.

This wholly diverted my thoughts from the design of removing my habitation, and I busied myself mightily, that day especially, in searching whether I could make any way into the ship; but I found nothing was to be expected of that kind, for all the inside of the ship was choked up with sand. However, as I had learned not to despair of anything, I resolved to pull everything to pieces that I could of the ship, concluding that everything I could get from her would be of some use or other to me.

Chapter 6

May 3. I began with my saw, and cut a piece of a beam through, which I thought held some of the upper part or quarter-deck together; and when I had cut it through, I cleared away the sand as well as I could from the side which lay highest; but, the tide coming in, I was obliged to give over for that time.

May 4. I went a-fishing but caught not one fish that I durst eat of, till I was weary of my sport; when, just going to leave off, I caught a young dolphin. I had made me a long line of some rope-yarn, but I had no hooks; yet I frequently caught fish enough, as much as I cared to eat; all which I dried in the sun, and ate them dry.

May 5. Worked on the wreck; cut another beam asunder; and brought three great fir planks off from the decks, which I tied together, and made to float on shore when the tide of flood came on.

May 6. Worked on the wreck; got several iron bolts out of her and other pieces of ironwork. Worked very hard, and came home very much tired, and had thoughts of giving it over.

May 7. Went to the wreck again, not with an intent to work, but found the weight of the wreck had broke itself down, the beams being cut; that several pieces of the ship seemed to lie loose, and the inside of the hold lay so open that I could see into it; but it was almost full of water and sand.

May 8. Went to the wreck and carried an iron crow to wrench up the deck, which lay now quite clear of the water or sand. I wrenched open two planks and brought them on shore also with the tide. I left the iron crow in the wreck for next day.

May 9. Went to the wreck, and with the crow made way into the body of the wreck, and felt several casks, and loosened them with the crow, but could not break them up. I felt also a roll of English lead, and could stir it, but it was too heavy to remove.

May 1–14. Went every day to the wreck and got a great many pieces of timber, and boards, or plank, and two or three hundredweight of iron.

May 15. I carried two hatchets to try if I could not cut a piece off the roll of lead by placing the edge of one hatchet and driving it with the other; but as it lay about a foot and a half in the water, I could not make any blow to drive the hatchet.

May 16. It had blown hard in the night, and the wreck appeared more broken by the force of the water; but I stayed so long in the woods to get pigeons for food that the tide prevented my going to the wreck that day.

May 17. I saw some pieces of the wreck blown on shore, at a great distance, near two miles off me, but resolved to see what they were, and found it was a piece of the head, but too heavy for me to bring away.

May 24. Every day, to this day, I worked on the wreck; and with hard labour I loosened some things so much with the crow that, the first flowing tide, several casks floated out, and two of the seamen's chests; but, the wind blowing from the shore, nothing came to land that day but pieces of timber and a hogshead, which had some Brazil pork in it; but the salt water and the sand had spoiled it. I continued this work every day to the 15th of June, except the time necessary to get food, which I always appointed, during this part of my employment, to be when the tide was up, that I might be ready when it was ebbed out; and by this time I had got timber and plank and ironwork enough to have built a good boat, if I had known how; and also I got, at several times and in several pieces, near one hundredweight of the sheet lead.

June 16. Going down to the seaside, I found a large tortoise or turtle. This was the first I had seen, which, it seems, was only my misfortune, not any defect of the place, or scarcity; for had I happened to be on the other side of the island, I might have had hundreds of them every day, as I found afterwards; but perhaps had paid dear enough for them.

June 17. I spent in cooking the turtle. I found in her three-score eggs; and her flesh was to me, at that time, the most savoury and pleasant that ever I tasted in my life, having had no flesh, but of goats and fowls, since I landed in this horrid place.

June 18. Rained all day, and I stayed within. I thought at this time the rain felt cold, and I was something chilly; which I knew was not usual in that latitude.

June 19. Very ill and shivering, as if the weather had been cold.

June 20. No rest all night; violent pains in my head, and feverish.

June 21. Very ill; frighted almost to death with the apprehensions of my sad condition—to be sick, and no help. Prayed to God, for the first time since the storm off Hull,[1] but scarce knew what I said, or why, my thoughts being all confused.

June 22. A little better; but under dreadful apprehensions of sickness.

June 23. Very bad again; cold and shivering, and then a violent headache.

June 24. Much better.

June 25. An ague very violent; the fit held me seven hours; cold fit and hot, with faint sweats after it.

June 26. Better; and having no victuals to eat, took my gun, but found myself very weak. However, I killed a she-goat, and with much difficulty got it home, and broiled some of it, and ate—I would fain have stewed it and made some broth, but had no pot.

June 27. The ague again so violent that I lay a-bed all day, and neither ate nor drank. I was ready to perish for thirst; but so weak, I had not strength to stand up, or to get myself any water to drink. Prayed to God again, but was light-headed; and when I was not, I was so ignorant that I knew not what to say; only I lay and cried, "Lord, look upon me! Lord, pity me! Lord, have mercy upon me!" I suppose I did nothing else for two or three hours; till, the fit wearing off, I fell asleep, and did not wake till far in the night. When I awoke I found myself much refreshed, but weak, and exceeding thirsty. However, as I had no water in my habitation, I was forced to lie till morning, and went to sleep again. In this second sleep I had this terrible dream: I thought that I was sitting on the ground on the outside of my wall, where I sat when the storm blew after the earthquake, and that I saw a man descend from a great black cloud, in a bright flame of fire, and light upon the ground. He was all over as bright as a flame, so that I could but just bear to look towards him; his countenance was most inexpressibly dreadful, impossible for words to describe. When he stepped upon the ground

[1] *storm off Hull* This storm occurred when he had first gone to sea, against his father's wishes.

with his feet, I thought the earth trembled, just as it had done before in the earthquake, and all the air looked, to my apprehension, as if it had been filled with flashes of fire. He was no sooner landed upon the earth but he moved forward towards me, with a long spear or weapon in his hand, to kill me; and when he came to a rising ground, at some distance, he spoke to me—or I heard a voice, so terrible that it is impossible to express the terror of it. All that I can say I understood was this: "Seeing all these things have not brought thee to repentance, now thou shalt die"; at which words I thought he lifted up the spear that was in his hand to kill me.

No one that shall ever read this account will expect that I should be able to describe the horrors of my soul at this terrible vision. I mean that even while it was a dream, I even dreamed of those horrors. Nor is it any more possible to describe the impression that remained upon my mind when I awaked and found it was but a dream.

I had, alas, no divine knowledge. What I had received by the good instruction of my father was then worn out by an uninterrupted series, for eight years, of seafaring wickedness, and a constant conversation with none but such as were, like myself, wicked and profane to the last degree. I do not remember that I had, in all that time, one thought that so much as tended either to looking upwards towards God, or inwards towards a reflection upon my own ways; but a certain stupidity of soul, without desire of good or conscience of evil, had entirely overwhelmed me; and I was all that the most hardened, unthinking, wicked creature among our common sailors can be supposed to be; not having the least sense either of the fear of God in danger, or of thankfulness to God in deliverance.

In the relating what is already past of my story, this will be the more easily believed when I shall add that, through all the variety of miseries that had to this day befallen me, I never had so much as one thought of it being the hand of God, or that it was a just punishment for my sin—my rebellious behaviour against my father, or my present sins, which were great—or so much as a punishment for the general course of my wicked life. When I was on the desperate expedition on the desert shores of Africa, I never had so much as one thought of what would become of me, or one wish to God to direct me whither I should go, or to keep me from the danger which apparently surrounded me, as well from voracious creatures as cruel savages. But I was merely thoughtless of a God or a Providence, acted like a mere brute, from the principles of nature and by the dictates of common sense only, and, indeed, hardly that.

When I was delivered and taken up at sea by the Portugal captain, well used, and dealt justly and honourably with, as well as charitably, I had not the least thankfulness in my thoughts. When again I was shipwrecked, ruined, and in danger of drowning on this island, I was as far from remorse, or looking on it as a judgment. I only said to myself often that I was an unfortunate dog, and born to be always miserable.

It is true, when I got on shore first here and found all my ship's crew drowned and myself spared, I was surprised with a kind of ecstasy, and some transports of soul which, had the grace of God assisted, might have come up to true thankfulness; but it ended where it began, in a mere common flight of joy, or, as I may say, being glad I was alive, without the least reflection upon the distinguished goodness of the hand which had preserved me, and had singled me out to be preserved when all the rest were destroyed, or an inquiry why Providence had been thus merciful unto me. Even just the same common sort of joy which seamen generally have after they are got safe ashore from a shipwreck, which they drown all in the next bowl of punch, and forget almost as soon as it is over; and all the rest of my life was like it.

Even when I was afterwards, on due consideration, made sensible of my condition—how I was cast on this dreadful place, out of the reach of human kind, out of all hope of relief or prospect of redemption—as soon as I saw but a prospect of living, and that I should not starve and perish for hunger, all the sense of my affliction wore off; and I began to be very easy, applied myself to the works proper for my preservation and supply, and was far enough from being afflicted at my condition, as a judgment from heaven, or as the hand of God against me, these were thoughts which very seldom entered my head.

The growing up of the corn, as is hinted in my journal, had at first some little influence upon me, and began to affect me with seriousness as long as I thought it had something miraculous in it; but as soon as ever that part of the thought was removed, all the impression that was raised from it wore off also, as I have noted already. Even the earthquake, though nothing could be more terrible in its nature, or more immediately directing to the invisible Power which alone directs such things, yet no sooner was the first fright over but the impression it had made went off also. I had no more sense of God or His judgments—much less of the present affliction of my circumstances being from His hand—than if I had been in the most prosperous condition of life. But now, when I began to be sick, and a leisurely view of the miseries of death came to place itself before me; when my spirits began to sink under the burden of a strong distemper, and nature was exhausted with the violence of the fever; conscience, that had slept so long, began to awake, and I began to reproach myself with my past life, in which I had so evidently, by uncommon wickedness, provoked the justice of God to lay me under uncommon strokes, and to deal with me in so vindictive a manner.

These reflections oppressed me for the second or third day of my distemper; and in the violence, as well of the fever as of the dreadful reproaches of my conscience, extorted some words from me like praying to God, though I cannot say they were either a prayer attended with desires or with hopes: it was rather the voice of mere fright and distress. My thoughts were confused, the convictions great upon my mind, and the horror of dying in such a miserable condition raised vapours into my head with the mere apprehensions; and in these hurries of my soul I knew not what my tongue might express. But it was rather exclamation, such as, "Lord, what a miserable creature am I! If I should be sick, I shall certainly die for want of help; and what will become of me!" Then the tears burst out of my eyes, and I could say no more for a good while.

In this interval the good advice of my father came to my mind, and presently his prediction, which I mentioned at the beginning of this story—*viz.* that if I did take this foolish step,[1] God would not bless me, and I would have leisure hereafter to reflect upon having neglected his counsel when there might be none to assist in my recovery. "Now," said I, aloud, "my dear father's words are come to pass; God's justice has overtaken me, and I have none to help or hear me. I rejected the voice of Providence, which had mercifully put me in a posture or station of life wherein I might have been happy and easy; but I would neither see it myself nor learn to know the blessing of it from my parents. I left them to mourn over my folly, and now I am left to mourn under the consequences of it. I abused their help and assistance, who would have lifted me in the world, and would have made everything easy to me; and now I have difficulties to struggle with, too great for even nature itself to support, and no assistance, no help, no comfort, no advice." Then I cried out, "Lord, be my help, for I am in great distress."

This was the first prayer, if I may call it so, that I had made for many years. But to return to my journal.

June 28. Having been somewhat refreshed with the sleep I had had, and the fit being entirely off, I got up; and though the fright and terror of my dream was very great, yet I considered that the fit of the ague would return again the next day, and now was my time to get something to refresh and support myself when I should be ill; and the first thing I did, I filled a large square case-bottle with water, and set it upon my table, in reach of my bed; and to take off the chill or aguish disposition of the water, I put about a quarter of a pint of rum into it, and mixed them together. Then I got me a piece of the goat's flesh and broiled it on the coals, but could eat very little. I walked about, but was very weak, and withal very sad and heavy-hearted under a sense of my miserable condition, dreading the return of my distemper the next day. At night I made my supper of three of the turtle's eggs, which I roasted in the ashes, and ate, as we call it, in the shell—and this was the first bit of meat I had ever asked God's blessing to, that I could remember, in my whole life.

After I had eaten I tried to walk, but found myself so weak that I could hardly carry a gun, for I never went out without that; so I went but a little way, and sat down upon the ground, looking out upon the sea, which was just before me, and very calm and smooth. As I sat here some such thoughts as these occurred to me: What is this earth and sea, of which I have seen so much? Whence is it produced? And what am I, and all the other creatures wild and tame, human and brutal? Whence are we? Sure we are all made by some secret Power, who formed the earth and sea, the air and sky. And who is that? Then it followed most naturally, it is God that has made all. Well, but then it came on

[1] *this foolish step* Of becoming a sailor and spending his life at sea.

strangely, if God has made all these things, He guides and governs them all, and all things that concern them; for the Power that could make all things must certainly have power to guide and direct them. If so, nothing can happen in the great circuit of His works, either without His knowledge or appointment.

And if nothing happens without His knowledge, He knows that I am here, and am in this dreadful condition; and if nothing happens without His appointment, He has appointed all this to befall me. Nothing occurred to my thought to contradict any of these conclusions, and therefore it rested upon me with the greater force, that it must needs be that God had appointed all this to befall me; that I was brought into this miserable circumstance by His direction, He having the sole power, not of me only, but of everything that happened in the world. Immediately it followed: Why has God done this to me? What have I done to be thus used?

My conscience presently checked me in that inquiry, as if I had blasphemed, and methought it spoke to me like a voice: "Wretch! dost *thou* ask what thou hast done? Look back upon a dreadful misspent life, and ask thyself what thou hast *not* done? Ask, why is it that thou wert not long ago destroyed? Why wert thou not drowned in Yarmouth Roads; killed in the fight when the ship was taken by the Sallee man-of-war; devoured by the wild beasts on the coast of Africa; or drowned *here*, when all the crew perished but thyself? Dost *thou* ask, what have I done?"

I was struck dumb with these reflections, as one astonished, and had not a word to say—no, not to answer to myself, but rose up pensive and sad, walked back to my retreat, and went up over my wall, as if I had been going to bed; but my thoughts were sadly disturbed, and I had no inclination to sleep; so I sat down in my chair and lighted my lamp, for it began to be dark. Now, as the apprehension of the return of my distemper terrified me very much, it occurred to my thought that the Brazilians take no physic but their tobacco for almost all distempers, and I had a piece of a roll of tobacco in one of the chests, which was quite cured, and some also that was green, and not quite cured.

I went, directed by Heaven no doubt; for in this chest I found a cure both for soul and body. I opened the chest, and found what I looked for, the tobacco; and, as the few books I had saved lay there too, I took out one of the Bibles which I mentioned before, and which to this time I had not found leisure or inclination to look into. I say, I took it out, and brought both that and the tobacco with me to the table. What use to make of the tobacco I knew not, in my distemper, or whether it was good for it or no; but I tried several experiments with it, as if I was resolved it should hit one way or other. I first took a piece of leaf and chewed it in my mouth, which, indeed, at first almost stupefied my brain, the tobacco being green and strong, and that I had not been much used to. Then I took some and steeped it an hour or two in some rum, and resolved to take a dose of it when I lay down; and lastly, I burnt some upon a pan of coals, and held my nose close over the smoke of it as long as I could bear it, as well for the heat as almost for suffocation. In the interval of this operation I took up the Bible and began to read; but my head was too much disturbed with the tobacco to bear reading, at least at that time; only, having opened the book casually, the first words that occurred to me were these, "Call on Me in the day of trouble, and I will deliver, and thou shalt glorify Me."

These words were very apt to my case, and made some impression upon my thoughts at the time of reading them, though not so much as they did afterwards; for, as for being *delivered*, the word had no sound, as I may say, to me; the thing was so remote, so impossible in my apprehension of things, that I began to say, as the children of Israel did when they were promised flesh to eat, "Can God spread a table in the wilderness?" So I began to say, "Can God Himself deliver me from this place?" And as it was not for many years that any hopes appeared, this prevailed very often upon my thoughts; but, however, the words made a great impression upon me, and I mused upon them very often. It grew now late, and the tobacco had, as I said, dozed my head so much that I inclined to sleep; so I left my lamp burning in the cave, lest I should want anything in the night, and went to bed. But before I lay down I did what I never had done in all my life—I kneeled down, and prayed to God to fulfil the promise to me, that if I called upon Him in the day of trouble, He would deliver me. After my broken and imperfect prayer was over, I drank the rum in which I had steeped the tobacco, which was so strong and rank of the tobacco that I could scarcely get it down; immediately upon this I went to bed. I found presently it flew up into my head violently; but I fell into a sound sleep and waked no more till, by the sun, it must necessarily be near three o'clock in the afternoon the next day—nay, to this hour I am partly of opinion that I slept all the next day and night, and till almost three the day after, for otherwise I know not how I should lose a day out of my reckoning in the days of the week, as it appeared some years after I had done; for if I had lost it by crossing and recrossing the line, I should have lost more than one day; but certainly I lost a day in my account, and never knew which way. Be that, however, one way or the other, when I awaked I found myself exceedingly refreshed, and my spirits lively and cheerful; when I got up I was stronger than I was the day before, and my stomach better, for I was hungry; and, in short, I had no fit the next day, but continued much altered for the better. This was the 29th.

The 30th was my well day[1] of course, and I went abroad with my gun, but did not care to travel too far. I killed a sea-fowl or two, something like a brandgoose,[2] and brought them home, but was not very forward to eat them; so I ate some more of the turtle's eggs, which were very good. This evening I renewed the medicine, which I had supposed did me good the day before—the tobacco steeped in rum; only I did not take so much as before, nor did I chew any of the leaf, or hold my head over the smoke; however, I was not so well the next day, which was the first of July, as I hoped I should have been; for I had a little spice of the cold fit, but it was not much.

July 2. I renewed the medicine all the three ways, and dosed myself with it as at first, and doubled the quantity which I drank.

July 3. I missed the fit for good and all, though I did not recover my full strength for some weeks after. While I was thus gathering strength, my thoughts ran exceedingly upon this Scripture, "I will deliver thee"; and the impossibility of my deliverance lay much upon my mind, in bar of my ever expecting it; but as I was discouraging myself with such thoughts, it occurred to my mind that I pored so much upon my deliverance from the main affliction that I disregarded the deliverance I had received, and I was, as it were, made to ask myself such questions as these—*viz.* Have I not been delivered, and wonderfully too, from sickness, from the most distressed condition that could be, and that was so frightful to me? and what notice had I taken of it? Had I done my part? God had delivered me, but I had not glorified Him—that is to say, I had not owned and been thankful for that as a deliverance; and how could I expect greater deliverance? This touched my heart very much; and immediately I knelt down and gave God thanks aloud for my recovery from my sickness.

July 4. In the morning I took the Bible, and, beginning at the New Testament, I began seriously to read it, and imposed upon myself to read a while every morning and every night; not tying myself to the number of chapters, but long as my thoughts should engage me. It was not long after I set seriously to this work till I found my heart more deeply and sincerely affected with the wickedness of my past life. The impression of my dream revived; and the words, "All these things have not brought thee to repentance," ran seriously through my thoughts. I was earnestly begging of God to give me repentance when it happened providentially, the very day that, reading the Scripture, I came to these words: "He is exalted a Prince and a Saviour, to give repentance and to give remission." I threw down the book; and, with my heart as well as my hands lifted up to heaven, in a kind of ecstasy of joy, I cried out aloud, "Jesus, thou Son of David! Jesus, thou exalted Prince and Saviour! give me repentance!"

This was the first time I could say, in the true sense of the words, that I prayed in all my life; for now I prayed with a sense of my condition, and a true Scripture view of hope, founded on the encouragement of the

[1] *well day* He is suffering from an ague that recurs every second day.

[2] *brandgoose* Smallest species of wild goose.

Word of God; and from this time, I may say, I began to hope that God would hear me.

Now I began to construe the words mentioned above, "Call on Me, and I will deliver thee," in a different sense from what I had ever done before; for then I had no notion of anything being called *deliverance* but my being delivered from the captivity I was in; for though I was indeed at large in the place, yet the island was certainly a prison to me, and that in the worst sense of the word. But now I learned to take it in another sense: now I looked back upon my past life with such horror, and my sins appeared so dreadful that my soul sought nothing of God but deliverance from the load of guilt that bore down all my comfort. As for my solitary life, it was nothing. I did not so much as pray to be delivered from it or think of it; it was all of no consideration in comparison to this. And I add this part here to hint to whoever shall read it that whenever they come to a true sense of things, they will find deliverance from sin a much greater blessing than deliverance from affliction. But, leaving this part, I return to my journal.

My condition began now to be, though not less miserable as to my way of living, yet much easier to my mind; and my thoughts being directed, by a constant reading the Scripture and praying to God, to things of a higher nature, I had a great deal of comfort within, which till now I knew nothing of. Also, my health and strength returned, I bestirred myself to furnish myself with everything that I wanted, and make my way of living as regular as I could.

From the 4th of July to the 14th I was chiefly employed in walking about with my gun in my hand, a little and a little at a time, as a man that was gathering up his strength after a fit of sickness; for it is hardly to be imagined how low I was, and to what weakness I was reduced. The application which I made use of was perfectly new, and perhaps which had never cured an ague before; neither can I recommend it to any to practice, by this experiment: and though it did carry off the fit, yet it rather contributed to weakening me; for I had frequent convulsions in my nerves and limbs for some time. I learned from it also this, in particular, that being abroad in the rainy season was the most pernicious thing to my health that could be, especially in those rains which came attended with storms and hurricanes of wind; for as the rain which came in the dry season was almost always accompanied with such storms, so I found that rain was much more dangerous than the rain which fell in September and October.

I had been now in this unhappy island above ten months; all possibility of deliverance from this condition seemed to be entirely taken from me, and I firmly believed that no human shape had ever set foot upon that place. Having now secured my habitation, as I thought, fully to my mind, I had a great desire to make a more perfect discovery of the island, and to see what other productions I might find which I yet knew nothing of.

—1719

In Context

Illustrating *Robinson Crusoe*

The first edition of *Robinson Crusoe* (1719) included only one illustration as a frontispiece; This illustration was reprinted numerous times over several decades—though there were some variants, such as that in the sixth edition of 1722. (Whereas the 1719 image shows a ship in full sail in good weather, the 1722 version portrays a ship foundering during a storm.) By the 1770s the book was neither widely read nor much esteemed in England, though it remained popular in France; in *Emile* (1762) Jean-Jacques Rousseau praised it as the finest work available on "natural education." In the 1780s and 1790s illustrated editions of *Robinson Crusoe* began to be issued with some frequency—as would remain the case throughout the nineteenth and twentieth centuries. The Clark and Pine image continued to exert an influence on many illustrators, but others departed from it entirely. A frequent focus of later illustrations is Crusoe becoming acquainted (after twenty-four years of solitude) with another human—the native whom he christens "Friday." The description of Friday in Defoe's text reads as follows:

> He was a comely, handsome fellow, perfectly well made, with straight, strong limbs, not too large; tall, and well-shaped; and, as I reckon, about twenty-six years of age. He had a very good countenance, not a fierce and surly aspect, but seemed to have something very manly in his face; and yet he had all the sweetness and softness of a European in his countenance, too, especially when he smiled. His hair was long and black, not curled like wool; his forehead very high and large; and a great vivacity and sparkling sharpness in his eyes. The colour of his skin was not quite black, but very tawny; and yet not an ugly, yellow, nauseous tawny, as the Brasilians and Virginians, and other natives of America are, but of a bright kind of a dun olive-colour, that had in it something very agreeable, though not very easy to describe. His face was round and plump; his nose small, not flat, like the negroes; a very good mouth, thin lips, and his fine teeth well set, and as white as ivory.

(John?) Clark and John Pine, frontispiece, 1719 edition.

Charles Ansell and Inigo Barlow, frontispiece, 1790.

George Cruikshank and Augustus Fox, frontispiece, 1831.

Alexander Fraser and Charles G. Lewis, *Robinson Crusoe reading the Bible to his Man Friday*, 1835.

John Butler Yeats, *Crusoe landing on the island*, 1895.

Charles Edmund Brock, *This Friday admired very much*, 1898.

from *A Journal of the Plague Year*[1]

It was now mid-July, and the plague, which had chiefly raged at the other end of the town, and, as I said before, in the parishes of St. Giles, St. Andrew's, Holborn, and towards Westminster, began to now come eastward towards the part where I lived. It was to be observed, indeed, that it did not come straight on towards us; for the city, that is to say, within the walls, was indifferently healthy still; nor was it got then very much over the water into Southwark; for though there died that week 1268 of all distempers, whereof it might be supposed above 900 died of the plague, yet there was but twenty-eight in the whole city, within the walls, and but nineteen in Southwark, Lambeth parish included; whereas in the parishes of St. Giles and St. Martin-in-the-Fields alone there died 421.

But we perceived the infection kept chiefly in the out-parishes, which being very populous, and fuller also of poor, the distemper found more to prey upon than in the city, as I shall observe afterwards. We perceived, I say, the distemper to draw our way, *viz.*[2] by the parishes of Clarkenwell, Cripplegate, Shoreditch, and Bishopsgate; which last two parishes joining to Aldgate, Whitechapel, and Stepney, the infection came at length to spread its utmost rage and violence in those parts, even when it abated at the western parishes where it began.

It was very strange to observe that in this particular week, from the 4th to the 11th of July, when, as I have

[1] *A Journal … Year* This piece of historical fiction was written in the early 1720s, when an outbreak of the plague threatened London. In the piece, the text's narrator (who resembles Defoe's uncle, Henry Foe, a London saddler in the parish of Aldgate) reflects back upon journal entries he wrote during 1665, the year of the great outbreak of bubonic plague in London, hoping to provide beneficial information for future generations.

[2] *viz.* Abbreviation of the Latin *videlicet*, meaning "namely; that is to say."

observed, there died near 400 of the plague in the two parishes of St. Martin and St. Giles-in-the-Fields only, there died in the parish of Aldgate but four, in the parish of Whitechapel three, in the parish of Stepney but one.

Likewise in the next week, from the 11th of July to the 18th, when the week's bill[1] was 1761, yet there died no more of the plague, on the whole Southwark side of the water, than sixteen.

But this face of things soon changed, and it began to thicken in Cripplegate parish especially, and in Clarkenwell; so that by the second week in August, Cripplegate parish alone buried 886, and Clarkenwell 155. Of the first, 850 might well be reckoned to die of the plague; and of the last, the bill itself said 145 were of the plague.

During the month of July and while, as I have observed, our part of the town seemed to be spared in comparison of the west part, I went ordinarily about the streets, as my business required, and particularly went generally once in a day, or in two days, into the city, to my brother's house, which he had given me charge of, and to see if it was safe; and, having the key in my pocket, I used to go into the house and over most of the rooms, to see that all was well; for though it be something wonderful to tell that any should have hearts so hardened in the midst of such a calamity as to rob and steal, yet certain it is that all sorts of villainies, and even levities and debaucheries, were then practised in the town as openly as ever—I will not say quite as frequently, because the numbers of people were many ways lessened.

But the city itself began now to be visited too, I mean within the walls; but the number of people there were indeed extremely lessened by so great a multitude having been gone into the country; and even all this month of July they continued to flee, though not in such multitudes as formerly. In August, indeed, they fled in such a manner that I began to think there would be really none but magistrates and servants left in the city.

As they fled now out of the city, so I should observe that the Court removed early, *viz.* in the month of June, and went to Oxford, where it pleased God to preserve them; and the distemper did not, as I heard of, so much as touch them, for which I cannot say that I ever saw they showed any great token of thankfulness, and hardly anything of reformation, though they did not want being told that their crying vices might without breach of charity be said to have gone far in bringing that terrible judgement upon the whole nation.

The face of London was now indeed strangely altered: I mean the whole mass of buildings, city, liberties, suburbs, Westminster, Southwark, and altogether; for as to the particular part called the city, or within the walls, that was not yet much infected. But in the whole the face of things, I say, was much altered. Sorrow and sadness sat upon every face; and though some parts were not yet overwhelmed, yet all looked deeply concerned; and, as we saw it apparently coming on, so every one looked on himself and his family as in the utmost danger. Were it possible to represent those times exactly to those that did not see them, and give the reader due ideas of the horror that everywhere presented itself, it must make just impressions upon their minds and fill them with surprise. London might well be said to be all in tears; the mourners did not go about the streets indeed, for nobody put on black or made a formal dress of mourning for their nearest friends; but the voice of mourners was truly heard in the streets. The shrieks of women and children at the windows and doors of their houses, where their dearest relations were perhaps dying, or just dead, were so frequent to be heard as we passed the streets that it was enough to pierce the stoutest heart in the world to hear them. Tears and lamentations were seen almost in every house, especially in the first part of the visitation; for towards the latter end men's hearts were hardened, and death was so always before their eyes that they did not so much concern themselves for the loss of their friends, expecting that themselves should be summoned the next hour.

Business led me out sometimes to the other end of the town, even when the sickness was chiefly there; and as the thing was new to me, as well as to everybody else, it was a most surprising thing to see those streets which were usually so thronged now grown desolate, and so few people to be seen in them that, if I had been a stranger and at a loss for my way, I might sometimes have gone the length of a whole street (I mean of the by-streets) and seen nobody to direct me except watchmen

[1] *the week's bill* I.e., the Bill of Mortality, a record of all London deaths published weekly.

set at the doors of such houses as were shut up, of which I shall speak presently.

One day, being at that part of the town on some special business, curiosity led me to observe things more than usually, and indeed I walked a great way where I had no business. I went up Holborn, and there the street was full of people, but they walked in the middle of the great street, neither on one side or other, because, as I suppose, they would not mingle with anybody that came out of houses, or meet with smells and scent from houses that might be infected.

The Inns of Court were all shut up; nor were very many of the lawyers in the Temple, or Lincoln's Inn, or Gray's Inn, to be seen there. Everybody was at peace; there was no occasion for lawyers; besides, it being in the time of the vacation too, they were generally gone into the country. Whole rows of houses in some places were shut close up, the inhabitants all fled, and only a watchman or two left.

When I speak of rows of houses being shut up, I do not mean shut up by the magistrates, but that great numbers of persons followed the Court, by the necessity of their employments and other dependences; and as others retired, really frighted with the distemper, it was a mere desolating of some of the streets. But the fright was not yet near so great in the city, abstractly so called, and particularly because, though they were at first in a most inexpressible consternation, yet as I have observed that the distemper intermitted often at first, so they were, as it were, alarmed and unalarmed again, and this several times, till it began to be familiar to them; and that even when it appeared violent, yet seeing it did not presently spread into the city, or the east and south parts, the people began to take courage, and to be, as I may say, a little hardened. It is true a vast many people fled, as I have observed, yet they were chiefly from the west end of the town, and from that we call the heart of the city: that is to say, among the wealthiest of the people, and such people as were unencumbered with trades and business. But of the rest, the generality stayed and seemed to abide the worst; so that in the place we call the Liberties, and in the suburbs, in Southwark, and in the east part, such as Wapping, Ratcliff, Stepney, Rotherhithe, and the like, the people generally stayed, except here and there a few wealthy families, who, as above, did not depend upon their business.

It must not be forgot here that the city and suburbs were prodigiously full of people at the time of this visitation, I mean at the time that it began; for though I have lived to see a further increase, and mighty throngs of people settling in London more than ever, yet we had always a notion that the numbers of people which—the wars being over, the armies disbanded, and the royal family and the monarchy being restored[1]—had flocked to London to settle in business, or to depend upon and attend the Court for rewards of services, preferments, and the like, was such that the town was computed to have in it above a hundred thousand people more than ever it held before; nay, some took upon them to say it had twice as many, because all the ruined families of the royal party flocked hither. All the old soldiers set up trades here, and abundance of families settled here. Again, the Court brought with them a great flux of pride, and new fashions. All people were grown gay and luxurious, and the joy of the Restoration had brought a vast many families to London.

... But I must go back again to the beginning of this surprising time. While the fears of the people were young, they were increased strangely by several odd accidents which, put altogether, it was really a wonder the whole body of the people did not rise as one man and abandon their dwellings, leaving the place as a space of ground designed by Heaven for an Aceldama,[2] doomed to be destroyed from the face of the earth, and that all that would be found in it would perish with it. I shall name but a few of these things; but sure they were so many, and so many wizards and cunning people[3] propagating them, that I have often wondered there was any (women especially) left behind.

In the first place, a blazing star or comet appeared for several months before the plague, as there did the

[1] *royal family ... restored* In 1660 the monarchy was restored after twenty years of turmoil, including civil war and the protectorate of Cromwell. Charles Stuart and his court returned from exile in France and Charles assumed the throne as Charles II.

[2] *Aceldama* Scene of slaughter or mass death; place with terrible associations. (From the field of that name near Jerusalem, which was purchased by priests with the money Judas received—and later returned to them—for betraying Jesus. The field was used as a burial ground for strangers.)

[3] *cunning people* People who possessed magical knowledge and skill.

year after another, a little before the fire.[1] The old women and the phlegmatic hypochondriac part of the other sex, whom I could almost call old women too, remarked (especially afterward, though not till both those judgements were over) that those two comets passed directly over the city, and that so very near the houses that it was plain they imported something peculiar to the city alone; that the comet before the pestilence was of a faint, dull, languid colour, and its motion very heavy, solemn, and slow; but that the comet before the fire was bright and sparkling, or, as others said, flaming, and its motion swift and furious; and that, accordingly, one foretold a heavy judgement, slow but severe, terrible and frightful, as was the plague; but the other foretold a stroke, sudden, swift, and fiery as the conflagration. Nay, so particular some people were that as they looked upon that comet preceding the fire, they fancied that they not only saw it pass swiftly and fiercely, and could perceive the motion with their eye, but even they heard it; that it made a rushing, mighty noise, fierce and terrible, though at a distance, and but just perceivable.

I saw both these stars and, I must confess, had so much of the common notion of such things in my head that I was apt to look upon them as the forerunners and warnings of God's judgements; and especially when, after the plague had followed the first. I yet saw another of the like kind. I could not but say God had not yet sufficiently scourged the city.

But I could not at the same time carry these things to the height that others did, knowing, too, that natural causes are assigned by the astronomers for such things, and that their motions and even their revolutions are calculated, or pretended to be calculated, so that they cannot be so perfectly called the forerunners or foretellers, much less the procurers, of such events as pestilence, war, fire, and the like.

But let my thoughts and the thoughts of the philosophers be, or have been, what they will, these things had a more than ordinary influence upon the minds of the common people, and they had almost universal melancholy apprehensions of some dreadful calamity and judgement coming upon the city; and this principally from the sight of this comet, and the little alarm that was given in December by two people dying at St. Giles's, as above.

The apprehensions of the people were likewise strangely increased by the error of the times; in which, I think, the people, from what principle I cannot imagine, were more addicted to prophecies and astrological conjurations, dreams, and old wives' tales than ever they were before or since. Whether this unhappy temper was originally raised by the follies of some people who got money by it—that is to say, by printing predictions and prognostications—I know not; but certain it is, books frighted them terribly, such as *Lilly's Almanack*, *Gadbury's Astrological Predictions*, *Poor Robin's Almanack*, and the like; also several pretended religious books, one entitled, *Come out of her, my People, lest you be Partaker of her Plagues*; another called *Fair Warning*; another, *Britain's Remembrancer*; and many such, all, or most part of which, foretold, directly or covertly, the ruin of the city. Nay, some were so enthusiastically bold as to run about the streets with their oral predictions, pretending they were sent to preach to the city; and one in particular, who, like Jonah to Nineveh, cried in the streets, "Yet forty days, and London shall be destroyed."[2]

... When the plague at first seized a family—that is to say, when anybody of the family had gone out and unwarily or otherwise catched the distemper and brought it home—it was certainly known by the family before it was known to the officers, who, as you will see by the order, were appointed to examine into the circumstances of all sick persons when they heard of their being sick.

In this interval between their being taken sick and the examiners coming, the master of the house had leisure and liberty to remove himself or all his family, if he knew whither to go, and many did so. But the great disaster was that many did thus after they were really infected themselves, and so carried the disease into the houses of those who were so hospitable as to receive them; which, it must be confessed, was very cruel and ungrateful.

And this was, in part, the reason of the general notion, or scandal rather, which went about of the

[1] *the fire* The Great Fire of London, in September 1666.

[2] *Yet forty ... destroyed* From Jonah 3.4, in which the prophet Jonah warns the people of Nineveh of their impending doom. They then repent and mend their evil ways, and God spares them.

temper of people infected—namely, that they did not take the least care or make any scruple of infecting others, though I cannot say but there might be some truth in it too, but not so general as was reported. What natural reason could be given for so wicked a thing at a time when they might conclude themselves just going to appear at the bar of Divine Justice I know not. I am very well satisfied that it cannot be reconciled to religion and principle any more than it can be to generosity and humanity, but I may speak of that again.

I am speaking now of people made desperate by the apprehensions of their being shut up, and their breaking out by stratagem or force, either before or after they were shut up, whose misery was not lessened when they were out, but sadly increased. On the other hand, many that thus got away had retreats to go to and other houses, where they locked themselves up and kept hid till the plague was over; and many families, foreseeing the approach of the distemper, laid up stores of provisions sufficient for their whole families, and shut themselves up, and that so entirely that they were neither seen or heard of till the infection was quite ceased, and then came abroad sound and well. I might recollect several such as these, and give you the particulars of their management; for doubtless it was the most effectual secure step that could be taken for such whose circumstances would not admit them to remove, or who had not retreats abroad proper for the case; for in being thus shut up they were as if they had been a hundred miles off. Nor do I remember that any one of those families miscarried. Among these, several Dutch merchants were particularly remarkable, who kept their houses like little garrisons besieged, suffering none to go in or out or come near them, particularly one in a court in Throgmorton Street whose house looked into Draper's Garden.[1]

But I come back to the case of families infected and shut up by the magistrates. The misery of those families is not to be expressed; and it was generally in such houses that we heard the most dismal shrieks and outcries of the poor people, terrified and even frighted to death by the sight of the condition of their dearest relations, and by the terror of being imprisoned as they were.

I remember, and while I am writing this story I think I hear the very sound of it, a certain lady had an only daughter, a young maiden about nineteen years old, and who was possessed of a very considerable fortune. They were only lodgers in the house where they were. The young woman, her mother, and the maid had been abroad on some occasion, I do not remember what, for the house was not shut up; but about two hours after they came home the young lady complained she was not well; in a quarter of an hour more she vomited and had a violent pain in her head. "Pray God," says her mother, in a terrible fright, "my child has not the distemper!" The pain in her head increasing, her mother ordered the bed to be warmed, and resolved to put her to bed, and prepared to give her things to sweat, which was the ordinary remedy to be taken when the first apprehensions of the distemper began.

While the bed was airing the mother undressed the young woman, and just as she was laid down in the bed, she, looking upon her body with a candle, immediately discovered the fatal tokens on the inside of her thighs. Her mother, not being able to contain herself, threw down her candle and shrieked out in such a frightful manner that it was enough to place horror upon the stoutest heart in the world; nor was it one scream or one cry, but the fright having seized her spirits, she fainted first, then recovered, then ran all over the house, up the stairs and down the stairs, like one distracted, and indeed really was distracted, and continued screeching and crying out for several hours void of all sense, or at least government of her senses, and, as I was told, never came thoroughly to herself again. As to the young maiden, she was a dead corpse from that moment, for the gangrene which occasions the spots had spread over her whole body, and she died in less than two hours. But still the mother continued crying out, not knowing anything more of her child, several hours after she was dead. It is so long ago that I am not certain, but I think the mother never recovered, but died in two or three weeks after.

This was an extraordinary case, and I am therefore the more particular in it because I came so much to the knowledge of it; but there were innumerable such-like cases, and it was seldom that the weekly bill came in but there were two or three put in, "frighted"; that is, that may well be called frighted to death. But besides those

[1] *Draper's Garden* Park next to Draper's Hall, the headquarters of a London livery company located in the heart of London.

who were so frighted as to die upon the spot, there were great numbers frighted to other extremes, some frighted out of their senses, some out of their memory, and some out of their understanding....

I went all the first part of the time freely about the streets, though not so freely as to run myself into apparent danger, except when they dug the great pit in the churchyard of our parish of Aldgate. A terrible pit it was, and I could not resist my curiosity to go and see it. As near as I may judge, it was about forty feet in length, and about fifteen or sixteen feet broad, and, at the time I first looked at it, about nine feet deep; but it was said they dug it near twenty feet deep afterwards in one part of it, till they could go no deeper for the water; for they had, it seems, dug several large pits before this. For though the plague was long a-coming to our parish, yet, when it did come, there was no parish in or about London where it raged with such violence as in the two parishes of Aldgate and Whitechapel.

I say they had dug several pits in another ground when the distemper began to spread in our parish, and especially when the dead-carts began to go about, which was not, in our parish, till the beginning of August. Into these pits they had put perhaps fifty or sixty bodies each; then they made larger holes wherein they buried all that the cart brought in a week, which, by the middle to the end of August, came to from 200 to 400 a week; and they could not well dig them larger, because of the order of the magistrates confining them to leave no bodies within six feet of the surface; and the water coming on at about seventeen or eighteen feet, they could not well, I say, put more in one pit. But now, at the beginning of September, the plague raging in a dreadful manner, and the number of burials in our parish increasing to more than was ever buried in any parish about London of no larger extent, they ordered this dreadful gulf to be dug—for such it was, rather than a pit.

They had supposed this pit would have supplied them for a month or more when they dug it, and some blamed the churchwardens for suffering such a frightful thing, telling them they were making preparations to bury the whole parish, and the like; but time made it appear the churchwardens knew the condition of the parish better than they did; for, the pit being finished the 4th of September, I think, they began to bury in it the 6th, and by the 20th, which was just two weeks, they had thrown into it 1,114 bodies when they were obliged to fill it up, the bodies being then come to lie within six feet of the surface. I doubt not but there may be some ancient persons alive in the parish who can justify the fact of this, and are able to show even in what place of the churchyard the pit lay better than I can. The mark of it also was many years to be seen in the churchyard on the surface, lying in length parallel with the passage which goes by the west wall of the churchyard out of Houndsditch, and turns east again into Whitechapel, coming out near the Three Nuns' Inn.

It was about the 10th of September that my curiosity led, or rather drove, me to go and see this pit again, when there had been near 400 people buried in it; and I was not content to see it in the day-time, as I had done before, for then there would have been nothing to have been seen but the loose earth; for all the bodies that were thrown in were immediately covered with earth by those they called the buriers, which at other times were called bearers;[1] but I resolved to go in the night and see some of them thrown in.

There was a strict order to prevent people coming to those pits, and that was only to prevent infection. But after some time that order was more necessary, for people that were infected and near their end, and delirious also, would run to those pits, wrapt in blankets or rugs, and throw themselves in, and, as they said, bury themselves. I cannot say that the officers suffered any willingly to lie there; but I have heard that in a great pit in Finsbury, in the parish of Cripplegate, it lying open then to the fields, for it was not then walled about, many came and threw themselves in, and expired there, before they threw any earth upon them; and that when they came to bury others and found them there, they were quite dead, though not cold.

This may serve a little to describe the dreadful condition of that day, though it is impossible to say anything that is able to give a true idea of it to those who did not see it, other than this—that it was indeed very, very, very dreadful, and such as no tongue can express.

[1] *buriers ... bearers* Bearers carried dead bodies to the pits at night, while during the day they brought the sick to plague-hospitals. Buriers, on the other hand (which the narrator confuses with bearers) arranged and buried the bodies in pits.

I got admittance into the churchyard by being acquainted with the sexton[1] who attended; who, though he did not refuse me at all, yet earnestly persuaded me not to go, telling me very seriously (for he was a good, religious, and sensible man) that it was indeed their business and duty to venture, and to run all hazards, and that in it they might hope to be preserved; but that I had no apparent call to it but my own curiosity, which, he said, he believed I would not pretend was sufficient to justify my running that hazard. I told him I had been pressed in my mind to go, and that perhaps it might be an instructing sight that might not be without its uses. "Nay," says the good man, "if you will venture upon that score, name of God go in; for, depend upon it, 'twill be a sermon to you, it may be the best that ever you heard in your life. 'Tis a speaking sight," says he, "and has a voice with it, and a loud one, to call us all to repentance"; and with that he opened the door and said, "Go, if you will."

His discourse had shocked my resolution a little, and I stood wavering for a good while, but just at that interval I saw two links[2] come over from the end of the Minories,[3] and heard the bellman,[4] and then appeared a dead-cart, as they called it, coming over the streets; so I could no longer resist my desire of seeing it, and went in. There was nobody, as I could perceive at first, in the churchyard, or going into it, but the buriers and the fellow that drove the cart, or rather led the horse and cart; but when they came up to the pit they saw a man go to and again, muffled up in a brown cloak, and making motions with his hands under his cloak, as if he was in great agony, and the buriers immediately gathered about him, supposing he was one of those poor delirious or desperate creatures that used to pretend,[5] as I have said, to bury themselves. He said nothing as he walked about, but two or three times groaned very deeply and loud, and sighed as he would break his heart.

When the buriers came up to him they soon found he was neither a person infected and desperate, as I have observed above, or a person distempered in mind, but one oppressed with a dreadful weight of grief indeed, having his wife and several of his children all in the cart that was just come in with him, and he followed in an agony and excess of sorrow. He mourned heartily, as it was easy to see, but with a kind of masculine grief that could not give itself vent by tears, and, calmly defying the buriers to let him alone, said he would only see the bodies thrown in and go away, so they left importuning him. But no sooner was the cart turned round and the bodies shot into the pit promiscuously, which was a surprise to him, for he at least expected they would have been decently laid in, though indeed he was afterwards convinced that was impracticable—I say, no sooner did he see the sight but he cried out aloud, unable to contain himself. I could not hear what he said, but he went backward two or three steps and fell down in a swoon. The buriers ran to him and took him up, and in a little while he came to himself, and they led him away to the Pie Tavern over against the end of Houndsditch, where, it seems, the man was known, and where they took care of him. He looked into the pit again as he went away, but the buriers had covered the bodies so immediately with throwing in earth, that though there was light enough—for there were lanterns, and candles in them, placed all night round the sides of the pit upon heaps of earth, seven or eight, or perhaps more—yet nothing could be seen.

This was a mournful scene indeed, and affected me almost as much as the rest; but the other was awful and full of terror. The cart had in it sixteen or seventeen bodies; some were wrapt up in linen sheets, some in rags, some little other than naked, or so loose that what covering they had fell from them in the shooting out of the cart, and they fell quite naked among the rest; but the matter was not much to them, or the indecency much to anyone else, seeing they were all dead, and were to be huddled together into the common grave of mankind, as we may call it; for here was no difference made, but poor and rich went together. There was no other way of burials, neither was it possible there should, for coffins were not to be had for the prodigious numbers that fell in such a calamity as this.

It was reported by way of scandal upon the buriers that if any corpse was delivered to them decently wound

[1] *sexton* Church official whose duties include caring for the church and its grounds and overseeing the digging of graves.

[2] *links* Torches; here, the boys hired to carry those torches.

[3] *the Minories* An Aldgate street.

[4] *bellman* Person who would ring a bell to announce the approach of the cart for burying the dead. In other times, the bellman would walk through the streets announcing the time and weather.

[5] *pretend* Try.

up, as we called it then, in a winding-sheet tied over the head and feet, which some did, and which was generally of good linen—I say, it was reported that the buriers were so wicked as to strip them in the cart and carry them quite naked to the ground. But as I cannot easily credit anything so vile among Christians, and at a time so filled with terrors as that was, I can only relate it and leave it undetermined....

We had at this time a great many frightful stories told us of nurses and watchmen who looked after the dying people; that is to say, hired nurses who attended infected people, using them barbarously, starving them, smothering them, or by other wicked means hastening their end—that is to say, murdering of them; and watchmen, being set to guard houses that were shut up when there has been but one person left, and perhaps that one lying sick, that they have broke in and murdered that body, and immediately thrown them out into the dead-cart! And so they have gone scarce cold to the grave.

I cannot say but that some such murders were committed, and I think two were sent to prison for it, but died before they could be tried; and I have heard that three others, at several times, were excused for murders of that kind; but I must say I believe nothing of its being so common a crime as some have since been pleased to say, nor did it seem to be so rational where the people were brought so low as not to be able to help themselves, for such seldom recovered, and there was no temptation to commit a murder, at least none equal to the fact, where they were sure persons would die in so short a time, and could not live.

That there were a great many robberies and wicked practices committed even in this dreadful time I do not deny. The power of avarice was so strong in some that they would run any hazard to steal and to plunder; and, particularly in houses where all the families or inhabitants have been dead and carried out, they would break in at all hazards, and without regard to the danger of infection, take even the clothes off the dead bodies and the bed-clothes from others where they lay dead.

This, I suppose, must be the case of a family in Houndsditch, where a man and his daughter, the rest of the family being, as I suppose, carried away before by the dead-cart, were found stark naked, one in one chamber and one in another, lying dead on the floor, and the clothes of the beds, from whence 'tis supposed they were rolled off by thieves, stolen and carried quite away.

It is indeed to be observed that the women were in all this calamity the most rash, fearless, and desperate creatures, and as there were vast numbers that went about as nurses to tend those that were sick, they committed a great many petty thieveries in the houses where they were employed; and some of them were publicly whipped for it, when perhaps they ought rather to have been hanged for examples, for numbers of houses were robbed on these occasions, till at length the parish officers were sent to recommend nurses to the sick, and always took an account whom it was they sent, so as that they might call them to account if the house had been abused where they were placed.

But these robberies extended chiefly to wearing-clothes, linen, and what rings or money they could come at when the person died who was under their care, but not to a general plunder of the houses; and I could give you an account of one of these nurses, who, several years after, being on her deathbed, confessed with the utmost horror the robberies she had committed at the time of her being a nurse, and by which she had enriched herself to a great degree. But as for murders, I do not find that there was ever any proof of the facts in the manner as it has been reported, except as above....

It was under this John Hayward's[1] care, and within his bounds, that the story of the piper, with which people have made themselves so merry, happened, and he assured me that it was true. It is said that it was a blind piper; but, as John told me, the fellow was not blind, but an ignorant, weak, poor man, and usually walked his rounds about ten o'clock at night and went piping along from door to door, and the people usually took him in at public-houses where they knew him, and would give him drink and victuals, and sometimes farthings; and he in return would pipe and sing and talk simply, which diverted the people; and thus he lived. It was but a very bad time for this diversion while things were as I have told, yet the poor fellow went about as

[1] *John Hayward* Friend of the narrator's brother and undersexton (i.e., gravedigger and bearer of the dead) for the parish of St. Stephen.

usual, but was almost starved; and when anybody asked how he did he would answer, the dead cart had not taken him yet, but that they had promised to call for him next week.

It happened one night that this poor fellow, whether somebody had given him too much drink or no—John Hayward said he had not drink in his house, but that they had given him a little more victuals than ordinary at a public-house in Coleman Street—and the poor fellow, having not usually had a bellyful for perhaps not a good while, was laid all along upon the top of a bulk or stall, and fast asleep, at a door in the street near London Wall, towards Cripplegate; and that upon the same bulk or stall the people of some house, in the alley of which the house was a corner, hearing a bell which they always rang before the cart came, had laid a body really dead of the plague just by him, thinking, too, that this poor fellow had been a dead body, as the other was, and laid there by some of the neighbours.

Accordingly, when John Hayward with his bell and the cart came along, finding two dead bodies lie upon the stall, they took them up with the instrument they used and threw them into the cart, and all this while the piper slept soundly.

From hence they passed along and took in other dead bodies, till, as honest John Hayward told me, they almost buried him alive in the cart; yet all this while he slept soundly. At length the cart came to the place where the bodies were to be thrown into the ground, which, as I do remember, was at Mount Mill; and as the cart usually stopped some time before they were ready to shoot out the melancholy load they had in it, as soon as the cart stopped the fellow awaked and struggled a little to get his head out from among the dead bodies, when, raising himself up in the cart, he called out. "Hey! where am I?" This frighted the fellow that attended about the work; but after some pause John Hayward, recovering himself, said, "Lord, bless us! There's somebody in the cart not quite dead!" So another called to him and said, "Who are you?" The fellow answered, "I am the poor piper. Where am I?" "Where are you?" says Hayward. "Why, you are in the dead-cart, and we are going to bury you." "But I an't dead though, am I?" says the piper, which made them laugh a little, though, as John said, they were heartily frighted at first; so they helped the poor fellow down, and he went about his business.

I know the story goes he set up his pipes in the cart and frighted the bearers and others so that they ran away; but John Hayward did not tell the story so, nor say anything of his piping at all; but that he was a poor piper, and that he was carried away as above, I am fully satisfied of the truth of.

It is to be noted here that the dead-carts in the city were not confined to particular parishes, but one cart went through several parishes, according as the number of dead presented; nor were they tied to carry the dead to their respective parishes, but many of the dead taken up in the city were carried to the burying-ground in the out-parts for want of room.

I have already mentioned the surprise that this judgement was at first among the people. I must be allowed to give some of my observations on the more serious and religious part. Surely never city, at least of this bulk and magnitude, was taken in a condition so perfectly unprepared for such a dreadful visitation, whether I am to speak of the civil preparations or religious. They were, indeed, as if they had had no warning, no expectation, no apprehensions, and consequently the least provision imaginable was made for it in a public way. For example, the Lord Mayor and sheriffs had made no provision as magistrates for the regulations which were to be observed. They had gone into no measures for relief of the poor. The citizens had no public magazines or storehouses for corn or meal for the subsistence of the poor, which if they had provided themselves, as in such cases is done abroad, many miserable families who were now reduced to the utmost distress would have been relieved, and that in a better manner than now could be done.

The stock of the city's money I can say but little to. The Chamber of London was said to be exceedingly rich, and it may be concluded that they were so, by the vast sums of money issued from thence in the rebuilding the public edifices after the fire of London, and in building new works, such as, for the first part, the Guildhall, Blackwell Hall, part of Leadenhall, half the Exchange, the Session House, the Compter, the prisons of Ludgate, Newgate, &c., several of the wharfs and stairs and landing-places on the river, all which were either burned down or damaged by the Great Fire of

London, the next year after the plague; and of the second sort, the Monument, Fleet Ditch with its bridges, and the Hospital of Bethlem or Bedlam,[1] &c. But possibly the managers of the city's credit at that time made more conscience of breaking in upon the orphan's money to show charity to the distressed citizens than the managers in the following years did to beautify the city and re-edify the buildings; though, in the first case, the losers would have thought their fortunes better bestowed, and the public faith of the city have been less subjected to scandal and reproach.

—1722

[1] *Bedlam* Hospital for the mentally ill (formally called the Hospital of St. Mary of Bethlehem).

Anne Finch, Countess of Winchilsea

1661 – 1720

Though she published only one volume of verse in her lifetime, Anne Finch managed her texts very carefully. (Her husband transcribed them formally in successive bound volumes.) She is justly regarded as one of the more significant of early eighteenth-century poets; her poems on married life, on women's friendship, and on nature have earned her a distinctive place in British literary history.

Finch was born into a distinguished family as the third child of Sir William Kingsmill and Anne Haslewood, but her childhood was marked by tragedy; her father died when she was only a few months old, her mother when she was three, and her stepfather when she was ten. Her father made provisions in his will for the education of his children, and Finch's work indicates that she was unusually learned—familiar with the classics, Greek and Roman mythology, English history and literature, some French and Italian (languages and literature), and the Bible. In 1682 Finch became a Maid of Honor to Mary of Modena, wife of James, Duke of York (who would later become King James II). At court, she met and, in 1684, married Captain Heneage Finch (1657–1726), who was gentleman to the bedchamber to the Duke of York. They both remained in service until the Glorious Revolution of 1688, when James II was deposed and fled to France. Finch's husband was accused of having plotted on James's behalf, and was arrested. He was acquitted after a year, but he remained a nonjuror—one who refused to take an oath of allegiance to the new monarchs William and Mary—and so was prevented from re-entering public life. Consequently, the Finches retired in 1690 to the country, to Eastwell Park in Kent, the home of her husband's nephew, the Earl of Winchilsea. When he died in 1712 Heneage Finch became the Earl of Winchilsea, which made Anne a Countess. They did not return permanently to London until 1708—and they continued even then to spend a good deal of time at Eastwell.

The couple appear to have lived contentedly in retirement in Kent, and much of Finch's best work dates from this period. Finch had been writing since the 1680s but she appears not to have circulated any of her works until the 1690s. Charles Gildon's 1701 *New Collection of Poems on Several Occasions* contains four of her pieces, and three pastorals appear in Jacob Tonson's *Poetical Miscellanies* (1709). The dramatist Nicolas Rowe praised her poetry in Gildon's collection, and Swift directed "Apollo Outwitted" to her in 1709. It was not until 1713, however, that Finch published *Miscellany Poems on Several Occasions, Written By a Lady*. She had become a Countess the year before the volume appeared, but as her poem "The Introduction" makes clear, publishing a book of poems was still a bold move for a woman. (Indeed, this was one of only a very few poetry collections published by a woman in the early part of the century.)

Finch's poetry is in large part written in heroic couplets, as was the fashion at the time. It reflects a sensitivity to nature, a delicacy towards political allegiances, and an appreciation of close personal relationships. While she can be extremely critical of marriage (and in particular its effect on women), her own marriage appears to have been happy. Her husband, whom she addresses as Daphnis or Flavio in her verse, was supportive of her writing and even transcribed poems for her. Finch did, however, suffer from what today we would categorize as depression and seems to have been quite ill in 1715. Her piece "The Spleen," which contemplates and analyzes depression, was her best known poem during her life. After her death in 1720 (the exact cause of which is unknown), her poetry continued to appear in collections for a time, but interest in her work waned in the latter half of the eighteenth-century. Wordsworth revived interest in Finch when, in his 1815 "Essay, Supplementary to the Preface," he noted that she was one of only two poets between the publication of Milton's *Paradise Lost* and Thomson's *The Seasons* (the other was Pope) to present a "new image of external nature." To see Finch primarily as a nature poet, however, is not to see her whole. Her range of genres and tones is unusually wide, and it is as much for her keen observations of the human as of the natural world that she is still read and remembered.

⌘⌘⌘

from *The Spleen*[1]

A Pindaric Poem

What art thou, Spleen, which every thing dost ape?
Thou Proteus[2] to abused mankind,
Who never yet thy real cause could find,
Or fix thee to remain in one continued shape.
Still varying thy perplexing form,
Now a dead sea thou'lt represent,
A calm of stupid discontent,
Then, dashing on the rocks wilt rage into a storm.
Trembling sometimes thou dost appear,
Dissolved into a panic fear;
On sleep intruding dost thy shadows spread,
Thy gloomy terrors round the silent bed,
And crowd with boding° dreams the melancholy head; *foreboding*
Or, when the midnight hour is told,
And drooping lids thou still dost waking hold,
Thy fond delusions cheat the eyes,
Before them antic spectres° dance, *ghosts*
Unusual fires their pointed heads advance,
And airy phantoms rise.
Such was the monstrous vision seen,
When Brutus (now beneath his cares oppressed,
And all Rome's fortunes rolling in his breast,
Before Philippi's latest field,
Before his fate did to Octavius lead)[3]
Was vanquished by the Spleen.

Falsely, the mortal part we blame
Of our depressed, and pond'rous frame,
Which, till the first degrading sin[4]
Let thee, its dull attendant, in,
Still with the other did comply,
Nor clogged the active soul, disposed to fly,
And range the mansions of its native sky.
Nor, whilst in his own heaven he dwelt,
Whilst man his paradise possessed,
His fertile garden in the fragrant East,[5]
And all united odors smelt,
No armed sweets, until thy reign,
Could shock the sense, or in the face
A flushed, unhandsome color place.
Now the jouquille[6] o'ercomes the feeble brain;
We faint beneath the aromatic pain,
Till some offensive scent thy pow'rs appease,
And pleasure we resign for short, and nauseous ease.

....

In vain to chase thee every art we try,
In vain all remedies apply,
In vain the Indian leaf° infuse, *tea*

[1] *Spleen* Melancholy or depression.

[2] *Proteus* Greek sea god who changes his shape at will.

[3] *Brutus ... Octavius* In Shakespeare's *Julius Caesar*, Brutus sees visions the night before Octavius kills him at Philippi.

[4] *first ... sin* Original sin, which was thought to cause decay and illness.

[5] *garden ... East* The Garden of Eden was thought to lie in the East.

[6] *jouquille* Sweet-smelling form of narcissus.

Or the parchèd Eastern berry° bruise; *coffee*
Some pass, in vain, those bounds, and nobler liquors use.
Now harmony, in vain, we bring,
Inspire the flute, and touch the string.
From harmony no help is had;
Music but soothes thee, if too sweetly sad,
And if too light, but turns thee gaily mad.
Though the physician's greatest gains,
Although his growing wealth he sees
Daily increased by ladies' fees,
Yet dost thou baffle all his studious pains.
Not skilful Lower[1] thy source could find,
Or through the well-dissected body trace
The secret, the mysterious ways,
By which thou dost surprise, and prey upon the mind.
Though in the search, too deep for humane thought,
With unsuccessful toil he wrought,
'Till thinking thee to've catched, himself by thee was caught,
Retained thy pris'ner, thy acknowledged slave,
And sunk beneath thy chain to a lamented grave.
—1701

The Introduction

Did I, my lines intend for public view,
How many censures, would their faults pursue,
Some would, because such words they do affect,
Cry they're insipid, empty, uncorrect.
And many, have attained, dull and untaught
The name of wit, only by finding fault.
True judges, might condemn their want of wit,
And all might say, they're by a woman writ.
Alas! a woman that attempts the pen,
Such an intruder on the rights of men,
Such a presumptuous creature, is esteemed,
The fault, can by no virtue be redeemed.
They tell us, we mistake our sex and way;
Good breeding, fashion, dancing, dressing, play
Are the accomplishments we should desire;
To write, or read, or think, or to enquire
Would cloud our beauty, and exhaust our time,
And interrupt the conquests of our prime;
Whilst the dull manage,° of a servile house *management*
Is held by some, our outmost art, and use.
Sure 'twas not ever thus, nor are we told
Fables, of women that excelled of old;
To whom, by the diffusive hand of heaven
Some share of wit, and poetry was given.
On that glad day, on which the Ark returned,[2]
The holy pledge, for which the land had mourned,
The joyful tribes, attend it on the way,
The Levites° do the sacred charge convey, *Judaic priests*
Whilst various instruments, before it play;
Here, holy virgins in the concert join,
The louder notes, to soften, and refine,
And with alternate verse, complete the hymn divine.
Lo! the young poet,[3] after God's own heart,
By Him inspired, and taught the muses' art,
Returned from conquest, a bright chorus meets,
That sing his slain ten thousand in the streets.[4]
In such loud numbers they his acts declare,
Proclaim the wonders, of his early war,
That Saul upon the vast applause does frown,[5]
And feels, its mighty thunder shake the crown.
What, can the threatened judgment now prolong?
Half of the kingdom is already gone;
The fairest half, whose influence guides the rest,
Have David's empire, o'er their hearts confessed.
A woman here, leads fainting Israel on,
She fights, she wins, she triumphs with a song,
Devout, majestic, for the subject fit,
And far above her arms, exalts her wit,
Then, to the peaceful, shady palm withdraws,
And rules the rescued nation, with her laws.[6]
How are we fall'n, fall'n by mistaken rules?
And education's, more than nature's fools,
Debarred from all improvements of the mind,
And to be dull, expected and designed;
And if some one would soar above the rest,
With warmer fancy, and ambition pressed,
So strong, th' opposing faction still appears,

[1] *Lower* Richard Lower (1631–91), noted London physician.

[2] *On ... returned* When David returned the ark of the covenant he was accompanied by musicians and singers (1 Chronicles 15).

[3] *young poet* David was held to be author of the psalms.

[4] *sing ... streets* See 1 Samuel 18.5–9.

[5] *Saul upon the vast applause does frown* Saul, unpopular king of Israel, feared that the people, led by the women, would come to want David chosen to replace him. See 1 Samuel 18.6–9.

[6] *A woman ... laws* Deborah, a judge in Israel (Judges 4).

The hopes to thrive, can ne'er outweigh the fears,
Be cautioned then my Muse, and still retired;
Nor be despised, aiming to be admired;
Conscious of wants, still with contracted wing,
To some few friends, and to thy sorrows sing;
For groves of laurel,[1] thou wert never meant;
Be dark enough thy shades, and be thou there content.
—1713

A Letter to Daphnis, April 2, 1685

This to the crown, and blessing of my life,
The much loved husband, of a happy wife;
To him, whose constant passion found the art
To win a stubborn, and ungrateful heart;
And to the world, by tend'rest proof discovers
They err, who say that husbands can't be lovers.
With such return of passion, as is due,
Daphnis I love, Daphnis my thoughts pursue,
Daphnis, my hopes, my joys, are bounded all in you:
Ev'n I, for Daphnis, and my promise sake,
What I in woman censure, undertake.
But this from love, not vanity, proceeds;
You know who writes; and I who 'tis that reads.
Judge not my passion, by my want of skill,
Many love well, though they express it ill;
And I your censure could with pleasure bear,
Would you but soon return, and speak it here.
—1713

To Mr. F., Now Earl of W.

Who going abroad, had desired Ardelia to write some verses upon whatever subject she thought fit, against his return in the evening

No sooner, Flavio, was you gone,
But, your injunction thought upon,
Ardelia took the pen;
Designing to perform the task,
Her Flavio did so kindly ask,
Ere he returned again.

Unto Parnassus[2] straight she sent,
And bid the messenger, that went
Unto the muses' court,
Assure them, she their aid did need,
And begged they'd use their utmost speed,
Because the time was short.

The hasty summons was allowed;
And being well-bred, they rose and bowed,
And said, they'd post away;[3]
That well they did Ardelia know,
And that no female's voice below
They sooner would obey:

That many of that rhyming train,
On like occasions, sought in vain
Their industry t'excite;
But for Ardelia all they'd leave:
Thus flatt'ring can the muse deceive,
And wheedle us to write.

Yet, since there was such haste required;
To know the subject 'twas desired,
On which they must infuse;
That they might temper words and rules,
And with their counsel carry tools,
As country-doctors use.

Wherefore to cut off all delays,
'Twas soon replied, a husband's praise
(Though in these looser times)
Ardelia gladly would rehearse
A husband's, who indulged her verse,
And now required her rhymes.

A husband! echoed all around:
And to Parnassus sure that sound
Had never yet been sent;
Amazement in each face was read,
In haste th' affrighted sisters fled,
And unto council went.

[1] *groves of laurel* Laurel was sacred to Apollo, the god of the arts, and is thus awarded to poets.

[2] *Parnassus* Greek mountain, sacred to Apollo and the Muses, and the home of the latter.

[3] *they'd post away* They would use relays of horses to travel faster.

Erato cried, since Grizel's[1] days,
Since Troy-town[2] pleased, and Chivey-chace,[3]
No such design was known;
And 'twas their business to take care,
It reached not to the public ear,
Or got about the town:

Nor came where evening beaux were met
O'er billets-doux° and chocolate, *love letters*
Lest it destroyed the house;° *playhouse*
For in that place, who could dispense° *excuse*
(That wore his clothes with common sense)
With mention of a spouse?

'Twas put unto the vote at last,
And in the negative it past,
None to her aid should move;
Yet since Ardelia was a friend,
Excuses 'twas agreed to send,
Which plausible might prove:

That Pegasus[4] of late had been
So often rid through thick and thin,
With neither fear nor wit;
In panegyric been so spurred
He could not from the stall be stirred,
Nor would endure the bit.

Melpomene[5] had given a bond,
By the new house[6] alone to stand,
And write of war and strife;
Thalia,[7] she had taken fees,
And stipends from the patentees,° *theater proprietors*
And durst not for her life.

Urania[8] only liked the choice;
Yet not to thwart the public voice,
She whisp'ring did impart:
They need no foreign aid invoke,
No help to draw a moving stroke,
Who dictate from the heart.

Enough! the pleased Ardelia cried;
And slighting every Muse beside,
Consulting now her breast,
Perceived that every tender thought,
Which from abroad she'd vainly sought,
Did there in silence rest:

And should unmoved that post maintain,
Till in his quick return again,
Met in some neighb'ring grove,
(Where vice nor vanity appear)
Her Flavio them alone might hear,
In all the sounds of love.

For since the world does so despise
Hymen's[9] endearments and its ties,
They should mysterious be;
Till we that pleasure too possess
(Which makes their fancied happiness)
Of stolen secrecy.

—1713

[1] *Erato* Muse of love poetry, one of the nine daughters of Zeus and Mnemosyne (Memory); *Grizel's* Griselda, the proverbial patient wife.

[2] *Troy-town* English ballad about the ancient city that was the site of a war between the Trojans and the Greeks.

[3] *Chivey-chace* "Chevy Chase," a fifteenth-century ballad.

[4] *Pegasus* Winged horse of Greek myth.

[5] *Melpomene* Muse of tragedy.

[6] *the new house* I.e., the new playhouse, probably the Haymarket Theatre (also confusingly known as the Queen's Theatre or the Opera House), which was licensed in December 1704 and opened in April 1705. The new theater's focus was to be opera, and since all operas of the time were virtual tragedies (essentially tragic plots with happy endings), the association with the Muse of tragedy is a natural one. The other theaters—run by the patentees, or proprietors—were most successful with comedy.

[7] *Thalia* Muse of comedy.

[8] *Urania* Muse of astronomy and heavenly love.

[9] *Hymen* God of marriage.

The Unequal Fetters

Could we stop the time that's flying
Or recall it when 'tis past,
Put far off the day of dying
Or make youth forever last,
To love would then be worth our cost.

But since we must lose those graces,
Which at first your hearts have won,
And you seek for in new faces
When our spring of life is done,
It would but urge our ruin on.

Free as nature's first intention
Was to make us, I'll be found,
Nor by subtle man's invention
Yield to be in fetters bound
By one that walks a freer round.

Marriage does but slightly tie Men,
Whilst close pris'ners we remain,
They, the larger slaves of Hymen,
Still are begging love again
At the full length of all their chain.

—1713

By neer resemblance that Bird betray'd[1]

By neer resemblance see that Bird betray'd
Who takes the well wrought Arras[2] for a shade.
There hopes to pearch and with a chearfull Tune
O're-passe the scortchings of the sultry Noon
But soon repuls'd by the obdurate Scean
How swift she turns but turns alas in vain
That piece a Grove this shews an ambient sky
Where immitated Fowl their pinnions° ply *wings*
Seeming to mount in flight and aiming still more high.
All she outstripps and with a moment's pride
Their understation silent does deride.
Till the dash'd cealing strikes her to the ground
No intercepting shrub to break the fall is found
Recovering breath the window next she gaines
Nor fears a stop from the transparent Panes.

O man what inspiration was thy Guide
Who taught thee Light and Air thus to divide
To lett in all the usefull beames of Day
Yett force as subtil winds without thy Sash to stay
T'extract from Embers by a strange device
Then pollish fair these flakes of sollid Ice
Which silver'd o're redouble all in place
And give thee back thy well or ill-complexion'd Face.
To colors blown exceed the gloomy Bowl
Which did the Wines full excellence controul
These shew the Body whilest you taste the soul.
Its Colour Sparkles motion letts thee see
Though yett th'excesse the Preacher warns to flee
Least men att length as clearly spy through thee.

But we degresse and leave th'imprison'd wretch
Now sinking low now on a loftyer stretch
Flutt'ring in endlesse cercles of dismay
Till some kind hand directs the certain way
Which through the casement an escape affoards
And leads to ample space the only Heav'n of Birds.

So here confin'd and but of female Clay
As much my soul mistook the rightful way
Whilst the soft breeze of Pleasure's tempting air
Made her° believe Felicity was there *the soul*
And basking in the warmth of early time
To vain Amusements dedicate her Prime
Ambition then alur'd her tow'ring Eye
For Paradice she heard was plac'd on high
Then thought the Court was all its glorious show
Was sure above the rest and Paradice below
There plac'd too soon the flaming sword[3] appear'd
Remov'd those Powers,[4] whom justly she rever'd

original spelling

[1] *By neer ... betray'd* Originally titled "Some occasional Reflections Digested (tho' not with great regularity) into a Poeme," this poem—a part of which is better known under the title "The Bird and the Arras"—appears in the original manuscript as it is printed here. It was later broken into three separate poems for publication in 1713.

[2] *Arras* Tapestry hung from a wall.

[3] *flaming sword* Cf. Genesis 3.24, in which God barred the way behind Adam and Eve when expelling them from Eden: "So he drove out the man; and he placed at the east of the garden of Eden Cherubims, and a flaming sword which turned every way, to keep the way of the tree of life."

[4] *those Powers* King James II and his queen, Mary of Modena.

Adher'd too in their Wreck, and in their Ruin shar'd.

original spelling

Now by the Wheels inevitable round[1]
With them thrown prostrate to the humble ground
No more she take's (instructed by that fall)
For fixt or worth her thought this rowling Ball
Nor feed a hope that boasts but mortal birth,
Or springs from man though fram'd of Royal earth
Tow'rds a more certain station she aspires
Unshaken by Revolts; and owns no lesse desires
But all in vain are Pray'rs extatick thoughts
Recover'd moments and retracted faults
Retirement which the World morossenesse calls
Abandon'd pleasures in Monastick walls
These but att distance towards that purpose tend
The lowly means to an exalted end
Which He must perfect who alotts her stay
And that accomplish'd will direct the way.
Pitty her restlesse cares and weary strife
And point some Issue to escaping Life
Which so dismiss'd no Pen or human speech
Th'ineffable Recesse can ever teach
Th'Expanse the Light the Harmony the Throng
The Brides attendance and the Bridal song
The numerous Mantions and th'immortal Tree
No Eye unpurg'd by Death must ever see
Or waves which through that wond'rous Citty rowl
Rest then content my too impatient Soul
Observe but here the easie Precepts given
Then wait with chearfull hope, till Heaven be known
in Heaven.

—1713

A Nocturnal Reverie

In such a night, when every louder wind
Is to its distant cavern safe confined;
And only gentle Zephyr[2] fans his wings,
And lonely Philomel,° still waking, sings; *nightingale*
Or from some tree, famed for the owl's delight,
She, hollowing clear, directs the wand'rer right:
In such a night, when passing clouds give place,
Or thinly veil the heav'n's mysterious face;
When in some river, overhung with green,
The waving moon and trembling leaves are seen;
When freshened grass now bears itself upright,
And makes cool banks to pleasing rest invite,
Whence springs the woodbind, and the bramble-rose,
And where the sleepy cowslip sheltered grows;
Whilst now a paler hue the foxglove takes,
Yet chequers still with red the dusky brakes
When scattered glow-worms, but in twilight fine,
Show trivial beauties watch their hour to shine;
Whilst Salisb'ry[3] stands the test of every light,
In perfect charms, and perfect virtue bright:
When odours, which declined repelling day,
Through temp'rate air uninterrupted stray;
When darkened groves their softest shadows wear,
And falling waters we distinctly hear;
When through the gloom more venerable shows
Some ancient fabric,° awful in repose, *building*
While sunburnt hills their swarthy looks conceal,
And swelling haycocks thicken up the vale:
When the loosed horse now, as his pasture leads,
Comes slowly grazing through th' adjoining meads,
Whose stealing pace, and lengthened shade we fear,
Till torn up forage in his teeth we hear:
When nibbling sheep at large pursue their food,
And unmolested kine° rechew the cud; *cattle*
When curlews cry beneath the village walls,
And to her straggling brood the partridge calls;
Their shortlived jubilee the creatures keep,
Which but endures, whilst tyrant-man does sleep;
When a sedate content the spirit feels,
And no fierce light disturb, whilst it reveals;
But silent musings urge the mind to seek
Something, too high for syllables to speak;
Till the free soul to a compos'dness charmed,
Finding the elements of rage disarmed,
O'er all below a solemn quiet grown,
Joys in th' inferior world, and thinks it like her own:
In such a night let me abroad remain,
Till morning breaks, and all's confused again;
Our cares, our toils, our clamours are renewed,
Or pleasures, seldom reached, again pursued.

—1713

[1] *Wheels ... round* Revolution of the wheel of fortune.

[2] *Zephyr* God of the west wind.

[3] *Salisb'ry* Anne Tufton, Countess of Salisbury.

Mary Astell

1666 – 1731

Astell was, as her biographer Ruth Perry has put it, one of the first women to "theorize about the politics of gender"; she not only argued that women were as capable as men of rationality and of reasoned argument, but also traced mechanisms and the effect of systemic bias against women in social structures. Astell's writing career coincided with a rapid increase in the availability of printed materials—and much of her writing takes the form of informed and reasoned responses to other contemporary publications on various public issues. She wrote numerous books and pamphlets, most of them reflecting her High Tory and Church of England convictions. It is her examination of the role of custom in women's lives in *A Serious Proposal to the Ladies* (1694 and 1697) and *Some Reflections upon Marriage* (1700) that has held the interest of scholars and readers, and prompted many to call her England's first feminist.

Born in 1666 to a coal-merchant family in Newcastle, Astell is believed to have been tutored by her uncle, Ralph Astell, a curate and poet who introduced her to the works of the Cambridge Platonists. Astell's father died when she was 12, and her uncle followed only a year later, leaving her without a dowry amid a predominately female household. At 21, Astell took the then-extraordinary step of setting out entirely independently as a young woman; she left Newcastle to settle in the London suburb of Chelsea, where she spent nearly all her remaining years. Unable to support herself when she first arrived, she applied for and received help from the Archbishop of Canterbury, William Sancroft, to whom out of gratitude she gave a copy of her manuscript poems. Sancroft also introduced her to Rich Wilkin, a royalist printer who handled her work until 1730. Always a voracious reader, Astell boldly wrote to Platonist John Norris regarding a possible inconsistency in the third volume of his *Discourses*, sparking a 10-month correspondence that Norris later printed as *Letters Concerning the Love of God* (1695).

In *A Serious Proposal to the Ladies* (1694), Astell encourages women to value a beautiful mind over a beautiful body, stressing that an authentic Christian life requires a clear understanding of the faith's tenets, not merely conformation to its practices. In order for women to serve God and improve their minds and souls, Astell recommends erecting a "Protestant monastery" where unmarried women could withdraw from the world, safe from temptation and gossip and free to pursue an education. When such an institution failed to materialize, she added Part Two of *A Serious Proposal* (1697), offering women detailed instructions on improving their reason on their own. Her recommendations reveal Astell's early grounding in Anglican and Christian Platonism, but she was also influenced by Cartesian theories which suggested that the capacity for logical thought and for understanding phenomena was not dependent on specialized training—anyone, man or woman, could learn to improve their reasoning abilities by fostering self-conscious thought. Astell eventually published a detailed outline of her philosophical beliefs, entitled *The Christian Religion as Profess'd by a Daughter of the Church of England* (1705), in response to the skepticism of Locke's *Reasonableness of Christianity* (1695).

Until her death in 1699, the notorious Hortense Mancini, Duchess of Mazarin, was one of Astell's Chelsea neighbors. She had published details of her divorce in her 1676 autobiography. Astell had read this autobiography, as well as the recently released transcripts of the lawsuit, and she subsequently wrote *Some Reflections upon Marriage* (1700) to counter the prevailing belief that woman's sole purpose was or should be to get and serve a husband. As a staunch religious conservative, Astell accepts a husband's authority over his wife in the same way that she accepts the sovereign's right to expect absolute obedience from his subjects, but in *Some Reflections* she encourages women to use good judgment in choosing "a monarch for life" and to consider that they may well be happier and more virtuous if they do not marry. Women cannot be too watchful, Astell warns, for men trick or pressure women into marriage with no thought for women's interests or well-being; thus, to protect themselves, women should be educated to enable them to make better marriage choices.

Astell's devout Anglicanism and staunch Toryism, as well as her satirical wit, would emerge again in three tracts published in 1704 that responded to works by Bishop White Kennet, James Owen, and Daniel Defoe. Her last published text was *Bart'lemy Fair: or, An Enquiry After Wit* (1709), an essay in response to the Earl of Shaftesbury's *A Letter Concerning Enthusiasm* (1708). Astell remained active in political circles, however, and suffered repeated questioning by Prime Minister Robert Walpole's agents in 1722 because of her alleged Jacobite sympathies. In 1709, Astell participated in a plan to open a charity school at Chelsea for daughters of hospital veterans; run entirely by women, the school survived until 1862. At 60, troubled by poor vision and financial worries, Astell moved in with Lady Catherine Jones, with whom she lived until her death from breast cancer at 65 in 1731.

⌘⌘⌘

from *A Serious Proposal to the Ladies*

Thus ignorance and a narrow education lay the foundation of vice, and imitation and custom rear it up. Custom, that merciless torrent that carries all before. And which indeed can be stemmed by none but such as have a great deal of prudence and a rooted virtue. For 'tis but decorous that she who is not capable of giving better rules should follow those she sees before her, lest she only change the instance and retain the absurdity. It would puzzle a considerate person to account for all that sin and folly that is in the world (which certainly has nothing in itself to recommend it), did not custom help to solve the difficulty. For virtue without question has on all accounts the pre-eminence of vice; 'tis abundantly more pleasant in the act, as well as more advantageous in the consequences, as any one who will but rightly use her reason, in a serious reflection on her self and the nature of things, may easily perceive. 'Tis custom therefore, that tyrant custom, which is the grand motive to all those irrational choices which we daily see made in the world, so very contrary to our present interest and pleasure, as well as to our future. We think it an unpardonable mistake not to do as our neighbours do, and part with our peace and pleasure as well as our innocence and virtue, merely in compliance with an unreasonable fashion. And having inured ourselves to folly, we know not how to quit it; we go on in vice, not because we find satisfaction in it, but because we are unacquainted with the joys of virtue.

Add to this the hurry and noise of the world, which does generally so busy and pre-engage us, that we have little time, and less inclination, to stand still and reflect on our own minds. Those impertinent[1] amusements which have seized us keep their hold so well, and so constantly buzz about our ears, that we cannot attend to the dictates of our reason, nor to the soft whispers and winning persuasives[2] of the divine Spirit by whose assistance, were we disposed to make use of it, we might shake off these follies and regain our freedom. But alas! to complete our misfortunes by a continual application to vanity and folly, we quite spoil the contexture[3] and frame of our minds, so loosen and dissipate, that nothing solid and substantial will stay in it. By a habitual inadvertency we render our selves incapable of any serious and improving thought, till our minds themselves become as light and frothy as those things they are conversant about. To all which, if we further add the great industry that bad people use to corrupt the good, and that unaccountable backwardness that appears in too many good persons, to stand up for and propagate the piety they profess (so strangely are things transposed that virtue puts on the blushes which belong to vice, and vice insults with the authority of virtue!); and we have a pretty fair account of the causes of our non-improvement.

[1] *impertinent* Inappropriate; out of place.

[2] *persuasives* Means of persuading.

[3] *contexture* Structure resulting from the arrangement of its elements.

When a poor young lady is taught to value herself on nothing but her clothes, and to think she is very fine when well accoutred. When she hears say that 'tis wisdom enough for her to know how to dress herself that she may become amiable in his eyes, to whom it appertains to be knowing and learned, who can blame her if she lay out her industry and money on such accomplishments, and sometimes extends it farther than her misinformer desires she should? When she sees the vain and the gay making parade in the world and attended with the courtship and admiration of all about them, no wonder that her tender eyes are dazzled with the pageantry; and wanting judgment to pass a due estimate on them and their admirers, longs to be such a fine and celebrated thing as they! What though she be sometimes told of another world; she has however a more lively perception of this, and may well think, that if her instructors were in earnest when they tell her of hereafter, they would not be so busied and concerned about what happens here. She is, it may be, taught the principles and duties of religion, but not acquainted with the reasons and grounds of them; being told 'tis enough for her to believe, to examine why and wherefore belongs not to her. And therefore, though her piety may be tall and spreading, yet because it wants foundation and root, the first rude temptation overthrows and blasts it, or perhaps the short lived gourd decays and withers of its own accord. But why should she be blamed for setting no great value on her soul, whose noblest faculty, her understanding, is rendered useless to her? Or censured for relinquishing a course of life, whose prerogatives she was never acquainted with, and though highly reasonable in itself, was put upon the embracing it with as little reason as she now forsakes it? For if her religion itself be taken up as the mode of the country, 'tis no strange thing that she lays it down again in conformity to the fashion. Whereas she whose reason is suffered to display itself, to inquire into the grounds and motives of religion, to make a disquisition of its graces, and [to] search out its hidden beauties; who is a Christian out of choice, not in conformity to those about her; and cleaves to piety because 'tis her wisdom, her interest, her joy, not because she has been accustomed to it; she who is not only eminently and unmoveably good, but able to give a reason why she is so; is too firm and stable to be moved by the pitiful allurements of sin, too wise and too well bottomed[1] to be undermined and supplanted by the strongest efforts of temptation. Doubtless a truly Christian life requires a clear understanding as well as regular affections, that both together may move the will to a direct choice of good and a steadfast adherence to it. For though the heart may be honest, it is but by chance that the will is right if the understanding be ignorant and cloudy. And what is the reason that we sometimes see persons falling off from their piety, but because 'twas their affections, not their judgment, that inclined them to be religious? Reason and truth are firm and immutable: she who bottoms on them is on sure ground; humour and inclination are sandy foundations, and she who is swayed by her affections more than by her judgment owes the happiness of her soul in a great measure to the temper of her body; her piety may perhaps blaze higher, but will not last long. For the affections are various and changeable, moved by every object, and the last comer easily undoes whatever its predecessor had done before it. Such persons are always in extremes: they are either violently good or quite cold and indifferent, a perpetual trouble to themselves and others by indecent raptures or unnecessary scruples; there is no beauty and order in their lives, all is rapid and unaccountable; they are now very furious in such a course, but they cannot well tell why, and anon[2] as violent in the other extreme. Having more heat than light, their zeal outruns their knowledge, and instead of representing piety as it is in itself, the most lovely and inviting thing imaginable, they expose it to the contempt and ridicule of the censorious world. Their devotion becomes ricketed,[3] starved, and contracted in some of its vital parts, and disproportioned and over-grown in less material instances; whilst one duty is over done to commute[4] for the neglect of another, and the mistaken person thinks the being often on her knees atones for all the miscarriages of her conversation, not considering that 'tis in vain to petition for those graces which we take no care to practice, and a mockery to adore those perfections we run counter to,

[1] *well bottomed* Founded on solid principles.

[2] *anon* Shortly.

[3] *ricketed* Weakened.

[4] *commute* Make up for.

and that the true end of all our prayers and external observances is to work our minds into a truly Christian temper, to obtain for us the empire of passions, and to reduce all irregular inclinations, that so we may be as like God in purity, charity, and all his imitable excellencies, as is consistent with the imperfection of a creature....

Now as to the proposal, it is to erect a monastery, or if you will (to avoid giving offence to the scrupulous and injudicious by names which, though innocent in themselves, have been abused by superstitious practices), we will call it a religious retirement, and such as shall have a double aspect, being not only a retreat from the world for those who desire that advantage, but likewise, an institution and previous discipline, to fit us to do the greatest good in it; such an institution as this (if I do not mightily deceive my self) would be the most probable method to amend the present and improve the future age. For here, those who are convinced of the emptiness of earthly enjoyments, who are sick of the vanity of the world and its impertinencies, may find more substantial and satisfying entertainments and need not be confined to what they justly loath. Those who are desirous to know and fortify their weak side first do good to themselves, that hereafter they may be capable of doing more good to others; or for their greater security are willing to avoid temptation, may get out of that danger which a continual stay in view of the enemy and the familiarity and unwearied application of the temptation may expose them to; and gain an opportunity to look into themselves, to be acquainted at home and no longer the greatest strangers to their own hearts. Such as are willing in a more peculiar and undisturbed manner to attend the great business they came into the world about, the service of God and improvement of their own minds, may find a convenient and blissful recess from the noise and hurry of the world. A world so cumbersome, so infectious, that although through the grace of God and their own strict watchfulness they are kept from sinking down into its corruptions, 'twill however damp[1] their flight to heaven, hinder them from attaining any eminent pitch of virtue.

You are therefore, ladies, invited into a place where you shall suffer no other confinement but to be kept out of the road of sin: you shall not be deprived of your grandeur, but only exchange the vain pomps and pageantry of the world, empty titles and forms of state, for the true and solid greatness of being able to despise them. You will only quit the chat of insignificant people for an ingenious conversation; the froth of flashy wit for real wisdom; idle tales for instructive discourses. The deceitful flatteries of those who, under pretence of loving and admiring you, really served their own base ends, for the seasonable reproofs and wholesome counsels of your hearty well-wishers and affectionate friends, which will procure you those perfections your feigned lovers pretended you had and kept you from obtaining. No uneasy task will be enjoined you, all your labour being only to prepare for the highest degrees of that glory, the very lowest of which is more than at present you are able to conceive, and the prospect of it sufficient to outweigh all the pains of religion, were there any in it, as really there is none. All that is required of you is only to be as happy as possibly you can, and to make sure of a felicity that will fill all the capacities of your souls! A happiness which, when once you have tasted, you will be fully convinced you could never do too much to obtain it; nor be too solicitous[2] to adorn your souls with such tempers and dispositions as will at present make you in some measure such holy and heavenly creatures, as you one day hope to be in a more perfect manner; without which qualifications you can neither reasonably expect nor are capable of enjoying the happiness of the life to come. Happy retreat! which will be the introducing you into such a paradise as your mother Eve forfeited, where you shall feast on pleasures that do not, like those of the world, disappoint your expectations, pall[3] your appetites, and by the disgust they give you, put you on the fruitless search after new delights, which when obtained are as empty as the former; but such as will make you truly happy now, and prepare you to be perfectly so hereafter. Here are no serpents to deceive you whilst you entertain yourselves in these delicious gardens. No provocations will be given in this amicable society, but to love and to good works,

[1] *damp* Hinder; discourage.

[2] *solicitous* Careful.

[3] *pall* Diminish.

which will afford such an entertaining employment that you will have as little inclination as leisure to pursue those follies which in the time of your ignorance passed with you under the name of love; although there are not in nature two more different things than true love and that brutish passion which pretends to ape it. Here will be no rivalling but for the love of God, no ambition but to procure His favour, to which nothing will more effectually recommend you than a great and dear affection to each other. Envy, that canker, will not here disturb your breasts; for how can she repine[1] at another's welfare who reckons it the greatest part of her own? No covetousness will gain admittance in this blest abode, but to amass huge treasures of good works, and to procure one of the brightest crowns of glory. You will not be solicitous to increase your fortunes, but enlarge your minds; esteeming no grandeur like being conformable[2] to the meek and humble Jesus. So that you only withdraw from the noise and trouble, the folly and temptation of the world, that you may more peaceably enjoy your selves, and all the innocent pleasures it is able to afford you, and particularly that which is worth all the rest, a noble, virtuous and disinterested friendship. And to complete all, that acme[3] of delight which the devout seraphic[4] soul enjoys when dead to the world, she devotes herself entirely to the contemplation and fruition of her beloved; when having disengaged herself from all those lets[5] which hindered her from without, she moves in a direct and vigorous motion towards her true and only good, whom now she embraces and acquiesces in, with such an unspeakable pleasure as is only intelligible to those who have tried and felt it, which we can no more describe to the dark and sensual part of mankind than we can the beauty of colours and harmony of sounds to the blind and deaf. In fine,[6] the place to which you are invited is a type[7] and antepast[8] of heaven, where your employment will be, as there, to magnify God, to love one another, and to communicate that useful knowledge, which by the due improvement of your time in study and contemplation you will obtain; and which when obtained, will afford you a much sweeter and more durable delight than all those pitiful diversions, those revellings and amusements, which now through your ignorance of better, appear the only grateful[9] and relishing[10] entertainments.

But because we were not made for ourselves, nor can by any means so effectually glorify God and do good to our own souls, as by doing offices of charity and beneficence to others; and to the intent, that every virtue, and the highest degrees of every virtue, may be exercised and promoted the most that may be; your retreat shall be so managed as not to exclude the good works of an active from the pleasure and serenity of a contemplative life, but by a due mixture of both retain all the advantages and avoid the inconveniences that attend either. It shall not so cut you off from the world as to hinder you from bettering and improving it, but rather qualify you to do it the greatest good, and be a seminary to stock the kingdom with pious and prudent ladies; whose good example, it is to be hoped, will so influence the rest of their sex that women may no longer pass for those little useless and impertinent animals, which the ill conduct of too many has caused them to be mistaken for.

We have hitherto considered our retirement only in relation to religion, which is indeed its main, I may say its only, design; nor can this be thought too contracting a word, since religion is the adequate business of our lives, and, largely considered, takes in all we have to do; nothing being a fit employment for a rational creature which has not either a direct or remote tendency to this great and only end. But because, as we have all along observed, religion never appears in its true beauty but when it is accompanied with wisdom and discretion, and that without a good understanding, we can scarce be truly, but never eminently good; being liable to a thousand seductions and mistakes; for even the men

[1] *repine* Complain.

[2] *conformable* Resembling.

[3] *acme* Highest point.

[4] *seraphic* In the Biblical Book of Isaiah seraphim are described as heavenly creatures with six wings hovering over the throne of God and are known for their intense love.

[5] *lets* Impediments.

[6] *In fine* To conclude.

[7] *type* Representation; symbol.

[8] *antepast* Food intended to sharpen the appetite before a meal.

[9] *grateful* Agreeable; pleasing.

[10] *relishing* Gratifying.

themselves, if they have not a competent degree of knowledge, they are carried about with every wind of doctrine. Therefore, one great end of this institution shall be to expel that cloud of ignorance which custom has involved us in, to furnish our minds with a stock of solid and useful knowledge that the souls of women may no longer be the only unadorned and neglected things. It is not intended that our religious should waste their time and trouble their heads about such unconcerning matters as the vogue of the world has turned up for learning, the impertinency of which has been excellently exposed by an ingenious pen,[1] but busy themselves in a serious enquiry after necessary and perfective truths, something which it concerns them to know, and which tends to their real interest and perfection, and what that is the excellent author just now mentioned will sufficiently inform them, such a course of study will neither be too troublesome nor out of the reach of a female virtuoso;[2] for it is not intended she should spend her hours in learning words but things, and therefore no more languages than are necessary to acquaint her with useful authors.[3] Nor need she trouble herself in turning over a great number of books, but take care to understand and digest a few well-chosen and good ones. Let her but obtain right ideas, and be truly acquainted with the nature of those objects that present themselves to her mind, and then no matter whether or no she be able to tell what fanciful people have said about them: and thoroughly to understand Christianity as professed by the Church of England will be sufficient to confirm her in the truth, though she have not a catalogue of those particular errors which oppose it. Indeed a learned education of the women will appear so unfashionable that I began to startle at the singularity of the proposition, but was extremely pleased when I found a late ingenious author (whose book I met with since the writing of this) agree with me in my opinion.[4] For speaking of the repute that learning was in about 150 years ago: "It was so very modish (says he) that the fair Sex seemed to believe that Greek and Latin added to their charms; and Plato and Aristotle untranslated, were frequent ornaments of their closets. One would think by the effects, that it was a proper way of educating them, since there are no accounts in history of so many great women in any one age, as are to be found between the years 15 and 1600."

For since God has given women as well as men intelligent souls, why should they be forbidden to improve them? Since He has not denied us the faculty of thinking, why should we not (at least in gratitude to Him) employ our thoughts on Himself, their noblest object, and not unworthily bestow them on trifles and gaieties and secular affairs? Being the soul was created for the contemplation of truth as well as for the fruition of good, is it not as cruel and unjust to preclude women from the knowledge of the one, as well as from the enjoyment of the other? Especially since the will is blind and cannot choose but by the direction of the understanding; or to speak more properly, since the soul always wills according as she understands, so that if she understands amiss, she wills amiss. And as exercise enlarges and exalts any faculty, so through want of using, it becomes cramped and lessened; if therefore we make little or no use of our understandings, we shall shortly have none to use; and the more contracted and unemployed the deliberating and directive power is, the more liable is the elective to[5] unworthy and mischievous options. What is it but the want of an ingenious education that renders the generality of feminine conversations so insipid and foolish and their solitude so insupportable? Learning is therefore necessary to render them more agreeable and useful in company, and to furnish them with becoming entertainments when alone that so they may not be driven to those miserable shifts[6] which too many make use of to put off their time, that precious talent that never lies on the hands of a judicious person. And since our happiness in the next world depends so far on those dispositions which we carry along with us out of this, that without a right

[1] *exposed ... pen* Reference to John Norris's *Reflections upon the Conduct of Human Life: With Reference to the Study of Learning and Knowledge* (1690), in which Norris outlines necessary knowledge for Christians and ladies.

[2] *virtuoso* Learned person interested in arts and sciences.

[3] *no more languages ... authors* In the *Preface* to *Reflections upon Marriage,* Astell suggests that men keep women ignorant of the original languages in which the Holy Scriptures are written.

[4] *I found ... opinion* Reference to William Wotton (1666–1727), an English scholar and the author of *Reflections upon Ancient and Modern Learning* (1694), quoted here by Astell.

[5] *elective to* Choosing of.

[6] *shifts* Expedients; stopgaps.

habitude[1] and temper of mind we are not capable of felicity; and seeing our beatitude consists in the contemplation of the divine truth and beauty, as well as in the fruition of his goodness, can ignorance be a fit preparative for heaven? Is it likely that she whose understanding has been busied about nothing but froth and trifles should be capable of delighting herself in noble and sublime truths? Let such therefore as deny us the improvement of our intellectuals[2] either take up his paradox, who said that women have no souls; which at this time of day, when they are allowed to brutes, would be as unphilosophical as it is unmannerly; or else let them permit us to cultivate and improve them. There is a sort of learning indeed which is worse than the greatest ignorance: a woman may study plays and romances all her days and be a great deal more knowing but never a jot the wiser. Such a knowledge as this serves only to instruct and put her forward in the practice of the greatest follies; yet how can they justly blame her, who forbid, or at least, [will not] afford opportunity of better? A rational mind will be employed, it will never be satisfied in doing nothing; and if you neglect to furnish it with good materials, 'tis like to take up with such as come to hand.

We pretend not that women should teach in the church, or usurp authority where it is not allowed them; permit us only to understand our own duty, and not be forced to take it upon trust from others; to be at least so far learned as to be able to form in our minds a true idea of Christianity, it being so very necessary to fence us against the danger of these last and perilous days,[3] in which deceivers, a part of whose character is to lead captive silly women, need not creep into houses[4] since they have authority to proclaim their errors on the house top.[5] And let us also acquire a true practical knowledge, such as will convince us of the absolute necessity of holy living as well as of right believing, and that no heresy is more dangerous than that of an ungodly and wicked life. And since the French tongue is understood by most ladies, methinks they may much better improve it by the study of philosophy (as I hear the French ladies do)—Descartes, Malebranche,[6] and others—than by reading idle novels and romances. 'Tis strange we should be so forward to imitate their fashions and fopperies, and have no regard to what is really imitable in them! And why shall it not be thought as genteel to understand French philosophy as to be accoutred in a French mode? Let therefore the famous Madame [Dacier],[7] etc., and our own incomparable Orinda,[8] excite the emulation of the English ladies.

The ladies, I'm sure, have no reason to dislike this proposal, but I know not how the men will resent it, to have their enclosure broke down, and women invited to taste of that tree of knowledge they have so long unjustly monopolized. But they must excuse me if I be as partial to my own sex as they are to theirs, and think women as capable of learning as men are, and that it becomes them as well. For I cannot imagine wherein the hurt lies, if instead of doing mischief to one another by an uncharitable and vain conversation, women be enabled to inform and instruct those of their own sex at least; the Holy Ghost having left it on record that Priscilla,[9] as well as her husband, catechised the eloquent Apollos, and the great Apostle found no fault with her. It will therefore be very proper for our ladies to spend part of their time in this retirement in adorning their minds with useful knowledge.

—1694

[1] *habitude* Disposition; temperament.

[2] *intellectuals* Intellect.

[3] *last ... days* Cf. 2 Timothy 3.1: "This know also, that in the last days perilous times shall come."

[4] *creep ... houses* Cf. 2 Timothy 3.6: "For of this sort are they which creep into houses, and lead captive silly women laden with sins, led away with divers lusts."

[5] *proclaim ... house top* Possible reference to either Matthew 10.27: "What I tell you in darkness, that speak ye in light: and what ye hear in the ear, that preach ye upon the housetops," or Luke 12.3: "Therefore whatsoever ye have spoken in darkness shall be heard in the light; and that which ye have spoken in the ear in closets shall be proclaimed upon the housetops."

[6] *Descartes, Malebranche* French philosophers René Descartes (1596–1650) and Nicolas Malebranche (1638-1715).

[7] *Madame Dacier* Anne Lefèvre Dacier (1654?–1729), French scholar, editor, and translator of such classical authors as Sappho, Aristophanes, and Homer.

[8] *Orinda* Katherine Fowler Philips (1631–64), an English poet known as the "Matchless Orinda" and the founder of the Society of Friendship, a literary group comprised mostly of women.

[9] *Priscilla* The wife of Aquila and a friend of St. Paul's, Priscilla worked alongside her husband as a tentmaker in Corinth: cf. Acts 18.2, Romans 16.3, and 2 Timothy 4.19. Acts 18.26 recounts how Aquila and Priscilla taught Apollos "the way of God more perfectly."

from *Reflections upon Marriage*

from The Preface

But the reflector, who hopes reflector is not bad English, now governor is happily of the feminine gender, had as good or better have said nothing; for people by being forbid, are only excited to a more curious enquiry. A certain ingenious gentleman (as she is informed) had the good nature to own these reflections, so far as to affirm that he had the original M.S.[1] in his closet, a proof she is not able to produce; and so to make himself responsible for all their faults, for which she returns him all due acknowledgment. However, the generality being of [the] opinion that a man would have had more prudence and manners than to have published such unseasonable truths, or to have betrayed the *arcana imperii*[2] of his sex, she humbly confesses that the contrivance and execution of this design, which is unfortunately accused of being so destructive to the government, of the men I mean, is entirely her own. She neither advised with friends, nor turned over ancient or modern authors, nor prudently submitted to the correction of such as are, or such as think they are good judges, but with an English spirit and genius[3] set out upon the forlorn hope, meaning no hurt to any body, nor designing any thing but the public good, and to retrieve, if possible, the native liberty, the rights, and privileges of the subject.

Far be it from her to stir up sedition of any sort, none can abhor it more; and she heartily wishes that our masters would pay their civil and ecclesiastical governors the same submission which they themselves exact from their domestic subjects. Nor can she imagine how she any way undermines the masculine empire, or blows the trumpet of rebellion to the moiety[4] of mankind. Is it by exhorting women not to expect to have their own will in any thing, but to be entirely submissive, when once they have made choice of a lord and master, though he happen not to be so wise, so kind, or even so just a governor as was expected? She did not indeed advise them to think his folly wisdom, nor his brutality that love and worship he promised in his matrimonial oath, for this required a flight of wit and sense much above her poor ability and proper only to masculine understandings. However she did not in any manner prompt them to resist, or to abdicate[5] the perjured[6] spouse, though the laws of God and the land make special provision for it, in a case wherein, as is to be feared, few men can truly plead not guilty.

'Tis true, through want of learning, and of that superior genius which men as men lay claim to, she was ignorant of the natural inferiority of our sex, which our masters lay down as a self-evident and fundamental truth. She saw nothing in the reason of things to make this either a principle or a conclusion, but much to the contrary; it being sedition at least, if not treason to assert it in this reign. For if, by the natural superiority of their sex, they mean that every man is by nature superior to every woman, which is the obvious meaning, and that which must be stuck to if they would speak sense, it would be a sin in any woman to have dominion over any man, and the greatest queen ought not to command but to obey her footman, because no municipal laws[7] can supersede or change the law of nature; so that if the dominion of the men be such, the Salic law,[8] as unjust as English men have ever thought it, ought to take place over all the earth, and the most glorious reigns in the English, Danish, Castilian,[9] and other annals were wicked violations of the law of nature!

If they mean that some men are superior to some women, this is no great discovery; had they turned the tables, they might have seen that some women are superior to some men. Or had they been pleased to remember their Oaths of Allegiance and Supremacy, they might have known that one woman is superior to all the men in these nations, or else they have sworn to

[1] *M.S.* Manuscript.

[2] *arcana imperii* Latin: state secrets.

[3] *genius* Disposition; character.

[4] *moiety* Half of two equal parts.

[5] *abdicate* Renounce.

[6] *perjured* Lied under oath.

[7] *municipal laws* Laws of a particular district, state, town, etc.

[8] *Salic law* French law that excluded women from inheriting the throne.

[9] *reigns … Castilian* Probably a reference to the influential reigns of Queen Elizabeth of England (1558–1603), Queen Margrethe I of Denmark (1387–1412), and Queen Isabella I of Castile (1474–1504).

very little purpose.[1] And it must not be supposed that their reason and religion would suffer[2] them to take oaths, contrary to the law of nature and reason of things.

By all which it appears, that our reflector's ignorance is very pitiable, it may be her misfortune but not her crime, especially since she is willing to be better informed, and hopes she shall never be so obstinate as to shut her eyes against the light of truth, which is not to be charged with novelty, howsoever late we may be blessed with the discovery. Nor can error, be it as ancient as it may, ever plead prescription against truth.[3] And since the only way to remove all doubts, to answer all objections, and to give the mind entire satisfaction, is not by affirming, but by proving, so that every one may see with their own eyes and judge according to the best of their own understandings, she hopes it is no presumption to insist on this natural right of judging for her self, and the rather, because by quitting it, we give up all the means of rational conviction. Allow us then as many glasses as you please to help our sight, and as many good arguments as you can afford to convince our understandings: but don't exact of us, we beseech you, to affirm that we see such things as are only the discovery of men who have quicker senses; or that we understand and know what we have by hearsay only; for to be so excessively complaisant[4] is neither to see nor to understand.

That the custom of the world has put women, generally speaking, into a state of subjection is not denied; but the right can no more be proved from the fact than the predominancy of vice can justify it. A certain great man has endeavoured to prove, by reasons not contemptible, that in the original state of things the woman was the superior, and that her subjection to the man is an effect of the Fall[5] and the punishment of her sin.[6] And that ingenious theorist Mr. Whiston[7] asserts that before the Fall there was a greater equality between the two sexes. However this be, 'tis certainly no arrogance in a woman to conclude that she was made for the service of God, and that this is her end. Because God made all things for himself, and a rational mind is too noble a being to be made for the sake and service of any creature. The service she at any time becomes obliged to pay to a man is only a business by the bye. Just as it may be any man's business and duty to keep hogs, he was not made for this, but if he hires himself out to such an employment, he ought conscientiously to perform it. Nor can any thing be concluded to the contrary from St. Paul's argument, I Cor. [11]. For he argues only for decency and order, according to the present custom and state of things. Taking his words strictly and literally, they prove too much, in that praying and [prophesying] in the Church are allowed the women, provided they do it with their head covered, as well as the men; and no inequality can be inferred from hence, neither from the gradation the apostle there uses, that the head of every man is Christ, and that the head of the woman is the man, and the head of Christ is God;[8] it being evident from the form of baptism that there is no natural inferiority among the Divine Persons,[9] but that they are in all things coequal. The apostle indeed adds that the man is the glory of God, and the woman the glory of the man,[10] etc. But what does he infer from hence? He says not a word of inequality or natural inferiority, but concludes that a woman ought to cover her head and a

[1] *Oaths ... purpose* As part of the Test Acts, a series of English laws designed to ensure that all public office holders were members of the Church of England, civil servants had to take oaths of allegiance to the sovereign. Astell reminds her readers that they have sworn to obey a female sovereign, Queen Anne (1665–1714).

[2] *suffer* Tolerate; allow.

[3] *prescription against truth* Custom resulting from long practice.

[4] *complaisant* Yielding.

[5] *the Fall* Christian doctrine of humanity's sinfulness brought about by Adam and Eve eating the forbidden fruit of the Tree of Knowledge in the Garden of Eden (see Genesis 3).

[6] *A certain great man ... her sin* Possibly an allusion to Chapter 20 of Hobbes's *Leviathan* (1660), "For in the condition of meer Nature, where there are no Matrimoniall lawes, it cannot be known who is the Father, unlesse it be declared by the Mother: and therefore the right of Dominion over the Child dependeth on her will, and is consequently hers."

[7] *Mr. Whiston* William Whiston (1667–1752), English divine, Cambridge professor, and author of *A New Theory of the Earth, From its Original, to the Consummation of All Things* (1696), in which he defended the Biblical book of Genesis using Newtonian theories.

[8] *the head ... God* Cf. 1 Corinthians 11.3: "But I would have you know, that the head of every man is Christ; and the head of the woman is the man; and the head of Christ is God."

[9] *Divine Persons* Members of the Trinity: Father, Son, and Holy Spirit.

[10] *man ... man* Reference to 1 Corinthians 11.7: "For a man indeed ought not to cover his head, forasmuch as he is the image and glory of God: but the woman is the glory of the man."

man ought not to cover his, and that even nature itself teaches us that if a man has long hair it is a shame unto him.[1] Whatever the apostle's argument proves in this place, nothing can be plainer than that there is much more said against the present fashion of men wearing long hair than for that supremacy they lay claim to. For by all that appears in the text, it is not so much a law of nature that women should obey men, as that men should not wear long hair. Now how can a Christian nation allow fashions contrary to the law of nature, forbidden by an apostle and declared by him to be a shame to man? Or if custom may make an alteration in one case it may in another, but what then becomes of the nature and reason of things? Besides, the conclusion the apostle draws from his argument concerning women, viz.[2] that they should have power on their heads because of the angels,[3] is so very obscure a text that the ingenious paraphrast[4] who pleads so much for the natural subjection of women ingenuously confesses that he does not understand it. Probably it refers to some custom among the Corinthians,[5] which being well known to them the apostle only hints at it, but which we are ignorant of and therefore apt to mistake him. 'Tis [likely] that the false apostle whom St. Paul writes against had led captive some of their rich and powerful but silly women,[6] who having as mean an opinion of the reason God had given them as any deceiver could desire, did not, like the noble minded Bereans, search the Scriptures whether those things were so,[7] but lazily took up with having men's persons in admiration and followed their leaders blindfold [along] the certain route to destruction. And it is also probable that the same cunning seducer employed these women to carry on his own designs, and putting them upon what he might not think fit to appear in himself, made them guilty of indecent behaviour in the church of Corinth. And therefore St. Paul thought it necessary to reprove them so severely in order to humble them; but this being done, he takes care in the conclusion to set the matter on a right foot, placing the two sexes on a level to keep men as much as might be from taking those advantages which people who have strength in their hands are apt to assume over those who cannot contend with them. For, says he, nevertheless, or notwithstanding the former argument, the man is not without the woman, nor the woman without the man, but all things of God.[8] The relation between the two sexes is mutual, and the dependence reciprocal, both of them depending entirely upon God, and upon Him only; which one would think is no great argument of the natural inferiority of either sex.

Our reflector is of [the] opinion that disputes of this kind, extending to human nature in general and not peculiar to those to whom the Word of God has been revealed, ought to be decided by natural reason only. And that the Holy Scriptures should not be [interested] in the present controversy, in which it determines nothing, any more than it does between the Copernican and Ptolomean systems.[9] The design of those holy books being to make us excellent moralists and perfect Christians, not great philosophers. And being writ for the vulgar as well as for the learned, they are accommodated

[1] *woman ought ... him* Reference to 1 Corinthians 11.14–15: "Doth not even nature itself teach you, that, if a man have long hair, it is a shame unto him? But if a woman have long hair, it is a glory to her: for her hair is given her for a covering."

[2] *viz.* Latin: *videlicet*; or, that is to say.

[3] *power ... angels* Reference to 1 Corinthians 11.10: "For this cause ought the woman to have power on her head because of the angels."

[4] *paraphrast* One who paraphrases.

[5] *Corinthians* Members of the Christian church at Corinth, located 81 km. southwest of Athens. Capital of Roman Greece, Corinth was famous for its cosmopolitan and licentious atmosphere.

[6] *false apostle ... women* Reference to 2 Timothy 3.6: "For of this sort are they which creep into houses, and lead captive silly women laden with sins, led away with divers lusts."

[7] *like the noble minded Bereans ... things were so* See Acts 17.10–11: "And the brethren immediately sent away Paul and Silas by night unto Berea: who coming thither went into the synagogue of the Jews. These were more noble than those in Thessalonica, in that they received word with all readiness of mind, and searched the scriptures daily, whether those things were so."

[8] *the man is not without... things of God* In 1 Corinthians 11.11-12: "Nevertheless neither is the man without the woman, neither the woman without the man, in the Lord. For as the woman is of the man, even so is the man also by the woman; but all things of God."

[9] *Copernican and Ptolomean systems* Nicholas Copernicus (1473–1543), Polish scientist considered the founder of modern astronomy, and author of *De Revolutionibus Orbium Coelestium* (1543), which outlined the modern theory of planetary motion based on the sun at the center; Claudius Ptolemy (c. 100–168), or Ptolomy, Greco-Egyptian mathematician and astronomer, and the author of *Almagest,* a 13–volume explanation of the heavens based on the earth at the center. Until his theories were supplanted by those of Copernicus, Ptolemy was considered the leading authority on astronomy.

to the common way of speech and the usage of the world; in which we have but a short probation, so that it matters not much what part we act, whether of governing or obeying, provided we perform it well with respect to the world to come.

One does not wonder indeed that when an adversary is drove to a nonplus[1] and reason declares against him, he flies to authority, especially to divine, which is infallible, and therefore ought not to be disputed. But scripture is not always on their side who make parade of it and, through their skill in languages and the tricks of the schools, wrest it from its genuine sense to their own inventions. And supposing, not granting, that it were apparently to the woman's disadvantage, no fair and generous adversary but would be ashamed to urge this advantage. Because women, without their own fault, are kept in ignorance of the original, wanting[2] languages and other helps to criticize on the sacred text, of which they know no more than men are pleased to impart in their translations. In short, they show their desire to maintain their hypotheses, but by no means their reverence to the sacred oracles[3] who engage them in such disputes. And therefore the blame be theirs who have unnecessarily introduced them in the present subject, and who by saying that the reflections were not agreeable to scripture, oblige the reflector to show that those who affirm it must either mistake her meaning, or the sense of holy scripture, or both, if they think what they say and do not find fault merely because they resolve to do so. For had she ever writ any thing contrary to those sacred truths, she would be the first in pronouncing its condemnation.

But what says the holy scripture? It speaks of women as in a state of subjection, and so it does of the Jews and Christians when under the dominion of the Chaldeans and Romans,[4] requiring of the one as well as of the other a quiet submission to them under whose power they lived. But will any one say that these had a natural superiority and right to dominion? That they had a superior understanding, or any pre-eminence, except what their greater strength acquired? Or that the others were subjected to their adversaries for any other reason but the punishment of their sins, and in order [for] their reformation? Or for the exercise of their virtue, and because the order of the world and the good of society required it?

If mankind had never sinned, reason would always have been obeyed; there would have been no struggle for dominion, and brutal power would not have prevailed. But in the lapsed state of mankind, and now that men will not be guided by their reason but by their appetites, and do not what they ought but what they can, the reason, or that which stands for it, the will and pleasure of the governor, is to be the reason of those who will not be guided by their own, and must take place for order's sake, although it should not be conformable to right reason. Nor can there be any society great or little, from empires down to private families, without a last resort to determine the affairs of that society by an irresistible sentence. Now unless this supremacy be fixed somewhere, there will be a perpetual contention[5] about it; such is the love of dominion, and let the reason of things be what it may, those who have least force, or cunning to supply it, will have the disadvantage. So that since women are acknowledged to have least bodily strength, their being commanded to obey is in pure kindness to them, and for their quiet and security, as well as for the exercise of their virtue. But does it follow that domestic governors have more sense than their subjects, any more than that other governors have? We do not find that any man thinks the worse of his own understanding because another has superior power, or concludes himself less capable of a post of honour and authority because he is not preferred[6] to it. How much time would lie on men's hands, how empty would the places of concourse[7] be, and how silent most companies, did men forbear to censure their governors—that is, in effect, to think themselves wiser. Indeed, government would be much more desirable than it is did it invest the possessor with a superior understanding as well as

[1] *nonplus* Puzzlement.

[2] *wanting* Lacking.

[3] *oracles* Those who expound upon or interpret the word of God.

[4] *Chaldeans* Under King Nebuchadnezzar, inhabitants of Chaldea, a region south of Babylon in modern-day Iraq, destroyed the Israelite Temple in Jerusalem and took many slaves back to Chaldea. See the Old Testament Books of 2 Kings 24.1–25, 2 Chronicles 36.5–21, Jeremiah 39.1–14, and Daniel 1.1–4.37; *Romans* By the time of Jesus, Rome governed the Kingdom of Judea through provincial governors, the most famous of which was Pontius Pilate.

[5] *contention* Dispute; controversy.

[6] *preferred* Advanced by another; promoted.

[7] *concourse* Meeting place.

power. And if mere power gives a right to rule, there can be no such thing as usurpation;[1] but a highway-man so long as he has strength to force, has also a right to require our obedience.[2]

Again, if absolute sovereignty be not necessary in a state, how comes it to be so in a family? Or if in a family why not in a state, since no reason can be alleged for the one that will not hold more strongly for the other? If the authority of the husband, so far as it extends, is sacred and inalienable, why not of the prince? The domestic sovereign is without dispute elected, and the stipulations and contract are mutual; is it not then partial in men to the last degree to contend for and practice that arbitrary dominion in their families, which they abhor and exclaim against in the state? For if arbitrary power is evil in itself, and an improper method of governing rational and free agents, it ought not to be practised anywhere; nor is it less but rather more mischievous in families than in kingdoms, by how much 100,000 tyrants are worse than one. What though a husband cannot deprive a wife of life without being responsible to the law, he may however do what is much more grievous to a generous mind: render life miserable, for which she has no redress, scarce pity, which is afforded to every other complainant. It being thought a wife's duty to suffer every thing without complaint. If all men are born free, how is it that all women are born slaves? As they must be if being subjected to the inconstant, uncertain, unknown, arbitrary will of men be the perfect condition of slavery? And if the essence of freedom consists, as our masters say it does, in having a standing rule to live by?[3] And why is slavery so much condemned and strove against in one case, and so highly applauded and held so necessary and so sacred in another?

'Tis true that God told Eve after the Fall that her husband should rule over her:[4] and so it is that he told Esau by the mouth of Isaac, his father, that he should serve his younger brother, and should in time, and when he was strong enough to do it, break the yoke from off his neck.[5] Now why one text should be a command any more than the other, and not both of them be predictions only; or why the former should prove Adam's natural right to rule, and much less every man's, any more than the latter is a proof of Jacob's right to rule, and of Esau's to rebel, one is yet to learn? The text in both cases foretelling what would be, but neither of them determining what ought to be.

But the scripture commands wives to submit themselves to their own husbands. True, for which St. Paul gives a mystical[6] reason (Ephesians 5.22, etc.) and St. Peter a prudential and charitable one (1 Peter 3.1–6), but neither of them derive that subjection from the law of nature. Nay St. Paul, as if he foresaw and meant to prevent this plea, giving directions for their conduct to women in general (1 Timothy 2.9–15) when he comes to speak of subjection, he changes his phrase from women which denotes the whole sex, to woman which in the New Testament is appropriated to a wife....

In a word, when we have reckoned up how many look no further than the making of their fortune, as they call it; who don't so much as propose to themselves any satisfaction in the woman to whom they plight[7] their faith, seeking only to be masters of her estate, that so they may have money enough to indulge all their irregular appetites; who think they are as good as can be expected, if they are but, according to the fashionable term, *civil husbands*; when we have taken the number of your giddy lovers, who are not more violent in their passion than they are certain to repent of it; when to these you have added such as marry without any thought at all, further than that it is the custom of the world, what others have done before them, that the family must be kept up, the ancient race preserved, and therefore their kind parents and guardians choose as they think convenient, without ever consulting the young ones' inclinations, who must be satisfied, or

[1] *usurpation* Unlawful occupation of another's place or property.

[2] *highway-man ... obedience* Reference to Section 119 of John Locke's *Second Treatise* (1690), in which Locke outlines how a person, born free, can be bound to civil authority by "tacit consent."

[3] *As they must ... standing rule to live by* References to Locke's *Two Treatises*, Book II, Sections 21–22, and Section 149.

[4] *husband ... her* See Genesis 3.16: "Unto the woman he said, I will greatly multiply thy sorrow and thy conception; in sorrow thou shalt bring forth children; and thy desire shall be to thy husband, and he shall rule over thee."

[5] *Esau ... neck* See Genesis 27.40: "And by thy sword shalt thou live, and shalt serve thy brother; and it shall come to pass when thou shalt have the dominion, that thou shalt break his yoke from off thy neck."

[6] *mystical* Spiritual.

[7] *plight* Pledge.

pretend so at least, upon pain of their displeasure, and that heavy consequence of it, forfeiture of their estate: These set aside, I fear there will be but a small remainder to marry out of better considerations; and even amongst the few that do, not one in a hundred takes care to deserve his choice.

But do the women never choose amiss? Are the men only in fault? That is not pretended, for he who will be just must be forced to acknowledge that neither sex are always in the right. A woman, indeed, can't properly be said to choose; all that is allowed her is to refuse or accept what is offered. And when we have made such reasonable allowances as are due to the sex, perhaps they may not appear so much in fault as one would at first imagine, and a generous spirit will find more occasion to pity than to reprove....

... And as men have little reason to expect happiness when they marry only for the love of money, wit, or beauty, as has been already shown, so much less can a woman expect a tolerable life when she goes upon these considerations. Let the business be carried as prudently as it can be on the woman's side, a reasonable man can't deny that she has by much the harder bargain, because she puts herself entirely into her husband's power, and if the matrimonial yoke be grievous, neither law nor custom afford her that redress which a man obtains. He who has sovereign power does not value the provocations of a rebellious subject, but knows how to subdue him with ease, and will make himself obeyed. But patience and submission are the only comforts that are left to a poor people who groan under tyranny, unless they are strong enough to break the yoke, to depose and abdicate, which I doubt[1] would not be allowed of here. For whatever may be said against passive obedience[2] in another case, I suppose there's no man but likes it very well in this; how much soever arbitrary power may be disliked on a throne, not Milton himself, nor B.H.——, nor any of the advocates of resistance,[3] would cry up liberty to poor *female slaves* or plead for the lawfulness of resisting a private tyranny.

If there be a disagreeableness of humours, this, in my mind, is harder to be borne than greater faults, as being a continual plague, and for the most part incurable. Other vices a man may grow weary of, or may be convinced of the evil of them, he may forsake them, or they him, but his humour and temper are seldom, if ever, put off, ill-nature sticks to him from his youth to his gray hairs, and a boy that's humorous and proud makes a peevish, positive,[4] and insolent old man. Now if this be the case, and the husband be full of himself, obstinately bent on his own way with or without reason, if he be one who must be always admired, always humoured, and yet scarce knows what will please him; if he has prosperity enough to keep him from considering and to furnish him with a train of flatterers and obsequious admirers; and learning and sense enough to make him a fop[5] in perfection, for a man can never be a complete coxcomb[6] unless he has a considerable share of these to value himself upon; what can the poor woman do? The husband is too wise to be advised, too good to be reformed, she must follow all his paces, and tread in all his unreasonable steps, or there is no peace, no quiet for her; she must obey with the greatest exactness, 'tis in vain to expect any manner of compliance on his side, and the more she complies, the more she may; his fantastical humours grow with her desire to gratify them, for age increases opinionatry[7] in some as well as it does experience in others....

If therefore it be a woman's hard fate to meet with a disagreeable temper, and of all others the haughty, imperious, and self-conceited are the most so, she is as unhappy as anything in this world can make her. For when a wife's temper does not please, if she makes her husband uneasy, he can find entertainments abroad; he has a hundred ways of relieving himself; but neither prudence nor duty will allow a woman to fly out: her

[1] *doubt* Fear.

[2] *passive obedience* Docile submission to a more powerful will; unquestioning obedience to authority. Originally theological, the term came to be increasingly applied to the monarchy during the sixteenth century.

[3] *Milton* John Milton, poet and political writer, who argues in *The Tenure of Kings and Magistrates* (1649) that the citizenry has the right to depose a tyrannical monarch; *B.H.——* Probable allusion to Bishop Benjamin Hoadly (1676–1761), who challenged the view that kings receive their legitimacy as rulers directly from God; *not Milton ... of resistance* The reference to B.H. and other "advocates" was added only in the fourth edition (1730) of the text; the first three editions mention Milton alone.

[4] *positive* Overconfident.

[5] *fop* Vain fool.

[6] *coxcomb* Vain man, excessively concerned with his appearance.

[7] *opinionatry* Excessive attachment to one's opinions.

business and entertainment are at home; and though he makes it ever so uneasy to her, she must be content and make her best on't. She who elects a monarch for life, who gives him an authority she cannot recall however he misapply it, who puts her fortune and person entirely in his power, nay, even the very desires of her heart, according to some learned casuists,[1] so as that it is not lawful to will or desire anything but what he approves and allows, had need be very sure that she does not make a fool her head, nor a vicious man her guide and pattern; she had best stay till she can meet with one who has the government of his own passions and has duly regulated his own desires, since he is to have such an absolute power over hers. But he who dotes on a face, he who makes money his idol, he who is charmed with vain and empty wit, gives no such evidence, either of wisdom or goodness, that a woman of any tolerable sense should care to venture herself to his conduct.

Indeed, your fine gentleman's actions are nowadays such that, did not custom and the dignity of his sex give weight and authority to them, a woman that thinks twice might bless herself and say, is this the Lord and Master to whom I am to promise love, honour, and obedience? What can be the object of love but amiable qualities, the image of the deity impressed upon a generous and godlike mind, a mind that is above this world, to be sure above all the vices, the tricks and baseness of it; a mind that is not full of itself, nor contracted to little private interests, but which, in imitation of that glorious pattern it endeavours to copy after, expands and diffuses itself to its utmost capacity in doing good? But this fine gentleman is quite of another strain; he is the reverse of this in every instance. He is, I confess, very fond of his own dear person, he sees very much in it to admire; his air and mien, his words and actions, every motion he makes declares it; but they must have a judgment of his size, every whit as shallow, and a partiality as great as his own, who can be of his mind. How then can I love? And if not love, much less honour. Love may arise from pity, or a generous desire to make that lovely which as yet is not so, when we see any hopes of success in our endeavours of improving it; but honour supposes some excellent qualities already, something worth our esteem, but alas there is nothing more contemptible than this trifle of a man, this mere outside, whose mind is as base and mean as his external pomp is glittering. His office or title apart, to which some ceremonious observance must be paid for order's sake, there's nothing in him that can command our respect. Strip him of equipage and fortune, and such things as only dazzle our eyes and imaginations, but don't in any measure affect our reason or cause a reverence in our hearts, and the poor creature sinks beneath our notice, because not supported by real worth. And if a woman can neither love nor honour, she does ill in promising to obey, since she is like to have a crooked rule to regulate her actions.

A mere obedience, such as is paid only to authority, and not out of love and a sense of the justice and reasonableness of the command, will be of an uncertain tenure. As it can't but be uneasy to the person who pays it, so he who receives it will be sometimes disappointed when he expects to find it; for that woman must be endowed with a wisdom and goodness much above what we suppose the sex capable of, I fear much greater than ever a man can pretend to, who can so constantly conquer her passions, and divest herself even of innocent self-love, as to give up the cause when she is in the right, and to submit her enlightened reason to the imperious dictates of a blind will and wild imagination, even when she clearly perceives the ill consequences of it, the imprudence, nay, folly and madness of such a conduct.

And if a woman runs such a risk when she marries prudently, according to the opinion of the world, that is, when she permits herself to be disposed of to a man equal to her in birth, education, and fortune, and as good as the most of his neighbours (for if none were to marry but men of strict virtue and honour, I doubt the world would be but thinly peopled), if at the very best her lot is hard, what can she expect who is sold, or any otherwise betrayed into mercenary hands, to one who is in all or most respects unequal to her? A lover who comes upon what is called equal terms makes no very advantageous proposal to the lady he courts, and to whom he seems to be an humble servant. For under many sounding compliments, words that have nothing in them, this is his true meaning: he wants one to manage his family, an housekeeper, one whose interest it will be not to wrong him, and in whom therefore he can put greater confidence than in any he can hire for money. One who may breed his children, taking all the

[1] *casuists* Those who engage in disingenuous reasoning.

care and trouble of their education, to preserve his name and family. One whose beauty, wit, or good humour and agreeable conversation will entertain him at home when he has been contradicted and disappointed abroad; who will do him that justice the ill-natured world denies him; that is, in anyone's language but his own, soothe his pride and flatter his vanity, by having always so much good sense as to be on his side, to conclude him in the right when others are so ignorant or so rude as to deny it. Who will not be blind to his merit nor contradict his will and pleasure, but make it her business, her very ambition to content him; whose softness and gentle compliance will calm his passions, to whom he may safely disclose his troublesome thoughts, and in her breast discharge his cares; whose duty, submission, and observance will heal those wounds other people's opposition or neglect have given him. In a word, one whom he can entirely govern, and consequently may form her to his will and liking, who must be his of life, and therefore cannot quit his service, let him treat her how he will. …

What then is to be done? How must a man choose, and what qualities must incline a woman to accept, that so our married couple may be as happy as that state can make them? This is no hard question; let the soul be principally considered, and regard had in the first place to a good understanding, a virtuous mind, and in all other respects let there be as much equality as may be. If they are good Christians and of suitable tempers all will be well; but I should be shrewdly tempted to suspect their Christianity who marry after any of those ways we have been speaking of, I dare venture to say, that they don't act according to the precepts of the Gospel, they neither show the wisdom of the serpent, nor the innocence of the dove,[1] they have neither so much government of themselves, nor so much charity for their neighbours, they neither take such care not to scandalize others, nor to avoid temptations themselves, are neither so much above this world, nor so affected with the next, as they would certainly be did the Christian religion operate in their hearts, did they rightly understand and sincerely practise it, or acted *indeed* according to the spirit of the Gospel.

But it is not enough to enter wisely into this state; care must be taken of our conduct afterwards. A woman will not want[2] being admonished of her duty; the custom of the world, economy, everything almost reminds her of it. Governors do not often suffer their subjects to forget obedience through their want of demanding it; perhaps husbands are but too forward on this occasion, and claim their right oftener and more imperiously than either discretion or good manners will justify, and might have both a more cheerful and constant obedience paid them if they were not so rigorous in exacting it. For there is a mutual stipulation, and love, honour, and worship, by which certainly civility and respect at least are meant, are as much the woman's due, as love, honour and obedience are the man's, and being the woman is said to be the weaker vessel, the man should be more careful not to grieve or offend her. Since her reason is supposed to be less, and her passions stronger than his, he should not give occasion to call that supposition in question by his pettish[3] carriage and needless provocations. Since he is the *man,* by which very word custom would have us understand not only greatest strength of body, but even greatest firmness and force of mind, he should not play the little master so much as to expect to be cockered,[4] nor run over to that side which the woman used to be ranked in; for, according to the wisdom of the Italians, *Will you? is spoken to sick folks.*[5]

Indeed subjection, according to the common notion of it, is not over easy; none of us, whether men or women, but have so good an opinion of our own conduct as to believe we are fit, if not to direct others, at least to govern ourselves. Nothing but a sound understanding and grace, the best improver of natural reason, can correct this opinion, truly humble us, and heartily reconcile us to obedience. This bitter cup therefore ought to be sweetened as much as may be; for authority may be preserved and government kept inviolable without that nauseous ostentation of power which serves to no end or purpose but to blow up the pride and vanity of those who have it, and to exasperate the spirits of such as must truckle under it.

Insolence 'tis true is never the effect of power but in weak and cowardly spirits who, wanting true *merit* and

[1] *wisdom of … the dove* In Matthew 10.16, Jesus instructs the apostles to be "wise as serpents, and innocent as doves."

[2] *want* Lack.

[3] *pettish* Childishly irritable.

[4] *cockered* Overly indulged.

[5] *Will you … sick folks* The first edition (1700) prints the phrase in its original Italian.

judgment to support themselves in that advantageous ground on which they stand, are ever appealing to their authority, and making a show of it to maintain their vanity and pride. A truly great mind and such as is fit to govern, though it may stand on its right with its equals, and modestly expect what is due to it even from its superiors, yet it never contends with its inferiors, nor makes use of its superiority but to do them good. So that considering the just dignity of man, his great wisdom so conspicuous on all occasions! the goodness of his temper and reasonableness of all his commands, which make it a woman's interest as well as duty to be observant and obedient in all things! that his prerogative is settled by an undoubted right and the prescription of many ages; it cannot be supposed that he should make frequent and insolent claims of an authority so well established and used with such moderation! nor give an impartial bystander (could such an one be found) any occasion from thence to suspect that he is inwardly conscious of the badness of his title; usurpers being always most desirous of recognitions and busy in imposing oaths, whereas a lawful prince contents himself with the usual methods and securities.

And since power does naturally puff up, and he who finds himself exalted seldom fails to think he *ought* to be so, it is more suitable to a man's wisdom and generosity to be mindful of his great obligations than to insist on his rights and prerogatives. Sweetness of temper and an obliging carriage are so justly due to a wife that a husband who must not be thought to want either understanding to know what is fit, nor goodness to perform it, can't be supposed not to show them. For setting aside the hazards of her person[1] to keep up his name and family, with all the pains and trouble that attend it, which may well be thought great enough to deserve all the respect and kindness that may be; setting this aside, though 'tis very considerable, a woman has so much the disadvantage in *most,* I was about to say in *all* things, that she makes a man the greatest compliment in the world when she condescends[2] to take him *for better for worse.*[3] She puts herself entirely in his power, leaves all that is dear to her, her friends and family, to espouse[4] his interests and follow his fortune, and makes it her business and duty to please him! What acknowledgments, what returns can he make? What gratitude can be sufficient for such obligations? She shows her good opinion of him by the great trust she reposes in him, and what a brute must he be who betrays that trust, or acts any way unworthy of it? Ingratitude is one of the basest vices, and if a man's soul is sunk so low as to be guilty of it towards her who has so generously obliged him, and who so entirely depends on him, if he can treat her disrespectfully, who has so fully testified her esteem of him, she must have a stock of virtue which he should blush to discern, if she can pay him that obedience of which he is so unworthy....

But how can a woman scruple[5] entire subjection, how can she forbear to admire the worth and excellency of the superior sex, if she at all considers it? Have not all the great actions that have been performed in the world been done by men? Have not they founded empires and overturned them? Do not they make laws and continually repeal and amend them? Their vast minds lay kingdoms waste, no bounds or measures can be prescribed to their desires. War and peace depend on them; they form cabals[6] and have the wisdom and courage to get over all these rubs,[7] the petty restraints which honour and conscience may lie[8] in the way of their desired grandeur. What is it they cannot do? They make worlds and ruin them, form systems of universal nature and dispute eternally about them; their pen gives worth to the most trifling controversy; nor can a fray be inconsiderable if they have drawn their swords in't. All that the wise man pronounces is an oracle, and every word the witty speaks, a jest. It is a woman's happiness to hear, admire, and praise them, especially if a little ill-nature keeps them at any time from bestowing due applauses on each other! And if she aspires no further, she is thought to be in her proper sphere of action; she is as wise and as good as can be expected from her!

[1] *hazards of her person* Risks to her body; i.e., dangers of childbirth.

[2] *condescends* In this context, willingly agrees.

[3] *for better for worse* The marriage service in the Book of Common Prayer of the Church of England asks the bride and groom to take each other "for better for worse ... till death us do part, according to God's holy ordinance."

[4] *espouse* Commit to.

[5] *scruple* Question or mistrust.

[6] *cabals* Covert political alliances.

[7] *rubs* Impediments.

[8] *these rubs ... may lie* Some editions read "these rubs which may lie."

She then who marries ought to lay it down for an indisputable maxim that her husband must govern absolutely and entirely, and that she has nothing else to do but to please and obey. She must not attempt to divide his authority, or so much as dispute it; to struggle with her yoke will only make it gall the more; but must believe him wise and good and in all respects the best, at least he must be so to her. She who can't do this is no way fit to be a wife, she may set up for that peculiar coronet[1] the ancient fathers talked of, but is not qualified to receive that great reward which attends the eminent exercise of humility and self-denial, patience and resignation, the duties that a wife is called to.

But some refractory[2] woman perhaps will say, how can this be? Is it possible for her to believe him wise and good who by a thousand demonstrations convinces her and all the world of the contrary? Did the bare name of husband confer sense on a man, and the mere being in authority infallibly qualify him for government, much might be done. But since a wise man and a husband are not terms convertible, and how loath soever one is to own it, matter of fact won't allow us to deny that the head many times stands in need of the inferior's brains to manage it, she must beg leave to be excused from such high thoughts of her sovereign, and if she submits to his power, it is not so much reason as necessity that compels her.

Now of how little force soever this objection may be in other respects, methinks it is strong enough to prove the necessity of a good education, and that men never mistake their true interest more than when they endeavour to keep women in ignorance. Could they indeed deprive them of their natural good sense at the same time they deny them the due improvement of it, they might compass their end; otherwise natural sense unassisted may run into a false track, and serve only to punish him justly, who would not allow it to be useful to himself or others. If man's authority be justly established, the more sense a woman has, the more reason she will find to submit to it; if according to the tradition of our fathers (who, having had *possession* of the pen, thought they had also the best *right* to it), women's understanding is but small, and men's partiality adds no weight to the observation, ought not the more care to be taken to improve them? How it agrees with the justice of men we inquire not, but certainly Heaven is abundantly more equitable than to enjoin women the hardest task and give them the least strength to perform it. And if men, learned, wise, and discreet as they are, who have, as is said, all the advantages of nature, and without controversy have or may have all the assistance of art, are so far from acquitting themselves as they ought, from living according to that reason and excellent understanding they so much boast of, can it be expected that a woman, who is reckoned silly enough in herself, at least comparatively, and whom men take care to make yet more so; can it be expected that she should constantly perform so difficult a duty as entire subjection, to which corrupt nature is so averse?

If the great and wise Cato,[3] a *man*, a man of no ordinary firmness and strength of mind, a man who was esteemed as an oracle, and by the philosophers and great men of his nation equalled even to the gods themselves; if he, with all his Stoical principles, was not able to bear the sight of a triumphant conqueror (who perhaps would have insulted, and perhaps would not), but out of a cowardly fear of an insult, ran to death to secure him from it; can it be thought that an ignorant weak woman should have the patience to bear a continued outrage and insolence all the days of her life? Unless you will suppose her a *very ass*, but then remember what the Italians say, to quote them once more, since being *very* husbands they may be presumed to have some authority in this case, *an ass though slow if provoked will kick*.[4]

We never see, or perhaps make sport with the ill effects of a bad education, till it comes to touch us home in the ill conduct of a sister, a daughter, or wife. Then the women must be blamed, their folly is exclaimed against, when all this while it was the wise man's fault, who did not set a better guard on those, who, according to him, stand in so much need of one. A young gentleman, as a celebrated author[5] tells us, ought above all things to be

[1] *peculiar coronet* I.e., nun's headpiece.

[2] *refractory* Headstrong, unmanageable.

[3] *Cato* Cato the Younger (95–46 BCE) was a Roman politician known for his adherence to the ethics of Stoic philosophy. He opposed Gaius Julius Caesar in the Great Roman Civil War, one of the wars through which Caesar established himself as dictator and brought an end to a period of republican government. When Cato learned that his side had been defeated, he committed suicide.

[4] *an ass ... will kick* The proverb is also included in Italian in the first (1700) and fourth (1730) editions of the *Reflections*.

[5] *celebrated author* John Locke, who states this opinion in *Some Thoughts Concerning Education* (1693), 94.

acquainted with the state of the world, the ways and humours, the follies, the cheats, the faults of the age he is fallen into; he should by degrees be informed of the vice in fashion, and warned of the application and design of those who will make it their business to corrupt him, should be told the arts they use, and the trains they lay, be prepared to be shocked by some and caressed by others; warned who are like to oppose, who to mislead, who to undermine, and who to serve him. He should be instructed how to know and distinguish them, where he should let them see and when dissemble the knowledge of them and their aims and workings....

And it is not less necessary that a young lady should receive the like instructions, whether or not her temptations be fewer, her reputation and honour however are to be more nicely preserved; they may be ruined by a little ignorance or indiscretion, and then though she has kept her innocence, and so is secured as to the next world, yet she is in a great measure lost to this. A woman cannot be too watchful, too apprehensive of her danger, nor keep at too great a distance from it, since man, whose wisdom and ingenuity is so much superior to hers! condescends for his interest sometimes, and sometimes by way of diversion, to lay snares for her. For though all men are *virtuosi*, philosophers and politicians, in comparison of the ignorant and illiterate women, yet they don't all pretend to be saints, and 'tis no great matter to them if women who were born to be their slaves be now and then ruined for their entertainment.

But according to the rate that young women are educated, according to the way their time is spent, they are destined to folly and impertinence, to say no worse, and which is yet more inhuman, they are blamed for that ill conduct they are not suffered to avoid, and reproached for those faults they are in a manner forced into; so that if Heaven has bestowed any sense on them, no other use is made of it than to leave them without excuse. So much and no more of the world is shown them as serves to weaken and corrupt their minds; to give them wrong notions and busy them in mean pursuits; to disturb, not to regulate their passions; to make them timorous and dependent, and, in a word, fit for nothing else but to act a farce for the diversion of their governors.

Even men themselves improve no otherwise than according to the aim they take and the end they propose; and he whose designs are but little and mean will be the same himself. Though ambition, as 'tis usually understood, is a foolish, not to say a base and pitiful vice, yet the aspirings of the soul after true glory are so much its nature that it seems to have forgot itself and to degenerate if it can forbear; and perhaps the great secret of education lies in affecting the soul with a lively sense of what is truly its perfection, and exciting the most ardent desires after it.

But, alas! what poor woman is ever taught that she should have a higher design than to get her a husband? Heaven will fall in of course; and if she makes but an obedient and dutiful wife, she cannot miss of it. A husband indeed is thought by both sexes so very valuable that scarce a man who can keep himself clean and make a bow, but thinks he is good enough to pretend to any woman; no matter for the difference of birth or fortune, a husband is such a wonder-working name as to make an equality, or something more, whenever it is pronounced.

And indeed were there no other proof of masculine wisdom, and what a much greater portion of ingenuity falls to the men than to the women's share, the address, the artifice, and management of a humble servant were a sufficient demonstration. What good conduct does he show! what patience exercise! what subtlety leave untried! what concealment of his faults! what parade of his virtues! what government of his passions! How deep is his policy in laying his designs at so great a distance, and working them up by such little accidents! How indefatigable is his industry, and how constant his watchfulness, not to slip any opportunity that may in the least contribute to his design! What a handsome set of disguises and pretences is he always furnished with! How concealed does he lie! how little pretend, till he is sure that his plot will take! And at the same time that he nourishes the hope of being Lord and Master, appears with all the modesty and submission of an humble and unpretending admirer.

—1700

Jonathan Swift

1667 – 1745

In *The Life of the Rev. Dr. Jonathan Swift* (1784), Thomas Sheridan called him "a man whose original genius and uncommon talents have raised him, in the general estimation, above all the writers of the age"—a list that included Defoe, Dryden, and Pope. If Swift's talents did indeed raise him above most writers of his time, he was entirely at one with his age in his penchant for satire, so notably illustrated in his most famous work, *Gulliver's Travels*. His aim in *Gulliver's Travels*, as he put it in a letter to Alexander Pope, was "to vex the world, not to divert it." Yet he understood that even the most pointed satire would often miss its mark. He once commented that satire "is a sort of glass, wherein beholders do generally discover everybody's face but their own." He held the glass up to hypocrites and bombasts of many forms, but he particularly loathed religious and political tyranny. *A Tale of a Tub* and "A Modest Proposal" are enduring protests against such oppression.

Swift was born in Ireland to Abigail Errick Swift; his English father died before he was born. At the age of one, Swift was kidnapped and taken to England by his nursemaid; he was not re-united with his mother until after he had reached the age of three. He studied at Kilkenny School and then moved on to Trinity College at the University of Dublin when he was fourteen. When he completed his education, he made what he thought would be a permanent move to England. There he took employment as secretary to retired politician Sir William Temple, through whom Swift made several lifelong friends.

During the 1690s Swift composed urban pastoral poetry, odes, and two early satires. *The Battle of the Books* was written in defense of Temple and against the "moderns" who were, in Swift's view, unwisely neglecting "ancient" modes of learning. In *A Tale of a Tub*, Swift mocked the religious and intellectual foolishness of the sort that prompts absurd flights of fancy. The narrative focuses on the adventures of three brothers of different religious persuasions, representing Roman Catholicism, Anglicanism, and Calvinism, but chapters of narrative alternate with inventively irrelevant digressions, including the famous "Digression in Praise of Digressions."

Swift seemed destined to keep returning, for one reason or another, to Ireland. He studied for the Anglican priesthood in Dublin from 1694 to 1696 before returning to Temple's service, but after his employer's death in 1699 he traveled to Ireland as secretary and chaplain to Earl Berkeley and was then appointed Vicar of Laracor in the Dublin area. He returned to England in 1707 as an emissary of the Irish clergy, seeking a reduction in tax on their incomes. Queen Anne had little sympathy, however; the pious but literal-minded queen had misread *A Tale of a Tub* as an attack on established religion rather than a defense of it. Swift's poem "The Windsor Prophecy" did not help matters, as the attack on the Duchess of Somerset, a Whiggish favorite of the Queen, further consolidated her opposition both to his causes and to him personally. Lacking promotion in England, Swift had little choice but to return to Ireland, where he was installed as Dean of St. Patrick's Cathedral in 1713. He was never to achieve his goal of holding high religious office in London.

In the early 1700s Swift began to distinguish himself by his political pamphleteering and his comical literary hoaxes, some of them published in Richard Steele's periodical *The Tatler* (which also published some of his best-known poems). In 1708, for example, he composed "An Argument Against Abolishing Christianity in England." Whatever his relation to authority in general, Swift was all his life a defender of the established religion, and his argument was really aimed against the Whig attempt to abolish certain forms of discrimination against Roman Catholics and Dissenters by repealing the Test Act, which imposed certain civil disabilities on those who refused Church of England sacraments. Swift's strategy was to conflate arguments against the Test Act with arguments against the Church itself, while opening a disturbing split in his argument between real or primitive Christianity (which is irrelevant, he says, because nobody practices it) and nominal Christianity.

While in Temple's service, Swift had tutored Temple's eight-year-old ward, Esther Johnson (or "Stella," as he would come to call her), and when she came of age he convinced her and a companion to live near him in Dublin. While separated from her when he was in England, he wrote her a series of letters that was published much later as *Journal to Stella* (written 1710–13). In the *Journal* Swift adopted a private, often obscure language—a "nursery talk" full of neologisms, irregular spellings, and novel grammatical usages. Swift's and Johnson's relationship endured to the end of her life in 1728 and was marked by an annual birthday poem; the survivors are some of his most charming poems. The dynamics of his emotional life remain obscure: he conducted a simultaneous relationship with "Vanessa" (Esther Vanhomrigh), who was a more rebellious character than Johnson and who followed him, without invitation, to Ireland from England. This relationship too produced a remarkable poem, *Cadenus and Vanessa*, in which Swift relates the story of their friendship from his own point of view, leaving its ending open.

Swift counted among his friends many of the leading lights of London's literary scene, including Joseph Addison (until politics divided the two), Alexander Pope, and John Gay, and counted his "banishment" to Ireland as "the greatest unhappiness" of his life. Although he made a number of return visits to England, after 1727 his home was "wretched Dublin, in miserable Ireland." Swift also suffered from undiagnosed Ménières disease, a debilitating inner-ear disease causing dizziness, headaches, depression, and deafness.

A preoccupation with death and decay lends a sharply pessimistic tone to Swift's later satires. Rereading these works several years later, Samuel Johnson despaired at ever discovering "by what depravity of intellect [Swift] took delight in revolting ideas from which almost every other mind shrinks with disgust." Swift was often accused of misanthropy, but in a letter to Alexander Pope he endeavored to counter the charge, insisting that while he had "ever hated all nations, professions, and communities," he did indeed love "individuals." Swift has often also been accused of misogyny on account of such poems as "The Lady's Dressing Room," in which a man is abruptly cured of his passion when he discovers his beloved's bedroom to be disgustingly squalid.

If Swift was embittered by Ireland, the nation, which remained entirely subject to English rule, was to benefit greatly by its association with him. Swift wrote numerous pamphlets and tracts in opposition to British policy, among them *A Modest Proposal* (1729), a brilliantly macabre send-up of English hard-heartedness toward the Irish and of the number-crunching approach to public policy, which puts economic utility first. In his *Proposal*, Swift recommends that the Irish could solve their problems of famine and overpopulation by raising their children for export as a food source for the English.

Swift often proudly anticipated public opposition to his views. Foreseeing the hostile reaction to his founding of St. Patrick's Hospital, Ireland's first mental asylum, he wrote *Verses on the Death of Dr. Swift* (1739), which predicts and responds to hostilities and objections. His legacy, he hoped, would be based not on fashionable and worldly expectations, but on his commitment to identifying and rooting out abuses. Translated from the Latin, the epitaph on his tomb in St. Patrick's Cathedral reads: "*Here is laid the body of Jonathan Swift, Doctor of Divinity, Dean of this Cathedral Church, where fierce indignation can no longer rend the heart. Go, traveller, and imitate if you can this earnest and dedicated champion of liberty. He died on the 19th day of October 1745 AD. Aged 78 years."*

⌘⌘⌘

The Progress of Beauty

When first Diana[1] leaves her bed,
Vapours and steams[2] her looks disgrace,
A frowzy° dirty-coloured red *shabby*
Sits on her cloudy wrinkled face:
But, by degrees, when mounted high,
Her artificial face appears
Down from her window in the sky,
Her spots are gone, her visage clears.
'Twixt earthly females and the moon,
All parallels exactly run;
If Celia should appear too soon,
Alas, the nymph° would be undone! *beautiful woman*
To see her from her pillow rise,
All reeking in a cloudy steam,
Cracked lips, foul teeth, and gummy eyes,
Poor Strephon,[3] how would he blaspheme!
Three colours, black, and red, and white,
So graceful in their proper place,
Remove them to a different light,
They form a frightful hideous face:
For instance, when the lily skips
Into the precincts of the rose,
And takes possession of the lips,
Leaving the purple to the nose.
So, Celia went entire to bed,
All her complexions safe and sound;
But, when she rose, white, black, and red,
Though still in sight, had changed their ground.
The black, which would not be confined,
A more inferior station seeks,
Leaving the fiery red behind,
And mingles in her muddy cheeks.
But Celia can with ease reduce,
By help of pencil, paint, and brush,
Each colour to its place and use,
And teach her cheeks again to blush.
She knows her early self no more;
But filled with admiration stands,
As other painters oft adore
The workmanship of their own hands.
Thus, after four important hours,
Celia's the wonder of her sex:
Say, which among the heav'nly pow'rs
Could cause such marvellous effects?
Venus,[4] indulgent to her kind,
Gave women all their hearts could wish,
When first she taught them where to find
White lead and Lusitanian dish.[5]
Love with white lead cements his wings;
White lead was sent us to repair
Two brightest, brittlest, earthly things,
A lady's face, and China-ware.[6]
She ventures now to lift the sash,
The window is her proper sphere:
Ah, lovely nymph! be not too rash,
Nor let the beaux approach too near:
Take pattern by your sister star,
Delude at once, and bless our sight;
When you are seen, be seen from far,
And chiefly choose to shine by night.
But, art no longer can prevail,
When the materials all are gone;
The best mechanic hand must fail,
Where nothing's left to work upon.
Matter, as wise logicians say,

[1] *Diana* Goddess of the moon.

[2] *Vapours* Exhalations from the organs, believed in the eighteenth century to cause a variety of physical and psychological ailments; *steams* Bad breath, perspiration, or other bodily excretions.

[3] *Strephon* Name commonly used in pastoral poetry for a young man in love.

[4] *Venus* Goddess of love and beauty.

[5] *White lead* Toxic lead-based pigment used as a cosmetic foundation; *Lusitanian dish* Cosmetic from Portugal.

[6] *China-ware* White lead was also used to glaze and repair porcelain.

Cannot without a form subsist;
And form, say I as well as they,
Must fail, if matter brings no grist.° *substance*
And this is fair Diana's case;
For all astrologers maintain,
Each night, a bit drops off her face,
When mortals say she's in her wane;
While Partrige[1] wisely shows the cause
Efficient of the moon's decay,
That Cancer with his pois'nous claws,[2]
Attacks her in the Milky Way:
But Gadbury,[3] in art profound,
From her pale cheeks pretends to show,
That swain° Endymion[4] is not found, *lover*
Or else, that Mercury's[5] her foe.
But, let the cause be what it will,
In half the month she looks so thin,
That Flamstead[6] can, with all his skill,
See but her forehead and her chin.
Yet, as she wastes, she grows discreet,
'Till midnight never shows her head;
So rotting Celia strolls the street,
When sober folks are all a-bed:
For sure if this be Luna's° fate, *the moon's*
Poor Celia, but of mortal race,
In vain expects a longer date
To the materials of her face.
When mercury her tresses mows,
To think of black-lead combs is vain;
No painting can restore a nose,
Nor will her teeth return again.
Ye pow'rs, who over love preside!
Since mortal beauties drop so soon,
If you would have us well supplied,
Send us new nymphs with each new moon.
—1719

[1] *Partrige* English astrologer John Partridge (1644–c. 1714).

[2] *Cancer with … pois'nous claws* The constellation Cancer is a crab.

[3] *Gadbury* English astrologer John Gadbury (1627–1704).

[4] *Endymion* Beautiful Greek youth of myth, lover to the moon.

[5] *Mercury's* Planet with astrological meaning, associated with the Roman god of the same name. Also a pun on the side effects of mercury poisoning; mercury compounds were used to treat venereal disease, and could cause tooth and hair loss, as well as rotting of the soft tissues of the face.

[6] *Flamstead* Astronomer John Flamsteed (1646–1719), director of the Royal Observatory.

A Description of a City Shower

Careful observers may foretell the hour
(By sure prognostics) when to dread a show'r.
While rain depends,° the pensive cat gives o'er *is imminent*
Her frolics, and pursues her tail no more.
Returning home at night you find the sink° *sewer*
Strike your offended sense with double stink.
If you be wise, then go not far to dine,
You spend in coach-hire more than save in wine.
A coming show'r your shooting[7] corns presage,
Old aches throb, your hollow tooth will rage.
Saunt'ring in coffee-house is Dulman seen;
He damns the climate and complains of spleen.[8]

Meanwhile the south,° rising with dabbled[9] wings, *south wind*
A sable cloud athwart the welkin° flings, *sky*
That swilled more liquor than it could contain,
And like a drunkard gives it up again.
Brisk Susan whips her linen from the rope,
While the first drizzling show'r is borne aslope:° *on an incline*
Such is that sprinkling which some careless quean° *hussy*
Flirts° on you from her mop, but not so clean: *flicks*
You fly, invoke the gods; then, turning, stop
To rail; she, singing, still whirls on her mop.
Nor yet the dust had shunned th' unequal strife,
But, aided by the wind, fought still for life,
And wafted with its foe by violent gust,
'Twas doubtful which was rain, and which was dust.
Ah! Where must needy poet seek for aid,
When dust and rain at once his coat invade?

[7] *shooting* I.e., beset by shooting pain.

[8] *spleen* Said to be the origin of melancholy feelings, "the spleen" was often used synonymously with "melancholia."

[9] *dabbled* Splashed with water or mud.

Sole coat, where dust cemented by the rain
Erects the nap,[1] and leaves a cloudy stain.

Now in contiguous drops the flood comes down,
Threat'ning with deluge this devoted° town. *doomed*
To shops in crowds the daggled° females fly, *bespattered*
Pretend to cheapen° goods, but nothing buy. *bargain for*
The templar spruce,[2] while every spout's abroach,° *streaming*
Stays till 'tis fair, yet seems to call a coach.
The tucked-up seamstress walks with hasty strides,
While streams run down her oiled umbrella's sides.
Here various kinds by various fortunes led,
Commence acquaintance underneath a shed.
Triumphant Tories, and desponding Whigs,
Forget their feuds,[3] and join to save their wigs.
Boxed in a chair° the beau impatient sits, *sedan chair*
While spouts run clatt'ring o'er the roof by fits,
And ever and anon with frightful din
The leather sounds;[4] he trembles from within.
So when Troy chairmen bore the wooden steed,
Pregnant with Greeks, impatient to be freed
(Those bully Greeks, who, as the moderns do,
Instead of paying chairmen, run them through),
Laocoon[5] struck the outside with his spear,
And each imprisoned hero quaked for fear.

Now from all parts the swelling kennels[6] flow,
And bear their trophies with them as they go:
Filths of all hues and odours seem to tell
What streets they sailed from, by the sight and smell.
They, as each torrent drives with rapid force
From Smithfield or St. Pulchre's shape their course,
And in huge confluent join at Snow Hill ridge,
Fall from the conduit prone to Holborn Bridge.[7]
Sweepings from butchers' stalls, dung, guts, and blood,
Drowned puppies, stinking sprats,[8] all drenched in mud,
Dead cats and turnip-tops come tumbling down the
flood.[9]

—1710

Stella's Birthday[10]

WRITTEN IN THE YEAR 1718[11]

Stella this day is thirty-four[12]
(We shan't dispute a year or more);
However, Stella, be not troubled,
Although thy size and years are doubled
Since first I saw thee at sixteen,[13]
The brightest virgin on the green.

[1] *nap* Rough surface layer of projecting threads on wooly surfaces.

[2] *templar* Law student; *spruce* Smartly dressed.

[3] *Triumphant Tories … feuds* In 1710 the Whig ministry fell and a Tory majority was elected to the House of Commons for the first time.

[4] *leather sounds* I.e., the rain pounds on the leather roof of the sedan chair.

[5] *Laocoon* Trojan priest who, according to Virgil's *Aeneid*, was suspicious of the horse and struck it with his spear. See *Aeneid* 2.40-53.

[6] *kennels* Open gutters that ran down the middle of streets. These were also used as sewers, into which all sorts of refuse could be dumped.

[7] *From Smithfield … Holborn Bridge* The drainage from the Smithfield cattle and sheep markets, which flowed down Cow Lane, met that from St. Sepulchre's Church, which flowed down Snow Hill, at the Holborn Conduit. The combined sewage ran into the Fleet River at Holborn Bridge.

[8] *sprats* Small fish.

[9] *Sweepings from … flood* According to the note, now attributed to Swift, in Faulkner's edition of Swift's *Works* (1735), this concluding triplet, with an alexandrine as the final line, is an imitation of a form popular with John Dryden and other Restoration poets. Swift claims his mockery of the established form (which he saw as the "mere effect of haste, idleness, and want of money") finally brought about its demise.

[10] *Stella's Birthday* This is the first of the series of poems Swift wrote to his dear friend Esther Johnson ("Stella") every year on her birthday (March 13) until her death in 1728. Swift plays upon the convention that the Poet Laureate would write a birthday ode for the monarch each year.

[11] *1718* Before 1751, when the calendar was reformed, the new year officially began on March 25, the Feast of the Annunciation. Because many people also recognized January 1 as the start of the new year, the year was often written according to both systems when the date fell between January 1 and March 24. Swift's poem was written in February or March of what we would recognize as 1719.

[12] *thirty-four* Johnson was really thirty-eight.

[13] *at sixteen* Johnson was actually eight when the two first met at Moor Park, Sir William's estate in Surrey. On his next visit to Moor Park, however, when she was 16, Swift first noticed that Johnson had bloomed into, as he said, a "beautiful, graceful, and agreeable" young woman.

So little is thy form declined,
Made up so largely in thy mind.

Oh, would it please the gods to split
Thy beauty, size, and years, and wit,
No age could furnish out a pair
Of nymphs so graceful, wise, and fair,
With half the lustre of your eyes,
With half your wit, your years, and size.
And then before it grew too late,
How should I beg of gentle fate
(That either nymph might have her swain°) *lover*
To split my worship too in twain.
—1728

Stella's Birthday (1727)[1]

This day, whate'er the fates decree,
Shall still be kept with joy by me;
This day then, let us not be told
That you are sick, and I grown old,
Nor think on our approaching ills,
And talk of spectacles and pills.
Tomorrow will be time enough
To hear such mortifying stuff.
Yet, since from reason may be brought
A better and more pleasing thought,
Which can, in spite of all decays,
Support a few remaining days,
From not the gravest of divines,° *clergymen, theologians*
Accept for once some serious lines.

Although we now can form no more
Long schemes of life, as heretofore,
Yet you, while time is running fast,
Can look with joy on what is past.

Were future happiness and pain[2]
A mere contrivance of the brain,
As atheists argue, to entice,
And fit their proselytes° for vice *converts*
(The only comfort they propose,
To have companions in their woes);
Grant this the case, yet sure 'tis hard,
That virtue, styled its own reward,
And by all sages understood
To be the chief of human good,
Should acting, die, nor leave behind
Some lasting pleasure in the mind,
Which by remembrance will assuage
Grief, sickness, poverty, and age,
And strongly shoot a radiant dart,
To shine through life's declining part.

Say, Stella, feel you no content,
Reflecting on a life well spent?
Your skilful hand employed to save
Despairing wretches from the grave;[3]
And then supporting with your store,
Those whom you dragged from death before
(So Providence on mortals waits,
Preserving what it first creates);
Your gen'rous boldness to defend
An innocent and absent friend;
That courage which can make you just,
To merit humbled in the dust;
The detestation you express
For vice in all its glitt'ring dress;
That patience under torturing pain,
Where stubborn Stoics would complain.

Shall these like empty shadows pass,
Or forms reflected from a glass?
Or mere chimeras[4] in the mind,
That fly and leave no marks behind?
Does not the body thrive and grow
By food of twenty years ago?
And, had it not been still supplied,
It must a thousand times have died.
Then who with reason can maintain,
That no effects of food remain?
And is not virtue in mankind
The nutriment that feeds the mind?

[1] *Stella's Birthday (1727)* The last of Swift's birthday poems to Esther Johnson ("Stella"), who died in 1728.

[2] *future happiness and pain* Reward or punishment in an afterlife.

[3] *Your skilful … grave* Johnson frequently nursed Swift when he was ill. She also helped care for the poor in her neighborhood.

[4] *chimeras* Wild fantasies; unreal creatures.

Upheld by each good action past,
And still continued by the last;
Then who with reason can pretend
That all effects of virtue end?

Believe me, Stella, when you show
That true contempt for things below,
Nor prize your life for other ends
Than merely to oblige your friends,
Your former actions claim their part,
And join to fortify your heart.
For virtue, in her daily race,
Like Janus[1] bears a double face,
Looks back with joy where she has gone,
And therefore goes with courage on.
She at your sickly couch will wait,
And guide you to a better state.

O then, whatever heav'n intends,
Take pity on your pitying friends;
Nor let your ills affect your mind,
To fancy they can be unkind.
Me, surely me, you ought to spare,
Who gladly would your suff'rings share,
Or give my scrap of life to you,
And think it far beneath your due;
You, to whose care so oft I owe,
That I'm alive to tell you so.
—1728

The Lady's Dressing Room[2]

Five hours (and who can do it less in?)
By haughty Celia spent in dressing;
The goddess from her chamber issues,
Arrayed in lace, brocade,[3] and tissues.
Strephon,[4] who found the room was void,
And Betty[5] otherwise employed,
Stole in, and took a strict survey
Of all the litter as it lay;
Whereof, to make the matter clear,
An *inventory* follows here.

And first, a dirty smock appeared,
Beneath the armpits well besmeared.
Strephon, the rogue, displayed it wide,
And turned it round on every side.
In such a case few words are best,
And Strephon bids us guess the rest,
But swears how damnably the men lie
In calling Celia sweet and cleanly.

Now listen while he next produces
The various combs for various uses,
Filled up with dirt so closely fixed,
No brush could force a way betwixt;
A paste of composition rare,
Sweat, dandruff, powder, lead,[6] and hair,
A forehead cloth with oil upon't
To smooth the wrinkles on her front;
Here alum flower[7] to stop the steams
Exhaled from sour unsavoury streams;
There night-gloves made of Tripsy's[8] hide,
Bequeathed by Tripsy when she died,
With puppy water,[9] beauty's help,
Distilled from Tripsy's darling whelp.
Here gallipots° and vials placed, *small ointment jars*
Some filled with washes, some with paste,
Some with pomatum,° paints, and slops, *hair ointment*

---

[1] *Janus* Roman god of gates, doorways, and beginnings and endings, after whom the month of January was named. He was depicted with two faces that looked in opposite directions, both forward and backward.

[2] *The Lady's Dressing Room* This poem provoked a biting response from Lady Mary Wortley Montagu. See her poem "The Reasons that Induced Dr. S. to Write a Poem Called The Lady's Dressing Room."

[3] *brocade* Fabric with a woven, raised pattern, usually in gold or silver.

[4] *Strephon* Name used commonly in pastoral poetry for a young swain.

[5] *Betty* Name used commonly to denote a servant.

[6] *powder* Used on the hair, not the face; *lead* White lead, a mixture used as a white face paint to lighten the skin.

[7] *alum flower* I.e., alum powder. The astringent mineral was used as an antiperspirant.

[8] *Tripsy* Celia's lapdog.

[9] *puppy water* Puppy urine, formerly used as a cosmetic.

And ointments good for scabby chops.
Hard by a filthy basin stands,
Fouled with the scouring of her hands;
The basin takes whatever comes,
The scrapings of her teeth and gums,
A nasty compound of all hues,
For here she spits, and here she spews.

But oh! it turned poor Strephon's bowels,
When he beheld and smelt the towels;
Begummed, bemattered, and beslimed;
With dirt, and sweat, and ear-wax grimed.
No object Strephon's eye escapes,
Here petticoats in frowzy heaps,
Nor be the handkerchiefs forgot,
All varnished o'er with snuff and snot.
The stockings why should I expose,
Stained with the moisture of her toes;
Or greasy coifs and pinners[1] reeking,
Which Celia slept at least a week in?
A pair of tweezers next he found
To pluck her brows in arches round,
Or hairs that sink the forehead low,
Or on her chin like bristles grow.

The virtues we must not let pass
Of Celia's magnifying glass;
When frighted Strephon cast his eye on't,
It showed the visage of a giant:
A glass that can to sight disclose
The smallest worm in Celia's nose,
And faithfully direct her nail
To squeeze it out from head to tail;
For catch it nicely by the head,
It must come out alive or dead.

Why, Strephon, will you tell the rest?
And must you needs describe the chest?
That careless wench! No creature warn her
To move it out from yonder corner,
But leave it standing full in sight,
For you to exercise your spite!
In vain the workman showed his wit
With rings and hinges counterfeit
To make it seem in this disguise
A cabinet to vulgar eyes,
Which Strephon ventured to look in,
Resolved to go through thick and thin;
He lifts the lid; there need no more,
He smelt it all the time before.

As from within Pandora's box,
When Epimethus oped the locks,
A sudden universal crew
Of human evils upward flew,
He still was comforted to find
That hope at last remained behind.[2]

So Strephon, lifting up the lid
To view what in the chest was hid,
The vapours flew from out the vent,
But Strephon cautious never meant
The bottom of the pan to grope,
And foul his hands in search of hope.

O ne'er may such a vile machine
Be once in Celia's chamber seen!
O may she better learn to keep
"Those secrets of the hoary deep"![3]

As mutton cutlets, prime of meat,
Which though with art you salt and beat,
As laws of cookery require,
And roast them at the clearest fire,
If from adown the hopeful chops
The fat upon a cinder drops,
To stinking smoke it turns the flame,
Pois'ning the flesh from whence it came,
And up exhales a greasy stench,
For which you curse the careless wench;
So things which must not be expressed,
When *plumped* into the reeking chest,

[1] *coifs* Close fitting caps; *pinners* Coifs with long flaps hanging down on either side.

[2] *As from … behind* Pandora, the first woman, according to Greek mythology, was given a box or jar that contained all the evils of the world. It was in fact Pandora, not her husband Epimetheus, who opened the box or jar and released all the evils of the world. Only hope remained inside.

[3] *Those … deep* See Milton's *Paradise Lost,* 2.891.

Send up an excremental smell
To taint the parts from which they fell,
The petticoats and gown perfume,
And waft a stink round every room.

Thus finishing his grand survey,
The swain° disgusted slunk away, *lover*
Repeating in his amorous fits,
"Oh! Celia, Celia, Celia shits!"

But Vengeance, goddess never sleeping,
Soon punished Strephon for his peeping.
His foul imagination links
Each dame he sees with all her stinks,
And, if unsav'ry odours fly,
Conceives a lady standing by.
All women his description fits,
And both ideas jump like wits,[1]
By vicious fancy coupled fast,
And still appearing in contrast.

I pity wretched Strephon, blind
To all the charms of womankind.
Should I the queen of love refuse
Because she rose from stinking ooze?[2]
To him that looks behind the scene,
Statira's but some pocky quean.[3]

When Celia in her glory shows,
If Strephon would but stop his nose,
Who now so impiously blasphemes
Her ointments, daubs, and paints and creams,
Her washes, slops, and every clout ° *cloth, rag*
With which she makes so foul a rout,
He soon would learn to think like me,
And bless his ravished eyes to see
Such order from confusion sprung,
Such gaudy tulips raised from dung.

—1732

[1] *jump like wits* Agree, coincide. An allusion to the proverb "Good wits jump"—i.e., "Great minds think alike."

[2] *queen ... ooze* Venus, the goddess of love, arose from the sea.

[3] *Statira* One of the heroines of Nathaniel Lee's *Rival Queens* (1677); *pocky* Covered in pockmarks, as a result either of syphilis or of smallpox; *quean* Harlot.

Verses on the Death of Dr Swift, D.S.P.D.[4]

OCCASIONED BY READING A MAXIM IN ROCHEFOUCAULD[5]

Dans l'adversité de nos meilleurs amis nous trouvons quelque chose, qui ne nous deplaist pas.

In the adversity of our best friends, we find something that doth not displease us.

As Rochefoucauld his maxims drew
From nature, I believe 'em true:
They argue° no corrupted mind *indicate*
In him; the fault is in mankind.

This maxim more than all the rest
Is thought too base for human breast:
"In all distresses of our friends
We first consult our private ends,
While Nature, kindly bent to ease us,
Points out some circumstance to please us."

If this perhaps your patience move° *exasperates*
Let reason and experience prove.

We all behold with envious eyes
Our equal raised above our size;
Who would not at a crowded show
Stand high himself, keep others low?
I love my friend as well as you,
But would not have him stop my view.
Then let me have the higher post;
I ask but for an inch at most.

If in a battle you should find
One whom you love of all mankind
Had some heroic action done,
A champion killed, or trophy won,
Rather than thus be overtopped,
Would you not wish his laurels[6] cropped?

[4] *D.S.P.D.* Dean of St. Patrick's Cathedral, Dublin.

[5] *Maxim in Rochefoucauld* François de la Rochefoucauld, whose *Reflections or Moral Aphorisms and Maxims* (1665) is made up of famously cynical, humorous observations.

[6] *laurels* In ancient Greece, laurel wreaths were given to victorious athletes, pre-eminent poets, and war heroes.

Dear honest Ned is in the gout,
Lies racked with pain, and you without:
How patiently you hear him groan!
How glad the case is not your own!

What poet would not grieve to see
His brethren write as well as he?
But rather than they should excel,
He'd wish his rivals all in hell.

Her end when Emulation misses,
She turns to envy, stings, and hisses:
The strongest friendship yields to pride,
Unless the odds be on our side.

Vain humankind! Fantastic race!
Thy various follies, who can trace?
Self-love, ambition, envy, pride,
Their empire in our hearts divide:
Give others riches, power, and station,
'Tis all on me a usurpation.
I have no title to aspire;
Yet, when you sink, I seem the higher.
In Pope,[1] I cannot read a line,
But with a sigh, I wish it mine:
When he can in one couplet fix
More sense than I can do in six,
It gives me such a jealous fit,
I cry, "Pox take him, and his wit."

Why must I be outdone by Gay[2]
In my own hum'rous biting way?

Arbuthnot[3] is no more my friend,
Who dares to irony pretend,
Which I was born to introduce,
Refined it first, and showed its use.

St. John, as well as Pulteney,[4] knows
That I had some repute for prose;
And, till they drove me out of date,
Could maul a minister of state.
If they have mortified my pride,
And made me throw my pen aside;
If with such talents Heav'n hath blest 'em,
Have I not reason to detest 'em?[5]

To all my foes, dear Fortune, send
Thy gifts, but never to my friend:
I tamely can endure the first,
But this° with envy makes me burst. *the latter*

Thus much may serve by way of proem;° *preamble*
Proceed we therefore to our poem.

The time is not remote when I
Must by the course of nature die;
When, I foresee, my special friends
Will try to find their private ends;
Though it is hardly understood
Which way my death can do them good,
Yet thus, methinks, I hear 'em speak:
"See how the Dean begins to break!
Poor gentleman, he droops apace;° *swiftly*
You plainly find it in his face.
That old vertigo in his head[6]
Will never leave him till he's dead.
Besides, his memory decays:
He recollects not what he says;
He cannot call his friends to mind;
Forgets the place where last he dined;

[1] *Pope* Alexander Pope (1688–1744), essayist, critic, satirist, and poet.

[2] *Gay* Poet and dramatist John Gay (1685–1732).

[3] *Arbuthnot* John Arbuthnot (1667–1735), Queen Anne's physician, satirist, and essayist.

[4] *St. John … Pulteney* Henry St. John, Lord Bolingbroke (1678–1751), was a Tory politician who was involved in the opposition to Sir Robert Walpole's Whig government. Among the opposition's members were a few disenchanted Whigs, including William Pulteney. The two helped put out a political paper, the *Craftsman*, that was in the style of Swift's own political pamphlets.

[5] *In Pope … detest 'em* Pope, Gay, and Arbuthnot were dear friends of Swift's. Along with Thomas Parnell, Swift himself, and occasionally Robert Harley, Earl of Oxford, they formed the Scriblerus Club, meeting from 1713 to 1714 with the purpose of satirizing "false tastes in learning."

[6] *old vertigo … head* Swift suffered from what is now known as Ménière's disease, characterized by dizziness, vertigo, ringing and pressure in the ears, and hearing loss.

Plies you with stories o'er and o'er,
He told them fifty times before.
How does he fancy we can sit
To hear his out-of-fashioned wit?
But he takes up with younger folks,
Who for his wine will bear his jokes.
Faith, he must make his stories shorter,
Or change his comrades once a quarter:
In half the time, he talks them round;
There must another set be found.

"For poetry, he's past his prime;
He takes an hour to find a rhyme.
His fire is out, his wit decayed,
His fancy sunk, his muse a jade.[1]
I'd have him throw away his pen,
But there's no talking to some men."

And then their tenderness appears
By adding largely to my years:
"He's older than he would be reckoned,
And well remembers Charles the Second.[2]

"He hardly drinks a pint of wine,
And that, I doubt,° is no good sign. *think*
His stomach° too begins to fail; *appetite*
Last year we thought him strong and hale,° *healthy*
But now he's quite another thing;
I wish he may hold out till spring."

Then hug themselves and reason thus:
"It is not yet so bad with us."

In such a case they talk in tropes,° *figures of speech*
And by their fears express their hopes.
Some great misfortune to portend,° *foretell*
No enemy can match a friend.
With all the kindness they profess,
The merit of a lucky guess
(When daily "How-d'ye's"° come of course, *how do you's*
And servants answer, "Worse and worse")
Would please 'em better than to tell
That, God be praised, the Dean is well.
Then he who prophesied the best
Approves° his foresight to the rest: *demonstrates*
"You know, I always feared the worst,
And often told you so at first."
He'd rather choose that I should die
Than his prediction prove a lie.
No one foretells I shall recover,
But all agree to give me over.

Yet should some neighbour feel a pain
Just in the parts where I complain,
How many a message would he send?
What hearty prayers that I should mend?
Enquire what regimen I kept,
What gave me ease, and how I slept?
And more lament, when I was dead,
Than all the sniv'llers round my bed.

My good companions, never fear,
For though you may mistake a year,
Though your prognostics run too fast,
They must be verified at last.

Behold the fatal day arrive!
"How is the Dean?"—"He's just alive."
Now the departing prayer is read;
"He hardly breathes."—"The Dean is dead."
Before the passing-bell[3] begun,
The news through half the town has run.
"O may we all for death prepare!
What has he left? And who's his heir?"
"I know no more than what the news is:
'Tis all bequeathed to public uses."
"To public use! A perfect whim!
What had the public done for him?
Mere envy, avarice, and pride!
He gave it all—but first he died.
And had the Dean, in all the nation,
No worthy friend, no poor relation?
So ready to do strangers good,
Forgetting his own flesh and blood?"

[1] *jade* Worn out, ill-tempered cart horse, here presented in contrast to the winged horse Pegasus, who in Greek mythology was associated with the Muses and poetic inspiration.

[2] *well remembers … Second* Swift was 18 when Charles II died in 1685.

[3] *passing-bell* Bell tolled after a person's death.

Now Grub Street[1] wits are all employed;
With elegies the town is cloyed:
Some paragraph in every paper
To curse the Dean or bless the Drapier.[2]

The doctors, tender of their fame,
Wisely on me lay all the blame:
"We must confess his case was nice,° *difficult*
But he would never take advice.
Had he been ruled, for aught appears,
He might have lived these twenty years;
For when we opened him, we found
That all his vital parts were sound."

From Dublin soon to London spread;
'Tis told at court, "The Dean is dead."

Kind Lady Suffolk, in the spleen,[3]
Runs laughing up to tell the Queen.
The Queen, so gracious, mild, and good,
Cries, "Is he gone? 'Tis time he should.
He's dead, you say? Why, let him rot;
I'm glad the medals were forgot.[4]
I promised them, I own, but when?
I only was a princess then,
But now, as consort of the King,
You know 'tis quite a different thing."

Now Chartres, at Sir Robert's levee,[5]
Tells with a sneer the tidings heavy.
"Why, is he dead without his shoes?"[6]
Cries Bob. "I'm sorry for the news.
Oh, were the wretch but living still,
And in his place my good friend Will;[7]
Or had a miter° on his head, *bishop's headdress*
Provided Bolingbroke were dead!"

Now Curll[8] his shop from rubbish drains;
Three genuine tomes of Swift's remains.
And then, to make them pass the glibber,[9]
Revised by Tibbalds, Moore, and Cibber.[10]
He'll treat me as he does my betters:
Publish my will, my life, my letters;
Revive the libels born to die,
Which Pope must bear, as well as I.

Here shift the scene to represent
How those I love, my death lament.
Poor Pope will grieve a month, and Gay
A week, and Arbuthnot a day.

St. John himself will scarce forbear
To bite his pen and drop a tear.
The rest will give a shrug and cry,
"I'm sorry; but we all must die."
Indifference clad in wisdom's guise,
All fortitude of mind supplies;
For how can stony bowels melt
In those who never pity felt?
When *we* are lashed, *they* kiss the rod,[11]
Resigning to the will of God.

1 *Grub Street* Street in London in which lived many writers who sold their services on a freelance basis. Gradually this became a term synonymous with "hack writers."

2 *Drapier* Under the name of M.B., a drapier, Swift had written a series of public letters persuading the Irish people to resist the British government's plan to introduce a new copper coin, Wood's half-pence, which would further debase Irish currency. For this he became a national hero.

3 *Lady Suffolk* Mistress of George II and close friend of Swift; *in the spleen* Depressed; melancholy (here meant ironically).

4 *medals were forgot* When Queen Caroline was still Princess of Wales she had promised Swift some medals; he had yet to receive them.

5 *Chartres* Colonel Francis Chartres, a moneylender, informer, and runner for Sir Robert Walpole. Chartres was a notorious scoundrel who was referred to as the "Rape-Master General" after having been convicted, at the age of 70, of having raped his maid. He was sentenced to death but pardoned by Sir Robert; *levee* Morning assembly or reception of visitors.

6 *dead … shoes* I.e., he died in bed, as opposed to being hanged (when he would have "died in his shoes").

7 *Will* William Pulteney.

8 *Curll* Edmund Curll, a bookseller who published pirated, forged, and falsely ascribed works, often scavenging memoirs, letters, and other personal documents after a person's death. Arbuthnot wrote that Curll's biographies were "one of the new terrors of death."

9 *pass the glibber* Sell more easily.

10 *Tibbalds* Lewis Theobold, a dramatist and editor of Shakespeare whom Pope had cast as King of the Dunces in his *Dunciad* (1728); *Moore* James Moore Smythe, another author and enemy of Pope; *Cibber* Colley Cibber, who was appointed Poet Laureate in 1730, and in 1743 was crowned next King of the Dunces in the new edition of Pope's *Dunciad*.

11 *kiss the rod* Accept the punishment submissively.

The fools, my juniors by a year,
Are tortured with suspense and fear—
Who wisely thought my age a screen,
When death approached, to stand between.
The screen removed, their hearts are trembling;
They mourn for me without dissembling.

My female friends, whose tender hearts
Have better learnt to act their parts,
Receive the news in doleful dumps,
"The Dean is dead (*and what is trumps*?),
Then Lord have mercy on his soul.
(*Ladies, I'll venture for the vole.*[1])
Six deans they say must bear the pall.
(*I wish I knew which king to call.*)"
"Madam, your husband will attend
The funeral of so good a friend?"
"No, madam, 'tis a shocking sight;
And he's engaged tomorrow night!
My Lady Club would take it ill
If he should fail her at quadrille.
He loved the Dean (*I lead a heart*),
But dearest friends, they say, must part.
His time was come; he ran his race;[2]
We hope he's in a better place."

Why do we grieve that friends should die?
No loss more easy to supply.
One year is past; a different scene;
No further mention of the Dean,
Who now, alas, no more is missed
Than if he never did exist.
Where's now this fav'rite of Apollo?[3]
Departed, and his works must follow,
Must undergo the common fate;
His kind of wit is out of date.

Some country squire to Lintot[4] goes,
Inquires for Swift in verse and prose.
Says Lintot, "I have heard the name;
He died a year ago."—"The same."
He searches all his shop in vain.
"Sir, you may find them in Duck Lane;[5]
I sent them with a load of books
Last Monday to the pastry-cook's.[6]
To fancy they could live a year!
I find you're but a stranger here.
The Dean was famous in his time,
And had a kind of knack at rhyme.
His way of writing now is past;
The town hath got a better taste.
I keep no antiquated stuff,
But spick and span I have enough.
Pray, do but give me leave to show 'em;
Here's Colley Cibber's birthday poem.[7]
This ode you never yet have seen,
By Stephen Duck,[8] upon the Queen.
Then here's a letter finely penned
Against the *Craftsman* and his friend;
It clearly shows that all reflection
On ministers is disaffection.
Next, here's Sir Robert's vindication,[9]
And Mr. Henley's last oration.[10]

---

[1] *vole* In the card game quadrille, a vole occurs when one wins all the tricks.

[2] *His time … his race* See 2 Timothy 4.6–7: "For I am now ready to be offered, and the time of my departure is at hand. I have fought a great fight, I have finished my course, I have kept my faith."

[3] *Apollo* God of music and poetry.

[4] *Lintot* Benard Lintot (1675–1736), London bookseller who had published some of Pope and Gay's work, and with whom Pope had quarreled.

[5] *Duck Lane* Street at the center of the secondhand book business where used and remaindered books were often sent.

[6] *pastry-cook's* Waste paper was used for wrapping pies or lining baking sheets and tins.

[7] *Colley … poem* Cibber, as Poet Laureate, was expected to compose a birthday ode to the monarch each year.

[8] *Stephen Duck* Referred to as the "thresher poet," Duck was a farm laborer turned poet who had gained favor with Queen Caroline and was even considered a possible candidate for Poet Laureate. He was a popular target for both Pope and Swift's ridicule.

[9] [Swift's note] Walpole hires a set of party scribblers who do nothing else but write in his defense.

[10] *Henley's last oration* John Henley was an independent preacher known as "Orator Henley." He gave lectures on a variety of matters, both theological and mundane, for which he charged a shilling for admission. Henley also edited the *Hyp Doctor*, a paper established in opposition to the *Craftsman*.

The hawkers° have not got 'em yet; *street sellers*
Your honour please to buy a set?

"Here's Woolston's tracts,[1] the twelfth edition;
'Tis read by every politician:
The country members,[2] when in town,
To all their boroughs send them down.
You never met a thing so smart;
The courtiers have them all by heart;
Those maids of honour (who can read)
Are taught to use them for their creed.
The rev'rend author's good intention
Hath been rewarded with a pension.
He doth an honour to his gown
By bravely running priestcraft down;
He shows, as sure as God's in Gloucester,[3]
That Jesus was a grand impostor,
That all his miracles were cheats,
Performed as jugglers do their feats.
The church had never such a writer;
A shame he hath not got a miter!"

Suppose me dead, and then suppose
A club assembled at the Rose,[4]
Where, from discourse of this and that,
I grow the subject of their chat;
And, while they toss my name about,
With favour some, and some without,
One quite indiff'rent in the cause
My character impartial draws:

"The Dean, if we believe report,
Was never ill received at court.
As for his works in verse and prose,
I own myself no judge of those,
Nor can I tell what critics thought 'em;
But this I know, all people bought 'em,
As with a moral view designed
To cure the vices of mankind.
His vein, ironically grave,
Exposed the fool and lashed the knave;
To steal a hint was never known,
But what he writ was all his own.

"He never thought an honour done him
Because a duke was proud to own him;
Would rather slip aside and choose
To talk with wits in dirty shoes;
Despised the fools with stars and garters,[5]
So often seen caressing Chartres.
He never courted men in station,
Nor persons had in admiration;
Of no man's greatness was afraid,
Because he sought for no man's aid.
Though trusted long in great affairs,
He gave himself no haughty airs;
Without regarding private ends,
Spent all his credit for his friends;
And only chose the wise and good—
No flatt'rers, no allies in blood;[6]
But succoured virtue in distress,
And seldom failed of good success,
As numbers in their hearts must own,
Who, but for him, had been unknown.

"With princes kept a due decorum,
But never stood in awe before 'em;
And to her Majesty, God bless her,
Would speak as free as to her dresser.[7]
She thought it his peculiar whim,
Nor took it ill as come from him.
He followed David's lesson just,
'In princes never put thy trust.'[8]
And, would you make him truly sour,
Provoke him with a slave in pow'r:

[1] *Woolston's tracts* Rev. Thomas Woolston was a freethinker who was tried for blasphemy in 1729, and whose sensational *Discourses on the Miracles of Our Savior* became extremely popular. He never received a pension, though Swift here predicts he would.

[2] *members* I.e., of Parliament.

[3] *as sure ... Gloucester* Proverbial. Gloucester was filled with monasteries.

[4] *the Rose* Fashionable tavern located across from the Drury Lane Theatre and frequented by playgoers.

[5] *stars and garters* Insignia of the Order of the Garter, the oldest and highest award for loyalty and military merit. Walpole received the Order in 1726.

[6] *allies in blood* Relatives.

[7] *dresser* Person who attends the Queen in her bedchamber and helps to dress her; here, most likely a reference specifically to Swift's friend Lady Suffolk.

[8] *David's ... trust* Cf. Psalm 146.3.

The Irish senate, if you named,
With what impatience he declaimed!
Fair LIBERTY was all his cry;
For her he stood prepared to die;
For her he boldly stood alone;
For her he oft exposed his own.
Two kingdoms, just as factions led,
Had set a price upon his head,
But not a traitor could be found
To sell him for six hundred pound.[1]

"Had he but spared his tongue and pen,
He might have rose like other men;
But pow'r was never in his thought,
And wealth he valued not a groat.[2]
Ingratitude he often found,
And pitied those who meant the wound,
But kept the tenor of his mind
To merit well of humankind,
Nor made a sacrifice of those
Who still were true, to please his foes.
He laboured many a fruitless hour
To reconcile his friends in pow'r;
Saw mischief by a faction brewing,
While they pursued each other's ruin.
But, finding vain was all his care,
He left the court in mere° despair.[3] *utter*

"And, oh, how short are human schemes!
Here ended all our golden dreams.
What St. John's skill in state affairs,
What Ormonde's[4] valour, Oxford's cares,
To save their sinking country lent,
Was all destroyed by one event.[5]
Too soon that precious life was ended,
On which alone our weal° depended. *well-being*
When up a dangerous faction starts,
With wrath and vengeance in their hearts;[6]
By solemn league and cov'nant bound,[7]
To ruin, slaughter, and confound;
To turn religion to a fable,
And make the government a Babel;
Pervert the law, disgrace the gown,
Corrupt the senate, rob the crown,
To sacrifice old England's glory,
And make her infamous in story.° *history*
When such a tempest shook the land,
How could unguarded virtue stand?

"With horror, grief, despair the Dean
Beheld the dire destructive scene:
His friends in exile or the Tower,[8]
Himself within the frown of power,
Pursued by base, envenomed pens,
Far to the land of slaves and fens;[9]
A servile race in folly nursed,
Who truckle° most when treated worst. *submit*

"By innocence and resolution
He bore continual persecution,
While numbers to preferment rose,
Whose merits were, to be his foes.
When *ev'n his own familiar friends*,
Intent upon their private ends,
Like renegadoes now he feels,
Against him lifting up their heels.[10]

[1] *Two kingdoms ... pound* In 1713 the Queen offered £300 to the person who could discover the author of a pamphlet entitled *Public Spirit of the Whigs*. In 1724 the Irish government offered a similar reward for the identity of the author of *The Drapier's Fourth Letter*. In both cases Swift's identity as author was widely known, but nobody came forward to identify him.

[2] *not a groat* I.e., not a bit. A groat was a silver coin equal in value to four pence, and was often referred to metaphorically to signify any very small sum.

[3] *To reconcile ... despair* The quarrel between two of Swift's close friends, Lord Bolingbroke and Robert Harley, Earl of Oxford, had divided the Tory ministry. The quarrel escalated until Queen Anne died on 1 August 1714 and the Whigs were restored to power.

[4] *Ormonde* James Butler, Duke of Ormonde, who was Captain-General of the English armies from 1712 until 1714, when he went into exile.

[5] *one event* The death of the Queen, who had supported the Tories.

[6] *dangerous faction ... hearts* The Whig party. After regaining power they commenced impeaching, banishing, and harassing those who had opposed them. Many libels were written against Swift in England, and it was even rumored there was a reward offered for his arrest.

[7] *solemn ... bound* Reference to the Solemn League and Covenant, which, in 1643, established Presbyterianism and provided for the suppression of Roman Catholicism.

[8] *the Tower* Tower of London, where the Earl of Oxford was sent by the Whigs. Bolingbroke had been exiled.

[9] *land ... fens* Ireland.

[10] *ev'n his own ... their heels* See Psalm 41.9.

"The Dean did by his pen defeat
An infamous destructive cheat;[1]
Taught fools their interest to know,
And gave them arms to ward the blow.
Envy hath owned it was his doing
To save that helpless land from ruin,
While they who at the steerage stood,[2]
And reaped the profit, sought his blood.

"To save them from their evil fate,
In him was held a crime of state.
A wicked monster on the bench,[3]
Whose fury blood could never quench,
As vile and profligate a villain
As modern Scroggs, or old Tresilian,[4]
Who long all justice had discarded,
Nor feared he God, nor man regarded,[5]
Vowed on the Dean his rage to vent,
And make him of his zeal repent.
But Heav'n his innocence defends;
The grateful people stand his friends:
Not strains of law, nor judges' frown,
Nor topics° brought to please the crown, *obscure points of law*
Nor witness hired, nor jury picked,
Prevail to bring him in convict.

"In exile, with a steady heart,
He spent his life's declining part;
Where folly, pride, and faction sway,
Remote from St. John, Pope, and Gay.

"His friendship there, to few confined,
Were always of the middling kind:
No fools of rank, a mongrel breed,
Who fain would pass for lords indeed;
Where titles give no right or power,
And peerage is a withered flower,
He would have held it a disgrace
If such a wretch had known his face.
On rural squires, that kingdom's bane,
He vented oft his wrath in vain;
Biennial squires[6] to market brought,
Who sell their souls and votes for naught;
The nation stripped, go joyful back
To rob the church, their tenants rack,[7]
Go snacks[8] with thieves and rapparees,° *highwaymen*
And keep the peace[9] to pick up fees;
In every job to have a share,
A jail or barrack to repair,
And turn the tax for public roads
Commodious to their own abodes.

"Perhaps I may allow the Dean
Had too much satire in his vein,
And seemed determined not to starve it,
Because no age could more deserve it.
Yet malice never was his aim;
He lashed the vice but spared the name.
No individual could resent
Where thousands equally were meant.
His satire points at no defect
But what all mortals may correct;
For he abhorred that senseless tribe
Who call it humour when they jibe:
He spared a hump or crooked nose
Whose owners set not up for beaux.
True, genuine dullness moved his pity,
Unless it offered to be witty.
Those who their ignorance confessed,
He ne'er offended with a jest;
But laughed to hear an idiot quote
A verse from Horace, learned by rote.

[1] *infamous ... cheat* England's plan to introduce Wood's copper half-pence into Ireland.

[2] *they who ... stood* Those who managed Ireland's affairs (literally, those who were at the helm).

[3] *wicked ... bench* William Whitshed, Chief Justice of Ireland, who in 1720 presided over the trial of the printer of Swift's anonymous pamphlet *The Universal Use of Irish Manufacture* and, in 1724, over that of the printer of Swift's fourth *Drapier's Letter*. In both cases he tried unsuccessfully to force the jury to return a verdict of guilty.

[4] *Scroggs* Sir William Scroggs, Lord Chief Justice who was involved in the trials surrounding the Popish Plot and who, in 1680, was impeached for misconduct; *Tresilian* Sir Robert Tresilian, who was Chief Justice in 1381 and who tried John Ball and his followers after the Peasant's Revolt. He was impeached and hanged for treason.

[5] *Nor ... regarded* See Luke 18.2.

[6] *Biennial squires* Members of the Irish Parliament, who met only once every two years and had little real power.

[7] *rack* Force to pay exorbitantly high rent, nearly equal to the value of the land (referred to as "rack-rent").

[8] *Go snacks* Share.

[9] *keep the peace* Serve as magistrates.

"He knew an hundred pleasant stories,
With all the turns of Whigs and Tories;
Was cheerful to his dying day,
And friends would let him have his way.

"He gave the little wealth he had
To build a house for fools and mad,[1]
And showed, by one satiric touch,
No nation wanted it so much.
That kingdom he hath left his debtor,
I wish it soon may have a better."

—1739 (WRITTEN IN 1731)

Gulliver's Travels

A cruel satire; a biting political allegory; a parodic travel narrative; a fantastical adventure with elements of proto-science fiction—*Gulliver's Travels* is each of these. It has appealed to a remarkably wide range of audiences over several centuries; it is a prominent focus of scholarly commentary, a presence in popular culture, and (in bowdlerized form) even a common children's book. The *Travels* was among the most popular bestsellers of its time; as Samuel Johnson would later record in his "Life of Swift," upon its first publication the book was "received with such avidity, that the price of the first edition was raised before a second could be made." It has never been out of print since.

On the surface, *Gulliver's Travels* appears as a parodic adventure story. Parodies of this kind were fairly common in the eighteenth century—no doubt in part because travel narratives themselves were so popular. Such works enticed readers with exciting adventures, exotic settings realistically described—and, almost invariably, a seafaring protagonist who embodied British colonial values. While he worked on his *Travels*, Swift complained about reading extensively in the genre, which he described as an "abundance of trash."

However much Swift may have detested typical travel narratives, mocking them was not the only object of his wit in this work; the parody travel narrative provides a structure for a much wider-ranging satire, a primary focus of which is early eighteenth-century British politics. A central figure here was the powerful Whig Robert Walpole, who possessed varying degrees of power throughout the 1710s and had become established in a position of political dominance by 1721—the year Swift began work on the *Travels*. Governing primarily through the influence he wielded as a favorite of the king and operating through political intrigue rather than through official channels, Walpole epitomized what Tories such as Swift considered the despicable corruption of government. Many of Walpole's political enemies were Swift's friends. Among these were Tories Lord Bolingbroke and Lord Oxford, who had negotiated an initially popular peace treaty with the French; branding this treaty as pro-French and pro-Catholic, Walpole had Oxford and Bolingbroke impeached for treason. This event is a particular object of the satire in *Gulliver's Travels*, especially in Book 1, but Swift also attacks Walpole and the state of British politics more generally. Among his targets are the enmity displayed by the English towards France (and vice versa), England's exploitative attitude toward Ireland, and the endless bickering between the High and Low tendencies within the Church of England.

Another subject of satire in the *Travels* is one Swift had previously attacked in his *Battle of the Books*: the rejection of ancient in favor of modern knowledge. He was particularly suspicious of the previous fifty years' developments in natural philosophy, in which Aristotle's classical methods had been largely replaced by an emphasis on experimentation. The Royal Society of London for Improving Natural Knowledge, an organization of experimenters at the forefront of these changes,

[1] *To build ... mad* In his will, Swift left a considerable sum to the city for the construction of Ireland's first mental hospital. St. Patrick's opened in 1757 and is still functioning today.

is caricatured in *Gulliver's Travels*; many of the experiments conducted at the Academy of Lagado in Book 3 are strikingly similar to some that were performed by Royal Society members. Members of the Royal Society attempted blood transfusion on dogs, and made use of bellows in experiments on the breathing of several animals. Scientific developments also influenced the text in other ways; the imagery of differing scale that Swift employs in Books 1 and 2 is deeply indebted to the invention of the microscope and the telescope in the previous century.

While scholars generally agree on the overall targets of the satire in *Gulliver's Travels*, there is no consensus as to what precise claims Swift is making in the text. Part of this ambiguity stems from the impossibility of equating the author's opinions with those of the narrator—a fictional character whose sanity at the end of the final book may be questioned. It has also proved impossible to establish a tidy allegorical correspondence between the story and any of the political events that inspired it; *Gulliver's Travels*' commentary on human nature cannot be reduced to a clever description of historical circumstances. In an angry letter to a translator who had altered the *Travels*' political content for publication in France, Swift said of his own work:

> If the books of Mr. Gulliver are calculated only for the British Isles, that traveler should pass for a very pitiful writer. The same vices, and the same follies reign everywhere, at least, in all the civilized countries of Europe, and the author who writes only for one city, one province, one realm, or even one century, so little deserves to be translated, that he does not deserve to be read. The partisans of this Gulliver, who remain in very great numbers here, maintain that his book will last as long as our language, for it derives its merit not from certain modes or manners of thinking and speaking, but from a series of observations on the imperfections, the follies, and the vices of man.

A Note on the Text

The manuscript of *Travels into Several Remote Nations of the World, in Four Parts*—as *Gulliver's Travels* was originally titled—was delivered in secret to London printer Benjamin Motte on an autumn night in 1726. The manuscript, which was later destroyed, was probably not in the handwriting of its author, whose real name did not appear on it; he had attributed the book to his protagonist, Lemuel Gulliver, and negotiated with the publisher by mail, posing as Gulliver's fictional cousin. Swift often published anonymously or under pseudonyms—even though, as in this case, it usually became widely known that he was the true author of the work. But even a thin cloak of anonymity allowed him to dissociate himself from the work on aesthetic grounds if he ever wished to do so—and also provided a means of protecting himself from legal retribution in case his barbed political content provoked a response from its powerful victims.

Unfortunately, Swift's efforts to distance himself from his work have left a legacy of confusion over textual matters. Because he did not communicate with Motte directly on the project, Swift was unable to review and correct the proofs, as would have been the usual practice. He spread the word that the printer had produced a "mangled and murdered" edition, full not only of typographical errors but also of more significant alterations. Did Motte, perhaps himself in fear of the law, edit out the most politically offensive passages? It may be that the first edition really was not representative of Swift's manuscript, but it is more likely that Swift created—or at least greatly exaggerated—the rumors of textual corruption as part of the charade to dissociate himself from the text. In 1735 Swift participated in the revision and correction of the text for a new printing by Dublin publisher George Faulkner; because of Swift's own complaints about the original printing, this later version is often used as the basis for modern editions of *Gulliver's Travels*. The following text, however, is based on the 1726 version, which was the first to amuse and unsettle the readers of early eighteenth-century London.

Gulliver's Travels

Illustration of *Captain Lemuel Gulliver*, printed as a frontispiece to the 1726 edition.

Map showing *Lilliput* as southwest of Sumatra, printed in the 1726 edition with no accompanying caption at the beginning of Part 1.

Part 1 – A Voyage to Lilliput

Chapter 1

(*The author gives some account of himself and family; his first inducements to travel. He is shipwrecked and swims for his life; gets safe on shore in the country of Lilliput; is made a prisoner and carried up the country.*)

My father had a small estate in Nottinghamshire; I was the third of five sons. He sent me to Emmanuel College in Cambridge at fourteen years old, where I resided three years and applied myself close to my studies; but the charge of maintaining me, although I had a very scanty allowance, being too great for a narrow fortune, I was bound apprentice to Mr. James Bates, an eminent surgeon in London, with whom I continued four years. And my father now and then sending me small sums of money, I laid them out in learning navigation and other parts of the mathematics useful to those who intend to travel, as I always believed it would be, some time or other, my fortune to do. When I left Mr. Bates, I went down to my father, where, by the assistance of him and my uncle John, and some other relations, I got forty pounds, and a promise of thirty pounds a year to maintain me at Leyden.[1] There I studied physic two years and seven months, knowing it would be useful in long voyages.

Soon after my return from Leyden, I was recommended by my good master Mr. Bates to be surgeon to the *Swallow*, Captain Abraham Pannel commander, with whom I continued three years and a half, making a voyage or two into the Levant[2] and some other parts. When I came back I resolved to settle in London, to which Mr. Bates, my master, encouraged me, and by him I was recommended to several patients. I took part of a small house in the Old Jury;[3] and, being advised to alter my condition,[4] I married Mrs.[5] Mary Burton, second daughter to Mr. Edmund Burton, hosier,[6] in Newgate Street, with whom I received four hundred pounds for a portion.[7]

But my good master Bates dying in two years after, and I having few friends, my business began to fail; for my conscience would not suffer me to imitate the bad practice of too many among my brethren. Having therefore consulted with my wife and some of my acquaintance, I determined to go again to sea. I was surgeon successively in two ships, and made several voyages, for six years, to the East and West Indies, by which I got some addition to my fortune. My hours of leisure I spent in reading the best authors, ancient and modern, being always provided with a good number of books; and when I was ashore, in observing the manners and dispositions of the people, as well as learning their language, wherein I had a great facility by the strength of my memory.

The last of these voyages not proving very fortunate, I grew weary of the sea, and intended to stay at home with my wife and family. I removed from the Old Jury to Fetter Lane, and from thence to Wapping, hoping to get business among the sailors; but it would not turn to account.[8] After three years expectation that things would mend, I accepted an advantageous offer from Captain William Prichard, master of the *Antelope*, who was making a voyage to the South Sea. We set sail from Bristol, May 4, 1699, and our voyage at first was very prosperous.

It would not be proper, for some reasons, to trouble the reader with the particulars of our adventures in those seas; let it suffice to inform him that in our passage from thence to the East Indies, we were driven by a violent storm to the north-west of Van Diemen's Land.[9] By an observation, we found ourselves in the latitude of 30 degrees 2 minutes south. Twelve of our crew were dead by immoderate labour and ill food; the rest were in a very weak condition. On the fifth of November, which was the beginning of summer in those parts, the weather being very hazy, the seamen spied a rock within half a cable's length[10] of the ship, but the wind was so strong that we were driven directly upon it, and immediately split. Six of the crew, of whom I was one, having let down the boat into the sea, made a shift to get clear of the ship and the rock. We rowed, by my computation, about three leagues,[11] till we were able to work no longer, being already spent with labour while we were in the ship. We therefore trusted ourselves to the mercy of the waves, and in about half an hour the boat was overset by a sudden flurry from the north. What became of my companions in the boat, as well as of those who escaped on the rock, or were left in the vessel, I cannot tell; but conclude they were all lost. For my own part, I swam as fortune directed me, and was pushed forward by wind and tide. I often let my legs drop, and could feel no bottom; but when I was almost gone, and able to struggle no longer, I found myself within my depth; and by this time the storm was much abated. The declivity was so small that I walked near a mile before I got to the shore, which I conjectured was about eight o'clock in the evening. I then advanced forward near half a mile,

[1] *Leyden* University in Holland noted for the study of medicine ("physic").

[2] *the Levant* Countries and islands of the eastern Mediterranean.

[3] *Old Jury* I.e., the "Old Jewry," a street in London inhabited largely by Jewish people before their expulsion in the thirteenth century.

[4] *alter my condition* I.e., from the single to the married state or "condition."

[5] *Mrs.* Pronounced "mistress," this title was applied to both married and unmarried women.

[6] *hosier* One who makes or sells stockings, socks, or men's clothing generally.

[7] *portion* Dowry.

[8] *turn to account* Result in profit.

[9] *Van Diemen's Land* Tasmania.

[10] *cable's length* 600 feet.

[11] *three leagues* Nine nautical miles.

but could not discover any sign of houses or inhabitants; at least, I was in so weak a condition that I did not observe them. I was extremely tired, and with that, and the heat of the weather, and about half a pint of brandy that I drank as I left the ship, I found myself much inclined to sleep. I lay down on the grass, which was very short and soft, where I slept sounder than ever I remembered to have done in my life, and, as I reckoned, about nine hours; for when I awaked, it was just day-light. I attempted to rise, but was not able to stir: for, as I happened to lie on my back, I found my arms and legs were strongly fastened on each side to the ground; and my hair, which was long and thick, tied down in the same manner. I likewise felt several slender ligatures across my body, from my armpits to my thighs. I could only look upwards; the sun began to grow hot, and the light offended my eyes. I heard a confused noise about me, but in the posture I lay, could see nothing except the sky. In a little time I felt something alive moving on my left leg, which advancing gently forward over my breast, came almost up to my chin; when, bending my eyes downwards as much as I could, I perceived it to be a human creature not six inches high,[1] with a bow and arrow in his hands and a quiver at his back. In the mean time, I felt at least forty more of the same kind (as I conjectured) following the first. I was in the utmost astonishment, and roared so loud that they all ran back in a fright; and some of them, as I was afterwards told, were hurt with the falls they got by leaping from my sides upon the ground. However, they soon returned, and one of them, who ventured so far as to get a full sight of my face, lifting up his hands and eyes by way of admiration,[2] cried out in a shrill but distinct voice, *Hekinah Degul*. The others repeated the same words several times, but then I knew not what they meant. I lay all this while, as the reader may believe, in great uneasiness. At length, struggling to get loose, I had the fortune to break the strings, and wrench out the pegs that fastened my left arm to the ground; for, by lifting it up to my face, I discovered the methods they had taken to bind me, and at the same time with a violent pull, which gave me excessive pain, I a little loosened the strings that tied down my hair on the left side, so that I was just able to turn my head about two inches. But the creatures ran off a second time, before I could seize them; whereupon there was a great shout in a very shrill accent, and after it ceased I heard one of them cry aloud, *Tolgo phonac*; when in an instant I felt above a hundred arrows discharged on my left hand, which pricked me like so many needles; and besides they shot another flight into the air, as we do bombs in Europe, whereof many, I suppose, fell on my body (though I felt them not), and some on my face, which I immediately covered with my left hand. When this shower of arrows was over, I fell a groaning with grief and pain; and then striving again to get loose, they discharged another volley larger than the first, and some of them attempted with spears to stick me in the sides; but by good luck I had on a buff jerkin,[3] which they could not pierce. I thought it the most prudent method to lie still, and my design was to continue so till night, when, my left hand being already loose, I could easily free myself. And as for the inhabitants, I had reason to believe I might be a match for the greatest army they could bring against me, if they were all of the same size with him that I saw. But fortune disposed otherwise of me. When the people observed I was quiet, they discharged no more arrows; but by the noise increasing, I knew their numbers were greater; and about four yards from me, over against my right ear, I heard a knocking for above an hour, like that of people at work; when turning my head that way, as well as the pegs and strings would permit me, I saw a stage erected about a foot and a half from the ground, capable of holding four of the inhabitants, with two or three ladders to mount it: from whence one of them, who seemed to be a person of quality, made me a long speech, whereof I understood not one syllable. But I should have mentioned that before the principal person began his oration, he cried out three times, *Langro dehul san* (these words and the former were afterwards repeated and explained to me); whereupon, immediately, about fifty of the inhabitants came and cut the strings that fastened the left side of my head, which gave me the liberty of turning it to the right, and of observing the person and gesture of him that was to speak. He appeared to be of a middle age, and taller than any of the other three who attended him, whereof one was a page that held up his train, and

[1] *six inches high* Everything in Lilliput is about one twelfth of the size it would be in Gulliver's world.

[2] *by way of admiration* In wonder.

[3] *buff jerkin* Military jacket made of thick leather.

seemed to be somewhat longer than my middle finger; the other two stood one on each side to support him. He acted every part of an orator, and I could observe many periods[1] of threatenings, and others of promises, pity, and kindness. I answered in a few words, but in the most submissive manner, lifting up my left hand, and both my eyes to the sun, as calling him for a witness; and being almost famished with hunger, having not eaten a morsel for some hours before I left the ship, I found the demands of nature so strong upon me, that I could not forbear showing my impatience (perhaps against the strict rules of decency) by putting my finger frequently to my mouth, to signify that I wanted food. The *Hurgo* (for so they call a great lord, as I afterwards learnt) understood me very well. He descended from the stage and commanded that several ladders should be applied to my sides, on which above a hundred of the inhabitants mounted and walked towards my mouth, laden with baskets full of meat, which had been provided and sent thither by the king's orders, upon the first intelligence he received of me. I observed there was the flesh of several animals, but could not distinguish them by the taste. There were shoulders, legs, and loins, shaped like those of mutton, and very well dressed, but smaller than the wings of a lark. I ate them by two or three at a mouthful, and took three loaves at a time, about the bigness of musket bullets. They supplied me as fast as they could, showing a thousand marks of wonder and astonishment at my bulk and appetite. I then made another sign, that I wanted drink. They found by my eating that a small quantity would not suffice me; and, being a most ingenious people, they slung up, with great dexterity, one of their largest hogsheads,[2] then rolled it towards my hand and beat out the top; I drank it off at a draught, which I might well do, for it did not hold half a pint, and tasted like a small wine[3] of Burgundy, but much more delicious. They brought me a second hogshead, which I drank in the same manner, and made signs for more; but they had none to give me. When I had performed these wonders, they shouted for joy, and danced upon my breast, repeating several times as they did at first, *Hekinah degul.* They made me a sign that I should throw down the two hogsheads, but first warning the people below to stand out of the way, crying aloud, *Borach mevolah*; and when they saw the vessels in the air, there was a universal shout of *Hekinah degul.* I confess I was often tempted, while they were passing backwards and forwards on my body, to seize forty or fifty of the first that came in my reach, and dash them against the ground. But the remembrance of what I had felt, which probably might not be the worst they could do, and the promise of honour I made them—for so I interpreted my submissive behaviour—soon drove out these imaginations. Besides, I now considered myself as bound, by the laws of hospitality, to a people who had treated me with so much expense and magnificence. However, in my thoughts I could not sufficiently wonder at the intrepidity of these diminutive mortals, who durst venture to mount and walk upon my body, while one of my hands was at liberty, without trembling at the very sight of so prodigious a creature as I must appear to them. After some time, when they observed that I made no more demands for meat, there appeared before me a person of high rank from his Imperial Majesty. His Excellency, having mounted on the small of my right leg, advanced forwards up to my face with about a dozen of his retinue; and producing his credentials under the Signet Royal, which he applied close to my eyes, spoke about ten minutes without any signs of anger, but with a kind of determinate resolution, often pointing forwards, which, as I afterwards found, was towards the capital city, about half a mile distant; whither it was agreed by his Majesty in council that I must be conveyed. I answered in few words, but to no purpose, and made a sign with my hand that was loose, putting it to the other (but over his excellency's head for fear of hurting him or his train) and then to my own head and body, to signify that I desired my liberty. It appeared that he understood me well enough, for he shook his head by way of disapprobation, and held his hand in a posture to show that I must be carried as a prisoner. However, he made other signs to let me understand that I should have meat and drink enough, and very good treatment. Whereupon I once more thought of attempting to break my bonds; but again, when I felt the smart of their arrows upon my face and hands, which were all in blisters, and many of the darts

[1] *periods* Sentences.

[2] *hogsheads* Large casks.

[3] *small wine* Wine of low alcoholic content; diluted wine.

still sticking in them, and observing likewise that the number of my enemies increased, I gave tokens to let them know that they might do with me what they pleased. Upon this, the *Hurgo* and his train withdrew with much civility and cheerful countenances. Soon after I heard a general shout, with frequent repetitions of the words, *Peplom selan*, and I felt great numbers of people on my left side relaxing the cords to such a degree that I was able to turn upon my right, and to ease myself with making water;[1] which I very plentifully did, to the great astonishment of the people, who, conjecturing by my motion what I was going to do, immediately opened to the right and left on that side, to avoid the torrent which fell with such noise and violence from me. But before this, they had daubed my face and both my hands with a sort of ointment, very pleasant to the smell, which, in a few minutes, removed all the smart of their arrows. These circumstances, added to the refreshment I had received by their victuals and drink, which were very nourishing, disposed me to sleep. I slept about eight hours, as I was afterwards assured; and it was no wonder, for the physicians, by the Emperor's order, had mingled a sleepy potion in the hogsheads of wine.

It seems that upon the first moment I was discovered sleeping on the ground after my landing, the Emperor had early notice of it by an express;[2] and determined in council, that I should be tied in the manner I have related (which was done in the night while I slept), that plenty of meat and drink should be sent to me, and a machine prepared to carry me to the capital city.

This resolution perhaps may appear very bold and dangerous, and I am confident would not be imitated by any prince in Europe on the like occasion. However, in my opinion, it was extremely prudent as well as generous: for, supposing these people had endeavoured to kill me with their spears and arrows while I was asleep, I should certainly have awaked with the first sense of smart, which might so far have roused my rage and strength as to have enabled me to break the strings wherewith I was tied; after which, as they were not able to make resistance, so they could expect no mercy.

These people are most excellent mathematicians, and arrived to a great perfection in mechanics by the countenance and encouragement of the Emperor, who is a renowned patron of learning. This prince has several machines fixed on wheels, for the carriage of trees and other great weights. He often builds his largest men of war, whereof some are nine feet long, in the woods where the timber grows, and has them carried on these engines[3] three or four hundred yards to the sea. Five hundred carpenters and engineers were immediately set at work to prepare the greatest engine they had. It was a frame of wood raised three inches from the ground, about seven feet long and four wide, moving upon twenty-two wheels. The shout I heard was upon the arrival of this engine, which, it seems, set out in four hours after my landing. It was brought parallel to me as I lay, but the principal difficulty was to raise and place me in this vehicle. Eighty poles, each of one foot high, were erected for this purpose, and very strong cords, of the bigness of packthread,[4] were fastened by hooks to many bandages which the workmen had girt round my neck, my hands, my body, and my legs. Nine hundred of the strongest men were employed to draw up these cords, by many pulleys fastened on the poles; and thus, in less than three hours, I was raised and slung into the engine, and there tied fast. All this I was told; for, while the operation was performing, I lay in a profound sleep, by the force of that soporiferous medicine infused into my liquor. Fifteen hundred of the Emperor's largest horses, each about four inches and a half high, were employed to draw me towards the metropolis, which, as I said, was half a mile distant.

About four hours after we began our journey, I awaked by a very ridiculous accident; for the carriage being stopped a while, to adjust something that was out of order, two or three of the young natives had the curiosity to see how I looked when I was asleep; they climbed up into the engine, and advancing very softly to my face, one of them, an officer in the guards, put the sharp end of his half-pike a good way up into my left nostril, which tickled my nose like a straw and made me sneeze violently; whereupon they stole off unperceived, and it was three weeks before I knew the cause of my waking so suddenly. We made a long march the remaining part of the day, and rested at night with five hundred guards on each side of me, half with torches, and

[1] *making water* Urinating.

[2] *express* Messenger.

[3] *engines* Mechanical devices.

[4] *packthread* Strong twine.

half with bows and arrows, ready to shoot me if I should offer to stir. The next morning at sunrise we continued our march, and arrived within two hundred yards of the city gates about noon. The Emperor and all his court came out to meet us, but his great officers would by no means suffer His Majesty to endanger his person by mounting on my body.

At the place where the carriage stopped there stood an ancient temple, esteemed to be the largest in the whole kingdom, which, having been polluted some years before by an unnatural murder, was, according to the zeal of those people, looked upon as profane, and therefore had been applied to common use, and all the ornaments and furniture carried away. In this edifice it was determined I should lodge. The great gate fronting to the north was about four feet high and almost two feet wide, through which I could easily creep. On each side of the gate was a small window not above six inches from the ground: into that on the left side, the King's smith conveyed fourscore and eleven chains, like those that hang to a lady's watch in Europe, and almost as large, which were locked to my left leg with six-and-thirty padlocks. Over against this temple, on the other side of the great highway, at twenty feet distance, there was a turret at least five feet high. Here the Emperor ascended, with many principal lords of his court, to have an opportunity of viewing me, as I was told, for I could not see them. It was reckoned that above a hundred thousand inhabitants came out of the town upon the same errand; and, in spite of my guards, I believe there could not be fewer than ten thousand, at several times, who mounted my body by the help of ladders. But a proclamation was soon issued to forbid it upon pain of death. When the workmen found it was impossible for me to break loose, they cut all the strings that bound me; whereupon I rose up, with as melancholy a disposition as ever I had in my life. But the noise and astonishment of the people at seeing me rise and walk are not to be expressed. The chains that held my left leg were about two yards long, and gave me not only the liberty of walking backwards and forwards in a semicircle, but, being fixed within four inches of the gate, allowed me to creep in, and lie at my full length in the temple.

CHAPTER 2

(*The Emperor of Lilliput, attended by several of the nobility, comes to see the author in his confinement. The Emperor's person and habit described. Learned men appointed to teach the author their language. He gains favour by his mild disposition. His pockets are searched, and his sword and pistols taken from him.*)

When I found myself on my feet, I looked about me, and must confess I never beheld a more entertaining prospect. The country around appeared like a continued garden, and the enclosed fields, which were generally forty feet square, resembled so many beds of flowers. These fields were intermingled with woods of half a stang,[1] and the tallest trees, as I could judge, appeared to be seven feet high. I viewed the town on my left hand, which looked like the painted scene of a city in a theatre.

I had been for some hours extremely pressed by the necessities of nature; which was no wonder, it being almost two days since I had last disburdened myself. I was under great difficulties between urgency and shame. The best expedient I could think on, was to creep into my house, which I accordingly did; and shutting the gate after me, I went as far as the length of my chain would suffer, and discharged my body of that uneasy load. But this was the only time I was ever guilty of so uncleanly an action; for which I cannot but hope the candid reader will give some allowance, after he has maturely and impartially considered my case, and the distress I was in. From this time my constant practice was, as soon as I rose, to perform that business in open air, at the full extent of my chain; and due care was taken every morning, before company came, that the offensive matter should be carried off in wheel-barrows by two servants appointed for that purpose. I would not have dwelt so long upon a circumstance that perhaps, at first sight, may appear not very momentous, if I had not thought it necessary to justify my character in point of cleanliness to the world; which, I am told, some of my maligners have been pleased, upon this and other occasions, to call in question.

When this adventure was at an end, I came back out of my house, having occasion for fresh air. The Emperor

[1] *stang* Quarter of an acre.

was already descended from the tower and advancing on horseback towards me, which had like to have cost him dear; for the beast, though very well trained, yet wholly unused to such a sight, which appeared as if a mountain moved before him, reared up on its hinder feet: but that prince, who is an excellent horseman, kept his seat till his attendants ran in and held the bridle, while His Majesty had time to dismount. When he alighted, he surveyed me round with great admiration, but kept beyond the length of my chain. He ordered his cooks and butlers, who were already prepared, to give me victuals and drink, which they pushed forward in a sort of vehicles upon wheels till I could reach them. I took these vehicles and soon emptied them all; twenty of them were filled with meat, and ten with liquor; each of the former afforded me two or three good mouthfuls, and I emptied the liquor of ten vessels, which was contained in earthen vials, into one vehicle, drinking it off at a draught; and so I did with the rest. The Empress, and young princes of the blood, of both sexes, attended by many ladies, sat at some distance in their chairs; but upon the accident that happened to the Emperor's horse, they alighted and came near his person, which I am now going to describe. He is taller by almost the breadth of my nail than any of his court, which alone is enough to strike an awe into the beholders. His features are strong and masculine, with an Austrian lip[1] and arched nose, his complexion olive, his countenance[2] erect, his body and limbs well proportioned, all his motions graceful, and his deportment majestic. He was then past his prime, being twenty-eight years and three quarters old, of which he had reigned about seven in great felicity, and generally victorious. For the better convenience of beholding him, I lay on my side, so that my face was parallel to his, and he stood but three yards off: however, I have had him since many times in my hand, and therefore cannot be deceived in the description. His dress was very plain and simple, and the fashion of it between the Asiatic and the European, but he had on his head a light helmet of gold, adorned with jewels, and a plume on the crest. He held his sword drawn in his hand to defend himself if I should happen to break loose; it was almost three inches long; the hilt and scabbard were gold enriched with diamonds. His voice was shrill, but very clear and articulate, and I could distinctly hear it when I stood up. The ladies and courtiers were all most magnificently clad, so that the spot they stood upon seemed to resemble a petticoat spread upon the ground, embroidered with figures of gold and silver. His Imperial Majesty spoke often to me, and I returned answers: but neither of us could understand a syllable. There were several of his priests and lawyers present (as I conjectured by their habits) who were commanded to address themselves to me; and I spoke to them in as many languages as I had the least smattering of, which were High and Low Dutch,[3] Latin, French, Spanish, Italian, and Lingua Franca,[4] but all to no purpose. After about two hours the court retired, and I was left with a strong guard to prevent the impertinence, and probably the malice, of the rabble, who were very impatient to crowd about me as near as they durst; and some of them had the impudence to shoot their arrows at me as I sat on the ground by the door of my house, whereof one very narrowly missed my left eye. But the colonel ordered six of the ringleaders to be seized, and thought no punishment so proper as to deliver them bound into my hands, which some of his soldiers accordingly did, pushing them forward with the butt-ends of their pikes into my reach. I took them all in my right hand, put five of them into my coat-pocket; and as to the sixth, I made a countenance as if I would eat him alive. The poor man squalled terribly, and the colonel and his officers were in much pain, especially when they saw me take out my penknife: but I soon put them out of fear; for, looking mildly, and immediately cutting the strings he was bound with, I set him gently on the ground, and away he ran. I treated the rest in the same manner, taking them one by one out of my pocket, and I observed both the soldiers and people were highly delighted at this mark of my clemency, which was represented very much to my advantage at court.

[1] *Austrian lip* Thick lower lip. This and the arched nose were features that were characteristic of Austria's Hapsburg family. The entire description of the Emperor may be a satiric representation of King George, who was stocky and ungainly.

[2] *countenance* Bearing.

[3] *High and Low Dutch* German and Dutch.

[4] *Lingua Franca* Mixed jargon, based primarily on Italian but containing elements of many Romance languages, used primarily by traders in the eastern Mediterranean.

Towards night I got with some difficulty into my house, where I lay on the ground, and continued to do so about a fortnight; during which time the Emperor gave orders to have a bed prepared for me. Six hundred beds of the common measure were brought in carriages and worked up in my house; a hundred and fifty of their beds, sewn together, made up the breadth and length, and these were four double, which, however, kept me but very indifferently from the hardness of the floor, that was of smooth stone. By the same computation they provided me with sheets, blankets, and coverlets, tolerable enough for one who had been so long inured to hardships as I.

As the news of my arrival spread through the kingdom, it brought prodigious numbers of rich, idle, and curious people to see me; so that the villages were almost emptied, and great neglect of tillage and household affairs must have ensued, if His Imperial Majesty had not provided, by several proclamations and orders of state, against this inconveniency. He directed that those who had already beheld me should return home, and not presume to come within fifty yards of my house without license from the court; whereby the secretaries of state got considerable fees.

In the meantime the Emperor held frequent councils to debate what course should be taken with me; and I was afterwards assured by a particular friend, a person of great quality, who was as much in the secret as any, that the court was under many difficulties concerning me. They apprehended[1] my breaking loose; that my diet would be very expensive, and might cause a famine. Sometimes they determined to starve me, or at least to shoot me in the face and hands with poisoned arrows, which would soon dispatch me; but again they considered that the stench of so large a carcass might produce a plague in the metropolis, and probably spread through the whole kingdom. In the midst of these consultations, several officers of the army went to the door of the great council-chamber, and two of them, being admitted, gave an account of my behaviour to the six criminals above-mentioned; which made so favourable an impression in the breast of His Majesty and the whole board in my behalf that an imperial commission was issued out, obliging all the villages nine hundred yards round the city to deliver in every morning six beeves,[2] forty sheep, and other victuals for my sustenance, together with a proportionable quantity of bread, and wine, and other liquors; for the due payment of which His Majesty gave assignments[3] upon his treasury; for this prince lives chiefly upon his own demesnes; seldom, except upon great occasions, raising any subsidies upon his subjects, who are bound to attend him in his wars at their own expense. An establishment was also made of six hundred persons to be my domestics, who had board-wages allowed for their maintenance, and tents built for them very conveniently on each side of my door. It was likewise ordered that three hundred tailors should make me a suit of clothes, after the fashion of the country; that six of His Majesty's greatest scholars should be employed to instruct me in their language; and lastly, that the Emperor's horses, and those of the nobility and troops of guards, should be frequently exercised in my sight, to accustom themselves to me. All these orders were duly put in execution, and in about three weeks I made a great progress in learning their language, during which time the Emperor frequently honoured me with his visits, and was pleased to assist my masters in teaching me. We began already to converse together in some sort; and the first words I learnt were to express my desire that he would please give me my liberty; which I every day repeated on my knees. His answer, as I could comprehend it, was that this must be a work of time, not to be thought on without the advice of his council, and that first I must *lumos kelmin pesso desmar lon emposo*; that is, swear a peace with him and his kingdom; however, that I should be used with all kindness. And he advised me to acquire, by my patience and discreet behaviour, the good opinion of himself and his subjects. He desired I would not take it ill if he gave orders to certain proper officers to search me; for probably I might carry about me several weapons, which must needs be dangerous things, if they answered the bulk of so prodigious a person. I said His Majesty should be satisfied, for I was ready to strip myself, and turn up my pockets before him. This I delivered part in words and part in signs. He replied that by the laws of the kingdom I must be searched by two of his officers; that he knew this could not be done without my con-

[1] *apprehended* Feared; were apprehensive of.

[2] *beeves* Oxen.

[3] *assignments* Legal documents transferring funds or property.

sent and assistance; and he had so good an opinion of my generosity and justice as to trust their persons in my hands; that whatever they took from me should be returned when I left the country, or paid for at the rate which I would set upon them. I took up the two officers in my hands, put them first into my coat-pockets, and then into every other pocket about me, except my two fobs, and another secret pocket which I had no mind should be searched, wherein I had some little necessaries that were of no consequence to any but myself. In one of my fobs[1] there was a silver watch, and in the other a small quantity of gold in a purse. These gentlemen, having pen, ink, and paper about them, made an exact inventory of everything they saw; and when they had done, desired I would set them down, that they might deliver it to the Emperor. This inventory I afterwards translated into English, and is, word for word, as follows.

Imprimis,[2] in the right coat-pocket of the great Man-Mountain (for so I interpret the words *Quinbus Flestrin*), after the strictest search, we found only one great piece of coarse cloth, large enough to be a foot-cloth for Your Majesty's chief room of state. In the left pocket we saw a huge silver chest, with a cover of the same metal, which we, the searchers, were not able to lift. We desired it should be opened, and one of us, stepping into it, found himself up to the mid leg in a sort of dust, some part whereof flying up to our faces, set us both a sneezing for several times together. In his right waistcoat-pocket we found a prodigious bundle of white thin substances, folded one over another, about the bigness of three men, tied with a strong cable and marked with black figures; which we humbly conceive to be writings, every letter almost half as large as the palm of our hands. In the left there was a sort of engine, from the back of which were extended twenty long poles, resembling the palisades before Your Majesty's court; wherewith we conjecture the Man-Mountain combs his head; for we did not always trouble him with questions because we found it a great difficulty to make him understand us. In the large pocket on the right side of his middle cover (so I translate the word *ranfulo*, by which they meant my breeches) we saw a hollow pillar of iron, about the length of a man, fastened to a strong piece of timber larger than the pillar; and upon one side of the pillar were huge pieces of iron sticking out, cut into strange figures, which we know not what to make of. In the left pocket, another engine of the same kind. In the smaller pocket on the right side were several round flat pieces of white and red metal, of different bulk; some of the white, which seemed to be silver, were so large and heavy that my comrade and I could hardly lift them. In the left pocket were two black pillars irregularly shaped: we could not, without difficulty, reach the top of them as we stood at the bottom of his pocket. One of them was covered, and seemed all of a piece, but at the upper end of the other there appeared a white round substance, about twice the bigness of our heads. Within each of these was enclosed a prodigious plate of steel; which, by our orders, we obliged him to show us, because we apprehended they might be dangerous engines. He took them out of their cases and told us that in his own country his practice was to shave his beard with one of these, and cut his meat with the other. There were two pockets which we could not enter: these he called his fobs; they were two large slits cut into the top of his middle cover, but squeezed close by the pressure of his belly. Out of the right fob hung a great silver chain with a wonderful kind of engine at the bottom. We directed him to draw out whatever was at the end of that chain, which appeared to be a globe, half silver, and half of some transparent metal; for, on the transparent side, we saw certain strange figures circularly drawn, and thought we could touch them, till we found our fingers stopped by the lucid substance. He put this engine into our ears, which made an incessant noise like that of a water-mill, and we conjecture it is either some unknown animal, or the god that he worships; but we are more inclined to the latter opinion because he assured us (if we understood him right, for he expressed himself very imperfectly) that he seldom did any thing without consulting it. He called it his oracle and said it pointed out the time for every action of his life. From the left fob he took out a net almost large enough for a fisherman, but contrived to open and shut like a purse, and served him for the same use: we found therein several massy pieces of yellow metal, which, if they be real gold, must be of immense value.

[1] *fobs* Small pockets in the waistband of pants, used for carrying valuables.

[2] *Imprimis* Latin: In the first place.

Having thus, in obedience to Your Majesty's commands, diligently searched all his pockets, we observed a girdle about his waist made of the hide of some prodigious animal, from which, on the left side, hung a sword of the length of five men; and on the right, a bag or pouch divided into two cells, each cell capable of holding three of Your Majesty's subjects. In one of these cells were several globes, or balls, of a most ponderous metal, about the bigness of our heads, and requiring a strong hand to lift them. The other cell contained a heap of certain black grains, but of no great bulk or weight, for we could hold above fifty of them in the palms of our hands.

This is an exact inventory of what we found about the body of the Man-Mountain, who used us with great civility and due respect to Your Majesty's commission. Signed and sealed on the fourth day of the eighty-ninth moon of your Majesty's auspicious reign.

CLEFREN FRELOCK, MARSI FRELOCK

When this inventory was read over to the Emperor, he directed me, although in very gentle terms, to deliver up the several particulars. He first called for my scimitar, which I took out, scabbard and all. In the meantime he ordered three thousand of his choicest troops (who then attended him) to surround me at a distance, with their bows and arrows just ready to discharge; but I did not observe it, for mine eyes were wholly fixed upon His Majesty. He then desired me to draw my scimitar, which, although it had got some rust by the sea water, was, in most parts, exceeding bright. I did so, and immediately all the troops gave a shout between terror and surprise; for the sun shone clear, and the reflection dazzled their eyes as I waved the scimitar to and fro in my hand. His Majesty, who is a most magnanimous prince, was less daunted than I could expect; he ordered me to return it into the scabbard and cast it on the ground as gently as I could, about six feet from the end of my chain. The next thing he demanded was one of the hollow iron pillars, by which he meant my pocket pistols. I drew it out and, at his desire, as well as I could, expressed to him the use of it; and charging it only with powder, which, by the closeness of my pouch, happened to escape wetting in the sea (an inconvenience against which all prudent mariners take special care to provide), I first cautioned the Emperor not to be afraid, and then I let it off in the air. The astonishment here was much greater than at the sight of my scimitar. Hundreds fell down as if they had been struck dead, and even the Emperor, although he stood his ground, could not recover himself for some time. I delivered up both my pistols in the same manner as I had done my scimitar, and then my pouch of powder and bullets, begging him that the former might be kept from fire, for it would kindle with the smallest spark and blow up his imperial palace into the air. I likewise delivered up my watch, which the Emperor was very curious to see, and commanded two of his tallest yeomen of the guards to bear it on a pole upon their shoulders, as draymen[1] in England do a barrel of ale. He was amazed at the continual noise it made and the motion of the minute-hand, which he could easily discern; for their sight is much more acute than ours. He asked the opinions of his learned men about it, which were various and remote, as the reader may well imagine without my repeating; although indeed I could not very perfectly understand them. I then gave up my silver and copper money, my purse with nine large pieces of gold, and some smaller ones; my knife and razor, my comb and silver snuff-box, my handkerchief and journal-book. My scimitar, pistols, and pouch were conveyed in carriages to His Majesty's stores, but the rest of my goods were returned me.

I had, as I before observed, one private pocket which escaped their search, wherein there was a pair of spectacles (which I sometimes use for the weakness of mine eyes), a pocket perspective,[2] and some other little conveniences; which, being of no consequence to the Emperor, I did not think myself bound in honour to discover, and I apprehended they might be lost or spoiled if I ventured them out of my possession.

[1] *draymen* At breweries, the workers who transport loads of beer, usually on low carts (or "drays").

[2] *perspective* Telescope.

CHAPTER 3

(*The author diverts the Emperor, and his nobility of both sexes, in a very uncommon manner. The diversions of the court of Lilliput described. The author has his liberty granted him upon certain conditions.*)

My gentleness and good behaviour had gained so far on the Emperor and his court, and indeed upon the army and people in general, that I began to conceive hopes of getting my liberty in a short time. I took all possible methods to cultivate this favourable disposition. The natives came, by degrees, to be less apprehensive of any danger from me. I would sometimes lie down and let five or six of them dance on my hand, and at last the boys and girls would venture to come and play at hide-and-seek in my hair. I had now made a good progress in understanding and speaking the language. The Emperor had a mind one day to entertain me with several of the country shows, wherein they exceed all nations I have known, both for dexterity and magnificence. I was diverted with none so much as that of the rope-dancers, performed upon a slender white thread extended about two feet and twelve inches from the ground. Upon which I shall desire liberty, with the reader's patience, to enlarge a little.

This diversion is only practised by those persons who are candidates for great employments, and high favour, at court. They are trained in this art from their youth, and are not always of noble birth or liberal education. When a great office is vacant, either by death or disgrace (which often happens), five or six of those candidates petition the Emperor to entertain His Majesty and the court with a dance on the rope; and whoever jumps the highest, without falling, succeeds in the office. Very often the chief ministers themselves are commanded to show their skill, and to convince the Emperor that they have not lost their faculty. Flimnap,[1] the Treasurer, is allowed to cut a caper on the straight rope, at least an inch higher than any other lord in the whole empire. I have seen him do the summerset[2] several times together, upon a trencher[3] fixed on a rope which is no thicker than a common packthread in England. My friend Reldresal, Principal Secretary for Private Affairs, is, in my opinion (if I am not partial) the second after the Treasurer. The rest of the great officers are much upon a par.

These diversions are often attended with fatal accidents, whereof great numbers are on record. I myself have seen two or three candidates break a limb. But the danger is much greater when the ministers themselves are commanded to show their dexterity; for, by contending to excel themselves and their fellows, they strain so far that there is hardly one of them who has not received a fall, and some of them two or three. I was assured that, a year or two before my arrival, Flimnap would infallibly have broke his neck if one of the King's cushions, that accidentally lay on the ground, had not weakened the force of his fall.[4]

There is likewise another diversion, which is only shown before the Emperor and Empress, and first minister, upon particular occasions. The Emperor lays on the table three fine silken threads[5] of six inches long. One is blue, the other red, and the third green. These threads are proposed as prizes for those persons whom the Emperor has a mind to distinguish by a peculiar mark of his favour. The ceremony is performed in His Majesty's great chamber of state, where the candidates are to undergo a trial of dexterity very different from the former, and such as I have not observed the least resemblance of in any other country of the new or old world. The Emperor holds a stick in his hands, both ends parallel to the horizon, while the candidates advancing, one by one, sometimes leap over the stick, sometimes creep under it backward and forward several times, according as the stick is advanced or depressed. Sometimes the Emperor holds one end of the stick, and his first minister the other; sometimes the minister has it entirely to himself. Whoever performs his part with most agility, and holds out the longest in leaping and creeping, is rewarded with the blue-col-

[1] *Flimnap* Thought to represent Whig Prime Minister Robert Walpole, who was notorious for his dexterous political acrobatics.

[2] *summerset* Somersault.

[3] *trencher* Flat board or platter.

[4] *Flimnap … fall* Walpole fell from power in 1717, but by cultivating the friendship of the Duchess of Kendal, one of the King's mistresses, he was restored to the King's favor.

[5] *three fine silken threads* These blue, red, and green ribbons are the colors, respectively, of the Order of the Garter, the Order of the Bath, and the Order of the Thistle. These highly coveted awards were conferred by the king for loyal service; Walpole was made a knight of the Garter in 1726.

oured silk; the red is given to the next, and the green to the third, which they all wear girt twice round about the middle; and you see few great persons about this court who are not adorned with one of these girdles.

The horses of the army and those of the royal stables, having been daily led before me, were no longer shy, but would come up to my very feet without starting. The riders would leap them over my hand as I held it on the ground, and one of the Emperor's huntsmen, upon a large courser, took my foot, shoe and all; which was indeed a prodigious leap. I had the good fortune to divert the Emperor one day after a very extraordinary manner. I desired he would order several sticks of two feet high, and the thickness of an ordinary cane, to be brought me; whereupon His Majesty commanded the master of his woods to give directions accordingly, and the next morning six woodmen arrived with as many carriages, drawn by eight horses to each. I took nine of these sticks and, fixing them firmly in the ground in a quadrangular figure, two feet and a half square, I took four other sticks and tied them parallel at each corner, about two feet from the ground. Then I fastened my handkerchief to the nine sticks that stood erect and extended it on all sides, till it was tight as the top of a drum, and the four parallel sticks, rising about five inches higher than the handkerchief, served as ledges on each side. When I had finished my work, I desired the Emperor to let a troop of his best horses, twenty-four in number, come and exercise upon this plain. His Majesty approved of the proposal, and I took them up, one by one, in my hands, ready mounted and armed, with the proper officers to exercise them. As soon as they got into order they divided into two parties, performed mock skirmishes, discharged blunt arrows, drew their swords, fled and pursued, attacked and retired, and in short discovered the best military discipline I ever beheld. The parallel sticks secured them and their horses from falling over the stage; and the Emperor was so much delighted that he ordered this entertainment to be repeated several days, and once was pleased to be lifted up and give the word of command; and with great difficulty persuaded even the Empress herself to let me hold her in her close chair[1] within two yards of the stage, when she was able to take a full view of the whole performance. It was my good fortune that no ill accident happened in these entertainments; only once a fiery horse, that belonged to one of the captains, pawing with his hoof struck a hole in my handkerchief, and his foot slipping, he overthrew his rider and himself; but I immediately relieved them both, and, covering the hole with one hand, I set down the troop with the other, in the same manner as I took them up. The horse that fell was strained in the left shoulder, but the rider got no hurt; and I repaired my handkerchief as well as I could; however, I would not trust to the strength of it anymore in such dangerous enterprises.

About two or three days before I was set at liberty, as I was entertaining the court with this kind of feat, there arrived an express to inform His Majesty that some of his subjects, riding near the place where I was first taken up, had seen a great black substance lying on the ground, very oddly shaped, extending its edges round as wide as His Majesty's bedchamber, and rising up in the middle as high as a man; that it was no living creature, as they at first apprehended, for it lay on the grass without motion, and some of them had walked round it several times; that, by mounting upon each other's shoulders, they had got to the top, which was flat and even, and, stamping upon it, they found that it was hollow within; that they humbly conceived it might be something belonging to the Man-Mountain, and if His Majesty pleased, they would undertake to bring it with only five horses. I presently knew what they meant, and was glad at heart to receive this intelligence. It seems, upon my first reaching the shore after our shipwreck I was in such confusion that, before I came to the place where I went to sleep, my hat, which I had fastened with a string to my head while I was rowing, and had stuck on all the time I was swimming, fell off after I came to land; the string, as I conjecture, breaking by some accident which I never observed, but thought my hat had been lost at sea. I entreated His Imperial Majesty to give orders it might be brought to me as soon as possible, describing to him the use and the nature of it, and the next day the wagoners arrived with it, but not in a very good condition. They had bored two holes in the brim, within an inch and half of the edge, and fastened two hooks in the holes; these hooks were tied by a long cord to the harness, and thus my hat was dragged along for above half an English mile; but, the ground in that

[1] *close chair* Closed sedan chair, normally carried on poles.

country being extremely smooth and level, it received less damage than I expected.

Two days after this adventure, the Emperor, having ordered that part of his army which quarters in and about his metropolis to be in readiness, took a fancy of diverting himself in a very singular manner. He desired I would stand like a colossus,[1] with my legs as far asunder as I conveniently could. He then commanded his general (who was an old experienced leader, and a great patron of mine) to draw up the troops in close order and march them under me; the foot[2] by twenty-four abreast, and the horse by sixteen, with drums beating, colours flying, and pikes advanced. This body consisted of three thousand foot, and a thousand horse. His Majesty gave orders, upon pain of death, that every soldier in his march should observe the strictest decency with regard to my person, which however could not prevent some of the younger officers from turning up their eyes as they passed under me; and, to confess the truth, my breeches were at that time in so ill a condition that they afforded some opportunities for laughter and admiration.

I had sent so many memorials and petitions for my liberty that His Majesty at length mentioned the matter, first in the cabinet and then in a full council, where it was opposed by none except Skyresh Bolgolam,[3] who was pleased, without any provocation, to be my mortal enemy. But it was carried against him by the whole board, and confirmed by the Emperor. That minister was *Galbet*, or Admiral of the Realm, very much in his master's confidence, and a person well versed in affairs, but of a morose and sour complexion. However, he was at length persuaded to comply; but prevailed that the articles and conditions upon which I should be set free, and to which I must swear, should be drawn up by himself. These articles were brought to me by Skyresh Bolgolam in person, attended by two under-secretaries and several persons of distinction. After they were read, I was demanded to swear to the performance of them, first in the manner of my own country, and afterwards in the method prescribed by their laws; which was to hold my right foot in my left hand, and to place the middle finger of my right hand on the crown of my head, and my thumb on the tip of my right ear. But because the reader may be curious to have some idea of the style and manner of expression peculiar to that people, as well as to know the article upon which I recovered my liberty, I have made a translation of the whole instrument, word for word, as near as I was able, which I here offer to the public.

Golbasto Momarem Evlame Gurdilo Shefin Mully Ully Gue, Most Mighty Emperor of Lilliput, Delight and Terror of the universe, whose dominions extend five thousand *blustrugs* (about twelve miles in circumference) to the extremities of the globe; Monarch of all Monarchs, taller than the sons of men, whose feet press down to the centre, and whose head strikes against the sun; at whose nod the princes of the earth shake their knees; pleasant as the spring, comfortable as the summer, fruitful as autumn, dreadful as winter. His Most Sublime Majesty proposes to the Man-Mountain, lately arrived at our celestial dominions, the following articles, which by a solemn oath he shall be obliged to perform.

First, the Man-Mountain shall not depart from our dominions without our license under our great seal.

Second, he shall not presume to come into our metropolis without our express order, at which time the inhabitants shall have two hours warning to keep within doors.

Third, the said Man-Mountain shall confine his walks to our principal high roads, and not offer to walk or lie down in a meadow or field of corn.

Fourthly, as he walks the said roads, he shall take the utmost care not to trample upon the bodies of any of our loving subjects, their horses or carriages, nor take any of our subjects into his hands without their own consent.

Fifthly, if an express requires extraordinary dispatch, the Man-Mountain shall be obliged to carry in his pocket the messenger and horse, a six days' journey once in every moon, and return the said messenger back (if so required) safe to our Imperial Presence.

[1] *colossus* Larger-than-life statue of a human. The most famous colossus was the bronze statue of Apollo, which was over one hundred feet high and stood astride the harbor of the city of Rhodes. It was one of the seven ancient wonders of the world; an earthquake destroyed it in 224 BCE.

[2] *foot* Foot soldiers.

[3] *Skyresh Bolgolam* Possibly the Earl of Nottingham, who was First Lord of the Admiralty from 1681 to 1684. Though Nottingham was himself a Tory, he was an enemy of Swift because he frequently opposed the Earl of Oxford's Tory government. He was nicknamed "Dismal" because of his sour demeanor. See Swift's poem "Toland's Invitation to Dismal."

Sixthly, he shall be our ally against our enemies in the island of Blefuscu, and do his utmost to destroy their fleet, which is now preparing to invade us.

Seventhly, that the said Man-Mountain shall, at his times of leisure, be aiding and assisting to our workmen, in helping to raise certain great stones towards covering the wall of the principal park and other our royal buildings.

Eighthly, that the said Man-Mountain shall, in two moons' time, deliver in an exact survey of the circumference of our dominions by a computation of his own paces round the coast.

Lastly, that, upon his solemn oath to observe all the above articles, the said Man-Mountain shall have a daily allowance of meat and drink sufficient for the support of 1724 of our subjects, with free access to our Royal Person, and other marks of our favour. Given at our palace at Belfaborac the twelfth day of the ninety-first moon of our reign.

I swore and subscribed to these articles with great cheerfulness and content, although some of them were not so honourable as I could have wished, which proceeded wholly from the malice of Skyresh Bolgolam, the High Admiral; whereupon my chains were immediately unlocked, and I was at full liberty. The Emperor himself, in person, did me the honour to be by at the whole ceremony. I made my acknowledgements by prostrating myself at His Majesty's feet, but he commanded me to rise, and after many gracious expressions, which, to avoid the censure of vanity, I shall not repeat, he added that he hoped I should prove a useful servant, and well deserve all the favours he had already conferred upon me, or might do for the future.

The reader may please to observe that in the last article of the recovery of my liberty, the Emperor stipulates to allow me a quantity of meat and drink sufficient for the support of 1724 Lilliputians. Some time after, asking a friend at court how they came to fix on that determinate number, he told me that His Majesty's mathematicians, having taken the height of my body by the help of a quadrant, and finding it to exceed theirs in the proportion of twelve to one, they concluded from the similarity of their bodies that mine must contain at least 1724 of theirs, and consequently would require as much food as was necessary to support that number of Lilliputians—by which the reader may conceive an idea of the ingenuity of that people, as well as the prudent and exact economy of so great a prince.

Chapter 4

(Mildendo, the metropolis of Lilliput, described, together with the Emperor's palace. A conversation between the author and a principal secretary, concerning the affairs of that empire. The author's offers to serve the Emperor in his wars.)

The first request I made after I had obtained my liberty was that I might have license to see Mildendo, the metropolis; which the Emperor easily granted me, but with a special charge to do no hurt either to the inhabitants or their houses. The people had notice by proclamation of my design to visit the town. The wall which encompassed it is two feet and a half high, and at least eleven inches broad, so that a coach and horses may be driven very safely round it, and it is flanked with strong towers at ten feet distance. I stepped over the great western gate and passed very gently, and sidling,[1] through the two principal streets, only in my short waistcoat, for fear of damaging the roofs and eaves of the houses with the skirts of my coat. I walked with the utmost circumspection, to avoid treading on any stragglers who might remain in the streets, although the orders were very strict that all people should keep in their houses, at their own peril. The garret windows and tops of houses were so crowded with spectators that I thought in all my travels I had not seen a more populous place. The city is an exact square, each side of the wall being five hundred feet long. The two great streets, which run across and divide it into four quarters, are five feet wide. The lanes and alleys, which I could not enter, but only view them as I passed, are from twelve to eighteen inches. The town is capable of holding five hundred thousand souls. The houses are from three to five stories; the shops and markets well provided.

The Emperor's palace is in the centre of the city where the two great streets meet. It is enclosed by a wall of two feet high and twenty feet distance from the buildings. I had His Majesty's permission to step over this wall, and, the space being so wide between that and

[1] *sidling* Moving sideways.

the palace, I could easily view it on every side. The outward court is a square of forty feet, and includes two other courts: in the inmost are the royal apartments, which I was very desirous to see, but found it extremely difficult; for the great gates, from one square into another, were but eighteen inches high and seven inches wide. Now the buildings of the outer court were at least five feet high, and it was impossible for me to stride over them without infinite damage to the pile,[1] though the walls were strongly built of hewn stone, and four inches thick. At the same time the Emperor had a great desire that I should see the magnificence of his palace, but this I was not able to do till three days after, which I spent in cutting down with my knife some of the largest trees in the royal park, about a hundred yards distant from the city. Of these trees I made two stools, each about three feet high, and strong enough to bear my weight. The people having received notice a second time, I went again through the city to the palace with my two stools in my hands. When I came to the side of the outer court, I stood upon one stool and took the other in my hand; this I lifted over the roof, and gently set it down on the space between the first and second court, which was eight feet wide. I then stepped over the building very conveniently from one stool to the other, and drew up the first after me with a hooked stick. By this contrivance I got into the inmost court, and, lying down upon my side, I applied my face to the windows of the middle stories, which were left open on purpose, and discovered the most splendid apartments that can be imagined. There I saw the Empress and the young princes in their several lodgings, with their chief attendants about them. Her Imperial Majesty was pleased to smile very graciously upon me, and gave me out of the window her hand to kiss.

But I shall not anticipate the reader with further descriptions of this kind, because I reserve them for a greater work, which is now almost ready for the press, containing a general description of this empire from its first erection through a long series of princes, with a particular account of their wars and politics, laws, learning, and religion; their plants and animals; their peculiar manners and customs, with other matters very curious and useful; my chief design at present being only to relate such events and transactions as happened to the public or to myself during a residence of about nine months in that empire.

One morning, about a fortnight after I had obtained my liberty, Reldresal, Principal Secretary (as they style him) of Private Affairs, came to my house attended only by one servant. He ordered his coach to wait at a distance, and desired I would give him an hour's audience, which I readily consented to on account of his quality and personal merits, as well as of the many good offices he had done me during my solicitations at court. I offered to lie down that he might the more conveniently reach my ear, but he chose rather to let me hold him in my hand during our conversation. He began with compliments on my liberty; said he might pretend to some merit in it; but, however, added that if it had not been for the present situation of things at court, perhaps I might not have obtained it so soon. For, said he, as flourishing a condition as we may appear to be in to foreigners, we labour under two mighty evils: a violent faction at home, and the danger of an invasion by a most potent enemy from abroad. As to the first, you are to understand that for about seventy moons past there have been two struggling parties in this empire, under the names of *Tramecksan* and *Slamecksan*,[2] from the high and low heels of their shoes, by which they distinguish themselves. It is alleged, indeed, that the high heels are most agreeable to our ancient constitution; but, however this be, His Majesty has determined to make use only of low heels in the administration of the government, and all offices in the gift of the crown, as you cannot but observe; and particularly that his Majesty's imperial heels are lower at least by a *drurr* than any of his court (*drurr* is a measure about the fourteenth part of an inch). The animosities between these two parties run so high that they will neither eat, nor drink, nor talk with each other. We compute the *Tramecksan*, or high heels, to exceed us in number, but the power is wholly on our side. We apprehend His Imperial High-

[1] *pile* Edifice.

[2] *Tramecksan and Slamecksan* Tory and Whig. Though both parties were Anglican, the Tories were the High Church party (which retained many elements of the Roman Catholic Church), while the Whigs were Low Church (which did not). George I and his ministry were Whigs, but in the last years of Queen Anne's reign a Tory ministry had ruled.

ness,[1] the heir to the crown, to have some tendency towards the high heels; at least, we can plainly discover that one of his heels is higher than the other, which gives him a hobble in his gait. Now, in the midst of these intestine disquiets, we are threatened with an invasion from the island of Blefuscu,[2] which is the other great empire of the universe, almost as large and powerful as this of His Majesty. For as to what we have heard you affirm, that there are other kingdoms and states in the world inhabited by human creatures as large as yourself, our philosophers[3] are in much doubt, and would rather conjecture that you dropped from the moon, or one of the stars, because it is certain that a hundred mortals of your bulk would in a short time destroy all the fruits and cattle of His Majesty's dominions. Besides, our histories of six thousand moons make no mention of any other regions than the two great empires of Lilliput and Blefuscu. Which two mighty powers have, as I was going to tell you, been engaged in a most obstinate war for six-and-thirty moons past. It began upon the following occasion. It is allowed on all hands that the primitive way of breaking eggs before we eat them was upon the larger end; but His present Majesty's grandfather, while he was a boy, going to eat an egg, and breaking it according to the ancient practice, happened to cut one of his fingers. Whereupon the Emperor his father published an edict commanding all his subjects, upon great penalties, to break the smaller end of their eggs. The people so highly resented this law that our histories tell us there have been six rebellions raised on that account; wherein one Emperor lost his life, and another his crown.[4] These civil commotions were constantly fomented by the monarchs of Blefuscu; and when they were quelled, the exiles always fled for refuge to that empire. It is computed that eleven thousand persons have at several times suffered death rather than submit to break their eggs at the smaller end. Many hundred large volumes have been published upon this controversy, but the books of the Big-Endians have been long forbidden, and the whole party rendered incapable by law of holding employments.[5] During the course of these troubles, the emperors of Blefuscu did frequently expostulate by their ambassadors, accusing us of making a schism in religion by offending against a fundamental doctrine of our great prophet Lustrog, in the fifty-fourth chapter of the *Blundecral* (which is their Alcoran). This, however, is thought to be a mere strain upon the text; for the words are these: "that all true believers break their eggs at the convenient end." And which is the convenient end, seems, in my humble opinion, to be left to every man's conscience, or at least in the power of the chief magistrate to determine. Now, the Big-Endian exiles have found so much credit in the Emperor of Blefuscu's court, and so much private assistance and encouragement from their party here at home, that a bloody war has been carried on between the two empires for six-and-thirty moons, with various success; during which time we have lost forty capital ships and a much greater number of smaller vessels, together with thirty thousand of our best seamen and soldiers; and the damage received by the enemy is reckoned to be somewhat greater than ours. However, they have now equipped a numerous fleet, and are just preparing to make a descent upon us; and His Imperial Majesty, placing great confidence in your valour and strength, has commanded me to lay this account of his affairs before you.

I desired the Secretary to present my humble duty to the Emperor, and to let him know that I thought it would not become me, who was a foreigner, to interfere with parties, but I was ready, with the hazard of my life, to defend his person and state against all invaders.

Chapter 5

(*The author, by an extraordinary stratagem, prevents an invasion. A high title of honour is conferred upon him. Ambassadors arrive from the Emperor of Blefuscu and sue for peace. The Empress's apartment on fire by an accident; the author instrumental in saving the rest of the palace.*)

[1] *His Imperial Highness* The Prince of Wales, later King George II. Though he seemed to have Tory leanings, as King he allowed the Whigs to retain power.

[2] *Blefuscu* France.

[3] *philosophers* Scientists.

[4] *It began … his crown* This is an allegorical description of the struggle between Catholics (Big-Endians) and Protestants (Little-Endians), beginning with Henry VIII, who broke with the Catholic Church. This struggle was a factor in the civil strife that saw Charles I beheaded and James II deposed.

[5] *whole party … employments* Catholics were prevented by the Test Acts of 1673 from holding office.

The empire of Blefuscu is an island situated to the north-east of Lilliput, from which it is parted only by a channel of eight hundred yards wide. I had not yet seen it, and upon this notice of an intended invasion, I avoided appearing on that side of the coast, for fear of being discovered by some of the enemy's ships, who had received no intelligence of me, all intercourse between the two empires having been strictly forbidden during the war, upon pain of death, and an embargo laid by our Emperor upon all vessels whatsoever. I communicated to His Majesty a project I had formed of seizing the enemy's whole fleet, which, as our scouts assured us, lay at anchor in the harbour, ready to sail with the first fair wind. I consulted the most experienced seamen upon the depth of the channel, which they had often plumbed; who told me that in the middle, at high-water, it was seventy *glumgluffs* deep, which is about six feet of European measure; and the rest of it fifty *glumgluffs* at most. I walked towards the north-east coast over against Blefuscu, where, lying down behind a hillock, I took out my small perspective glass and viewed the enemy's fleet at anchor, consisting of about fifty men of war and a great number of transports. I then came back to my house and gave orders (for which I had a warrant) for a great quantity of the strongest cable and bars of iron. The cable was about as thick as packthread and the bars of the length and size of a knitting-needle. I trebled the cable to make it stronger, and for the same reason I twisted three of the iron bars together, bending the extremities into a hook. Having thus fixed fifty hooks to as many cables, I went back to the north-east coast and, putting off my coat, shoes, and stockings, walked into the sea in my leather jerkin, about half an hour before high water. I waded with what haste I could, and swam in the middle about thirty yards till I felt ground. I arrived at the fleet in less than half an hour. The enemy was so frightened when they saw me that they leaped out of their ships and swam to shore, where there could not be fewer than thirty thousand souls. I then took my tackling and, fastening a hook to the hole at the prow of each, I tied all the cords together at the end. While I was thus employed, the enemy discharged several thousand arrows, many of which stuck in my hands and face, and, beside the excessive smart, gave me much disturbance in my work. My greatest apprehension was for mine eyes, which I should have infallibly lost if I had not suddenly thought of an expedient. I kept, among other little necessaries, a pair of spectacles in a private pocket, which, as I observed before, had escaped the Emperor's searchers. These I took out and fastened as strongly as I could upon my nose, and thus armed, went on boldly with my work in spite of the enemy's arrows, many of which struck against the glasses of my spectacles, but without any other effect further than a little to discompose them. I had now fastened all the hooks, and, taking the knot in my hand, began to pull; but not a ship would stir, for they were all too fast held by their anchors, so that the boldest part of my enterprise remained. I therefore let go the cord and, leaving the hooks fixed to the ships, I resolutely cut with my knife the cables that fastened the anchors, receiving about two hundred shots in my face and hands. Then I took up the knotted end of the cables, to which my hooks were tied, and with great ease drew fifty of the enemy's largest men of war after me.

The Blefuscudians, who had not the least imagination of what I intended, were at first confounded with astonishment. They had seen me cut the cables, and thought my design was only to let the ships run adrift or fall foul on each other; but when they perceived the whole fleet moving in order, and saw me pulling at the end, they set up such a scream of grief and despair as it is almost impossible to describe or conceive. When I had got out of danger, I stopped awhile to pick out the arrows that stuck in my hands and face, and rubbed on some of the same ointment that was given me at my first arrival, as I have formerly mentioned. I then took off my spectacles, and, waiting about an hour till the tide was a little fallen, I waded through the middle with my cargo and arrived safe at the royal port of Lilliput.

The Emperor and his whole court stood on the shore, expecting the issue of this great adventure. They saw the ships move forward in a large half-moon, but could not discern me, who was up to my breast in water. When I advanced to the middle of the channel they were yet more in pain because I was under water to my neck. The Emperor concluded me to be drowned, and that the enemy's fleet was approaching in a hostile manner. But he was soon eased of his fears; for the channel growing shallower every step I made, I came in a short time within hearing, and, holding up the end of the cable by which the fleet was fastened, I cried in a loud voice, "Long live the most puissant king of Lilliput!" This great prince received me at my landing with all possible encomiums,[1] and created me a *Nardac* upon the spot, which is the highest title of honour among them.

His Majesty desired I would take some other opportunity of bringing all the rest of his enemy's ships into his ports. And so unmeasureable is the ambition of princes that he seemed to think of nothing less than reducing the whole empire of Blefuscu into a province, and governing it, by a viceroy; of destroying the Big-Endian exiles and compelling that people to break the smaller end of their eggs, by which he would remain the sole monarch of the whole world. But I endeavoured to divert him from this design by many arguments drawn from the topics of policy as well as justice; and I plainly protested that I would never be an instrument of bringing a free and brave people into slavery. And, when the matter was debated in council, the wisest part of the ministry were of my opinion.

This open bold declaration of mine was so opposite to the schemes and politics of His Imperial Majesty that he could never forgive me. He mentioned it in a very artful manner at council, where I was told that some of the wisest appeared, at least by their silence, to be of my opinion; but others, who were my secret enemies, could not forbear some expressions which by a side-wind[2] reflected on me. And from this time began an intrigue between His Majesty and a junto[3] of ministers maliciously bent against me, which broke out in less than two months, and had like to have ended in my utter destruction. Of so little weight are the greatest services to princes, when put into the balance with a refusal to gratify their passions.

About three weeks after this exploit there arrived a solemn embassy from Blefuscu with humble offers of a peace, which was soon concluded upon conditions very advantageous to our Emperor, wherewith I shall not trouble the reader. There were six ambassadors with a train of about five hundred persons, and their entry was very magnificent, suitable to the grandeur of their master and the importance of their business. When their treaty[4] was finished, wherein I did them several good offices by the credit I now had, or at least appeared to have, at court, their Excellencies, who were privately told how much I had been their friend, made me a visit in form.[5] They began with many compliments upon my valour and generosity, invited me to that kingdom in the Emperor their master's name, and desired me to show them some proofs of my prodigious strength, of which they had heard so many wonders; wherein I readily obliged them, but shall not trouble the reader with the particulars.

When I had for some time entertained Their Excellencies to their infinite satisfaction and surprise, I desired they would do me the honour to present my most humble respects to the Emperor their master, the renown of whose virtues had so justly filled the whole world with admiration, and whose royal person I resolved to attend, before I returned to my own country. Accordingly, the next time I had the honour to see our Emperor, I desired his general license to wait on the Blefuscudian monarch, which he was pleased to grant me, as I could perceive, in a very cold manner; but could not guess the reason till I had a whisper from a certain person that Flimnap and Bolgolam had represented my intercourse with those ambassadors as a mark of disaffection, from which I am sure my heart was wholly free. And this was the first time I began to conceive some imperfect idea of courts and ministers.

It is to be observed that these ambassadors spoke to me by an interpreter, the languages of both empires differing as much from each other as any two in Europe, and each nation priding itself upon the antiquity, beauty, and energy of their own tongue, with an avowed contempt for that of their neighbour. Yet our Emperor, standing upon the advantage he had got by the seizure of their fleet, obliged them to deliver their credentials, and make their speech, in the Lilliputian tongue. And it must be confessed that from the great intercourse of trade and commerce between both realms, from the continual reception of exiles which is mutual among them, and from the custom, in each empire, to send

[1] *encomiums* Panegyrics; expressions of praise.

[2] *by a side-wind* Indirectly.

[3] *junto* Political body; faction.

[4] *treaty* The Treaty of Utrecht, negotiated by Tory ministers, ended England's war with France in 1713. These same ministers, including Bolingbroke and Oxford, were later accused of weakness by the Whigs and driven from public life.

[5] *visit in form* Formal diplomatic visit.

their young nobility and richer gentry to the other, in order to polish themselves by seeing the world and understanding men and manners, there are few persons of distinction, or merchants, or seamen, who dwell in the maritime parts, but what can hold conversation in both tongues; as I found some weeks after, when I went to pay my respects to the Emperor of Blefuscu, which, in the midst of great misfortunes, through the malice of my enemies, proved a very happy adventure to me, as I shall relate in its proper place.

The reader may remember that when I signed those articles upon which I recovered my liberty, there were some which I disliked upon account of their being too servile; neither could anything but an extreme necessity have forced me to submit. But being now a *Nardac* of the highest rank in that empire, such offices were looked upon as below my dignity, and the Emperor (to do him justice) never once mentioned them to me. However, it was not long before I had an opportunity of doing His Majesty, at least as I then thought, a most signal[1] service. I was alarmed at midnight with the cries of many hundred people at my door; by which, being suddenly awaked, I was in some kind of terror. I heard the word *Burglum* repeated incessantly; several of the Emperor's court, making their way through the crowd, entreated me to come immediately to the palace, where Her Imperial Majesty's apartment was on fire, by the carelessness of a maid of honour, who fell asleep while she was reading a romance. I got up in an instant; and orders being given to clear the way before me, and it being likewise a moonshine night, I made a shift to get to the palace without trampling on any of the people. I found they had already applied ladders to the walls of the apartment, and were well provided with buckets, but the water was at some distance. These buckets were about the size of large thimbles, and the poor people supplied me with them as fast as they could, but the flame was so violent that they did little good. I might easily have stifled it with my coat, which I unfortunately left behind me for haste, and came away only in my leather jerkin. The case seemed wholly desperate and deplorable; and this magnificent palace would have infallibly been burnt down to the ground, if, by a presence of mind unusual to me, I had not suddenly thought of an expedient. I had the evening before drunk plentifully of a most delicious wine called *glimigrim* (the Blefuscudians call it *flunec*, but ours is esteemed the better sort), which is very diuretic. By the luckiest chance in the world, I had not discharged myself of any part of it. The heat I had contracted by coming very near the flames, and by labouring to quench them, made the wine begin to operate by urine, which I voided in such a quantity, and applied so well to the proper places, that in three minutes the fire was wholly extinguished, and the rest of that noble pile, which had cost so many ages in erecting, preserved from destruction.

It was now daylight, and I returned to my house without waiting to congratulate with the Emperor because, although I had done a very eminent piece of service, yet I could not tell how His Majesty might resent the manner by which I had performed it: for, by the fundamental laws of the realm, it is capital[2] in any person, of what quality soever, to make water within the precincts of the palace. But I was a little comforted by a message from His Majesty that he would give orders to the Grand Justiciary for passing my pardon in form; which, however, I could not obtain. And I was privately assured that the Empress,[3] conceiving the greatest abhorrence of what I had done, removed to the most distant side of the court, firmly resolved that those buildings should never be repaired for her use; and, in the presence of her chief confidents, could not forbear vowing revenge.

CHAPTER 6

(*Of the inhabitants of Lilliput; their learning, laws, and customs; the manner of educating their children. The author's way of living in that country. His vindication of a great lady.*)

Although I intend to leave the description of this empire to a particular treatise, yet in the meantime I am content to gratify the curious reader with some general ideas. As the common size of the natives is somewhat under six inches high, so there is an exact

[1] *signal* Notable.

[2] *capital* Capital crime, punishable by death.

[3] *the Empress* Here a reference to Queen Anne, who was supposedly so offended by the coarseness of Swift's work *A Tale of a Tub* that she refused to grant him a bishopric.

proportion in all other animals, as well as plants and trees. For instance, the tallest horses and oxen are between four and five inches in height; the sheep an inch and half, more or less; their geese about the bigness of a sparrow; and so the several gradations downwards till you come to the smallest, which to my sight were almost invisible. But nature has adapted the eyes of the Lilliputians to all objects proper for their view; they see with great exactness, but at no great distance. And, to show the sharpness of their sight towards objects that are near, I have been much pleased with observing a cook pulling[1] a lark, which was not so large as a common fly, and a young girl threading an invisible needle with invisible silk. Their tallest trees are about seven feet high—I mean some of those in the great royal park, the tops whereof I could but just reach with my fist clenched. The other vegetables are in the same proportion, but this I leave to the reader's imagination.

I shall say but little at present of their learning, which for many ages has flourished in all its branches among them: but their manner of writing is very peculiar, being neither from the left to the right, like the Europeans; nor from the right to the left, like the Arabians; nor from up to down, like the Chinese; nor from down to up, like the Cascagians;[2] but aslant, from one corner of the paper to the other, like ladies in England.

They bury their dead with their heads directly downward because they hold an opinion that in eleven thousand moons they are all to rise again; in which period the earth (which they conceive to be flat) will turn upside down, and by this means they shall, at their resurrection, be found ready standing on their feet. The learned among them confess the absurdity of this doctrine, but the practice still continues, in compliance to the vulgar.

There are some laws and customs in this empire very peculiar; and if they were not so directly contrary to those of my own dear country, I should be tempted to say a little in their justification. It is only to be wished they were as well executed. The first I shall mention relates to informers. All crimes against the state are punished here with the utmost severity; but, if the person accused makes his innocence plainly to appear upon his trial, the accuser is immediately put to an ignominious death; and out of his goods or lands the innocent person is quadruply recompensed for the loss of his time, for the danger he underwent, for the hardship of his imprisonment, and for all the charges he has been at in making his defence. Or, if that fund be deficient, it is largely supplied by the crown. The Emperor also confers on him some public mark of his favour, and proclamation is made of his innocence through the whole city.

They look upon fraud as a greater crime than theft, and therefore seldom fail to punish it with death; for they allege that care and vigilance, with a very common understanding, may preserve a man's goods from thieves, but honesty has no defence against superior cunning. And, since it is necessary that there should be a perpetual intercourse of buying and selling, and dealing upon credit, where fraud is permitted and connived at,[3] or has no law to punish it, the honest dealer is always undone, and the knave gets the advantage. I remember when I was once interceding with the Emperor for a criminal who had wronged his master of a great sum of money, which he had received by order and ran away with; and, happening to tell His Majesty, by way of extenuation, that it was only a breach of trust, the Emperor thought it monstrous in me to offer as a defence the greatest aggravation of the crime; and truly I had little to say in return, farther than the common answer that different nations had different customs; for, I confess, I was heartily ashamed.

Although we usually call reward and punishment the two hinges upon which all government turns, yet I could never observe this maxim to be put in practice by any nation except that of Lilliput. Whoever can there bring sufficient proof that he has strictly observed the laws of his country for seventy-three moons has a claim to certain privileges, according to his quality[4] or condition of life, with a proportionable sum of money out of a fund appropriated for that use. He likewise acquires the title of *Snilpall*, or *Legal*, which is added to his name, but does not descend to his posterity. And these people thought it a prodigious defect of policy among us when I told them that our laws were enforced only by penalties, without any mention of reward. It is upon this

[1] *pulling* Plucking.

[2] *Cascagians* Invented by Swift.

[3] *connived at* Indulged or overlooked.

[4] *quality* Rank; position.

account that the image of Justice, in their courts of judicature, is formed with six eyes, two before, as many behind, and on each side one, to signify circumspection; with a bag of gold open in her right hand, and a sword sheathed in her left, to show she is more disposed to reward than to punish.

In choosing persons for all employments, they have more regard to good morals than to great abilities; for, since government is necessary to mankind, they believe that the common size of human understanding is fitted to some station or other; and that Providence never intended to make the management of public affairs a mystery to be comprehended only by a few persons of sublime genius, of which there seldom are three born in an age; but they suppose truth, justice, temperance, and the like, to be in every man's power; the practice of which virtues, assisted by experience and a good intention, would qualify any man for the service of his country, except where a course of study is required. But they thought the want of moral virtues was so far from being supplied by superior endowments of the mind that employments could never be put into such dangerous hands as those of persons so qualified; and, at least, that the mistakes committed by ignorance in a virtuous disposition would never be of such fatal consequence to the public weal[1] as the practices of a man whose inclinations led him to be corrupt, and who had great abilities to manage, to multiply, and defend his corruptions.

In like manner, the disbelief of a Divine Providence renders a man incapable of holding any public station; for, since Kings avow themselves to be the deputies of Providence, the Lilliputians think nothing can be more absurd than for a prince to employ such men as disown the authority under which he acts.

In relating these and the following laws, I would only be understood to mean the original institutions, and not the most scandalous corruptions, into which these people are fallen by the degenerate nature of man. For, as to that infamous practice of acquiring great employments by dancing on the ropes, or badges of favour and distinction by leaping over sticks and creeping under them, the reader is to observe that they were first introduced by the grandfather of the Emperor now reigning, and grew to the present height by the gradual increase of party and faction.

Ingratitude is among them a capital crime, as we read it to have been in some other countries; for they reason thus, that whoever makes ill returns to his benefactor must needs be a common enemy to the rest of mankind, from whom he has received no obligation, and therefore such a man is not fit to live.

Their notions relating to the duties of parents and children differ extremely from ours. For, since the conjunction of male and female is founded upon the great law of nature, in order to propagate and continue the species, the Lilliputians will needs have it that men and women are joined together, like other animals, by the motives of concupiscence; and that their tenderness towards their young proceeds from the like natural principle, for which reason they will never allow that a child is under any obligation to his father for begetting him, or to his mother for bringing him into the world; which, considering the miseries of human life, was neither a benefit in itself, nor intended so by his parents, whose thoughts, in their love encounters, were otherwise employed. Upon these and the like reasonings, their opinion is that parents are the last of all others to be trusted with the education of their own children; and therefore they have in every town public nurseries, where all parents, except cottagers[2] and labourers, are obliged to send their infants of both sexes to be reared and educated when they come to the age of twenty moons, at which time they are supposed to have some rudiments of docility.[3] These schools are of several kinds, suited to different qualities and both sexes. They have certain professors well skilled in preparing children for such a condition of life as befits the rank of their parents, and their own capacities as well as inclinations. I shall first say something of the male nurseries, and then of the female.

The nurseries for males of noble or eminent birth are provided with grave and learned professors and their several deputies. The clothes and food of the children are plain and simple. They are bred up in the principles of honour, justice, courage, modesty, clemency, religion, and love of their country; they are always employed in some business, except in the times of eating and sleeping, which are very short, and two hours for diversions consisting of bodily exercises. They are dressed by men

[1] *public weal* Public well-being; common good.

[2] *cottagers* Country dwellers.

[3] *docility* Ability to be taught.

till four years of age, and then are obliged to dress themselves, although their quality be ever so great; and the women attendant, who are aged proportionably to ours at fifty, perform only the most menial offices. They are never suffered to converse with servants, but go together in smaller or greater numbers to take their diversions, and always in the presence of a professor or one of his deputies, whereby they avoid those early bad impressions of folly and vice to which our children are subject. Their parents are suffered to see them only twice a year; the visit is not to last above an hour; they are allowed to kiss the child at meeting and parting, but a professor, who always stands by on those occasions, will not suffer them to whisper, or use any fondling expressions, or bring any presents of toys, sweetmeats,[1] and the like.

The pension from each family for the education and entertainment[2] of a child, upon failure of due payment, is levied by the Emperor's officers.

The nurseries for children of ordinary gentlemen, merchants, traders, and handicrafts are managed proportionably after the same manner; only those designed for trades are put out apprentices at eleven years old, whereas those of persons of quality continue in their exercises till fifteen, which answers to twenty-one with us; but the confinement is gradually lessened for the last three years.

In the female nurseries, the young girls of quality are educated much like the males, only they are dressed by orderly servants of their own sex, but always in the presence of a professor or deputy, till they come to dress themselves, which is at five years old. And if it be found that these nurses ever presume to entertain the girls with frightful or foolish stories, or the common follies practised by chambermaids among us, they are publicly whipped thrice about the city, imprisoned for a year, and banished for life to the most desolate part of the country. Thus the young ladies are as much ashamed of being cowards and fools as the men and despise all personal ornaments, beyond decency and cleanliness; neither did I perceive any difference in their education made by their difference of sex, only that the exercises of the females were not altogether so robust; and that some rules were given them relating to domestic life; and a smaller compass of learning was enjoined them. For their maxim is that among peoples of quality, a wife should be always a reasonable and agreeable companion, because she cannot always be young. When the girls are twelve years old, which among them is the marriageable age, their parents or guardians take them home, with great expressions of gratitude to the professors, and seldom without tears of the young lady and her companions.

In the nurseries of females of the meaner sort, the children are instructed in all kinds of works proper for their sex and their several degrees:[3] those intended for apprentices are dismissed at seven years old, the rest are kept to eleven.

The meaner families who have children at these nurseries are obliged, besides their annual pension, which is as low as possible, to return to the steward of the nursery a small monthly share of their gettings, to be a portion for the child; and therefore all parents are limited in their expenses by the law. For the Lilliputians think nothing can be more unjust than that people, in subservience to their own appetites, should bring children into the world, and leave the burden of supporting them on the public. As to persons of quality, they give security to appropriate a certain sum for each child, suitable to their condition; and these funds are always managed with good husbandry and the most exact justice.

The cottagers and labourers keep their children at home, their business being only to till and cultivate the earth, and therefore their education is of little consequence to the public; but the old and diseased among them are supported by hospitals, for begging is a trade unknown in this empire.

And here it may perhaps divert the curious reader to give some account of my domestic[4] and my manner of living in this country during a residence of nine months and thirteen days. Having a head mechanically turned, and being likewise forced by necessity, I had made for myself a table and chair, convenient enough, out of the largest trees in the royal park. Two hundred seamstresses were employed to make me shirts, and linen for my bed and table, all of the strongest and coarsest kind they could get; which, however, they were forced to quilt together in several folds, for the thickest was some

[1] *sweetmeats* Sweet foods, such as pastries, cakes, or candies.

[2] *entertainment* Sustenance; maintenance.

[3] *several degrees* Various social stations.

[4] *domestic* Household arrangements.

degrees finer than lawn.[1] Their linen is usually three inches wide, and three feet make a piece. The seamstresses took my measure as I lay on the ground, one standing at my neck and another at my mid-leg, with a strong cord extended that each held by the end, while a third measured the length of the cord with a rule of an inch long. Then they measured my right thumb, and desired no more; for, by a mathematical computation that twice round the thumb is once round the wrist, and so on to the neck and the waist, and by the help of my old shirt, which I displayed on the ground before them for a pattern, they fitted me exactly. Three hundred tailors were employed in the same manner to make me clothes; but they had another contrivance for taking my measure. I kneeled down, and they raised a ladder from the ground to my neck; upon this ladder one of them mounted, and let fall a plumb-line from my collar to the floor, which just answered the length of my coat; but my waist and arms I measured myself. When my clothes were finished, which was done in my house (for the largest of theirs would not have been able to hold them), they looked like the patchwork made by the ladies in England, only that mine were all of a colour.

I had three hundred cooks to dress my victuals in little convenient huts built about my house, where they and their families lived and prepared me two dishes apiece. I took up twenty waiters in my hand and placed them on the table; a hundred more attended below on the ground, some with dishes of meat, and some with barrels of wine and other liquors slung on their shoulders; all which the waiters above drew up as I wanted, in a very ingenious manner, by certain cords—as we draw the bucket up a well in Europe. A dish of their meat was a good mouthful, and a barrel of their liquor a reasonable draught. Their mutton yields to ours, but their beef is excellent. I have had a sirloin so large that I have been forced to make three bites of it, but this is rare. My servants were astonished to see me eat it bones and all, as in our country we do the leg of a lark. Their geese and turkeys I usually ate at a mouthful, and I confess they far exceed ours. Of their smaller fowl I could take up twenty or thirty at the end of my knife.

One day His Imperial Majesty, being informed of my way of living, desired that himself and his royal consort, with the young princes of the blood of both sexes, might have the happiness (as he was pleased to call it) of dining with me. They came accordingly, and I placed them in chairs of state on my table, just over against me, with their guards about them. Flimnap, the Lord High Treasurer, attended there likewise, with his white staff;[2] and I observed he often looked on me with a sour countenance, which I would not seem to regard, but ate more than usual, in honour to my dear country, as well as to fill the court with admiration. I have some private reasons to believe that this visit from His Majesty gave Flimnap an opportunity of doing me ill offices to his master. That minister had always been my secret enemy, though he outwardly caressed me more than was usual to the moroseness of his nature. He represented to the Emperor the low condition of his treasury: that he was forced to take up money at a great discount; that exchequer bills[3] would not circulate under nine per cent below par; that I had cost His Majesty above a million and a half of *sprugs* (their greatest gold coin, about the bigness of a spangle); and, upon the whole, that it would be advisable in the Emperor to take the first fair occasion of dismissing me.

I am here obliged to vindicate the reputation of an excellent lady who was an innocent sufferer upon my account. The Treasurer took a fancy to be jealous of his wife, from the malice of some evil tongues, who informed him that Her Grace had taken a violent affection for my person; and the court scandal ran for some time that she once came privately to my lodging. This I solemnly declare to be a most infamous falsehood, without any grounds farther than that Her Grace was pleased to treat me with all innocent marks of freedom and friendship. I own she came often to my house, but always publicly, nor ever without three more in the coach, who were usually her sister, and young daughter, and some particular acquaintance; but this was common to many other ladies of the court. And I still appeal to my servants round, whether they at any time saw a coach at my door without knowing what persons were in it. On those occasions, when a servant had given me notice, my custom was to go immediately to the door and, after paying my respects, to take up the coach and two horses very carefully in my hands (for, if there were

[1] *lawn* Type of very fine linen.

[2] *white staff* Lord treasurer's symbol of office.

[3] *exchequer bills* Bills of credit issued by Parliament.

six horses, the postillion[1] always unharnessed four) and place them on a table, where I had fixed a movable rim quite round, of five inches high, to prevent accidents. And I have often had four coaches and horses at once on my table full of company, while I sat in my chair leaning my face towards them; and when I was engaged with one set, the coachmen would gently drive the others round my table. I have passed many an afternoon very agreeably in these conversations. But I defy the Treasurer, or his two informers (I will name them, and let them make the best of it), Clustril and Drunlo, to prove that any person ever came to me *incognito*, except the Secretary Reldresal, who was sent by express command of His Imperial Majesty, as I have before related. I should not have dwelt so long upon this particular if it had not been a point wherein the reputation of a great lady is so nearly concerned, to say nothing of my own; though I then had the honour to be a *Nardac*, which the Treasurer himself is not; for all the world knows that he is only a *Clumglum*, a title inferior by one degree, as that of a marquis is to a duke in England; yet I allow he preceded me in right of his post. These false informations, which I afterwards came to the knowledge of by an accident not proper to mention, made the Treasurer show his lady for some time an ill countenance, and me a worse; and although he was at last undeceived and reconciled to her, yet I lost all credit with him, and found my interest decline very fast with the Emperor himself, who was indeed too much governed by that favourite.

Chapter 7

(*The author, being informed of a design to accuse him of high treason, makes his escape to Blefuscu. His reception there.*)

Before I proceed to give an account of my leaving this kingdom, it may be proper to inform the reader of a private intrigue which had been for two months forming against me.

I had been hitherto, all my life, a stranger to courts, for which I was unqualified by the meanness of my condition.[2] I had indeed heard and read enough of the dispositions of great princes and ministers, but never expected to have found such terrible effects of them in so remote a country, governed, as I thought, by very different maxims from those in Europe.

When I was just preparing to pay my attendance on the Emperor of Blefuscu, a considerable person at court (to whom I had been very serviceable at a time when he lay under the highest displeasure of His Imperial Majesty) came to my house very privately at night in a close chair, and, without sending his name, desired admittance. The chairmen were dismissed. I put the chair, with his lordship in it, into my coat-pocket: and, giving orders to a trusty servant to say I was indisposed and gone to sleep, I fastened the door of my house, placed the chair on the table, according to my usual custom, and sat down by it. After the common salutations were over, observing His Lordship's countenance full of concern, and inquiring into the reason, he desired I would hear him with patience, in a matter that highly concerned my honour and my life. His speech was to the following effect, for I took notes of it as soon as he left me.

You are to know (said he) that several committees of council have been lately called in the most private manner on your account; and it is but two days since His Majesty came to a full resolution.

You are very sensible that Skyresh Bolgolam (*Galbet*, or High Admiral) has been your mortal enemy almost ever since your arrival. His original reasons I know not, but his hatred is increased since your great success against Blefuscu, by which his glory as Admiral is much obscured. This lord, in conjunction with Flimnap the High Treasurer, whose enmity against you is notorious on account of his lady; Limtoc the General; Lalcon the Chamberlain; and Balmuff the Grand Justiciary, have prepared articles of impeachment against you, for treason and other capital crimes.[3]

This preface made me so impatient, being conscious of my own merits and innocence, that I was going to interrupt, when he entreated me to be silent, and thus proceeded:

Out of gratitude for the favours you have done me, I procured information of the whole proceedings and a

[1] *postillion* One who guides the first pair of horses.

[2] *meanness … condition* Low rank.

[3] *treason … crimes* After the Whigs regained power, both Oxford and Bolingbroke were accused of being Jacobite sympathizers and were impeached for treason.

copy of the articles, wherein I venture my head for your service.

Articles of Impeachment against QUINBUS FLESTRIN (*the* Man-Mountain.)

ARTICLE 1

Whereas, by a statute made in the reign of His Imperial Majesty Calin Deffar Plune, it is enacted that whoever shall make water within the precincts of the royal palace shall be liable to the pains and penalties of high-treason; notwithstanding, the said Quinbus Flestrin, in open breach of the said law, under colour of extinguishing the fire kindled in the apartment of His Majesty's most dear imperial consort, did maliciously, traitorously, and devilishly, by discharge of his urine, put out the said fire kindled in the said apartment, lying and being within the precincts of the said royal palace, against the statute in that case provided, etc., against the duty, etc.

ARTICLE 2

That the said Quinbus Flestrin, having brought the imperial fleet of Blefuscu into the royal port, and being afterwards commanded by His Imperial Majesty to seize all the other ships of the said empire of Blefuscu, and reduce that empire to a province, to be governed by a viceroy from hence, and to destroy and put to death not only all the Big-Endian exiles, but likewise all the people of that empire who would not immediately forsake the Big-Endian heresy, he, the said Flestrin, like a false traitor against His Most Auspicious, Serene, Imperial Majesty, did petition to be excused from the said service, upon pretence of unwillingness to force the consciences, or destroy the liberties and lives of an innocent people.

ARTICLE 3

That, whereas certain ambassadors arrived from the court of Blefuscu to sue for peace in His Majesty's court, he, the said Flestrin, did, like a false traitor, aid, abet, comfort, and divert the said ambassadors, although he knew them to be servants to a prince who was lately an open enemy to His Imperial Majesty, and in an open war against His said Majesty.

ARTICLE 4

That the said Quinbus Flestrin, contrary to the duty of a faithful subject, is now preparing to make a voyage to the court and empire of Blefuscu, for which he has received only verbal license from His Imperial Majesty; and, under colour of the said license, does falsely and traitorously intend to take the said voyage, and thereby to aid, comfort, and abet the Emperor of Blefuscu, so late an enemy, and in open war with His Imperial Majesty aforesaid.

There are some other articles, but these are the most important, of which I have read you an abstract.

In the several debates upon this impeachment, it must be confessed that His Majesty gave many marks of his great lenity, often urging the services you had done him, and endeavouring to extenuate your crimes. The Treasurer and Admiral insisted that you should be put to the most painful and ignominious death, by setting fire to your house at night, and the General was to attend with twenty thousand men, armed with poisoned arrows, to shoot you on the face and hands. Some of your servants were to have private orders to strew a poisonous juice on your shirts and sheets, which would soon make you tear your own flesh and die in the utmost torture. The General came into the same opinion, so that for a long time there was a majority against you. But His Majesty resolving, if possible, to spare your life, at last brought off[1] the Chamberlain.

Upon this incident, Reldresal, Principal Secretary for Private Affairs, who always approved himself your true friend, was commanded by the Emperor to deliver his opinion, which he accordingly did; and therein justified the good thoughts you have of him. He allowed your crimes to be great, but that still there was room for mercy, the most commendable virtue in a prince, and for which His Majesty was so justly celebrated. He said the friendship between you and him was so well known to the world that perhaps the most honourable board might think him partial; however, in obedience to the command he had received, he would freely offer his sentiments. That if His Majesty, in consideration of your services, and pursuant to his own merciful disposition, would please to spare your life, and only give orders to

[1] *brought off* Won over from his former position.

put out both your eyes, he humbly conceived that by this expedient justice might in some measure be satisfied, and all the world would applaud the lenity of the Emperor, as well as the fair and generous proceedings of those who have the honour to be his counsellors. That the loss of your eyes would be no impediment to your bodily strength, by which you might still be useful to His Majesty; that blindness is an addition to courage, by concealing dangers from us; that the fear you had for your eyes was the greatest difficulty in bringing over the enemy's fleet; and it would be sufficient for you to see by the eyes of the ministers, since the greatest princes do no more.

This proposal was received with the utmost disapprobation by the whole board. Bolgolam, the Admiral, could not preserve his temper, but, rising up in fury, said he wondered how the Secretary durst presume to give his opinion for preserving the life of a traitor; that the services you had performed were, by all true reasons of state, the great aggravation of your crimes; that you, who were able to extinguish the fire by discharge of urine in Her Majesty's apartment (which he mentioned with horror) might, at another time, raise an inundation by the same means, to drown the whole palace; and the same strength which enabled you to bring over the enemy's fleet might serve, upon the first discontent, to carry it back; that he had good reasons to think you were a Big-Endian in your heart; and, as treason begins in the heart before it appears in overt acts, so he accused you as a traitor on that account, and therefore insisted you should be put to death.

The Treasurer was of the same opinion. He showed to what straits His Majesty's revenue was reduced by the charge of maintaining you, which would soon grow insupportable; that the Secretary's expedient of putting out your eyes was so far from being a remedy against this evil that it would probably increase it, as is manifest from the common practice of blinding some kind of fowls, after which they fed the faster, and grew sooner fat; that His sacred Majesty and the council, who are your judges, were in their own consciences fully convinced of your guilt, which was a sufficient argument to condemn you to death, without the formal proofs required by the strict letter of the law.

But His Imperial Majesty, fully determined against capital punishment, was graciously pleased to say that since the council thought the loss of your eyes too easy a censure, some other way may be inflicted hereafter. And your friend the Secretary, humbly desiring to be heard again, in answer to what the Treasurer had objected concerning the great charge His Majesty was at in maintaining you, said that his Excellency, who had the sole disposal of the Emperor's revenue, might easily provide against that evil by gradually lessening your establishment; by which, for want of sufficient food, you would grow weak and faint, and lose your appetite, and consequently decay and consume in a few months; neither would the stench of your carcass be then so dangerous, when it should become more than half diminished; and immediately upon your death five or six thousand of His Majesty's subjects might, in two or three days, cut your flesh from your bones, take it away by cart-loads, and bury it in distant parts to prevent infection, leaving the skeleton as a monument of admiration to posterity.

Thus, by the great friendship of the Secretary, the whole affair was compromised. It was strictly enjoined that the project of starving you by degrees should be kept a secret; but the sentence of putting out your eyes was entered on the books; none dissenting except Bolgolam the Admiral, who, being a creature of the Empress, was perpetually instigated by Her Majesty to insist upon your death, she having borne perpetual malice against you on account of that infamous and illegal method you took to extinguish the fire in her apartment.

In three days your friend the Secretary will be directed to come to your house and read before you the articles of impeachment; and then to signify the great lenity and favour of His Majesty and council, whereby you are only condemned to the loss of your eyes, which His Majesty does not question you will gratefully and humbly submit to; and twenty of His Majesty's surgeons will attend, in order to see the operation well performed, by discharging very sharp-pointed arrows into the balls of your eyes as you lie on the ground.

I leave to your prudence what measures you will take, and to avoid suspicion I must immediately return in as private a manner as I came.

His Lordship did so, and I remained alone, under many doubts and perplexities of mind.

It was a custom introduced by this prince and his

ministry (very different, as I have been assured, from the practice of former times) that after the court had decreed any cruel execution, either to gratify the monarch's resentment or the malice of a favourite, the Emperor always made a speech to his whole council, expressing his great lenity and tenderness, as qualities known and confessed by all the world. This speech was immediately published throughout the kingdom; nor did anything terrify the people so much as those encomiums on His Majesty's mercy, because it was observed that the more these praises were enlarged and insisted on, the more inhuman was the punishment, and the sufferer more innocent. Yet, as to myself, I must confess, having never been designed for a courtier either by my birth or education, I was so ill a judge of things that I could not discover the lenity and favour of this sentence, but conceived it (perhaps erroneously) rather to be rigorous than gentle. I sometimes thought of standing my trial, for, although I could not deny the facts alleged in the several articles, yet I hoped they would admit of some extenuation. But having in my life perused many state trials, which I ever observed to terminate as the judges thought fit to direct, I durst not rely on so dangerous a decision in so critical a juncture, and against such powerful enemies. Once I was strongly bent upon resistance, for, while I had liberty the whole strength of that empire could hardly subdue me, and I might easily with stones pelt the metropolis to pieces; but I soon rejected that project with horror, by remembering the oath I had made to the Emperor, the favours I received from him, and the high title of *Nardac* he conferred upon me. Neither had I so soon learned the gratitude of courtiers to persuade myself that his Majesty's present severities acquitted me of all past obligations.

At last I fixed upon a resolution, for which it is probable I may incur some censure, and not unjustly; for I confess I owe the preserving of mine eyes, and consequently my liberty, to my own great rashness and want of experience; because, if I had then known the nature of princes and ministers, which I have since observed in many other courts, and their methods of treating criminals less obnoxious than myself, I should, with great alacrity and readiness, have submitted to so easy a punishment. But hurried on by the precipitancy of youth, and having his Imperial Majesty's license to pay my attendance upon the Emperor of Blefuscu, I took this opportunity, before the three days were elapsed, to send a letter to my friend the Secretary, signifying my resolution of setting out that morning for Blefuscu,[1] pursuant to the leave I had got; and, without waiting for an answer, I went to that side of the island where our fleet lay. I seized a large man of war, tied a cable to the prow, and, lifting up the anchors, I stripped myself, put my clothes (together with my coverlet, which I carried under my arm) into the vessel, and, drawing it after me, between wading and swimming arrived at the royal port of Blefuscu, where the people had long expected me. They lent me two guides to direct me to the capital city, which is of the same name. I held them in my hands till I came within two hundred yards of the gate, and desired them to signify my arrival to one of the secretaries, and let him know I there waited His Majesty's command. I had an answer in about an hour, that His Majesty, attended by the royal family and great officers of the court, was coming out to receive me. I advanced a hundred yards. The Emperor and his train alighted from their horses, the Empress and ladies from their coaches, and I did not perceive they were in any fright or concern. I lay on the ground to kiss His Majesty's and the Empress's hands. I told His Majesty that I was come according to my promise, and with the license of the Emperor my master, to have the honour of seeing so mighty a monarch, and to offer him any service in my power, consistent with my duty to my own prince; not mentioning a word of my disgrace because I had hitherto no regular information of it, and might suppose myself wholly ignorant of any such design; neither could I reasonably conceive that the Emperor would discover the secret while I was out of his power; wherein, however, it soon appeared I was deceived.

I shall not trouble the reader with the particular account of my reception at this court, which was suitable to the generosity of so great a prince; nor of the difficulties I was in for want of a house and bed, being forced to lie on the ground, wrapped up in my coverlet.

[1] *setting out … Blefuscu* Similarly, Bolingbroke fled to France in order to avoid his trial for treason.

CHAPTER 8

(*The author, by a lucky accident, finds means to leave Blefuscu; and, after some difficulties, returns safe to his native country.*)

Three days after my arrival, walking out of curiosity to the northeast coast of the island, I observed, about half a league off in the sea, somewhat that looked like a boat overturned. I pulled off my shoes and stockings, and, wading two or three hundred yards, I found the object to approach nearer by force of the tide; and then plainly saw it to be a real boat, which I supposed might by some tempest have been driven from a ship. Whereupon I returned immediately towards the city, and desired His Imperial Majesty to lend me twenty of the tallest vessels he had left after the loss of his fleet, and three thousand seamen under the command of his Vice Admiral. This fleet sailed round while I went back the shortest way to the coast where I first discovered the boat. I found the tide had driven it still nearer. The seamen were all provided with cordage, which I had beforehand twisted to a sufficient strength. When the ships came up, I stripped myself and waded till I came within a hundred yards of the boat, after which I was forced to swim till I got up to it. The seamen threw me the end of the cord, which I fastened to a hole in the fore-part of the boat, and the other end to a man of war. But I found all my labour to little purpose; for, being out of my depth, I was not able to work. In this necessity I was forced to swim behind, and push the boat forwards, as often as I could, with one of my hands; and the tide favouring me, I advanced so far that I could just hold up my chin and feel the ground. I rested two or three minutes, and then gave the boat another shove, and so on till the sea was no higher than my armpits; and now, the most laborious part being over, I took out my other cables, which were stowed in one of the ships, and fastened them first to the boat, and then to nine of the vessels which attended me. The wind being favourable, the seamen towed, and I shoved, until we arrived within forty yards of the shore; and, waiting till the tide was out, I got dry to the boat, and by the assistance of two thousand men with ropes and engines, I made a shift to turn it on its bottom, and found it was but little damaged.

I shall not trouble the reader with the difficulties I was under by the help of certain paddles, which cost me ten days making, to get my boat to the royal port of Blefuscu, where a mighty concourse of people appeared upon my arrival, full of wonder at the sight of so prodigious a vessel. I told the Emperor that my good fortune had thrown this boat in my way to carry me to some place whence I might return into my native country, and begged His Majesty's orders for getting materials to fit it up, together with his license to depart, which, after some kind expostulations, he was pleased to grant.

I did very much wonder, in all this time, not to have heard of any express relating to me from our Emperor to the court of Blefuscu. But I was afterward given privately to understand that his Imperial Majesty, never imagining I had the least notice of his designs, believed I was only gone to Blefuscu in performance of my promise, according to the license he had given me, which was well known at our court, and would return in a few days, when the ceremony was ended. But he was at last in pain at my long absence; and after consulting with the Treasurer and the rest of that cabal, a person of quality was dispatched with the copy of the articles against me. This envoy had instructions to represent to the monarch of Blefuscu the great lenity of his master, who was content to punish me no farther than with the loss of mine eyes; that I had fled from justice; and if I did not return in two hours, I should be deprived of my title of *Nardac* and declared a traitor. The envoy further added that in order to maintain the peace and amity between both empires, his master expected that his brother of Blefuscu would give orders to have me sent back to Lilliput, bound hand and foot, to be punished as a traitor.

The Emperor of Blefuscu, having taken three days to consult, returned an answer consisting of many civilities and excuses. He said that, as for sending me bound, his brother knew it was impossible; that, although I had deprived him of his fleet, yet he owed great obligations to me for many good offices I had done him in making the peace; that however, both Their Majesties would soon be made easy, for I had found a prodigious vessel on the shore, able to carry me on the sea, which he had given orders to fit up, with my own assistance and direction; and he hoped in a few weeks both empires would be freed from so insupportable an encumbrance.

With this answer the envoy returned to Lilliput, and the Monarch of Blefuscu related to me all that had passed, offering me at the same time (but under the strictest confidence) his gracious protection if I would continue in his service; wherein, although I believed him sincere, yet I resolved never more to put any confidence in princes or ministers where I could possibly avoid it; and therefore, with all due acknowledgments for his favourable intentions, I humbly begged to be excused. I told him that since fortune, whether good or evil, had thrown a vessel in my way, I was resolved to venture myself on the ocean, rather than be an occasion of difference between two such mighty monarchs. Neither did I find the Emperor at all displeased; and I discovered, by a certain accident, that he was very glad of my resolution, and so were most of his ministers.

These considerations moved me to hasten my departure somewhat sooner than I intended; to which the court, impatient to have me gone, very readily contributed. Five hundred workmen were employed to make two sails to my boat, according to my directions, by quilting thirteen folds of their strongest linen together. I was at the pains of making ropes and cables by twisting ten, twenty, or thirty of the thickest and strongest of theirs. A great stone that I happened to find, after a long search by the seashore, served me for an anchor. I had the tallow of three hundred cows for greasing my boat, and other uses. I was at incredible pains in cutting down some of the largest timber-trees for oars and masts, wherein I was, however, much assisted by His Majesty's ship-carpenters, who helped me in smoothing them after I had done the rough work.

In about a month, when all was prepared, I sent to receive His Majesty's commands and to take my leave. The Emperor and royal family came out of the palace; I lay down on my face to kiss his hand, which he very graciously gave me—so did the Empress and young Princes of the Blood. His Majesty presented me with fifty purses of two hundred *sprugs* apiece, together with his picture at full length, which I put immediately into one of my gloves to keep it from being hurt. The ceremonies at my departure were too many to trouble the reader with at this time.

I stored the boat with the carcasses of a hundred oxen and three hundred sheep, with bread and drink proportionable, and as much meat ready dressed as four hundred cooks could provide. I took with me six cows and two bulls alive, with as many ewes and rams, intending to carry them into my own country and propagate the breed. And to feed them on board I had a good bundle of hay and a bag of corn.[1] I would gladly have taken a dozen of the natives, but this was a thing the Emperor would by no means permit; and, besides a diligent search into my pockets, His Majesty engaged my honour not to carry away any of his subjects, although with their own consent and desire.

Having thus prepared all things as well as I was able, I set sail on the twenty-fourth day of September, 1701, at six in the morning; and when I had gone about four leagues to the northward, the wind being at southeast, at six in the evening I descried a small island about half a league to the north-west. I advanced forward and cast anchor on the lee-side of the island, which seemed to be uninhabited. I then took some refreshment and went to my rest. I slept well and, as I conjectured, at least six hours, for I found the day broke in two hours after I awaked. It was a clear night. I ate my breakfast before the sun was up; and, heaving anchor, the wind being favourable, I steered the same course that I had done the day before, wherein I was directed by my pocket compass. My intention was to reach, if possible, one of those islands which I had reason to believe lay to the northeast of Van Diemen's Land. I discovered nothing all that day; but upon the next, about three in the afternoon, when I had by my computation made twenty-four leagues from Blefuscu, I descried a sail steering to the southeast; my course was due east. I hailed her, but could get no answer; yet I found I gained upon her, for the wind slackened. I made all the sail I could, and in half an hour she spied me, then hung out her ancient[2] and discharged a gun. It is not easy to express the joy I was in upon the unexpected hope of once more seeing my beloved country, and the dear pledges[3] I left in it. The ship slackened her sails, and I came up with her between five and six in the evening, September 26th;

---

[1] *corn* Cereal grain such as wheat, barley, or rye.

[2] *ancient* Flag; insignia.

[3] *pledges* Children (i.e., Gulliver's children).

but my heart leaped within me to see her English colours. I put my cows and sheep into my coat-pockets and got on board with all my little cargo of provisions. The vessel was an English merchantman, returning from Japan by the North and South Seas;[1] the Captain, Mr. John Biddel of Deptford, a very civil man and an excellent sailor. We were now in the latitude of 30 degrees south; there were about fifty men in the ship; and here I met an old comrade of mine, one Peter Williams, who gave me a good character to the Captain. This gentleman treated me with kindness, and desired I would let him know what place I came from last, and whither I was bound; which I did in a few words, but he thought I was raving, and that the dangers I underwent had disturbed my head; whereupon I took my black cattle and sheep out of my pocket, which, after great astonishment, clearly convinced him of my veracity. I then showed him the gold given me by the Emperor of Blefuscu, together with His Majesty's picture at full length, and some other rarities of that country. I gave him two purses of two hundreds *sprugs* each and promised, when we arrived in England, to make him a present of a cow and a sheep big with young.

I shall not trouble the reader with a particular account of this voyage, which was very prosperous for the most part. We arrived in the Downs[2] on the 13th of April, 1702. I had only one misfortune, that the rats on board carried away one of my sheep; I found her bones in a hole, picked clean from the flesh. The rest of my cattle I got safe ashore, and set them a grazing in a bowling-green at Greenwich, where the fineness of the grass made them feed very heartily, though I had always feared the contrary; neither could I possibly have preserved them in so long a voyage if the Captain had not allowed me some of his best biscuit, which, rubbed to powder and mingled with water, was their constant food. The short time I continued in England, I made a considerable profit by showing my cattle to many persons of quality and others; and before I began my second voyage, I sold them for six hundred pounds. Since my last return I find the breed is considerably increased, especially the sheep, which I hope will prove much to the advantage of the woollen manufacture by the fineness of the fleeces.

I stayed but two months with my wife and family, for my insatiable desire of seeing foreign countries would suffer me to continue no longer. I left fifteen hundred pounds with my wife, and fixed her in a good house at Redriff. My remaining stock I carried with me, part in money and part in goods, in hopes to improve my fortunes. My eldest uncle John had left me an estate in land, near Epping, of about thirty pounds a-year, and I had a long lease of the Black Bull in Fetter Lane, which yielded me as much more, so that I was not in any danger of leaving my family upon the parish.[3] My son Johnny, named so after his uncle, was at the grammar school, and a towardly[4] child. My daughter Betty (who is now well married, and has children) was then at her needlework. I took leave of my wife, and boy and girl, with tears on both sides, and went on board the *Adventure*, a merchant-ship of three hundred tons, bound for Surat,[5] Captain John Nicholas of Liverpool, Commander. But my account of this voyage must be referred to the second part of my travels.

Part 2 – A Voyage to Brobdingnag

Chapter 1

(*A great storm described; the longboat sent to fetch water; the author goes with it to discover the country. He is left on shore, is seized by one of the natives and carried to a farmer's house. His reception, with several accidents that happened there. A description of the inhabitants.*)

Having been condemned by nature and fortune to active and restless life, in two months after my return I again left my native country, and took shipping in the Downs on the 20th day of June, 1702, in the *Adventure*, Captain John Nicholas, a Cornish man, Commander, bound for Surat. We had a very prosperous gale till we arrived at the Cape of Good Hope, where we landed for fresh water, but discovering a leak, we unshipped our goods and wintered there; for the Captain falling sick of an ague, we could not leave the

[1] *North and South Seas* North and South Pacific.

[2] *the Downs* Area of water off the coast of Kent.

[3] *upon the parish* The parish was responsible for taking care of the poor.

[4] *towardly* Promising.

[5] *Surat* Port in India, located on the Gulf of Cambay.

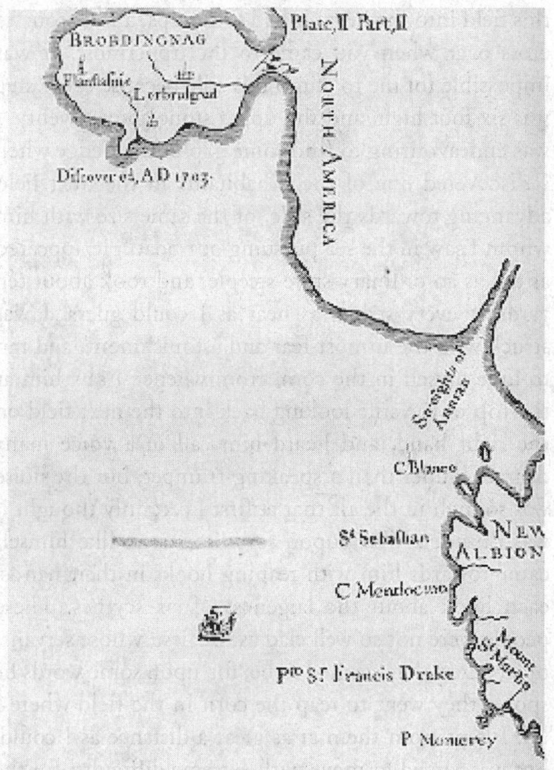

Map showing Brobdingnag in relation to North America, printed in the 1726 edition with no accompanying caption at the beginning of Part 2.

Cape till the end of March. We then set sail, and had a good voyage till we passed the Straits of Madagascar; but having got northward of that island, and to about five degrees south latitude, the winds, which in those seas are observed to blow a constant equal gale between the north and west from the beginning of December to the beginning of May, on the 19th of April began to blow with much greater violence and more westerly than usual, continuing so for twenty days together, during which time we were driven a little to the east of the Molucca Islands and about three degrees northward of the Line,[1] as our Captain found by an observation he took the 2nd of May, at which time the wind ceased, and it was a perfect calm, whereat I was not a little rejoiced. But he, being a man well experienced in the navigation of those seas, bid us all prepare against a storm, which accordingly happened the day following: for the southern wind, called the southern monsoon, began to set in.

Finding it was likely to overblow, we took in our spritsail and stood by to hand the foresail; but making foul weather, we looked the guns were all fast, and handed the mizzen. The ship lay very broad off, so we thought it better spooning before the sea than trying or hulling. We reefed the foresail and set him, and hauled aft the foresheet; the helm was hard a-weather. The ship wore bravely. We belayed the fore-downhaul; but the sail was split, and we hauled down the yard, and got the sail into the ship, and unbound all the things clear of it. It was a very fierce storm; the sea broke strange and dangerous. We hauled off upon the lanyard of the whipstaff, and helped the man at the helm. We would not get down our topmast, but let all stand, because she scudded before the sea very well, and we knew that the topmast being aloft, the ship was the wholesomer, and made better way through the sea, seeing we had searoom. When the storm was over, we set foresail and mainsail, and brought the ship to. Then we set the mizzen, main topsail, and the fore topsail. Our course was east-northeast, the wind was at southwest. We got the starboard tacks aboard; we cast off our weather braces and lifts; we set in the lee braces, and hauled forward by the weather-bowlings,[2] and hauled them tight, and belayed them, and hauled over the mizzen tack to windward, and kept her full and by as near as she would lie.[3]

During this storm, which was followed by a strong wind west-southwest, we were carried, by my computation, about five hundred leagues to the east, so that the oldest sailor on board could not tell in what part of the world we were. Our provisions held out well, our ship was staunch, and our crew all in good health; but we lay in the utmost distress for water. We thought it best to hold on the same course, rather than turn more northerly, which might have brought us to the northwest part of Great Tartary[4] and into the Frozen Sea.[5]

[1] *Line* Equator.

[2] *weather-bowlings* I.e., bowlines.

[3] *Finding it.... would lie* This paragraph is meant to satirize the then-prevalent use of nautical jargon in popular accounts of voyages. It is taken almost verbatim from Samuel Sturmy's *Mariner's Magazine.*

[4] *Great Tartary* Siberia.

[5] *Frozen Sea* Arctic Ocean.

On the 16th day of June, 1703, a boy on the top-mast discovered land. On the 17th, we came in full view of a great island or continent (for we knew not whether), on the south side whereof was a small neck of land jutting out into the sea, and a creek too shallow to hold a ship of above one hundred tons. We cast anchor within a league of this creek, and our captain sent a dozen of his men well armed in the long-boat, with vessels for water, if any could be found. I desired his leave to go with them, that I might see the country and make what discoveries I could. When we came to land we saw no river or spring, nor any sign of inhabitants. Our men therefore wandered on the shore to find out some fresh water near the sea, and I walked alone about a mile on the other side, where I observed the country all barren and rocky. I now began to be weary, and seeing nothing to entertain my curiosity, I returned gently down towards the creek; and the sea being full in my view, I saw our men already got into the boat, and rowing for life to the ship. I was going to holler after them, although it had been to little purpose, when I observed a huge creature walking after them in the sea as fast as he could; he waded not much deeper than his knees, and took prodigious strides, but our men had the start of him half a league, and the sea thereabouts being full of sharp-pointed rocks, the monster was not able to overtake the boat. This I was afterwards told, for I durst not stay to see the issue of the adventure; but ran as fast as I could the way I first went, and then climbed up a steep hill, which gave me some prospect of the country. I found it fully cultivated; but that which first surprised me was the length of the grass, which, in those grounds that seemed to be kept for hay, was about twenty feet high.[1]

I fell into a high road, for so I took it to be, though it served to the inhabitants only as a footpath through a field of barley. Here I walked on for some time, but could see little on either side, it being now near harvest, and the corn rising at least forty feet. I was an hour walking to the end of this field, which was fenced in with a hedge of at least one hundred and twenty feet high, and the trees so lofty that I could make no computation of their altitude. There was a stile to pass from this field into the next. It had four steps, and a stone to cross over when you came to the uppermost. It was impossible for me to climb this stile because every step was six foot high, and the upper stone above twenty. I was endeavouring to find some gap in the hedge when I discovered one of the inhabitants in the next field advancing towards the stile, of the same size with him whom I saw in the sea pursuing our boat. He appeared as tall as an ordinary spire-steeple, and took about ten yards at every stride, as near as I could guess. I was struck with the utmost fear and astonishment, and ran to hide myself in the corn, from whence I saw him at the top of the stile looking back into the next field on the right hand, and heard him call in a voice many degrees louder than a speaking-trumpet; but the noise was so high in the air that at first I certainly thought it was thunder. Whereupon seven monsters like himself came towards him with reaping hooks in their hands, each hook about the largeness of six scythes. These people were not so well clad as the first, whose servants or labourers they seemed to be; for, upon some words he spoke, they went to reap the corn in the field where I lay. I kept from them at as great a distance as I could, but was forced to move with extreme difficulty, for the stalks of the corn were sometimes not above a foot distant, so that I could hardly squeeze my body betwixt them. However, I made a shift to go forward till I came to a part of the field where the corn had been laid[2] by the rain and wind. Here it was impossible for me to advance a step, for the stalks were so interwoven that I could not creep through, and the beards of the fallen ears so strong and pointed that they pierced through my clothes into my flesh. At the same time I heard the reapers not a hundred yards behind me. Being quite dispirited with toil, and wholly overcome by grief and despair, I lay down between two ridges and heartily wished I might there end my days. I bemoaned my desolate widow and fatherless children; I lamented my own folly and wilfulness in attempting a second voyage, against the advice of all my friends and relations. In this terrible agitation of mind I could not forbear thinking of Lilliput, whose inhabitants looked upon me as the greatest prodigy that ever appeared in the world; where I was able to draw an imperial fleet in my hand, and perform those other actions which will be recorded

[1] *twenty feet high* While in Lilliput the scale to our world is roughly 1 to 12, in Brobdingnag it is approximately (though less consistently) 12 to 1.

[2] *laid* Knocked flat.

forever in the chronicles of that empire, while posterity shall hardly believe them, although attested by millions. I reflected what a mortification it must prove to me to appear as inconsiderable in this nation as one single Lilliputian would be among us. But this I conceived was to be the least of my misfortunes; for, as human creatures are observed to be more savage and cruel in proportion to their bulk, what could I expect but to be a morsel in the mouth of the first among these enormous barbarians that should happen to seize me? Undoubtedly philosophers are in the right when they tell us that nothing is great or little otherwise than by comparison. It might have pleased fortune to have let the Lilliputians find some nation where the people were as diminutive with respect to them as they were to me. And who knows but that even this prodigious race of mortals might be equally overmatched in some distant part of the world, whereof we have yet no discovery.

Scared and confounded as I was, I could not forbear going on with these reflections when one of the reapers, approaching within ten yards of the ridge where I lay, made me apprehend that with the next step I should be squashed to death under his foot, or cut in two with his reaping-hook. And therefore, when he was again about to move, I screamed as loud as fear could make me. Whereupon the huge creature trod short, and, looking round about under him for some time, at last espied me as I lay on the ground. He considered awhile, with the caution of one who endeavours to lay hold on a small dangerous animal in such a manner that it shall not be able either to scratch or bite him, as I myself have sometimes done with a weasel in England. At length he ventured to take me behind, by the middle, between his forefinger and thumb, and brought me within three yards of his eyes, that he might behold my shape more perfectly. I guessed his meaning, and my good fortune gave me so much presence of mind that I resolved not to struggle in the least as he held me in the air above sixty feet from the ground, although he grievously pinched my sides for fear I should slip through his fingers. All I ventured was to raise mine eyes towards the sun, and place my hands together in a supplicating posture, and to speak some words in a humble melancholy tone, suitable to the condition I then was in. For I apprehended every moment that he would dash me against the ground, as we usually do any little hateful animal which we have a mind to destroy. But my good star would have it that he appeared pleased with my voice and gestures, and began to look upon me as a curiosity, much wondering to hear me pronounce articulate words, although he could not understand them. In the meantime I was not able to forbear groaning and shedding tears and turning my head towards my sides, letting him know, as well as I could, how cruelly I was hurt by the pressure of his thumb and finger. He seemed to apprehend my meaning; for, lifting up the lappet[1] of his coat, he put me gently into it, and immediately ran along with me to his master, who was a substantial[2] farmer, and the same person I had first seen in the field.

The farmer, having (as I suppose by their talk) received such an account of me as his servant could give him, took a piece of a small straw, about the size of a walking-staff, and therewith lifted up the lappets of my coat, which it seems he thought to be some kind of covering that nature had given me. He blew my hairs aside to take a better view of my face. He called his hinds[3] about him and asked them, as I afterwards learned, whether they had ever seen in the fields any little creature that resembled me. He then placed me softly on the ground upon all four, but I got immediately up and walked slowly backward and forward, to let those people see I had no intent to run away. They all sat down in a circle about me, the better to observe my motions. I pulled off my hat and made a low bow towards the farmer; I fell on my knees, and lifted up my hands and eyes, and spoke several words as loud as I could; I took a purse of gold out of my pocket and humbly presented it to him. He received it on the palm of his hand, then applied it close to his eye to see what it was, and afterwards turned it several times with the point of a pin (which he took out of his sleeve), but could make nothing of it. Whereupon I made a sign that he should place his hand on the ground. I then took the purse, and, opening it, poured all the gold into his palm. There were six Spanish pieces of four pistoles each, beside twenty or thirty smaller coins. I saw him wet the tip of his little finger upon his tongue and take

[1] *lappet* Flap or fold; lapel.

[2] *substantial* Well established, well-to-do.

[3] *hinds* Servants, farm workers.

up one of my largest pieces, and then another, but he seemed to be wholly ignorant what they were. He made me a sign to put them again into my purse, and the purse again into my pocket, which, after offering it to him several times, I thought it best to do.

The farmer by this time was convinced I must be a rational creature. He spoke often to me, but the sound of his voice pierced my ears like that of a water mill, yet his words were articulate enough. I answered as loud as I could in several languages, and he often laid his ear within two yards of me, but all in vain, for we were wholly unintelligible to each other. He then sent his servants to their work and, taking his handkerchief out of his pocket, he doubled and spread it on his left hand, which he placed flat on the ground with the palm upward, making me a sign to step into it, as I could easily do, for it was not above a foot in thickness. I thought it my part to obey, and, for fear of falling, laid myself at full length upon the handkerchief, with the remainder of which he lapped me up to the head for further security, and in this manner carried me home to his house. There he called his wife, and showed me to her, but she screamed and ran back, as women in England do at the sight of a toad or a spider. However, when she had a while seen my behaviour, and how well I observed the signs her husband made, she was soon reconciled, and by degrees grew extremely tender of me.

It was about twelve at noon, and a servant brought in dinner. It was only one substantial dish of meat (fit for the plain condition of a husbandman[1]) in a dish of about four-and-twenty foot diameter. The company were the farmer and his wife, three children, and an old grandmother. When they were sat down, the farmer placed me at some distance from him on the table, which was thirty feet high from the floor. I was in a terrible fright, and kept as far as I could from the edge, for fear of falling. The wife minced a bit of meat, then crumbled some bread on a trencher and placed it before me. I made her a low bow, took out my knife and fork, and fell to eat, which gave them exceeding delight. The mistress sent her maid for a small dram cup, which held about two gallons, and filled it with drink; I took up the vessel with much difficulty in both hands, and in a most respectful manner drank to her ladyship's health, expressing the words as loud as I could in English, which made the company laugh so heartily that I was almost deafened with the noise. This liquor tasted like a small[2] cider, and was not unpleasant. Then the master made me a sign to come to his trencher side; but as I walked on the table, being in great surprise all the time, as the indulgent reader will easily conceive and excuse, I happened to stumble against a crust, and fell flat on my face, but received no hurt. I got up immediately, and observing the good people to be in much concern, I took my hat (which I held under my arm out of good manners) and waving it over my head, made three huzzas to show I had got no mischief by my fall. But advancing forward towards my master (as I shall henceforth call him), his youngest son, who sat next to him, an arch boy of about ten years old, took me up by the legs and held me so high in the air, that I trembled every limb; but his father snatched me from him, and at the same time gave him such a box on the left ear as would have felled an European troop of horse to the earth, ordering him to be taken from the table. But being afraid the boy might owe me a spite, and well remembering how mischievous all children among us naturally are to sparrows, rabbits, young kittens, and puppy dogs, I fell on my knees and, pointing to the boy, made my master to understand, as well as I could, that I desired his son might be pardoned. The father complied, and the lad took his seat again, whereupon I went to him and kissed his hand, which my master took, and made him stroke me gently with it.

In the midst of dinner, my mistress's favourite cat leaped into her lap. I heard a noise behind me like that of a dozen stocking-weavers at work, and, turning my head, I found it proceeded from the purring of that animal, who seemed to be three times larger than an ox, as I computed by the view of her head and one of her paws while her mistress was feeding and stroking her. The fierceness of this creature's countenance altogether discomposed me, though I stood at the farther end of the table, above fifty feet off, and although my mistress held her fast for fear she might give a spring and seize me in her talons. But it happened there was no danger, for the cat took not the least notice of me when my master placed me within three yards of her. And as I have been always told, and found true by experience in my travels, that flying or discovering fear before a fierce

[1] *husbandman* Farmer.

[2] *small* Weak, of low alcohol content.

animal is a certain way to make it pursue or attack you, so I resolved in this dangerous juncture to show no manner of concern. I walked with intrepidity five or six times before the very head of the cat, and came within half a yard of her; whereupon she drew herself back, as if she were more afraid of me. I had less apprehension concerning the dogs, whereof three or four came into the room, as it is usual in farmers' houses; one of which was a mastiff, equal in bulk to four elephants, and another a greyhound, somewhat taller than the mastiff but not so large.

When dinner was almost done, the nurse came in with a child of a year old in her arms, who immediately spied me and began a squall that you might have heard from London Bridge to Chelsea, after the usual oratory of infants, to get me for a plaything. The mother, out of pure indulgence, took me up and put me towards the child, who presently seized me by the middle and got my head into his mouth, where I roared so loud that the urchin was frightened and let me drop, and I should infallibly have broke my neck if the mother had not held her apron under me. The nurse, to quiet her babe, made use of a rattle which was a kind of hollow vessel filled with great stones, and fastened by a cable to the child's waist; but all in vain; so that she was forced to apply the last remedy by giving it suck. I must confess no object ever disgusted me so much as the sight of her monstrous breast, which I cannot tell what to compare with so as to give the curious reader an idea of its bulk, shape, and colour. It stood prominent six feet, and could not be less than sixteen in circumference. The nipple was about half the bigness of my head, and the hue both of that and the dug[1] so varied with spots, pimples, and freckles, that nothing could appear more nauseous: for I had a near sight of her, she sitting down the more conveniently to give suck, and I standing on the table. This made me reflect upon the fair skins of our English ladies, who appear so beautiful to us only because they are of our own size, and their defects not to be seen but through a magnifying glass, where we find by experiment that the smoothest and whitest skins look rough, and coarse, and ill-coloured.

I remember when I was at Lilliput the complexion of those diminutive people appeared to me the fairest in the world; and, talking upon this subject with a person of learning there, who was an intimate friend of mine, he said that my face appeared much fairer and smoother when he looked on me from the ground than it did upon a nearer view, when I took him up in my hand and brought him close, which he confessed was at first a very shocking sight. He said he could discover great holes in my skin, that the stumps of my beard were ten times stronger than the bristles of a boar, and my complexion made up of several colours altogether disagreeable—although I must beg leave to say for myself that I am as fair as most of my sex and country, and very little sunburnt by all my travels. On the other side, discoursing of the ladies in that Emperor's court, he used to tell me one had freckles, another too wide a mouth, a third too large a nose; nothing of which I was able to distinguish. I confess this reflection was obvious enough, which however I could not forbear, lest the reader might think those vast creatures were actually deformed; for I must do them the justice to say, they are a comely race of people, and particularly the features of my master's countenance, although he was but a farmer, when I beheld him from the height of sixty feet, appeared very well proportioned.

When dinner was done my master went out to his labourers and, as I could discover by his voice and gesture, gave his wife strict charge to take care of me. I was very much tired and disposed to sleep, which my mistress perceiving, she put me on her own bed and covered me with a clean white handkerchief, but larger and coarser than the mainsail of a man-of-war.

I slept about two hours, and dreamt I was at home with my wife and children, which aggravated my sorrows when I awaked and found myself alone in a vast room between two and three hundred feet wide, and above two hundred high, lying in a bed twenty yards wide. My mistress was gone about her household affairs, and had locked me in. The bed was eight yards from the floor. Some natural necessities required me to get down; I durst not presume to call, and if I had, it would have been in vain with such a voice as mine at so great a distance from the room where I lay to the kitchen where the family kept. While I was under these circumstances, two rats crept up the curtains and ran smelling backwards and forwards on the bed. One of them came up almost to my face, whereupon I rose in a fright and

[1] *dug* Breast.

drew out my hanger[1] to defend myself. These horrible animals had the boldness to attack me on both sides, and one of them held his forefeet at my collar, but I had the good fortune to rip up his belly before he could do me any mischief. He fell down at my feet, and the other, seeing the fate of his comrade, made his escape, but not without one good wound on the back, which I gave him as he fled, and made the blood run trickling from him. After this exploit I walked gently to and fro on the bed to recover my breath and loss of spirits. These creatures were of the size of a large mastiff, but infinitely more nimble and fierce, so that if I had taken off my belt before I went to sleep, I must have infallibly been torn to pieces and devoured. I measured the tail of the dead rat and found it to be two yards long, wanting an inch; but it went against my stomach to drag the carcass off the bed, where it lay still bleeding. I observed it had yet some life, but with a strong slash across the neck I thoroughly dispatched it.

Soon after my mistress came into the room, who seeing me all bloody, ran and took me up in her hand. I pointed to the dead rat, smiling and making other signs to show I was not hurt, whereat she was extremely rejoiced, calling the maid to take up the dead rat with a pair of tongs and throw it out of the window. Then she set me on a table, where I showed her my hanger all bloody and, wiping it on the lappet of my coat, returned it to the scabbard. I was pressed to do more than one thing, which another could not do for me, and therefore endeavoured to make my mistress understand that I desired to be set down on the floor; which after she had done, my bashfulness would not suffer me to express myself farther than by pointing to the door and bowing several times. The good woman with much difficulty at last perceived what I would be at and, taking me up again in her hand, walked into the garden, where she set me down. I went on one side about two hundred yards and, beckoning to her not to look or to follow me, I hid myself between two leaves of sorrel, and there discharged the necessities of nature.

I hope the gentle reader will excuse me for dwelling on these and the like particulars, which, however insignificant they may appear to groveling, vulgar minds, yet will certainly help a philosopher to enlarge his thoughts and imagination, and apply them to the benefit of public as well as private life, which was my sole design in presenting this and other accounts of my travels to the world; wherein I have been chiefly studious of truth, without affecting any ornaments of learning or of style. But the whole scene of this voyage made so strong an impression on my mind, and is so deeply fixed in my memory, that in committing it to paper I did not omit one material circumstance; however, upon a strict review I blotted out several passages of less moment which were in my first copy, for fear of being censured as tedious and trifling, whereof travellers are often, perhaps not without justice, accused.

CHAPTER 2

(*A description of the farmer's daughter. The author carried to a market town, and then to the metropolis. The particulars of his journey.*)

My mistress had a daughter of nine years old, a child of towardly parts[2] for her age, very dexterous at her needle and skilful in dressing her baby.[3] Her mother and she contrived to fit up the baby's cradle for me against night: the cradle was put into a small drawer of a cabinet, and the drawer placed upon a hanging shelf for fear of the rats. This was my bed all the time I stayed with those people, though made more convenient by degrees as I began to learn their language and make my wants known. This young girl was so handy that after I had once or twice pulled off my clothes before her, she was able to dress and undress me, though I never gave her that trouble when she would let me do either myself. She made me seven shirts, and some other linen, of as fine cloth as could be got, which indeed was coarser than sackcloth; and these she constantly washed for me with her own hands. She was likewise my schoolmistress to teach me the language: when I pointed to anything, she told me the name of it in her own tongue, so that in a few days I was able to call for whatever I had a mind to. She was very good-natured, and not above forty feet high, being little for her age. She gave me the name of *Grildrig*, which the family took up, and afterwards the whole kingdom. The word imports what the Latins call

[1] *hanger* Short sword hung from the belt.

[2] *towardly parts* Promising abilities.

[3] *baby* Doll.

nanunculus, the Italians *homunceletino*,[1] and the English *mannikin*. To her I chiefly owe my preservation in that country: we never parted while I was there; I called her my *Glumdalclitch*, or little nurse, and should be guilty of great ingratitude if I omitted this honourable mention of her care and affection towards me, which I heartily wish it lay in my power to requite as she deserves, instead of being the innocent but unhappy instrument of her disgrace, as I have too much reason to fear.

It now began to be known and talked of in the neighbourhood that my master had found a strange animal in the field, about the bigness of a *splacknuck*, but exactly shaped in every part like a human creature, which it likewise imitated in all its actions: seemed to speak in a little language of its own, had already learned several words of theirs, went erect upon two legs, was tame and gentle, would come when it was called, do whatever it was bid, had the finest limbs in the world, and a complexion fairer than a nobleman's daughter of three years old. Another farmer who lived hard by, and was a particular friend of my master, came on a visit on purpose to inquire into the truth of this story. I was immediately produced and placed upon a table, where I walked as I was commanded, drew my hanger, put it up again, made my reverence to my master's guest, asked him in his own language how he did, and told him he was welcome, just as my little nurse had instructed me. This man, who was old and dim-sighted, put on his spectacles to behold me better, at which I could not forbear laughing very heartily, for his eyes appeared like the full moon shining into a chamber at two windows. Our people, who discovered the cause of my mirth, bore me company in laughing, at which the old fellow was fool enough to be angry and out of countenance. He had the character of a great miser, and, to my misfortune, he well deserved it by the cursed advice he gave my master to show me as a sight upon a market-day in the next town, which was half an hour's riding, about two-and-twenty miles from our house. I guessed there was some mischief when I observed my master and his friend whispering together, sometimes pointing at me; and my fears made me fancy that I overheard and understood some of their words. But the next morning Glumdalclitch, my little nurse, told me the whole matter, which she had cunningly picked out from her mother. The poor girl laid me on her bosom and fell a-weeping with shame and grief. She apprehended some mischief would happen to me from rude vulgar folks, who might squeeze me to death, or break one of my limbs by taking me in their hands. She had also observed how modest I was in my nature, how nicely I regarded my honour, and what an indignity I should conceive it to be exposed for money as a public spectacle to the meanest of the people. She said her papa and mamma had promised that Grildrig should be hers, but now she found they meant to serve her as they did last year, when they pretended to give her a lamb, and yet as soon as it was fat sold it to a butcher. For my own part, I may truly affirm that I was less concerned than my nurse. I had a strong hope, which never left me, that I should one day recover my liberty: and as to the ignominy of being carried about for a monster, I considered myself to be a perfect stranger in the country, and that such a misfortune could never be charged upon me as a reproach if ever I should return to England, since the King of Great Britain himself, in my condition, must have undergone the same distress.

My master, pursuant to the advice of his friend, carried me in a box the next market day to the neighbouring town, and took along with him his little daughter, my nurse, upon a pillion[2] behind him. The box was close on every side, with a little door for me to go in and out and a few gimlet holes[3] to let in air. The girl had been so careful as to put the quilt of her baby's bed into it for me to lie down on. However, I was terribly shaken and discomposed in this journey, though it was but of half an hour, for the horse went about forty feet at every step and trotted so high that the agitation was equal to the rising and falling of a ship in a great storm, but much more frequent. Our journey was somewhat farther than from London to St. Alban's.[4] My master alighted at an inn which he used to frequent; and after consulting awhile with the inn-keeper, and making some necessary preparations, he hired the *grultrud*, or crier, to give notice through the town of a strange

[1] *Latins ... homunceletino* These words are Swift's own inventions.

[2] *pillion* Cushion attached to the back of a saddle on which a second person could sit.

[3] *gimlet holes* Holes made by a gimlet, a sharp piercing or boring tool.

[4] *from London to St. Alban's* A distance of approximately 20 miles.

creature to be seen at the Sign of the Green Eagle, not so big as a *splacknuck* (an animal in that country very finely shaped, about six feet long), and in every part of the body resembling a human creature; could speak several words and perform a hundred diverting tricks.

I was placed upon a table in the largest room of the inn, which might be near three hundred feet square. My little nurse stood on a low stool close to the table to take care of me and direct what I should do. My master, to avoid a crowd, would suffer only thirty people at a time to see me. I walked about on the table as the girl commanded; she asked me questions, as far as she knew my understanding of the language reached, and I answered them as loud as I could. I turned about several times to the company, paid my humble respects, said they were welcome, and used some other speeches I had been taught. I took up a thimble filled with liquor, which Glumdalclitch had given me for a cup, and drank their health. I drew out my hanger and flourished with it after the manner of fencers in England. My nurse gave me a part of a straw, which I exercised as a pike, having learnt the art in my youth. I was that day shown to twelve sets of company, and as often forced to act over again the same fopperies, till I was half dead with weariness and vexation; for those who had seen me made such wonderful reports that the people were ready to break down the doors to come in. My master for his own interest would not suffer any one to touch me except my nurse; and, to prevent danger, benches were set round the table at such a distance as to put me out of every body's reach. However, an unlucky schoolboy aimed a hazelnut directly at my head, which very narrowly missed me; otherwise, it came with so much violence that it would have infallibly knocked out my brains, for it was almost as large as a small pumpion.[1] But I had the satisfaction to see the young rogue well beaten and turned out of the room.

My master gave public notice that he would show me again the next market day, and in the meantime he prepared a convenient vehicle for me, which he had reason enough to do, for I was so tired with my first journey, and with entertaining company for eight hours together, that I could hardly stand upon my legs or speak a word. It was at least three days before I recovered my strength; and that I might have no rest at home, all the neighbouring gentlemen from a hundred miles round, hearing of my fame, came to see me at my master's own house. There could not be fewer than thirty persons with their wives and children (for the country is very populous), and my master demanded the rate of a full room whenever he showed me at home, although it were only to a single family, so that for some time I had but little ease every day of the week (except Wednesday, which is their Sabbath), although I were not carried to the town.

My master, finding how profitable I was likely to be, resolved to carry me to the most considerable cities of the kingdom. Having therefore provided himself with all things necessary for a long journey, and settled his affairs at home, he took leave of his wife; and upon the 17th of August, 1703, about two months after my arrival, we set out for the metropolis, situated near the middle of that empire, and about three thousand miles distance from our house. My master made his daughter Glumdalclitch ride behind him. She carried me on her lap in a box tied about her waist. The girl had lined it on all sides with the softest cloth she could get, well quilted underneath, furnished it with her baby's bed, provided me with linen and other necessaries, and made everything as convenient as she could. We had no other company but a boy of the house, who rode after us with the luggage.

My master's design was to show me in all the towns by the way, and to step out of the road for fifty or a hundred miles to any village or person of quality's house where he might expect custom. We made easy journeys of not above seven or eight score miles a-day, for Glumdalclitch, on purpose to spare me, complained she was tired with the trotting of the horse. She often took me out of my box at my own desire, to give me air and show me the country, but always held me fast by leading strings.[2] We passed over five or six rivers many degrees broader and deeper than the Nile or the Ganges, and there was hardly a rivulet so small as the Thames at London Bridge. We were ten weeks in our journey, and I was shown in eighteen large towns, besides many villages and private families.

On the 26th day of October we arrived at the metropolis, called in their language *Lorbrulgrud*, or

[1] *pumpion* Pumpkin.

[2] *leading strings* Strings that were attached to small children in order to guide and support them while they were learning to walk.

Pride of the Universe. My master took a lodging in the principal street of the city, not far from the royal palace, and put out bills[1] in the usual form, containing an exact description of my person and parts. He hired a large room between three and four hundred feet wide. He provided a table sixty feet in diameter, upon which I was to act my part, and palisadoed[2] it round three feet from the edge, and as many high, to prevent my falling over. I was shown ten times a day to the wonder and satisfaction of all people. I could now speak the language tolerably well, and perfectly understood every word that was spoken to me. Besides, I had learnt their alphabet, and could make a shift to explain a sentence here and there; for Glumdalclitch had been my instructor while we were at home, and at leisure hours during our journey. She carried a little book in her pocket, not much larger than a Sanson's *Atlas*;[3] it was a common treatise for the use of young girls, giving a short account of their religion. Out of this she taught me my letters and interpreted the words.

CHAPTER 3

(*The author sent for to court. The Queen buys him of his master the farmer, and presents him to the King. He disputes with His Majesty's great scholars. An apartment at court provided for the author. He is in high favour with the Queen. He stands up for the honour of his own country. His quarrels with the Queen's dwarf.*)

The frequent labours I underwent every day made in a few weeks a very considerable change in my health: the more my master got by me, the more insatiable he grew. I had quite lost my stomach, and was almost reduced to a skeleton. The farmer observed it and, concluding I must soon die, resolved to make as good a hand of me as he could. While he was thus reasoning and resolving with himself, a *sardral*, or gentleman usher, came from court, commanding my master to carry me immediately thither for the diversion of the Queen and her ladies. Some of the latter had already been to see me and reported strange things of my beauty, behaviour, and good sense. Her Majesty and those who attended her were beyond measure delighted with my demeanour. I fell on my knees and begged the honour of kissing her Imperial foot; but this gracious princess held out her little finger towards me after I was set on the table, which I embraced in both my arms, and put the tip of it with the utmost respect to my lip. She made me some general questions about my country and my travels, which I answered as distinctly and in as few words as I could. She asked whether I could be content to live at court. I bowed down to the board of the table, and humbly answered that I was my master's slave, but, if I were at my own disposal, I should be proud to devote my life to Her Majesty's service. She then asked my master whether he was willing to sell me at a good price. He, who apprehended I could not live a month, was ready enough to part with me, and demanded a thousand pieces of gold, which were ordered him on the spot, each piece being about the bigness of eight hundred moidores;[4] but, allowing for the proportion of all things between that country and Europe, and the high price of gold among them, was hardly so great a sum as a thousand guineas would be in England. I then said to the Queen, since I was now Her Majesty's most humble creature and vassal, I must beg the favour that Glumdalclitch, who had always tended me with so much care and kindness, and understood to do it so well, might be admitted into her service and continue to be my nurse and instructor. Her Majesty agreed to my petition and easily got the farmer's consent, who was glad enough to have his daughter preferred at court, and the poor girl herself was not able to hide her joy. My late master withdrew, bidding me farewell and saying he had left me in a good service; to which I replied not a word, only making him a slight bow.

The Queen observed my coldness and, when the farmer was gone out of the apartment, asked me the reason. I made bold to tell Her Majesty that I owed no other obligation to my late master than his not dashing out the brains of a poor harmless creature, found by chance in his fields; which obligation was amply recompensed by the gain he had made in showing me through half the kingdom, and the price he had now sold me for. That the life I had since led was laborious enough to kill

[1] *bills* Advertisements.

[2] *palisadoed* Enclosed; fenced in.

[3] *Sanson's Atlas* Book approximately 20 inches by 20 inches. Sanson was a French cartographer whose atlases were made in the largest possible book size.

[4] *moidores* Portuguese gold coins.

an animal of ten times my strength. That my health was much impaired by the continual drudgery of entertaining the rabble every hour of the day; and that if my master had not thought my life in danger, Her Majesty would not have got so cheap a bargain. But as I was out of all fear of being ill-treated under the protection of so great and good an Empress, the Ornament of Nature, the Darling of the World, the Delight of her Subjects, the Phoenix of the Creation, so I hoped my late master's apprehensions would appear to be groundless, for I already found my spirits revive by the influence of her most august presence.

This was the sum of my speech, delivered with great improprieties and hesitation. The latter part was altogether framed in the style peculiar to that people, whereof I learned some phrases from Glumdalclitch while she was carrying me to court.

The Queen, giving great allowance for my defectiveness in speaking, was, however, surprised at so much wit and good sense in so diminutive an animal. She took me in her own hand and carried me to the King, who was then retired to his cabinet.[1] His Majesty, a prince of much gravity, and austere countenance, not well observing my shape at first view, asked the Queen after a cold manner how long it was since she grew fond of a *splacknuck*; for such it seems he took me to be, as I lay upon my breast in Her Majesty's right hand. But this princess, who has an infinite deal of wit and humour, set me gently on my feet upon the scrutore[2] and commanded me to give His Majesty an account of myself, which I did in a very few words; and Glumdalclitch, who attended at the cabinet door and could not endure I should be out of her sight, being admitted, confirmed all that had passed from my arrival at her father's house.

The King, although he be as learned a person as any in his dominions, had been educated in the study of philosophy,[3] and particularly mathematics; yet when he observed my shape exactly, and saw me walk erect, before I began to speak, conceived I might be a piece of clockwork (which is in that country arrived to a very great perfection) contrived by some ingenious artist.[4] But when he heard my voice, and found what I delivered to be regular and rational, he could not conceal his astonishment. He was by no means satisfied with the relation I gave him of the manner I came into his kingdom, but thought it a story concerted between Glumdalclitch and her father, who had taught me a set of words to make me sell at a better price. Upon this imagination, he put several other questions to me, and still received rational answers no otherwise defective than by a foreign accent and an imperfect knowledge in the language, with some rustic phrases which I had learned at the farmer's house, and did not suit the polite style of a court.

His Majesty sent for three great scholars, who were then in their weekly waiting (according to the custom in that country). These gentlemen, after they had a while examined my shape with much nicety, were of different opinions concerning me. They all agreed that I could not be produced according to the regular laws of nature because I was not framed with a capacity of preserving my life, either by swiftness, or climbing of trees, or digging holes in the earth. They observed by my teeth, which they viewed with great exactness, that I was a carnivorous animal; yet most quadrupeds being an overmatch for me, and field mice, with some others, too nimble, they could not imagine how I should be able to support myself, unless I fed upon snails and other insects, which they offered, by many learned arguments, to evince that I could not possibly do. One of these virtuosi seemed to think that I might be an embryo, or abortive birth. But this opinion was rejected by the other two, who observed my limbs to be perfect and finished; and that I had lived several years, as it was manifest from my beard, the stumps whereof they plainly discovered through a magnifying glass. They would not allow me to be a dwarf because my littleness was beyond all degrees of comparison; for the Queen's favourite dwarf, the smallest ever known in that kingdom, was near thirty feet high. After much debate, they concluded unanimously that I was only *relplum scalcath*, which is interpreted literally, *lusus naturae*;[5] a determination exactly agreeable to the modern philosophy of Europe, whose professors, disdaining the old evasion of occult causes, whereby the followers of Aristotle endea-

[1] *cabinet* Boudoir, private chamber or apartment.

[2] *scrutore* Escritoire, a small writing desk.

[3] *philosophy* Science, or natural philosophy.

[4] *artist* Artisan, craftsman.

[5] *lusus naturae* Freak of nature. Swift here is criticizing those who referred to all things unfamiliar as resulting from "occult causes."

voured in vain to disguise their ignorance, have invented this wonderful solution of all difficulties, to the unspeakable advancement of human knowledge.

After this decisive conclusion, I entreated to be heard a word or two. I applied myself to the King, and assured His Majesty that I came from a country which abounded with several millions of both sexes, and of my own stature; where the animals, trees, and houses were all in proportion, and where, by consequence, I might be as able to defend myself and to find sustenance as any of His Majesty's subjects could do here; which I took for a full answer to those gentlemen's arguments. To this they only replied with a smile of contempt, saying that the farmer had instructed me very well in my lesson. The King, who had a much better understanding, dismissing his learned men, sent for the farmer, who by good fortune was not yet gone out of town. Having therefore first examined him privately, and then confronted him with me and the young girl, His Majesty began to think that what we told him might possibly be true. He desired the Queen to order that a particular care should be taken of me; and was of opinion that Glumdalclitch should still continue in her office of tending me, because he observed we had a great affection for each other. A convenient apartment was provided for her at court; she had a sort of governess appointed to take care of her education, a maid to dress her, and two other servants for menial offices; but the care of me was wholly appropriated to herself. The Queen commanded her own cabinet-maker to contrive a box that might serve me for a bedchamber, after the model that Glumdalclitch and I should agree upon. This man was a most ingenious artist and, according to my direction, in three weeks finished for me a wooden chamber of sixteen feet square and twelve high, with sash-windows, a door, and two closets, like a London bedchamber. The board that made the ceiling was to be lifted up and down by two hinges, to put in a bed ready furnished by Her Majesty's upholsterer, which Glumdalclitch took out every day to air, made it with her own hands, and, letting it down at night, locked up the roof over me. A nice[1] workman, who was famous for little curiosities, undertook to make me two chairs, with backs and frames, of a substance not unlike ivory, and two tables, with a cabinet to put my things in. The room was quilted on all sides, as well as the floor and the ceiling, to prevent any accident from the carelessness of those who carried me, and to break the force of a jolt when I went in a coach. I desired a lock for my door to prevent rats and mice from coming in. The smith, after several attempts, made the smallest that ever was seen among them, for I have known a larger at the gate of a gentleman's house in England. I made a shift to[2] keep the key in a pocket of my own, fearing Glumdalclitch might lose it. The Queen likewise ordered the thinnest silks that could be gotten, to make me clothes, not much thicker than an English blanket, very cumbersome till I was accustomed to them. They were after the fashion of the kingdom, partly resembling the Persian and partly the Chinese, and are a very grave and decent habit.

The Queen became so fond of my company that she could not dine without me. I had a table placed upon the same at which Her Majesty ate, just at her left elbow, and a chair to sit on. Glumdalclitch stood on a stool on the floor near my table, to assist and take care of me. I had an entire set of silver dishes and plates, and other necessaries, which, in proportion to those of the Queen, were not much bigger than what I have seen in a London toy-shop for the furniture of a baby-house: these my little nurse kept in her pocket in a silver box and gave me at meals as I wanted them, always cleaning them herself. No person dined with the Queen but the two princesses royal, the eldest sixteen years old, and the younger at that time thirteen and a month. Her Majesty used to put a bit of meat upon one of my dishes, out of which I carved for myself, and her diversion was to see me eat in miniature. For the Queen (who had indeed but a weak stomach) took up at one mouthful as much as a dozen English farmers could eat at a meal, which to me was for some time a very nauseous sight. She would crunch the wing of a lark, bones and all, between her teeth, although it were nine times as large as that of a full-grown turkey; and put a bit of bread into her mouth as big as two twelve-penny loaves. She drank out of a golden cup, above a hogshead at a draught. Her knives were twice as long as a scythe set straight upon the handle. The spoons, forks, and other instruments were all in the same proportion. I remember when Glumdalclitch carried me, out of curiosity, to see some of the

[1] *nice* Precise.

[2] *made a shift to* Contrived to, succeeded with difficulty in.

tables at court, where ten or a dozen of those enormous knives and forks were lifted up together, I thought I had never till then beheld so terrible a sight.

It is the custom that every Wednesday (which, as I have observed, is their Sabbath) the King and Queen, with the royal issue of both sexes, dine together in the apartment of His Majesty, to whom I was now become a great favourite; and at these times my little chair and table were placed at his left hand, before one of the salt-cellars. This prince took a pleasure in conversing with me, inquiring into the manners, religion, laws, government, and learning of Europe; wherein I gave him the best account I was able. His apprehension was so clear, and his judgment so exact, that he made very wise reflections and observations upon all I said. But I confess that after I had been a little too copious in talking of my own beloved country, of our trade and wars by sea and land, of our schisms in religion and parties in the state, the prejudices of his education prevailed so far that he could not forbear taking me up in his right hand, and stroking me gently with the other, after a hearty fit of laughing, asked me whether I were a Whig or Tory. Then, turning to his first minister, who waited behind him with a white staff near as tall as the mainmast of the *Royal Sovereign*,[1] he observed how contemptible a thing was human grandeur, which could be mimicked by such diminutive insects as I. "And yet," says he, "I dare engage,[2] these creatures have their titles and distinctions of honour; they contrive little nests and burrows that they call houses and cities; they make a figure in dress and equipage; they love, they fight, they dispute, they cheat, they betray!" And thus he continued on, while my colour came and went several times with indignation to hear our noble country, the mistress of arts and arms; the scourge of France; the arbitress of Europe; the seat of virtue, piety, honour, and truth; the pride and envy of the world, so contemptuously treated.

But as I was not in a condition to resent injuries, so upon mature thoughts I began to doubt whether I was injured or no. For, after having been accustomed several months to the sight and converse of this people, and observed every object upon which I cast mine eyes to be of proportionable magnitude, the horror I had at first conceived from their bulk and aspect was so far worn off that if I had then beheld a company of English lords and ladies in their finery and birthday clothes,[3] acting their several parts in the most courtly manner of strutting, and bowing, and prating, to say the truth, I should have been strongly tempted to laugh as much at them as this King and his grandees did at me. Neither indeed could I forbear smiling at myself when the Queen used to place me upon her hand towards a looking-glass, by which both our persons appeared before me in full view together; and there could be nothing more ridiculous than the comparison, so that I really began to imagine myself dwindled many degrees below my usual size.

Nothing angered and mortified me so much as the Queen's dwarf, who, being of the lowest stature that was ever in that country (for I verily think he was not full thirty feet high) became so insolent at seeing a creature so much beneath him that he would always affect to swagger and look big as he passed by me in the Queen's antechamber, while I was standing on some table talking with the lords or ladies of the court, and he seldom failed of a smart word or two upon my littleness, against which I could only revenge myself by calling him brother, challenging him to wrestle, and such repartees as are usually in the mouths of court pages. One day at dinner this malicious little cub was so nettled with something I had said to him that, raising himself upon the frame of Her Majesty's chair, he took me up by the middle as I was sitting down, not thinking any harm, and let me drop into a large silver bowl of cream, and then ran away as fast as he could. I fell over head and ears, and if I had not been a good swimmer it might have gone very hard with me; for Glumdalclitch in that instant happened to be at the other end of the room, and the Queen was in such a fright that she wanted presence of mind to assist me. But my little nurse ran to my relief and took me out, after I had swallowed above a quart of cream. I was put to bed: however, I received no other damage than the loss of a suit of clothes, which was utterly spoiled. The dwarf was soundly whipped, and, as a further punishment, forced to drink up the bowl of cream into which he had thrown me; neither was he ever restored to favour; for soon after the Queen bestowed him on a lady of high quality, so that I saw

[1] *Royal Sovereign* One of the tallest ships in the English navy, with a main mast over 100 feet high.

[2] *dare engage* Believe.

[3] *birthday clothes* Dress worn by courtiers for the monarch's birthday celebration.

him no more, to my very great satisfaction; for I could not tell to what extremities such a malicious urchin might have carried his resentment.

He had before served me a scurvy trick, which set the Queen a laughing, although at the same time she was heartily vexed, and would have immediately cashiered[1] him if I had not been so generous as to intercede. Her Majesty had taken a marrow bone upon her plate and, after knocking out the marrow, placed the bone again in the dish erect, as it stood before; the dwarf, watching his opportunity, while Glumdalclitch was gone to the side-board, mounted the stool that she stood on to take care of me at meals, took me up in both hands and, squeezing my legs together, wedged them into the marrow bone above my waist, where I stuck for some time and made a very ridiculous figure. I believe it was near a minute before any one knew what was become of me, for I thought it below me to cry out. But, as princes seldom get their meat hot, my legs were not scalded, only my stockings and breeches in a sad condition. The dwarf at my entreaty had no other punishment than a sound whipping.

I was frequently rallied[2] by the Queen upon account of my fearfulness, and she used to ask me whether the people of my country were as great cowards as myself. The occasion was this. The kingdom is much pestered with flies in summer, and these odious insects, each of them as big as a Dunstable[3] lark, hardly gave me any rest while I sat at dinner, with their continual humming and buzzing about mine ears. They would sometimes alight upon my victuals and leave their loathsome excrement or spawn behind, which to me was very visible, though not to the natives of that country, whose large optics were not so acute as mine in viewing smaller objects. Sometimes they would fix upon my nose or forehead, where they stung me to the quick, smelling very offensively; and I could easily trace that viscous matter, which our naturalists tell us enables those creatures to walk with their feet upwards upon a ceiling. I had much ado to defend myself against these detestable animals, and could not forbear starting when they came on my face. It was the common practice of the dwarf to catch a number of these insects in his hand, as schoolboys do among us, and let them out suddenly under my nose, on purpose to frighten me and divert the Queen. My remedy was to cut them in pieces with my knife as they flew in the air, wherein my dexterity was much admired.

I remember one morning when Glumdalclitch had set me in a box upon a window, as she usually did in fair days to give me air (for I durst not venture to let the box be hung on a nail out of the window, as we do with cages in England), after I had lifted up one of my sashes, and sat down at my table to eat a piece of sweet cake for my breakfast, above twenty wasps, allured by the smell, came flying into the room, humming louder than the drones of as many bagpipes. Some of them seized my cake and carried it piecemeal away; others flew about my head and face, confounding me with the noise and putting me in the utmost terror of their stings. However, I had the courage to rise and draw my hanger, and attack them in the air. I dispatched four of them, but the rest got away, and I presently shut my window. These insects were as large as partridges; I took out their stings, found them an inch and a half long and as sharp as needles. I carefully preserved them all and, having since shown them with some other curiosities in several parts of Europe, upon my return to England I gave three of them to Gresham College,[4] and kept the fourth for myself.

CHAPTER 4

(*The country described. A proposal for correcting modern maps. The King's palace, and some account of the metropolis. The author's way of travelling. The chief temple described.*)

I now intend to give the reader a short description of this country, as far as I travelled in it, which was not above two thousand miles round Lorbrulgrud, the metropolis. For the Queen, whom I always attended, never went farther when she accompanied the King in his progresses, and there staid till His Majesty returned from viewing his frontiers. The whole extent of this prince's dominions reaches about six thousand miles in length, and from three to five in breadth. From whence

[1] *cashiered* Dismissed from service.

[2] *rallied* Teased.

[3] *Dunstable* City north of London. Larks were a popular food.

[4] *Gresham College* Home of the Royal Society of England (a prestigious scientific organization) and of their museum.

I cannot but conclude that our geographers of Europe are in a great error by supposing nothing but sea between Japan and California; for it was ever my opinion that there must be a balance of earth to counterpoise the great continent of Tartary; and therefore they ought to correct their maps and charts by joining this vast tract of land to the northwest parts of America, wherein I shall be ready to lend them my assistance.

The kingdom is a peninsula, terminated to the northeast by a ridge of mountains thirty miles high, which are altogether impassable by reason of the volcanoes upon the tops. Neither do the most learned know what sort of mortals inhabit beyond those mountains, or whether they be inhabited at all. On the three other sides it is bounded by the ocean. There is not one seaport in the whole kingdom, and those parts of the coasts into which the rivers issue are so full of pointed rocks, and the sea generally so rough, that there is no venturing with the smallest of their boats; so that these people are wholly excluded from any commerce with the rest of the world. But the large rivers are full of vessels and abound with excellent fish, for they seldom get any from the sea because the sea fish are of the same size with those in Europe, and consequently not worth catching; whereby it is manifest that nature, in the production of plants and animals of so extraordinary a bulk, is wholly confined to this continent, of which I leave the reasons to be determined by philosophers. However, now and then they take a whale that happens to be dashed against the rocks, which the common people feed on heartily. These whales I have known so large that a man could hardly carry one upon his shoulders; and sometimes for curiosity they are brought in hampers to Lorbrulgrud; I saw one of them in a dish at the King's table, which passed for a rarity, but I did not observe he was fond of it; for I think indeed the bigness disgusted him, although I have seen one somewhat larger in Greenland.

The country is well inhabited, for it contains fifty-one cities, near a hundred walled towns, and a great number of villages. To satisfy my curious reader, it may be sufficient to describe Lorbrulgrud. This city stands upon almost two equal parts on each side the river that passes through. It contains above eighty thousand houses and about six hundred thousand inhabitants. It is in length three *glomglungs* (which make about fifty-four English miles), and two and a half in breadth, as I measured it myself in the royal map made by the King's order, which was laid on the ground on purpose for me, and extended a hundred feet. I paced the diameter and circumference several times barefoot and, computing by the scale, measured it pretty exactly.

The King's palace is no regular edifice, but a heap of buildings about seven miles round. The chief rooms are generally two hundred and forty feet high, and broad and long in proportion. A coach was allowed to Glumdalclitch and me, wherein her governess frequently took her out to see the town or go among the shops; and I was always of the party, carried in my box, although the girl at my own desire would often take me out and hold me in her hand, that I might more conveniently view the houses and the people as we passed along the streets. I reckoned our coach to be about a square of Westminster-hall,[1] but not altogether so high: however, I cannot be very exact. One day the governess ordered our coachman to stop at several shops, where the beggars, watching their opportunity, crowded to the sides of the coach and gave me the most horrible spectacle that ever a European eye beheld. There was a woman with a cancer in her breast, swelled to a monstrous size, full of holes, in two or three of which I could have easily crept and covered my whole body. There was a fellow with a wen[2] in his neck larger than five woolpacks,[3] and another with a couple of wooden legs, each about twenty feet high. But the most hateful sight of all was the lice crawling on their clothes. I could see distinctly the limbs of these vermin with my naked eye, much better than those of a European louse through a microscope, and their snouts, with which they rooted like swine. They were the first I had ever beheld, and I should have been curious enough to dissect one of them if I had had proper instruments, which I unluckily left behind me in the ship, although, indeed, the sight was so nauseous that it perfectly turned my stomach.

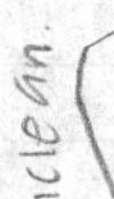

Besides the large box in which I was usually carried, the Queen ordered a smaller one to be made for me, of about twelve feet square and ten high, for the conve-

[1] *Westminster-hall* Massive hall where the law courts then sat, now part of the English Parliament. It is approximately 290 feet long and 68 feet wide. Swift seems to mean the square of this area.

[2] *wen* Protuberance.

[3] *woolpacks* Large bags for transporting wool.

nience of travelling, because the other was somewhat too large for Glumdalclitch's lap, and cumbersome in the coach; it was made by the same artist, whom I directed in the whole contrivance. This travelling-closet was an exact square, with a window in the middle of three of the squares, and each window was latticed with iron wire on the outside, to prevent accidents in long journeys. On the fourth side, which had no window, two strong staples were fixed, through which the person that carried me, when I had a mind to be on horseback, put a leathern belt, and buckled it about his waist. This was always the office of some grave trusty servant, in whom I could confide, whether I attended the King and Queen in their progresses, or were disposed to see the gardens, or pay a visit to some great lady or minister of state in the court, when Glumdalclitch happened to be out of order;[1] for I soon began to be known and esteemed among the greatest officers—I suppose more upon account of Their Majesties' favour than any merit of my own. In journeys, when I was weary of the coach, a servant on horseback would buckle on my box and place it upon a cushion before him; and there I had a full prospect of the country on three sides from my three windows. I had in this closet a field bed and a hammock hung from the ceiling, two chairs and a table, neatly screwed to the floor to prevent being tossed about by the agitation of the horse or the coach. And, having been long used to sea voyages, those motions, although sometimes very violent, did not much discompose me.

Whenever I had a mind to see the town, it was always in my travelling closet, which Glumdalclitch held in her lap in a kind of open sedan, after the fashion of the country, borne by four men and attended by two others in the Queen's livery. The people, who had often heard of me, were very curious to crowd about the sedan, and the girl was complaisant enough to make the bearers stop, and to take me in her hand that I might be more conveniently seen.

I was very desirous to see the chief temple, and particularly the tower belonging to it, which is reckoned the highest in the kingdom. Accordingly, one day my nurse carried me thither, but I may truly say I came back disappointed; for the height is not above three thousand feet, reckoning from the ground to the highest pinnacle top, which, allowing for the difference between the size of those people and us in Europe, is no great matter for admiration, nor at all equal in proportion (if I rightly remember) to Salisbury steeple.[2] But, not to detract from a nation to which, during my life, I shall acknowledge myself extremely obliged, it must be allowed that whatever this famous tower wants in height, is amply made up in beauty and strength. For the walls are near a hundred feet thick, built of hewn stone, whereof each is about forty feet square, and adorned on all sides with statues of gods and emperors cut in marble, larger than the life, placed in their several niches. I measured a little finger which had fallen down from one of these statues and lay unperceived among some rubbish, and found it exactly four feet and an inch in length. Glumdalclitch wrapped it up in her handkerchief and carried it home in her pocket to keep among other trinkets, of which the girl was very fond, as children at her age usually are.

The King's kitchen is indeed a noble building, vaulted at top, and about six hundred feet high. The great oven is not so wide by ten paces as the cupola at St. Paul's[3]—for I measured the latter on purpose after my return. But if I should describe the kitchen grate, the prodigious pots and kettles, the joints of meat turning on the spits, with many other particulars, perhaps I should be hardly believed; at least a severe critic would be apt to think I enlarged a little, as travellers are often suspected to do. To avoid which censure, I fear I have run too much into the other extreme, and that if this treatise should happen to be translated into the language of Brobdingnag (which is the general name of that kingdom) and transmitted thither, the King and his people would have reason to complain that I had done them an injury by a false and diminutive representation.

His Majesty seldom keeps above six hundred horses in his stables; they are generally from fifty-four to sixty foot high. But when he goes abroad on solemn days, he is attended, for state, by a military guard of five hundred horse, which indeed I thought was the most splendid sight that could be ever beheld, till I saw part of his

[1] *out of order* Indisposed.

[2] *Salisbury steeple* At 404 feet high, the steeple of Salisbury Cathedral is the tallest in England.

[3] *the cupola at St. Paul's* Dome of St. Paul's Cathedral, London, approximately 112 feet in diameter.

army in battalia,[1] whereof I shall find another occasion to speak.

CHAPTER 5

(*Several adventures that happened to the author. The execution of a criminal. The author shows his skill in navigation.*)

I should have lived happy enough in that country if my littleness had not exposed me to several ridiculous and troublesome accidents, some of which I shall venture to relate. Glumdalclitch often carried me into the gardens of the court in my smaller box, and would sometimes take me out of it, and hold me in her hand or set me down to walk. I remember, before the dwarf left the Queen, he followed us one day into those gardens, and my nurse having set me down, he and I being close together near some dwarf apple trees, I must needs show my wit by a silly allusion between him and the trees, which happens to hold in their language as it does in ours. Whereupon, the malicious rogue, watching his opportunity, when I was walking under one of them, shook it directly over my head, by which a dozen apples, each of them near as large as a Bristol barrel,[2] came tumbling about my ears; one of them hit me on the back as I chanced to stoop, and knocked me down flat on my face; but I received no other hurt, and the dwarf was pardoned at my desire, because I had given the provocation.

Another day, Glumdalclitch left me on a smooth grassplot to divert myself while she walked at some distance with her governess. In the meantime, there suddenly fell such a violent shower of hail that I was immediately by the force of it struck to the ground; and when I was down the hailstones gave me such cruel bangs all over the body, as if I had been pelted with tennis balls; however, I made a shift to creep on all four and shelter myself by lying flat on my face on the lee-side of a border of lemon thyme, but so bruised from head to foot that I could not go abroad in ten days. Neither is this at all to be wondered at because, nature in that country observing the same proportion through all her operations, a hailstone is near eighteen hundred times as large as one in Europe; which I can assert upon experience, having been so curious as to weigh and measure them.

But a more dangerous accident happened to me in the same garden when my little nurse, believing she had put me in a secure place (which I often entreated her to do, that I might enjoy my own thoughts), and having left my box at home to avoid the trouble of carrying it, went to another part of the garden with her governess and some ladies of her acquaintance. While she was absent and out of hearing, a small white spaniel that belonged to one of the chief gardeners, having got by accident into the garden, happened to range near the place where I lay. The dog, following the scent, came directly up and, taking me in his mouth, ran straight to his master, wagging his tail, and set me gently on the ground. By good fortune he had been so well taught that I was carried between his teeth without the least hurt, or even tearing my clothes. But the poor gardener, who knew me well and had a great kindness for me, was in a terrible fright. He gently took me up in both his hands and asked me how I did, but I was so amazed and out of breath that I could not speak a word. In a few minutes I came to myself, and he carried me safe to my little nurse, who by this time had returned to the place where she left me, and was in cruel agonies when I did not appear, nor answer when she called. She severely reprimanded the gardener on account of his dog; but the thing was hushed up and never known at court, for the girl was afraid of the Queen's anger, and truly, as to myself, I thought it would not be for my reputation that such a story should go about.

This accident absolutely determined Glumdalclitch never to trust me abroad for the future out of her sight. I had been long afraid of this resolution and therefore concealed from her some little unlucky adventures that happened in those times when I was left by myself. Once, a kite[3] hovering over the garden made a stoop[4] at me, and if I had not resolutely drawn my hanger and run under a thick espalier,[5] he would have certainly

[1] *in battalia* In their battle array.

[2] *Bristol barrel* Barrel holding roughly 40 gallons. Barrels varied in size depending on where they came from, and those from Bristol, a major industrial center, were among the largest.

[3] *kite* Bird of prey of the falcon family.

[4] *stoop* Swoop.

[5] *espalier* Trees trained to grow upon lattice-work or stakes.

carried me away in his talons. Another time, walking to the top of a fresh mole-hill, I fell to my neck in the hole through which that animal had cast up the earth, and coined some lie, not worth remembering, to excuse myself for spoiling my clothes. I likewise broke my right shin against the shell of a snail, which I happened to stumble over as I was walking alone and thinking on poor England.

I cannot tell whether I were more pleased or mortified to observe in those solitary walks that the smaller birds did not appear to be at all afraid of me, but would hop about within a yard distance, looking for worms and other food, with as much indifference and security as if no creature at all were near them. I remember a thrush had the confidence to snatch out of my hand, with his bill, a piece of cake that Glumdalclitch had just given me for my breakfast. When I attempted to catch any of these birds, they would boldly turn against me, endeavouring to peck my fingers, which I durst not venture within their reach; and then they would hop back, unconcerned, to hunt for worms or snails, as they did before. But one day I took a thick cudgel and threw it with all my strength so luckily at a linnet that I knocked him down and, seizing him by the neck with both my hands, ran with him in triumph to my nurse. However, the bird—who had only been stunned—recovering himself, gave me so many boxes with his wings on both sides of my head and body, though I held him at arm's length and was out of the reach of his claws, that I was twenty times thinking to let him go. But I was soon relieved by one of our servants, who wrung off the bird's neck, and I had him next day for dinner, by the Queen's command. This linnet, as near as I can remember, seemed to be somewhat larger than an English swan.

The Maids of Honour often invited Glumdalclitch to their apartments, and desired she would bring me along with her, on purpose to have the pleasure of seeing and touching me. They would often strip me naked from top to toe and lay me at full length in their bosoms; wherewith I was much disgusted because, to say the truth, a very offensive smell came from their skins; which I do not mention or intend to the disadvantage of those excellent ladies, for whom I have all manner of respect; but I conceive that my sense was more acute in proportion to my littleness, and that those illustrious persons were no more disagreeable to their lovers, or to each other, than people of the same quality are with us in England. And, after all, I found their natural smell was much more supportable than when they used perfumes, under which I immediately swooned away. I cannot forget that an intimate friend of mine in Lilliput took the freedom in a warm day, when I had used a good deal of exercise, to complain of a strong smell about me, although I am as little faulty that way as most of my sex; but I suppose his faculty of smelling was as nice[1] with regard to me as mine was to that of this people. Upon this point, I cannot forbear doing justice to the Queen my mistress and Glumdalclitch my nurse, whose persons were as sweet as those of any lady in England.

That which gave me most uneasiness among these Maids of Honour (when my nurse carried me to visit them) was to see them use me without any manner of ceremony, like a creature who had no sort of consequence. For they would strip themselves to the skin and put on their smocks in my presence, while I was placed on their toilet[2] directly before their naked bodies, which I am sure to me was very far from being a tempting sight, or from giving me any other emotions than those of horror and disgust. Their skins appeared so coarse and uneven, so variously coloured, when I saw them near, with a mole here and there as broad as a trencher, and hairs hanging from it thicker than packthreads, to say nothing farther concerning the rest of their persons. Neither did they at all scruple, while I was by, to discharge what they had drank, to the quantity of at least two hogsheads, in a vessel that held above three tuns. The handsomest among these Maids of Honour, a pleasant, frolicsome girl of sixteen, would sometimes set me astride upon one of her nipples, with many other tricks, wherein the reader will excuse me for not being over particular. But I was so much displeased that I entreated Glumdalclitch to contrive some excuse for not seeing that young lady any more.

One day a young gentleman who was nephew to my nurse's governess came and pressed them both to see an execution. It was of a man who had murdered one of that gentleman's intimate acquaintance. Glumdalclitch was prevailed on to be of the company, very much against her inclination, for she was naturally tender-

[1] *nice* Sharp.

[2] *toilet* Dressing table.

hearted; and, as for myself, although I abhorred such kind of spectacles, yet my curiosity tempted me to see something that I thought must be extraordinary. The malefactor was fixed in a chair upon a scaffold erected for that purpose, and his head cut off at one blow with a sword of about forty feet long. The veins and arteries spouted up such a prodigious quantity of blood, and so high in the air, that the great *jet d'eau* at Versailles[1] was not equal to it for the time it lasted; and the head, when it fell on the scaffold floor, gave such a bounce as made me start, although I was at least half an English mile distant.

The Queen, who often used to hear me talk of my sea voyages, and took all occasions to divert me when I was melancholy, asked me whether I understood how to handle a sail or an oar, and whether a little exercise of rowing might not be convenient for my health? I answered that I understood both very well. For although my proper employment had been to be surgeon or doctor to the ship, yet often, upon a pinch, I was forced to work like a common mariner. But I could not see how this could be done in their country, where the smallest wherry[2] was equal to a first-rate man of war among us; and such a boat as I could manage would never live in any of their rivers. Her Majesty said, if I would contrive[3] a boat, her own joiner[4] should make it, and she would provide a place for me to sail in. The fellow was an ingenious workman and, by my instructions, in ten days finished a pleasure boat with all its tackling, able conveniently to hold eight Europeans. When it was finished, the Queen was so delighted that she ran with it in her lap to the King, who ordered it to be put into a cistern full of water, with me in it, by way of trial; where I could not manage my two sculls, or little oars, for want of room. But the Queen had before contrived another project. She ordered the joiner to make a wooden trough of three hundred feet long, fifty broad, and eight deep; which, being well pitched to prevent leaking, was placed on the floor along the wall in an outer room of the palace. It had a cock[5] near the bottom to let out the water when it began to grow stale; and two servants could easily fill it in half an hour. Here I often used to row for my own diversion, as well as that of the Queen and her ladies, who thought themselves well entertained with my skill and agility. Sometimes I would put up my sail, and then my business was only to steer while the ladies gave me a gale with their fans; and when they were weary some of their pages would blow my sail forward with their breath, while I showed my art by steering starboard or larboard as I pleased. When I had done, Glumdalclitch always carried back my boat into her closet[6] and hung it on a nail to dry.

In this exercise I once met an accident which had like to have cost me my life; for, one of the pages having put my boat into the trough, the governess who attended Glumdalclitch very officiously[7] lifted me up to place me in the boat; but I happened to slip through her fingers, and should infallibly have fallen down forty feet upon the floor if, by the luckiest chance in the world, I had not been stopped by a corking-pin that stuck in the good gentlewoman's stomacher,[8] the head of the pin passing between my shirt and the waistband of my breeches. And thus I was held by the middle in the air until Glumdalclitch ran to my relief.

Another time, one of the servants, whose office it was to fill my trough every third day with fresh water, was so careless as to let a huge frog (not perceiving it) slip out of his pail. The frog lay concealed till I was put into my boat, but then, seeing a resting-place, climbed up and made it lean so much on one side that I was forced to balance it with all my weight on the other to prevent overturning. When the frog was got in, it hopped at once half the length of the boat, and then over my head, backward and forward, daubing my face and clothes with its odious slime. The largeness of its features made it appear the most deformed animal that can be conceived. However, I desired Glumdalclitch to let me deal with it alone. I banged it a good while with one of my sculls, and at last forced it to leap out of the boat.

[1] *jet … Versailles* Largest fountain in Louis XIV's palace gardens at Versailles sprayed its water nearly 70 feet in the air.

[2] *wherry* Small, light rowboat.

[3] *contrive* Devise; invent.

[4] *joiner* Carpenter.

[5] *cock* Tap; spout.

[6] *closet* Small, private inner chamber.

[7] *officiously* Eagerly; dutifully.

[8] *corking-pin* Large pin; *stomacher* Ornamental chest-covering for women, often decorated with jewels.

But the greatest danger I ever underwent in that kingdom was from a monkey who belonged to one of the clerks of the kitchen. Glumdalclitch had locked me up in her closet while she went somewhere upon business or a visit. The weather being very warm, the closet window was left open, as well as the windows and the door of my bigger box, in which I usually lived because of its largeness and conveniency. As I sat quietly meditating at my table, I heard something bounce in at the closet window and skip about from one side to the other, whereat, although I was much alarmed, yet I ventured to look out, but not stirring from my seat; and then I saw this frolicsome animal frisking and leaping up and down, till at last he came to my box, which he seemed to view with great pleasure and curiosity, peeping in at the door and every window. I retreated to the farther corner of my room, or box; but the monkey, looking in at every side, put me in such a fright that I wanted presence of mind to conceal myself under the bed, as I might easily have done. After some time spent in peeping, grinning, and chattering, he at last espied me and, reaching one of his paws in at the door, as a cat does when she plays with a mouse, although I often shifted place to avoid him, he at length seized the lappet of my coat (which being made of that country silk, was very thick and strong) and dragged me out. He took me up in his right forefoot and held me as a nurse does a child she is going to suckle, just as I have seen the same sort of creature do with a kitten in Europe; and when I offered to struggle he squeezed me so hard that I thought it more prudent to submit. I have good reason to believe that he took me for a young one of his own species, by his often stroking my face very gently with his other paw. In these diversions he was interrupted by a noise at the closet door, as if somebody were opening it, whereupon he suddenly leaped up to the window at which he had come in, and thence upon the leads and gutters, walking upon three legs and holding me in the fourth, till he clambered up to a roof that was next to ours. I heard Glumdalclitch give a shriek at the moment he was carrying me out. The poor girl was almost distracted;[1] that quarter of the palace was all in an uproar; the servants ran for ladders; the monkey was seen by hundreds in the court, sitting upon the ridge of a building, holding me like a baby in one of his forepaws and feeding me with the other by cramming into my mouth some victuals he had squeezed out of the bag on one side of his chaps,[2] and patting me when I would not eat; whereat many of the rabble below could not forbear laughing; neither do I think they justly ought to be blamed, for without question the sight was ridiculous enough to everybody but myself. Some of the people threw up stones, hoping to drive the monkey down, but this was strictly forbidden, or else very probably my brains had been dashed out.

The ladders were now applied, and mounted by several men; which the monkey observing, and finding himself almost encompassed, not being able to make speed enough with his three legs, let me drop on a ridge tile and made his escape. Here I sat for some time, five hundred yards from the ground, expecting every moment to be blown down by the wind, or to fall by my own giddiness, and come tumbling over and over from the ridge to the eaves. But an honest lad, one of my nurse's footmen, climbed up and, putting me into his breeches pocket, brought me down safe.

I was almost choked with the filthy stuff the monkey had crammed down my throat, but my dear little nurse picked it out of my mouth with a small needle, and then I fell a vomiting, which gave me great relief. Yet I was so weak and bruised in the sides with the squeezes given me by this odious animal that I was forced to keep my bed a fortnight. The King, Queen, and all the court sent every day to inquire after my health, and Her Majesty made me several visits during my sickness. The monkey was killed, and an order made that no such animal should be kept about the palace.

When I attended the King after my recovery, to return him thanks for his favours, he was pleased to rally me a good deal upon this adventure. He asked me what my thoughts and speculations were while I lay in the monkey's paw, how I liked the victuals he gave me, his manner of feeding, and whether the fresh air on the roof had sharpened my stomach. He desired to know what I would have done upon such an occasion in my own country. I told His Majesty that in Europe we had no monkeys except such as were brought for curiosity from other places, and so small that I could deal with a dozen of them together if they presumed to attack me. And as for that monstrous animal with whom I was so lately

[1] *distracted* Frantic.

[2] *chaps* Cheeks.

engaged (it was indeed as large as an elephant), if my fears had suffered me to think so far as to make use of my hanger (looking fiercely, and clapping my hand on the hilt, as I spoke) when he poked his paw into my chamber, perhaps I should have given him such a wound as would have made him glad to withdraw it with more haste than he put it in. This I delivered in a firm tone, like a person who was jealous lest his courage should be called in question. However, my speech produced nothing else beside a loud laughter, which all the respect due to His Majesty from those about him could not make them contain. This made me reflect how vain an attempt it is for a man to endeavour to do himself honour among those who are out of all degree of equality or comparison with him. And yet I have seen the moral of my own behaviour very frequent in England since my return; where a little contemptible varlet, without the least title to birth, person, wit, or common sense, shall presume to look with importance, and put himself upon a foot with the greatest persons of the kingdom.

I was every day furnishing the court with some ridiculous story, and Glumdalclitch, although she loved me to excess, yet was arch enough to inform the Queen whenever I committed any folly that she thought would be diverting to Her Majesty. The girl, who had been out of order, was carried by her governess to take the air about an hour's distance, or thirty miles from town. They alighted out of the coach near a small footpath in a field, and, Glumdalclitch setting down my travelling box, I went out of it to walk. There was a cow dung in the path, and I must need try my activity by attempting to leap over it. I took a run, but unfortunately jumped short, and found myself just in the middle up to my knees. I waded through with some difficulty, and one of the footmen wiped me as clean as he could with his handkerchief, for I was filthily bemired, and my nurse confined me to my box till we returned home, where the Queen was soon informed of what had passed, and the footmen spread it about the court, so that all the mirth for some days was at my expense.

Chapter 6

(*Several contrivances of the author to please the King and Queen. He shows his skill in music. The King inquires into the state of England, which the author relates to him. The King's observations thereon.*)

I used to attend the King's levee[1] once or twice a week, and had often seen him under the barber's hand, which indeed was at first very terrible to behold, for the razor was almost twice as long as an ordinary scythe. His Majesty, according to the custom of the country, was only shaved twice a-week. I once prevailed on the barber to give me some of the suds or lather, out of which I picked forty or fifty of the strongest stumps of hair. I then took a piece of fine wood and cut it like the back of a comb, making several holes in it at equal distances with as small a needle as I could get from Glumdalclitch. I fixed in the stumps so artificially,[2] scraping and sloping them with my knife toward the points, that I made a very tolerable comb; which was a seasonable supply,[3] my own being so much broken in the teeth that it was almost useless; neither did I know any artist in that country so nice and exact as would undertake to make me another.

And this puts me in mind of an amusement wherein I spent many of my leisure hours. I desired the Queen's woman to save for me the combings of Her Majesty's hair, whereof in time I got a good quantity; and consulting with my friend the cabinet-maker, who had received general orders to do little jobs for me, I directed him to make two chair-frames, no larger than those I had in my box, and to bore little holes with a fine awl round those parts where I designed the backs and seats; through these holes I wove the strongest hairs I could pick out, just after the manner of cane chairs in England. When they were finished, I made a present of them to Her Majesty; who kept them in her cabinet and used to show them for curiosities, as indeed they were the wonder of everyone that beheld them. The Queen would have me sit upon one of these chairs, but I absolutely refused to obey her, protesting I would rather

[1] *levee* Morning reception of visitors, which was sometimes held as one dressed for the day.

[2] *artificially* With artifice; skillfully.

[3] *seasonable supply* Opportune provision.

die a thousand deaths than place a dishonourable part of my body on those precious hairs that once adorned Her Majesty's head. Of these hairs (as I had always a mechanical genius) I likewise made a neat little purse, about five feet long, with Her Majesty's name deciphered in gold letters, which I gave to Glumdalclitch, by the Queen's consent. To say the truth, it was more for show than use, being not of strength to bear the weight of the larger coins, and therefore she kept nothing in it but some little toys that girls are fond of.

The King, who delighted in music, had frequent concerts at court, to which I was sometimes carried, and set in my box on a table to hear them; but the noise was so great that I could hardly distinguish the tunes. I am confident that all the drums and trumpets of a royal army, beating and sounding together just at your ears, could not equal it. My practice was to have my box removed from the place where the performers sat, as far as I could, then to shut the doors and windows of it, and draw the window curtains, after which I found their music not disagreeable.

I had learned in my youth to play a little upon the spinet.[1] Glumdalclitch kept one in her chamber, and a master attended twice a week to teach her: I called it a spinet because it somewhat resembled that instrument, and was played upon in the same manner. A fancy came into my head that I would entertain the King and Queen with an English tune upon this instrument. But this appeared extremely difficult, for the spinet was near sixty feet long, each key being almost a foot wide, so that with my arms extended I could not reach to above five keys, and to press them down required a good smart stroke with my fist, which would be too great a labour and to no purpose. The method I contrived was this: I prepared two round sticks about the bigness of common cudgels; they were thicker at one end than the other, and I covered the thicker ends with pieces of a mouse's skin, that by rapping on them I might neither damage the tops of the keys nor interrupt the sound. Before the spinet a bench was placed about four feet below the keys, and I was put upon the bench. I ran sideling upon it, that way and this, as fast as I could, banging the proper keys with my two sticks, and made a shift to play a jig, to the great satisfaction of both their majesties; but it was the most violent exercise I ever underwent; and yet I could not strike above sixteen keys, nor consequently play the bass and treble together as other artists do, which was a great disadvantage to my performance.

The King, who, as I before observed, was a prince of excellent understanding, would frequently order that I should be brought in my box and set upon the table in his closet. He would then command me to bring one of my chairs out of the box and sit down within three yards' distance upon the top of the cabinet, which brought me almost to a level with his face. In this manner I had several conversations with him. I one day took the freedom to tell His Majesty that the contempt he discovered towards Europe and the rest of the world did not seem answerable to those excellent qualities of mind that he was master of; that reason did not extend itself with the bulk of the body; on the contrary, we observed in our country that the tallest persons were usually the least provided with it; that, among other animals, bees and ants had the reputation of more industry, art, and sagacity than many of the larger kinds; and that, as inconsiderable as he took me to be, I hoped I might live to do His Majesty some signal service. The King heard me with attention, and began to conceive a much better opinion of me than he had ever before. He desired I would give him as exact an account of the government of England as I possibly could because, as fond as princes commonly are of their own customs (for so he conjectured of other monarchs, by my former discourses), he should be glad to hear of anything that might deserve imitation.

Imagine with thyself, courteous reader, how often I then wished for the tongue of Demosthenes or Cicero,[2] that might have enabled me to celebrate the praise of my own dear native country in a style equal to its merits and felicity.

I began my discourse by informing His Majesty that our dominions consisted of two islands, which composed three mighty kingdoms under one sovereign, beside our plantations[3] in America. I dwelt long upon the fertility of our soil and the temperature[4] of our climate. I then spoke at large upon the constitution of an English Parliament, partly made up of an illustrious body called the House of Peers—persons of the noblest

[1] *spinet* Musical instrument resembling a harpsichord.

[2] *Demosthenes or Cicero* Greek and Roman orators.

[3] *plantations* Colonies.

[4] *temperature* Temperate nature.

blood and of the most ancient and ample patrimonies. I described that extraordinary care always taken of their education in arts and arms to qualify them for being counsellors both to the King and kingdom; to have a share in the legislature; to be members of the Highest Court of Judicature, whence there can be no appeal; and to be champions always ready for the defence of their prince and country by their valour, conduct, and fidelity. That these were the ornament and bulwark of the kingdom, worthy followers of their most renowned ancestors, whose honour had been the reward of their virtue, from which their posterity were never once known to degenerate. To these were joined several holy persons, as part of that assembly under the title of bishops, whose peculiar business is to take care of religion and of those who instruct the people therein. These were searched and sought out through the whole nation, by the prince and his wisest counsellors, among such of the priesthood as were most deservedly distinguished by the sanctity of their lives and the depth of their erudition, who were indeed the spiritual fathers of the clergy and the people.

That the other part of the Parliament consisted of an assembly called the House of Commons, who were all principal gentlemen freely picked and culled out by the people themselves, for their great abilities and love of their country, to represent the wisdom of the whole nation. And that these two bodies made up the most august assembly in Europe, to whom, in conjunction with the prince, the whole legislature is committed.

I then descended to the Courts of Justice, over which the judges, those venerable sages and interpreters of the law, presided for determining the disputed rights and properties of men, as well as for the punishment of vice and protection of innocence. I mentioned the prudent management of our treasury, the valour and achievements of our forces by sea and land. I computed the number of our people by reckoning how many millions there might be of each religious sect or political party among us. I did not omit even our sports and pastimes, or any other particular which I thought might redound to the honour of my country. And I finished all with a brief historical account of affairs and events in England for about a hundred years past.

This conversation was not ended under five audiences, each of several hours; and the King heard the whole with great attention, frequently taking notes of what I spoke, as well as memorandums of what questions he intended to ask me.

When I had put an end to these long discourses, His Majesty, in a sixth audience, consulting his notes, proposed many doubts, queries, and objections upon every article. He asked what methods were used to cultivate the minds and bodies of our young nobility, and in what kind of business they commonly spent the first and teachable parts of their lives. What course was taken to supply that assembly when any noble family became extinct. What qualifications were necessary in those who are to be created new lords. Whether the humour[1] of the prince, a sum of money to a court lady, or a design of strengthening a party opposite to the public interest ever happened to be the motive in those advancements. What share of knowledge these lords had in the laws of their country, and how they came by it, so as to enable them to decide the properties of their fellow subjects in the last resort. Whether they were always so free from avarice, partialities, or want that a bribe, or some other sinister view, could have no place among them. Whether those holy lords I spoke of were always promoted to that rank upon account of their knowledge in religious matters, and the sanctity of their lives; had never been compliers with the times while they were common priests, or slavish prostitute chaplains to some nobleman whose opinions they continued servilely to follow after they were admitted into that assembly?

He then desired to know what Arts were practised in electing those whom I called Commoners. Whether, a Stranger with a strong Purse might not influence the vulgar Voters to chuse him before their own Landlord, or the most considerable Gentleman in the Neighbourhood. How it came to pass, that People were so violently bent upon getting into this Assembly, which I allowed to be a great Trouble and Expence, often to the Ruin of their Families, without any Salary or Pension: Because this appeared such an exalted strain of Virtue and publick Spirit, that his Majesty seemed to doubt it might possibly not be always sincere: And he desired to know whether such zealous Gentlemen could have any Views of refunding themselves for the Charges and Trouble they were at, by sacrificing the Publick Good to

original spelling

[1] *humour* Idle fancy.

original spelling

the Designs of a weak and vicious Prince, in Conjunction with a corrupted Ministry. He multiplied his Questions, and sifted[1] me thoroughly upon every part of this Head,[2] proposing numberless Enquiries and Objections, which I think it not prudent or convenient to repeat.

Upon what I said in relation to our Courts of Justice, His Majesty desired to be satisfied in several points, and this I was the better able to do, having been formerly almost ruined by a long suit in Chancery,[3] which was decreed for me with costs. He asked what time was usually spent in determining between right and wrong, and what degree of expense. Whether advocates and orators had liberty to plead in causes manifestly known to be unjust, vexatious, or oppressive. Whether party in religion or politics were observed to be of any weight in the scale of justice. Whether those pleading orators were persons educated in the general knowledge of equity, or only in provincial, national, and other local customs. Whether they or their judges had any part in penning those laws which they assumed the liberty of interpreting, and glossing upon at their pleasure. Whether they had ever, at different times, pleaded for and against the same cause, and cited precedents to prove contrary opinions. Whether they were a rich or a poor corporation. Whether they received any pecuniary reward for pleading or delivering their opinions. And particularly, whether they were ever admitted as members in the lower senate.

He fell next upon the management of our Treasury, and said he thought my memory had failed me, because I computed our taxes at about five or six millions a year, and when I came to mention the issues,[4] he found they sometimes amounted to more than double; for the notes he had taken were very particular in this point because he hoped, as he told me, that the knowledge of our conduct might be useful to him, and he could not be deceived in his calculations. But if what I told him were true, he was still at a loss how a kingdom could run out of its estate, like a private person. He asked me who were our creditors, and where we found money to pay them. He wondered to hear me talk of such chargeable and expensive wars; that certainly we must be a quarrelsome people, or live among very bad neighbours, and that our generals must needs be richer than our kings.[5] He asked what business we had out of our own islands, unless upon the score of trade or treaty, or to defend the coasts with our fleet. Above all, he was amazed to hear me talk of a mercenary standing army[6] in the midst of peace, and among a free people. He said, if we were governed by our own consent in the persons of our representatives, he could not imagine of whom we were afraid, or against whom we were to fight; and would hear my opinion whether a private man's house might not be better defended by himself, his children and family than by half-a-dozen rascals, picked up at a venture in the streets for small wages, who might get a hundred times more by cutting their throats.

original spelling

He laughed at my odd kind of Arithmetick, as he was pleased to call it, in reckoning the Numbers of our People by a Computation drawn from the several Sects among us in Religion and Politicks. He said, he knew no Reason, why those who entertain Opinions prejudicial to the Publick, should be obliged to Change, or should not be obliged to Conceal them. And as it was Tyranny in any Government to require the first, so it was Weakness not to enforce the second: for a Man may be allowed to keep Poisons in his closet, but not to vend them about for Cordials.[7]

He observed that among the diversions of our nobility and gentry, I had mentioned gaming.[8] He desired to know at what age this entertainment was usually taken up and when it was laid down; how much of their time it employed; whether it ever went so high as to affect their fortunes; whether mean, vicious people, by their dexterity in that art, might not arrive at great riches, and sometimes keep our very nobles in depend-

[1] *sifted* Investigated; questioned.

[2] *Head* Topic.

[3] *Chancery* Court of the Lord Chancellor, ranking below only the House of Lords in legal authority.

[4] *issues* Expenditures.

[5] *our generals ... kings* One of Swift's enemies, the Duke of Marlborough, amassed an enormous fortune while serving as Captain General.

[6] *standing army* A standing army without the approval of Parliament had been illegal since the declaration of the Bill of Rights in 1689, but one still existed. Swift and the Tories were strongly opposed to this.

[7] *Cordials* Medicines, food, or beverages (usually alcoholic) that stimulate or invigorate the heart; restoratives.

[8] *gaming* Gambling.

ence, as well as habituate them to vile companions, wholly take them from the improvement of their minds, and force them, by the losses they received, to learn and practise that infamous dexterity upon others.

He was perfectly astonished with the historical account I gave him of our affairs during the last century, protesting it was only a heap of conspiracies, rebellions, murders, massacres, revolutions, banishments—the very worst effects that avarice, faction, hypocrisy, perfidiousness, cruelty, rage, madness, hatred, envy, lust, malice, and ambition could produce.

original spelling

His Majesty in another audience, was at the Pains to recapitulate the Sum of all I had spoken, compared the Questions he made with the Answers I had given; then taking me into his Hands, and stroking me gently, delivered himself in these Words, which I shall never forget, nor the manner he spoke them in: "My little friend *Grildrig*; you have made a most admirable Panegyrick upon your Country. You have clearly proved that Ignorance, Idleness, and Vice are the proper Ingredients for qualifying a Legislator. That Laws are best explained, interpreted, and applied by those whose Interest and Abilities lye in perverting, confounding, and eluding them. I observe among you some Lines of an Institution, which in its Original might have been tolerable, but these half erased, and the rest wholly blurred and blotted by Corruptions. It doth not appear from all you have said how any one Virtue is required towards the Procurement of any one Station among you, much less that Men are ennobled on Account of their Virtue, that Priests are advanced for their Piety or Learning, Soldiers for their Conduct or Valour, Judges for their Integrity, Senators for the Love of their Country, or Counsellors for their Wisdom. As for yourself (continued the King) who have spent the greatest part of your Life in travelling, I am well disposed to hope you may hitherto have escaped many Vices of your Country. But by what I have gathered from your own Relation, and the Answers I have with much Pains wringed and extorted from you, I cannot but conclude the Bulk of your Natives, to be the most pernicious Race of little odious Vermin that Nature ever suffered to crawl upon the Surface of the Earth."

Chapter 7

(The author's love of his country. He makes a proposal of much advantage to the King, which is rejected. The King's great ignorance in politics. The learning of that country very imperfect and confined. The laws, and military affairs, and parties in the state.)

Nothing but an extreme love of truth could have hindered me from concealing this part of my story. It was in vain to discover my resentments, which were always turned into ridicule, and I was forced to rest with patience while my noble and beloved country was so injuriously treated. I am as heartily sorry as any of my readers can possibly be that such an occasion was given, but this prince happened to be so curious and inquisitive upon every particular that it could not consist either with gratitude or good manners to refuse giving him what satisfaction I was able. Yet thus much I may be allowed to say in my own vindication, that I artfully eluded many of his questions, and gave to every point a more favourable turn by many degrees than the strictness of truth would allow. For I have always borne that laudable partiality to my own country which Dionysius Halicarnassensis,[1] with so much justice, recommends to an historian. I would hide the frailties and deformities of my political mother and place her virtues and beauties in the most advantageous light. This was my sincere endeavour in those many discourses I had with that monarch, although it unfortunately failed of success.

But great allowances should be given to a King who lives wholly secluded from the rest of the world, and must therefore be altogether unacquainted with the manners and customs that most prevail in other nations, the want of which knowledge will ever produce many prejudices, and a certain narrowness of thinking, from which we and the politer countries of Europe are wholly exempted. And it would be hard indeed if so remote a prince's notions of virtue and vice were to be offered as a standard for all mankind.

To confirm what I have now said, and further to show the miserable effects of a confined education, I shall here insert a passage which will hardly obtain

[1] *Dionysius Halicarnassensis* Dionysius Halicarnassus was a Greek historian who wrote a twenty-volume history of Rome that extolled the Romans' virtues and accomplishments in an effort to reconcile the Greeks to the idea of being enslaved.

belief. In hopes to ingratiate myself further into His Majesty's favour, I told him of an invention discovered between three and four hundred years ago, to make a certain powder, into a heap of which, the smallest spark of fire falling, would kindle the whole in a moment, although it were as big as a mountain, and make it all fly up in the air together, with a noise and agitation greater than thunder. That a proper quantity of this powder rammed into a hollow tube of brass or iron, according to its bigness, would drive a ball of iron or lead with such violence and speed as nothing was able to sustain its force. That the largest balls thus discharged would not only destroy whole ranks of an army at once, but batter the strongest walls to the ground; sink down ships, with a thousand men in each, to the bottom of the sea; and, when linked together by a chain, would cut through masts and rigging, divide hundreds of bodies in the middle, and lay all waste before them. That we often put this powder into large hollow balls of iron and discharged them by an engine into some city we were besieging, which would rip up the pavements, tear the houses to pieces, burst and throw splinters on every side, dashing out the brains of all who came near. That I knew the ingredients very well, which were cheap and common; I understood the manner of compounding them, and could direct his workmen how to make those tubes, of a size proportionable to all other things in His Majesty's kingdom, and the largest need not be above a hundred feet long; twenty or thirty of which tubes, charged with the proper quantity of powder and balls, would batter down the walls of the strongest town in his dominions in a few hours, or destroy the whole metropolis, if ever it should pretend to dispute his absolute commands. This I humbly offered to His Majesty as a small tribute of acknowledgment in turn for so many marks that I had received of his royal favour and protection.

The King was struck with horror at the description I had given of those terrible engines and the proposal I had made. He was amazed how so impotent and grovelling an insect as I (these were his expressions) could entertain such inhuman ideas, and in so familiar a manner as to appear wholly unmoved at all the scenes of blood and desolation which I had painted as the common effects of those destructive machines; whereof (he said) some evil genius, enemy to mankind, must have been the first contriver. As for himself, he protested that although few things delighted him so much as new discoveries in art or in nature, yet he would rather lose half his kingdom than be privy to such a secret, which he commanded me, as I valued my life, never to mention any more.

A strange effect of narrow principles and short views! That a prince possessed of every quality which procures veneration, love, and esteem; of strong parts, great wisdom, and profound learning; endued with admirable talents for government, and almost adored by his subjects, should, from a nice, unnecessary scruple, whereof in Europe we can have no conception, let slip an opportunity put into his hands that would have made him absolute master of the lives, the liberties, and the fortunes of his people! Neither do I say this with the least intention to detract from the many virtues of that excellent King, whose character, I am sensible, will on this account be very much lessened in the opinion of an English reader: but I take this defect among them to have risen from their ignorance, by not having hitherto reduced politics into a science, as the more acute wits of Europe have done. For, I remember very well, in a discourse one day with the King, when I happened to say there were several thousand books among us written upon the art of government, it gave him (directly contrary to my intention) a very mean opinion of our understandings. He professed both to abominate and despise all mystery, refinement, and intrigue, either in a prince or a minister. He could not tell what I meant by secrets of state, where an enemy or some rival nation were not in the case. He confined the knowledge of governing within very narrow bounds: to common sense and reason, to justice and lenity, to the speedy determination of civil and criminal causes, with some other obvious topics which are not worth considering. And he gave it for his opinion that whoever could make two ears of corn or two blades of grass to grow upon a spot of ground where only one grew before would deserve better of mankind, and do more essential service to his country, than the whole race of politicians put together.

The learning of this people is very defective, consisting only in morality, history, poetry, and mathematics, wherein they must be allowed to excel. But the last of these is wholly applied to what may be useful in life—to the improvement of agriculture and all mechanical arts—so that among us it would be little esteemed. And as to ideas, entities, abstractions, and transcendentals, I could never drive the least conception into their heads.

No law in that country must exceed in words the number of letters in their alphabet, which consists only of two and twenty. But indeed few of them extend even to that length. They are expressed in the most plain and simple terms, wherein those people are not mercurial enough to discover above one interpretation. And to write a comment upon any law is a capital crime. As to the decision of civil causes, or proceedings against criminals, their precedents are so few that they have little reason to boast of any extraordinary skill in either.

They have had the art of printing as well as the Chinese, time out of mind. But their libraries are not very large; for that of the King, which is reckoned the largest, does not amount to above a thousand volumes placed in a gallery of twelve hundred feet long, from whence I had liberty to borrow what books I pleased. The Queen's joiner had contrived in one of Glumdalclitch's rooms a kind of wooden machine five-and-twenty foot high, formed like a standing ladder; the steps were each fifty feet long. It was indeed a moveable pair of stairs, the lowest end placed at ten feet distance from the wall of the chamber. The book I had a mind to read was put up leaning against the wall. I first mounted to the upper step of the ladder and, turning my face towards the book, began at the top of the page, and so walking to the right and left about eight or ten paces according to the length of the lines, till I had gotten a little below the level of mine eyes, and then descending gradually till I came to the bottom; after which I mounted again and began the other page in the same manner, and so turned over the leaf, which I could easily do with both my hands, for it was as thick and stiff as a pasteboard, and in the largest folios not above eighteen or twenty feet long.

Their style is clear, masculine, and smooth, but not florid; for they avoid nothing more than multiplying unnecessary words or using various expressions. I have perused many of their books, especially those in history and morality. Among the rest, I was much diverted with a little old treatise which always lay in Glumdalclitch's bed chamber, and belonged to her governess, a grave, elderly gentlewoman who dealt in writings of morality and devotion. The book treats of the weakness of human kind, and is in little esteem, except among the women and the vulgar. However, I was curious to see what an author of that country could say upon such a subject. This writer went through all the usual topics of European moralists: showing how diminutive, contemptible, and helpless an animal was man in his own nature; how unable to defend himself from inclemencies of the air or the fury of wild beasts; how much he was excelled by one creature in strength, by another in speed, by a third in foresight, by a fourth in industry. He added, that nature was degenerated in these latter declining ages of the world, and could now produce only small abortive births in comparison of those in ancient times. He said it was very reasonable to think not only that the species of men were originally much larger, but also that there must have been giants in former ages; which, as it is asserted by history and tradition, so it has been confirmed by huge bones and skulls, casually dug up in several parts of the kingdom, far exceeding the common dwindled race of men in our days. He argued that the very laws of nature absolutely required we should have been made in the beginning of a size more large and robust, not so liable to destruction from every little accident of a tile falling from a house, or a stone cast from the hand of a boy, or being drowned in a little brook. From this way of reasoning, the author drew several moral applications, useful in the conduct of life but needless here to repeat. For my own part, I could not avoid reflecting how universally this talent was spread, of drawing lectures in morality, or indeed rather matter of discontent and repining, from the quarrels we raise with nature. And I believe, upon a strict inquiry, those quarrels might be shown as ill-grounded among us as they are among that people.

As to their military affairs, they boast that the King's army consists of a hundred and seventy-six thousand foot and thirty-two thousand horse: if that may be called an army which is made up of tradesmen in the several cities, and farmers in the country, whose commanders are only the nobility and gentry, without pay or reward. They are indeed perfect enough in their exercises and under very good discipline, wherein I saw no great merit; for how should it be otherwise, where every farmer is under the command of his own landlord, and every citizen under that of the principal men in his own city, chosen after the manner of Venice, by ballot?[1]

I have often seen the militia of Lorbrulgrud drawn out to exercise in a great field near the city, of twenty miles square. They were in all not above twenty-five thousand foot and six thousand horse, but it was impossible for me to compute their number, considering the space of ground they took up. A cavalier mounted on a large steed might be about ninety feet high. I have seen this whole body of horse, upon a word of command, draw their swords at once and brandish them in the air. Imagination can figure nothing so grand, so surprising, and so astonishing! It looked as if ten thousand flashes of lightning were darting at the same time from every quarter of the sky.

I was curious to know how this prince, to whose dominions there is no access from any other country, came to think of armies, or to teach his people the practice of military discipline. But I was soon informed both by conversation and reading their histories. For in the course of many ages, they have been troubled with the same disease to which the whole race of mankind is subject: the nobility often contending for power, the people for liberty, and the King for absolute dominion. All which, however happily tempered by the laws of that kingdom, have been sometimes violated by each of the three parties, and have more than once occasioned civil wars, the last whereof was happily put an end to by this prince's grandfather in a general composition;[2] and the militia, then settled with common consent, has been ever since kept in the strictest duty.

Chapter 8

(*The King and Queen make a progress to the frontiers. The author attends them. The manner in which he leaves the country very particularly related. He returns to England.*)

I had always a strong impulse that I should some time recover my liberty, though it was impossible to conjecture by what means, or to form any project with the least hope of succeeding. The ship in which I sailed was the first ever known to be driven within sight of that coast, and the King had given strict orders that if at any time another appeared, it should be taken ashore and with all its crew and passengers brought in a tumbril[3] to Lorbrulgrud. He was strongly bent to get me a woman of my own size, by whom I might propagate the breed; but I think I should rather have died than undergone the disgrace of leaving a posterity to be kept in cages like tame canary-birds, and perhaps in time sold about the kingdom to persons of quality for curiosities. I was indeed treated with much kindness: I was the favourite of a great King and Queen and the delight of the whole court, but it was upon such a foot as ill became the dignity of humankind. I could never forget those domestic pledges I had left behind me. I wanted to be among people with whom I could converse upon even terms, and walk about the streets and fields without being afraid of being trod to death like a frog or a young puppy. But my deliverance came sooner than I expected, and in a manner not very common; the whole story and circumstances of which I shall faithfully relate.

I had now been two years in this country; and about the beginning of the third, Glumdalclitch and I attended the King and Queen in a progress to the south coast of the kingdom. I was carried, as usual, in my travelling-box, which, as I have already described, was a very convenient closet of twelve feet wide. And I had ordered a hammock to be fixed by silken ropes from the four corners at the top, to break the jolts when a servant carried me before him on horseback, as I sometimes desired; and would often sleep in my hammock while we were upon the road. On the roof of my closet, not directly over the middle of the hammock, I ordered the joiner to cut out a hole of a foot square, to give me air in hot weather as I slept; which hole I shut at pleasure with a board that drew backward and forward through a groove.

When we came to our journey's end, the King thought proper to pass a few days at a palace he has near Flanflasnic, a city within eighteen English miles of the seaside. Glumdalclitch and I were much fatigued. I had gotten a small cold, but the poor girl was so ill as to be confined to her chamber. I longed to see the ocean, which must be the only scene of my escape, if ever it should happen. I pretended to be worse than I really

[1] *if that may ... by ballot* This description of the army strongly resembles the idea for a trained militia of citizens advocated by Swift and the Tories.

[2] *composition* Treaty or mutual agreement for the settlement of political differences.

[3] *tumbril* Cart resembling a wheelbarrow that was used in farming; a dung cart.

was, and desired leave to take the fresh air of the sea with a page whom I was very fond of, and who had sometimes been trusted with me. I shall never forget with what unwillingness Glumdalclitch consented, nor the strict charge she gave the page to be careful of me, bursting at the same time into a flood of tears, as if she had some forboding of what was to happen. The boy took me out in my box about half an hour's walk from the palace towards the rocks on the sea-shore. I ordered him to set me down and, lifting up one of my sashes,[1] cast many a wistful melancholy look towards the sea. I found myself not very well, and told the page that I had a mind to take a nap in my hammock, which I hoped would do me good. I got in, and the boy shut the window close down to keep out the cold. I soon fell asleep, and all I can conjecture is that while I slept, the page, thinking no danger could happen, went among the rocks to look for birds' eggs, having before observed him from my window searching about and picking up one or two in the clefts. Be that as it will, I found myself suddenly awaked with a violent pull upon the ring which was fastened at the top of my box for the conveniency of carriage. I felt my box raised very high in the air, and then borne forward with prodigious speed. The first jolt had like to have shaken me out of my hammock, but afterward the motion was easy enough. I called out several times, as loud as I could raise my voice, but all to no purpose. I looked towards my windows and could see nothing but the clouds and sky. I heard a noise just over my head like the clapping of wings, and then began to perceive the woeful condition I was in; that some eagle had got the ring of my box in his beak, with an intent to let it fall on a rock, like a tortoise in a shell, and then pick out my body and devour it. For the sagacity and smell of this bird enables him to discover his quarry at a great distance, although better concealed than I could be within a two-inch board.

In a little time I observed the noise and flutter of wings to increase very fast, and my box was tossed up and down like a sign in a windy day. I heard several bangs or buffets, as I thought, given to the eagle (for such I am certain it must have been that held the ring of my box in his beak), and then all on a sudden felt myself falling perpendicularly down for above a minute, but with such incredible swiftness that I almost lost my breath. My fall was stopped by a terrible squash[2] that sounded louder to my ears than the cataract of Niagara; after which I was quite in the dark for another minute, and then my box began to rise so high that I could see light from the tops of the windows. I now perceived I was fallen into the sea. My box, by the weight of my body, the goods that were in, and the broad plates of iron fixed for strength at the four corners of the top and bottom, floated about five feet deep in water. I did then, and do now, suppose that the eagle which flew away with my box was pursued by two or three others, and forced to let me drop while he defended himself against the rest, who hoped to share in the prey. The plates of iron fastened at the bottom of the box (for those were the strongest) preserved the balance while it fell, and hindered it from being broken on the surface of the water. Every joint of it was well grooved, and the door did not move on hinges, but up and down like a sash, which kept my closet so tight that very little water came in. I got with much difficulty out of my hammock, having first ventured to draw back the slip-board on the roof already mentioned, contrived on purpose to let in air, for want of which I found myself almost stifled.

How often did I then wish myself with my dear Glumdalclitch, from whom one single hour had so far divided me! And I may say with truth that in the midst of my own misfortunes I could not forbear lamenting my poor nurse, the grief she would suffer for my loss, the displeasure of the Queen, and the ruin of her fortune. Perhaps many travellers have not been under greater difficulties and distress than I was at this juncture, expecting every moment to see my box dashed to pieces, or at least overset by the first violent blast or rising wave. A breach in one single pane of glass would have been immediate death, nor could any thing have preserved the windows but the strong lattice wires placed on the outside against accidents in travelling. I saw the water ooze in at several crannies, although the leaks were not considerable, and I endeavoured to stop them as well as I could. I was not able to lift up the roof of my closet, which otherwise I certainly should have done, and sat on the top of it, where I might at least preserve myself some hours longer than by being shut up (as I may call it) in the hold. Or if I escaped these dangers for a day or two, what could I expect but a

[1] *sashes* I.e., window-sashes.

[2] *squash* Splash.

miserable death of cold and hunger? I was four hours under these circumstances, expecting and indeed wishing every moment to be my last.

I have already told the reader that there were two strong staples fixed upon that side of my box which had no window, and into which the servant, who used to carry me on horseback, would put a leathern belt, and buckle it about his waist. Being in this disconsolate state, I heard, or at least thought I heard, some kind of grating noise on that side of my box where the staples were fixed; and soon after I began to fancy that the box was pulled or towed along the sea; for I now and then felt a sort of tugging, which made the waves rise near the tops of my windows, leaving me almost in the dark. This gave me some faint hopes of relief, although I was not able to imagine how it could be brought about. I ventured to unscrew one of my chairs, which were always fastened to the floor; and, having made a hard shift to screw it down again directly under the slipping-board that I had lately opened, I mounted on the chair and, putting my mouth as near as I could to the hole, I called for help in a loud voice, and in all the languages I understood. I then fastened my handkerchief to a stick I usually carried and, thrusting it up the hole, waved it several times in the air, that if any boat or ship were near, the seamen might conjecture some unhappy mortal to be shut up in the box.

I found no effect from all I could do, but plainly perceived my closet to be moved along; and in the space of an hour or better, that side of the box where the staples were, and had no windows, struck against something that was hard. I apprehended it to be a rock, and found myself tossed more than ever. I plainly heard a noise upon the cover of my closet, like that of a cable, and the grating of it as it passed through the ring. I then found myself hoisted up, by degrees, at least three feet higher than I was before. Whereupon I again thrust up my stick and handkerchief, calling for help till I was almost hoarse. In return to which, I heard a great shout repeated three times, giving me such transports of joy as are not to be conceived but by those who feel them. I now heard a trampling over my head, and somebody calling through the hole with a loud voice, in the English tongue, "If there be any body below, let them speak." I answered, I was an Englishman, drawn by ill fortune into the greatest calamity that ever any creature underwent, and begged, by all that was moving, to be delivered out of the dungeon I was in. The voice replied, I was safe, for my box was fastened to their ship, and the carpenter should immediately come and saw a hole in the cover large enough to pull me out. I answered, that was needless and would take up too much time; for there was no more to be done, but let one of the crew put his finger into the ring and take the box out of the sea into the ship, and so into the captain's cabin. Some of them, upon hearing me talk so wildly, thought I was mad; others laughed, for indeed it never came into my head that I was now got among people of my own stature and strength. The carpenter came, and in a few minutes sawed a passage about four feet square, then let down a small ladder, upon which I mounted, and thence was taken into the ship in a very weak condition.

The sailors were all in amazement, and asked me a thousand questions, which I had no inclination to answer. I was equally confounded at the sight of so many pigmies, for such I took them to be, after having so long accustomed mine eyes to the monstrous objects I had left. But the Captain, Mr. Thomas Wilcocks, an honest worthy Shropshire man, observing I was ready to faint, took me into his cabin, gave me a cordial to comfort me, and made me turn in upon his own bed, advising me to take a little rest, of which I had great need. Before I went to sleep, I gave him to understand that I had some valuable furniture in my box, too good to be lost: a fine hammock, a handsome field-bed, two chairs, a table, and a cabinet; that my closet was hung on all sides, or rather quilted, with silk and cotton; that if he would let one of the crew bring my closet into his cabin, I would open it there before him and show him my goods. The Captain, hearing me utter these absurdities, concluded I was raving; however (I suppose to pacify me), he promised to give order as I desired and, going upon deck, sent some of his men down into my closet, whence (as I afterwards found) they drew up all my goods and stripped off the quilting; but the chairs, cabinet, and bedstead, being screwed to the floor, were much damaged by the ignorance of the seamen, who tore them up by force. Then they knocked off some of the boards for the use of the ship, and when they had got all they had a mind for, let the hull drop into the sea, which by reason of many breaches made in the bottom and sides, sunk to rights.[1] And indeed, I was glad not to have been a spectator of the havoc they made, because I am confident it would have sensibly touched me by bringing former passages into my mind, which I had rather forgot.

I slept some hours, but perpetually disturbed with dreams of the place I had left and the dangers I had escaped. However, upon waking I found myself much recovered. It was now about eight o'clock at night, and the Captain ordered supper immediately, thinking I had already fasted too long. He entertained me with great kindness, observing me not to look wildly or talk inconsistently; and, when we were left alone, desired I would give him a relation of my travels, and by what accident I came to be set adrift in that monstrous wooden chest. He said that about twelve o'clock at noon, as he was looking through his glass, he spied it at a distance and thought it was a sail, which he had a mind to make,[2] being not much out of his course, in hopes of buying some biscuit, his own beginning to fall short. That upon coming nearer and finding his error, he sent out his longboat to discover what it was; that his men came back in a fright, swearing they had seen a swimming house. That he laughed at their folly and went himself in the boat, ordering his men to take a strong cable along with them. That the weather being calm, he rowed round me several times, observed my windows and wire lattices that defended them. That he discovered two staples upon one side, which was all of boards, without any passage for light. He then commanded his men to row up to that side and, fastening a cable to one of the staples, ordered them to tow my chest, as they called it, toward the ship. When it was there he gave directions to fasten another cable to the ring fixed in the cover, and to raise up my chest with pulleys, which all the sailors were not able to do above two or three feet. He said they saw my stick and handkerchief thrust out of the hole, and concluded that some unhappy man must be shut up in the cavity. I asked whether he or the crew had seen any prodigious birds in the air about the time he first discovered me. To which he answered that, discoursing this matter with the sailors while I was asleep, one of them said he had observed three eagles flying towards the north, but remarked nothing of their being larger than the usual size (which I suppose must be imputed to the great height they were at), and he could not guess the reason of my question. I then asked the Captain how far he reckoned we might be from land. He said by the best computation he could make we were at least a hundred leagues. I assured him that he must be mistaken by almost half, for I had not left the country whence I came above two hours before I dropped into the sea. Whereupon he began again to think that my brain was disturbed, of which he gave me a hint, and advised me to go to bed in a cabin he had provided. I assured him I was well refreshed with his good entertainment and company, and as much in my senses as ever I was in my life. He then grew serious, and desired to ask me freely whether I were not troubled in my mind by the consciousness of some enormous crime, for which I was punished at the command of some prince, by exposing me in that chest, as great criminals in other countries have been forced to sea in a leaky vessel without provisions; for although he should be sorry to have taken so ill[3] a man into his ship, yet he would engage his word to set me safe ashore in the first port where we arrived. He added that his suspicions were much increased by some very absurd speeches I had delivered at first to his sailors, and afterwards to himself, in relation to my closet or chest, as well as by my odd looks and behaviour while I was at supper.

I begged his patience to hear me tell my story, which I faithfully did from the last time I left England to the moment he first discovered me. And as truth always forces its way into rational minds, so this honest worthy gentleman, who had some tincture of learning and very good sense, was immediately convinced of my candour and veracity. But further to confirm all I had said, I entreated him to give order that my cabinet should be brought, of which I had the key in my pocket (for he had already informed me how the seamen disposed of my closet). I opened it in his own presence and showed him the small collection of rarities I made in the country from which I had been so strangely delivered. There was the comb I had contrived out of the stumps of the King's beard, and another of the same materials, but fixed into a paring of Her Majesty's thumbnail, which served for the back. There was a collection of needles and pins from a foot to half a yard long; four wasp-

[1] *sunk to rights* Sunk straight down, all at once.

[2] *make* Reach.

[3] *ill* Evil.

stings, like joiner's tacks; some combings of the Queen's hair; a gold ring which one day she made me a present of in a most obliging manner, taking it from her little finger and throwing it over my head like a collar. I desired the Captain would please to accept this ring in return for his civilities, which he absolutely refused. I showed him a corn that I had cut off with my own hand from a Maid of Honour's toe; it was about the bigness of Kentish pippin,[1] and grown so hard that when I returned to England I got it hollowed into a cup and set in silver. Lastly, I desired him to see the breeches I had then on, which were made of a mouse's skin.

I could force nothing on him but a footman's tooth, which I observed him to examine with great curiosity, and found he had a fancy for it. He received it with abundance of thanks, more than such a trifle could deserve. It was drawn by an unskilful surgeon in a mistake from one of Glumdalclitch's men, who was afflicted with the toothache, but it was as sound as any in his head. I got it cleaned and put it into my cabinet. It was about a foot long, and four inches in diameter.

The Captain was very well satisfied with this plain relation I had given him, and said he hoped when we returned to England, I would oblige the world by putting it on paper and making it public. My answer was that we were overstocked with books of travels; that nothing could now pass which was not extraordinary; wherein I doubted some authors less consulted truth than their own vanity or interest, or the diversion of ignorant readers; that my story could contain little beside common events, without those ornamental descriptions of strange plants, trees, birds, and other animals, or of the barbarous customs and idolatry of savage people, with which most writers abound. However, I thanked him for his good opinion and promised to take the matter into my thoughts.

He said he wondered at one thing very much, which was, to hear me speak so loud, asking me whether the King or Queen of that country were thick of hearing. I told him it was what I had been used to for above two years past, and that I admired[2] as much at the voices of him and his men, who seemed to me only to whisper, and yet I could hear them well enough. But, when I spoke in that country, it was like a man talking in the streets to another looking out from the top of a steeple, unless when I was placed on a table or held in any person's hand. I told him I had likewise observed another thing, that when I first got into the ship and the sailors stood all about me, I thought they were the most little contemptible creatures I had ever beheld. For indeed, while I was in that prince's country I could never endure to look in a glass, after mine eyes had been accustomed to such prodigious objects, because the comparison gave me so despicable a conceit[3] of myself. The Captain said that while we were at supper, he observed me to look at every thing with a sort of wonder, and that I often seemed hardly able to contain my laughter, which he knew not well how to take, but imputed it to some disorder in my brain. I answered, it was very true; and I wondered how I could forbear, when I saw his dishes of the size of a silver three-pence, a leg of pork hardly a mouthful, a cup not so big as a nut-shell; and so I went on, describing the rest of his household stuff and provisions after the same manner. For, although the Queen had ordered a little equipage of all things necessary for me while I was in her service, yet my ideas were wholly taken up with what I saw on every side of me, and I winked at[4] my own littleness as people do at their own faults. The captain understood my raillery very well, and merrily replied with the old English proverb that he doubted[5] mine eyes were bigger than my belly, for he did not observe my stomach so good, although I had fasted all day; and, continuing in his mirth, protested he would have gladly given a hundred pounds to have seen my closet in the eagle's bill, and afterwards in its fall from so great a height into the sea; which would certainly have been a most astonishing object, worthy to have the description of it transmitted to future ages; and the comparison of Phaëton[6] was so obvious that he could not forbear applying it, although I did not much admire the conceit.

---

[1] *pippin* Small apple.

[2] *admired* Marveled.

[3] *conceit* Opinion; notion.

[4] *winked at* Overlooked.

[5] *doubted* Suspected.

[6] *Phaëton* Son of Helios (later Apollo, the Greek sun god) who one day attempted to drive the chariot of the sun for his father, but instead drove too close to the earth and nearly scorched it. He was struck down by Zeus's thunderbolt and drowned in the river Eridanus.

The Captain, having been at Tonquin,[1] was in his return to England driven northeastward to the latitude of 44 degrees, and longitude of 143. But meeting a trade wind two days after I came on board him, we sailed southward a long time and, coasting New Holland,[2] kept our course west-southwest, and then south-southwest till we doubled the Cape of Good Hope. Our voyage was very prosperous, but I shall not trouble the reader with a journal of it. The Captain called in at one or two ports and sent in his longboat for provisions and fresh water, but I never went out of the ship till we came into the Downs, which was on the third day of June, 1706, about nine months after my escape. I offered to leave my goods in security for payment of my freight, but the captain protested he would not receive one farthing. We took a kind leave of each other, and I made him promise he would come to see me at my house in Redriff. I hired a horse and guide for five shillings, which I borrowed of the Captain.

As I was on the road, observing the littleness of the houses, the trees, the cattle, and the people, I began to think myself in Lilliput. I was afraid of trampling on every traveller I met, and often called aloud to have them stand out of the way, so that I had like to have gotten one or two broken heads for my impertinence.

When I came to my own house, for which I was forced to inquire, one of the servants opening the door, I bent down to go in (like a goose under a gate) for fear of striking my head. My wife run out to embrace me, but I stooped lower than her knees, thinking she could otherwise never be able to reach my mouth. My daughter kneeled to ask my blessing, but I could not see her till she arose, having been so long used to stand with my head and eyes erect to above sixty feet; and then I went to take her up with one hand by the waist. I looked down upon the servants, and one or two friends who were in the house, as if they had been pigmies and I a giant. I told my wife she had been too thrifty, for I found she had starved herself and her daughter to nothing. In short, I behaved myself so unaccountably that they were all of the Captain's opinion when he first saw me, and concluded I had lost my wits. This I mention as an instance of the great power of habit and prejudice.

In a little time, I and my family and friends came to a right understanding; but my wife protested I should never go to sea any more, although my evil destiny so ordered that she had not power to hinder me, as the reader may know hereafter. In the meantime, I here conclude the second part of my unfortunate voyages.

Part 3 — A Voyage to Laputa, Balnibarbi, Luggnagg, Glubbdubdrib, and Japan

Chapter 1

(*The author sets out on his third voyage, is taken by pirates. The malice of a Dutchman. His arrival at an island. He is received into Laputa.*)

I had not been at home above ten days, when Captain William Robinson, a Cornish man, Commander of the *Hopewell*, a stout ship of three hundred tons, came to my house. I had formerly been surgeon of another ship where he was master, and a fourth part owner, in a voyage to the Levant;[3] he had always treated me more like a brother than an inferior officer, and hearing of my arrival made me a visit, as I apprehended only out of friendship, for nothing passed more than what is usual after long absences. But repeating his visits often, expressing his joy to find me in good health, asking whether I were now settled for life, adding that he intended a voyage to the East Indies in two months; at last he plainly invited me, though with some apologies, to be surgeon of the ship; that I should have another surgeon under me besides our two mates; that my salary should be double to the usual pay; and that having experienced my knowledge in sea-affairs to be at least equal to his, he would enter into any engagement to follow my advice, as much as if I had share in the command.

He said so many other obliging things, and I knew him to be so honest a man, that I could not reject his proposal; the thirst I had of seeing the world, notwithstanding my past misfortunes, continuing as violent as

[1] *Tonquin* Tonkin, a region in the north of present-day Vietnam.

[2] *New Holland* Australia.

[3] *Levant* Eastern Mediterranean coastal region between Greece and Egypt.

ever. The only difficulty that remained, was to persuade my wife, whose consent however I at last obtained by the prospect of advantage she proposed[1] to her children.

We set out the 5th day of August, 1706, and arrived at Fort St. George[2] the 11th of April, 1707. We stayed there three weeks to refresh our crew, many of whom were sick. From thence we went to Tonquin, where the Captain resolved to continue some time, because many of the goods he intended to buy were not ready, nor could he expect to be dispatched in several months. Therefore, in hopes to defray some of the charges he must be at, he bought a sloop,[3] loaded it with several sorts of goods, wherewith the Tonquinese usually trade to the neighbouring islands, and putting fourteen men on board, whereof three were of the country, he appointed me master of the sloop, and gave me power to traffic for two months, while he transacted his affairs at Tonquin.

We had not sailed above three days, when a great storm arising, we were driven five days to the north-north-east, and then to the east: after which we had fair weather, but still with a pretty strong gale from the west. Upon the tenth day we were chased by two pirates,[4] who soon overtook us; for my sloop was so deep loaden, that she sailed very slow; neither were we in a condition to defend ourselves.

We were boarded about the same time by both the pirates, who entered furiously at the head of their men, but finding us all prostrate upon our faces (for so I gave order), they pinioned us with strong ropes, and setting a guard upon us, went to search the sloop.

I observed among them a Dutchman, who seemed to be of some authority, though he was not Commander of either ship. He knew us by our countenances to be Englishmen, and jabbering to us in his own language, swore we should be tied back to back, and thrown into the sea.

I spoke Dutch tolerably well; I told him who we were, and begged him in consideration of our being Christians and Protestants, of neighbouring countries, in strict alliance,[5] that he would move the Captains to take some pity on us. This inflamed his rage; he repeated his threatenings, and turning to his companions, spoke with great vehemence, in the Japanese language, as I suppose, often using the word *Christianos*.

The largest of the two pirate ships was commanded by a Japanese Captain, who spoke a little Dutch, but very imperfectly. He came up to me, and after several questions, which I answered in great humility, he said we should not die. I made the Captain a very low bow, and then turning to the Dutchman, said, I was sorry to find more mercy in a heathen, than in a brother Christian. But I had soon reason to repent those foolish words: for that malicious reprobate, having been endeavoured in vain to persuade both the Captains that I might be thrown into the sea (which they would not yield to after the promise made me, that I should not die), however prevailed so far as to have a punishment inflicted on me, worse in all human appearance than death itself. My men were sent by an equal division into both the pirate ships, and my sloop new manned. As to myself, it was determined that I should be set a-drift in a small canoe, with paddles and a sail, and four days provisions, which last the Japanese Captain was so kind to double out of his own stores, and would permit no man to search me. I got down into the canoe, while the Dutchman standing upon the deck, loaded me with all the curses and injurious terms his language could afford.

About an hour before we saw the pirates, I had taken an observation, and found we were in the latitude of 46 N. and of longitude 183. When I was at some distance from the pirates, I discovered by my pocket-glass several islands to the south-east. I set up my sail, the wind being fair, with a design to reach the nearest of those islands, which I made a shift to do in about three hours. It was all rocky; however, I got many birds' eggs, and striking fire, I kindled some heath[6] and dry seaweed, by which I roasted my eggs. I eat no other supper, being resolved to spare my provisions as much as I could. I passed the night under the shelter of a rock, strowing some heath under me, and slept pretty well.

The next day I sailed to another island, and thence to a third and fourth, sometimes using my sail, and

[1] *proposed* Expected.

[2] *Fort St. George* Now called Madras, this was the first British fortress in India.

[3] *sloop* Small sailing ship.

[4] *pirates* Pirate ships.

[5] *strict alliance* The Dutch and English had formed the Grand Alliance (1701) against France but remained commercial rivals.

[6] *heath* Heather.

sometimes my paddles. But not to trouble the reader with a particular account of my distresses, let it suffice, that on the fifth day I arrived at the last island in my sight, which lay south-south-east to the former.

This island was at a greater distance than I expected, and I did not reach it in less than five hours. I encompassed it almost round, before I could find a convenient place to land in, which was a small creek, about three times the wideness of my canoe. I found the island to be all rocky, only a little intermingled with tufts of grass, and sweet-smelling herbs. I took out my small provisions, and after having refreshed myself, I secured the remainder in a cave, whereof there were great numbers. I gathered plenty of eggs upon the rocks, and got a quantity of dry sea-weed, and parched grass, which I designed to kindle the next day, and roast my eggs as well as I could (for I had about me my flint, steel, match, and burning-glass). I lay all night in the cave where I had lodged my provisions. My bed was the same dry grass and sea-weed which I intended for fuel. I slept very little, for the disquiets of my mind prevailed over my weariness, and kept me awake. I considered how impossible it was to preserve my life in so desolate a place, and how miserable my end must be. Yet I found myself so listless and desponding, that I had not the heart to rise; and before I could get spirits enough to creep out of my cave, the day was far advanced. I walked a while among the rocks; the sky was perfectly clear, and the sun so hot, that I was forced to turn my face from it: when all on a sudden it became obscured, as I thought, in a manner very different from what happens by the interposition of a cloud. I turned back, and perceived a vast opaque body between me and the sun, moving forwards towards the island: it seemed to be about two miles high, and hid the sun six or seven minutes, but I did not observe the air to be much colder, or the sky more darkened, than if I had stood under the shade of a mountain. As it approached nearer over the place where I was, it appeared to be a firm substance, the bottom flat, smooth, and shining very bright from the reflection of the sea below. I stood upon a height about two hundred yards from the shore, and saw this vast body descending almost to a parallel with me, at less than an English mile distance. I took out my pocket perspective,[1] and could plainly discover numbers of people moving up and down the sides of it, which appeared to be sloping, but what those people were doing, I was not able to distinguish.

The natural love of life gave me some inward motions of joy, and I was ready to entertain a hope that this adventure[2] might some way or other help to deliver me from the desolate place and condition I was in. But at the same time the reader can hardly conceive my astonishment, to behold an island in the air, inhabited by men, who were able (as it should seem) to raise or sink, or put it into a progressive motion, as they pleased. But not being at that time in a disposition to philosophise upon this phenomenon, I rather chose to observe what course the island would take, because it seemed for a while to stand still. Yet soon after, it advanced nearer, and I could see the sides of it encompassed with several gradations of galleries and stairs, at certain intervals, to descend from one to the other. In the lowest gallery, I beheld some people fishing with long angling rods, and others looking on. I waved my cap (for my hat was long since worn out) and my handkerchief towards the island; and upon its nearer approach, I called and shouted with the utmost strength of my voice; and then looking circumspectly, I beheld a crowd gather to that side which was most in my view. I found by their pointing towards me and to each other, that they plainly discovered me, although they made no return to my shouting. But I could see four or five men running in great haste up the stairs to the top of the island, who then disappeared. I happened rightly to conjecture, that these were sent for orders to some person in authority upon this occasion.

The number of people increased, and in less than half an hour, the island was moved and raised in such a manner, that the lowest gallery appeared in a parallel of less than an hundred yards distance from the height where I stood. I then put myself into the most supplicating postures, and spoke in the humblest accent, but received no answer. Those who stood nearest over against me, seemed to be persons of distinction, as I supposed by their habit. They conferred earnestly with each other, looking often upon me. At length one of them called out in a clear, polite, smooth dialect, not unlike in sound to the Italian; and therefore I returned an answer in that language, hoping at least that the

[1] *pocket perspective* Small spyglass.

[2] *adventure* Chance event or occurrence.

cadence might be more agreeable to his ears. Although neither of us understood the other, yet my meaning was easily known, for the people saw the distress I was in.

They made signs for me to come down from the rock, and go towards the shore, which I accordingly did; and the flying island being raised to a convenient height, the verge directly over me, a chain was let down from the lowest gallery, with a seat fastened to the bottom, to which I fixed myself, and was drawn up by pulleys.

CHAPTER 2

(*The humours*[1] *and dispositions of the Laputians described. An account of their learning. Of the King and his court. The author's reception there. The inhabitants subject to fear and disquietudes. An account of the women.*)

At my alighting I was surrounded by a crowd of people, but those who stood nearest seemed to be of better quality. They beheld me with all the marks and circumstances of wonder; neither, indeed, was I much in their debt, having never till then seen a race of mortals so singular in their shapes, habits, and countenances. Their heads were all reclined either to the right or the left; one of their eyes turned inward, and the other directly up to the zenith.[2] Their outward garments were adorned with the figures of suns, moons, and stars, interwoven with those of fiddles, flutes, harps, trumpets, guitars, harpsichords, and many other instruments of music, unknown to us in Europe.[3] I observed here and there many in the habit of servants, with a blown bladder fastened like a flail to the end of a short stick, which they carried in their hands. In each bladder was a small quantity of dried pease, or little pebbles (as I was afterwards informed). With these bladders they now and then flapped the mouths and ears of those who stood near them, of which practice I could not then conceive the meaning; it seems, the minds of these people are so taken up with intense speculations, that they neither can speak, nor attend to the discourses of others, without being roused by some external taction[4] upon the organs of speech and hearing; for which reason, those persons who are able to afford it always keep a flapper (the original is *climenole*) in their family, as one of their domestics, nor ever walk abroad or make visits without him. And the business of this officer is, when two or more persons are in company, gently to strike with his bladder the mouth of him who is to speak, and the right ear of him or them to whom the speaker addresseth himself. This flapper is likewise employed diligently to attend his master in his walks, and upon occasion to give him a soft flap on his eyes, because he is always so wrapped up in cogitation,[5] that he is in manifest danger of falling down every precipice, and bouncing his head against every post, and in the streets, of justling[6] others, or being justled himself into the kennel.[7]

It was necessary to give the reader this information, without which he would be at the same loss with me, to understand the proceedings of these people, as they conducted me up the stairs, to the top of the island, and from thence to the royal palace. While we were ascending, they forgot several times what they were about, and left me to myself, till their memories were again roused by their flappers; for they appeared altogether unmoved by the sight of my foreign habit and countenance, and by the shouts of the vulgar, whose thoughts and minds were more disengaged.

At last we entered the palace, and proceeded into the chamber of presence, where I saw the King seated on his throne, attended on each side by persons of prime quality. Before the throne, was a large table filled with globes and spheres, and mathematical instruments of all kinds.[8] His Majesty took not the least notice of us, although our entrance was not without sufficient noise, by the concourse of all persons belonging to the court. But he was then deep in a problem, and we attended at least an hour, before he could solve it. There stood by him on each side, a young page, with flaps in their hands, and when they saw he was at leisure, one of them

[1] *humours* Tendencies.

[2] *zenith* The sky directly overhead.

[3] *Their outward ... in Europe* The Laputians are a parody of contemporary speculative science that contained abstract theories of science, mathematics, and music.

[4] *taction* Act of touching.

[5] *cogitation* Act of reflection or thinking.

[6] *justling* Jostling.

[7] *kennel* Gutter.

[8] *Before the throne ... all kinds* King George I (1660–1727) was a patron of science and music.

gently struck his mouth, and the other his right ear; at which he started like one awaked on the sudden, and looking towards me, and the company I was in, recollected the occasion of our coming, whereof he had been informed before. He spoke some words, whereupon immediately a young man with a flap came up to my side, and flapped me gently on the right ear; but I made signs, as well as I could, that I had no occasion for such an instrument; which, as I afterwards found, gave his Majesty and the whole court a very mean opinion of my understanding. The King, as far as I could conjecture, asked me several questions, and I addressed myself to him in all the languages I had. When it was found that I could neither understand nor be understood, I was conducted by his order to an apartment in his palace (this prince being distinguished above all his predecessors for his hospitality to strangers),[1] where two servants were appointed to attend me. My dinner was brought, and four persons of quality, whom I remembered to have seen very near the King's person, did me the honour to dine with me. We had two courses, of three dishes each. In the first course, there was a shoulder of mutton, cut into an equilateral triangle, a piece of beef into a rhomboides, and a pudding into a cycloid. The second course was two ducks, trussed up into the form of fiddles; sausages and puddings resembling flutes and haut-boys,[2] and a breast of veal in the shape of a harp. The servants cut our bread into cones, cylinders, parallelograms, and several other mathematical figures.

While we were at dinner, I made bold to ask the names of several things in their language; and those noble persons, by the assistance of their flappers, delighted to give me answers, hoping to raise my admiration of their great abilities, if I could be brought to converse with them. I was soon able to call for bread and drink, or whatever else I wanted.

After dinner my company withdrew, and a person was sent to me by the King's order, attended by a flapper. He brought with him pen, ink, and paper, and three or four books, giving me to understand by signs, that he was sent to teach me the language. We sat together four hours, in which time I wrote down a great number of words in columns, with the translations over against them. I likewise made a shift to learn several short sentences. For my tutor would order one of my servants to fetch something, to turn about, to make a bow, to sit, or stand, or walk, and the like. Then I took down the sentence in writing. He showed me also in one of his books, the figures of the sun, moon, and stars, the zodiac, the tropics, and polar circles, together with the denominations of many planes and solids. He gave me the names and descriptions of all the musical instruments, and the general terms of art[3] in playing on each of them. After he had left me, I placed all my words with their interpretations in alphabetical order. And thus in a few days, by the help of a very faithful memory, I got some insight into their language.

The word, which I interpret the *Flying* or *Floating Island*,[4] is in the original *Laputa*, whereof I could never learn the true etymology. *Lap* in the old obsolete language signifieth *high*, and *untuh*, a *governor*, from which they say, by corruption, was derived *Laputa*, from *Lapuntuh*. But I do not approve of this derivation, which seems to be a little strained. I ventured to offer to the learned among them a conjecture of my own, that *Laputa* was *quasi lap outed*; *lap* signifying properly the dancing of the sunbeams in the sea, and *outed*, a wing, which however I shall not obtrude, but submit to the judicious reader.[5]

Those to whom the King had entrusted me, observing how ill I was clad, ordered a tailor to come next morning, and take my measure for a suit of clothes. This operator did his office after a different manner from those of his trade in Europe. He first took my altitude by a quadrant, and then with a rule and compasses, described the dimensions and outlines of my whole body, all which he entered upon paper, and in six days brought my clothes very ill made, and quite out of shape, by happening to mistake a figure in the calcula-

[1] *this prince ... strangers* George I caused controversy by filling his court with visitors from Hanover.

[2] *haut-boys* Oboes.

[3] *terms of art* Technical terms.

[4] *Floating Island* Cf. Sir William Temple, "Memoirs," 454: "our counsels and conduct were like those of a floating island, driven one way or t'other, according to the winds or tides." Temple was referring to English foreign policy under Charles II (r. 1660–85).

[5] *Lap ... reader* Swift's mock solemnity here is thought to be a satire of editor Richard Bentley who was disliked by Swift and his circle. Part of the joke is that Gulliver ignores the most obvious meaning of *Laputa* (or *la puta*): "the whore" in Spanish.

tion.[1] But my comfort was, that I observed such accidents very frequent, and little regarded.

During my confinement for want of clothes, and by an indisposition that held me some days longer, I much enlarged my dictionary; and when I went next to court, was able to understand many things the King spoke, and to return him some kind of answers. His Majesty had given orders that the island should move north-east and by east, to the vertical point over Lagado, the metropolis of the whole kingdom below upon the firm earth. It was about ninety leagues distant, and our voyage lasted four days and an half. I was not in the least sensible of the progressive motion made in the air by the island. On the second morning about eleven o'clock, the King himself in person, attended by his nobility, courtiers, and officers, having prepared all their musical instruments, played on them for three hours without intermission, so that I was quite stunned with the noise; neither could I possibly guess the meaning, till my tutor informed me. He said that the people of their island had their ears adapted to hear the music of the spheres,[2] which always played at certain periods, and the Court was now prepared to bear their part in whatever instrument they most excelled.

In our journey towards Lagado, the capital city, his Majesty ordered that the island should stop over certain towns and villages, from whence he might receive the petitions of his subjects. And to this purpose several packthreads were let down with small weights at the bottom. On these packthreads the people strung their petitions, which mounted up directly like scraps of paper fastened by school-boys at the end of the string that holds their kite.[3] Sometimes we received wine and victuals from below, which were drawn up by pulleys.

The knowledge I had in mathematics gave me great assistance in acquiring their phraseology, which depended much upon that science and music; and in the latter I was not unskilled. Their ideas are perpetually conversant in lines and figures. If they would, for example, praise the beauty of a woman, or any other animal, they describe it by rhombs, circles, parallelograms, ellipses, and other geometrical terms, or by words of art drawn from music, needless here to repeat. I observed in the King's kitchen all sorts of mathematical and musical instruments, after the figures of which they cut up the joints that were served to his Majesty's table.

Their houses are very ill built, the walls bevil,[4] without one right angle in any apartment, and this defect ariseth from the contempt they bear to practical geometry which they despise as vulgar and mechanic, those instructions they give being too refined for the intellectuals of their work-men, which occasions perpetual mistakes. And although they are dexterous enough upon a piece of paper in the management of the rule, the pencil, and the divider, yet in the common actions and behaviour of life, I have not seen a more clumsy, awkward, and unhandy people, nor so slow and perplexed in their conceptions upon all other subjects, except those of mathematics and music. They are very bad reasoners, and vehemently given to opposition, unless when they happen to be of the right opinion, which is seldom their case. Imagination, fancy, and invention, they are wholly strangers to, nor have any words in their language by which those ideas can be expressed; the whole compass of their thoughts and mind being shut up within the two forementioned sciences.

Most of them, and especially those who deal in the astronomical part, have great faith in judicial astrology,[5] although they are ashamed to own it publicly. But what I chiefly admired,[6] and thought altogether unaccountable, was the strong disposition I observed in them towards news and politics, perpetually enquiring into public affairs, giving their judgments in matters of state, and passionately disputing every inch of a party opinion. I have indeed observed the same disposition among

[1] *by happening ... calculation* Refers to unsuccessful contemporary efforts to determine the altitude of the sun, moon, stars, and mountains, by mathematical instruments. Also a reference to a controversy in which a printer erroneously added an extra zero in Isaac Newton's (1643–1727) calculation of the distance of the earth from the sun.

[2] *music of the spheres* According to ancient philosophers, the harmonious sounds made as the spheres carried the sun, moon, and planets in their motions.

[3] *On these packthreads ... kite* George I was notoriously remote from his subjects; he spent much of his time in Hanover. Therefore, those who wanted to see him would literally have to "go fly a kite."

[4] *bevil* Slant.

[5] *judicial astrology* Study of how human affairs are influenced by the stars.

[6] *admired* Wondered at.

most of the mathematicians I have known in Europe,[1] although I could never discover the least analogy between the two sciences; unless those people suppose, that because the smallest circle hath as many degrees as the largest, therefore the regulation and management of the world require no more abilities than the handling and turning of a globe. But I rather take this quality to spring from a very common infirmity of human nature, inclining us to be more curious and conceited[2] in matters where we have least concern, and for which we are least adapted either by study or nature.

These people are under continual disquietudes, never enjoying a minute's peace of mind; and their disturbances proceed from causes which very little affect the rest of mortals. Their apprehensions arise from several changes they dread in the celestial bodies. For instance; that the earth, by the continual approaches of the sun towards it, must in course of time be absorbed, or swallowed up.[3] That the face of the sun will by degrees be encrusted with its own effluvia,[4] and give no more light to the world. That the earth very narrowly escaped a brush from the tail of the last comet, which would have infallibly reduced it to ashes; and that the next, which they have calculated for one and thirty years hence, will probably destroy us.[5] For, if in its perihelion[6] it should approach within a certain degree of the sun (as by their calculations they have reason to dread), it will receive a degree of heat ten thousand times more intense than that of red-hot glowing iron; and in its absence from the sun, carry a blazing tail ten hundred thousand and fourteen miles long; through which if the earth should pass at the distance of one hundred thousand miles from the nucleus or main body of the comet, it must in its passage be set on fire, and reduced to ashes. That the sun daily spending its rays without any nutriment to supply them, will at last be wholly consumed and annihilated; which must be attended with the destruction of this earth, and of all the planets that receive their light from it.

They are so perpetually alarmed with the apprehensions of these and the like impending dangers, that they can neither sleep quietly in their beds, nor have any relish for the common pleasures or amusements of life. When they meet an acquaintance in the morning, the first question is about the sun's health, how he looked at his setting and rising, and what hopes they have to avoid the stroke of the approaching comet. This conversation they are apt to run into with the same temper that boys discover, in delighting to hear terrible stories of spirits and hobgoblins, which they greedily listen to, and dare not go to bed for fear.

The women of the island have abundance of vivacity: they contemn[7] their husbands, and are exceedingly fond of strangers, whereof there is always a considerable number from the continent below, attending at court, either upon affairs of the several towns and corporations[8] or their own particular occasions, but are much despised, because they want[9] the same endowments. Among these the ladies choose their gallants:[10] but the vexation is, that they act with too much ease and security, for the husband is always so rapt in speculation, that the mistress and lover may proceed to the greatest familiarities before his face, if he be but provided with paper and implements, and without his flapper at his side.

The wives and daughters lament their confinement to the island, although I think it the most delicious spot of ground in the world; and although they live in the greatest plenty and magnificence, and are allowed to do whatever they please, they long to see the world, and take the diversions of the metropolis, which they are not allowed to do without a particular licence from the King; and this is not easy to be obtained, because the people of quality have found, by frequent experience, how hard it is to persuade their women to return from

[1] *the same disposition … Europe* Many mathematicians in England at the time, such as Newton, supported the Whig party.

[2] *conceited* Opinionated.

[3] *the earth … swallowed up* All of the possible disasters that frighten the Laputans were possible ramifications of Newton's theories suggested by English scientists. Newton's theories of planetary motion suggested that any change to the balance between the speed with which the earth rotated around the sun would result in the earth falling into the sun.

[4] *effluvia* Sunspots.

[5] *the earth … destroy us* Refers to Halley's Comet, which some astronomers feared would strike the earth on its next appearance.

[6] *perihelion* Point in the orbit of a comet where it is nearest to the sun.

[7] *contemn* To treat with contempt.

[8] *corporations* Municipal authorities.

[9] *want* Lack.

[10] *gallants* Lovers, paramours.

once people go below, they are changed

below. I was told that a great court lady, who had several children, is married to the prime minister, the richest subject in the kingdom, a very graceful person, extremely fond of her, and lives in the finest palace of the island, went down to Lagado, on the pretence of health, there hid herself for several months, till the King sent a warrant to search for her, and she was found in an obscure eating-house all in rags, having pawned her clothes to maintain an old deformed footman, who beat her every day, and in whose company she was taken much against her will. And although her husband received her with all possible kindness, and without the least reproach, she soon after contrived to steal down again with all her jewels, to the same gallant, and hath not been heard of since.

This may perhaps pass with the reader rather for an European or English story, than for one of a country so remote. But he may please to consider, that the caprices of womankind are not limited by any climate or nation, and that they are much more uniform than can be easily imagined.

In about a month's time I had made a tolerable proficiency in their language, and was able to answer most of the King's questions, when I had the honour to attend him. His Majesty discovered not the least curiosity to enquire into the laws, government, history, religion, or manners of the countries where I had been, but confined his questions to the state of mathematics, and received the account I gave him with great contempt and indifference, though often roused by his flapper on each side.

CHAPTER 3

(*A phenomenon solved*[1] *by modern philosophy and astronomy. The Laputians' great improvements in the latter. The King's method of suppressing insurrections.*)

I desired leave of this prince to see the curiosities of the island, which he was graciously pleased to grant and ordered my tutor to attend me. I chiefly wanted to know to what cause in art, or in nature, it owed its several motions, whereof I will now give a philosophical account to the reader.

The Flying or Floating Island is exactly circular, its diameter 7837 yards, or about four miles and an half,[2] and consequently contains ten thousand acres. It is three hundred yards thick. The bottom or under surface, which appears to those who view it below, is one even regular plate of adamant,[3] shooting up to the height of about two hundred yards. Above it lie the several minerals in their usual order, and over all is a coat of rich mould, ten or twelve foot deep. The declivity[4] of the upper surface, from the circumference to the centre, is the natural cause why all the dews and rains which fall upon the island, are conveyed in small rivulets toward the middle, where they are emptied into four large basins, each of about half a mile in circuit, and two hundred yards distant from the centre. From these basins the water is continually exhaled by the sun in the day-time, which effectually prevents their overflowing. Besides, as it is in the power of the monarch to raise the island above the region of clouds and vapours, he can prevent the falling of dews and rains whenever he pleases. For the highest clouds cannot rise above two miles, as naturalists agree, at least they were never known to do so in that country.

At the centre of the island there is a chasm about fifty yards in diameter, from whence the astronomers descend into a large dome, which is therefore called *Flandona Gagnole*, or the Astronomer's Cave,[5] situated at the depth of an hundred yards beneath the upper surface of the adamant. In this cave are twenty lamps continually burning, which from the reflection of the adamant cast a strong light into every part. The place is stored with great variety of sextants, quadrants, telescopes, astrolabes, and other astronomical instruments. But the greatest curiosity, upon which the fate of the island depends, is a loadstone of a prodigious size, in shape resembling a weaver's shuttle. It is in length six

---

[1] *A phenomenon solved* Here Swift is satirizing the language of some Royal Society papers.

[2] *its diameter ... half* Probably modeled on the terrella (little earth), a spherical loadstone used by scientists to investigate the magnetic action of the earth. One such terrella, with a diameter of four and a half inches (Laputa is four and a half miles in diameter), appeared in the exhibits of the Royal Society.

[3] *adamant* Name of a supposed mineral which was a combination of a diamond and a loadstone or magnet.

[4] *declivity* Downward slope.

[5] *Astronomer's Cave* The description here is thought to be based on the cave in the Royal Observatory in Paris.

yards, and in the thickest part at least three yards over.[1] This magnet is sustained by a very strong axle of adamant passing through its middle, upon which it plays, and is poised so exactly that the weakest hand can turn it. It is hooped round with an hollow cylinder of adamant, four foot deep, as many thick, and twelve yards in diameter, placed horizontally, and supported by eight adamantine feet, each six yards high. In the middle of the concave side there is a groove twelve inches deep, in which the extremities of the axle are lodged, and turned round as there is occasion.

The stone cannot be moved from its place by any force, because the hoop and its feet are one continued piece with that body of adamant which constitutes the bottom of the island.

By means of this loadstone,[2] the island is made to rise and fall, and move from one place to another. For, with respect to that part of the earth over which the monarch presides, the stone is endued at one of its sides[3] with an attractive power, and at the other with a repulsive. Upon placing the magnet erect with its attracting end towards the earth, the island descends; but when the repelling extremity points downwards, the island mounts directly upwards. When the position of the stone is oblique, the motion of the island is so too. For in this magnet the forces always act in lines parallel to its direction.

By this oblique motion, the island is conveyed to different parts of the monarch's dominions. To explain the manner of its progress, let *A B* represent a line drawn across the dominions of Balnibarbi, let the line *c d* represent the loadstone, of which let *d* be the repelling end, and *c* the attracting end, the island being over *C*; let the stone be placed in the position *c d*, with its repelling end downwards; then the island will be driven upwards obliquely towards *D*. When it is arrived at *D*, let the stone be turned upon its axle, till its attracting end points towards *E*, and then the island will be carried obliquely towards *E*; where if the stone be again turned upon its axle till it stands in the position *E F*, with its repelling point downwards, the island will rise obliquely towards *F*, where by directing the attracting end towards *G*, the island may be carried to *G*, and from *G* to *H*, by turning the stone, so as to make its repelling extremity to point directly downwards. And thus by changing the situation of the stone as often as there is occasion, the island is made to rise and fall by turns in an oblique direction, and by those alternate risings and fallings (the obliquity being not considerable) is conveyed from one part of the dominions to the other.

But it must be observed, that this island cannot move beyond the extent of the dominions below, nor can it rise above the height of four miles. For which the astronomers (who have written large systems concerning the stone) assign the following reason: that the magnetic virtue does not extend beyond the distance of four miles, and that the mineral which acts upon the stone in the bowels of the earth, and in the sea about six leagues distant from the shore, is not diffused through the whole globe, but terminated with the limits of the King's dominions; and it was easy from the great advantage of such a superior situation, for a prince to bring under his obedience whatever country lay within the attraction of that magnet.

When the stone is put parallel to the plane of the horizon, the island standeth still; for in that case, the extremities of it being at equal distance from the earth, act with equal force, the one in drawing downwards, the other in pushing upwards, and consequently no motion can ensue.

This loadstone is under the care of certain astronomers, who from time to time give it such positions as the monarch directs. They spend the greatest part of their lives in observing the celestial bodies, which they do by the assistance of glasses far excelling ours in goodness. For although their largest telescopes do not exceed three feet, they magnify much more than those of an hundred among us, and show the stars with greater clearness. This advantage hath enabled them to extend their discoveries much further than our astronomers in Europe; for they have made a catalogue of ten thousand fixed stars, whereas the largest of ours do not contain above one third part of that number.[4] They have likewise discovered two lesser stars, or satellites, which revolve about Mars, whereof the innermost is

[1] *over* Across.

[2] *By means of this loadstone* Swift uses theories presented in William Gilbert's *De Magnete* (1600) to describe the movement and navigation of Laputa.

[3] *sides* Poles.

[4] *they have made ... number* In *British Catalogue of Stars* (1725) John Flamsteed listed 2935 stars.

distant from the centre of the primary planet exactly three of his diameters, and the outermost five; the former revolves in the space of ten hours, and the latter in twenty-one and an half; so that the squares of their periodical times are very near in the same proportion with the cubes of their distance from the centre of Mars, which evidently shows them to be governed by the same law of gravitation, that influences the other heavenly bodies.

They have observed ninety-three different comets,[1] and settled their periods with great exactness. If this be true (and they affirm it with great confidence), it is much to be wished that their observations were made public, whereby the theory of comets, which at present is very lame and defective, might be brought to the same perfection with other parts of astronomy.

The King would be the most absolute prince in the universe, if he could but prevail on a ministry to join with him; but these having their estates below on the continent, and considering that the office of a favourite hath a very uncertain tenure, would never consent to the enslaving their country.

If any town should engage in rebellion or mutiny, fall into violent factions, or refuse to pay the usual tribute, the King hath two methods of reducing them to obedience. The first and the mildest course is by keeping the island hovering over such a town, and the lands about it, whereby he can deprive them of the benefit of the sun and the rain, and consequently afflict the inhabitants with dearth and diseases. And if the crime deserve it, they are at the same time pelted from above with great stones, against which they have no defence but by creeping into cellars or caves, while the roofs of their houses are beaten to pieces. But if they still continue obstinate, or offer to raise insurrections, he proceeds to the last remedy, by letting the island drop directly upon their heads, which makes a universal destruction both of houses and men. However, this is an extremity to which the prince is seldom driven, neither, indeed, is he willing to put it in execution, nor dare his ministers advise him to an action, which as it would render them odious to the people, so it would be a great damage to their own estates, which lie all below, for the island is the King's demesne.

But there is still indeed a more weighty reason, why the kings of this country have been always averse from executing so terrible an action, unless upon the utmost necessity. For if the town intended to be destroyed should have in it any tall rocks, as it generally falls out in the larger cities, a situation probably chosen at first with a view to prevent such a catastrophe; or if it abound in high spires, or pillars of stone, a sudden fall might endanger the bottom or under surface of the island, which, although it consists, as I have said, of one entire adamant two hundred yards thick, might happen to crack by too great a choque,[2] or burst by approaching too near the fires from the houses below, as the backs both of iron and stone will often do in our chimneys. Of all this the people are well apprised, and understand how far to carry their obstinacy, where their liberty or property is concerned. And the King, when he is highest provoked, and most determined to press a city to rubbish, orders the island to descend with great gentleness, out of a pretence of tenderness to his people, but indeed for fear of breaking the adamantine bottom; in which case, it is the opinion of all their philosophers, that the loadstone could no longer hold it up, and the whole mass would fall to the ground.

About three years before my arrival among them, while the King was in his progress over his dominions, there happened an extraordinary accident[3] which had like to have put a period to the fate of that monarchy, at least as it is now instituted. Lindalino,[4] the second city in the kingdom, was the first his Majesty visited in his progress. Three days after his departure the inhabitants, who had often complained of great oppressions, shut the town gates, seized on the governor, and with incredible

[1] *They have observed ... comets* In 1704 Edmund Halley had only identified twenty-four comets.

[2] *choque* Sudden and violent blow or impact.

[3] *About three years ... accident* The incident recounted here relates to the William Wood scandal which began in 1723, three years before *Gulliver's Travels*'s publication in 1726. Wood bribed the Duchess of Kendal to procure a patent authorizing him to supply £100,800 worth of copper coins for Ireland, without the consultation of the Irish Parliament. The coins, protested the Irish Parliament, would be disastrous for Ireland's economy. Adding their voices in opposition to the plan were James Maculla, who published a pamphlet entitled *Ireland's Consternation*, and Swift, who anonymously published *Drapier's Letters* calling for Irish resistance. In 1725, the patent was withdrawn.

[4] *Lindalino* Scholars have interpreted this name as a coded form of Dublin, i.e., double lin.

speed and labour erected four large towers,[1] one at every corner of the city (which is an exact square), equal in height to a strong pointed rock[2] that stands directly in the centre of the city. Upon the top of each tower, as well as upon the rock, they fixed a great loadstone, and in case their design should fail, they had provided a vast quantity of the most combustible fuel,[3] hoping to burst therewith the adamantine bottom of the island, if the loadstone project should miscarry.

It was eight months[4] before the King had perfect notice that the Lindalinians were in rebellion. He then commanded that the island should be wafted over the city. The people were unanimous, and had laid in store of provisions, and a great river runs through the middle of the town. The King hovered over them several days to deprive them of the sun and the rain. He ordered many packthreads to be let down, yet not a person offered to send up a petition, but instead thereof, very bold demands, the redress of all their grievances, great immunities, the choice of their own governor, and other the like exorbitances. Upon which his Majesty commanded all the inhabitants of the island to cast great stones from the lower gallery into the town; but the citizens had provided against this mischief by conveying their persons and effects into the four towers, and other strong buildings, and vaults underground.

The King being now determined to reduce this proud people, ordered that the island should descend gently within forty yards of the top of the towers and rock. This was accordingly done; but the officers employed in that work found the descent much speedier than usual, and by turning the loadstone could not without great difficulty keep it in a firm position, but found the island inclining to fall. They sent the King immediate intelligence of this astonishing event, and begged his Majesty's permission to raise the island higher; the King consented, a general council was called, and the officers of the loadstone ordered to attend. One of the oldest and expertest among them obtained leave to try an experiment. He took a strong line of an hundred yards, and the island being raised over the town above the attracting power they had felt, he fastened a piece of adamant to the end of his line, which had in it a mixture of iron mineral, of the same nature with that whereof the bottom or lower surface of the island is composed, and from the lower gallery let it down slowly towards the top of the towers. The adamant was not descended four yards, before the officer felt it drawn so strongly downwards, that he could hardly pull it back. He then threw down several small pieces of adamant, and observed that they were all violently attracted by the top of the tower. The same experiment was made on the other three towers, and on the rock with the same effect.

This incident broke entirely the King's measures, and (to dwell no longer on other circumstances) he was forced to give the town their own conditions.

I was assured by a great minister, that if the island had descended so near the town as not to be able to raise itself, the citizens were determined to fix it for ever, to kill the King and all his servants, and entirely change the government.

By a fundamental law of this realm, neither the king, nor either of his two eldest sons, are permitted to leave the island;[5] nor the queen, till she is past child-bearing.

CHAPTER 4

(*The author leaves Laputa; is conveyed to Balnibarbi, arrives at the metropolis. A description of the metropolis, and the country adjoining. The author hospitably received by a great Lord. His conversation with that Lord.*)

Although I cannot say that I was ill treated in this island, yet I must confess I thought myself too much neglected, not without some degree of contempt.

[1] *four large towers* These towers represent the four main agencies of Irish local government: the Privy Council, the Grand Jury, and the two houses of the Irish Parliament.

[2] *a strong pointed rock* Refers to the Irish Church, symbolized by St. Patrick's Cathedral, of which Swift was dean.

[3] *most combustible fuel* The incendiary pamphlets of Swift and the Irish Parliament's resolutions.

[4] *eight months* Eight months after Maculla's pamphlet was published, the King summoned the Lord-Lieutenant of Ireland to London to report on the Irish situation.

[5] *By a fundamental ... island* Refers to the Act of Settlement (1701), forbidding the King to leave England without permission from Parliament. In order to freely visit Hanover, George I persuaded Parliament to remove this law in 1716. His frequent absences were the cause of much bitterness among his subjects.

For neither prince nor people appeared to be curious in any part of knowledge, except mathematics and music, wherein I was far their inferior, and upon that account very little regarded.

On the other side, after having seen all the curiosities of the island, I was very desirous to leave it, being heartily weary of those people. They were indeed excellent in two sciences for which I have great esteem, and wherein I am not unversed; but at the same time so abstracted and involved in speculation, that I never met with such disagreeable companions. I conversed only with women, tradesmen, flappers, and court-pages, during two months of my abode there, by which, at last, I rendered myself extremely contemptible; yet these were the only people from whom I could ever receive a reasonable answer.

I had obtained, by hard study, a good degree of knowledge in their language; I was weary of being confined to an island where I received so little countenance,[1] and resolved to leave it with the first opportunity.

There was a great lord at court, nearly related to the King, and for that reason alone used with respect. He was universally reckoned the most ignorant and stupid person among them. He had performed many eminent services for the crown, had great natural and acquired parts, adorned with integrity and honour, but so ill an ear for music, that his detractors reported he had been often known to beat time in the wrong place; neither could his tutors, without extreme difficulty, teach him to demonstrate the most easy proposition in the mathematics. He was pleased to show me many marks of favour, often did me the honour of a visit, desired to be informed in the affairs of Europe, the laws and customs, the manners and learning of the several countries where I had travelled. He listened to me with great attention, and made very wise observations on all I spoke. He had two flappers attending him for state, but never made use of them except at court, and in visits of ceremony, and would always command them to withdraw when we were alone together.

I entreated this illustrious person to intercede in my behalf with his Majesty for leave to depart, which he accordingly did, as he was pleased to tell me, with regret: for indeed he had made me several offers very advantageous, which, however, I refused with expressions of the highest acknowledgment.

On the 16th day of February I took leave of his Majesty and the court. The King made me a present to the value of about two hundred pounds English, and my protector his kinsman as much more, together with a letter of recommendation to a friend of his in Lagado, the metropolis. The island being then hovering over a mountain about two miles from it, I was let down from the lowest gallery, in the same manner as I had been taken up.

The continent, as far as it is subject to the monarch of the Flying Island, passes under the general name of *Balnibarbi*, and the metropolis, as I said before, is called *Lagado*. I felt some little satisfaction in finding myself on firm ground. I walked to the city without any concern, being clad like one of the natives, and sufficiently instructed to converse with them. I soon found out the person's house to whom I was recommended, presented my letter from his friend the grandee in the island, and was received with much kindness. This great lord, whose name was Munodi, ordered me an apartment in his own house, where I continued during my stay, and was entertained in a most hospitable manner.

The next morning after my arrival, he took me in his chariot to see the town, which is about half the bigness of London, but the houses very strangely built, and most of them out of repair. The people in the streets walked fast, looked wild, their eyes fixed, and were generally in rags. We passed through one of the town gates, and went about three miles into the country, where I saw many labourers working with several sorts of tools in the ground, but was not able to conjecture what they were about; neither did I observe any expectation either of corn or grass, although the soil appeared to be excellent. I could not forbear admiring at these odd appearances both in town and country, and I made bold to desire my conductor, that he would be pleased to explain to me what could be meant by so many busy heads, hands, and faces, both in the streets and the fields, because I did not discover any good effects they produced; but on the contrary, I never knew a soil so unhappily cultivated, houses so ill contrived and so ruinous, or a people whose countenances and habit expressed so much misery and want.[2]

[1] *countenance* Favor or encouragement.

[2] *I never knew ... want* It has been suggested that Swift is alluding here to the situation in Ireland under British rule.

This Lord Munodi was a person of the first rank, and had been some years Governor of Lagado; but by a cabal of ministers was discharged for insufficiency.[1] However, the King treated him with tenderness, as a well-meaning man, but of a low contemptible understanding.

When I gave that free censure of the country and its inhabitants, he made no further answer than by telling me, that I had not been long enough among them to form a judgment; and that the different nations of the world had different customs, with other common topics to the same purpose. But when we returned to his palace, he asked me how I liked the building, what absurdities I observed, and what quarrel I had with the dress or looks of his domestics. This he might safely do, because every thing about him was magnificent, regular, and polite.[2] I answered that his Excellency's prudence, quality, and fortune, had exempted him from those defects, which folly and beggary had produced in others. He said if I would go with him to his country-house, about twenty miles distant, where his estate lay, there would be more leisure for this kind of conversation. I told his Excellency that I was entirely at his disposal; and accordingly we set out next morning.

During our journey, he made me observe the several methods used by farmers in managing their lands, which to me were wholly unaccountable; for, except in some very few places, I could not discover one ear of corn or blade of grass. But, in three hours travelling, the scene was wholly altered; we came into a most beautiful country; farmers' houses at small distances, neatly built; the fields enclosed, containing vineyards, corn-grounds, and meadows. Neither do I remember to have seen a more delightful prospect. His Excellency observed my countenance to clear up; he told me, with a sigh, that there his estate began, and would continue the same, till we should come to his house. That his countrymen ridiculed and despised him for managing his affairs no better, and for setting so ill an example to the kingdom, which however was followed by very few, such as were old, and wilful, and weak like himself.

We came at length to the house, which was indeed a noble structure, built according to the best rules of ancient architecture. The fountains, gardens, walks, avenues, and groves, were all disposed with exact judgment and taste. I gave due praises to every thing I saw, whereof his Excellency took not the least notice till after supper, when, there being no third companion, he told me with a very melancholy air, that he doubted he must throw down his houses in town and country, to rebuild them after the present mode, destroy all his plantations, and cast others into such a form as modern usage required, and give the same directions to all his tenants, unless he would submit to incur the censure, of pride, singularity, affectation, ignorance, caprice, and perhaps increase his Majesty's displeasure.

That the admiration I appeared to be under, would cease or diminish when he had informed me of some particulars, which probably I never heard of at court, the people there being too much taken up in their own speculations, to have regard to what passed here below.

The sum of his discourse was to this effect. That about forty years ago, certain persons went up to Laputa, either upon business or diversion, and, after five months continuance, came back with a very little smattering in mathematics, but full of volatile spirits acquired in that airy region. That these persons upon their return began to dislike the management of every thing below, and fell into schemes of putting all arts, sciences, languages, and mechanics upon a new foot. To this end they procured a royal patent for erecting an Academy of Projectors[3] in Lagado; and the humour prevailed so strongly among the people, that there is not a town of any consequence in the kingdom without such an academy. In these colleges, the professors contrive new rules and methods of agriculture and building, and new instruments and tools for all trades and manufactures, whereby, as they undertake, one man shall do the work of ten; a palace may be built in a week, of materials so durable as to last for ever without repairing. All the fruits of the earth shall come to maturity at whatever season we think fit to choose, and increase an hundred fold more than they do at present,[4] with

[1] *insufficiency* Incompetence.

[2] *polite* Elegant.

[3] *Projectors* Inventors, experimenters. Swift's depiction of the Academy is based largely on the Royal Society, founded in 1662 for the purpose of scientific experimentation. Despite numerous successes, the Royal Society had a reputation for peculiar failed experiments.

[4] *All the fruits … present* Cf. Francis Bacon, *New Atlantis*, 158: "And we make (by art) … trees and flowers to come earlier or later than their seasons; and to come up and bear more speedily than by their natural course they do."

innumerable other happy proposals. The only inconvenience is, that none of these projects are yet brought to perfection, and in the mean time, the whole country lies miserably waste, the houses in ruins, and the people without food or clothes. By all which, instead of being discouraged, they are fifty times more violently bent upon prosecuting their schemes, driven equally on by hope and despair: that as for himself, being not of an enterprising spirit, he was content to go on in the old forms, to live in the houses his ancestors had built, and act as they did in every part of life without innovation. That some few other persons of quality and gentry had done the same, but were looked on with an eye of contempt and ill will, as enemies to art, ignorant, and ill commonwealth's-men, preferring their own ease and sloth before the general improvement of their country.

His Lordship added, that he would not by any further particulars prevent the pleasure I should certainly take in viewing the grand Academy, whither he was resolved I should go. He only desired me to observe a ruined building upon the side of a mountain about three miles distant, of which he gave me this account. That he had a very convenient mill within half a mile of his house, turned by a current from a large river, and sufficient for his own family, as well as a great number of his tenants. That about seven years ago, a club of those projectors came to him with proposals to destroy this mill, and build another on the side of that mountain, on the long ridge whereof a long canal must be cut for a repository of water, to be conveyed up by pipes and engines to supply the mill: because the wind and air upon a height agitated the water, and thereby made it fitter for motion: and because the water descending down a reclivity would turn the mill with half the current of a river whose course is more upon a level. He said, that being then not very well with the court, and pressed by many of his friends, he complied with the proposal; and after employing an hundred men for two years, the work miscarried, the projectors went off, laying the blame entirely upon him, railing at him ever since, and putting others upon the same experiment, with equal assurance of success, as well as equal disappointment.

In a few days we came back to town, and his Excellency, considering the bad character he had in the Academy, would not go with me himself, but recommended me to a friend of his to bear me company thither. My lord was pleased to represent me as a great admirer of projects, and a person of much curiosity and easy belief; which, indeed, was not without truth; for I had myself been a sort of projector in my younger days.

CHAPTER 5

(*The author permitted to see the Grand Academy of Lagado. The Academy largely described. The arts wherein the professors employ themselves.*)

This Academy is not an entire single building, but a continuation of several houses on both sides of a street, which growing waste[1] was purchased and applied to that use.

I was received very kindly by the Warden, and went for many days to the Academy. Every room hath in it one or more projectors, and I believe I could not be[2] in fewer than five hundred rooms.[3]

The first man I saw was of a meagre aspect, with sooty hands and face, his hair and beard long, ragged and singed in several places. His clothes, shirt, and skin, were all of the same colour. He had been eight years upon a project for extracting sun-beams out of cucumbers,[4] which were to be put into vials hermetically sealed, and let out to warm the air in raw inclement summers. He told me, he did not doubt, in eight years more, he should be able to supply the Governor's gardens with sunshine at a reasonable rate; but he complained that his stock was low, and entreated me to give him something as an encouragement to ingenuity, especially since this had been a very dear season for cucumbers. I made him a small present, for my lord had furnished me with money on purpose, because he knew their practice of begging from all who go to see them.

I went into another chamber, but was ready to hasten back, being almost overcome with a horrible stink. My conductor pressed me forward, conjuring me in a whisper to give no offence, which would be highly

[1] *growing waste* Falling into disuse.

[2] *could not be* Could not have been.

[3] *five hundred rooms* Swift is here parodying the Royal Society's ambitious plans for expansion.

[4] *project ... cucumbers* English botanist Stephen Hales (1677–1761) had been investigating sunlight's role in plant respiration.

resented, and therefore I durst not so much as stop my nose. The projector of this cell was the most ancient student of the Academy; his face and beard were of a pale yellow; his hands and clothes daubed over with filth. When I was presented to him, he gave me a close embrace (a compliment I could well have excused). His employment from his first coming into the Academy, was an operation to reduce human excrement to its original food, by separating the several parts, removing the tincture[1] which it receives from the gall, making the odour exhale, and scumming off the saliva. He had a weekly allowance from the society, of a vessel filled with human ordure,[2] about the bigness of a Bristol barrel.[3]

I saw another at work to calcine[4] ice into gunpowder, who likewise showed me a treatise he had written concerning the malleability of fire,[5] which he intended to publish.

There was a most ingenious architect who had contrived a new method for building houses, by beginning at the roof, and working downwards to the foundation, which he justified to me by the like practice of those two prudent insects, the bee and the spider.

There was a man born blind,[6] who had several apprentices in his own condition: their employment was to mix colours for painters, which their master taught them to distinguish by feeling and smelling. It was indeed my misfortune to find them at that time not very perfect in their lessons, and the professor himself happened to be generally mistaken: this artist is much encouraged and esteemed by the whole fraternity.

In another apartment I was highly pleased with a projector, who had found a device for ploughing the ground with hogs, to save the charges of ploughs, cattle, and labour. The method is this: in an acre of ground you bury, at six inches distance and eight deep, a quantity of acorns, dates, chestnuts, and other mast[7] or vegetables whereof these animals are fondest; then you drive six hundred or more of them into the field, where in a few days they will root up the whole ground in search of their food, and make it fit for sowing, at the same time manuring it with their dung. It is true, upon experiment they found the charge and trouble very great, and they had little or no crop. However, it is not doubted that this invention may be capable of great improvement.

I went into another room, where the walls and ceiling were all hung round with cobwebs, except a narrow passage for the artist[8] to go in and out. At my entrance he called aloud to me not to disturb his webs. He lamented the fatal mistake the world had been so long in of using silk-worms, while we had such plenty of domestic insects, who infinitely excelled the former, because they understood how to weave as well as spin. And he proposed farther, that by employing spiders, the charge of dying silks should be wholly saved, whereof I was fully convinced when he showed me a vast number of flies most beautifully coloured, wherewith he fed his spiders, assuring us, that the webs would take a tincture from them; and as he had them in all hues, he hoped to fit everybody's fancy, as soon as he could find proper food for the flies, of certain gums, oils, and other glutinous matter to give a strength and consistence to the threads.

There was an astronomer who had undertaken to place a sun-dial upon the great weathercock on the town-house,[9] by adjusting the annual and diurnal[10] motions of the earth and sun, so as to answer and coincide with all accidental turnings by the wind.

I was complaining of a small fit of colic, upon which my conductor led me into a room, where a great physician resided, who was famous for curing that disease by contrary operations from the same instrument. He had

[1] *tincture* Coloring.

[2] *ordure* Excrement.

[3] *Bristol barrel* Barrel holding about 37 gallons.

[4] *calcine* Reduce by burning to essential substance.

[5] *malleability of fire* Cf. François Rabelais, *Gargantua and Pantagruel*, 5.22; "Others were cutting fire with a knife, and drawing up water in a net."

[6] *a man born blind* In *Experiments and Observations upon Colours* (1665), Robert Boyle described a blind man who could distinguish colors by touch.

[7] *mast* Nuts that have fallen to the ground and are used to feed pigs.

[8] *the artist* Possible models for this character include a Frenchman named M. Bon, who proposed that spider webs could be used to spin silk, and an Englishman named Wall, who argued that the excrement of ants that were fed on certain types of sap could be used as dye.

[9] *town-house* Town hall.

[10] *diurnal* Daily.

a large pair of bellows with a long slender muzzle of ivory. This he conveyed eight inches up the anus, and drawing in the wind, he affirmed he could make the guts as lank as a dried bladder. But when the disease was more stubborn and violent, he let in the muzzle while the bellows were full of wind, which he discharged into the body of the patient, then withdrew the instrument to replenish it, clapping his thumb strongly against the orifice of the fundament; and this being repeated three or four times, the adventitious wind would rush out, bringing the noxious along with it (like water put into a pump), and the patient recover. I saw him try both experiments upon a dog,[1] but could not discern any effect from the former. After the latter, the animal was ready to burst, and made so violent a discharge, as was very offensive to me and my companions. The dog died on the spot, and we left the doctor endeavouring to recover him by the same operation.

I visited many other apartments, but shall not trouble my reader with all the curiosities I observed, being studious of brevity.

I had hitherto seen only one side of the Academy, the other being appropriated to the advancers of speculative learning, of whom I shall say something when I have mentioned one illustrious person more, who is called among them the universal artist.[2] He told us he had been thirty years employing his thoughts for the improvement of human life. He had two large rooms full of wonderful curiosities, and fifty men at work. Some were condensing air into a dry tangible substance, by extracting the nitre,[3] and letting the aqueous or fluid particles percolate; others softening marble for pillows and pincushions; others petrifying the hoofs of a living horse to preserve them from foundering. The artist himself was at that time busy upon two great designs; the first, to sow land with chaff,[4] wherein he affirmed the true seminal virtue to be contained, as he demonstrated by several experiments which I was not skilful enough to comprehend. The other was, by a certain composition of gums, minerals, and vegetables outwardly applied, to prevent the growth of wool upon two young lambs; and he hoped in a reasonable time to propagate the breed of naked sheep all over the kingdom.

We crossed a walk to the other part of the Academy, where, as I have already said, the projectors in speculative learning resided.

The first professor I saw was in a very large room, with forty pupils about him. After salutation, observing me to look earnestly upon a frame, which took up the greatest part of both the length and breadth of the room, he said perhaps I might wonder to see him employed in a project for improving speculative knowledge by practical and mechanical operations. But the world would soon be sensible[5] of its usefulness, and he flattered himself that a more noble exalted thought never sprang in any other man's head. Every one knew how laborious the usual method is of attaining to arts and sciences; whereas, by his contrivance, the most ignorant person at a reasonable charge, and with a little bodily labour, may write books in philosophy, poetry, politics, law, mathematics, and theology, without the least assistance from genius or study. He then led me to the frame, about the sides whereof all his pupils stood in ranks. It was twenty foot square, placed in the middle of the room. The superficies[6] was composed of several bits of wood, about the bigness of a die, but some larger than others. They were all linked together by slender wires. These bits of wood were covered on every square with paper pasted on them, and on these papers were written all the words of their language, in their several moods, tenses, and declensions, but without any order. The professor then desired me to observe, for he was going to set his engine[7] at work. The pupils at his command took each of them hold of an iron handle, whereof there were forty fixed round the edges of the frame, and giving them a sudden turn, the whole disposition[8] of the words was entirely changed. He then

[1] *I saw him … dog* In 1667 Robert Hooke (1635–1703) performed an experiment in which he blew air into the windpipe of a dog with a pair of bellows and produced artificial respiration.

[2] *the universal artist* Swift may be alluding to Robert Boyle (1627–91), who studied marble, petrifaction, agriculture, sheep breeding, and the nature of air.

[3] *nitre* Air was thought to contain a nitrous substance.

[4] *chaff* Seed casings from grains such as wheat. Figuratively, something that is worthless.

[5] *sensible* Aware.

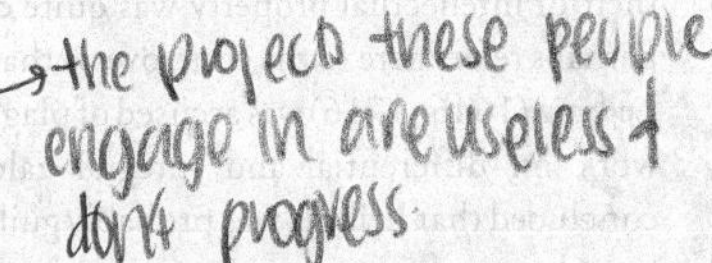

→the projects these people
engage in are useless +
don't progress

[6] *superficies* Surface.

[7] *engine* Machine.

[8] *disposition* Arrangement.

commanded six and thirty of the lads to read the several lines softly as they appeared upon the frame; and where they found three or four words together that might make part of a sentence, they dictated to the four remaining boys who were scribes. This work was repeated three or four times, and at every turn the engine was so contrived, that the words shifted into new places, as the square bits of wood moved upside down.

Six hours a day the young students were employed in this labour, and the professor showed me several volumes in large folio already collected, of broken sentences, which he intended to piece together, and out of those rich materials to give the world a complete body of all arts and sciences; which, however, might be still improved, and much expedited, if the public would raise a fund for making and employing five hundred such frames in Lagado, and oblige the managers to contribute in common their several[1] collections.

He assured me, that this invention had employed all his thoughts from his youth, that he had emptied the whole vocabulary into his frame, and made the strictest computation of the general proportion there is in books between the numbers of particles, nouns, and verbs, and other parts of speech.

I made my humblest acknowledgment to this illustrious person for his great communicativeness, and promised if ever I had the good fortune to return to my native country, that I would do him justice, as the sole inventor of this wonderful machine; the form and contrivance of which I desired leave to delineate upon paper, as in the figure here annexed. I told him,

although it were the custom of our learned in Europe to steal inventions from each other,[2] who had thereby at least this advantage, that it became a controversy which was the right owner, yet I would take such caution, that he should have the honour entire without a rival.

We next went to the school of languages, where three professors sat in consultation upon improving that

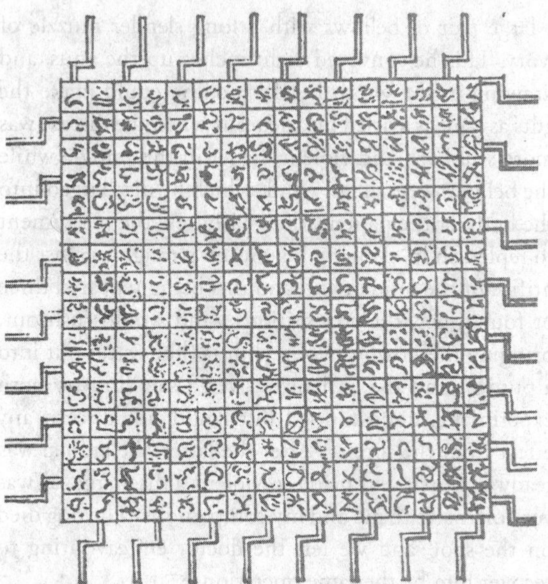

A project for a computer.

of their own country.[3]

The first project was to shorten discourse by cutting polysyllables into one, and leaving out verbs and participles, because in reality all things imaginable are but nouns.

The other project was a scheme for entirely abolishing all words whatsoever; and this was urged as a great advantage in point of health as well as brevity. For it is plain, that every word we speak is in some degree a diminution of our lungs by corrosion, and consequently contributes to the shortening of our lives. An expedient was therefore offered, that since words are only names for *things*, it would be more convenient for all men to carry about them such things as were necessary to express the particular business they are to discourse on.[4] And this invention would certainly have taken place, to the great ease as well as health of the subject, if the women, in conjunction with the vulgar and illiterate, had not threatened to raise a rebellion, unless they

[1] *several* Separate, individual.

[2] *steal inventions from each other* Because there was no patent law, theft of intellectual property was quite common at this time. Swift perhaps refers here to the controversy that had arisen when Gottfried Leibniz (1646–1716) was accused of plagiarizing from Newton in his work on differential and integral calculus. The Royal Society concluded that Leibniz was probably guilty, but modern scholarship has shown that each scientist arrived at the same conclusion independently.

[3] *three professors … own country* In this passage Swift alludes to a proposal from scientists of the time for a philosophical language that would create a more precise scientific discourse by eradicating the discrepancy between words and objects.

[4] *that since words … discourse on* Swift alludes to John Locke's theory of language, set out in *An Essay Concerning Human Understanding* (1690), which posits that words only indirectly stand for objects.

might be allowed the liberty to speak with their tongues, after the manner of their ancestors; such constant irreconcilable enemies to science are the common people. However, many of the most learned and wise adhere to the new scheme of expressing themselves by things, which hath only this inconvenience attending it, that if a man's business be very great, and of various kinds, he must be obliged in proportion to carry a greater bundle of things upon his back, unless he can afford one or two strong servants to attend him. I have often beheld two of those sages almost sinking under the weight of their packs, like pedlars among us; who, when they met in the streets, would lay down their loads, open their sacks, and hold conversation for an hour together; then put up their implements, help each other to resume their burthens, and take their leave.

But for short conversations a man may carry implements in his pockets and under his arms, enough to supply him, and in his house he cannot be at a loss. Therefore the room where company meet who practice this art, is full of all things ready at hand,[1] requisite to furnish matter for this kind of artificial converse.

Another great advantage proposed by this invention, was that it would serve as an universal language[2] to be understood in all civilised nations, whose goods and utensils are generally of the same kind, or nearly resembling, so that their uses might easily be comprehended. And thus ambassadors would be qualified to treat with foreign princes or ministers of state, to whose tongues they were utter strangers.

I was at the mathematical school, where the master taught his pupils after a method scarce imaginable to us in Europe. The proposition and demonstration were fairly written on a thin wafer, with ink composed of a cephalic tincture.[3] This the student was to swallow upon a fasting stomach, and for three days following eat nothing but bread and water. As the wafer digested, the tincture mounted to his brain, bearing the proposition along with it. But the success hath not hitherto been answerable, partly by some error in the *quantum* or composition, and partly by the perverseness of lads, to whom this bolus[4] is so nauseous, that they generally steal aside, and discharge it upwards before it can operate; neither have they been yet persuaded to use so long an abstinence as the prescription requires.

CHAPTER 6

(*A further account of the Academy. The author proposes some improvements, which are honourably received.*)

In the school of political projectors I was but ill entertained, the professors appearing in my judgment wholly out of their senses, which is a scene that never fails to make me melancholy. These unhappy people were proposing schemes for persuading monarchs to choose favourites upon the score of their wisdom, capacity, and virtue; of teaching ministers to consult the public good; of rewarding merit, great abilities, eminent services; of instructing princes to know their true interest by placing it on the same foundation with that of their people; of choosing for employments persons qualified to exercise them; with many other wild impossible chimaeras,[5] that never entered before into the heart of man to conceive, and confirmed in me the old observation, that there is nothing so extravagant and irrational which some philosophers have not maintained for truth.

But, however, I shall so far do justice to this part of the Academy, as to acknowledge that all of them were not so visionary. There was a most ingenious doctor who seemed to be perfectly versed in the whole nature and system of government. This illustrious person had very usefully employed his studies in finding out effectual remedies for all diseases and corruptions, to which the several kinds of public administration are subject by the vices or infirmities of those who govern, as well as by the licentiousness of those who are to obey. For instance; whereas all writers and reasoners have agreed, that there is a strict universal resemblance between the natural and the political body; can there be any thing more evident, than that the health of both must be

[1] *full of all things ready at hand* Swift is here satirizing the Royal Society's attempt to collect one sample of every object in the world.

[2] *an universal language* Alludes to George Dalgarno's *Ars Signorum, vulgo Character Universalis, et Lingua Philosophica* (1661) and Bishop John Wilkins's *Essay Towards a Real Character and a Philosophical Language* (1668). These authors built new languages by allocating symbols or letters to groups of things and ideas.

[3] *cephalic tincture* Medicine for the head.

[4] *quantum* Quantity; *bolus* Extra-large round pill.

[5] *chimaeras* Mythological fire-breathing monsters said to be part goat, part lion, and part serpent. Figuratively, fanciful ideas.

preserved, and the diseases cured by the same prescriptions? It is allowed, that senates and great councils are often troubled with redundant, ebullient, and other peccant humours,[1] with many diseases of the head, and more of the heart; with strong convulsions, with grievous contractions of the nerves and sinews in both hands, but especially the right; with spleen, flatus,[2] vertigos, and deliriums; with scrofulous tumours full of foetid purulent matter; with sour frothy ructations,[3] with canine appetites and crudeness of digestion, besides many others needless to mention. This doctor therefore proposed, that upon the meeting of a senate, certain physicians should attend at the three first days of their sitting, and at the close of each day's debate, feel the pulses of every senator; after which, having maturely considered, and consulted upon the nature of the several maladies, and the methods of cure, they should on the fourth day return to the senate house, attended by their apothecaries stored with proper medicines; and before the members sat, administer to each of them lenitives, aperitives, abstersives, corrosives, restringents, palliatives, laxatives, cephalagics, icterics, apophlegmatics, acoustics,[4] as their several cases required; and according as these medicines should operate; repeat, alter, or omit them at the next meeting.

This project could not be of any great expense to the public, and would, in my poor opinion, be of much use for the dispatch of business in those countries where senates have any share in the legislative power; beget unanimity, shorten debates, open a few mouths which are now closed, and close many more which are now open; curb the petulancy of the young, and correct the positiveness of the old; rouse the stupid, and damp the pert.[5]

[1] *ebullient* Agitated; *peccant humours* Fluids of a harmful nature. According to archaic theory, health depended on maintaining a balance between humors or bodily fluids: black bile, blood, choler, and phlegm.

[2] *spleen* Depression, melancholia; *flatus* Morbid inflammation and swelling.

[3] *ructations* Belches.

[4] *lenitives* soothing drugs; *aperitives* Laxatives; *abstersives* Purgatives; *corrosives* Substances which burn tissue; *restringents* Drugs to restrain the action of the bowels; *cephalagics* Remedies for headache; *icterics* Remedies for jaundice; *apophlegmatics* Phlegm-removers; *acoustics* Cures for deafness.

[5] *pert* Impertinent.

Again; because it is a general complaint, that the favourites of princes are troubled with short and weak memories; the same doctor proposed, that whoever attended a first minister, after having told his business with the utmost brevity and in the plainest words, should at his departure give the said minister a tweak by the nose, or a kick in the belly, or tread on his corns, or lug him thrice by both ears, or run a pin into his breech, or pinch his arm black and blue, to prevent forgetfulness; and at every levee day repeat the same operation, till the business were done or absolutely refused.

He likewise directed, that every senator in the great council of a nation, after he had delivered his opinion, and argued in the defence of it, should be obliged to give his vote directly contrary; because if that were done, the result would infallibly terminate in the good of the public.

When parties in a state are violent, he offered a wonderful contrivance to reconcile them. The method is this. You take a hundred leaders of each party, you dispose them into couples of such whose heads are nearest of a size; then let two nice operators saw off the occiput[6] of each couple at the same time, in such a manner that the brain may be equally divided. Let the occiputs thus cut off be interchanged, applying each to the head of his opposite party-man. It seems indeed to be a work that requireth some exactness, but the professor assured us, that if it were dexterously performed, the cure would be infallible. For he argued thus; that the two half brains being left to debate the matter between themselves within the space of one skull, would soon come to a good understanding, and produce that moderation, as well as regularity of thinking, so much to be wished for in the heads of those, who imagine they came into the world only to watch and govern its motion: and as to the difference of brains in quantity or quality, among those who are directors in faction, the doctor assured us from his own knowledge, that it was a perfect trifle.

I heard a very warm debate between two professors, about the most commodious[7] and effectual ways and means of raising money without grieving the subject. The first affirmed the justest method would be to lay a certain tax upon vices and folly, and the sum fixed upon every man, to be rated after the fairest manner by a jury

[6] *occiput* Area located at the back of the head.

[7] *commodious* Convenient.

of his neighbours. The second was of an opinion directly contrary, to tax those qualities of body and mind for which men chiefly value themselves, the rate to be more or less according to the degrees of excelling, the decision whereof should be left entirely to their own breast. The highest tax was upon men who are the greatest favourites of the other sex, and the assessments according to the number and natures of the favours they have received; for which they are allowed to be their own vouchers. Wit, valour, and politeness were likewise proposed to be largely taxed, and collected in the same manner, by every person's giving his own word for the quantum of what he possessed. But as to honour, justice, wisdom, and learning, they should not be taxed at all, because they are qualifications of so singular a kind, that no man will either allow them to his neighbour, or value them in himself.

The women were proposed to be taxed according to their beauty and skill in dressing, wherein they had the same privilege with the men, to be determined by their own judgment. But constancy, chastity, good sense, and good nature were not rated, because they would not bear the charge of collecting.

To keep senators in the interest of the crown, it was proposed that the members should raffle for employments, every man first taking an oath, and giving security that he would vote for the court, whether he won or no; after which the losers had in their turn the liberty of raffling upon the next vacancy. Thus hope and expectation would be kept alive, none would complain of broken promises, but impute their disappointments wholly to fortune, whose shoulders are broader and stronger than those of a ministry.

Another professor showed me a large paper of instructions for discovering plots and conspiracies against the government. He advised great statesmen to examine into the diet of all suspected persons; their times of eating; upon which side they lay in bed; with which hand they wiped their posteriors; to take a strict view of their excrements, and, from the colour, the odour, the taste, the consistence, the crudeness of maturity of digestion, form a judgment of their thoughts and designs. Because men are never so serious, thoughtful, and intent, as when they are at stool,[1] which he found by frequent experiment; for in such conjunctures, when he used merely as a trial to consider which was the best way of murdering the king, his ordure would have a tincture of green, but quite different when he thought only of raising an insurrection or burning the metropolis.

The whole discourse was written with great acuteness, containing many observations both curious and useful for politicians, but as I conceived not altogether complete. This I ventured to tell the author, and offered if he pleased to supply him with some additions. He received my proposition with more compliance than is usual among writers, especially those of the projecting species, professing he would be glad to receive farther information.

I told him, that in the kingdom of Tribnia, by the natives called Langden,[2] where I had sojourned some time in my travels, the bulk of the people consist in a manner wholly of discoverers, witnesses, informers, accusers, prosecutors, evidencers, swearers, together with their several subservient and subaltern instruments, all under the colours and conduct of ministers of state and their deputies. The plots in that kingdom are usually the workmanship of those persons who desire to raise their own characters of profound politicians,[3] to restore new vigour to a crazy administration, to stifle or divert general discontents, to fill their pockets with forfeitures,[4] and raise or sink the opinion of public credit,[5] as either shall best answer their private advantage. It is first agreed and settled among them, what suspected persons shall be accused of a plot; then, effectual care is taken to secure all their letters and papers, and put the criminals in chains. These papers are delivered to a set of artists, very dexterous in finding out the mysterious meanings

[1] *at stool* Defecating. This passage alludes to the trial of Bishop Atterbury, who was accused of participating in a Jacobite plot to capture the royal family in 1722. Papers used as evidence were reportedly found in his private lavatory.

[2] *Tribnia ... Langden* Anagrams for Britain and England respectively.

[3] *The plots ... politicians* The Whigs accused the Tories of concocting Jacobite plots.

[4] *fill their pockets with forfeitures* The English government seized the estates of the leaders of the 1715 rebellion.

[5] *opinion of public credit* Cost of government bonds.

of words, syllables, and letters. For instance, they can discover a close-stool to signify a privy council; a flock of geese, a senate; a lame dog, an invader;[1] a codshead, a ——; the plague, a standing army; a buzzard, a prime minister; the gout, a high priest; a gibbet, a secretary of state; a chamber-pot, a committee of grandees; a sieve, a court lady; a broom, a revolution; a mouse-trap, an employment; a bottomless pit, the treasury; a sink, the court; a cap and bells, a favourite; a broken reed, a court of justice; an empty tun, a general; a running sore, the administration.

When this method fails, they have two others more effectual, which the learned among them call acrostics and anagrams. First they can decipher all initial letters into political meanings. Thus, *N.* shall signify a plot; *B.* a regiment of horse; *L.* a fleet at sea; or secondly by transposing the letters of the alphabet in any suspected paper they can discover the deepest designs of a discontented party. So, for example, if I should say in a letter to a friend, *Our Brother* Tom *has just got the piles*, a skilful decipherer would discover, that the same letters which compose that sentence, may be analysed into the following words; *Resist, a plot is brought home; The tour*. And this is the anagrammatic method.

The professor made me great acknowledgments for communicating these observations, and promised to make honourable mention of me in his treatise.

I saw nothing in this country that could invite me to a longer continuance, and began to think of returning home to England.

Chapter 7

(*The author leaves Lagado, arrives at Maldonada. No ship ready. He takes a short voyage to Glubbdubdrib. His reception by the Governor.*)

The continent of which this kingdom is a part, extends itself, as I have reason to believe, eastward to that unknown tract of America, westward of California, and north to the Pacific Ocean, which is not above a hundred and fifty miles from Lagado; where there is a good port and much commerce with the great island of Luggnagg, situated to the north-west about 29 degrees north latitude, and 140 longitude. This island of Luggnagg stands south-eastwards of Japan, about an hundred leagues distant. There is a strict alliance between the Japanese Emperor and the King of Luggnagg, which affords frequent opportunities of sailing from one island to the other. I determined therefore to direct my course this way, in order to my return to Europe. I hired two mules with a guide to show me the way, and carry my small baggage. I took leave of my noble protector, who had shown me so much favour, and made me a generous present at my departure.

My journey was without any accident or adventure worth relating. When I arrived at the port of Maldonada (for so it is called), there was no ship in the harbour bound for Luggnagg, nor likely to be in some time. The town is about as large as Portsmouth. I soon fell into some acquaintance, and was very hospitably received. A gentleman of distinction said to me, that since the ships bound for Luggnagg could not be ready in less than a month, it might be no disagreeable amusement for me to take a trip to the little island of Glubbdubdrib, about five leagues off to the south-west. He offered himself and a friend to accompany me, and that I should be provided with a small convenient barque for the voyage.

Glubbdubdrib, as nearly as I can interpret the word, signifies the Island of *Sorcerers* or *Magicians.* It is about one third as large as the Isle of Wight, and extremely fruitful: it is governed by the head of a certain tribe, who are all magicians. This tribe marries only among each other, and the eldest in succession is Prince or Governor. He hath a noble palace, and a park of about three thousand acres, surrounded by a wall of hewn stone twenty foot high. In this park are several small enclosures for cattle, corn, and gardening.

The Governor and his family are served and attended by domestics of a kind somewhat unusual. By his skill in necromancy, he hath a power of calling whom he pleaseth from the dead, and commanding their service for twenty-four hours, but no longer; nor can he call the same persons up again in less than three months, except upon very extraordinary occasions.

When we arrived at the island, which was about eleven in the morning, one of the gentlemen who accompanied me, went to the Governor, and desired

[1] *a lame dog, an invader* Swift refers to Atterbury's trial and the use as evidence of letters; Atterbury mentions a lame dog named Harlequin that had been given to him from France. This mention of Harlequin was suggested to be a form of code.

admittance for a stranger, who came on purpose to have the honour of attending on his Highness. This was immediately granted, and we all three entered the gate of the palace between two rows of guards, armed and dressed after a very antic[1] manner, and something in their countenances that made my flesh creep with a horror I cannot express. We passed through several apartments, between servants of the same sort, ranked on each side as before, till we came to the chamber of presence, where after three profound obeisances, and a few general questions, we were permitted to sit on three stools near the lowest step of his Highness's throne. He understood the language of Balnibarbi, although it were different from that of his island. He desired me to give him some account of my travels; and, to let me see that I should be treated without ceremony, he dismissed all his attendants with a turn of his finger, at which to my great astonishment they vanished in an instant, like visions in a dream, when we awake on a sudden. I could not recover myself in some time, till the Governor assured me that I should receive no hurt; and observing my two companions to be under no concern, who had been often entertained in the same manner, I began to take courage, and related to his Highness a short history of my several adventures, yet not without some hesitation, and frequently looking behind me to the place where I had seen those domestic spectres. I had the honour to dine with the Governor, where a new set of ghosts served up the meat, and waited at table. I now observed myself to be less terrified than I had been in the morning. I stayed till sunset, but humbly desired his Highness to excuse me for not accepting his invitation of lodging in the palace. My two friends and I lay at a private house in the town adjoining, which is the capital of this little island; and the next morning we returned to pay our duty to the Governor, as he was pleased to command us.

After this manner we continued in the island for ten days, most part of every day with the Governor, and at night in our lodging. I soon grew so familiarized to the sight of spirits, that after the third or fourth time they gave me no emotion at all; or, if I had any apprehensions left, my curiosity prevailed over them. For his Highness the Governor ordered me to call up whatever persons I would choose to name, and in whatever numbers among all the dead from the beginning of the world to the present time, and command them to answer any questions I should think fit to ask; with this condition, that my questions must be confined within the compass of the times they lived in. And one thing I might depend upon, that they would certainly tell me the truth, for lying was a talent of no use in the lower world.

I made my humble acknowledgments to his Highness for so great a favour. We were in a chamber, from whence there was a fair prospect into the park. And because my first inclination was to be entertained with scenes of pomp and magnificence, I desired to see Alexander the Great, at the head of his army just after the battle of Arbela;[2] which upon a motion of the Governor's finger immediately appeared in a large field under the window, where we stood. Alexander was called up into the room: it was with great difficulty that I understood his Greek, and had but little of my own. He assured me upon his honour that he was not poisoned, but died of a fever by excessive drinking.[3]

Next I saw Hannibal passing the Alps, who told me he had not a drop of vinegar in his camp.[4]

I saw Caesar and Pompey at the head of their troops, just ready to engage.[5] I saw the former in his last great triumph. I desired that the senate of Rome might appear before me in one large chamber, and a modern representative, in counterview, in another. The first seemed to be an assembly of heroes and demi-gods; the other a knot of pedlars, pickpockets, highway-men, and bullies.

---

[1] *antic* Gross, bizarre.

[2] *the battle of Arbela* Battle of Gaugamela (331 BCE), in which Macedonian leader Alexander the Great (356–323 BCE) defeated Darius (380–330 BCE) and thereby conquered Mesopotamia and Babylon.

[3] *Alexander ... drinking* Allusion to the historical theory that Alexander was poisoned by his cup-bearer. Ancient historian, Plutarch (c. 46–127) argues he died after excessive drinking, but adds that he may have drunk heavily due to a fever which made him extremely thirsty.

[4] *Hannibal ... his camp* Reference to first-century BCE historian Livy's story that while making his famous crossing of the Alps, Hannibal (247–182/3 BCE) lit fires onto which he poured vinegar to soften and then cut through the rocks in his way.

[5] *I saw Caesar ... engage* Reference to the battle of Pharsalia, at which Gaius Julius Caesar (100–44 BCE) defeated Gnaeus Pompeius Magnus (Pompey) (106–48 BCE).

The Governor at my request gave the sign for Caesar and Brutus[1] to advance towards us. I was struck with a profound veneration at the sight of Brutus, and could easily discover the most consummate virtue, the greatest intrepidity and firmness of mind, the truest love of his country, and general benevolence for mankind in every lineament of his countenance. I observed with much pleasure, that these two persons were in good intelligence with each other, and Caesar freely confessed to me, that the greatest actions of his own life were not equal by many degrees to the glory of taking it away. I had the honour to have much conversation with Brutus; and was told, that his ancestors Junius, Socrates, Epaminondas, Cato the younger, Sir Thomas More,[2] and himself were perpetually together: a sextumvirate[3] to which all the ages of the world cannot add a seventh.

It would be tedious to trouble the reader with relating what vast numbers of illustrious persons were called up, to gratify that insatiable desire I had to see the world in every period of antiquity placed before me. I chiefly fed my eyes with beholding the destroyers of tyrants and usurpers, and the restorers of liberty to oppressed and injured nations. But it is impossible to express the satisfaction I received in my own mind, after such a manner as to make it a suitable entertainment to the reader.

CHAPTER 8

(*A further account of Glubbdubdrib. Ancient and modern history corrected.*)

Having a desire to see those ancients, who were most renowned for wit and learning, I set apart one day on purpose. I proposed that Homer and Aristotle[4] might appear at the head of all their commentators; but these were so numerous that some hundreds were forced to attend in the court, and outward rooms of the palace. I knew and could distinguish those two heroes at first sight, not only from the crowd, but from each other. Homer was the taller and comelier person of the two, walked very erect for one of his age, and his eyes were the most quick and piercing I ever beheld. Aristotle stooped much, and made use of a staff. His visage was meagre, his hair lank and thin, and his voice hollow. I soon discovered that both of them were perfect strangers to the rest of the company, and had never seen or heard of them before. And I had a whisper from a ghost, who shall be nameless, that these commentators always kept in the most distant quarters from their principals in the lower world, through a consciousness of shame and guilt, because they had so horribly misrepresented the meaning of those authors to posterity. I introduced Didymus and Eustathius[5] to Homer, and prevailed on him to treat them better than perhaps they deserved; for he soon found they wanted a genius to enter into the spirit of a poet. But Aristotle was out of all patience with the account I gave him of Scotus and Ramus,[6] as I presented them to him; and he asked them whether the rest of the tribe were as great dunces as themselves.

I then desired the Governor to call up Descartes and Gassendi,[7] with whom I prevailed to explain their systems to Aristotle. This great philosopher freely acknowledged his own mistakes in natural philosophy, because he proceeded in many things upon conjecture, as all men must do; and he found, that Gassendi, who

[1] *Brutus* Marcus Julius Brutus (85–42 BCE), one of the group who assassinated Julius Caesar.

[2] *Junius* Lucius Junius Brutus, founder of the Roman Republic (509 BCE) who led an uprising against the Tarquins and expelled them from Rome as revenge for the rape of Lucretia; *Socrates* (469–399 BCE) Influential Athenian philosopher; *Epaminondas* Theban general and politician (c. 420–362 BCE); *Cato the younger* Marcius Porcius Cato (95–46 BCE), a Stoic known for his integrity and refusal of taking bribes, who defended the Roman Republic against Julius Caesar; *Sir Thomas More* English politician (and author of *Utopia*) who refused to acknowledge Henry VIII as the head of the English Church and was executed as punishment (d. 1535).

[3] *sextumvirate* Group of six men.

[4] *Homer* (c. 700 BCE) Greek poet and author of the *Iliad* and the *Odyssey*; *Aristotle* (384–322 BCE) Greek philosopher.

[5] *Didymus* (c. 65 BCE–10 CE) An Alexandrian scholar, known for his commentary on Homer; *Eustathius* Archbishop of Thessalonica, author of a *Commentary on the Iliad and Odyssey* (d. 1194).

[6] *Scotus* John Duns Scotus (c. 1265–c. 1308), philosopher, theologian, and author of a commentary on Aristotle. The word *dunce* has its origin in mockery of Duns Scotus's views; *Ramus* Pierre la Ramée (1515–72), humanist, educational reformer, and a famous opponent of the Aristotelian system.

[7] *Descartes* René Descartes (1596–1650), French philosopher and mathematician; *Gassendi* Pierre Gassendi (1592–1655), French mathematician, astronomer, and philosopher. He opposed the theories of Aristotle and Descartes, and tried to reconcile the atomic physics of Epicurus with Christianity.

had made the doctrine of Epicurus[1] as palatable as he could, and the *vortices* of Descartes,[2] were equally exploded. He predicted the same fate to *attraction*, whereof the present learned are such zealous asserters. He said, that new systems of nature were but new fashions, which would vary in every age; and even those who pretend to demonstrate them from mathematical principles, would flourish but a short period of time, and be out of vogue when that was determined.[3]

I spent five days in conversing with many others of the ancient learned. I saw most of the first Roman emperors. I prevailed on the Governor to call up Eliogabalus's cooks[4] to dress us a dinner, but they could not show us much of their skill, for want of materials. A helot[5] of Agesilaus[6] made us a dish of Spartan broth, but I was not able to get down a second spoonful.

The two gentlemen who conducted me to the island, were pressed by their private affairs to return in three days, which I employed in seeing some of the modern dead, who had made the greatest figure for two or three hundred years past in our own and other countries of Europe; and having been always a great admirer of old illustrious families, I desired the Governor would call up a dozen or two of kings with their ancestors in order for eight or nine generations. But my disappointment was grievous and unexpected. For, instead of a long train with royal diadems,[7] I saw in one family two fiddlers, three spruce courtiers, and an Italian prelate. In another, a barber, an abbot, and two cardinals. I have too great a veneration for crowned heads to dwell any longer on so nice a subject. But as to counts, marquesses, dukes, earls, and the like, I was not so scrupulous. And I confess it was not without some pleasure that I found myself able to trace the particular features, by which certain families are distinguished, up to their originals. I could plainly discover from whence one family derives a long chin, why a second hath abounded with knaves for two generations, and fools for two more; why a third happened to be crack-brained, and a fourth to be sharpers. Whence it came what Polydore Virgil[8] says of a certain great house, *Nec vir fortis, nec foemina casta.*[9] How cruelty, falsehood, and cowardice grew to be characteristics by which certain families are distinguished as much as by their coat of arms. Who first brought the pox[10] into a noble house, which hath lineally descended in scrofulous tumours to their posterity. Neither could I wonder at all this, when I saw such an interruption of lineages by pages, lackeys, valets, coachmen, gamesters, fiddlers, players, captains, and pickpockets.

I was chiefly disgusted with modern history. For having strictly examined all the persons of greatest name in the courts of princes, for an hundred years past, I found how the world had been misled by prostitute writers, to ascribe the greatest exploits in war to cowards, the wisest counsel to fools, sincerity to flatterers, Roman virtue to betrayers of their country, piety to atheists, chastity to sodomites, truth to informers. How many innocent and excellent persons had been condemned to death or banishment, by the practising of great ministers upon[11] the corruption of judges, and the malice of factions. How many villains had been exalted to the highest places of trust, power, dignity, and profit: how great a share in the motions and events of courts, councils, and senates might be challenged by bawds, whores, pimps, parasites, and buffoons. How low an opinion I had of human wisdom and integrity, when I was truly informed of the springs and motives of great enterprises and revolutions in the world, and of the contemptible accidents to which they owed their success.

[1] *doctrine of Epicurus* Greek philosopher Epicurus (341–270 BCE) taught that life should be lived in avoidance of pain and in pursuit of pleasure. He postulated that the gods were completely indifferent to the actions of humans.

[2] *the vortices of Descartes* Descartes's theory postulated that heavenly bodies were moved about in "vortices" or whirlpools of material particles.

[3] *determined* Ended.

[4] *Eliogabalus's cooks* Heliogabalus (c. 203–222), an emperor of Rome, was notorious for his extravagant luxury and decadence.

[5] *helot* One of a Spartan class of serfs.

[6] *Agesilaus* King of Sparta (c. 398–361 BCE) who was known for his hardiness and frugality.

[7] *diadems* Jeweled crowns.

[8] *Polydore Virgil* Italian-born English historian, author of *A History of England* (1534).

[9] *Nec vir fortis, nec foemina casta* "Neither a brave man, nor a chaste woman."

[10] *the pox* Syphilis.

[11] *by the practising of great ministers upon* By means of great ministers taking advantage of.

Here I discovered the roguery and ignorance of those who pretend to write *anecdotes*, or secret history, who send so many kings to their graves with a cup of poison; will repeat the discourse between a prince and chief minister, where no witness was by; unlock the thoughts and cabinets of ambassadors and secretaries of state, and have the perpetual misfortune to be mistaken. Here I discovered the true causes of many great events that have surprised the world, how a whore can govern the back-stairs, the back-stairs a council, and the council a senate. A general confessed in my presence, that he got a victory purely by the force of cowardice and ill conduct; and an admiral, that for want of proper intelligence, he beat the enemy to whom he intended to betray the fleet. Three kings protested to me, that in their whole reigns they never did once prefer any person of merit, unless by mistake or treachery of some minister in whom they confided: neither would they do it if they were to live again: and they showed with great strength of reason, that the royal throne could not be supported without corruption, because that positive, confident, restive temper, which virtue infused into man, was a perpetual clog to public business.

I had the curiosity to enquire in a particular manner, by what method great numbers had procured to themselves high titles of honour, and prodigious estates; and I confined my enquiry to a very modern period: however, without grating upon present times, because I would be sure to give no offence even to foreigners (for I hope the reader need not be told that I do not in the least intend my own country in what I say upon this occasion), a great number of persons concerned were called up, and upon a very slight examination, discovered such a scene of infamy, that I cannot reflect upon it without some seriousness. Perjury, oppression, subornation, fraud, pandarism, and the like infirmities,[1] were amongst the most excusable arts they had to mention, and for these I gave, as it was reasonable, great allowance. But when some confessed they owed their greatness and wealth to sodomy or incest; others to the prostituting of their own wives and daughters; others to the betraying their country or their prince; some to poisoning, more to the perverting of justice in order to destroy the innocent: I hope I may be pardoned if these discoveries inclined me a little to abate of that profound veneration which I am naturally apt to pay to persons of high rank, who ought to be treated with the utmost respect due to their sublime dignity, by us their inferiors.

I had often read of some great services done to princes and states, and desired to see the persons by whom those services were performed. Upon enquiry I was told that their names were to be found on no record, except a few of them whom history hath represented as the vilest rogues and traitors. As to the rest, I had never once heard of them. They all appeared with dejected looks, and in the meanest habit, most of them telling me they died in poverty and disgrace, and the rest on a scaffold or a gibbet.

Among others there was one person whose case appeared a little singular. He had a youth about eighteen years old standing by his side. He told me he had for many years been commander of a ship, and in the sea fight at Actium,[2] had the good fortune to break through the enemy's great line of battle, sink three of their capital ships, and take a fourth, which was the sole cause of Antony's flight, and of the victory that ensued; that the youth standing by him, his only son, was killed in the action. He added, that upon the confidence of some merit, the war being at an end, he went to Rome, and solicited at the court of Augustus to be preferred to a greater ship, whose commander had been killed; but without any regard to his pretensions, it was given to a youth who had never seen the sea, the son of Libertina,[3] who waited on one of the emperor's mistresses. Returning back to his own vessel, he was charged with neglect of duty, and the ship given to a favourite page of Publicola, the vice-admiral; whereupon he retired to a poor farm at a great distance from Rome, and there ended his life. I was so curious to know the truth of this story, that I desired Agrippa[4] might be called, who was admiral in that fight. He appeared, and confirmed the whole account, but with much more advantage to the captain, whose modesty had extenuated or concealed a great part of his merit.

I was surprised to find corruption grown so high and so quick in that empire, by the force of luxury so lately

[1] *infirmities* Weaknesses.

[2] *Actium* Naval battle in 31 BCE in which Antony (80–30 BCE) and Cleopatra (69–30 BCE) were defeated by Octavius Caesar (63 BCE–14 CE).

[3] *Libertina* Woman who was formerly a slave.

[4] *Agrippa* Marcus Vipsanius Agrippa (c. 62–12 BCE).

introduced, which made me less wonder at many parallel cases in other countries, where vices of all kinds have reigned so much longer, and where the whole praise as well as pillage hath been engrossed by the chief commander, who perhaps had the least title to either.

As every person called up made exactly the same appearance he had done in the world, it gave me melancholy reflections to observe how much the race of human kind was degenerated among us, within these hundred years past. How the pox under all its consequences and denominations had altered every lineament of an English countenance, shortened the size of bodies, unbraced the nerves, relaxed the sinews and muscles, introduced a sallow complexion, and rendered the flesh loose and rancid.

I descended so low as to desire some English yeomen of the old stamp might be summoned to appear, once so famous for the simplicity of their manners, diet, and dress, for justice in their dealings, for their true spirit of liberty, for their valour and love of their country. Neither could I be wholly unmoved after comparing the living with the dead, when I considered how all these pure native virtues were prostituted for a piece of money by their grandchildren, who in selling their votes, and managing[1] at elections, have acquired every vice and corruption that can possibly be learned in a court.

CHAPTER 9

(*The author returns to Maldonada. Sails to the Kingdom of Luggnagg. The author confined. He is sent for to court. The manner of his admittance. The King's great lenity to his subjects.*)

The day of our departure being come, I took leave of his Highness the Governor of Glubbdubdrib, and returned with my two companions to Maldonada, where after a fortnight's waiting, a ship was ready to sail for Luggnagg. The two gentlemen, and some others, were so generous and kind as to furnish me with provisions, and see me on board. I was a month in this voyage. We had one violent storm, and were under a necessity of steering westward to get into the trade wind, which holds for about sixty leagues. On the 21st of April, 1708, we sailed into the river of Clumegnig, which is a seaport town, at the south-east point of Luggnagg. We cast anchor within a league of the town, and made a signal for a pilot. Two of them came on board in less than half an hour, by whom we were guided between certain shoals and rocks, which are very dangerous in the passage to a large basin, where a fleet may ride in safety within a cable's length of the town wall.

Some of our sailors, whether out of treachery or inadvertence, had informed the pilots that I was a stranger and a great traveller, whereof these gave notice to a custom-house officer, by whom I was examined very strictly upon my landing. This officer spoke to me in the language of Balnibarbi, which by the force of much commerce is generally understood in that town, especially by seamen, and those employed in the customs. I gave him a short account of some particulars, and made my story as plausible and consistent as I could; but I thought it necessary to disguise my country, and call myself an Hollander, because my intentions were for Japan, and I knew the Dutch were the only Europeans permitted to enter into that kingdom.[2] I therefore told the officer, that having been shipwrecked on the coast of Balnibarbi, and cast on a rock, I was received up into Laputa, or the Flying Island (of which he had often heard), and was now endeavouring to get to Japan, from whence I might find a convenience[3] of returning to my own country. The officer said, I must be confined till he could receive orders from court, for which he would write immediately, and hoped to receive an answer in a fortnight. I was carried to a convenient lodging, with a sentry placed at the door; however I had the liberty of a large garden, and was treated with humanity enough, being maintained all the time at the King's charge. I was invited by several persons, chiefly out of curiosity, because it was reported that I came from countries very remote of which they had never heard.

[1] *managing* Securing influence by questionable methods such as bribery or flattery.

[2] *I knew the Dutch … kingdom* Japan closed its borders to all Europeans, except the Dutch, in 1638 as a response to both missionary activity and the revolt of Christians in Shimabara. Dutch sailors could still visit Japan but were subject to extreme restrictions and forbidden to display any outward signs of Christianity.

[3] *a convenience* Convenient method.

I hired a young man who came in the same ship to be an interpreter; he was a native of Luggnagg, but had lived some years at Maldonada, and was a perfect master of both languages. By his assistance I was able to hold a conversation with those who came to visit me; but this consisted only of their questions, and my answers.

The dispatch came from court about the time we expected. It contained a warrant for conducting me and my retinue to Traldragdubh or Trildrogdrib, for it is pronounced both ways as near as I can remember, by a party of ten horse. All my retinue was that poor lad for an interpreter, whom I persuaded into my service, and at my humble request, we had each of us a mule to ride on. A messenger was dispatched half a day's journey before us, to give the King notice of my approach, and to desire that his Majesty would please to appoint a day and hour, when it would be his gracious pleasure that I might have the honour to *lick the dust before his footstool*.[1] This is the court style, and I found it to be more than matter of form. For upon my admittance two days after my arrival, I was commanded to crawl on my belly, and lick the floor as I advanced; but on account of my being a stranger, care was taken to have it made so clean that the dust was not offensive. However, this was a peculiar grace, not allowed to any but persons of the highest rank, when they desire an admittance. Nay, sometimes the floor is strewed with dust on purpose, when the person to be admitted happens to have powerful enemies at court. And I have seen a great lord with his mouth so crammed, that when he had crept to the proper distance from the throne, he was not able to speak a word. Neither is there any remedy, because it is capital for those who receive an audience to spit or wipe their mouths in his Majesty's presence. There is indeed another custom, which I cannot altogether approve of. When the King hath a mind to put any of his nobles to death in a gentle indulgent manner, he commands to have the floor strowed with a certain brown powder, of a deadly composition, which being licked up infallibly kills him in twenty-four hours. But in justice to this prince's great clemency, and the care he hath of his subjects' lives (wherein it were much to be wished that the monarchs of Europe would imitate him), it must be mentioned for his honour, that strict orders are given to have the infected parts of the floor well washed after every such execution; which if his domestics neglect, they are in danger of incurring his royal displeasure. I myself heard him give directions, that one of his pages should be whipped, whose turn it was to give notice about washing the floor after an execution, but maliciously had omitted it; by which neglect a young lord of great hopes coming to an audience, was unfortunately poisoned, although the King at that time had no design against his life. But this good prince was so gracious, as to forgive the poor page his whipping, upon promise that he would do so no more, without special orders.

To return from this digression; when I had crept within four yards of the throne, I raised myself gently upon my knees, and then striking my forehead seven times on the ground, I pronounced the following words, as they had been taught me the night before, *Ickpling glofffthrobb squutserumm blhiop mlashnalt zwin tnodbalkuffh slhiophad gurdlubh asht*. This is the compliment established by the laws of the land for all persons admitted to the King's presence. It may be rendered into English thus: *May your Celestial Majesty outlive the sun, eleven moons and a half*. To this the King returned some answer, which although I could not understand, yet I replied as I had been directed: *Fluft drin yalerick dwuldom prastrad mirpush*, which properly signifies, *My tongue is in the mouth of my friend*, and by this expression was meant that I desired leave to bring my interpreter; whereupon the young man already mentioned was accordingly introduced, by whose intervention I answered as many questions as his Majesty could put in above an hour. I spoke in the Balnibarbian tongue, and my interpreter delivered my meaning in that of Luggnagg.

The King was much delighted with my company, and ordered his *Bliffmarklub*, or High Chamberlain, to appoint a lodging in the court for me and my interpreter, with a daily allowance for my table, and a large purse of gold for my common expenses.

I stayed three months in this country out of perfect obedience to his Majesty, who was pleased highly to favour me, and made me very honourable offers. But I thought it more consistent with prudence and justice to pass the remainder of my days with my wife and family.

[1] *lick the dust before his footstool* Cf. Isaiah, 49.23: "they shall bow down to thee and lick up the dust of thy feet." The passage may also allude to descriptions of meetings with the Siamese and Japanese rulers who required subjects to crawl towards them.

CHAPTER 10

(*The Luggnaggians commended. A particular description of the Struldbrugs, with many conversations between the author and some eminent persons upon that subject.*)

The Luggnaggians are a polite and generous people, and although they are not without some share of that pride which is peculiar to all Eastern countries, yet they show themselves courteous to strangers, especially such who are countenanced by the court. I had many acquaintance among persons of the best fashion, and being always attended by my interpreter, the conversation we had was not disagreeable.

One day in much good company I was asked by a person of quality, whether I had seen any of their *struldbrugs*, or *immortals*. I said I had not, and desired he would explain to me what he meant by such an appellation applied to a mortal creature. He told me, that sometimes, though very rarely, a child happened to be born in a family with a red circular spot in the forehead, directly over the left eyebrow, which was an infallible mark that it should never die. The spot, as he described it, was about the compass of a silver threepence, but in the course of time grew larger, and changed its colour; for at twelve years old it became green, so continued till five and twenty, then turned to a deep blue; at five and forty it grew coal black, and as large as an English shilling, but never admitted any further alteration. He said these births were so rare, that he did not believe they could be above eleven hundred *struldbrugs* of both sexes in the whole kingdom, of which he computed about fifty in the metropolis, and among the rest a young girl born about three years ago. That these productions were not peculiar to any family, but a mere effect of chance; and the children of the *struldbrugs* themselves, were equally mortal with the rest of the people.

I freely own myself to have been struck with inexpressible delight upon hearing this account: and the person who gave it me happening to understand the Balnibarbian language, which I spoke very well, I could not forbear breaking out into expressions perhaps a little too extravagant. I cried out as in a rapture; Happy nation where every child hath at least a chance of being immortal! Happy people who enjoy so many living examples of ancient virtue, and have masters ready to instruct them in the wisdom of all former ages! but, happiest beyond all comparison are those excellent *struldbrugs*, who being born exempt from that universal calamity of human nature, have their minds free and disengaged, without the weight and depression of spirits caused by the continual apprehension of death. I discovered my admiration that I had not observed any of these illustrious persons at court; the black spot on the forehead being so remarkable a distinction, that I could not have easily overlooked it: and it was impossible that his Majesty, a most judicious prince, should not provide himself with a good number of such wise and able counsellors. Yet perhaps the virtue of those reverend sages was too strict for the corrupt and libertine manners of a court. And we often find by experience that young men are too opinionative and volatile to be guided by the sober dictates of their seniors. However, since the King was pleased to allow me access to his royal person, I was resolved upon the very first occasion to deliver my opinion to him on this matter freely, and at large by the help of my interpreter; and whether he would please to take my advice or no, yet in one thing I was determined, that his Majesty having frequently offered me an establishment in this country, I would with great thankfulness accept the favour, and pass my life here in the conversation of those superior beings the *struldbrugs*, if they would please to admit me.

The gentleman to whom I addressed my discourse, because (as I have already observed) he spoke the language of Balnibarbi, said to me with sort of a smile, which usually ariseth from pity to the ignorant, that he was glad of any occasion to keep me among them, and desired my permission to explain to the company what I had spoke. He did so, and they talked together for some time in their own language, whereof I understood not a syllable, neither could I observe by their countenances what impression my discourse had made on them. After a short silence, the same person told me, that his friends and mine (so he thought fit to express himself) were very much pleased with the judicious remarks I had made on the great happiness and advantages of immortal life; and they were desirous to know in a particular manner, what scheme of living I should have formed to myself, if it had fallen to my lot to have been born a *struldbrug*.

I answered, it was easy to be eloquent on so copious and delightful a subject, especially to me who have been often apt to amuse myself with visions of what I should do if I were a king, or a great lord: and upon this very case I had frequently run over the whole system how I should employ myself, and pass the time if I were sure to live for ever.

That, if it had been my good fortune to come into the world a *struldbrug*, as soon as I could discover my own happiness by understanding the difference between life and death, I would first resolve by all arts and methods whatsoever to procure myself riches. In the pursuit of which by thrift and management, I might reasonably expect in about two hundred years, to be the wealthiest man in the kingdom. In the second place, I would from my earliest youth apply myself to the study of arts and sciences, by which I should arrive in time to excel all others in learning. Lastly, I would carefully record every action and event of consequence that happened in the public, impartially draw the characters of the several successions of princes and great ministers of state, with my own observations on every point. I would exactly set down the several changes in customs, language, fashions of dress, diet, and diversions. By all which acquirements, I should be a living treasury of knowledge and wisdom, and certainly become the oracle of the nation.

I would never marry after threescore, but live in an hospitable manner, yet still on the saving side. I would entertain myself in forming and directing the minds of hopeful young men, by convincing them from my own remembrance, experience, and observation, fortified by numerous examples, of the usefulness of virtue in public and private life. But my choice and constant companions should be a set of my own immortal brotherhood, among whom I would elect a dozen from the most ancient down to my own contemporaries. Where any of these wanted fortunes, I would provide them with convenient lodges round my own estate, and have some of them always at my table, only mingling a few of the most valuable among you mortals, whom length of time would harden me to lose with little or no reluctance, and treat your posterity after the same manner; just as a man diverts himself with the annual succession of pinks and tulips in his garden, without regretting the loss of those which withered the preceding year.

These *struldbrugs* and I would mutually communicate our observations and memorials through the course of time, remark the several gradations by which corruption steals into the world, and oppose it in every step, by giving perpetual warning and instruction to mankind; which, added to the strong influence of our own example, would probably prevent that continual degeneracy of human nature so justly complained of in all ages.

Add to all this, the pleasure of seeing the various revolutions of states and empires, the changes in the lower and upper world,[1] ancient cities in ruins, and obscure villages become the seats of kings. Famous rivers lessening into shallow brooks, the ocean leaving one coast dry, and overwhelming another: the discovery of many countries yet unknown. Barbarity over-running the politest nations, and the most barbarous become civilized. I should then see the discovery of the longitude, the perpetual motion, the universal medicine,[2] and many other great inventions brought to the utmost perfection.

What wonderful discoveries should we make in astronomy, by outliving and confirming our own predictions, by observing the progress and returns of comets, with the changes of motion in the sun, moon, and stars.

I enlarged upon many other topics, which the natural desire of endless life and sublunary[3] happiness could easily furnish me with. When I had ended, and the sum of my discourse had been interpreted as before, to the rest of the company, there was a good deal of talk among them in the language of the country, not without some laughter at my expense. At last the same gentleman who had been my interpreter said, he was desired by the rest to set me right in a few mistakes, which I had fallen into through the common imbecility of human nature, and upon that allowance was less answerable for them. That this breed of *struldbrugs* was peculiar to their country, for there were no such people either in Balnibarbi or Japan, where he had the honour to be ambassador from his Majesty, and found the

[1] *the lower and upper world* Earth and heavens.

[2] *the discovery … medicine* Gulliver mentions several scientific pursuits that Swift thought impossible and ridiculous, such as a method for determining longitude at sea, a perpetual motion machine, and one drug to cure all diseases.

[3] *sublunary* Earthly.

natives in both those kingdoms very hard to believe[1] that the fact was possible; and it appeared from my astonishment when he first mentioned the matter to me, that I received it as a thing wholly new, and scarcely to be credited. That in the two kingdoms above mentioned, where during his residence he had conversed very much, he observed long life to be the universal desire and wish of mankind. That whoever had one foot in the grave, was sure to hold back the other as strongly as he could. That the oldest had still hopes of living one day longer, and looked on death as the greatest evil, from which nature always prompted him to retreat; only in this island of Luggnagg the appetite for living was not so eager, from the continual example of the *struldbrugs* before their eyes.

That the system of living contrived by me was unreasonable and unjust, because it supposed a perpetuity of youth, health, and vigour, which no man could be so foolish to hope, however extravagant he may be in his wishes. That the question therefore was not whether a man would chose to be always in the prime of youth, attended with prosperity and health, but how he would pass a perpetual life under all the usual disadvantages which old age brings along with it. For although few men will avow their desires of being immortal upon such hard conditions, yet in the two kingdoms before mentioned of Balnibarbi and Japan, he observed that every man desired to put off death for some time longer, let it approach ever so late; and he rarely heard of any man who died willingly, except he were incited by the extremity of grief or torture. And he appealed to me whether in those countries I had travelled as well as my own, I had not observed the same general disposition.

After this preface, he gave me a particular account of the *struldbrugs* among them. He said they commonly acted like mortals, till about thirty years old, after which by degrees they grew melancholy and dejected, increasing in both till they came to fourscore. This he learned from their own confession: for otherwise there not being above two or three of that species born in an age, they were too few to form a general observation by. When they came to fourscore years, which is reckoned the extremity of living in this country, they had not only all the follies and infirmities of other old men, but many more which arose from the dreadful prospect of never dying. They were not only opinionative, peevish, covetous, morose, vain, talkative, but uncapable of friendship, and dead to all natural affection, which never descended below their grandchildren. Envy and impotent desires are their prevailing passions. But those objects against which their envy seems principally directed, are the vices of the younger sort, and the deaths of the old. By reflecting on the former, they find themselves cut off from all possibility of pleasure; and whenever they see a funeral, they lament and repine that others have gone to a harbour of rest, to which they themselves never can hope to arrive. They have no remembrance of anything but what they learned and observed in their youth and middle age, and even that is very imperfect. And for the truth or particulars of any fact, it is safer to depend on common traditions than upon their best recollections. The least miserable among them appear to be those who turn to dotage, and entirely lose their memories; these meet with more pity and assistance, because they want many bad qualities which abound in others.

If a *struldbrug* happen to marry one of his own kind, the marriage is dissolved of course by the courtesy of the kingdom, as soon as the younger of the two comes to be fourscore. For the law thinks it a reasonable indulgence, that those who are condemned without any fault of their own to a perpetual continuance in the world, should not have their misery doubled by the load of a wife.

As soon as they have completed the term of eighty years, they are looked on as dead in law; their heirs immediately succeed to their estates, only a small pittance is reserved for their support, and the poor ones are maintained at the public charge. After that period they are held incapable of any employment of trust or profit, they cannot purchase lands or take leases, neither are they allowed to be witnesses in any cause, either civil or criminal, not even for the decision of meers[2] and bounds.

At ninety they lose their teeth and hair, they have at that age no distinction of taste, but eat and drink whatever they can get, without relish or appetite. The diseases they were subject to still continue without increasing or diminishing. In talking they forget the common appellation of things, and the names of

[1] *to believe* To convince.

[2] *meers* Property lines.

persons, even of those who are their nearest friends and relations. For the same reason, they never can amuse themselves with reading, because their memory will not serve to carry them from the beginning of a sentence to the end; and by this defect they are deprived of the only entertainment whereof they might otherwise be capable.

The language of this country being always upon the flux, the *struldbrugs* of one age do not understand those of another, neither are they able after two hundred years to hold any conversation (farther than by a few general words) with their neighbours the mortals; and thus they lie under the disadvantage of living like foreigners in their own country.

This was the account given me of the *struldbrugs*, as near as I can remember. I afterwards saw five or six of different ages, the youngest not above two hundred years old, who were brought to me at several times by some of my friends; but although they were told that I was a great traveller, and had seen all the world, they had not the least curiosity to ask me a question; only desired I would give them *slumskudask*, or a token of remembrance, which is a modest way of begging, to avoid the law that strictly forbids it, because they are provided for by the public, although indeed with a very scanty allowance.

They are despised and hated by all sorts of people; when one of them is born, it is reckoned ominous, and their birth is recorded very particularly: so that you may know their age by consulting the registry, which however hath not been kept above a thousand years past, or at least hath been destroyed by time or public disturbances. But the usual way of computing how old they are, is by asking them what kings or great persons they can remember, and then consulting history, for infallibly the last prince in their mind did not begin his reign after they were fourscore years old.

They were the most mortifying sight I ever beheld, and the women more horrible than the men. Besides the usual deformities in extreme old age, they acquired an additional ghastliness in proportion to their number of years, which is not to be described; and among half a dozen, I soon distinguished which was the eldest, although there was not above a century or two between them.

The reader will easily believe, that from what I had heard and seen, my keen appetite for perpetuity of life was much abated. I grew heartily ashamed of the pleasing visions I had formed, and thought no tyrant could invent a death into which I would not run with pleasure from such a life. The King heard of all that had passed between me and my friends upon this occasion, and rallied[1] me very pleasantly, wishing I would send a couple of *struldbrugs* to my own country, to arm our people against the fear of death; but this it seems is forbidden by the fundamental laws of the kingdom, or else I should have been well content with the trouble and expense of transporting them.

I could not but agree that the laws of this kingdom, relating to the *struldbrugs*, were founded upon the strongest reasons, and such as any other country would be under the necessity of enacting in the like circumstances. Otherwise, as avarice is the necessary consequent of old age, those immortals would in time become proprietors of the whole nation, and engross[2] the civil power, which, for want of abilities to manage, must end in the ruin of the public.

Chapter II

(*The author leaves Luggnagg, and sails to Japan. From thence he returns in a Dutch ship to Amsterdam, and from Amsterdam to England.*)

I thought this account of the *struldbrugs* might be some entertainment to the reader, because it seems to be a little out of the common way; at least, I do not remember to have met the like in any book of travels that hath come to my hands: and if I am deceived, my excuse must be that it is necessary for travellers, who describe the same country, very often to agree in dwelling on the same particulars, without deserving the censure of having borrowed or transcribed from those who wrote before them.

There is indeed a perpetual commerce between this kingdom and the great empire of Japan, and it is very probable that the Japanese authors may have given some account of the *struldbrugs*; but my stay in Japan was so short, and I was so entirely a stranger to that language, that I was not qualified to make any enquiries. But I

[1] *rallied* Teased.

[2] *engross* Monopolize.

hope the Dutch, upon this notice, will be curious and able enough to supply my defects.

His Majesty having often pressed me to accept some employment in his court, and finding me absolutely determined to return to my native country, was pleased to give me his licence to depart, and honoured me with a letter of recommendation under his own hand to the Emperor of Japan. He likewise presented me with four hundred forty-four large pieces of gold (this nation delighting in even numbers), and a red diamond which I sold in England for eleven hundred pounds.

On the 6th day of May, 1709, I took a solemn leave of his Majesty, and all my friends. This prince was so gracious as to order a guard to conduct me to Glanguenstald, which is a royal port to the south-west part of the island. In six days I found a vessel ready to carry me to Japan, and spent fifteen days in the voyage. We landed at a small port-town called Xamoschi, situated on the south-east part of Japan; the town lies on the western point, where there is a narrow strait, leading northward into a long arm of the sea, upon the north-west part of which, Yedo[1] the metropolis stands. At landing, I showed the custom-house officers my letter from the King of Luggnagg to his Imperial Majesty. They knew the seal perfectly well; it was as broad as the palm of my hand. The impression was, *a King lifting up a lame beggar from the earth*.[2] The magistrates of the town hearing of my letter, received me as a public minister. They provided me with carriages and servants, and bore my charges to Yedo, where I was admitted to an audience, and delivered my letter, which was opened with great ceremony, and explained to the Emperor by an interpreter, who then gave me notice by his Majesty's order, that I should signify my request, and, whatever it were, it should be granted for the sake of his royal brother of Luggnagg. This interpreter was a person employed to transact affairs with the Hollanders; he soon conjectured by my countenance that I was an European, and therefore repeated his Majesty's commands in Low Dutch,[3] which he spoke perfectly well. I answered (as I had before determined), that I was a Dutch merchant, shipwrecked in a very remote country, from whence I had travelled by sea and land to Luggnagg, and then took shipping for Japan, where I knew my countrymen often traded, and with some of these I hoped to get an opportunity of returning into Europe: I therefore most humbly entreated his royal favour, to give order, that I should be conducted in safety to Nangasac.[4] To this I added another petition, that for the sake of my patron the King of Luggnagg, his Majesty would condescend to excuse my performing the ceremony imposed on my countrymen, of trampling upon the crucifix,[5] because I had been thrown into his kingdom by my misfortunes, without any intention of trading. When this latter petition was interpreted to the Emperor, he seemed a little surprised, and said, he believed I was the first of my countrymen who ever made any scruple in this point, and that he began to doubt whether I was a real Hollander, or no, but rather suspected I must be a Christian.[6] However, for the reasons I had offered, but chiefly to gratify the King of Luggnagg by an uncommon mark of his favour, he would comply with the singularity of my humour; but the affair must be managed with dexterity, and his officers should be commanded to let me pass as it were by forgetfulness. For he assured me, that if the secret should be discovered by my countrymen, the Dutch, they would cut my throat in the voyage. I returned my thanks by the interpreter for so unusual a favour, and some troops being at that time on their march to Nangasac, the commanding officer had orders to convey me safe thither, with particular instructions about the business of the crucifix.

On the 9th day of June, 1709, I arrived at Nangasac, after a very long and troublesome journey. I soon fell into the company of some Dutch sailors belonging to the *Amboyna*,[7] of Amsterdam, a stout ship of 450 tons.

[1] *Yedo* Renamed Tokyo in 1868.

[2] *a King ... earth* Luggnagg is thought to be Swift's satirical portrayal of France, and this seal to represent Louis XIV situating his illegitimate son in the line for the throne.

[3] *Low Dutch* Dutch.

[4] *Nangasac* Nagasaki, which contained a Dutch colony.

[5] *trampling upon the crucifix* Japanese rulers had devised this test to identify Japanese Christians (which, contrary to Gulliver's statements, was not applied to the Dutch). The penalty for not trampling the crucifix when required to do so was death.

[6] *I was the first ... Christian* Refers to the fact that some Dutch traders willingly accepted the Japanese ban on outward signs of Christianity.

[7] *Amboyna* Name of a Dutch-controlled colony in the East Indies. In 1623, despite trading treaties between the English and Dutch, ten Englishmen were tortured and executed in Amboyna by the Dutch under dubious claims of treason.

I had lived long in Holland, pursuing my studies at Leyden, and I spoke Dutch well. The seamen soon knew from whence I came last: they were curious to enquire into my voyages and course of life. I made up a story as short and probable as I could, but concealed the greatest part. I knew many persons in Holland; I was able to invent names for my parents, whom I pretended to be obscure people in the province of Guelderland. I would have given the captain (one Theodorus Vangrult) what he pleased to ask for my voyage to Holland; but understanding I was a surgeon, he was contented to take half the usual rate, on condition that I would serve him in the way of my calling. Before we took shipping, I was often asked by some of the crew, whether I had performed the ceremony above-mentioned. I evaded the question by general answers, that I had satisfied the Emperor and court in all particulars. However, a malicious rogue of a skipper[1] went to an officer, and pointing to me, told him I had not yet trampled on the crucifix: but the other, who had received instructions to let me pass, gave the rascal twenty strokes on the shoulders with a bamboo, after which I was no more troubled with such questions.

Nothing happened worth mentioning in this voyage. We sailed with a fair wind to the Cape of Good Hope, where we stayed only to take in fresh water. On the 10th of April, 1710, we arrived safe at Amsterdam, having lost only three men by sickness in the voyage, and a fourth who fell from the foremast into the sea, not far from the coast of Guinea. From Amsterdam I soon after set sail for England in a small vessel belonging to that city.

On the 16th of April we put in at the Downs. I landed the next morning, and saw once more my native country after an absence of five years and six months complete. I went straight to Redriff, where I arrived the same day at two in the afternoon, and found my wife and family in good health.

[1] *skipper* Ship's boy.

PART 4 –
A VOYAGE TO THE COUNTRY OF THE HOUYHNHNMS[2]

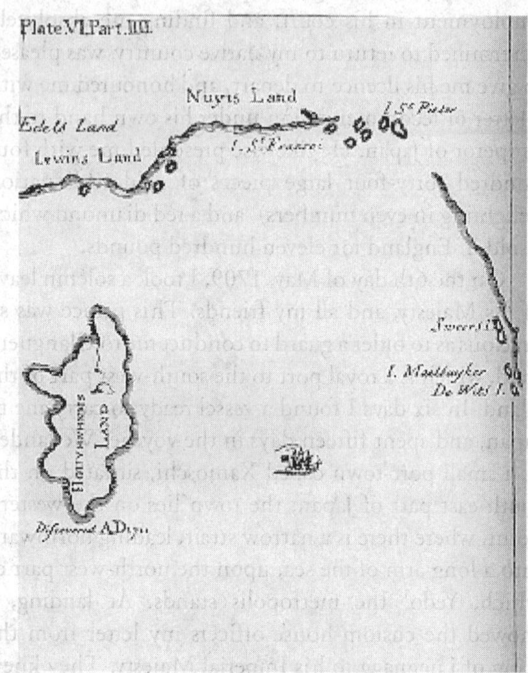

Map showing the location of "Houyhnhnms Land," printed in the 1726 edition with no accompanying caption at the beginning of Part 4.

CHAPTER 1

(*The author sets out as Captain of a ship. His men conspire against him, confine him a long time to his cabin, and set him on shore in an unknown land. He travels up into the country. The Yahoos, a strange sort of animal, described. The author meets two Houyhnhnms.*)

I continued at home with my wife and children about five months, in a very happy condition, if I could have learned the lesson of knowing when I was well. I left my poor wife big with child[3] and accepted an advantageous offer made me to be Captain of the *Adventure*, a stout merchantman of 350 tons; for I understood navigation well and, being grown weary of

[2] *HOUYHNHNMS* Pronounced "hwhin-hims," the name is meant to mimic the sound of a horse's whinny.

[3] *big with child* Pregnant.

a surgeon's employment at sea, which, however, I could exercise upon occasion, I took a skilful young man of that calling, one Robert Purefoy, into my ship. We set sail from Portsmouth upon the 7th day of September, 1710; on the 14th we met with Captain Pocock of Bristol, at Teneriffe,[1] who was going to the bay of Campeche[2] to cut logwood. On the 16th he was parted from us by a storm; I heard since my return that his ship foundered, and none escaped but one cabin boy. He was an honest man and a good sailor, but a little too positive in his own opinions, which was the cause of his destruction, as it has been with several others. For if he had followed my advice, he might at this time have been safe at home with his family as well as myself.

I had several men who died in my ship of calentures,[3] so that I was forced to get recruits out of Barbados and the Leeward Islands, where I touched[4] by the direction of the merchants who employed me; which I had soon too much cause to repent, for I found afterwards that most of them had been buccaneers. I had fifty hands onboard, and my orders were that I should trade with the Indians in the South Sea, and make what discoveries I could. These rogues whom I had picked up debauched my other men, and they all formed a conspiracy to seize the ship and secure me; which they did one morning, rushing into my cabin and binding me hand and foot, threatening to throw me overboard if I offered to stir. I told them I was their prisoner and would submit. This they made me swear to do, and then they unbound me, only fastening one of my legs with a chain near my bed, and placed a sentry at my door with his piece charged, who was commanded to shoot me dead if I attempted my liberty. They sent me down victuals and drink, and took the government of the ship to themselves. Their design was to turn pirates and plunder the Spaniards, which they could not do till they got more men. But first they resolved to sell the goods in the ship, and then go to Madagascar for recruits, several among them having died since my confinement. They sailed many weeks and traded with the Indians, but I knew not what course they took, being kept a close prisoner in my cabin and expecting nothing less than to be murdered, as they often threatened me.

Upon the 9th day of May, 1711, one James Welch came down to my cabin and said he had orders from the Captain to set me ashore. I expostulated with him, but in vain; neither would he so much as tell me who their new Captain was. They forced me into the longboat, letting me put on my best suit of clothes, which were as good as new, and take a small bundle of linen, but no arms except my hanger; and they were so civil as not to search my pockets, into which I conveyed what money I had, with some other little necessaries. They rowed about a league and then set me down on a strand.[5] I desired them to tell me what country it was. They all swore they knew no more than myself, but said that the Captain (as they called him) was resolved, after they had sold the lading,[6] to get rid of me in the first place where they could discover land. They pushed off immediately, advising me to make haste for fear of being overtaken by the tide, and so bade me farewell.

In this desolate condition I advanced forward, and soon got upon firm ground, where I sat down on a bank to rest myself and consider what I had best do. When I was a little refreshed I went up into the country, resolving to deliver myself to the first savages I should meet, and purchase my life from them by some bracelets, glass rings, and other toys,[7] which sailors usually provide themselves with in those voyages, and whereof I had some about me. The land was divided by long rows of trees, not regularly planted, but naturally growing; there was great plenty of grass and several fields of oats. I walked very circumspectly, for fear of being surprised, or suddenly shot with an arrow from behind or on either side. I fell into a beaten road, where I saw many tracks of human feet, and some of cows, but most of horses. At last I beheld several animals in a field, and one or two of the same kind sitting in trees. Their shape was very singular and deformed, which a little discomposed me, so that I lay down behind a thicket to observe them better. Some of them, coming forward near the place where I lay, gave me an opportunity of distinctly

[1] *Teneriffe* Largest of the Canary Islands.

[2] *bay of Campeche* The southernmost part of the Gulf of Mexico.

[3] *calentures* Tropical fever, common among sailors, which causes delirium.

[4] *touched* Landed for a short stay.

[5] *strand* Shore.

[6] *lading* Freight; cargo.

[7] *toys* Trinkets.

marking their form. Their heads and breasts were covered with a thick hair, some frizzled and others lank; they had beards like goats, and a long ridge of hair down their backs and the fore parts of their legs and feet; but the rest of their bodies was bare, so that I might see their skins, which were of a brown buff colour. They had no tails, nor any hair at all on their buttocks, except about the anus, which I presume nature had placed there to defend them as they sat on the ground, for this posture they used, as well as lying down, and often stood on their hind feet. They climbed high trees as nimbly as a squirrel, for they had strong extended claws before and behind, terminating in sharp points, and hooked. They would often spring, and bound, and leap with prodigious agility. The females were not so large as the males; they had long lank hair on their heads but none on their faces, nor anything more than a sort of down on the rest of their bodies, except about the anus and pudenda. The dugs hung between their fore feet and often reached almost to the ground as they walked. The hair of both sexes was of several colours: brown, red, black, and yellow. Upon the whole, I never beheld in all my travels so disagreeable an animal, or one against which I naturally conceived so strong an antipathy. So that, thinking I had seen enough, full of contempt and aversion, I got up and pursued the beaten road, hoping it might direct me to the cabin of some Indian. I had not got far when I met one of these creatures full in my way, and coming up directly to me. The ugly monster, when he saw me, distorted several ways every feature of his visage, and stared as at an object he had never seen before; then, approaching nearer, lifted up his forepaw, whether out of curiosity or mischief I could not tell; but I drew my hanger and gave him a good blow with the flat side of it, for I durst not strike with the edge, fearing the inhabitants might be provoked against me if they should come to know that I had killed or maimed any of their cattle. When the beast felt the smart, he drew back, and roared so loud that a herd of at least forty came flocking about me from the next field, howling and making odious faces; but I ran to the body of a tree and, leaning my back against it, kept them off by waving my hanger. Several of this cursed brood, getting hold of the branches behind, leaped up into the tree, whence they began to discharge their excrements on my head; however, I escaped pretty well by sticking close to the stem of the tree, but was almost stifled with the filth, which fell about me on every side.

In the midst of this distress, I observed them all to run away on a sudden as fast as they could; at which I ventured to leave the tree and pursue the road, wondering what it was that could put them into this fright. But looking on my left hand, I saw a horse walking softly in the field; which, my persecutors having sooner discovered, was the cause of their flight. The horse started a little when he came near me, but soon, recovering himself, looked full in my face with manifest tokens of wonder; he viewed my hands and feet, walking round me several times. I would have pursued my journey, but he placed himself directly in the way, yet looking with a very mild aspect, never offering the least violence. We stood gazing at each other for some time; at last I took the boldness to reach my hand towards his neck with a design to stroke it, using the common style and whistle of jockeys when they are going to handle a strange horse. But this animal seemed to receive my civilities with disdain, shook his head and bent his brows, softly raising up his right forefoot to remove my hand. Then he neighed three or four times, but in so different a cadence that I almost began to think he was speaking to himself in some language of his own.

While he and I were thus employed, another horse came up, who applying himself to the first in a very formal manner, they gently struck each other's right hoof before, neighing several times by turns, and varying the sound, which seemed to be almost articulate. They went some paces off, as if it were to confer together, walking side by side, backward and forward, like persons deliberating upon some affair of weight, but often turning their eyes towards me, as it were to watch that I might not escape. I was amazed to see such actions and behaviour in brute beasts, and concluded with myself that if the inhabitants of this country were endued with a proportionable degree of reason, they must needs be the wisest people upon earth. This thought gave me so much comfort that I resolved to go forward until I could discover some house or village, or meet with any of the natives, leaving the two horses to discourse together as they pleased. But the first, who was a dapple gray, observing me to steal off, neighed after me in so expressive a tone that I fancied myself to understand what he meant; whereupon I turned back and came near to him to expect[1] his farther commands; but concealing my fear as much as I could, for I began to be in some pain how this adventure might terminate; and the reader will easily believe I did not much like my present situation.

The two horses came up close to me, looking with great earnestness upon my face and hands. The gray steed rubbed my hat all round with his right forehoof, and discomposed it so much that I was forced to adjust it better by taking it off and settling it again; whereat both he and his companion (who was a brown bay) appeared to be much surprised. The latter felt the lappet of my coat, and, finding it to hang loose about me, they both looked with new signs of wonder. He stroked my right hand, seeming to admire the softness and colour, but he squeezed it so hard between his hoof and his pastern[2] that I was forced to roar; after which they both touched me with all possible tenderness. They were under great perplexity about my shoes and stockings, which they felt very often, neighing to each other, and using various gestures not unlike those of a philosopher, when he would attempt to solve some new and difficult phenomenon.

Upon the whole, the behaviour of these animals was so orderly and rational, so acute and judicious, that I at last concluded they must needs be magicians who had thus metamorphosed themselves upon some design and, seeing a stranger in the way, resolved to divert themselves with him; or perhaps were really amazed at the sight of a man so very different in habit, feature, and complexion from those who might probably live in so remote a climate. Upon the strength of this reasoning, I ventured to address them in the following manner: "Gentlemen, if you be conjurers, as I have good cause to believe, you can understand my language; therefore I make bold to let your worships know that I am a poor distressed Englishman, driven by his misfortunes upon your coast; and I entreat one of you to let me ride upon his back, as if he were a real horse, to some house or village where I can be relieved. In return of which favour, I will make you a present of this knife and bracelet" (taking them out of my pocket). The two creatures stood silent while I spoke, seeming to listen with great attention, and when I had ended they neighed frequently towards each other, as if they were engaged in serious conversation. I plainly observed that their language expressed the passions very well, and the words might, with little pains, be resolved into an alphabet more easily than the Chinese.

I could frequently distinguish the word *Yahoo*, which was repeated by each of them several times; and although it was impossible for me to conjecture what it meant, yet while the two horses were busy in conversation, I endeavoured to practise this word upon my tongue; and as soon as they were silent, I boldly pronounced *Yahoo* in a loud voice, imitating at the same time, as near as I could, the neighing of a horse; at which they were both visibly surprised, and the gray repeated the same word twice, as if he meant to teach me the right accent; wherein I spoke after him as well as I could, and found myself perceivably to improve every time, although very far from any degree of perfection. Then the bay tried me with a second word, much harder to be pronounced; but reducing it to the English orthography, may be spelt thus, *Houyhnhnm*. I did not succeed in this so well as in the former; but after two or three farther trials I had better fortune; and they both appeared amazed at my capacity.

After some further discourse, which I then conjectured might relate to me, the two friends took their leaves, with the same compliment of striking each other's hoof, and the gray made me signs that I should walk before him; wherein I thought it prudent to comply till I could find a better director. When I offered to slacken my pace, he would cry "*Hhuun, hhuun*." I guessed his meaning, and gave him to understand as well as I could that I was weary, and not able to walk faster; upon which he would stand awhile to let me rest.

Chapter 2

(*The author conducted by a Houyhnhnm to his house. The house described. The author's reception. The food of the Houyhnhnms. The author in distress for want of meat. Is at last relieved. His manner of feeding in this country.*)

Having travelled about three miles, we came to a long kind of building, made of timber stuck in the

[1] *expect* Wait for.

[2] *pastern* Part between the lower leg and the hoof, the equivalent of the ankle.

ground and wattled[1] across; the roof was low and covered with straw. I now began to be a little comforted, and took out some toys, which travellers usually carry for presents to the savage Indians of America and other parts, in hopes the people of the house would be thereby encouraged to receive me kindly. The horse made me a sign to go in first; it was a large room with a smooth clay floor, and a rack and manger extending the whole length on one side. There were three nags and two mares, not eating, but some of them sitting down upon their hams, which I very much wondered at; but wondered more to see the rest employed in domestic business. The last seemed but ordinary cattle;[2] however, this confirmed my first opinion, that a people who could so far civilize brute animals must needs excel in wisdom all the nations of the world. The gray came in just after, and thereby prevented any ill treatment which the others might have given me. He neighed to them several times in a style of authority, and received answers.

Beyond this room there were three others, reaching the length of the house, to which you passed through three doors opposite to each other, in the manner of a vista.[3] We went through the second room towards the third. Here the gray walked in first, beckoning me to attend.[4] I waited in the second room, and got ready my presents for the master and mistress of the house; they were two knives, three bracelets of false pearls, a small looking-glass, and a bead necklace. The horse neighed three or four times, and I waited to hear some answers in a human voice, but I heard no other returns than in the same dialect, only one or two a little shriller than his. I began to think that this house must belong to some person of great note among them, because there appeared so much ceremony before I could gain admittance. But, that a man of quality should be served all by horses, was beyond my comprehension. I feared my brain was disturbed by my sufferings and misfortunes. I roused myself and looked about me in the room where I was left alone; this was furnished like the first, only after a more elegant manner. I rubbed my eyes often, but the same objects still occurred. I pinched my arms and sides to awake myself, hoping I might be in a dream. I then absolutely concluded that all these appearances could be nothing else but necromancy and magic. But I had no time to pursue these reflections, for the gray horse came to the door and made me a sign to follow him into the third room, where I saw a very comely mare, together with a colt and foal, sitting on their haunches upon mats of straw, not unartfully made, and perfectly neat and clean.

The mare, soon after my entrance, rose from her mat, and coming up close, after having nicely observed my hands and face, gave me a most contemptuous look; then turning to the horse, I heard the word *Yahoo* often repeated betwixt them; the meaning of which word I could not then comprehend, although it was the first I had learned to pronounce. But I was soon better informed, to my everlasting mortification; for the horse, beckoning to me with his head and repeating the word *hhuun, hhuun*, as he did upon the road, which I understood was to attend him, led me out into a kind of court, where was another building at some distance from the house. Here we entered, and I saw three of those detestable creatures, which I first met after my landing, feeding upon roots and the flesh of some animals, which I afterwards found to be that of asses and dogs, and now and then a cow dead by accident or disease. They were all tied by the neck with strong withes,[5] fastened to a beam; they held their food between the claws of their forefeet, and tore it with their teeth.

The master horse ordered a sorrel nag, one of his servants, to untie the largest of these animals and take him into the yard. The beast and I were brought close together, and by our countenances diligently compared both by master and servant, who thereupon repeated several times the word *Yahoo*. My horror and astonishment are not to be described when I observed in this abominable animal a perfect human figure: the face of it indeed was flat and broad, the nose depressed, the lips large, and the mouth wide; but these differences are common to all savage nations, where the lineaments of the countenance are distorted by the natives suffering their infants to lie grovelling on the earth, or by carrying them on their backs, nuzzling with their face against the mothers' shoulders. The forefeet of the Yahoo differed

[1] *wattled* Made of woven sticks or branches.

[2] *cattle* Horses.

[3] *vista* Long and narrow passage.

[4] *attend* Wait.

[5] *withes* Shackles or bands made of twigs twisted together.

from my hands in nothing else but the length of the nails, the coarseness and brownness of the palms, and the hairiness on the backs. There was the same resemblance between our feet, with the same differences; which I knew very well, though the horses did not because of my shoes and stockings; the same in every part of our bodies except as to hairiness and colour, which I have already described.

The great difficulty that seemed to stick with the two horses was to see the rest of my body so very different from that of a Yahoo, for which I was obliged to my clothes, whereof they had no conception. The sorrel nag offered me a root, which he held (after their manner, as we shall describe in its proper place) between his hoof and pastern; I took it in my hand, and, having smelt it, returned it to him again as civilly as I could. He brought out of the Yahoos' kennel a piece of ass's flesh, but it smelt so offensively that I turned from it with loathing. He then threw it to the Yahoo, by whom it was greedily devoured. He afterwards showed me a wisp of hay and a fetlock full of oats, but I shook my head to signify that neither of these were food for me. And indeed I now apprehended that I must absolutely starve if I did not get to some of my own species; for as to those filthy Yahoos, although there were few greater lovers of mankind, at that time, than myself, yet I confess I never saw any sensitive being so detestable on all accounts; and the more I came near them the more hateful they grew, while I stayed in that country. This the master horse observed by my behaviour, and therefore sent the *Yahoo* back to his kennel. He then put his forehoof to his mouth, at which I was much surprised, although he did it with ease, and with a motion that appeared perfectly natural, and made other signs to know what I would eat; but I could not return him such an answer as he was able to apprehend; and if he had understood me, I did not see how it was possible to contrive any way for finding myself nourishment. While we were thus engaged, I observed a cow passing by, whereupon I pointed to her and expressed a desire to go and milk her. This had its effect; for he led me back into the house and ordered a mare-servant to open a room, where a good store of milk lay in earthen and wooden vessels, after a very orderly and cleanly manner. She gave me a large bowlful, of which I drank very heartily, and found myself well refreshed.

About noon, I saw coming towards the house a kind of vehicle drawn like a sledge by four Yahoos. There was in it an old steed, who seemed to be of quality; he alighted with his hind feet forward, having by accident got a hurt in his left forefoot. He came to dine with our horse, who received him with great civility. They dined in the best room, and had oats boiled in milk for the second course, which the old horse ate warm, but the rest cold. Their mangers were placed circular in the middle of the room and divided into several partitions, round which they sat on their haunches upon bosses of straw. In the middle was a large rack with angles answering to every partition of the manger; so that each horse and mare ate their own hay, and their own mash of oats and milk, with much decency and regularity. The behaviour of the young colt and foal appeared very modest, and that of the master and mistress extremely cheerful and complaisant to their guest. The gray ordered me to stand by him, and much discourse passed between him and his friend concerning me, as I found by the stranger's often looking on me, and the frequent repetition of the word Yahoo.

I happened to wear my gloves, which the master gray observing, seemed perplexed, discovering signs of wonder what I had done to my forefeet. He put his hoof three or four times to them, as if he would signify that I should reduce them to their former shape, which I presently did, pulling off both my gloves and putting them into my pocket. This occasioned farther talk; and I saw the company was pleased with my behaviour, whereof I soon found the good effects. I was ordered to speak the few words I understood; and while they were at dinner, the master taught me the names for oats, milk, fire, water, and some others, which I could readily pronounce after him, having from my youth a great facility in learning languages.

When dinner was done, the master horse took me aside, and by signs and words made me understand the concern he was in that I had nothing to eat. Oats in their tongue are called *hlunnh*. This word I pronounced two or three times; for although I had refused them at first, yet, upon second thoughts, I considered that I could contrive to make of them a kind of bread, which might be sufficient, with milk, to keep me alive till I could make my escape to some other country, and to creatures of my own species. The horse immediately ordered a white mare servant of his family to bring me a good quantity of oats in a sort of wooden tray. These I heated before the fire as well as I could, and rubbed them till the husks came off, which I made a shift to winnow from the grain. I ground and beat them between two stones, then took water and made them into a paste or cake, which I toasted at the fire and ate warm with milk. It was at first a very insipid diet, though common enough in many parts of Europe, but grew tolerable by time; and having been often reduced to hard fare in my life, this was not the first experiment I had made how easily nature is satisfied. And I cannot but observe that I never had one hour's sickness while I stayed in this island. It is true, I sometimes made a shift to catch a rabbit or bird by springes[1] made of Yahoo's hairs; and I often gathered wholesome herbs, which I boiled and ate as salads with my bread; and now and then, for a rarity, I made a little butter, and drank the whey. I was at first at a great loss for salt, but custom soon reconciled me to the want of it; and I am confident that the frequent use of salt among us is an effect of luxury, and was first introduced only as a provocative to drink, except where it is necessary for preserving flesh in long voyages, or in places remote from great markets; for we observe no animal to be fond of it but man, and as to myself, when I left this country it was a great while before I could endure the taste of it in anything that I ate.

This is enough to say upon the subject of my diet, wherewith other travellers fill their books, as if the readers were personally concerned whether we fare well or ill. However, it was necessary to mention this matter, lest the world should think it impossible that I could find sustenance for three years in such a country, and among such inhabitants.

When it grew towards evening, the master horse ordered a place for me to lodge in; it was but six yards from the house and separated from the stable of the Yahoos. Here I got some straw and, covering myself with my own clothes, slept very sound. But I was in a short time better accommodated, as the reader shall know hereafter, when I come to treat more particularly about my way of living.

[1] *springes* Snares.

CHAPTER 3

(*The author studies to learn the language. The Houyhnhnm, his master, assists in teaching him. The language described. Several Houyhnhnms of quality come out of curiosity to see the author. He gives his master a short account of his voyage.*)

My principal endeavour was to learn the language, which my master (for so I shall henceforth call him), and his children, and every servant of his house, were desirous to teach me; for they looked upon it as a prodigy, that a brute animal should discover such marks of a rational creature. I pointed to everything and inquired the name of it, which I wrote down in my journal-book when I was alone, and corrected my bad accent by desiring those of the family to pronounce it often. In this employment, a sorrel nag, one of the under servants, was very ready to assist me.

In speaking, they pronounced through the nose and throat, and their language approaches nearest to the High Dutch, or German, of any I know in Europe; but is much more graceful and significant.[2] The Emperor Charles V made almost the same observation when he said that if he were to speak to his horse, it should be in High Dutch.[3]

The curiosity and impatience of my master were so great that he spent many hours of his leisure to instruct me. He was convinced (as he afterwards told me) that I must be a Yahoo; but my teachableness, civility, and cleanliness astonished him; which were qualities altogether opposite to those animals. He was most perplexed about my clothes, reasoning sometimes with himself whether they were a part of my body; for I never pulled them off till the family were asleep, and got them on before they waked in the morning. My master was eager to learn whence I came; how I acquired those appearances of reason, which I discovered in all my actions; and to know my story from my own mouth, which he hoped he should soon do by the great proficiency I made in learning and pronouncing their words and

[2] *significant* Expressive.

[3] *Emperor Charles … High Dutch* Charles V, Emperor of Rome, King of Spain, and ruler of parts of Italy and the Netherlands, apparently said that he would speak to his God in Spanish, his mistress in Italian, and his horse in German.

sentences. To help my memory, I formed all I learned into the English alphabet and writ the words down with the translations. This last, after some time, I ventured to do in my master's presence. It cost me much trouble to explain to him what I was doing; for the inhabitants have not the least idea of books or literature.

In about ten weeks time I was able to understand most of his questions, and in three months could give him some tolerable answers. He was extremely curious to know from what part of the country I came, and how I was taught to imitate a rational creature; because the Yahoos (whom he saw I exactly resembled in my head, hands, and face, that were only visible), with some appearance of cunning, and the strongest disposition to mischief, were observed to be the most unteachable of all brutes. I answered that I came over the sea, from a far place, with many others of my own kind, in a great hollow vessel made of the bodies of trees; that my companions forced me to land on this coast and then left me to shift for myself. It was with some difficulty, and by the help of many signs, that I brought him to understand me. He replied that I must needs be mistaken, or that I *said the thing which was not*; for they have no word in their language to express lying or falsehood. He knew it was impossible that there could be a country beyond the sea, or that a parcel of brutes could move a wooden vessel whither they pleased upon water. He was sure no Houyhnhnm alive could make such a vessel, nor would trust Yahoos to manage it.

The word Houyhnhnm in their tongue signifies a horse and, in its etymology, the perfection of nature. I told my master that I was at a loss for expression, but would improve as fast as I could, and hoped, in a short time, I should be able to tell him wonders. He was pleased to direct his own mare, his colt and foal, and the servants of the family to take all opportunities of instructing me; and every day, for two or three hours, he was at the same pains himself. Several horses and mares of quality in the neighbourhood came often to our house upon the report spread of a wonderful Yahoo that could speak like a Houyhnhnm, and seemed, in his words and actions, to discover some glimmerings of reason. These delighted to converse with me; they put many questions, and received such answers as I was able to return. By all these advantages I made so great a progress that in five months from my arrival I understood whatever was spoken, and could express myself tolerably well.

The Houyhnhnms, who came to visit my master out of a design of seeing and talking with me, could hardly believe me to be a right Yahoo because my body had a different covering from others of my kind. They were astonished to observe me without the usual hair or skin, except on my head, face, and hands; but I discovered that secret to my master upon an accident which happened about a fortnight before.

I have already told the reader that every night when the family were gone to bed, it was my custom to strip and cover myself with my clothes. It happened one morning early that my master sent for me by the sorrel nag, who was his valet. When he came I was fast asleep, my clothes fallen off on one side, and my shirt above my waist. I awaked at the noise he made, and observed him to deliver his message in some disorder; after which he went to my master, and in a great fright gave him a very confused account of what he had seen. This I presently discovered; for, going as soon as I was dressed to pay my attendance upon his honour, he asked me the meaning of what his servant had reported, that I was not the same thing when I slept as I appeared to be at other times; that his valet assured him, some part of me was white, some yellow, at least not so white, and some brown.

I had hitherto concealed the secret of my dress in order to distinguish myself, as much as possible, from that cursed race of Yahoos; but now I found it in vain to do so any longer. Besides, I considered that my clothes and shoes would soon wear out, which already were in a declining condition, and must be supplied by some contrivance from the hides of Yahoos, or other brutes; whereby the whole secret would be known. I therefore told my master that in the country from whence I came, those of my kind always covered their bodies with the hairs of certain animals prepared by art, as well for decency as to avoid the inclemencies of air, both hot and cold; of which, as to my own person, I would give him immediate conviction, if he pleased to command me; only desiring his excuse if I did not expose those parts that nature taught us to conceal. He said my discourse was all very strange, but especially the last part; for he could not understand why nature should teach us to conceal what nature had given; that neither himself nor family were ashamed of any parts of their bodies; but, however, I might do as I pleased. Whereupon I first unbuttoned my coat and pulled it off. I did the same with my waistcoat. I drew off my shoes, stockings, and breeches. I let my shirt down to my waist, and drew up the bottom, fastening it like a girdle about my middle to hide my nakedness.

My master observed the whole performance with great signs of curiosity and admiration. He took up all my clothes in his pastern, one piece after another, and examined them diligently; he then stroked my body very gently, and looked round me several times; after which, he said it was plain I must be a perfect Yahoo; but that I differed very much from the rest of my species in the softness, whiteness, and smoothness of my skin; my want of hair in several parts of my body; the shape and shortness of my claws behind and before; and my affectation of walking continually on my two hinder feet. He desired to see no more, and gave me leave to put on my clothes again, for I was shuddering with cold.

I expressed my uneasiness at his giving me so often the appellation of Yahoo, an odious animal for which I had so utter a hatred and contempt. I begged he would forbear applying that word to me, and make the same order in his family and among his friends whom he suffered to see me. I requested likewise that the secret of my having a false covering to my body might be known to none but himself, at least as long as my present clothing should last; for as to what the sorrel nag, his valet, had observed, his honour might command him to conceal it.

All this my master very graciously consented to; and thus the secret was kept till my clothes began to wear out, which I was forced to supply by several contrivances that shall hereafter be mentioned. In the meantime, he desired I would go on with my utmost diligence to learn their language, because he was more astonished at my capacity for speech and reason than at the figure of my body, whether it were covered or not; adding that he waited with some impatience to hear the wonders which I promised to tell him.

Thenceforward he doubled the pains he had been at to instruct me; he brought me into all company, and made them treat me with civility; because, as he told them privately, this would put me into good humour, and make me more diverting.

Every day when I waited on him, beside the trouble he was at in teaching, he would ask me several questions concerning myself, which I answered as well as I could, and by these means he had already received some general ideas, though very imperfect. It would be tedious to relate the several steps by which I advanced to a more regular conversation; but the first account I gave of myself in any order and length was to this purpose:

That I came from a very far country, as I already had attempted to tell him, with about fifty more of my own species; that we travelled upon the seas in a great hollow vessel made of wood, and larger than his honour's house. I described the ship to him in the best terms I could, and explained, by the help of my handkerchief displayed, how it was driven forward by the wind. That upon a quarrel among us, I was set on shore on this coast, where I walked forward, without knowing whither, till he delivered me from the persecution of those execrable Yahoos. He asked me who made the ship, and how it was possible that the Houyhnhnms of my country would leave it to the management of brutes? My answer was that I durst proceed no further in my relation unless he would give me his word and honour that he would not be offended, and then I would tell him the wonders I had so often promised. He agreed; and I went on by assuring him that the ship was made by creatures like myself, who in all the countries I had travelled, as well as in my own, were the only governing rational animals; and that upon my arrival hither, I was as much astonished to see the Houyhnhnms act like rational beings as he or his friends could be in finding some marks of reason in a creature he was pleased to call a Yahoo; to which I owned my resemblance in every part, but could not account for their degenerate and brutal nature. I said farther, that if good fortune ever restored me to my native country, to relate my travels hither, as I resolved to do, everybody would believe that I said the thing that was not, that I invented the story out of my own head; and (with all possible respect to himself, his family, and friends, and under his promise of not being offended) our countrymen would hardly think it probable that a Houyhnhnm should be the presiding creature of a nation, and a Yahoo the brute.

Chapter 4

(*The Houyhnhnm's notion of truth and falsehood. The author's discourse disapproved by his master. The author gives a more particular account of himself and the accidents of his voyage.*)

My master heard me with great appearances of uneasiness in his countenance; because doubting or not believing are so little known in this country that the inhabitants cannot tell how to behave themselves under such circumstances. And I remember in frequent discourses with my master concerning the nature of manhood[1] in other parts of the world, having occasion to talk of lying and false representation, it was with much difficulty that he comprehended what I meant, although he had otherwise a most acute judgment. For he argued thus: that the use of speech was to make us understand one another, and to receive information of facts; now if anyone *said the thing which was not*, these ends were defeated, because I cannot properly be said to understand him; and I am so far from receiving information that he leaves me worse than in ignorance; for I am led to believe a thing black when it is white, and short when it is long. And these were all the notions he had concerning that faculty of lying, so perfectly well understood, and so universally practiced, among human creatures.

To return from this digression; when I asserted that the Yahoos were the only governing animals in my country, which my master said was altogether past his conception, he desired to know whether we had Houyhnhnms among us, and what was their employment? I told him we had great numbers; that in summer they grazed in the fields and in winter were kept in houses with hay and oats, where Yahoo servants were employed to rub their skins smooth, comb their manes, pick their feet, serve them with food, and make their beds. I understand you well, said my master; it is now very plain from all you have spoken that whatever share of reason the Yahoos pretend to, the Houyhnhnms are your masters; I heartily wish our Yahoos would be so tractable. I begged his honour would please to excuse me from proceeding any further, because I was very certain that the account he expected from me would be highly displeasing. But he insisted in commanding me to let him know the best and the worst. I told him he should be obeyed. I owned that the Houyhnhnms among us, whom we called horses, were the most generous[2] and comely animals we had; that they excelled in strength and swiftness; and, when they belonged to persons of quality, were employed in travelling, racing, or drawing chariots; they were treated with much kindness and care, till they fell into diseases or became foundered[3] in the feet; but then they were sold, and used to all kind of drudgery till they died; after which their skins were stripped and sold for what they were worth, and their bodies left to be devoured by dogs and birds of prey. But the common race of horses had not so good fortune, being kept by farmers and carriers, and other mean people, who put them to greater labour, and fed them worse. I described, as well as I could, our way of riding; the shape and use of a bridle, a saddle, a spur, and a whip; of harness and wheels. I added that we fastened plates of a certain hard substance, called iron, at the bottom of their feet to preserve their hoofs from being broken by the stony ways on which we often travelled.

My master, after some expressions of great indignation, wondered how we dared to venture upon a Houyhnhnm's back; for he was sure that the weakest servant in his house would be able to shake off the strongest Yahoo; or, by lying down and rolling on his back, squeeze the brute to death. I answered that our horses were trained up from three or four years old to the several uses we intended them for; that if any of them proved intolerably vicious, they were employed for carriages; that they were severely beaten while they were young for any mischievous tricks; that the males, designed for the common use of riding or draught, were generally castrated about two years after their birth, to take down their spirits and make them more tame and gentle; that they were indeed sensible of rewards and punishments, but his honour would please to consider that they had not the least tincture of reason, any more than the Yahoos in this country.

It put me to the pains of many circumlocutions to give my master a right idea of what I spoke; for their language does not abound in variety of words, because

[1] *nature of manhood* Human nature.

[2] *generous* Noble; of noble birth.

[3] *foundered* Lamed.

their wants and passions are fewer than among us. But it is impossible to express his noble resentment at our savage treatment of the Houyhnhnm race; particularly after I had explained the manner and use of castrating horses among us, to hinder them from propagating their kind and to render them more servile. He said, if it were possible there could be any country where Yahoos alone were endued with reason, they certainly must be the governing animal, because reason in time will always prevail against brutal strength. But, considering the frame of our bodies, and especially of mine, he thought no creature of equal bulk was so ill-contrived for employing that reason in the common offices of life; whereupon he desired to know whether those among whom I lived resembled me or the Yahoos of his country? I assured him that I was as well shaped as most of my age; but the younger, and the females, were much more soft and tender, and the skins of the latter generally as white as milk. He said I differed indeed from other Yahoos, being much more cleanly, and not altogether so deformed; but, in point of real advantage, he thought I differed for the worse: that my nails were of no use either to my fore or hinder feet; as to my forefeet, he could not properly call them by that name, for he never observed me to walk upon them; that they were too soft to bear the ground; that I generally went with them uncovered; neither was the covering I sometimes wore on them of the same shape, or so strong as that on my feet behind; that I could not walk with any security, for if either of my hinder feet slipped, I must inevitably fail. He then began to find fault with other parts of my body: the flatness of my face; the prominence of my nose; mine eyes placed directly in front, so that I could not look on either side without turning my head; that I was not able to feed myself without lifting one of my forefeet to my mouth, and therefore nature had placed those joints to answer that necessity. He knew not what could be the use of those several clefts and divisions in my feet behind; that these were too soft to bear the hardness and sharpness of stones without a covering made from the skin of some other brute; that my whole body wanted a fence against heat and cold, which I was forced to put on and off every day, with tediousness and trouble; and lastly, that he observed every animal in this country naturally to abhor the Yahoos, whom the weaker avoided and the stronger drove from them. So that, supposing us to have the gift of reason, he could not see how it were possible to cure that natural antipathy which every creature discovered against us; nor, consequently, how we could tame and render them serviceable. However, he would (as he said) debate the matter no farther, because he was more desirous to know my own story, the country where I was born, and the several actions and events of my life before I came hither.

I assured him how extremely desirous I was that he should be satisfied on every point; but I doubted much whether it would be possible for me to explain myself on several subjects, whereof his honour could have no conception; because I saw nothing in his country to which I could resemble them; that, however, I would do my best, and strive to express myself by similitudes, humbly desiring his assistance when I wanted proper words; which he was pleased to promise me.

I said, my birth was of honest parents, in an island called England, which was remote from his country as many days' journey as the strongest of his honour's servants could travel in the annual course of the sun; that I was bred a surgeon, whose trade it is to cure wounds and hurts in the body gotten by accident or violence; that my country was governed by a female man, whom we called queen; that I left it to get riches, whereby I might maintain myself and family when I should return; that in my last voyage I was commander of the ship, and had about fifty Yahoos under me, many of which died at sea, and I was forced to supply them by others picked out from several nations; that our ship was twice in danger of being sunk, the first time by a great storm, and the second by striking against a rock. Here my master interposed by asking me how I could persuade strangers out of different countries to venture with me after the losses I had sustained and the hazards I had run? I said, they were fellows of desperate fortunes, forced to fly from the places of their birth on account of their poverty or their crimes. Some were undone by lawsuits; others spent all they had in drinking, whoring, and gaming; others fled for treason; many for murder, theft, poisoning, robbery, perjury, forgery, coining false money, for committing rapes or sodomy; for flying from their colours[1] or deserting to the enemy; and most of them had broken prison; none of these

[1] *flying from their colours* Deserting from their regiments.

durst return to their native countries, for fear of being hanged or of starving in a jail; and therefore they were under the necessity of seeking a livelihood in other places.

During this discourse, my master was pleased to interrupt me several times. I had made use of many circumlocutions in describing to him the nature of the several crimes for which most of our crew had been forced to fly their country. This labour took up several days' conversation before he was able to comprehend me. He was wholly at a loss to know what could be the use or necessity of practising those vices. To clear up which, I endeavoured to give some ideas of the desire of power and riches; of the terrible effects of lust, intemperance, malice, and envy. All this I was forced to define and describe by putting of cases[1] and making of suppositions. After which, like one whose imagination was struck with something never seen or heard of before, he would lift up his eyes with amazement and indignation. Power, government, war, law, punishment, and a thousand other things had no terms wherein that language could express them, which made the difficulty almost insuperable to give my master any conception of what I meant. But, being of an excellent understanding, much improved by contemplation and converse, he at last arrived at a competent knowledge of what human nature, in our parts of the world, is capable to perform, and desired I would give him some particular account of that land which we call Europe, but especially of my own country.

CHAPTER 5

(*The author, at his master's command, informs him of the state of England. The causes of war among the princes of Europe. The author begins to explain the English Constitution.*)

The reader may please to observe that the following extract of many conversations I had with my master contains a summary of the most material points, which were discoursed at several times for above two years; his honour often desiring fuller satisfaction as I farther improved in the Houyhnhnm tongue. I laid before him, as well as I could, the whole state of Europe; I discoursed of trade and manufactures, of arts and sciences; and the answers I gave to all the questions he made, as they arose upon several subjects, were a fund of conversation not to be exhausted. But I shall here only set down the substance of what passed between us concerning my own country, reducing it in order as well as I can, without any regard to time or other circumstances, while I strictly adhere to truth. My only concern is that I shall hardly be able to do justice to my master's arguments and expressions, which must needs suffer by my want of capacity, as well as by a translation into our barbarous English.

In obedience, therefore, to his honour's commands, I related to him the Revolution under the Prince of Orange; the long war with France entered into by the said prince and renewed by his successor, the present Queen, wherein the greatest powers of Christendom were engaged, and which still continued.[2] I computed, at his request, that about a million of Yahoos might have been killed in the whole progress of it, and perhaps a hundred or more cities taken, and five times as many ships burnt or sunk.

He asked me, what were the usual causes or motives that made one country go to war with another? I answered, they were innumerable; but I should only mention a few of the chief. Sometimes the ambition of princes, who never think they have land or people enough to govern; sometimes the corruption of ministers, who engage their master in a war in order to stifle or divert the clamour of the subjects against their evil administration. Difference in opinions has cost many millions of lives: for instance, whether flesh be bread, or bread be flesh; whether the juice of a certain berry be blood or wine; whether whistling be a vice or a virtue; whether it be better to kiss a post, or throw it into the fire; what is the best colour for a coat, whether black, white, red, or gray; and whether it should be long or short, narrow or wide, dirty or clean;[3] with many more.

[1] *putting of cases* Presenting the circumstances and grounds upon which a claim rests (legal terminology).

[2] *the Revolution ... still continued* Gulliver describes the Glorious Revolution of 1688, in which the Catholic King James II was deposed and the Protestant William of Orange crowned King, and the war between France and the Protestant allies that continued until the Peace of Utrecht, 1713.

[3] *whether flesh ... or clean* These differences in opinion, all of which occur between different denominations of Christians, are over transubstantiation, the place of music in church ("whistling"), worship of the crucifix and other icons, and the proper style of vestments.

Neither are any wars so furious and bloody, or of so long a continuance, as those occasioned by difference in opinion, especially if it be in things indifferent.[1]

Sometimes the quarrel between two princes is to decide which of them shall dispossess a third of his dominions, where neither of them pretend to any right. Sometimes one prince quarrels with another for fear the other should quarrel with him. Sometimes a war is entered upon because the enemy is too strong; and sometimes because he is too weak. Sometimes our neighbours want the things which we have, or have the things which we want, and we both fight, till they take ours or give us theirs. It is a very justifiable cause of a war to invade a country after the people have been wasted by famine, destroyed by pestilence, or embroiled by factions among themselves. It is justifiable to enter into war against our nearest ally when one of his towns lies convenient for us, or a territory of land that would render our dominions round and complete. If a prince sends forces into a nation where the people are poor and ignorant, he may lawfully put half of them to death, and make slaves of the rest, in order to civilize and reduce[2] them from their barbarous way of living. It is a very kingly, honourable, and frequent practice, when one prince desires the assistance of another to secure him against an invasion, that the assistant, when he has driven out the invader, should seize on the dominions himself and kill, imprison, or banish the prince he came to relieve. Alliance by blood or marriage, is a frequent cause of war between princes; and the nearer the kindred is, the greater their disposition to quarrel. Poor nations are hungry, and rich nations are proud; and pride and hunger will ever be at variance. For these reasons, the trade of a soldier is held the most honourable of all others, because a soldier is a Yahoo hired to kill, in cold blood, as many of his own species, who have never offended him, as possibly he can.

There is likewise a kind of beggarly princes in Europe, not able to make war by themselves, who hire out their troops to richer nations for so much a day to each man; of which they keep three-fourths to themselves, and it is the best part of their maintenance; such are those in many northern parts of Europe.[3]

"What you have told me," said my master, "upon the subject of war, does indeed discover most admirably the effects of that reason you pretend to; however, it is happy that the shame is greater than the danger; and that nature has left you utterly incapable of doing much mischief. For, your mouths lying flat with your faces, you can hardly bite each other to any purpose, unless by consent. Then as to the claws upon your feet before and behind, they are so short and tender that one of our Yahoos would drive a dozen of yours before him. And therefore, in recounting the numbers of those who have been killed in battle, I cannot but think you have said the thing which is not."

I could not forbear shaking my head and smiling a little at his ignorance. And being no stranger to the art of war, I gave him a description of cannons, culverins,[4] muskets, carabines,[5] pistols, bullets, powder, swords, bayonets, battles, sieges, retreats, attacks, undermines, countermines,[6] bombardments, sea fights, ships sunk with a thousand men, twenty thousand killed on each side, dying groans, limbs flying in the air, smoke, noise, confusion, trampling to death under horses' feet, flight, pursuit, victory, fields strewed with carcasses left for food to dogs and wolves and birds of prey, plundering, stripping, ravishing, burning, and destroying. And to set forth the valour of my own dear countrymen, I assured him that I had seen them blow up a hundred enemies at once in a siege, and as many in a ship, and beheld the dead bodies drop down in pieces from the clouds, to the great diversion of all the spectators.

I was going on to more particulars when my master commanded me silence. He said, whoever understood the nature of Yahoos might easily believe it possible for so vile an animal to be capable of every action I had named, if their strength and cunning equalled their malice. But, as my discourse had increased his abhor-

[1] *indifferent* Of no consequence, unimportant.

[2] *reduce* Reform, convert.

[3] *beggarly princes ... Europe* George I, as Elector of Hanover, hired German mercenaries to defend his kingdom.

[4] *culverins* Large cannons.

[5] *carabines* Short firearms.

[6] *undermines* Mines placed underneath fortress walls; *countermines* Mines or excavations made by the defenders of a fortress to intercept the undermines.

rence of the whole species, so he found it gave him a disturbance in his mind to which he was wholly a stranger before. He thought his ears, being used to such abominable words, might, by degrees, admit them with less detestation. That, although he hated the Yahoos of this country, yet he no more blamed them for their odious qualities than he did a gnnayh (a bird of prey) for its cruelty, or a sharp stone for cutting his hoof. But when a creature pretending to reason could be capable of such enormities, he dreaded lest the corruption of that faculty might be worse than brutality itself. He seemed therefore confident that, instead of reason, we were only possessed of some quality fitted to increase our natural vices; as the reflection from a troubled stream returns the image of an ill-shapen body not only larger, but more distorted.

He added that he had heard too much upon the subject of war, both in this and some former discourses. There was another point which a little perplexed him at present. I had informed him that some of our crew left their country on account of being ruined by law; that I had already explained the meaning of the word, but he was at a loss how it should come to pass that the law, which was intended for every man's preservation, should be any man's ruin. Therefore he desired to be further satisfied what I meant by law, and the dispensers thereof, according to the present practice in my own country, because he thought nature and reason were sufficient guides for a reasonable animal, as we pretended to be, in showing us what he ought to do, and what to avoid.

I assured his honour that the law was a science in which I had not much conversed, further than by employing advocates, in vain, upon some injustices that had been done me; however, I would give him all the satisfaction I was able.

I said there was a society of men among us, bred up from their youth in the art of proving, by words multiplied for the purpose, that white is black, and black is white, according as they are paid. To this society all the rest of the people are slaves.

For example, if my neighbour has a mind to my cow, he has a lawyer to prove that he ought to have my cow from me. I must then hire another to defend my right, it being against all rules of law that any man should be allowed to speak for himself. Now, in this case, I, who am the right owner, lie under two great disadvantages. First, my lawyer, being practised almost from his cradle in defending falsehood, is quite out of his element when he would be an advocate for justice, which is an unnatural office he always attempts with great awkwardness, if not with ill-will. The second disadvantage is that my lawyer must proceed with great caution, or else he will be reprimanded by the judges, and abhorred by his brethren, as one that would lessen the practice of the law. And therefore I have but two methods to preserve my cow. The first is to gain over my adversary's lawyer with a double fee, who will then betray his client by insinuating that he hath justice on his side. The second way is for my lawyer to make my cause appear as unjust as he can, by allowing the cow to belong to my adversary; and this, if it be skillfully done, will certainly bespeak[1] the favour of the bench.

Now, your honour is to know that these judges are persons appointed to decide all controversies of property, as well as for the trial of criminals, and picked out from the most dexterous lawyers who are grown old or lazy; and, having been biased all their lives against truth and equity, lie under such a fatal necessity of favouring fraud, perjury, and oppression, that I have known some of them refuse a large bribe from the side where justice lay, rather than injure the faculty[2] by doing anything unbecoming their nature or their office.

It is a maxim among these lawyers that whatever has been done before may legally be done again; and therefore they take special care to record all the decisions formerly made against common justice and the general reason of mankind. These, under the name of precedents, they produce as authorities to justify the most iniquitous opinions; and the judges never fail of directing accordingly.

In pleading, they studiously avoid entering into the merits of the cause; but are loud, violent, and tedious in dwelling upon all circumstances which are not to the purpose. For instance, in the case already mentioned, they never desire to know what claim or title my adversary has to my cow; but whether the said cow were red or black; her horns long or short; whether the field I graze her in be round or square; whether she was milked at home or abroad; what diseases she is subject to, and

[1] *bespeak* Engage; gain.

[2] *faculty* Profession.

the like. After which they consult precedents, adjourn the cause from time to time, and in ten, twenty, or thirty years come to an issue.[1]

It is likewise to be observed that this society has a peculiar cant and jargon of their own, that no other mortal can understand, and wherein all their laws are written, which they take special care to multiply; whereby they have wholly confounded the very essence of truth and falsehood, of right and wrong; so that it will take thirty years to decide whether the field left me by my ancestors for six generations belongs to me or to a stranger three hundred miles off.

In the trial of persons accused for crimes against the state, the method is much more short and commendable: the judge first sends to sound the disposition of those in power; after which he can easily hang or save a criminal, strictly preserving all due forms of law.

Here my master, interposing, said it was a pity that creatures endowed with such prodigious abilities of mind as these lawyers, by the description I gave of them, must certainly be, were not rather encouraged to be instructors of others in wisdom and knowledge. In answer to which I assured his honour that in all points out of their own trade they were usually the most ignorant and stupid generation among us, the most despicable in common conversation, avowed enemies to all knowledge and learning, and equally disposed to pervert the general reason of mankind in every other subject of discourse as in that of their own profession.

CHAPTER 6

(*A continuation of the state of England under Queen Anne. The character of a first minister in the courts of Europe.*)

My master was yet wholly at a loss to understand what motives could incite this race of lawyers to perplex, disquiet, and weary themselves by engaging in a confederacy of injustice, merely for the sake of injuring their fellow animals; neither could he comprehend what I meant in saying they did it for hire. Whereupon I was at much pains to describe to him the use of money, the materials it was made of, and the value of the metals; that when a Yahoo had got a great store of this precious substance, he was able to purchase whatever he had a mind to: the finest clothing, the noblest houses, great tracts of land, the most costly meats and drinks, and have his choice of the most beautiful females. Therefore since money alone was able to perform all these feats, our Yahoos thought they could never have enough of it to spend or to save, as they found themselves inclined from their natural bent either to profusion or avarice. That the rich man enjoyed the fruit of the poor man's labour, and the latter were a thousand to one in proportion to the former. That the bulk of our people were forced to live miserably by labouring every day for small wages, to make a few live plentifully. I enlarged myself much on these and many other particulars to the same purpose; but his honour was still to seek,[2] for he went upon a supposition that all animals had a title to their share in the productions of the earth, and especially those who presided over the rest. Therefore he desired I would let him know what these costly meats were, and how any of us happened to want[3] them. Whereupon I enumerated as many sorts as came into my head, with the various methods of dressing them, which could not be done without sending vessels by sea to every part of the world, as well for liquors to drink as for sauces and innumerable other conveniences. I assured him that this whole globe of earth must be at least three times gone round before one of our better female Yahoos could get her breakfast, or a cup to put it in. He said, "That must needs be a miserable country which cannot furnish food for its own inhabitants." But what he chiefly wondered at was how such vast tracts of ground as I described should be wholly without fresh water, and the people put to the necessity of sending over the sea for drink. I replied that England (the dear place of my nativity) was computed to produce three times the quantity of food more than its inhabitants are able to consume, as well as liquors extracted from grain, or pressed out of the fruit of certain trees, which made excellent drink, and the same proportion in every other convenience of life. But, in order to feed the luxury and intemperance of the males and the vanity of the females, we sent away the greatest part of our necessary things to other countries, from whence, in return, we brought the materials of diseases,

[1] *to an issue* To a judgment.

[2] *still to seek* Still unable to comprehend.

[3] *want* Lack.

folly, and vice, to spend among ourselves. Hence it follows of necessity that vast numbers of our people are compelled to seek their livelihood by begging, robbing, stealing, cheating, pimping, forswearing,[1] flattering, suborning,[2] forging, gaming, lying, fawning, hectoring, voting, scribbling, stargazing, poisoning, whoring, canting,[3] libelling, freethinking,[4] and the like occupations; every one of which terms I was at much pains to make him understand.

That wine was not imported among us from foreign countries to supply the want of water or other drinks, but because it was a sort of liquid which made us merry by putting us out of our senses; diverted all melancholy thoughts, begat wild extravagant imaginations in the brain, raised our hopes and banished our fears, suspended every office of reason for a time, and deprived us of the use of our limbs, until we fell into a profound sleep; although it must be confessed that we always awoke sick and dispirited; and that the use of this liquor filled us with diseases which made our lives uncomfortable and short.

But beside all this, the bulk of our people supported themselves by furnishing the necessities or conveniences of life to the rich and to each other. For instance, when I am at home and dressed as I ought to be, I carry on my body the workmanship of a hundred tradesmen; the building and furniture of my house employ as many more, and five times the number to adorn my wife.

I was going on to tell him of another sort of people, who get their livelihood by attending the sick; having upon some occasions informed his honour that many of my crew had died of diseases. But here it was with the utmost difficulty that I brought him to apprehend what I meant. He could easily conceive that a Houyhnhnm grew weak and heavy a few days before his death, or by some accident might hurt a limb; but that nature, who works all things to perfection, should suffer any pains to breed in our bodies, he thought impossible, and desired to know the reason of so unaccountable an evil. I told him we fed on a thousand things which operated contrary to each other; that we ate when we were not hungry and drank without the provocation of thirst; that we sat whole nights drinking strong liquors without eating a bit, which disposed us to sloth, inflamed our bodies, and precipitated or prevented digestion; that prostitute female Yahoos acquired a certain malady which bred rottenness in the bones of those who fell into their embraces; that this and many other diseases were propagated from father to son, so that great numbers came into the world with complicated maladies upon them; that it would be endless to give him a catalogue of all diseases incident to human bodies, for they would not be fewer than five or six hundred, spread over every limb and joint—in short, every part, external and intestine, having diseases appropriated to itself. To remedy which, there was a sort of people bred up among us in the profession, or pretence, of curing the sick. And because I had some skill in the faculty, I would, in gratitude to his honour, let him know the whole mystery and method by which they proceed.

Their fundamental is that all diseases arise from repletion; from whence they conclude that a great evacuation of the body is necessary, either through the natural passage or upwards at the mouth. Their next business is from herbs, minerals, gums, oils, shells, salts, juices, sea-weed, excrements, barks of trees, serpents, toads, frogs, spiders, dead men's flesh and bones, birds, beasts, and fishes, to form a composition for smell and taste the most abominable, nauseous, and detestable they can possibly contrive, which the stomach immediately rejects with loathing, and this they call a vomit. Or else from the same storehouse, with some other poisonous additions, they command us to take in at the orifice above or below (just as the physician then happens to be disposed) a medicine equally annoying and disgustful to the bowels; which, relaxing the belly, drives down all before it; and this they call a purge, or a clyster. For nature (as the physicians allege) having intended the superior anterior orifice only for the intromission of solids and liquids, and the inferior posterior for ejection, these artists ingeniously considering that in all diseases nature is forced out of her seat; therefore, to replace her in it, the body must be treated in a manner directly contrary, by interchanging the use of each orifice: forcing solids and liquids in at the anus, and making evacuations at the mouth.

[1] *forswearing* Committing perjury.

[2] *suborning* Bribing.

[3] *canting* Speaking in professional or technical language; using jargon.

[4] *freethinking* Rejecting any religious belief or authority.

But, besides real diseases, we are subject to many that are only imaginary, for which the physicians have invented imaginary cures; these have their several names, and so have the drugs that are proper for them; and with these our female Yahoos are always infested.

One great excellency in this tribe is their skill at prognostics, wherein they seldom fail; their predictions in real diseases, when they rise to any degree of malignity, generally portending death (which is always in their power when recovery is not); and therefore, upon any unexpected signs of amendment after they have pronounced their sentence, rather than be accused as false prophets, they know how to approve[1] their sagacity to the world by a seasonable dose.

They are likewise of special use to husbands and wives who are grown weary of their mates; to eldest sons, to great ministers of state, and often to princes.

I had formerly, upon occasion, discoursed with my master upon the nature of government in general, and particularly of our own excellent constitution, deservedly the wonder and envy of the whole world. But having here accidentally mentioned a minister of state, he commanded me, some time after, to inform him what species of Yahoo I particularly meant by that appellation.

I told him that a first or chief minister of state, who was the person I intended to describe, was the creature wholly exempt from joy and grief, love and hatred, pity and anger; at least, makes use of no other passions but a violent desire of wealth, power, and titles; that he applies his words to all uses except to the indication of his mind; that he never tells a truth but with an intent that you should take it for a lie; nor a lie but with a design that you should take it for a truth; that those he speaks worst of behind their backs are in the surest way of preferment; and whenever he begins to praise you to others, or to yourself, you are from that day forlorn. The worst mark you can receive is a promise, especially when it is confirmed with an oath; after which every wise man retires and gives over all hopes.

There are three methods by which a man may rise to be chief minister. The first is by knowing how, with prudence, to dispose of a wife, a daughter, or a sister; the second, by betraying or undermining his predecessor; and the third is by a furious zeal, in public assemblies, against the corruptions of the court. But a wise prince would rather choose to employ those who practise the last of these methods, because such zealots prove always the most obsequious and subservient to the will and passions of their master. That these ministers, having all employments at their disposal, preserve themselves in power by bribing the majority of a senate or great council; and at last, by an expedient called an Act of Indemnity[2] (whereof I described the nature to him), they secure themselves from after reckonings and retire from the public, laden with the spoils of the nation.

The palace of a chief minister is a seminary to breed up others in his own trade; the pages, lackeys, and porters, by imitating their master, become ministers of state in their several districts, and learn to excel in the three principal ingredients, of insolence, lying, and bribery. Accordingly, they have a subaltern court paid to them by persons of the best rank; and sometimes, by the force of dexterity and impudence, arrive, through several gradations, to be successors to their lord.

He is usually governed by a decayed wench, or favourite footman, who are the tunnels through which all graces are conveyed, and may properly be called, in the last resort, the governors of the kingdom.

One day my master, having heard me mention the nobility of my country, was pleased to make me a compliment which I could not pretend to deserve: that he was sure I must have been born of some noble family, because I far exceeded in shape, colour, and cleanliness, all the Yahoos of his nation, although I seemed to fail in strength and agility, which must be imputed to my different way of living from those other brutes; and besides I was not only endowed with the faculty of speech, but likewise with some rudiments of reason, to a degree that, with all his acquaintance, I passed for a prodigy.

He made me observe that among the Houyhnhnms, the white, the sorrel, and the iron gray were not so exactly shaped as the bay, the dapple gray, and the black; nor born with equal talents of mind, or a capacity to improve them; and therefore continued always in the condition of servants, without ever aspiring to match

[1] *approve* Demonstrate.

[2] *Act of Indemnity* Act that protects ministers from being prosecuted for illegal or unconstitutional activities undertaken, presumably with good intent, while in office.

out of[1] their own race, which in that country would be reckoned monstrous and unnatural.

I made his honour my most humble acknowledgments for the good opinion he was pleased to conceive of me, but assured him at the same time that my birth was of the lower sort, having been born of plain, honest parents, who were just able to give me a tolerable education; that nobility, among us, was altogether a different thing from the idea he had of it; that our young noblemen are bred from their childhood in idleness and luxury; that, as soon as years will permit, they consume their vigour, and contract odious diseases among lewd females; and when their fortunes are almost ruined, they marry some woman of mean birth, disagreeable person, and unsound constitution (merely for the sake of money), whom they hate and despise. That the productions of such marriages are generally scrofulous,[2] rickety, or deformed children; by which means the family seldom continues above three generations, unless the wife takes care to provide a healthy father among her neighbours or domestics, in order to improve and continue the breed. That a weak, diseased body, a meagre countenance and sallow complexion, are the true marks of noble blood; and a healthy robust appearance is so disgraceful in a man of quality that the world concludes his real father to have been a groom or a coachman. The imperfections of his mind run parallel with those of his body, being a composition of spleen,[3] dullness, ignorance, caprice, sensuality, and pride.

Without the consent of this illustrious body, no law can be enacted, repealed, or altered; and these nobles have likewise the decision of all our possessions, without appeal.

Chapter 7

(*The author's great love of his native country. His master's observations upon the constitution and administration of England, as described by the author, with parallel cases and comparisons. His master's observations upon human nature.*)

The reader may be disposed to wonder how I could prevail on myself to give so free a representation of my own species among a race of mortals who are already too apt to conceive the vilest opinion of humankind, from that entire congruity between me and their Yahoos. But I must freely confess that the many virtues of those excellent quadrupeds, placed in opposite view to human corruptions, had so far opened my eyes and enlarged my understanding that I began to view the actions and passions of man in a very different light, and to think the honour of my own kind not worth managing;[4] which, besides, it was impossible for me to do before a person of so acute a judgment as my master, who daily convinced me of a thousand faults in myself, whereof I had not the least perception before, and which, with us, would never be numbered even among human infirmities. I had likewise learned, from his example, an utter detestation of all falsehood or disguise; and truth appeared so amiable to me that I determined upon sacrificing every thing to it.

Let me deal so candidly with the reader as to confess that there was yet a much stronger motive for the freedom I took in my representation of things. I had not yet been a year in this country before I contracted such a love and veneration for the inhabitants that I entered on a firm resolution never to return to humankind, but to pass the rest of my life among these admirable Houyhnhnms in the contemplation and practice of every virtue, where I could have no example or incitement to vice. But it was decreed by fortune, my perpetual enemy, that so great a felicity should not fall to my share. However, it is now some comfort to reflect that in what I said of my countrymen, I extenuated their faults as much as I durst before so strict an examiner; and upon every article gave as favourable a turn as the matter would bear. For, indeed, who is there alive that will not be swayed by his bias and partiality to the place of his birth?

I have related the substance of several conversations I had with my master during the greatest part of the time I had the honour to be in his service; but have indeed, for brevity sake, omitted much more than is here set down.

When I had answered all his questions, and his curiosity seemed to be fully satisfied, he sent for me one

[1] *match out of* Choose a mate from outside of.

[2] *scrofulous* Infected with scrofula, a disease characterized by the inflammation and degeneration of the lymph nodes.

[3] *spleen* Melancholia, ill-humor, irritability.

[4] *managing* Looking after.

morning early, and commanded me to sit down at some distance (an honour which he had never before conferred upon me). He said he had been very seriously considering my whole story, as far as it related both to myself and my country; that he looked upon us as a sort of animals, to whose share, by what accident he could not conjecture, some small pittance of reason had fallen, whereof we made no other use than by its assistance to aggravate our natural corruptions and to acquire new ones, which nature had not given us. That we disarmed ourselves of the few abilities she had bestowed; had been very successful in multiplying our original wants, and seemed to spend our whole lives in vain endeavours to supply them by our own inventions. That, as to myself, it was manifest I had neither the strength nor agility of a common Yahoo; that I walked infirmly on my hinder feet; had found out a contrivance to make my claws of no use or defence, and to remove the hair from my chin, which was intended as a shelter from the sun and the weather; lastly, that I could neither run with speed nor climb trees like my brethren (as he called them), the Yahoos in his country.

That our institutions of government and law were plainly owing to our gross defects in reason and, by consequence, in virtue, because reason alone is sufficient to govern a rational creature; which was, therefore, a character we had no pretence to challenge, even from the account I had given of my own people; although he manifestly perceived that, in order to favour them, I had concealed many particulars, and often *said the thing which was not*.

He was the more confirmed in this opinion because he observed that, as I agreed in every feature of my body with other Yahoos, except where it was to my real disadvantage in point of strength, speed, and activity, the shortness of my claws, and some other particulars where nature had no part; so from the representation I had given him of our lives, our manners, and our actions, he found as near a resemblance in the disposition of our minds. He said the Yahoos were known to hate one another more than they did any different species of animals; and the reason usually assigned was the odiousness of their own shapes, which all could see in the rest, but not in themselves. He had therefore begun to think it not unwise in us to cover our bodies, and by that invention conceal many of our deformities from each other, which would else be hardly supportable. But he now found he had been mistaken, and that the dissensions of those brutes in his country were owing to the same cause with ours, as I had described them. For if (said he) you throw among five Yahoos as much food as would be sufficient for fifty, they will, instead of eating peaceably, fall together by the ears, each single one impatient to have all to itself; and therefore a servant was usually employed to stand by while they were feeding abroad, and those kept at home were tied at a distance from each other. That if a cow died of age or accident before a Houyhnhnm could secure it for his own Yahoos, those in the neighbourhood would come in herds to seize it, and then would ensue such a battle as I had described, with terrible wounds made by their claws on both sides, although they seldom were able to kill one another, for want of such convenient instruments of death as we had invented. At other times the like battles have been fought between the Yahoos of several neighbourhoods without any visible cause; those of one district watching all opportunities to surprise the next before they are prepared. But if they find their project has miscarried, they return home and, for want of enemies, engage in what I call a civil war among themselves.

That in some fields of his country there are certain shining stones of several colours, whereof the Yahoos are violently fond; and when part of these stones is fixed in the earth, as it sometimes happens, they will dig with their claws for whole days to get them out, and then carry them away and hide them by heaps in their kennels; but still looking round with great caution, for fear their comrades should find out their treasure. My master said he could never discover the reason of this unnatural appetite, or how these stones could be of any use to a Yahoo; but now he believed it might proceed from the same principle of avarice which I had ascribed to mankind. That he had once, by way of experiment, privately removed a heap of these stones from the place where one of his Yahoos had buried it; whereupon the sordid animal, missing his treasure, by his loud lamenting brought the whole herd to the place, there miserably howled, then fell to biting and tearing the rest; began to pine away, would neither eat, nor sleep, nor work till he ordered a servant privately to convey the stones into the same hole and hide them as before; which, when his

Yahoo had found, he presently recovered his spirits and good humour, but took good care to remove them to a better hiding place, and has ever since been a very serviceable brute.

My master further assured me, which I also observed myself, that in the fields where the shining stones abound, the fiercest and most frequent battles are fought, occasioned by perpetual inroads of the neighbouring Yahoos.

He said it was common, when two Yahoos discovered such a stone in a field, and were contending which of them should be the proprietor, a third would take the advantage, and carry it away from them both; which my master would needs contend to have some kind of resemblance with our suits at law; wherein I thought it for our credit not to undeceive him; since the decision he mentioned was much more equitable than many decrees among us, because the plaintiff and defendant there lost nothing beside the stone they contended for: whereas our courts of equity would never have dismissed the cause, while either of them had any thing left.

My master, continuing his discourse, said there was nothing that rendered the Yahoos more odious than their undistinguishing appetite to devour every thing that came in their way, whether herbs, roots, berries, the corrupted flesh of animals, or all mingled together; and it was peculiar in their temper that they were fonder of what they could get by rapine or stealth at a greater distance, than much better food provided for them at home. If their prey held out, they would eat till they were ready to burst; after which nature had pointed out to them a certain root that gave them a general evacuation.

There was also another kind of root, very juicy, but somewhat rare and difficult to be found, which the Yahoos sought for with much eagerness, and would suck it with great delight; it produced in them the same effects that wine has upon us. It would make them sometimes hug, and sometimes tear one another; they would howl, and grin, and chatter, and reel, and tumble, and then fall asleep in the mud.

I did indeed observe that the Yahoos were the only animals in this country subject to any diseases; which, however, were much fewer than horses have among us, and contracted not by any ill-treatment they meet with, but by the nastiness and greediness of that sordid brute. Neither has their language any more than a general appellation for those maladies, which is borrowed from the name of the beast, and called *hnea-yahoo*, or Yahoo's evil; and the cure prescribed is a mixture of their own dung and urine, forcibly put down the Yahoo's throat. This I have since often known to have been taken with success, and do here freely recommend it to my countrymen for the public good, as an admirable specific against all diseases produced by repletion.

As to learning, government, arts, manufactures, and the like, my master confessed he could find little or no resemblance between the Yahoos of that country and those in ours; for he only meant to observe what parity there was in our natures. He had heard, indeed, some curious Houyhnhnms observe that in most herds there was a sort of ruling Yahoo (as among us there is generally some leading or principal stag in a park), who was always more deformed in body, and mischievous in disposition, than any of the rest; that this leader had usually a favourite as like himself as he could get, whose employment was to lick his master's feet and posteriors and drive the female Yahoos to his kennel; for which he was now and then rewarded with a piece of ass's flesh. This favourite is hated by the whole herd, and therefore, to protect himself, keeps always near the person of his leader. He usually continues in office till a worse can be found; but the very moment he is discarded, his successor, at the head of all the Yahoos in that district, young and old, male and female, come in a body, and discharge their excrements upon him from head to foot. But how far this might be applicable to our courts and favourites, and ministers of state, my master said I could best determine.

I durst make no return to this malicious insinuation, which debased human understanding below the sagacity of a common hound, who has judgment enough to distinguish and follow the cry of the ablest dog in the pack, without being ever mistaken.

My master told me there were some qualities remarkable in the Yahoos which he had not observed me to mention, or at least very slightly, in the accounts I had given of humankind. He said those animals, like other brutes, had their females in common; but in this they differed, that the she-Yahoo would admit the males while she was pregnant; and that the hes would quarrel and fight with the females as fiercely as with each other.

Both which practices were such degrees of infamous brutality as no other sensitive creature ever arrived at.

Another thing he wondered at in the Yahoos was their strange disposition to nastiness and dirt; whereas there appears to be a natural love of cleanliness in all other animals. As to the two former accusations, I was glad to let them pass without any reply, because I had not a word to offer upon them in defence of my species, which otherwise I certainly had done from my own inclinations. But I could have easily vindicated humankind from the imputation of singularity upon the last article, if there had been any swine in that country (as unluckily for me there were not), which, although it may be a sweeter quadruped than a Yahoo, cannot, I humbly conceive, in justice pretend to more cleanliness; and so his honour himself must have owned, if he had seen their filthy way of feeding and their custom of wallowing and sleeping in the mud.

My master likewise mentioned another quality which his servants had discovered in several Yahoos, and to him was wholly unaccountable. He said a fancy would sometimes take a Yahoo to retire into a corner, to lie down, and howl, and groan, and spurn away all that came near him, although he were young and fat, wanted neither food nor water, nor did the servant imagine what could possibly ail him. And the only remedy they found was to set him to hard work, after which he would infallibly come to himself. To this I was silent out of partiality to my own kind; yet here I could plainly discover the true seeds of spleen, which only seizes on the lazy, the luxurious, and the rich; who, if they were forced to undergo the same regimen, I would undertake for the cure.

His honour had further observed that a female Yahoo would often stand behind a bank or a bush to gaze on the young males passing by, and then appear, and hide, using many antic gestures and grimaces, at which time it was observed that she had a most offensive smell; and when any of the males advanced, would slowly retire, looking often back, and, with a counterfeit show of fear, run off into some convenient place where she knew the male would follow her.

At other times, if a female stranger came among them, three or four of her own sex would get about her, and stare and chatter, and grin, and smell her all over, and then turn off with gestures that seemed to express contempt and disdain.

Perhaps my master might refine a little in these speculations, which he had drawn from what he observed himself, or had been told him by others; however, I could not reflect without some amazement, and much sorrow, that the rudiments of lewdness, coquetry, censure, and scandal should have place by instinct in womankind.

I expected every moment that my master would accuse the Yahoos of those unnatural appetites in both sexes, so common among us. But nature, it seems, has not been so expert a schoolmistress; and these politer pleasures are entirely the productions of art and reason on our side of the globe.

CHAPTER 8

they are vulgar people-

(*The author relates several particulars of the Yahoos. The great virtues of the Houyhnhnms. The education and exercise of their youth. Their general assembly.*)

As I ought to have understood human nature much better than I supposed it possible for my master to do, so it was easy to apply the character he gave of the Yahoos to myself and my countrymen; and I believed I could yet make further discoveries from my own observation. I therefore often begged his honour to let me go among the herds of Yahoos in the neighbourhood; to which he always very graciously consented, being perfectly convinced that the hatred I bore these brutes would never suffer me to be corrupted by them; and his honour ordered one of his servants, a strong sorrel nag, very honest and good-natured, to be my guard; without whose protection I durst not undertake such adventures. For I have already told the reader how much I was pestered by these odious animals upon my first arrival; and I afterwards failed very narrowly three or four times of falling into their clutches when I happened to stray at any distance without my hanger. And I have reason to believe they had some imagination that I was of their own species, which I often assisted myself by stripping up my sleeves and showing my naked arms and breasts in their sight, when my protector was with me. At which times they would approach as near as they durst, and imitate my actions after the manner of monkeys, but ever with great signs of hatred; as a tame jackdaw[1] with cap and stockings is always persecuted by the wild ones when he happens to be got among them.

They are prodigiously nimble from their infancy. However, I once caught a young male of three years old and endeavoured, by all marks of tenderness, to make it quiet; but the little imp fell a-squalling, and scratching, and biting with such violence that I was forced to let it go; and it was high time, for a whole troop of old ones came about us at the noise; but, finding the cub was safe (for away it ran), and my sorrel nag being by, they durst not venture near us. I observed the young animal's flesh to smell very rank, and the stink was somewhat between a weasel and a fox, but much more disagreeable. I forgot another circumstance (and perhaps I might have the reader's pardon if it were wholly omitted), that while I held the odious vermin in my hands, it voided its filthy excrements of a yellow liquid substance all over my clothes; but by good fortune there was a small brook hard by, where I washed myself as clean as I could; although I durst not come into my master's presence until I were sufficiently aired.

By what I could discover, the Yahoos appear to be the most unteachable of all animals, their capacity never reaching higher than to draw or carry burdens. Yet I am of opinion, this defect arises chiefly from a perverse, restive[2] disposition; for they are cunning, malicious, treacherous, and revengeful. They are strong and hardy, but of a cowardly spirit, and, by consequence, insolent, abject, and cruel. It is observed that the red-haired of both sexes are more libidinous and mischievous than the rest, whom yet they much exceed in strength and activity.

The Houyhnhnms keep the Yahoos for present use in huts not far from the house; but the rest are sent abroad to certain fields, where they dig up roots, eat several kinds of herbs, and search about for carrion, or sometimes catch weasels and *luhimuhs* (a sort of wild rat), which they greedily devour. Nature has taught them to dig deep holes with their nails on the side of a rising ground, wherein they lie by themselves; only the kennels of the females are larger, sufficient to hold two or three cubs.

They swim from their infancy like frogs, and are able to continue long under water, where they often take fish, which the females carry home to their young. And, upon this occasion, I hope the reader will pardon my relating an odd adventure.

Being one day abroad with my protector the sorrel nag, and the weather exceeding hot, I entreated him to let me bathe in a river that was near. He consented, and I immediately stripped myself stark naked and went down softly into the stream. It happened that a young female Yahoo, standing behind a bank, saw the whole proceeding, and, inflamed by desire (as the nag and I conjectured), came running with all speed and leaped into the water within five yards of the place where I bathed. I was never in my life so terribly frightened. The nag was grazing at some distance, not suspecting any harm. She embraced me after a most fulsome manner. I roared as loud as I could, and the nag came galloping towards me, whereupon she quitted her grasp with the utmost reluctancy, and leaped upon the opposite bank, where she stood gazing and howling all the time I was putting on my clothes.

This was a matter of diversion to my master and his family, as well as of mortification to myself. For now I could no longer deny that I was a real Yahoo in every limb and feature, since the females had a natural propensity to me as one of their own species. Neither was the hair of this brute of a red colour (which might have been some excuse for an appetite a little irregular), but black as a sloe,[3] and her countenance did not make an appearance altogether so hideous as the rest of her kind; for I think she could not be above eleven years old.

Having lived three years in this country, the reader, I suppose, will expect that I should, like other travellers, give him some account of the manners and customs of its inhabitants, which it was indeed my principal study to learn.

As these noble *Houyhnhnms* are endowed by nature with a general disposition to all virtues, and have no conceptions or ideas of what is evil in a rational creature, so their grand maxim is to cultivate reason, and to be wholly governed by it. Neither is reason among them a point problematical—as with us, where men can argue with plausibility on both sides of the question—but strikes you with immediate conviction; as it must needs

[1] *jackdaw* Small crow that is easily tamed and trained to imitate speech.

[2] *restive* Obstinate.

[3] *sloe* Small, sour, wild plum.

do, where it is not mingled, obscured, or discoloured by passion and interest. I remember it was with extreme difficulty that I could bring my master to understand the meaning of the word "opinion," or how a point could be disputable; because reason taught us to affirm or deny only where we are certain; and beyond our knowledge we cannot do either. So that controversies, wranglings, disputes, and positiveness in false or dubious propositions are evils unknown among the Houyhnhnms. In the like manner, when I used to explain to him our several systems of natural philosophy,[1] he would laugh that a creature pretending to reason should value itself upon the knowledge of other people's conjectures, and in things where that knowledge, if it were certain, could be of no use. Wherein he agreed entirely with the sentiments of Socrates, as Plato delivers them,[2] which I mention as the highest honour I can do that prince of philosophers. I have often since reflected what destruction such doctrine would make in the libraries of Europe, and how many paths of fame would be then shut up in the learned world.

Friendship and benevolence are the two principal virtues among the Houyhnhnms; and these not confined to particular objects, but universal to the whole race; for a stranger from the remotest part is equally treated with the nearest neighbour, and wherever he goes, looks upon himself as at home. They preserve decency and civility in the highest degrees, but are altogether ignorant of ceremony. They have no fondness for their colts or foals, but the care they take in educating them proceeds entirely from the dictates of reason. And I observed my master to show the same affection to his neighbour's issue that he had for his own. They will have it that nature teaches them to love the whole species, and it is reason only that makes a distinction of persons, where there is a superior degree of virtue.

When the matron Houyhnhnms have produced one of each sex, they no longer accompany with[3] their consorts, except they lose one of their issue by some casualty, which very seldom happens; but in such a case they meet again; or when the like accident befalls a person whose wife is past bearing, some other couple bestow on him one of their own colts, and then go together a second time, until the mother is pregnant. This caution is necessary to prevent the country from being overburdened with numbers. But the race of inferior Houyhnhnms, bred up to be servants, is not so strictly limited upon this article: these are allowed to produce three of each sex, to be domestics in the noble families.

In their marriages they are exactly careful to choose such colours as will not make any disagreeable mixture in the breed. Strength is chiefly valued in the male, and comeliness in the female; not upon the account of love, but to preserve the race from degenerating; for where a female happens to excel in strength, a consort is chosen with regard to comeliness. Courtship, love, presents, jointures,[4] settlements, have no place in their thoughts, or terms whereby to express them in their language. The young couple meet and are joined merely because it is the determination of their parents and friends; it is what they see done everyday, and they look upon it as one of the necessary actions of a reasonable being. But the violation of marriage, or any other unchastity, was never heard of; and the married pair pass their lives with the same friendship and mutual benevolence that they bear to all others of the same species who come in their way, without jealousy, fondness, quarrelling, or discontent.

In educating the youth of both sexes their method is admirable, and highly deserves our imitation. These are not suffered to taste a grain of oats, except upon certain days, till eighteen years old; nor milk but very rarely; and in summer they graze two hours in the morning, and as many in the evening, which their parents likewise observe; but the servants are not allowed above half that time, and a great part of their grass is brought home, which they eat at the most convenient hours, when they can be best spared from work.

Temperance, industry, exercise, and cleanliness are the lessons equally enjoined to the young ones of both sexes; and my master thought it monstrous in us to give the females a different kind of education from the

[1] *natural philosophy* Science.

[2] *sentiments of ... them* Socrates believed that only ethics, or human nature, was worth studying, because in studying the physical world we cannot know anything for certain, but can only form opinions and conjectures.

[3] *accompany with* Have sexual intercourse with.

[4] *jointures* Sum of money brought into a marriage by the wife and reserved for her sole ownership after her husband's death. A husband could not legally spend his wife's jointure without first obtaining her permission.

males, except in some articles of domestic management; whereby, as he truly observed, one half of our natives were good for nothing but bringing children into the world; and to trust the care of our children to such useless animals, he said was yet a greater instance of brutality.

But the Houyhnhnms train up their youth to strength, speed, and hardiness by exercising them in running races up and down steep hills and over hard stony grounds; and when they are all in a sweat, they are ordered to leap over head and ears into a pond or river. Four times a year the youth of a certain district meet to show their proficiency in running and leaping, and other feats of strength and agility; where the victor is rewarded with a song in his or her praise. On this festival, the servants drive a herd of Yahoos into the field, laden with hay, and oats, and milk, for a repast to the Houyhnhnms; after which these brutes are immediately driven back again, for fear of being noisome to the assembly.

Every fourth year, at the vernal equinox, there is a representative council of the whole nation, which meets in a plain about twenty miles from our house, and continues about five or six days. Here they inquire into the state and condition of the several districts; whether they abound or be deficient in hay, or oats, or cows, or Yahoos; and wherever there is any want (which is but seldom) it is immediately supplied by unanimous consent and contribution. Here likewise the regulation of children is settled: as, for instance, if a Houyhnhnm has two males, he changes one of them with another that has two females; and when a child has been lost by any casualty, where the mother is past breeding, it is determined what family in the district shall breed another to supply the loss.

CHAPTER 9

(*A grand debate at the general assembly of the Houyhnhnms, and how it was determined. The learning of the Houyhnhnms. Their buildings. Their manner of burials. The defectiveness of their language.*)

One of these grand assemblies was held in my time, about three months before my departure, whither my master went as the representative of our district. In this council was resumed their old debate, and indeed the only debate that ever happened in their country; whereof my master, after his return, gave me a very particular account.

The question to be debated was whether the Yahoos should be exterminated from the face of the earth. One of the members for the affirmative offered several arguments of great strength and weight, alleging that, as the Yahoos were the most filthy, noisome, and deformed animals which nature ever produced, so they were the most restive and indocible,[1] mischievous and malicious; they would privately suck the teats of the Houyhnhnms' cows, kill and devour their cats, trample down their oats and grass, if they were not continually watched, and commit a thousand other extravagancies. He took notice of a general tradition that Yahoos had not been always in their country, but that many ages ago two of these brutes appeared together upon a mountain; whether produced by the heat of the sun upon corrupted mud and slime, or from the ooze and froth of the sea, was never known; that these Yahoos engendered, and their brood in a short time grew so numerous as to overrun and infest the whole nation. That the Houyhnhnms, to get rid of this evil, made a general hunting, and at last enclosed the whole herd; and, destroying the older, every Houyhnhnm kept two young ones in a kennel, and brought them to such a degree of tameness as an animal so savage by nature can be capable of acquiring, using them for draught and carriage. That there seemed to be much truth in this tradition, and that those creatures could not be *yinhniamshy* (or aborigines of the land), because of the violent hatred the Houyhnhnms, as well as all other animals, bore them, which, although their evil disposition sufficiently deserved, could never have arrived at so high a degree if they had been aborigines, or else they would have long since been rooted out. That the inhabitants, taking a fancy to use the service of the Yahoos, had very imprudently neglected to cultivate the breed of asses, which are a comely animal, easily kept, more tame and orderly, without any offensive smell, strong enough for labour, although they yield to the other in agility of body; and, if their braying be no agreeable sound, it is far preferable to the horrible howlings of the Yahoos.

[1] *indocible* Incapable of being taught.

Several others declared their sentiments to the same purpose, when my master proposed an expedient to the assembly, whereof he had indeed borrowed the hint from me. He approved of the tradition mentioned by the honourable member who spoke before, and affirmed that the two Yahoos said to be seen first among them had been driven thither over the sea; that, coming to land and being forsaken by their companions, they retired to the mountains and, degenerating by degrees, became in process of time much more savage than those of their own species in the country whence these two originals came. The reason of this assertion was that he had now in his possession a certain wonderful Yahoo (meaning myself) which most of them had heard of, and many of them had seen. He then related to them how he first found me; that my body was all covered with an artificial composure of the skins and hairs of other animals; that I spoke in a language of my own, and had thoroughly learned theirs; that I had related to him the accidents which brought me thither; that when he saw me without my covering, I was an exact Yahoo in every part, only of a whiter colour, less hairy, and with shorter claws. He added how I had endeavoured to persuade him that in my own and other countries the Yahoos acted as the governing, rational animal, and held the Houyhnhnms in servitude; that he observed in me all the qualities of a Yahoo, only a little more civilized by some tincture of reason, which, however, was in a degree as far inferior to the Houyhnhnm race as the Yahoos of their country were to me; that, among other things, I mentioned a custom we had of castrating Houyhnhnms when they were young, in order to render them tame; that the operation was easy and safe; that it was no shame to learn wisdom from brutes, as industry is taught by the ant, and building by the swallow (for so I translate the word *lyhannh*, although it be a much larger fowl). That this invention might be practised upon the younger Yahoos here, which, besides rendering them tractable and fitter for use, would in an age put an end to the whole species without destroying life. That in the mean time the Houyhnhnms should be exhorted to cultivate the breed of asses, which, as they are in all respects more valuable brutes, so they have this advantage, to be fit for service at five years old, which the others are not till twelve.

This was all my master thought fit to tell me at that time of what passed in the grand council. But he was pleased to conceal one particular, which related personally to myself, whereof I soon felt the unhappy effect, as the reader will know in its proper place, and whence I date all the succeeding misfortunes of my life.

The Houyhnhnms have no letters, and consequently their knowledge is all traditional. But there happening few events of any moment among a people so well united, naturally disposed to every virtue, wholly governed by reason, and cut off from all commerce with other nations, the historical part is easily preserved without burdening their memories. I have already observed that they are subject to no diseases, and therefore can have no need of physicians. However, they have excellent medicines, composed of herbs, to cure accidental bruises and cuts in the pastern or frog of the foot by sharp stones, as well as other maims and hurts in the several parts of the body.

They calculate the year by the revolution of the sun and moon, but use no subdivisions into weeks. They are well enough acquainted with the motions of those two luminaries, and understand the nature of eclipses; and this is the utmost progress of their astronomy.

In poetry they must be allowed to excel all other mortals; wherein the justness of their similes and the minuteness, as well as exactness, of their descriptions are indeed inimitable. Their verses abound very much in both of these, and usually contain either some exalted notions of friendship and benevolence or the praises of those who were victors in races and other bodily exercises. Their buildings, although very rude and simple, are not inconvenient, but well contrived to defend them from all injuries of cold and heat. They have a kind of tree which at forty years old loosens in the root and falls with the first storm; it grows very straight and, being pointed like stakes with a sharp stone (for the Houyhnhnms know not the use of iron), they stick them erect in the ground, about ten inches asunder, and then weave in oat straw, or sometimes wattles, betwixt them. The roof is made after the same manner, and so are the doors.

The Houyhnhnms use the hollow part between the pastern and the hoof of their forefeet as we do our hands, and this with greater dexterity than I could at first imagine. I have seen a white mare of our family thread a needle (which I lent her on purpose) with that joint. They milk their cows, reap their oats, and do all the work which requires hands in the same manner. They have a kind of hard flints, which, by grinding against other stones, they form into instruments that serve instead of wedges, axes, and hammers. With tools made of these flints, they likewise cut their hay and reap their oats, which there grow naturally in several fields. The Yahoos draw home the sheaves in carriages, and the servants tread them in certain covered huts to get out the grain, which is kept in stores. They make a rude kind of earthen and wooden vessels, and bake the former in the sun.

If they can avoid casualties, they die only of old age, and are buried in the obscurest places that can be found, their friends and relations expressing neither joy nor grief at their departure; nor does the dying person discover the least regret that he is leaving the world, any more than if he were upon returning home from a visit to one of his neighbours. I remember my master having once made an appointment with a friend and his family to come to his house upon some affair of importance; on the day fixed, the mistress and her two children came very late; she made two excuses, first for her husband, who, as she said, happened that very morning to *lhnuwnh*. The word is strongly expressive in their language, but not easily rendered into English; it signifies, *to retire to his first Mother*. Her excuse for not coming sooner was that, her husband dying late in the morning, she was a good while consulting her servants about a convenient place where his body should be laid; and I observed she behaved herself at our house as cheerfully as the rest. She died about three months after.

They live generally to seventy or seventy-five years, very seldom to fourscore. Some weeks before their death they feel a gradual decay, but without pain. During this time they are much visited by their friends because they cannot go abroad with their usual ease and satisfaction. However, about ten days before their death, which they seldom fail in computing, they return the visits that have been made them by those who are nearest in the neighbourhood, being carried in a convenient sledge drawn by Yahoos; which vehicle they use, not only upon this occasion, but when they grow old, upon long journeys, or when they are lamed by any accident. And therefore, when the dying Houyhnhnms return those visits, they take a solemn leave of their friends, as if they were going to some remote part of the country where they designed to pass the rest of their lives.

I know not whether it may be worth observing that the Houyhnhnms have no word in their language to express any thing that is evil, except what they borrow from the deformities or ill qualities of the Yahoos. Thus they denote the folly of a servant, an omission of a child, a stone that cuts their feet, a continuance of foul or unseasonable weather, and the like, by adding to each the epithet of Yahoo. For instance, *hhnm Yahoo*, *whnaholm Yahoo*, *ynlhmndwihlma Yahoo*, and an ill-contrived house, *ynholmhnmrohlnw* Yahoo.

I could with great pleasure enlarge further upon the manners and virtues of this excellent people; but, intending in a short time to publish a volume by itself, expressly upon that subject, I refer the reader thither; and, in the meantime, proceed to relate my own sad catastrophe.

CHAPTER 10

(*The author's economy*[1] *and happy life among the Houyhnhnms. His great improvement in virtue by conversing with them. Their conversations. The author has notice given him by his master that he must depart from the country. He falls into a swoon for grief, but submits. He contrives and finishes a canoe by the help of a fellow-servant, and puts to sea at a venture.*)

I had settled my little economy to my own heart's content. My master had ordered a room to be made for me after their manner, about six yards from the house, the sides and floors of which I plastered with clay and covered with rush mats of my own contriving. I had beaten hemp, which there grows wild, and made of it a sort of ticking;[2] this I filled with the feathers of several birds I had taken with springes made of Yahoos' hairs, and were excellent food. I had worked two chairs with my knife, the sorrel nag helping me in the grosser[3] and more laborious part. When my clothes were worn to rags, I made myself others with the skins of rabbits, and of a certain beautiful animal about the same size, called

[1] *economy* Means of managing a household.

[2] *ticking* Strong material used to make mattress or pillow coverings.

[3] *grosser* Larger; heavier.

nnuhnoh, the skin of which is covered with a fine down. Of these I also made very tolerable stockings. I soled my shoes with wood, which I cut from a tree and fitted to the upper leather; and when this was worn out, I supplied it with the skins of Yahoos dried in the sun. I often got honey out of hollow trees, which I mingled with water, or ate with my bread. No man could more verify the truth of these two maxims, that *Nature is very easily satisfied*, and that *Necessity is the mother of invention*. I enjoyed perfect health of body and tranquillity of mind; I did not feel the treachery or inconstancy of a friend, nor the injuries of a secret or open enemy. I had no occasion of bribing, flattering, or pimping to procure the favour of any great man, or of his minion; I wanted no fence against fraud or oppression; here was neither physician to destroy my body, nor lawyer to ruin my fortune; no informer to watch my words and actions or forge accusations against me for hire; here were no gibers, censurers, backbiters, pickpockets, highwaymen, housebreakers, attorneys, bawds, buffoons, gamesters, politicians, wits, splenetics, tedious talkers, controvertists, ravishers, murderers, robbers, virtuosos;[1] no leaders or followers of party and faction; no encouragers to vice by seducement or examples; no dungeon, axes, gibbets, whipping-posts, or pillories; no cheating shopkeepers or mechanics; no pride, vanity, or affectation; no fops, bullies, drunkards, strolling whores, or poxes; no ranting, lewd, expensive wives; no stupid, proud pedants; no importunate, overbearing, quarrelsome, noisy, roaring, empty, conceited, swearing companions; no scoundrels raised from the dust upon the merit of their vices, or nobility thrown into it on account of their virtues; no lords, fiddlers, judges, or dancing masters.[2]

I had the favour of being admitted to several Houyhnhnms who came to visit or dine with my master; where his honour graciously suffered me to wait in the room and listen to their discourse. Both he and his company would often descend to ask me questions and receive my answers. I had also sometimes the honour of attending my master in his visits to others. I never presumed to speak, except in answer to a question; and then I did it with inward regret, because it was a loss of so much time for improving myself; but I was infinitely delighted with the station of an humble auditor in such conversations, where nothing passed but what was useful, expressed in the fewest and most significant words; where, as I have already said, the greatest decency was observed, without the least degree of ceremony; where no person spoke without being pleased himself, and pleasing his companions; where there was no interruption, tediousness, heat, or difference of sentiments. They have a notion that when people are met together, a short silence does much improve conversation. This I found to be true; for during those little intermissions of talk, new ideas would arise in their minds, which very much enlivened the discourse. Their subjects are generally on friendship and benevolence; on order and economy; sometimes upon the visible operations of nature, or ancient traditions; upon the bounds and limits of virtue; upon the unerring rules of reason, or upon some determinations to be taken at the next great assembly; and often upon the various excellences of poetry. I may add, without vanity, that my presence often gave them sufficient matter for discourse because it afforded my master an occasion of letting his friends into the history of me and my country, upon which they were all pleased to descant in a manner not very advantageous to humankind; and for that reason I shall not repeat what they said; only I may be allowed to observe that his honour, to my great admiration, appeared to understand the nature of Yahoos much better than myself. He went through all our vices and follies, and discovered many which I had never mentioned to him, by only supposing what qualities a Yahoo of their country, with a small proportion of reason, might be capable of exerting; and concluded, with too much probability, how vile, as well as miserable, such a creature must be.

I freely confess that all the little knowledge I have of any value was acquired by the lectures I received from my master, and from hearing the discourses of him and his friends; to which I should be prouder to listen than to dictate to the greatest and wisest assembly in Europe. I admired the strength, comeliness, and speed of the inhabitants; and such a constellation of virtues in such amiable persons produced in me the highest veneration. At first, indeed, I did not feel that natural awe which the Yahoos and all other animals bear toward them; but it

[1] *virtuosos* Those who have special interest in or knowledge of particular aspects of the arts or sciences.

[2] *dancing masters* Those who taught the art of dancing, a skill essential for social advancement.

grew upon me by degrees, much sooner than I imagined, and was mingled with a respectful love and gratitude, that they would condescend to distinguish me from the rest of my species.

When I thought of my family, my friends, my countrymen, or the human race in general, I considered them as they really were, Yahoos in shape and disposition, perhaps a little more civilized, and qualified with the gift of speech; but making no other use of reason than to improve and multiply those vices whereof their brethren in this country had only the share that nature allotted them. When I happened to behold the reflection of my own form in a lake or fountain, I turned away my face in horror and detestation of myself, and could better endure the sight of a common Yahoo than of my own person. By conversing with the Houyhnhnms, and looking upon them with delight, I fell to imitate their gait and gesture, which is now grown into a habit; and my friends often tell me in a blunt way that I trot like a horse; which, however, I take for a great compliment. Neither shall I disown that in speaking I am apt to fall into the voice and manner of the Houyhnhnms, and hear myself ridiculed on that account without the least mortification.

In the midst of all this happiness, and when I looked upon myself to be fully settled for life, my master sent for me one morning a little earlier than his usual hour. I observed by his countenance that he was in some perplexity, and at a loss how to begin what he had to speak. After a short silence, he told me, he did not know how I would take what he was going to say; that, in the last general assembly, when the affair of the Yahoos was entered upon, the representatives had taken offence at his keeping a Yahoo (meaning myself) in his family, more like a Houyhnhnm than a brute animal. That he was known frequently to converse with me, as if he could receive some advantage or pleasure in my company; that such a practice was not agreeable to reason or nature, or a thing ever heard of before among them. The assembly did therefore exhort him either to employ me like the rest of my species, or command me to swim back to the place whence I came. That the first of these expedients was utterly rejected by all the Houyhnhnms who had ever seen me at his house or their own; for they alleged that because I had some rudiments of reason, added to the natural pravity[1] of those animals, it was to be feared I might be able to seduce them into the woody and mountainous parts of the country, and bring them in troops by night to destroy the Houyhnhnms' cattle, as being naturally of the ravenous kind, and averse from labour.

My master added that he was daily pressed by the Houyhnhnms of the neighbourhood to have the assembly's exhortation executed, which he could not put off much longer. He doubted it would be impossible for me to swim to another country; and therefore wished I would contrive some sort of vehicle resembling those I had described to him, that might carry me on the sea; in which work I should have the assistance of his own servants, as well as those of his neighbours. He concluded that, for his own part, he could have been content to keep me in his service as long as I lived, because he found I had cured myself of some bad habits and dispositions by endeavouring, as far as my inferior nature was capable, to imitate the Houyhnhnms.

I should here observe to the reader that a decree of the general assembly in this country is expressed by the word *hnhloayn*, which signifies an exhortation, as near as I can render it; for they have no conception how a rational creature can be compelled, but only advised or exhorted, because no person can disobey reason without giving up his claim to be a rational creature.

I was struck with the utmost grief and despair at my master's discourse; and, being unable to support the agonies I was under, I fell into a swoon at his feet. When I came to myself, he told me that he concluded I had been dead (for these people are subject to no such imbecilities of nature). I answered in a faint voice that death would have been too great a happiness; that although I could not blame the assembly's exhortation or the urgency of his friends, yet, in my weak and corrupt judgment, I thought it might consist with reason to have been less rigorous. That I could not swim a league, and probably the nearest land to theirs might be distant above a hundred; that many materials, necessary for making a small vessel to carry me off, were wholly wanting in this country; which, however, I would attempt in obedience and gratitude to his honour, although I concluded the thing to be impossible,

[1] *pravity* Depravity.

and therefore looked on myself as already devoted[1] to destruction. That the certain prospect of an unnatural death was the least of my evils; for, supposing I should escape with life by some strange adventure, how could I think with temper[2] of passing my days among Yahoos, and relapsing into my old corruptions, for want of examples to lead and keep me within the paths of virtue. That I knew too well upon what solid reasons all the determinations of the wise Houyhnhnms were founded, not to be shaken by arguments of mine, a miserable Yahoo; and therefore, after presenting him with my humble thanks for the offer of his servants' assistance in making a vessel, and desiring a reasonable time for so difficult a work, I told him I would endeavour to preserve a wretched being; and, if ever I returned to England, was not without hopes of being useful to my own species by celebrating the praises of the renowned Houyhnhnms, and proposing their virtues to the imitation of mankind.

My master in a few words made me a very gracious reply, allowed me the space of two months to finish my boat, and ordered the sorrel nag, my fellow servant (for so at this distance I may presume to call him), to follow my instruction, because I told my master that his help would be sufficient, and I knew he had a tenderness for me.

In his company my first business was to go to that part of the coast where my rebellious crew had ordered me to be set on shore. I got upon a height, and, looking on every side into the sea, fancied I saw a small island toward the northeast. I took out my pocket glass, and could then clearly distinguish it above five leagues off, as I computed; but it appeared to the sorrel nag to be only a blue cloud; for, as he had no conception of any country beside his own, so he could not be as expert in distinguishing remote objects at sea, as we who so much converse in that element.

After I had discovered this island, I considered no further; but resolved it should, if possible, be the first place of my banishment, leaving the consequence to fortune.

I returned home and, consulting with the sorrel nag, we went into a copse at some distance, where I with my knife, and he with a sharp flint fastened very artificially, after their manner, to a wooden handle, cut down several oak wattles about the thickness of a walking staff, and some larger pieces. But I shall not trouble the reader with a particular description of my own mechanics; let it suffice to say that in six weeks time, with the help of the sorrel nag, who performed the parts that required most labour, I finished a sort of Indian canoe, but much larger, covering it with the skins of Yahoos, well stitched together with hempen threads of my own making. My sail was likewise composed of the skins of the same animal; but I made use of the youngest I could get, the older being too tough and thick; and I likewise provided myself with four paddles. I laid in a stock of boiled flesh of rabbits and fowls, and took with me two vessels, one filled with milk and the other with water.

I tried my canoe in a large pond near my master's house, and then corrected in it what was amiss, stopping all the chinks with Yahoos' tallow till I found it staunch[3] and able to bear me and my freight. And, when it was as complete as I could possibly make it, I had it drawn on a carriage very gently by Yahoos, to the seaside, under the conduct of the sorrel nag and another servant.

When all was ready, and the day came for my departure, I took leave of my master and lady, and the whole family, my eyes flowing with tears and my heart quite sunk with grief. But his honour, out of curiosity, and perhaps (if I may speak without vanity) partly out of kindness, was determined to see me in my canoe, and got several of his neighbouring friends to accompany him. I was forced to wait above an hour for the tide, and then, observing the wind very fortunately bearing toward the island to which I intended to steer my course, I took a second leave of my master; but as I was going to prostrate myself to kiss his hoof, he did me the honour to raise it gently to my mouth. I am not ignorant how much I have been censured for mentioning this last particular. Detractors are pleased to think it improbable that so illustrious a person should descend to give so great a mark of distinction to a creature so inferior as I. Neither have I forgotten how apt some travellers are to boast of extraordinary favours they have received. But, if these censurers were better acquainted with the noble and courteous disposition of the Houyhnhnms, they would soon change their opinion.

I paid my respects to the rest of the Houyhnhnms in his honour's company; then, getting into my canoe, I pushed off from shore.

[1] *devoted* Doomed.

[2] *temper* Composure.

[3] *staunch* Watertight.

CHAPTER II

(*The author's dangerous voyage. He arrives at New Holland, hoping to settle there. Is wounded with an arrow by one of the natives. Is seized and carried by force into a Portuguese ship. The great civilities of the Captain. The author arrives at England.*)

I began this desperate voyage on February 15, 1714–15,[1] at nine o'clock in the morning. The wind was very favourable; however, I made use at first only of my paddles; but considering I should soon be weary, and that the wind might chop about,[2] I ventured to set up my little sail; and thus, with the help of the tide, I went at the rate of a league and a half an hour, as near as I could guess. My master and his friends continued on the shore till I was almost out of sight; and I often heard the sorrel nag (who always loved me) crying out, *Hnuy illa nyha, majah Yahoo* ("Take care of thyself, gentle Yahoo").

My design was, if possible, to discover some small island uninhabited, yet sufficient by my labour to furnish me with the necessaries of life, which I would have thought a greater happiness than to be first minister in the politest court of Europe, so horrible was the idea I conceived of returning to live in the society and under the government of Yahoos. For in such a solitude as I desired, I could at least enjoy my own thoughts, and reflect with delight on the virtues of those inimitable Houyhnhnms, without any opportunity of degenerating into the vices and corruptions of my own species.

The reader may remember what I related when my crew conspired against me and confined me to my cabin: how I continued there several weeks without knowing what course we took; and when I was put ashore in the longboat, how the sailors told me with oaths, whether true or false, that they knew not in what part of the world we were. However, I did then believe us to be about 10 degrees southward of the Cape of Good Hope, or about 45 degrees southern latitude, as I gathered from some general words I overheard among them, being, I supposed, to the southeast in their intended voyage to Madagascar. And although this were little better than conjecture, yet I resolved to steer my course eastward, hoping to reach the southwest coast of New Holland,[3] and perhaps some such island as I desired lying westward of it. The wind was full west, and by six in the evening I computed I had gone eastward at least eighteen leagues when I spied a very small island about half a league off, which I soon reached. It was nothing but a rock with one creek, naturally arched by the force of tempests. Here I put in my canoe, and, climbing a part of the rock, I could plainly discover land to the east, extending from south to north. I lay all night in my canoe, and, repeating my voyage early in the morning, I arrived in seven hours to the southeast point of New Holland. This confirmed me in the opinion I have long entertained that the maps and charts place this country at least three degrees more to the east than it really is; which thought I communicated many years ago to my worthy friend, Mr. Herman Moll,[4] and gave him my reasons for it, although he has rather chosen to follow other authors.

I saw no inhabitants in the place where I landed, and, being unarmed, I was afraid of venturing far into the country. I found some shellfish on the shore and ate them raw, not daring to kindle a fire for fear of being discovered by the natives. I continued three days feeding on oysters and limpets,[5] to save my own provisions; and I fortunately found a brook of excellent water, which gave me great relief.

On the fourth day, venturing out early a little too far, I saw twenty or thirty natives upon a height, not above five hundred yards from me. They were stark naked men, women, and children round a fire, as I could discover by the smoke. One of them spied me and gave notice to the rest; five of them advanced toward me, leaving the women and children at the fire. I made what haste I could to the shore, and, getting into my canoe, shoved off. The savages, observing me retreat, ran after me; and, before I could get far enough into the sea,

[1] *1714–15* Before the Gregorian calendar was adopted in 1752, the new year officially began on March 25. However, since many people also considered the new year to begin on January 1, the dates between January 1 and March 24, inclusive, were written according to both systems. Thus Gulliver leaves on February 15, 1715, according to our calendar.

[2] *chop about* Suddenly change direction.

[3] *New Holland* Australia.

[4] *Mr. Herman Moll* Dutch cartographer (1678–1732) who prepared the maps for the early editions of *Gulliver's Travels*.

[5] *limpets* Mollusks.

discharged an arrow which wounded me deeply on the inside of my left knee. (I shall carry the mark to my grave.) I apprehended the arrow might be poisoned, and, paddling out of the reach of their darts (being a calm day), I made a shift to suck the wound and dress it as well as I could.

I was at a loss what to do, for I durst not return to the same landing place, but stood to[1] the north, and was forced to paddle; for the wind, though very gentle, was against me, blowing northwest. As I was looking about for a secure landing-place, I saw a sail to the north-northeast, which appearing every minute more visible, I was in some doubt whether I should wait for them or no; but at last my detestation of the Yahoo race prevailed; and, turning my canoe, I sailed and paddled together to the south, and got into the same creek whence I set out in the morning, choosing rather to trust myself among these barbarians than live with European Yahoos. I drew up my canoe as close as I could to the shore, and hid myself behind a stone by the little brook, which, as I have already said, was excellent water.

The ship came within half a league of this creek, and sent her longboat with vessels to take in fresh water (for the place, it seems, was very well known), but I did not observe it till the boat was almost on shore, and it was too late to seek another hiding-place. The seamen at their landing observed my canoe and, rummaging it all over, easily conjectured that the owner could not be far off. Four of them, well armed, searched every cranny and lurking-hole till at last they found me flat on my face behind the stone. They gazed awhile in admiration at my strange uncouth dress; my coat made of skins, my wooden-soled shoes, and my furred stockings; from whence, however, they concluded I was not a native of the place, who all go naked. One of the seamen in Portuguese bid me rise, and asked who I was. I understood that language very well and, getting upon my feet, said I was a poor Yahoo banished from the Houyhnhnms, and desired they would please to let me depart. They admired to hear me answer them in their own tongue, and saw by my complexion I must be a European; but were at a loss to know what I meant by Yahoos and Houyhnhnms, and at the same time fell a laughing at my strange tone in speaking, which resembled the neighing of a horse. I trembled all the while betwixt fear and hatred. I again desired leave to depart, and was gently moving to my canoe; but they laid hold of me, desiring to know, what country I was of? whence I came? with many other questions. I told them I was born in England, from whence I came about five years ago, and then their country and ours were at peace. I therefore hoped they would not treat me as an enemy, since I meant them no harm, but was a poor Yahoo seeking some desolate place where to pass the remainder of his unfortunate life.

When they began to talk, I thought I never heard or saw any thing more unnatural; for it appeared to me as monstrous as if a dog or a cow should speak in England, or a Yahoo in Houyhnhnmland. The honest Portuguese were equally amazed at my strange dress and the odd manner of delivering my words, which, however, they understood very well. They spoke to me with great humanity, and said they were sure the Captain would carry me *gratis*[2] to Lisbon, from whence I might return to my own country; that two of the seamen would go back to the ship to inform the Captain of what they had seen, and receive his orders; in the meantime, unless I would give my solemn oath not to fly, they would secure me by force. I thought it best to comply with their proposal. They were very curious to know my story, but I gave them very little satisfaction, and they all conjectured that my misfortunes had impaired my reason. In two hours the boat, which went laden with vessels of water, returned with the Captain's command to fetch me on board. I fell on my knees to preserve my liberty; but all was in vain, and the men, having tied me with cords, heaved me into the boat, from whence I was taken into the ship, and from thence into the Captain's cabin.

His name was Pedro de Mendez; he was a very courteous and generous person. He entreated me to give some account of myself, and desired to know what I would eat or drink; said I should be used as well as himself, and spoke so many obliging things that I wondered to find such civilities from a Yahoo. However, I remained silent and sullen; I was ready to faint at the very smell of him and his men. At last I desired something to eat out of my own canoe; but he ordered me a chicken and some excellent wine, and then directed that

[1] *stood to* Steered towards.

[2] *gratis* Latin: free of charge.

I should be put to bed in a very clean cabin. I would not undress myself, but lay on the bedclothes, and in half an hour stole out, when I thought the crew was at dinner; and, getting to the side of the ship, was going to leap into the sea and swim for my life, rather than continue among Yahoos. But one of the seamen prevented me, and, having informed the Captain, I was chained to my cabin.

After dinner Don Pedro came to me and desired to know my reason for so desperate an attempt; assured me he only meant to do me all the service he was able; and spoke so very movingly that at last I descended to treat him like an animal which had some little portion of reason. I gave him a very short relation of my voyage, of the conspiracy against me by my own men, of the country where they set me on shore, and of my five years residence there. All which he looked upon as if it were a dream or a vision; whereat I took great offence; for I had quite forgot the faculty of lying, so peculiar to Yahoos in all countries where they preside, and consequently their disposition of suspecting truth in others of their own species. I asked him whether it were the custom in his country to *say the thing that was not*? I assured him I had almost forgot what he meant by falsehood, and if I had lived a thousand years in Houyhnhnmland, I should never have heard a lie from the meanest servant. That I was altogether indifferent whether he believed me or not; but, however, in return for his favours, I would give so much allowance to the corruption of his nature as to answer any objection he would please to make, and then he might easily discover the truth.

The Captain, a wise man, after many endeavours to catch me tripping in some part of my story, at last began to have a better opinion of my veracity. But he added that since I professed so inviolable an attachment to truth, I must give him my word and honour to bear him company in this voyage without attempting anything against my life; or else he would continue me a prisoner till we arrived at Lisbon. I gave him the promise he required; but at the same time protested that I would suffer the greatest hardships rather than return to live among Yahoos.

Our voyage passed without any considerable accident. In gratitude to the Captain, I sometimes sat with him at his earnest request, and strove to conceal my antipathy against humankind, although it often broke out; which he suffered to pass without observation. But the greatest part of the day I confined myself to my cabin, to avoid seeing any of the crew. The Captain had often entreated me to strip myself of my savage dress, and offered to lend me the best suit of clothes he had. This I would not be prevailed on to accept, abhorring to cover myself with anything that had been on the back of a Yahoo. I only desired he would lend me two clean shirts, which, having been washed since he wore them, I believed would not so much defile me. These I changed every second day, and washed them myself.

We arrived at Lisbon, Nov. 5, 1715. At our landing, the Captain forced me to cover myself with his cloak to prevent the rabble from crowding about me. I was conveyed to his own house; and at my earnest request he led me up to the highest room backwards.[1] I conjured[2] him to conceal from all persons what I had told him of the Houyhnhnms, because the least hint of such a story would not only draw numbers of people to see me, but probably put me in danger of being imprisoned, or burnt by the Inquisition. The Captain persuaded me to accept a suit of clothes newly made; but I would not suffer the tailor to take my measure; however, Don Pedro being almost of my size, they fitted me well enough. He accoutred me with other necessaries, all new, which I aired for twenty-four hours before I would use them.

The Captain had no wife, nor above three servants, none of which were suffered to attend at meals; and his whole deportment was so obliging, added to very good human understanding, that I really began to tolerate his company. He gained so far upon me that I ventured to look out of the back window. By degrees I was brought into another room, from whence I peeped into the street, but drew my head back in a fright. In a week's time he seduced me down to the door. I found my terror gradually lessened, but my hatred and contempt seemed to increase. I was at last bold enough to walk the street in his company, but kept my nose well stopped with rue,[3] or sometimes with tobacco.

In ten days, Don Pedro, to whom I had given some account of my domestic affairs, put it upon me as a matter of honour and conscience that I ought to return

[1] *backwards* At the rear of the house.

[2] *conjured* Entreated.

[3] *rue* Strong-smelling leaves of the rue, a shrub.

to my native country, and live at home with my wife and children. He told me there was an English ship in the port just ready to sail, and he would furnish me with all things necessary. It would be tedious to repeat his arguments and my contradictions. He said it was altogether impossible to find such a solitary island as I desired to live in; but I might command in my own house, and pass my time in a manner as recluse as I pleased.

I complied at last, finding I could not do better. I left Lisbon the 24th day of November, in an English merchantman, but who was the master I never inquired. Don Pedro accompanied me to the ship and lent me twenty pounds. He took kind leave of me, and embraced me at parting, which I bore as well as I could. During this last voyage I had no commerce with the master or any of his men; but, pretending I was sick, kept close in my cabin. On the fifth of December, 1715, we cast anchor in the Downs, about nine in the morning, and at three in the afternoon I got safe to my house at Redriff.

My wife and family received me with great surprise and joy, because they concluded me certainly dead; but I must freely confess the sight of them filled me only with hatred, disgust, and contempt, and the more by reflecting on the near alliance I had to them. For although, since my unfortunate exile from the Houyhnhnm country, I had compelled myself to tolerate the sight of Yahoos, and to converse with Don Pedro de Mendez, yet my memory and imagination were perpetually filled with the virtues and ideas of those exalted Houyhnhnms. And when I began to consider that by copulating with one of the Yahoo species I had become a parent of more, it struck me with the utmost shame, confusion, and horror.

As soon as I entered the house, my wife took me in her arms and kissed me; at which, having not been used to the touch of that odious animal for so many years, I fell into a swoon for almost an hour. At the time I am writing, it is five years since my last return to England. During the first year, I could not endure my wife or children in my presence; the very smell of them was intolerable, much less could I suffer them to eat in the same room. To this hour they dare not presume to touch my bread or drink out of the same cup, neither was I ever able to let one of them take me by the hand. The first money I laid out was to buy two young stone-horses,[1] which I keep in a good stable; and next to them, the groom is my greatest favourite, for I feel my spirits revived by the smell he contracts in the stable. My horses understand me tolerably well; I converse with them at least four hours every day. They are strangers to bridle or saddle; they live in great amity with me and friendship to each other.

Chapter 12

(*The author's veracity. His design in publishing this work. His censure of those travellers who swerve from the truth. The author clears himself from any sinister ends in writing. An objection answered. The method of planting colonies. His native country commended. The right of the Crown to those countries described by the author is justified. The difficulty of conquering them. The author takes his last leave of the reader; proposes his manner of living for the future; gives good advice, and concludes.*)

Thus, gentle reader, I have given thee a faithful history of my travels for sixteen years and above seven months; wherein I have not been so studious of ornament as of truth. I could perhaps, like others, have astonished thee with strange improbable tales; but I rather chose to relate plain matter of fact, in the simplest manner and style, because my principal design was to inform, and not to amuse thee.

It is easy for us who travel into remote countries, which are seldom visited by Englishmen or other Europeans, to form descriptions of wonderful animals both at sea and land. Whereas a traveller's chief aim should be to make men wiser and better, and to improve their minds by the bad, as well as good, example of what they deliver concerning foreign places.

I could heartily wish a law was enacted that every traveller, before he were permitted to publish his voyages, should be obliged to make oath before the Lord High Chancellor that all he intended to print was absolutely true to the best of his knowledge; for then the world would no longer be deceived, as it usually is, while some writers, to make their works pass the better upon the public, impose the grossest falsities on the unwary reader. I have perused several books of travels

[1] *stone-horses* Stallions.

with great delight in my younger days; but having since gone over most parts of the globe, and been able to contradict many fabulous accounts from my own observation, it has given me a great disgust against this part of reading, and some indignation to see the credulity of mankind so impudently abused. Therefore, since my acquaintance were pleased to think my poor endeavours might not be unacceptable to my country, I imposed on myself, as a maxim never to be swerved from, that I would strictly adhere to truth; neither indeed can I be ever under the least temptation to vary from it while I retain in my mind the lectures and example of my noble master and the other illustrious Houyhnhnms of whom I had so long the honour to be an humble hearer.

—Nec si miserum Fortuna Sinonem
Finxit, vanum etiam, mendacemque improba finget.[1]

I know very well how little reputation is to be got by writings which require neither genius nor learning, nor indeed any other talent except a good memory or an exact journal. I know likewise that writers of travels, like dictionary-makers, are sunk into oblivion by the weight and bulk of those who come last, and therefore lie uppermost. And it is highly probable that such travellers who shall hereafter visit the countries described in this work of mine, may, by detecting my errors (if there be any) and adding many new discoveries of their own, jostle me out of vogue and stand in my place, making the world forget that ever I was an author. This indeed would be too great a mortification if I wrote for fame; but, as my sole intention was the public good, I cannot be altogether disappointed. For who can read of the virtues I have mentioned in the glorious Houyhnhnms without being ashamed of his own vices, when he considers himself as the reasoning, governing animal of his country? I shall say nothing of those remote nations where Yahoos preside; among which the least corrupted are the Brobdingnagians, whose wise maxims in morality and government it would be our happiness to observe. But I forbear descanting further, and rather leave the judicious reader to his own remarks and application.

I am not a little pleased that this work of mine can possibly meet with no censurers; for what objections can be made against a writer who relates only plain facts that happened in such distant countries where we have not the least interest with respect either to trade or negotiations? I have carefully avoided every fault with which common writers of travels are often too justly charged. Besides, I meddle not the least with any party, but write without passion, prejudice, or ill-will against any man, or number of men, whatsoever. I write for the noblest end, to inform and instruct mankind, over whom I may, without breach of modesty, pretend to some superiority, from the advantages I received by conversing so long among the most accomplished Houyhnhnms. I write without any view to profit or praise. I never suffer a word to pass that may look like reflection,[2] or possibly give the least offence, even to those who are most ready to take it. So that I hope I may with justice pronounce myself an author perfectly blameless; against whom the tribes of answerers, considerers, observers, reflectors, detectors, remarkers will never be able to find matter for exercising their talents.

I confess it was whispered to me that I was bound in duty, as a subject of England, to have given in a memorial[3] to a secretary of state at my first coming over, because whatever lands are discovered by a subject belong to the Crown. But I doubt whether our conquests in the countries I treat of would be as easy as those of Ferdinando Cortez over the naked Americans. The Lilliputians, I think, are hardly worth the charge of a fleet and army to reduce them; and I question whether it might be prudent or safe to attempt the Brobdingnagians; or whether an English army would be much at their ease with the Flying Island[4] over their heads. The Houyhnhnms indeed appear not to be so well prepared for war, a science to which they are perfect strangers, and especially against missive weapons. However, supposing myself to be a minister of state, I could never give my advice for invading them. Their prudence, unanimity, unacquaintedness with fear, and their love of their country would amply supply all defects in the

[1] *Nec ... finget* Latin: Nor, if cruel Fortune has made Sinon miserable, will she also make him false and a liar. See Virgil's *Aeneid*, 2.79–80. Sinon spoke these words to the Trojans when convincing them to accept the Greeks' gift of a wooden horse.

[2] *reflection* Imputation, accusation.

[3] *memorial* Record of events that is submitted to the government.

[4] *Flying Island* Reference to Part 3 of *Gulliver's Travels*, "A Voyage to Laputa," which is included in this anthology.

military art. Imagine twenty thousand of them breaking into the midst of an European army, confounding the ranks, overturning the carriages, battering the warriors' faces into mummy[1] by terrible yerks[2] from their hinder hoofs; for they would well deserve the character given to Augustus, *Recalcitrat undique tutus.*[3] But, instead of proposals for conquering that magnanimous nation, I rather wish they were in a capacity or disposition to send a sufficient number of their inhabitants for civilizing Europe, by teaching us the first principles of honour, justice, truth, temperance, public spirit, fortitude, chastity, friendship, benevolence, and fidelity. The names of all which virtues are still retained among us in most languages, and are to be met with in modern, as well as ancient authors; which I am able to assert from my own small reading.

But I had another reason which made me less forward[4] to enlarge His Majesty's dominions by my discoveries. To say the truth, I had conceived a few scruples with relation to the distributive justice of princes upon those occasions. For instance, a crew of pirates are driven by a storm they know not whither; at length a boy discovers land from the topmast; they go on shore to rob and plunder; they see a harmless people, are entertained with kindness; they give the country a new name; they take formal possession of it for their king; they set up a rotten plank or a stone for a memorial; they murder two or three dozen of the natives, bring away a couple more by force for a sample; return home, and get their pardon. Here commences a new dominion acquired with a title by divine right. Ships are sent with the first opportunity; the natives driven out or destroyed; their princes tortured to discover their gold; a free license given to all acts of inhumanity and lust, the earth reeking with the blood of its inhabitants. And this execrable crew of butchers, employed in so pious an expedition, is a modern colony, sent to convert and civilize an idolatrous and barbarous people!

But this description, I confess, does by no means affect the British nation, who may be an example to the whole world for their wisdom, care, and justice in planting colonies; their liberal endowments for the advancement of religion and learning; their choice of devout and able pastors to propagate Christianity; their caution in stocking their provinces with people of sober lives and conversations from this the mother kingdom; their strict regard to the distribution of justice, in supplying the civil administration through all their colonies with officers of the greatest abilities, utter strangers to corruption; and, to crown all, by sending the most vigilant and virtuous governors, who have no other views than the happiness of the people over whom they preside, and the honour of the king their master.

But, as those countries which I have described do not appear to have any desire of being conquered and enslaved, murdered or driven out by colonies, nor abound either in gold, silver, sugar, or tobacco, I did humbly conceive they were by no means proper objects of our zeal, our valour, or our interest. However, if those whom it more concerns think fit to be of another opinion, I am ready to depose, when I shall be lawfully called, that no European did ever visit those countries before me. I mean, if the inhabitants ought to be believed, unless a dispute may arise concerning the two Yahoos said to have been seen many years ago upon a mountain in Houyhnhnmland.

But, as to the formality of taking possession in my sovereign's name, it never came once into my thoughts; and if it had, yet, as my affairs then stood, I should perhaps in point of prudence and self-preservation have put it off to a better opportunity.

Having thus answered the only objection that can ever be raised against me as a traveller, I here take a final leave of all my courteous readers, and return to enjoy my own speculations in my little garden at Redriff; to apply those excellent lessons of virtue which I learned among the Houyhnhnms; to instruct the Yahoos of my own family as far as I shall find them docible animals; to behold my figure often in a glass, and thus, if possible, habituate myself by time to tolerate the sight of a human creature; to lament the brutality to Houyhnhnms in my own country, but always treat their persons with respect, for the sake of my noble master, his family, his friends, and the whole Houyhnhnm race, whom these of ours have the honour to resemble in all their lineaments, however their intellectuals[5] came to degenerate.

[1] *mummy* Pulp.

[2] *yerks* Blows.

[3] *Recalcitrat undique tutus* Latin: He kicks backwards, protected on all sides.

[4] *forward* Eager.

[5] *intellectuals* Intellects.

I began last week to permit my wife to sit at dinner with me, at the farthest end of a long table, and to answer (but with the utmost brevity) the few questions I asked her. Yet, the smell of a Yahoo continuing very offensive, I always keep my nose well stopped with rue, lavender, or tobacco leaves. And, although it be hard for a man late in life to remove old habits, I am not altogether out of hopes in some time to suffer a neighbour Yahoo in my company without the apprehensions I am yet under of his teeth or his claws.

My reconcilement to the Yahoo kind in general might not be so difficult if they would be content with those vices and follies only which nature has entitled them to. I am not in the least provoked at the sight of a lawyer, a pickpocket, a colonel, a fool, a lord, a gamester, a politician, a whoremonger, a physician, an evidence,[1] a suborner, an attorney, a traitor, or the like; this is all according to the due course of things. But when I behold a lump of deformity and diseases, both in body and mind, smitten with pride, it immediately breaks all the measures of my patience; neither shall I be ever able to comprehend how such an animal, and such a vice, could tally together. The wise and virtuous Houyhnhnms, who abound in all excellences that can adorn a rational creature, have no name for this vice in their language, which has no terms to express anything that is evil, except those whereby they describe the detestable qualities of their Yahoos, among which they were not able to distinguish this of pride, for want of thoroughly understanding human nature as it shows itself in other countries where that animal presides. But I, who had more experience, could plainly observe some rudiments of it among the wild Yahoos.

But the Houyhnhnms, who live under the government of reason, are no more proud of the good qualities they possess than I should be for not wanting a leg or an arm; which no man in his wits would boast of, although he must be miserable without them. I dwell the longer upon this subject from the desire I have to make the society of an English Yahoo by any means not insupportable; and therefore I here entreat those who have any tincture of this absurd vice, that they will not presume to come in my sight.

—1726

In Context

Gulliver's Travels in Its Time

The letters excerpted below give some sense of Swift's own feelings about *Gulliver's Travels* and of the reactions the work provoked.

from Letter from Swift to Alexander Pope, 29 September 1725

Sir,

… My letter you saw to Lord Bolingbroke has shown you the situation I am in, and the company I keep, if I do not forget some of its contents, but I am now returning to the noble scene of Dublin, into the *grand monde*,[2] for fear of burying my parts, to signalise myself among curates and vicars, and correct all corruptions crept in relating to the weight of bread and butter, through those dominions where I govern. I have employed my time, besides ditching, in finishing, correcting, amending, and transcribing my *Travels*, in four parts complete, newly augmented, and intended for the press, when the world shall deserve them, or rather when a printer shall be found brave enough to venture his

[1] *evidence* Witness.

[2] *grand monde* High society.

ears.[1] I like the scheme of our meeting after distresses and dispersions; but the chief end I propose to myself in all my labours is to vex the world rather than divert it; and if I could compass that design, without hurting my own person or fortune, I would be the most indefatigable writer you have ever seen, without reading. I am exceedingly pleased that you have done with translations. Lord Treasurer Oxford[2] often lamented that a rascally world should lay you under a necessity of misemploying your genius for so long a time. But since you will now be so much better employed, when you think of the world give it one lash the more at my request. I have ever hated all nations, professions, and communities, and all my love is toward individuals: for instance, I hate the tribe of lawyers, but I love Counsellor Such-a-one, and Judge Such-a-one: so with physicians—I will not speak of my own trade—soldiers, English, Scotch, French, and the rest. But principally I hate and detest that animal called man, although I heartily love John, Peter, Thomas, and so forth. This is the system upon which I have governed myself many years, but do not tell, and so I shall go on till I have done with them. I have got materials toward a treatise, proving the falsity of that definition *animal rationale*,[3] and to show it would be only *rationis capax*.[4] Upon this great foundation of misanthropy, though not in Timon's[5] manner, the whole building of my *Travels* is erected; and I never will have peace of mind till all honest men are of my opinion. By consequence you are to embrace it immediately, and procure that all who deserve my esteem may do so too. The matter is so clear that it will admit of no dispute; nay, I will hold a hundred pounds that you and I agree in the point. …

I have almost done with harridans,[6] and shall soon become old enough to fall in love with girls of fourteen. The lady whom you describe to live at court, to be deaf, and no party woman, I take to be mythology, but know not how to moralise it. She cannot be Mercy, for Mercy is neither deaf, nor lives at Court. Justice is blind, and perhaps deaf, but neither is she a Court lady. Fortune is both blind and deaf, and a Court lady, but then she is a most damnable party woman, and will never make me easy, as you promise. It must be Riches, which answers all your description. I am glad she visits you, but my voice is so weak that I doubt she will never hear me.

Mr. Lewis sent me an account of Dr. Arbuthnot's[7] illness, which is a very sensible affliction to me, who, by living so long out of the world, have lost that hardness of heart contracted by years and general conversation. I am daily losing friends, and neither seeking nor getting others. Oh! if the world had but a dozen Arbuthnots in it, I would burn my *Travels*. …

from Letter from Swift to Alexander Pope, 26 November 1725

… Drown the world! I am not content with despising it, but I would anger it, if I could with safety. I wish there were a hospital[8] built for its despisers, where one might act with safety, and it need not be a large building, only I would have it well endowed. …

[1] *venture his ears* I.e., risk having his ears cut off. One punishment for printing seditious libel was to have the ears cropped.

[2] *Lord Treasurer Oxford* Robert Harley, Earl of Oxford (1661–1724).

[3] *animal rationale* Latin: rational animal.

[4] *rationis capax* Latin: capable of reason. I.e., not a rational animal, but only an animal capable of reason.

[5] *Timon* Greek Skeptic philosopher Timon of Philius (c. 320–c. 230 BCE), author of satires, who displayed a deep distrust of humankind and its "truths."

[6] *harridans* Hags, shrewish old women.

[7] *Dr. Arbuthnot* John Arbuthnot (1667–1735), Scottish physician, scientist, and satirist.

[8] *hospital* Refuge.

I desire you and all my friends will take a special care that my disaffection to the world may not be imputed to my age, for I have credible witnesses ready to depose, that it has never varied from the twenty-first to the f—ty-eighth year of my life; pray fill that blank charitably.[1] I tell you after all, that I do not hate mankind: it is *vous autres*[2] who hate them, because you would have them reasonable animals, and are angry for being disappointed. I have always rejected that definition, and made another of my own. I am no more angry with ——[3] than I was with the kite[4] that last week flew away with one of my chickens; and yet I was pleased when one of my servants shot him two days after. …

Letter from "Richard Sympson" to Benjamin Motte,[5] 8 August 1726

My cousin, Mr. Lemuel Gulliver, entrusted me some years ago with a copy of his travels, whereof that which I here send you is about a fourth part, for I shortened them very much as you will find in my "Preface to the Reader." I have shown them to several persons of great judgment and distinction, who are confident they will sell very well; and, although some parts of this and the following volumes may be thought in one or two places to be a little satirical, yet it is agreed they will give no offence; but in that you must judge for yourself, and take the advice of your friends, and if they or you be of another opinion, you may let me know it when you return these papers, which I expect shall be in three days at furthest. The good report I have received of you makes me put so great a trust into your hands, which I hope you will give me no reason to repent, and in that confidence I require that you will never suffer these papers to be once out of your sight.

As the printing these Travels will probably be of great value to you, so, as a manager for my friend and cousin, I expect you will give a due consideration for it, because I know the author intends the profit for the use of poor sea-men, and I am advised to say that two hundred pounds is the least sum I will receive on his account; but if it shall happen that the sale will not answer as I expect and believe, then whatever shall be thought too much even upon your own word, shall be duly repaid.

Perhaps you will think this a strange way of proceeding to a man of trade, but since I begin with so great a trust to you, whom I never saw, I think it not hard that you should trust me as much; therefore if after three days' reading and consulting these papers you think it proper to stand to my agreement, you may begin to print them, and the subsequent parts shall be all sent to you one after another in less than a week, provided that immediately upon your resolution to print them you do within three days deliver a bank-bill of two hundred pounds, wrapped up so as to make a parcel, to the hand from whence you receive this, who will come in the same manner exactly at nine o'clock on Thursday, which will be the 11th instant.

If you do not approve of this proposal, deliver these papers to the person who will come on Thursday. If you choose rather to send the papers, make no other proposal of your own, but just barely write on a piece of paper that you do not accept my offer. I am, sir,

Your humble servant,

Richard Sympson

---

[1] *fill … charitably* Swift was turning 58 that year.

[2] *vous autres* French: you others.

[3] —— Sir Robert Walpole, Whig prime minister of England from 1721 to 1742.

[4] *kite* Bird of prey.

[5] *Richard Sympson* Fictional cousin of Lemuel Gulliver. Swift disguised himself as Gulliver's cousin in order to remain anonymous; he had John Gay write out the letter so that no one would recognize his handwriting; *Benjamin Motte* Publisher of *Gulliver's Travels*.

from Letter from John Gay and Alexander Pope to Swift, 17 November 1726

About ten days ago a book was published here of the travels of one Gulliver, which hath been the conversation of the whole town ever since: the whole impression sold in a week, and nothing is more diverting than to hear the different opinions people give of it, though all agree in liking it extremely. It is generally said that you are the author; but I am told, the bookseller declares, he knows not from what hand it came. From the highest to the lowest it is universally read, from the cabinet-council to the nursery. The politicians to a man agree, that it is free from particular reflections, but that the satire on general societies of men is too severe. Not but we now and then meet with people of greater perspicuity, who are in search for particular applications in every leaf; and it is highly probable we shall have keys[1] published to give light into Gulliver's design. Your Lord ——[2] is the person who least approves it, blaming it as a design of evil consequence to depreciate human nature, at which it cannot be wondered that he takes most offence, being himself the most accomplished of his species, and so losing more than any other of that praise which is due both to the dignity and virtue of a man. Your friend, my Lord Harcourt, commends it very much, though he thinks in some places the matter too far carried. The Duchess Dowager of Marlborough is in raptures at it; she says she can dream of nothing else since she read it; she declares, that she hath now found out, that her whole life hath been lost in caressing the worst part of mankind, and treating the best as her foes; and that if she knew Gulliver, though he had been the worst enemy she ever had, she would give up her present acquaintance for his friendship.

You may see by this, that you are not much injured by being supposed the author of this piece. If you are, you have disobliged us, and two or three of your best friends, in not giving us the least hint of it while you were with us; and in particular Dr. Arbuthnot, who says it is ten thousand pities he had not known it, he could have added such abundance of things upon every subject. Among lady critics, some have found out that Mr. Gulliver had a particular malice to maids of honour. Those of them who frequent the Church, say, his design is impious, and that it is an insult on Providence depreciating the works of the Creator. Notwithstanding, I am told the Princess[3] has read it with great pleasure. As to other critics, they think the flying island[4] is the least entertaining; and so great an opinion the town have of the impossibility of Gulliver's writing at all below himself it is agreed that part was not writ by the same hand, though this has its defenders too. It has passed Lords and Commons, *nemine contradicente*;[5] and the whole town, men, women, and children are quite full of it. Perhaps I may all this time be talking to you of a book you have never seen, and which has not yet reached Ireland. If it has not, I believe what we have said will be sufficient to recommend it to your reading, and that you will order me to send it to you. But it will be much better to come over yourself, and read it here, where you will have the pleasure of variety of commentators, to explain the difficult passages to you.

… We are strangely surprised to hear that the bells in Ireland ring[6] without your money. I hope you do not write the thing that is not. We are afraid that B— has been guilty of that crime, that you, like a Houyhnhnm, have treated him as a Yahoo, and discarded him your service. I fear you do not understand these modish terms, which every creature now understands but yourself. … You fancy we

[1] *keys* I.e., books that explain the allusions to incidents and identities of persons represented in works of veiled meaning.

[2] *Lord ——* Bolingbroke.

[3] *the Princess* Caroline, Princess of Wales, wife of the future George II.

[4] *flying island* From Part 3.

[5] *nemine contradicente* Latin: with no opposition.

[6] *bells in Ireland ring* There was a public celebration in Ireland upon Swift's return to Dublin.

envy you, but you are mistaken; we envy those you are with, for we cannot envy the man we love. Adieu.

from Letter from Alexander Pope to Swift, 26 November 1726

... I congratulate you first upon what you call your cousin's wonderful book, which is *publica trita manu* at present, and I prophecy will be hereafter the admiration of all men. That countenance with which it is received by some statesmen is delightful. I wish I could tell you how every single man looks upon it, to observe which has been my whole diversion this fortnight. I have never been a night in London, since you left me, till now for this very end, and indeed it has fully answered my expectations.

I find no considerable man very angry at the book. Some, indeed, think it rather too bold, and too general a satire; but none that I hear of accuse it of particular reflections—I mean no persons of consequence, or good judgment; the mob of critics, you know, always are desirous to apply satire to those that they envy for being above them—so that you needed not to have been so secret upon this head. Motte received the copy, he tells me, he knew not from whence, nor from whom, dropped at his house in the dark, from a hackney coach. By computing the time, I found it was after you left England, so for my part, I suspend my judgment. ...

... I question not, many men would be of your intimacy, that you might be of their interest; but God forbid an honest or witty man should be of any, but that of his country. They have scoundrels enough to write for their passions and their designs; let us write for truth, for honour, and for posterity. If you must needs write about politics at all—but perhaps it is full as wise to play the fool any other way—surely it ought to be so as to preserve the dignity and integrity of your character with those times to come, which will most impartially judge of you. ...

A Modest Proposal

For Preventing the Children of Poor People in Ireland from Being a Burden to Their Parents or the Country, and for Making Them Beneficial to the Public

It is a melancholy object to those who walk through this great town,[1] or travel in the country, when they see the streets, the roads, and cabin doors crowded with beggars of the female sex, followed by three, four, or six children, all in rags and importuning every passenger[2] for an alms. These mothers, instead of being able to work for their honest livelihood, are forced to employ all their time in strolling[3] to beg sustenance for their helpless infants, who, as they grow up, either turn thieves for want of work, or leave their dear native country to fight for the Pretender in Spain, or sell themselves to the Barbados.[4]

I think it is agreed by all parties that this prodigious number of children in the arms, or on the backs, or at the heels of their mothers, and frequently of their fathers, is, in the present deplorable state of the kingdom, a very great additional grievance; and therefore, whoever could find out a fair, cheap, and easy method of making these children sound and useful members of the commonwealth would deserve so well of the public as to have his statue set up for a preserver of the nation.

But my intention is very far from being confined to provide only for the children of professed beggars; it is

[1] *this great town* I.e., Dublin.

[2] *passenger* Passerby.

[3] *strolling* Wandering, roving.

[4] *the Pretender* James Francis Edward Stuart, son of James II who was deposed from the throne in the Glorious Revolution due to his overt Catholicism. Catholic Ireland was loyal to Stuart, and the Irish were often recruited by France and Spain to fight against England; *Barbados* Because of the extreme poverty in Ireland, many Irish people emigrated to the West Indies, selling their labor to sugar plantations in advance to pay for the voyage.

of a much greater extent, and shall take in the whole number of infants at a certain age who are born of parents in effect as little able to support them as those who demand our charity in the streets.

As to my own part, having turned my thoughts for many years upon this important subject and maturely weighed the several schemes of other projectors,[1] I have always found them grossly mistaken in their computation. 'Tis true, a child just dropped from its dam may be supported by her milk for a solar year with little other nourishment, at most not above the value of two shillings, which the mother may certainly get, or the value in scraps, by her lawful occupation of begging; and it is exactly at one year old that I propose to provide for them in such a manner as, instead of being a charge upon their parents or the parish, or wanting food and raiment for the rest of their lives, they shall on the contrary contribute to the feeding, and partly to the clothing, of many thousands.

There is likewise another great advantage in my scheme, that it will prevent those abortions, and that horrid practice of women murdering their bastard children, alas, too frequent among us, sacrificing the poor innocent babes, I doubt,[2] more to avoid the expense than the shame, which would move tears and pity in the most savage and inhuman breast.

The number of souls in this kingdom being usually reckoned one million and a half, of these I calculate there may be about two hundred thousand couple whose wives are breeders, from which number I subtract thirty thousand couples who are able to maintain children, although I apprehend there cannot be as many under the present distresses of the kingdom; but this being granted, there will remain one hundred and seventy thousand breeders.

I again subtract fifty thousand for those women who miscarry, or whose children die by accident or disease within the year. There only remain one hundred and twenty thousand children of poor parents annually born. The question therefore is how this number shall be reared and provided for, which, as I have already said, under the present situation of affairs is utterly impossible by all the methods hitherto proposed. For we can neither employ them in handicraft or agriculture; we neither build houses (I mean in the country) nor cultivate land.[3] They can very seldom pick up a livelihood by stealing till they arrive at six years old, except where they are of towardly parts,[4] although I confess they learn the rudiments much earlier, during which time they can however be properly looked upon only as probationers,[5] as I have been informed by a principal gentleman in the county of Cavan, who protested to me that he never knew above one or two instances under the age of six, even in a part of the kingdom so renowned for the quickest proficiency in that art.

I am assured by our merchants that a boy or a girl before twelve years old is no saleable commodity; and even when they come to this age, they will not yield above three pounds, or three pounds and half a crown at most, on the Exchange,[6] which cannot turn to account[7] either to the parents or the kingdom, the charge of nutriment and rags having been at least four times that value.

I shall now therefore humbly propose my own thoughts, which I hope will not be liable to the least objection.

I have been assured by a very knowing American[8] of my acquaintance in London that a young healthy child well nursed is at a year old a most delicious, nourishing, and wholesome food, whether stewed, roasted, baked, or boiled; and I make no doubt that it will equally serve in a fricassee or a ragout.[9]

I do therefore humbly offer it to public consideration that of the hundred and twenty thousand children already computed, twenty thousand may be reserved for breed, whereof only one fourth part to be males, which is more than we allow to sheep, black cattle, or swine, and my reason is that these children are seldom the fruits of marriage, a circumstance not much regarded by our savages; therefore, one male will be sufficient to

[1] *projectors* Those who design or propose experiments or projects.

[2] *doubt* Fear.

[3] *neither build ... land* The British placed numerous restrictions on the Irish agricultural industry, retaining the majority of land for the grazing of sheep. The vast estates of British absentee landlords further contributed to Ireland's poverty.

[4] *towardly parts* Promising; exceptionally able.

[5] *probationers* Novices.

[6] *on the Exchange* At the market.

[7] *turn to account* Result in profit.

[8] *American* I.e., Native American.

[9] *fricassee or a ragout* Stews.

serve four females. That the remaining hundred thousand may at a year old be offered in sale to the persons of quality and fortune through the kingdom, always advising the mother to let them suck plentifully of the last month, so as to render them plump and fat for a good table. A child will make two dishes at an entertainment for friends, and when the family dines alone, the fore or hind quarter will make a reasonable dish, and seasoned with a little pepper or salt will be very good boiled on the fourth day, especially in winter.

I have reckoned upon a medium that a child just born will weigh twelve pounds, and in a solar year if tolerably nursed increase to twenty-eight pounds.

I grant this food will be somewhat dear,[1] and therefore very proper for landlords, who, as they have already devoured most of the parents, seem to have the best title to the children.

Infants' flesh will be in season throughout the year, but more plentiful in March, and a little before and after. For we are told by a grave author,[2] an eminent French physician, that, fish being a prolific diet,[3] there are more children born in Roman Catholic countries about nine months after Lent than at any other season; therefore, reckoning a year after Lent, the markets will be more glutted than usual because the number of popish infants is at least three to one in this kingdom, and therefore it will have one other collateral advantage by lessening the number of papists among us.

I have already computed the charge of nursing a beggar's child (in which list I reckon all cottagers,[4] labourers, and four fifths of the farmers) to be about two shillings per annum, rags included, and I believe no gentleman would repine[5] to give ten shillings for the carcass of a good fat child, which, as I have said, will make four dishes of excellent nutritive meat when he hath only some particular friend or his own family to dine with him. Thus the Esquire[6] will learn to be a good landlord and grow popular among his tenants; the mother will have eight shillings net profit and be fit for work till she produces another child.

Those who are more thrifty (as I must confess the times require) may flay the carcass, the skin of which, artificially[7] dressed, will make admirable gloves for ladies and summer boots for fine gentlemen.

As to our city of Dublin, shambles[8] may be appointed for this purpose in the most convenient parts of it, and butchers we may be assured will not be wanting, although I rather recommend buying the children alive and dressing them hot from the knife, as we do roasting pigs.

A very worthy person, a true lover of his country, and whose virtues I highly esteem, was lately pleased, in discoursing on this matter, to offer a refinement upon my scheme. He said that, many gentlemen of this kingdom having of late destroyed their deer, he conceived that the want of venison might be well supplied by the bodies of young lads and maidens, not exceeding fourteen years of age nor under twelve, so great a number of both sexes in every county being now ready to starve for want of work and service; and these to be disposed of by their parents if alive, or otherwise by their nearest relations. But with due deference to so excellent a friend and so deserving a patriot, I cannot be altogether in his sentiments; for as to the males, my American acquaintance assured me from frequent experience that their flesh was generally tough and lean, like that of our schoolboys, by continual exercise, and their taste disagreeable, and to fatten them would not answer the charge. Then as to the females, it would, I think with humble submission, be a loss to the public because they soon would become breeders themselves. And besides, it is not improbable that some scrupulous people might be apt to censure such a practice (although indeed very unjustly) as a little bordering upon cruelty, which, I confess, hath always been with me the strongest objection against any project, however well intended.

But in order to justify my friend, he confessed that this expedient was put into his head by the famous Psalmanazar,[9] a native of the island of Formosa, who

[1] *dear* Expensive.

[2] *grave author* Sixteenth-century satirist François Rabelais. See his *Gargantua and Pantagruel*.

[3] *prolific diet* Causing increased fertility.

[4] *cottagers* Country dwellers.

[5] *repine* Complain or express discontent.

[6] *Esquire* Commoner; person without any other title.

[7] *artificially* Artfully, skillfully.

[8] *shambles* Slaughterhouses.

[9] *Psalmanazar* George Psalmanazar (1679?–1763), a French adventurer who pretended to be a Formosan and published an account of Formosan customs, *Historical and Geographical Description of Formosa* (1704), which was later exposed as fraudulent. The

came from thence to London above twenty years ago, and in conversation told my friend that in his country, when any young person happened to be put to death the executioner sold the carcass to persons of quality as a prime dainty, and that in his time the body of a plump girl of fifteen, who was crucified for an attempt to poison the emperor, was sold to his Imperial Majesty's Prime Minister of State and other great Mandarins of the court, in joints from the gibbet,[1] at four hundred crowns. Neither indeed can I deny that if the same use were made of several plump young girls in this town who, without one single groat[2] to their fortunes, cannot stir abroad without a chair,[3] and appear at the playhouse and assemblies in foreign fineries which they never will pay for, the kingdom would not be the worse.

Some persons of a desponding spirit are in great concern about that vast number of poor people who are aged, diseased, or maimed, and I have been desired to employ my thoughts what course may be taken to ease the nation of so grievous an encumbrance. But I am not in the least pain upon that matter because it is very well known that they are every day dying and rotting by cold and famine, and filth and vermin, as fast as can be reasonably expected. And as to the younger labourers, they are now in almost as hopeful a condition. They cannot get work, and consequently pine away for want of nourishment to a degree that if at any time they are accidentally hired to common labour, they have not strength to perform it; and thus the country and themselves are happily delivered from the evils to come.

I have too long digressed, and therefore shall return to my subject. I think the advantages by the proposal which I have made are obvious and many, as well as of the highest importance.

For first, as I have already observed, it would greatly lessen the number of papists, with whom we are yearly overrun, being the principal breeders of the nation as well as our most dangerous enemies, and who stay at home on purpose with a design to deliver the kingdom to the Pretender, hoping to take their advantage by the absence of so many good Protestants, who have chosen rather to leave their country than stay at home and pay tithes against their conscience to an Episcopal curate.

Secondly, the poorer tenants will have something valuable of their own, which by law may be made liable to distress[4] and help to pay their landlord's rent, their corn and cattle being already seized, and money a thing unknown.

Thirdly, whereas the maintenance of an hundred thousand children from two years old and upwards cannot be computed at less than ten shillings apiece per annum, the nation's stock will be thereby increased fifty thousand pounds per annum, besides the profit of a new dish introduced to the tables of all gentlemen of fortune in the kingdom who have any refinement in taste, and the money will circulate among ourselves, the goods being entirely of our own growth and manufacture.

Fourthly, the constant breeders, besides the gain of eight shillings sterling per annum by the sale of their children, will be rid of the charge of maintaining them after the first year.

Fifthly, this food would likewise bring great customs to taverns, where the vintners will certainly be so prudent as to procure the best receipts[5] for dressing it to perfection, and consequently have their houses frequented by all the fine gentlemen who justly value themselves upon their knowledge in good eating. And a skilful cook who understands how to oblige his guests will contrive to make it as expensive as they please.

Sixthly, this would be a great inducement to marriage, which all wise nations have either encouraged by rewards or enforced by laws and penalties. It would increase the care and tenderness of mothers toward their children, when they were sure of a settlement for life to the poor babes, provided in some sort by the public, to their annual profit instead of expense. We should soon see an honest emulation[6] among the married women, which of them could bring the fattest child to market. Men would become as fond of their wives during the time of their pregnancy as they are now of their mares in

story Swift recounts here is found in the second edition of Psalmanazar's work.

[1] *gibbet* Gallows.

[2] *groat* Silver coin equal in value to four pence. It was removed from circulation in 1662, and thereafter "a groat" was used metaphorically to signify any very small sum.

[3] *chair* Sedan chair, which seated one person and was carried on poles by two men.

[4] *distress* Seizure of property for the payment of debt.

[5] *receipts* Recipes.

[6] *emulation* Rivalry.

foal, their cows in calf, or sows when they are ready to farrow, nor offer to beat or kick them (as it is too frequent a practice) for fear of a miscarriage.

Many other advantages might be enumerated: for instance, the addition of some thousand carcasses in our exportation of barreled beef; the propagation of swine's flesh and improvement in the art of making good bacon, so much wanted among us by the great destruction of pigs, too frequent at our tables, which are no way comparable in taste or magnificence to a well-grown, fat yearling child, which, roasted whole, will make a considerable figure at a Lord Mayor's feast or any other public entertainment. But this and many others I omit, being studious of brevity.

Supposing that one thousand families in this city would be constant customers for infants' flesh, besides others who might have it at merry-meetings, particularly weddings and christenings, I compute that Dublin would take off annually about twenty thousand carcasses, and the rest of the kingdom (where probably they will be sold somewhat cheaper) the remaining eighty thousand.

I can think of no one objection that will possibly be raised against this proposal, unless it should be urged that the number of people will be thereby much lessened in the kingdom. This I freely own, and it was indeed one principal design in offering it to the world. I desire the reader will observe that I calculate my remedy for this one individual kingdom of Ireland, and for no other that ever was, is, or, I think, ever can be upon earth. Therefore let no man talk to me of other expedients:[1] of taxing our absentees at five shillings a pound; of using neither clothes nor household furniture, except what is of our own growth and manufacture; of utterly rejecting the materials and instruments that promote foreign luxury; of curing the expensiveness of pride, vanity, idleness, and gaming[2] in our women; of introducing a vein of parsimony, prudence, and temperance; of learning to love our country, wherein we differ even from Laplanders and the inhabitants of Topinamboo;[3] of quitting our animosities and factions, nor act any longer like the Jews, who were murdering one another at the very moment their city was taken;[4] of being a little cautious not to sell our country and consciences for nothing; of teaching landlords to have at least one degree of mercy toward their tenants; lastly, of putting a spirit of honesty, industry, and skill into our shopkeepers, who, if a resolution could now be taken to buy only our native goods, would immediately unite to cheat and exact upon us in the price, the measure, and the goodness, nor could ever yet be brought to make one fair proposal of just dealing, though often in earnest invited to it.

Therefore I repeat, let no man talk to me of these and the like expedients till he hath at least some glimpse of hope that there will ever be some hearty and sincere attempt to put them in practice.

But as to myself, having been wearied out for many years with offering vain, idle, visionary thoughts, and at length utterly despairing of success, I fortunately fell upon this proposal, which, as it is wholly new, so it hath something solid and real, of no expense and little trouble, full in our own power, and whereby we can incur no danger in disobliging England. For this kind of commodity will not bear exportation, the flesh being of too tender a consistence to admit a long continuance in salt, although perhaps I could name a country[5] which would be glad to eat up our whole nation without it.

After all, I am not so violently bent upon my own opinion as to reject any offer, proposed by wise men, which shall be found equally innocent, cheap, easy, and effectual. But before something of that kind shall be advanced in contradiction to my scheme, and offering a better, I desire the author or authors will be pleased maturely to consider two points.

First, as things now stand, how they will be able to find food and raiment for one hundred thousand useless mouths and backs.

And secondly, there being a round million of creatures in human figure throughout this kingdom whose whole subsistence, put into a common stock,

[1] *other expedients* All of which Swift had already proposed in earnest attempts to remedy Ireland's poverty. See, for example, his *Proposal for the Universal Use of Irish Manufactures*. In early editions the following proposals were italicized to show the suspension of Swift's ironic tone.

[2] *gaming* Gambling.

[3] *Topinamboo* District in Brazil.

[4] *Jews … was taken* According to the history of Flavius Joseph, Roman Emperor Titus's invasion and capture of Jerusalem in 70 BCE was aided by the fact that factional fighting had divided the city.

[5] *a country* I.e., England.

would leave them in debt two million of pounds sterling, adding those who are beggars by profession to the bulk of farmers, cottagers, and labourers with their wives and children, who are beggars in effect.

I desire those politicians who dislike my overture, and may perhaps be so bold to attempt an answer, that they will first ask the parents of these mortals whether they would not at this day think it a great happiness to have been sold for food at a year old in the manner I prescribe, and thereby have avoided such a perpetual scene of misfortunes as they have since gone through by the oppression of landlords, the impossibility of paying rent without money or trade, the want of common sustenance, with neither house nor clothes to cover them from the inclemencies of the weather, and the most inevitable prospect of entailing[1] the like or greater miseries upon their breed forever.

I profess in the sincerity of my heart that I have not the least personal interest in endeavoring to promote this necessary work, having no other motive than the public good of my country by advancing our trade, providing for infants, relieving the poor, and giving some pleasure to the rich. I have no children by which I can propose to get a single penny, the youngest being nine years old, and my wife past childbearing.

—1729

In Context

Sermons and Tracts: Backgrounds to *A Modest Proposal*

Before adopting a bitingly satirical approach toward the oppression of Ireland in *A Modest Proposal*, Swift wrote several sermons and tracts on the subject; two of these are excerpted below.

from Jonathan Swift, "Causes of the Wretched Condition of Ireland" (1726)

It is a very melancholy reflection, that such a country as ours, which is capable of producing all things necessary, and most things convenient for life, sufficient for the support of four times the number of its inhabitants, should yet lie under the heaviest load of misery and want, our streets crowded with beggars, so many of our lower sort of tradesmen, labourers, and artificers, not able to find clothes and food for their families.

I think it may therefore be of some use to lay before you the chief causes of this wretched condition we are in, and then it will be easier to assign what remedies are in our power towards removing, at least, some part of these evils.

For it is ever to be lamented, that we lie under many disadvantages, not by our own faults, which are peculiar to ourselves, and which no other nation under heaven hath any reason to complain of.

I shall, therefore, first mention some causes of our miseries, which I doubt are not to be remedied, until God shall put it in the hearts of those who are the stronger, to allow us the common rights and privileges of brethren, fellow subjects, and even of mankind.

The first cause of our misery is the intolerable hardships we lie under in every branch of our trade, by which we are become as *hewers of wood, and drawers of water*[2] to our rigorous neighbours.

The second cause of our miserable state is the folly, the vanity, and ingratitude of those vast numbers, who think themselves too good to live in the country which gave them birth, and still gives them bread, and rather choose to pass their days, and consume their wealth, and draw out the very vitals of their mother kingdom, among those who heartily despise them.

[1] *entailing* Bestowing, conferring.

[2] *hewers … water* Those who perform menial tasks (from Joshua 9.21).

These I have but lightly touched on, because I fear they are not to be redressed, and, besides, I am very sensible how ready some people are to take offence at the honest truth; and, for that reason, I shall omit several other grievances, under which we are long likely to groan.

I shall therefore go on to relate some other causes of this nation's poverty, by which, if they continue much longer, it must infallibly sink to utter ruin.

The first is that monstrous pride and vanity in both sexes, especially the weaker sex, who, in the midst of poverty, are suffered to run into all kind of expense and extravagance in dress, and particularly priding themselves to wear nothing but what cometh from abroad, disdaining the growth or manufacture of their own country, in those articles where they can be better served at home with half the expense; and this is grown to such a height, that they will carry the whole yearly rent of a good estate at once on their body. And, as there is in that sex a spirit of envy, by which they cannot endure to see others in a better habit than themselves, so those, whose fortunes can hardly support their families in the necessaries of life, will needs vie with the richest and greatest amongst us, to the ruin of themselves and their posterity.

Neither are the men less guilty of this pernicious folly, who, in imitation of a gaudiness and foppery of dress, introduced of late years into our neighbouring kingdom, (as fools are apt to imitate only the defects of their betters) cannot find materials in their own country worthy to adorn their bodies of clay, while their minds are naked of every valuable quality.

Thus our tradesmen and shopkeepers, who deal in home-goods, are left in a starving condition, and only those encouraged who ruin the kingdom by importing among us foreign vanities.

Another cause of our low condition is our great luxury, the chief support of which is the materials of it brought to the nation in exchange for the few valuable things left us, whereby so many thousand families want the very necessaries of life.

Thirdly, in most parts of this kingdom the natives are from their infancy so given up to idleness and sloth, that they often choose to beg or steal, rather than support themselves with their own labour; they marry without the least view or thought of being able to make any provision for their families; and whereas, in all industrious nations, children are looked on as a help to their parents, with us, for want of being early trained to work, they are an intolerable burthen at home, and a grievous charge upon the public, as appeareth from the vast number of ragged and naked children in town and country, led about by strolling women, trained up in ignorance and all manner of vice.

Lastly, a great cause of this nation's misery, is that Egyptian bondage of cruel, oppressing, covetous landlords, expecting that all who live under them should *make bricks without straw*,[1] who grieve and envy when they see a tenant of their own in a whole coat, or able to afford one comfortable meal in a month, by which the spirits of the people are broken, and made for slavery; the farmers and cottagers, almost through the whole kingdom, being to all intents and purposes as real beggars, as any of those to whom we give our charity in the streets. And these cruel landlords are every day unpeopling their kingdom, by forbidding their miserable tenants to till the earth, against common reason and justice, and contrary to the practice and prudence of all other nations, by which numberless families have been forced either to leave the kingdom, or stroll about, and increase the number of our thieves and beggars.

[1] *Egyptian bondage … bricks without straw* From Exodus 5.5–7, recalling the burdens laid upon the Israelites by the Pharaoh of Egypt.

from Jonathan Swift, *A Short View of the State of Ireland* (1727)

I am assured that it hath, for some time, been practised as a method of making men's court, when they are asked about the rate of lands, the abilities of tenants, the state of trade and manufacture in this kingdom, and how their rents are paid, to answer that in their neighbourhood, all things are in a flourishing condition, the rent and purchase of land every day increasing. And if a gentleman happens to be a little more sincere in his representations, besides being looked on as not well affected, he is sure to have a dozen contradictors at his elbow. I think it is no manner of secret why these questions are so *cordially* asked, or so *obligingly* answered.

But since, with regard to the affairs of this kingdom, I have been using all endeavours to subdue my indignation, to which, indeed, I am not provoked by any personal interest, being not the owner of one spot of ground in the whole island; I shall only enumerate by rules generally known, and never contradicted, what are the true causes of any countries flourishing and growing rich, and then examine what effects arise from those causes in the kingdom of Ireland.

The first cause of a kingdom's thriving, is the fruitfulness of the soil, to produce the necessaries and conveniences of life, not only sufficient for the inhabitants, but for exportation into other countries.

The second, is the industry of the people, in working up all their native commodities, to the last degree of manufacture.

The third, is the conveniency of safe ports and havens, to carry out their own goods, as much manufactured, and bring in those of others, as little manufactured, as the nature of mutual commerce will allow.

The fourth is, that the natives should, as much as possible, export and import their goods in vessels of their own timber, made in their own country.

The fifth, is the privilege of a free trade in all foreign countries which will permit them, except to those who are in war with their own prince or state.

The sixth, is, by being governed only by laws made with their own consent, for otherwise they are not a free people. And therefore, all appeals for justice, or applications for favour or preferment, to another country, are so many grievous impoverishments.

The seventh is, by improvement of land, encouragement of agriculture, and thereby increasing the number of their people, without which, any country, however blessed by nature, must continue poor.

The eighth, is the residence of the prince, or chief administrator of the civil power.

The ninth, is the concourse of foreigners for education, curiosity, or pleasure, or as to a general mart of trade.

The tenth, is by disposing all offices of honour, profit, or trust, only to the natives, or at least with very few exceptions, where strangers have long inhabited the country, and are supposed to understand, and regard the interest of it as their own.

The eleventh, is when the rents of lands, and profits of employments, are spent in the country which produced them, and not in another, the former of which will certainly happen, where the love of our native country prevails.

The twelfth, is by the public revenues being all spent and employed at home, except on the occasions of a foreign war.

The thirteenth is, where the people are not obliged, unless they find it for their own interest or conveniency, to receive any monies, except of their own coinage by a public mint, after the manner of all civilized nations.

The fourteenth, is a disposition of the people of a country to wear their own manufactures, and import as few incitements to luxury, either in clothes, furniture, food, or drink, as they possibly can live conveniently without.

There are many other causes of a nation's thriving, which I cannot at present recollect, but without advantage from at least some of these, after turning my thoughts a long time, I am not able to discover from whence our wealth proceeds, and therefore would gladly be better informed. In the meantime, I will here examine what share falls to Ireland of these causes, or of the effects and consequences.

It is not my intention to complain, but barely to relate facts; and the matter is not of small importance. For it is allowed, that a man who lives in a solitary house, far from help, is not wise in endeavouring to acquire, in the neighbourhood, the reputation of being rich, because those who come for gold, will go off with pewter and brass, rather than return empty. And in the common practice of the world, those who possess most wealth, make the least parade, which they leave to others, who have nothing else to bear them out, in showing their faces on the exchange.

As to the first cause of a nation's riches, being the fertility of the soil, as well as temperature of climate, we have no reason to complain, for, although the quantity of unprofitable land in this kingdom, reckoning bog, and rock, and barren mountain, be double in proportion to what it is in England; yet the native productions which both kingdoms deal in, are very near on equality in point of goodness, and might, with the same encouragement, be as well manufactured. I except mines and minerals, in some of which, however, we are only defective in point of skill and industry.

In the second, which is the industry of the people, our misfortune is not altogether owing to our own fault, but to a million of discouragements.

The conveniency of ports and havens, which nature hath bestowed so liberally on this kingdom, is of no more use to us, than a beautiful prospect to a man shut up in a dungeon.

As to shipping of its own, Ireland is so utterly unprovided, that of all the excellent timber cut down within these fifty or sixty years, it can hardly be said, that the nation hath received the benefit of one valuable house to dwell in, or one ship to trade with.

Ireland is the only kingdom I ever heard or read of, either in ancient or modern story, which was denied the liberty of exporting their native commodities and manufactures, wherever they pleased, except to countries at war with their own prince or state. Yet this privilege, by the superiority of mere power, is refused us, in the most momentous parts of commerce, besides an act of navigation, to which we never consented, pinned down upon us, and rigorously executed, and a thousand other unexampled circumstances, as grievous, as they are invidious to mention. To go on to the rest.

It is too well known, that we are forced to obey some laws we never consented to, which is a condition I must not call by its true uncontroverted name, for fear of Lord Chief Justice Whitshed's[1] ghost, with his *Libertas & natale Solum*,[2] written as a motto on his coach, as it stood at the door of the court, while he was perjuring himself to betray both. Thus, we are in the condition of patients, who have physic[3] sent them by doctors at a distance, strangers to their constitution and the nature of their disease. And thus, we are forced to pay five hundred percent, to decide our properties, in all which, we have likewise the honour to be distinguished from the whole race of mankind.

As to improvement of land, those few who attempt that, or planting, through covetousness, or want of skill, generally leave things worse than they were, neither succeeding in trees nor hedges, and by running into the fancy of grazing, after the manner of the Scythians,[4] are every day depopulating the country.

---

[1] *Lord Chief Justice Whitshed* William Whitshed (1671–1727), outspoken judge (who died the year this tract was written) at the trial of the printer of Swift's *Drapier's Letters*, a pamphlet urging the Irish to wear only clothing manufactured in Ireland. Whitshed urged the grand jury to indict the printer, but the members refused to do so.

[2] *Libertas & natale Solum* Latin: Liberty and my native country.

[3] *physic* Medicine.

[4] *Scythians* Ancient nomadic people of Eurasia whose principal trade was grain.

We are so far from having a king to reside among us, that even the viceroy[1] is generally absent four-fifths of his time in the government.

No strangers from other countries make this a part of their travels, where they can expect to see nothing but scenes of misery and desolation.

Those who have the misfortune to be born here, have the least title to any considerable employment, to which they are seldom preferred, but upon a political consideration.

One third part of the rents of Ireland is spent in England, which, with the profit of employments, pensions, appeals, journeys of pleasure or health, education at the Inns of Court,[2] and both universities, remittances at pleasure, the pay of all superior officers in the army, and other incidents, will amount to a full half of the income of the whole kingdom, all clear profit to England.

We are denied the liberty of coining gold, silver, or even copper. In the Isle of Man,[3] they coin their own silver; every petty prince, vassal to the emperor, can coin what money he pleaseth. And in this, as in most of the articles already mentioned, we are an exception to all other states or monarchies that were ever known in the world.

As to the last, or fourteenth article, we take special care to act diametrically contrary to it in the whole course of our lives. Both sexes, but especially the women, despise and abhor to wear any of their own manufactures, even those which are better made than in other countries, particularly a sort of silk plaid, through which the workmen are forced to run a sort of gold thread that it may pass for Indian. Even ale and potatoes are imported from England, as well as corn. And our foreign trade is little more than importation of French wine, for which I am told we pay ready money.

Now, if all this be true, upon which I could easily enlarge, I would be glad to know by what secret method it is, that we grow a rich and flourishing people, without *Liberty*, *Trade*, *Manufactures*, *Inhabitants*, *Money*, or the *Privilege of Coining*, without *Industry*, *Labour*, or *Improvement of Lands*, and with more than half the rent and profits of the whole kingdom annually exported, for which we receive not a single farthing.

---

1 *viceroy* Governor.

2 *Inns of Court* Buildings in London where people are educated in the law and admitted to the bar.

3 *Isle of Man* Island off the shore of Great Britain in the Irish Sea.

Joseph Addison

1672 – 1719

Joseph Addison was born in Wiltshire to Anglican clergyman Lancelot and Jane Addison in 1672. A lifelong Whig whose commitment to state service directly influenced his literary endeavors, Addison was an unabashedly didactic writer; his poems, plays, and pamphlets champion the Whig cause with varying degrees of subtlety, their tone ranging from gentle humor to outright propaganda. Not surprisingly, his publications earned him government favor; *The Campaign* (1704), his timely poem celebrating the Duke of Marlborough's victory over the French at Blenheim, for example, ensured his appointment as a Commissioner of Appeal in Excise. Although his literary reputation has declined somewhat in the past century, Addison is still regarded as an important figure in the history of English prose, and is remembered in particular for his journalistic partnership with Richard Steele. Displaying a mastery of what Samuel Johnson labeled "an English style, familiar but not coarse, and elegant but not ostentatious," the graceful and fluid style of Addison's essays is still upheld as a model of writing excellence.

Addison met Richard Steele in 1686 at London's Charterhouse School. The following year, Addison entered Queen's College, Oxford; he later moved to Magdalen College at the same university, where he took his B.A. in 1691 and his M.A. in 1693. Noted for his proficiency in Latin verse and his interest in science during his university years, Addison also published several English poems dedicated to prominent Whigs. He was awarded a fellowship at Magdalen in 1698, and soon after received a grant to travel in Europe in preparation for civil service. His grant ended with King William's death in 1702, and Addison returned to England soon after. He later fashioned his continental experiences into a travel book entitled *Remarks upon Several Parts of Italy* (1705).

Addison soon became involved in London literary and political circles. He joined the Kit-Kat Club, a group of Whig writers (then the official opposition) and supporters whose members included Steele, Jonathan Swift, and William Congreve, and tried his hand at various forms of writing. Addison made several attempts to write for the stage, although only one of his plays, *Cato* (1713), was a commercial success.

Addison's first foray into elected politics was short-lived; he won the seat of Lostwithiel in Cornwall in 1708, but lost it after only a year. His next attempt was more successful: he served as Member of Parliament for Malmesbury from 1710 until his death in 1719. Late in 1708, Addison was appointed to act as secretary to Lord Wharton, Lord Lieutenant of Ireland—an alliance that would lead to roles as Irish Privy Councillor and Keeper of Records in Dublin Castle. When the Whig government was defeated in 1710, Addison's income was drastically reduced, but he again benefitted from his staunch support of the Whig cause after the government was re-established in 1715 under the new monarch, George I: he served as Chief Secretary for Ireland in 1715, Commissioner of Trade in 1716, and Secretary of State in 1717.

The first significant Addison-Steele collaboration was Steele's hugely popular *The Tatler*, a thrice-weekly paper launched by Steele, who hoped that the journal's articles would have the effect of reforming public manners and morals. Ostensibly edited and authored by the fictional Isaac Bickerstaff, a character created by Swift, the paper appeared from April 1709 to January 1711. *The Tatler* published reports from various fashionable clubs and coffee houses around London: White's Chocolate House handled entertainment, Will's Coffee House dealt with poetry, the Grecian Club tackled education, and St. James's Coffee House covered foreign and domestic news. Addison contributed—either solely or in collaboration with others—to approximately twenty percent of *The Tatler*'s 271 issues; his main interests were generally confined to the classics, religion, and citizenship, while Steele concentrated on the theater, politics, and manners.

The Spectator was launched in March 1711, only a few months after the final *Tatler* issue. Published six days a week, *The Spectator* employed a fictional writer-editor (called simply Mr. Spectator) who reported on the news of the day overheard in polite society. Addison was considerably more involved with *The Spectator* than he had been with *The Tatler,* writing approximately half of the 555 issues. Addison and Steele relied on a variety of innovative literary devices to meet the demand for interesting material, including introducing a hugely popular club of fictional characters who offered different points of view to the journal's readers. Along with social criticism, *The Spectator* tackled philosophy and science, and Addison wrote essays on literary topics such as Milton's *Paradise Lost*, the nature of tragedy, and the pleasures of the imagination. *The Spectator* initially ceased publication in December 1712, but Addison revived it between June and December 1714 with a second series consisting of 80 issues.

Addison's final significant collaboration with Steele was *The Guardian*, of which 175 issues were published between March and October 1713. Like *The Tatler* and *The Spectator*, *The Guardian* utilized a fictional writer-editor (this time called Nestor Ironside) who reported on the conversations and activities of his relatives, the Lizard family. Sadly, Addison's friendship with Steele began to deteriorate late in 1713 by divisions within the Whig party; a few years later, the two men were drawn into a bitter dispute concerning political measures under the new monarch, and their relationship was effectively severed. Addison's personal circumstances underwent a significant change relatively late in life; in 1716, he married Charlotte, Countess of Warwick, who bore him a daughter, Charlotte, in January 1719. Addison did not live to see his child's first birthday; he died in June 1719, and was buried in Westminster Abbey. A collected edition of his works was published two years later in 1721.

⌘⌘⌘

from *The Spectator*

No. 285,[1] Saturday, 26 January 1712
[On the Language of *Paradise Lost*]

Ne quicunque Deus, quicunque adhibebitur heros,
Regali conspectus in auro nuper & ostro,
Migret in Obscuras humili sermone tabernas:
Aut dum vitat humum, nubes & inania captet.[2]

Horace

Having already treated of the fable, the characters, and sentiments in the *Paradise Lost*, we are in the last place to consider the language; and as the learned world is very much divided upon Milton as to this point, I hope they will excuse me if I appear particular in any of my opinions, and incline to those who judge the most advantageously of the author.

[1] *No. 285* Addison's 18 essays on Milton's *Paradise Lost* appeared in the *Spectator*'s Saturday issues starting on 5 January 1712 and ending on 3 May 1712. This essay is the fourth in the series.

[2] *Ne ... captet* Latin: from Horace's *Ars Poetica*: "That none who shall be exhibited as a god, none who is introduced as a hero lately conspicuous in regal purple and gold, may deviate into the low style of obscure, mechanical shops; or, ... while he avoids the ground, affect cloudy mist and empty jargon" (227–30); *Horace* Quintus Horatius Flaccus (65–8 BCE), Roman poet, author of *Ars Poetica*, an epistle on the art of poetry that greatly influenced Western poets.

It is requisite that the language of an heroic poem should be both perspicuous[1] and sublime.[2] In proportion as either of these two qualities are wanting, the language is imperfect. Perspicuity is the first and most necessary qualification; insomuch, that a good-natured reader sometimes overlooks a little slip even in the grammar or syntax[3] where it is impossible for him to mistake the poet's sense. Of this kind is that passage in Milton, wherein he speaks of Satan.

... God and his Son except,
Created thing nought valu'd he nor shunn'd.[4]

And that in which he describes Adam and Eve.

Adam the goodliest man of men since born
His Sons, the fairest of her Daughters *Eve*.[5]

It is plain, that in the former of these passages, according to the natural syntax, the divine persons mentioned in the first line are represented as created beings; and that in the other, Adam and Eve are confounded with their sons and daughters. Such little blemishes as these, when the thought is great and natural, we should, with Horace, impute[6] to a pardonable inadvertency,[7] or to the weakness of human nature, which cannot attend to each minute particular, and give the last finishing to every circumstance in so long a work. The ancient critics therefore, who were acted[8] by a spirit of candour, rather than that of cavilling,[9] invented certain figures of speech on purpose to palliate[10] little errors of this nature in the writings of those authors, who had so many greater beauties to atone for them.

If clearness and perspicuity were only to be consulted, the poet would have nothing else to do but to clothe his thoughts in the most plain and natural expressions. But, since it often happens, that the most obvious phrases, and those which are used in ordinary conversation, become too familiar to the ear, and contract a kind of meanness[11] by passing through the mouths of the vulgar,[12] a poet should take particular care to guard himself against idiomatic ways of speaking. Ovid and Lucan[13] have many poornesses of expression upon this account, as taking up with the first phrases that offered, without putting themselves to the trouble of looking after such as would not only be natural, but also elevated and sublime. Milton has but a few failings in this kind, of which, however, you may meet with some instances, as in the following passages.

Embryos, and Idiots, Eremites and Friars
White, Black and Grey, with all their trumpery.
Here Pilgrims roam ...[14]
... A while discourse they hold;
No fear lest Dinner cool; when thus began
Our Author ...[15]
Who of all Ages to succeed, but feeling
The evil on him brought by me, will curse
My Head; Ill fare our Ancestor impure,
For this we may thank *Adam* ...[16]

The great masters in composition know very well that many an elegant phrase becomes improper for a poet or an orator when it has been debased by common use. For this reason the works of ancient authors, which are written in dead languages, have a great advantage over those which are written in languages that are now spoken. Were there any mean phrases or idioms in

[1] *perspicuous* Easily understood.

[2] *It is requisite ... sublime* Reference to Aristotle's *Poetics* Chapter 22.

[3] *syntax* Arrangement of words by which a sentence's meaning is established.

[4] *God ... shunn'd* From *Paradise Lost* 2.678–79.

[5] *Adam ... Eve* From *Paradise Lost* 4.323–24.

[6] *impute* Consider to be caused by.

[7] *Such ... inadvertency* Reference to Horace's *Ars Poetica* 351–53.

[8] *acted* I.e., motivated, inspired.

[9] *cavilling* Petty fault-finding.

[10] *palliate* Excuse.

[11] *meanness* Vulgarity.

[12] *vulgar* Common people.

[13] *Ovid* Latin poet (43 BCE–18 CE), author of *Amores*, *Ars Amatoria*, and *Metamorphoses*, a compendium of classical myths in verse; *Lucan* Latin poet (39–65 CE), author of *Bellum Civile*, an epic that recounts the civil war between Caesar and Pompey.

[14] *Embryos ... roam* From *Paradise Lost* 3.474–76.

[15] *A while ... Author* From *Paradise Lost* 5.395–97.

[16] *Who ... Adam* From *Paradise Lost* 10.733–36.

Virgil and Homer,[1] they would not shock the ear of the most delicate modern reader, so much as they would have done that of an old Greek or Roman, because we never hear them pronounced in our streets or in ordinary conversation.

It is not therefore sufficient that the language of an epic poem be perspicuous, unless it be also sublime. To this end it ought to deviate from the common forms and ordinary phrases of speech. The judgment of a poet very much discovers itself in shunning the common roads of expression without falling into such ways of speech as may seem stiff and unnatural; he must not swell into a false sublime by endeavouring to avoid the other extreme. Among the Greeks, Aeschylus, and sometimes Sophocles,[2] were guilty of this fault; among the Latins, Claudian and Statius;[3] and among our own countrymen, Shakespeare and Lee.[4] In these authors the affectation of greatness often hurts the perspicuity of the style, as in many others the endeavour after perspicuity prejudices its greatness.

Aristotle[5] has observed that the idiomatic style may be avoided, and the sublime formed, by the following methods.[6] First, by the use of metaphors: such are those in Milton.

Imparadis'd in one another's arms,[7]
... and in his hand a Reed
Stood waving tipt with fire; ...[8]
The grassy Clods now Calv'd ...[9]
Spangl'd with eyes ...[10]

In these and innumerable other instances, the metaphors are very bold but just; I must however observe that the metaphors are not thick sown in Milton, which always savours too much of wit; that they never clash with one another, which as Aristotle observes, turns a sentence into a kind of an enigma or riddle;[11] and that he seldom has recourse to them where the proper and natural words will do as well.

Another way of raising the language, and giving it a poetical turn, is to make use of the idioms of other tongues.[12] Virgil is full of the Greek forms of speech, which the critics call hellenisms, as Horace in his Odes abounds with them much more than Virgil. I need not mention the several dialects which Homer has made use of for this end. Milton, in conformity with the practice of the ancient poets, and with Aristotle's rule, has infused a great many latinisms, as well as graecisms, and sometimes hebraisms,[13] into the language of his poem, as towards the beginning of it.

Nor did they not perceive the evil plight
In which they were, or the fierce pains not feel;
Yet to their General's Voice they soon obey'd ...[14]
... who shall tempt with wand'ring feet
The dark unbottom'd infinite Abyss
And through the palpable obscure find out
His uncouth way, or spread his aery flight
Upborne with indefatigable wings
Over the vast abrupt ...[15]

---

[1] *Virgil* Roman poet (70–19 BCE), author of *The Aeneid*, an epic detailing the life of Aeneas, who embodied the Roman virtues, and *The Georgics*, poems recounting the joy of rural and farming life; *Homer* Greek poet (c. 700 BCE), putative author of *The Iliad*, an account of the Greeks' war with the Trojans, and *The Odyssey*, Odysseus's journey home after the war's end.

[2] *Aeschylus* Greek dramatist (525–456 BCE), author of approximately 80 plays including *Prometheus Bound* and *The Oresteia*; *Sophocles* Greek dramatist and politician (c. 496–406 BCE), author of such tragedies as *Oedipus Tyrannus, Electra,* and *Antigone.*

[3] *Claudian* Latin poet (c. 370–404 CE), author of several epics including *Rape of Proserpine*; *Statius* Latin poet (c. 45–96 CE), favorite of the Emperor Domitian, author of a collection of poems entitled *Silvae* and several epics.

[4] *Lee* Nathaniel Lee (c. 1653–92), English playwright and actor, author of such verse plays as *Sophonisba* and *Nero*, as well as the blank verse tragedy *The Rival Queens.*

[5] *Aristotle* Greek philosopher and student of Plato (384–322 BCE), founder of a school and library in Athens in 335 BCE, tutor to Alexander the Great, and author of such influential philosophical works as *De Anima, De Poetica, Rhetoric,* and *Physics.*

[6] *Aristotle ... methods* Reference to Aristotle's *Poetics* Chapter 22.

[7] *Imparadis'd ... arms* From *Paradise Lost* 4.506.

[8] *and ... fire* From *Paradise Lost* 6.579–80.

[9] *The ... Calv'd* From *Paradise Lost* 7.463.

[10] *Spangl'd ... eyes* From *Paradise Lost* 11.130.

[11] *enigma or riddle* Reference to Aristotle's *Poetics* Chapter 22.

[12] *idioms ... tongues* Reference to Aristotle's *Poetics* Chapter 22.

[13] *graecisms ... hebraisms* Features or qualities of the Greek or Hebrew language employed in other languages.

[14] *Nor ... obey'd* From *Paradise Lost* 1.335–37.

[15] *who ... abrupt* From *Paradise Lost* 2.404–09.

... So both ascend
In the Visions of God ...[1]

Under this head may be reckoned the placing the adjective after the substantive,[2] the transposition of words, the turning the adjective into a substantive, with several other foreign modes of speech, which this poet has naturalized to give his verse the greater sound, and throw it out of prose.

The third method mentioned by Aristotle, is what agrees with the genius of the Greek language more than with that of any other tongue, and is therefore more used by Homer than by any other poet. I mean the lengthening of a phrase by the addition of words, which may either be inserted or omitted, as also by the extending or contracting of particular words by the insertion or omission of certain syllables.[3] Milton has put in practice this method of raising his language, as far as the nature of our tongue will permit, as in the passage abovementioned, eremite, for what is hermit, in common discourse. If you observe the measure of his verse, he has with great judgment suppressed a syllable in several words, and shortened those of two syllables into one, by which method, besides the abovementioned advantage, he has given a greater variety to his numbers. But this practice is more particularly remarkable in the names of persons and of countries, as Beelzebub, Hessebon, and in many other particulars, wherein he has either changed the name, or made use of that which is not the most commonly known, that he might the better depart from the language of the vulgar.

The same reason recommended to him several old words, which also makes his poem appear the more venerable,[4] and gives it a greater air of antiquity.

I must likewise take notice that there are in Milton several words of his own coining, as Cerberean, miscreated, Hell-doom'd, embryon Atoms,[5] and many others. If the reader is offended at this liberty in our English poet, I would recommend him to a discourse in Plutarch,[6] which shows us how frequently Homer has made use of the same liberty.

Milton, by the above-mentioned helps, and by the choice of the noblest words and phrases which our tongue would afford him, has carried our language to a greater height than any of the English poets have ever done before or after him, and made the sublimity of his style equal to that of his sentiments.

I have been the more particular in these observations on Milton's style because it is that part of him in which he appears the most singular. The remarks I have here made upon the practice of other poets, with my observations out of Aristotle, will perhaps alleviate the prejudice which some have taken to his poem upon this account; though after all, I must confess, that I think his style, though admirable in general, is in some places too much stiffened and obscured by the frequent use of those methods, which Aristotle has prescribed for the raising of it.

This redundancy of those several ways of speech which Aristotle calls foreign language, and with which Milton has so very much enriched, and in some places darkened the language of his poem, was the more proper for his use because his poem is written in blank verse. Rhyme, without any other assistance, throws the language off from prose, and very often makes an indifferent phrase pass unregarded; but where the verse is not built upon rhymes, there pomp of sound and energy of expression are indispensably necessary to support the style and keep it from falling into the flatness of prose.

Those who have not a taste for this elevation of style, and are apt to ridicule a poet when he goes out of the common forms of expression, would do well to see how Aristotle has treated an ancient author, called Euclid,[7] for his insipid mirth upon this occasion. Mr. Dryden used to call this sort of men his prose-critics.

I should, under this head of the language, consider Milton's numbers,[8] in which he has made use of several elisions[9] that are not customary among other English

[1] *So ... God* From *Paradise Lost* 11.376–77.

[2] *substantive* Noun.

[3] *The third ... syllables* Reference to Aristotle's *Poetics*, Chapter 22.

[4] *venerable* Older.

[5] *Cerberean ... embryon Atoms* From *Paradise Lost* 2.655, 683, 697, and 900; Addison is not correct about Milton's coining "miscreated;" the word appears in Spenser's *The Faerie Queene*, I.ii.3.1.

[6] *Plutarch* Greek biographer (46–120 CE), author of *The Parallel Lives*, a collection of paired biographies of prominent Greeks and Romans; *The Life and Poetry of Homer* was wrongly attributed to Plutarch.

[7] *Euclid* Greek mathematician (c. 300 BCE), author of *Elements of Geometry*; Addison refers to *Ars Poetica* Chapter 22.

[8] *numbers* Meter.

[9] *elisions* Alterations in pronunciation by suppressing some syllables or letters.

poets, as may be particularly observed in his cutting off the letter Y when it precedes a vowel.[1] This, and some other innovations in the measure[2] of his verse, has varied his numbers in such a manner as makes them incapable of satiating the ear and cloying[3] the reader; which the same uniform measure would certainly have done, and which the perpetual returns of rhyme never fail to do in long narrative poems. I shall close these reflections upon the language of *Paradise Lost* with observing that Milton has copied after Homer, rather than Virgil, in the length of his periods,[4] the copiousness of his phrases, and the running of his verses into one another.

No. 414, Wednesday, 25 June 1712
[Nature, Art, Gardens]

... Alterius sic
Altera poscit opem res et conjurat amice.[5]
Horace

If we consider the works of *nature* and *art,* as they are qualified to entertain the imagination, we shall find the last very defective, in comparison of the former; for though they may sometimes appear as beautiful or strange, they can have nothing in them of that vastness and immensity which afford so great an entertainment to the mind of the beholder. The one may be as polite and delicate as the other, but can never show herself so august and magnificent in the design. There is something more bold and masterly in the rough careless strokes of nature than in the nice touches and embellishments of art. The beauties of the most stately garden or palace lie in a narrow compass;[6] the imagination immediately runs them over and requires something else to gratify her; but, in the wide fields of nature, the sight wanders up and down without confinement, and is fed with an infinite variety of images, without any certain stint or number. For this reason we always find the poet in love with a country life, where nature appears in the greatest perfection and furnishes out all those scenes that are most apt to delight the imagination.

Scriptorum chorus omnis amat nemus et fugit urbes.[7]
Horace

Hic secura quies, et nescia fallere vita,
Dives opum variarum; hic latis otia fundis,
Speluncae, vivique lacus, hic frigida tempe,
Mugitusque boum, mollesque sub arbore somni.[8]
Virgil

But though there are several of these wild scenes that are more delightful than any artificial shows, yet we find the works of nature still more pleasant the more they resemble those of art. For in this case our pleasure arises from a double principle: from the agreeableness of the objects to the eye and from their similitude to other objects; we are pleased as well with comparing their beauties as with surveying them, and can represent them to our minds either as copies or originals. Hence it is that we take delight in a prospect[9] which is well laid out and diversified with fields and meadows, woods and rivers, in those accidental landscapes of trees, clouds and cities that are sometimes found in the veins of marble, in the curious fret-work[10] of rocks and grottos, and, in a word, in anything that hath such a variety or regularity as may seem the effect of design, in what we call the works of chance.

If the products of nature rise in value, according as they more or less resemble those of art, we may be sure that artificial works receive a greater advantage from their resemblance of such as are natural; because here the similitude is not only pleasant, but the pattern more perfect. The prettiest landscape I ever saw was one

1 *cutting ... vowel* In fact, Milton rarely omits the letter "y" at the end of a word, though he often omits vowels in this way (e.g. "th'shame;" "T'whom;" "th'attempt;" "th' advent'rous bands").

2 *measure* Rhythm.

3 *cloying* Sickening through excess.

4 *periods* Complete sentences.

5 *Alterius ... amice* Latin: from Horace's *Ars Poetica*, "So much does the one require the assistance of the other, and so amicably do they conspire" (410–11).

6 *compass* Boundary, enclosed limits of space.

7 *Scriptorum ... urbes* Latin: from Horace's *Epistles*, "The whole poetic chorus loves the groves and flees the city" (2.2.77).

8 *Hic ... somni* Latin: from Virgil's *Georgics*, "Unvex'd with Quarrels, undisturb'd with Noise, / The Country King his peaceful Realm enjoys: / Cool Grots, and living Lakes, the Flow'ry Pride / Of Meads, and Streams that thro' the Valley glide; / And shady Groves that easie Sleep invite, / And after toilsome Days, a soft repose at Night" (2.467–70).

9 *prospect* View of the landscape.

10 *fret-work* Decorative carving consisting of intersecting lines.

drawn on the walls of a dark room, which stood opposite on one side to a navigable river, and on the other to a park.[1] The experiment is very common in optics. Here you might discover the waves and fluctuations of the water in strong and proper colors with the picture of a ship entering at one end and sailing by degrees through the whole piece. On another there appeared the green shadows of trees, waving to and fro with the wind, and herds of deer among them in miniature, leaping about upon the wall. I must confess, the novelty of such a sight may be one occasion of its pleasantness to the imagination, but certainly the chief reason is its near resemblance to nature, as it does not only, like other pictures, give the color and figure, but the motion of the things it represents.

We have before observed that there is generally in nature something more grand and august than what we meet with in the curiosities of art. When, therefore, we see this imitated in any measure, it gives us a nobler and more exalted kind of pleasure than what we receive from the nicer[2] and more accurate productions of art. On this account our English gardens are not so entertaining to the fancy as those in France and Italy, where we see a large extent of ground covered over with an agreeable mixture of garden and forest which represent everywhere an artificial rudeness[3] much more charming than that neatness and elegancy which we meet with in those of our own country. It might, indeed, be of ill consequence to the public, as well as unprofitable to private persons, to alienate so much ground from pasturage and the plow in many parts of a country that is so well peopled, and cultivated to a far greater advantage. But why may not a whole estate be thrown into a kind of garden by frequent plantations[4] that may turn as much to the profit as the pleasure of the owner? A marsh overgrown with willows, or a mountain shaded with oaks, are not only more beautiful, but more beneficial, than when they lie bare and unadorned. Fields of corn[5] make a pleasant prospect, and if the walks were a little taken care of that lie between them, if the natural embroidery of the meadows were helped and improved by some small additions of art, and the several rows of hedges set off by trees and flowers that the soil was capable of receiving, a man might make a pretty landscape of his own possessions.

Writers who have given us an account of China tell us the inhabitants of that country laugh at the plantations of our Europeans which are laid out by the rule and line; because, they say, any one may place trees in equal rows and uniform figures. They choose rather to show a genius in works of this nature, and therefore always conceal the art by which they direct themselves. They have a word, it seems, in their language, by which they express the particular beauty of a plantation that thus strikes the imagination at first sight without discovering what it is that has so agreeable an effect. Our British gardeners, on the contrary, instead of humoring nature, love to deviate from it as much as possible. Our trees rise in cones, globes, and pyramids. We see the marks of the scissors upon every plant and bush. I do not know whether I am singular in my opinion, but, for my own part, I would rather look upon a tree in all its luxuriancy and diffusion of boughs and branches than when it is thus cut and trimmed into a mathematical figure; and I cannot but fancy that an orchard in flower looks infinitely more delightful than all the little labyrinths of the most finished parterre.[6] But as our great modelers of gardens have their magazines[7] of plants to dispose of, it is very natural for them to tear up all the beautiful plantations of fruit trees and contrive a plan that may most turn to their own profit—in taking off[8] their evergreens, and the like moveable plants, with which their shops are plentifully stocked.

—1712

[1] *The prettiest … park* Reference to a camera obscura, a dark room or box into which light is directed through a lens; images placed on the lens would be replicated on the walls of the room or box.

[2] *nicer* More refined, cultured.

[3] *rudeness* Primitive or unrefined state.

[4] *plantations* Planted lands.

[5] *corn* Grain.

[6] *parterre* Formal arrangement of flower beds in a level area.

[7] *magazines* Storehouses for goods.

[8] *taking off* Selling out.

Alexander Pope

1688 – 1744

Alexander Pope may have been speaking generally when he wrote, "The life of a wit is a warfare upon earth," but the statement is particularly applicable to his own life. In the highly competitive literary society of the time, one's rivals were quick to exploit any perceived weaknesses—personal or literary—and Pope was an easy target in many respects. As a result of tuberculosis of the bone (Pott's disease) contracted in his youth, Pope's spine was severely curved, and he only grew to four foot six. He was a Catholic, and as such was denied most of the privileges of British citizenship, including the right to vote and the right to inherit land. Pope was also a Tory, which, in the politically charged climate of Robert Walpole's Whig government, resulted in further persecution. Pope's rivals interpreted his Catholicism as evidence of treasonous Jacobitism, his Tory sympathies as proof of disloyalty to his King and Parliament, and his disabled body as a sign of a malignant and twisted soul. Given this hostile environment it is surprising that Pope did not abandon his literary ambitions altogether. Instead, using the worst qualities of his society to his advantage, Pope built a reputation for himself as a satirist of civil follies and a champion of truth and moral virtue. Declaring that "the proper study of mankind is man," he based his enormously successful literary career on social commentary, and on the documentation of contemporary experience.

Pope was born in London in 1688, the same year that a new Act of Parliament prohibited Catholics from living within ten miles of that city. Pope was privately educated (his religion also prevented him from attending schools); he read widely in his father's library and designed for himself an apprenticeship of translation and imitation of classical poets.

From the start Pope aspired to poetic greatness. His first independent publication, *An Essay on Criticism* (1711), sought to compress and comment upon all previous critical work concerning poetry. It was an unusual kind of production—an essay, written in verse, on the criticism of verse—that took the essays of Horace as its model. This ambitious and densely woven poem brought him his first personal attack: poet and dramatist John Dennis, finding himself cited as an example of a bad critic, issued a reply calling Pope a "hunch-backed toad." But the poem also brought Pope to the attention of prominent literary figures, including Richard Steele and Joseph Addison, whose influential "little senate" of Whig writers held court at Button's coffee house.

Political differences soon severed this new connection, however, and Pope later discovered that Addison was behind a plot to discredit his scholarship. Luckily he had developed other, more lasting friendships with Henry St. John (Lord Bolingbroke), Francis Atterbury (Bishop of Rochester, later imprisoned by Walpole as a Jacobite leader), Martha Blount (to whom Pope addressed his *Epistle to a Lady*, 1735), and John Caryll. Caryll's cousin Lord Petre became the subject of one of the most famous courtship scandals of the century when he snipped a lock of hair from the head of Arabella Fermor. She and her family took offense, and the situation had escalated into a feud when Caryll asked Pope to intervene by "laughing them together again" with a poem. The result, *The Rape of the Lock*, uses the inversion of the mock-heroic form to do justice to both the weight and the triviality of the event. The first published version (1712) succeeded in its objective of restoring good humor to the families, and the later release of the extended, five-canto poem (1714) charmed wider audiences with its imaginative play.

Pope's more famous group of friends were his fellow members of the Scriblerus Club, formed in 1714 by Pope, Jonathan Swift, John Gay, Dr. John Arbuthnot, Robert Harley (Lord Oxford), Thomas Parnell, and Lord Bolingbroke. The members focused upon an invented learned fool, Martinus Scriblerus, to whose work they attributed all that was tedious, narrow-minded, and pedantic in contemporary scholarship. The origins of Swift's *Gulliver's Travels* (1726), Pope's *The Dunciad* (1728), Gay's *The Beggar's Opera* (1728)—generally seen as the greatest satires of their age—may all be traced to the Club.

In 1714 Pope began using his refined translation skills to produce a verse translation of Homer's *Iliad* (1715–20); paid for by subscription and released in volumes, the translation made him enough money to acquire an estate in Twickenham. This estate provided a lifelong haven from the turmoil of the London literary and political scenes, and a removed position from which to write. With both his reputation as a poet and his financial well-being secured, Pope turned to higher philosophical and political writing—he also now began his work as a damaging satirist.

The Dunciad (1728–43) was Pope's most biting and direct satiric attack on his enemies. Structured as an ironic epic of praise to hack writers, it presented the most ludicrous and low quality writing of his contemporaries and some of his own early work, as a praiseworthy example of ideal literature. The piece starred Lewis Theobald—the scholar who had argued that Pope's edition of Shakespeare was erratic and unreliable—as King of the Dunces (crowned by the Goddess Dullness). Pope expanded and altered *The Dunciad* over time, keeping pace with the changing literary scene he attacked. *The New Dunciad* saw a new poet laureate, Colley Cibber, replace Theobald as anti-hero.

Often, Pope's most brilliant and humorous satiric passages are those that take incontrovertible facts about his subjects and pervert them to form desperately damaging pictures—as he does in his portrayal of Lord Hervey in the "Epistle to Arbuthnot," for example. The ferocity of these attacks, however, leads many readers to question what could possibly have warranted such animosity—particularly considering that attacks on some, such as Lady Mary Wortley Montagu, were pursued through an entire sequence of his greatest satires, published over the span of several years. The majority of his satires, however, convey an impression of pettiness, mediocrity, and dullness as forces capable of destroying culture. To Pope, low, vulgar, sensational art was not merely bad in an aesthetic sense; it was also immoral and could corrupt society if allowed to spread unchecked.

In contrast to his satire, Pope intended his *Essay on Man* (1733–34), he told Swift, to be "a book to make mankind look upon his life with comfort and pleasure, and put morality into good humour." An ambitious essay in verse, the poem analyzes aspects of human nature, and discusses humanity's place in the universe. Its first three epistles (there were four in total) were published anonymously to avoid the censure of his enemies, whose numbers had substantially increased since *The Dunciad* first appeared.

The *Essay on Man* was followed by Pope's *Imitations of Horace* (1733–40) and his *Moral Essays, or Epistles to Several Persons* (1731–35), many of which are also written in the Horatian mode. Bolingbroke had pointed out how well the Roman poet's lightly satirical style suited Pope's own purposes, and the poems written in this manner have been generally regarded as among the most finely crafted and carefully controlled of Pope's career. The "Epistle to Dr. Arbuthnot" (1735), perhaps his most famous, replies to all those who had attacked his "Person, Morals, and Family," defends his use of satire, and gives a controlled, carefully shaped account of his literary development.

By the time of his death in 1744, Pope had proven himself a master of a wide range of modes—among them pastoral, lyric, and mock-heroic. The diversity of Pope's poetic success is particularly remarkable given that almost all his poetry was composed in heroic couplets. Within this regular form of rhyming pairs of iambic pentameter lines, Pope was able to vary the mood and tone of his work enormously, and to convey the richness of the society he saw around him. Pope died at his villa in Twickenham, surrounded by numerous friends.

⌘⌘⌘

from *An Essay on Criticism*

An Essay on Criticism established Pope as a leading poet of his day. Samuel Johnson, in his biography of Pope, declared that even if Pope "had written nothing else," *An Essay on Criticism* "would have placed him among the first critics and the first poets, as it exhibits every mode of excellence that can embellish or dignify didactic composition." The poem reflects the range of Pope's reading, including all the well-known English, French, and Latin poets, as well as many Greek poets in the original. Pope's discursive essay in verse is in the tradition of Horace's *Ars Poetica* (*The Art of Poetry*) and French poet Nicolas Boileau's *Art Poétique* (1674). Like these poems, the *Essay on Criticism* uses simple and conversational language. It draws together a range of historical and intellectual knowledge, but does not aim for novelty; instead, it attempts to express generally accepted doctrines in a pleasing style, setting out precepts in language that exemplifies the precepts themselves. Covering topics from divinity to freedom of the press to everyday follies, the poem is characterized by its lively style, by its wide range of comic expression, and by its use of maxim and epigram. Many phrases in the poem have become proverbial—notable among them, line 625, "For fools rush in where angels fear to tread," and line 525, "To err is human, to forgive, divine."

An Essay on Criticism consists of three parts. The first describes an Edenic, golden era of art and criticism exemplified by Homer and other classical writers, considered to be especially well placed to observe Nature directly and reflect it in their art. The subject of the poem's second part is the decay and disorder Pope observes in the criticism of his day, which he attributes very largely to the divisive, egotistic nature of critics. The third part sets out a means of reformation through virtue, and a restoration of the ideals set out in Part 1. Although Pope's goals are generally conciliatory, and he attempts to accommodate seemingly conflicting artistic values and views, there were nonetheless several people who took offense to parts of the poem. Many of Pope's fellow Catholics objected to his critical representation of their Church, and Pope's mocking allusions to dramatist John Dennis (1658–1734) sparked a public feud between the two that would last through both of their careers—the first of many such literary feuds Pope's writing would instigate.

from *An Essay on Criticism*[1]

PART I

'Tis hard to say, if greater want of skill
Appear in writing or in judging ill;
But of the two less dang'rous is th'offense
To tire our patience than mislead our sense.
Some few in that, but numbers err in this,
Ten censure wrong for one who writes amiss;
A fool might once himself alone expose,
Now one in verse makes many more in prose.
'Tis with our judgments as our watches, none
Go just alike, yet each believes his own.
In poets as true genius is but rare,
True taste as seldom is the critic's share;
Both must alike from Heav'n derive their light,
These born to judge, as well as those to write.
Let such teach others who themselves excel,
And censure freely who have written well.
Authors are partial to their wit, 'tis true,
But are not critics to their judgment too?
Yet if we look more closely, we shall find
Most have the seeds of judgment in their mind:
Nature affords at least a glimm'ring light;
The lines, though touched but faintly, are drawn right.

[1] *An Essay on Criticism* The complete text is available on the website component of the anthology (www.broadviewpress.com/babl).

But as the slightest sketch, if justly traced,
Is by ill colouring but the more disgraced,
So by false learning is good sense defaced:
Some are bewildered in the maze of schools,
And some made coxcombs Nature meant but fools.
In search of wit these lose their common sense,
And then turn critics in their own defence:
Each burns alike, who can, or cannot write,
Or° with a rival's, or an eunuch's spite. *either*
All fools have still an itching to deride,
And fain would be upon the laughing side.
If Maevius[1] scribble in Apollo's[2] spite,
There are who judge still worse than he can write.
  Some have at first for wits, then poets passed,
Turned critics next, and proved plain fools at last.
Some neither can for wits nor critics pass,
As heavy mules are neither horse nor ass.
Those half-learned witlings, num'rous in our isle,
As half-formed insects on the banks of Nile;
Unfinished things, one knows not what to call,
Their generation's so equivocal:
To tell° 'em would a hundred tongues require, *count*
Or one vain wit's, that might a hundred tire.
  But you who seek to give and merit fame,
And justly bear a critic's noble name,
Be sure yourself and your own reach to know,
How far your genius, taste, and learning go;
Launch not beyond your depth, but be discreet,
And mark that point where sense and dullness meet.
  Nature to all things fixed the limits fit,
And wisely curbed proud man's pretending° wit. *aspiring*
As on the land while here the ocean gains,
In other parts it leaves wide sandy plains;
Thus in the soul while memory prevails,
The solid pow'r of understanding fails;
Where beams of warm imagination play,
The memory's soft figures melt away.
One science only will one genius fit,
So vast is art,° so narrow human wit: *scholarship*
Not only bounded to peculiar arts,
But oft in those confined to single parts.
Like kings we lose the conquests gained before,
By vain ambition still° to make them more; *always*
Each might his sev'ral province well command,
Would all but stoop to what they understand.
  First follow Nature, and your judgment frame
By her just standard, which is still the same;
Unerring Nature, still divinely bright,
One clear, unchanged, and universal light,
Life, force, and beauty must to all impart.
At once the source, and end, and test of art.
Art from that fund each just supply provides,
Works without show, and without pomp presides.
In some fair body thus th'informing° soul *animating*
With spirits feeds, with vigour fills the whole,
Each motion guides, and every nerve sustains;
Itself unseen, but in th'effects remains.
Some, to whom Heav'n in wit has been profuse,
Want as much more to turn it to its use;
For wit and judgment often are at strife,
Though meant each other's aid, like man and wife.
'Tis more to guide than spur the Muse's steed,
Restrain his fury than provoke his speed;
The wingèd courser,[3] like a gen'rous° horse, *thoroughbred*
Shows most true mettle° when you check his course. *character*
  Those rules of old discovered, not devised,
Are Nature still, but Nature methodized;
Nature, like liberty, is but restrained
By the same laws which first herself ordained.

· · · ·

  You then whose judgment the right course would steer,
Know well each ancient's proper character;
His fable,° subject, scope° in every page; *story, plot / purpose*
Religion, country, genius of his age:
Without all these at once before your eyes,
Cavil you may, but never criticize.
Be Homer's[4] works your study and delight,
Read them by day, and meditate by night;
Thence form your judgment, thence your maxims bring,

[1] *Maevius* Notorious critic of the Augustan age who attacked, among others, Virgil (70–19 BCE) and Horace (65–8 BCE).

[2] *Apollo* In classical mythology, the god of poetry and the arts, among other things.

[3] *courser* I.e., Pegasus, a winged horse of classical mythology associated with Muses and poetic inspiration.

[4] *Homer* Ancient Greek epic poet (c. 8th century BCE).

And trace the Muses upward to their spring.
Still with itself compared, his text peruse;
And let your comment be the Mantuan Muse.
When first young Maro[1] in his boundless mind
A work t' outlast immortal Rome designed,
Perhaps he seemed above the critic's law,
And but from Nature's fountains scorned to draw;
But when t'examine every part he came,
Nature and Homer were, he found, the same.
Convinced, amazed, he checks the bold design,
And rules as strict his laboured work confine
As if the Stagirite[2] o'erlooked each line.
Learn hence for ancient rules a just esteem;
To copy Nature is to copy them.
Some beauties yet no precepts can declare,
For there's a happiness as well as care.
Music resembles poetry, in each
Are nameless graces which no methods teach,
And which a master-hand alone can reach.
If, where the rules not far enough extend
(Since rules were made but to promote their end)
Some lucky license answers to the full
Th'intent proposed, that license is a rule.

. . . . . .

Still green with bays each ancient altar stands
Above the reach of sacrilegious hands,
Secure from flames, from envy's fiercer rage,
Destructive war, and all-involving age.
See, from each clime the learned their incense bring!
Here in all tongues consenting° paeans[3] ring! *in harmony*
In praise so just let every voice be joined,
And fill the gen'ral chorus of mankind.
Hail, bards triumphant! born in happier days,
Immortal heirs of universal praise!
Whose honours with increase of ages grow,
As streams roll down, enlarging as they flow;
Nations unborn your mighty names shall sound,
And worlds applaud that must not yet be found!
Oh, may some spark of your celestial fire,
The last, the meanest of your sons inspire
(That on weak wings, from far, pursues your flights,
Glows while he reads, but trembles as he writes)
To teach vain wits a science little known,
T'admire superior sense, and doubt their own!

PART 2

Of all the causes which conspire to blind
Man's erring judgment, and misguide the mind
What the weak head with strongest bias rules,
Is pride, the never-failing vice of fools.
Whatever Nature has in worth denied,
She gives in large recruits° of needful pride; *supplies*
For as in bodies, thus in souls, we find
What wants in blood and spirits, swelled with wind:
Pride, where wit fails, steps in to our defence,
And fills up all the mighty void of sense.
If once right reason drives that cloud away,
Truth breaks upon us with resistless day.
Trust not yourself: but your defects to know,
Make use of every friend—and every foe.
A little learning is a dang'rous thing;
Drink deep, or taste not the Pierian[4] spring.
There shallow draughts intoxicate the brain,
And drinking largely sobers us again.

. . . . . .

Whoever thinks a faultless piece to see,
Thinks what ne'er was, nor is, nor e'er shall be.
In every work regard the writer's end,
Since none can compass more than they intend;
And if the means be just, the conduct true,
Applause, in spite of trivial faults, is due.
As men of breeding, sometimes men of wit,
T'avoid great errors must the less commit,
Neglect the rules each verbal° critic lays, *pedantic, petty*
For not to know some trifles is a praise.
Most critics, fond of some subservient art,
Still make the whole depend upon a part:
They talk of principles, but notions prize,
And all to one loved folly sacrifice.

[1] *Mantuan Muse ... Maro* I.e., Virgil, classical Roman poet, who was born near Mantua; also known as "Maro."

[2] *Stagirite* I.e., Aristotle (384–322 BCE), ancient Greek philosopher who was born in Stagira. He was the author of the *Poetics*, which was (incorrectly) supposed to have established strict rules for tragedies, governing place and time as well as action.

[3] *paeans* Triumphal or grateful songs.

[4] *Pierian* Sacred spring to the Muses.

Once on a time La Mancha's knight,[1] they say,
A certain bard encount'ring on the way,
Discoursed in terms as just, with looks as sage,
As e'er could Dennis,[2] of the Grecian stage;
Concluding all were desp'rate sots and fools
Who durst depart from Aristotle's rules.[3]
Our author, happy in a judge so nice,
Produced his play, and begged the knight's advice;
Made him observe the subject and the plot,
The manners, passions, unities; what not?
All which, exact to rule, were brought about,
Were but a combat in the lists left out.
"What! leave the combat out?" exclaims the knight.
"Yes, or we must renounce the Stagirite."
"Not so, by Heav'n!" he answers in a rage,
"Knights, squires, and steeds must enter on the stage."
"So vast a throng the stage can ne'er contain."
"Then build a new, or act it in a plain."

Thus critics of less judgment than caprice,
Curious,° not knowing, not exact, but nice,° *particular* / *fastidious*
Form short ideas, and offend in arts
(As most in manners) by a love to parts.

Some to conceit alone their taste confine,
And glitt'ring thoughts struck out at every line;
Pleased with a work where nothing's just or fit,
One glaring chaos and wild heap of wit.
Poets like painters, thus unskilled to trace
The naked nature and the living grace,
With gold and jewels cover every part,
And hide with ornaments their want of art.
True wit is Nature to advantage dressed,
What oft was thought, but ne'er so well expressed;
Something, whose truth convinced at sight we find,
That gives us back the image of our mind.
As shades more sweetly recommend the light,
So modest plainness sets off sprightly wit;
For works may have more wit than does 'em good,
As bodies perish through excess of blood.

Others for language all their care express,
And value books, as women men, for dress.
Their praise is still—"the style is excellent";
The sense they humbly take upon content.
Words are like leaves; and where they most abound,
Much fruit of sense beneath is rarely found.
False eloquence, like the prismatic glass,
Its gaudy colours spreads on every place;
The face of Nature we no more survey,
All glares alike, without distinction gay.
But true expression, like th'unchanging sun,
Clears and improves whate'er it shines upon;
It gilds all objects, but it alters none.
Expression is the dress of thought, and still
Appears more decent as more suitable.
A vile conceit in pompous words expressed
Is like a clown° in regal purple dressed *peasant, rustic*
For diff'rent styles with diff'rent subjects sort,
As several garbs with country, town, and court.
Some by old words to fame have made pretence,
Ancients in phrase, mere moderns in their sense:
Such laboured nothings, in so strange a style,
Amaze th' unlearn'd, and make the learned smile;
Unlucky as Fungoso[4] in the play,
These sparks with awkward vanity display
What the fine gentleman wore yesterday;
And but so mimic ancient wits at best,
As apes our grandsires in their doublets dressed.
In words as fashions the same rule will hold,
Alike fantastic if too new or old:
Be not the first by whom the new are tried,
Nor yet the last to lay the old aside.

But most by numbers° judge a poet's song, *versification*
And smooth or rough, with them, is right or wrong.
In the bright Muse though thousand charms conspire,
Her voice is all these tuneful fools admire,
Who haunt Parnassus but to please their ear,
Not mend their minds; as some to church repair,
Not for the doctrine, but the music there.
These equal syllables alone require,
Though oft the ear the open vowels tire,
While expletives their feeble aid do join,
And ten low words oft creep in one dull line:

[1] *La Mancha's knight* I.e., the eponymous hero of Miguel de Cervantes's *Don Quixote* (1605–15).

[2] *Dennis* John Dennis (1658–1734), neo-classical literary critic with whom Pope feuded.

[3] *Aristotle's rules* I.e., the dramatic unities of time, place, and action.

[4] *Fungoso* Character from Ben Jonson's *Every Man out of His Humour* (1518).

While they ring round the same unvaried chimes,
With sure returns of still expected rhymes:
Where'er you find "the cooling western breeze,"
In the next line, it "whispers through the trees";
If crystal streams "with pleasing murmurs creep,"
The reader's threatened (not in vain) with "sleep";
Then, at the last and only couplet fraught
With some unmeaning thing they call a thought,
A needless Alexandrine[1] ends the song
That, like a wounded snake, drags its slow length along.
Leave such to tune their own dull rhymes, and know
What's roundly smooth or languishingly slow;
And praise the easy vigour of a line
Where Denham's strength and Waller's sweetness join.[2]
True ease in writing comes from art, not chance,
As those move easiest who have learned to dance.
'Tis not enough no harshness gives offence,
The sound must seem an echo to the sense:
Soft is the strain when Zephyr° gently blows, *the west wind*
And the smooth stream in smoother numbers flows;
But when loud surges lash the sounding shore,
The hoarse, rough verse should like the torrent roar.
When Ajax[3] strives some rock's vast weight to throw,
The line too labours, and the words move slow;
Not so when swift Camilla[4] scours the plain,
Flies o'er th'unbending corn, and skims along the
main.° *sea*
Hear how Timotheus'[5] varied lays surprise,
And bid alternate passions fall and rise!
While, at each change, the son of Libyan Jove[6]
Now burns with glory, and then melts with love;
Now his fierce eyes with sparkling fury glow,
Now sighs steal out, and tears begin to flow:
Persians and Greeks like° turns of *similar*
nature° found, *feelings*
And the world's victor stood subdued by sound!
The pow'r of music all our hearts allow,
And what Timotheus was, is Dryden[7] now.
Avoid extremes, and shun the fault of such
Who still are pleased too little or too much.
At every trifle scorn to take offence,
That always shows great pride, or little sense;
Those heads, as stomachs, are not sure the best,
Which nauseate all, and nothing can digest.
Yet let not each gay turn thy rapture move,
For fools admire,° but men of sense approve: *marvel at*
As things seem large which we through mists descry,
Dullness is ever apt to magnify.

. . . . .

Some ne'er advance a judgment of their own,
But catch the spreading notion of the town;
They reason and conclude by precedent,
And own stale nonsense which they ne'er invent.
Some judge of authors names, not works, and then
Nor praise nor blame the writings, but the men.
Of all this servile herd, the worst is he
That in proud dullness joins with quality.° *people of rank*
A constant critic at the great man's board,
To fetch and carry nonsense for my Lord.
What woeful stuff this madrigal[8] would be,
In some starved hackney[9] sonneteer, or me?
But let a lord once own the happy lines,
How the wit brightens! how the style refines!
Before his sacred name flies every fault,
And each exalted stanza teems with thought!
The vulgar thus through imitation err;
As oft the learn'd by being singular;
So much they scorn the crowd, that if the throng
By chance go right, they purposely go wrong:
So schismatics the plain believers quit,
And are but damned for having too much wit.

[1] *Alexandrine* Line of poetry with twelve syllables (as has line 357).

[2] *Denham's strength ... join* Sir John Denham (1614/15–69), poet and courtier; Edmund Waller (1608–87), poet and politician. Both poets were known for their smooth, easy style.

[3] *Ajax* The "greater Ajax" of Homer's *Illiad,* who is proverbially strong.

[4] *Camilla* In classical mythology, a warrior virgin; she appears in Book 7 of Virgil's *Aeneid.*

[5] *Timotheus* Greek poet and musician (4th century BCE) who played for Alexander the Great (356–323 BCE).

[6] *Libyan Jove* I.e., Alexander the Great (356–323 BCE), Macedonian military leader; when he visited the oracle of Zeus Ammon ("Libyan Jove"), he was proclaimed son of the god.

[7] *Dryden* John Dryden (1631–1700), leading poet, playwright, and critic of the Restoration.

[8] *madrigal* Short lyric, especially one set to music.

[9] *hackney* Doing or ready to do work for hire.

Some praise at morning what they blame at night;
But always think the last opinion right.
A muse by these is like a mistress used,
This hour she's idolized, the next abused;
While their weak heads, like towns unfortified,
'Twixt sense and nonsense daily change their side.
Ask them the cause; they're wiser still, they say;
And still° tomorrow's wiser than today. *always*
We think our fathers fools, so wise we grow;
Our wiser sons, no doubt, will think us so.

. . . .

Of old, those met rewards who could excel,
And such were praised who but endeavoured well.
Though triumphs were to gen'rals only due,
Crowns were reserved to grace the soldiers too.
Now, they who reach Parnassus' lofty crown,
Employ their pains to spurn° some others down; *kick*
And while self-love each jealous writer rules,
Contending wits become the sport of fools;
But still the worst with most regret commend,
For each ill author is as bad a friend.
To what base ends, and by what abject ways,
Are mortals urged through sacred lust of praise!
Ah ne'er so dire a thirst of glory boast,
Nor in the critic let the man be lost.
Good-nature and good-sense must ever join;
To err is human, to forgive, divine,
But if in noble minds some dregs remain
Not yet purged off, of spleen° and sour disdain; *spite*
Discharge that rage on more provoking crimes,
Nor fear a dearth in these flagitious° times. *extremely wicked*
No pardon vile obscenity should find,
Though wit and art conspire to move your mind;
But dullness with obscenity must prove
As shameful sure as impotence in love.

. . . .

Part 3

Learn then what morals critics ought to show,
For 'tis but half a judge's task, to know.
'Tis not enough, taste, judgment, learning, join;
In all you speak, let truth and
candour° shine: *openness of mind*
That not alone what to your sense is due
All may allow; but seek your friendship too.
Be silent always when you doubt your sense;
And speak, though sure, with seeming diffidence:
Some positive, persisting fops we know,
Who, if once wrong, will needs be always so;
But you, with pleasure own your errors past,
And make each day a critic° on the last. *critique*
'Tis not enough, your counsel still be true;
Blunt truths more mischief than nice falsehoods do;
Men must be taught as if you taught them not,
And things unknown proposed as things forgot.
Without good breeding, truth is disapproved;
That only makes superior sense belov'd.

. . . . . .

The bookful blockhead, ignorantly read,
With loads of learned lumber in his head,
With his own tongue still edifies his ears,
And always list'ning to himself appears.
All books he reads, and all he reads assails,
From Dryden's *Fables* down to Durfey's *Tales*.[1]
With him, most authors steal their works, or buy;
Garth[2] did not write his own *Dispensary*.
Name a new play, and he's the poet's friend,
Nay showed his faults—but when would poets mend?
No place so sacred from such fops is barred,
Nor is Paul's church more safe than Paul's church yard:[3]
Nay, fly to altars; there they'll talk you dead:
For fools rush in where angels fear to tread.
Distrustful sense with modest caution speaks,
It still looks home, and short excursions makes;
But rattling nonsense in full volleys breaks,
And never shocked,° and never turned aside, *stopped*
Bursts out, resistless, with a thund'ring tide.
But where's the man, who counsel can bestow,
Still pleased to teach, and yet not proud to know?
Unbiased, or° by favour, or by spite: *either*

[1] *Dryden's Fables … Durfey's Tales* John Dryden's *Fables, Ancient and Modern* (1700) and Thomas D'Urfey's *Tales Tragical and Comical* (1704). D'Urfey's *Tales* is a poor imitation of Dryden's *Fables*.

[2] *Garth* Samuel Garth's *Dispensary* (1699) was closely modeled on Nicolas Boileau's *Le Lutrin* (1674); Garth's critics accused him of plagiarism.

[3] *Paul's church … Paul's church yard* The former was used as a place for business meetings, and the latter was close to the booksellers' quarter.

Not dully prepossessed, nor blindly right;
Though learn'd, well-bred; and though well-bred, sincere;
Modestly bold, and humanly severe:
Who to a friend his faults can freely show,
And gladly praise the merit of a foe?
Blest with a taste exact, yet unconfined;
A knowledge both of books and human kind;
Gen'rous° converse;° a soul exempt from pride; *well-bred / conversation*
And love to praise, with reason on his side?
 Such once were critics; such the happy few,
Athens and Rome in better ages knew.

. . . .

—1711

Windsor-Forest

TO THE RIGHT HONOURABLE
GEORGE LORD LANSDOWN[1]

Non injussa cano: te nostrae, Vare, myricae
Te nemus omne canet; nec Phoebo gratior ulla est
Quam sibi quae Vari praescripsit pagina nomen.[2]

VIRG.

Thy forests, Windsor![3] and thy green retreats,
At once the monarch's and the Muse's seats,
Invite my lays.[4] Be present, sylvan maids![5]
Unlock your springs and open all your shades.
Granville commands, "Your aid, O Muses, bring!"
What Muse for Granville can refuse to sing?
 The groves of Eden, vanished now so long,
Live in description, and look green in song.[6]
These, were my breast inspired with equal flame,
Like them in beauty, should be like in fame.
Here hills and vales, the woodland and the plain,
Here earth and water seem to strive again,
Not Chaos-like together crushed and bruised,
But as the world, harmoniously confused:
Where order in variety we see,
And where, though all things differ, all agree.
Here waving groves a chequered scene display,
And part admit and part exclude the day,
As some coy nymph° her lover's warm address *maiden*
Nor quite indulges, nor can quite repress.
There, interspersed in lawns[7] and opening glades,
Thin trees arise that shun each other's shades.
Here in full light the russet plains extend;
There, wrapped in clouds, the bluish hills ascend:
Ev'n the wild heath displays her purple dyes,[8]
And 'midst the desert[9] fruitful fields arise
That, crowned with tufted trees[10] and springing corn,
Like verdant isles the sable waste adorn.
Let India boast her plants, nor envy we
The weeping amber or the balmy tree
While by our oaks the precious loads are borne,[11]
And realms commanded which those trees adorn.
Not proud Olympus[12] yields a nobler sight,

[1] *George Lord Lansdown* George Granville, Baron Lansdown, was a minor poet and playwright, as well as the Tory Secretary of War under Queen Anne. In this latter role he was partially responsible for the British victory in the War of Spanish Succession and for the long-awaited peace that followed. Lansdown admired Pope's poetry and had encouraged him to compose a poem celebrating the Peace of Utrecht that ended the war.

[2] *Non ... nomen* From Virgil's *Eclogues* 6.9-12: "I do not sing unbidden: all the grove of our tamarisks shall sing of you, Varus; nor is any page more pleasing to Phoebus than that which is prefixed with the name of Varus"; *tamarisk* Evergreen shrub sacred to the god Apollo, one of whose names is "Phoebus."

[3] *Thy forests, Windsor* Windsor Castle, originally built by William I, served as the country home ("seat") of the royal family and the meeting place of the Knights of the Garter. Pope also refers to the surrounding forest as the seat of the muses because it had been the home of seventeenth-century poets John Denham and Abraham Cowley. Pope himself grew up in Windsor Forest, in the town of Binfield.

[4] *lays* Songs, and therefore, poems.

[5] *sylvan maids* Spirits or nymphs of the woods ("sylvan" meaning "of the woods").

[6] *in description* I.e., in the Bible; *song* Milton's *Paradise Lost.*

[7] *lawns* Open spaces between woods.

[8] *her purple dyes* Heather, which covered the moors in late summer.

[9] *desert* Originally signifying any uninhabited or uncultivated region.

[10] *tufted trees* Trees growing in clumps.

[11] *oaks ... borne* Oak was used to make the English ships that traded with and conquered distant territories.

[12] *Olympus* Mount Olympus, home of the gods.

Though gods assembled grace his tow'ring height,
Than what more humble mountains offer here,
Where, in their blessings, all those gods appear.
See Pan with flocks, with fruits Pomona crowned,
Here blushing Flora paints th' enameled ground,[1]
Here Ceres' gifts in waving prospect stand,[2]
And nodding tempt the joyful reaper's hand;
Rich Industry sits smiling on the plains,
And Peace and Plenty tell, a Stuart[3] reigns.
    Not thus the land appeared in ages past,[4]
A dreary desert and a gloomy waste,
To savage beasts and savage laws[5] a prey,
And kings more furious and severe than they:
Who claimed the skies, dispeopled° air and floods, *depopulated*
The lonely lords of empty wilds and woods.
Cities laid waste; they stormed the dens and caves
(For wiser brutes were backward° to be slaves). *reluctant*
What could be free when lawless beasts obeyed,
And ev'n the elements a tyrant swayed?
In vain kind seasons swelled the teeming grain,
Soft show'rs distilled, and suns grew warm in vain;
The swain° with tears his frustrate labour yields, *farmer*
And famished dies amidst his ripened fields.[6]
What wonder then, a beast or subject slain
Were equal crimes in a despotic reign;
Both doomed alike, for sportive tyrants bled,
But while the subject starved, the beast was fed.
Proud Nimrod[7] first the bloody chase began,
A mighty hunter, and his prey was man.
Our haughty Norman boasts that barb'rous name,
And makes his trembling slaves the royal game.
The fields are ravished from th' industrious swains,
From men their cities, and from gods their fanes.° *temples*
The leveled towns with weeds lie covered o'er,
The hollow winds through naked temples roar;
Round broken columns clasping ivy twined;
O'er heaps of ruin stalked the stately hind;° *female deer*
The fox obscene° to gaping tombs retires, *disgusting*
And savage howlings fill the sacred quires.° *choir stalls*
Awed by his nobles, by his commons° cursed, *commoners*
Th' oppressor ruled tyrannic where he durst,
Stretched o'er the poor, and church, his iron rod,
And served alike his vassals and his God.
Whom ev'n the Saxon spared, and bloody Dane,
The wanton victims of his sport remain.
But see the man who spacious regions gave
A waste for beasts, himself denied a grave![8]
Stretched on the lawn his second hope[9] survey,
At once the chaser and at once the prey.
Lo Rufus,[10] tugging at the deadly dart,
Bleeds in the forest, like a wounded hart.° *male deer*
Succeeding monarchs heard the subject's cries,
Nor saw displeased the peaceful cottage rise.
Then gath'ring flocks on unknown[11] mountains fed,
O'er sandy wilds were yellow harvests spread,
The forests wondered at th' unusual grain,
And secret transport[12] touched the conscious[13] swain.
Fair Liberty, Britannia's goddess, rears
Her cheerful head, and leads the golden years.

---

[1] *enameled ground* Metaphor for nature derived from the process of coating metal with enamel to produce jewel-like decoration.

[2] *Pan ... stand* Together these gods are responsible for the land's natural abundance. Pan rules over shepherds and flocks; Pomona is the goddess of fruit trees; Flora of flowers; and Ceres of crops and the harvest.

[3] *a Stuart* I.e., Queen Anne.

[4] *in ages past* Pope begins by describing the land in Norman times, specifically during the reign of William the Conqueror, who converted much forest land into private royal hunting grounds, taking over many local towns to do so. When several members of the King's family died in New Forest (in Hampshire) the people viewed the deaths as divine retribution for the damage inflicted upon the environment and the community.

[5] *savage laws* The Forest Laws, under which anyone bilking game in any of the royal hunting preserves were severely punished.

[6] *famished ... fields* Because his crops were grown to feed animals, not people.

[7] *Nimrod* Described in Genesis as a "mighty hunter," he was also seen as a despot.

[8] *spacious regions ... grave* The site selected for the king's burial was owned by a knight who objected to the grave being placed on his land.

[9] [Pope's note] Richard, second son of William the Conqueror. [Richard was killed by a stag while hunting in New Forest.]

[10] *Rufus* Nickname of William II, who was killed in New Forest by a fellow hunter's arrow.

[11] *unknown* Unfamiliar (because formerly forbidden to the flocks).

[12] *transport* Joy.

[13] *conscious* Aware; witnessing.

Ye vig'rous swains! while youth ferments your blood[1]
And purer spirits swell the sprightly flood,
Now range the hills, the gameful woods beset,
Wind° the shrill horn, or spread the waving net. *blow*
When milder autumn summer's heat succeeds,
And in the new-shorn field the partridge feeds,
Before his lord the ready spaniel bounds;
Panting with hope, he tries the furrowed grounds,
But when the tainted[2] gales the game betray,
Couched° close he lies, and meditates the prey; *pressed down*
Secure they trust th' unfaithful field, beset,
Till hov'ring o'er 'em sweeps the swelling net.
Thus (if small things we may with great compare)
When Albion[3] sends her eager sons to war,
Some thoughtless town with ease and plenty blest,
Near, and more near, the closing lines invest;
Sudden they seize th' amazed, defenceless prize,
And high in air Britannia's standard flies.
See! from the brake° the whirring pheasant springs, *thicket*
And mounts exulting on triumphant wings;
Short is his joy! he feels the fiery wound,
Flutters in blood, and panting beats the ground.
Ah! what avail his glossy, varying dyes,
His purple crest, and scarlet-circled eyes,
The vivid green his shining plumes unfold,
His painted wings, and breast that flames with gold?
Nor yet, when moist Arcturus[4] clouds the sky,
The woods and fields their pleasing toils deny.
To plains with well-breathed beagles we repair,
And trace the mazes of the circling hare.
(Beasts, urged by us, their fellow beasts pursue,
And learn of man each other to undo.)
With slaught'ring guns th' unwearied fowler roves
When frosts have whitened all the naked groves;
Where doves in flocks the leafless trees o'ershade,
And lonely woodcocks haunt the watery glade.
He lifts the tube° and levels with his eye; *gun*
Straight a short thunder breaks the frozen sky.
Oft, as in airy rings they skim the heath,
The clam'rous lapwings feel the leaden death:
Oft as the mounting larks their notes prepare,
They fall, and leave their little lives in air.
In genial° spring, beneath the quiv'ring shade *generative*
Where cooling vapours breathe along the mead,
The patient fisher takes his silent stand,
Intent, his angle trembling in his hand;
With looks unmoved, he hopes the scaly breed,
And eyes the dancing cork and bending reed.
Our plenteous streams a various race supply:
The bright-eyed perch with fins of Tyrian dye,[5]
The silver eel, in shining volumes° rolled, *coils*
The yellow carp, in scales bedropped with gold,
Swift trouts, diversified with crimson stains,
And pikes, the tyrants of the wat'ry plains.
Now Cancer glows with Phoebus' fiery car;[6]
The youth rush eager to the sylvan war;
Swarm o'er the lawns, the forest walks surround,
Rouse the fleet hart,° and cheer the opening hound.[7] *deer*
Th' impatient courser° pants in every vein *horse*
And, pawing, seems to beat the distant plain;
Hills, vales, and floods appear already crossed,
And, ere he starts, a thousand steps are lost.
See! the bold youth strain up the threatening steep,
Rush through the thickets, down the valleys sweep,
Hang o'er their coursers' heads with eager speed,
And earth rolls back beneath the flying steed.
Let old Arcadia boast her ample plain,
Th' Immortal Huntress, and her virgin train;
Nor envy, Windsor! since thy shades have seen
As bright a goddess, and as chaste a Queen;
Whose care, like hers, protects the sylvan reign,
The earth's fair light, and empress of the main.[8]

---

[1] *youth ... blood* Refined substances, called "spirits," were thought to permeate the blood. Animal spirits (as opposed to vital and natural spirits) were those responsible for quickening the blood and animating the body to exercise.

[2] *tainted* Carrying the animal's scent.

[3] *Albion* England. Pope recalls recent British conquests, probably specifically the capture of Gibralter.

[4] *Arcturus* Star that, when it rose with the sun in September, was thought to bring bad weather in classical antiquity.

[5] *Tyrian dye* Purple or crimson dye originally made in Tyre, the ancient capital of Phoenicia.

[6] *Now ... car* On June 22 the sun (referred to as the chariot, or "car," of the sun god, Phoebus Apollo) enters the constellation of Cancer.

[7] *opening hound* Hunting dog that leads the hunt with its cry.

[8] *As bright ... main* Pope claims Queen Anne is as chaste and as skilled a huntress (Queen Anne took an interest in hunting) as Diana, the virgin goddess of the hunt. In addition, as ruler of the seas (the "main"), Queen Anne held a power comparable to that of Diana, who

Here too, 'tis sung of old, Diana strayed,
And Cynthus'[1] top forsook for Windsor shade;
Here was she seen o'er airy wastes to rove,
Seek the clear spring, or haunt the pathless grove;
Here, armed with silver bows, in early dawn
Her buskined° virgins traced the dewy lawn. *booted*
Above the rest a rural nymph was famed,
Thy offspring, Thames! the fair Lodona named[2]
(Lodona's fate, in long oblivion cast,
The Muse shall sing, and what she sings shall last),
Scarce could the goddess from her nymph be known,
But by the crescent° and the golden zone.[3] *crescent moon*
She scorned the praise of beauty, and the care;
A belt her waist, a fillet° binds her hair, *ribbon*
A painted quiver on her shoulder sounds,
And with her dart the flying deer she wounds.
It chanced, as eager of the chase the maid
Beyond the forest's verdant limits strayed,
Pan saw and loved, and, burning with desire,
Pursued her flight; her flight increased his fire.
Not half so swift the trembling doves can fly
When the fierce eagle cleaves the liquid° sky; *clear*
Not half so swiftly the fierce eagle moves
When through the clouds he drives the trembling doves;
As from the god she flew with furious pace,
Or as the god, more furious, urged the chase.
Now fainting, sinking, pale, the nymph appears;
Now close behind his sounding steps she hears;
And now his shadow reached her as she run
(His shadow lengthened by the setting sun),
And now his shorter breath with sultry air
Pants on her neck, and fans her parting hair.
In vain on Father Thames she calls for aid,
Nor could Diana help her injured maid.
Faint, breathless, thus she prayed, nor prayed in vain:
"Ah, Cynthia!° ah—though banished from thy train, *Diana*
Let me, O let me, to the shades repair,
My native shades—there weep, and murmur there,"
She said, and melting as in tears she lay,
In a soft, silver stream dissolved away.
The silver stream her virgin coldness keeps,
Forever murmurs, and forever weeps;
Still bears the name the hapless virgin bore,
And bathes the forest where she ranged before.
In her chaste current oft the goddess laves,° *bathes*
And with celestial tears augments the waves.
Oft in her glass the musing shepherd spies
The headlong mountains and the downward skies,
The wat'ry landscape of the pendant[4] woods,
And absent° trees that tremble in the floods; *nonexistent, illusory*
In the clear azure gleam the flocks are seen,
And floating forests paint the waves with green.
Through the fair scene roll slow the lingering streams,
Then foaming pour along, and rush into the Thames.
Thou too, great father of the British floods![5]
With joyful pride survey'st our lofty woods,
Where tow'ring oaks their growing honours rear,
And future navies on thy shores appear.
Not Neptune's[6] self from all his streams receives
A wealthier tribute than to thine he gives.
No seas so rich, so gay no banks appear,
No lake so gentle, and no spring so clear.
Nor Po so swells the fabling poet's lays
While, led along the skies, his current strays,[7]
As thine, which visits Windsor's famed abodes
To grace the mansion of our earthly gods.
Nor all his stars above a lustre show
Like the bright beauties on thy banks below,
Where Jove, subdued° by mortal passion still, *overcome*
Might change Olympus for a nobler hill.
Happy the man whom this bright court approves,
His sov'reign favours, and his country loves;
Happy next him who to these shades retires,
Whom Nature charms, and whom the Muse inspires,
Whom humbler joys of home-felt quiet please,
Successive study, exercise, and ease.
He gathers health from herbs the forest yields,
And of their fragrant physic° spoils° the fields: *medicine / strips*
With chemic art exalts° the min'ral pow'rs, *intensifies, distills*

was also goddess of the moon, and therefore controlled the tides.

[1] *Cynthus* Mount Cynthus, Diana's birthplace.

[2] *offspring ... named* The river Loddon is a tributary of the Thames.

[3] *zone* Belt.

[4] *pendant* Downward-hanging.

[5] *great ... floods* The Thames.

[6] *Neptune* God of the sea.

[7] *Po ... strays* Both Virgil and Ovid referred to the river Po as the Eridanus, which is both a river in classical mythology and a constellation of the southern hemisphere that resembles a winding river.

And draws° the aromatic souls of flow'rs. *extracts*
Now marks the course of rolling orbs on high;
O'er figured worlds[1] now travels with his eye.
Of ancient writ unlocks the learned store,
Consults the dead, and lives past ages o'er.
Or, wand'ring thoughtful in the silent wood,
Attends the duties of the wise and good;
T' observe a mean,[2] be to himself a friend,
To follow Nature, and regard his end.
Or looks on heav'n with more than mortal eyes,
Bids his free soul expatiate° in the skies, *wander freely*
Amid her kindred stars[3] familiar roam,
Survey the region, and confess her home!
Such was the life great Scipio[4] once admired,
Thus Atticus, and Trumbull[5] thus retired.
  Ye sacred Nine![6] that all my soul possess,
Whose raptures fire me, and whose visions bless,
Bear me, oh bear me to sequestered scenes,
The bow'ry mazes and surrounding greens;
To Thames's banks, which fragrant breezes fill,
Or where ye Muses sport on Cooper's Hill.[7]
(On Cooper's Hill eternal wreaths shall grow,
While lasts the mountain, or while Thames shall flow.)
I seem through consecrated walks to rove,
I hear soft music die along the grove;
Led by the sound I roam from shade to shade,
By god-like poets venerable made:
Here his first lays majestic Denham sung;
There the last numbers flowed from Cowley's tongue.[8]
O early lost! what tears the river shed
When the sad pomp along his banks was led?[9]
His drooping swans on every note expire,[10]
And on his willows hung each Muse's lyre.
  Since Fate relentless stopped their heav'nly voice,
No more the forests ring, or groves rejoice;
Who now shall charm the shades where Cowley strung
His living harp, and lofty Denham sung?
But hark! the groves rejoice, the forest rings!
Are these revived? or is it Granville sings?
  'Tis yours, my Lord, to bless our soft retreats,
And call the muses to their ancient seats;
To paint anew the flow'ry sylvan scenes,
To crown the forests with immortal greens,
Make Windsor hills in lofty numbers rise,
And lift her turrets nearer to the skies;
To sing those honours you deserve to wear,
And add new lustre to her silver star.[11]
  Here noble Surrey[12] felt the sacred rage,
Surrey, the Granville of a former age:
Matchless his pen, victorious was his lance;
Bold in the lists, and graceful in the dance;
In the same shades the Cupids tuned his lyre,
To the same notes of love and soft desire;
Fair Geraldine, bright object of his vow,
Then filled the groves, as heav'nly Myra now.[13]
  Oh wouldst thou sing what heroes Windsor bore,

---

[1] *figured worlds* I.e., represented on a globe or map.

[2] *observe a mean* Maintain a balance.

[3] *kindred stars* Souls were formerly thought to be made of the same substance as the stars.

[4] *Scipio* Scipio Africanus defeated Hannibal in the Second Punic War, but declined all offers of political distinction that he subsequently received, preferring to pass the remainder of his life cultivating his estate.

[5] *Atticus* Titus Pomponius, a philosopher and friend of Cicero who retired to a life of study in Athens in order to avoid the political controversies of Rome; *Trumbull* William Trumbull, who was Secretary of State under William III until he retired to Windsor Forest, where he acted as Pope's mentor.

[6] *sacred Nine* The nine Muses.

[7] *Cooper's Hill* Located near the Thames, this hill was celebrated in John Denham's poem "Cooper's Hill." Pope refers to Denham in the following two lines.

[8] [Pope's note] Mr. Cowley died at the Chertsey, on the borders of the Forest, and was from thence conveyed to Westminster.

[9] *early lost ... led* When Cowley died (at the age of 49) his body was floated down the river to London by barge.

[10] *drooping swans ... expire* Swans were said to sing just before their deaths.

[11] *silver star* Worn by members of the Order of the Garter. Granville was never admitted to the Order, though Pope here suggests he should be.

[12] [Pope's note] Henry Howard, Earl of Surrey, one of the first refiners of the English poetry, who flourished in the time of Henry VIII for his sonnets. [Surrey spent time at Windsor Castle as a young man, and it is believed that he later wrote many of his love poems while imprisoned there.]

[13] *Fair ... now* Geraldine and Myra are the fictional names given to the women to whom Surrey and Granville, respectively, directed their love poems.

What kings first breathed upon her winding shore,[1]
Or raise old warriors whose adored remains
In weeping[2] vaults her hallowed earth contains!
With Edward's acts[3] adorn the shining page,
Stretch his long triumphs down through every age,
Draw monarchs chained, and Crécy's glorious field,
The lilies blazing on the regal shield.
Then, from her roofs when Verrio's colours[4] fall,
And leave inanimate the naked wall,
Still in thy song should vanquished France appear,
And bleed forever under Britain's spear.

Let softer strains ill-fated Henry mourn,
And palms eternal flourish round his urn.
Here o'er the martyr-king the marble weeps,
And fast beside him, once-feared Edward sleeps;
Whom not th' extended Albion could contain,
From old Belerium to the Northern Main,
The grave unites; where ev'n the great find rest,
And blended lie th' oppressor and th' oppressed![5]

Make sacred Charles's's[6] tomb forever known
(Obscure the place, and uninscribed the stone)
Oh, fact° accursed! What tears has Albion shed, *crime*
Heav'ns! what new wounds, and how her old have bled?
She saw her sons with purple deaths expire,
Her sacred domes° involved in rolling fire, *churches*
A dreadful series of intestine° wars,[7] *civil*
Inglorious triumphs, and dishonest° scars. *shameful*
At length great ANNA[8] said—"Let discord cease!"
She said, the world obeyed, and all was peace![9]

In that blest moment, from his oozy bed
Old Father Thames advanced his rev'rend head.
His tresses dropped with dews, and o'er the stream
His shining horns diffused a golden gleam.
Graved on his urn appeared the moon, that guides
His swelling waters and alternate tides;
The figured streams in waves of silver rolled,
And on their banks Augusta° rose in gold. *London*
Around his throne the sea-born brothers[10] stood,
Who swell, with tributary urns, his flood.
First the famed authors of his ancient name,
The winding Isis, and the fruitful Thame;[11]
The Kennet swift, for silver eels renowned;
The Loddon slow, with verdant alders crowned;
Colne, whose dark streams his flow'ry islands lave;
And chalky Wey, that rolls a milky wave.
The blue, transparent Vandalis° appears; *Wandle*
The gulphy° Lee his sedgy° tresses rears; *eddying / reedy*
And sullen Mole, that hides his diving flood;[12]
And silent Darent, stained with Danish blood.[13]

High in the midst, upon his urn reclined
(His sea-green mantle waving with the wind),
The god appeared; he turned his azure eyes
Where Windsor domes and pompous turrets rise,
Then bowed and spoke; the winds forget to roar,
And the hushed waves glide softly to the shore.

Hail sacred peace! hail long-expected days,
That Thames's glory to the stars shall raise!

---

[1] *winding shore* The word "Windsor" is said to derive from "winding shore," or "winding bank."

[2] *weeping* As a result of condensation that collects and runs down the surfaces of stone in damp places.

[3] *Edward's acts* King Edward III defeated the French at Crécy (line 305) and took captive, at different times, the kings of both France and Scotland. When he assumed the title of King of France, he added the French emblem of the lily to the English coat of arms (line 306).

[4] *Verrio's colours* Murals depicting the surrender of France to King Edward were painted on the Windsor Castle ceilings by artist Antonio Verrio.

[5] *Let ... th' oppressed* When Edward, Duke of York, proclaimed himself King Edward IV, King Henry VI was forced to become a fugitive. He hid in northern Britain until Edward eventually captured and murdered him. Henry has since been regarded by many as a saint and a martyr (the "palms eternal," line 312, are a symbol of martyrdom). Eventually both kings were buried in St. George's Chapel in Windsor Castle.

[6] *Charles* Charles I, who was executed by the Puritans, was buried, without any service, in an unmarked tomb in St. George's Chapel.

[7] *She saw ... wars* Some people believed the Great Plague (1665), the Great Fire (1666), and the Revolution of 1688 to be divine retribution for the murder of Charles I.

[8] *great ANNA* I.e., Queen Anne.

[9] *peace* With the forthcoming Treaty of Utrecht.

[10] *sea-born brothers* According to classical mythology, all rivers were the offspring of the sea gods Oceanus and Tethys.

[11] *famed ... Thame* The Thames was said to be the son of the rivers Thame and Isis.

[12] *diving flood* Part of the river Mole flows underground.

[13] *Darent ... blood* Reference to the defeat of the Danes at the battle of Otford, which occurred not far from the banks of the Darent.

Though Tiber's streams immortal Rome behold,
Though foaming Hermus[1] swells with tides of gold,
From Heav'n itself though sev'nfold Nilus[2] flows,
And harvests on a hundred realms bestows;
These now no more shall be the Muse's themes,
Lost in my fame, as in the sea their streams.
Let Volga's banks with iron squadrons shine,[3]
And groves of lances glitter on the Rhine,
Let barb'rous Ganges[4] arm a servile train;
Be mine the blessings of a peaceful reign.
No more my sons shall dye with British blood
Red Iber's[5] sands, or Ister's[6] foaming flood;
Safe on my shore each unmolested swain
Shall tend the flocks, or reap the bearded grain;
The shady empire shall retain no trace
Of war or blood, but in the sylvan chase,
The trumpets sleep while cheerful horns are blown,
And arms employed on birds and beasts alone.
Behold! th' ascending villas[7] on my side
Project long shadows o'er the crystal tide.
Behold! Augusta's glitt'ring spires increase,
And temples rise,[8] the beauteous works of peace.
I see, I see where two fair cities[9] bend
Their ample bow, a new Whitehall ascend![10]
There, mighty nations shall inquire their doom,[11]
The world's great oracle in times to come;
There kings shall sue, and suppliant states be seen
Once more[12] to bend before a British Queen.
Thy trees, fair Windsor! now shall leave their woods,
And half thy forests rush into my floods,
Bear Britain's thunder, and her cross[13] display
To the bright regions of the rising day;
Tempt° icy seas, where scarce the waters roll, *risk*
Where clearer flames glow round the frozen pole;
Or under southern skies exalt their sails,
Led by new stars, and born by spicy gales!
For me the balm shall bleed, and amber flow;
The coral redden, and the ruby glow;
The pearly shell its lucid globe enfold,
And Phoebus warm the ripening ore[14] to gold.
The time shall come when, free as seas or wind,
Unbounded Thames[15] shall flow for all mankind;
Whole nations enter with each swelling tide,
And seas but join the regions they divide.
Earth's distant ends our glory shall behold,
And the new world launch forth to seek the old.
Then ships of uncouth° form shall stem the tide, *strange*
And feathered people[16] crowd my wealthy side,
And naked youths and painted chiefs admire
Our speech, our colour, and our strange attire!
Oh, stretch thy reign, fair Peace! from shore to shore,
Till Conquest cease, and Slav'ry be no more;
Till the freed Indians[17] in their native groves
Reap their own fruits, and woo their sable loves;
Peru once more a race of kings[18] behold,

[1] *Hermus* Italian river celebrated by Virgil, the sands of which were fabled to be made of gold.

[2] *From … Nilus* Because the source of the Nile was still unknown at the time, it was commonly said to flow from heaven. Ovid referred to the Nile as "sevenfold" because of its delta, which gave it many mouths.

[3] *Volga … shine* Allusion to Russia's defeat of Charles XII of Sweden in 1709.

[4] *barb'rous Ganges* Reference to the recent Mogul wars.

[5] *Iber* Ebro river in Spain, where England and the Allies gained a victory at Sargossa in 1710.

[6] *Ister* Danube. The Duke of Marlborough had achieved Britain's greatest recent victory at Blenheim in 1704.

[7] *th' ascending villas* New homes being built along the Thames.

[8] *temples rise* To accommodate the growing population, Queen Anne recommended that 50 new churches be built; only 12 were ultimately constructed.

[9] *two fair cities* London and Westminster, located above and below a bend ("bow") in the river Thames.

[10] *new … ascend* There were plans (never carried out) to restore Whitehall Palace, a former residence of the British monarchs that had burned down in 1698.

[11] *doom* Fate. See Isaiah 60.

[12] *Once more* As they did during the reign of Elizabeth I.

[13] *her cross* Red cross of St. George on the Union Jack, Britain's flag. Britain's wooden ships are here depicted spreading British rule and commerce across the globe.

[14] *ripening ore* It was believed that the sun caused precious metals to grow and ripen in the ground.

[15] [Pope's note] A wish that London may be a free port. [Many objected to the current customs duties, believing they limited international trade.]

[16] *feathered people* In 1710 four Iroquois chiefs had visited England and been granted a public audience with the queen.

[17] *freed Indians* From Spanish tyranny.

[18] *race of kings* Incas.

And other Mexico's be roofed with gold.
Exiled by thee from earth to deepest hell,
In brazen bonds shall barb'rous Discord dwell;
Gigantic Pride, pale Terror, gloomy Care,
And mad Ambition shall attend her there.
There purple Vengeance, bathed in gore, retires,
Her weapons blunted, and extinct her fires;
There hateful Envy her own snakes shall feel,
And Persecution mourn her broken wheel;[1]
There Faction roar, Rebellion bite her chain,
And gasping Furies thirst for blood in vain.
Here cease thy flight, nor with unhallowed lays
Touch the fair fame of Albion's golden days.
The thoughts of gods let Granville's verse recite,
And bring the scenes of opening fate to light.
My humble Muse, in unambitious strains,
Paints the green forests and the flow'ry plains,
Where Peace descending bids her olives spring,
And scatters blessings from her dove-like wing.
Ev'n I more sweetly pass my careless days,
Pleased in the silent shade with empty praise;
Enough for me that to the listening swains
First in these fields I sung the sylvan strains.
—1713

The Rape of the Lock: An Heroi-Comical Poem in Five Cantos

TO MRS. ARABELLA FERMOR[2]

Madam,

It will be in vain to deny that I have some regard for this piece, since I dedicate it to you. Yet you may bear me witness, it was intended only to divert a few young ladies, who have good sense and good humour enough, to laugh not only at their sex's little unguarded follies, but at their own. But, as it was communicated with the air of a secret, it soon found its way into the world. An imperfect copy having been offered to a bookseller,[3] you had the good nature for my sake to consent to the publication of one more correct; this I was forced to before I had executed half my design, for the machinery was entirely wanting to complete it.

The machinery, Madam, is a term invented by the critics to signify that part which the deities, angels, or demons are made to act in a poem; for the ancient poets are in one respect like many modern ladies: let an action be never so trivial in itself, they always make it appear of the utmost importance. These machines I determined to raise on a very new and odd foundation, the Rosicrucian[4] doctrine of spirits.

I know how disagreeable it is to make use of hard words before a lady, but 'tis so much the concern of a poet to have his works understood, and particularly by your sex, that you must give me leave to explain two or three difficult terms.

The Rosicrucians are a people I must bring you acquainted with. The best account I know of them is in a French book called *Le Comte de Gabalis*,[5] which both in its title and size is so like a novel that many of the fair sex have read it for one by mistake. According to these gentlemen, the four elements are inhabited by spirits, which they call Sylphs, Gnomes, Nymphs, and Salamanders.[6] The Gnomes, or demons of earth, delight in mischief, but the Sylphs, whose habitation is in the air, are the best-conditioned creatures imaginable. For they say any mortals may enjoy the most intimate familiarities with these gentle spirits, upon a condition very easy to all true adepts, an inviolate preservation of chastity.

As to the following cantos, all the passages of them are as fabulous[7] as the vision at the beginning, or the transformation at the end (except the loss of your hair,

[1] *wheel* Instrument of torture.

[2] *MRS. ARABELLA FERMOR* Arabella Fermor was the daughter of a prominent Catholic family. She was celebrated for her beauty. Lord Robert Petre snipped off a lock of her hair, occasioning Pope's poem. Mrs. was a title of respect for married or unmarried women.

[3] *bookseller* Publisher.

[4] *Rosicrucian* Religious sect, originating in Germany, which existed in the seventeenth and eighteenth centuries. Its members were devoted to the study of arcane philosophy and mystical doctrines.

[5] *Le Comte de Gabalis* Written by Abbé de Monfaucon de Villars and published in 1670, this was a lighthearted exploration of Rosicrucian philosophy. It was printed in duodecimo (about five by eight inches), a common size for novels and other inexpensive books.

[6] *Salamanders* Salamanders were believed to be able to withstand, and live in, fire.

[7] *fabulous* Mythical, fictional.

which I always mention with reverence). The human persons are as fictitious as the airy ones, and the character of Belinda, as it is now managed, resembles you in nothing but in beauty.

If this poem had as many graces as there are in your person, or in your mind, yet I could never hope it should pass through the world half so uncensured as you have done. But let its fortune be what it will, mine is happy enough, to have given me this occasion of assuring you that I am, with the truest esteem,

Madam,

Your most obedient humble servant.

A. POPE

Canto 1. Illustration from the 1714 edition. The other four illustrations from this edition are reproduced below.

CANTO 1

What dire offence from am'rous causes springs,
What mighty contests rise from trivial things,
I sing—This verse to Caryll, Muse! is due;
This, ev'n Belinda may vouchsafe to view:
Slight is the subject, but not so the praise,
If she inspire, and he approve my lays.° *verses*
Say what strange motive, Goddess! could compel
A well-bred lord t' assault a gentle belle?
Oh say what stranger cause, yet unexplored,° *undiscovered*
Could make a gentle belle reject a lord?
In tasks so bold can little men engage,
And in soft bosoms dwells such mighty rage?
Sol° through white curtains shot a tim'rous ray, *sun*
And oped those eyes that must eclipse the day;
Now lapdogs give themselves the rousing shake,
And sleepless lovers, just at twelve, awake:
Thrice rung the bell, the slipper knocked the ground,[1]
And the pressed watch[2] returned a silver sound.
Belinda still her downy pillow pressed,
Her guardian Sylph prolonged the balmy rest.
'Twas he had summoned to her silent bed
The morning dream[3] that hovered o'er her head.
A youth more glitt'ring than a birthnight beau[4]
(That ev'n in slumber caused her cheek to glow)
Seemed to her ear his winning lips to lay,
And thus in whispers said, or seemed to say:
"Fairest of mortals, thou distinguished care
Of thousand bright inhabitants of air!
If e'er one vision touched thy infant thought,
Of all the nurse and all the priest have taught,
Of airy elves by moonlight shadows seen,
The silver token, and the circled green,[5]

[1] *slipper ... ground* She bangs her slipper on the floor to summon the maid.

[2] *pressed watch* "Repeater" watches would chime the time, to the nearest quarter hour, when the stem was pressed.

[3] *morning dream* Morning dreams were believed to be particularly portentous.

[4] *birthnight beau* On the birthday of the sovereign, members of the court dressed in their most lavish attire.

[5] *silver token* Fairies were said to skim the cream from the top of jugs of milk left overnight, leaving a silver coin in its place; *circled green* Rings in the grass that were said to be produced by dancing fairies.

Or virgins visited by angel pow'rs,
With golden crowns and wreaths of heav'nly flow'rs,
Hear and believe! thy own importance know,
Nor bound thy narrow views to things below.
Some secret truths, from learned pride concealed,
To maids alone and children are revealed.
What though no credit doubting wits may give?
The fair and innocent shall still believe.
Know then, unnumbered spirits round thee fly,
The light militia of the lower sky;
These, though unseen, are ever on the wing,
Hang o'er the box, and hover round the Ring.[1]
Think what an equipage° thou hast in air, *retinue with vehicles*
And view with scorn two pages and a chair.° *sedan chair*
As now your own, our beings were of old,
And once enclosed in woman's beauteous mold;
Thence, by a soft transition, we repair
From earthly vehicles to these of air.
Think not, when woman's transient breath is fled,
That all her vanities at once are dead:
Succeeding vanities she still regards,
And though she plays no more, o'erlooks the cards.
Her joy in gilded chariots, when alive,
And love of ombre,[2] after death survive.
For when the fair in all their pride expire,
To their first elements[3] their souls retire:
The sprites[4] of fiery termagants[5] in flame
Mount up, and take a Salamander's name.
Soft yielding minds to water glide away,
And sip, with Nymphs, their elemental tea.
The graver prude sinks downward to a Gnome,
In search of mischief still on earth to roam.
The light coquettes in Sylphs aloft repair,
And sport and flutter in the fields of air.
"Know further yet, whoever fair and chaste
Rejects mankind, is by some Sylph embraced:
For spirits, freed from mortal laws, with ease
Assume what sexes and what shapes they please.[6]
What guards the purity of melting maids
In courtly balls, and midnight masquerades,
Safe from the treach'rous friend, the daring spark,° *suitor*
The glance by day, the whisper in the dark,
When kind occasion prompts their warm desires,
When music softens, and when dancing fires?
'Tis but their Sylph, the wise celestials know,
Though *honour* is the word with men below.
"Some nymphs° there are, too conscious of their face, *maidens*
For life predestined to the Gnomes' embrace.
These swell their prospects and exalt their pride
When offers are disdained, and love denied.
Then gay ideas° crowd the vacant brain, *images*
While peers° and dukes, and all their sweeping train, *nobles*
And garters, stars, and coronets[7] appear,
And in soft sounds, 'your Grace' salutes their ear.
'Tis these that early taint the female soul,
Instruct the eyes of young coquettes to roll,
Teach infant cheeks a bidden blush to know,
And little hearts to flutter at a beau.
"Oft, when the world imagine women stray,
The Sylphs through mystic mazes guide their way,
Through all the giddy circle they pursue,
And old impertinence expel by new.
What tender maid but must a victim fall
To one man's treat,° but for another's ball? *feast*
When Florio speaks, what virgin could withstand,
If gentle Damon did not squeeze her hand?
With varying vanities, from ev'ry part,
They shift the moving toyshop[8] of their heart;
Where wigs with wigs, with sword-knots[9] sword-knots strive,

[1] *box* Private compartment in a theater; *the Ring* Circular drive that divides Hyde Park from Kensington Gardens.

[2] *ombre* A popular card game.

[3] *first elements* All things on earth had been thought to be made from the four elements (earth, air, fire, and water), and one of these four elements had been thought to be predominant in the temperament of each person.

[4] *sprites* Spirits.

[5] *termagants* Quarrelsome, turbulent, or hot-tempered women.

[6] *spirits … please* Cf. Milton's *Paradise Lost*, 1.423–24, "For spirits when they please / Can either sex assume, or both." This is one of many allusions to Milton's epic poem.

[7] *garters, stars, and coronets* Emblems of noble ranks.

[8] *toyshop* Store that sold not only toys but various trinkets, accessories, and ornaments.

[9] *sword-knots* Fashionable men of society wore ribbons knotted around the hilts of their swords. They also wore wigs.

Beaux banish beaux, and coaches coaches drive.
This erring mortals levity may call,
Oh blind to truth! the sylphs contrive it all.
"Of these am I, who thy protection claim,
A watchful sprite, and Ariel is my name.
Late, as I ranged the crystal wilds of air,
In the clear mirror of thy ruling star
I saw, alas! some dread event impend,
Ere to the main° this morning sun descend; *sea*
But Heav'n reveals not what, or how, or where:
Warned by thy Sylph, oh pious maid beware!
This to disclose is all thy guardian can:
Beware of all, but most beware of man!"
He said; when Shock,[1] who thought she slept too long,
Leaped up, and waked his mistress with his tongue.
'Twas then, Belinda, if report say true,
Thy eyes first opened on a billet-doux;° *love letter*
Wounds, charms, and ardors were no sooner read,
But all the vision vanished from thy head.
And now, unveiled, the toilet° stands displayed, *dressing table*
Each silver vase in mystic order laid.
First, robed in white, the nymph intent adores,
With head uncovered, the cosmetic pow'rs.
A heav'nly image in the glass appears,
To that she bends, to that her eyes she rears.° *lifts*
Th' inferior priestess,[2] at her altar's side,
Trembling begins the sacred rites of pride.
Unnumbered treasures ope at once, and here
The various off'rings of the world appear;
From each she nicely culls with curious toil,
And decks the goddess with the glitt'ring spoil.
This casket India's glowing gems unlocks,
And all Arabia breathes from yonder box.
The tortoise here and elephant unite,
Transformed to combs, the speckled and the white.
Here files of pins extend their shining rows,
Puffs, powders, patches,[3] Bibles, billet-doux.
Now awful° beauty puts on all its arms; *awe-inspiring*
The fair each moment rises in her charms,
Repairs her smiles, awakens ev'ry grace,
And calls forth all the wonders of her face;
Sees by degrees a purer blush arise,
And keener lightnings quicken in her eyes.[4]
The busy Sylphs surround their darling care,
These set the head, and those divide the hair,
Some fold the sleeve, whilst others plait the gown;
And Betty's praised for labours not her own.

CANTO 2

Not with more glories, in th' ethereal plain,
The sun first rises o'er the purpled main,
Than issuing forth, the rival of his beams

[1] *Shock* Belinda's lapdog, named after a popular breed of long-haired, Icelandic toy poodle called the "shough," or "shock."

[2] *Th' inferior priestess* Betty, Belinda's maid.

[3] *patches* Artificial beauty marks made of silk or plaster cut into various shapes and placed on the face, either for decoration or to hide an imperfection.

[4] *keener ... eyes* As a result of drops of belladonna, or deadly nightshade, which enlarges the pupils.

Launched on the bosom of the silver Thames.[1]
Fair nymphs and well-dressed youths around her shone,
But every eye was fixed on her alone.
On her white breast a sparkling cross she wore,
Which Jews might kiss, and infidels adore.
Her lively looks a sprightly mind disclose,
Quick as her eyes, and as unfixed as those:
Favours to none, to all she smiles extends;
Oft she rejects, but never once offends.
Bright as the sun, her eyes the gazers strike,
And, like the sun, they shine on all alike.
Yet graceful ease, and sweetness void of pride,
Might hide her faults, if belles had faults to hide:
If to her share some female errors fall,
Look on her face, and you'll forget 'em all.
This nymph, to the destruction of mankind,
Nourished two locks, which graceful hung behind
In equal curls, and well conspired to deck
With shining ringlets the smooth iv'ry neck.
Love in these labyrinths his slaves detains,
And mighty hearts are held in slender chains;
With hairy springes° we the birds betray; *snares*
Slight lines of hair surprise the finny prey;
Fair tresses man's imperial race ensnare,
And beauty draws us with a single hair.
Th' adventurous Baron the bright locks admired;
He saw, he wished, and to the prize aspired.
Resolved to win, he meditates the way,
By force to ravish, or by fraud betray;
For when success a lover's toil attends,
Few ask if fraud or force attained his ends.
For this, ere Phoebus[2] rose, he had implored
Propitious Heav'n, and every pow'r adored,° *worshiped*
But chiefly Love—to Love an altar built,
Of twelve vast French romances, neatly gilt.
There lay three garters, half a pair of gloves,
And all the trophies of his former loves.
With tender billet-doux he lights the pyre,
And breathes three am'rous sighs to raise the fire.
Then prostrate falls, and begs with ardent eyes
Soon to obtain, and long possess the prize:
The pow'rs gave ear, and granted half his prayer;
The rest the winds dispersed in empty air.
But now secure the painted vessel glides,
The sunbeams trembling on the floating tides,
While melting music steals upon the sky,
And softened sounds along the waters die.
Smooth flow the waves, the zephyrs gently play,
Belinda smiled, and all the world was gay.
All but the Sylph—with careful thoughts oppressed,
Th' impending woe sat heavy on his breast.
He summons strait his denizens of air;
The lucid squadrons round the sails repair:
Soft o'er the shrouds[3] aerial whispers breathe
That seemed but zephyrs° to the train beneath. *mild breezes*
Some to the sun their insect-wings unfold,
Waft on the breeze, or sink in clouds of gold.
Transparent forms, too fine for mortal sight,
Their fluid bodies half dissolved in light,
Loose to the wind their airy garments flew,
Thin glitt'ring textures of the filmy dew,
Dipped in the richest tincture of the skies,
Where light disports in ever-mingling dyes,
While every beam new transient colours flings,
Colours that change whene'er they wave their wings.
Amid the circle, on the gilded mast,
Superior by the head, was Ariel placed;
His purple pinions° op'ning to the sun, *wings*
He raised his azure wand, and thus begun:
"Ye Sylphs and Sylphids, to your chief give ear!
Fays, Fairies, Genii, Elves, and Demons, hear!
Ye know the spheres and various tasks assigned,
By laws eternal, to th' aerial kind.
Some in the fields of purest ether[4] play,
And bask and whiten in the blaze of day.
Some guide the course of wand'ring orbs on high,
Or roll the planets through the boundless sky.
Some, less refined, beneath the moon's pale light
Pursue the stars that shoot athwart the night,
Or suck the mists in grosser[5] air below,
Or dip their pinions in the painted bow,
Or brew fierce tempests on the wintry main,

[1] *Launched ... Thames* Belinda voyages upstream to Hampton Court for the day. By taking a boat she avoids the crowds and filth in the streets.

[2] *Phoebus* One of the names of Apollo, god of the sun.

[3] *shrouds* Ropes that brace the mast of the ship.

[4] *ether* Clear regions above the moon.

[5] *grosser* Material, as opposed to ethereal, realms.

Or o'er the glebe[1] distill the kindly rain.
Others on earth o'er human race preside,
Watch all their ways, and all their actions guide:
Of these the chief the care of nations own,
And guard with arms divine the British Throne.
"Our humbler province is to tend the fair,
Not a less pleasing, though less glorious care:
To save the powder from too rude a gale,
Nor let th' imprisoned essences° exhale; *perfumes*
To draw fresh colours from the vernal flow'rs;
To steal from rainbows ere they drop in show'rs
A brighter wash;[2] to curl their waving hairs,
Assist their blushes, and inspire their airs;
Nay, oft in dreams invention we bestow,
To change a flounce, or add a furbelo.° *pleated trim*
"This day, black omens threat the brightest fair
That e'er deserved a watchful spirit's care;
Some dire disaster, or by force or slight,
But what, or where, the Fates have wrapped in night.
Whether the nymph shall break Diana's law,[3]
Or some frail China jar receive a flaw,
Or stain her honour, or her new brocade,
Forget her prayers, or miss a masquerade,
Or lose her heart, or necklace, at a ball;
Or whether Heav'n has doomed that Shock must fall.
Haste then, ye spirits! To your charge repair:
The flutt'ring fan be Zephyretta's care;
The drops° to thee, Brillante, we consign; *diamond earrings*
And, Momentilla, let the watch be thine;
Do thou, Crispissa,[4] tend her fav'rite lock;
Ariel himself shall be the guard of Shock.
"To fifty chosen Sylphs, of special note,
We trust th' important charge, the petticoat:
Oft have we known that sev'nfold fence[5] to fail,
Though stiff with hoops, and armed with ribs of whale.
Form a strong line about the silver bound,
And guard the wide circumference around.
"Whatever spirit, careless of his charge,
His post neglects, or leaves the fair at large,
Shall feel sharp vengeance soon o'ertake his sins,
Be stopped in vials, or transfixed with pins,
Or plunged in lakes of bitter washes lie,
Or wedged whole ages in a bodkin's[6] eye;
Gums and pomatums° shall his flight restrain, *hair ointments*
While clogged he beats his silken wings in vain,
Or alum styptics[7] with contracting pow'r
Shrink his thin essence like a riveled° flow'r. *shriveled*
Or, as Ixion[8] fixed, the wretch shall feel
The giddy motion of the whirling mill,
In fumes of burning chocolate shall glow,
And tremble at the sea that froths below!"
He spoke; the spirits from the sails descend;
Some, orb in orb, around the nymph extend;
Some thread the mazy° ringlets of her hair; *maze-like*
Some hang upon the pendants of her ear.
With beating hearts the dire event they wait,
Anxious, and trembling for the birth of fate.

CANTO 3

Close by those meads forever crowned with flow'rs,
Where Thames with pride surveys his rising tow'rs,
There stands a structure of majestic frame,[9]
Which from the neighb'ring Hampton takes its name.
Here Britain's statesmen oft the fall foredoom
Of foreign tyrants, and of nymphs at home;
Here thou, great Anna! whom three realms obey,
Dost sometimes counsel take—and sometimes tea.
Hither the heroes and the nymphs resort,
To taste awhile the pleasures of a court;
In various talk th' instructive hours they passed,
Who gave the ball, or paid the visit last;

[1] *glebe* Fields.

[2] *wash* Liquid cosmetic.

[3] *break Diana's law* Lose her virginity (Diana was the Roman goddess of chastity).

[4] *Crispissa* From *crispere*, the Latin verb meaning "to curl."

[5] *sev'nfold fence* Allusion to Achilles's "sevenfold shield" in *The Iliad*.

[6] *bodkin* Blunt needle with both a large and a small eye, used to draw ribbon through a hem.

[7] *alum styptics* Astringent substances applied to cuts to contract tissue and stop bleeding.

[8] *Ixion* Zeus punished Ixion, who had attempted to seduce Hera, by tying him to a continuously revolving wheel in Hades. Here the wheel would be that of a machine that beats hot chocolate to a froth.

[9] *structure … majestic frame* Hampton Court, largest of Queen Anne's residences, located about 12 miles up the Thames from London.

One speaks the glory of the British Queen,
And one describes a charming Indian screen;
A third interprets motions, looks, and eyes;
At every word a reputation dies.
Snuff, or the fan, supply each pause of chat,
With singing, laughing, ogling, and all that.
    Meanwhile, declining from the noon of day,
The sun obliquely shoots his burning ray;
The hungry judges soon the sentence sign,
And wretches hang that jurymen may dine;
The merchant from th' Exchange[1] returns in peace,
And the long labours of the toilette cease.
Belinda now, whom thirst of fame invites,
Burns to encounter two adventurous knights
At ombre,[2] singly to decide their doom,
And swells her breast with conquests yet to come.
Straight the three bands prepare in arms to join,
Each band the number of the sacred nine.[3]
Soon as she spreads her hand, th' aerial guard
Descend, and sit on each important card:
First Ariel perched upon a Matadore,[4]
Then each according to the rank they bore;
For Sylphs, yet mindful of their ancient race,
Are, as when women, wondrous fond of place.° *social status*
    Behold, four Kings in majesty revered,
With hoary whiskers and a forky beard;
And four fair Queens whose hands sustain a flow'r,
Th' expressive emblem of their softer pow'r;
Four Knaves in garbs succinct,[5] a trusty band,
Caps on their heads, and halberds[6] in their hand;
And parti-coloured troops, a shining train,
Draw forth to combat on the velvet plain.
    The skilful nymph reviews her force with care;
"Let Spades be trumps!" she said, and trumps they were.
    Now move to war her sable Matadores,
In show like leaders of the swarthy Moors.
Spadillio first, unconquerable lord!
Led off two captive trumps, and swept the board.
As many more Manillio forced to yield,
And marched a victor from the verdant field.
Him Basto followed, but, his fate more hard,
Gained but one trump and one plebeian card.
With his broad sabre next, a chief in years,
The hoary Majesty of Spades appears,
Puts forth one manly leg, to sight revealed,
The rest his many-coloured robe concealed.
The rebel Knave, who dares his prince engage,
Proves the just victim of his royal rage.

[1] *th' Exchange* The Royal Exchange, located in the commercial center of London, was the principal market where merchants traded and where bankers and brokers met to do business.

[2] *ombre* In the game of ombre that Belinda plays against the two men, Pope conveys an accurate sense of the game, the rules of which are similar to those of bridge. Each of the three players receives 9 cards from the 40 that are used (8s, 9s, and 10s are discarded). Belinda, as the challenger, or "ombre" (from the Spanish *hombre*, "man"), names the trumps. To win, she must make more tricks than either of the other two. For a complete description of the game, see Geoffrey Tillotson's Twickenham edition of Pope's poems, volume 2.

[3] *sacred nine* Muses.

[4] *Matadore* Matadores are the three highest cards of the game. When spades are trump, as they are here, the highest card is the ace of spades ("Spadillio"), followed by the two of spades ("Manillio"), and then the ace of clubs ("Basto").

[5] *succinct* Brief, short. The knaves are wearing short tunics.

[6] *halberds* Weapons that combined the spear and battle axe.

Ev'n mighty Pam,[1] that kings and queens o'erthrew,
And mowed down armies in the fights of Loo,
Sad chance of war! now, destitute of aid,
Falls undistinguished by the victor Spade!
Thus far both armies to Belinda yield;
Now to the Baron fate inclines the field.
His warlike Amazon[2] her host invades,
Th' imperial consort of the crown of Spades.
The Club's black tyrant first her victim died,
Spite of his haughty mien° and barb'rous pride. *look*
What boots° the regal circle on his head, *avails*
His giant limbs in state unwieldy spread?
That long behind he trails his pompous robe,
And of all monarchs only grasps the globe?
The Baron now his Diamonds pours apace;
Th' embroidered King, who shows but half his face,
And his refulgent Queen, with pow'rs combined,
Of broken troops an easy conquest find.
Clubs, Diamonds, Hearts, in wild disorder seen,
With throngs promiscuous strew the level green.
Thus when dispersed a routed army runs,
Of Asia's troops, and Afric's sable sons,
With like confusion diff'rent nations fly,
Of various habit, and of various dye,
The pierced battalions disunited fall
In heaps on heaps; one fate o'erwhelms them all.
The Knave of Diamonds tries his wily arts,
And wins (oh, shameful chance!) the Queen of Hearts.
At this, the blood the virgin's cheek forsook,
A livid paleness spreads o'er all her look;
She sees, and trembles at th' approaching ill,
Just in the jaws of ruin, and Codille.[3]
And now (as oft in some distempered state)
On one nice trick depends the gen'ral fate.
An Ace of Hearts steps forth: the King unseen
Lurked in her hand, and mourned his captive Queen.
He springs to vengeance with an eager pace,
And falls like thunder on the prostrate Ace.
The nymph, exulting, fills with shouts the sky;
The walls, the woods, and long canals reply.

O thoughtless mortals! ever blind to fate,
Too soon dejected, and too soon elate!
Sudden these honours shall be snatched away,
And cursed forever this victorious day.
For lo! the board with cups and spoons is crowned,
The berries crackle, and the mill turns round.[4]
On shining altars of Japan[5] they raise
The silver lamp; the fiery spirits blaze.
From silver spouts the grateful liquors glide,
While China's earth[6] receives the smoking tide.
At once they gratify their scent and taste,
And frequent cups prolong the rich repast.
Straight hover round the fair her airy band;
Some, as she sipped, the fuming liquor fanned,
Some o'er her lap their careful plumes displayed,
Trembling, and conscious of the rich brocade.
Coffee (which makes the politician wise,
And see through all things with his half-shut eyes)
Sent up in vapours to the Baron's brain
New stratagems, the radiant lock to gain.
Ah, cease, rash youth! desist ere 'tis too late,
Fear the just gods, and think of Scylla's[7] fate!
Changed to a bird, and sent to flit in air,
She dearly pays for Nisus' injured hair!
But when to mischief mortals bend their will,
How soon they find fit instruments of ill!
Just then, Clarissa drew with tempting grace
A two-edged weapon° from her shining case; *pair of scissors*
So ladies in romance assist their knight,
Present the spear, and arm him for the fight.
He takes the gift with rev'rence, and extends
The little engine° on his fingers' ends; *instrument*
This just behind Belinda's neck he spread,
As o'er the fragrant steams she bends her head.
Swift to the lock a thousand sprites repair,
A thousand wings, by turns, blow back the hair,

[1] *Pam* Jack (knave) of clubs, the highest card in Loo, another popular card game.

[2] *Amazon* Female warrior; here, the Queen of Spades.

[3] *Codille* Defeat of the ombre.

[4] *berries ... round* Coffee beans ("berries") roasted and then ground.

[5] *altars of Japan* I.e., lacquered, or "japanned" tables, highly decorated and varnished tables. The style originated in Japan.

[6] *China's earth* China cups.

[7] *Scylla* According to Ovid's *Metamorphoses*, Scylla was turned into a seabird by her father, King Nisus, after she cut off his purple lock of hair (on which the kingdom's safety depended) to please her lover, Minos, who was besieging the city.

And thrice they twitched the diamond in her ear;
Thrice she looked back, and thrice the foe drew near.
Just in that instant, anxious Ariel sought
The close recesses of the virgin's thought;
As on the nosegay in her breast reclined,
He watched th' ideas rising in her mind.
Sudden he viewed, in spite of all her art,
An earthly lover lurking at her heart.
Amazed, confused, he found his pow'r expired,
Resigned to fate, and with a sigh retired.
The Peer now spreads the glitt'ring forfex° *scissors*
wide,
T' enclose the lock; now joins it, to divide.
Ev'n then, before the fatal engine closed,
A wretched Sylph too fondly interposed;
Fate urged the sheers, and cut the Sylph in twain
(But airy substance soon unites again).
The meeting points the sacred hair dissever
From the fair head, forever and forever!
Then flashed the living lightning from her eyes,
And screams of horror rend th' affrighted skies.
Not louder shrieks to pitying heav'n are cast,
When husbands or when lapdogs breathe their last,
Or when rich china vessels, fall'n from high,
In glitt'ring dust and painted fragments lie!
"Let wreaths of triumph now my temples twine,"
The victor cried, "the glorious prize is mine!
While fish in streams, or birds delight in air,
Or in a coach and six the British fair,
As long as *Atalantis*[1] shall be read,
Or the small pillow grace a lady's bed,
While visits shall be paid on solemn days,
When num'rous wax-lights in bright order blaze,
While nymphs take treats, or assignations give,
So long my honour, name, and praise shall live!
"What time would spare, from steel receives its date,
And monuments, like men, submit to fate!
Steel could the labour of the Gods destroy,
And strike to dust th' imperial towers of Troy;
Steel could the works of mortal pride confound,
And hew triumphal arches to the ground.
What wonder then, fair nymph! thy hairs should feel
The conqu'ring force of unresisted steel?"

CANTO 4

But anxious cares the pensive nymph oppressed,
And secret passions laboured in her breast.
Not youthful kings in battle seized alive,
Not scornful virgins who their charms survive,
Not ardent lovers robbed of all their bliss,
Not ancient ladies when refused a kiss,
Not tyrants fierce that unrepenting die,
Not Cynthia when her manteau's pinned awry,
Ev'r felt such rage, resentment, and despair,
As thou, sad virgin! for thy ravished hair.
For, that sad moment when the sylphs withdrew,
And Ariel weeping from Belinda flew,
Umbriel, a dusky, melancholy sprite
As ever sullied the fair face of light,
Down to the central earth, his proper scene,

[1] *Atalantis* Delarivier Manley's *New Atalantis* was an enormously creative rendering of the latest political scandals and social intrigues, which she recreated as fiction.

Repaired to search the gloomy Cave of Spleen.[1]
  Swift on his sooty pinions flits the Gnome,
And in a vapour reached the dismal dome.
No cheerful breeze this sullen region knows,
The dreaded east[2] is all the wind that blows.
Here, in a grotto, sheltered close from air,
And screened in shades from day's detested glare,
She sighs forever on her pensive bed,
Pain at her side, and megrim° at her head. *migraine*
  Two handmaids wait the throne: alike in place,
But diff'ring far in figure and in face.
Here stood Ill-Nature like an ancient maid,
Her wrinkled form in black and white arrayed;
With store of prayers for mornings, nights, and noons
Her hand is filled; her bosom with lampoons.
  There Affectation, with a sickly mien,° *appearance*
Shows in her cheek the roses of eighteen,
Practised to lisp, and hang the head aside,
Faints into airs, and languishes with pride;
On the rich quilt sinks with becoming woe,
Wrapped in a gown, for sickness and for show.
The fair ones feel such maladies as these,
When each new nightdress gives a new disease.
  A constant vapour o'er the palace flies,
Strange phantoms rising as the mists arise;
Dreadful as hermit's dreams in haunted shades,
Or bright as visions of expiring maids.
Now glaring fiends and snakes on rolling spires,° *coils*
Pale spectres, gaping tombs, and purple fires;
Now lakes of liquid gold, Elysian scenes,
And crystal domes, and angels in machines.[3]
  Unnumbered throngs on every side are seen
Of bodies changed to various forms by spleen.
Here living teapots stand, one arm held out,
One bent; the handle this, and that the spout.
A pipkin° there like Homer's tripod[4] walks; *small earthen pot*
Here sighs a jar, and there a goose pye[5] talks;
Men prove with child, as pow'rful fancy works,
And maids turned bottles call aloud for corks.
  Safe passed the Gnome through this fantastic band,
A branch of healing spleenwort[6] in his hand.
Then thus addressed the pow'r: "Hail, wayward Queen!
Who rule the sex to fifty from fifteen,
Parent of vapors and of female wit,
Who give th' hysteric or poetic fit,
On various tempers act by various ways,
Make some take physic,° others scribble plays; *medicine*
Who cause the proud their visits to delay,
And send the godly in a pet,[7] to pray.
A nymph there is that all thy pow'r disdains,
And thousands more in equal mirth maintains.
But oh! if e'er thy Gnome could spoil a grace,
Or raise a pimple on a beauteous face,
Like citron-waters[8] matrons' cheeks inflame,
Or change complexions at a losing game;
If e'er with airy horns[9] I planted heads,
Or rumpled petticoats, or tumbled beds,
Or caused suspicion when no soul was rude,
Or discomposed the headdress of a prude,
Or e'er to costive lapdog gave disease,
Which not the tears of brightest eyes could ease—
Hear me, and touch Belinda with chagrin;
That single act gives half the world the spleen."
  The Goddess with a discontented air
Seems to reject him, though she grants his prayer.
A wondrous bag with both her hands she binds,

[1] *Cave of Spleen* The spleen was thought to be the seat of melancholy or morose feelings, and "spleen" became a term used to cover any number of complaints including headaches, depression, irritability, hallucinations, or hypochondria.

[2] *dreaded east* An east wind was thought to bring on attacks of spleen (also called "the vapors").

[3] *machines* Contraptions used in theater to lower actors playing gods onto the stage from above. This convention from ancient Greek drama is reflected in the term *Deus ex machina* (Latin: God from the machine), referring to a divine intervention or another plot twist that immediately resolves a seemingly unsolvable problem within a work of fiction.

[4] *Homer's tripod* In Homer's *Illiad* (Book 18), Vulcan makes three-legged stools that move by themselves.

[5] [Pope's note] Alludes to a real fact, a Lady of distinction imagin'd herself in this condition.

[6] *spleenwort* Herb said to cure ailments of the spleen. Here it is reminiscent of the golden bough that Aeneas carries for protection on his journey to the underworld (*Aeneid*, Book 6).

[7] *pet* Fit of ill-humor.

[8] *citron-waters* Lemon-flavored brandy-based liquor.

[9] *horns* Sign of a cuckold. The horns here are "airy" because the wife's infidelity is only imagined by her jealous husband.

Like that where once Ulysses held the winds;[1]
There she collects the force of female lungs:
Sighs, sobs, and passions, and the war of tongues.
A vial next she fills with fainting fears,
Soft sorrows, melting griefs, and flowing tears.
The Gnome rejoicing bears her gifts away,
Spreads his black wings, and slowly mounts to day.
    Sunk in Thalestris'[2] arms the nymph he found,
Her eyes dejected and her hair unbound.
Full o'er their heads the swelling bag he rent,
And all the Furies issued at the vent.
Belinda burns with more than mortal ire,
And fierce Thalestris fans the rising fire.
"O wretched maid!" she spread her hands, and cried
(While Hampton's echoes, "Wretched maid!" replied),
"Was it for this you took such constant care
The bodkin, comb, and essence to prepare?
For this your locks in paper durance[3] bound,
For this with tort'ring irons wreathed around?
For this with fillets strained your tender head,
And bravely bore the double loads of lead?
Gods! shall the ravisher display your hair,
While the fops envy, and the ladies stare!
Honour forbid! at whose unrivaled shrine
Ease, pleasure, virtue, all, our sex resign.
Methinks already I your tears survey,
Already hear the horrid things they say,
Already see you a degraded toast,[4]
And all your honour in a whisper lost!
How shall I, then, your helpless fame defend?
'Twill then be infamy to seem your friend!
And shall this prize, th' inestimable prize,
Exposed through crystal to the gazing eyes,
And heightened by the diamond's circling rays,
On that rapacious hand forever blaze?[5]
Sooner shall grass in Hyde Park Circus[6] grow,
And wits take lodgings in the sound of Bow;[7]
Sooner let earth, air, sea, to chaos fall,
Men, monkeys, lapdogs, parrots, perish all!"
    She said; then raging to Sir Plume repairs,
And bids her beau demand the precious hairs
(Sir Plume, of amber snuffbox justly vain,
And the nice conduct of a clouded° cane). *marbled*
With earnest eyes and round unthinking face,
He first the snuffbox opened, then the case,
And thus broke out—"My Lord, why, what the devil?
Z—ds!° damn the lock! 'fore Gad, you must *zounds*
    be civil!
Plague on't! 'tis past a jest—nay prithee, pox!
Give her the hair"—he spoke, and rapped his box.
    "It grieves me much," replied the Peer again,
"Who speaks so well should ever speak in vain.
But by this lock, this sacred lock I swear
(Which never more shall join its parted hair;
Which never more its honours shall renew,
Clipped from the lovely head where late it grew)
That while my nostrils draw the vital air,
This hand, which won it, shall forever wear."
He spoke, and, speaking, in proud triumph spread
The long-contended honours of her head.
    But Umbriel, hateful Gnome! forbears not so;
He breaks the vial whence the sorrows flow.
Then see! the nymph in beauteous grief appears,
Her eyes half languishing, half drowned in tears;
On her heaved bosom hung her drooping head,
Which with a sigh she raised, and thus she said:
    "Forever cursed be this detested day,
Which snatched my best, my fav'rite curl away!
Happy! ah ten times happy had I been,
If Hampton Court these eyes had never seen!
Yet am not I the first mistaken maid
By love of courts to num'rous ills betrayed.
Oh, had I rather unadmired remained
In some lone isle, or distant northern land;

[1] *Ulysses … winds* In Homer's *Odyssey*, Aeolus, keeper of the winds, gives Odysseus a bag filled with wind to help him sail home to Ithaca. Believing that the bag is filled with riches, Odysseus's men greedily open it and unleash a hurricane.

[2] *Thalestris* Queen of the Amazons; here, suggesting a fierce, pugnacious woman.

[3] *paper durance* Curling papers, which were fastened to the hair with strips of hot lead. The head was then encircled by a fillet, or thin crown.

[4] *toast* Woman whose health is drunk. Since toasting a woman implied familiarity with her, it was detrimental to a lady's reputation if it was done too frequently, or by too many men.

[5] *Exposed … blaze* I.e., the Baron will set the hair in a ring.

[6] *Hyde Park Circus* Another name for the Ring road in Hyde Park.

[7] *in the sound of Bow* Within the sound of the church bells of St. Mary-le-Bow in Cheapside, an unfashionable part of town.

Where the gilt chariot never marks the way,
Where none learn ombre, none e'er taste bohea![1]
There kept my charms concealed from mortal eye,
Like roses that in deserts bloom and die.
What moved my mind with youthful lords to roam?
Oh, had I stayed and said my prayers at home!
'Twas this the morning omens seemed to tell;
Thrice from my trembling hand the patch box fell;
The tott'ring china shook without a wind,
Nay, Poll[2] sat mute, and Shock was most unkind!
A Sylph too warned me of the threats of fate,
In mystic visions, now believed too late!
See the poor remnants of these slighted hairs!
My hands shall rend what ev'n thy rapine spares.
These, in two sable ringlets taught to break,
Once gave new beauties to the snowy neck.
The sister lock now sits uncouth, alone,
And in its fellow's fate foresees its own;
Uncurled it hangs, the fatal shears demands,
And tempts once more thy sacrilegious hands.
Oh, hadst thou, cruel! been content to seize
Hairs less in sight, or any hairs but these!"

CANTO 5

She said; the pitying audience melt in tears,
But Fate and Jove[3] had stopped the Baron's ears.
In vain Thalestris with reproach assails,
For who can move when fair Belinda fails?
Not half so fixed the Trojan could remain,
While Anna begged and Dido raged in vain.[4]
Then grave Clarissa[5] graceful waved her fan;
Silence ensued, and thus the nymph began:

"Say, why are beauties praised and honoured most,
The wise man's passion, and the vain man's toast?
Why decked with all that land and sea afford,
Why angels called, and angel-like adored?
Why round our coaches crowd the white-gloved beaux,
Why bows the side box from its inmost rows?
How vain are all these glories, all our pains,
Unless good sense preserve what beauty gains;
That men may say, when we the front box grace,
'Behold the first in virtue, as in face!'
Oh! if to dance all night, and dress all day,
Charmed the smallpox, or chased old age away,
Who would not scorn what housewife's cares produce,
Or who would learn one earthly thing of use?
To patch, nay ogle, might become a saint,
Nor could it sure be such a sin to paint.
But since, alas! frail beauty must decay,
Curled or uncurled, since locks will turn to grey;
Since painted, or not painted, all shall fade,
And she who scorns a man must die a maid;

---

[1] *bohea* Expensive Chinese black tea.

[2] *Poll* Belinda's parrot.

[3] *Jove* King of the gods (Roman).

[4] *the Trojan … vain* Commanded by the gods, Aeneas left his distraught lover, Dido, to found the city of Rome. Dido's sister Anna begged him to return, but he refused.

[5] [Pope's note] A new character introduced in the subsequent editions to open more clearly the moral of the poem, in a parody of the speech of Sarpedon to Glaucus in Homer. [Cf. *Iliad* 12, in which Sarpedon reflects on glory and urges Glaucus to join the attack on Troy.]

What then remains but well our pow'r to use,
And keep good humour still, whate'er we lose?
And trust me, dear! good humour can prevail,
When airs and flights and screams and scolding fail.
Beauties in vain their pretty eyes may roll;
Charms strike the sight, but merit wins the soul."
So spoke the dame, but no applause ensued;[1]
Belinda frowned, Thalestris called her prude.
"To arms, to arms!" the fierce virago[2] cries,
And swift as lightning to the combat flies.
All side in parties, and begin th' attack;
Fans clap, silks rustle, and tough whalebones crack;
Heroes' and heroines' shouts confus'dly rise,
And base and treble voices strike the skies.
No common weapons in their hands are found;
Like Gods they fight, nor dread a mortal wound.
So when bold Homer makes the Gods engage,
And heav'nly breasts with human passions rage;
'Gainst Pallas, Mars; Latona, Hermes[3] arms;
And all Olympus rings with loud alarms.
Jove's thunder roars, heav'n trembles all around;
Blue Neptune storms, the bellowing deeps resound;
Earth shakes her nodding tow'rs, the ground gives way,
And the pale ghosts start at the flash of day!
Triumphant Umbriel on a sconce's[4] height
Clapped his glad wings, and sat to view the fight.
Propped on their bodkin spears, the sprites survey
The growing combat, or assist the fray.
While through the press enraged Thalestris flies,
And scatters deaths around from both her eyes,
A beau and witling° perished in the throng— *inferior wit*
One died in metaphor, and one in song.
"O cruel nymph! a living death I bear,"
Cried Dapperwit, and sunk beside his chair.
A mournful glance Sir Fopling upwards cast,
"Those eyes are made so killing"—was his last.
Thus on Maeander's flow'ry margin lies
Th' expiring swan, and as he sings he dies.[5]
When bold Sir Plume had drawn Clarissa down,
Chloe stepped in, and killed him with a frown;
She smiled to see the doughty° hero slain, *valiant*
But at her smile the beau revived again.
Now Jove suspends his golden scales[6] in air,
Weighs the men's wits against the lady's hair;
The doubtful beam long nods from side to side;
At length the wits mount up, the hairs subside.
See, fierce Belinda on the Baron flies
With more than usual lightning in her eyes;
Nor feared the chief th' unequal fight to try,
Who sought no more than on his foe to die.[7]
But this bold lord, with manly strength endued,
She with one finger and a thumb subdued:
Just where the breath of life his nostrils drew,
A charge of snuff the wily virgin threw;
The Gnomes direct, to every atom just,
The pungent grains of titillating dust.
Sudden, with starting tears each eye o'erflows,
And the high dome re-echoes to his nose.
"Now meet thy fate," incensed Belinda cried,
And drew a deadly bodkin[8] from her side.
(The same, his ancient personage to deck,
Her great-great-grandsire wore about his neck
In three seal rings;[9] which after, melted down,
Formed a vast buckle for his widow's gown.
Her infant grandame's whistle next it grew,
The bells she jingled, and the whistle blew;
Then in a bodkin graced her mother's hairs,
Which long she wore, and now Belinda wears.)
"Boast not my fall," he cried, "insulting foe!
Thou by some other shalt be laid as low.
Nor think to die dejects my lofty mind;
All that I dread is leaving you behind!
Rather than so, ah let me still survive,
And burn in Cupid's flames—but burn alive."

[1] [Pope's note] It is a verse frequently repeated in Homer after any speech, "So spoke ——, and all the heroes applauded."

[2] *virago* Female warrior.

[3] *Pallas* Athena, goddess of wisdom; *Mars* God of war; *Latona* Mother of Apollo and Diana; goddess of light; *Hermes* Amongst other attributions, god of deceit.

[4] *sconce* Wall bracket for holding a candle; also a small fort or earthwork.

[5] *Maeander ... dies* River in Phrygia (present-day Turkey). Swans were said to sing before their deaths.

[6] *golden scales* Used by the god to weigh the fates of mortals, particularly in battle.

[7] *to die* Metaphorically, to experience an orgasm.

[8] *bodkin* Here, a sharp hairpin. (A bodkin was formerly also a name for a dagger.)

[9] *seal rings* Rings used to imprint the wax that seals an envelope.

"Restore the lock!" she cries, and all around,
"Restore the lock!" the vaulted roofs rebound.
Not fierce Othello in so loud a strain
Roared for the handkerchief that caused his pain.[1]
But see how oft ambitious aims are crossed,
And chiefs contend 'till all the prize is lost!
The lock, obtained with guilt and kept with pain,
In every place is sought, but sought in vain;
With such a prize no mortal must be blessed,
So Heav'n decrees! with Heav'n who can contest?
Some thought it mounted to the lunar sphere,
Since all things lost on earth are treasured there.
There heroes' wits are kept in pond'rous vases,
And beaux' in snuffboxes and tweezer cases.
There broken vows and deathbed alms are found,
And lovers' hearts with ends of ribbon bound;
The courtier's promises, and sick man's prayers,
The smiles of harlots, and the tears of heirs,
Cages for gnats, and chains to yoke a flea,
Dried butterflies, and tomes of casuistry.[2]
But trust the Muse—she saw it upward rise,
Though marked by none but quick poetic eyes
(So Rome's great founder[3] to the heav'ns withdrew,
To Proculus alone confessed in view);
A sudden star, it shot through liquid° air, *transparent*
And drew behind a radiant trail of hair.
Not Berenice's[4] locks first rose so bright,
The heav'ns bespangling with disheveled light.
The Sylphs behold it kindling as it flies,
And, pleased, pursue its progress through the skies.
This the beau monde shall from the Mall[5] survey,
And hail with music its propitious ray.
This the blessed lover shall for Venus take,
And send up vows from Rosamonda's Lake.[6]
This Partridge[7] soon shall view in cloudless skies
When next he looks through Galileo's eyes;[8]
And hence th' egregious wizard shall foredoom
The fate of Louis, and the fall of Rome.
Then cease, bright nymph! to mourn thy ravished hair,
Which adds new glory to the shining sphere!
Not all the tresses that fair head can boast
Shall draw such envy as the lock you lost.
For, after all the murders of your eye,
When, after millions slain, yourself shall die;
When those fair suns shall set, as set they must,
And all those tresses shall be laid in dust;
This lock the Muse shall consecrate to fame,
And 'midst the stars inscribe Belinda's name!
—1717 (original, two-canto version published 1712)

[1] *fierce Othello … pain* See Shakespeare's *Othello* 3.4.

[2] *casuistry* The application of general rules of ethics or morality to specific matters of conscience (often through minutely detailed, yet ultimately false or evasive reasoning).

[3] *Rome's great founder* Romulus, who was apparently transported from earth in a storm cloud, never to be seen again except by Proculus, who claimed Romulus came to him in a vision from heaven.

[4] *Berenice* Berenice dedicated a lock of her hair to Aphrodite to ensure her husband's safe return from war. She placed the lock in Aphrodite's temple, but it disappeared the next day, and was reputed to have ascended to the heavens, where it became a new constellation.

[5] *the Mall* Walk in St. James's Park.

Elegy to the Memory of an Unfortunate Lady

What beck'ning ghost, along the moonlight shade
Invites my step, and points to yonder glade?
'Tis she!—but why that bleeding bosom gored,
Why dimly gleams the visionary sword?
Oh ever beauteous, ever friendly! tell,
Is it in heav'n a crime to love too well?
To bear too tender, or too firm a heart,
To act a lover's or a Roman's part?[9]
Is there no bright reversion[10] in the sky
For those who greatly think, or bravely die?
Why bade ye else, ye pow'rs, her soul aspire
Above the vulgar flight of low desire?
Ambition first sprung from your blest abodes,

[6] *Rosamonda's Lake* Pond in St. James's Park that is associated with unhappy lovers. (According to legend, Rosamond was Henry II's mistress and was murdered by his queen.)

[7] [Pope's note] John Partridge was a ridiculous star-gazer who, in his almanacs every year, never failed to predict the downfall of the Pope, and the King of France, then at war with the English.

[8] *Galileo's eyes* Telescope.

[9] *act a … Roman's part* Commit suicide.

[10] *reversion* Inheritance.

The glorious fault of angels and of gods;
Thence to their images on earth it flows,
And in the breasts of kings and heroes glows!
Most souls, 'tis true, but peep out once an age,
Dull sullen pris'ners in the body's cage;
Dim lights of life that burn a length of years,
Useless, unseen, as lamps in sepulchres;
Like eastern kings a lazy state they keep,
And close confined to their own palace sleep.
    From these perhaps (ere nature bade her die)
Fate snatched her early to the pitying sky.
As into air the purer spirits flow,
And sep'rate from their kindred dregs below,[1]
So flew the soul to its congenial place,
Nor left one virtue to redeem her race.
    But thou, false guardian of a charge too good,
Thou, mean deserter of thy brother's blood!
See on these ruby lips the trembling breath,
These cheeks, now fading at the blast of death.
Cold is that breast which warmed the world before,
And those love-darting eyes must roll no more.
Thus, if eternal justice rules the ball,[2]
Thus shall your wives, and thus your children fall.
On all the line a sudden vengeance waits,
And frequent hearses shall besiege your gates;
There passengers° shall stand, and pointing say *passers-by*
(While the long fun'rals[3] blacken all the way),
"Lo, these were they whose souls the Furies[4] steeled,
And cursed with hearts unknowing how to yield."
Thus unlamented pass the proud away—
The gaze of fools, and pageant of a day!
So perish all whose breast ne'er learned to glow
For others' good, or melt at others' woe.
    What can atone (oh ever-injured shade!)
Thy fate unpitied, and thy rites unpaid?
No friend's complaint, no kind domestic tear
Pleased thy pale ghost, or graced thy mournful bier.
By foreign hands thy dying eyes were closed;
By foreign hands thy decent limbs composed;
By foreign hands thy humble grave adorned;
By strangers honoured, and by strangers mourned!
What though[5] no friends in sable weeds appear,
Grieve for an hour, perhaps, then mourn a year,
And bear about the mockery of woe
To midnight dances, and the public show?
What though no weeping loves° thy ashes grace, *cupids*
Nor polished marble emulate thy face?
What though no sacred earth allow thee room,
Nor hallowed dirge be muttered o'er thy tomb?[6]
Yet shall thy grave with rising flow'rs be dressed,
And the green turf lie lightly[7] on thy breast;
There shall the morn her earliest tears bestow,
There the first roses of the year shall blow;° *bloom*
While angels with their silver wings o'ershade
The ground, now sacred by thy relics° made. *remains*
    So peaceful rests, without a stone, a name,
What once had beauty, titles, wealth, and fame;
How loved, how honoured once, avails thee not,
To whom related, or by whom begot;
A heap of dust alone remains of thee,
'Tis all thou art, and all the proud shall be!
    Poets themselves must fall, like those they sung,
Deaf the praised ear, and mute the tuneful tongue.
Ev'n he whose soul now melts in mournful lays
Shall shortly want the gen'rous tear he pays;
Then from his closing eyes thy form shall part,
And the last pang shall tear thee from his heart;
Life's idle business at one gasp be o'er,
The muse forgot, and thou beloved no more!
—1717

[1] *into air ... below* This image of the separation of purer parts from "dregs" is taken from chemistry.

[2] *the ball* Earth, often shown as an orb in the hands of a personified Justice.

[3] *fun'rals* Funeral processions.

[4] *Furies* Erinyes or Eumenides, the three vengeful goddesses of Greek mythology who pursue and punish those who break natural laws (for example, by killing a family member or committing suicide).

[5] *What though* What does it matter if.

[6] *What though ... tomb* Those who committed suicide could not be buried in consecrated ground.

[7] *turf lie lightly* From a popular Roman epitaph, "May the earth lie lightly on you" (*Sit tibi terra levis*).

Eloisa to Abelard[1]

The Argument

Abelard and Eloisa flourished in the twelfth century; they were two of the most distinguished persons of their age in learning and beauty, but for nothing more famous than for their unfortunate passion. After a long course of calamities, they retired each to a several[2] convent, and consecrated the remainder of their days to religion. It was many years after this separation that a letter of Abelard's to a friend, which contained the history of his misfortunes, fell into the hands of Eloisa. This awakening all her tenderness occasioned those celebrated letters (out of which the following is partly extracted) which give so lively a picture of the struggles of grace and nature, virtue and passion.

In these deep solitudes and awful cells,
Where heav'nly-pensive contemplation dwells,
And ever-musing melancholy reigns;
What means this tumult in a vestal's[3] veins?
Why rove my thoughts beyond this last retreat?
Why feels my heart its long-forgotten heat?
Yet, yet I love!—From Abelard it[4] came,
And Eloisa yet must kiss the name.
  Dear fatal[5] name! rest ever unrevealed,
Nor pass these lips in holy silence sealed.
Hide it, my heart, within that close disguise,
Where, mixed with God's, his loved idea° lies. *mental image*
O write it not, my hand—the name appears
Already written—wash it out, my tears!
In vain lost Eloisa weeps and prays,
Her heart still dictates, and her hand obeys.
  Relentless walls! whose darksome round contains
Repentant sighs, and voluntary pains:
Ye rugged rocks! which holy knees have worn;
Ye grots and caverns shagged with horrid° thorn! *bristling*
Shrines! where their vigils pale-eyed virgins keep,
And pitying saints, whose statues learn to weep![6]
Though cold like you, unmoved, and silent grown,
I have not yet forgot myself to stone.
All is not Heav'n's while Abelard has part,
Still rebel nature holds out half my heart;
Nor prayers nor fasts its stubborn pulse restrain,
Nor tears, for ages taught to flow in vain.
  Soon as thy letters trembling I unclose,
That well-known name awakens all my woes.
Oh name forever sad! forever dear!
Still breathed in sighs, still ushered with a tear.
I tremble too, where'er my own I find,
Some dire misfortune follows close behind.
Line after line my gushing eyes o'erflow,
Led through a sad variety of woe:
Now warm in love, now with'ring in thy bloom,
Lost in a convent's solitary gloom!
There stern religion quenched th' unwilling flame,
There died the best of passions, love and fame.[7]
  Yet write, oh write me all, that I may join
Griefs to thy griefs, and echo sighs to thine.
Nor foes nor fortune take this pow'r away;
And is my Abelard less kind than they?
Tears still are mine, and those I need not spare,
Love but demands what else were shed in prayer;
No happier task these faded eyes pursue,
To read and weep is all they now can do.
  Then share thy pain, allow that sad relief;
Ah, more than share it! Give me all thy grief.
Heav'n first taught letters for some wretch's aid,
Some banished lover, or some captive maid;

[1] *Eloisa to Abelard* Peter or Pierre Abelard was a French philosopher and theologian who, in 1117, at the age of 38, fell in love with his 17-year-old pupil, Héloise. They became lovers and she gave birth to his child, and the two were secretly married. Héloise's uncle, enraged at Abelard's actions, hired a gang of thugs to attack and castrate him. The two lovers separated, Héloise entering a convent and Abelard a monastery. Both devoted their lives to God and went on to successful careers in the church. Several years later the two exchanged a series of letters in Latin, which were published in 1616. A romanticized French version appeared in 1687, and in 1713 this was translated into English. It was upon the English translation that Pope based his poem.

[2] *several* Separate.

[3] *vestal* In ancient Rome, vestal virgins were those devoted to the service of Vesta, goddess of the hearth, and to the maintenance of her sacred fire. "Vestal" later became synonymous with "virgin" or "nun."

[4] *it* I.e., the letter.

[5] *fatal* Name that has determined Eloisa's destiny, or fate.

[6] *learn to weep* Stone statues placed in damp places collect condensation, which then runs down their surfaces.

[7] *fame* Good reputation. Abelard's disgrace had ruined his good name and his professional ambitions.

They live, they speak, they breathe what love inspires,
Warm from the soul, and faithful to its fires,
The virgin's wish without her fears impart,
Excuse[1] the blush, and pour out all the heart,
Speed the soft intercourse from soul to soul,
And waft a sigh from Indus to the Pole.

Thou know'st how guiltless first I met thy flame,
When love approached me under friendship's name;
My fancy formed thee of angelic kind,
Some emanation of th' all-beauteous Mind.[2]
Those smiling eyes, attemp'ring° every ray, *soothing*
Shone sweetly lambent° with celestial day: *radiant*
Guiltless I gazed; heav'n listened while you sung;
And truths divine came mended from that tongue.[3]
From lips like those what precept failed to move?
Too soon they taught me 'twas no sin to love.
Back through the paths of pleasing sense I ran,
Nor wished an angel whom I loved a man.
Dim and remote the joys of saints I see,
Nor envy them that heav'n I lose for thee.

How oft, when pressed to marriage, have I said,
Curse on all laws but those which love has made!
Love, free as air, at sight of human ties
Spreads his light wings, and in a moment flies.
Let wealth, let honour, wait the wedded dame,
August her deed, and sacred be her fame;
Before true passion all those views remove,° *disappear*
Fame, wealth, and honour! what are you to love?
The jealous god,[4] when we profane his fires,
Those restless passions in revenge inspires,
And bids them make mistaken mortals groan,
Who seek in love for aught but love alone.
Should at my feet the world's great master[5] fall,
Himself, his throne, his world, I'd scorn 'em all:
Not Caesar's empress would I deign to prove;° *become*
No, make me mistress to the man I love;
If there be yet another name, more free,
More fond than mistress, make me that to thee!
Oh happy state! when souls each other draw,
When love is liberty, and nature, law:
All then is full, possessing, and possessed,
No craving void left aching in the breast:
Ev'n thought meets thought ere from the lips it part,
And each warm wish springs mutual from the heart.
This sure is bliss (if bliss on earth there be)
And once the lot of Abelard and me.

Alas how changed! What sudden horrors rise!
A naked lover bound and bleeding lies!
Where, where was Eloise? Her voice, her hand,
Her poniard,° had opposed the dire command. *dagger*
Barbarian, stay! that bloody stroke restrain;
The crime was common,° common be the pain.[6] *shared*
I can no more; by shame, by rage suppressed,
Let tears and burning blushes speak the rest.

Canst thou forget that sad, that solemn day,
When victims at yon altar's foot we lay?
Canst thou forget what tears that moment fell,
When, warm in youth, I bade the world farewell?
As with cold lips I kissed the sacred veil,
The shrines all trembled, and the lamps grew pale:
Heav'n scarce believed the conquest it surveyed,
And saints with wonder heard the vows I made.
Yet then, to those dread altars as I drew,
Not on the Cross my eyes were fixed, but you;
Not grace, or zeal, love only was my call,
And if I lose thy love, I lose my all.
Come! with thy looks, thy words, relieve my woe;
Those still at least are left thee to bestow.
Still on that breast enamoured let me lie,
Still drink delicious poison from thy eye,
Pant on thy lip, and to thy heart be pressed;
Give all thou canst—and let me dream the rest.
Ah no! instruct me other joys to prize,
With other beauties charm my partial eyes,
Full in my view set all the bright abode,
And make my soul quit Abelard for God.

Ah think at least thy flock deserves thy care,
Plants of thy hand, and children of thy prayer.
From the false world in early youth they fled,
By thee to mountains, wilds, and deserts led.

[1] *Excuse* Remove the need for.

[2] *all-beauteous Mind* God.

[3] [Pope's note] He was her preceptor in philosophy and divinity.

[4] *jealous god* Cupid.

[5] *world's greatest master* Most likely a reference to Alexander the Great.

[6] *pain* Punishment.

You raised these hallowed walls;[1] the desert smiled,
And paradise was opened in the wild.
No weeping orphan saw his father's stores
Our shrines irradiate,° or emblaze the floors; *adorn*
No silver saints, by dying misers giv'n,
Here bribed the rage of ill-requited heav'n:
But such plain roofs as piety could raise,
And only vocal with the Maker's praise.
In these lone walls (their day's eternal bound)
These moss-grown domes with spiry turrets crowned,
Where awful arches make a noon-day night,
And the dim windows shed a solemn light,
Thy eyes diffused a reconciling ray,
And gleams of glory brightened all the day.
But now no face divine contentment wears,
'Tis all blank sadness, or continual tears.
See how the force of others' prayers I try
(Oh pious fraud of am'rous charity!),
But why should I on others' prayers depend?
Come thou, my father, brother, husband, friend!
Ah let thy handmaid, sister, daughter move,
And, all those tender names in one, thy love!
The darksome pines that o'er yon rocks reclined
Wave high, and murmur to the hollow wind,
The wand'ring streams that shine between the hills,
The grots that echo to the tinkling rills,
The dying gales that pant upon the trees,
The lakes that quiver to the curling breeze;
No more these scenes my meditation aid,
Or lull to rest the visionary[2] maid.
But o'er the twilight groves and dusky caves,
Long-sounding isles° and intermingled graves, *aisles*
Black Melancholy sits, and round her throws
A death-like silence, and a dread repose:
Her gloomy presence saddens all the scene,
Shades every flow'r, and darkens every green,
Deepens the murmur of the falling floods,
And breathes a browner horror on the woods.

Yet here for ever, ever must I stay;
Sad proof how well a lover can obey!
Death, only death, can break the lasting chain;
And here ev'n then, shall my cold dust remain,
Here all its frailties, all its flames resign,
And wait 'till 'tis no sin to mix with thine.

Ah wretch! believed the spouse of God in vain,
Confessed within the slave of love and man.
Assist me heav'n! But whence arose that prayer?
Sprung it from piety, or from despair?
Ev'n here, where frozen chastity retires,
Love finds an altar for forbidden fires.
I ought to grieve, but cannot what I ought;
I mourn the lover, not lament the fault;
I view my crime, but kindle at the view,
Repent old pleasures, and solicit new;
Now turned to heav'n, I weep my past offence,
Now think of thee, and curse my innocence.
Of all affliction taught a lover yet,
'Tis sure the hardest science[3] to forget!
How shall I lose the sin, yet keep the sense,[4]
And love th' offender, yet detest th' offence?
How the dear object from the crime remove,
Or how distinguish penitence from love?
Unequal[5] task! a passion to resign,
For hearts so touched, so pierced, so lost as mine.
Ere such a soul regains its peaceful state,
How often must it love, how often hate!
How often hope, despair, resent, regret,
Conceal, disdain—do all things but forget.
But let heav'n seize it, all at once 'tis fired,
Not touched, but rapt; not wakened, but inspired!
Oh come! Oh teach me nature to subdue,
Renounce my love, my life, my self—and you.
Fill my fond heart with God alone, for He
Alone can rival, can succeed to thee.

How happy is the blameless vestal's lot!
The world forgetting, by the world forgot.
Eternal sunshine of the spotless mind!
Each prayer accepted, and each wish resigned;
Labour and rest, that equal periods keep;
"Obedient slumbers that can wake and weep;"[6]

[1] *You … walls* When Abelard became abbot of St. Gildas-de-Rhuys, he gave Paraclete, the hermitage where he had originally established his monastic school, to Héloise. She and her religious community had recently been evicted from their property. It was shortly after this that the two began their correspondence.

[2] *visionary* Dreamy.

[3] *science* Kind of knowledge.

[4] *sense* Meaning both "sensation" and "faculty of perception."

[5] *Unequal* Excessive.

[6] *Obedient … weep* From Richard Crashaw's *Description of a Religious House* (1648).

Desires composed, affections ever ev'n;
Tears that delight, and sighs that waft to heav'n.
Grace shines around her with serenest beams,
And whisp'ring angels prompt her golden dreams.
For her th' unfading rose of Eden blooms,
And wings of seraphs shed divine perfumes;
For her the Spouse° prepares the bridal ring;[1] *Christ*
For her white virgins hymenaeals° sing; *wedding hymns*
To sounds of heav'nly harps she dies away,
And melts in visions of eternal day.
Far other dreams my erring soul employ,
Far other raptures, of unholy joy:
When at the close of each sad, sorrowing day,
Fancy restores what vengeance snatched away,
Then conscience sleeps, and leaving nature free,
All my loose soul unbounded springs to thee.
O curst, dear horrors of all-conscious° night! *all-knowing*
How glowing guilt exalts° the keen delight! *heightens, intensifies*
Provoking daemons all restraint remove,
And stir within me every source of love.
I hear thee, view thee, gaze o'er all thy charms,
And round thy phantom glue my clasping arms.
I wake—no more I hear, no more I view,
The phantom flies me, as unkind as you.
I call aloud; it hears not what I say;
I stretch my empty arms; it glides away.
To dream once more I close my willing eyes;
Ye soft illusions, dear deceits, arise!
Alas, no more!—methinks we wand'ring go
Through dreary wastes, and weep each other's woe,
Where round some mould'ring tower pale ivy creeps,
And low-browed rocks hang nodding o'er the deeps.
Sudden you mount! You beckon from the skies;
Clouds interpose, waves roar, and winds arise.
I shriek, start up, the same sad prospect find,
And wake to all the griefs I left behind.
For thee the fates, severely kind, ordain
A cool suspense from pleasure and from pain;
Thy life a long, dead calm of fixed repose;
No pulse that riots, and no blood that glows.
Still as the sea, ere winds were taught to blow,
Or moving spirit bade the waters flow;
Soft as the slumbers of a saint forgiv'n,
And mild as opening gleams of promised heav'n.
Come, Abelard! for what hast thou to dread?
The torch of Venus burns not for the dead.
Nature stands checked; religion disapproves;
Ev'n thou art cold—yet Eloisa loves.
Ah hopeless, lasting flames! like those that burn
To light the dead, and warm th' unfruitful urn.[2]
What scenes appear where'er I turn my view,
The dear ideas, where I fly, pursue,
Rise in the grove, before the altar rise,
Stain all my soul, and wanton in my eyes!
I waste the matin lamp[3] in sighs for thee,
Thy image steals between my God and me,
Thy voice I seem in every hymn to hear,
With every bead[4] I drop too soft a tear.
When from the censer clouds of fragrance roll,[5]
And swelling organs lift the rising soul,
One thought of thee puts all the pomp to flight,
Priests, tapers, temples, swim before my sight:
In seas of flame my plunging soul is drowned,
While altars blaze, and angels tremble round.
While prostrate here in humble grief I lie,
Kind,° virtuous drops just gath'ring in my eye, *natural*
While praying, trembling, in the dust I roll,
And dawning grace is op'ning on my soul:
Come, if thou dar'st, all charming as thou art!
Oppose thyself to heav'n; dispute° my heart; *contend for*
Come, with one glance of those deluding eyes
Blot out each bright idea of the skies;
Take back that grace, those sorrows, and those tears,
Take back my fruitless penitence and prayers,
Snatch me, just mounting, from the blest abode,
Assist the fiends and tear me from my God!
No, fly me, fly me! far as pole from pole;
Rise Alps between us, and whole oceans roll!
Ah come not, write not, think not once of me,
Nor share one pang of all I felt for thee.
Thy oaths I quit,° thy memory resign; *release you from*
Forget, renounce me, hate whate'er was mine.

[1] *bridal ring* Certain orders of nuns wear a wedding ring to symbolize their marriage to Christ.

[2] *like those ... urn* The ancient Romans kept lamps perpetually burning in their tombs.

[3] *matin lamp* Light used for the dawn service.

[4] *bead* I.e., rosary bead.

[5] *censer ... fragrance roll* Incense was burned and its smoke diffused by the swinging of a container called a censer.

Fair eyes, and tempting looks (which yet I view!)
Long loved, adored ideas! all adieu!
O grace serene! oh virtue heav'nly fair!
Divine oblivion of low-thoughted care!
Fresh blooming hope, gay daughter of the sky!
And faith, our early immortality![1]
Enter, each mild, each amicable guest;
Receive, and wrap me in eternal rest!
See in her cell sad Eloisa spread,
Propped on some tomb, a neighbour of the dead!
In each low wind methinks a spirit calls,
And more than echoes talk along the walls.
Here, as I watched the dying lamps around,
From yonder shrine I heard a hollow sound.
"Come, sister, come! (it said, or seemed to say)
Thy place is here, sad sister, come away!
Once like thyself, I trembled, wept, and prayed,
Love's victim then, though now a sainted maid:
But all is calm in this eternal sleep;
Here grief forgets to groan, and love to weep,
Ev'n superstition loses every fear:
For God, not man, absolves our frailties here."
I come, I come! Prepare your roseate bow'rs,
Celestial palms, and ever-blooming flow'rs.
Thither, where sinners may have rest, I go,
Where flames refined in breasts seraphic glow.
Thou, Abelard, the last sad office[2] pay,
And smooth my passage to the realms of day;
See my lips tremble, and my eyeballs roll,
Suck my last breath, and catch my flying soul![3]
Ah no—in sacred vestments may'st thou stand,
The hallowed taper trembling in thy hand,
Present the Cross before my lifted eye,
Teach me at once, and learn of° me to die. *from*
Ah then, thy once-loved Eloisa see!
It will be then no crime to gaze on me.
See from my cheek the transient roses fly!
See the last sparkle languish in my eye!
Till every motion, pulse, and breath, be o'er;
And ev'n my Abelard be loved no more.
O death all-eloquent! you only prove
What dust we doat on, when 'tis man we love.
Then too, when fate shall thy fair frame destroy,
(That cause of all my guilt, and all my joy)
In trance ecstatic may thy pangs be drowned,
Bright clouds descend, and angels watch thee round,
From op'ning skies may streaming glories shine,
And saints embrace thee with a love like mine.
May one kind grave unite each hapless name,[4]
And graft my love immortal on thy fame!
Then, ages hence, when all my woes are o'er,
When this rebellious heart shall beat no more;
If ever chance two wand'ring lovers brings
To Paraclete's white walls and silver springs,
O'er the pale marble shall they join their heads,
And drink the falling tears each other sheds;
Then sadly say, with mutual pity moved,
"Oh may we never love as these have loved!"
From the full choir when loud Hosannas[5] rise,
And swell the pomp of dreadful sacrifice,[6]
Amid that scene, if some relenting eye
Glance on the stone where our cold relics lie,
Devotion's self shall steal a thought from heav'n,
One human tear shall drop, and be forgiv'n.
And sure if fate some future bard shall join
In sad similitude of griefs to mine,
Condemned whole years in absence to deplore,° *mourn*
And image charms he must behold no more;
Such if there be, who loves so long, so well,
Let him our sad, our tender story tell;[7]
The well-sung woes will sooth my pensive ghost;
He best can paint 'em, who shall feel 'em most.

—1717

[1] *faith ... immortality* I.e., faith in an afterlife provides the first experience of immortality.

[2] *last sad office* Last rites.

[3] *Suck ... soul* It was commonly believed that at the time of death the soul left the body through the mouth.

[4] [Pope's note] Abelard and Eloisa were interred in the same grave, or in monuments adjoining, in the monastery of the Paraclete. He died in the year 1142, she in 1163.

[5] *Hosannas* Exclamations of praise.

[6] *dreadful sacrifice* Term for the celebration of the Eucharist (mass), in which Christ's sacrifice is reenacted.

[7] *future bard ... tell* Pope is referring to himself. Though these lines are not confession or autobiographical fact, he probably hints at his feelings for Lady Mary Wortley Montagu, who was in Turkey with her husband at the time. This was well before Pope's fascination with her had turned to enmity.

from *An Essay on Man*

The Design

Having proposed to write some pieces on Human Life and Manners, such as, to use my Lord Bacon's expression, "come home to men's business and bosoms," I thought it more satisfactory to begin with considering Man in the abstract, his nature and his state: since to prove any moral duty, to enforce any moral precept, or to examine the perfection or imperfection of any creature whatsoever, it is necessary first to know what condition and relation it is placed in, and what is the proper end and purpose of its being.

The science of Human Nature is, like all other sciences, reduced to a few clear points: there are not many certain truths in this world. It is therefore in the anatomy of the mind, as in that of the body; more good will accrue to mankind by attending to the large, open, and perceptible parts, than by studying too much such finer nerves and vessels, the conformations and uses of which will for ever escape our observation. The disputes are all upon these last; and, I will venture to say, they have less sharpened the wits than the hearts of men against each other, and have diminished the practice more than advanced the theory of morality. If I could flatter myself that this Essay has any merit, it is in steering betwixt the extremes of doctrines seemingly opposite, in passing over terms utterly unintelligible and in forming a temperate, yet not inconsistent, and a short, yet not imperfect, system of ethics.

This I might have done in prose; but I chose verse, and even rhyme, for two reasons. The one will appear obvious; that principles, maxims, or precepts, so written, both strike the reader more strongly at first, and are more easily retained by him afterwards: the other may seem odd, but it is true: I found I could express them more shortly this way than in prose itself; and nothing is more certain than that much of the force as well as grace of arguments or instructions depends on their conciseness. I was unable to treat this part of my subject more in detail without becoming dry and tedious; or more poetically without sacrificing perspicuity to ornament, without wandering from the precision, or breaking the chain of reasoning. If any man can unite all these without diminution of any of them, I freely confess he will compass a thing above my capacity.

What is now published is only to be considered as a general Map of Man, marking out no more than the greater parts, their extent, their limits, and their connection, but leaving the particular to be more fully delineated in the charts which are to follow; consequently these epistles in their progress (if I have health and leisure to make any progress) will be less dry, and more susceptible of poetical ornament. I am here only opening the fountains, and clearing the passage: to deduce the rivers, to follow them in their course, and to observe their effects, may be a task more agreeable.

Epistle 1

Awake, my St. John![1] leave all meaner things
To low ambition, and the pride of kings.
Let us (since life can little more supply
Than just to look about us and to die)
Expatiate[2] free o'er all this scene of man;
A mighty maze! but not without a plan;
A wild, where weeds and flow'rs promiscuous shoot,
Or garden, tempting with forbidden fruit.
Together let us beat[3] this ample field,
Try what the open, what the covert[4] yield;
The latent tracts, the giddy heights, explore
Of all who blindly creep, or sightless soar;
Eye Nature's walks, shoot Folly as it flies,

---

[1] *St. John* Henry St. John, Lord Bolingbroke, to whom Pope addressed all four epistles of the *Essay on Man*. Bolingbroke served as Secretary of State under the Tory administration of 1710–14, but fled to France in order to avoid being charged with treason when George I ascended the throne. He was pardoned in 1723 and returned to England, where he involved himself in the opposition to Robert Walpole's Whig government and continued his philosophical writing.

[2] *Expatiate* Meaning both to speak at length and to wander.

[3] *beat* Hunting term, meaning to flush game out from fields.

[4] *covert* Thick brush that could provide shelter to game.

And catch the Manners living as they rise;
Laugh where we must, be candid° where we can, *generous*
But vindicate the ways of God to man.

Say first, of God above or man below,
What can we reason, but from what we know?
Of man, what see we but his station here,
From which to reason, or to which refer?
Through worlds unnumbered though the God be known,
'Tis ours to trace him only in our own.
He, who through vast immensity can pierce,
See worlds on worlds compose one universe,
Observe how system° into system runs, *solar system*
What other planets circle other suns,
What varied being peoples every star,
May tell why Heav'n has made us as we are.
But of this frame the bearings, and the ties,
The strong connections, nice dependencies,
Gradations just, has thy pervading soul
Looked through? or can a part contain the whole?
Is the great chain—that draws all to agree
And, drawn, supports°—upheld by God, or thee? *sustains*

Presumptuous man! the reason wouldst thou find
Why formed so weak, so little, and so blind!
First, if thou canst, the harder reason guess,
Why formed no weaker, blinder, and no less!
Ask of thy mother earth why oaks are made
Taller or stronger than the weeds they shade?
Or ask of yonder argent fields above° *night sky*
Why Jove's satellites[1] are less than Jove?
Of systems possible, if 'tis confessed
That wisdom infinite must form the best,
Where all must full, or not coherent, be,[2]
And all that rises, rise in due degree;
Then, in the scale of reas'ning life, 'tis plain
There must be, somewhere, such a rank[3] as man,
And all the question (wrangle e'er so long)
Is only this, if God has placed him wrong?

[1] *Jove's satellites* Jupiter's moons. The last "e" in "satellites" is here pronounced, making this a four-syllable word. (Pope uses the Latin pronunciation.)

[2] *Where ... be* The Great Chain of Being cannot contain any gaps; each level must be filled.

[3] *such a rank* I.e., one made up of rational animals.

Respecting man, whatever wrong we call,
May, must be right, as relative to all.
In human works, though laboured on with pain,
A thousand movements scarce one purpose gain;
In God's, one single can its end produce,
Yet serves to second too some other use.
So man, who here seems principal alone,
Perhaps acts second to some sphere unknown,
Touches some wheel, or verges to some goal;
'Tis but a part we see, and not a whole.
When the proud steed shall know why man restrains
His fiery course, or drives him o'er the plains;
When the dull ox, why now he breaks the clod,
Is now a victim, and now Egypt's god:[4]
Then shall man's pride and dullness comprehend
His actions', passions', being's use and end;
Why doing, suff'ring, checked, impelled; and why
This hour a slave, the next a deity.
Then say not man's imperfect, Heav'n in fault;
Say rather, man's as perfect as he ought;
His knowledge measured to his state and place,
His time a moment, and a point his space.
If to be perfect in a certain sphere,
What matter soon or late, or here or there?
The blest today is as completely so
As who began a thousand years ago.

Heav'n from all creatures hides the book of Fate,
All but the page prescribed, their present state;
From brutes what men, from men what spirits know,
Or who could suffer being here below?
The lamb thy riot° dooms to bleed today, *extravagance*
Had he thy reason, would he skip and play?
Pleased to the last, he crops the flow'ry food,
And licks the hand just raised to shed his blood.
Oh, blindness to the future! kindly giv'n,
That each may fill the circle marked by Heav'n;
Who sees with equal eye, as God of all,
A hero perish or a sparrow fall,
Atoms or systems into ruin hurled,

[4] *Egypt's god* The Egyptians worshiped Apis, the sacred bull of Memphis, as a god.

And now a bubble burst, and now a world.
Hope humbly then; with trembling pinions° *wings* soar;
Wait the great teacher, Death, and God adore!
What future bliss, he gives not thee to know,
But gives that hope to be thy blessing now.
Hope springs eternal in the human breast:
Man never is, but always to be blest:
The soul, uneasy and confined from home,[1]
Rests and expatiates° in a life to come. *roams*
Lo! the poor Indian, whose untutored mind
Sees God in clouds, or hears him in the wind;
His soul proud science never taught to stray
Far as the solar walk, or Milky Way;
Yet simple Nature to his hope has giv'n,
Behind the cloud-topped hill, an humbler heav'n;
Some safer world in depth of woods embraced,
Some happier island in the wat'ry waste,
Where slaves once more their native land behold,
No fiends torment, no Christians thirst for gold!
To be, contents his natural desire,
He asks no angel's wing, no seraph's fire;
But thinks, admitted to that equal° sky, *egalitarian*
His faithful dog shall bear him company.

Go, wiser thou! and in thy scale of sense
Weigh thy opinion against Providence;
Call imperfection what thou fancy'st such,
Say, here he gives too little, there too much;
Destroy all creatures for thy sport or gust,° *taste*
Yet cry, if man's unhappy, God's unjust;
If man alone engross not Heav'n's high care,
Alone made perfect here, immortal there:
Snatch from his hand the balance[2] and the rod,
Rejudge his justice, be the God of God!
In pride, in reas'ning pride, our error lies;
All quit their sphere and rush into the skies.
Pride still is aiming at the blest abodes,
Men would be angels, angels would be gods.
Aspiring to be gods, if angels fell,
Aspiring to be angels, men rebel;
And who but wishes to invert the laws
Of order, sins against th' Eternal Cause.

Ask for what end the heav'nly bodies shine;
Earth for whose use? Pride answers, "'Tis for mine.
For me kind Nature wakes her genial° pow'r, *generative*
Suckles each herb, and spreads out every flow'r;
Annual, for me the grape, the rose renew
The juice nectareous, and the balmy dew;
For me the mine a thousand treasures brings;
For me health gushes from a thousand springs;
Seas roll to waft me, suns to light me rise;
My footstool earth, my canopy[3] the skies."
But errs not Nature from this gracious end,
From burning suns when livid deaths descend,[4]
When earthquakes swallow, or when tempests sweep
Towns to one grave, whole nations to the deep?
"No," 'tis replied, "the first Almighty cause
Acts not by partial, but by gen'ral laws;
Th' exceptions few; some change since all began,
And what created perfect?"—Why then man?
If the great end be human happiness,
Then Nature deviates; and can man do less?
As much that end a constant course requires
Of show'rs and sunshine, as of man's desires;
As much eternal springs and cloudless skies
As men forever temp'rate, calm, and wise.
If plagues or earthquakes break not Heav'n's design,
Why then a Borgia or a Catiline?[5]
Who knows but he whose hand the lightning forms,
Who heaves old ocean, and who wings the storms,
Pours fierce ambition in a Caesar's mind,
Or turns young Ammon[6] loose to scourge mankind?
From pride, from pride our very reas'ning springs;
Account for moral as for nat'ral things:

[1] *from home* I.e., away from its heavenly home.

[2] *balance* Scales of justice.

[3] *canopy* Covering suspended above a throne.

[4] *From ... descend* Incidences of pestilence and fever increased during the hottest months.

[5] *Borgia* The Borgias were a Renaissance Italian family notorious for the cruelty of their crimes; *Cataline* Lucius Sergius Cataline, the greedy Roman conspirator who was publicly denounced by Cicero for plotting against the republic.

[6] *Ammon* Alexander the Great.

Why charge we Heav'n in those, in these[1] acquit?
In both, to reason right is to submit.
Better for us, perhaps it might appear,
Were there[2] all harmony, all virtue here;
That never air or ocean felt the wind;
That never passion discomposed the mind:
But ALL subsists by elemental strife,
And passions are the elements of life.
The gen'ral order, since the whole began,
Is kept in Nature, and is kept in man.

What would this man? Now upward will he soar,
And, little less than angel, would be more;
Now looking downwards, just as grieved appears
To want the strength of bulls, the fur of bears.
Made for his use all creatures if he call,
Say what their use, had he the pow'rs of all?
Nature to these, without profusion kind,
The proper organs, proper pow'rs assigned;
Each seeming want compensated of course,[3]
Here with degrees of swiftness, there of force;[4]
All in exact proportion to the state;
Nothing to add, and nothing to abate.
Each beast, each insect, happy in its own;
Is Heav'n unkind to man, and man alone?
Shall he alone, whom rational we call,
Be pleased with nothing, if not blest with all?
The bliss of man (could pride that blessing find)
Is not to act or think beyond mankind;
No pow'rs of body or of soul to share,
But what his nature and his state can bear.
Why has not man a microscopic eye?
For this plain reason, man is not a fly.
Say what the use, were finer optics giv'n,
To inspect a mite, not comprehend the heav'n?
Or touch, if tremblingly alive all o'er,
To smart and agonize at every pore?
Or quick effluvia[5] darting through the brain,
Die of a rose in aromatic pain?
If nature thundered in his op'ning ears,
And stunned him with the music of the spheres,[6]
How would he wish that Heav'n had left him still
The whisp'ring zephyr,° and the purling rill? *breeze*
Who finds not Providence all good and wise,
Alike in what it gives, and what denies?

Far as creation's ample range extends,
The scale of sensual, mental pow'rs ascends:
Mark how it mounts to man's imperial race
From the green myriads in the peopled grass:
What modes of sight betwixt each wide extreme,
The mole's dim curtain, and the lynx's beam:[7]
Of smell, the headlong lioness between,
And hound sagacious on the tainted[8] green:
Of hearing, from the life that fills the flood
To that which warbles through the vernal wood:
The spider's touch, how exquisitely fine!
Feels at each thread, and lives along the line:
In the nice° bee, what sense so subtly true *precise*
From pois'nous herbs extracts the healing dew:[9]
How instinct varies in the grov'lling swine
Compared, half-reas'ning elephant, with thine:
'Twixt that and reason, what a nice barrier;
Forever sep'rate, yet forever near!
Remembrance and reflection how allied;
What thin partitions sense from thought divide:
And middle natures, how they long to join,
Yet never pass th' insuperable line!
Without this just gradation, could they be
Subjected these to those, or all to thee?
The pow'rs of all subdued by thee alone,
Is not thy reason all these pow'rs in one?

---

[1] *in those* The former; *in these* The latter.

[2] *there* I.e., in the natural realm (whereas "here" indicates the moral realm of man).

[3] *of course* Naturally; as a matter of course.

[4] [Pope's note] It is a certain axiom in the anatomy of creatures, that in proportion as they are formed for strength, their swiftness is lessened; or as they are formed for swiftness, their strength is lessened.

[5] *effluvia* Sensory perceptions were thought to result from "effluvia," minuscule particles which bombarded the pores in streams.

[6] *music of the spheres* Music believed to be made by the planets which only angels could hear.

[7] *mole's ... beam* A popular theory of the time held that sight depended upon beams of light emitted from the eye.

[8] *sagacious* Possessing an acute sense of smell; *tainted* I.e., with the scent of the hunted animal.

[9] *healing dew* Honey, which was often used for medicinal purposes.

See, through this air, this ocean, and this earth,
All matter quick,[1] and bursting into birth.
Above, how high progressive life may go!
Around, how wide! how deep extend below!
Vast Chain of Being, which from God began,
Natures ethereal, human, angel, man,
Beast, bird, fish, insect, what no eye can see,
No glass[2] can reach! from infinite to thee,
From thee to nothing!—On superior pow'rs
Were we to press, inferior might on ours:
Or in the full creation leave a void,
Where, one step broken, the great scale's destroyed:
From Nature's chain whatever link you strike,
Tenth or ten thousandth, breaks the chain alike.
And if each system in gradation roll,
Alike essential to th' amazing whole,
The least confusion but in one, not all
That system only, but the whole, must fall.
Let earth unbalanced from her orbit fly,
Planets and suns run lawless through the sky;
Let ruling angels from their spheres be hurled,
Being on being wrecked, and world on world,
Heav'n's whole foundations to their centre nod,
And Nature tremble to the throne of God:
All this dread order break—for whom? for thee?
Vile worm!—oh, madness, pride, impiety!

What if the foot, ordained the dust to tread,
Or hand to toil, aspired to be the head?
What if the head, the eye, or ear repined
To serve mere engines° to the ruling mind? *instruments*
Just as absurd for any part to claim
To be another, in this gen'ral frame:
Just as absurd to mourn the tasks or pains
The great directing Mind of All ordains.
All are but parts of one stupendous whole,
Whose body Nature is, and God the soul;
That, changed through all, and yet in all the same,
Great in the earth, as in th' ethereal frame,
Warms in the sun, refreshes in the breeze,
Glows in the stars, and blossoms in the trees;
Lives through all life, extends through all extent,
Spreads undivided, operates unspent,
Breathes in our soul, informs our mortal part,
As full, as perfect in a hair as heart;
As full, as perfect in vile man that mourns,
As the rapt seraph that adores and burns;[3]
To him no high, no low, no great, no small;
He fills, he bounds, connects, and equals° all. *makes equal*

Cease then, nor ORDER imperfection name;
Our proper bliss depends on what we blame.
Know thy own point: this kind, this due degree
Of blindness, weakness, Heav'n bestows on thee.
Submit—in this, or any other sphere,
Secure to be as blest as thou canst bear:
Safe in the hand of one disposing pow'r,
Or in the natal, or the mortal hour.[4]
All Nature is but art unknown to thee;
All chance, direction which thou canst not see;
All discord, harmony not understood;
All partial evil, universal good:
And, spite of pride, in erring reason's spite,
One truth is clear: Whatever IS, is RIGHT.

Epistle 2

Know then thyself, presume not God to scan;° *judge*
The proper study of mankind is man.
Placed on this isthmus of a middle state,
A being darkly wise, and rudely great:
With too much knowledge for the skeptic side,
With too much weakness for the Stoic's pride,
He hangs between; in doubt to act or rest,
In doubt to deem himself a God or beast,
In doubt his mind or body to prefer,
Born but to die, and reas'ning but to err;
Alike in ignorance, his reason such,
Whether he thinks too little, or too much:
Chaos of thought and passion, all confused;
Still by himself abused, or disabused;
Created half to rise, and half to fall;

[1] *quick* Stirring with life.

[2] *glass* Telescope or microscope.

[3] *burns* With holy love. Seraphs, the highest of the nine orders of angels, were generally depicted in flame. Their name comes from the root of a Greek word meaning "to burn."

[4] *mortal hour* Hour of death.

Great lord of all things, yet a prey to all;
Sole judge of truth, in endless error hurled:
The glory, jest, and riddle of the world!
Go, wonderous creature! Mount where science guides;
Go, measure earth, weigh air, and state the tides;
Instruct the planets in what orbs to run,
Correct old time, and regulate the sun;
Go, soar with Plato to th' empyreal sphere,[1]
To the first good, first perfect, and first fair;
Or tread the mazy° round his foll'wers trod, *labyrinthine*
And quitting sense[2] call imitating God;
As Eastern priests in giddy circles run,[3]
And turn their heads to imitate the sun.
Go teach eternal wisdom how to rule—
Then drop into thyself, and be a fool!
Superior beings, when of late they saw
A mortal man unfold all Nature's law,
Admired such wisdom in an earthly shape,
And showed a Newton[4] as we show an ape.
Could he, whose rules the rapid comet bind,
Describe or fix one movement of his mind?
Who saw its fires here rise, and there descend,
Explain his own beginning, or his end?
Alas, what wonder! Man's superior part
Unchecked may rise, and climb from art to art,
But when his own great work is but begun,
What reason weaves, by passion is undone.
Trace science, then, with modesty thy guide;
First strip off all her equipage of pride,
Deduct what is but vanity, or dress,
Or learning's luxury, or idleness,
Or tricks to show the stretch of human brain,
Mere curious pleasure, or ingenious pain;
Expunge the whole, or lop th' excrescent parts
Of all, our vices have created arts.
Then see how little the remaining sum,
Which served the past, and must the times to come!
Two principles in human nature reign:
Self-love, to urge, and reason, to restrain;
Nor this a good, nor that a bad we call,
Each works its end, to move or govern all;
And to their proper operation still
Ascribe all good; to their improper, ill.
Self-love, the spring of motion, acts° the soul; *activates*
Reason's comparing balance rules the whole.
Man, but for that, no action could attend,
And, but for this, were active to no end:
Fixed like a plant on his peculiar° spot, *particular*
To draw nutrition, propagate, and rot;
Or, meteor-like, flame lawless through the void,
Destroying others, by himself destroyed.
Most strength the moving principle requires;
Active its task, it prompts, impels, inspires.
Sedate and quiet the comparing lies,
Formed but to check, delib'rate, and advise.
Self-love still stronger, as its objects nigh;
Reason's at distance, and in prospect lie.
That sees immediate good by present sense;
Reason, the future and the consequence.
Thicker than arguments, temptations throng,
At best more watchful this, but that more strong.
The action of the stronger to suspend
Reason still use, to reason still attend:
Attention, habit and experience gains,
Each strengthens reason, and self-love restrains.
Let subtle schoolmen[5] teach these friends to fight,
More studious to divide than to unite,
And grace and virtue, sense and reason split,
With all the rash dexterity of wit:
Wits, just like fools, at war about a name,
Have full as oft no meaning, or the same.
Self-love and reason to one end aspire,
Pain their aversion, pleasure their desire;
But greedy that its object would devour,
This, taste the honey, and not wound the flow'r:

[1] *empyreal sphere* Highest heavens.

[2] *quitting sense* Leaving the body, as in a trance, with a pun on abandoning good sense.

[3] *priests ... run* Reference to dervishes, Muslim friars of various orders, some of which are known for their fantastic practices, such as whirling (hence the term "whirling dervish").

[4] *Newton* Physicist and mathematician Sir Isaac Newton (1642-1727).

[5] *schoolmen* Experts in formal logic and theology, particularly as taught in universities.

Pleasure, or wrong or rightly understood,
Our greatest evil or our greatest good.

Modes of self-love the passions we may call;
'Tis real good, or seeming, moves them all;
But since not every good we can divide,° *share*
And reason bids us for our own provide,
Passions, though selfish, if their means be fair,
List° under reason, and deserve her care; *enlist*
Those, that imparted,[1] court a nobler aim,
Exalt their kind, and take some virtue's name.
In lazy apathy let Stoics boast
Their virtue fixed; 'tis fixed as in a frost—
Contracted all, retiring to the breast;
But strength of mind is exercise, not rest:
The rising tempest puts in act the soul,
Parts it may ravage, but preserves the whole.
On life's vast ocean diversely we sail,
Reason the card,° but passion is the gale; *mariner's chart*
Nor God alone in the still calm we find,
He mounts the storm, and walks upon the wind.
Passions, like elements, though born to fight,
Yet mixed and softened, in his° work unite:[2] *God's*
These 'tis enough to temper and employ;
But what composes man, can man destroy?
Suffice that reason keep to Nature's road,
Subject, compound them, follow her and God.
Love, Hope, and Joy, fair pleasure's smiling train,
Hate, Fear, and Grief, the family of pain;
These, mixed with art, and to due bounds confined,
Make and maintain the balance of the mind—
The lights and shades, whose well accorded strife
Gives all the strength and colour of our life.
Pleasures are ever in our hands or eyes,
And when in act they cease, in prospect rise;
Present to grasp, and future still to find,
The whole employ of body and of mind.
All spread their charms, but charm not all alike;
On diff'rent senses diff'rent objects strike;
Hence diff'rent passions more or less inflame,
As strong or weak, the organs of the frame;[3]
And hence one master passion in the breast,
Like Aaron's serpent,[4] swallows up the rest.
As man, perhaps, the moment of his breath,
Receives the lurking principle of death;
The young disease, that must subdue at length,
Grows with his growth, and strengthens with his strength:[5]
So, cast and mingled with his very frame,
The mind's disease, its ruling passion, came;
Each vital humour, which should feed the whole,
Soon flows to this in body and in soul.
Whatever warms the heart or fills the head,
As the mind opens, and its functions spread,
Imagination plies her dang'rous art,
And pours it all upon the peccant[6] part.
Nature its mother, habit is its nurse;
Wit, spirit, faculties but make it worse;
Reason itself but gives it edge and pow'r,
As Heav'n's blest beam turns vinegar more sour.
We, wretched subjects though to lawful sway
In this weak queen,[7] some fav'rite still obey.
Ah! if she lend not arms, as well as rules,
What can she more than tell us we are fools?
Teach us to mourn our nature, not to mend,
A sharp accuser, but a helpless° friend! *unhelpful*
Or from a judge turn pleader, to persuade
The choice we make, or justify it made;
Proud of an easy conquest all along,
She but removes weak passions for the strong:

[1] *Those, that imparted* I.e., the passions, when imbued with reason.

[2] *Passions … unite* The four elements of the universe (earth, air, fire, and water) had been traditionally believed to correspond to four humors (melancholy, blood, choler, and phlegm), of which, in different proportions, all human constitutions were thought to be formed. By the eighteenth century these notions were no longer taken as literal truth, but they retained their currency as metaphors.

[3] *Hence … frame* Different passions were thought to reside in and dominate different organs of the body.

[4] *Aaron's serpent* Exodus 7.10–12 relates the story of Aaron, who cast down his rod before the Pharaoh and turned it into a snake. The Egyptian magicians did the same, but Aaron's serpent devoured theirs.

[5] *As man … strength* It was believed that the origin of some diseases was communicated to the foetus in the womb.

[6] *peccant* Diseased.

[7] *weak queen* Reason.

So, when small humors gather to a gout,[1]
The doctor fancies he has driv'n them out.
Yes, Nature's road must ever be preferred;
Reason is here no guide, but still a guard:
'Tis hers to rectify, not overthrow,
And treat this passion more as friend than foe.
A mightier pow'r the strong direction sends,
And sev'ral men impels to sev'ral ends;
Like varying winds, by other passions tossed,[2]
This drives them constant to a certain coast.
Let pow'r or knowledge, gold or glory, please,
Or (oft more strong than all) the love of ease;
Through life 'tis followed, ev'n at life's expense;
The merchant's toil, the sage's indolence,
The monk's humility, the hero's pride,
All, all alike, find reason on their side.
Th' eternal art,[3] educing good from ill,
Grafts on this passion our best principle.
'Tis thus the mercury of man is fixed:
Strong grows the virtue with his nature mixed;
The dross° cements what else were too refined, *impurity*
And in one interest body acts with mind.
As fruits ungrateful° to the planter's care *unresponsive*
On savage stocks inserted learn to bear,[4]
The surest virtues thus from passions shoot,
Wild nature's vigor working at the root.
What crops of wit and honesty appear
From spleen, from obstinacy, hate, or fear!
See anger zeal and fortitude supply;
Ev'n av'rice, prudence; sloth, philosophy;
Lust, through some certain strainers well refined,
Is gentle love, and charms all womankind;
Envy, to which th' ignoble mind's a slave,
Is emulation in the learned or brave;
Nor virtue, male or female, can we name,
But what will grow on pride, or grow on shame.
Thus Nature gives us (let it check our pride)
The virtue nearest to our vice allied;
Reason the bias turns to good from ill,
And Nero reigns a Titus,[5] if he will.
The fiery soul abhorred in Catiline,
In Decius charms, in Curtius[6] is divine.
The same ambition can destroy or save,
And make a patriot as it makes a knave.

This light and darkness, in our chaos joined,
What shall divide? The God within the mind.[7]
Extremes in nature equal ends produce,
In man they join to some mysterious use;
Though each by turns the other's bound invade,
As, in some well-wrought picture, light and shade,
And oft so mix, the diff'rence is too nice° *subtle*
Where ends the virtue, or begins the vice.
Fools! who from hence into the notion fall
That vice or virtue there is none at all.
If white and black blend, soften, and unite
A thousand ways, is there no black or white?
Ask your own heart, and nothing is so plain;
'Tis to mistake them costs the time and pain.

Vice is a monster of so frightful mien,
As, to be hated, needs but to be seen;
Yet seen too oft, familiar with her face,
We first endure, then pity, then embrace;
But where th' extreme of vice, was ne'er agreed.

[1] *gout* Thought to result from the body's attempt to rid itself of a redundancy of humors.

[2] *A mightier … tossed* I.e., God (the "mightier pow'r") ensures that there are people of various temperaments and inclinations to carry out the assorted tasks necessary to the world's work.

[3] *eternal art* Providence.

[4] *fruits … bear* Grafts inserted in the stem of a wild plant.

[5] *Nero* Emperor of Rome who ordered his mother and sister murdered, and whose notorious cruelty and debauchery caused several revolts among his people, eventually leading him to commit suicide; *Titus* Celebrated as one of the most benevolent Roman emperors, he did much to alleviate the suffering and increase the happiness of his people. He is perhaps best known for the construction of the Roman Colosseum.

[6] *Decius* Roman consul who died defending his army against the Goths; *Curtius* According to Livy, in 445 BCE lightning struck near the Roman Forum, creating a large chasm. After an oracle claimed that the hole could be closed by Rome's most precious possession, Marcus Curtius jumped into it, wearing full armor and riding a fine horse. The chasm closed immediately.

[7] *This light … mind* Cf. Genesis 1.4.

Ask, "Where's the North?" At York, 'tis on the Tweed;[1]
In Scotland, at the Orcades;° and there, *Orkney Islands*
At Greenland, Zembla,[2] or the Lord knows where:
No creature owns° it in the first degree, *admits to*
But thinks his neighbour farther gone than he—
Ev'n those who dwell beneath its very zone,
Or° never feel the rage, or° never own. *either / or*
What happier natures shrink at with affright,
The hard[3] inhabitant contends is right.

Virtuous and vicious every man must be,
Few in th' extreme, but all in the degree;
The rogue and fool by fits is fair and wise,
And ev'n the best, by fits, what they despise.
'Tis but by parts we follow good or ill,
For, vice or virtue, self directs it still;
Each individual seeks a sev'ral° goal, *separate*
But Heav'n's great view is one, and that the whole
That counter-works each folly and caprice;
That disappoints th' effect of every vice
That happy frailties to all ranks applied—
Shame to the virgin, to the matron pride,
Fear to the statesman, rashness to the chief,
To kings presumption, and to crowds belief—
That virtue's ends from vanity can raise,
Which seeks no int'rest, no reward but praise;
And build on wants, and on defects of mind,
The joy, the peace, the glory of mankind.
Heav'n forming each on other to depend,
A master, or a servant, or a friend,
Bids each on other for assistance call,
'Till one man's weakness grows the strength of all.
Wants, frailties, passions closer still ally
The common int'rest, or endear the tie.
To these we owe true friendship, love sincere,
Each home-felt joy that life inherits here;
Yet from the same we learn, in its decline,
Those joys, those loves, those int'rests to resign:
Taught half by reason, half by mere decay,
To welcome death, and calmly pass away.
Whate'er the passion, knowledge, fame, or pelf,° *wealth*
Not one will change his neighbor with himself.
The learn'd is happy nature to explore,
The fool is happy that he knows no more;
The rich is happy in the plenty giv'n,
The poor contents him with the care of heav'n.
See the blind beggar dance, the cripple sing,
The sot° a hero, lunatic a king; *drunkard*
The starving chemist° in his golden views *alchemist*
Supremely blest, the poet in his muse.
See some strange comfort every state attend,
And pride bestowed on all, a common friend.
See some fit passion every age supply;
Hope travels through, nor quits us when we die.
Behold the child, by Nature's kindly law
Pleased with a rattle, tickled with a straw;
Some livelier plaything gives his youth delight,
A little louder, but as empty quite:
Scarves, garters,[4] gold amuse his riper stage,
And beads[5] and prayer-books are the toys of age:
Pleased with this bauble still, as that before,
'Till tired he sleeps, and life's poor play is o'er!
Meanwhile, opinion gilds with varying rays
Those painted clouds that beautify our days;
Each want of happiness by hope supplied,
And each vacuity of sense by pride.
These build as fast as knowledge can destroy;
In folly's cup still laughs the bubble, joy;
One prospect lost, another still we gain,
And not a vanity is giv'n in vain.
Ev'n mean self-love becomes, by force divine,
The scale to measure others' wants by thine.
See! and confess, one comfort still must rise;
'Tis this: though man's a fool, yet GOD IS WISE.
—1733

[1] *Tweed* River in southern Scotland.

[2] *Zembla* Novaya Zemlya, an archipelago off the Arctic coast of Russia.

[3] *hard* Hardened (i.e., to vice, as an inhabitant of the Arctic climate would be to the cold).

[4] *Scarves* Worn by Doctors of Divinity; *garters* Badges of the Knights of the Garter.

[5] *beads* Rosaries.

An Epistle from Mr. Pope to Dr. Arbuthnot[1]

Neque sermonibus vulgi dederis te, nec in Praemiis humanis spem posueris rerum tuarum: suis te oportet illecebris ipsa Virtus trahat ad verum decus. Quid de te alii loquantur, ipsi videant, sed loquentur tamen.[2]

TULLY [*De Re Publica,* Lib. VI, cap. XXIII].

ADVERTISEMENT

This paper is a sort of bill of complaint, begun many years since, and drawn up by snatches, as the several occasions offered. I had no thoughts of publishing it till it pleased some persons of rank and fortune (the authors of *Verses to the Imitator of Horace*, and of an *Epistle to a Doctor of Divinity from a Nobleman at Hampton Court*)[3] to attack, in a very extraordinary manner, not only my writings (of which, being public, the public judge) but my person, morals, and family, whereof, to those who know me not, a truer information may be requisite. Being divided between the necessity to say something of myself, and my own laziness to undertake so awkward a task, I thought it the shortest way to put the last hand to this epistle. If it have anything pleasing, it will be that by which I am most desirous to please, the truth and the sentiment; and if anything offensive, it will be only to those I am least sorry to offend, the vicious or the ungenerous.

Many will know their own pictures in it, there being not a circumstance but what is true; but I have for the most part spared their names, and they may escape being laughed at if they please.

I would have some of them know, it was owing to the request of the learned and candid friend to whom it is inscribed that I make not as free use of theirs as they have done of mine. However, I shall have this advantage and honour on my side, that whereas, by their proceeding, any abuse may be directed at any man, no injury can possibly be done by mine, since a nameless character can never be found out but by its truth and likeness.

Shut, shut the door, good John![4] (fatigued I said)
Tie up the knocker, say I'm sick, I'm dead.
The Dog Star[5] rages! nay 'tis past a doubt,
All Bedlam, or Parnassus,[6] is let out:
Fire in each eye, and papers in each hand,
They rave, recite, and madden round the land.
What walls can guard me, or what shades can hide?
They pierce my thickets, through my grot[7] they glide,
By land, by water, they renew the charge,
They stop the chariot, and they board the barge.[8]
No place is sacred, not the church is free,
Ev'n Sunday shines no Sabbath day to me:
Then from the Mint[9] walks forth the man of rhyme,
Happy! to catch me just at dinner time.
Is there a parson, much bemused in beer,[10]
A maudlin poetess, a rhyming peer,° *member of the nobility*

[1] *Dr. Arbuthnot* Formerly Queen Anne's physician, Arbuthnot was a close friend of Swift and a fellow member of the Scriblerus Club. Pope was spurred to complete this poem, which he had worked on intermittently for several years, when he learned that Arbuthnot was terminally ill. The poem, completed seven weeks before Arbuthnot's death, was, Pope declared, "the best memorial I can leave, both of my friendship to you, and to my character."

[2] *Neque.... tamen* Latin: "You will neither give yourself to the gossip of the vulgar, nor place your hope in the rewards of men for the success of your affairs. Virtue herself, by her own allure, should lead you to true honor. What others may say of you, regard as their concern, for they will say it nevertheless." From *De Re Publica* 6.23, by Marcus Tullius Cicero ("Tully").

[3] *authors ... Court* Lady Mary Wortley Montagu and John, Lord Hervey, respectively.

[4] *John* John Serle, Pope's gardener and servant.

[5] *Dog Star* Sirius, the brightest star in the constellation Canis Major. In late summer Sirius sets with the sun, and it is therefore associated with maddening heat. Late summer was also when poetry recitals were held in ancient Rome.

[6] *Bedlam* The Hospital of St. Mary's of Bethlehem, a London hospital for the insane; *Parnassus* Mountain in Greece that, according to myth, was sacred to Apollo and the Muses, and was therefore seen as the home of artistic inspiration.

[7] *my grot* On Pope's property in Twickenham an underground passage connected his house with his garden, which lay on the opposite side of the road. He decorated this passage and turned it into a beautiful grotto that functioned as a subterranean retreat.

[8] *board the barge* Twickenham was on the Thames, enabling Pope to travel to London by barge.

[9] *the Mint* Area in London that was a sanctuary for debtors—they could not be arrested while within its boundaries. Debtors could not be arrested anywhere on Sundays.

[10] *parson ... beer* Probably a reference to Poet Laureate Laurence Eusden (the words "bemused in" play on his name), who was a parson and notorious for his heavy drinking.

A clerk, foredoomed his father's soul to cross,
Who pens a stanza when he should engross?[1]
Is there who, locked from ink and paper, scrawls
With desp'rate charcoal round his darkened walls?
All fly to Twit'nam° and, in humble strain, *Twickenham*
Apply to me to keep them mad or vain.
Arthur,[2] whose giddy son neglects the laws,
Imputes to me and my damned works the cause;
Poor Cornus[3] sees his frantic wife elope,
And curses wit, and poetry, and Pope.
  Friend to my life (which did not you prolong,
The world had wanted many an idle song)
What drop or nostrum° can this plague remove? *remedy*
Or which must end me, a fool's wrath or love?
A dire dilemma! Either way I'm sped,° *dispatched, destroyed*
If foes, they write, if friends, they read me dead.
Seized and tied down to judge, how wretched I!
Who can't be silent, and who will not lie;
To laugh were want of goodness and of grace,
And to be grave exceeds all pow'r of face.
I sit with sad civility, I read
With honest anguish and an aching head,
And drop at last, but in unwilling ears,
This saving counsel, "Keep your piece nine years."[4]
  "Nine years!" cries he, who, high in Drury Lane,[5]
Lulled by soft zephyrs° through the broken pane, *breezes*
Rhymes ere he wakes, and prints before term[6] ends,
Obliged by hunger and request of friends:
"The piece you think is incorrect: why, take it;
I'm all submission; what you'd have it, make it."
  Three things another's modest wishes bound,
My friendship, and a prologue, and ten pound.
  Pitholeon[7] sends to me: "You know his Grace.
I want a patron; ask him for a place."° *job*
Pitholeon libeled me—"but here's a letter
Informs you, sir, 'twas when he knew no better.
Dare you refuse him? Curll[8] invites to dine;
He'll write a *Journal*, or he'll turn divine."[9]
  Bless me! a packet.—"'Tis a stranger sues,
A virgin tragedy, an orphan muse."
If I dislike it, "Furies, death, and rage!"
If I approve, "Commend it to the stage."
There (thank my stars) my whole commission ends;
The play'rs and I are, luckily, no friends.
Fired that the house° reject him, "'Sdeath, *playhouse*
  I'll print it
And shame the fools—your int'rest, sir, with Lintot."[10]
Lintot, dull rogue, will think your price too much.
"Not, sir, if you revise it, and retouch."
All my demurs but double his attacks;
At last he whispers, "Do, and we go snacks."° *shares*
Glad of a quarrel, straight I clap the door,
Sir, let me see your works and you no more.
  'Tis sung, when Midas' ears[11] began to spring
(Midas, a sacred person and a king),
His very minister, who spied them first,
(Some say his queen) was forced to speak, or burst.
And is not mine, my friend, a sorer case,

[1] *engross* Write in legal form; write out legal documents.

[2] *Arthur* Arthur Moore, a business man and Member of Parliament whose son, James Moore Smythe, was a writer, and one Pope scorned. Pope later accused him of stealing lines from his *Epistle to a Lady* for use in a play.

[3] *Cornus* From *cornu*, the Latin word for "horn," which was the emblem of the cuckold.

[4] *Keep … years* I.e., before publishing it. This advice is taken from Horace's *Ars Poetica*, line 388.

[5] *high in Drury Lane* In a garret on Drury Lane, a street known for its theater but also for its squalid living quarters, which were home to many prostitutes and criminals.

[6] *term* Period during which the law courts were in session. The publishing seasons coincided with these legal terms.

[7] [Pope's note] The name taken from a foolish poet at Rhodes, who pretended much to Greek. [This was a reference to Leonard Welsted, mentioned again on line 375, with whom Pope had quarreled.]

[8] *Curll* Edmund Curll, an unethical publisher who was notorious for publishing pirated, forged, and falsely ascribed works. He was one of Pope's primary adversaries and a frequent object of his attacks.

[9] *write … divine* I.e., he will attack Pope in an article in the *London Journal* or will write a theological treatise.

[10] *Lintot* Bernard Lintot, the publisher who had issued Pope's early work, including his edition of Homer, but with whom Pope had since quarreled. Lintot, with Curll, figures in Pope's satire *The Dunciad*.

[11] *Midas' ears* King Midas of Lydia was given ass's ears by the god Apollo when he claimed to prefer Pan's rustic flute playing to the refined melodies of Apollo's lyre. Depending upon the version of the story, the secret of Midas's ears (which he hid under a turban) was first discovered by either the king's wife or his barber. The discoverer of the secret, unable to sleep, whispered the story either into a hole in the earth or a bed of reeds. Here Pope's references to the queen, minister, and king are allusions to Queen Caroline, first minister Robert Walpole, and King George II.

When every coxcomb° perks them in my face? *fool*
"Good friend, forbear! You deal in dang'rous things;
I'd never name queens, ministers, or kings.
Keep close to ears, and those let asses prick;
'Tis nothing"—Nothing? if they bite and kick?
Out with it, *Dunciad*! Let the secret pass,
That secret to each fool, that he's an ass:
The truth once told (and wherefore should we lie?)
The Queen of Midas slept, and so may I.
    You think this cruel? Take it for a rule,
No creature smarts so little as a fool.
Let peals of laughter, Codrus,[1] round thee break,
Thou unconcerned canst hear the mighty crack.
Pit, box, and gall'ry[2] in convulsions hurled,
Thou stand'st unshook amidst a bursting world.
Who shames a scribbler? Break one cobweb through,
He spins the slight, self-pleasing thread anew:
Destroy his fib or sophistry, in vain;
The creature's at his dirty work again;
Throned in the centre of his thin designs,
Proud of a vast extent of flimsy lines.
Whom have I hurt? Has poet yet, or peer,
Lost the arched eyebrow or Parnassian sneer?
And has not Colley[3] still his lord and whore?
His butchers Henley? his freemasons Moore?[4]
Does not one table Bavius[5] still admit?
Still to one bishop Philips[6] seem a wit?
Still Sappho[7]—"Hold! for God's sake—you'll offend.
No names—be calm—learn prudence of a friend:
I too could write, and I am twice as tall,
But foes like these!"—One flatt'rer's worse than all;
Of all mad creatures, if the learn'd are right,
It is the slaver kills, and not the bite.
A fool quite angry is quite innocent;
Alas! 'tis ten times worse when they repent.

    One dedicates in high heroic prose,
And ridicules beyond a hundred foes;
One from all Grub Street[8] will my fame defend,
And, more abusive, calls himself my friend.
This prints my letters,[9] that expects a bribe,
And others roar aloud, "Subscribe, subscribe."[10]
    There are, who to my person pay their court:
I cough like Horace, and though lean, am short;
Ammon's great son[11] one shoulder had too high,
Such Ovid's nose,[12] and "Sir! you have an eye—"
Go on, obliging creatures, make me see
All that disgraced my betters, met in me.
Say for my comfort, languishing in bed,
"Just so immortal Maro° held his head"; *Virgil*
And when I die, be sure you let me know
Great Homer died three thousand years ago.

    Why did I write? What sin to me unknown
Dipped me in ink, my parents', or my own?
As yet a child, nor yet a fool to fame,
I lisped in numbers,° for the numbers came. *meter*
I left no calling for this idle trade,
No duty broke, no father disobeyed.
The muse but served to ease some friend, not wife,
To help me through this long disease, my life,
To second, Arbuthnot! thy art and care,
And teach the being you preserved, to bear.° *endure*

    But why then publish? Granville the polite,
And knowing Walsh, would tell me I could write;
Well-natured Garth inflamed with early praise,

[1] *Codrus* Fictional poet ridiculed by both Virgil and Juvenal.

[2] *Pit, box, and gall'ry* Sections of the theater.

[3] *Colley* Colley Cibber, Poet Laureate, who figured as King of the Dunces in the new edition of Pope's *Dunciad*.

[4] *Henley* John Henley was an independent preacher who gave sensational orations on a variety of matters, both theological and mundane, for which he charged a shilling for admission. His oratory was set up in one of London's primary meat markets, and in 1729 he had given a sermon that claimed to trace the religious history and use of the butcher's calling; *Moore* James Moore Smythe, who was a freemason.

[5] *Bavius* Poet who attacked Virgil and Horace.

[6] *Philips* Ambrose Philips, a rival poet who served as secretary to Hugh Boulter, Archbishop of Armagh.

[7] *Sappho* Famous lyric poet of ancient Greece; also, Pope's poetic nickname for Lady Montagu.

[8] *Grub Street* Collective term for literary hack writers, taken from the street in London of that name, where many such writers lived.

[9] *prints my letters* Curll published an unauthorized version of Pope's letters in 1726.

[10] *subscribe* Books were sometimes printed by subscription.

[11] *Ammon's great son* Alexander the Great.

[12] *Ovid's nose* Ovid's family name was Naso (from the Latin *nasus*, meaning "nose").

And Congreve loved, and Swift endured my lays;° *verses*
The courtly Talbot, Somers, Sheffield read,
Ev'n mitred Rochester would nod the head,
And St. John's self (great Dryden's friends before)
With open arms received one poet more.[1]
Happy my studies, when by these approved!
Happier their author, when by these belov'd!
From these the world will judge of men and books,
Not from the Burnets, Oldmixons, and Cookes.[2]
Soft were my numbers; who could take offence
While pure description held the place of sense?
Like gentle Fanny's[3] was my flow'ry theme,
A painted mistress, or a purling stream.
Yet then did Gildon[4] draw his venal quill;
I wished the man a dinner, and sat still.
Yet then did Dennis[5] rave in furious fret;
I never answered, I was not in debt.
If want provoked, or madness made them print,
I waged no war with Bedlam or the Mint.
Did some more sober critic come abroad?
If wrong, I smiled; if right, I kissed the rod.[6]
Pains, reading, study are their just pretence,
And all they want is spirit, taste, and sense.
Commas and points they set exactly right,
And 'twere a sin to rob them of their mite.[7]
Yet ne'er one sprig of laurel[8] graced these
ribalds,° *abusive rascals*
From slashing Bentley down to piddling Tibbalds.[9]
Each wight[10] who reads not, and but scans and spells,
Each word-catcher that lives on syllables,
Ev'n such small critics some regard may claim,
Preserved in Milton's or in Shakespeare's name.
Pretty! in amber to observe the forms
Of hairs, or straws, or dirt, or grubs, or worms;
The things, we know, are neither rich nor rare,
But wonder how the devil they got there?
Were others angry? I excused them too;
Well might they rage; I gave them but their due.
A man's true merit 'tis not hard to find,
But each man's secret standard in his mind.
That casting weight[11] pride adds to emptiness,
This, who can gratify? for who can guess?
The bard[12] whom pilfered pastorals renown,
Who turns a Persian tale for half a crown,[13]
Just writes to make his barrenness appear,
And strains from hard-bound brains eight lines a year:
He who, still wanting though he lives on theft,
Steals much, spends little, yet has nothing left;
And he who now to sense, now nonsense leaning,
Means not, but blunders round about a meaning;
And he whose fustian's[14] so sublimely bad,

[1] *Granville ... more* This list of men—intended to establish Pope as a preeminent poet and Dryden's successor—names friends and supporters of Dryden who had also encouraged the young Pope. George Granville, William Walsh, and Sir Samuel Garth were all poets of note; William Congreve was a playwright; Charles Talbot, Duke of Shrewsbury; Lord Somers; and John Sheffield, Duke of Buckingham, were all statesmen and patrons. Francis Atterbury, Bishop of Rochester, and Henry St. John, Lord Bolingbroke, were both close friends of Pope.

[2] *Burnets, Oldmixons, and Cookes* Three writers who had attacked Pope in print. In his note Pope calls them "authors of secret and scandalous history."

[3] *Fanny* Lord Fanny was one of Pope's nicknames for John, Lord Hervey, a favorite of the Queen and a known bisexual whose effeminate manner and appearance were frequently commented upon.

[4] *Gildon* Charles Gildon, a critic and writer who had occasionally condemned Pope's writing, at the instigation (Pope believed) of Joseph Addison, one of Pope's rivals; it is for this reason that Pope accuses Gildon of having a corrupt, or mercenary, pen.

[5] *Dennis* John Dennis, another critic who had attacked Pope, though only after Pope had mocked him in his *Essay on Criticism*.

[6] *kissed the rod* Accepted the criticism.

[7] *mite* Very small or insignificant amount of money.

[8] *laurel* Wreaths of laurel (sacred to Apollo) were used to crown celebrated poets in ancient Greece and Rome.

[9] *Bentley* Richard Bentley, a great classical scholar who, however, earned ridicule for his edition of Milton's *Paradise Lost*, in which he arbitrarily placed in square brackets numerous passages that he felt were not up to Milton's standard, claiming they must have been slipped in by an amanuensis, without the blind poet's knowledge; *Tibbalds* Lewis Theobald, a scholar who used his expertise in Elizabethan literature to expose errors in Pope's edition of Shakespeare.

[10] *wight* Human being (usually a contemptuous or belittling term).

[11] *casting weight* Weight that tips the scale one way or the other; deciding factor.

[12] *bard* Ambrose Philips, part of whose *Fifth Pastoral* Pope claimed was plagiarized from the work of an Italian poet. Philips had also published *Persian Tales*, a book of translated stories.

[13] *half a crown* The fee usually charged by a prostitute.

[14] *fustian* Inflated, lofty, and pompous language.

It is not poetry, but prose run mad:
All these, my modest satire bade translate,
And owned that nine such poets made a Tate.[1]
How did they fume, and stamp, and roar, and chafe!
And swear, not Addison himself was safe.
Peace to all such! But were there one[2] whose fires
True genius kindles, and fair fame inspires,
Blessed with each talent and each art to please,
And born to write, converse, and live with ease:
Should such a man, too fond to rule alone,
Bear, like the Turk,[3] no brother near the throne;
View him with scornful, yet with jealous eyes,
And hate for arts that caused himself to rise;
Damn with faint praise, assent with civil leer,
And, without sneering, teach the rest to sneer;
Willing to wound, and yet afraid to strike,
Just hint a fault, and hesitate dislike;
Alike reserved to blame or to commend,
A tim'rous foe, and a suspicious friend;
Dreading ev'n fools; by flatterers besieged,
And so obliging that he ne'er obliged;
Like Cato, give his little senate laws,[4]
And sit attentive to his own applause;
While wits and templars[5] every sentence raise,
And wonder with a foolish face of praise.
Who but must laugh, if such a man there be?
Who would not weep, if Atticus were he!
What though my name stood rubric° on the walls? *written in red*
Or plastered posts, with claps,° in capitals?[6] *placards*
Or smoking forth,[7] a hundred hawkers'° load, *street vendors'*
On wings of winds came flying all abroad?
I sought no homage from the race that write;
I kept, like Asian monarchs, from their sight:
Poems I heeded (now berhymed so long)
No more than thou, great George! a birthday song.[8]
I ne'er with wits or witlings passed my days
To spread about the itch of verse and praise;
Nor like a puppy daggled° through the town *traipsed, taken*
To fetch and carry sing-song up and down;
Nor at rehearsals sweat, and mouthed, and cried,
With handkerchief and orange[9] at my side;
But sick of fops, and poetry, and prate,
To Bufo left the whole Castalian[10] state.
Proud as Apollo on his forked hill,
Sat full-blown Bufo, puffed by every quill;
Fed with soft dedication all day long,
Horace and he went hand in hand in song.
His library (where busts of poets dead,
And a true Pindar, stood without a head)[11]
Received of wits an undistinguished race,
Who first his judgment asked, and then a place:
Much they extolled his pictures, much his seat,° *estate*
And flattered every day, and some days eat;° *ate*
Till grown more frugal in his riper days,
He paid some bards with port, and some with praise;

[1] *nine ... Tate* Nahum Tate, poet and dramatist, was poet laureate from 1692 to 1715. He was best known for his rewriting of Shakespeare's *King Lear*, in which he provided a happy ending. Pope is here playing on the expression "It takes nine tailors to make a man."

[2] *one* Joseph Addison, whose writing and wit Pope admired, but with whom Pope had quarreled after he discovered Addison had been behind a plot to discredit his edition of Homer's *Iliad*. His satirical nickname for Addison here, as elsewhere, is Atticus, after the Roman philosopher of that name, who was a friend of Cicero and a man renowned for his wisdom, generosity, and love of truth.

[3] *like the Turk* It was a popular stereotype at the time that Turkish monarchs would murder any kinsmen, particularly brothers, who could become rivals to the throne.

[4] *Cato ... laws* Addison had written an immensely popular tragedy about Cato, the virtuous Roman senator who chose to commit suicide rather than submit to Caesar's tyrannical authority, for which Pope had composed the prologue. This line, which satirically echoes one from that prologue, mocks the "little senate" of fellow Whig writers over whom Addison ruled during regular meetings at Button's Coffee House.

[5] *templars* Law students or young lawyers, some of whom had literary aspirations.

[6] *What though ... capitals* Allusions to publishers' methods of advertising new books.

[7] *smoking forth* I.e., hot off the press.

[8] *great George ... song* Each year the Poet Laureate was required to compose a birthday ode for the monarch.

[9] *orange* Oranges were commonly sold in theaters.

[10] *Bufo* Latin for "toad"; Bufo is the name given to a certain type of vain, tasteless, and self-absorbed patron; *Castalian* Castalia was the spring on Mount Parnassus that was sacred to Apollo and the Muses. It ran between the two peaks of the mountain (the "forked hill" of line 231), one of which was sacred to Apollo, the other to Bacchus.

[11] *busts ... head* Pope is mocking those who displayed headless busts and claim them to belong to statues of great poets.

To some a dry rehearsal[1] was assigned,
And others (harder still) he paid in kind.[2]
Dryden alone (what wonder?) came not nigh,
Dryden alone escaped this judging eye:
But still the great have kindness in reserve;
He helped to bury whom he helped to starve.[3]
 May some choice patron bless each gray goose quill!
May every Bavius have his Bufo still!
So when a statesman wants a day's defence,
Or envy holds a whole week's war with sense,
Or simple pride for flatt'ry makes demands,
May dunce by dunce be whistled off my hands!
Blessed be the great! for those they take away,
And those they left me—for they left me Gay;[4]
Left me to see neglected genius bloom,
Neglected die, and tell it on his tomb;
Of all thy blameless life the sole return
My verse, and Queensb'ry weeping o'er thy urn!
Oh let me live my own, and die so too!
("To live and die is all I have to do"):[5]
Maintain a poet's dignity and ease,
And see what friends, and read what books I please;
Above a patron, though I condescend
Sometimes to call a minister my friend.
I was not born for courts or great affairs;
I pay my debts, believe, and say my prayers,
Can sleep without a poem in my head,
Nor know if Dennis be alive or dead.
 Why am I asked what next shall see the light?
Heav'ns! was I born for nothing but to write?
Has life no joys for me? or (to be grave)
Have I no friend to serve, no soul to save?
"I found him close with Swift"—"Indeed? No doubt"
(Cries prating Balbus[6]) "something will come out."
'Tis all in vain, deny it as I will.
"No, such a genius never can lie still,"
And then for mine obligingly mistakes
The first lampoon Sir Will or Bubo[7] makes.
Poor guiltless I! and can I choose but smile,
When every coxcomb knows me by my style?
 Cursed be the verse, how well soe'er it flow,
That tends to make one worthy man my foe,
Give virtue scandal, innocence a fear,
Or from the soft-eyed virgin steal a tear!
But he who hurts a harmless neighbour's peace,
Insults fall'n worth, or beauty in distress,
Who loves a lie, lame slander helps about,
Who writes a libel, or who copies out:
That fop whose pride affects a patron's name,
Yet absent, wounds an author's honest fame;
Who can your merit selfishly approve,
And show the sense of it without the love;
Who has the vanity to call you friend,
Yet wants the honour, injured, to defend;
Who tells whate'er you think, whate'er you say,
And, if he lie not, must at least betray:
Who to the Dean and silver bell can swear,
And sees at Cannons what was never there:[8]
Who reads but with a lust to misapply,
Make satire a lampoon, and fiction lie.
A lash like mine no honest man shall dread,
But all such babbling blockheads in his stead.
 Let Sporus[9] tremble—"What? that thing of silk,
Sporus, that mere white curd of ass's milk?
Satire or sense, alas! can Sporus feel?

[1] *dry rehearsal* Recitation of poetry that was not rewarded with alcohol.

[2] *paid in kind* I.e., Bufo paid them by reciting his own poetry.

[3] [Pope's note] Mr. Dryden, after having lived in exigencies, had a magnificent funeral bestowed upon him by the contributions of several persons of quality.

[4] *Gay* John Gay, a close friend of Pope, Swift, and Addison and a fellow member of the Scriblerus Club. Though Gay was the author of several popular works, including *The Beggar's Opera*, he failed to win patronage until, toward the end of his life, he was taken under the protection of the Duke and Duchess of Queensberry.

[5] *To live ... do* Line 94 of John Denham's *Of Prudence*.

[6] *Balbus* Latin: Stammering.

[7] *Sir Will or Bubo* Sir William Yonge, a minor poet and political pawn of Walpole, and Bubb Dodington, a wealthy, extravagant, and corrupt politician who made a show of being a patron of the arts.

[8] *Who ... there* In Pope's *Epistle to Burlington*, his description of Timon's villa was mistaken (perhaps intentionally) for a satire of Cannons, the estate of the Duke of Chandos. The description of Timon's villa, unlike the real Cannons, had a chapel with a silver bell and a Dean.

[9] *Sporus* Sporus was a boy whom Roman Emperor Nero favored. He had him castrated and then married him in a large, public ceremony. Here Sporus is meant to represent Lord Hervey, a favorite of the Queen and a man whose effeminate manners and appearance were frequently commented upon.

Who breaks a butterfly upon a wheel?"[1]
Yet let me flap this bug with gilded wings,
This painted[2] child of dirt, that stinks and stings;
Whose buzz the witty and the fair annoys,
Yet wit ne'er tastes, and beauty ne'er enjoys;
So well-bred spaniels civilly delight
In mumbling of the game they dare not bite.
Eternal smiles his emptiness betray,
As shallow streams run dimpling all the way.
Whether in florid impotence he speaks,
And, as the prompter[3] breathes, the puppet squeaks;
Or at the ear of Eve,[4] familiar toad,
Half froth, half venom, spits himself abroad,
In puns, or politics, or tales, or lies,
Or spite, or smut, or rhymes, or blasphemies.
His wit all seesaw between that and this,
Now high, now low, now master up, now miss,
And he himself one vile antithesis.
Amphibious thing! that acting either part,
The trifling head or the corrupted heart,
Fop at the toilet,° flatt'rer at the board,[5] *dressing table*
Now trips a lady, and now struts a lord.
Eve's tempter thus the rabbins° have expressed, *rabbis*
A cherub's face, a reptile all the rest;
Beauty that shocks you, parts that none will trust,
Wit that can creep, and pride that licks the dust.
Not fortune's worshipper, nor fashion's fool,
Not lucre's madman, nor ambition's tool,
Not proud, nor servile, be one poet's praise
That, if he pleased, he pleased by manly ways:
That flatt'ry, even to kings, he held a shame,
And thought a lie in verse or prose the same:
That not in fancy's maze he wandered long,
But stooped[6] to truth, and moralized his song:
That not for fame, but virtue's better end,
He stood° the furious foe, the timid friend, *withstood*
The damning critic, half-approving wit,
The coxcomb hit, or fearing to be hit;
Laughed at the loss of friends he never had,
The dull, the proud, the wicked, and the mad;
The distant threats of vengeance on his head,
The blow unfelt, the tear he never shed;
The tale revived, the lie so oft o'erthrown,
Th' imputed trash, and dullness not his own;
The morals blackened when the writings 'scape,
The libeled person, and the pictured shape;[7]
Abuse on all he loved, or loved him, spread,
A friend in exile, or a father dead;
The whisper that to greatness still too near,
Perhaps yet vibrates on his Sovereign's ear—
Welcome for thee, fair virtue! all the past:
For thee, fair virtue! welcome ev'n the last!
"But why insult the poor, affront the great?"
A knave's a knave, to me, in every state;
Alike my scorn, if he succeed or fail,
Sporus at court, or Japhet[8] in a jail,
A hireling scribbler, or a hireling peer,
Knight of the Post corrupt, or of the Shire,[9]
If on a pillory, or near a throne,
He gain his prince's ear, or lose his own.
Yet soft by nature, more a dupe than wit,
Sappho can tell you how this man was bit:[10]
This dreaded sat'rist Dennis will confess
Foe to his pride, but friend to his distress:[11]
So humble, he has knocked at Tibbald's door,
Has drunk with Cibber, nay has rhymed for Moore.
Full ten years slandered, did he once reply?

[1] *wheel* I.e., of torture.

[2] *painted* Lord Hervey was known to wear makeup.

[3] *the prompter* Walpole.

[4] *Eve* Queen Caroline. Cf. Milton's *Paradise Lost*, 4.799, in which the devil is described in this position.

[5] *board* Dining table.

[6] *stooped* Swooped, as a falcon does when it catches sight of its prey.

[7] *the pictured shape* Some caricatures of Pope showed him as a hunchbacked ape.

[8] *Japhet* Japhet Crook, a notorious forger who obtained several thousand pounds and two estates through forged deeds and wills before he was discovered, whereupon he was placed in the pillory, his ears were cut off, and he was locked in prison.

[9] *Knight ... Shire* A Knight of the Post made a living by giving false evidence; a Knight of the Shire represented his county in Parliament.

[10] *bit* Deceived.

[11] *Dennis ... distress* Near the end of his life Dennis fell into debt. In addition to publicly supporting Dennis's works, Pope helped to organize a benefit performance in his honor and contributed a prologue to the play that was performed.

Three thousand suns went down on Welsted's lie.[1]
To please a mistress one aspersed his life;
He lashed him not, but let her be his wife.
Let Budgell charge low Grub Street on his quill,
And write whate'er he pleased, except his will;[2]
Let the two Curlls of town and court[3] abuse
His father, mother, body, soul, and muse.
Yet why? that father held it for a rule
It was a sin to call our neighbour fool;
That harmless mother thought no wife a whore—
Hear this, and spare his family, James More!
Unspotted names, and memorable long,
If there be force in virtue, or in song.
  Of gentle blood (part shed in honour's cause,
While yet in Britain honour had applause)
Each parent sprung—"What fortune, pray?"—Their own,
And better got than Bestia's[4] from the throne.
Born to no pride, inheriting no strife,
Nor marrying discord in a noble wife,
Stranger to civil and religious rage,
The good man walked innoxious° through his age. *doing no harm*
No courts he saw, no suits would ever try,
Nor dared an oath,[5] nor hazarded a lie.
Unlearned, he knew no schoolman's subtle art,
No language but the language of the heart.
By nature honest, by experience wise,
Healthy by temp'rance and by exercise;
His life, though long, to sickness passed unknown;
His death was instant, and without a groan.
Oh grant me thus to live, and thus to die!
Who sprung from kings shall know less joy than I.
  O friend! may each domestic bliss be thine!
Be no unpleasing melancholy mine:
Me, let the tender office long engage
To rock the cradle of reposing age,
With lenient° arts extend a mother's breath, *soothing*
Make languor smile, and smooth the bed of death,
Explore the thought, explain the asking eye,
And keep a while one parent from the sky!
On cares like these if length of days attend,
May Heav'n, to bless those days, preserve my friend,
Preserve him social, cheerful, and serene,
And just as rich as when he served a Queen!
Whether that blessing be denied, or giv'n,
Thus far was right—the rest belongs to Heav'n.
—1735 (WRITTEN 1731–34)

[1] *Welsted's lie* Leonard Welsted, who, according to Pope, claimed Pope had "occasioned a lady's death." Welsted was also one of those who maintained that Pope's *Epistle to Burlington* satirized the Duke of Chandos.

[2] *Budgell ... will* An article in the *Grub Street Journal* accused Eustace Budgell of forging the will of Matthew Tindal. Budgell believed (wrongly) that Pope had written the article.

[3] *two Curlls ... court* The Curll of the court is Lord Hervey; the other is Edmund Curll, the publisher.

[4] *Bestia* Corrupt Roman politician of the second century BCE. Here the name is probably meant to signify the Duke of Marlborough, who became rich by winning the favor of Queen Anne.

[5] *dared an oath* Pope's father refused both to renounce his Catholicism and to take oaths against the Pope. As a result, he was denied many of the rights of citizenship, including the rights to vote, attend schools, and inherit property.

Epistle 2. To a Lady[6]

Of the Characters of Women[7]

from *Moral Essays*

ARGUMENT

Of the characters of women (considered only as contradistinguished from the other sex). That these are yet more inconsistent and incomprehensible than those of men, of which instances are given even from such characters as are plainest and most strongly marked, as in the affected, verses 7, etc.; the soft-natured, 29; the cunning, 45; the whimsical, 53; the wits and refiners, 87; the stupid and silly, 101. How contrarieties run through them all.

But though the particular characters of this sex are more various than those of men, the general characteristic as to the ruling passion is more uniform and confined. In what that lies, and whence it proceeds, 207, etc. Men are best known in public life, women in private, 199. What are the aims and the fate of the sex,

[6] *To a Lady* Martha Blount, whom Pope had known since childhood and who was his closest female friend.

[7] [Pope's note] Of the characters of women, treating of this sex only as contradistinguished from the other.

both as to power and pleasure? 219, 231, etc. Advice for their true interest, 249. The picture of an esteemable woman, made up of the best kind of contrarieties, 269, etc.

Nothing so true as what you once let fall:[1]
"Most women have no characters at all."
Matter too soft a lasting mark to bear,
And best distinguished by black, brown, or fair.
How many pictures of one nymph we view,
All how unlike each other, all how true!
Arcadia's Countess, here in ermined pride,[2]
Is there Pastora[3] by a fountain side.
Here Fannia,[4] leering on her own good man,
And there a naked Leda with a swan.[5]
Let then the fair one beautifully cry
In Magdalene's[6] loose hair and lifted eye,
Or dressed in smiles of sweet Cecilia[7] shine,[8]
With simp'ring angels, palms, and harps divine;
Whether the charmer sinner it, or saint it,
If folly grows romantic, I must paint it.
Come then, the colours and the ground[9] prepare!
Dip in the rainbow, trick[10] her off in air,
Choose a firm cloud before it fall, and in it
Catch, ere she change, the Cynthia[11] of this minute.
Rufa,[12] whose eye, quick-glancing o'er the park,[13]
Attracts each light gay meteor of a spark,° *beau*
Agrees as ill with Rufa studying Locke[14]
As Sappho's[15] diamonds with her dirty smock,
Or Sappho at her toilet's° greasy task *dressing table's*
With Sappho fragrant at an evening masque:° *masquerade*
So morning insects, that in muck begun,
Shine, buzz, and fly-blow° in the setting sun. *lay eggs*
How soft is Silia! fearful to offend,
The frail one's advocate, the weak one's friend;
To her, Calista proved her conduct nice,[16]
And good Simplicius° asks of her advice. *simpleton*
Sudden, she storms! she raves! You tip the wink,[17]
But spare your censure—Silia does not drink.
All eyes may see from what the change arose,
All eyes may see—a pimple on her nose.[18]
Papillia,[19] wedded to her doting spark,
Sighs for the shades—"How charming is a park!"
A park is purchased, but the fair he sees
All bathed in tears—"Oh odious, odious trees!"
Ladies, like variegated tulips, show
'Tis to their changes that their charms they owe;
Their happy spots the nice° admirer take, *discerning*

[1] [Pope's note] That these particular Characters are not so strongly mark'd as those of Men, seldom so fixed, and still more inconsistent with themselves.

[2] *Arcadia's Countess* Mary, Countess of Pembroke. Mary's brother, Sir Philip Sidney, had written a romance entitled *The Countess of Pembroke's Arcadia*, which he dedicated to her; *ermined pride* In her formal state robes.

[3] *Pastora* I.e., as a shepherdess. It was fashionable for ladies of distinction to have themselves painted in a variety of guises.

[4] *Fannia* Infamous Roman adulteress.

[5] *Leda … swan* Leda was raped by Zeus, who came to her in the form of a swan. Leda's daughter from this union was Helen of Troy.

[6] *Magdalene* Mary Magdalene, who was believed to be first a prostitute and then Jesus's follower, was a common subject of paintings.

[7] *Cecilia* Patron saint of music.

[8] [Pope's note] Attitudes in which several ladies affected to be drawn, and sometimes one lady in them all.—The poet's politeness and complaisance to the sex is observable in this instance, amongst others, that, whereas in the *Characters of Men* he has sometimes made use of real names, in the *Characters of Women* always fictitious.

[9] *ground* Background color, or the preliminary layer of paint on the canvas.

[10] *trick* Sketch an outline.

[11] *Cynthia* Goddess of the moon, which was associated with mutability and instability.

[12] *Rufa* Red-haired. Redheads were believed to be especially wanton and lascivious.

[13] [Pope's note] Instances of contrarieties given even from such Characters as are most strongly mark'd and seemingly therefore most consistent. As I. In the *Affected*, v. 21 &c.

[14] *Locke* John Locke, English philosopher, author of *Essay Concerning Human Understanding*.

[15] *Sappho* Famous lyric poet of ancient Greece; also, Pope's poetic name for Lady Mary Wortley Montagu, a former friend of his and a frequent subject of his satire.

[16] *Callista* Literally meaning "fairest," but also suggesting Callisto, an Arcadian nymph made pregnant by Zeus, and therefore implying a lack of chastity; *proved … nice* I.e., was able to justify herself.

[17] *tip the wink* Wink at someone as a sign of warning.

[18] [Pope's note] Contrarieties in the *Soft-natured*.

[19] *Papillia* From *papilio*, the Latin for "butterfly."

Fine by defect, and delicately weak.
'Twas thus Calypso[1] once each heart alarmed,
Awed without virtue, without beauty charmed;
Her tongue bewitched as oddly as her eyes,
Less wit than mimic, more a wit than wise;
Strange graces still, and stranger flights she had,
Was just not ugly, and was just not mad;
Yet ne'er so sure our passion to create,
As when she touched the brink of all we hate.[2]
    Narcissa's[3] nature, tolerably mild,
To make a wash[4] would hardly stew a child,
Has ev'n been proved to grant a lover's prayer,
And paid a tradesman once to make him stare;
Gave alms at Easter, in a Christian trim,° *guise*
And made a widow happy for a whim.
Why then declare good nature is her scorn,
When 'tis by that alone she can be born?
Why pique all mortals, yet affect a name?
A fool to pleasure, and a slave to fame:
Now deep in Taylor and the Book of Martyrs,[5]
Now drinking citron with his Grace and Chartres.[6]
Now conscience chills her, and now passion burns,
And atheism and religion take their turns:
A very heathen in the carnal part,
Yet still a sad, good Christian at her heart.[7]
    See sin in state, majestically drunk,
Proud as a peeress,° prouder as a punk;° *noblewoman / prostitute*
Chaste to her husband, frank[8] to all beside,
A teeming mistress but a barren bride.
What then? let blood and body bear the fault,
Her head's untouched, that noble seat of thought:
Such this day's doctrine—in another fit
She sins with poets through pure love of wit.
What has not fired her bosom or her brain?
Caesar and Tall-boy, Charles[9] and Charlemagne.
As Helluo,[10] late dictator of the feast,
The nose of haut-gout[11] and the tip° of taste, *epitome*
Critiqued your wine and analyzed your meat,
Yet on plain pudding deigned at home to eat;
So Philomedé,[12] lect'ring all mankind
On the soft passion, and the taste refined,
Th' address,[13] the delicacy—stoops at once,
And makes her hearty meal upon a dunce.
    Flavia's a wit, has too much sense to pray,[14]
To toast our wants and wishes is her way;
Nor asks of God, but of her stars to give
The mighty blessing, "while we live, to live."
Then all for death, that opiate of the soul!
Lucretia's dagger, Rosamonda's bowl.[15]
Say, what can cause such impotence of mind?
A spark too fickle, or a spouse too kind.
Wise wretch! with pleasures too refined to please,
With too much spirit to be e'er at ease,
With too much quickness ever to be taught,
With too much thinking to have common thought;[16]
Who purchase pain with all that joy can give,

[1] *Calypso* In Homer's *Odyssey*, Calypso is a sea-nymph who bewitches Odysseus and his men and keeps them on her island for seven years.

[2] [Pope's note] Contrarieties in the *Cunning* and *Artful*.

[3] *Narcissa* Meant to indicate a female version of the Greek Narcissus, who fell in love with his own image in a pond.

[4] *wash* Liquid cosmetic or lotion.

[5] *Taylor* Bishop Jeremy Taylor, author of popular devotional works such as *Holy Living* and *Holy Dying*; *Book of Martyrs* By John Foxe, another widely-read work.

[6] *citron* Lemon-flavored brandy; *his Grace* Probably Philip, Duke of Wharton, who was president of the Hell-Fire Club; *Chartres* Colonel Francis Chartres, a moneylender, an informer, and a notorious scoundrel who was referred to as the "Rape-Master General" after having been convicted, at the age of 70, of raping his maid.

[7] [Pope's note] IV. In the *Whimsical*.

[8] *frank* Free (here in a sexual sense).

[9] *Tall-boy* The foolish, slow-witted lover in Richard Broome's *The Jovial Crew*; *Charles* Standard name for a footman.

[10] *Helluo* Latin: Glutton.

[11] *nose of haut-gout* Connoisseur of strong flavors.

[12] *Philomedé* The name has been taken to literally mean "a lover of the Medes," or one with exotic tastes. Because Pope originally suppressed this section, he most likely had a real woman in mind, though it is uncertain who that may be.

[13] *address* Manner of speaking, deportment.

[14] [Pope's note] V. In the *Lewd* and *Vicious*.

[15] *Lucretia* The Roman wife who committed suicide after being raped by Sextus, son of Tarquinius Superbus, the last king of Rome; *Rosamonda's bowl* Mistress of Henry II who was supposedly killed by Queen Eleanor of Aquitaine, who forced her to drink from a poisoned bowl.

[16] *common thought* Common sense.

And die of nothing but a rage to live.[1]
 Turn then from wits, and look on Simo's[2] mate,
No ass so meek, no ass so obstinate;
Or her that owns her faults, but never mends,
Because she's honest, and the best of friends;
Or her whose life the church and scandal share,
Forever in a passion or a prayer;
Or her who laughs at hell, but (like her Grace)
Cries, "Ah! how charming if there's no such place!";
Or who in sweet vicissitude appears
Of mirth and opium, ratafie[3] and tears,
The daily anodyne,° and nightly draught, *painkiller*
To kill those foes to fair ones, time and thought.
Woman and fool are two hard things to hit,
For true no-meaning puzzles more than wit.
 But what are these to great Atossa's[4] mind?
Scarce once herself, by turns all womankind!
Who, with herself or others, from her birth
Finds all her life one warfare upon earth:
Shines in exposing knaves and painting fools,
Yet is whate'er she hates and ridicules.
No thought advances, but her eddy° brain *swirling*
Whisks it about, and down it goes again.
Full sixty years the world has been her trade,
The wisest fool much time has ever made.
From loveless youth to unrespected age,
No passion gratified except her rage.
So much the fury still out-ran the wit,
The pleasure missed her, and the scandal hit.
Who breaks with her, provokes revenge from hell,
But he's a bolder man who dares be well:[5]
Her every turn with violence pursued,
Nor more a storm her hate than gratitude.
To that each passion turns, or soon or late;
Love, if it makes her yield, must make her hate.
Superiors? death! and equals? what a curse!
But an inferior not dependent? worse.
Offend her, and she knows not to forgive;
Oblige her, and she'll hate you while you live;
But die, and she'll adore you—then the bust
And temple rise—then fall again to dust.[6]
Last night, her lord was all that's good and great,
A knave this morning, and his will a cheat.
Strange! by the means defeated of the ends,
By spirit robbed of pow'r, by warmth of friends,
By wealth of followers! without one distress,
Sick of herself through very selfishness!
Atossa, cursed with every granted prayer,
Childless with all her children, wants an heir.
To heirs unknown descends th' unguarded store,
Or wanders, heav'n-directed, to the poor.
 Pictures like these, dear Madam, to design
Asks no firm hand, and no unerring line;
Some wand'ring touch, or some reflected light,
Some flying stroke alone can hit 'em right:
For how should equal° colours do the knack?° *uniform / trick*
Chameleons who can paint in white and black?
 "Yet Chloe[7] sure was formed without a spot—"
Nature in her then erred not, but forgot.
"With every pleasing, every prudent part,
Say, what can Chloe want?"—She wants a heart.
She speaks, behaves, and acts just as she ought,
But never, never, reached one gen'rous thought.
Virtue she finds too painful an endeavour,
Content to dwell in decencies forever.
So very reasonable, so unmoved,
As never yet to love, or to be loved.
She, while her lover pants upon her breast,
Can mark the figures on an Indian chest;
And when she sees her friend in deep despair,

[1] [Pope's note] VI. Contrarieties in the Witty and Refin'd.

[2] *Simo* I.e., an ape-like man (from *simius*, the Latin for "ape").

[3] *ratafie* Fruit-flavored brandy.

[4] *Atossa* Persian queen, daughter of Cyrus the Great. Here the character seems to be a satire on the Duchess of Buckingham, the eccentric daughter of James II. She bore the Duke five children, but all of them predeceased her, and she spent years involved in legal battles with the Duke's illegitimate children over the contents of his will. She was known for the violence of her rages, and eventually was declared insane. Pope had edited her husband's posthumous works at her request, but she quarreled with him over some of his attempted revisions.

[5] *be well* Get along well with her.

[6] *bust … dust* The Duchess ordered ornate monuments built in memory of her husband and son.

[7] *Chloe* From the Greek word for "blooming," this name is normally given to women of simplicity and beauty. Here she is said to have some characteristics in common with Pope's friend the Countess of Suffolk.

Observes how much a chintz exceeds mohair.[1]
Forbid it, heav'n, a favour or a debt
She e'er should cancel—but she may forget.
Safe is your secret still in Chloe's ear,
But none of Chloe's shall you ever hear.
Of all her dears she never slandered one,
But cares not if a thousand are undone.
Would Chloe know if you're alive or dead?
She bids her footman put it in her head.
Chloe is prudent—would you too be wise?
Then never break your heart when Chloe dies.
 One certain portrait may (I grant) be seen,
Which heav'n has varnished out,[2] and made a Queen:[3]
The same forever![4] and described by all
With truth and goodness, as with crown and ball.[5]
Poets heap virtues, painters gems at will,
And show their zeal, and hide their want of skill.
'Tis well—but, artists! who can paint or write,
To draw the naked is your true delight:
That robe of quality so struts and swells,
None see what parts of nature it conceals.
Th' exactest° traits of body or of mind, *most perfect*
We owe to models of an humble kind.
If Queensberry[6] to strip there's no compelling,
'Tis from a handmaid we must take a Helen.[7]
From peer or bishop 'tis no easy thing
To draw the man who loves his God or King;
Alas! I copy (or my draught° would fail) *drawing*
From honest Mah'met, or plain Parson Hale.[8]

 But grant, in public men sometimes are shown,[9]
A woman's seen in private life alone;
Our bolder talents in full light displayed,
Your virtues open fairest in the shade.
Bred to disguise, in public 'tis you hide;
There, none distinguish 'twixt your shame or pride,
Weakness or delicacy; all so nice° *subtle*
That each may seem a virtue, or a vice.
 In men we various ruling passions find,[10]
In women, two almost divide the kind;
Those, only fixed, they first or last obey,
The love of pleasure, and the love of sway.° *power*
 That,° nature gives; and where the lesson taught[11] *the former*
Is but to please, can pleasure seem a fault?
Experience, this;° by man's oppression cursed, *the latter*
They seek the second not to lose the first.
 Men, some to business, some to pleasure take,
But every woman is at heart a rake;[12]
Men, some to quiet, some to public strife,
But every lady would be queen for life.
 Yet mark the fate of a whole sex of queens![13]
Pow'r all their end, but beauty all the means.
In youth they conquer with so wild a rage
As leaves them scarce a subject in their age;
For foreign glory, foreign joy, they roam,
No thought of peace or happiness at home.
But wisdom's triumph is well-timed retreat,
As hard a science to the fair as great!

[1] *chintz* Painted calico imported from India; *mohair* Here not the original fabric made from the angora goat, but a silk imitation.

[2] *varnished out* Completed with a coat of varnish.

[3] *Queen* Caroline, wife of George II, whom Pope disliked as a result of her Whig sympathies.

[4] *The same forever* This was the motto of Elizabeth I and of Queen Anne (in Latin, *semper eadem*).

[5] *ball* Golden orb, a symbol of the sovereign's earthly authority.

[6] *Queensberry* Catherine Hyde, the Duchess of Queensberry, who is said to have been one of the most beautiful women of the eighteenth century. She and her husband were the patrons of Pope's friend John Gay.

[7] *a Helen* Beautiful as Helen of Troy, whose legendary good looks sparked the Trojan War.

[8] *Mah'met* Turkish servant to George I who was captured at the siege of Buda; *Parson Hale* Pope's friend and neighbor Dr. Stephen Hales, a clergyman and famous plant physiologist. Hales had witnessed Pope's will.

[9] [Pope's note] In the former Editions, between this and the foregoing lines, a want of Connection might be perceived, occasioned by the omission of certain *Examples* and *Illustrations* to the Maxims laid down; and tho' some of these have since been found, viz. the Characters of *Philomedé, Atossa, Chloe,* and some verses following, others are still wanting, nor can we answer that these are exactly inserted.

[10] [Pope's note] The former part having shewn, that the *particular Characters* of Women are more various than those of Men, it is nevertheless observ'd, that the *general* Characteristic of the sex, as to the *ruling Passion,* is more uniform.

[11] [Pope's note] This is occasioned partly by their *Nature,* partly by their *Education,* and in some degree by *Necessity.*

[12] *rake* Person of loose habits and morals.

[13] [Pope's note] What are the *Aims* and the *Fate* of this Sex?—I. As to *Power.*

Beauties, like tyrants, old and friendless grown,
Yet hate to rest, and dread to be alone;
Worn out in public, weary every eye,
Nor leave one sigh behind them when they die.
  Pleasures the sex, as children birds, pursue,[1]
Still out of reach, yet never out of view;
Sure, if they catch, to spoil the toy at most,
To covet flying, and regret when lost.
At last, to follies youth could scarce defend,
'Tis half their age's prudence to pretend;
Ashamed to own they gave delight before,
Reduced to feign it, when they give no more.
As hags° hold sabbaths, less for joy than spite, *witches*
So these their merry, miserable night;
Still round and round the ghosts of beauty glide,
And haunt the places where their honour died.
  See how the world its veterans rewards!
A youth of frolics, an old age of cards;
Fair to no purpose, artful to no end,
Young without lovers, old without a friend;
A fop their passion, but their prize a sot,
Alive, ridiculous, and dead, forgot!
  Ah, friend! to dazzle let the vain design,[2]
To raise the thought and touch the heart, be thine!
That charm shall grow, while what fatigues the Ring[3]
Flaunts and goes down, an unregarded thing.
So when the sun's broad beam has tired the sight,
All mild ascends the moon's more sober light;
Serene in virgin modesty she shines,
And unobserved the glaring orb declines.
  Oh! blest with temper,° whose unclouded ray *equanimity*
Can make tomorrow cheerful as today;
She who can love a sister's charms, or hear
Sighs for a daughter with unwounded ear;
She who ne'er answers till a husband cools,
Or, if she rules him, never shows she rules;
Charms by accepting, by submitting sways,
Yet has her humour most when she obeys;
Lets fops or fortune fly which way they will;
Disdains all loss of tickets,° or codille;[4] *lottery tickets*
Spleen, vapours, or smallpox,[5] above them all,
And mistress of herself, though China fall.
  And yet, believe me, good as well as ill,[6]
Woman's at best a contradiction still.
Heav'n, when it strives to polish all it can
Its last best work, but forms a softer man;
Picks from each sex to make its fav'rite blest,
Your love of pleasure, our desire of rest;
Blends, in exception to all gen'ral rules,
Your taste of follies with our scorn of fools,
Reserve with frankness, art with truth allied,
Courage with softness, modesty with pride,
Fixed principles with fancy ever new;
Shakes all together, and produces—you.
  Be this a woman's fame; with this unblest,
Toasts[7] live a scorn, and queens may die a jest.
This Phoebus promised (I forget the year[8])
When those blue eyes first opened on the sphere;
Ascendant[9] Phoebus watched that hour with care,
Averted half your parents simple prayer,
And gave you beauty, but denied the pelf[10]
Which buys your sex a tyrant[11] o'er itself.
The gen'rous God, who wit and gold refines,[12]
And ripens spirits as he ripens mines,
Kept dross[13] for duchesses, the world shall know it,
To you gave sense, good-humour, and a poet.
—1735

[1] [Pope's note] II. As to *Pleasure.*

[2] [Pope's note] Advice for their true Interest.

[3] *the Ring* Circular drive around Hyde Park.

[4] *codille* Term for the defeat of the challenger in the popular card game of ombre.

[5] *Spleen* Term for a variety of complaints, including melancholy, ill-humor, and irritability; *vapours* Fits of spleen; *smallpox* Common and often fatal disease at the time. Martha Blount had contracted it several years earlier, and her face was scarred as a result.

[6] [Pope's note] The Picture of an estimable Woman, with the best kinds of contrarieties.

[7] *Toasts* Women whose beauty was celebrated with toasts.

[8] *the year* Martha Blount was born in 1690.

[9] *Ascendant* Astrological term for the sign of the zodiac that was rising above the horizon (and therefore had a dominant influence) at the time of birth.

[10] *pelf* Wealth. Martha Blount's parents could not afford to provide her with a dowry.

[11] *tyrant* I.e., a husband.

[12] *gen'rous God … refines* As god of both poetry and the sun, Phoebus Apollo could refine wits as well as gold (precious metals were thought by some to grow and ripen in the earth).

[13] *dross* Discarded impurities.

Epistle 4. To Richard Boyle, Earl of Burlington[1]

Of the Use of Riches

from *Moral Essays*

ARGUMENT

The vanity of expense in people of wealth and quality. The abuse of the word taste, verse 13. That the first principle and foundation, in this as in everything else, is good sense, verse 40. The chief proof of it is to follow nature even in works of mere luxury and elegance. Instanced in architecture and gardening, where all must be adapted to the genius[2] and use of the place, and the beauties not forced into it, but resulting from it, verse 50. How men are disappointed in their most expensive undertakings, for want of this true foundation, without which nothing can please long, if at all: and the best examples and rules will but be perverted into something burdensome or ridiculous, verse 65, etc., to 92. A description of the false taste of magnificence; the first grand error of which is to imagine that greatness consists in the size and dimension, instead of the proportion and harmony of the whole, verse 97, and the second, either in joining together parts incoherent, or too minutely resembling, or in the repetition of the same too frequently, verse 105, etc. A word or two of false taste in books, in music, in painting, even in preaching and prayer, and lastly in entertainments, verse 133, etc. Yet Providence is justified in giving wealth to be squandered in this manner, since it is dispersed to the poor and laborious part of mankind, verse 169 (recurring to what is laid down in the first book, Epistle 2.,[3] and in the Epistle preceding this,[4] verse 159, etc.). What are the proper objects of magnificence, and a proper field for the expense of great men, verse 177, etc., and finally, the great and public works which become a prince, verse 191 to the end.

'Tis strange, the miser should his cares employ
To gain those riches he can ne'er enjoy:
Is it less strange, the prodigal° should waste *recklessly extravagant*
His wealth to purchase what he ne'er can taste?
Not for himself he sees, or hears, or eats;
Artists must choose his pictures, music, meats:
He buys for Topham,[5] drawings and designs,
For Pembroke,[6] statues, dirty gods,[7] and coins;
Rare monkish manuscripts for Hearne[8] alone,
And books for Mead, and butterflies for Sloane.[9]
Think we all these are for himself? no more
Than his fine wife, alas! or finer whore.

For what his Virro[10] painted, built, and planted?
Only to show, how many tastes he wanted.[11]
What brought Sir Visto's[12] ill got wealth to waste?
Some daemon whispered, "Visto! have a taste."
Heav'n visits with a taste the wealthy fool,

---

[1] *Richard Boyle, Earl of Burlington* Richard Boyle, Third Earl of Burlington (1694–1753), a close friend to Pope. He was a skilled architect and influential proponent of Roman classicism in contrast to the much more ornate baroque style that was dominant at the time.

[2] *genius* I.e., local guardian spirit of classical mythology; also a location's particular character.

[3] *first book, Epistle 2* Epistle 2 of *Essay on Man.*

[4] *the Epistle preceding this* Epistle 3, addressed to Allen, Lord Bathurst (1685–1775). Epistle 3 was also given the subtitle *Of the Use of Riches*.

[5] [Pope's note] A gentleman famous for a judicious collection of drawings. [Richard Topham (d. 1735).]

[6] *Pembroke* Thomas Herbert, eighth Earl of Pembroke (1656–1733), a politician and also an art and coin collector.

[7] *dirty gods* Antiquities, dirty from having been dug from the ground.

[8] *Hearne* Thomas Hearne (1678–1735), medievalist known for his editions of historical texts.

[9] [Pope's note] Two eminent physicians; the one had an excellent library; the other the finest collection in Europe of natural curiosities; both men of great learning and humanity. [Richard Mead (1673–1754) was Pope's physician and treated George II; Sir Hans Sloane (1660–1753) was President of the Royal College of Physicians. Sloane's collection became the basis of the British Museum.]

[10] *Virro* Character in Juvenal's fifth Satire (c. 100 CE); a greedy, contemptible patron who is a terrible host to his guests of lower class.

[11] *wanted* Pun on the word's two meanings; i.e., "desired" and "lacked."

[12] *Visto* Italian: Vista, the view at the end of a tree-lined avenue. Used as a name, "Visto" suggests an interest in landscaping.

And needs no rod but Ripley[1] with a rule.[2]
See! sportive fate, to punish awkward pride,
Bids Bubo[3] build, and sends him such a guide:
A standing sermon, at each year's expense,
That never coxcomb° reached magnificence! *fool*

You[4] show us, Rome was glorious, not profuse,
And pompous buildings once were things of use.
Yet shall (my Lord) your just, your noble rules
Fill half the land with imitating fools;
Who random drawings from your sheets shall take,
And of one beauty many blunders make;
Load some vain church with old theatric state,[5]
Turn arcs of triumph to a garden gate;
Reverse your ornaments, and hang them all
On some patched dog-hole eked with° ends of wall; *stuck to*
Then clap four slices of pilaster° on't, *ornamental column*
That laced with bits of rustic,[6] makes a front.° *formal entrance*
Or call the winds through long arcades to roar,
Proud to catch cold at a Venetian door;[7]
Conscious they act a true Palladian part,
And, if they starve,[8] they starve by rules of art.

Oft have you hinted to your brother peer,
A certain truth, which many buy too dear:
Something there is more needful than expense,
And something previous ev'n to taste—'tis sense:
Good sense, which only is the gift of Heav'n,
And though no science, fairly worth the sev'n:[9]
A light, which in yourself you must perceive;
Jones and Le Nôtre[10] have it not to give.

To build, to plant, whatever you intend,
To rear the column, or the arch to bend,
To swell the terrace, or to sink the grot;[11]
In all, let nature never be forgot.
But treat the goddess like a modest fair,
Nor overdress, nor leave her wholly bare;
Let not each beauty ev'rywhere be spied,
Where half the skill is decently° to hide. *appropriately*
He gains all points, who pleasingly confounds,
Surprises, varies, and conceals the bounds.

Consult the genius of the place in all;
That tells the waters or° to rise, or fall; *either*
Or helps th'ambitious hill the heav'ns to scale,
Or scoops in circling theatres the vale;
Calls in the country, catches opening glades,
Joins willing woods, and varies shades from shades,
Now breaks, or now directs, th'intending lines;[12]
Paints as you plant, and, as you work, designs.

Still follow sense, of ev'ry art the soul,
Parts answ'ring parts shall slide into a whole,
Spontaneous beauties all around advance,
Start ev'n from difficulty, strike from chance;

[1] [Pope's note] This man was a carpenter, employed by a first minister [Sir Robert Walpole (1676–1745), a politician of great influence], who raised him to an architect, without any genius in art, and after some wretched proofs of his insufficiency in public buildings, made him comptroller of the board of works. [Thomas Ripley (1682–1758) was head administrator of the Office of Works, which oversaw the design and construction of royal buildings.]

[2] *no rod … a rule* A pun on "rule," meaning both a carpenter's ruler used as a rod for punishment and an architectural principle misused by the incompetent architect Ripley.

[3] *Bubo* Latin: Owl. Pope's derisive nickname for George Bubb Dodington (1691–1762), who spent an extravagant sum on his family mansion.

[4] [Pope's note] The Earl of Burlington was then publishing the *Designs of Inigo Jones*, and the *Antiquities of Rome* by Palladio. [Both were important works in Italian-style Renaissance architecture; Andrea Palladio (1508–80) played a central role in the development of the style, and Inigo Jones (1573–1652) was the first architect to employ it in Britain.]

[5] *old theatric state* I.e., architectural details inappropriately borrowed from Roman amphitheaters.

[6] *rustic* Stone with rough surface texture common in Renaissance architecture.

[7] *Venetian door* Invention of Palladio; an arched opening framed by rectangular windows.

[8] *starve* I.e., starve as a result of having overspent on an impractical building.

[9] *the sev'n* The seven liberal arts as defined by medieval scholars.

[10] [Pope's note] Inigo Jones, the celebrated architect, and M. Le Nôtre [André Le Nôtre (1613–1700)], the designer of the best gardens of France.

[11] *grot* Grotto; a constructed cave.

[12] *intending lines* Lines important to the architectural composition.

Nature shall join you; time shall make it grow
A work to wonder at—perhaps a Stowe.[1]

Without it, proud Versailles![2] thy glory falls;
And Nero's terraces[3] desert their walls:
The vast parterres[4] a thousand hands shall make,
Lo! Cobham[5] comes, and floats° them with a lake: *floods*
Or cut wide views through mountains to the plain,
You'll wish your hill or sheltered seat again.[6]
Ev'n in an ornament its place remark,° *consider*
Nor in an hermitage set Dr. Clarke.[7]

Behold Villario's[8] ten years' toil complete;
His quincunx darkens, his espaliers[9] meet;
The wood supports the plain, the parts unite,
And strength of shade contends with strength of light;
A waving glow his bloomy beds display,
Blushing in bright diversities of day,
With silver-quiv'ring rills° meandered o'er— *small streams*
Enjoy them, you! Villario can no more;
Tired of the scene parterres and fountains yield,
He finds at last he better likes a field.

Through his young woods how pleased Sabinus[10] strayed,
Or sat delighted in the thick'ning shade,
With annual joy the redd'ning shoots to greet,
Or see the stretching branches long to meet!
His son's fine taste an op'ner vista loves,
Foe to the dryads° of his father's groves; *tree spirits*
One boundless green, or flourished carpet views,[11]
With all the mournful family of yews;[12]
The thriving plants ignoble broomsticks made,
Now sweep those alleys they were born to shade.

At Timon's villa[13] let us pass a day,
Where all cry out, "What sums are thrown away!"
So proud, so grand of that stupendous air,
Soft and agreeable come never there.
Greatness, with Timon, dwells in such a draught
As brings all Brobdingnag[14] before your thought.

[1] [Pope's note] The seat and gardens of the Lord Viscount Cobham in Buckinghamshire. [Richard Temple (1645–1749), Viscount Cobham, was a politician and distinguished soldier, as well as a friend of Pope.]

[2] *Versailles* The palace of Louis XIV (1638–1715). Its landscaping, designed by André Le Nôtre, was among the finest examples of the French formal garden style.

[3] *Nero's terraces* The Golden House of Roman Emperor Nero (37–68 CE) overlooked an extensive artificial landscape.

[4] *parterres* Flower-beds for formal plantings, often in curlicued shapes like a paisley pattern ("flourished carpets"). Intentionally artificial in appearance, therefore bad.

[5] *Cobham* Richard Temple, Viscount Cobham.

[6] [Pope's note] This was done in Hertfordshire, by a wealthy citizen, at the expense of above £5,000 by which means (merely to overlook a dead plain) he let in the north wind upon his house and parterre, which were before adorned and defended by beautiful woods.

[7] *Nor in … Dr. Clarke* Reference to the bizarrely ornate Hermitage, a garden building in Richmond Park. Queen Caroline (1683–1737), who commissioned the building, filled it with an eclectic collection of objects including sculptures of notable people; one of these was a bust of the philosopher Samuel Clarke (1675–1729).

[8] *Villario* Invented character whose name is probably a modified form of "villa."

[9] *quincunx* Geometric grouping of five trees; *espaliers* Shrubs grown flat against a trellis.

[10] *Sabinus* A reference to "Father Sabinus, planter of the vine," mentioned in the *Aeneid* (Book 8). Sabinus's son appears to be an invented character.

[11] [Pope's note] The two extremes in parterres, which are equally faulty; a *boundless green*, large and naked as a field, or a *flourished carpet*, where the greatness and nobleness of the piece is lessened by being divided into too many parts, with scrolled work and beds, of which the examples are frequent.

[12] [Pope's note] Touches upon the ill taste of those who are so fond of evergreens (particularly yews, which are the most tonsile [easiest to shape by pruning]) as to destroy the nobler forest trees, to make way for such little ornaments as pyramids of dark green continually repeated, not unlike a funeral procession.

[13] [Pope's note] This description is intended to comprise the principles of a false taste of magnificence, and to exemplify what was said before, that nothing but a good sense can attain it. [There is debate as to whether Pope in this section is referring to a particular individual, a combination of individuals, or simply an invented character. Possible targets of Pope's mockery include James Brydges, first Duke of Chandos (1673–1744), and Robert Walpole, whose ostentatious homes Pope found distasteful. The name "Timon" may be a reference to the extravagant Timon of Athens, who became a misanthrope when he ran out of money and his friends abandoned him.]

[14] *Brobdingnag* Land of the giants in Jonathan Swift's *Gulliver's Travels* (1726), where the objects are so enormous that people of normal size cannot use them.

To compass this, his building is a town,
His pond an ocean, his parterre a down:° *upland countryside*
Who but must laugh, the master when he sees,
A puny insect, shiv'ring at a breeze!
Lo, what huge heaps of littleness around!
The whole, a laboured quarry above ground.
Two cupids squirt before: a lake behind
Improves the keenness of the Northern wind.
His gardens next your admiration call,
On ev'ry side you look, behold the wall!
No pleasing intricacies intervene,
No artful wildness to perplex the scene;
Grove nods at grove, each alley has a brother,
And half the platform just reflects the other.
The suff'ring eye inverted Nature sees,
Trees cut to statues, statues thick as trees;[1]
With here a fountain, never to be played;
And there a summerhouse, that knows no shade;
Here Amphitrite[2] sails through myrtle bow'rs;
There gladiators fight, or die in flow'rs;[3]
Unwatered see the drooping sea horse mourn,
And swallows roost in Nilus' dusty urn.[4]

My Lord advances with majestic mien,
Smit° with the mighty pleasure, to be seen: *struck*
But soft—by regular approach—not yet—
First through the length of yon hot terrace sweat;
And when up ten steep slopes you've dragged your thighs,
Just at his study door he'll bless your eyes.

His study! with what authors is it stored?
In books, not authors, curious is my Lord;[5]
To all their dated backs he turns you round:
These Aldus printed, those Du Sueil[6] has bound.
Lo, some are vellum,[7] and the rest as good
For all his Lordship knows, but they are wood.
For Locke or Milton 'tis in vain to look,
These shelves admit not any modern book.

And now the chapel's silver bell you hear,
That summons you to all the pride of prayer:
Light quirks of music, broken and uneven,[8]
Make the soul dance upon a jig to heaven.
On painted ceilings[9] you devoutly stare,
Where sprawl the saints of Verrio or Laguerre,[10]
On gilded clouds in fair expansion lie,
And bring all paradise before your eye.
To rest, the cushion and soft dean invite,
Who never mentions Hell to ears polite.[11]

But hark! the chiming clocks to dinner call;
A hundred footsteps scrape the marble hall:
The rich buffet well-coloured serpents grace,
And gaping Tritons spew to wash your face.[12]
Is this a dinner?[13] this a genial room?
No, 'tis a temple, and a hecatomb.° *ritual slaughter*

---

[1] *Trees ... trees* I.e., trees sculpted into topiaries and an overabundance of statues.

[2] *Amphitrite* Sea goddess.

[3] [Pope's note] The two [often duplicated] statues of the *Gladiator pugnans* [fighting] and *Gladiator moriens* [dying].

[4] *Nilus' dusty urn* As god of the Nile, Nilus ought to have water flowing from his urn.

[5] [Pope's note] The false taste in books; a satire on the vanity of collecting them, more frequent in men of fortune than the study to understand them. Many delight chiefly in the elegance of the print, or of the binding; some have carried it so far, as to cause the upper shelves to be filled with painted books of wood....

[6] *Aldus* Aldus Manutius (1450–1515), leading printer of Renaissance Venice; *Du Sueil* Augustin Du Sueil (1673–1746), famous French bookbinder.

[7] *vellum* Good quality parchment.

[8] [Pope's note] The false taste in music, improper to the subjects, as of light airs in churches, often practised by organists, etc.

[9] [Pope's note] And in painting (from which even Italy is not free) of naked figures in churches, etc., which has obliged some popes to put draperies on some of those of the best masters.

[10] *Verrio or Laguerre* Antonio Verrio (1639–1707) or Louis Laguerre (1663–1721); both artists had, according to Pope's notes, "painted many ceilings."

[11] [Pope's note] This is a fact; a reverend Dean of Peterborough, preaching at court, threatened the sinner with punishment in "a place which he thought it not decent to name in so polite an assembly."

[12] [Pope's note] Taxes the incongruity of ornaments (though sometimes practised by the ancients) where an open mouth ejects the water into a fountain, or where the shocking images of serpents, etc., are introduced in grottos or buffets; *Tritons* Sea gods, half human and half fish.

[13] [Pope's note] The proud festivals of some men are here set forth to ridicule where pride destroys the ease, and formal regularity all the pleasurable enjoyment of the entertainment.

A solemn sacrifice, performed in state,
You drink by measure, and to minutes eat.
So quick retires each flying course, you'd swear
Sancho's dread doctor and his wand were there.[1]
Between each act the trembling salvers ring,
From soup to sweet wine, and God bless the King.[2]
In plenty starving, tantalized in state,
And complaisantly helped to all I hate,
Treated, caressed, and tired, I take my leave,
Sick of his civil pride from morn to eve;
I curse such lavish cost, and little skill,
And swear no day was ever passed so ill.

Yet hence the poor are clothed, the hungry fed;[3]
Health to himself, and to his infants bread
The lab'rer bears: What his hard heart denies,
His charitable vanity supplies.

Another age shall see the golden ear[4]
Embrown the slope, and nod on the parterre,
Deep harvests bury all his pride has planned,
And laughing Ceres[5] reassume the land.

Who then shall grace, or who improve the soil?
Who plants like Bathurst, or who builds like Boyle.[6]
'Tis use alone that sanctifies expense,
And splendour borrows all her rays from sense.

His father's acres who enjoys in peace,
Or makes his neighbours glad, if he increase:
Whose cheerful tenants bless their yearly toil,
Yet to their Lord owe more than to the soil;
Whose ample lawns are not ashamed to feed
The milky heifer and deserving steed;
Whose rising forests, not for pride or show,
But future buildings, future navies, grow:
Let his plantations stretch from down to down,
First shade a country, and then raise a town.

You too proceed! make falling° arts your care, *degenerating*
Erect new wonders, and the old repair;
Jones and Palladio to themselves restore,
And be whate'er Vitruvius[7] was before:
Till kings call forth th'ideas of your mind,
Proud to accomplish what such hands designed,
Bid harbours open, public ways extend,
Bid temples, worthier of the God, ascend;
Bid the broad arch the dang'rous flood contain,
The mole° projected break the roaring main;[8] *breakwater*
Back to his bounds their subject sea command,
And roll obedient rivers through the land;
These honours, peace to happy Britain brings,
These are imperial works, and worthy kings.
—1731, 1735

[1] *Sancho's ... there* In *Don Quixote*, Part 2 (1615), just as the ravenous Sancho is about to eat a meal, his doctor taps every dish on the table with his wand, prompting servants to carry away the food.

[2] *From soup ... the King* I.e., from the beginning to the end of the meal, which concludes with a toast to the king.

[3] [Pope's note] The moral of the whole, where Providence is justified in giving wealth to those that squander it in this manner. A bad taste employs more hands and diffuses expense more than a good one....

[4] *golden ear* I.e., of wheat.

[5] *Ceres* Roman goddess of agriculture, and of grain crops in particular.

[6] *Bathurst* Allen, Lord Bathurst, a politician and avid gardener. The Epistle that precedes this one in *Moral Essays* is addressed to him; *Boyle* Richard Boyle, to whom the present Epistle is addressed.

[7] *Vitruvius* Marcus Vitruvius Pollio (c. 85–c. 15 BCE), Roman architect whose treatise *Ten Books on Architecture* was a standard reference work for architects after the Renaissance.

[8] *Bid harbours ... roaring main* In a note, Pope explains that when the first version of the poem was published in 1731, "some of the new-built churches, by the act of Queen Anne, were ready to fall, being founded in boggy land," and "[m]any of the highways throughout England were hardly passable." In a similar display of governmental incompetence, a proposal to build a much-needed bridge at Westminster was initially rejected, and when it was finally passed "the execution was left to the carpenter [Ripley] who would have made it a wooden one." Eventually, however, the bridge was built in stone, with Richard Boyle as a commissioner.

Lady Mary Wortley Montagu

1689 – 1762

In keeping with expectations for women of her station, Lady Mary Wortley Montagu never published under her own name, but was nonetheless one of the most celebrated and admired female writers of her age. She is known today mainly for her letters, but wrote in a variety of genres, including poetry, fiction, and essays. Twentieth-century feminist literary critics have recovered and explored Montagu's writings on female sexual desire, gender relations, and her feminist critique of marriage. Unconventional, erudite, and independent, she referred to herself as "a sister of the quill."

Montagu was born Mary Pierrepont in London in 1689; her father, the Whig Evelyn Pierrepont, became an earl when she was one year old. At three years of age she lost her mother (born Lady Mary Fielding), whom she later imagined to have been a model of female forbearance at the hands of a libertine husband. The eldest of four children, in her youth Mary was surrounded by some of the leading figures of the London literary scene, including Joseph Addison, Richard Steele, and William Congreve. She also formed close friendships in her teenage years with a circle of upper- and middle-class literary women. As was standard for a young woman of her social and economic position, she was trained by a governess in the conventional accomplishments of a lady's curriculum, but Montagu's intellectual ambitions were broader. She duly embarked on a secret, self-directed education in Latin in her father's study; everyone around her assumed she was locked away reading novels. In 1712 she eloped with Edward Wortley Montagu, a Whig Member of Parliament, against the wishes of her father, who had intended her for another suitor to whom she objected. The couple had two children. In late 1715 Montagu barely survived a serious bout of smallpox. The disease had killed her only brother a few years earlier, and it left her severely scarred. Less than a year after her recovery she left for Constantinople with her husband, who had been appointed British Ambassador to Turkey.

Montagu's most memorable writing grew out of her experiences in what was then the Ottoman Empire. Fascinated by the cultures of Islamic Europe, Turkey, and the Mediterranean, she was an observant and sensitive traveler, and her letters home—to her sister, to Alexander Pope, and others—show the range of her curiosity, and include descriptions and insights into everyday life, religious issues, and literary matters. At Sofia in Bulgaria she visited the famed women's public baths, which she describes with a frankness and admiration unusual for a western visitor. Upon her return to England she edited and compiled what she called her *Embassy Letters* for publication after her death.

Montagu's sojourn in Turkey had a lasting impact not only in the world of letters but also in the field of public health. Having narrowly escaped death by smallpox herself, Montagu had her five-year-old son inoculated against the disease at Constantinople. Later, in 1721, the first inoculation in England was performed on her three-year-old daughter, and Montagu became a strong advocate of a procedure that was treated with great prejudice and suspicion by the English medical establishment. She was heavily criticized for promoting the practice, and she published "A Plain Account of

Inoculating the Smallpox" (1722), in which she castigates the medical profession for its blind self-interest, pseudonymously in a newspaper.

Montagu's "Six Town Eclogues," written in 1715 and 1716, have been widely admired. The poems (some of which were attributed to Pope and Gay) are biting, satirical, and studded with references to actual persons and their intrigues. Each of this series of six poems is written not in a rustic voice (as is traditional in the eclogue) but in that of a member or members of London "society." Among Montagu's many epistolary poems, the "Epistle from Mrs. Yonge to Her Husband" is the complaint of a divorced wife whose philandering husband profits financially from the dissolution of the marriage.

Other significant writings include her essay #573 of Addison and Steele's *Spectator* (she was the only female contributor, and remained anonymous), and her own political periodical, *The Nonsense of Common-Sense* (1737–38). Montagu's learning, outspokenness, and refusal to conform to the conventions of "female" behavior made her an easy target in a male-dominated literary scene. Beginning in 1728, Alexander Pope, her former correspondent, admirer, and occasional collaborator, launched a smear campaign against Montagu, the exact reasons for which remain unclear. Montagu responded to these attacks by ridiculing Pope's appearance, intellectual abilities, and writing. Their quarrel, all of it carried on in print, lasted on his side until after she left England.

In the 1730s the Montagus' marriage began to fail. In 1736 Montagu fell in love with the much younger bisexual Italian writer Francesco Algarotti, and launched an ardent epistolary relationship with him that lasted for five years. In 1739 she left London to reside in Italy, secretly intending to live with Algarotti. In Venice she conducted a salon, a regular social gathering of Venetian nobility, intelligentsia, and visiting luminaries. For the last twenty-five years of her life she lived mainly in Italy, but conducted various travels in Europe, including a kind of Grand Tour (traditionally a rite reserved for upper-class young men) in the early 1740s.

Near the end of her life Montagu returned to England. Back in London she received many visits by people who regarded her as a kind of living legend, a well-traveled woman of letters who had never refrained from asserting her own voice, nor from conducting herself according to her own rules. Her later prose writings, chiefly letters and fiction, are at last beginning to receive critical attention. She died of breast cancer in London in 1762 and was buried in Grosvenor Chapel in Hanover Square.

⌘⌘⌘

Saturday;
The Small Pox[1]

Flavia

The wretched Flavia on her couch reclined,
Thus breathed the anguish of a wounded mind.
A glass reversed in her right hand she bore,
For now she shunned the face she sought before.
How am I changed! Alas, how am I grown
A frightful spectre, to myself unknown!
Where's my complexion, where the radiant bloom
That promised happiness for years to come?
Then, with what pleasure I this face surveyed!
To look once more, my visits oft delayed!
Charmed with the view, a fresher red would rise,
And a new life shot sparkling from my eyes.
Ah, faithless glass, my wonted° bloom restore!
Alas, I rave! That bloom is now no more!
The greatest good the gods on men bestow,
Ev'n youth itself to me is useless now.
There was a time (Oh, that I could forget!)
When opera tickets poured before my feet,

wonted: accustomed

[1] *Saturday … Pox* From *Six Town Eclogues.*

And at the Ring,[1] where brightest beauties shine,
The earliest cherries of the park were mine.
Witness, oh Lilly![2] And thou, Motteux,[3] tell
How much Japan[4] these eyes have made you sell!
With what contempt you saw me oft despise
The humble offer of the raffled prize.
For at each raffle still the prize I bore,
With scorn rejected, or with triumph wore.
Now beauty's fled, and presents are no more.
　For me, the patriot has the house[5] forsook,
And left debates to catch a passing look;
For me, the soldier has soft verses writ;
For me, the beau has aimed to be a wit;
For me, the wit to nonsense was betrayed;
The gamester° has for me his dun delayed　*gambler*
And overseen the card I would have paid.[6]
The bold and haughty, by success made vain,
Awed by my eyes has trembled to complain.
The bashful squire, touched with a wish unknown,
Has dared to speak with spirit not his own.
Fired by one wish, all did alike adore;
Now beauty's fled, and lovers are no more.
　As round the room I turn my weeping eyes,
New unaffected scenes of sorrow rise.
Far from my sight that killing picture bear,
The face disfigure, or the canvas tear!
That picture, which with pride I used to show,
The lost resemblance but upbraids me now.
And thou, my toilette, where I oft have sate,
While hours unheeded passed in deep debate
How curls should fall, or where a patch[7] to place,
If blue or scarlet best became my face,
Now on some happier nymph° thy aid bestow.　*maiden*
On fairer heads, ye useless jewels, glow!
No borrowed lustre can my charms restore;
Beauty is fled, and dress[8] is now no more.
　Ye meaner beauties, I permit you, shine;
Go triumph in the hearts that once were mine.
But 'midst your triumphs, with confusion know
'Tis to my ruin all your charms ye owe.
Would pitying heav'n restore my wonted mien,[9]
You still might move unthought of and unseen—
But oh, how vain, how wretched is the boast
Of beauty faded and of Empire lost!
What now is left but weeping to deplore
My beauty fled and Empire now no more!
　Ye cruel chemists, what withheld your aid?
Could no pomatums[10] save a trembling maid?
How false and triffling is that art you boast;
No art can give me back my beauty lost!
In tears surrounded by my friends I lay,
Masked o'er and trembling at the light of day.
Mirmillo[11] came, my fortune to deplore
(A golden headed cane, well carried, he bore);
Cordials, he cried, my spirits must restore—
Beauty is fled, and spirit is no more!
Galen the Grave, officious Squirt,[12] was there
With fruitless grief and unavailing care;

[1] *the Ring* West Carriage Drive, a circular drive that divides Hyde Park from Kensington Gardens. The most fashionable members of society would drive around the Ring, displaying themselves in their coaches.

[2] *Lilly* Charles Lillie, a celebrated perfumer and seller of snuff who owned a shop in the Strand. Lillie was also a printer of *The Tatler* and *The Spectator*.

[3] *Motteux* Peter Anthony Motteux, who described himself in a letter to the *Spectator* No. 288 as "an author turned dealer." Motteux was a former playwright and translator who went into business, establishing an East India warehouse in London, from which he sold tea, fabrics, china, fans, and other Indian and Chinese goods.

[4] *Japan* Word used loosely to refer to several common products of Japan at the time, including Japanese porcelain and silk.

[5] *house* House of Parliament.

[6] *gamester ... paid* Rather than immediately demanding the money due to him (his dun), the gambler was underwriting Flavia's next bet.

[7] *patch* Piece of silk or plaster, cut in various ornamental shapes (stars, half-moons, etc.), and put on the face either to hide a scar or imperfection, or simply as decoration.

[8] *dress* Act of adorning oneself.

[9] *mien* Expression or appearance of the face.

[10] *pomatums* Pomades, scented ointments for the skin.

[11] *Mirmillo* Sir Hans Sloane, a distinguished physician and the president of the Royal Society from 1727 to 1741.

[12] *Galen the Grave* Galen was John Gay's nickname for Dr. John Woodward, a natural historian, geologist, and physician whose work *The State of Physic and of Diseases* (1718) condemned the popular treatment of smallpox; *Squirt* Character in Samuel Garth's famous poem *The Dispensary* (1699), often referred to as "officious Squirt."

Machaon[1] too, the great Machaon, known
By his red cloak and his superior frown.
"And why," he cried, "this grief and this despair?
You shall again be well, again be fair,
Believe my oath" (with that an oath he swore)
False was his oath! My beauty is no more.
Cease, hapless maid; no more thy tale pursue,
Forsake mankind and bid the world adieu.
Monarchs and beauties rule with equal sway;
All strive to serve, and glory to obey.
Alike unpitied when deposed they grow,
Men mock the idol of their former vow.
Adieu, ye parks in some obscure recess,
Where gentle streams will weep at my distress,
Where no false friend will in my grief take part,
And mourn my ruin with a joyful heart.
There let me live in some deserted place,
There hide in shades this lost, inglorious face.
Ye operas, circles, I no more must view!
My toilette, patches, all the world, adieu!
—1716

The Reasons that Induced Dr. S. to Write a Poem Called The Lady's Dressing Room[2]

The Doctor in a clean starched band,° *clerical collar*
His golden snuff box in his hand,
With care his diamond ring displays
And artful shows its various rays,
While grave he stalks down——Street,
His dearest Betty——to meet.
Long had he waited for this hour,
Nor gained admittance to the bow'r,
Had joked and punned, and swore and writ,
Tried all his gallantry and wit,
Had told her oft what part he bore
In Oxford's schemes in days of yore,
But bawdy,° politics, nor satire *lewd talk*
Could move this dull hard-hearted creature.
Jenny, her maid, could taste° a rhyme *appreciate*
And, grieved to see him lose his time,
Had kindly whispered in his ear,
"For twice two pound you enter here;
My lady vows without that sum
It is in vain you write or come."
The destined off'ring now he brought
And, in a paradise of thought,
With a low bow approached the dame,
Who smiling heard him preach his flame.
His gold she takes (such proofs as these
Convince most unbelieving shes)
And in her trunk rose up to lock it
(Too wise to trust it in her pocket)
And then, returned with blushing grace,
Expects the doctor's warm embrace.
But now this is the proper place
Where morals stare me in the face,
And for the sake of fine expression
I'm forced to make a small digression.
Alas, for wretched humankind,
With learning mad, with wisdom blind!
The ox thinks he's for saddle fit
(As long ago friend Horace writ[3])
And men their talents still mistaking,
The stutterer fancies his is speaking.
With admiration oft we see
Hard features heightened by toupee,
The beau affects the politician,
Wit is the citizen's[4] ambition,
Poor Pope philosophy displays on
With so much rhyme and little reason,
And though he argues ne'er so long
That all is right, his head is wrong.[5]
None strive to know their proper merit
But strain for wisdom, beauty, spirit,
And lose the praise that is their due
While they've th' impossible in view.

[1] *Machaon* Hero of *The Dispensary*; here Garth, Lady Mary's family doctor.

[2] *The Reasons … Room* This poem is a response to Jonathan Swift's "The Lady's Dressing Room" (1732). Its original title was "The Dean's Provocation for Writing the Lady's Dressing Room."

[3] *ox … Horace writ* Horace, *Epistles* 1.14.43: "The ox desires the saddle."

[4] *citizen* As distinguished from a member of the gentry or nobility; a tradesman.

[5] *That all … wrong* Cf. Pope's *Essay on Man* (1733), which concludes, "One truth is clear, 'Whatever *is*, is right.'"

So have I seen the injudicious heir
To add one window the whole house impair.
Instinct the hound does better teach,
Who never undertook to preach;
The frighted hare from dogs does run
But not attempts to bear a gun.
Here many noble thoughts occur
But I prolixity abhor,
And will pursue th' instructive tale
To show the wise in some things fail.
The rev'rend lover with surprise
Peeps in her bubbies,° and her eyes, *breasts*
And kisses both, and tries—and tries.
The evening in this hellish play,
Beside his guineas thrown away,
Provoked the priest to that degree
He swore, "The fault is not in me.
Your damned close stool[1] so near my nose,
Your dirty smock, and stinking toes
Would make a Hercules as tame
As any beau that you can name."
The nymph grown furious roared, "By God!
The blame lies all in sixty odd,"[2]
And scornful pointing to the door
Cried, "Fumbler, see my face no more."
"With all my heart I'll go away,
But nothing done, I'll nothing pay.
Give back the money." "How," cried she,
"Would you palm such a cheat on me!
For poor four pound to roar and bellow—
Why sure you want some new Prunella?"[3]
"I'll be revenged, you saucy quean"° *whore*
(Replies the disappointed Dean),
"I'll so describe your dressing room
The very Irish shall not come."
She answered short, "I'm glad you'll write.
You'll furnish paper when I shite."
—1734

[1] *close stool* Chamber pot enclosed in a stool or box.

[2] *in sixty odd* I.e., in his old age.

[3] *Prunella* Name commonly ascribed at the time to a prostitute or promiscuous woman; also, a type of cloth used to make clergymen's robes.

The Lover: A Ballad

At length, by so much importunity pressed,
Take, (Molly[4]), at once, the inside of my breast;
This stupid indiff'rence so often you blame
Is not owing to nature, to fear, or to shame;
I am not as cold as a Virgin in lead,
Nor is Sunday's sermon so strong in my head;
I know but too well how time flies along,
That we live but few years and yet fewer are young.

But I hate to be cheated, and never will buy
Long years of repentance for moments of joy.
Oh, was there a man (but where shall I find
Good sense and good nature so equally joined?)
Would value his pleasure, contribute to mine,
Not meanly would boast, nor lewdly design,
Not over severe, yet not stupidly vain,
For I would have the power though not give the pain;

No pedant yet learnèd, not rakehelly[5] gay
Or laughing because he has nothing to say,
To all my whole sex obliging and free,
Yet never be fond of any but me;
In public preserve the decorums are just,
And show in his eyes he is true to his trust,
Then rarely approach, and respectfully bow,
Yet not fulsomely pert, nor yet foppishly low.

But when the long hours of public are past
And we meet with champagne and a chicken at last,
May every fond pleasure that hour endear,
Be banished afar both discretion and fear,
Forgetting or scorning the airs of the crowd
He may cease to be formal, and I to be proud,
Till lost in the joy we confess that we live,
And he may be rude, and yet I may forgive.

And that my delight may be solidly fixed,
Let the friend and the lover be handsomely mixed,
In whose tender bosom my soul might confide,

[4] *Molly* Maria Skerrett, a friend of Montagu's and the mistress of Prime Minister Robert Walpole.

[5] *rakehelly* In the manner of a rascal or scoundrel.

Whose kindness can sooth me, whose counsel could guide.
From such a dear lover as here I describe
No danger should fright me, no millions should bribe;
But till this astonishing creature I know,
As I long have lived chaste, I will keep myself so.

I never will share with the wanton coquette,
Or be caught by a vain affectation of wit.
The toasters[1] and songsters may try all their art
But never shall enter the pass of my heart.
I loathe the lewd rake,[2] the dressed fopling° despise; *fool*
Before such pursuers the nice° virgin flies; *fastidious*
And as Ovid has sweetly in parables told
We harden like trees, and like rivers are cold.[3]
—1747

Epistle from Mrs. Y[onge][4] to Her Husband

Think not this paper comes with vain pretense
To move your pity, or to mourn th' offense.
Too well I know that hard obdurate heart;
No softening mercy there will take my part,
Nor can a woman's arguments prevail,
When even your patron's wise example fails.[5]
But this last privilege I still retain;
Th' oppressed and injured always may complain.
Too, too severely laws of honor bind
The weak submissive sex of womankind.
If sighs have gained or force compelled our hand,
Deceived by art, or urged by stern command,
Whatever motive binds the fatal tie,
The judging world expects our constancy.
Just heaven! (for sure in heaven does justice reign,
Though tricks below that sacred name profane)
To you appealing I submit my cause,
Nor fear a judgment from impartial laws.
All bargains but conditional are made;
The purchase void, the creditor unpaid;
Defrauded servants are from service free;
A wounded slave regains his liberty.
For wives ill used no remedy remains,
To daily racks condemned, and to eternal chains.
From whence is this unjust distinction grown?
Are we not formed with passions like your own?
Nature with equal fire our souls endued,
Our minds as haughty, and as warm our blood;
O'er the wide world your pleasures you pursue,
The change is justified by something new;
But we must sigh in silence—and be true.
Our sex's weakness you expose and blame
(Of every prating[6] fop the common theme),
Yet from this weakness you suppose is due
Sublimer virtue than your Cato[7] knew.
Had heaven designed us trials so severe,
It would have formed our tempers then to bear.
And I have borne (oh, what have I not borne!)
The pang of jealousy, the insults of scorn.
Wearied at length, I from your sight remove,
And place my future hopes in secret love.
In the gay bloom of glowing youth retired,
I quit the woman's joy to be admired,
With that small pension your hard heart allows,
Renounce your fortune, and release your vows.
To custom (though unjust) so much is due;
I hide my frailty from the public view.
My conscience clear, yet sensible of shame,
My life I hazard, to preserve my fame.[8]
And I prefer this low inglorious state
To vile dependence on the thing I hate—

[1] *toasters* Those who propose toasts; i.e., admirers of women.

[2] *rake* Seducer of women.

[3] *as Ovid ... cold* In Ovid's *Metamorphoses*, the virgin Daphne is turned into a laurel tree to escape the advances of the god Apollo, while Arethusa prefers being transformed into a fountain to surrendering to the pursuits of the god Alpheus.

[4] *Mrs. Y[onge]* After Mrs. Yonge and her husband, infamous libertine William Yonge, were separated, she began an affair with another man. Though Mr. Yonge had had numerous affairs throughout their marriage, he successfully sued his wife's lover for damages and then filed for divorce. In a public, well-attended trial, Mr. Yonge was granted not only his divorce but also the majority of his ex-wife's fortune.

[5] *When ... fails* Prime Minister Robert Walpole also engaged in extra-marital affairs, but, unlike Yonge, he endured it when his wife did the same.

[6] *prating* Chattering, talking too much.

[7] *Cato* Roman politician Marcus Porcius Cato, an opponent of Caesar's who, after Caesar's victory, committed suicide rather than submit to his tyrannical authority.

[8] *fame* Good name or character.

But you pursue me to this last retreat.
Dragged into light, my tender crime is shown
And every circumstance of fondness known.
Beneath the shelter of the law you stand,
And urge my ruin with a cruel hand,
While to my fault thus rigidly severe,
Tamely submissive to the man you fear.[1]
    This wretched outcast, this abandoned wife,
Has yet this joy to sweeten shameful life:
By your mean conduct, infamously loose,
You are at once my accuser and excuse.
Let me be damned by the censorious prude
(Stupidly dull, or spiritually lewd),
My hapless case will surely pity find
From every just and reasonable mind.
When to the final sentence I submit,
The lips condemn me, but their souls acquit.
    No more my husband, to your pleasures go,
The sweets of your recovered freedom know.
Go: court the brittle friendship of the great,
Smile at his board,° or at his levee[2] wait; *dining table*
And when dismissed, to madam's toilet[3] fly,
More than her chambermaids or glasses,° lie, *mirrors*
Tell her how young she looks, how heavenly fair,
Admire the lilies and the roses there.
Your high ambition may be gratified,
Some cousin of her own be made your bride,
And you the father of a glorious race
Endowed with Ch—l's strength and Low—r's face.[4]
—1977 (written 1724)

[1] *the man you fear* Sir Robert Walpole.

[2] *levee* Assembly or reception of visitors.

[3] *toilet* Dressing room, where it was fashionable for women of distinction to receive visitors as they were finishing their toilet.

[4] *Endowed ... face* References to General Charles Churchill, who was thought to have had an affair with Lady Walpole, and Anthony Lowther, a well-known ladies' man.

The Spectator No. 573[5]

[FROM THE PRESIDENT OF THE WIDOW'S CLUB]

Wednesday, 28 July 1714

Castigata remordent.[6]

Juvenal

My paper on the club of widows has brought me in several letters, and, among the rest, a long one from Mrs. President, as follows.

Smart Sir,

You are pleased to be very merry, as you imagine, with us widows, and you seem to ground your satire on our receiving consolation so soon after the death of our dears, and the number we are pleased to admit for our companions. But you never reflect what husbands we have buried, and how short a sorrow the loss of them was capable of occasioning. For my own part, Mrs. President as you call me, my first husband I was married to at fourteen by my uncle and guardian (as I afterwards discovered) by way of sale for the third part of my fortune. This fellow looked upon me as a mere child he might breed up after his own fancy. If he kissed my chambermaid before my face, I was supposed so ignorant, how could I think there was any hurt in it? When he came home roaring drunk at five in the morning, 'twas the custom of all men that live in the world. I was not to see a penny of money, for, poor thing, how could I manage it? He took a handsome cousin of his into the house (as he said) to be my housekeeper and to govern my servants, for how should I know how to rule a family? And while she had what money she pleased, which was but reasonable for the trouble she was at for my good, I was not to be so censorious as to dislike familiarity and kindness between near relations. I was too great a coward to contend, but not so ignorant a child to be thus imposed upon. I resented his contempt as I ought to do, and as most poor, passive, blinded wives do, till it pleased heaven to take away my tyrant,

[5] *Spectator, No. 573* Response to Addison's essay no. 561, which mocked widows who remarry. The essay gave a satiric description of a club of widows whose president is considering taking her seventh husband.

[6] *Castigata remordent* Latin: "Chastised, they bite back" (from Juvenal's *Satires* 2.35).

who left me free possession of my own land and a large jointure.[1] My youth and money brought me many lovers, and several endeavoured to establish an interest in[2] my heart while my husband was in his last sickness. The honourable Edward Waitfort was one of the first who addressed to me, advised to it by a cousin of his that was my intimate friend and knew to a penny what I was worth. Mr. Waitfort is a very agreeable man, and everybody would like him as well as he does himself if they did not plainly see that his esteem and love is all taken up, and by such an object as 'tis impossible to get the better of—I mean himself. He made no doubt of marrying me within four or five months, and begun to proceed with such an assured, easy air that piqued my pride not to banish him. Quite contrary, out of pure malice I heard his first declaration with so much innocent surprise, and blushed so prettily, I perceived it touched his very heart, and he thought me the best-natured silly poor thing upon earth. When a man has such a notion of a woman, he loves her better than he thinks he does. I was overjoyed to be thus revenged on him for designing on my fortune. And, finding 'twas in my power to make his heart ache, I resolved to complete my conquest, and entertained several other pretenders. The first impression of my undesigning innocence was so strong in his head, he attributed all my followers to the inevitable force of my charms, and from several blushes and side glances concluded himself the favourite. And when I used him like a dog for my diversion he thought it was all prudence and fear, and pitied the violence I did my own inclinations, to comply with my friends, when I married Sir Nicholas Fribble, of sixty years of age. You know, sir, the case of Mrs. Medlar;[3] I hope you would not have had me cry out my eyes for such a husband. I shed tears enough for my widowhood a week after my marriage, and when he was put in his grave, reckoning he had been two years dead, and myself a widow of that standing, I married three weeks afterwards John Sturdy, Esq., his next heir. I had indeed some thoughts of taking Mr. Waitfort, but I found he could stay, and besides he thought it indecent to ask me to marry again till my year was out. So, privately resolving him for my fourth, I took Mr. Sturdy for the present. Would you believe it, sir, Mr. Sturdy was just five and twenty, about six foot high, and the stoutest fox-hunter in the county, and I believe I wished ten thousand times for my old Fribble again. He was following his dogs all the day, and all the night keeping them up at table with him and his companions; however, I think myself obliged to them for leading him a chase in which he broke his neck. Mr. Waitfort begun his addresses anew, and I verily believe I had married him now, but there was a young officer in the guards that had debauched[4] two or three of my acquaintance, and I could not forbear being a little vain of his courtship. Mr. Waitfort heard of it and read me such an insolent lecture upon the conduct of women, I married the officer that very day out of pure spite to him. Half an hour after I was married I received a penitential letter from the honourable Mr. Edward Waitfort in which he begged pardon for his passion as proceeding from the violence of his love. I triumphed when I read it and could not help, out of the pride of my heart, showing it to my new spouse, and we were very merry together upon it. Alas, my mirth lasted a short time. My young husband was very much in debt when I married him, and his first action afterwards was to set up a gilt chariot and six,[5] in fine trappings before and behind. I had married so hastily I had not the prudence to reserve my estate in my own hands. My ready money[6] was lost in two nights at the Groom Porter's,[7] and my diamond necklace, which was stole I did not know how, I met in the street upon Jenny Wheadle's neck. My plate[8] vanished piece by piece, and I had been reduced to downright pewter if my officer had not been deliciously killed in a duel by a fellow that had cheated him of five

[1] *jointure* Estate that becomes the possession of a woman upon the death of her husband.

[2] *interest in* Claim upon.

[3] *Mrs. Medlar* One of the widows in the club. She took a man of sixty as her third husband, but was allowed to retain her status as a widow because the marriage remained unconsummated.

[4] *debauched* Seduced.

[5] *chariot and six* Type of light, four-wheeled carriage that had a coach box and only back seats, drawn by six horses.

[6] *ready money* Cash, money immediately available.

[7] *Groom Porter's* Gaming house run by the Groom-Porter, an officer of the English Royal Household whose main duty was the regulation of all matters connected with gambling within the court.

[8] *plate* Silverware.

hundred pounds and afterwards, at his own request, satisfied[1] him and me too by running him through the body. Mr. Waitfort was still in love and told me so again; to prevent all fears of ill-usage he desired me to reserve everything in my own hands.[2] But now my acquaintance begun to wish me joy of his constancy, my charms were declining, and I could not resist the delight I took in showing the young flirts about town, it was yet in my power to give pain to a man of sense. This and some private hopes he would hang himself—and what a glory would it be for me, and how I should be envied—made me accept of being third wife to my Lord Friday. I proposed,[3] from my rank and his estate, to live in all the joys of pride; but how was I mistaken? He was neither extravagant, nor ill-natured, nor debauched; I suffered however more with him than with all my others. He was splenatic.[4] I was forced to sit whole days harkening to his imaginary ails. It was impossible to tell what would please him; what he liked when the sun shined made him sick when it rained. He had no distemper, but lived in constant fear of them all. My good genius dictated to me to bring him acquainted with Doctor Gruel. From that day he was always contented because he had names for all his complaints; the good doctor furnished him with reasons for all his pains and prescriptions for every fancy that troubled him. In hot weather he lived upon juleps and let blood to prevent fevers; when it grew cloudy he generally apprehended a consumption. To shorten the history of this wretched part of my life, he ruined a good constitution by endeavouring to mend it, and took several medicines which ended in taking the grand remedy, which cured both him and me of all our uneasinesses. After his death I did not expect to hear any more of Mr. Waitfort. I knew he had renounced me to all his friends and been very witty upon my choice, which he affected to talk of with great indifferency. I gave over thinking of him, being told that he was engaging with a pretty woman and a great fortune. It vexed me a little, but not enough to make me neglect the advice of my cousin Wishwell, that came to see me the day my lord went into the country with Russell.[5] She told me experimentally, nothing put an unfaithful lover and a dead husband so soon out of one's head as a new one, and at the same time proposed to me a kinsman of hers. "You understand enough of the world," said she, "to know money is the most valuable consideration. He is very rich and, I'm sure, cannot live long; he has a cough that must carry him off soon." I knew afterwards she had given the selfsame character of me to him. But, however, I was so much persuaded by her, I hastened on the match for fear he should die before the time came. He had the same fears and was so pressing I married him in a fortnight, resolving to keep it private a fortnight longer. During this fortnight Mr. Waitfort came to make me a visit. He told me he had waited on me sooner, but had that respect for me, he would not interrupt me in the first day of my affliction for my dead lord; that as soon as he heard I was at liberty to make another choice, he had broke off a match very advantageous for his fortune just upon the point of conclusion, and was forty times more in love with me than ever. I never received more pleasure in my life than from this declaration, but I composed my face to a grave air and said the news of his engagement had touched me to the heart, that in a rash, jealous fit I had married a man I could never have thought on if I had not lost all hopes of him. Good-natured Mr. Waitfort had like to have dropped down dead at hearing this, but went from me with such an air as plainly showed me he laid all the blame upon himself, and hated those friends that had advised him to the fatal application. He seemed as much touched by my misfortune as his own, for he had not the least doubt I was still passionately in love with him. The truth of the story is, my new husband gave me reason to repent I had not staid for him. He had married me for my money, and I soon found he loved money to distraction; there was nothing he would not

[1] *satisfied* The technical term for answering a challenge to a duel was "giving satisfaction."

[2] *reserve … hands* I.e., take legal steps, while she was a widow and had civil rights, to preserve her property from the use of any future husbands.

[3] *proposed* Anticipated, expected.

[4] *splenatic* Suffering from excessive moroseness, depression, and irritability. The spleen was seen as the origin of melancholy feelings.

[5] *the day … Russell* Probably an elaborate reference to the day Lord Friday died. Lord William Russell was one of the leaders of the "country party," an opposition party to the court of Charles II, and in 1683 he was executed for treason.

do to get it, nothing he would not suffer to preserve it. The smallest expense kept him awake whole nights, and when he paid a bill, 'twas with as many sighs and after as many delays as a man that endures the loss of a limb. I heard nothing but reproofs for extravagancy, whatever I did. I saw very well that he would have starved me but for losing my jointures,[1] and he suffered agonies between the grief of seeing me have so good a stomach, and the fear that if he made me fast it might prejudice my health. I did not doubt he would have broke my heart if I did not break his, which was allowable by the law of self-defense. The way was very easy. I resolved to spend as much money as I could, and, before he was aware of the stroke, appeared before him in a two thousand pound diamond necklace. He said nothing, but went quietly to his chamber and, as it is thought, composed himself with a dose of opium. I behaved myself so well upon the occasion that to this day I believe he died of an apoplexy. Mr. Waitfort was resolved not to be too late this time, and I heard from him in two days. I am almost out of my weed[2] at this present writing, and very doubtful whether I'll marry him or no. I do not think of a seventh for the ridiculous reason you mention,[3] but out of pure morality, that I think so much constancy should be rewarded, though I may not do it after all perhaps. I do not believe all the unreasonable malice of mankind can give a pretence why I should have been constant to the memory of any of the deceased or have spent much time in grieving for an insolent, insignificant, negligent, extravagant, splenetic, or covetous husband. My first insulted me, my second was nothing to me, my third disgusted me, the fourth would have ruined me, the fifth tormented me, and the sixth would have starved me. If the other ladies you name would thus give in their husbands' pictures, at length you would see they have had as little reason as myself to lose their hours in weeping and wailing.

—1714

[1] *losing my jointures* The property would have reverted to the writer's former husbands' heirs.

[2] *weed* Widow's weeds; heavy, black garments of mourning.

[3] *ridiculous ... mention* In Addison's essay he had facetiously suggested, "there is as much virtue in the touch of a seventh husband as of a seventh son." Seventh sons had long been thought to possess peculiar powers, including a healing touch.

A Plain Account of the Inoculating of the Smallpox by a Turkey[4] Merchant[5]

Out of compassion to the numbers abused and deluded by the knavery[6] and ignorance of physicians, I am determined to give a true account of the manner of inoculating the smallpox as it is practised at Constantinople with constant success, and without any ill consequence whatever. I shall sell no drugs, nor take no fees, could I persuade people of the safety and reasonableness of this easy operation. 'Tis no way my interest[7] (according to the common acceptation of that word) to convince the world of their errors; that is, I shall get nothing by it but the private satisfaction of having done good to mankind, and I know nobody that reckons that satisfaction any part of their interest.

The matter[8] ought to be taken from a young person of a sound constitution and the best sort[9] of the smallpox, when 'tis turned of the height. The old nurse who is the general surgeon upon this occasion at Constantinople takes it in a nut shell, which holds enough to infect 50 people—contrary to the infamous practice here, which is to fill the blood with such a quantity of that matter as often endangers the life, and never fails of making the distemper[10] more violent than it need to be. She opens the arms, and sometimes legs, with a small rip of a needle, and with the point of the same needle takes

[4] *Turkey* Turkish.

[5] *A ... Merchant* This article was published anonymously in *The Flying-Post* in September of 1722 and never attributed to Montagu, though she was a strong advocate of this procedure and had been instrumental in introducing its practice to England. Montagu herself had been severely scarred by smallpox in 1715, and when she accompanied her husband on his ambassadorship in Constantinople she was struck by the Turkish practice of inoculating against the virus using the pus from the sores of the infected. Her son was inoculated in Turkey, and her daughter became the first person to be inoculated in Great Britain.

[6] *knavery* Dishonesty, trickery.

[7] *'Tis ... interest* It is in no way to my advantage.

[8] *matter* That is, the pus from the sores that are characteristic of smallpox.

[9] *best sort* There are various strains of smallpox, some with less severe symptoms than others.

[10] *distemper* Illness or ailment.

as much of the matter as will lie upon it, and mixes it with that drop of blood that follows the little incision. The wounds are bound up with a small nut still over them, which is thrown off in 12 or 16 hours, and the inflammation appears, more or less, as the blood is more or less disposed to receive the infection. From that time the patient is confined to a warm chamber and a low diet, being utterly forbid wine or flesh meat. The eruption generally appears the 7 or 8th day afterwards. They give no cordials to heighten the fever and, leaving Nature to herself, never fail of the good success which generally follows a rational way of acting upon all occasions. And the murders that have been committed on two unfortunate persons[1] that have died under this operation has been wholly occasioned by the preparatives given by our learned physicians, of whom I have too good an opinion not to suppose they knew what they did by weakening bodies that were to go through a distemper. I am confirmed in this opinion by the unfair accounts that were given in the public papers of their deaths. I believe 'tis much to be doubted if purges, or any violent method, ever brings the body into a moderate temper,[2] which may always be done by a cool diet and regular hours. But as I am not of the College,[3] I will not pretend to dispute with those gentlemen concerning their general practice in other distempers; but they must give me leave to tell them from my own knowledge, witnessed by every one of our Company[4] that has ever resided at Constantinople, and several thousands of those there that have happily undergone this operation, that their long preparations only serve to destroy the strength of body necessary to throw off the infection. The miserable gashes that they give people in the arms may endanger the loss of them, and the vast quantity they throw in of that infectious matter may possibly give them the worst kind of smallpox, and the cordials that they pour down their throats may increase the fever to such a degree as may put an end to their lives. And after some few more sacrifices of this kind it may be hoped this terrible design against the revenue of the College may be entirely defeated, and those worthy members receive two guineas a day, as before, of the wretches that send for them in that distemper.

Since I writ this, I have read some queries, published in the *St. James's Evening Post,* stated in a very unfair manner, most of the facts there mentioned being utterly false. However, I never will deny but 'tis in the power of a surgeon to make an ulcer[5] with the help of lancet[6] and plaster,[7] and of a doctor to kill by prescriptions.

—1722

[1] *two unfortunate persons* The two-year old son of the Earl of Sunderland and an adolescent servant of Lord Bathurst.

[2] *moderate temper* Proper, healthy condition.

[3] *the College* Royal College of Physicians.

[4] *our Company* Levant Company, a British merchant company that controlled much of the trade in Turkey and paid the salaries of the British ambassadors there.

Selected Letters

TO WORTLEY[8]

[28 March 1710]

Perhaps you'll be surprised at this letter; I have had many debates with myself before I could resolve on it.[9] I know it is not acting in form, but I do not look upon you as I do upon the rest of the world, and by what I do for you, you are not to judge my manner of acting with others. You are brother to a woman I tenderly loved.[10] My protestations of friendship are not like other people's: I never speak but what I mean, and when I say I love, it is forever. I had that real concern for Mrs. Wortley; I look with some regard on everyone

[5] *ulcer* Open sore.

[6] *lancet* Surgical knife used at this time in England to make the incision for the smallpox virus.

[7] *plaster* Substance applied an injury to heal the wound or administer medicine.

[8] *Wortley* Edward Wortley Montagu.

[9] *Perhaps ... it* It was forbidden for women to write to men or to have any private interactions with potential suitors—though they often did, surreptitiously. This letter begins a lengthy secret correspondence between the two that continued, with occasional interruptions, until their elopement in August of 1712.

[10] *woman ... loved* Anne Wortley, who had died the previous month. The two women had been friends and correspondents for some time, though in the last months before her death Anne's letters to Lady Montagu were dictated to her by her brother Edward, who used them as a surreptitious means of courtship. It was Anne's death that finally prompted him to write Lady Mary directly.

that is related to her. This and my long acquaintance with you may in some measure excuse what I am now doing.

I am surprised at one of the "Tatlers" you sent me.[1] Is it possible to have any sort of esteem for a person one believes capable of having such trifling inclinations? Mr. Bickerstaff has very wrong notions of our sex. I can say there are some of us that despise charms of show, and all the pageantry of greatness, perhaps with more ease than any of the philosophers. In contemning the world, they seem to take pains to contemn it. We despise it without taking the pains to read lessons of morality to make us do it. At least I know I have always looked upon it with contempt, without being at the expense of one serious reflection to oblige me to it. I carry the matter yet farther. Was I to choose of £2,000 a year or twenty thousand, the first would be my choice. There is something of an unavoidable *embarras* in making what is called a great figure in the world, [that] takes off from the happiness of life. I hate the noise and hurry inseparable from great estates and titles, and look upon both as blessings that ought only to be given to fools, for 'tis only to them that they are blessings.

The pretty fellows you speak of I own entertain me sometimes, but is it impossible to be diverted with what one despises? I can laugh at a puppet show at the same time I know there is nothing in it worth my attention or regard. General notions are generally wrong; ignorance and folly are thought the best foundations for virtue, as if not knowing what a good wife is was necessary to make one so. I confess that can never be my way of reasoning, as I always forgive an injury when I think it not done out of malice; I can never think myself obliged by what is done without design. Give me leave to say it (I know it sounds vain): I know how to make a man of sense happy, but then that man must resolve to contribute something towards it himself. I have so much esteem for you I should be very sorry to hear you was unhappy, but for the world I would not be the instrument of making you so, which (of the humour you are) is hardly to be avoided if I am your wife. You distrust me. I can neither be easy nor loved where I am distrusted, nor do I believe your passion for me is what you pretend it; at least I'm sure, was I in love I could not talk as you do.

Few women would have spoke so plainly as I have done, but to dissemble is among the things I never do. I take more pains to approve my conduct to myself than to the world, and would not have to accuse myself of a minute's deceit. I wish I loved you enough to devote myself to be forever miserable for the pleasure of a day or two's happiness. I cannot resolve upon it—You must think otherwise of me or not at all.

I don't enjoin you to burn this letter; I know you will.[2] 'Tis the first I ever writ to one of your sex and shall be the last. You must never expect another; I resolve against all correspondence of this kind. My resolutions are seldom made and never broken.

To Philippa Mundy[3]

25 September [1711]

Really, my dear Philippa, though nobody can have more exalted notions of Paradise[4] than myself, yet if Hell is very tempting, I cannot advise you to resist it, since virtue, in this wicked world, is seldom anything but its own reward. I guess Mr. Chester[5] to be the man; in point of prudence (contrary to point of pleasure) you ought not refuse him. I give you better counsel than I can take myself, for I have that aversion to Hell, I shall resist it all my life (though without hope of Paradise),

[1] *one … me* The *Tatler* article is no. 143 (9 March 1710), which urges men to curb women's excessive fondness for expensive equipage.

[2] *I don't … will* Not only did he not burn the letter, he wrote out a copy to keep as well.

[3] *Philippa Mundy* Close friend of Lady Mary's since adolescence.

[4] *Paradise* Montagu, her sister Frances, and Mundy used a number of code words when speaking of their intimate concerns surrounding courtship and marriage. "Paradise" meant a marriage for love (though rarely did any woman expect to have such luck); "Hell" was a forced marriage to a man one found distasteful; and "Limbo," the most common occurrence, was a marriage of relative indifference. For Lady Mary, Edward Wortley Montagu was a "Limbo."

[5] *Mr. Chester* William Chester was a close friend of Burrell Massingberd, who had begun to court Mundy roughly a year earlier. Chester was serving as go-between. Mundy originally conceived of Massingberd as a "Hell," but changed her mind after the two became acquainted through a secret correspondence that he initiated in an attempt to win her favor. They were married in 1714.

and I am very well convinced I shall never go to Hell, except 'tis to lead apes there.[1]

I pray for the success of your endeavors to come to London, where I hope we shall meet, and I be happy in discoursing with you with that freedom I would discourse with nobody else. You need not doubt my fidelity; I never take notice to[2] anybody when I receive a letter from you, to avoid enquiries.

Dear Phil, write me longer letters, and be assured, to my little power I will faithfully serve you. My friendship is more sincere than the generality of our sex's, and I would do anything that you could imagine of service to you.

I've had a general hunting day last Tuesday, where we had 20 ladies well dressed and mounted, and more men. The day was concluded with a ball. I rid and danced with a view of exercise, and that is all—how dull that is!

Dear Phil, adieu. I'm obliged by your confidence, and you shall never repent it.

To Philippa Mundy

[c. 2 November 1711]

I am glad, dear Phil, that you begin to find peace in this world. I despair of it, God knows; the Devil to pull, and a father to drive, and yet—I don't believe I shall go to Hell for all that, though I have no more hope of Paradise than if I was dead and buried a 1,000 fathom. To say truth, I have been this 10 days in debate whether I should hang or marry, in which time I have cried some 2 hours every day, and knocked my head against the wall some 15 times; 'tis yet doubtful which way my resolution will finally carry me——

So much for my own affairs; as to my advice concerning yours, you know it already. Scruples and demurs are as fatal to some young women as the flesh and Devil to others, and there are some proverbs written for our edification, as "faint heart, etc.," "nothing venture nothing have," and more of the same nature. You know where you may have a faithful messenger—I say no more; you understand me.

Dear Phil, infuse into me notions of moderate happiness. I am yet so miserable to be incapable of Limbo, and such an infidel I cannot persuade myself there is any such place in the creation. I rave of nothing but fire and brimstone, God help me. For you, if you do abandon hopes of the pretty Paradise you once placed your Heaven in, however, may you find another flowing with milk and honey, as charming, as enchanting, and every way worthy of such a lovely Eve.

To Wortley

[c. 26 July 1712]

I am going to write you a plain long letter. What I have *already* told you is nothing but the truth. I have no reason to believe I am going to be otherwise confined than by my duty, but I, that know my own mind, know that is enough to make me miserable. I see all the misfortune of marrying where it is impossible to love. I am going to confess a weakness [that] may perhaps add to your contempt of me. I wanted courage to resist at first the will of my relations, but as every day added to my fears, those at last grew strong enough to make me venture the disobliging them. A harsh word damps my spirits to a degree of silencing all I have to say. I knew the folly of my own temper, and took the method of writing to the disposer of me.[3] I said everything in this letter I thought proper to move him, and proffered in atonement for not marrying whom he would,[4] never to marry at all. He did not think fit to answer this letter, but sent for me to him. He told me he was very much surprised that I did not depend on his judgment for my future happiness, that he knew nothing I had to complain of, etc., that he did not doubt I had some other fancy in my head which encouraged me to this disobedience, but he assured me if I refused a settlement he has provided for me, he gave me his word, whatever proposals were made him, he would never so much as enter into a treaty with any other; that if I founded any hopes

[1] *except ... there* "To lead apes into hell" was the proverbial fate of women who died without marrying. [Cf. Shakespeare's *Taming of the Shrew* 2.1.]

[2] *take notice to* Mention to.

[3] *disposer of me* Her father.

[4] *whom he would* Her father wished her to marry Clotworthy Skeffington, an M.P. and the heir of Viscount Massereene.

upon his death, I should find myself mistaken—he never intended to leave me any thing but an annuity of £400; that though another would proceed in this manner, after I had given so just a pretence for it, yet he had goodness to leave my destiny yet in my own choice; and at the same time commanded me to communicate my design to my relations and ask their advice.

As hard as this may sound, it did not shock my resolution. I was pleased to think at any price I had it in my power to be free from a man I hated. I told my intention to all my nearest relations; I was surprised at their blaming it to the greatest degree. I was told they were sorry I would ruin myself, but if I was so unreasonable they could not blame my f[ather], whatever he inflicted on me. I objected I did not love him. They made answer they found no necessity of loving; if I lived well with him, that was all was required of me, and that if I considered this town I should find very few women in love with their husbands, and yet a many happy. It was in vain to dispute with such prudent people; they looked upon me as a little romantic, and I found it impossible to persuade them that living in London at liberty was not the height of happiness. However, they could not change my thoughts, though I found I was to expect no protection from them. When I was to give my final answer to [my Father] I told him that I preferred a single life to any other, and if he pleased to permit me, I would take that resolution. He replied, he could not hinder my resolutions, but I should not pretend after that to please him, since pleasing him was only to be done by obedience; that if I would disobey, I knew the consequences—he would not fail to confine me where I might repent at leisure; that he had also consulted my relations and found them all agreeing in his sentiments.

He spoke this in a manner hindered my answering. I retired to my chamber, where I writ a letter to let him know my aversion to the man proposed was too great to be overcome, that I should be miserable beyond all things could be imagined, but I was in his hands, and he might dispose of me as he thought fit. He was perfectly satisfied with this answer, and proceeded as if I had given a willing consent. —I forgot to tell you he named you, and said if I thought that way I was very much mistaken, that if he had no other engagements, yet he would never have agreed to your proposals, having no inclination to see his grandchildren beggars.[1]

I do not speak this to endeavor to alter your opinion, but to show the improbability of his agreeing to it. I confess I am entirely of your mind. I reckon it among the absurdities of custom that a man must be obliged to settle his whole estate on an eldest son, beyond his power to recall, whatever he proves to be, and make himself unable to make happy a younger child that may deserve to be so. If I had an estate myself, I should not make such ridiculous settlements, and I cannot blame you for being in the right.

I have told you all my affairs with a plain sincerity. I have avoided to move your compassion, and I have said nothing of what I suffer; and I have not persuaded you to a treaty which I am sure my family will never agree to. I can have no fortune without an entire obedience.

Whatever your business is, may it end to your satisfaction. I think of the public as you do. As little as that is a woman's care, it may be permitted into the number of a woman's fears. But wretched as I am, I have no more to fear for myself. I have still a concern for my friends, and I am in pain for your danger. I am far from taking ill what you say. I never valued myself as the daughter of——, and ever despised those that esteemed me on that account. With pleasure I could barter all that, and change to be any country gentleman's daughter that would have reason enough to make happiness in privacy.

My letter is too long. I beg your pardon. You may see by the situation of my affairs 'tis without design.

From Wortley

[13 August 1712]

Before you are to leave Acton, the post will go out but thrice, and I cannot omit using it every time. I have now done disputing with you. Say what you please to

[1] *I forgot ... beggars* Wortley had entered into negotiations with Montagu's father, Lord Dorchester, two years before this, but these had collapsed, largely because Wortley refused to guarantee his eldest son would be his unconditional heir, preferring instead to choose the most worthy of his offspring.

the contrary, I will go to Acton at the hour you named and stand near the summer house which looks upon the great road that goes into the town.[1] Whatever you may tell me in the meantime I cannot be assured how you will stand affected then; you must judge for both of us. A mistake may be fatal. I am yours till you turn me away.

To Wortley

[15 August 1712]
Friday, 7 o'clock

If I think till tomorrow after the same manner I have thought ever since I saw you, the wisest thing I can do is to do whatever you please. 'Tis an odd thing to confess, but I fear nothing so much as a change in my mind when there can be none in my condition. My thoughts of you are capable of improvement both ways. I am more susceptible of gratitude than anybody living. You may manage in a manner to make me passionately fond of you. Should you use me ill, can I answer that I should be able to hinder myself from reflecting back on the sacrifice I had made? An engagement for my whole life is no trifle, and should we both be so happy as to find we liked one another, yet even years of exquisite happiness, when they are past, could not pay me for a whole life of misery to come. I think perhaps farther than I have occasion to think, but in an affair like this, all possible as well as all probable events are to be foreseen, since a mistake is not to be retrieved. In my present opinion, I think that if I was yours and you used me well, nothing could be added to my misfortune should I lose you. But when I suffer my reason to speak, it tells me that in any circumstance of life (wretched or happy) there is a certain proportion of money, as the world is made, absolutely necessary to the living in it. I have never yet found myself in any straits of fortune, and am hardly able to imagine the misery arising from it. Should I find myself 20 year hence your widow, without a competency to maintain me in a manner suitable in some degree to my education, I shall not then be so old I may not possibly live 20 year longer without what is requisite to make life easy. Happiness is what I should not think of.

After all these prudent considerations, the bias of my heart is in your favour. I hate the man they propose to me. If I did not hate him, my reason would tell me he is not capable of either being my friend or my companion. I have an esteem for you, with a mixture of more kindness than I imagined. That kindness would persuade me to abandon all things for you—my fame,[2] my family, the settlement they have provided for me—and rather embark with you through all the hazards of perhaps finding myself reduced to the last extremes of want (which would be heavier on me than any other body) than enjoy the certainty of a plentiful fortune with another. I can think with pleasure of giving you with my first declaration of love the sincerest proof of it. I read over some of your first letters, and I form romantic scenes to myself of love and solitude. I did not believe I was capable of thinking this way, but I find 'tis in your power to make me think what you please.

One would think this letter were determined, yet I know not what I shall do. I know if I do not venture all things to have you, I shall repent it.

To Wortley

[15 August 1712]
Friday Night

I tremble for what we are doing. Are you sure you will love me forever? Shall we never repent? I fear, and I hope. I foresee all that will happen on this occasion. I shall incense my family to the highest degree. The generality of the world will blame my conduct, and the relations and friends of—— will invent a thousand stories of me, yet 'tis possible you may recompense everything to me. In this letter (which I am fond of) you promise me all that I wish.—Since I writ so far, I received your Friday letter. I will be only yours, and I will do what you please.

[1] *Say what ... town* After months of debate, negotiation, and hesitation, Wortley and Montagu had decided to elope. He was to arrange to have a coach waiting outside her brother's house in Acton (where the family would be visiting) for her escape.

[2] *fame* Good reputation or character.

[*Postscript*] You shall hear from me again tomorrow, not to contradict but to give some directions. My resolution is taken—love me and use me well.

To Lady Mar[1]

17 November [1716]

O.S.[2] November 17, Prague

I hope my dear sister wants no new proof of my sincere affection for her, but I'm sure if you did I could not give you a stronger than writing at this time, after 3 days—or, more properly speaking, 3 nights and days—hard post travelling.

The kingdom of Bohemia is the most desert[3] of any I have seen in Germany; the villages so poor and the post-houses[4] so miserable, clean straw and fair water are blessings not always to be found, and better accommodation not to be hoped. Though I carried my own bed with me, I could not sometimes find a place to set it up in, and I rather chose to travel all night, as cold as it is, wrapped up in my furs, than go into the common stoves,[5] which are filled with a mixture of all sort of ill scents.

This town was once the royal seat of the Bohemian kings, and is still the capital of the kingdom. There are yet some remains of its former splendour, being one of the largest towns in Germany, but for the most part old built and thinly inhabited, which makes the houses very cheap, and those people of quality who cannot easily bear the expence of Vienna choose to reside here, where they have assemblies, music, and all other diversions (those of a court excepted) at very moderate rates, all things being here in great abundance, especially the best wild fowl I ever tasted. I have already been visited by some of the most considerable ladies, whose relations I knew at Vienna. They are dressed after the fashions there, as people at Exeter imitate those of London—that is, their imitation is more excessive than the original—and 'tis not easy to describe what extraordinary figures they make. The person is so much lost between headdress and petticoat, they have as much occasion to write upon their backs, "This is a woman," for the information of travellers, as ever signpost painter had to write, "This is a bear."[6]

I will not forget to write to you again from Dresden and Leipzig, being much more solicitous to content your curiosity than to indulge my own repose. I am, etc.

[1] *Lady Mar* Montagu's sister, Frances, who had married the earl of Mar in July of 1714. These and the following letters to Lady Mar are from two manuscript books that Montagu kept, detailing her travels abroad with her husband, who in 1716 was appointed Ambassador to Turkey and given the diplomatic mission of ending the current war between the Austrians and the Turks. The manuscripts, which she intended for posthumous publication, were epistolary travel books that combined and condensed the actual letters she sent—keeping the identities of her correspondents veiled (this letter was originally addressed to "the Countess——").

[2] *O.S.* Old style of dating, according to the Julian system used in England. The date according to the Gregorian calendar (used in Continental Europe) would be 11 days later.

[3] *desert* Desolate, uncultivated.

[4] *post-houses* Inns.

[5] *common stoves* Public rooms with heating stoves (not known in England).

To Lady——

1 April [1717]

Adrianople, Ap. 1, O.S.

I am now got into a new world, where everything I see appears to me a change of scene, and I write to your ladyship with some content of mind, hoping at least that you will find the charm of novelty in my letters and no longer reproach me that I tell you nothing extraordinary. I won't trouble you with a relation of our tedious journey, but I must not omit what I saw remarkable at Sofia, one of the most beautiful towns in the Turkish empire and famous for its hot baths, that are resorted to

[6] *The person ... bear* Reference to *Tatler* no. 18 (21 May 1709), which laments the poor skills of both the painters and the writers of signs, so that passers-by can neither make sense of the picture nor read the writing below, which is often filled with spelling and grammatical errors. The article gives as an example a man who was lost for hours looking for a certain tavern, which had the sign of a bear outside. He passed it several times, but because the writing below the unrecognizable picture of the bear read, "This is a beer," he believed he had the wrong place.

both for diversion and health.[1] I stopped here one day on purpose to see them. Designing to go incognito, I hired a Turkish coach. These *voitures* are not at all like ours, but much more convenient for the country, the heat being so great that glasses would be very troublesome. They are made a good deal in the manner of the Dutch coaches, having wooden lattices painted and gilded, the inside being painted with baskets and nosegays of flowers, intermixed commonly with little poetical mottos. They are covered all over with scarlet cloth, lined with silk, and very often richly embrodiered and fringed. This covering entirely hides the persons in them, but may be thrown back at pleasure and the ladies peep through the lattices. They hold four people very conveniently, seated on cushions, but not raised.

In one of these covered wagons I went to the bagnio[2] about ten o'clock. It was already full of women. It is built of stone in the shape of a dome, with no windows but in the roof, which gives light enough. There was five of these domes joined together, the outmost being less than the rest and serving only as a hall where the porteress stood at the door. Ladies of quality generally give this woman the value of a crown or 10 shillings, and I did not forget that ceremony. The next room is a very large one, paved with marble, and all round it raised two sofas of marble, one above another. There were four fountains of cold water in this room, falling first into marble basins and then running on the floor in little channels made for that purpose, which carried the streams into the next room, something less than this, with the same sort of marble sofas, but so hot with steams of sulphur proceeding from the baths joining to it, 'twas impossible to stay there with one's clothes on. The two other domes were the hot baths, one of which had cocks[3] of cold water turning into it to temper it to what degree of warmth the bathers have a mind to.

I was in my travelling habit, which is a riding dress, and certainly appeared very extraordinary to them, yet there was not one of them that showed the least surprise or impertinent curiosity, but received me with all the obliging civility possible. I know no European court where the ladies would have behaved themselves in so polite a manner to a stranger.

I believe in the whole there were 200 women, and yet none of those disdainful smiles or satiric whispers that never fail in our assemblies when anybody appears that is not dressed exactly in fashion. They repeated over and over to me, *Uzelle, pek uzelle*, which is nothing but "charming, very charming." The first sofas were covered with cushions and rich carpets, on which sat the ladies, and on the second their slaves behind them, but without any distinction of rank by their dress, all being in the state of nature, that is, in plain English, stark naked, without any beauty or defect concealed, yet there was not the least wanton smile or immodest gesture amongst them. They walked and moved with the same majestic grace which Milton describes of our general mother.[4] There were many amongst them as exactly proportioned as ever any goddess was drawn by the pencil of Guido or Titian,[5] and most of their skins shiningly white, only adorned by their beautiful hair divided into many tresses hanging on their shoulders, braided either with pearl or riband,[6] perfectly representing the figures of the Graces.[7] I was here convinced of the truth of a reflection that I had often made, that if 'twas the fashion to go naked, the face would be hardly observed. I perceived that the ladies with the finest skins and most delicate shapes had the greatest share of my admiration, though their faces were sometimes less beautiful than those of their companions. To tell you the truth, I had wickedness enough to wish secretly that Mr. Jervas[8] could have been there invisible. I fancy it would have very much improved his art to see so many fine women naked in different postures, some in conversation, some working, others drinking coffee or sherbet, and many negligently lying

[1] *hot baths ... health* Springs, whose temperatures are around 45°C, said to heal a variety of ailments, from skin complaints to digestive, respiratory, and circulatory difficulties.

[2] *bagnio* Bath.

[3] *cocks* Taps.

[4] *Milton ... mother* I.e., Eve, in *Paradise Lost*, Book 4.

[5] *Guido or Titian* Guido Reni and Tiziano Vecellio, two celebrated Italian painters.

[6] *riband* Ribbon.

[7] *the Graces* The three sister goddesses of Greek mythology who dispense beauty, joy, and charm.

[8] *Mr. Jervas* Painter and one of Montagu and Alexander Pope's circle. French painter Jean Auguste Dominique Ingres's painting "Le Bain Turc," now hanging in the Louvre, was based on Montagu's description here.

on their cushions while their slaves (generally pretty girls of 17 or 18) were employed in braiding their hair in several pretty manners. In short, 'tis the women's coffee-house, where all the news of the town is told, scandal invented, etc. They generally take this diversion once a week, and stay there at least four or five hours without getting cold by immediate coming out of the hot bath into the cool room, which was very surprising to me. The lady that seemed the most considerable amongst them entreated me to sit by her and would fain have undressed me for the bath. I excused myself with some difficulty, they being all so earnest in persuading me. I was at last forced to open my skirt and show them my stays,[1] which satisfied them very well, for I saw they believed I was so locked up in that machine[2] that it was not in my own power to open it, which contrivance they attributed to my husband. I was charmed with their civility and beauty and should have been very glad to pass more time with them, but, Mr. W[ortley] resolving to pursue his journey the next morning early, I was in haste to see the ruins of Justinian's church,[3] which did not afford me so agreeable a prospect as I had left, being little more than a heap of stones.

Adieu, Madam. I am sure I have now entertained you with an account of such a sight as you never saw in your life, and what no book of travels could inform you of. 'Tis no less than death for a man to be found in one of these places.

To Lady Mar

1 April [1717]

Adrianople, Ap. 1, O.S.

I wish to God, dear sister, that you was as regular in letting me have the pleasure of knowing what passes on your side of the globe as I am careful in endeavouring to amuse you by the account of all I see that I think you care to hear of. You content yourself with telling me over and over that the town is very dull. It may possibly be dull to you when every day does not present you with something new, but for me that am in arrear at least two months news, all that seems very stale with you would be fresh and sweet here; pray let me into more particulars. I will try to awaken your gratitude by giving you a full and true relation of the novelties of this place, none of which would surprise you more than a sight of my person as I am now in my Turkish habit, though I believe you would be of my opinion, that 'tis admirably becoming. I intend to send you my picture; in the meantime accept of it here.

The first piece of my dress is a pair of drawers, very full, that reach to my shoes and conceal the legs more modestly than your petticoats. They are of a thin, rose-colour damask brocaded with silver flowers, my shoes of white kid leather embroidered with gold. Over this hangs my smock of a fine white silk gauze edged with embroidery. This smock has wide sleeves hanging half way down the arm and is closed at the neck with a diamond button, but the shape and colour of the bosom very well to be distinguished through it. The *antery* is a waistcoat made close to the shape, of white and gold damask, with very long sleeves falling back and fringed with deep gold fringe, and should have diamond or pearl buttons. My caftan, of the same stuff with my drawers, is a robe exactly fitted to my shape and reaching to my feet, with very long, strait falling sleeves. Over this is the girdle of about four fingers broad, which all that can afford have entirely of diamonds or other precious stones. Those that will not be at that expense have it of exquisite embroidery on satin, but it must be fastened before with a clasp of diamonds. The *curdee* is a loose robe they throw off or put on according to the weather, being of a rich brocade (mine is green and gold) either lined with ermine or sables; the sleeves reach very little below the shoulders. The headdress is composed of a cap called *talpock*, which is in winter of fine velvet embroidered with pearls or diamonds and in summer of a light shining silver stuff. This is fixed on one side of the head, hanging a little way down with a gold tassel and bound on either with a circle of diamonds (as I have seen several) or a rich embroidered handkerchief. On the other side of the head the hair is

---

[1] *stays* Undergarment stiffened with whalebone, made of two separate pieces that laced together and extended from the thighs to the chest.

[2] *machine* Structure.

[3] *Justinian's church* The Church of St. Sofia, which was founded by Emperor Justinian in the sixth century and from which the capital city took its name.

laid flat, and here the ladies are at liberty to show their fancies, some putting flowers, others a plume of heron's feathers, and, in short, what they please, but the most general fashion is a large bouquet of jewels made like natural flowers, that is, the buds of pearl, the roses of different coloured rubies, the jasmines of diamonds, jonquils of topazes, etc., so well set and enameled 'tis hard to imagine anything of that kind so beautiful. The hair hangs at its full length behind, divided into tresses braided with pearl or riband, which is always in great quantity.

I never saw in my life so many fine heads of hair. I have counted 110 of these tresses of one lady's, all natural; but it must be owned that every beauty is more common here than with us. 'Tis surprising to see a young woman that is not very handsome. They have naturally the most beautiful complexions in the world and generally large black eyes. I can assure you with great truth that the court of England (though I believe it the fairest in Christendom) cannot show so many beauties as are under our protection here. They generally shape their eyebrows, and the Greeks and Turks have a custom of putting round their eyes on the inside a black tincture that, at a distance or by candlelight, adds very much to the blackness of them. I fancy many of our ladies would be overjoyed to know this secret, but 'tis too visible by day. They dye their nails rose colour; I own I cannot enough accustom myself to this fashion to find any beauty in it.

As to their morality or good conduct, I can say like Arlequin, 'tis just as 'tis with you,[1] and the Turkish ladies don't commit one sin the less for not being Christians. Now I am a little acquainted with their ways, I cannot forbear admiring either the exemplary discretion or extreme stupidity of all the writers that have given accounts of them. 'Tis very easy to see they have more liberty than we have, no woman of what rank soever being permitted to go in the streets without two muslins, one that covers her face, all but her eyes, and another that hides the whole dress of her head and hangs half way down her back; and their shapes are wholly concealed by a thing they call a *ferigée*, which no woman of any sort appears without. This has straight sleeves that reaches to their fingers' ends, and it laps all round them, not unlike a riding hood. In winter 'tis of cloth, and in summer, plain stuff or silk. You may guess how effectually this disguises them, that there is no distinguishing the great lady from her slave, and 'tis impossible for the most jealous husband to know his wife when he meets her, and no man dare either touch or follow a woman in the street.

This perpetual masquerade gives them entire liberty of following their inclinations without danger of discovery. The most usual method of intrigue is to send an appointment to the lover to meet the lady at a Jew's shop,[2] which are as notoriously convenient as our Indian houses,[3] and yet even those that don't make that use of them do not scruple to go to buy penn'orths and tumble over[4] rich goods, which are chiefly to be found amongst that sort of people. The great ladies seldom let their gallants know who they are, and 'tis so difficult to find it out that they can very seldom guess at her name they have corresponded with above half a year together. You may easily imagine the number of faithful wives very small in a country where they have nothing to fear from their lovers' indiscretion, since we see so many that have the courage to expose themselves to that in this world and all the threatened punishment of the next, which is never preached to the Turkish damsels. Neither have they much to apprehend from the resentment of their husbands, those ladies that are rich having all their money in their own hands, which they take with them upon a divorce, with an addition which he is obliged to give them. Upon the whole, I look upon the Turkish women as the only free people in the empire. The very *Divan*[5] pays a respect to them, and the *Grand Signior*[6]

[1] *like Arlequin ... you* In Aphra Behn's comedy *The Emperor of the Moon*, the character Harlequin pretends to be a visitor from the moon and describes the morals and customs of his imaginary home, which turn out to be just as corrupt as those on earth.

[2] *Jew's shop* From the medieval period until the twentieth century, Jews were restricted in many countries, either by law or by custom, to a very limited number of professions, notably moneylending, tailoring, and certain types of retailing.

[3] *Indian houses* Stores selling goods from India and the Far East.

[4] *penn'orths* From pennyworths, the amounts (of various things) that could be bought for a penny—i.e., any good buy; *tumble over* Browse through.

[5] *Divan* Member of the privy council.

[6] *Grand Signior* Sultan.

himself, when a *Bashaw*[1] is executed, never violates the privileges of the harem (or women's apartment), which remains unsearched entire to the widow. They are queens of their slaves, which the husband has no permission so much as to look upon, except it be an old woman or two that his lady chooses. 'Tis true their law permits them four wives, but there is no instance of a man of quality that makes use of this liberty, or of a woman of rank that would suffer it. When a husband happens to be inconstant (as those things will happen) he keeps his mistress in a house apart and visits her as privately as he can, just as 'tis with you. Amongst all the great men here I only know the *Tefterdar* (i.e., treasurer) that keeps a number of she slaves for his own use (that is, on his own side of the house, for a slave once given to serve a lady is entirely at her disposal), and he is spoke of as a libertine, or what we should call a rake, and his wife won't see him, though she continues to live in his house.

Thus you see, dear sister, the manners of mankind do not differ so widely as our voyage writers would make us believe. Perhaps it would be more entertaining to add a few surprising customs of my own invention, but nothing seems to me so agreeable as truth, and I believe nothing so acceptable to you. I conclude with repeating the great truth of my being, dear sister, etc.

To [Sarah Chiswell][2]

1 April [1717]
Adrianople, Ap. 1, O.S.

In my opinion, dear S[arah], I ought rather to quarrel with you for not answering my Nijmegen[3] letter of August till December than to excuse my not writing again till now.

I am sure there is on my side a very good excuse for silence, having gone such tiresome land journeys, though I don't find the conclusion of them so bad as you seem to imagine. I am very easy here and not in the solitude you fancy me; the great quantity of Greek, French, English, and Italians that are under our protection make their court to me from morning till night, and I'll assure you are many of them very fine ladies, for there is no possibility for a Christian to live easily under this government but by the protection of an ambassador, and the richer they are the greater their danger.

Those dreadful stories you have heard of the plague have very little foundation in truth. I own I have much ado to reconcile myself to the sound of a word which has always given me such terrible ideas, though I am convinced there is little more in it than a fever, as a proof of which we passed through two or three towns most violently infected. In the very next house where we lay, in one of them,[4] two persons died of it. Luckily for me, I was so well deceived that I knew nothing of the matter, and I was made believe that our second cook, who fell ill there, had only a great cold. However, we left our doctor to take care of him, and yesterday they both arrived here in good health, and I am now let into the secret that he has had the plague. There are many that 'scape of it, neither is the air ever infected. I am persuaded it would be as easy to root it out here as out of Italy and France, but it does so little mischief, they are not very solicitous about it and are content to suffer this distemper instead of our variety, which they are utterly unacquainted with.

Apropos of distempers, I am going to tell you a thing that I am sure will make you wish yourself here. The smallpox, so fatal and so general amongst us,[5] is here entirely harmless by the invention of engrafting (which is the term they give it). There is a set of old women who make it their business to perform the operation. Every autumn in the month of September, when the great heat is abated, people send to one another to know if any of their family has a mind to have the smallpox. They make parties for this purpose, and when they are met (commonly 15 or 16 together) the old woman comes with a nutshell full of the matter of the best sort[6]

[1] *Bashaw* Pasha, a title given to military commanders and governors of provinces.

[2] *Sarah Chiswell* Montagu's friend since childhood.

[3] *Nijmegen* City of the eastern Netherlands near the German border.

[4] *one of them* I.e., one of those towns.

[5] *so general amongst us* Montagu herself barely survived a bout of smallpox in 1715 and was left severely scarred.

[6] *the matter* Pus from the smallpox sores; *best sort* There are various strains of smallpox, some of which have less severe symptoms and are less dangerous than others.

of smallpox and asks what veins you please to have opened. She immediately rips open that you offer to her with a large needle (which gives you no more pain than a common scratch) and puts into the vein as much venom as can lie upon the head of her needle, and after binds up the little wound with a hollow bit of shell, and in this manner opens four or five veins. The Grecians have commonly the superstition of opening one in the middle of the forehead, in each arm, and on the breast to mark the sign of the cross, but this has a very ill effect, all these wounds leaving little scars, and is not done by those that are not superstitious, who choose to have them in the legs or that part of the arm that is concealed. The children or young patients play together all the rest of the day and are in perfect health till the eighth. Then the fever begins to seize them and they keep their beds two days, very seldom three. They have very rarely above twenty or thirty in their faces, which never mark, and in eight days time they are as well as before their illness. Where they are wounded there remains running sores during the distemper, which I don't doubt is a great relief to it. Every year thousands undergo this operation, and the French ambassador says pleasantly that they take the smallpox here by way of diversion, as they take the waters in other countries. There is no example of any one that has died in it, and you may believe I am very well satisfied of the safety of the experiment, since I intend to try it on my dear little son.[1] I am patriot enough to take pains to bring this useful invention into fashion in England, and I should not fail to write to some of our doctors very particularly about it if I knew any one of them that I thought had virtue enough to destroy such a considerable branch of their revenue for the good of mankind. But that distemper is too beneficial to them not to expose to all their resentment the hardy wight[2] that should undertake to put an end to it. Perhaps if I live to return I may, however, have courage to war with them.[3] Upon this occasion, admire the heroism in the heart of your friend, etc.

TO ALEXANDER POPE

[September 1718]

Dover, November 1

I have this minute received a letter of yours, sent me from Paris.[4] I believe and hope I shall very soon see both you and Mr. Congreve,[5] but as I am here in an inn where we stay to regulate our march to London, bag and baggage, I shall employ some of my leisure time in answering that part of yours that seems to require an answer.

I must applaud your good nature in supposing that your pastoral lovers (vulgarly called haymakers) would have lived in everlasting joy and harmony if the lightning had not interrupted their scheme of happiness. I see no reason to imagine that John Hughes and Sarah Drew were either wiser or more virtuous than their neighbours. That a well-set man of twenty-five should have a fancy to marry a brown woman of eighteen is nothing marvellous, and I cannot help thinking that had they married, their lives would have passed in the common tract with their fellow parishioners. His endeavoring to shield her from the storm was a natural action and what he would have certainly done for his horse if he had been in the same situation. Neither am I of opinion that their sudden death was a reward of their mutual virtue. You know the Jews were reproved for thinking a village destroyed by fire more wicked than those that had escaped the thunder. Time and chance

[1] *since ... son* Montagu's son was inoculated in Turkey in 1718.

[2] *wight* Creature.

[3] *Perhaps ... them* Montagu did succeed in bringing the procedure back to England, and in 1721 her infant daughter was the first person to be inoculated there. The operation was not quite as safe in England as in Turkey, largely because the physicians modified the procedure, making it more rigorous and damaging, and the entire process was the subject of much controversy. Montagu worked extensively to prevent the procedure being rendered riskier and to dispel the public's prejudice against it (see *A Plain Account of the Inoculating of the Smallpox by a Turkey Merchant*).

[4] *letter ... Paris* Pope's letter, sent abroad on 1 September, was forwarded back to England, where Montagu had recently arrived. In the letter he relates the story of two lovers, John Hewet and Sarah Drew, who were struck by lightning while seeking shelter from a thunderstorm; he also includes two epitaphs he composed on the subject and some personal pressure on her to react sentimentally.

[5] *Congreve* English poet and dramatist William Congreve, a former disciple of Dryden, a friend of Addison and Steele, and one of Montagu's most regular correspondents.

happen to all men. Since you desire me to try my skill in an epitaph, I think the following lines perhaps more just, though not so poetical as yours:

Here lies John Hughes and Sarah Drew;
Perhaps you'll say, what's that to you?
Believe me, friend, much may be said
On this poor couple that are dead.
On Sunday next they should have married,
But see how oddly things are carried.
On Thursday last it rained and lightened;
These tender lovers, sadly frightened,
Sheltered beneath the cocking hay
In hopes to pass the storm away.
But the bold thunder found them out
(Commissioned for that end no doubt)
And seizing on their trembling breath,
Consigned them to the shades of death.
Who knows if 'twas not kindly done?
For had they seen the next year's sun,
A beaten wife and cuckold swain° *young man*
Had jointly cursed the marriage chain.
Now they are happy in their doom,
For P[ope] has wrote upon their tomb.

I confess these sentiments are not altogether so heroic as yours, but I hope you will forgive them in favor of the two last lines. You see how much I esteem the honour you have done them, though I am not very impatient to have the same and had rather continue to be your stupid living humble servant than be celebrated by all the pens in Europe.

I would write to Mr. C[ongreve] but suppose you will read this to him if he enquires after me.

To Lady Mar

[September 1727]

This is a vile world, dear sister, and I can easily comprehend that whither one is at Paris or London one is stifled with a certain mixture of fool and knave that most people are composed of. I would have patience with a parcel of polite rascals or your downright honest fools. But father Adam shines through his whole progeny; he first ate the apple like a sot and then turned informer like a scoundrel. So much for our inside. Then our outward is so liable to ugliness and distempers that we are perpetually plagued with feeling our own decays and seeing other people's—yet six penn'orth of common sense divided amongst a whole nation would make our lives roll away glib enough. But then we make laws and we follow customs; by the first we cut off our own pleasures, and by the second we are answerable for the faults and extravagancies of others. All these things and 500 more convince me (as I have the most profound adoration for the Author of Nature) that we are here in an actual state of punishment. I am satisfied I have been damned ever since I was born, and in submission to divine justice don't at all doubt but I deserved it in some pre-existent state. I am very willing to soften the word damned and hope I am only in purgatory, and that after whining and grunting here a certain number of years I shall be translated to some more happy sphere where virtue will be natural and custom reasonable; that is, in short, where common sense will reign.

I grow very devout, as you see, and place all my hopes in the next life, being totally persuaded of the nothingness of this. Don't you remember how miserable we were in the little parlor at Thorsby? We thought marrying would put us at once into possession of all we wanted; then came being with child, etc., and you see what comes of being with child.[1]

Though after all I am still of opinion that 'tis extremely silly to submit to ill fortune; one should pluck up a spirit and live upon cordials when one can have no other nourishment. These are my present endeavors, and I run about though I have 5,000 pins and needles running into my heart. I try to console with a small damsel who is at present everything that I like, but alas, she is yet in a white frock. At 14 she may run away with the butler. There's one of the blessed consequences of great disappointment; you are not only hurt by the thing present, but it cuts off all future hopes and makes your very expectations melancholy. *Quelle vie!*

[1] *you see … child* The source of Montagu's distress is her fourteen-year-old son, Edward Wortley Montagu, junior, who had run away. He had boarded a ship bound for Gibraltar, and despite his parents' extensive searches and offers of a reward, he could not be found. He was finally returned the following January.

To Lady Bute[1]

5 January [1748]

Dear Child,

I am glad to hear that yourself and family are in good health. As to the alteration you say you find in the world, it is only owing to your being better acquainted with it. I have never, in all my various travels, seen but two sorts or people (and those very like one another): I mean men and women, who always have been, and ever will be, the same. The same vices and the same follies have been the fruit of all ages, though sometimes under different names. I remember (when I returned from Turkey) meeting with the same affectation of youth amongst my acquaintance that you now mention amongst yours, and I do not doubt but your daughter will find the same twenty years hence amongst hers. One of the greatest happinesses of youth is the ignorance of evil, though it is often the ground of great indiscretions, and sometimes the active part of life is over before an honest mind finds out how one ought to act in such a world as this. I am as much removed from it as it is possible to be on this side the grave, which is from my own inclination, for I might have even here a great deal of company, the way of living in this province[2] being what I believe it is now in the sociable part of Scotland and was in England a hundred years ago.

I had a visit in the beginning of these holidays of thirty horse of ladies and gentlemen with their servants (by the way, the ladies all ride like the late Duchess of Cleveland).[3] They came with the kind intent of staying with me at least a fortnight, though I had never seen any of them before; but they were all neighbours within ten mile round. I could not avoid entertaining them at supper, and by good luck had a large quantity of game in the house, which with the help of my poultry furnished out a plentiful table. I sent for the fiddles, and they were so obliging to dance all night, and even dine with me next day, though none of them had been in bed, and were much disappointed I did not press them to stay, it being the fashion to go in troops to one another's houses, hunting and dancing together, a month in each castle. I have not yet returned any of their visits, nor do not intend it of some time, to avoid this expensive hospitality. The trouble of it is not very great, they not expecting any ceremony. I left the room about one o'clock, and they continued their ball in the saloon above stairs without being at all offended at my departure. The greatest diversion I had was to see a lady of my own age comfortably dancing with her own husband some years older, and I can assure you she jumps and gallops with the best of them.

May you always be as well satisfied with your family as you are at present, and your children return in your age the tender care you have of their infancy. I know no greater happiness that can be wished for you by your most affectionate mother,

M. Wortley.

Brescia, Jan. 5

My compliments to Lord Bute and blessing to my grandchildren.

To Lady Bute

19 February [1750]

My Dear Child,

I gave you some general thoughts on the education of your children in my last letter, but, fearing you should think I neglected your request by answering it with too much conciseness, I am resolved to add to it what little I know on that subject, and which may perhaps be useful to you in a concern with which you seem so nearly affected.

People commonly educate their children as they build their houses, according to some plan they think beautiful, without considering whither it is suited to the purposes for which they are designed. Almost all girls of quality are educated as if they were to be great ladies, which is often as little to be expected as an immoderate heat of the sun in the north of Scotland. You should teach yours to confine their desires to probabilities, to be

[1] *Lady Bute* Montagu's daughter, formerly Mary Wortley Montagu, who married the Earl of Bute in 1736.

[2] *the way … province* Montagu, who was essentially separated from her husband (their marriage had turned out to be less successful than they had hoped), had moved to Italy in 1739. At the time she was residing in Brescia.

[3] *ladies all … Cleveland* I.e., astride their horses, rather than sidesaddle.

as useful as is possible to themselves, and to think privacy (as it is) the happiest state of life.

I do not doubt your giving them all the instructions necessary to form them to a virtuous life, but 'tis a fatal mistake to do this without proper restrictions. Vices are often hid under the name of virtues, and the practise of them followed by the worst of consequences. Sincerity, friendship, piety, disinterestedness, and generosity are all great virtues, but pursued without discretion become criminal. I have seen ladies indulge their own ill humour by being very rude and impertinent, and think they deserved approbation by saying, "I love to speak truth." One of your acquaintance made a ball the next day after her mother died, to show she was sincere. I believe your own reflection will furnish you with but too many examples of the ill effects of the rest of the sentiments I have mentioned, when too warmly embraced. They are generally recommended to young people without limits or distinction, and this prejudice hurries them into great misfortunes while they are applauding themselves in the noble practise (as they fancy) of very eminent virtues.

I cannot help adding (out of my real affection to you), I wish you would moderate that fondness you have for your children. I do not mean you should abate any part of your care, or not do your duty to them in its utmost extent, but I would have you early prepare yourself for disappointments, which are heavy in proportion to their being surprising. It is hardly possible in such a number that none should be unhappy. Prepare yourself against a misfortune of that kind. I confess there is hardly any more difficult to support, yet it is certain imagination has a great share in the pain of it, and it is more in our power (than it is commonly believed) to soften whatever ills are founded or augmented by fancy. Strictly speaking, there is but one real evil: I mean acute pain. All other complaints are so considerably diminished by time that it is plain the grief is owing to our passion, since the sensation of it vanishes when that is over.

There is another mistake I forgot to mention usual in mothers. If any of their daughters are beauties, they take great pains to persuade them that they are ugly, or at least that they think so, which the young woman never fails to believe springs from envy, and is (perhaps) not much in the wrong. I would, if possible, give them a just notion of their figure and show them how far it is valuable. Every advantage has its price, and may be either over or undervalued. It is the common doctrine of (what are called) good books to inspire a contempt of beauty, riches, greatness, etc., which has done as much mischief amongst the young of our sex as an over eager desire of them. They should look on these things as blessings where they are bestowed, though not necessaries that it is impossible to be happy without. I am persuaded the ruin of Lady Frances Meadows[1] was in great measure owing to the notions given her by the sillily[2] good people that had the care of her.[3] 'Tis true her circumstances and your daughters' are very different. They should be taught to be content with privacy, and yet not neglect good fortune if it should be offered them.

I am afraid I have tired you with my instructions. I do not give them as believing my age has furnished me with superior wisdom, but in compliance with your desire, and being fond of every opportunity that gives a proof of the tenderness with which I am ever your affectionate mother,

M. Wortley.

I should be glad you sent me the third volume of architecture, and with it any other entertaining books. I have seen the Duchess of Marlborough's, but should be glad of the *Apology for a Late Resignation*.[4] As to the ale, 'tis now so late in the year it is impossible it should come good.

You do not mention your father. My last letter from him told me he intended soon for England.[5] I am afraid

[1] *Lady Frances Meadows* Formerly Lady Frances Pierrepont, the orphaned daughter of Montagu's brother. She had been temporarily in Montagu's care, but had eloped—against the wishes of Montagu and the rest of the family—with Philip Meadows in 1734.

[2] *sillily* Foolishly.

[3] *the ruin ... her* Lady Frances Meadows was raised by her great-aunt Lady Cheyne.

[4] *Duchess of Marlborough's* Political testament of the Duchess of Marlborough, *An Account of the Conduct of the Dowager Duchess of Marlborough, from her first coming to Court to the year 1710*; *Apology ... Resignation* Anonymous defense of Secretary of State Chesterfield's resignation.

[5] *My last ... England* Montagu's husband had been in France for several months.

several of mine to him have miscarried, though directed as he ordered.

I have asked you so often the price of raw silk[1] that I am weary of repeating it. However, I once more beg you would send me that information.

To Wortley

10 October [1753]

I think I now know why our correspondence is so miserably interrupted and so many of my letters lost to and from England, but I am no happier in the discovery than a man that has found out his complaints proceed from a stone in the kidneys. I know the cause but am entirely ignorant of the remedy, and must suffer my uneasiness with what patience I can.

An old priest made me a visit as I was folding my last packet to my daughter. Observing it to be large, he told me I had done a great deal of business that morning. I made answer, I had done no business at all; I had only wrote to my daughter on family affairs or such trifles as make up women's conversation. He said gravely, people like your Excellenza do not use to write long letters upon trifles. I assured him that if he understood English I would let him read my letter. He replied (with a mysterious smile), if I did understand English, I should not understand what you have written, except you would give me the key, which I durst not presume to ask. What key? (said I, staring); there is not one cypher beside the date. He answered, cyphers were only used by novices in politics, and it was very easy to write intelligibly under feigned names of persons and places to a correspondent in such a manner as should be almost impossible to be understood by anybody else.

Thus I suppose my innocent epistles are severely scrutinized, and when I talk of my grandchildren they are fancied to represent all the potentates of Europe. This is very provoking. I confess there are good reasons for extraordinary caution at this juncture, but 'tis very hard I cannot pass for being as insignificant as I really am.

The house at Acton was certainly left to Lady Carolina; and whatever Lady Anne[2] left, so little (when divided it [sic] 5 parts) it is not worth enquiring for, especially after so long silence.

I heartily congratulate you on the recovery of your sight. It is a blessing I prefer to life, and will seek for glasses whenever I am in a place where they are sold.

To Lady Bute

[30 November (?) 1753]

My dear Child,

I received your agreeable letter of Sept. 24 yesterday, Nov. 29, and am very glad our daughter (for I think she belongs to us both) turns out so much to your satisfaction; may she ever do so. I hope she has by this time received my token. I am afraid I have lost some of your letters. In last April you wrote me word the box directed to me was to set out in a week's time. Since that I have had no news of it, and apprehend very much that the bill which I suppose you sent me has miscarried. If so, I am in danger of losing the cargo.

You please me extremely in saying my letters are of any entertainment to you. I would contribute to your happiness in every shape I can, but in my solitude there are so few subjects present themselves, it is not easy to find one that would amuse you, though as I believe you have some leisure hours at Kenwood, when anything new is welcome, I will venture to tell you a small history in which I had some share.

I have already informed you of the divisions and subdivisions of estates in this country, by which you will imagine there is a numerous gentry of great names and little fortunes. Six of those families inhabit this town. You may fancy this forms a sort of society, but far from it, as there is not one of them that does not think (for some reason or other) they are far superior to all the rest. There is such a settled aversion amongst them, they avoid one another with the utmost care, and hardly ever meet except by chance at the castle (as they call my

[1] *raw silk* Montagu owned a farm on which she raised silk worms, and she was hoping to sell the silk in England.

[2] *The house … Carolina* In his will, Montagu's father, the Duke of Kingston, left this house to his second wife; *Lady Anne* Montagu's half sister.

house),[1] where their regard for me obliges them to behave civilly, but it is with an affected coldness that is downright disagreeable, and hinders me from seeing any of them often.

I was quietly reading in my closet[2] when I was interrupted by the chambermaid of the Signora Laura Bono, who flung herself at my feet and, in an agony of sobs and tears, begged me for the love of the Holy Madonna to hasten to her master's house, where the two brothers would certainly murder one another if my presence did not stop their fury. I was very much surprised, having always heard them spoke of as a pattern of fraternal union. However, I made all possible speed thither, without staying for hoods or attendance. I was soon there (the house touching my garden wall) and was directed to the bedchamber by the noise of oaths and execrations, but on opening the door was astonished to a degree you may better guess than I describe, by seeing the Signora Laura prostrate on the ground, melting in tears, and her husband standing with a drawn stiletto[3] in his hand, swearing she should never see tomorrow's sun. I was soon let into the secret.

The good man, having business of consequence at Brescia, went thither early in the morning, but as he expected his chief tenant to pay his rent that day, he left orders with his wife that if the farmer (who lived two mile off) came himself or sent any of his sons, she should take care to make him very welcome. She obeyed him with great punctuality. The money coming in the hand of a handsome lad of eighteen, she did not only admit him to her own table and produce the best wine in the cellar, but resolved to give him *chère entière*.[4] While she was exercising this generous hospitality, the husband met midway the gentleman he intended to visit, who was posting to another side of the country. They agreed on another appointment, and he returned to his own house, where, giving his horse to be led round to the stable by the servant that accompanied him, he opened his door with the *passe-partout* key,[5] and proceeded to his chamber without meeting anybody, where he found his beloved spouse asleep on the bed with her gallant. The opening of the door waked them. The young fellow immediately leaped out of the window, which looked into the garden and was open (it being summer), and escaped over the fields, leaving his breeches on a chair by the bedside, a very striking circumstance. In short, the case was such I do not think the Queen of Fairies herself could have found an excuse, though Chaucer tells us she has made a solemn promise to leave none of her sex unfurnished with one, to all eternity.[6] As to the poor criminal, she had nothing to say for herself but what I dare swear you will hear from your youngest daughter if ever you catch her stealing of sweetmeats: pray, pray, she would do so no more, and indeed it was the first time.

This last article found no credit with me. I can not be persuaded that any woman who had lived virtuous till forty (for such was her age) could suddenly be endowed with such consummate impudence to solicit a youth at first sight, there being no probability, his age and station considered, that he would have made any attempt of that kind. I must confess I was wicked enough to think the unblemished reputation she had hitherto maintained, and did not fail to put us in mind of, was owing to a series of such frolics; and to say truth, they are the only amours that can reasonably hope to remain undiscovered. Ladies that can resolve to make love thus *ex tempore*[7] may pass unobserved, especially if they can content themselves with low life, where fear may oblige their favourites to secrecy. There wants only a very lewd constitution, a very bad heart, and a moderate understanding to make this conduct easy, and I do not doubt it has been practiced by many prudes beside her I am now speaking of.

You may be sure I did not communicate these reflections. The first word I spoke was to desire Signor Carlo to sheath his poniard, not being pleased with its glittering. He did so very readily, begging my pardon for

[1] *castle ... house* Because Montagu's home stood on the site of an old castle.

[2] *closet* Inner chamber or private room or study.

[3] *stiletto* Short, thick dagger.

[4] *chère entière* French: complete repast. Here, with a sexual connotation. Cf. John Cleland's *Fanny Hill*, Part 10.

[5] *passe-partout key* Master key.

[6] *Queen ... eternity* In "The Merchant's Tale" of Chaucer's *Canterbury Tales*.

[7] *ex tempore* Without premeditation.

not having done it on my first appearance, saying he did not know what he did; and indeed he had the countenance and gesture of a man distracted. I did not endeavor a defense that seemed to me impossible, but represented to him as well as I could the crime of a murder which, if he could justify before men, was still a crying sin before God, the disgrace he would bring on himself and posterity, and irreparable injury he would do his eldest daughter (a pretty girl of 15 that I knew he was extreme fond of). I added that if he thought it proper to part from his lady he might easily find a pretext for it some months hence, and that it was as much his interest as hers to conceal this affair from the knowledge of the world. I could not presently make him taste these reasons, and was forced to stay there near five hours (almost from five to ten at night) before I durst leave them together, which I would not do till he had sworn in the most serious manner he would make no future attempt on her life. I was content with his oath, knowing him to be very devout, and found I was not mistaken.

How the matter was made up between them afterwards I know not, but 'tis now two year since it happened, and all appearances remaining as if it had never been. The secret is in very few hands; his brother, being at that time at Brescia, I believe knows nothing of it to this day. The chambermaid and myself have preserved the strictest silence, and the lady retains the satisfaction of insulting all her acquaintance on the foundation of a spotless character that only she can boast in the parish, where she is most heartily hated, from these airs of impertinent virtue and another very essential reason, being the best dressed woman amongst them, though one of the plainest in her figure.

The discretion of the chambermaid in fetching me, which possibly saved her mistress's life, and her taciturnity since, I fancy appears very remarkable to you, and is what would certainly never happen in England. The first part of her behavior deserves great praise, coming of her own accord, and inventing so decent an excuse for her admittance; but her silence may be attributed to her knowing very well that any servant that presumes to talk of his master will most certainly be incapable of talking at all in a short time, their lives being entirely in the power of their superiors. I do not mean by law but by custom, which has full as much force. If one of them was killed, it would either never be enquired into at all or very slightly passed over; yet it seldom happens, and I know no instance of it, which I think is owing to the great submission of domestics, who are sensible of their dependence, and the national temper not being hasty and never enflamed by wine, drunkenness being a vice abandoned to the vulgar and spoke of with greater detestation than murder, which is mentioned with as little concern as a drinking bout in England, and is almost as frequent. It was extreme shocking to me at my first coming, and still gives me a sort of horror, though custom has in some degree familiarized it to my imagination. Robbery would be pursued with great vivacity and punished with the utmost rigour, therefore is very rare, though stealing is in daily practice; but as all the peasants are suffered the use of firearms, the slightest provocation is sufficient to shoot, and they see one of their own species lie dead before them with as little remorse as a hare or a partridge; and, when revenge spurs them on, with much more pleasure. A dissertation on this subject would engage me in a discourse not proper for the post.

My compliments to Lord Bute. His kindness to you ought to obtain the friendship of all that love you. My blessing to your little ones. Think of me as ever your most affectionate mother,

M. Wortley.

Have you received my letter to my sister Mar?

TO SIR JAMES STEUART[1]

[14 November 1758]

This letter will be solely to you, and I desire you would not communicate it to Lady Fanny. She is the best woman in the world, and I would by no means make her uneasy, but there will be such strange things in it that the Talmud or the Revelations are not half so mysterious. What these prodigies portend, God knows, but I never should have suspected half the wonders I see

[1] *James Steuart* Scottish lawyer who, along with his wife, Lady Fanny, had resided briefly in Italy, where the couple developed a close friendship with Montagu. They were now settled in Germany.

before my eyes, and am convinced of the necessity of the repeal of the Witch Act[1] (as it is commonly called). I mean, to speak correctly, the tacit permission given to witches, so scandalous to all good Christians, though I tremble to think of it for my own interests. It is certain the British Islands have always been strangely addicted to this diabolical intercourse, of which I dare swear you know many instances; but since this public encouragement given to it, I am afraid there will not be an old woman in the nation entirely free from suspicion. The Devil rages more powerfully than ever: you will believe me when I assure you the great and learned English minister is turned Methodist, several duels have been fought in the Place of Saint Marc for the charms of his excellent lady, and I have been seen flying in the air in the figure of Julian Cox,[2] whose history is related with so much candour and truth by the pious pen of Joseph Glanville, chaplain to King Charles. I know you young rakes make a jest of all those things, but I think no good body can doubt of a relation so well attested. She was about 70 years old (very near my age), and the whole sworn to before Judge Archer, 1663: very well worth reading but rather too long for a letter.

You know (wretch that I am) 'tis one of my wicked maxims to make the best of a bad bargain, and I have said publicly that every period of life has its privileges and that even the most despicable creatures alive may find some pleasures. Now observe this comment: who are the most despicable creatures? Certainly, old women. What pleasure can an old woman take? Only witchcraft. I think this argument as clear as any of the devout Bishop of Cloyne's's[3] metaphysics; this being decided in a full congregation of saints, only such atheists as you and Lady Fanny can deny it. I own all the facts, as many witches have done before me, and go every night in a public manner astride upon a black cat to a meeting where you are suspected to appear. This last article is not sworn to, it being doubtful in what manner our clandestine midnight correspondence is carried on. Some think it treasonable, others lewd (don't tell Lady Fanny), but all agree there was something very odd and unaccountable in such sudden likings. I confess, as I said before, it is witchcraft. You won't wonder I do not sign (notwithstanding all my impudence) such dangerous truths. Who knows the consequence? The Devil is said to desert his votaries.

P.S. Fribourg, who you enquire after so kindly, is turned beau garçon and actually kept by the finest lady in Venice. Doctor Moro robs on the highway, and Antonio[4] sings at the opera. Would you desire better witchcraft? This to be continued.

Nota bene.[5] You have dispossessed me of the real devils who haunted me: I mean the nine Muses.

[1] *Witch Act* Under George II a new Witch Act ended the practice that had been instituted by James I of hanging those convicted of witchcraft. Instead, convicted witches could be imprisoned for up to a year and forced to stand in the pillory.

[2] *Julian Cox* Woman who was executed as a witch in 1663.

[3] *Bishop of Cloyne* Philosopher George Berkeley.

[4] *Fribourg* Montagu's servant; *Doctor Moro* Montagu's secretary; *Antonio* Eighty-six year old head of a Venetian family and a friend of Montagu's.

[5] *Nota bene* Observe particularly.

Eliza Haywood

1693 – 1756

One of the most prolific writers of the eighteenth century is also one of the most elusive. Little is known of Eliza Haywood's private life, yet she produced more than 80 titles and wrote some of the most popular works of the first half of the century. Her fame began in 1719 when she published *Love in Excess; or, the Fatal Inquiry*, an amorous tale of adventure that became one of the best selling books of the early eighteenth century.

Born in London as Eliza Fowler, probably but not certainly in 1693, Haywood left London and married by 1714, when she began a theater apprenticeship in Dublin under the name Eliza Haywood. We know that she had two children (precisely when is unknown), and that her marriage had ended by 1717 when she returned to England and toured with various theater companies. One of her few letters suggests that she began writing to support herself and her children.

Love in Excess began a writing career that progressed at an astonishing pace: Haywood averaged five titles a year in the 1720s and produced two collected editions by 1725. From 1721 until 1724 she had a romantic relationship with the poet Richard Savage, and from 1724 probably until her death she lived with William Hatchett, a minor playwright and actor. Little else is known of her domestic life. Her first biographer, David Erskine Baker, claimed in 1764 that she deliberately obscured her history: "from a supposition of some improper liberties being taken with her character after death, by the intermixture of truth and falsehood with her history, she laid a solemn injunction on a person who was well acquainted with all the particulars of it, not to communicate to any one the least circumstance relating to her."

Although the details of Haywood's personal life remain vague, her public persona was well known. Her dozens of amorous fictions published in the 1720s and 1730s found a wide audience; she was dubbed the "Great arbitress of passion" by one contemporary poet, and "Mrs. Novel" by Henry Fielding (in his 1730 play *The Author's Farce*). *Fantomina* is representative of this early fiction. First published in her 1725 collection *Secret Histories, Novels, and Poems*, it explores male inconstancy, female agency, and sexual adventure, as well as the social repercussions of such adventure.

In the 1730s the pace of Haywood's fiction writing slowed as she returned to the theater. From 1729 to 1737 she wrote or co-wrote several plays and acted in at least six. Collaborating with William Hatchett, she produced the successful *Opera of Operas* in 1733, a musical adaptation of Fielding's *Tragedy of Tragedies.* During this period she also anonymously published *The Adventures of Eovaii, Princess of Ivajeo* (1736), a satire of English politics and—in particular—of Sir Robert Walpole, Prime Minister from 1721 to 1742. In subsequent years she translated works from French, wrote a 1741 parody of *Pamela*, became a publisher herself, continued to act in the theater, and in 1749 wrote a controversial political pamphlet that led to her arrest (though not her prosecution).

In the last fifteen years of her life, Haywood's writing became more domestic, moral, and didactic. Novels such as *The History of Miss Betsy Thoughtless* (1751) and *The History of Jemmy and Jenny Jessamy* (1753) endeavor not only to entertain readers but also to instruct them in such matters as courtship and marriage. She also published the first periodical written for women, *The Female*

Spectator, which appeared in 24 installments from April 1744 to May 1746 and touched on philosophical, political, and scientific, as well as literary, matters. In 1756 she began a new periodical entitled *The Young Lady*, but she announced in an early issue that she was too ill to continue with the journal. She died shortly thereafter, on 25 February 1756.

It was typical of the time that, however widely a woman writer might be read, she would also be criticized for having made writing her profession. In *The Dunciad* (1728) for example, Alexander Pope satirized those he considered to be hack writers, and castigated Haywood in particular. But other contemporaries acknowledged her talent, and present-day critics are increasingly recognizing her important contribution to the development of the novel. Haywood was one of the earliest novelists to explore inner states and feelings. Her reputation may well continue to grow: scholars continue to attribute newly-found titles to this prolific pioneer of the novel.

Fantomina: or, Love in a Maze

Eliza Haywood was first famous as an author of amatory fiction, her work raising the popularity of an already popular genre; *Fantomina: or, Love in a Maze* (1725) was one of her many novels of this kind. Although amatory fictions were read by both genders, such works were considered to be books by and for women, focusing on what was thought to be the female reader's greatest interest: sexual and romantic love. In their real lives, the women readers of books like *Fantomina* were disadvantaged by the sexual mores of the time. Celibacy before marriage was the rule—but it was a rule not enforced for men, while a woman discovered to have broken it faced disgrace. Social success (and financial stability) also required that an unmarried woman attract a husband without appearing improperly forward—and without attracting socially dangerous sexual advances. Amatory fictions offered imaginary escape from these confining expectations, but they also illustrated the dangers facing women who transgressed; the stories were presented as means of moral instruction. Whatever delight a reader might take in accounts of scandalous sexuality would be tempered by the story line. Unhappy consequences were inevitably imposed on women characters who acted upon their desires.

While its engagement with romance and sexuality certainly places *Fantomina* in the genre of amatory fiction, the work toys with the expectations of its eighteenth-century readers. Many amatory fictions—including some of Haywood's own—follow a formula in which an innocent woman becomes the passive victim of a deceitful, experienced man. In this formula, the seducer, having captured the woman's virtue, quickly tires of and abandons her; she weeps and protests, but is helpless to prevent him. In *Fantomina*, the unnamed heroine takes an atypically active role in orchestrating her own seduction, and her use of careful deception and disguise complicates the usual pattern of innocence betrayed.

An eighteenth-century audience may also have found *Fantomina* shockingly unclear in the moral attitude it displays toward its characters. The unnamed heroine's unwanted pregnancy and banishment to a French monastery may look like onerous consequences to present-day readers, but the heroine gets off lightly by the standards of the genre; usually, such amatory fictions ended with the heroine's repentance, death, or abject misery, with explicit didactic commentary from the narrator to emphasize the moral point. Some eighteenth-century readers may well have interpreted *Fantomina*'s ending as a just punishment for the heroine. But others might have entertained the thought that banishment to a convent would not necessarily mean an end to the sexual life of a literary character; nuns are a common subject in pornographic writing of the period, and in a number of amatory works of the period, lovers escape from convents.

It is worth noting that the heroine of *Fantomina* is only able to escape the social consequences of her actions for as long as she does because she has financial and personal freedom almost unheard-of for a real woman in the 1720s. The first three disguises she adopts—a well-off woman raped by a suitor and abandoned to a likely fate of prostitution, a maid exploited by her employer, and a widow at risk of poverty because inheritance laws do not protect her rights—provide a somewhat more realistic vision of women's circumstances in the period.

Haywood called *Fantomina* a "Masquerade Novel," and its central theme of disguise reflects the early eighteenth century's preoccupation with masks. Beginning in the late seventeenth century, women often wore masks to the theater; soon after, they began to wear them with elaborate costumes to masquerade balls, which reached a height of popularity in the 1720s. The concealed identity that masks represented offered women a respite from social conventions, allowing them to act relatively freely without fear for their reputations. For men, masked women possessed the allure of mystery; as William Wycherley dryly observed, "a woman masked, like a covered dish, gives a man curiosity and appetite." Perhaps not surprisingly, masquerades were an object of moral condemnation and quickly became associated with unsavory sexuality; at the time Haywood was writing *Fantomina*, the mask was widely considered a symbol of prostitution.

⌘⌘⌘

Fantomina: or, Love in a Maze

In love the victors from the vanquished fly.
They fly that wound, and they pursue that die.[1]

WALLER.

A young lady of distinguished birth, beauty, wit, and spirit happened to be in a box[2] one night at the playhouse, where, though there were a great number of celebrated toasts,[3] she perceived several gentlemen extremely pleased themselves with entertaining a woman who sat in a corner of the pit and, by her air and manner of receiving them, might easily be known to be one of those who come there for no other purpose than to create acquaintance with as many as seem desirous of it. She could not help testifying her contempt of men who, regardless either of the play or circle,[4] threw away their time in such a manner to some ladies that sat by her. But they, either less surprised by being more accustomed to such sights than she—who had been bred for the most part in the country—or not of a disposition to consider anything very deeply, took but little notice of it. She still thought of it, however, and the longer she reflected on it, the greater was her wonder that men, some of whom she knew were accounted to have wit, should have tastes so very depraved. This excited a curiosity in her to know in what manner these creatures were addressed. She was young, a stranger to the world and, consequently, to the dangers of it, and, having nobody in town at that time to whom she was obliged to be accountable for her actions, did in everything as her inclinations or humours[5] rendered most agreeable to her. Therefore she thought it not in the least a fault to put in practice a little whim which came immediately into her head, to dress herself as near as she could in the fashion of those women who make sale of their favours and set herself in the way of being accosted as such a one, having at that time no other aim than the gratification of an innocent curiosity. She no sooner designed this frolic than she put it in execution and, muffling her hoods over her face, went the next night into the gallery-box[6] and, practicing as much as she had observed at that distance the behaviour of that woman, was not long before she found her disguise had answered the ends she wore it for. A crowd of purchasers of all degrees and capacities were in a moment gathered about her, each endeavouring to out-bid the other in offering her a price for her embraces. She listened to them all and was not a little diverted in her mind at the disappointment she should give to so many, each of which

[1] *"In love ... die"* Edmund Waller, "To A.H., of the Different Successes of Their Loves" (1645), ll. 27–28.

[2] *box* Private compartment at a theater.

[3] *celebrated toasts* Beautiful women (toasted with drinks by men).

[4] *circle* I.e., dress circle; the lower gallery, with the most expensive seats.

[5] *humours* Temperaments.

[6] *gallery-box* Box in the higher and less expensive gallery.

thought himself secure of gaining her. She was told by them all that she was the most lovely woman in the world, and some cried, "Gad, she is mighty like my fine Lady Such-a-one"—naming her own name. She was naturally vain and received no small pleasure in hearing herself praised, though in the person of another and a supposed prostitute, but she dispatched as soon as she could all that had hitherto attacked her when she saw the accomplished Beauplaisir was making his way through the crowd as fast as he was able, to reach the bench she sat on. She had often seen him in the drawing room;[1] had talked with him (but then her quality and reputed virtue kept him from using her with that freedom she now expected he would do); and had discovered something in him which had made her often think she should not be displeased if he would abate some part of his reserve. Now was the time to have her wishes answered. He looked in her face and fancied, as many others had done, that she very much resembled that lady whom she really was, but the vast disparity there appeared between their characters prevented him from entertaining even the most distant thought that they could be the same. He addressed her at first with the usual salutations of her pretended profession, as, "Are you engaged, Madam? Will you permit me to wait on you home after the play? By Heaven, you are a fine girl! How long have you used this house?" and such like questions. But, perceiving she had a turn of wit and a genteel manner in her raillery[2] beyond what is frequently to be found among those wretches who are for the most part gentlewomen but by necessity, few of them having had an education suitable to what they affect to appear, he changed the form of his conversation and showed her it was not because he understood no better that he had made use of expressions so little polite. In fine,[3] they were infinitely charmed with each other. He was transported[4] to find so much beauty and wit in a woman who he doubted not but on very easy terms he might enjoy, and she found a vast deal of pleasure in conversing with him in this free and unrestrained manner. They passed their time all the play with an equal satisfaction, but when it was over, she found herself involved in a difficulty which before never entered into her head, but which she knew not well how to get over. The passion he professed for her was not of that humble nature which can be content with distant adorations. He resolved not to part from her without the gratifications of those desires she had inspired and, presuming on the liberties which her supposed function allowed of, told her she must either go with him to some convenient house of his procuring or permit him to wait on her to her own lodgings. Never had she been in such a dilemma. Three or four times did she open her mouth to confess her real quality,[5] but the influence of her ill stars prevented it by putting an excuse into her head which did the business as well, and at the same time did not take from her the power of seeing and entertaining him a second time with the same freedom she had done this. She told him she was under obligations to a man who maintained her and whom she durst not disappoint, having promised to meet him that night at a house hard by.[6] This story, so like what those ladies sometimes tell, was not at all suspected by Beauplaisir. And, assuring her he would be far from doing her a prejudice, he desired that in return for the pain he should suffer in being deprived of her company that night, that she would order her affairs so as not to render him unhappy the next. She gave a solemn promise to be in the same box on the morrow evening, and they took leave of each other—he to the tavern to drown the remembrance of his disappointment, she in a hackney-chair[7] hurried home to indulge contemplation on the frolic she had taken, designing nothing less on her first reflections than to keep the promise she had made him, and hugging herself with joy that she had the good luck to come off undiscovered.

But these cogitations[8] were but of a short continuance; they vanished with the hurry of her spirits and were succeeded by others vastly different and ruinous. All the charms of Beauplaisir came fresh into her mind; she languished, she almost died for another opportunity of conversing with him, and not all the admonitions of

[1] *drawing room* Court assembly.

[2] *raillery* Banter.

[3] *In fine* In short.

[4] *transported* Enraptured.

[5] *quality* High social status.

[6] *hard by* Near by.

[7] *hackney-chair* One-seated vehicle for hire, carried on poles.

[8] *cogitations* Thoughts.

her discretion were effectual to oblige her to deny laying hold of that which offered itself the next night. She depended on the strength of her virtue to bear her safe through trials more dangerous than she apprehended this to be, and never having been addressed by him as Lady, was resolved to receive his devoirs as a town-mistress,[1] imagining a world of satisfaction to herself in engaging him in the character of such a one, and in observing the surprise he would be in to find himself refused by a woman who he supposed granted her favours without exception. Strange and unaccountable were the whimsies she was possessed of, wild and incoherent her desires, unfixed and undetermined her resolutions, but in that of seeing Beauplaisir in the manner she had lately done. As for her proceedings with him, or how a second time to escape him without discovering who she was, she could neither assure herself, nor whether or not in the last extremity she would do so. Bent, however, on meeting him, whatever should be the consequence, she went out some hours before the time of going to the playhouse and took lodgings in a house not very far from it, intending that, if he should insist on passing some part of the night with her, to carry him there, thinking she might with more security to her honour entertain him at a place where she was mistress than at any of his own choosing.

The appointed hour being arrived, she had the satisfaction to find his love in his assiduity.[2] He was there before her, and nothing could be more tender than the manner in which he accosted her. But from the first moment she came in to that of the play being done, he continued to assure her no consideration should prevail with him to part from her again, as she had done the night before, and she rejoiced to think she had taken that precaution of providing herself with a lodging to which she thought she might invite him without running any risk, either of her virtue or reputation. Having told him she would admit of his accompanying her home, he seemed perfectly satisfied and, leading her to the place, which was not above twenty houses distant, would have ordered a collation[3] to be brought after them. But she would not permit it, telling him she was not one of those who suffered themselves to be treated at their own lodgings, and as soon she was come in, sent a servant belonging to the house to provide a very handsome supper and wine, and everything was served to table in a manner which showed the director neither wanted[4] money, nor was ignorant how it should be laid out.

This proceeding, though it did not take from him the opinion that she was what she appeared to be, yet it gave him thoughts of her which he had not before. He believed her a mistress, but believed her to be one of a superior rank, and began to imagine the possession of her would be much more expensive than at first he had expected. But, not being of a humour to grudge anything for his pleasures, he gave himself no farther trouble than what were occasioned by fears of not having money enough to reach her price about him.

Supper being over, which was intermixed with a vast deal of amorous conversation, he began to explain himself more than he had done, and both by his words and behaviour let her know he would not be denied that happiness the freedoms she allowed had made him hope. It was in vain she would have retracted the encouragement she had given; in vain she endeavoured to delay till the next meeting the fulfilling of his wishes. She had now gone too far to retreat. He was bold; he was resolute; she, fearful, confused, altogether unprepared to resist in such encounters, and rendered more so by the extreme liking she had to him. Shocked, however, at the apprehension of really losing her honour, she struggled all she could, and was just going to reveal the whole secret of her name and quality when the thoughts of the liberty he had taken with her, and those he still continued to prosecute, prevented her with representing the danger of being exposed and the whole affair made a theme for public ridicule. Thus much, indeed, she told him: that she was a virgin and had assumed this manner of behaviour only to engage him. But that he little regarded, or if he had, would have been far from obliging him to desist. Nay, in the present burning eagerness of desire, 'tis probable that had he been acquainted both

[1] *receive … town-mistress* To receive his addresses as a prostitute would.

[2] *in his assiduity* In devoted attendance.

[3] *collation* Light meal.

[4] *wanted* Lacked.

with who and what she really was, the knowledge of her birth would not have influenced him with respect sufficient to have curbed the wild exuberance of his luxurious[1] wishes, or made him in that longing—that impatient moment—change the form of his addresses. In fine, she was undone, and he gained a victory so highly rapturous that, had he known over whom, scarce could he have triumphed more. Her tears, however, and the distraction she appeared in after the ruinous ecstasy was past, as it heightened his wonder, so it abated his satisfaction. He could not imagine for what reason a woman who, if she intended not to be a mistress, had counterfeited the part of one and taken so much pains to engage him, should lament a consequence which she could not but expect—and, till the last test, seemed inclinable to grant—and was both surprised and troubled at the mystery. He omitted nothing that he thought might make her easy and, still retaining an opinion that the hope of interest[2] had been the chief motive which had led her to act in the manner she had done (and believing that she might know so little of him as to suppose, now she had nothing left to give he might not make that recompence she expected for her favours), to put her out of that pain, he pulled out of his pocket a purse of gold, entreating her to accept of that as an earnest of what he intended to do for her, assuring her with ten thousand protestations that he would spare nothing which his whole estate could purchase to procure her content and happiness. This treatment made her quite forget the part she had assumed and, throwing it from her with an air of disdain, "Is this a reward," said she, "for condescensions such as I have yielded to? Can all the wealth you are possessed of make a reparation for my loss of honour? Oh no, I am undone beyond the power of heaven itself to help me!" She uttered many more such exclamations, which the amazed Beauplaisir heard without being able to reply to, till, by degrees sinking from that rage of temper, her eyes resumed their softening glances and, guessing at the consternation he was in, "No, my dear Beauplaisir," added she, "your love alone can compensate for the shame you have involved me in. Be you sincere and constant, and I hereafter shall, perhaps, be satisfied with my fate and forgive myself the folly that betrayed me to you."

Beauplaisir thought he could not have a better opportunity than these words gave him of enquiring who she was and wherefore she had feigned herself to be of a profession which he was now convinced she was not. And after he had made her a thousand vows of an affection as inviolable and ardent[3] as she could wish to find in him, entreated she would inform him by what means his happiness had been brought about, and also to whom he was indebted for the bliss he had enjoyed. Some remains of yet unextinguished modesty and sense of shame made her blush exceedingly at this demand. But, recollecting herself in a little time, she told him so much of the truth as to what related to the frolic she had taken of satisfying her curiosity in what manner mistresses of the sort she appeared to be were treated by those who addressed them, but forbore discovering her true name and quality for the reasons she had done before—resolving, if he boasted of this affair he should not have it in his power to touch her character. She therefore said she was the daughter of a country gentleman who was come to town to buy clothes and that she was called Fantomina. He had no reason to distrust the truth of this story and was therefore satisfied with it, but did not doubt by the beginning of her conduct but that in the end she would be in reality the thing she so artfully had counterfeited, and had good nature enough to pity the misfortunes he imagined would be her lot. But to tell her so or offer his advice in that point was not his business, at least as yet.

They parted not till towards morning, and she obliged him to a willing vow of visiting her the next day at three in the afternoon. It was too late for her to go home that night; therefore, she contented herself with lying there. In the morning she sent for the woman of the house to come up to her and, easily perceiving by her manner that she was a woman who might be influenced by gifts, made her a present of a couple of broad pieces[4] and desired her that if the gentleman who had been there the night before should ask any questions

[1] *luxurious* Concerned with extravagant pleasures.

[2] *interest* Profit.

[3] *ardent* Passionate.

[4] *broad pieces* Coins worth twenty shillings each, a substantial sum for a prostitute but not for a gentlewoman.

concerning her, that he should be told she was lately come out of the country, had lodged there about a fortnight,[1] and that her name was Fantomina. "I shall," also added she, "lie but seldom here, nor, indeed, ever come but in those times when I expect to meet him. I would therefore have you order it so that he may think I am but just gone out if he should happen by any accident to call when I am not here, for I would not for the world have him imagine I do not constantly lodge here." The landlady assured her she would do everything as she desired and gave her to understand she wanted not the gift of secrecy.

Everything being ordered at this home for the security of her reputation, she repaired to the other, where she easily excused to an unsuspecting aunt, with whom she boarded, her having been abroad all night, saying she went with a gentleman and his lady in a barge to a little country seat[2] of theirs up the river, all of them designing to return the same evening, but that one of the bargemen happening to be taken ill on the sudden, and no other waterman to be got that night, they were obliged to tarry till morning. Thus did this lady's wit and vivacity assist her in all but where it was most needful. She had discernment to foresee and avoid all those ills which might attend the loss of her reputation, but was wholly blind to those of the ruin of her virtue, and, having managed her affairs so as to secure the one, grew perfectly easy with the remembrance she had forfeited the other. The more she reflected on the merits of Beauplaisir, the more she excused herself for what she had done. And the prospect of that continued bliss she expected to share with him took from her all remorse for having engaged in an affair which promised her so much satisfaction, and in which she found not the least danger of misfortune. "If he is really," said she, to herself, "the faithful, the constant lover he has sworn to be, how charming will be our amour? And if he should be false, grow satiated like other men, I shall but, at the worst, have the private vexation of knowing I have lost him—the intrigue being a secret, my disgrace will be so too. I shall hear no whispers as I pass, 'She is forsaken.' The odious word *forsaken* will never wound my ears, nor will my wrongs excite either the mirth or pity of the talking world. It will not be even in the power of my undoer himself to triumph over me. And while he laughs at and perhaps despises the fond, the yielding Fantomina, he will revere and esteem the virtuous, the reserved Lady." In this manner did she applaud her own conduct and exult with the imagination that she had more prudence than all her sex beside. And it must be confessed indeed that she preserved an oeconomy[3] in the management of this intrigue beyond what almost any woman but herself ever did: in the first place, by making no person in the world a confidante in it, and in the next, in concealing from Beauplaisir himself the knowledge who she was. For though she met him three or four days in a week at that lodging she had taken for that purpose, yet as much as he employed her time and thoughts, she was never missed from any assembly she had been accustomed to frequent. The business of her love has engrossed her till six in the evening, and before seven she has been dressed in a different habit[4] and in another place. Slippers and a nightgown[5] loosely flowing has been the garb in which he has left the languishing Fantomina; laced and adorned with all the blaze of jewels has he, in less than an hour after, beheld at the royal chapel, the palace gardens, drawing room, opera, or play, the haughty, awe-inspiring lady. A thousand times has he stood amazed at the prodigious likeness between his little mistress and this court beauty, but was still as far from imagining they were the same as he was the first hour he had accosted her in the playhouse, though it is not impossible but that her resemblance to this celebrated lady might keep his inclination alive something longer than otherwise they would have been, and that it was to the thoughts of this as he supposed unenjoyed charmer she owed in great measure the vigour of his latter caresses.

But he varied not so much from his sex as to be able to prolong desire to any great length after possession. The rifled charms of Fantomina soon lost their poignancy[6] and grew tasteless and insipid. And when, the

[1] *fortnight* Two weeks.

[2] *seat* Residence.

[3] *oeconomy* Frugal and judicious conduct; discretion.

[4] *habit* Outfit.

[5] *nightgown* Evening dress.

[6] *poignancy* I.e., intensity.

season of the year inviting the company to the Bath,[1] she offered to accompany him, he made an excuse to go without her. She easily perceived his coldness and the reason why he pretended her going would be inconvenient, and endured as much from the discovery as any of her sex could do. She dissembled it, however, before him, and took her leave of him with the show of no other concern than his absence occasioned. But this she did to take from him all suspicion of her following him, as she intended and had already laid a scheme for. From her first finding out that he designed to leave her behind, she plainly saw it was for no other reason than that being tired of her conversation, he was willing to be at liberty to pursue new conquests and, wisely considering that complaints,[2] tears, swoonings, and all the extravagancies which women make use of in such cases have little prevailance over a heart inclined to rove, and only serve to render those who practice them more contemptible by robbing them of that beauty which alone can bring back the fugitive lover, she resolved to take another course. And, remembering the height of transport[3] she enjoyed when the agreeable Beauplaisir kneeled at her feet, imploring her first favours, she longed to prove[4] the same again. Not but a woman of her beauty and accomplishments might have beheld a thousand in that condition Beauplaisir had been, but with her sex's modesty she had not also thrown off another virtue equally valuable, though generally unfortunate: constancy. She loved Beauplaisir. It was only he whose solicitations could give her pleasure and, had she seen the whole species despairing, dying for her sake, it might, perhaps, have been a satisfaction to her pride, but none to her more tender inclination. Her design was once more to engage him. To hear him sigh, to see him languish, to feel the strenuous pressures of his eager arms, to be compelled, to be sweetly forced to what she wished with equal ardour was what she wanted and what she had formed a stratagem[5] to obtain, in which she promised herself success.

She no sooner heard he had left the town than, making a pretence to her aunt that she was going to visit a relation in the country, she went towards Bath, attended but by two servants who she found reasons to quarrel with on the road and discharged. Clothing herself in a habit she had brought with her, she forsook the coach and went into a wagon, in which equipage she arrived at Bath. The dress she was in was a round-eared cap, a short red petticoat, and a little jacket of grey stuff.[6] All the rest of her accoutrements were answerable to these, and, joined with a broad country dialect, a rude[7] unpolished air (which she, having been bred in these parts, knew very well how to imitate), with her hair and eyebrows blacked, made it impossible for her to be known or taken for any other than what she seemed. Thus disguised did she offer herself to service in the house where Beauplaisir lodged, having made it her business to find out immediately where he was. Notwithstanding this metamorphosis she was still extremely pretty, and the mistress of the house, happening at that time to want a maid, was very glad of the opportunity of taking her. She was presently received into the family and had a post in it such as she would have chosen had she been left at her liberty: that of making the gentlemen's beds, getting them their breakfasts, and waiting on them in their chambers. Fortune in this exploit was extremely on her side. There were no others of the male sex in the house than an old gentleman who had lost the use of his limbs with the rheumatism and had come thither for the benefit of the waters,[8] and her beloved Beauplaisir, so that she was in no apprehensions of any amorous violence but where she wished to find it. Nor were her designs disappointed. He was fired with the first sight of her, and though he did not presently take any farther notice of her than giving her two or three hearty kisses, yet she, who now understood that language but too well, easily saw they were the prelude to more substantial joys. Coming the next morning to bring his chocolate as he had ordered, he caught her by

[1] *Bath* Resort town and social center for the upper classes.

[2] *complaints* Sorrowful utterances.

[3] *height of transport* Ecstasy.

[4] *prove* Experience.

[5] *stratagem* Scheme.

[6] *The dress … grey stuff* Garments associated with the country; *stuff* Fashionable wool fabric.

[7] *rude* Simple.

[8] *benefit of the waters* Hot springs of Bath.

the pretty leg—which the shortness of her petticoat did not in the least oppose—then, pulling her gently to him, asked her how long she had been at service, how many sweethearts she had, if she had ever been in love, and many other such questions befitting one of the degree she appeared to be, all which she answered with such seeming innocence as more inflamed the amorous heart of him who talked to her. He compelled her to sit in his lap and, gazing on her blushing beauties, which, if possible, received addition from her plain and rural dress, he soon lost the power of containing himself. His wild desires burst out in all his words and actions. He called her "little angel," "cherubim"; swore he must enjoy her though death were to be the consequence; devoured her lips, her breasts with greedy kisses; held to his burning bosom her half-yielding, half-reluctant body; nor suffered her to get loose till he had ravaged all and glutted each rapacious sense with the sweet beauties of the pretty Celia—for that was the name she bore in this second expedition. Generous as liberality itself to all who gave him joy this way, he gave her a handsome sum of gold, which she durst not now refuse for fear of creating some mistrust and losing the heart she so lately had regained. Therefore, taking it with an humble curtsy and a well counterfeited show of surprise and joy, she cried, "O law, Sir! What must I do for all this?" He laughed at her simplicity and, kissing her again, though less fervently than he had done before, bade her not be out of the way when he came home at night. She promised she would not, and very obediently kept her word.

His stay at Bath exceeded not a month, but in that time his supposed country lass had persecuted him so much with her fondness that, in spite of the eagerness with which he first enjoyed her, he was at last grown more weary of her than he had been of Fantomina; which, she perceiving, would not be troublesome but, quitting her service, remained privately in the town till she heard he was on his return, and in that time provided herself of another disguise to carry on a third plot, which her inventing brain had furnished her with, once more to renew his twice-decayed ardours. The dress she had ordered to be made was such as widows wear in their first mourning, which, together with the most afflicted and penitential countenance that ever was seen, was no small alteration to her who used to seem all gaiety. To add to this, her hair, which she was accustomed to wear very loose, both when Fantomina and Celia, was now tied back so strait,[1] and her pinners[2] coming so very forward, that there was none of it to be seen. In fine, her habit and her air[3] were so much changed that she was not more difficult to be known in the rude country girl than she was now in the sorrowful widow.

She knew that Beauplaisir came alone in his chariot[4] to Bath, and in the time of her being servant in the house where he lodged, heard nothing of any body that was to accompany him to London, and hoped he would return in the same manner he had gone. She therefore hired horses and a man to attend her to an inn about ten miles on this side Bath, where, having discharged them, she waited till the chariot should come by, which when it did, and she saw that he was alone in it, she called to him that drove it to stop a moment and, going to the door, saluted the master with these words:

The Distress'd and Wretched, Sir, (*said she*,) never fail to excite Compassion in a generous Mind; and I hope I am not deceiv'd in my Opinion that yours is such:—You have the Appearance of a Gentleman, and cannot, when you hear my Story, refuse that Assistance which is in your Power to give to an unhappy Woman, who without it, may be render'd the most miserable of all created Beings.

IT would not be very easy to represent the Surprise, so odd an Address created in the Mind of him to whom it was made.—She had not the Appearance of one who wanted Charity; and what other Favour she requir'd he cou'd not conceive: But telling her, she might command any Thing in his Power, gave her Encouragement to declare herself in this Manner: You may judge, (*resumed she*,) by the melancholy Garb I am in, that I have lately lost all that ought to be valuable to Womankind; but it is impossible for you to guess the Greatness of my Misfortune, unless you had known my Husband, who

original spelling

[1] *strait* Tightly drawn.

[2] *pinners* Flaps attached to a cap, also called a pinner, that is worn pinned to the head, especially by upper-class women.

[3] *her habit and her air* Her dress and appearance.

[4] *chariot* Lightweight four-wheeled carriage with seats in the back only.

original spelling

was Master of every Perfection to endear him to a Wife's Affections.—But, notwithstanding, I look on myself as the most unhappy of my Sex in out-living him, I must so far obey the Dictates of my Discretion, as to take care of the little Fortune he left: behind him, which being in the Hands of a Brother of his in *London*, will be all carry'd off to *Holland*, where he is going to settle; if I reach not the Town before he leaves it, I am undone for ever.—To which End I left *Bristol*, the Place where we liv'd, hoping to get a Place in the Stage at *Bath*, but they were all taken up before I came; and being, by a Hurt I got in a Fall, render'd incapable of travelling any long Journey on Horseback, I have no Way to go to *London*, and must be inevitably ruin'd in the Loss of all I have on Earth, without you have good Nature enough to admit me to take Part of your Chariot.

Here the feigned widow ended her sorrowful tale, which had been several times interrupted by a parenthesis of sighs and groans, and Beauplaisir, with a complaisant and tender air, assured her of his readiness to serve her in things of much greater consequence than what she desired of him, and told her it would be an impossibility of denying a place in his chariot to a lady who he could not behold without yielding one in his heart. She answered the compliments he made her but with tears, which seemed to stream in such abundance from her eyes that she could not keep her handkerchief from her face one moment. Being come into the chariot, Beauplaisir said a thousand handsome things to persuade her from giving way to so violent a grief, which, he told her, would not only be destructive to her beauty, but likewise her health. But all his endeavours for consolement appeared ineffectual, and he began to think he should have but a dull journey in the company of one who seemed so obstinately devoted to the memory of her dead husband that there was no getting a word from her on any other theme. But, bethinking himself of the celebrated story of the Ephesian matron,[1] it came into his head to make trial whether she who seemed equally susceptible of sorrow might not also be so too of love. And, having began a discourse on almost every other topic, and finding her still incapable of answering, he resolved to put it to the proof if this would have no more effect to rouse her sleeping spirits. With a gay air, therefore, though accompanied with the greatest modesty and respect, he turned the conversation, as though without design, on that joy-giving passion, and soon discovered that was indeed the subject she was best pleased to be entertained with. For, on his giving her a hint to begin upon, never any tongue run more voluble[2] than hers on the prodigious power it had to influence the souls of those possessed of it to actions even the most distant from their intentions, principles, or humours. From that she passed to a description of the happiness of mutual affection, the unspeakable ecstasy of those who meet with equal ardency, and represented it in colours so lively, and disclosed by the gestures (with which her words were accompanied) and the accent of her voice so true a feeling of what she said that Beauplaisir, without being as stupid as he was really the contrary, could not avoid perceiving there were seeds of fire not yet extinguished in this fair widow's soul, which wanted but the kindling breath of tender sighs to light into a blaze. He now thought himself as fortunate as some moments before he had the reverse, and doubted not but that before they parted he should find a way to dry the tears of this lovely mourner to the satisfaction of them both. He did not, however, offer, as he had done to Fantomina and Celia, to urge his passion directly to her, but by a thousand little softening artifices, which he well knew how to use, gave her leave to guess he was enamoured. When they came to the inn where they were to lie, he declared himself somewhat more freely and, perceiving she did not resent it past forgiveness, grew more encroaching still. He now took the liberty of kissing away her tears and catching the sighs as they issued from her lips; telling her if grief was infectious, he was resolved to have his share; protesting he would gladly exchange passions with her and be content to bear her load of sorrow, if she would as willingly ease the burden of his love. She said little in answer to the

[1] *celebrated story ... matron* The story originates in Petronius (d. 65 CE; see *Satyricon*, "Eumolpus," 111–12) and was adapted in 1659 by Sir Walter Charlton. In it, a woman famous for her chastity has sex with a soldier whom she encounters while mourning by the tomb of her recently deceased husband.

[2] *voluble* Fluently.

strenuous pressures with which at last he ventured to enfold her, but not thinking it decent for the character she had assumed to yield so suddenly, and unable to deny both his and her own inclinations, she counterfeited a fainting and fell motionless upon his breast. He had no great notion that she was in a real fit, and the room they supped in happening to have a bed in it, he took her in his arms and laid her on it, believing that whatever her distemper was, that was the most proper place to convey her to. He laid himself down by her and endeavoured to bring her to herself, and she was too grateful to her kind physician at her returning sense to remove from the posture he had put her in, without his leave.

It may perhaps seem strange that Beauplaisir should in such near intimacies continue still deceived. I know there are men who will swear it is an impossibility, and that no disguise could hinder them from knowing a woman they had once enjoyed. In answer to these scruples, I can only say that besides the alteration which the change of dress made in her, she was so admirably skilled in the art of feigning that she had the power of putting on almost what face she pleased, and knew so exactly how to form her behaviour to the character she represented that all the comedians at both playhouses[1] are infinitely short of her performances. She could vary her very glances, tune her voice to accents the most different imaginable from those in which she spoke when she appeared herself. These aids from nature, joined to the wiles of art and the distance between the places where the imagined Fantomina and Celia were, might very well prevent his having any thought that they were the same, or that the fair widow was either of them. It never so much as entered his head, and, though he did fancy he observed in the face of the latter, features which were not altogether unknown to him, yet he could not recollect when or where he had known them. And, being told by her that from her birth she had never removed from Bristol, a place where he never was, he rejected the belief of having seen her and supposed his mind had been deluded by an idea of some other whom she might have a resemblance of.

They passed the time of their journey in as much happiness as the most luxurious gratification of wild desires could make them, and when they came to the end of it, parted not without a mutual promise of seeing each other often. He told her to what place she should direct a letter to him, and she assured him she would send to let him know where to come to her as soon as she was fixed in lodgings.

She kept her promise and, charmed with the continuance of his eager fondness,[2] went not home but into private lodgings, whence she wrote to him to visit her the first opportunity and enquire for the widow Bloomer. She had no sooner dispatched this billet than she repaired to the house where she had lodged as Fantomina, charging the people if Beauplaisir should come there, not to let him know she had been out of town. From thence she wrote to him, in a different hand, a long letter of complaint that he had been so cruel in not sending one letter to her all the time he had been absent, entreated to see him, and concluded with subscribing herself his unalterably affectionate Fantomina. She received in one day answers to both these. The first contained these lines:

To the charming Mrs. Bloomer

It would be impossible, my angel, for me to express the thousandth part of that infinity of transport the sight of your dear letter gave me. Never was woman formed to charm like you. Never did any look like you, write like you, bless like you; nor did ever man adore as I do. Since yesterday we parted, I have seemed a body without a soul, and had you not by this inspiring billet[3] *gave me new life, I know not what by tomorrow I should have been. I will be with you this evening about five. O'tis an age till then! But the cursed formalities of duty oblige me to dine with my Lord, who never rises from table till that hour. Therefore, adieu till then, sweet lovely mistress of the soul and all the faculties of*

Your most faithful,

BEAUPLAISIR.

[1] *comedians at both playhouses* Actors staged by the licensed theaters at Drury Lane and Covent Garden, London.

[2] *eager fondness* Infatuation.

[3] *billet* Note.

The other was in this manner:

To the lovely FANTOMINA

If you were half so sensible as you ought of your own power of charming, you would be assured that to be unfaithful or unkind to you would be among the things that are in their very natures impossibilities. It was my misfortune, not my fault, that you were not persecuted every post with a declaration of my unchanging passion. But I had unluckily forgot the name of the woman at whose house you are, and knew not how to form a direction that it might come safe to your hands. And indeed, the reflection how you might misconstrue my silence brought me to town some weeks sooner than I intended. If you knew how I have languished to renew those blessings I am permitted to enjoy in your society, you would rather pity than condemn

Your ever faithful,

BEAUPLAISIR.

P.S. *I fear I cannot see you till tomorrow; some business has unluckily fallen out that will engross my hours till then. Once more, my dear, adieu.*

"Traitor!" cried she as soon as she had read them. "'Tis thus our silly, fond, believing sex are served when they put faith in man. So had I been deceived and cheated, had I like the rest believed, and sat down mourning in absence, and vainly waiting recovered tendernesses. How do some women," continued she, "make their life a hell, burning in fruitless expectations and dreaming out their days in hopes and fears, then wake at last to all the horror of despair? But I have outwitted even the most subtle of the deceiving kind, and while he thinks to fool me, he is himself the only beguiled person."

She made herself, most certainly, extremely happy in the reflection on the success of her stratagems and, while the knowledge of his inconstancy and levity of nature kept her from having that real tenderness for him she would else have had, she found the means of gratifying the inclination she had for his agreeable person in as full a manner as she could wish. She had all the sweets of love, but as yet had tasted none of the gall,[1] and was in a state of contentment which might be envied by the more delicate.

[1] *gall* Bitterness.

When the expected hour arrived, she found that her lover had lost no part of the fervency[2] with which he had parted from her. But when the next day she received him as Fantomina, she perceived a prodigious difference, which led her again into reflections on the unaccountableness of men's fancies, who still prefer the last conquest only because it is the last. Here was an evident proof of it, for there could not be a difference in merit because they were the same person, but the widow Bloomer was a more new acquaintance than Fantomina, and therefore esteemed more valuable. This, indeed, must be said of Beauplaisir, that he had a greater share of good nature than most of his sex, who, for the most part, when they are weary of an intrigue, break it entirely off without any regard to the despair of the abandoned nymph.[3] Though he retained no more than a bare pity and complaisance for Fantomina, yet, believing she loved him to an excess, he would not entirely forsake her, though the continuance of his visits was now become rather a penance than a pleasure.

The widow Bloomer triumphed some time longer over the heart of this inconstant, but at length her sway was at an end, and she sunk in this character to the same degree of tastelessness[4] as she had done before in that of Fantomina and Celia. She presently perceived it, but bore it as she had always done, it being but what she expected. She had prepared herself for it and had another project in embryo which she soon ripened into action. She did not, indeed, complete it altogether so suddenly as she had done the others, by reason there must be persons employed in it, and the aversion she had to any confidantes in her affairs, and the caution with which she had hitherto acted, and which she was still determined to continue, made it very difficult for her to find a way without breaking through that resolution to compass what she wished. She got over the difficulty at last, however, by proceeding in a manner if possible more extraordinary than all her former behaviour. Muffling herself up in her hood one day, she went into the park about the hour when there are a great

[2] *fervency* Passion.

[3] *nymph* Young woman.

[4] *tastelessness* Dullness.

many necessitous[1] gentlemen who think themselves above doing what they call "little things for a maintenance" walking in the Mall[2] to take a chameleon treat and fill their stomachs with air instead of meat.[3] Two of those, who by their physiognomy[4] she thought most proper for her purpose, she beckoned to come to her and, taking them into a walk more remote from company, began to communicate the business she had with them in these words: "I am sensible, Gentlemen," said she, "that, through the blindness of fortune and partiality of the world, merit frequently goes unrewarded, and that those of the best pretensions[5] meet with the least encouragement. I ask your pardon," continued she, perceiving they seemed surprised, "if I am mistaken in the notion that you two may, perhaps, be of the number of those who have reason to complain of the injustice of fate. But if you are such as I take you for, I have a proposal to make you which may be of some little advantage to you." Neither of them made any immediate answer, but appeared buried in consideration for some moments. At length, "We should, doubtless, Madam," said one of them, "willingly come into any measures to oblige you, provided they are such as may bring us into no danger, either as to our persons or reputations." "That which I require of you," resumed she, "has nothing in it criminal. All that I desire is secrecy in what you are entrusted, and to disguise yourselves in such a manner as you cannot be known if hereafter seen by the person on whom you are to impose. In fine, the business is only an innocent frolic, but if blazed abroad,[6] might be taken for too great a freedom in me. Therefore, if you resolve to assist me, here are five pieces to drink my health and assure you that I have not discoursed you on an affair I design not to proceed in. And when it is accomplished fifty more lie ready for your acceptance." These words and, above all, the money, which was a sum which 'tis probable they had not seen of a long time, made them immediately assent to all she desired and press for the beginning of their employment. But things were not yet ripe for execution, and she told them that the next day they should be let into the secret, charging them to meet her in the same place at an hour she appointed. 'Tis hard to say which of these parties went away best pleased—they, that fortune had sent them so unexpected a windfall, or she, that she had found persons who appeared so well qualified to serve her.

Indefatigable in the pursuit of whatsoever her humour was bent upon, she had no sooner left her new-engaged emissaries than she went in search of a house for the completing her project. She pitched on one very large and magnificently furnished, which she hired by the week, giving them the money beforehand to prevent any inquiries. The next day she repaired to the park, where she met the punctual 'squires of low degree, and, ordering them to follow her to the house she had taken, told them they must condescend to appear like servants, and gave each of them a very rich livery.[7] Then, writing a letter to Beauplaisir in a character vastly different from either of those she had made use of as Fantomina or the fair widow Bloomer, ordered one of them to deliver it into his own hands, to bring back an answer, and to be careful that he sifted out nothing of the truth. "I do not fear," said she, "that you should discover to him who I am, because that is a secret of which you yourselves are ignorant, but I would have you be so careful in your replies that he may not think the concealment springs from any other reasons than your great integrity to your trust. Seem, therefore, to know my whole affairs, and let your refusing to make him partaker in the secret appear to be only the effect of your zeal for my interest and reputation." Promises of entire fidelity on the one side and reward on the other being passed, the messenger made what haste he could to the house of Beauplaisir and, being there told where he might find him, performed exactly the injunction that had been given him. But never astonishment exceeding that which Beauplaisir felt at the reading this billet, in which he found these lines:

To the all-conquering Beauplaisir

[1] *necessitous* In need of money, indigent.

[2] *the Mall* Fashionable pedestrian concourse in St. James's Park, London.

[3] *to take ... meat* The chameleon was believed to live on air.

[4] *physiognomy* Facial appearance.

[5] *pretensions* Claims (here, to merit).

[6] *blazed abroad* Made widely known.

[7] *livery* Uniform.

I imagine not that 'tis a new thing to you to be told you are the greatest charm in nature to our sex. I shall, therefore, not to fill up my letter with any impertinent praises on your wit or person, only tell you that I am infinite in love with both and, if you have a heart not too deeply engaged, should think myself the happiest of my sex in being capable of inspiring it with some tenderness. There is but one thing in my power to refuse you, which is the knowledge of my name, which, believing the sight of my face will render no secret, you must not take it ill that I conceal from you. The bearer of this is a person I can trust. Send by him your answer, but endeavour not to dive into the meaning of this mystery, which will be impossible for you to unravel and at the same time very much disoblige me. But, that you may be in no apprehensions of being imposed on by a woman unworthy of your regard, I will venture to assure you the first and greatest men in the kingdom would think themselves blessed to have that influence over me you have, though unknown to yourself, acquired. But I need not go about to raise your curiosity by giving you any idea of what my person is. If you think fit to be satisfied, resolve to visit me tomorrow about three in the afternoon, and, though my face is hid, you shall not want sufficient demonstration that she who takes these unusual measures to commence a friendship with you is neither old nor deformed. Till then I am,

Yours,

Incognita.

He had scarce come to the conclusion before he asked the person who brought it from what place he came, the name of the lady he served, if she were a wife or widow, and several other questions directly opposite to the directions of the letter. But silence would have availed him as much as did all those testimonies of curiosity. No *Italian bravo*[1] employed in a business of the like nature performed his office with more artifice,[2] and the impatient enquirer was convinced that nothing but doing as he was desired could give him any light into the character of the woman who declared so violent a passion for him. And, little fearing any consequence which could ensue from such an encounter, he resolved to rest satisfied till he was informed of everything from herself, not imagining this Incognita varied so much from the generality of her sex as to be able to refuse the knowledge of anything to the man she loved with that transcendency of passion she professed, and which his many successes with the ladies gave him encouragement enough to believe. He therefore took pen and paper, and answered her letter in terms tender enough for a man who had never seen the person to whom he wrote. The words were as follows:

To the obliging and witty Incognita

Though to tell me I am happy enough to be liked by a woman such as by your manner of writing I imagine you to be is an honour which I can never sufficiently acknowledge, yet I know not how I am able to content myself with admiring the wonders of your wit alone. I am certain a soul like yours must shine in your eyes with a vivacity which must bless all they look on. I shall, however, endeavour to restrain myself in those bounds you are pleased to set me, till by the knowledge of my inviolable fidelity I may be thought worthy of gazing on that heaven I am now but to enjoy in contemplation. You need not doubt my glad compliance with your obliging summons. There is a charm in your lines which gives too sweet an idea of their lovely author to be resisted. I am all impatient for the blissful moment which is to throw me at your feet and give me an opportunity of convincing you that I am,

Your everlasting slave,

Beauplaisir.

Nothing could be more pleased than she to whom it was directed at the receipt of this letter. But when she was told how inquisitive he had been concerning her character and circumstances, she could not forbear laughing heartily to think of the tricks she had played him and applauding her own strength of genius and force of resolution, which by such unthought-of ways could triumph over her lover's inconstancy and render that very temper which to other women is the greatest curse a means to make herself more blessed. "Had he been faithful to me," said she to herself, "either as Fantomina, or Celia, or the widow Bloomer, the most violent passion, if it does not change its object, in time will wither. Possession naturally abates the vigour of

[1] *Italian bravo* Hired soldier; here, a spy.

[2] *artifice* Cunning.

desire, and I should have had at best but a cold, insipid, husband-like lover in my arms. But by these arts of passing on him as a new mistress whenever the ardour (which alone makes love a blessing) begins to diminish for the former one, I have him always raving, wild, impatient, longing, dying. O that all neglected wives and fond abandoned nymphs would take this method! Men would be caught in their own snare and have no cause to scorn our easy, weeping, wailing sex!" Thus did she pride herself, as if secure she never should have any reason to repent the present gaiety of her humour. The hour drawing near in which he was to come, she dressed herself in as magnificent a manner as if she were to be that night at a ball at court, endeavouring to repair the want of those beauties which the vizard[1] should conceal by setting forth the others with the greatest care and exactness. Her fine shape and air and neck appeared to great advantage, and by that which was to be seen of her one might believe the rest to be perfectly agreeable. Beauplaisir was prodigiously charmed, as well with her appearance as with the manner she entertained him. But, though he was wild with impatience for the sight of a face which belonged to so exquisite a body, yet he would not immediately press for it, believing before he left her he should easily obtain that satisfaction. A noble collation being over, he began to sue for[2] the performance of her promise of granting everything he could ask, excepting the sight of her face and knowledge of her name. It would have been a ridiculous piece of affectation in her to have seemed coy in complying with what she herself had been the first in desiring. She yielded without even a show of reluctance. And if there be any true felicity in an amour such as theirs, both here enjoyed it to the full. But not in the height of all their mutual raptures could he prevail on her to satisfy his curiosity with the sight of her face. She told him that she hoped he knew so much of her as might serve to convince him she was not unworthy of his tenderest regard, and if he could not content himself with that which she was willing to reveal, and which was the conditions of their meeting, dear as he was to her she would rather part with him forever than consent to gratify an inquisitiveness which, in her opinion, had no business with his love. It was in vain that he endeavoured to make her sensible of her mistake and that this restraint was the greatest enemy imaginable to the happiness of them both. She was not to be persuaded, and he was obliged to desist his solicitations, though determined in his mind to compass what he so ardently desired before he left the house. He then turned the discourse wholly on the violence of the passion he had for her, and expressed the greatest discontent in the world at the apprehensions of being separated; swore he could dwell forever in her arms, and with such an undeniable earnestness pressed to be permitted to tarry with her the whole night that had she been less charmed with his renewed eagerness of desire, she scarce would have had the power of refusing him. But in granting this request she was not without a thought that he had another reason for making it besides the extremity of his passion, and had it immediately in her head how to disappoint him.

The hours of repose being arrived, he begged she would retire to her chamber, to which she consented but obliged him to go to bed first, which he did not much oppose because he supposed she would not lie in her mask and doubted not but the morning's dawn would bring the wished discovery. The two imagined servants ushered him to his new lodging, where he lay some moments in all the perplexity imaginable at the oddness of this adventure. But she suffered not these cogitations to be of any long continuance. She came, but came in the dark, which, being no more than he expected by the former part of her proceedings, he said nothing of. But as much satisfaction as he found in her embraces, nothing ever longed for the approach of day with more impatience than he did. At last it came, but how great was his disappointment when, by the noises he heard in the street—the hurry of the coaches and the cries of penny-merchants[3]—he was convinced it was night nowhere but with him? He was still in the same darkness as before, for she had taken care to blind the windows in such a manner that not the least chink was left to let in day. He complained of her behaviour in terms that she would not have been able to resist yielding to if she had not been certain it would have been the

[1] *vizard* Mask worn at a masquerade ball.

[2] *to sue for* Beg for, ask for.

[3] *penny-merchants* Street merchants selling cheap goods.

ruin of her passion. She therefore answered him only as she had done before and, getting out of the bed from him, flew out of the room with too much swiftness for him to have overtaken her if he had attempted it. The moment she left him, the two attendants entered the chamber and, plucking down the implements which had screened him from the knowledge of that which he so much desired to find out, restored his eyes once more to day. They attended to assist him in dressing, brought him tea, and by their obsequiousness let him see there was but one thing which the mistress of them would not gladly oblige him in. He was so much out of humour, however, at the disappointment of his curiosity that he resolved never to make a second visit. Finding her in an outer room, he made no scruple of expressing the sense he had of the little trust she reposed in him, and at last plainly told her he could not submit to receive obligations from a lady who thought him uncapable of keeping a secret which she made no difficulty of letting her servants into. He resented; he once more entreated; he said all that man could do to prevail on her to unfold the mystery. But all his adjurations[1] were fruitless, and he went out of the house determined never to re-enter it till she should pay the price of his company with the discovery of her face and circumstances. She suffered him to go with this resolution and doubted not but he would recede from it when he reflected on the happy moments they had passed together. But if he did not, she comforted herself with the design of forming some other stratagem with which to impose on him a fourth time.

She kept the house and her gentlemen-equipage for about a fortnight, in which time she continued to write to him as Fantomina and the widow Bloomer, and received the visits he sometimes made to each. But his behaviour to both was grown so cold that she began to grow as weary of receiving his now insipid caresses as he was of offering them. She was beginning to think in what manner she should drop these two characters when the sudden arrival of her mother, who had been some time in a foreign country, obliged her to put an immediate stop to the course of her whimsical adventures. That lady, who was severely virtuous, did not approve of many things she had been told of the conduct of her daughter. And though it was not in the power of any person in the world to inform her of the truth of what she had been guilty of, yet she heard enough to make her keep her afterwards in a restraint little agreeable to her humour and the liberties to which she had been accustomed.

But this confinement was not the greatest part of the trouble of this now afflicted lady. She found the consequences of her amorous follies would be, without almost a miracle, impossible to be concealed: she was with child. And though she would easily have found means to have screened even this from the knowledge of the world had she been at liberty to have acted with the same unquestionable authority over herself as she did before the coming of her mother, yet now all her invention was at a loss for a stratagem to impose on a woman of her penetration.[2] By eating little, lacing prodigious strait, and the advantage of a great hoop-petticoat, however, her bigness was not taken notice of, and perhaps she would not have been suspected till the time of her going into the country, where her mother designed to send her and from whence she intended to make her escape to some place where she might be delivered with secrecy, if the time of it had not happened much sooner than she expected. A ball being at court, the good old lady was willing she should partake of the diversion of it as a farewell to the town. It was there she was seized with those pangs which none in her condition are exempt from. She could not conceal the sudden rack[3] which all at once invaded her, or, had her tongue been mute, her wildly rolling eyes, the distortion of her features, and the convulsions which shook her whole frame in spite of her would have revealed she laboured under some terrible shock of nature. Everybody was surprised; everybody was concerned; but few guessed at the occasion. Her mother grieved beyond expression, doubted not but she was struck with the hand of death, and ordered her to be carried home in a chair while herself followed in another. A physician was immediately sent for, but he, presently perceiving what was her distemper, called the old lady aside and told her

[1] *adjurations* Entreaties.

[2] *penetration* Discernment; mental acuteness.

[3] *rack* Pain.

it was not a doctor of his sex but one of her own her daughter stood in need of. Never was astonishment and horror greater than that which seized the soul of this afflicted parent at these words. She could not for a time believe the truth of what she heard, but he insisting on it and conjuring her to send for a midwife, she was at length convinced of it. All the pity and tenderness she had been for some moment before possessed of now vanished and were succeeded by an adequate shame and indignation. She flew to the bed where her daughter was lying and, telling her what she had been informed of and which she was now far from doubting, commanded her to reveal the name of the person whose insinuations had drawn her to this dishonour. It was a great while before she could be brought to confess anything, and much longer before she could be prevailed on to name the man whom she so fatally had loved. But the rack of nature growing more fierce, and the enraged old lady protesting no help should be afforded her while she persisted in her obstinacy, she, with great difficulty and hesitation in her speech, at last pronounced the name of Beauplaisir. She had no sooner satisfied her weeping mother than that sorrowful lady sent messengers at the same time for a midwife and for that gentleman who had occasioned the other's being wanted. He happened by accident to be at home and immediately obeyed the summons, though prodigiously surprised what business a lady so much a stranger to him could have to impart. But how much greater was his amazement when, taking him into her closet, she there acquainted him with her daughter's misfortune, of the discovery she had made, and how far he was concerned in it? All the idea one can form of wild astonishment was mean to what he felt. He assured her that the young lady her daughter was a person whom he had never more than at a distance admired, that he had indeed spoke to her in public company, but that he never had a thought which tended to her dishonour. His denials, if possible, added to the indignation she was before inflamed with. She had no longer patience and, carrying him into the chamber where she was just delivered of a fine girl, cried out, "I will not be imposed on. The truth by one of you shall be revealed." Beauplaisir, being brought to the bedside, was beginning to address himself to the lady in it to beg she would clear the mistake her mother was involved in, when she, covering herself with the clothes and ready to die a second time with the inward agitations of her soul, shrieked out, "Oh, I am undone! I cannot live and bear this shame!" But the old lady, believing that now or never was the time to dive into the bottom of this mystery, forcing her to rear her head, told her she should not hope to escape the scrutiny of a parent she had dishonoured in such a manner and, pointing to Beauplaisir, "Is this the gentleman," said she, "to whom you owe your ruin? Or have you deceived me by a fictitious tale?"

"Oh no!" resumed the trembling creature, "He is indeed the innocent cause of my undoing. Promise me your pardon," continued she, "and I will relate the means." Here she ceased, expecting what she would reply, which, on hearing Beauplaisir cry out, "What mean you, Madam? I your undoing, who never harboured the least design on you in my life?" she did in these words: "Though the injury you have done your family," said she, "is of a nature which cannot justly hope forgiveness, yet be assured, I shall much sooner excuse you when satisfied of the truth than while I am kept in a suspense if possible as vexatious as the crime[1] itself is to me." Encouraged by this, she related the whole truth. And 'tis difficult to determine if Beauplaisir or the lady were most surprised at what they heard—he, that he should have been blinded so often by her artifices, or she, that so young a creature should have the skill to make use of them. Both sat for some time in a profound reverie, till at length she broke it first in these words: "Pardon, Sir," said she, "the trouble I have given you. I must confess it was with a design to oblige you to repair the supposed injury you had done this unfortunate girl by marrying her, but now I know not what to say. The blame is wholly hers, and I have nothing to request further of you than that you will not divulge the distracted folly she has been guilty of." He answered her in terms perfectly polite, but made no offer of that which perhaps she expected, though could not, now informed of her daughter's proceedings, demand. He assured her, however, that if she would commit the newborn lady to his care, he would discharge it faithfully. But neither of them would consent to that, and he took his leave, full of cogitations more confused than ever he

[1] *crime* Morally odious act.

had known in his whole life. He continued to visit there to enquire after her health every day, but the old lady perceiving there was nothing likely to ensue from these civilities but perhaps a renewing of the crime, she entreated him to refrain, and as soon as her daughter was in a condition, sent her to a monastery in France, the abbess of which had been her particular friend. And thus ended an intrigue which, considering the time it lasted, was as full of variety as any, perhaps, that many ages has produced.

—1725

IN CONTEXT

The Eighteenth-Century Sexual Imagination

from *A Present for a Servant-Maid* (1743)

Eliza Haywood wrote extensively on romantic and sexual themes not only in her fiction and drama but also in a variety of nonfictional prose contexts. Among the most interesting of these works is *A Present for a Servant-Maid*, which was published anonymously in 1743. It went through several editions and was widely imitated. The work presents advice for young female servants and devotes a considerable amount of attention to the difficulties they are likely to face at the hands of the gentlemen in the households in which they work.

Dear Girls,

I think there cannot be a greater service done to the commonwealth (of which you are a numerous body) than to lay down some general rules for your behaviour, which, if observed, will make your condition as happy to yourselves as it is necessary to others. Nothing can be more melancholy than to hear continual complaints for faults which a very little reflection would render it almost as easy for you to avoid as to commit; most of the mistakes laid to your charge proceeding at first only from a certain indolence and inactivity of the mind, but, if not rectified in time, become habitual and difficult to be thrown off.

As the first step therefore towards being happy in service, you should never enter into a place[1] but with a view of *staying in it*; to which end I think it highly necessary that (as no mistress worth serving will take you without a character[2]) you should also make some enquiry into the place before you suffer yourself to be hired. There are some houses which appear well by *day*, that it would be little safe for a modest maid to sleep in at *night*: I do not mean those coffeehouses, bagnios, &c. which some parts of the town, particularly Covent Garden,[3] abounds with; for in those the very aspect of the persons who keep them are sufficient to show what manner of trade they follow. But houses which have no public show of business, are richly furnished, and where the mistress has an air of the strictest modesty, and perhaps affects a double purity of behaviour, yet under such roofs, and under the sanction of such women as I have described, are too frequently acted such scenes of debauchery as would startle even the owners of some common brothels. Great regard is therefore to be had to the character of the persons who recommend you, and the manner in which you heard of the place; for

[1] *place* Position (of employment).

[2] *character* I.e., a letter of character reference.

[3] *Covent Garden* Where many brothels were located.

those sort of people have commonly their emissaries at inns, watching the coming in of the wagons, and, if they find any pretty girls who come to town to go to service, presently hire them in the name of some person of condition, and by this means the innocent young creature, while she thanks God for her good fortune in being so immediately provided for, is ensnared into the service of the Devil. Here temptations of all kinds are offered her; she is not treated as a servant but a guest; her country habit is immediately stripped off, and a gay modish one put on in the stead; and then the designed victim, willing or unwilling, is exposed to sale to the first lewd supporter of her mistress's grandeur that comes to the house. If she refuses the shameful business for which she was hired, and prefers the preservation of her virtue to all the promises can be made her, which way can she escape? She is immediately confined, close watched, threatened, and at last forced to compliance. Then, by a continued prostitution withered in her bloom, she becomes despised, no longer affords any advantage to the wretch who betrayed her, and is turned out to infamy and beggary, perhaps too with the most loathsome of all diseases, which ends her miserable days in an hospital or workhouse, in case she can be admitted, though some have not had even that favour, but found their deathbed on a dunghill.

… This town at present abounds with such variety of allurements that a young heart cannot be too much upon its guard. It is those expensive ones, I mean, which drain your purse as well as waste your time: such as plays, the Wells,[1] and gardens, and other public shows and entertainments; places which it becomes nobody to be seen often at, and more especially young women in your station. All things that are invented merely for the gratification of luxury, and are of no other service than temporary delight, ought to be shunned by those who have their bread to get. Nor is it any excuse for you that a friend gives you tickets and it costs you nothing; it costs you at least what is more precious than money—your time; not only what you pass in seeing the entertainments, but what the idea and memory of them will take up. They are a kind of delicious poison to the mind, which pleasingly intoxicates and destroys all relish for any thing beside. If you could content yourselves with one sight and no more of any, or even all, these shows, or could you answer that they would engross your thoughts no longer than while you were spectators, the curiosity might be excusable. But it rarely happens that you have this command over yourselves; the music, the dances, the gay clothes and scenes make too strong an impression on the senses not to leave such traces behind as are entirely inconsistent either with good housewifery or the duties of your place. Avoid, therefore, such dangerous amusements.…

Temptations from your Master: Being so much under his command, and obliged to attend him at any hour and at any place he is pleased to call you will lay you under difficulties to avoid his importunities, which it must be confessed are not easy to surmount; yet a steady resolution will enable you; and as a vigorous resistance is less to be expected in your station, your persevering may, perhaps, in time oblige him to desist and acknowledge you have more reason than himself: it is a duty, however, owing to yourself to endeavour it.

Behaviour to him, if a single man: If he happens to be a single man, and is consequently under less restraint, be as careful as you can, opportunities will not be wanting to prosecute his aim; and, as you cannot avoid hearing what he says, must humbly, and in the most modest terms you can, remonstrate to him the sin and shame he would involve you in; and omit nothing to make him sensible how cruel it is to go about to betray a person whom it is his duty to protect. Add that nothing shall ever prevail on you to forfeit your virtue; and take care that all your looks and gestures correspond with what you say: let no wanton smile or light coquette air give him room to suspect you are not so much displeased

[1] *the Wells* Several locations of popular springs, such as Epsom Wells and Lambeth Wells, also offered other entertainments, such as gambling or concerts, in addition to their spas.

with the inclination he has for you as you would seem; for if he once imagines you deny but for the sake of form, it will the more inflame him, and render him more pressing than ever. Let your answers, therefore, be delivered with the greatest sedateness. Show that you are truly sorry, and more ashamed than vain that he finds anything in you to like....

If a married man: Greater caution is still to be observed if he is a married man. As soon as he gives you the least intimation of his design, either by word or action, you ought to keep as much as possible out of his way in order to prevent his declaring himself more plainly; and if, in spite of all your care, he find an opportunity of telling you his mind, you must remonstrate the wrong he would do his wife, and how much he demeans both himself and her by making such an offer to his own servant. If this is ineffectual and he continues to persecute you still, watching you wherever you go, both abroad and at home, and is so troublesome in his importunities that you cannot do your business quietly and regularly, your only way then is to give warning; but be very careful not to let your mistress know the motive of it. That is a point too tender to be touched upon even in the most distant manner, much less plainly told. Such a discovery would not only give her an infinite uneasiness (for in such cases the innocent suffer for the crimes of the guilty), but turn the inclination your master had for you into the extremest hatred. He may endeavour to clear himself by throwing the odium on you, for those who are unjust in one thing will be so in others; and you cannot expect that he who does not scruple to wrong his wife, and indeed his own soul, will make any to take away your reputation, when he imagines his own will be secured by it. He may pretend you threw yourself in his way when he was in liquor, or that, having taken notice of some indecencies in your carriage, and suspecting you were a loose creature, he had only talked a little idly to you as a trial how you would behave; and that it was because he did not persist as you expected, and offer you money, that you had made the discovery—partly out of malice, and partly to give yourself an air of virtue. But though he should not be altogether so unjust and cruel, nor allege any thing of this kind against you, it would be a thing which you never ought to forgive yourself for, if by any imprudent hint you gave occasion for a breach of that amity and confidence which is the greatest blessing of the married state, and when once dissolved, continual jarring and mutual discontent are the unfailing consequence.

from *Venus in the Cloister; or, The Nun in Her Smock* (1725)

At the end of *Fantomina* Haywood refers to the heroine being sent "to a monastery in France." For eighteenth-century readers, such a reference would almost certainly have carried with it connotations of debauchery; sexual activities in French nunneries were a frequent topic in the erotic fiction of the period. One of the best-known examples is *Vénus dans le cloitre, ou la Religieuse en chemise,* a French pornographic novel originally printed in 1683 and translated into English as *Venus in the Cloister* in 1725. The following excerpt is related by Angelica, a 20-year-old nun; she is discussing the activities of Eugenia, another woman in the same nunnery.

Angel. I'll tell thee: I thought I saw one of the workmen enter her cell, and, tripping softly along the dormitory, I made up to her door, which having a large chink between the boards, I saw what I tell you. The first thing I beheld was Eugenia all naked with Frederick sitting by her, holding in his hand—which extremely surprised me, imagining to myself that she could never enjoy the excess of pleasure I afterwards found she did.

Said I to myself, "Lord! what pain must poor Eugenia undergo? How is it possible he should not tear her to pieces?" These were my thoughts, but I suppose he treated her very gently on account of her youth, for she was but bare fifteen. While I was thus busied in my thoughts, I heard Frederick say, "Eugenia, my dear, turn upon your back;" which after she had done, he got up and put his—into her—for my part I was quite frightened when I heard her cry out as if she were in excessive pain. This gave me, as thou may'st well imagine, a great deal of uneasiness, for I did not dare to come in for fear of surprising of them, which might have had perhaps but very ill consequences. However, a moment after I saw her move her legs and embrace her lover with both her arms after such an extraordinary manner as sufficiently expressed the utmost satisfaction.

Frederick was no less pleased with this encounter. "Ha!" said he, "what pleasure does thou give me!" In short, after endeavouring to exceed each other in the amorous combat, they softly sighed, and then for some small space reposed as in an ecstasy. And to show thee what love Eugenia had for her lover, I must tell thee that, notwithstanding this pleasing trance, she could not help now and then giving him many a kiss, nay, I think she kissed him all over, and spoke to him the kindest things in the world, which sufficiently convinced me what excess of joy she then received. This raised a desire in me to taste the same love potion, and indeed I even grew distracted with strong unknown longings and desires. I could not help thinking of it all night, and slept not a moment till the morning, and, by a lucky accident, fortune, who favoured my desires, gave me some consolation.

Print Culture, Stage Culture

CONTEXTS

With the Restoration of the monarchy in 1660 came the reopening of the theater, in whatever buildings could be found, and Charles II's issue of licenses for two playhouses and companies. The major innovations were the proscenium arch (though much action still took place on an apron stage in front of the curtain), movable scenery, and women instead of boys playing the female roles. The new stage scenery took the form of painted flats trundled on and off in grooves in the stage, so that successive scenes—say, in the park, in the street, and indoors—would each be visually represented instead of entirely imagined by the audience. Theater managers sought increasingly ornate, complex scenery to accompany their productions. This was especially so for tragedy, which was often set in exotic locations and extreme circumstances, unlike comedy, which represented the life and society known by experience to the spectators. Updated versions of old plays were popular, and writers assumed a free hand in reshaping the originals. One of the era's most popular productions was Poet Laureate Nahum Tate's version of Shakespeare's *King Lear*, which held the stage for 150 years after its first performance in 1681, after the original had twice been revived unsuccessfully. The excerpt of Tate's *Lear* reprinted here gives a sense of the ways in which Tate changed the original text. While in the parallel scene in Shakespeare's *Lear*, Cordelia is executed after she and Lear are captured, and Lear then dies of grief, here both characters live and see their kingdom restored. Tate also removed the role of the Fool from the play entirely and undercut the character of Cordelia by having her fall in love with Edgar at the opening of the action, so that she has less to lose in defying her father, and acts largely in the interests of her future husband. Tate's *Lear* affirms that, even in the face of enormous adversity, "truth and virtue shall succeed at last." When Cordelia says, "Then there are gods, and virtue is their care," she is asserting precisely the kind of belief that is at least temporarily shaken by Shakespeare's play.

Restoration audiences liked to see good triumph in their tragedies and rightful government restored. In comedy they liked to see the love-lives of the young and fashionable, with a central couple bringing their courtship to a successful conclusion (often overcoming the opposition of their elders to do so). Heroines had to be chaste, but were independent-minded and outspoken; now that they were played by women, there was more mileage for the playwright in disguising them in men's clothes or giving them narrow escapes from rape. Heroes were generally anything but chaste, and sowed their wild oats in plenty before declaring their love to the heroine. To non-theater-goers these comedies were widely seen as licentious and morally suspect, holding up the antics of a small, privileged, and decadent class for admiration. This same class dominated the audiences of Restoration theater—groups of men, and women escorted by men attended, and Colley Cibber (actor, dramatist, theater manager, and later Poet Laureate) notes below, some women wore masks to the theater so that their reaction to bawdy or irreligious language or to overtly sexual scenes could not be observed.

Many middle-class people disapproved of the theater as a playground for the dissipated and irreligious upper classes. Of these, some wanted reform, and others wanted outright suppression. One of the most vociferous objectors to the theater was Jeremy Collier (1650–1726), a clergyman whose pamphlet *A Short View of the Immorality and Profaneness of the English Stage*, excerpted here, attacks writers such as William Congreve, William Wycherley, and John Dryden for their characters' sexual freedom and profane dialogue, and for bringing women and especially clergymen into disrespect. While Collier's *Short View* sparked many replies (particularly from those, such as Congreve, whom he had singled out) and much heated debate, he continued to voice his opinions in a series of pamphlets in the next decade: *A Defense of the Short View* (1698), *A Second Defense of the Short View* (1700), *A Dissuasive from the Playhouse* (1703), and *A Further Vindication of the Short View* (1707).

The excerpt below from a *Spectator* article by Joseph Addison describes the rise in England of what became another form of theater popular among the upper classes, the opera. This new genre, imported from Italy, received mixed reactions in eighteenth-century England. Many were delighted by the music, the star system among the singers, and the elaborate and expensive settings, but others could not understand the appeal of a libretto written in a language incomprehensible to its audience.

During the 1730s the theater became an important vehicle for political satire. John Gay and Henry Fielding set out to attack the government through stage works that proved highly popular. Robert Walpole's government responded to this challenge with the Licensing Act of 1737, the legal language of which is excerpted here. This decreed that all plays were subject to censorship by the office of the Lord Chamberlain, which had to pre-approve anything that would be acted. The act also re-stated the monopoly of the two licensed (or "patent") theaters, Drury Lane and Covent Garden. Both before and after the Act some venues circumvented this decree with illegitimate performances of burlettas, or by adding music to plays and charging admission for the music, rather than for the play. But for the moment the Licensing Act tightened up enforcement, through inspectors who would patrol London to ensure the law was not being broken. Although the Patent Act that limited theater numbers was dropped in 1843, the Lord Chamberlain retained the function of censoring plays until 1968, and movies are still licensed for public showing in most jurisdictions.

While the Licensing Act made life harder for playwrights, the Statute of Anne (1710) was designed to clarify the position of the industry of printing and bookselling (as "publishing" was then generally called). This statute, considered to be the first piece of copyright legislation, both established the "sole right and liberty" of booksellers and printers to sell the new works they had issued, and appeared to place a clear limit (in most cases, 14 years) on that right. In practice (as discussed in the general introduction to this period), it was not until the decision of the House of Lords in *Donaldson v. Beckett* in 1774, that the 14-year limit became a reality. Samuel Johnson's comments on the latter, recorded in Boswell's *Life of Samuel Johnson*, suggest some of its subsequent effects on the book trade.

The next two excerpts given below are responses to the proliferation of other forms of printed material in the late seventeenth and eighteenth centuries. In *Tatler* number 224 Joseph Addison comments on the growth of the advertising industry, while Samuel Johnson, in an article from his *Idler*, gives a disparaging view of the standards of reporting in England's weekly papers (of which, in 1760, there were over 150).

During this period women began to make up a significant percentage of the nation's numerous writers. Clara Reeve's *The Progress of Romance* (1785) was the first literary history of what we now call the novel. The excerpt chosen contains her discussion of three of the most notorious women writers of previous generations: Aphra Behn, Delarivier Manley, and Eliza Haywood. Since the time of their writing (especially that of Behn), fiction, like the stage, had acquired different conventions and become more frequently didactic. The excerpt chosen from Reeve reflects the way comment on women's writing tended to slide into comment on their lives, but her championship of Behn is remarkable given that by this date Behn was generally regarded as disreputable and her work corrupting.

James Lackington, a self-educated bookseller known for his commitment to selling books at the cheapest possible prices, estimated in 1792 that the reading public had quadrupled in the previous twenty years. In this excerpt from his *Memoirs*, he celebrates the increase in reading among women and "the lower classes of the community," and applauds booksellers (that is, publishers) as advancers of knowledge.

As the final passage in this section demonstrates, the eighteenth century's political climate was highly charged. The press in Britain had greater freedom than it did in absolute monarchies like that of France, or religious governments like that of colonial Massachusetts, but any work considered offensive or politically dangerous could be censored under the law of Seditious Libel. Daniel Defoe, Delarivier Manley, and Thomas Paine were among those charged with libel during the period; publishers, however, generally took the brunt of the blame for the production of such works, as is evident in the excerpt below of the trial of Paine's publisher, Thomas Williams.

⌘⌘⌘

from Nahum Tate, *The History of King Lear* (1681)

from ACT 5

(*Scene, a prison.*)

... (*Kent brought in.*)

LEAR. Who are you?
My eyes are none o' th' best, I'll tell you straight;
Oh Albany! Well, sir, we are your captives,
And you are come to see death pass upon us.
Why this delay? Or is 't your Highness' pleasure
To give us first the torture? Say ye so?
Why here's old Kent and I, as tough a pair
As e'er bore tyrant's stroke—but my Cordelia,
My poor Cordelia here, O pity!
ALBANY. Take off their chains. Though injured Majesty,
The Wheel of Fortune now has made her circle,
And blessings yet stand 'twixt thy grave and thee.
LEAR. Com'st though, inhuman Lord, to sooth us back
To a fool's paradise of hope, to make
Our doom more wretched? Go to,[1] we are too well
Acquainted with misfortune to be gulled° *deceived*
With lying hope; no, we will hope no more.
ALBANY. I have a tale t'unfold so full of wonder
As cannot meet an easy faith;
But by that Royal injured head 'tis true.
KENT. What would your Highness?
ALBANY. Know the noble Edgar
Impeached Lord Edmund since the fight, of treason,
And dared him for the proof to fight combat,
In which the gods confirmed his charge by conquest;
I left ev'n now the traitor wounded mortally.
LEAR. And whither ends this story?
ALBANY. E'er they fought
Lord Edgar gave into my hands this paper,
A blacker scroll of treason, and of lust,
Than can be found in the records of Hell;
There, sacred sir, behold the characters
Of Goneril, the worst of daughters, but
More vicious wife.
CORDELIA. Could there be yet addition to their guilt?
What will not they that wrong a father do?
ALBANY. Since then my injuries, Lear, fall in with thine:
I have resolved the same redress for both.
KENT. What says my Lord?
CORDELIA. Speak, for me thought I heard
The charming voice of a descending god.
ALBANY. The troops by Edmund raised, I have disbanded;
Those that remain are under my command.
What comfort may be brought to cheer your age
And heal your savage wrongs, shall be applied;
For to your Majesty we do resign
Your kingdom, save what part yourself conferred
On us in marriage.
KENT. Hear you that, my liege?
CORDELIA. Then there are gods, and virtue is their care.
LEAR. Is't possible?
Let the spheres stop their course, the sun make halt,
The winds be hushed, the seas and fountains rest;
All nature pause, and listen to the change.
Where is my Kent, my Cajus?[2]
KENT. Here, my liege.
LEAR. Why, I have news that will recall thy youth;

[1] *Go to* Come on.

[2] *Cajus* I.e., Caius. Kent had assumed the name of Caius while he was disguised.

Ha! Didst thou hear't, or did th'inspiring gods
Whisper to me alone? Old Lear shall be
A king again.
KENT. The Prince, that like a god has power, has said it.
LEAR. Cordelia then shall be a queen, mark that:
Cordelia shall be queen; winds catch the sound
And bear it on your rosy wings to heaven.
Cordelia is a queen.

(*Re-enter Edgar with Gloucester.*)

ALBANY. Look, Sir, where pious Edgar comes
Leading his eye-less father: O my liege!
His wondrous story will deserve your leisure:
What he has done and suffered for your sake,
What for the fair Cordelia's.
GLOUCESTER. Where is my liege? Conduct me to his knees to hail
His second birth of empire; my dear Edgar
Has, with himself, revealed the King's blest restoration.
LEAR. My poor dark Gloucester;
GLOUCESTER. O let me kiss that once more sceptred hand!
LEAR. Hold, thou mistak'st the Majesty, kneel here;
Cordelia has our pow'r, Cordelia's queen.
Speak, is not that the noble suff'ring Edgar?
GLOUCESTER. My pious son, more dear than my lost eyes.
LEAR. I wronged him too, but here's the fair amends.
EDGAR. Your leave, my liege, for an unwelcome message.
Edmund (but that's a trifle) is expired;
What more will touch you, your imperious daughters
Goneril and haughty Regan, both are dead,
Each by the other poisoned at a banquet;
This, dying, they confessed.
CORDELIA. O fatal period of ill-governed life!
LEAR. Ungrateful as they were, my heart feels yet
A pang of nature for their wretched fall—
But, Edgar, I defer thy joys too long:
Thou serv'dst distressed Cordelia; take her crowned:
Th'imperial grace fresh blooming on her brow;
Nay, Gloucester, thou hast here a father's right;
Thy helping hand t'heap blessings on their head.
KENT. Old Kent throws in his hearty wishes too.
EDGAR. The gods and you too largely recompence
What I have done; the gift strikes merit dumb.
CORDELIA. Nor do I blush to own my self o'er-paid
For all my suff'rings past.
GLOUCESTER. Now, gentle gods, give Gloucester his discharge.
LEAR. No, Gloucester, thou hast business yet for life;
Thou, Kent, and I, retired to some cool cell
Will gently pass our short reserves of time
In calm reflections on our fortunes past,
Cheered with relation of the prosperous reign
Of this celestial pair; thus our remains
Shall in an even course of thought be past,
Enjoy the present hour, nor fear the last.
EDGAR. Our drooping country now erects her head,
Peace spreads her balmy wings, and plenty blooms.
Divine Cordelia, all the gods can witness
How much thy love to Empire I prefer!
Thy bright example shall convince the world
(Whatever storms of fortune are decreed)
That truth and virtue shall at last succeed.

(*Exeunt Omnes.*)[1]

from Colley Cibber, *An Apology for the Life of Mr. Colley Cibber* (1740)

… But while our authors took these extraordinary liberties with their wit, I remember the ladies were then observed to be decently afraid of venturing bare-faced to a new comedy, 'till they had been assured they might do it without the risk of an insult to their modesty—or, if their curiosity were too strong for their patience, they took care, at least, to save appearances, and rarely came upon the first days of acting but in masks (then daily worn, and admitted in the pit, the side boxes, and gallery), which custom, however, had so many ill consequences attending it, that it has been abolished these many years.[2]

---

[1] *Exeunt Omnes* Latin: Exit all.

[2] *masks … years* Masks came to denote prostitutes.

from Jeremy Collier, *A Short View of the Immorality and Profaneness of the English Stage* (1698)

INTRODUCTION

The business of plays is to recommend virtue and discountenance vice; to show the uncertainty of human greatness, the sudden turns of fate, and the unhappy conclusions of violence and injustice; 'tis to expose the singularities of pride and fancy, to make folly and falsehood contemptible, and to bring everything that is ill under infamy and neglect. This design has been oddly pursued by the English stage. Our poets write with a different view and are gone into another interest. 'Tis true, were their intentions fair, they might be serviceable to this purpose. They have in a great measure the springs of thought and inclination in their power. Show, music, action, and rhetoric are moving entertainments; and, rightly employed, would be very significant. But force and motion are things indifferent, and the use lies chiefly in the application. These advantages are now in the enemy's hand and under a very dangerous management. Like cannon seized, they are pointed the wrong way; and by the strength of the defense, the mischief is made the greater. That this complaint is not unreasonable I shall endeavor to prove by showing the misbehavior of the stage with respect to morality and religion. Their liberties in the following particulars are intolerable, *viz.*,[1] their smuttiness of expression; their swearing, profaneness, and lewd application of Scripture; their abuse of the clergy, their making their top characters libertines and giving them success in their debauchery. This charge, with some other irregularities, I shall make good against the stage and show both the novelty and scandal of the practice. And, first, I shall begin with the rankness and indecency of their language....

from CHAPTER 1: THE IMMODESTY OF THE STAGE

... To argue the matter more at large.

Smuttiness is a fault in behavior as well as in religion. 'Tis a very coarse diversion, the entertainment of those who are generally least both in sense and station. The looser part of the mob have no true relish of decency and honor, and want education and thought to furnish out a genteel conversation. Barrenness of fancy makes them often take up with those scandalous liberties. A vicious imagination may blot a great deal of paper at this rate with ease enough. And 'tis possible convenience may sometimes invite to the expedient. The modern poets seem to use smut as the old ones did machines,[2] to relieve a fainting invention. When Pegasus[3] is jaded and would stand still, he is apt like other tits[4] to run into every puddle.

Obscenity in any company is a rustic, uncreditable talent, but among women 'tis particularly rude. Such talk would be very affrontive in conversation and not endured by any lady of reputation. Whence, then, comes it to pass that those liberties which disoblige so much in conversation should entertain upon the stage? Do women leave all the regards to decency and conscience behind them when they come to the playhouse? Or does the place transform their inclinations and turn their former aversions into pleasure? Or were their pretenses to sobriety elsewhere nothing but hypocrisy and grimace? Such suppositions as these are all satire and invective. They are rude imputations upon the whole sex. To treat the ladies with such stuff is no better than taking their money to abuse them. It supposes their imagination vicious and their memories ill-furnished, that they are practiced in the language of the stews[5] and pleased with the scenes of brutishness. When at the same time the customs of education and the laws of decency are so very cautious and reserved in regard to women—I say so very reserved—that 'tis almost a fault for them to understand they are ill-used. They can't discover their disgust without disadvantage, nor blush without disservice to their modesty. To appear with any skill in such cant looks as if they had fallen upon ill conversation or managed their curiosity amiss. In a word, he that treats the ladies with such discourse must conclude either that they like it or they do not. To

[1] *viz.* Abbreviation of Latin word "videlicit," meaning "that is to say."

[2] *machines* Moveable contrivances for the production of effects.

[3] *Pegasus* Winged horse of the gods.

[4] *tits* Small or low-grade horses; nags.

[5] *stews* Brothels.

suppose the first is a gross reflection upon their virtue. And as for the latter case, it entertains them with their own aversion, which is ill-nature, and ill-manners enough in all conscience. And in this particular custom and conscience, the forms of breeding and the maxims of religion are on the same side. In other instances vice is often too fashionable. But here a man can't be a sinner without being a clown.[1]

In this respect the stage is faulty to a scandalous degree of nauseousness and aggravation. For:

The poets make women speak smuttily. Of this the places before-mentioned are sufficient evidence, and if there was occasion they might be multiplied to a much greater number. Indeed the comedies are seldom clear of these blemishes. And sometimes you have them in tragedy....

They represent their single ladies and persons of condition under these disorders of liberty. This makes the irregularity still more monstrous and a greater contradiction to Nature and probability. But rather than not be vicious, they will venture to spoil a character....

They have oftentimes not so much as the poor refuge of a double meaning to fly to. So that you are under a necessity either of taking ribaldry or nonsense. And when the sentence has two handles, the worst is generally turned to the audience. The matter is so contrived that the smut and scum of the thought now arises uppermost, and, like a picture drawn to sight, looks always upon the company.

And which is still more extraordinary, the prologues and epilogues are sometimes scandalous to the last degree.... Now here, properly speaking, the actors quit the stage and remove from fiction into life. Here they converse with the boxes and pit and address directly to the audience. These preliminary and concluding parts are designed to justify the conduct of the play, and bespeak the favor of the company. Upon such occasions one would imagine, if ever, the ladies should be used with respect and the measures of decency observed. But here we have lewdness without shame or example. Here the poet exceeds himself. Here are such strains as would turn the stomach of an ordinary debauchee and be almost nauseous in the stews. And to make it the more agreeable, women are commonly picked out for this service. Thus the poet courts the good opinion of the audience. This is the dessert he regales the ladies with at the close of the entertainment. It seems, he thinks, they have admirable palates! Nothing can be a greater breach of manners than such liberties as these. If a man would study to outrage quality and virtue, he could not do it more effectually. But:

Smut is still more insufferable with respect to religion. The heathen religion was in a great measure a mystery of iniquity. Lewdness was consecrated in the temples as well as practiced in the stews. Their deities were great examples of vice and worshipped with their own inclination. 'Tis no wonder therefore their poetry should be tinctured with their belief, and that the stage should borrow some of the liberties of their theology. This made Mercury's procuring and Jupiter's adultery the more passable in *Amphitryon*.[2] Upon this score, Gimnausium is less monstrous in praying the gods to send her store of gallants. And thus Chaerea defends his adventure by the precedent of Jupiter and Danae. But the Christian religion is quite of another complexion. Both its precepts and authorities are the highest discouragement to licentiousness. It forbids the remotest tendencies to evil, banishes the follies of conversation, and obliges us to sobriety of thought. That which might pass for raillery and entertainment in heathenism is detestable in Christianity. The restraint of the precept and the quality of the Deity and the expectations of futurity quite alter the case....

from CHAPTER 4: THE STAGE-POETS MAKE THEIR PRINCIPAL PERSONS VICIOUS AND REWARD THEM AT THE END OF THE PLAY

... Indeed, to make delight the main business of comedy is an unreasonable and dangerous principle, opens the way to all licentiousness, and confounds the distinction between mirth and madness. For if diversion is the chief end, it must be had at any price. No serviceable expedient must be refused, though never so scandalous. And thus the worst things are said, and the best abused; religion is insulted, and the most serious matters turned

[1] *clown* Oaf.

[2] *Amphitryon* Play by third-century BCE Roman comic playwright Plautus. Collier also refers here to plays by Roman comic playwright Terence (second century BCE).

into ridicule! As if the blind side of an audience ought to be caressed, and their folly and atheism entertained in the first place. Yes, if the palate is pleased, no matter though the body is poisoned! For can one die of an easier disease than diversion? But raillery apart, certainly mirth and laughing without respect to the cause are not such supreme satisfactions! A man has sometimes pleasure in losing his wits. Frenzy and possession will shake the lungs and brighten the face; and yet I suppose they are not much to be coveted. However, now we know the reason of the profaneness and obscenity of the stage, of their hellish cursing and swearing, and in short of their great industry to make God and goodness contemptible. 'Tis all to satisfy the company and make people laugh! A most admirable justification. What can be more engaging to an audience than to see a poet thus atheistically brave? To see him charge up to the cannon's mouth and defy the vengeance of Heaven to serve them? Besides, there may be somewhat of convenience in the case. To fetch diversion out of innocence is no such easy matter. There's no succeeding, it may be, in this method, without sweat and drudging. Clean wit, inoffensive humour, and handsome contrivance require time and thought. And who would be at this expense when the purchase is so cheap another way? 'Tis possible a poet may not always have sense enough by him for such an occasion. And since we are upon supposals, it may be the audience is not to be gained without straining a point and giving a loose to conscience. And when people are sick, are they not to be humoured? In fine, we must make them laugh, right or wrong, for delight is the chief end of comedy. Delight! He should have said debauchery. That's the English of the word and the consequence of the practice. But the original design of comedy was otherwise. And granting it was not so, what then? If the ends of things were naught,[1] they must be mended. Mischief is the chief end of malice, would it be then a blemish in ill nature to change temper and relent into goodness? The chief end of a madman, it may be, is to fire a house; must we not therefore bind him in his bed? To conclude. If delight without restraint or distinction, without conscience or shame, is the supreme law of comedy, 'twere well if we had less on't. Arbitrary pleasure is more dangerous than arbitrary power. Nothing is more brutal than to be abandoned to appetite; and nothing more wretched than to serve in such a design....

[1] *naught* I.e., wicked.

from Joseph Addison, *The Spectator* No. 18 (21 March 1711)

... Equitis quoque jam migravit ab aure voluptas
Omnis ad incertos oculos & gaudia vana.[2]

—HORACE

It is my design in this paper to deliver down to posterity a faithful account of the Italian opera, and of the gradual progress which it has made upon the English stage. For there is no question but our great grandchildren will be very curious to know the reason why their forefathers used to sit together like an audience of foreigners in their own country, and to hear whole plays acted before them in a tongue which they did not understand.

Arsinoe[3] was the first opera that gave us a taste of Italian music. The great success this opera met with produced some attempts of forming pieces upon Italian plans, which should give a more natural and reasonable entertainment than what can be met with in the elaborate trifles of that nation. This alarmed the poetasters and fiddlers of the town, who were used to deal in a more ordinary kind of ware; and therefore laid down an established rule, which is received as such to this day, *that nothing is capable of being well set to music, that is not nonsense*.

This maxim was no sooner received, but we immediately fell to translating the Italian operas; and as there was no great danger of hurting the sense of those extraordinary pieces, our authors would often make words of their own which were entirely foreign to the meaning of the passages they pretended to translate; their chief care being to make the numbers[4] of the English verse answer to those of the Italian, that both of

[2] *Equitis ... vana* Latin: "But now our nobles too are fops and vain, / Neglect the sense but love the Painted Scene." (Horace, Epistles 2.1. 87–88, translated by Creech.)

[3] *Arsinoe* Thomas Clayton's opera, *Arsinoe, Queen of Cyprus* (1705).

[4] *numbers* Metrical feet.

them might go to the same tune. Thus the famous song in *Camilla*,[1]

Barbara si t'intendo, &c.
Barbarous woman, yes, I know your meaning,

which expresses the resentments of an angry lover, was translated into that English lamentation

Frail are a lover's hopes, &c.

And it was pleasant enough to see the most refined persons of the British nation dying away and languishing to notes that were filled with a spirit of rage and indignation. It happened also very frequently, where the sense was rightly translated, the necessary transposition of words which were drawn out of the phrase of one tongue into that of another made the music appear very absurd in one tongue, that was very natural in the other. I remember an Italian verse that ran thus word for word,

And turned my rage into pity;

which the English for rhyme's sake translated,

And into pity turned my rage.

By this means, the soft notes that were adapted to pity in the Italian fell upon the word *rage* in the English; and the angry sounds that were tuned to rage in the original, were made to express pity in the translation. It oftentimes happened, likewise, that the finest notes in the air fell upon the most insignificant words in the sentence. I have known the word *and* pursued through the whole gamut, have been entertained with many a melodious *the*, and have heard the most beautiful graces, quavers, and divisions bestowed upon *then*, *for*, and *from*; to the eternal honour of our English particles.[2]

The next step to our refinement was the introducing of Italian actors into our opera; who sung their parts in their own language, at the same time that our countrymen performed theirs in our native tongue. The king or hero of the play generally spoke in Italian, and his slaves answered him in English; the lover frequently made his court, and gained the heart of his princess, in a language which she did not understand. One would have thought it very difficult to have carried on dialogues after this manner, without an interpreter between the persons that conversed together; but this was the state of the English stage for about three years.

At length the audience grew tired of understanding half the opera, and therefore, to ease themselves entirely of the fatigue of thinking, have so order'd it at present that the whole opera is performed in an unknown tongue. We no longer understand the language of our own stage; insomuch that I have often been afraid, when I have seen our Italian performers chattering in the vehemence of action, that they have been calling us names, and abusing us among themselves; but I hope, since we do put such an entire confidence in them, they will not talk against us before our faces, though they may do it with the same safety as if it were behind our backs. In the meantime I cannot forbear thinking how naturally an historian who writes two or three hundred years hence, and does not know the taste of his wise forefathers, will make the following reflection, *In the beginning of the eighteenth century the Italian tongue was so well understood in England that operas were acted on the public stage in that language.*

Once scarce knows how to be serious in the confutation of an absurdity that shows itself at the first sight. It does not want any great measure of sense to see the ridicule of this monstrous practice; but what makes it the more astonishing, it is not the taste of the rabble, but of persons of the greatest politeness, which has established it....

from *The Licensing Act of 1737*

...And be it further enacted by the authority aforesaid that from and after the said twenty-fourth day of June, one thousand, seven hundred and thirty seven, no person shall for hire, gain, or reward act, perform, represent, or cause to be acted, performed, or represented any new interlude, tragedy, comedy opera, play, farce, or other part added to any old interlude, tragedy,

[1] *Camilla* Italian opera first performed with an English libretto in 1706.

[2] *particles* Prepositions; insignificant parts of speech.

comedy, opera, play, farce, or other entertainment of the stage, or any new prologue or epilogue unless a true copy thereof be sent to the Lord Chamberlain of the King's household for the time being,[1] fourteen days at least before the acting, representing, or performing thereof, together with an account of the playhouse or other place where the same shall be and the time when the same is intended to be first acted, represented, or performed, signed by the master or manager, or one of the masters or managers of such playhouse or place, or company of actors therein.

4. And be it enacted by the authority aforesaid that from and after the said twenty-fourth day of June, one thousand, seven hundred and thirty seven, it shall and may be lawful to and for the said Lord Chamberlain for the time being, from time to time, and when and as often as he shall think fit, to prohibit the acting, performing or representing any interlude, tragedy, comedy, opera, play, farce or other entertainment of the stage, or any act, scene or part thereof, or any prologue or epilogue. And in case any person or persons shall for hire, gain or reward act, perform or represent, or cause to be acted, performed or represented, any interlude, tragedy, comedy, opera, play, farce or other entertainment of the stage, or any act, scene, or part thereof, or any prologue or epilogue, contrary to such prohibition as aforesaid; every person so offending shall for every such offence forfeit the sum of fifty pounds and every grant, licence, and authority (in any case there be any such) by or under which the said master or masters or manager or managers set up, formed, or continued such playhouse, or such company of actors, shall cease, determine and become absolutely void to all intents and purposes whatsoever.

5. Provided always that no person or persons shall be authorised by virtue of any letters patent from His Majesty, his heirs, successors or predecessors, or by the licence of the Lord Chamberlain of His Majesty's household for the time being, to act, represent, or perform for hire, gain, or reward, any interlude, tragedy, comedy, opera, play, farce, or other entertainment of the stage, or any part or parts therein, in any part of Great Britain, except in the City of Westminster and within the liberties thereof, and in such places where His Majesty, his heirs or successors, shall in their royal persons reside, and during such residence only....

from *The Statute of Anne* (1710)

An act for the encouragement of learning, by vesting the copies[2] of printed books in the authors or purchasers of such copies, during the times therein mentioned.

Whereas printers, booksellers, and other persons have of late frequently taken the liberty of printing, reprinting, and publishing, or causing to be printed, reprinted, and published, books and other writings, without the consent of the authors or proprietors of such books and writings, to their very great detriment, and too often to the ruin of them and their families: for preventing therefore such practices for the future, and for the encouragement of learned men to compose and write useful books, may it please Your Majesty that it may be enacted, and be it enacted by the Queen's most excellent Majesty, by and with the advice and consent of the Lords spiritual and temporal, and Commons in this present Parliament assembled, and by the authority of the same, that from and after the tenth day of April, one thousand seven hundred and ten, the author of any book or books already printed, who hath not transferred to any other the copy or copies of such book or books, share or shares thereof, or the bookseller or booksellers, printer or printers, or other person or persons, who hath or have purchased or acquired the copy or copies of any book or books, in order to print or reprint the same, shall have the sole right and liberty of printing such book and books for the term of one and twenty years, to commence from the said tenth day of April, and no longer; and that the author of any book or books already composed and not printed and published, or that shall hereafter be composed, and his assignee, or assigns, shall have the sole liberty of printing and reprinting such book and books for the term of fourteen years, to commence from the day of the first publishing the same, and no longer; and that if any other bookseller, printer,

[1] *for the time being* Currently holding office.

[2] *copies* Copyright.

or other person whatsoever, from and after the tenth day of April, one thousand seven hundred and ten, within the times granted and limited by this act, as aforesaid, shall print, reprint, or import, or cause to be printed, reprinted, or imported any such book or books, without the consent of the proprietor or proprietors thereof first had and obtained in writing, signed in the presence of two or more credible witnesses; or knowing the same to be so printed or reprinted, without the consent of the proprietors, shall sell, publish, or expose to sale, or cause to be sold, published, or exposed to sale, any such book or books, without such consent first had and obtained, as aforesaid, then such offender or offenders shall forfeit such book or books, and all and every sheet or sheets, being part of such book or books, to the proprietor or proprietors of the copy thereof, who shall forthwith damask[1] and make waste-paper of them. And further, that every such offender or offenders shall forfeit one penny for every sheet which shall be found in his, her, or their custody, either printed or printing, published or exposed to sale, contrary to the true intent and meaning of this act, the one moiety thereof to the Queen's most excellent Majesty, Her heirs and successors, and the other moiety thereof to any person or persons that shall sue for the same, to be recovered in any of Her Majesty's Courts of Record at Westminster, by action of debt, bill, plaint, or information, in which no wager of law, essoign,[2] privilege, or protection, or more than one imparlance,[3] shall be allowed.

And whereas many persons may through ignorance offend against this act, unless some provision be made whereby the property in every such book, as is intended by this act to be secured to the proprietor or proprietors thereof, may be ascertained, as likewise the consent of such proprietor or proprietors for the printing or reprinting of such book or books may from time to time be known; be it therefore further enacted by the authority aforesaid, that nothing in this act contained shall be construed to extend to subject any bookseller, printer, or other person whatsoever, to the forfeitures or penalties therein mentioned, for or by reason of the printing or reprinting of any book or books without such consent as aforesaid, unless the title to the copy of such book or books hereafter published shall, before such publication be entered in the register-book of the Company of Stationers, in such manner as hath been usual, which register-book shall at all times be kept at the hall of the said Company, and unless such consent of the proprietor or proprietors be in like manner entered, as aforesaid, for every of which several entries, six pence shall be paid, and no more; which said register-book may, at all reasonable and convenient times, be resorted to, and inspected by any bookseller, printer, or other person, for the purposes before mentioned, oned,[4] without any fee or reward; and the clerk of the said Company of Stationers, shall, when and as often as thereunto required, give a certificate under his hand of such entry or entries, and for every such certificate, may take a fee not exceeding six pence....

Provided always, and it is hereby enacted, that nine copies of each book or books, upon the best paper, that from and after the said tenth day of April, one thousand seven hundred and ten, shall be printed and published, as aforesaid, or reprinted and published with additions, shall, by the printer and printers thereof, be delivered to the warehouse-keeper of the said Company of Stationers for the time being, at the Hall of the said Company, before such publication made, for the use of the Royal Library, the libraries of the Universities of Oxford and Cambridge, the libraries of the four universities in Scotland, the library of Sion College in London, and the library commonly called the library belonging to the Faculty of Advocates at Edinburgh respectively.[5] ...

Provided nevertheless, that all actions, suits, bills, indictments, or informations for any offence that shall be committed against this act, shall be brought, sued, and commenced within three months next after such offence committed, or else the same shall be void and of none effect.

[1] *damask* Deface.

[2] *essoign* Excuse for non-appearance in court at an appointed time.

[3] *imparlance* Extension of time granted to allow the negotiation of an amicable settlement.

[4] *oned* Joined; united.

[5] *nine copies ... respectively* This confirmed and extended to Scotland a law of 1662 which gave the copyright libraries or libraries of record their status. The Bodleian Library at Oxford already had such an agreement, negotiated in 1610. The Royal Library later became the nucleus of the British Library.

Provided always, that after the expiration of the said term of fourteen years, the sole right of printing or disposing of copies shall return to the authors thereof, if they are then living, for another term of fourteen years.

from James Boswell, *The Life of Samuel Johnson* (1791)

[20 July 1763]

Mr. Alexander Donaldson, bookseller of Edinburgh, had for some time opened a shop in London, and sold his cheap editions of the most popular English books, in defiance of the supposed common-law right of literary property. Johnson, though he concurred in the opinion which was afterwards sanctioned by a judgment of the House of Lords, that there was no such right,[1] was at this time very angry that the booksellers of London, for whom he uniformly professed much regard, should suffer from an invasion of what they had ever considered to be secure, and he was loud and violent against Mr. Donaldson. "He is a fellow who takes advantage of the law to injure his brethren; for, notwithstanding that the statute secures only fourteen years of exclusive right, it has always been understood by *the trade* that he who buys the copyright of a book from the author obtains a perpetual property;[2] and upon that belief, numberless bargains are made to transfer that property after the expiration of the statutory term. Now Donaldson, I say, takes advantage here, of people who have really an equitable title from usage; and if we consider how few of the books, of which they buy the property, succeed so well as to bring profit, we should be of opinion that the term of fourteen years is too short; it should be sixty years." DEMPSTER. "Donaldson, sir, is anxious for the encouragement of literature. He reduces the price of books, so that poor students may buy them." JOHNSON (laughing). "Well, sir, allowing that to be his motive, he is no better than Robin Hood, who robbed the rich in order to give to the poor."

It is remarkable that when the great question concerning literary property came to be ultimately tried before the supreme tribunal of this country, in consequence of the very spirited exertions of Mr. Donaldson, Dr. Johnson was zealous against a perpetuity; but he thought that the term of the exclusive right of authors should be considerably enlarged. He was then for granting a hundred years.[3]

Joseph Addison, *The Tatler* No. 224 (14 September 1710)

Materiam superabat Opus.[4]
—Ovid.

From my own apartment, September 13.

It is my custom, in a dearth of news, to entertain myself with those collections of advertisements that appear at the end of all our public prints.[5] These I consider as accounts of news from the little world, in the same manner that the foregoing parts of the paper are from the great. If in one we hear that a sovereign prince is fled from his capital city, in the other we hear of a tradesman who hath shut up his shop and run away. If in one we find the victory of a general, in the other we

[1] *in defiance ... no such right* In the 1769 case of Millar *v.* Taylor, the court ruled that a common-law right of literary property still existed, despite the Statute of Anne's changes in statutory law. In other words, when the statutory rights granted by the Statute of Anne expired, common-law rights would remain in effect, thus preventing works from ever entering the public domain. *Donaldson v. Beckett*, in 1774, overturned Millar *v.* Taylor by deciding that the Statute of Anne, which granted the author possession of copyright for the period of 14 years, had completely exploded the previous protection of literary property under common law. In other words, if the copyright of the author, or the publisher who had purchased the copyright, had expired, he or she could not sue another bookseller, such as Donaldson, for reprinting.

[2] *he who buys ... property* Reference to the custom of the time of perpetual copyright, according to which booksellers would buy and sell copyrights of books from earlier centuries—such as Shakespeare, Milton, John Dryden, and Aphra Behn—although they did not technically own these copyrights.

[3] *He was ... years* The present-day duration of copyright in Britain and the United States is the life of the author plus seventy years, and in Canada it is the life of the author plus fifty years.

[4] *Materiam superabat Opus* Latin: "The craftsmanship will surpass the material." From Ovid, *Metamorphoses* 2.5.

[5] *those collections ... prints* Here Addison is referring to personal advertisements, though he goes on to discuss commercial advertising in the following paragraphs.

see the desertion of a private soldier. I must confess, I have a certain weakness in my temper that is often very much affected by these little domestic occurrences, and have frequently been caught with tears in my eyes over a melancholy advertisement. But to consider this subject in its most ridiculous lights, advertisements are of great use to the vulgar; first of all, as they are instruments of ambition. A man that is by no means big enough for the *Gazette*[1] may easily creep into the advertisements; by which means we often see an apothecary in the same paper of news with a plenipotentiary,[2] or a running-footman with an ambassador. An advertisement from Piccadilly goes down to posterity with an article from Madrid; and John Bartlett of Goodman's Fields is celebrated in the same paper with the Emperor of Germany. Thus the fable tells us that the wren mounted as high as the eagle by getting upon his back.

A second use which this sort of writings have been turned to of late years has been the management of controversy, insomuch that above half the advertisements one meets with now-a-days are purely polemical. The inventors of strops[3] for razors have written against one another this way for several years, and that with great bitterness; as the whole argument pro and con in the case of the morning-gowns is still carried on after the same manner. I need not mention the several proprietors of *Dr. Anderson's Pills*; nor take notice of the many satirical works of this nature so frequently published by Dr. Clark, who has had the confidence to advertise upon that learned knight, my very worthy friend, Sir William Read.[4] But I shall not interpose in their quarrel; Sir William can give him his own in advertisements that, in the judgment of the impartial, are as well penned as the Doctor's.

The third and last use of these writings is to inform the world where they may be furnished with almost every thing that is necessary for life. If a man has pains in his head, colics[5] in his bowels, or spots in his clothes, he may here meet with proper cures and remedies. If a man would recover a wife or a horse that is stolen or strayed; if he wants new sermons, electuaries,[6] ass's milk, or anything else, either for his body or his mind, this is the place to look for them in.

The great art in writing advertisements is the finding out a proper method to catch the reader's eye; without which, a good thing may pass over unobserved, or be lost among commissions of bankruptcy. Asterisks and hands[7] were formerly of great use for this purpose. Of late years, the *N.B.*[8] has been much in fashion; as also little cuts and figures,[9] the invention of which we must ascribe to the author of spring-trusses.[10] I must not here omit the blind Italian[11] character, which being scarce legible, always fixes and detains the eye, and gives the curious reader something like the satisfaction of prying into a secret.

But the great skill in an advertiser is chiefly seen in the style which he makes use of. He is to mention *the universal esteem, or general reputation,* of things that were never heard of. If he is a physician or astrologer, he must change his lodgings frequently, and (though he never saw anybody in them besides his own family) give public notice of it, *For the information of the nobility and gentry.* Since I am thus usefully employed in writing criticisms on the works of these diminutive authors, I must not pass over in silence an advertisement which has lately made its appearance, and is written altogether in a Ciceronian[12] manner. It was sent to me, with five shillings, to be inserted among my advertisements; but as it is a pattern of good writing in this way, I shall give it a place in the body of my paper.

[1] *Gazette* England's official newspaper, a record of military and political events, whose advertisements largely consisted of bankruptcy notices. The paper was, at the time, edited by Addison's friend and partner Richard Steele.

[2] *plenipotentiary* Envoy given absolute authority to act as he or she sees fit in a particular matter.

[3] *strops* Strips of leather for sharpening razors.

[4] *Sir William Read* Ophthalmologist to Queen Anne, who was knighted in 1705 for curing soldiers and sailors of blindness.

[5] *colics* I.e., pains.

[6] *electuaries* Medicinal pastes mixed with honey, preserve, or syrup.

[7] *hands* I.e., figures of hands drawn with their forefingers pointing.

[8] *N.B.* For *nota bene* (Latin: note well).

[9] *cuts and figures* I.e., illustrations and diagrams.

[10] *spring-trusses* Surgical appliances for applying pressure to a wound or hernia.

[11] *Italian* Italic.

[12] *Ciceronian* I.e., using inflated rhetoric. (Cicero was a celebrated Roman orator of the first century BCE.)

> The highest compounded spirit of lavender, the most glorious (if the expression may be used) enlivening scent and flavour that can possibly be, which so raptures the spirits, delights the gust,[1] and gives such airs to the countenance, as are not to be imagined but by those that have tried it. The meanest sort of the thing is admired by most gentlemen and ladies; but this far more, as by far it exceeds it, to the gaining among all a more than common esteem. It is sold (in neat flint bottles fit for the pocket) only at the Golden Key in Warton's Court near Holborn Bars, for 3s. 6d.[2] with directions.

At the same time that I recommend the several flowers in which this spirit of lavender is wrapped up (if the expression may be used), I cannot excuse my fellow labourers for admitting into their papers several uncleanly advertisements, not at all proper to appear in the works of polite writers. Among these I must reckon the *Carminative Wind-expelling Pills.* If the Doctor had called them only his Carminative Pills, he had been as cleanly as one could have wished; but the second word entirely destroys the decency of the first. There are other absurdities of this nature so very gross that I dare not mention them; and shall therefore dismiss this subject with a public admonition to Michael Parrot, that he do not presume any more to mention a certain worm he knows of, which, by the way, has grown seven foot in my memory; for, if I am not much mistaken, it is the same that was but nine foot long about six months ago.

By the remarks I have here made, it plainly appears that a collection of advertisements is a kind of miscellany,[3] the writers of which, contrary to all authors, except men of quality,[4] give money to the booksellers who publish their copies. The genius of the bookseller is chiefly shown in his method of ranging and digesting these little tracts. The last paper I took up in my hands places them in the following order:

> The True Spanish Blacking for Shoes, &c.
> The Beautifying Cream for the Face, &c.
> Pease and Plasters, &c.
> Nectar and Ambrosia, &c.
> Four Freehold Tenements of 15. l.[5] per Annum, &c.
> The Present State of England, &c.[6]
> Annotations upon the *Tatler*, &c.
> A Commission of Bankrupt being awarded against B.L., Bookseller, *&c.*

[1] *gust* Sense of taste.

[2] *3s. 6d.* Three shillings and six pence.

[3] *miscellany* I.e., anthology.

[4] *men of quality* A dig at upper-class vanity authors.

from Samuel Johnson, *The Idler* No. 30 (11 November 1758)

... No species of literary men has lately been so much multiplied as the writers of news. Not many years ago the nation was content with one *Gazette*;[7] but now we have not only in the metropolis papers for every morning and every evening, but almost every large town has its weekly historian, who regularly circulates his periodical intelligence,[8] and fills the villages of his district with conjectures on the events of war, and with debates on the true interest of Europe.

To write news in its perfection requires such a combination of qualities that a man completely fitted for the task is not always to be found. In Sir Henry Wotton's[9] jocular definition, "An ambassador" is said to be "a man of virtue sent abroad to tell lies for the advantage of his country"; a news-writer is "a man without virtue, who writes lies at home for his own profit." To these compositions is required neither genius nor knowledge, neither industry nor sprightliness; but contempt of shame and indifference to truth are absolutely necessary. He who, by a long familiarity with infamy, has obtained these qualities, may confidently tell today what he intends to contradict tomorrow; he may affirm fearlessly what he knows that he shall be obliged to recant, and may write letters from Amsterdam or Dresden to himself.

[5] *l.* Pounds.

[6] *The Present State of England, &c.* An annual publication.

[7] *Gazette* England's official newspaper.

[8] *intelligence* Information.

[9] *Henry Wotton* Diplomat and writer (1568–1639).

In a time of war the nation is always of one mind, eager to hear something good of themselves and ill of the enemy. At this time the task of news-writers is easy; they have nothing to do but to tell that a battle is expected, and afterwards that a battle has been fought, in which we and our friends, whether conquering or conquered, did all, and our enemies did nothing.

Scarce anything awakens attention like a tale of cruelty. The writer of news never fails in the intermission of action to tell how the enemies murdered children and ravished virgins; and, if the scene of action be somewhat distant, scalps half the inhabitants of a province.

Among the calamities of war may be justly numbered the diminution of the love of truth, by the falsehoods which interest dictates and credulity encourages. A peace will equally leave the warrior and relater of wars destitute of employment; and I know not whether more is to be dreaded from streets filled with soldiers accustomed to plunder, or from garrets filled with scribblers accustomed to lie.

from Clara Reeve, *The Progress of Romance, through Times, Countries, Manners; with Remarks on the Good and Bad Effects of it, on them Respectively; in a Course of Evening Conversations* (1785)

EVENING 7

EUPHRASIA. … Among our early novel-writers we must reckon Mrs. Behn. There are strong marks of genius in all this lady's works, but unhappily, there are some parts of them very improper to be read by, or recommended to, virtuous minds, and especially to youth. She wrote in an age, and to a court of licentious manners, and perhaps we ought to ascribe to these causes the loose turn of her stories. Let us do justice to her merits, and cast the veil of compassion over her faults. She died in the year 1689, and lies buried in the cloisters of Westminster Abbey. The inscription will show how high she stood in estimation at that time.

HORTENSIUS. Are you not partial to the sex of this genius, when you excuse in her what you would not to a man?

EUPHRASIA. Perhaps I may, and you must excuse me if I am so, especially as this lady had many fine and amiable qualities, besides her genius for writing.

SOPHRONIA. Pray let her rest in peace—you were speaking of the inscription on her monument, I do not remember it.

EUPHRASIA. It is as follows:

Mrs. APHRA BEHN, 1689.
Here lies a proof that wit can never be
Defence enough against mortality.

Let me add that Mrs. Behn will not be forgotten so long as the tragedy of *Oroonoko*[1] is acted; it was from her story of that illustrious African that Mr. Southern wrote that play, and the most affecting parts of it are taken almost literally from her.

HORTENSIUS. Peace be to her manes![2] I shall not disturb her, or her works.

EUPHRASIA. I shall not recommend them to your perusal, Hortensius.

The next female writer of this class is Mrs. Manley,[3] whose works are still more exceptionable than Mrs. Behn's, and as much inferior to them in point of merit. She hoarded up all the public and private scandal within her reach, and poured it forth, in a work too well known in the last age, though almost forgotten in the present; a work that partakes of the style of the romance, and the novel. I forbear the name, and further observations on it, as Mrs. Manley's works are sinking gradually into oblivion. I am sorry to say they were once in fashion, which obliges me to mention them, otherwise I had rather be spared the pain of disgracing an author of my own sex.

SOPHRONIA. It must be confessed that these books of the last age were of worse tendency than any of those of the present.

[1] *tragedy of Oroonoko* Thomas Southerne's stage adaptation of Aphra Behn's *Oroonoko*, first performed in 1695, was tremendously popular in the eighteenth century.

[2] *manes* Spirit.

[3] *Manley* Delarivier Manley, author of several *romans à clef* (which described and sometimes exaggerated the vices of actual people, mostly those in power, who appeared under fictitious names), including *The New Atalantis* (1709), for which she was arrested, and which is referred to here.

EUPHRASIA. My dear friend, there were bad books at all times, for those who sought for them. Let us pass them over in silence.

HORTENSIUS. No, not yet. Let me help your memory to one more lady-author of the same class—Mrs. Haywood. She has the same claim upon you as those you have last mentioned.

EUPHRASIA. I had intended to have mentioned Mrs. Haywood, though in a different way, but I find you will not suffer any part of her character to escape you.

HORTENSIUS. Why should she be spared any more than the others?

EUPHRASIA. Because she repented of her faults, and employed the latter part of her life in expiating the offences of the former. There is reason to believe that the examples of the two ladies we have spoken of seduced Mrs. Haywood into the same track; she certainly wrote some amorous novels in her youth,[1] and also two books of the same kind as Mrs. Manley's capital work, all of which I hope are forgotten.

HORTENSIUS. I fear they will not be so fortunate; they will be known to posterity by the infamous immortality conferred upon them by Pope in his *Dunciad*.[2]

EUPHRASIA. Mr. Pope was severe in his castigations, but let us be just to merit of every kind. Mrs. Haywood had the singular good fortune to recover a lost reputation, and the yet greater honour to atone for her errors. She devoted the remainder of her life and labours to the service of virtue. Mrs. Haywood was one of the most voluminous female writers that ever England produced, none of her latter works are destitute of merit, though they do not rise to the highest pitch of excellence. *Betsy Thoughtless*[3] is reckoned her best novel; but those works by which she is most likely to be known to posterity, are the *Female Spectator*, and the *Invisible Spy*.[4] This lady died so lately as the year 1758.

SOPHRONIA. I have heard it often said that Mr. Pope was too severe in his treatment of this lady; it was supposed that she had given some private offence, which he resented publicly as was too much his way.

HORTENSIUS. That is very likely, for he was not of a forgiving disposition. If I have been too severe also, you ladies must forgive me in behalf of your sex.

EUPHRASIA. Truth is sometimes severe. Mrs. Haywood's wit and ingenuity were never denied. I would be the last to vindicate her faults, but the first to celebrate her return to virtue, and her atonement for them.

SOPHRONIA. May her first writings be forgotten, and the last survive to do her honour!

from James Lackington, *Memoirs of the Forty-Five First Years of the Life of James Lackington, Bookseller* (1792)

I cannot help observing that the sale of books in general has increased prodigiously within the last twenty years. According to the best estimation I have been able to make, I suppose that more than four times the number of books are sold now than were sold twenty years since. The poorer sort of farmers, and even the poor country people in general, who before that period spent their winter evenings in relating stories of witches, ghosts, hobgoblins, &c, now shorten the winter nights by hearing their sons and daughters read tales, romances, &c; and on entering their houses, you may see *Tom Jones, Roderick Random*,[5] and other entertaining books, stuck up on their bacon racks, &c. If John goes to town with a load of hay, he is charged to be sure not to forget to bring home "Peregrine Pickle's Adven-

[1] *amorous novels … youth* Of the list of Haywood's amorous "novels," the best known today may be *Love in Excess* (1719) and *Fantomina* (1725).

[2] *Pope in his Dunciad* Alexander's Pope's mock epic attack on Grub-Street writers, *The Dunciad*, features Eliza Haywood, with "two babes of love close clinging to her waist," as the prize in a pissing contest between rival booksellers Edmund Curll and William Chetwood.

[3] *Betsy Thoughtless* Haywood's *The History of Miss Betsy Thoughtless* (1751) was probably her best known work. In this didactic work, the heroine learns to behave better before being rewarded by true love. The morality evident in the novel probably does not represent repentance on the part of the author, but a successful shift to keep with what the market then, a generation after her earliest works, demanded.

[4] *Female … Spy* Haywood's *The Female Spectator*, a highly successful periodical that she began in 1744, and *The Invisible Spy* (1755), a political tale.

[5] *Tom … Random* I.e., *The History of Tom Jones* (1749), by Henry Fielding, and *The Adventures of Roderick Random* (1748), by Tobias Smollett.

tures";[1] and when Dolly is sent to market to sell her eggs, she is commissioned to purchase "The History of Pamela Andrews."[2] In short, all ranks and degrees now read. But the most rapid increase of the sale of books has been since the termination of the late war.[3]

A number of book-clubs are also formed in every part of England, where each member subscribes a certain sum quarterly to purchase books; in some of these clubs the books, after they have been read by all the subscribers, are sold among them to the highest bidders, and the money produced by such sale is expended in fresh purchases, by which prudent and judicious mode each member has it in his power to become possessed of the work of any particular author he may judge deserving a superior degree of attention; and the members at large enjoy the advantage of a continual succession of different publications, instead of being restricted to a repeated perusal of the same authors; which must have been the case with many, if so rational a plan had not been adopted.

I have been informed that when circulating libraries were first opened, the booksellers were much alarmed, and their rapid increase added to their fears, and led them to think that the sale of books would be much diminished by such libraries. But experience has proved that the sale of books, so far from being diminished by them, has been greatly promoted, as from those repositories many thousand families have been cheaply supplied with books, by which the taste for reading has become much more general, and thousands of books are purchased every year by such as have first borrowed them at those libraries, and after reading, approving of them, become purchasers.

Circulating libraries have also greatly contributed towards the amusement and cultivation of the other sex; by far the greatest part of ladies have now a taste for books.

"——Learning, once the man's exclusive pride,
Seems verging fast towards the female side."[4]

It is true that I do not, with Miss Mary Wollstonecraft, "earnestly wish to see the distinction of sex confounded in society," not even with her exception, "unless where love animates the behaviour."[5] And yet I differ widely from those gentlemen who would prevent the ladies from acquiring a taste for books; and as yet I have never seen any solid reason advanced why ladies should not polish their understandings, and render themselves fit companions for men of sense. And I have often thought that one great reason why some gentlemen spend all their leisure hours abroad,[6] is, for want of rational companions at home; for, if a gentleman happens to marry a fine lady, as justly painted by Miss Wollstonecraft, or the square elbow family drudge, as drawn to the life by the same hand, I must confess that I see no great inducement that he has to desire the company of his wife, as she scarce can be called a rational companion, or one fit to be entrusted with the education of her children; and even Rousseau is obliged to acknowledge that it "is a melancholy thing for a father of a family, who is fond of home, to be obliged to be always wrapped up in himself, and to have nobody about him to whom he can impart his sentiments."[7] Lord Lyttleton advises well in the two following lines:

"Do you, my fair, endeavour to possess
An elegance of mind, as well as dress."[8]

[1] *Peregrine Pickle's Adventures* Tobias Smollett's *The Adventures of Peregrine Pickle* (1751).

[2] *The History … Andrews* Samuel Richardson's *Pamela, or Virtue Rewarded* (1740).

[3] *late war* American Revolution.

[4] *Learning … side* From William Cowper's *The Progress of Error* (1782), lines 429–30.

[5] *earnestly wish … behaviour* From Mary Wollstonecraft's *A Vindication of the Rights of Woman* (1792), Chapter 4.

[6] *abroad* I.e., out of the house.

[7] *Rousseau … sentiments* Lackington is reflecting received wisdom when he supposes that the justification for educating women is not their own benefit but that of men. Here he quotes a passage from French philosopher Jean-Jacques Rousseau's *Émile* (1762) that Wollstonecraft also cites to support her argument that educated men would be happiest with compatible companions. Rousseau generally believed that women's education should be limited in order to maintain their innocence.

[8] *Do you … dress* From *Advice to a Lady* (1733), lines 27–28, by First Baron Lord Lyttleton, a patron of literature.

I cannot help thinking that the reason why some of the eastern nations treat the ladies with such contempt, and look upon them in such a degrading point of view, is owing to their marrying them when mere children, both as to age and understanding, which last being entirely neglected, they seldom are capable of rational conversation, and of course are neglected and despised. But this is not the case with English ladies;[1] they now in general read, not only novels, although many of that class are excellent productions, and tend to polish both the heart and head; but they also read the best books in the English language, and many read the best works in various languages; and there are some thousands of ladies who come to my shop that know as well what books to choose, and are as well acquainted with works of taste and genius as any gentlemen in the kingdom, notwithstanding the sneer against novel-readers, &c.

The Sunday-schools are spreading very fast in most parts of England, which will accelerate the diffusion of knowledge among the lower classes of the community and in a very few years exceedingly increase the sale of books. Here permit me earnestly to call on every honest bookseller (I trust my call will not be in vain) as well as on every friend to the extension of knowledge, to unite (as *you* I am confident will) in a hearty Amen.

[1] *But this ... ladies* Here Lackington reflects another common line of thinking—that Asian and Middle-Eastern nations were inferior because of their supposedly inferior treatment of women.

from Thomas Erskine, *Speech as Prosecution in the Seditious-Libel Trial of Thomas Williams for Publishing* Age of Reason, *by Thomas Paine* (1797)

A free and unlicensed press, in the just and legal sense of the expression, has led to all the blessings both of religion and government, which Great Britain or any part of the world at this moment enjoys, and it is calculated to advance mankind to still higher degrees of civilization and happiness. But this freedom, like every other, must be limited to be enjoyed, and like every human advantage, may be defeated by its abuse. An intellectual book, however erroneous, addressed to the intellectual world upon so profound and complicated a subject, can never work the mischief which this Indictment is calculated to repress. Such works will only incite the minds of men enlightened by study, to a closer investigation of a subject well worthy of their deepest and continued contemplation. The powers of the mind are given for human improvement in the progress of human existence. The changes produced by such reciprocations of lights and intelligences are certain in their progressions, and make their way imperceptibly, by the final and irresistible power of truth. But this book has no such object, and no such capacity: it presents no arguments to the wise and enlightened. On the contrary, it treats the faith and opinions of the wisest with the most shocking contempt, and stirs up men, without the advantages of learning, or sober thinking, to a total disbelief of every thing hitherto held sacred; and consequently to a rejection of all the laws and ordinances of the state, which stand only upon the assumption of their truth.

Eighteenth-Century Periodicals and Prints

CONTEXTS

The English periodical was a new medium at the beginning of the eighteenth century, one that quickly began to play a prominent role in the formation of popular taste and political opinion—and in the shaping of English literature. Although the first English "news sheets" were printed in the seventeenth century, the eighteenth century saw the development and flourishing of two influential forms—the periodical essay and the magazine.

The variety of readers that periodicals attracted was unprecedented. Although their primary audience was urban and middle class, periodicals also found readers in the aristocracy and the laboring class, and they had a significant audience outside London. Even those who were illiterate could have access to periodicals, which were often read aloud to groups of people. Men gathered in coffeehouses, chocolate houses, and clubs to read and discuss the latest issues of the leading periodicals; both men and women discussed them at home. Even periodicals such as *The Female Spectator* and *The Female Tatler*, which were presented as specifically tailored to women, in fact had a mixed gender audience. But if reading periodicals was an activity available to both genders, writing them was far less so; between 1700 and 1770, when periodical titles abounded, only five women are known to have authored their own. (Writings by three of these—Eliza Haywood, Mary Wortley Montagu, and Frances Brooke—are included below.)

The periodicals themselves varied enormously in content, offering political opinion, social commentary, critical reviews, fiction, poetry, advertising, and more. Some individual publications were specialized, but others were wildly eclectic in their selection of content. Periodicals were differentiated from other media by their patterns of creation and consumption; they were written quickly and issued often. Each periodical was planned for release on a regular basis—daily, weekly, or monthly. Some were printed on one large sheet, others on several sheets of paper. They tended to be disposable, and were often reused as scrap paper—although the best ones were sometimes shared and reread until the paper fell apart. Successful periodicals were often granted an afterlife as bound books; many collectors had their individual issues bound together, and printers continued to re-issue and sell old titles in the form of annuals or complete collections. Sometimes these compilations were more widely read than the initial run had been; in collected form, some successful periodicals were still being reprinted and sold in the nineteenth century.

The nature of the periodical tended in several ways to broaden the exchange of ideas. Writers were encouraged to exchange ideas with their audiences, and to engage with other periodicals and other forms of literature. Many periodicals published readers' letters—both real and fictional ones—and often responses to the letters as well. Periodicals advertised and reviewed books and theatrical performances, thereby helping to shape the new genre of literary criticism.

Periodical writers drew inspiration from, commented upon, and even unapologetically stole from each other. They also exchanged arguments. Every political periodical—and even most that were not explicitly political—had an agenda and a party affiliation, and both authors and readers believed in the power of public opinion to affect government behavior. Political writers could be vicious, often adopting a wittily abusive style in their efforts to entertain readers and sell more papers—but they also tended to be cautious, veiling attacks in a variety of ways in the hope of avoiding arrest for "seditious libel."[1] Other essayists focused less on politics than on social commentary, styling themselves as defenders of public morality or of good taste—though these sorts of argument could also carry implicit political messages. Some periodical writers engaged in non-political insult contests, abusing personal enemies and lampooning writers whose work they held in contempt.

There were many who held low opinions of certain periodicals, and many who viewed the genre as a whole with distaste. Members of the privileged classes frequently expressed disdain for periodical readers and writers, who were often (though by no means exclusively) middle class; periodicals were relatively inexpensive reading material, and during the eighteenth century they became one of the best ways for a working writer to earn a living. Periodicals were closely associated with the image of the "Grub Street hack," living in one of the shabby garrets above the publishing houses of Grub Street and prostituting his meager skills, churning out writing without regard to political truth or artistic merit.

Periodical writing was indeed driven by deadlines and market demands, and the quality was extremely varied. Nonetheless, many of the era's major literary figures were accomplished periodical writers: Daniel Defoe, Jonathan Swift, Eliza Haywood, Samuel Johnson, Samuel Richardson, Oliver Goldsmith, and Mary Wortley Montagu, among many others, all worked in the medium.

Of all the writers who contributed to the genre, the first names associated with the eighteenth-century periodical are those of Richard Steele and Joseph Addison, who early in the century authored two extraordinarily influential publications: *The Tatler* (1709–11) and *The Spectator* (1711–12). Although the two friends worked on both periodicals, *The Tatler* was primarily Steele's work, while *The Spectator* is more closely associated with Addison; both were instrumental in developing a conventional style and format used by many periodical authors of the century. One of Richard Steele's major innovations was to adopt a persona; he wrote many pieces as Isaac Bickerstaff, Esquire, whose character he developed as that of an observant and likeable old man. Political writers had long been making use of pseudonyms—Steele's originality lay in going beyond the mere use of a different name; by developing Bickerstaff's personality, he made his social commentary more appealing to readers. The highlight of each issue of *The Tatler* was a personal musing ostensibly written by Bickerstaff. These pieces originated as a short feature but were so popular that they came to occupy most of the paper, evolving into a new form; Bickerstaff's "lucubrations" were unified essays, written in a persona, and intended both to entertain and to morally improve their audience.

When *The Tatler* concluded, Addison and Steele fully embraced this new form in their new project, *The Spectator*. Each issue of *The Spectator* features a single essay (usually criticism or social commentary) written in the persona of the witty, eccentric Mr. Spectator, a quiet man who wanders London's public places, himself unnoticed, observing all that happens in the city. *The Spectator* was even more successful than its predecessor; Addison estimated that 60,000 people—one tenth of London's population—read each daily issue. Because *The Tatler* and *The Spectator* were so popular, and continued to sell in compilation throughout the century (*The Tatler* sold more than 25 editions before 1800), they inspired many imitations by authors hoping for similar commercial success.

The printer Edward Cave played an equally important role in the development of periodicals as the founder of the first successful "magazine." *The Gentleman's Magazine*, which Cave first issued in 1731, made a monthly selection from other periodical publications from essays in verse to weather information, from serialized short stories to obituaries, into a single monthly volume with something of interest for any general reader. Cave used the word "magazine"—the original meaning of which was "storehouse"—to describe this miscellany. His venture was a popular success, and many printers imitated his new format; they borrowed from its title as well, and many other "magazines" were born.

[1] *seditious libel* E.g., Henry Haines, printer of the opposition journal, *The Craftsman*, was arrested in 1737 for material written about George II. He was tried and sentenced in 1738 and fined two thousand pounds.

Content in these periodicals was indeed varied. Items published in the popular *British Magazine* during the first few months of 1760, for example, included "A letter concerning a new Method for sweetening Seawater," "A Translation of a Speech made by the Dutch ambassador to the King," "An accurate Map of Louisiana and the Territory in Dispute Between the English and the French," "Description of the Rattlesnake Plant in Louisiana," the sheet music for "Retirement: A New Song," and a set of "New Mathematical Questions"—all this in addition to political essays, fiction, and a good deal else.

While periodicals addressed political and social subjects through written language, political prints addressed similar topics through satirical images. Political prints (the term "political cartoon" would not be coined until the nineteenth century) were sometimes included as inserts in magazines or bound in print collections, but most were sold as individual sheets. These tended to be more expensive than periodicals and to be issued in smaller numbers. Like periodicals they generally had many more readers than buyers, since they were circulated in coffeehouses and displayed to all who passed by print-shop windows. Not all resonated with a wide audience, however; some were accessible only to viewers with a sophisticated understanding of current events.

⌘⌘⌘

from Joseph Addison,[1] *The Tatler* No. 155 [The Political Upholsterer] (6 April 1710)

Like other miscellaneous articles in *The Tatler*, this essay is addressed from the apartment of Isaac Bickerstaff. Through the persona of the elderly Bickerstaff, writers for *The Tatler* often adopt a light, mocking attitude toward human failings; John Gay once commented that "Bickerstaff ventured to tell the town that they were a parcel of fops, fools, and vain coquettes, but in such a manner as even pleased them." The following essay discusses a Londoner's obsession with following the news.

——Aliena negotia curat
Excussus propriis.[2]——

HORACE

From My Own Apartment, April 5.

There lived some years since within my neighbourhood a very grave person, an upholsterer, who seemed a man of more than ordinary application to business. He was a very early riser, and was often abroad two or three hours before any of his neighbours. He had a particular carefulness in the knitting of his brows, and a kind of impatience in all his motions that plainly discovered he was always intent on matters of importance. Upon my enquiry into his life and conversation, I found him to be the greatest newsmonger[3] in our quarter; that he rose before day to read the *Post-Man*;[4] and that he would take two or three turns to the other end of the town before his neighbours were up, to see if there were any Dutch mails[5] come in. He had a wife and several children, but was much more inquisitive to know what passed in Poland than in his own family, and was in greater pain and anxiety of mind for King Augustus's[6]

[1] *Joseph Addison* Richard Steele founded *The Tatler* and wrote most of the issues himself, but he also printed work by other writers. Steele's close friend Joseph Addison was the most frequent contributor.

[2] *Aliena negotia … propriis* Latin: "He looks after other people's business, having lost his own" (altered from Horace, *Satires* 2.3.19–20).

[3] *newsmonger* Here, political gossip.

[4] *Post-Man* Popular Whig newspaper, issued in the morning.

[5] *Dutch mails* I.e., foreign news; nearby nations sent weekly ships to London bearing mail, including international news correspondence.

[6] *King Augustus* King Frederick Augustus I of Poland (1670– 1733), who participated in the Great Northern War (1700–21) against King Charles XII of Sweden. Charles defeated and [continued …]

welfare than that of his nearest relations. He looked extremely thin in a dearth of news, and never enjoyed himself in a westerly wind.[1] This indefatigable kind of life was the ruin of his shop; for about the time that his favourite prince[2] left the crown of Poland, he broke and disappeared.

This man and his affairs had been long out of my mind, till about three days ago, as I was walking in St. James's Park,[3] I heard somebody at a distance hemming after me: and who should it be but my old neighbour the upholsterer? I saw he was reduced to extreme poverty, by certain shabby superfluities in his dress: for notwithstanding that it was a very sultry day for the time of the year, he wore a loose greatcoat and a muff, with a long campaign wig out of curl; to which he had added the ornament of a pair of black garters buckled under the knee.[4] Upon his coming up to me, I was going to enquire into his present circumstances, but was prevented by his asking me with a whisper whether the last letters brought any accounts that one might rely upon from Bender?[5] I told him none that I heard of, and asked him whether he had yet married his eldest daughter? He told me no. "But pray," says he, "tell me sincerely, what are your thoughts of the King of Sweden?" For though his wife and children were starving, I found his chief concern at present was for this great monarch. I told him that I looked upon him as one of the first heroes of the age. "But pray," says he, "do you think there is anything in the story of his wound?" And finding me surprised at the question, "Nay," says he, "I only propose it to you." I answered that I thought there was no reason to doubt of it. "But why in the heel," says he, "more than in any other part of the body?" "Because," says I, "the bullet chanced to light there."

This extraordinary dialogue was no sooner ended but he began to launch out into a long dissertation upon the affairs of the North; and after having spent some time on them, he told me he was in a great perplexity how to reconcile the *Supplement* with the *English Post*, and had been just now examining what the other papers say upon the same subject. "The *Daily Courant*," says he, "has these words: *We have advices from very good hands that a certain Prince has some matters of great importance under consideration.* This is very mysterious, but the *Post-Boy* leaves us more in the dark; for he tells us *That there are private intimations of measures taken by a certain Prince, which time will bring to light.* Now the *Post-Man*," says he, "who uses[6] to be very clear, refers to the same news in these words, *The late conduct of a certain Prince affords great matter of speculation.* This certain Prince," says the upholsterer, "whom they are all so cautions of naming, I take to be——" Upon which, though there was nobody near us, he whispered something in my ear, which I did not hear, or think worth my while to make him repeat.

We were now to the upper end of the Mall,[7] where were 3 or 4 very odd fellows sitting together upon the bench....

I at length took my leave of the company, and was going away; but had not been gone 30 yards before the upholsterer hemmed again after me. Upon his advancing towards me with a whisper, I expected to hear some secret piece of news which he had not thought fit to communicate to the bench; but instead of that, he desired me[8] in my ear to lend him half a crown.[9] In compassion to so needy a statesman, and to dissipate the confusion I found he was in, I told him, if he pleased, I would give him five shillings, to receive five pounds of him when the Great Turk was driven out of Constantinople;[10] which he very readily accepted, but not before

deposed Frederick, but Frederick regained his crown in 1709 when the tide turned against Sweden. Sweden eventually lost the war to Russia and its allies.

[1] *westerly wind* Such a wind would delay the arrival of the foreign news.

[2] *his favourite prince* I.e., Frederick Augustus I.

[3] *St. James's Park* Fashionable park in London.

[4] *campaign wig* Wig with full, decorative curls; *black garters ... the knee* These were extremely unfashionable at the time.

[5] *Bender* Town in the Ottoman Empire to which Charles XII of Sweden fled in 1709 after a major defeat in the Great Northern War. He remained there for five years.

[6] *uses* I.e., tends.

[7] *Mall* Pall Mall, a promenade in St. James's Park.

[8] *desired me* Requested of me.

[9] *half a crown* Two and a half shillings.

[10] *Constantinople* Capital of the Ottoman Empire, a participant in the Great Northern War.

he had laid down to me the impossibility of such an event as the affairs of Europe now stand.

This paper I design for the particular benefit of those worthy citizens who live more in a coffeehouse than in their shops, and whose thoughts are so taken up with the affairs of the Allies that they forget their customers.

from *The Female Tatler* No. 1 [Introduction, Advertisement] (8 July 1709)

Inspired by *The Tatler*, many periodicals attempted to share in its popularity; *The Female Tatler* (1709–10) was one that succeeded. Through the persona of "Mrs. Crackenthorpe, a lady that knows every thing," *The Female Tatler* entertained its audience—both men and women readers—with scandal and social commentary.

As its eighteenth-century readers did, present-day scholars are still speculating about the authorship of *The Female Tatler*; the writer most frequently suggested as the creator of Mrs. Crackenthorpe is pamphleteer and novelist Delarivier Manley. A male author is also a possibility; it was not unusual for men to adopt female personae in writing periodicals that were, like this one, more social than political in content.

The early success of *The Female Tatler* was clearly marked by the springing up of a rival after eighteen numbers. The original publisher, Benjamin Bragge, faced an alternative *Female Tatler* issued by Abigail Baldwin. Each claimed to be the original confronting an imposter: the Baldwin colophon claims that Crackenthorpe found herself in dispute with her original publisher.

[INTRODUCTION]

I hope Isaac Bickerstaff, Esq.,[1] will not think I invade his property by undertaking a paper of this kind, since tatling was ever adjudged peculiar to our sex; my design is not to rival his performance, or in the least prejudice the reputation he has deservedly gained. But as more ridiculous things are done every day than ten such papers can relate, I desire leave to prate a little to the town, and try what diversion my intelligence can give 'em. My acquaintance, which is a very great part of the town (for I am intimate with everybody at first sight) have encouraged me to this attempt by saying I have the character of knowing everybody's actions, and have sometimes pretended to declare people's intentions, 'tis true, I have twice a week a very great assembly of both sexes, from his Grace my Lord Duke to Mr. Sagathy the spruce mercer[2] in the city; and from her Grace my Lady Duchess to Mrs. Topsail, the sea captain's wife at Wapping;[3] not that my drawing room ever had the least ill character, though a foolish baronet once called it the Scandal Office. But as I am courteous to all persons, and strangers have the same respect paid 'em as my former acquaintance, half the nation visits me, where I have a true history of the world; and to oblige those who are absent from me, by turns, shall endeavour to give it 'em again. I shall date all my advices from my own apartment, which comprehends White's, Will's, the Grecian, Garraway's in Exchange Alley, and all the India houses within the bills of mortality.[4] Since grave statesmen, airy beaus, lawyers, cits,[5] poets, and parsons, and ladies of all degrees assemble there, each person delivers himself according to his talent, which gives me a superficial smattering for all of 'em. The variety of our conversation affords general satisfaction; books are canvassed, removals at court suggested, law cases disputed, the price of stocks told, the beaus and ladies inform us of new fashions, and the first long pocket that was seen in town received its reputation from being approved of at Mrs. Crackenthorpe's drawing room. But when we get into general tittle-tattle, 'tis every little story that happens to get air; those of quality are as liable

[1] *Isaac Bickerstaff, Esq.* Persona adopted by Richard Steele as author of *The Tatler*.

[2] *Sagathy* Fine fabric similar to serge; *mercer* Seller of fine fabrics.

[3] *Wapping* Riverside community of sailors and shipbuilders near London.

[4] *I shall … of mortality* Refers to the organization of *The Tatler*, in which most articles supposedly come from London's popular coffeehouses, with the rest addressed from Bickerstaff's "own apartment"; *White's, Will's … Exchange Alley* London coffee or chocolate houses; *India houses* Shops selling goods imported from India or the East Indies; *within the … of mortality* I.e., within the district of London (the area for which the city keeps a record of births and deaths).

[5] *beaus* Fashionable men; *cits* Urban businesspeople.

to reflection as their inferiors, and seldom any person obliges the company with a new piece of scandal, but 'tis repaid him with above twenty more. And though to support my visiting days, I am forced to act the good Lady Praise-all myself, yet the moment any visitor retires to give place to a fresh comer in, someone of the company breaks out into (if a gentleman), "Really, Mrs. Crackenthorpe, Sir Charles is mighty good company, would he not rail at people so behind their backs. Pray what estate has he?" Says another, "I hear but small, and they say damnably dipped."[1] (If a lady) "Cousin Crackenthorpe, d'you think that lady handsome, she's horrid silly however, and not a bit genteel; but what a load of jewels she had on." "Ay," says another, "they say she lies in 'em;[2] I don't believe her earrings were right." As to particular stories, I shall begin my second paper with them; but in that, and every following piece, as I find encouragement to proceed, shall be very careful, unjustly or ungenteely, not to reflect upon any person whatsoever, but gently to correct the vices and vanities which some of distinction, as well as others, willfully commit....

I would entreat those who are not particularly acquainted with me, that they would not imagine I write this paper merely for the profit that may accrue to me by it; for all that I have the honour to be intimate with, know that I have an estate of 300 *l. per an.*[3] and always kept two maids and a footman; but if I should happen to succeed beyond my expectation, it might so far advance my fortune that I may be able to keep a coach as well as my sister Micklethwait. I shall follow Mr. Bickerstaff's method to get a footing into the world, and deliver the first paper gratis.[4] Afterwards those that will receive them at the price of 1 *d.*[5] will in some measure repay the charge and trouble of such an undertaking; and to prevent mistakes, which may happen by people's enquiring for either of the *Tatlers*, I shall publish mine the contrary days, *viz.* Mondays, Wednesdays, and Fridays.[6]

PHOEBE CRACKENTHORPE.

[ADVERTISEMENT]

A gentleman who can give a very good account of his family would accept a place of about 500 l. per an. *provided it requires little or no attendance, he never having had any great genius to business; he is willing to reside as a companion to some nobleman at his seat in the country, during the summer season, provided he has a chariot to attend him everywhere, and a handsome allowance for clothes and pocket money; or would accompany him to Tunbridge, or the Bath,*[7] *having his charges born.*[8] *He is not much inclined to go abroad, but if the government would send him in a distinguishing post to any pleasant part of Europe, he might be induced to accept of the same, out of a general disposition he has to serve his country.*

Richard Steele, *The Spectator* No. 11 [Inkle and Yarico] (13 March 1711)

The story of Inkle and Yarico first appeared as an anecdote in *A True & Exact History of the Island of Barbados* (1657), the Englishman Richard Ligon's autobiographical account of Barbadian life. Toward the end of the century—decades after it was first retold in the *Spectator* essay below—Inkle and Yarico were revived again as a popular subject for abolitionist poets and playwrights. One version, a musical comedy by George Colman, was among the most popular plays of the late eighteenth century; in this and many later versions, the story is altered so that Yarico is African, and in the end Inkle chooses not to sell her, the lovers reconciling instead.

Dat veniam corvis, vexat censura columbas.[9]

JUVENAL

[1] *damnably dipped* Heavily mortgaged.

[2] *she lies in 'em* I.e., they are fake.

[3] *l. per an.* Pounds per year.

[4] *gratis* Free.

[5] *1 d.* One penny.

[6] *to prevent ... and Fridays* The original *Tatler* was issued on Tuesdays, Thursdays, and Saturdays; *viz.* Abbreviation of the Latin *videlicet*, meaning "namely" or "that is to say."

[7] *Tunbridge, or the Bath* Popular English spa resorts.

[8] *his charges born* I.e., the cost paid by his employer.

[9] *Dat veniam ... columbas* Latin: "[The censor] absolves the raven and harasses the doves" (Juvenal, *Satires* 2.63).

Arietta is visited by all persons of both sexes who have any pretence to wit and gallantry. She is in that time of life which is neither affected with the follies of youth or infirmities of age; and her conversation is so mixed with gaiety and prudence that she is agreeable both to the young and the old. Her behaviour is very frank, without being in the least blameable; and as she is out of the tract of any amorous or ambitious pursuits of her own, her visitants entertain her with accounts of themselves very freely, whether they concern their passions or their interests. I made her a visit this afternoon, having been formerly introduced to the honour of her acquaintance by my friend Will Honeycomb,[1] who has prevailed upon her to admit me sometimes into her assembly, as a civil, inoffensive man. I found her accompanied with one person only, a commonplace talker, who, upon my entrance, rose, and after a very slight civility sat down again, then, turning to Arietta, pursued his discourse, which I found was upon the old topic of constancy in love. He went on with great facility in repeating what he talks every day of his life; and, with the ornaments of insignificant laughs and gestures, enforced his arguments by quotations out of plays and songs which allude to the perjuries of the fair and the general levity[2] of women. Methought he strove to shine more than ordinarily in his talkative way, that he might insult my silence and distinguish himself before a woman of Arietta's taste and understanding. She had often an inclination to interrupt him, but could find no opportunity 'till the larum[3] ceased of itself; which it did not 'till he had repeated and murdered the celebrated story of the Ephesian matron.[4]

Arietta seemed to regard this piece of raillery[5] as an outrage done to her sex; as indeed I have always observed that women, whether out of a nicer regard to their honour, or what other reason I cannot tell, are more sensibly touched with those general aspersions which are cast upon their sex than men are by what is said of theirs.

When she had a little recovered herself from the serious anger she was in, she replied in the following manner.

Sir, when I consider how perfectly new all you have said on this subject is, and that the story you have given us is not quite two thousand years old, I cannot but think it a piece of presumption to dispute with you: but your quotations put me in mind of the fable of the lion and the man. The man, walking with that noble animal, showed him in the ostentation of human superiority a sign of a man killing a lion. Upon which the lion said very justly, "We lions are none of us painters, else we could show a hundred men killed by lions, for one lion killed by a man." You men are writers, and can represent us women as unbecoming as you please in your works, while we are unable to return the injury. You have twice or thrice observed in your discourse that hypocrisy is the very foundation of our education, and that an ability to dissemble our affections is a professed part of our breeding. These and such other reflections are sprinkled up and down the writings of all ages, by authors who leave behind them memorials of their resentment against the scorn of particular women, in invectives against the whole sex. Such a writer, I doubt not, was the celebrated Petronius, who invented the pleasant aggravations of the frailty of the Ephesian lady; but when we consider this question between the sexes, which has been either a point of dispute or raillery ever since there were men and women, let us take facts from plain people, and from such as have not either ambition or capacity to embellish their narrations with any beauties of imagination. I was the other day amusing myself with Ligon's *Account of Barbados*; and, in answer to your well-wrought tale, I will give you (as it dwells upon my memory) out of that honest traveller, in his fifty-fifth page, the history of Inkle and Yarico.

---

[1] *Will Honeycomb* Mr. Spectator is helped in his observations by members of his club, who are delineated as fictional characters. Will Honeycomb is one of them and so is Roger de Coverley, the crusty Tory squire or rural landowner, whose character enables Addison to voice a political mindset which was very far from his own.

[2] *perjuries of the fair* Deceitful behavior of women; *levity* I.e., lack of seriousness.

[3] *larum* Noise.

[4] *story of the Ephesian matron* From Petronius's *Satyricon* (first century CE). A widow, grieving the death of her husband, decides to starve herself to death in his tomb. She is discovered by a soldier, who convinces her to eat and then seduces her. Infatuated with his new lover, the soldier neglects his duties; he has been stationed to guard the crucified corpses of criminals, and one of the corpses is stolen. The widow offers her husband's body to replace the criminal's so the soldier will not be punished for abandoning his post.

[5] *raillery* Banter.

Mr. Thomas Inkle of London, aged twenty years, embarked in the Downs[1] on the good ship called the *Achilles*, bound for the West Indies, on the 16th of June, 1647, in order to improve his fortune by trade and merchandise.[2] Our adventurer was the third son of an eminent citizen, who had taken particular care to instil into his mind an early love of gain, by making him a perfect master of numbers, and consequently giving him a quick view of loss and advantage, and preventing the natural impulses of his passions by prepossession towards his interests. With a mind thus turned, young Inkle had a person every way agreeable, a ruddy vigour in his countenance, strength in his limbs, with ringlets of fair hair loosely flowing on his shoulders. It happened in the course of the voyage that the *Achilles*, in some distress, put into a creek on the main of America, in search of provisions; the youth, who is the hero of my story, among others, went ashore on this occasion. From their first landing they were observed by a party of Indians, who hid themselves in the woods for that purpose. The English unadvisedly marched a great distance from the shore into the country, and were intercepted by the natives, who slew the greatest number of them. Our adventurer escaped, among others, by flying into a forest. Upon his coming into a remote and pathless part of the wood, he threw himself, breathless, on a little hillock, when an Indian maid rushed from a thicket behind him. After the first surprise, they appeared mutually agreeable to each other. If the European was highly charmed with the limbs, features, and wild graces of the naked American, the American was no less taken with the dress, complexion, and shape of an European, covered from head to foot. The Indian grew immediately enamoured of him, and consequently solicitous[3] for his preservation; she therefore conveyed him to a cave, where she gave him a delicious repast of fruits and led him to a stream to slake his thirst. In the midst of these good offices, she would sometimes play with his hair, and delight in the opposition of its colour to that of her fingers; then open his bosom, then laugh at him for covering it. She was, it seems, a person of distinction, for she every day came to him in a different dress, of the most beautiful shells, bugles,[4] and braids. She likewise brought him a great many spoils, which her other lovers had presented to her, so that his cave was richly adorned with all the spotted skins of beasts and most particoloured[5] feathers of fowls which that world afforded. To make his confinement more tolerable, she would carry him in the dusk of the evening, or by the favour of moon-light, to unfrequented groves and solitudes,[6] and show him where to lie down in safety and sleep amidst the falls of waters and melody of nightingales. Her part was to watch and hold him in her arms, for fear of her countrymen, and wake on occasions to consult his safety. In this manner did the lovers pass away their time, till they had learned a language of their own, in which the voyager communicated to his mistress how happy he should be to have her in his country, where she should be clothed in such silks as his waistcoat was made of, and be carried in houses drawn by horses, without being exposed to wind or weather. All this he promised her the enjoyment of, without such fears and alarms as they were there tormented with. In this tender correspondence these lovers lived for several months, when Yarico, instructed by her lover, discovered a vessel on the coast, to which she made signals; and in the night, with the utmost joy and satisfaction, accompanied him to a ships' crew of his countrymen, bound for Barbados. When a vessel from the main[7] arrives in that island, it seems the planters come down to the shore, where there is an immediate market of the Indians and other slaves, as with us of horses and oxen.

To be short, Mr. Thomas Inkle, now coming into English territories, began seriously to reflect upon his loss of time, and to weigh with himself how many days' interest of his money he had lost during his stay with Yarico. This thought made the young man very pensive, and careful what account he should be able to give his friends of his voyage. Upon which considerations, the prudent and frugal young man sold Yarico to a Barbadian merchant; notwithstanding that the poor girl, to

[1] *the Downs* Site of a major English port.

[2] *merchandise* Commerce.

[3] *solicitous* Anxious.

[4] *bugles* Long, round beads.

[5] *particoloured* Multicolored.

[6] *solitudes* Unoccupied places.

[7] *main* Ocean.

incline him to commiserate her condition, told him that she was with child by him. But he only made use of that information to rise in his demands upon the purchaser.

I was so touched with this story (which I think should be always a counterpart to the Ephesian matron) that I left the room with tears in my eyes; which a woman of Arietta's good sense did, I am sure, take for greater applause than any compliments I could make her.

Joseph Addison, *The Spectator* No. 112 [Sir Roger at Church] (19 July 1711)

The essays in *The Spectator* are populated by Mr. Spectator's fictional friends, including a scholar, a city merchant, a military captain, a womanizer, and a clergyman. Number 112 features *The Spectator*'s best known character, Sir Roger de Coverley, an eccentric Tory gentleman who is the squire of a country estate.

A facsimile of the issue is included on the next two pages. *The Spectator* was printed in the format typical for periodicals in the early part of the century: two columns on both sides of a single sheet, with advertising at the end. All issues of *The Spectator* begin with a quotation; number 112 begins with a line attributed to the Greek philosopher Pythagoras. It means "first worship the immortal gods as the law ordains."

from Joseph Addison, *The Spectator* No. 127 [On the Hoop Petticoat] (26 July 1711)

The beginning of the eighteenth century saw the invention of the hoop petticoat, an undergarment containing a framework of whalebone, cane, or wire that was worn to enlarge a woman's skirts. Although they were expensive, cumbersome, and mercilessly mocked by contemporary satirists—as in the *Spectator* essay below—they remained fashionable into the 1780s.

Quantum est in rebus inane?[1]

PERS.

It is our custom at Sir Roger's,[2] upon the coming in of the post, to sit about a pot of coffee and hear the old knight read *Dyer's Letter*;[3] which he does with his spectacles upon his nose, and in an audible voice, smiling very often at those little strokes of satire which are so frequent in the writings of that author. I afterwards communicate to the knight such packets as I receive under the quality of SPECTATOR.[4] The following letter chancing to please him more than ordinary, I shall publish it at his request.

Mr. SPECTATOR,

You have diverted the town almost a whole month at the expense of the country;[5] it is now high time that you should give the country their revenge. Since your withdrawing from this place, the fair sex are run into great extravagancies. Their petticoats, which began to heave and swell before you left us, are now blown up into a most enormous concave, and rise every day more and more: in a word, sir, since our women know themselves to be out of the eye of the SPECTATOR, they will be kept within no compass. You praised them a little too soon for the modesty of their head-dresses;[6] for as the humour[7] of a sick person is often driven out of one limb into another, their superfluity of ornaments, instead of

[1] *Quantum … inane* Latin: "How much emptiness is in the world" (Persius, *Satires* 1.1).

[2] *Sir Roger* Mr. Spectator's fictional friend Sir Roger de Coverley, a lovable country squire.

[3] *Dyer's Letter* A long-running newsletter commonly read by Tory country gentlemen (such as Sir Roger), *Dyer's Weekly Letter* was known for fabricating stories and was often mocked by Addison and other Whigs.

[4] *such packets … of SPECTATOR* I.e., letters to the editor of *The Spectator*. Addison and Steele published both real and fictional letters; the following letter is Addison's work.

[5] *You have … the country* In issue number 106, Mr. Spectator accepts an invitation to spend a month in the country, and he remains there until number 133. Many of the essays during this period focus on life in the country (see number 127 above, and number 119 in the "Town and Country" Contexts section elsewhere in this volume).

[6] *You praised … head-dresses* In number 98, Mr. Spectator declares himself pleased that the fashion for extravagant, tall hairstyles has passed.

[7] *humour* In early eighteenth-century medicine, one of four governing substances that control the body. Disease was still thought to result from an imbalance in the humors.

Numb. CXII.

The SPECTATOR.

Ἀθανάτους μὲν πρῶτα θεοὺς, νόμῳ ὡς διάκειται,
Τιμᾶ ——. Pyth.

Monday, July 9. 1711.

I Am always very well pleased with a Country *Sunday*; and think, if keeping holy the Seventh Day had been only a human Institution, it would have been the best Method that could have been thought of for the polishing and civilizing of Mankind. It is certain the Country-People would soon degenerate into a kind of Savages and Barbarians, were there not such frequent Returns of a stated Time, in which the whole Village meet together with their best Faces, and in their cleanliest Dress, to converse with one another upon indifferent Subjects, hear their Duties explained to them, and join together in Adoration of the supreme Being. *Sunday* clears away the Rust of the whole Week, not only as it refreshes in their Minds the Notions of Religion, but as it puts both the Sexes upon appearing in their most agreeable Forms, and exerting all such Qualities as are apt to give them a Figure in the Eye of the Village. A Country-Fellow distinguishes himself as much in the *Church-yard*, as a Citizen does upon the *Change*, the whole Parish-Politicks being generally discuss'd in that Place either after Sermon or before the Bell rings.

My Friend Sir Roger being a good Churchman, has beautified the Inside of his Church with several Texts of his own chusing: He has likewise given a handsom Pulpit-Cloth, and railed in the Communion-Table at his own Expence. He has often told me that at his coming to his Estate he found the Parish very irregular; and that in order to make them kneel and join in the Responses, he gave every one of them a Hassock and a Common-prayer Book; and at the same Time employed an itinerant Singing-Master, who goes about the Country for that Purpose, to instruct them rightly in the Tunes of the Psalms; upon which they now very much value themselves, and indeed out-do most of the Country Churches that I have ever heard.

As Sir Roger is Landlord to the whole Congregation, he keeps them in very good Order, and will suffer no Body to sleep in it besides himself; for if by Chance he has been surprized into a short Nap at Sermon, upon recovering out of it he stands up and looks about him, and if he sees any Body else nodding, either wakes them himself, or sends his Servant to them. Several other of the old Knight's Particularities break out upon these Occasions: Sometimes he will be lengthening out a Verse in the Singing-Psalms half a Minute after the rest of the Congregation have done with it; sometimes, when he is pleased with the Matter of his Devotion, he pronounces *Amen* three or four times to the same Prayer; and sometimes stands up when every Body else is upon their Knees, to count the Congregation, or see if any of his Tenants are missing.

I was Yesterday very much surprized to hear my old Friend, in the Midst of the Service, calling out to one *John Mathews* to mind what he was about, and not disturb the Congregation. This *John Mathews* it seems is remarkable for being an idle Fellow, and at that Time was kicking his Heels for his Diversion. This Authority of the Knight, though exerted in that odd Manner which accompanies him in all Circumstances of Life, has a very good Effect upon the Parish, who are not polite enough to see any thing ridiculous in his Behaviour; besides that, the general good Sense and Worthiness of his Character, make his Friends observe these little Singularities as Foils that rather set off than blemish his good Qualities.

As soon as the Sermon is finished, no Body presumes to stir till Sir Roger is gone out of the Church. The Knight walks from his Seat in the Chancel, between a double Row of his Tenants, that stand bowing to him on each Side; and every now and then inquires how such an one's Wife or Mother, or Son, or Father do whom he does not see

see at Church; which is understood as a secret Reprimand to the Person that is absent.

The Chaplain has often told me, that upon a Catechizing-day, when Sir ROGER has been pleased with a Boy that answers well, he has ordered a Bible to be given him next Day for his Encouragement; and sometimes accompanies it with a Flitch of Bacon to his Mother. Sir ROGER has likewise added five Pounds a Year to the Clerk's Place; and that he may encourage the young Fellows to make themselves perfect in the Church-Service, has promised upon the Death of the present Incumbent, who is very old, to bestow it according to Merit.

The fair Understanding between Sir ROGER and his Chaplain, and their mutual Concurrence in doing Good, is the more remarkable, because the very next Village is famous for the Differences and Contentions that rise between the Parson and the 'Squire, who live in a perpetual State of War. The Parson is always preaching at the 'Squire, and the 'Squire to be revenged on the Parson never comes to Church. The 'Squire has made all his Tenants Atheists and Tithe-Stealers; while the Parson instructs them every *Sunday* in the Dignity of his Order, and insinuates to them in almost every Sermon, that he is a better Man than his Patron. In short, Matters are come to such an Extremity, that the 'Squire has not said his Prayers either in publick or private this half Year; and that the Parson threatens him, if he does not mend his Manners, to pray for him in the Face of the whole Congregation.

Feuds of this Nature, though too frequent in the Country, are very fatal to the ordinary People; who are so used to be dazled with Riches, that they pay as much Deference to the Understanding of a Man of an Estate, as of a Man of Learning; and are very hardly brought to regard any Truth, how important soever it may be, that is preached to them, when they know there are several Men of five hundred a Year who do not believe it.

LONDON: Printed for *Sam. Buckley*, at the *Dolphin* in *Little-Britain*; and Sold by *A. Baldwin* in *Warwick-Lane*; where Advertisements are taken in; as also by *Charles Lillie*, Perfumer, at the Corner of *Beauford-Buildings* in

being entirely banished, seems only fallen from their heads upon their lower parts. What they have lost in height they make up in breadth and, contrary to all rules of architecture, widen the foundations at the same time that they shorten the superstructure. Were they, like Spanish jennets,[1] to impregnate by the wind, they could not have thought on a more proper invention. But as we do not yet hear any particular use in this petticoat, or that it contains anything more than what was supposed to be in those of a scantier make, we are wonderfully at a loss about it.

The women give out, in defense of these wide bottoms, that they are airy, and very proper for the season; but this I look upon to be only a pretence, and a piece of art, for it is well known we have not had a more moderate summer these many years, so that it is certain the heat they complain of cannot be in the weather. Besides, I would fain ask these tender-constitutioned ladies why they should require more cooling than their mothers before them.

I find several speculative persons are of opinion that our sex has of late years been very saucy, and that the hoop petticoat is made use of to keep us at a distance. It is most certain that a woman's honour cannot be better entrenched than after this manner, in circle within circle, amidst such a variety of outworks and lines of circumvallation.[2] A female who is thus invested in whalebone is sufficiently secured against the approaches of an ill-bred fellow, and might as well think of Sir George Etheridge's way of making love in a tub,[3] as in the midst of so many hoops.

Among these various conjectures, there are men of superstitious tempers who look upon the hoop petticoat as a kind of prodigy.[4] Some will have it that it portends the downfall of the French King, and observe that the farthingale appeared in England a little before the ruin of the Spanish Monarchy.[5] Others are of opinion that it foretells battle and bloodshed, and believe it of the same prognostication as the tail of a blazing star. For my part, I am apt to think it is a sign that multitudes are coming into the world rather than going out of it.[6]

The first time I saw a lady dressed in one of these petticoats, I could not forbear blaming her in my own thoughts for walking abroad when she was *so near her time*,[7] but soon recovered myself out of my error when I found all the modish part of the sex as *far gone* as herself. It is generally thought some crafty women have thus betrayed their companions into hoops, that they might make them accessory to their own concealments, and by that means escape the censure of the world,[8] as wary generals have sometimes dressed two or three dozen of their friends in their own habit,[9] that they might not draw upon themselves any particular attacks from the enemy. The strutting petticoat smoothes all distinctions, levels the mother with the daughter, and sets maids and matrons, wives and widows, upon the same bottom. In the meanwhile, I cannot but be troubled to see so many well-shaped innocent virgins bloated up and walking up and down like big-bellied women.

Should this fashion get among the ordinary people, our public ways would be so crowded that we should want street-room. Several congregations of the best fashion find themselves already very much straitened, and if the mode increase I wish it may not drive many ordinary women into meetings and conventicles.[10]

[1] *jennets* Spanish horses. In his *Natural History*, the ancient Roman author Pliny describes Spanish horses conceiving offspring by facing the west wind (8.67).

[2] *outworks* Outer defensive structures; *circumvallation* Surrounding fortification.

[3] *Sir George ... a tub* In George Etherege's play *The Comical Revenge; or, Love in a Tub* (1664), a degenerate Frenchman is made to wear a large barrel.

[4] *prodigy* I.e., omen.

[5] *farthingale* Stiffened petticoat shaped by a wire or whalebone frame. It became popular in the English court in the mid-sixteenth century; *ruin of ... Monarchy* The Spanish monarchy went bankrupt in 1557.

[6] *a sign that ... of it* I.e., a sign of many impending births, as all the wearers of hoop petticoats must be pregnant.

[7] *so near her time* So far along in her pregnancy.

[8] *It is ... the world* This may be a serious assertion; the origins of the hoop petticoat were not known, and one rumored possibility was that the style was originated by a woman who needed to conceal an illegitimate pregnancy.

[9] *habit* I.e., uniform.

[10] *straitened* Narrowly confined; *mode* Fashion; *meetings and conventicles* Secret meetings of religious nonconformists (into which people would be forced because there was no room in the churches).

Should our sex at the same time take it into their heads to wear trunk breeches[1] (as who knows what their indignation at this female treatment may drive them to) a man and his wife would fill a whole pew.

You know, sir, it is recorded of Alexander the Great[2] that in his Indian expedition he buried several suits of armour which by his directions were made much too big for any of his soldiers, in order to give posterity an extraordinary idea of him, and make them believe he had commanded an army of giants. I am persuaded that if one of the present petticoats happens to be hung up in any repository of curiosities, it will lead into the same error the generations that lie some removes from us—unless we can believe our posterity will think so disrespectfully of their great-grandmothers, that they made themselves monstrous to appear amiable.

When I survey this new-fashioned rotunda[3] in all its parts, I cannot but think of the old philosopher who after having entered into an Egyptian temple and looked about for the idol of the place, at length discovered a little black monkey enshrined in the midst of it, upon which he could not forbear crying out (to the great scandal of the worshippers), "What a magnificent palace is here for such a ridiculous inhabitant!"

Though you have taken a resolution in one of your papers to avoid descending to particularities of dress, I believe you will not think it below you, on so extraordinary an occasion, to unhoop the fair sex and cure this fashionable timpani that is got among them. I am apt to think the petticoat will shrink of its own accord at your first coming to town; at least a touch of your pen will make it contract itself, like the sensitive plant,[4] and by that means oblige several who are either terrified or astonished at this portentous novelty, and among the rest,

Your humble servant, &c.

[1] *trunk breeches* Men's hose covering the upper half of the legs, padded or folded so that the fabric puffed out from the body. This style was fashionable in the last half of the sixteenth century.

[2] *Alexander the Great* Ancient king who conquered a vast empire stretching from Greece to India.

[3] *rotunda* Round building, usually with a dome.

[4] *sensitive plant* Plant with leaves that fold up when they are touched.

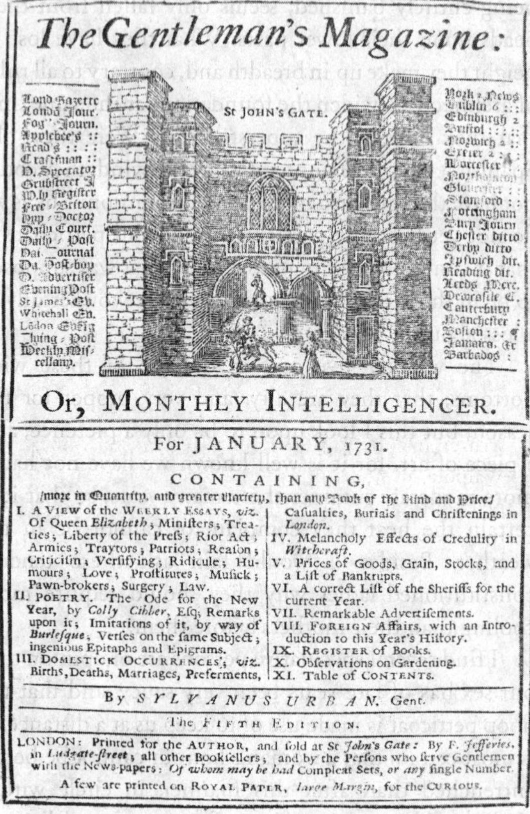

The Gentleman's Magazine:

Lond Gazette
Londō Jour.
Fog's Journ.
Applebee's
Read's
Craftſman
D. Spectator
Grubſtreet J.
W.ly Regiſter
Free-Briton
Hyp-Doctor
Daily Court.
Daily-Poſt
Dai. Journal
Da. Poſt-boy
D. Advertiſer
Evening Poſt
St James's Ev.
Whitehall Ev.
Lōdon Ev&g
Flying-Poſt
Weekly Miſcellany.

St JOHN'S GATE.

York 2 News
Dublin 6
Edinburgh 2
Briſtol
Norwich 2
Exeter 2
Worceſter
Northampton
Glouceſter
Stamford
Nottingham
Bury Journ
Cheſter ditto
Derby ditto
Ipſwich dit.
Reading dit.
Leeds Merc.
Newcaſtle C.
Canterbury
Mancheſter
Boſton
Jamaica, &c
Barbados

Or, MONTHLY INTELLIGENCER.

For JANUARY, 1731.

CONTAINING,

(more in Quantity, and greater Variety, than any Book of the Kind and Price.)

I. A VIEW of the WEEKLY ESSAYS, *viz.* Of Queen *Elizabeth*; Miniſters; Treaties; Liberty of the Preſs; Riot Act; Armies; Traytors; Patriots; Reaſon; Criticiſm; Verſifying; Ridicule; Humours; Love; Proſtitutes; Muſick; Pawn-brokers; Surgery; Law.

II. POETRY. The Ode for the New Year, by *Colly Cibber*, Eſq; Remarks upon it; Imitations of it, by way of *Burleſque*; Verſes on the ſame Subject; ingenious Epitaphs and Epigrams.

III. DOMESTICK OCCURRENCES; *viz.* Births, Deaths, Marriages, Preferments, Caſualties, Burials and Chriſtenings in *London*.

IV. Melancholy Effects of Credulity in *Witchcraft*.

V. Prices of Goods, Grain, Stocks, and a Liſt of Bankrupts.

VI. A correct Liſt of the Sheriffs for the current Year.

VII. Remarkable Advertiſements.

VIII. FOREIGN Affairs, with an Introduction to this Year's Hiſtory.

IX. REGISTER of Books.

X. Obſervations on Gardening.

XI. Table of CONTENTS.

By *SYLVANUS URBAN*, Gent.

The FIFTH EDITION.

LONDON: Printed for the AUTHOR, and ſold at St *John's Gate*: By F. *Jefferies*, in *Ludgate-ſtreet*; all other Bookſellers; and by the Perſons who ſerve Gentlemen with the News-papers: *Of whom may be had* Compleat Sets, *or any* ſingle Number.

A few are printed on ROYAL PAPER, *large Margin*, for the CURIOUS.

Cover of the first issue of *The Gentleman's Magazine*, January 1731. The first successful periodical that was truly miscellaneous in content, *The Gentleman's Magazine* began a trend of general-interest journals that eventually resulted in the development of magazines as they exist today. The *Magazine*'s founder, printer Edward Cave, employed his own writers for original articles, but he also filled his pages with material taken from newspapers, recent books, and other periodicals. The title page lists some of the publications he used as sources, arrayed on either side of a picture of the gatehouse where the magazine was created and sold.

The Gentleman's Magazine reigned for some time as the most widely circulated periodical in print. By 1741, ten years after the first issue was released, Samuel Johnson (who wrote for the magazine) reported that it was "read as far as the English language extends." It continued publication until 1914.

Lady Mary Wortley Montagu, *The Nonsense of Common-Sense* No. 5 [On Publishing] (17 January 1738)

Lady Mary Wortley Montagu is believed to have been the first woman to write one of the many political essay periodicals published in London during the eighteenth century—and the only one to do so before 1770. She concealed her unconventional female authorship by writing anonymously. Her anonymity was so successful that she was not identified as the author of *The Nonsense of Common-Sense* (1737–38) until the twentieth century.

The Nonsense of Common-Sense, which was written in support of Whig Prime Minister Robert Walpole, was part of a vicious print war that took place during his administration (1721–42), in which the pro-Walpole and Opposition papers engaged in endless argument and insult. Many pro-government writers were paid by Walpole or his supporters, but Montagu did not write for bribes. She was among those who genuinely admired and supported Walpole's politics. Like many politically affiliated periodicals, *The Nonsense of Common-Sense* claimed to offer "short essays of morality, without any touch of politics"; while some essays do in fact discuss political policy directly, numerous others do not. All, however, attack the anti-Walpole papers. The article below, for instance, was likely written in response to recent Opposition articles defending the nobility of the free press and arguing against government interference. The "*Common-Sense*" referred to in the title was London's most popular anti-Walpole periodical; the author's political stance would thus have been apparent to her readers.

I have seen the world in a great variety of lights, but till very lately never saw it in the light of an author, nor was sensible what difficulties those poor creatures are obliged to struggle with. I always believed we enjoyed at present the liberty of the press, and I was confirmed in this opinion by observing that some people even abused that liberty to a degree of licentiousness; and, without respect to the highest characters or a due regard to moral truth, endeavoured to raise laughter and get readers by the severest, and sometimes by the most unjust raillery.[1] This provoked me to handle a weapon very new to me, and take up my pen in defence of good nature and good breeding. I very well foresaw that so innocent a design would meet with but small applause; and, as I declared in my first paper, I did not expect to be supported by any party. I was not ignorant, if my ultimate intention had been the sale of my writings, that I chose a very wrong plan. The herd of readers only seek for gratifications of their own envy; and as Mr. Dryden has said somewhere,

> The reader's malice helps the writer's out.[2]

It is very easy to be witty in marking out the frailties of particular men, or at least to appear so to those who are willing to believe the pleasure they receive from a libel rather rises from the author's wit than their own ill-nature; when God knows, a very small portion of the first, with a large quantity of the other, will put off the coarsest style and the most trite conceits that were ever wrote by —— or ——. I was sensible of this, yet I thought that an honest indifferent subject of England might utter his own natural sentiments without any molestation whatever; and that the worst misfortune would be the censure of being very dull, when he confined himself to antiquated morals without satire, puns, or double entendres.

You shall hear by a plain story how much I was mistaken. I carried my paper with great innocence to the first printer come into my head, not enquiring what party or principle he was of; believing it ought to be as indifferent to me as the religion of my shoemaker, when I bespeak a pair of shoes, supposing he would follow my orders upon being paid for his labour. He read it over with great earnestness, and being charmed with the novelty, gave me many thanks for choosing him for the publisher; and assured me with very significant gestures, it was lucky that I did not go to any of his brethren, who would have used me ill. I did not trouble myself with enquiring what he meant, but desired him to print away, and a few days after, carried him my second

---

[1] *raillery* Ridicule.

[2] *The reader's ... writer's out* From "On Mr. Hobbs," a poem written by John Sheffield (1647–1721); it was included in the anthology *Miscellany Poems* (1684), edited by John Dryden.

paper. I then found him in a very different temper; he told me in a great fright that he had not questioned[1] I intended to write against the ministry. That his bread depended on that set of people. That he was told by some of my readers that I was on the other side, which he never could have supposed a gentleman of my appearance to be. That the Court[2] writers were a parcel of miserable hirelings; and he should be undone if he was thought to be employed by them. I could not help laughing at his scruples,[3] and had the patience to read over my paper three times to him, and endeavour to make him comprehend that there was not one party-stroke from one end to the other of it. He sighed, shook his head, and murmured several times to himself, "This will never take"; and then turning short upon me, said, "Sir, what if you clapt in a home reflection or two about Sir ———? I own it is very hard to find anything new to say against him. A little dash against Squire ———, his competitor, might sell too." When he found me not willing to comply with these projects, "But, Sir," added he vehemently, "here is no waggery:[4] If you are obstinately bent not to be read by the politicians on either side, you should try to please the ladies and fine gentlemen of the age. A joke now and then would be very acceptable; if you have none of your own, though that's strange methinks, there are a great many of Durphy's plays and Tom Brown's epistles[5] that you may steal from safely, they being mostly out of print. I have a collection by me at your service." I gave him thanks for this courteous offer, but utterly refused making use of it; and told him my intention was to write to those that could admit of plain reasoning, without any touches of that kind. That I was not yet persuaded that there was not still a considerable number of honest men and modest women in the nation, and it was to them I dedicated my labours. With some other persuasions, and the money paid beforehand, I prevailed on him to promise to print my last paper, though, I saw, he left me with a visible discontent in his countenance, and a great contempt for my whimsical way of thinking.

However, my paper appears the Tuesday following, but to my great surprise, my printer had thrown in a little bawdy at the end of a paragraph that no way led to any idea of that sort.[6] You may imagine how much I was provoked; I blotted it out of the few copies I sent to my friends, and immediately sent for the fellow to expostulate with him, but found him as much out of humour as myself. "I'll assure you, Sir," said he, in a heat, "I have done all I could for the service of your paper; but it is a damned ministerial thing,[7] and the hawkers refuse to sell it, and the coffee-houses will not take it in, and if you will rail at nobody, nor put in no feigned names that everybody may understand,[8] all the bawdy in the *Dunciad*[9] will not carry it off. Here's a paper," continued he, pulling the *Common Sense* of December 31 out of his pocket. "I'll engage this shall be read all over the kingdom. Do but observe how wittily this polite author rallies Mr. Henley in his affliction.[10] What a charming jest he makes of all sentiments of friendship and conjugal affection. Then there is something very sly in the sneers upon the words piety, affability, and sincerity."[11] He had gone on much farther in his praise of this paper, with which he was delighted, but that finding myself beginning to be angry, I told him coldly that he should be no longer troubled with mine; and that I found myself entirely unqualified to be an author according to his taste.

---

[1] *not questioned* Assumed.

[2] *Court* I.e., pro-Walpole.

[3] *scruples* Hesitations.

[4] *waggery* Joke.

[5] *Durphy's … epistles* Thomas D'Urfey (1653–1723) and Tom Brown (1663–1704) were both writers known for coarse wit.

[6] *bawdy* Smut or sexual innuendo; *thrown in … that sort* The unnecessary lewd comment was inserted into *The Nonsense of Common-Sense* No. 2.

[7] *damned ministerial thing* Piece written in support of Walpole's ministry.

[8] *nor put … may understand* When writers insulted well-known public figures, they often gave their targets false names with obvious meanings.

[9] *Dunciad* Satire by Alexander Pope (1688–1744). Pope was a major contributor to anti-Walpole literature, as well as Montagu's personal enemy; Pope and Montagu insulted each other mercilessly in their writings.

[10] *rallies Mr. … his affliction* The 31 December 1737 issue of *Common-Sense* targets the pro-Walpole writer John Henley, ridiculing him for his emotional reaction to his wife's recent death.

[11] *piety, affability, and sincerity* Words used in the *Common-Sense* article's cynical description of Henley's late wife.

After he was gone, I began seriously to consider the injustice and ill consequence of the paper he recommended. I look upon tenderness and grief as the excrescences[1] of virtue. They are only to be found in the humane and honest mind. As only such a one is capable of the impression of a sincere friendship, divested of all interested[2] views, the sincerity of such a friendship never appears in so strong a light as by the marks of respect and the tears we pay to the ashes of a dead friend, from whom we can expect no return. Whatever services are done, or professions made, to a living friend, even those to one in distress, as rarely as they happen, may possibly be in a view of receiving some pleasure or future advantage from them, since nobody is thrown so low by fortune but some accident may make them useful to those even in the highest rank; but when the expressions of our love can never reach their knowledge, they can only proceed from a heart truly touched, a real gratitude for past obligations, and are real effects of love and esteem.

How amiable appears to me a heart capable of such an attachment! How rare it is to see a friendship continued for a length of years without decay! It is natural for weak minds to grow weary of any engagement that lasts long; and it is beyond the power of merit to fix a light or engage a selfish man. 'Tis, in my opinion, the best measure we can take of anyone's value, to know how far they are capable of being a friend. I could, on this occasion, quote the greatest authors of antiquity; few have ever been capable of such friendships as they have described, but hitherto all have seemed, at best, to respect those who could feel such disinterested[3] and delicate sentiments. We are now in an age that they are become the objects of ridicule, and we are told we are to laugh at the most legitimate sorrow, and despise the noblest proofs of the noblest mind.

My head being full of these thoughts, I could not help throwing some of them together, which I intended to publish, and carried them to a declared printer on the Court side,[4] not with any view of listing myself under him, but despairing of prevailing with any others to print for me. I confess I was used with more civility. My paper was courteously read over, but returned with, "Sir, I can print nothing against the ministry." "This is not against any ministry," answered I, "either past, present, or future." "Why, I own," said he, "it is very well couched, and I cannot directly point where the sting lies; but it must be so, for I never heard of any volunteers in their service, and you are not recommended to me by any considerable person;[5] but if it should be so, and that you desire to be taken notice of, in order to be taken in,[6] let me tell you, Sir, it is taking bread out of other men's mouths; and between, you and I, Sir, considering their number, there is not too much comes to every man's share." I interrupted him by saying this was only intended to be a moral paper. "A moral paper," cried he, starting, "And how do you expect to get money by it?" "I do not propose to get money by it," said I. Upon which he turned from me with the air of compassionate contempt with which good-natured people look upon those they suppose *non compos mentis*.[7]

I am now convinced by these trials that the liberty of the press is as much blocked up by the combination of the printers, pamphlet-sellers, authors, &c., or perhaps more, than it would be by an Act of Parliament; and that without bribery, or some methods tantamount to it, it is as impossible for a man to express his thoughts to the public as it would be for one honest fishmonger to retail turbots[8] in a plentiful season below the price fixed on them by the trade. I have with much ado prevailed on an obscure printer to print this plain story;[9] and the poor fellow is half frighted out of his wits for fear his

---

[1] *excrescences* Natural outgrowths.

[2] *interested* I.e., self-interested.

[3] *disinterested* Not self-interested.

[4] *declared printer … Court side* Printer that openly states a pro-Walpole stance.

[5] *I never … considerable person* I.e., no one writes for Walpole unless they have been paid, and no one wealthy enough to have bribed you has recommended you to me.

[6] *to be taken in* To be enlisted as a paid pro-Walpole writer.

[7] *non compos mentis* Latin: not of sound mind.

[8] *turbots* Flatfish.

[9] *prevailed on … plain story* This statement is a fiction; all the numbers of *The Nonsense of Common-Sense* were issued by the same printer.

fraternity should find out he dares print without their permission.

N.B.[1] Whereas we have been informed that gentlemen have sent to several booksellers and pamphlet-shops for this paper, and have had for answer, they had none of them, nor could find any of them; we are therefore obliged to give gentlemen notice that when they receive any such answer, it is only because the bookseller or pamphlet-seller will not be at the pains to send for what they want; for the publisher of this paper, where everyone may be supplied, is well known to all the booksellers and pamphlet-sellers in town. In all such cases it would be easy for gentlemen to insist upon being supplied with whatever they want by those they usually deal with; for every bookseller and pamphlet-seller must know where to find anything just published and often advertised.

from Eliza Haywood, *The Female Spectator* Book 1 [Erminia] (April 1744)

Eliza Haywood was one of the most popular novelists of the eighteenth century, but her periodical *The Female Spectator* (1744–46), published anonymously, was even more successful than her novels. Like the earlier *Spectator* referred to in the title, its stated purpose was the moral improvement of its readers. *The Female Spectator* was issued monthly—less often than many other essay periodicals—and was relatively longer, printed in books instead of on unbound sheets. Each issue contained one long, loosely organized essay blending social commentary with personal advice; letters from real or imaginary readers; and morally instructive stories such as the one below.

… [Erminia] and her brother were the only issue of a very happy marriage, and both shared equally the tenderness of their indulgent parents. They were educated in the strictest rudiments of piety and virtue, and had something so innately good in their dispositions as made the practice of those duties which to others seem most severe, to them a pleasure. The family lived in the country and came not to London but once in two or three years, and then stayed but a short time, till, the young gentleman having finished his studies at Cambridge, it was thought proper he should see more of the world than he could possibly do in that retired[2] part. But fearing he should fall into the vices of the age, in case he were left too much to himself, they resolved on removing to town in order to have him still under their own eye.…

Soon after their arrival winter came on, and wherever either [Erminia] or her brother went, nothing was talked on but the masquerade; neither of them had ever seen one, and the eagerness they observed in others excited a curiosity in them. Their parents would not oppose the inclination they expressed, and consented they should go together, but gave their son a strict charge to be watchful over his sister, and never to quit sight of her till he brought her home to them again. Though this was an entertainment unknown in England in their gay time of life, and, consequently, they were strangers to the methods practised at it, yet having heard somewhat of the dangers, they repeated over and over the same injunction to the young gentleman, who assured them he would take the same care as if themselves were present.

Alas! he little knew how impracticable it was to keep his promise; they were no sooner entered than both were bewildered amidst the promiscuous[3] assembly—the strange habits,[4] the hurry, the confusion quite distracted their attention. They kept close to each other, indeed, for some time, but were soon separated by a crowd that came rushing between them, some accosting the brother, others the sister. Those who talked to them easily found they were strangers to the conversation of the place, and whispering it about, our young country gentry served as butts[5] for the company to level all the arrows of their wit against.

Erminia had lost her brother for a considerable time, and was encompassed by persons of both sexes whose mode of speech was neither pleasing to her, nor did she know how to answer; at last, the sight of a blue

[1] *N.B.* Abbreviation of the Latin *nota bene*, meaning "note well."

[2] *retired* Secluded.

[3] *promiscuous* Indiscriminately mixed.

[4] *habits* Costumes.

[5] *butts* Targets.

domino,[1] which was the habit he went in, revived her, and she ran to the person who wore it, and catching fast hold of him, "Dear brother," (cried she) "let us go home, I have been frighted to death by those noisy people yonder. I wonder what pleasure anybody can take in being here."

The person she accosted made no reply, but taking her under the arm, conducted her out as she had desired, and went with her into a hackney coach. Little suspecting the accident that had befallen her, she attended not to what orders he gave the coachman, and, glad to find herself out of a place which for her had so few charms, entertained her supposed brother with a repetition of what had been said to her till the coach stopped at the door of a great house. As it was not yet light, she distinguished it not from their own, and innocently jumped out, and was within the entry before she discovered her mistake; but as soon as she did, "Bless me," (cried she) "where have you brought me, brother?" She followed him, however, upstairs, where he, pulling off his vizard, discovered[2] a face she had never seen before.

Never was surprise and terror greater than that which now seized the heart of this unfortunate young lady. She wept, she prayed, she conjured him by everything that is called sacred or worthy of veneration, to suffer her to depart. But he was one to whom, had she been less beautiful, her innocence was a sufficient charm. The more averse and shocked she seemed at the rude behaviour with which he immediately began to treat her, the more were his desires inflamed, and, having her in his power, and in a house where all her shrieks and cries were as unavailing as her tears and entreaties, he satiated, by the most barbarous force, his base inclinations, and for a moment's joy to himself was the eternal ruin of a poor creature whose ignorance of the world and the artifices of mankind alone had betrayed to him.

The cruel conquest gained, he was at a loss how to dispose of his prey; a thousand times she begged he would complete the villainy he had begun, and kill the wretch he had made; but this was what neither his safety, nor perhaps his principle, wicked as he was, would permit him to do. He easily found she was a girl of condition, and doubted not but she had friends who would revenge the injury had been done her, could they by any means discover the author; he therefore, after having in vain endeavoured to pacify her and prevail on her to comply with his desires of holding a secret correspondence with him, compelled her to let him bind a handkerchief over her eyes, that she might not be able to describe either the house or street where she had been abused; then put her into a hackney coach, which he ordered to drive into an obscure, dirty lane in the Strand,[3] near the water side, where he made her be let down, and immediately drove away with all the speed the horses could make....

[Erminia returns to her family and is persuaded to tell them what has happened to her.]

Never was so disconsolate a family, and the more so, as they could by no means discover the brutal author of their misfortune; the precautions he had taken rendered all their search in vain, and when some days after they prevailed on Erminia to go with them in a coach almost throughout all London, yet could she not point out either the house or street where her ravisher had carried her.

To fill the measure of her woes, a young gentleman arrived in town who long had loved her, and had the approbation[4] of her friends, and for whom she also felt all of that passion that can inspire a virtuous mind; he had by some business been prevented from accompanying the family in their removal, but was now come full of the hopes of having his desires completed by a happy marriage with the sweet Erminia.

Melancholy reverse of fate! Instead of being received with open arms and that cheerful welcome he had been accustomed to and had reason to expect, the most heavy gloom appeared on all the faces of those he was permitted to see; but Erminia no sooner heard of his arrival than she shut herself up in her chamber, and would by no means be prevailed upon to appear before him. To excuse her absence, they told him she was indisposed;

[1] *domino* Costume commonly worn at masquerades, comprised of a hooded cloak and a mask.

[2] *vizard* Mask; *discovered* Uncovered.

[3] *the Strand* London street known in the eighteenth century for its theaters, taverns, and brothels.

[4] *approbation* Approval.

but this seemed all pretence, because the freedom with which they had always lived together might very well have allowed him the privilege of visiting her in her chamber. He complained of this alteration in their behaviour, and doubted not, at first, but it was occasioned by the preference they gave to some new rival. The true reason, however, could not be kept so much a secret, but that it was whispered about, and he soon got a hint of it. How sensible a shock it must give him may easily be conceived, but he got the better of it, and after a very little reflection went to her father, told him the afflicting news he had heard, but withal assured him that as his love for Erminia was chiefly founded on her virtue, an act of force could not be esteemed any breach of it, and was still ready to marry her, if she would consent.

This generosity charmed the whole family, but Erminia could not think of accepting the offer; the more she found him worthy of her affections in her state of innocence, the less could she support the shame of being his in the condition she now was. She told her parents that she had taken a firm resolution never to marry, and begged their permission to retire to an aunt, who was married to an old clergyman and lived in one of the most remote counties in England. Dear as her presence was, they found something so truly noble in her way of thinking that they would not oppose it; and even her lover, in spite of himself, could not forbear applauding what gave a thousand daggers to his heart.

Erminia in a short time departed for her country residence; nothing was ever more mournful than the leave she took of her parents and brother; but not all the entreaties of her lover, by messages and letters, could gain so far upon her modesty as to prevail on her to see him; she sent him, however, a letter full of the most tender acknowledgements of his love and generosity, and with this he was obliged to be content.

It is not every woman would have resented such an injury in the same manner with Erminia, and it must be confessed that her notions of honour and virtue had somewhat superlatively delicate in them. What a loss then to the world to be deprived of so amiable an example, as she would have doubtless proved, of conjugal truth, tenderness, and a strict observance of every duty that men so much desire to find in her they make a partner for life. How can her brutal ravisher reflect, as it is impossible but he sometimes must, on the mischiefs he has occasioned, without horrors such as must render life a burden! Though he yet is hid in darkness, and left no traces by which the public may point the villain out and treat him with the abhorrence he deserves, his own thoughts must surely be the avengers of his crime and make him more truly wretched than any exterior punishment could do....

Samuel Johnson, *The Rambler* No. 148 [On Parental Tyranny] (17 August 1751)

Samuel Johnson's essays in *The Rambler* (1750–52) did a great deal to establish his reputation for insightful and incisive writing. While most essay periodicals aimed to be witty and accessible, *The Rambler* adopted an elevated vocabulary and an intensely thoughtful tone. Initially *The Rambler* achieved a modest circulation of 500 copies per twice-weekly issue, but its collected editions were extremely popular in both the eighteenth and nineteenth centuries.

Me pater saevis oneret catenis,
Quod viro clemens misero peperci:
Me vel extremis Numidarum in agros
Classe releget.

—HORACE, *Odes*, 3.11.45–48

Me let my father load with chains,
Or banish to Numidia's farthest plains!
My crime, that I, a loyal wife,
In kind compassion saved my husband's life.[1]

—FRANCIS

Politicians remark that no oppression is so heavy or lasting as that which is inflicted by the perversion and exorbitance of legal authority. The robber may be seized and the invader repelled whenever they are found; they who pretend no right but that of force may by force be punished or

[1] *Me let ... husband's life* The speaker of this ode is Hypermnestra, a daughter of the mythological king Danaüs. Danaüs was compelled to marry his daughters to the sons of his enemy; he complied, but told his daughters to kill their new husbands on their wedding night. All his daughters complied except Hypermnestra; *Numidia* Ancient kingdom in North Africa.

552 A Song for two Voices. As sung at both Playhouses.
God save great GEORGE our king, Long live our noble king,
God save great GEORGE our king, Long live our noble king,
God save the king. Send him vic - to - ri - ous, Happy and glo - ri - ous,
God save, the king. Send him vic - to - ri - ous, Happy and glo - ri - ous,
Long to reign o - ver us, God save the king.
Long to reign o - ver us, God save the king.
2.
O Lord our God arise,
Scatter his enemies,
And make them fall;
Confound their politics,
Frustrate their knavish tricks,
On him our hopes we fix,
O save us all.
3.
Thy choicest gifts in store
On George be pleas'd to pour,
Long may he reign;
May he defend our laws,
And ever give us cause,
To say with heart and voice
God save the king.

"God Save Our Lord the King: A New Song Set for Two Voices," from *The Gentleman's Magazine*, October 1745. Eighteenth-century magazines often brought together what to a present-day mind may seem quite disparate materials. Alongside the text of a political speech, a list of new books, or a scientific article, an issue of a magazine might also include a song.

The inclusion of music as well as lyrics when songs were published in periodicals was a common practice; one notable example is the publication of this early version of "God Save the King" in *The Gentleman's Magazine*. Though scholars dispute the provenance of the anthem, the version that was regarded as "a new song" in 1745—and that *The Gentleman's Magazine* helped to popularize—is very close to the tune (and the words) that came to be accepted in the nineteenth century as the unofficial national anthem. The words of the second and third stanzas as printed here remain, with only small modifications ("on her we pour" for "on George we pour," etc.), those of the standard version of "God Save the Queen"—though they are only rarely sung.

suppressed. But when plunder bears the name of impost,[1] and murder is perpetrated by a judicial sentence, fortitude is intimidated and wisdom confounded; resistance shrinks from an alliance with rebellion, and the villain remains secure in the robes of the magistrate.

Equally dangerous and equally detestable are the cruelties often exercised in private families under the venerable sanction of parental authority; the power which we are taught to honour from the first moments of reason; which is guarded from insult and violation by all that can impress awe upon the mind of man; and which therefore may wanton[2] in cruelty without control, and trample the bounds of right with innumerable transgressions, before duty and piety will dare to seek redress, or think themselves at liberty to recur to any other means of deliverance than supplications by which insolence is elated, and tears by which cruelty is gratified.

It was for a long time imagined by the Romans that no son could be the murderer of his father, and they had therefore no punishment appropriated to parricide.[3] They seem likewise to have believed with equal confidence that no father could be cruel to his child, and therefore they allowed every man the supreme judicature[4] in his own house, and put the lives of his offspring into his hands. But experience informed them by degrees that they had determined too hastily in favour of human nature; they found that instinct and habit were not able to contend with avarice or malice; that the nearest relation might be violated; and that power, to whomsoever entrusted, might be ill employed. They were therefore obliged to supply and to change their institutions, to deter the parricide by a new law, and to transfer capital punishments from the parent to the magistrate.

There are indeed many houses which it is impossible to enter familiarly without discovering that parents are by no means exempt from the intoxications of dominion; and that he who is in no danger of hearing remonstrances[5] but from his own conscience will seldom be long without the art of controlling his convictions and modifying justice by his own will.

If in any situation the heart were inaccessible to malignity,[6] it might be supposed to be sufficiently secured by parental relation. To have voluntarily become to any being the occasion of its existence produces an obligation to make that existence happy. To see helpless infancy stretching out her hands and pouring out her cries in testimony of dependence, without any powers to alarm jealousy, or any guilt to alienate affection, must surely awaken tenderness in every human mind; and tenderness once excited will be hourly increased by the natural contagion of felicity, by the repercussion[7] of communicated pleasure, by the consciousness of the dignity of benefaction. I believe no generous or benevolent man can see the vilest animal courting his regard, and shrinking at his anger, playing his gambols of delight before him, calling on him in distress, and flying to him in danger, without more kindness than he can persuade himself to feel for the wild and unsocial inhabitants of the air and water. We naturally endear to ourselves those to whom we impart any kind of pleasure, because we imagine their affection and esteem secured to us by the benefits which they receive.

There is indeed another method by which the pride of superiority may be likewise gratified. He that has extinguished all the sensations of humanity, and has no longer any satisfaction in the reflection that he is loved as the distributor of happiness, may please himself with exciting terror as the inflictor of pain; he may delight his solitude with contemplating the extent of his power and the force of his commands, in imagining the desires that flutter on the tongue which is forbidden to utter them, or the discontent which preys on the heart in which fear confines it; he may amuse himself with new contrivances of detection, multiplications of prohibition, and varieties of punishment, and swell with exultation when he considers how little of the homage that he receives he owes to choice.

1 *impost* Tax.

2 *wanton* Revel freely.

3 *parricide* Killing of a parent.

4 *judicature* Legal authority.

5 *remonstrances* Rebukes.

6 *malignity* Evil.

7 *repercussion* I.e., return.

That princes of this character have been known, the history of all absolute kingdoms will inform us; and since, as Aristotle observes, ἡ οἰκονομικὴ μοναρχία,[1] "the government of a family is naturally monarchical," it is, like other monarchies, too often arbitrarily administered. The regal and parental tyrant differ only in the extent of their dominions and the number of their slaves. The same passions cause the same miseries; except that seldom any prince, however despotic, has so far shaken off all awe of the public eye as to venture upon those freaks of injustice which are sometimes indulged under the secrecy of a private dwelling. Capricious injunctions, partial decisions, unequal allotments, distributions of reward not by merit but by fancy, and punishments regulated not by the degree of the offence but by the humour of the judge, are too frequent where no power is known but that of a father.

That he delights in the misery of others no man will confess, and yet what other motive can make a father cruel? The king may be instigated by one man to the destruction of another; he may sometimes think himself endangered by the virtues of a subject; he may dread the successful general or the popular orator; his avarice may point out golden confiscations; and his guilt may whisper that he can only be secure by cutting off all power of revenge.

But what can a parent hope from the oppression of those who were born to his protection, of those who can disturb him with no competition, who can enrich him with no spoils? Why cowards are cruel may be easily discovered; but for what reason not more infamous than cowardice can that man delight in oppression who has nothing to fear?

The unjustifiable severity of a parent is loaded with this aggravation, that those whom he injures are always in his sight. The injustice of a prince is often exercised upon those of whom he never had any personal or particular knowledge; and the sentence which he pronounces, whether of banishment, imprisonment, or death, removes from his view the man whom he condemns. But the domestic oppressor dooms himself to gaze upon those faces which he clouds with terror and with sorrow, and beholds every moment the effects of his own barbarities. He that can bear to give continual pain to those who surround him, and can walk with satisfaction in the gloom of his own presence; he that can see submissive misery without relenting, and meet without emotion the eye that implores mercy or demands justice, will scarcely be amended by remonstrance or admonition; he has found means of stopping the avenues of tenderness, and arming his heart against the force of reason.

Even though[2] no consideration should be paid to the great law of social beings by which every individual is commanded to consult the happiness of others, yet the harsh parent is less to be vindicated than any other criminal, because he less provides for the happiness of himself. Every man, however little he loves others, would willingly be loved; every man hopes to live long, and therefore hopes for that time at which he shall sink back to imbecility, and must depend for ease and cheerfulness upon the officiousness[3] of others. But how has he obviated[4] the inconveniencies of old age who alienates from him the assistance of his children, and whose bed must be surrounded in the last hours, in the hours of languor and dejection, of impatience and of pain, by strangers to whom his life is indifferent, or by enemies to whom his death is desirable?

Piety will indeed in good minds overcome provocation, and those who have been harassed by brutality will forget the injuries which they have suffered so far as to perform the last duties with alacrity and zeal. But surely no resentment can be equally painful with kindness thus undeserved, nor can severer punishment be imprecated[5] upon a man not wholly lost in meanness and stupidity than, through the tediousness of decrepitude, to be reproached by the kindness of his own children, to receive not the tribute but the alms of attendance, and to owe every relief of his miseries not to gratitude but to mercy.

[1] ἡ οἰκονομικὴ μοναρχία From *Politics* 1.2.

[2] *though* I.e., if.

[3] *officiousness* I.e., helpfulness.

[4] *obviated* Averted.

[5] *imprecated* Called for (with ill will, as one would call for a curse).

from Samuel Richardson, *The Rambler* No. 97 [Change in the Manners of Women] (19 February 1751)

Although Samuel Johnson wrote almost all of the *Ramblers* himself—an impressive accomplishment, especially considering he was also hard at work on his *Dictionary* at the time—a few issues were written by friends in his literary circle. The author of the letter below is Samuel Richardson, famous as the author of the epistolary novels *Pamela* (1741) and *Clarissa* (1748).

TO THE RAMBLER.

SIR,

When the *Spectator* was first published in single papers,[1] it gave me so much pleasure that it is one of the favourite amusements of my age to recollect it; and when I reflect on the foibles of those times, as described in that useful work, and compare them with the vices now reigning among us, I cannot but wish that you would oftener take cognizance of the manners of the better half of the human species, that if your precepts and observations be carried down to posterity, the *Spectators* may show to the rising generation what were the fashionable follies of their grandmothers, the *Rambler* of their mothers, and that from both they may draw instruction and warning.

When I read those *Spectators* which took notice of the misbehaviour of young women at church, by which they vainly hope to attract admirers, I used to pronounce such forward young women SEEKERS, in order to distinguish them by a mark of infamy from those who had patience and decency to stay till they were sought.

But I have lived to see such a change in the manners of women that I would now be willing to compound with them for that name, although I then thought it disgraceful enough if they would deserve no worse; since now they are too generally given up to negligence of domestic business, to idle amusements, and to wicked rackets,[2] without any settled view at all but of squandering time.

In the time of the *Spectator*, excepting sometimes an appearance in the ring,[3] sometimes at a good and chosen play, sometimes on a visit at the house of a grave relation, the young ladies contented themselves to be found employed in domestic duties; for then routs, drums,[4] balls, assemblies, and such like markets for women were not known.

Modesty and diffidence, gentleness and meekness, were looked upon as the appropriate virtues and characteristic graces of the sex. And if a forward spirit pushed itself into notice, it was exposed in print as it deserved.

The churches were almost the only places where single women were to be seen by strangers. Men went thither expecting to see them, and perhaps too much for that only purpose.

But some good often resulted, however improper might be their motives. Both sexes were in the way of[5] their duty. The man must be abandoned indeed, who loves not goodness in another; nor were the young fellows of that age so wholly lost to a sense of right as pride and conceit has since made them affect to be. When, therefore, they saw a fair-one whose decent behaviour and cheerful piety showed her earnest in her first duties, they had the less doubt, judging politically only, that she would have a conscientious regard to her second.[6]

With what ardour have I seen watched for the rising of a kneeling beauty; and what additional charms has devotion given to her recommunicated features?

The men were often the better for what they heard. Even a Saul was once found prophesying among the

[1] *single papers* Individual issues, as opposed to the collected issues that were published later.

[2] *rackets* Lively parties and other social excitements.

[3] *the ring* Circular path for coaches in Hyde Park; wealthy people traveled the circuit in order to be seen by others.

[4] *routs* Large house parties; *drums* Tea parties.

[5] *in the way of* I.e., acting according to.

[6] *first duties* I.e, to God; *politically* Judiciously; *her second* I.e., her duties to her husband.

prophets whom he had set out to destroy.[1] To a man thus put into good humour by a pleasing object, religion itself looked more amiably. The MEN SEEKERS of the *Spectator*'s time loved the holy place for the object's sake, and loved the object for her suitable behaviour in it.

Reverence mingled with their love, and they thought that a young lady of such good principles must be addressed only by the man who at least made a show of good principles, whether his heart was yet quite right or not.

Nor did the young lady's behaviour, at any time of the service, lessen this reverence. Her eyes were her own, her ears the preacher's. Women are always most observed when they seem themselves least to observe, or to lay out for observation. The eye of a respectful lover loves rather to receive confidence from the withdrawn eye of the fair one, than to find itself obliged to retreat. When a young gentleman's affection was thus laudably engaged, he pursued its natural dictates; keeping[2] then was a rare, at least a secret and scandalous vice, and a wife was the summit of his wishes. Rejection was now dreaded, and pre-engagement apprehended. A woman whom he loved, he was ready to think must be admired by all the world. His fears, his uncertainties increased his love.

Every enquiry he made into the lady's domestic excellence, which, when a wife is to be chosen, will surely not be neglected, confirmed him in his choice. He opens his heart to a common friend, and honestly discovers[3] the state of his fortune. His friend applies to those of the young lady, whose parents, if they approve his proposals, disclose them to their daughter.

She perhaps is not an absolute stranger to the passion of the young gentleman. His eyes, his assiduities,[4] his constant attendance at a church, whither, till of late, he used seldom to come, and a thousand little observances that he paid her, had very probably first forced her to regard, and then inclined her to favour him.

That a young lady should be in love, and the love of the young gentleman undeclared, is an heterodoxy[5] which prudence, and even policy, must not allow. But thus applied to, she is all resignation[6] to her parents. Charming resignation, which inclination opposes not.

Her relations applaud her for her duty; friends meet; points are adjusted; delightful perturbations, and hopes, and a few lover's fears, fill up the tedious space till an interview is granted; for the young lady had not made herself cheap at public places.

The time of interview arrives. She is modestly reserved; he is not confident. He declares his passion; the consciousness of her own worth, and his application to her parents, take from her any doubt of his sincerity; and she owns herself obliged to him for his good opinion. The enquiries of her friends into his character have taught her that his good opinion deserves to be valued.

She tacitly allows of his future visits; he renews them; the regard of each for the other is confirmed; and when he presses for the favour of her hand, he receives a declaration of an entire acquiescence with her duty, and a modest acknowledgement of esteem for him.

He applies to her parents therefore for a near day; and thinks himself under obligation to them for the cheerful and affectionate manner with which they receive his agreeable application.

With this prospect of future happiness, the marriage is celebrated. Gratulations pour in from every quarter. Parents and relations on both sides, brought acquainted in the course of the courtship, can receive the happy couple with countenances illumined, and joyful hearts.

The brothers, the sisters, the friends of one family, are the brothers, the sisters, the friends of the other. Their two families, thus made one, are the world to the young couple.

Their home is the place of their principal delight, nor do they ever occasionally quit it but they find the pleasure of returning to it augmented in proportion to the time of their absence from it.

Oh, Mr. RAMBLER! forgive the talkativeness of an old man! When I courted and married my Laetitia, then a blooming beauty, everything passed just so! But how

[1] *Even a ... to destroy* The apostle Paul (born with the name Saul) persecuted the early Christians until he had a vision and converted to Christianity himself.

[2] *keeping* I.e., keeping a mistress.

[3] *discovers* Reveals.

[4] *assiduities* Constant courtesies.

[5] *heterodoxy* Thing opposed to accepted opinion.

[6] *resignation* Obedience.

is the case now? The ladies, maidens, wives, and widows are engrossed by places of open resort and general entertainment, which fill every quarter of the metropolis, and being constantly frequented, make home irksome. Breakfasting-places, dining-places; routs, drums, concerts, balls, plays, operas, masquerades for the evening, and even for all night, and lately, public sales of the goods of broken[1] housekeepers, which the general dissoluteness of manners has contributed to make very frequent, come in as another seasonable relief to these modern time killers.

In the summer there are in every country town assemblies; Tunbridge, Bath, Cheltenham, Scarborough![2] What expense of dress and equipage is required to qualify the frequenters for such emulous[3] appearance?

By the natural infection of example, the lowest people have places of sixpenny resort, and gaming tables for pence. Thus servants are now induced to fraud and dishonesty to support extravagance and supply their losses.

As to the ladies who frequent those public places, they are not ashamed to show their faces wherever men dare go, nor blush to try[4] who shall stare most impudently, or who shall laugh loudest on the public walks.

The men who would make good husbands, if they visit those places, are frighted at wedlock and resolve to live single, except[5] they are bought at a very high price. They can be spectators of all that passes, and, if they please, more than spectators, at the expense of others. The companion of an evening and the companion for life require very different qualifications.

Two thousand pounds in the last age, with a domestic wife, would go farther than ten thousand in this. Yet settlements are expected that often, to a mercantile man especially, sink a fortune into uselessness; and pin-money[6] is stipulated for, which makes a wife independent, and destroys love by putting it out of a man's power to lay any obligation upon her that might engage gratitude and kindle affection. When to all this the card-tables are added, how can a prudent man think of marrying?

And when the worthy men know not where to find wives, must not the sex be left to the foplings, the coxcombs, the libertines[7] of the age, whom they help to make such? And need even these wretches marry to enjoy the conversation of those who render their company so cheap?

And what, after all, is the benefit which the gay coquette[8] obtains by her flutters? As she is approachable by every man without requiring, I will not say incense[9] or adoration, but even common complaisance, every fop treats her as upon the level, looks upon her light airs as invitations, and is on the watch to take the advantage. She has companions indeed, but no lovers; for love is respectful and timorous; and where, among all her followers, will she find a husband?

Set, dear Sir, before the youthful, the gay, the inconsiderate, the contempt as well as the danger to which they are exposed. At one time or other, women not utterly thoughtless will be convinced of the justice of your censure, and the charity of your instruction.

But should your expostulations and reproofs have no effect upon those who are far gone in fashionable folly, they may be retailed[10] from their mouths to their nieces (marriage will not often have entitled these to daughters) when they, the meteors of a day, find themselves elbowed off the stage of vanity by other flutterers—for the most admired women cannot have many Tunbridge, many Bath seasons to blaze in, since even fine faces, often seen, are less regarded than new faces—the proper punishment of showy girls for rendering themselves so impoliticly cheap.

I am, SIR,

Your sincere admirer, &c.

[1] *broken* I.e., bankrupt.

[2] *Tunbridge ... Scarborough* Popular resort towns.

[3] *equipage* Carriage and attendants; *emulous* Rivalrous; motivated by competition to follow trends.

[4] *try* Compete as to.

[5] *except* Unless.

[6] *pin-money* Allowance given by a husband to his wife.

[7] *foplings ... libertines* Vain, hedonistic men.

[8] *coquette* Flirt.

[9] *incense* Praise.

[10] *retailed* Related.

Samuel Johnson, *The Rambler* No. 114 [On Capital Punishment] (20 April 1751)

Samuel Johnson's famous essay on capital punishment was written at a time when the number of capital crimes in English law was increasing rapidly. In 1688 there were 50 crimes that could incur the death penalty under English law; by 1765 there were more than three times that many. It became a capital offense not only to commit murder or treason but also to shoplift, to cut down trees in a garden, or to pick pocket more than a shilling. However, not everyone who committed such crimes was killed. Judges and juries were reluctant to convict minor criminals of capital crimes—even when they were obviously guilty—and many of those who were sentenced to death received royal pardons before the sentence was carried out.

——— *Audi,*
Nulla unquam de morte hominis cunctatio longa est.
—Juvenal, *Satires*, 6.220–21

——— When man's life is in debate,
The judge can ne'er too long deliberate.
—Dryden

Power and superiority are so flattering and delightful that, fraught with temptation and exposed to danger as they are, scarcely any virtue is so cautious, or any prudence so timorous, as to decline them. Even those that have most reverence for the laws of right are pleased with showing that not fear, but choice, regulates their behavior; and would be thought to comply, rather than obey. We love to overlook the boundaries which we do not wish to pass; and, as the Roman satirist[1] remarks, he that has no design to take the life of another, is yet glad to have it in his hands.

From the same principle, tending yet more to degeneracy and corruption, proceeds the desire of investing lawful authority with terror, and governing by force rather than persuasion. Pride is unwilling to believe the necessity of assigning any other reason than her own will, and would rather maintain the most equitable claims by violence and penalties than descend from the dignity of command to dispute and expostulation.

It may, I think, be suspected that this political arrogance has sometimes found its way into legislative assemblies and mingled with deliberations upon property and life. A slight perusal of the laws by which the measures of vindictive and coercive justice are established will discover so many disproportions between crimes and punishments, such capricious distinctions of guilt, and such confusion of remissness[2] and severity, as can scarcely be believed to have been produced by public wisdom, sincerely and calmly studious of public happiness.

The learned, the judicious, the pious Boerhaave[3] relates that he never saw a criminal dragged to execution without asking himself, "Who knows whether this man is not less culpable than me?" On the days when the prisons of this city are emptied into the grave, let every spectator of the dreadful procession put the same question to his own heart. Few among those that crowd in thousands to the legal massacre and look with carelessness, perhaps with triumph, on the utmost exacerbations of human misery, would then be able to return without horror and dejection. For who can congratulate himself upon a life passed without some act more mischievous to the peace or prosperity of others than the theft of a piece of money?

It has been always the practice, when any particular species of robbery becomes prevalent and common, to endeavour its suppression by capital denunciations.[4] Thus, one generation of malefactors[5] is commonly cut off, and their successors are frighted into new expedients; the art of thievery is augmented with greater variety of fraud, and subtilized to higher degrees of dexterity and more occult[6] methods of conveyance. The law then renews the pursuit in the heat of anger, and overtakes the offender again with death. By this practice, capital inflictions are multiplied, and crimes very

[1] *Roman satirist* Juvenal, in his *Satires* 10.96–97.

[2] *remissness* Negligence.

[3] *Boerhaave* Doctor and intellectual Herman Boerhaave (1668–1738), whom Johnson greatly admired.

[4] *by capital denunciations* I.e., by trying criminals for capital offenses.

[5] *malefactors* Criminals.

[6] *occult* Secret.

different in their degrees of enormity are equally subjected to the severest punishment that man has the power of exercising upon man.

The lawgiver is undoubtedly allowed to estimate the malignity[1] of an offence not merely by the loss or pain which single acts may produce, but by the general alarm and anxiety arising from the fear of mischief and insecurity of possession. He therefore exercises the right which societies are supposed to have over the lives of those that compose them, not simply to punish a transgression, but to maintain order and preserve quiet; he enforces those laws with severity that are most in danger of violation, as the commander of a garrison doubles the guard on that side which is threatened by the enemy.

This method has been long tried, but tried with so little success that rapine[2] and violence are hourly increasing. Yet few seem willing to despair of its efficacy, and of those who employ their speculations upon the present corruption of the people, some propose the introduction of more horrid, lingering and terrific punishments; some are inclined to accelerate the executions; some to discourage pardons; and all seem to think that lenity has given confidence to wickedness, and that we can only be rescued from the talons of robbery by inflexible rigour and sanguinary[3] justice.

Yet since the right of setting an uncertain and arbitrary value upon life has been disputed, and since experience of past times gives us little reason to hope that any reformation will be effected by a periodical havoc[4] of our fellow beings, perhaps it will not be useless to consider what consequences might arise from relaxations of the law and a more rational and equitable adaptation of penalties to offences.

Death is, as one of the ancients observes, τὸ τ ν φοβερ ν φοβερώτατον, "of dreadful things the most dreadful"; an evil beyond which nothing can be threatened by sublunary[5] power, or feared from human enmity or vengeance. This terror should, therefore, be reserved as the last resort of authority, as the strongest and most operative of prohibitory sanctions, and placed before the treasure of life, to guard from invasion what cannot be restored. To equal robbery with murder is to reduce murder to robbery, to confound in common minds the gradations of iniquity, and incite the commission of a greater crime to prevent the detection of a less. If only murder were punished with death, very few robbers would stain their hands in blood; but when by the last act of cruelty no new danger is incurred, and greater security may be obtained, upon what principle shall we bid them forbear?

It may be urged that the sentence is often mitigated to simple robbery;[6] but surely this is to confess that our laws are unreasonable in our own opinion; and, indeed, it may be observed that all but murderers have, at their last hour, the common sensations of mankind pleading in their favour.

From this conviction of the inequality of the punishment to the offence proceeds the frequent solicitation of pardons. They who would rejoice at the correction of a thief are yet shocked at the thought of destroying him. His crime shrinks to nothing, compared with his misery; and severity defeats itself by exciting pity.

The gibbet,[7] indeed, certainly disables those who die upon it from infesting the community; but their death seems not to contribute more to the reformation of their associates than any other method of separation. A thief seldom passes much of his time in recollection or anticipation, but from robbery hastens to riot, and from riot to robbery; nor, when the grave closes upon his companion, has any other care than to find another.

The frequency of capital punishments therefore rarely hinders the commission of a crime, but naturally and commonly prevents its detection, and is, if we proceed only upon prudential principles, chiefly for that reason to be avoided. Whatever may be urged by casuists[8] or politicians, the greater part of mankind, as

[1] *malignity* Evil nature.

[2] *rapine* Plunder.

[3] *sanguinary* Bloody.

[4] *havoc* Devastation.

[5] *sublunary* Of the material world.

[6] *simple robbery* I.e., petty larceny. Grand larceny (theft of anything with a value over one shilling) was punishable by death, while petty larceny (under one shilling) incurred lesser punishments; judges often deliberately underestimated the cost of stolen goods for this reason.

[7] *gibbet* Gallows. Hanging was the most common method of execution.

[8] *casuists* People who reason cleverly but misleadingly.

they can never think that to pick the pocket and to pierce the heart is equally criminal, will scarcely believe that two malefactors so different in guilt can be justly doomed to the same punishment; nor is the necessity of submitting the conscience to human laws so plainly evinced, so clearly stated, or so generally allowed, but that the pious, the tender, and the just, will always scruple to concur with the community in an act which their private judgment cannot approve.

He who knows not how often rigorous laws produce total impunity, and how many crimes are concealed and forgotten for fear of hurrying the offender to that state in which there is no repentance, has conversed very little with mankind. And whatever epithets of reproach or contempt this compassion may incur from those who confound cruelty with firmness, I know not whether any wise man would wish it less powerful, or less extensive.

If those whom the wisdom of our laws has condemned to die had been detected in their rudiments[1] of robbery, they might by proper discipline and useful labour have been disentangled from their habits; they might have escaped all the temptations to subsequent crimes, and passed their days in reparation and penitence; and detected they might all have been, had the prosecutors been certain that their lives would have been spared. I believe every thief will confess that he has been more than once seized and dismissed; and that he has sometimes ventured upon capital crimes because he knew that those whom he injured would rather connive at his escape than cloud their minds with the horrors of his death.

All laws against wickedness are ineffectual unless some will inform, and some will prosecute; but till we mitigate the penalties for mere violations of property, information will always be hated, and prosecution dreaded. The heart of a good man cannot but recoil at the thought of punishing a slight injury with death; especially when he remembers that the thief might have procured safety by another crime, from which he was restrained only by his remaining virtue.

The obligations to assist the exercise of public justice are indeed strong; but they will certainly be overpowered by tenderness for life. What is punished with severity contrary to our ideas of adequate retribution will be seldom discovered;[2] and multitudes will be suffered to advance from crime to crime till they deserve death, because if they had been sooner prosecuted, they would have suffered death before they deserved it.

This scheme of invigorating the laws by relaxation, and extirpating[3] wickedness by lenity, is so remote from common practice that I might reasonably fear to expose it to the public, could it be supported only by my own observations: I shall, therefore, by ascribing it to its author, Sir Thomas More,[4] endeavour to procure it that attention which I wish always paid to prudence, to justice, and to mercy.

from Henry Fielding, *The Covent-Garden Journal* No. 6 [Mortality of Print] (21 January 1752)

Although he is much better known as a popular playwright and comic novelist, Henry Fielding also enjoyed success as a periodical essayist. His fourth and last periodical, *The Covent-Garden Journal* (January–November 1752) is the only one that is not primarily political in nature; the essays predominantly address morality and taste, although Fielding also includes a column informing readers about his activities as a magistrate.

Quam multi tineas pascunt, blattasque diserti!
Et redimunt soli carmina docta coci!
Nescio quid plus est quod donat secula chartis,
Victurus genium debet habere liber.[5] MART. LIB. 6.

How many fear the moth's and bookworm's rage,
And pastry-cooks, sole buyers in this age?
What can these murderers of wit control?
To be immortal, books must have a soul.

[1] *rudiments* Beginnings.

[2] *discovered* Revealed.

[3] *extirpating* Eliminating.

[4] *Sir Thomas More* In the fictional society of More's *Utopia* (1516), capital punishment is used in very few circumstances.

[5] *Quam multi … liber* From the Latin poet Martial, *Epigrams* 6.61. The translation follows.

There are no human productions to which time seems so bitter and malicious an enemy as to the works of the learned: for though all the pride and boast of art must sooner or later yield to this great destroyer; though all the labours of the architect, the statuary,[1] and the painter, must share the same mortality with their authors; yet, with these, time acts in a gentler and milder manner, allows them generally a reasonable period of existence, and brings them to an end by a gradual and imperceptible decay: so that they may seem rather cut off by the fatal laws of necessity than to be destroyed by any such act of violence as this cruel tyrant daily executes on us writers.

It is true, indeed, there are some exceptions to this rule; some few works of learning have not only equalled, but far exceeded, all other human labours in their duration; but alas! how very few are these compared to that vast number which have been swallowed up by this great destroyer. Many of them cut off in their very prime; others in their early youth; and others, again, at their very birth; so that they can scarce be said ever to have been.

And, as to the few that remain to us, is not their long existence to be attributed to their own unconquerable spirit, rather to the weakness than to the mercy of time? Have not many of their authors foreseen, and foretold, the endeavours which would be exerted to destroy them, and have boldly asserted their just claim to immortality, in defiance of all the malice, all the cunning, and all the power of time?

Indeed, when we consider the many various engines which have been employed for this destructive purpose, it will be matter of wonder that any of the writings of antiquity have been able to make their escape. This might almost lead us into a belief that the writers were really possessed of that divinity to which some of them pretended, especially as those which seem to have had the best pretensions to this divinity have been almost the only ones which have escaped into our hands.

And here, not to mention those great engines of destruction which Ovid so boldly defies, such as swords, and fire, and the devouring moths of antiquity,[2] how many cunning methods hath the malice of time invented, of later days, to extirpate[3] the works for the learned, and to convert the invention of paper, and even of printing, to the total abolition of those very works which they were so ingeniously calculated to perpetuate.

The first of these, decency will permit me barely to hint to the reader. It is the application of it to a use for which parchment and vellum,[4] the ancient repositories of learning, would have been utterly unfit. To this cunning invention of time, therefore, printing and paper have chiefly betrayed the learned; nor can I see, without indignation, the booksellers, those great enemies of authors, endeavouring by all their sinister arts to propagate so destructive a method: for what is commoner than to see books advertised to be printed *on a superfine, delicate, soft paper*, and again, *very proper to be had in all families*, a plain insinuation to what use they are adapted, according to these lines.

Lintot's for gen'ral use are fit,
For some folks read, but all folks[5]—.

By this abominable method, the whole works of several modern authors have been so obliterated that the most curious searcher into antiquity, hereafter, will never be able to wipe off the injuries of time.

And, yet, so truly do the booksellers verify that old observation, *dulcis odor lucri ex re qualibet*,[6] that they are daily publishing several works manifestly calculated for this use only; nay, I am told, that one of them is, by

[1] *statuary* I.e., sculptor.

[2] *Ovid* Roman poet (43 BCE–17 CE), famous for his *Metamorphoses*; *Ovid so ... antiquity* Near the end of his *Metamorphoses*, Ovid declares that he has "finished a work that neither Jove's rage, nor fire, nor the sword, nor fast-devouring time can wipe away" (15.871–72).

[3] *extirpate* Eliminate.

[4] *parchment and vellum* Stiff writing sheets made from animal skin.

[5] *Lintot* Bernard Lintot (1675–1736), London bookseller who printed the work of major literary figures; *Lintot's ... ———* From Alexander Pope, "Verses to Be Prefixed before Bernard Lintot's New Miscellany" (1712). Lintot was Pope's printer for a time, but Pope wrote the "Verses to Be Prefixed" after the two had a falling out.

[6] *dulcis ... qualibet* Latin: "money smells good, wherever it comes from" (Juvenal, *Satires* 14.204–05).

means of a proper translator, preparing the whole works of Plato for the b—.

Next to the booksellers are the trunk-makers,[1] a set of men who have of late years made the most intolerable depredations[2] on modern learning. The ingenious Hogarth hath very finely satirized this by representing several of the most valuable productions of these times on the way to the trunk-maker.[3] If these persons would line a trunk with a whole pamphlet, they might possibly do more good than harm; for then, perhaps, the works of last year might be found in our trunks, when they were possibly to be found nowhere else, but so far from this, they seem to take a delight in dismembering authors; and in placing their several limbs together in the most absurd manner. Thus while the bottom of a trunk contains a piece of poetry, the top presents us with a sheet of romance, and the sides and ends are adorned with mangled libels of various kinds.

The third species of these depredators are the pastry cooks. What indignation must it raise in a lover of the moderns, to see some of their best performances stained with the juice of gooseberries, currants, and damascenes![4] But what concern must the author himself feel on such an occasion; when he beholds those writings which were calculated to support the glorious cause of disaffection or infidelity, humbled to the ignoble purpose of supporting a tart or a custard! So, according to the poet,

> Great Alexander dead, and turned to clay,
> May stop a hole to keep the wind away.[5]

But, besides the injuries done to learning by this method, there is another mischief which these pastry cooks may thus propagate in the society: for many of these wondrous performances are calculated only for the use and inspection of the few, and are by no means proper food for the mouths of babes and sucklings. For instance, that the Christian religion is a mere cheat and imposition on the public, nay, that the very being of a God is a matter of great doubt and incertainty,[6] are discoveries of too deep a nature to perplex the minds [of] children with; and it is better, perhaps, till they come to a certain age, that they should believe quite the opposite doctrines. Again, as children are taught to obey and honour their superiors, and to keep their tongues from evil-speaking, lying, and slandering, to what good purposes can it tend to show them that the very contrary is daily practiced and suffered and supported in the world? Is not this to confound their understandings, and almost sufficient to make them neglect their learning? Lastly, there are certain *arcana naturæ*,[7] in disclosing which the moderns have made great progress; now whatever merit there may be in such denudations of nature, if I may so express myself, and however exquisite a relish they may afford to *very* adult persons of both sexes in their closets,[8] they are surely too speculative and mysterious for the contemplation of the young and tender, into whose hands tarts and pies are most likely to fall.

Now as these three subjects, namely, infidelity, scurrility,[9] and indecency, have principally exercised the pens of the moderns, I hope for the future, pastry cooks will be more cautious than they have lately been. In short, if they have no regard to learning, they will have some, I hope, to morality.

The same caution may be given to grocers and chandlers;[10] both of whom are too apt to sell their figs, raisins, and sugar to children, without enough considering the poisonous vehicle in which they are conveyed. At the waste paper market, the cheapness of the commodity is only considered; and it is easy to see with what goods that market is likely to abound; since though the press hath lately swarmed with libels against our religion and government, there is not a single writer of any

[1] *trunk-makers* Scrap pages were used as lining for trunks.

[2] *depredations* Destructive attacks.

[3] *The ingenious … trunk-maker* See Hogarth's *Beer Street*, in the online portion of this "Contexts" section.

[4] *damascenes* Dark-colored plums.

[5] *Great Alexander … wind away* Altered from Shakespeare's *Hamlet* 5.1.213–14.

[6] *the Christian … and incertainty* Refers to the writings of skeptics who expressed equivocal or atheistic opinions about religion; Fielding had a low opinion of these thinkers.

[7] *arcana naturæ* Latin: secrets of nature, here meaning scientific information about reproduction.

[8] *closets* Private rooms.

[9] *scurrility* Coarse abusiveness.

[10] *chandlers* Sellers of household goods.

reputation in this kingdom who hath attempted to draw his pen against either.

But to return to that subject from which I seem to have a little digressed. How melancholy a consideration must it be to a modern author that the labours, I might call them the offspring, of his brain are liable to so many various kinds of destruction that what Tibullus says of the numerous avenues to death may be here applied.

—*Leti mille repente viæ.*[1]

To Death there are a thousand sudden ways.

For my own part, I never walk into Mrs. Dodd's shop,[2] and survey all that vast and formidable host of papers and pamphlets arranged on her shelves, but the noble lamentation of Xerxes occurs to my mind; who, when he reviewed his army on the banks of the Hellespont, is said to have grieved, for that not one of all those hundreds of thousands would be living an hundred years from that time.[3] In the same manner have I said to myself, "How dreadful a thought is it that of all these numerous and learned works, none will survive to the next year?" But, within that time,

———All will become,
Martyrs to pies, and relics of the b[4]—.

I was led into these reflections by an accident which happened to me the other day, and which all lovers of antiquity will esteem a very fortunate one. Having had the curiosity to examine a written paper, in which my baker enclosed me two hot rolls, I have rescued from oblivion one of the most valuable fragments that I believe is now to be found in the world. I have ordered it to be fairly transcribed, and shall very soon present it to my readers, with my best endeavours, by a short comment, to illustrate a piece which appears to have remained to us from the most distant and obscure ages.[5]

[1] *Leti mille repente viæ* From the Latin poet Tibullus, *Elegies* 1.3.50; the translation follows.

[2] *Mrs. Dodd's shop* Well-known shop selling news and political pamphlets, including *The Covent-Garden Journal.*

[3] *when he ... that time* Xerxes I of Persia (519–465 BCE), on his way to invade Greece with a vast army, crossed the Hellespont, a strait in Turkey. (See the Greek historian Herodotus, *Histories* 7.45–46.)

[4] *All will ... the b—* Refers to a passage in John Dryden's poem *Mac Flecknoe* (1682), a satirical attack on bad writing: "From dusty shops neglected authors come, / Martyrs of pies and relics of the bum."

[5] *I have rescued ... obscure ages* Issue No. 8 of *The Covent-Garden Journal* includes a religious debate conducted by a contemporary society of atheists and skeptics, presented as a poorly translated ancient work.

from Frances Brooke, *The Old Maid* No. 13 [The Foundling Hospital] (7 February 1756)

Frances Brooke, who spent some years in Canada and is widely considered the first novelist in Canadian literature, established her literary reputation years before that, when she was still in London, as the author of *The Old Maid* (1755–56). She wrote *The Old Maid* in the persona of the elderly "Mary Singleton, Spinster"; Brooke herself, however, was in her early thirties; she married during the run of the periodical. *The Old Maid* offers theatrical criticism and political observations alongside social commentary and stories; many issues focus on the lives of Mary Singleton, her niece Julia, and Julia's friend Rosara.

The following article discusses the funding of the Foundling Hospital, a London home for orphaned and abandoned children. At the time Brooke was writing, the Foundling Hospital was overwhelmed by children whose mothers could not support them, and the institution chose applicants by lottery, admitting only a fraction of those in need.

——— Poor babes!
Some powerful spirit instruct the kites[6] and ravens
To be your nurses! Wolves and bears, they say,
Casting their savageness aside, have done
Like offices of pity.[7]

Winter's Tale.

Julia and I made a visit the other day to the Foundling Hospital, where I often indulge her and myself with a sight which must give pleasure to every mind which

[6] *kites* Birds of prey similar to hawks.

[7] *Poor babes ... of pity* From Shakespeare, *Winter's Tale* 2.3.221–25.

has any tincture of humanity, that of a number of unfortunate innocents saved from an untimely death, or what is worse, from being trained up in abandoned principles and under profligate examples, to lead a wretched and pernicious[1] life, proceeding in pain and misery, and ending in infamy and horror; but are here educated in a manner the most proper to their condition and birth, and put into the way to be happy themselves, and useful to society. My niece, from a mistaken generosity, was very desirous of giving something to the little creatures, who, as usual, came round us; but as I think the prohibition of this a very wise regulation, I prevented her, and directed her bounty to the box appointed to receive the charities of such whose hearts are touched with benevolence at a sight which, I should think, would melt the soul of a savage.

It is surprising to me that so useful, so politic, and as long as there are vices or extreme poverty in the world, so necessary a foundation, should be left to the chance of private and uncertain donations, the consequence of which is that three parts in four of those who are brought there to be provided for are rejected; when, to answer the very end of its institution, it requires that all should be taken in. I will charitably suppose that no motive but the fear of shame, or the extremity of want, can operate so powerfully upon a mother as to counterwork the force of nature, and the instinctive fondness every creature has for its offspring, to such a degree as to instigate her to destroy the babe who is a dearer part of herself, and the object, as I have been told, of the most pleasing of the human affections. And I am afraid this hospital will have very little effect towards preventing such dreadful crimes when the parents of these unhappy infants know it is more than three to one that they are returned to them again: nay perhaps the despair and rage of disappointment in such whose application has been unsuccessful may more effectually condemn their unhappy infants to the grave than if no such foundation was in being.

The strange unfeeling carelessness of the gay part of the world, and the ill-judged severity of the more regular, have hitherto prevented such a provision from being made as is necessary to render this hospital of general use; nor can it ever answer the noble purposes for which it is intended till some certain revenue is settled on it, sufficient to enable the governors to raise and support a building extensive enough to receive all who are offered, in the same manner as at Paris and Madrid.[2]

It has been said by people who, though perhaps well-meaning, appear totally ignorant of human nature, that this provision is an encouragement to vice: but it is not, I think, to be supposed that any person who gives way to a criminal passion thinks at all of the consequences of so destructive a folly; if they did, they would certainly avoid a conduct of which shame, remorse, and sorrow are the unavoidable effects. I am inclined to believe the parting with a child is a very severe punishment to the mother, however abandoned; and if there be any so savage as to want[3] the soft sensations of tenderness for their offspring and, without reluctance and the strongest necessity, to give them up forever to the care of others, their own consciences will be their tormentors, and we may

> Leave them to Heaven
> And to the thorns that in their bosom lodge
> To goad and sting them.[4]

But if this be not sufficient to obviate[5] the objection, let those who think it of importance but turn their thoughts to the infinite variety of sudden and unforeseen distress in this vast metropolis, by which the parents of a legitimate offspring, at least the more tender and helpless parent, by the death or unavoidable absence of the other, may be reduced to an incapacity of supporting a newborn infant, and they will perceive at once the extreme charity and usefulness of such a foundation as this, without supposing it intended besides for the reception of such unhappy babes as owe their birth to their parents' guilt and folly.

As there is no nation in the world more justly renowned for generosity and humanity than this, I hope a British senate will not think this affair of too little moment to be taken into consideration; and at this

[1] *profligate* Degenerate; *pernicious* Wicked.

[2] *Paris and Madrid* Both cities had large orphanages.

[3] *want* Lack.

[4] *Leave them … sting them* Altered from Shakespeare, *Hamlet* 1.5.86–88.

[5] *obviate* Invalidate.

time, especially since it seems necessary to chastise the insolence and perfidiousness of our aspiring neighbours the French,[1] it cannot sure be ill policy to endeavour at so obvious a means of providing some supply for the loss of such numbers of our countrymen as a war must inevitably take off.

It is extremely melancholy to reflect upon the many unhappy infants who are daily found exposed in the streets, and the greater number who are destroyed almost before they see the light: one cannot think without the extremest horror on those whose bodies were found putrified in the river about a year since,[2] and who I am afraid were not all destroyed by parish nurses,[3] though that is too often the fate of such as escape the hands of their mothers.

I hope every gentleman who has the honour of being entrusted by his country with a seat in parliament, whatever may be his political principles, will heartily concur in endeavouring to prevent such shocking accidents for the future, by increasing some way or other a fund which is at present so very insufficient to answer the purpose of this foundation, and only serves to show what good it might do if the revenue was plentiful and certain. He that has not humanity enough to exert himself in behalf of deserted innocence, scarcely deserves the name of a man: and whose patriotism will not rouse him to endeavour to raise and increase this hospital to a sufficiency to receive all who are brought to it, much less deserves the name of a Briton: as under the plan laid down and pursued by the governors, it must prove an excellent seminary[4] for seamen and soldiers, and supply our fleets and armies with much stronger bodies and braver spirits than are to be met with amongst the lazy, drunken, debauched vagabonds in the streets.

I am a woman, and politics are not my province, nor does it become me to dictate to my superiors, but I hope wiser heads will think further on so interesting a subject, and pardon a hint which comes from a heart warm with the love of that country which, of all others, deserves best to be loved, and melting with pity for these abandoned helpless objects of our compassion....

Oliver Goldsmith, Letter 3, *The Public Ledger* No. 15 [The Citizen of the World Observes British Fashion] (29 January 1760)

Irish poet, comic playwright, and novelist Oliver Goldsmith began his writing career selling essays and articles to London periodicals. Among these projects was a series of letters in the voice of the fictional character Lien Chi Altangi, a Chinese traveler who has come to Britain seeking to broaden his horizons. Lien Chi's letters to home detail his experiences and observations of Britain. The letters were originally printed, without a title or introduction, twice a week in *The Public Ledger* (from 1760–61); afterwards, they were collected and revised as *The Citizen of the World; or, Letters from a Chinese Philosopher Residing in London to His Friends in the East* (1762).

To the care of Fipsihi, Tartarean[5] *resident in Moscow; to be forwarded by the Russian caravan to Fum Hoam, first president of the ceremonial academy at Pekin*[6] *in China.*

Think not, O thou guide of my youth, that absence can impair my respect, or that interposing trackless deserts can blot your reverend figure from my memory. The farther I travel I feel the pain of separation with more reluctance; those ties that bind me to my native country, and you, are still unbroken, while, by every remove, I only drag a greater length of chain.

Could I find aught worth transmitting from so remote a region as this to which I have wandered, I

[1] *it seems ... the French* The Seven Years' War, a conflict involving France, England, and several other European powers, was already in progress. England's official declaration of war was not issued until May of 1756, but the French and English colonies in North America had been fighting since 1754.

[2] *bodies were ... year since* Drowning one's child in the Thames was the most common form of infanticide.

[3] *parish nurses* The countryside wet-nurses who took in babies for money were often too poor themselves to provide proper care. In the worst cases, these wet-nurses practiced deliberate infanticide or allowed babies to die from neglect.

[4] *seminary* School.

[5] *Tartarean* Of the Tartars, a Russian ethnic group.

[6] *Pekin* I.e., Beijing.

should gladly send it; but instead of this, you must be contented with a renewal of my former professions, and an imperfect account of a people with whom I yet am but superficially acquainted. The remarks of a man who has been but three days in the country can only be those obvious circumstances which force themselves upon the imagination: I consider myself here as a newly-created being introduced into a new world, every object strikes with wonder and surprise. The imagination, still unsatiated, seems the only active principle of the mind. The most trifling occurrence gives pleasure till the gloss of novelty is worn away, nor till we have ceased wondering can we possibly grow wise; it is then we call the reasoning principle to our aid, and compare those objects with each other which we before examined without reflection.

Behold me then in London, gazing at the strangers, and they at me; it seems they find somewhat absurd in my figure; and had I been never from home, it is possible I might find an infinite fund of ridicule in theirs; but by long travelling I am taught to laugh at folly alone, and to find nothing truly ridiculous but vice. When I had just quitted my native country, and crossed the Chinese wall, I thought every deviation from the customs and manners of China was a departing from nature. I smiled at the blue lips and red foreheads of the Tongusas; I could hardly contain when I saw the Daures dress their heads with horns; the Ostiacs powder their hair with red earth; and the Calmuck[1] beauties trick out in all the finery of sheep-skin. But I soon perceived that the ridicule lay not in them, but in me, and that I falsely condemned others of absurdity because they happened to differ from my standard of perfection, which was founded in prejudice or partiality.

I find no pleasure therefore in taxing the English with departing from nature in their external appearance, which is all I yet know of their character; it is possible they only endeavour to improve her simple plan, since every extravagance in our dress proceeds from a desire of becoming more beautiful than nature made us. This is so harmless a vanity that I not only pardon but approve it; a desire to be more excellent than others is what actually makes us so, and, as thousands find a livelihood in society by such appetites, none but the ignorant inveigh against them.

You are not insensible, most reverend Fum Hoam, what numberless trades, even among the Chinese, subsist by the harmless pride of each other. Your nose-borers, feet-swathers, tooth-stainers, eyebrow pluckers,[2] would all want[3] bread, should their neighbours happen to want vanity. Those vanities, however, employ much fewer hands in China than in England; a fine gentleman, or a fine lady, here dressed up to the fashion, seem scarcely to have a single limb or feature as nature has left it; they call in to their assistance fancy on every occasion, and think themselves finest when they most depart from what they really are.

To make a fine gentleman, several trades are required, but chiefly a barber. You have undoubtedly heard of the Jewish champion all whose strength lay in his hair;[4] one would think that the English were for placing all wisdom there: in order to appear a wise man, nothing more is requisite than to borrow hair from the heads of all his neighbours, and clap it like a bush on his own. The distributors of their laws[5] stick on such quantities that it is almost impossible, even in idea, to distinguish between their heads and the hair.

Those whom I have been now describing affect the gravity of the lion; those I am going to describe more resemble the tricks of the monkey. The barber, who still seems master of the ceremonies, cuts their hair, not round the edges as with us, but close to the crown; and

---

[1] *Tongusas* Evenki people of Northern China and Russia; *Daures* Daur people of Northern China; *Ostiacs* Khanty people of western Siberia; *Calmuck* Kalmyk people of eastern Russia.

[2] *nose-borers* I.e., nose piercers; such piercings were in fact an Indian, not a Chinese tradition; *feet-swathers* I.e., foot binders; *tooth-stainers* Refers to the tradition of coating teeth with black enamel, which was practiced in Japan and Vietnam, but not in China; *eyebrow pluckers* Refers to the eighteenth-century Chinese fashion of very thin eyebrows.

[3] *want* Lack.

[4] *Jewish … his hair* Samson, a biblical hero who is granted supernatural strength by God. He loses his strength when his hair is cut.

[5] *distributors of their laws* Judges and other legal officials customarily wore wigs as part of their court attire.

then with a composition of meal and hog's lard,[1] plasters the whole in such a manner as to make it impossible to distinguish whether he wears a cap or a plaster; still to make the picture more perfectly striking, conceive the tail of some beast, a pig's tail for instance, appended to the back of his head, and reaching down to the place where other tails are generally seen to begin.[2] Thus betailed and bepowdered, he fancies he improves in beauty, dresses up his hard-featured face in smiles, and attempts to look hideously tender. Thus equipped, he is qualified to make love,[3] and hopes for success more from the powder on the outside of his head than the sentiments within.

Yet when you consider what sort of a creature the fine lady is to whom he pays his addresses, it is not strange to find him thus equipped in order to please her. She is herself every whit as fond of powder, and tails, and ribbons, and hog's lard as he; to speak my secret sentiments, most reverend Fum, the ladies here are horribly ugly; I can hardly endure the sight of them; they no way resemble the beauties of China. The Europeans have a quite different idea of beauty from us; when I reflect on the small-footed perfections of thy charming daughter, how is it possible I should have eyes for any other personal excellence: how very broad her face; how very short her nose; how very little her eyes; how thin her lips; and how black her teeth; the snow on the tops of Bao is not fairer than her cheek; and her eyebrows are small as a thread of the finest silk. Here a lady with such perfections would be frightful; Dutch and Chinese beauties I own have some resemblance, but English ladies are entirely different; red cheeks, big eyes, and teeth of a most odious whiteness are everywhere to be seen—and then such masculine feet as actually serve *some* of them for walking![4]

Yet uncivil as nature has been, they seem resolved to outdo her in unkindness: they use white powder, blue powder, and black powder, but never red powder, as among the Tartars, in their hair. They paint their faces not less than the Calmucks, and stick on with spittle little black patches[5] on every part of the face, except on the tip of the nose, which I have never seen with a patch on it. You'll have a better idea of their manner of placing these spots when I have finished a map of an English face patched up to the fashion, which, perhaps, I shall shortly send to add to your curious collection of beasts, medals, and monsters.

Thus far I have seen, and I have now one of their own authors before me, who tells me something strange, and which I can hardly believe. His words are to this effect: "Most ladies in this country have two faces: one face to sleep in, and another to show in company; the first face is generally reserved for the husband and family at home, the other put on to please strangers abroad: this last is always made at the toilet, where whim, the looking-glass, and the toad-eater[6] sit in council, and settle the complexion of the day."

I can't ascertain the truth of this remark; however, they seem to me to act upon very odd principles upon another occasion, since they wear more clothes within doors than without, and a lady who seems to shudder at a breeze in her own apartment appears half naked in public. Adieu,

LIEN CHI ALTANGI.

[1] *meal and hog's lard* Flour was used as hair powder; lard was used as a pomade to make the hair powder stick.

[2] *conceive the … to begin* A greased ponytail was often part of the men's powdered hairstyle.

[3] *make love* I.e., make overtures of love.

[4] *such masculine … for walking* Refers to the practice of foot-binding (which made walking painful and sometimes impossible for Chinese women of the period) in comparison with the uncomfortable and impractical women's shoes then in fashion in London.

[5] *little black patches* Beauty patches, cut into small shapes and worn on the face as decoration or to hide blemishes.

[6] *toad-eater* Poor woman who relies on socially superior relatives for support, and so must court their favor and tolerate their insults; someone who is willing to do anything—even eat a toad—to gain approval.

Prints

BUBBLE CARDS
The Headlong Fools Plunge into South Sea Water.
But the. Sly Long-heads Wade with Caution ater.
The First are Drowning but the Wise Last
Venture no Deeper than the knees or Waist.

Carrington Bowles (printer), South Sea Bubble card, 1720. In the early eighteenth century a frenzy of stock market speculation known as the South Sea Bubble bankrupted businesses and individuals—from small companies and middle-class investors to banks and wealthy aristocrats. At the center of this economic disaster was the South Sea Company. Formed a few years before the conclusion of the War of Spanish Succession (1701–14), the Company was founded on an agreement with the British government: in exchange for taking on the national debt Britain had accumulated during the war, the South Sea Company received a monopoly on trade with the Spanish colonies in South America. The South Sea Company did not find the trade very profitable, but it was very successful in creating the appearance of profitability and increasing the price of its shares. The price peaked in 1720 when, as part of a general surge in stock buying, the cost of South Sea shares climbed from £128 in January to £1050 in June. At this point, people began to sell, and prices plummeted back down to £175 in September, bringing financial ruin to those who had invested too liberally.

The South Sea Bubble was a favorite subject for satirists; prints, poems, and even plates and playing cards referencing the Bubble abounded. The accompanying print is from a 1720 collage of images satirizing the speculation mania (and similar manias that occurred around the same time in other European nations). In it, climbing investors fall from the high branches of a tree into the dangerous waters of the South Sea. The caption reads: "The headlong fools plunge into South Sea water / But the sly long-heads wade with caution after. / The first are drowning but the wise last— / Venture no deeper than the knees or waist."

William Hogarth, *Night*, 1738. This is the last in a series of engravings titled *The Four Times of the Day*. The setting is Charing Cross Road, identifiable by the equestrian statue of Charles I visible in the background. The bonfire in the foreground, the candles in the windows, and the oak leaves decorating the street mark this as the celebration of May 29th, the anniversary of Charles II's restoration to the throne. In the foreground, a drunken freemason with a cut on his forehead leans on the waiter who is escorting him home; the drunk is probably Sir Thomas de Veil, a magistrate very unpopular for advocating the taxation of gin. A maid is "accidentally" emptying a chamber pot onto his head, and behind him a barkeeper is pouring gin into a barrel. On the other side of the picture, the "Salisbury flying coach" is overturning; "Salisbury" refers to James Cecil, sixth Earl of Salisbury, who had inherited a powerful political title but led a degenerate life, and was known for his frequent driving accidents. The signs on the street are for the Rummer Tavern and the Cardigan's Head, both brothels, and a barber conducting surgery can be seen through the window of his shop. Beneath the window, a homeless family crouches for shelter; the son is a link-boy, who carries a torch to light the dark streets for pedestrians. In the background, a tenant is leaving home with all his possessions in a cart, taking advantage of the cover of night to escape his landlord. Far in the distance, smoke billows from a house on fire—a likely occurrence on a night of such riotous festivity.

Benjamin Franklin, *Join, or Die*, 1754. Originally printed by Benjamin Franklin in his *Pennsylvania Gazette*, this may be the first political print to appear in an American newspaper. The woodcut shows a snake sliced into pieces, with initials indicating eleven of the Thirteen Colonies: South Carolina, North Carolina, Virginia, Maryland, Pennsylvania, New Jersey, New York, and the four colonies of New England. It was printed at the beginning of the Seven Years' War in North America, when representatives from the Colonies were about to meet to discuss their conduct of the war. One subject of discussion would be Franklin's "Albany Plan," a proposal to create a unified government to serve the Colonies' common interests, especially those of defense. Franklin printed the woodcut with an article asserting the importance of unity during war; if the Thirteen Colonies were not well-organized in the conduct of the war, he argued, they would lose to their French and Native American enemies. *Join, or Die* was recycled during the American Revolution—contrary to Franklin's own moderate opinions—as a symbol of unified military action against the British. (For more material related to Franklin and to North America in general, see the "Transatlantic Currents" section elsewhere in this volume.)

Matthew Darly and Mary Darly (printers), *A Mungo Macaroni*, 1772. This print was part of the Darlys' series of "macaroni" caricatures. The macaroni was a brief cultural phenomenon lasting from 1764 to 1774; macaronis were wealthy men who dressed and acted with outrageous flamboyance, inspired by the fashions of continental Europe. They were often ridiculed in satires of the day. One subject of this particular caricature is Julius Soubise (1754–98), who was born to a slave mother in the Caribbean. As a child, he was taken to England and given to the Duchess of Queensbury, who freed him, educated him in aristocratic fashion, and gave him extravagant financial support. He charmed the London social scene, becoming one of the most well-known black people in London, and a notorious macaroni.

"Mungo" was a racial slur then in vogue. It referred to a character recently popularized in the British theater, a hardworking black slave named Mungo who amused eighteenth-century audiences by complaining and talking back to his master. The name was also applied to the (white) MP Jeremiah Dyson, who was seen as a lackey for his party; first called "Mungo" in a parliamentary debate, he was often caricatured as a black man—and sometimes specifically as Soubise. This cartoon may target Dyson and Soubise simultaneously. ("A Mungo Macaroni," from *Macaronis, Characters, Caricatures &c* by M. Darly, Volume 4, 1772. Copyright © The Trustees of the British Museum.)

William White (printer), *The Horse America Throwing His Master*, 1779. This drawing depicts a rider (King George III) being thrown from the back of a horse (America), as he tries to whip the horse with a medley of swords, bayonets, and other weapons. In the background is a rebel soldier bearing a flag in support of the thirteen colonies. This cartoon was printed and sold in London, where popular opinion regarding the American Revolutionary War was divided; among the urban public, support for the American rebels was at times as strong as support for the government.

James Gillray, *United Irishmen upon Duty*, 1798. This image was printed during the Irish Rebellion (May–September 1798, an armed attempt by the Society of United Irishmen to establish Ireland as an independent republic. The United Irishmen were inspired by the inclusive, egalitarian ideals of the French and American Revolutions, and had military support from the French. The rebellion failed, and tens of thousands died—with the vast majority of the casualties on the rebel side. The government's political response to the rebellion was also brutal; the 1801 Act of Union increased English power over Ireland, dissolving the Irish legislature and unifying Ireland with England, Scotland, and Wales to form the United Kingdom.

In the above scene, United Irishmen loot a burning farmhouse. On the left, one rebel has his arms around a woman whose child has fallen to the ground, while another rebel, bearing a dagger, pushes inside. Above the doorway, domesticated doves are escaping from their dovecote. In the foreground, a rebel has raised his bloody sword to kill a farmer; on the sword is written "LIBERTY." On the rebel's hat is a cocade bearing the colors of the French Revolution, as well as green leaves symbolizing his allegiance to the United Irishmen. A dead mastiff is at his feet. To the right, piglets chase after their mother as she is carried away by another rebel. A road packed with sheep leads to a military camp flying a French flag, on which the word "EQUALITY" is written. Near the camp is a town on fire. ("United Irishmen upon Duty," print by James Gillray. Published 1798 by Hannah Humphrey).

James Thomson

1700 – 1748

Author of *The Seasons*, an innovative nature poem which became the eighteenth century's most popular work of poetry, James Thomson also published other poems and six plays. A member of a literary circle consisting of English and Scottish writers, many of whom played an active part in the opposition politics of the day, Thomson is perhaps now most often remembered for writing the words of what has become Britain's unofficial anthem, "Rule Britannia." This originated as a song in *Alfred, A Masque* (1740), which Thomson wrote with David Mallet to celebrate the birth of the Prince of Wales's first child, Princess Augusta. It is *The Seasons*, however, that secured his place as a leading poet of the early eighteenth century, as an influence on the Romantic poets of the late eighteenth and early nineteenth centuries, and as a major figure in Scottish literary tradition.

The son of a Presbyterian minister, James Thomson was born on 11 September 1700 and lived in Southdean in the south of Scotland until 1715. His early education included instruction in the Shorter Catechism and the Bible from his father, traditional Border songs and ballads from his mother, and the classics at Jedburgh Grammar School—all influences which surface in his work. After his father's death in 1716, Thomson's family moved to Edinburgh where James studied at the University of Edinburgh. Although Thomson completed the requisite four years, he did not take his degree. Planning to become a minister, he subsequently entered Divinity Hall in 1719 to begin a six-year course of study; that, too, he abandoned just before completion, moving to London in 1725.

Once in London, Thomson turned his attention more seriously to writing—*Winter* appeared in April 1726, and was an immediate publishing sensation. Thomson followed it with *Summer* (1727) and *Spring* (1728); "Autumn" first appeared as part of the collected *The Seasons* in 1730. In form *The Seasons* is a georgic, a poem about agricultural labor, the countryside, and the wealth produced there. The genre takes its name from Virgil's *Georgics*, written in Latin in the first century BCE and designed both as a farming manual for army veterans (who were issued with land as part of their retirement package) and also as a celebration of the natural riches produced by the land. This offered Thomson the opportunity to write on man's experience of Nature. Thomson returned repeatedly to *The Seasons*, publishing new editions in 1744 and again in 1746, each time increasing the poem's political and scientific content; the final version is substantially larger than that published in 1730.

During the years he was writing *The Seasons*, Thomson also worked as a tutor, initially to the son of a Scottish peer, Lord Binning. By May 1726 he was employed as a private tutor at a school run by hymn-writer and educator Isaac Watts, having already published *Winter* in April 1726; he remained at the school until November 1730, by which time he had published one play, *Sophonisba* (1730), a tribute to Newton entitled *A Poem Sacred to the Memory of Sir Isaac Newton* (1727), and the remaining three seasons: *Summer* (1727), *Spring* (1728), and "Autumn" as part of the collected *Seasons* (1730).

In November 1730, Thomson accompanied the son of his patron, Lord Charles Talbot, on a grand tour of France and Italy that lasted over a year. His Continental experiences spawned another ambitious, albeit less-successful poem, *Liberty*, the five books of which follow the goddess of Liberty throughout the history of the civilized world (1735–36).

By 1735, Thomson had moved to Richmond, just outside of London, where he eventually met and fell in love with fellow-Scotswoman Elizabeth Young, sister-in-law of a neighbor. Thomson courted her for three years, and was devastated by her final refusal in 1745; some have suggested that the strength of his feelings over this relationship lent force to the writing of his most romantic and successful play, *Tancred and Sigismunda* (1745). Thomson's final poem, *The Castle of Indolence* (1748), written in Spenserian stanzas, was the product of fifteen years' labor. It explores the seductive qualities of idleness, and many critics have found ambivalence in its ultimate celebration of the regenerating force of hard work. The poet was acknowledged to be intimately familiar with the subject-matter of the poem; he was as well known for his indolence and his love of food and drink as he was for his generosity and good humor.

Thomson did not live to see his last play, *Coriolanus* (1746), performed on stage in 1749, for he died of a fever weeks before his forty-eighth birthday on 27 August 1748. In 1762 his friends and admirers, including George III, memorialized him by erecting a monument in Westminster Abbey's Poets' Corner, funded by the proceeds of a posthumous edition of his collected *Works* (1762).

⌘⌘⌘

Winter[1]

See! Winter comes, to rule the varied year,
Sullen, and sad; with all his rising train,° *group of attendants*
Vapours, and clouds, and storms: Be these my theme,
These, that exalt the soul to solemn thought,
And heavenly musing. Welcome kindred glooms!
Wished, wint'ry, horrors, hail! With frequent foot,
Pleased, have I, in my cheerful morn of life,[2]
When, nursed by careless solitude, I lived,
And sung of Nature with unceasing joy,
Pleased, have I wandered through your rough domains;
Trod the pure, virgin snows, my self as pure:
Heard the winds roar, and the big torrent burst:
Or seen the deep, fermenting tempest brewed,
In the red, evening sky. Thus passed the time,
Till, through the opening chambers of the south,[3]
Looked out the joyous Spring, looked out, and smiled.

Thee too, inspirer of the toiling swain![4]
Fair Autumn, yellow robed! I'll sing of thee,
Of thy last, tempered days, and sunny calms;
When all the golden hours are on the wing,
Attending thy retreat, and round thy wain,° *wagon*
Slow-rolling, onward to the southern sky.

Behold! the well-poised hornet, hovering, hangs,
With quivering pinions,° in the genial blaze; *wings*
Flies off, in airy circles: then returns,
And hums, and dances to the beating ray.
Nor shall the man, that, musing, walks alone,
And, heedless, strays within his radiant lists,° *enclosed spaces*
Go unchastised away. Sometimes, a fleece
Of clouds, wide-scattering, with a lucid° veil, *bright, clear*
Soft, shadow o'er th' unruffled face of heaven;
And, through their dewy sluices,[5] shed the sun,
With tempered influence down. Then is the time
For those, whom Wisdom and whom Nature charm,
To steal themselves from the degenerate crowd,
And soar above this little scene of things:
To tread low-thoughted Vice beneath their feet:

[1] *Winter* Published in 1726, this is the first version of *Winter* and the first of the *Seasons* poems to appear.

[2] *morn of life* Youth.

[3] *chambers of the south* Reference to the southern sky in Job 9.9: "Which maketh Arcturus, Orion, and Pleiades, and the chambers of the south."

[4] *swain* Country laborer, often a shepherd.

[5] *sluices* Structures designed to regulate water.

To lay their passions in a gentle calm,
And woo lone Quiet, in her silent walks.

Now, solitary, and in pensive guise,
Oft let me wander o'er the russet mead,° *meadow*
Or through the pining grove; where scarce is heard
One dying strain to cheer the woodman's toil:
Sad Philomel,[1] perchance, pours forth her plaint,° *lamentation*
Far, through the withering copse.° *small wood*
Meanwhile, the leaves
That, late, the forest clad with lively green,
Nipped by the drizzly night, and sallow-hued,
Fall, wavering, through the air; or shower amain,° *at full speed*
Urged by the breeze, that sobs amid the boughs.
Then list'ning hares forsake the rustling woods,
And, starting at the frequent noise, escape
To the rough stubble, and the rushy fen.° *marsh*
Then woodcocks, o'er the fluctuating main,[2]
That glimmers to the glimpses of the moon,
Stretch their long voyage to the woodland glade:
Where, wheeling with uncertain flight, they mock
The nimble fowler's° aim. Now Nature droops; *bird hunter's*
Languish the living herbs with pale decay:
And all the various family of flowers
Their sunny robes resign. The falling fruits,
Through the still night, forsake the parent-bough,
That, in the first grey glances of the dawn,
Looks wild, and wonders at the wintry waste.° *desolate land*

The year, yet pleasing, but declining fast,
Soft, o'er the secret soul, in gentle gales,
A philosophic melancholy breathes,
And bears the swelling thought aloft to heaven.
Then forming fancy rouses to conceive,
What never mingled with the vulgar's° dream: *uneducated*
Then wake the tender pang, the pitying tear,
The sigh for suffering worth, the wish preferred° *put forward*
For humankind, the joy to see them blessed,
And all the social offspring of the heart!

Oh! bear me then to high, embowering[3] shades;
To twilight groves, and visionary vales;
To weeping grottos,° and to hoary[4] caves;
Where angel-forms are seen, and voices heard,
Sighed in low whispers, that abstract the soul,
From outward sense, far into worlds remote.

Now, when the western sun withdraws the day,
And humid evening, gliding o'er the sky,
In her chill progress checks the straggling beams,
And robs them of their gathered, vapoury prey,
Where marshes stagnate, and where rivers wind,
Cluster the rolling fogs, and swim along
The dusky-mantled lawn:° then slow descend, *open land*
Once more to mingle with their wat'ry friends.
The vivid stars shine out, in radiant files;
And boundless ether[5] glows; till the fair moon
Shows her broad visage, in the crimsoned east;
Now, stooping, seems to kiss the passing cloud:
Now, o'er the pure cerulean,° rides sublime. *sky-blue*
Wide the pale deluge floats, with silver waves,
O'er the skied[6] mountain, to the low-laid vale;
From the white rocks, with dim reflection, gleams,
And faintly glitters through the waving shades.

All night, abundant dews, unnoted, fall,
And, at return of morning, silver o'er
The face of Mother Earth; from every branch
Depending,° tremble the translucent gems, *dangling*
And, quivering, seem to fall away, yet cling,
And sparkle in the sun, whose rising eye,
With fogs bedimmed, portends a beauteous day.

Now, giddy Youth, whom headlong passions fire,
Rouse the wild game, and stain the guiltless grove,
With violence, and death; yet call it sport,
To scatter ruin through the realms of love,

[1] *Philomel* Nightingale. The daughter of the King of Athens, Philomela was transformed into a nightingale after being pursued and raped by her brother-in-law, Tereus, King of Thrace.

[2] *main* Wide expanse.

[3] *embowering* Enclosed in trees.

[4] *hoary* White or grey with mold.

[5] *ether* Upper regions of space; the substance that comprises all the space beyond the moon.

[6] *skied* Appearing to reach the sky.

And peace, that thinks no ill: But these, the Muse,[1]
Whose charity, unlimited, extends
As wide as Nature works, disdains to sing,
Returning to her nobler theme in view—

For, see! where Winter comes, himself, confessed,° *revealed*
Striding the gloomy blast. First rains obscure
Drive through the mingling skies, with tempest foul;
Beat on the mountain's brow, and shake the woods,
That, sounding, wave below. The dreary plain
Lies overwhelmed, and lost. The bellying clouds
Combine, and deepening into night, shut up
The day's fair face. The wanderers of heaven,[2]
Each to his home, retire; save those that love
To take their pastime in the troubled air,
And, skimming, flutter round the dimply flood.
The cattle, from th' untasted fields, return,
And ask, with meaning low,° their wonted° stalls; *moo* *customary*
Or ruminate[3] in the contiguous° shade: *neighboring*
Thither, the household, feathery people crowd,
The crested cock, with all his female train,
Pensive, and wet. Meanwhile, the cottage swain
Hangs o'er th' enlivening blaze, and, taleful,° there *talkative*
Recounts his simple frolic: much he talks,
And much he laughs, nor wrecks the storm that blows
Without, and rattles on his humble roof.

At last, the muddy deluge pours along,
Resistless, roaring; dreadful down it comes
From the chapt° mountain, and the mossy wild, *fissured*
Tumbling through rocks abrupt, and sounding far:
Then o'er the sanded valley, floating, spreads,
Calm, sluggish, silent; till again constrained,
Betwixt two meeting hills, it bursts a way,
Where rocks and woods o'erhang the turbid° stream. *muddy*
There gathering triple force, rapid, and deep,
It boils, and wheels, and foams, and thunders through.

Nature! great parent! whose directing hand
Rolls round the seasons of the changeful year,
How mighty! how majestic are thy works!
With what a pleasing dread they swell the soul,
That sees, astonished! and, astonished, sings!
You too, ye Winds! that now begin to blow,
With boisterous sweep, I raise my voice to you.
Where are your stores,° ye viewless beings! say! *possessions*
Where your aerial magazines° reserved *warehouses*
Against the day of tempest perilous?
In what untraveled country of the air,
Hushed in still silence, sleep you, when 'tis calm?

Late, in the lowering[4] sky, red, fiery streaks
Begin to flush about; the reeling clouds
Stagger with dizzy aim, as doubting yet
Which master to obey: while rising, slow,
Sad, in the leaden-coloured east, the moon
Wears a bleak circle round her sullied orb.
Then issues forth the storm, with loud control,
And the thin fabric of the pillared air
O'erturns, at once. Prone, on th' uncertain main,
Descends th' ethereal force, and plows its waves,
With dreadful rift: from the mid-deep appears,
Surge after surge, the rising, wat'ry war.
Whitening, the angry billows roll immense,
And roar their terrors through the shuddering soul
Of feeble Man, amidst their fury caught,
And dashed upon his fate: Then, o'er the cliff,
Where dwells the sea-mew,° unconfined, they fly, *seagull*
And, hurrying, swallow up the sterile shore.

The mountain growls; and all its sturdy sons
Stoop to the bottom of the rocks they shade:
Lone, on its midnight-side, and all aghast,
The dark, wayfaring stranger, breathless, toils,
And climbs against the blast—
Low waves the rooted forest, vexed,° and sheds *disturbed*
What of its leafy honours yet remains.
Thus, struggling through the dissipated grove,
The whirling tempest raves along the plain;
And, on the cottage thatched or lordly dome° *mansion*
Keen-fastening, shakes 'em to the solid base.

[1] *Muse* The Muses were nine daughters of Zeus and Mnemosyne, each of whom presided over and provided inspiration for an aspect of learning or the arts.

[2] *wanderers of heaven* Wild birds.

[3] *ruminate* Meaning both "chew the cud" and "meditate."

[4] *lowering* Dark and threatening.

Sleep, frighted, flies; the hollow chimney howls,
The windows rattle, and the hinges creak.

Then too, they say, through all the burdened air
Long groans are heard, shrill sounds, and distant sighs,
That, murmured by the demon of the night,
Warn the devoted wretch of woe, and death!
Wild uproar lords it wide: the clouds commixed,
With stars, swift-gliding, sweep along the sky.
All nature reels. But hark! the Almighty speaks:
Instant, the chidden° storm begins to pant, *rebuked*
And dies, at once, into a noiseless calm.

As yet, 'tis midnight's reign; the weary clouds,
Slow-meeting, mingle into solid gloom:
Now, while the drowsy world lies lost in sleep,
Let me associate with the low-browed Night,
And Contemplation, her sedate compeer;° *companion*
Let me shake off th' intrusive cares of day,
And lay the meddling senses all aside.

And now, ye lying vanities of life!
You ever-tempting, ever-cheating train!
Where are you now? and what is your amount?° *significance*
Vexation, disappointment, and remorse.
Sad, sickening thought! and yet, deluded Man,
A scene of wild, disjointed visions past,
And broken slumbers, rises, still resolved,
With new-flushed hopes, to run your giddy round.

Father of light, and life! Thou Good Supreme!
O! teach me what is good! teach me thy self!
Save me from folly, vanity and vice,
From every low pursuit! and feed my soul,
With knowledge, conscious peace, and virtue pure,
Sacred, substantial, never-fading bliss!

Lo! from the livid east, or piercing north,
Thick clouds ascend, in whose capacious womb
A vapoury deluge lies, to snow congealed:
Heavy, they roll their fleecy world along;
And the sky saddens with th' impending storm.
Through the hushed air, the whitening shower descends,
At first, thin-wavering; till, at last, the flakes
Fall broad, and wide, and fast, dimming the day
With a continual flow. See! sudden, hoared,
The woods beneath the stainless burden bow,
Blackening, along the mazy° stream it melts; *winding*
Earth's universal face, deep-hid, and chill,
Is all one dazzling waste. The labourer-ox
Stands covered o'er with snow, and then demands
The fruit of all his toil. The fowls of heaven,
Tamed by the cruel season, crowd around
The winnowing[1] store, and claim the little boon,° *favor*
That Providence allows. The foodless wilds
Pour forth their brown inhabitants; the hare,
Though timorous° of heart, and hard beset *fearful*
By death in various forms—dark snares, and dogs,
And more unpitying men—the garden seeks,
Urged on by fearless want. The bleating kind° *sheep*
Eye the bleak heavens, and next, the glistening Earth,
With looks of dumb despair; then sad, dispersed,
Dig for the withered herb, through heaps of snow.

Now, shepherds, to your helpless charge be kind;
Baffle° the raging year, and fill their pens *defeat*
With food, at will: lodge them below the blast,
And watch them strict; for from the bellowing east,
In this dire season, oft the whirlwind's wing
Sweeps up the burden of whole wintry plains
In one fierce blast, and o'er th' unhappy flocks,
Lodged in the hollow of two neighbouring hills,
The billowy tempest whelms;° till, upwards urged, *buries*
The valley to a shining mountain swells,
That curls its wreaths amid the freezing sky.

Now, all amid the rigours of the year,
In the wild depth of Winter, while without
The ceaseless winds blow keen, be my retreat
A rural, sheltered, solitary scene;
Where ruddy fire and beaming tapers° join *candles*
To chase the cheerless gloom: there let me sit,
And hold high converse with the mighty dead,
Sages of ancient time, as gods revered,
As gods beneficent, who blest mankind
With arts, and arms, and humanized a world,
Roused at th' inspiring thought—I throw aside

[1] *winnowing* Exposed to the wind so that the chaff is separated from the heavier grain.

The long-lived volume,[1] and, deep-musing, hail
The sacred shades, that, slowly-rising, pass
Before my wondering eyes—First, Socrates,[2]
Truth's early champion, martyr for his God:
Solon,[3] the next, who built his commonweal,° *commonwealth*
On equity's firm base: Lycurgus,[4] then,
Severely good, and him of rugged Rome,
Numa,[5] who softened her° rapacious° sons. *Rome's / greedy*
Cimon[6] sweet-souled, and Aristides[7] just.
Unconquered Cato,[8] virtuous in extreme;
With that attempered° hero,[9] mild, and firm, *well-balanced*
Who wept the brother, while the tyrant bled.
Scipio,[10] the humane warrior, gently brave,
Fair learning's friend, who early sought the shade,
To dwell, with innocence and truth, retired.
And, equal to the best, the Theban,[11] he
Who, single, raised his country into fame.
Thousands behind, the boast of Greece and Rome,
Whom virtue owns, the tribute of a verse
Demand, but who can count the stars of heaven?
Who sing their influence on this lower world?
But see who yonder comes! nor comes alone,
With sober state, and of majestic mien,° *bearing*
The Sister-Muses in his train—'tis he!
Maro![12] the best of poets, and of men!
Great Homer[13] too appears, of daring wing!
Parent of song! and, equal, by this side,
The British Muse,[14] joined hand in hand, they walk,
Darkling,° nor miss their way to fame's ascent. *in the dark*

Society divine! Immortal minds!
Still visit thus my nights, for you reserved,
And mount my soaring soul to deeds like yours.
Silence! thou lonely power! the door be thine:
See, on the hallowed hour, that none intrude,
Save Lycidas,[15] the friend with sense refined,
Learning digested well, exalted faith,
Unstudied wit, and humour ever gay.

[1] *long-lived volume* Reference to *Parallel Lives,* a collection of paired biographies of prominent Greeks and Romans by Plutarch, Greek biographer (c. 46–120 CE).

[2] *Socrates* Greek philosopher (469–399 BCE) who considered the knowledge of one's self as the highest good; he was forced to drink poisonous hemlock after being convicted of corrupting Athens' youth and perpetuating religious heresies.

[3] *Solon* Athenian statesman (c. 639–c. 559 BCE) whose humane legal reforms contributed to the end of serfdom in Attica and established the democratic basis of the Athenian state.

[4] *Lycurgus* Although it is unclear whether he actually existed, Lycurgus is traditionally held to be the founder of the Spartan constitution.

[5] *Numa* Numa Pompilius (7th century BCE), second king of Rome after Romulus, believed to be responsible for the Roman ceremonial laws and religious rites that encouraged peace in the city.

[6] *Cimon* Athenian general and statesman (c. 510–449 BCE), remembered for both his military success against the Persians and his powerful influence in government.

[7] *Aristides* Athenian general and statesman (d. c. 468 BCE), known as Aristides the Just, who contributed significantly to Cimon's military success against the Persians.

[8] *Cato* Marcus Porcius Cato (95–46 BCE), Roman statesman known for his incorruptibility and honesty, who opposed Julius Caesar and was subsequently exiled; Cato marched six days across the African desert to join his allies in Utica after which he realized the futility of his campaign; he chose suicide rather than surrender to Caesar.

[9] *attempered hero* Timoleon, Greek statesman and military leader (d. c. 337 BCE) who successfully fought against the tyrants of Syracuse, where he subsequently set up a democratic government; when Timoleon's brother, Timophanes, attempted to declare himself the absolute ruler of their city, Corinth, Timoleon assisted in his brother's assassination, weeping all the while.

[10] *Scipio* Publius Cornelius Scipio Africanus (236–183 BCE), Roman general who conquered Spain and Carthage and defeated Hannibal in the Punic Wars.

[11] *the Theban* Possibly Pelopidas (d. 364 BCE), Theban general who rescued Thebes from Sparta in 379 BCE, or Epaminondas (c. 420–362 BCE), famous Greek military tactician under whom Pelopidas served.

[12] *Maro* Publius Virgilius Maro, or Virgil, Roman poet (70–19 BCE), author of *The Aeneid,* an epic detailing the life of Aeneas, mythical father of the Roman people, who embodied the Roman virtues, and *The Georgics,* poems recounting the joy of rural and farming life.

[13] *Homer* Greek poet (c. 700 BCE), putative author of *The Iliad,* an account of the Greeks' war with the Trojans, and *The Odyssey,* which tells the story of Odysseus's journey home after the war's end; Homer was believed to have been blind.

[14] *British Muse* John Milton (1608–74), English poet famous for such works as *Paradise Lost, Comus,* and *Paradise Regained.*

[15] *Lycidas* In his pastoral elegy *Lycidas* (1638), Milton laments the drowning death of his school fellow, Edward King; Thomson may be referring to his friend David Mallet, with whom he wrote the masque *Alfred* (1740).

Clear frost succeeds, and through the blue serene,
For sight too fine, the ethereal nitre[1] flies,
To bake the glebe,° and bind the slippery flood. *soil*
This of the wintry season is the prime;
Pure are the days, and lustrous are the nights,
Brightened with starry worlds, till then unseen.
Meanwhile, the Orient, darkly red, breathes forth
An icy gale, that, in its mid career,
Arrests the bickering° stream. The nightly sky *noisy*
And all her glowing constellations pour
Their rigid influence down: it freezes on
Till Morn, late-rising, o'er the drooping world
Lifts her pale eye, unjoyous: then appears
The various labour of the silent night,
The pendant icicle, the frost-work fair,
Where thousand figures rise, the crusted snow,
Though white, made whiter, by the fining° north. *refining*
On blithesome° frolics bent, the youthful swains, *sprightly*
While every work of man is laid at rest,
Rush o'er the wat'ry plains, and, shuddering, view
The fearful deeps below: or with the gun,
And faithful spaniel, range the ravaged fields,
And, adding to the ruins of the year,
Distress the feathery, or the footed game.

But hark! the nightly winds, with hollow voice,
Blow, blustering, from the south—the frost subdued,
Gradual, resolves into a weeping thaw.
Spotted, the mountains shine: loose sleet descends,
And floods the country round: the rivers swell,
Impatient for the day. Those sullen seas,
That wash th' ungenial° pole, will rest no more *inhospitable*
Beneath the shackles of the mighty north;
But, rousing all their waves, resistless heave,
And hark! the length'ning roar, continuous, runs
Athwart° the rifted main; at once it bursts, *side to side*
And piles a thousand mountains to the clouds!
Ill fares the bark,° the wretches' last resort, *boat*
That, lost amid the floating fragments, moors
Beneath the shelter of an icy isle;
While night o'erwhelms the sea, and horror looks
More horrible. Can human hearts endure
Th' assembled mischiefs that besiege them round:
Unlist'ning hunger, fainting weariness,
The roar of winds, and waves, the crush of ice,
Now ceasing, now renewed with louder rage,
And bellowing round the main: nations remote,
Shook from their midnight-slumbers, deem they hear
Portentous thunder in the troubled sky.
More to embroil the deep, Leviathan[2]
And his unwieldy train, in horrid sport,
Tempest the loosened brine; while, through the gloom,
Far from the dire, inhospitable shore,
The lion's rage, the wolf's sad howl is heard,
And all the fell° society of night. *cruel*
Yet Providence, that ever-waking eye,
Looks down, with pity, on the fruitless toil
Of mortals, lost to hope, and lights° them safe *causes to arrive*
Through all this dreary labyrinth of fate.

'Tis done! dread Winter has subdued the year,
And reigns, tremendous, o'er the desert plains!
How dead the vegetable kingdom lies!
How dumb the tuneful! Horror wide extends
His solitary empire. Now, fond Man!
Behold thy pictured life: pass some few years,
Thy flow'ring Spring, thy short-lived Summer's strength,
Thy sober Autumn, fading into age,
And pale, concluding, Winter shuts thy scene,
And shrouds thee in the grave—where now, are fled
Those dreams of greatness? those unsolid hopes
Of happiness? those longings after fame?
Those restless cares? those busy, bustling days?
Those nights of secret guilt? those veering thoughts,
Flutt'ring 'twixt good and ill, that shared thy life?
All, now, are vanished! Virtue, sole, survives,
Immortal, mankind's never-failing friend,
His guide to happiness on high—and see!
'Tis come, the glorious morn! the second birth
Of Heaven, and Earth! Awakening Nature hears
Th' Almighty trumpet's voice, and starts to life,
Renewed, unfading. Now, th' eternal scheme,
That dark perplexity, that mystic maze,
Which sight could never trace, nor heart conceive,
To reason's eye, refined, clears up apace.° *speedily*
Angels and men, astonished, pause—and dread

[1] *ethereal nitre* Substance believed to exist in air or plants and to cause various phenomena.

[2] *Leviathan* Monster of the deep mentioned in Job 41.

To travel through the depths of Providence,
Untried, unbounded. Ye vain learned! see,
And, prostrate in the dust, adore that power,
And goodness, oft arraigned.° See now the cause, *accused of a fault*
Why conscious worth, oppressed, in secret long
Mourned, unregarded: why the good man's share
In life was gall, and bitterness of soul:
Why the lone widow, and her orphans, pined,
In starving solitude; while luxury,
In palaces, lay prompting her low thought
To form unreal wants: why heaven-born faith,
And charity, prime grace! wore the red marks
Of persecution's scourge:° why licensed pain, *whip*
That cruel spoiler, that embosomed° foe, *embraced*
Embittered all our bliss. Ye good distressed!
Ye noble few! that, here, unbending, stand
Beneath life's pressures—yet a little while,
And all your woes are past. Time swiftly fleets,
And wished eternity, approaching, brings
Life undecaying, love without allay,
Pure flowing joy, and happiness sincere.
—1726

Rule, Britannia[1]

When Britain first, at Heaven's command,
Arose from out the azure main;° *sea*
This was the charter of the land,
And guardian angels sung this strain:
"Rule, Britannia, rule the waves;
Britons never will be slaves."

The nations not so blessed as thee
Must, in their turns, to tyrants fall:
While thou shalt flourish great and free,
The dread and envy of them all.
"Rule," etc.

Still more majestic shalt thou rise,
More dreadful, from each foreign stroke:
As the loud blast that tears the skies
Serves but to root thy native oak.
"Rule," etc.

Thee haughty tyrants ne'er shall tame:
All their attempts to bend thee down
Will but arouse thy generous flame,
But work their woe, and thy renown.
"Rule," etc.

To thee belongs the rural reign;
Thy cities shall with commerce shine:
All thine shall be the subject main,
And every shore it circles thine.
"Rule," etc.

The Muses, still° with freedom found, *always*
Shall to thy happy coast repair:
Blessed isle! with matchless beauty crowned,
And manly hearts to guard the fair.
"Rule, Britannia, rule the waves;
Britons never will be slaves."
—1740

[1] *Rule, Britannia* From Thomson's masque *Alfred* (1740), first performed for the Prince and Princess of Wales. This song became so popular that it has come to be considered the unofficial national anthem of Britain ("Britannia" was the original name given to England and Wales by the Romans).

Henry Fielding

1707 – 1754

Best known today as the father of the comic novel in English, Henry Fielding had a wide-ranging professional career that also included successful turns as a playwright, journalist, and Justice of the Peace for Middlesex and Westminster. Before even considering prose fiction, Fielding enjoyed a decade of fame as one of the most prodigious, innovative, and controversial playwrights of his day. At various points in his career, he contributed to and edited periodicals distinguished for their sharp political commentary and humorous reflections on the state of contemporary literature and culture. In his later life, his fairness and tough-on-crime attitude as the chief magistrate of London won him admiration from those who wished to combat the disorder and corruption of the city. Among his many achievements, Fielding helped to establish the "Bow Street Runners," a group that undertook raids to break up gangs of street robbers; it was an important precursor to the Metropolitan Police Service still operating in the London area today.

The oldest of seven children, Henry Fielding had a tumultuous childhood. His mother died a week before his eleventh birthday, and his father, a colonel who had expensive tastes and small means, lost custody of Henry and his siblings to their maternal grandmother after selling off much of their inheritance to pay his debts and finance an early remarriage. Given such a family situation, Fielding, despite being the eldest child and heir, was forced to make a living for himself.

Witty, passionate, and an excellent conversationalist with a strong sense of humor, the young Fielding chose playwriting as a promising career. London at the time boasted many playhouses and a large theatrical market; a talented playwright could do very well—and Fielding would become arguably the most popular playwright of the 1730s. After seeing his first play, *Love in Several Masques*, produced in 1728, Fielding left London temporarily to study in Holland at the University of Leiden. Upon his return, he staged four successful plays in one year (1730): *The Temple Beau, The Author's Farce, Tom Thumb*, and *Rape upon Rape: or, The Justice Caught in His Own Trap*. He went on to complete more than twenty-five plays in less than ten years, almost all of which were staged—an extraordinary output for an author still in his twenties through most of this period. While many critics, both in his own time and in later periods, found his work uneven, George Bernard Shaw (1856–1950) praised him as "the greatest dramatist, with the single exception of Shakespeare, produced in England between the Middle Ages and the nineteenth century." From 1732 to 1733, Fielding was the leading playwright of the Drury Lane Theatre, then the largest and most prestigious of London's theaters. In 1736 he took over management of the Little Theatre in the Haymarket, where he wrote plays for his own company of comedians.

A number of Fielding's plays were conventional five-act comedies in which he attempted to treat serious social themes, writing in the tradition of the master comedic playwrights he admired (such as Molière, William Congreve, George Farquhar, and William Wycherley); perhaps the most notable of these is *The Modern Husband* (1732). Far more successful, however, were his farces, ballad operas, and dramatic satires, which experimented with form, incorporated songs, and lambasted well-known personalities of the day. Among the most remarkable of these is *The Author's Farce*, Fielding's first smash hit, which satirized London's theatrical world by dramatizing the efforts of one Harry Luckless to become a successful dramatist. Luckless's puppet play, *The Pleasures of the Town*, is eventually staged—with actors performing the roles of the puppets—but success of this sort is uncertain and unstable; in the play's third and final act, the boundary between the world of the puppet play and the "real" world of *The Author's Farce* collapses, as Luckless is revealed to be related to his wooden characters.

Fielding also targeted government corruption and mismanagement, and at times he viciously criticized chief minister Sir Robert Walpole (although his political allegiances varied dramatically throughout his career). His *Grub Street Opera*, which mocked the royal family as well as both political parties, was notoriously withdrawn from the Haymarket Theatre before its opening night in 1731, likely because of political pressure. Fielding's playwriting career ended when the Stage Licensing Act of 1737 required that all plays be approved by a government examiner before they were produced, effectively censoring all theatrical work. It was widely suggested that the act was provoked in large part by the "seditious" content of Fielding's plays, and contemporaries claimed that the act was passed to silence one man. While that may be something of an exaggeration, there can be no doubt that he had touched a nerve.

Forced to make a career change, Fielding decided to pursue law, and in 1740 he was called to the bar. During the next few years he was plagued by financial trouble (and even briefly arrested for debt) as he built a career as a lawyer. He made money during this time by (anonymously) publishing satiric essays in anti-Walpole periodicals, establishing his own journal, and taking on several miscellaneous writing projects. One such project would change the direction of the rest of his career: *An Apology for the Life of Mrs. Shamela Andrews* (1741). This pamphlet-length parody of Samuel Richardson's first novel, *Pamela, or Virtue Rewarded* (1740), mocked its epistolary style and heavily moralistic tone. Though Fielding's little work was only one of many "anti-Pamelas" printed in the wake of *Pamela*'s publication, his was particularly well received, and he was prompted to try his hand at comic prose fiction in a more earnest fashion. The result was *Joseph Andrews* (1742), supposedly a history of Pamela's virtuous brother Joseph, written, according to its title page, in imitation of Miguel de Cervantes, author of *Don Quixote*. Like Cervantes's work—and unlike *Pamela* and *Shamela*—*Joseph Andrews* is written as a sustained (albeit highly episodic) narrative rather than an extended exchange of letters. Fielding described the work in his preface as a "comic epic-poem in prose," a form he declared himself unable to "remember to have seen hitherto attempted in our language."

Fielding published his next novel, *Tom Jones* (1749), seven years after the success of *Joseph Andrews*. Readers embraced the book with such enthusiasm that at first the publisher struggled to keep up; the first print run sold out before its publication date, and three more editions—totaling a remarkable 10,000 copies—were printed before the end of the year. Considered Fielding's masterpiece, this picaresque novel details the hilarious episodes that lead to a foundling's coming into fortune. Yet the novel's most characteristic feature is its self-consciously chatty and intrusive narrator, who never misses an opportunity to digress on ethical quandaries or critical issues, and who never lets the reader forget who is telling the story. *Tom Jones* and *Joseph Andrews* together established the tradition of the comic novel in English.

Fielding completed one last novel, *Amelia* (1751), a story of a troubled marriage that contains elements of social protest. He also applied his wit to moral and literary commentary in the *Covent-Garden Journal* (1752), a new periodical that he sustained for almost a year while writing much of its content himself. However, much of his later life was taken up with his work as a magistrate. In 1753, in declining health as a result of cirrhosis of the liver, Fielding retired from public service. The following year he sailed to Portugal in the hopes of recovering his health. He died there, near Lisbon, where he was buried. His final journey is described with humor and pathos in *The Journal of a Voyage to Lisbon*, posthumously published in 1755.

⌘⌘⌘

The Tragedy of Tragedies: or, the Life and Death of Tom Thumb the Great

One of the greatest successes of Fielding's early playwriting career was *Tom Thumb*, a two-act play originally added as an afterpiece to *The Author's Farce*; when it was first performed in 1730, it ran to full houses for forty-one nights. Fielding began to revise the play during its initial run, and would eventually turn it into *The Tragedy of Tragedies*. With an added third act and the addition of the character of Glumdalca, *The Tragedy of Tragedies* is similar to the original *Tom Thumb* up to about halfway through the second act, but almost all the material past this point is new. In its revised and expanded version, the play is a parody of the heroic drama that has all the elements of the extravagant genre it mocks, including a superhuman hero (though of miniature size), a captive princess (of enormous size), a heroic battle (accompanied by thunder and lightning), and two (ridiculously convoluted) love triangles. By the time Fielding staged and published *The Tragedy of Tragedies*, heroic plays were no longer popular in the English theater—indeed, most of his specific targets are more than thirty years old. Fielding, however, revived the old-fashioned genre in order to direct his satire more generally at the misuses and abuses of language, exploiting the overwrought style of plays like John Dryden's *Aureng-Zebe* (1675) and John Banks's *The Albion Queens* (1704) to expose any writing that allows words to get in the way of meaning.

Heroic drama also facilitated Fielding's ridicule of false scholarship. *The Tragedy of Tragedies* was put forward as the work not of Henry Fielding, but of "H. Scriblerus Secundus," a pen name Fielding adopted for several of his plays, thereby placing himself in the tradition of Jonathan Swift, John Gay, and, especially, Alexander Pope, who founded the so-called Scriblerus Club in 1714 in an attempt to satirize "all false tastes in learning." Like the Scriblerians, Fielding attacks mindless pedantry and inflated writing, imitating the format of Pope's *Dunciad Variorum* (1729) in an ironic preface and in copious notes (written in the voice of Scriblerus for printed editions of the play) that treat *The Life and Death of Tom Thumb the Great* as a work of sublime genius, and which mock-learnedly identify more than forty plays whose best lines are ostensibly borrowed from the tragedy. The number of words in the annotations outnumber those in the playtext two to one, and Fielding's main joke is discovered in the disjunction between the play's silly plot and frivolous characters, and the extraordinary lengths to which Scriblerus Secundus goes to explain them.

The Tragedy of Tragedies first appeared on the stage in 1731. The play enjoyed five seasons of immense popularity and went on to inspire numerous adaptations. It even became a favorite choice for amateur domestic performances, particularly by and for children. Novelist Frances Burney recounts playing Huncamunca in one such performance, and Charles Dickens's son Henry played Tom Thumb in another.

NOTE ON THE TEXT

In the original 1731 edition of *The Tragedy of Tragedies*, the commentary of H. Scriblerus Secundus appeared as lettered footnotes at the base of the printed page. So as to avoid confusion with modern editorial commentary, the lettered notes have been printed in the right column of the present edition, parallel with the playtext appearing in the left column. Numbered editor's notes appear at the base of the page. The studied nature of the 1731 text suggests that Fielding was working and citing from printed editions of the more than forty plays parodied in *The Tragedy of Tragedies*. For this reason, the editorial notes assign each play a date of first publication, instead of a date of first performance.

The Tragedy of Tragedies, or, the Life and Death of Tom Thumb the Great

H. SCRIBLERUS SECUNDUS, HIS PREFACE

The town hath seldom been more divided in its opinion than concerning the merit of the following scenes. Whilst some publicly affirmed that no author could produce so fine a piece but Mr. P——,[1] others have with as much vehemence insisted that no one could write anything so bad, but Mr. F——.[2]

Nor can we wonder at this dissention about its merit, when the learned world have not unanimously decided even the very nature of this tragedy. For though most of the universities in Europe have honoured it with the name of *egregium & maximi pretii opus, tragœdiis tam antiquis quam novis longe anteponendum*;[3] nay, Dr. B—— hath pronounced, *citiùs Maevii Æneadem quam Scribleri istius tragœdiam hanc crediderim, cujus autorem Senecam ipsum tradidisse haud dubitârim*;[4] and the great Professor Burman hath styled Tom Thumb, *heroum omnium tragicorum facilè principem*.[5] Nay, though it hath, among other languages, been translated into Dutch, and celebrated with great applause at Amsterdam (where burlesque[6] never came) by the title of *Mynheer Vander Thumb*, the burgomasters[7] receiving it with that reverent and silent attention which becometh an audience at a deep tragedy. Notwithstanding all this, there have not been wanting[8] some who have represented these scenes in a ludicrous light; and Mr. D——[9] hath been heard to say, with some concern, that he wondered a tragical and Christian nation would permit a representation on its theatre so visibly designed to ridicule and extirpate everything that is great and solemn among us.

This learned critic and his followers were led into so great an error by that surreptitious and piratical copy which stole last year into the world;[10] with what injustice and prejudice to our author, I hope will be acknowledged by everyone who shall happily peruse this genuine and original copy. Nor can I help remarking, to the great praise of our author, that, however imperfect the former was, still did even that faint resemblance of the true *Tom Thumb* contain sufficient beauties to give it a run of upwards of forty nights, to the politest audiences. But, notwithstanding that applause which it received from all the best judges, it was as severely censured by some few bad ones, and, I believe, rather maliciously than ignorantly, reported to have been intended a burlesque on the loftiest parts of tragedy, and designed to banish what we generally call fine things from the stage.

Now, if I can set my country right in an affair of this importance, I shall lightly esteem any labour which it may cost. And this I the rather undertake, first, as it is indeed in some measure incumbent on me to vindicate myself from that surreptitious copy before mentioned, published by some ill-meaning people under my name.

[1] *Mr. P——* Poet Alexander Pope (1688–1744), who adopted the ironic persona of "Martinus Scriblerus" for a number of his satires on dullness and false learning.

[2] *Mr. F——* Henry Fielding.

[3] *egregium … anteponendum* Latin: a distinguished work of the greatest value, to be rated as by far the best tragedy, ancient or modern.

[4] *Dr. B——* Classical scholar Dr. Richard Bentley (1662–1742), who was considered a tasteless pedant by Pope and Jonathan Swift, both of whom mocked him in their work; *citiùs … dubitârim* Latin: "I would sooner have believed the *Aeneid* to be by Maevius than that this tragedy, which I would not hesitate to ascribe to Seneca himself, could be the work of one like Scriblerus." The *Aeneid* was written in the first century BCE by the Roman poet Virgil, whose famous epic was belittled by a second-rate critic named Maevius; Seneca the Younger was a first-century CE Roman philosopher and dramatist, best known for violent tragedies adapted from the Greek.

[5] *Professor Burman* Dutch classical scholar Pieter Burmann (1688–1744), under whom Fielding studied from 1728 to 1729; *heroum … principem* Latin: of all tragic heroes, easily the foremost.

[6] *burlesque* Type of comedy in which distortion is used to evoke ridicule and laughter, either by treating a lofty subject in a trivial manner, or, as in Fielding's *Tragedy*, treating a low subject in an exaggerated manner.

[7] *burgomasters* Dutch.

[8] *wanting* Lacking.

[9] *Mr. D——* John Dennis (1657–1734), an irascible critic and playwright with whom Pope frequently quarreled.

[10] *that surreptitious … world* Scriblerus Secundus is made to suggest that *Tom Thumb*, the original two-act play that Fielding published in 1730 (a second edition of which was published that same year under Scriblerus's name), was a pirated, inaccurate copy of *The Tragedy of Tragedies*.

Secondly, as knowing myself more capable of doing justice to our author than any other man, as I have given myself more pains to arrive at a thorough understanding of this little piece, having for ten years together read nothing else; in which time, I think I may modestly presume, with the help of my English dictionary, to comprehend all the meanings of every word in it.

But should any error of my pen awaken *Clariss.* Bentleium[1] to enlighten the world with his annotations on our author, I shall not think that the least reward or happiness arising to me from these my endeavours.

I shall waive at present, what hath caused such feuds in the learned world: whether this piece was originally written by Shakespeare,[2] though certainly that, were it true, must add a considerable share to its merit; especially with such who are so generous as to buy and to commend what they never read, from an implicit faith in the author only: a faith which our age abounds in as much as it can be called deficient in any other.

Let it suffice that the *Tragedy of Tragedies*, or, *The Life and Death of Tom Thumb*, was written in the reign of Queen Elizabeth.[3] Nor can the objection made by Mr. D——, that the tragedy must then have been antecedent to the history, have any weight, when we consider that though the *History of Tom Thumb*, printed by and for Edward M——r, at the Looking-Glass on London-Bridge,[4] be of a later date, still must we suppose this history to have been transcribed from some other, unless we suppose the writer thereof to be inspired: a gift very faintly contended for by the writers of our age. As to this history's not bearing the stamp of second, third, or fourth edition, I see but little in that objection, editions being very uncertain lights to judge of books by. And perhaps Mr. M——r may have joined twenty editions in one, as Mr. C——l[5] hath ere now divided one into twenty.

Nor doth the other argument, drawn from the little care our author hath taken to keep up to the letter of the history, carry any greater force. Are there not instances of plays wherein the history is so perverted that we can know the heroes whom they celebrate by no other marks than their names? Nay, do we not find the same character placed by different poets in such different lights that we can discover not the least sameness, or even likeness in the features? The Sophonisba of Mairet, and of Lee, is a tender, passionate, amorous mistress of Massinissa; Corneille and Mr. Thomson give her no other passion but the love of her country, and make her as cool in her affection to Massinissa, as to Syphax.[6] In the two latter, she resembles the character of Queen Elizabeth; in the two former she is the picture of Mary, Queen of Scotland.[7] In short, the one Sophonisba is as different from the other as the Brutus of Voltaire is from the Marius Jun. of Otway; or as the Minerva is from the Venus[8] of the ancients.

---

[1] *Clariss. Bentleium* Abbreviation for the Latin *clarissimum*, meaning "most illustrious" Bentley, a mocking imitation of learned forms of address.

[2] *Shakespeare* During the early part of the eighteenth century, William Shakespeare (1564–1616) was particularly well known for his tragedies, which were performed regularly at the patent theaters.

[3] *the reign of Queen Elizabeth* Elizabeth I reigned from 1558 to 1603. By dating *The Life and Death of Tom Thumb* to the Elizabethan period, and having Scriblerus Secundus claim that works published as early as 1613 and as late as 1731 borrowed from the tragedy, Fielding pokes fun at bad historical scholarship.

[4] *Edward … Bridge* Edward Midwinter was a publisher of cheap, popular print works. The location of his shop on London Bridge was a highly undesirable one.

[5] *Mr. C—l* Edmund Curll (1675–1747), an unscrupulous publisher and antagonist of Pope, who notoriously multiplied "new" editions of a work by replacing the title page of the first edition with a fresh one. Scriblerus Secundus suggests that Edward Midwinter could have done the opposite by collapsing several editions into one.

[6] *The Sophonisba … Syphax* Sophonisba was a Carthaginian noblewoman married to Syphax, King of Numidia, who was defeated by Massinissa, a Numidian prince in alliance with Rome, in 203 BCE. Massinissa subsequently fell in love with Sophonisba, but rather than see her return to Rome a captive, he convinced her to kill herself by drinking poison. This story was the subject of numerous plays and operas, several of which Scriblerus Secundus references here: Jean Mairet's *Sophonisbe* (1634), Nathaniel Lee's *Sophonisba* (1676), Pierre Corneille's *Sophonisbe* (1663), and James Thomson's *The Tragedy of Sophonisba* (1730), which the notes usually identify as the "new" *Sophonisba*.

[7] *Mary, Queen of Scotland* Queen Mary I of Scotland was forced to abdicate the Scottish throne in 1567, and was later executed as a traitor for attempting to assassinate Queen Elizabeth of England, whose kingdom she sought to inherit.

[8] *Brutus of … Otway* Brutus and Marius Junior each appear in a different play set in Augustan Rome: *Brutus* (1730) by Voltaire and *The History and Fall of Caius Marius* (1680) by Thomas Otway, respectively; *Minerva … Venus* Minerva and Venus were Roman goddesses; Minerva was associated with wisdom and war, and Venus with love and beauty.

Let us now proceed to a regular examination of the tragedy before us, in which I shall treat separately of the fable, the moral, the characters, the sentiments, and the diction.[1]

And first of the fable, which I take to be the most simple imaginable; and, to use the words of an eminent author, "One, regular and uniform, not charged with a multiplicity of incidents, and yet affording several revolutions of fortune; by which the passions may be excited, varied, and driven to their full tumult of emotion."[2] Nor is the action of this tragedy less great than uniform. The spring of all is the love of Tom Thumb for Huncamunca; which causeth the quarrel between their Majesties in the first act; the passion of Lord Grizzle in the second; the rebellion, fall of Lord Grizzle and Glumdalca, devouring of Tom Thumb by the cow, and that bloody catastrophe in the third.

Nor is the moral of this excellent tragedy less noble than the fable; it teaches these two instructive lessons, *viz.*[3] that human happiness is exceeding transient, and that death is the certain end of all men; the former whereof is inculcated by the fatal end of Tom Thumb; the latter, by that of all the other personages.

The characters are, I think, sufficiently described in the *Dramatis Personae*; and I believe we shall find few plays where greater care is taken to maintain them throughout, and to preserve in every speech that characteristical mark which distinguishes them from each other. "But (says Mr. D——) how well doth the character of Tom Thumb, whom we must call the hero of this tragedy, if it hath any hero, agree with the precepts of Aristotle, who defineth tragedy to be the imitation of a short but perfect action, containing a just greatness in itself, etc.[4] What greatness can be in a fellow whom history relateth to have been no higher than a span?"[5] This gentleman seemeth to think, with Sergeant Kite,[6] that the greatness of a man's soul is in proportion to that of his body, the contrary of which is affirmed by our English physognominical writers. Besides, if I understand Aristotle right, he speaketh only of the greatness of the action, and not of the person.

As for the sentiments and the diction, which now only remain to be spoken to; I thought I could afford them no stronger justification than by producing parallel passages out of the best of our English writers. Whether this sameness of thought and expression which I have quoted from them proceeded from an agreement in their way of thinking, or whether they have borrowed from our author, I leave the reader to determine. I shall adventure to affirm this of the sentiments of our author; that they are generally the most familiar which I have ever met with, and at the same time delivered with the highest dignity of phrase; which brings me to speak of his diction. Here I shall only beg one postulatum,[7] *viz.* that the greatest perfection of the language of a tragedy is that it is not to be understood; which granted (as I think it must be), it will necessarily follow that the only way to avoid this is by being too high or too low for the understanding, which will comprehend everything within its reach. Those two extremities of style Mr. Dryden illustrates by the familiar image of two inns,[8] which I shall term the aerial and the subterrestrial.

Horace goeth farther, and showeth when it is proper to call at one of these inns, and when at the other:

[1] *Let us now … and the diction* In his preliminary commentary on *The Dunciad Variorum* (1729), Martinus Scriblerus examines Pope's mock-epic poem under similar heads. Both Pope and Fielding parody the stiff formalism of French neoclassical critics like René Rapin (1621–87) and René Le Bossu (1631–80), and of English exponents like Dennis.

[2] *One, regular … emotion* From the preface to Thomson's *Sophonisba*, mentioned above.

[3] *viz.* Short for the Latin *videlicet*, meaning "that is to say," or "namely."

[4] *Aristotle … itself, etc.* Dennis's reference is to Aristotle's *Poetics* (1449b).

[5] *span* The distance from the tip of the thumb to that of the little finger.

[6] *Sergeant Kite* A character in George Farquhar's 1706 comedy, *The Recruiting Officer*. In an attempt to attract new recruits, Kite contends in the first scene of the play that "he that has the good fortune to be born six foot high, was born to be a great man."

[7] *postulatum* Fundamental principle.

[8] *Mr. Dryden … two inns* In his essay "Of Heroic Plays" (1672), poet, playwright, and critic John Dryden (1631–1700) argues against those who recognize that serious plays should transcend the prose of ordinary conversation, but who do not admit that rhyming poetry is best for the stage; such people, he says, are lodging themselves "in the open field between two inns," because they "have lost that which [they] call natural, and have not required the last perfection of art."

Telephus & Peleus, cùm pauper & exul uterque,
Projicit ampullas & sesquipedalia verba.[1]

That he approveth of the *sesquipedalia verba* is plain; for had not *Telephus & Peleus* used this sort of diction in prosperity, they could not have dropped it in adversity. The aerial inn, therefore (says Horace) is proper only to be frequented by princes and other great men, in the highest affluence of fortune; the subterrestrial is appointed for the entertainment of the poorer sort of people only, whom Horace advises,

——dolere sermone pedestri.[2]

The true meaning of both which citations is that bombast is the proper language for joy, and doggerel[3] for grief, the latter of which is literally implied in the *sermo pedestris*, as the former is in the *sesquipedalia verba.*

Cicero recommendeth the former of these: *quid est tam furiosum vel tragicum quàm verborum sonitus inanis, nullâ subjectâ sententiâ neque scientiâ.*[4] What can be so proper for tragedy as a set of big sounding words, so contrived together as to convey no meaning; which I shall one day or other prove to be the sublime of Longinus.[5] Ovid declareth absolutely for the latter inn:

Omne genus scripti gravitate tragaedia vincit.[6]

Tragedy hath of all writings the greatest share in the *bathos,*[7] which is the profound of Scriblerus.[8]

I shall not presume to determine which of these two styles be properer for tragedy. It sufficeth that our author excelleth in both. He is very rarely within sight through the whole play, either rising higher than the eye of your understanding can soar, or sinking lower than it careth to stoop. But here it may perhaps be observed that I have given more frequent instances of authors who have imitated him in the sublime than in the contrary. To which I answer, first, bombast being properly a redundancy of genius, instances of nature occur in poets whose names do more honour to our author than the writers in the doggerel, which proceeds from a cool, calm, weighty way of thinking. Instances whereof are most frequently to be found in authors of a lower class. Secondly, that the works of such authors are difficultly found at all. Thirdly, that it is a very hard task to read them, in order to extract these flowers from them. And lastly, it is very often difficult to transplant them at all; they being like some flowers of a very nice nature, which will flourish in no soil but their own: For it is easy to transcribe a thought, but not the want of one. *The Earl of Essex,*[9] for instance, is a little garden of choice rarities, whence you can scarce transplant one line so as to preserve its original beauty. This must account to the reader for his missing the names of several of his acquaintance, which he had certainly found here, had I ever read their works; for which, if I have not a just esteem, I can at least say with Cicero, *quae non contemno,*

[1] *Telephus … verba* Latin: "Both Telephus and Peleus, as paupers and in exile, abandoned bombast and six-foot long words." From the *Ars Poetica* of the first-century BCE Roman poet Horace.

[2] *dolere … pedestri* Latin: "grieve in ordinary prose." Again, from the *Ars Poetica.*

[3] *bombast* Inflated language used to describe a commonplace subject; *doggerel* Irregular or badly composed comic verse.

[4] *quid est … scientiâ* A very loose paraphrase of first-century BCE Roman orator Cicero's *De Oratore* (*On the Orator*). The original translates as: "for what savors so much of madness as the empty sound of words, even the choicest and most eloquent, when there is no sense or knowledge contained in them?" Scriblerus Secundus provides a translation of his misquotation, which inverts the meaning of the original.

[5] *Longinus* Third-century CE Greek rhetorician who is conventionally ascribed authorship of *On the Sublime*, a treatise that argues that good writing is that which achieves "elevation," rising above the ordinary in both style and subject.

[6] *Omne … vincit* Latin: "Tragedy surpasses all other kinds of writing in the matter of seriousness." From first-century BCE Roman poet Ovid's *Tristia* (*Sorrows*).

[7] *bathos* Unintentional descent from the elevated to the commonplace; anticlimax.

[8] *Scriblerus* Martinus Scriblerus, the "author" of Pope's *Peri Bathous; or, The Art of Sinking in Poetry* (1728). The following paragraph echoes that treatise's humorous defense of the *bathos* as the opposite extreme of the sublime.

[9] *The Earl of Essex* *The Unhappy Favourite: Or the Earl of Essex* (1682), by John Banks, who was known for the dramatic sentimentality—but not necessarily the good quality—of his plays.

quippè quae nunquam legerim.[1] However, that the reader may meet with due satisfaction in this point, I have a young commentator from the university who is reading over all the modern tragedies at five shillings a dozen, and collecting all that they have stole from our author, which shall shortly be added as an appendix to this work.

Dramatis Personae

Men

King Arthur, *a passionate sort of king, husband to Queen Dollalolla, of whom he stands a little in fear; father to Huncamunca, whom he is very fond of; and in love with Glumdalca.*

Tom Thumb the Great, *a little hero with a great soul, something violent in his temper, which is a little abated by his love for Huncamunca.*

Ghost of Gaffer[2] Thumb, *a whimsical sort of ghost.*

Lord Grizzle, *extremely zealous for the liberty of the subject,*[3] *very choleric*[4] *in his temper, and in love with Huncamunca.*

Merlin, *a conjurer, and in some sort father to Tom Thumb.*

Noodle *and* Doodle, *courtiers in place,*[5] *and consequently of that party that is uppermost.*

Foodle, *a courtier that is out of place, and consequently of that party that is undermost.*

Bailiff *and* Follower, *of the party of the plaintiff.*

Parson, *of the side of the church.*

Women

Queen Dollalolla, *wife to King Arthur, and mother to Huncamunca, a woman entirely faultless, saving that she is a little given to drink, a little too much a virago*[6] *towards her husband, and in love with Tom Thumb.*

The Princess Huncamunca, *daughter to their Majesties King Arthur and Queen Dollalolla, of a very sweet, gentle, and amorous disposition, equally in love with Lord Grizzle and Tom Thumb, and desirous to be married to them both.*

Glumdalca, *of the giants, a captive Queen, beloved by the King, but in love with Tom Thumb.*

Cleora, *maid of honour, in love with Noodle.*

Mustacha, *maid of honour, in love with Doodle.*

Courtiers, Guards, Rebels, Drums, Trumpets, Thunder and Lightning.

[1] *quae … legerim* Latin: "those that I do not despise, because I have never read them." From *Tusculan Disputations*, where Cicero speaks of books by would-be philosophers.

[2] *Gaffer* Title of respect given to elderly men, similar to "Master," but indicating a lower rank.

[3] *zealous for … the subject* Passionate about individual liberties.

[4] *choleric* Hot-tempered.

[5] *courtiers in place* Court attendants in government.

[6] *virago* Overbearing, quarrelsome woman.

Scene: *The court of King Arthur, and a plain thereabouts.*

ACT I, SCENE I. THE PALACE.

(*Doodle, Noodle.*)

DOODLE. Sure, such a[a] day as this was never seen!
The sun himself, on this auspicious day,
Shines, like a beau in a new birthday suit:
This down the seams embroidered, that the beams.
All nature wears one universal grin.
NOODLE. This day, O Mr. Doodle, is a day
Indeed, [b] a day we never saw before.
The mighty [c] Thomas Thumb victorious comes;
Millions of giants crowd his chariot wheels,

[a] Corneille[1] recommends some very remarkable day, wherein to fix the action of a tragedy. This the best of our tragical writers have understood to mean a day remarkable for the serenity of the sky, or what we generally call a fine summer's day: so that according to this their exposition, the same months are proper for tragedy, which are proper for pastoral. Most of our celebrated English tragedies,[2] as *Cato, Mariamne, Tamerlane,* &c. begin with their observations on the morning. Lee seems to have come the nearest to this beautiful description of our authors:

> The morning dawns with an unwonted crimson,
> The flowers all odorous seem, the garden birds
> Sing louder, and the laughing sun ascends
> The gaudy earth with an unusual brightness,
> All nature smiles. *Caes. Borg.*

Massinissa in the new *Sophonisba* is also a favourite of the sun:

> ——————The sun too seems
> As conscious of my joy with broader eye
> To look abroad the world, and all things smile
> Like Sophonisba.

Memnon in the *Persian Princess* makes the sun decline rising, that he may not peep on objects, which would profane his brightness.

> ——————The morning rises slow,
> And all those ruddy streaks that used to paint
> The day's approach are lost in clouds as if
> The horrors of the night had sent 'em back
> To warn the sun he should not leave the sea,
> To peep, &c.

[b] This line is highly conformable to the beautiful simplicity of the ancients. It hath been copied by almost every modern:[3]

> Not to be is not to be in woe. *State of Innocence.*
> Love is not sin but where 'tis sinful love. *Don Sebastian.*
> Nature is nature, Laelius. *Sophonisba.*
> Men are but men, we did not make ourselves. *Revenge.*

[c] Dr. B——y reads "the mighty Tall-mast Thumb." Mr. D——s "the mighty Thumping Thumb." Mr. T——d[4] reads "Thundering." I think "Thomas" more agreeable to the great simplicity so apparent in our author.

---

[1] *Corneille* Innovative French tragedian and critic, Pierre Corneille (1606–84), in his *Discours des trios unites* (1660).

[2] *celebrated English tragedies* Scriblerus Secundus alludes to Joseph Addison's *Cato* (1713), Elijah Fenton's *Mariamne* (1723), and Nicholas Rowe's *Tamerlane* (1702), and quotes lines from Lee's *Caesar Borgia* (1680), Thomson's *The Tragedy of Sophonisba* (1730), and Lewis Theobald's *The Persian Princess* (1715).

[3] *every modern* The lines are "copied by" (i.e., parodies of) Dryden's *Don Sebastian* (1690), Thomson's *Sophonisba,* and Edward Young's *The Revenge* (1721).

[4] *Dr. B——y* Bentley; *reads* Asserts that the correct text says (with the implication that the present text is flawed); *Mr. D——s* Dennis; *Mr. T——d* Theobald. The note ridicules critics who "over-read" texts, straining to explain them in the most artful way possible.

[d] Giants! to whom the giants in Guildhall[1]
Are infant dwarfs. They frown, and foam, and roar,
While Thumb regardless of their noise rides on.
So some cock-sparrow° in a farmer's yard, *male sparrow*
Hops at the head of an huge flock of turkeys.
DOODLE. When Goody[2] Thumb first brought this
Thomas forth,
The genius of our land triumphant reigned;
Then, then, oh Arthur! did thy genius reign.
NOODLE. They tell me it is [e] whispered in the books
Of all our sages that this mighty hero,
By Merlin's art° begot, hath not a bone *sorcery*
Within his skin, but is a lump of gristle.
DOODLE. Then 'tis a gristle of no mortal kind,
Some God, my Noodle, stepped into the place
Of Gaffer Thumb, and more than[f] half begot
This mighty Tom.

[d] That learned historian Mr. S——n in the third number of his criticism on our author, takes great pains to explode this passage. "It is," says he, "difficult to guess what giants are here meant, unless the Giant Despair in the *Pilgrim's Progress*, or the Giant Greatness[3] in *The Royal Villain*; for I have heard of no other sort of giants in the reign of King Arthur." Petrus Burmanus makes three Tom Thumbs, one whereof he supposes to have been the same person whom the Greeks called Hercules, and that by these giants are to be understood the centaurs slain by that hero. Another Tom Thumb he contends to have been no other than the Hermes Trismegistus of the ancients. The third Tom Thumb he places under the reign of King Arthur, to which third Tom Thumb, says he, the actions of the other two were attributed. Now though I know that this opinion is supported by an assertion of Justus Lipsius, "*Thomam illum Thumbum non alium quam Herculem fuisse satis constat*";[4] yet shall I venture to oppose one line of Mr. Midwinter against them all:

In Arthur's court Tom Thumb did live.[5]

But then, says Dr. B——y, if we place Tom Thumb in the court of King Arthur, it will be proper to place that court out of Britain, where no giants were ever heard of. Spenser, in his *Fairy Queen*, is of another opinion, where describing Albion he says,

——Far within a salvage nation dwelt
Of hideous giants.

And in the same canto,

Then Elfar, who two brethren giants had,
The one of which had two Heads——
The other three.[6]

Risum teneatis, Amici.[7]

[e] To whisper in books, says Mr. D——s, is errant nonsense. I am afraid this learned man does not sufficiently understand the extensive meaning of the word "whisper." If he had rightly understood what is meant by the "senses whisp'ring the soul" in *The Persian Princess*, or what "whisp'ring like winds" is in *Aureng-Zebe*, or "like thunder"[8] in another author, he would have understood this. Emmeline in Dryden sees a voice, but she was born blind, which is an excuse Panthea cannot plead in *Cyrus*, who hears a sight:

————Your description will surpass
All fiction, painting, or dumb show of horror,
That ever ears yet heard, or eyes beheld.

When Mr. D——s understands these he will understand whisp'ring in books.

[f] —Some ruffian stepped into his father's place,
And more than half begot him. *Mary Q. of Scots*.[9]

[1] *Guildhall* The seat of government in London, where two carved giants, Gog and Magog, sit on pedestals.

[2] *Goody* I.e., Mrs.

[3] *Mr. S——n* Nathaniel Salmon (1675–1742), antiquarian and critic; *Giant Despair* Character in John Bunyan's 1678 religious allegory; *Giant Greatness* Referring to the line "swell this unknown ill to giant greatness" in Theobald's *Persian Princess*, subtitled *The Royal Villain*.

[4] *Petrus Burmanus* Pieter Burmann; *Hermes Trismegistus* "Thrice-Great Hermes," a divine author to whom a collection of alchemical texts were attributed; *Justus Lipsius* Joose Lips (1547–1606), Belgian philologist; *Thomam … constat* Latin: "Thomas Thumb, who it is agreed was none other than Hercules."

[5] *In Arthur's … live* Quotation from a lost chapbook edition of *The Famous History of Tom Thumb*, published by Midwinter.

[6] *Far within … three* From *The Faerie Queene* (1590–96), Book II Canto X.

[7] *Risum … Amici* Latin: "Restrain your laughter, friends," from Horace's *Ars Poetica*.

[8] *senses whisp'ring* Theobald, *The Persian Princess*; *whisp'ring like winds* Dryden, *Aureng-Zebe* (1675); *like thunder* Perhaps Benjamin Martyn, *Timoleon* (1730). Emmeline appears in Dryden's *King Arthur: or, The British Worthy* (1691), and Panthea in Banks's *Cyrus the Great: or, The Tragedy of Love* (1696).

[9] *Mary Q. of Scots* Banks, *The Albion Queens: or, The Death of Mary Queen of Scotland* (1704).

NOODLE. [g] Sure he was sent express
From Heav'n, to be the pillar of our state.
Though small his body be, so very small,
A chairman's leg is more than twice as large;
Yet is his soul like any mountain big,
And as a mountain once brought forth a mouse,
[h] So doth this mouse contain a mighty mountain.
DOODLE. Mountain indeed! So terrible his name,
[i] The giant nurses frighten children with it;
And cry "Tom Thumb is come, and if you are
Naughty, will surely take the child away."
NOODLE. But hark! [j] these trumpets speak the King's approach.
DOODLE. He comes most luckily for my petition.

(*Flourish.*)

ACT 1, SCENE 2

(*King, Queen, Grizzle, Noodle, Doodle, Foodle.*)

KING. [k] Let nothing but a face of joy appear;
The man who frowns this day shall lose his head,
That he may have no face to frown withal.
Smile, Dollalolla—Ha! what wrinkled sorrow,
[l] Hangs, sits, lies, frowns upon thy knitted brow?
Whence flow those tears fast down thy blubbered cheeks,
Like a swollen gutter, gushing through the streets?
QUEEN. [m] Excess of joy, my Lord, I've heard folks say,
Gives tears as certain as excess of grief.

[g] ——For Ulamar seems sent express from heaven,
To civilize this rugged Indian clime. *Liberty Asserted.*[1]

[h] "*Omne majus continet in se minus, sed minus non in se majus continere potest,*" says Scaliger[2] in *Thumbo*,—I suppose he would have cavilled at these beautiful lines in *The Earl of Essex*:

Thy most inveterate soul,
That looks through the foul prison of thy body.

And at those of Dryden,

The palace is without too well designed,
Conduct me in, for I will view thy mind. *Aureng-Zebe.*

[i] Mr. Banks hath copied this almost verbatim:

It was enough to say, here's Essex come,
And nurses stilled their children with the fright. *E. of Essex.*

[j] The trumpet in a tragedy is generally as much as to say enter King: which makes Mr. Banks in one of his plays[3] call it "the trumpet's formal sound."

[k] Phraortes in *The Captives*[4] seems to have been acquainted with King Arthur.

Proclaim a festival for seven days' space,
Let the court shine in all its pomp and lustre,
Let all our streets resound with shouts of joy;
Let music's care-dispelling voice be heard,
The sumptuous banquet, and the flowing goblet
Shall warm the cheek, and fill the heart with gladness.
Astarbe shall sit mistress of the feast.

[l] Repentance frowns on thy contracted brow. *Sophonisba.*
Hung on his clouded brow, I marked despair. *Ibid.*
——A sullen gloom
Scowls on his brow. *Busiris.*[5]

[m] Plato is of this opinion, and so is Mr. Banks;

Behold these tears sprung from fresh pain and joy. *E. of Essex.*

---

[1] *Liberty Asserted* By Dennis (1704).

[2] *Omne … potest* Latin: "The greater contains the lesser, but the lesser does not contain the greater"; *Scaliger* Julius Caesar Scaliger (1484–1558), French classicist regularly cited during this period for his commentaries on ancient literary texts. *Thumbo* and the quoted lines are of Fielding's invention.

[3] *in one of his plays* Banks, *Cyrus the Great.*

[4] *The Captives* By John Gay (1724).

[5] *Busiris* By Edward Young (1719).

KING. If it be so, let all men cry for joy,
[n] 'Till my whole court be drowned with their tears;
Nay, till they overflow my utmost land,
And leave me nothing but the sea to rule.
DOODLE. My Liege, I a petition have here got.
KING. Petition me no petitions, sir, today;
Let other hours be set apart for business.
Today it is our pleasure to be [o] drunk,
And this our Queen shall be as drunk as We.
QUEEN. (Though I already [p] half seas over am)
If the capacious goblet overflow
With arrack-punch[1] —'fore George![2] I'll see it out;
Of rum and brandy, I'll not taste a drop.
KING. Though rack,° in punch, eight shillings be a quart, *arrack*
And rum and brandy be no more than six,
Rather than quarrel, you shall have your will.

(*Trumpets.*)

But, ha! the warrior comes; the great Tom Thumb;
The little hero, giant-killing boy,
Preserver of my kingdom, is arrived.

ACT I, SCENE 3

(*Tom Thumb, to them with Officers, Prisoners, and Attendants.*)

KING. [q] Oh! welcome most, most welcome to my arms.
What gratitude can thank away the debt
Your valour lays upon me?
QUEEN. (*Aside.*) [r] Oh! ye Gods!

[n] These floods are very frequent in the tragic authors.
Near to some murmuring brook I'll lay me down,
Whose waters if they should too shallow flow,
My tears shall swell them up till I will drown. Lee's *Sophonisba.*
Pouring forth tears at such a lavish rate,
That were the world on fire, they might have drowned
The wrath of heav'n, and quenched the mighty ruin. *Mithridates.*
One Author changes the Waters of Grief to those of Joy,
——These Tears that sprung from Tides of Grief
Are now augmented to a Flood of Joy. *Cyrus the Great.*
Another
Turns all the streams of hate, and makes them flow
In pity's channel. *Royal Villain.*
One drowns himself:
——Pity like a torrent pours me down,
Now I am drowning all within a deluge. *Anna Bullen.*[3]
Cyrus drowns the whole world:
Our swelling grief [...]
Shall melt into a deluge, and the world
Shall drown in tears. *Cyrus the Great.*

[o] An expression vastly beneath the dignity of tragedy, says Mr. D——s, yet we find the word he cavils at in the mouth of Mithridates less properly used and applied to a more terrible idea;
I would be drunk with death. *Mithrid.*
The author of the new *Sophonisba* taketh hold of this monosyllable, and uses it pretty much to the same purpose,
The Carthaginian sword with Roman blood
Was drunk.
I would ask Mr. D——s which gives him the best idea, a drunken King, or a drunken sword?
Mr. Tate dresses up King Arthur's resolution in heroics,
Merry, my Lord, o'th'Captain's humour right,
I am resolved to be dead drunk tonight.
Lee also uses this charming Word;
Love's the drunkenness of the mind. *Gloriana.*[4]

[p] Dryden hath borrowed this, and applied it improperly:
I'm half seas o'er in death. *Cleom.*[5]

[q] This figure is in great use among the tragedians;
'Tis therefore, therefore 'tis. *Victim.*[6]
I long repent, repent and long again. *Busiris.*

[r] A tragical exclamation.

[1] *arrack-punch* Sweet flavored liquor.

[2] *'fore George* An oath, like "by George!", referring to St. George, the patron saint of England.

[3] *Mithridates* Lee, *Mithridates, King of Pontus* (1678); *Anna Bullen* Banks, *Virtue Betrayed: or, Anna Bullen* (1682).

[4] *Mr. Tate* Nahum Tate in *Injured Love: or, The Cruel Husband* (1707); *Gloriana* By Lee (1676).

[5] *Cleom.* Dryden, *Cleomenes, The Spartan Hero* (1692).

[6] *Victim* By Charles Johnson (1714).

TOM THUMB. When I'm not thanked at all, I'm
thanked enough,
[s] I've done my duty, and I've done no more.
QUEEN. (*Aside.*) Was ever such a Godlike creature seen!
KING. Thy modesty's a [t] candle to thy merit,
It shines itself, and shows thy merit too.
But say, my boy, where did'st thou leave the giants?
TOM THUMB. My Liege, without° the castle gates they stand, *outside*
The castle gates too low for their admittance.
KING. What look they like?
TOM THUMB. Like nothing but themselves.
QUEEN. (*Aside.*) [u] And sure thou art like nothing but thy self.
KING. Enough! the vast idea fills my soul.
I see them, yes, I see them now before me:
The monstrous, ugly, barb'rous sons of whores.
But, ha! What form majestic strikes our eyes?
[v] So perfect that it seems to have been drawn
By all the Gods in council: So fair she is,
That surely at her birth the council paused,
And then at length cried out, "This is a Woman!"
TOM THUMB. Then were the Gods mistaken. She is not
A woman, but a giantess—whom we
[w] With much ado, have made a shift to haul
Within the town [x]: for she is, by a foot,
Shorter than all her subject giants were.
GLUMDALCA. We yesterday were both a queen and wife,
One hundred thousand giants owned our sway,[1]
Twenty whereof were married to our self.
QUEEN. Oh! happy state of giantism—where husbands
Like mushrooms grow, whilst hapless we are forced
To be content, nay, happy thought with one.
GLUMDALCA. But then to lose them all in one black day,
That the same sun, which rising, saw me wife
To twenty giants, setting, should behold

[s] This Line is copied verbatim in *The Captives.*

[t] We find a candlestick for this candle in two celebrated authors;

——————Each star withdraws
His golden head and burns within the socket. *Nero.*[2]
A soul grown old and sunk into the socket. *Sebastian.*

[u] This simile occurs very frequently among the dramatic writers of both kinds.

[v] Mr. Lee hath stolen this thought from our author;

——This perfect face, drawn by the gods in council,
Which they were long a making. *Lu. Jun. Brut.*
——At his birth, the heavenly council paused,
And then at last cried out, this is a man!

Dryden hath improved this hint to the utmost perfection:

So perfect, that the very gods who formed you, wondered
At their own skill, and cried, a lucky hit
Has mended our design! Their envy hindered,
Or you had been immortal, and a pattern,
When heaven would work for ostentation sake,
To copy out again. *All for Love.*

Banks prefers the works of Michelangelo to that of the gods;

A pattern for the gods to make a man by,
Or Michelangelo to form a statue.[3]

[w] It is impossible, says Mr. W——,[4] sufficiently to admire this natural easy line.

[x] This tragedy, which in most points resembles the ancients, differs from them in this: that it assigns the same honour to lowness of stature which they did to height. The gods and heroes in Homer and Virgil are continually described higher by the head than their followers, the contrary of which is observed by our author. In short, to exceed on either side is equally admirable, and a man of three foot is as wonderful a sight as a man of nine.

[1] *owned our sway* Our sovereign power possessed.

[2] *Nero* By Lee (1675).

[3] *Lu. Jun. Brut* Lee, *Lucius Junius Brutus; Father of his Country* (1680); *At his birth … this is a man!* From Lee and Dryden, *The Duke of Guise* (1683); *All for Love* By Dryden (1678); *A pattern … a statue* From Banks, *The Earl of Essex.*

[4] *Mr. W——* The identity of Mr. W—— remains uncertain, but the note might refer to poet and critic Leonard Welsted (1688–1747), who wrote effusively about poetical spirit and easy grace, and who was ridiculed by Pope in both *Peri Bathous* and *The Dunciad Variorum.*

Me widowed of them all. [y] My worn out heart,
That ship, leaks fast, and the great heavy lading,° *cargo*
My soul, will quickly sink.

QUEEN. Madam, believe,
I view your sorrows with a woman's eye;
But learn to bear them with what strength you may,
Tomorrow we will have our grenadiers[1]
Drawn out before you, and you then shall choose
What husbands you think fit.

GLUMDALCA. [z] Madam, I am
Your most obedient, and most humble servant.

KING. Think, mighty princess, think this court your own,
Nor think the landlord me, this house my inn;
Call for whate'er you will, you'll nothing pay.
[aa] I feel a sudden pain within my breast,
Nor know I whether it arise from love,
Or only the wind-colic.[2] Time must show.
Oh, Thumb! What do we to thy valour owe?
Ask some reward, great as we can bestow.

TOM THUMB. [bb] I ask not kingdoms, I can conquer those,
I ask not money, money I've enough;
For what I've done, and what I mean to do,
For giants slain, and giants yet unborn,
Which I will slay—if this be called a debt,
Take my receipt in full—I ask but this,
[cc] To sun myself in Huncamunca's eyes.

KING. (*Aside.*) Prodigious bold request.

QUEEN. (*Aside.*) [dd] Be still my soul.

TOM THUMB. [ee] My heart is at the threshold of your mouth,
And waits its answer there—Oh! do not frown,
I've tried, to reason's tune, to tune my soul,
But love did over-wind and crack the string.
Though Jove[3] in thunder had cried out, YOU SHAN'T,
I should have loved her still—for oh, strange fate,
Then when I loved her least, I loved her most.

[y]
My blood leaks fast, and the great heavy lading
My soul will quickly sink. *Mithrid.*
My soul is like a ship. *Injured Love.*

[z] This well-bred line seems to be copied in *The Persian Princess*;
To be your humblest, and most faithful slave.

[aa] This doubt of the King puts me in mind of a passage in *The Captives*, where the noise of feet is mistaken for the rustling of leaves,
———Methinks I hear
The sound of feet. […]
No, 'twas the wind that shook yon cypress boughs.

[bb] Mr. Dryden seems to have had this passage in his eye in the first page of *Love Triumphant.*[4]

[cc] Don Carlos in *The Revenge* suns himself in the charms of his mistress,
While in the lustre of her charms I lay.

[dd] A tragical phrase much in use.

[ee] This speech hath been taken to pieces by several tragical authors who seem to have rifled it and shared its beauties among them.
My soul waits at the portal of thy breast,
To ravish from thy lips the welcome news. *Anna Bullen.*
My soul stands listening at my ears. *Cyrus the Great.*
Love to his tune my jarring heart would bring,
But reason overwinds and cracks the string. *D. of Guise.*
———I should have loved,
Though Jove in muttering thunder had forbid it. New *Sophonisba.*
And when it (my Heart) wild resolves to love no more,
Then is the triumph of excessive love. *Ibidem.*[5]

[1] *grenadiers* Tallest and best soldiers in a regiment.

[2] *wind-colic* Colic (stomach pains) caused by gas.

[3] *Jove* In Roman mythology, father of the gods.

[4] *Love Triumphant* Dryden, *Love Triumphant: or, Nature Will Prevail* (1694). Fielding seems to have cited the wrong play; he probably means to refer to *The Indian Queen* (1665), a heroic play by Dryden and Robert Howard in which the ruler of the Incas offers a reward to his general, who asks to marry the princess.

[5] *Ibidem.* Latin: "In the same place."

KING. It is resolved—the Princess is your own.
TOM THUMB. [ff] Oh! happy, happy, happy, happy, Thumb!
QUEEN. Consider, sir, reward your soldier's merit,
But give not Huncamunca to Tom Thumb.
KING. Tom Thumb! Odzooks,[1] my wide extended realm
Knows not a name so glorious as Tom Thumb.
Let Macedonia, Alexander boast,
Let Rome her Caesar's and her Scipio's show,
Her Messieurs France, let Holland boast Mynheers,
Ireland her Os, her Macs[2] let Scotland boast,
Let England boast no other than Tom Thumb.
QUEEN. Though greater yet his boasted merit was,
He shall not have my daughter, that is pos'.° *positive*
KING. Ha! sayest thou Dollalolla?
QUEEN. I say he shan't.
KING. [gg] Then by our royal self we swear you lie.
QUEEN. [hh] Who but a dog, who but a dog,
Would use me as thou dost? Me, who have lain
[ii] These twenty years so loving by thy side.
But I will be revenged. I'll hang myself,
Then tremble all who did this match persuade,
[jj] For riding on a cat,[3] from high I'll fall,
And squirt down royal vengeance on you all.
FOODLE. [kk] Her Majesty the Queen is in a passion.
KING. [ll] Be she, or be she not—I'll to the girl
And pave thy way, oh Thumb—Now, by our self,
We were indeed a pretty king of clouts,
To truckle° to her will—For when by force *submit*
Or art the wife her husband over-reaches,
Give him the petticoat, and her the breeches.

[1] *Odzooks* Expression of surprise euphemistically substituting "od" for "god."

[2] *Alexander* Alexander the Great, Greek king of Macedon in the fourth century BCE; *Caesar* Julius Caesar, legendary Roman general of the first century BCE; *Scipio* Scipio Africanus, Roman general who defeated Hannibal in the Second Punic War (in 202 BCE); *Messieurs* French form of polite address, equivalent to "Misters"; *Mynheers* The Dutch equivalent of "Messieurs"; *Os* I.e., surnames starting with "O," common in Ireland and meaning "son of"; *Macs* Surnames starting with "Mac," common in Scotland and meaning "son of."

[3] *cat* Moveable structure used in sieges.

[4] *No by my self* In the quoted line, the speaker swears on his own person.

[5] *Banks* In *Virtue Betrayed: or, Anna Bullen*.

[6] *Conquest of Granada* In two parts, by Dryden (1672). These lines are actually from Dryden's *The Indian Emperor* (1667).

[ff] Massinissa is one fourth less happy than Tom Thumb.

Oh! happy, happy, happy. New *Sophonisba*.

[gg] No by my self.[4] *Anna Bullen*.

[hh] ——————Who caused
This dreadful revolution in my fate?
ULAMAR. Who but a dog, who but a dog. *Liberty Asserted*.

[ii] ——————A bride,
Who twenty years lay loving by your side. Banks.[5]

[jj] For borne upon a cloud, from high I'll fall,
And rain down royal vengeance on you all. *Albion Queen*.

[kk] An information very like this we have in *The Tragedy of Love*, where Cyrus having stormed in the most violent manner, Cyaxares observes very calmly,

Why, nephew Cyrus—you are moved.

[ll] 'Tis in your choice,
Love me, or love me not! *Conquest of Granada*.[6]

Tom Thumb. [mm] Whisper, ye winds, that Huncamunca's mine;
Echoes repeat that Huncamunca's mine!
The dreadful business of the war is o'er,
And beauty, heavenly beauty! crowns my toils,
I've thrown the bloody garment now aside,
And hymeneal° sweets invite my bride. *marital*
So when some chimney-sweeper, all the day,
Hath through dark paths pursued the sooty way,
At night, to wash his hands and face he flies,
And in his t'other shirt with his Brickdusta lies.

[mm] There is not one beauty in this charming speech but hath been borrowed by almost every tragic writer.

Act 1, Scene 4

(*Grizzle solus.*[1])

Grizzle. [nn] Where art thou Grizzle? where are now thy glories?
Where are the drums that wakened thee to honour?
Greatness is a laced coat from Monmouth Street,
Which Fortune lends us for a day to wear,
Tomorrow puts it on another's back.
The spiteful sun but yesterday surveyed
His rival, high as Saint Paul's cupola;
Now may he see me as Fleet-Ditch[2] laid low.

[nn] Mr. Banks has (I wish I could not say too servilely) imitated this of Grizzle in his *Earl of Essex*.
Where art thou Essex, &c.[3]

[1] *solus* Latin: alone.

[2] *Monmouth Street* Location of many used-clothing stores in eighteenth-century London; *Saint Paul's cupola* The dome of Saint Paul's Cathedral, one of the most admired works of architecture of the time; *Fleet-Ditch* Colloquial name for the Fleet River, which ran down into the Thames at Blackfriars Bridge and which was transformed by pollution into an open sewer—a low point, topographically and culturally.

[3] *Where art thou Essex, &c.* The original lines from *The Earl of Essex* are parodied at length in Grizzle's soliloquy:
Where art thou Essex! Where are now thy Glories! …
The early songs that every morning waked thee; …
Yesterday's sun saw his great rival thus,
The spiteful planet saw me thus adored,
And some tall-built pyramid, whose height
And golden top confronts him in his sky
He tumbles down with lightning in his rage
So on a sudden he has snatched my garlands.

ACT 1, SCENE 5

(*Queen, Grizzle.*)

QUEEN. °° Teach me to scold, prodigious-minded Grizzle.
Mountain of treason, ugly as the devil,
Teach this confounded hateful mouth of mine
To spout forth words malicious as thyself,
Words which might shame all Billingsgate[1] to speak.

GRIZZLE. Far be it from my pride to think my tongue
Your royal lips can in that art instruct,
Wherein you so excel. But may I ask,
Without offence, wherefore my Queen would scold?

QUEEN. Wherefore, oh! Blood and thunder! han't you heard
(What every corner of the court resounds)
That little Thumb will be a great man[2] made.

GRIZZLE. I heard it, I confess—for who, alas!
PP Can always stop his ears—but would my teeth,
By grinding knives, had first been set on edge.

QUEEN. Would I had heard at the still noon of night,[3]
The hallaloo[4] of fire in every street!
Odsbobs! I have a mind to hang myself,
To think I should a grandmother be made,
By such a rascal. Sure the King forgets,
When in a pudding, by his mother put,
The bastard, by a tinker, on a stile° *window frame*
Was dropped.—O, good Lord Grizzle! can I bear
To see him, from a pudding, mount the throne?
Or can, oh can! my Huncamunca bear,
To take a pudding's offspring to her arms?

°° The Countess of Nottingham in *The Earl of Essex* is apparently acquainted with Dollalolla.[5]

PP Grizzle was not probably possessed of that glue, of which Mr. Banks speaks in his *Cyrus*.

> I'll glue my ears to ev'ry word.

[1] *Billingsgate* Area of London by the Thames where the fishmongers lived; the reference is to the proverbially sharp tongues of fishwives.

[2] *great man* Possibly a satiric swipe at Robert Walpole, England's chief minister through the 1730s, who was sarcastically referred to as a "Great Man," and who was responsible for the Stage Licensing Act of 1737, which effectively ended Fielding's dramatic career.

[3] *noon of night* Midnight.

[4] *hallaloo* Cry to come help.

[5] *Countess of Nottingham ... Dollalolla* The implication is that Banks's character borrows her well-known complaint from Dollalolla:

> Help me to rail, prodigious minded Burleigh,
> Prince of bold English councils, teach me how
> This hateful breast of mine may dart forth words
> Keen as thy wit, malicious as thy person.

GRIZZLE. Oh horror! horror! horror! cease my Queen,
[qq] Thy voice, like twenty screech-owls, wracks my brain.
QUEEN. Then rouse thy spirit—we may yet prevent
This hated match—
GRIZZLE. We will [rr]; not fate itself,
Should it conspire with Thomas Thumb, should cause it.
I'll swim through seas; I'll ride upon the clouds;
I'll dig the earth; I'll blow out ev'ry fire;
I'll rave; I'll rant; I'll rise; I'll rush; I'll roar;
Fierce as the man whom [ss] smiling dolphins bore,
From the prosaic to poetic shore.
I'll tear the scoundrel into twenty pieces.
QUEEN. Oh, no! prevent the match, but hurt him not;
For though I would not have him have my daughter,
Yet can we kill the man that killed the giants?
GRIZZLE. I tell you, madam, it was all a trick.
He made the giants first, and then he killed them;
As fox hunters bring foxes to the wood,
And then with hounds they drive them out again.
QUEEN. How! have you seen no giants? Are there not
Now, in the yard, ten thousand proper giants?
GRIZZLE. [tt] Indeed, I cannot positively tell,
But firmly do believe there is not one.
QUEEN. Hence! from my sight! thou traitor, hie° *go*
away;
By all my stars! Thou enviest Tom Thumb.
Go, sirrah! go, [uu] hie away! hie!—thou art
A setting dog, be gone.
GRIZZLE. Madam, I go.
Tom Thumb shall feel the vengeance you have raised:
So, when two dogs are fighting in the streets,
With a third dog one of the two dogs meets,
With angry teeth he bites him to the bone,
And this dog smarts for what that dog had done.

[qq] Screech-owls, dark ravens and amphibious monsters,
Are screaming in that voice. *Mary Q. of Scots.*

[rr] The reader may see all the beauties of this speech in a late ode called the *Naval Lyric.*[1]

[ss] This epithet to a dolphin doth not give one so clear an idea as were to be wished, a smiling fish seeming a little more difficult to be imagined than a flying fish. Mr. Dryden is of opinion, that smiling is the property of reason, and that no irrational creature can smile.

Smiles not allowed to beasts from reason
move. *State of Innocence.*

[tt] These lines are written in the same key with those in *The Earl of Essex*;

Why say'st thou so, I love thee well, indeed
I do, and thou shalt find by this, 'tis true.

Or with this in Cyrus;

The most heroic mind that ever was.

And with above half of the modern tragedies.

[uu] Aristotle in that excellent work of his which is very justly styled his masterpiece,[2] earnestly recommends using the terms of art, however coarse or even indecent they may be. Mr. Tate is of the same opinion.

BRACHIANO. Do not, like young hawks, fetch a course about,
Your game flies fair.
FRANCISCO. Do not fear it.
He answers you in your own hawking phrase. *Injured Love.*

I think these two great authorities are sufficient to justify Dollalolla in the use of the phrase "hie away hie" when in the same line she says she is speaking to a setting dog.

[1] *Naval Lyric* Young's *Imperium Pelagi* (*Empire of the Sea*): *A Naval Lyric* (1730) makes extensive use of alliteration and repetition. It also mentions a smiling dolphin.

[2] *masterpiece* An imaginary citation from Aristotle's *Poetics*, which contains no such recommendation. Given the privileging of the "indecent," there may also be a pun on "*Aristotle's Masterpiece*," a notorious manual of sex that circulated in the late seventeenth and eighteenth century. Its authorship is unclear.

ACT 1, SCENE 6

(*Queen sola.*)

QUEEN. And whither shall I go? Alack-a-day!
I love Tom Thumb—but must not tell him so;
For what's a woman, when her virtue's gone?
A coat without its lace; wig out of buckle;
A stocking with a hole in't—I can't live
Without my virtue, or without Tom Thumb.
[vv] Then let me weigh them in two equal scales,
In this scale put my virtue, that, Tom Thumb.
Alas! Tom Thumb is heavier than my virtue.
But hold!—perhaps I may be left a widow:
This match prevented, then Tom Thumb is mine:
In that dear hope, I will forget my pain.
So, when some wench to Tothill-Bridewell's sent,
With beating hemp, and flogging[1] she's content:
She hopes in time to ease her present pain,
At length is free, and walks the streets again.

ACT 2, SCENE 1. THE STREET.

(*Bailiff, Follower.*)

BAILIFF. Come on, my trusty follower, come on,
This day discharge thy duty, and at night
A double mug of beer, and beer shall glad thee.
Stand here by me, this way must Noodle pass.
FOLLOWER. No more, no more, oh bailiff! every word
Inspires my soul with virtue.—Oh! I long
To meet the enemy in the street—and nab him;
To lay arresting hands upon his back,
And drag him trembling to the sponging-house.[2]
BAILIFF. There, when I have him, I will sponge upon him.[3]

[vv] We meet with such another pair of scales in Dryden's *King Arthur*.

Arthur and Oswald, and their different fates,
Are weighing now within the scales of heav'n.

Also in *Sebastian*.

This hour my lot is weighing in the scales.

---

[1] *Tothill-Bridewell* Prison in London; *beating hemp* Work for women prisoners sentenced to hard labor; *flogging* Typical punishment for prisoners who did not work hard enough.

[2] *sponging-house* Bailiff's house, where suspected criminals would be held until their trial.

[3] *sponge upon him* Press him for money; force him to pay for his keep.

[ww] Oh! glorious thought! By the sun, moon, and stars,
I will enjoy it, though it be in thought!
Yes, yes, my follower, I will enjoy it.
FOLLOWER. Enjoy it then some other time, for now
Our prey approaches.
BAILIFF. Let us retire.

ACT 2, SCENE 2

(*Tom Thumb, Noodle, Bailiff, Follower.*)

TOM THUMB. Trust me my Noodle, I am wondrous sick;
For though I love the gentle Huncamunca,
Yet at the thought of marriage, I grow pale;
For oh!— [xx] but swear thoul't keep it ever secret,
I will unfold a tale will make thee stare.
NOODLE. I swear by lovely Huncamunca's charms.
TOM THUMB. Then know —[yy] my grand-mamma hath often said,
Tom Thumb, beware of marriage.
NOODLE. Sir, I blush
To think a warrior great in arms as you
Should be affrighted by his grand-mamma;
Can an old woman's empty dreams deter
The blooming hero from the virgin's arms?
Think of the joy that will your soul alarm,° *rouse, excite*
When in her fond embraces clasped you lie,
While on her panting breast dissolved in bliss,
You pour out all Tom Thumb in every kiss.
TOM THUMB. Oh! Noodle, thou hast fired my eager soul;
Spite° of my grandmother, she shall be mine; *in spite*
I'll hug, caress, I'll eat her up with love.
Whole days, and nights, and years shall be too short
For our enjoyment, every sun shall rise
[zz] Blushing, to see us in our bed together.
NOODLE. Oh, sir! this purpose of your soul pursue.
BAILIFF. Oh, sir! I have an action against you.
NOODLE. At whose suit is it?
BAILIFF. At your tailor's, sir.
Your tailor put this warrant in my hands,
And I arrest you, sir, at his commands.

[ww] Mr. Rowe is generally imagined to have taken some hints from this scene in his character of Bajazet;[1] but as he, of all the tragic writers, bears the least resemblance to our author in his diction, I am unwilling to imagine he would condescend to copy him in this particular.

[xx] This method of surprising an audience by raising their expectation to the highest pitch, and then baulking it, hath been practised with great success by most of our tragical authors.

[yy] Almeyda in *Sebastian* is in the same distress;
Sometimes methinks I hear the groan of ghosts,
Thin hollow sounds and lamentable screams;
Then, like a dying echo from afar,
My mother's voice that cries, wed not Almeyda!
Forewarned, Almeyda, marriage is thy crime.

[zz] As very well he may if he hath any modesty in him, says Mr. D——s. The Author of *Busiris* is extremely zealous to prevent the sun's blushing at any indecent object; and therefore on all such occasions he addresses himself to the sun, and desires him to keep out of the way.
Rise never more, O sun! let night prevail,
Eternal darkness close the world's wide scene. *Busiris.*
Sun hide thy face and put the world in mourning. *Ibid.*

Mr. Banks makes the sun perform the office of Hymen; and therefore not likely to be disgusted at such a sight:
The sun sets forth like a gay brideman[2] with you. *Mary Q. of Scots.*

[1] *Bajazet* In Act II of *Tamerlane*, the villain Bajazet exclaims: "Oh, glorious thought! by heav'n I will enjoy it, / Though but in fancy."

[2] *brideman* Bridegroom's attendant.

TOM THUMB. Ha! Dogs! Arrest my friend before my face!
Think you Tom Thumb will suffer this disgrace!
But let vain cowards threaten by their word,
Tom Thumb shall show his anger by his sword.

(*Kills the Bailiff and his Follower.*)

BAILIFF. Oh, I am slain!
FOLLOWER. I am murdered also,
And to the shades, the dismal shades below,
My bailiff's faithful follower, I go.
NOODLE. [aaa] Go then to Hell, like rascals as you are,
And give our service to the bailiffs there.
TOM THUMB. Thus perish all the bailiffs in the land,
Till debtors at noon-day shall walk the streets,
And no one fear a bailiff or his writ.

ACT 2, SCENE 3.
THE PRINCESS HUNCAMUNCA'S APARTMENT.

(*Huncamunca, Cleora, Mustacha.*)

HUNCAMUNCA. [bbb] Give me some music—see that it be sad.
CLEORA. (*Sings.*) Cupid, ease a love-sick maid,
Bring thy quiver to her aid;
With equal ardour wound the swain:° *sweetheart*
Beauty should never sigh in vain.
Let him feel the pleasing smart,
Drive thy arrow through his heart;
When one you wound, you then destroy;
When both you kill, you kill with joy.
HUNCAMUNCA. [ccc] O, Tom Thumb! Tom Thumb! wherefore art thou Tom Thumb?
Why had'st thou not been born of royal race?
Why had not mighty Bantam[1] been thy father?

[1] *Bantam* In Fielding's earlier play, *The Author's Farce* (1730), the impecunious poet and playwright Luckless is relieved of his woes when he is implausibly discovered to be the lost heir to the throne of Bantam, a center of trade in the north-west of Java that had long signified exotic opulence.

[2] *Anthony ... same words* In Dryden's *All for Love*.

[3] *Otway's Marius* *The History and Fall of Caius Marius* borrows heavily from *Romeo and Juliet*, although Shakespeare's play had not been mounted on the London stage since the early 1660s. Part of the joke is that, for all his pedantry, Scriblerus Secundus is blind to obvious Shakespearean allusion.

[aaa] Nourmahal sends the same message to Heaven;

For I would have you, when you upwards move,
Speak kindly of us to our friends above. *Aureng-Zebe.*

We find another to Hell, in *The Persian Princess*;

Villain, get thee down
To Hell, and tell them that the fray's begun.

[bbb] Anthony gives the same command in the same words.[2]

[ccc] Oh! Marius, Marius; wherefore art thou Marius? Otway's *Marius*.[3]

Or else the King of Brentford, old or new?[1]

MUSTACHA. I am surprised that your Highness can give yourself a moment's uneasiness about that little insignificant fellow, [ddd] Tom Thumb the Great—One properer for a play-thing, than a husband. Were he my husband, his horns should be as long as his body. If you had fallen in love with a grenadier, I should not have wondered at it—If you had fallen in love with something; but to fall in love with nothing!

HUNCAMUNCA. Cease, my Mustacha, on thy duty cease.
The zephyr,° when in flow'ry vales it plays, *west wind*
Is not so soft, so sweet as Thummy's breath.
The dove is not so gentle to its mate.

MUSTACHA. The dove is every bit as proper for a husband—Alas! Madam, there's not a beau about the court looks so little like a man—He is a perfect butterfly, a thing without substance, and almost without shadow too.

HUNCAMUNCA. This rudeness is unseasonable, desist;
Or, I shall think this railing° *complaining*
comes from love.
Tom Thumb's a creature of that charming form,
That no one can abuse, unless they love him.

MUSTACHA. Madam, the King.

ACT 2, SCENE 4

KING. Let all but Huncamunca leave the room.

(*Exit Cleora and Mustacha.*)

Daughter, I have observed of late some grief,
Unusual in your countenance—your eyes,
[eee] That, like two open windows, used to show
The lovely beauty of the rooms within,
Have now two blinds before them—What is the cause?
Say, have you not enough of meat and drink?
We've given strict orders not to have you stinted.

[ddd] Nothing is more common than these seeming contradictions; such as,

Haughty weakness. *Victim.*
Great small world. *Noah's Flood.*[2]

[eee] Lee hath improved this metaphor.

Dost thou not view joy peeping from my eyes,
The casements opened wide to gaze on thee;
So Rome's glad citizens to windows rise,
When they some young triumpher fain would see. *Gloriana.*

---

[1] *King of … new* Brentford was a proverbially squalid village west of London, in which it was said two rival kings (the "old" and "new") quarreled over succession. Fielding alludes to the play-within-a-play in his burlesque predecessor, Buckingham's *The Rehearsal* (1672), which takes the attempted usurpation of the Kingdom of Brentford as its subject.

[2] *Noah's Flood* By Edward Ecclestone (1679).

HUNCAMUNCA. Alas! my Lord, I value not myself,
That once I eat two fowls and half a pig;
[fff] Small is that praise; but oh! a maid may want,
What she can neither eat nor drink.
KING. What's that?
HUNCAMUNCA. [ggg] O spare my blushes; but I mean a husband.
KING. If that be all, I have provided one,
A husband great in arms, whose warlike sword
Streams with the yellow blood of slaughtered giants.
Whose name in *terra incognita*[1] is known,
Whose valour, wisdom, virtue make a noise,
Great as the kettle-drums of twenty armies.
HUNCAMUNCA. Whom does my royal father mean?
KING. Tom Thumb.
HUNCAMUNCA. Is it possible?
KING. Ha! the window-blinds are gone,
[hhh] A country dance of joy is in your face,
Your eyes spit fire, your cheeks grow red as beef.
HUNCAMUNCA. O, there's a magic music in that sound,
Enough to turn me into beef indeed.
Yes, I will own, since licensed by your word,
I'll own Tom Thumb the cause of all my grief.
For him I've sighed, I've wept, I've gnawed my sheets.
KING. Oh! thou shalt gnaw thy tender sheets no more,
A husband thou shalt have to mumble now.
HUNCAMUNCA. Oh! happy sound! henceforth, let no one tell,
That Huncamunca shall lead apes in Hell.[2]
Oh! I am overjoyed!
KING. I see thou art.
[iii] Joy lightens in thy eyes, and thunders from thy brows;
Transports,° like lightning, dart along thy soul, *fits of ecstasy*
As small-shot° through a hedge. *musket bullets*
HUNCAMUNCA. Oh! say not small.
KING. This happy news shall on our tongue ride post,[3]

[fff] Almahide hath the same contempt for these appetites;

To eat and drink can no perfection be. *Conquest of Granada.*

The Earl of Essex is of a different opinion, and seems to place the chief happiness of a General therein.

Were but commanders half so well rewarded,
Then they might eat. Banks's *Earl of Essex.*

But if we may believe one who knows more than either—the Devil himself—we shall find eating to be an affair of more moment than is generally imagined.

Gods are immortal only by their
food. Lucifer in *The State of Innocence.*

[ggg] This expression is enough of itself (says Mr. D——s) utterly to destroy the character of Huncamunca; yet we find a woman of no abandoned character in Dryden, adventuring farther and thus excusing herself;

To speak our wishes first, forbid it pride,
Forbid it modesty: true, they forbid it,
But nature does not, when we are athirst
Or hungry, will imperious nature stay,
Nor eat, nor drink, before 'tis bid fall on. *Cleomenes.*

Cassandra speaks before she is asked. Huncamunca afterwards. Cassandra speaks her wishes to her lover, Huncamunca only to her father.

[hhh] Her eyes resistless magic bear,
Angels I see, and gods are dancing there. Lee's *Sophonisba.*

[iii] Mr. Dennis in that excellent tragedy called *Liberty Asserted*, which is thought to have given so great a stroke to the late French King, hath frequent imitations of this beautiful speech of King Arthur;

Conquest lightning in his eyes, and thund'ring in his arm.
Joy lightened in her eyes.
Joys like lightning dart along my soul.[4]

---

[1] *terra incognita* Latin: unknown territory.

[2] *lead apes in Hell* Proverbial fate of unmarried women.

[3] *ride post* Practice of carrying mail with the greatest possible speed, stopping at each interval, or post, along the road only to change to a fresh horse.

[4] *Liberty Asserted … my soul* It was said that Dennis so greatly overestimated the political impact of his anti-French play that he feared abduction by the French government.

Our self will bear the happy news to Thumb.
Yet think not, daughter, that your powerful charms
Must still detain the hero from his arms;
Various his duty, various his delight;
Now is his turn to kiss, and now to fight;
And now to kiss again. So mighty [jjj] Jove,
When with excessive thundering tired above,
Comes down to earth, and takes a bit[1]—and then,
Flies to his trade of thundering, back again.

ACT 2, SCENE 5

(*Grizzle, Huncamunca.*)

[kkk] GRIZZLE. Oh, Huncamunca, Huncamunca, oh,
Thy pouting breasts, like kettle-drums of brass,
Beat everlasting loud alarms of joy;
As bright as brass they are, and oh, as hard;
Oh Huncamunca, Huncamunca! oh!
HUNCAMUNCA. Ha! do'st thou know me, princess as I am,
[lll] That thus of me you dare to make your game.
GRIZZLE. Oh Huncamunca, well I know that you
A princess are, and a king's daughter too.
But love no meanness scorns, no grandeur fears,
Love often lords into the cellar bears,
And bids the sturdy porter come upstairs.
For what's too high for love, or what's too low?
Oh Huncamunca, Huncamunca, oh!
HUNCAMUNCA. But granting all you say of love were true,
My love, alas! is to another due!
In vain, to me a-suitoring you come;
For I'm already promised to Tom Thumb.
GRIZZLE. And can my princess such a durgen° wed, *dwarf*
One fitter for your pocket than your bed!
Advised by me, the worthless baby shun,
Or you will ne'er be brought to bed of one.
Oh take me to thy arms and never flinch,
Who am a man by Jupiter ev'ry inch.

[jjj] Jove with excessive thund'ring tired above,
Comes down for ease, enjoys a nymph, and then
Mounts dreadful, and to thund'ring goes again. *Gloriana.*

[kkk] This beautiful Line, which ought, says Mr. W——, to be written in gold, is imitated in the new *Sophonisba*;

Oh! Sophonisba, Sophonisba, oh!
Oh! Narva, Narva, oh!

The author of a song called *Duke upon Duke*,[2] hath improved it:

Alas! O Nick, O Nick, alas!

Where, by the help of a little false spelling, you have two meanings in the repeated words.

[lll] Edith, in *The Bloody Brother*,[3] speaks to her lover in the same familiar language.

Your grace is full of game.

---

[1] *So mighty Jove ... a bit* In Roman mythology, Jove would often assume the form of some animal and, in that form, rape a mortal woman.

[2] *Duke upon Duke* A 1720 broadside ballad, partly written by Pope, commemorating a quarrel between Sir John Guise (1677–1732) and Nicholas Lechmere (1675–1727).

[3] *The Bloody Brother* By John Fletcher, Phillip Massinger, and others (1639).

[mmm] Then while in joys together lost we lie
I'll press thy soul while gods stand wishing by.
HUNCAMUNCA. If, sir, what you insinuate you prove,
All obstacles of promise you remove;
For all engagements to a man must fall,
Whene'er that man is proved no man at all.
GRIZZLE. Oh let him seek some dwarf, some fairy miss,
Where no joint-stool[1] must lift him to the kiss.
But by the stars and glory, you appear
Much fitter for a Prussian grenadier;
One globe alone on Atlas'[2] shoulders rests,
Two globes are less than Huncamunca's breasts:
The milky way is not so white, that's flat,
And sure thy breasts are full as large as that.
HUNCAMUNCA. Oh, sir, so strong your eloquence I find,
It is impossible to be unkind.
GRIZZLE. Ah! speak that o'er again, and let the [nnn] sound
From one pole to another pole rebound;
The earth and sky each be a battledore[3]
And keep the sound, that shuttlecock, up an hour;
To Doctors Commons[4] for a license I,
Swift as an arrow from a bow, will fly.
HUNCAMUNCA. Oh no! lest some disaster we should meet,
'Twere better to be married at the Fleet.[5]
GRIZZLE. Forbid it, all ye powers, a princess should
By that vile place contaminate her blood;
My quick return shall to my charmer prove,
I travel on the [ooo] post-horses[6] of love.
HUNCAMUNCA. Those post-horses to me will seem too slow,
Though they should fly swift as the gods, when they
Ride on behind that post-boy, opportunity.

[mmm] Traverse the glitt'ring chambers of the sky,
Borne on a cloud in view of fate I'll lie,
And press her soul while gods stand wishing by. *Hannibal.*[7]

[nnn] Let the four winds from distant corners meet,
And on their wings first bear it into France;
Then back again to Edina's proud walls,
Till victim to the sound th'aspiring city falls. *Albion Queens.*

[ooo] I do not remember any metaphors so frequent in the tragic poets as those borrowed from riding post;

The gods and opportunity ride post. *Hannibal.*
———Let's rush together,
For death rides post. *Duke of Guise.*[8]
Destruction gallops to thy murder post. *Gloriana.*

---

[1] *joint-stool* High rectangular seat common around eighteenth-century dinner tables.

[2] *Atlas* Ancient god who supposedly held up the pillars of the universe.

[3] *battledore* Racket used in playing "battledore and shuttlecock," an early version of badminton in which two players hit a shuttlecock, a cork with feathers attached to it, back and forth without letting it drop.

[4] *Doctors Commons* College for lawyers where one could get a marriage license quickly.

[5] *married at the Fleet* I.e., married in secret, without a license, by a disreputable clergyman (such as one imprisoned in the Fleet Street prison).

[6] *post-horses* Horses kept for riding post.

[7] *Hannibal* Alternate title of Lee's *Sophonisba.*

[8] *Duke of Guise* These lines actually appear in Lee's *Caesar Borgia.*

ACT 2, SCENE 6

(*Tom Thumb, Huncamunca.*)

TOM THUMB. Where is my Princess, where's my Huncamunca?
Where are those eyes, those cardmatches[1] of love,
That [ppp] light up all with love my waxen soul?
Where is that face which artful nature made
[qqq] In the same moulds where Venus' self was cast?
HUNCAMUNCA. [rrr] Oh! What is music to the ear that's deaf,
Or a goose-pie to him that has no taste?
What are these praises now to me, since I
Am promised to another?
TOM THUMB. Ha! promised.
HUNCAMUNCA. Too sure; it's written in the book of fate.
TOM THUMB. [sss] Then I will tear away the leaf
Wherein it's writ, or if fate won't allow
So large a gap within its journal-book,
I'll blot it out at least.

ACT 2, SCENE 7

(*Glumdalca, Tom Thumb, Huncamunca.*)

GLUMDALCA. [ttt] I need not ask if you are Huncamunca,
Your brandy nose[2] proclaims—
HUNCAMUNCA. I am a princess;
Nor need I ask who you are.
GLUMDALCA. A giantess;
The queen of those who made and unmade queens.
HUNCAMUNCA. The man whose chief ambition is to be
My sweetheart hath destroyed these mighty giants.

[ppp] This image too very often occurs;

—Bright as when thy eye
First lighted up our loves. *Aureng-Zebe.*
This not a crown alone lights up my name. *Busiris.*

[qqq] There is great dissension among the poets concerning the method of making man. One tells his mistress that the mould she was made in being lost, Heaven cannot form such another. Lucifer in Dryden gives a merry description of his own formation;

Whom Heaven neglecting, made and scarce designed,
But threw me in for number to the rest. *State of Innocence.*

In one place, the same poet supposes man to be made of metal;

I was formed
Of that coarse metal, which when she was made,
The gods threw by for rubbish. *All for Love.*

In another, of dough;

When the gods moulded up the paste of man,
Some of their clay was left upon their hands,
And so they made Egyptians. *Cleomenes.*

In another of clay;

—Rubbish of remaining clay. *Sebastian.*

One makes the soul of wax;

Her waxen soul begins to melt apace. *Anna Bullen.*

Another of flint;

Sure our two souls have somewhere been acquainted
In former beings, or struck out together,
One spark to Afric flew, and one to Portugal. *Sebastian.*

To omit the great quantities of iron, brazen and leaden souls which are so plenty in modern authors—I cannot omit the dress of a soul as we find it in Dryden;

Souls shirted but with air. *King Arthur.*

Nor can I pass by a particular sort of soul in a particular sort of description, in the new *Sophonisba.*

Ye mysterious powers,
—Whether through your gloomy depths I wander,
Or on the mountains walk; give me the calm,
The steady smiling soul, where wisdom sheds
Eternal sunshine, and eternal joy.

[rrr] This line Mr. Banks has plundered entire in his *Anna Bullen.*

[sss]

Good Heaven, the Book of Fate before me lay,
But to tear out the journal of that day.
Or if the order of the world below,
Will not the gap of one whole day allow,
Give me that minute when she made
her vow. *Conquest of Granada.*

[ttt] I know some of the commentators have imagined, that Mr. Dryden, in the altercative scene[3] between Cleopatra and Octavia, a scene which Mr. Addison inveighs against with great bitterness, is much beholden to our author. How just this their observation is, I will not presume to determine.

[1] *cardmatches* Pieces of card dipped in melted sulphur.

[2] *brandy nose* Enlarged and reddened nose with a deformed appearance, associated with alcoholism.

[3] *the altercative scene* The exchange between Cleopatra and Octavia, the romantic rivals for Antony, appears in Act III Scene I of *All for Love*; *Mr. Addison.* Addison had claimed in *The Guardian* No. 110 (17 July 1713) that anyone reading the scene would "be amazed to hear a Roman lady's mouth filled with such obscene raillery."

GLUMDALCA. Your sweetheart? dost thou think the man who once
Hath worn my easy chains, will e'er wear thine?
HUNCAMUNCA. Well may your chains be easy, since if fame
Says true, they have been tried on twenty husbands.
uuu The glove or boot, so many times pulled on,
May well sit easy on the hand or foot.
GLUMDALCA. I glory in the number, and when I
Sit poorly down, like thee, content with one,
Heaven change this face for one as bad as thine.
HUNCAMUNCA. Let me see nearer what this beauty is
That captivates the heart of men by scores.° *twenties*

(*Holds a candle to her face.*)

Oh! Heaven, thou art as ugly as the devil.
GLUMDALCA. You'd give the best of shoes within your shop,
To be but half so handsome.
HUNCAMUNCA. Since you come
vvv To that, I'll put my beauty to the test;
Tom Thumb, I'm yours, if you with me will go.
GLUMDALCA. Oh! stay, Tom Thumb, and you alone shall fill
That bed where twenty giants used to lie.
TOM THUMB. In the balcony that o'er-hangs the stage,
I've seen a whore two 'prentices° engage; *apprentices*
One half a crown does in his fingers hold,
The other shows a little piece of gold;
She the half guinea wisely does purloin,
And leaves the larger and the baser coin.[1]

(*Exeunt*[2] *all but Glumdalca.*)

GLUMDALCA. Left, scorned, and loathed for such a chit[3] as this;
www I feel the storm that's rising in my mind,

uuu A cobbling poet indeed, says Mr. D. and yet I believe we may find as monstrous images in the tragic authors: I'll put down one;

Untie your folded thoughts, and let them dangle loose as a Bride's hair. *Injured Love.*

Which lines seem to have as much title to a milliner's shop, as our author's to a shoemaker's.

vvv Mr. L——[4] takes occasion in this place to commend the great care of our author to preserve the metre of blank verse, in which Shakespeare, Johnson and Fletcher were so notoriously negligent; and the moderns, in imitation of our author, so laudably observant;

——————Then does
Your Majesty believe that he can be
A traitor! *Earl of Essex.*

Every page of *Sophonisba* gives us instances of this excellence.

www Love mounts and rolls about my stormy mind. *Aureng-Zebe.*
Tempests and whirlwinds through my bosom move. *Cleom.*

[1] *half a crown* Silver coin worth two and a half shillings; *half guinea* Gold coin smaller than a half crown, worth about ten shillings; *purloin* Steal; *baser* Inferior.

[2] *Exeunt* Exit.

[3] *chit* Childish, disrespectful young girl.

[4] *Mr. L——* Mr. L——'s identity is uncertain.

Tempests and whirlwinds rise, and roll and roar.
I'm all within a hurricane, as if
[xxx] The world's four winds[1] were pent within my
carcass.
[yyy] Confusion, horror, murder, guts and death.

ACT 2, SCENE 8

(*King, Glumdalca.*)

KING. [zzz] Sure never was so sad a king as I,
[aaaa] My life is worn as ragged as a coat
A beggar wears; a prince should put it off,
[bbbb] To love a captive and a giantess.
Oh love! Oh love! how great a king art thou!
My tongue's thy trumpet, and thou trumpetest,
Unknown to me, within me. [cccc] Oh Glumdalca!
Heaven thee designed a giantess to make,
But an angelic soul was shuffled in.
[dddd] I am a multitude of walking griefs,
And only on her lips the balm is found,
[eeee] To spread a plaster[2] that might cure them all.
GLUMDALCA. What do I hear?
KING. What do I see?
GLUMDALCA. Oh!
KING. Ah!
[ffff] GLUMDALCA. Ah wretched queen!

[xxx] With such a furious tempest on his brow,
As if the world's four winds were pent within
His blust'ring carcass. *Anna Bullen.*

[yyy] *Verba tragica.*[3]

[zzz] This speech hath been terribly mauled by the poets.

[aaaa] ———My life is worn to rags;
Not worth a Prince's wearing. *Love Triumph.*

[bbbb] Must I beg the pity of my slave?
Must a King beg! But love's a greater king,
A tyrant, nay a devil that possesses me.
He tunes the organ of my voice and speaks,
Unknown to me, within me. *Sebastian.*

[cccc] When thou wer't formed, Heaven did a man begin;
But a brute soul by Chance was shuffled in. *Aureng-Zebe.*

[dddd] ———I am a multitude
Of walking griefs. New *Sophonisba.*[4]

[eeee] I will take thy scorpion blood,
And lay it to my grief till I have ease. *Anna Bullen.*

[ffff] Our Author, who everywhere shows his great penetration into human nature, here outdoes himself: where a less judicious poet would have raised a long scene of whining love. He who understood the passions better, and that so violent an affection as this must be too big for utterance, chooses rather to send his characters off in this sullen and doleful manner: in which admirable conduct he is imitated by the author of the justly celebrated *Eurydice.*[5] Dr. Young seems to point at this violence of passion;

———————Passion chokes
Their words, and they're the statues of despair.[6]

And Seneca tells us, "*curae leves loquuntur, ingentes stupent.*"[7] The story of the Egyptian King in Herodotus is too well known to need to be inserted; I refer the more curious reader to the excellent Montaigne, who hath written an essay on this subject.[8]

[1] *world's four winds* I.e., winds from the four corners of the earth.

[2] *plaster* Medicinal substance, usually spread on a bandage.

[3] *Verba tragica* Latin: Language of tragedy.

[4] *New Sophonisba* This line does not occur in Thomson's play, but in Francis Beaumont and John Fletcher's *The Maid's Tragedy* (1613).

[5] *Eurydice* By David Mallet (1731), in which a stage direction reads: "Eurydice kneels to Periander, who after looking on her for some time with emotion, breaks away without speaking."

[6] *Passion chokes … of despair* Lines taken from *Busiris.*

[7] *curae … stupent* Latin: "light cares speak, great ones are speechless"; from Seneca's first-century CE tragedy, *Phaedra.*

[8] *story of the Egyptian King* In Herodotus' *Histories*, the king Psammenitus does not cry to see his daughter enslaved and his son executed, but the suffering of a friend moves him to tears; he explains that his own misery is too great to express; *excellent Montaigne … this subject* In his essay "*De la Tristesse*" ("Of Sorrow"), Montaigne retells this story and gives other examples of "that melancholic, dumb, and deaf stupefaction which benumbs all our faculties when oppressed with accidents greater than we are able to bear."

KING. Oh! Wretched king!
[gggg] GLUMDALCA. Ah!
KING. Oh!

ACT 2, SCENE 9

(*Tom Thumb, Huncamunca, Parson.*)

PARSON. Happy's the wooing that's not long adoing;
For if I guess aright, Tom Thumb this night
Shall give a being to a new Tom Thumb.
TOM THUMB. It shall be my endeavour so to do.
HUNCAMUNCA. Oh! fie upon you, sir, you make me blush.
TOM THUMB. It is the virgin's sign, and suits you well:
[hhhh] I know not where, nor how, nor what I am,
[iiii] I'm so transported, I have lost myself.
HUNCAMUNCA. Forbid it, all ye stars, for you're so small
That, were you lost, you'd find yourself no more.
So the unhappy seamstress once, they say,
Her needle in a pottle,[1] lost, of hay;
In vain she looked, and looked, and made her moan,
For ah, the needle was forever gone.
PARSON. Long may they live, and love, and propagate,
Till the whole land be peopled with Tom Thumbs.
[jjjj] So when the Cheshire cheese[2] a maggot breeds,
Another and another still succeeds.
By thousands, and ten thousands they increase,
Till one continued maggot fills the rotten cheese.

[1] *pottle* Half-gallon container.

[2] *Cheshire cheese* Cheese from the English county of Cheshire.

[3] *Don Carlos* By Otway (1676). The lines actually occur in John Gay's *The What D'Ye Call It* (1715), a farce mocking contemporary theater that seems also to have influenced Fielding's *Tragedy*.

[4] *Medea* By Charles Johnson (1730).

[5] *Assist me … against me* Lines taken from *The Conquest of Granada*.

[6] *solecism* Mistake in grammar or absurdity, or a breach of good manners or social propriety.

[7] *Welsh* Cheese was supposedly the favorite food of any Welshman.

[gggg] To part is Death——
——'Tis Death to part.
——————Ah.
——————Oh. *Don Carlos.*[3]

[hhhh] Nor know I whether.
What am I, who or where. *Busiris.*
I was I know not what, and am I know not how. *Gloriana.*

[iiii] To understand sufficiently the beauty of this passage, it will be necessary that we comprehend every man to contain two selves. I shall not attempt to prove this from philosophy which the poets make so plainly evident.

One runs away from the other;
Let me demand your Majesty,
Why fly you from yourself? *Duke of Guise.*

In a 2d, one self is a guardian to the other;

Leave me the care of me. *Conquest of Granada.*

Again,

Myself am to myself less near. *Ibid.*

In the same, the first self is proud of the second;

I myself am proud of me. *State of Innocence.*

In a 3d, distrustful of him;

Fain I would tell, but whisper it in mine ear,
That none besides might hear, nay not myself. *Earl of Essex.*

In a 4th, honours him;

I honour Rome,
But honour too myself. *Sophonisba.*

In a 5th, at variance with him;

Leave me not thus at variance with myself. *Busiris.*

Again, in a 6th:

I find myself divided from myself. *Medea.*[4]
She seemed the sad effigies of herself. Banks's *Albion Queens.*
Assist me, Zulema, if thou would'st be
The friend thou seemest, assist me against me.[5]

From all which it appears, that there are two selves; and therefore Tom Thumb's losing himself is no such solecism[6] as it hath been represented by men, rather ambitious of criticizing than qualified to criticize.

[jjjj] Mr. F—— imagines this Parson to have been a Welsh[7] one from his simile.

ACT 2, SCENE 10

(*Noodle, Grizzle and then Huncanmunca.*)

NOODLE. [kkkk] Sure nature means to break her solid
 chain,[1]
Or else unfix the world, and in a rage,
To hurl it from its axle-tree and hinges;
All things are so confused, the King's in love,
The Queen is drunk, the Princess married is.
GRIZZLE. Oh! Noodle, hast thou Huncamunca seen?
NOODLE. I've seen a thousand sights this day, where none
Are by the wonderful bitch herself outdone,
The King, the Queen, and all the court are sights.
GRIZZLE. [llll] D——n your delay, you trifler, are you
 drunk, ha?
I will not hear one word but Huncamunca.
NOODLE. By this time she is married to Tom Thumb.
GRIZZLE. [mmmm] My Huncamunca.
NOODLE. Your Huncamunca.
Tom Thumb's Huncamunca, every man's
 Huncamunca.
GRIZZLE. If this be true all womankind are damned.
NOODLE. If it be not, may I be so myself.
GRIZZLE. See where she comes! I'll not believe a word
Against that face, upon whose [nnnn] ample brow,
Sits innocence with majesty enthroned.
GRIZZLE. Where has my Huncamunca been? See here
The licence in my hand!
HUNCAMUNCA. Alas! Tom Thumb.
GRIZZLE. Why dost thou mention him?
HUNCAMUNCA. Ah me! Tom Thumb.
GRIZZLE. What means my lovely Huncamunca?
HUNCAMUNCA. Hum!
GRIZZLE. Oh! Speak.
HUNCAMUNCA. Hum!
GRIZZLE. Ha! Your every word is "Hum."

[kkkk] Our author hath been plundered here according to custom;
Great nature break thy chain that links together
The fabric of the world and make a chaos
Like that within my soul. *Love Triumphant.*
———Startle nature, unfix the globe,
And hurl it from its axle-tree and hinges. *Albion Queens.*
The tott'ring Earth seems sliding off its props.[2]

[llll] D——n your delay, ye torturers proceed,
I will not hear one word but Almahide. *Conq. of Granada.*

[mmmm] Mr. Dryden hath imitated this in *All for Love*.[3]

[nnnn] This Miltonic style abounds in the new *Sophonisba.*
—And on her ample brow
Sat majesty.

[1] *her solid chain* The great chain of being, a common poetic image of natural order.

[2] *The tott'ring ... its props* Lines taken from *The Persian Princess.*

[3] *Mr. Dryden ... All for Love* Scriblerus Secundus has in mind the exchange in Act 4 Scene 1, where Anthony asks "My Cleopatra?" and Ventidius replies, "Your Cleopatra; / Dollabella's Cleopatra / Every man's Cleopatra."

[oooo] You force me still to answer you Tom Thumb.
Tom Thumb, I'm on the rack, I'm in a flame,
[pppp] Tom Thumb, Tom Thumb, Tom Thumb, you love the name;
So pleasing is that sound, that were you dumb
You still would find a voice to cry "Tom Thumb."

HUNCAMUNCA. Oh! Be not hasty to proclaim my doom,
My ample heart for more than one has room,
A maid like me, heaven formed at least for two;
[qqqq] I married him, and now I'll marry you.

GRIZZLE. Ha! dost thou own thy falsehood to my face?
Think'st thou that I will share thy husband's place,
Since to that office one cannot suffice,
And since you scorn to dine one single dish on,
Go, get your husband put into commission,[1]
Commissioners to discharge (ye gods) it fine is,
The duty of a husband to your Highness;
Yet think not long I will my rival bear,
Or unrevenged the slighted willow[2] wear;
The gloomy, brooding tempest, now confined
Within the hollow caverns of my mind,
In dreadful whirl shall roll along the coasts,
Shall thin the land of all the men it boasts,
[rrrr] And cram up ev'ry chink of hell with ghosts.
[ssss] So have I seen, in some dark winter's day,
A sudden storm rush down the sky's highway,
Sweep through the streets with terrible ding dong,
Gush through the spouts, and wash whole crowds along.
The crowded shops, the thronging vermin screen,[3]
Together cram the dirty and the clean,
And not one shoe-boy in the street is seen.

[oooo] Your ev'ry answer still so ends in that,
You force me still to answer you Morat. *Aureng-Zebe.*

[pppp] Morat, Morat, Morat, you love the name. *Aureng-Zebe.*

[qqqq] Here is a sentiment for the virtuous Huncamunca (says Mr. D——s) and yet with the leave of this great man, the virtuous Panthea in *Cyrus* hath an heart every whit as ample;

For two I must confess are Gods to me,
Which is my Abradatus first, and thee. *Cyrus the Great.*

Nor is the Lady in *Love Triumphant* more reserved, though not so intelligible;

——I am so divided,
That I grieve most for both, and love both most.[4]

[rrrr] A ridiculous supposition to anyone who considers the great and extensive largeness of Hell, says a commentator: but not so to those who consider the great expansion of immaterial substance. Mr. Banks makes one soul to be so expanded that Heaven could not contain it;

The Heavens are all too narrow for her soul. *Virtue Betrayed.*

The Persian Princess hath a passage not unlike the author of this;

We will send such shoals of murdered slaves,
Shall glut Hell's empty regions.

This threatens to fill Hell even though it were empty; Lord Grizzle only to fill up the chinks, supposing the rest already full.

[ssss] Mr. Addison is generally thought to have had this simile in his eye when he wrote that beautiful one at the end of the third act of his *Cato*.[5]

---

[1] *get your … into commission* I.e., have his duties taken over by a commissioning body.

[2] *slighted willow* The willow was a symbol of unrequited love.

[3] *thronging vermin screen* A reference to the fact that few people in the eighteenth century bathed; instead they covered lice and dirt with powder and wigs.

[4] *I am … love both most* The lines actually appear in *Cleomenes*.

[5] *the third act of his Cato* The reference is actually to the end of the second act of Addison's play:

So, where our wide Numidian wastes extend,
Sudden, th'impetuous hurricanes descend,
Wheel through the air, in circling eddies play,
Tear up the sands, and sweep whole plains away.
The helpless traveller with wild surprise
Sees the dry desert all around him rise
And smothered in the dusty whirlwind dies.

HUNCAMUNCA. Oh! fatal rashness should his fury slay,
My hapless bridegroom on his wedding day;
I, who this morn, of two chose which to wed,
May go again this night alone to bed;
[tttt] So have I seen some wild unsettled fool,
Who had her choice of this, and that joint-stool;
To give the preference to either, loath
And fondly coveting to sit on both:
While the two stools her sitting part confound,
Between 'em both fall squat upon the ground.

ACT 3, SCENE 1. KING ARTHUR'S PALACE.

([uuuu] *Ghost solus.*)

GHOST. Hail! ye black horrors of midnight's midnoon!
Ye fairies, goblins, bats and screech-owls, hail!
And oh! ye mortal watchmen, whose hoarse throats[1]
Th'immortal ghosts dread croakings counterfeit,° *imitate*
All hail!—Ye dancing phantoms, who by day
Are some condemned to fast, some feast in fire;[2]
Now play in church-yards, skipping o'er the graves,
To the [vvvv] loud music of the silent bell,
All hail!

[tttt] This beautiful simile is founded on a proverb which does honour to the English language;

Between two stools the breech falls to the ground.

I am not so pleased with any written remains of the ancients as with those little aphorisms which verbal tradition hath delivered down to us under the title of proverbs. It were to be wished that instead of filling their pages with the fabulous theology of the pagans, our modern poets would think it worth their while to enrich their works with the proverbial sayings of their ancestors. Mr. Dryden hath chronicled one in heroic;

Two ifs scarce make one possibility. *Conquest of Granada.*

My Lord Bacon is of opinion that whatever is known of arts and sciences might be proved to have lurked in the proverbs of Solomon. I am of the same opinion in relation to those abovementioned: at least I am confident that a more perfect system of ethics, as well as economy, might be compiled out of them, than is at present extant, either in the works of the ancient philosophers, or those more valuable, as more voluminous, ones of the modern divines.[3]

[uuuu] Of all the particulars in which the modern stage falls short of the ancient, there is none so much to be lamented as the great scarcity of ghosts in the latter. Whence this proceeds, I will not presume to determine. Some are of opinion that the moderns are unequal to that sublime language which a ghost ought to speak. One says ludicrously that ghosts are out of fashion; another that they are properer for comedy; forgetting, I suppose, that Aristotle hath told us that a ghost is the soul of tragedy; for so I render the Ψυχή ὁ μῦθος τῆς τραγωδίας, which M. Dacier,[4] amongst others, hath mistaken, I suppose misled by not understanding the *fabula* of the Latins, which signifies a ghost as well as a fable.

——*Te premet nox, fabulæque manes.*[5] Hor.

Of all the ghosts that have ever appeared on the stage, a very learned and judicious foreign critic gives the preference to this of our author. These are his words, speaking of this tragedy:

——*Nec quidquam in illâ admirabilius quam phasma quoddam horrendum, quod omnibus aliis spectris, quibuscum scatet anglorum tragœdia, longè (pace D——isii V. Doctiss. dixerim) prætulerim.*[6]

[vvvv] We have already given instances of this figure.

[1] *hoarse throats* Watchmen would be hoarse from calling out each hour, from sunset to sunrise.

[2] *some condemned ... fire* One proverbial idea of Hell was of a place of extremes—there would either be too much food or none, for example.

[3] *My Lord Bacon ... modern divines* Scriblerus Secundus learnedly alludes to Book II of *The Advancement of Learning* (1605), where Francis Bacon (1561–1626) explains "we may see in those aphorisms which have place amongst divine writings composed by Solomon the King, of whom the Scriptures testify, that his heart was as the sands of the sea, encompassing the world, and all worldly matters; we see, I say, not a few profound and excellent cautions, precepts, positions, extending to much variety of occasions."

[4] Ψυχή ὁ μῦθος τῆς τραγωδίας Greek: "plot is the soul of tragedy," with a pun on "μῦθος," which also means "fable"; *M. Dacier* André Dacier (1651–1722), French classical scholar and translator whose version of Aristotle's *Poetics* was published in England in 1705.

[5] *Te premet nox, fabulæque manes* Latin: "The fabled ghosts and night will press upon you." The lines are taken from the first-century BCE *Odes* of Horace.

[6] *Nec quidquam ... prætulerim* Latin: "Nothing is so admirable as a certain dreadful phantasm, which is much preferable (do not be offended, D[ennis]issi, most learned man) to all the other ghosts with which English tragedy overflows."

ACT 3, SCENE 2

(*King, and Ghost.*)

KING. What noise is this? What villain dares,
At this dread hour, with feet and voice profane,
Disturb our royal walls?
GHOST. One who defies
Thy empty power to hurt him; [wwww] one who dares
Walk in thy bedchamber.
KING. Presumptuous slave!
Thou diest!
GHOST. Threaten others with that word,
[xxxx] I am a ghost, and am already dead.
KING. Ye stars! 'tis well; were thy last hour to come,
This moment had been it; [yyyy] yet by thy shroud[1]
I'll pull thee backward, squeeze thee to a bladder,[2]
'Till thou dost groan thy nothingness away.

(*Ghost retires.*)

Thou fliest! 'Tis well.
[zzzz] I thought what was the courage of a ghost!
Yet, dare not, on thy life—Why say I that,
Since life thou hast not?—Dare not walk again,
Within these walls, on pain of the Red Sea.[3]
For, if henceforth I ever find thee here,
As sure, sure as a gun, I'll have thee laid—
GHOST. Were the Red Sea a sea of Holland's gin,[4]
The liquor (when alive) whose very smell
I did detest, did loathe—yet for the sake
Of Thomas Thumb, I would be laid therein.

[wwww] Almanzor reasons in the same manner;

——A ghost I'll be,
And from a ghost, you know, no place is free. *Conq. of Granada.*

[xxxx] The man who writ this wretched pun (says Mr. D.) would have picked your pocket: which he proceeds to show not only bad in itself, but doubly so on so solemn an occasion.[5] And yet in that excellent play of *Liberty Asserted*, we find something very much resembling a pun in the mouth of a mistress, who is parting with the lover she is fond of;

ULAMAR. Oh, mortal woe! one kiss, and then farewell.
IRENE. The gods have given to others to fare well.
O miserably must Irene fare.

Agamemnon, in *The Victim*, is full as facetious on the most solemn occasion, that of sacrificing his daughter;

Yes, Daughter, yes; you will assist the priest;
Yes, you must offer up your——vows for Greece.

[yyyy] I'll pull thee backwards by thy shroud to light,
Or else, I'll squeeze thee like a bladder, there,
And make thee groan thyself away to air. *Conquest of Granada.*
Snatch me, ye Gods, this moment into nothing. *Cyrus the Great.*

[zzzz] So, art thou gone? Thou canst no conquest boast,
I thought what was the courage of a ghost. *Conquest of Granada.*

King Arthur seems to be as brave a fellow as Almanzor, who says most heroically,

In spite of Ghosts, I'll on.[6]

---

[1] *shroud* Sheet in which a corpse is wrapped for burial.

[2] *to a bladder* I.e., like an inflated bag.

[3] *Red Sea* Sea between Africa and Asia; one of the places where ghosts could supposedly be successfully imprisoned, or in which they feared drowning.

[4] *Holland's gin* Cheap gin made in Holland. It was popular among the laboring classes because of its price.

[5] *The man ... an occasion* Dennis once responded to a terrible pun, "the man that will make such an execrable pun as that in my company, would pick my pocket." In *The Dunciad Variorum*, Pope similarly references this anecdote in order to expose ironically Dennis's own use of puns.

[6] *In spite ... I'll on* This line is actually spoken by Oedipus in Lee and Dryden's *Oedipus* (1679).

KING. Ha! said you?
GHOST. Yes, my liege, I said Tom Thumb,
Whose father's ghost I am—once not unknown
To mighty Arthur. But, I see, 'tis true,
The dearest friend, when dead, we all forget.
KING. 'Tis he, it is the honest Gaffer Thumb.
Oh, let me press thee in my eager arms,
Thou best of ghosts! Thou something more than ghost!
GHOST. Would I were something more, that we again
Might feel each other in the warm embrace.
But now I have th' advantage of my king,
[aaaaa] For I feel thee, whilst thou dost not feel me.
KING. But say, [bbbbb] thou dearest air, Oh! say, what dread,
Important business sends thee back to earth?
GHOST. Oh! then prepare to hear—which, but to hear,
Is full enough to send thy spirit hence.
Thy subjects up in arms, by Grizzle led,
Will, ere the rosy fingered morn shall ope° *open*
The shutters of the sky, before the gate
Of this thy royal palace, swarming spread:
[ccccc] So have I seen[1] the bees in clusters swarm,
So have I seen the stars in frosty nights,
So have I seen the sand in windy days,
So have I seen the ghosts on Pluto's shore,[2]
So have I seen the flowers in spring arise,
So have I seen the leaves in autumn fall,
So have I seen the fruits in summer smile,
So have I seen the snow in winter frown.
KING. Damn all thou'st seen!—Dost thou, beneath the shape
Of Gaffer Thumb, come hither to abuse me,
With similies to keep me on the rack?
Hence—or by all the torments of thy hell,
[ddddd] I'll run thee through the body, though thou'st none.
GHOST. Arthur, beware; I must this moment hence,
Not frighted by your voice, but by the cocks;
Arthur beware, beware, beware, beware!
Strive to avert thy yet impending fate;
For if thou'rt killed today
Tomorrow all thy care will come too late.

[1] *So have I seen* This exaggerated verbal formula is intended to parody the reliance of contemporary tragedies on overwrought and distracting similes.

[2] *Pluto's shore* Pluto was the classical god of the underworld. The shore referred to is that of the River Styx, across which souls of the dead would be transported into Hades.

[3] *I have ... I know not* These lines are taken from *King Arthur*.

[aaaaa] The ghost of Lausaria in *Cyrus* is a plain copy of this, and is therefore worth reading.

Ah, Cyrus!
Thou may'st as well grasp water, or fleet air,
As think of touching my immortal shade. *Cyrus the Great.*

[bbbbb] Thou better part of heavenly air. *Conquest of Granada.*

[ccccc] A string of similes (says one) proper to be hung up in the cabinet of a prince.

[ddddd] This passage hath been understood several different ways by the commentators. For my part, I find it difficult to understand it at all. Mr. Dryden says,

I have heard something how two bodies meet,
But how two souls join, I know not.[3]

So that 'till the body of a spirit be better understood, it will be difficult to understand how it is possible to run him through it.

ACT 3, SCENE 3

(*King solus.*)

KING. Oh stay, and leave me not uncertain thus!
And whilst thou tellest me what's like my fate,
Oh, teach me how I may avert it too!
Curst be the man who first a simile made!
Curst, ev'ry bard who writes! So have I seen
Those whose comparisons are just and true,
And those who liken things not like at all.
The devil is happy, that the whole creation
Can furnish out no simile to his fortune.

ACT 3, SCENE 4

(*King, Queen.*)

QUEEN. What is the cause, my Arthur, that you steal
Thus silently from Dollalolla's breast?
Why dost thou leave me in the [eeeee] dark alone,
When well thou knowest I am afraid of spirits?
KING. Oh, Dollalolla! Do not blame my love;
I hoped the fumes of last night's punch had laid
Thy lovely eyelids fast. But, oh! I find
There is no power in drams[1] to quiet wives;
Each morn, as the returning sun, they wake,
And shine upon their husbands.
QUEEN. Think, oh think!
What a surprise it must be to the sun,
Rising, to find the vanished world away.
What less can be the wretched wife's surprise,
When, stretching out her arms to fold thee fast,
She folds her useless bolster in her arms.
[fffff] Think, think on that—Oh! think, think well on that.
I do remember also to have read
[ggggg] In Dryden's Ovid's *Metamorphosis*,[2]
That Jove in form inanimate did lie
With beauteous Danae; and trust me, Love,
[hhhhh] I feared the bolster might have been a Jove.

[1] *drams* Small draughts of liquor or medicine.

[2] *Dryden's Ovid's Metamorphosis* Though Dryden did translate several tales from Ovid's *Metamorphoses*, he did not translate the one alluded to here, in which Jove rapes the nymph Danaë in the form of a shower of gold.

[eeeee] Cydaria is of the same fearful temper with Dollalolla;
I never durst in darkness be alone. *Ind. Emp.*

[fffff] Think well of this, think that, think every way. *Sophonisba.*

[ggggg] These quotations are more usual in the comic than in the tragic writers.

[hhhhh] This distress (says Mr. D——) I must allow to be extremely beautiful, and tends to heighten the virtuous character of Dollalolla, who is so exceeding delicate that she is in the highest apprehension from the inanimate embrace of a bolster. An example worthy of imitation from all our writers of tragedy.

KING. Come to my arms, most virtuous of thy sex;
Oh Dollalolla! were all wives like thee,
So many husbands never had worn horns.[1]
Should Huncamunca of thy worth partake,
Tom Thumb indeed were blest. Oh fatal name!
For didst thou know one quarter what I know,
Then would'st thou know—Alas! what thou would'st know!
QUEEN. What can I gather hence? Why dost thou speak
Like men who carry raree-shows[2] about,
Now you shall see, gentlemen, what you shall see?
O tell me more, or thou hast told too much.

ACT 3, SCENE 5

(*King, Queen, Noodle.*)

NOODLE. Long life attend your Majesties serene,
Great Arthur, King, and Dollalolla, Queen!
Lord Grizzle, with a bold, rebellious crowd,
Advances to the palace, threatening loud,
Unless the Princess be delivered straight,
And the victorious Thumb, without his pate,° *head*
They are resolved to batter down the gate.

ACT 3, SCENE 6

(*King, Queen, Huncamunca, Noodle.*)

KING. See where the Princess comes! Where is Tom Thumb?
HUNCAMUNCA. Oh! Sir, about an hour and half ago
He sallied out to encounter with the foe,
And swore, unless his fate had him misled,
From Grizzle's shoulders to cut off his head,
And serve't up with your chocolate in bed.
KING. 'Tis well, I find one devil told us both.
Come Dollalolla, Huncamunca, come,
Within we'll wait for the victorious Thumb;
In peace and safety we secure may stay,
While to his arm we trust the bloody fray;

---

[1] *horns* The proverbial sign of a cuckold, a man whose wife has been unfaithful.

[2] *raree-shows* Peep shows contained in portable boxes, into which customers could look for a fee.

Though men and giants should conspire with gods,
iiiii He is alone equal to all these odds.
QUEEN. He is, indeed, a jjjjj helmet to us all,
While he supports, we need not fear to fall;
His arm dispatches all things to our wish,
And serves up every foe's head in a dish.
Void is the mistress of the house of care,
While the good cook presents the bill of fare;[1]
Whether the cod, that northern king of fish,
Or duck, or goose, or pig, adorn the dish.
No fears the number of her guests afford,
But at her hour she sees the dinner on the board.° *sideboard*

ACT 3, SCENE 7. A PLAIN.

(*Lord Grizzle, Foodle, and Rebels.*)

GRIZZLE. Thus far our arms with victory are crowned;
For though we have not fought, yet we have found
kkkkk No enemy to fight withal.
FOODLE. Yet I,
Methinks, would willingly avoid this day,
lllll This first of April, to engage our foes.
GRIZZLE. This day, of all the days of th' year, I'd choose,
For on this day my grandmother was born.
Gods! I will make Tom Thumb an April fool;
mmmmm Will teach his wit an errand it ne'er knew,
And send it post to the Elysian shades.
FOODLE. I'm glad to find our army is so stout,
Nor does it move my wonder less than joy.
GRIZZLE. nnnnn What friends we have, and how we came so strong,
I'll softly tell you as we march along.

iiiii "*Credat Judaeus Apelles. Non ego*"[2] (Says Mr. D.) "For, passing over the absurdity of being equal to odds, can we possibly suppose a little insignificant fellow—I say again, a little insignificant fellow, able to vie with a strength which all the Sampsons and Hercules's of antiquity would be unable to encounter." I shall refer this incredulous critic to Mr. Dryden's defence of his Almanzor[3]; and lest that should not satisfy him, I shall quote a few lines from the speech of a much braver fellow than Almanzor, Mr. Johnson's Achilles;

Though human race rise in embattled hosts
To force her from my arms—Oh! son of Atreus!
By that immortal pow'r, whose deathless spirit
Informs this earth, I will oppose them all. *Victim.*

jjjjj "I have heard of being supported by a staff" (says Mr. D.) "but never of being supported by an helmet." I believe he never heard of sailing with wings, which he may read in no less a poet than Mr. Dryden;

Unless we borrow wings, and sail through air.[4] *Love Triumphant.*

What will he say to a kneeling valley?

——————I'll stand
Like a safe valley, that low bends the knee
To some aspiring mountain. *Injured Love.*

I am ashamed of so ignorant a carper, who doth not know that an epithet in tragedy is very often no other than an expletive.[5] Do not we read in the new *Sophonisba* of grinding chains, blue plagues, white occasions, and blue serenity? Nay, 'tis not the adjective only, but sometimes half a sentence is put by way of expletive, as, "beauty pointed high with spirit," in the same play—and, "in the lap of blessing, to be most curst," in the *Revenge.*

kkkkk A victory like that of Almanzor.
Almanzor is victorious without fight. *Conq. of Granada.*

lllll Well have we chose an happy day for fight,
For every man in course of time has found
Some days are lucky, some unfortunate. *K. Arthur.*

mmmmm We read of such another in Lee;
Teach his rude wit a flight she never made,
And sent her post to the Elysian shade. *Gloriana.*

nnnnn These lines are copied verbatim in *The Indian Emperor.*

[1] *bill of fare* List of dishes to be served; menu.

[2] *Credat … Non ego* Latin: "Apelles the Jew may believe you, but I do not." The passage is taken from Book I of Horace's *Satires* and had proverbial familiarity.

[3] *defence of his Almanzor* Dryden responded to the criticism that his hero "performs impossibilities" in the essay "Of Heroic Plays," prefixed to *The Conquest of Granada.*

[4] *Unless we … through air* This line actually appears in *King Arthur.*

[5] *carper* Petty critic; *epithet* Descriptive term; *expletive* Meaningless filler word.

ACT 3, SCENE 8

(*Tom Thumb, Glumdalca cum suis.*[1])

(*Thunder and Lightning.*)

TOM THUMB. Oh, Noodle! hast thou seen a day like
 this?
ooooo The unborn thunder rumbles o'er our heads,
ppppp As if the gods meant to unhinge the world;
And heaven and earth in wild confusion hurl;
Yet will I boldly tread the tottering ball.
MERLIN. Tom Thumb!
TOM THUMB. What voice is this I hear?
MERLIN. Tom Thumb!
TOM THUMB. Again it calls.
MERLIN. Tom Thumb!
GLUMDALCA. It calls again.
TOM THUMB. Appear, whoe'er thou art, I fear thee not.
MERLIN. Thou hast no cause to fear; I am thy friend,
Merlin by name, a conjuror by trade,
And to my art thou dost thy being owe.
TOM THUMB. How!
MERLIN. Hear then the mystic getting of Tom Thumb.
qqqqq *His father was a ploughman plain,*
 His mother milked the cow;
And yet the way to get a son,
 This couple knew not how.
Until such time the good old man
 To learned Merlin goes,
And there to him, in great distress,
 In secret manner shows;
How in his heart he wished to have
 A child, in time to come,
To be his heir, though it might be
 No bigger than his thumb:
Of which old Merlin was foretold,
 That he his wish should have;
And so a son of stature small,
 The charmer to him gave.
Thou'st heard the past, look up and see the future.

ooooo Unborn thunder rolling in a cloud. *Conq. of Gran.*

ppppp Were Heaven and Earth in wild confusion hurled,
Should the rash Gods unhinge the rolling world,
Undaunted, would I tread the tott'ring ball,
Crushed, but unconquered, in the dreadful
 Fall. *Female Warrior.*[2]

qqqqq See *The History of Tom Thumb*,[3] page 2.

[1] *cum suis* Latin: with associates.

[2] *Female Warrior* Charles Hopkins, *Friendship Improved: or, The Female Warrior* (1700).

[3] *History of Tom Thumb* The text given here follows that found in contemporary versions of the Tom Thumb story.

TOM THUMB. [rrrrr] Lost in amazement's gulf, my senses sink;
See there, Glumdalca, see another [sssss] me?
GLUMDALCA. O sight of horror! See, you are devoured
By the expanded jaws of a red cow.
MERLIN. Let not these sights deter thy noble mind,
[ttttt] For lo! a sight more glorious courts thy eyes;
See from afar a theatre arise;
There, ages yet unborn shall tribute pay
To the heroic actions of this day:
Then buskin tragedy[1] at length shall choose
Thy name the best supporter of her muse.[2]
TOM THUMB. Enough; let every warlike music sound,
We fall contented, if we fall renowned.

ACT 3, SCENE 9

(*Lord Grizzle, Foodle, Rebels on one side. Tom Thumb, Glumdalca on the other.*)

FOODLE. At length the enemy advances nigh,
[uuuuu] I hear them with my ear, and see them with my eye.
GRIZZLE. Draw all your swords, for liberty we fight,
[vvvvv] And liberty the mustard is of life.
TOM THUMB. Are you the man whom men famed Grizzle name?
GRIZZLE. [wwwww] Are you the much more famed Tom Thumb?
TOM THUMB. The same.
GRIZZLE. Come on, our worth upon ourselves we'll prove,
For liberty I fight.
TOM THUMB. And I for love.

(*A bloody engagement between the two armies here, drums beating, trumpets sounding, thunder and lightning. They fight off and on several times. Some fall. Grizzle and Glumdalca remain.*)

[1] *buskin tragedy* Tragedy in the Athenian dramatic tradition.

[2] *muse* Figure of inspiration for poetry or art, so called after the nine Muses, classical goddesses who presided over the arts and learning.

[rrrrr] ———Amazement swallows up my sense,
And in th'impetuous whirl of circling fate
Drinks down my reason. *Pers. Princess.*

[sssss] ———I have outfaced myself,
What! am I two? Is there another me? *K. Arthur.*

[ttttt] The character of Merlin is wonderful throughout, but most so in this prophetic part. We find several of these prophecies in the tragic authors, who frequently take this opportunity to pay a compliment to their country, and sometimes to their prince. None but our author (who seems to have detested the least appearance of flattery) would have passed by such an opportunity of being a political prophet.

[uuuuu] I saw the villain, Myron, with these eyes I saw him. *Busiris.* In both which places it is intimated that it is sometimes possible to see with other eyes than your own.

[vvvvv] "This mustard" (says Mr. D.) "is enough to turn one's stomach: I would be glad to know what idea the author had in his head when he wrote it." This will be, I believe, best explained by a line of Mr. Dennis;
And gave him liberty, the salt of life. *Liberty Asserted.*
The understanding that can digest the one will not rise at the other.

[wwwww] HANNIBAL. Are you the Chief whom men famed Scipio call?
SCIPIO. Are you the much more famous Hannibal? *Hannib.*

Glumdalca. Turn, coward, turn, nor from a woman fly.
Grizzle. Away—thou art too ignoble for my arm.
Glumdalca. Have at thy heart.
Grizzle. Nay then, I thrust at thine.
Glumdalca You push too well, you've run me through the guts,
And I am dead.
Grizzle. Then there's an end of one.
Tom Thumb. When thou art dead, then there's an end of two,
[xxxxx] Villain.
Grizzle. Tom Thumb!
Tom Thumb. Rebel!
Grizzle. Tom Thumb!
Tom Thumb. Hell!
Grizzle. Huncamunca!
Tom Thumb. Thou hast it there.
Grizzle. Too sure I feel it.
Tom Thumb. To hell then, like a rebel as you are,
And give my service to the rebels there.
Grizzle. Triumph not, Thumb, nor think thou shalt enjoy
Thy Huncamunca undisturbed, I'll send
[yyyyy] My ghost to fetch her to the other world;
[zzzzz] It shall but bait at heaven, and then return.
[aaaaaa] But, ha! I feel death rumbling in my brains,
[bbbbbb] Some kinder spright knocks softly at my soul,
And gently whispers it to haste away:
I come, I come, most willingly I come.
[cccccc] So, when some city wife, for country air,
To Hampstead, or to Highgate[1] does repair;
Her, to make haste, her husband does implore,
And cries, "My dear, the coach is at the door."
With equal wish, desirous to be gone,
She gets into the coach, and then she cries—"Drive on!"
Tom Thumb. With those last words [dddddd] he vomited his soul,
Which, [eeeeee] like whipped cream, the Devil will swallow down.
Bear off the body, and cut off the head,

[xxxxx] Dr. Young seems to have copied this engagement in his *Busiris*:

Myron. Villain!
Memnon. Myron!
Myron. Rebel!
Memnon. Myron!
Myron. Hell!
Memnon. Mandane!

[yyyyy] This last speech of my Lord Grizzle hath been of great service to our poets;

———I'll hold it fast
As life, and when life's gone, I'll hold this last;
And if thou tak'st it from me when I'm slain,
I'll send my ghost, and fetch it back again. *Conquest of Granada.*

[zzzzz] My soul should with such speed obey,
It should not bait at Heaven to stop its way.[2]

Lee seems to have had this last in his eye;

'Twas not my purpose, Sir, to tarry there,
I would but go to Heaven to take the air. *Gloriana.*

[aaaaaa] A rising vapour rumbling in my brains. *Cleomenes.*

[bbbbbb] Some kind sprite knocks softly at my soul,
To tell me fate's at hand.[3]

[cccccc] Mr. Dryden seems to have had this simile in his eye when he says,

My soul is packing up, and just on wing. *Conquest of Granada.*

[dddddd] And in a purple vomit poured his soul. *Cleomenes.*

[eeeeee] The Devil swallows vulgar souls
Like whipped cream. *Sebastian.*

[1] *Hampstead … Highgate* Two villages then located just outside of London.

[2] *My soul … stop its way* Lines taken again from *The Conquest of Granada.*

[3] *Some kind … at hand* Lines taken from *Don Sebastian.*

Which I will to the King in triumph lug;
Rebellion's dead, and now I'll go to breakfast.

ACT 3, SCENE 10

(*King, Queen, Huncamunca, and Courtiers.*)

KING. Open the prisons, set the wretched free,
And bid our treasurer disburse six pounds
To pay their debts. Let no-one weep today.
Come, Dollalolla; [ffffff] Curse that odious name!
It is so long, it asks an hour to speak it.
By heavens! I'll change it into Doll, or Loll,
Or any other civil monosyllable
That will not tire my tongue. —Come, sit thee down.
Here seated, let us view the dancer's sports;
Bid 'em advance. This is the wedding day
Of Princess Huncamunca and Tom Thumb;
Tom Thumb! who wins two victories [gggggg] today,
And this way marches, bearing Grizzle's head.

(*A dance here.*)

NOODLE. Oh! monstrous, dreadful, terrible, oh! Oh!
Deaf be my ears, forever blind my eyes!
Dumb be my tongue! Feet lame! All senses lost!
[hhhhhh] Howl wolves, grunt bears, hiss snakes, shriek all ye ghosts!
KING. What does the blockhead mean?
NOODLE. I mean, my liege,
[iiiiii] Only to grace my tale with decent horror;
Whilst from my garret, twice two stories high,
I looked abroad into the streets below;
I saw Tom Thumb attended by the mob,
Twice twenty shoe boys, twice two dozen links,

[ffffff] How I could curse my name of Ptolemy!
It is so long, it asks an hour to write it.
By Heav'n! I'll change it into Jove, or Mars,
Or any other civil monosyllable,
That will not tire my hand. *Cleomenes.*

[gggggg] Here is a visible conjunction of two days in one, by which our author may have either intended an emblem of a wedding; or to insinuate that men in the honeymoon are apt to imagine time shorter than it is. It brings into my mind a passage in the comedy called *The Coffee-House Politician*;[1]

We will celebrate this day at my house tomorrow.

[hhhhhh] These beautiful phrases are all to be found in one single speech of *King Arthur,*[2] *or The British Worthy.*

[iiiiii] I was but teaching him to grace his tale
With decent horror. *Cleomenes.*

[1] *The Coffee-House Politician* By Fielding (1730) himself. The ridiculous line was the result of a composing error: "To-morrow" was supposed to begin the next sentence.

[2] *one single speech of King Arthur* Scriblerus Secundus alludes to a speech in Act III, Scene I:

But straight a rumbling sound, like bellowing winds,
Rose and grew loud; confused with howls of wolves,
And grunts of bears, and dreadful hiss of snakes;
Shrieks more than human ...

Chairmen and porters, hackney-coachmen,[1] whores;
Aloft he bore the grizzly head of Grizzle;
When of a sudden through the streets there came
A cow, of larger than the usual size,
And in a moment—guess, oh! guess the rest!
And in a moment swallowed up Tom Thumb.

KING. Shut up again the prisons, bid my treasurer
Not give three farthings out—hang all the culprits,
Guilty or not—no matter—ravish virgins,
Go bid the schoolmasters whip all their boys;
Let lawyers, parsons, and physicians loose
To rob, impose on, and to kill the world.

NOODLE. Her Majesty the Queen is in a swoon.

QUEEN. Not so much in a swoon, but I have still
Strength to reward the messenger of ill news.

(*Kills Noodle.*)

NOODLE. Oh! I am slain.

CLEORA. My lover's killed, I will revenge him so.

(*Kills the Queen.*)

HUNCAMUNCA. My Mamma killed! vile murderess, beware.

(*Kills Cleora.*)

DOODLE. This for an old grudge, to thy heart.

(*Kills Huncamunca.*)

MUSTACHA. And this
I drive to thine, Oh Doodle! for a new one.

(*Kills Doodle.*)

KING. Ha! Murderess vile, take that!

(*Kills Mustacha.*)

[1] *links* Torch-bearers; boys who carried the links, torches to light people along the streets; *hackney-coachmen* Those who drive hackney coaches, or coaches for hire.

jjjjj And take thou this.

(*Kills himself, and falls.*)

So when the child whom nurse from danger guards,
Sends Jack for mustard[1] with a pack of cards;
Kings, queens and knaves° throw one another down, *male servants*
'Till the whole pack lies scattered and o'erthrown;
So all our pack upon the floor is cast,
And all I boast is—that I fall the last.

(*Dies.*)

FINIS
—1731

jjjjjj We may say with Dryden,

> Death did at length so many slain forget,
> And left the tale, and took them by the great.[2]

I know of no tragedy which comes nearer to this charming and bloody catastrophe than *Cleomenes*, where the curtain covers five principal characters dead on the stage. These lines too,

> I ask no questions then, of who killed who?
> The bodies tell the story as they lie.

seem to have belonged more properly to this scene of our author—nor can I help imagining they were originally his. *The Rival Ladies*[3] too seem beholden to this scene;

> We're now a chain of lovers linked in death,
> Julia goes first, Gonsalvo hangs on her,
> And Angelina hangs upon Gonsalvo,
> As I on Angelina.

No scene, I believe, ever received greater honours than this. It was applauded by several encores, a word very unusual in tragedy—and it was very difficult for the actors to escape without a second slaughter. This I take to be a lively assurance of that fierce spirit of liberty which remains among us, and which Mr. Dryden in his *Essay on Dramatic Poetry*[4] hath observed: "Whether custom" (says he) "hath so insinuated itself into our countrymen, or nature hath so formed them to fierceness, I know not, but they will scarcely suffer combats and other objects of horror to be taken from them." And indeed I am for having them encouraged in this martial disposition; nor do I believe our victories over the French have been owing to anything more than to those bloody spectacles daily exhibited in our tragedies, of which the French stage is so entirely clear.[5]

---

[1] *Sends Jack for mustard* Plays "52 Pickup."

[2] *Death did … by the great* Lines taken from *The Conquest of Granada*.

[3] *The Rival Ladies* By Dryden (1664).

[4] *Essay on Dramatic Poetry* Dryden's essay *Of Dramatic Poesy* (1668), a critical symposium in which several characters debate English drama past and present, was influential for its lively defense of the use of rhyme, its comparison of the English and French theater, and its praise of Shakespeare.

[5] *nor do I … so entirely clear* French playwrights, following classical tradition, tended to locate violence offstage.

Samuel Johnson

1709 – 1784

Samuel Johnson, the legendary eighteenth-century figure, has been referred to as a "great talker," "great moralist," "great man of letters," "great Cham of literature," and even, "a great man who looked like an idiot." One nineteenth-century British scholar declared that the reputation of Johnson's genius was such that he had come to embody for the English "all that we admire in ourselves." Johnson's rise from poverty and obscurity, his quick wit and forceful personality, his dedication to practical common sense and morality, his insatiable pursuit of knowledge, and his use of that knowledge for the cultural advancement of the English have all played a part in making him one of the most celebrated literary figures in British history.

The first three decades of Johnson's life gave little indication that he would one day claim such greatness. He was a premature, unhealthy infant who was not expected to survive childhood. He contracted scrofula soon after birth, the result of which was deep facial scarring, deafness in one ear, and blindness in one eye. As he grew older he suffered from a variety of nervous tics that caused him to twitch and mutter a good deal; until he began speaking, which he did with extraordinary eloquence, people often assumed him to be suffering from some mental disability. He was also prone to depression and was plagued by a series of anxieties, the most pervasive of which was an overwhelming fear of madness. This was strongest, according to James Boswell, "*at the very time* when he was giving proofs of a more than ordinary soundness of judgment and vigour."

Johnson excelled in school, however, and supplemented his education with voracious reading at home. His father was a bookseller, and Johnson chose his books indiscriminately from the available stacks. He arrived at Oxford one of the most qualified students the university had seen; nevertheless, his parents' meager funds did not allow him to stay through his second year. After a brief teaching post, a failed attempt to start a school, and several years of paralyzing depression, Johnson and his wife Tetty (whom he had married in 1735), moved to London.

In London Johnson joined the hundreds of others who earned their living by anonymous hack writing. As his poem *London* (1738) attests, "Slow rises worth, by poverty depressed." Johnson's career was helped along by his writing for *Gentleman's Magazine*, one of the most successful of London's journals. He also gained valuable employment compiling an annotated catalogue of the library of Edward Harley, Lord Oxford, for its purchaser, Thomas Osborne—a job that helped him to become a scholar who, as Adam Smith later claimed, "knew more books than any man alive."

In 1749, Johnson, who was becoming known for his extraordinary erudition, was hired by a group of London booksellers to compile the first comprehensive English dictionary. *The Dictionary of the English Language* (1755)—the first edition of which required nine years and the help of six assistants to complete—set the standard for all future dictionaries in the sheer volume of words it defined (40,000 in total), the various shades of meaning it distinguished, the logic and clarity of those definitions, and the hundreds of thousands of literary quotations (many of which Johnson wrote out from memory) that served as examples. Though Johnson's whimsical definition of lexicographer reads "a writer of dictionaries, a harmless drudge," many of the decisions he made in forming his dictionary became central tenets of modern lexicography. In particular, his choice to make the dictionary descriptive (a catalogue of all known words and their various uses) rather than prescriptive (a selective list to instruct in the proper use of the language and eliminate "low" or "vulgar" words) decisively shaped the role that dictionaries would play in the future development of the language.

During these years, "Dictionary Johnson" composed essays as a nightly diversion from the "drudgery" of lexicography. Over 200 of the moral, critical, and intellectual explorations he compiled were published in a periodical he produced twice weekly (frequently dashing off articles at the very last minute, with the printer's messenger waiting by his side), called *The Rambler* (1750–52). The practical wisdom and stark clarity of these essays won favor with readers, as did Johnson's careful study and description of human nature, his ability to apply reason to experience, and his celebrations of moral strength and virtue. He later resumed his essay writing with the lighter and more humorous weekly periodical *The Idler* (1758–60). *Rasselas, Prince of Abyssinia* (1759) broadened Johnson's reputation as a moralist. This work of fiction—part novel, part moral parable—tells the story of various characters who leave their idyllic home to embark on a fruitless search for one "choice of life" that will bring them endless happiness. The wit and compassion evident in this tale of the insatiability of the human mind made it Johnson's most enduringly popular work, and led Boswell to claim that he was not satisfied unless he reread it at least once a year.

In the latter half of the eighteenth century Johnson at last attained professional and financial security. For his dictionary work Oxford awarded him an honorary Master's degree in 1755 (followed in 1765 by a Doctorate of Law from Trinity College and in 1775 by a Doctorate of Civil Law, also from Oxford), and George III granted him an annual pension of £300. In 1765, after eight years of toil, he completed his edition of Shakespeare, which, with its preface, became an influential contribution to Shakespeare scholarship.

For a time after the death of his wife in 1752, Johnson led a rather solitary existence. Within a few years, however, he had met aspiring writer James Boswell and brewer Henry Thrale and his wife, Hester Thrale (later Piozzi), and had begun to travel for the first time in his life—with the Thrales to France and Wales and with Boswell to Scotland and the Hebrides. By now renowned for his powers of conversation, Johnson eventually found himself at the center of a large circle of leading men (which included painter Sir Joshua Reynolds, politician Edmund Burke, writer Oliver Goldsmith, and actor David Garrick), whose weekly discussions were motivated largely by a desire to hear Johnson talk.

Johnson's last major project was his *Lives of the English Poets* (1779–81). Asked by a group of publishers to write brief introductions to a small edition of English poets, Johnson so enjoyed the project that his pieces expanded beyond mere prefaces into comprehensive critical and historical texts. The publishers, recognizing that these 52 biographies and literary commentaries were powerful works of scholarship in their own right, released them as an independent text. The *Lives* demonstrates Johnson's belief in "the dignity and usefulness of biography" not merely as a source of historical information about a particular figure, but also as a revealing means of documenting human passions and desires with universal significance. He insisted that his biographies give detailed and truthful accounts of his subjects' vices as well as their virtues. For Johnson, it was the minute particularities of the subject that held the essence of each life. Johnson's theories of biography also had an impact on the deeply personal, intimately detailed biographies of him that his friends—most notably Boswell, but also Hester Thrale Piozzi—released after his death.

A few years before his death in 1784 Johnson observed, as he told Boswell, that "there is hardly a day in which there is not something about me in the papers." Historical research has confirmed the accuracy of this remark—Johnson's travel plans, various ailments, and movements about town were constantly reported. If there was no news to record, anecdotes were recycled or even invented. The force of Johnson's personality had captured the attention of the public, and the man who had once professed himself a "retired and uncourtly scholar" had become an integral part of the daily life of a nation. Johnson suffered a stroke in 1783 from which he never fully recovered; he died on 13 December 1784 and was buried in Westminster Abbey a week later.

[Please note that additional work by Johnson appears in the "Early Eighteenth-Century Periodicals" section elsewhere in this volume.]

⌘⌘⌘

The Vanity of Human Wishes

The Tenth Satire of Juvenal Imitated[1]

Let Observation, with extensive view,
Survey mankind, from China to Peru;
Remark each anxious toil, each eager strife,
And watch the busy scenes of crowded life;
Then say how hope and fear, desire and hate,
O'erspread with snares the clouded maze of fate,
Where wav'ring man, betrayed by vent'rous pride,
To tread the dreary paths without a guide,
As treach'rous phantoms in the mist delude,
Shuns fancied ills, or chases airy° good; *imaginary*
How rarely reason guides the stubborn choice,
Rules the bold hand, or prompts the suppliant voice;
How nations sink, by darling schemes oppressed,
When vengeance listens to the fool's request.
Fate wings with every wish th'afflictive dart,
Each gift of nature, and each grace of art,
With fatal heat impetuous courage glows,
With fatal sweetness elocution flows,
Impeachment stops the speaker's pow'rful breath,
And restless fire precipitates on death.
But scarce observed, the knowing and the bold
Fall in the gen'ral massacre of gold;
Wide-wasting pest! that rages unconfined,
And crowds with crimes the records of mankind;
For gold his sword the hireling ruffian draws,
For gold the hireling judge distorts the laws;
Wealth heaped on wealth, nor truth nor safety buys,
The dangers gather as the treasures rise.
Let hist'ry tell where rival kings command,
And dubious title shakes the madded land,
When statutes glean the refuse of the sword,
How much more safe the vassal than the lord;
Low skulks the hind° beneath the rage of pow'r, *farm-worker*
And leaves the wealthy traitor in the Tow'r,[2]
Untouched his cottage, and his slumbers sound,
Though confiscation's vultures hover round.
The needy traveler, secure and gay,
Walks the wild heath, and sings his toil away.
Does envy seize thee? crush th'upbraiding joy,
Increase his riches and his peace destroy;
Now fears in dire vicissitude invade,
The rustling brake° alarms, and quiv'ring shade, *thicket*
Nor light nor darkness bring his pain relief,
One shows the plunder, and one hides the thief.
Yet still one gen'ral cry the skies assails,
And gain and grandeur load the tainted gales;
Few know the toiling statesman's fear or care,
Th' insidious rival and the gaping heir.
Once more, Democritus,[3] arise on earth,
With cheerful wisdom and instructive mirth,
See motley[4] life in modern trappings dressed,
And feed with varied fools th'eternal jest:
Thou who couldst laugh where want enchained caprice,
Toil crushed conceit, and man was of a piece;
Where wealth unloved without a mourner died,
And scarce a sycophant was fed by pride;
Where ne'er was known the form of mock debate,
Or seen a new-made mayor's unwieldy state;
Where change of fav'rites made no change of laws,
And senates heard before they judged a cause;
How wouldst thou shake at Britain's modish tribe,
Dart the quick taunt, and edge the piercing gibe?
Attentive truth and nature to descry,° *perceive*
And pierce each scene with philosophic eye.
To thee were solemn toys or empty show,

[1] *The Vanity … Imitated* In his imitation of Juvenal's satire of human ambition and failure, Johnson replaces the ancient Roman examples with modern ones and adds a background of Christian theology.

[2] *Tow'r* The Tower of London, where those accused of treason were imprisoned.

[3] *Democritus* Philosopher of ancient Greece who is occasionally called "the laughing philosopher" because of his response to the follies of humanity.

[4] *motley* Multicolored (a reference to the brightly-colored clothing worn by jesters and fools).

The robes of pleasure and the veils of woe:
All aid the farce, and all thy mirth maintain,
Whose joys are causeless, or whose griefs are vain.
Such was the scorn that filled the sage's mind,
Renewed at ev'ry glance on humankind;
How just that scorn ere yet thy voice declare,
Search every state, and canvass° every prayer. *scrutinize*
Unnumbered suppliants crowd Preferment's gate,
Athirst for wealth, and burning to be great;
Delusive Fortune hears th'incessant call,
They mount, they shine, evaporate, and fall.
On every stage the foes of peace attend,
Hate dogs their flight, and insult mocks their end.
Love ends with hope, the sinking statesman's door
Pours in the morning worshiper[1] no more;
For growing names the weekly scribbler lies,
To growing wealth the dedicator flies,
From ev'ry room descends the painted face,
That hung the bright Palladium[2] of the place,
And smoked in kitchens, or in auctions sold,
To better features yields the frame of gold;
For now no more we trace in ev'ry line
Heroic worth, benevolence divine:
The form distorted justifies the fall,
And detestation rids th'indignant wall.
But will not Britain hear the last appeal,
Sign her foes' doom, or guard her fav'rites' zeal?
Through Freedom's sons no more remonstrance rings,
Degrading nobles and controlling kings;
Our supple tribes repress their patriot throats,
And ask no questions but the price of votes;
With weekly libels and septennial ale,[3]
Their wish is full to riot and to rail.
In full-blown dignity, see Wolsey[4] stand,
Law in his voice, and fortune in his hand:
To him the church, the realm, their pow'rs consign,
Through him the rays of regal bounty shine,
Turned by his nod the stream of honor flows,
His smile alone security bestows:
Still to new heights his restless wishes tow'r,
Claim leads to claim, and pow'r advances pow'r;
Till conquest unresisted ceased to please,
And rights submitted, left him none to seize.
At length his sov'reign frowns—the train of state
Mark the keen glance, and watch the sign to hate.
Where'er he turns he meets a stranger's eye,
His suppliants scorn him, and his followers fly;
At once is lost the pride of awful state,
The golden canopy, the glitt'ring plate,
The regal palace, the luxurious board,
The liv'ried army, and the menial lord.
With age, with cares, with maladies oppressed,
He seeks the refuge of monastic rest.
Grief aids disease, remembered folly stings,
And his last sighs reproach the faith of kings.
Speak thou, whose thoughts at humble peace repine,
Shall Wolsey's wealth, with Wolsey's end be thine?
Or liv'st thou now, with safer pride content,
The wisest justice on the banks of Trent?[5]
For why did Wolsey near the steeps° of fate, *precipices*
On weak foundations raise th'enormous weight?
Why but to sink beneath misfortune's blow,
With louder ruin to the gulfs below?
What gave great Villiers to th'assassin's knife,
And fixed disease on Harley's[6] closing life?
What murdered Wentworth, and what exiled Hyde,[7]
By kings protected, and to kings allied?
What but their wish indulged in courts to shine,
And pow'r too great to keep, or to resign?
When first the college rolls receive his name,
The young enthusiast quits his ease for fame;
Through all his veins the fever of renown
Burns from the strong contagion of the gown;[8]

[1] *morning worshiper* Men of state would receive visitors and supplicants at morning receptions, or levees.

[2] *Palladium* Statue of Pallas Athena that was worshiped in Troy and which protected the city.

[3] *septennial ale* Those running for Parliament would give away free ale at the elections (usually held every seven years).

[4] *Wolsey* Lord Chancellor to Henry VIII until imprisoned for failing to obtain the King's divorce from Catherine of Aragon.

[5] *Trent* River that flows northeasterly through the center of England.

[6] *Villiers* George Villiers, first duke of Buckingham and a favorite of King James I. He was stabbed to death by an army officer in 1628; *Harley* Robert Harley, first earl of Oxford and powerful politician and statesman (1661–1724).

[7] *Wentworth* First earl of Stafford and advisor to Charles I who was executed in 1641 at the beginning of the civil war; *Hyde* First earl of Clarendon who was Lord Chancellor to Charles II but was impeached in 1667 and forced to flee to France.

[8] *gown* Scholarly robe.

O'er Bodley's dome[1] his future labors spread,
And Bacon's[2] mansion trembles o'er his head.
Are these thy views? proceed, illustrious youth,
And virtue guard thee to the throne of Truth!
Yet should thy soul indulge the gen'rous heat,
Till captive Science yields her last retreat;
Should Reason guide thee with her brightest ray,
And pour on misty Doubt resistless day;
Should no false Kindness lure to loose delight,
Nor Praise relax, nor Difficulty fright;
Should tempting Novelty thy cell refrain,° *avoid*
And Sloth effuse her opiate fumes in vain;
Should Beauty blunt on fops her fatal dart,
Nor claim the triumph of a lettered heart;
Should no disease thy torpid veins invade,
Nor Melancholy's phantoms haunt thy shade;° *spirit*
Yet hope not life from grief or danger free,
Nor think the doom of man reversed for thee:
Deign on the passing world to turn thine eyes,
And pause awhile from letters, to be wise;
There mark what ills the scholar's life assail,
Toil, envy, want, the patron, and the jail.
See nations slowly wise, and meanly just,
To buried merit raise the tardy bust.
If dreams yet flatter, once again attend,
Hear Lydiat's life, and Galileo's end.[3]
Nor deem, when learning her last prize bestows,
The glitt'ring eminence exempt from foes;
See when the vulgar 'scape, despised or awed,
Rebellion's vengeful talons seize on Laud.[4]
From meaner minds, though smaller fines content,
The plundered palace or sequestered rent;
Marked out by dangerous parts° he meets the shock, *talents*
And fatal Learning leads him to the block:
Around his tomb let Art and Genius weep,
But hear his death, ye blockheads, hear and sleep.

The festal blazes, the triumphal show,
The ravished standard, and the captive foe,
The senate's thanks, the gazette's pompous tale,
With force resistless o'er the brave prevail.
Such bribes the rapid Greek[5] o'er Asia whirled,
For such the steady Romans shook the world;
For such in distant lands the Britons shine,
And stain with blood the Danube or the Rhine;
This pow'r has praise, that virtue scarce can warm,
Till fame supplies the universal charm.
Yet Reason frowns on War's unequal game,
Where wasted nations raise a single name,
And mortgaged states their grandsires' wreaths[6] regret,
From age to age in everlasting debt;
Wreaths which at last the dear-bought right convey
To rust on medals, or on stones decay.
On what foundation stands the warrior's pride,
How just his hopes let Swedish Charles[7] decide;
A frame of adamant, a soul of fire,
No dangers fright him, and no labors tire;
O'er love, o'er fear, extends his wide domain,
Unconquered lord of pleasure and of pain;
No joys to him pacific scepters yield,
War sounds the trump, he rushes to the field;
Behold surrounding kings their pow'r combine,
And one capitulate, and one resign;[8]
Peace courts his hand, but spreads her charms in vain;
"Think nothing gained," he cries, "till nought remain,
On Moscow's walls till Gothic[9] standards fly,
And all be mine beneath the polar sky."
The march begins in military state,
And nations on his eye suspended wait;
Stern Famine guards the solitary coast,
And Winter barricades the realms of Frost;
He comes, not want and cold his course delay—
Hide, blushing Glory, hide Pultowa's[10] day:

[1] *Bodley's dome* Bodleian Library at Oxford University.

[2] [Johnson's note] There is a tradition that the study of Friar Bacon, built on an arch over the bridge, will fall when a man greater than Bacon shall pass under it. [Roger Bacon was a noted medieval philosopher, and the bridge referred to is Folly Bridge, at Oxford, which was demolished in 1779.]

[3] *Lydiat's life* The mathematician Lydiat lived a life of poverty and was imprisoned for debt; *Galileo's end* Galileo died condemned of heresy as a result of his philosophical claims.

[4] *Laud* William Laud, archbishop of Canterbury during the reign of Charles I, executed for treason in 1645.

[5] *the rapid Greek* Alexander the Great.

[6] *wreaths* I.e., victory.

[7] *Swedish Charles* Charles XII of Sweden (1682–1718), a power-hungry king who, when he was defeated by the Russians, attempted to form an alliance with the Turks. Upon his return to Sweden he invaded Norway and was killed in battle.

[8] *And one … resign* Frederick IV of Demark yielded to Charles, and Augustus II of Poland was deposed.

[9] *Gothic* Here, Swedish.

[10] *Pultowa* Location of Peter the Great's defeat of Charles in 1709.

The vanquished hero leaves his broken bands,
And shows his miseries in distant lands;
Condemned a needy supplicant to wait,
While ladies interpose, and slaves debate.
But did not Chance at length her error mend?
Did no subverted empire mark his end?
Did rival monarchs give the fatal wound?
Or hostile millions press him to the ground?
His fall was destined to a barren strand,
A petty fortress, and a dubious hand;[1]
He left the name, at which the world grew pale,
To point a moral, or adorn a tale.
All times their scenes of pompous woes afford,
From Persia's tyrant to Bavaria's lord.[2]
In gay hostility, and barb'rous pride,
With half mankind embattled at his side,
Great Xerxes comes to seize the certain prey,
And starves exhausted regions in his way;
Attendant Flattery counts his myriads o'er,
Till counted myriads soothe his pride no more;
Fresh praise is tried till madness fires his mind,
The waves he lashes, and enchains the wind;
New pow'rs are claimed, new pow'rs are still bestowed,
Till rude resistance lops the spreading god;
The daring Greeks deride the martial show,
And heap their valleys with the gaudy foe;
Th'insulted sea with humbler thoughts he gains,
A single skiff to speed his flight remains;
Th'encumbered oar scarce leaves the dreaded coast
Through purple billows and a floating host.
The bold Bavarian, in a luckless hour,
Tries the dread summits of Cesarean power,
With unexpected legions bursts away,
And sees defenseless realms receive his sway;
Short sway! fair Austria spreads her mournful charms,
The queen, the beauty, sets the world in arms;
From hill to hill the beacon's rousing blaze
Spreads wide the hope of plunder and of praise;
The fierce Croatian, and the wild Hussar,[3]
And all the sons of ravage crowd the war;
The baffled prince in honor's flattering bloom
Of hasty greatness finds the fatal doom,
His foes' derision, and his subjects' blame,
And steals to death from anguish and from shame.
Enlarge my life with multitude of days,
In health, in sickness, thus the suppliant prays;
Hides from himself his state, and shuns to know,
That life protracted is protracted woe.
Time hovers o'er, impatient to destroy,
And shuts up all the passages of joy:
In vain their gifts the bounteous seasons pour,
The fruit autumnal, and the vernal flow'r,
With listless eyes the dotard views the store,
He views, and wonders that they please no more;
Now pall the tasteless meats, and joyless wines,
And Luxury° with sighs her slave resigns. *pleasure*
Approach, ye minstrels, try the soothing strain,
Diffuse the tuneful lenitives° of pain: *palliatives*
No sounds alas would touch th'impervious ear,
Though dancing mountains witnessed Orpheus[4] near;
Nor lute nor lyre his feeble pow'rs attend,
Nor sweeter music of a virtuous friend,
But everlasting dictates crowd his tongue,
Perversely grave, or positively wrong.
The still returning tale, and ling'ring jest,
Perplex the fawning niece and pampered guest,
While growing hopes scarce awe the gathering sneer,
And scarce a legacy can bribe to hear;
The watchful guests still hint the last offense,
The daughter's petulance, the son's expense,
Improve° his heady rage with treach'rous skill, *increase*
And mold his passions till they make his will.
Unnumbered maladies his joints invade,
Lay siege to life and press the dire blockade;
But unextinguished Avarice still remains,
And dreaded losses aggravate his pains;
He turns, with anxious heart and crippled hands,
His bonds of debt, and mortgages of lands;
Or views his coffers with suspicious eyes,
Unlocks his gold, and counts it till he dies.
But grant, the virtues of a temp'rate prime

[1] *dubious hand* It was believed that Charles was shot in battle by one of his own men.

[2] *Persia's tyrant … Bavaria's lord* References to Xerxes and Charles Albert. Xerxes was the Persian king who invaded Greece using a bridge of ships to cross the Hellespont. After a storm broke up the bridge, he ordered his men to whip the wind and waves with chains. Charles Albert, Elector of Bavaria, was defeated by Maria Theresa of Austria in the War of the Austrian Succession (1740–48).

[3] *Hussar* Hungarian light cavalry.

[4] *Orpheus* Musician of Greek mythology who was able to make mountains move with his music.

Bless with an age exempt from scorn or crime;
An age that melts with unperceived decay,
And glides in modest innocence away;
Whose peaceful day Benevolence endears,
Whose night congratulating Conscience cheers;
The gen'ral favorite as the gen'ral friend:
Such age there is, and who shall wish its end?
Yet ev'n on this her load Misfortune flings,
To press the weary minutes' flagging wings:
New sorrow rises as the day returns,
A sister sickens, or a daughter mourns.
Now kindred Merit fills the sable bier,
Now lacerated Friendship claims a tear.
Year chases year, decay pursues decay,
Still drops some joy from with'ring life away;
New forms arise, and different views engage,
Superfluous lags the vet'ran[1] on the stage,
Till pitying Nature signs the last release,
And bids afflicted worth retire to peace.
But few there are whom hours like these await,
Who set unclouded in the gulfs of fate.
From Lydia's monarch[2] should the search descend,
By Solon cautioned to regard his end,
In life's last scene what prodigies surprise,
Fears of the brave, and follies of the wise?
From Marlborough's[3] eyes the streams of dotage flow,
And Swift[4] expires a driveler and a show.
The teeming° mother, anxious for her race,° *pregnant* / *offspring*
Begs for each birth the fortune of a face:
Yet Vane could tell what ills from beauty spring;
And Sedley[5] cursed the form that pleased a king.
Ye nymphs of rosy lips and radiant eyes,
Whom Pleasure keeps too busy to be wise,
Whom Joys with soft varieties invite,
By day the frolic, and the dance by night,
Who frown with vanity, who smile with art,
And ask the latest fashion of the heart,
What care, what rules your heedless charms shall save,
Each nymph your rival, and each youth your slave?
Against your fame with fondness hate combines,
The rival batters, and the lover mines.
With distant voice neglected Virtue calls,
Less heard and less, the faint remonstrance falls;
Tired with contempt, she quits the slipp'ry reign,
And Pride and Prudence take her seat in vain.
In crowd at once, where none the pass defend,
The harmless Freedom, and the private Friend.
The guardians yield, by force superior plied;
By Interest,° Prudence; and by Flattery, Pride. *self-interest*
Now beauty falls betrayed, despised, distressed,
And hissing Infamy proclaims the rest.
Where then shall Hope and Fear their objects find?
Must dull Suspense corrupt the stagnant mind?
Must helpless man, in ignorance sedate,
Roll darkling[6] down the torrent of his fate?
Must no dislike alarm, no wishes rise,
No cries attempt the mercies of the skies?
Inquirer, cease, petitions yet remain,
Which Heav'n may hear, nor deem religion vain.
Still raise for good the supplicating voice,
But leave to Heav'n the measure and the choice,
Safe in his power, whose eyes discern afar
The secret ambush of a specious prayer.
Implore his aid, in his decisions rest,
Secure whate'er he gives, he gives the best.
Yet when the sense of sacred presence fires,
And strong devotion to the skies aspires,
Pour forth thy fervors for a healthful mind,
Obedient passions, and a will resigned;
For love, which scarce collective° man can fill; *as a whole*
For patience sov'reign o'er transmuted ill;
For faith, that panting for a happier seat,
Counts death kind Nature's signal of retreat:
These goods for man the laws of Heav'n ordain,
These goods he grants, who grants the power to gain;
With these celestial wisdom calms the mind,
And makes the happiness she does not find.

—1749

[1] *vet'ran* Of life, rather than of war.

[2] *Lydia's monarch* Croesus, the wealthy sixth-century BCE king of Lydia who was cautioned by the Athenian philosopher Solon that no man should count himself happy until he reached the end of his life. Later, Croesus was overthrown by King Cyrus of Persia.

[3] *Marlborough* John Churchill, first duke of Marlborough, was a great general during the War of Spanish Succession, but he was debilitated by two strokes before his death in 1722.

[4] *Swift* Poet Jonathan Swift became senile before his death, and it is believed that following his demise his servants were bribed to put him on display and allow souvenir hunters to take hairs from his head.

[5] *Vane … Sedley* Anne Vane and Catherine Sedley were the mistresses of Frederick, prince of Wales, and James II respectively.

[6] *darkling* In the dark.

On the Death of Dr. Robert Levett[1]

Condemned to Hope's delusive mine,
As on we toil from day to day,
By sudden blasts, or slow decline,
Our social comforts drop away.

Well tried through many a varying year,
See Levett to the grave descend;
Officious,° innocent, sincere, *kind*
Of every friendless name the friend.

Yet still he fills affection's eye,
Obscurely° wise, and coarsely kind; *quietly*
Nor, lettered° arrogance, deny *scholarly*
Thy praise to merit unrefined.

When fainting nature called for aid,
And hovering Death prepared the blow,
His vigorous remedy displayed
The power of art without the show.

In misery's darkest caverns known,
His useful care was ever nigh,
Where hopeless Anguish poured his groan,
And lonely want retired to die.

No summons mocked by chill delay,
No petty gain disdained by pride,
The modest wants of every day
The toil of every day supplied.

His virtues walked their narrow round,
Nor made a pause, nor left a void;
And sure th' Eternal Master found
The single talent well employed.[2]

The busy day, the peaceful night,
Unfelt, uncounted, glided by;
His frame was firm, his powers were bright,
Though now his eightieth year was nigh.

Then with no throbbing fiery pain,
No cold gradations of decay,
Death broke at once the vital chain,
And freed his soul the nearest way.

—1783

[1] *Dr. Robert Levett* Medical practitioner who worked among London's poor. In later life he resided with Johnson, and died in 1782 at the age of 76.

[2] *single … employed* Cf. the parable of the talents (Matthew 25.14–30).

The Rambler No. 4

[ON FICTION]

Saturday, 31 March 1750

Simul et jucunda et idonea dicere vitae.
—Horace, *Ars Poetica*, line 334

And join both profit and delight in one.
—Creech

The works of fiction with which the present generation seems more particularly delighted are such as exhibit life in its true state, diversified only by accidents that daily happen in the world, and influenced by passions and qualities which are really to be found in conversing with mankind.

This kind of writing may be termed not improperly the comedy of romance, and is to be conducted nearly by the rules of comic poetry. Its province is to bring about natural events by easy means, and to keep up curiosity without the help of wonder: it is therefore precluded from the machines[3] and expedients of the heroic romance, and can neither employ giants to snatch away a lady from the nuptial rites, nor knights to bring her back from captivity; it can neither bewilder its personages in deserts, nor lodge them in imaginary castles.

I remember a remark made by Scaliger upon Pontanus,[4] that all his writings are filled with the same images; and that if you take from him his lilies and his roses, his satyrs and his dryads, he will have nothing left that can be called poetry. In like manner, almost all the fictions of the last age will vanish if you deprive them of a hermit and a wood, a battle and a shipwreck.

Why this wild strain of imagination found reception so long in polite and learned ages, it is not easy to conceive; but we cannot wonder that, while readers

[3] *machines* Unnatural agents or devices that advance the plot.

[4] *Scaliger upon Pontanus* In his *Poetics* (1561), influential Renaissance humanist Julius Caesar Scaliger criticizes the Latin poetry of Italian poet Giovanni Pontano (1426–1503).

could be procured, the authors were willing to continue it: for when a man had by practice gained some fluency of language, he had no further care than to retire to his closet,[1] let loose his invention, and heat his mind with incredibilities; a book was thus produced without fear of criticism, without the toil of study, without knowledge of nature, or acquaintance with life.

The task of our present writers is very different; it requires, together with that learning which is to be gained from books, that experience which can never be attained by solitary diligence, but must arise from general converse and accurate observation of the living world. Their performances have, as Horace expresses it, *plus oneris quantum veniae minus*, little indulgence, and therefore more difficulty.[2] They are engaged in portraits of which everyone knows the original, and can detect any deviation from exactness of resemblance. Other writings are safe, except from the malice of learning, but these are in danger from every common reader; as the slipper ill executed was censured by a shoemaker who happened to stop in his way at the Venus of Apelles.[3] But the fear of not being approved as just copiers of human manners is not the most important concern that an author of this sort ought to have before him. These books are written chiefly to the young, the ignorant, and the idle, to whom they serve as lectures of conduct and introductions into life. They are the entertainment of minds unfurnished with ideas, and therefore easily susceptible of impressions; not fixed by principles, and therefore easily following the current of fancy; not informed by experience, and consequently open to every false suggestion and partial account.

That the highest degree of reverence should be paid to youth, and that nothing indecent should be suffered to approach their eyes or ears, are precepts extorted by sense and virtue from an ancient writer,[4] by no means eminent for chastity of thought. The same kind, though not the same degree of caution, is required in everything which is laid before them, to secure them from unjust prejudices, perverse opinions, and incongruous combinations of images.

In the romances formerly written, every transaction and sentiment was so remote from all that passes among men that the reader was in very little danger of making any applications to himself; the virtues and crimes were equally beyond his sphere of activity; and he amused himself with heroes and with traitors, deliverers and persecutors, as with beings of another species, whose actions were regulated upon motives of their own, and who had neither faults nor excellencies in common with himself.

But when an adventurer is leveled with the rest of the world, and acts in such scenes of the universal drama, as may be the lot of any other man, young spectators fix their eyes upon him with closer attention, and hope by observing his behavior and success to regulate their own practices, when they shall be engaged in the like part.

For this reason these familiar histories may perhaps be made of greater use than the solemnities of professed morality, and convey the knowledge of vice and virtue with more efficacy than axioms and definitions. But if the power of example is so great as to take possession of the memory by a kind of violence, and produce effects almost without the intervention of the will, care ought to be taken that, when the choice is unrestrained, the best examples only should be exhibited; and that which is likely to operate so strongly should not be mischievous or uncertain in its effects.

The chief advantage which these fictions have over real life is that their authors are at liberty, though not to invent, yet to select objects, and to cull from the mass of mankind those individuals upon which the attention ought most to be employed; as a diamond, though it cannot be made, may be polished by art, and placed in such a situation as to display that lustre which before was buried among common stones.

It is justly considered as the greatest excellency of art to imitate nature; but it is necessary to distinguish those parts of nature which are most proper for imitation: greater care is still required in representing life, which is so often discolored by passion, or deformed by wickedness. If the world be promiscuously[5] described, I cannot see of what use it can be to read the account; or

[1] *closet* Private study.

[2] *Horace … difficulty* From *Epistles* 2.1.170.

[3] *slipper … Apelles* The fourth-century Greek painter Apelles was praised for the verisimilitude of his works. This story of a shoemaker finding fault with Venus's slipper (prompting Apelles to correct the painting) comes from the *Natural History* of Pliny the Elder.

[4] *an ancient writer* Roman satirist Juvenal, in his *Satires*, 14.1–58.

[5] *promiscuously* Indiscriminately.

why it may not be as safe to turn the eye immediately upon mankind, as upon a mirror which shows all that presents itself without discrimination.

It is therefore not a sufficient vindication of a character that it is drawn as it appears, for many characters ought never to be drawn; nor of a narrative, that the train of events is agreeable to observation and experience, for that observation which is called knowledge of the world will be found much more frequently to make men cunning than good. The purpose of these writings is surely not only to show mankind, but to provide that they may be seen hereafter with less hazard; to teach the means of avoiding the snares which are laid by Treachery for Innocence, without infusing any wish for that superiority with which the betrayer flatters his vanity; to give the power of counteracting fraud, without the temptation to practice it; to initiate youth by mock encounters in the art of necessary defense, and to increase prudence without impairing virtue.

Many writers, for the sake of following nature, so mingle good and bad qualities in their principal personages, that they are both equally conspicuous; and as we accompany them through their adventures with delight, and are led by degrees to interest ourselves in their favor, we lose the abhorrence of their faults, because they do not hinder our pleasure, or, perhaps, regard them with some kindness for being united with so much merit.

There have been men indeed splendidly wicked, whose endowments threw a brightness on their crimes, and whom scarce any villainy made perfectly detestable, because they never could be wholly divested of their excellencies; but such have been in all ages the great corrupters of the world, and their resemblance ought no more to be preserved, than the art of murdering without pain.

Some have advanced, without due attention to the consequences of this notion, that certain virtues have their correspondent faults, and therefore that to exhibit either apart is to deviate from probability. Thus men are observed by Swift to be "grateful in the same degree as they are resentful."[1] This principle, with others of the same kind, supposes man to act from a brute impulse, and pursue a certain degree of inclination, without any choice of the object; for otherwise, though it should be allowed that gratitude and resentment arise from the same constitution of the passions, it follows not that they will be equally indulged when reason is consulted; yet unless that consequence be admitted, this sagacious maxim becomes an empty sound, without any relation to practice or to life.

Nor is it evident that even the first motions[2] to these effects are always in the same proportion. For pride, which produces quickness of resentment, will obstruct gratitude by unwillingness to admit that inferiority which obligation implies; and it is very unlikely that he who cannot think he receives a favor will acknowledge or repay it.

It is of the utmost importance to mankind that positions of this tendency should be laid open and confuted; for while men consider good and evil as springing from the same root, they will spare the one for the sake of the other and, in judging, if not of others at least of themselves, will be apt to estimate their virtues by their vices. To this fatal error all those will contribute who confound the colors of right and wrong, and, instead of helping to settle their boundaries, mix them with so much art that no common mind is able to disunite them.

In narratives where historical veracity has no place, I cannot discover why there should not be exhibited the most perfect idea of virtue; of virtue not angelical, nor above probability, for what we cannot credit we shall never imitate, but the highest and purest that humanity can reach, which, exercized in such trials as the various revolutions of things shall bring upon it, may, by conquering some calamities, and enduring others, teach us what we may hope, and what we can perform. Vice, for vice is necessary to be shown, should always disgust; nor should the graces of gaiety, or the dignity of courage, be so united with it as to reconcile it to the mind. Wherever it appears, it should raise hatred by the malignity of its practices, and contempt by the meanness of its stratagems; for while it is supported by either parts or spirit, it will be seldom heartily abhorred. The Roman tyrant[3] was content to be hated, if he was but feared; and there are thousands of the readers of romances willing to be thought wicked, if they may be allowed to be wits. It is therefore to be steadily incul-

[1] *Swift ... resentful* This comment was made by Pope in the *Miscellanies* he wrote with Swift.

[2] *motions* Impulses.

[3] *The Roman tyrant* Caligula (12–43 CE), as reported by the Roman historian Suetonis in his *Lives of the Caesars.*

cated that virtue is the highest proof of understanding, and the only solid basis of greatness; and that vice is the natural consequence of narrow thoughts, that it begins in mistake, and ends in ignominy.

The Rambler No. 12

[CRUELTY OF EMPLOYERS]

Saturday, 28 April 1750

Miserum parva stipe focilat, ut pudibundos
Exercere sales inter convivia possit. ...
... Tu mitis, & acri
Asperitate carens, positoque per omnia fastu,
Inter ut aequales unus numeraris amicos,
Obsequiumque doces, & amorem quaeris amando.
— Lucan, *Carmen ad Pisonem*, lines 114–15, 117–20

Unlike the ribald whose licentious jest,
Pollutes his banquet and insults his guest;
From wealth and grandeur easy to descend,
Thou joy'st to lose the master in the friend:
We round thy board the cheerful menials see,
Gay with the smile of bland equality;
No social care the gracious lord disdains;
Love prompts to love, and rev'rence rev'rence gains.

To the Rambler

Sir,

As you seem to have devoted your labours to virtue, I cannot forbear to inform you of one species of cruelty, with which the life of a man of letters perhaps does not often make him acquainted; and which, as it seems to produce no other advantage to those that practise it than a short gratification of thoughtless vanity, may become less common when it has been once exposed in its various forms and its full magnitude.

I am the daughter of a country gentleman whose family is numerous, and whose estate, not at first sufficient to supply us with affluence, has been lately so much impaired by an unsuccessful lawsuit that all the younger children are obliged to try such means as their education affords them for procuring the necessaries of life. Distress and curiosity concurred to bring me to London, where I was received by a relation with the coldness which misfortune generally finds. A week, a long week, I lived with my cousin, before the most vigilant enquiry could procure us the least hopes of a place, in which time I was much better qualified to bear all the vexations of servitude. The first two days she was content to pity me, and only wish'd I had not been quite so well bred, but people must comply with their circumstances. This lenity, however, was soon at an end; and, for the remaining part of the week, I heard every hour of the pride of my family, the obstinacy of my father, and of people better born than myself that were common servants.

At last, on Saturday noon, she told me with very visible satisfaction that Mrs. Bombasine,[1] the great silk-mercer's lady, wanted a maid, and a fine place it would be, for there would be nothing to do but to clean my mistress's room, get up her linen, dress the young ladies, wait at tea in the morning, take care of a little miss just come from nurse, and then sit down to my needle. But madam was a woman of great spirit and would not be contradicted, and therefore I should take care, for good places were not easily to be got.

With these cautions, I waited on Madam Bombasine, of whom the first sight gave me no ravishing ideas. She was two yards round the waist, her voice was at once loud and squeaking, and her face brought to my mind the picture of the full moon. "Are you the young woman," says she, "that are come to offer yourself? It is strange when people of substance want a servant, how soon it is the town-talk. But they know they shall have a belly-full that live with me. Not like people at the other end of the town, we dine at one o'clock. But I never take anybody without a character; what friends do you come of?" I then told her that my father was a gentleman, and that we had been unfortunate.—"A great misfortune, indeed, to come to me and have three meals a-day! So your father was a gentleman, and you are a gentlewoman I suppose—such gentlewomen!" "Madam, I did not mean to claim any exemptions, I only answered your enquiry—" "Such gentlewomen! People should set their children to good trades, and keep them off the parish. Pray go to the other end of the town, there are gentlewomen, if they would pay their debts: I am sure we have lost enough by gentlewomen." Upon this, her broad face grew broader with triumph, and I was afraid she would have taken me for the

[1] *Bombasine* Twilled or corded dress material made of silk and wool.

pleasure of continuing her insult; but happily the next word was, "Pray, Mrs. Gentlewoman, troop down stairs." You may believe I obeyed her.

I returned and met with a better reception from my cousin than I expected; for while I was out, she had heard that Mrs. Standish,[1] whose husband had lately been raised from a clerk in an office to be commissioner of the excise, had taken a fine house and wanted a maid. To Mrs. Standish I went, and, after having waited six hours, was at last admitted to the top of the stairs, when she came out of her room, with two of her company. There was a smell of punch. "So, young woman, you want a place, whence do you come?" "From the country, madam." "Yes, they all come out of the country. And what brought you to town, a bastard? Where do you lodge? At the Seven-Dials? What, you never heard of the foundling house?" Upon this, they all laughed so obstreperously that I took the opportunity of sneaking off in the tumult.

I then heard of a place at an elderly lady's. She was at cards; but in two hours, I was told, she would speak to me. She asked me if I could keep an account, and ordered me to write. I wrote two lines out of some book that lay by her. She wondered what people meant, to breed up poor girls to write at that rate. "I suppose, Mrs. Flirt, if I was to see your work, it would be fine stuff! You may walk. I will not have love-letters written from my house to every young fellow in the street."

Two days after, I went on the same pursuit to Lady Lofty, dressed, as I was directed, in what little ornaments I had, because she had lately got a place at court. Upon the first sight of me, she turns to the woman that showed me in, "Is this the lady that wants a place? Pray what place would you have, miss? a maid of honour's place? Servants now a-days!" "Madam, I heard you wanted—" "Wanted what? Somebody finer than myself! A pretty servant indeed—I should be afraid to speak to her—I suppose, Mrs. Minx, these fine hands cannot bear wetting—A servant indeed! Pray move off—I am resolved to be the head person in this house—You are ready dressed, the taverns will be open."

I went to enquire for the next place in a clean linen gown, and heard the servant tell his lady, there was a young woman, but he saw she would not do. I was brought up, however. "Are you the trollop that has the impudence to come for my place? What, you have hired that nasty gown and are come to steal a better." "Madam, I have another, but being obliged to walk—" "Then these are your manners, with your blushes and your courtesies, to come to me in your worst gown." "Madam, give me leave to wait upon you in my other." "Wait on me, you saucy slut! Then you are sure of coming—I could not let such a drab come near me—Here, you girl that came up with her, have you touched her? If you have, wash your hands before you dress me.—Such trollops! Get you down. What, whimpering? Pray walk."

I went away with tears; for my cousin had lost all patience. However she told me that, having a respect for my relations, she was willing to keep me out of the street, and would let me have another week.

The first day of this week I saw two places. At one I was asked where I had lived, and, upon my answer, was told by the lady that people should qualify themselves in ordinary places, for she should never have done if she was to follow girls about. At the other house I was a smirking hussy, and that sweet face I might make money of—For her part, it was a rule with her never to take any creature that thought herself handsome.

The three next days were spent in Lady Bluff's entry, where I waited six hours every day for the pleasure of seeing the servants peep at me and go away laughing—"Madam will stretch her small shanks in the entry; she will know the house again"—At sun-set the two first days I was told, that my lady would see me to-morrow; and on the third, that her woman stayed.

My week was now near its end, and I had no hopes of a place. My relation, who always laid upon me the blame of every miscarriage, told me that I must learn to humble myself, and that all great ladies had particular ways; that if I went on in that manner, she could not tell who would keep me; she had known many, that had refused places, sell their clothes and beg in the streets.

It was to no purpose that the refusal was declared by me to be never on my side; I was reasoning against interest, and against stupidity; and therefore I comforted myself with the hope of succeeding better in my next attempt, and went to Mrs. Courtly, a very fine lady who had routs[2] at her house and saw the best company in town.

[1] *Standish* Inkstand.

[2] *routs* Fashionable evening parties or receptions.

I had not waited two hours before I was called up and found Mr. Courtly and his lady at piquet, in the height of good humour. This I looked on as a favourable sign, and stood at the lower end of the room in expectation of the common questions. At last Mr. Courtly called out, after a whisper, "Stand facing the light, that one may see you." I changed my place, and blushed. They frequently turned their eyes upon me, and seemed to discover many subjects of merriment; for at every look they whispered, and laughed with the most violent agitations of delight. At last Mr. Courtly cried out, "Is that colour your own, child?" "Yes," says the lady, "if she has not robbed the kitchen hearth." This was so happy a conceit that it renewed the storm of laughter, and they threw down their cards in hopes of better sport. The lady then called me to her, and began with an affected gravity to enquire what I could do. "But first, turn about, and let us see your fine shape; Well, what are you fit for, Mrs. Mum?[1] You would find your tongue, I suppose, in the kitchen." "No, no," says Mr. Courtly, "the girl's a good girl yet, but I am afraid a brisk young fellow, with fine tags on his shoulder—Come, child, hold up your head; what? you have stole nothing—" "Not yet," says the lady, "but she hopes to steal your heart quickly." Here was a laugh of happiness and triumph, prolonged by the confusion which I could no longer repress. At last the lady recollected herself: "Stole? no—but if I had her, I should watch her; for that downcast eye—Why cannot you look people in the face?" "Steal?" says her husband, "she would steal nothing but, perhaps, a few ribbands before they were left off by her lady." "Sir," answered I, "why should you, by supposing me a thief, insult one from whom you had received no injury?" "Insult," says the lady; "are you come here to be a servant, you saucy baggage, and talk of insulting? What will this world come to, if a gentleman may not jest with a servant? Well, such servants! pray be gone, and see when you will have the honour to be so insulted again. Servants insulted—a fine time. Insulted! Get down stairs, you slut, or the footman shall insult you."

The last day of the last week was now coming, and my kind cousin talked of sending me down in the wagon to preserve me from bad courses. But in the morning she came and told me that she had one trial more for me; Euphemia wanted a maid, and perhaps I might do for her; for, like me, she must fall her crest,[2] being forced to lay down her chariot upon the loss of half her fortune by bad securities, and, with her way of giving her money to everybody that pretended to want it, she could have little beforehand; therefore I might serve her; for, with all her fine sense, she must not pretend to be nice.[3]

I went immediately, and met at the door a young gentlewoman who told me she had herself been hired that morning, but that she was ordered to bring any that offered up stairs. I was accordingly introduced to Euphemia, who, when I came in, laid down her book, and told me, that she sent for me not to gratify an idle curiosity, but lest my disappointment might be made still more grating by incivility; that she was in pain to deny anything, much more what was no favour; that she saw nothing in my appearance which did not make her wish for my company; but that another, whose claims might perhaps be equal, had come before me. The thought of being so near to such a place, and missing it, brought tears into my eyes, and my sobs hindered me from returning my acknowledgments. She rose up confused, and supposing by my concern that I was distressed, placed me by her, and made me tell her my story: which when she had heard, she put two guineas in my hand, ordering me to lodge near her, and make use of her table till she could provide for me. I am now under her protection, and know not how to shew my gratitude better than by giving this account to the Rambler.

—Zosima

The Rambler No. 60

[ON BIOGRAPHY]

Saturday, 13 October 1750

Quid sit pulchrum, quid turpe, quid utile, quid non,
Plenius et melius Chrysippo et Crantore dicit.

—Horace, *Epistles*, 1.2.3–4

Whose works the beautiful and base contain;
Of vice and virtue more instructive rules,

[1] *Mum* I.e., silent.

[2] *fall her crest* Lower her pride.

[3] *nice* Particular, fastidious.

Than all the sober sages of the schools.
—Francis

All joy or sorrow for the happiness or calamities of others is produced by an act of the imagination that realizes the event however fictitious, or approximates it[1] however remote, by placing us, for a time, in the condition of him whose fortune we contemplate; so that we feel, while the deception lasts, whatever motions would be excited by the same good or evil happening to ourselves.

Our passions are therefore more strongly moved, in proportion as we can more readily adopt the pains or pleasures proposed to our minds, by recognizing them as once our own, or considering them as naturally incident to our state of life. It is not easy for the most artful writer to give us an interest in happiness or misery which we think ourselves never likely to feel, and with which we have never yet been made acquainted. Histories of the downfall of kingdoms and revolutions of empires are read with great tranquility; the imperial tragedy pleases common auditors only by its pomp of ornament and grandeur of ideas; and the man whose faculties have been engrossed by business, and whose heart never fluttered but at the rise or fall of stocks, wonders how the attention can be seized, or the affections agitated, by a tale of love.

Those parallel circumstances and kindred images to which we readily conform our minds are, above all other writings, to be found in narratives of the lives of particular persons; and therefore no species of writing seems more worthy of cultivation than biography, since none can be more delightful or more useful, none can more certainly enchain the heart by irresistible interest, or more widely diffuse instruction to every diversity of condition.

The general and rapid narratives of history, which involve a thousand fortunes in the business of a day and complicate innumerable incidents in one great transaction, afford few lessons applicable to private life, which derives its comforts and its wretchedness from the right or wrong management of things which nothing but their frequency makes considerable, *Parva, si non fiant quotidie*,[2] says Pliny, and which can have no place in those relations[3] which never descend below the consultation of senates, the motions of armies, and the schemes of conspirators.

I have often thought that there has rarely passed a life of which a judicious and faithful narrative would not be useful. For, not only every man has, in the mighty mass of the world, great numbers in the same condition with himself, to whom his mistakes and miscarriages, escapes and expedients, would be of immediate and apparent use; but there is such an uniformity in the state of man, considered apart from adventitious and separable decorations and disguises, that there is scarce any possibility of good or ill, but is common to humankind. A great part of the time of those who are placed at the greatest distance by fortune, or by temper, must unavoidably pass in the same manner; and though, when the claims of nature are satisfied, caprice, and vanity, and accident begin to produce discriminations and peculiarities, yet the eye is not very heedful or quick which cannot discover the same causes still terminating their influence in the same effects, though sometimes accelerated, sometimes retarded, or perplexed by multiplied combinations. We are all prompted by the same motives, all deceived by the same fallacies, all animated by hope, obstructed by danger, entangled by desire, and seduced by pleasure.

It is frequently objected to relations of particular lives that they are not distinguished by any striking or wonderful vicissitudes. The scholar who passed his life among his books, the merchant who conducted only his own affairs, the priest whose sphere of action was not extended beyond that of his duty, are considered as no proper objects of public regard, however they might have excelled in their several stations, whatever might have been their learning, integrity, and piety. But this notion arises from false measures of excellence and dignity and must be eradicated by considering that, in the esteem of uncorrupted reason, what is of most use is of most value.

It is, indeed, not improper to take honest advantages of prejudice, and to gain attention by a celebrated name; but the business of the biographer is often to pass

[1] *approximates it* Brings it near.

[2] *Parva … quotidie* Latin: "Small matters, if they did not occur every day" (Pliny the Younger, *Epistles* 3.1).

[3] *relations* Narratives.

slightly over those performances and incidents which produce vulgar greatness, to lead the thoughts into domestic privacies and display the minute details of daily life, where exterior appendages are cast aside and men excel each other only by prudence and by virtue. The account of Thuanus[1] is, with great propriety, said by its author to have been written that it might lay open to posterity the private and familiar character of that man, *cuius ingenium et candorem ex ipsius scriptis sunt olim semper miraturi*,[2] whose candor and genius will to the end of time be by his writings preserved in admiration.

There are many invisible circumstances which, whether we read as inquirers after natural or moral knowledge, whether we intend to enlarge our science[3] or increase our virtue, are more important than public occurrences. Thus Sallust,[4] the great master of nature, has not forgot, in his account of Catiline, to remark that "his walk was now quick, and again slow," as an indication of a mind revolving something with violent commotion. Thus the story of Melancthon[5] affords a striking lecture on the value of time by informing us that when he made an appointment, he expected not only the hour, but the minute to be fixed, that the day might not run out in the idleness of suspense; and all the plans and enterprises of De Witt[6] are now of less importance to the world than that part of his personal character which represents him as "careful of his health, and negligent of his life."

But biography has often been allotted to writers who seem very little acquainted with the nature of their task, or very negligent about the performance. They rarely afford any other account than might be collected from public papers, but imagine themselves writing a life when they exhibit a chronological series of actions or preferments; and so little regard the manners or behavior of their heroes that more knowledge may be gained of a man's real character by a short conversation with one of his servants than from a formal and studied narrative, begun with his pedigree and ended with his funeral.

If now and then they condescend to inform the world of particular facts, they are not always so happy as to select the most important. I know not well what advantage posterity can receive from the only circumstance by which Tickell[7] has distinguished Addison from the rest of mankind, the irregularity of his pulse: nor can I think myself overpaid for the time spent in reading the life of Malherb,[8] by being enabled to relate, after the learned biographer, that Malherb had two predominant opinions: one, that the looseness of a single woman might destroy all her boast of ancient descent; the other, that the French beggars made use very improperly and barbarously of the phrase "noble gentleman," because either word included the sense of both.

There are, indeed, some natural reasons why these narratives are often written by such as were not likely to give much instruction or delight, and why most accounts of particular persons are barren and useless. If a life be delayed till interest and envy are at an end, we may hope for impartiality, but must expect little intelligence; for the incidents which give excellence to biography are of a volatile and evanescent kind, such as soon escape the memory and are rarely transmitted by tradition. We know how few can portray a living acquaintance, except by his most prominent and observable particularities and the grosser features of his mind; and it may be easily imagined how much of this little knowledge may be lost in imparting it, and how soon a succession of copies will lose all resemblance of the original.

If the biographer writes from personal knowledge, and makes haste to gratify the public curiosity, there is danger lest his interest, his fear, his gratitude, or his tenderness overpower his fidelity and tempt him to

---

[1] *The account of Thuanus* Nicolas Rigout's commentary on French historian Jacques-Auguste de Thou's *History of His Own Time* (1604–20).

[2] *cuius … miraturi* Johnson translates the Latin in the words that follow.

[3] *science* Knowledge.

[4] *Sallust* First-century BCE Roman historian who wrote a history of Roman politician Catiline's conspiracy against the Republic.

[5] *Melancthon* Protestant theologian (1497–1560), a biography of whom was written by Joachim Camerarius.

[6] *De Witt* Famous Dutch statesman (1625–72). The quotation following is from Sir William Temple's "Essay upon the Cure of the Gout" (1680).

[7] *Tickell* Thomas Tickell's life of the essayist Joseph Addison was published in 1721.

[8] *Malherb* François de Malherbe (1555–1628), French poet whose biography was written by his friend the Marquis de Racan and published in 1651.

conceal, if not to invent. There are many who think it an act of piety to hide the faults or failings of their friends, even when they can no longer suffer by their detection; we therefore see whole ranks of characters adorned with uniform panegyric, and not to be known from one another, but by extrinsic and casual circumstances. "Let me remember," says Hale, "when I find myself inclined to pity a criminal, that there is likewise a pity due to the country."[1] If we owe regard to the memory of the dead, there is yet more respect to be paid to knowledge, to virtue, and to truth.

The Rambler No. 155

[On Becoming Acquainted with Our Real Characters]

Tuesday, 10 September 1751

Steriles transmisimus annos,
Haec aevi mihi prima dies, haec limina vitae.
—Statins, *Silvae*, 4.2.12-13

Our barren years are past;
Be this of life the first, of sloth the last.
—Elphinston

No weakness of the human mind has more frequently incurred animadversion than the negligence with which men overlook their own faults, however flagrant, and the easiness with which they pardon them, however frequently repeated.

It seems generally believed that, as the eye cannot see itself, the mind has no faculties by which it can contemplate its own state, and that therefore we have not means of becoming acquainted with our real characters; an opinion which, like innumerable other postulates, an enquirer finds himself inclined to admit upon very little evidence because it affords a ready solution of many difficulties. It will explain why the greatest abilities frequently fail to promote the happiness of those who possess them; why those who can distinguish with the utmost nicety the boundaries of vice and virtue suffer them to be confounded in their own conduct; why the active and vigilant resign their affairs implicitly to the management of others; and why the cautious and fearful make hourly approaches towards ruin, without one sigh of solicitude or struggle for escape.

When a position teems thus with commodious consequences, who can without regret confess it to be false? Yet it is certain that declaimers have indulged a disposition to describe the dominion of the passions as extended beyond the limits that nature assigned. Self-love is often rather arrogant than blind; it does not hide our faults from ourselves, but persuades us that they escape the notice of others, and disposes us to resent censures lest we should confess them to be just. We are secretly conscious of defects and vices which we hope to conceal from the public eye, and please ourselves with innumerable impostures by which, in reality, nobody is deceived.

In proof of the dimness of our internal sight, or the general inability of man to determine rightly concerning his own character, it is common to urge the success of the most absurd and incredible flattery, and the resentment always raised by advice, however soft, benevolent, and reasonable. But flattery, if its operation be nearly examined, will be found to owe its acceptance not to our ignorance but knowledge of our failures, and to delight us rather as it consoles our wants than displays our possessions. He that shall solicit the favour of his patron by praising him for qualities which he can find in himself will be defeated by the more daring panegyrist who enriches him with adscititious[2] excellence. Just praise is only a debt, but flattery is a present. The acknowledgement of those virtues on which conscience congratulates us is a tribute that we can at any time exact with confidence, but the celebration of those which we only feign, or desire without any vigorous endeavours to attain them, is received as a confession of sovereignty over regions never conquered, as a favourable decision of disputable claims, and is more welcome as it is more gratuitous.

Advice is offensive, not because it lays us open to unexpected regret, or convicts us of any fault which had escaped our notice, but because it shows us that we are known to others as well as to ourselves; and the officious monitor is persecuted with hatred, not because his accusation is false, but because he assumes that superior-

[1] *Let … country* From *Life and Death of Sir Matthew Hale* (1682), by Gilbert Burnet.

[2] *adscititious* In his *Dictionary*, Johnson defines this as, "taken in to complete something else, though originally extrinsic; supplemental; additional."

ity which we are not willing to grant him, and has dared to detect what we desired to conceal.

For this reason advice is commonly ineffectual. If those who follow the call of their desires without enquiry whither they are going had deviated ignorantly from the paths of wisdom and were rushing upon dangers unforeseen, they would readily listen to information that recalls them from their errors, and catch the first alarm by which destruction or infamy is denounced. Few that wander in the wrong way mistake it for the right; they only find it more smooth and flowery, and indulge their own choice rather than approve it: therefore few are persuaded to quit it by admonition or reproof, since it impresses no new conviction, nor confers any powers of action or resistance. He that is gravely informed how soon profusion will annihilate his fortune hears with little advantage what he knew before, and catches at the next occasion of expence, because advice has no force to suppress his vanity. He that is told how certainly intemperance will hurry him to the grave runs with his usual speed to a new course of luxury, because his reason is not invigorated, nor his appetite weakened.

The mischief of flattery is not that it persuades any man that he is what he is not, but that it suppresses the influence of honest ambition by raising an opinion that honour may be gained without the toil of merit; and the benefit of advice arises commonly, not from any new light imparted to the mind, but from the discovery which it affords of the public suffrages. He that could withstand conscience is frighted at infamy, and shame prevails when reason was defeated.

As we all know our own faults, and know them commonly with many aggravations which human perspicacity cannot discover, there is, perhaps, no man, however hardened by impudence or dissipated by levity, sheltered by hypocrisy, or blasted by disgrace, who does not intend some time to review his conduct, and to regulate the remainder of his life by the laws of virtue. New temptations indeed attack him, new invitations are offered by pleasure and interest, and the hour of reformation is always delayed; every delay gives vice another opportunity of fortifying itself by habit; and the change of manners, though sincerely intended and rationally planned, is referred to the time when some craving passion shall be fully gratified, or some powerful allurement cease its importunity.

Thus procrastination is accumulated on procrastination, and one impediment succeeds another, till age shatters our resolution, or death intercepts the project of amendment. Such is often the end of salutary purposes, after they have long delighted the imagination and appeased that disquiet which every mind feels from known misconduct, when the attention is not diverted by business or by pleasure.

Nothing surely can be more unworthy of a reasonable nature than to continue in a state so opposite to real happiness as that all the peace of solitude and felicity of meditation must arise from resolutions of forsaking it. Yet the world will often afford examples of men who pass months and years in a continual war with their own convictions, and are daily dragged by habit or betrayed by passion into practices which they closed and opened their eyes with purposes to avoid; purposes which, though settled on conviction, the first impulse of momentary desire totally overthrows.

The influence of custom is indeed such that to conquer it will require the utmost efforts of fortitude and virtue, nor can I think any man more worthy of veneration and renown than those who have burst the shackles of habitual vice. This victory, however, has different degrees of glory as of difficulty; it is more heroic as the objects of guilty gratification are more familiar, and the recurrence of solicitation more frequent. He that, from experience of the folly of ambition, resigns his offices, may set himself free at once from temptation to squander his life in courts, because he cannot regain his former station. He who is enslaved by an amorous passion may quit his tyrant in disgust, and absence will without the help of reason overcome by degrees the desire of returning. But those appetites to which every place affords their proper object, and which require no preparatory measures or gradual advances, are more tenaciously adhesive; the wish is so near the enjoyment that compliance often precedes consideration, and before the powers of reason can be summoned, the time for employing them is past.

Indolence is therefore one of the vices from which those whom it once infects are seldom reformed. Every other species of luxury operates upon some appetite that is quickly satiated, and requires some concurrence of art or accident which every place will not supply; but the desire of ease acts equally at all hours, and the longer it is indulged is the more increased. To do nothing is in every man's power; we can never want an opportunity of omitting duties. The lapse to indolence is soft and imperceptible because it is only a mere cessation of activity; but the return to diligence is difficult because it implies a change from rest to motion, from privation to reality.

Facilis descensus Averni:
Noctes atque dies patet atri janua Ditis:
Sed revocare gradum, superasque evadere ad auras,
Hoc opus, hic labor est.
—*Aeneid*, 6.126–29

The gates of Hell are open night and day;
Smooth the descent, and easy is the way:
But, to return, and view the cheerful skies;
In this, the task and mighty labour lies.
—Dryden

Of this vice, as of all others, every man who indulges it is conscious; we all know our own state, if we could be induced to consider it; and it might perhaps be useful to the conquest of all these ensnarers of the mind if at certain stated days life was reviewed. Many things necessary are omitted because we vainly imagine that they may be always performed, and what cannot be done without pain will for ever be delayed if the time of doing it be left unsettled. No corruption is great but by long negligence, which can scarcely prevail in a mind regularly and frequently awakened by periodical remorse. He that thus breaks his life into parts will find in himself a desire to distinguish every stage of his existence by some improvement, and delight himself with the approach of the day of recollection, as of the time which is to begin a new series of virtue and felicity.

The Idler No. 26[1]

[BETTY BROOM]

Saturday, 14 October 1758

Mr. Idler,

I never thought that I should write anything to be printed; but having lately seen your first essay, which was sent down into the kitchen with a great bundle of gazettes and useless papers, I find that you are willing to admit any correspondent, and therefore hope you will not reject me. If you publish my letter, it may encourage others in the same condition with myself to tell their stories, which may be perhaps as useful as those of great ladies.

I am a poor girl. I was bred in the country at a charity school maintained by the contributions of wealthy neighbours. The ladies our patronesses visited us from time to time, examined how we were taught, and saw that our clothes were clean. We lived happily enough, and were instructed to be thankful to those at whose cost we were educated. I was always the favourite of my mistress; she used to call me to read and show my copybook to all strangers, who never dismissed me without commendation, and very seldom without a shilling.

At last the chief of our subscribers, having passed a winter in London, came down full of an opinion new and strange to the whole country. She held it little less than criminal to teach poor girls to read and write. They who are born to poverty, she said, are born to ignorance, and will work the harder the less they know. She told her friends that London was in confusion by the insolence of servants, that scarcely a wench was to be got "for all work," since education had made such numbers of fine ladies that nobody would now accept a lower title than that of a waiting maid, or something that might qualify her to wear laced shoes and long ruffles and to sit at work in the parlour window. But she was resolved, for her part, to spoil no more girls; those who were to live by their hands should neither read nor write out of her pocket; the world was bad enough already, and she would have no part in making it worse.

She was for a short time warmly opposed; but she persevered in her notions, and withdrew her subscrip-

[1] *Idler No. 26* In his *Life of Johnson*, Boswell claims that this story of Betty Broom is based on a tale of a charity-school student recounted to Johnson by a friend, Mrs. Ann Hedges Gardiner.

tion. Few listen without a desire of conviction to those who advise them to spare their money. Her example and her arguments gained ground daily, and in less than a year the whole parish was convinced that the nation would be ruined if the children of the poor were taught to read and write.

Our school was now dissolved; my mistress kissed me when we parted and told me that, being old and helpless, she could not assist me, advised me to seek a service, and charged me not to forget what I had learned.

My reputation for scholarship, which had hitherto recommended me to favour, was, by the adherents to the new opinion, considered as a crime; and when I offered myself to any mistress, I had no other answer than, "Sure, child, you would not work; hard work is not fit for a penwoman; a scrubbing-brush would spoil your hand, child!"

I could not live at home; and while I was considering to what I should betake me, one of the girls, who had gone from our school to London, came down in a silk gown and told her acquaintance how well she lived, what fine things she saw, and what great wages she received. I resolved to try my fortune, and took my passage in the next week's wagon to London. I had no snares laid for me at my arrival, but came safe to a sister of my mistress, who undertook to get me a place. She knew only the families of mean tradesmen; and I, having no high opinion of my own qualifications, was willing to accept the first offer.

My first mistress was wife of a working watchmaker, who earned more than was sufficient to keep his family in decency and plenty, but it was their constant practice to hire a chaise[1] on Sunday, and spend half the wages of the week on Richmond Hill;[2] of Monday he commonly lay half in bed, and spent the other half in merriment; Tuesday and Wednesday consumed the rest of his money; and three days every week were passed in extremity of want by us who were left at home, while my master lived on trust at an alehouse. You may be sure that of the sufferers the maid suffered most, and I left them after three months rather than be starved.

I was then maid to a hatter's wife. There was no want to be dreaded, for they lived in perpetual luxury. My mistress was a diligent woman, and rose early in the morning to set the journeymen to work; my master was a man much beloved by his neighbours, and sat at one club or other every night. I was obliged to wait on my master at night, and on my mistress in the morning. He seldom came home before two, and she rose at five. I could no more live without sleep than without food, and therefore entreated them to look out for another servant.

My next removal was to a linen draper's, who had six children. My mistress, when I first entered the house, informed me that I must never contradict the children, nor suffer them to cry. I had no desire to offend, and readily promised to do my best. But when I gave them their breakfast I could not help all first; when I was playing with one in my lap, I was forced to keep the rest in expectation. That which was not gratified always resented the injury with a loud outcry, which put my mistress in a fury at me, and procured sugar plums to the child. I could not keep six children quiet who were bribed to be clamorous, and was therefore dismissed as a girl honest, but not good-natured.

I then lived with a couple that kept a petty shop of remnants and cheap linen. I was qualified to make a bill, or keep a book, and being therefore often called, at a busy time, to serve the customers, expected that I should now be happy in proportion as I was useful. But my mistress appropriated every day part of the profit to some private use, and, as she grew bolder in her theft, at last deducted such sums that my master began to wonder how he sold so much and gained so little. She pretended to assist his enquiries and began, very gravely, to hope that "Betty was honest, and yet those sharp girls were apt to be light fingered." You will believe that I did not stay there much longer.

The rest of my story I will tell you in another letter, and only beg to be informed, in some paper, for which of my places, except perhaps the last, I was disqualified by my skill in reading and writing.

I am, Sir,

Your very humble servant,

Betty Broom

---

[1] *chaise* Carriage for traveling.

[2] *Richmond Hill* Fashionable area of London located near the banks of the Thames.

The Idler No. 29

[BETTY BROOM, CONT.]

Saturday, 4 November 1758

To The Idler

Sir,

I have often observed that friends are lost by discontinuance of intercourse without any offence on either part, and have long known that it is more dangerous to be forgotten than to be blamed; I therefore make haste to send you the rest of my story, lest by the delay of another fortnight the name of Betty Broom might be no longer remembered by you or your readers.

Having left the last place in haste to avoid the charge or the suspicion of theft, I had not secured another service, and was forced to take a lodging in a back street. I had now got good clothes. The woman who lived in the garret opposite to mine was very officious, and offered to take care of my room and clean it while I went round to my acquaintance to enquire for a mistress. I knew not why she was so kind, nor how I could recompense her, but in a few days I missed some of my linen, went to another lodging, and resolved not to have another friend in the next garret.

In six weeks I became under-maid at the house of a mercer[1] in Cornhill, whose son was his apprentice. The young gentleman used to sit late at the tavern, without the knowledge of his father, and I was ordered by my mistress to let him in silently to his bed under the counter, and to be very careful to take away his candle. The hours which I was obliged to watch, whilst the rest of the family was in bed, I considered as supernumerary, and having no business assigned for them, thought myself at liberty to spend them my own way: I kept myself awake with a book, and for some time liked my state the better for this opportunity of reading. At last, the upper-maid found my book and showed it to my mistress, who told me that wenches like me might spend their time better; that she never knew any of the readers that had good designs in their heads; that she could always find something else to do with her time than to puzzle over books; and did not like that such a fine lady should sit up for her young master.

This was the first time that I found it thought criminal or dangerous to know how to read. I was dismissed decently, lest I should tell tales, and had a small gratuity above my wages.

I then lived with a gentlewoman of a small fortune. This was the only happy part of my life; my mistress, for whom public diversions were too expensive, spent her time with books, and was pleased to find a maid who could partake her amusements. I rose early in the morning that I might have time in the afternoon to read or listen, and was suffered to tell my opinion or express my delight. Thus fifteen months stole away, in which I did not repine that I was born to servitude. But a burning fever seized my mistress, of whom I shall say no more than that her servant wept upon her grave.

I had lived in a kind of luxury, which made me very unfit for another place, and was rather too delicate for the conversation of a kitchen; so that when I was hired in the family of an East India director, my behaviour was so different, as they said, from that of a common servant that they concluded me a gentlewoman in disguise and turned me out in three weeks on suspicion of some design which they could not comprehend.

I then fled for refuge to the other end of the town, where I hoped to find no obstruction from my new accomplishments, and was hired under the housekeeper in a splendid family. Here I was too wise for the maids, and too nice for the footmen; yet I might have lived on without much uneasiness had not my mistress, the housekeeper, who used to employ me in buying necessaries for the family, found a bill which I had made of one day's expences. I suppose it did not quite agree with her own book, for she fiercely declared her resolution that there should be no pen and ink in that kitchen but her own.

She had the justice, or the prudence, not to injure my reputation; and I was easily admitted into another house in the neighbourhood, where my business was to sweep the rooms and make the beds. Here I was, for some time, the favourite of Mrs. Simper, my lady's woman, who could not bear the vulgar girls and was happy in the attendance of a young woman of some education. Mrs. Simper loved a novel, though she could not read hard words, and therefore when her lady was abroad we always laid hold on her books. At last, my abilities became so much celebrated that the house-

---

[1] *mercer* Dealer in textile fabrics.

steward used to employ me in keeping his accounts. Mrs. Simper then found out that my sauciness was grown to such a height that nobody could endure it, and told my lady that there never had been a room well swept since Betty Broom came into the house.

I was then hired by a consumptive lady, who wanted a maid that could read and write. I attended her four years, and though she was never pleased, yet when I declared my resolution to leave her she burst into tears and told me that I must bear the peevishness of a sick-bed, and I should find myself remembered in her will. I complied, and a codicil was added in my favour; but in less than a week, when I set her gruel before her I laid the spoon on the left side, and she threw her will into the fire. In two days she made another, which she burnt in the same manner because she could not eat her chicken. A third was made and destroyed because she heard a mouse within the wainscot and was sure that I should suffer her to be carried away alive. After this I was for some time out of favour, but as her illness grew upon her, resentment and sullenness gave way to kinder sentiments. She died and left me five hundred pounds; with this fortune I am going to settle in my native parish, where I resolve to spend some hours every day in teaching poor girls to read and write.

I am, Sir,

Your humble servant,

Betty Broom

The Idler No. 31

[ON IDLENESS]

Saturday, 18 November 1758

Many moralists have remarked that pride has, of all human vices, the widest dominion, appears in the greatest multiplicity of forms, and lies hid under the greatest variety of disguises; of disguises, which, like the moon's "veil of brightness," are both its "luster and its shade,"[1] and betray it to others, though they hide it from ourselves.

It is not my intention to degrade pride from this pre-eminence of mischief, yet I know not whether idleness may not maintain a very doubtful and obstinate competition.

There are some that profess idleness in its full dignity, who call themselves the Idle, as Busiris in the play "calls himself the Proud";[2] who boast that they do nothing, and thank their stars that they have nothing to do; who sleep every night till they can sleep no longer, and rise only that exercise may enable them to sleep again; who prolong the reign of darkness by double curtains, and never see the sun but to "tell him how they hate his beams";[3] whose whole labor is to vary the postures of indulgence, and whose day differs from their night but as a couch or chair differs from a bed.

These are the true and open votaries of idleness, for whom she weaves the garlands of poppies, and into whose cup she pours the waters of oblivion; who exist in a state of unruffled stupidity,[4] forgetting and forgotten; who have long ceased to live, and at whose death the survivors can only say that they have ceased to breathe.

But idleness predominates in many lives where it is not suspected, for being a vice which terminates in itself, it may be enjoyed without injury to others, and is therefore not watched like fraud, which endangers property, or like pride, which naturally seeks its gratifications in another's inferiority. Idleness is a silent and peaceful quality that neither raises envy by ostentation, nor hatred by opposition; and therefore nobody is busy to censure or detect it.

As pride sometimes is hid under humility, idleness is often covered by turbulence and hurry. He that neglects his known duty and real employment, naturally endeavors to crowd his mind with something that may bar out the remembrance of his own folly, and does any thing but what he ought to do with eager diligence, that he may keep himself in his own favor.

Some are always in a state of preparation, occupied in previous measures, forming plans, accumulating materials, and providing for the main affair. These are certainly under the secret power of idleness. Nothing is to be expected from the workman whose tools are forever to be sought. I was once told by a great master that no man ever excelled in painting who was emi-

[1] *veil ... shade* From Samuel Butler's *Hudibras* (1663–78), 2.1.907–08.

[2] *Busiris ... Proud* From the play *Busiris* (1719), 1.1.13, by Edward Young.

[3] *tell ... beams* Satan in Milton's *Paradise Lost*, 4.37.

[4] *stupidity* Stupor.

nently curious[1] about pencils[2] and colors.

There are others to whom idleness dictates another expedient, by which life may be passed unprofitably away without the tediousness of many vacant hours. The art is to fill the day with petty business, to have always something in hand which may raise curiosity, but not solicitude, and keep the mind in a state of action, but not of labor.

This art has for many years been practiced by my old friend Sober,[3] with wonderful success. Sober is a man of strong desires and quick imagination, so exactly balanced by the love of ease that they can seldom stimulate him to any difficult undertaking; they have, however, so much power that they will not suffer him to lie quite at rest, and though they do not make him sufficiently useful to others, they make him at least weary of himself.

Mr. Sober's chief pleasure is conversation; there is no end of his talk or his attention; to speak or to hear is equally pleasing; for he still fancies that he is teaching or learning something, and is free for the time from his own reproaches.

But there is one time at night when he must go home, that his friends may sleep; and another time in the morning, when all the world agrees to shut out interruption. These are the moments of which poor Sober trembles at the thought. But the misery of these tiresome intervals he has many means of alleviating. He has persuaded himself that the manual arts are undeservedly overlooked; he has observed in many trades the effects of close thought and just ratiocination. From speculation he proceeded to practice, and supplied himself with the tools of a carpenter, with which he mended his coal-box very successfully, and which he still continues to employ, as he finds occasion.

He has attempted at other times the crafts of the shoemaker, tinman, plumber, and potter; in all these arts he has failed, and resolves to qualify himself for them by better information. But his daily amusement is chemistry. He has a small furnace, which he employs in distillation, and which has long been the solace of his life. He draws oils and waters, and essences and spirits, which he knows to be of no use; sits and counts the drops as they come from his retort, and forgets that, while a drop is falling, a moment flies away.

Poor Sober! I have often teased him with reproof, and he has often promised reformation; for no man is so much open to conviction as the idler, but there is none on whom it operates so little. What will be the effect of this paper I know not; perhaps he will read it and laugh, and light the fire in his furnace; but my hope is that he will quit his trifles and betake himself to rational and useful diligence.

The Idler No. 49

[WILL MARVEL]

Saturday, 24 March 1759

I supped three nights ago with my friend Will Marvel. His affairs obliged him lately to take a journey into Devonshire, from which he has just returned. He knows me to be a very patient hearer, and was glad of my company, as it gave him an opportunity of disburthening himself by a minute relation of the casualties of his expedition.

Will is not one of those who go out and return with nothing to tell. He has a story of his travels, which will strike a homebred citizen with horror, and has in ten days suffered so often the extremes of terror and joy that he is in doubt whether he shall ever again expose either his body or mind to such danger and fatigue.

When he left London the morning was bright, and a fair day was promised. But Will is born to struggle with difficulties. That happened to him which has sometimes, perhaps, happened to others. Before he had gone more than ten miles it began to rain. What course was to be taken! His soul disdained to turn back. He did what the king of Prussia might have done, he flapped his hat, buttoned up his cape, and went forwards, fortifying his mind by the stoical consolation that whatever is violent will be short.

His constancy was not long tried; at the distance of about half a mile he saw an inn, which he entered wet and weary, and found civil treatment and proper refreshment. After a respite of about two hours he looked abroad and, seeing the sky clear, called for his

[1] *curious* Fastidious.

[2] *pencils* Paintbrushes.

[3] *old friend Sober* Many of Johnson's friends believed the description of Sober was meant to be autobiographical.

horse and passed the first stage without any other memorable accident.

Will considered that labour must be relieved by pleasure, and that the strength which great undertakings require must be maintained by copious nutriment; he therefore ordered himself an elegant supper, drank two bottles of claret, and passed the beginning of the night in sound sleep; but, waking before light, was forewarned of the troubles of the next day by a shower beating against his windows with such violence as to threaten the dissolution of nature. When he arose he found what he expected, that the country was under water. He joined himself, however, to a company that was travelling the same way, and came safely to the place of dinner, though every step of his horse dashed the mud into the air.

In the afternoon, having parted from his company, he set forward alone, and passed many collections of water of which it was impossible to guess the depth, and which he now cannot review without some censure of his own rashness; but what a man undertakes he must perform, and Marvel hates a coward at his heart.

Few that lie warm in their beds think what others undergo who have perhaps been as tenderly educated, and have as acute sensations as themselves. My friend was now to lodge the second night almost fifty miles from home, in a house which he never had seen before, among people to whom he was totally a stranger, not knowing whether the next man he should meet would prove good or bad; but seeing an inn of a good appearance, he rode resolutely into the yard, and knowing that respect is often paid in proportion as it is claimed, delivered his injunction to the hostler with spirit and, entering the house, called vigorously about him.

On the third day up rose the sun and Mr. Marvel. His troubles and his dangers were now such as he wishes no other man ever to encounter. The ways were less frequented, and the country more thinly inhabited. He rode many a lonely hour through mire and water, and met not a single soul for two miles together with whom he could exchange a word. He cannot deny that, looking round upon the dreary region and seeing nothing but bleak fields and naked trees, hills obscured by fogs, and flats covered with inundations, he did for some time suffer melancholy to prevail upon him, and wished himself again safe at home. One comfort he had, which was to consider that none of his friends were in the same distress, for whom, if they had been with him, he should have suffered more than for himself; he could not forbear sometimes to consider how happily the Idler is settled in an easier condition, who, surrounded like him with terrors, could have done nothing but lie down and die.

Amidst these reflections he came to a town and found a dinner, which disposed him to more cheerful sentiments: but the joys of life are short, and its miseries are long; he mounted and travelled fifteen miles more through dirt and desolation.

At last the sun set, and all the horrors of darkness came upon him. He then repented the weak indulgence by which he had gratified himself at noon with too long an interval of rest: yet he went forward along a path which he could no longer see, sometimes rushing suddenly into water, and sometimes encumbered with stiff clay, ignorant whither he was going, and uncertain whether his next step might not be the last.

In this dismal gloom of nocturnal peregrination his horse unexpectedly stood still. Marvel had heard many relations of the instinct of horses, and was in doubt what danger might be at hand. Sometimes he fancied that he was on the bank of a river still and deep, and sometimes that a dead body lay across the track. He sat still awhile to recollect his thoughts; and as he was about to alight and explore the darkness, out stepped a man with a lantern, and opened the turnpike.[1] He hired a guide to the town, arrived in safety, and slept in quiet.

The rest of his journey was nothing but danger. He climbed and descended precipices on which vulgar mortals tremble to look; he passed marshes like the "Serbonian bog, where armies whole have sunk";[2] he forded rivers where the current roared like the eagre of the Severn;[3] or ventured himself on bridges that trembled under him, from which he looked down on foaming whirlpools, or dreadful abysses; he wandered over houseless heaths, amidst all the rage of the elements, with the snow driving in his face and the tempest howling in his ears.

[1] *turnpike* Bar across the road to stop travelers and collect tolls.

[2] *Serbonian ... sunk* From Milton's *Paradise Lost*.

[3] *eagre* Tidal wave; *Severn* The longest river in England, flowing through Wales and England into the Bristol channel.

Such are the colours in which Marvel paints his adventures. He has accustomed himself to sounding words and hyperbolical images till he has lost the power of true description. In a road through which the heaviest carriages pass without difficulty, and the post-boy every day and night goes and returns, he meets with hardships like those which are endured in Siberian deserts, and misses nothing of romantic danger but a giant and a dragon. When his dreadful story is told in proper terms, it is only that the way was dirty in winter, and that he experienced the common vicissitudes of rain and sunshine.

The Idler No. 81

[ON NATIVE AMERICANS]

Saturday, 3 November 1759

As the English army was passing towards Quebec[1] along a soft savanna between a mountain and a lake, one of the petty chiefs of the inland regions stood upon a rock surrounded by his clan, and from behind the shelter of the bushes contemplated the art and regularity of European war. It was evening, the tents were pitched, he observed the security with which the troops rested in the night, and the order with which the march was renewed in the morning. He continued to pursue them with his eye till they could be seen no longer, and then stood for some time silent and pensive.

Then turning to his followers,[2] "My children," said he, "I have often heard from men hoary with long life, that there was a time when our ancestors were absolute lords of the woods, the meadows, and the lakes, wherever the eye can reach or the foot can pass. They fished and hunted, feasted and danced, and when they were weary lay down under the first thicket, without danger and without fear. They changed their habitations as the seasons required, convenience prompted, or curiosity allured them, and sometimes gathered the fruits of the mountain, and sometimes sported in canoes along the coast.

"Many years and ages are supposed to have been thus passed in plenty and security; when at last a new race of men entered our country from the great ocean. They enclosed themselves in habitations of stone, which our ancestors could neither enter by violence, nor destroy by fire. They issued from those fastnesses, sometimes covered like the armadillo with shells, from which the lance rebounded on the striker, and sometimes carried by mighty beasts which had never been seen in our vales or forests, of such strength and swiftness that flight and opposition were vain alike. Those invaders ranged over the continent, slaughtering in their rage those that resisted, and those that submitted, in their mirth. Of those that remained, some were buried in caverns and condemned to dig metals for their masters; some were employed in tilling the ground, of which foreign tyrants devour the produce; and when the sword and the mines have destroyed the natives, they supply their place by human beings of another colour, brought from some distant country to perish here under toil and torture.

"Some there are who boast their humanity, and content themselves to seize our chases[3] and fisheries, who drive us from every track of ground where fertility and pleasantness invite them to settle, and make no war upon us except when we intrude upon our own lands.

"Others pretend to have purchased a right of residence and tyranny; but surely the insolence of such bargains is more offensive than the avowed and open dominion of force. What reward can induce the possessor of a country to admit a stranger more powerful than himself? Fraud or terror must operate in such contracts; either they promised protection which they never have afforded, or instruction which they never imparted. We hoped to be secured by their favour from some other evil, or to learn the arts of Europe, by which we might be able to secure ourselves. Their power they have never exerted in our defence, and their arts they have studiously concealed from us. Their treaties are only to deceive, and their traffic only to defraud us. They have a written law among them, of which they boast as derived from Him who made the earth and sea, and by which they profess to believe that man will be made happy when life shall forsake him. Why is not this law communicated to us? It is concealed because it is

[1] *As ... Quebec* The English defeated the French in Quebec in October of 1759.

[2] *Then ... followers* The basis for this speech may have been one given by the chief of the Micmac that had been printed in *London Magazine* the previous year.

[3] *chases* Hunting grounds.

violated. For how can they preach it to an Indian nation when I am told that one of its first precepts forbids them to do to others what they would not that others should do to them.

"But the time perhaps is now approaching when the pride of usurpation shall be crushed, and the cruelties of invasion shall be revenged. The sons of rapacity have now drawn their swords upon each other and referred their claims to the decision of war; let us look unconcerned upon the slaughter, and remember that the death of every European delivers the country from a tyrant and a robber; for what is the claim of either nation but the claim of the vulture to the leveret,[1] of the tiger to the fawn? Let them then continue to dispute their title to regions which they cannot people, to purchase by danger and blood the empty dignity of dominion over mountains which they will never climb, and rivers which they will never pass. Let us endeavour, in the meantime, to learn their discipline, and to forge their weapons; and when they shall be weakened with mutual slaughter, let us rush down upon them, force their remains to take shelter in their ships, and reign once more in our native country."

from *A Dictionary of the English Language*

from The Preface

It is the fate of those who toil at the lower employments of life to be rather driven by the fear of evil than attracted by the prospect of good; to be exposed to censure without hope of praise; to be disgraced by miscarriage, or punished for neglect, where success would have been without applause, and diligence without reward.

Among these unhappy mortals is the writer of dictionaries, whom mankind have considered not as the pupil, but the slave, of science, the pioneer[2] of literature, doomed only to remove rubbish and clear obstructions from the paths through which learning and genius press forward to conquest and glory, without bestowing a smile on the humble drudge that facilitates their progress. Every other author may aspire to praise: the lexicographer can only hope to escape reproach—and even this negative recompense has been yet granted to very few.

I have, notwithstanding this discouragement, attempted a dictionary of the English language, which, while it was employed in the cultivation of every species of literature, has itself been hitherto neglected, suffered to spread, under the direction of chance, into wild exuberance, resigned to the tyranny of time and fashion, and exposed to the corruptions of ignorance and caprices of innovation.

When I took the first survey of my undertaking, I found our speech copious without order, and energetic without rules: wherever I turned my view, there was perplexity to be disentangled and confusion to be regulated; choice was to be made out of boundless variety, without any established principle of selection; adulterations were to be detected, without a settled test of purity; and modes of expression to be rejected or received, without the suffrages of any writers of classical reputation or acknowledged authority.

Having therefore no assistance but from general grammar, I applied myself to the perusal of our writers; and, noting whatever might be of use to ascertain or illustrate any word or phrase, accumulated in time the materials of a dictionary, which, by degrees, I reduced to method, establishing to myself, in the progress of the work, such rules as experience and analogy suggested to me—experience, which practice and observation were continually increasing, and analogy, which, though in some words obscure, was evident in others.

In adjusting the orthography, which has been to this time unsettled and fortuitous, I found it necessary to distinguish those irregularities that are inherent in our tongue, and perhaps coeval with it, from others which the ignorance or negligence of later writers has produced. Every language has its anomalies which, though inconvenient and in themselves once unnecessary, must be tolerated among the imperfections of human things, and which require only to be registered that they may not be increased, and ascertained that they may not be confounded. But every language has likewise its improprieties and absurdities which it is the duty of the lexicographer to correct or proscribe.

... When we see men grow old and die at a certain time one after another, from century to century, we

[1] *leveret* Young hare (under a year old).

[2] *pioneer* Soldier who builds roads and fortifications, removes obstructions, and otherwise prepares the way for a traveling army.

laugh at the elixir that promises to prolong life to a thousand years; and with equal justice may the lexicographer be derided, who, being able to produce no example of a nation that has preserved their words and phrases from mutability, shall imagine that his dictionary can embalm his language and secure it from corruption and decay, that it is in his power to change sublunary nature, and clear the world at once from folly, vanity, and affectation.

With this hope, however, academies have been instituted to guard the avenues of their languages, to retain fugitives, and repulse intruders. But their vigilance and activity have hitherto been vain: sounds are too volatile and subtle for legal restraints; to enchain syllables, and to lash the wind, are equally the undertakings of pride, unwilling to measure its desires by its strength. The French language has visibly changed under the inspection of the academy;[1] the style of Amelot's translation of Father Paul is observed by Le Courayer to be *un peu passé*;[2] and no Italian will maintain that the diction of any modern writer is not perceptibly different from that of Boccace, Machiavel, or Caro.[3]

Total and sudden transformations of a language seldom happen: conquests and migrations are now very rare. But there are other causes of change which, though slow in their operation and invisible in their progress, are perhaps as much superior to human resistance as the revolutions of the sky or intumescence of the tide. Commerce, however necessary, however lucrative, as it depraves the manners, corrupts the language; they that have frequent intercourse with strangers, to whom they endeavour to accommodate themselves, must in time learn a mingled dialect, like the jargon which serves the traffickers on the Mediterranean and Indian coasts. This will not always be confined to the exchange, the warehouse, or the port, but will be communicated by degrees to other ranks of the people, and be at last incorporated with the current speech.

There are likewise internal causes equally forcible. The language most likely to continue long without alteration would be that of a nation raised a little, and but a little, above barbarity, secluded from strangers, and totally employed in procuring the conveniences of life, either without books or, like some of the Mahometan countries, with very few: men thus busied and unlearned, having only such words as common use requires, would perhaps long continue to express the same notions by the same signs. But no such constancy can be expected in a people polished by arts, and classed by subordination, where one part of the community is sustained and accommodated by the labour of the other. Those who have much leisure to think will always be enlarging the stock of ideas, and every increase of knowledge, whether real or fancied, will produce new words or combinations of words. When the mind is unchained from necessity, it will range after convenience; when it is left at large in the fields of speculation, it will shift opinions; as any custom is disused, the words that expressed it must perish with it; as any opinion grows popular, it will innovate speech in the same proportion as it alters practice.

As, by the cultivation of various sciences, a language is amplified, it will be more furnished with words deflected from their original sense: the geometrician will talk of a courtier's *zenith,* or the *eccentric* virtue of a wild hero,[4] and the physician of *sanguine* expectations and *phlegmatic* delays.[5] Copiousness of speech will give opportunities to capricious choice, by which some words will be preferred and others degraded; vicissitudes of fashion will enforce the use of new, or extend the

[1] *The French ... academy* The Académie française, founded in 1635, was commissioned to purify and preserve the French language. The Académie published its dictionary in 1634.

[2] *style ... passé* Father Paul Sarpi was the author of the *History of the Council of Trent,* published in Italian in 1619. In 1739 Father Pierre François Le Courayer produced a new French translation of this work, replacing the 1683 translation by Amelot de la Houssaye, which Le Courayer referred to as "a bit outdated."

[3] *Boccace* Giovanni Boccaccio, the fourteenth-century author of the *Decameron*; *Machiavel* Fifteenth-century political philosopher Niccolò Machiavelli; *Caro* Annibale Caro, a fifteenth-century writer of pastoral romance.

[4] *the geometrician ... hero* "Zenith" and "eccentric" were formerly used solely as geometrical or astronomical terms, meaning "the point of the heavens directly above" and "not concentric (with another circle), or "not perfectly circular," respectively.

[5] *physician ... delays* "Sanguine" and "phlegmatic" were physicians' terms describing the predominance in the body of blood or phlegm, respectively. These terms were later used to describe the temperaments associated with these two humors: those who are sanguine are said to be hopeful and courageous, while those who are phlegmatic are sluggish and apathetic.

signification of known, terms. The tropes[1] of poetry will make hourly encroachments, and the metaphorical will become the current sense; pronunciation will be varied by levity or ignorance, and the pen must at length comply with the tongue; illiterate writers will at one time or other, by public infatuation, rise into renown, who, not knowing the original import of words, will use them with colloquial licentiousness, confound distinction, and forget propriety. As politeness increases some expressions will be considered as too gross and vulgar for the delicate, others as too formal and ceremonious for the gay and airy: new phrases are therefore adopted which must, for the same reasons, be in time dismissed. Swift, in his petty treatise on the English language,[2] allows that new words must sometimes be introduced but proposes that none should be suffered to become obsolete. But what makes a word obsolete, more than general agreement to forbear it? and how shall it be continued, when it conveys an offensive idea, or recalled again to the mouths of mankind, when it has once become unfamiliar by disuse, and unpleasing by unfamiliarity?

There is another cause of alteration more prevalent than any other, which yet in the present state of the world cannot be obviated. A mixture of two languages will produce a third distinct from both, and they will always be mixed where the chief part of education, and the most conspicuous accomplishment, is skill in ancient or in foreign tongues. He that has long cultivated another language will find its words and combinations crowd upon his memory, and haste or negligence, refinement or affectation, will obtrude borrowed terms and exotic expressions.

[Selected Entries]

Asthma. A frequent, difficult, and short respiration, joined with a hissing sound and a cough, especially in the night-time, and when the body is in a prone posture; because then the contents of the lower belly bear so against the diaphragm, as to lessen the capacity of the breast, whereby the lungs have less room to move. Quincy.

Bat. An animal having the body of a mouse and the wings of a bird; not with feathers, but with a sort of skin which is extended. It lays no eggs, but brings forth its young alive, and suckles them. It never grows tame, feeds upon flies, insects, and fatty substances, such as candles, oil, and cheese; and appears only in the summer evenings, when the weather is fine. Calmet.

Booby. (A word of no certain etymology. Henshaw thinks it a corruption of *bull-beef*[3] ridiculously; Skinner imagines it to be derived from *bobo*, foolish, Span. Junius finds *bowbard* to be an old Scottish word for a *coward*, a *contemptible fellow*; from which he naturally deduces *booby*; but the original of *bowbard* is not known.) A dull, heavy, stupid fellow; a lubber.

Comedy. A dramatic representation of the lighter faults of mankind.

Epic. Narrative; comprising narrations, not acted, but rehearsed. It is usually supposed to be heroic, or to contain one great action achieved by a hero.

Lexicographer. A writer of dictionaries; a harmless drudge, that busies himself in tracing the original, and detailing the signification of words.

Novel. A small tale, generally of love.

Nowadays. (This word, though common and used by the best writers, is perhaps barbarous.) In the present age.

Oats. A grain, which in England is generally given to horses, but in Scotland supports the people.

To partialize. To make partial. A word, perhaps, peculiar to Shakespeare, and not unworthy of general use.

Such neighbour-nearness to our sacred blood
Should nothing privilege him, nor *partialize*
Th'unstooping firmness of my upright soul.
Shakespeare.

[1] *tropes* Figures of speech in which words are used in senses other than those that are accepted or standard.

[2] *Swift … language* Jonathan Swift's *A Proposal for Correcting, Improving, and Ascertaining the English Tongue* (1712); *petty* Small.

[3] *bull-beef* Literally, the flesh of bulls; also a term of abuse.

Pastoral. A poem in which any action or passion is represented by its effects upon a country life; or according to the common practice in which speakers take upon them the character of shepherds; an idyll; a bucolic.

Patriot. One whose ruling passion is the love of his country. It is sometimes used for a factious disturber of the government.

Patron. One who countenances, supports, or protects. Commonly a wretch who supports with insolence, and is paid with flattery.

Precarious. Dependent; uncertain, because depending on the will of another; held by courtesy; changeable or alienable at the pleasure of another. No word is more unskilfully used than this with its derivatives. It is used for *uncertain* in all its senses; but it only means uncertain, as dependent on others: thus there are authors who mention the *precariousness* of an *account,* of the *weather,* of a *die.*

Rapport. Relation; reference; proportion. A word introduced by the innovator, Temple,[1] but not copied by others.

Reputeless. Disreputable; disgraceful. A word not inelegant, but out of use.

Opinion, that did help me to the crown,
Had left me in reputeless banishment,
A fellow of no mark nor livelihood.
Shakespeare *Henry IV.*

Romance. A military fable of the middle ages; a tale of wild adventures in war and love.

Romantic: (I) Resembling the tales of romances; wild.
(2) Improbable; false.
(3) Fanciful; full of wild scenery.

Sonnet. A short poem consisting of fourteen lines, of which the rhymes are adjusted by a particular rule. It is not very suitable to the English language, and has not been used by any man of eminence since Milton.

Sonnetteer. A small poet, in contempt.

Stockjobber. A low wretch who gets money by buying and selling shares in the funds.

Tory. One who adheres to the ancient constitution of the state, and the apostolical hierarchy of the church of England, opposed to a Whig.

Vastidity. Wideness; immensity. A barbarous word.

Perpetual durance,
Through all the world's *vastidity.* Shakespeare.

Vaulty. Arched; concave. A bad word.

I will kiss thy detestable bones,
And put my eye-balls in thy *vaulty* brows,
And ring these fingers with thy houshold worms.
Shakespeare.

Whig. The name of a faction.

—1755

from The Preface to *The Works of William Shakespeare*

Nothing can please many, and please long, but just representations of general nature. Particular manners can be known to few, and therefore few only can judge how nearly they are copied. The irregular combinations of fanciful invention may delight a while, by that novelty of which the common satiety of life sends us all in quest; but the pleasures of sudden wonder are soon exhausted, and the mind can only repose on the stability of truth.

Shakespeare is, above all writers, at least above all modern writers, the poet of nature, the poet that holds up to his readers a faithful mirror of manners and of life. His characters are not modified by the customs of particular places, unpracticed by the rest of the world; by the peculiarities of studies or professions, which can operate but upon small numbers; or by the accidents of transient fashions or temporary opinions: they are the

[1] *Temple* Sir William Temple, seventeenth-century English diplomat and author, perhaps best known for his essay *Of Ancient and Modern Learning* (1690).

genuine progeny of common humanity, such as the world will always supply, and observation will always find. His persons act and speak by the influence of those general passions and principles by which all minds are agitated, and the whole system of life is continued in motion. In the writings of other poets a character is too often an individual; in those of Shakespeare it is commonly a species.

It is from this wide extension of design that so much instruction is derived. It is this which fills the plays of Shakespeare with practical axioms and domestic wisdom. It was said of Euripides[1] that every verse was a precept, and it may be said of Shakespeare that from his Works may be collected a system of civil and economical[2] prudence. Yet his real power is not shown in the splendour of particular passages, but by the progress of his fable,[3] and the tenor of his dialogue; and he that tries to recommend him by select quotations will succeed like the pedant in *Hierocles*,[4] who, when he offered his house to sale, carried a brick in his pocket as a specimen.

It will not easily be imagined how much Shakespeare excels in accommodating his sentiments to real life, but by comparing him with other authors. It was observed of the ancient schools of declamation that the more diligently they were frequented, the more was the student disqualified for the world, because he found nothing there which he should ever meet in any other place. The same remark may be applied to every stage but that of Shakespeare. The theatre, when it is under any other direction, is peopled by such characters as were never seen conversing in a language which was never heard, upon topics which will never arise in the commerce of mankind. But the dialogue of this author is often so evidently determined by the incident which produces it, and is pursued with so much ease and simplicity, that it seems scarcely to claim the merit of fiction, but to have been gleaned by diligent selection out of common conversation, and common occurrences. Upon every other stage the universal agent is love, by whose power all good and evil is distributed, and every action quickened or retarded. To bring a lover, a lady, and a rival into the fable; to entangle them in contradictory obligations, perplex them with oppositions of interest, and harass them with violence of desires inconsistent with each other; to make them meet in rapture and part in agony; to fill their mouths with hyperbolical joy and outrageous sorrow; to distress them as nothing human ever was distressed; to deliver them as nothing human ever was delivered, is the business of a modern dramatist. For this, probability is violated, life is misrepresented, and language is depraved.[5] But love is only one of many passions, and as it has no great influence upon the sum of life, it has little operation in the dramas of a poet, who caught his ideas from the living world, and exhibited only what he saw before him. He knew that any other passion, as it was regular or exorbitant, was a cause of happiness or calamity.

Characters thus ample and general were not easily discriminated and preserved, yet perhaps no poet ever kept his personages more distinct from each other. I will not say with Pope[6] that every speech may be assigned to the proper speaker, because many speeches there are which have nothing characteristical; but perhaps, though some may be equally adapted to every person, it will be difficult to find any that can be properly transferred from the present possessor to another claimant. The choice is right, when there is reason for choice.

Other dramatists can only gain attention by hyperbolical or aggravated characters, by fabulous and unexampled excellence or depravity, as the writers of barbarous romances invigorated the reader by a giant and a dwarf; and he that should form his expectations of human affairs from the play, or from the tale, would be equally deceived. Shakespeare has no heroes; his scenes are occupied only by men, who act and speak as the reader thinks that he should himself have spoken or acted on the same occasion. Even where the agency is supernatural, the dialogue is level with life. Other writers disguise the most natural passions and most frequent incidents; so that he who contemplates them in the book will not know them in the world: Shakespeare

[1] *Euripides* Greek tragic poet of the fifth century BCE. The opinion is that of Cicero, stated in his *Letters to His Friends*, 16.8.

[2] *economical* Johnson defines this in his *Dictionary* as "pertaining to the regulation of a household."

[3] *fable* Defined by Johnson as "the series or contexture of events which constitute a poem epic or dramatic."

[4] *Hierocles* Alexandrian philosopher of the fifth century CE.

[5] *depraved* Debased.

[6] *Pope* Alexander Pope, in the preface to his edition of Shakespeare's plays (1725).

approximates[1] the remote, and familiarizes the wonderful; the event which he represents will not happen, but if it were possible, its effects would probably be such as he has assigned; and it may be said that he has not only shown human nature as it acts in real exigencies, but as it would be found in trials to which it cannot be exposed.

This therefore is the praise of Shakespeare, that his drama is the mirror of life; that he who has mazed[2] his imagination in following the phantoms which other writers raise up before him, may here be cured of his delirious ecstasies by reading human sentiment in human language; by scenes from which a hermit may estimate the transactions of the world, and a confessor[3] predict the progress of the passions.

His adherence to general nature has exposed him to the censure of critics, who form their judgements upon narrower principles. Dennis and Rymer[4] think his Romans not sufficiently Roman; and Voltaire[5] censures his kings as not completely royal. Dennis is offended that Menenius, a senator of Rome, should play the buffoon; and Voltaire perhaps thinks decency violated when the Danish usurper is represented as a drunkard.[6] But Shakespeare always makes nature predominate over accident; and if he preserves the essential character, is not very careful of distinctions superinduced and adventitious. His story requires Romans or kings, but he thinks only on men. He knew that Rome, like every other city, had men of all dispositions; and, wanting a buffoon, he went into the senate-house for that which the senate-house would certainly have afforded him. He was inclined to show a usurper and a murderer not only odious but despicable; he therefore added drunkenness to his other qualities, knowing that kings love wine like other men, and that wine exerts its natural power upon kings. These are the petty cavils of petty minds; a poet overlooks the casual distinction of country and condition, as a painter, satisfied with the figure, neglects the drapery.

The censure which he has incurred by mixing comic and tragic scenes, as it extends to all his works, deserves more consideration. Let the fact be first stated, and then examined.

Shakespeare's plays are not in the rigorous and critical sense either tragedies or comedies, but compositions of a distinct kind; exhibiting the real state of sublunary nature, which partakes of good and evil, joy and sorrow, mingled with endless variety of proportion and innumerable modes of combination; and expressing the course of the world, in which the loss of one is the gain of another; in which, at the same time, the reveller is hasting to his wine, and the mourner burying his friend; in which the malignity of one is sometimes defeated by the frolic of another; and many mischiefs and many benefits are done and hindered without design.

Out of this chaos of mingled purposes and casualties[7] the ancient poets, according to the laws which custom had prescribed, selected some the crimes of men, and some their absurdities; some the momentous vicissitudes of life, and some the lighter occurrences; some the terrors of distress, and some the gaieties of prosperity. Thus rose the two modes of imitation, known by the names of *tragedy* and *comedy*, compositions intended to promote different ends by contrary means, and considered as so little allied, that I do not recollect among the Greeks or Romans a single writer who attempted both.

Shakespeare has united the powers of exciting laughter and sorrow not only in one mind but in one composition. Almost all his plays are divided between serious and ludicrous characters, and, in the successive evolutions of the design, sometimes produce seriousness and sorrow, and sometimes levity and laughter.

That this is a practice contrary to the rules of criticism[8] will be readily allowed, but there is always an appeal open from criticism to nature. The end of writing is to instruct; the end of poetry is to instruct by

[1] *approximates* Brings near.

[2] *mazed* Bewildered.

[3] *confessor* I.e., a priest.

[4] *Dennis and Rymer* John Dennis, playwright and literary critic, author of *An Essay on the Genius and Writing of Shakespeare* (1712), and Thomas Rymer, historian and drama critic, author of *A Short View of Tragedy* (1693).

[5] *Voltaire* French philosopher; this criticism of Shakespeare occurs in his *Appeal to All the Nations of Europe* (1761).

[6] *Dennis is ... drunkard* References to Menenius of *Coriolanus*, who describes himself as a buffoon in 2.1, and to King Claudius in *Hamlet*.

[7] *casualties* Chance occurrences.

[8] *rules of criticism* Set forth by Horace and Sir Philip Sidney, among others.

pleasing.[1] That the mingled drama may convey all the instruction of tragedy or comedy cannot be denied, because it includes both in its alternations of exhibition, and approaches nearer than either to the appearance of life by showing how great machinations and slender designs may promote or obviate one another, and the high and the low co-operate in the general system by unavoidable concatenation.[2]

It is objected that by this change of scenes the passions are interrupted in their progression, and that the principal event, being not advanced by a due gradation of preparatory incidents, wants at last the power to move, which constitutes the perfection of dramatic poetry. This reasoning is so specious, that it is received as true even by those who in daily experience feel it to be false. The interchanges of mingled scenes seldom fail to produce the intended vicissitudes of passion. Fiction cannot move so much, but that the attention may be easily transferred; and though it must be allowed that pleasing melancholy be sometimes interrupted by unwelcome levity, yet let it be considered likewise, that melancholy is often not pleasing, and that the disturbance of one man may be the relief of another; that different auditors have different habitudes; and that, upon the whole, all pleasure consists in variety.

The players, who in their edition divided our author's works into comedies, histories, and tragedies, seem not to have distinguished the three kinds, by any very exact or definite ideas.

An action which ended happily to the principal persons, however serious or distressful through its intermediate incidents, in their opinion constituted a comedy. This idea of a comedy continued long amongst us, and plays were written, which, by changing the catastrophe, were tragedies today and comedies tomorrow.

Tragedy was not in those times a poem of more general dignity or elevation than comedy; it required only a calamitous conclusion, with which the common criticism of that age was satisfied, whatever lighter pleasure it afforded in its progress.

History was a series of actions, with no other than chronological succession, independent of each other, and without any tendency to introduce or regulate the conclusion. It is not always very nicely distinguished from tragedy. There is not much nearer approach to unity of action in the tragedy of *Antony and Cleopatra,* than in the history of *Richard the Second.* But a history might be continued through many plays; as it had no plan, it had no limits.

Through all these denominations of the drama, Shakespeare's mode of composition is the same; an interchange of seriousness and merriment, by which the mind is softened at one time, and exhilarated at another. But whatever be his purpose, whether to gladden or depress, or to conduct the story, without vehemence or emotion, through tracts of easy and familiar dialogue, he never fails to attain his purpose; as he commands us, we laugh or mourn, or sit silent with quiet expectation, in tranquillity without indifference.

When Shakespeare's plan is understood, most of the criticisms of Rymer and Voltaire vanish away. The play of *Hamlet* is opened, without impropriety, by two sentinels; Iago bellows at Brabantio's window, without injury to the scheme of the play, though in terms which a modern audience would not easily endure; the character of Polonius is seasonable and useful; and the gravediggers themselves may be heard with applause.[3]

Shakespeare engaged in the dramatic poetry with the world open before him; the rules of the ancients were yet known to few; the public judgement was unformed; he had no example of such fame as might force him upon imitation, nor critics of such authority as might restrain his extravagance. He therefore indulged his natural disposition, and his disposition, as Rymer has remarked, led him to comedy. In tragedy he often writes with great appearance of toil and study, what is written at last with little felicity; but in his comic scenes, he seems to produce, without labour, what no labour can improve. In tragedy he is always struggling after some occasion to be comic, but in comedy he seems to repose, or to luxuriate, as in a mode of thinking congenial to his nature. In his tragic scenes there is always something wanting, but his comedy often surpasses expectation or desire. His comedy pleases by the thoughts and the

[1] *The end ... pleasing* An idea that originated from Horace's *Art of Poetry*: "The poet's aim is either to profit or to please, or to blend in one the delightful and the useful."

[2] *concatenation* Linkage, union.

[3] *Iago ... applause* Iago is a character in *Othello.* Polonius and the gravediggers are characters in *Hamlet.*

language, and his tragedy for the greater part by incident and action. His tragedy seems to be skill, his comedy to be instinct.

The force of his comic scenes has suffered little diminution from the changes made by a century and a half, in manners or in words. As his personages act upon principles arising from genuine passion, very little modified by particular forms, their pleasures and vexations are communicable to all times and to all places; they are natural, and therefore durable; the adventitious peculiarities of personal habits are only superficial dyes, bright and pleasing for a little while, yet soon fading to a dim tinct, without any remains of former lustre; but the discriminations of true passion are the colours of nature; they pervade the whole mass, and can only perish with the body that exhibits them. The accidental compositions of heterogeneous modes are dissolved by the chance which combined them; but the uniform simplicity of primitive qualities neither admits increase, nor suffers decay. The sand heaped by one flood is scattered by another, but the rock always continues in its place. The stream of time, which is continually washing the dissoluble fabrics of other poets, passes without injury by the adamant of Shakespeare.

If there be, what I believe there is, in every nation a style which never becomes obsolete, a certain mode of phraseology so consonant and congenial to the analogy[1] and principles of its respective language as to remain settled and unaltered; this style is probably to be sought in the common intercourse of life, among those who speak only to be understood, without ambition of elegance. The polite are always catching modish innovations, and the learned depart from established forms of speech in hope of finding or making better; those who wish for distinction forsake the vulgar,[2] when the vulgar is right; but there is a conversation above grossness and below refinement where propriety resides, and where this poet seems to have gathered his comic dialogue. He is therefore more agreeable to the ears of the present age than any other author equally remote, and among his other excellencies deserves to be studied as one of the original masters of our language.

These observations are to be considered not as unexceptionably constant, but as containing general and predominant truth. Shakespeare's familiar dialogue is affirmed to be smooth and clear, yet not wholly without ruggedness or difficulty; as a country may be eminently fruitful, though it has spots unfit for cultivation. His characters are praised as natural though their sentiments are sometimes forced and their actions improbable, as the earth upon the whole is spherical though its surface is varied with protuberances and cavities.

Shakespeare with his excellencies has likewise faults, and faults sufficient to obscure and overwhelm any other merit. I shall show them in the proportion in which they appear to me, without envious malignity or superstitious veneration. No question can be more innocently discussed than a dead poet's pretensions to renown; and little regard is due to that bigotry which sets candour higher than truth.

His first defect is that to which may be imputed most of the evil in books or in men. He sacrifices virtue to convenience, and is so much more careful to please than to instruct that he seems to write without any moral purpose. From his writings indeed a system of social duty may be selected, for he that thinks reasonably must think morally; but his precepts and axioms drop casually from him; he makes no just distribution of good or evil, nor is always careful to show in the virtuous a disapprobation of the wicked; he carries his persons indifferently through right and wrong, and at the close dismisses them without further care, and leaves their examples to operate by chance. This fault the barbarity of his age cannot extenuate; for it is always a writer's duty to make the world better, and justice is a virtue independent on time or place.

The plots are often so loosely formed that a very slight consideration may improve them, and so carelessly pursued, that he seems not always fully to comprehend his own design. He omits opportunities of instructing or delighting which the train of his story seems to force upon him, and apparently rejects those exhibitions which would be more affecting for the sake of those which are more easy.

It may be observed that in many of his plays the latter part is evidently neglected. When he found himself near the end of his work, and in view of his reward, he shortened the labour to snatch the profit. He therefore remits his efforts where he should most

[1] *analogy* Formative processes.

[2] *vulgar* Common.

vigorously exert them, and his catastrophe[1] is improbably produced or imperfectly represented.

He had no regard to distinction of time or place, but gives to one age or nation, without scruple, the customs, institutions, and opinions of another, at the expense not only of likelihood, but of possibility. These faults Pope has endeavoured, with more zeal than judgement, to transfer to his imagined interpolators.[2] We need not wonder to find Hector quoting Aristotle when we see the loves of Theseus and Hippolyta combined with the Gothic mythology of fairies.[3] Shakespeare, indeed, was not the only violator of chronology, for in the same age Sidney,[4] who wanted not the advantages of learning, has, in his *Arcadia,* confounded the pastoral with the feudal times, the days of innocence, quiet, and security, with those of turbulence, violence, and adventure.

In his comic scenes he is seldom very successful when he engages his characters in reciprocations of smartness and contests of sarcasm; their jests are commonly gross and their pleasantry licentious; neither his gentlemen nor his ladies have much delicacy, nor are sufficiently distinguished from his clowns[5] by any appearance of refined manners. Whether he represented the real conversation of his time is not easy to determine; the reign of Elizabeth is commonly supposed to have been a time of stateliness, formality, and reserve; yet perhaps the relaxations of that severity were not very elegant. There must, however, have been always some modes of gaiety preferable to others, and a writer ought to choose the best.

In tragedy his performance seems constantly to be worse, as his labour is more. The effusions of passion which exigence forces out are for the most part striking and energetic; but whenever he solicits his invention, or strains his faculties, the offspring of his throes is tumour, meanness,[6] tediousness, and obscurity.

In narration he affects a disproportionate pomp of diction and a wearisome train of circumlocution, and tells the incident imperfectly in many words which might have been more plainly delivered in few. Narration in dramatic poetry is naturally tedious, as it is unanimated and inactive and obstructs the progress of the action; it should therefore always be rapid and enlivened by frequent interruption. Shakespeare found it an encumbrance and, instead of lightening it by brevity, endeavoured to recommend it by dignity and splendour.

His declamations or set speeches are commonly cold and weak, for his power was the power of nature; when he endeavoured, like other tragic writers, to catch opportunities of amplification and, instead of inquiring what the occasion demanded, to show how much his stores of knowledge could supply, he seldom escapes without the pity or resentment of his reader....

The objection arising[7] from the impossibility of passing the first hour at Alexandria and the next at Rome supposes that when the play opens the spectator really imagines himself at Alexandria and believes that his walk to the theatre has been a voyage to Egypt, and that he lives in the days of Antony and Cleopatra. Surely he that imagines this may imagine more. He that can take the stage at one time for the palace of the Ptolemies may take it in half an hour for the promontory of Actium. Delusion, if delusion be admitted, has no certain limitation; if the spectator can be once persuaded that his old acquaintance are Alexander and Caesar, that a room illuminated with candles is the plain of Pharsalia or the bank of Granicus,[8] he is in a state of elevation above the reach of reason, or of truth, and from the heights of empyrean poetry may despise the circumscriptions of terrestrial nature. There is no reason why a

[1] *catastrophe* Conclusion.

[2] *his imagined interpolators* I.e., those who published his plays. In his preface, Pope claimed that many of the faults in Shakespeare's plays were introduced by publishers, not by the writer himself.

[3] *We need ... fairies* Hector quotes Aristotle in *Troilus and Cressida*, 2.2.166–67; in *A Midsummer Night's Dream*, the characters of Theseus and Hippolyta parallel those of Oberon and Titania, the King and Queen of the fairies.

[4] *Sidney* Sir Philip Sidney, English poet and courtier.

[5] *clowns* Yokels.

[6] *tumour* Turgidity of language or style; *meanness* Baseness.

[7] *The objection arising* This and the following paragraphs reference the classical unities, a set of three guidelines for structuring plays. According to the unities, a play should have unity of action (it should focus on a single plot), unity of time (the whole play should be set in a single day), and unity of place (the action should occur in a single setting). These rules, developed from commends made by Aristotle, were embraced by neoclassical critics.

[8] *plain of ... Granicus* Locations of the victories of Julius Caesar and Alexander the Great, respectively.

mind thus wandering in ecstasy should count the clock, or why an hour should not be a century in that calenture[1] of the brains that can make the stage a field.

The truth is that the spectators are always in their senses and know, from the first act to the last, that the stage is only a stage and that the players are only players. They came to hear a certain number of lines recited with just gesture and elegant modulation. The lines relate to some action, and an action must be in some place; but the different actions that complete a story may be in places very remote from each other; and where is the absurdity of allowing that space to represent first Athens and then Sicily which was always known to be neither Sicily nor Athens, but a modern theatre?

By supposition, as place is introduced time may be extended; the time required by the fable elapses for the most part between the acts; for, of so much of the action as is represented, the real and poetical duration is the same. If in the first act preparations for war against Mithridates are represented to be made in Rome, the event of the war may without absurdity be represented, in the castastrophe, as happening in Pontus; we know that there is neither war nor preparation for war; we know that we are neither in Rome nor Pontus; that neither Mithridates nor Lucullus[2] are before us. The drama exhibits successive imitations of successive actions, and why may not the second imitation represent an action that happened years after the first if it be so connected with it that nothing but time can be supposed to intervene? Time is, of all modes of existence, most obsequious to the imagination; a lapse of years is as easily conceived as a passage of hours. In contemplation we easily contract the time of real actions, and therefore willingly permit it to be contracted when we only see their imitation.

It will be asked how the drama moves if it is not credited. It is credited with all the credit due to a drama. It is credited, whenever it moves, as a just picture of a real original, as representing to the auditor what he would himself feel if he were to do or suffer what is there feigned to be suffered or to be done. The reflection that strikes the heart is not that the evils before us are real evils, but that they are evils to which we ourselves may be exposed. If there be any fallacy, it is not that we fancy the players, but that we fancy ourselves unhappy for a moment; but we rather lament the possibility than suppose the presence of misery, as a mother weeps over her babe when she remembers that death may take it from her. The delight of tragedy proceeds from our consciousness of fiction; if we thought murders and treasons real, they would please no more.

Imitations produce pain or pleasure not because they are mistaken for realities, but because they bring realities to mind. When the imagination is recreated[3] by a painted landscape, the trees are not supposed capable to give us shade, or the fountains coolness; but we consider how we should be pleased with such fountains playing beside us and such woods waving over us. We are agitated in reading the history of *Henry the Fifth*, yet no man takes his book for the field of Agincourt.[4] A dramatic exhibition is a book recited with concomitants that increase or diminish its effect. Familiar[5] comedy is often more powerful in the theatre than on the page; imperial tragedy is always less. The humour of Petruchio may be heightened by grimace; but what voice or what gesture can hope to add dignity or force to the soliloquy of Cato?[6]

A play read affects the mind like a play acted. It is therefore evident that the action is not supposed to be real, and it follows that between the acts a longer or shorter time may be allowed to pass, and that no more account of space or duration is to be taken by the auditor of a drama than by the reader of a narrative, before whom may pass in an hour the life of a hero or the revolutions of an empire.

Whether Shakespeare knew the unities[7] and rejected them by design, or deviated from them by happy

---

[1] *calenture* Fever.

[2] *Mithridates … Lucullus* King of Pontus and his Roman opponent, both of whom are characters in the tragedy *Mithridates* (1678) by Nathaniel Lee.

[3] *recreated* Enlivened.

[4] *field of Agincourt* Site of Henry V's 1415 defeat of French troops, depicted in Act 4 of Shakespeare's *Henry V.*

[5] *Familiar* Domestic.

[6] *Petruchio* Protagonist of *The Taming of the Shrew*; *Cato* Protagonist of Joseph Addison's *Cato* (1713), who contemplates suicide in a famous soliloquy (5.1).

[7] *the unities* The classical unities, a set of three guidelines for structuring plays (see note above).

ignorance, it is, I think, impossible to decide and useless to inquire. We may reasonably suppose that when he rose to notice he did not want[1] the counsels and admonitions of scholars and critics, and that he at last deliberately persisted in a practice which he might have begun by chance. As nothing is essential to the fable but unity of action, and as the unities of time and place arise evidently from false assumptions, and, by circumscribing the extent of the drama, lessen its variety, I cannot think it much to be lamented that they were not known by him, or not observed; nor, if such another poet could arise, should I very vehemently reproach him that his first act passed at Venice, and his next in Cyprus.[2] Such violations of rules merely positive[3] become the comprehensive genius of Shakespeare, and such censures are suitable to the minute and slender criticism of Voltaire:

Non usque adeo permiscuit imis
Longus summa dies, ut non, si voce Metelli
Serventur leges, malint a Caesare tolli.[4]

Yet when I speak thus slightly of dramatic rules, I cannot but recollect how much wit and learning may be produced against me; before such authorities I am afraid to stand, not that I think the present question one of those that are to be decided by mere authority, but because it is to be suspected that these precepts have not been so easily received but for better reasons than I have yet been able to find. The result of my inquiries, in which it would be ludicrous to boast of impartiality, is that the unities of time and place are not essential to a just drama, that though they may sometimes conduce to pleasure, they are always to be sacrificed to the nobler beauties of variety and instruction; and that a play, written with nice observation of critical rules, is to be contemplated as an elaborate curiosity, as the product of superfluous and ostentatious art, by which is shown rather what is possible than what is necessary.

He that, without diminution of any other excellence, shall preserve all the unities unbroken deserves the like applause with the architect who shall display all the orders[5] of architecture in a citadel without any deduction from its strength; but the principal beauty of a citadel is to exclude the enemy, and the greatest graces of a play are to copy nature and instruct life.

—1765

from *Lives of the English Poets*

from JOHN MILTON

I am now to examine *Paradise Lost*, a poem which, considered with respect to design, may claim the first place, and with respect to performance the second,[6] among the productions of the human mind.

By the general consent of critics the first praise of genius is due to the writer of an epic poem, as it requires an assemblage of all the powers which are singly sufficient for other compositions. Poetry is the art of uniting pleasure with truth, by calling imagination to the help of reason. Epic poetry undertakes to teach the most important truths by the most pleasing precepts, and therefore relates some great event in the most affecting manner. History must supply the writer with the rudiments of narration, which he must improve and exalt by a nobler art, must animate by dramatic energy, and diversify by retrospection and anticipation; morality must teach him the exact bounds and different shades of vice and virtue; from policy and the practice of life he has to learn the discriminations of character and the tendency of the passions, either single or combined; and physiology must supply him with illustrations and images. To put these materials to poetical use is required an imagination capable of painting nature and realizing fiction. Nor is he yet a poet till he has attained the whole extension of his language, distinguished all the delicacies of phrase, and all the colours of words, and learned to adjust their different sounds to all the varieties of metrical modulation.

[1] *want* Lack.

[2] *first act … Cyprus* As in the first two acts of *Othello*.

[3] *positive* Proceeding from custom and arbitrarily instituted.

[4] *Non … tolli* Latin: "The course of time does not bring such confusion that the laws would not rather be trampled upon by a Caesar than saved by a Metellus." From Lucan's *Pharsalia* (3.138–40), an epic poem of the Roman civil wars. Metellus was a minor Roman politician.

[5] *all the orders* I.e., Doric, Ionic, and Corinthian.

[6] *second* With Homer's *Iliad* presumably ranked first.

Bossu[1] is of opinion that the poet's first work is to find a *moral*, which his fable is afterwards to illustrate and establish. This seems to have been the process only of Milton: the moral of other poems is incidental and consequent; in Milton's only it is essential and intrinsic. His purpose was the most useful and the most arduous: "to vindicate the ways of God to man";[2] to show the reasonableness of religion, and the necessity of obedience to the Divine Law.

To convey this moral there must be a *fable*, a narration artfully constructed so as to excite curiosity and surprise expectation. In this part of his work Milton must be confessed to have equalled every other poet. He has involved in his account of the Fall of Man the events which preceded, and those that were to follow it: he has interwoven the whole system of theology with such propriety that every part appears to be necessary, and scarcely any recital is wished shorter for the sake of quickening the progress of the main action.

The subject of an epic poem is naturally an event of great importance. That of Milton is not the destruction of a city, the conduct of a colony, or the foundation of an empire. His subject is the fate of worlds, the revolutions of heaven and of earth; rebellion against the Supreme King raised by the highest order of created beings; the overthrow of their host and the punishment of their crime; the creation of a new race of reasonable creatures; their original happiness and innocence, their forfeiture of immortality, and their restoration to hope and peace.

Great events can be hastened or retarded only by persons of elevated dignity. Before the greatness displayed in Milton's poem all other greatness shrinks away. The weakest of his agents are the highest and noblest of human beings, the original parents of mankind; with whose actions the elements consented, on whose rectitude or deviation of will depended the state of terrestrial nature and the condition of all the future inhabitants of the globe. Of the other agents in the poem the chief are such as it is irreverence to name on slight occasions. The rest were lower powers;

> of which the least could wield
> Those elements, and arm him with the force
> Of all their regions;[3]

powers which only the control of Omnipotence restrains from laying creation waste and filling the vast expanse of space with ruin and confusion. To display the motives and actions of beings thus superior, so far as human reason can examine them or human imagination represent them, is the task which this mighty poet has undertaken and performed.

In the examination of epic poems much speculation is commonly employed upon the *characters*. The characters in the *Paradise Lost* which admit of examination are those of angels and of man; of angels good and evil, of man in his innocent and sinful state.

Among the angels the virtue of Raphael is mild and placid, of easy condescension and free communication; that of Michael is regal and lofty, and, as may seem, attentive to the dignity of his own nature. Abdiel and Gabriel appear occasionally and act as every incident requires; the solitary fidelity of Abdiel is very amiably painted.

Of the evil angels the characters are more diversified. To Satan, as Addison observes, such sentiments are given as suit "the most exalted and most depraved being."[4] Milton has been censured by Clarke[5] for the impiety which sometimes breaks from Satan's mouth. For there are thoughts, as he justly remarks, which no observation of character can justify, because no good man would willingly permit them to pass, however transiently, through his own mind. To make Satan speak as a rebel, without any such expressions as might taint the reader's imagination, was indeed one of the great difficulties in Milton's undertaking, and I cannot but think that he has extricated himself with great happiness. There is in Satan's speeches little that can give pain to a pious ear. The language of rebellion cannot be the same with that of obedience. The malignity of Satan foams in haughtiness and obstinacy; but his expressions are commonly general, and no otherwise offensive than as they are wicked.

---

[1] *Bossu* French abbot René le Bossu. The opinion referred to is expressed in his *Treatise on the Epic Poem* (1675).

[2] *to vindicate ... man* A misquote of *Paradise Lost* 1.26, "justify the ways of God to men." Alexander Pope's *Essay on Man*, however, hoped to "vindicate the ways of God to man" (1.16).

[3] *of which ... regions* From *Paradise Lost* 6.221–23.

[4] *the most ... being* From essay no. 303 in *The Spectator*.

[5] *Clarke* John Clarke, who criticizes Milton in his *Essay upon Study* (1731).

The other chiefs of the celestial rebellion are very judiciously discriminated in the first and second books; and the ferocious character of Moloch appears, both in the battle and the council, with exact consistency.

To Adam and to Eve are given during their innocence such sentiments as innocence can generate and utter. Their love is pure benevolence and mutual veneration; their repasts are without luxury and their diligence without toil. Their addresses to their Maker have little more than the voice of admiration and gratitude. Fruition left them nothing to ask, and Innocence left them nothing to fear.

But with guilt enter distrust and discord, mutual accusation, and stubborn self-defence; they regard each other with alienated minds and dread their Creator as the avenger of their transgression. At last they seek shelter in his mercy, soften to repentance, and melt in supplication. Both before and after the Fall the superiority of Adam is diligently sustained.

Of the *probable* and the *marvellous*, two parts of a vulgar[1] epic poem which immerge[2] the critic in deep consideration, the *Paradise Lost* requires little to be said. It contains the history of a miracle, of Creation and Redemption; it displays the power and the mercy of the Supreme Being: the probable therefore is marvellous, and the marvellous is probable. The substance of the narrative is truth; and as truth allows no choice, it is, like necessity, superior to rule. To the accidental or adventitious parts, as to every thing human, some slight exceptions may be made. But the main fabric is immovably supported.…

In Milton every line breathes sanctity of thought and purity of manners, except when the train of the narration requires the introduction of the rebellious spirits; and even they are compelled to acknowledge their subjection to God in such a manner as excites reverence and confirms piety.

Of human beings there are but two; but those two are the parents of mankind, venerable before their fall for dignity and innocence, and amiable after it for repentance and submission. In their first state their affection is tender without weakness and their pity sublime without presumption. When they have sinned they show how discord begins in mutual frailty, and how it ought to cease in mutual forbearance; how confidence of the divine favour is forfeited by sin, and how hope of pardon may be obtained by penitence and prayer. A state of innocence we can only conceive, if indeed in our present misery it be possible to conceive it; but the sentiments and worship proper to a fallen and offending being we have all to learn, as we have all to practise.

The poet, whatever be done, is always great. Our progenitors in their first state conversed with angels; even when folly and sin had degraded them they had not in their humiliation "the port of mean suitors;"[3] and they rise again to reverential regard when we find that their prayers were heard.

As human passions did not enter the world before the Fall, there is in the *Paradise Lost* little opportunity for the pathetic; but what little there is has not been lost. That passion which is peculiar to rational nature, the anguish arising from the consciousness of transgression and the horrors attending the sense of the Divine Displeasure, are very justly described and forcibly impressed. But the passions are moved only on one occasion; sublimity is the general and prevailing quality of this poem—sublimity variously modified, sometimes descriptive, sometimes argumentative.[4]…

Milton would not have excelled in dramatic writing; he knew human nature only in the gross, and had never studied the shades of character, nor the combinations of concurring or the perplexity of contending passions. He had read much and knew what books could teach; but had mingled little in the world, and was deficient in the knowledge which experience must confer.

Through all his greater works there prevails an uniform peculiarity of *diction*, a mode and cast of expression which bears little resemblance to that of any former writer, and which is so far removed from common use that an unlearned reader when he first opens his book finds himself surprised by a new language.

This novelty has been, by those who can find nothing wrong in Milton, imputed to his laborious endeavours after words suitable to the grandeur of his ideas. "Our language," says Addison, "sunk under

[1] *vulgar* Common, familiar.

[2] *immerge* Immerse.

[3] *the port … suitors* From *Paradise Lost* 11.8–9.

[4] *argumentative* I.e., contributing to the argument, or theme, of the poem.

him."[1] But the truth is that, both in prose and verse, he had formed his style by a perverse and pedantic principle. He was desirous to use English words with a foreign idiom. This in all his prose is discovered and condemned, for there judgement operates freely, neither softened by the beauty nor awed by the dignity of his thoughts; but such is the power of his poetry that his call is obeyed without resistance, the reader feels himself in captivity to a higher and a nobler mind, and criticism sinks in admiration.

Milton's style was not modified by his subject: what is shown with greater extent in *Paradise Lost* may be found in *Comus*.[2] One source of his peculiarity was his familiarity with the Tuscan poets: the disposition of his words is, I think, frequently Italian; perhaps sometimes combined with other tongues. Of him, at last, may be said what Jonson says of Spenser, that "he wrote no language,"[3] but has formed what Butler calls "a Babylonish dialect,"[4] in itself harsh and barbarous, but made by exalted genius and extensive learning the vehicle of so much instruction and so much pleasure that, like other lovers, we find grace in its deformity.

Whatever be the faults of his diction he cannot want the praise of copiousness and variety; he was master of his language in its full extent, and has selected the melodious words with such diligence that from his book alone the art of English poetry might be learned.

After his diction something must be said of his versification. "The measure," he says, "is the English heroic verse without rhyme."[5] Of this mode he had many examples among the Italians, and some in his own country. The Earl of Surrey[6] is said to have translated one of Virgil's books without rhyme, and besides our tragedies a few short poems had appeared in blank verse; particularly one tending to reconcile the nation to Raleigh's wild attempt upon Guiana,[7] and probably written by Raleigh himself. These petty performances cannot be supposed to have much influenced Milton, who more probably took his hint from Trisino's *Italia Liberata*;[8] and, finding blank verse easier than rhyme, was desirous of persuading himself that it is better.

"Rhyme," he says, and says truly, "is no necessary adjunct of true poetry."[9] But perhaps of poetry as a mental operation metre or music is no necessary adjunct; it is however by the music of metre that poetry has been discriminated in all languages, and in languages melodiously constructed with a due proportion of long and short syllables metre is sufficient. But one language cannot communicate its rules to another; where metre is scanty and imperfect some help is necessary. The music of the English heroic line strikes the ear so faintly that it is easily lost, unless all the syllables of every line cooperate together; this cooperation can be only obtained by the preservation of every verse unmingled with another as a distinct system of sounds, and this distinctness is obtained and preserved by the artifice of rhyme. The variety of pauses, so much boasted by the lovers of blank verse, changes the measures of an English poet to the periods of a declaimer; and there are only a few skilful and happy readers of Milton who enable their audience to perceive where the lines end or begin. "Blank verse," said an ingenious critic,[10] "seems to be verse only to the eye."

Poetry may subsist without rhyme, but English poetry will not often please; nor can rhyme ever be safely spared but where the subject is able to support itself. Blank verse makes some approach to that which is called the "lapidary style,"[11] has neither the easiness of prose nor the melody of numbers, and therefore tires by long continuance. Of the Italian writers without rhyme, whom Milton alleges as precedents, not one is popular; what reason could urge in its defence has been confuted by the ear.

[1] *Our … him* From *Spectator* no. 297.

[2] *Comus* Masque by Milton.

[3] *Jonson … language* Poet Ben Jonson in his *Timber, or Discoveries* (1640), no. 116.

[4] *Butler … dialect* Seventeenth-century poet Samuel Butler, in his satire *Hudibras* (1663), 1.1.93.

[5] *The measure … rhyme* From Milton's preface to *Paradise Lost*.

[6] *Earl of Surrey* Henry Howard (1517–47), who completed blank-verse translations of books 2 and 4 of Virgil's *Aeneid*.

[7] *Raleigh's … Guiana* Sir Walter Ralegh had, in 1595, led a search in Venezuela for the fabled Eldorado. The poem referred to is "Of Guiana, an Epic Song" (1596), actually by George Chapman.

[8] *Trisino's Italia Liberata* The epic poem *Italy Delivered from the Goths* (1547–48) by Giovanni Giorgio.

[9] *Rhyme … poetry* From the preface to *Paradise Lost*.

[10] *ingenious critic* In his *Life of Johnson* 4.43, Boswell says this statement was made by art critic William Locke (1732–1810).

[11] *lapidary style* Style characteristic of monument inscriptions.

But, whatever be the advantage of rhyme, I cannot prevail on myself to wish that Milton had been a rhymer, for I cannot wish his work to be other than it is; yet like other heroes he is to be admired rather than imitated. He that thinks himself capable of astonishing may write blank verse, but those that hope only to please must condescend to rhyme.

The highest praise of genius is original invention. Milton cannot be said to have contrived the structure of an epic poem, and therefore owes reverence to that vigour and amplitude of mind to which all generations must be indebted for the art of poetical narration, for the texture of the fable, the variation of incidents, the interposition of dialogue, and all the stratagems that surprise and enchain attention. But of all the borrowers from Homer, Milton is perhaps the least indebted. He was naturally a thinker for himself, confident of his own abilities and disdainful of help or hindrance; he did not refuse admission to the thoughts or images of his predecessors, but he did not seek them. From his contemporaries he neither courted nor received support; there is in his writings nothing by which the pride of other authors might be gratified or favour gained, no exchange of praise nor solicitation of support. His great works were performed under discountenance and in blindness, but difficulties vanished at his touch; he was born for whatever is arduous; and his work is not the greatest of heroic poems, only because it is not the first. —1779

from ALEXANDER POPE

The person of Pope is well known not to have been formed by the nicest model. He has, in his account of the "Little Club,"[1] compared himself to a spider, and by another is described as protuberant behind and before. He is said to have been beautiful in his infancy; but he was of a constitution originally feeble and weak, and, as bodies of a tender frame are easily distorted, his deformity was probably in part the effect of his application. His stature was so low that to bring him to a level with common tables it was necessary to raise his seat. But his face was not displeasing, and his eyes were animated and vivid.

By natural deformity or accidental distortion his vital functions were so much disordered that his life was a "long disease."[2] His most frequent assailant was the headache, which he used to relieve by inhaling the steam of coffee, which he very frequently required.

Most of what can be told concerning his petty peculiarities was communicated by a female domestic of the Earl of Oxford, who knew him perhaps after the middle of life. He was then so weak as to stand in perpetual need of female attendance; extremely sensible of cold, so that he wore a kind of fur doublet under a shirt of very coarse warm linen with fine sleeves. When he rose he was invested in a bodice made of stiff canvas, being scarce able to hold himself erect till they were laced, and he then put on a flannel waistcoat. One side was contracted. His legs were so slender that he enlarged their bulk with three pair of stockings, which were drawn on and off by the maid; for he was not able to dress or undress himself, and neither went to bed nor rose without help. His weakness made it very difficult for him to be clean.

His hair had fallen almost all away, and he used to dine sometimes with Lord Oxford, privately, in a velvet cap. His dress of ceremony was black, with a tie-wig and a little sword ...

His declaration that his care for his works ceased at their publication was not strictly true. His parental attention never abandoned them; what he found amiss in the first edition, he silently corrected in those that followed. He appears to have revised the *Iliad* and freed it from some of its imperfections, and the *Essay on Criticism* received many improvements after its first appearance. It will seldom be found that he altered without adding clearness, elegance, or vigour. Pope had perhaps the judgement of Dryden; but Dryden certainly wanted the diligence of Pope.

In acquired knowledge the superiority must be allowed to Dryden, whose education was more scholastic[3] and who before he became an author had been allowed more time for study, with better means of information. His mind has a larger range, and he collects his images and illustrations from a more exten-

[1] *his account ... Club* Pope's account appears in *Guardian* no. 92.

[2] *long disease* From Pope's "Epistle to Dr. Arbuthnot," line 132: "This long disease, my life."

[3] *scholastic* Systematic; also, pertaining to formal logic.

sive circumference of science. Dryden knew more of man in his general nature, and Pope in his local manners. The notions of Dryden were formed by comprehensive speculation, and those of Pope by minute attention. There is more dignity in the knowledge of Dryden, and more certainty in that of Pope.

Poetry was not the sole praise of either, for both excelled likewise in prose; but Pope did not borrow his prose from his predecessor. The style of Dryden is capricious and varied, that of Pope is cautious and uniform; Dryden obeys the motions of his own mind, Pope constrains his mind to his own rules of composition. Dryden is sometimes vehement and rapid; Pope is always smooth, uniform, and gentle. Dryden's page is a natural field, rising into inequalities, and diversified by the varied exuberance of abundant vegetation; Pope's is a velvet lawn, shaven by the scythe, and levelled by the roller.

Of genius, that power which constitutes a poet; that quality without which judgement is cold and knowledge is inert; that energy which collects, combines, amplifies, and animates—the superiority must, with some hesitation, be allowed to Dryden. It is not to be inferred that of this poetical vigour Pope had only a little, because Dryden had more, for every other writer since Milton must give place to Pope; and even of Dryden it must be said that if he has brighter paragraphs, he has not better poems. Dryden's performances were always hasty, either excited by some external occasion, or extorted by domestic necessity; he composed without consideration, and published without correction. What his mind could supply at call, or gather in one excursion, was all that he sought, and all that he gave. The dilatory caution of Pope enabled him to condense his sentiments, to multiply his images, and to accumulate all that study might produce, or chance might supply. If the flights of Dryden therefore are higher, Pope continues longer on the wing. If of Dryden's fire the blaze is brighter, of Pope's the heat is more regular and constant. Dryden often surpasses expectation, and Pope never falls below it. Dryden is read with frequent astonishment, and Pope with perpetual delight.…

Of *The Dunciad* the hint is confessedly taken from Dryden's *MacFlecknoe*, but the plan is so enlarged and diversified as justly to claim the praise of an original, and affords perhaps the best specimen that has yet appeared of personal satire ludicrously pompous.

That the design was moral, whatever the author might tell either his readers or himself, I am not convinced. The first motive was the desire of revenging the contempt with which Theobald had treated his *Shakespeare*,[1] and regaining the honour which he had lost, by crushing his opponent. Theobald was not of bulk enough to fill a poem, and therefore it was necessary to find other enemies with other names, at whose expense he might divert the public.

In this design there was petulance and malignity enough; but I cannot think it very criminal. An author places himself uncalled before the tribunal of criticism, and solicits fame at the hazard of disgrace. Dullness or deformity are not culpable in themselves, but may be very justly reproached when they pretend to the honour of wit or the influence of beauty. If bad writers were to pass without reprehension what should restrain them? *Impune diem consumpserit ingens "Telephus"*;[2] and upon bad writers only will censure have much effect. The satire which brought Theobald and Moore into contempt dropped impotent from Bentley like the javelin of Priam.[3]

All truth is valuable, and satirical criticism may be considered as useful when it rectifies error and improves judgement: he that refines the public taste is a public benefactor.

The beauties of this poem are well known; its chief fault is the grossness of its images. Pope and Swift had an unnatural delight in ideas physically impure, such as every other tongue utters with unwillingness, and of which every ear shrinks from the mention.

[1] *Theobald … Shakespeare* Pope made Lewis Theobald, a Shakespeare scholar who had pointed out several errors in Pope's edition of Shakespeare, the hero of his biting satire *The Dunciad*.

[2] *Impune … Telephus* Latin: "Shall an interminable *Telephus* consume an entire day with impunity?" (Juvenal's *Satires* 1.4–5). *Telephus* was a fifth-century BCE play by the Greek dramatist Euripides.

[3] *Moore* James Moore Smythe, who Pope claimed had stolen lines from his *Epistle to a Lady* for use in a play; *Bentley* Richard Bentley, a classical scholar who in 1732 produced a controversial edition of Milton's *Paradise Lost*. Pope satirizes him in both *The Dunciad* and "An Epistle to Dr. Arbuthnot"; *Priam* King of Troy at the time of the Trojan War. He attempted to kill Neoptolemus, son of Achilles, but his feeble attempt was in vain, and he was then slain by Neoptolemus.

But even this fault, offensive as it is, may be forgiven for the excellence of other passages, such as the formation and dissolution of Moore, the account of the Traveller, the misfortune of the Florist, and the crowded thoughts and stately numbers which dignify the concluding paragraph.

The alterations which have been made in *The Dunciad*, not always for the better, require that it should be published, as in the last collection,[1] with all its variations.

The *Essay on Man* was a work of great labour and long consideration, but certainly not the happiest of Pope's performances. The subject is perhaps not very proper for poetry, and the poet was not sufficiently master of his subject; metaphysical morality was to him a new study, he was proud of his acquisitions, and, supposing himself master of great secrets, was in haste to teach what he had not learned. Thus he tells us, in the first Epistle, that from the nature of the Supreme Being may be deduced an order of beings such as mankind, because Infinite Excellence can do only what is best. He finds out that these beings must be "somewhere," and that "all the question is whether man be in a wrong place."[2] Surely if, according to the poet's Leibnitzian reasoning,[3] we may infer that man ought to be only because he is, we may allow that his place is the right place, because he has it. Supreme Wisdom is not less infallible in disposing than in creating. But what is meant by "somewhere" and "place" and "wrong place" it had been vain to ask Pope, who probably had never asked himself.

Having exalted himself into the chair of wisdom he tells us much that every man knows, and much that he does not know himself; that we see but little, and that the order of the universe is beyond our comprehension, an opinion not very uncommon; and that there is a chain of subordinate beings "from infinite to nothing," of which himself and his readers are equally ignorant. But he gives us one comfort which, without his help, he supposes unattainable, in the position "that though we are fools, yet God is wise."

This *Essay* affords an egregious instance of the predominance of genius, the dazzling splendour of imagery, and the seductive powers of eloquence. Never were penury of knowledge and vulgarity of sentiment so happily disguised. The reader feels his mind full, though he learns nothing; and when he meets it in its new array no longer knows the talk of his mother and his nurse. When these wonder-working sounds sink into sense and the doctrine of the *Essay*, disrobed of its ornaments, is left to the powers of its naked excellence, what shall we discover? That we are, in comparison with our Creator, very weak and ignorant; that we do not uphold the chain of existence; and that we could not make one another with more skill than we are made. We may learn yet more: that the arts of human life were copied from the instinctive operations of other animals; that if the world be made for man, it may be said that man was made for geese. To these profound principles of natural knowledge are added some moral instructions equally new: that self-interest well understood will produce social concord; that men are mutual gainers by mutual benefits; that evil is sometimes balanced by good; that human advantages are unstable and fallacious, of uncertain duration and doubtful effect; that our true honour is not to have a great part, but to act it well; that virtue only is our own; and that happiness is always in our power.

Surely a man of no very comprehensive search may venture to say that he has heard all this before, but it was never till now recommended by such a blaze of embellishment or such sweetness of melody. The vigorous contraction of some thoughts, the luxuriant amplification of others, the incidental illustrations, and sometimes the dignity, sometimes the softness of the verses, enchain philosophy, suspend criticism, and oppress judgement by overpowering pleasure.

This is true of many paragraphs; yet if I had undertaken to exemplify Pope's felicity of composition before a rigid critic I should not select the *Essay on Man*, for it contains more lines unsuccessfully laboured, more harshness of diction, more thoughts imperfectly expressed, more levity without elegance, and more heaviness without strength, than will easily be found in all his other works.

—1781

[1] *last collection* Published by Warburton in 1751.

[2] *somewhere ... place* From *Essay on Man* 1.47–50.

[3] *Leibnitzian reasoning* Reasoning of the sort used by German philosopher and mathematician Gottfried Wilhelm Leibnitz, who is known for his belief that this is necessarily "the best of all possible worlds."

Letters

To the Right Honourable
The Earl of Chesterfield[1]

7 February 1755

My Lord,

I have been lately informed, by the proprietor of *The World*,[2] that two papers, in which my Dictionary is recommended to the public, were written by your Lordship. To be so distinguished is an honour which, being very little accustomed to favours from the great, I know not well how to receive, or in what terms to acknowledge.

When, upon some slight encouragement, I first visited your Lordship, I was overpowered, like the rest of mankind, by the enchantment of your address,[3] and could not forbear to wish that I might boast myself *le vainqueur du vainqueur de la terre*;[4]—that I might obtain that regard for which I saw the world contending. But I found my attendance so little encouraged that neither pride nor modesty would suffer me to continue it. When I had once addressed your Lordship in public, I had exhausted all the art of pleasing which a retired and uncourtly scholar can possess. I had done all that I could; and no man is well pleased to have his all neglected, be it ever so little.

Seven years, my lord, have now passed since I waited in your outward room, or was repulsed from your door; during which time I have been pushing on my work through difficulties of which it is useless to complain, and have brought it, at last, to the verge of publication, without one act of assistance, one word of encouragement, or one smile of favour. Such treatment I did not expect, for I never had a patron before.

The shepherd in Virgil grew at last acquainted with Love, and found him a native of the rocks.[5] Is not a patron, my lord, one who looks with unconcern on a man struggling for life in the water, and, when he has reached ground, encumbers him with help? The notice which you have been pleased to take of my labours, had it been early, had been kind; but it has been delayed till I am indifferent, and cannot enjoy it: till I am solitary, and cannot impart it; till I am known, and do not want it. I hope it is no very cynical asperity[6] not to confess obligations where no benefit has been received, or to be unwilling that the public should consider me as owing that to a patron, which Providence has enabled me to do for myself.

Having carried on my work thus far with so little obligation to any favourer of learning, I shall not be disappointed though I should conclude it, if less be possible, with less; for I have been long wakened from that dream of hope, in which I once boasted myself with so much exultation,

My Lord,
Your Lordship's most humble,
most obedient servant,
SAMUEL JOHNSON

[1] *Earl of Chesterfield* Philip Stanhope (1694–1773), fourth Earl of Chesterfield, a politician who placed great value on cultural refinement. Seeking patronage, Johnson went to him with a plan for the *Dictionary*; Chesterfield donated only £10 and, Johnson felt, treated him rudely. Seven years later when the *Dictionary* was about to be published, Chesterfield wrote two articles in support of it, associating himself with the *Dictionary* as Johnson's advocate—a position Johnson thought he had done nothing to deserve.

[2] *The World* Periodical founded by Robert Dodsley, who published many of Johnson's works and helped to finance the *Dictionary*. Chesterfield's essays on the *Dictionary* appeared in *The World*.

[3] *enchantment of your address* Social manner.

[4] *le vainqueur … la terre* French: "the conqueror of the conqueror of the earth." From the first line of *Alaric* (1656), an epic by Georges de Scudéry.

[5] *The shepherd … the rocks* In Virgil's *Eclogues* 8.44–46 a shepherd, in despair because his lover has left him for a rich man, describes love as an inhuman boy born from the "harsh rocks" of a mountain.

[6] *asperity* Bitter discourtesy.

To MRS. THRALE[1]

10 July 1780
London

Dear Madam

If Mr. Thrale eats but half his usual quantity, he can hardly eat too much.[2] It were better however to have some rule, and some security. Last week I saw flesh but twice, and I think fish once, the rest was pease.[3]

You are afraid, you say, lest I extenuate[4] myself too fast, and are an enemy to violence: but did you never hear nor read, dear Madam, that every man has his genius, and that the great rule by which all excellence is attained, and all success procured, is to follow genius; and have you not observed in all our conversations that my genius is always in extremes; that I am very noisy, or very silent; very gloomy, or very merry; very sour, or very kind? And would you have me cross my genius, when it leads me sometimes to voracity and sometimes to abstinence? You know that the oracle[5] said follow your genius. When we get together again (but when, alas, will that be?) you can manage me, and spare me the solicitude of managing myself.

Poor Miss Owen[6] called on me on Saturday, with that fond and tender application which is natural to misery, when it looks to everybody for that help which nobody can give. I was melted; and soothed and counselled her as well as I could, and am to visit her tomorrow.

She gave a very honourable account of my dear Queeney and says of my master[7] that she thinks his manner and temper more altered than his looks, but of this alteration she could give no particular account; and all that she could say ended in this, that he is now sleepy in the morning. I do not wonder at the scantiness of her narration, she is too busy within to turn her eyes abroad.

I am glad that Pepys[8] is come, but hope that resolute temperance will make him unnecessary. I doubt he can do no good to poor Mr. Scrase.[9]

I stay at home to work, and yet do not work diligently; nor can tell when I shall have done, nor perhaps does anybody but myself wish me to have done; for what can they hope I shall do better? yet I wish the work was over, and I was at liberty. And what would I do if I was at liberty? Would I go to see Mrs. Aston and Mrs. Porter,[10] and see the old places, and sigh to find that my old friends are gone? Would I recall plans of life which I never brought into practice, and hopes of excellence which I once presumed, and never have attained? Would I compare what I now am with what I once expected to have been? Is it reasonable to wish for suggestions of shame, and opportunities of sorrow?

If you please, Madam, we will have an end of this, and contrive some other wishes. I wish I had you in an evening, and I wish I had you in a morning; and I wish I could have a little talk, and see a little frolic. For all this I must stay, but life will not stay.

I will end my letter and go to Blackmore's Life, when I have told you that

I am, &c,

SAM. JOHNSON.

To MRS. THRALE

19 June 1783
Bolt Court, Fleet Street

Dear Madam

I am sitting down in no cheerful solitude to write a narrative which would once have affected you with tenderness and sorrow, but which you will perhaps pass over now with the careless glance of frigid indifference. For this diminution of regard, however, I know not whether I ought to blame you, who may have reasons

[1] *To Mrs. Thrale* Hester Thrale, close friend of Johnson.

[2] *If ... much* Thrale's husband, Henry, had recently suffered numerous strokes, and his health was continually deteriorating. Nevertheless, he continued to eat what both his doctors believed was an unhealthy amount of food.

[3] *pease* Mashed peas.

[4] *extenuate* Spread or make slim. Johnson was then working on his *Lives of the Poets.*

[5] *the oracle* Persius, Roman satirical poet of the first century CE.

[6] *Miss Owen* Distant cousin and close childhood friend of Mrs. Thrale.

[7] *Queeney* The Thrales's eldest child; *my master* I.e., Henry Thrale.

[8] *Pepys* One of the physicians who treated Mr. Thrale.

[9] *Mr. Scrase* Friend of the Thrales.

[10] *Mrs. Aston and Mrs. Porter* Johnson's friend and his step-daughter, respectively. The former lived at Lichfield and the second at Stow Hill in Lichfield.

which I cannot know, and I do not blame myself, who have for a great part of human life done you what good I could, and have never done you evil.

I had been disordered in the usual way, and had been relieved by the usual methods, by opium and cathartics, but had rather lessened my dose of opium.

On Monday the 16th I sat for my picture, and walked a considerable way with little inconvenience. In the afternoon and evening I felt myself light and easy, and began to plan schemes of life. Thus I went to bed, and in a short time waked and sat up, as has been long my custom, when I felt a confusion and indistinctness in my head, which lasted I suppose about half a minute; I was alarmed, and prayed God that however he might afflict my body, he would spare my understanding. This prayer, that I might try the integrity of my faculties, I made in Latin verse. The lines were not very good, but I knew them not to be very good: I made them easily, and concluded myself to be unimpaired in my faculties. Soon after I perceived that I had suffered a paralytic stroke, and that my speech was taken from me. I had no pain, and so little dejection in this dreadful state, that I wondered at my own apathy, and considered that perhaps death itself when it should come would excite less horror than seems now to attend it.

In order to rouse the vocal organs I took two drams. Wine has been celebrated for the production of eloquence. I put myself into violent motion, and I think repeated it; but all was vain. I then went to bed, and, strange as it may seem, I think, slept. When I saw light, it was time to contrive what I should do. Though God stopped my speech he left me my hand, I enjoyed a mercy which was not granted to my dear friend Lawrence,[1] who now perhaps overlooks me as I am writing, and rejoices that I have what he wanted. My first note was necessarily to my servant, who came in talking, and could not immediately comprehend why he should read what I put into his hands.

I then wrote a card to Mr Allen,[2] that I might have a discreet friend at hand to act as occasion should require. In penning this note I had some difficulty; my hand, I knew not how nor why, made wrong letters. I then wrote to Dr. Taylor to come to me, and bring Dr. Heberden, and I sent to Dr. Brocklesby, who is my neighbour. My physicians are very friendly and very disinterested, and give me great hopes, but you may imagine my situation. I have so far recovered my vocal powers as to repeat the Lord's Prayer with no very imperfect articulation. My memory, I hope, yet remains as it was; but such an attack produces solicitude for the safety of every faculty.

How this will be received by you I know not. I hope you will sympathize with me; but perhaps My mistress gracious, mild, and good, Cries! Is he dumb? 'Tis time he shou'd.[3]

But can this be possible? I hope it cannot. I hope that what, when I could speak, I spoke of you, and to you, will be in a sober and serious hour remembered by you; and surely it cannot be remembered but with some degree of kindness. I have loved you with virtuous affection; I have honoured you with sincere esteem. Let not all our endearments be forgotten, but let me have in this great distress your pity and your prayers. You see I yet turn to you with my complaints as a settled and unalienable friend; do not, do not drive me from you, for I have not deserved either neglect or hatred.

To the girls, who do not write often, for Susy has written only once, and Miss Thrale owes me a letter,[4] I earnestly recommend, as their guardian and friend, that they remember their Creator in the days of their youth.

I suppose you may wish to know how my disease is treated by the physicians. They put a blister upon my back, and two from my ear to my throat, one on a side. The blister on the back has done little, and those on the throat have not risen. I bullied and bounced (it sticks to our last sand)[5] and compelled the apothecary to make his salve according to the *Edinburgh Dispensatory*,[6] that it might adhere better. I have two on now of my own

[1] *Lawrence* Dr. Thomas Lawrence, who had been Johnson's physician for several years, and who had died earlier that month.

[2] *Mr Allen* Johnson's landlord and neighbor.

[3] *My … shou'd* Paraphrase of lines 181–82 of Jonathan Swift's *Verses on the Death of Dr. Swift*: "The Queen, so gracious, mild and good, / Cries, 'Is he gone? 'tis time he should.'"

[4] *the girls … letter* Johnson had been made guardian of the Thrales' children after Henry Thrale's death. Here he mentions two of the daughters, Susanna Arabella and Queeney, the eldest (who is therefore referred to as "Miss Thrale").

[5] *it … sand* Reference to Alexander Pope's *Epistles to Several Persons*, Epistle 1.225, in which he says that a person's ruling passion continues until the end of his life.

[6] *Dispensatory* Book describing the preparation of medicines.

prescription. They likewise give me salt of hartshorn,[1] which I take with no great confidence, but am satisfied that what can be done is done for me.

O God! give me comfort and confidence in Thee: forgive my sins; and if it be Thy good pleasure, relieve my diseases for Jesus Christ's sake. Amen.

I am almost ashamed of this querulous letter, but now it is written, let it go.

I am, &c.,

SAM. JOHNSON.

To Mrs. Thrale

2 July 1784

Madam

If I interpret your letter right, you are ignominiously married;[2] if it is yet undone, let us once more talk together. If you have abandoned your children and your religion, God forgive your wickedness; if you have forfeited your fame[3] and your country, may your folly do no further mischief. If the last act is yet to do, I who have loved you, esteemed you, reverenced you, and served you, I who long thought you the first of humankind, entreat that, before your fate is irrevocable, I may once more see you. I was, I once was,

Madam, most truly yours,

SAM. JOHNSON

I will come down, if you permit it.

To Mrs. Thrale

8 July 1784

London[4]

Dear Madam

What you have done, however I may lament it, I have no pretence to resent, as it has not been injurious to me: I therefore breathe out one sigh more of tenderness, perhaps useless, but at least sincere.

I wish that God may grant you every blessing, that you may be happy in this world for its short continuance, and eternally happy in a better state; and whatever I can contribute to your happiness I am very ready to repay for that kindness which soothed twenty years of a life radically wretched.

Do not think slightly of the advice which I now presume to offer. Prevail upon Mr. Piozzi to settle in England. You may live here with more dignity than in Italy, and with more security. Your rank will be higher, and your fortune more under your own eye. I desire not to detail all my reasons, but every argument of prudence and interest is for England, and only some phantoms of imagination seduce you to Italy.

I am afraid however that my counsel is vain, yet I have eased my heart by giving it.

When Queen Mary[5] took the resolution of sheltering herself in England, the Archbishop of St. Andrew's, attempting to dissuade her, attended on her journey and, when they came to the irremeable[6] stream that separated the two kingdoms, walked by her side into the water, in the middle of which he seized her bridle, and, with earnestness proportioned to her danger and his own affection, pressed her to return. The Queen went forward.—If the parallel reaches thus far, may it go no further. The tears stand in my eyes.

I am going into Derbyshire, and hope to be followed by your good wishes, for I am, with great affection,

Your, &c,

SAM. JOHNSON

Any letters that come for me hither will be sent me.

[1] *salts of hartshorn* Smelling salts.

[2] *If … married* Mrs. Thrale had written to Johnson to inform him that she intended to marry Gabriel Piozzi, an Italian musician. Because Piozzi was Roman Catholic and, as a result of his profession, was seen as her social inferior, and because Hester Thrale was a mature woman not needing or seeking financial support, the marriage was a scandalous one, and it resulted in strained relations between Hester Thrale Piozzi and her family and friends.

[3] *fame* Good reputation or character.

[4] *8 July … London* Johnson's former letter to Hester Thrale had brought him a severe and dignified letter of reproof.

[5] *Queen Mary* Mary, Queen of Scots, who sought refuge in England from the rebellion in Scotland. In England she was imprisoned and executed for conspiracy against Queen Elizabeth.

[6] *irremeable* Through which there is no return.

Thomas Gray

1716 – 1771

One of the most celebrated poems in the English language, Gray's "Elegy Written in a Country Churchyard" was written by a man who shunned celebrity and considered himself more a scholar than a poet. Thomas Gray published only a small body of work, but found a wide readership and excited considerable commentary. In the decades immediately following his death, writers such as Johnson, Wordsworth, and Coleridge recognized Gray's importance, and his work continues to be acknowledged as pivotal in the literature of the eighteenth century.

Gray was the fifth of twelve children born to Philip Gray, a scrivener, and Dorothy Antrobus, a milliner. His childhood was not a happy one; none of his siblings survived past infancy, and his mentally unstable father abused his mother. With his mother financing his education, Gray went to Eton in 1725 and spent some of the happiest years of his life in companionship with Horace Walpole (son of the prime minister, Sir Robert Walpole), Richard West, and Thomas Ashton. Interested in reading, poetry and Latin studies (at which Gray became very proficient), the boys formed a "quadruple alliance," in allusion to the 1718 European treaty of that name. After Eton, Gray, Walpole, and Ashton entered the University of Cambridge, while West went to the University of Oxford, but Gray cared for neither the society nor the studies at Cambridge, and he left without a degree in 1738. In 1739, Walpole invited him on an extended tour of the continent. They visited France, Switzerland, and Italy, but then in 1741 they quarrelled, parted, and subsequently remained estranged for several years. Gray returned to Cambridge and corresponded frequently with Richard West, whose health was poor and whose death in 1742 stunned Gray, inspiring not only his "Sonnet on the Death of Mr. Richard West" but elements of his other elegiac poetry as well.

In November 1745, Walpole and Gray were finally reconciled, an event that was central to Gray's literary career, as Walpole would become instrumental in publishing Gray's poetry. Three poems, "Ode on a Distant Prospect of Eton College," "Ode on the Spring" and "Ode on the Death of a Favourite Cat, Drowned in a Tub of Gold Fishes" (written about a cat of Walpole's), appeared anonymously in the 1748 *Miscellany* of Robert Dodsley, the leading London publisher. Gray had also for several years been working on the "Elegy," and in 1750 he sent the finished poem to Walpole, who circulated it in manuscript. This circulation soon forced Gray to publish the poem. He received word of an impending unauthorized version, so he released the poem himself on 15 February 1751, published on its own under the title *An Elegy Wrote in a Country Church Yard.*

Drawing on traditions that included landscape poetry, the funeral elegy, and graveyard poetry, the "Elegy" drew immediate and widespread praise from both critics and readers. It went through 12 editions by 1763, appeared in several periodicals, was imitated, parodied, and translated into numerous languages, and became arguably the most quoted poem in the English language. The reasons for its popularity were—and still are—as intriguing a subject as the poem itself. Besides simply being an excellently written piece, the poem represents the age: its style embodies neoclassical restraint while its themes echo the sentiments of sensibility, the movement in the mid-century towards the expression of "universal feelings." Samuel Johnson highlighted this characteristic of the poem when he concluded, "I rejoice to concur with the common reader… The Church-yard abounds with images which find a mirrour in every mind, and with sentiments to which every bosom returns an echo."

After the success of the *Elegy*, Dodsley published Gray's first collected edition of poems with illustrations by Richard Bentley (1753), and Gray turned to writing more elaborate poetry. In 1757, he was offered the Poet Laureateship, which he declined, and he published two Pindaric odes, "The Progress of Poesy" and "The Bard"—complex, allusive poems that puzzled many readers (and were parodied in two odes to "Oblivion" and "Obscurity"). In later years he studied more and wrote less, took walking tours, and, in 1768, accepted a professorship of modern history at Cambridge. He never married, and his most passionate relationships were with men. In 1769 he met and became devoted to a young Swiss nobleman, Charles Victor de Bonstetten. Gray planned to visit de Bonstetten in Switzerland, but he was taken suddenly ill before he could make the trip; he died in July 1771.

Gray is in many ways a study in contrasts. He is a transitional figure, poised between classicism and romanticism, and his poetry expresses universal themes that are often accompanied by a technically complex style. Because he read widely, he amassed a vast amount of knowledge that makes many of his poems highly allusive. His notebooks record volumes of material from such varied studies as Norse literature, botany, entomology, music, painting, and architecture. Despite his scholarship, he took only one degree (a baccalaureate in civil law, a subject he disliked), never delivered a lecture, and—for such a well-known poet—wrote very little. In temperament, he described himself as melancholic and others described him as socially withdrawn. His letters, however, reveal a superior intellect, a lively wit, and an understanding of his own literary challenges. In sending Walpole the "Elegy," Gray told him to "look upon it in the light of a thing with an end to it; a merit that most of my writings have wanted and are like to want."

⌘⌘⌘

Ode on a Distant Prospect of Eton College[1]

Ye distant spires, ye antique tow'rs,
That crown the wat'ry glade,
Where grateful Science° still adores *learning*
Her Henry's holy shade;[2]
And ye that from the stately brow
Of Windsor's heights th' expanse below
Of grove, of lawn, of mead° survey, *meadow*
Whose turf, whose shade, whose flow'rs among
Wanders the hoary Thames along
His silver-winding way.

Ah, happy hills, ah, pleasing shade,
Ah, fields belov'd in vain,
Where once my careless childhood strayed,
A stranger yet to pain!
I feel the gales, that from ye blow,
A momentary bliss bestow,
As waving fresh their gladsome wing,
My weary soul they seem to soothe,
And, redolent of joy and youth,
To breathe a second spring.

Say, Father Thames, for thou hast seen
Full many a sprightly race
Disporting on thy margent° green *riverbank*
The paths of pleasure trace,
Who foremost now delight to cleave
With pliant arm thy glassy wave?
The captive linnet which enthrall?
What idle progeny succeed
To chase the rolling circle's[3] speed,
Or urge the flying ball?

While some on earnest business bent
Their murm'ring labours ply

[1] *Eton College* School for boys that Gray attended from 1725 to 1734.

[2] *Henry's ... shade* The ghost of Henry VI (reigned 1422–61, 1470–71), who founded Eton in 1440. A bronze statue of him was erected at Eton shortly before Gray arrived.

[3] *circle* Hoop.

'Gainst graver hours, that bring constraint
To sweeten liberty:
Some bold adventurers disdain
The limits of their little reign,
And unknown regions dare descry:
Still as they run they look behind,
They hear a voice in every wind,
And snatch a fearful joy.

Gay hope is theirs by fancy fed,
Less pleasing when possessed;
The tear forgot as soon as shed,
The sunshine of the breast:
Theirs buxom° health of rosy hue, *vigorous*
Wild wit, invention ever-new,
And lively cheer of vigour born;
The thoughtless day, the easy night,
The spirits pure, the slumbers light,
That fly th' approach of morn.

Alas, regardless of their doom,
The little victims play!
No sense have they of ills to come,
Nor care beyond today:
Yet see how all around 'em wait
The ministers of human fate,
And black Misfortune's baleful train!
Ah, show them where in ambush stand
To seize their prey the murd'rous band!
Ah, tell them, they are men!

These shall the fury Passions tear,
The vultures of the mind,
Disdainful Anger, pallid Fear,
And Shame that skulks behind;
Or pining Love shall waste their youth,
Or Jealousy with rankling tooth,
That inly° gnaws the secret heart, *inwardly*
And Envy wan, and faded Care,
Grim-visaged comfortless Despair,
And Sorrow's piercing dart.

Ambition this shall tempt to rise,
Then whirl the wretch from high,
To bitter Scorn a sacrifice,
And grinning Infamy.
The stings of Falsehood those shall try,
And hard Unkindness' altered eye,
That mocks the tear it forced to flow;
And keen Remorse with blood defiled,
And moody Madness laughing wild
Amid severest woe.

Lo, in the vale of years beneath
A grisly troop are seen,
The painful family of Death,
More hideous than their Queen:
This racks the joints, this fires the veins,
That every lab'ring sinew strains,
Those in the deeper vitals rage:
Lo, Poverty, to fill the band,
That numbs the soul with icy hand,
And slow-consuming Age.

To each his suff'rings: all are men,
Condemned alike to groan;
The tender for another's pain,
Th' unfeeling for his own.
Yet ah! why should they know their fate?
Since sorrow never comes too late,
And happiness too swiftly flies.
Thought would destroy their paradise.
No more; where ignorance is bliss,
'Tis folly to be wise.
—1747

Ode on the Death of a Favourite Cat, Drowned in a Tub of Gold Fishes[1]

'Twas on a lofty vase's side,
Where China's gayest art had dyed
The azure flow'rs, that blow;° *bloom*
Demurest of the tabby kind,
The pensive Selima reclined,
Gazed on the lake below.

Her conscious tail her joy declared;
The fair round face, the snowy beard,
The velvet of her paws,

[1] *Ode … Fishes* Written on Horace Walpole's request, after Selima, one of his cats, drowned in a blue-and-white oriental china cistern.

Her coat that with the tortoise vies,
Her ears of jet and emerald eyes,
She saw; and purred applause.

Still had she gazed; but 'midst the tide
Two angel forms were seen to glide,
The genii of the stream:
Their scaly armour's Tyrian[1] hue
Through richest purple to the view
Betrayed a golden gleam.

The hapless nymph with wonder saw:
A whisker first and then a claw,
With many an ardent wish,
She stretched in vain to reach the prize.
What female heart can gold despise?
What cat's averse to fish?

Presumptuous maid! with looks intent
Again she stretched, again she bent,
Nor knew the gulf between.
(Malignant Fate sat by and smiled)
The slipp'ry verge her feet beguiled,
She tumbled headlong in.

Eight times emerging from the flood
She mewed to every wat'ry god,
Some speedy aid to send.
No dolphin came, no Nereid[2] stirred:
Nor cruel Tom nor Susan[3] heard.
A fav'rite has no friend!

From hence, ye beauties, undeceived,
Know, one false step is ne'er retrieved,
And be with caution bold.
Not all that tempts your wand'ring eyes
And heedless hearts is lawful prize;
Nor all that glisters[4] gold.
—1748

[1] *Tyrian* Purple or crimson, as in the dye made from mollusks in the ancient city of Tyre.

[2] *dolphin* In mythology, rescuer of the bard Arion; *Nereid* Sea nymph, daughter of Nereus the sea god.

[3] *Tom ... Susan* Servants.

[4] *glisters* Glitters, glistens. Cf. Shakespeare's *Merchant of Venice* 2.7.65.

Sonnet on the Death of Mr. Richard West[5]

In vain to me the smiling Mornings shine,
And reddening Phoebus[6] lifts his golden fire,
The birds in vain their amorous descant join,
Or cheerful fields resume their green attire;
These ears, alas! for other notes repine,° *long for*
A different object do these eyes require;
My lonely anguish melts no heart but mine;
And in my breast the imperfect joys expire.
Yet Morning smiles the busy race to cheer,
And new-born pleasure brings to happier men,
The fields to all their wonted° tribute bear; *usual*
To warm their little loves the birds complain;
I fruitless mourn to him that cannot hear,
And weep the more because I weep in vain.
—1775 (WRITTEN 1742)

Elegy Written in a Country Churchyard

The curfew tolls the knell[7] of parting day,
The lowing herd wind slowly o'er the lea,[8]
The plowman homeward plods his weary way,
And leaves the world to darkness and to me.

Now fades the glimm'ring landscape on the sight,
And all the air a solemn stillness holds,
Save where the beetle wheels his droning flight,
And drowsy tinklings lull the distant folds;

Save that from yonder ivy-mantled tow'r
The moping owl does to the moon complain

[5] *Richard West* Friend of Gray's who died suddenly in 1742 at age 25. Gray and West had been friends since they were boys at Eton College. The text of this poem is that of the 1742 manuscript copy.

[6] *Phoebus* By-name for Apollo, who is often referred to poetically as the sun god.

[7] *curfew* From the French for "cover your fire," a medieval regulation that decreed that at an appointed hour (indicated by the ringing of a bell) all fires had to be covered and houses shut up for the night. The practice of ringing a bell at a certain hour of the evening (usually eight o'clock) persists in many towns; *knell* Sound made by a bell, especially one struck after a death.

[8] *lea* Meadow or area of grassland.

Of such as, wand'ring near her secret bow'r,
Molest her ancient solitary reign.

Beneath those rugged elms, that yew-tree's shade,
Where heaves the turf in many a mould'ring heap,
Each in his narrow cell for ever laid,
The rude° forefathers of the hamlet sleep. *unlearned*

The breezy call of incense-breathing morn,
The swallow twitt'ring from the straw-built shed,
The cock's shrill clarion or the echoing horn,
No more shall rouse them from their lowly bed.

For them no more the blazing hearth shall burn,
Or busy housewife ply her evening care:
No children run to lisp their sire's return,
Or climb his knees the envied kiss to share.

Oft did the harvest to their sickle yield,
Their furrow oft the stubborn glebe° has broke; *soil*
How jocund° did they drive their team afield! *merrily*
How bowed the woods beneath their sturdy stroke!

Let not Ambition mock their useful toil,
Their homely joys, and destiny obscure;
Nor Grandeur hear, with a disdainful smile,
The short and simple annals of the poor.

The boast of heraldry, the pomp of pow'r,
And all that beauty, all that wealth e'er gave,
Awaits alike th' inevitable hour.
The paths of glory lead but to the grave.

Nor you, ye Proud, impute to these the fault,
If Mem'ry o'er their tomb no trophies raise,
Where through the long-drawn aisle and fretted[1] vault
The pealing anthem swells the note of praise.

Can storied urn or animated bust
Back to its mansion call the fleeting breath?
Can Honour's voice provoke the silent dust,
Or Flatt'ry soothe the dull cold ear of Death?

Perhaps in this neglected spot is laid
Some heart once pregnant with celestial fire;
Hands that the rod of empire might have swayed,
Or waked to ecstasy the living lyre.

But Knowledge to their eyes her ample page
Rich with the spoils of time did ne'er unroll;
Chill Penury repressed their noble rage,[2]
And froze the genial current of the soul.

Full many a gem of purest ray serene
The dark unfathomed caves of ocean bear:
Full many a flow'r is born to blush unseen
And waste its sweetness on the desert air.

Some village-Hampden[3] that with dauntless breast
The little tyrant of his fields withstood;
Some mute inglorious Milton[4] here may rest,
Some Cromwell[5] guiltless of his country's blood.

Th' applause of list'ning senates to command,
The threats of pain and ruin to despise,
To scatter plenty o'er a smiling land,
And read their hist'ry in a nation's eyes,

Their lot forbade: nor circumscribed alone
Their growing virtues, but their crimes confined;
Forbade to wade through slaughter to a throne,
And shut the gates of mercy on mankind,

The struggling pangs of conscious truth to hide,
To quench the blushes of ingenuous shame,
Or heap the shrine of Luxury and Pride
With incense kindled at the Muse's flame.[6]

---

[1] *fretted* Carved with decorative patterns.

[2] *rage* Ardor, enthusiasm.

[3] *Hampden* John Hampden (1594–1643), member of Parliament who defied Charles I and died early in the ensuing civil war.

[4] *Milton* John Milton (1608–74), English poet, dramatist.

[5] *Cromwell* Oliver Cromwell (1599–1658), Commander-in-Chief and then Lord Protector of England during the republican or commonwealth period (1649–60).

[6] *With … flame* After this line, the earliest extant draft of the poem contains four stanzas that appear to be an earlier ending to the poem:

The thoughtless World to Majesty may bow
Exalt the brave, and idolize Success
But more to Innocence their Safety owe
Than Power and Genius e'er conspired to bless

And thou, who mindful of the unhonour'd Dead
Dost in these Notes their artless Tale relate

Cont.

Far from the madding crowd's ignoble strife,
Their sober wishes never learned to stray;
Along the cool sequestered vale of life
They kept the noiseless tenor of their way.

Yet ev'n these bones from insult to protect
Some frail memorial still erected nigh,
With uncouth rhymes and shapeless sculpture decked,
Implores the passing tribute of a sigh.

Their name, their years, spelt by th' unlettered muse,
The place of fame and elegy supply:
And many a holy text around she strews,
That teach the rustic moralist to die.

For who to dumb Forgetfulness a prey,
This pleasing anxious being e'er resigned,
Left the warm precincts of the cheerful day,
Nor cast one longing ling'ring look behind?

On some fond breast the parting soul relies,
Some pious drops the closing eye requires;
Ev'n from the tomb the voice of nature cries,
Ev'n in our ashes live their wonted fires.

For thee who, mindful of th' unhonoured dead,
Dost in these lines their artless tale relate;
If chance, by lonely Contemplation led,
Some kindred spirit shall inquire thy fate,

Haply some hoary-headed swain may say,
"Oft have we seen him at the peep of dawn
Brushing with hasty steps the dews away
To meet the sun upon the upland lawn.

"There at the foot of yonder nodding beech
That wreathes its old fantastic roots so high,
His listless length at noontide would he stretch,
And pore upon the brook that babbles by.

"Hard by yon wood, now smiling as in scorn,
Mutt'ring his wayward fancies he would rove,
Now drooping, woeful wan, like one forlorn,
Or crazed with care, or crossed in hopeless love.

"One morn I missed him on the customed hill,
Along the heath and near his fav'rite tree;
Another came; nor yet beside the rill,
Nor up the lawn, nor at the wood was he;

"The next with dirges due in sad array
Slow through the church-way path we saw him borne.
Approach and read (for thou can'st read) the lay,
Graved on the stone beneath yon aged thorn."

THE EPITAPH

Here rests his head upon the lap of earth
A youth to fortune and to fame unknown.
Fair Science° frowned not on his humble birth, learning
And Melancholy marked him for her own.

Large was his bounty and his soul sincere,
Heav'n did a recompense as largely send:
He gave to Mis'ry all he had, a tear,
He gained from Heav'n ('twas all he wished) a friend.

No farther seek his merits to disclose,
Or draw his frailties from their dread abode,
(There they alike in trembling hope repose)
The bosom of his Father and his God.

—1751

By Night and lonely Contemplation led
To linger in the gloomy Walks of Fate

Hark how the sacred Calm, that broods around
Bids ev'ry fierce tumultuous Passion cease
In still small Accents whisp'ring from the Ground
A grateful Earnest of eternal Peace

No more with Reason and thyself at strife;
Give anxious Cares and endless Wishes room
But thro' the cool sequester'd Vale of Life
Pursue the silent Tenor of thy Doom.

Popular Ballads

In general terms, the ballad is a song that tells a story in a popular style, which, traditionally, relied on oral tradition for transmission. In the Middle Ages, ballads were generally composed to accompany a dance; in the earliest recorded ballads, which date back to the fifteenth century, this connection is evident in the form of the couplet with a refrain in alternate lines. Dancers would sing the refrain in time with their dancing. The common quatrain form of alternating four- and three-beat lines also has its origins in the Middle Ages. Ballads tended to originate in feudal castles, manor houses, and village communities and expressed a particularly local point of view, and were composed in local dialects. Country ballads often preserve aspects of an earlier way of life that had, even at the time of their composition, disappeared from all but isolated, rural communities. Scottish ballads in particular, such as "Tam Lin," demonstrate the strong, lingering presence of pre-Christian belief in practices and entities such as magic, fairies, and ghosts.

Ballads are generally highly formulaic; phrases and images are often not only repeated throughout a single ballad, but also shared in common among different ballads. The same theme, such as the lover's late-night visit, may be expressed in almost identical words and meter in various ballads. Singers, who could usually not read but had excellent memories, relied on such formulas to express aspects of the story in time-honored ways. The meter of a ballad controls its rhetoric, phrasing, and the shape of its dialogue. It is also linked to the ballad's highly dramatic style; the story must be told in sharp flashes that fit into its short stanza form.

Ballads tend to be of uncertain age and authorship. Even those ballads that were composed around a particular event in history, and that may have originated as a written text, soon entered oral tradition and began to change as they traveled from place to place. Each singer was thus both a transmitter and a composer, as ballads would change with each singing. Versions of any one ballad would differ from village to village, with no version representing an "authentic" or "superior" version. "Mary Hamilton," for example, exists in over thirty known versions, and its exact historical origins remain unknown.

One of the first major collectors of ballads was Bishop Thomas Percy, who published his three-volume *Reliques of Ancient English Poetry* in 1765. In eighteenth-century Scotland a number of poets, including Robert Burns and Sir Walter Scott, took an active interest in old ballads, often going back to the numerous old versions and editing or combining them, or even composing new works in the traditional style. Scott, whose *Minstrelsy of the Scottish Border* (1802–03) was extremely popular, often went directly to the sources of the ballads, copying them down as they were dictated to him. In the Romantic period many scholars and poets began the study and imitation of balladry; Wordsworth, Coleridge, and Keats were among those who returned to the ballad for its simple, "natural" style.

⌘⌘⌘

Robin Hood and Alan a Dale

1

Come listen to me, you gallants so free,
All you that love mirth for to hear,
And I will you tell of a bold outlaw,
That lived in Nottinghamshire.

2

As Robin Hood in the forest stood,
All under the green-wood tree,

There was he ware° of a brave young man, *aware*
As fine as fine might be.

3

The youngster was clothed in scarlet red,
In scarlet fine and gay,
And he did frisk it° over the plain, *frolic*
And chanted a roundelay.[1]

4

As Robin Hood next morning stood,
Amongst the leaves so gay,
There did he espy the same young man
Come drooping along the way.

5

The scarlet he wore the day before,
It was clean cast away;
And every step he fetcht a sigh,
"Alack and a well a day!"[2]

6

Then steppèd forth brave Little John,
And Much the miller's son,
Which made the young man bend his bow,
When as he saw them come.

7

"Stand off, stand off!" the young man said,
"What is your will with me?"
"You must come before our master straight,
Under yon green-wood tree."

8

And when he came bold Robin before,
Robin askt him courteously,
"O hast thou any money to spare,
For my merry men and me?"

9

"I have no money," the young man said,
"But five shillings and a ring;
And that I have kept this seven long years,
To have it at my wedding.

10

"Yesterday I should have married a maid,
But she is now from me tane,° *taken*
And chosen to be an old knight's delight,
Whereby my poor heart is slain."

11

"What is thy name?" then said Robin Hood,
"Come tell me, without any fail."
"By the faith of my body," then said the young man
"My name it is Alan a Dale."

12

"What wilt thou give me," said Robin Hood,
"In ready gold or fee,
To help thee to thy true-love again,
And deliver her unto thee?"

13

"I have no money," then quoth° the young man, *said*
"No ready gold nor fee,
But I will swear upon a book
Thy true servant for to be."

14

"But how many miles to thy true-love?
Come tell me without any guile."
"By the faith of my body," then said the young man,
"It is but five little mile."

15

Then Robin he hasted over the plain,
He did neither stint nor lin,[3]
Until he came unto the church
Where Alan should keep his wedding.

16

"What dost thou do here?" the Bishop he said,
"I prithee now tell to me."
"I am a bold harper," quoth Robin Hood,
"And the best in the north country."

[1] *roundelay* Short, simple song with a refrain.

[2] *well a day* Welladay, an expression of lamentation.

[3] *stint* Turn aside from a pursuit; *lin* Stop.

17

"O welcome, O welcome!" the Bishop he said,
"That musick best pleaseth me."
"You shall have no musick," quoth Robin Hood,
"Till the bride and the bridegroom I see."

18

With that came in a wealthy knight,
Which was both grave and old,
And after him a finikin° lass, *dainty*
Did shine like glistering gold.

19

"This is no fit match," quoth bold Robin Hood,
"That you do seem to make here;
For since we are come unto the church,
The bride she shall chuse her own dear."

20

Then Robin Hood put his horn to his mouth,
And blew blasts two or three;
When four and twenty bowmen bold
Come leaping over the lee.

21

And when they came into the churchyard,
Marching all on a row,
The first man was Alan a Dale,
To give bold Robin his bow.

22

"This is thy true-love," Robin he said,
"Young Alan, as I hear say;
And you shall be married at this same time,
Before we depart away."

23

"That shall not be," the Bishop he said,
"For thy word it shall not stand;
They shall be three times askt in the church,
As the law is of our land."[1]

24

Robin Hood pull'd off the Bishop's coat,
And put it upon Little John;
"By the faith of my body," then Robin said,
"This cloath doth make thee a man."

25

When Little John went into the quire,° *chancel*
The people began for to laugh;
He askt them seven times in the church,
Least three should not be enough.

26

"Who gives me this maid?" then said Little John;
Quoth Robin, "That do I!
And he that doth take her from Alan a Dale
Full dearly he shall her buy."

27

And thus having ended this merry wedding,
The bride lookt as fresh as a queen,
And so they return'd to the merry green-wood,
Amongst the leaves so green.

—1723

Edward, Edward

1

"Why does your brand° sae° drop° *sword / so / drip*
wi' blude,° *blood*
Edward, Edward?
Why does your brand sae drop wi' blude,
And why sae sad gang° ye, O?" *go*
"O I hae kill'd my hawk sae° gude,° *so / good*
Mither, mither;
O I hae kill'd my hawk sae gude,
And I had nae° mair° but he, O." *no / more*

2

"Your hawk's blude was never sae red,
Edward, Edward;
Your hawk's blude was never sae red,
My dear son, I tell thee, O."
"O I hae kill'd my red-roan steed,

[1] *They shall be ... land* This "calling the bans" on three successive Sundays gave the public an opportunity to object to a marriage, as a guard against, for instance, bigamy.

Mither, mither;
O I hae kill'd my red-roan steed,
That erst° was sae fair and free, O." *formerly*

3

"Your steed was auld,° and ye hae got mair, *old*
Edward, Edward;
Your steed was auld, and ye hae got mair;
Some other dule ye dree,[1] O."
"O I hae kill'd my father dear,
Mither, mither;
O I hae kill'd my father dear,
Alas, and wae° is me, O!" *woe*

4

"And whatten° penance will ye dree for that, *what*
Edward, Edward?
Whatten penance will ye dree for that?
My dear son, now tell me, O."
"I'll set my feet in yonder boat,
Mither, mither;
I'll set my feet in yonder boat,
And I'll fare over the sea, O."

5

"And what will ye do wi' your tow'rs and your ha',° *hall*
Edward, Edward?
And what will ye do wi' your tow'rs and your ha',
That were sae fair to see, O?"
"I'll let them stand till they doun° fa',° *down / fall*
Mither, mither;
I'll let them stand till they doun fa',
For here never mair maun° I be, O." *must*

6

"And what will ye leave to your bairns° and your wife, *children*
Edward, Edward?
And what will ye leave to your bairns and your wife,
When ye gang owre the sea, O?"
"The warld's room:° let them beg through life, *world's space*
Mither, mither;
For them never mair will I see, O."

7

"And what will ye leave to your ain° mither dear, *own*
Edward, Edward?
And what will ye leave to your ain mither dear,
My dear son, now tell me, O?"
"The curse of hell frae° me sall° ye bear, *from / shall*
Mither, mither;
The curse of hell frae me sall ye bear:
Sic° counsels ye gave to me, O!" *such*
—1765

[1] *dule ye dree* Grief you suffer.

Tam Lin

1

"O I forbid you, maidens a',° *all*
That wear gowd° on your hair, *gold*
To come or gae by Carterhaugh,
For young Tam Lin is there.

2

"For even about that knight's middle
O' siller° bells are nine; *silver*
And nae° maid comes to Carterhaugh *no*
And a maid returns again."

3

Fair Janet sat in her bonny bower,
Sewing her silken seam,
And wish'd to be in Carterhaugh
Amang the leaves sae° green. *so*

4

She's lat her seam fa'° to her feet, *fall*
The needle to her tae,° *toe*
And she's awa' to Carterhaugh
As fast as she could gae.

5

And she has kilted° her green kirtle° *tuck up / skirt*
A little abune° her knee; *above*

And she has braided her yellow hair
A little abune her bree;° *brow*
And she has gaen for Carterbaugh
As fast as she can hie.° *hasten*

6

She hadna pu'd° a rose, a rose, *pulled*
A rose but barely ane,° *one*
When up and started young Tam Lin;
Says, "Ladye, let alane.° *alone*

7

"What gars° ye pu'° the rose, Janet? *makes / pull*
What gars ye break the tree?
What gars ye come to Carterhaugh
Without the leave o' me?"

8

"Weel may I pu' the rose," she says,
"And ask no leave at thee;
For Carterhaugh it is my ain,° *own*
My daddy gave it me."

9

He's ta'en her by the milk-white hand,
And by the grass-green sleeve,
He's led her to the fairy ground
At her he askd nae leave.

10

Janet has kilted her green kirtle
A little abune her knee,
And she has snooded[1] her yellow hair
A little abune her bree,° *brow*
And she is to her father's ha'° *hall*
As fast as she can hie.

11

But when she came to her father's ha',
She look'd sae wan and pale,
They thought the lady had gotten a fright,
Or with sickness she did ail.

12

Four and twenty ladies fair
Were playing at the ba',[2]
And out then came fair Janet
Ance° the flower amang them a'. *once*

13

Four and twenty ladies fair
Were playing at the chess,
And out then came fair Janet
As green as onie° glass. *any*

14

Out then spak' an auld grey knight
'Lay owre the Castle wa',
And says, "Alas, fair Janet!
For thee we'll be blamèd a'."

15

"Hauld your tongue, ye auld-faced knight,
Some ill death may ye die!
Father my bairn° on whom I will, *child*
I'll father nane° on thee. *none*

16

"O if my love were an earthly knight,
As he is an elfin gay,
I wadna gie° my ain true-love *give*
For nae laird° that ye hae.° *lord / have*

17

"The steed that my true-love rides on
Is fleeter° nor° the wind; *faster / than*
Wi' siller he is shod before,
Wi' burning gold behind."

18

Out then spak' her brither dear—
He meant to do her harm:
"There grows an herb in Carterbaugh
Will twine° you an' the bairn." *sunder*

[1] *snooded* Fastened in a snood, a hair-band worn by young, unmarried women.

[2] *ba'* Ball, a game.

19

Janet has kilted her green kirtle
A little abune her knee,
And she has snooded her yellow hair
A little abune her bree,
And she's awa' to Carterhaugh
As fast as she can hie.

20

She hadna pu'd a leaf, a leaf,
A leaf but only twae,° *two*
When up and started young Tam Lin,
Says, "Ladye, thou's° pu' nae mae.° *thou shall / more*

21

"How dar' ye pu' a leaf?" he says,
"How dar' ye break the tree,
How dar' ye scathe° my babe," he says, *harm*
"That's between you and me?"

22

"O tell me, tell me, Tam," she says,
"For His sake that died on tree,[1]
If ye were ever in holy chapel
Or sain'd° in Christentie?" *baptized*

23

"The truth I'll tell to thee, Janet,
Ae° word I winna° lee°; *one / will not / lie*
A knight me got,° and a lady me bore, *begot*
As well as they did thee.

24

"Roxburgh he was my grandfather,
Took me with him to bide;° *remain*
And ance° it fell upon a day, *once*
As hunting I did ride,

25

"There came a wind out o' the north,
A sharp wind an' a snell,° *cold*
A dead sleep it came over me
And frae° my horse I fell; *from*
And the Queen o' Fairies she took me
In yon green hill to dwell.

26

"And pleasant is the fairy land
For those that in it dwell,
But ay° at end of seven years *always*
They pay a teind° to hell; *tithe*
I am sae fair and fu' o' flesh
I'm fear'd 'twill be mysell.

27

"But the night is Hallowe'en,[2] Janet,
The morn is Hallowday;
Then win me, win me, an° ye will, *if*
For weel I wat° ye may. *know*

28

"The night it is gude Hallowe'en,
The fairy folk do ride,
And they that wad° their true-love win, *would*
At Miles Cross they maun° bide.°" *must / wait*

29

"But how should I you ken,° Tam Lin, *know*
How should I borrow° you, *ransom*
Amang a pack of uncouth° knights *unknown*
The like I never saw?"

30

"You'll do you down to Miles Cross
Between twel' hours and ane,
And fill your hands o' the holy water
And cast your compass roun'.[3]

31

"The first company that passes by,
Say na,° and let them gae; *nothing*

[1] *For ... tree* Christ.

[2] *Hallowe'en* Hallowe'en was originally the Celtic celebration of the new year, which is why Tam Lin refers to it as the end of a seven-year period. It was also a night when the realms of the dead and the living would intermingle.

[3] *cast ... roun'* I.e., sprinkle it all around you.

The neist° company that passes by, *next*
Say na, and do right sae;° *same*
The third company that passes by,
Then I'll be ane o' thae.° *those*

32

"O first let pass the black, ladye,
And syne° let pass the brown; *next*
But quickly run to the milk-white steed,
Pu' ye his rider down.

33

"For some ride on the black, ladye,
And some ride on the brown;
But I ride on a milk-white steed,
A gowd star en my crown:
Because I was an earthly knight
They gie me that renown.

34

"My right hand will be gloved, ladye,
My left hand will be bare,
And thae's the tokens I gie thee:
Nae doubt I will be there.

35

"Ye'll tak' my horse then by the head
And let the bridle fa';
The Queen o' Elfin she'll cry out
'True Tam Lin he's awa'!'

36

"They'll turn me in your arms, ladye,
An aske° but and[1] a snake; *lizard*
But hauld me fast, let me na gae,
To be your warldis° make.° *worldly / mate*

37

"They'll turn me in your arms, ladye,
But and a deer so wild;
But hauld me fast, let me na gae,
The father o' your child.

38

"They'll shape me in your arms, ladye,
A hot iron at the fire;
But hauld me fast, let me na go,
To be your heart's desire.

39

"They'll shape me last in your arms, Janet,
A mother-naked[2] man;
Cast your green mantle over me,
And sae will I be won."

40

Janet has kilted her green kirtle
A little abune the knee;
And she has snooded her yellow hair
A little abune her bree,
And she is on to Miles Cross
As fast as she can hie.

41

About the dead hour o' the night
She heard the bridles ring;
And Janet was as glad at that
As any earthly thing.

42

And first gaed by the black, black steed,
And syne gaed by the brown;
But fast she gript the milk-white steed
And pu'd the rider down.

43

She's pu'd him frae the milk-white steed,
An' loot° the bridle fa' *let*
And up there rase° an eldritch° cry, *rose / unearthly*
"True Tam Lin he's awa'!"

44

They shaped him in her arms twa
An aske but and a snake;
But aye she grips and hau'ds hint fast
To be her warldis make.

[1] *but and* And also.

[2] *mother-naked* I.e., naked as a baby at birth.

45

They shaped him in her arms twa
But and a deer sae wild;
But aye she grips and hau'ds him fast,
The father o' her child.

46

They shaped him in her arms twa
A hot iron at the fire;
But aye she grips and hau'ds him fast
To be her heart's desire.

47

They shaped him in her arms at last
A mother-naked man;
She cast her mantle over him,
And sae her love she wan.° *won*

48

Up then spak' the Queen o' Fairies,
Out o' a bush o' broom,[1]
"She that has borrow'd young Tam Lin
Has gotten a stately groom."

49

Out then spak' the Queen o' Fairies,
And an angry woman was she,
"She's ta'en awa' the bonniest knight
In a' my companie!"

50

"But what I ken this night, Tam Lin,
Gin° I had kent yestreen,° *if / yesterday evening*
I wad° ta'en out thy heart o' flesh, *would have*
And put in a heart o' stane.

51

"And adieu, Tam Lin! But gin I had kent
A ladye wad borrow'd thee,
I wad ta'en out thy twa grey e'en° *eyes*
Put in twa e'en o' tree.° *wood*

52

"And had I the wit° yestreen, yestreen, *knowledge*
That I have coft° this day, *bought*
I'd paid my teind seven times to hell
Ere you had been won away!"
—1769

The Death of Robin Hood

1

When Robin Hood and Little John
Down a-down, a-down, a-down
Went o'er yon bank of broom,
Said Robin Hood bold to Little John,
"We have shot for many a pound."
Hey, down, a-down, a-down!

2

"But I am not able to shoot one shot more,
My broad arrows will not flee;
But I have a cousin lives down below,
Please God, she will bleed me.

3

"I will never eat nor drink," he said,
"Nor meat will do me good,
Till I have been to merry Kirkleys
My veins for to let blood.

4

"The dame prior is my aunt's daughter,
And nigh unto my kin;
I know she wo'ld me no harm this day,
For all the world to win."

5

"That I rede° not," said Little John *advise*
"Master, by th'assent of me,
Without half a hundred of your best bowmen
You take to go with yee."

[1] *broom* Type of shrub, common on English heaths, that bears large yellow flowers.

6

"An thou be afear'd, thou Little John,
At home I rede thee be."
"An you be wroth, my deare master
You shall never hear more of me."

7

Now Robin is gone to merry Kirkleys
And knocked upon the pin;° *door*
Up then rose Dame Priorèss
And let good Robin in.

8

Then Robin gave to Dame Priorèss
Twenty pound in gold,
And bade her spend while that did last,
She sho'ld have more when she wo'ld.

9

"Will you please to sit down, cousin Robin,
And drink some beer with me?"
"No, I will neither eat nor drink
Till I am blooded by thee."

10

Down then came Dame Priorèss
Down she came in that ilk,[1]
With a pair of blood-irons in her hands,
Were wrappèd all in silk.

11

"Set a chafing-dish to the fire," she said,
"And strip thou up thy sleeve."
I hold him but an unwise man
That will no warning 'leeve!° *believe*

12

She laid the blood-irons to Robin's vein,
Alack, the more pitye!
And pierc'd the vein, and let out the blood
That full red was to see.

13

And first it bled the thick, thick blood,
And afterwards the thin,
And well then wist° good Robin Hood *knew*
Treason there was within.

14

And there she blooded bold Robin Hood
While one drop of blood wou'd run;
There did he bleed the live-long day,
Until the next at noon.

15

He bethought him then of a casement[2] there,
Being lockèd up in the room;
But was so weak he could not leap,
He could not get him down.

16

He bethought him then of his bugle-horn,
That hung low down to his knee;
He set his horn unto his mouth,
And blew out weak blasts three.

17

Then Little John he heard the horn
Where he sat under a tree:
"I fear my master is now near dead,
He blows so wearily."

18

Little John is gone to merry Kirkleys,
As fast as he can dree°; *bear*
And when he came to merry Kirkleys,
He broke locks two or three:

19

Until he came bold Robin to see,
Then he fell on his knee;
"A boon, a boon!" cries Little John,
"Master, I beg of thee!"

[1] *in that ilk* In that same moment.

[2] *casement* Frame that opens on hinges and forms part of a window.

20

"What is that boon," said Robin Hood,
"Little John, thou begs of me?"
"It is to burn fair Kirkleys-hall,
And all their nunnerye."

21

"Now nay, now nay," quoth° Robin Hood, *said*
"That boon I'll not grant thee;
I never hurt woman in all my life,
Nor men in their company.

22

"I never hurt maid in all my time,
Nor at mine end shall it be;
But give me my bent bow in my hand,
And a broad arrow I'll let flee;
And where this arrow is taken up
There shall my grave digg'd be.

23

"But lay me a greed sod under my head,
And another at my feet;
And lay my bent bow at my side,
Which was my music sweet;
And make my grave of gravel and green,
Which is most right and meet.

24

"Let me have length and breadth enough,
And under my head a sod;
That they may say when I am dead,
—Here lies bold Robin Hood!"

—1786

A Lyke-Wake[1] Dirge

1

This ae° nighte, this ae nighte, *one*
—Every nighte and alle,
Fire and fleet[2] and candle-lighte,
And Christe receive thy saule.° *soul*

2

When thou from hence away art past,
—Every nighte and alle,
To Whinny-muir[3] thou com'st at last:
And Christe receive thy saule.

3

If ever thou gavest hosen° and shoon,° *socks / shoes*
—Every nighte and alle,
Sit thee down and put them on:
And Christe receive thy saule.

4

If hosen and shoon thou ne'er gav'st nane° *none*
—Every nighte and alle,
The whinnes[4] sall° prick thee to the bare *shall*
bane;° *bone*
And Christe receive thy saule.

5

From whinny-muir when thou may'st pass,
—Every nighte and alle,
To Brig o' Dread[5] thou com'st at last;
And Christe receive thy saule.

6

From Brig o' Dread when thou may'st pass,
—Every nighte and alle,
To Purgatory fire thou com'st at last;
And Christe receive thy saule.

[1] *Lyke-Wake* Watch kept overnight over a dead body.

[2] *fleet* Floor. "Sleet" has also been proposed as an alternate reading.

[3] *Whinny-muir* Waiting-area where souls go before the journey to Purgatory. It was conceived of as a sort of moor full of prickly gorse furze. Here the soul would be examined for its generosity in life (such as the giving of clothing to the poor) and rewarded or punished accordingly.

[4] *whinnes* Prickly shrubs; heather or furze.

[5] *Brig o' Dread* Bridge of Dread, from which wicked souls fall into Hell on their way to Purgatory. Here, as in Whinny-muir, the soul is rewarded for previous generosity or punished for wickedness.

7

If ever thou gavest meat or drink,
—Every nighte and alle,
The fire sall never make thee shrink;
And Christe receive thy saule.

8

If meat or drink thou ne'er gav'st nane,
—Every nighte and alle,
The fire will burn thee to the bare bane;
And Christe receive thy saule.

9

This ae nighte, this ae nighte,
—Every nighte and alle,
Fire and fleet and candle-lighte,
And Christe receive thy saule.

—1802

Mary Hamilton[1]

Word's gane° to the kitchen, *gone*
And word's gane to the ha,° *hall*
That Marie Hamilton gangs° wi bairn° *goes / child*
To the hichest° Stewart of a'.° *highest / all*

He's courted her in the kitchen,
He's courted her in the ha,
He's courted her in the laigh° cellar, *low*
And that was warst of a'.

She's tyed it in her apron
And she's thrown it in the sea;
Says, "Sink ye, swim ye, bonny wee babe!
You'l neer get mair° o me." *more*

Down then cam the auld° queen, *old*
Goud° tassels tying her hair: *gold*
"O Marie, where's the bonny wee babe
That I heard greet° sae° sair?°" *cry out / so / sore*

"There never was a babe intill° my room, *in*
As little designs to be;
It was but a touch o my sair side,
Come oer my fair bodie."

"O Marie, put on your robes o black,
Or else your robes o brown,
For ye maun° gang° wi me the night, *must / go*
To see fair Edinbro town."

"I winna put on my robes o black,
Nor yet my robes o brown;
But I'll put on my robes o white,
To shine through Edinbro town."

When she gaed up the Cannogate,[2]
She laughd loud laughters three;
But whan she cam down the Cannogate
The tear blinded her ee.° *eye*

When she gaed up the Parliament stair,
The heel cam aff her shee;° *shoe*
And lang or° she cam down again *before*
She was condemnd to dee.

When she cam down the Cannogate,
The Cannogate sae free,
Many a ladie lookd oer her window,
Weeping for this ladie.

"Ye need nae weep for me," she says,
"Ye need nae weep for me;
For had I not slain mine own sweet babe,
This death I wadna° dee. *would not*

[1] *Mary Hamilton* Scottish maid-of-honor to the Empress Catherine, wife of Peter the Great. She had an affair with Ivan Orlof, an aide to the Czar, and murdered their illegitimate child. As punishment she was tortured and decapitated. This story is conflated here with that of a French woman who was one of the four Maries, a term for maids of honor as well as the given name of each, who served Mary, Queen of Scots. She had a child by the Queen's apothecary and murdered it, for which she was hanged in Edinburgh.

[2] *Cannogate* I.e., Cannongate, main thoroughfare in downtown Edinburgh on which is located Cannongate Tollbooth, which contained the courthouse and prison.

"Bring me a bottle of wine," she says,
"The best that eer ye hae,
That I may drink to my weil-wishers,
And they may drink to me.

"Here's a health to the jolly sailors,
That sail upon the main;° *sea*
Let them never let on to my father and mother
But what I'm coming hame.° *home*

"Here's a health to the jolly sailors,
That sail upon the sea;
Let them never let on to my father and mother
That I cam here to dee.

"Oh little did my mother think,
The day she cradled me,
What lands I was to travel through,
What death I was to dee.

"Oh little did my father think,
The day he held up me,
What lands I was to travel through,
What death I was to dee.

"Last night I washd the queen's feet,
And gently laid her down;
And a' the thanks I've gotten the nicht° *tonight*
To be hangd in Edinbro town!

"Last nicht there was four Maries,
The nicht there'l be but three;
There was Marie Seton, and Marie Beton,
And Marie Carmichael, and me."[1]

—1802, 1824

[1] *Mary Seton … me* The surnames on record of the four women who served Mary Stuart, Queen of Scots, are Seton, Beaton, Fleming, and Livingston.

Christopher Smart

1722 – 1771

Christopher Smart produced several works of highly original poetry in the late 1750s and early 1760s. He also spent five of those years in a lunatic asylum, and much of the critical attention paid to Smart has centered on debates over the nature of his madness and the extent of its effect on his work. Whatever Smart's state, however, the poems themselves—particularly *Jubilate Agno* and *A Song to David*—have generally been recognized as boldly experimental and extremely influential. They have served as models for a variety of modern writers, including Anne Sexton, Alan Ginsberg, Edith Sitwell, Benjamin Britten, and Eli Mandel.

The son of a steward, Smart was born on 11 April 1722 at Shipbourne, Kent. He was educated at Cambridge, where he distinguished himself for his heavy drinking and inability to manage money (his friends once had to bail him out of debtors' prison), as well as for his academic excellence and prize-winning poetry.

Smart gave up a potential career at Cambridge to seek fame as a poet in London. There he made a living as a hack writer, contributing occasional pieces to various journals. He and the publisher John Newbery (whose step-daughter, Anna Maria Carnan, Smart married in 1753) started the journal *The Midwife: or the Old Woman's Magazine*, in which Smart wrote miscellaneous jokes, puns, and satirical pieces as the vastly popular Mary Midnight.

In 1756 Smart began to be overwhelmed by irrepressibly strong religious convictions. He would fall upon his knees and pray whenever the urge came upon him—in St. James's Park, in the Mall, in the streets—and oblige his friends to join him, often dragging them away from their dinners or out of their beds to do so. In 1757 Smart's family placed him in the London madhouse St. Luke's Hospital, where he was pronounced incurable. He was confined for most of the following six years.

Smart's most productive period occurred following his release in 1763. He completed many of the poems he had begun while confined, including his renowned *A Song to David* (1763), generally judged to be his greatest poem, and *Translations of the Psalms of David* (1765). Smart also translated the complete works of Horace into verse (a translation that remains highly regarded today). Tainted by his reputation as a madman, however, he was rarely taken seriously as a poet. In 1770 his debts caught up with him, and he was imprisoned in the King's Bench Prison. There he wrote his final poems, *Hymns for the Amusement of Children*, and remained until his death in 1771.

The surviving fragments of Smart's poem *Jubilate Agno* (*Rejoice in the Lamb*) were not printed until 1939, and these survived only because friends of the poet William Cowper had kept the manuscript, hoping to use it to better understand Cowper's own mental illness. Smart wrote *Jubilate Agno*, his ecstatic celebration of the omnipresence of the Divine Being, a few lines a day over a period of four years (1759–63) of confinement in the madhouse. As something of a journal of praise, it provides insight into his daily activities there. But in its experiments in poetic techniques it also moves toward an entirely new form of poetry. Like *A Song to David*, *Jubilate Agno* rejects the influences of Milton, Dryden, and Pope that had been evident in Smart's earlier poetry. Instead, with its alternating sections of lines beginning with "Let" and "For," it appears to draw on traditional Hebrew poetry, and resembles response readings such as those found in the Psalter, the Litany, and other texts in the *Book of Common Prayer*.

Although the story of Smart's life of confinement and death in prison is an unhappy one, his poetry is infused with an irrepressible sense of joy. In the most famous section of *Jubilate Agno*, "My Cat Jeoffry," Smart lovingly praises his cat, his sole companion in confinement. With witty wordplay and obscure scholarly references, Smart celebrates Jeoffry both as a source of comfort and love and as one of God's creatures, proof of his divine plan.

⌘⌘⌘

from *Jubilate Agno*
[MY CAT JEOFFRY]

For I will consider my Cat Jeoffry.
For he is the servant of the Living God duly and daily serving him.
For at the first glance of the glory of God in the East[1] he worships in his way.
For is this done by wreathing his body seven times round with elegant quickness.
For then he leaps up to catch the musk, which is the blessing of God upon his prayer.
For he rolls upon prank[2] to work it in.
For having done duty and received blessing he begins to consider himself.
For this he performs in ten degrees.
For first he looks upon his forepaws to see if they are clean.
For secondly he kicks up behind to clear away there.
For thirdly he works it upon stretch with the forepaws extended.
For fourthly he sharpens his paws by wood.
For fifthly he washes himself.
For Sixthly he rolls upon wash.
For Seventhly he fleas himself, that he may not be interrupted upon the beat.
For Eighthly he rubs himself against a post.
For Ninthly he looks up for his instructions.
For Tenthly he goes in quest of food.
For having considered God and himself he will consider his neighbor.
For if he meets another cat he will kiss her in kindness.
For when he takes his prey he plays with it to give it a chance.
For one mouse in seven escapes by his dallying.
For when his day's work is done his business more properly begins.
For he keeps the Lord's watch in the night against the adversary.
For he counteracts the powers of darkness by his electrical skin[3] & glaring eyes.
For he counteracts the Devil, who is death, by brisking about[4] the life.
For in his morning orisons he loves the sun and the sun loves him.
For he is of the tribe of Tiger.
For the Cherub Cat is a term of the Angel Tiger.[5]
For he has the subtlety and hissing of a serpent, which in goodness he suppresses.
For he will not do destruction if he is well fed, neither will he spit without provocation.
For he purrs in thankfulness, when God tells him he's a good Cat.
For he is an instrument for the children to learn benevolence upon.
For every house is incomplete without him & a blessing is lacking in the spirit.
For the Lord commanded Moses concerning the cats at

[1] *glory ... East* Sunrise.

[2] *upon prank* For a frolic; for a trick.

[3] *electrical skin* An article in *The Gentleman's Magazine* 24 (1754) stated that cats have a natural electricity greater than that of any other animal.

[4] *brisking about* Moving about briskly.

[5] *Cherub ... Tiger* Smart is referring to the fact that a cherub is a small angel, as a cat is a small tiger.

the departure of the Children of Israel from Egypt.[1]
For every family had one cat at least in the bag.
For the English Cats are the best in Europe.
For he is the cleanest in the use of his forepaws of any quadruped.
For the dexterity of his defence is an instance of the love of God to him exceedingly.
For he is the quickest to his mark of any creature.
For he is tenacious of his point.
For he is a mixture of gravity and waggery.[2]
For he knows that God is his Saviour.
For there is nothing sweeter than his peace when at rest.
For there is nothing brisker than his life when in motion.
For he is of the Lord's poor and so indeed is he called by benevolence perpetually—Poor Jeoffry! poor Jeoffry! the rat has bit thy throat.
For I bless the name of the Lord Jesus that Jeoffry is better.
For the divine spirit comes about his body to sustain it in compleat° cat. *complete*
For his tongue is exceeding pure so that it has in purity what it wants in music.
For he is docile and can learn certain things.
For he can set up with gravity, which is patience upon approbation.
For he can fetch and carry, which is patience in employment.
For he can jump over a stick, which is patience upon proof positive.
For he can spraggle° upon waggle[3] at the word of command. *sprawl*
For he can jump from an eminence into his master's bosom.
For he can catch the cork and toss it again.
For he is hated by the hypocrite and miser.
For the former is afraid of detection.
For the latter refuses the charge.
For he camels his back to bear the first notion of business.
For he is good to think on, if a man would express himself neatly.
For he made a great figure in Egypt for his signal services.
For he killed the Ichneumon-rat[4] very pernicious by land.
For his ears are so acute that they sting again.[5]
For from this proceeds the passing quickness of his attention.
For by stroking of him I have found out electricity.
For I perceived God's light about him both wax and fire.
For the Electrical fire is the spiritual substance, which God sends from heaven to sustain the bodies both of man and beast.
For God has blessed him in the variety of his movements.
For, though he cannot fly, he is an excellent clamberer.
For his motions upon the face of the earth are more than any other quadruped.
For he can tread to all the measures upon the music.
For he can swim for life.
For he can creep.

—1939 (WRITTEN 1759–63)

[1] *Lord ... Egypt* The Lord commanded the children of Israel to take their flocks and herds with them upon departure (Exodus 13.32).

[2] *waggery* Mischievous jocularity.

[3] *upon waggle* While wiggling about.

[4] *Ichneumon-rat* Mongoose-like carnivorous mammal domesticated and revered by the ancient Egyptians for its ability to find and destroy the eggs of crocodiles and other dangerous reptiles.

[5] *again* In response.

TRANSATLANTIC CURRENTS

CONTEXTS

British and New World literatures have tended for centuries to be studied and taught in isolation from each other. Recently, however, both scholarship and pedagogy have begun to focus more frequently on the connections between Britain, Africa, and the Americas. There are of course necessary cultural distinctions to be made between, for instance, a tropical plantation, a barely established North American frontier settlement, and the fully developed urban bustle of London—but there are also connections to be acknowledged, as the flow of economic goods, people, and ideas across the sea in multiple directions influenced the development of literature in English on all shores of the Atlantic.

The slave trade was essential to the continued interchange; British merchants had become heavily engaged in the trade halfway through the seventeenth century, and their involvement continued to grow past the end of the eighteenth century. The trade operated in a loosely triangular form: ships transported manufactured goods from Europe to Africa to exchange for slaves; the slaves were brought to the Caribbean, where they were forced to engage in the production of luxury commodities such as sugar and tobacco; these products were then brought back to Europe for sale. The British colonies in North America also purchased slaves from Africa and traded with the Caribbean, exporting wood and food and importing luxury goods. Demand for slaves prompted the transportation of vast numbers of people: in the eighteenth century alone, about 6,500,000 slaves were traded, of whom an estimated 2,500,000 were shipped by British traders. This exchange created extraordinary economic growth for Britain and its colonies. And, in the latter half of the eighteenth century, the traffic of goods and people spawned intellectual and literary connections as authors, political campaigners, and theologians expressed their moral outrage over Britain's role in the slave trade and the treatment of slaves in British colonies.[1] As a result of growing opposition, the British slave trade would be outlawed in 1807, and all slaves in Britain and its colonies would be legally freed in 1834. (Anti-slavery laws were passed slightly earlier in Upper and Lower Canada and in some northern American states, with other states gradually following suit until official nationwide emancipation was achieved in 1865.)

While Africans were brought to the Americas by force, others came freely from England, Scotland, and Ireland. In rural areas, high rents and failing industry, combined with the promise of relatively cheap land and well-paid employment in the Americas, encouraged those who could afford the cost of travel to leave their homes behind—bringing to North America their families, their cultural influence, and their agricultural skills. Migrants from urban centers were more likely to travel individually; most of these were tradespeople or unskilled young men with few prospects at home. Although the English language and a blend of English, Scottish, and Irish culture dominated in the colonies, there were also regions with high concentrations of German, Dutch, and other settlers from continental Europe.

With settlement came conflict, both old and new. From the late seventeenth century to the 1760s, France and Britain engaged in a series of four wars, and their North American possessions fought each

[1] See the Contexts section "The Abolition of Slavery," available in this anthology's online component, for more material on the British anti-slavery movement.

other whenever the colonial powers did. England's self-image was deeply invested in the outcomes of its overseas battles; a mythology grew up around the death of General Wolfe, for example, in the wake of his defeat of French forces at Quebec, a moment which came to be seen as emblematic of the empire's glory. Pre-existing European conflicts blended with the conflicts of the New World. Colonists attempted to displace native people from useful land but also wanted to take advantage of the trade opportunities and military strength that alliances with tribes could afford.[1] The intercolonial wars of this period in North America are often called the French and Indian Wars, a somewhat misleading name, given that Native people participated on both sides. Greater numbers allied with the French in the hope of preventing further British expansion, but their hopes were disappointed when the French, in negotiating peace with Britain in 1763, ceded these tribes' territories without consulting them. Throughout the eighteenth century relations between colonists and Native people continued to be strained; while treaties were sometimes negotiated and alliances sometimes honored, that was far from the norm. Tribes often defended themselves with violence—both alongside their colonial allies and independently during times of peace between the colonies.

As the eighteenth century progressed and the Thirteen Colonies became more self-sufficient economically, they began as well to develop a more distinct sense of political identity. In the last half of the century, when the British government imposed a series of taxes and other legislation on the colonists without consulting local government in the Colonies, American dissenters responded with a cry of "no taxation without representation." Their argument was that, as Englishmen, they had a right to participate in the decisions of the British Parliament. This disagreement also created turmoil on the opposite side of the Atlantic, with the British pressed to define their political identity as an imperial power. In England, those defending the authority of the crown outnumbered those advocating concessions to the Colonies; although the British were forced to repeal the Stamp Act (the most controversial piece of legislation), they passed the Declaratory Act, a statement of their right to make law for the Colonies unilaterally. Opposition in the Colonies intensified, the British government passed increasingly invasive legislation, and the hostilities escalated into armed conflict; the Revolutionary War, which began in 1775, ended officially with American independence in 1783.

This did not, of course, end North America's relationship with Great Britain. The colonies of British North America (the eastern part of present-day Canada) still belonged to the empire, which continued to expand its territory to the west. And even the newly-formed United States of America remained far more closely tied to Britain, both economically and culturally, than to any other nation.

⌘⌘⌘

[1] See Samuel Johnson's imagining of a native perspective on colonization in *The Idler* No. 81 elsewhere in this anthology.

Slavery

from Richard Ligon, *A True & Exact History of the Island of Barbados* (1657)

In 1647, Richard Ligon found himself without money or opportunity in England and traveled to Barbados in the hope that his fortunes would change. They did not; a fever prompted his return to England in 1650, and he was thrown into debtors' prison shortly after his arrival home. His descriptions of life in Barbados shed valuable light on the early development of slavery in Britain's colonies—and on the development of the racist ideology that supported the institution.

The island is divided into three sorts of men, *viz.*[1] masters, servants, and slaves. The slaves and their posterity, being subject to their masters forever, are kept and preserved with greater care than the servants, who are theirs but for five years,[2] according to the law of the island....

It has been accounted a strange thing that the negroes, being more than double the numbers of the Christians that are there—and they accounted a bloody people, where they think they have power or advantages, and the more bloody by how much they are more fearful than others—that these should not commit some horrid massacre upon the Christians, thereby to enfranchise[3] themselves, and become masters of the island. But there are three reasons that take away this wonder; the one is, they are not suffered to touch or handle any weapons; the other, that they are held in such awe and slavery as they are fearful to appear in any daring act; and seeing the mustering of our men and hearing their gunshot (that which nothing is more terrible to them), their spirits are subjugated to so low a condition as they dare not look up to any bold attempt. Besides these, there is a third reason, which stops all designs of that kind, and that is, they are fetched from several parts of Africa, who speak several languages, and by that means one of them understands not another: for some of them are fetched from Guinny and Binny, some from Cutchew, some from Angola, and some from the River of Gambra.[4] And in some of these places where petty kingdoms are, they sell their subjects and such as they take in battle, whom they make slaves; and some mean men sell their servants, their children, and sometimes their wives; and think all good traffic[5] for such commodities as our merchants send them.

When they are brought to us, the planters buy them out of the ship, where they find them stark naked, and therefore cannot be deceived in any outward infirmity. They choose them as they do horses in a market; the strongest, youthfulest, and most beautiful yield the greatest prices. Thirty pound sterling is a price for the best man negro; and twenty-five, twenty-six, or twenty-seven pound for a woman; the children are at easier rates. And we buy them so as the sexes may be equal; for, if they have more men than women, the men who are unmarried will come to their masters and complain that they cannot live without wives, and desire him,[6] they may have wives. And he tells them that the next ship that comes, he will buy them wives, which satisfies them for the present; and so they expect the good time: which the master performing with them, the bravest fellow is to choose first, and so in order, as they are in place; and every one of them knows his better, and gives him the precedence, as cows do one another in passing through a narrow gate; for the most of them are as near beasts as may be, setting their souls aside. Religion they know none; yet most of them acknowledge a God, as appears by their motion and gestures: for, if one of them do another wrong, and he cannot revenge himself, he looks up to heaven for vengeance and holds up both his hands, as if the power must come from thence, that must do him right. Chaste they are as any people under

[1] *viz.* Abbreviation of the Latin *videlicet*, meaning "namely."

[2] *the servants ... five years* At this time, it was a common practice for people to contract themselves as indentured servants, legally committing to a set number of years of unpaid labor, in exchange for passage to the Americas.

[3] *enfranchise* Free.

[4] *Guinny ... Gambra* Places ranging along much of Africa's west coast, including Guinea, Benin, the Gambia River, and Cacheu (in present day Guinea-Bissau).

[5] *good traffic* Reasonable trade.

[6] *desire him* I.e., request of him that.

the sun; for, when the men and women are together naked, they never cast their eyes towards the parts that ought to be covered; and those amongst us that have breeches and petticoats, I never saw so much as a kiss, or embrace, or a wanton glance with their eyes between them. Jealous they are of their wives, and hold it for a great injury and scorn if another man make the least courtship to his wife....

[While I was using a compass] this negro Sambo comes to me, and seeing the needle wag, desired to know the reason of its stirring, and whether it were alive: I told him no, but it stood upon a point, and for a while it would stir, but by and by stand still, which he observed and found it to be true. The next question was why it stood one way and would not remove to any other point. I told him that it would stand no way but north and south, and upon that showed him the four cardinal points of the compass, east, west, north, south, which he presently learnt by heart and promised me never to forget it. His last question was why it would stand north. I gave this reason, because of the huge rocks of loadstone that were in the north part of the world, which had a quality to draw iron to it; and this needle, being of iron touched with a loadstone, it would always stand that way.

This point of philosophy was a little too hard for him, and so he stood in a strange muse;[1] which to put him out of, I bade him reach his axe and put it near to the compass, and remove it about; and, as he did so, the needle turned with it, which put him in the greatest admiration that ever I saw a man, and so quite gave over his questions, and desired me[2] that he might be made a Christian; for he thought to be a Christian was to be endued with all those knowledges he wanted.

I promised to do my best endeavour; and when I came home, spoke to the master of the plantation, and told him that poor Sambo desired much to be a Christian. But his answer was that the people of that island were governed by the laws of England, and by those laws we could not make a Christian a slave. I told him my request was far different from that, for I desired him to make a slave a Christian. His answer was that it was true, there was a great difference in that; but, being once a Christian, he could no more account him a slave, and so lose the hold they had of them as slaves by making them Christians; and by that means should open such a gap as all the planters in the island would curse him. So I was struck mute, and poor Sambo kept out of the Church; as ingenious, as honest, and as good a natured poor soul, as ever wore black, or ate green....

Though there be a mark set upon these people which will hardly ever be wiped off, as of their cruelties when they have advantages, and of their fearfulness and falseness; yet no rule so general but hath his[3] exception: for I believe, and I have strong motives to cause me to be of that persuasion, that there are as honest, faithful, and conscionable people amongst them as amongst those of Europe or any other part of the world....

[1] *muse* Act of reflection or musing.

[2] *desired me* Requested of me.

[3] *his* Its.

from John Woolman, "Considerations on the Keeping of Negroes" (1754)

One of the first prominent Quakers to publicly oppose slavery, John Woolman was influential in increasing anti-slavery sentiment among Quakers, who came to play a significant role in the abolition movement. Born in New Jersey, he traveled to preach in the colonies and eventually in England. He abstained from using sugar, dyed clothing, and other products of slave labor.

"Forasmuch as ye did it to the least of these my brethren, ye did it unto me."

—Matthew 25.40

As many times there are different motives to the same action, and one does that from a generous heart which another does for selfish ends; the like may be said in this case.

There are various circumstances among those that keep negroes, and different ways by which they fall under their care; and I doubt not, there are many well disposed persons amongst them who desire rather to manage wisely and justly in this difficult matter, than to make gain of it.

But the general disadvantage which these poor negroes lie under in an enlightened Christian country having often filled me with real sadness, I now think it my duty, through Divine aid, to offer some thoughts thereon to the consideration of others.

When we remember that all nations are of one blood, (Gen. 3.20)[1] that in this world we are but sojourners, that we are subject to the like afflictions and infirmities of body, the like disorders and frailties in mind, the like temptations, the same death, and the same judgment, and that the all-wise Being is Judge and Lord over us all, it seems to raise an idea of general brotherhood, and a disposition easy to be touched with a feeling of each other's afflictions; but when we forget those things, and look chiefly at our outward circumstances, in this and some ages past, constantly retaining in our minds the distinction between us and them, with respect to our knowledge and improvement in things Divine, natural and artificial, our breasts being apt to be filled with fond notions of superiority, there is danger of erring in our conduct toward them.

We allow them to be of the same species with ourselves; odds is, we are in a higher station, and enjoy greater favour than they. And when it is thus that our heavenly Father endoweth some of his children with distinguished gifts, they are intended for good ends; but if those thus gifted are thereby lifted up above their brethren, not considering themselves as debtors to the weak, nor behaving themselves as faithful stewards, none who judge impartially can suppose them free from ingratitude.

When a people dwell under the liberal distribution of favours from heaven, it behooves them carefully to inspect their ways, and consider the purposes for which those favours are bestowed, lest, through forgetfulness of God and misusing his gifts, they incur his heavy displeasure, whose judgments are just and equal, who exalteth and humbleth to the dust, as he seeth meet....

To prevent such an error, let us calmly consider their circumstance; and the better to do it, make their case ours. Suppose then that our ancestors and we had been exposed to constant servitude, in the more servile and inferior employments of life; that we had been destitute of the help of reading and good company; that amongst ourselves we had had but few wise and pious instructors; that the religious amongst our superiors seldom took notice of us; that while others in ease had plentifully heaped up the fruit of our labour, we had received barely enough to relieve nature; and being wholly at the command of others, had generally been treated as a contemptible, ignorant part of mankind; should we, in that case, be less abject than they now are? Again, if oppression be so hard to bear that a wise man is made mad by it, Eccl. 7.7,[2] then a series of oppressions, altering the behaviour and manners of a people is what may reasonably be expected.

When our property is taken contrary to our mind, by means appearing to us unjust, it is only through Divine influence, and the enlargement of heart from thence proceeding, that we can love our reputed oppressors. If the negroes fall short in this, an uneasy, if not a disconsolate disposition will be awakened, and remain like seeds in their minds, producing sloth and other habits which appear odious to us; and with which, had they been free men, they would not perhaps have been chargeable. These and other circumstances, rightly considered, will lessen the too great disparity which some make between us and them.

Integrity of heart has appeared in some of them; so that if we continue in the word of Christ, and our conduct towards them be seasoned with his love, we may hope to see the good effect of it. This, in a good degree, is the case with some into whose hands they have fallen; but that too many treat them otherwise, not seeming conscious of any neglect, is, alas! too evident.

When self-love presides in our minds, our opinions are biased in our own favour; and in this condition, being concerned with a people so situated that they have no voice to plead their own cause, there is danger of using ourselves to an undisturbed partiality, until, by long custom, the mind becomes reconciled with it, and the judgment itself infected....

"[Christ] hath laid down the best criterion by which mankind ought to judge of their own conduct, and others judge for them of theirs, one towards another,

[1] *Gen. 3.20* "And Adam called his wife's name Eve, because she was the mother of all living."

[2] *Eccl. 7.7* "Surely oppression maketh a wise man mad; and a gift destroyeth the heart."

viz.[1] 'Whatsoever ye would that men should do unto you, do ye even so to them.'[2] I take it that all men by nature are equally entitled to the equity of this rule, and under the indispensable obligations of it. One man ought not to look upon another man or society of men as so far beneath him that he should not put himself in their place, in all his actions towards them, and bring all to this test, *viz.* How should I approve of this conduct, were I in their circumstance, and they in mine?"[3] ...

It may be objected that there is the cost of purchase, and risk of their lives to them who possess [slaves], and therefore it is needful that they make the best use of their time. In a practice just and reasonable, such objections may have weight; but if the work be wrong from the beginning, there is little or no force in them. If I purchase a man who has never forfeited his liberty, the natural right of freedom is in him; and shall I keep him and his posterity in servitude and ignorance? "How should I approve of this conduct, were I in his circumstances, and he in mine?" ...

If we, by the operation of the Spirit of Christ, become heirs with him in the kingdom of his Father and are redeemed from the alluring counterfeit joys of this world, and the joy of Christ remain in us; to suppose that one in this happy condition can, for the sake of earthly riches, not only deprive his fellow-creatures of the sweetness of freedom, which, rightly used, is one of the greatest temporal blessings, but therewith neglect using proper means for their acquaintance with the Holy Scriptures and the advantage of true religion, seems at least a contradiction to reason....

To conclude, it is a great truth most certain that a life guided by wisdom from above, agreeably with justice, equity and mercy, is throughout consistent and amiable, and truly beneficial to society; the serenity and calmness of mind in it affords an unparalleled comfort in this life, and the end of it is blessed.

And it is no less true that they who in the midst of high favours remain ungrateful, and under all the advantages that a Christian can desire are selfish, earthly and sensual, do miss the true fountain of happiness and wander in a maze of dark anxiety, where all their treasures are insufficient to quiet their minds: hence, from an insatiable craving, they neglect doing good with what they have acquired, and too often add oppression to vanity, that they may compass[4] more.

Hannah More, "Slavery: A Poem" (1788)

Hannah More was already a very successful playwright when she became involved with England's circle of prominent abolitionist campaigners. Composed at the request of the Society for the Abolition of the Slave Trade in support of a parliamentary debate on the subject, "Slavery: A Poem" was widely circulated by anti-slavery committees.

If heaven has into being deigned to call
Thy light, O LIBERTY! to shine on all;
Bright intellectual sun! why does thy ray
To earth distribute only partial day?
Since no resisting cause from spirit flows
Thy penetrating essence to oppose;
No obstacles by nature's hand impress,
Thy subtle and ethereal beams arrest;
Nor motion's laws can speed thy active course,
Nor strong repulsion's pow'rs obstruct thy force;
Since there is no convexity in MIND,[5]
Why are thy genial beams to parts confined?
While the chill North with thy bright ray is blest,
Why should fell darkness half the South invest?
Was it decreed, fair freedom! at thy birth,
That thou should'st ne'er irradiate° all the earth? *cast light on*
While Britain basks in thy full blaze of light,
Why lies sad Afric quenched in total night?
Thee only, sober Goddess! I attest,
In smiles chastised, and decent graces drest.
Not that unlicensed monster of the crowd,
Whose roar terrific bursts in peals so loud,

[1] *viz.* Abbreviation of the Latin *videlicet*, meaning "namely," or "that is to say."

[2] *Whatsoever ye ... to them* See Matthew 7.12.

[3] *[Christ] hath ... I in mine?* From Quaker writer Alexander Arscott's treatise *Some Considerations Relating to the Present State of the Christian Religion, Part Third* (1734).

[4] *compass* Attain.

[5] *Since there ... in MIND* Since the realm of thought is not curved like the earth.

Deaf'ning the ear of peace: fierce faction's tool;
Of rash sedition born, and mad misrule;
Whose stubborn mouth, rejecting reason's rein,
No strength can govern, and no skill restrain;
Whose magic cries the frantic vulgar draw
To spurn at order, and to outrage law;
To tread on grave authority and pow'r,
And shake the work of ages in an hour:
Convulsed° her voice, and pestilent her breath, *agitated*
She raves of mercy, while she deals out death:
Each blast is fate; she darts from either hand
Red conflagration° o'er th'astonished land; *inferno*
Clamouring for peace, she rends the air with noise,
And to reform a part, the whole destroys.
  O, plaintive Southerne![1] whose impassioned strain
So oft has waked my languid Muse in vain!
Now, when congenial° themes her cares engage, *similar*
She burns to emulate thy glowing page;
Her failing efforts mock her fond° desires, *foolish*
She shares thy feelings, not partakes thy fires.
Strange pow'r of song! the strain that warms the heart
Seems the same inspiration to impart;
Touched by the kindling energy alone,
We think the flame which melts us is our own;
Deceived, for genius we mistake delight,
Charmed as we read, we fancy we can write.
  Though not to me, sweet bard, thy pow'rs belong
Fair Truth, a hallowed guide! inspires my song.
Here Art would weave her gayest flow'rs in vain,
For Truth the bright invention would disdain.
For no fictitious ills these numbers flow,
But living anguish, and substantial woe;
No individual griefs my bosom melt,
For millions feel what Oronoko felt:
Fired by no single wrongs, the countless host
I mourn, by rapine° dragged from Afric's coast. *plunder*
  Perish th'illiberal thought which would debase
The native genius of the sable° race! *dark*
Perish the proud philosophy, which sought
To rob them of the pow'rs of equal thought!
Does then th'immortal principle within
Change with the casual colour of a skin?
Does matter govern spirit? or is mind
Degraded by the form to which 'tis joined?
  No: they have heads to think, and hearts to feel,
And souls to act, with firm, though erring, zeal;
For they have keen affections, kind desires,
Love strong as death, and active patriot fires;
All the rude energy, the fervid flame,
Of high-souled passion, and ingenuous shame:
Strong, but luxuriant virtues boldly shoot
From the wild vigour of a savage root.
  Nor weak their sense of honour's proud control,
For pride is virtue in a pagan soul;
A sense of worth, a conscience of desert,° *deserving praise*
A high, unbroken haughtiness of heart:
That self-same stuff which erst° proud empires swayed, *once*
Of which the conquerors of the world were made.
Capricious fate of man! that very pride
In Afric scourged, in Rome was deified.
  No muse, O Quashi![2] shall thy deeds relate,
No statue snatch thee from oblivious fate!
For thou wast born where never gentle Muse
On valour's grave the flow'rs of genius strews;
And thou wast born where no recording page
Plucks the fair deed from time's devouring rage.
Had fortune placed thee on some happier coast,
Where polished souls heroic virtue boast,
To thee, who sought'st a voluntary grave,
Th'uninjured honours of thy name to save,

[1] [More's note] Author of the tragedy of Oronoko. [Aphra Behn wrote the original *Oroonoko* (1688), about an African prince who became a British slave, but Thomas Southerne's stage adaptation (1695) was better known.]

[2] [More's note] It is a point of honour among negroes of high spirit to die rather than to suffer their glossy skin to bear the mark of the whip. Qua-shi had somehow offended his master, a young planter with whom he had been bred up in the endearing intimacy of a play-fellow. His services had been faithful; his attachment affectionate. The master resolved to punish him, and pursued him for that purpose. In trying to escape Qua-shi stumbled and fell; the master fell upon him; they wrestled long with doubtful victory; at length Qua-shi got uppermost, and, being firmly seated on his master's breast, he secured his legs with one hand, and with the other drew a sharp knife; then said, "Master, I have been bred up with you from a child; I have loved you as myself: in return, you have condemned me to a punishment of which I must ever have borne the marks: thus only can I avoid them"; so saying, he drew the knife with all his strength across his own throat, and fell down dead, without a groan, on his master's body. [More cites the source of this story as James Ramsay's *Essay on the Treatment and Conversion of African Slaves in the British Sugar Colonies* (1784).]

Whose generous arm thy barbarous master spared,
Altars had smoked, and temples had been reared.
Whene'er to Afric's shores I turn my eyes,
Horrors of deepest, deadliest guilt arise;
I see, by more than fancy's mirror shown,
The burning village, and the blazing town:
See the dire victim torn from social life,
The shrieking babe, the agonizing wife!
She, wretch forlorn! is dragged by hostile hands,
To distant tyrants sold, in distant lands!
Transmitted miseries, and successive chains,
The sole sad heritage her child obtains!
Ev'n this last wretched boon their foes deny,
To weep together, or together die.
By felon hands, by one relentless stroke,
See the fond links of feeling nature broke!
The fibres twisting round a parent's heart,
Torn from their grasp, and bleeding as they part.
Hold, murderers, hold! not aggravate distress;
Respect the passions you yourselves possess;
Ev'n you, of ruffian heart, and ruthless hand,
Love your own offspring, love your native land.
Ah! leave them holy Freedom's cheering smile,
The heav'n-taught fondness for the parent soil;
Revere affections mingled with our frame,
In every nature, every clime the same;
In all, these feelings equal sway maintain;
In all the love of HOME and FREEDOM reign:
And Tempe's vale, and parched Angola's[1] sand,
One equal fondness of their sons command.
Th'unconquered savage laughs at pain and toil,
Basking in freedom's beams which gild his native soil.
Does thirst of empire, does desire of fame,
(For these are specious crimes) our rage inflame?
No: sordid lust of gold their fate controls,
The basest appetite of basest souls;
Gold, better gained, by what their ripening sky,
Their fertile fields, their arts[2] and mines supply.
What wrongs, what injuries does oppression plead
To smooth the horror of th'unnatural deed?
What strange offence, what aggravated sin?
They stand convicted—of a darker skin!
Barbarians, hold! th'opprobious° commerce spare, *disgraceful*
Respect his sacred image which they bear:[3]
Though dark and savage, ignorant and blind,
They claim the common privilege of kind;
Let Malice strip them of each other plea,[4]
They still are men, and men should still be free.
Insulted Reason loaths th'inverted trade[5]—
Dire change! the agent is the purchase made!
Perplexed, the baffled Muse involves° the tale; *confuses*
Nature confounded, well may language fail!
The outraged Goddess with abhorrent eyes
Sees MAN the traffic, SOULS the merchandise!
Plead not, in reason's palpable abuse,
Their sense of feeling callous and obtuse:[6]
From heads to hearts lies nature's plain appeal,
Though few can reason, all mankind can feel.
Though wit may boast a livelier dread of shame,
A loftier sense of wrong refinement claim;
Though polished manners may fresh wants invent,
And nice° distinctions nicer souls torment; *fine*
Though these on finer spirits heavier fall,
Yet natural evils are the same to all.
Though wounds there are which reason's force may heal,
There needs no logic sure to make us feel.
The nerve, howe'er untutored, can sustain
A sharp, unutterable sense of pain;
As exquisitely fashioned in a slave,
As where unequal fate a sceptre[7] gave.
Sense is as keen where Congo's[8] sons preside,
As where proud Tiber[9] rolls his classic tide.
Rhetoric or verse may point the feeling line,

[1] *Tempe's vale* River valley in Greece; *Angola* Portuguese colony in sub-Saharan Africa.

[2] [More's note] Besides many valuable productions of the soil, cloths and carpets of exquisite manufacture are brought from the coast of Guinea.

[3] *Respect … bear* I.e., respect the fact that they are made in God's image.

[4] *each other plea* Every other argument.

[5] *th'inverted trade* The opposite trade; the use of white slaves by black people.

[6] [More's note] Nothing is more frequent than this cruel and stupid argument, that they do not feel the miseries inflicted on them as Europeans would do.

[7] *sceptre* Ornamental rod that is a symbol of royal authority.

[8] *Congo* River in Central Africa.

[9] *Tiber* River in Italy that passes through Rome.

They do not whet° sensation, but define. *sharpen*
Did ever slave less feel the galling° chain, *chafing*
When Zeno[1] proved there was no ill in pain?
Their miseries philosophic quirks deride,
Slaves groan in pangs disowned by Stoic pride.
　When the fierce Sun darts vertical his beams,
And thirst and hunger mix their wild extremes;
When the sharp iron[2] wounds his inmost soul,
And his strained eyes in burning anguish roll;
Will the parched negro find, ere he expire,
No pain in hunger, and no heat in fire?
　For him, when fate his tortured frame destroys,
What hope of present fame, or future joys?
For this, have heroes shortened nature's date;
For that, have martyrs gladly met their fate;
But him, forlorn, no hero's pride sustains,
No martyr's blissful visions soothe his pains;
Sullen, he mingles with his kindred dust,
For he has learned to dread the Christian's trust;
To him what mercy can that pow'r display,
Whose servants murder, and whose sons betray?
Savage! thy venial° error I deplore, *excusable*
They are not Christians who infest thy shore.
　O thou sad spirit, whose preposterous yoke
The great deliverer death, at length, has broke!
Released from misery, and escaped from care,
Go meet that mercy man denied thee here.
In thy dark home, sure refuge of th'opressed,
The wicked vex not, and the weary rest.
And, if some notions, vague and undefined,
Of future terrors have assailed thy mind;
If such thy masters have presumed to teach,
As terrors only they are prone to preach;
(For should they paint eternal mercy's reign,
Where were th'oppressor's rod, the captive's chain?)
If, then, thy troubled soul has learned to dread
The dark unknown thy trembling footsteps tread;
On HIM, who made thee what thou art, depend;
HE, who withholds the means, accepts the end.
Not thine the reckoning dire of LIGHT abused,
KNOWLEDGE disgraced, and LIBERTY misused;
On thee no awful judge incensed shall sit
For parts perverted, and dishonoured wit.
Where ignorance will be found the surest plea,
How many learn'd and wise shall envy thee!
　And thou, WHITE SAVAGE! whether lust of gold,
Or lust of conquest, rule thee uncontrolled!
Hero, or robber!—by whatever name
Thou plead thy impious claim to wealth or fame;
Whether inferior mischiefs be thy boast,
A petty tyrant rifling Gambia's coast:
Or bolder carnage track thy crimson way,
Kings dispossessed, and provinces thy prey;
Panting to tame wide earth's remotest bound;
All Cortez[3] murdered, all Columbus found;
O'er plundered realms to reign, detested Lord,
Make millions wretched, and thyself abhorred;——
In reason's eye, in wisdom's fair account,
Your sum of glory boasts a like amount;
The means may differ, but the end's the same;
Conquest is pillage with a nobler name.
Who makes the sum of human blessings less,
Or sinks the stock of general happiness,
No solid fame shall grace, no true renown,
His life shall blazon,° or his memory crown. *adorn*
　Had those advent'rous spirits who explore
Through ocean's trackless wastes, the far-sought shore;
Whether of wealth insatiate,° or of pow'r, *endlessly greedy*
Conquerors who waste, or ruffians who devour:
Had these possessed, O COOK![4] thy gentle mind,
Thy love of arts, thy love of humankind;
Had these pursued thy mild and liberal plan,
DISCOVERERS had not been a curse to man!
Then, blessed philanthropy! thy social hands
Had linked dissevered° worlds in brothers' bands; *divided*

[1] *Zeno* Zeno of Citum (334 BCE–262 BCE), founder of Stoicism, a philosophy asserting that a wise person can be happy under any circumstances.

[2] [More's note] This is not said figuratively. The writer of these lines has seen a complete set of chains, fitted to every separate limb of these unhappy, innocent men; together with instruments for wrenching open the jaws, contrived with such cruelty as would shock the humanity of an inquisitor.

[3] *Cortez* Hérnan Cortés (1485–1547), a Spanish Conquistador whose expedition to Mexico resulted in the fall of the Aztec Empire.

[4] *COOK* Captain James Cook (1728–79), British explorer and cartographer who mapped many places that were previously unknown to or uncharted by Europeans. Although his discoveries prompted further colonization, Cook himself was friendly and sympathetic toward the indigenous peoples of all the places he visited.

Careless, if colour, or if clime° divide; *climate*
Then, loved, and loving, man had lived, and died.
The purest wreaths which hang on glory's shrine,
For empires founded, peaceful PENN![1] are thine;
No blood-stained laurels[2] crowned thy virtuous toil,
No slaughtered natives drenched thy fair-earned soil.
Still thy meek spirit in thy flock[3] survives,
Consistent still, *their* doctrines rule their lives;
Thy followers only have effaced the shame
Inscribed by SLAVERY on the Christian name.
Shall Britain, where the soul of freedom reigns,
Forge chains for others she herself disdains?
Forbid it, Heaven! O let the nations know
The liberty she loves she will bestow;
Not to herself the glorious gift confined,
She spreads the blessing wide as humankind;
And, scorning narrow views of time and place,
Bids all be free in earth's extended space.
What page of human annals can record
A deed so bright as human rights restored?
O may that god-like deed, that shining page,
Redeem OUR fame, and consecrate OUR age!
And see, the cherub° Mercy from above, *angel*
Descending softly, quits the sphere of love!
On feeling hearts she sheds celestial dew,
And breathes her spirit o'er th'enlightened few;
From soul to soul the spreading influence steals,
Till every breast the soft contagion feels.
She bears, exulting, to the burning shore
The loveliest office angel ever bore;
To vindicate the pow'r in Heaven adored,
To still the clank of chains, and sheathe the sword;
To cheer the mourner, and with soothing hands
From bursting hearts unbind th'oppressor's bands;
To raise the lustre of the Christian name,
And clear the foulest blot° that dims its fame. *stain*
As the mild Spirit hovers o'er the coast,
A fresher hue the withered landscapes boast;
Her healing smiles the ruined scenes repair,
And blasted Nature wears a joyous air.
She spreads her blest commission from above,
Stamped with the sacred characters of love;
She tears the banner stained with blood and tears,
And, LIBERTY! thy shining standard rears!
As the bright ensign's° glory she displays, *flag's*
See pale OPPRESSION faints beneath the blaze!
The giant dies! no more his frown appalls,
The chain untouched, drops off; the fetter° falls. *shackle*
Astonished echo tells the vocal shore,
Opression's fall'n, and slavery is no more!
The dusky myriads° crowd the sultry[4] plain, *multitudes*
And hail that mercy long invoked in vain.
Victorious pow'r! she bursts their two-fold bands,
And FAITH and FREEDOM spring from Mercy's hands.

[1] *PENN* William Penn (1644–1718), an influential Quaker and the founder of Pennsylvania, attempted to live peacefully with the Lenape, its aboriginal inhabitants.

[2] *laurels* Victories; accomplishments. Crowns made of leaves of the bay laurel were awarded in ancient Greece as a symbol of victory or poetic achievement.

[3] [More's note] The Quakers have emancipated all their slaves throughout America.

[4] *sultry* Hot and humid, i.e., from hot work.

Ann Yearsley, "A Poem on the Inhumanity of the Slave-Trade" (1788)

Ann Yearsley, a laboring-class milkwoman, was saved from near-destitution when Hannah More discovered her poetic abilities and became her patron. By the time Yearsley and More wrote their major abolitionist poems, both of which were published in the same year, the friendship had ended over disagreements as to how Yearsley's profits should be managed.

Bristol,[5] thine heart hath throbbed to glory.—Slaves,
E'en Christian slaves, have shook their chains, and gazed
With wonder and amazement on thee. Hence
Ye grov'ling souls, who think the term I give,
Of Christian slave, a paradox! to *you*
I do not turn, but leave you to conception
Narrow; with that be blest, nor dare to stretch
Your shackled souls along the course of Freedom.

[5] *Bristol* A major port for marine trade and Yearsley's hometown; Bristol experienced great economic growth as a result of slavery.

Yet, Bristol, list!° nor deem Lactilla's[1] soul *listen*
Lessened by distance; snatch her rustic thought,
Her crude ideas, from their panting state,
And let them fly in wide expansion; lend
Thine energy, so little understood
By the rude million, and I'll dare the strain
Of Heav'n-born Liberty till Nature moves
Obedient to her voice. Alas! my friend,
Strong rapture dies within the soul, while Pow'r
Drags on his bleeding victims. Custom,[2] Law,
Ye blessings, and ye curses of mankind,
What evils do ye cause? We feel enslaved,
Yet move in your direction. Custom, thou
Wilt preach up filial piety; thy sons
Will groan, and stare with impudence at Heav'n,
As if they did abjure° the act, where Sin *renounce*
Sits full on Inhumanity; the church
They fill with mouthing, vap'rous sighs and tears,
Which, like the guileful crocodile's,[3] oft fall,
Nor fall, but at the cost of human bliss.
Custom, thou hast undone us! led us far
From God-like probity,° from truth, *moral integrity*
and heaven.
But come, ye souls who feel for human woe,
Though dressed in savage guise! Approach, thou son,
Whose heart would shudder at a father's chains,
And melt o'er thy loved brother as he lies
Gasping in torment undeserved. Oh, sight
Horrid and insupportable! far worse
Than an immediate, an heroic death;
Yet to this sight I summon thee. Approach,
Thou slave of avarice, that canst see the maid
Weep o'er her inky sire! Spare me, thou God
Of all-indulgent Mercy, if I scorn
This gloomy wretch, and turn my tearful eye
To more enlightened beings. Yes, my tear
Shall hang on the green furze,[4] like pearly dew
Upon the blossom of the morn. My song
Shall teach sad Philomel[5] a louder note,
When Nature swells her woe. O'er suff'ring man
My soul with sorrow bends! Then come, ye few
Who feel a more than cold, material essence;
Here ye may vent your sighs, till the bleak North
Find its adherents aided.—Ah, no more!
The dingy youth comes on, sullen in chains;
He smiles on the rough sailor, who aloud
Strikes at the spacious heav'n, the earth, the sea,
In breath too blasphemous; yet not to him
Blasphemous, for he dreads not either:—lost
In dear internal imagery, the soul
Of Indian Luco[6] rises to his eyes,
Silent, not inexpressive: the strong beams
With eager wildness yet drink in the view
Of his too humble home, where he had left
His mourning father, and his Incilanda.
Curse on the toils spread by a Christian hand
To rob the Indian of his freedom! Curse
On him who from a bending parent steals
His dear support of age, his darling child;
Perhaps a son, or a more tender daughter,
Who might have closed his eyelids, as the spark
Of life gently retired. Oh, thou poor world!
Thou fleeting good to individuals! see
How much for thee they care, how wide they ope
Their helpless arms to clasp thee; vapour thou!
More swift than passing wind! thou leav'st them nought
Amid th'unreal scene, but a scant grave.
I know the crafty merchant will oppose
The plea of nature to my strain, and urge
His toils are for his children: the soft plea
Dissolves my soul—but when I sell a son,
Thou God of nature, let it be my own!
Behold that Christian! see what horrid joy
Lights up his moody features, while he grasps
The wished-for gold, purchase of human blood!
Away, thou seller of mankind! Bring on

[1] *Lactilla* Yearsley often refers to herself by this name, a reference to her work as a milkwoman.

[2] *Custom* Tradition; practices dictated by cultural habit.

[3] *crocodile* It was said that crocodiles cry as they devour their prey.

[4] *furze* Gorse, a prickly shrub.

[5] *Philomel* In Greek mythology, Philomela was raped by King Tereus and swore to tell the world of the injustice done to her. In some versions, the gods turned her into a nightingale (a bird known for its mournful song).

[6] *Indian Luco* Luco appears at times to be of African, and at others to be of Caribbean origin; such ambiguous portrayals of Africans and New World aboriginals were not uncommon in the eighteenth century.

Thy daughter to this market! bring thy wife!
Thine aged mother, though of little worth,
With all thy ruddy boys! Sell them, thou wretch,
And swell the price of Luco![1] Why that start?
Why gaze as thou wouldst fright me from my challenge
With look of anguish? Is it Nature strains
Thine heart-strings at the image? Yes, my charge
Is full against her, and she rends thy soul,
While I but strike upon thy pityless ear,
Fearing her rights are violated.—Speak,
Astound the voice of Justice! bid thy tears
Melt the unpitying pow'r, while thus she claims
The pledges of thy love. Oh, throw thine arm
Around thy little ones, and loudly plead
Thou canst not sell thy children.—Yet, beware
Lest Luco's groan be heard; should that prevail,
Justice will scorn thee in her turn, and hold
Thine act against thy prayer. Why clasp, she cries,
That blooming youth? Is it because thou lov'st him?
Why Luco was belov'd: then wilt thou feel,
Thou selfish Christian, for thy private woe,
Yet cause such pangs to him that is a father?
Whence comes thy right to barter for thy fellows?
Where are thy statutes? Whose the iron pen
That gave thee precedent? Give me the seal
Of virtue, or religion, for thy trade,
And I will ne'er upbraid thee; but if force
Superior, hard brutality alone
Become thy boast, hence to some savage haunt,
Nor claim protection from my social laws.
    Luco is gone; his little brothers weep,
While his fond mother climbs the hoary° rock *ancient*
Whose point o'er-hangs the main.° No Luco there, *sea*
No sound, save the hoarse billows.° On she roves, *waves*
With love, fear, hope, holding alternate rage
In her too anxious bosom. Dreary main!
Thy murmurs now are riot, while she stands
List'ning to ev'ry breeze, waiting the step
Of gentle Luco. Ah, return! return!
Too hapless mother, thy indulgent arms
Shall never clasp thy fettered Luco more.
See Incilanda! artless maid, my soul
Keeps pace with thee, and mourns. Now o'er the hill
She creeps, with timid foot, while Sol[2] embrowns
The bosom of the isle, to where she left
Her faithful lover: here the well-known cave,
By nature formed amid the rock, endears
The image of her Luco; here his pipe,
Formed of the polished cane,° neglected lies, *plant stem*
No more to vibrate;° here the useless dart, *produce sound*
The twanging bow, and the fierce panther's skin,
Salute the virgin's eye. But where is Luco?
He comes not down the steep, though he had vowed,
When the sun's beams at noon should sidelong gild
The cave's wide entrance, he would swift descend
To bless his Incilanda. Ten pale moons
Had glided by, since to his generous breast
He clasped the tender maid, and whispered love.
Oh, mutual sentiment! thou dang'rous bliss!
So exquisite, that Heav'n had been unjust
Had it bestowed less exquisite of ill;
When thou art held no more, thy pangs are deep,
Thy joys convulsive to the soul; yet all
Are meant to smooth th'uneven road of life.
    For Incilanda, Luco ranged the wild,
Holding her image to his panting heart;
For her he strained the bow, for her he stripped
The bird of beauteous plumage; happy hour,
When with these guiltless trophies he adorned
The brow of her he loved. Her gentle breast
With gratitude was filled, nor knew she aught
Of language strong enough to paint her soul,
Or ease the great emotion; whilst her eye
Pursued the gen'rous Luco to the field,
And glowed with rapture at his wished return.
    Ah, sweet suspense! betwixt the mingled cares
Of friendship, love, and gratitude, so mixed,
That ev'n the soul may cheat herself.—Down, down,
Intruding Memory! bid thy struggles cease,
At this soft scene of innate war. What sounds
Break on her ear? She, starting, whispers "Luco."
Be still, fond maid; list to the tardy step
Of leaden-footed woe. A father comes,
But not to seek his son, who from the deck
Had breathed a last adieu: no, he shuts out
The soft, fallacious gleam of hope, and turns
Within upon the mind: horrid and dark

[1] *swell the … of Luco* I.e., profit even more than you would have by selling Luco alone.

[2] *Sol* In Roman mythology, the god of the sun.

Are his wild, unenlightened pow'rs: no ray
Of forced philosophy to calm his soul,
But all the anarchy of wounded nature.
    Now he arraigns his country's gods, who sit,
In his bright fancy, far beyond the hills,
Unriveting the chains of slaves: his heart
Beats quick with stubborn fury, while he doubts
Their justice to his child. Weeping old man,
Hate not a Christian's God, whose record holds
Thine injured Luco's name. Frighted he starts,
Blasphemes the Deity, whose altars rise
Upon the Indian's helpless neck, and sinks,
Despising comfort, till by grief and age
His angry spirit is forced out. Oh, guide,
Ye angel-forms, this joyless shade to worlds
Where the poor Indian, with the sage, is proved
The work of a Creator. Pause not here,
Distracted maid! ah, leave the breathless form,
On whose cold cheek thy tears so swiftly fall,
Too unavailing! On this stone, she cries,
My Luco sat, and to the wand'ring stars
Pointed my eye, while from his gentle tongue
Fell old traditions of his country's woe.
Where now shall Incilanda seek him? Hence,
Defenceless mourner, ere the dreary night
Wrap thee in added horror. Oh, Despair,
How eagerly thou rend'st the heart! She pines
In anguish deep, and sullen: Luco's form
Pursues her, lives in restless thought, and chides
Soft consolation. Banished from his arms,
She seeks the cold embrace of death; her soul
Escapes in one sad sigh. Too hapless° maid! *unfortunate*
Yet happier far than he thou lov'dst; his tear,
His sigh, his groan avail not, for they plead
Most weakly with a Christian. Sink, thou wretch,
Whose act shall on the cheek of Albion's° sons *England's*
Throw Shame's red blush: thou, who hast
    frighted° far *scared away*
Those simple wretches from thy God, and taught
Their erring minds to mourn his partial love,[1]
Profusely poured on thee, while they are left
Neglected to thy mercy. Thus deceived,
How doubly dark must be their road to death!
    Luco is borne around the neighb'ring isles,
Losing the knowledge of his native shore
Amid the pathless wave; destined to plant
The sweet luxuriant cane.° He strives to please, *sugarcane*
Nor once complains, but greatly° smothers grief. *nobly*
His hands are blistered, and his feet are worn,
Till ev'ry stroke dealt by his mattock[2] gives
Keen agony to life; while from his breast
The sigh arises, burdened with the name
Of Incilanda. Time inures the youth,
His limbs grow nervous, strained by willing toil;
And resignation, or a calm despair,
(Most useful either) lulls him to repose.
    A Christian renegade, that from his soul
Abjures the tenets of our schools, nor dreads
A future punishment, nor hopes for mercy,
Had fled from England, to avoid those laws
Which must have made his life a retribution
To violated justice, and had gained,
By fawning guile, the confidence (ill placed)
Of Luco's master. O'er the slave he stands
With knotted whip, lest fainting nature shun
The task too arduous, while his cruel soul,
Unnat'ral, ever feeds, with gross delight,
Upon his suff'rings. Many slaves there were,
But none who could suppress the sigh, and bend,
So quietly as Luco: long he bore
The stripes, that from his manly bosom drew
The sanguine° stream (too little prized); *bloody*
    at length
Hope fled his soul, giving her struggles o'er,
And he resolved to die. The sun had reached
His zenith—pausing faintly, Luco stood,
Leaning upon his hoe, while mem'ry brought,
In piteous imag'ry, his aged father,
His poor fond mother, and his faithful maid:
The mental group in wildest motion set
Fruitless imagination; fury, grief,
Alternate shame, the sense of insult, all
Conspire to aid the inward storm; yet words
Were no relief, he stood in silent woe.
    Gorgon, remorseless Christian, saw the slave

[1] [Yearsley's note] Indians have been often heard to say, in their complaining moments, "God Almighty no love us well; he be good to buckera [white people]; he bid buckera burn us; he no burn buckera."

[2] *mattock* Tool for digging.

Stand musing, 'mid the ranks, and, stealing soft
Behind the studious Luco, struck his cheek
With a too-heavy whip, that reached his eye,
Making it dark forever. Luco turned,
In strongest agony, and with his hoe
Struck the rude Christian on the forehead. Pride,
With hateful malice, seize on Gorgon's soul,
By nature fierce; while Luco sought the beach,
And plunged beneath the wave; but near him lay
A planter's barge, whose seamen grasped his hair
Dragging to life a wretch who wished to die.
Rumour now spreads the tale, while Gorgon's breath
Envenomed, aids her blast: imputed crimes
Oppose the plea of Luco, till he scorns
Even a just defence, and stands prepared.
The planters, conscious that to fear alone
They owe their cruel pow'r, resolve to blend
New torment with the pangs of death, and hold
Their victims high in dreadful view, to fright
The wretched number left. Luco is chained
To a huge tree, his fellow-slaves are ranged
To share the horrid sight; fuel is placed
In an increasing train, some paces back,
To kindle slowly, and approach the youth,
With more than native terror. See, it burns!
He gazes on the growing flame, and calls
For "water, water!" The small boon's denied.
E'en Christians throng each other, to behold
The different alterations of his face,
As the hot death approaches. (Oh, shame, shame
Upon the followers of Jesus! shame
On him that dares avow a God!) He writhes,
While down his breast glide the unpitied tears,
And in their sockets strain their scorched balls.
"Burn, burn me quick! I cannot die!" he cries:
"Bring fire more close!" The planters heed him not,
But still prolonging Luco's torture, threat° *threaten*
Their trembling slaves around. His lips are dry,
His senses seem to quiver, ere they quit
His frame for ever, rallying strong, then driv'n
From the tremendous conflict. Sight no more
Is Luco's, his parched tongue is ever mute;
Yet in his soul his Incilanda stays,
Till both escape together. Turn, my muse,
From this sad scene; lead Bristol's milder soul
To where the solitary spirit roves,
Wrapt in the robe of innocence, to shades
Where pity breathing in the gale, dissolves
The mind, when fancy paints such real woe.
Now speak, ye Christians (who for gain enslave
A soul like Luco's, tearing her[1] from joy
In life's short vale; and if there be a hell,
As ye believe, to that ye thrust her down,
A blind, involuntary victim), where
Is your true essence of religion? where
Your proofs of righteousness, when ye conceal
The knowledge of the deity from those
Who would adore him fervently? Your God
Ye rob of worshippers, his altars keep
Unhailed, while driving from the sacred font[2]
The eager slave, lest he should hope in Jesus.
Is this your piety? Are these your laws,
Whereby the glory of the Godhead spreads
O'er barb'rous climes? Ye hypocrites, disown
The Christian name, nor shame its cause: yet where
Shall souls like yours find welcome? Would the Turk,
Pagan, or wildest Arab, ope their arms
To gain such proselytes?° No; he that owns *converts*
The name of Mussulman° would start, and shun *Muslim*
Your worse than serpent touch; he frees his slave
Who turns to Mahomet.[3] The Spaniard[4] stands
Your brighter contrast; he condemns the youth
Forever to the mine; but ere the wretch
Sinks to the deep domain, the hand of faith
Bathes his faint temples in the sacred stream,
Bidding his spirit hope. Briton, dost thou
Act up to this? If so, bring on thy slaves
To Calv'ry's mount,[5] raise high their kindred souls
To him who died to save them: this alone
Will teach them calmly to obey thy rage,
And deem a life of misery but a day,
To long eternity. Ah, think how soon

[1] *her* I.e., the soul.

[2] *sacred font* Bowl of water for baptism.

[3] [Yearsley's note] The Turk gives freedom to his slave on condition that he embraces Mahometism [Islam].

[4] [Yearsley's note] The Spaniard, immediately on purchasing an Indian, gives him baptism.

[5] *Calv'ry's mount* Mount Calvary is where Christ was crucified (See Luke 23.33).

Thine head shall on earth's dreary pillow lie,
With thy poor slaves, each silent, and unknown
To his once furious neighbour. Think how swift
The sands of time ebb out, for him and thee.
Why groans that Indian youth, in burning chains
Suspended o'er the beach? The lab'ring sun
Strikes from his full meridian° on the slave *height*
Whose arms are blistered by the heated iron,
Which still corroding, seeks the bone. What crime
Merits so dire a death?[1] Another gasps
With strongest agony, while life declines
From recent amputation. Gracious God!
Why thus in mercy let thy whirlwinds sleep
O'er a vile race of Christians, who profane
Thy glorious attributes? Sweep them from earth,
Or check their cruel pow'r: the savage tribes
Are angels when compared to brutes like these.
  Advance, ye Christians, and oppose my strain:
Who dares condemn it? Prove from laws divine,
From deep philosophy, or social love,
That ye derive your privilege. I scorn
The cry of Av'rice, or the trade that drains
A fellow-creature's blood: bid Commerce plead
Her public good, her nation's many wants,
Her sons thrown idly on the beach, forbade
To seize the image of their God and sell it:[2]—
I'll hear her voice, and Virtue's hundred tongues
Shall sound against her. Hath our public good
Fell rapine° for its basis? Must our wants *barbarous plunder*
Find their supply in murder? Shall the sons
Of Commerce shiv'ring stand, if not employed
Worse than the midnight robber? Curses fall
On the destructive system that shall need
Such base supports! Doth England need them? No;
Her laws, with prudence, hang the meagre thief
That from his neighbour steals a slender sum,
Though famine drove him on. O'er him the priest,
Beneath the fatal tree, laments the crime,
Approves the law, and bids him calmly die.
Say, doth this law, that dooms the thief, protect
The wretch who makes another's life his prey,
By hellish force to take it at his will?
Is this an English law, whose guidance fails
When crimes are swelled to magnitude so vast,
That Justice dare not scan them? Or does Law
Bid Justice an eternal distance keep
From England's great tribunal, when the slave
Calls loud on Justice only? Speak, ye few
Who fill Britannia's senate, and are deemed
The fathers of your country! Boast your laws,
Defend the honour of a land so fall'n,
That Fame from ev'ry battlement is flown,
And Heathens start, e'en at a Christian's name.
  Hail, social love! true soul of order, hail!
Thy softest emanations, pity, grief,
Lively emotion, sudden joy, and pangs,
Too deep for language, are thy own: then rise,
Thou gentle angel! spread thy silken wings
O'er drowsy man, breathe in his soul, and give
Her God-like pow'rs thy animating force,
To banish Inhumanity. Oh, loose
The fetters of his mind, enlarge his views,
Break down for him the bound° of avarice, lift *limit*
His feeble faculties beyond a world
To which he soon must prove a stranger! Spread
Before his ravished eye the varied tints
Of future glory; bid them live to Fame,
Whose banners wave forever. Thus inspired,
All that is great, and good, and sweetly mild,
Shall fill his noble bosom. He shall melt,
Yea, by thy sympathy unseen, shall feel
Another's pang: for the lamenting maid
His heart shall heave a sigh; with the old slave
(Whose head is bent with sorrow) he shall cast
His eye back on the joys of youth, and say,

[1] [Yearsley's note] A Coromantin slave in Jamaica (who had frequently escaped to the mountains) was, a few years since, doomed to have his leg cut off. A young practitioner from England (after the surgeon of the estate had refused to be an executioner) undertook the operation, but after the removal of the limb, on the slave's exclaiming, "You buckera! God Almighty made dat leg; you cut it off! You put it on again?" was so shocked that the other surgeon was obliged to take up [close] the [blood] vessels, apply the dressings, &c. The Negro suffered without a groan, called for his pipe, and calmly smoked, till the absence of his attendant gave him an opportunity of tearing off his bandages, when he bled to death in an instant.

Many will call this act of the Negro's stubbornness; under such circumstances, I dare give it a more glorious epithet, and that is *fortitude*. [Coromantins, from the Gold Coast, were often mentioned in anti-slavery writings as exemplars of defiant courage.]

[2] *Her sons ... sell it* Commerce's complaint is that the slave traders will be unemployed if they are unable to sell people.

"Thou once couldst feel, as I do, love's pure bliss;
Parental fondness, and the dear returns
Of filial tenderness were thine, till torn
From the dissolving scene."—Oh, social love,
Thou universal good, thou that canst fill
The vacuum of immensity, and live
In endless void! thou that in motion first
Set'st the long lazy atoms,° by thy force *particles*
Quickly assimilating, and restrained
By strong attraction; touch the soul of man;
Subdue him; make a fellow-creature's woe
His own by heart-felt sympathy, whilst wealth
Is made subservient to his soft disease.
And when thou hast to high perfection wrought
This mighty work, say, "such is Bristol's soul."

Immigration to America

from William Moraley, *The Infortunate: The Voyage and Adventures of William Moraley, an Indentured Servant* (1743)

About half of the Europeans who came in search of opportunity in the British colonies of North America were indentured servants, people who sold their freedom and their labor for a term of years in exchange for the cost of travel to the New World. One of these was William Moraley, who chose to immigrate after his father's death left him impoverished. Although his decision to write an autobiography was atypical of someone of his class, Moraley—an individual without extensive family ties, not wholly destitute but without promising employment—was in other ways typical of the migrants who left England's urban centers in the eighteenth century. It was also a common experience (and became even more so in the nineteenth century) for migrants to America to return to Britain after a few years, sometimes with their fortunes made but frequently in disappointment. Still others, even more unfortunate than Moraley, never managed to save enough for passage home.

... [N]ot caring what became of me, it entered my head to leave England and sell myself for a term of years into the American plantations. Accordingly I repaired to the Royal Exchange, to inform myself, by the printed advertisements fixed against the walls, of the ships bound to America; where musing by myself, a man accosted me in the following manner. "Sir," said he, "I have for some time observed you, and fancy your condition of life is altered for the worse, and guess you have been in better circumstances; but if you will take my advice, I'll make it my business to find out some way which may be of service to you. Perhaps you may imagine I have a design to inveigle[1] you, but I assure you I have none; and if you will accept a mug of beer, I will impart what I have to propose to you." The man appearing sincere, I gave ear to him.

I was dressed at that time in a very odd manner. I had on a red rug coat[2] with black lining, black buttons and button holes, and black lace upon the pockets and facing; an old worn out tie wig,[3] which had not been combed out for above a fortnight;[4] an unshaven beard; a torn shirt that had not been washed for above a month; bad shoes; and stockings all full of holes.

After he had shaved me, he proposed to me an American voyage, and said there was a ship at Limehouse dock that would sail for Pennsylvania in three or four days. "Sir," said I, "a person like me, oppressed by Dame Fortune, need not care where he goes. All places are alike to me; and I am very willing to accept of your offer, if I could have some view of bettering my condition of life, though I might have expected a better fate than to be forced to leave my native country. But adverse fortune is become familiar to me, by a series of misfortunes; so had rather leave a place where I have no prospect of advancing myself, than to continue here where I have no friends to relieve me. Besides, in a distant place, not being known, no person can reflect on me for any ill management, which oftentimes discourages one's friends from supporting one, knowing the ill use that is made of their support."

"Sir," says the person, "I'm entirely of your way of thinking, and believe you will better yourself by following my advice. I will recommend you to the

[1] *inveigle* Deceitfully persuade.

[2] *rug coat* Coat made of coarse wool.

[3] *tie wig* Wig tied in the back with ribbon.

[4] *fortnight* Two weeks.

captain, who is bound for Philadelphia, in Pennsylvania, a country producing everything necessary for the support of life; and when your time is expired, you will be free to live in any of the Provinces of America."

Then he asked me, if I was bred to any business. I told him watchmaking was my occupation. He said he was afraid I would not do for any other business, that being of little service to the Americans; the useful trades being bricklayers, shoemakers, barbers, carpenters, joiners, smiths, weavers, bakers, tanners, and husbandmen[1] more useful than all the rest. They bind themselves for four years; but if I would consent to bind myself for five, he said he would undertake to get me admitted. Those men brokers have generally for their pains three half crowns, given them by the masters of those vessels which they are employed for.

After we had drank two pints of beer, he paid the reckoning.[2] I absolutely agreed to go, and to that intent we went before Sir Robert Bailis, Lord Mayor, where I was sworn as not being a married person or an apprentice by indenture. He paid for my oath one shilling, a perquisite of[3] his clerk. From thence we went to London Bridge, to a stationer's shop, and there an Indenture of Servitude was drawn, which I signed. After this we took boat at Billingsgate, steered our course for Limehouse, where we arrived about eleven o'clock in the forenoon. The ship was named the *Bonetta*, of about 200 tons. …

I observed several of my brother adventurers seemed very dejected, from whence I guessed they repented of their rashness. Soon after, dinner was brought on the table, which consisted of stewed mutton chops. I was very glad I had an opportunity of trying the temper of my tusks,[4] for I had not eaten meat for four days. I ate very heartily and washed down the mutton with about two quarts of small beer.[5] I began to think myself happy, being in a way to eat; and on this account became insensible of the condition I had brought myself to. In the afternoon, the master and mate being absent, I ventured into the cabin and, peeping into a chest, discovered a large quantity of raisins, of which I made free with about two pound, and pocketed them for my own use. Besides, the small beer stood upon deck and was free of us at all times, so that laying all reflections aside, I comforted myself with the hopes of living well all the voyage, but was soon made sensible to the contrary when we set out to sea.

[On the voyage]

…[W]e were stinted in our allowance, being joined together in messes: five to each mess. Three biscuits were given to each man for the day, and a small piece of salt beef no bigger than a penny chop of mutton. Some days we had stockfish,[6] when every man was obliged to beat his share with a maul[7] to make it tender, with a little stinking butter for sauce.

Every morning and evening a captain called every one of us to the cabin door, where we received a thimble full of bad brandy. We were obliged to turn out every four hours, with the sailors, to watch; which was to prevent our falling sick by herding under deck.

In our voyage we observed little worth taking notice of till we were in latitude 33, when the sun was intensely hot, which so parched our bodies, having but a scanty allowance of water, not above three quarts to each mess. We attempted to drink the salt water, but it increased our thirst. Sometimes, but rarely, it rained, when we set our hats upon deck to catch the water; but it sliding down the sails gave it the taste of tar. …

[In Pennsylvania]

My master employed me in his business: I continued satisfied with him for sometime; but being desirous to settle at Philadelphia during the rest of my servitude, I declared to him, I would stay no longer and desired him to dispose of me to some other master. … This demand made him cross to me, and I attempted an escape, but was taken and put into prison; but was soon released, with a promise to satisfy my demand. About a fortnight after, we went to the Mayor of Philadelphia—his name was Griffith, a man of exact justice, though an Irishman

[1] *husbandmen* Farmers.

[2] *reckoning* Cost.

[3] *perquisite of* Gratuity for.

[4] *temper of my tusks* I.e., condition of my teeth.

[5] *small beer* Thin beer containing little alcohol.

[6] *stockfish* Air dried, unsalted fish.

[7] *maul* Hammer.

—who reconciled us; so I returned back to Burlington, and continued with him three years, he forgiving me the other two: I was ever after perfectly pleased with my master's behaviour to me, which was generous....

The condition of bought servants is very hard, notwithstanding their indentures are made in England, wherein it is expressly stipulated that they shall have at their arrival all the necessaries specified in those indentures to be given them by their future masters, such as clothes, meat, and drink. Yet upon complaint made to a magistrate against the master for nonperformance, the master is generally heard before the servant, and it is ten to one if he does not get his licks for his pains, as I have experienced upon the like occasion, to my cost.

If they endeavour to escape, which is next to impossible, there being a reward for taking up any person who travels without a pass, which is extended all over the British Colonies, their masters immediately issue out a reward for the apprehending them, from thirty shillings to five pound, as they think proper, and this generally brings them back again. Printed and written advertisements are also set up against the trees and public places in the town, besides those in the newspapers. Notwithstanding these difficulties, they are perpetually running away, but seldom escape, for a hot pursuit being made brings them back, when a justice settles the expenses, and the servant is obliged to serve a longer time....

At last ... the time of my servitude expired, and I became free. 'Tis impossible to express the satisfaction I found at being released from the precarious humour and dependence of my master. He accoutered[1] me in an indifferent manner, and gave me my discharge to find out a new way of living. I then went to Philadelphia and served one Edmund Lewis, a brisk young clock-maker; but he being unsettled, and of a roving temper (like master, like man!), I left him, and lived with Mr. Graham, a watch-maker, newly arrived, and nephew to the famous Mr. Graham in Fleet Street.[2] With him I continued ten weeks at ten shillings per week wages, and my board found me;[3] but he designing to settle at Antigua,[4] I left him.

Then I roamed about like a Roving Tartar[5] for the convenience of grazing, and for three weeks had no abiding place. In the nights I was forced to skulk about the extremity of the town, where I lay in a hayloft....

But this life not being likely to last long, ... I set my wits to work how to get home. But not presently hearing of a ship bound for England, I was reduced to such extremity that I looked like a picture of bad luck, and so thin that you might have seen my ribs through my skin, and I was greatly afraid of a consumption.[6] However, having some acquaintance in the country, I went about cleaning clocks and watches, and followed the occupation of a tinker; but not being well versed in that trade, where I mended one hole I was sure to make another....

I now began to be heartily tired with these ramblings, and endeavoured to make friends with masters of ships in order to get my passage. One morning, as I was forging a horseshoe, a grave Quaker, one Thomas Wetheril of Workington in Cumberland, told me he found the business I followed would do little for me, and advised me to return home, where he heard I had considerable relations. He said he had recommended me to Capt. Peel, whose ship then lay at the key and would sail in about five weeks.

I, who had before resolved to embrace the first opportunity that offered, readily entered into his measures, immediately left the horse shoe unfinished and went to the ship.

from Lady Lucan, "On the Present State of Ireland" (1768)

The British were highly alarmed by the numbers of migrants leaving Ireland in the late seventeenth and eighteenth centuries. The causes of emigration were apparent to English poet Margaret Bingham, Countess of Lucan, who observed firsthand the

[1] *accoutered* Equipped.

[2] *famous ... Fleet Street* George Graham (1675–1751), accomplished London clock-maker and inventor.

[3] *my board found me* My food and lodging provided to me.

[4] *Antigua* Island in the Caribbean.

[5] *Roving Tartar* Desert nomad.

[6] *consumption* Lung infection.

widespread poverty that weighed on the nation. While a series of climate-induced famines exacerbated the suffering of the poor, political mismanagement by the English government was a much larger problem. Legislation prevented the advancement of Ireland's industry while allowing England to exploit its resources, and absentee landlords living in England charged unreasonable rents to their poor tenants, drawing large amounts of money out of the Irish economy. The poorest Irish people were generally not, however, the ones to migrate; most of those who could afford to leave were the relatively well-off Scotch-Irish, who exerted strong cultural influence in colonial America, especially in the Appalachian region. The Irish poor would emigrate in vast numbers later on, prompted by the Great Famine of the nineteenth century.

See! with what pale and mournful look appears,
England! Thy faithful sister drowned in tears.
Thus wronged Hibernia° sues to Britain's throne: *Ireland*
Where is thy justice, where thy wisdom flown?
In me a suff'ring, loyal, people see,
Harassed and torn, by wanton tyranny.
Hear this, ye great, as from the feast ye rise,
Which every plundered element supplies!
Hear when fatigued, not nourished, ye have dined,
The food of thousands to its roots confined![1]
Eternal fasts that know no taste of bread;
Nor where who sows the corn, by corn is fed.

[1] [Lucan's note] The situation of these miserable people in the province that I am most acquainted with is truly lamentable. The lower class never eat meat or bread, not even on Christmas Day (when the poor of all other countries make a feast), but are confined to potatoes for food, and to water for their drink. A working man, who labours from six o'clock in the morning to six in the evening, has nothing to support him but roots and water; four pence is the price of a day labourer in Connaught; in other parts I believe it is something more, but a very trifle. Let his majesty ask those who have had the curiosity to visit the interior parts of the country; let him ask one of the lords of his bed-chamber, who lately made a tour through Ireland, and he will find that I do not exaggerate.—As to their cottages, such is their wretched poverty, that it is a known fact, the cottager frequently pulls it down to exempt himself from paying the hearth tax, which is two shillings only, but which he is absolutely unable to pay; and he and his family remain exposed to all the inclemencies of the open air, until the time of collecting this cruel tax is passed....

Throughout the year, no feast e'er crowns his
board,° *table*
Four pence a day, ah! what can that afford?
So poor their country where they strive to live,
No ampler pay can starving farmers give.
Did you not blast us with a jealous eye,
Our industry and arts with yours would vie.
Nature's best face in our soft clime is shown,
And commerce here would gladly fix her throne.
E'en might that commerce far as India roam,
No Irish soul would chain that wealth at home.
Fools that ye are, to you that wealth would roll,
And, lodestone° like, you would attract the *magnet*
whole.
But you are swayed by narrow policy,
And in a friend a hated rival see.
Our journals show with how profuse a hand
Hibernan senates give, on your demand;
Freely they give, nor aught from you require,
But justice, only justice they desire.
Your gratitude unlike our bounty flows;
Our idleness this truth too plainly shows;
One trade alone, your jealousy affords,[2]
(To paint such mighty folly, grant me words!)
One trade alone, is to this people given,
Though blessed with every requisite by Heaven.
And when for taxes, pensions, loud you cry,
Like fools you stop the means of your supply.
To English marts alone our wool must speed,[3]
And sinks or swells its value as they bid.
What free born souls will such oppression bear?

[2] [Lucan's note] The linen is the only trade carried on to any extent in Ireland, and this is unjustly cramped by English policy and acts of parliament....

[3] [Lucan's note] Ireland is not suffered to export any sort of woollen goods, even to those foreign markets where the English woollen manufactures are not sent. There are a variety of woollen and mixed goods which they are inclined to make in Ireland, ... which England does not run into, and which would be a most advantageous trade to Ireland. The French have beat out the English in several foreign markets, particularly in the Levant and Turkey, by making these goods; and they make them, shame to the English Parliament and ministry! with Irish smuggled wool. As to the inland woollen trade of Ireland, it is encumbered with every disadvantage, and receives every check that can be laid upon it; it is controlled and taxed so that a pair of knit woollen stockings, the labour of old age! cannot be exposed to sale without first paying a duty....

We sell to France, prevent us if you dare.
Thus laws too strict are ever useless made,
And enemies and rivals get your trade.
For us in vain our flocks their fleeces bear;
A sad reward for all the shepherd's care.
To card[1] or spin, the careful housewife fears,
She trembling draws the fleece, and spins with tears.
Early and late her weary hours are spent,
And much she toils to pay the landlord's rent.
But when to public sale her work she'd send,
A cruel seizure does her labours end.
Oh! Charlotte,[2] lend a while thy sacred ear,
While I recount the griefs thy subjects bear....
Oh! deign to tell our tale, we ask no more.
Thus shall our pious king our suff'rings hear,
And modest truth attain a monarch's ear.
Bred in a faith, they guard their souls sincere.[3]
For right or wrong, that faith to them is dear:
'Tis what their fathers and forefathers taught,
For which they suffered or for which they fought;
No wonder then, though wrapped in error's night,
They breed their sons in what they think is right,
Various religions, still they deem the same;
'Tis virtue always diff'ring but in name.
Our gavel laws,[4] few converts can create,
The persecuted soul grows obstinate.
A land of liberty can this be called,
Where by such tyrant laws we are enthralled?
That snatch the weapon from the father's hand,
His home exposing to the ruffian band?
Ah! wretched parents, little you foresee
Of gavel laws, the sad calamity;
Laws still accursed by the good and wise,
That teach the son his father to despise;
Most cruel laws, that can such acts approve,
Ah! sad return of our paternal love,
That from all ties of brotherhood deters,
And him, that's first a hypocrite prefers....
Ireland awake! Raise up thy drooping head,
Look to these laws, their consequences dread!...
Since toleration is Britannia's pride,
Why, by such cruel laws, is Ireland tied?
Beware ye senators, look round in time,
Rebellion is not fixed to any clime;
For 'twould be strange, a most unnat'ral thing,
That he who hates his sire should love his king.
In trade, religion, every way oppressed,
You'll find, too late, such wrongs must be redressed.
Those riches in America you've lost,[5]
May soon again be found on Ireland's coast:
Open our ports at once with generous minds,
Let commerce be as free as waves and winds;
Seize quick the time, for now, consider well,
Whole quarters of the world at once rebel.

[1] *card* Prepare wool for spinning, i.e., by combing, parting, and straightening it with an iron-toothed comb called a card.

[2] *Charlotte* Queen Charlotte (1744–1818) of the United Kingdom.

[3] *Bred in ... souls sincere* Lucan's footnote explains that the majority of Ireland's inhabitants were Roman Catholics, and that as such their rights were heavily restricted by the penal laws; for instance, Catholics could not purchase property or hold public office. Although Lucan was not alone in citing the penal laws as a major cause of increasing Irish emigration, the extent to which the laws actually had that effect is now contested. Some of the Irish emigrants in the eighteenth century were Catholics, but most were Scotch-Irish Presbyterians, who were also affected by some, but not all, of the penal laws.

[4] *gavel laws* Part of the penal laws drawn from the Celtic tradition of Gavelkind, in which, upon the death of a father, his estate was shared equally among his sons. The gavel laws forced Catholics to undertake this practice—unless the eldest son converted to Protestantism, in which case he would inherit everything.

from Commissioners of the Customs in Scotland, *Report of the Examination of the Emigrants from the Counties of Caithness and Sutherland on Board the Ship* Bachelor of Leith *Bound to Wilmington in North Carolina* (1774)

British policymakers were equally concerned about the levels of emigration from Ireland and from Scotland; it was widely believed that before long the rural areas of both countries would be emptied of able laborers. Causes of emigration from Scotland were for the most part similar to those in Ireland: economic instability, unreasonably high rents, and the anticipation of greater opportunity in North

[5] *Those riches ... you've lost* Although the American Revolutionary War would not begin for a few more years, in 1768 opposition to British rule of the colonies was growing increasingly violent and pronounced.

America. Anxiety surrounding emigration prompted the gathering of reports such as the one excerpted below, in which emigrants explain their reasons for leaving Scotland behind.

John Catanach, aged fifty years, by trade a farmer, married, hath 4 children from 19 to 7 years old; resided last at Chabster in the parish of Rae in the county of Caithness, upon the estate of Mr. Alexander Nicolson, minister at Thurso; intends to go to Wilmington, North Carolina; left his own country because crops failed, bread became dear, the rents of his possession were raised from two to five pounds sterling; besides his pasture or common grounds were taken up by placing new tenants thereon, especially the grounds adjacent to his farm, which were the only grounds on which his cattle pastured. That this method of parking and placing tenants on the pasture grounds rendered his farm useless; his cattle died for want of grass, and his corn farm was unfit to support his family after paying the extravagant tack duty.[1] That beside the rise of rents and scarcity of bread, the landlord exacted arbitrary and oppressive services, such as obliging the declarant to labour up his ground, cast, win, lead and stack his peats;[2] mow, win and lead his hay, and cut his corn and lead it in the yard, which took up about 30 or 40 days of his servants and horses each year, without the least acknowledgment for it, and without victuals,[3] save the men that mowed the hay, who got their dinner only. That he was induced to emigrate by advices received from his friends in America; that provisions are extremely plenty and cheap, and the price of labour very high, so that people who are temperate and laborious have every chance of bettering their circumstances. Adds that the price of bread in the country he hath left is greatly enhanced by distilling,[4] that being for so long a time so scarce and dear,[5] and the price of cattle at the same time reduced full one half while the rents of lands have been raised nearly in the same proportion, all the smaller farms must inevitably be ruined.

James Duncan, aged twenty-seven years, by trade a farmer, married, hath two children, one five years the other 9 months old. Resided last at Mondle in the parish of Farr in the shire of Sutherland, upon the estate of Sutherland, intends to go to Wilmington in North Carolina; left his own country because crops failed him for several years, and among the last years of his labouring he scarce reaped any crop; bread became dear and the price of cattle so much reduced that one cow's price could only buy a boll of meal.[6] That the people on the estate of Sutherland were often supplied with meal from Caithness, but the farmers there had of late stopped the sale of their meal, because it rendered them a much greater profit by distilling. That he could find no employment at home whereby he could support his family. That he has very promising prospects by the advices from his friends in Carolina, as they have bettered their circumstances greatly since they went there by their labours. Lands being cheap and good provisions plenty, and the price of labour very encouraging.

William Sutherland aged twenty-four, married, left an only child at home. Resided last in the parish of Latheron and county of Caithness, upon the estate of John Sutherland of Forse. Goes to Carolina because he lost his cattle in 1772, and for a farm of 40/ rent, was obliged to perform with his family and his horses so many and so arbitrary services to his landlord at all times of the year, but especially in seed time and harvest, that he could not, in two years he possessed it, raise as much corn and[7] serve his family for six months. That, his little stock daily decreasing, he was encouraged to go to Carolina by the assurances of the fertility of the land, which yields three crops a year, by which means provisions are extremely cheap, wheat being sold at 3 shillings a boll, potatoes at 1 shilling, so that one man's labour will maintain a family of twenty persons. He has no money, therefore proposes to employ himself as a day labourer; his wife can spin and sew, and he has heard of many going out in the same way who are now substantial

[1] *tack duty* Lease payment.

[2] *labour up his ground* I.e., work his land; *cast* Cut; *win* Dry; *lead* Carry; *peats* Squares of bog soil used as fuel.

[3] *victuals* Food.

[4] *the price ... distilling* I.e., the price of bread has increased because people are using their grain for alcohol instead.

[5] *dear* Expensive.

[6] *boll* Six bushels of ground grain, equivalent to about 360 pounds of wheat; *meal* The ground part of grain that is edible.

[7] *as much corn and* Enough corn to.

farmers. At any rate he comforts himself in the hopes that he cannot be any worse than he has been at home.

Gilbert Stuart, *The Skater* (1782). Born in Rhode Island, Stuart traveled to England to launch his artistic career. He was apprenticed to another transatlantic artist, Benjamin West, until acclaim for this work, *The Skater*, established him as a popular success. The subject is Scottish politician William Grant, and the work was painted in London (Westminster Abbey is visible in the background). Stuart later returned to the United States, where he painted many important figures of early American politics; his 1796 portrait of George Washington is now reproduced on the American dollar bill.

from Benjamin Franklin, *Information to Those Who Would Remove to America* (1782)

Many persons in Europe, having directly or by letters expressed to the writer of this, who is well acquainted with North America, their desire of transporting and establishing themselves in that country, but who appear to have formed, through ignorance, mistaken ideas and expectations of what is to be obtained there; he thinks it may be useful, and prevent inconvenient, expensive, and fruitless removals and voyages of improper persons, if he gives some clearer and truer notions of that part of the world than appear to have hitherto prevailed.

He finds it is imagined by numbers that the inhabitants of North America are rich, capable of rewarding and disposed to reward all sorts of ingenuity; that they are at the same time ignorant of all the sciences, and, consequently, that strangers, possessing talents in the *belles-lettres*,[1] fine arts, &c., must be highly esteemed, and so well paid as to become easily rich themselves; that there are also abundance of profitable offices to be disposed of, which the natives are not qualified to fill; and that, having few persons of family[2] among them, strangers of birth must be greatly respected, and of course easily obtain the best of those offices, which will make all their fortunes; that the governments too, to encourage emigrations from Europe, not only pay the expense of personal transportation, but give lands *gratis*[3] to strangers, with negroes to work for them, utensils of husbandry,[4] and stocks of cattle. These are all wild imaginations; and those who go to America with expectations founded upon them will surely find themselves disappointed.

The truth is that though there are in that country few people so miserable as the poor of Europe, there are also very few that in Europe would be called rich; it is rather a general happy mediocrity[5] that prevails. There are few great proprietors of the soil, and few tenants;

[1] *belles-lettres* Literary writing.

[2] *persons of family* People born into a high social class.

[3] *gratis* Latin: free.

[4] *husbandry* Farming.

[5] *mediocrity* Averageness.

most people cultivate their own lands or follow some handicraft or merchandise; very few rich enough to live idly upon their rents or incomes, or to pay the high prices given in Europe for paintings, statues, architecture, and the other works of art that are more curious than useful. Hence the natural geniuses that have arisen in America with such talents have uniformly quitted that country for Europe, where they can be more suitably rewarded. It is true that letters and mathematical knowledge are in esteem there, but they are at the same time more common than is apprehended; there being already existing nine colleges or universities, *viz.*[1] four in New England, and one in each of the provinces of New York, New Jersey, Pennsylvania, Maryland, and Virginia, all furnished with learned professors; besides a number of smaller academies; these educate many of their youth in the languages, and those sciences that qualify men for the professions of divinity, law, or physic.[2] Strangers indeed are by no means excluded from exercising those professions; and the quick increase of inhabitants everywhere gives them a chance of employ, which they have in common with the natives. Of civil offices or employments, there are few; no superfluous ones, as in Europe; and it is a rule established in some of the states that no office should be so profitable as to make it desirable. The 36th article of the constitution of Pennsylvania runs expressly in these words: "As every freeman, to preserve his independence (if he has not a sufficient estate), ought to have some profession, calling, trade, or farm, whereby he may honestly subsist, there can be no necessity for, nor use in, establishing offices of profit; the usual effects of which are dependence and servility, unbecoming freemen, in the possessors and expectants; faction, contention, corruption, and disorder among the people. Wherefore, whenever an office, through increase of fees or otherwise, becomes so profitable as to occasion many to apply for it, the profits ought to be lessened by the legislature."

These ideas prevailing more or less in all the United States, it cannot be worth any man's while, who has a means of living at home, to expatriate himself in hopes of obtaining a profitable civil office in America; and as to military offices, they are at an end with the war, the armies being disbanded. Much less is it advisable for a person to go thither who has no other quality to recommend him but his birth. In Europe it has indeed its value; but it is a commodity that cannot be carried to a worse market than that of America, where people do not inquire concerning a stranger, *What is he?* but, *What can he do?* If he has any useful art, he is welcome; and if he exercises it, and behaves well, he will be respected by all that know him; but a mere man of quality who, on that account, wants to live upon the public by some office or salary will be despised and disregarded. The husbandman is in honor there, and even the mechanic, because their employments are useful. The people have a saying that God Almighty is himself a mechanic, the greatest in the universe; and he is respected and admired more for the variety, ingenuity, and utility of his handiworks than for the antiquity of his family. They are pleased with the observation of a negro, and frequently mention it, that *Boccarorra* (meaning the white men) *make de black man workee, make de horse workee, make de ox workee, make ebery ting workee; only de hog. He, de hog, no workee; he eat, he drink, he walk about, he go to sleep when he please, he libb like a gentleman.* According to these opinions of the Americans, one of them would think himself more obliged to a genealogist who could prove for him that his ancestors and relations for ten generations had been ploughmen, smiths, carpenters, turners, weavers, tanners, or even shoemakers, and consequently that they were useful members of society; than if he could only prove that they were gentlemen, doing nothing of value, but living idly on the labour of others, mere *fruges consumere nati*,[3] and otherwise good for nothing, till by their death their estates, like the carcass of the negro's gentleman-hog, come to be cut up.

With regard to encouragements for strangers from government, they are really only what are derived from good laws and liberty. Strangers are welcome because there is room enough for them all, and therefore the old inhabitants are not jealous of them; the laws protect them sufficiently so that they have no need of the patronage of great men; and everyone will enjoy securely

[1] *viz.* Abbreviation of the Latin *videlicet*, meaning "namely" or "that is to say."

[2] *physic* Medical practice.

[3] *fruges consumere nati* Latin: born to consume the fruits (of the earth).

the profits of his industry. But if he does not bring a fortune with him, he must work and be industrious to live. One or two years' residence gives him all the rights of a citizen; but the government does not at present, whatever it may have done in former times, hire people to become settlers by paying their passages, giving land, negroes, utensils, stock, or any other kind of emolument[1] whatsoever. In short, America is the land of labour, and by no means what the English call *Lubberland*,[2] and the French *Pays de Cocagne*,[3] where the streets are said to be paved with half-peck[4] loaves, the houses tiled with pancakes, and where the fowls fly about ready roasted, crying, *Come eat me!*

Who then are the kind of persons to whom an emigration to America may be advantageous? And what are the advantages they may reasonably expect?

Land being cheap in that country, from the vast forests still void of inhabitants, and not likely to be occupied in an age to come, insomuch that the propriety of an hundred acres of fertile soil full of wood may be obtained near the frontiers, in many places, for eight or ten guineas,[5] hearty young labouring men who understand the husbandry of corn and cattle, which is nearly the same in that country as in Europe, may easily establish themselves there. A little money saved of the good wages they receive there, while they work for others, enables them to buy the land and begin their plantation, in which they are assisted by the goodwill of their neighbours, and some credit. Multitudes of poor people from England, Ireland, Scotland, and Germany have by this means in a few years become wealthy farmers, who, in their own countries, where all the lands are fully occupied and the wages of labour low, could never have emerged from the poor condition wherein they were born.

From the salubrity[6] of the air, the healthiness of the climate, the plenty of good provisions, and the encouragement to early marriages by the certainty of subsistence in cultivating the earth, the increase of inhabitants by natural generation is very rapid in America, and becomes still more so by the accession of strangers; hence there is a continual demand for more artisans of all the necessary and useful kinds, to supply those cultivators of the earth with houses, and with furniture and utensils of the grosser sorts, which cannot so well be brought from Europe. Tolerably good workmen in any of those mechanic arts are sure to find employ, and to be well paid for their work, there being no restraints preventing strangers from exercising any art they understand, nor any permission necessary. If they are poor, they begin first as servants or journeymen; and if they are sober, industrious, and frugal, they soon become masters, establish themselves in business, marry, raise families, and become respectable citizens....

from J. Hector St. John de Crèvecoeur, *Letters from an American Farmer* (1782)

Michel-Guillaume-Jean de Crèvecoeur was born in France into a family of minor nobility. He immigrated to New France and, after the English victory in the Seven Years' War, anglicized his name to J. Hector St. John de Crèvecoeur and became a citizen of New York. He first published *Letters from an American Farmer* in England, but it was read throughout Europe and Ameria, and its success prompted several editions and translations. Works of a similar tone, idealizing life in the colonies (and often written with a view to encouraging immigration) remained popular through to the late nineteenth century—though accounts that presented a less rosy view of the immigrant experience also gained wide currency.

I wish I could be acquainted with the feelings and thoughts which must agitate the heart and present themselves to the mind of an enlightened Englishman when he first lands on this continent. He must greatly rejoice that he lived at a time to see this fair country

[1] *emolument* Payment or benefit.

[2] *Lubberland* The 1685 ballad "Invitation to Lubberland" describes a place of laziness and vice where the streets are "paved with pudding-pies" and the roofs tiled with pancakes.

[3] *Pays de Cocagne* French: Land of Plenty.

[4] *half-peck* I.e., large.

[5] *guineas* In the late 1700s, an average American wage-earner would be paid one guinea in about two weeks.

[6] *salubrity* Health-promoting quality.

discovered and settled; he must necessarily feel a share of national pride when he views the chain of settlements which embellishes these extended shores. When he says to himself, this is the work of my countrymen, who, when convulsed by factions, afflicted by a variety of miseries and wants, restless and impatient, took refuge here. They brought along with them their national genius,[1] to which they principally owe what liberty they enjoy and what substance they possess. Here he sees the industry of his native country displayed in a new manner, and traces in their works the embryos of all the arts, sciences, and ingenuity which flourish in Europe. Here he beholds fair cities, substantial villages, extensive fields, an immense country filled with decent houses, good roads, orchards, meadows, and bridges, where an hundred years ago all was wild, woody and uncultivated! What a train of pleasing ideas this fair spectacle must suggest; it is a prospect which must inspire a good citizen with the most heartfelt pleasure. The difficulty consists in the manner of viewing so extensive a scene. He is arrived on a new continent; a modern society offers itself to his contemplation, different from what he had hitherto seen. It is not composed, as in Europe, of great lords who possess everything and of a herd of people who have nothing. Here are no aristocratical families, no courts, no kings, no bishops, no ecclesiastical dominion, no invisible power giving to a few a very visible one; no great manufacturers employing thousands, no great refinements of luxury. The rich and the poor are not so far removed from each other as they are in Europe. Some few towns excepted, we are all tillers of the earth, from Nova Scotia to West Florida. We are a people of cultivators, scattered over an immense territory communicating with each other by means of good roads and navigable rivers, united by the silken bands of mild government, all respecting the laws, without dreading their power, because they are equitable. We are all animated with the spirit of an industry which is unfettered and unrestrained, because each person works for himself. If he travels through our rural districts he views not the hostile castle and the haughty mansion, contrasted with the clay-built hut and miserable cabin, where cattle and men help to keep each other warm, and dwell in meanness, smoke, and indigence.[2] A pleasing uniformity of decent competence appears throughout our habitations. The meanest of our log-houses is a dry and comfortable habitation. Lawyer or merchant are the fairest titles our towns afford; that of a farmer is the only appellation of the rural inhabitants of our country. It must take some time ere he can reconcile himself to our dictionary, which is but short in words of dignity and names of honour. There, on a Sunday, he sees a congregation of respectable farmers and their wives, all clad in neat homespun,[3] well mounted, or riding in their own humble wagons. There is not among them an esquire, saving the unlettered magistrate.[4] There he sees a parson as simple as his flock, a farmer who does not riot[5] on the labour of others. We have no princes, for whom we toil, starve, and bleed: we are the most perfect society now existing in the world. Here man is free as he ought to be; nor is this pleasing equality so transitory as many others are. Many ages will not see the shores of our great lakes replenished with inland nations, nor the unknown bounds of North America entirely peopled. Who can tell how far it extends? Who can tell the millions of men whom it will feed and contain? for no European foot has as yet travelled half the extent of this mighty continent! The next wish of this traveller will be to know whence came all these people? they are mixture of English, Scotch, Irish, French, Dutch, Germans, and Swedes. From this promiscuous[6] breed, that race now called Americans have arisen. The eastern provinces must indeed be excepted, as being the unmixed descendants of Englishmen.…

In this great American asylum, the poor of Europe have by some means met together, and in consequence of various causes; to what purpose should they ask one another what countrymen they are? Alas, two thirds of them had no country. Can a wretch who wanders about, who works and starves, whose life is a continual scene of

[1] *genius* Particular spirit.

[2] *indigence* Destitution.

[3] *homespun* Clothing made from yarn spun at home.

[4] *esquire* Member of the gentry; *magistrate* Local court judge, usually a member of the gentry.

[5] *riot* Make merry; live indulgently.

[6] *promiscuous* Varied.

sore affliction or pinching penury;[1] can that man call England or any other kingdom his country? A country that had no bread for him, whose fields procured him no harvest; who met with nothing but the frowns of the rich, the severity of the laws, with jails and punishments; who owned not a single foot of the extensive surface of this planet? No! urged by a variety of motives, here they came. Everything has tended to regenerate them; new laws, a new mode of living, a new social system; here they are become men: in Europe they were as so many useless plants, wanting vegetative mould[2] and refreshing showers; they withered, and were mowed down by want, hunger, and war; but now by the power of transplantation, like all other plants they have taken root and flourished! Formerly they were not numbered in any civil lists of their country, except in those of the poor; here they rank as citizens. By what invisible power has this surprising metamorphosis been performed? By that of the laws and that of their industry. The laws, the indulgent laws, protect them as they arrive, stamping on them the symbol of adoption; they receive ample rewards for their labours; these accumulated rewards procure them lands; those lands confer on them the title of freemen, and to that title every benefit is affixed which men can possibly require. This is the great operation daily performed by our laws. From whence proceed these laws? From our government. Whence the government? It is derived from the original genius and strong desire of the people ratified and confirmed by the crown. This is the great chain which links us all, this is the picture which every province exhibits, Nova Scotia excepted....

What attachment can a poor European emigrant have for a country where he had nothing? The knowledge of the language, the love of a few kindred as poor as himself, were the only cords that tied him; his country is now that which gives him land, bread, protection, and consequence: *Ubi panis ibi patria*,[3] is the motto of all emigrants. What then is the American, this new man? He is either an European, or the descendant of an European, hence that strange mixture of blood, which you will find in no other country. I could point out to you a family whose grandfather was an Englishman, whose wife was Dutch, whose son married a French woman, and whose present four sons have now four wives of different nations. *He* is an American, who leaving behind him all his ancient prejudices and manners, receives new ones from the new mode of life he has embraced, the new government he obeys, and the new rank he holds.

He becomes an American by being received in the broad lap of our great *Alma Mater*.[4] Here individuals of all nations are melted into a new race of men, whose labours and posterity will one day cause great changes in the world. Americans are the western pilgrims, who are carrying along with them that great mass of arts, sciences, vigour, and industry which began long since in the east; they will finish the great circle. The Americans were once scattered all over Europe; here they are incorporated into one of the finest systems of population which has ever appeared, and which will hereafter become distinct by the power of the different climates they inhabit. The American ought therefore to love this country much better than that wherein either he or his forefathers were born. Here the rewards of his industry follow with equal steps the progress of his labour; his labour is founded on the basis of nature, SELF-INTEREST; can it want a stronger allurement? Wives and children, who before in vain demanded of him a morsel of bread, now, fat and frolicsome, gladly help their father to clear those fields whence exuberant crops are to arise to feed and to clothe them all; without any part being claimed, either by a despotic prince, a rich abbot, or a mighty lord. Here, religion demands but little of him; a small voluntary salary to the minister, and gratitude to God; can he refuse these? The American is a new man, who acts upon new principles; he must therefore entertain new ideas, and form new opinions. From involuntary idleness, servile dependence, penury, and useless labour, he has passed to toils of a very different nature, rewarded by ample subsistence.—This is an American.

[1] *pinching penury* I.e., penny-pinching destitution.

[2] *wanting ... mould* I.e., lacking fertilization.

[3] *Ubi panis ibi patria* Latin: Where there is bread, there is my homeland.

[4] *Alma Mater* Latin: Bountiful Mother.

from Anonymous, *Look Before You Leap* (1796)

Through the eighteenth and into the nineteenth century, persuasive writers strove to counter the excessive optimism of works promoting immigration to America. While their negative assessments were often based on fact, such was not always the case. Selfless honesty was generally not their primary motivation; concerned that Britain was losing its skilled laborers to the enticing possibilities of the New World, these writers tended to overstate the dangers and difficulties of immigrant life. Some even lied outright; the following is from the introduction to a supposedly "genuine collection of letters" from immigrant tradespeople. A contemporary review suspiciously remarked that the letters contained contradictory facts, as well as attempts at literary flair and philosophical contemplation "not such as those who use the chisel, the trowel, and the brush are likely to make in letters to their wives or friends."

from THE PREFACE

In America, the condition of society is extremely different from what it is in England, and those persons who have enjoyed the social pleasures and mixed intercourse of the metropolis, and of other great towns in this country, will find themselves very uncomfortable and dissatisfied when experiencing a different scene on the Western continent.

Such persons as have built their expectations on finding affluence and ease will meet with a familiar disappointment. What prospect is there of such extraordinary happiness in a country not matured and enriched by commerce, in a new discovered land, occupied in the interior by inhospitable savages and ravaged on the exterior by a late unmerciful war.

Let me now proceed to ask every artisan, mechanic, &c. who may peruse the succeeding letters what particular advantage he finds in them to engage his attention? What superiority of gratification over that enjoyed by persons of the same condition with himself in his own country? Has he found out that the Americans will press down to the shore, and receive him with open arms on his first landing, and vie with each other who shall be most profuse in rendering him offices of kindness and humanity? Does he find that easy complacency and friendly attention, which the canting crimp[1] has taught him to believe is the prominent characteristic of the Virginians? Has he met with the so much boasted encouragement and protection which was to raise him to the most astonishing degrees of preferment?

Does he hear from these experimental adventurers enrapturing accounts of an hospitable country, the fruits of whose luxurious soil are extensively distributed amongst its inhabitants to supply their wants and increase their comforts?

Does he hear of a wholesome climate congenial to the health and longevity of an Englishman, or of an unsettled and inauspicious atmosphere, the fatal effects of which so frequently destroy the most athletic and robust?

Does he find a mechanic can obtain a greater surplus from his earnings, when he has placed the expenses of his board, lodgings, washing, wearing apparel, and other incidents against the receipt of his income?

In fine,[2] does he remark any grateful sensations, any pleasing retrospect experienced by those persons who have quitted this country?

Where is the comfort they enjoy? What is the enchanting prospect before them? If he finds none of these blessings, friendships, gratifications, and prospects, for Heaven's sake! why, wretched as it is, quit his native country and plunge himself precipitately into another, infinitely more unlikely to procure him lasting enjoyment.

It has been well remarked that those who attempt and expect perfect happiness in this world are pursuing the ideal phantom of a sanguine[3] imagination. This may be well applied to the vain expectations raised in the minds of such credulous persons as seek superior comfort and felicity on the continent of America. They are pursuing that which it is not in the power of the country to bestow, and will most certainly be left the disappointed dupes of their own chimerical ideas.

The publisher is well aware of the obloquy[4] that will be cast upon this publication by the innumerable host

---

[1] *canting crimp* I.e., recruiter who lies to trick his victims into immigrating.

[2] *In fine* I.e., in conclusion.

[3] *sanguine* Optimistic.

[4] *obloquy* Public reproach.

of American kidnappers, and he well knows it will be their studied task and serious endeavour to controvert his assertions and to prove them fallacious.... He knows they will confidently ask, If America be the place you have represented, what is the reason that, out of so many thousands who cross the Atlantic, so very few return? To this he as confidently answers. Many unfortunate speculators who have emigrated to America dare not return. The majority of those needy adventurers that have gone the same road cannot return; and many of those who have possessed the means have, alas! been snatched to that bourne from which no traveller returns.[1] The majority of those who have escaped the devouring jaws of death, and have had it in their power, *have* returned, injured in their finances and disappointed in their prospects, cursing the authors of their misery and their own credulity in becoming the passive dupes of such abominable duplicity.

General Wolfe and the Fall of Quebec

from "Anecdotes Relating to the Battle of Quebec" (March 1760)

The year after General Wolfe's much-celebrated capture of Quebec City, the capital of New France, the following retelling of events from a British soldier's perspective was printed in *The British Magazine*.

On the evening that preceded the battle, two French deserters were carried on board one of our men of war,[2] which lay near the north shore, commanded by Capt. Smith; and gave him intelligence that the garrison of Quebec expected that night to receive a convoy of provisions to be sent down the river in boats by Mons. de Bougainville,[3] who commanded a detached body above the town to watch the motions of General Wolfe. From this body to near the place where our troops landed, sentries were posted along shore, to challenge the boats and vessels as they should pass and give the alarm occasionally.[4] One of our captains embarked in the first boat, which was followed by the rest in a string, hugging the north shore. Being questioned by the first sentry, and understanding French perfectly well, answered to the *Qui vit*,[5] which is the challenging word, *la France*; then he asked *a quel regiment*, to what regiment; and the captain replying softly, *de la Reine*, which he knew was one of those under Bougainville, the sentry cried *passe*; and allowed all the boats to pass without further question, in full belief that they were the expected convoy. In the same manner the other sentries were deceived; though one, more wary than the rest, came running down to the shore, and called, *pourquoy est que vous ne parlez plus haut?* Why don't you speak with an audible voice? The English captain, whose presence of mind cannot be sufficiently admired, answered without hesitation, *Tai toi, soutre ou nous serons attrappeés*. "Hush, fool! or we shall be discovered and taken." Thus satisfied, the Frenchman retired, and our troops landed a little farther down without opposition. The first boat was piloted by a midshipman, who mistaking the landing-place in the dark, ordered the men to row past it; but the same captain who had acted so discreetly before insisted upon his being mistaken, and commanded the rowers to put ashore at the destined place, which he knew from having been formerly posted with his company on the opposite side of the river. This was another providential escape; for had the boats overshot the landing-place, confusion would have ensued, and in all probability the opportunity would have been lost.

The two French deserters, on board of Capt. Smith, perceiving our boats gliding down the river in the dark, began to shout and make a noise, declaring they were part of the convoy; and the captain, who was not acquainted with the intended attack, believing their information, had already given orders to point his guns at our own troops, when General Wolfe, in person, rowing alongside of him, prevented the discharge; which not only might have been fatal to our soldiers, but would have infallibly frustrated the design.

[1] *bourne* Boundary; *been snatched ... traveller returns* I.e., died.

[2] *men of war* Sailing ships armed with cannons.

[3] *Mons. de Bougainville* Louis Antoine de Bougainville (1729–1811), French admiral, who commanded an elite troop in the defense of Quebec City.

[4] *occasionally* I.e., at appropriate times.

[5] *Qui vit* French: Who lives?

The common path that slanted up the hill from the landing-place was rendered impassable by ditches, which the enemy had dug across in several parts, and a kind of entrenchment near the top, defended by a piquet-guard.[1] Mr. Wolfe, having formed the men as they landed, divided them into detachments and ordered them to ascend the hill on both sides of the path. Though it was extremely steep and dangerous, the men scrambled up with surprising alacrity and expedition; the summit was first gained by the detachment under the command of the captain aforementioned. The French piquets threw in a straggling fire, which did little or no execution; then they retired with precipitation,[2] and the rest of our army assembled without further trouble....

Advanced parties from both sides piqueered[3] for some hours, and a great many of our officers and soldiers were wounded by a body of burghers[4] from Quebec, selected as good marksmen, who lay concealed in a field of corn opposite to our right. It was from these skulkers that General Wolfe received both his wounds, as he gave directions in the front of the line. The fatal ball took place just as the enemy were advancing to the charge; being unable to stand, he leaned upon the shoulder of a lieutenant, who sat down for that purpose. The French, after a very ineffectual fire, gave way immediately; upon which the lieutenant exclaimed, "They run!" "Who run?" cried the gallant Wolfe with great eagerness. "The enemy," replied the other. "What!" said the general, "do the rascals run already? Then I die happy." So saying, the glorious youth expired.

The action began about nine in the morning and was over in a few minutes, so that the courage of the English army was altogether disappointed; and such was the spirit of the soldiers, that they were mortified because they had not a better opportunity of showing their discipline and valour. All the officers agree that a finer body of troops was never seen.

[1] *piquet-guard* Soldiers guarding the hilltop; the initial English landing party intended to defeat this guard to clear the way for the rest of the army.

[2] *precipitation* Sudden haste.

[3] *piqueered* Skirmished.

[4] *burghers* Townspeople.

from Horace Walpole, *Memoirs of the Last Ten Years of the Reign of King George II* (1822)

Horace Walpole (1717–97) was a Member of Parliament, but is much better remembered for his influence on gothic literature and architecture. His posthumously published *Memoirs of the Reign of George II* includes an account of the fall of Quebec that differs in several respects from that in *The British Magazine.*

... [A] desponding letter [was] received from General Wolfe before Quebec,[5] on the 14th of October. He had found the enterprise infinitely more difficult than he had conceived, the country strong from every circumstance of situation: the French had a superior army, had called in every Canadian capable of bearing arms; twenty-two ship-loads of provisions had escaped Admiral Durell[6] and got into the town; Amherst[7] was not come up; and, above all, Montcalm,[8] the French general, had shown that he understood the natural strength of the country, had posted himself in the most advantageous situation, and was not to be drawn from it by any stratagem which Wolfe, assisted by the steady cooperation of our fleet, could put in practice. Wolfe himself was languishing with the stone[9] and a complication of disorders, which fatigue and disappointment had brought upon him. Townshend[10] and other officers had crossed him in his plans, but he had not yielded. Himself had been one of the warmest censurers of the

[5] *before Quebec* Before the Battle of Quebec, also known as the Battle of the Plains of Abraham.

[6] *twenty-two ... Admiral Durell* Vice-Admiral Philip Durell (1707–66) had arrived too late to intercept the expected delivery of supplies from France.

[7] *Amherst* Lord Jeffery Amherst (1717–97), military commander-in-chief in North America, had planned to join Wolfe but was delayed establishing a military foothold on Lake Champlain.

[8] *Montcalm* Louis-Joseph de Montcalm-Gazon (1712–59), commander of the French forces in North America.

[9] *the stone* Kidney stones.

[10] *Townshend* George Townshend (1724–1807), later a Field Marshal and Marquess, would take command of the British forces after Wolfe's death. He thought Wolfe incompetent and disapproved of his decisions.

miscarried expedition to Rochfort;[1] and he had received this high command upon the assurance that no dangers or difficulties should discourage him. His army wasted before his eyes by sickness; the season advanced fast which must put an end to his attempts; he had no choice remaining but in variety of difficulties. In the most artful terms that could be framed he left the nation uncertain whether he meant to prepare an excuse for desisting, or to claim the melancholy merit of having sacrificed himself without a prospect of success.

Three days after, an express arrived that Quebec was taken—a conquest heightened by the preceding gloom and despair. The rapidity with which our arms had prevailed in every quarter of the globe made us presume that Canada could not fail of being added to our acquisitions; and however arduously won, it would have sunk in value if the transient cloud that overcast the dawn of this glory had not made it burst forth with redoubled lustre. The incidents of dramatic fiction could not be conducted with more address to lead an audience from despondency to sudden exaltation, than accident prepared to excite the passions of a whole people. They despaired—they triumphed—and they wept—for Wolfe had fallen in the hour of victory! Joy, grief, curiosity, astonishment, were painted in every countenance: the more they enquired, the higher their admiration rose. Not an incident but was heroic and affecting!

Wolfe, between persuasion of the impracticability, unwillingness to leave any attempt untried that could be proposed, and worn out with anxiety of mind and body, had determined to make one last effort above the town. He embarked his forces at one in the morning, and passed the French sentinels in silence that were posed along the shore. The current carried them beyond the destined spot. They found themselves at the foot of a precipice, esteemed so impracticable that only a slight guard of one hundred and fifty men defended it. Had there been a path, the night was too dark to discover it. The troops, whom nothing could discourage, for these difficulties could not, pulled themselves and one another up by stumps and boughs of trees. The guard, hearing a rustling, fired down the precipice at random, as our men did up into the air; but terrified by the strangeness of the attempt, the French piquet[2] fled....

Daybreak discovered our forces in possession of the eminence.[3] Montcalm could not credit it when reported to him, but it was too late to doubt when nothing but a battle could save the town. Even then he held our attempt so desperate that, being shown the position of the English, he said, "*Oui, je les vois où ils ne doivent pas être.*"[4] Forced to quit his entrenchments, he said, "*S'il faut donc combattre, je vais le ecraser.*"[5] He prepared for engagement after lining the bushes with detachments of Indians. Our men, according to orders, reserved their fire with a patience and tranquility equal to the resolution they had exerted in clambering the precipice—but when they gave it, it took place with such terrible slaughter of the enemy that half an hour decided the day. The French fled precipitately,[6] and Montcalm, endeavouring to rally them, was killed on the spot....

The fall of Wolfe was noble indeed. He received a wound in the head, but covered it from his soldiers with his handkerchief. A second ball struck him in the belly; that too he dissembled.[7] A third hitting him in the breast, he sunk under the anguish and was carried behind the ranks. Yet, fast as life ebbed out, his whole anxiety centred on the fortune of the day. He begged to be borne nearer to the action, but his sight being dimmed by the approach of death, he entreated to be told what they who supported him saw: he was answered that the enemy gave ground. He eagerly repeated the question, heard the enemy was totally routed, cried "I am satisfied"—and expired.

[1] *Rochfort* Wolfe had participated in a 1757 attack on Rochefort, France, in which, despite initial success, the commander chose to withdraw.

[2] *piquet* Guarding force.

[3] *eminence* High ground.

[4] *Oui ... être* French: Yes, I see them where they should not be.

[5] *S'il faut ... ecraser* French: If we must fight, I will crush them.

[6] *precipitately* Hastily.

[7] *dissembled* Disguised.

Colonists and Native People

William Wordsworth, "Complaint of a Forsaken Indian Woman" (1798)

In this poem (first published in *Lyrical Ballads*) Wordsworth addresses a subject that was common in poetry of the late eighteenth century: the image of the dying Indian.

When a Northern Indian, from sickness, is unable to continue his journey with his companions, he is left behind, covered over with deer-skins, and is supplied with water, food, and fuel if the situation of the place will afford it. He is informed of the track which his companions intend to pursue, and if he is unable to follow or overtake them, he perishes alone in the desert; unless he should have the good fortune to fall in with some other tribes of Indians. It is unnecessary to add that the females are equally, or still more, exposed to the same fate. See that very interesting work Hearne's *Journey from Hudson's Bay to the Northern Ocean.*[1] When the northern lights, as the same writer informs us, vary their position in the air, they make a rustling and a crackling noise. This circumstance is alluded to in the first stanza of the following poem.

Before I see another day,
Oh let my body die away!
In sleep I heard the northern gleams;
The stars they were among my dreams;
In sleep I did behold the skies,
I saw the crackling flashes drive;
And yet they are upon my eyes,
And yet I am alive.
Before I see another day,
Oh let my body die away!

My fire is dead: it knew no pain;
Yet is it dead, and I remain.
All stiff with ice the ashes lie;
And they are dead, and I will die.
When I was well, I wished to live,
For clothes, for warmth, for food, and fire;
But they to me no joy can give,
No pleasure now, and no desire.
Then here contented will I lie;
Alone I cannot fear to die.

Alas! you might have dragged me on
Another day, a single one!
Too soon despair o'er me prevailed;
Too soon my heartless spirit failed;
When you were gone my limbs were stronger;
And Oh how grievously I rue,
That, afterwards, a little longer,
My friends, I did not follow you!
For strong and without pain I lay,
My friends, when you were gone away.

My child! they gave thee to another,
A woman who was not thy mother.
When from my arms my babe they took,
On me how strangely did he look!
Through his whole body something ran,
A most strange something did I see;
—As if he strove to be a man,
That he might pull the sledge for me.
And then he stretched his arms, how wild!
Oh mercy! like a little child.

My little joy! my little pride!
In two days more I must have died.
Then do not weep and grieve for me;
I feel I must have died with thee.
Oh wind, that o'er my head art flying,
The way my friends their course did bend,
I should not feel the pain of dying,
Could I with thee a message send.
Too soon, my friends, you went away;
For I had many things to say.

I'll follow you across the snow,
You travel heavily and slow:
In spite of all my weary pain,
I'll look upon your tents again.
My fire is dead, and snowy white

[1] *Hearne's ... Ocean* Explorer Samuel Hearne (1745–92) documented his experiences in *A Journey from Prince of Wales's Fort in Hudson's Bay to the Northern Ocean*, published posthumously in 1795.

The water which beside it stood;
The wolf has come to me tonight,
And he has stolen away my food.
Forever left alone am I,
Then wherefore should I fear to die?

My journey will be shortly run,
I shall not see another sun,
I cannot lift my limbs to know
If they have any life or no.
My poor forsaken child! if I
For once could have thee close to me,
With happy heart I then would die,
And my last thoughts would happy be.
I feel my body die away,
I shall not see another day.

Benjamin West, *William Penn's Treaty with the Indians when he founded the Province of Pennsylvania in North America* (1771). Born in Pennsylvania, West was living in England when he painted this and the other large history paintings for which he is best known. The subject is William Penn, Quaker philosopher and founder of Pennsylvania, who was renowned for his unusually good relationship with the Lenape Indians of the region. Unlike other early settlers, who saw no need to compensate native people for their land, Penn negotiated an exchange with the Lenape, trading goods for signed documents ceding land to the colonists. Historians quite rightly point out that Penn and his settlers displaced the Lenape and forced them to conform to the needs of the colony; nevertheless, the relationship between the Pennsylvanians and the Lenape was remarkably peaceful for the period and was seen as representative of ideal Indian-settler relations. (See the color insert in this bound volume for another example of Benjamin West's work.)

from Susannah Johnson, *The Captive American, or A Narrative of the Suffering of Mrs. Johnson During Four Years Captivity with the Indians and French* (1797)

The Seven Years' War was a global conflict involving France, Austria, and other allies fighting against Britain, Prussia, and their allies, both in Europe and through their colonial possessions in North and South America, Africa, India, and the Philippines. Susannah Johnson was living in present-day Charlestown, New Hampshire, during the early escalation of the North American conflict that would become part of this war. She and her family were captured by a raiding party of Abenaki Indians, who were allied with the French, having been largely forced out of New Hampshire by English colonization. The Abenaki held her captive for a few months before selling her to French settlers; when she was finally released, more than three years had passed since her capture. Years later, Johnson dictated her story to a local lawyer, and it became one of the most widely read works in the popular genre of Indian captivity narratives.

from the INTRODUCTION

During ... the Cape Breton War,[1] the town of No. 4[2] could hardly be said to be inhabited; some adventurers had made a beginning, but few were considered as belonging to the town. Captain Stevens, whose valour is recorded as an instance of consummate generalship, part of the time kept the fort, which afforded a shelter to the enterprising settlers in times of imminent danger. But even his vigilance did not save the town from numerous scenes of carnage. At the commencement of the peace in 1749, the enterprising spirit of New England rose superior to the dangers of the forest, and they began to venture innovation. The Indians, still thirsty for plunder and rapine,[3] and regardless of the peace which their masters, the French, had concluded, kept up a flying warfare and committed several outrages upon lives and property; this kept the increasing inhabitants in a state of alarm for three or four years; most of the time they performed their daily work without molestation, but retreated to the fort at each returning night.

Our country has so long been exposed to the Indian wars that recitals of exploits and sufferings, of escapes and deliverances, have become both numerous and trite. The air of novelty will not be attempted in the following pages; simple facts, unadorned, are what the reader must expect; pity for my sufferings, and admiration at my safe return, is all that my history can excite....

from CHAPTER 1

Everyone "was tremblingly alive" with fear. The Indians were reported to be on their march for our destruction, and our distance from sources of information gave full latitude for exaggerations of news before it reached our ears. The fears of the night were horrible beyond description, and even the light of day was far from dispelling painful anxiety. While looking from the windows of my log house, and seeing my neighbours tread cautiously by each hedge and hillock, lest some secreted savage might start forth to take their scalp, my fears would baffle description. Alarms grew greater and greater, till our apprehensions were too strongly confirmed by the news of the capture of Mr. Malony's family, on Merrimack River: this reached us about the 20th of August. Imagination now saw and heard a thousand Indians; and I never went round my own house without first looking with trembling caution by each corner, to see if a tomahawk was not raised for my destruction....

On the evening of the 29th of August our house was visited by a party of neighbours who spent the time very cheerfully with watermelons and flip[4] till midnight; they all then retired in high spirits, except a spruce young spark, who tarried to keep company with my sister. We then went to bed with feelings well tuned for sleep, and rested with fine composure till midway between daybreak and sunrise, when we were roused by neighbour Labarree's knocking at the door, who had shouldered his

[1] *Cape Breton War* More commonly known as King George's War, the North American component of the War of the Austrian Succession, one of several conflicts between the major powers of Europe that spread to their colonies.

[2] *No. 4* Present day Charlestown, New Hampshire.

[3] *rapine* Pillage.

[4] *flip* Hot alcoholic beverage.

ax to do a day's work for my husband. Mr. Johnson slipped on his jacket and trousers, and stepped to the door to let him in. But by opening the door he opened a scene—terrible to describe!—Indians! Indians! were the first words I heard; he sprang to his guns, but Labarree, heedless of danger, instead of closing the door to keep them out, began to rally our hired men upstairs for not rising earlier. But in an instant a crowd of savages, fixed horribly for war, rushed furiously in. I screamed, and begged my friends to ask for quarters.[1] By this time they were all over the house, some upstairs, some hauling my sister out of bed; another had hold of me, and one was approaching Mr. Johnson, who stood in the middle of the floor to deliver himself up; but the Indian supposing that he would make resistance, and be more than his match, went to the door and brought three of his comrades, and the four bound him. I was led to the door, fainting and trembling; there stood my friend Labarree bound; Ebenezer Farnsworth, whom they found up in his chamber, they were putting in the same situation; and, to complete the shocking scene, my three little children were driven naked to the place where I stood. On viewing myself, I found that I too was naked. An Indian had purloined three gowns who, on seeing my situation, gave me the whole. I asked another for a petticoat, but he refused it. After what little plunder their hurry would allow them to get was confusedly bundled up, we were ordered to march. After going about twenty roods,[2] we fell behind a rising ground, where we halted to pack the things in a better manner; while there, a savage went back, as we supposed, to fire the buildings. Farnsworth proposed to my husband to go back with him, to get a quantity of pork from the cellar to help us on the journey; but Mr. Johnson prudently replied that by that means the Indians might find the rum, and in a fit of intoxication kill us all....

We all arrived safe on the other side of the river about four o'clock in the afternoon; a fire was kindled, and some of the stolen kettles were hung over it and filled with porridge. The savages took delight in viewing their spoil, which amounted to forty or fifty pounds in value. They then, with a truly savage yell, gave their war whoop and bade defiance to danger. As we tarried an hour in this place, I had time to reflect on our miserable situation. Captives, in the power of unmerciful savages, without provision and almost without clothes, in a wilderness where we must sojourn as long as the children of Israel did, for aught we knew; and, what added to our distress, not one of our savage masters could understand a word of English....

The fifth day's journey was an unvaried scene of fatigue. The Indians sent out two or three hunting parties, who returned without game. As we had in the morning consumed the last morsel of our meal, everyone now began to be seriously alarmed, and hunger, with all its horrors, looked us earnestly in the face. At night, we found the waters that run into Lake Champlain, which was over the height of land; before dark we halted, and the Indians, by help of their punck,[3] which they carried in horns, made a fire. They soon adopted a plan to relieve their hunger: the horse was shot, and his flesh was in a few minutes broiling on embers, and they, with native gluttony, satiated their craving appetites. To use the term politeness in the management of this repast may be thought a burlesque, yet their offering the prisoners the best parts of the horse certainly bordered on civility; an epicure could not have catered nicer slices, nor, in that situation, served them up with more neatness. Appetite is said to be the best sauce, yet our abundance of it did not render savoury this novel steak. My children, however, ate too much, which made them very unwell for a number of days. Broth was made for me and my child,[4] which was rendered almost a luxury by the seasoning of roots. After supper, countenances began to brighten; those who had relished the meal exhibited new strength, and those who had only snuffed its effluvia[5] confessed themselves regaled. The evening was employed in drying and smoking what remained for future use. The night was a scene of distressing fears to me, and my extreme weakness had affected my mind to such a degree that every difficulty appeared doubly terrible. By the assistance of Scoggin,[6] I had been

[1] *quarters* Mercy.

[2] *twenty roods* Almost 14 miles.

[3] *punck* Tinder.

[4] *my child* Johnson was in a late stage of pregnancy when she was taken, and her baby was born during the journey.

[5] *effluvia* Unpleasant smell.

[6] *Scoggin* Name of the horse.

brought so far, yet so great was my debility, that every hour I was taken off and laid on the ground, to keep me from expiring. But now, alas! this conveyance was no more. To walk it was impossible. Inevitable death in the midst of woods one hundred miles wide appeared to be my only portion.

from CHAPTER 3

In the morning of the sixth day, the Indians exerted themselves to prepare one of their greatest dainties. The marrow bones of old Scoggin were pounded for a soup, and every root, both sweet and bitter, that the woods afforded was thrown in to give it a flavour. Each one partook of as much as his feelings would allow. The war whoop then resounded, with an infernal yell, and we began to fix for a march. My fate was unknown till my master brought some bark and tied my petticoats as high as he supposed would be convenient for walking, and ordered me to "munch."[1] With scarce strength to stand alone, I went on half a mile with my little son and three Indians. The rest were advanced. My power to move then failed, the world grew dark, and I dropped down. I had sight enough to see an Indian lift his hatchet over my head, while my son screamed, "Ma'am do go, for they will kill you!" As I fainted, my last thought was that I should presently be in a world of spirits. When I awoke, my master was talking angrily with the savage who had threatened my life. By his gestures, I could learn that he charged him with not acting the honourable part of a warrior, by an attempt to destroy the prize of a brother. A whoop was given for the halt. My master helped me to the rest of the company, where a council was held, the result of which was that my husband should walk by my side and help me along....

from CHAPTER 4

Whenever the warriors return from an excursion against an enemy, their return to the tribe or village must be designated by warlike ceremonial; the captives or spoil which may happen to crown their valour must be conducted in triumphant form and decorated to every possible advantage. For this end, we must now submit to painting; their vermilion,[2] with which they were ever supplied, was mixed with bear's grease, and every cheek, chin, and forehead must have a dash. We then rowed on within a mile of the town, where we stopped at a French house to dine; the prisoners were served with soup meagre[3] and bread. After dinner, two savages proceeded to the village to carry the glad tidings of our arrival. The whole atmosphere soon resounded from every quarter, with whoops, yells, shrieks, and screams. St. Francis, from the noise that came from it, might be supposed the centre of Pandemonium.[4] Our masters were not backward, they made every response they possibly could. The whole time we were sailing from the French house, the noise was direful to be heard. Two hours before sunset, we came to the landing at the village. No sooner had we landed than the yelling in the town was redoubled, and a cloud of savages of all sizes and sexes soon appeared running towards us; when they reached the boats, they formed themselves into a long parade, leaving a small space through which we must pass. Each Indian took his prisoner by the hand, and after ordering him to sing the war-song, began to march through the gauntlet. We expected a severe beating before we got through, but were agreeably disappointed when we found that each Indian only gave us a tap on the shoulder. We were led directly into the houses, each taking his prisoner to his own wigwam.... My new home was not the most agreeable; a large wigwam without a floor, with a fire in the centre, and only a few water vessels and dishes to eat from made of birch bark, and tools for cookery, made clumsily of wood, for furniture,[5] will not be thought a pleasing residence for one accustomed to civilized life.

from CHAPTER 5

Hasty pudding was presently brought forward for supper. A spacious bowl of wood, well filled, was placed in a central spot, and each one drew near with a wooden spoon. As the Indians never use seats, nor have any in their wigwams, my awkwardness in taking my position was a matter of no small amusement to my new com-

[1] *munch* March, pronounced with an accent.

[2] *vermilion* Bright red pigment.

[3] *soup meagre* Green vegetable soup.

[4] *Pandemonium* Capital of Hell in Milton's *Paradise Lost.*

[5] *furniture* Equipment.

panions. The squaws first fall upon their knees and then sit back upon their heels. This was a posture that I could not imitate. To sit in any other was thought by them indelicate and unpolite. But I advanced to my pudding with the best grace I could, not, however, escaping some of their funny remarks. When the hour for sleep came on (for it would be improper to call it bedtime, where beds were not) I was pointed to a platform, raised half a yard, where, upon a board covered with a blanket, I was to pass the night. The Indians threw themselves down in various parts of the building in a manner that more resembled cows in a shed than human beings in a house.…

It was now the 15th day of October. Forty-five days had passed since my captivity, and no prospect but what was darkened with clouds of misfortune. The uneasiness occasioned by indolence[1] was in some measure relieved by the privilege of making shirts for my brother.[2] At night and morn, I was allowed to milk the cows. The rest of the time I strolled gloomily about, looking sometimes into an unsociable wigwam, at others sauntering into the bushes, and walking on the banks of brooks. Once I went to a French house three miles distant to visit some friends of my brother's family, where I was entertained politely a week. At another time I went with a party to fish, accompanied by a number of squaws. My weakness obliged me to rest often, which gave my companions a poor opinion of me; but they showed no other resentment than calling me "no good squaw," which was the only reproach my sister ever gave when I displeased her. All the French inhabitants I formed an acquaintance with treated me with that civility which distinguishes the nation; once in particular, being almost distracted with an aching tooth, I was carried to a French physician across the river for relief. They prevailed on the Indians to let me visit them a day or two, during which time their marked attention and generosity claim my warmest gratitude. At parting, they expressed their earnest wishes to have me visit them again.

St. Francis contained about thirty wigwams, which were thrown disorderly into a clump. There was a church, in which mass was held every night and morning, and every Sunday; the hearers were summoned by a bell; and attendance was pretty general. Ceremonies were performed by a French friar, who lived in the midst of them for the salvation of their souls. He appeared to be in that place what the legislative branch is in civil governments, and the grand sachem the executive. The inhabitants lived in perfect harmony, holding most of their property in common. They were prone to indolence when at home, and not remarkable for neatness. They were extremely modest and apparently averse to airs of courtship. Necessity was the only thing that called them to action; this induced them to plant their corn and to undergo the fatigues of hunting. Perhaps I am wrong in calling necessity the only motive; revenge, which prompts them to war, has great power. I had a numerous retinue of relations, which I visited daily; but my brother's house being one of the most decent in the village, I fared full as well at home. Among my connections was a little brother Sabaties, who brought the cows for me, and took particular notice of my child. He was a sprightly little fellow, and often amused me with feats performed with his bow and arrow.…

In justice to the Indians, I ought to remark that they never treated me with cruelty to a wanton degree: few people have survived a situation like mine, and few have fallen into the savages disposed to more lenity and patience. Modesty has ever been a characteristic of every savage tribe, a truth which the whole of my family will join to corroborate to the extent of their knowledge. As they are aptly called the children of nature, those who have profited by refinement and education ought to abate part of the prejudice which prompts them to look with an eye of censure on this untutored race. Can it be said of civilized conquerors that they in the main are willing to share with their prisoners the last ration of food when famine stares them in the face? Do they ever adopt an enemy and salute him by the tender name of brother? And I am justified in doubting whether, if I had fallen into the hands of French soldiery, so much assiduity[3] would have been shown to preserve my life.

[1] *indolence* Idleness.

[2] *my brother* The Abenaki family holding Johnson captive has adopted her.

[3] *assiduity* Concerted attention.

American Independence

from Edmund Burke, "Speech on Conciliation with the Colonies" (22 March 1775)

One English writer and politician very largely sympathetic to the cause of the American colonies in the 1770s was the Irish-born British politician Edmund Burke—later to become a prominent opponent of the French Revolution. Burke's approach took the continuity of history and circumstance into account at least as much as it did abstract principles. As these excerpts from an influential 1775 speech indicate, Burke saw the cause of the American colonies as emerging naturally from their English traditions; in contrast, he saw the French Revolution as a violent rupture with the past.[1]

... I have in my hand two accounts: one a comparative state of the export trade of England to its colonies, as it stood in the year 1704, and as it stood in the year 1772; the other a state of the export trade of this country to its colonies alone, as it stood in 1772, compared with the whole trade of England to all parts of the world (the colonies included) in the year 1704....

The export trade to the colonies consists of three great branches: the African—which, terminating almost wholly in the colonies, must be put to the account of their commerce—the West Indian, and the North American. All these are so interwoven that the attempt to separate them would tear to pieces the contexture of the whole, and, if not entirely destroy, would very much depreciate the value of all the parts. I therefore consider these three denominations to be, what in effect they are, one trade.

The trade to the colonies, taken on the export side, at the beginning of this century, that is, in the year 1704, stood thus:—

Exports to North America and the West Indies.	£483,265
To Africa.	£86,665
	£569,930

In the year 1772, which I take as a middle year between the highest and lowest of those lately laid on your table, the account was as follows:—

To North America and the West Indies.	£4,791,734
To Africa.	£866,398
To which, if you add the export trade from Scotland, which had in 1704 no existence.	£364,000
	£6,022,132

From five hundred and odd thousand, it has grown to six millions. It has increased no less than twelve-fold.... But this is not all. Examine my second account. See how the export trade to the colonies alone in 1772 stood in the other point of view; that is, as compared to the whole trade of England in 1704:—

The whole export trade of England, including that to the colonies, in 1704.	£6,509,000
Export to the colonies alone, in 1772.	£6,024,000
Difference.	£485,000

The trade with America alone is now within less than £500,000 of being equal to what this great commercial nation, England, carried on at the beginning of this century with the whole world! ...

America, gentlemen say, is a noble object. It is an object well worth fighting for. Certainly it is, if fighting a people be the best way of gaining them. Gentlemen in this respect will be led to their choice of means by their complexions[2] and their habits. Those who understand the military art will of course have some predilection for it. Those who wield the thunder of the state may have more confidence in the efficacy of arms. But I confess, possibly for want of this knowledge, my opinion is much more in favour of prudent management than of force; considering force not as an odious, but a feeble instrument for preserving a people so numerous, so active, so growing, so spirited as this, in a profitable and subordinate connection with us.

First, Sir, permit me to observe that the use of force alone is but temporary. It may subdue for a moment, but it does not remove the necessity of subduing again;

---

[1] *French Revolution ... the past* For Burke's and other opinions on the French Revolution, see "Contexts: The French Revolution and the Napoleonic Era" (in the online component of this anthology, volume 4).

[2] *complexions* Personal attitudes.

and a nation is not governed which is perpetually to be conquered.

My next objection is its uncertainty. Terror is not always the effect of force, and an armament is not a victory. If you do not succeed, you are without resource; for, conciliation failing, force remains; but, force failing, no further hope of reconciliation is left. Power and authority are sometimes bought by kindness; but they can never be begged as alms by an impoverished and defeated violence.

A further objection to force is that you impair the object by your very endeavors to preserve it. The thing you fought for is not the thing which you recover; but depreciated, sunk, wasted, and consumed in the contest. Nothing less will content me than whole America. I do not choose to consume its strength along with our own, because in all parts it is the British strength that I consume. I do not choose to be caught by a foreign enemy at the end of this exhausting conflict, and still less in the midst of it. I may escape; but I can make no insurance against such an event. Let me add, that I do not choose wholly to break the American spirit, because it is the spirit that has made the country.

Lastly, we have no sort of experience in favour of force as an instrument in the rule of our colonies. Their growth and their utility has been owing to methods altogether different. Our ancient indulgence has been said to be pursued to a fault. It may be so. But we know, if feeling is evidence, that our fault was more tolerable than our attempt to mend it; and our sin far more salutary[1] than our penitence.

These, Sir, are my reasons for not entertaining that high opinion of untried force by which many gentlemen, for whose sentiments in other particulars I have great respect, seem to be so greatly captivated. But there is still behind a third consideration concerning this object which serves to determine my opinion on the sort of policy which ought to be pursued in the management of America, even more than its population and its commerce—I mean its temper and character.

In this character of the Americans, a love of freedom is the predominating feature which marks and distinguishes the whole; and as an ardent is always a jealous affection, your colonies become suspicious, restive, and untractable[2] whenever they see the least attempt to wrest from them by force, or shuffle from them by chicane,[3] what they think the only advantage worth living for. This fierce spirit of liberty is stronger in the English colonies probably than in any other people of the earth, and this from a great variety of powerful causes; which, to understand the true temper of their minds and the direction which this spirit takes, it will not be amiss to lay open somewhat more largely.

First, the people of the colonies are descendants of Englishmen. England, Sir, is a nation which still, I hope, respects, and formerly adored, her freedom. The colonists emigrated from you when this part of your character was most predominant, and they took this bias and direction the moment they parted from your hands. They are therefore not only devoted to liberty, but to liberty according to English ideas and on English principles. Abstract liberty, like other mere abstractions, is not to be found. Liberty inheres in some sensible object; and every nation has formed to itself some favorite point, which by way of eminence becomes the criterion of their happiness. It happened, you know, Sir, that the great contests for freedom in this country were from the earliest times chiefly upon the question of taxing.… The colonies draw from [England], as with their life-blood, these ideas and principles. Their love of liberty, as with you, fixed and attached on this specific point of taxing. Liberty might be safe, or might be endangered, in twenty other particulars, without their being much pleased or alarmed. Here they felt its pulse; and as they found that beat, they thought themselves sick or sound. I do not say whether they were right or wrong in applying your general arguments to their own case. It is not easy, indeed, to make a monopoly of theorems and corollaries.[4] The fact is that they did thus apply those general arguments; and your mode of governing them, whether through lenity or indolence,[5] through wisdom or mistake, confirmed them in the

[1] *salutary* Beneficial.

[2] *untractable* Difficult to manage.

[3] *chicane* Deceit.

[4] *theorems and corollaries* Established propositions and what can be reasoned from them.

[5] *indolence* Laziness.

imagination that they, as well as you, had an interest in these common principles.

…

The Americans will have no interest contrary to the grandeur and glory of England when they are not oppressed by the weight of it; and they will rather be inclined to respect the acts of a superintending legislature when they see them the acts of that power which is itself the security, not the rival, of their secondary importance. In this assurance my mind most perfectly acquiesces, and I confess I feel not the least alarm from the discontents which are to arise from putting people at their ease, nor do I apprehend the destruction of this empire from giving, by an act of free grace and indulgence, to two millions of my fellow-citizens some share of those rights upon which I have always been taught to value myself.…

from Benjamin Franklin,[1] *The Autobiography of Benjamin Franklin* (1793)

Benjamin Franklin was a remarkable polymath—in addition to playing a major political role in the American Revolution, he was also a successful book printer, author, inventor, and scientist, among other things. Instrumental in the foundation of the United States, he was also influential in Europe; he acted as a negotiator with the British government and as a diplomat to France, where he was hugely popular. In the following excerpt from his *Autobiography*, he describes a journey to England at the beginning of the Revolution; fighting had just begun when his ship left the American coast.

The Assembly finally, finding the proprietaries[2] obstinately persisted in manacling their deputies with instructions inconsistent not only with the privileges of the people, but with the service of the Crown, resolved to petition the king against them, and appointed me their agent to go over to England, to present and support the petition.…

In the morning it was found by the soundings, &c., that we were near our port, but a thick fog hid the land from our sight. About nine o'clock the fog began to rise, and seemed to be lifted up from the water like the curtain at a play-house, discovering underneath the town of Falmouth, the vessels in its harbor, and the fields that surrounded it. A most pleasing spectacle to those who had been so long without any other prospects than the uniform view of a vacant ocean! And it gave us the more pleasure as we were now free from the anxieties which the state of war occasioned.

I set out immediately, with my son, for London, and we only stopped a little by the way to view Stonehenge on Salisbury Plain, and Lord Pembroke's house and gardens, with his very curious antiquities at Wilton.[3]

We arrived in London the 27th of July, 1775. As soon as I was settled in a lodging Mr. Charles had provided for me, I went to visit Dr. Fothergill, to whom I was strongly recommended, and whose counsel respecting my proceedings I was advised to obtain. He was against an immediate complaint to government, and thought the proprietaries should first be personally applied to, who might possibly be induced by the interposition and persuasion of some private friends to accommodate matters amicably. I then waited on my old friend and correspondent Mr. Peter Collinson, who told me that John Hanbury, the great Virginia merchant, had requested to be informed when I should arrive, that he might carry me to Lord Granville's, who was then President of the Council, and wished to see me as soon as possible. I agreed to go with him the next morning. Accordingly Mr. Hanbury called for me and took me in his carriage to that nobleman's, who received me with great civility; and after some questions respecting the present state of affairs in America and discourse thereupon, he said to me: "You Americans have wrong ideas of the nature of your constitution; you contend that the king's instructions to his governors are not laws, and think yourselves at liberty to regard or disregard them at your own discretion. But those instructions are not like the pocket instructions given to a minister going abroad, for regulating his conduct in some trifling

[1] *from Benjamin Franklin* Further selections from Franklin are available in the website component of this anthology.

[2] *the proprietaries* The Penn family, which had been granted governing rights to Pennsylvania by royal charter.

[3] *Lord Pembroke … Wilton* Wilton, the seat of the Earls of Pembroke, was (and is) renowned as a beautiful country estate.

point of ceremony. They are first drawn up by judges learned in the laws; they are then considered, debated, and perhaps amended in Council, after which they are signed by the king. They are then, so far as relates to you, the law of the land, for THE KING IS THE LEGISLATOR OF THE COLONIES." I told his lordship this was new doctrine to me. I had always understood from our charters that our laws were to be made by our Assemblies, to be presented indeed to the king for his royal assent, but that being once given the king could not repeal or alter them. And as the Assemblies could not make permanent laws without his assent, so neither could he make a law for them without theirs. He assured me I was totally mistaken. I did not think so, however. And his lordship's conversation having a little alarmed me as to what might be the sentiments of the Court concerning us, I wrote it down as soon as I returned to my lodgings. I recollected that about 20 years before, a clause in a bill brought into Parliament by the ministry had proposed to make the king's instructions laws in the colonies, but the clause was thrown out by the Commons, for which we adored them as our friends and friends of liberty, till by their conduct towards us in 1765 it seemed that they had refused that point of sovereignty to the king only that they might reserve it for themselves.

from Richard Price, *Observations on the Nature of Civil Liberty, the Principles of Government, and the Justice and Policy of the War with America* (1776)

British preacher and writer Richard Price never left the British Isles, but his ideas influenced the political relationship between England and America on both sides. His pamphlets in support of the American Revolution were at the center of the English debate surrounding policy toward the Thirteen Colonies, and the first, excerpted below, played a role in encouraging the Americans to declare their independence.

from PART 2

Though clearly decided in my own judgment on this subject, I am inclined to make great allowances for the different judgments of others. We have been so used to speak of the colonies as *our* colonies, and to think of them as in a state of subordination to us, and as holding their existence in America only for our use, that it is no wonder the prejudices of many are alarmed when they find a different doctrine maintained. The meanest[1] person among us is disposed to look upon himself as having a body of subjects in America, and to be offended at the denial of his right to make laws for them, though perhaps he does not know what colour they are of, or what language they talk. Such are the natural prejudices of this country. But the time is coming, I hope, when the unreasonableness of them will be seen, and more just sentiments prevail....

from SECTION 1, *Of the Justice of the War with America*

The enquiry whether the war with the colonies is a just war will be best determined by stating the power over them, which it is the end of the war to maintain; and this cannot be better done than in the words of an act of parliament, made on purpose to define it. That act, it is well known, declares, "That this kingdom has power, and of right ought to have power to make laws and statutes to bind the colonies, and people of America, in all cases whatever."[2] Dreadful power indeed! I defy anyone to express slavery in stronger language. It is the same with[3] declaring "that we have a right to do with them what we please."...

But, probably, most persons will be for using milder language; and for saying no more than that the united legislatures of England and Scotland have of right power to tax the colonies, and a supremacy of legislature over America. But this comes to the same. If it means anything, it means that the property and the legislations of the colonies are subject to the absolute discretion of Great Britain, and ought of right to be so. The nature of the thing admits of no limitation. The colonies can never be admitted to be judges how far the authority over them in

[1] *meanest* Most inferior; of lowest social status.

[2] *That this ... whatever* Paraphrased passage from the Declaratory Act (1766), which stated that the British government "had, hath, and of right ought to have, full power and authority to make laws and statutes of sufficient force and validity to bind the colonies and people of America, subjects of the crown of Great Britain, in all cases whatsoever."

[3] *same with* Same as.

these cases shall extend. This would be to destroy it entirely. If any part of their property is subject to our discretion, the whole must be so. If we have a right to interfere at all in their internal legislations, we have a right to interfere as far as we think proper. It is self-evident that this leaves them nothing they can call their own....

Much has been said of "the superiority of the British state." But what gives us our superiority? Is it our wealth? This never confers real dignity. On the contrary its effect is always to debase, intoxicate, and corrupt. Is it the number of our people? The colonies will soon be equal to us in number. Is it our knowledge and virtue? They are probably equally knowing and more virtuous. There are names among them that will not stoop to any names among the philosophers and politicians of this island....

from SECTION 3, *Of the Policy of the War with America*

[W]hat deserves particular consideration here is that this [war] is a contest from which no advantages can possibly be derived. Not a revenue, for the provinces of America, when desolated, will afford no revenue, or, if they should, the expense of subduing them and keeping them in subjection will much exceed that revenue. Not any of the advantages of trade, for it is a folly, next to insanity, to think trade can be promoted by impoverishing our customers and fixing in their minds an everlasting abhorrence of us. It remains, therefore, that this war can have no other object than the extension of power. Miserable reflection! To sheath our swords in the bowels of our brethren and spread misery and ruin among a happy people for no other end than to oblige them to acknowledge our supremacy. How horrid! This is the cursed ambition that led a Caesar and an Alexander,[1] and many other mad conquerors, to attack peaceful communities and to lay waste the earth.

But a worse principle than even this influences some among us. Pride and the love of dominion are principles hateful enough, but blind resentment and the desire of revenge are infernal principles. And these, I am afraid, have no small share at present in guiding our public conduct. One cannot help indeed being astonished at the virulence with which some speak on the present occasion against the Colonies. For what have they done? Have they crossed the ocean and invaded us? Have they attempted to take from us the fruits of our labour and to overturn that form of government which we hold so sacred? This cannot be pretended. On the contrary, this is what we have done to them. We have transported ourselves to their peaceful retreats and employed our fleets and armies to stop up their ports, to destroy their commerce, to seize their effects, and to burn their towns. Would we but let them alone and suffer them to enjoy in security their property and governments, instead of disturbing us they would thank and bless us. And yet it is we who imagine ourselves ill-used. The truth is, we expected to find them a cowardly rabble who would lie quietly at our feet, and they have disappointed us. They have risen in their own defence and repelled force by force. They deny the plenitude of our power over them and insist upon being treated as free communities. It is this that has provoked us and kindled our governors into rage....

Thomas Jefferson, "A Declaration by the Representatives of the United States of America, in General Congress Assembled"[2] (1776)

The American Revolutionary War had already begun when the Second Continental Congress, an assembly of delegates from the Thirteen Colonies, gathered to perform the functions of government, orchestrating the conduct of the war and the confederation of the colonies as a nation independent from the British Empire. Needing to provide an official explanation for the decision to sever allegiances to Great Britain, Congress appointed a committee of five people—including Thomas Jefferson, Benjamin Franklin, and John Adams—to draft a Declaration of Independence enumerating the American grievances against the Crown and the ideological justifications for rejecting British rule. The draft was edited by Congress and then immediately printed and distributed throughout the colonies; one copy was sent to England.

[1] *Caesar* Julius Caesar, first-century BCE Roman general and statesman who helped form the Roman Empire and led the first Roman invasion of Britain; *Alexander* Alexander the Great, a fourth-century BCE Macedonian king who excelled as a military commander and who formed one of the largest ancient empires.

[2] *A Declaration ... Congress Assembled* The final version is titled "The unanimous Declaration of the thirteen united States of America."

The following text is the first complete draft of the Declaration, written by Thomas Jefferson and incorporating changes by other members of the drafting committee; it differs in a few major and many minor respects from the version that Congress eventually adopted. These changes highlight some of the tensions in America over the ideological content of the Declaration; for example, Congress altered Jefferson's expressions of disappointment in the British Empire and completely removed a paragraph relating to slavery. The most significant differences between the draft and final versions are indicated below in footnotes.

When in the course of human events it becomes necessary for a people to advance from that subordination in which they have hitherto remained,[1] and to assume among the powers of the earth the equal and independent station to which the laws of nature and of nature's God entitle them, a decent respect to the opinions of mankind requires that they should declare the causes which impel them to the change.

We hold these truths to be self-evident; that all men are created equal and independent; that from that equal creation they derive rights inherent and inalienable, among which are the preservation of life, and liberty, and the pursuit of happiness;[2] that to secure these ends, governments are instituted among men, deriving their just powers from the consent of the governed; that whenever any form of government shall become destructive of these ends, it is the right of the people to alter or to abolish it, and to institute new government, laying its foundation on such principles and organizing its power in such form as to them shall seem most likely to effect their safety and happiness. Prudence indeed will dictate that governments long established should not be changed for light and transient causes: and accordingly all experience hath shown that mankind are more disposed to suffer while evils are sufferable, than to right themselves by abolishing the forms to which they are accustomed. But when a long train of abuses and usurpations, begun at a distinguished period, and pursuing invariably the same object, evinces a design to reduce them to absolute despotism, it is their right, it is their duty, to throw off such government and to provide new guards for future security. Such has been the patient sufferance of the colonies; and such is now the necessity which constrains them to expunge their former systems of government. The history of his present majesty[3] is a history of unremitting injuries and usurpations, among which no one fact stands single or solitary to contradict the uniform tenor of the rest,[4] all of which have in direct object the establishment of an absolute tyranny over these states. To prove this, let facts be submitted to a candid world, for the truth of which we pledge a faith yet unsullied by falsehood.[5]

He has refused his assent to laws the most wholesome and necessary for the public good.

He has forbidden his governors to pass laws of immediate and pressing importance, unless suspended in their operation till his assent should be obtained; and when so suspended, he has neglected utterly to attend to them.

He has refused to pass other laws for the accommodation of large districts of people unless those people would relinquish the right of representation in the legislature, a right inestimable to them and formidable to tyrants only:[6]

He has dissolved Representative Houses repeatedly and continually, for opposing with manly firmness his invasions on the rights of the people:

[1] *to advance … hitherto remained* The final version reads "to dissolve the political bands which have connected them with another."

[2] *created equal … of happiness* The final version reads "created equal, that they are endowed by their Creator with certain unalienable rights, that among these are life, liberty, and the pursuit of happiness."

[3] *his present majesty* The final version reads "the present King of Great Britain."

[4] *among which … the rest* These words are removed from the final version.

[5] *for the truth … by falsehood* These words are removed from the final version.

[6] *He has refused … tyrants only* In 1774, the elected government of the province of Quebec was replaced with an appointed one, and the new government refused to pass important laws until the people of Quebec stopped agitating for a return to the representative system. Similar changes were made to the government of Massachusetts; *tyrants only* In the final version, here is added the following complaint: "He has called together legislative bodies at places unusual, uncomfortable, and distant from the depository of their public records, for the sole purpose of fatiguing them into compliance with his measures." As retribution for the Boston Tea Party, the governor of Massachusetts forced its assembly to move to Salem, but kept the public records in Boston.

He has refused for a long time after such dissolutions to cause others to be elected, whereby the legislative powers, incapable of annihilation, have returned to the people at large for their exercise,[1] the state remaining in the meantime exposed to all the dangers of invasion from without and convulsions within:

He has endeavoured to prevent the population of these states; for that purpose obstructing the laws for naturalization for foreigners; refusing to pass others to encourage their migrations hither; and raising the conditions of new appropriations of lands:[2]

He has suffered the administration of justice totally to cease in some of these colonies,[3] refusing his assent to laws for establishing judiciary powers:

He has made our judges dependent on his will alone for the tenure of their offices and amount of their salaries:

He has erected a multitude of new offices by a self-assumed power,[4] and sent hither swarms of officers to harass our people and eat out their substance:

He has kept among us in times of peace standing armies and ships of war:[5]

He has affected to render the military independent of and superior to the civil power:[6]

He has combined with others to subject us to a jurisdiction foreign to our constitutions and unacknowledged by our laws; giving his assent to their pretended acts of legislation:

For quartering large bodies of armed troops among us;

For protecting them by a mock-trial from punishment for any murders which they should commit on the inhabitants of these states;

For cutting off our trade with all parts of the world;

For imposing taxes on us without our consent;

For depriving us of the benefits of trial by jury;

For transporting us beyond seas to be tried for pretended offenses;[7]

For taking away our charters,[8] and altering fundamentally the forms of our governments;

For suspending our own legislatures and declaring themselves invested with power to legislate for us in all cases whatsoever:

He has abdicated government here, withdrawing his governors, and declaring us out of his allegiance and protection:[9]

He has plundered our seas, ravaged our coasts, burnt our towns and destroyed the lives of our people:

He is at this time transporting large armies of foreign mercenaries[10] to complete the works of death, desolation and tyranny, already begun with circumstances of cruelty and perfidy unworthy the head[11] of a civilized nation:

He has endeavoured to bring on the inhabitants of our frontiers the merciless Indian savages, whose known rule of warfare is an undistinguished destruction of all ages, sexes, and conditions of existence:

[1] *the legislative … their exercise* I.e., because the people's right to good laws cannot be extinguished, but the government is prevented from exercising it on their behalf, the people are justified in undertaking government for themselves.

[2] *raising the conditions … of lands* I.e., making it more difficult for new immigrants to obtain frontier land, thus discouraging immigration.

[3] *suffered the … these colonies* The final version reads "obstructed the administration of justice, by."

[4] *by a self-assumed power* These words are removed from the final version.

[5] *and ships of war* The final version reads "without the consent of our legislatures."

[6] *He has affected … civil power* By an order of the King, the power of the military commander-in-chief for the colonies superseded the power of all civil government in America.

[7] *For transporting … pretended offenses* A 1774 Massachusetts bill entitled the magistrate to send accused criminals to England to be tried; of course, before the trial occurred, it could not be determined whether a transported prisoner was innocent or guilty; *pretended offenses* Here, the following complaint is added in the final version: "For abolishing the free system of English laws in a neighbouring province, establishing therein an arbitrary government, and enlarging its boundaries so as to render it at once an example and fit instrument for introducing the same absolute rule into these colonies." The 1774 changes to the government of Quebec were seen as a means to appease the powerful Catholics there, in order to ensure the province's military allegiance in case of an American rebellion.

[8] *our charters* In the final version, here is added "abolishing our most valuable laws."

[9] *withdrawing his … and protection* The final version reads "by declaring us out of his protection and waging war against us."

[10] *foreign mercenaries* The British hired many thousands of German soldiers to help fight the American rebels.

[11] *unworthy the head* The final version reads "scarcely paralleled in the most barbarous ages, and totally unworthy the head."

He has incited treasonable insurrections in our fellow-citizens, with the allurements of forfeiture and confiscation of our property:[1]

He has waged cruel war against human nature itself, violating its most sacred rights of life and liberty in the persons of a distant people who never offended him, captivating and carrying them into slavery in another hemisphere, or to incur miserable death in their transportation thither. This piratical warfare, the opprobrium of infidel powers, is the warfare of the CHRISTIAN king of Great Britain. Determined to keep open a market where MEN should be bought and sold, he has prostituted his negative for suppressing every legislative attempt to prohibit or to restrain this execrable commerce:[2] and that this assemblage of horrors might want no fact of distinguished dye,[3] he is now exciting those very people to rise in arms among us,[4] and to purchase that liberty of which he has deprived them by murdering the people upon whom he also obtruded them: thus paying off former crimes committed against the liberties of one people with crimes which he urges them to commit against the lives of another.[5]

In every stage of these oppressions we have petitioned for redress in the most humble terms; our repeated petitions have been answered by repeated injury. A prince whose character is thus marked by every act which may define a tyrant is unfit to be the ruler of a people who mean to be free.[6] Future ages will scarce believe that the hardiness of one man adventured, within the short compass of twelve years only, on so many acts of tyranny without a mask, over a people fostered and fixed in principles of liberty.[7]

Nor have we been wanting in attentions to our British brethren. We have warned them from time to time of attempts by their legislature to extend a jurisdiction over these our states.[8] We have reminded them of the circumstances of our emigration and settlement here, no one of which could warrant so strange a pretension:[9] that these were effected at the expense of our own blood and treasure, unassisted by the wealth or the strength of Great Britain: that in constituting indeed our several forms of government, we had adopted one common king, thereby laying a foundation for perpetual league and amity with them: but that submission to their parliament was no part of our constitution, nor ever in idea, if history may be credited: and[10] we appealed to their native justice and magnanimity, as well as to the ties of our common kindred to disavow these usurpations which were likely to[11] interrupt our correspondence and connection. They too have been deaf to the voice of justice and of consanguinity,[12] and when occasions have been given them, by the regular course of their laws, of removing from their councils the disturbers of our harmony, they have by their free election re-established them in power. At this very time too they are permitting their chief magistrate to send over not only soldiers of our common blood, but Scotch and foreign mercenaries to invade and deluge us in blood. These facts have given the last stab to agonizing affection, and manly spirit bids us to renounce forever these unfeeling brethren. We must endeavour to forget our former love for them, and to hold them as we hold the rest of mankind, enemies in war, in peace friends. We

[1] *He has endeavoured ... our property* The final version reads: "He has constrained our fellow citizens taken captive on the high seas to bear arms against their country, to become the executioners of their friends and brethren, or to fall themselves by their hands.

"He has excited domestic insurrections among us, and has endeavoured to bring on the inhabitants of our frontiers the merciless Indian savages, whose known rule of warfare is an undistinguished destruction of all ages, sexes and conditions."

[2] *prostituted his ... execrable commerce* The king had vetoed resolutions against the slave trade—primarily at the insistence of slave-owners in the southern colonies.

[3] *want no ... distinguished dye* I.e., lack no equally reprehensible element.

[4] *he is now ... among us* The British government offered freedom to slaves who escaped their rebel masters and joined the war on the British side.

[5] *He has waged ... of another* This paragraph does not appear in the final version.

[6] *a people ... be free* The final version reads: "a free people."

[7] *Future ages ... of liberty* This sentence does not appear in the final version.

[8] *a jurisdiction ... our states* The final version reads: "an unwarrantable jurisdiction over us."

[9] *so strange a pretension* I.e., the notion that the people of the Thirteen Colonies were subject to the English Parliament as opposed to their own.

[10] *no one of which ... credited: and* These words do not appear in the final version.

[11] *were likely to* The final version reads: "would inevitably."

[12] *consanguinity* Commonality of blood.

might have been a free and a great people together; but a communication of grandeur and of freedom it seems is below their dignity. Be it so, since they will have it; the road to happiness and to glory is open to us too; we will climb it apart from them, and acquiesce in the necessity which denounces our eternal separation![1]

We therefore the representatives of the United States of America in General Congress assembled[2] do, in the name and by authority of the good people of these states, reject and renounce all allegiance and subjection to the kings of Great Britain and all others who may hereafter claim by, through, or under them; we utterly dissolve and break off all political connection which may have heretofore subsisted between us and the people or parliament of Great Britain; and finally we do assert and declare these colonies to be free and independent states,[3] and that as free and independent states they shall hereafter[4] have full power to levy war, conclude peace, contract alliances, establish commerce, and to do all other acts and things which independent states may of right do. And for the support of this declaration[5] we mutually pledge to each other our lives, our fortunes, and our sacred honour.

from Thomas Paine, *The American Crisis* (1777)

Born in England, Thomas Paine immigrated to the Thirteen Colonies in 1774 and became a citizen of Pennsylvania just in time for the beginning of the Revolutionary War. His bestselling pamphlets *Common Sense* and *The American Crisis* were hugely important in exciting public opinion in support of the war. He later returned to England, where he wrote *Rights of Man* in support of the French Revolution.[6]

NUMBER 1

These are the times that try men's souls. The summer soldier and the sunshine patriot will, in this crisis, shrink from the service of his country, but he that stands it now deserves the love and thanks of man and woman. Tyranny, like hell, is not easily conquered; yet we have this consolation with us, that the harder the conflict, the more glorious the triumph. What we obtain too cheap, we esteem too lightly; 'tis dearness only that gives everything its value. Heaven knows how to set a proper price upon its goods; and it would be strange indeed, if so celestial an article as freedom should not be highly rated. Britain, with an army to enforce her tyranny, has declared, that she has a right (not only to tax) but "to bind us in all cases whatsoever,"[7] and if being bound in that manner is not slavery, then is there not such a thing as slavery upon earth. Even the expression is impious, for so unlimited a power can belong only to GOD.

Whether the independence of the Continent was declared too soon, or delayed too long, I will not now enter into as an argument; my own simple opinion is that had it been eight months earlier, it would have been much better. We did not make a proper use of last winter, neither could we, while we were in a dependent state. However, the fault, if it were one, was all our own; we have none to blame but ourselves. But no great deal is lost yet; all that Howe[8] has been doing for this month past is rather a ravage than a conquest, which the spirit of the Jersies[9] a year ago would have quickly repulsed,

[1] *and when occasions ... eternal separation* The final version reads: "We must, therefore, acquiesce in the necessity which denounces our separation, and hold them, as we hold the rest of mankind, enemies in war, in peace friends."

[2] *assembled* In the final version, here is added "appealing to the supreme judge of the world for the rectitude of our intentions."

[3] *of these states ... independent states* The final version reads: "of these colonies, solemnly publish and declare that these united colonies are, and of right ought to be, free and independent states; that they are absolved from all allegiance to the British Crown, and that all political connection between them and the state of Great Britain is and ought to be totally dissolved."

[4] *shall hereafter* These words do not appear in the final version.

[5] *declaration* In the final version, here is added "with a firm reliance on the protection of divine Providence."

[6] *Rights of ... Revolution* See Paine's *Rights of Man*, excerpted in the online component of this anthology, volume 4.

[7] *to bind ... whatsoever* Reference to a statement made in the Declaratory Act (1766): "[the British government] had, hath, and of right ought to have, full power and authority to make laws and statutes of sufficient force and validity to bind the colonies and people of America, subjects of the crown of Great Britain, in all cases whatsoever."

[8] *Howe* Sir William Howe (1729–1814), commander of the British forces during the War of Independence.

[9] *Jersies* Colonies of East and West Jersey; Paine is referring to Washington's successful surprise attack on Christmas Day of the previous year.

and which time and a little resolution will soon recover.

I have as little superstition in me as any man living, but my secret opinion has ever been, and still is, that GOD almighty will not give up a people to military destruction, or leave them unsupported to perish, who had so earnestly and so repeatedly sought to avoid the calamities of war by every decent method which wisdom could invent. Neither have I so much of the infidel in me as to suppose that He has relinquished the government of the world, and given us up to the care of devils; and as I do not, I cannot see on what grounds the king of Britain can look up to Heaven for help against us: a common murderer, a highwayman, or a housebreaker, has as good a pretence as he.

John Singleton Copley, *The Death of Major Peirson, 6 January 1781* (1783). France provided unofficial assistance to the Americans from the beginning of the Revolutionary War, but by the end of the war it was openly fighting against the English, as were Spain and the Dutch Republic. Battles related to the Revolutionary War occurred in India, the West Indies, and even in Europe; this painting depicts the results of a battle on the island of Jersey, a British possession off the coast of France. The governor of Jersey surrendered after an attack by the French, but British major Francis Peirson refused to accept the surrender and organized the defeat of the French forces. He died early in the battle and never learned of his success, but this painting depicts him dying at the moment of victory. The artist, John Singleton Copley, was born in New England and painted portraits there before immigrating to England, where he painted this and other historical works. (See the color insert in this bound volume for another important example.)

from Richard Price, *Observations on the Importance of the American Revolution* (1785)

OF THE IMPORTANCE OF THE REVOLUTION WHICH HAS ESTABLISHED THE INDEPENDENCE OF THE UNITED STATES

Having, from pure conviction, taken a warm part in favour of the British colonies (now the United States of America) during the late war and been exposed, in consequence of this, to much abuse and some danger, it must be supposed that I have been waiting for the issue[1] with anxiety. I am thankful that my anxiety is removed and that I have been spared to be a witness to that very issue of the war which has been all along the object of my wishes. With heartfelt satisfaction I see the revolution in favour of universal liberty which has taken place in America, a revolution which opens a new prospect in human affairs and begins a new era in the history of mankind, a revolution by which Britons themselves will be the greatest gainers, if wise enough to improve properly the check that has been given to the despotism of their ministers, and to catch the flame of virtuous liberty which has saved their American brethren.

The late war, in its commencement and progress, did great good by disseminating just sentiments of the rights of mankind and the nature of legitimate government, by exciting a spirit of resistance to tyranny which has emancipated one European country and is likely to emancipate others, and by occasioning the establishment in America of forms of government more equitable and more liberal than any that the world has yet known. But, in its termination, the war has done still greater good by preserving the new governments from that destruction in which they must have been involved, had Britain conquered, by providing, in a sequestrated continent possessed of many singular advantages, a place of refuge for oppressed men in every region of the world, and by laying the foundation there of an empire which may be the seat of liberty, science and virtue, and from whence there is reason to hope these sacred blessings will spread till they become universal and the time arrives when kings and priests shall have no more power to oppress, and that ignominious slavery which has hitherto debased the world exterminated. I therefore think I see the hand of providence in the late war working for the general good.

Reason, as well as tradition and revelation, lead us to expect that a more improved and happy state of human affairs will take place before the consummation of all things.[2] The world has hitherto been gradually improving. Light and knowledge have been gaining ground, and human life at present, compared with what it once was, is much the same that a youth approaching to manhood is compared with an infant....

OF THE NEGRO TRADE AND SLAVERY

The negro trade cannot be censured in language too severe. It is a traffic which, as it has been hitherto carried on, is shocking to humanity, cruel, wicked, and diabolical. I am happy to find that the United States are entering into measures for discountenancing[3] it and for abolishing the odious slavery which it has introduced. Till they have done this, it will not appear they deserve the liberty for which they have been contending. For it is self-evident that if there are any men whom they have a right to hold in slavery, there may be others who have had a right to hold them in slavery. I am sensible, however, that this is a work which they cannot accomplish at once. The emancipation of the negroes must, I suppose, be left in some measure to be the effect of time and of manners. But nothing can excuse the United States if it is not done with as much speed, and at the same time with as much effect, as their particular circumstances and situation will allow. I rejoice that on this occasion I can recommend to them the example of my own country. In Britain, a negro becomes a freeman the moment he sets his foot on British ground.[4]

[1] *issue* I.e., the resolution of the conflict.

[2] *consummation of all things* End of the world as foretold in the Bible.

[3] *discountenancing* Discouraging.

[4] *In Britain ... British ground* Reference to a 1772 court ruling (Somersett's Case) that effectively outlawed the keeping of slaves in England. English people, however, continued to own slaves in other parts of the British Empire.

Oliver Goldsmith

1730 – 1774

Oliver Goldsmith arguably displayed less early promise than any of the leading figures of English literary history, yet eventually produced some of the most important writing of his time.

Goldsmith was probably born in 1730 in a small village in Ireland, the fifth of eight children born to Charles Goldsmith, a poor rural Anglican minister, and his wife Ann. The family was originally English, but had been settled in Ireland for several generations. At the age of two Goldsmith moved with his family to Lissoy in County Westmeath, in the center of Ireland, a village that was to appear under different names in his later writing.

He attended various schools but was never an outstanding student. His academic career did not improve when he entered Trinity College, Dublin, in 1745; he was ranked lowest on the list of those who had passed the entrance exam. Because his family had little money, Goldsmith served while at Trinity as a sizar—a student who helped to pay for his tuition and lodging by waiting on tables and performing other services for wealthier students. At one point he ran away from college after being caught hosting a rowdy party in his rooms, but he was escorted back by his brother. Goldsmith graduated from Trinity in 1750, again at the bottom of his class.

After he graduated, his relatives urged him to follow his father's lead and enter the clergy, but his application for ordination was rejected. Over the next ten years there followed a series of abortive attempts at finding a career. He tried tutoring and then returned to new studies himself, this time at law. When that did not suit, Goldsmith attempted to emigrate to America, but he missed his departure time, and the ship left without him. He chose finally to study medicine, funded by relatives. He studied in Edinburgh for a while, but then left to continue his studies at the University of Leyden, Holland, in 1754. Goldsmith stayed in Leyden until his money ran out, then wandered for two years through France, Switzerland, Germany, and Italy, earning his living teaching English, gambling, and performing songs for villagers. In 1756 he returned to England with no money, but with a medical degree ostensibly completed somewhere in Europe. He tried to practice medicine for a while, but was ultimately unsuccessful.

Goldsmith's fortunes changed when he began writing for *The Monthly Review*, a London periodical. Over the next few years, Goldsmith earned his living as a hack writer, dashing off reviews and critical essays for a number of London periodicals. His first real writing success came in 1759 with the publication of a short book, *An Enquiry into the Present State of Polite Learning in Europe*, a treatise lamenting the demise of the patronage system for artists. He also wrote a series of popular and lucrative history books. Goldsmith was a socially awkward man and never married, but in the London literary world he found himself part of an artistic and intellectual circle called the Club, where he mingled with influential men such as Samuel Johnson, David Garrick, Edmund Burke, and Edward Gibbon.

Over the next dozen years Goldsmith displayed extraordinary range as a writer. His novel *The Vicar of Wakefield* (1766), a tale of fine moral sensibility about a clergyman and his family who suffer every possible kind of adversity and bad luck, became one of the most widely read and influential works of eighteenth-century fiction. (Critics are still in disagreement as to how far the calamities in this book can be seen as comic.) He wrote two popular comedies, *The Good-Natured Man* (1768) and *She Stoops to Conquer* (1773); like Sheridan's *The School for Scandal* both mock the "weeping sentimental comedy so much in fashion at present" (to borrow the phrasing Goldsmith used in his influential "An Essay on the Theatre"). Goldsmith's plays vie with those of Sheridan as the most popular late-eighteenth century plays for today's stage. Of his works in verse the most substantial are the philosophic poem *The Traveller* (1764) and *The Deserted Village* (1770).

The Deserted Village is very much a product of Goldsmith's time and place. He wrote on the cusp of a major social and economic transition in England, when the labor force was beginning to move from agriculture to industry. This transition was expedited by the British government, which passed a number of Acts of Enclosure between 1760 and 1830—legislation that privatized common pasturelands for purchase by major landowners. These changes in ownership created severe hardship for many agricultural laborers, who had relied on supplementing their wages by keeping livestock and gathering firewood for heating and cooking on common land. As a result, many laborers left their villages and either moved to the cities to look for work in factories or as servants, or emigrated to British colonies. Such was the context for Goldsmith's elegiac poem.

Goldsmith made a significant amount of money from his writing. He lived extravagantly, however, spending on himself, giving away a good deal of money to others, and struggling constantly with debt; Samuel Johnson memorably said of Goldsmith: "no man was more foolish when he had not a pen in his hand, or more wise when he had." He still owed £2000, a very large sum during a time when a modest income was £70 a year, when he died of a fever on 4 April 1774. He was buried in the grounds of the Church of St. Mary (known as The Temple) in London.

⌘⌘⌘

The Deserted Village

Sweet Auburn![1] loveliest village of the plain,
Where health and plenty cheered the labouring swain,° *countryman*
Where smiling spring its earliest visit paid,
And parting summer's lingering blooms delayed:
Dear lovely bowers of innocence and ease,
Seats of my youth, when every sport could please,
How often have I loitered o'er thy green,
Where humble happiness endeared each scene;
How often have I paused on every charm,
The sheltered cot,° the cultivated farm, *cottage*
The never-failing brook, the busy mill,
The decent church that topped the neighbouring hill,
The hawthorn bush, with seats beneath the shade,
For talking age and whisp'ring lovers made;
How often have I blessed the coming day,
When toil remitting lent its turn to play,
And all the village train,° from labour free, *people, retinue*
Led up° their sports beneath the spreading tree, *began*
While many a pastime circled in the shade,
The young contending as the old surveyed;
And many a gambol frolicked o'er the ground,
And sleights of art and feats of strength went round;
And still, as each repeated pleasure tired,
Succeeding sports the mirthful band inspired;
The dancing pair that simply sought renown
By holding out to tire each other down;
The swain mistrustless° of his smutted face, *unsuspecting*
While secret laughter tittered round the place;
The bashful virgin's sidelong looks of love,
The matron's glance that would those looks reprove:
These were thy charms, sweet village! Sports like these,
With sweet succession, taught e'en toil to please;

[1] *Auburn* There is an Auburn in Wiltshire and one in Lincolnshire, though it is likely that Goldsmith's town is meant to be fictitious.

These round thy bowers their cheerful influence shed,
These were thy charms—But all these charms are fled.
Sweet smiling village, loveliest of the lawn,° *glade*
Thy sports are fled, and all thy charms withdrawn;
Amidst thy bowers the tyrant's hand is seen,
And desolation saddens all thy green:
One only master grasps the whole domain,
And half a tillage[1] stints° thy smiling plain. *confines*
No more thy glassy brook reflects the day,
But, choked with sedges,[2] works its weedy way;
Along thy glades, a solitary guest,
The hollow-sounding bittern[3] guards its nest;
Amidst thy desert walks the lapwing flies,
And tires their echoes with unvaried cries.
Sunk are thy bowers, in shapeless ruin all,
And the long grass o'ertops the mold'ring wall;
And trembling, shrinking from the spoiler's hand,
Far, far away, thy children leave the land.
Ill fares the land, to hastening ills a prey,
Where wealth accumulates, and men decay.
Princes and lords may flourish, or may fade;
A breath can make them, as a breath has made;
But a bold peasantry, their country's pride,
When once destroyed, can never be supplied.
A time there was, ere England's griefs began,
When every rood° of ground maintained its man; *quarter acre*
For him light labour spread her wholesome store,
Just gave what life required, but gave no more:
His best companions, innocence and health;
And his best riches, ignorance of wealth.
But times are altered; trade's unfeeling train
Usurp the land and dispossess the swain;
Along the lawn, where scattered hamlets rose,
Unwieldy wealth and cumbrous pomp repose;
And every want to opulence allied,
And every pang that folly pays to pride.
Those gentle hours that plenty bade to bloom,
Those calm desires that asked but little room,
Those healthful sports that graced the peaceful scene,
Lived in each look, and brightened all the green;
These, far departing, seek a kinder shore,
And rural mirth and manners are no more.
Sweet Auburn! parent of the blissful hour,
Thy glades forlorn confess the tyrant's power.
Here, as I take my solitary rounds,
Amidst thy tangling walks and ruined grounds,
And, many a year elapsed, return to view
Where once the cottage stood, the hawthorn grew,
Remembrance wakes with all her busy train,
Swells at my breast, and turns the past to pain.
In all my wand'rings round this world of care,
In all my griefs—and God has giv'n my share—
I still had hopes my latest hours to crown,
Amidst these humble bowers to lay me down;
To husband out life's taper[4] at the close,
And keep the flame from wasting by repose.
I still had hopes, for pride attends us still,
Amidst the swains to show my book-learned skill,
Around my fire an evening group to draw,
And tell of all I felt and all I saw;
And, as a hare whom hounds and horns pursue
Pants to the place from whence at first she flew,
I still had hopes, my long vexations past,
Here to return—and die at home at last.
O blessed retirement, friend to life's decline,
Retreats from care that never must be mine,
How happy he who crowns in shades like these,
A youth of labour with an age of ease;
Who quits a world where strong temptations try,
And, since 'tis hard to combat, learns to fly!
For him no wretches, born to work and weep,
Explore the mine, or tempt the dang'rous deep;
No surly porter stands in guilty state
To spurn imploring famine from the gate;
But on he moves to meet his latter end,
Angels around befriending virtue's friend;
Bends to the grave with unperceived decay,
While Resignation gently slopes the way;
And, all his prospects bright'ning to the last,
His Heav'n commences ere the world be past!
Sweet was the sound when oft at evening's close
Up yonder hill the village murmur rose.
There, as I passed with careless steps and slow,
The mingling notes came softened from below;

[1] *tillage* Area of tilled land.

[2] *sedges* Coarse, rush-like plants that grow together en masse in wet places.

[3] *bittern* Small, heron-like bird known for its booming call.

[4] *To husband out* To economize something, use something frugally so that it lasts a long time; *taper* Candle.

The swain responsive as the milkmaid sung,
The sober herd that lowed to meet their young,
The noisy geese that gabbled o'er the pool,
The playful children just let loose from school,
The watchdog's voice that bayed the whisp'ring wind,
And the loud laugh that spoke the vacant[1] mind;
These all in sweet confusion sought the shade,
And filled each pause the nightingale had made.
But now the sounds of population fail,
No cheerful murmurs fluctuate in the gale,
No busy steps the grass-grown footway tread,
For all the bloomy flush of life is fled.
All but yon widowed, solitary thing
That feebly bends beside the plashy° spring; *swampy*
She, wretched matron, forced, in age, for bread,
To strip the brook, with mantling° cresses[2] spread, *enveloping*
To pick her wintry faggot° from the thorn, *firewood*
To seek her nightly shed, and weep till morn;
She only left of all the harmless train,
The sad historian of the pensive plain.
Near yonder copse, where once the garden smiled,
And still where many a garden flower grows wild,
There, where a few torn shrubs the place disclose,
The village preacher's modest mansion rose.
A man he was to all the country dear,
And passing rich with forty pounds a year;
Remote from towns he ran his godly race,
Nor e'er had changed, nor wished to change his place;
Unpractised he to fawn, or seek for power
By doctrines fashioned to the varying hour;
Far other aims his heart had learned to prize,
More skilled to raise the wretched than to rise.
His house was known to all the vagrant train;
He chid their wand'rings but relieved their pain;
The long remembered beggar was his guest,
Whose beard descending swept his aged breast;
The ruined spendthrift, now no longer proud,
Claimed kindred there, and had his claims allowed;
The broken soldier, kindly bade to stay,
Sate by his fire and talked the night away;
Wept o'er his wounds, or tales of sorrow done,
Shouldered his crutch, and showed how fields were won.
Pleased with his guests, the good man learned to glow,
And quite forgot their vices in their woe;
Careless their merits, or their faults to scan,
His pity gave ere charity began.
Thus to relieve the wretched was his pride,
And e'en his failings leaned to Virtue's side;
But in his duty prompt at every call,
He watched and wept, he prayed and felt, for all;
And, as a bird each fond endearment tries,
To tempt its new-fledged offspring to the skies,
He tried each art, reproved each dull delay,
Allured to brighter worlds, and led the way.
Beside the bed where parting life was laid,
And sorrow, guilt, and pain, by turns dismayed,
The rev'rend champion stood. At his control,
Despair and anguish fled the struggling soul;
Comfort came down the trembling wretch to raise,
And his last falt'ring accents whispered praise.
At church, with meek and unaffected grace,
His looks adorned the venerable place;
Truth from his lips prevailed with double sway,
And fools, who came to scoff, remained to pray.
The service past, around the pious man,
With steady zeal each honest rustic ran;
E'en children followed with endearing wile,
And plucked his gown to share the good man's smile.
His ready smile a parent's warmth expressed,
Their welfare pleased him, and their cares distressed;
To them his heart, his love, his griefs were given,
But all his serious thoughts had rest in Heaven.
As some tall cliff that lifts its awful form,
Swells from the vale, and midway leaves the storm,
Though round its breast the rolling clouds are spread,
Eternal sunshine settles on its head.
Beside yon straggling fence that skirts the way,
With blossomed furze[3] unprofitably gay,
There, in his noisy mansion, skilled to rule,
The village master taught his little school.
A man severe he was, and stern to view;
I knew him well, and every truant knew;
Well had the boding tremblers learned to trace
The day's disasters in his morning face;
Full well they laughed with counterfeited glee,
At all his jokes, for many a joke had he;
Full well the busy whisper circling round,

[1] *vacant* Idle, free from anxiety.

[2] *cresses* Type of water plant with edible leaves.

[3] *furze* Gorse, a prickly plant with yellow flowers.

Conveyed the dismal tidings when he frowned;
Yet he was kind, or if severe in aught,
The love he bore to learning was in fault;
The village all declared how much he knew;
'Twas certain he could write, and cipher° too: *do arithmetic*
Lands he could measure, terms and tides[1] presage,
And ev'n the story ran that he could gauge.[2]
In arguing too, the parson owned his skill,
For, ev'n though vanquished, he could argue still;
While words of learned length and thundering sound
Amazed the gazing rustics ranged around;
And still they gazed, and still the wonder grew,
That one small head could carry all he knew.
    But past is all his fame. The very spot
Where many a time he triumphed, is forgot.
Near yonder thorn, that lifts its head on high,
Where once the signpost caught the passing eye,
Low lies that house where nut-brown draughts[3] inspired,
Where greybeard Mirth and smiling Toil retired,
Where village statesmen talked with looks profound,
And news much older than their ale went round.
Imagination fondly stoops to trace
The parlour splendours of that festive place:
The whitewashed wall, the nicely-sanded floor,
The varnished clock that clicked behind the door;
The chest contrived a double debt to pay,
A bed by night, a chest of drawers by day;
The pictures placed for ornament and use,
The twelve good rules, the royal game of goose;[4]
The hearth, except when winter chilled the day,
With aspen boughs, and flowers, and fennel gay,
While broken teacups, wisely kept for show,
Ranged o'er the chimney, glistened in a row.
    Vain transitory splendours! Could not all
Reprieve the tottering mansion from its fall!
Obscure it sinks, nor shall it more impart
An hour's importance to the poor man's heart;
Thither no more the peasant shall repair
To sweet oblivion of his daily care;
No more the farmer's news, the barber's tale,
No more the woodman's ballad shall prevail;
No more the smith his dusky brow shall clear,
Relax his pond'rous strength, and lean to hear;
The host himself no longer shall be found
Careful to see the mantling bliss[5] go round;
Nor the coy maid, half willing to be pressed,
Shall kiss the cup to pass it to the rest.
    Yes! let the rich deride, the proud disdain,
These simple blessings of the lowly train,
To me more dear, congenial to my heart,
One native charm, than all the gloss of art;
Spontaneous joys, where nature has its play,
The soul adopts, and owns their first-born sway;
Lightly they frolic o'er the vacant mind,
Unenvied, unmolested, unconfined.
But the long pomp, the midnight masquerade,
With all the freaks of wanton wealth arrayed,
In these, ere triflers half their wish obtain,
The toiling pleasure sickens into pain;
And, e'en while fashion's brightest arts decoy,
The heart distrusting asks, if this be joy.
    Ye friends to truth, ye statesmen, who survey
The rich man's joys increase, the poor's decay,
'Tis yours to judge how wide the limits stand
Between a splendid and a happy land.
Proud swells the tide with loads of freighted ore,
And shouting Folly hails them from her shore;
Hoards e'en beyond the miser's wish abound,
And rich men flock from all the world around.
Yet count our gains. This wealth is but a name
That leaves our useful products still the same.
Not so the loss. The man of wealth and pride
Takes up a space that many poor supplied;
Space for his lake, his park's extended bounds,
Space for his horses, equipage, and hounds;
The robe that wraps his limbs in silken sloth
Has robbed the neighb'ring fields of half their growth;
His seat, where solitary sports are seen,
Indignant spurns the cottage from the green;
Around the world each needful product flies,
For all the luxuries the world supplies.

[1] *terms* Fixed days on which rent, wages, and other dues were to be paid; *tides* Festivals and anniversaries of the church, which fell on different days each year.

[2] *gauge* Determine the capacity of casks, barrels, or other vessels.

[3] *house* Inn; *draughts* Beer.

[4] *twelve good rules* Rules of good conduct, attributed to Charles I, that were commonly displayed on posters in taverns; *goose* Popular board game played with dice.

[5] *mantling bliss* Foaming ale.

While thus the land adorned for pleasure all
In barren splendor feebly waits the fall.
As some fair female unadorned and plain,
Secure to please while youth confirms her reign,
Slights every borrowed charm that dress supplies,
Nor shares with art the triumph of her eyes;
But when those charms are past, for charms are frail,
When time advances, and when lovers fail,
She then shines forth, solicitous to bless,
In all the glaring impotence of dress;
Thus fares the land, by luxury betrayed;
In nature's simplest charms at first arrayed;
But verging to decline, its splendours rise,
Its vistas strike, its palaces surprise;
While scourged by famine from the smiling land,
The mournful peasant leads his humble band;
And while he sinks without one arm to save,
The country blooms—a garden, and a grave.
Where then, ah where, shall poverty reside,
To 'scape the pressure of contiguous pride?
If to some common's fenceless limits strayed,
He drives his flock to pick the scanty blade,
Those fenceless fields the sons of wealth divide,
And ev'n the bare-worn common is denied.
If to the city sped—what waits him there?
To see profusion that he must not share;
To see ten thousand baneful arts combined
To pamper luxury, and thin mankind;
To see those joys the sons of pleasure know,
Extorted from his fellow-creature's woe.
Here, while the courtier glitters in brocade,
There the pale artist° plies his sickly trade; *artisan*
Here, while the proud their long drawn pomps display,
There the black gibbet° glooms beside the way. *gallows*
The dome where Pleasure holds her midnight reign,
Here, richly decked, admits the gorgeous train;
Tumultuous grandeur crowds the blazing square,
The rattling chariots clash, the torches glare.
Sure, scenes like these no troubles e'er annoy!
Sure these denote one universal joy!
Are these thy serious thoughts?—Ah, turn thine eyes
Where the poor houseless shiv'ring female lies.
She once, perhaps, in village plenty blessed,
Has wept at tales of innocence distressed;
Her modest looks the cottage might adorn,
Sweet as the primrose peeps beneath the thorn;
Now lost to all; her friends, her virtue fled,
Near her betrayer's door she lays her head,
And pinched with cold and shrinking from the shower,
With heavy heart deplores that luckless hour,
When idly first, ambitious of the town,
She left her wheel° and robes of country brown. *spinning wheel*
Do thine, sweet Auburn, thine, the loveliest train,
Do thy fair tribes participate her pain?
Ev'n now, perhaps, by cold and hunger led,
At proud men's doors they ask a little bread!
Ah, no. To distant climes, a dreary scene,
Where half the convex world intrudes between,
Through torrid tracts with fainting steps they go,
Where wild Altama[1] murmurs to their woe.
Far different there from all that charm'd before,
The various terrors of that horrid shore;
Those blazing suns that dart a downward ray,
And fiercely shed intolerable day;
Those matted woods where birds forget to sing,
But silent bats in drowsy clusters cling;
Those pois'nous fields with rank luxuriance crowned,
Where the dark scorpion gathers death around;
Where at each step the stranger fears to wake
The rattling terrors of the vengeful snake;
Where crouching tigers[2] wait their hapless prey,
And savage men, more murd'rous still than they;
While oft in whirls the mad tornado flies,
Mingling the ravaged landscape with the skies.
Far different these from every former scene,
The cooling brook, the grassy-vested green,
The breezy covert of the warbling grove,
That only sheltered thefts of harmless love.
Good Heaven! what sorrows gloom'd that parting day
That called them from their native walks away;
When the poor exiles, every pleasure past,
Hung round their bowers, and fondly looked their last,
And took a long farewell, and wished in vain
For seats like these beyond the western main;
And, shudd'ring still to face the distant deep,
Returned and wept, and still returned to weep.

---

[1] *Altama* Altamaha River, in the southeast of what was then the British colony of Georgia.

[2] *tigers* Goldsmith does not mean the tiger, which is native to Asia, but the American cougar, or puma.

The good old sire, the first prepared to go
To new-found worlds, and wept for others' woe.
But for himself, in conscious virtue brave,
He only wished for worlds beyond the grave.
His lovely daughter, lovelier in her tears,
The fond companion of his helpless years,
Silent went next, neglectful of her charms,
And left a lover's for a father's arms:
With louder plaints the mother spoke her woes,
And blest the cot where every pleasure rose;
And kissed her thoughtless babes with many a tear,
And clasped them close in sorrow doubly dear;
Whilst her fond husband strove to lend relief
In all the silent manliness of grief.
O, luxury! thou curst by Heaven's decree,
How ill exchanged are things like these for thee!
How do thy potions, with insidious joy,
Diffuse their pleasures only to destroy!
Kingdoms, by thee, to sickly greatness grown,
Boast of a florid vigour not their own.
At every draught more large and large they grow,
A bloated mass of rank unwieldy woe;
Till, sapped their strength, and every part unsound,
Down, down they sink, and spread a ruin round.
Ev'n now the devastation is begun,
And half the business of destruction done;
Ev'n now, methinks, as pond'ring here I stand,
I see the rural Virtues leave the land.
Down where yon anchoring vessel spreads the sail,
That idly waiting flaps with every gale,
Downward they move, a melancholy band,
Pass from the shore, and darken all the strand.
Contented Toil, and hospitable Care,
And kind connubial Tenderness are there;
And Piety, with wishes placed above,
And steady Loyalty, and faithful Love.
And thou, sweet Poetry, thou loveliest maid,
Still first to fly where sensual joys invade;
Unfit in these degenerate times of shame,
To catch the heart, or strike for honest fame;
Dear charming Nymph, neglected and decried,
My shame in crowds, my solitary pride;
Thou source of all my bliss, and all my woe,
That found'st me poor at first, and keep'st me so;
Thou guide by which the nobler arts excel,
Thou nurse of every virtue, fare thee well.
Farewell, and O! where'er thy voice be tried,
On Torno's cliffs, or Pambamarca's[1] side,
Whether where equinoctial fervours[2] glow,
Or winter wraps the polar world in snow,
Still let thy voice, prevailing over time,
Redress the rigours of th' inclement clime;
Aid slighted truth with thy persuasive strain
Teach erring man to spurn the rage of gain;
Teach him, that states of native strength possessed,
Though very poor, may still be very blessed;
That Trade's proud empire hastes to swift decay,
As ocean sweeps the laboured mole[3] away;
While self-dependent power can time defy,
As rocks resist the billows and the sky.[4]
—1770

[1] *Torno* Torne, a river in northern Sweden; *Pambamarca* A mountain in Ecuador.

[2] *equinoctial fervours* The heat of the tropics.

[3] *laboured mole* Laboriously constructed breakwater or pier.

[4] *That Trade's ... sky* These last four lines were added by Samuel Johnson.

William Cowper

1731 – 1800

William Cowper (pronounced Cooper) had an enormous readership during his generation, even though he spent most of his life in seclusion in the countryside, where he wrote the poems and letters for which he is best remembered. The inspiration for his best-known work came from his friend Lady Austen. When Cowper complained to her that he had nothing to write about, she suggested that he compose a poem in blank verse about his sofa. "The Sofa" did indeed become Book I of *The Task* (1785), engendering an extended work that is almost epic in its breadth of subject matter and style (while its domestic focus and absence of narrative are the very reverse of epic). *The Task* comprises six books, beginning with a playful narrative about the evolution of furniture, written in mock-heroic, Miltonic style. It moves on to myriad other subjects, including a meditation on the immorality of slavery (a subject about which the author felt passionately) and an extended celebration of domestic and rural life. Cowper is at his finest when meditating upon the significance of commonplace items and the details of lush, pastoral scenes, using unadorned language that has sometimes been said to foreshadow the style of the later Romantics. Indeed, Samuel Taylor Coleridge called Cowper "the best modern poet." In addition to *The Task*, he remains known for his varied range of short poems, for his comic narrative "The Diverting History of John Gilpin," and for the astonishing contrasts between his outwardly ordinary life and his inner despair.

Cowper was born in Berkampstead, Hertfordshire, to the Reverend John Cowper and Ann Donne, whose family claimed a kinship with the poet John Donne. She died when Cowper was only six, and he believed that his later problems with depression stemmed partly from this premature loss. Cowper's early difficulties were aggravated by the relentless bullying he suffered at the hands of his schoolmates in school. He eventually studied law, a profession ill-suited to him and which he never practiced. When a relative tried to help him procure a position as Clerk of the Journals in the House of Lords, Cowper was thrown into terror at the prospect of the interview he would be required to attend. This caused his first suicide attempt, upon which he was incarcerated in an asylum. During this period Cowper wrote "Lines Written During a Period of Insanity," which describes his growing fear of the wrath of God for the "sin" he had committed against the Holy Ghost: "Him [Satan] the vindictive rod of angry justice / Sent quick and howling to the centre headlong; / I, fed with judgement, in a fleshly tomb, am / Buried above ground." Although Cowper would eventually find some respite from his despair upon his conversion to Evangelicalism, when he lost his first ecstatic religious feelings he was convinced he was damned, and his despondency returned, increased.

In 1765 Cowper moved to the home of Reverend Morley and Mary Unwin in Huntingdon. After Morley Unwin died two years later, Cowper moved with Mary and her children to Olney; he lived with her for the rest of his life. He wrote two famous paeans to Mary—"My Mary" and "To Mary Unwin"; she in turn devotedly nursed him through his depressions and encouraged his literary work. In Olney he came under the influence of John Newton, a fiery Evangelical preacher and ex-slave trader, who helped stoke his religious angst. During the period in which Cowper was still under Newton's sway, the two co-authored the hauntingly beautiful *Olney Hymns* (written in 1771–72 and published in 1779), which include Newton's "Amazing Grace" and Cowper's "Oh for a closer walk with God" and "God moves in a mysterious way."

Although he spent his years in Olney and later in Weston Underwood in isolation, Cowper became one of the most celebrated poets of his time. His 1782 volume *Poems by William Cowper, of the Inner Temple, Esq.*, which included eight satires, was received with great enthusiasm, ironically enough, for its "cheerfulness of spirit." 1785 saw publication of *The Task*, Cowper's *tour de force*, again with a very favorable response (including, it was said, from the Royal Family). His later works include a translation of Homer's *The Iliad* (1791).

Upon leaving Olney, Cowper continued to write long and evocative letters to friends; these letters have since become famous for their descriptive beauty and the simplicity of their language. Mary Unwin's prolonged illness and her death in 1796 again pushed Cowper to the limits of his sanity, and he spent the remainder of his life as an invalid, dying in 1800. Before he died, though, he wrote "The Castaway," a powerful poem that likens his own situation, in which he expected his soul to perish in damnation, to that of a sailor swept overboard who can see his "floating home" but knows that it is powerless to stop for him and that he will drown. The poem speaks to its author's sense of being cast out from the community of the saved; it has remained one of his best-known works.

⌘⌘⌘

Light Shining Out of Darkness

God moves in a mysterious way,
His wonders to perform;
He plants his footsteps in the sea,
And rides upon the storm.

Deep in unfathomable mines
Of never failing skill;
He treasures up his bright designs,
And works his Sovereign Will.

Ye fearful Saints fresh courage take,
The clouds ye so much dread
Are big with Mercy, and shall break
In blessings on your head.

Judge not the Lord by feeble sense,
But trust him for his Grace;
Behind a frowning Providence,
He hides a smiling face.

His purposes will ripen fast,
Unfolding every hour;
The bud may have a bitter taste,
But *wait*, to *smell the flower*.

Blind unbelief is sure to err,
And scan his work in vain;
God is his own Interpreter,
And he will make it plain.

—1772

from *The Task*

ADVERTISEMENT

The history of the following production is briefly this. A lady, fond of blank verse, demanded a poem of that kind from the author, and gave him the sofa for a subject. He obeyed; and having much leisure, connected another subject with it; and pursuing the train of thought which his situation and turn of mind led him, brought forth at length, instead of the trifle which he at first intended, a serious affair—a Volume.

In the poem, on the subject of education he would be very sorry to stand suspected of having aimed his censure at any particular school. His objections are such as naturally apply themselves to schools in general. If there were not, as for the most part there is, wilful neglect in those who manage them, and an omission even of such discipline as they are susceptible of, the objects are yet too numerous for minute attention; and the aching hearts of ten thousand parents mourning under the bitterest disappointments, attest the truth of the allegation. His quarrel therefore is with the mischief at large, and not with any particular instance of it.

from Book 1: The Sofa

I sing the sofa. I, who lately sang
Truth, Hope, and Charity,[1] and touched with awe
The solemn chords, and with a trembling hand,
Escaped with pain from that advent'rous flight,
Now seek repose upon an humbler theme;
The theme though humble, yet august and proud
Th' occasion—for the Fair[2] commands the song.
   Time was, when clothing sumptuous or for use,
Save their own painted skins, our sires had none.
As yet black breeches were not; satin smooth,
Or velvet soft, or plush with shaggy pile:
The hardy chief upon the rugged rock
Washed by the sea, or on the grav'ly bank
Thrown up by wintry torrents roaring loud,
Fearless of wrong, reposed his weary strength.
Those barb'rous ages past, succeeded next
The birth-day of invention; weak at first,
Dull in design, and clumsy to perform.
Joint-stools were then created; on three legs
Upborn they stood. Three legs upholding firm
A massy slab, in fashion square or round.
On such a stool immortal Alfred[3] sat,
And swayed the sceptre of his infant realms:
And such in ancient halls and mansions drear
May still be seen; but perforated sore,
And drilled in holes, the solid oak is found,
By worms voracious eating through and through.
   At length a generation more refined
Improved the simple plan; made three legs four,
Gave them a twisted form vermicular,° *wormlike*
And o'er the seat, with plenteous wadding stuffed,
Induced a splendid cover, green and blue,
Yellow and red, of tap'stry richly wrought,
And woven close, or needle-work sublime.
There might ye see the peony spread wide,
The full-blown rose, the shepherd and his lass,
Lap-dog and lambkin with black staring eyes,
And parrots with twin cherries in their beak.
   Now came the cane from India, smooth and bright
With Nature's varnish; severed into stripes
That interlaced each other, these supplied
Of texture firm a lattice-work, that braced
The new machine, and it became a chair.
But restless was the chair; the back erect
Distressed the weary loins, that felt no ease;
The slipp'ry seat betrayed the sliding part
That press'd it, and the feet hung dangling down,
Anxious in vain to find the distant floor.
These for the rich: the rest, whom fate had placed
In modest mediocrity, content
With base materials, sat on well-tanned hides,
Obdurate and unyielding, glassy smooth,
With here and there a tuft of crimson yarn,
Or scarlet crewel,° in the cushion fixt; *embroidery yarn*
If cushion might be called, what harder seemed
Than the firm oak of which the frame was formed.
No want of timber then was felt or feared
In Albion's° happy isle. The lumber stood *England's*
Pond'rous and fixt by its own massy weight.
But elbows still were wanting; these, some say,
An alderman of Cripplegate contrived:
And some ascribe th' invention to a priest
Burly and big, and studious of his ease.
But, rude at first, and not with easy slope
Receding wide, they pressed against the ribs,
And bruised the side; and, elevated high,
Taught the raised shoulders to invade the ears.
Long time elapsed or e'er our rugged sires
Complained, though incommodiously pent in,
And ill at ease behind. The ladies first
'Gan murmur, as became the softer sex.
Ingenious fancy, never better pleased
Than when employed t' accommodate the fair,

[1] *Truth, Hope, and Charity* Cowper wrote a series of satires, three of which were named *Truth, Hope,* and *Charity.*

[2] *the Fair* A woman, or women. Here, one woman, she who asked for the poem (see "Advertised").

[3] *Alfred* King Alfred the Great of England (849–99).

Heard the sweet moan with pity, and devised
The soft settee; one elbow at each end,
And in the midst an elbow it received,
United yet divided, twain at once.
So sit two kings of Brentford[1] on one throne;
And so two citizens who take the air,
Close packed, and smiling, in a chaise and one.
But relaxation of the languid frame,
By soft recumbency of outstretched limbs,
Was bliss reserved for happier days. So slow
The growth of what is excellent; so hard
T' attain perfection in this nether world.
Thus first necessity invented stools,
Convenience next suggested elbow-chairs,
And luxury th' accomplished Sofa last.
 The nurse sleeps sweetly, hired to watch the sick,
Whom snoring she disturbs. As sweetly he,
Who quits the coach-box at the midnight hour
To sleep within the carriage more secure,
His legs depending at the open door.
Sweet sleep enjoys the curate in his desk,
The tedious rector drawling o'er his head;
And sweet the clerk below. But neither sleep
Of lazy nurse, who snores the sick man dead,
Nor his who quits the box at midnight hour
To slumber in the carriage more secure,
Nor sleep enjoyed by curate in his desk,
Nor yet the dozings of the clerk, are sweet,
Compared with the repose the SOFA yields.
 Oh may I live exempted (while I live
Guiltless of pampered appetite obscene)
From pangs arthritic, that infest the toe
Of libertine excess. The SOFA suits
The gouty limb, 'tis true; but gouty limb,
Though on a SOFA, may I never feel:
For I have loved the rural walk through lanes
Of grassy swarth, close cropped by nibbling sheep,
And skirted thick with intertexture firm
Of thorny boughs; have loved the rural walk
O'er hills, through valleys, and by rivers' brink,
E'er since a truant boy I passed my bounds
T' enjoy a ramble on the banks of Thames;
And still remember, nor without regret
Of hours that sorrow since has much endeared,
How oft, my slice of pocket store consumed,
Still hung'ring, pennyless and far from home,
I fed on scarlet hips and stony haws,[2]
Or blushing crabs, or berries, that emboss
The bramble, black as jet, or sloes[3] austere.
Hard fare! but such as boyish appetite
Disdains not; nor the palate, undepraved
By culinary arts, unsav'ry deems.
No SOFA then awaited my return;
Nor SOFA then I needed. Youth repairs
His wasted spirits quickly, by long toil
Incurring short fatigue; and, though our years
As life declines speed rapidly away,
And not a year but pilfers as he goes
Some youthful grace that age would gladly keep;
A tooth or auburn lock, and by degrees
Their length and colour from the locks they spare;
Th' elastic spring of an unwearied foot
That mounts the stile with ease, or leaps the fence,
That play of lungs, inhaling and again
Respiring freely the fresh air, that makes
Swift pace or steep ascent no toil to me,
Mine have not pilfered yet; nor yet impaired
My relish of fair prospect; scenes that soothed
Or charmed me young, no longer young, I find
Still soothing and of pow'r to charm me still.
And witness, dear companion of my walks,
Whose arm this twentieth winter I perceive
Fast locked in mine, with pleasure such as love,
Confirmed by long experience of thy worth
And well-tried virtues, could alone inspire—
Witness a joy that thou hast doubled long.
Thou know'st my praise of nature most sincere,
And that my raptures are not conjured up
To serve occasions of poetic pomp,
But genuine, and art partner of them all.
How oft upon yon eminence our pace
Has slackened to a pause, and we have born
The ruffling wind, scarce conscious that it blew,
While admiration, feeding at the eye,
And still unsated, dwelt upon the scene.
Thence with what pleasure have we just discerned

[1] *two kings of Brentford* From George Villiers, Duke of Buckingham's satiric play *The Rehearsal* (1671).

[2] *scarlet hips and stony haws* Rosehips and hawthorn fruit.

[3] *sloes* Dark plumlike fruit of the blackthorn.

The distant plough slow moving, and beside
His lab'ring team, that swerved not from the track,
The sturdy swain diminished to a boy!
Here Ouse,[1] slow winding through a level plain
Of spacious meads with cattle sprinkled o'er,
Conducts the eye along its sinuous course
Delighted. There, fast rooted in their bank,
Stand, never overlooked, our fav'rite elms,
That screen the herdsman's solitary hut;
While far beyond, and overthwart° the stream *opposite*
That, as with molten glass, inlays the vale,
The sloping land recedes into the clouds;
Displaying on its varied side the grace
Of hedge-row beauties numberless, square tow'r,
Tall spire, from which the sound of cheerful bells
Just undulates upon the list'ning ear,
Groves, heaths, and smoking villages, remote.
Scenes must be beautiful, which, daily viewed,
Please daily, and whose novelty survives
Long knowledge and the scrutiny of years.
Praise justly due to those that I describe.
  Nor rural sights alone, but rural sounds,
Exhilarate the spirit, and restore
The tone of languid Nature. Mighty winds,
That sweep the skirt of some far-spreading wood
Of ancient growth, make music not unlike
The dash of ocean on his winding shore,
And lull the spirit while they fill the mind;
Unnumbered branches waving in the blast,
And all their leaves fast flutt'ring, all at once.
Nor less composure waits upon the roar
Of distant floods, or on the softer voice
Of neighb'ring fountain, or of rills that slip
Through the cleft rock, and, chiming as they fall
Upon loose pebbles, lose themselves at length
In matted grass, that with a livelier green
Betrays the secret of their silent course.
Nature inanimate employs sweet sounds,
But animated nature sweeter still,
To sooth and satisfy the human ear.
Ten thousand warblers cheer the day, and one
The live-long night: nor these alone, whose notes
Nice fingered art must emulate in vain,
But cawing rooks, and kites[2] that swim sublime
In still repeated circles, screaming loud,
The jay, the pie, and ev'n the boding owl
That hails the rising moon, have charms for me.
Sounds inharmonious in themselves and harsh,
Yet heard in scenes where peace for ever reigns,
And only there, please highly for their sake....

from Book 6: The Winter Walk at Noon

... The night was winter in his roughest mood;
The morning sharp and clear. But now at noon
Upon the southern side of the slant hills,
And where the woods fence off the northern blast,
The season smiles, resigning all its rage,
And has the warmth of May. The vault° is blue *sky*
Without a cloud, and white without a speck
The dazzling splendour of the scene below.
Again the harmony comes o'er the vale;
And through the trees I view th' embattled tow'r
Whence all the music. I again perceive
The soothing influence of the wafted strains,
And settle in soft musings as I tread
The walk, still verdant, under oaks and elms,
Whose outspread branches overarch the glade.
The roof, though moveable through all its length
As the wind sways it, has yet well sufficed,
And, intercepting in their silent fall
The frequent flakes, has kept a path for me.
No noise is here, or none that hinders thought.
The redbreast warbles still, but is content
With slender notes, and more than half suppressed:
Pleased with his solitude, and flitting light
From spray to spray, where'er he rests he shakes
From many a twig the pendent drops of ice,
That tinkle in the withered leaves below.
Stillness, accompanied with sounds so soft,
Charms more than silence. Meditation here
May think down hours to moments. Here the heart
May give an useful lesson to the head,
And learning wiser grow without his books.
Knowledge and wisdom, far from being one,
Have oft-times no connection. Knowledge dwells
In heads replete with thoughts of other men;

[1] *Ouse* River in England.

[2] *rooks* Crow-like birds; *kites* Hawks.

Wisdom in minds attentive to their own.
Knowledge, a rude unprofitable mass,
The mere materials with which wisdom builds,
Till smoothed and squared and fitted to its place,
Does but encumber whom it seems t' enrich.
Knowledge is proud that he has learned so much;
Wisdom is humble that he knows no more.
Books are not seldom talismans and spells,
By which the magic art of shrewder wits
Holds an unthinking multitude enthralled.
Some to the fascination of a name
Surrender judgment, hood-winked. Some the style
Infatuates, and through labyrinths and wilds
Of error leads them by a tune entranced.
While sloth seduces more, too weak to bear
The insupportable fatigue of thought,
And swallowing, therefore, without pause or choice,
The total grist° unsifted, husks and all. *grain*
But trees, and rivulets whose rapid course
Defies the check of winter, haunts of deer,
And sheep-walks populous with bleating lambs,
And lanes in which the primrose ere her time
Peeps through the moss that clothes the hawthorn root,
Deceive no student. Wisdom there, and truth,
Not shy, as in the world, and to be won
By slow solicitation, seize at once
The roving thought, and fix it on themselves.
 What prodigies can pow'r divine perform
More grand than it produces year by year,
And all in sight of inattentive man?
Familiar with th' effect we slight the cause,
And, in the constancy of nature's course,
The regular return of genial months,
And renovation of a faded world,
See nought to wonder at. Should God again,
As once in Gibeon,[1] interrupt the race
Of the undeviating and punctual sun,
How would the world admire! but speaks it less
An agency divine, to make him know
His moment when to sink and when to rise,
Age after age, than to arrest his course?
All we behold is miracle; but, seen
So duly, all is miracle in vain.
Where now the vital energy that moved,
While summer was, the pure and subtle lymph[2]
Through th' imperceptible meand'ring veins
Of leaf and flow'r? It sleeps; and th' icy touch
Of unprolific winter has impressed
A cold stagnation on th' intestine° tide. *confined*
But let the months go round, a few short months,
And all shall be restored. These naked shoots,
Barren as lances, among which the wind
Makes wintry music, sighing as it goes,
Shall put their graceful foliage on again,
And, more aspiring, and with ampler spread,
Shall boast new charms, and more than they have lost.
Then, each in its peculiar honours clad,
Shall publish, even to the distant eye,
Its family and tribe. Laburnum, rich
In streaming gold; syringa, iv'ry pure;
The scentless and the scented rose; this red
And of an humbler growth, the other tall,
And throwing up into the darkest gloom
Of neighb'ring cypress, or more sable yew,
Her silver globes, light as the foamy surf
That the wind severs from the broken wave;
The lilac, various in array, now white,
Now sanguine, and her beauteous head now set
With purple spikes pyramidal, as if,
Studious of ornament, yet unresolved
Which hue she most approved, she chose them all;
Copious of flow'rs the woodbine, pale and wan,
But well compensating her sickly looks
With never-cloying odours, early and late;
Hypericum, all bloom, so thick a swarm
Of flow'rs, like flies clothing her slender rods,
That scarce a leaf appears; mezerion, too,
Though leafless, well attired, and thick beset
With blushing wreaths, investing every spray;
Althaea with the purple eye; the broom,
Yellow and bright, as bullion unalloyed,
Her blossoms and, luxuriant above all,

[1] *Gibeon* Ancient city north of Jerusalem, now el-Jib. From Joshua 10.13: "And the sun stood still [over Gibeon], and the moon stayed, until the people had avenged themselves upon their enemies."

[2] *lymph* In the second half of the eighteenth century, British physicians such as William Hunter and William Hewson, in studying the circulation and properties of human blood, noted the way in which the lymphatic system has connections with blood vessels, and concluded that the lymphatic system plays a key part in the absorption of nutrients.

The jasmine, throwing wide her elegant sweets,
The deep dark green of whose unvarnished leaf
Makes more conspicuous, and illumines more
The bright profusion of her scattered stars.—
These have been, and these shall be in their day;
And all this uniform, uncoloured scene,
Shall be dismantled of its fleecy load,
And flush into variety again.
From dearth to plenty, and from death to life,
Is Nature's progress when she lectures man
In heav'nly truth; evincing, as she makes
The grand transition, that there lives and works
A soul in all things, and that soul is God.
The beauties of the wilderness are his,
That make so gay the solitary place
Where no eye sees them. And the fairer forms
That cultivation glories in, are his.
He sets the bright procession on its way,
And marshals all the order of the year;
He marks the bounds which winter may not pass,
And blunts his pointed fury; in its case,
Russet and rude, folds up the tender germ,
Uninjured, with inimitable art;
And, ere one flow'ry season fades and dies,
Designs the blooming wonders of the next.
    Some say that, in the origin of things,
When all creation started into birth,
The infant elements received a law,
From which they swerve not since. That under force
Of that controlling ordinance they move,
And need not his immediate hand, who first
Prescribed their course, to regulate it now.
Thus dream they, and contrive to save a God
Th' incumbrance of his own concerns, and spare
The great Artificer of all that moves
The stress of a continual act, the pain
Of unremitted vigilance and care,
As too laborious and severe a task.
So man, the moth, is not afraid, it seems,
To span omnipotence, and measure might
That knows no measure, by the scanty rule
And standard of his own, that is today,
And is not ere tomorrow's sun go down!
But how should matter occupy a charge
Dull as it is, and satisfy a law
So vast in its demands, unless impelled
To ceaseless service by a ceaseless force,
And under pressure of some conscious cause?
The Lord of all, himself through all diffused,
Sustains, and is the life of all that lives.
Nature is but a name for an effect,
Whose cause is God. He feeds the secret fire
By which the mighty process is maintained,
Who sleeps not, is not weary; in whose sight
Slow circling ages are as transient days;
Whose work is without labour; whose designs
No flaw deforms, no difficulty thwarts;
And whose beneficence no charge exhausts.
Him blind antiquity profaned, not served,
With self-taught rites, and under various names,
Female and male, Pomona, Pales, Pan,
And Flora, and Vertumnus;[1] peopling earth
With tutelary° goddesses and gods *protective*
That were not; and commending, as they would,
To each some province, garden, field, or grove.
But all are under one. One spirit—His
Who wore the platted° thorns with bleeding brows— *braided*
Rules universal nature. Not a flow'r
But shows some touch, in freckle, streak, or stain,
Of his unrivalled pencil. He inspires
Their balmy odours, and imparts their hues,
And bathes their eyes with nectar, and includes,
In grains as countless as the sea-side sands,
The forms with which he sprinkles all the earth.
Happy who walks with him! whom what he finds
Of flavour or of scent in fruit or flow'r,
Or what he views of beautiful or grand
In nature, from the broad majestic oak
To the green blade that twinkles in the sun,
Prompts with remembrance of a present God!
His presence, who made all so fair, perceived,
Makes all still fairer. As with him no scene
Is dreary, so with him all seasons please.
Though winter had been none, had man been true,
And earth be punished for its tenant's sake,
Yet not in vengeance; as this smiling sky,

[1] *Pomona* Roman goddess of fruit trees; *Pales* Roman goddess of shepherds, flocks, and cattle; *Pan* Greek god of shepherds and flocks; *Flora* Roman goddess of blossoming spring flowers; *Vertumnus* Roman god of fruit trees, gardens, and seasons.

So soon succeeding such an angry night,
And these dissolving snows, and this clear stream
Recov'ring fast its liquid music, prove....
—1785

The Castaway[1]

Obscurest night involved the sky,
   Th' Atlantic billows roared,
When such a destined wretch as I,
   Washed headlong from on board,
Of friends, of hope, of all bereft,
His floating home forever left.

No braver chief could Albion° boast   *England*
   Than he with whom he went,
Nor ever ship left Albion's coast,
   With warmer wishes sent.
He loved them both, but both in vain,
Nor him beheld, nor her again.

Not long beneath the whelming brine,
   Expert to swim, he lay;
Nor soon he felt his strength decline,
   Or courage die away;
But waged with death a lasting strife,
Supported by despair of life.

He shouted; nor his friends had failed
   To check the vessel's course,
But so the furious blast prevailed,
   That, pitiless perforce,
They left their outcast mate behind,
And scudded still before the wind.

Some succor yet they could afford;
   And, such as storms allow,
The cask, the coop,° the floated cord,°   *basket / rope*
   Delayed not to bestow.
But he (they knew) nor ship, nor shore,
Whate'er they gave, should visit more.

Nor, cruel as it seemed, could he
   Their haste himself condemn,
Aware that flight, in such a sea,
   Alone could rescue them;
Yet bitter felt it still to die
Deserted, and his friends so nigh.

He long survives, who lives an hour
   In ocean, self-upheld;
And so long he, with unspent pow'r,
   His destiny repelled;
And ever, as the minutes flew,
Entreated help, or cried, "Adieu!"

At length, his transient respite past,
   His comrades, who before
Had heard his voice in every blast,
   Could catch the sound no more.
For then, by toil subdued, he drank
The stifling wave, and then he sank.

No poet wept him; but the page
   Of narrative sincere,
That tells his name, his worth, his age,
   Is wet with Anson's tear.
And tears by bards or heroes shed
Alike immortalize the dead.

I therefore purpose not, or dream,
   Descanting on his fate,
To give the melancholy theme
   A more enduring date:
But misery still delights to trace
Its semblance in another's case.

No voice divine the storm allayed,[2]
   No light propitious shone,
When, snatched from all effectual aid,
   We perished, each alone;
But I beneath a rougher sea,
And whelmed in deeper gulfs than he.
—1803

[1] *The Castaway* Based upon an occurrence documented in Lord George Anson's *Voyage Round the World* (1748), in which a sailor on Anson's ship was tossed overboard in a fierce storm and could not be rescued.

[2] *No voice ... allayed* See Matthew 8.26.

The Retired Cat

A poet's cat, sedate and grave
As poet well could wish to have,
Was much addicted to inquire
For nooks to which she might retire,
And where, secure as mouse in chink,
She might repose, or sit and think.
I know not where she caught the trick—
Nature perhaps herself had cast her
In such a mould *philosophique*,
Or else she learned it of her master.
Sometimes ascending, debonair,
An apple tree or lofty pear,
Lodged with convenience in the fork,
She watched the gardener at his work;
Sometimes her ease and solace sought
In an old empty wat'ring pot;
There, wanting nothing save a fan
To seem some nymph in her sedan,
Apparelled in exactest sort,
And ready to be borne to court.

But love of change, it seems, has place
Not only in our wiser race;
Cats also feel, as well as we,
That passion's force, and so did she.
Her climbing, she began to find,
Exposed her too much to the wind,
And the old utensil of tin
Was cold and comfortless within:
She therefore wished instead of those
Some place of more serene repose,
Where neither cold might come, nor air
Too rudely wanton with her hair,
And sought it in the likeliest mode
Within her master's snug abode.

A drawer, it chanced, at bottom lined
With linen of the softest kind,
With such as merchants introduce
From India, for the ladies' use—
A drawer impending o'er the rest,
Half open in the topmost chest,
Of depth enough, and none to spare,
Invited her to slumber there;
Puss with delight beyond expression
Surveyed the scene, and took possession.
Recumbent at her ease ere long,
And lulled by her own humdrum song,
She left the cares of life behind,
And slept as she would sleep her last,
When in came, housewifely inclined
The chambermaid, and shut it fast;
By no malignity impelled,
But all unconscious whom it held.

Awakened by the shock, cried Puss,
"Was ever cat attended thus!
The open drawer was left, I see,
Merely to prove a nest for me.
For soon as I was well composed,
Then came the maid, and it was closed.
How smooth these kerchiefs, and how sweet!
Oh, what a delicate retreat!
I will resign myself to rest
Till Sol,° declining in the west, *the sun*
Shall call to supper, when, no doubt,
Susan will come and let me out."

The evening came, the sun descended,
And puss remained still unattended.
The night rolled tardily away
(With her indeed 'twas never day),
The sprightly morn her course renewed,
The evening gray again ensued,
And puss came into mind no more
Than if entombed the day before.
With hunger pinched, and pinched for room,
She now presaged approaching doom,
Nor slept a single wink, or purred,
Conscious of jeopardy incurred.

That night, by chance, the poet watching
Heard an inexplicable scratching;
His noble heart went pit-a-pat
And to himself he said, "What's that?"
He drew the curtain at his side,
And forth he peeped, but nothing spied;
Yet, by his ear directed, guessed

Something imprisoned in the chest,
And, doubtful what, with prudent care
Resolved it should continue there.
At length a voice which well he knew,
A long and melancholy mew,
Saluting his poetic ears,
Consoled him, and dispelled his fears:
He left his bed, he trod the floor,
He 'gan in haste the drawers explore,
The lowest first, and without stop
The rest in order to the top;
For 'tis a truth well known to most,
That whatsoever thing is lost,
We seek it, ere it come to light,
In every cranny but the right.
Forth skipped the cat, not now replete
As erst° with airy self-conceit, *before*
Nor in her own fond apprehension
A theme for all the world's attention,
But modest, sober, cured of all
Her notions hyperbolical,
And wishing for a place of rest
Anything rather than a chest.
Then stepped the poet into bed,
With this reflection in his head:

MORAL

Beware of too sublime a sense
Of your own worth and consequence.
The man who dreams himself so great,
And his importance of such weight,
That all around in all that's done
Must move and act for him alone,
Will learn in school of tribulation
The folly of his expectation.
—1803

On the Loss of the Royal George[1]

Toll for the brave!
The brave that are no more!
All sunk beneath the wave
Fast by their native shore.

Eight hundred of the brave,
Whose courage well was tried,
Had made the vessel heel,
And laid her on her side.

A land breeze shook the shrouds,
And she was overset;
Down went the Royal George,
With all her crew complete.

Toll for the brave!
Brave Kempenfelt is gone;
His last sea fight is fought,
His work of glory done.

It was not in the battle,
No tempest gave the shock,
She sprang no fatal leak,
She ran upon no rock.

His sword was in its sheath,
His fingers held the pen,
When Kempenfelt went down
With twice four hundred men.

Weigh the vessel up,
Once dreaded by our foes;
And mingle with our cup
The tears that England owes.

Her timbers yet are sound,
And she may float again
Full charged with England's thunder,
And plough the distant main.

[1] *Loss of the Royal George* In 1782 the *Royal George,* flagship of a fleet commanded by Rear-Admiral Kempenfelt, sank in anchorage at Portsmouth, resulting in numerous deaths. The exact toll has never been determined; estimates range from 900 to 1200.

But Kempenfelt is gone,
His victories are o'er;
And he and his eight hundred
Shall plough the wave no more.
—1803 (written 1782)

My Mary[1]

The twentieth year is well nigh past
Since first our sky was overcast;[2]
Ah, would that this might be the last!
My Mary!

Thy spirits have a fainter flow,
I see thee daily weaker grow;
'Twas my distress that brought thee low,
My Mary!

Thy needles, once a shining store,
For my sake restless heretofore,
Now rust disused, and shine no more;
My Mary!

For though thou gladly would'st fulfil
The same kind office for me still,
Thy sight now seconds not thy will,
My Mary!

But well thou play'dst the housewife's part,
And all thy threads with magic art
Have wound themselves about this heart,
My Mary!

Thy indistinct expressions seem
Like language uttered in a dream;
Yet me they charm, whate'er the theme,
My Mary!

Thy silver locks, once auburn bright,
Are still more lovely in my sight
Than golden beams of orient light,
My Mary!

For could I view nor them nor thee,
What sight worth seeing could I see?
The sun would rise in vain for me.
My Mary!

Partakers of thy sad decline,
Thy hands their little force resign;
Yet, gently pressed, press gently mine,
My Mary!

Such feebleness of limbs thou prov'st,
That now at every step thou mov'st
Upheld by two; yet still thou lov'st,
My Mary!

And still to love, though pressed with ill,
In wintry age to feel no chill,
With me is to be lovely still,
My Mary!

But ah! by constant heed I know
How oft the sadness that I show
Transforms thy smiles to looks of woe,
My Mary!

And should my future lot be cast
With much resemblance of the past,
Thy worn-out heart will break at last—
My Mary!
—1803 (written 1793)

[1] *Mary* Cowper wrote this poem in 1793, the year his longtime companion, Mary Unwin, suffered a paralytic stroke.

[2] *Twentieth year ... overcast* Cowper suffered from mental illness, which had prevented the two from marrying many years previous.

Laboring-Class Poets

From the late medieval period onwards, many English poets wrote pastoral poems that celebrated a vision of idyllic rural happiness. It was not until the eighteenth century, however, that poets with first-hand knowledge of rural labor began to find their own voices. The poets represented here are all rural laborers who found their way into print—generally with the help of friends or patrons. Mary Leapor, for example, was a kitchen worker whose writings came to the attention of Bridget Fremantle, a well-educated daughter of a rector who arranged for the publication of two posthumous volumes of Leapor's *Poems on Several Occasions.* Stephen Duck's *Poems on Several Subjects*, which included "The Thresher's Labour," was commissioned as a work "on his own labours." Mary Collier, in contrast, published her work at her own expense. Collier was a washerwoman who was spurred to write by Duck's insinuation, in his "Thresher's Labour," that men work harder than women. Collier's poem responds directly to Duck's, presenting many of the events narrated in his work—such as the preparation of hay stacks, the walk home at the end of the day, and the evening meal—from the women's point of view.

Servants, such as Mary Leapor and Elizabeth Hands, often had no formal education and read what their parents had managed to procure or what they could find in their employers' libraries. Nevertheless, these writers' works show signs of extensive reading. Leapor often imitated the style of Alexander Pope; her "Epistle to a Lady," for example, takes its title from Pope's work of that name. Elizabeth Hands also acquired proficiency in a number of different poetic genres, including the epistle, ode, pastoral, and elegy. These poets occasionally achieved considerable reputations. Duck, who was often referred to as the "Thresher Poet," became the most widely known, after he acquired the financial support of Queen Caroline. Unfortunately, such popularity was rarely sustained for long. The female writers in particular were generally forgotten after their deaths and have only been rediscovered in the twentieth century.

⌘⌘⌘

STEPHEN DUCK

The Thresher's Labour[1]

The grateful tribute of these rural lays,
Which to her patron's[2] hand the Muse[3] conveys,
Deign to accept; 'tis just she tribute bring
To him whose bounty gives her life to sing;
To him whose generous favours tune her voice,
And bid her 'midst her poverty rejoice.
Inspired by these, she dares herself prepare,
To sing the toils of each revolving year:
Those endless toils, which always grow anew,
And the poor thresher's destined to pursue;
Even these with pleasure can the Muse rehearse,
When you, and gratitude, command the verse.

Soon as the harvest hath laid bare the plains,
And barns well filled reward the farmer's pains;
What corn° each sheaf will yield, intent to hear, *grain*
And guess from thence the profits of the year;
Or else impending ruin to prevent,
By paying, timely, threat'ning Landlord's rent,
He calls his threshers forth: around we stand,
With deep attention waiting his command.
To each our tasks he readily divides,
And pointing, to our different stations guides.
As he directs, to different barns we go;
Here two for wheat, and there for barley two.
But first, to show what he expects to find,
These words, or words like these, disclose his mind:
"So dry the corn was carried from the field,
"So easily 'twill thresh, so well 'twill yield;
"Sure large day's work I well may hope for now;
"Come, strip, and try, let's see what you can do."
Divested of our clothes, with flail in hand,
At a just distance, front to front we stand;
And first the threshall's° gently swung, to prove, *flail*
Whether with just exactness it will move:
That once secure, more quick we whirl them round,
From the strong planks our crab-tree staves° *rods*
rebound,
And echoing barns return the rattling sound.
Now in the air our knotty weapons fly;
And now with equal force descend from high:
Down one, one up, so well they keep the time,
The Cyclops'[4] hammers could not truer chime;
Nor with more heavy strokes could Aetna groan,
When Vulcan forged the arms for Thetis' son.[5]
In briny streams our sweat descends apace,
Drops from our locks, or trickles down our face.
No intermission in our works we know;
The noisy threshall must for ever go.
Their master absent, others safely play;
The sleeping threshall doth it self betray.
Nor yet the tedious labour to beguile,
And make the passing minutes sweetly smile.
Can we, like shepherds, tell a merry tale?
The voice is lost, drowned by the noisy flail.
But we may think——Alas! what pleasing thing
Here to the mind can the dull fancy bring?
The eye beholds no pleasant object here;
No cheerful sound diverts the list'ning ear.
The shepherd well may tune his voice to sing,
Inspired by all the beauties of the spring:
No fountains murmur here, no lambkins play,
No linets warble, and no fields look gay;
'Tis all a dull and melancholy scene,
Fit only to provoke the Muse's spleen.° *ill-humor*

[1] *The Thresher's Labour* The present text is that of the original 1730 version of Duck's poem. There has been some critical controversy over the textual history of this poem, but scholarly work by William Christmas and others has established both that the 1730, unauthorized version was by Duck himself and that this 1730 version (rather than Duck's revised, authorized version of 1736) was the one to which Mary Collier was responding in her 1739 poem "The Woman's Labour: To Mr. Stephen Duck." For purposes of comparison, the full text of Duck's 1736 version is provided as part of the website component of this anthology. The publishers are grateful for editorial advice provided by Dr. Christmas on these textual matters.

[2] *her patron* Probably a reference to Reverend Stanley, who suggested this autobiographical topic to Duck.

[3] *Muse* One of the nine daughters of Zeus and Mnemosyne, each of whom presides over, and provides inspiration for, a different aspect of the arts and sciences.

[4] *Cyclops* According to classical mythology, three one-eyed Titans who forged thunderbolts for the god Zeus.

[5] *Aetna* Volcanic mountain in Sicily (also spelled "Etna") where the forge of Vulcan, the classical god of fire and metalworking, was supposedly located; *Thetis' son* Achilles, the famous warrior of the *Iliad*, whose armor was forged by Vulcan.

When sooty peas we thresh, you scarce can know
Our native colour, as from work we go;
The sweat, and dust, and suffocating smoke,
Make us so much like Ethiopians look:
We scare our wives, when evening brings us home;
And frighted infants think the bugbear[1] come.
Week after week we this dull task pursue,
Unless when winnowing[2] days produce a new;
A new indeed, but frequently a worse,
The threshall yields but to the master's curse:
He counts the bushels, counts how much a day,
Then swears we've idled half our time away.
"Why look ye, rogues! D'ye think that this will do?
"Your neighbours thresh as much again as you."
Now in our hands we wish our noisy tools,
To drown the hated names of rogues and fools;
But wanting those, we just like school-boys look,
When th' angry master views the blotted book:
They cry their ink was faulty, and their pen;
We, "The corn threshes bad, 'twas cut too green."
But now the Winter hides his hoary° head, *white*
And Nature's face is with new beauty spread;
The Spring appears, and kind refreshing showers
New clothe the field with grass, and deck with flowers.
Next her, the ripening Summer presses on,
And Sol begins his longest stage to run.
Before the door our welcome master stands,
And tells us the ripe grass requires our hands.
The long much-wished intelligence imparts
Life to our looks, and spirit to our hearts:
We wish the happy season may be fair,
And joyful, long to breathe in opener air.
This change of labour seems to give much ease;
And does, at least, imagination please.
With thoughts of happiness our joy's complete;
There's always bitter mingled with the sweet.
When Morn does through the eastern windows peep,
Straight from our beds we start, and shake off sleep;
This new employ with eager haste to prove,
This new employ becomes so much our love;
Alas! that human joys should change so soon,
Even this may bear another face at noon!
The birds salute us as to work we go,
And a new life seems in our breasts to glow.
Across one's shoulder hangs a scythe well steeled,
The weapon destined to unclothe the field;
T'other supports the whetstone, scrip,[3] and beer;
That for our scythes, and these ourselves to cheer.
And now the field designed our strength to try
Appears, and meets at last our longing eye;
The grass and ground each cheerfully surveys,
Willing to see which way th' advantage lays.
As the best man, each claims the foremost place,
And our first work seems but a sportive race:
With rapid force our well-whet blades we drive,
Strain every nerve, and blow for blow we give;
Though but this eminence the foremost gains,
Only t'excel the rest in toil and pains.
But when the scorching sun is mounted high,
And no kind barns with friendly shades are nigh,
Our weary scythes entangle in the grass,
And streams of sweat run trickling down apace;
Our sportive labour we too late lament,
And wish that strength again, we vainly spent.
Thus in the morn a courser° I have seen, *horse*
With headlong fury scour the level green,
Or mount the hills, if hills are in his way,
As if no labour could his fire allay,
'Till the meridian sun with sultry heat,
And piercing beams hath bathed his sides in sweat;
The lengthened chase scarce able to sustain,
He measures back the hills and dales with pain.
With heat and labour tired, our scythes we quit,
Search out a shady tree, and down we sit;
From scrip and bottle hope new strength to gain;
But scrip and bottle too are tried in vain.
Down our parched throats we scarce the bread can get,
And quite o'er-spent with toil, but faintly eat;
Nor can the bottle only answer all,
Alas! the bottle and the beer's too small.[4]
Our time slides on, we move from off the grass,
And each again betakes him to his place.
Not eager now, as late, our strength to prove,
But all contented regular to move:
Often we whet,° as often view the sun, *sharpen*

[1] *bugbear* Imaginary creature; hobgoblin.

[2] *winnowing* The process of exposing grain to the wind so that the chaff and other refuse are blown away.

[3] *whetstone* Stone used to sharpen blades; *scrip* Satchel.

[4] *small* Small beer is of low alcoholic content.

To see how near his tedious race is run;
At length he veils his radiant face from sight,
And bids the weary traveller goodnight:
Homewards we move, but so much spent with toil,
We walk but slow, and rest at every stile.
Our good expecting wives, who think we stay,° *delay*
Got to the door, soon eye us in the way;
Then from the pot the dumpling's catched° *taken*
  in haste,
And homely by its side the bacon's placed.
Supper and sleep by morn new strength supply,
And out we set again our works to try:
But not so early quite, nor quite so fast,
As to our cost we did the morning past.
Soon as the rising sun hath drank the dew,
Another scene is opened to our view;
Our master comes, and at his heels a throng
Of prattling females, armed with rake and prong,
Prepared, whil'st he is here, to make his hay;
Or, if he turns his back, prepared to play.
But here, or gone, sure of this comfort still,
Here's company, so they may chat their fill:
And were their hands as active as their tongues,
How nimbly then would move their rakes and prongs?
The grass again is spread upon the ground,
'Till not a vacant place is to be found;
And while the piercing sun-beams on it shine,
The haymakers have time allowed to dine.
That soon dispatched, they still sit on the ground,
And the brisk chat renewed, a-fresh goes round:
All talk at once, but seeming all to fear,
That all they speak so well, the rest won't hear;
By quick degrees so high their notes they strain,
That standers-by can naught distinguish plain:
So loud their speech, and so confused their noise,
Scarce puzzled echo can return a voice;
Yet spite of this, they bravely all go on,
Each scorns to be, or seem to be, outdone,
'Till (unobserved before) a louring[1] sky,
Fraught with black clouds, proclaims a shower nigh;
The tattling crowd can scarce their garments gain,
Before descends the thick impetuous rain.
Their noisy prattle all at once is done,
And to the hedge they all for shelter run.

  Thus have I seen on a bright summer's day,
On some green brake° a flock of sparrows play; *thicket*
From twig to twig, from bush to bush they fly,
And with continued chirping fill the sky;
But on a sudden, if a storm appears,
Their chirping noise no longer dins your ears;
They fly for shelter to the thickest bush,
There silent sit, and all at once is hush.
But better fate succeeds this rainy day,
And little labour serves to make the hay;
Fast as 'tis cut, so kindly shines the sun,
Turned once or twice, the pleasing work is done.
Next day the cocks[2] appear in equal rows,
Which the glad master in safe ricks° bestows. *stacks*

  But now the field we must no longer range,
And yet, hard fate! still work for work we change.
Back to the barns again in haste we're sent,
Where lately so much time we pensive spent:
Not pensive now; we bless the friendly shade,
And to avoid the parching sun are glad.
But few days here we're destined to remain,
Before our master calls us forth again:
"For harvest now," says he, "yourselves prepare,
"The ripened harvest now demands your care.
"Early next morn I shall disturb your rest,
"Get all things ready, and be quickly drest."
Strict to his word, scarce the next dawn appears,
Before his hasty summons fills our ears.
Obedient to his call, straight up we get,
And finding soon our company complete,
With him, our guide, we to the wheat-field go;
He, to appoint, and we, the work to do.
Ye reapers, cast your eyes around the field,
And view the scene its different beauties yield;
Then look again with a more tender eye,
To think how soon it must in ruin lie.
For once set in, where-e'er our blows we deal,
There's no resisting of the well-whet steel:
But here or there, where-e'er our course we bend,
Sure desolation does our steps attend.
Thus, when Arabia's sons, in hopes of prey,
To some more fertile country take their way;
How beauteous all things in the morn appear,

[1] *louring* Looking dark and threatening.

[2] *cocks* Hay-cocks, conical heaps of hay.

There villages, and pleasing cots° are here; *cottages*
So many pleasing objects meet the sight,
The ravished eye could willing gaze 'till night.
But long e'er then, where-e'er their troops have past,
Those pleasant prospects lie a gloomy waste.

The morning past, we sweat beneath the sun,
And but uneasily our work goes on.
Before us we perplexing thistles find,
And corn blown adverse with the ruffling wind.
Behind our backs the female gleaners[1] wait,
Who sometimes stoop, and sometimes hold a chat.
Each morn we early rise, go late to bed,
And lab'ring hard, a painful life we lead:
For Toils, scarce ever ceasing, press us now,
Rest never does, but on the Sabbath, show,
And barely that, our master will allow.
Nor, when asleep, are we secure from pain,
We then perform our labours o'er again:
Our mimic° fancy always restless seems, *imitative*
And what we act awake, she acts in dreams.
Hard fate! Our labours even in sleep don't cease,
Scarce Hercules[2] e'er felt such toils as these.
At length in rows stands up the well-dried corn,
A grateful scene, and ready for the barn.
Our well-pleased master views the sight with joy,
And we for carrying, all our force employ.
Confusion soon o'er all the field appears,
And stunning clamours fill the workmen's ears;
The bells, and clashing whips, alternate sound,
And rattling wagons thunder o'er the ground.
The wheat got in, the peas, and other grain,
Share the same fate, and soon leave bare the plain.
In noisy triumph the last load moves on,
And loud huzzas° proclaim the harvest done. *cheers*
Our master, joyful at the welcome sight,
Invites us all to feast with him at night.
A table plentifully spread we find,
And jugs of humming beer to cheer the mind;
Which he, too generous, pushes on so fast,
We think no toils to come, nor mind the past.

[1] *gleaners* Those who pick up the ears of corn after the reapers.

[2] *Hercules* According to classical mythology, the heroic son of Zeus and Alcmene who performed twelve nearly impossible labors in order to gain immortality.

But the next morning soon reveals the cheat,
When the same toils we must again repeat:
To the same barns again must back return,
To labour there for room for next year's corn.

Thus, as the year's revolving course goes round,
No respite from our labour can be found:
Like Sisyphus,[3] our work is never done;
Continually rolls back the restless stone.
Now growing labours still succeed the past,
And growing always new, must always last.
—1730

MARY COLLIER

The Woman's Labour:
To Mr. Stephen Duck

Immortal bard![4] Thou favorite of the nine![5]
Enriched by peers, advanced by Caroline![6]
Deign to look down on one that's poor and low
Remembering you yourself was lately so;
Accept these lines. Alas! What can you have
From her, who ever was, and's still a slave?
No learning ever was bestowed on me;
My life was always spent in drudgery:
And not alone; alas! with grief I find,
It is the portion of poor woman-kind.
Oft have I thought as on my bed I lay,
Eased from the tiresome labours of the day,
Our first extraction from a mass refined,
Could never be for slavery designed;
Till time and custom by degrees destroyed

[3] *Sisyphus* King of Corinth who, as punishment for his cruelty, was condemned in the afterlife to continually roll a boulder up a hill in Hades (the classical underworld). Whenever the boulder neared the top, it would fall down again.

[4] *Immortal bard!* I.e., Stephen Duck.

[5] *the nine* I.e., the nine Muses, one of whom Duck invokes at the beginning of his poem.

[6] *Caroline* Queen Caroline, who provided Duck with an annuity and a house in which to live after his work was brought to her attention. She made him a yeoman of the guard in 1733, and then keeper of the Queen's Library in Merlin Cave in 1735.

That happy state our sex at first enjoyed.
When men had used their utmost care and toil,
Their recompence was but a female smile;
When they by arts or arms were rendered great,
They laid their trophies at a woman's feet;
They, in those days, unto our sex did bring
Their hearts, their all, a free-will offering;
And as from us their being they derive,
They back again should all due homage give.

Jove, once descending from the clouds, did drop
In show'rs of gold on lovely Danae's lap;[1]
The sweet-tongued poets, in those generous days,
Unto our shrine still offered up their lays:° *verses*
But now, alas! that Golden Age is past,
We are the objects of your scorn at last.
And you, great Duck, upon whose happy brow
The Muses seem to fix the garland[2] now,
In your late poem boldly did declare
Alcides'° labours can't with yours compare; *Hercules'*
And of your annual task have much to say,
Of threshing, reaping, mowing corn and hay;
Boasting your daily toil, and nightly dream,
But can't conclude your never-dying theme,
And let our hapless sex in silence lie
Forgotten, and in dark oblivion die;
But on our abject state you throw your scorn,
And women wrong, your verses to adorn.
You of hay-making speak a word or two,
As if our sex but little work could do:
This makes the honest farmer smiling say,
He'll seek for women still to make his hay;
For if his back be turned, their work they mind
As well as men, as far as he can find.
For my own part, I many a summer's day
Have spent in throwing, turning, making hay;
But ne'er could see, what you have lately found,
Our wages paid for sitting on the ground.
'Tis true, that when our morning's work is done,
And all our grass exposed unto the sun,
While that his scorching beams do on it shine,
As well as you, we have a time to dine:
I hope, that since we freely toil and sweat
To earn our bread, you'll give us time to eat.
That over, soon we must get up again,
And nimbly turn our hay upon the plain;
Nay, rake and prow[3] it in, the case is clear;
Or how should cocks° in equal rows appear? *haystacks*
But if you'd have what you have wrote believed,
I find, that you to hear us talk are grieved:
In this, I hope, you do not speak your mind,
For none but Turks, that ever I could find,
Have mutes to serve them, or did e'er deny
Their slaves, at work to chat it merrily.
Since you have liberty to speak your mind,
And are to talk, as well as we, inclined
Why should you thus repine, because that we,
Like you, enjoy that pleasing liberty?
What! would you lord it quite, and take away
The only privilege our sex enjoy?

When ev'ning does approach, we homeward hie,
And our domestic toils incessant ply:
Against your coming home prepare to get
Our work all done, our house in order set;
Bacon and *dumpling* in the pot we boil,
Our beds we make, our swine we feed the while;
Then wait at door to see you coming home,
And set the table out against° you come: *in preparation*
Early next morning we on you attend;
Our children dress and feed, their clothes we mend;
And in the field our daily task renew,
Soon as the rising sun has dried the dew.

When harvest comes, into the field we go,
And help to reap the wheat as well as you;
Or else we go the ears of corn to glean;° *gather*
No labour scorning, be it e'er so mean;
But in the work we freely bear a part,
And what we can, perform with all our heart.
To get a living we so willing are,
Our tender babes into the field we bear,

[1] *Jove ... lap* Danaë was a princess of Argos who, according to classical mythology, was imprisoned in her chamber by her father after a prophecy declared that Danaë's offspring would later murder him. Jove, king of the gods, visited Danaë in her chamber in the form of a golden shower that fell on her lap, impregnating her with her son Perseus.

[2] *garland* Crowns of laurels were conferred upon poets in ancient Greece as a mark of honor.

[3] *prow* Draw.

And wrap them in our clothes to keep them warm,
While round about we gather up the corn;
And often unto them our course do bend,
To keep them safe, that nothing them offend:
Our children that are able, bear a share
In gleaning corn, such is our frugal care.
When night comes on, unto our home we go,
Our corn we carry, and our infant too;
Weary, alas! but 'tis not worth our while
Once to complain, or *rest at ev'ry stile*;
We must make haste, for when we home are come,
Alas! we find our work but just begun;
So many things for our attendance call,
Had we ten hands, we could employ them all.
Our children put to bed, with greatest care
We all things for your coming home prepare:
You sup, and go to bed without delay,
And rest yourselves till the ensuing day;
While we, alas! but little sleep can have,
Because our froward[1] children cry and rave;
Yet, without fail, soon as day-light doth spring,
We in the field again our work begin
And there, with all our strength, our toil renew,
Till Titan's[2] golden rays have dried the dew;
Then home we go unto our children dear,
Dress, feed, and bring them to the field with care.
Were this your case, you justly might complain
That day nor night you are secure from pain;
Those mighty troubles which perplex your mind,
(Thistles before, and females come behind)
Would vanish soon, and quickly disappear,
Were you, like us, encumbered thus with care.
What you would have of us we do not know:
We oft take up the corn that you do mow;
We cut the peas, and always ready are
In every work to take our proper share;
And from the time that harvest doth begin,
Until the corn be cut and carried in,
Our toil and labour's daily so extreme,
That we have hardly ever time to dream.

The harvest ended, respite none we find;
The hardest of our toil is still behind:
Hard labour we most cheerfully pursue,
And out, abroad, a charing[3] often go:
Of which I now will briefly tell in part,
What fully to declare is past my art;
So many hardships daily we go through,
I boldly say, the like *you* never knew.

When bright Orion glitters in the skies
In Winter nights, then early we must rise;
The weather ne'er so bad, wind, rain, or snow,
Our work appointed, we must rise and go;
While you on easy beds may lie and sleep,
Till light does through your chamber-windows peep.
When to the house we come where we should go,
How to get in, alas! we do not know:
The maid quite tired with work the day before,
O'ercome with sleep; we standing at the door
Oppressed with cold, and often call in vain,
Ere to our work we can admittance gain:
But when from wind and weather we get in,
Briskly with courage we our work begin;
Heaps of fine linen we before us view,
Whereon to lay our strength and patience too;
Cambrics and muslins,[4] which our ladies wear,
Laces and edgings, costly, fine, and rare,
Which must be washed with utmost skill and care;
With Holland[5] shirts, ruffles, and fringes too,
Fashions which our fore-fathers never knew.
For several hours here we work and slave,
Before we can one glimpse of daylight have;
We labour hard before the morning's past,
Because we fear the time runs on too fast.

At length bright Sol° illuminates the skies, *sun*
And summons drowsy mortals to arise;
Then comes our mistress to us without fail,
And in her hand, perhaps, a mug of ale
To cheer our hearts, and also to inform
Herself, what work is done that very morn;
Lays her commands upon us, that we mind
Her linen well, nor leave the dirt behind:

[1] *froward* Peevish.

[2] *Titan* I.e., the sun.

[3] *charing* Working at odd cleaning or housekeeping jobs.

[4] *Cambrics* Fine linens of a type made in Cambray in Flanders; *muslins* Light-weight cotton fabrics.

[5] *Holland* Type of linen cloth originally made in Holland.

Not this alone, but also to take care
We don't her cambrics nor her ruffles tear;
And these most strictly does of us require,
To save her soap, and sparing be of fire;
Tells us her charge° is great, nay furthermore, *expense*
Her clothes are fewer than the time before.
Now we drive on, resolved our strength to try,
And what we can, we do most willingly;
Until with heat and work, 'tis often known,
Not only sweat, but blood runs trickling down
Our wrists and fingers; still our work demands
The constant action of our lab'ring hands.

Now night comes on, from whence you have relief,
But that, alas! does but increase our grief;
With heavy hearts we often view the sun,
Fearing he'll set before our work is done;
For either in the morning, or at night,
We piece[1] the summer's day with candle-light.
Though we all day with care our work attend,
Such is our fate, we know not when 'twill end:
When ev'ning's come, you homeward take your way,
We, till our work is done, are forced to stay;
And after all our toil and labour past,
Six-pence or eight-pence pays us off at last;
For all our pains, no prospect can we see
Attend us, but old age and poverty.

The washing is not all we have to do:
We oft change work for work as well as you.
Our mistress of her pewter doth complain,
And 'tis our part to make it clean again.
This work, though very hard and tiresome too,
Is not the worst we hapless females do:
When night comes on, and we quite weary are,
We scarce can count what falls unto our share;
Pots, kettles, sauce-pans, skillets, we may see,
Skimmers and ladles, and such trumpery,° *trifles*
Brought in to make complete our slavery.
Though early in the morning 'tis begun,
'Tis often very late before we've done;
Alas! our labours never know an end;
On brass and iron we our strength must spend;
Our tender hands and fingers scratch and tear:
All this, and more, with patience we must bear.
Coloured with dirt and filth we now appear;
Your threshing sooty peas will not come near.
All the perfections woman once could boast,
Are quite obscured, and altogether lost.

Once more our mistress sends to let us know
She wants our help, because the beer runs low:
Then in much haste for brewing we prepare,
The vessels clean, and scald with greatest care;
Often at midnight, from our bed we rise;
At other times, ev'n that will not suffice;
Our work at ev'ning oft we do begin,
And ere we've done, the night comes on again.
Water we pump, the copper[2] we must fill,
Or tend the fire; for if we e'er stand still,
Like you, when threshing, we a watch must keep,
Our wort[3] boils over if we dare to sleep.

But to rehearse all labour is in vain,
Of which we very justly might complain:
For us, you see, but little rest is found;
Our toil increases as the year runs round.
While you to Sisyphus[4] yourselves compare,
With Danaus' daughters[5] we may claim a share;
For while *he* labours hard against the hill,
Bottomless tubs of water *they* must fill.

So the industrious bees do hourly strive
To bring their loads of honey to the hive;
Their sordid° owners always reap the gains, *covetous*
And poorly recompense their toil and pains.
—1739

[1] *piece* Eke out.

[2] *copper* Large copper vessel for brewing or washing dishes or laundry.

[3] *wort* A malt infusion that, after fermentation, becomes beer.

[4] *Sisyphus* King of Corinth who, as punishment for his cruelty, was condemned in the afterlife to continually roll a boulder up a hill in Hades (the classical underworld). Whenever the boulder neared the top, it would fall down again

[5] *Danaus' daughters* The Danaides, the fifty daughter of Danaus, King of Argos, who, at their father's command, murdered their husbands on their wedding nights. As punishment, in Hades they were forced to constantly fill leaky vessels with water.

MARY LEAPOR

An Epistle to a Lady

In vain, dear Madam, yes in vain you strive;
Alas! to make your luckless Mira[1] thrive,
For Tycho and Copernicus[2] agree,
No golden planet bent its rays on me.

'Tis twenty winters, if it is no more;
To speak the truth it may be twenty four.
As many springs their 'pointed space have run,
Since Mira's eyes first opened on the sun.
'Twas when the flocks on slabby hillocks lie,
And the cold fishes[3] rule the wat'ry sky:
But though these eyes the learned page explore,
And turn the pond'rous volumes o'er and o'er,
I find no comfort from their systems' flow,
But am dejected more as more I know.
Hope shines a while, but like a vapour flies,
(The fate of all the curious and the wise)
For, ah! cold Saturn[4] triumphed on that day,
And frowning Sol[5] denied his golden ray.

You see I'm learned, and I show't the more,
That none may wonder when they find me poor.
Yet Mira dreams, as slumbering poets may,
And rolls in treasures till the breaking day:
While books and pictures in bright order rise,
And painted parlours swim before her eyes:
Till the shrill clock impertinently rings,
And the soft visions move their shining wings:
Then Mira wakes—her pictures are no more,
And through her fingers slides the vanished ore.
Convinced too soon, her eye unwilling falls
On the blue curtains and the dusty walls:
She wakes, alas! to business and to woes,
To sweep her kitchen, and to mend her clothes.

But see pale sickness with her languid eyes,
At whose appearance all delusion flies:
The world recedes, its vanities decline,
Clorinda's features seem as faint as mine!
Gay robes no more the aching sight admires,
Wit grates the ear, and melting music tires:
Its wonted° pleasures with each sense decay, *accustomed*
Books please no more, and paintings fade away,
The sliding joys in misty vapours end:
Yet let me still, ah! let me grasp a friend:
And when each joy, when each loved object flies,
Be you the last that leaves my closing eyes.

But how will this dismantled soul appear,
When stripped of all it lately held so dear,
Forced from its prison of expiring clay,
Afraid and shiv'ring at the doubtful way.

Yet did these eyes a dying parent see,
Loosed from all cares except a thought for me,
Without a tear resign her short'ning breath,
And dauntless meet the ling'ring stroke of death.
Then at th' Almighty's sentence shall I mourn:
"Of dust thou art, to dust shalt thou return."[6]
Or shall I wish to stretch the line of fate,
That the dull years may bear a longer date,
To share the follies of succeeding times
With more vexations and with deeper crimes:
Ah no—though Heav'n brings near the final day,
For such a life I will not, dare not pray;
But let the tear for future mercy flow,
And fall resigned beneath the mighty blow.
Nor I alone—for through the spacious ball,
With me will numbers of all ages fall:
And the same day that Mira yields her breath,
Thousands may enter through the gates of death.
—1748

[1] *Mira* Leapor's poetic name for herself.

[2] *Tycho and Copernicus* Danish astronomer Tycho Brahe (1546–1601) and Polish astronomer Nicholas Copernicus (1473–1543), whose Copernican system formed the basis of modern astronomy.

[3] *cold fishes* I.e., the constellation Pisces, which rules the sky in late winter, early spring.

[4] *Saturn* Then thought to be the outermost planet of the solar system, Saturn was said to bring about melancholy or dullness.

[5] *Sol* Sun.

[6] *Of dust … return* Cf. Genesis 3.19: "For dust thou art, and unto dust thou shalt return." The phrase is used in Christian burial services.

To a Gentleman with a Manuscript Play

As some grave matron bred on rural downs,
Who at the mention of a top-knot frowns,
And the proud minxes of the market-towns;
Whose humble senses are not much refined,
But used to labour with a cheerful mind;
Clad in plain coifs and gown of russet hue,
With home-spun aprons of a decent blue;
From the white curds extracts the greener whey,
Nor dreams of fashion, poetry, or play;
From wicked verse she turns her cautious eyes,
And wonders people can delight in lies:
At length her landlord, the right noble squire,
Takes her young daughter at her own desire;
Prefers the damsel to attend his spouse,
And she with joy resigns her brindled[1] cows:
For London now prepares the smiling dame,
While her sad mother trembles at the name.
But O! what griefs attend the parting leave,
No Muse[2] can paint 'em, nor no heart conceive:
In vain her spouse or friendly neighbour tries,
To quell the sorrows in her streaming eyes:
Rossell she fears will slight her jersey gown,
And wear white aprons in the sinful town;
On the pure ghost of Win'fred then she calls,
To guard her child within its guilty walls.

So this rude babe I to your mercy yield,
Rough as the soil of some untillaged field:
Can nature please? Not 'till she's well refined,
Reforming art should follow close behind;
But that proud dame with me disdains to dwell,
And far she flies—ah far from Mira's[3] cell.
What then remains? What hope for me or mine,
But the kind of silence of forgetful time?
To save us from the sly buffooning leer,
The spiteful grimace, and the scornful sneer;
The threat'ning critic with his dreadful rules,
The wit's keen satire and the burst of fools.

The wretched villain pinioned up on high,[4]
Two hours pendant 'twixt the earth and sky,
With eggs and turnips whirling round his pate,° *skull*
Is but an emblem of an author's fate.
A dread example to the rhyming fry,[5]
So poets tell me, but I hope they lie:
The world's good-natured, if it is not crossed,
But wits are often saucy to their cost.

Though unassured, yet not in deep despair,
I trust this infant to its patron's care:
Ah, let your roofs the simple vagrants shield,
I ask no more than charity may yield,
Some little corner in the friendly dome,
(Lest the loose varlet° be induced to roam) *rascal*
Where the cold storms may hover round in vain,
The chilling snow or penetrating rain;
Where the fierce rat (all dreadful) never climbs,
Nor the sleek mouse, sad foe to Mira's rhymes.

But I have done—for who implores a friend
With long petitions, justly may offend:
To no straight bounds good-nature is confined;
And who shall dictate to a gen'rous mind?
Which not content in narrow space to roll,
Like the broad ocean spreads from pole to pole:
While the glad nations bless the ample tide,
And wasted treasures o'er its surface glide:
That still waves on, regardless of the praise,
As you perhaps of Mira's idle lays.° *verses*
—1748

[1] *brindled* Streaked; tabby.

[2] *Muse* One of the nine daughters of Zeus and Mnemosyne, each of whom presides over, and provides inspiration for, a different aspect of the arts and sciences.

[3] *Mira* Leapor's poetic name for herself.

[4] *The wretched ... on high* This line describes the fate of a criminal condemned to stand in the pillory.

[5] *fry* Group of insignificant beings.

Crumble Hall

When friends or fortune frown on Mira's[1] lay,° *verse*
Or gloomy vapours hide the lamp of day;
With low'ring° forehead, and with aching limbs, *scowling*
Oppressed with headache, and eternal whims,
Sad Mira vows to quit the darling crime:
Yet takes her farewell, and repents, in rhyme.

But see (more charming than Armida's[2] wiles)
The sun returns, and Artemisia smiles:
Then in a trice the resolutions fly;
And who so frolic as the Muse[3] and I?
We sing once more, obedient to her call;
Once more we sing; and 'tis of Crumble Hall;
That Crumble Hall, whose hospitable door
Has fed the stranger, and relieved the poor;
Whose Gothic towers, and whose rusty spires,
Were known of old to knights, and hungry squires.
There powdered° beef, and warden pies,[4] were found; *salted*
And pudden dwelt within her spacious bound:
Pork, peas, and bacon (good old English fare!),
With tainted[5] ven'son, and with hunted hare:
With humming[6] beer her vats were wont to flow,
And ruddy nectar[7] in her vaults to glow.
Here came the wights,° who battled for renown, *people*
The sable friar, and the russet clown:° *country person*
The loaded tables sent a sav'ry gale,
And the brown bowls were crowned with simp'ring° ale; *simmering*
While the guests ravaged° on the smoking store,° *wreaked havoc* / *provisions, provender*
Till their stretched girdles would contain no more.

Of this rude palace might a poet sing
From cold December to returning spring;
Tell how the building spreads on either hand,
And two grim giants o'er the portals stand;
Whose grizzled beards are neither combed nor shorn,
But look severe, and horribly adorn.° *adorned*

Then step within—there stands a goodly row
Of oaken pillars—where a gallant show
Of mimic pears and carved pomegranates twine,
With the plump clusters of the spreading vine.
Strange forms above present themselves to view;
Some mouths that grin, some smile, and some that spew.
Here a soft maid or infant seems to cry:
Here stares a tyrant, with distorted eye.
The roof—no Cyclops[8] e'er could reach so high:
Not Polypheme, though formed for dreadful harms,
The top could measure with extended arms.
Here the pleased spider plants her peaceful loom:
Here weaves secure, nor dreads the hated broom.
But at the head (and furbished once a year)
The herald's mystic compliments appear:° *coat of arms*
Round the fierce dragon *Honi Soit*[9] twines,
And Royal Edward o'er the chimney shines.

Safely the mice through yon dark passage run,
Where the dim windows ne'er admit the sun.
Along each wall the stranger blindly feels;
And (trembling) dreads a spectre at his heels.

The sav'ry kitchen much attention calls:
Westphalia[10] hams adorn the sable walls:
The fires blaze; the greasy pavements° fry; *stone floors*
And steaming odours from the kettles fly.

[1] *Mira* Leapor's poetic name for herself.

[2] *Armida* Beautiful sorceress and seductress in sixteenth-century Italian poet Torquato Tasso's epic poem *Gerusalemme liberatta* (*Jerusalem Delivered*).

[3] *Muse* One of the nine daughters of Zeus and Mnemosyne, each of whom presides over, and provides inspiration for, a different aspect of the arts and sciences.

[4] *warden pies* Pies made from warden pears, a type of baking pear.

[5] *tainted* Aged game meat.

[6] *humming* Strong; frothing.

[7] *ruddy nectar* I.e., cider.

[8] *Cyclops* Race of one-eyed, man-eating giants who, according to Greek mythology, forged thunderbolts for the god Zeus. In Homer's *Odyssey*, Odysseus blinds Polypheme, the leader of the Cyclops.

[9] *Honi Soit* The first words of the French motto of the English Order of the Garter (created by King Edward III in 1348), "Honi soit qui mal y pense" (Shame to the person who thinks evil of it).

[10] *Westphalia* Region in western Germany.

See! yon brown parlour on the left appears,
For nothing famous, but its leathern chairs,
Whose shining nails like polished armour glow,
And the dull clock beats audible and slow.

But on the right we spy a room more fair:
The form—'tis neither long, nor round, nor square—
The walls how lofty, and the floor how wide,
We leave for learned Quadrus to decide.
Gay China bowls o'er the broad chimney shine,
Whose long description would be too sublime:
And much might of the tapestry be sung:
But we're content to say, "The parlour's hung."

We count the stairs, and to the right ascend,
Where on the walls the gorgeous colours blend.
There doughty George[1] bestrides the goodly steed;
The dragon's slaughtered, and the virgin freed:
And there (but lately rescued from their fears)
The nymph and serious Ptolemy appears:
Their awkward limbs unwieldy are displayed;
And, like a milk-wench, glares the royal maid.

From hence we turn to more familiar rooms;
Whose hangings ne'er were wrought in Grecian looms:
Yet the soft stools, and eke° the lazy chair, *also*
To sleep invite the weary, and the fair.

Shall we proceed? Yes, if you'll break the wall:
If not, return, and tread once more the hall.
Up ten stone steps now please to drag your toes,
And a brick passage will succeed to those.
Here the strong doors were aptly framed to hold
Sir Wary's person, and Sir Wary's gold.
Here Biron sleeps, with books encircled round;
And him you'd guess a student most profound.
Not so—in form the dusty volumes stand:
There's few that wear the mark of Biron's hand.

Would you go further?—Stay a little then:
Back through the passage—down the steps again;
Through yon dark room—be careful how you tread
Up these steep stairs,—or you may break your head.

These rooms are furnished amiably, and full:
Old shoes, and sheep-ticks bred in stacks of wool;
Grey Dobbin's[2] gears, and drenching-horns[3]
enow;° *enough*
Wheel-spokes, the irons of a tattered plough.

No farther—yes, a little higher, pray:
At yon small door you'll find the beams of day,
While the hot leads return the scorching ray.
Here a gay prospect meets the ravished eye:
Meads, fields, and groves, in beauteous order lie.
From hence the Muse precipitant is hurled,
And drags down Mira to the nether world.

Thus far the palace—yet there still remain
Unsung the gardens, and the menial
train.° *household servants*
Its groves anon—its people first we sing:
Hear, Artemisia, hear the song we bring.
Sophronia first in verse shall learn to chime,
And keep her station, though in Mira's rhyme;
Sophronia sage! whose learned knuckles know
To form round cheese-cakes of the pliant dough;
To bruise the curd, and through her fingers squeeze
Ambrosial butter with the tempered cheese:
Sweet tarts and pudden, too, her skill declare;
And the soft jellies, hid from baneful air.

O'er the warm kettles, and the sav'ry steams,
Grave Colinettus of his oxen dreams:
Then, starting, anxious for his new-mown hay,
Runs headlong out to view the doubtful day:
But dinner calls with more prevailing charms;
And surly Gruffo in his awkward arms
Bears the tall jug, and turns a glaring eye,
As though he feared some insurrection nigh
From the fierce crew, that gaping stand a-dry.

O'er-stuffed with beef; with cabbage much too full,
And dumpling too (fit emblem of his skull!)
With mouth wide open, but with closing eyes
Unwieldy Roger on the table lies.

[1] *George* Saint George, patron saint of the Order of the Garter, who is said to have slain a dragon to rescue a damsel in distress.

[2] *Dobbin* Typical name for a farm horse.

[3] *drenching-horns* Instruments used to administer medicine to horses.

His able lungs discharge a rattling sound:
Prince barks, Spot howls, and the tall roofs rebound.
Him Urs'la views; and with dejected eyes,
"Ah! Roger, ah!" the mournful maiden cries:
"Is wretched Urs'la then your care no more,
That, while I sigh, thus you can sleep and snore?
Ingrateful Roger! wilt thou leave me now?
For you these furrows mark my fading brow;
For you my pigs resign their morning due;
My hungry chickens lose their meat for you;
And, was it not, ah! was it not for thee,
No goodly pottage[1] would be dressed by me.
For thee these hands wind up the whirling jack,[2]
Or place the spit across the sloping rack.
I baste the mutton with a cheerful heart,
Because I know my Roger will have part."

Thus she—but now her dish-kettle began
To boil and blubber with the foaming bran.
The greasy apron round her hips she ties,
And to each plate the scalding clout° applies: *cloth*
The purging bath each glowing dish refines,
And once again the polished pewter shines.

Now to those meads° let frolic fancy rove, *meadows*
Where o'er yon waters nods a pendant grove;
In whose clear waves the pictured boughs are seen,
With fairer blossoms, and a brighter green.
Soft flow'ry banks the spreading lakes divide:
Sharp-pointed flags adorn each tender side.
See! the pleased swans along the surface play;
Where yon cool willows meet the scorching ray,
When fierce Orion[3] gives too warm a day.

But, hark! what scream the wond'ring ear invades!
The dryads° howling for their threatened shades: *wood-nymphs*
Round the dear grove each nymph distracted flies
(Though not discovered but with poet's eyes);
And shall those shades, where Philomela's[4] strain
Has oft to slumber lulled the hapless swain;° *country laborer*
Where turtles° used to clasp their silken wings; *turtle-doves*
Whose rev'rend oaks have known a hundred springs;
Shall these ignobly from their roots be torn,
And perish shameful, as the abject thorn;
While the slow car° bears off their aged limbs, *wagon*
To clear the way for slopes, and modern whims;
Where banished nature leaves a barren gloom,
And awkward art supplies the vacant room?
Yet (or the Muse for vengeance calls in vain)
The injured nymphs shall haunt the ravaged plain.
Strange sounds and forms shall tease the gloomy green;
And fairy-elves by Urs'la shall be seen:
Their new-built parlour shall with echoes ring,
And in their hall shall doleful crickets sing.

Then cease, Diracto, stay thy desp'rate hand;
And let the grove, if not the parlour, stand.

—1751

Elizabeth Hands

On the Supposition of an Advertisement Appearing in a Morning Paper, of the Publication of a Volume of Poems, by a Servant Maid

The tea-kettle bubbled, the tea things were set,
The candles were lighted, the ladies were met;
The how d'ye's were over, and entering bustle,
The company seated, and silks ceased to rustle:
The great Mrs. Consequence opened her fan;
And thus the discourse in an instant began
(All affected reserve, and formality scorning):
"I suppose you all saw in the paper this morning,
A volume of poems advertised—'tis said
They're produced by the pen of a poor servant maid."

[1] *pottage* Type of thick soup.

[2] *jack* Machine for turning the spit for roasting meat, usually wound up like a watch.

[3] *Orion* Probably a reference to Sirius, the dog star, also known as Orion's hound. The prominence of this star in the sky during most of the summer in Egypt led the ancients to believe the star was responsible for the extreme heat of the late summer days, which have since become known as the "dog days" of summer.

[4] *Philomela* Princess of classical myth who was turned into a nightingale.

"A servant write verses!" says Madam Du Bloom;
"Pray what is the subject? A mop, or a broom?"
"He, he, he," says Miss Flounce; "I suppose we shall see
An ode on a dishclout°—what else can it be?" *dishcloth*
Says Miss Coquettilla, "Why ladies so tart?° *acrimonious*
Perhaps Tom the footman has fired her heart;
And she'll tell us how charming he looks in new clothes,
And how nimble his hand moves in brushing the shoes;
Or how the last time that he went to Mayfair,[1]
He bought her some sweethearts of ginger-bread ware."
"For my part I think," says old lady Marr-joy,
"A servant might find herself other employ:
Was she mine I'd employ her as long as 'twas light,
And send her to bed without candle at night."
"Why so?" says Miss Rhymer, displeased; "I protest
'Tis pity a genius should be so depressed!"
"What ideas can such low-bred creatures conceive,"
Says Mrs. Noworthy, and laughed in her sleeve.
Says old Miss Prudella, "If servants can tell
How to write to their mothers, to say they are well,
And read of a Sunday the Duty of Man,[2]
Which is more I believe than one half of them can,
I think 'tis much properer they should rest there,
Than be reaching at things so much out of their sphere."
Says old Mrs. Candour, "I've now got a maid
That's the plague of my life—a young gossiping jade;[3]
There's no end of the people that after her come,
And whenever I'm out, she is never at home;
I'd rather ten times she would sit down and write,
Than gossip all over the town every night."
"Some whimsical trollop most like," says Miss Prim,
"Has been scribbling of the nonsense, just out of a whim,
And conscious it neither is witty or pretty,
Conceals her true name, and ascribes it to Betty."[4]
"I once had a servant myself," says Miss Pines,
"That wrote on a wedding, some very good lines."
Says Mrs. Domestic, "and when they were done,
I can't see for my part, what use they were *on*;
Had she wrote a receipt,° to've instructed you how *recipe*
To warm a cold breast of veal, like a ragout,
Or to make cowslip wine that would pass for Champagne;
It might have been useful, again and again."
On the sofa was old lady Pedigree placed,
She owned that for poetry she had no taste,
That the study of heraldry was more in fashion,
And boasted she knew all the crests in the nation.
Says Mrs. Routella, "Tom, take out the urn,
And stir up the fire, you see it don't burn."
The tea things removed, and the tea-table gone,
The card-tables brought, and the cards laid thereon,
The ladies ambitious for each other's crown,
Like courtiers contending for honours sat down.
—1789

[1] *Mayfair* Fair held in May, especially one held near Hyde Park Corner in London. Now only used in reference to a district of London in the West End.

[2] *Duty of Man* I.e., *The Whole Duty of Man*, a popular devotional work, written by Samuel von Pufendorf and translated into English by Richard Allestree, available throughout the eighteenth and nineteenth centuries.

[3] *jade* Term of reprobation applied to women, similar to "hussy."

[4] *Betty* Typical name for a serving girl or housemaid.

Town and Country

CONTEXTS

During the late seventeenth and early eighteenth centuries, London solidified its position as Europe's largest city and became a multicultural center. The bustling, industrious city was filthy and dangerous, with people of every class pressed together on its crowded streets—but, as John Gay explains in his poem *Trivia: or, the Art of Walking the Streets of London*, it afforded many delights for those with the wisdom to navigate it cleanly and safely. Londoners could purchase the products of international travel and trade, which increased as the British Empire expanded and navigation improved. Goods and people moved more easily through the nation. At the center of city life was a growing class of people: the merchant middle class. Joseph Addison's *Spectator* article number 69 and Daniel Defoe's "On Trade" both celebrate England's status as a leader in international commerce and expound upon the many benefits trade had brought. For these writers, England's success in trade was one of numerous proofs that it was the greatest nation in the world. The following pieces, from *The Female Tatler*, offer a glimpse into the world of consumers (particularly the female consumers) and of those merchants who provide goods for them.

Coffee-houses proliferated in the eighteenth century (it was estimated London had 3000 by the end of the century) and provided a forum for many business transactions. While some customers met there for idle conversation or to read the news, many merchants and insurance brokers also used them as a place in which to conduct business; some even listed their business addresses as coffee-shops. Two pamphlets excerpted below provide contrasting views of the coffee-house. The first paints the coffee-house as a place where fools and pretenders to wit congregate, while the other presents an idealized portrait of the coffee-shop as a haven of intellectual debate, where men improve their minds through open and unregulated conversation. Richard Steele's *Spectator* article number 155, written from the point of view of a female proprietor of a coffee-house, presents a portrait of coffee-houses that falls somewhere in between, and highlights the ways in which changes in class structure also led to shifts in gender roles—and to confusion as to the proper role for women of the merchant class.

The following four selections also comment on changing roles, values, and tastes. William Hogarth's series of prints, *Marriage A-la-Mode*, shows a merchant who marries his daughter off to the son of an aristocrat; the series portrays the tensions between the declining aristocracy and the rising middle class, both of whom are regarded as greedy and morally suspect. Addison's *Spectator* article number 119 comments on the differences in manners and dress between residents of the country and city. While Addison disparages affluent country dwellers, John Gay caricatures the rural lower class in *The Shepherd's Week*, a burlesque of the pastoral singing-match. The poem, Gay's first piece of writing for the Scriblerus Club—a group formed to satirize the pretentious and talentless writers and critics of London's literary scene—seeks to mock the pastoral poetry of Ambrose Philips, who had recently been targeted by Gay's fellow Scriblerian, Alexander Pope. Influenced by her friends in the Scriblerus Club, Lady Mary Wortley Montagu similarly sends up the pastoral tradition in her *Six Town*

Eclogues. The eclogue traditionally featured country shepherds declaring their love for country maids or music; here, Montagu uses the form to criticize the frivolity and immorality of urban social practices.

The landscape of both town and country changed substantially over the course of this period. Farms became larger, more complex, and more standardized in organization, as is evident from the picture on the cover of John Worlidge's *Systema Agriculturae*. London, which had incurred extensive damage in the Great Fire of 1666, was rebuilt, with many improvements, under the direction of Charles II. The London monument commemorating the Great Fire, shown below, was designed by Christopher Wren and Robert Hooke and constructed between 1671 and 1677. Town planning also became more of a consideration in the eighteenth century, and a number of fashionable squares (such as Bloomsbury Square, also shown below) were constructed as part of a massive expansion, mostly westward, which lasted throughout the eighteenth century.

Landscape gardening became a passion in the eighteenth century; designers attempted to create beautiful, artfully designed landscapes that combined all the most pleasing elements of nature, without betraying any sense of the artifice required to create them. This marked a change from the gardens of the previous century, which were openly artificial, with perfectly symmetrical arrangements and bushes and trees sculpted into a variety of geometric shapes. In London, numerous landscaped parks provided beautiful ponds, grottoes, temples, and fountains for citizens to admire as they walked the paths. Pleasure gardens, of which Vauxhall was the most popular, also offered other entertainment, including masquerades, concerts, ballets, opera, and firework displays. These forerunners of the modern theme park grew in popularity from the middle of the seventeenth century on.

Addison, in his *Spectator* article number 414 (even before any of the great names in landscape gardening had become active), discusses landscape as a source of pleasure and presents some ideals for landscape gardeners to keep in mind. *A View at Stourhead* shows one admired garden. Another landscape painting, *View of the Temple Pond at Beachborough Manor*, shows the private grounds of a manor in Kent, and the drawing of Alexander Pope's grotto and garden shows one of the most famous grounds of the eighteenth century. In Pope's view (as his letter explains), part of the beauty of his grounds is the seeming lack of artifice in their construction. Such landscapes were, in the eighteenth century, seen as possessing the power to move a viewer to strong emotions. John Dyer praises both natural and human-made landscapes in *The Fleece*, a poem celebrating the wool industry and describing in detail many towns and regions of England. The poem marked a new genre of descriptive, local poetry; Romantic poet William Wordsworth later praised it for its "living landscape." Edmund Burke, who takes up many of the ideas explored by Addison earlier, articulates in his *Philosophical Enquiry into the Origin of Our Ideas of the Sublime and the Beautiful* the effects many English people sought in landscape. For Burke, those objects which we cannot tame or control inspire the most powerful feelings in us; the sense of awe they produce is even stronger than the sense of pleasure produced by beauty. Burke's presentation of the sublime is more original than his presentation of the beautiful, and the former concept became increasingly significant in the Romantic period.

⌘⌘⌘

from John Gay, *Trivia:*[1] *or, the Art of Walking the Streets of London* (1716)

from Book 1
Of the Implements for Walking the Streets, and Signs of the Weather.

Through winter streets to steer your course aright,
How to walk clean by day, and safe by night,
How jostling crowds, with prudence, to decline,
When to assert the wall,[2] and when resign,
I sing: thou Trivia, goddess, aid my song,
Through spacious streets conduct thy bard along;
By thee transported, I securely stray
Where winding alleys lead the doubtful way,
The silent court, and op'ning square explore,
And long perplexing lanes untrod before.
To pave thy realm, and smooth the broken ways,
Earth from her womb a flinty tribute pays;
For thee, the sturdy pavior[3] thumps the ground,
Whilst every stroke his lab'ring lungs resound;
For thee, the scavenger bids kennels° glide *gutters*
Within their bounds, and heaps of dirt subside.
My youthful bosom burns with thirst of fame,
From the great theme to build a glorious name,
To tread in paths to ancient bards unknown,
And bind my temples with a civic crown;
But more, my country's love demands the lays,° *lyric poems*
My country's be the profit, mine the praise.

When the black youth[4] at chosen stands rejoice,
And "clean your shoes" resounds from ev'ry voice;
When late their miry° sides stage-coaches show, *muddy*
And their stiff horses through the town move slow;
When all the Mall[5] in leafy ruin lies,
And damsels first renew their oyster cries:[6]
Then let the prudent walker shoes provide,
Not of the Spanish or Morocco hide;[7]
The wooden heel may raise the dancer's bound,
And with the 'scalloped top his step be crowned:
Let firm, well-hammered soles protect thy feet
Through freezing snows, and rains, and soaking sleet.
Should the big laste[8] extend the shoe too wide,
Each stone will wrench th'unwary step aside:
The sudden turn may stretch the swelling vein,
Thy cracking joint unhinge, or ankle sprain;
And when too short the modish° shoes are worn,[9] *fashionable*
You'll judge the seasons by your shooting corn.

Nor should it prove thy less important care,
To chose a proper coat for winter's wear.
Now in thy trunk thy doily[10] habit° fold, *garment*
The silken drugget[11] ill can fence the cold;
The frieze's[12] spongy nap[13] is soaked with rain,
And show'rs soon drench the camlet's[14] cockled° grain. *puckered*
True Witney broadcloth[15] with its shag unshorn,
Unpierced is in the lasting tempest worn:
Be this the horseman's fence; for who would wear
Amid the town the spoils of Russia's bear?
Within the Roquelaure's[16] clasp thy hands are pent,
Hands that, stretched forth, invading harms prevent.
Let the looped Bavaroy[17] the fop[18] embrace,

[1] *Trivia* Here, a goddess of streets. "Trivia" was an epithet given to any goddess whose temple sat at the junction of three roads.

[2] *the wall* I.e., side of the walkway next to the wall, the inner side.

[3] *pavior* Person who lays paving.

[4] *black youth* I.e., shoe shiners.

[5] *the Mall* A walkway in St. James's Park, London, bordered by trees.

[6] *oyster cries* I.e., cries to buy oysters.

[7] *Spanish or Morocco hide* Costly delicate leather.

[8] *laste* Model of the foot used by shoemakers to construct shoes.

[9] *Should the big … are worn* At this point in the century, men's fashions had changed from sturdy, high-heeled shoes to shorter, wider shoes.

[10] *doily* Woolen fabric popular for summer wear.

[11] *drugget* Cheap, coarse fabric, often half silk and half wool.

[12] *frieze* Heavy, fuzzy woolen fabric generally made in Ireland.

[13] *nap* Layer of rough fibers projecting from the surface of a fabric.

[14] *camlet* Expensive Asian fabric (and its European imitations) usually made from goat hair.

[15] *Witney broadcloth* Heavy, water-repellent woolen cloth for which Witney, Oxfordshire, was famous.

[16] *Roquelaure* Fashionable men's cloak, knee length and with a cape collar.

[17] *Bavaroy* Type of cloak.

[18] *fop* Overdressed, vain man.

Or his deep cloak be spattered o'er with lace.
That garment best the winter's rage defends,
Whose shapeless form in ample plaits° depends; *pleats*
Thy various names in various counties known,
Yet held in all the true surtout° alone: *overcoat*
Be thine of Kersey[1] firm, though small the cost,
Then brave unwet the rain, unchilled the frost.

If the strong cane support thy walking hand,
Chairmen[2] no longer shall the wall command;
Even sturdy car-men[3] shall thy nod obey,
And rattling coaches stop to make thee way:
This shall direct thy cautious tread aright,
Though not one glaring lamp enliven night.
Let beaus their canes with amber tipped produce,
Be theirs for empty show, but thine for use.
In gilded chariots while they loll° at ease, *recline*
And lazily ensure a life's disease;
While softer chairs the tawdry load convey
To Court, to White's,[4] Assemblies, or the play;
Rose-complexioned health thy steps attends,
And exercise thy lasting youth defends.
Imprudent men Heav'n's choicest gifts profane.
Thus some beneath their arm support the cane;
The dirty point oft checks the careless pace,
And miry spots thy clean cravat disgrace:
O! may I never such misfortune meet,
May no such vicious walkers crowd the street,
May providence o'er-shade me with her wings,
While the bold Muse experienced danger sings.

Not that I wander from my native home,
And tempting perils foreign cities roam.
Let Paris be the theme of Gallia's° muse, *France's*
Where slavery treads the streets in wooden shoes;
Nor do I rove in Belgia's° frozen clime, *Belgium's*
And teach the clumsy boor to skate in rhyme,
Where, if the warmer clouds in rain descend,
No miry ways industrious steps offend,
The rushing floods from sloping pavements pours,
And blackens the canals with dirty show'rs.
Let others Naples' smoother streets rehearse,
And with proud Roman structures grace their verse,
Where frequent murders wake the night with groans,
And blood in purple torrents dyes the stones;
Nor shall the Muse through narrow Venice stray,
Where gondolas their painted oars display.
O happy streets to rumbling wheels unknown,
No carts, no coaches shake the floating town!
Thus was of old Britannia's city blessed,
Ere pride and luxury her sons possessed:
Coaches and chariots yet unfashioned lay,
Nor late invented chairs perplexed the way:
Then the proud lady tripped along the town,
And tucked up petticoats secured her gown,
Her rosy cheek with distant visits glowed,
And exercise unartful charms bestowed;
But since in braided gold her foot is bound,
And a long trailing manteau° sweeps the ground, *gown*
Her shoe disdains the street; the lazy fair,° *fair girl*
With narrow step affects a limping air.
Now gaudy pride corrupts the lavish age,
And the streets flame with glaring equipage;
The tricking gamester insolently rides,
With loves and graces[5] on his chariot's sides;
In saucy° state the griping broker sits, *insolent*
And laughs at honesty, and trudging
    wits°: *men of intelligence*
For you, O honest men, these useful lays
The Muse prepares; I seek no other praise.

…

from Book 2

Of Walking the Streets by Day.

Thus far the Muse has traced in useful lays
The proper implements for wintry ways;
Has taught the walker, with judicious eyes,
To read the various warnings of the skies.
Now venture, Muse, from home to range the town,
And for the public safety risk thy own.

[1] *Kersey* Coarse woolen cloth named after the town in Suffolk.

[2] *Chairmen* Those who carry sedan chairs, a common mode of transportation for the upper class.

[3] *car-men* Drivers of chariots.

[4] *White's* Expensive London chocolate house.

[5] *loves and graces* Goddesses commonly depicted in decorative art; refers to the custom of ostentatiously painting chariots.

For ease and for dispatch, the morning's best;
No tides of passengers the street molest.
You'll see a draggled damsel, here and there,
From Billingsgate[1] her fishy traffic bear;
On doors the sallow milk-maid chalks° her gains; *tallies*
Ah! how unlike the milk-maid of the plains!
Before proud gates attending asses[2] bray,
Or arrogate° with solemn pace° the way; *claim* / *manner of stepping*
These grave physicians with their milky cheer,
The love-sick maid and dwindling beau repair;
Here rows of drummers stand in martial file,
And with their vellum[3]-thunder shake the pile,
To greet the new-made bride. Are sounds like these
The proper prelude to a state of peace?
Now industry awakes her busy sons,
Full charged with news the breathless hawker runs:
Shops open, coaches roll, carts shake the ground,
And all the streets with passing cries resound.

If clothed in black, you tread the busy town
Or if distinguished by the rev'rend gown,
Three trades avoid; oft in the mingling press,° *crowd*
The barber's apron soils the sable dress;
Shun the perfumer's touch with cautious eye,
Nor let the baker's step advance too nigh;
Ye walkers too that youthful colours wear,
Three sullying trades avoid with equal care:
The little chimney-sweeper skulks along,
And marks with sooty stains the heedless throng;
When small-coal° murmurs in the hoarser throat, *charcoal*
From smutty dangers guard thy threatened coat:
The dust-man's[4] cart offends thy clothes and eyes,
When through the street a cloud of ashes flies;
But whether black or lighter dyes are worn,
The chandler's° basket, on his shoulder borne, *candle-maker's*
With tallow spots thy coat; resign the way,
To shun the surly butcher's greasy tray,
Butchers, whose hands are dyed with blood's foul stain,
And always foremost in the hangman's train.
Let due civilities be strictly paid.
The wall surrender to the hooded maid;
Nor let thy sturdy elbow's hasty rage
Jostle the feeble steps of trembling age;
And when the porter bends beneath his load,
And pants for breath, clear thou the crowded road.
But, above all, the groping blind direct,
And from the pressing throng the lame protect.
You'll sometimes meet a fop, of nicest tread,
Whose mantling° peruke° veils his empty head; *covering* / *wig*
At every step he dreads the wall to lose,
And risks, to save° a coach, his red-heeled shoes; *reserve*
Him, like the miller, pass with caution by,
Lest from his shoulder clouds of powder fly.
But when the bully, with assuming pace,
Cocks his broad hat, edged round with tarnished lace,
Yield not the way; defy his strutting pride,
And thrust him to the muddy kennel's side;
He never turns again, nor dares oppose,
But mutters coward curses as he goes.

If drawn by business to a street unknown,
Let the sworn porter point thee through the town;
Be sure observe the signs, for signs remain,
Like faithful landmarks to the walking train.° *body of people*
Seek not from 'prentices° to learn the way, *apprentices*
Those fabling boys will turn thy steps astray;
Ask the grave tradesman to direct thee right,
He ne'er deceives, but when he profits by't.

Where famed St. Giles's[5] ancient limits spread,
An inrailed column rears its lofty head,
Here to sev'n streets sev'n dials count the day,
And from each other catch the circling ray.
Here oft the peasant, with enquiring face,
Bewildered, trudges on from place to place;
He dwells on every sign with stupid gaze,

[1] *Billingsgate* Famous London fish market.

[2] *asses* In the eighteenth century, asses' milk was in high demand for its cosmetic and medicinal properties; asses could be brought to the milk-buyer's door for a fee.

[3] *vellum* Skin used to cover drums.

[4] *dust-man* Collector who disposes of the ashes from domestic coal fires.

[5] *St. Giles* Parish in London at whose center is a large open area, from which seven streets radiate. In the eighteenth century, a large column stood at the intersection of these seven streets and a sundial faced each street.

Enters the narrow alley's doubtful maze,
Tries every winding court and street in vain,
And doubles o'er his weary steps again.
Thus hardy Theseus, with intrepid feet,
Traversed the dang'rous labyrinth of Crete;[1]
But still the wand'ring passes forced his stay,
Till Ariadne's clue unwinds the way.
But do not thou, like that bold chief, confide
Thy vent'rous° footsteps to a female guide; *adventurous*
She'll lead thee with delusive smiles along,
Dive in thy fob,° and drop thee in the throng. *watch-pocket*

When waggish° boys the stunted besom° *mischievous / broom*
ply
To rid the slabby pavement, pass not by
Ere thou hast held their hands; some heedless flirt
Will over-spread thy calves with spatt'ring dirt.
Where porters hogsheads° roll from *casks (of wine)*
carts aslope,
Or brewers down steep cellars stretch the rope,
Where counted billets° are by car-men tossed, *bills of fare*
Stay thy rash steps, and walk without° the post.[2] *outside*

What though the gath'ring mire thy feet besmear,
The voice of industry is always near.
Hark! the boy calls thee to his destined stand,
And the shoe shines beneath his oily hand.
Here let the Muse, fatigued amid the throng,
Adorn her precepts with digressive song;
Of shirtless youths the secret rise to trace,
And show the parent of the sable race.

Like mortal man, great Jove[3] (grown fond of change)
Of old was wont° this nether world to range *accustomed*
To seek amours; the vice the monarch loved
Soon through the wide ethereal court improved,
And ev'n the proudest goddess now and then
Would lodge a night among the sons of men;
To vulgar deities descends the fashion,
Each, like her betters, had her earthly passion.
Then Cloacina[4] (goddess of the tide,
Whose sable streams beneath the city glide)
Indulged the modish flame; the town she roved,
A mortal scavenger she saw, she loved;
The muddy spots that dried upon his face,
Like female patches,[5] heightened every grace:
She gazed; she sighed. For love can beauties spy
In what seems faults to every common eye.

Now had the watchman walked his second round;
When Cloacina hears the rumbling sound
Of her brown lover's cart, for well she knows
That pleasing thunder: swift the goddess rose,
And through the streets pursued the distant noise,
Her bosom panting with expected joys.
With the night wandering harlot's airs she passed,
Brushed near his side, and wanton glances cast;
In the black form of cinder wench she came,
When love, the hour, the place had banished shame;
To the dark alley arm in arm they move:
O may no link-boy[6] interrupt their love!

When the pale moon had nine times filled her space,
The pregnant goddess (cautious of disgrace)
Descends to earth; but sought no midwife's aid,
Nor 'midst her anguish to Lucina[7] prayed;
No cheerful gossip wished the mother joy,
Alone, beneath a bulk[8] she dropt the boy.

The child through various risks in years improved,
At first a beggar's brat, compassion moved;

[1] *Theseus … Crete* A reference to the myth of Theseus, who was imprisoned in a labyrinth by King Minos of Crete. Theseus killed the minotaur in the labyrinth and was able to escape with the help of the King's daughter, Ariadne, who left him thread to lead him out of the maze.

[2] *post* A line of posts marked the edge of the pavement on most London streets.

[3] *Jove* King of the Roman gods.

[4] [Gay's note] Cloacina was a Goddess whose image Tatius (a king of the Sabines [a tribe of central Italy]) found in the common shore, and not knowing what Goddess it was, he called it Cloacina, from the place in which it was found, and paid to it divine honours.… [Cloacina was goddess of the *cloacae*, the sewers of Rome.]

[5] *patches* Pieces of black silk cut into decorative shapes and worn on the face.

[6] *link-boy* Hired torch-carrier who lights the way for pedestrians at night.

[7] *Lucina* Roman goddess of childbirth.

[8] *bulk* Stall or frame projecting from a shop-front.

His infant tongue soon learnt the canting° art, *begging*
Knew all the prayers and whines to touch the heart.

O happy unowned youths, your limbs can bear
The scorching dog star[1] and the winter's air,
While the rich infant, nursed with care and pain,
Thirsts with each heat, and coughs with every rain!

The goddess long had marked the child's distress,
And long had sought his suff'rings to redress;
She prays the gods to take the fondling's[2] part,
To teach his hands some beneficial art
Practised in streets: the gods her suit allowed,
And made him useful to the walking crowd,
To cleanse the miry feet, and o'er the shoe
With nimble skill the glossy black renew.
Each power contributes to relieve the poor:
With the strong bristles of the mighty boar
Diana forms his brush; the god of day
A tripod gives, amid the crowded way
To raise the dirty foot, and ease his toil;
Kind Neptune fills his vase with fetid oil
Pressed from th'enormous whale; the god of fire,[3]
From whose dominions smoky clouds aspire,
Among these gen'rous presents joins his part,
And aids with soot the new japanning° art: *lacquering*
Pleased, she receives the gifts; she downward glides,
Lights in Fleet-ditch,[4] and shoots beneath the tides.

Now dawns the morn, the sturdy lad awakes,
Leaps from his stall, his tangled hair he shakes.
Then leaning o'er the rails he musing stood,
And viewed below the black canal of mud,
Where common shores° a lulling murmur keep, *sewers*
Whose torrents rush Holborn's[5] fatal steep:
Pensive through idleness, tears flowed apace,
Which eased his loaded heart, and washed his face;
At length he sighing cried: "That boy was blest,
Whose infant lips have drained a mother's breast;
But happier far are those (if such be known)
Whom both a father and a mother own:
But I, alas! had fortune's utmost scorn,
Who ne'er knew parent, was an orphan born!
Some boys are rich by birth beyond all wants,
Beloved by uncles, and kind good old aunts;
When time comes round a Christmas box they bear,
And one day makes them rich for all the year.
Had I the precepts of a father learned,
Perhaps I then the coachman's fare had earned,
For lesser boys can drive; I thirsty stand
And see the double flagon[6] charge their hand,
See them puff off the froth, and gulp amain,° *without delay*
While with dry tongue I lick my lips in vain."

While thus he fervent prays, the heaving tide
In widened circles beats on either side;
The goddess rose amid the inmost round,
With withered turnip-tops her temples crowned;
Low reached her dripping tresses, lank, and black
As the smooth jet, or glossy raven's back;
Around her waste a circling eel was twined,
Which bound her robe that hung in rags behind.
Now beck'ning to the boy, she thus begun,
"Thy prayers are granted; weep no more, my son:
Go thrive. At some frequented corner stand;
This brush I give thee, grasp it in thy hand.
Temper the soot within this vase of oil,
And let the little tripod aid thy toil;
On this methinks I see the walking crew
At thy request support the miry shoe,
The foot grows black that was with dirt embrowned,
And in thy pockets jingling halfpence sound."
The goddess plunges swift beneath the flood,
And dashes all around her showers of mud;
The youth straight chose his post; the labour plied
Where branching streets from Charing Cross divide;

[1] *dog star* Sirius, the bright star whose prominence during the summer months was believed to be responsible for the additional heat.

[2] *fondling* Much loved one.

[3] *Diana* Goddess of the hunt; *god of day* Apollo, god of the sun; *Neptune* God of the sea; *god of fire* Vulcan, who was also god of volcanoes.

[4] *Fleet-ditch* A large open sewer running from Fleet Street into the Thames.

[5] *Holborn* Area in central London.

[6] *flagon* Vessel of alcohol.

His treble voice resounds along the Mews,
And Whitehall[1] echoes, "Clean your honour's shoes."

Like the sweet ballad, this amusing lay
Too long detains the walker on his way;
The busy city asks instructive song.

Where elevated o'er the gaping crowd,
Clasped in the board the perjured head is bowed,
Betimes retreat; here, thick as hailstones pour,
Turnips, and half-hatched eggs (a mingled show'r)
Among the rabble rain: some random throw
May with the trickling yolk thy cheek o'erflow;

Though expedition bids, yet never stray
Where no ranged posts defend the rugged way.
Here laden carts with thund'ring wagons meet,
Wheels clash with wheels, and bar the narrow street;
The lashing whip resounds, the horses strain,
And blood in anguish bursts the swelling vein.
O barb'rous men, your cruel breasts assuage,
Why vent ye on the generous steed your rage?
Does not his service earn your daily bread?
Your wives, your children, by his labours fed!
If, as the Samian[2] taught, the soul revives,
And, shifting seats, in other bodies lives,
Severe shall be the brutal coachman's change,
Doomed in a hackney-horse the town to range:
Car-men, transformed, the groaning load shall draw
Whom other tyrants with the lash shall awe.
…

O roving Muse, recall that wondrous year,
When winter reigned in bleak Britannia's air;
When hoary Thames, with frosted osiers° crowned, *willows*
Was three long moons in icy fetters bound,
The waterman, forlorn along the shore,
Pensive reclines upon his useless oar,
See harnessed steeds desert the stony town;
And wander roads unstable, not their own:
Wheels o'er the hardened waters smoothly glide,
And raze,° with whitened tracks, the slippery tide. *scrape, mark*
Here the fat cook plies high the blazing fire,
And scarce the spit can turn the steer entire.
Booths sudden hide the Thames, long streets appear,
And num'rous games proclaim the crowded fair.
So when a general bids the martial train[3]
Spread their encampments o'er the spacious plain;
Thick-rising camps a canvas city build,
And the loud dice resound through all the field.
'Twas here the matron found a doleful fate:
Let elegiac lay the woe relate,
Soft as the breath of distant flutes, at hours
When silent ev'ning closes up the flow'rs;
Lulling as falling water's hollow noise;
Indulging grief, like Philomela's[4] voice.

Doll every day had walked these treacherous roads;
Her neck grew warped beneath the autumnal loads
Of various fruit; she now a basket bore;
That head, alas! shall basket bear no more.
Each booth she frequent passed, in quest of gain,
And boys with pleasure heard her shrilling strain.
Ah Doll! all mortals must resign their breath,
And industry itself submit to death!
The crackling crystal yields, she sinks, she dies,
Her head, chopped off, from her lost shoulders flies;
"Pippins,"° she cried, but Death her voice confounds, *Apples*
And pip-pip-pip along the ice resounds.
So when the Thracian furies Orpheus tore,
And left his bleeding trunk deformed with gore,
His severed head floats down the silver tide,
His yet warm tongue for his lost consort cried;
Eurydice with quivering voice he mourned,

[1] *Charing Cross* Intersection of the Strand, Whitehall, and Cockspur Street; considered the center of London; *Mews* I.e., King's Mews, the stables of the royal family, then located at Charing Cross; *Whitehall* Street where many government buildings are located.

[2] *the Samian* Philosopher and mathematician Pythagoras, who was born c. 570 BCE on the island of Samos. Pythagoras believed in the reincarnation of the soul until it attained immortality.

[3] *martial train* I.e., the soldiers and artillery for battle.

[4] *Philomela* According to classical myth, Philomela was turned into a nightingale after being raped by her brother-in-law; she expressed her grief through birdsong.

And Heber's banks Eurydice returned.[1]

But now the western gale the flood unbinds,
And black'ning clouds move on with warmer winds,
The wooden town its frail foundation leaves,
And Thames' full urn° rolls down his plenteous waves; *stream*
From every penthouse streams the fleeting snow,
And with dissolving frost the pavements flow.
…

O ye associate walkers, O my friends,
Upon your state what happiness attends!
What, though no coach to frequent visit rolls,
Nor for your shilling chairmen sling their poles;
Yet still your nerves rheumatic pains defy,
Nor lazy jaundice dulls your saffron° eye; *yellow*
No wasting cough discharges sounds of death,
Nor wheezing asthma heaves in vain for breath;
Nor from your restless couch is heard the groan
Of burning gout,[2] or sedentary stone.° *gall stone*
Let others in the jolting coach confide,
Or in the leaky boat the Thames divide;
Or, boxed within the chair, contemn the street,
And trust their safety to another's feet,
Still let me walk; for oft the sudden gale
Ruffles the tide, and shifts the dang'rous sail.
Then shall the passenger too late deplore
Then whelming° billow,° and the faithless oar; *capsizing / swell*
The drunken chair-man in the kennel spurns,° *stumbles*
The glasses shatters, and his charge o'erturns.
Who can recount the coach's various harms,
The legs disjointed, and the broken arms?

I've seen a beau, in some ill-fated hour,
When o'er the stones choked kennels swell the show'r,
In gilded chariot loll; he with disdain
Views spattered passengers all drenched in rain;
With mud filled high, the rumbling cart draws near,
Now rule thy prancing steeds, laced charioteer!
The dust-man lashes on with spiteful rage,
His pond'rous spokes thy painted wheel engage,
Crushed is thy pride, down falls the shrieking beau,
The slabby pavement crystal fragments strow,° *scatter*
Black floods of mire th'embroidered coat disgrace,
And mud enwraps the honours of his face.
So when dread Jove the son of Phoebus[3] hurled,
Scarred with dark thunder, to the nether world;
The headstrong coursers° tore the silver reins, *horses*
And the sun's beamy ruin gilds the plains.

If the pale walker pant with weakening ills,
His sickly hand is stored with friendly bills;
From hence he learns the seventh-born doctor's fame,
From hence he learns the cheapest tailor's name.

Shall the large mutton smoke upon your boards?
Such, Newgate's copious market best affords.
Wouldst thou with mighty beef augment thy meal?
Seek Leaden Hall; St. James's sends thee veal;
Thames Street gives cheeses; Covent Garden fruits;
Moorfield old books; and Monmouth Street old suits.
Hence may'st thou well supply the wants of life,
Support thy family, and clothe thy wife.

Volumes on sheltered stalls expanded lie,
And various science lures the learned eye;
The bending shelves with pond'rous scholiasts[4] groan,
And deep divines to modern shops unknown:
Here, like the bee, that on industrious wing
Collects the various odours of the spring,
Walkers, at leisure, learning's flowers may spoil,° *loot*
Nor watch the wasting of the midnight oil,

[1] *So when … returned* A reference to the myth of Orpheus, a celebrated poet and musician who traveled to the underworld to win back his wife, Eurydice, from Hades. He was allowed to bring her back to earth on the condition that he not look back at her on the walk up from the underworld. When he did accidentally, Eurydice was pulled back to Hades. According to Ovid, Orpheus refused the love of women after Eurydice's death. For this he was supposedly ripped to shreds, either by jealous women or by the furies, three avenging goddesses. As Orpheus's head and lyre floated down the river Hebrus, they continued to make mournful music.

[2] *gout* Disease characterized by inflammation of the joints.

[3] *son of Phoebus* Asclepius, son of Phoebus Apollo (god of the sun) from a mortal woman. Asclepius was a famed healer, but he incurred Jove's rage when he used his gift to bring back the dead. As punishment, Jove killed him with a thunderbolt.

[4] *scholiasts* Those who comment upon classical writers.

May morals snatch from Plutarch's[1] tattered page,
A mildewed Bacon, or Stageira's sage.[2]
Here saunt'ring 'prentices o'er Otway weep,
O'er Congreve smile, or over D——[3] sleep;
Pleased seamstresses the Lock's famed rape[4] unfold,
And squirts read Garth, 'till apozems[5] grow cold.

O Lintot,[6] let my labours obvious lie,
Ranged° on thy stall, for every curious eye; *arranged*
So shall the poor these precepts gratis° know, *for free*
And to my verse their future safeties owe.

What walker shall his mean ambition fix
On the false lustre of a coach and six?[7]
Let the vain virgin, lured by glaring show,
Sigh for the liveries° of th'embroidered beau. *garb*

See yon bright chariot on its braces swing,
With Flanders mares,[8] and on an arched spring;
That wretch, to gain an equipage and place,
Betrayed his sister to a lewd embrace.
This coach, that with the blazoned 'scutcheon° glows, *shield*
Vain of his unknown race, the coxcomb° shows. *vain fool*
Here the bribed lawyer, sunk in velvet, sleeps;
The starving orphan, as he passes, weeps;
There flames a fool, begirt° with tinselled slaves, *surrounded*
Who wastes the wealth of a whole race of knaves.
That other, with a clust'ring train° behind, *retinue*
Owes his new honours to a sordid mind.
This next in court fidelity excels,
The public rifles,° and his country sells. *gambles*
May the proud chariot never be my fate,
If purchased at so mean, so dear a rate;
O rather give me sweet content on foot,
Wrapped in my virtue, and a good surtout!° *overcoat*

from Book 3

Of Walking the Streets by Night.

…

Where Lincoln's Inn,[9] wide space, is railed around,
Cross not with vent'rous step; there oft is found
The lurking thief, who while the daylight shone,
Made the walls echo with his begging tone:
That crutch which late° compassion moved, shall wound *recently*
Thy bleeding head, and fell thee to the ground.
Though thou art tempted by the link-man's call,
Yet trust him not along the lonely wall;
In the midway he'll quench the flaming brand,
And share the booty with the pilf'ring band.
Still keep the public streets, where oily rays,
Shot from the crystal lamp, o'erspread the ways.
Happy Augusta!° Law-defended town! *London*
Here no dark lanterns shade the villain's frown;
No Spanish jealousies thy lanes infest,
Nor Roman vengeance stabs th'unwary breast;
Here tyranny ne'er lifts her purple[10] hand,
But liberty and justice guard the land;
No bravos° here profess the bloody trade, *assassins*
Nor is the Church the murd'rer's refuge made.

[1] *Plutarch* Greek historian and essayist of the first century CE.

[2] *Bacon* Francis Bacon (1561–1626), English author, scientist, and philosopher; *Stageira's sage* Greek philosopher Aristotle, who was born in the village of Stageira.

[3] *Otway* Playwright and poet Thomas Otway (1652–85); *Congreve* William Congreve, another well-known playwright and poet (1670–1729); *D——* John Dryden, celebrated poet and critic (1631–1700).

[4] *the Lock's famed rape* I.e., Alexander Pope's poem *The Rape of the Lock* (1712).

[5] *squirts* I.e., apothecaries' delivery boys; a reference to the errand boy in Garth's poem *The Dispensary*; *Garth* Physician and poet Samuel Garth (1661–1719); *apozems* Medicinal infusions.

[6] *Lintot* Barnaby Bernard Lintot, a leading publisher of authors such as Pope, Congreve, Dryden, and Gay.

[7] *coach and six* Large carriage pulled by six horses.

[8] *Flanders mares* Large horses needed to pull heavy carriages.

[9] *Lincoln's Inn* London's largest city square.

[10] *purple* Color symbolizing royalty.

Joseph Addison, *The Spectator* No. 69 (19 May 1711)

Hic segetes, illic veniunt felicius uvæ:
Arborei foetus alibi, atque injussa virescunt
Gramina. Nonne vides, croceos ut Tmolus odores,
India mittit ebur, molles sua thura Sabæi?
At Chalybes nudi ferrum, virosaque Pontus
Castorea, Eliadum palmas Epirus equarum?
Continuo has leges æternaque fœdera certis
Imposuit Natura locis ...[1] —VIRGIL

There is no place in the town which I so much love to frequent as the Royal Exchange. It gives me a secret satisfaction, and, in some measure, gratifies my vanity, as I am an Englishman, to see so rich an assembly of countrymen and foreigners consulting together upon the private business of mankind, and making this metropolis a kind of emporium for the whole earth. I must confess I look upon high-change[2] to be a great council, in which all considerable nations have their representatives. Factors[3] in the trading world are what ambassadors are in the politic world; they negotiate affairs, conclude treaties, and maintain a good correspondence between those wealthy societies of men that are divided from one another by seas and oceans, or live on the different extremities of a continent. I have often been pleased to hear disputes adjusted between an inhabitant of Japan and an alderman of London, or to see a subject of the Great Mogul[4] entering into a league with one of the Czar of Muscovy.[5] I am infinitely delighted in mixing with these several ministers of commerce, as they are distinguished by their different walks and different languages. Sometimes I am jostled among a body of Armenians; sometimes I am lost in a crowd of Jews, and sometimes make one in a group of Dutch-men. I am a Dane, Swede, or Frenchman at different times, or rather fancy myself like the old philosopher[6] who, upon being asked what country-man he was, replied that he was a citizen of the world.

Though I very frequently visit this busy multitude of people, I am known to nobody there but my friend Sir Andrew, who often smiles upon me as he sees me bustling in the crowd, but at the same time connives at

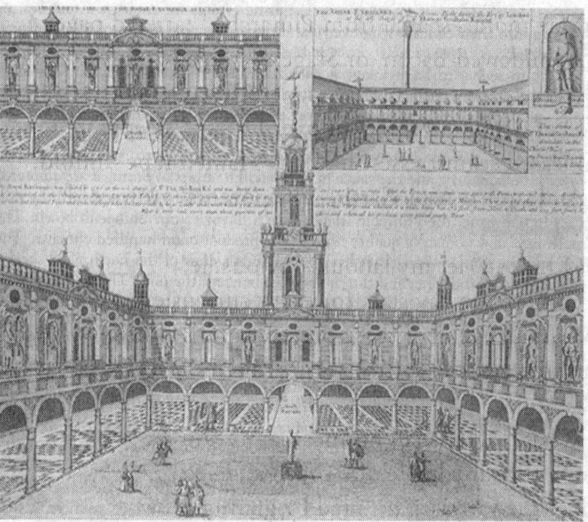

The Royal Exchange, by Sutton Nicholls (1712).The Royal Exchange, located in London's financial district, was a meeting place for merchants and businessmen. As shown in this picture, the Exchange consisted of a quadrangle of shops (of which there were nearly 200) set around a large open courtyard, where merchants would meet and make deals. The Exchange became a major site of commerce as early as 1570. The picture in the top right corner shows the original Exchange, which was destroyed by the Great Fire of London in 1666. It was rebuilt in 1669 in a more ornate, intricate style. Within each of the second-floor arches stands the statue of a king, and in the center of the courtyard is a statue of Charles II dressed as a Roman emperor. This statue highlighted the perceived similarities between contemporary Britain and the Roman Empire during the reign of Augustus Caesar, the first Roman Emperor.

[1] *Hic ... locis* Latin: "Grain grows more plentifully here, grapes there. In other places trees grow laden with fruit, and grasses grow unbidden. Do you not see how Tmolus sends us its saffron perfumes; India her ivory; the soft Sabeans their frankincense; but the naked Chalybes send us iron, the Pontus pungent beaver oil, and Epirus prize-winning Olympic horses? These are the continual law and eternal covenants Nature has imposed on certain places." From Virgil's *Georgics* 1.54–61.

[2] *high-change* Peak trading period at the Exchange.

[3] *Factors* Mercantile agents; commission merchants.

[4] *Great Mogul* Ruler of India.

[5] *Muscovy* I.e., Russia.

[6] *old philosopher* Diogenes the Cynic, a Greek philosopher of the fourth century BCE who rejected conventional comforts and the concepts of personal property and personal happiness.

my presence without taking any further notice of me. There is indeed a merchant of Egypt who just knows me by sight, having formerly remitted me some money to Grand Cairo; but as I am not versed in the modern Coptic, our conferences go no further than a bow and a grimace.[1]

This grand scene of business gives me an infinite variety of solid and substantial entertainments. As I am a great lover of mankind, my heart naturally overflows with pleasure at the sight of a prosperous and happy multitude, insomuch that at many public solemnities I cannot forbear expressing my joy with tears that have stolen down my cheeks. For this reason I am wonderfully delighted to see such a body of men thriving in their own private fortunes, and at the same time promoting the public stock; or, in other words, raising estates for their own families by bringing into their country whatever is wanting, and carrying out of it whatever is superfluous.

Nature seems to have taken a particular care to disseminate her blessings among the different regions of the world, with an eye to this mutual intercourse and traffic among mankind, that the natives of the several parts of the globe might have a kind of dependence upon one another, and be united together by their common interest. Almost every degree produces something peculiar to it. The food often grows in one country, and the sauce in another. The fruits of Portugal are corrected by the products of Barbados; the infusion of a China plant sweetened with the pith of an Indian cane; the Philippic islands give a flavour to our European bowls. The single dress of a woman of quality is often the product of an hundred climates. The muff and the fan come together from the different ends of the earth. The scarf is sent from the torrid zone, and the tippet[2] from beneath the pole. The brocade petticoat rises out of the mines of Peru, and the diamond necklace out of the bowels of Indostan.

If we consider our own country in its natural prospect, without any of the benefits and advantages of commerce, what a barren uncomfortable spot of earth falls to our share! Natural historians tell us that no fruit grows originally among us, besides hips and haws, acorns and pig-nuts,[3] with other delicacies of the like nature; that our climate of itself, and without the assistances of art, can make no further advances towards a plum than to a sloe,[4] and carries an apple to no greater a perfection than a crab; that our melons, our peaches, our figs, our apricots, and cherries, are strangers among us, imported in different ages and naturalized in our English gardens; and that they would all degenerate and fall away into the trash of our own country if they were wholly neglected by the planter, and left to the mercy of our sun and soil. Nor has traffic more enriched our vegetable world than it has improved the whole face of nature among us. Our ships are laden with the harvest of every climate; our tables are stored with spices, and oils, and wines; our rooms are filled with pyramids of China and adorned with the workmanship of Japan; our morning's draught[5] comes to us from the remotest corners of the earth; we repair our bodies by the drugs of America, and repose ourselves under Indian canopies. My friend Sir Andrew calls the vineyards of France our gardens, the Spice Islands[6] our hotbeds, the Persians our silk-weavers, and the Chinese our potters. Nature indeed furnishes us with the bare necessaries of life, but traffic gives us a great variety of what is useful, and at the same time supplies us with everything that is convenient and ornamental. Nor is it the least part of this our happiness, that whilst we enjoy the remotest products of the north and south, we are free from those extremities of weather which give them birth; that our eyes are refreshed with the green fields of Britain at the same time that our palates are feasted with fruits that rise between the tropics.

For these reasons there are not more useful members in a commonwealth than merchants. They knit mankind together in a mutual intercourse of good offices, distribute the gifts of nature, find work for the poor, add wealth to the rich and magnificence to the great. Our English merchant converts the tin of his own country into gold and exchanges his wool for rubies. The

[1] *grimace* Affected expression of politeness.

[2] *tippet* Cape or short cloak made of fur or wool.

[3] *hips* Fruits of the wild rose bush; *haws* Fruits of the hawthorn tree; *pig-nuts* Nuts of the broom hickory tree.

[4] *sloe* Small bitter fruit of the blackthorn bush.

[5] *draught* Drink.

[6] *Spice Islands* Islands in Indonesia.

Mahometans are clothed in our British manufacture, and the inhabitants of the frozen zone warmed with the fleeces of our sheep.

When I have been upon the 'Change, I have often fancied one of our old kings standing in person, where he is represented in effigy, and looking down upon the wealthy concourse of people with which that place is every day filled. In this case, how would he be surprised to hear all the languages of Europe spoken in this little spot of his former dominions, and to see so many private men, who in his time would have been the vassals of some powerful baron, negotiating like princes for greater sums of money than were formerly to be met with in the Royal Treasury! Trade, without enlarging the British territories, has given us a kind of additional Empire: it has multiplied the number of the rich, made our landed estates infinitely more valuable than they were formerly, and added to them an accession of other estates as valuable as the lands themselves.

from Daniel Defoe, "On Trade" (from *The Complete English Tradesman*), Letter 22, "Of the Dignity of Trade in England More Than in Other Countries" (1726)

Sir,

It is said of England by way of distinction, and we all value ourselves upon it, that it is a trading country; and King Charles II, who was perhaps the prince of all the kings that ever reigned in England, that best understood the country and the people that he governed, used to say that the tradesmen were the only gentry in England. His Majesty spoke it merrily, but it had a happy signification in it, such as was peculiar to the best genius of that prince, who, though he was not the bright governor, was the best acquainted with the world of all the princes of his age, if not of all the men in it; and though it be a digression, give me leave, after having quoted the King, to add three short observations of my own in favour of England and of the people and trade of it, and yet without the least partiality to our own country.

1. We are not only a trading country, but the greatest trading country in the world.
2. Our climate is the most agreeable climate in the world to live in.
3. Our Englishmen are the stoutest and best men (I mean what we call men of their hands) in the world.

These are great things to advance in our own favour, and yet to pretend not to be partial to; and therefore I shall give my reasons, which I think support my opinion, and they shall be as short as the heads themselves, that I may not go too much off from my subject.

1. We are the greatest trading country in the world because we have the greatest exportation of the growth and product of our land, and of the manufacture and labour of our people; and the greatest importation and consumption of the growth, product, and manufactures of other countries from abroad, of any nation in the world.

2. Our climate is the best and most agreeable because a man can be more out of doors in England than in other countries. This was King Charles the Second's reason for it, and I cannot name it without doing justice to His Majesty in it.

3. Our men are the stoutest and best because, strip them naked from the waist upwards, and give them no weapons at all but their hands and heels, and turn them into a room, or stage, and lock them in with the like number of other men of any nation, man for man, and they shall beat the best men you shall find in the world.

From this digression, which I hope will not be disagreeable, as it is not very tedious, I come back to my first observation, that England is a trading country; and two things I offer from that head.

First, our tradesmen are not, as in other countries, the meanest[1] of our people.

Secondly, some of the greatest, and best, and most flourishing families—among not the gentry only, but even the nobility—have been raised from

[1] *not … the meanest* I.e., not the most inferior, or not inferior.

trade, owe their beginning, their wealth, and their estates to trade; and I may add,

Thirdly, those families are not at all ashamed of their original,[1] and indeed have no occasion to be ashamed of it.

It is true that in England we have a numerous and an illustrious nobility and gentry; and it is true also that not so many of those families have raised themselves by the sword as in other nations, though we have not been without men of fame in the field too.

But trade and learning has been the two chief steps by which our gentlemen have raised their relations and have built their fortunes; and from which they have ascended up to the prodigious height, both in wealth and number, which we see them now risen to.

As so many of our noble and wealthy families are raised by, and derive from trade, so it is true, and indeed it cannot well be otherwise, that many of the younger branches of our gentry, and even of the nobility itself, have descended again into the spring from whence they flowed, and have become tradesmen; and thence it is that, as I said above, our tradesmen in England are not, as it generally is in other countries, always of the meanest of our people.

Indeed, I might have added here that trade itself in England is not, as it generally is in other countries, the meanest thing the men can turn their hand to; but, on the contrary, trade is the readiest way for men to raise their fortunes and families; and therefore it is a field of men of figure and of good families to enter upon.

> *N.B.* By trade we must be understood to include navigation and foreign discoveries, because they are, generally speaking, all promoted and carried on by trade, and even by tradesmen, as well as merchants; and the tradesmen are at this time as much concerned in shipping (as owners) as the merchants, only the latter may be said to be the chief employers of the shipping.

Having thus done a particular piece of justice to ourselves, in the value we put upon trade and tradesmen in England, it reflects very much upon the understandings of those refined heads who pretend to depreciate that part of the nation, which is so infinitely superior in number and in wealth to the families who call themselves gentry, and so infinitely more numerous....

Let anyone who is acquainted with England look but abroad into the several counties, especially near London, or within fifty miles of it: how are the ancient families worn out by time and family misfortunes, and the estates possessed by a new race of tradesmen, grown up into families of gentry, and established by the immense wealth, gained, as I may say, behind the counter; that is, in the shop, the warehouse, and the counting-house? How are the sons of tradesmen ranked among the prime of the gentry? How are the daughters of tradesmen at this time adorned with the ducal coronets, and seen riding in the coaches of the best of the nobility? Nay, many of our trading gentlemen at this time refuse to be ennobled, scorn being knighted, and content themselves with being known to be rated among the richest commoners in the nation. And it must be acknowledged that whatever they be as to court-breeding and to manners, they, generally speaking, come behind none of the gentry in knowledge of the world....

from *The Female Tatler*[2] No. 9 (25–27 July 1709)

This afternoon, some ladies, having an opinion of my fancy in clothes, desired me to accompany 'em to Ludgate Hill,[3] which I take to be as agreeable an amusement as a lady can pass away three or four hours in. The shops are perfect gilded theatres: the variety of wrought silks, so many changes of fine scenes, and the mercers[4] are the performers in the opera, and instead of "Viviture

[1] *original* Origin.

[2] *The Female Tatler* This popular periodical was published on Mondays, Wednesdays, and Fridays (alternating with Steele's *The Tatler*) from 8 July 1709 to 31 March 1710. There has been much debate concerning authorship of the periodical; see above in the section "Contexts: Eighteenth-Century Periodicals and Prints."

[3] *Ludgate Hill* Street in the City where many shops were located.

[4] *mercers* Those who run shops that sell fabric.

Ingenio,"[1] you have in gold capitals "No Trust by Retail." They are the sweetest, fairest, nicest dished out creatures, and by their elegant address and soft speeches, you would guess 'em to be Italians. As people glance within their doors, they salute 'em with "Garden silks, ladies, Italian silks, brocades, tissues, cloth of silver, or cloth of gold, very fine Mantua silks, any right Geneva velvet, English velvet, velvets embossed"; and to the meaner sort, "Fine thread satins, both striped and plain, fine mohairs, silk satinets, burdets,[2] perfianets, Norwich crepes, auterines, silks for hoods and scarves—any camlets, drudgets, or sagathies;[3] gentlemen, nightgowns ready made, shalloons, durances[4] and right Scotch plaids."

We went into a shop which had three partners, two of 'em were to flourish out their silks and, after an obliging smile and a pretty mouth made, Cicero-like,[5] to expatiate on their goodness; and the other's sole business was to be gentleman-usher of the shop, to stand completely dressed at the door, bow to all the coaches that pass by, and hand ladies out and in.

We saw abundance of gay fancies fit for sea captains' wives, sheriffs' feasts, and Taunton-Dean[6] ladies—"This, madam, is wonderful charming"—"This, madam, is so diverting a silk"—"This, madam—my stars! how cool it looks." "But this, madam, ye gods, would I had ten thousand yards of it" (then gathers up a sleeve and places it to our shoulders), "It suits your ladyship's face wonderfully well." When we had pleased ourselves, and bid him ten shillings a yard for what he asked fifteen: "Fan me, ye winds, your ladyship rallies[7] me! Should I part with it at such a price, the weavers would rise upon the very shop—Was you at the park last night, madam?—Your ladyship shall abate me sixpence—Have you read *The Tatler* today, pretty lady? A smart fellow I'll assure you."

But being tired with his impertinence, as very ridiculous things soon cloy people, we agreed the point. He whipped us off twenty-eight yards with as much dexterity as Young G——y shall dash you out glasses of wine, and Mr. Fantast at the door reconveyed us into the coach.

These fellows are positively the greatest fops[8] in the kingdom; they have their toilets,[9] and their fine night-gowns, their chocolate in a morning, and their green-tea two hours after, turkey polts for their dinner, and then perfumes, washes, and clean linen equip 'em for the parade. 'Tis fit those whose professions invite the ladies should appear decent before 'em. But if some women of note would not countenance their foppery, and cry, "Really Mr. Farendine, you are too well bred, and have too good an air for a tradesman, but a mercer is a genteel calling. Suppose you had been bred a soap-boiler" … "Fogh!" says he. "Oh filthy!" says she; nor invite 'em to collations,[10] and be seen in a hackney coach with 'em, they'd leave off their conceited niceties and keep within the sphere of industry. For sure, no composition can be more ridiculous than a creature made up of beau and business. Our sex indeed have a might[11] ascendant, and those poor animals may be a little excused, when some women shall have power to coin fops and fools out of the greatest statesmen and politicians.

from *The Female Tatler* No. 67 (7–9 December 1709)

Arabella's Day

Emilia and I, having at an India house[12] muddled away a little of our own money, were sitting to observe the variety of the company that frequent those

[1] *Viviture Ingenio* Latin: Long live genius.

[2] *silk satinets* Materials made of imitation satin, or satin and cotton combined; *burdets* Cotton fabrics.

[3] *camlet* Eastern fabric made of silk and goat hair; *drudgets* Felted wools; *sagathies* Woolen fabrics.

[4] *shalloons* Worsted twill fabrics; *durances* Stout, durable cloths.

[5] *Cicero-like* In a rhetorical style reminiscent of that of the famous Roman orator Cicero.

[6] *Taunton-Dean* Fertile vale in Somerset in which the ancient town of Taunton is located, where wool and silk were manufactured.

[7] *rallies* Teases, jokes with.

[8] *fops* People over-attentive to their appearance.

[9] *toilets* Dressing table covered with cosmetics.

[10] *collations* Meals.

[11] *might* I.e., mighty.

[12] *India house* Shop selling goods imported from the East Indies and or the Indian subcontinent.

places, and how different their fancies were in pictures, fans, china, and such fashionable impertinences. Lady Praise-All surveyed the nick-nackatory with an amazement, as if she had received a new sense—these cups were charming, those stones unparalleled, and such prodigious jars were never heard of—everything was displaced to oblige her ladyship's curiosity, who protested she shouldn't grudge to spend an estate on things so prodigiously fine, drank a gallon of tea, and marched off without laying out a sixpence. Mrs. Trifleton came so full of commissions from ladies in the country that we thought she would have emptied the warehouse, and stared at the handsome prentice as if she expected to have him into the bargain. She wanted finer things than were ever made, and, could they have been had, would have demanded them cheaper than they were bought. She bid three half crowns for a two-guinea fan, wanted chocolate, all nut, for eighteen pence a pound, and beat down the best Imperial tea to the price of Sage o' Virtue.[1] Japan work[2] she thought at an excessive rate, China images were idolatrous, India pictures were the foolishest things; she'd have had them given her a dozen. At last, having positive orders from my Lady Smoak and Sot of Exeter to buy her a stone spitting-pot, she shook her head at the dearness of it, and ordered them to set it down to her.

Mrs. Honeysuckle was two hours pleasing herself in a paper nosegay, and Mrs. Delf employed five people to match her grout cup.[3] On a sudden, stops a leathern conveniency at the door, with four fellows of the world behind it, in the gayest liveries I ever saw, out of which comes a couple of quality Quakers.[4] They moved in, like disdainful duchesses who complain of corns if they walk but cross a room, rolled about their sanctified eyes, as if it were condescension in them to appear upon earth, and with abundance of reluctancy, one of them vouchsafed us a bow, instead of a curtsey. Emilia and I were not a little pleased to remark the pride and singularity in dress, speech, and behavior in that sect of people summed up in these two statues....

[1] *Sage o' Virtue* Inexpensive type of herbal tea.

[2] *Japan work* Varnished or lacquered articles such as trays, tables, serving vessels, etc.

[3] *grout cup* Porridge bowl.

[4] *Quakers* Members of the Society of Friends, a radical Protestant sect, who dressed plainly and sought to avoid worldly vanities, but were often wealthy business people.

from Anonymous, *The Character of a Coffee-House, with the Symptoms of a Town-Wit* (1673)

A coffee-house is a lay conventicle,[5] good-fellowship turned Puritan, ill-husbandry[6] in masquerade, whither people come, after toping[7] all day, to purchase, at the expense of their last penny, the repute of sober companions: a rota-room[8] that, like Noah's ark, receives animals of every sort, from the precise diminutive band,[9] to the hectoring cravat and cuffs in folio;[10] a nursery for training up the smaller fry of virtuosi in confident tattling, or a cabal of kittling critics[11] that have only learned to spit and mew; a mint of intelligence that, to make each man his pennyworth,[12] draws out into petty parcels what the merchant receives in bullion.[13] He that comes often saves twopence a week in *Gazettes*,[14] and has his news and his coffee for the same charge, as at a threepenny ordinary they give in broth to your chop of mutton. It is an exchange where haberdashers of political small-wares meet and mutually abuse each other, and the public, with bottomless stories, and heedless notions; the rendezvous of idle pamphlets, and persons more idly employed to read them; a high court of justice, where every little fellow in a camlet[15] cloak takes upon him to transpose affairs both in Church and state, to show reasons against Acts of Parliament, and condemn the decrees of general councils....

[5] *conventicle* Clandestine or illegal meeting, usually religious.

[6] *ill-husbandry* Poor management of resources.

[7] *toping* Drinking.

[8] *rota-room* Room for political meetings.

[9] *band* Clergyman.

[10] *in folio* In large size.

[11] *kittling critics* Baby critic (a grown-up critic is a cat, of spit and mew).

[12] *pennyworth* A good bargain.

[13] *bullion* Lump of gold or silver.

[14] *Gazettes* The *Gazette* was the official government newspaper.

[15] *camlet* Fine fabric made of Angora goat hair.

The room stinks of tobacco worse than the Hell of brimstone, and is as full of smoke as their heads that frequent it, whose humours are as various as those of Bedlam,[1] and their discourse oft-times as heathenish and dull as their liquors....

As you have a hodge-podge of drinks, such too is your company, for each man seems a leveller,[2] and ranks and files himself as he lists, without regard to degrees or order; so that often you may see a silly fop and a worshipful justice, a griping rook[3] and a grave citizen, a worthy lawyer and an errant pickpocket, a reverend non-conformist and a canting mountebank,[4] all blended together to compose an olio[5] of impertinence....

The arch-devil wherewith this smoke-hole is haunted is the town-wit, one that plays *rex*[6] wherever he comes, and makes as much hurry as Robin Goodfellow[7] of old amongst our granams'[8] milkbowls. He is a kind of a squib[9] on a rope, a meteor composed of self-conceit and noise, that by blazing and crackling engages the wonder of the ignorant, till on a sudden he vanishes and leaves a stench, if not infection, behind him. He is too often the stain of a good family, and by his debauched life blots the noble coat of his ancestors....

He is so refractory to divinity that morality itself cannot hold him; he affirms humane nature knows no such things as principles of good and evil, and will swear all women are whores, though his mother and sister both stand by. Whatever is sacred or serious he seeks to render ridiculous, and thinks government and religion fit objects for his idle and fantastic buffoonery. His humor is proud and assuming, as if he would palliate his ignorance by scoffing at what he understands not, and therefore with a pert and pragmatic scorn depreciates all things of nobler moment....

By means of some small scraps of learning matched with a far greater stock of confidence, a voluble tongue, and bold delivery, he has the ill-luck to be celebrated by the vulgar for a man of parts,[10] which opinion gains credit to his insolences, and sets him on further extravagances to maintain his title of a wit by continuing his practice of fooling, whereas all his mighty parts are summed up in this inventory....

from Anonymous, *Coffee-Houses Vindicated* (1675)

... It is older than Aristotle, and will be true, when Hobbes is forgot, that man is a sociable creature, and delights in company. Now, whither shall a person, wearied with hard study, or the laborious turmoils of a tedious day, repair to refresh himself? Or where can young gentlemen, or shop-keepers, more innocently and advantageously spend an hour or two in the evening, than at a coffee-house? Where they shall be sure to meet company, and, by the custom of the house, not such as at other places, stingy and reserved to themselves, but free and communicative; where every man may modestly begin his story, and propose to, or answer another, as he thinks fit. Discourse is *pabulum animi, cos ingenii*, the mind's best diet,[11] and the great whetstone and incentive of ingenuity; by that we come to know men better than by their physiognomy. *Loquere, ut te videam*, speak, that I may see you, was the philosopher's adage. To read men is acknowledged more useful than books; but where is there a better library for that study, generally, than here, amongst such a variety of humors, all expressing themselves on diverse subjects, according to their respective abilities?

[1] *Bedlam* From the Hospital of St. Mary of Bethlehem, a term meaning an insane asylum.

[2] *leveller* One who would "level" all men to the same rank.

[3] *rook* Con artist.

[4] *mountebank* Charlatan, generally a street performer.

[5] *olio* Medley; hodgepodge.

[6] *rex* Latin: king.

[7] *Robin Goodfellow* Sprite who, according to English folk legend, played tricks such as curdling milk.

[8] *granams'* I.e., grandams', or grandmothers'.

[9] *squib* Firework.

[10] *parts* Abilities.

[11] *diet* Food, nourishment.

from Richard Steele, *The Spectator* No. 155 (28 August 1711)

… Mr. Spectator,[1]

I keep a coffee-house, and am one of those whom you have thought fit to mention as an idol[2] some time ago. I suffered a good deal of raillery upon that occasion, but shall heartily forgive you, who were the cause of it, if you will do me justice in another point. What I ask of you is to acquaint my customers (who are otherwise very good ones) that I am unavoidably hasped[3] in my bar, and cannot help hearing the improper discourses they are pleased to entertain me with. They strive who shall say the most immodest things in my hearing. At the same time half a dozen of them loll at the bar staring just in my face, ready to interpret my looks and gestures according to their own imaginations. In this passive condition I know not where to cast my eyes, place my hands, or to what to employ myself in. But this confusion is to be a jest, and I hear them say in the end, with an insipid air of mirth and subtlety, "Let her alone, she knows as well as we for all she looks so." Good Mr. Spectator, persuade gentlemen that this is out of all decency. Say it is possible a woman may be modest, and yet keep a public house. Be pleased to argue that, in truth, the affront is more unpardonable because I am obliged to suffer it, and cannot fly from it. I do assure you, sir, the cheerfulness of life, which would rise from the honest gain I have, is utterly lost to me from the endless, flat, impertinent pleasantries which I hear from morning to night. In a word, it is too much for me to bear, and I desire you to acquaint them that I will keep pen and ink at the bar and write down all they say to me, and send it to you for the press. It is possible when they see how empty they speak, without the advantage of an impudent countenance and gesture, will appear, they may come to some sense of themselves and the insults they are guilty of towards me. I am,

Sir,
Your most humble servant,
The Idol

This representation is so just that it is hard to speak of it without an indignation which perhaps would appear too elevated to such as can be guilty of this inhumane treatment, where they see they affront a modest, plain, and ingenuous behavior. This correspondent is not the only sufferer in this kind, for I have long letter both from the Royal and New Exchange[4] on the same subject. They tell me that a young fop[5] cannot buy a pair of gloves but he is at the same time straining for some ingenious ribaldry to say to the young woman who helps them on. It is not small addition to the calamity that the rogues buy as hard[6] as the plainest and modestest customers they have; besides which, they loll upon their counters half an hour longer than they need, to drive away other customers, who are to share their impertinencies with the milliner, or go to another shop. Letters from 'Change Alley are full of the same evil, and the girls tell me except I can chase some eminent merchants from their shops, they shall in a short time fail.…

[1] *Mr. Spectator* This is a fictitious letter Steele has written from the point of view of a female merchant.

[2] *idol* According to Spectator no. 73, a female who, in an attempt to seduce men, is "wholly taken up in the adorning of her person."

[3] *hasped* Confined.

[4] *Royal Exchange* Business and financial center that housed nearly 200 shops; *New Exchange* Collection of stalls in the Strand, built in 1608–09, where many fashionable goods were sold. It was destroyed in 1737.

[5] *fop* Fool.

[6] *buy as hard* Drive as hard a bargain.

William Hogarth, *Marriage A-la-Mode* (1745).

Plate 1.

This scene depicts the cementing of the marriage contract between the son of a lord and the daughter of a merchant. Lord Squanderfield sits on the left with his family tree in his hand (indicating he is descended from William, Duke of Normandy, i.e., William the Conqueror). He is lame as a result of gout, and he has run out of money. Construction on his new mansion (seen out the window) has stopped, and a usurer, standing at the center of the table, is already taking some of the lord's newly acquired money as payment for a mortgage. The merchant, sitting opposite the lord, examines the marriage contract. The new couple sit on the couch together, entirely ignoring one another. The groom is examining himself in the mirror; the bride is staring off into space, polishing her wedding ring in a handkerchief, while lawyer Silvertongue leans over her and sharpens his pen. The pair of dogs chained to one another on the floor (one of whom has a coronet on his back) reflects the state of the young couple. The pictures on the wall depict various scenes of disaster and death from the Bible and mythology. The head of Medusa gazes over the room with a look of horror and disgust.

Plate 2.

The clock indicates it is 1:20 a.m. The couple sit in separate chairs ignoring one another; evidently they have spent the night independently. We may infer that the husband has been out with a mistress and in a fight; a small dog pulls a woman's cap out of his pocket, and his broken sword lies at his feet. The wife has had guests over to play cards. Candles are still burning in the other room (one of them has set fire to the back of a chair), and scattered cards and a book on the card game whist lie by the wife's feet. The wife stretches out her leg seductively, attempting to attract her husband's attention, but he takes no notice of her and merely stares off into space, exhausted. A servant holds a stack of unpaid bills in his hand. The mantle is cluttered with little statues; in a picture above it Cupid plays the bagpipes and his bow lies broken beside him. In the other room, mirrors line the walls, with the exception of one portrait, covered up because of its lewdness. A naked foot can just be seen at its edge.

Plate 3.

The husband visits a quack, an unqualified pretender to medical knowledge, in search of a cure for venereal disease. The pills he holds out to the quack, while playfully threatening him with a cane, have not worked, and the tearful young girl who stands between his legs has been infected. The woman standing between the two men may be the quack's wife, another of the nobleman's mistresses, the girl's mother, or the keeper of the house of prostitution where the girl works. On the left we can see the doorway into the quack's laboratory. A variety of strange and threatening machines, experiments, and human and animal parts are evident throughout the room.

Plate 4.

Meanwhile, the wife entertains guests in her bedchamber (a fashion known as "attending a toilet") as she dresses for the day. As a hairdresser does her hair, she talks to the lawyer, Silvertongue, whose portrait is also visible on the right-hand wall. The other paintings show scenes of unnatural seduction in classical mythology. The coronets in the room indicate that the old Earl has died, and his son is now Earl. Hanging from the chair is a child's rattle, indicating that the countess has had a child, who must be in the care of servants. In the center of the picture a black servant laughs at the affectations of the guests. Another servant, a small boy, points to the statue of Actaeon, whose horns are a sign of a cuckold (a man whose wife has been unfaithful to him). This suggests the nature of the conversation behind him.

Plate 5.

The Earl, having heard of the affair between his wife and the lawyer, has barged into their meeting place and surprised them, and challenged the lawyer to a duel. The lawyer has mortally wounded him and now flees out the window in his shirt as the landlord and watchman enter the door. The kneeling wife begs her husband's forgiveness. Masks strewn on the floor indicate the adulterous couple have been at a masquerade. A tapestry on the wall depicts the judgment of Solomon. A painting above the countess shows a prostitute with a squirrel in her hand. Above the doorway, a painting shows St. Luke, patron saint of artists, recording the scene.

Plate 6.

The countess has committed suicide by taking an overdose of laudanum; the empty bottle lies on the floor. Next to it is "Counseller Silvertongue's Last Dying Speech," indicating that the cause of her suicide is her lover's having been hanged for killing her husband. The doctor can be seen leaving at the far right. The countess's father, to whose bare house (evidence of a miserly lifestyle) she has returned, removes the wedding ring from her finger. A starving dog steals the pig's head from the table. An apothecary berates a servant who evidently supplied the laudanum. A female servant holds the countess's only child, a daughter (the Earl has no heir), to kiss her dead mother's cheek. The child's leg brace and patch designed to cover some skin eruption are evidence that she has inherited her father's venereal disease.

Joseph Addison, *The Spectator* No. 119 (17 July 1711)

Urbem quam dicunt Romam, Melibœe, putavi
Stultus ego huic nostræ similem ...[1] —VIRGIL

The first and most obvious reflections which arise in a man who changes the city for the country are upon the different manners of the people whom he meets within those two different scenes of life. By manners I do not mean morals, but behaviour and good breeding as they show themselves in the town and in the country.

And here, in the first place, I must observe a very great revolution that has happened in the article of good breeding. Several obliging deferences, condescensions, and submissions, with many outward forms and ceremonies that accompany them, were first of all brought up among the politer part of mankind who lived in courts and cities, and distinguished themselves from the rustic part of the species (who on all occasions acted bluntly and naturally) by such a mutual complaisance and intercourse of civilities. These forms of conversation by degrees multiplied and grew troublesome; the modish world found too great a constraint in them, and have therefore thrown most of them aside. Conversation, like the Romish Religion,[2] was so encumbered with show and ceremony that it stood in need of a reformation to retrench its superfluities and restore it to its natural good sense and beauty. At present, therefore, an unconstrained carriage and a certain openness of behaviour are the height of good breeding. The fashionable world is grown free and easy; our manners sit more loose upon us. Nothing is so modish as an agreeable negligence. In a word, good breeding shows itself most where to an ordinary eye it appears the least.

If, after this, we look on the people of mode in the country, we find in them the manners of the last age. They have no sooner fetched themselves up to the fashion of the polite world, but the town has dropped them, and are nearer to the first state of nature than to those refinements which formerly reigned in the court, and still prevail in the country. One may now know a man that never conversed in the world by his excess of good breeding. A polite country squire shall make you as many bows in half an hour as would serve a courtier for a week. There is infinitely more to-do about place and precedence in a meeting of Justices' wives than in an assembly of Duchesses.

This rural politeness is very troublesome to a man of my temper, who generally take the chair that is next me, and walk first or last, in the front or in the rear, as chance directs. I have known my friend Sir Roger's[3] dinner almost cold before the company could adjust the ceremonial and be prevailed upon to sit down; and have heartily pitied my old friend when I have seen him forced to pick and cull his guests, as they sat at the several parts of his table, that he might drink their healths according to their respective ranks and qualities. Honest Will Wimble, who I should have thought had been altogether uninfected with ceremony, gives me abundance of trouble in this particular; though he has been fishing all the morning, he will not help himself at dinner 'till I am served. When we are going out of the hall he runs behind me, and last night, as we were walking in the fields, stopped short at a stile till I came up to it, and upon my making signs to him to get over, told me, with a serious smile, that sure I believed they had no manners in the country.

There has happened another revolution in the point of good breeding, which relates to the conversation among men of mode, and which I cannot but look upon as very extraordinary. It was certainly one of the first distinctions of a well-bred man to express everything that had the most remote appearance of being obscene in modest terms and distant phrases, whilst the clown, who had no such delicacy of conception and expression, clothed his ideas in those plain homely terms that are the most obvious and natural. This kind of good manners was perhaps carried to an excess, so as to make conversation too stiff, formal, and precise; for which reason (as hypocrisy in one age is generally succeeded by atheism in another), conversation is in a great measure relapsed into the first extreme, so that at present several of our men of the town, and particularly those who have been polished in France, make use of

[1] *Urbem ... similem* Latin: "Fool that I was, I thought Imperial Rome was like Mantua." From Virgil's *Eclogues* 1.19–20.

[2] *Romish Religion* I.e., Roman Catholicism.

[3] *Sir Roger* Sir Roger de Coverley, a recurring character in the Spectator Club, is a Tory country gentleman.

the most coarse uncivilized words in our language, and utter themselves often in such a manner as a clown would blush to hear.

This infamous piece of good breeding, which reigns among the coxcombs of the town, has not yet made its way into the country; and as it is impossible for such an irrational way of conversation to last long among a people that make any profession of religion, or show of modesty, if the country gentlemen get into it they will certainly be left in the lurch. Their good breeding will come too late to them, and they will be thought a parcel of lewd clowns, while they fancy themselves talking together like men of wit and pleasure.

As the two points of good breeding which I have hitherto insisted upon regard behaviour and conversation, there is a third which turns upon dress. In this too the country are very much behind hand. The rural beaux are not yet got out of the fashion that took place at the time of the Revolution, but ride about the country in red coats and laced hats, while the women in many parts are still trying to outvie one another in the height of their head-dresses.

But a friend of mine, who is now upon the Western Circuit,[1] having promised to give me an account of the several modes and fashions that prevail in the different parts of the nation through which he passes, I shall defer the enlarging upon this last topic till I have received a letter from him, which I expect every post.

Illustration from John Worlidge's *Systema Agriculturae*, fourth edition (1687). Worlidge's *Systema Agriculturae* was a highly influential, comprehensive treatise on husbandry, or the management of a farm. First published in 1675, the book was re-issued several times in the late seventeenth and early eighteenth centuries, indicating the importance of the agricultural developments brought about by the era's scientific advances. As this illustration shows, the ideal farm was very neatly and systematically laid out, with trim hedges symmetrically dividing plots of land and well-ordered trees and gardens providing pleasing decoration.

[1] *Circuit* Journey of judges, lawyers, etc. through appointed areas for the purpose of holding of court.

The Monument of LONDON in remembrance of the dreadfull Fire in 1666.
Its Height is 202 feet
Printed for John Bowles at the Black Horse in Cornhill.
Collone de LONDRES elevé pour une Perpetuelle Resouvenance de L'incendre
Generalle de cette Ville en 1666. En Haut 202 Pieds.

The Monument of London, in Remembrance of the Dreadful Fire in 1666 (1752). London Monument is located in City of London district, near the north end of London Bridge. The Great Fire started approximately 60 meters from this point. The monument is 61 meters tall (at the time, it was the tallest free-standing stone structure in the world) and, as seen in the picture, it has an observation deck near its pinnacle to which visitors could climb up through a winding staircase in the shaft of the monument. The central shaft was also meant for use as a zenith telescope and in gravity and pendulum experiments; the shaft connects to an underground laboratory, in which observers could work. The inscription on the monument reads, in part, "The burning of this Protestant City was begun and carried on by the treachery and malice of the Popish faction...." As Alexander Pope pointed out, this perpetuated the false accusation that the fire had been deliberately started by disaffected Roman Catholics. The inscription was removed in 1685 after the Catholic King James II came to the throne, reappeared in 1689 when Protestant rulers came back to the throne, and was finally permanently removed in 1831.

View of Bloomsbury Square, drawn by E. Dayes (1787). The popularity of Bloomsbury Square, constructed in the seventeenth century, led to the design of many such squares, including Bedford Square and Russell Square, in the following century. Fashionable gentry and members of the aristocracy constructed their houses around the square.

In the early twentieth century, Bloomsbury became famous for the numerous writers and artists that lived in the area, including Virginia Woolf, Duncan Grant, and Lytton Strachey.

Richard Wilson, *Croome Court, Worcestershire*, 1758–59. Wilson earned his living largely by painting views of country estates commissioned by their aristocratic owners.

from John Gay, *The Shepherd's Week*: "The Shepherd's Week 1. Monday; or, the Squabble" (1714)

(*Lobbin Clout, Cuddy, Cloddipole.*)

LOBBIN CLOUT.

Thy younglings,° Cuddy, are but just awake; *youngsters*
No thrustles° shrill the bramblebush forsake; *thrushes*
No chirping lark the welkin[1] sheen° invokes; *bright*
No damsel yet the swelling udder strokes;
O'er yonder hill does scant° the dawn appear, *hardly*
Then why does Cuddy leave his cot so rear°? *early*

CUDDY.

Ah Lobbin Clout! I ween° my plight is guessed, *think*
For he that loves, a stranger is to rest;
If swains° belie° not, thou hast proved the smart,° *lovers / deceive* *injury*
And Blouzelinda's mistress of thy heart.
This rising rear betokeneth° well thy mind, *shows*
Those arms are folded for thy Blouzelind.
And well, I trow,° our piteous plights agree, *believe*
Thee Blouzelinda smites, Buxoma me.

LOBBIN CLOUT.

Ah Blouzelind! I love thee more by half
Than does° their fawns, or cows the new-fallen calf: *female deer*
Woe worth the tongue! may blisters sore it gall,° *irritate*
That names Buxoma, Blouzelind withal.

CUDDY.

Hold, witless° Lobbin Clout, I thee advise, *foolish*
Lest blisters sore on thy own tongue arise.
Lo yonder Cloddipole, the blithesome° swain,[2] *cheerful*
The wisest lout° of all the neighbouring plain. *bumpkin*
From Cloddipole we learnt to read the skies,
To know when hail will fall, or winds arise.
He taught us erst° the heifers' tails to view, *some time ago*
When stuck aloft, that show'rs would strait° ensue; *immediately*
He first that useful secret did explain,
That pricking corns[3] foretold the gath'ring rain.
When swallows fleet° soar high and sport° in air, *swift / play*
He told us that the welkin° would be clear. *sky*
Let Cloddipole then hear us twain° rehearse, *two*
And praise his sweetheart in alternate verse.
I'll wager this same oaken staff with thee,
That Cloddipole shall give the prize to me.

LOBBIN CLOUT.

See this tobacco pouch that's lined with hair,
Made of the skin of sleekest fallow deer.[4]
This pouch, that's tied with tape of reddest hue,
I'll wager, that the prize shall be my due.

CUDDY.

Begin thy carols then, thou vaunting° slouch, *bragging*
Be thine the oaken staff, or mine the pouch.

LOBBIN CLOUT.

My Blouzelinda is the blithest° lass, *most cheery*
Than primrose sweeter, or the clover-grass.
Fair is the king-cup° that in meadow blows, *buttercup*
Fair is the daisy that beside her grows,
Fair is the gillyflow'r,° of gardens sweet, *clove*
Fair is the marigold, for pottage° meet.° *soup / fitting*
But Blouzelind's than gillyflow'r more fair,
Than daisy, marigold, or king-cup rare.

CUDDY.

My brown Buxoma is the featest° maid, *prettiest*
That e'er at Wake[5] delightsome gambol° played. *frolic*
Clean as young lambkins° or the goose's down, *little lambs*
And like the goldfinch in her Sunday gown.
The witless lambs may sport upon the plain,
The frisking kid delight the gaping swain,
The wanton calf may skip with many a bound,
And my cur° Tray play deftest feats around; *dog*
But neither lamb nor kid, nor calf nor Tray,
Dance like Buxoma on the first of May.

[1] *welkin* Sky. Gay defines some of his archaic words in footnotes; here, his definitions have been incorporated into the editor's annotations.

[2] *swain* Rural young man.

[3] *pricking corns* Increased pain in sore places on the feet.

[4] *fallow deer* Mottled deer common in England.

[5] *Wake* Village festival held on the evening before a saint's day.

LOBBIN CLOUT.
Sweet is my toil when Blouzelind is near,
Of her bereft 'tis winter all the year.
With her no sultry summer's heat I know;
In winter, when she's nigh, with love I glow.
Come Blouzelinda, ease thy swain's desire,
My summer's shadow and my winter's fire!

CUDDY.
As with Buxoma once I worked at hay,
Ev'n noon-tide labour seemed an holiday;
And holidays, if haply° she were gone, *by chance*
Like worky-days I wished would soon be done.
Eftsoons,° O sweetheart kind, my love repay, *very soon*
And all the year shall then be holiday.

LOBBIN CLOUT.
As Blouzelinda in a gamesome° mood, *playful*
Behind a haycock° loudly laughing stood, *haystack*
I slyly ran, and snatched a hasty kiss,
She wiped her lips, nor took it much amiss.
Believe me, Cuddy, while I'm bold to say,
Her breath was sweeter than the ripened hay.

CUDDY.
As my Buxoma in a morning fair,
With gentle finger stroked her milky care,[1]
I quaintly° stole a kiss; at first, 'tis true, *archly*
She frowned, yet after granted one or two.
Lobbin, I swear, believe who will my vows,
Her breath by far excelled the breathing cows.

LOBBIN CLOUT.
Leek to the Welch, to Dutchmen butter's dear,
Of Irish swains potato is the cheer;
Oats for their feasts the Scottish shepherds grind,
Sweet turnips are the food of Blouzelind.
While she loves turnips, butter I'll despise,
Nor leeks nor oatmeal nor potato prize.

CUDDY.
In good roast beef my landlord sticks his knife,
The capon fat delights his dainty wife,
Pudding our parson eats, the squire loves hare,
But white-pot[2] thick is my Buxoma's fare.
While she loves white-pot, capon ne'er shall be,
Nor hare, nor beef, nor pudding, food for me.[3]

LOBBIN CLOUT.
As once I played at blindman's-buff,[4] it hapt
About my eyes the towel thick was wrapt.
I missed the swains, and seized on Blouzelind.
True speaks that ancient proverb, Love is blind.

CUDDY.
As at hot-cockles[5] once I laid me down,
And felt the weighty hand of many a clown;
Buxoma gave a gentle tap, and I
Quick rose, and read soft mischief in her eye.

LOBBIN CLOUT.
On two near elms, the slackened cord I hung,
Now high, now low my Blouzelinda swung.
With the rude wind her rumpled garment rose,
And showed her taper° leg, and scarlet hose. *tapering*

CUDDY.
Across the fallen oak the plank I laid,
And myself poised against the tott'ring maid,
High leapt the plank; adown Buxoma fell;
I spied—but faithful sweethearts never tell.

LOBBIN CLOUT.
This riddle, Cuddy, if thou canst, explain,
This wily riddle puzzles ev'ry swain.
What flower is that which bears the Virgin's name,
The richest metal joined with the same?[6]

[1] *stroked her milky care* I.e., milked the cows.

[2] *white-pot* Type of pudding made with rice and milk.

[3] *Leek to … for me* In an author's note, Gay quotes Virgil's pastoral *Eclogues* 7: "Dearest is the poplar to Alcides, the vine to Bacchus, the myrtle to fair Venus, and his own laurel to Phoebus. Phyllis loves hazels. And while Phyllis loves them, neither myrtle nor laurel of Phoebus shall outvie the hazels."

[4] *blindman's-buff* Game in which one person, blindfolded, has to catch and identify one of the surrounding players.

[5] *hot-cockles* Game in which one player lies face down and tries to guess the identity of the player who hits him or her on the back.

[6] *What flower … same* The answer is the marigold.

CUDDY.
Answer, thou carle,° and judge this riddle right, *peasant*
I'll frankly own thee for a cunning wight.° *creature*
What flower is that which royal honour craves,
Adjoin the Virgin, and 'tis strown on graves.[1]

CLODDIPOLE.
Forbear, contending louts, give o'er your strains,
An oaken staff each merits for his pains.[2]
But see the sunbeams bright to labour warn,
And gild the thatch of Goodman Hodges' barn.
Your herds for want of water stand adry,
They're weary of your songs—and so am I.

from Lady Mary Wortley Montagu, *Six Town Eclogues* (1747)

TUESDAY.
St. James's Coffee-House.

(*Silliander and Patch.*)

SILLIANDER and PATCH.
Thou so many favours hast received,
Wondrous to tell, and hard to be believed,
Oh! H——d,[3] to my lays attention lend,
Hear how two lovers boastingly contend;
Like thee successful, such their bloomy youth,
Renowned alike for gallantry and truth.

St. James's bell[4] had tolled some wretches in,
As tattered riding-hoods alone could sin,
The happier sinners now their charms put out,
And to their manteaus° their complexions suit: *gowns*
The opera queens had finished half their faces,
And city-dames already taken places;
Fops° of all kinds to see the lion,[5] run; *vain fools*
The beauties stay till the first act's begun,
And beaux step home to put fresh linen on.
No well-dressed youth in coffee-house remained,
But pensive Patch, who on the window leaned;
And Silliander, that alert and gay,
First picked his teeth, and then began to say.

SILLIANDER.
Why all these sighs, ah! why so pensive grown?
Some cause there is why thus you sit alone.
Does hapless° passion all this sorrow move? *unlucky*
Or dost thou envy, where the ladies love?

PATCH.
If, whom they love, my envy must pursue,
'Tis sure, at least, I never envy you.

SILLIANDER.
No, I'm unhappy, you are in the right,
'Tis you they favour, and 'tis me they slight.
Yet I could tell, but that I hate to boast,
A club of ladies where 'tis me they toast.

PATCH.
Toasting does seldom any favour prove;
Like us, they never toast the thing they love.
A certain Duke one night my health begun;
With cheerful pledges round the room it run,
Till the young Silvia, pressed to drink it too,
Started, and vowed she knew not what to do:
What, drink a fellow's health! she died with shame,
Yet blushed whenever she pronounced my name.

SILLIANDER.
Ill fates pursue me, may I never find
The dice propitious, or the ladies kind,
If fair Miss Flippy's fan I did not tear,
And one from me she condescends to wear.

[1] *What flower ... graves* The answer is rosemary. In an author's note, Gay quotes one of a pair of similar riddles in Virgil's *Eclogues* 3: "Say in what lands grow flowers inscribed with the names of kings."

[2] *An oaken ... his pains* In an author's note, Gay quotes from the closing stanza of *Eclogues* 3, in which Palaemon, the judge of a contest of singing between two rivals, concludes the match without bestowing the prize: "You deserve the heifer, and so does he."

[3] *H——d* Charles Howard (d. 1765), a family friend of Montagu's.

[4] *St. James's bell* The clock bell would likely be striking 6, the time the curtain usually rose at the opera.

[5] *the lion* Francesco Mancini's opera *Hydaspes*, which was produced in London in 1710, featured a scene in which a lion was killed.

Patch.
Women are always ready to receive;
'Tis then a favour when the sex will give.
A lady (but she is too great to name)
Beauteous in person, spotless is her fame,
With gentle strugglings let me force this ring;
Another day may give another thing.

Silliander.
I could say something—see this billet-doux°— *love-letter*
And as for presents—look upon my shoe—
These buckles were not forced, nor half a theft,
But a young Countess fondly made the gift.

Patch.
My Countess is more nice,° more artful too, *lascivious*
Affects to fly that I may fierce pursue:
This snuff box, which I begged, she still denied,
And when I strove to snatch it, seemed to hide;
She laughed and fled, and as I sought to seize,
With affectation crammed it down her stays:° *bodice*
Yet hoped she did not place it there unseen,
I pressed her breasts, and pulled it from between.

Silliander.
Last night, as I stood ogling of her Grace,
Drinking delicious poison from her face,
The soft enchantress did that face decline,
Nor ever raised her eyes to meet with mine;
With sudden art some secret did pretend,
Leaned cross two chairs to whisper to a friend,
While the stiff whalebone with the motion rose,
And thousand beauties to my sight expose.

Patch.
Early this morn (but I was asked to come)
I drank bohea° in Caelia's dressing-room: *black tea*
Warm from her bed, to me alone within,
Her night-gown fastened with a single pin;
Her night-clothes tumbled with resistless grace,
And her bright hair played careless round her face;
Reaching the kettle, made her gown unpin,
She wore no waistcoat, and her shift[1] was thin.

[1] *waistcoat* Expensive and showy undergarment worn by women underneath a gown, but so that it could be partially seen; *shift* Chemise, another type of female undergarment.

Silliander.
See Titiana driving to the park,
Hark! let us follow, 'tis not yet too dark;
In her all beauties of the spring are seen,
Her cheeks are rosy, and her mantle° green. *gown*

Patch.
See, Tintoretta to the opera goes!
Haste, or the crowd will not permit our bows;
In her the glory of the heavens we view,
Her eyes are star-like, and her mantle blue.

Silliander.
What colour does in Caelia's stockings shine?
Reveal that secret, and the prize is thine.

Patch.
What are her garters! Tell me if you can;
I'll freely own thee for the happier man.

Thus Patch continued his heroic strain,
While Silliander but contends in vain.
After a conquest so important gained,
Unrivaled Patch in every ruelle[2] reigned.

Thursday.
The Basset-Table.[3]

(*Smilinda, Cardelia.*)

Cardelia.
The basset-table spread, the tallier[4] come,
Why stays Smilinda in the dressing-room?
Rise, pensive nymph! The tallier stays for you.

Smilinda.
Ah! Madam, since my Sharper is untrue,
I joyless make my once ador'd alpieu.[5]
I saw him stand behind Ombrelia's chair,

[2] *ruelle* Bedroom in which ladies held morning receptions of fashionable people.

[3] *Basset-Table* Table for playing basset, a now obsolete card game played for large sums of money in high society.

[4] *tallier* Person in charge of the money.

[5] *alpieu* Decision to raise the stake after a win.

And whisper with that soft deluding air,
And those feigned sighs that cheat the list'ning fair—

CARDELIA.
Is this the cause of your romantic strains?
A mightier grief my heavy heart sustains.
As you by love, so I by fortune crossed,
In one bad deal three septlevas[1] I lost.

SMILINDA.
Is that a grief which you compare with mine?
With ease the smiles of fortune I resign.
Would all my gold in one bad deal were gone,
Were lovely Sharper mine, and mine alone.

CARDELIA.
A lover lost is but a common care,
And prudent nymphs against the change prepare.
The queen of clubs thrice lost! Oh, who could guess
This fatal stroke, this unforeseen distress!

SMILINDA.
See Betty Loveit, very à propos!
She all the pains of love and play does know,
Deeply experienced many years ago.
Dear Betty shall th'important point decide,
Betty, who oft the pains of each has tried:
Impartial, she shall say who suffers most,
By cards' ill-usage, or by lovers lost.

LOVEIT.
Tell, tell your griefs; attentive will I stay,
Though time is precious, and I want some tea.

CARDELIA.
Behold this equipage by Mathers[2] wrought
With fifty guineas (a great pen'orth!°) bought! *bargain*
See on the tooth-pick Mars and Cupid[3] strive,
And both the struggling figures seem to live.
Upon the bottom see the Queen's bright face;
A myrtle foliage round the thimble case;
Jove,[4] Jove himself does on the scissors shine,
The metal and the workmanship divine.

SMILINDA.
This snuff-box once the pledge of Sharper's love,
When rival beauties for the present strove,
(At Corticelli's[5] he the raffle won,
There first his passion was in public shown;
Hazardia blushed, and turned her head aside,
A rival's envy all in vain to hide)
This snuff-box—on the hinge see diamonds shine;
This snuff-box will I stake, the prize is mine.

CARDELIA.
Alas! far lesser losses than I bear,
Have made a soldier sigh, a lover swear:
But oh! what makes the disappointment hard,
'Twas my own Lord who drew the fatal card!
In complaisance I took the queen he gave,
Though my own secret wish was for the knave:
The knave won son ecart[6] that I had chose,
And the next pull° my septleva I lose. *draw*

SMILINDA.
But ah! what aggravates the killing smart,° *wound*
The cruel thought that stabs me to the heart,
This cursed Ombrelia, this undoing fair,
By whose vile arts this heavy grief I bear,
She, at whose name I shed these spiteful tears,
She owes to me, the very charms she wears:
An awkward thing when first she came to town,
Her shape unfinished and her face unknown;
She was my friend, I taught her first to spread
Upon her sallow cheeks enlivening red,
I introduced her to the park and plays,
And by my interest Cosins[7] made her stays°; *bodice*
Ungrateful wretch! with mimic airs grown pert,° *impertinent*
She dares to steal my favourite lover's heart.

[1] *septlevas* Opportunities to make seven times what is staked.

[2] *equipage* Collection of articles for personal use; *Mathers* Renowned gold engraver.

[3] *Mars and Cupid* Gods of war and love, respectively.

[4] *Jove* King of the Roman gods.

[5] *Corticelli's* Indian warehouse and popular meeting place.

[6] *son ecart* Card with an immediate effect on the game.

[7] *Cosins* Fashionable London bodice-maker.

CARDELIA.
Wretch that I was! how often have I swore,
When Winnall tallied, I would punt° no more! *play*
I know the bite, yet to my ruin run,
And see the folly which I cannot shun.

SMILINDA.
How many maids have Sharper's vows deceived?
How many cursed the moment they believed?
Yet, his known falsehood could no warning prove:
Ah! what are warnings to a maid in love!

CARDELIA.
But of what marble must that breast be formed,
Can gaze on basset, and remain unwarmed?
When kings, queens, knaves are set in decent rank,
Exposed in glorious heaps the tempting bank!
Guineas, half-guineas, all the shining train,
The winner's pleasure and the loser's pain;
In bright confusion open rouleaus[1] lie,
They strike the soul, and glitter in the eye;
Fired by the sight, all reason I disdain,
My passions rise, and will not bear the rein:
Look upon basset, you who reason boast,
And see if reason may not there be lost!

SMILINDA.
What more than marble must that breast compose,
That listens coldly to my Sharper's vows!
Then when he trembles, when his blushes rise,
When awful love seems melting in his eyes!
With eager beats his Mechlin cravat[2] moves:
He loves, I whisper to myself, He loves!
Such unfeigned passion in his look appears,
I lose all mem'ry of my former fears;
My panting heart confesses all his charms;
I yield at once, and sink into his arms.
Think of that moment, you who prudence boast!
For such a moment, prudence well were lost.

CARDELIA.
At the Groom-porter's,[3] battered bullies play;
Some Dukes at Marybon[4] bowl time away:
But who the bowl or rattling dice compares
To basset's heavenly joys and pleasing cares?

SMILINDA.
Soft Simplicetta dotes upon a beau;
Prudina likes a man, and laughs at show:
Their several graces in my Sharper meet;
Strong as the footman, as the master sweet.

LOVEIT.
Cease your contention, which has been too long,
I grow impatient, and the tea grows strong:
Attend, and yield to what I now decide,
The equipage shall grace Smilinda's side;
The snuff-box to Cardelia I decree;
So leave complaining, and begin your tea.

from Joseph Addison, *The Spectator* No. 414 (25 June 1712)

... Alterius sic
Altera poscit opem res et conjurat amice.[5] —HORACE

If we consider the works of nature and art, as they are qualified to entertain the imagination, we shall find the last very defective in comparison of the former; for though they may sometimes appear as beautiful or strange, they can have nothing in them of that vastness and immensity which afford so great an entertainment to the mind of the beholder. The one may be as polite and delicate as the other, but can never show herself so august and magnificent in the design. There is something more bold and masterly in the rough careless strokes of nature than in the nice touches and embellishments of art. The beauties of the most stately garden or palace lie in a narrow compass; the imagination immedi-

[1] *rouleaus* Rolls of guineas.

[2] *Mechlin cravat* Fashionable lace necktie.

[3] *Groom-porter* Royal officer in charge of regulating gaming within the court.

[4] *Marybon* Marylebone Gardens, where bowling greens and other forms of entertainment were located.

[5] *Alterius ... amice* Latin: "Each demands assistance of the other and swears to be the other's friend." From Horace, *Ars Poetica* 410–11.

ately runs them over and requires something else to gratify her. But in the wide fields of nature the sight wanders up and down without confinement, and is fed with an infinite variety of images, without any certain stint or number. For this reason we always find the poet in love with a country life, where nature appears in the greatest perfection, and furnishes out all those scenes that are most apt to delight the imagination.

Scriptorum chorus omnis amat nemus et fugit urbes.[1]
—Horace

Hic secura quits, et nescia fallere vita,
Dives opum variorum; hic latis otia fundis,
Speluncae, vivique lacus, hic frigida tempe,
Mugitusque bourn, mollesque sub arbore somni.[2]—Virgil

But though there are several of these wild scenes that are more delightful than any artificial shows, yet we find the works of nature still more pleasant the more they resemble those of art. For in this case our pleasure arises from a double principle; from the agreeableness of the objects to the eye, and from their similitude to other objects. We are pleased as well with comparing their beauties as with surveying them, and can represent them to our minds either as copies or originals. Hence it is that we take delight in a prospect which is well laid out, and diversified with fields and meadows, woods and rivers, in those accidental landscapes of trees, clouds, and cities, that are sometimes found in the veins of marble, in the curious fret-work of rocks and grottos, and, in a word, in anything that hath such a variety or regularity as may seem the effect of design, in what we call the works of chance....

Writers who have given us an account of China tell us the inhabitants of that country laugh at the plantations of our Europeans, which are laid out by the rule and line; because, they say, any one may place trees in equal rows and uniform figures. They choose rather to show a genius in works of this nature, and therefore always conceal the art by which they direct themselves. They have a word, it seems, in their language, by which they express the particular beauty of a plantation that thus strikes the imagination at first sight, without discovering what it is that has so agreeable an effect. Our British gardeners, on the contrary, instead of humoring nature, love to deviate from it as much as possible. Our trees rise in cones, globes, and pyramids. We see the marks of the scissors upon every plant and bush. I do not know whether I am singular in my opinion, but, for my own part, I would rather look upon a tree in all its luxuriancy and diffusion of boughs and branches than when it is thus cut and trimmed into a mathematical figure; and cannot but fancy that an orchard in flower looks infinitely more delightful than all the little labyrinths of the most finished parterre.[3] But as our great modelers of gardens have their magazines[4] of plants to dispose of, it is very natural for them to tear up all the beautiful plantations of fruit trees and contrive a plan that may most turn to their own profit, in taking off[5] their evergreens, and the like moveable plants, with which their shops are plentifully stocked....

[1] *Scriptorum ... urbes* Latin: "Each writer loves the grove and flees the city." From Horace, *Epistles* 2.2.77.

[2] *Hic ... somni* Latin:
Unvexed with quarrels, undisturbed with noise,
The country king his peaceful realm enjoys:
Cool grots, and living lakes, the flow'ry pride
Of meads, and streams that through the valley glide,
And shady groves that easy sleep invite,
And after toilsome days, a soft repose at night.
(from Virgil, *Georgics* 2.467–70. Translated by Dryden.)

[3] *parterre* Flat space containing ornamental arrangements of flowerbeds.

[4] *magazines* Warehouses.

[5] *taking off* Getting rid of.

Francis Nicholson, *A View at Stourhead*, showing one of the popular landscape parks of the eighteenth century. Stourhead was renowned for its classical temples and grottoes, all carefully planned for the effect they would have on a visitor following the path around the lake.

Sketch of Alexander Pope's garden by William Kent (c. 1725–30).

Poet Alexander Pope's gardens and the underground grotto that connected the two parts of his property were known for their beauty. The grotto had been a necessary construction, since the Twickenham property was cut through the middle by a busy road to London, and the tunnel was a means of connecting the two parts without needing to cross among traffic or to have gates opening on the road. This embellished sketch of Pope's garden shows, in the center, the small arch that leads down into the grotto and then out onto the bank of the Thames, on which Pope's house stood.

from Alexander Pope, Letter to Edward Blount

2 June 1725

… I have put the last hand to my works of this kind, in happily finishing the subterraneous way and grotto; I there found a spring of the clearest water, which falls in a perpetual rill that echoes through the cavern day and night. From the river Thames you see through my arch up a walk of the wilderness to a kind of open temple, wholly composed of shells in the rustic manner, and from that distance under the temple you look down through a sloping arcade of trees, and see the sails on the river passing suddenly and vanishing, as through a perspective glass. When you shut the doors of this grotto, it becomes on the instant, from a luminous room, a *camera obscura*;[1] on the walls of which all the objects of the river, hills, woods, and boats are forming a moving picture in their visible radiations. And when you have a mind to light it up, it affords you a very different scene: it is finished with shells interspersed with pieces of looking glass in angular forms; and in the ceiling is a star of the same material, at which when a lamp (of an orbicular figure of thin alabaster) is hung in the middle, a thousand pointed rays glitter and are reflected over the place. There are—connected to this grotto by a narrower passage—two porches, with niches and seats; one toward the river, of smooth stones, full of light and open; the other toward the arch of trees, rough with shells, flints, and iron ore. The bottom is paved with simple pebble, as the adjoining walk up the wilderness to the temple is to be cockleshells, in the natural taste, agreeing not ill with the little dripping murmur, and the aquatic idea of the whole place. It wants nothing to complete it but a good statue with an inscription....

You'll think I have been very poetical in this description, but it is pretty near the truth. I wish you were here to bear testimony to how little it owes to art, either the place itself, or the image I give of it.

from John Dyer, *The Fleece* (1757)

from BOOK I

The care of sheep, the labours of the loom,
And arts of trade, I sing. Ye rural nymphs,
Ye swains,° and princely merchants, aid the verse. *country laborers*
And ye, high-trusted guardians of our isle,
Whom public voice approves, or lot of birth
To the great charge assigns: ye good, of all
Degrees, all sects, be present to my song.
So may distress, and wretchedness, and want,
The wide felicities of labour learn:
So may the proud attempts of restless Gaul° *France*
From our strong borders, like a broken wave,
In empty foam retire. But chiefly thou,
The people's shepherd, eminently placed
Over the num'rous swains of ev'ry vale,
With well-permitted pow'r and watchful eye,
On each gay field to shed beneficence,
Celestial office! Thou protect the song.

On spacious airy downs,[2] the gentle hills,
With grass and thyme o'erspread, and clover wild,
Where smiling Phoebus[3] tempers every breeze,
The fairest flocks rejoice: they, nor of halt,° *a limp*
Hydropic tumours,[4] nor of rot,° complain; *foot-rot*
Evils deformed and foul: nor with hoarse cough
Disturb the music of the past'ral pipe:
But, crowding to the note, with silence soft
The close-wov'n carpet graze; where nature blends
Flowrets and herbage of minutest size,
Innoxious° luxury. Wide airy downs *guiltless*
Are health's gay walks to shepherd and to sheep.

All arid soils, with sand, or chalky flint,
Or shells diluvian[5] mingled; and the turf,
That mantles° over rocks of brittle stone, *covers*
Be thy regard: and where low-tufted broom,[6]
Or box,[7] or berried juniper arise;
Or the tall growth of glossy-rinded° beech; *barked*
And where the burrowing rabbit turns the dust;
And where the dappled deer delights to bound.

Such are the downs of Banstead,[8] edged with woods
And tow'ry villas; such Dorcestrian[9] fields,

[1] *camera obscura* Latin: dark vault, or chamber. An instrument consisting of a dark box into which light is emitted through a double lens, causing an image of external objects to be projected on a surface. Pope refers to the way in which the light reflected from objects outside is projected onto the walls of the grotto, forming images of these objects.

[2] *downs* Areas of open, elevated land.

[3] *Phoebus* Apollo, god of the sun.

[4] *Hydropic tumours* Dropsy, swelling caused by accumulations of water in connective tissue.

[5] *diluvian* Of a flood.

[6] *broom* Shrub with yellow flowers, common on English pastures.

[7] *box* Small evergreen shrub.

[8] *Banstead* Town just south of London.

[9] *Dorcestrian* Pertaining to Dorcester, in Dorset, in the southwest of England. The town is in the Frome River Valley, south of the Dorset Downs.

Whose flocks innum'rous whiten all the land:
Such those slow-climbing wilds, that lead the step
Insensibly to Dover's[1] windy cliff,
Tremendous height! and such the clovered lawns
And sunny mounts° of beauteous Normanton,[2] *hills*
Health's cheerful haunt, and the selected walk
Of Heathcote's leisure: such the spacious plain
Of Sarum,[3] spread like ocean's boundless round,
Where solitary Stonehenge, grey with moss,
Ruin of ages, nods ...

How erring oft the judgment in its hate,
Or fond desire! Those slow-descending showers,
Those hov'ring fogs, that bathe our growing vales
In deep November (loathed by trifling Gaul,
Effeminate), are gifts the Pleiads[4] shed,
Britannia's handmaids. As the bev'rage falls,
Her hills rejoice, her valleys laugh and sing.

Hail noble Albion°! Where no golden mines, *England*
No soft perfumes, nor oils, nor myrtle bow'rs,° *arbors*
The vig'rous frame and lofty heart of man
Enervate:° round whose stern cerulean° *weaken / deep blue*
brows
White-winged snow, and cloud, and pearly rain,
Frequent attend, with solemn majesty:
Rich queen of mists and vapours! These thy sons
With their cool arms compress, and twist their nerves
For deeds of excellence and high renown.
Thus formed, our Edwards, Henrys,[5] Churchills, Blakes,
Our Lockes, our Newtons, and our Miltons,[6] rose.

See the sun gleams; the living pastures rise,
After the nurture of the fallen show'r,
How beautiful! How blue th'ethereal vault,
How verdurous° the lawns, how clear the brooks! *green*
Such noble warlike steeds, such herds of kine,° *cattle*
So sleek, so vast; such spacious flocks of sheep,
Like flakes of gold illumining the green,
What other paradise adorn but thine,
Britannia? Happy, if thy sons would know
Their happiness. To these thy naval streams,
Thy frequent towns superb of busy trade,
And ports magnific add, and stately ships
Innumerous. But whither strays my muse?
Pleased, like a traveller upon the strand° *coast*
Arrived of bright Augusta:° wild he roves *London*
From deck to deck, through groves immense of masts;
'Mong crowds, bales,[7] cars,° the wealth of *chariots*
either Ind;[8]
Through wharfs, and squares, and palaces, and domes,
In sweet surprise; unable yet to fix
His raptured mind, or scan in ordered course
Each object singly; with discov'ries new
His native country studious to enrich....

from Edmund Burke, *A Philosophical Enquiry into the Origin of Our Ideas of the Sublime and the Beautiful* (1757)

Of the Sublime

Whatever is fitted in any sort to excite the ideas of pain and danger, that is to say, whatever is in any sort terrible, or is conversant about terrible objects, or operates in a manner analogous to terror, is a source of the *sublime*; that is, it is productive of the strongest emotion which the mind is capable of feeling. I say the strongest emotion because I am satisfied the ideas of pain are much more powerful than those which enter on the part of pleasure. Without all doubt, the torments which we may be made to suffer are much greater in

[1] *Dover* Port town in southeast England; known for its chalk cliffs, commonly referred to as "the white cliffs of Dover."

[2] *Normanton* Small parish that consists of a large park of about 400 acres. In the mid-eighteenth century Sir Gilbert Heathcote demolished Normanton's church and village to form the park.

[3] *Sarum* Site of England's earliest settlement, dating to about 3000 BCE.

[4] *Pleiads* In Greek mythology, the seven daughters of Atlas and Pleione, who were turned into stars; their arrival in the sky indicates the coming of winter.

[5] *Edwards, Henrys* Past kings of England, several of whom have had the names Edward or Henry.

[6] *Churchills ... Miltons* References to, in order, politician John Churchill, first duke of Marlborough (1650–1722); Admiral Robert Blake (1598–1657); philosopher John Locke (1632–1704); mathematician and physicist Sir Isaac Newton (1643–1727); and poet John Milton (1562–1647), author of *Paradise Lost*.

[7] *bales* Bundles of merchandise.

[8] *either Ind* The East or West Indies.

their effect on the body and mind than any pleasures which the most learned voluptuary could suggest, or than the liveliest imagination and the most sound and exquisitely sensible body could enjoy. Nay, I am in great doubt whether any man could be found who would earn a life of the most perfect satisfaction at the price of ending it in the torments which justice inflicted in a few hours on the late unfortunate regicide in France.[1] But as pain is stronger in its operation than pleasure, so death is in general a much more affecting idea than pain; because there are very few pains, however exquisite, which are not preferred to death; nay, what generally makes pain itself, if I may say so, more painful, is that it is considered as an emissary of this king of terrors. When danger or pain press too nearly, they are incapable of giving any delight, and are simply terrible; but at certain distances, and with certain modifications, they may be, and they are delightful, as we every day experience. The cause of this I shall endeavor to investigate hereafter.

Of the Passion Caused by the Sublime

The passion caused by the great and sublime in nature, when those causes operate most powerfully, is astonishment; and astonishment is that state of the soul in which all its motions are suspended, with some degree of horror. In this case the mind is so entirely filled with its object that it cannot entertain any other, nor by consequence reason on that object which employs it. Hence arises the great power of the sublime, that far from being produced by them, it anticipates our reasonings, and hurries us on by an irresistible force. Astonishment, as I have said, is the effect of the sublime in its highest degree; the inferior effects are admiration, reverence, and respect....

The Sublime and Beautiful Compared

On closing this general view of beauty, it naturally occurs, that we should compare it with the sublime; and in this comparison there appears a remarkable contrast. For sublime objects are vast in their dimensions, beautiful ones comparatively small; beauty should be smooth and polished; the great, rugged and negligent. Beauty should shun the right line, yet deviate from it insensibly; the great in many cases loves the right line, and when it deviates, it often makes a strong deviation. Beauty should not be obscure; the great ought to be dark and gloomy. Beauty should be light and delicate; the great ought to be solid, and even massive. They are indeed ideas of a very different nature, one being founded on pain, the other on pleasure; and however they may vary afterwards from the direct nature of their causes, yet these causes keep up an eternal distinction between them, a distinction never to be forgotten by any whose business it is to affect the passions. In the infinite variety of natural combinations we must expect to find the qualities of things the most remote imaginable from each other united in the same object.

We must expect also to find combinations of the same kind in the works of art. But when we consider the power of an object upon our passions, we must know that when anything is intended to affect the mind by the force of some predominant property, the affection produced is like to be the more uniform and perfect if all the other properties or qualities of the object be of the same nature, and tending to the same design as the principal;

> If black and white blend, soften, and unite,
> A thousand ways, are there no black and white?[2]

If the qualities of the sublime and beautiful are sometimes found united, does this prove that they are the same? Does it prove that they are any way allied? Does it prove even that they are not opposite and contradictory? Black and white may soften, may blend, but they are not therefore the same. Nor when they are so softened and blended with each other, or with different colors, is the power of black as black, or of white as white, so strong as when each stands uniform and distinguished....

[1] *late ... France* Reference to Francis Damiens (1714–57), who was tortured and executed for attempting to assassinate King Louis XV.

[2] *If ... white* Cf. Alexander Pope's *Essay on Man* 2.213–14.

Hester Thrale Piozzi

1741 – 1821

During the course of her adult life Hester Thrale Piozzi occupied two vastly different identities. First, as Hester Thrale, she was a brewer's wife and skilled hostess whose diaries and letters continue to be a source of important biographical information concerning the group of established literati whom she and her husband frequently entertained. After her second marriage, as Hester Piozzi, she became a publishing author in her own right whose lifestyle and writing—both atypical of women at the time—were subjects of much controversy.

Piozzi was born Hester Lynch Salusbury in remote northwest Wales in 1741. Both her parents were descended from old Welsh families of high standing, and they raised their daughter as a gentlewoman—educating her in etiquette, horsemanship, Spanish, Italian, Latin, and rhetoric—though they were by no means wealthy. In fact, it was due to their continued financial concerns that Mrs. Salusbury persuaded her daughter to marry Southwark entrepreneur Henry Thrale. At 22 Thrale, later Piozzi—formerly active and independent—found her duties limited to the frequent birthing of her children (she bore twelve, though only three survived to adulthood); the management of her husband's brewery; and the entertainment of his guests.

In this last role Thrale—thanks to her intelligence, education, and powers of conversation—was particularly adept. Her home became the social center for a number of major literary figures of the time, Samuel Johnson chief among them. Thrale formed a close friendship with Johnson, who was soon established with his own apartment in her home. Johnson in turn encouraged Thrale's scholarship and writing, and helped her to publish several of her poems. During her first marriage Thrale was constantly writing. She published only rarely but composed a number of private poems, penned hundreds of letters, recorded her thoughts and anecdotes in a six-volume commonplace-book—entitled *Thraliana* (1942)—and detailed the progress and education of her children in *A Family Book* (1977).

In *Thraliana* Thale declares, "I have always sacrificed my own choice to that of others … because I am a woman of superior understanding, and must not for the world degrade myself from my situation in life." This attitude eventually changed about three years after the death of Henry Thrale in 1781, when she shocked London society by marrying Italian musician Gabriel Piozzi. The marriage was scandalous: her new husband was a foreigner, a Catholic, and of a social order considered much lower than her own. In addition, her impulsive, passionate decision and subsequent departure to Italy marked a complete break from the traditional role she had previously occupied with such skill and propriety. The marriage was unfathomable to those who knew her, and as a result of it she lost her social status and most of her friendships—including that with Dr. Johnson. (Thrale, now Hester Piozzi, had kept her marriage a secret from Johnson and when he found out he wrote her a furious letter, in which genuine concern for her is overshadowed by jealousy and hurt. She sent a dignified reply, and he apologized, but the friendship did not recover. These letters appear earlier in this volume.)

Piozzi was never again either entirely welcome or comfortable in London society, but she was finally free to pursue her own interests, and in her new diary she declared herself happier than she had ever been. After Dr. Johnson's death in 1784, she compiled and published (from Italy, therefore without access to her notes) a biography, *Anecdotes of Samuel Johnson* (1786), whose first printing sold out on the evening of its release. (Johnson was a popular figure, and tremendous curiosity had long surrounded their relationship. Some had even expected her to marry Johnson.) *Letters to and From the Late Samuel Johnson* followed two years later. Encouraged by her early success, Piozzi experimented with a variety of modes and genres, producing work that reveals the extent of her intellect, and ambition. *Observations and Reflections Made in the Course of a Journey Through France, Italy, and Germany* (1789) assumes an authority, informality, and directness unusual to women's travel literature of the time. *British Synonymy* (1794, billed as an attempt to help foreigners like her second husband with the prodigal wealth of the English language) presents a detailed and playful explanation of over 1180 synonyms; and *Retrospection* (1801), Piozzi's most ambitious undertaking, provides a history of the West from the birth of Christ onward.

Observations and *British Synonymy* enjoyed a brief success, but in all three of these later publications Piozzi was censured for having exceeded the proper bounds for the feminine pursuit of knowledge. The serious topics she addressed and the scholarly methods she adopted, combined with her conversational tone, attempts at light humor, and feminine humility, puzzled readers. Perhaps had she led a more conventional life this unconventionality in her writing could have been viewed with a more forgiving eye. Instead, her work only provided further ammunition for the sort of mocking, satirical attack to which she had been subject since her second marriage. Piozzi continued to write until her death in 1821. She left her last big work, "Lyford Redivivus or A Grandame's Garrulity," a study of proper names, unpublished, and printed nothing more but one or two pamphlets.

⌘⌘⌘

from *Hester Thrale's Journal*

31 December 1773

I am now come to the end of the year 1773, during the last six months of which I have suffered the loss of a parent, a child, & the almost certain hopes of an ample fortune,[1] in the full expectation of which I had been bred up from twelve years old. In the midst of this distress I have brought a baby,[2] which seems to be in some measure affected by my vexations; he is heavy, stupid, & drowsy, though very large, and what those who do not observe him as I do call a fine boy. But I see no wit sparkle in his eyes like the mother in Gay's fables.[3] What is most singular is my own recovery from a scene of sorrow & trouble scarcely to be equalled—from the loss of the finest girl I almost ever saw,[4] & the cutting mortification of seeing my estate snatched from me in a manner most base & vile by wretches whom I despise. My uncle too, upon whose lap I lived for 20 years (the happiest I have known) is now wholly lost to me, & injuriously as he has treated me I half regret him. I had depended upon ending my days at dear Offley, where they first began to be agreeable, & had relied upon enjoying the society of my *new* friends, where I had once been merry with my *old* ones. I had indulged the vanity of thinking how I should enrich my family,

[1] *hopes ... fortune* Hester Thrale's uncle, Sir Thomas Salusbury (1708–73) had apparently promised his estate, Offley Place, to Thrale several years earlier. In his will, however, he left the property to his widow.

[2] *brought a baby* Ralph (1773–75), Thrale's second son.

[3] *Gay's fables* *Fifty-One Fables in Verse* (1727) by John Gay, British poet and playwright (1685–1732).

[4] *finest girl ... saw* Hester Thrale's daughter Lucy, who died at age four.

how my husband would double his attention, my children their duty, & my acquaintance their flattery.

How I should manage when possessed of the Hertfordshire estate was the chief enquiry of my solitary hours, & many a delightful moment has been spent in recalling the beloved places to my view where I once was happy in the favour of all my relations, friends, & admirers. Whose disappointment then can surpass mine? And grievous & heavy I confess it is for to bear! But I hope it has kindled no bad passions in my breast—I have not neglected my duties because my heart was full, nor appeared less cheerful before those who have no business to partake my concerns. I have never failed to hear the same stated lessons I ever heard, nor suffered the children to be neglected because I was miserable. As I have now no soothing friend to tell my grief to, it will perhaps sink the sooner into insensibility. Dr. Johnson is very kind as can be, & I ought to be thankful that Mr. Thrale does not, as most husbands would, aggravate by insult and anger the sorrows of my mind. It however happily for me operates upon him quite another way: he would rather be without the estate I believe, than hold it of *a wife*. He therefore bids me keep up my spirits, for that we do not want it, & that he would never have lived at Offley if we had had it, &c.

So farewell to all I formerly loved—to my mother, my house in Hertfordshire, my lovely Lucy, and to this accursed year 1773.

30 September 1774

I returned safe home from my long tour;[1] brought Queeney safe back; called on my girls at Kensington, whom I found quite well (I had no time to examine mental improvements); and got in good time to Streatham where Harry met & rejoiced over us very kindly. He is wonderfully grown & seems in perfect health, though having lost a few teeth gives him an odd look. But he appears happy & cheerful, and full of spirits. Little Ralph is more visibly improved than any of them, except Susan,[2] who now commences both wit and beauty forsooth. She is in no respect the same child she was two or three years ago, so that if she did not grow very like Harry, I tell Mrs. Cumyns, I should think she had changed her. Everything, however, happens to perplex *me*, & now that I hoped to come home & be quiet, examine my children & see what deficiencies could be supplied, and enjoy a little quiet after the hurrying life I have been leading of late, here is the general election broke out—deuce take it!—and my attendance is wanted in the Borough.[3]

2 October 1774

Before I launch into this new confusion, let me mention a word of my little ones. Queeney kept her birthday running about Hagley Park. She was pretty well all the journey, except a severe cold & cough whilst we were at Ashburne, & now & then a slight touch of the worms, but nothing really formidable. Upon the whole she has been active, intrepid, and observing, & though we may have lost some Italian, we have, I think, gained some images which will make more than amends. Nothing escapes this girl's penetration, nothing intimidates her courage, nothing flutters her fancy. Mean inns, or splendid apartments—for we have experienced both—find her mind always prepared to enjoy the one & to defy the other. Mr. Johnson tells how she wished to see a storm when we crossed over to Anglesey, & how she rode 15 miles once on a single hard trotting in the night among the mountains of Snowdon. These are certainly noble qualities and great performances for a girl scarce ten years old, yet is Queeney no very desirable companion....

Sullen, malicious, & perverse, desirous of tormenting *me* even by hurting herself, & resolute to utter nothing in my hearing that might give credit to either of us, she often tells me what she thought on such an occasion, what she *could* have said, &c. when we are alone, but has an affectation of playing the Agnes[4] when we are in company together. However, when my back

[1] *long tour* Mr. and Mrs. Thrale, Johnson, and Queeney, the Thrales's daughter, had been traveling in Wales since the beginning of July.

[2] *Harry ... Susan* Harry, Ralph, and Susan, the Thrales's other children.

[3] *general election ... Borough* Henry Thrale was running for re-election as member of Parliament for Southwark, and Piozzi was helping him to campaign.

[4] *playing the Agnes* Agnes, the heroine of Molière's *L'École des Femmes*, a clinging, helpless sort of woman.

is turned, & she sees no danger of giving me any delight, her tongue is voluble enough, I find, & her manner so particularly pleasing that a young fellow who saw her in Derbyshire half a dozen times persuaded his foolish father at his return to propose him to marry her, protesting he would rather wait seven years for Miss Thrale than have any other girl he ever saw in his life—an early conquest I must confess! So much for Hetty, or Queeney, or Niggey as we called her …

Ralph is most exceedingly come on—grown vastly handsome, & much more intelligent, has a healthy colour in his cheeks, & promises mighty well indeed. He makes no effort to talk, however, but Nurse is beginning to set him on his feet. She is not a little proud of him.

Harry is the very best boy in the world; has minded his business as if I had been watching him. I shall make Mr. Jones[1] a present—I see there has been great pains taken on both sides, and no faults found on either. That is sweet.

The girls do very well as to health, and Mrs. Cumyns[2] writes me wonderful accounts of Susan's prowess in the literary way—so wonderful indeed that I do not believe them. But when this odious election is over I shall see. The truth is Susan is so changed in her face & figure that if every thing else keeps pace, all she says may be true. I used to joke with my poor mother & say Susan would become the pillar of the family perhaps, as everything happens contrary to one's expectations (little thinking it however). But, as Goneril says in King Lear, "Jesters do oft prove prophets!"[3]

Now for this filthy election! I must leave Queeney to the care of Mr. Baretti,[4] I believe, or him to hers, & she must keep house here at Streatham while I go fight the opposition in the Borough. Oh my sweet mother, how every thing makes your loss more heavy! …

On Thursday the 21st they all[5] rose well & lively, & Queeney went with me to fetch her sister[6] from school for a week. She[7] seemed sullen all the way there & back, but not sick, so I huffed[8] her & we got home in good time to dress for dinner, when we expected Sir Robert Cotton & the Davenants. Harry, however, had seen a play of his friend Murphy's[9] advertised, & teased me so to let him see it that I could not resist his importunity, and treated[10] one of our principal clerks to go with him. He came home at 12 o'clock half mad with delight, and in such spirits, health, & happiness that nothing ever exceeded. Queeney, however, drooped all afternoon; complained of the headache. Mr. Thrale was so cross at my giving Harry leave to go to the play, instead of showing him to Sir Robert, that I passed an uneasy time of it, and could not enjoy the praises given to Susan, I was so fretted about the two eldest. When Harry came home so happy, however, all was forgotten, & he went to rest in perfect tranquillity. Queeney, however, felt hot, & I was not at all pleased with her. But on Friday morning the boy rose quite cheerful & did our little business with great alacrity. Count Manucci[11] came to breakfast by appointment. We were all to go show him the Tower[12] forsooth, so Queeney made light of her illness & pressed me to take her too. There was one of the ships bound for Boston now in the river with our beer aboard.[13] Harry ran to see the blaze in the morning, & coming back to the Compting house, "I see," says he to our 1st clerk, "I see your porter is good, Mr. Perkins, for it *burns* special well." Well by this time we set out

[1] *Mr. Jones* John Jones, a cousin who had watched Harry while the Thrales were in Wales.

[2] *Mrs. Cumyns* Old friend of Piozzi's who kept a school in Kensington Square.

[3] *Goneril … prophets* See Shakespeare's *King Lear* 5.3.72; however, the speaker is Regan.

[4] *Mr. Baretti* Italian writer and scholar, a close friend of the Thrales and Queeney's Italian tutor.

[5] *they all* I.e., Queeney, Harry, and Sophie Thrale.

[6] *her sister* I.e., Susan.

[7] *She* I.e., Queeney.

[8] *huffed* Scolded, chided.

[9] *of his friend Murphy's* Arthur Murphy, playwright (1727–1805).

[10] *treated* Paid for.

[11] *Count Manucci* The Count of Florence, whom the Thrales had met in Paris the year before.

[12] *Tower* Tower of London.

[13] *ships … aboard* This ship was on fire.

for the Tower, Papa & Manucci & the children & I. Queeney was not half well, but Harry continued in high spirits, both among the lions & the arms, repeating passages from the English History, examining the artillery, & getting into every mortar till he was as black as the ground. Count Manucci observed his pranks, & said he must be a soldier with him, but Harry would not fight for the Grand Duke of Tuscany because he was a papist. "And look here," said he, showing the instruments of torture to the Count, "what those Spanish papists intended for *us.*" From this place we drove to Moore's Carpet Manufactory, where the boy was still active, attentive, & lively. But as Queeney's looks betrayed the sickness she would fain have concealed, we drove homewards, taking in our way Brooke's Menagerie, where I just stopped to speak about my peafowl. Here Harry was happy again with a lion intended for a show, who was remarkably tame, & a monkey so beautiful & gentle that I was as much pleased with him as the children. Here we met a Mr. Hervey, who took notice of the boy, how *well* he looked. "Yes," said I, "if the dirt were scraped off him." It was now time to get home, & Harry, after saying how hungry he was, instantly pounced (as he called it) on a piece of cold mutton & spent the afternoon among us all recounting the pleasures of the day. He went to bed that night as perfectly well as ever I saw man, woman, or child in my life. Queeney, however, took some rhubarb & went on drooping & felt feverish. I looked at her two or three times in the night too, & found her hot & feverish. But her dear brother slept as cool & comfortable as possible, & on the morning of the next fatal day, Saturday, 23rd of March, 1776, he rose in perfect health; went to the baker for his roll and watched the drawing it out of the oven; carried it to Bachelors' Hall (as he called it), where the young clerks live down the brewhouse yard. There he got butter & cooked a merry breakfast among them. After this he returned with two penny cakes he had bought for the little girls, & distributed them between them in his pleasant manner for minuets that he made them dance. I was all this while waiting on Queeney, who seemed far from well, & I was once very impatient at the noise the maids & children made in the nursery by laughing excessively at his antic tricks. By this time I came down to my dressing room to tutor Sophy till the clock struck ten, which is my regular breakfast hour. I had scarce made the tea when Moll came to tell me Queeney was better, & Harry making a figure of 5:10[1] (so we always called his manner of twisting about when anything ailed him). When I got to the nursery, there was Harry crying as if he had been whipped instead of ill, so I reproved him for making such a bustle about nothing & said, "See how differently your sister behaves," who, though in earnest far from well, had begged to make breakfast for Papa & Mr. Baretti while I was employed above. The next thing I did was to send for Mr. Lawrence of York Buildings, to whom Nurse was always partial. My note expressed to him that both the eldest children were ill, but Hetty *worst.* Presently however, finding the boy inclined to vomit, I administered a large wine glass of emetic wine, which however did nothing *any way*, though he drank small liquids with avidity. And now seeing his sickness increase, & his countenance begin to alter, I sent out Sam with orders not to come back without *some* physician—Jebb, Bromfield, Pinkstan, or Lawrence of Essex Street, whichever he could find. In the meantime I plunged Harry into water as hot as could easily be borne, up to his middle, & had just taken him out of the tub & laid him in a warm bed when Jebb came & gave him 1st hot wine, then usquebaugh,[2] then Daffy's Elixir,[3] so fast that it alarmed me—though I had no notion of *death*, having seen him so perfectly well at 9 o'clock. He then had poultices made with mustard put to his feet, & strong broth & wine clysters[4] injected, but we could get no evacuation *any* way, & the inclination to vomit still continuing, Jebb gave him 5 grains of ipecacuanha[5] & then drove away to call Heberden's help. The child all this while spoke well & brisk; sat upright to talk with the Drs.; said he had no pain now but his breath was short. This I attributed to the hot things he had taken, & thought Jebb in my heart far more officious than wise. I was, however, all confusion, distress, & perplex-

[1] *figure of 5:10* Knee-chest position.

[2] *usquebaugh* Whiskey.

[3] *Daffy's Elixir* Medicine for infants, often mixed with gin.

[4] *clysters* Enemas.

[5] *ipecacuanha* Root of a South American plant, useful as a purgative or emetic.

ity, & Mr. Thrale bid me not cry so, for I should look like a hag when I went to court next day. He often saw Harry in the course of the morning and apprehended no danger at all—no more did Baretti, who said he should be whipped for frightening his mother for nothing. Queeney had for some time been laid down on her own bed, & got up fancying herself better. But soon a universal shriek called us all together to Harry's bedside, where he struggled a moment—thrusting his finger down his throat to excite vomiting—& then turning to Nurse said very distinctly, "Don't scream so, I *know* I must die."

This however I did not hear....

23 July 1776

Sophia Thrale is five Years old today; She Has read three Epistles & three Gospels: I do not make her get much by heart: the thing is—I have really listened to Babies Learning till I am half stupefied—& all my pains have answered so poorly—I have no heart to battle with Sophy: She would probably learn very well, if I had the Spirit of teaching I once had, as She is docile & stout; able to bear buffeting & Confinement, & has withal reasonable good parts & a great Desire to please. but I will not make her Life miserable as I suppose it will be short—not for want of Health indeed, for no Girl can have better, but Harry & Lucy are dead, & why Should Sophy live? The Instructions I labor'd to give *them*—what did they end in? The Grave—& every recollection brings only new Regret. Sophy shall read well, & learn her Prayers; & take her Chance for more, when I can get it for her. at Present I can not begin battling with Babies—/ have already spent my whole Youth at it & lost my Reward at last....

original spelling

No peace saith my God for the wicked! no quiet Gestation for me! on Sunday Night the 3rd of Sept. Mr. Thrale told me he had an Ailment, & shewed me a Testicle swelled to an immense Size: I had no Notion but of a *Cancer*—Poor Fool! & press'd him to have the best help that could be got—no he would have only Gregory—a drunken crazy Fellow that his Father had known: however when I pressed him with an honest earnestness and kind Voice to have Hawkins, Potts or some eminent hand—he said it was nothing dangerous with a Smile; but that since I had an Aversion to Mr. Gregory he would send for one Osborne; a sort of half Quack, whose Name I have sometimes read in the papers as possessing the Receipts of a M: Daran a famous Practitioner in the *Venereal* Way: I now began to understand where I was, and to perceive that my poor Father's Prophecy was verified who said If you marry that Scoundrel he will catch the Pox, & for your Amusement set you to make his Pultices. This is now literally made out; & I am preparing Pultices as he said, and Fomenting[1] this elegant Ailment every Night & Morning for an Hour together on my Knees, & receiving for my Reward such Impatient Expressions as disagreable Confinement happens to dictate. however tis well tis no worse—he has I am pretty sure not given it me, and I am now pregnant & may bring a healthy Boy who knows? All my Concern is lest it *should* after all prove a Schirrus[2]—my Master denies it's being the other Thing very resolutely, & says he has felt it ever since he jumped from the Chaise between Rouen & Paris exactly this Time Twelvemonth: if this should be true we are all undone, undone indeed! for it can end in nothing but a Cancer, & I know but too well the Dreadful Consequence of that most fatal Disease—Yet I will *hope* it may be only a Venereal Complaint, if so there is no Danger to be sure & this Osborne may manage it rightly.

My poor Heart which is ever beating for some *Family* Cause, is now more than ever oppressed: if he dies—the Band is burst, and we are all turned a Drift—but I will hope better things, & I saw the Surgeon smile yesterday, & charge him to live remarkably low—abstaining from Wine Spice &c. denials in such Cases are never to be regarded—I do think it is only a Consequence of Folly & Vice, no real & dangerous Disease.

original spelling

7 January 1777

I have now begun a new year in my children's book; may it prove a fortunate one to them or it cannot be so to me. All is well with them at present, and I go on myself as usual in my pregnancy, but with more atten-

[1] *Fomenting* Bathing with warm medicinal substances.

[2] *Schirrus* Tumor.

tion to every sensation, as I consider it of unusual importance. The truth is I did pray earnestly for a son, and I am strangely prepossessed with a notion that God has heard my prayers. But perhaps like poor Rachel[1] I may pay my own life for it. Well, no matter! I shall leave a son of my own to inherit my paternal estate, & for the rest Mr. Thrale may provide himself with children & choose a wife where he will. It is not his principle to lament much for the dead, so my loss will not break *his* heart, & as for Queeney, I defy him to find her a mother she will *appear* to like less than her own. Miss Owen[2] is very likely to be my successor; we often joke about it, & such jests have always some earnest in them. She would not wrong my girls, I dare say, and if I have a boy I should leave him a certain provision. Mr. Thrale would probably be partial to *her* children in point of personal fondness—but that is a very small affair, and I doubt not his equitable proceeding to them all in the main business of life. My master has not yet set about ridding himself of his hydrocele[3] for good & all; however, it is almost inclined to go away of itself, and will be cured with great ease in a constitution so perfect as his. Poor Mr. Johnson would have the greatest loss of me, and he would be the most sensible of his loss. He would willingly write my epitaph, I am sure, if my husband would treat me with a monument, which I do believe he would, too, if anybody would press him to it before the first year was out. After *that* he would be married again, & his second lady would perhaps make objections. So if I *do* die this time, then,

"Farewell light and life, and thou blest sun serene!"[4]

—1977

[1] *poor Rachel* Rachel, the wife of Jacob, died giving birth to Benjamin (see Genesis 35.18).

[2] *Miss Owen* Distant cousin and close childhood friend of Hester Thrale's.

[3] *hydrocele* Swelling or accumulation of fluid.

[4] *Farewell ... serene* Unidentified.

Olaudah Equiano or Gustavus Vassa

1745 – 1797

Olaudah Equiano's *The Interesting Narrative of the Life of Olaudah Equiano* was the first slave narrative written in English, and he is viewed by many as the originator of the genre. As such, his work is seen as the beginning of black literary tradition. His narrative became a central document for the abolitionist movement, showing readers the horrors of slavery while also demonstrating the eloquence of a native-born African who had been educated in the Western tradition, and displaying to the devout that black people were as capable of spiritual enlightenment as were whites.

Until recently Equiano's account of his early years was generally taken at face value; it was accepted that he had been born into the Ibo nation; that he had been kidnaped at the age of eleven and enslaved for some time in Africa; and that he was eventually brought across the Atlantic as a slave. In an important 1999 article and then in his 2005 biography of Equiano, historian Vincent Carretta challenged his account, citing two newly-discovered documents indicating that Equiano had been born not in Africa, but in Carolina. The issue may never be entirely resolved, but Carretta's arguments are now widely accepted. It is significant, however, that neither Carretta nor other scholars have challenged the authenticity of the information Equiano provides about life in Africa, the passage across the Atlantic, and so on; if Equiano himself was indeed born an American slave, he would have obtained such information directly from his fellow slaves. At issue, then, is not the fundamental reality of the account Equiano provides, but only whether the early part of his narrative represents a first-hand account or an act of creative imagination based on first-hand research.

Equiano's account of his life following his purchase by the British naval captain Michael Henry Pascal is not in dispute. As a slave to Pascal (who renamed him "Gustavus Vassa") Equiano began his career as a seaman. For the next ten or eleven years, Equiano traveled widely to the Mediterranean, Europe, and the Americas, and was engaged in several battles during the Seven Years' War (1756–63). Despite his years of service, Pascal sold Equiano for £40 to the Quaker Robert King, from whom Equiano was eventually able to buy his freedom in 1766.

After securing his freedom, Equiano settled in England. While slavery was still permitted in England's overseas colonies, it was frowned on at home, and there was a relatively large black population (10,000–20,000). Because he had most often been enslaved to British men, and because he had been baptized into the Anglican Church in 1759, Equiano considered himself "almost an Englishman." He had been taught to read and write while still a slave and he now used these skills to highlight the position of slaves and to petition for the abolition of slavery. He worked with several prominent abolitionists, including Granville Sharpe and William Wilberforce. When his narrative was published in 1789 it was widely read, and it became influential in furthering the abolitionists' cause. Equiano married in 1792 and had two daughters before he died in 1797.

⌘⌘⌘

from *The Interesting Narrative of the Life of Olaudah Equiano, or Gustavus Vassa, the African. Written by Himself*

Chapter I

The author's account of his country, and their manners and customs—Administration of justice—Embrenche—Marriage ceremony, and public entertainments—Mode of living—Dress—Manufactures Buildings—Commerce—Agriculture—War and religion—Superstition of the natives—Funeral ceremonies of the priests or magicians—Curious mode of discovering poison—Some hints concerning the origin of the author's countrymen, with the opinions of different writers on that subject.

I believe it is difficult for those who publish their own memoirs to escape the imputation of vanity; nor is this the only disadvantage under which they labour: it is also their misfortune that what is uncommon is rarely, if ever, believed, and what is obvious we are apt to turn from with disgust, and to charge the writer with impertinence. People generally think those memoirs only worthy to be read or remembered which abound in great or striking events, those, in short, which in a high degree excite either admiration or pity: all others they consign to contempt and oblivion. It is therefore, I confess, not a little hazardous in a private and obscure individual, and a stranger too, thus to solicit the indulgent attention of the public; especially when I own I offer here the history of neither a saint, a hero, nor a tyrant. I believe there are few events in my life which have not happened to many: it is true the incidents of it are numerous; and, did I consider myself an European, I might say my sufferings were great: but when I compare my lot with that of most of my countrymen, I regard myself as a particular favourite of Heaven, and acknowledge the mercies of Providence in every occurrence of my life. If then the following narrative does not appear sufficiently interesting to engage general attention, let my motive be some excuse for its publication. I am not so foolishly vain as to expect from it either immortality or literary reputation. If it affords any satisfaction to my numerous friends, at whose request it has been written, or in the smallest degree promotes the interests of humanity, the ends for which it was undertaken will be fully attained, and every wish of my heart gratified. Let it therefore be remembered that, in wishing to avoid censure, I do not aspire to praise.

That part of Africa, known by the name of Guinea, to which the trade for slaves is carried on, extends along the coast above 3400 miles, from the Senegal to Angola, and includes a variety of kingdoms. Of these the most considerable is the kingdom of Benin,[1] both as to extent and wealth, the richness and cultivation of the soil, the power of its king, and the number and warlike disposition of the inhabitants. It is situated nearly under the line,[2] and extends along the coast about 170 miles, but runs back into the interior part of Africa to a distance hitherto I believe unexplored by any traveller; and seems only terminated at length by the empire of Abyssinia, near 1500 miles from its beginning. This kingdom is divided into many provinces or districts: in one of the most remote and fertile of which, called Eboe, I was born, in the year 1745, in a charming fruitful vale named Essaka. The distance of this province from the capital of Benin and the sea coast must be very considerable; for I had never heard of white men or Europeans, nor of the sea. And our subjection to the king of Benin was little more than nominal, for every transaction of the government, as far as my slender observation extended, was conducted by the chiefs or elders of the place. The manners and government of a people who have little commerce with other countries are generally very simple, and the history of what passes in one family or village may serve as a specimen of a nation. My father was one of those elders or chiefs I have spoken of, and was styled Embrenche; a term, as I remember, importing the highest distinction, and signifying in our language a *mark* of grandeur. This mark is conferred on the person entitled to it by cutting the skin across at the top of the forehead, and drawing it down to the eyebrows; and while it is in this situation applying a warm hand,

[1] *kingdom of Benin* This kingdom extended over part of present-day Nigeria as well as present-day Benin.

[2] *under the line* South of the equator.

and rubbing it until it shrinks up into a thick weal[1] across the lower part of the forehead. Most of the judges and senators were thus marked; my father had long borne it. I had seen it conferred on one of my brothers, and I was also *destined* to receive it by my parents. Those Embrenche, or chief men, decided disputes and punished crimes, for which purpose they always assembled together. The proceedings were generally short, and in most cases the law of retaliation prevailed. I remember a man was brought before my father and the other judges for kidnapping a boy; and, although he was the son of a chief or senator, he was condemned to make recompense by a man or woman slave. Adultery, however, was sometimes punished with slavery or death, a punishment which I believe is inflicted on it throughout most of the nations of Africa, so sacred among them is the honour of the marriage bed, and so jealous are they of the fidelity of their wives. Of this I recollect an instance: a woman was convicted before the judges of adultery, and delivered over, as the custom was, to her husband to be punished. Accordingly he determined to put her to death; but it being found, just before her execution, that she had an infant at her breast; and no woman being prevailed on to perform the part of a nurse, she was spared on account of the child. The men, however, do not preserve the same constancy to their wives which they expect from them; for they indulge in a plurality, though seldom in more than two. Their mode of marriage is thus: both parties are usually betrothed when young by their parents (though I have known the males to betroth themselves). On this occasion a feast is prepared, and the bride and bridegroom stand up in the midst of all their friends, who are assembled for the purpose, while he declares she is thenceforth to be looked upon as his wife, and that no other person is to pay any addresses to her. This is also immediately proclaimed in the vicinity, on which the bride retires from the assembly. Some time after she is brought home to her husband, and then another feast is made, to which the relations of both parties are invited. Her parents then deliver her to the bridegroom, accompanied with a number of blessings, and at the same time they tie round her waist a cotton string of the thickness of a goose-quill, which none but married women are permitted to wear: she is now considered as completely his wife; and at this time the dowry is given to the new married pair, which generally consists of portions of land, slaves, and cattle, household goods, and implements of husbandry. These are offered by the friends of both parties; besides which the parents of the bridegroom present gifts to those of the bride, whose property she is looked upon before marriage; but after it she is esteemed the sole property of her husband. The ceremony being now ended, the festival begins, which is celebrated with bonfires, and loud acclamations of joy, accompanied with music and dancing.

We are almost a nation of dancers, musicians, and poets. Thus every great event, such as a triumphant return from battle or other cause of public rejoicing, is celebrated in public dances, which are accompanied with songs and music suited to the occasion. The assembly is separated into four divisions which dance either apart or in succession, and each with a character peculiar to itself. The first division contains the married men, who in their dances frequently exhibit feats of arms, and the representation of a battle. To these succeed the married women, who dance in the second division. The young men occupy the third; and the maidens the fourth. Each represents some interesting scene of real life, such as a great achievement, domestic employment, a pathetic story, or some rural sport; and as the subject is generally founded on some recent event, it is therefore ever new. This gives our dances a spirit and variety which I have scarcely seen elsewhere.[2] We have many musical instruments, particularly drums of different kinds, a piece of music which resembles a guitar, and another much like a stickado.[3] These last are chiefly used by betrothed virgins, who play on them on all grand festivals.

As our manners are simple, our luxuries are few. The dress of both sexes is nearly the same. It generally consists of a long piece of calico, or muslin, wrapped loosely round the body, somewhat in the form of a highland plaid. This is usually dyed blue, which is our

[1] *weal* Mark; welt.

[2] [Equiano's note] When I was in Smyrna I have frequently seen the Greeks dance after this manner.

[3] *stickado* Musical instrument similar to a xylophone.

favourite colour. It is extracted from a berry, and is brighter and richer than any I have seen in Europe. Besides this, our women of distinction wear golden ornaments; which they dispose with some profusion on their arms and legs. When our women are not employed with the men in tillage, their usual occupation is spinning and weaving cotton, which they afterwards dye and make it into garments. They also manufacture earthen vessels, of which we have many kinds. Among the rest tobacco pipes, made after the same fashion, and used in the same manner, as those in Turkey.[1]

Our manner of living is entirely plain; for as yet the natives are unacquainted with those refinements in cookery which debauch the taste: bullocks, goats, and poultry supply the greatest part of their food. These constitute likewise the principal wealth of the country, and the chief articles of its commerce. The flesh is usually stewed in a pan; to make it savoury we sometimes use also pepper and other spices, and we have salt made of wood ashes. Our vegetables are mostly plantains, eadas, yams, beans, and Indian corn.[2] The head of the family usually eats alone; his wives and slaves have also their separate tables. Before we taste food we always wash our hands: indeed our cleanliness on all occasions is extreme; but on this it is an indispensable ceremony. After washing, libation is made by pouring out a small portion of the drink in a certain place, for the spirits of departed relations, which the natives suppose to preside over their conduct and guard them from evil. They are totally unacquainted with strong or spirituous liquours, and their principal beverage is palm wine. This is gotten from a tree of that name by tapping it at the top and fastening a large gourd to it; and sometimes one tree will yield three or four gallons in a night. When just drawn it is of a most delicious sweetness; but in a few days it acquires a tartish and more spirituous flavour, though I never saw any one intoxicated by it. The same tree also produces nuts and oil. Our principal luxury is in perfumes; one sort of these is an odoriferous wood of delicious fragrance; the other a kind of earth, a small portion of which thrown into the fire diffuses a most powerful odour.[3] We beat this wood into powder, and mix it with palm oil; with which both men and women perfume themselves.

In our buildings we study convenience rather than ornament. Each master of a family has a large square piece of ground, surrounded with a moat or fence, or enclosed with a wall made of red earth tempered, which, when dry, is as hard as brick. Within this are his houses to accommodate his family and slaves, which, if numerous, frequently present the appearance of a village. In the middle stands the principal building, appropriated to the sole use of the master and consisting of two apartments, in one of which he sits in the day with his family; the other is left apart for the reception of his friends. He has besides these a distinct apartment in which he sleeps, together with his male children. On each side are the apartments of his wives, who have also their separate day and night houses. The habitations of the slaves and their families are distributed throughout the rest of the enclosure. These houses never exceed one story in height; they are always built of wood, or stakes driven into the ground, crossed with wattles and neatly plastered within and without. The roof is thatched with reeds. Our dayhouses are left open at the sides; but those in which we sleep are always covered and plastered in the inside with a composition mixed with cow-dung, to keep off the different insects which annoy us during the night. The walls and floors also of these are generally covered with mats. Our beds consist of a platform, raised three or four feet from the ground, on which are laid skins and different parts of a spongy tree called plantain. Our covering is calico or muslin, the same as our dress. The usual seats are a few logs of wood, but we have benches, which are generally perfumed, to accommodate strangers. These compose the greater part of our household furniture. Houses so constructed and furnished require but little skill to erect them. Every man is a sufficient architect for the purpose. The whole neighbourhood afford their unanimous assistance in building them and in return receive, and expect, no other recompense than a feast.

[1] [Equiano's note] The bowl is earthen, curiously figured, to which a long reed is fixed as a tube. This tube is sometimes so long as to be borne by one, and frequently out of grandeur by two boys.

[2] *Indian corn* Maize; corn.

[3] [Equiano's note] When I was in Smyrna I saw the same kind of earth, and brought some of it with me to England; it resembles musk in strength, but is more delicious in scent, and is not unlike the smell of a rose.

As we live in a country where nature is prodigal of her favours, our wants are few and easily supplied; of course, we have few manufactures. They consist for the most part of calicoes, earthen ware, ornaments, and instruments of war and husbandry. But these make no part of our commerce, the principal articles of which, as I have observed, are provisions. In such a state money is of little use; however, we have some small pieces of coin, if I may call them such. They are made something like an anchor, but I do not remember either their value or denomination. We have also markets, at which I have been frequently with my mother. These are sometimes visited by stout mahogany-coloured men from the south west of us: we call them Oye-Eboe, which term signifies "red men living at a distance." They generally bring us firearms, gunpowder, hats, beads, and dried fish. The last we esteemed a great rarity, as our waters were only brooks and springs. These articles they barter with us for odoriferous woods and earth, and our salt of wood ashes. They always carry slaves through our land; but the strictest account is exacted of their manner of procuring them before they are suffered to pass. Sometimes indeed we sold slaves to them, but they were only prisoners of war, or such among us as had been convicted of kidnapping, or adultery, and some other crimes which we esteemed heinous. This practice of kidnapping induces me to think that, notwithstanding all our strictness, their principal business among us was to trepan[1] our people. I remember too they carried great sacks along with them, which not long after I had an opportunity of fatally seeing applied to that infamous purpose.

Our land is uncommonly rich and fruitful, and produces all kinds of vegetables in great abundance. We have plenty of Indian corn, and vast quantities of cotton and tobacco. Our pineapples grow without culture; they are about the size of the largest sugar-loaf,[2] and finely flavoured. We have also spices of different kinds, particularly pepper, and a variety of delicious fruits which I have never seen in Europe, together with gums of various kinds, and honey in abundance. All our industry is exerted to improve those blessings of nature. Agriculture is our chief employment, and everyone, even the children and women, are engaged in it. Thus we are all habituated to labour from our earliest years. Everyone contributes something to the common stock, and as we are unacquainted with idleness, we have no beggars. The benefits of such a mode of living are obvious. The West India planters prefer the slaves of Benin or Eboe to those of any other part of Guinea, for their hardiness, intelligence, integrity, and zeal. Those benefits are felt by us in the general healthiness of the people, and in their vigour and activity; I might have added too in their comeliness.[3] Deformity is indeed unknown amongst us—I mean that of shape. Numbers of the natives of Eboe now in London might be brought in support of this assertion: for, in regard to complexion, ideas of beauty are wholly relative. I remember while in Africa to have seen three negro children who were tawny, and another quite white, who were universally regarded by myself and the natives in general, as far as related to their complexions, as deformed. Our women too were in my eyes at least uncommonly graceful, alert, and modest to a degree of bashfulness; nor do I remember to have ever heard of an instance of incontinence[4] amongst them before marriage. They are also remarkably cheerful. Indeed cheerfulness and affability are two of the leading characteristics of our nation.

Our tillage is exercised in a large plain or common some hours' walk from our dwellings, and all the neighbours resort thither in a body. They use no beasts of husbandry, and their only instruments are hoes, axes, shovels, and beaks, or pointed iron to dig with. Sometimes we are visited by locusts, which come in large clouds, so as to darken the air, and destroy our harvest. This however happens rarely, but when it does, a famine is produced by it. I remember an instance or two wherein this happened. This common is often the theatre of war; and therefore when our people go out to till their land, they not only go in a body, but generally take their arms with them for fear of a surprise; and when they apprehend an invasion they guard the avenue to their dwellings by driving sticks into the ground, which are so sharp at one end as to pierce the foot, and are generally dipped in poison. From what I can recol-

[1] *trepan* Trick.

[2] *sugar-loaf* A variety of pineapple popular in England at the time.

[3] *comeliness* Pleasing appearance; beauty of form.

[4] *incontinence* Unchastity.

lect of these battles, they appear to have been irruptions[1] of one little state or district on the other, to obtain prisoners or booty. Perhaps they were incited to this by those traders who brought the European goods I mentioned amongst us. Such a mode of obtaining slaves in Africa is common, and I believe more are procured this way, and by kidnapping, than any other.[2] When a trader wants slaves, he applies to a chief for them, and tempts him with his wares. It is not extraordinary if on this occasion he yields to the temptation with as little firmness and accepts the price of his fellow creatures' liberty with as little reluctance as the enlightened merchant. Accordingly he falls on his neighbours, and a desperate battle ensues. If he prevails and takes prisoners, he gratifies his avarice by selling them; but, if his party be vanquished, and he falls into the hands of the enemy, he is put to death: for, as he has been known to foment[3] their quarrels, it is thought dangerous to let him survive, and no ransom can save him, though all other prisoners may be redeemed. We have firearms, bows and arrows, broad two-edged swords and javelins; we have shields also which cover a man from head to foot. All are taught the use of these weapons; even our women are warriors, and march boldly out to fight along with the men. Our whole district is a kind of militia: on a certain signal given, such as the firing of a gun at night, they all rise in arms and rush upon their enemy. It is perhaps something remarkable that when our people march to the field a red flag or banner is borne before them. I was once a witness to a battle in our common. We had been all at work in it one day as usual when our people were suddenly attacked. I climbed a tree at some distance, from which I beheld the fight. There were many women as well as men on both sides; among others my mother was there, and armed with a broad sword. After fighting for a considerable time with great fury, and after many had been killed, our people obtained the victory and took their enemy's chief prisoner. He was carried off in great triumph, and, though he offered a large ransom for his life, he was put to death. A virgin of note among our enemies had been slain in the battle, and her arm was exposed in our market-place, where our trophies were always exhibited. The spoils were divided according to the merit of the warriors. Those prisoners which were not sold or redeemed we kept as slaves: but how different was their condition from that of the slaves in the West Indies! With us they do no more work than other members of the community, even their masters; their food, clothing, and lodging were nearly the same as theirs (except that they were not permitted to eat with those who were free-born), and there was scarce any other difference between them than a superior degree of importance which the head of a family possesses in our state, and that authority which, as such, he exercises over every part of his household. Some of these slaves have even slaves under them as their own property and for their own use.

As to religion, the natives believe that there is one Creator of all things, and that he lives in the sun and is girded round with a belt; that he may never eat or drink; but, according to some, he smokes a pipe, which is our own favourite luxury. They believe he governs events, especially our deaths or captivity; but, as for the doctrine of eternity, I do not remember to have ever heard of it: some however believe in the transmigration of souls in a certain degree. Those spirits which are not transmigrated, such as our dear friends or relations, they believe always attend them and guard them from the bad spirits or their foes. For this reason they always before eating, as I have observed, put some small portion of the meat, and pour some of their drink, on the ground for them; and they often make oblations of the blood of beasts or fowls at their graves. I was very fond of my mother, and almost constantly with her. When she went to make these oblations at her mother's tomb, which was a kind of small solitary thatched house, I sometimes attended her. There she made her libations and spent most of the night in cries and lamentations. I have been often extremely terrified on these occasions. The loneliness of the place, the darkness of the night, and the ceremony of libation, naturally awful and gloomy, were heightened by my mother's lamentations; and these, concurring with the cries of doleful birds by which these places were frequented, gave an inexpressible terror to the scene.

[1] *irruptions* Invasions.

[2] [Equiano's note] See Benezet's "Account of Africa" throughout.

[3] *foment* Stir up.

We compute the year from the day on which the sun crosses the line, and on its setting that evening there is a general shout throughout the land—at least, I can speak from my own knowledge, throughout our vicinity. The people at the same time make a great noise with rattles, not unlike the basket rattles used by children here, though much larger, and hold up their hands to heaven for a blessing. It is then the greatest offerings are made, and those children whom our wise men foretell will be fortunate are then presented to different people. I remember many used to come to see me, and I was carried about to others for that purpose. They have many offerings, particularly at full moons, generally two at harvest before the fruits are taken out of the ground; and when any young animals are killed, sometimes they offer up part of them as a sacrifice. These offerings, when made by one of the heads of a family, serve for the whole. I remember we often had them at my father's and my uncle's, and their families have been present. Some of our offerings are eaten with bitter herbs. We had a saying among us to any one of a cross temper, that "if they were to be eaten, they should be eaten with bitter herbs."

We practised circumcision like the Jews, and made offerings and feasts on that occasion in the same manner as they did. Like them also, our children were named from some event, some circumstance or fancied foreboding, at the time of their birth. I was named *Olaudah*, which, in our language, signifies "vicissitude" or "fortunate," also, one favoured, and having a loud voice and well spoken. I remember we never polluted the name of the object of our adoration; on the contrary, it was always mentioned with the greatest reverence; and we were totally unacquainted with swearing, and all those terms of abuse and reproach which find their way so readily and copiously into the languages of more civilized people. The only expressions of that kind I remember were "May you rot," or "May you swell," or "May a beast take you."

I have before remarked that the natives of this part of Africa are extremely cleanly. This necessary habit of decency was with us a part of religion, and therefore we had many purifications and washings; indeed almost as many and used on the same occasions, if my recollection does not fail me, as the Jews. Those that touched the dead at any time were obliged to wash and purify themselves before they could enter a dwelling-house. Every woman too, at certain times, was forbidden to come into a dwelling-house, or touch any person or any thing we ate. I was so fond of my mother I could not keep from her or avoid touching her at some of those periods, in consequence of which I was obliged to be kept out with her, in a little house made for that purpose, till offering was made, and then we were purified.

Though we had no places of public worship, we had priests and magicians, or wise men. I do not remember whether they had different offices, or whether they were united in the same persons, but they were held in great reverence by the people. They calculated our time and foretold events, as their name imported, for we called them Ah-affoe-way-cah, which signifies "calculators" or "yearly men," our year being called Ah-affoe. They wore their beards, and when they died they were succeeded by their sons. Most of their implements and things of value were interred along with them. Pipes and tobacco were also put into the grave with the corpse, which was always perfumed and ornamented, and animals were offered in sacrifice to them. None accompanied their funerals but those of the same profession or tribe. These buried them after sunset, and always returned from the grave by a different way from that which they went.

These magicians were also our doctors or physicians. They practised bleeding by cupping, and were very successful in healing wounds and expelling poisons. They had likewise some extraordinary method of discovering jealousy, theft, and poisoning; the success of which no doubt they derived from their unbounded influence over the credulity and superstition of the people. I do not remember what those methods were, except that as to poisoning: I recollect an instance or two, which I hope it will not be deemed impertinent here to insert, as it may serve as a kind of specimen of the rest, and is still used by the negroes in the West Indies. A virgin had been poisoned, but it was not known by whom. The doctors ordered the corpse to be taken up by some persons and carried to the grave. As soon as the bearers had raised it on their shoulders, they seemed seized with some sudden impulse, and ran to and fro unable to stop themselves. At last, after having passed through a number of thorns and prickly bushes unhurt, the corpse fell from them close to a house, and defaced it in the fall; and, the owner being taken up, he immediately confessed the poisoning.[1]

The natives are extremely cautious about poison. When they buy any eatable the seller kisses it all round before the buyer, to show him it is not poisoned; and the same is done when any meat or drink is presented, particularly to a stranger. We have serpents of different kinds, some of which are esteemed ominous when they appear in our houses, and these we never molest. I remember two of those ominous snakes, each of which was as thick as the calf of a man's leg, and in colour resembling a dolphin in the water, crept at different times into my mother's night-house, where I always lay with her, and coiled themselves into folds, and each time they crowed like a cock. I was desired by some of our wise men to touch these, that I might be interested in the good omens, which I did, for they were quite harmless and would tamely suffer themselves to be handled; and then they were put into a large open earthen pan and set on one side of the highway. Some of our snakes, however, were poisonous: one of them crossed the road one day when I was standing on it, and passed between my feet without offering to touch me, to the great surprise of many who saw it; and these incidents were accounted by the wise men, and therefore by my mother and the rest of the people, as remarkable omens in my favour.

Such is the imperfect sketch my memory has furnished me with of the manners and customs of a people among whom I first drew my breath. And here I cannot forbear suggesting what has long struck me very forcibly, namely, the strong analogy which even by this sketch, imperfect as it is, appears to prevail in the manners and customs of my countrymen and those of the Jews before they reached the Land of Promise, and particularly the patriarchs while they were yet in that pastoral state which is described in Genesis—an analogy which alone would induce me to think that the one people had sprung from the other. Indeed this is the opinion of Dr. Gill,[2] who, in his commentary on Genesis, very ably deduces the pedigree of the Africans from Afer and Afra, the descendants of Abraham by Keturah, his wife and concubine (for both these titles are applied to her). It is also conformable to the sentiments of Dr. John Clarke, formerly Dean of Sarum, in his *Truth of the Christian Religion*:[3] both these authors concur in ascribing to us this original. The reasonings of these gentlemen are still further confirmed by the scripture chronology; and if any further corroboration were required, this resemblance in so many respects is a strong evidence in support of the opinion. Like the Israelites in their primitive state, our government was conducted by our chiefs or judges, our wise men and elders; and the head of a family with us enjoyed a similar authority over his household with that which is ascribed to Abraham and the other patriarchs. The law of retaliation obtained almost universally with us as with them; and even their religion appeared to have shed upon us a ray of its glory, though broken and spent in its passage, or eclipsed by the cloud with which time, tradition, and ignorance might have enveloped it; for we had our circumcision (a rule I believe peculiar to that people); we had also our sacrifices and burnt-offerings, our washings and purifications, on the same occasions as they had.

As to the difference of colour between the Eboan Africans and the modern Jews, I shall not presume to account for it. It is a subject which has engaged the pens of men of both genius and learning, and is far above my

[1] [Equiano's note] An instance of this kind happened at Montserrat in the West Indies in the year 1763. I then belonged to the Charming Sally, Capt. Doran. The chief mate, Mr. Mansfield, and some of the crew, being one day on shore, were present at the burying of a poisoned negro girl. Though they had often heard of the circumstance of the running in such cases, and had even seen it, they imagined it to be a trick of the corpse-bearers. The mate therefore desired two of the sailors to take up the coffin and carry it to the grave. The sailors, who were all of the same opinion, readily obeyed; but they had scarcely raised it to their shoulders before they began to run furiously about, quite unable to direct themselves, till at last, without intention, they came to the hut of him who had poisoned the girl. The coffin then immediately fell from their shoulders against the hut, and damaged part of the wall. The owner of the hut was taken into custody on this, and confessed the poisoning. I give this story as it was related by the mate and crew on their return to the ship. The credit which is due to it I leave with the reader.

[2] *Dr. Gill* John Gill (1697–1771), the Baptist author of *An Exposition of the Old Testament, in which Are Recorded the Original of Mankind, of the Several Nations of the World, and of the Jewish Nation in Particular....* (1788).

[3] *Dr. John ... Religion* John Clarke (1682–1757) published a translation of a seventeenth-century religious work by Hugo Grotius, *The Truth of the Christian Religion* (1627), in 1786.

strength. The most able and Reverend Mr. T. Clarkson, however, in his much admired *Essay on the Slavery and Commerce of the Human Species*, has ascertained the cause in a manner that at once solves every objection on that account and, on my mind at least, has produced the fullest conviction. I shall therefore refer to that performance for the theory, contenting myself with extracting a fact as related by Dr. Mitchel.[1] "The Spaniards, who have inhabited America, under the torrid zone, for any time, are become as dark coloured as our native Indians of Virginia; of which *I myself have been a witness*." There is also another instance of a Portuguese settlement at Mitomba, a river in Sierra Leona, where the inhabitants are bred from a mixture of the first Portuguese discoverers with the natives, and are now become, in their complexion, and in the wooly quality of their hair, perfect negroes, retaining however a smattering of the Portuguese language.

These instances, and a great many more which might be adduced, while they show how the complexions of the same persons vary in different climates, it is hoped may tend also to remove the prejudice that some conceive against the natives of Africa on account of their colour. Surely the minds of the Spaniards did not change with their complexions! Are there not causes enough to which the apparent inferiority of an African may be ascribed, without limiting the goodness of God, and supposing he forbore to stamp understanding on certainly his own image, because "carved in ebony"?[2] Might it not naturally be ascribed to their situation?

When they come among Europeans, they are ignorant of their language, religion, manners, and customs. Are any pains taken to teach them these? Are they treated as men? Does not slavery itself depress the mind, and extinguish all its fire and every noble sentiment? But, above all, what advantages do not a refined people possess over those who are rude and uncultivated. Let the polished and haughty European recollect that his ancestors were once, like the Africans, uncivilized, and even barbarous. Did Nature make *them* inferior to their sons? And should *they too* have been made slaves? Every rational mind answers, No. Let such reflections as these melt the pride of their superiority into sympathy for the wants and miseries of their sable brethren, and compel them to acknowledge that understanding is not confined to feature or colour. If, when they look round the world, they feel exultation, let it be tempered with benevolence to others, and gratitude to God, "who hath made of one blood all nations of men for to dwell on all the face of the earth;[3] and whose wisdom is not our wisdom, neither are our ways his ways."

CHAPTER 2

The author's birth and parentage—His being kidnapped with his sister—Their separation—Surprise at meeting again—Are finally separated—Account of the different places and incidents the author met with till his arrival on the coast—The effect the sight of a slave ship had on him —He sails for the West Indies—Horrors of a slave ship—Arrives at Barbadoes, where the cargo is sold and dispersed.

I hope the reader will not think I have trespassed on his patience in introducing myself to him with some account of the manners and customs of my country.[4] They had been implanted in me with great care, and made an impression on my mind which time could not erase, and which all the adversity and variety of fortune I have since experienced served only to rivet and record; for, whether the love of one's country be real or imaginary, or a lesson of reason, or an instinct of nature, I still look back with pleasure on the first scenes of my life, though that pleasure has been for the most part mingled with sorrow.

I have already acquainted the reader with the time and place of my birth. My father, besides many slaves, had a numerous family, of which seven lived to grow up, including myself and a sister, who was the only daughter. As I was the youngest of the sons, I became, of course, the greatest favourite with my mother, and was always with her; and she used to take particular pains to form my mind. I was trained up from my

[1] [Equiano's note] Philos. Trans. No. 476, Sect. 4, cited by Mr. Clarkson, p. 205.

[2] *carved in ebony* Cf. *The Holy and Profane State*, 2.20 (1642): "But our captain counts the Image of God nevertheless his image, cut in ebony as if done in ivory."

[3] [Equiano's note] Acts, c. 17 v. 26.

[4] *my country* Equiano says he was born in Essaka, a country located in the interior of present-day Nigeria.

earliest years in the art of war; my daily exercise was shooting and throwing javelins, and my mother adorned me with emblems after the manner of our greatest warriors. In this way I grew up till I was turned the age of eleven, when an end was put to my happiness in the following manner. Generally, when the grown people in the neighbourhood were gone far in the fields to labour, the children assembled together in some of the neighbours' premises to play; and commonly some of us used to get up a tree to look out for any assailant or kidnapper that might come upon us; for they sometimes took those opportunities of our parents' absence to attack and carry off as many as they could seize. One day, as I was watching at the top of a tree in our yard, I saw one of those people come into the yard of our next neighbour but one, to kidnap, there being many stout young people in it. Immediately on this I gave the alarm of the rogue, and he was surrounded by the stoutest of them, who entangled him with cords, so that he could not escape till some of the grown people came and secured him. But alas! ere long it was my fate to be thus attacked, and to be carried off, when none of the grown people were nigh. One day, when all our people were gone out to their works as usual, and only I and my dear sister were left to mind the house, two men and a woman got over our walls and in a moment seized us both, and, without giving us time to cry out or make resistance, they stopped our mouths and ran off with us into the nearest wood. Here they tied our hands and continued to carry us as far as they could, till night came on, when we reached a small house where the robbers halted for refreshment and spent the night. We were then unbound, but were unable to take any food; and, being quite overpowered by fatigue and grief, our only relief was some sleep, which allayed our misfortune for a short time.

The next morning we left the house and continued travelling all the day. For a long time we had kept the woods, but at last we came into a road, which I believed I knew. I had now some hopes of being delivered, for we had advanced but a little way before I discovered some people at a distance, on which I began to cry out for their assistance. But my cries had no other effect than to make them tie me faster and stop my mouth, and then they put me into a large sack. They also stopped my sister's mouth and tied her hands, and in this manner we proceeded till we were out of the sight of these people. When we went to rest the following night they offered us some victuals, but we refused it, and the only comfort we had was in being in one another's arms all that night, and bathing each other with our tears. But alas! we were soon deprived of even the small comfort of weeping together. The next day proved a day of greater sorrow than I had yet experienced, for my sister and I were then separated while we lay clasped in each other's arms. It was in vain that we besought them not to part us; she was torn from me and immediately carried away, while I was left in a state of distraction not to be described. I cried and grieved continually, and for several days I did not eat anything but what they forced into my mouth.

At length, after many days travelling, during which I had often changed masters, I got into the hands of a chieftain in a very pleasant country. This man had two wives and some children, and they all used me extremely well, and did all they could to comfort me—particularly the first wife, who was something like my mother. Although I was a great many days' journey from my father's house, yet these people spoke exactly the same language with us. This first master of mine, as I may call him, was a smith,[1] and my principal employment was working his bellows, which were the same kind as I had seen in my vicinity. They were in some respects not unlike the stoves here in gentlemen's kitchens, and were covered over with leather; and in the middle of that leather a stick was fixed, and a person stood up and worked it in the same manner as is done to pump water out of a cask with a hand pump. I believe it was gold he worked, for it was of a lovely bright yellow colour, and was worn by the women on their wrists and ankles.

I was there I suppose about a month, and they at last used to trust me some little distance from the house. This liberty I used in embracing every opportunity to inquire the way to my own home; and I also sometimes, for the same purpose, went with the maidens in the cool of the evenings to bring pitchers of water from the springs for the use of the house. I had also remarked where the sun rose in the morning and set in the evening as I had travelled along, and I had observed that my father's house was towards the rising of the sun. I

[1] *smith* One who works with metals.

therefore determined to seize the first opportunity of making my escape, and to shape my course for that quarter; for I was quite oppressed and weighed down by grief after my mother and friends; and my love of liberty, ever great, was strengthened by the mortifying circumstance of not daring to eat with the free-born children, although I was mostly their companion.

While I was projecting my escape, one day an unlucky event happened which quite disconcerted my plan and put an end to my hopes. I used to be sometimes employed in assisting an elderly woman slave to cook and take care of the poultry, and one morning while I was feeding some chickens, I happened to toss a small pebble at one of them, which hit it on the middle and directly killed it. The old slave, having soon after missed the chicken, inquired after it; and on my relating the accident (for I told her the truth, because my mother would never suffer me to tell a lie), she flew into a violent passion, threatened that I should suffer for it, and, my master being out, she immediately went and told her mistress what I had done. This alarmed me very much, and I expected an instant flogging, which to me was uncommonly dreadful, for I had seldom been beaten at home. I therefore resolved to fly, and accordingly I ran into a thicket that was hard by and hid myself in the bushes. Soon afterwards my mistress and the slave returned, and, not seeing me, they searched all the house; but, not finding me, and I not making answer when they called to me, they thought I had run away, and the whole neighbourhood was raised in the pursuit of me. In that part of the country (as in ours) the houses and villages were skirted with woods, or shrubberies, and the bushes were so thick that a man could readily conceal himself in them so as to elude the strictest search. The neighbours continued the whole day looking for me, and several times many of them came within a few yards of the place where I lay hid. I then gave myself up for lost entirely and expected every moment, when I heard a rustling among the trees, to be found out and punished by my master. But they never discovered me, though they were often so near that I even heard their conjectures as they were looking about for me; and I now learned from them that any attempt to return home would be hopeless. Most of them supposed I had fled towards home, but the distance was so great, and the way so intricate, that they thought I could never reach it, and that I should be lost in the woods. When I heard this I was seized with a violent panic and abandoned myself to despair. Night too began to approach, and aggravated all my fears. I had before entertained hopes of getting home, and I had determined when it should be dark to make the attempt; but I was now convinced it was fruitless, and I began to consider that, if possibly I could escape all other animals, I could not those of the human kind, and that, not knowing the way, I must perish in the woods. Thus was I like the hunted deer:

> Ev'ry leaf and ev'ry whisp'ring breath
> Conveyed a foe, and ev'ry foe a death.[1]

I heard frequent rustlings among the leaves, and, being pretty sure they were snakes, I expected every instant to be stung by them. This increased my anguish, and the horror of my situation became now quite insupportable. I at length quitted the thicket, very faint and hungry, for I had not eaten or drank anything all the day, and crept to my master's kitchen, from whence I set out at first, and which was an open shed, and laid myself down in the ashes with an anxious wish for death to relieve me from all my pains. I was scarcely awake in the morning when the old woman slave, who was the first up, came to light the fire and saw me in the fireplace. She was very much surprised to see me, and could scarcely believe her own eyes. She now promised to intercede for me, and went for her master, who soon after came and, having slightly reprimanded me, ordered me to be taken care of and not to be ill-treated.

Soon after this my master's only daughter, and child by his first wife, sickened and died, which affected him so much that for some time he was almost frantic, and really would have killed himself, had he not been watched and prevented. However, in a small time afterwards he recovered, and I was again sold. I was now carried to the left of the sun's rising, through many different countries and a number of large woods. The people I was sold to used to carry me very often, when I was tired, either on their

[1] *Ev'ry ... death* Cf. lines 287–88 of John Denham's "Cooper's Hill": "Now every leaf, and every moving breath / Presents a foe, and every foe a death."

shoulders or on their backs. I saw many convenient, well built sheds along the roads, at proper distances to accommodate the merchants and travellers, who lay in those buildings along with their wives, who often accompany them; and they always go well armed.

From the time I left my own nation, I always found somebody that understood me, till I came to the sea coast. The languages of different nations did not totally differ, nor were they so copious as those of the Europeans, particularly the English. They were therefore easily learned, and while I was journeying thus through Africa I acquired two or three different tongues. In this manner I had been travelling for a considerable time when one evening, to my great surprise, whom should I see brought to the house where I was but my dear sister! As soon as she saw me she gave a loud shriek and ran into my arms. I was quite overpowered: neither of us could speak, but for a considerable time clung to each other in mutual embraces, unable to do any thing but weep. Our meeting affected all who saw us; and indeed I must acknowledge, in honour of those sable destroyers of human rights, that I never met with any ill treatment, or saw any offered to their slaves, except tying them when necessary, to keep them from running away. When these people knew we were brother and sister they indulged us together, and the man to whom I supposed we belonged lay with us, he in the middle, while she and I held one another by the hands across his breast all night; and thus for a while we forgot our misfortunes in the joy of being together. But even this small comfort was soon to have an end, for scarcely had the fatal morning appeared when she was again torn from me forever! I was now more miserable, if possible, than before. The small relief which her presence gave me from pain was gone, and the wretchedness of my situation was redoubled by my anxiety after her fate and my apprehensions lest her sufferings should be greater than mine, when I could not be with her to alleviate them. Yes, thou dear partner of all my childish sports! thou sharer of my joys and sorrows! happy should I have ever esteemed myself to encounter every misery for you, and to procure your freedom by the sacrifice of my own. Though you were early forced from my arms, your image has been always riveted in my heart, from which neither time nor fortune have been able to remove it; so that, while the thoughts of your sufferings have damped my prosperity, they have mingled with adversity and increased its bitterness. To that Heaven which protects the weak from the strong, I commit the care of your innocence and virtues, if they have not already received their full reward, and if your youth and delicacy have not long since fallen victims to the violence of the African trader, the pestilential stench of a Guinea ship,[1] the seasoning in the European colonies, or the lash and lust of a brutal and unrelenting overseer.

I did not long remain after my sister. I was again sold and carried through a number of places, till, after travelling a considerable time, I came to a town called Tinmah, in the most beautiful country I had yet seen in Africa. It was extremely rich, and there were many rivulets which flowed through it and supplied a large pond in the centre of the town, where the people washed. Here I first saw and tasted cocoa-nuts, which I thought superior to any nuts I had ever tasted before; and the trees, which were loaded, were also interspersed amongst the houses, which had commodious shades adjoining and were in the same manner as ours, the insides being neatly plastered and whitewashed. Here I also saw and tasted for the first time sugar cane. Their money consisted of little white shells the size of the fingernail. I was sold here for one hundred and seventy-two of them by a merchant who lived, and brought me, there. I had been about two or three days at his house when a wealthy widow, a neighbour of his, came there one evening and brought with her an only son, a young gentleman about my own age and size. Here they saw me; and, having taken a fancy to me, I was bought of the merchant and went home with them. Her house and premises were situated close to one of those rivulets I have mentioned, and were the finest I ever saw in Africa: they were very extensive, and she had a number of slaves to attend her. The next day I was washed and perfumed, and when mealtime came I was led into the presence of my mistress, and ate and drank before her with her son. This filled me with astonishment, and I could scarce help expressing my surprise that the young gentleman should suffer me, who was bound, to eat with him, who was free; and not only so, but that he would not at any time either eat or drink till I had taken first, because I

[1] *Guinea ship* Slave ship from Guinea.

was the eldest (which was agreeable to our custom). Indeed, everything here, and all their treatment of me, made me forget that I was a slave. The language of these people resembled ours so nearly that we understood each other perfectly. They had also the very same customs as we. There were likewise slaves daily to attend us, while my young master and I with other boys sported with our darts and bows and arrows, as I had been used to do at home. In this resemblance to my former happy state I passed about two months; and I now began to think I was to be adopted into the family, and was beginning to be reconciled to my situation and to forget by degrees my misfortunes, when all at once the delusion vanished; for, without the least previous knowledge, one morning early, while my dear master and companion was still asleep, I was wakened out of my reverie to fresh sorrow, and hurried away even amongst the uncircumcised.[1]

Thus at the very moment I dreamed of the greatest happiness I found myself most miserable, and it seemed as if fortune wished to give me this taste of joy only to render the reverse more poignant. The change I now experienced was as painful as it was sudden and unexpected. It was a change indeed from a state of bliss to a scene which is inexpressible by me, as it discovered to me an element I had never before beheld, and till then had no idea of, and wherein such instances of hardship and cruelty continually occurred, as I can never reflect on but with horror.

All the nations and people I had hitherto passed through resembled our own in their manners, customs, and language, but I came at length to a country, the inhabitants of which differed from us in all those particulars. I was very much struck with this difference, especially when I came among a people who did not circumcise, and ate without washing their hands. They cooked also in iron pots, and had European cutlasses and cross bows, which were unknown to us, and fought with their fists amongst themselves. Their women were not so modest as ours, for they ate and drank and slept with their men. But, above all, I was amazed to see no sacrifices or offerings among them. In some of those places the people ornamented themselves with scars, and likewise filed their teeth very sharp. They wanted sometimes to ornament me in the same manner, but I would not suffer them, hoping that I might sometime be among a people who did not thus disfigure themselves, as I thought they did. At last I came to the banks of a large river which was covered with canoes, in which the people appeared to live with their household utensils and provisions of all kinds. I was beyond measure astonished at this, as I had never before seen any water larger than a pond or a rivulet, and my surprise was mingled with no small fear when I was put into one of these canoes and we began to paddle and move along the river. We continued going on thus till night; and when we came to land and made fires on the banks, each family by themselves, some dragged their canoes on shore, others stayed and cooked in theirs and laid in them all night. Those on the land had mats, of which they made tents, some in the shape of little houses. In these we slept, and after the morning meal we embarked again and proceeded as before. I was often very much astonished to see some of the women, as well as the men, jump into the water, dive to the bottom, come up again, and swim about.

Thus I continued to travel, sometimes by land, sometimes by water, through different countries and various nations, till, at the end of six or seven months after I had been kidnapped, I arrived at the seacoast. It would be tedious and uninteresting to relate all the incidents which befell me during this journey, and which I have not yet forgotten; of the various hands I passed through, and the manners and customs of all the different people among whom I lived. I shall therefore only observe that in all the places where I was the soil was exceedingly rich; the pumpkins, eadas,[2] plantains, yams, etc., etc., were in great abundance, and of incredible size. There were also vast quantities of different gums, though not used for any purpose, and everywhere a great deal of tobacco. The cotton even grew quite wild, and there was plenty of redwood. I saw no mechanics[3] whatever in all the way, except such as I have mentioned. The chief employment in all these countries was agriculture, and both the males and females, as with us, were brought up to it, and trained in the arts of war.

[1] *uncircumcised* I.e., heathens, foreigners.

[2] *eadas* Clearly a fruit or vegetable, but what sort is uncertain.

[3] *mechanics* Artisans.

The first object which saluted my eyes when I arrived on the coast was the sea, and a slave ship, which was then riding at anchor and waiting for its cargo. These filled me with astonishment, which was soon converted into terror when I was carried on board. I was immediately handled and tossed up, to see if I were sound, by some of the crew; and I was now persuaded that I had gotten into a world of bad spirits, and that they were going to kill me. Their complexions, too, differing so much from ours, their long hair, and the language they spoke (which was very different from any I had ever heard) united to confirm me in this belief. Indeed, such were the horrors of my views and fears at the moment that, if ten thousand worlds had been my own, I would have freely parted with them all to have exchanged my condition with that of the meanest slave in my own country. When I looked round the ship, too, and saw a large furnace or copper boiling, and a multitude of black people of every description chained together, every one of their countenances expressing dejection and sorrow, I no longer doubted of my fate; and, quite overpowered with horror and anguish, I fell motionless on the deck and fainted. When I recovered a little I found some black people about me who I believed were some of those who brought me on board and had been receiving their pay; they talked to me in order to cheer me, but all in vain. I asked them if we were not to be eaten by those white men with horrible looks, red faces, and loose hair. They told me I was not, and one of the crew brought me a small portion of spirituous liquor in a wine glass; but, being afraid of him, I would not take it out of his hand. One of the blacks therefore took it from him and gave it to me, and I took a little down my palate, which, instead of reviving me as they thought it would, threw me into the greatest consternation at the strange feeling it produced, having never tasted any such liquor before.

Soon after this the blacks who brought me on board went off, and left me abandoned to despair. I now saw myself deprived of all chance of returning to my native country, or even the least glimpse of hope of gaining the shore, which I now considered as friendly; and I even wished for my former slavery in preference to my present situation, which was filled with horrors of every kind, still heightened by my ignorance of what I was to undergo. I was not long suffered to indulge my grief; I was soon put down under the decks, and there I received such a salutation in my nostrils as I had never experienced in my life; so that, with the loathsomeness of the stench and crying together, I became so sick and low that I was not able to eat, nor had I the least desire to taste anything. I now wished for the last friend, death, to relieve me; but soon, to my grief, two of the white men offered me eatables; and, on my refusing to eat, one of them held me fast by the hands and laid me across, I think, the windlass,[1] and tied my feet while the other flogged me severely. I had never experienced anything of this kind before; and although, not being used to the water, I naturally feared that element the first time I saw it, yet nevertheless, could I have got over the nettings, I would have jumped over the side. But I could not, and besides, the crew used to watch us very closely who were not chained down to the decks, lest we should leap into the water, and I have seen some of these poor African prisoners most severely cut for attempting to do so, and hourly whipped for not eating. This indeed was often the case with myself.

In a little time after, amongst the poor chained men I found some of my own nation, which in a small degree gave ease to my mind. I inquired of these what was to be done with us; they gave me to understand we were to be carried to these white people's country to work for them. I then was a little revived and thought, if it were no worse than working, my situation was not so desperate. But still I feared I should be put to death; the white people looked and acted, as I thought, in so savage a manner—for I had never seen among any people such instances of brutal cruelty, and this not only shown towards us blacks, but also to some of the whites themselves. One white man in particular I saw, when we were permitted to be on deck, flogged so unmercifully with a large rope near the foremast that he died in consequence of it, and they tossed him over the side as they would have done a brute.[2] This made me fear these people the more, and I expected nothing less than to be treated in the same manner. I could not help expressing

[1] *windlass* On board ship, a mechanical contrivance used for winding ropes or chains.

[2] *brute* Animal.

my fears and apprehensions to some of my countrymen. I asked them if these people had no country, but lived in this hollow place (the ship). They told me they did not, but came from a distant one. "Then," said I, "how comes it in all our country we never heard of them?" They told me because they lived so very far off. I then asked, where were their women? had they any like themselves? I was told they had. "And why," said I, "do we not see them?" They answered, because they were left behind. I asked how the vessel could go. They told me they could not tell, but that there were cloths put upon the masts by the help of the ropes I saw, and then the vessel went on; and the white men had some spell or magic they put in the water when they liked in order to stop the vessel. I was exceedingly amazed at this account, and really thought they were spirits. I therefore wished much to be from amongst them, for I expected they would sacrifice me. But my wishes were vain, for we were so quartered that it was impossible for any of us to make our escape.

While we stayed on the coast I was mostly on deck, and one day, to my great astonishment, I saw one of these vessels coming in with the sails up. As soon as the whites saw it, they gave a great shout, at which we were amazed; and the more so as the vessel appeared larger by approaching nearer. At last she came to an anchor in my sight, and when the anchor was let go I and my countrymen who saw it were lost in astonishment to observe the vessel stop, and were now convinced it was done by magic. Soon after this the other ship got her boats out, and they came on board of us, and the people of both ships seemed very glad to see each other. Several of the strangers also shook hands with us black people and made motions with their hands, signifying, I suppose, we were to go to their country; but we did not understand them. At last, when the ship we were in had got in all her cargo, they made ready with many fearful noises, and we were all put under deck, so that we could not see how they managed the vessel. But this disappointment was the least of my sorrow. The stench of the hold while we were on the coast was so intolerably loathsome that it was dangerous to remain there for any time, and some of us had been permitted to stay on the deck for the fresh air, but now that the whole ship's cargo were confined together, it became absolutely pestilential. The closeness of the place and the heat of the climate, added to the number in the ship, which was so crowded that each had scarcely room to turn himself, almost suffocated us. This produced copious perspirations, so that the air soon became unfit for respiration from a variety of loathsome smells, and brought on a sickness among the slaves, of which many died, thus falling victims to the improvident avarice, as I may call it, of their purchasers. This wretched situation was again aggravated by the galling[1] of the chains, now become insupportable, and the filth of the necessary tubs, into which the children often fell, and were almost suffocated. The shrieks of the women and the groans of the dying rendered the whole a scene of horror almost inconceivable. Happily perhaps for myself, I was soon reduced so low here that it was thought necessary to keep me almost always on deck; and from my extreme youth I was not put in fetters. In this situation I expected every hour to share the fate of my companions, some of whom were almost daily brought upon deck at the point of death, which I began to hope would soon put an end to my miseries. Often did I think many of the inhabitants of the deep much more happy than myself. I envied them the freedom they enjoyed, and as often wished I could change my condition for theirs. Every circumstance I met with served only to render my state more painful and heighten my apprehensions and my opinion of the cruelty of the whites. One day they had taken a number of fishes; and when they had killed and satisfied themselves with as many as they thought fit, to our astonishment who were on the deck, rather than give any of them to us to eat as we expected, they tossed the remaining fish into the sea again, although we begged and prayed for some as well as we could, but in vain; and some of my countrymen, being pressed by hunger, took an opportunity, when they thought no one saw them, of trying to get a little privately; but they were discovered, and the attempt procured them some very severe floggings.

One day, when we had a smooth sea and moderate wind, two of my wearied countrymen who were chained together (I was near them at the time), preferring death to such a life of misery, somehow made through the nettings and jumped into the sea. Immediately another

[1] *galling* Chafing.

quite dejected fellow, who, on account of his illness, was suffered to be out of irons, also followed their example; and I believe many more would very soon have done the same if they had not been prevented by the ship's crew, who were instantly alarmed. Those of us that were the most active were in a moment put down under the deck, and there was such a noise and confusion amongst the people of the ship as I never heard before, to stop her and get the boat out to go after the slaves. However, two of the wretches were drowned; but they got the other, and afterwards flogged him unmercifully for thus attempting to prefer death to slavery.

In this manner we continued to undergo more hardships than I can now relate, hardships which are inseparable from this accursed trade. Many a time we were near suffocation from the want of fresh air, which we were often without for whole days together. This, and the stench of the necessary tubs, carried off many. During our passage I first saw flying fishes, which surprised me very much: they used frequently to fly across the ship, and many of them fell on the deck. I also now first saw the use of the quadrant;[1] I had often with astonishment seen the mariners make observations with it, and I could not think what it meant. They at last took notice of my surprise, and one of them, willing to increase it, as well as to gratify my curiosity, made me one day look through it. The clouds appeared to me to be land, which disappeared as they passed along. This heightened my wonder, and I was now more persuaded than ever that I was in another world, and that everything about me was magic.

At last we came in sight of the island of Barbados, at which the whites on board gave a great shout and made many signs of joy to us. We did not know what to think of this, but as the vessel drew nearer we plainly saw the harbour and other ships of different kinds and sizes, and we soon anchored amongst them off Bridgetown. Many merchants and planters now came on board, though it was in the evening. They put us in separate parcels and examined us attentively. They also made us jump, and pointed to the land, signifying we were to go there. We thought by this we should be eaten by these ugly men, as they appeared to us; and, when soon after we were all put down under the deck again, there was much dread and trembling among us, and nothing but bitter cries to be heard all the night from these apprehensions, insomuch that at last the white people got some old slaves from the land to pacify us. They told us we were not to be eaten, but to work, and were soon to go on land, where we should see many of our country people. This report eased us much; and sure enough, soon after we were landed, there came to us Africans of all languages. We were conducted immediately to the merchant's yard, where we were all pent up together like so many sheep in a fold, without regard to sex or age. As every object was new to me, everything I saw filled me with surprise. What struck me first was that the houses were built with stories, and in every other respect different from those in Africa. But I was still more astonished on seeing people on horseback. I did not know what this could mean, and indeed I thought these people were full of nothing but magical arts. While I was in this astonishment, one of my fellow prisoners spoke to a countryman of his about the horses, who said they were the same kind they had in their country. I understood them, though they were from a distant part of Africa, and I thought it odd I had not seen any horses there; but afterwards, when I came to converse with different Africans, I found they had many horses amongst them, and much larger than those I then saw.

We were not many days in the merchant's custody before we were sold after their usual manner, which is this: on a signal given (as the beat of a drum), the buyers rush at once into the yard where the slaves are confined, and make choice of that parcel they like best. The noise and clamour with which this is attended, and the eagerness visible in the countenances of the buyers, serve not a little to increase the apprehensions of the terrified Africans, who may well be supposed to consider them as the ministers of that destruction to which they think themselves devoted. In this manner, without scruple, are relations and friends separated, most of them never to see each other again. I remember in the vessel in which I was brought over, in the men's apartment there were several brothers who, in the sale, were sold in different lots; and it was very moving on this occasion to see and hear their cries at parting. O ye nominal Christians![2] Might not an African ask you, "Learned you this from

[1] *quadrant* Instrument used for taking altitudes.

[2] *nominal Christians* I.e., Christians in name only.

your God, who says unto you, 'Do unto all men as you would men should do unto you'? Is it not enough that we are torn from our country and friends to toil for your luxury and lust of gain? Must every tender feeling be likewise sacrificed to your avarice? Are the dearest friends and relations, now rendered more dear by their separation from their kindred, still to be parted from each other, and thus prevented from cheering the gloom of slavery with the small comfort of being together and mingling their sufferings and sorrows? Why are parents to lose their children, brothers their sisters, or husbands their wives?" Surely this is a new refinement in cruelty, which, while it has no advantage to atone for it, thus aggravates distress and adds fresh horrors even to the wretchedness of slavery.

—1789

In Context

Reactions to Olaudah Equiano's Work

Reactions to the publication of Equiano's *Interesting Narrative* varied widely. At one extreme *The Oracle* and *The Star* attempted to discredit the work by asserting that Equiano had been born and bred in Santa Cruz in the West Indies rather than in Africa. (The writer of the piece in *The Oracle* went on to cast slurs against abolitionist William Wilberforce as well, falsely asserting that Wilberforce himself had an interest in a slave-owning plantation.) Excerpts from some of the reactions to Equiano's work in other journals are reproduced below; the comments in *The Analytic Review* may be of particular interest in that they were written by Mary Wollstonecraft.

from *The Analytic Review*, May 1789

The life of an African, written by himself, is certainly a curiosity, as it has been a favourite philosophic[1] whim to degrade the numerous nations, on whom the sun-beams more directly dart, below the common level of humanity, and hastily to conclude that nature, by making them inferior to the rest of the human race, designed to stamp them with a mark of slavery. How they were shaded down, from the fresh colour of northern rustics, to the sable hue seen on the African sands, is not our task to inquire, nor do we intend to draw a parallel between the abilities of a negro and European mechanic;[2] we shall only observe, that if these volumes do not exhibit extraordinary intellectual powers, sufficient to wipe off the stigma, yet the activity and ingenuity, which conspicuously appear in the character of Gustavus, place him on a par with the general mass of men, who fill the subordinate stations in a more civilized society than that which he was thrown into at his birth.

from *The Gentleman's Magazine*, June 1789

Among other contrivances (and perhaps one of the most innocent) to interest the national humanity in favour of the Negro slaves, one of them here writes his own history, as formerly another of them published his correspondence. These memoirs, written in a very unequal style, place

[1] *philosophic* Scientific.

[2] *mechanic* Manual laborer.

the writer on a par with the general mass of men in the subordinate stations of civilized society, and prove that there is no general rule without an exception.

from *The Monthly Review*, June 1789

We entertain no doubt of the general authenticity of this very intelligent African's story; though it is not improbable that some English writer has assisted him in the compilement, or, at least, the correction of his book; for it is sufficiently well-written. The *Narrative* wears an honest face; and we have conceived a good opinion of the man, from the artless manner in which he has detailed the variety of adventures and vicissitudes which have fallen to his lot. His publication appears very seasonable, at a time when negro-slavery is the subject of public investigation; and it seems calculated to increase the odium that has been excited against the West-India planters, on account of the cruelties that some are said to have exercised on their slaves, many instances of which are here detailed.

from *The General Magazine and Impartial Review*, July 1789

This is "a round unvarnished tale"[1] of the chequered adventures of an African, who early in life, was torn from his native country, by those savage dealers in a traffic disgraceful to humanity, and which has fixed a stain on the legislature of Britain. The *Narrative* appears to be written with much truth and simplicity. The author's account of the manners of the natives of his own province (Ebo) is interesting and pleasing; and the reader, unless perchance he is either a West-India planter, or Liverpool merchant, will find his humanity often severely wounded by the shameless barbarity practised towards the author's hapless countrymen in all our colonies; if he feel as he ought, the oppressed and the oppressors will equally excite his pity and indignation. That so unjust, so iniquitous a commerce may be abolished is our ardent wish; and we heartily join in our author's prayer, "That the God of Heaven may inspire the hearts of our Representatives in Parliament, with peculiar benevolence on that important day when so interesting a question is to be discussed; when thousands, in consequence of their determination, are to look for happiness or misery!"

[1] *a round unvarnished tale* Cf. William Shakespeare, *Othello* 1.3.89.

Richard Brinsley Sheridan
1751 – 1816

Richard Brinsley Sheridan emerged as the quintessential voice of the late eighteenth-century English theater. Writing in the style that had been pioneered a century earlier by Restoration playwrights (though without the overtly sexual innuendo that permeates many of the plays of the earlier period), Sheridan created light yet pointed comedies of sexual politics. His plays were wildly popular with audiences of his time—and two of them have remained popular ever since.

Sheridan was born in Dublin on 20 October 1751. He was the second surviving son of Thomas and Frances Sheridan, both of whom were successful theater professionals. Sheridan first attended school in Dublin, was home-schooled, and then attended Harrow School when the family moved to England. He left school at age 17, but continued his education with a tutor and through private lessons in elocution given by his father. He began writing at an early age, producing translations, poems, political pamphlets, and dramatic works; none of these juvenilia were published or produced.

In 1771 Sheridan met a 16-year-old soprano named Elizabeth Ann Linley. He became one of her suitors, but was judged unfit by the young woman's father, composer Thomas Linley. Elizabeth was being stalked by a married man, Captain Thomas Mathews, who had repeatedly threatened to assault her. She confided the matter to Sheridan; the two of them eloped to France, and were secretly married. Elizabeth stayed for a time in a convent in France, while Sheridan returned to England. He dueled twice with Mathews. In the first duel, Sheridan was victorious and forced Mathews to apologize for his actions. However, Mathews soon withdrew his apology, and the two dueled again on 2 July 1772. This time Sheridan was severely wounded by Mathews, who fled to France.

Sheridan recovered from his injuries and returned to his studies, enrolling at Waltham Abbey, Essex, where he focused his attentions on mathematics. In 1773 he entered the Middle Temple to study law. Elizabeth's father finally deemed him suitable for his daughter; the two were publicly married on 13 April 1773.

At this time, Sheridan's writing career began in earnest. His first comedy, *The Rivals*, was produced at Covent Garden Theatre on 17 January 1775. Echoing Sheridan's own story, one of the play's main storylines concerns multiple suitors of a young lady, and its final, climactic scene revolves around a duel. Its first performance was not particularly well received. The play was judged to be too long, and the performance of the actor playing the supporting role of Sir Lucius O'Trigger was, by all accounts, poor. Performances were cancelled for a week and a half while Sheridan edited the script and replaced the actor. The play was performed again on 28 January, this time to great acclaim.

After the success of *The Rivals*, Sheridan entered into a highly productive period. All of his best-known works were completed before he turned 27. His next play, a farce entitled *St. Patrick's Day, or the Scheming Lieutenant*, opened on 2 May 1775. In November of the same year, he wrote and produced a comic opera, *The Duenna*, with financial and musical help from his new father-in-law. The show opened at Covent Garden Theatre on 21 November 1775 and played 75 performances—an unusually long run at the time.

Buoyed by the success of *The Duenna*, Sheridan made plans for a new financial venture: the purchase in 1776 of Drury Lane Theatre from the famous actor and manager David Garrick. He bought a half-share in the theater with his partners, one of whom was his father-in-law, and bought the entire theater outright two years later.

On 8 May 1777, Sheridan produced his next play at Drury Lane, a comedy entitled *The School for Scandal.* Although there is considerable evidence that the last portions of the script were hastily prepared, the show was a tremendous success. With this play perhaps more than any other, Sheridan breathed new life into the comic form, combining rapier-like wit with broad farce in satirizing the hypocrisy and artifice of a clique of scandalmongers. As many of his contemporaries had also begun to do, Sheridan populated the play with members of the newly influential merchant classes, rather than characters of the court. The play deals with the machinations of half a dozen delightfully dubious characters that caricature eighteenth-century London society, newly invigorated as it was by social mobility, trade, and commerce. Dressing rooms and tea parlors, libraries and picture galleries provide the right blend of settings for gossip and a variety of social schemes. Sheridan followed up with *The Critic*, which opened on 30 October 1779. This play, a self-referential comedy about the world of the theater that includes a highly entertaining play-within-a-play, was a much more modest success. Sheridan's finances were in good order, however; *The School for Scandal* continued to play to full houses.

After *The Critic*, Sheridan's writing career slowed. He made notes for a new comedy called *Affectation*, but this was never written nor performed. He produced one more work in 1799, a tragedy entitled *Pizarro*, but it had little impact.

After he had finished writing plays, Sheridan turned to politics while continuing to manage Drury Lane. In 1780 he became Member of Parliament for Stafford. His election was controversial—his first speech in Parliament was in his own defense against bribery charges. Nevertheless, Sheridan developed a reputation as both a fine orator and a radical liberal while in Parliament. He spoke out in favor of the French Revolution and criticized Britain's war against the newly independent American colonies. As a token of gratitude, the American Congress later offered him a gift of £20,000, but Sheridan turned down the money, fearing that he would be seen as disloyal.

Sheridan remained in politics until 1812, when he was defeated in a bid for re-election. By then he had racked up considerable debt. Drury Lane had proved to be something of a financial sinkhole: it had been refurbished for safety reasons in 1791, and then rebuilt after a fire in 1809, both times at significant expense. Sheridan's second wife, Hester Jane Ogle, whom he married in 1795, had a taste for extravagance, which further increased his debt. As a Member of Parliament Sheridan was protected from his creditors, but when he became a private citizen they came looking for payment, and in 1813 he was arrested. He was released when a close friend paid off his creditors, but he died in abject poverty on 7 July 1816. Despite his low estate he was buried with great pomp in Westminster Abbey six days later.

⌘⌘⌘

The School for Scandal

PROLOGUE

Spoken by Mr. King[1]
Written by D. Garrick,[2]
Esq.

A School for Scandal! tell me, I beseech you,
Needs there a school this modish° [fashionable] art to teach you?
No need of lessons now, the knowing think—
We might as well be taught to eat and drink.
Caused by a dearth of scandal, should the vapours[3]
Distress our fair ones—let 'em read the papers;
Their pow'rful mixtures such disorders hit;
Crave what they will, there's *quantum sufficit.*[4]
"Lord!" cries my Lady Wormwood (who loves tattle,
And puts much salt and pepper in her prattle),
Just ris'n at noon, all night at cards when threshing
Strong tea and scandal—"Bless me, how refreshing!
Give me the papers, Lisp—how bold and free! (*Sips.*)
Last night Lord L—— (*Sips.*) *was caught with Lady D*—
For aching heads what charming sal volatile![5] (*Sips.*)
If Mrs. B.—— *will still continue flirting,*
We hope she'll DRAW, *or we'll* UNDRAW *the curtain.*
Fine satire, poz°—in public all abuse it, [positively]
But, by ourselves (*Sips.*), our praise we can't refuse it.
Now, Lisp, *read you*—there, at that dash and star."[6]
"Yes, ma'am.—A *certain Lord had best beware,*
Who lives not twenty miles from Grosv'nor Square;[7]
For should he Lady W—— *find willing,*
WORMWOOD *is bitter*"—"Oh! that's me! the villain!
Throw it behind the fire, and never more
Let that vile paper come within my door."—
Thus at our friends we laugh, who feel the dart;
To reach our feelings, we ourselves must smart.
Is our young bard so young, to think that he
Can stop the full spring-tide of calumny?
Knows he the world so little, and its trade?
Alas! the devil is sooner raised than laid.
So strong, so swift, the monster there's no gagging:
Cut Scandal's head off—still the tongue is wagging.
Proud of your smiles once lavishly bestowed,
Again your young Don Quixote[8] takes the road:
To show his gratitude, he draws his pen,
And seeks this hydra,[9] Scandal, in his den.
For your applause all perils he would through—
He'll fight—that's *write*—a cavalliero[10] true,
Till every drop of blood—that's *ink*—is spilt for you.

DRAMATIS PERSONAE

[MEN]	[WOMEN]
Sir Peter Teazle	Lady Teazle
Sir Oliver Surface	Lady Sneerwell
Joseph Surface	Mrs. Candour
Charles Surface	Maria
Snake	
Rowley	
Moses	
Careless	
Sir Toby Bumper[11]	
Trip	
Sir Benjamin Backbite	
Crabtree	
[Servants]	

[1] *Mr. King* Actor Thomas King (1730–1805), who appeared in the play's original cast as Peter Teazle.

[2] *D. Garrick* Famous actor and theater manager David Garrick (1717–79).

[3] *the vapours* State of depression or ill health.

[4] *quantum sufficit* Latin: sufficient quantity (i.e., enough to satisfy the readers).

[5] *sal volatile* Substance used in smelling salts.

[6] *dash and star* In eighteenth-century print media, dashes and asterisks marked places where a name or other identifying detail had been withheld.

[7] *Grosv'nor Square* Grosvenor Square, site of aristocratic residences in London's West End.

[8] *Don Quixote* Title character of a Spanish comic romance (1605, 1615) by Miguel de Cervantes. The idealistic Quixote reads too many romances and believes himself to be a chivalric hero.

[9] *hydra* Greek mythological monster that has multiple heads and grows two more whenever one is cut off.

[10] *cavalliero* Spanish: knight or gentleman.

[11] *Bumper* Full glass of alcohol used for a toast.

ACT 1, SCENE 1. [Lady Sneerwell's house.][1]

(*Lady Sneerwell at the dressing table; Mr. Snake drinking chocolate.*)

LADY SNEERWELL. The paragraphs you say, Mr. Snake, were all inserted?

SNAKE. They were, madam, and as I copied them myself in a feigned hand, there can be no suspicion whence they came.

LADY SNEERWELL. Did you circulate the report of Lady Brittle's intrigue with Captain Boastall?

SNAKE. That is in as fine a train as your ladyship could wish; in the common course of things, I think it must reach Mrs. Clackit's ears within four-and-twenty hours, and then you know the business is as good as done.

LADY SNEERWELL. Why truly, Mrs. Clackit has a very pretty talent and a great deal of industry.

SNAKE. True, madam, and has been tolerably successful in her day. To my knowledge she has been the cause of six matches being broken off and three sons being disinherited, of four forced elopements, as many close confinements,[2] nine separate maintenances,[3] and two divorces. Nay, I have more than once traced her causing a tête-à-tête in the *Town and Country Magazine*[4] when the parties perhaps had never seen each others' faces before in the course of their lives.

LADY SNEERWELL. She certainly has talents, but her manner is gross.[5]

SNAKE. 'Tis very true: she generally designs well, has a free tongue and a bold invention, but her colouring is too dark and her outline often extravagant. She wants[6] that delicacy of hint and mellowness of sneer which distinguishes your ladyship's scandal.

LADY SNEERWELL. Ah! You are partial, Snake.

SNAKE. Not in the least: everybody allows that Lady Sneerwell can do more with a word or a look than many can with the most laboured detail, even when they happen to have a little truth on their side to support it.

LADY SNEERWELL. Yes, my dear Snake, and I am no hypocrite to deny the satisfaction I reap from the success of my efforts. Wounded myself in the early part of my life by the envenomed tongue of slander, I confess I have since known no pleasure equal to the reducing others to the level of my own reputation.

SNAKE. Nothing can be more natural. But Lady Sneerwell, there is one affair in which you have lately employed me wherein I confess I am at a loss to guess your motives.

LADY SNEERWELL. I conceive you mean with respect to my neighbour, Sir Peter Teazle, and his family?

SNAKE. I do. Here are two young men to whom Sir Peter has acted as a kind of guardian since their father's death: the eldest possessing the most amiable character and universally well spoken of; the youngest the most dissipated and extravagant young fellow in the kingdom, without friends or character. The former an avowed admirer of your ladyship's and apparently your favourite; the latter attached to Maria, Sir Peter's ward, and confessedly beloved by her. Now on the face of these circumstances, it is utterly unaccountable to me why you, the widow of a City knight[7] with a good jointure,[8] should not close with the passion of a man of such character and expectation as Mr. Surface, and more so, why you should be so uncommonly earnest to destroy the mutual attachment between his brother Charles and Maria.

LADY SNEERWELL. Then at once to unravel this mystery, I must inform you that love has no share whatever in the intercourse between Mr. Surface and me.

SNAKE. No!

LADY SNEERWELL. His real attachment is to Maria or her fortune, but finding in his brother a favoured rival, he has been obliged to mask his pretensions and profit by my assistance.

---

[1] *[Lady Sneerwell's House.]* Stage directions not appearing in the original play have been added in square brackets.

[2] *close confinements* Secret childbirths.

[3] *separate maintenances* Living allowances given by one member of a separated couple to the other; in the eighteenth century, a maintenance was provided by the husband.

[4] *Town and Country Magazine* Gossip periodical publicizing high-society scandals.

[5] *gross* Unrefined.

[6] *wants* Lacks.

[7] *City knight* I.e., knighted London merchant; *City* City of London, the oldest area of London and the location of its business centers.

[8] *jointure* Estate left to a widow by her husband to provide for her until the end of her life.

SNAKE. Yet still I am more puzzled why you should interest yourself in his success.

LADY SNEERWELL. Heavens, how dull you are! Cannot you surmise the weakness which I hitherto through shame have concealed even from you? Must I confess that Charles, that libertine, that extravagant, that bankrupt in fortune and reputation, that he it is for whom I am thus anxious and malicious and to gain whom I would sacrifice everything?

SNAKE. Now, indeed your conduct appears consistent, but how came you and Mr.[1] Surface so confidential?

LADY SNEERWELL. For our mutual interest. I have found him out a long time since. I know him to be artful, selfish, and malicious—in short, a sentimental knave[2]—while with Sir Peter, and indeed with all his acquaintance, he passes for a miracle of prudence, good sense, and benevolence.

SNAKE. Nay, Sir Peter vows he has not his equal in England, and above all he praises him as a Man of Sentiment.[3]

LADY SNEERWELL. True, and with the assistance of sentiments and hypocrisy, he has brought him entirely into his interest with regard to Maria, while poor Charles has no friend in the house, though I fear he has a powerful one in Maria's heart, against whom we must direct our schemes.

(*Enter servant.*)

SERVANT. Mr. Surface.

LADY SNEERWELL. Show him up.

(*Exit servant.*)

He generally calls about this time; I don't wonder at people's giving him to me for a lover.

(*Enter Joseph Surface.*)

JOSEPH SURFACE. My dear Lady Sneerwell, how do you do today? Mr. Snake, your most obedient.

LADY SNEERWELL. Snake has just been arraigning me on our mutual attachment, but I have informed him of our real views. You know how useful he has been to us, and believe me, the confidence is not ill placed.

JOSEPH SURFACE. Madam, it is impossible for me to suspect a man of Mr. Snake's sensibility and discernment.

LADY SNEERWELL. Well, well, no compliments now, but tell me when you saw your mistress, Maria, or what is more material to me, your brother.

JOSEPH SURFACE. I have not seen either since I left you, but I can inform you that they never meet. Some of your stories have taken a good effect on Maria.

LADY SNEERWELL. Ah my dear Snake, the merit of this belongs to you.—But do your brother's distresses increase?

JOSEPH SURFACE. Every hour. I am told he has had another execution[4] in his house yesterday; in short, his dissipation and extravagance exceed everything I ever heard of.

LADY SNEERWELL. Poor Charles!

JOSEPH SURFACE. True, madam, notwithstanding his vices, one cannot help feeling for him. Aye, poor Charles indeed. I am sure I wish it was in my power to be of any essential service to him. For the man who does not share in the distresses of a brother, even though merited by his own misconduct, deserves—

LADY SNEERWELL. Oh Lud![5] You are going to be moral and forget that you are among friends.

JOSEPH SURFACE. Egad that's true. I'll keep that sentiment till I see Sir Peter. However, it is certainly a charity to rescue Maria from such a libertine, who, if he is to be reclaimed, can be so only by one of your ladyship's superior accomplishments and understanding.

SNAKE. I believe, Lady Sneerwell, here's company coming; I'll go and copy the letter I mentioned to you.—Mr. Surface, your most obedient. (*Exit.*)

JOSEPH SURFACE. Sir, your very devoted—Lady Sneerwell, I am very sorry you have put any further confidence in that fellow.

---

[1] *Mr.* I.e., the older of the two Surface brothers.

[2] *sentimental knave* I.e., a hypocrite who expresses respectably moral sentiments.

[3] *Man of Sentiment* Phrase with a double meaning; it could mean that Joseph Surface is "sentimental" in the sense used above, or that he is virtuously sympathetic.

[4] *execution* Legal acquisition of a debtor's possessions in lieu of an unpaid debt.

[5] *Lud* Swear word meaning "Lord."

LADY SNEERWELL. Why so?

JOSEPH SURFACE. I have lately detected him in frequent conference with old Rowley, who was formerly my father's steward and has never, you know, been a friend of mine.

LADY SNEERWELL. And do you think he would betray us?

JOSEPH SURFACE. Nothing more likely, take my word for it, Lady Sneerwell, that fellow has not virtue enough to be faithful or constant even to his own villainy.—Hah, Maria!

(*Enter Maria.*)

LADY SNEERWELL. Maria, my dear, how do you do? What's the matter?

MARIA. Oh, there's that disagreeable lover of mine, Sir Benjamin Backbite, has just called at my guardian's with his odious uncle Crabtree, so I slipped out and ran hither to avoid them.

LADY SNEERWELL. Is that all?

JOSEPH SURFACE. If my brother Charles had been of the party, madam, perhaps you would not have been so much alarmed.

LADY SNEERWELL. Nay now, you are severe, for I dare swear the truth of the matter is, Maria heard you were here.—But my dear, what has Sir Benjamin done that you should avoid him so?

MARIA. Oh, he has done nothing, but 'tis for what he has said. His conversation is a perpetual libel on all his acquaintance.

JOSEPH SURFACE. Aye, and the worst of it is, there is no advantage in not knowing him, for he'll abuse a stranger just as soon as his best friend, and his uncle is as bad.

LADY SNEERWELL. Nay, but we should make allowance: Sir Benjamin is a wit and a poet.

MARIA. For my part I own, madam, wit loses its respect with me when I see it in company with malice.—What do you think, Mr. Surface?

JOSEPH SURFACE. Certainly, madam, to smile at the jest which plants a thorn in another's breast is to become a principal in the mischief.

LADY SNEERWELL. Pshaw! There's no possibility of being witty without a little ill nature; malice of a good thing is the barb which makes it stick.—What's your opinion, Mr. Surface?

JOSEPH SURFACE. To be sure, madam, that conversation where the spirit of raillery[1] is suppressed will ever appear tedious and insipid.

MARIA. Well, I'll not debate how far scandal may be allowable, but in a man I am sure it is always contemptible. We have pride, envy, rivalship, and a thousand little motives to depreciate each other, but the male slanderer must have the cowardice of a woman before he can traduce one.

(*Enter servant.*)

SERVANT. Madam, Mrs. Candour is below and, if your ladyship's at leisure, will leave her carriage.

LADY SNEERWELL. Beg her to walk in.

(*Exit servant.*)

Now Maria, however, here is a character to your taste, for though Mrs. Candour is a little talkative, everybody allows her to be the best natured and best sort of woman.

MARIA. Yet with a very gross affectation of good nature and benevolence, she does more mischief than the direct malice of old Crabtree.

JOSEPH SURFACE. I'faith, 'tis very true, Lady Sneerwell. Whenever I hear the current running against the characters of my friends, I never think them in such danger as when Candour undertakes their defence.

LADY SNEERWELL. Hush! Here she is.

(*Enter Mrs. Candour.*)

MRS. CANDOUR. My dear Lady Sneerwell, how have you been this century? Mr. Surface, what news do you hear, though indeed it is no matter, for I think one hears nothing else but scandal.

JOSEPH SURFACE. Just so indeed, madam.

MRS. CANDOUR. Ah! Maria, child, is the whole affair off between you and Charles? His extravagance, I presume; the Town[2] talks of nothing else.

MARIA. I am very sorry, ma'am, the Town have so little to do.

---

[1] *raillery* Teasing.

[2] *the Town* I.e., London high society.

MRS. CANDOUR. True, true, child, but there is no stopping people's tongues. I own I was hurt to hear it, as indeed I was to learn from the same quarter that your guardian, Sir Peter, and Lady Teazle have not agreed lately so well as could be wished.

MARIA. 'Tis strangely impertinent for people to busy themselves so. I'm sure such reports are—

MRS. CANDOUR. Very true, child, but what's to be done? People will talk, there's no preventing it. Why it was but yesterday I was told that Miss Gadabout had eloped with Sir Filagree Flirt—but Lord, there is no minding what one hears—though to be sure I had this from very good authority.

MARIA. Such reports are highly scandalous.

MRS. CANDOUR. So they are, child—shameful! shameful! But the world is so censorious no character escapes. Lord now! Who would have suspected your friend Miss Prim of an indiscretion? Yet such is the ill nature of people that they say her uncle stopped her last week just as she was stepping into the York diligence[1] with her dancing master.

MARIA. I'll answer for it, there are no grounds for the report.

MRS. CANDOUR. Oh, no foundation in the world, I dare swear, no more probably than for the story circulated last month of Mrs. Festino's affair with Colonel Cassino,[2] though to be sure that matter was never rightly cleared up.

JOSEPH SURFACE. The license of invention some people take is monstrous indeed!

MARIA. 'Tis so, but in my opinion those who report such things are equally culpable.

MRS. CANDOUR. To be sure they are: tale bearers are as bad as tale makers; 'tis an old observation and a very true one. But what's to be done, as I said before? How will you prevent people from talking? Today Mrs. Clackit assured me Mr. and Mrs. Honeymoon were at last become mere man and wife like the rest of her acquaintance. She likewise hinted that a certain widow in the next street had got rid of her dropsy[3] and recovered her shape in a most surprising manner, and the same time Miss Tattle, who was by, affirmed that Lord Buffalo had discovered his lady at a house of no extraordinary fame and that Sir Harry Bouquet and Tom Saunter were to measure swords on a similar provocation. But Lord, do you think I would report these things? No, no, tale-bearers, as I said before, are just as bad as tale-makers.

JOSEPH SURFACE. Oh Mrs. Candour, if everybody had your forbearance and good nature!

MRS. CANDOUR. I confess, Mr. Surface, I cannot bear to hear people attacked behind their backs, and when ugly circumstances come out against one's acquaintances, I own I always love to think the best. By the bye, I hope 'tis not true that your brother is absolutely ruined.

JOSEPH SURFACE. I am afraid his circumstances are very bad indeed, madam.

MRS. CANDOUR. Ah, I heard so, but you must tell him to keep up his spirits: Sir Thomas Splint, Captain Quinzes, and Mr. Nickit, all up,[4] I hear, within this week, so if Charles is undone, he will find half his acquaintances ruined too, and that, you know, is a consolation.

JOSEPH SURFACE. Doubtless, ma'am, a very great one.

(*Enter servant.*)

SERVANT. Mr. Crabtree and Sir Benjamin Backbite. (*Exit.*)

LADY SNEERWELL. So Maria, you see your lover pursues you. Positively you shan't escape.

(*Enter Crabtree and Sir Benjamin Backbite.*)

CRABTREE. Lady Sneerwell, I kiss your hands.—Mrs. Candour, I don't believe you are acquainted with my nephew, Sir Benjamin Backbite. Egad ma'am, he has a pretty wit and is a pretty poet too.—Isn't he, Lady Sneerwell?

SIR BENJAMIN. Oh fie, Uncle!

CRABTREE. Nay, egad 'tis true: I'll back him at a rebus or a charade[5] against the best rhymer in the kingdom.

[1] *York diligence* Public horse-drawn coach to York.

[2] *Festino* Italian: Party; *Cassino* Italian: Dance hall; also the name of a card game.

[3] *dropsy* Swelling caused by accumulation of fluid (here used as a cover for pregnancy).

[4] *Quinzes* French card game; *all up* Completely broke.

[5] *rebus* Puzzle in which players must decode a message made up of pictures and letters; *charade* Riddle involving wordplay.

Has your ladyship heard the epigram he wrote last week on Lady Frizzle's feather catching fire! Do, Benjamin, repeat it, or the charade you made last night extempore at Mrs. Drowzy's conversazione.[1] Come now, your first is the name of a fish, your second a great naval commander—and—

SIR BENJAMIN. Uncle—now—prithee!

CRABTREE. I'faith, madam, 'twould surprise you to hear how ready he is at these things.

LADY SNEERWELL. I wonder, Sir Benjamin, you never publish anything.

SIR BENJAMIN. To say truth, ma'am, 'tis very vulgar to print, and as my little productions are mostly satires and lampoons on particular people, I find they circulate more by giving copies in confidence to the friends of the parties; however, I have some love elegies which, when favoured with this lady's smiles, I mean to give to the public.

CRABTREE. 'Fore Heaven, ma'am, they'll immortalize you; you'll be handed down to posterity like Petrarch's Laura or Waller's Sacharissa.[2]

SIR BENJAMIN. Yes madam, I think you will like them when you shall see them on a beautiful quarto page,[3] where a neat rivulet of text shall murmur through a meadow of margin. 'Fore gad, they will be the most elegant things of their kind—

CRABTREE. But ladies, that's true. Have you heard the news?

MRS. CANDOUR. What, sir, do you mean the report of—

CRABTREE. No ma'am, that's not it. Miss Nicely is going to be married to her own footman.

MRS. CANDOUR. Impossible!

CRABTREE. Ask Sir Benjamin.

SIR BENJAMIN. 'Tis very true, ma'am: everything is fixed and the wedding livery bespoke.

CRABTREE. Yes, and they do say there were pressing reasons for it.

LADY SNEERWELL. Why, I have heard something of this before.

MRS. CANDOUR. It can't be, and I wonder anyone should believe such a story of so prudent a lady as Miss Nicely.

SIR BENJAMIN. Oh Lud ma'am, that's the very reason 'twas believed at once. She has always been so cautious and so reserved that everybody was sure there was some reason for it at bottom.

MRS. CANDOUR. Why, to be sure a tale of scandal is as fatal to the credit of a prudent lady of her stamp as a fever is generally to those of the strongest constitutions. But there is a sort of puny, sickly reputation that is always ailing yet will outlive the robuster character of a hundred prudes.

SIR BENJAMIN. True madam, there are valetudinarians[4] in reputation as well as constitution, who, being conscious of their weak part, avoid the least breath of air and supply their want of stamina by care and circumspection.

MRS. CANDOUR. Well, but this may be all a mistake. You know, Sir Benjamin, very trifling circumstances often give rise to the most injurious tales.

CRABTREE. That they do, I'll be sworn, ma'am. Did you ever hear how Miss Piper came to lose her lover and her character last summer at Tunbridge?[5] Sir Benjamin, you remember it?

SIR BENJAMIN. Oh, to be sure! The most whimsical circumstance—

LADY SNEERWELL. How was it pray?

CRABTREE. Why, one evening at Mrs. Ponto's assembly[6] the conversation happened to turn on the difficulty of breeding Nova Scotia sheep in this country; says a lady in company, "I have known instances of it, for Miss Laetitia Piper, a first cousin of mine, had a Nova Scotia sheep that produced her twins." "What!" cries the Dowager Lady Dundizzy (who you know is as deaf as a post) "has Miss Laetitia Piper had twins?" This mistake, as you may imagine, threw the whole company into a fit

[1] *conversazione* Small party intended for refined intellectual conversation.

[2] *Laura* Subject of the love sonnets of Francesco Petrarch (1304–74); *Waller's Sacharissa* In the 1630s Edmund Waller wrote a series of poems to Lady Dorothy Sidney (referred to in the poems as "Sacharissa"), which were extremely popular in the seventeenth and eighteenth centuries.

[3] *on a … quarto page* I.e., in print; quarto books are produced using large sheets of paper folded to produce four pages each.

[4] *valetudinarians* Unhealthy people, or people who go to great lengths to preserve their health.

[5] *Tunbridge* Tunbridge Wells, a fashionable resort town.

[6] *assembly* I.e., party.

of laughter; however, 'twas the next day reported, and in a few days believed by the whole Town, that Miss Laetitia Piper had actually been brought to bed of a fine boy and a girl, and in less than a week there were people who could name the father and the farmhouse where the babies were put out to nurse.[1]

LADY SNEERWELL. Strange indeed.

CRABTREE. Matter of fact, I assure you.—Oh Lud, Mr. Surface, pray is it true that your Uncle Sir Oliver is coming home?

JOSEPH SURFACE. Not that I know of, indeed sir.

CRABTREE. He has been in the East Indies a long time; you can scarcely remember him, I believe. Sad comfort whenever he returns to hear how your brother has gone on.

JOSEPH SURFACE. Charles has been imprudent, sir, to be sure, but I hope no busy people have already prejudiced Sir Oliver against him; he may reform.

SIR BENJAMIN. To be sure he may. For my part I never believed him so utterly void of principle as people say, and though he has lost all his friends, I am told nobody is better spoken of by the Jews.[2]

CRABTREE. That's true, egad Nephew. If the old Jewry was a ward,[3] I believe Charles would be an alderman. No man more popular there. 'Fore gad, I hear he pays as many annuities as the Irish tontine[4] and that whenever he's sick they have prayers for the recovery of his health in the synagogue.

SIR BENJAMIN. Yet no man lives in greater splendour. They tell me when he entertains his friends, he can sit down to dinner with a dozen of his own securities, have a score of tradesman in the anti-chamber and an officer behind every guest's chair.

JOSEPH SURFACE. This may be entertainment to you, gentlemen, but you pay very little regard to the feelings of a brother.

MARIA. [*Aside.*] Their malice is intolerable.—Lady Sneerwell, I must wish you a good morning—I'm not very well. (*Exit.*)

MRS. CANDOUR. Oh dear, she changes colour very much.

LADY SNEERWELL. Do Mrs. Candour follow her, she may want assistance.

MRS. CANDOUR. That I will with all my soul, ma'am. Poor dear creature, who knows what her situation may be? (*Exit.*)

LADY SNEERWELL. 'Twas nothing but that she could not bear to hear Charles reflected on, notwithstanding their difference.

SIR BENJAMIN. The young lady's penchant is obvious.

CRABTREE. But Benjamin, you mustn't give up the pursuit for that. Follow her and put her into good humour, repeat her some of your verses. Come, I'll assist you.

SIR BENJAMIN. Mr. Surface, I did not mean to hurt you, but depend on't, your brother is utterly undone.[5]

CRABTREE. Oh Lud! Aye! undone as ever man was, can't raise a guinea.[6]

SIR BENJAMIN. Everything sold, I am told, that was moveable.[7]

CRABTREE. I have seen one that was at his house: not a thing left but some empty bottles that were overlooked and the family pictures, which I believe are framed in the wainscot.[8]

SIR BENJAMIN. And I am very sorry to hear also some bad stories against him. (*Going.*)

CRABTREE. Oh, he has done many mean[9] things, that's certain.

SIR BENJAMIN. But however, as he's your brother—(*Going.*)

---

1 *put out to nurse* Sent to live in the country with a wet nurse.

2 *nobody ... Jews* Refers to the stereotypical association between Jews and moneylending. Moneylending was a common profession for Jewish people, as social and legal discrimination prevented them from working in most professions, while religious doctrine forbade Christians from making loans for profit (a prohibition not always obeyed in practice).

3 *old Jewry* Street in the City where many moneylenders' offices were located; *ward* Region of a city that elects an alderman as its representative in the city government.

4 *tontine* Money-raising method in which a large group of participants contribute funds, for which they receive annuities (periodic payments) that increase as the other participants die. The Irish Parliament undertook several tontines in the latter half of the eighteenth century.

5 *utterly undone* Financially ruined.

6 *guinea* Coin worth slightly more than a pound.

7 *moveable* I.e., not land or buildings.

8 *framed in the wainscot* I.e., embedded in the wall paneling.

9 *mean* Base, contemptible.

CRABTREE. We'll tell you all another opportunity.

(*Exeunt Sir Benjamin and Crabtree.*)

LADY SNEERWELL. Ha, ha, ha! 'tis very hard for them to leave a subject they have not quite run down.

JOSEPH SURFACE. And I believe their abuse was no more acceptable to your ladyship than Maria.

LADY SNEERWELL. I doubt[1] her affections are further engaged than we imagined. But the family are to be here this evening, so you may as well dine where you are, and we shall have an opportunity of observing further; in the meantime, I'll go and plot mischief, and you shall study sentiments.

(*Exeunt.*)

ACT 1, SCENE 2. Sir Peter Teazle's house.

(*Enter Sir Peter.*)

SIR PETER. When an old bachelor takes a young wife, what is he to expect? 'Tis now six months since Lady Teazle made me the happiest of men, and I have been the miserablest dog ever since. We tiffed a little going to church and came to a quarrel before the bells were done ringing. I was more than once nearly choked with gall during the honeymoon and had lost all comfort in life before my friends had done wishing me joy. Yet I chose with caution: a girl bred wholly in the country, who never knew luxury beyond one silk gown nor dissipation above the annual gala of a race ball. Yet now she plays her part in all the extravagant fopperies of the fashion and the Town with as ready a grace as if she had never seen a bush nor a grass plot out of Grosvenor Square. I am sneered at by my old acquaintance, paragraphed in the newspapers; she dissipates my fortune and contradicts all humours. Yet the worst of it is, I doubt I love her, or I should never bear all this; however, I'll never be weak enough to own it.

(*Enter Rowley.*)

ROWLEY. Oh Sir Peter, your servant. How is it with you, sir?

SIR PETER. Very bad, Master Rowley, very bad. I meet with nothing but crosses and vexations.

ROWLEY. What can have happened to trouble you since yesterday?

SIR PETER. A good question to a married man.

ROWLEY. Nay, I'm sure Sir Peter, your lady can't be the cause of your uneasiness.

SIR PETER. Why, has anyone told you she was dead?

ROWLEY. Come, come, Sir Peter, you love her, notwithstanding your tempers don't exactly agree.

SIR PETER. But the fault is entirely hers, Master Rowley. I am myself the sweetest tempered man alive and hate a teasing temper, and so I tell her an hundred times a day.

ROWLEY. Indeed!

SIR PETER. Aye, and what is very extraordinary, in all our disputes she is always in the wrong. But Lady Sneerwell and the set she meets at her house encourage the perverseness of her disposition. Then to complete my vexations, Maria, my ward, whom I ought to have the power of a father over, is determined to turn rebel too and absolutely refuses the man whom I have long resolved on for her husband, meaning, I suppose, to bestow herself on his profligate brother.

ROWLEY. You know, Sir Peter, I have always taken the liberty to differ with you on the subject of these two young gentlemen. I only wish you may not be deceived in your opinion of the elder; for Charles, my life on't, he will retrieve his errors yet. Their worthy father, once my honoured master, was at his years nearly as wild a spark, but when he died, he did not leave a more benevolent heart to lament his loss.

SIR PETER. You are wrong, Master Rowley. On their father's death you know I acted as a kind of guardian to them both 'till their uncle Sir Oliver's eastern liberality[2] gave them an early independence. Of course, no person could have more opportunities of judging of their hearts, and I was never mistaken in my life. Joseph is indeed a model for the young men of the age: he is a man of sentiment and acts up to the sentiments he professes. But for the other, take my word for't, if he had any grains of virtue by descent, he has dissipated

[1] *doubt* Fear or suspect.

[2] *eastern liberality* I.e., generosity; Sir Oliver acquired his wealth in Southeast Asia.

them with the rest of his inheritance. Ah, my old friend Sir Oliver will be deeply mortified when he finds how part of his bounty has been misapplied.

ROWLEY. I am sorry to find you so violent against the young man because this may be the most critical period of his fortune; I came hither with news that will surprise you.

SIR PETER. What? let me hear.

ROWLEY. Sir Oliver is arrived and at this moment in Town.

SIR PETER. How! You astonish me! I thought you did not expect him this month.

ROWLEY. I did not, but his passage has been remarkably quick.

SIR PETER. Egad, I shall rejoice to see my old friend; 'tis sixteen years since we met. We have had many a day together. But does he still enjoin us not to inform his nephews of his arrival?

ROWLEY. Most strictly. He means before it is known to make some trial of their dispositions.

SIR PETER. Ah, there needs no art to discover their merits; however, he shall have his way. But pray, does he know I am married?

ROWLEY. Yes, and will soon wish you joy.

SIR PETER. What, as we drink health to a friend in a consumption?[1] Ah! Oliver will laugh at me. We used to rail at[2] matrimony together, but he has been steady to his text. Well, he must be at my house though. I'll instantly give orders for his reception. But Master Rowley, don't drop a word that Lady Teazle and I disagree.

ROWLEY. By no means—

SIR PETER. For I should never be able to stand Noll's[3] jokes, so I'd have him think, Lord forgive me, that we are a very happy couple.

ROWLEY. I understand you. But then you must be very careful not to differ while he's in the house with you.

SIR PETER. Egad, and so we must—and that's impossible. Ah Master Rowley, when an old bachelor marries a young wife, he deserves—no, the crime carries the punishment along with it.

(*Exeunt.*)

[1] *in a consumption* With a wasting disease such as tuberculosis.

[2] *rail at* Make fun of.

[3] *Noll* Contracted form of "Oliver."

ACT 2, SCENE 1. Sir Peter Teazle's house.

(*Enter Sir Peter and Lady Teazle.*)

SIR PETER. Lady Teazle, Lady Teazle, I'll not bear it.

LADY TEAZLE. Sir Peter, Sir Peter, you may bear it or not, as you please, but I ought to have my own way in everything, and what's more, I will too. What, though I was educated in the country, I know very well that women of fashion in London are accountable to nobody after they are married.

SIR PETER. Very well, ma'am, very well, so a husband is to have no influence, no authority?

LADY TEAZLE. Authority! No, to be sure. If you wanted authority over me, you should have adopted me and not married me; I am sure you were old enough.

SIR PETER. Old enough! Aye, there it is, well, well, Lady Teazle, though my life may be made unhappy by your temper, I'll not be ruined by your extravagance.

LADY TEAZLE. My extravagance? I'm sure I'm not more extravagant than a woman of fashion ought to be.

SIR PETER. No, no, madam, you shall throw away no more sums on such unmeaning luxury. 'Slife,[4] to spend as much to furnish your dressing room with flowers in winter, as would suffice to turn the Pantheon into a greenhouse and give a fête champêtre[5] at Christmas.

LADY TEAZLE. Lord, Sir Peter, am I to blame because flowers are dear[6] in cold weather; you should find fault with the climate and not with me. For my part I am sure I wish it were spring all the year round and that roses grew under our feet.

SIR PETER. 'Oons[7] madam! If you had been born to this, I should not wonder at your talking thus, but you forget what your situation was when I married you.

LADY TEAZLE. No, no, I don't: 'twas a very disagreeable one, or I should never have married you.

SIR PETER. Yes, yes, madam, you were then somewhat in an humbler style: the daughter of a plain country squire.

[4] *'Slife* Swear word meaning "God's life."

[5] *Pantheon* Neoclassical building of impressive size, constructed in London in the late eighteenth century as a site for fashionable entertainment; *fête champêtre* French: garden party.

[6] *dear* Costly.

[7] *'Oons* Contraction of "Zounds," a swear word meaning "God's wounds."

Recollect, Lady Teazle, when I first saw you sitting at your tambour in a pretty figured[1] linen gown, with a bunch of keys by your side, your hair combed smoothly over a roll, and your apartment hung round with fruits in worsted of your own working.

LADY TEAZLE. Oh yes, I remember it very well, and a curious life I led! My daily occupation: to inspect the dairy, superintend the poultry, make extracts from the family receipt[2] book, and comb my aunt Deborah's lapdog.

SIR PETER. Yes, yes, madam, 'twas so indeed.

LADY TEAZLE. And then you know my evening amusements: to draw patterns for ruffles which I had not the materials to make, to play Pope Joan with the curate, read a sermon to my aunt, or be stuck down to an old spinet[3] to strum my father to sleep after a fox chase.

SIR PETER. I am glad you have so good a memory. Yes madam, these were the recreations I took you from. But now you must have your coach, vis-à-vis, and three powdered footmen before your chair[4]—and in summer a pair of white cats to draw you to Kensington Gardens.[5] No recollection I suppose when you were content to ride double behind the butler on a docked coach horse?[6]

LADY TEAZLE. No, I swear I never did that, I deny the butler and the coach horse.

SIR PETER. This, madam, was your situation, and what have I not done for you? I have made you a woman of fashion, of fortune, of rank; in short, I have made you *my wife*.

LADY TEAZLE. Well then, and there is but one thing more you can make me to add to the obligation—and that is—

SIR PETER. My widow, I suppose?

LADY TEAZLE. Hem, hem!

SIR PETER. Thank you, madam, but don't flatter yourself, for though your ill conduct may disturb my peace, it shall never break my heart, I promise you; however, I am equally obliged to you for the hint.

LADY TEAZLE. Then why will you endeavour to make yourself so disagreeable to me and thwart me in every little elegant expense?

SIR PETER. 'Slife madam, I say, had you any of these elegant expenses when you married me?

LADY TEAZLE. Lord, Sir Peter, would you have me be out of fashion?

SIR PETER. The fashion indeed! What had you to do with the fashion when you married me?

LADY TEAZLE. For my part I should think you would like to have your wife thought a woman of taste.

SIR PETER. Aye, there again—taste—Zounds, Madam! You had no taste when you married me.

LADY TEAZLE. That's very true indeed, Sir Peter, and after having married you, I should never pretend to taste again, I allow. But now Sir Peter, if we have finished our daily jangle, I presume I may go to my engagement at Lady Sneerwell's?

SIR PETER. Aye, there's another precious circumstance, a charming set of acquaintance you have made there.

LADY TEAZLE. Nay Sir Peter, they are people of rank and fortune, and remarkably tenacious of reputation.

SIR PETER. Yes, egad, they are tenacious of reputation with a vengeance! For they don't choose anybody should have a character but themselves. Such a crew! Ah! Many a wretch has rid on a hurdle[7] who has done less mischief than these utterers of forged tales, coiners of scandal, and clippers[8] of reputation.

LADY TEAZLE. What, would you restrain the freedom of speech?

SIR PETER. Oh, they have made you just as bad as any one of the society.

[1] *tambour* Round frame used for embroidery; *pretty figured* With pretty designs.

[2] *receipt* Recipe.

[3] *Pope Joan* Card game for three players; *spinet* Small harpsichord.

[4] *vis-à vis* Two-person carriage in which the passengers sit facing each other; *chair* Sedan chair, carried on poles by servants as a mode of transport.

[5] *cats* Presumably a slang term meaning "horses" or "ponies"; *Kensington Gardens* Fashionable London park. Members of high society traveled "the Ring," a path between Kensington Gardens and nearby Hyde Park, in order to display themselves and their carriages.

[6] *docked coach horse* Large horse intended for heavy labor; working horses' tails were "docked" (cropped short) to keep them from getting caught in equipment.

[7] *hurdle* Frame to which criminals were tied before being pulled by horse to their execution.

[8] *clippers* Refers to the criminal practice of "clipping," devaluing a coin by shaving small amounts of precious metal from its edges. Like forgery, clipping was punishable by execution.

LADY TEAZLE. Why I believe I do bear a part with a tolerable grace, but I vow I have no malice against the people I abuse. When I say an ill-natured thing, 'tis out of pure good humour, and I take for granted they'll deal exactly in the same manner with me. But Sir Peter, you know you promised to come to Lady Sneerwell's too.

SIR PETER. Well, well, I'll call in just to look after my own character.

LADY TEAZLE. Then, indeed, you must make haste after me or you'll be too late. So goodbye to you. (*Exit.*)

SIR PETER. So! I have gained much by my intended expostulations. Yet with what a charming air she contradicts everything I say and how pleasingly she shows her contempt of my authority. Well, though I can't make her love me, there is great satisfaction in quarrelling with her, and I think she never appears to such advantage as when she's doing everything in her power to plague me.

(*Exit.*)

ACT 2, SCENE 2. Lady Sneerwell's house.

(*Lady Sneerwell, Mrs. Candour, Crabtree, Sir Benjamin Backbite, and Joseph Surface discovered;*[1] *servants attending with tea.*)

LADY SNEERWELL. Nay, positively we will have it.

JOSEPH SURFACE. Yes, yes, the epigram, by all means.

SIR BENJAMIN. Oh plague on't, Uncle, 'tis mere nonsense.

CRABTREE. No, no, 'fore gad, very clever for an extempore.

SIR BENJAMIN. But ladies, you should be acquainted with the circumstance. You must know that one day last week, as Lady Betty Curricle[2] was taking the dust in Hyde Park in a sort of duodecimo phaeton,[3] she desired me to write some verses on her ponies, upon which I took out my pocket book and in one moment produced the following:

Sure never were seen two such beautiful ponies,
Other horses are clowns, and these macaronies;[4]
Nay, to give them this title I'm sure is not wrong,
Their legs are so slim, and their tails are so long.

CRABTREE. There ladies, done in the smack of a whip and on horseback too.

JOSEPH SURFACE. A very Phoebus[5] mounted indeed, Sir Benjamin.

SIR BENJAMIN. Oh dear sir, trifles, trifles!

(*Enter Lady Teazle and Maria.*)

MRS. CANDOUR. I must have a copy.

LADY SNEERWELL. Lady Teazle, I hope we shall see Sir Peter.

LADY TEAZLE. I believe he'll wait on your ladyship presently.

LADY SNEERWELL. Maria my dear, you look grave. Come, you shall sit down to piquet[6] with Mr. Surface.

MARIA. I take very little pleasure in cards; however, I'll do as your ladyship pleases.

LADY TEAZLE. [*Aside.*] I am surprised Mr. Surface should sit down with her. I thought he would have embraced this opportunity of speaking to me before Sir Peter came.

MRS. CANDOUR. Now, I'll die but you are so scandalous, I'll foreswear your society.

LADY TEAZLE. What's the matter, Mrs. Candour?

MRS. CANDOUR. They'll not allow our friend, Miss Vermillion, to be handsome.

LADY SNEERWELL. Oh surely, she's a pretty woman.

CRABTREE. I'm very glad you think so, madam.

MRS. CANDOUR. She has a charming, fresh colour.

LADY TEAZLE. Yes, when it is fresh put on.

MRS. CANDOUR. Oh fie! I'll swear her colour is natural. I have seen it come and go.

LADY TEAZLE. I dare swear you have, ma'am; it goes off at night and comes again in the morning.

MRS. CANDOUR. Ha, ha, ha! How I hate to hear you talk so. But surely now, her sister *is* or *was* very handsome.

---

[1] *discovered* Revealed.

[2] *Curricle* Small carriage.

[3] *duodecimo phaeton* Very small open carriage pulled by two horses.

[4] *macaronies* Flamboyantly fashionable men.

[5] *Phoebus* Name applied to the Greek god Apollo in his role as sun god. He rides his chariot across the sky to bring sunlight to the earth.

[6] *piquet* Two-player card game.

CRABTREE. Who, Mrs. Evergreen? Oh Lord! She's six-and-fifty if she's an hour.

MRS. CANDOUR. Now positively you wrong her, fifty-two or fifty-three is the utmost, and I don't think she looks more.

SIR BENJAMIN. Oh there's no judging by her looks, unless one could see her face.

LADY SNEERWELL. Well, well, if Mrs. Evergreen does take some pains to repair the ravages of time, you must allow she effects it with great ingenuity, and surely that's better than the careless manner in which the Widow Ochre caulks her wrinkles.

SIR BENJAMIN. Nay now Lady Sneerwell, you are severe upon the widow. Come, come, it is not that the widow paints so ill, but when she has finished her face, she joins it on so badly to her neck that she looks like a mended statue in which the connoisseur discovers at once that the head is modern though the trunk's antique.

CRABTREE. Ha, ha, ha! Well said, Nephew.

MRS. CANDOUR. Well, you make me laugh, but I vow I hate you for't. What do you think of Miss Simper?

SIR BENJAMIN. Why, she has very pretty teeth.

LADY TEAZLE. Yes, and on that account when she is neither speaking nor laughing, which very seldom happens, she never absolutely shuts her mouth but leaves it always on ajar as it were.

MRS. CANDOUR. How can you be so ill-natured?

LADY TEAZLE. I'll allow that's better than the pains Mrs. Prim takes to conceal her losses in front. She draws her mouth till it positively resembles the aperture of a poor box,[1] and all her words appear to slide out edgeways.

LADY SNEERWELL. Very well, Lady Teazle, I see you can be a little severe.

LADY TEAZLE. In defence of a friend it is but justice.—But here comes Sir Peter to spoil our pleasantry.

(*Enter Sir Peter.*)

SIR PETER. Ladies, your most obedient—Mercy on me, here is the whole set: a character dead at every word, I suppose.

MRS. CANDOUR. I am rejoiced you are come, Sir Peter; they have been so censorious, they'll allow good qualities to nobody, not even good nature to our friend, Mrs. Pursey.

LADY TEAZLE. What, the fat dowager who was at Mrs. Codille's[2] last night?

MRS. CANDOUR. Nay, her bulk is her misfortune, and when she takes such pains to get rid of it, you ought not to reflect on her.

LADY SNEERWELL. That's very true, indeed.

LADY TEAZLE. Yes, I know she almost lives upon acids and small whey, laces herself by pulleys, and often in the hottest noon in summer you may see her on a little, squat pony with her hair plaited up behind like a drummer and puffing around the Ring in a full trot.

MRS. CANDOUR. I thank you, Lady Teazle, for defending her.

SIR PETER. Yes, a good defence, truly.

MRS. CANDOUR. But Sir Benjamin is as censorious as Miss Sallow.

CRABTREE. Yes, and she is a curious being to pretend to be censorious, an awkward gawky without any one good point under heaven.

MRS. CANDOUR. Positively you shall not be so severe. Miss Sallow is a relation of mine by marriage, and as for her person, great allowance is to be made, for let me tell you, a woman labours under many disadvantages who tries to pass for a girl at six-and-thirty.

LADY SNEERWELL. Though surely she *is* handsome still, and for the weakness in her eyes, considering how much she reads by candlelight, it is not to be wondered at.

MRS. CANDOUR. True, and then as to her manner, upon my word I think it is particularly graceful, considering she never had the least education, for you know her mother was a Welsh milliner[3] and her father a sugar baker at Bristol.

SIR BENJAMIN. Ah, you are both of you too good-natured.

SIR PETER. Yes, damned good-natured—this is their own relation, mercy on me!

SIR BENJAMIN. And Mrs. Candour is of so moral a turn.

MRS. CANDOUR. Well, I will never join in ridiculing a friend. And so I constantly tell my cousin Ogle, and you

[1] *aperture of a poor box* Narrow slit in the top of a box used for charity collection.

[2] *Codille* Term used in Ombre, a popular card game.

[3] *milliner* Hat-maker.

well know what pretensions she has to be critical in beauty.

CRABTREE. Oh, to be sure, she has herself the oddest countenance that ever was seen; 'tis a collection of features from all the different countries of the globe.

SIR BENJAMIN. She has indeed an Irish front.

CRABTREE. Caledonian[1] locks.

SIR BENJAMIN. Dutch nose.

CRABTREE. Austrian lip.[2]

SIR BENJAMIN. Complexion of a Spaniard.

CRABTREE. And teeth *à la chinoise*.[3]

SIR BENJAMIN. In short, her face resembles a table d'hôte at Spa,[4] where no two guests are of a nation.

CRABTREE. Or a congress at the close of a general war, where all the members, even to her eyes, appear to have a different interest, and her nose and chin are the only parties likely to join issue.

MRS. CANDOUR. Ha, ha, ha!

SIR PETER. Mercy on my life! A person they dine with twice a week.

MRS. CANDOUR. Nay, but I vow you shall not carry the laugh off so, for give me leave to say that Mrs. Ogle—

SIR PETER. Madam, madam, I beg your pardon, there is no stopping these good gentlemen's tongues, but when I tell you, Mrs. Candour, that the lady they are abusing is a particular friend of mine, I hope you'll not take her part.

LADY SNEERWELL. Well said, Sir Peter, but you are a cruel creature: too phlegmatic[5] yourself for a jest and too peevish to allow it in others.

SIR PETER. Ah madam, true wit is more nearly allied to good nature than your ladyship is aware of.

LADY TEAZLE. True, Sir Peter, I believe they are so near of kin they can never be united.

SIR BENJAMIN. Oh! Rather, ma'am, suppose them man and wife, because one so seldom sees them together.

LADY TEAZLE. But Sir Peter is such an enemy to scandal, I believe he would have it put down[6] by Parliament.

SIR PETER. 'Fore Heaven, madam, if they were to consider the sporting with reputation of as much importance as the poaching on manors[7] and pass an Act for the Preservation of Fame, I believe many would thank them for the bill.

LADY SNEERWELL. Oh Lud! Sir Peter, would you deprive us of our privileges?

SIR PETER. Aye madam, and then no person should be permitted to kill characters or run down reputations but qualified old maids and disappointed widows.

LADY SNEERWELL. Go, you monster!

MRS. CANDOUR. But sure you would not be quite so severe on those who only report what they hear?

SIR PETER. Yes madam, I would have law-merchant[8] for them too, and in all cases of slander currency, whenever the drawer of the lie was not to be found, the injured party should have a right to come on any of the endorsers.

CRABTREE. Well, for my part, I believe there never was a scandalous tale without some foundation.

LADY SNEERWELL. Come ladies, shall we sit down to cards in the next room?

(*Enter servant, who whispers to Sir Peter.*)

SIR PETER. I'll be with them directly.

[*Exit servant.*]

[*Aside.*] I'll get away unperceived. (*Going.*)

LADY SNEERWELL. Sir Peter, you are not leaving us?

SIR PETER. Your ladyship must excuse me; I'm called away by particular business—but I'll leave my character behind me. (*Exit.*)

SIR BENJAMIN. Well certainly, Lady Teazle, that lord of yours is a strange being. I would tell you some stories of him that would make you laugh heartily, if he wasn't your husband.

[1] *Caledonian* Scottish.

[2] *Austrian lip* Lip deformity also known as "Hapsburg lip" because of its prevalence among the Hapsburgs, an Austrian royal family that held power in several European nations.

[3] *à la chinoise* French: in Chinese style. A tradition of coating teeth with black enamel was practiced in Japan and Vietnam, but not in China.

[4] *table d'hôte at Spa* Table shared by tourists in the Belgian resort town of Spa.

[5] *phlegmatic* Sluggish and apathetic.

[6] *put down* I.e., made illegal.

[7] *poaching on manors* Game preservation laws were severe, forbidding all but the most wealthy and propertied individuals to hunt.

[8] *law-merchant* Assemblage of laws and customs governing mercantile transactions.

LADY TEAZLE. Oh pray don't mind that, come, do, let's hear them.

(*They retire. Joseph Surface and Maria come forward.*)

JOSEPH SURFACE. Maria, I see you have no satisfaction in this society.

MARIA. How is it possible I should? If to raise malicious smiles at the infirmities and misfortunes of those who have never injured us be the province of wit or humour, Heaven grant me a double portion of dullness.

JOSEPH SURFACE. Yet they appear more ill-natured than they are; they have no malice at heart.

MARIA. Then is their conduct more inexcusable, for in my opinion, nothing but a depravity of heart could tempt them to such practices.

JOSEPH SURFACE. But can you, Maria, feel thus for others and be unkind to me alone; is hope to be denied the tenderest passion?

MARIA. Why will you distress me by renewing the subject?

JOSEPH SURFACE. Ah Maria! You would not treat me thus and oppose your guardian's, Sir Peter's, will but that I see that profligate Charles is still a favoured rival.

MARIA. Ungenerously urged! But whatever my sentiments of that unfortunate young man are, be assured I shall not feel more bound to give him up because his distresses have lost him the regard even of a brother.

(*Lady Teazle returns.*)

JOSEPH SURFACE. [*Kneeling.*] Nay, but Maria, do not leave me with a frown. By all that's honest, I swear—(*Aside.*) Gad's life, here is Lady Teazle.—You must not, no, you shall not, for though I have the greatest regard for Lady Teazle—

MARIA. Lady Teazle!

JOSEPH SURFACE. Yet were Sir Peter once to suspect—

LADY TEAZLE. [*Aside.*] What's this, pray? Does he take her for me?—Child, you are wanted in the next room.

(*Exit Maria.*)

What's all this, pray?

JOSEPH SURFACE. Oh, the most unlucky circumstance in nature. Maria has somehow suspected the tender concern which I have for your happiness and threatened to acquaint Sir Peter with her suspicions, and I was just endeavouring to reason with her when you came.

LADY TEAZLE. Indeed! But you seemed to adopt a very tender method of reasoning: Do you usually argue on your knees?

JOSEPH SURFACE. Oh, she's a child, and I thought a little bombast—But Lady Teazle, when are you to give me your judgment on my library[1] as you promised?

LADY TEAZLE. No, no, I begin to think it would be imprudent, and you know I admit you as a lover no further than fashion requires.

JOSEPH SURFACE. True, a mere platonic cicisbeo,[2] what every wife is entitled to.

LADY TEAZLE. Certainly, one must not be out of the fashion; however, I have so many of my country prejudices left that though Sir Peter's ill humour may vex me ever so, it shall never provoke me to—

JOSEPH SURFACE. The only revenge in your power. Well, I applaud your moderation.

LADY TEAZLE. Go, you are an insinuating wretch. But we shall be missed; let us join the company.

JOSEPH SURFACE. But we had best not return together.

LADY TEAZLE. Well, don't stay, for Maria shan't come to hear any more of your reasoning, I promise you. (*Exit.*)

JOSEPH SURFACE. A curious dilemma, truly, my politics have run me into: I wanted at first only to ingratiate myself with Lady Teazle that she might not be my enemy with Maria, and I have, I don't know how, become her serious lover! Sincerely, I begin to wish I had never made such a point of gaining so very good a character, for it has led me into so many rogueries that I doubt I shall be exposed at last.

(*Exit.*)

[1] *give me … my library* Literally, "examine the books in my library"; also a sexual innuendo.

[2] *cicisbeo* Italian term for a married woman's male companion or escort.

ACT 2, SCENE 3. Sir Peter Teazle's house.

(*Enter Rowley and Sir Oliver.*)

SIR OLIVER. Ha, ha, ha! and so my old friend is married, hey! A young wife out of the country, ha, ha, ha! That he should have stood bluff[1] to old bachelor so long, and sink into husband at last.

ROWLEY. But you must not rally him on the subject, Sir Oliver; 'tis a tender point I assure you, though he has been married only seven months.

SIR OLIVER. Then he has been just half a year on the stool of repentance. Poor Peter! But you say he has entirely given up Charles? Never sees him, hey?

ROWLEY. His prejudice against him is astonishing and, I'm sure, greatly increased by a jealousy of him with Lady Teazle, which he has been industriously led into by a scandalous society in the neighbourhood, who have contributed not a little to Charles's ill name, whereas the truth is, I believe, if the lady is partial to either of them, his brother is the favourite.

SIR OLIVER. Aye, I know there is a set of malicious, prating, prudent gossips, both male and female, who murder characters to kill time and will rob a young fellow of his good name before he has years to know the value of it. But I am not to be prejudiced against my nephew by such, I promise you; no, no, if Charles has done nothing false or mean, I shall compound for his extravagance.

ROWLEY. Then my life on't, you will reclaim him. Ah sir, it gives me new life to find that your heart is not turned against him and that the son of my good old master has one friend, however, left.

SIR OLIVER. What, shall I forget, Master Rowley, when I was at his years myself? Egad, my brother and I were neither very prudent youths, and yet I believe you have not seen many better men than your old master was.

ROWLEY. Sir, 'tis this reflection gives me assurance that Charles may yet be a credit to his family.—But here comes Sir Peter.

SIR OLIVER. Egad, so he does. Mercy on me! he's greatly altered and seems to have a settled, married look! One may read husband in his face at this distance.

(*Enter Sir Peter.*)

SIR PETER. Hah! Sir Oliver, my old friend, welcome to England a thousand times.

SIR OLIVER. Thank you, thank you, Sir Peter. And i'faith, I'm as glad to find you well, believe me.

SIR PETER. Ah! 'Tis a long time since we met: sixteen years, I doubt, Sir Oliver, and many a cross accident in the time.

SIR OLIVER. Aye, I have had my share. But what, I find you are married, hey, my old boy! Well, well, it can't be helped, and so I wish you joy with all my heart.

SIR PETER. Thank you, thank you, Sir Oliver. Yes, I have entered into the happy state—but we'll not talk of that now.

SIR OLIVER. True, true, Sir Peter, old friends should not begin on grievances at first meeting, no, no, no.

ROWLEY. (*To Sir Oliver.*) Take care, pray sir.

SIR OLIVER. So, one of my nephews I find is a wild, extravagant young rogue, hey!

SIR PETER. Wild! Ah my old friend, I grieve for your disappointment there: he's a lost young man indeed. However, his brother will make you amends; Joseph is indeed what a youth should be. Everybody in the world speaks well of him.

SIR OLIVER. I am sorry to hear it: he has too good a character to be an honest fellow. Everybody speaks well of him! Pshaw! Then he has bowed as low to knaves and fools as to the honest dignity of genius or virtue.

SIR PETER. What, Sir Oliver, do you blame him for not making enemies?

SIR OLIVER. Yes, if he has merit enough to deserve them.

SIR PETER. Well, well, you'll be convinced when you know him. 'Tis edification to hear him converse. He possesses the noblest sentiments.

SIR OLIVER. Oh plague of his sentiments! If he salutes[2] me with a scrap of morality in his mouth, I shall be sick directly. But, however, don't mistake me, Sir Peter, I don't mean to defend Charles's errors, but before I form my judgment of either of them, I intend to make a trial of their hearts, and my friend Rowley and I have planned something for the purpose.

[1] *bluff* Unfalteringly.

[2] *salutes* Kisses in greeting.

ROWLEY. And Sir Peter shall own he has been for once mistaken.

SIR PETER. Oh, my life on Joseph's honour.

SIR OLIVER. Well, come, give us a bottle of good wine, and we'll drink your lady's good health and tell you all our scheme.

SIR PETER. Allons[1] then.

SIR OLIVER. And don't, Sir Peter, be so severe against your old friend's son. 'Odd's[2] my life! I'm not sorry that he has run out of the course a little. For my part, I hate to see prudence clinging to the green suckers of youth. 'Tis like ivy round a sapling and spoils the growth of the tree.

(*Exeunt.*)

ACT 3, SCENE 1. Sir Peter Teazle's house.

(*Enter Sir Peter, Sir Oliver, and Rowley.*)

SIR PETER. Well then, we will see this fellow first and have our wine afterwards. But how is this, Master Rowley? I don't see the gist of your scheme.

ROWLEY. Why sir, this Mr. Stanley, whom I was speaking of, is nearly related to them by their mother. He was once a merchant in Dublin but has been ruined by a series of undeserved misfortunes. He has applied by letter since his confinement both to Mr. Surface and Charles. From the former he has received nothing but evasive promises of future service, while Charles has done all that his extravagance has left him power to do, and he is at this time endeavouring to raise a sum of money, part of which in the midst of his own distresses, I know, he intends for the service of poor Stanley.

SIR OLIVER. Ah! He is my brother's son.

SIR PETER. Well, but how is Sir Oliver personally to—

ROWLEY. Why sir, I will inform Charles and his brother that Stanley has obtained permission to apply in person to his friends, and as they have neither of them ever seen him, let Sir Oliver assume the character, and he will have a fair opportunity of judging at least of the benevolence of their dispositions. And believe me, sir, you will find in the youngest brother one, who in the midst of folly and dissipation, has still, as our immortal bard expresses it,

A tear for pity and a hand
Open as day for melting charity.[3]

SIR PETER. Pshaw! What signifies his having an open hand or a purse either when he has nothing left to give? Well, well, make the trial if you please, but where is the fellow whom you brought for Sir Oliver to examine relative to Charles's affairs?

ROWLEY. Below, waiting his commands, and no one can give him better intelligence.—This, Sir Oliver, is a friendly Jew, who to do him justice, has done everything in his power to bring your nephew to a proper sense of his extravagance.

SIR PETER. Pray, let us have him in.

ROWLEY. Desire Mr. Moses to walk upstairs.

SIR PETER. But pray, why should you suppose he will speak the truth?

ROWLEY. Oh, I have convinced him he has no chance of recovering certain sums advanced to Charles but through the bounty of Sir Oliver, who he knows is arrived, so that you may depend on his fidelity to his own interest. I have also another evidence[4] in my power, one Snake, whom I have detected in a matter little short of forgery, and shall shortly produce him to remove some of *your* prejudices, Sir Peter, relative to Charles and Lady Teazle.

SIR PETER. I have heard too much on that subject.

ROWLEY. Here comes the honest Israelite.

(*Enter Moses.*)

ROWLEY. This is Sir Oliver.

SIR OLIVER. Sir, I understand you have lately had great dealings with my nephew, Charles?

MOSES. Yes, Sir Oliver. I done all my power for him, but he was ruined before he came to me for assistance.

SIR OLIVER. That was unlucky, truly, for you have had no opportunity of showing your talents.

MOSES. None at all. I had not the pleasure of knowing his distresses till he was some thousands worse than nothing.

---

[1] *Allons* French: We shall go.

[2] *'Odd's* Swear word meaning "God's."

[3] *A tear … charity* From Shakespeare, *2 Henry IV* 4.4.31–32.

[4] *evidence* I.e., giver of evidence.

SIR OLIVER. Unfortunate indeed! But I suppose you have done all in your power for him, honest Moses?

MOSES. Yes, he knows that. This very evening I was to have brought him a gentleman from the City, who does not know him and will, I believe, advance him some money.

SIR PETER. What, one Charles never had money from before?

MOSES. Yes, Mr. Premium, of Crutched Friars,[1] formerly a broker.

SIR PETER. Egad, Sir Oliver, a thought strikes me.—Charles, you say, doesn't know Mr. Premium?

MOSES. Not at all.

SIR PETER. Now then, Sir Oliver, you may have an opportunity of satisfying yourself better than by an old romancing tale of a poor relation.—Go with my friend, Moses, and present Mr. Premium.—And then I'll answer for't, you will see your nephew in all his glory.

SIR OLIVER. Egad, I like this idea better than the other, and I may visit Joseph afterwards as old Stanley.

SIR PETER. True, so you may.

ROWLEY. Well, this is taking Charles at a disadvantage to be sure; however, Moses, you understand Sir Peter and will be faithful.

MOSES. You may depend upon me. This is near the time I was to have gone.

SIR OLIVER. I'll accompany you as soon as you please, Moses, but hold, I forgot one thing: How the plague shall I be able to pass for a Jew?

MOSES. There is no need: the principal[2] is Christian.

SIR OLIVER. Is he? I am sorry to hear it. But then again, an't I too smartly dressed to look like a moneylender?

SIR PETER. Not at all. 'Twould not be out of character if you went in your own carriage, would it, Moses?

MOSES. Not in the least.

SIR OLIVER. Well, but how must I talk? There's certainly some cant of usury and mode of treating that I ought to know.

SIR PETER. Oh, there's not much to learn. The great point, as I take it, is to be exorbitant enough in your demands, hey Moses?

MOSES. Yes, that's a very great point.

SIR OLIVER. I'll answer for't; I'll not be wanting in that. I'll ask him eight, or ten percent, upon the loan, at least.

MOSES. If you ask him no more than that, you'll be discovered immediately.

SIR OLIVER. Hey, what a plague! How much then?

MOSES. That depends upon circumstances; if he appears not very anxious for the supply, you should require only forty or fifty percent, but if you find him in great distress and want the monies very bad, you may ask him double.

SIR PETER. A good, honest trade you are learning, Sir Oliver.

SIR OLIVER. Truly, I think so, and not unprofitable.

MOSES. Then, you know, you haven't the monies yourself but are forced to borrow them for him of a friend.

SIR OLIVER. Oh! I borrow it of a friend, do I?

MOSES. Yes, and your friend is an unconscionable dog, but you can't help it.

SIR OLIVER. My friend is an unconscionable dog, is he?

MOSES. Yes, and he himself has not the monies by him but is forced to sell stock at a great loss.

SIR OLIVER. He's forced to sell stock at a great loss, is he? Well, that's very kind of him.

SIR PETER. I'faith, Sir Oliver, Mr. Premium I mean, you'll soon be master of the trade.

SIR OLIVER. Right, right! Well, Moses shall give me further instructions as we go together.

SIR PETER. You will not have much time, for your nephew lives hard by.

SIR OLIVER. Oh, never fear, my tutor appears so able that, though Charles lived in the next street, it must be my own fault if I'm not a complete rogue before I turn the corner.

(*Exeunt Sir Oliver and Moses.*)

SIR PETER. So now I think Sir Oliver will be convinced you are partial, Rowley, and would have prepared Charles for the other plot.

ROWLEY. No, upon my word, Sir Peter.

SIR PETER. Well, go bring me this Snake, and I'll hear what he has to say presently.—I see Maria and want to speak with her.

(*Exit Rowley.*)

[1] *Crutched Friars* Street in London.

[2] *principal* I.e., the broker for whom Moses is acting as an agent.

I should be glad to be convinced my suspicions of Lady Teazle and Charles were unjust. I have never yet opened my mind on this subject to my friend Joseph; I am determined I will do it: he will give me his opinion sincerely.

(*Enter Maria.*)

SIR PETER. So child, has Mr. Surface returned with you?

MARIA. No sir, he was engaged.

SIR PETER. Well Maria, do you not reflect the more you converse with that amiable young man what return his partiality for you deserves?

MARIA. Indeed, Sir Peter, your frequent importunity on this subject distresses me extremely; you compel me to declare that I know no man who has ever paid me a particular attention whom I would not prefer to Mr. Surface.

SIR PETER. So, here's perverseness! No, no, Maria, 'tis Charles only whom you would prefer; 'tis evident his vices and follies have won your heart.

MARIA. This is unkind, sir. You know I have obeyed you in neither seeing nor corresponding with him. I have heard enough to convince me that he is unworthy my regard, yet I cannot think it culpable if, while my understanding severely condemns his vices, my heart suggests some pity for his distresses.

SIR PETER. Well, well, pity him as much as you please, but give your heart and hand to a worthier object.

MARIA. Never to his brother.

SIR PETER. Go, perverse and obstinate! But take care, madam, you have never yet known what the authority of a guardian is; do not compel me to inform you of it.

MARIA. I can only say you shall not have just reason. 'Tis true, by my father's will I am for a short period bound to regard you as his substitute but must cease to think you so when you would compel me to be miserable. (*Exit.*)

SIR PETER. Was there ever man so crossed[1] as I am! Everything conspiring to fret me. I had not been involved in matrimony a fortnight[2] before her father, a hale and hearty man, died, on purpose, I believe, for the pleasure of plaguing me with the care of his daughter. But here comes my helpmate. She appears in great good humour. How happy I should be if I could tease her into loving me, though but a little.

(*Enter Lady Teazle.*)

LADY TEAZLE. Lud! Sir Peter, I hope you haven't been quarrelling with Maria? It isn't using me well to be ill-humoured when I'm not by.

SIR PETER. Ah! Lady Teazle, you might have the power to make me good-humoured at all times.

LADY TEAZLE. I am sure I wish I had, for I want you to be in a charming, sweet temper at this moment. Do be good-humoured now and let me have two hundred pounds, will you?

SIR PETER. Two hundred pounds! What, an't I to be in a good humour without paying for it? But speak to me thus, and i'faith, there's nothing I would refuse you. You shall have it but seal me a bond[3] for the repayment.

LADY TEAZLE. Oh no! There's my note of hand[4] will do as well.

SIR PETER. And you shall no longer reproach me with not giving you an independent settlement—I mean shortly to surprise you—but shall we always live thus, hey?

LADY TEAZLE. If you please. I'm sure I do not care how soon we leave off quarrelling, provided you'll own you were tired first.

SIR PETER. Well then, let our future contest be who shall be most obliging.

LADY TEAZLE. I assure you, Sir Peter, good nature becomes you; you look now as you did before we were married! When you used to walk with me under the elms and tell me stories of what a gallant you were in your youth, and chuck me under the chin, you would, and ask me if I thought I could love an old fellow who would deny me nothing, didn't you?

SIR PETER. Yes, yes, and you were as kind and attentive—

LADY TEAZLE. Aye, so I was and would always take your part when my acquaintance used to abuse you and turn you into ridicule.

[1] *crossed* Unlucky in fate.

[2] *a fortnight* Two weeks.

[3] *bond* Formal promise of repayment on a loan; Sir Peter is playfully requesting a kiss.

[4] *note of hand* Literally, a signed note; in performance, Lady Teazle would hold out her hand for Sir Peter to kiss.

SIR PETER. Indeed!

LADY TEAZLE. Aye, and when my cousin Sophy called you a stiff, peevish old bachelor and laughed at me for thinking of marrying one who might be my father, I have always defended you and said I didn't think you so ugly by any means.

SIR PETER. Thank you!

LADY TEAZLE. And that I dared say you would make a very good sort of a husband.

SIR PETER. And you prophesied right, and we shall certainly now be the happiest couple—

LADY TEAZLE. And never differ again.

SIR PETER. No, never—though at the same time indeed, my dear Lady Teazle, you must watch your temper very narrowly, for in all our little quarrels, my dear—if you recollect, my love, you always began first.

LADY TEAZLE. I beg pardon, my dear Sir Peter, indeed you always gave the provocation.

SIR PETER. Now see my angel, contradicting isn't the way to keep friends.

LADY TEAZLE. Then don't you begin it, my love.

SIR PETER. There now—you—you are going on, you don't perceive, my life, that you are just doing the very thing which you know always makes me angry.

LADY TEAZLE. Nay, you know if you will be angry without any reason—

SIR PETER. There now, you want to quarrel again.

LADY TEAZLE. No, I'm sure I don't, but if you will be so peevish—

SIR PETER. There, *now* who begins first?

LADY TEAZLE. Why, you, to be sure. I said nothing, but there's no bearing your temper.

SIR PETER. No, no, madam, the fault is in your own temper.

LADY TEAZLE. Aye, you are just what my cousin Sophy said you would be—

SIR PETER. Your cousin Sophy is a forward, impertinent Gypsy.

LADY TEAZLE. And you a great bear to abuse my relations.

SIR PETER. Now may all the plagues of marriage be doubled on me if ever I try to be friends with you any more.

LADY TEAZLE. So much the better.

SIR PETER. No, no, madam, 'tis evident you never cared a pin for me, and I was a madman to marry you: a pert, rural coquette[1] that had refused half the honest squires in the neighbourhood.

LADY TEAZLE. And I am sure I was a fool to marry you: an old, dangling bachelor, who was single at fifty only because he never could meet with anyone who would have him.

SIR PETER. Aye, aye, madam, but you were pleased enough to listen to me: you never had such an offer before.

LADY TEAZLE. No! Didn't I refuse Sir Tivy Terrier, who everybody said would have been a better match? For his estate is just as good as yours, and he has broke his neck since we have been married.

SIR PETER. Oh, oh, oh! I have done with you, madam. You are unfeeling, ungrateful—but there is an end of everything. I believe you capable of anything that's bad. Yes madam, I now believe the report relative to you and Charles, madam. Madam—yes, madam, you and Charles, not without grounds.

LADY TEAZLE. Take care, Sir Peter. You had better not insinuate any such thing. I'll not be suspected without a cause, I promise you.

SIR PETER. Very well, madam, very well, a separate maintenance as soon as you please—yes madam, or a divorce. I'll make an example of myself for the benefit of all old bachelors. Let us separate, madam.

LADY TEAZLE. Agreed, agreed. And now my dear Sir Peter, we are of a mind once more; we may be the happiest couple and never differ again, you know, ha, ha! Well, you are going to be in a passion, I see, and I shall only interrupt you, so bye bye. (*Exit.*)

SIR PETER. Plagues and tortures! Can't I make her angry either? Oh, I am the miserablest fellow! But I'll not bear her presuming to keep her temper. No, she may break my heart, but she shall not keep her temper.

(*Exit.*)

[1] *coquette* Flirt.

ACT 3, SCENE 2. A chamber in Charles's house.

(*Enter Trip, Moses, and Sir Oliver.*)

TRIP. Here master, master, if you will stay a moment, I'll try whether—what's the gentleman's name?

SIR OLIVER. [*Aside.*] Mr. Moses, what is my name?

MOSES. Mr. Premium.

TRIP. Premium—very well. (*Exit taking snuff.*)

SIR OLIVER. To judge by the servants, one would believe the master was ruined. But what! Sure this was my brother's house!

MOSES. Yes sir, Mr. Charles bought it of Mr. Joseph, with the furniture, pictures, etcetera, just as the old gentleman left it. Sir Peter thought it a great piece of extravagance in him.

SIR OLIVER. In my mind the other's economy in selling it him was more reprehensible by half.

(*Enter Trip.*)

TRIP. My master says you must wait, gentleman, he has company and can't speak with you yet.

SIR OLIVER. If he knew who it was wanted to see him, perhaps he wouldn't have sent such a message.

TRIP. Yes, yes, sir, he knows you are here; I didn't forget little Premium, no, no, no.

SIR OLIVER. Very well, and I pray sir, what may be your name?

TRIP. Trip, sir, my name is Trip, at your service.

SIR OLIVER. Well then Mr. Trip, you have a pleasant sort of place here I guess?

TRIP. Why yes, here are three or four of us pass our time agreeably enough, but then our wages are sometimes a little in arrear, and not very good either, but fifty pounds a year and find our own bags[1] and bouquets.

SIR OLIVER. Bags and bouquets! Halters and bastinadoes.[2]

TRIP. But apropos, Moses! Have you been able to get me that little bill discounted?[3]

SIR OLIVER. [*Aside.*] Wants to raise money too—mercy on me—has his distresses, I warrant, like a lord, and affects creditors and duns.[4]

MOSES. 'Twas not to be done indeed, Mr. Trip.

TRIP. Good lack! You surprise me. My friend Brush has endorsed it, and I thought, when he puts his mark to the back of the bill, 'twas as good as cash.

MOSES. No, 'twouldn't do.

TRIP. A small sum—but twenty pounds. Harkee, Moses, do you think you could get it me by way of annuity?[5]

SIR OLIVER. [*Aside.*] An annuity! Ha, ha, ha! A footman raise money by annuity! Well done, luxury, egad!

MOSES. But you must insure your place.

TRIP. Oh, with all my heart I'll insure my place—and my life too if you please.

SIR OLIVER. [*Aside.*] It's more than I would your neck.

MOSES. But is there nothing you could deposit?

TRIP. Why nothing capital of my master's wardrobe has dropped lately,[6] but I could give you a mortgage on some of his winter clothes, with equity and redemption before November, or you shall have the reversion of the French velvet or a post-obit[7] on the blue and silver—these, I should think, Moses, with a few pair of point[8] ruffles, as a collateral security, hey my little fellow?

MOSES. Well, well—

(*Bell rings.*)

TRIP. Egad, I heard the bell. I believe, gentlemen, I can now introduce you.—Don't forget the annuity, little Moses.—This way, gentlemen.—Insure my place, you know!

SIR OLIVER. [*Aside.*] If the man be the shadow of the master, this is the temple of dissipation indeed!

(*Exeunt.*)

---

[1] *bags* Wigs.

[2] *Halters* Hangings; *bastinadoes* Canings of the feet.

[3] *bill* I.e., bill of exchange, a document similar to a check in which one party promises to pay the holder at a specified date, usually some months in the future; *discounted* Sold for a reduced amount of immediate cash.

[4] *duns* Debt collectors. Sir Oliver is suggesting that Trip is too low-class to have debt of this kind.

[5] *annuity* Annual payment, usually obtained by way of an investment or insurance agreement.

[6] *my master's … dropped lately* As a senior servant, Trip would sometimes receive hand-me-down clothing from Charles Surface.

[7] *reversion* I.e., ownership rights after the current owner's death; *post-obit* Loan agreement in which repayment is postponed until the death of a person from whom the borrower expects to inherit.

[8] *point* I.e., lace.

ACT 3, SCENE 3.

(*Charles, Careless, Sir Toby Bumper, etc. discovered at a table drinking wine.*)

CHARLES. 'Fore Heaven 'tis true, there's the great degeneracy of the age: many of our acquaintance have taste, spirit, and politeness, but plague on't, they won't drink.

CARELESS. It is so indeed, Charles; they give into all the substantial luxuries of the table and abstain from nothing but wine and wit.

CHARLES. Oh certainly, society suffers by it intolerably, for now instead of the social spirit of raillery that used to mantle over a glass of bright burgundy, their conversation is become just like the spa-water[1] they drink, which has all the pertness and flatulence of champagne without its spirit or flavour.

FIRST GENTLEMAN. But what are they to do, who love play better than wine?

CARELESS. True, there's Harry diets himself for gaming and is now under a hazard[2] regimen.

CHARLES. Then he'll have the worst of it. What! You wouldn't train a horse for the course by keeping him from corn?[3] For my part, egad, I am now never so successful as when I am a little merry; let me throw on a bottle of champagne, and I never lose, at least I never feel my losses, which is exactly the same thing.

SECOND GENTLEMAN. Aye, that I believe.

CHARLES. And then, what man can pretend to be a believer in love who is an abjurer of wine? 'Tis the test by which the lover knows his own heart. Fill a dozen bumpers to a dozen beauties, and she that floats at top is the maid that has bewitched you.

CARELESS. Now then, Charles, be honest and give us your real favourite.

CHARLES. Why, I have withheld her only in compassion to you; if I toast her, you must give a round of her peers, which is impossible on earth.

CARELESS. Oh, then we'll find some canonized vestals[4] or heathen goddesses that will do, I warrant.

CHARLES. Here then, bumpers, you rogues, bumpers. Maria, Maria!

FIRST GENTLEMAN. Maria who?

CHARLES. Oh damn the surname, 'tis too formal to be registered in love's calendar.—But now, Sir Toby, beware, we must have beauty's superlative.

CARELESS. Nay, never study, Sir Toby; we'll stand to the toast though your mistress should want an eye, and you know you have a song will excuse you.

SIR TOBY. Egad, so I have, and I'll give him the song instead of the lady.

[Song and Chorus.]

Here's to the maiden of bashful fifteen;
  Here's to the widow of fifty;
Here's to the flaunting, extravagant quean,° *whore*
  And here's to the housewife that's thrifty.

[Chorus.]

Let the toast pass,
Drink to the lass,
I'll warrant she'll prove an excuse for the glass.

Here's to the charmer whose dimples we prize;
  Now to the maid who has none, sir;
Here's to the girl with a pair of blue eyes,
  And here's to the nymph[5] with but one, sir.
    Let the toast pass, etc.

Here's to the maid with a bosom of snow;
  Now to her that's as brown as a berry;
Here's to the wife with her face full of woe,
  And now for the damsel that's merry.
    Let the toast pass, etc.

For let them be clumsy or let them be slim,
  Young or ancient I care not a feather;
So fill a pint bumper quite up to the brim,
  And let us e'en toast them together.
    Let the toast pass, etc.

ALL. Bravo, Bravo!

(*Enter Trip, who whispers to Charles.*)

[1] *spa-water* Water from a mineral spring.

[2] *hazard* Complicated dice game.

[3] *corn* Food grain, such as oats.

[4] *vestals* I.e., virgins.

[5] *nymph* Young woman.

CHARLES. Gentlemen, you must excuse me a little.—Careless, take the chair, will you?

CARELESS. Nay prithee Charles, what now? This is one of your peerless beauties, I suppose, has dropped in by chance.

CHARLES. No, faith, to tell you the truth, 'tis a Jew and a broker who are come by appointment.

CARELESS. Oh damn it, let's have the Jew in.

FIRST GENTLEMAN. Aye, and the broker too, by all means.

SECOND GENTLEMAN. Yes, yes, the Jew and the broker.

CHARLES. Egad, with all my heart.—Trip, bid the gentlemen walk in, (*Exit Trip.*) though there's one of them a stranger, I can assure you.

CARELESS. Charles, let us give them some generous burgundy, and perhaps they'll grow conscientious.

CHARLES. Oh hang 'em, no, wine does but draw forth the natural qualities of a man, and to make them drink would only be to whet their knavery.

(*Enter Trip, Sir Oliver, and Moses.*)

CHARLES. So, honest Moses, walk in, walk in pray, Mr. Premium. That's the gentleman's name, isn't it, Moses?

MOSES. Yes sir.

CHARLES. Set chairs, Trip.—Sit down, Mr. Premium.—Glasses, Trip.—Sit down, Moses.—Come, Mr. Premium, I'll give you a sentiment: here's success to usury.—Moses, fill the gentleman a bumper.

MOSES. Success to usury.

CARELESS. Right, Moses, usury is prudence and industry and deserves to succeed.

SIR OLIVER. Then here's all the success it deserves.

CARELESS. No, no, that won't do, Mr. Premium. You have demurred to the toast and must drink it in a pint-bumper.

FIRST GENTLEMAN. A pint bumper at least.

MOSES. Oh pray sir, consider Mr. Premium's a gentleman.

CARELESS. And therefore loves good wine.

SECOND GENTLEMAN. Give Moses a quart-glass; this is mutiny and a high contempt of the chair.

CARELESS. Here now for't. I'll see justice done to the last drop of my bottle.

SIR OLIVER. Nay, pray gentlemen, I did not expect this usage.

CHARLES. No, hang it, Careless, you shan't. Mr. Premium's a stranger.

SIR OLIVER. [*Aside.*] 'Odd, I wish I was well out of their company.

CARELESS. Plague on them, then. If they won't drink, we'll not sit down with them. Come Harry, the dice are in the next room. Charles, you'll join us when you've finished your business with these gentlemen.

(*Exeunt Sir Toby and gentlemen.*)

CHARLES. I will, I will. Careless!

CARELESS. Well.

CHARLES. Perhaps I may want you.

CARELESS. Oh, you know I am always ready; word, note, or bond, 'tis all the same to me. (*Exit.*)

MOSES. Sir, this is Mr. Premium, a gentleman of the strictest honour and secrecy and always performs what he undertakes. Mr. Premium, this is—

CHARLES. Pshaw! Have done.—Sir, my friend Moses is a very honest fellow but a little slow at expression; he'll be an hour giving us our titles. Mr. Premium, the plain state of the matter is this: I am an extravagant young fellow who wants money to borrow; you I take to be a prudent old fellow who has got money to lend. I am blockhead enough to give fifty per cent[1] sooner than not have it, and *you*, I presume, are rogue enough to take an hundred if you can get it. Now sir, you see we are acquainted at once and may proceed to business without any further ceremony.

SIR OLIVER. [*Aside.*] Exceeding frank, upon my word.—I see, sir, you are not a man of many compliments.

CHARLES. Oh no, sir, plain dealing in business I always think best.

SIR OLIVER. Sir, I like you the better for't. However, you are mistaken in one thing: I have no money to lend. But I believe I could procure some of a friend, but then he's an unconscionable dog, isn't he, Moses? and must sell stock to accommodate you, mustn't he, Moses?

MOSES. Yes indeed. You know I always speak the truth and scorn to tell a lie.

[1] *give fifty per cent* I.e., pay 50 per cent interest on the borrowed money.

CHARLES. Right! People that speak the truth generally do.—But these are trifles, Mr. Premium. What, I know money isn't to be bought without paying for't.

SIR OLIVER. Well, but what security could you give? You have no land, I suppose?

CHARLES. Not a mole-hill nor a twig but what's in beau-pots[1] out at the window.

SIR OLIVER. Nor any stock, I presume?

CHARLES. Nothing but livestock, and that's only a few pointers and ponies. But pray, Mr. Premium, are you acquainted at all with any of my connections?

SIR OLIVER. Why to say truth, I am.

CHARLES. Then you must know that I have a devilish rich uncle in the East Indies, Sir Oliver Surface, from whom I have the greatest expectations.

SIR OLIVER. That you have a wealthy uncle, I have heard, but how your expectations will turn out is more, I believe, than you can tell.

CHARLES. Oh no! There can be no doubt; they tell me I'm a prodigious favourite and that he talks of leaving me everything.

SIR OLIVER. Indeed! This is the first I have heard of it.

CHARLES. Yes, yes, 'tis just so. Moses knows 'tis true, don't you, Moses?

MOSES. Oh yes, I'll swear to it.

SIR OLIVER. [*Aside.*] Egad, they'll persuade me presently I'm at Bengal.

CHARLES. Now I propose, Mr. Premium, if it is agreeable to you, to grant you a post-obit on Sir Oliver's life, though at the same time the old fellow has been so liberal to me that I give you my word I should be very sorry to hear anything had happened to him.

SIR OLIVER. Not more than I should, I assure you. But the bond you mention happens to be just the worst security you could offer me, for I might live to an hundred and never recover the principal.

CHARLES. Oh, yes you would, the moment Sir Oliver dies you know you would come on me for the money.

SIR OLIVER. Then I believe I should be the most unwelcome dun you ever had in your life.

CHARLES. What, I suppose you are afraid Sir Oliver is too good a life?

SIR OLIVER. No indeed, I am not though I have heard he is as hale and healthy as any man of his years in Christendom.

CHARLES. There again you are misinformed; no, no, the climate has hurt him considerably. Poor Uncle Oliver! Yes, he breaks apace, I am told, and so much altered lately that his nearest relations would not know him.

SIR OLIVER. No? Ha, ha, ha! So much altered lately that his relations would not know him, ha, ha, ha! That's droll, egad, ha, ha, ha!

CHARLES. Ha, ha, ha! You're glad to hear that, little Premium?

SIR OLIVER. No, no, I am not.

CHARLES. Yes, yes, you are, ha, ha, ha! You know that mends your chance.

SIR OLIVER. But I'm told Sir Oliver is coming over; nay, some say he is actually arrived.

CHARLES. Pshaw! Sure I must know better than you whether he's coming or not; no, no, rely on't, he is at this moment at Calcutta, isn't he, Moses?

MOSES. Yes, certainly.

SIR OLIVER. Very true, as you say, you must know better than I, though I have it from pretty good authority, haven't I, Moses?

MOSES. Yes, most undoubted.

SIR OLIVER. But sir, as I understand you want a few hundreds immediately, is there nothing you would dispose of?

CHARLES. How do you mean?

SIR OLIVER. For instance, now, I have heard that your father left behind him a great quantity of massy old plate.[2]

CHARLES. Oh, Lud! That's gone long ago; Moses can tell you how better than I.

SIR OLIVER. [*Aside.*] Good lack! All the family race-cups and corporation bowls![3]—Then it was also supposed his library was one of the most valuable and complete.

CHARLES. Yes, yes, so it was, vastly too much so for a private gentleman; for my part I was always of a communicative disposition, so I thought it was a shame to keep so much knowledge to myself.

SIR OLIVER. [*Aside.*] Mercy on me! Learning that had run in the family like an heirloom.—Pray, what are become of the books?

[1] *beau-pots* Containers of flowers.

[2] *plate* Silver plate.

[3] *race-cups* Trophies for horse racing; *corporation bowls* Bowls given by the city in recognition of service.

CHARLES. You must inquire of the auctioneer, Master Premium, for I don't believe even Moses can direct you there.

MOSES. I know nothing of books.

SIR OLIVER. So, so, nothing of the family property left, I suppose?

CHARLES. Not much indeed, unless you have a mind to the family pictures. I have got a room full of ancestors above, and if you have taste for old paintings, egad, you shall have them a bargain.

SIR OLIVER. Hey, the devil! Sure you won't sell your forefathers, would you?

CHARLES. Every man of them to the best bidder.

SIR OLIVER. What, your great uncles and aunts?

CHARLES. Yes, and my grandfathers and grandmothers too.

SIR OLIVER. [*Aside.*] Now I give him up.—What the plague, have you no bowels for your kindred? 'Odd's life! Do you take me for Shylock[1] in the play, that you would raise money of me on your own flesh and blood?

CHARLES. Nay, my little broker, don't be angry. What need you care, if you have your money's worth?

SIR OLIVER. Well, I'll be the purchaser; I think I can dispose of the family canvas. [*Aside.*] Oh! I'll never forgive him this—never.

(*Enter Careless.*)

CARELESS. Come Charles, what keeps you?

CHARLES. I can't come yet, i'faith; we are going to have a sale above. Here's little Premium will buy all my ancestors.

CARELESS. Oh, burn your ancestors!

CHARLES. No, he may do that afterwards, if he pleases. Stay, Careless, we want you; egad, you shall be auctioneer, so come along with us.

CARELESS. Oh, have with you, if that's the case; I can handle a hammer as well as a dice-box. A-going, a-going,[2] etcetera.

SIR OLIVER. [*Aside.*] Oh the profligates!

CHARLES. Come, Moses. You shall be appraiser, if we want one.—Gad's life, little Premium, you don't seem to like the business?

SIR OLIVER. Oh, yes, I do vastly, ha, ha! Yes, yes, I think it a rare joke to sell one's family by auction, ha, ha! (*Aside.*) Oh the prodigal!

CHARLES. To be sure! When a man wants money, where the plague should he get assistance if he can't make free with his own relations?

SIR OLIVER. [*Aside.*] I'll never forgive him! Never, never! (*Exeunt.*)

ACT 4, SCENE 1. Picture room at Charles's house.

(*Enter Charles, Sir Oliver, Moses, and Careless.*)

CHARLES. Walk in, gentlemen, walk in pray. Here they are, the family of the Surfaces up to the Conquest.[3]

SIR OLIVER. And in my opinion, a goodly collection.

CHARLES. Aye, aye, they are done in the true spirit of portrait painting, no volunteer grace or expression, not like the works of your modern Raphael,[4] who gives you the strongest resemblance yet contrives to make your own portrait independent of you, so that you may sink the original and not hurt the pictures. No, no, the merit of these is the inveterate likeness: all stiff and awkward as the originals and like nothing in human nature beside.

SIR OLIVER. Ah! We shall never see such figures of men again.

CHARLES. I hope not. Well, you see, Master Premium, what a domestic character I am; here I sit of an evening surrounded by my family. But come, go to your pulpit, Mr. Auctioneer. Here's an old gouty chair[5] of my grandfather's will answer the purpose.

CARELESS. Aye, aye, this will do, but Charles, I have ne'er a hammer, and what's an auctioneer without his hammer?

[1] *Shylock* Moneylender in Shakespeare's *The Merchant of Venice.* In Shakespeare's play, Shylock gives a loan on the condition that, if he is not repaid by a specified time, he is entitled to a pound of flesh from the person who guaranteed the loan.

[2] *A-going, a-going* Auctioneer's call.

[3] *up to the Conquest* I.e., as far back as the eleventh century; the Norman Conquest was in 1066.

[4] *modern Raphael* Phrase Sheridan used elsewhere to refer to his friend Sir Joshua Reynolds (1723–92), an influential portrait painter. Raphael (1483–1520) was a major painter of the Italian Renaissance.

[5] *gouty chair* Chair made for someone with gout.

CHARLES. Egad, that's true. What parchment do we have here? Richard, heir to Thomas[1]—Oh, our genealogy in full.—Here Careless, you shall have no common bit of mahogany; here's the family tree for you, you rogue. This shall be your hammer, and now you may knock down my ancestors with their own pedigree.

SIR OLIVER. [*Aside.*] What an unnatural rogue! An *ex post facto*[2] parricide!

CARELESS. Yes, yes, here's a list of your generation, indeed. 'Faith, Charles, this is the most convenient thing you could have found for the business, for 'twill serve not only as a hammer but a catalogue into the bargain. But come, begin, a-going, a-going, a-going—

CHARLES. Bravo, Careless! Well, here's my great uncle, Sir Richard Raveline,[3] a marvellous good general in his day, I assure you; he served in all the Duke of Marlborough's wars and got that cut over his eye at the Battle of Malplaquet.[4] What say you, Mr. Premium, look at him, there's a hero: not cut out of his feathers as your modern clipped captains are but enveloped in wig and regimentals as a general should be. What do you bid?

SIR OLIVER. (*Aside to Moses.*) Bid him speak.

MOSES. Mr. Premium would have you speak.

CHARLES. Why, then he shall have him for ten pounds, and I'm sure that's not dear for a staff officer.

SIR OLIVER. [*Aside.*] Heaven deliver me! His famous uncle Richard for ten pounds!—Very well, sir, I take him at that.

CHARLES. Careless, knock down my Uncle Richard. Here now is a maiden sister of his, my great aunt Deborah, done by Kneller[5] in his best manner and esteemed a very formidable likeness; there she is, you see, a shepherdess feeding her flock. You shall have her at five pounds ten; the sheep are worth the money.

SIR OLIVER. [*Aside.*] Ah, poor Deborah! A woman who set such a value on herself.—Five pounds ten, she is mine.

CHARLES. Knock down my Aunt Deborah. This now is a grandfather of my mother's, a learned judge, well-known on the western circuit. What do you rate him at, Moses?

MOSES. Four guineas.

CHARLES. Four guineas! Gad's life, you don't bid me the price of his wig.—Mr. Premium, you have more respect for the woolsack.[6] Do let us knock his lordship down at fifteen.

SIR OLIVER. By all means.

CARELESS. Gone.

CHARLES. And there are two brothers of his, William and Walter Blunt, Esquires, both members of Parliament and noted speakers, and what's very extraordinary, I believe this is the first time they were ever bought and sold.

SIR OLIVER. That is very extraordinary indeed! I'll take them at your own price for the honour of Parliament.

CARELESS. Well said, little Premium; I'll knock them down at forty.

CHARLES. Here's a jolly fellow. I don't know what relation, but he was Mayor of Norwich. Take him at eight pounds.

SIR OLIVER. No, no, six will do for the mayor.

CHARLES. Come, make it guineas, and I'll throw you the two aldermen into the bargain.

SIR OLIVER. They are mine.

CHARLES. Careless, knock down the mayor and aldermen. But plague on't, we shall be all day retailing in this manner. Do let us deal wholesale. What say you, Premium, give me three hundred pounds, and take all that remains on each side in the lump.

SIR OLIVER. Well, well, anything to accommodate you; they are mine. But there is one portrait which you have always passed over.

CARELESS. What! That little ill-looking fellow over the settee?

SIR OLIVER. Yes sir, I mean that, though I don't think him so ill-looking a little fellow by any means.

CHARLES. What, that! Oh, that's my Uncle Oliver; 'twas done before he went to India.

CARELESS. Your Uncle Oliver! Gad, then you'll never be friends, Charles. That now to me is as stern a looking

[1] *Richard, heir to Thomas* Reference to the playwright's own family tree—Richard Brinsley Sheridan's father was named Thomas.

[2] *ex post facto* Latin: after the fact.

[3] *Raveline* Suggestive of "ravelin," a form of fortification.

[4] *Battle of Malplaquet* High-casualty battle (1709) in the War of the Spanish Succession (1701–14).

[5] *Kneller* Sir Godfrey Kneller (1646–1723), a painter famous for his portraits of English nobility and prominent intellectuals.

[6] *woolsack* I.e., the office of the Lord Chancellor in the House of Lords; his seat was made of a large sack of wool.

rogue as ever I saw: an unforgiving eye and a damned disinheriting countenance. An inveterate knave, depend on't. Don't you think so, little Premium?

SIR OLIVER. Upon my soul, sir, I do not. I think it as honest a looking face as any in the room, dead or alive.—But I suppose your Uncle Oliver goes with the rest of the lumber.[1]

CHARLES. No, hang it, I'll not part with poor Noll; the old fellow has been very good to me, and egad, I'll keep his picture while I've a room to put it in.

SIR OLIVER. [*Aside.*] The rogue's my nephew after all!—But sir, I have somehow taken a fancy to that picture.

CHARLES. I'm sorry for't, for you certainly will not have it. 'Oons! Haven't you got enough of 'em?

SIR OLIVER. [*Aside.*] I forgive him everything!—But sir, when I take a whim in my head, I don't value money. I'll give you as much for that as for all the rest.

CHARLES. Don't tease me, Master Broker, I tell you I'll not part with it, and there's an end on't.

SIR OLIVER. [*Aside.*] How like his father the dog is. Well, well, I have done. I did perceive it before, but I never saw such a resemblance.—Well sir, here's a draft for the sum.

CHARLES. Why, 'tis for eight hundred pounds.

SIR OLIVER. You will not let Oliver go?

CHARLES. Zounds! No, I tell you once more.

SIR OLIVER. Then never mind the difference; we'll balance another time. But give me your hand on the bargain. You are an honest fellow, Charles. I beg pardon for being so free.—Come, Moses.

CHARLES. [*Aside.*] Egad, this is a whimsical old fellow!—But harkee, Premium, you'll prepare lodgings for these gentlemen?

SIR OLIVER. Yes, yes, I'll send for them in a day or two.

CHARLES. But hold, do now send a genteel conveyance for them, for I assure you they were most of them used to ride in their own carriages.

SIR OLIVER. I will, I will, for all but—Oliver.

CHARLES. Aye, all but the little nabob.[2]

SIR OLIVER. You're fixed!

CHARLES. Peremptorily.

SIR OLIVER. [*Aside.*] A dear extravagant rogue.—Good day. Come, Moses, let me hear now who dares call him profligate.

(*Exeunt Sir Oliver and Moses.*)

CARELESS. Why this is the oddest genius of the sort I ever saw.

CHARLES. Egad, he's the prince of brokers, I think. I wonder how the devil Moses got acquainted with so honest a fellow? But hark! Here's Rowley. Do, Careless, say that I'll join the company in a moment.

CARELESS. I will. But don't now let that old blockhead persuade you to squander any of that money on old musty debts or any such nonsense, for tradesmen, Charles, are the most exorbitant fellows.

CHARLES. Very true, and paying them is only encouraging them.

CARELESS. Nothing else.

CHARLES. Aye, aye, never fear.

(*Exit Careless.*)

So, this was an odd fellow indeed—let me see—two thirds of this, five hundred and thirty odd pounds are mine by right. Fore Heaven, I find one's ancestors are more valuable relations than I took them for! Ladies and gentlemen, your most obedient and very grateful humble servant.

(*Enter Rowley.*)

Hah! Old Rowley, egad, you are just come in time to take leave of your old acquaintance.

ROWLEY. Yes, I heard they were going, but I wonder you can have such spirits under so many distresses.

CHARLES. Why, there's the point: my distresses are so many that I can't afford to part with my spirits. But I shall be rich and splenetic[3] all in good time; however, I suppose that you are surprised that I am not more sorrowful at parting with so many near relations. To be sure, 'tis very affecting, but rot 'em, you see they never move a muscle, so why should I?

[1] *lumber* Household clutter filling up storage space.

[2] *nabob* British person who became rich working for the East India Company, a powerful British trading company that dominated the government of India during the late eighteenth and early nineteenth centuries.

[3] *splenetic* Ill-humored.

ROWLEY. There's no making you serious a moment.

CHARLES. Yes, faith I am so now. Here, my honest Rowley, here, get me this changed directly and take a hundred pounds of it immediately to old Stanley.

ROWLEY. A hundred pounds! Consider only—

CHARLES. Gad's life, don't talk about. Poor Stanley's wants are pressing, and if you don't make haste, we shall have someone call that has a better right to the money.

ROWLEY. Ah! there's the point. I never will cease dunning you with the old proverb—

CHARLES. "Be just before you're generous." Hey! Why, so I would if I could, but justice is an old, lame, hobbling beldam,[1] and I can't get her to keep pace with generosity for the soul of me.

ROWLEY. Yet Charles, believe me, one hour's reflection—

CHARLES. Aye, aye, it is very true, but harkee, Rowley, while I have, by heaven I will give. So damn your economy and now for hazard.

(*Exeunt.*)

ACT 4, SCENE 2. The parlour.

(*Enter Sir Oliver and Moses.*)

MOSES. Well sir, I think, as Sir Peter said, you have seen Mr. Charles in high glory; 'tis great pity he's so extravagant.

SIR OLIVER. True, but he wouldn't sell my picture.

MOSES. And loves wine and women so much.

SIR OLIVER. But he wouldn't sell my picture.

MOSES. And game so deep.

SIR OLIVER. But he wouldn't sell my picture.—Oh, here's Rowley.

(*Enter Rowley.*)

ROWLEY. Oh Sir Oliver, I find you have made a purchase.

SIR OLIVER. Yes, yes, our young rake has parted with his ancestors like old tapestry.

ROWLEY. And here has he commissioned me to redeliver you a part of the purchase money, I mean, though, in your necessitous character of Old Stanley.

MOSES. Ah! There is the pity of all, he's so damned charitable.

ROWLEY. And I left a hosier and two tailors in the hall, who I'm sure won't be paid, and this hundred would satisfy them.

SIR OLIVER. Well, well, I'll pay his debts and his benevolence too. But now I'm no more a broker, and you shall introduce me to the brother as Old Stanley.

ROWLEY. Not yet a while. Sir Peter, I know, means to call there about this time.

(*Enter Trip.*)

TRIP. Oh gentlemen, I beg pardon for not showing you out. This way, gentlemen.—Moses, a word—

(*Exeunt Trip and Moses.*)

SIR OLIVER. There's a fellow for you. Would you believe it, that puppy intercepted the Jew on our coming and wanted to raise money before he got to his master.

ROWLEY. Indeed!

SIR OLIVER. Yes, they are now planning an annuity business. Ah Master Rowley, in my days servants were content with the follies of their masters when they were worn a little threadbare, but now they have their vices like their birthday clothes,[2] with the gloss on.

(*Exeunt.*)

ACT 4, SCENE 3. A library.

(*Enter Joseph Surface and servant.*)

JOSEPH SURFACE. No letter from Lady Teazle?

SERVANT. No sir.

JOSEPH SURFACE. I am surprised she has not sent if she is prevented from coming. Sir Peter certainly does not suspect me, yet I wish I may not lose the heiress through the scrape I have drawn myself in with the wife. However, Charles's imprudence and bad character are great points in my favour.

[1] *beldam* Elderly woman.

[2] *birthday clothes* New, ornate clothing worn by those attending the king's birthday celebrations.

[*Knock within.*]

SERVANT. Sir, I believe that must be Lady Teazle.

JOSEPH SURFACE. Hold! See whether it is or not before you go to the door; I have a particular message for you if it should be my brother.

SERVANT. 'Tis her ladyship, sir, she always leaves her chair at the milliner's in the next street.

JOSEPH SURFACE. Stay, stay, draw that screen before the window; that will do. My opposite neighbour is a maiden lady of a curious temper.

(*Servant draws the screen, and exit.*)

I have a difficult hand to play in this affair. Lady Teazle has lately suspected my views on Maria, but she must by no means be let into that secret, at least till I have her more in my power.

(*Enter Lady Teazle.*)

LADY TEAZLE. What, sentiment in soliloquy! Have you been very impatient now? O Lud, don't pretend to look grave. I vow I couldn't come before.

JOSEPH SURFACE. Oh madam! Punctuality is a species of constancy—very unfashionable quality in a lady.

LADY TEAZLE. Upon my word, you ought to pity me. Do you know that Sir Peter is grown so ill-natured of late and so jealous of Charles too? That's the best of the story, isn't it?

JOSEPH SURFACE. (*Aside.*) I am glad my scandalous friends keep that up.

LADY TEAZLE. I'm sure I wish he would let Maria marry him, and then perhaps he would be convinced. Don't you, Mr. Surface?

JOSEPH SURFACE. (*Aside.*) Indeed I do not.—Oh, certainly I do, for then my dear Lady Teazle would also be convinced how wrong her suspicions were of my having any design on the silly girl.

LADY TEAZLE. Well, well, I'm inclined to believe you, but isn't it provoking to have the most ill-natured things said to one. There is my friend Lady Sneerwell has circulated I don't how many scandalous tales of me—and all without any foundation too. That's what vexes me.

JOSEPH SURFACE. Aye madam, that is the provoking circumstance—without foundation; yes, yes, there's the mortification indeed. For when a scandalous story is believed against one, there certainly is no comfort like the consciousness of having deserved it.

LADY TEAZLE. No, to be sure. Then I'd forgive their malice. But to attack *me*, who am really so innocent and who never says an ill-natured thing of anybody, that is, of my friends—and then Sir Peter too to have him so peevish and so suspicious—when I know the integrity of my own heart—indeed 'tis monstrous.

JOSEPH SURFACE. But my dear Lady Teazle, 'tis your own fault if you suffer it. When a husband entertains a groundless suspicion of his wife and withdraws his confidence from her, the original compact is broke, and she owes it to the honour of her sex to endeavour to outwit him.

LADY TEAZLE. Indeed! So that if he suspects me without cause, it follows that the best way of curing his jealousy is to give him reason for't?

JOSEPH SURFACE. Undoubtedly, for your husband should never be deceived in you, and in that case it becomes *you* to become frail in compliment to his discernment.

LADY TEAZLE. To be sure what you say is very reasonable, and when the consciousness of my own innocence—

JOSEPH SURFACE. Ah, my dear madam, there is the great mistake; 'tis this very conscious innocence that is of the greatest prejudice to you. What is it makes you negligent of forms and careless of the world's opinion? Why, the consciousness of your innocence. What makes you thoughtless in your conduct and apt to run into a thousand little imprudences? Why, the consciousness of your innocence. What makes you impatient of Sir Peter's temper, and outrageous at his suspicions? Why, the consciousness of your own innocence.

LADY TEAZLE. 'Tis very true.

JOSEPH SURFACE. Now my dear Lady Teazle, if you would but once make a trifling faux-pas, you can't conceive how cautious you would grow and how ready to humour and agree with your husband.

LADY TEAZLE. Do you think so?

JOSEPH SURFACE. Oh, I'm sure on't. And then you'd find all scandal would cease at once, for in short, your character at present is like a person in a plethora:[1] absolutely dying of too much health.

LADY TEAZLE. Why, if my understanding were once convinced—

JOSEPH SURFACE. Oh certainly, madam. Your understanding *should* be convinced—yes, yes. Heaven forbid I should persuade you to do anything you thought wrong—no, no. I have too much honour to desire it.

LADY TEAZLE. Don't you think we may as well leave honour out of the argument.

JOSEPH SURFACE. Ah! The ill effects of your country education I see still remain with you.

LADY TEAZLE. I doubt they do, indeed, and I will fairly own to you that, if I could be persuaded to do wrong, it would be Sir Peter's ill usage sooner than your honourable logic after all.

JOSEPH SURFACE. Then by this hand which he is unworthy of—

(*Enter Servant.*)

'Sdeath,[2] you blockhead, what do you want?

SERVANT. I beg pardon, sir, but I thought you wouldn't choose Sir Peter's coming upstairs without announcing him.

JOSEPH SURFACE. Sir Peter, 'oons, and the devil!

LADY TEAZLE. Sir Peter! Oh Lud, I'm ruined! I'm ruined!

SERVANT. Sir, 'twasn't I let him in.

LADY TEAZLE. Oh! I'm undone. What will become of me now, Mr. Logic? Oh mercy, he's on the stairs! I'll get behind here, and if ever I'm so imprudent again! (*Goes behind the screen.*)

JOSEPH SURFACE. Give me a book.

(*Enter Sir Peter.*)

SIR PETER. Aye, ever improving himself.—Mr. Surface! Mr. Surface!

JOSEPH SURFACE. Oh my dear Sir Peter, I beg your pardon, (*Gaping and throwing away the book.*) I have been dozing over a stupid book. Well, I am much obliged to you for this call. You have not been here, I believe, since I fitted up this room. Books, you know, are the only things I am a coxcomb[3] in.

SIR PETER. 'Tis very neat indeed. Well, well, that's proper, and you make even your screen a source of knowledge: hung, I perceive, with maps.

JOSEPH SURFACE. Oh yes, I find great use in that screen.

SIR PETER. I dare say you must, certainly, when you want to find anything in a hurry.

JOSEPH SURFACE. (*Aside.*) Aye, or to hide anything in a hurry either.

SIR PETER. Well, I have a little private business.

JOSEPH SURFACE. You needn't stay.

SERVANT. No sir. (*Exit.*)

JOSEPH SURFACE. Here's a chair, Sir Peter. I beg—

SIR PETER. Well now we are alone, there is a subject, my dear friend, on which I wish to unburden my mind to you, a point of greatest moment to my peace—in short, my good friend, Lady Teazle's conduct of late has made me very unhappy.

JOSEPH SURFACE. Indeed, I am sorry to hear it.

SIR PETER. Yes, 'tis but too plain she has not the least regard for me, but what's worse, I have pretty good authority to suppose that she must have formed an attachment to another.

JOSEPH SURFACE. Indeed! You astonish me!

SIR PETER. Yes, and between ourselves, I think I have discovered the person.

JOSEPH SURFACE. How! You alarm me exceedingly!

SIR PETER. Ah my dear friend, I knew you would sympathize with me!

JOSEPH SURFACE. Yes, believe me, Sir Peter, such a discovery would distress me just as much as it would you.

SIR PETER. I am convinced of it. Ah, it is a happiness to have a friend whom one can trust even with one's family secrets. But have you no guess who I mean?

JOSEPH SURFACE. I haven't the most distant idea. It can't be Sir Benjamin Backbite?

SIR PETER. Oh, no. What say you to Charles?

JOSEPH SURFACE. My brother! Impossible!

SIR PETER. It's very true.

JOSEPH SURFACE. Oh no, Sir Peter, you must not credit the scandalous insinuation you hear. No, no, Charles, to be sure, has been charged many things of this kind, but

[1] *plethora* Sickness thought to be caused by an overabundance of blood.

[2] *'Sdeath* Swear word meaning "God's death."

[3] *coxcomb* Dandy; excessively showy man.

I can never think he could meditate[1] so gross an injury.

SIR PETER. Ah, my dear friend! The goodness of your own heart misleads you; you judge of others by yourself.

JOSEPH SURFACE. Certainly, Sir Peter, the heart that is conscious of its own integrity is ever slow to credit another's baseness.

SIR PETER. True, but your brother has no sentiment; you never hear him talk so.

JOSEPH SURFACE. Yet I can't but think that Lady Teazle herself has too much principle.

SIR PETER. Aye, but what's her principle against the flattery of a handsome, lively, young fellow.

JOSEPH SURFACE. That's very true.

SIR PETER. And then you know the difference of our ages makes it highly improbable that she should have any violent affection for me, and if she were to be frail, and I were to make it public, why the Town would only laugh at me, the foolish old bachelor who had married a girl.

JOSEPH SURFACE. That's true. To be sure, they would laugh.

SIR PETER. Laugh, aye, and make ballads and paragraphs and the devil knows what of me.

JOSEPH SURFACE. No, you must never make it public.

SIR PETER. But then again, that the nephew of my old friend, Sir Oliver, should be the person to do such a wrong hurts one more nearly.

JOSEPH SURFACE. Aye, there's the point: When ingratitude barbs the dart of injury, the wound has double danger in it.

SIR PETER. Aye, I that was in a manner left his guardian, in whose house he has been so often entertained, who never in my life denied him my advice.

JOSEPH SURFACE. Oh 'tis not to be credited. There may be a man capable of such baseness to be sure, but for my part, till you can give me positive proofs, I cannot but doubt it; however, if this should be proved on him, he is no longer a brother of mine. I disclaim kindred with him. For the man who can break through the laws of hospitality and attempt the wife of his friend deserves to be branded as the pest of society.

SIR PETER. What a difference there is between you! What noble sentiments!

JOSEPH SURFACE. Yet I cannot suspect Lady Teazle's honour.

SIR PETER. I am sure I wish to think well of her and to remove all ground of quarrel between us. She has lately reproached me more than once with having made no settlement on her, and in our last quarrel she almost hinted that she would not break her heart if I was dead. Now as we seem to differ in our ideas of expense, I have resolved she shall be her own mistress in that respect for the future, and if I were to die, she shall find that I have not been inattentive to her interests while living. Here, my friend, are the drafts of two deeds which I wish to have your opinion on: by one, she will enjoy eight hundred a year, independent, while I live, and by the other, the bulk of my fortune after my death.

JOSEPH SURFACE. This conduct, Sir Peter, is indeed truly generous! (*Aside.*) I wish it may not corrupt my pupil.

SIR PETER. Yes, I am determined she shall have no cause to complain, though I would not have her acquainted with the latter instance of my affection yet awhile.

JOSEPH SURFACE. [*Aside.*] Nor I, if I could help it.

SIR PETER. And now, my dear friend, if you please, we will talk over the situation of your hopes with Maria.

JOSEPH SURFACE. [*Softly.*] No, no, Sir Peter, another time if you please.

SIR PETER. I am sensibly chagrined at the little progress you seem to make in her affections—

JOSEPH SURFACE. (*Softly.*) I beg you will not mention it, sir. What are my disappointments when your happiness is in debate. [*Aside.*] 'Sdeath, I shall be ruined every way.

SIR PETER. And though you are so averse to my acquainting Lady Teazle with your passion, I am sure she is not your enemy in the affair.

JOSEPH SURFACE. Pray Sir Peter, oblige me—I am really too much affected by the subject we have been talking to bestow a thought on my own concerns. The man who is entrusted with his friend's distresses—can never—Well, sir—

(*Enter Servant.*)

SERVANT. Your brother, sir, is speaking to a gentleman in the street and says he knows you are within.

JOSEPH SURFACE. 'Sdeath! Blockhead, I am not within; I am out for the day.

SIR PETER. Stay, hold, a thought has struck me: you shall be at home.

[1] *meditate* Consider.

JOSEPH SURFACE. Well, well, let him up. (*Exit Servant.*) (*Aside.*) He'll interrupt Sir Peter, however.

SIR PETER. Now my good friend, oblige me, I entreat you: before Charles comes, let me conceal myself somewhere; then do you tax him on the point we have been talking on, and his answers may satisfy me at once.

JOSEPH SURFACE. Oh fie, Sir Peter! Would you have me join in so mean a trick—to trepan[1] my brother too—

SIR PETER. Nay, you tell me you are sure he's innocent; if so, you do him the greatest service in giving him an opportunity to clear himself, and you will set my heart at rest. Come, you shall not refuse me. Here behind this screen will be—Hey! What the devil! There seems to be one listener already. I'll swear I saw a petticoat.

JOSEPH SURFACE. Ha, ha, ha! Well, this is ridiculous enough. I'll tell you, Sir Peter, though I hold a man of intrigue to be a most despicable character, yet you know it does not follow that one is to be an absolute Joseph[2] either. Harkee, 'tis a little French milliner, a silly[3] rogue that plagues me, and having some character, on your coming in she ran behind the screen.

SIR PETER. Ah, you rogue. But egad, she has overheard all I have been saying of my wife.

JOSEPH SURFACE. Oh, 'twill never go any farther, you may depend on't.

SIR PETER. No! Then i'faith, let her hear it out. Here's a closet will do as well.

JOSEPH SURFACE. Well, go in then.

SIR PETER. Sly rogue, sly rogue! (*Goes into the closet.*)

JOSEPH SURFACE. A narrow escape indeed, and a curious situation I am in, to part man and wife in this manner.

LADY TEAZLE. (*Peeping out.*) Couldn't I steal off?

JOSEPH SURFACE. Keep close, my angel.

SIR PETER. (*Peeping out.*) Joseph, tax him home.

JOSEPH SURFACE. Back, my dear friend.

LADY TEAZLE. Couldn't you lock Sir Peter in?

JOSEPH SURFACE. Lie still, my life.

SIR PETER. You are sure the little milliner won't blab?

JOSEPH SURFACE. In, in, my dear Sir Peter. Foregad, I wish I had a key to the door.

(*Enter Charles.*)

CHARLES. Holla, brother! What has been the matter? Your fellow wouldn't let me up at first. What, have you had a Jew or a wench with you?

JOSEPH SURFACE. Neither brother, I assure you.

CHARLES. And what has made Sir Peter steal off? I thought he had been with you.

JOSEPH SURFACE. He was, brother, but hearing you were coming, he did not choose to stay.

CHARLES. What! Was the old gentleman afraid I wanted to borrow money of him?

JOSEPH SURFACE. No, sir. But I am sorry to find, Charles, that you have lately given that worthy man grounds for great uneasiness.

CHARLES. Yes, yes, they tell me I do that to a great many worthy men, but how so pray?

JOSEPH SURFACE. To be plain with you, brother, he thinks you are endeavouring to gain Lady Teazle's affections from him.

CHARLES. Who I? Oh Lud! Not I, upon my word. Ha, ha, ha! So the old fellow has found out that he has got a young wife, has he?

JOSEPH SURFACE. This is no subject to jest upon, brother. He who can laugh—

CHARLES. True, true, as you were going to say—then seriously, I never had the least idea of what you charge me with, upon my honour.

JOSEPH SURFACE. Well, well, it will give Sir Peter great satisfaction to hear it.

CHARLES. To be sure, I once thought the lady seemed to have taken a fancy to me, but upon my soul, I never gave the least encouragement; besides, you know my attachment to Maria.

JOSEPH SURFACE. But sure brother, if Lady Teazle had betrayed the fondest partiality for you—

CHARLES. Why, look ye Joseph, I hope I shall never deliberately do a dishonourable action—but if a pretty woman were purposely to throw herself in my way—and that pretty woman married to a man old enough to be her father—

JOSEPH SURFACE. Well!

CHARLES. Why, I believe I should be obliged to borrow a little of your morality, that's all. But brother, do you know now that you surprise me exceedingly by naming

[1] *trepan* I.e., trick into confessing his behavior.

[2] *Joseph* Biblical figure who is propositioned by his master's wife and refuses her.

[3] *silly* Simple, insignificant.

me with Lady Teazle, for 'faith, I always understood *you* were her favourite.

JOSEPH SURFACE. For shame, Charles, this retort is foolish.

CHARLES. Nay, I swear I have seen you exchange such significant glances.

JOSEPH SURFACE. Nay, nay sir, this is no jest.

CHARLES. Egad, I'm serious, don't you remember one day when I called here—

JOSEPH SURFACE. Nay prithee Charles—

CHARLES. And found you together—

JOSEPH SURFACE. Zounds sir! I insist—

CHARLES. And another time when your servant—

JOSEPH SURFACE. Brother, brother, a word with you. (*Aside.*) Gad I must stop him.

CHARLES. Informed me, I say, that—

JOSEPH SURFACE. Hush! I beg your pardon, but Sir Peter has overheard all we have been saying; I knew you would clear yourself, or I should not have consented.

CHARLES. How! Sir Peter! Where is he?

JOSEPH SURFACE. Softly—there. (*Points to the closet.*)

CHARLES. Oh! 'Fore Heaven, I'll have him out.—Sir Peter, come forth.

JOSEPH SURFACE. No, no.

CHARLES. I say, Sir Peter, come into court. (*Pulls in Sir Peter.*) What, my old guardian! What! Turned inquisitor, and taking evidence incog?[1]

SIR PETER. Give me your hand, Charles, I believe I have suspected you wrongfully. But you mustn't be angry with Joseph—'twas my plan.

CHARLES. Indeed!

SIR PETER. But I acquit you. I promise you, I don't think near so ill of you as I did. What I have heard has given me great satisfaction.

CHARLES. Egad then! 'twas lucky you didn't hear any more.—Wasn't it, Joseph?

SIR PETER. Ah! You would have retorted on him.

CHARLES. Aye, aye, that was a joke.

SIR PETER. Yes, yes, I know his honour too well.

CHARLES. But you might as well have suspected *him* as me in this matter for all that.—Mightn't he, Joseph?

SIR PETER. Well, well, I believe you.

JOSEPH SURFACE. (*Aside.*) I wish they were both well out of the room.

[1] *incog* Incognito.

SIR PETER. And in future perhaps we may not be such strangers.

(*Enter servant who speaks to Joseph Surface.*)

SERVANT. Sir, Lady Sneerwell is below and says she will come up.

JOSEPH SURFACE. (*To the servant.*) Lady Sneerwell—Gad's life! She mustn't come here.—Gentlemen, I beg pardon—I must wait on you downstairs—here is a person come on particular business.

CHARLES. Well, well, you can see him in another room; Sir Peter and I have not met for a long time, and I have something to say to him.

JOSEPH SURFACE. [*Aside.*] They must not be left together. I'll send Lady Sneerwell away directly.—Sir Peter, not a word of the French milliner.

SIR PETER. Oh not for the world!

(*Exit Joseph Surface* [*and servant*].)

Ah Charles, if you associated more with your brother, one might indeed hope for your reformation. He is a man of sentiment. Well, there's nothing so noble as a man of sentiment.

CHARLES. Pshaw, he is too moral by half and so apprehensive of his good name, as he calls it, that I suppose he would as soon let a priest into his house as a wench.

SIR PETER. No, no, come, come, you wrong him. No, no, Joseph is no rake, but he is no such saint in that respect either. (*Aside.*) I have a great mind to tell him; we should have such a laugh.

CHARLES. Oh, hang him! He's a very anchorite—a young hermit!

SIR PETER. Hark ye, you must not abuse him; he may chance to hear of it again, I promise.

CHARLES. Why, you won't tell him?

SIR PETER. No—but—this way—[*Aside.*] Egad, I'll tell him.—Hark ye, have you a mind to have a good laugh against Joseph?

CHARLES. I should like it of all things.

SIR PETER. Then, faith, we will. [*Aside.*] I'll be quit with him for discovering[2] me. (*Whispers.*) He had a girl with him when I called.

[2] *discovering* Revealing.

Performance of *The School for Scandal*, 1778. This engraving shows actors who appeared in the first production of *The School for Scandal*, staged at Drury Lane Theatre in 1777; an inscription below the original image describes "Mrs. Abingdon, Mr. King, Mr. Smith and Mr. Palmer in the Characters of Lady Teazle, Sir Peter Teaszle, Charles and Joseph Surface." The moment depicted is from a well-known portion of the play that is often referred to as the screen scene (Act 4, Scene 3).

Charles. What, Joseph! You jest.

SIR PETER. Hush! A little French milliner—and the best of the jest is—she's in the room now.

CHARLES. The devil she is! (*Looking at the closet.*)

SIR PETER. Hush I tell you! (*Points to the screen.*)

CHARLES. Behind the screen? 'Odd's life! Let us unveil her.

SIR PETER. No, no, he's coming, you shan't indeed.

CHARLES. Oh egad, we'll have a peep at the little milliner!

SIR PETER. No, not for the world—Joseph will never forgive me.

CHARLES. I'll stand by you.

SIR PETER. 'Odd's life! Here he is.

(*Joseph enters as Charles throws down the screen.*)

CHARLES. Lady Teazle, by all that's wonderful!

SIR PETER. Lady Teazle, by all that's damnable!

CHARLES. Sir Peter, this is one of the smartest French milliners I ever saw. Egad, you seem all to have been diverting yourselves at hide and seek. And I don't see who is out of the secret.—Shall I beg your ladyship to inform me? Not a word!—Brother, will you please to explain this matter? What, is morality dumb too?—Sir Peter, though I found you in the dark, perhaps you are not so now. All mute! Well, though I can make nothing of this affair, I suppose you perfectly understand one another, so I shall leave you to yourselves. (*going*) Brother, I am sorry to find you have given that worthy man grounds for so much uneasiness.—Sir Peter, there's nothing in the world so noble as a man of sentiment! (*Exit.*)

JOSEPH SURFACE. Sir Peter, notwithstanding I confess that appearances are against me, if you will afford me your patience, I make no doubt but I shall explain everything to your satisfaction.

SIR PETER. If you please, sir.

JOSEPH SURFACE. The fact is, sir—that Lady Teazle, knowing my pretensions to your ward, Maria—I say, sir, Lady Teazle being apprehensive of the jealousy of your temper and knowing my friendship to the family—she, sir, I say, called here, in order that I might explain those pretensions—but on your coming, being apprehensive as I said of your jealousy—she withdrew—and this, you may depend on't, is the whole truth of the matter.

SIR PETER. A very clear account upon my word, and I dare swear the lady will vouch for every article of it.

LADY TEAZLE. For not one word of it, Sir Peter.

SIR PETER. How! Don't you think it worthwhile to agree in the lie?

LADY TEAZLE. There is not one syllable of truth in what that gentleman has told you.

SIR PETER. I believe you, upon my soul, madam.

JOSEPH SURFACE. 'Sdeath, madam, will you betray me?

LADY TEAZLE. Good Mr. Hypocrite, by your leave, I will speak for myself.

SIR PETER. Aye, let her alone, sir; you'll find she'll make a better story than you without prompting.

LADY TEAZLE. Hear me, Sir Peter, I came hither on no matter relating to your ward and even ignorant of this gentleman's pretensions to her. But I came here seduced by his insidious arguments, at least to listen to his pretended passion, if not to sacrifice your honour to his baseness.

SIR PETER. Now I believe the truth is coming indeed.

JOSEPH SURFACE. The woman's mad.

LADY TEAZLE. No sir, she has recovered her senses, and your own arts have furnished her with the means.—Sir Peter, I do not expect you to credit me, but the tenderness you expressed for me, when I'm sure you could not think I was a witness to it, has penetrated so to my heart that, had I left the place without the shame of the discovery, my future life should have spoken the sincerity of my gratitude. As for that smoothed-tongue hypocrite, who would have seduced the wife of his too credulous friend while he affected honourable addresses to his ward, I behold him now in a light so truly despicable that I never again shall respect myself for having listened to him. (*Exit.*)

JOSEPH SURFACE. Notwithstanding all this, Sir Peter, Heaven knows—

SIR PETER. That you are a villain, and so I leave you to your conscience.

JOSEPH SURFACE. You are too rash, Sir Peter—you shall hear me—the man who shuts out conviction by refusing to—

SIR PETER. Oh, damn your sentiment!

(*Exeunt.*)

ACT 5, SCENE 1. A library.

(*Enter Joseph Surface and servant.*)

JOSEPH SURFACE. Mr. Stanley! and why should you think I would see him? You must know he comes to ask something.

SERVANT. Sir, I should not have let him in, but that Mr. Rowley came to the door with him.

JOSEPH SURFACE. Pshaw! Blockhead! To suppose that I should now be in a temper to receive visits from poor relations! Well, why don't you show the fellow up?

SERVANT. I will, sir. Why sir, it wasn't my fault that Sir Peter discovered my lady. (*Exit.*)

JOSEPH SURFACE. Go, fool. Sure, Fortune never played a man of my policy such a trick before. My character with Sir Peter, my hopes with Maria, destroyed in a moment! I am in a rare humour to listen to other people's distresses! I shan't be able to bestow even a benevolent sentiment on Stanley.—Oh, here he comes, and Rowley with him. I must try to recover myself and put a little charity into my face, however. (*Exit.*)

(*Enter Sir Oliver and Rowley.*)

SIR OLIVER. What, does he avoid us? That was he, was it not?

ROWLEY. It was, sir, but I doubt you are come a little too abruptly. His nerves are so weak that the sight of a poor relation may be too much for him. I should have gone first to break you to him.

SIR OLIVER. A plague of his nerves! Yet this is he whom Sir Peter extols as a man of the most benevolent way of thinking.

ROWLEY. As to his way of thinking, I cannot pretend to decide, for to do him justice, he appears to have as much speculative benevolence as any private gentleman in the kingdom, though he is seldom so sensual as to indulge himself in the exercise of it.

SIR OLIVER. Yet has a string of charitable sentiments, I suppose, at his fingers' ends.

ROWLEY. Or rather at his tongue's end, Sir Oliver, for I believe there is no sentiment he has more faith in than that "Charity begins at home."

SIR OLIVER. And his, I presume, is of that domestic sort,

it never stirs abroad at all.

ROWLEY. I doubt you'll find it so. But he's coming. I must not seem to interrupt you, and you know, immediately as you leave him, I come in to announce your arrival in your real character.

SIR OLIVER. True, and afterwards you'll meet me at Sir Peter's.

ROWLEY. Without losing a moment. (*Exit.*)

SIR OLIVER. So! I don't like the complaisance of his features.

(*Enter Joseph Surface.*)

JOSEPH SURFACE. Sir, I beg you ten thousand pardons for keeping you a moment waiting. Mr. Stanley, I presume?

SIR OLIVER. At your service, sir.

JOSEPH SURFACE. Sir, I beg you will do me the honour to sit down. I entreat you, sir.

SIR OLIVER. Dear sir, there's no occasion. (*Aside.*) Too civil by half.

JOSEPH SURFACE. I have not the pleasure of knowing you, Mr. Stanley, but I am extremely happy to see you look so well. You were nearly related to my mother, Mr. Stanley, I think?

SIR OLIVER. I was, sir, so nearly that my present poverty, I fear, may do discredit to her wealthy children, else I should not have presumed to trouble you.

JOSEPH SURFACE. Dear sir, there needs no apology. He that is in distress, though a stranger, has a right to claim kindred with the wealthy. I'm sure I wish I was of that class and had it in my power to offer you even a small relief.

SIR OLIVER. If your uncle Sir Oliver was here, I should have a friend.

JOSEPH SURFACE. I wish he was, sir, with all my heart. You should not want an advocate with him, believe me Sir.

SIR OLIVER. I should not need one; my distresses would recommend me. But I imagined his bounty had enabled you to become the agent of his charity.

JOSEPH SURFACE. My dear sir, you are strangely misinformed. Sir Oliver is a worthy man, a very worthy sort of a man, but avarice, Mr. Stanley, is the vice of the age. I will tell you, my good sir, in confidence, what he has done for me has been a mere nothing, though people, I know, have thought otherwise, and for my part, I never chose to contradict the report.

SIR OLIVER. What! Has he never transmitted you bullion, rupees, pagodas?[1]

JOSEPH SURFACE. Oh dear sir! Nothing of the kind. No, no, a few presents now and then, china, shawls, congou tea, avadavats, and India crackers,[2] little more, believe me.

SIR OLIVER. [*Aside.*] Here's gratitude for twelve thousand pounds! Avadavats and India crackers!

JOSEPH SURFACE. Then, my dear sir, you have heard, I doubt not, of the extravagance of my brother; there are very few would credit what I have done for that unfortunate young man.

SIR OLIVER. (*Aside.*) Not I, for one.

JOSEPH SURFACE. The sums I have lent him—Indeed I have been exceedingly to blame. It was an amiable weakness; however, I don't pretend to defend it, and now I feel it doubly culpable since it has deprived me of the power of serving you, Mr. Stanley, as my heart directs.

SIR OLIVER. [*Aside.*] Dissembler!—Then, sir, you cannot assist me.

JOSEPH SURFACE. At present it grieves me to say I cannot, but whenever I have the ability, you may depend upon hearing from me.

SIR OLIVER. I am extremely sorry—

JOSEPH SURFACE. Not more than I am, believe me; to pity without the power to relieve is still more painful than to ask and be denied.

SIR OLIVER. Kind sir, your most obedient humble servant.

JOSEPH SURFACE. You leave me deeply affected, Mr. Stanley—William, be ready to open the door.

SIR OLIVER. Oh dear sir, no ceremony!

JOSEPH SURFACE. Your very obedient.

SIR OLIVER. Sir, your most obsequious.

JOSEPH SURFACE. You may depend upon hearing from me, whenever I can be of service.

SIR OLIVER. Sweet sir, you are too good.

JOSEPH SURFACE. In the meantime, I wish you health and spirits.

---

[1] *bullion* Unminted gold or silver; *rupees, pagodas* Indian money.

[2] *congou tea* Chinese black tea; *avadavats* South Asian birds often kept as pets; *India crackers* I.e., firecrackers.

SIR OLIVER. Your ever grateful and perpetual humble servant.

JOSEPH SURFACE. Sir, yours as sincerely.

SIR OLIVER. Now I'm satisfied. (*Exit.*)

JOSEPH SURFACE. This is one of the bad effects of a good character. It invites application from the unfortunate, and there needs no small degree of address to gain the reputation of benevolence without incurring the expense. The silver ore of pure charity is an expensive article in the catalogue of a man's good qualities, whereas the sentimental French plate I use instead of it makes just as good a show and pays no tax.

(*Enter Rowley.*)

ROWLEY. Mr. Surface, your servant. I was apprehensive of interrupting you, though my business demands immediate action, as this note will inform you.

JOSEPH SURFACE. Always happy to see Mr. Rowley. (*Aside.*) A rascal!—How! Sir Oliver Surface, my uncle, arrived!

ROWLEY. He is indeed—we have just parted—quite well after a speedy voyage, and impatient to embrace his worthy nephew.

JOSEPH SURFACE. I am astonished!—William, stop Mr. Stanley if he's not gone.

ROWLEY. Oh he's out of reach, I believe.

JOSEPH SURFACE. Why didn't you let me know this when you came in together?

ROWLEY. I thought you had particular business, but I must be gone to inform your brother and appoint him here to meet his uncle. He will be with you in a quarter of an hour.

JOSEPH SURFACE. So he says. Well, I'm strangely overjoyed at his coming. (*Aside.*) Never was anything, to be sure, so damned unlucky.

ROWLEY. You will be delighted to see how well he looks.

JOSEPH SURFACE. Oh, I am rejoiced to hear it. (*aside*) Just at this time.

ROWLEY. I will tell him how impatient you expect him. (*Exit.*)

JOSEPH SURFACE. Do, do, pray give my best duty and affection.—Indeed, I cannot express the sensations I feel at the thought of seeing him. Certainly his coming just at this time is the cruellest piece of ill fortune.

(*Exit.*)

ACT 5, SCENE 2. Sir Peter Teazle's house.

(*Enter Mrs. Candour and maid.*)

MAID. Indeed, ma'am, my lady will see nobody at present.

MRS. CANDOUR. Did you tell her it was her friend, Mrs. Candour?

MAID. Yes ma'am, but she begs you will excuse her.

MRS. CANDOUR. Do go again. I shall be glad to see her only for a moment, for I'm sure she must be in great distress. (*Exit maid.*) Dear heart, how provoking! I'm not mistress of half the circumstances. We shall have the whole affair in the newspapers with the names of the parties at full length before I have dropped the story at a dozen houses. (*Enter Sir Benjamin Backbite.*) Oh dear, Sir Benjamin! You have heard I suppose—

SIR BENJAMIN. Of Lady Teazle and Mr. Surface.

MRS. CANDOUR. And Sir Peter's discovery.

SIR BENJAMIN. Oh, the strangest piece of business, to be sure!

MRS. CANDOUR. Well, I never was so surprised in my life. I am sorry for all parties indeed!

SIR BENJAMIN. Now, I don't pity Sir Peter at all; he was so extravagantly partial to Mr. Surface.

MRS. CANDOUR. Mr. Surface! Why, 'twas with Charles Lady Teazle was detected.

SIR BENJAMIN. No such thing. Mr. Surface is the gallant.

MRS. CANDOUR. No, no, Charles is the man. 'Twas Mr. Surface brought Sir Peter on purpose to discover them.

SIR BENJAMIN. I tell you I have it from one—

MRS. CANDOUR. And I have it from one—

SIR BENJAMIN. Who had it from one—who had it—

MRS. CANDOUR. From one immediately—but here's Lady Sneerwell; perhaps she knows the whole affair.

(*Enter Lady Sneerwell.*)

LADY SNEERWELL. So my dear Mrs. Candour, here's a sad affair of our friend Teazle.

MRS. CANDOUR. Aye, my dear friend, who could have thought it.

LADY SNEERWELL. Well, there's no trusting to appearances, though indeed she was always too lively for me.

Mrs. Candour. To be sure, her manners were a little too free, but she was very young.

Lady Sneerwell. And had indeed some good qualities.

Mrs. Candour. She had indeed—but have you heard the particulars?

Lady Sneerwell. No, but everybody says that Mr. Surface—

Sir Benjamin. Aye, there I told you, Mr. Surface was the man.

Mrs. Candour. No, no indeed, the assignation was with Charles.

Lady Sneerwell. With Charles! You alarm me, Mrs. Candour.

Mrs. Candour. Yes, yes, he was the lover; Mr. Surface, to do him justice, was only the informer.

Sir Benjamin. Well, I'll not dispute with you, Mrs. Candour. Be it which it may, I hope that Sir Peter's wound will not—

Mrs. Candour. Sir Peter's wound! Oh mercy, I did not hear a word of their fighting.

Lady Sneerwell. Nor I a syllable.

Sir Benjamin. No! What, no mention of the duel!

Mrs. Candour. Not a word.

Sir Benjamin. Oh Lord! Yes, yes, they fought before they left the room.

Lady Sneerwell. Pray, let us hear.

Mrs. Candour. Aye, do oblige us with the duel.

Sir Benjamin. "Sir," says Sir Peter, immediately after the discovery, "you are a most ungrateful fellow"—

Mrs. Candour. Aye, to Charles.

Sir Benjamin. No, no, to Mr. Surface—"a most ungrateful fellow, and old as I am, sir," says he, "I insist on immediate satisfaction."

Mrs. Candour. Aye, that must have been to Charles, for 'tis very unlikely Mr. Surface should go fight in his own house.

Sir Benjamin. Gad's life, madam, not at all—"giving me immediate satisfaction"—on this, madam, Lady Teazle, seeing Sir Peter in such danger, ran out of the room in strong hysterics and Charles after her, calling for hartshorn[1] and water; then madam, they began to fight with swords—

(*Enter Crabtree.*)

Crabtree. With pistols, Nephew, I have it from undoubted authority.

Mrs. Candour. Oh Mr. Crabtree, then it's all true.

Crabtree. Too true indeed, ma'am, and Sir Peter is dangerously wounded.

Sir Benjamin. By a thrust in segoon,[2] quite through his left side.

Crabtree. By a bullet lodged in the thorax.

Mrs. Candour. Mercy on me, poor Sir Peter!

Crabtree. Yes ma'am, though Charles would have avoided the matter if he could.

Mrs. Candour. I knew Charles was the person.

Sir Benjamin. My uncle, I see, knows nothing of the matter.

Crabtree. But Sir Peter taxed him with the basest ingratitude.

Sir Benjamin. That I told you, you know.

Crabtree. Do, Nephew, let me speak—and insisted on immediate satisfaction.

Sir Benjamin. Just as I said.

Crabtree. 'Odd's life! Nephew, allow others to know something too—a pair of pistols lay on the bureau (for Mr. Surface, it seems, had come the night before late from Salt Hill where he had been to see the Montem[3] with a friend who has a son at Eton), so unluckily the pistols were left charged.

Sir Benjamin. I heard nothing of this.

Crabtree. Sir Peter forced Charles to take one, and they fired, it seems, pretty nearly together; Charles's shot took place as I tell you, and Sir Peter's missed. But what is very extraordinary, the ball struck against a little bronze Shakespeare that stood over the chimneypiece, grazed out of the window at a right angle, and wounded the postman, who was just coming to the door with a double letter[4] from Northamptonshire.

Sir Benjamin. My uncle's account is more circumstantial,[5] I must confess—but I believe mine is the true one for all that.

[1] *hartshorn* Smelling salt made from a deer's (hart's) horn.

[2] *segoon* Seconde, a position in fencing.

[3] *Montem* Customary trek in which the students at Eton boys' school walked to Salt Hill, two miles away, requesting money from the people they passed.

[4] *double letter* Two-page letter.

[5] *circumstantial* Detailed.

LADY SNEERWELL. [*Aside*,] I am more interested in this affair than they imagine and must have better information. (*Exit*.)

SIR BENJAMIN. Ah! Lady Sneerwell's alarm is very easily accounted for.

CRABTREE. Yes, yes, they certainly *do* say—but that's neither here nor there.

MRS. CANDOUR. But pray, where is Sir Peter at present?

CRABTREE. Oh, they brought him home, and he is now in the house, though the servants are ordered to deny it.

MRS. CANDOUR. I believe so, and Lady Teazle, I suppose, attending him.

CRABTREE. Yes, yes, I saw one of the Faculty[1] enter just before me.

SIR BENJAMIN. Hey! Who comes here?

CRABTREE. Oh this is he! Physician, depend on't.

MRS. CANDOUR. Oh certainly, it must be the physician—and now we shall know.

(*Enter Sir Oliver*.)

CRABTREE. Well, Doctor, what hopes?

MRS. CANDOUR. Aye Doctor, how's your patient?

SIR BENJAMIN. Now Doctor, isn't it a wound with a small sword?

CRABTREE. A bullet lodged in the thorax, for a hundred.

SIR OLIVER. Doctor! A wound with a small sword and a bullet in the thorax! What, are you mad, good people?

SIR BENJAMIN. Perhaps, sir, you are not a doctor?

SIR OLIVER. Truly, I am to thank you for my degrees if I am.

CRABTREE. Only a friend of Sir Peter's then, I presume. But sir, you must have heard of his accident?

SIR OLIVER. Not a word.

CRABTREE. Not of his being dangerously wounded?

SIR OLIVER. The devil he is!

SIR BENJAMIN. Run through the body!

CRABTREE. Shot in the breast.

SIR BENJAMIN. By one Mr. Surface.

CRABTREE. Aye, by the younger.

SIR OLIVER. Hey! What the plague! You seem to differ strangely in your accounts. However, you agree that Sir Peter is dangerously wounded?

SIR BENJAMIN. Oh yes, we agree in that.

CRABTREE. Yes, yes, I believe there can be no doubt of that.

SIR OLIVER. Then upon my word, for a person in that situation, he is the most imprudent man alive, for here he comes walking as if nothing at all was the matter.

(*Enter Sir Peter*.)

'Odd's heart! Sir Peter, you are come in good time, I promise you, for we had just given you over.

SIR BENJAMIN. Egad Uncle, this is the most sudden recovery—

SIR OLIVER. Why man, what do you do out of your bed, with a small sword through your body and a bullet lodged in your thorax?

SIR PETER. A small sword and a bullet?

SIR OLIVER. Aye, these gentlemen would have killed you without law or physic and wanted to dub me a doctor to make me an accomplice.

SIR PETER. Why, what is all this?

SIR BENJAMIN. We rejoice, Sir Peter, that the story of the duel is not true and are sincerely sorry for your other misfortunes.

SIR PETER. [*Aside*.] So, it's all over the Town already.

CRABTREE. Though, Sir Peter, you were certainly vastly to blame to marry at all at your years.

SIR PETER. What business is that of yours, sir?

MRS. CANDOUR. Though indeed, as Sir Peter made so good a husband, he's very much to be pitied.

SIR PETER. Plague on your pity, ma'am, I desire none of it.

SIR BENJAMIN. However, Sir Peter, you mustn't mind the laughing and jests you will meet with on the occasion.

SIR PETER. Sir, I desire to be master of my own house.

CRABTREE. 'Tis no uncommon case—that's one comfort.

SIR PETER. I insist on being left to myself; without ceremony, I insist on your leaving my house directly.

MRS. CANDOUR. Well, well, we are going—and depend on't, we'll make the best report of you we can.

SIR PETER. Leave my house.

CRABTREE. And tell how hard you have been treated.

SIR PETER. Leave my house.

SIR BENJAMIN. And how patiently you bear it.

[1] *one of the Faculty* I.e., a medical doctor.

SIR PETER. Leave my house—

(*Exeunt Mrs. Candour, Sir Benjamin, and Crabtree.*)

Fiends! Vipers! Furies! Oh that their own venom would choke them.

SIR OLIVER. They are very provoking indeed, Sir Peter.

(*Enter Rowley.*)

ROWLEY. I heard high words. What has ruffled you, Sir Peter?

SIR PETER. Pshaw! What signifies asking? Do I ever pass a day without my vexations?

SIR OLIVER. Well, I'm not inquisitive. I come only to tell you that I have seen both my nephews in the manner we proposed.

SIR PETER. A precious couple they are!

ROWLEY. Yes, and Sir Oliver is convinced that your judgement was right, Sir Peter.

SIR OLIVER. Yes, I find Joseph is indeed the man after all.

ROWLEY. Aye, as Sir Peter says, he's a man of sentiment.

SIR OLIVER. And acts up to the sentiments he professes.

ROWLEY. It's certainly edification to hear him talk!

SIR OLIVER. Oh, he's a model for the young men of the age! But how's this, Sir Peter? You don't join in your friend Joseph's praise, as I expected.

SIR PETER. Sir Oliver, we live in a damned, wicked world, and the fewer we praise, the better.

ROWLEY. What, do you say so, Sir Peter, who never were mistaken in your life?

SIR PETER. Pshaw! Plague on you both. I see by your sneering you have heard the whole affair. I shall go mad among you.

ROWLEY. Then, to fret you no longer, Sir Peter, we are indeed acquainted with it all. I met Lady Teazle coming from Mr. Surface's so humbled that she deigned to request me to be her advocate with you.

SIR PETER. And does Sir Oliver know all too?

SIR OLIVER. Every circumstance.

SIR PETER. What, of the closet—and the screen, hey?

SIR OLIVER. Yes, yes, and the little French milliner! Oh, I have been vastly diverted with the story—ha, ha!

SIR PETER. 'Twas very pleasant.

SIR OLIVER. I never laughed more in my life, I assure you, ha, ha, ha!

SIR PETER. Oh, vastly diverting, ha, ha, ha!

ROWLEY. To be sure, Joseph with his sentiments—ha, ha, ha!

SIR PETER. Yes, yes, his sentiments—ha, ha, ha! A hypocritical villain!

SIR OLIVER. Aye, and that rogue Charles to pull Sir Peter out of the closet—ha, ha, ha!

SIR PETER. Ha, ha!—'twas devilish entertaining, to be sure.

SIR OLIVER. Ha, ha! Egad, Sir Peter, I should like to have seen your face when the screen was thrown down—ha, ha, ha!

SIR PETER. Yes, yes, my face when the screen was thrown down—ha, ha! Oh, I must never show my head again.

SIR OLIVER. But come, come, it isn't fair to laugh at you neither, my old friend, though upon my soul I can't help it.

SIR PETER. Oh pray, don't restrain your mirth on my account; it doesn't hurt me at all. I laugh at the whole affair myself. Yes, yes, I think being a standing jest for all one's acquaintances a very happy situation. Oh yes, and then of a morning to read the paragraphs about Lady T. and Sir P. will be so entertaining. I shall certainly leave town tomorrow and never look mankind in the face again.

ROWLEY. Without affectation, Sir Peter, you may despise the ridicule of fools. But I see Lady Teazle going towards the next room; I am sure you must desire a reconciliation as much as she does.

SIR OLIVER. Perhaps my being here prevents her coming to you. Well, I'll leave honest Rowley to mediate between you—but he must bring you all presently to Mr. Surface's, where I am now returning, if not to reclaim a libertine, at least to expose hypocrisy. (*Exit.*)

SIR PETER. Ah! I'll be present at your discovering yourself there with all my heart, though 'tis a vile, unlucky place for discoveries.

ROWLEY. We'll follow.

SIR PETER. She's not coming here, you see, Rowley.

ROWLEY. No. But she has left the door of that room open, you perceive. She's in tears.

SIR PETER. Certainly a little mortification appears very becoming in a wife. Don't you think 'twill do her good to let her pine a little?

ROWLEY. Oh! This is ungenerous in you.

SIR PETER. Well, I know not what to think. You remember, Rowley, the letter I found of hers evidently intended for Charles.

ROWLEY. Oh mere forgery, Sir Peter, laid in your way on purpose; this is one of the points I intend Snake shall give you conviction on.

SIR PETER. I wish I was once satisfied of that.—She looks this way. What a remarkably elegant turn of the head she has.—Rowley, I'll go to her.

ROWLEY. Certainly.

SIR PETER. Though when 'tis known we are reconciled, people will laugh at me ten times more.

ROWLEY. Let them laugh, and retort their malice only by showing you are happy in spite of it.

SIR PETER. I'faith, so I will, and if I am not mistaken we may be the happiest couple in the country.

ROWLEY. Nay Sir Peter, he who once lays aside suspicion—

SIR PETER. Hold, Master Rowley! If you have any regard for me, never let me hear you utter anything like a sentiment. I have had enough of *them* to serve me the rest of my life.

(*Exeunt.*)

ACT 5, SCENE 3. The library.

(*Enter Joseph Surface and Lady Sneerwell.*)

LADY SNEERWELL. Impossible! Will not Sir Peter immediately be reconciled to Charles and of consequence no longer oppose his union with Maria? The thought is distraction to me.

JOSEPH SURFACE. Can passion furnish a remedy?

LADY SNEERWELL. No, nor cunning either. Oh, I was a fool! an idiot! to league with such a blunderer.

JOSEPH SURFACE. Sure Lady Sneerwell, I am the greatest sufferer, yet you see I bear the accident with calmness.

LADY SNEERWELL. Because the disappointment doesn't reach your heart; your interest only attached you to Maria. Had you felt for her what I have felt for that ungrateful libertine, neither your temper nor hypocrisy could prevent your showing the sharpness of your vexation.

JOSEPH SURFACE. But why should your reproaches fall on me for this disappointment?

LADY SNEERWELL. Are you not the cause of it? What had you to do to bate in your pursuit of Maria, to pervert Lady Teazle by the way? Had you not a sufficient field for your roguery in blinding Sir Peter and supplanting your brother? I hate such an avarice of crimes; 'tis an unfair monopoly and never prospers.

JOSEPH SURFACE. Well, I admit I have been to blame. I confess I have deviated from the direct road of wrong, but I don't think we are so totally defeated either.

LADY SNEERWELL. No?

JOSEPH SURFACE. You tell me you have made a trial of Snake since we met and that you still believe him faithful to us?

LADY SNEERWELL. I do believe so.

JOSEPH SURFACE. And that he has undertaken, should it be necessary, to swear and prove that Charles is at this time contracted by vows and honour to your ladyship, which some of his former letters to you will serve to support.

LADY SNEERWELL. This indeed might have assisted.

JOSEPH SURFACE. Come, come, it is not too late yet.

(*Knocking.*)

But hark! This is probably my uncle, Sir Oliver. Retire to that room and we'll consult farther when he's gone.

LADY SNEERWELL. I have no diffidence of your abilities, only to be constant to one roguery at a time. (*Exit.*)

JOSEPH SURFACE. I will, I will—So, 'tis confounded hard after such bad fortune to be baited by one's confederate in evil. Well, at all events my character is so much better than Charles's that I certainly—Hey! What! This is not Sir Oliver but old Stanley again. Plague on't that he should return to tease me just now. We shall have Sir Oliver come and find him here and—

(*Enter Sir Oliver.*)

Gad's life, Mr. Stanley, you have come back to plague me at this time? You must not stay, upon my word.

SIR OLIVER. Sir, I hear your uncle Sir Oliver is expected here, and though he has been so penurious to you, I'll try what he will do for me.

JOSEPH SURFACE. Sir, 'tis impossible for you to stay now. So I must beg you, come any other time, and I promise you, you shall be assisted.

SIR OLIVER. No. Sir Oliver and I must be acquainted.

JOSEPH SURFACE. Zounds sir, then I insist on your quitting the room directly.

SIR OLIVER. Nay sir—

JOSEPH SURFACE. Sir, I insist on't.—Here William, show this gentleman out.—Since you compel me, sir—not one moment—this is such insolence—

(*Enter Charles.*)

CHARLES. Heyday! What's the matter? What the devil, have you got hold of my little broker here? Zounds, don't hurt little Premium! What's the matter, my little fellow?

JOSEPH SURFACE. So he has been with you too, has he?

CHARLES. To be sure he has. Why, 'tis as honest a little—But sure, Joseph, you have not been borrowing money too, have you?

JOSEPH SURFACE. Borrowing! No. But Brother, you know here we expect Sir Oliver every—

CHARLES. Oh gad! That's true. Noll mustn't find the little broker here, to be sure.

JOSEPH SURFACE. Yet Mr. Stanley insists—

CHARLES. Stanley! Why, his name is Premium.

JOSEPH SURFACE. No, no, Stanley.

CHARLES. No, no, Premium.

JOSEPH SURFACE. Well, no matter which—but—

CHARLES. Aye, aye, Stanley or Premium, 'tis the same thing, as you say, for I suppose he goes by half an hundred names, besides A and B at the coffee house.[1]

(*Knocking.*)

JOSEPH SURFACE. 'Sdeath! Here's Sir Oliver at the door. Now I beg, Mr. Stanley—

CHARLES. Aye, aye, and I beg, Mr. Premium—

SIR OLIVER. Gentlemen—

JOSEPH SURFACE. Sir, by Heaven you shall go.

CHARLES. Aye, out with him certainly.

SIR OLIVER. This violence—

JOSEPH SURFACE. 'Tis your own fault.

CHARLES. Out with him to be sure.

(*Both forcing Sir Oliver out. Enter Sir Peter, Lady Teazle, Maria and Rowley.*)

SIR PETER. My old friend, Sir Oliver, hey! What in the name of wonder! Here are dutiful nephews! assault their uncle at the first visit.

LADY TEAZLE. Indeed, Sir Oliver, 'twas well we came in to rescue you.

ROWLEY. Truly it was, for I perceive, Sir Oliver, the character of Old Stanley was not a protection to you.

SIR OLIVER. No, nor of Premium either: the necessities of the former couldn't extort a shilling from that benevolent gentleman, and with the other I stood a chance of faring worse than my ancestors and being knocked down without being bid for.

JOSEPH SURFACE. Charles!

CHARLES. Joseph!

JOSEPH SURFACE. 'Tis now complete.

CHARLES. Very.

SIR OLIVER. Sir Peter, my friend, and Rowley too, look on that elder nephew of mine. You know what he has already received from my bounty, and you know also how gladly I would have regarded half my fortune as held in trust for him. Judge then my disappointment in discovering him to be destitute of truth, charity, and gratitude.

SIR PETER. Sir Oliver, I should be more surprised at this declaration if I had not myself found him to be selfish, treacherous, and hypocritical.

LADY TEAZLE. And if the gentleman pleads not guilty to these, pray let him call me to his character.

SIR PETER. Then I believe we need add no more. If he knows himself, he will consider it as the most perfect punishment that he is known by the world.

CHARLES. [*Aside.*] If they talk this way to honesty, what will they say to me by and by?

[1] *A and … coffee house* Anonymous newspaper advertisements sometimes gave the advertiser's initials as "A.B." and directed readers to a coffee house where they could respond to the posting.

SIR OLIVER. As for that prodigal his brother there—

CHARLES. [*Aside.*] Aye, now comes my turn—the damned family pictures will ruin me.

JOSEPH SURFACE. Sir Oliver! Uncle! If you will honour me with a hearing.

SIR OLIVER. (*Turns from him with contempt.*) Pshaw!

CHARLES. (*Aside.*) Now if Joseph would make one of his long speeches, I might recollect myself a little.

SIR OLIVER. I suppose you would undertake to justify yourself entirely.

JOSEPH SURFACE. I trust I could.

SIR OLIVER. Pshaw. Nay, if you desert your roguery in its distress and try to be justified, you have even less principle than I thought you had. (*To Charles.*) Well sir, and you could justify yourself too, I suppose.

CHARLES. Not that I know of, Sir.

SIR OLIVER. What, little Premium has been let too much into the secret, I presume.

CHARLES. True, sir, but they were family secrets and should never be mentioned again, you know.

ROWLEY. Come, Sir Oliver, I know you cannot speak of Charles's follies with anger.

SIR OLIVER. 'Odd's heart! No more I can, nor with gravity either.—Sir Peter, do you know the rogue bargained with me for all his ancestors: sold me judges and generals by the foot, and maiden aunts as cheap as broken china.

CHARLES. To be sure, Sir Oliver, I did make free with the family canvas, that's the truth on't; my ancestors may certainly rise in evidence against me, there's no denying. But believe me sincere when I tell you, and upon my soul I would not say it if it was not, that, if I do not appear mortified at the exposure of my follies, it is because I feel at this moment the warmest satisfaction in seeing *you*, my liberal benefactor.

SIR OLIVER. Charles, I believe you, give me your hand: the ill-looking little fellow over the settee has made your peace.

CHARLES. Then sir, my gratitude to the original is still increased.

LADY TEAZLE. Yet I believe, Sir Oliver, there is one whom Charles is still more anxious to be reconciled to.

SIR OLIVER. Oh, I have heard of his attachment there, and with the young lady's pardon, if I construe right that blush—

SIR PETER. Well, child, speak your sentiments.

MARIA. Sir, I have little to say but that I shall rejoice to hear that he is happy; for me, whatever claim I had to his attention, I willingly resign it to one who has a better title.

CHARLES. How Maria!

SIR PETER. Heyday! What's the mystery now? While he appeared an incorrigible rake, you would give your hand to no one else, and now that he's likely to reform, I warrant you won't have him.

MARIA. His own heart and Lady Sneerwell's knows the cause.

CHARLES. Lady Sneerwell!

JOSEPH SURFACE. Brother, it is with great concern I am obliged to speak on this point, but my regard to justice obliges me, and Lady Sneerwell's injuries can no longer be concealed. (*Goes to the door.*)

(*Enter Lady Sneerwell.*)

ALL. Lady Sneerwell!!!

SIR PETER. So! Another French milliner. Egad, he has one in every room in the house, I suppose.

LADY SNEERWELL. Ungrateful Charles! Well may you be surprised and feel for the indelicate situation which your perfidy has forced me into.

CHARLES. Pray, Uncle, is this another plot of yours, for as I have life, I don't understand it.

JOSEPH SURFACE. I believe, sir, there is but the evidence of one person more necessary to make it extremely clear.

SIR PETER. And that person, I imagine, is Mr. Snake.—Rowley, you were perfectly right to bring him with us, and pray let him appear.

ROWLEY. Walk in, Mr. Snake.

(*Enter Snake.*)

I thought his testimony might be wanted; however, it happens unluckily that he comes to confront Lady Sneerwell and not to support her.

LADY SNEERWELL. A villain! treacherous to me at last. Speak fellow, have you conspired against me?

SNAKE. I beg your ladyship ten thousand pardons: You paid me extremely liberally for the lie in question, but I have unfortunately been offered double the sum to speak the truth.

SIR PETER. Plot and counterplot.

LADY SNEERWELL. The torments of shame and disappointment on you all.

LADY TEAZLE. Hold, Lady Sneerwell, before you go, let me thank you for the trouble you and that gentleman have taken in writing letters to me from Charles and answering them yourself. And let me also request you to make my respects to the Scandalous College, of which you are president, and inform them that Lady Teazle, licentiate, begs leave to return the diploma they granted her—as she leaves off practice and kills characters no longer.

LADY SNEERWELL. You too, madam—provoking—insolent—may your husband live these fifty years. (*Exit.*)

LADY TEAZLE. What a malicious creature it is!

SIR PETER. Hey! What, not for her last wish?

LADY TEAZLE. Oh, no.

SIR OLIVER. Well sir, what have you to say now?

JOSEPH SURFACE. Sir, I am so confounded that Lady Sneerwell could be guilty of suborning Mr. Snake in this manner to impose on us all that I know not what to say; however, lest her revengeful spirit should prompt her to injure my brother, I had certainly better follow her directly. (*Exit.*)

SIR PETER. Moral to the last drop.

SIR OLIVER. Aye, and marry her, Joseph, if you can, oil and vinegar, egad you'll do very well together.

ROWLEY. I believe we have no more occasion for Mr. Snake at present.

SNAKE. Before I go, I beg pardon once for all for whatever uneasiness I have been the humble instrument of causing to the parties present.

SIR PETER. Well, well, you have made atonement by a good deed at last.

SNAKE. But I must request of the company that it shall never be known.

SIR PETER. Hey! What the plague, are you ashamed of having done a right thing once in your life.

SNAKE. Ah sir, consider I live by the badness of my character. I have nothing but my infamy to depend on, and if it were once known that I had been betrayed into an honest action, I should lose every friend I have in the world. (*Exit.*)

SIR PETER. Here's a precious rogue.

SIR OLIVER. Well, well, we'll not traduce you by saying any thing to your praise, never fear.

LADY TEAZLE. See, Sir Oliver, there needs no persuasion now to reconcile your nephew and Maria.

SIR OLIVER. Aye, aye, that's as it should be, and egad, we'll have the wedding tomorrow morning.

CHARLES. Thank you, my dear uncle.

SIR PETER. What, you rogue! Don't you ask the girl's consent first?

CHARLES. I have done that a long time—a minute—ago, and she looked—yes.

MARIA. For shame, Charles.—I protest, Sir Peter, there has not been a word.

SIR OLIVER. Well then, the fewer the better. May your love for each other never know abatement.

SIR PETER. And may you live as happily together as Lady Teazle and I—intend to do.

CHARLES. Rowley, my old friend, I am sure you congratulate me, and I suspect that I owe you much.

SIR OLIVER. You do indeed, Charles.

ROWLEY. If my efforts to serve you had not succeeded, you would have been in my debt for the attempt, but deserve to be happy, and you overpay me.

SIR PETER. Aye! Honest Rowley always said you would reform.

CHARLES. Why as to reforming, Sir Peter, I'll make no promises—and that I take to be a proof that I intend to set about it. But here shall be my monitor, my gentle guide. Ah! can I leave the virtuous path those eyes illumine? (*To the audience.*)

For thou, dear maid, shouldst waive thy beauty's sway.
Thou still must rule because I will obey.
An humbled fugitive from folly view—
No sanctuary near but love and you.
You can indeed each anxious fear remove,
For even scandal dies if you approve.

[*Exeunt.*]

THE END.

EPILOGUE

Written by G. Colman,[1] Esq.
Spoken by Mrs. Abington[2]

I, who was late so volatile and gay,
Like a trade-wind must now blow all one way,
Bend all my cares, my studies, and my vows,
To one old rusty weathercock—my spouse!
So wills our virtuous bard—the motley Bayes[3]
Of crying epilogues and laughing plays!
  Old bachelors, who marry smart young wives,
Learn from our play to regulate your lives:
Each bring his dear to town, all faults upon her—
London will prove the very source of honour.
Plunged fairly in, like a cold bath it serves,
When principles relax, to brace the nerves.
  Such is my case—and yet I might deplore
That the gay dream of dissipation's o'er;
And say, ye fair, was ever lively wife,
Born with a genius for the highest life,
Like me untimely blasted in her bloom,
Like me condemned to such a dismal doom?
Save money—when I just knew how to waste it!
Leave London—just as I began to taste it!
Must I then watch the early crowing cock,
The melancholy ticking of a clock;
In the lone rustic hall for ever pounded,
With dogs, cats, rats, and squalling brats surrounded?
With humble curates can I now retire,
(While good Sir Peter boozes with the squire)
And at backgammon mortify my soul,
That pants for loo,[4] or flutters at a vole?[5]
Seven's the main![6] Dear sound!—that must expire,
Lost at hot cockles,[7] round a Christmas fire!
The transient hour of fashion too soon spent,
Farewell the tranquil mind, farewell content!
Farewell the plumèd head, the cushioned tête,[8]
That takes the cushion from its proper seat!
That spirit-stirring drum!—card drums° I mean, *parties*
Spadille—odd trick—pam—basto—king and queen![9]
And you, ye knockers, that, with brazen throat,
The welcome visitors' approach denote;
Farewell! all quality of high renown,
Pride, pomp, and circumstance of glorious town!
Farewell! your revels I partake no more,
And Lady Teazle's occupation's o'er!
All this I told our bard°—he smiled, and said 'twas clear, *playwright*
I ought to play deep tragedy next year.
Meanwhile he drew wise morals from his play,
And in these solemn periods stalked away:—
"Blest were the fair like you; her faults who stopped,
And closed her follies when the curtain dropped!
No more in vice or error to engage,
Or play the fool at large on life's great stage."

—1777

[1] *G. Colman* George Colman the Elder (1732–99), English theater manager and playwright.

[2] *Mrs. Abington* Actress Frances Abington (1737–1815), who appeared in the play's original cast as Lady Teazle.

[3] *Bayes* Playwright. "Bayes" is the name of the playwright character mocked in the Duke of Buckingham's *The Rehearsal* (1671).

[4] *loo* Gambling card game.

[5] *vole* Round of cards in which the same player wins every trick.

[6] *Seven's the main* Phrase that might be spoken by a player of hazard; the choice of main affects what dice rolls win and lose during the caster's turn.

[7] *hot cockles* Unsophisticated game, often played by families at Christmas, in which a player is blindfolded and hit from behind, and must then guess who did it.

[8] *cushioned tête* Padded head; padding was used to add volume to elaborate hairstyles.

[9] *Spadille … king and queen* Terms from popular card games.

Phillis Wheatley

1753 – 1784

Phillis Wheatley was the first author of African descent to publish a book of poetry, *Poems on Various Subjects, Religious and Moral* (London, 1773). During her life she gained an international readership on both sides of the Atlantic. Born in Africa and kidnapped by slave traders when she was six or seven years old, Wheatley was purchased by an evangelical family in Boston who taught her to read. She immersed herself in Biblical and classical traditions and soon taught herself to write, publishing her first poem in a Rhode Island newspaper when she was a young teenager. A deeply religious poet who drew on John Milton and Alexander Pope, Wheatley was praised in her time by Voltaire, Benjamin Franklin, and George Washington. She is best known for writing about her experience of slavery and the slave trade, including the controversial poem "On Being Brought from Africa to America." More recently, scholars have come to recognize and appreciate the wide diversity of Wheatley's work, including elegies, lyrics, hymns, and narrative poems inspired by the Old Testament and Ovid's *Metamorphoses*. Long recognized as the founding author of the African American literary tradition, she is now also considered one of the most important poets of colonial North America.

Wheatley was probably born in 1753 near the West coast of sub-Saharan Africa, although the precise place and date of her birth are unknown. She was brought to Boston in 1761 on the slave ship *Phillis*, after which her new masters, John and Susanna Wheatley, saw fit to name her. She first became famous in 1770 after the transatlantic reprinting of her elegy for George Whitefield, a founder of Methodism who preached frequently in North America and believed in the spiritual equality of Africans. Wheatley soon advertised in Boston for subscriptions to a book of twenty-eight poems but was unable to gather enough support for publication; Great Britain, however, proved friendlier ground. While visiting London with her master's son, Nathaniel, in the summer of 1773, Wheatley helped arrange for her book's publication under the patronage of Selina Hastings, the Countess of Huntingdon, a Methodist leader to whom Whitefield had been personal chaplain. Wheatley was welcomed in London by many prominent historical figures, including Benjamin Franklin, Granville Sharp (the famous abolitionist), the Earl of Dartmouth (for whom Dartmouth College had been named), and Sir Brook Watson, eventual Lord Mayor of London. She wrote effusively of how she had been welcomed in London: "I was received in England with such kindness, complaisance, and so many marks of esteem and real friendship as astonishes me on the reflection." Wheatley soon returned to Boston, however, to care for her ailing mistress.

As a poet, Wheatley was particularly adept at the heroic couplet, the dominant poetic form of the eighteenth century. Her devotion to Protestant Christianity is revealed in elegies that exhort surviving relatives to seek comfort in the glory of salvation. As with Milton before her, Wheatley mingled biblical references with frequent allusions to Greek and Roman myth, often invoking the Muses to her aid. A few meditative poems explore the workings of the mind ("On Recollection," "On Imagination"), while more explicitly political poems such as "To the Right Honourable William, Earl of Dartmouth" display her commitment to freedom and equality. Wheatley's letters to prominent individuals and personal friends—including Obour Tanner, an enslaved black woman living in Newport, Rhode Island—address her religious faith, her transatlantic travels, the sale of her book of poems, and her strident anti-slavery beliefs.

Wheatley's poetry challenged Western culture's racist belief that people of African descent were inferior to whites—even that Africans were less than fully human. Her patrons and publishers rightly assumed that many readers would be incredulous that a slave and native of Africa could have written a volume of poetry. *Poems on Various Subjects* thus includes a preface by Wheatley's master verifying her authorship, and an attestation of her poetic abilities signed by eighteen prominent Bostonians, including Thomas Hutchison, Governor of Massachusetts, and John Hancock, future signer of the Declaration of Independence. The book also contained a frontispiece depicting Wheatley at her writing desk in humble servant's attire. Her poetic achievement remained an important touchstone in debates about race and slavery well into the nineteenth century.

Immediately after *Poems on Various Subjects* was published, many readers expressed outrage that such an accomplished poet was still enslaved. Responding to this pressure, John Wheatley manumitted Phillis in 1773. Throughout the period of the American Revolution she continued to write poems—among them a panegyric to George Washington. The war disrupted the transatlantic network of Methodist patrons that had supported her early career, however, and she never garnered enough support to publish a second book. She married John Peters, a free black man, in 1778, and died in 1784.

Wheatley was later adopted as an icon of the anti-slavery movement when abolitionists in Boston published a new edition of her book in 1834.

⌘⌘⌘

To Maecenas[1]

Maecenas, you, beneath the myrtle shade,
Read o'er what poets sung, and shepherds played.
What felt those poets but you feel the same?
Does not your soul possess the sacred flame?
Their noble strains° your equal genius shares *verses*
In softer language, and diviner airs.

While Homer[2] paints lo! circumfused° *dispersed*
in air,
Celestial Gods in mortal forms appear;
Swift as they move hear each recess rebound,
Heav'n quakes, earth trembles, and the shores resound.
Great Sire of verse, before my mortal eyes,
The lightnings blaze across the vaulted skies,
And, as the thunder shakes the heav'nly plains,
A deep-felt horror thrills through all my veins.
Where gentler strains demand thy graceful song,
The length'ning line moves languishing along.
When great Patroclus courts Achilles'[3] aid,
The grateful tribute of my tears is paid;
Prone on the shore he feels the pangs of love,
And stern Pelides[4] tend'rest passions move.

Great Maro's[5] strain in heav'nly numbers flows,
The Nine[6] inspire, and all the bosom glows.
O could I rival thine and Virgil's page,

[1] *Maecenas* Wealthy Roman patron (d. 8 BCE) and the dedicatee of poems by Horace (56–8 BCE) and Virgil (70–19 BCE), including *The Georgics* (36–29 BCE).

[2] *Homer* Ancient Greek poet, traditionally believed to be the author of the *Iliad* and *Odyssey*. Wheatley read Homer in a popular English translation by Alexander Pope (1688–1744).

[3] *Patroclus* In the *Iliad*, the character who pleads with *Achilles*, the great Greek warrior, to return to battle.

[4] *Pelides* Another name in the *Iliad* for Achilles, the son of Peleus.

[5] *Maro* A common name for Virgil.

[6] *Nine* The Muses, nine goddesses who preside over the arts.

Or claim the Muses with the Mantuan Sage;[1]
Soon the same beauties should my mind adorn,
And the same ardors in my soul should burn:
Then should my song in bolder notes arise,
And all my numbers pleasingly surprize;
But here I sit, and mourn a grov'ling mind,
That fain would mount, and ride upon the wind.

Not you, my friend, these plaintive strains become,
Not you, whose bosom is the Muses home;
When they from tow'ring Helicon[2] retire,
They fan in you the bright immortal fire,
But I less happy, cannot raise the song,
The fault'ring music dies upon my tongue.

The happier Terence[3] all the choir inspir'd,
His soul replenished, and his bosom fir'd;
But say, ye Muses, why this partial grace,
To one alone of Afric's sable race;
From age to age transmitting thus his name
With the first glory in the rolls of fame?

Thy virtues, great Maecenas! shall be sung
In praise of Him, from those virtues sprung:
While blooming wreaths around thy temples spread,
I'll snatch a laurel from thine honoured head,
While you indulgent smile upon the deed.

As long as Thames[4] in streams majestic flows,
Or Naiads[5] in their oozy beds repose,
While Phoebus[6] reigns above the starry train,
While bright Aurora[7] purples o'er the main,
So long, great Sir, the muse thy praise shall sing,
So long thy praise shall make Parnassus[8] ring:
Then grant, Maecenas, thy paternal rays,
Hear me propitious,° and defend my lays. *with favor*
—1773

[1] *Mantuan Sage* Another name for Virgil, born in Mantua.

[2] *Helicon* A mountain sacred to the Muses.

[3] [Wheatley's note] He was an African by birth. [Terence was a dramatist (d. c. 159 BCE) born in Carthage, in North Africa, who lived for a time as a slave in Rome.]

[4] *Thames* The great river that flows through London.

[5] *Naiads* Nymphs dwelling in springs and rivers.

[6] *Phoebus* Apollo, god of the sun.

[7] *Aurora* Goddess of the dawn.

[8] *Parnassus* A sacred mountain in Greece associated with Apollo and the Muses.

To the King's Most Excellent Majesty[9]

Your subjects hope, dread Sire—
The crown upon your brows may flourish long,
And that your arm may in your God be strong!
O may your sceptre num'rous nations sway,
And all with love and readiness obey!

But how shall we the British king reward!
Rule thou in peace, our father, and our lord!
Midst the remembrance of thy favours past,
The meanest peasants most admire the last.[10]
May George, belov'd by all the nations round,
Live with heav'ns choicest constant blessings crown'd!

Great God, direct, and guard him from on high,
And from his head let ev'ry evil fly!
And may each clime with equal gladness see
A monarch's smile can set his subjects free!
—1773 (WRITTEN 1768)

On Being Brought from Africa to America

'Twas mercy brought me from my Pagan land,
Taught my benighted soul to understand
That there's a God, that there's a Saviour too:
Once I redemption neither sought nor knew.
Some view our sable race with scornful eye,
"Their colour is a diabolic die."

[9] *To the King's … Majesty* As Wheatley's note to line 9 indicates, this poem celebrates the repeal by King George III (1738–1820) of the Stamp Act, a controversial measure that taxed printed material (such as newspapers and legal documents) throughout the American colonies. It was repealed in 1766.

[10] [Wheatley's note] The Repeal of the Stamp Act.

Remember, *Christians, Negros,* black as Cain,[1]
May be refined and join th' angelic train.
—1773

To the Right Honourable William, Earl of Dartmouth, His Majesty's Principal Secretary of State for North-America[2]

Hail, happy day, when, smiling like the morn,
Fair Freedom rose, New-England to adorn:
The northern clime beneath her genial ray,
Dartmouth, congratulates thy blissful sway:
Elate with hope her race no longer mourns,
Each soul expands, each grateful bosom burns,
While in thine hand with pleasure we behold
The silken reins, and Freedom's charms unfold.
Long lost to realms beneath the northern skies
She shines supreme, while hated faction dies:
Soon as appeared the Goddess° long desired, *Freedom*
Sick at the view, she° languished and expired; *faction*
Thus from the splendors of the morning light
The owl in sadness seeks the caves of night.

No more, America, in mournful strain
Of wrongs, and grievance unredressed complain,
No longer shall thou dread the iron chain,
Which wanton Tyranny with lawless hand
Had made, and with it meant t' enslave the land.

[1] *Cain* The oldest son of Adam and Eve, who kills his younger brother, Abel, in Genesis 4. As punishment, God exiled Cain from Eden and set a mark of sin upon him. Some in Wheatley's time believed this mark took the form of dark skin, and attempted to justify slavery on the grounds that Africans were descended from Cain.

[2] *William ... North-America* William Legge (1731–1801), Second Earl of Dartmouth, in 1772 appointed Secretary of State for the Colonies by Lord North (1732–92). Dartmouth's support for the repeal of the Stamp Act in 1766 had earned him a favorable reputation among colonists angered by British taxation policies; expectations upon his appointment were therefore high. Wheatley initially wrote this poem at the instigation of Thomas Wooldridge, who suggested Dartmouth's appointment as a subject when he visited the Wheatleys in Boston in October 1772. Wheatley revised the poem for its inclusion in *Poems on Various Subjects*; that is the version printed here.

Should you, my lord, while you peruse my song,
Wonder from whence my love of freedom sprung,
Whence flow these wishes for the common good,
By feeling hearts alone best understood,
I, young in life, by seeming cruel fate
Was snatch'd from Afric's fancy'd happy seat:
What pangs excruciating must molest,° *disturb*
What sorrows labour in my parent's breast?
Steeled° was that soul and by no misery moved *hardened*
That from a father seized his babe belov'd:
Such, such my case.[3] And can I then but pray
Others may never feel tyrannic sway?

For favours past, great Sir, our thanks are due,
And thee we ask thy favours to renew,
Since in thy pow'r, as in thy will before,
To soothe the griefs, which thou did'st once deplore.
May heav'nly grace the sacred sanction° give *blessing*
To all thy works, and thou forever live
Not only on the wings of fleeting fame,
Though praise immortal crowns the patriot's name,
But to conduct to heav'n's refulgent° *radiant*
fane,° *temple*
May fiery coursers° sweep th' ethereal plain, *horses*
And bear thee upwards to that blest abode,
Where, like the prophet, thou shalt find thy God.
—1773

To S.M. a Young African Painter,[4] *on Seeing His Works*

To show the lab'ring bosom's deep intent,
And thought in living characters to paint,
When first thy pencil did those beauties give,
And breathing figures learnt from thee to live,
How did those prospects give my soul delight,
A new creation rushing on my sight?
Still, wond'rous youth! each noble path pursue,
On deathless glories fix thine ardent view:

[3] *Steeled ... my case* Wheatley references being stolen from her father's arms by a stoic slave trader unmoved by his abominable task.

[4] *To S.M. ... African Painter* This poem is addressed to Scipio Moorhead, an enslaved black painter working in Boston in the 1760s and 1770s.

Still may the painter's and the poet's fire
To aid thy pencil, and thy verse conspire![1]
And may the charms of each seraphic° theme *angelic*
Conduct thy footsteps to immortal fame!
High to the blissful wonders of the skies
Elate thy soul, and raise thy wishful eyes.
Thrice happy, when exalted to survey
That splendid city,° crowned with endless day, *heaven*
Whose twice fixed gates on radiant hinges ring:
Celestial Salem[2] blooms in endless spring.

Calm and serene thy moments glide along,
And may the muse inspire each future song!
Still, with the sweets of contemplation bless'd,
May peace with balmy wings your soul invest!
But when these shades of time are chased away,
And darkness ends in everlasting day,
On what seraphic° pinions° shall we move, *angelic / wings*
And view the landscapes in the realms above?
There shall thy tongue in heav'nly murmurs flow,
And there my muse with heav'nly transport glow:
No more to tell of Damon's[3] tender sighs,
Or rising radiance of Aurora's[4] eyes,
For nobler themes demand a nobler strain,° *song*
And purer language on th'ethereal plain.
Cease, gentle muse! the solemn gloom of night
Now seals the fair creation from my sight.
—1773

[1] *To aid … conspire* Wheatley declares that the artist and the poet "conspire," i.e., cooperate with one another, in mutual appreciation.

[2] *Salem* Hebrew for "peace" and another name for the heavenly Jerusalem.

[3] *Damon* Generic name in pastoral poetry for a farmer, dating back to Virgil.

[4] *Aurora* Goddess of the dawn.

A Farewell to America. To Mrs. S.W.[5]

1

Adieu, New-England's smiling meads,° *meadows*
Adieu, the flow'ry plain:
I leave thine op'ning charms, O spring,
And tempt the roaring main.° *sea*

2

In vain for me the flow'rets rise,
And boast their gaudy pride,
While here beneath the northern skies
I mourn for health denied.

3

Celestial maid of rosy hue,[6]
O let me feel thy reign!
I languish till thy face I view,
Thy vanish'd joys regain.

4

Susanna mourns, nor can I bear
To see the crystal show'r,
Or mark the tender falling tear
At sad departure's hour;

5

Not unregarding can I see
Her soul with grief opprest:
But let no sighs, no groans for me,
Steal from her pensive breast.

6

In vain the feather'd warblers sing,
In vain the garden blooms,
And on the bosom of the spring
Breathes out her sweet perfumes

[5] *S.W.* Susanna Wheatley, the poet's mistress. This poem commemorates Wheatley's transatlantic voyage to London, where she traveled both for her health and to oversee the publication of *Poems on Various Subjects,* in which this poem was printed. Susanna Wheatley stayed behind in Boston.

[6] *Celestial … hue* The New England sun.

7

While for Britannia's° distant shore *Great Britain's*
We sweep the liquid plain,
And with astonish'd eyes explore
The wide-extended main.

8

Lo! Health appears! celestial dame!
Complacent and serene,
With Hebe's[1] mantle o'er her Frame,
With soul-delighting mein.° *strength*

9

To mark the vale where London lies
With misty vapours crown'd,
Which cloud Aurora's[2] thousand dyes,° *colors*
And veil her charms around,

10

Why, Phoebus,[3] moves thy car so slow?
So slow thy rising ray?
Give us the famous town to view,
Thou glorious king of day!

11

For thee, Britannia, I resign
New-England's smiling fields
To view again her charms divine,
What joy the prospect yields!

12

But thou! Temptation hence away,
With all thy fatal train° *consequences*
Nor once seduce my soul away,
By thine enchanting strain.° *music*

13

Thrice happy they, whose heav'nly shield
Secures their souls from harms,
And fell temptation on the field defeat
Of all its pow'r disarms!

—1773

---

[1] *Hebe* Greek goddess of youth.

[2] *Aurora* Goddess of the dawn.

[3] *Phoebus* Apollo, god of the sun.

A Funeral Poem on the Death of C.E., An Infant of Twelve Months

Through airy roads he wings his instant flight
To purer regions of celestial light;
Enlarged he sees unnumbered systems roll,
Beneath him sees the universal whole;
Planets on planets run their destined round,
And circling wonders fill the vast profound.
Th'ethereal now, and now th' empyreal skies
With growing splendours strike his wond'ring eyes:
The angels view him with delight unknown,
Press his soft hand, and seat him on the throne;
Then, smiling thus: "To this divine abode,
The seat of saints, of seraphs, and of God,
Thrice welcome thou." The raptured babe replies:
"Thanks to my God, who snatched me to the skies,
Ere vice triumphant had possessed my heart,
Ere yet the tempter had beguiled my heart,
Ere yet on sin's base actions I was bent,
Ere yet I knew temptation's dire intent,
Ere yet the lash for horrid crimes I felt,
Ere vanity had led my way to guilt;
But, soon arrived at my celestial goal,
Full glories rush on my expanding soul."
Joyful he spoke: exulting cherubs round
Clapt their glad wings; the heav'nly vaults resound.

Say, parents, why this unavailing moan?
Why heave your pensive bosoms with the groan?
To Charles, the happy subject of my song,
A brighter world, and nobler strains belong.
Say, would you tear him from the realms above,
By thoughtless wishes and prepost'rous love?
Doth his felicity increase your pain?
Or could you welcome to this world again
The heir of bliss? With a superior air
Methinks he answers with a smile severe,
"Thrones and dominions cannot tempt me there."
But still you cry, "Can we the sigh forbear,
And still and still must we not pour the tear?
Our only hope, more dear than vital breath,
Twelve moons revolved, becomes the prey of death;
Delightful infant, nightly visions give
Thee to our arms, and we with joy receive;

We fain would clasp the phantom to our breast,
The phantom flies, and leaves the soul unblest."

To yon bright regions let your faith ascend;
Prepare to meet your dearest infant friend
In pleasures without measure, without end.
—1773

On the Death of the Rev. Mr. George Whitefield. 1770

Phillis Wheatley revised her poems throughout her career and especially for her 1773 book *Poems on Various Subjects, Religious and Moral.* Many important poems exist in earlier versions, including "To the Right Honourable William, Earl of Dartmouth" and "Farewell to America." Wheatley significantly revised the poem that first brought her transatlantic fame, her elegy for George Whitefield, the Methodist minister. Whitefield toured the American colonies multiple times, delivering sermons outdoors to thousands of people during the Great Awakening of the 1730s and 1740s. He was well known as a philanthropist and advocate for the spiritual equality of black people, although, notably, he was not an abolitionist. Wheatley's elegy circulated as a broadside and was reprinted widely in Britain and North America. Included here are two versions: the first published within weeks of Whitefield's death in 1770, and the later version published in *Poems on Various Subjects*. In the book version, Wheatley's poem is divorced from its initial context to fit with the other poems in the collection: the long headnote from the broadside, included here, was replaced in the book with a brief title and the date of its original publication. Wheatley also shortened the poem by over a dozen lines; made many subtle changes to her language ("Inflame the soul" in line 8, for example, becomes "Inflame the heart"); and cut a passage about the Boston Massacre.

An elegiac poem, on the death of that celebrated divine, and eminent servant of Jesus Christ, the late Reverend, and pious George Whitefield, Chaplain to the Right Honorable the Countess of Huntingdon,[1] *&c. &c., who made his exit from this transitory state, to dwell in the celestial realms of bliss, on Lord's Day, 30th of September, 1770, when he was seized with a fit of the asthma, at Newbury-Port, near Boston, in New England. In which is a condolatory address to his truly noble benefactress, the worthy and pious Lady Huntingdon—and the Orphan-Children in Georgia;*[1] *who, with many thousands, are left, by the death of this great man, to lament the loss of a father, friend, and benefactor.*

By Phillis, a servant girl[2] of 17 years of age, belonging to Mr. J. Wheatley, of Boston:—and has been but 9 years in this country from Africa.

[No break occurs here in the 1773 version; line 16 follows on directly.]

[1] *Countess of Huntingdon* Selina Hastings (1707–91), an evangelical who founded the "Huntingdon Connexion," a group of radical Methodists who broke from the Church of England in 1782. Whitefield was her personal Chaplain at the time of his death.

Hail happy saint on thy immortal throne!
To thee complaints of grievance are unknown;
We hear no more the music of thy tongue,
Thy wonted° auditories° cease to throng. *usual / audiences*
Thy lessons in unequalled° accents flowed! *unparalleled*
While emulation in each bosom glowed;
Thou didst, in strains of eloquence refined,
Inflame the soul, and captivate the mind.
Unhappy we, the setting sun deplore!
Which once was splendid, but it shines no more.
He leaves this earth for Heaven's unmeasured height:
And worlds unknown, receive him from our fight;
There Whitefield wings, with rapid course his way,
And sails to Zion°, through vast seas of day. *heaven, or the promised land*

When his Americans were burdened sore,° *with much suffering*
When streets were crimsoned with their guiltless gore![3]
Unrivaled friendship in his breast now strove:
The fruit thereof was charity and love
Towards America—couldst thou do more
Than leave thy native home, the British shore,
To cross the great Atlantic's wat'ry road,
To see America's distressed abode?
Thy prayers, great saint, and thy incessant cries,
Have pierced the bosom of thy native skies!
Thou moon hast seen, and ye bright stars of light
Have witness been of his requests by night!
He prayed that grace in every heart might dwell:
He longed to see America excel;
He charged its youth to let the grace divine
Arise, and in their future actions shine;
He offered that he did himself receive,
A greater gift not God himself can give:
He urged the need of Him to every one;
It was no less than God's co-equal Son!

Hail, happy saint, on thine immortal throne,
Possesed of glory, life, and bliss unknown;
We hear no more the music of thy tongue,
Thy wonted° auditories° cease to throng. *usual / audiences*
Thy sermons in unequalled° accents flowed, *unparalleled*
And ev'ry bosom with devotion glowed;
Thou didst in strains of eloquence refined
Inflame the heart, and captivate the mind.
Unhappy we the setting sun deplore,
So glorious once, but ah! it shines no more.

Behold the prophet in his tow'ring flight!
He leaves the earth for heav'n's unmeasured height,
And worlds unknown receive him from our fight.
There Whitefield wings with rapid course his way,
And sails to Zion° through vast seas of day. *heaven, or the promised land*

Thy prayers, great saint, and thine incessant cries
Have pierced the bosom of thy native skies.
Thou moon hast seen, and all the stars of light,
How he has wrestled with his God by night.
He prayed that grace in ev'ry heart might dwell,
He longed to see America excel;
He charged its youth that ev'ry grace divine
Should with full lustre in their conduct shine;
That Saviour, which his soul did first receive,
The greatest gift that ev'n a God can give,
He freely offered to the num'rous throng,
That on his lips with list'ning pleasure hung.

---

[1] *Orphan-Children in Georgia* Whitefield founded an orphanage in Bethesda, Georgia, in 1738, and throughout his career solicited funds for its upkeep.

[2] *servant girl* In Boston at this time "servant" was a common euphemism for "slave."

[3] *streets … gore* A reference to the Boston Massacre on 5 March 1770, which Whitefield condemned. British troops fired without orders into a group of civilians, killing three and setting off a firestorm of anti-British sentiment in the colonies.

Take Him ye wretched for your only good;
Take Him ye starving souls to be your food.
Ye thirsty, come to this life giving stream:
Ye preachers, take him for your joyful theme:
Take Him, "my dear Americans," he said,
Be your complaints in his kind bosom laid:
Take Him ye Africans, he longs for you;
Impartial Saviour, is his title due;
If you will choose to walk in grace's road,
You shall be sons, and kings, and priests to God.

Great Countess! We Americans revere
Thy name, and thus condole° thy grief sincere: *sympathize with*
We mourn with thee, that tomb obscurely placed,
In which thy Chaplain undisturbed doth rest.
New England sure, doth feel the orphan's smart;[1]
Reveals the true sensations of his heart:
Since this fair Sun, withdraws his golden rays,
No more to brighten these distressful days!
His lonely Tabernacle, sees no more
A Whitefield landing on the British shore:
Then let us view him in yon azure skies:
Let every mind with this loved object rise.
No more can he exert his lab'ring breath,
Seized by the cruel messenger of death.
What can his dear America return?
But drop a tear upon his happy urn,
Thou tomb, shalt safe retain thy sacred trust,
Till life divine re-animate his dust.
—1770

"Take him, ye wretched, for your only good,
Take him ye starving sinners, for your food;
Ye thirsty, come to this life-giving stream,
Ye preachers, take him for your joyful theme;
Take him my dear Americans, he said,
Be your complaints on his kind bosom laid:
Take him, ye Africans, he longs for you,
Impartial Saviour is his title due:
Washed in the fountain of redeeming blood,
You shall be sons, and kings, and priests to God."

Great Countess,[2] we Americans revere
Thy name, and mingle in thy grief sincere;
New England deeply feels, the Orphans mourn,
Their more than father will no more return.
But, though arrested by the hand of death,
Whitefield no more exerts his lab'ring breath,
Yet let us view him in th' eternal skies,
Let ev'ry heart to this bright vision rise;
While the tomb safe retains its sacred trust,
Till life divine re-animates his dust.
—1773

[1] *smart* Suffering. A reference to the orphanage Whitefield supported in Georgia.

[2] [Wheatley's note] The Countess of Huntingdon, to whom Mr. Whitefield was Chaplain.

IN CONTEXT

Letters Concerning Black or Slave Writers

The authenticity of a collection of poems by a slave was bound to be contested in eighteenth-century England—and even more so in eighteenth-century America. Of the following documents, the first two were the result of the inquisition in Boston that had been convened to judge Wheatley's capability of writing the works in question and were included in the prefatory materials to the first edition of her *Poems* (1773). Among those who praised her work was George Washington, who pronounced Wheatley a person "favored by the Muses, and to whom Nature has been ... liberal and beneficent in her dispensations." Thomas Jefferson was among those unconvinced; eight years later he set out his conclusions on the relative abilities of blacks and whites in *Notes on the State of Virginia*, excerpted below.

Copy of a Letter sent by the Author's Master to the Publisher, Boston [14 November 1772]

Phillis was brought from Africa to America in the Year 1761, between seven and eight years of age. Without any assistance from school education, and by only what she was taught in the family, she, in sixteen months time from her arrival, attained the English language, to which she was an utter stranger before, to such a degree as to read any, the most difficult parts of the sacred writings, to the great astonishment of all who heard her.

As to her writing, her own curiosity led her to it; and this she learnt in so short a time, that in the year 1765, she wrote a letter to the Rev. Mr. Occom, the Indian minister, while in England.

She has a great inclination to learn the Latin tongue, and has made some progress in it.

This relation is given by her master, who bought her, and with whom she now lives.

John Wheatley

from *The Massachusetts Gazette and Boston Post Boy and Advertisers* [21 March 1774][1]

The following is an extract of a letter from Phillis, a negro girl of Mr. Wheatley's of this town, to the Rev. Samson Occom, which we are desired to insert as a specimen of her ingenuity.

Reverend and Honoured Sir,

I have this day received your obliging kind epistle, and am greatly satisfied with your reasons respecting the negroes, and think highly reasonable what you offer in vindication of their natural rights: those that invade them cannot be insensible that the divine light is chasing away the thick darkness which broods over the land of Africa; and the chaos which has reigned so long, is converting into beautiful order, and reveals more and more clearly, the glorious dispensation of civil and religious liberty, which are so inseparably united, that there is little or no enjoyment of one without the other: otherwise, perhaps, the Israelites had been less solicitous for their freedom from Egyptian slavery; I

[1] *21 March 1774* Dated 11 February 1774, this letter was first printed in the *Connecticut Gazette* on 11 March 1774, and thereafter in at least 11 New England papers including *The Massachusetts Gazette and Boston Post Boy and Advertisers* (21 March 1774), which carried the headnote: "The following is an extract of a letter from Phillis, a Negro Girl of Mr. Wheatley's of this Town, to the Rev. Samson Occom, which we are desired to insert as a specimen of her ingenuity."

do not say they would have been contented without it, by no means, for in every human breast, God has implanted a principle, which we call love of freedom; it is impatient of oppression, and pants for deliverance; and by the leave of our modern Egyptians I will assert, that the same principle lives in us. God grants deliverance in his own way and time, and get him honour upon all those whose avarice impels them to countenance and help forward the calamities of their fellow creatures. This I desire not for their hurt, but to convince them of the strange absurdity of their conduct whose words and actions are so diametrically opposite. How well the cry for liberty, and the reverse disposition for the exercise of oppressive power over others agree—I humbly think it does not require the penetration of a philosopher to determine.

from Thomas Jefferson, *Notes on the State of Virginia* [1784]

The first difference[1] which strikes us is that of colour.… [T]he difference is fixed in nature, and is as real as if its seat and cause were better known to us. And is this difference of no importance? Is it not the foundation of a greater or less share of beauty in the two races? Are not the fine mixtures of red and white, the expressions of every passion by greater or less suffusions of colour in the one, preferable to that eternal monotony, which reigns in the countenances, that immoveable veil of black which covers all emotions of the other race? Add to these, flowing hair, a more elegant symmetry of form, their own judgment in favour of the whites, declared by their preference of them, as uniformly as is the preference of the Oranootan for the black women over those of his own species.… Comparing them by their faculties of memory, reason, and imagination, it appears to me, that in memory they are equal to the whites; in reason much inferior, as I think one could scarcely be found capable of tracing and comprehending the investigations of Euclid;[2] and that in imagination they are dull, tasteless, and anomalous. It would be unfair to follow them to Africa for this investigation. We will consider them here, on the same stage with the whites, and where the facts are not apocryphal on which a judgment is to be formed. It will be right to make great allowances for the difference of condition, of education, of conversation, of the sphere in which they move. Many millions of them have been brought to, and born in America. Most of them indeed have been confined to tillage, to their own homes, and their own society: yet many have been so situated, that they might have availed themselves of the conversation of their masters; many have been brought up to the handicraft arts, and from the circumstance have always been associated with the whites.… But never yet could I find that a black had uttered a thought above the level of plain narration; never see even an elementary trait of painting or sculpture. In music they are more generally gifted than the whites with accurate ears for tune and time, and they have been found capable of imagining a small catch.[3] Whether they will be equal to the composition of a more extensive run of melody, or of complicated harmony, is yet to be proved. Misery is often the parent of the most affecting touches of poetry. Among the blacks is misery enough, God knows, but no poetry.

---

[1] *The first difference* I.e., between blacks and whites.

[2] *Euclid* Greek mathematician (fl. 300 BCE).

[3] *catch* Type of guitar.

Reading Poetry

WHAT IS A POEM?

Most of us know what a poem is when we see one. Still, even poets find it difficult to define a poem, or poetry. In a lecture on "The Name and Nature of Poetry" (1933), the English poet A.E. Housman stated that he could "no more define poetry than a terrier can define a rat"; however, he added, "we both recognize the object by the symptoms which it provokes in us." Housman knew he was in the presence of poetry if he experienced a shiver down the spine, or "a constriction of the throat and a precipitation of water to the eyes." Implicit in Housman's response is a recognition that we have to go beyond mere formal characteristics—stanzas, rhymes, rhythms—if we want to know what poetry is, or why it differs from prose. Poetry both represents and *creates* emotions in a highly condensed way. Therefore, any definition of the genre needs to consider, as much as possible, the impact of poetry on us as readers or listeners.

Worth consideration too is the role of the listener or reader not only as passive recipient of a poem, but also as an active participant in its performance. Poetry is among other things the locus for a communicative exchange. A section below deals with the sub-genre of performance poetry, but in a very real sense all poetry is subject to performance. Poems are to be read aloud as well as on the page, and both in sensing meaning and in expressing sound the reader plays a vital role in bringing a poem to life, no matter how long dead its author may be; as W.H. Auden wrote memorably of his fellow poet W.B. Yeats, "the words of a dead man / Are modified in the guts of the living."

For some readers, poetry is, in William Wordsworth's phrase, "the breath and finer spirit of all knowledge" ("Preface" to the *Lyrical Ballads*). They look to poetry for insights into the nature of human experience, and expect elevated thought in carefully wrought language. In contrast, other readers distrust poetry that seems moralistic or didactic. "We hate poetry that has a palpable design upon us," wrote John Keats to his friend J.H. Reynolds; rather, poetry should be "great & unobtrusive, a thing which enters into one's soul, and does not startle it or amaze it with itself but with its subject." The American poet Archibald MacLeish took Keats's idea a step further: in his poem "Ars Poetica" he suggested that "A poem should not mean / But be." MacLeish was not suggesting that a poem should lack meaning, but rather that meaning should inhere in the poem's expressive and sensuous qualities, not in some explicit statement or versified idea.

Whatever we look for in a poem, the infinitude of forms, styles, and subjects that make up the body of literature we call "poetry" is, in the end, impossible to capture in a definition that would satisfy all readers. All we can do, perhaps, is to agree that a poem is a discourse that is characterized by a heightened attention to language, form, and rhythm, by an expressiveness that works through figurative rather than literal modes, and by a capacity to stimulate our imagination and arouse our feelings.

THE LANGUAGE OF POETRY

To speak of "the language of poetry" implies that poets make use of a vocabulary that is somehow different from the language of everyday life. In fact, all language has the capacity to be "poetic," if by poetry we understand a use of language to which some special importance is attached. The ritualistic utterances of religious ceremonies sometimes have this force; so do the skipping rhymes of children in the schoolyard. We can distinguish such uses of language from the kind of writing we find in, say, a computer user's manual: the author of the manual can describe a given function in a variety of ways, whereas the magic of the skipping rhyme can be invoked only by getting the right words in the right order. So with the poet: he or she chooses particular words in a particular order; the *way* the poet speaks is as important to our understanding as what is said. This doesn't mean that an instruction manual couldn't have poetic qualities—indeed, modern poets have created "found" poems from even less likely materials—but it does mean that in poetry there is an intimate relation amongst language, form, and meaning, and that the writer deliberately structures and manipulates language to achieve very particular ends.

THE BEST WORDS IN THE BEST ORDER

Wordsworth provides us with a useful example of the way that poetry can invest quite ordinary words with a high emotional charge:

No motion has she now, no force,
She neither hears nor sees;
Rolled round in earth's diurnal course
With rocks, and stones, and trees.

To paraphrase the content of this stanza from "A Slumber Did My Spirit Seal," "she" is dead and buried. But the language and structures used here give this prosaic idea great impact. For example, the regular iambic meter of the two last lines conveys something of the inexorable motion of the earth and of Lucy embedded in it; the monosyllabic last line is a grim reminder of her oneness with objects in nature; the repeated negatives in the first two lines drive home the irreparable destructiveness of death; the alliteration in the third and fourth lines gives a tangible suggestion of roundness, circularity, repetition in terms of the earth's shape and motion, suggesting a cycle in which death is perhaps followed by renewal. Even the unusual word "diurnal" (which would not have seemed so unusual to Wordsworth's readers) seems "right" in this context; it lends more weight to the notion of the earth's perpetual movement than its mundane synonym "daily" (which, besides, would not scan here). It is difficult to imagine a change of any kind to these lines; they exemplify another attempted definition of poetry, this time by Wordsworth's friend Samuel Taylor Coleridge: "the best words in the best order" (*Table Talk*, 1827).

POETIC DICTION AND THE ELEVATED STYLE

Wordsworth's diction in the "Lucy" poem cited above is a model of clarity; he has chosen language that, in its simplicity and bluntness, conveys the strength of the speaker's feelings far more strongly than an elaborate description of grief in more conventionally "poetic" language might have done. Wordsworth, disturbed by what he felt was a deadness and artificiality in the poetry of his day, sought to "choose incidents and situations from common life" and to describe them in "a selection of language really used by men" ("Preface" to *Lyrical Ballads*). His plan might seem an implicit reproach of the "raised" style, the elevated diction of epic poetry we associate with John Milton's *Paradise Lost*:

Anon out of the earth a fabric huge
Rose like an exhalation, with the sound
Of dulcet symphonies and voices sweet,

Built like a temple, where pilasters round
Were set, and Doric pillars overlaid
With golden architrave; nor did there want
Cornice or frieze, with bossy sculptures graven;
The roof was fretted gold.

(*Paradise Lost* I.710–17)

At first glance this passage, with its Latinate vocabulary and convoluted syntax, might seem guilty of inflated language and pretentiousness. However, Milton's description of the devils' palace in Hell deliberately seeks to distance us from its subject in order to emphasize the scale and sublimity of the spectacle, far removed from ordinary human experience. In other words, language and style in *Paradise Lost* are well adapted to suit a particular purpose, just as they are in "A Slumber Did My Spirit Seal," though on a wholly different scale. Wordsworth criticized the poetry of his day, not because of its elevation, but because the raised style was too often out of touch with its subject; in his view, the words did not bear any significant relation to the "truths" they were attempting to depict.

"PLAIN" LANGUAGE IN POETRY

Since Wordsworth's time, writers have been conscious of a need to narrow the apparent gap between "poetic" language and the language of everyday life. In much of the poetry of the past century, especially free verse, we can observe a growing approximation to speech—even to conversation—in the diction and rhythms of poetry. This may have something to do with the changed role of the poet, who today has discarded the mantle of teacher or prophet that was assumed by poets of earlier times, and who is ready to admit all fields of experience and endeavor as appropriate for poetry. The modern poet looks squarely at life, and can often find a provoking beauty in even the meanest of objects.

We should not assume, however, that a greater concern with the "ordinary," with simplicity, naturalness, and clarity, means a reduction in complexity or suggestiveness. A piece such as Stevie Smith's "Mother, Among the Dustbins," for all the casual and playful domesticity of some of its lines, skillfully evokes a range of emotions and sense impressions defying simple paraphrase.

IMAGERY, SYMBOLISM, AND FIGURES OF SPEECH

The language of poetry is grounded in the objects and phenomena that create sensory impressions. Sometimes the poet renders these impressions quite literally, in a series of *images* that seek to recreate a scene in the reader's mind:

Only a man harrowing clods
In a slow silent walk
With an old horse that stumbles and nods
Half asleep as they stalk.

Only thin smoke without flame
From the heaps of couch-grass;
Yet this will go onward the same
Though Dynasties pass.

Yonder a maid and her wight
Come whispering by:
War's annals will cloud into night
Ere their story die.
(Thomas Hardy, "In Time of 'The Breaking of Nations'")

Here, the objects of everyday life are re-created with sensory details designed to evoke in us the sensations or responses felt by the speaker viewing the scene. At the same time, the writer invests the objects with such significance that the poem's meaning extends beyond the literal to the symbolic: that is, the images come to stand for something much larger than the objects they represent. Hardy's poem moves from the presentation of stark images of rural life to a sense of their timelessness. By the last stanza we see the ploughman, the burning grass, and the maid and her companion as symbols of recurring human actions and motives that defy the struggles and conflicts of history.

IMAGISM

The juxtaposition of clear, forceful images is associated particularly with the Imagist movement that flourished at the beginning of the twentieth century. Its chief representatives (in their early work) were the American poets H.D. and Ezra Pound, who defined an image as "that which represents an intellectual and emotional complex in an instant of time." Pound's two-line poem "In a Station of the Metro" provides a good example of the Imagists' goal of representing emotions or impressions through the use of concentrated images:

The apparition of these faces in the crowd,
Petals on a wet, black bough.

As in a Japanese *haiku*, a form that strongly influenced the Imagists, the poem uses sharp, clear, concrete details to evoke both a sensory impression and the emotion or the atmosphere of the scene. Though the Imagist movement itself lasted only a short time (from about 1912 to 1917), it had a far-reaching influence on modern poets such as T.S. Eliot and William Carlos Williams.

FIGURES OF SPEECH

Imagery often works together with figurative expression to extend and deepen the meaning or impact of a poem. "Figurative" language means language that is metaphorical, not literal or referential. Through "figures of speech" such as metaphor and simile, metonymy, synecdoche, and personification, the writer may alter the ordinary, denotative meanings of words in order to convey greater force and vividness to ideas or impressions, often by showing likenesses between unlike things.

With *simile*, the poet makes an explicit comparison between the subject (called the *tenor*) and another object or idea (known as the *vehicle*), using "as" or "like":

It is a beauteous evening, calm and free,
The holy time is quiet as a Nun
Breathless with adoration. …

In this opening to a sonnet, Wordsworth uses a visual image of a nun in devout prayer to convey in concrete terms the less tangible idea of evening as a "holy time." The comparison also introduces an emotional dimension, conveying something of the feeling that the scene induces in the poet. The simile can thus illuminate and expand meaning in a compact way. The poet may also extend the simile to elaborate at length on any points of likeness.

In *metaphor*, the comparison between tenor and vehicle is implied: connectives such as "like" are omitted, and a kind of identity is created between the subject and the term with which it is being compared. Thus in John Donne's "The Good-Morrow," a lover asserts the endless joy that he and his beloved find in each other:

> My face in thine eye, thine in mine appears,
> And true plain hearts do in the faces rest;
> Where can we find two better hemispheres,
> Without sharp north, without declining west?

Here the lovers are transformed into "hemispheres," each of them a half of the world not subject to the usual natural phenomena of wintry cold ("sharp north") or the coming of night ("declining west"). Thus, they form a perfect world in balance, in which the normal processes of decay or decline have been arrested. Donne renders the abstract idea of a love that defies change in pictorial and physical terms, making it more real and accessible to us. The images here are all the more arresting for the degree of concentration involved; it is not merely the absence of "like" or "as" that gives the metaphor such direct power, but the fusion of distinct images and emotions into a new idea.

Personification is the figure of speech in which the writer endows abstract ideas, inanimate objects, or animals with human characteristics. In other words, it is a type of implied metaphorical comparison in which aspects of a non-human subject are compared to the feelings, appearance, or actions of a human being. In the second stanza of his ode "To Autumn," Keats personifies the concept of autumnal harvesting in the form of a woman, "sitting careless on a granary floor, / Thy hair soft-lifted by the winnowing wind." Personification may also help to create a mood, as when Thomas Gray attributes human feelings to a hooting owl in "Elegy Written in a Country Churchyard"; using such words as "moping" and "complain," Gray invests the bird's cries with the quality of human melancholy:

> … from yonder ivy-mantled tow'r
> The moping owl does to the moon complain
> Of such, as wand'ring near her secret bow'r,
> Molest her ancient solitary reign.

In his book *Modern Painters* (1856), the English critic John Ruskin criticized such attribution of human feelings to objects in nature. Calling this device the "pathetic fallacy," he objected to what he saw as an irrational distortion of reality, producing "a falseness in all our impressions of external things." Modern criticism, with a distrust of any notions of an objective "reality," tends to use Ruskin's term as a neutral label simply to describe instances of extended personification of natural objects.

Apostrophe, which is closely related to personification, has the speaker directly addressing a non-human object or idea as if it were a sentient human listener. Blake's "The Sick Rose," Shelley's "Ode to the West Wind," and his ode "To a Sky-Lark" all employ apostrophe, personifying the object addressed. Keats's "Ode on a Grecian Urn" begins by apostrophizing the urn ("Thou still unravish'd bride of quietness"), then addresses it in a series of questions and reflections through which the speaker attempts to unravel the urn's mysteries.

Apostrophe also appeals to or addresses a person who is absent or dead. W.H. Auden's lament "In Memory of W.B. Yeats" apostrophizes both the earth in which Yeats is to be buried ("Earth, receive an honoured guest") and the dead poet himself ("Follow, poet, follow right / To the bottom of the night ..."). Religious prayers offer an illustration of the usefulness of apostrophe, since they are direct appeals from an earth-bound supplicant to an invisible god. The suggestion of strong emotion associated with such appeals is a common feature of apostrophe in poetry also, especially poetry with a religious theme, like Donne's "Holy Sonnets" (e.g., "Batter My Heart, Three-Personed God").

Metonymy and *synecdoche* are two closely related figures of speech that further illustrate the power of metaphorical language to convey meaning more intensely and vividly than is possible with prosaic statement. *Metonymy* (from the Greek, meaning "change of name") involves referring to an object or concept by substituting the name of another object or concept with which it is usually associated: for example, we might speak of "the Crown" when we mean the monarch, or describe the US executive branch as "the White House." When the writer uses only part of something to signify the whole, or an individual to represent a class, we have an instance of *synecdoche*: T.S. Eliot provides an example in "The Love Song of J. Alfred Prufrock" when a crab is described as "a pair of ragged claws." Similarly, synecdoche is present in Milton's contemptuous term "blind mouths" to describe the "corrupted clergy" he attacks in "Lycidas."

Dylan Thomas employs both metonymy and synecdoche in his poem "The Hand That Signed the Paper":

The hand that signed the paper felled a city;
Five sovereign fingers taxed the breath,
Doubled the globe of dead and halved a country;
These five kings did a king to death.

The mighty hand leads to a sloping shoulder,
The finger joints are cramped with chalk;
A goose's quill has put an end to murder
That put an end to talk.

The hand that signed the treaty bred a fever,
And famine grew, and locusts came;
Great is the hand that holds dominion over
Man by a scribbled name.

The five kings count the dead but do not soften
The crusted wound nor stroke the brow;
A hand rules pity as a hand rules heaven;
Hands have no tears to flow.

The "hand" of the poem is evidently a synecdoche for a great king who enters into treaties with friends and foes to wage wars, conquer kingdoms, and extend his personal power—all at the expense of his suffering subjects. The "goose quill" of the second stanza is a metonymy, standing for the pen used to sign the treaty or the death warrant that brings the war to an end.

Thomas's poem is an excellent example of the power of figurative language, which, by its vividness and concentrated force, can add layers of meaning to a poem, make abstract ideas concrete, and intensify the poem's emotional impact.

THE POEM AS PERFORMANCE: WRITER AND PERSON

Poetry is always dramatic. Sometimes the drama is explicit, as in Robert Browning's monologues, in which we hear the voice of a participant in a dialogue; in "My Last Duchess" we are present as the Duke reflects on the portrait of his late wife for the benefit of a visitor who has come to negotiate on behalf of the woman who is to become the Duke's next wife. Or we listen with amusement and pity as the dying Bishop addresses his venal and unsympathetic sons and tries to bargain with them for a fine burial ("The Bishop Orders His Tomb at St. Praxed's"). In such poems, the notion of a speaking voice is paramount: the speaker is a personage in a play, and the poem a means of conveying plot and character.

Sometimes the drama is less apparent, and takes the form of a plea, or a compliment, or an argument addressed to a silent listener. In Donne's "The Flea" we can infer from the poem the situation that has called it forth: a lover's advances are being rejected by his beloved, and his poem is an argument intended to overcome her reluctance by means of wit and logic. We can see a similar example in Marvell's "To His Coy Mistress": here the very shape of the poem, its three-paragraph structure, corresponds to the stages of the speaker's argument as he presents an apparently irrefutable line of reasoning. Much love poetry has this kind of background as its inspiration; the yearnings or lamentations of the lover are part of an imagined scene, not merely versified reflections about an abstraction called "love."

Meditative or reflective poetry can be dramatic too. Donne's "Holy Sonnets" are pleas from a tormented soul struggling to find its god; Tennyson's "In Memoriam" follows the agonized workings of a mind tracing a path from grief and anger to acceptance and renewed hope.

We should never assume that the speaker, the "I" of the poem, is simply a voice for the writer's own views. The speaker in W.H. Auden's "To an Unknown Citizen," presenting a summary of the dead citizen's life, appears to be an official spokesperson for the society which the citizen served ("Our report on his union"; "Our researchers ..." etc.). The speaker's words are laudatory, yet we perceive immediately that Auden's own views of this society are anything but approving. The speaker seems satisfied with the highly regimented nature of his society, one in which every aspect of the individual's life is under scrutiny and subject to correction. The only things necessary to the happiness of the "Modern Man," it seems, are "A phonograph, a radio, a car, and a frigidaire." The tone here is subtly ironic, an irony created by the gap between the imagined speaker's perception and the real feelings of the writer.

PERFORMANCE POETRY

Poetry began as an oral art, passed on in the form of chants, myths, ballads, and legends recited to an audience of listeners rather than readers. Even today, the dramatic qualities of a poem may extend beyond written text. "Performance poets" combine poetry and stagecraft in presenting their work to live audiences. Dramatic uses of voice, rhythm, body movement, music, and sometimes other visual effects make the "text" of the poem multi-dimensional. For example, Edith Sitwell's poem-sequence *Façade* (1922) was originally set to music: Sitwell read from behind a screen, while a live orchestra played. This performance was designed to enhance the verbal and rhythmic qualities of her poetry:

Beneath the flat and paper sky
The sun, a demon's eye
Glowed through the air, that mask of glass;
All wand'ring sounds that pass

Seemed out of tune, as if the light
Were fiddle-strings pulled tight.
The market-square with spire and bell
Clanged out the hour in Hell.

By performing their poetry, writers can also convey cultural values and traditions. The cultural aspect of performance is central to Black poetry, which originates in a highly oral tradition of folklore and storytelling. From its roots in Africa, this oral tradition has been manifested in the songs and stories of slaves, in spirituals, in the jazz rhythms of the Twenties and the Thirties and in the rebelliousness of reggae and of rap. Even when it remains "on the page," much Black poetry written in the oral tradition has a compelling rhythmic quality. The lines below from Linton Kwesi Johnson's "Mi Revalueshanary Fren," for example, blur the line between spoken poetry and song. Johnson often performs his "dub poetry" against reggae musical backings.

yes, people powa jus a showa evry howa
an evrybady claim dem democratic
but some a wolf an some a sheep
an dat is problematic

The chorus of Johnson's poems, with its constant repetitions, digs deeply into the roots of African song and chant. Its performance qualities become clearer when the poem is read aloud:

Husak
e ad to go
Honnicka
e ad to go
Chowcheskhu
e ad to go
Just like apartied
will av to go

To perform a poem is one way to see and hear poetry as multi-dimensional, cultural, historical, and often also political. Performance is also another way to discover how poetic "meaning" can be constructed in the dynamic relation between speaker and listener.

TONE: THE SPEAKER'S ATTITUDE

In understanding poetry, it is helpful to imagine a poem as having a "voice." The voice may be close to the poet's own, or that of an imagined character, a *persona* adopted by the poet. The tone of the voice will reveal the speaker's attitude to the subject, thus helping to shape our understanding and response. In speech we can indicate our feelings by raising or lowering our voices, and we can accompany words with physical actions. In writing, we must try to convey the tonal inflections of the speaking voice through devices of language and rhythm, through imagery and figures of speech, and through allusions and contrasts.

THE IRONIC TONE

Housman's poem "Terence, This Is Stupid Stuff" offers a useful example of ways in which manipulating tone can reinforce meaning. When Housman, presenting himself in the poem as "Terence," imagines himself to be criticized for writing gloomy poems, his response to his critics takes the form of an ironic alternative: perhaps they should stick to drinking ale:

Oh, many a peer of England brews
Livelier liquor than the Muse,
And malt does more than Milton can
To justify God's ways to man.

The tone here is one of heavy scorn. The speaker is impatient with those who refuse to look at the realities of life and death, and who prefer to take refuge in simple-minded pleasure. The ludicrous comparisons, first between the brewers who have been made peers of England and the classical Muse of poetry, then between malt and Milton, create a sense of disproportion and ironic tension; the explicit allusion to *Paradise Lost* ("To justify God's ways to man") helps to drive home the poet's bitter recognition that his auditors are part of that fallen world depicted by Milton, yet unable or unwilling to acknowledge their harsh condition. The three couplets that follow offer a series of contrasts: in each case, the first line sets up a pleasant expectation and the second dashes it with a blunt reminder of reality:

Ale, man, ale's the stuff to drink
For fellows whom it hurts to think:
Look into the pewter pot
To see the world as the world's not.
And faith, 'tis pleasant till 'tis past:
The mischief is that 'twill not last.

These are all jabs at the "sterling lads" who would prefer to lie in "lovely muck" and not think about the way the world is. Housman's sardonic advice is all the more pointed for its sharp and ironic tone.

POETIC FORMS

In poetry, language is intimately related to form, which is the structuring of words within identifiable patterns. In prose we speak of phrases, sentences, and paragraphs; in poetry, we identify structures by lines, stanzas, or complete forms such as the sonnet or the ode (though poetry in complete or blank verse has paragraphs of variable length, not formal stanzas: see below).

Rightly handled, the form enhances expression and meaning, just as a frame can define and enhance a painting or photograph. Unlike the photo frame, however, form in poetry is an integral part of the whole work. At one end of the scale, the term "form" may describe the *epic*, the lengthy narrative governed by such conventions as division into books, a lofty style, and the interplay between human and supernatural characters. At the other end lies the *epigram*, a witty and pointed saying whose distinguishing characteristic is its brevity, as in Alexander Pope's famous couplet,

I am his Highness' dog at Kew;
Pray tell me sir, whose dog are you?

Between the epic and the epigram lie many other poetic forms, such as the sonnet, the ballad, or the ode. "Form" may also describe stanzaic patterns like *couplets* and *quatrains.*

"FIXED FORM" POEMS

The best-known poetic form is probably the sonnet, the fourteen-line poem inherited from Italy (the word itself is from the Italian *sonetto*, little song or sound). Within those fourteen lines, whether the poet chooses the "Petrarchan" rhyme scheme or the "English" form (see below in the section on "Rhyme"), the challenge is to develop an idea or situation that must find its statement and its resolution within the strict confines of the sonnet frame. Typically, there is an initial idea, description, or statement of feeling, followed by a "turn" in the thought that takes the reader by surprise, or that casts the situation in an unexpected light. Thus in Sonnet 130, "My Mistress' Eyes Are Nothing Like the Sun," William Shakespeare spends the first three quatrains apparently disparaging his lover in a series of unfavorable comparisons—"If snow be white, why then her breasts are dun"—but in the closing couplet his point becomes clear:

And yet, by heaven, I think my love as rare
As any she belied with false compare.

In other words, the speaker's disparaging comparisons have really been parodies of sentimental clichés which falsify reality; his mistress has no need of the exaggerations or distortions of conventional love poetry.

Other foreign forms borrowed and adapted by English-language poets include the *ghazal* and the *pantoum*. The *ghazal*, strongly associated with classical Urdu literature, originated in Persia and Arabia and was brought to the Indian subcontinent in the twelfth century. It consists of a series of couplets held together by a refrain, a simple rhyme scheme (a/a, b/a, c/a, d/a...), and a common rhythm, but only loosely related in theme or subject. Some English-language practitioners of the form have captured the epigrammatic quality of the ghazal, but most do not adhere to the strict pattern of the classical form.

The *pantoum*, based on a Malaysian form, was imported into English poetry via the work of nineteenth-century French poets. Typically it presents a series of quatrains rhyming *abab*, linked by a pattern of repetition in which the second and fourth lines of a quatrain become the first and third lines of the stanza that follows. In the poem's final stanza, the pattern is reversed: the second line repeats the third line of the first stanza, and the last line repeats the poem's opening line, thus creating the effect of a loop.

Similar to the pantoum in the circularity of its structure is the *villanelle*, originally a French form, with five *tercets* and a concluding *quatrain* held together by only two rhymes (aba, aba, aba, aba, aba, abaa) and by a refrain that repeats the first line at lines 6, 12, and 18, while the third line of the first tercet reappears as lines 9, 15, and 19. With its interlocking rhymes and elaborate repetitions, the villanelle can create a variety of tonal effects, ranging from lighthearted parody to the sonorous and earnest exhortation of Dylan Thomas's "Do Not Go Gentle into That Good Night."

STANZAIC FORMS

Recurring formal groupings of lines within a poem are usually described as "stanzas." Both the recurring and the formal aspects of stanzaic forms are important; it is a common misconception to think that any group of lines in a poem, if it is set off by line spaces, constitutes a stanza. If such a group of lines is not patterned as one of a recurring group sharing similar formal characteristics, however, then it may be more appropriate to refer to such irregular groupings in the way we do for prose—as paragraphs. A ballad is typically divided into stanzas; a prose poem or a poem written in free verse, on the other hand, will rarely be divided into stanzas.

A stanza may be identified by the number of lines and the patterns of rhyme repeated in each grouping. One of the simpler traditional forms is the *ballad stanza*, with its alternating four and three-foot lines and its *abcb* rhyme scheme. Drawing on this form's association with medieval ballads and legends, Keats produces the eerie mystery of "La Belle Dame Sans Merci":

I saw pale kings and princes too,
Pale warriors, death-pale were they all;
They cried—"La Belle Dame sans Merci
Hath thee in thrall!"

Such imitations are a form of literary allusion; Keats uses a traditional stanza form to remind us of poems like "Sir Patrick Spens" or "Barbara Allen" to dramatize the painful thralldom of love by placing it within a well-known tradition of ballad narratives with similar forms and themes.

The four-line stanza, or *quatrain*, may be used for a variety of effects: from the elegiac solemnity of Gray's "Elegy Written in a Country Churchyard" to the apparent lightness and simplicity of some of Emily Dickinson's poems. Tennyson used a rhyming quatrain to such good effect in *In Memoriam* that the form he employed (four lines of iambic tetrameter rhyming *abba*) is known as the "In Memoriam stanza."

Other commonly used forms of stanza include the *rhyming couplet*, *terza rima*, *ottava rima*, *rhyme royal*, and the *Spenserian stanza*. Each of these is a rhetorical unit within a longer whole, rather like a paragraph within an essay. The poet's choice among such forms is dictated, at least in part, by the effects that each may produce. Thus the *rhyming couplet* often expresses a complete statement within two lines, creating a sense of density of thought, of coherence and closure; it is particularly effective where the writer wishes to set up contrasts, or to achieve the witty compactness of epigram:

Of all mad creatures, if the learn'd are right,
It is the slaver kills, and not the bite.
A fool quite angry is quite innocent:
Alas! 'tis ten times worse when they repent.

(from Pope, "Epistle to Dr. Arbuthnot")

Ottava rima, as its Italian name implies, is an eight-line stanza, with the rhyme scheme *abababcc*. Like the sonnet, it is long enough to allow the development of a single thought in some detail and complexity, with a concluding couplet that may extend the central idea or cast it in a wholly unexpected light. W.B. Yeats uses this stanza form in "Sailing to Byzantium" and "Among Schoolchildren." Though much used by Renaissance poets, it is particularly associated with George Gordon, Lord Byron's *Don Juan*, in which the poet exploits to the full its potential for devastating irony and bathos. It is long enough to allow the development of a single thought in some detail and complexity; the concluding couplet can then, sonnet-like, turn that thought upon its head, or cast it in a wholly unexpected light:

Sagest of women, even of widows, she
    Resolved that Juan should be quite a paragon,
And worthy of the noblest pedigree
    (His sire was of Castile, his dam from Aragon).
Then for accomplishments of chivalry,
    In case our lord the king should go to war again,
He learned the arts of riding, fencing, gunnery,
And how to scale a fortress—or a nunnery.
(*Don Juan* I.38)

FREE VERSE

Not all writers want the order and symmetry—some might say the restraints and limitations—of traditional forms, and many have turned to *free verse* as a means of liberating their thoughts and feelings. Deriving its name from the French "vers libre" made popular by the French Symbolistes at the end of the nineteenth century, free verse is characterized by irregularity of meter, line length, and rhyme. This does not mean that it is without pattern; rather, it tends to follow more closely than other forms the unforced rhythms and accents of natural speech, making calculated use of spacing, line breaks, and "cadences," the rhythmic units that govern phrasing in speech.

Free verse is not a modern invention. Milton was an early practitioner, as was Blake; however, it was the great modern writers of free verse—first Walt Whitman, then Pound, Eliot, and William Carlos Williams (interestingly, all Americans, at least originally)—who gave this form a fluidity and flexibility that could free the imagination to deal with any kind of feeling or experience. Perhaps because it depends so much more than traditional forms upon the individual intuitions of the poet, it is the form of poetic structure most commonly found today. The best practitioners recognize that free verse, like any other kind of poetry, demands clarity, precision, and a close connection between technique and meaning.

PROSE POETRY

At the furthest extreme from traditional forms lies poetry written in prose. Contradictory as this label may seem, the two have much in common. Prose has at its disposal all the figurative devices available to poetry, such as metaphor, personification, or apostrophe; it may use structuring devices such as verbal repetition or parallel syntactical structures; it can draw on the same tonal range, from pathos to irony. The difference is that prose poetry accomplishes its ends in sentences and paragraphs, rather than lines or stanzas. First given prominence by the French poet Charles Baudelaire (*Petits Poèmes en prose*, 1862), the form is much used to present fragments of heightened sensation, conveyed through vivid or impressionistic description. It draws upon such prosaic forms as journal entries, lists, even footnotes. Prose poetry should be distinguished from "poetic prose," which may be found in a variety of settings (from the King James Bible to the fiction of Jeanette Winterson); the distinction—which not all critics would accept—appears to lie in the writer's intention.

Christan Bök's *Eunoia* is an interesting example of the ways in which a writer of prose poetry may try to balance the demands of each medium. *Eunoia* is an avowedly experimental work in which each chapter is restricted to the use of a single vowel. The text is governed by a series of rules described by the author in an afterword; they include a requirement that all chapters "must allude to the art of writing. All sentences must accent internal rhyme through the use of syntactical parallelism. The text must exhaust the lexicon for each vowel, citing at least 98% of the available repertoire…." Having imposed such constraints upon the language and form of the work, Bök then sets himself the task of showing that "even under such improbable conditions of duress, language can still express an uncanny, if not sublime, thought." The result is a surrealistic narrative that blends poetic and linguistic devices to almost hypnotic effect.

THE POEM AS A MATERIAL OBJECT

Both free verse and prose poetry pay attention in different ways to the poem as a living thing on the printed page. But the way in which poetry is presented in material form is an important part of the existence of almost any form of poetry. In the six volumes of this anthology the material form of the poem is highlighted by the inclusion of a number of facsimile reproductions of poems of other eras in their earliest extant material form.

RHYTHM AND SCANSION

When we read poetry, we often become aware of a pattern of rhythm within a line or set of lines. The formal analysis of that rhythmic pattern, or "meter," is called *scansion.* The verb "to scan" may carry different meanings, depending upon the context: if the *critic* "scans" a line, he or she is attempting to determine the metrical pattern in which it is cast; if the *line* "scans," we are making the observation that the line conforms to particular metrical rules. Whatever the context, the process of scansion is based on the premise that a line of verse is built on a pattern of stresses, a recurring set of more or less regular beats established by the alternation of light and heavy accents in syllables and words. The rhythmic pattern so distinguished in a given poem is said to be the "meter" of that poem. If we find it impossible to identify any specific metrical pattern, the poem is probably an example of free verse.

QUANTITATIVE, SYLLABIC, AND ACCENTUAL-SYLLABIC VERSE

Although we owe much of our terminology for analyzing or describing poetry to the Greeks and Romans, the foundation of our metrical system is quite different from theirs. They measured a line of verse by the duration of sound ("quantity") in each syllable, and by the combination of short and long syllables. Such poetry is known as *quantitative* verse.

Unlike Greek or Latin, English is a heavily accented language. Thus poetry of the Anglo-Saxon period, such as *Beowulf,* was *accentual*: that is, the lines were based on a fixed number of accents, or stresses, regardless of the number of syllables in the line:

Oft Scyld Scefing   sceapena þreatum
monegum maegþum   meodosetla ofteah.

Few modern poets have written in the accentual tradition. A notable exception was Gerard Manley Hopkins, who based his line on a pattern of strong stresses that he called "sprung rhythm." Hopkins experimented with rhythms and stresses that approximate the accentual quality of natural speech; the result is a line that is emphatic, abrupt, even harsh in its forcefulness:

I caught this morning morning's minion, kingdom of daylight's dauphin, dapple-dawn-drawn
Falcon, in his riding
Of the rolling level underneath him steady air ....

(from "The Windhover")

Under the influence of French poetry, following the Norman invasion of the eleventh century, English writers were introduced to *syllabic* prosody: that is, poetry in which the number of syllables is the determining factor in the length of any line, regardless of the number of stresses or their placement. A few modern writers have successfully produced syllabic poetry.

However, the accentual patterns of English, in speech as well as in poetry, were too strongly ingrained to disappear. Instead, the native accentual practice combined with the imported syllabic conventions to produce the *accentual-syllabic* line, in which the writer works with combinations of stressed and unstressed syllables in lines of equal syllabic length. Geoffrey Chaucer was the first great writer to employ the accentual-syllabic line in English poetry:

x / / x x / x /x / x
Ther was also a Nonne, a Prioresse,
x / x /x x / x x /
That of hir smiling was ful simple and coy.
x / x / x / x / x /
Hir gretteste ooth was but by saintè Loy,
x / x / x / x / x / x
And she was clepèd Madame Eglantine.
(from *The Canterbury Tales*)

The fundamental pattern here is the ten-syllable line (although the convention of sounding the final "e" at the end of a line in Middle English verse sometimes produces eleven syllables). Each line contains five stressed syllables, each of which alternates with one or two unstressed syllables. This was to become the predominant meter of poetry in English until the general adoption of free verse in the twentieth century.

IDENTIFYING POETIC METER

Conventionally, meter is established by dividing a line into roughly equal parts, based on the rise and fall of the rhythmic beats. Each of these divisions, conventionally marked by a bar, is known as a "foot," and within the foot there will be a combination of stressed and unstressed syllables, indicated by the prosodic symbols / (stressed) and x (unstressed).

x / x / x / x /
I know | that I | shall meet | my fate
/ x x / x / x /
Somewhere | among | the clouds | above ...
(from Yeats, "An Irish Airman Foresees His Death")

To describe the meter used in a poem, we must first determine what kind of foot predominates, and then count the number of feet in each line. To describe the resultant meter we use terminology borrowed from classical prosody. In identifying the meter of English verse we commonly apply the following labels:

iambic (x /): a foot with one weak stress followed by one strong stress

x / x / x / x / x /
("Look home | ward, Ang | el, now, | and melt | with ruth")

trochaic (/ x): strong followed by weak

/ x / x / x /
("Ty-ger! | Ty-ger! | burning | bright")

anapaestic (x x /): two weak stresses, followed by a strong

x x / x x / x x /
("I have passed | with a nod | of the head")

dactylic (/ x x): strong stress followed by two weak

/ x x / x x /
("Hickory | dickory | dock")

spondaic (/ /): two strong stresses

/ / / x / x / x
("If hate | killed men,| Brother | Lawrence,
/ / / x / x /
God's blood,| would not | mine kill | you?")

We also use classical terms to describe the number of feet in a line. Thus, a line with one foot is *monometer*; with two feet, *dimeter*; three feet, *trimeter*; four feet, *tetrameter*; five feet, *pentameter*; and six feet, *hexameter*.

Scansion of the two lines from Yeats's "Irish Airman" quoted above shows that the predominant foot is iambic (x /), that there are four feet to each line, and that the poem is therefore written in *iambic tetrameters*. The first foot of the second line, however, may be read as a trochee ("Somewhere"); the variation upon the iambic norm here is an example of *substitution*, a means whereby the writer may avoid the monotony that would result from adhering too closely to a set rhythm. We very quickly build up an expectation about the dominant meter of a poem; the poet will sometimes disturb that expectation by changing the beat, and so through substitution create a pleasurable tension in our awareness.

The prevailing meter in English poetry is iambic, since the natural rhythm of spoken English is predominantly iambic. Nonetheless, poets may employ other rhythms where it suits their purpose. Thus W.H. Auden can create a solemn tone by the use of a trochaic meter (/ x):

/ x / x / x /
Earth, receive an honoured guest;
/ x / x / x /
William Yeats is laid to rest:
/ x / x / x /
Let the Irish vessel lie
/ x / x / x x
Emptied of its poetry.

The same meter may be much less funereal, as in Ben Jonson's song "To Celia ":

/ x / x / x /
Come, my Celia, let us prove,
/ x / x / x /
While we may, the sports of love.
/ x / x / x / x
Time will not be ours forever;
/ x / x / x / x
He, at length, our good will sever.

The sense of greater pace in this last example derives in part from the more staccato phrasing, and also from the greater use of monosyllabic words. A more obviously lilting, dancing effect is obtained from anapaestic rhythm (x x /):

x / x x / x x / x x /
I sprang to the stirrup, and Joris, and he;
x / x x / x x / x x /
I galloped, Dirck galloped, we galloped all three.
/ / x x / x x / x x /
"Good speed!" cried the watch, as the gatebolts undrew;
/ / x x / xx / xx /
"Speed!" echoed the wall to us galloping through.
(from Browning, "How They Brought the Good News from Ghent to Aix")

Coleridge wittily captured the varying effects of different meters in "Metrical Feet: Lesson for a Boy," which the poet wrote for his sons, and in which he marked the stresses himself:

/ x / x / x /
Trochee trips from long to short;
x / x / x / x /
From long to long in solemn sort
/ / x / / / x / / x
Slow Spondee stalks; strong foot! yet ill able
/ x x / x x / x x / x x
Ever to come up with Dactyl trisyllable.
x / x / x / x /
Iambics march from short to long:—
x x / x x / x x / x x /
With a leap and a bound the swift Anapaests throng....

A meter which often deals with serious themes is unrhymed iambic pentameter, also known as *blank verse.* This is the meter of Shakespeare's plays, notably his great tragedies; it is the meter, too, of Milton's *Paradise Lost,* to which it lends a desired sonority and magnificence; and of Wordsworth's "Lines Composed a Few Miles above Tintern Abbey," where the flexibility of the meter allows the writer to move by turns from description, to narration, to philosophical reflection.

RHYME, CONSONANCE, ASSONANCE, AND ALLITERATION

Perhaps the most obvious sign of poetic form is rhyme: that is, the repetition of syllables with the same or similar sounds. If the rhyme words are placed at the end of the line, they are known as *end-rhymes.* The opening stanza of Housman's "To an Athlete Dying Young" has two pairs of end-rhymes:

The time you won your town the *race*
We chaired you through the market-*place*;
Man and boy stood cheering *by*,
And home we brought you shoulder-*high*.

Words rhyming within a line are *internal rhymes*, as in the first and third lines of this stanza from Coleridge's "The Rime of the Ancient Mariner":

The fair breeze *blew*, the white foam *flew*
The furrow followed free;
We were the *first* that ever *burst*
Into that silent sea.

When, as is usually the case, the rhyme occurs in a stressed syllable, it is known as a *masculine rhyme*; if the rhyming word ends in an unstressed syllable, it is referred to as *feminine*. The difference is apparent in the opening stanzas of Alfred Tennyson's poem "The Lady of Shalott," where the first stanza establishes the basic iambic meter with strong stresses on the rhyming words:

On either side the river *lie*
Long fields of barley and of *rye*,
That clothe the wold and meet the *sky*;
And through the field the road runs *by*
To many-towered Camelot ...

In the second stanza Tennyson changes to trochaic lines, ending in unstressed syllables and feminine rhymes:

Willows whiten, aspens *quiver*,
Little breezes dusk and *shiver*
Through the wave that runs *forever*
By the island in the *river*
Flowing down to Camelot.

Not only does Tennyson avoid monotony here by his shift to feminine rhymes, he also darkens the mood by using words that imply a contrast with the bright warmth of day—"quiver," "dusk," "shiver"—in preparation for the introduction of the "silent isle" that embowers the Lady.

NEAR RHYMES

Most of the rhymes in "The Lady of Shalott" are exact, or "*perfect*" rhymes. However, in the second of the stanzas just quoted, it is evident that "forever" at the end of the third line is not a "perfect" rhyme; rather, it is an instance of "*near*" or "*slant*" rhyme. Such "*imperfect*" rhymes are quite deliberate; indeed, two stanzas later we find the rhyming sequence "early," "barley," "cheerly," and "clearly," followed by the rhymes "weary," "airy," and "fairy." As with the introduction of feminine rhymes, such divergences from one dominant pattern prevent monotony and avoid a too-mechanical sing-song effect.

More importantly, near-rhymes have an oddly unsettling effect, perhaps because they both raise and frustrate our expectation of a perfect rhyme. Their use certainly gives added emphasis to the words at the end of these chilling lines from Wilfred Owen's "Strange Meeting":

For by my glee might many men have laughed,
And of my weeping something had been left,
Which must die now. I mean the truth untold,
The pity of war, the pity war distilled.
Now men will go content with what we spoiled,
Or, discontent, boil bloody, and be spilled.

CONSONANCE AND ASSONANCE

In Owen's poem, the near-rhymes "laughed / left" and "spoiled / spilled" are good examples of *consonance*, which pairs words with similar consonants but different intervening vowels. Other examples from Owen's poem include "groined / groaned," "hall / Hell," "years / yours," and "mystery / mastery."

Related to consonance as a linking device is *assonance*, the echoing of similar vowel sounds in the stressed syllables of words with differing consonants (lane/hail, penitent/reticence). A device favored particularly by descriptive poets, it appears often in the work of the English Romantics, especially Shelley and Keats, and their great Victorian successor Tennyson, all of whom had a good ear for the musical quality of language. In the following passage, Tennyson makes effective use of repeated "o" and "ow" sounds to suggest the soft moaning of the wind as it spreads the seed of the lotos plant:

The Lotos blooms below the barren peak,
The Lotos blows by every winding creek;
All day the wind breathes low with mellower tone;
Through every hollow cave and alley lone
Round and round the spicy downs the yellow Lotos dust is blown.

(from "The Lotos-Eaters")

ALLITERATION

Alliteration connects words which have the same initial consonant. Like consonance and rhyme, alliteration adds emphasis, throwing individual words into strong relief, and lending force to rhythm. This is especially evident in the work of Gerard Manley Hopkins, where alliteration works in conjunction with the heavy stresses of *sprung rhythm*:

Brute beauty and valour and act, oh, air, pride, plume, here
Buckle! AND the fire that breaks from thee then, a billion
Times told lovelier, more dangerous, O my chevalier!

(from "The Windhover")

Like assonance, alliteration is useful in descriptive poetry, reinforcing an impression or mood through repeated sounds:

Thou on whose stream, 'mid the steep sky's commotion,
Loose clouds like Earth's decaying leaves are shed,
Shook from the tangled boughs of Heaven and Ocean ....

(from Percy Shelley, "Ode to the West Wind")

The repetition of "s" and "sh" sounds conveys the rushing sound of a wind that drives everything before it. This effect is also an example of *onomatopoeia*, a figure of speech in which the sound of the words seems to echo the sense.

RHYME AND POETIC STRUCTURE

Rhyme may play a central role in the structure of a poem. This is particularly apparent in the *sonnet* form, where the expression of the thought is heavily influenced by the poet's choice of rhyme-scheme. The "English" or "Shakespearean" sonnet has three quatrains rhyming *abab*, *cdcd*, *efef*, and concludes with a rhyming couplet, *gg*. This pattern lends itself well to the statement and restatement of an idea, as we find, for example, in Shakespeare's sonnet "That time of year thou mayst in me behold." Each of the quatrains presents an image of decline or decay—a tree in winter, the coming of night, a dying fire; the closing couplet then relates these images to the thought of an impending separation and attendant feelings of loss.

The organization of the "Italian" or "Petrarchan" sonnet, by contrast, hinges on a rhyme scheme that creates two parts, an eight-line section (the *octave*) typically rhyming *abbaabba*, and a concluding six-line section (the *sestet*) rhyming *cdecde* or some other variation. In the octave, the writer describes a thought or feeling; in the sestet, the writer may elaborate upon that thought, or may introduce a sudden "turn" or change of direction. A good example of the Italian form is Donne's "Batter My Heart, Three-Personed God."

The rhyming pattern established at the beginning of a poem is usually followed throughout; thus the opening sets up an expectation in the reader, which the poet may sometimes play on by means of an unexpected or surprising rhyme. This is especially evident in comic verse, where peculiar or unexpected rhymes can contribute a great deal to the comic effect:

I shoot the Hippopotamus
with bullets made of platinum,
Because if I use leaden ones
his hide is sure to flatten 'em.

(Hilaire Belloc, "The Hippopotamus")

Finally, one of the most obvious yet important aspects of rhyme is its sound. It acts as a kind of musical punctuation, lending verse an added resonance and beauty. And as anyone who has ever had to learn poetry by heart will testify, the sound of rhyme is a powerful aid to memorization and recall, from helping a child to learn numbers—

One, two,
Buckle my shoe,
Three, four,
Knock at the door—

—to selling toothpaste through an advertising jingle in which the use of rhyme drives home the identity of a product:

You'll wonder where the yellow went,
When you brush your teeth with Pepsodent.

OTHER FORMS WITH INTERLOCKING RHYMES

Other forms besides the sonnet depend upon rhyme for their structural integrity. These include the *rondeau*, a poem of thirteen lines in three stanzas, with two half lines acting as a refrain, and having only two rhymes. The linking effect of rhyme is also essential to the three-line stanza called *terza rima,* the form chosen by Shelley for his "Ode to the West Wind," where the rhyme scheme (*aba*, *bcb*, *cdc*, etc.) gives a strong sense of forward movement. But a poet need not be limited to particular forms to use interlocking rhyme schemes.

THE POET'S TASK

The poet's task, in Sir Philip Sidney's view, is to move us to virtue and well-doing by coming to us with

> words set in delightful proportion, either accompanied with, or prepared for, the well-enchanting skill of music; and with a tale forsooth he cometh unto you, with a tale which holdeth children from play, and old men from the chimney corner; and pretending no more, doth intend the winning of the mind from wickedness to virtue: even as the child is often brought to take most wholesome things by hiding them in such other as have a pleasant taste.
>
> (*The Defence of Poesy*, 1593)

Modern poets have been less preoccupied with the didactic or moral force of poetry, its capacity to win the mind to virtue; nonetheless, like their Renaissance counterparts, they view poetry as a means to understanding, a point of light in an otherwise dark universe. To Robert Frost, a poem "begins in delight and ends in wisdom":

> It begins in delight, it inclines to the impulse, it assumes direction with the first line laid down, it runs a course of lucky events, and ends in a clarification of life—not necessarily a great clarification, such as sects and cults are founded on, but in a momentary stay against confusion.
>
> ("The Figure a Poem Makes," *Collected Poems*, 1939)

Rhyme and meter are important tools at the poet's disposal, and can be valuable aids in developing thought as well as in creating rhythmic or musical effects. However, the technical skills needed to turn a good line or create metrical complexities should not be confused with the ability to write good poetry. Sidney wryly observes in his *Defence of Poesy* that "there have been many excellent poets that never versified, and now swarm many versifiers that need never answer to the name of poets.…[I]t is not rhyming and versing that maketh a poet, no more than a long gown maketh an advocate." Technical virtuosity may arouse our admiration, but something else is needed to bring that "constriction of the throat and … precipitation of water to the eyes" that A.E. Housman speaks about. What that "something" is will always elude definition, and is perhaps best left for readers and listeners to determine for themselves through their own encounters with poetry.

Maps

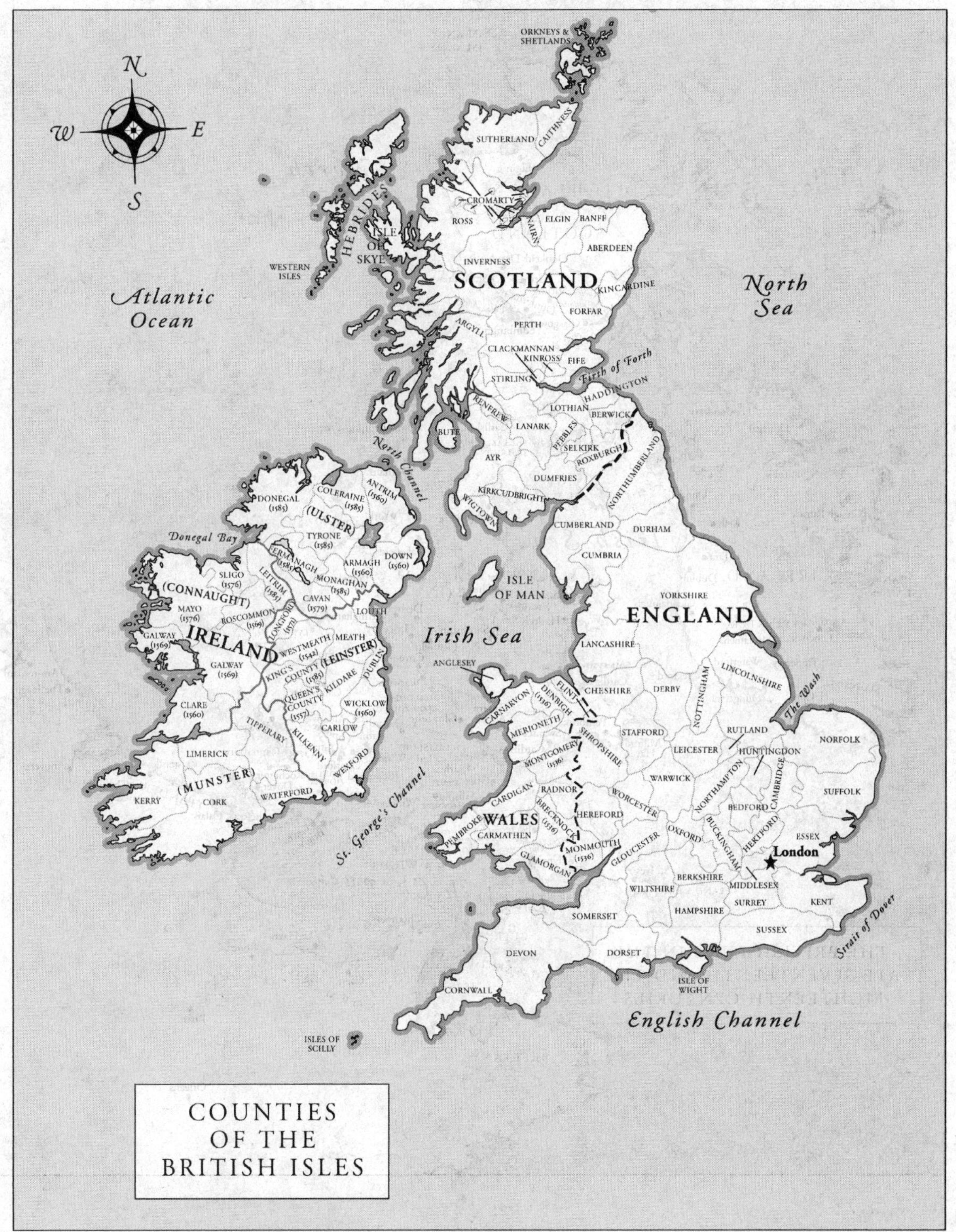

COUNTIES OF THE BRITISH ISLES

THE BRITISH ISLES IN THE LATE SEVENTEENTH AND THE EIGHTEENTH CENTURIES

THE LONDON AREA
Finchley
Harrow
EPPING
FOREST
Twyford
Abbey
London
Tower
Westminster
Chelsea
Woolwich
Greenwich
Battersea
Deptford
Richmond
Twickenham
Dartford
Kingston
Wimbledon
Sydenham
Hampton
Court
Merton

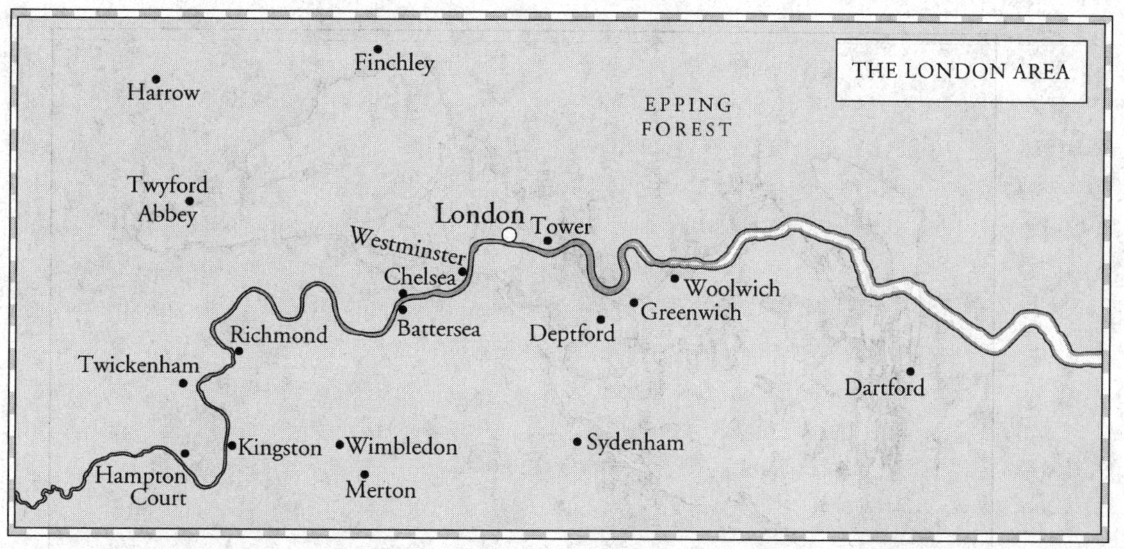

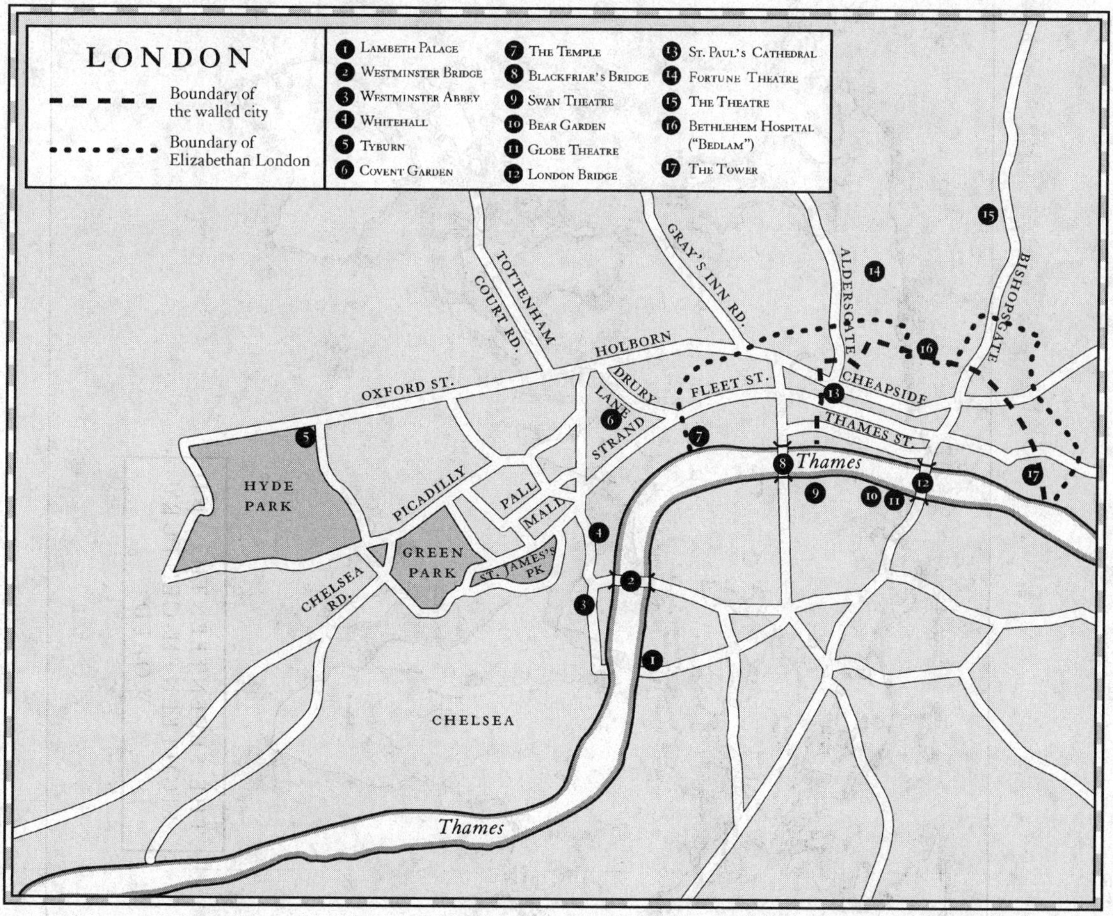

LONDON
Boundary of the walled city
Boundary of Elizabethan London
1 Lambeth Palace
2 Westminster Bridge
3 Westminster Abbey
4 Whitehall
5 Tyburn
6 Covent Garden
7 The Temple
8 Blackfriar's Bridge
9 Swan Theatre
10 Bear Garden
11 Globe Theatre
12 London Bridge
13 St. Paul's Cathedral
14 Fortune Theatre
15 The Theatre
16 Bethlehem Hospital ("Bedlam")
17 The Tower
TOTTENHAM COURT RD.
GRAY'S INN RD.
ALDERSGATE
BISHOPSGATE
HOLBORN
OXFORD ST.
DRURY LANE
FLEET ST.
CHEAPSIDE
THAMES ST.
STRAND
Thames
HYDE PARK
PICADILLY
PALL MALL
GREEN PARK
ST. JAMES'S PK
CHELSEA RD.
CHELSEA
Thames

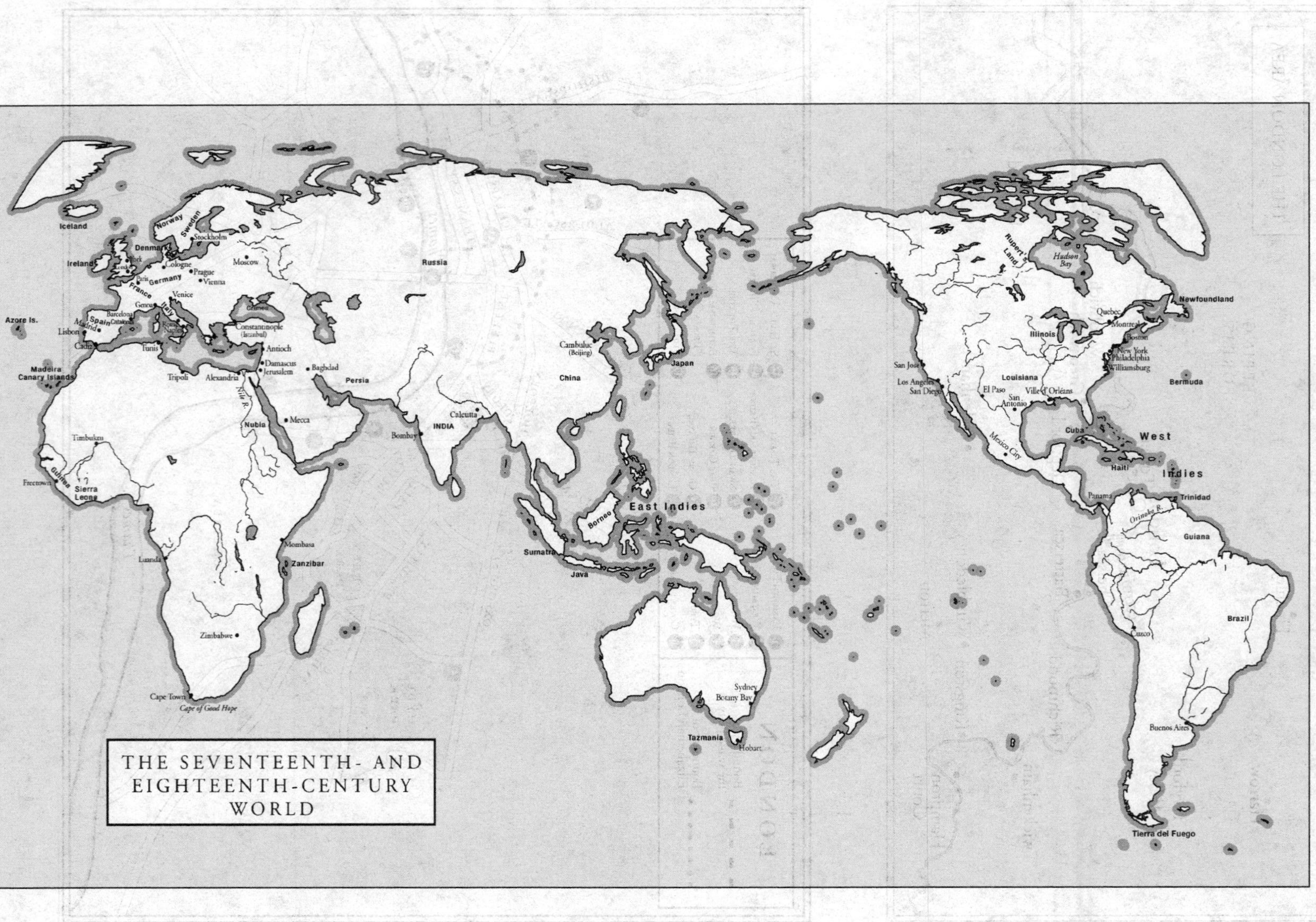
THE SEVENTEENTH- AND EIGHTEENTH-CENTURY WORLD
Iceland
Ireland
Norway
Sweden
Denmark
Stockholm
York
Cologne
Paris
Germany
Prague
Vienna
Moscow
France
Venice
Genoa
Italy
Barcelona
Spain
Madrid
Lisbon
Cadiz
Azore Is.
Madeira
Canary Islands
Tunis
Tripoli
Alexandria
Constantinople
(Istanbul)
Antioch
Damascus
Jerusalem
Baghdad
Persia
Mecca
Nubia
Nile R.
Russia
Bombay
INDIA
Calcutta
Cambuluc
(Beijing)
China
Japan
Sumatra
Java
Borneo
East Indies
Timbuktu
Freetown
Guinea
Sierra Leone
Luanda
Mombasa
Zanzibar
Zimbabwe
Cape Town
Cape of Good Hope
Sydney
Botany Bay
Tazmania
Hobart
Rupert's Land
Hudson Bay
Newfoundland
Quebec
Montreal
Boston
New York
Philadelphia
Williamsburg
Illinois
Louisiana
Bermuda
San Jose
Los Angeles
San Diego
El Paso
San Antonio
Ville d'Orléans
Mexico City
Cuba
Haiti
West Indies
Panama
Trinidad
Orinoko R.
Guiana
Cuzco
Brazil
Buenos Aires
Tierra del Fuego

Monarchs and Prime Ministers

MONARCHS

House of Wessex	
Egbert (Ecgberht)	829–39
Æthelwulf	839–58
Æthelbald	858–60
Æthelbert	860–66
Æthelred I	866–71
Alfred the Great	871–99
Edward the Elder	899–924
Athelstan	924–40
Edmund I	940–46
Edred (Eadred)	946–55
Edwy (Eadwig)	955–59
Edgar	959–75
Edward the Martyr	975–78
Æthelred II (the Unready)	978–1016
Edmund II (Ironside)	1016

Danish Line	
Canute (Cnut)	1016–35
Harold I (Harefoot)	1035–40
Hardecanute	1040–42

Wessex Line, Restored	
Edward the Confessor	1042–66
Harold II	1066

Norman Line	
William I (the Conqueror)	1066–87
William II (Rufus)	1087–1100
Henry I (Beauclerc)	1100–35
Stephen	1135–54

Harold II

William I

MONARCHS

PLANTAGENET, ANGEVIN LINE

Henry II	1154–89
Richard I (Coeur de Lion)	1189–99
John (Lackland)	1199–1216
Henry III	1216–72
Edward I (Longshanks)	1272–1307
Edward II	1307–27
Edward III	1327–77
Richard II	1377–99

Henry VIII

PLANTAGENET, LANCASTRIAN LINE

Henry IV	1399–1413
Henry V	1413–22
Henry VI	1422–61

PLANTAGENET, YORKIST LINE

Edward IV	1461–83
Edward V	1483
Richard III	1483–85

HOUSE OF TUDOR

Henry VII	1485–1509
Henry VIII	1509–47
Edward VI	1547–53
Mary I	1553–58
Elizabeth I	1558–1603

Mary I

HOUSE OF STUART

James I	1603–25
Charles I	1625–49
(The Commonwealth)	1649–60
Oliver Cromwell	1649–58
Richard Cromwell	1658–59

MONARCHS

HOUSE OF STUART, RESTORED

Charles II	1660–85
James II	1685–88

HOUSE OF ORANGE AND STUART

William III and Mary II	1689–94
William III	1694–1702

HOUSE OF STUART

Anne	1702–14

HOUSE OF BRUNSWICK, HANOVER LINE

George I	1714–27
George II	1727–60
George III	1760–1820

George III

George, Prince of Wales, Prince Regent

PRIME MINISTERS

Sir Robert Walpole (Whig)	1721–42
Earl of Wilmington (Whig)	1742–43
Henry Pelham (Whig)	1743–54
Duke of Newcastle (Whig)	1754–56
Duke of Devonshire (Whig)	1756–57
Duke of Newcastle (Whig)	1757–62
Earl of Bute (Tory)	1762–63
George Grenville (Whig)	1763–65
Marquess of Rockingham (Whig)	1765–66
William Pitt the Elder (Earl of Chatham) (Whig)	1766–68
Duke of Grafton (Whig)	1768–70
Frederick North (Lord North) (Tory)	1770–82
Marquess of Rockingham (Whig)	1782
Earl of Shelburne (Whig)	1782–83
Duke of Portland	1783
William Pitt the Younger (Tory)	1783–1801
Henry Addington (Tory)	1801–04
William Pitt the Younger (Tory)	1804–06
William Wyndham Grenville (Baron Grenville) (Whig)	1806–07

MONARCHS

George, Prince of Wales, Prince Regent	1811–20
George IV	1820–30
William IV	1830–37
Victoria	1837–1901

Victoria

HOUSE OF SAXE-COBURG-GOTHA

Edward VII	1901–10

HOUSE OF WINDSOR

George V	1910–36

PRIME MINISTERS

Duke of Portland (Whig)	1807–09
Spencer Perceval (Tory)	1809–12
Earl of Liverpool (Tory)	1812–27
George Canning (Tory)	1827
Viscount Goderich (Tory)	1827–28
Duke of Wellington (Tory)	1828–30
Earl Grey (Whig)	1830–34
Viscount Melbourne (Whig)	1834
Sir Robert Peel (Tory)	1834–35
Viscount Melbourne (Whig)	1835–41
Sir Robert Peel (Tory)	1841–46
Lord John Russell (later Earl) (Liberal)	1846–52
Earl of Derby (Con.)	1852
Earl of Aberdeen (Con.)	1852–55
Viscount Palmerston (Lib.)	1855–58
Earl of Derby (Con.)	1858–59
Viscount Palmerston (Lib.)	1859–65
Earl Russell (Liberal)	1865–66
Earl of Derby (Con.)	1866–68
Benjamin Disraeli (Con.)	1868
William Gladstone (Lib.)	1868–74
Benjamin Disraeli (Con.)	1874–80
William Gladstone (Lib.)	1880–85
Marquess of Salisbury (Con.)	1885–86
William Gladstone (Lib.)	1886
Marquess of Salisbury (Con.)	1886–92
William Gladstone (Lib.)	1892–94
Earl of Rosebery (Lib.)	1894–95
Marquess of Salisbury (Con.)	1895–1902
Arthur Balfour (Con.)	1902–05
Sir Henry Campbell-Bannerman (Lib.)	1905–08
Herbert Asquith (Lib.)	1908–15
Herbert Asquith (Lib.)	1915–16

MONARCHS		PRIME MINISTERS	
		David Lloyd George	1916–22
		Andrew Bonar Law (Con.)	1922–23
		Stanley Baldwin (Con.)	1923–24
		James Ramsay MacDonald (Labour)	1924
		Stanley Baldwin (Con.)	1924–29
		James Ramsay MacDonald (Labour)	1929–31
		James Ramsay MacDonald (Labour)	1931–35
Edward VIII	1936	Stanley Baldwin (Con.)	1935–37
George VI	1936–52	Neville Chamberlain (Con.)	1937–40
		Winston Churchill (Con.)	1940–45
		Winston Churchill (Con.)	1945
		Clement Attlee (Labour)	1945–51
Elizabeth II	1952–	Sir Winston Churchill (Con.)	1951–55
		Sir Anthony Eden (Con.)	1955–57
		Harold Macmillan (Con.)	1957–63
		Sir Alex Douglas-Home (Con.)	1963–64
		Harold Wilson (Labour)	1964–70
		Edward Heath (Con.)	1970–74
		Harold Wilson (Labour)	1974–76
		James Callaghan (Labour)	1976–79
		Margaret Thatcher (Con.)	1979–90
		John Major (Con.)	1990–97
		Tony Blair (Labour)	1997–2007
		Gordon Brown (Labour)	2007–10
		David Cameron (Con.)	2010–16
		Theresa May (Con.)	2016–

Winston Churchill

Glossary of Terms

Accent: the natural emphasis (stress) speakers place on a syllable.

Accentual Verse: poetry in which a line is measured only by the number of accents or stresses, not by the number of syllables.

Accentual-Syllabic Verse: the most common metrical system in traditional English verse, in which a line is measured by the number of syllables and by the pattern of accented (stressed) and unaccented (unstressed) syllables.

Aesthetes: members of a late nineteenth-century movement that valued "art for art's sake"—for its purely aesthetic qualities, as opposed to valuing art for the moral content it may convey, for the intellectual stimulation it may provide, or for a range of other qualities.

Alexandrine: a line of verse that is 12 syllables long. In English verse, the alexandrine is always an iambic hexameter: that is, it has six iambic feet. The most-often quoted example is the second line in a couplet from Alexander Pope's "Essay on Criticism" (1711): "A needless Alexandrine ends the song / That, like a wounded snake, drags its slow length along." See also *Spenserian stanza.*

Allegory: a narrative with both a literal meaning and secondary, often symbolic meaning or meanings. Allegory frequently employs personification to give concrete embodiment to abstract concepts or entities, such as feelings or personal qualities. It may also present one set of characters or events in the guise of another, using implied parallels for the purposes of satire or political comment, as in John Dryden's poem "Absalom and Achitophel."

Alliteration: the grouping of words with the same initial consonant (e.g., "break, blow, burn, and make me new"). The repetition of sound acts as a connector. See also *assonance* and *consonance.*

Alliterative Verse: poetry that employs alliteration of stressed syllables in each line as its chief structural principle.

Allusion: a reference, often indirect or unidentified, to a person, thing, or event. A reference in one literary work to another literary work, whether to its content or its form, also constitutes an allusion.

Ambiguity: an "opening" of language created by the writer to allow for multiple meanings or differing interpretations. In literature, ambiguity may be deliberately employed by the writer to enrich meaning; this differs from any unintentional, unwanted, ambiguity in non-literary prose.

Amphibrach: a metrical foot with three syllables, the second of which is stressed: x / x (e.g., sensation).

Analogy: a broad term that refers to our processes of noting similarities among things or events. Specific forms of analogy in poetry include *simile* and *metaphor* (see below).

Anapaest: a metrical foot containing two unstressed syllables followed by one stressed syllable: xx / (e.g., underneath, intervene).

Anglican Church / Church of England: formed after Henry VIII's break with Rome in the 1530s, the Church of England had acquired a permanently Protestant cast by the 1570s. There has remained considerable variation within the Church, however, with distinctions often drawn among High Church, Broad Church, and Latitudinarian. At one extreme High Church Anglicans (some of whom prefer to be known as "Anglo-Catholics") prefer relatively elaborate church rituals not dissimilar in form to those of the Roman Catholic Church and place considerable emphasis on church hierarchy, while in the other direction Latitudinarians prefer relatively informal religious services and tend far more towards egalitarianism.

Antistrophe: from Greek drama, the chorus's countermovement or reply to an initial movement (*strophe*). See *ode* below.

Apostrophe: a figure of speech (a trope; see *figures of speech* below) in which a writer directly addresses an object—or a dead or absent person—as if the imagined audience were actually listening.

Archetype: in literature and mythology, a recurring idea, symbol, motif, character, or place. To some scholars and psychologists, an archetype represents universal human thought-patterns or experiences.

Assonance: the repetition of identical or similar vowel sounds in stressed syllables in which the surrounding consonants are different: for example, "shame" and "fate"; "gale" and "cage"; or the long "i" sounds in "Beside the pumice isle..."

Aubade: a lyric poem that greets or laments the arrival of dawn.

Ballad: a folk song, or a poem originally recited to an audience, which tells a dramatic story based on legend or history.

Ballad Stanza: a quatrain with alternating four-stress and three-stress lines, rhyming *abcb*. A variant is "common measure," in which the alternating lines are strictly iambic, and rhyme *abab*.

Ballade: a fixed form most commonly characterized by only three rhymes, with an 8-line stanza rhyming *ababbcbc* and an envoy rhyming *bcbc*. Both Chaucer and Dante Gabriel Rossetti ("Ballad of the Dead Ladies") adopted this form.

Baroque: powerful and heavily ornamented in style. "Baroque" is a term from the history of visual art and of music that is sometimes also used to describe certain literary styles, such as that of Richard Crashaw.

Bathos: an anticlimactic effect brought about by a writer's descent from an elevated subject or tone to the ordinary or trivial.

Benedictine Rule: set of instructions for monastic communities, composed by Saint Benedict of Nursia (died c. 457).

Blank Verse: unrhymed lines written in iambic pentameter, a form introduced to English verse by Henry Howard, Earl of Surrey, in his translation of parts of Virgil's *Aeneid* in 1547.

Bombast: inappropriately inflated or grandiose language.

Broadside: individual sheet of paper printed on only one side. From the sixteenth through to the eighteenth centuries broadsides of a variety of different sorts (e.g., ballads, political tracts, short satires) were sold on the streets.

Broken Rhyme: in which a multi-syllable word is split at the end of a line and continued onto the next, to allow an end-rhyme with the split syllable.

Burlesque: satire of a particularly exaggerated sort, particularly that which ridicules its subject by emphasizing its vulgar or ridiculous aspects.

Caesura: a pause or break in a line of verse occurring where a phrase, clause, or sentence ends, and indicated in scansion by the mark II. If it occurs in the middle of the line, it is known as a "medial" caesura.

Canon: in literature, those works that are commonly accepted as possessing authority or importance. In practice, "canonical" texts or authors are those that are discussed most frequently by scholars and taught most frequently in university courses.

Canto: a sub-section of a long (usually epic) poem.

Canzone: a short song or poem, with stanzas of equal length and an envoy.

Carpe Diem: Latin (from Horace) meaning "seize the day." The idea of enjoying the moment is a common one in Renaissance love poetry. See, for example, Marvell's "To His Coy Mistress."

Catalexis: the omission of unstressed syllables from a line of verse (such a line is referred to as "catalectic"). In iambic verse it is usually the first syllable of the line that is omitted; in trochaic, the last. For example, in the first stanza of Housman's "To an Athlete Dying Young" the third line is catalectic: i.e., it has dropped the first, unstressed syllable called for by the poem's iambic tetrameter form: "The time you won your town the race / We chaired you through the market-place; / Man and boy stood cheering by, / And home we brought you shoulder-high."

Catharsis: the arousal through the performance of a dramatic tragedy of "emotions of pity and fear" to a point where "purgation" or "purification" occurs and the feelings are released or transformed. The concept was developed by Aristotle in his *Poetics* from an ancient Greek medical concept, and adapted by him into an aesthetic principle.

Chiasmus: a figure of speech (a scheme) that reverses word order in successive parallel clauses. If the word order is A-B-C in the first clause, it becomes C-B-A in the second: for example, Donne's line "She is all states, and all princes, I" ("The Sun Rising") incorporates this reversal (though with an ellipsis).

Classical: originating in or relating to ancient Greek or Roman culture. As commonly conceived, *classical* implies a strong sense of formal order. The term *neoclassical* is often used with reference to literature of the Restoration and eighteenth century that was strongly influenced by ancient Greek and Roman models.

Closet Drama: a play (typically in verse) written for private performance. The term came into use in the first half of the nineteenth century.

Colored Narrative: alternative term for *free indirect discourse.*

Comedy: as a literary term, used originally to denote that class of ancient Greek drama in which the action ends happily. More broadly the term has been used to describe a wide variety of literary forms of a more or less light-hearted character.

***Commedia dell'arte*:** largely improvised comic performances conducted by masked performers and involving considerable physical activity. The genre of *commedia dell'arte* originated in Italy in the sixteenth century; it was influential throughout Europe for more than two centuries thereafter.

Commonwealth: from the fifteenth century, a term roughly equivalent to the modern "state," but tending to emphasize the commonality of interests among all citizens. In the seventeenth century Britain was named a commonwealth under Oliver Cromwell. In the twentieth century, the term came to be applied to associations of many nations; the British Commonwealth became the successor to the British Empire.

Conceit: an unusually elaborate metaphor or simile that extends beyond its original tenor and vehicle, sometimes becoming a "master" analogy for the entire poem (see, for example, Donne's "The Flea," and Robert Frost's sonnet "She is as in a field a silken tent"). Ingenious or fanciful images and comparisons were especially popular with the metaphysical poets of the seventeenth century, giving rise to the term "metaphysical conceit."

Concrete Poetry: an experimental form, most popular during the 1950s and 60s, in which the printed type itself forms a visual image of the poem's key words or ideas. See also *pattern poetry, assonance.*

Connotation: the implied, often unspoken meaning(s) of a given word, as distinct from its denotation, or literal meaning. Connotations may have highly emotional undertones and are usually culturally specific.

Conservative Party: See *Political Parties.*

Consonance: the pairing of words with similar initial and ending consonants, but with different vowel sounds (live/love, wander/wonder). See also *alliteration.*

Convention: aesthetic approach, technique, or practice accepted as characteristic and appropriate for a particular form. It is a convention of certain sorts of plays, for example, that the characters speak in blank verse, of other sorts of plays that characters speak in rhymed couplets, and of still other sorts of dramatic performances that characters frequently break into song to express their feelings.

Couplet: a pair of rhyming lines, usually in the same meter. If they form a complete unit of thought and are grammatically complete, the lines are known as a closed couplet. See also *heroic couplet* below.

Dactyl: a metrical foot containing one strong stress followed by two weak stresses: / xx (e.g., muttering, helplessly). A minor form known as "double dactyls" makes use of this meter for humorous purposes, e.g., "Jiggery pokery" or "Higgledy piggledy."

Denotation: See *connotation* above.

Devolution: process through which a degree of political power was transferred in the late twentieth and early twenty-first centuries from the British government to assemblies in Scotland and in Wales.

Dialogue: words spoken by characters to one another. (When a character is addressing him or her self or the audience directly, the words spoken are referred to as a *monologue.*)

Diction: word choice. Whether the diction of a literary work (or of a literary character) is colloquial, conversational, formal, or of some other type contributes significantly to the tone of the text as well as to characterization.

Didacticism: aesthetic approach emphasizing moral instruction.

Dimeter: a poetic line containing two metrical feet.

Dirge: a song or poem that mourns someone's death. See also *elegy* and *lament* below.

Disestablishmentarianism: movement opposing an official state-supported religion, in particular the Church of England in that role.

Dissonance: harsh, unmusical sounds or rhythms which poets may use deliberately to achieve certain effects.

Dramatic Irony: this form of irony occurs when the audience's reception of a speech by a character on the stage is affected by the possession by the audience of information not available to the character.

Dramatic Monologue: a lyric poem that takes the form of an utterance by a single person addressing a silent listener. The speaker may be an historical personage (as in some of Robert Browning's dramatic monologues), a figure drawn from myth or legend (as in some of Tennyson's), or an entirely imagined figure, as in Webster's "A Castaway."

Dub Poetry: a form of protest poetry originating in Jamaica, with its roots in dance rhythms, especially reggae, and often accompanied in performance by drums and music. See also *rap*.

Duple Foot: a duple foot of poetry has two syllables. The possible duple forms are iamb (in which the stress is on the second of the two syllables), trochee (in which the stress is on the first of the two syllables), spondee (in which both are stressed equally), and pyrrhic (in which both syllables are unstressed).

Eclogue: now generally used simply as an alternative name for a pastoral poem. In classical times and in the early modern period, however, an *eclogue* (or *idyll*) was a specific type of pastoral poem—a dialogue or dramatic monologue involving rustic characters. (The other main sub-genre of the pastoral was the *georgic*.)

Elegiac Stanza: a quatrain of iambic pentameters rhyming *abab*, often used in poems meditating on death or sorrow. The best-known example is Thomas Gray's "Elegy Written in a Country Churchyard."

Elegy: a poem which formally mourns the death of a particular person (e.g., Tennyson's "In Memoriam") or in which the poet meditates on other serious subjects (e.g., Gray's "Elegy"). See also *dirge*.

Elision: omitting or suppressing a letter or an unstressed syllable at the beginning or end of a word, so that a line of verse may conform to a given metrical scheme. For example, the three syllables at the beginning of Shakespeare's sonnet 129 are reduced to two by the omission of the first vowel: "Th' expense of spirit in a waste of shame." See also *syncope*.

Ellipsis: the omission of a word or words necessary for the complete grammatical construction of a sentence, but not necessary for our understanding of the sentence.

End-rhyme: See *rhyme*.

End-stopped: a line of poetry is said to be end-stopped when the end of the line coincides with a natural pause in the syntax, such as the conclusion of a sentence; e.g., in this couplet from Pope's "Essay on Criticism," both lines are end-stopped: "A little learning is a dangerous thing; / Drink deep, or taste not the Pierian spring." Compare this with *enjambement*.

Enjambement: the "running-on" of the sense from one line of poetry to the next, with no pause created by punctuation or syntax. (The more commonly found alternative is referred to as an *end-stopped line*.)

Envoy (Envoi): a stanza or half-stanza that forms the conclusion of certain French poetic forms, such as the *sestina* or the *ballade*. It often sums up or comments upon what has gone before.

Epic: a lengthy narrative poem, often divided into books and sub-divided into cantos. It generally celebrates heroic deeds or events, and the style tends to be lofty and grand. Examples in English include Spenser's *The Faerie Queene* and Milton's *Paradise Lost*.

Epic Simile: an elaborate simile, developed at such length that the vehicle of the comparison momentarily displaces the primary subject with which it is being compared.

Epigram: a very short poem, sometimes in closed couplet form, characterized by pointed wit.

Epigraph: a quotation placed at the beginning of a discourse to indicate or foreshadow the theme.

Epiphany: a moment at which matters of significance are suddenly illuminated for a literary character (or for the reader), typically triggered by something small and seemingly of little import. The term first came into wide currency in connection with the fiction of James Joyce.

Episodic Plot: plot comprising a variety of episodes that are only loosely connected by threads of story material (as opposed to plots that present one or more continually unfolding narratives where successive episodes build one on another).

Epithalamion: a poem celebrating a wedding. The best-known example in English is probably Edmund Spenser's "Epithalamion" (1595).

Eulogy: text expressing praise, especially for a distinguished person recently deceased.

Euphemism: mode of expression through which aspects of reality considered to be vulgar, crudely physical, or unpleasant are referred to indirectly rather than named explicitly. A variety of euphemisms exist for the processes of urination and defecation; *passed away* is often used as a euphemism for *died.* (The word *euphemism* has the same root as *Euphuism* (see below), but has taken on a different meaning.)

Euphony: pleasant, musical sounds or rhythms—the opposite of dissonance.

Euphuism: in the late sixteenth century John Lyly published a prose romance, *Euphues*, which employed a style that featured long sentences filled with balanced phrases and clauses, many of them adding little to the content. This highly mannered style was popular in the court of Elizabeth I for a few years following the publication of Lyly's famous work, and the style became known as *Euphuism*.

European Union (EU): group of nations formed in 1993 as the successor to the European Economic Community (Common Market). Britain first applied for membership in the latter in 1961; at first its efforts to join were blocked by the French government, but in 1973 Prime Minister Edward Heath successfully negotiated Britain's entry into the group. Britain resisted some moves towards full integration with the European community, in particular retaining its own currency when other European nations adopted the Euro on 1 January 2002. In 2016, the United Kingdom held a referendum and voted to leave the European Union altogether.

Exchequer: in earlier eras, the central royal financial office, responsible for receiving and keeping track of crown revenues. In later eras, part of the bureaucracy equivalent to the Ministry of Finance in Canada or the Treasury in the United States (the modern post of Chancellor of the Exchequer is equivalent to the American post of Secretary of the Treasury, the Canadian post of Minister of Finance, or the Australian post of Treasurer).

Exposition: the setting out of material in an ordered form, either in speech or in writing. In a play those parts of the action that do not occur on stage but are rather recounted by the characters are frequently described as being presented in exposition. Similarly, when the background narrative is filled in near the beginning of a novel, such material is often described as having been presented in exposition. Somewhat confusingly, however, the term "expository prose" is usually used with reference not to fiction but to the setting forth of arguments or descriptions in the context of essays or other works of prose non-fiction.

Eye-rhyme: See *rhyme* below.

Feminine Ending: the ending of a line of poetry on an "extra," and, especially, on an unstressed syllable. See, for example, the first line of Keat's "Ode on a Grecian Urn": "A thing of beauty is a joy forever," a line of iambic pentameter in which the final foot is an amphibrach rather than an iamb.

Feminine Rhyme: See *rhyme* below.

Figures of Speech: deliberate, highly concentrated uses of language to achieve particular purposes or effects on an audience. There are two kinds of figures: schemes and tropes. Schemes involve changes in word-sound and word-order, such as *alliteration* and *chiasmus.* Tropes play on our understandings of words to extend, alter, or transform meaning, as in *metaphor* and *personification.*

First-Person Narrative: narrative recounted using *I* and *me.* See also *narrative perspective.*

Fixed Forms: the term applied to a number of poetic forms and stanzaic patterns, many derived from French models, such as *ballade, rondeau, sestina, triolet,* and *villanelle.* Other "fixed forms" include the *sonnet, rhyme royal, haiku,* and *ottava rima.*

Folio: largest of several sizes of book page commonly used in the first few centuries after the introduction of the printing press. A folio size results from very large paper being folded in half. Paper size during this period was not standardized; though a typical folio page was about 15 inches high, some could be more than twice that height. When the same sheet is folded twice a quarto is produced, and when it is folded 3 times an octavo.

Foot: a unit of a line of verse which contains a particular combination of stressed and unstressed syllables. Dividing a line into metrical feet (*iambs, trochees,* etc.), then counting the number of feet per line, is part of *scansion.* See also *meter.*

Franklin: in the late medieval period, a landholder of free status, but ranking below the gentry.

Free Indirect Discourse: in prose fiction, commentary in which a seemingly objective and omniscient narrative voice assumes the point of view of one or more characters. When we hear through the third person narrative voice of Jane Austen's *Pride and Prejudice*, for example, that Mr. Darcy "was the proudest, most disagreeable man in the world, and every body hoped that he would never come there again," the narrative voice has assumed the point of view of "every body" in the community; we as readers are not meant to take it that Mr. Darcy is indeed the most disagreeable man in the world. Similarly, in the following passage from the same novel, we are likely to take it as being the view of the character Charlotte that marriage is "the only honourable provision for well-educated young women of small fortune," not to take it to be an objective statement of perceived truth on the part of the novel's third person narrative voice:

> [Charlotte's] reflections were in general satisfactory. Mr. Collins to be sure was neither sensible nor agreeable; his society was irksome, and his attachment to her must be imaginary. But still he would be her husband. Without thinking highly either of men or of matrimony, marriage had always been her object; it was the only honourable provision for well-educated young women of small fortune, and however uncertain of giving happiness, must be their pleasantest preservative from want.

The term free indirect discourse may also be applied to situations in which it may not be entirely clear if the thoughts expressed emanate from the character, the narrator, or some combination of the two. (In the above-quoted passage expressing Charlotte's thoughts, indeed, some might argue that the statement concerning marriage should be taken as the expression of a belief that the narrative voice shares, at least in part.)

Free Verse: poetry that does not follow any regular meter, line length, or rhyming scheme. In many respects, though, free verse follows the complex natural "rules" and rhythmic patterns (or cadences) of speech.

Gaelic: Celtic language, variants of which are spoken in Ireland and Scotland.

Genre: a particular literary form. The concept of genre may be used with different levels of generality. At the most general, poetry, drama, and prose fiction are distinguished as separate genres. At a lower level of generality various sub-genres are frequently distinguished, such as (within drama) comedy and tragedy, or, at a still lower level of generality, Elizabethan domestic tragedy, Edwardian drawing-room comedy, and so on.

Georgic: (from Virgil's *Georgics*) a poem that celebrates the natural wealth of the countryside and advises how to cultivate and live in harmony with it. Pope's *Windsor Forest* and James Thomson's *Seasons* are classed as georgics. They were often said to make up, with eclogues, the two alliterative forms of pastoral poetry.

Ghazal: derived from Persian and Indian precedents, the ghazal presents a series of thoughts in closed couplets joined by a simple rhyme-scheme: *aa ba ca da*, etc.

Gothic: in architecture and the visual arts, a term used to describe styles prevalent from the twelfth to the fourteenth centuries, but in literature a term used to describe work with a sinister or grotesque tone that seeks to evoke a sense of terror on the part of the reader or audience. Gothic literature originated as a genre in the eighteenth century with works such as Horace Walpole's *The Castle of Otranto*. To some extent the notion of the medieval itself then carried with it associations of the dark and the grotesque, but from the beginning an element of intentional exaggeration (sometimes verging on self-parody) attached itself to the genre. The Gothic trend of youth culture that began in the late twentieth century is less clearly associated with the medieval, but shares with the various varieties of Gothic literature (from Walpole in the eighteenth century, to Bram Stoker in the early twentieth, to Stephen King and Anne Rice in the late twentieth) a fondness for the sensational and the grotesque, as well as a propensity to self-parody.

Guilds: non-clerical associations that arose in the late Anglo-Saxon period, devoted both to social purposes (such as the organization of feasts for the members) and to piety. In the later medieval period guilds developed strong associations with particular occupations.

Haiku: a Japanese form, using three unrhymed lines of five, seven, and five syllables. Conventionally, it uses precise, concentrated images to suggest states of feeling.

Heptameter: a line containing seven metrical feet.

Heroic Couplet: a pair of rhymed iambic pentameters, so called because the form was much used in seventeenth- and eighteenth-century poems and plays on heroic subjects.

Hexameter: a line containing six metrical feet.

Home Rule: movement dedicated to making Ireland politically independent from Britain.

Horatian Ode: inspired by the work of the Roman poet Horace, an ode that is usually calm and meditative in tone, and homostrophic (i.e., having regular stanzas) in form. Keats's odes are English examples.

House of Commons: elected legislative body, in Britain currently consisting of six hundred and fifty members of Parliament. See also *Parliament.*

House of Lords: the "Upper House" of the British Houses of Parliament. Since the nineteenth century the House of Lords has been far less powerful than the elected House of Commons. The House of Lords is currently made up of both hereditary peers (Lords whose title is passed on from generation to generation) and life peers. As a result of legislation enacted by the Labour government of Tony Blair, the role of hereditary peers in Parliament is being phased out.

Humors: the four humors were believed in until the sixteenth and seventeenth centuries to be elements in the makeup of all humans; a person's temperament was thought to be determined by the way in which the humors were combined. When the *choleric* humor was dominant, the person would tend towards anger; when the *sanguine* humor was dominant, towards pleasant affability; when the *phlegmatic* humor was dominant, towards a cool and calm attitude and/or a lack of feeling or enthusiasm; and when the *melancholic* humor was dominant, towards withdrawal and melancholy.

Hymn: a song whose theme is usually religious, in praise of divinity. Literary hymns may praise more secular subjects.

Hyperbole: a *figure of speech* (a trope) that deliberately exaggerates or inflates meaning to achieve particular effects, such as the irony in A.E. Housman's claim (from "Terence, This Is Stupid Stuff") that "malt does more than Milton can / To justify God's ways to man."

Iamb: the most common metrical foot in English verse, containing one unstressed syllable followed by a stressed syllable: x / (e.g., between, achieve).

Idyll: traditionally, a short pastoral poem that idealizes country life, conveying impressions of innocence and happiness.

Image: the recreation in words of objects perceived by the senses, sometimes thought of as "pictures," although other senses besides sight are involved. Besides this literal application, the term also refers more generally to the descriptive effects of figurative language, especially in *metaphor* and *simile*.

Imagism: a poetic movement that was popular mainly in the second decade of the twentieth century. The goal of Imagist poets (such as H.D. and Ezra Pound in their early work) was to represent emotions or impressions through highly concentrated imagery.

Incantation: a chant or recitation of words that are believed to have magical power. A poem can achieve an "incantatory" effect through a compelling rhyme scheme and other repetitive patterns.

In Memoriam Stanza: a four-line stanza in iambic tetrameter, rhyming *abba*: the type of stanza used by Tennyson in *In Memoriam*.

Interlocking Rhyme: See *rhyme*.

Internal Rhyme: See *rhyme*.

Irony: a subtle form of humor in which a statement is understood to convey a quite different (and often entirely opposite) meaning. A writer achieves this by carefully making sure that the statement occurs in a context which undermines or twists the statement's "literal" meaning. *Hyperbole* and *litotes* are often used for ironic effect. *Sarcasm* is a particularly strong or crude form of irony (usually spoken), in which the meaning is conveyed largely by the tone of voice adopted; something said sarcastically is meant clearly to imply its opposite.

Labour Party: See *Political Parties*.

Lament: a poem which expresses profound regret or grief either because of a death, or because of the loss of a former, happier state.

Language Poetry: a movement that defies the usual lyric and narrative conventions of poetry, and that challenges the structures and codes of everyday language. Often seen as both politically and aesthetically subversive, its roots lie in the works of modernist writers like Ezra Pound and Gertrude Stein.

Liberal Party: See *Political Parties*.

Litotes: a *figure of speech* (a trope) in which a writer deliberately uses understatement to highlight the importance of an argument, or to convey an ironic attitude.

Liturgical Drama: drama based on and/or incorporating text from the liturgy—the text recited during religious services.

Lollard: member of the group of radical Christians that took its inspiration from the ideas of John Wyclif (c. 1330–84). The Lollards, in many ways precursors of the Protestant Reformation, advocated making the Bible available to all, and dedication to the principles of evangelical poverty in imitation of Christ.

Luddites: protestors against the mechanization of industry on the grounds that it was leading to the loss of employment and to an increase in poverty. In the years 1811 to 1816 there were several Luddite protests in which machines were destroyed.

Lyric: a poem, usually short, expressing an individual speaker's feelings or private thoughts. Originally a song performed with accompaniment on a lyre, the lyric poem is often noted for musicality of rhyme and rhythm. The lyric genre includes a variety of forms, including the *sonnet*, the *ode*, the *elegy*, the *madrigal*, the *aubade*, the *dramatic monologue*, and the *hymn*.

Madrigal: a lyric poem, usually short and focusing on pastoral or romantic themes. A madrigal is often set to music.

Masculine Ending: a metrical line ending on a stressed syllable. *Masculine Rhyme*: see *rhyme*.

Masque: an entertainment typically combining music and dance, with a limited script, extravagant costumes and sets, and often incorporating spectacular special effects. Masques, which were performed before court audiences in the early seventeenth century, often focused on royal themes and frequently drew on classical mythology.

Mass: within Christianity, a church service that includes the sacrament of the Eucharist (Holy Communion), in which bread and wine are consumed which are believed by those of many Christian denominations to have been transubstantiated into the body and blood of Christ. Anglicans (Episcopalians) are more likely to believe the bread and wine merely symbolizes the body and blood.

Melodrama: originally a term used to describe nineteenth-century plays featuring sensational story lines and a crude separation of characters into moral categories, with the pure and virtuous pitted against evil villains. Early melodramas employed background music throughout the action of the play as a means of heightening the emotional response of the audience. By extension, certain sorts of prose fictions or poems are often described as having melodramatic elements.

Metaphor: a *figure of speech* (in this case, a trope) in which a comparison is made or identity is asserted between two unrelated things or actions without the use of "like" or "as." The primary subject is known as the *tenor*; to illuminate its nature, the writer links it to wholly different images, ideas, or actions referred to as the *vehicle*. Unlike a *simile*, which is a direct comparison of two things, a metaphor "fuses" the separate qualities of two things, creating a new idea. For example, Shakespeare's "Let slip the dogs of war" is a metaphorical statement. The tenor, or primary subject, is "war"; the vehicle of the metaphor is the image of hunting dogs released from their leash. The line fuses the idea of war with the qualities of ravening bloodlust associated with hunting dogs.

Metaphysical Poets: a group of seventeenth-century English poets, notably Donne, Cowley, Marvell, and Herbert, who employed unusual difficult imagery and *conceits* (see above) in order to develop intellectual and religious themes. The term was first applied to these writers to mark as far-fetched their use of philosophical and scientific ideas in a poetic context.

Meter: the pattern of stresses, syllables, and pauses that constitutes the regular rhythm of a line of verse. The meter of a poem written in the English accentual-syllabic tradition is determined by identifying the stressed and unstressed syllables in a line of verse, and grouping them into recurring units known as feet. See *accent*, *accentual-syllabic*, *caesura*, *elision*, and *scansion*. For some of the better known meters, see *iamb*, *trochee*, *dactyl*, *anapaest*, and *spondee*. See also *monometer*, *dimeter*, *trimeter*, *tetrameter*, *pentameter*, and *hexameter*.

Methodist: Protestant denomination formed in the eighteenth century as part of the religious movement led by John and Charles Wesley. Originally a movement within the Church of England, Methodism entailed enthusiastic evangelism, a strong emphasis on free will, and a strict regimen of Christian living.

Metonymy: a *figure of speech* (a trope), meaning "change of name," in which a writer refers to an object or idea by substituting the name of another object or idea closely associated with it: for example, the substitution of "crown" for monarchy, "the press" for journalism, or "the pen" for writing. *Synecdoche* (see below) is a kind of metonymy.

Mock-heroic: a style applying the elevated diction and vocabulary of epic poetry to low or ridiculous subjects. An example is Alexander Pope's "The Rape of the Lock."

Monologue: words spoken by a character to him or herself or to an audience directly.

Monometer: a line containing one metrical foot.

Mood: this can describe the writer's attitude, implied or expressed, towards the subject (see *tone* below); or it may refer to the atmosphere that a writer creates in a passage of description or narration.

Motif: an idea, image, action, or plot element that recurs throughout a literary work, creating new levels of meaning and strengthening structural coherence. The term is taken from music, where it describes recurring melodies or themes. See also *theme*.

Narrative Perspective: in fiction, the point of view from which the story is narrated. A first-person narrative is recounted using *I* and *me*, whereas a third person narrative is recounted using *he*, *she*, *they*, and so on. When a narrative is written in the third person and the narrative voice evidently "knows" all that is being done and thought, the story is typically described as being recounted by an "omniscient narrator."

Neoclassical: adapted from or substantially influenced by the cultures of ancient Greece and Rome. The term *neoclassical* is often used to describe the ideals of Restoration and eighteenth-century writers and artists who looked to ancient Greek and Roman civilization for models.

Nobility: privileged class, the members of which are distinguished by the holding of titles. Dukes, Marquesses, Earls, Viscounts, and Barons (in that order of precedence) are all holders of hereditary titles—that is to say, in the British patrilineal tradition, titles passed on from generation to generation to the eldest son. The title of Baronet, also hereditary, was added to this list by James I. Holders of non-hereditary titles include Knights and Dames.

Nonconformist: general term used to describe one who does not subscribe to the Church of England.

Nonsense Verse: light, humorous poetry which contradicts logic, plays with the absurd, and invents words for amusing effects. Lewis Carroll is one of the best-known practitioners of nonsense verse.

Octave: also known as "octet," the first eight lines in an Italian/Petrarchan sonnet, rhyming *abbaabba*. See also *sestet* and *sonnet*.

Octosyllabic: a line of poetry with eight syllables, as in iambic tetrameter.

Ode: originally a classical poetic form, used by the Greeks and Romans to convey serious themes. English poetry has evolved three main forms of ode: the Pindaric (imitative of the odes of the Greek poet Pindar); the Horatian (modeled on the work of the Roman writer Horace); and the irregular ode. The Pindaric ode was an irregular stanza in English, has a tripartite structure of *strophe*, *antistrophe*, and *epode* (meaning turn, counterturn, and stand), modeled on the songs and movements of the Chorus in Greek drama. The Horatian ode is more personal, reflective, and literary, and employs a pattern of repeated stanzas. The irregular ode, as its name implies, avoids a recurrent stanza pattern, and is sometimes irregular in line length also (see, for example, Wordsworth's "Ode: Intimations of Immortality").

Onomatopoeia: a *figure of speech* (a scheme) in which a word "imitates" a sound, or in which the sound of a word seems to reflect its meaning.

Ottava Rima: an eight-line stanza, usually in iambic pentameter, with the rhyme scheme *abababcc*. For an example, see Byron's *Don Juan*, or Yeats's "Sailing to Byzantium."

Oxymoron: a *figure of speech* (a trope) in which two words whose meanings seem contradictory are placed together, a paradox: for example, the phrase "darkness visible," from Milton's *Paradise Lost*.

Paean: a triumphant, celebratory song, often associated with a military victory.

Pale: in the medieval period, term for a protective zone around a fortress. As of the year 1500 three of these had been set up to guard frontiers of territory controlled by England—surrounding Calais in France, Berwick-upon-Tweed on the Scottish frontier, and Dublin in Ireland. The Dublin Pale was the largest of the three, and the term remained in use for a longer period there.

Pantoum: a poem in linked quatrains that rhyme *abab*. The second and fourth lines of one stanza are repeated as the first and third lines of the stanza that follows. In the final stanza the pattern is reversed: the second line repeats the third line of the first stanza, the fourth and final line repeats the first line of the first stanza.

Parliament: in Britain, the legislative body, comprising both the House of Commons and the House of Lords. Since the eighteenth century, the most powerful figure in the British government has been the Prime Minister rather than the monarch, the House of Commons has been the dominant body in Parliament, and members of the House of Commons have been organized in political parties. Since the mid-nineteenth century the effective executive in the British Parliamentary system has been the Cabinet, each member of which is typically in charge of a department of government. Unlike the American system, the British Parliamentary system (sometimes called the "Westminster system," after the location of the Houses of Parliament) brings together the executive and legislative functions of government, with the Prime Minister leading the government party in the House of Commons as well as directing the cabinet. By convention it is understood that the House of Lords will not contravene the wishes of the House of Commons in any fundamental way, though the "Upper House," as it is often referred to, may sometimes modify or reject legislation.

Parody: a close, usually mocking imitation of a particular literary work, or of the well-known style of a particular author, in order to expose or magnify weaknesses. Parody is a form of satire—that is, humor that may ridicule and scorn its object.

Pastiche: a discourse which borrows or imitates other writers' characters, forms, style, or ideas. Unlike a parody, a pastiche is usually intended as a compliment to the original writer.

Pastoral: in general, pertaining to country life; in prose, drama, and poetry, a stylized type of writing that idealizes the lives and innocence of country people, particularly shepherds and shepherdesses. Also see *eclogue, georgic, idyll,* above.

Pastoral Elegy: a poem in which the poet uses the pastoral style to lament the death of a friend, usually represented as a shepherd. Milton's "Lycidas" provides a good example of the form, including its use of such conventions as an invocation of the muse and a procession of mourners.

Pathetic Fallacy: a form of personification in which inanimate objects are given human emotions: for example, rain clouds "weeping." The word "fallacy" in this connection is intended to suggest the distortion of reality or the false emotion that may result from an exaggerated use of personification.

Pathos: the emotional quality of a discourse; or the ability of a discourse to appeal to our emotions. It is usually applied to the mood conveyed by images of pain, suffering, or loss that arouse feelings of pity or sorrow in the reader.

Pattern Poetry: a predecessor of modern concrete poetry, in which the shape of the poem on the page is intended to suggest or imitate an aspect of the poem's subject. George Herbert's "Easter Wings" is an example of pattern poetry.

Penny Dreadful: Victorian term for a cheap and poorly produced work of short fiction, usually of a sensational nature.

Pentameter: a line of verse containing five metrical feet.

Performance Poetry: poetry composed primarily for oral performance, often very theatrical in nature. See also *dub poetry* and *rap*.

Persona: the assumed identity or "speaking voice" that a writer projects in a discourse. The term "persona" literally means "mask." Even when a writer speaks in the first person, we should be aware that the attitudes or opinions we hear may not necessarily be those of the writer in real life.

Personification: a *figure of speech* (a trope), also known as "prosopopoeia," in which a writer refers to inanimate objects, ideas, or animals as if they were human, or creates a human figure to represent an abstract entity such as Philosophy or Peace.

Petrarchan Sonnet: the earliest form of the sonnet, also known as the Italian sonnet, with an 8-line octave and a six-line sestet. The Petrarchan sonnet traditionally focuses on love and descriptions of physical beauty.

Phoneme: a linguistic term denoting the smallest unit of sound that it is possible to distinguish. The words *fun* and *phone* each have three phonemes, though one has three letters and one has five. (Each makes up a single syllable.)

Pindaric: See *ode*.

Plot: the organization of story materials within a literary work. The order in which story material is presented (especially causes and consequences); the inclusion of elements that allow or encourage the reader or audience to form expectations as to what is likely to happen; the decision to present some story material through exposition rather than in more extended form as part of the main action of the narrative—all these are matters of plotting.

Political Parties: the party names "Whig" and "Tory" began to be used in the late seventeenth century; before that time members of the House of Commons acted individually or through shifting and very informal factions. At first the Whigs and Tories had little formal organization either, but by the mid-eighteenth century parties had acknowledged leaders, and the leader of the party with the largest number of members in the House of Commons had begun to be recognized as the Prime Minister. The Tories evolved into the modern Conservative Party, and the Whigs into the Liberal Party. In the late nineteenth century the Labour Party was formed in an effort to provide better representation in Parliament for the working class, and since the 1920s Labour and the Conservatives have alternated as the party of government, with the Liberals reduced to third-party status. (Since 1988, when the Liberals merged with a breakaway faction from Labour known as the Social Democrats, this third party has been named the Liberal Democrats.)

Pre-Raphaelites: originally a group of Victorian artists and writers, formed in 1848. Their goal was to revive what they considered the simpler, fresher, more natural art that existed before Raphael (1483–1520). The poet Dante Gabriel Rossetti was one of the founders of the group.

Presbyterian: term applied to a group of Protestants (primarily English and Scottish) who advocated replacing the traditional hierarchical church in which bishops and archbishops governed lower level members of the clergy with a system in which all presbyters (or ministers) would be equal. The Presbyterians, originally led by John Knox, were strongly influenced by the ideas of John Calvin.

Prose Poem: a poetic discourse that uses prose formats (e.g., it may use margins and paragraphs rather than line breaks or stanzas) yet is written with the kind of attention to language, rhythm, and cadence that characterizes verse.

Prosody: the study and analysis of meter, rhythm, rhyme, stanzaic pattern, and other devices of versification.

Protagonist: the central character in a literary work.

Prothalamion: a wedding song; a term coined by the poet Edmund Spenser, adapted from "epithalamion" (see above).

Public School: See *schools* below.

Pun: a play on words, in which a word with two or more distinct meanings, or two words with similar sounds, may create humorous ambiguities. Also known as *paranomasia*.

Puritan: term, originally applied only in a derogatory fashion but later widely accepted as descriptive, referring to those in England who favored religious reforms that went beyond those instituted as part of the Protestant Reformation, or, more generally, who were more forceful and uncompromising in pressing for religious purity both within the Church and in society as a whole.

Pyrrhic: a metrical foot containing two weak stresses: xx.

Quadrivium: group of four academic subjects (arithmetic, astronomy, geometry, and music) that made up part of the university coursework in the Middle Ages. They were studied after the more basic subjects of the *Trivium.*

Quantitative Meter: a metrical system used by Greek and Roman poets, in which a line of verse was measured by the "quantity," or length of sound of each syllable. A foot was measured in terms of syllables classed as long or short.

Quantity: duration of syllables in poetry. The line "There is a Garden in her face" (the first line from the poem of the same name by Thomas Campion) is characterized by the short quantities of the syllables. The last line of Thomas Hardy's "During Wind and Rain" has the same number of syllables as the line by Campion, but the quantities of the syllables are much longer—in other words, the line takes much longer to say: "Down their carved names the rain drop ploughs."

Quatrain: a four-line stanza, usually rhymed.

Quintet: a five-line stanza. Sometimes given as *quintain.*

Rap: originally coined to describe informal conversation, "rap" now usually describes a style of performance poetry in which a poet will chant rhymed verse, sometimes improvised and usually with musical accompaniment that has a heavy beat.

Realism: as a literary term, the presentation through literature of material closely resembling real life. As notions both of what constitutes "real life" and of how it may be most faithfully represented in literature have varied widely, "realism" has taken a variety of meanings. The term *naturalistic* has sometimes been used as a synonym for *realistic*; *naturalism* originated in the nineteenth century as a term denoting a form of realism focusing in particular on grim, unpleasant, or ugly aspects of the real.

Refrain: one or more words or lines repeated at regular points throughout a poem, often at the end of each stanza or group of stanzas. Sometimes a whole stanza may be repeated to create a refrain, like the chorus in a song.

Reggae: a style of heavily rhythmic music from the West Indies with lyrics that are colloquial in language and often anti-establishment in content and flavor. First popularized in the 1960s and 1970s, reggae has had a lasting influence on performance poetry, rap, and dub.

Rhetoric: in classical Greece and Rome, the art of persuasion and public speaking. From the Middle Ages onwards, the study of rhetoric gave greater attention to style, particularly figures of speech. Today in poetics, the term rhetoric may encompass not only figures of speech, but also the persuasive effects of forms, sounds, and word choices.

Rhyme: the repetition of identical or similar sounds, usually in pairs and generally at the ends of metrical lines.

End-rhyme: a rhyming word or syllable at the end of a line.

Eye Rhyme: rhyming that pairs words whose spellings are alike but whose pronunciations are different: for example, though/slough.

Feminine Rhyme: a two-syllable (also known as "double") rhyme. The first syllable is stressed and the second unstressed: for example, hasty/tasty. See also *triple rhyme* below.

Interlocking Rhyme: the repetition of rhymes from one stanza to the next, creating links that add to the poem's continuity and coherence. Examples may be found in Shelley's use of *terza rima* in "Ode to the West Wind" and in Dylan Thomas's villanelle "Do Not Go Gentle into That Good Night."

Internal Rhyme: the placement of rhyming words within lines so that at least two words in a line rhyme with each other.

Masculine Rhyme: a correspondence of sound between the final stressed syllables at the end of two or more lines, as in grieve / leave, arr-i've / sur-vive.

Slant Rhyme: an imperfect or partial rhyme (also known as "near" or "half" rhyme) in which the final consonants of stressed syllables match but the vowel sounds do not. E.g., spoiled / spilled, taint / stint.

Triple Rhyme: a three-syllable rhyme in which the first syllable of each rhyme-word is stressed and the other two unstressed (e.g., lottery / coterie).

True Rhyme: a rhyme in which everything but the initial consonant matches perfectly in sound and spelling.

Rhyme Royal: a stanza of seven iambic pentameters, with a rhyme-scheme of *ababbcc*. This is also known as the Chaucerian stanza, as Chaucer was the first English poet to use this form. See also *septet.*

Rhythm: in speech, the arrangement of stressed and unstressed syllables creates units of sound. In song or verse, these units usually form a regular rhythmic pattern, a kind of beat, described in prosody as *meter*.

Romanticism: a major social and cultural movement, originating in Europe, that shaped much of Western artistic thought in the late eighteenth and nineteenth centuries. Opposing the ideal of controlled, rational order of the Enlightenment, Romanticism emphasizes the importance of spontaneous self-expression, emotion, and personal experience in producing art. In Romanticism, the "natural" is privileged over the conventional or the artificial.

Rondeau: a fifteen-line poem, generally octosyllabic, with only two rhymes throughout its three stanzas, and an unrhymed refrain at the end of the ninth and fifteenth lines, repeating part of the opening line.

Sarcasm: See *irony.*

Satire: literary work designed to make fun of or seriously criticize its subject. According to many literary theories of the Renaissance and neoclassical periods, the ridicule through satire of a certain sort of behavior may function for the reader or audience as a corrective of such behavior.

Scansion: the formal analysis of patterns of rhythm and rhyme in poetry. Each line of verse will have a certain number of fairly regular "beats" consisting of alternating stressed and unstressed syllables. To "scan" a poem is to count the beats in each line, to mark stressed and unstressed syllables and indicate their combination into "feet," to note pauses, and to identify rhyme schemes with letters of the alphabet.

Scheme: See *figures of speech.*

Schools: in the sixteenth and seventeenth centuries the different forms of school in England included Cathedral schools (often founded with a view to the education of members of the choir); grammar schools (often founded by towns or by guilds, and teaching a much broader curriculum than the modern sense of "grammar" might suggest; private schools, operated by private individuals out of private residences; and public schools, which (like the private schools and the grammar schools) operated independent of any church authority, but unlike the grammar schools and private schools were organized as independent charities, and often offered free education. Over the centuries certain of these public schools, while remaining not-for-profit institutions, began to accept fee-paying students and to adopt standards that made them more and more exclusive. In the eighteenth and nineteenth century attendance at such prestigious public boarding schools as Eton, Westminster, and Winchester had become almost exclusively the preserve of the upper classes; by the nineteenth century such "public" schools were the equivalent of private schools in North America. A few girls attended some early grammar schools, but the greater part of this educational system was for boys only. Though a number of individuals of earlier periods were concerned to increase the number of private schools for girls, the movement to create a parallel girls' system of public schools and grammar schools dates from the later nineteenth century.

Septet: a stanza containing seven lines.

Serf: in the medieval period, a person of unfree status, typically engaged in working the land.

Sestet: a six-line stanza that forms the second grouping of lines in an Italian / Petrarchan sonnet, following the octave. See *sonnet* and *sestina.*

Sestina: an elaborate unrhymed poem with six six-line stanzas and a three-line envoy.

Shire: originally a multiple estate; since the late medieval period a larger territory forming an administrative unit—also referred to as a county.

Simile: a *figure of speech* (a trope) which makes an explicit comparison between a particular object and another object or idea that is similar in some (often unexpected) way. A simile always uses "like" or "as" to signal the connection. Compare with *metaphor* above.

Sonnet: a highly structured lyric poem, which normally has fourteen lines of iambic pentameter. We can distinguish four major variations of the sonnet.

> **Italian/Petrarchan:** named for the fourteenth-century Italian poet Petrarch, has an octave rhyming *abbaabba*, and a sestet rhyming *cdecde*, or *cdcdcd* (other arrangements are possible here). Usually, a turn in argument takes place between octave and sestet.

Miltonic: developed by Milton and similar to the Petrarchan in rhyme scheme, but eliminating the turn after the octave, thus giving greater unity to the poem's structure of thought.

Shakespearean: often called the English sonnet, this form has three quatrains and a couplet. The quatrains rhyme internally but do not interlock: *abab cdcd efef gg*. The turn may occur after the second quatrain, but is usually revealed in the final couplet. Shakespeare's sonnets are the best-known examples of this form.

Spenserian: after Edmund Spenser, who developed the form in his sonnet cycle *Amoretti*. This sonnet form has three quatrains linked through interlocking rhyme, and a separately rhyming couplet: *abab bcbc cdcd ee*.

Speaker: in the late medieval period, a member of the Commons in Parliament who spoke on behalf of that entire group. (The Commons first elected a Speaker in 1376.) In later eras the role of Speaker became one of chairing debates in the House of Commons and arbitrating disputes over matters of procedure.

Spenserian Stanza: a nine-line stanza, with eight iambic pentameters and a concluding alexandrine, rhyming *ababbcbcc*.

Spondee: a metrical foot containing two strong stressed syllables: // (e.g., blind mouths).

Sprung Rhythm: a modern variation of accentual verse, created by the English poet Gerard Manley Hopkins, in which rhythms are determined largely by the number of strong stresses in a line, without regard to the number of unstressed syllables. Hopkins felt that sprung rhythm more closely approximated the natural rhythms of speech than did conventional poetry.

Stanza: any lines of verse that are grouped together in a poem and separated from other similarly structured groups by a space. In metrical poetry, stanzas share metrical and rhyming patterns; however, stanzas may also be formed on the basis of thought, as in irregular odes. Conventional stanza forms include the *tercet*, the *quatrain*, *rhyme royal*, the *Spenserian stanza*, the *ballad stanza*, and *ottava rima*.

Stream of Consciousness: narrative technique that attempts to convey in prose fiction a sense of the progression of the full range of thoughts and sensations occurring within a character's mind. Twentieth-century pioneers in the use of the stream of consciousness technique include Dorothy Richardson, Virginia Woolf, and James Joyce.

Stress: See *accent*.

Strophe: the first stanza in a Pindaric ode. This is followed by an *antistrophe* (see above), which presents the same metrical pattern and rhyme scheme, and finally by an *epode*, differing in meter from the preceding stanzas. Upon completion of this "triad," the entire sequence can recur. *Strophe* may also describe a stanza or other subdivision in other kinds of poem.

Sublime: a concept, most popular in eighteenth-century England, of the qualities of grandeur, power, and awe that may be inherent in or produced by undomesticated nature or great art. The sublime was thought of as higher and loftier than something that is merely beautiful.

Subplot: a line of story that is subordinate to the main storyline of a narrative. (Note that properly speaking a subplot is a category of story material, not of plot.)

Substitution: a deliberate change from the dominant pattern of stresses in a line of verse to create emphasis or variation. Thus the first line of Shakespeare's sonnet "'Shall I compare thee to a summer's day?'" is decidedly iambic in meter (x / x / x / x / x /), whereas the second line substitutes a trochee (/ x) in the opening foot: "Thou art more lovely and more temperate."

Subtext: implied or suggested meaning of a passage of text, or of an entire work.

Syllabic Verse: poetry in which the length of a line is measured solely by the number of syllables, regardless of accents or patterns of stress.

Syllable: vocal sound or group of sounds forming a unit of speech; a syllable may be formed with a single effort of articulation. Some syllables consist of a single phoneme (e.g., the word *I*, or the first syllable in the word *u*-ni-ty) but others may be made up of several phonemes (as with one-syllable words such as *lengths*, *splurged*, and *through*). By contrast, the much shorter words *ago*, *any*, and *open* each have two syllables.

Symbol: a word, image, or idea that represents something more, or other, than for what it at first appears to stand. Like metaphor, the symbol extends meaning; but while the tenor and vehicle of metaphor are bound in a specific relationship, a symbol may have a range of connotations. For example, the image of a rose may call forth associations of love, passion, transience, fragility, youth and beauty, among others. Depending upon the context, such an image could be interpreted in a variety of ways, as in Blake's lyric, "The Sick Rose." Though this power of symbolic representation characterizes all language, poetry most particularly endows the concrete imagery evoked through language with a larger meaning. Such meaning is implied rather than explicitly stated; indeed, much of the power of symbolic language lies in the reader's ability to make meaningful sense of it.

Syncope: in poetry, the dropping of a letter or syllable from the middle of a word, as in "trav'ler." Such a contraction allows a line to stay within a metrical scheme. See also *catalexis* and *elision*.

Synecdoche: a kind of *metonymy* in which a writer substitutes the name of a part of something to signify the whole: for example, "sail" for ship or "hand" for a member of the ship's crew.

Tercet: a group, or stanza, of three lines, often linked by an interlocking rhyme scheme as in *terza rima*. See also *triplet*.

Terza Rima: an arrangement of tercets interlocked by a rhyme scheme of *aba bcb cdc ded*, etc., and ending with a couplet that rhymes with the second-last line of the final tercet (for example, *efe*, *ff*). See, for example, Percy Shelley's "Ode to the West Wind."

Tetrameter: a line of poetry containing four metrical feet.

Theme: the governing idea of a discourse, conveyed through the development of the subject, and through the recurrence of certain words, sounds, or metrical patterns. See also *motif*.

Third-Person Narrative: See *narrative perspective*.

Tone: the writer's attitude toward a given subject or audience, as expressed through an authorial persona or "voice." Tone can be projected through particular choices of wording, imagery, figures of speech, and rhythmic devices. Compare *mood.*

Tories: See *Political Parties.*

Tragedy: in the traditional definition originating in discussions of ancient Greek drama, a serious narrative recounting the downfall of the protagonist. More loosely, the term has been applied to a wide variety of literary forms in which the tone is predominantly a dark one and the narrative does not end happily.

Transcendentalism: a philosophical movement that influenced such Victorian writers as Thomas Carlyle and Robert Browning. Also a mode of Romantic thought, Transcendentalism places the supernatural and the natural within one great Unity and believes that each individual person embodies aspects of the divine.

Trimeter: a line of poetry containing three metrical feet.

Triolet: a French form in which the first line appears three times in a poem of only eight lines. The first line is repeated at lines 4 and 7; the second line is repeated in line 8. The triolet has only two rhymes: *abaaabab.*

Triple Foot: poetic foot of three syllables. The possible varieties of triple foot are the anapest (in which two unstressed syllables are followed by a stressed syllable), the dactyl (in which a stressed syllable is followed by two unstressed lines), and the mollossus (in which all three syllables are stressed equally). English poetry tends to use duple rhythms far more frequently than triple rhythms.

Triplet: a group of three lines with the same end-rhyme, much used by eighteenth-century poets to vary or punctuate the flow of couplets. See also *tercet.*

Trivium: group of three academic subjects (dialectic, grammar, and rhetoric) that were part of the university curriculum in the Middle Ages. Their study precedes that of the more advanced subjects of the *quadrivium.*

Trochee: a metrical foot containing one strong stress followed by one weak stress: / x (heaven, lover).

Trope: any figure of speech that plays on our understandings of words to extend, alter, or transform "literal" meaning. Common tropes include *metaphor*, *simile*, *personification*, *hyperbole*, *metonymy*, *oxymoron*, *synecdoche*, and *irony*. See also *figures of speech*, above.

Turn (Italian "volta"): the point in a *sonnet* where the mood or argument changes. The turn may occur between the octave and sestet, i.e., after the eighth line, or in the final couplet, depending on the kind of sonnet.

Unities: Many literary theorists of the late sixteenth through late eighteenth centuries held that a play should ideally be presented as representing a single place, and confining the action to a single day and a single dominant event. They disapproved of plots involving gaps or long periods of time, shifts in place, or subplots. These concepts, which came to be referred to as the unities of space, time, and action, were based on a misreading of classical authorities (principally of Aristotle).

Vers de societé: literally, "verse about society." The term originated with poetry written by aristocrats and upper-middle-class poets that specifically disavows the ambition of creating "high art" while treating the concerns of their own group in verse forms that demonstrate a high degree of formal control (e.g., artful rhymes, surprising turns of diction).

Vers libre: See *free verse* above.

Verse: a general term for works of poetry, usually referring to poems that incorporate some kind of metrical structure. The term may also describe a line of poetry, though more frequently it is applied to a stanza.

Villanelle: a poem usually consisting of 19 lines, with five 3-line stanzas (tercets) rhyming *aba*, and a concluding quatrain rhyming *abaa*. The first and third lines of the first tercet are repeated at fixed intervals throughout the rest of the poem. See, for example, Dylan Thomas's "Do Not Go Gentle into That Good Night."

Whigs: See *Political Parties*.

Workhouse: public institution in which the poor were provided with a minimal level of sustenance and with lodging in exchange for work performed. Early workhouses were typically administered by individual parishes. In 1834 a unified system covering all of England and Wales was put into effect.

Zeugma: a *figure of speech* (trope) in which one word links or "yokes" two others in the same sentence, often to comic or ironic effect. For example, a verb may govern two objects, as in Pope's line "Or stain her honour, or her new brocade."

Permissions Acknowledgments

Burney, Frances. "The Witlings." Reproduced with the permission of Peter Sabor and Geoffrey Sill. (sites.broadviewpress.com/bablonline)

Haywood, Eliza. "Fantomina." Reproduced with the permission of Margaret Case, Alexander Pettit, and Anna C. Patchias. (p. 632)

Piozzi, Hester Lynch Salusbury Thrale. Reprinted by permission of the publisher from THE THRALES OF STREATHAM PARK, edited by Mary Hyde, pp. 85–86, 105–07, 149–152, 163, 165–67, 175, Cambridge, Mass.: Harvard University Press, Copyright © 1976, 1977 by Mary Hyde. (p. 946)

Sheridan, Richard Brinsley. "The School for Scandal," edited by Mita Choudhury. Reproduced with permission of the editor. (p.972)

Walpole, Horace. "The Castle of Otranto." Reproduced with the permission of Frederick Frank. (sites.broadviewpress.com/bablonline)

Wycherley, William. "The Country Wife," edited by Peggy Thompson. Reproduced with permission of the editor. (p.239)

Illustration Credits

Anonymous. Portrait of Dido Elizabeth Belle and Lady Elizabeth Murray, c. 1777. From the collection of the Earl of Mansfield, Scone Palace, Perth, Scotland. (color insert)

Anonymous, 1778. Scene from "School for Scandal" being performed in Drury Lane Theatre, London: four actors on stage, the audience watching from boxes on either side. Copyright © The British Museum.

Darly, Matthew. A Mungo Macaroni. From *Macaronies, Characters, Caricatures &c* by M Darly. [1772] (Vol.4). Copyright © The Trustees of the British Museum. (p. 706)

Gillray, James. United Irishmen Upon Duty. Copyright © The Trustees of the British Museum. (p. 707)

Cover and Page LVI: Reproduced by permission of the TATE Gallery © Tate, London 2005.

Page 32: Reproduced by permission of the National Portrait Gallery, London. [Bunyan]

Page 69: Reproduced by permission of the National Portrait Gallery, London. [Dryden]

Page 112: Reproduced by permission of the National Portrait Gallery, London. [Pepys]

Page 196: Reproduced by permission of the National Portrait Gallery, London. [Behn]

Page 290: Reproduced by permission of the National Portrait Gallery, London. [Wilmot]

Page 348: Reproduced by permission of the National Portrait Gallery, London. [Finch]

Page 533: Reproduced by permission of the National Portrait Gallery, London. [Addison]

Page 540: Reproduced by permission of the National Portrait Gallery, London. [Pope]

Page 708: Reproduced by permission of the National Portrait Gallery, London. [Thomson]

Page 804: Reproduced by permission of the National Portrait Gallery, London. [Gray]

(sites.broadviewpress.com/bablonline): Reproduced by permission of the National Portrait Gallery, London. [Walpole]

Page 822: Reproduced by permission of the National Portrait Gallery, London. [Smart]

Page 945: Reproduced by permission of the National Portrait Gallery, London. [Piozzi]

Page 1004: James Roberts. (1753–1809). Frances Abingdon, Thomas King, John Palmer and William Smith in *School for Scandal*, 1776, by R.B. Sheridan. Photo: The Garrick Club / The Art Archive at Art Resource, NY.

(sites.broadviewpress.com/bablonline): Reproduced by permission of the National Portrait Gallery, London. [Burney]

(sites.broadviewpress.com/bablonline): [Photograph of Strawberry Hill:] Reproduced by permission of Frederick Frank.

Information on all translations used is provided in footnotes at the beginning of selections. Copyright permission to reproduce material translated or edited for this anthology and material reproduced or adapted here that originally appeared in other books published by Broadview Press may be sought from Broadview.

The publisher has endeavored to contact rights holders of all copyright material and would appreciate receiving any information as to errors or omissions.

Index of First Lines

A milk-white hair-lace wound up all her hairs 3
A poet's cat, sedate and grave 887
A School for Scandal! tell me, I beseech you 972
A trader I am to the African shore (Website)
Adieu, New England's smiling meads 1020
All human things are subject to decay 87
All my past life is mine no more 294
Armed with thy sad last gift—the pow'r to die (Website)
As Rochefoucauld his maxims drew 381
As some brave admiral, in former war 295
As some grave matron bred on rural downs 899
At length, by so much importunity pressed 606
Awake, my St. John! leave all meaner things 575
Before I see another day 855
Betwixt two ridges of plowed land lay Wat 4
Bristol, thine heart hath throbbed to glory.—Slaves, 834
But anxious cares the pensive nymph oppressed 563
By neer resemblance see that Bird betray'd 353
Careful observers may foretell the hour 376
Cease, Wilberforce, to urge thy generous aim! (Website)
Chloe, in verse by your command I write 296
Close by those meads forever crowned with flow'rs 560
Come, gentle Spring, ethereal mildness, come (Website)
Come listen to me, you gallants so free 810
Condemn me not for making such a coil 3
Condemned by fate to wayward curse (Website)
Condemned to Hope's delusive mine 766
Could we stop the time that's flying 353
Crowned with the sickle and the wheaten sheaf (Website)
Dark was the dawn, and o'er the deep (Website)
Did I, my lines intend for public view 350
Dim, as the borrowed beams of moon and stars 90
Fair lovely maid, or if that title be 200
Farewell, too little and too lately known 91
Five hours (and who can do it less in?) 379
For I will consider my Cat Jeoffry 823
From brightening fields of ether fair-disclosed (Website)
From harmony, from heav'nly harmony 92
God bless our good and gracious King 300
God moves in a mysterious way 880
Hail, happy day, when, smiling like the morn 1019
Hail, happy saint! on thine immortal throne 1023
Hark! 'tis the twanging horn! o'er yonder bridge (Website)
How doth the little busy bee 182
I sing the sofa. I, who lately sang 881
I' th' isle of Britain, long since famous grown 291
If heaven has into being deigned to call 830
Immortal bard! Thou favorite of the nine! 894
In pious times, ere priestcraft did begin 72
In such a night, when every louder wind 354
In these deep solitudes and awful cells 570
In vain, dear Madam, yes in vain you strive 898
In vain to me the smiling Mornings shine 807
Know then thyself, presume not God to scan 579
Let Observation, with extensive view 761
Maecenas, you, beneath the myrtle shade 1017
Naked she lay, clasped in my longing arms 299
No sooner, Flavio, was you gone 351
Not with more glories, in th' ethereal plain 559
Nothing so true as what you once let fall: 592
Now you, the vigorous, who daily here 289
O I forbid you, maidens a' 813
O Love, how thou art tired out with rhyme! 3
Obscurest night involved the sky 886
Oh for a lodge in some vast wilderness (Website)
Old as I am, for ladies' love unfit 93
One day the amorous Lysander 197
Our God, our help in ages past 183
Poets, like cudgeled bullies, never do 239
Reading my verses, I like't them so well 3
Ruin seize thee, ruthless King (Website)
Science! thou fair effusive ray 180
See! Winter comes, to rule the varied year 709
See! with what pale and mournful look appears 843
Shall the great soul of Newton quit this Earth 179
Shall the poor AFRICAN, the passive Slave (Website)
She said; the pitying audience melt in tears 566
Shut, shut the door, good John! (fatigued I said) 584
Stella this day is thirty-four 377
Sweet Auburn! loveliest village of the plain 873
The care of sheep, the labours of the loom 942
The curfew tolls the knell of parting day 807
The devil take this cursed plotting age (Website)
The Doctor in a clean starched band 605
The grateful tribute of these rural lays 891
The tea-kettle bubbled, the tea things were set 902
The twentieth year is well nigh past 889
The wretched Flavia on her couch reclined 603
Think not this paper comes with vain pretense 607
This ae nighte, this ae nighte 819
This day, whate'er the fates decree 378

This to the crown, and blessing of my life 351
Thou so many favours hast received 935
Thou, to whom the world unknown (Website)
Through airy roads he wings his instant flight 1021
Through winter streets to steer your course aright 906
Thy forests, Windsor! and thy green retreats 548
Thy Plains, O Abram! And thy pleasing views (Website)
Thy younglings, Cuddy, are but just awake 933
Tis hard to say, if greater want of skill 542
'Tis strange, the miser should his cares employ 597
To show the lab'ring bosom's deep intent 1019
Toll for the brave! 888
'Twas mercy brought me from my pagan land 1018
'Twas on a lofty vase's side 806
Were I (who to my cost already am 292
What art thou, Spleen, which every thing dost ape? 349
What beck'ning ghost, along the moonlight shade 568
What bodies else but Man's did Nature make 3
What dire offence from am'rous causes springs 556
When at the first I took my pen in hand 34
When Britain first, at Heaven's command 715
When first Diana leaves her bed 375
When friends or fortune frown on Mira's lay 900
When Robin Hood and Little John 817
Whilst happy I triumphant stood 199
Why does your brand sae drop wi' blude 812
Why should our damned tyrants oblige us to live 283
Word's gane to the kitchen 820
Ye distant spires, ye antique tow'rs 805
Your subjects hope, dread Sire— 1018

Index of Authors and Titles

Absalom and Achitophel 72
Abram's Plains (Website)
Account of a Very Odd Monstrous Calf, An 149
Account of Another Experiment of Transfusion, *viz.* Of Bleeding a Mangy into a Sound Dog 150
Account of Some Observations Made by a Young Gentleman Who Was Born Blind, An 151
Account of the Slave Trade on the Coast of Africa (Website)
Addison, Joseph 533, 657, 661, 670, 676, 914, 928, 938
African, The (Website)
Akenside, Mark 180
Against Idleness and Mischief 182
American, Crisis, The 869
Analytic Review, The 968
Anecdotes Relating to the Battle of Quebec 852
Apology for the Life of Mr. Colley Cibber, An 654
Apology of Negro Slavery, An (Website)
Arabella's Day 715
Astell, Mary 190, 355
Aubrey, John (Website)
Autobiography of Benjamin Franklin, from The 153, 863
Autumn (Website)
Barbauld, Anna Laetitia (Website)
Bard, The (Website)
Beggar's Opera, The (Website)
Behn, Aphra 196
Bicknell, John and Thomas Day (Website)
Bolingbroke (Website)
Boswell, James 185, 661 (Website)
Boudier de Villemert, Pierre Joseph (Website)
Boyle, Robert 149
Brief Lives, from (Website)
Brooke, Frances 698 (Website)
Bryan, Margaret 181
Bunyan, John 32
Burke, Edmund 861, 943
Burney, Frances (Website)
By neer resemblance that Bird betray'd 353
Captive American, The 857
Cary, Thomas (Website)
Castaway, The 886
Castle of Otranto, The (Website)
Causes of the Wretched Condition of Ireland 528
Cavendish, Margaret 1; 167
Character of a Coffee-House, The 919
Chesselden, Will 151
Cibber, Colley 654
Clarkson, Thomas (Website)
Coffee-Houses Vindicated 920
Coleridge, Samuel Taylor (Website)
Collier, Jeremy 655
Collier, Mary 894
Collins, William (Website)
Compendious System of Astronomy, from A 181
Complaint of a Forsaken Indian Woman 855
Consideration on the Keeping of Negroes 828
Continuation of the Observations on Mr. Oldcastle's Remarks upon the English History, A (Website)
Convent of Pleasure, The 13
Cooke, Ebenezer (Website)
Country Wife, The 239
Covent-Garden Journal, The, No. 4, (Website)
Covent-Garden Journal, The, No. 6 695
Covent-Garden Journal, The, No. 31 (Website)
Cowper, William 879 (Website)
Coxe, Thomas 150
Credulity, Superstition, and Fanaticism: A Medley 187
Crumble Hall 900
Cugoano, Quobna Ottobah (Website)
Cymon and Iphigenia, from Boccace 93
Darwin, Erasmus 189
Death of Robin Hood, The 817
Declaration by the Representatives of the United States of America, in General Congress Assembled, A 865
Defoe, Daniel 302, 916 (website)
Description of a City Shower, A 376
Description of a New World, Called the Blazing World, The 6
Deserted Village, The 873
Dialogue Betwixt the Body and the Mind, A 3
Diary, The 114
Dictionary of the English Language, A 783
Disabled Debauchee, The 295
Disappointment, The 197
Drake, Judith 192

Dryden, John 69
Duck, Stephen 891
Dyer, John 942
Dying Negro, A Poem, The (Website)
Earle, William (Website)
Edward, Edward 812
Elegy to the Memory of an Unfortunate Lady 568
Elegy Written in a Country Churchyard 807
Eloisa to Abelard 570
Enquiry Concerning Human Understanding, An 183
Epistle 2. To a Lady 591
Epistle 4. To Richard Boyle, Earl of Burlington 597
Epistle from Mr. Pope to Dr. Arbuthnot, An 584
Epistle from Mrs. Y[onege] to Her Husband 607
Epistle from Mrs. Yonge to Her Husband 490
Epistle to a Lady, An 898
Epistle to William Wilberforce, Esq., on the Rejection of the Bill for Abolishing the Slave Trade (Website)
Equiano, Olaudah or Gustavus Vassa 952
Erskine, Thomas 667
Essay Concerning Human Understanding, An 159
Essay in Defense of the Female Sex, An 192
Essay of Dramatic Poesy, An 101
Essay on Criticism, An 542 (complete text Website)
Essay on Man, An 575
Essay on the Theatre, An 860
Evening 7 546
Excuse for so Much Writ upon My Verses, An 3
Experiments and Observations on Different Kinds of Air, from 155
Falconbridge, Alexander (Website)
Fantomina: or, Love in a Maze 632
Farewell to America: To Mrs. S.W., A 1020
Feigned Courtesans, The (Website)
Female Spectator, The, Book 1 684 (Website)
Female Spectator, The, No. 10 194
Female Tatler, The, No. 1 672
Female Tatler, The, No. 9 917
Female Tatler, The, No. 67 918
Fénelon, François (Website)
Fielding, Henry 695, 716 (Website)
Finch, Anne, Countess of Winchilsea 348
Fleece, The 942
Franklin, Benjamin 153, 182, 846, 863 (Website)
Funeral Poem on the Death of C.E., an Infant of Twelve Months, A 1021
Gay, John 906, 933 (Website)
General Magazine and Impartial Review, The 969
Gentleman's Magazine, The 968
Gleaner Contemplates the Future Prospects of Women in this 'Enlightened Age' (Website)
Goldsmith, Oliver 700, 872
Grasmere Journal, The (Website)
Gray, Thomas 804 (Website)
Gulliver's Travels 389
Hands, Elizabeth 902
Haywood, Eliza 630 (Webiste)
Hazlitt, William (Website)
Hester Thrale's Journal 946
History of King Lear, The 653
History of the Rise, Progress and Accomplishment of the Abolition of the African Slave Trade (Website)
History of the Royal Society of London 146
Hogarth, William 187, 922
Hooke, Robert 161
Hughes, John (Website)
Hume, David 183
Hunting of the Hare, The 4
Hymn to Science 180
I believe it is difficult for those who publish their own memoirs (Website)
Idler, The, No. 26 [Betty Broom] 776
Idler, The, No. 29 [Betty Broom, cont.] 778
Idler, The, No. 30 663
Idler, The, No. 31 [On Idleness] 779
Idler, The, No. 49 [Will Marvel] 780
Idler, The, No. 81 [On Native Americans] 782
Idler, The, No. 82 [On Beauty] (Website)
Imperfect Enjoyment, The 299
Impromptu on Charles II 300
Information to Those Who Would Remove to America 846
Infortunate, The 840
Interesting Narrative of the Life of Olaudah Equiano, The 953
Introduction, The 350
"Introduction" to the 1811 edition of The Castle of Otranto 672
Jefferson, Thomas 865, 1026
Johnson, Samuel 663, 686, 759 (Website)
Johnson, Susannah 857
Journal of A West India Proprietor (Website)
Journal of the Plague Year, A 338
Journey to Pennsylvania (Website)
Jubilate Agno 823
Lackington, James 665

Lady Lucan 842
Lady's Dressing Room, The 379
Lady's Museum, The (Website)
Leapor, Mary 898
Letter from Artemisia in the Town to Chloe in the Country, A 296
Letter from William Penn … to the Committee of the Free Society of Traders of that Province Residing in London (Website)
Letter of Mr. Isaac Newton … Concerning His New Theory about Light and Colour 151
Letter to Daphnis, April 2, 1685, A 351
Letter to Edward Blount 941
Letter to Richard Bentley 177
Letter to Sir Joseph Priestley 182
Letters [Frances Burney] (Website)
Letters [Samuel Johnson] 800
Letters [Lady Mary Wortley Montagu] 612
Letters [Hester Thrale Piozzi] (Website)
Letters from an American Farmer 848
Lewis, Matthew Gregory (Website)
Licensing Act of 1737, The 658
Life and Remarkable Adventures of Israel R. Potter (Website)
Life of Samuel Johnson, The 661 (Website)
Light Shining Out of Darkness 880
Ligon, Richard 827
Lives of the English Poets 793
Locke, John 159
London Journal (Website)
Look Before You Leap 851
Lover: A Ballad, The 606
Love and Life: A Song 294
Loves of the Plants, from 189
Lyke-Wake Dirge, A 819
Mac Flecknoe 87
Man Frail, and God Eternal 183
Marriage A-la-Mode 922
Mary Hamilton 820
Memoirs of the Forty-Five First Years of the Life of James Lackington 665
Memoirs of the Last Ten Years of the Reign of King George II 853
Micrographia, from 161
Micromegas, from 171
Mittelberger, Gottlieb (Website)
Modest Proposal, A 523
Montagu, Lady Mary Wortley 602, 681, 935
Monthly Review, The 969 (Website)
Moraley, William 840
More, Hannah 830
Murray, Judith Sargent (Website)
My Mary 889
Narrative of the Captivity and Restoration of Mrs. Mary Rowlandson, A (Website)
Nature, Art, Gardens 432
Negro Girl, The (Website)
Newton, Isaac 151; 177 (Website)
Nicholls, Rev. Robert Boncher (Website)
Nocturnal Reverie, A 354
Nonsense of Common-Sense No. 5, The 681
Notes on the State of Virginia 1026
North-Briton, The, No. 45 [The King's Speech] (Website)
Obi; or, the History of Three-Fingered Jack (Website)
Observations, Occasioned by the Attempts Made in England to Effect the Abolition of the Slave Trade (Website)
Observations on the Importance of the American Revolution 870
Observations on the Nature of Civil Liberty 864
Observations upon Experimental Philosophy, To Which Is Added, The Description of a New Blazing World, from 167
Occom, Samson (Website)
Ode on a Distant Prospect of Eton College 805
Ode on the Death of a Favourite Cat, Drowned in a Tub of Goldfish 806
Ode to Fear (Website)
Of the Importance of the Education of Daughters (Website)
Of the Studies Proper for Women (Website)
Of the Theme of Love 3
Old Maid, The, No. 18 (Website)
Old Maid, The, No. 113 698
On a Juniper Tree, Cut Down to Make Busks 199
On Being Brought from Africa to America 1018
On the Death of Dr. Robert Levett 766
On the Death of the Reverend Mr. George Whitefield 1022
On the English Novelists (Website)
On the Loss of the Royal George 888
On the Present State of Ireland 842
On the Slave Trade (Website)
On the Supposition of an Advertisement Appearing in a Morning Paper 902

On Trade 916
Oroonoko: or, The Royal Slave. A True History 201
Paine, Thomas 869
Penn, William (Website)
Pepys, Samuel 112
Philosophical Enquiry into the Origin of Our Ideas of the Sublime and the Beautiful, A 943
Philosophical Transactions 149
Pilgrim's Progress, The 34
Piozzi, Hester Thrale 945
Pitt, James (Website)
Plain Account of the Inoculating of the Smallpox, A 611
Poem on the Inhumanity of the Slave-Trade, A 834
Poem Sacred to the Memory of Sir Isaac Newton, A 179
Poetess's Hasty Resolution, The 3
Pope, Alexander 540, 941
Potter, Israel (Website)
Preface to The Works of William Shakespeare, The 786
Present for a Servant-Maid, A 647
Price, Richard 864, 870
Priestley, Joseph 155
Print and Stage Culture 533
Progress of Beauty, The 375
Public Ledger, The, No. 15 [The Citizen of the World Observes British Fashion] 700
Rambler, The, No. 4 [On Fiction] 766
Rambler, The, No. 12. [Cruelty of Employers] 769
Rambler, The, No. 60 [On Biography] 771
Rambler, The, No. 97 690
Rambler, The, No. 114 693
Rambler, The, No. 155 [On Becoming Acquainted With Our Real Characters] 774
Rambler, The, No. 170 (Website)
Rape of the Lock, The 555
Reasons that Induced Dr. S. to Write a Poem Called The Lady's Dressing Room, The 605
Reeve, Clara 664
Reflections upon Marriage 297
Religio Laici 90
Remarks Concerning the Savages of North America (Website)
Remarks on the History of England: Letter 5 (Website)
Report on the Examination of the Emigrants from the Counties of Caithness and Sutherland on board the Ship Bachelor of Leith bound to Wilmington in North Carolina 844
Retired Cat, The 887
Reynolds, Sir Joshua (Website)
Richardson, Samuel 690
Robin Hood and Alan a Dale 810
Robinson Crusoe 309
Robinson, Mary (Website)
Rowlandson, Mary (Website)
Rule, Britannia 715
Satire against Reason and Mankind, A 292
Satire On Charles II, A 291
Saturday. The Small Pox 603
School for Scandal, The 972
Scott, Sir Walter (Website)
Seasons, The 709 (Website)
Serious Proposal to the Ladies, A 190, 356
Sheridan, Richard Brinsley 970
Shepherd's Week, The 933
Short Narrative of My Life, A (Website)
Short View of the Immorality and Profaneness of the English Stage, A 655
Short View of the State of Ireland, A 530
Slave Trader's Journal, A (Website)
Slavery: A Poem 830
Smart, Christopher 822
Sociable Letters 11
Some Reflections Upon Marriage 362
Song for St. Cecilia's Day, A 92
Sonnet on the Death of Mr. Richard West 807
Sotweed Factor, The (Website)
Spectator, The, No. 7 186
Spectator, The, No. 11 673
Spectator, The, No. 18 657
Spectator, The, No. 69 914
Spectator, The, No. 112 676
Spectator, The, No. 119 928
Spectator, The, No. 155 921
Spectator, The, No. 285 534
Spectator, The, No. 302 (Website)
Spectator, The, No. 414 538, 938
Spectator, The, No. 573 608
Speech as Prosecution in the Seditious-Libel Trial of Thomas Williams 667
Speech on Conciliation with the Colonies 861
Speech to the House of Commons (Website)
Spleen: A Pindaric Poem, The 349
Sprat, Thomas 146
Spring (Website)
St. John Crèvecoeur, J. Hector 848
Statute of Anne, The 659
Steele, Richard 673, 921 (Website)

Stella's Birthday (1727) 378
Stella's Birthday, written in the year 1718 377
Summer (Website)
Sweet Meat Has Sour Sauce (Website)
Swift, Jonathan 373
Tam Lin 813
Task, The 880 (Website)
Tate, Nahum 651
Tatler, The, No. 21 (Website)
Tatler, The, No. 155 670
Tatler, The, No. 224 661
Taxation No Tyranny (Website)
Thomson, James 179, **708** (Website)
Thoughts and Sentiments on the Evil and Wicked Traffic of the Slavery and Commerce of the Human Species (Website)
Thoughts on the Slavery of Negroes, as It Affects the British Colonies in the West Indies (Website)
Thresher's Labour, The 891 (Website)
'Tis hard to say, if greater want of skill (Website)
To a Gentleman with a Manuscript Play 899
To Maecenas 1017
To Mr. F., Now Earl of W. 351
To My Fair Clarinda 200
To S.M. a Young African Painter, on Seeing His Works 1019
To the King's Most Excellent Majesty 1018
To the Memory of Mr. Oldham 91
To the Right Honorable William Earl of Dartsmouth 1019
Town Eclogues 935
Tragedy of Tragedies, The 718
Trials Proposed by Mr. Oyle to Dr. Lower to Be Made by Him for the Improvement of Transfusing Blood out of One Live Animal into Another 149
Trivia 906
True & Exact History of the Island of Barbados, A 827
True Relation of My Birth, Breeding, and Life, A (Website)
True Relation of the Apparition of One Mrs. Veal, A 304
Turnball, Gordon (Website)
Unequal Fetters, The 353
Vanity of Human Wishes, The 761
Venus in the Cloister; or, The Nun in Her Smock 649
Verses on the Death of Dr Swift, D.S.P.D. 381
Vindication of the Rights of Men, A (Website)
Voltaire, 171
Walpole, Horace 853 (Website)
Warburton, William (Website)
Watts, Isaac 182
Weekly Review of the Affairs of France, A (Website)
Wheatley, Phillis 1016 (Website)
Wilberforce, William (Website)
Wilkes, John (Website)
Will and Testament (Website)
Wilmot, John, Earl of Rochester 290
Windsor-Forest 548
Winter 709
Witlings, The (Website)
Wollstonecraft, Mary (Website)
Woman Drest by Age, A 3
Woman's Labour, The 894
Woolman, John 828
Wordsworth, Dorothy (Website)
Wordsworth, William 855
Wycherley, William 238
Yearsley, Ann 834